The *Enhanced* Guide for Occupational Exploration

Revised Second Edition

Descriptions for the 2,800 Most Important Jobs

Compiled by Marilyn Maze and Donald Mayall

Based on information from the U.S. Department of Labor and Other Sources
With Introductory Chapters by J. Michael Farr

The *Enhanced* Guide for Occupational Exploration
Revised Second Edition
Descriptions for the 2,800 Most Important Jobs

©1995, JIST Works, Inc., Indianapolis, IN

Library of Congress Cataloging-in-Publication Data
Maze, Marilyn.
    The enhanced guide for occupational exploration : descriptions for the
2,800 most important jobs / complied by Marilyn Maze and Donald Mayall : with
introductory materials by J. Michael Farr. – 2nd ed., rev.
    p.   cm.
        "Based on information from the U.S. Department of Labor,
Department of commerce, Census Bureau, and other sources."
    Includes index.
    ISBN 1-56370-207-X
        1. Vocational Interests–United States.   2. Vocational guidance–
United States.   I. Mayall, Donald, 1932-   II. United States Dept. of
Labor.   III. Title
HF 5382.M37   1995   95-12097
331.7'0973–dc20   CIP

Disclaimer of liability: The authors and publisher have been careful to obtain reliable and accurate information in this work but can accept no responsibility for any omissions or errors in fact nor for any decisions
made or actions taken as a result of the information provided. As in all things, we humbly suggest that you
accept your own judgment regarding career and life decisions as the ultimate human authority.

JIST Works, Inc.
8902 Otis Avenue
Indianapolis, IN 46216
Phone: 1-800-648-JIST · FAX: 1-800-JIST-FAX
E-mail: jistworks@aol.com   World Wide Web address: http://www.jist.com

ISBN: 1-56370-207-X

About This Book

This book represents the first time that such a wide variety of information on all the major occupations has been assembled in one place. The fact that it was done without government funding is noteworthy, although it would not have been possible without access to the computerized data files of the U.S. Department of Labor and other government sources. In that sense, it is the result of positive collaboration between the public and private sectors.

The first edition of this book has become a standard career reference since its introduction in 1991. Thousands of copies have been sold since that time and it is widely used in libraries, schools, and other places as an easy-to-use source of accurate information on an enormous number of specific job titles. This edition keeps the same organizational structure and allows you to find jobs within 12 major interest areas and increasingly specific groupings of related jobs. This system, originally developed by the U.S. Department of Labor, makes it very simple to find clusters of jobs with similar characteristics. This system, as well as the helpful information provided for each grouping, and the occupational descriptions themselves, make this book an ideal tool for career exploration, considering educational alternatives, or identifying alternative job targets—as well as other uses.

New Features in This Revision

While we have kept many features of the original edition that were so well received, this new revision includes a variety of improvements.

More jobs: We have increased the number of job descriptions to 2,800 from the previous edition's count of 2,500. This is a very large number of jobs and includes those held by more than 95 percent of the workforce.

New information: We dropped some of the outmoded jobs included in the previous edition and added 793 new descriptions. In addition, 805 descriptions have been revised.

Based on the latest government data: All the descriptions in this edition are based on the current edition of the *Dictionary of Occupational Titles.* Some of the occupational data details incorporate more recent updates that are not published elsewhere.

New selection criteria: We have improved our selection criteria. This edition now eliminates obsolete jobs, includes highly technical and newly created ones, and emphasizes those employing the most people.

New one-page Code Abbreviation Key: A new one-page Code Abbreviations Key has been included that makes occupational code interpretation much easier. Please feel free to photocopy it. We have included a variety of new codification changes that have not been published elsewhere.

As the labor market progresses, new jobs are created and old ones change. We hope that future editions of this book continue to reflect these changes and that it continues to be a helpful resource to the many people who use it.

© 1995, JIST Works, Inc. ● Indianapolis, IN

Table of Contents

Provides a more detailed review of the sources and interpretation of the occupational descriptions and the codes provided for each. Sections include: The Narrative Section of the Occupational Descriptions and Detailed Descriptions of the Data Categories and Codes.

OCCUPATIONAL DESCRIPTIONS

This section is the major component of this book. It provides descriptions of 2,800 jobs organized within increasingly specific clusters of related jobs. The occupations are arranged in clusters of related jobs, listed within the numeric sections that follow. In addition to the descriptions themselves, there is a narrative section at the beginning of each major cluster of jobs that describes what these jobs have in common. These brief narratives allow you to gain an overview of each job cluster before looking more closely at specific jobs listed within each. It provides an effective method for exploring career alternatives in a simple and efficient manner.

Following are the titles of the 12 major occupational interest areas into which each of the 2,800 jobs are organized, along with the numeric section of the book where these jobs begin. The Brief Definitions of the 12 Interest Areas on page ix and the Summary List of Interest Areas, Work Groups and Subgroups, beginning on page xi, provides additional details on how the jobs in this book are organized.

The 2,800 jobs described in this book are listed in alphabetical order along with their related *DOT* (*Dictionary of Occupational Titles*) and *GOE* (*Guide for Occupational Exploration*) numbers. If you know the title of a job, you can look it up here.

This appendix consists of two sections. The first is an alphabetical listing of industries along with their related abbreviations as used in this book. The second lists clusters of related industries and provides industry codes for each.

Organizes the 2,800 jobs that are described in this book within major industry groups where they are most often found. Useful for finding jobs within an industry with which you are already familiar or for considering a change to a different industry.

Organizes all 2,800 jobs by the amount of education typically required to obtain that job. This is a helpful appendix to see what other jobs your current level of education may qualify you for or to consider jobs requiring additional education or training.

This appendix lists jobs arranged by the amount of skill needed in working with data, people, and things. Use this list to locate jobs that require the combination of those skills that you want to use in your work.

The Occupational Employment Statistics (OES) coding system is widely used in government publications. This code is provided as part of each job description and this appendix lists the codes and their related occupations.

These codes tell you what materials (M), products (P), subject matter (SM), or services (S) you must be familiar with in order to do each job listed in this book. This appendix is a complete listing of the code numbers and their related meanings.

These codes specify which tasks or skills you must perform in each job. The appendix provides a listing of the code numbers and their related meanings.

An Introduction to the *EGOE*

The *Enhanced Guide for Occupational Exploration* (often referred to as the *Enhanced GOE* or *EGOE*) is a significant new resource for job seekers, career changers, students, and vocational counselors. Containing 2,800 occupational descriptions, it covers more than 95 percent of all workers in the U.S. economy. Its cross-referencing systems allow you to find jobs by skills, interests, education required, industry, and many other criteria.

This book has been carefully researched and compiled to provide useful information. Some of the information provided is not available in any other published source, and the variety of information provided on each occupation had never been gathered in one book before. Each occupational description and related information codes is based on expert analysis of the latest computerized databases provided by the U.S. Department of Labor.

The Earlier Editions

To understand the importance of the *EGOE*, it is useful to know its predecessors. The original *Guide for Occupational Exploration* (often referred to as the *GOE* throughout this work) was published by the U.S. Department of Labor in 1979. A second edition, with significant improvements by Dr. Thomas Harrington and Dr. Arthur O'Shea, was published by another source in the mid-1980s. Each of these books organized more than 12,000 occupations into logical clusters and provided a number of ways to cross-reference them.

Designed to help job seekers, career changers, students, and others explore career alternatives, these older editions were widely used by vocational counselors. They allowed users to access the huge variety of occupational choices in a rational and useful way. But both books had limitations caused by the huge number of occupations listed. The first major limitation was that neither edition contained descriptions of the more than 12,000 job titles they listed. Finding descriptions required users to refer to another U.S. Department of Labor publication, the *Dictionary of Occupational Titles* (often called the *DOT* or D.O.T.). This approach is understandable since the original GOE was more than 700 pages and providing even brief descriptions for each occupation would have made it an unmanageable 2,000 pages or so.

Another limitation of the early editions of the *GOE* was that, for many people, there were too many occupations listed. Many were highly specialized occupations that have very few people employed in them. In fact, more than 90 percent of the workforce are employed in fewer than 2,000 of the more than 12,000 occupations listed. Since the early *GOE* did not differentiate the more important occupations from the less important ones, the book was difficult for many to use.

One other limitation of the early editions of the *GOE* was that many people wanted specific information that was not provided. For example, most individuals would want to know how much training is required for a specific job and its salary range. Vocational counselors and clients would also need information on a variety of other measures such as work field codes, temperaments, or stress and physical requirements codes. Yet the information was not available without reference to a variety of other hard-to-obtain governmental and other information sources. In some cases, the information was not readily available at all.

This book, *The Enhanced Guide for Occupational Exploration*, (*EGOE*) was designed to correct the major limitations of the early editions of the *GOE*. We did a careful analysis of more than 12,000 occupations to identify the 2,800 jobs included in this book. Few people would be interested in the occupations that have been excluded as they employ very few people or are highly specialized. Each of the selected jobs has a narrative description as well as substantial additional information. We used sophisticated computer techniques to develop the descriptions of jobs included in this book. Data for each occupation was obtained from a variety of published and unpublished sources and includes information that had previously been available only by combing through a variety of reference books. In some cases, information has been included that has not been previously published at all. Additional details on selection criteria and sources of data are provided in the first two chapters.

The 2,800 occupations selected for this book are arranged in the same useful clusters found in the original *GOE*. A series of indices is also provided to cross-reference the various jobs listed in a variety of helpful ways.

The New *Complete Guide for Occupational Exploration*

Since the publication of the first edition of the *EGOE*, a thorough revision of the original *GOE* has been published by JIST. Titled *The Complete Guide for Occupational Exploration (CGOE)*, it includes all 12,741 job titles included in the current edition of the *Dictionary of Occupational Titles*. Using the same organizational structure as the original *GOE*, the new *CGOE* also provides a variety of coded information for each title as well as a career exploration section, a variety of cross-referencing systems, and other useful features. While space limitations did not permit the inclusion of job descriptions, the *CGOE* has become another standard career reference that is useful for those wanting a complete listing of all jobs within the various *GOE* groupings.

This new edition of the *EGOE*, like the *CGOE*, will remain important career reference tools for years to come.

Brief Definitions of the 12 Interest Areas

The U.S. Department of Labor has divided all jobs into 12 major groupings based on interests. These are the same groupings used in the original *Guide for Occupational Exploration* and are frequently used in other career information systems. Brief definitions of these 12 interest areas are provided below. Additional information on these interest areas and their more specific subgroupings are provided later in the book.

One way to approach career exploration or job seeking is to look for the interest areas that you like best or in which you have previous experience or training. These groups then define the clusters of jobs worthy of additional exploration.

Look over the brief descriptions that follow. They are the same 12 groupings provided in the Table of Contents. They provide the basic structure for organizing occupations throughout this book.

The 12 Interest Areas

01 Artistic:

Interest in creative expression of feelings or ideas.

04 Protective:

Interest in the use of authority to protect people and property.

02 Scientific:

Interest in discovering, collecting, and analyzing information about the natural world and in applying scientific research findings to problems in medicine, life sciences, and natural sciences.

05 Mechanical:

Interest in applying mechanical principles to practical situations, using machines, hand tools, or techniques.

03 Plants and Animals:

Interest in activities involving plants and animals, usually in an outdoor setting.

06 Industrial:

Interest in repetitive, concrete, organized activities in a factory setting.

07 Business Detail:

Interest in organized, clearly defined
activities requiring accuracy and
attention to detail, primarily in
an office setting.

10 Humanitarian:

Interest in helping others with their
mental, spiritual, social, physical, or
vocational needs.

08 Selling:

Interest in bringing others to a
point of view through personal
persuasion, using sales and
promotion techniques.

11 Leading-Influencing:

Interest in leading and influencing
others through activities involving
high-level verbal
or numerical abilities.

09 Accommodating:

Interest in catering to the wishes
of others, usually on a
one-on-one basis.

12 Physical Performing:

Interest in physical activities
performed before an audience.

Summary List of Interest Areas, Work Groups, and Subgroups

The 12 major interest areas are further divided into 66 work groups and 350 even more specific subgroups of related jobs. This structure is presented in the summary table that follows. Each of the increasingly specific interest areas, work groups, and subgroups have brief narratives at the beginning of their respective sections in the book. These narratives provide an overview of the jobs in that cluster, followed by descriptions of the jobs that fit into the various groupings.

Because each of the 2,800 jobs in this book is organized within increasingly specific clusters of related jobs, any job is easy to find in the numerical sequence of its GOE number. To explore options, simply identify one of the 12 major interest areas that appeals to you and continue to explore subgroupings that interest you. You should study jobs listed in these clusters more carefully. Note that a system of number codes is used for the various groupings. Called "GOE Codes" these numbers are used throughout this book, with a unique "GOE number" assigned to each occupation. You can use these numbers to cross-reference other occupational information systems that use the same organizational structure.

Summary List of Interest Areas, Work Groups, and Subgroups

01 Artistic

01.01	**Literary Arts**
01.01-01	Editing
01.01-02	Creative Writing
01.01-03	Critiquing
01.02	**Visual Arts**
01.02-01	Instructing and Appraising
01.02-02	Studio Art
01.02-03	Commercial Art
01.03	**Performing Arts: Drama**
01.03-01	Instructing & Directing
01.03-02	Performing
01.03-03	Narrating & Announcing
01.04	**Performing Arts: Music**
01.04-01	Instructing & Directing
01.04-02	Composing & Arranging
01.04-03	Vocal Performing
01.04-04	Instrumental Performing
01.05	**Performing Arts: Dance**
01.05-01	Instructing & Choreography
01.05-02	Performing
01.06	**Craft Arts**
01.06-01	Graphic Arts & Related Crafts
01.06-02	Arts & Crafts
01.06-03	Hand Lettering, Painting & Decorating
01.07	**Elemental Arts**
01.07-01	Psychic Science
01.07-02	Announcing
01.07-03	Entertaining
01.08	**Modeling**
01.08-01	Personal Appearance

02 Scientific

02.01	**Physical Sciences**
02.01-01	Theoretical Research
02.01-02	Technology
02.02	**Life Sciences**
02.02-01	Animal Specialization
02.02-02	Plant Specialization
02.02-03	Plant & Animal Specialization
02.02-04	Food Research
02.03	**Medical Sciences**
02.03-01	Medicine & Surgery
02.03-02	Dentistry
02.03-03	Veterinary Medicine
02.03-04	Health Specialties
02.04	**Laboratory Technology**
02.04-01	Physical Sciences
02.04-02	Life Sciences

03 Plants and Animals

03.01	**Managerial Work: Plants and Animals**
03.01-01	Farming
03.01-02	Specialty Breeding
03.01-03	Specialty Cropping
03.01-04	Forestry & Logging
03.02	**General Supervision: Plants and Animals**
03.02-01	Farming
03.02-02	Forestry & Logging
03.02-03	Nursery & Groundskeeping
03.02-04	Services
03.03	**Animal Training and Service**
03.03-01	Animal Training
03.03-02	Animal Service
03.04	**Elemental Work: Plants and Animals**
03.04-01	Farming
03.04-02	Forestry & Logging
03.04-03	Hunting & Fishing
03.04-04	Nursery & Groundskeeping
03.04-05	Services

04 Protective

04.01	**Safety and Law Enforcement**
04.01-01	Managing
04.01-02	Investigating
04.02	**Security Services**
04.02-01	Detention
04.02-02	Property & People
04.02-03	Law & Order
04.02-04	Emergency Responding

05 Mechanical

05.01	**Engineering**
05.01-01	Research
05.01-02	Environmental Protection
05.01-03	Systems Design
05.01-04	Testing & Quality Control
05.01-05	Sales Engineering
05.01-06	Work Planning & Utilization
05.01-07	Design
05.01-08	General Engineering
05.02	**Managerial Work: Mechanical**
05.02-01	Research
05.02-02	Maintenance & Construction
05.02-03	Processing & Manufacturing
05.02-04	Communications
05.02-05	Mining, Logging, and Petroleum Production

Summary List of Codes Used in This Book

As you start reading the actual job descriptions beginning on page 29, it may help to return to these pages that contain a quick reference guide to interpret the occupational codes used. You can photocopy the one-page Code Abbreviations Key at the end of chapter 1 to help interpret the many codes provided for the job descriptions. More thorough descriptions of these codes are provided in chapter 2.

The GOE Number: Refers to the unique job classification system used in the *Guide for Occupational Exploration*. This six-digit number groups occupations into 12 basic categories based on interest factors.

The DOT Number: Consists of nine digits. The first three numbers refer to the occupational classification system used by the *Dictionary of Occupation Titles*. The fourth through sixth digits refer to skills required for the job relative to data, people, and things, while the last three numbers further categorize each job within an occupational group. Because knowing what skills each job requires is useful, the fourth through sixth digits of the DOT number is interpreted below.

DOT Code, 4th Digit = Data (high = 0, low = 6)

0 = Synthesizing	**2** = Analyzing	**4** = Computing
1 = Coordinating	**3** = Compiling	**5** = Copying
		6 = Comparing

DOT Code, 5th Digit = People (high = 0, low = 8)

0 = Mentoring	**3** = Supervising	**6** = Speaking-Signaling
1 = Negotiating	**4** = Diverting	**7** = Serving
2 = Instructing	**5** = Persuading	**8** = Taking Instruction-Helping

DOT Code, 6th Digit = Things (high = 0, low = 7)

0 = Setting Up	**3** = Driving-Operating	**6** = Feeding-Offbearing
1 = Precision Working	**4** = Manipulating	**7** = Handling
2 = Operating-Controlling	**5** = Tending	

The OES Code: Explains the Occupational Employment Statistics category in which the occupation belongs. Helpful for looking up the occupations in government reports.

The GED Code: Refers to general educational development required for the job. There are six levels in each of the following areas: Reasoning (R), Math (M), and Language (L). The higher the number, the more complex the skill required to do that job.

The SVP Code: Stands for "Specific Vocational Preparation" and refers to the time in years, months, or days required to demonstrate standard proficiency in a job.

The Academic Codes (Ed and Eng): Refer to the educational degrees required and knowledge and proficiency in the English language.

Ed Codes:
M = Master's degree or above
B = Bachelor's degree
A = Associate degree or apprenticeship
H = High school diploma or GED
N = No diploma

Eng Codes
G = Understanding English grammar
S = Simple communication in English
N = No communication in English

The Work Field Code: A three-digit code that refers to groups of occupations clustered together based on similar techniques, related skills, and overall socioeconomic objectives. For a full listing of these codes and corresponding categories refer to Appendix H.

The MPSMS Code: This three-digit code classifies jobs by materials, products, subject matter, and services. Appendix G lists the specific job categories.

The Aptitudes Codes: Refers to aptitudes required in specific areas measured on a rating scale (high = 1 to low = 5), relative to the total population.

G = General Learning Ability	**P =** Form Perception	**M =** Manual Dexterity
V = Verbal Aptitude	**Q =** Clerical Perception	**E =** Eye-Hand-Foot Coordination
N = Numerical Aptitude	**K =** Motor Coordination	**C =** Color Discrimination
S = Spatial Aptitude	**F =** Finger Dexterity	

The Temperaments Code: Defined as adaptability requirements placed on workers.

D = DIRECTING, Controlling or Planning Activities of Others
R = Performing REPETITIVE or Short-Cycle Work
I = INFLUENCING People in Their Opinions, Attitudes, and Judgments
V = Performing a VARIETY of Duties
E = EXPRESSING Personal Feelings
A = Working ALONE or Apart in Physical Isolation from Others
S = Performing Effectively Under STRESS
T = Attaining Precise Set Limits, TOLERANCES, and Standards
U = Working UNDER Specific Instructions
P = Dealing with PEOPLE
J = Making JUDGMENTS and Decisions

The Physical Demands Code:

Strength Rating Codes (Stg):

Following are descriptions of the five terms in which the Strength Factor is expressed:

S = Sedentary Work	**M =** Medium Work	**V =** Very Heavy Work
L = Light Work	**H =** Heavy Work	

Other Physical Demands Ratings Codes:

All other physical demand factors are coded to represent the presence and frequency of the activity in the work situation as follows:

Const = Continuously	Activity exists two-thirds or more of the time
Freq = Frequently	Activity exists from one-third to two-thirds of the time
Occas = Occasionally	Activity exists up to one-third of the time
Never	Condition does not exist or is rarely needed

Following are the other physical demand factors; if a code letter is not shown for an *EGOE* title, then that activity never occurs for that occupation.

C = Climbing	**R =** Reaching	**M =** Tasting/Smelling
B = Balancing	**H =** Handling	**N =** Near Acuity
S = Stooping	**I =** Fingering	**F =** Far Acuity
K = Kneeling	**E =** Feeling	**D =** Depth Perception
O = Crouching	**T =** Talking	**A =** Accommodation
W = Crawling	**G =** Hearing	**X =** Color Vision
		V = Field of Vision

The Work Environment Code: These codes provide information on the types of work environments found in a given job.

Noise Intensity Level (Noise)

The noise intensity level to which the worker is exposed in the job environment. This factor is expressed by one of five letters:

VQ = Very Quiet   **Q** = Quiet   **N** = Normal   **L** = Loud   **V** = Very Loud

All other environmental condition factors are coded with a letter that represents the presence and frequency of the condition in the work situation as follows:

Const = Continuously	Activity exists two-thirds or more of the time
Freq = Frequently	Activity exists from one-third to two-thirds of the time
Occas = Occasionally	Activity exists up to one-third of the time
Never	Condition does not exist or is rarely needed

Following are the other environmental conditions; if a code letter is not shown for an *EGOE* title, then that condition never occurs for that occupation.

W = Exposure to Weather
C = Extreme Cold
H = Extreme Heat
U = Wet and/or Humid

V = Vibration
A = Atmospheric Conditions
M = Proximity to Moving Mechanical Parts
E = Exposure to Electrical Shock
D = Working in High, Exposed Places
R = Exposure to Radiation

X = Working with Explosives
T = Exposure to Toxic or Caustic Chemicals
O = Other Environmental Conditions

The Salary Code: Occupations are assigned to one of five salary categories based on expected starting salary (high = 5, low = 1).

1 = Lowest, below $14,000 per year
2 = Moderately low, $14,000 to $16,999 per year
3 = Mid-range, $17,000 to $20,999 per year
4 = Moderately high $21,000 to $27,999 per year
5 = Highest, $28,000 per year and above

The Outlook Code: Occupations are assigned to one of five employment outlook categories based on the average length of time it takes before finding employment in this field (low = 1, high = 5).

1 = Lowest—can take more than a year
2 = Moderately low—can take a few months to a year
3 = Mid-range—can be found in a few months
4 = Moderately high—can be found in a couple of weeks
5 = Highest—employment can be found quickly

Chapter 1
How to Use This Book

This chapter provides background information on how *The Enhanced Guide for Occupational Exploration* was developed and how it can best be used. Chapter 2 provides additional information on interpreting the occupational codes used in each occupational description.

Note: At various times throughout this book we use the words "occupation" and "job" interchangeably. Some argue that the two words have different meanings but, for our purposes, they will mean the same thing.

Who Should Use This Book?

The Enhanced Guide for Occupational Exploration EGOE was created to serve the needs of two primary groups of people. The first group includes people trying to explore career alternatives or find a job. The second group consists of vocational counselors, business people, and other professionals needing access to the specialized information provided in this book.

Few people are able to identify the "best" jobs for them from among the many thousands of job titles that exist. They have difficulty relating their interests, skills, potentials, experiences, and preferences to appropriate occupations. For them, this book offers a well-organized and thorough guide to finding various occupations that most closely match their criteria.

Vocational counselors and other professionals also need access to information about occupations to help their clients make good career decisions, to classify jobs for documentation purposes, or to obtain technical information on various occupational characteristics and requirements.

This book will help both groups. By providing descriptions for the jobs that an overwhelming majority of the people actually work in, it becomes a unique and valuable resource. The use of a simple and logical clustering of related jobs allows a novice to access one or more of the 2,800 jobs in an orderly and easy-to-understand manner. The addition of technical data and codes from a variety of previously hard-to obtain sources provides information of great value to novices and professional vocational counselors alike. The various appendices that provide additional information and ways to access the many listed jobs can prove to be invaluable to many.

How the Book Is Organized

The major portion of the *EGOE* consists of detailed descriptions of 2,800 occupations. They are grouped into increasingly specific clusters of related occupations to provide a helpful way to find and explore career alternatives. The basic organizational structure consists of 12 major interest areas, 66 work groups, and 350 subgroups of related occupations. This is the same structure developed by the U.S. Department of Labor and used in the original *Guide for Occupational Exploration*. It is a very useful structure for finding clusters of related occupations.

There are also several appendices at the end of this book. These allow you to look up the 2,800 listed jobs in a variety of helpful ways. The appendices also provide additional information regarding the classification of occupations. This technical information will be of particular interest to vocational counselors and other professionals, though some job seekers may also find it of interest. Look at the Table of Contents at the beginning of this book for a list of the appendices and brief descriptions of their content.

The 12 Major Interest Areas

If you have not yet read the sections of this book titled "Brief Definitions of the 12 Interest Areas" and "Summary List of Interest Areas, Work Groups, and Subgroups," please look up their location in the Table of Contents and refer to them to best understand what follows.

All 2,800 of the jobs listed in the *EGOE* are grouped within one of 12 major occupational categories called interest areas. These 12 interest areas correspond to the major occupational interest factors identified in research conducted by the Division of Testing in the U.S. Employment Service. The interest areas are identified by the first two digits used in the six-digit numerical *GOE* code system applied to each occupation described in this book. For example, the first two digits of the *GOE* number 01.01.01 refer to the "Artistic" interest area, one of the 12 major interest areas.

The 66 More Specific Work Groups

Each major interest area is further divided into 66 work groups. Jobs within each work group involve the same general type of work and require the same general capabilities of the worker. Each group has its own unique four-digit code and title. For example, in the number 01.01.01, the first two digits refer to the "Artistic" interest area, while the second two digits refer to the "Literary Arts" work group. The number of work groups within each interest area varies from two to twelve.

The 350 Subgroups

Within each work group, jobs are further divided into 350 subgroups to make it easier to distinguish among similar jobs. Each subgroup has its own unique six-digit code and title. In the example 01.01.01, the last two digits refer to the subgroup titled "Editing." Specific occupations or jobs are then listed under this subgroup.

An integral part of every job title is its industry designation. Because the same job in a different industry may have very different duties and working conditions, the industry is listed in parentheses after each job title. If the duties and working conditions are similar in several industries, these industries may be listed together following a single job title. When duties and/or working conditions differ significantly, separate definitions may be provided, each with a different industry designation.

Tips for Finding a Particular Job or Job Cluster

The grouping of jobs by increasingly specific clusters makes it easy to find a specific job beginning with the major interest area in which it would be found. Use the Table of Contents to identify the major interest areas, or find the more specific work group or subgroup on pages xi through xiii. You can also look up the specific title in the alphabetical listing in Appendix A or use another appendix to look up occupations in a variety of other useful ways.

A Sample Occupational Description

Each of the 2,800 occupational descriptions found in this book provides a substantial amount of useful information. Some of the information is in coded form. While this is not as easy to interpret, we wanted to include lots of additional information and using some codes allowed us to pack more information into a reasonable number of pages. Some of the coded information is of use to professional career counselors; other information would be of interest to a person considering career options or looking for a job.

Below is a sample job description along with a brief analysis of what each section of the description means to help you understand how each occupational description is organized. Comments on each of the numbered sections are provided following the sample description. While most components of each occupational description are readily understood, you will need to familiarize yourself with the coding system for those codes that interest you.

A Brief Review of the Elements of a Job Description

Below are brief definitions of the various elements contained in each job description. Additional details on interpreting each element is provided later in this chapter.

1. **Occupational (or "Job") Title:** This is the formal name of the occupation as provided by the U.S. Department of Labor. It is the same title as listed in the current edition of the *Dictionary of Occupational Titles (DOT)* or, for newer titles, in the Department of Labor's computer database.

2. **Industry Designation:** This is the industry in which the occupation is most commonly found. Additional details are provided in chapter 2, and Appendix B provides listings of the industries alphabetically and by subject area.

3. *DOT* **Code Number:** This is the code number assigned to this occupational title by the U.S. Department of Labor in the *Dictionary of Occupational Titles*. This number provides important information about each job and it also allows you to cross-reference the job to a variety of other career information systems. More information on elements of the *DOT* number is provided in the next chapter.

4. **OES Code Number:** The Occupational Employment Statistics (OES) coding system is widely used in government publications. This code can help you cross-reference to other occupational information sources. Additional information on the OES codes are provided in chapter 2, and Appendix F provides a listing of the codes and their related occupations.

5. **Alternate Job Titles:** Following the OES code, you will typically see one or more additional job titles in all capital letters. These titles are used by some employers instead of the main *DOT* title. When an alternate title is not used, none (of course) will be provided.

6. **Narrative Description:** This brief description outlines the basic duties and responsibilities of the job. These descriptions are those found in the *Dictionary of Occupational Titles* and are packed with carefully structured information. The "lead statement" summarizes the entire occupation. "Task element statements" indicate how the worker actually carries out his or her duties. "May" items indicate that some workers in different establishments ("may") perform one or more of the varied tasks listed. Additional information on how the descriptions are structured is contained in chapter 2.

7. **GED Codes:** These codes refer to the "General Educational Development" required to handle this job in Reasoning (R), Math (M), and Language (L). On a scale of 1 to 6, the higher the number, the higher the level required in that category. Additional information on interpreting these codes is provided in chapter 2.

8. **SVP Code:** Refers to the "Specific Vocational Preparation" required for entry into the job. It provides information on how much job-specific training is required to handle the job. On a scale of 1 to 9, the higher the number, the higher the level of training required for that job. Additional information for interpreting this code is provided in chapter 2.

9. **Academic Codes:** Refers to the degrees typically required for the job. The first element of this code, "Ed," refers to the Educational degree or certification typically required for entry into this occupation. The "Eng" component of the code refers to the job's require-

ments for communicating in the English language. Additional information for interpreting this code is provided in chapter 2.

10. **Work Field Code Number:** Work Fields are intended to help you find jobs that use the skills you enjoy using. Look through the list in Appendix H and pick the ones you want to use in your work. These skills are sometimes called "specific content skills" because they are used only in specific types of jobs. For example, if "knitting" is one of your skills, you could easily find jobs that require that skill.

11. **MPSMS Code Numbers:** These codes tell you what Materials, Products, Subject Matter, or Services you must know about in order to do the job. Additional information for interpreting these codes is provided in chapter 2, and Appendix G provides a complete listing of the MPSMS code numbers and their related meanings.

12. **Aptitudes Codes:** These codes refer to various work-related aptitudes including: General Learning Ability (G), Verbal Aptitude (V), Numerical Aptitude (N), Spatial Aptitude (S), Form Perception (P), Clerical Perception (Q), Motor Coordination (K), Finger Dexterity (F), Manual Dexterity (M), Eye-Hand-Foot Coordination (E), and Color Discrimination (C). On a scale of 1 to 5, the lower the number, the higher the level required for the job in each of the categories provided. Additional information for interpreting these codes is provided in chapter 2.

13. **Temperaments Codes:** These letter codes indicate that for this job a particular personality characteristic is required of the worker. These codes are described in chapter 2.

14. **Physical Requirements Codes:** These codes refer to job requirements for Strength and other physical requirements. Additional information for interpreting these codes is provided in chapter 2.

15. **Work Environment Codes:** These codes provide information on the types of work environments that are typically found or that must be endured for each job. Additional information for interpreting these codes is provided in chapter 2.

16. **Salary Code:** The salary code provides information on the average salary range expected for the job. On a scale of 1 to 5, the higher the number, the higher the salary. Additional information for interpreting this code is provided in chapter 2.

17. **Outlook Code:** This code provides a measure of how much the job is in demand by indicating how long it takes, on average, to find this type of job. On a scale of 1 to 5, the lower the number, the longer it takes (on average) to obtain this type of job. Additional information for interpreting this code is provided in chapter 2.

As you can see, we have provided a substantial amount of information for each occupation described in this book. The use of codes allows us to provide all of this information in a compact and useful format.

How We Selected Jobs to Include

The *EGOE* uses standard job titles that are defined by the U.S. Department of Labor and listed in the *Dictionary of Occupational Titles*. As anyone who has ever tried to use the *DOT* knows, it has a great many job titles—more than 20,000. Many titles are unfamiliar and even curious-sounding to most readers. This is because the *DOT* attempts to describe the entire work world throughout the United States. It thus includes jobs which are held by only a few people; are limited to a single industry or geographic location; or are only available through occupation-specific internal promotion ladders. For the vast majority of people entering the labor market or considering an occupational change, these jobs are not realistic alternatives.

To overcome this shortcoming, the 2,800 most important occupations from the *DOT* have been selected for inclusion in the *EGOE*. These occupations represent more than 95 percent of the jobs in which people actually work. As a group, these jobs offer realistic alternatives for those entering the job market, recent graduates from training or educational programs, job changers, and job seekers. The criteria for selecting jobs to include are listed below.

1. **There is a significant labor market for the job.** Many of the occupations in the *DOT* employ very few people. Some of the jobs have always been small, while others have been shrinking since they were studied. For example, how many people today work in ice plants, manufacturing ice? There are 10 separate occupations in the *DOT* for people who manufacture ice. At one time this was a major industry, but today it is very small and highly mechanized. These and other jobs which are shrinking or found only in limited locations—have been excluded from this book.

2. **The occupation is an "access point" for people who have been working in other fields or are just starting to work.** Some jobs can only be reached by promotion from within an establishment or by highly specific training, education, or experience. This book does not include many of these jobs. If you are planning a significant occupational change, you need to know which occupations are "access points" since these are the jobs offering the most opportunity for initial entry into a field and eventual promotion.

It is important to understand the difference between "access points" and "entry-level" occupations. Entry-level jobs can be done by people with very little training or experience. Many times these people are just starting their work life. Although significant numbers of the occupations in this book are entry-level (that is, they can be obtained by a person with little specialized education or training), many do require job-related training or experience and some require substantial preparation. But these jobs do not necessarily require experience in the same company or organization, and may not need to be in the same industry. Instead, these jobs are access points, jobs where a person with the necessary training or experience can get an initial job with an organization.

This book contains virtually all of the titles commonly regarded as "career fields." They are described in the *Occupational Outlook Handbook (OOH)*, a standard career reference book published by the U.S. Department of Labor. All of the traditional professional pursuits such as engineering, law, science, health, teaching, business, and "the arts" are represented. Also included are all apprenticeable trades and technical fields that require any kind of specialized training or certificate program. All clerical and service jobs for which there are significant labor markets, and the more common sales jobs are also included. Entry-level jobs are included for every industrial category of national significance.

Occupations That Are Not Included

Not included in this book are many upper-level specialties in the professions which normally require becoming competent in a related lower-level profession. Thus, "physician" is included but not cardiologist, anesthesiologist, or some other medical specialties. Most high-level, highly specialized positions in administration and management are excluded as are highly specialized sales titles such as sewing machine salesperson or veterinarian supplies sales representative. Also not included are many specialized supervisory jobs and other jobs that can be obtained only by promotion from lower level jobs where skills are learned on-the-job.

Sources of Data Used in This Book

A variety of sources have been used to obtain the information provided for each job listed in this book. The primary sources include various publications and databases of the U.S. Department of Labor. This section provides a brief overview of the sources of information used. More detailed information will be provided in the next chapter.

The U.S. Department of Labor

The U.S. Department of Labor (DOL) is an agency of the federal government. For many years it has collected and analyzed labor market information and is considered to be the most authoritative—and sometimes only—source of key information on jobs and labor market data.

The DOL has compiled a large amount of information about occupations, including descriptions and "worker traits"—those traits of people who are successful working in each occupation. Some of the information in the DOL database has been published by the U.S. Government and is available in any Government Printing Office bookstore, but other information is either unpublished or not readily available. We have assembled data from a variety of sources and used sophisticated computer procedures to select information that we felt would be the most helpful to most users. This book represents the first time this has been done.

The narrative descriptions for each of the 2,800 jobs in this book are based on those contained in the current edition of the *Dictionary of Occupational Titles (DOT)* as published by the Department of Labor. The descriptions include all the *DOT's* definitions, titles, alternate titles, and industry titles. The DOL updates this database of occupations every two months and the information provided in this book is the newest information that was available at the time of the publication of this book. This means that some of the descriptions and related information is more recent than that published in the current *DOT*.

In addition to the narrative descriptions, a substantial amount of additional information is provided for each of the listed jobs. This data was also obtained from current *DOT* and other databases and may differ from the format used in older data sources published by the DOL.

The Guide for Occupational Exploration (GOE) was originally published by the DOL in 1979 to help students and career changers find occupations more easily. We have used the *GOE's* system of organizing jobs into increasingly specific groupings because it works so well. In 1991, the DOL published the *Revised Fourth Edition* of the *DOT* in which GOE numbers and selected characteristics follow each occupational definition. However, the GOE number is of little use unless the meanings of the GOE numbers are also readily available. The arrangement of occupations in the *DOT* is according to occupational level and work task. While adding the GOE number to this complex classification structure is somewhat helpful, many people involved in career exploration find the GOE classification system more helpful as an organizing principal for occupations. In this volume, the description of a GOE number begins each section and the definitions of related occupations follow.

Other Worker Traits provided in the *EGOE* have not been published in any government publication, including Aptitudes, Temperaments, Work Fields, MPSMS (Materials, Products, Subject

Occupational Selection Comparison

The graph of Employment by Industry shows the percentage of people working in the major industry clusters in the United States in 1992 and percentages projected for these industry clusters in the year 2005. The graph of the Titles by Industry shows the percentage of titles in the *EGOE* and in the *DOT* in these same industry clusters. It is apparent from comparing these two graphs that the occupations selected for inclusion in the *EGOE* are far more representative of the jobs available in the United States than are the occupations in the *DOT*.

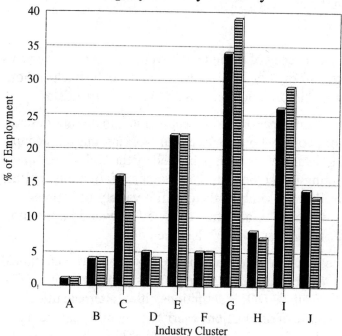

Employment by Industry

Industry Clusters

A Agriculture, Forestry, & Fishing
B Mining & Construction
C Manufacturing
D Transportation & Utilities
E Trade
F Finance, Insurance, & Real Estate
G Services
H Government
I Professional & Kindred
J Clerical
K Any Industry

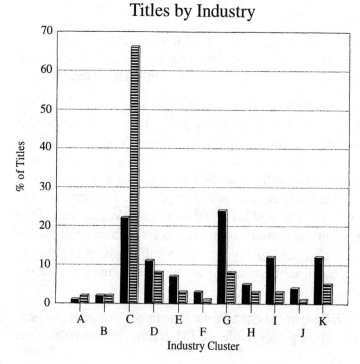

Titles by Industry

Matter, and Services), and OES (Occupational Employment Statistics) codes. These code numbers are available in computerized form from the North Carolina Occupational Analysis Field Center, and appear in printed form in *The Worker Traits Data Book* compiled by Don Mayall and published by JIST in 1994. The *EGOE* is this first book to provide these codes in printed format along with each occupational description.

Instructions for analyzing jobs and explanations of the coding used in the revised fourth edition of the *DOT* was published by the DOL in *The Revised Handbook for Analyzing Jobs* in 1991. This volume includes accurate, updated descriptions of all of the coding systems used in the *EGOE*.

In summary, the *EGOE* brings together for the first time many informational elements that have been scattered in a bewildering array of books printed in various years. In this one volume you will find much of the occupational information that the DOL has painstakingly maintained for 40 years, in a format that can readily be used by people who need it.

Other Sources of Data

In addition to the information provided by the Department of Labor, this book contains information that has been developed by the authors and is not published anywhere else. This proprietary information includes the categories of education, English proficiency, salary, and outlook that are provided for each job listed in this book. To construct these measures, we used a variety of DOL and other governmental sources including:

- *Dictionary of Occupational Titles*
- *Occupational Outlook Handbook*
- *Guide for Occupational Exploration*
- *The Handbook for Analyzing Jobs*
- *Outlook 1992-2005* (DOL, 1992)
- *Standard Occupational Classification Manual* (U.S. Department of Commerce, 1977)
- *Standard Industrial Classification Manual* (Office of Management and Budget, 1987)

The OES (Occupational Employment Statistics) codes provided in this book were obtained from the Bureau of Labor Statistics. The OES codification system changed in 1990 and the new codes are included here. Until now, published lists of these codes had not been readily available.

In addition, we incorporated information from want ads, private industry surveys (like those done by Chambers of Commerce, etc.), and placement statistics from schools and colleges.

Perhaps the most useful additions are indicators for Salary and Outlook. Each occupation has a salary indicator, on a scale from 1 to 5, to let you know approximately how much you could expect to earn on that job. And each occupation has an outlook indicator to give you an estimate of how hard or easy it will be to find a job in this field. Other special information about the academic, physical, and stress-related demands of the occupations are also included.

Tips for Using the Book
without Counselor Assistance

The Enhanced Guide for Occupational Exploration is a unique and valuable book for vocational counselors as it provides the most often wanted information for most jobs in one location. It is arranged in such a way to make it a useful tool for exploring career and job search alternatives for individuals as well.

If you need help deciding what kind of work you should choose, you can use the *EGOE* to help you plan your career, identify jobs you qualify for, consider jobs requiring additional training or education, or move up within your organization or field. Your task is to find not just any job, but one you can do well and that will be satisfying to you.

To find the right kind of job for you, you need two types of information:

1. **Information about yourself.** You need to know the kind of work you would like to do and whether you are able to do such work. If you can't do it now, can you learn to do it through an educational or training program?

2. **Information about occupations that sound interesting to you.** What does the worker do on such jobs? What knowledge and skills must the worker have? What training is required?

The *EGOE* clusters occupations into major interest areas and work groups within each major interest area. These work groups are then further divided into subgroups of similar jobs with specific jobs then listed within each subgroup.

A rational and easy-to-use system of code numbers allows jobs to be organized and hence easy to find within this book. This system, developed by the U.S. Department of Labor, was used in the original *GOE* and retained for this book because of its practical value. Rather than trying to explore the impossibly large world of job options, this book allows you to identify those areas of work in which you have the strongest interest and, within the interest areas, those work groups that are most closely related to your interests, skills, aptitudes, education, training, and physical abilities.

The Enhanced Guide for Occupational Exploration helps you locate and learn about occupations that relate to your interests and abilities. When you use it properly, you will be better prepared to plan your career or seek employment. You will learn about many jobs, including some you never knew existed. Listed below is a logical approach to using the *EGOE*.

Step 1. Think About Your Interests

What kind of work would you most like to do? Did you know that all jobs have been organized into groups according to the interests of the workers?

Some workers like to help others. Some would rather work with their hands or tools. Others prefer artistic work, or writing, selling, clerical, or other types of work. The *EGOE* uses a system developed by the U.S. Department of Labor to organize all its jobs into 12 areas based on the interests of workers. Each of these 12 interest areas has been given a name, a code number, and a brief description. In order to learn more about the relationship of your interests to occupations, turn to the "Brief Definitions of the 12 Interest Areas" on page ix and read the titles and descriptions of each interest area. Select one or more that you would like to explore.

Step 2. Select One or More Work Groups to Explore

In order to know which work groups to explore, you need to decide whether you would find satisfaction in work activities such as those required by occupations in the group. To do this, turn to the "Summary List of Interest Areas, Work Groups, and Subgroups" on pages xi-xiii. Under each major interest area, notice that there are various clusters of jobs listed in bold letters. These are called work groups. Listed beneath each of these are even more specific subgroups of similar occupations.

As you identify work groups that you would like to learn more about, note the numbers listed next to each. You can use these numbers to learn more about each of these work groups. Simply look for the narrative descriptions in the occupational descriptions section. All descriptions are listed in numerical order within each interest area and work group. Each work group has a brief description of the types of jobs within that group. You can also find descriptions for each of the subgroups using the numbers provided in a similar way.

Many of the jobs listed in the interest areas you have selected may require knowledge and skills that you do not have or would have difficulty acquiring. There should be some occupations, however, that fit your interests and that you can do or can learn to do.

It may be helpful to note that the work groups within each interest area begin with those requiring higher levels of education, training, or experience. For example, in the Artistic interest area, Literary Arts (including Editing and Creative Writing) and Visual Arts (including Instructing and Studio Arts) are listed first, while the Modeling work group is listed last. This same arrangement is used in listing jobs within subgroups, making it easier to identify entry-level jobs.

Step 3. Explore the Work Groups You Selected

To explore a work group, look up its description and read it very carefully. As you read about a group, you may discover that it is not what you thought it would be and that you are not interested in it. Or you may find that the training or other requirements are more difficult than you want. As you discover this, drop this group from further consideration and go on to the next group.

In some cases, you could consider jobs that require substantial training or education as a long-term objective. Don't eliminate such a job if it is one that interests you. You may need to consider related or other jobs while you continue or return to school, gain experience, or get additional training.

Step 4. Explore Subgroups and Specific Occupations

Once you have learned more about the work groups and subgroups that interest you, look at the job descriptions that are listed within each category. Each work group contains occupations that have been organized into subgroups. Each subgroup is identified by a six-digit code and a title, plus a list of all the occupations assigned to it.

After you have studied a work group description and decided that you are interested in considering it further, you should examine its subgroup occupations to see if one or more of them appear to match your interests and qualifications better than the others. The various subgroups are also listed on pages xi through xiii of this book. Look over these subgroups carefully. Since the job descriptions in this book are arranged in order of their GOE numbers, the numbers accompanying the various subgroups will tell you where to find these jobs described.

Look over the job descriptions within that subgroup carefully and give particular attention to any that appear to most closely match your interests and qualifications.

Step 5. Create a Plan of Action

Once you have identified groups of jobs that interest you, you need to decide what to do next. Perhaps you can qualify for some of these jobs with your present qualifications, while others will require additional training, education, or experience.

Your next step may be clear to you. Perhaps your exploration has identified some jobs that you will begin looking for right away using your present qualifications. Or some other plan is obvious to you. But if you are still not sure about what you want to do, you can probably be helped by a vocational counselor or by a course or program designed for people who want assistance in career planning.

Many Schools may offer career planning assistance services to graduates. Most areas also have government-funded programs that provide these services, as do local colleges and universities. Look in the *Yellow Pages* of the phone book under "Career and Vocational Counseling" or ask your librarian for help in locating these resources.

Because the descriptions in this book are brief, you may want additional information on one or more of them before you make a decision on what to do. Longer descriptions for 250 of the most popular jobs can be found in the *Occupational Outlook Handbook*. This is a book published by the U.S. Department of Labor and available in most libraries and schools. Your librarian will also be able to help you find additional books, journals, magazine articles, and other information on many jobs. The library will also have a variety of books to help you find sources of training or education for many occupations.

You should also consider visiting with people who have the kinds of jobs that interest you to obtain firsthand information. School or vocational counselors will often be able to provide you with additional information on resources for deciding on job or training objectives as well. For important decisions such as career planning, it is difficult to have *too much* information.

Where the Jobs Are

The labor market has changed rapidly over the last decade and is projected to continue to change in the years to come. In some cases the changes have been dramatic, yet many people are not fully aware of how these changes affect them. For example, there are far more women in the workforce today and they tend to work for longer periods of time. And there are many millions of new workers that have been absorbed into the labor force. Many factors have also affected the types of jobs and the training required to handle them.

Jobs are constantly changing. Companies go out of business and new ones start. Plants close down and relocate in countries with lower salaries. New technology makes old ways of doing things obsolete.

While the labor force has expanded, the number of manufacturing jobs has actually declined. As a result, many relatively unskilled people have lost these jobs and have had a difficult time finding replacement jobs that pay as well. But many new manufacturing jobs have also been created, though they often require more training and education than the manufacturing jobs that have been lost.

Virtually all of the increase in our new jobs have been in the "service" economy in sectors such as medicine; business services; and technical, professional and managerial jobs. Many of these jobs pay well but require special training and advanced education.

Not all of the new jobs in the service sector require special training, but those that do not typically pay lower wages. For example, entry-level jobs in transportation, hotels, restaurants, entertainment, amusement parks, and recreation do not typically pay well. In some areas, there is a shortage of workers who are willing to work for low wages, so older people, those with little education or education deficits, people that don't speak English well, and people with disabilities are finding jobs more easily. For some people who work hard and accept responsibility in these jobs, it is possible to move up into jobs that pay well, or start their own business.

Also included in the service industry are medical services such as hospitals, clinics, homes for the elderly, and drug rehabilitation centers. Medical and social services are growing rapidly due to improvements in medical services and because modern medicine is able to keep people alive longer. Jobs in this industry range from janitors and orderlies to nurses and counselors to doctors and hospital administrators. This industry offers a variety of salaries, training requirements, and responsibility levels.

Business services of all kinds are another service sector that is growing rapidly. These jobs include banking, accounting, insurance, and data processing. Many of the new jobs in business require using a computer or professional skills. Many of these jobs require good academic skills and special training and pay quite well. People who can type accurately and use correct English can usually find clerical jobs quite easily. Clerical salaries are typically lower than salaries in manufacturing, but there is opportunity for moving up and good skills are rewarded with higher salaries.

Another area of rapid growth is retail trade. The number of stores is growing fast. Clerks, salespeople, and managers are needed for these businesses. Starting salaries tend to be low. People who work hard and accept responsibility for their department or other employees may be promoted fairly quickly into jobs with good salaries.

For people who want higher salaries, opportunities are good for managers, technicians, and information processors. People who are dependable, willing to work long hours, and able to convince others to work hard, are always in demand for promotion to management positions. People who can understand machines (computers, sophisticated measurement devices, office machines, telephones, etc.) and design, program, or repair them can earn excellent wages. People who have the ability to read and understand information, to recognize and summarize important information, and to write or speak clearly can find a variety of jobs, from trainers to technical writers to graphic artists. All of these areas are growing quickly.

It seems clear that people in today's labor market can benefit from special training more than ever before. There is a clear relationship between earnings and the amount of training and education you have. Career planning has become an essential survival skill in the new economy and the *EGOE* can help you explore career alternatives that use your skills and experiences to their best effect. It can help you identify jobs that use the skills you already have or help you more clearly define a long-term objective to prepare for a career that is both interesting and rewarding.

Using the *EGOE* Codes Key

On the next page you will find a summary of the codes used for each of the occupations described in the *EGOE*. It is a handy reference sheet to help you interpret the various codes used in the occupational descriptions. Please feel free to photocopy it for use with this book. Each of the codes will be described in more detail in chapter 2.

Code Abbreviations Key

GED   General Educational Development
R   Reasoning Development
6 = Using abstract concepts, symbols (formulas, musical notes, etc.), or scientific theories to solve problems.
5 = Defining problems, collecting data, and drawing conclusions about abstract and concrete problems.
4 = Interpreting instructions. Using logic to solve concrete problems.
3 = Using common sense while following instructions. Solving problems by trying solutions that worked before.
2 = Following detailed instructions. Choosing the right solution to problems based on rules.
1 = Following one- or two-step instructions. Dealing with problems when they fit simple rules.

M   Mathematical Development
6 = Advanced calculus, modern algebra, or statistics
5 = Linear algebra, calculus, or statistics
4 = Algebra, geometry, or shop math
3 = Business math, simple algebra, or simple geometry
2 = Multiplying, dividing, fractions, or reading graphs
1 = Adding, subtracting, making change, or measuring

L   Language Development
6 = Creating literature or technical reports, or teaching or supervising those who do.
5 = Understanding and enjoying literature or poetry, or making speeches.
4 = Reading novels or manuals, writing business letters, or speaking in panel discussions.
3 = Reading novels or rules, writing reports with proper grammar, or speaking correctly in public.
2 = Reading instructions and using the dictionary, cursive writing, or speaking clearly.
1 = Reading slowly, printing, or speaking simply.

SVP   Specific Vocational Preparation

9 = Over 10 years	4 = 3 to 6 months
8 = 4 to 10 years	3 = 1 to 3 months
7 = 2 to 4 years	2 = Up to 30 days
6 = 1 to 2 years	1 = Short demonstration only
5 = 6 months to 1 year	

Academic Demands
Ed   Educational Requirements
M = Master's degree or above
B = Bachelor's degree
A = Associate degree or apprenticeship
H = High school Diploma or GED
N = No diploma

Eng   English Proficiency
G = Understanding English grammar
S = Simple communication in English
N = No communication in English

Work Fields: See Appendix H

MPSMS: See Appendix G

Temperaments
D = Directing or supervising others
R = Doing repetitive work
S = Working under stress
I = Influencing or persuading others
T = Doing precise work, to close tolerances
J = Making judgments and decisions
V = Changing tasks often, varied duties
P = Working with people
U = Working under specific instructions
A = Working alone or apart from others
E = Expressing feelings

Aptitudes
Scale: 1 = Top 10%   4 = Lower 33%
          2 = Top 33%   5 = Lower 10%
          3 = Middle 33%

G = **General learning ability.** Catching on to things quickly. Understanding instructions easily. Closely related to doing well in school.
V = **Verbal aptitude.** Understanding the meaning of words and using them effectively. Understanding what others say to you. Knowing how to use grammar and write properly.
N = **Numerical aptitude.** Understanding numbers and doing arithmetic quickly and accurately.
S = **Spatial aptitude.** Understanding drawings or visualizing plans.
P = **Form perception.** Seeing slight differences in shapes and objects.
Q = **Clerical perception.** Proof-reading: finding errors in words or numbers.
K = **Motor coordination.** Moving quickly and accurately when you see something happen.
F = **Finger dexterity.** Moving fingers and working with small things quickly and accurately.
M = **Manual dexterity.** Moving hands quickly and accurately. Placing and turning things.
E = **Eye-hand-foot coordination.** Moving limbs accurately when you see something happen.
C = **Color discrimination.** Seeing differences in colors and shades.

Physical Demands
Stg   Strength
V =   Very Heavy (no restrictions)
H =   Heavy (100 pounds maximum)
M =   Medium (50 pounds maximum)
L =   Light (20 pounds maximum)
S =   Sedentary (10 pounds maximum)

Scale: Constantly   Occasionally   Frequently   Never

C =	Climbing	T =	Talking
B =	Balancing	G =	Hearing
S =	Stooping	M =	Tasting/Smelling
K =	Kneeling	N =	Near Acuity
O =	Crouching	F =	Far Acuity
W =	Crawling	D =	Depth Perception
R =	Reaching	A =	Accommodation
H =	Handling	X =	Color Vision
I =	Fingering	V =	Field of Vision
E =	Feeling		

Work Environment
Noise
V =   Very Loud   Q =   Quiet
L =   Loud   VQ = Very Quiet
N =   Normal

Scale: Constantly   Occasionally   Frequently   Never

W = Exposure to weather	E = Exposure to electrical shock
C = Extreme cold parts	D = Working in high, exposed places
H = Extreme heat	R = Exposure to radiation
U = Wet and/or humid	X = Working with explosives
V = Vibration	T = Exposure to toxic or caustic
A = Atmospheric conditions	chemicals
M = Proximity to moving,	O = Other hazards
mechanical parts	

Salary (in 1995)
1 = Below $14,000 per year   3 = $17,000 to $20,999 per year
2 = $14,000 to $16,999 per year   4 = $21,000 to $27,999 per year
                5 = $28,000 per year and above

Outlook: Time needed to find a job (on an average)
1 = Over a year   2 = 3 months to a year   3 = 1 to 2 months
                4 = About 2 weeks   5 = A few days

Chapter 2
Detailed Information on the Narrative and Codes Used in the Occupational Descriptions

This chapter provides detailed information on the various codes used in the occupations described in this book. Some of the codes may be of limited use to you but of great importance to others. For this reason, pay more attention to understanding the codes of greatest interest to you.

We have attempted to provide a nontechnical review of the structure, terms, and codes used in this book and believe that this is enough to satisfy most users. To obtain a more technical understanding of the many complex issues incorporated into the various codification systems covered will require additional reading and we will refer you to additional sources as appropriate.

As you read the material in this chapter, it will be helpful to refer to a sample occupational description. An annotated sample description is on page 3, although any description found in this book will have similar elements. Each element of the descriptions will be covered in the material that follows. As you will soon discover, the descriptions provide a substantial amount of information in coded form. You will find it less overwhelming if you pay the most attention to the information of most importance to you. And keep in mind that the one-page *EGOE* occupational Code Abbreviations Key at the end of chapter 1 will help you remember what the various codes mean.

The Narrative Section of the Occupational Descriptions

The narrative section of each job description is based on the descriptions used in the *Dictionary of Occupational Titles* (*DOT*), published by the U.S. Department of Labor. This section reviews the narrative section only, other elements are covered later in this chapter.

The Lead Statement: Each narrative description opens with a "lead statement" as the first sentence following the alternative titles (if any) and is followed by a colon (:). This lead statement summarizes the entire occupation. It offers essential information such as:

- worker actions
- the objective or purpose of worker actions
- machines, tools, equipment, or work aids used by the worker
- materials used, products made, subject matter dealt with, or services rendered
- instructions followed or judgments made

Task Element Statements: Following the lead statement are task element statements indicating the specific tasks the worker performs to accomplish the overall job purpose described in the lead statement. These statements indicate how the worker actually carries out his or her duties.

"May" Items: Many definitions contain one or more sentences beginning with the word "May." They describe duties required of workers in this occupation in some establishments but not in others. The word "may" does *not* indicate that a worker will sometimes perform this task, but rather some workers in different establishments generally perform one or more of the varied tasks listed.

Should you wish to know more about how the narrative descriptions are devised, you can find additional details in the *Dictionary of Occupational Titles*.

Detailed Descriptions of the Data Categories and Codes

This section describes the nonnarrative component of each job description. This will provide sufficient information to satisfy most users in interpreting the occupational descriptions. If you wish to obtain additional and more detailed information on the source and meanings of the codes used in classifying jobs, you will need to refer to other reference materials. Many of the codes are described in more detail in *The Revised Handbook for Analyzing Jobs* published by the U.S. Department of Labor. This and other references will be mentioned as appropriate.

You should also note that, while every precaution has been taken to assure the accuracy of the data used in this book, some errors may exist. Local conditions may vary substantially from the national information used in the descriptions. There are also often significant differences in the duties and requirements for jobs with the same titles found in different organizations. For these and other reasons, the occupational descriptions and the data they contain should only be considered guidelines in making any decision. The information in the rest of this chapter will help you interpret the data categories and codes used in each occupational description.

Industry Designation:

Following the occupational title in each description is an industry name in parentheses. Think of this as part of the title. You will sometimes see the same title used in more than one occupation and with different definitions. This is not an error since different industries often require different tasks, even though it may use the same job title.

We decided to include abbreviated industry names in the occupational descriptions rather than the less readily understood numeric codes. Each occupation has up to four industries listed, indicating the industries where the occupation is most often (but not always) found. The industry designation system is the same as that used in the *DOT* and other Department of Labor publications. In cases where an occupation is found in many industries, the industry is assigned a cross-industry designation. For example, clerical occupations are found in most industries, so a broad "clerical" designation is used for these jobs. Other cross-industry designations include "professional and kindred" and "any industry."

In Appendix B you will find two lists of industries. The first list is an alphabetical listing of industries along with their related abbreviations as used in this book. The second list organizes each industry within clusters of related industries and provides the DOL industry designation code for use in cross-referencing other career information systems.

DOT (*Dictionary of Occupational Titles*) Code:

The U.S. Department of Labor (DOL) has done extensive research into the types of jobs in the U.S. economy. They have described more than 12,000 different jobs and identified more than 20,000 job titles (the difference in numbers is because some of the jobs have alternative names). Several classification systems have been used to organize these jobs into some rational order. One of the systems used by the DOL assigns a unique number to each job. This number is called the *DOT* number because it is the major classification system used in the *Dictionary of Occupational Titles* (*DOT*), published by the Department of Labor. The *DOT* number is often used for cross-referencing jobs in most career information systems.

Besides this use, the number also provides substantial information on the occupation it refers to. Each *DOT* number consists of nine digits such as 132.037-022 (for the job titled "EDITOR, PUBLICATIONS"). The first three numbers refer to that occupation's major occupational category (the first digit), division (the second digit), and group (the third digit). Because this classification system is not followed in the *EGOE*, we have not provided additional details on this part of the *DOT* code number. Details are described in the *DOT* itself.

The *DOT* number's fourth through sixth digits refer to skills required for the job in relation to data, people, and things. Because of the value of this information, we have provided additional information here to help you interpret the meaning of this part of the *DOT* code number.

The last three numbers are simply a unique number given to each job within a group and are assigned sequentially.

Definitions of Data, People, and Things Skills

The middle three digits of the *DOT* number refer to the highest level of skill required in that job in relation to data, to people, and to things. The lower the number, the higher the level of skill required. By analyzing these numbers, you can determine the highest level of skill required for each of the jobs listed in this book.

Knowing what skills the job requires is useful information. It can help you identify jobs that require the skills you already have or want to develop. Appendix E arranges the 2,800 jobs described in this book into various combinations of skills required to do that job. This can be very helpful, especially if you are looking for jobs in unfamiliar fields requiring skills you have used in the past. Following are the definitions for the various skills and their related numbers as used in the *DOT* numbering system.

Data (high = 0, low = 6)

This refers to the fourth digit in the *DOT* code number.

0 = Synthesizing: Putting ideas and facts together in new ways to explain how things work. Developing new ideas and theories.

1 = Coordinating: Organizing things. Planning projects. Deciding in which order things must be done. Checking to be sure the steps are done on time and correctly.

2 = Analyzing: Studying information to find out what it means. Deciding what could be done to solve a problem.

3 = Compiling: Collecting, arranging, or combining facts about data, people, or things and reporting the results.

4 = Computing: Using arithmetic. Reporting the results or following instructions based on the results.

5 = Copying: Writing, listing, or entering numbers or letters exactly as seen.

6 = Comparing: Deciding if data, people, or things are alike or different. Using rules to decide how different they are.

People (high = 0, low = 8)

This refers the fifth digit in the *DOT* code number.

0 = Mentoring: Helping people deal with problems. May give legal, scientific, clinical, spiritual, or other professional advice.

1 = Negotiating: Talking over ideas, information, and opinions with others until all agree on solutions.

2 = Instructing: Teaching people (or animals) by explaining, showing, or watching them practice. Giving advice on a topic that you know a great deal about.

3 = Supervising: Directing workers by giving orders and explaining duties. Making sure they do the work on time. Helping everyone work together.

4 = Diverting: Amusing others. Saying or doing things that people find interesting. May work on a stage, radio, TV, or movie.

5 = Persuading: Winning others over to a product, service, or point of view.

6 = Speaking-Signaling: Talking or making motions so people can understand you and getting an answer from them. Telling people what to do in a way that they understand.

7 = Serving: Helping people or animals. Carrying out their wants or wishes right away.

8 = Taking Instructions-Helping: Doing what you are told. Following orders without deciding if they are right or wrong.

Things (high = 0, low = 7)

This refers to the sixth digit in the *DOT* code number.

0 = Setting Up: Changing parts on machines so they can do different tasks. Fixing them if they break down. Knowing how to operate several different machines.

1 = Precision Working: Being responsible for making things that fit exact rules or standards. Deciding which tools or materials to use to make them correctly.

2 = Operating-Controlling: Starting, stopping, and watching machines or equipment to be sure they are doing the right thing. Watching gages, dials, etc. and changing valves or controls as needed.

3 = Driving-Operating: Steering or guiding machines or tools. Estimating distance, speed, and direction.

4 = Manipulating: Moving, guiding, placing, or working things using your body or tools. Selecting tools, objects, or materials.

5 = Tending: Starting, stopping, and watching machines work. Watching timers or gages. Making changes based on rules.

6 = Feeding-Offbearing: Filling up or emptying machines which are running automatically or run by other workers.

7 = Handling: Moving or carrying things.

The OES (Occupational Employment Statistics) Code:

The Bureau of Labor Statistics, a part of the U.S. Department of Labor, publishes Occupational Employment Statistics (OES). Data is collected from a variety of sources, including the census, public employment agencies, and other surveys. Experts study past and present employment data, as well as economic trends, and prepare "projections"—expected numbers of workers needed for each occupation during the next 10 to 15 years. Current numbers of workers and projections of future employment are published for each of about 500 OES categories.

This code number explains in which OES category the occupation belongs. You can use it to find information about the size of the occupation and salaries in government reports. These reports are updated annually (or more often) by the branch of your state government which serves unemployed people. In general, these agencies are called employment security offices, but in each state they have a different name. If you ask at these offices, you can obtain current information about salaries and outlook for the OES occupational groups. Refer to Appendix F for a complete list of the OES codes in numerical order along with their related occupational category.

The GED (General Educational Development) Code:

The GED code refers to education of a general nature which does not have a specific occupational objective. Ordinarily, such education is obtained in elementary school, high school, or college, but it can also be obtained through self-study and experience. The codes used in the occupational descriptions refer to the "General Educational Development" required to handle this job in Reasoning (R), Math (M), and Language (L). Additional information on this code system can be found in the *Handbook for Analyzing Jobs*. Use the following information to interpret the numeric codes used for each of these three major categories.

Reasoning Development (high = 6, low = 1)

Level 6 = Using abstract concepts, symbols (formulas, musical notes, etc.), and scientific theories to solve problems.

Level 5 = Defining problems, collecting data, and drawing conclusions about all kinds of problems.

Level 4 = Interpreting instructions. Using logic to solve concrete problems.

Level 3 = Using common sense while following instructions. Solving problems by trying solutions that have worked before.

Level 2 = Following detailed instructions. Choosing the right solution to problems based on rules.

Level 1 = Following one- or two-step instructions. Dealing with problems when they fit simple rules.

Mathematical Development (high = 6, low = 1)

Level 6 = Using advanced calculus, modern algebra, or statistics.

Level 5 = Using linear algebra, calculus, or statistics.

Level 4 = Using algebra, geometry, or shop math.

Level 3 = Using business math, simple algebra, or simple geometry.

Level 2 = Multiplying, dividing, using fractions, or reading graphs.

Level 1 = Adding, subtracting, making change, or measuring.

Language Development (high = 6, low = 1)

Level 6 = Creating literature or technical reports, or teaching or supervising those who do.

Level 5 = Understanding and enjoying literature or poetry, or making speeches.

Level 4 = Reading novels or manuals, writing summaries or business letters, or speaking before an audience as part of a group.

Level 3 = Reading novels or rules, writing reports with proper grammar, or speaking correctly in public.

Level 2 = Reading instructions and using the dictionary, writing with proper punctuation, or speaking clearly.

Level 1 = Reading up to 2,500 words, printing simple sentences, or speaking using normal correct order.

The SVP (Specific Vocational Preparation) Code:

SVP stands for "Specific Vocational Preparation" and refers to the time required to learn the techniques, acquire the information, and develop the facility needed for average performance in a specific job. The training may be acquired in a school; on the job; or in a military, institutional, or vocational environment. Additional information on this code system can be found in the *Handbook for Analyzing Jobs.*

The SVP code is a bit confusing for most people. It does not indicate how many years it will take you to reach the job. Instead, it tells you how long you would have to train if you were to receive the training without pausing to work. Since many jobs can only be reached by on-the-job experience (managers, for example) it is hard to determine how much time it would take for the training if you never stopped to work. Consider, for example, the difference between a two-year associate's degree and an apprenticeship. It is generally assumed that one year of college is equal to two years of apprenticeship, since apprentices spend a lot of time working between the learning experiences.

Use the SVP coding system to compare the amount of training needed between two different jobs. You should be more careful in using it to determine how much education is required. Some of your prior training may help you to qualify for the job faster. Or you may need to slow down and practice the skills you are learning before you complete the training. So these codes may not apply directly to you. But they will help you to determine which jobs require a lot of training and which jobs can be entered with very little training.

The SVP codes used in this book are as follows:

Specific Vocational Preparation (SVP) (high = 9, low = 1)

9 = Over 10 years

8 = Over 4 years up to 10 years

7 = Over 2 years up to 4 years

6 = Over 1 year up to 2 years

5 = Over 6 months up to 1 year

4 = Over 3 months up to 6 months

3 = Over 30 days up to 3 months

2 = Beyond a short demonstration up to 30 days

1 = Short demonstration only

Academic Codes (Ed and Eng):

The "Ed" (Educational Degree or Certification) Code:

The academic code has two components. The first component, "Ed," refers to the educational degree or certification typically required for entry into this occupation. In some fields the educational requirements are clearly defined, while in others they are ambiguous. For example, a movie producer usually has a college education, but a talented individual without this education would be accepted into this field. Thus, the minimum educational level for this occupation is much lower than the average education level. The education code indicates the minimum education accepted for entry into this type of work. If you do not have the educational background necessary for a particular job and lack the time, preparation, ability, temperament, or other resources needed to get that education, then this job will not be available to you.

There is no single satisfactory source of data on the educational requirements of occupations. In many cases the education required is a direct function of the level of difficulty and complexity of the work and is closely related to the General Educational Development (GED) factors in the *DOT* database. In other cases, educational attainment such as receipt of a high school diploma, college degree, or completion of an apprenticeship or certificate program is often used as screening criteria in government agencies and large private enterprises—and there is no close relationship between educational attainment and complexity of the job.

Educational codes used in this book are based on data in the *Occupational Outlook Handbook* (published by the DOL), newspaper want ads, civil service job announcements, and similar sources for all occupations where such information was available. The remaining occupations were then coded based upon GED levels. Adjustments to this coding were made for occupations in which screening requirements were known to be a significant factor such as appriceable skilled trades, white-collar clerical jobs in certain industries, health and social service jobs, and technical jobs in fields with certificate training programs.

The "Ed" Codes used in this book are as follows:

M = Master's degree or above: A Master of Arts, Master of Science, Ph.D., Ed.D., MD, DDS, or other similar professional degree based upon collegiate education beyond the four-year bachelor's degree is required.

B = Bachelor's degree: A Bachelor of Arts or a Bachelor of Science or similar four-year college degree is required.

A = Associate degree or apprenticeship: An Associate of Arts or Sciences or completion of a certificate program at a postsecondary collegiate institution or completion of a formal apprenticeship program is required.

H = High school diploma or GED: A high school diploma or the equivalent is required. Postsecondary or technical school courses of less than two years duration may also be required.

N = No diploma: While a high school diploma is very useful in getting any job, some occupations do not actually require a high school diploma or GED.

The "Eng" (English Language Proficiency) Code:

The "Eng" code is another characteristic that is coded within the academic code section of each job description.

Many jobs require knowledge of and proficiency in the English language. For example, you must be fluent in English to answer correspondence, understand instructions, contracts, or specifications written in English. You must be fluent in English to respond to inquiries from the public, or to explain things to others where English is normally spoken. In some jobs there is no substantial need for language proficiency. These are situations where work routines can be picked up through observation, where instructions are available in other languages, or coworkers are available to translate instructions. In other jobs, training obtained in another language (in another country) may be effectively used in this country.

The occupations in this book were coded on the level of English proficiency required by using the DOL database indicators on levels of language development, the relationship with the People Worker Function, the Dealing with People temperament, and the description of the occupation.

The "Eng" Codes used are as follows:

G = **Understanding English Grammar:** Knows English grammar and vocabulary of over 5,000 words; can understand and communicate using nontechnical written or spoken English. Examples include most professional, clerical, and sales representative jobs.

S = **Simple Communication in English:** Knows enough English words and phrases to respond to simple communications in English from coworkers or the public. Examples include sales clerk, taxi driver, and carpenters with limited amounts of public contact.

N = **No Communication in English:** While speaking English is always useful in getting a job, there are some jobs that can be done effectively without English proficiency at either of the two previous levels.

The Work Field Code:

This is a numeric code referring to groups of occupations clustered together based on similar technology, related skills, and overall socioeconomic objective. Although every job requires many different skills, the skills within a work field tend to be quite specific and relate very closely to the occupation. They are usually not easily "transferable" to other work fields and are often used only in a small number of occupations.

There are 96 work fields and all the jobs in the economy have been classified into one or more of them. Each work field has a title, definition, and three-digit code number. The work fields are also organized into groups on the basis of similar overall objectives. Additional information on this code system can be found in the *Handbook for Analyzing Jobs*.

The work fields are arranged numerically in Appendix H. These are also available in *The Revised Handbook for Analyzing Jobs*.

The MPSMS (Materials, Products, Subject Matter, and Services) Code:

This category answers the question "What do you do it with?" This includes: (a) basic materials being processed, such as fabric, metal, or wood; (b) final products being made, such as automobiles or baskets; (c) data, when being dealt with or applied, such as insurance or physics; and (d) services, such as barbering or dentistry.

This system of codes consists of 334 categories organized into 48 groups, each designated by a three-digit code. A code ending in 9 designates a "Not Elsewhere Classified" (N.E.C.) category. Additional information on this code system can be found in *The Revised Handbook for Analyzing Jobs*.

The MPSMS code list is provided in Appendix G and contains a complete listing of the MPSMS codes in numerical order.

The Aptitudes Codes:

These codes refer to aptitudes required in General Learning Ability (G), Verbal Aptitude (V), Numerical Aptitude (N), Spatial Aptitude (S), Form Perception (P), Clerical Perception (Q), Motor Coordination (K), Finger Dexterity (F), Manual Dexterity (M), Eye-Hand-Foot Coordination (E) and Color Discrimination (C).

Aptitudes are defined as the specific capacities or abilities required of an individual in order to facilitate the learning of some task or job duty. Aptitudes are often measured through the administration of tests such as the GATB (General Aptitude Test Battery), administered under the direction of the U.S. Employment Service. Various studies have been conducted to determine the level of aptitudes to assure success in various jobs. Additional information on this code system can be found in the *Handbook for Analyzing Jobs*.

Following is information needed to interpret this code in the occupational descriptions. The following scale applies to all aptitudes:

Aptitude Codes (high = 1, low = 5)

1 = The top 10 percent of the population. This segment of the population possesses an extremely high degree of the aptitude.

2 = The highest third exclusive of the top 10 percent of the population. This segment of the population possesses an above average or high degree of the aptitude.

3 = The middle third of the population. This segment of the population possesses a medium degree of the aptitude, ranging from slightly below to slightly above average.

4 = The lowest third exclusive of the bottom 10 percent of the population. This segment of the population possesses a below average or low degree of the aptitude.

5 = The lowest 10 percent of the population. This segment of the population possesses a negligible degree of the aptitude.

Definitions of the Aptitudes

G = General Learning Ability: Catching on to things quickly. Understanding instructions easily. Reasoning and making judgments. (Closely related to doing well in school.)

V = Verbal Aptitude: Understanding the meaning of words and using them effectively. Understanding what others say to you. Knowing how to use grammar and write properly.

N = Numerical Aptitude: Understanding numbers and doing arithmetic quickly and accurately.

S = Spatial Aptitude: Understanding drawings or visualizing plans. (Used in such tasks as blueprint reading and in solving geometry problems.)

P = Form Perception: Seeing slight differences in shapes and objects. Noticing differences in shapes, widths, or lengths.

Q = Clerical Perception: Proof-reading—finding errors in words or numbers quickly.

K = Motor Coordination: Moving quickly and accurately when you see something happen.

F = Finger Dexterity: Moving fingers and working with small things quickly and accurately.

M = Manual Dexterity: Moving hands quickly and accurately. Placing and turning things.

E = Eye-Hand-Foot Coordination: Moving hands and feet accurately when you see something happen.

C = Color Discrimination: Seeing slight differences in colors or shades. Knowing when colors match or contrast.

The Temperaments Codes:

Temperaments are defined as the adaptability requirements placed on the worker by specific types of job-worker situations. Often described as "personality requirements," many employers specify which of these traits they do or do not want in a person they hire. They is often predictors of employee success in the job since many job failures are more the result of an inability to adjust to a work situation than to an inability to do the required tasks.

The occupational descriptions include one or more of the following letter codes if that temperament is important to have in the occupation described. If one or more of the codes are missing from a given occupational description, that temperament is not considered as important to have for that occupation.

D =   **DIRECTING, Controlling, or Planning Activities of Others:** Taking responsibility for telling others what to do or planning their tasks (not your own work). Making rules and decisions that others must follow.

R =   **Performing REPETITIVE or Short-Cycle Work:** Doing the same task or following the same steps over again many times each day.

I =   **INFLUENCING People in Their Opinions, Attitudes, and Judgments:** Getting them to do the things you want them to do.

V =   **Performing a VARIETY of Duties:** Being able to change tasks quickly. Doing many different types of work during a day.

E =   **EXPRESSING Personal Feelings:** Creating art or criticizing the art of others. Using imagination and creativity.

A =   **Working ALONE or Apart in Physical Isolation from Others:** For long periods of time you don't see other people face-to-face.

S =   **Working Effectively under STRESS:** Working under stress caused by emergencies, danger, or criticism. Working very fast or concentrating very hard.

T =   **Attaining Precise Set Limits, TOLERANCES, and Standards:** Being very precise in making things, doing arithmetic, recording data, or inspecting things.

U =   **Working UNDER Specific Instructions:** There is little or no room for independent action or judgment.

P =   **Dealing with PEOPLE:** Working together with others or helping them (more than just giving or receiving instructions).

J =   **Making JUDGMENTS and Decisions:** Making decisions based on what you see, hear, smell, or touch.

The Physical Requirements Codes:

These codes refer to job requirements for strength and other physical demands of a particular job.

Strength Codes

The physical demands rating for strength reflects the estimated overall strength requirement of the job, expressed using the first letter corresponding to the particular strength rating. It represents the strength requirements that are considered to be important for average, successful work performance.

The strength rating is expressed by one of five terms: Sedentary (S), Light (L), Medium (M), Heavy (H), and Very Heavy (V). In order to determine the overall rating, an evaluation is made of the worker's involvement in the following activities:

a. Standing, Walking, Sitting

Standing: Remaining on one's feet in an upright position at a work station without moving about.

Walking: Moving about on foot.

Sitting: Remaining in a seated position.

b. Lifting, Carrying, Pushing, Pulling

Lifting: Raising or lowering an object from one level to another (includes upward pulling).

Carrying: Transporting an object, usually holding it in the hands or arms, or on the shoulder.

Pushing: Exerting force upon an object so that the object moves away from the force (includes slapping, striking, kicking, and treadle actions).

Pulling: Exerting force upon an object so that the object moves toward the force (includes jerking).

Lifting, pushing, and pulling are evaluated in terms of both intensity and duration. Consideration is given to the weight handled, position of the worker's body, and the aid given by helpers or mechanical equipment. Carrying is most often evaluated in terms of duration, weight carried, and distance carried.

Estimating the strength factor rating for an occupation requires the exercise of care on the part of occupational analysts in evaluating the force and physical effort a worker must exert. For instance, if the worker is in a crouching position, it may be much more difficult to push an object than if pushed at waist height. Also, if the worker is required to lift and carry continuously or push and pull objects over long distances, the worker may exert as much physical effort as is required to similarly move objects twice as heavy, but less frequently and/or over shorter distances.

c. Controls

Controls entail the use of one or both arms or hands (hand/arm) and/or one or both feet or legs (foot/leg) to move controls on machinery or equipment. Controls include but are not limited to: buttons, knobs, pedals, levers, and cranks.

Strength (Stg) Ratings Codes

Following are descriptions of the five terms in which the strength factor is expressed:

S = Sedentary Work: Exerting up to 10 pounds of force occasionally (occasionally: activity or condition exists up to one-third of the time) and/or a negligible amount of force frequently (frequently: activity or condition exists from one-third to two-thirds of the time) to lift, carry, push, pull, or otherwise move objects, including the human body. Sedentary work involves sitting most of the time, but may involve walking or standing for brief periods of time. Jobs are sedentary if walking and standing are required only occasionally and all other sedentary criteria are met.

L = Light Work: Exerting up to 20 pounds of force occasionally, and/or up to 10 pounds of force frequently, and/or a negligible amount of force constantly (constantly: activity or condition exists two-thirds or more of the time) to move objects. Physical demand requirements are in excess of those for Sedentary Work. Even though the weight lifted may be only a negligible amount, a job should be rated Light Work: (1) when it requires walking or standing to a significant degree; or (2) when it requires sitting most of the time but entails pushing and/or pulling of arm or leg controls; and/or (3) when the job requires working at a production rate pace entailing the constant pushing and/or pulling of materials even though the weight of those materials is negligible.

Note: The constant stress and strain of maintaining a production rate pace, especially in an industrial setting, can be and is physically demanding of a worker even though the amount of force exerted is negligible.

M = Medium Work: Exerting 20 to 50 pounds of force occasionally, and/or 10 to 25 pounds of force frequently, and/or greater than negligible up to 10 pounds of force constantly to move objects. Physical demand requirements are in excess of those for Light Work.

H = Heavy Work: Exerting 50 to 100 pounds of force occasionally, and/or 25 to 50 pounds of force frequently, and/or 10 to 20 pounds of force constantly to move objects. Physical demand requirements are in excess of those for Medium Work.

V = Very Heavy Work: Exerting in excess of 100 pounds of force occasionally, and/or in excess of 50 pounds of force frequently, and/or in excess of 20 pounds of force constantly to move objects. Physical demand requirements are in excess of those for Heavy Work.

Other Physical Demands Ratings Codes

All other physical demand factors are coded to represent the presence and frequency of the requirement in the work situation as follows:

Const = Continuously Condition exists two-thirds or more of the time
Freq = Frequently Condition exists from one-third to two-thirds of the time
Occas = Occasionally Condition exists up to one-third of the time
Never Condition does not exist or is rarely needed

Following are the other physical demand factors. If a code letter is not shown for an *EGOE* title, then that requirement never occurs for that occupation.

C = Climbing: Ascending or descending ladders, stairs, scaffolding, ramps, poles, and the like, using feet and legs or hands and arms. Body agility is emphasized.

B = Balancing: Maintaining body equilibrium to prevent falling when walking, standing, crouching; or running on narrow, slippery, or erratically moving surfaces; or maintaining body equilibrium when performing gymnastic feats.

S = Stooping: Bending body downward and forward by bending spine at the waist, requiring full use of the lower extremities and back muscles.

K = Kneeling: Bending legs at knees to rest on knee or knees.

O = Crouching: Bending body downward and forward by bending legs and spine.

W = Crawling: Moving about on hands and knees or hands and feet.

R = Reaching: Extending hand(s) and arm(s) in any direction.

H = Handling: Seizing, holding, grasping, turning or otherwise working with hand or hands. Fingers are involved only to the extent that they are an extension of the hand, such as to turn a switch or shift automatics gears.

I = Fingering: Picking, pinching, or otherwise working primarily with fingers rather than with the whole hand or arm as in handling.

E = Feeling: Perceiving attributes of objects, such as size, shape, temperature, or texture, by touching with skin, particularly that of fingertips.

T = Talking: Expressing or exchanging ideas by means of the spoken word to impart oral information to clients or to the public and to convey detailed spoken instructions to other workers accurately, loudly, or quickly.

G = Hearing: Perceiving the nature of sounds by ear.

M = Tasting/Smelling: Distinguishing, with a degree of accuracy, differences or similarities in intensity or quality of flavors or odors, or recognizing particular flavors or odors, using tongue or nose.

N = **Near Acuity:** Clarity of vision at 20 inches or less.

F = **Far Acuity:** Clarity of vision at 20 feet or more.

D = **Depth Perception:** Three-dimensional vision. Ability to judge distances and spatial relationships so as to see objects where and as they actually are.

A = **Accommodation:** Adjustment of lens of eye to bring an object into sharp focus. This factor is required when doing near point work at varying distances from the eye.

X = **Color Vision:** Ability to identify and distinguish colors.

V = **Field of Vision:** Observing an area that can be seen up and down or to the right or left while eyes are fixed on a given point.

The Work Environment Code:

These codes provide information on the types of work environments that are found in a given job and must be accepted by the worker.

Noise Intensity Level (Noise)

The noise intensity level to which the worker is exposed in the job environment. This factor is expressed by one of five levels:

VQ = Very Quiet

Q = Quiet

N = Moderate

L = Loud

V = Very Loud

Other Work Environment Codes

All other environmental condition factors are coded to indicate the presence and frequency of the condition in the work situation as follows:

Const = Continuously   Condition exists two-thirds or more of the time

Freq = Frequently   Condition exists from one-third to two-thirds of the time

Occas = Occasionally   Condition exists up to one-third of the time

Never   Condition does not exist or is rarely needed

Following are the other work environment factors. If a code letter is not shown for an *EGOE* title, then that activity never occurs for that occupation.

W = **Exposure to Weather:** Exposure to outside atmospheric conditions.

C = **Extreme Cold:** Exposure to nonweather-related cold temperatures.

H = **Extreme Heat:** Exposure to nonweather-related hot temperatures.

U = **Wet and/or Humid:** Contact with water or other liquids or exposure to nonweather-related humid conditions.

V = **Vibration:** Exposure to a shaking object or surface.

A = **Atmospheric Conditions:** Exposure to conditions such as fumes, noxious odors, dusts, mists, gases, and poor ventilation, that affect the respiratory system, eyes, or skin.

M = **Proximity to Moving Mechanical Parts:** Exposure to possible bodily injury from moving mechanical parts of equipment, tools, or machinery.

E = **Exposure to Electrical Shock:** Exposure to possible bodily injury from electrical shock.

D = **Working in High, Exposed Places:** Exposure to possible bodily injury from falling.

R = **Exposure to Radiation:** Exposure to possible bodily harm from radiation.

X = **Working with Explosives:** Exposure to possible injury from explosions.

T = **Exposure to Toxic or Caustic Chemicals:** Exposure to possible bodily injury from toxic or caustic chemicals.

O = **Other Environmental Conditions:** Other conditions not defined above.

The Salary Code:

Occupations in the *EGOE* are assigned one of five pay ranges based on the expected starting salary for a qualified worker. These codes are based on data in the *Occupational Outlook Handbook*, numerous wage and salary surveys, want ads, and many other sources. They reflect pay information as of June, 1994. Please note that these are starting salaries for workers with training but no experience. In some cases, wages increase rapidly with experience. In other cases, wages change little as the worker stays longer in the job. The salaries indicated below are national averages. Salaries in your community may differ.

Salary Code (low = 1, high = 5)

1 = **Lowest:** Below $14,000 per year
2 = **Moderately Low:** $14,000 to $16,999 per year
3 = **Mid-Range:** $17,000 to $20,999 per year
4 = **Moderately High:** $21,000 to $27,999 per year
5 = **Highest:** $28,000 per year and above

The Outlook Code:

Each *EGOE* occupation is assigned one of five employment outlook categories based upon the length of time that a qualified but inexperienced job seeker could expect to spend before finding employment in the specified field. This data is based on national averages. The time you spend looking for a job will depend on conditions in your community including when you are looking, your skills, and how well you are able to impress possible employers. It is also important to note that higher-paying jobs and those requiring advanced education or credentials typically take longer to find but are often more stable.

These codes are based on the *Occupational Outlook Handbook*, *Projections of Employment*, educational program completion statistics, want ads, and many other data sources. Due to the delay in compiling data, the projections used here were about one year old at the time this book was published. Generally, this data does not change rapidly from year to year and should provide useful guidelines for years to come. However, conditions in your community may differ for some jobs due to local conditions.

Outlook Code (low = 1, high = 5)

1 = **Lowest:** Finding employment can take over a year
2 = **Moderately Low:** Finding employment can take from a few months to a year
3 = **Mid Range:** Employment can be found within a few months
4 = **Moderately High:** Employment can be found within a couple of weeks
5 = **Highest:** In many areas, employment can be found quickly

Artistic 01

An interest in creative expression of feelings or ideas. You can satisfy this interest in several of the creative or performing arts fields. You may enjoy literature. Perhaps writing or editing would appeal to you. You may prefer to work in the performing arts. You could direct or perform in drama, music, or dance. You may enjoy the visual arts. You could become a critic in painting, sculpture, or ceramics. You may want to use your hands to create or decorate products. Or you may prefer to model clothes or develop acts for entertainment.

Literary Arts 01.01

Workers in this group write, edit, or direct the publication of prose or poetry. They find employment on newspapers or magazines, in radio and television studios, and in the theater and motion picture industries. Some writers are self-employed and sell stories, plays, and other forms of literary composition to publishers.

✓ What kind of work would you do?

Your work activities would depend upon your specific job. For example, you might:

- write plays or scripts for movies.
- write short stories, poems, or novels.
- edit the work of creative writers.
- write dialogue for television programs.
- write reviews of literature, musical performances, and other artistic work.
- select writers and subject matter for television productions

✓ What skills and abilities do you need for this kind of work?

To do this kind of work, you must be able to:

- present personal views or interpretations relating to such subjects as politics, social conditions, religion, or plays or other writings.
- deal with various kinds of people.
- make decisions based on personal judgment.
- influence the opinion of people through words.

✓ How do you know if you would like or could learn to do this kind of work?

The following questions may give you clues about yourself as you consider this group of jobs.

- Have you written a book review for a class? Do you enjoy others reading your interpretations?
- Have you written an original story? Can you create original characters or situations that interest and entertain others?
- Have you developed publicity posters for a garage sale, fund drive, or community activity? Can you select words that spark people's curiosity and interest?
- Have you written poems for an English class or for poetry contests? Do you enjoy expressing personal thoughts and feelings in this type of writing?
- Have you written for or edited a school newspaper, union bulletin, or company newsletter? Can you edit and improve the writing of others?
- Have you told ghost stories around a campfire or other setting? Were they interesting and entertaining to others?

✓ How can you prepare for and enter this kind of work?

Occupations in this group usually require education and/or training extending from two to over ten years, depending upon the specific kind of work. Experience in writing is usually required for employment. Writing for weekly or monthly newspapers or magazines can be helpful in getting jobs with large newspapers or advertising agencies. Employers often require samples of published writing. Editing jobs usually require several years experience as a writer.

Courses in English grammar and composition, as well as literature, are basic high school subjects. Community colleges and universities offer programs that prepare people for this kind of work. Courses in journalism, English, and creative writing provide necessary skills. Some occupations require proficiency in one or more foreign languages; while others require a knowledge of political science, art, drama, or other subjects. For example, a person wishing to become a critic must have in-depth knowledge of the subject to be criticized, art, music, or the like. This knowledge can be acquired through courses at colleges or universities; specialized schools, such as art institutes; or performing arts little theaters or playhouses.

Self-employed or free-lance writers sometimes use literary agents to help them find publishers. These agents may help the writer prepare material for publication. Publishers occasionally hire experienced free-lance writers to write about a particular subject.

✓ What else should you consider about these jobs?

Most new workers in writing occupations start with routine assignments such as writing headlines. Only in establishments where few writers are employed is the newcomer given creative writing assignments.

Some jobs are available for part-time workers. Free-lance writers sometimes prepare advertising copy or serve as local correspondents for daily newspapers.

If you think you would like to do this kind of work, look at the job descriptions listed below.

■ ■ ■

GOE: 01.01.01
Editing

CONTINUITY DIRECTOR (radio-tv broad.) ● DOT #132.037-010 ● OES: 34001 ● Alternate titles: EDITOR, CONTINUITY AND SCRIPT. Coordinates activities of continuity department of radio or television station: Assigns duties to staff and freelance writers. Supervises staff writers preparing program continuity and scripts for broadcasting, and edits material to ensure conformance with company policy, laws, and regulations. May be responsible for nonmusical copyright material. May read book or script of television programs and commercials or view and listen to videotapes to detect and recommend deletion of vulgar, immoral, libelous, or misleading statements, applying knowledge of Federal Communications Commission and station standards and regulations. May supervise administrative research workers and employees receiving and examining program ideas and scripts suggested by public for station or network presentation. ● **GED:** R5, M2, L5 ● **SVP:** 4-10 yrs ● **Academic:** Ed=A, Eng=G ● **Work Field:** 261 ● **MPSMS:** 863, 864, 869 ● **Aptitudes:** G2, V1, N3, S4, P4, Q3, K4, F4, M4, E5, C5 ● **Temperaments:** D, J, P ● **Physical:** Stg=S; Freq: T, G, N, A Occas: R, H, I ● **Work Env:** Noise=N; ● **Salary:** 5 ● **Outlook:** 3

EDITOR, PUBLICATIONS (print. & pub.) ● DOT #132.037-022 ● OES: 34001 ● Formulates policy; plans, coordinates, and directs editorial activities; and supervises workers who assist in selecting and preparing material for publication in magazines, trade journals, house organs, and related publications: Confers with executives, department heads, and editorial staff to formulate policy, coordinate department activities, establish production schedules, solve publication problems, and discuss makeup plans and organizational changes. Determines theme of issue and gathers related material. Writes or assigns staff members or freelance writers to write articles, reports, editorials, reviews, and other material. Reads and evaluates material submitted for publication consideration. Secures graphic material from picture sources and assigns artists and photographers to produce pictures and illustrations. Assigns staff member, or personally interviews individuals and attends gatherings, to obtain items for publication, verify facts, and clarify information. Assigns research and other editorial duties to assistants. Organizes material, plans overall and individual page layouts, and selects type. Marks dummy pages to indicate position and size of printed and graphic material. Reviews final proofs and approves or makes changes. Reviews and evaluates work of staff members and makes recommendations and changes. May perform related editorial duties listed under EDITORIAL ASSISTANT (print. & pub.). May direct activities of production, circulation, or promotion personnel. May prepare news or public relations releases, special brochures, and similar materials. May be designated according to type of publication worked on as Communications Manager (print. & pub.); Editor, Farm Journal (print. & pub.); Editor, House Organ (print. & pub.); Editor, Magazine (print. & pub.); Editor, Trade Journal (print. & pub.); Industrial Editor (print. & pub.). ● **GED:** R6, M3, L6 ● **SVP:** 4-10 yrs ● **Academic:** Ed=B, Eng=G ● **Work Field:** 261, 264, 295 ● **MPSMS:** 757 ● **Aptitudes:** G1, V1, N3, S3, P3, Q3, K3, F4, M4, E5, C5 ● **Temperaments:** D, F, J, P ● **Physical:** Stg=S; Freq: R, H, T, G, N, A Occas: I ● **Work Env:** Noise=N; ● **Salary:** 4 ● **Outlook:** 3

FILM OR VIDEOTAPE EDITOR (motion picture) ● DOT #962.262-010 ● OES: 39998 ● Alternate titles: CUTTER. Edits motion picture film, television or cable television video tape, and sound tracks: Evaluates and selects scenes in terms of dramatic and entertainment value and story continuity. Trims film segments to specified lengths and reassembles segments in sequence that presents story with maximum effect, or edits video tape, using editing equipment. Reviews assembled film or edited video tape on screen or monitor and makes corrections. Confers with supervisory personnel and others concerning filming of scenes. May specialize in particular field of film or video editing, such as feature, news, sound, sound effects, or music. ● **GED:** R5, M2, L4 ● **SVP:** 4-10 yrs ● **Academic:** Ed=A, Eng=G ● **Work Field:** 261, 281 ● **MPSMS:** 864, 869, 911 ● **Aptitudes:** G2, V2, N3, S3, P2, Q4, K4, F3, M3, E5, C3 ● **Temperaments:** F, J, T ● **Physical:** Stg=L; Freq: R, H, I, T, G, X Occas: N ● **Work Env:** Noise=N; ● **Salary:** 3 ● **Outlook:** 1

PRODUCER (motion picture) ● DOT #187.167-174 ● OES: 34056 ● Coordinates activities of personnel engaged in writing, directing, editing, and producing motion pictures: Reviews synopses and scripts and directs adaptation for screen. Determines treatment and scope of proposed productions and establishes departmental operating budgets. Selects principal members of cast and key production staff members. Reviews filmed scenes of each day's shooting, orders retakes, and approves final editing of filmed productions. Conducts meetings with DIRECTOR, MOTION PICTURE (motion picture), SCREEN WRITER (motion picture; radio-tv broad.), and other staff members to discuss production progress and results. ● **GED:** R6, M5, L6 ● **SVP:** 4-10 yrs ● **Academic:** Ed=B, Eng=G ● **Work Field:** 295, 297 ● **MPSMS:** 754 ● **Aptitudes:** G1, V2, N2, S2, P4, Q4, K4, F4, M4, E5, C5 ● **Temperaments:** D, J, P ● **Physical:** Stg=S; Freq: R, H, I, T, G, N Occas: F, D, A, X, V ● **Work Env:** Noise=N; ● **Salary:** 5 ● **Outlook:** 3

SUPERVISING FILM-OR-VIDEOTAPE EDITOR (motion picture) ● DOT #962.132-010 ● OES: 39998 ● Supervises and coordinates activities of workers engaged in editing and assembling filmed scenes photographed by others: Reviews edited and assembled film on screen or edited videotape on monitor, to detect errors. Studies script and confers with producers and directors concerning layout or editing techniques to increase dramatic or entertainment value of production. Trims film segments to specified lengths and assembles segments in sequence that presents story with maximum effect, or edits videotape to correct errors, using editing equipment. Performs other duties as described under SUPERVISOR (any industry) Master Title. May operate studio or portable, shoulder-mounted camera [CAMERA OPERATOR (motion picture; radio-tv broad.) 143.062-022]. May be designated according to specialty as Supervising Editor, Feature (motion picture; radio-tv broad.); Supervising Editor, News Reel (radio-tv broad.); Supervising Editor, Trailer (motion picture; radio-tv broad.). ● **GED:** R5, M3, L5 ● **SVP:** 4-10 yrs ● **Academic:** Ed=A, Eng=G ● **Work Field:** 211, 264, 281 ● **MPSMS:** 864, 869, 911 ● **Aptitudes:** G2, V2, N2, S3, P3, Q3, K4, F3, M4, E5, C3 ● **Temperaments:** D, F, J, P, V ● **Physical:** Stg=M; Freq: R, H, I, T, G, X Occas: S, O, N, D, A ● **Work Env:** Noise=N; ● **Salary:** 3 ● **Outlook:** 3

GOE: 01.01.02
Creative Writing

BIOGRAPHER (profess. & kin.) ● DOT #052.067-010 ● OES: 34001 ● Specializes in reconstruction in narrative form of career or phase in life of individual: Assembles biographical material from sources, such as news accounts, diaries, personal papers and correspondence, written accounts of events in which subject participated, and consultation with associates and relatives of subject. Portrays character and behavior of subject on basis of historical environment and application of psychological analysis, relating subject's activities to pertinent events during subject's lifetime [WRITER, PROSE, FICTION AND NONFICTION (profess. & kin.)]. ● **GED:** R5, M2, L5 ● **SVP:** 2-4 yrs ● **Academic:** Ed=A, Eng=G ● **Work Field:** 251 ● **MPSMS:** 743 ● **Aptitudes:** G2, V2, N3, S4, P4, Q2, K4, F4, M4, E5, C5 ● **Temperaments:** D, J ● **Physical:** Stg=S; Freq: T, G ● **Work Env:** Noise=Q; ● **Salary:** 4 ● **Outlook:** 1

COPY WRITER (profess. & kin.) ● DOT #131.067-014 ● OES: 34001 ● Writes advertising copy for use by publication or broadcast media to promote sale of goods and services: Consults with sales media, and marketing representatives to obtain information on product or service and discuss style and length of advertising copy. Obtains additional background and current development information through research and interview. Reviews advertising trends, consumer surveys, and other data regarding marketing of specific and related goods and services to formulate presentation approach. Writes preliminary draft of copy and sends to supervisor for approval. Corrects and revises copy as necessary. May write articles, bulletins, sales letters, speeches, and other related informative and promotional material. May enter information into computer to prepare advertising copy. ● **GED:** R5, M2, L5 ● **SVP:** 2-4 yrs ● **Academic:** Ed=A, Eng=G ● **Work Field:** 261 ● **MPSMS:** 896 ● **Aptitudes:** G2, V1, N3, S4, P3, Q3, K3, F4, M4, E5, C5 ● **Temperaments:** F, I, J, P ● **Physical:** Stg=S; Freq: T, G Occas: R, H, I, N, A ● **Work Env:** Noise=N; ● **Salary:** 3 ● **Outlook:** 3

CROSSWORD-PUZZLE MAKER (print. & pub.) ● DOT #139.087-010 ● OES: 39998 ● Devises and creates crossword puzzles: Draws form setting up numbered blank squares for insertion of words and black squares to complete design. Fits words, whose spelling coincides vertically and horizontally, into blank areas and composes short definitions numbered correspondingly with matching series of blank squares. Sets up filled puzzle as key to solution. May originate puzzles for specific purposes, such as advertisements or holiday specialities. ● **GED:** R5, M2, L5 ● **SVP:** 1-2 yrs ● **Academic:** Ed=N, Eng=G ● **Work Field:** 261 ● **MPSMS:** 757 ● **Aptitudes:** G2, V3, N3, S3, P4, Q3, K4, F4, M4, E5, C5 ● **Temperaments:** F, T ● **Physical:** Stg=S; Freq: R, H, N Occas: I ● **Work Env:** Noise=Q; ● **Salary:** 4 ● **Outlook:** 1

EDITORIAL WRITER (print. & pub.) ● DOT #131.067-022 ● OES: 34001 ● Writes comments on topics of reader interest to stimulate or mold public opinion, in accordance with viewpoints and policies of publication: Prepares assigned or unassigned articles from knowledge of topic and editorial position of publication, supplemented by additional study and research. Submits and discusses copy with editor for approval. May specialize in one or more fields, such as international affairs, fiscal matters, or national or local politics. May participate in conferences of editorial policy committee to recommend topics and position to be taken by publication on specific public issues. ● **GED:** R5, M3, L5 ● **SVP:** 4-10 yrs ● **Academic:** Ed=A, Eng=G ● **Work Field:** 261 ● **MPSMS:** 757 ● **Aptitudes:** G1, V1, N3, S4, P3, Q3, K3, F4, M4, E5, C5 ● **Temperaments:** F, I, J, P, V ● **Physical:** Stg=S; Freq: R, H, I, N, A Occas: T, G ● **Work Env:** Noise=Q; ● **Salary:** 3 ● **Outlook:** 3

HUMORIST (profess. & kin.) ● DOT #131.067-026 ● OES: 34001 ● Writes humorous material for publication or performance: Selects topic according to personal preference or assignment. Writes and makes changes and revisions to material until it meets personal standards. Submits material for approval and confers with client regarding additional changes or revisions. May conduct research to obtain factual information regarding subject matter. May specialize in writing comedy routines, gags, or special material for entertainers and be designated Gag Writer (profess. & kin.). May write comedy shows for presentation on radio or television and be designated Comedy Writer (profess. & kin.). May work as a member of writing team and be assigned to develop segment of comedy show. ● **GED:** R6, M2, L6 ● **SVP:** 4-10 yrs ● **Academic:** Ed=N, Eng=G ● **Work Field:** 261 ● **MPSMS:** 860, 759 ● **Aptitudes:** G1, V1, N4, S4, P4, Q3, K4, F4, M4, E5, C5 ● **Temperaments:** F, J, P ● **Physical:** Stg=S; Freq: R, H, N Occas: I, T, G ● **Work Env:** Noise=Q; ● **Salary:** 5 ● **Outlook:** 1

LIBRETTIST (profess. & kin.) ● DOT #131.067-030 ● OES: 34001 ● Composes text for opera, musical play, or extended choral work, fitting words to music composed by another. Adapts text to accommodate musical requirements of COMPOSER (profess. & kin.) and SINGER (amuse. & rec.; motion picture; radio-tv broad.). ● **GED:** R6, M2, L6 ● **SVP:** 2-4 yrs ● **Academic:** Ed=N, Eng=G ● **Work Field:** 261 ● **MPSMS:** 756, 759 ● **Aptitudes:** G1, V1, N4, S4, P4, Q3, K4, F3, M4, E5, C5 ● **Temperaments:** F, J ● **Physical:** Stg=S; Freq: R, H, T, G, N Occas: I ● **Work Env:** Noise=Q; ● **Salary:** 4 ● **Outlook:** 1

LYRICIST (profess. & kin.) ● DOT #131.067-034 ● OES: 34001 ● Alternate titles: LYRIC WRITER; SONG WRITER. Writes words to be sung or spoken to accompaniment of music. Expresses sentiment, ideas, or narration, usually in verse, to fit music. ● **GED:** R6, M2, L6 ● **SVP:** 2-4 yrs ● **Academic:** Ed=N, Eng=G ● **Work Field:** 261 ● **MPSMS:** 756, 757 ● **Aptitudes:** G1, V2, N4, S4, P4, Q4, K4, F4, M4, E5, C5 ● **Temperaments:** F, J ● **Physical:** Stg=S; Freq: T, G ● **Work Env:** Noise=Q; ● **Salary:** 4 ● **Outlook:** 1

PLAYWRIGHT (profess. & kin.) ● DOT #131.067-038 ● OES: 34001 ● Alternate titles: DRAMATIST. Writes original plays, such as tragedies, comedies, or dramas, or adapts themes from fictional, historical, or narrative sources, for dramatic presentation: Writes plays, usually involving action, conflict, purpose, and resolution, to depict series of events from imaginary or real life. Writes dialogue and describes action to be followed during enactment of play. Revises script during rehearsals and preparation for initial showing. ● **GED:** R6, M2, L6 ● **SVP:** 4-10 yrs ● **Academic:** Ed=N, Eng=G ● **Work Field:** 261 ● **MPSMS:** 754, 757 ● **Aptitudes:** G1, V1, N4, S4, P4, Q4, K4, F4, M4, E5, C5 ● **Temperaments:** F, J ● **Physical:** Stg=S; Freq: R, H, I, T, G, N Occas: F, D, A, X, V ● **Work Env:** Noise=N; ● **Salary:** 5 ● **Outlook:** 1

SCREEN WRITER (motion picture) ● DOT #131.067-050 ● OES: 34001 ● Alternate titles: SCENARIO WRITER; SCRIPT WRITER. Writes scripts for motion pictures or television: Selects subject and theme for script based on personal interests or assignment. Conducts research to obtain accurate factual background information and authentic detail. Writes plot outline, narrative synopsis, or treatment and submits for approval. Confers with PRODUCER (motion picture) 187.167-174 or PRODUCER (radio-tv broad.) 159.117-010 and DIRECTOR, MOTION PICTURE (motion picture) 159.067-010 or DIRECTOR, TELEVISION (radio-tv broad.) 159.067-014 regarding script development, revisions, and other changes. Writes one or more drafts of script. May work in collaboration with other writers. May adapt books or plays into scripts for use in television or motion picture production. May write continuity or comedy routines. May specialize in particular type of script or writing. ● **GED:** R6, M2, L6 ● **SVP:** 2-4 yrs ● **Academic:** Ed=H, Eng=G ● **Work Field:** 261 ● **MPSMS:** 754 ● **Aptitudes:** G1, V1, N4, S4, P4, Q4, K4, F4, M4, E5, C5 ● **Temperaments:** F, J, P ● **Physical:** Stg=S; Freq: I, T, G, N Occas: R, H ● **Work Env:** Noise=Q; ● **Salary:** 4 ● **Outlook:** 1

WRITER, PROSE, FICTION AND NONFICTION (profess. & kin.)
● DOT #131.067-046 ● OES: 34001 ● Alternate titles: WRITER. Writes original prose material for publication: Selects subject matter based on personal interest or receives specific assignment from publisher. Conducts research and makes notes to retain ideas, develop factual information, and obtain authentic detail. Organizes material and plans arrangement or outline. Develops factors, such as theme, plot, order, characterization, and story line. Writes draft of manuscript. Reviews, revises, and corrects it and submits material for publication. Confers with publisher's representative regarding manuscript changes. May specialize in one or more styles or types of writing, such as descriptive or critical interpretations or analyses, essays, magazine articles, short stories, novels, and biographies. ● **GED:** R6, M3, L6 ● **SVP:** 4-10 yrs ● **Academic:** Ed=H, Eng=G ● **Work Field:** 261 ● **MPSMS:** 757 ● **Aptitudes:** G1, V1, N3, S4, P4, Q4, K4, F4, M4, E5, C5 ● **Temperaments:** F, J ● **Physical:** Stg=S; Freq: R, H, I, N Occas: T, G ● **Work Env:** Noise=Q; ● **Salary:** 2 ● **Outlook:** 1

Visual Arts   01.02

Workers in this group create original works of art or do commercial art work, using such techniques as drawing, painting, photographing, and sculpturing to express or interpret ideas or to illustrate various written materials. Some visual artists design products, settings, or graphics (such as advertisements or book covers), and oversee the work of other artists or craftsmen who produce or install them. Others teach art, or appraise or restore paintings and other fine art objects. Advertising agencies, printing and publishing firms, television and motion picture studios, museums and restoration laboratories employ visual artists. They also work for manufacturers and in retail and wholesale trade. Many are self-employed, operating their own commercial art studios or doing free-lance work.

✓ What kind of work would you do?

Your work activities would depend upon your specific job. For example, you might:

- paint or sketch portraits, landscapes, or other subjects in oils, watercolors, or charcoals.
- design and supervise the construction of scenery for plays.
- plan the arrangement of advertising materials for a department store.
- examine oil paintings to determine the need for restoration, and use scientific and artistic techniques to restore them to their original appearance.
- design and cut original patterns for women's clothing.
- sculpture a statue or other work of art.
- draw accurate and precise pictures of diseased body organs to illustrate articles in medical journals.
- photograph subjects to prepare a photo story.

✓ What skills and abilities do you need for this kind of work?

To do this kind of work, you must be able to:

- understand and apply artistic principles and techniques.
- visualize how the final product will look from rough sketches or work drawings.
- use paint brushes, pens, charcoal, or sculpturing tools skillfully, to produce accurate plans for displays or scenery, illustrations for written materials, or original works of art.
- choose the most appropriate equipment to express an idea or create a particular effect.
- tell whether a work of art is the 'real thing' or a fake by examining it and using various chemical tests, knowledge of art history, and familiarity with the characteristics of the style of various artists.

✓ How do you know if you would like or could learn to do this kind of work?

The following questions may give you clues about yourselves as you consider this group of jobs.

- Have you taken courses in drawing or sketching? Were any of your works selected for display or entry in competition?
- Have you helped paint scenery for amateur plays? Can you select the proper color combinations to achieve a desired effect?
- Have you taken photographs of family, friends, or activities? Do you think they were of good quality and pleasing to the eye?
- Have you viewed art galleries and shows? Do you try to judge the quality of paintings or sculptures?
- Have you worked with modeling clay? Do you enjoy creating original designs in clay?

✓ How can you prepare for and enter this kind of work?

Occupations in this group usually require education and/or training extending from two years up to and over ten years, depending upon the specific kind of work. A common method of preparation is to obtain a four-year degree with a major in fine arts or commercial art. Some artists earn a two- or three-year certificate at an art institute. Programs include the study of art history and critique as well as instruction in techniques.

Small advertising agencies, department stores, and photography studios sometimes hire workers with vocational school or junior college background. These workers are assigned tasks according to their ability. They are usually provided on-the-job training to improve their skills.

Industrial designing jobs require artistic and engineering skills to make scale drawings and to illustrate technical information. Jobs in restoring and appraising art objects usually require a background in art history, chemistry, and similar subjects.

Free-lance visual artists usually have experience as illustrators, designers, art restorers, or photographers. These workers must be well-known for their work and have contact with potential buyers. Samples of their work are used to show their skills to customers.

Administrative and supervisory jobs in the visual arts require extensive experience in the field.

✓ *What else should you consider about these jobs?*

Most visual artists depend upon some sort of commercial art or design work for financial security. Few can afford to be artists with no regular income.

People who can use a variety of techniques and art media have more opportunities for employment than those who specialize in one area.

If you think you would like to do this kind of work, look at the job titles listed below.

■ ■ ■

GOE: 01.02.01
Instructing & Appraising

APPRAISER, ART (profess. & kin.) ● DOT #191.287-014 ● OES: 49998 ● Examines works of art, such as paintings, sculpture, and antiques, to determine their authenticity and value: Examines work for color values, style of brushstroke, esthetic correctness, and other characteristics, to establish art period or identify artist. Judges authenticity and value, based on knowledge of art history, materials employed, techniques of individual artists, and current market. May illuminate work with quartz light to determine whether discoloration is present. May x ray painting and perform chemical tests on paint sample to detect forgery or to authenticate work. May specialize in particular categories of art or in specific types of artistic articles appraised. ● **GED:** R5, M4, L4 ● **SVP:** 4-10 yrs ● **Academic:** Ed=A, Eng=G ● **Work Field:** 211 ● **MPSMS:** 539, 751 ● **Aptitudes:** G2, V2, N4, S3, P2, Q4, K4, F4, M4, E4, C1 ● **Temperaments:** J ● **Physical:** Stg=L; Const: N, X Freq: F, A Occas: B, R, H ● **Work Env:** Noise=Q; ● **Salary:** 3 ● **Outlook:** 2

GOE: 01.02.02
Studio Art

QUICK SKETCH ARTIST (amuse. & rec.) ● DOT #149.041-010 ● OES: 34035 ● Sketches likeness of customers: Poses subject to accentuate most pleasing features and draws likeness, using pencil, charcoal, pastels, or other medium. May draw sketch from photograph. May only draw exaggerated likenesses and be designated Caricaturist (amuse. & rec.). May be identified according to medium worked in. ● **GED:** R5, M1, L3 ● **SVP:** 1-2 yrs ● **Academic:** Ed=A, Eng=S ● **Work Field:** 262 ● **MPSMS:** 752 ● **Aptitudes:** G2, V3, N4, S2, P2, Q4, K2, F2, M2, E5, C2 ● **Temperaments:** F, J ● **Physical:** Stg=S; Const: I, N Freq: R, H, X Occas: F, V ● **Work Env:** Noise=VQ; Freq: W ● **Salary:** 3 ● **Outlook:** 1

GOE: 01.02.03
Commercial Art

ART DIRECTOR (motion picture) ● DOT #142.061-062 ● OES: 34038 ● Formulates design concepts, selects locations and settings, and directs and coordinates set design, construction, and erection activities to produce sets for motion picture and television productions: Reads script and confers with heads of production and direction to establish budget, schedules, and determine setting requirement. Conducts research and consults experts to establish architectural styles which accurately depict given periods and locations. Conducts search for suitable locations and constructed sets. Assigns assistants and staff members to complete design ideas and prepare sketches, illustrations, and detailed drawings of sets. Directs design and production of graphics or animation to produce graphics or animation for on-air programs. Estimates construction costs and presents plans and estimates for approval. Directs and coordinates set construction, erection, and decoration activities to ensure that they conform to design, budget, and schedule requirements. Reviews budget and expenditures reports to monitor costs. May make rough drawings of design concepts. May formulate design concepts for costumes, makeup, photographic effects, titles, and related production items. ● **GED:** R5, M3, L5 ● **SVP:** 4-10 yrs ● **Academic:** Ed=B, Eng=S ● **Work Field:** 264 ● **MPSMS:** 759, 864 ● **Aptitudes:** G1, V2, N3, S2, P2, Q4, K2, F2, M3, E5, C2 ● **Temperaments:** D, F, J, P ● **Physical:** Stg=S; Freq: H, T, G, N, D, X Occas: R, I, F ● **Work Env:** Noise=N; ● **Salary:** 5 ● **Outlook:** 1

ART DIRECTOR (profess. & kin.) ● DOT #141.031-010 ● OES: 34038 ● Formulates concepts and supervises workers engaged in executing layout designs for art work and copy to be presented by visual communications media, such as magazines, books, newspapers, television, posters, and packaging: Reviews illustrative material and confers with client or individual responsible for presentation regarding budget, background information, objectives, presentation approaches, styles, techniques, and related production factors. Formulates basic layout design concept and conducts research to select and secure suitable illustrative material, or conceives and assigns production of material and detail to artists and photographers. Assigns and directs staff members to develop design concepts into art layouts and prepare layouts for printing. Reviews, approves, and presents final layouts to client or department head for approval. May perform duties of GRAPHIC DESIGNER (profess. & kin.) to design art layouts. May mark up, paste up, and finish layouts to prepare layouts for printing. May draw illustrations. May prepare detailed story board showing sequence and timing of story development when producing material for television. May specialize in particular field, media, or type of layout. ● **GED:** R5, M3, L5 ● **SVP:** 4-10 yrs ● **Academic:** Ed=A, Eng=G ● **Work Field:** 264 ● **MPSMS:** 752, 860, 896 ● **Aptitudes:** G2, V2, N3, S2, P2, Q3, K3, F3, M3, E5, C2 ● **Temperaments:** D, F, I, J, P ● **Physical:** Stg=S; Freq: R, H, T, G, N, D, X Occas: I, A ● **Work Env:** Noise=Q; ● **Salary:** 4 ● **Outlook:** 2

AUDIOVISUAL PRODUCTION SPECIALIST (profess. & kin.) ● DOT #149.061-010 ● OES: 39998 ● Alternate titles: INSTRUC-

TIONAL TECHNOLOGY SPECIALIST. Plans and produces audio, visual, and audiovisual material for communication and learning: Develops production ideas based on assignment or generates own ideas based on objectives and personal interest. Conducts research or utilizes knowledge and training to determine format, approach, content, level, and medium which will be most effective, meet objectives, and remain within budget. Plans and develops, or directs assistants to develop, preproduction ideas into outlines, scripts, continuity, story boards, and graphics. Executes, or directs assistants to execute, rough and finished graphics and graphic designs. Locates and secures settings, properties, effects, and other production necessities. Directs and coordinates activities of assistants and other personnel during production. May review, evaluate, and direct modifications to material produced independently by other personnel. May set up, adjust, and operate equipment, such as cameras, sound mixers, and recorders during production. May perform narration or present announcements. May construct and place in position properties, sets, lighting equipment, and other equipment. May develop manuals, texts, workbooks, or related materials for use in conjunction with production materials. May conduct training sessions on selection, use, and design of audiovisual materials, and operation of presentation equipment. May perform duties listed under DIRECTOR, INSTRUCTIONAL MATERIAL (education) 099.167-018. ● **GED:** R5, M4, L5 ● **SVP:** 2-4 yrs ● **Academic:** Ed=B, Eng=G ● **Work Field:** 201, 261, 264 ● **MPSMS:** 752, 753 ● **Aptitudes:** G2, V2, N3, S2, P2, Q2, K2, F3, M3, E5, C3 ● **Temperaments:** D, F, I, J, P ● **Physical:** Stg=L; Freq: R, H, I, T, G, N Occas: A, X ● **Work Env:** Noise=N; ● **Salary:** 4 ● **Outlook:** 3

CAMERA OPERATOR (motion picture) ● DOT #143.062-022 ● OES: 34026 ● Photographs various subjects and subject material, using motion picture, television broadcasting, or video recording cameras and equipment, utilizing knowledge of motion picture, television broadcasting, or video recording techniques, limitations, and advantages to photograph scenes: Resolves problems presented by exposure control, subject and camera movement, changes in subject distance during filming, and related variables. May receive directives from PRODUCER (radio-tv broad.) 159.117-010 or DIRECTOR, TELEVISION (radio-tv broad.) 159.067-014 over headset. May set up and operate dollies, cranes, camera mounting heads, power zooms, and related motion picture, television broadcasting, or video recording equipment and accessories. May maintain or repair equipment and accessories. May specialize in particular subject material or field, such as medical, scientific, news, or commercial. May photograph action on motion picture or television sets and locations, using shoulder held camera, and be designated Camera Operator, Second (motion picture; radio-tv broad.) or photograph special effects and be designated Camera Operator, Special Effects (motion picture; radio-tv broad.). May specialize in operation of television cameras and be designated Camera Operator, Television (radio-tv broad.). May specialize in operation of motion picture cameras and be designated Photographer, Motion Picture (motion picture). ● **GED:** R4, M3, L4 ● **SVP:** 2-4 yrs ● **Academic:** Ed=H, Eng=S ● **Work Field:** 201 ● **MPSMS:** 753, 864, 911 ● **Aptitudes:** G2, V3, N3, S2, P2, Q4, K3, F3, M3, E5, C2 ● **Temperaments:** J, P, T ● **Physical:** Stg=M; Freq: H, G, D, A, X Occas: S, O, R, I, T ● **Work Env:** Noise=N; Occas: W ● **Salary:** 3 ● **Outlook:** 2

CARTOONIST (print. & pub.) ● DOT #141.061-010 ● OES: 34035 ● Draws cartoons for publications to amuse readers and interpret or illustrate news highlights, advertising, stories, or articles: Develops personal ideas or reads written material to develop ideas from context. Discusses ideas with editor or publisher's representative or sketches cartoon drawing and submits drawing for approval. Makes changes and corrections as necessary and finishes drawing. May develop and draw comic strips. May be designated according to type of cartoons drawn as Editorial Cartoonist (print. & pub.); Sports Cartoonist (print. & pub.). ● **GED:** R5, M2, L4 ● **SVP:** 2-4 yrs ● **Academic:** Ed=N, Eng=G ● **Work Field:** 262 ● **MPSMS:** 752, 757 ● **Aptitudes:** G2, V2, N4, S2, P2, Q4, K2, F1, M2, E5, C2 ● **Temperaments:** F, I, J ● **Physical:** Stg=S; Const: R, H, I, N Occas: A ● **Work Env:** Noise=Q; ● **Salary:** 4 ● **Outlook:** 1

COMMERCIAL DESIGNER (profess. & kin.) ● DOT #141.061-038 ● OES: 34038 ● Creates and designs graphic material for use as ornamentation, illustration, advertising, or cosmetic on manufactured materials and packaging: Receives assignment from customer or supervisor. Studies traditional, period, and contemporary design styles and motifs to obtain perspective. Reviews marketing trends and preferences of target and related markets. Integrates findings with personal interests, knowledge of design, and limitations presented by methods and materials. Creates, draws, modifies, and changes design to achieve desired effect. Confers with customer or supervisor regarding approval or desired changes to design. May be required to have specialized knowledge of material designed. May prepare original artwork and design model. May perform related duties, such as fabricating silk screens, drawing full size patterns, or cutting stencils. May work with specific items, such as signs, packaging, wallpaper, ceramics, tile, glassware, monograms, crests, emblems, or embroidery. See INDUSTRIAL DESIGNER (profess. & kin.) 142.061-026 for workers who design both product form and associated graphic materials. ● **GED:** R5, M3, L4 ● **SVP:** 2-4 yrs ● **Academic:** Ed=A, Eng=S ● **Work Field:** 264, 262 ● **MPSMS:** 889, 752 ● **Aptitudes:** G2, V2, N3, S2, P2, Q3, K3, F2, M3, E5, C2 ● **Temperaments:** F, J ● **Physical:** Stg=S; Const: R, H, N, D, A, X Freq: I, T, G Occas: V ● **Work Env:** Noise=Q; ● **Salary:** 5 ● **Outlook:** 3

DIRECTOR OF PHOTOGRAPHY (motion picture) ● DOT #143.062-010 ● OES: 34026 ● Alternate titles: CAMERA OPERATOR, FIRST; CAMERA OPERATOR, HEAD; CINEMATOGRAPHER. Plans, directs, and coordinates motion picture filming: Confers with DIRECTOR, MOTION PICTURE (motion picture) regarding interpretation of scene and desired effects. Observes set or location and reviews drawings and other information relating to natural or artificial conditions to determine filming and lighting requirements. Reads charts and computes ratios to determine required lighting, film, shutter angles, filter factors, camera distance, depth of field and focus, angles of view, and other variables to produce desired effects. Confers with ELECTRICIAN, CHIEF (motion picture) to establish lighting requirements. Selects cameras, accessories, equipment, and film stock, utilizing knowledge of filming techniques, filming requirements, and computations. Instructs camera operators regarding camera setup, angles, distances, movement, and other variables and signals cues for starting and stopping filming. Surveys set or location for potential problems, observes effects of lighting, measures lighting levels, and coordinates necessary changes prior to filming. Views film after processing and makes adjustments, as necessary, to achieve desired effects. May direct television productions which utilize electronic cameras. May specialize in special effects and be designated Director Of Photography, Special Effects (motion picture; radio-tv broad.). ● **GED:** R5, M4, L4 ● **SVP:** 4-10 yrs ● **Academic:** Ed=B, Eng=S ● **Work Field:** 201 ● **MPSMS:** 911, 753 ● **Aptitudes:** G2, V2, N2, S2, P2, Q4, K4, F4, M4, E5, C1 ● **Temperaments:** D, F, J ● **Physical:** Stg=L; Const: N, F Freq: T, G, D, X, V Occas: A ● **Work Env:** Noise=N; Occas: W ● **Salary:** 5 ● **Outlook:** 1

DISPLAY DESIGNER (profess. & kin.) ● DOT #142.051-010 ● OES: 34038 ● Alternate titles: DISPLAY AND BANNER DESIGNER; FLAG DECORATOR AND DESIGNER. Designs displays, using paper, cloth, plastic, and other material to decorate streets, fairgrounds, buildings, and other places for celebrations, fairs, and special occasions: Confers with client regarding budget, theme, materials, colors, emblem styles, and related factors. Plans display and sketches rough design for client's approval. Selects stock decorations or directs construction according to design concepts. May construct decorations. May direct and supervise workers who put up decorations. May design, draw, paint, or sketch backgrounds and fixtures made of wood, cardboard, paper, plaster, canvas, or other material for use in windows or interior displays and be designated Display Artist (profess. & kin.). May specialize in designing outdoor displays and be designated Display Designer, Outside (profess. & kin.). ● **GED:** R5, M3, L4 ● **SVP:** 2-4 yrs ● **Academic:** Ed=A, Eng=G ● **Work Field:** 264, 262 ● **MPSMS:** 752, 889 ● **Aptitudes:** G2, V3, N3, S2, P2, Q4, K3, F2, M3, E4, C2 ● **Temperaments:** F, J ● **Physical:** Stg=S; Freq: R, H, I, N, F, D, X ● **Work Env:** Noise=Q; Occas: W ● **Salary:** 4 ● **Outlook:** 3

DISPLAYER, MERCHANDISE (retail trade) ● DOT #298.081-010 ● OES: 39998 ● Alternate titles: DECORATOR, STORE; DISPLAY TRIMMER. Displays merchandise, such as clothes, accessories, and furniture, in windows, showcases, and on sales floor of retail store to attract attention of prospective customers: Originates display ideas or follows suggestions or schedule of MANAGER, DISPLAY (retail trade) and constructs or assembles prefabricated display properties from wood, fabric, glass, paper, and plastic, using handtools. Arranges properties, mannequins, furniture, merchandise, and backdrop according to prearranged plan or own ideas. Places price and descriptive signs on backdrop, fixtures, merchandise, or floor. May dress mannequins for use in displays and be designated Model Dresser (retail trade). May be designated according to area trimmed or decorated as Showcase Trimmer (retail trade); Window Dresser (retail trade). ● **GED:** R4, M3, L3 ● **SVP:** 1-2 yrs ● **Academic:** Ed=H, Eng=S ● **Work Field:** 264 ● **MPSMS:** 889 ● **Aptitudes:** G2, V3, N3, S2, P2, Q4, K4, F4, M3, E4, C2 ● **Temperaments:** F, I, J ● **Physical:** Stg=M; Freq: S, R, H, I, N, F, D, A, X, V Occas: K, O, W, E ● **Work Env:** Noise=N; ● **Salary:** 4 ● **Outlook:** 3

EXHIBIT ARTIST (museums) ● DOT #149.261-010 ● OES: 34035 ● Produces artwork for use in permanent or temporary exhibit settings of museum, zoo, or similar establishment, performing any combination of following duties to prepare exhibit setting and accessories for installation: Confers with professional museum personnel to discuss objectives of exhibits and type of artwork needed. Makes scale drawing of exhibit design, indicating size, position, and general outlines of artwork needed for use of installation and other fabrication personnel. Paints scenic, panoramic, or abstract composition on canvas, board, burlap, or other material to be used as background or component of exhibit, following layout prepared by designer. Paints or stencils exhibit titles and legends on boards, or cuts letters from plastic or plywood to form title and legend copy, and mounts letters on panel or board, using adhesives or handtools. Photographs persons, artifacts, scenes, plants, or other objects, and develops negatives to obtain prints to be used in exhibits. Enlarges, intensifies, or otherwise modifies prints, according to exhibit design specifications. Fashions exhibit accessories, such as human figures, tree parts, or relief maps, from clay, plastic, wood, fiberglass, papier mache, or other materials, using hands, handtools, or molding equipment to cut, carve, scrape, mold, or otherwise shape material to specified dimensions. Brushes or sprays protective or decorative finish on completed background panels, informational legends, and exhibit accessories. Maintains files of photographs, paintings, and accessories for use in exhibits. ● **GED:** R5, M3, L4 ● **SVP:** 1-2 yrs ● **Academic:** Ed=N, Eng=G ● **Work Field:** 262, 264, 102 ● **MPSMS:** 939, 919 ● **Aptitudes:** G2, V2, N3, S2, P2, Q4, K2, F2, M2, E5, C2 ● **Temperaments:** F, J, V ● **Physical:** Stg=L; Freq: R, H, I, N, D, A, X Occas: S, O, E, T, G, F ● **Work Env:** Noise=N; ● **Salary:** 4 ● **Outlook:** 2

EXHIBIT DESIGNER (museums) ● DOT #142.061-058 ● OES: 34038 ● Plans, designs, and oversees construction and installation of permanent and temporary exhibits and displays: Confers with administrative, curatorial, and exhibit staff members to determine theme, content, interpretive or informational purpose, and planned location of exhibit, to discuss budget, promotion, and time limitations, and to plan production schedule for fabrication and installation of exhibit components. Prepares preliminary drawings of proposed exhibit, including detailed construction, layout, and special effect diagrams and material specifications, for final drawing rendition by other personnel, basing design and specifications on knowledge of artistic and technical concepts, principles, and techniques. Submits plan for approval, and adapts plan as needed to serve intended purpose or to conform to budget or fabrication restrictions. Oversees preparation of artwork and construction of exhibit components to ensure intended interpretation of concepts and conformance to structural and material specifications. Arranges for acquisition of specimens or graphics or building of exhibit structures by outside contractors as needed to complete exhibit. Inspects installed exhibit for conformance to specifications and satisfactory operation of special effects components. Oversees placement of collection objects or informational materials in exhibit framework. ● **GED:** R5, M4, L5 ● **SVP:** 2-4 yrs ● **Academic:** Ed=A, Eng=S ● **Work Field:** 295, 264 ● **MPSMS:** 889, 931, 933 ● **Aptitudes:** G2, V2, N3, S2, P2, Q3, K3, F3, M4, E5, C2 ● **Temperaments:** D, F, J, P ● **Physical:** Stg=S; Freq: R, H, I, T, G, N, D, X Occas: A ● **Work Env:** Noise=N; ● **Salary:** 3 ● **Outlook:** 2

FASHION ARTIST (retail trade) ● DOT #141.061-014 ● OES: 34035 ● Draws or paints apparel and accessory illustrations for newspaper or related advertisements: Positions garment, accessory, or model to accentuate desired sales features. Renders drawing of garment or accessory, complementary articles, and background, using various art media and materials. May use models, props, and settings to accentuate subject materials. May draw lettering. ● **GED:** R5, M2, L4 ● **SVP:** 2-4 yrs

● **Academic:** Ed=A, Eng=S ● **Work Field:** 262 ● **MPSMS:** 752 ● **Aptitudes:** G2, V2, N3, S2, P1, Q3, K2, F1, M2, E5, C2 ● **Temperaments:** F, J ● **Physical:** Stg=S; Const: R, H Freq: I, N, D, X Occas: T, G ● **Work Env:** Noise=Q; ● **Salary:** 3 ● **Outlook:** 1

FASHION DESIGNER (profess. & kin.) ● DOT #142.061-018 ● OES: 34038 ● Alternate titles: CLOTHES DESIGNER. Designs men's, women's, and children's clothing and accessories: Analyzes fashion trends and predictions, confers with sales and management executives, compares leather, fabrics, and other apparel materials, and integrates findings with personal interests, tastes, and knowledge of design to create new designs for clothing, shoes, handbags, and other accessories. Sketches rough and detailed drawings of apparel and writes specifications describing factors, such as color scheme, construction, and type of material to be used. Confers with and coordinates activities of workers who draw and cut patterns and construct garments to fabricate sample garment. Examines sample garment on and off model and modifies design as necessary to achieve desired effect. May draw pattern for article designed, using measuring and drawing instruments. May cut patterns. May construct sample, using sewing equipment. May arrange for showing of sample garments at sales meetings or fashion shows. May attend fashion and fabric shows to observe new fashions and materials. May be identified according to specific group designed for, such as men, women, or children or areas of specialization, such as sportswear, coats, dresses, suits, lingerie, or swimwear. May design custom garments for clients and be designated Custom Garment Designer (retail trade). May conduct research and design authentic period, country, or social class costumes to be worn by film, television, concert, stage, and other performers and be designated Costume Designer (profess. & kin.). May design, fabricate, repair, and sell leather articles and be designated Leather Crafter (leather prod.). May design, copy, or modify clothing accessories and be designated according to article designed as Handbag Designer (leather prod.); Hat Designer (hat & cap); or Shoe Designer (boot & shoe). ● **GED:** R5, M3, L4 ● **SVP:** 2-4 yrs ● **Academic:** Ed=A, Eng=G ● **Work Field:** 264 ● **MPSMS:** 440, 520, 752 ● **Aptitudes:** G2, V2, N3, S2, P2, Q3, K2, F2, M3, E5, C2 ● **Temperaments:** F, J, T, V ● **Physical:** Stg=L; Freq: R, H, I, N, D, A, X Occas: E, T, G ● **Work Env:** Noise=N; ● **Salary:** 3 ● **Outlook:** 1

FLORAL DESIGNER (retail trade) ● DOT #142.081-010 ● OES: 34038 ● Alternate titles: FLORIST. Designs and fashions live, cut, dried, and artificial floral and foliar arrangements for events, such as holidays, anniversaries, weddings, balls, and funerals: Confers with client regarding price and type of arrangement desired. Plans arrangement according to client's requirements and costs, utilizing knowledge of design and properties of materials, or selects appropriate standard design pattern. Selects flora and foliage necessary for arrangement. Trims material and arranges bouquets, sprays, wreaths, dish gardens, terrariums, and other items, using wire, pins, floral tape, foam, trimmers, cutters, shapers, and other materials and tools. May decorate buildings, halls, churches, or other facilities where events are planned. May pack and wrap completed arrangements. May estimate costs and price arrangements. May conduct classes or demonstrations. May instruct and direct other workers. May arrange according to standard designs or under instruction of designer and be designated Floral Arranger (retail trade). ● **GED:** R4, M3, L3 ● **SVP:** 1-2 yrs ● **Academic:** Ed=H, Eng=S ● **Work Field:** 264 ● **MPSMS:** 889, 310 ● **Aptitudes:** G3, V3, N3, S3, P2, Q3, K3, F2, M2, E5, C2 ● **Temperaments:** F, J ● **Physical:** Stg=L; Const: R, H, I, N, X Freq: D ● **Work Env:** Noise=Q; ● **Salary:** 2 ● **Outlook:** 2

FURNITURE DESIGNER (furniture) ● DOT #142.061-022 ● OES: 34038 ● Designs furniture for manufacture, according to knowledge of design trends, offerings of competition, production costs, capability of production facilities, and characteristics of company's market: Confers with production, design, and sales personnel to obtain design suggestions and customer orders. Evaluates orders and proposals to determine feasibility of producing item. Sketches freehand design of article. Obtains approval from customer, design committee, or authorized company officials, and originates scale or full size drawing, using drawing instruments. Prepares itemized production requirements to produce item. Traces drawing on material for use in production of blueprints, using drawing instruments. Prepares or directs preparation of blueprints containing manufacturing specifications, such as dimensions, kind of wood, and upholstery fabrics to be used in manufacturing article. Attends staff conference with plant personnel to explain and resolve production requirements. May design and prepare detailed drawings of jigs, fixtures, forms, or tools required to be used in production. May plan modifications for completed furniture to conform to changes in design trends and increase customer acceptance. May design custom pieces or styles according to specific period or country. May build or oversee construction of models or prototypes. May design fixtures and equipment, such as counters and display cases, and be designated Fixture Designer (furniture). ● **GED:** R5, M4, L4 ● **SVP:** 2-4 yrs ● **Academic:** Ed=A, Eng=G ● **Work Field:** 264 ● **MPSMS:** 460 ● **Aptitudes:** G2, V3, N2, S2, P2, Q3, K3, F2, M3, E5, C2 ● **Temperaments:** F, J ● **Physical:** Stg=S; Const: R, H, I, N, X Freq: T, G, D ● **Work Env:** Noise=N; ● **Salary:** 3 ● **Outlook:** 2

GRAPHIC DESIGNER (profess. & kin.) ● DOT #141.061-018 ● OES: 34035 ● Alternate titles: LAYOUT ARTIST. Designs art and copy layouts for material to be presented by visual communications media such as books, magazines, newspapers, television, and packaging: Studies illustrations and photographs to plan presentation of material, product, or service. Determines size and arrangement of illustrative material and copy, selects style and size of type, and arranges layout based upon available space, knowledge of layout principles, and esthetic design concepts. Draws sample of finished layout and presents sample to ART DIRECTOR (profess. & kin.) 141.031-010 for approval. Prepares notes and instructions for workers who assemble and prepare final layouts for printing. Reviews final layout and suggests improvements as needed. May prepare illustrations or rough sketches of material according to instructions of client or supervisor. May prepare series of drawings to illustrate sequence and timing of story development for television production. May mark up, paste, and assemble final layouts to prepare layouts for printer. May specialize in particular field, medium, or type of layout. May produce still and animated graphic formats for on-air and taped portions of television news broadcasts, using electronic video equipment. May photograph layouts, using camera, to make layout prints for supervisor or client. May develop negatives and prints, using negative and print developing equipment, tools and work aids to produce layout photographs for client or supervisor. May key information into computer equipment to create layouts for client or supervisor. ● **GED:** R5, M3, L4 ● **SVP:** 2-4 yrs ● **Academic:** Ed=A, Eng=G ● **Work Field:** 264 ● **MPSMS:** 752, 860, 890 ● **Aptitudes:** G2, V2, N3, S2, P2, Q3, K3, F3, M3, E5, C2 ● **Temperaments:** F, J ● **Physical:** Stg=S; Freq: R, H, I, N, A, X Occas: T, G, D ● **Work Env:** Noise=N; ● **Salary:** 3 ● **Outlook:** 2

ILLUSTRATOR (profess. & kin.) ● DOT #141.061-022 ● OES: 34035 ● Alternate titles: ARTIST; COMMERCIAL ARTIST; GRAPHIC ARTIST. Draws or paints illustrations for use by various media to explain or adorn printed or spoken word: Studies layouts, sketches of proposed illustrations, and related materials to become familiar with assignment. Determines style, technique, and medium best suited to produce desired effects and conform with reproduction requirements, or receives specific instructions regarding these variables. Formulates concept and renders illustration and detail from models, sketches, memory, and imagination. Discusses illustration at various stages of completion and makes changes as necessary. May select type, draw lettering, lay out material, or perform related duties. May be identified according to specific style, technique, medium, subject material or combination of variables. May draw or paint graphic material and lettering to be used for title, background, screen advertising, commercial logo, and other visual layouts for motion picture production and television programming and be designated Title Artist (motion picture; radio-tv broad.). ● **GED:** R5, M2, L4 ● **SVP:** 2-4 yrs ● **Academic:** Ed=A, Eng=S ● **Work Field:** 262 ● **MPSMS:** 752 ● **Aptitudes:** G2, V2, N3, S1, P1, Q3, K2, F1, M2, E5, C1 ● **Temperaments:** F, J ● **Physical:** Stg=S; Freq: R, H, I, N, D, A, X ● **Work Env:** Noise=Q; ● **Salary:** 4 ● **Outlook:** 3

ILLUSTRATOR, MEDICAL AND SCIENTIFIC (profess. & kin.) ● DOT #141.061-026 ● OES: 34035 ● Alternate titles: ARTIST, SCIENTIFIC. Creates illustrations, graphics, and three dimensional models to demonstrate medical or biological subjects, using variety of artistic techniques: Develops drawings, paintings, diagrams, and models of medical or biological subjects in fields such as anatomy, physiology, histology, pathology, or in surgical procedures, for use in publications, exhibits, consultations, research, and teaching activities. Completes illustrations in pen and ink, oil, monochromatic wash, watercolor, car-

bon dust, and mixed media. Constructs or advises in construction of models in plaster, wax, plastics, and other materials. Devises visual aids, such as films, video tapes, charts, and computer graphics, to assist in teaching and research programs. ● **GED:** R5, M4, L5 ● **SVP:** 2-4 yrs ● **Academic:** Ed=A, Eng=G ● **Work Field:** 262, 264 ● **MPSMS:** 752 ● **Aptitudes:** G2, V2, N3, S1, P1, Q3, K2, F1, M2, E5, C1 ● **Temperaments:** F, J, T ● **Physical:** Stg=S; Freq: R, H, I, N, X Occas: S, K, O, E, T, G, A ● **Work Env:** Noise=Q; ● **Salary:** 4 ● **Outlook:** 4

INDUSTRIAL DESIGNER (profess. & kin.) ● DOT #142.061-026 ● OES: 34038 ● Originates and develops ideas to design the form of manufactured products: Reads publications, attends showings, and consults with engineering, marketing, production, and sales representatives to establish design concepts. Evaluates design ideas based on factors such as appealing appearance, design-function relationships, serviceability, materials and methods engineering, application, budget, price, production costs, methods of production, market characteristics, and client specifications. Integrates findings and concepts and sketches design ideas. Presents design to client or design committee and discusses need for modification and change. May design product packaging and graphics for advertising. May build simulated model, using hand and power tools and various materials. May prepare illustrations. May prepare or coordinate preparation of working drawings from sketches and design specifications. May design products for custom applications. May be required to have specialized product knowledge. Usually specializes in specific product or type of product including, but not limited to hardware, motor vehicle exteriors and interiors, scientific instruments, industrial equipment, luggage, jewelry, housewares, toys, or novelties and is designated accordingly. ● **GED:** R5, M4, L4 ● **SVP:** 2-4 yrs ● **Academic:** Ed=B, Eng=G ● **Work Field:** 264 ● **MPSMS:** 700, 759, 889 ● **Aptitudes:** G2, V2, N3, S2, P2, Q3, K3, F2, M3, E5, C2 ● **Temperaments:** F, J, P ● **Physical:** Stg=S; Freq: R, H, I, T, G, N, X Occas: D, A ● **Work Env:** Noise=Q; ● **Salary:** 4 ● **Outlook:** 2

INTERIOR DESIGNER (profess. & kin.) ● DOT #142.051-014 ● OES: 34041 ● Plans, designs, and furnishes interior environments of residential, commercial, and industrial buildings: Confers with client to determine architectural preferences, purpose and function of environment, budget, types of construction, equipment to be installed, and other factors which affect planning interior environments. Integrates findings with knowledge of interior design and formulates environmental plan to be practical, esthetic, and conducive to intended purposes, such as raising productivity, selling merchandise, or improving life style of occupants. Advises client on interior design factors, such as space planning, layout and utilization of furnishings and equipment, color schemes, and color coordination. Renders design ideas in form of paste ups, drawings, or illustrations, estimates material requirements and costs, and presents design to client for approval. Selects or designs and purchases furnishings, art works, and accessories. Subcontracts fabrication, installation, and arrangement of carpeting, fixtures, accessories, draperies, paint and wall coverings, art work, furniture, and related items. May plan and design interior environments for boats, planes, buses, trains, and other enclosed spaces. May specialize in particular field, style, or phase of interior design. May specialize in decorative aspects of interior design and be designated Interior Decorator (profess. & kin.). ● **GED:** R5, M3, L4 ● **SVP:** 2-4 yrs ● **Academic:** Ed=A, Eng=G ● **Work Field:** 264 ● **MPSMS:** 889 ● **Aptitudes:** G2, V2, N3, S2, P2, Q3, K3, F2, M3, E5, C2 ● **Temperaments:** D, F, I, J, P ● **Physical:** Stg=L; Freq: R, H, T, G, N, D, X Occas: C, S, K, O, I, F, A, V ● **Work Env:** Noise=N; ● **Salary:** 3 ● **Outlook:** 1

MANAGER, DISPLAY (retail trade) ● DOT #142.031-014 ● OES: 34038 ● Develops advertising displays for window or interior use and supervises and coordinates activities of workers engaged in laying out and assembling displays: Consults with advertising and sales officials to ascertain type of merchandise to be featured and time and place for each display. Develops layout and selects theme, colors, and props to be used. Oversees requisitioning and construction of decorative props from such materials as wood, plastics, paper, and glass. Plans lighting arrangement and selects coloring medium. May design store fixtures. May prepare sketches or floor plans of proposed displays. May develop merchandise displays at special exhibits, such as trade shows. ● **GED:** R5, M3, L4 ● **SVP:** 2-4 yrs ● **Academic:** Ed=A, Eng=S ● **Work Field:** 264, 292 ● **MPSMS:** 889 ● **Aptitudes:** G2, V2, N3, S2, P2, Q4, K3, F4, M4, E5, C2 ● **Temperaments:** D, F, J, P ● **Physical:** Stg=L; Freq: R, H, T, G, N, D, A, X, V Occas: I ● **Work Env:** Noise=N; ● **Salary:** 4 ● **Outlook:** 3

OPTICAL-EFFECTS-CAMERA OPERATOR (motion picture) ●
DOT #143.260-010 ● OES: 34026 ● Sets up and operates optical printers
and related equipment to produce fades, dissolves, superimpositions,
and other optical effects required in motion pictures, applying knowledge of optical effects printing and photography: Reads work order
and count sheet to ascertain optical effects specifications and location
of subject material on original photography film. Analyzes specifications to determine work procedures, sequence of operations, and machine setup, using knowledge of optical effects techniques and
procedures. Loads camera of optical effects printer with magazine of
unexposed film stock. Mounts original photography film in transport
and masking mechanism of optical-printer projector and moves film
into designated position for optical effect, using counter and film markings to determine placement. Adjusts camera position, lens position,
mask opening, lens aperture, focus, shutter angle, film transport speed,
and related controls, using precision measuring instruments and knowledge of optical effects techniques to determine settings. Selects designated color and neutral density filters and mounts in filter holder to
control light and intensity. Sets controls in automatic or manual mode,
moves control to start camera, and observes printer operation and footage counter during filming. Adjusts controls during filming operation
when operating in manual mode, and stops camera when designated
counter reading is observed. Moves controls to rewind camera film and
original photography film and repeats select portions or entire operation number of times necessary to produce designated effect. Sets up
and operates animation and matte cameras and related equipment to
photograph artwork, such as titles and painted mattes. Sets up and operates single pass optical printers when enlarging or reducing film or
performing related operations. Sets up and operates subtitle camera
and related equipment to photograph film subtitles. Examines frames
of film exposed with different combinations of color filters (wedges) to
select optimum color balance based on experience and judgment. ●
GED: R4, M3, L3 ● **SVP:** 2-4 yrs ● **Academic:** Ed=H, Eng=G ●
Work Field: 201 ● **MPSMS:** 753, 911 ● **Aptitudes:** G2, V3, N3, S3,
P3, Q3, K3, F3, M3, E4, C2 ● **Temperaments:** J, T ● **Physical:** Stg=L;
Freq: R, H, I, N, A, X Occas: S, O, T, G, F, D ● **Work Env:** Noise=N;
● **Salary:** 4 ● **Outlook:** 3

PACKAGE DESIGNER (profess. & kin.) ● DOT #142.081-018 ● OES:
34038 ● Designs containers for products, such as foods, beverages, toiletries, cigarettes, and medicines: Confers with representatives of engineering,
marketing, management, and other departments to determine packaging
requirements and type of product market. Sketches design of container for
specific product, considering factors, such as convenience in handling and
storing, distinctiveness for identification by consumer, and simplicity to
minimize production costs. Renders design, including exterior markings
and labels, using paints and brushes. Typically fabricates model in paper,
wood, glass, plastic, or metal, depending on material to be used in package.
Makes changes or modifications required by approving authority. ● **GED:**
R5, M3, L4 ● **SVP:** 2-4 yrs ● **Academic:** Ed=A, Eng=G ● **Work Field:**
264 ● **MPSMS:** 889, 752 ● **Aptitudes:** G2, V2, N3, S2, P2, Q3, K3, F2,
M3, E5, C2 ● **Temperaments:** F, J ● **Physical:** Stg=S; Const: N, X Freq:
R, H, I, D ● **Work Env:** Noise=Q; ● **Salary:** 3 ● **Outlook:** 2

PHOTOGRAPHER, STILL (profess. & kin.) ● DOT #143.062-030 ●
OES: 34023 ● Alternate titles: COMMERCIAL PHOTOGRAPHER. Photographs subjects, using still cameras, color or black-and-white film, and
variety of photographic accessories: Selects and assembles equipment according to subject material, anticipated conditions, and knowledge of function and limitations of various types of cameras, lenses, films, and accessories.
Views subject and setting and plans composition, camera position, and camera
angle to produce desired effect. Arranges subject material, poses subject, or
maneuvers into position to take candid photo. Estimates or measures light
level, using light meter or creates artificial lighting with flash units, lights,
and lighting equipment. Adjusts lens aperture and shutter speed based on
combination of factors, such as lighting, depth of field, subject motion, and
film speed. Determines subject-to-lens distance, using tape measure, range
finder, ground glass, or reflex viewing system to adjust focus. Positions
camera and trips shutter to expose film. May calculate variables, such as
exposure time, exposure interval, filter effect, and color temperature using
tables, standard formulas, and mechanical or electronic measuring instruments. May make adjustments to camera, lens, or equipment to compensate
for factors, such as distorted perspective and parallax. May design, build,
arrange, or secure properties and settings to be used as background for
subject material. May direct activities of other workers. May mix chemicals, process film and photographic paper, and make contact and enlarged

prints. May spot and retouch prints and negatives. May conceive and plan
photographic sequence for effective presentation. May specialize in particular type of photography, such as illustrative, fashion, architectural, or
portrait. May be required to have detailed knowledge of use and character-
istics of various types of film, including specialty films, such as infrared. ●
GED: R4, M3, L4 ● **SVP:** 2-4 yrs ● **Academic:** Ed=H, Eng=S ● **Work
Field:** 201 ● **MPSMS:** 753 ● **Aptitudes:** G2, V3, N3, S2, P2, Q4, K3, F3,
M3, E5, C2 ● **Temperaments:** F, J, P ● **Physical:** Stg=L; Freq: R, H, I, N,
F, D, A, X, V Occas: S, K, T, G ● **Work Env:** Noise=N; Occas: W ●
Salary: 4 ● **Outlook:** 1

PHOTOJOURNALIST (print. & pub.) ● DOT #143.062-034 ● OES:
34023 ● Alternate titles: PHOTOGRAPHER, NEWS. Photographs
newsworthy events, locations, people, or other illustrative or educational material for use in publications or telecasts, using still cameras:
Travels to assigned location and takes pictures. Develops negatives and
prints film. Submits negatives and pictures to editorial personnel. Usually specializes in one phase of photography, as news, sports, special
features, or as freelance photographer. ● **GED:** R4, M2, L4 ● **SVP:** 2-4
yrs ● **Academic:** Ed=H, Eng=G ● **Work Field:** 201, 202 ● **MPSMS:** 753,
757 ● **Aptitudes:** G3, V3, N3, S2, P2, Q3, K3, F3, M3, E5, C5 ● **Temperaments:** F, J, P ● **Physical:** Stg=L; Const: R, H, I Freq: T, G, N, F, D, A, X,
V ● **Work Env:** Noise=N; Freq: W ● **Salary:** 5 ● **Outlook:** 2

POLICE ARTIST (government ser.) ● DOT #141.061-034 ● OES:
34035 ● Alternate titles: FORENSIC ARTIST. Sketches likenesses of
criminal suspects, according to descriptions of victims and witnesses,
and prepares schematic drawings depicting scenes of crimes: Interviews
crime victims and witnesses to obtain descriptive information concerning physical build, sex, nationality, facial features, and related characteristics of unidentified suspect. Prepares series of simple line drawings
conforming to description of suspect and presents drawings to informant for selection of sketch that most resembles suspect. Questions
informant to obtain additional descriptive information and draws and
verifies details of features to improve resemblance of conception to
recollection of informant. Measures distances and sketches layout of
crime scene, or develops sketches from photographs and measurements
taken at scene of crime by other police personnel to prepare schematic
drawing of scene of crime. ● **GED:** R5, M3, L4 ● **SVP:** 2-4 yrs ●
Academic: Ed=A, Eng=G ● **Work Field:** 262 ● **MPSMS:** 759, 951 ●
Aptitudes: G2, V2, N3, S2, P2, Q3, K2, F2, M2, E5, C3 ● **Temperaments:** J, P, T ● **Physical:** Stg=L; Freq: R, H, I, T, G, N, F, D, A, X, V
● **Work Env:** Noise=N; ● **Salary:** 4 ● **Outlook:** 3

SET DECORATOR (motion picture) ● DOT #142.061-042 ● OES:
34038 ● Selects decorations and coordinates activities of workers who
decorate sets for motion picture or television production: Reads script
to determine decoration requirements. Selects furniture, draperies, pictures, lamps, and rugs for decorative quality and appearance on film.
Gives directions to GRIP (motion picture; radio-tv broad.) in placing
items on set. Examines dressed sets to ensure props and scenery do not
interfere with moovements of cast or view of camera. ● **GED:** R5, M2,
L4 ● **SVP:** 4-10 yrs ● **Academic:** Ed=A, Eng=G ● **Work Field:** 264 ●
MPSMS: 759 ● **Aptitudes:** G2, V2, N3, S2, P2, Q4, K4, F4, M4, E5,
C1 ● **Temperaments:** D, F, J, P ● **Physical:** Stg=S; Freq: T, G, N, D,
X Occas: F ● **Work Env:** Noise=N; ● **Salary:** 4 ● **Outlook:** 1

SET DESIGNER (amuse. & rec.) ● DOT #142.061-050 ● OES: 34038
● Alternate titles: SCENIC DESIGNER; THEATRICAL-SCENIC
DESIGNER. Designs sets for theatrical productions: Confers with play's
director regarding interpretation and set requirements. Conducts research to determine appropriate architectural and furnishing styles. Integrates requirements, interpretation, research, design concepts, and
practical considerations regarding factors, such as mobility, interchange-
ability, and budget to plan sets. Renders drawing or illustration of design concept, estimates costs, and presents drawing for approval.
Prepares working drawings of floor plan, front elevation, scenery, and
properties to be constructed. Prepares charts to indicate where items,
such as curtains and borders are to be hung. Oversees building of sets,
furniture, and properties. May build scale models from cardboard, plaster, or sponge. May design stage lighting to achieve dramatic or decorative effects. ● **GED:** R5, M3, L4 ● **SVP:** 4-10 yrs ● **Academic:**
Ed=A, Eng=G ● **Work Field:** 264 ● **MPSMS:** 701, 912 ● **Aptitudes:**
G2, V2, N3, S1, P2, Q4, K2, F2, M3, E5, C2 ● **Temperaments:** D, F,
J, P, T ● **Physical:** Stg=L; Freq: R, H, I, E, T, G, N, F, D, A, X, V ●
Work Env: Noise=N; ● **Salary:** 4 ● **Outlook:** 1

SET DESIGNER (motion picture) ● DOT #142.061-046 ● OES: 34038 ● Designs motion picture or television production sets, signs, props, or scenic effects, and prepares scale drawings for use in construction, modification, or alteration: Confers with ART DIRECTOR (motion picture; radio-tv broad.) 142.061-062 and reviews illustrations to determine set requirements and discuss preliminary design ideas. Integrates requirements and concepts to conceive set design. Prepares rough draft and scale working drawings of set [DRAFTER (profess. & kin.) Master Title]. Presents drawings for approval and makes changes and corrections as directed. May design miniature motion picture or television production sets used in filming backgrounds, titles, and special effects and be designated Miniature Set Designer (motion picture; radio-tv broad.). May purchase construction materials and ready made props to ensure availability for use by freelance workers. May schedule times television production sets and props are to be used, and coordinate setup and storage of television production sets and props. ● **GED:** R5, M3, L4 ● **SVP:** 4-10 yrs ● **Academic:** Ed=A, Eng=G ● **Work Field:** 242, 264 ● **MPSMS:** 752, 864, 911 ● **Aptitudes:** G2, V2, N3, S2, P2, Q4, K2, F2, M3, E5, C2 ● **Temperaments:** F, J, T, V ● **Physical:** Stg=L; Freq: T, G, N, X Occas: C, R, H, I, F, D, A ● **Work Env:** Noise=N; ● **Salary:** 4 ● **Outlook:** 1

TELEVISION TECHNICIAN (radio-tv broad.) ● DOT #194.062-010 ● OES: 34028 ● Alternate titles: PRODUCTION ASSISTANT;

PRODUCTION TECHNICIAN. Performs any combination of following duties to record and transmit broadcasts: Operates studio and mini-television (portable, shoulder-mounted) cameras [CAMERA OPERATOR (motion picture; radio-tv broad.) 143.062-022]. Controls console to regulate transmission of television scenes [VIDEO OPERATOR (radio-tv broad.) 194.282-010]. Produces educational and training films and video tapes [COMMUNICATIONS TECHNICIAN (education) 962.362-010]. Sets up and controls television production equipment, such as cameras [CAMERA OPERATOR (radio-tv broad.)], lights [LIGHT TECHNICIAN (motion picture; radio-tv broad.) 962.362-014], microphones and microphone booms [MICROPHONE-BOOM OPERATOR (motion picture; radio-tv broad.) 962.384-010], and recording equipment [RECORDIST (motion picture) 962.382-010], in studio and at locations outside of studio, to record or transmit broadcasts. Performs preventive and minor equipment maintenance, using work tools. Maintains log to record equipment usage and location of equipment. May perform duties of other related occupations depending upon specific production needs of individual airwave or closed-circuit station where workers must be able to set up and operate equipment. ● **GED:** R5, M4, L5 ● **SVP:** 2-4 yrs ● **Academic:** Ed=A, Eng=G ● **Work Field:** 201, 281 ● **MPSMS:** 864, 869 ● **Aptitudes:** G2, V2, N3, S2, P2, Q3, K3, F3, M3, E4, C3 ● **Temperaments:** F, J, P, T, V ● **Physical:** Stg=H; Freq: R, H, T, G Occas: S, O, I, N, F, D, A, X, V ● **Work Env:** Noise=N; Occas: W ● **Salary:** 3 ● **Outlook:** 2

Artistic   01

Performing Arts: Drama   01.03

Workers in this group produce, direct, and perform in dramatic productions and similar forms of entertainment. They also tech acting, choose performers for particular roles, and perform other 'behind-the-scenes' work to make productions run smoothly. They are employed by motion picture, television, and radio studios, and by stock companies, theaters and other places where plays or floor shows are presented. Schools and colleges hire performing artists both to teach drama and to produce and direct student productions. Full time employment in this field is found at educational institutions, at studios which have staff announcers, disc jockeys, and regularly scheduled 'talk shows' or dramatic presentations. However, most performing artists are not permanently employed, and must audition for roles in both short-term and long-run productions.

✓ What kind of work would you do?

Your work activities would depend upon your specific job. For example, you might:

- do a pantomime, using only body movements and facial expressions.
- instruct students in the basic techniques of acting.
- direct actors and other workers involved in a play or motion picture.
- select, announce, and play popular records at a radio station.
- perform a comic monologue on a television variety show or in a night club.

✓ What skills and abilities do you need for this kind of work?

To do this kind of work, you must be able to:

- perform before an audience with poise and self-confidence.
- interpret roles, and express ideas and emotions through body motions, facial expressions, and voice inflections.
- understand the ideas that the author of a script is trying to get across, and demonstrate to others methods of moving or speaking to convey these ideas to an audience.
- speak clearly and loudly.
- memorize dialogue and respond to cues promptly.
- maintain physical and mental energy through long hours of rehearsal and performance.

✓ How do you know if you would like or could learn to do this kind of work?

The following questions may give you clues about yourself as you consider this group of jobs.

- Have you performed in a play? Do you enjoy performing before an audience?
- Have you spoken on radio or television? Are you able to control your voice and is it pleasing when electronically amplified?
- Have you memorized a long passage? Can you recite from memory before an audience?

✓ How can you prepare for and enter this kind of work?

Occupations in this group usually require education and/or training extending from one year to over ten years, depending upon the specific kind of work. Because of the strong competition for jobs, workers in this group must have both training and experience. Initial training and experience are available in speech classes, debate programs, and school or community plays. Four-year degrees and advanced study in drama or communications provide additional training. Courses in speech, pantomime, directing, and acting are a part of these programs. Colleges also provide opportunities for experience in acting, announcing, and directing. Special acting schools offer professional training in the dramatic arts.

Experience in numerous productions is very important, including both amateur and paid jobs. Dinner theaters, summer theaters, repertory groups, and local radio and television stations provide valuable experiences.

Jobs in directing require extensive acting experience or experience in directing amateur productions. Dramatic coaching and college level teaching usually require advanced degrees in dramatics. Professional experience in acting, directing, or play production is also helpful. Teachers of high school courses in drama, speech, or communications must meet specific educational and licensing requirements.

✓ *What else should you consider about these jobs?*

Dramatic artists are often required to meet demanding work schedules. These schedules may require early or late hours for rehearsals and performances. Memorizing sessions require individual study. In addition, frequent travel may be necessary.

Work assignments sometimes depend upon an individual's voice or physical appearance. Distinctive features are assets which are in much demand.

If you think you would like to do this kind of work, look at the job titles listed below.

■ ■ ■

GOE: 01.03.01
Instructing & Directing, Drama

COMMUNICATIONS TECHNICIAN (education) ● DOT #962.362-010 ● OES: 39998 ● Performs a variety of duties involved in producing motion picture film in audio-visual department of educational institution: Selects areas and locations for filming motion pictures according to specifications. Sets up lighting equipment. Selects picture and sound takes to conform film to script. Assists in designing and building sets for film production. Requisitions props. Edits and splices motion picture film. Operates projectors, video tape recorders, and sound recording equipment to inspect and preview film for clients. Packages and ships film. ● **GED:** R4, M2, L3 ● **SVP:** 2-4 yrs ● **Academic:** Ed=H, Eng=G ● **Work Field:** 281, 111 ● **MPSMS:** 911 ● **Aptitudes:** G3, V3, N3, S3, P2, Q3, K3, F3, M3, E4, C3 ● **Temperaments:** J ● **Physical:** Stg=L; Freq: R, H, I, N, D, X Occas: T, G, A ● **Work Env:** Noise=L; Freq: W ● **Salary:** 4 ● **Outlook:** 3

DIRECTOR, MOTION PICTURE (motion picture) ● DOT #159.067-010 ● OES: 34056 ● Reads and interprets script, conducts rehearsals, and directs activities of cast and technical crew for motion picture film: Confers with ART DIRECTOR (motion picture; radio-tv broad.) to ensure that music, sets, scenic effects, and costumes conform to script interpretation. Confers with DIRECTOR OF PHOTOGRAPHY (motion picture) to explain details of scene to be photographed and to consider utilization of miniatures, stock film, inserts, transparencies, backgrounds, or trick shots. Schedules sequences of scenes to be filmed for each day of shooting, grouping scenes together according to set and cast of characters. Rehearses cast and suggests changes, using knowledge of acting, voice, and movement to elicit best possible performance. Informs technicians of scenery, lights, props, and other equipment desired. Approves scenery, costumes, choreography, and music. Directs cast, DIRECTOR OF PHOTOGRAPHY (motion picture; radio-tv broad.), and other technicians during rehearsals and final filming. May audition and select cast. May cut and edit film. May direct film on set in studio or on location. May direct film for television. ● **GED:** R5, M4, L5 ● **SVP:** 4-10 yrs ● **Academic:** Ed=A, Eng=G ● **Work Field:** 295 ● **MPSMS:** 911 ● **Aptitudes:** G1, V2, N3, S3, P3, Q3, K4, F4, M4, E5, C5 ● **Temperaments:** D, J, P, V ● **Physical:** Stg=S; Freq: T, G, N, X Occas: R, H, F ● **Work Env:** Noise=Q; Occas: W ● **Salary:** 5 ● **Outlook:** 1

DIRECTOR, STAGE (amuse. & rec.) ● DOT #150.067-010 ● OES: 34056 ● Interprets script, directs technicians, and conducts rehearsals to create stage presentation: Confers with PLAYWRIGHT (profess. & kin.) and PRODUCER (amuse. & rec.) to discuss script changes. Confers with MANAGER, STAGE (amuse. & rec.) to coordinate production plans. Rehearses cast in individual roles to elicit best possible performance. Suggests changes, such as voice and movement, to develop performance based on script interpretation and using knowledge of acting techniques. Approves scenic and costume designs, sound, special effects, and choreography. May select cast. May select SET DESIGNER (amuse. & rec.). ● **GED:** R5, M3, L5 ● **SVP:** 4-10 yrs ● **Academic:** Ed=H, Eng=G ● **Work Field:** 295 ● **MPSMS:** 754 ● **Aptitudes:** G1, V2, N4, S2, P3, Q3, K4, F4, M4, E4, C3 ● **Temperaments:** D, F, J, P, V ● **Physical:** Stg=L; Const: T, G Freq: N, F, D, A, X, V ● **Work Env:** Noise=N; ● **Salary:** 5 ● **Outlook:** 2

MANAGER, STAGE (amuse. & rec.) ● DOT #159.167-018 ● OES: 34056 ● Coordinates production plans and directs activities of stage crew and performers during rehearsals and performance: Confers with DIRECTOR, STAGE (amuse. & rec.) 150.067-010 concerning production plans. Arranges conference times for cast, crew, and DIRECTOR, STAGE (amuse. & rec.), and disseminates general information about production. Reads script during each performance and gives cues for curtain, lights, sound effects, and prompting performers. Interprets stage-set diagrams to determine stage layout. Supervises stage crew engaged in placing scenery and properties. Devises emergency substitutes for stage equipment or properties. Keeps records to advise PRODUCER (amuse. & rec.) 187.167-178 on matters of time, attendance, and employee benefits. Compiles cue words and phrases to form prompt book. Directs activities of one or more assistants. May instruct understudy, replacement, or extra. May call performers at specified interval before curtain time. May operate production equipment to transmit or record performance. ● **GED:** R4, M3, L4 ● **SVP:** 2-4 yrs ● **Academic:** Ed=H, Eng=G ● **Work Field:** 295 ● **MPSMS:** 910, 864, 869 ● **Aptitudes:** G2, V2, N3, S3, P4, Q3, K4, F3, M3, E4, C4 ● **Temperaments:** D, J, P, V ● **Physical:** Stg=L; Const: T, G Freq: R, H, N Occas: I, D, A, X, V ● **Work Env:** Noise=N; ● **Salary:** 4 ● **Outlook:** 2

PRODUCER (amuse. & rec.) ● DOT #187.167-178 ● OES: 34056 ● Selects play for stage performance, arranges finances, and coordinates play production activities: Reads manuscripts and selects play on basis of plot, timeliness, and quality of writing. Sells shares to investors to finance production. Hires DIRECTOR, STAGE (amuse. & rec.); MANAGER, STAGE (amuse. & rec.), cast, and crew. Formulates business management policies and coordinates production schedules. Suggests or approves changes in script and staging. Arbitrates personnel disputes. May direct production of play [DIRECTOR, STAGE (amuse. & rec.)]. May produce shows for special occasions, such as fund-raising events or testimonial banquets. ● **GED:** R5, M4, L5 ● **SVP:** 2-4 yrs ● **Academic:** Ed=B, Eng=G ● **Work Field:** 295, 297 ● **MPSMS:** 754 ● **Aptitudes:** G2, V2, N3, S4, P2, Q4, K4, F4, M4, E5, C4 ● **Temperaments:** D, J, P, V ● **Physical:** Stg=L; Freq: T, G, N Occas: R, H, I, X ● **Work Env:** Noise=N; ● **Salary:** 5 ● **Outlook:** 1

PRODUCER (radio-tv broad.) ● DOT #159.117-010 ● OES: 34056 ● Alternate titles: ASSOCIATE PRODUCER. Plans and coordinates various aspects of radio, television, or cable television programs: Interviews and selects SCREEN WRITERS (motion picture; radio-tv broad.) 131.067-050 and cast principals from staff members or outside talent. Outlines program to be produced to SCREEN WRITERS (motion picture; radio-tv broad.) and evaluates finished script. Composes or edits program script to meet management or other requirements, using typewriter or computer terminal. Coordinates various aspects of production, such as audio work, scenes, music, timing, camera work, and script writing. Gives instructions to staff to schedule broadcast and to develop and coordinate details to obtain desired production. Reviews production to ensure objectives are attained. Views taped program to select scenes to be used for promotional purposes, using video equipment. Listens to audio tape recording to verify program, script, or sound effects conform to broadcast standards, using audio equipment. May obtain costumes, props, music, or other equipment or personnel to complete production. May represent television network, acting as liaison to independent producer of television series produced for network broadcast. May review budget and expenditures for programs or commercial productions for conformance to budgetary restrictions. May coordinate production details to produce live television programs from locations distant from station. May be designated according to level of responsibility and by type of show produced as Executive Producer (radio-tv broad.); or by type of media as Radio Producer (radio-tv broad.); Television Producer (radio-tv broad.). ● **GED:** R6, M4, L6 ● **SVP:** 4-10 yrs ● **Academic:** Ed=B, Eng=S ● **Work Field:** 295 ● **MPSMS:** 863, 864, 869 ● **Aptitudes:** G1, V1, N3, S4, P3, Q4, K4, F4, M4, E5, C4 ● **Temperaments:** D, F, J, P, V ● **Physical:** Stg=L; Freq: H, T, G Occas: R, I, N, D, A, X, V ● **Work Env:** Noise=N; ● **Salary:** 5 ● **Outlook:** 1

SUPERVISOR, SHOW OPERATIONS (amuse. & rec.) ● DOT #969.137-014 ● OES: 39998 ● Supervises and coordinates activities of performers and technicians in amusement or theme park: Reviews and adjusts performance schedule to ensure number of performances meets anticipated attendance. Arranges shift assignments of performers and technicians. Talks to guests in person or by telephone to answer questions and resolve complaints. Performs other duties as described under SUPERVISOR (any industry) Master Title. ● **GED:** R4, M4, L4 ● **SVP:** 1-2 yrs ● **Academic:** Ed=N, Eng=G ● **Work Field:** 297 ● **MPSMS:** 919 ● **Aptitudes:** G2, V2, N3, S3, P3, Q3, K4, F4, M4, E5, C5 ● **Temperaments:** D, P, V ● **Physical:** Stg=L; Freq: T, G, N Occas: S, R, H, I ● **Work Env:** Noise=N; ● **Salary:** 4 ● **Outlook:** 2

GOE: 01.03.02
Performing, Drama

ACTOR (amuse. & rec.) ● DOT #150.047-010 ● OES: 34056 ● Portrays role in dramatic production to interpret character or present characterization to audience: Rehearses part to learn lines and cues as directed. Interprets serious or comic role by speech, gesture, and body movement to entertain or inform audience for stage, motion picture, television, radio, or other media production. May write or adapt own material. May dance and sing. May direct self and others in production [DIRECTOR, MOTION PICTURE (motion picture); DIRECTOR, STAGE (amuse. & rec.)]. May read from script or book, utilizing minimum number of stage properties and relying mainly on changes of voice and inflection to hold audience's attention and be designated Dramatic Reader (amuse. & rec.). May be designated according to gender of worker or type of role portrayed as Actress (amuse. & rec.); Character Actor (amuse. & rec.); Character Actress (amuse. & rec.); Ingenue (amuse. & rec.); Juvenile (amuse. & rec.). ● **GED:** R5, M2, L5 ● **SVP:** 2-4 yrs ● **Academic:** Ed=A, Eng=G ● **Work Field:** 297 ●

MPSMS: 754 ● **Aptitudes:** G2, V2, N5, S3, P3, Q5, K4, F4, M4, E3, C5 ● **Temperaments:** F, J, P, V ● **Physical:** Stg=L; Const: T, G ● **Work Env:** Noise=N; ● **Salary:** 2 ● **Outlook:** 1

CLOWN (amuse. & rec.) ● DOT #159.047-010 ● OES: 34056 ● Dresses in comical costume and makeup and performs original or stock comedy routines to entertain audience. ● **GED:** R4, M2, L3 ● **SVP:** 1-2 yrs ● **Academic:** Ed=N, Eng=N ● **Work Field:** 297 ● **MPSMS:** 919 ● **Aptitudes:** G3, V3, N4, S3, P4, Q5, K2, F3, M2, E2, C4 ● **Temperaments:** I, J, P, T ● **Physical:** Stg=L; Freq: C, B, R, H, T, G, F, V ● **Work Env:** Noise=N; Occas: W ● **Salary:** 4 ● **Outlook:** 1

COMEDIAN (amuse. & rec.) ● DOT #159.047-014 ● OES: 34056 ● Alternate titles: COMIC. Attempts to make audience laugh by telling jokes, delivering comic lines, singing humorous songs, performing comedy dances or walks, or facial contortions, wearing funny costumes, or resorting to any similar device to amuse audience. May do impersonations [IMPERSONATOR (amuse. & rec.)]. ● **GED:** R5, M2, L4 ● **SVP:** 6 mos-1 yr ● **Academic:** Ed=N, Eng=G ● **Work Field:** 297 ● **MPSMS:** 919 ● **Aptitudes:** G3, V2, N4, S3, P4, Q4, K3, F4, M4, E5, C5 ● **Temperaments:** F, P, V ● **Physical:** Stg=L; Const: T, G ● **Work Env:** Noise=N; ● **Salary:** 3 ● **Outlook:** 1

IMPERSONATOR (amuse. & rec.) ● DOT #159.047-018 ● OES: 34056 ● Alternate titles: IMITATOR; MIMIC. Entertains by impersonating another person, or type of person, or animal, or some inanimate object, usually by copying mannerisms, form, expression, dress, voice, or sound of character or thing impersonated. May be designated according to character impersonated as Animal Impersonator (amuse. & rec.); Female Impersonator (amuse. & rec.); Male Impersonator (amuse. & rec.). ● **GED:** R4, M2, L4 ● **SVP:** 1-2 yrs ● **Academic:** Ed=N, Eng=G ● **Work Field:** 297 ● **MPSMS:** 969, 919 ● **Aptitudes:** G2, V2, N4, S3, P4, Q4, K4, F4, M4, E4, C5 ● **Temperaments:** F, P ● **Physical:** Stg=L; Const: T, G ● **Work Env:** Noise=N; ● **Salary:** 4 ● **Outlook:** 1

INTERPRETER, DEAF (profess. & kin.) ● DOT #137.267-014 ● OES: 39998 ● Alternate titles: TRANSLATOR, DEAF. Provides translation between spoken and manual (sign language) communication: Translates spoken material into sign language for understanding of deaf. Interprets sign language of deaf into oral or written language for hearing individuals or others not conversant in sign language. May translate late television news and other broadcasts for deaf viewers. ● **GED:** R4, M3, L4 ● **SVP:** 6 mos-1 yr ● **Academic:** Ed=H, Eng=G ● **Work Field:** 282 ● **MPSMS:** 869 ● **Aptitudes:** G3, V2, N4, S4, P3, Q3, K2, F3, M3, E5, C5 ● **Temperaments:** J, P ● **Physical:** Stg=L; Freq: R, H, I, T, G, N ● **Work Env:** Noise=N; ● **Salary:** 4 ● **Outlook:** 4

PUPPETEER (amuse. & rec.) ● DOT #159.041-014 ● OES: 34056 ● Originates puppet shows, designs and constructs puppets and moves controls of puppets to animate them for entertainment of audience: Studies media for ideas that relate to fads, stories, plays, and seasonal themes and confers with other staff to develop ideas for new show. Writes or adapts script for use in puppet theater. Sketches designs for puppets based on script. Constructs hand, string, rod, and shadow puppets from materials, such as wood, papier mache, styrofoam, wires, metal, and rubber, using handtools and machine tools. Sews clothing for puppets by hand or machine. Animates puppets, using string, wire, rod, fingers or hand from position above, below, or at level with stage. Talks or sings during performance to give illusion of voice to puppets. May operate audio equipment, such as tape deck, during performance and simultaneously move puppet's mouth in synchronization with music to create illusion of singing. ● **GED:** R4, M3, L4 ● **SVP:** 4-10 yrs ● **Academic:** Ed=N, Eng=G ● **Work Field:** 261, 264, 297 ● **MPSMS:** 919 ● **Aptitudes:** G2, V2, N3, S3, P2, Q4, K2, F2, M2, E3, C2 ● **Temperaments:** J, P, S, T ● **Physical:** Stg=L; Freq: B, S, K, O, R, H, I, T, G, D, X, V Occas: C, W, E, N, A ● **Work Env:** Noise=N; ● **Salary:** 2 ● **Outlook:** 1

GOE: 01.03.03
Narrating & Announcing

ANNOUNCER (radio-tv broad.) ● DOT #159.147-010 ● OES: 34010 ● Alternate titles: RADIO BOARD OPERATOR-ANNOUNCER.

Announces radio and television programs to audience: Memorizes script, reads, or ad-libs to identify station, introduce and close shows, and announce station breaks, commercials, or public service information. Cues worker to transmit program from network central station or other pick-up points according to schedule. Reads news flashes to keep audience informed of important events. May rewrite news bulletin from wire service teletype to fit specific time slot. May describe public event such as parade or convention. May interview guest, such as sport or other public personality, and moderate panel or discussion show to entertain audience. May keep daily program log. May operate control console (radio board). May perform additional duties in small stations, such as operating radio transmitter [TRANSMITTER OPERATOR (radio-tv broad.) 193.262-038], selling time, or writing advertising copy. May be designated according to media as Radio Announcer (radio-tv broad.); Television Announcer (radio-tv broad.). May announce program of local interest and be designated Local Announcer (radio-tv broad.). May announce program for transmission over network and affiliated stations and be designated Network Announcer (radio-tv broad.). May announce in foreign language for international broadcast and be designated Announcer, International Broadcast (radio-tv broad.). May describe sporting event during game from direct observation or announce sports news received at station for radio or television broadcasting and be designated Sports Announcer (radio-tv broad.). ● **GED:** R5, M3, L4 ● **SVP:** 1-2 yrs ● **Academic:** Ed=A, Eng=G ● **Work Field:** 282, 297 ● **MPSMS:** 863, 864, 869 ● **Aptitudes:** G2, V2, N3, S4, P4, Q3, K4, F4, M4, E5, C5 ● **Temperaments:** J, P, T, V ● **Physical:** Stg=L; Freq: T, G Occas: R, H, I, N ● **Work Env:** Noise=N; ● **Salary:** 4 ● **Outlook:** 1

DISC JOCKEY (radio-tv broad.) ● DOT #159.147-014 ● OES: 34010 ● Announces radio program of musical selections: Selects phonograph or tape recording to be played based on program specialty, knowledge of audience taste, or listening audience requests. Comments on music and other matters of interest to audience, such as weather, time, or traffic conditions. May interview musical personalities. May interview members of listening audience who telephone musical requests. May specialize in one type of music, such as classical, pop, rock, or country and western. May write entries onto log to provide information on all elements aired during broadcast, such as musical selections and station promotions. May be designated Combination Operator (radio-tv broad.) when operating transmitter or control console. ● **GED:** R5, M3, L5 ● **SVP:** 6 mos-1 yr ● **Academic:** Ed=A, Eng=S ● **Work Field:** 282, 297 ● **MPSMS:** 863 ● **Aptitudes:** G2, V2, N3, S4, P4, Q3, K4, F3, M4, E5, C5 ● **Temperaments:** P, V ● **Physical:** Stg=L; Const: G Freq: H Occas: R, I, T ● **Work Env:** Noise=N; ● **Salary:** 5 ● **Outlook:** 1

NARRATOR (motion picture) ● DOT #150.147-010 ● OES: 34056 ● Alternate titles: MOTION-PICTURE COMMENTATOR. Makes explanatory comments to accompany action parts of motion picture: Reads from script and speaks into microphone as film is being projected, timing comments to fit action portrayed. May write script. ● **GED:** R5, M2, L5 ● **SVP:** 6 mos-1 yr ● **Academic:** Ed=A, Eng=G ● **Work Field:** 297 ● **MPSMS:** 911 ● **Aptitudes:** G2, V2, N3, S4, P4, Q4, K4, F4, M4, E5, C5 ● **Temperaments:** F, J ● **Physical:** Stg=L; Const: T, G ● **Work Env:** Noise=Q; ● **Salary:** 4 ● **Outlook:** 3

PROGRAM COORDINATOR (amuse. & rec.) ● DOT #139.167-010 ● OES: 34056 ● Coordinates activities of amusement park educational department to present educational scripts during animal performances: Reviews educational materials to gather information for scripts. Confers with animal trainer to verify format of performance, and writes script to coincide with performance, or reviews scripts prepared by department researchers for suggested changes in format. Prepares brochures containing information, such as time of performances, theme of performances, and map of park facilities. Reads reservation log to determine information, such as name of visiting groups, size of groups, and time of arrival. Greets visitors, passes out brochures, answers questions, and escorts visitors to site of performance. May introduce trainer to audience and present memorized script during performance over speaker system and be designated Narrator (amuse. & rec.). ● **GED:** R4, M2, L4 ● **SVP:** 4-10 yrs ● **Academic:** Ed=H, Eng=G ● **Work Field:** 295, 261 ● **MPSMS:** 931 ● **Aptitudes:** G2, V2, N3, S4, P4, Q2, K4, F4, M4, E5, C5 ● **Temperaments:** D, I, J, P ● **Physical:** Stg=L; Const: R, H Freq: I, T, G, N Occas: S, K, F, A, V ● **Work Env:** Noise=N; ● **Salary:** 3 ● **Outlook:** 2

SHOW HOST/HOSTESS (radio-tv broad.) ● DOT #159.147-018 ● OES: 34010 ● Alternate titles: GAME SHOW HOST/HOSTESS; TALENT; TALK SHOW HOST/HOSTESS. Performs any combination of following duties to broadcast program over television or radio: Discusses and prepares program content with PRODUCER (radio-tv broad.) 159.117-010 and assistants. Interviews show guests about their lives, their work, or topics of current interest. Discusses various topics over telephone with viewers or listeners. Asks questions of contestants, or manages play of game, to enable contestants to win prizes. Describes or demonstrates products that viewers may purchase by telephoning show or by mail, or may purchase in stores. Acts as Host/Hostess at civic, charitable, or promotional events that are broadcast over television or radio. ● **GED:** R5, M3, L5 ● **SVP:** 1-2 yrs ● **Academic:** Ed=N, Eng=G ● **Work Field:** 282, 297 ● **MPSMS:** 863, 864, 869 ● **Aptitudes:** G2, V2, N3, S4, P4, Q3, K4, F4, M4, E5, C5 ● **Temperaments:** P, V ● **Physical:** Stg=L; Const: T, G Occas: R, H, I, N, F, V ● **Work Env:** Noise=N; Occas: W ● **Salary:** 2 ● **Outlook:** 1

Performing Arts: Music   **01.04**

Workers in this group sing or play instruments, teach, or direct vocal or instrumental music. They compose, arrange, or orchestrate musical compositions, and plan the presentation of concerts. They work for motion picture studios, television and radio networks or local stations, recording studios, night clubs, and other places where musical entertainment is provided regularly. They may be employed by orchestras, bands, or choral groups which give scheduled performances or are hired for special events. Composers, arrangers, and orchestrators work for music publishing companies and firms in the recording and entertainment fields. Schools and colleges hire musicians to teach and direct vocal and instrumental music. Many musicians are self-employed, and like all performing artists, must audition for parts in musical productions or for employment with an orchestra or other performing group.

✓ What kind of work would you do?

Your work activities would depend upon your specific job. For example, you might:

- direct a choir, orchestra, or band.
- sing in a professional choir.
- play a musical instrument in a band.
- sing several solos in a concert.
- prepare the musical score for all instruments in an orchestra.
- compose an original music number.
- select and arrange a program of music.

- give private voice or instrument lessons.
- What skills and abilities do you need for this kind of work?

To do this kind of work, you must be able to:

- spend long hours developing and perfecting your talent, and, even after becoming extremely skilled, continue to practice daily.
- perform before an audience with poise and self-assurance.
- recognize and follow music symbols and oral or written instructions for interpreting music properly.
- understand the qualities of various musical instruments and consider these in orchestrating or arranging compositions to create desired effects.
- apply standard musical theories and techniques to direct performances of vocal or instrumental groups.
- use your hands and fingers skillfully to play an instrument.

✓ How do you know if you would like or could learn to do this kind of work?

The following questions may give you clues about yourself as you consider this group of jobs.

- Have you sung in school choruses or church choirs? Does your voice blend well with others? Do you enjoy singing in public?
- Have you had lessons in singing or playing a musical instrument? Have you played in a school band or orchestra? Can you read music?
- Have you composed a song or music for an instrument? Did others enjoy it?
- Have you sung or played with a rock or country group?

✓ How can you prepare for an enter this kind of work?

Occupations in this group usually require education and/or training extending from two years to over ten years, depending upon the specific kind of work. Professional instrumental musicians usually receive initial training while in elementary school. They

continue studying throughout most of their working life. Several hours of practice each day is a continuing requirement for the development and maintenance of the needed skills.

Professional vocal musicians usually start formal training in high school or whenever their voices mature. School music groups and programs provide good initial training. Daily individual or group practice is a continuing requirement for vocal musicians.

Although some persons with fine natural singing voices or self-developed skill in playing an instrument may find work—or even achieve great success—in popular rock, country, or jazz music, they are the rare exceptions. Study in college, at a music conservatory, or with private teachers is recommended for people who want to become professional musicians. Courses in music theory, composition, and conducting are required in addition to technical instruction. Arrangers, composers, and conductors need extensive training in these subjects.

Membership in a musical group is considered valuable experience and preparation for musicians. This experience is also helpful for people studying for solo performances.

Employment as a professional musician is usually dependent upon the skill and experience of the individual. Teachers in public schools and colleges are required to meet specific educational and licensing requirements.

✓ What else should you consider about these jobs?

Vocal musicians sometimes have a shorter working life than instrumentalists. Voice quality may change with age or the personal singing style may become outdated. Singers who can also dance or act may have more job opportunities.

Some instrumentalists are required to have the ability to play several different instruments

If you think you would like to do this kind of work, look at the job titles listed below.

■ ■ ■

GOE: 01.04.01
Instructing & Directing, Music

ARTIST AND REPERTOIRE MANAGER (amuse. & rec.) ● DOT #159.167-010 ● OES: 34056 ● Selects recording artists and musical selections for production of phonograph records: Auditions recording artist or record to select most appropriate talent for each recording, using knowledge of vocal and instrumental technique and familiarity with popular taste in music. May direct recording sessions. May promote record sales by personal appearances and contacts with broad-

casting personalities. ● **GED:** R4, M3, L4 ● **SVP:** 2-4 yrs ● **Academic:** Ed=H, Eng=G ● **Work Field:** 295 ● **MPSMS:** 869 ● **Aptitudes:** G2, V2, N4, S4, P4, Q4, K4, F4, M4, E5, C5 ● **Temperaments:** D, F, I, J, P ● **Physical:** Stg=L; Const: T, G ● **Work Env:** Noise=Q; ● **Salary:** 5 ● **Outlook:** 1

TEACHER, MUSIC (education) ● DOT #152.021-010 ● OES: 31317 ● Alternate titles: MUSIC INSTRUCTOR. Teaches individuals or groups instrumental or vocal music in public or private school: Plans daily classroom work based on teaching outline prepared for course of study to meet curriculum requirements. Evaluates students' interests, aptitudes, temperament, and individual characteristics to determine suitable instrument for beginner. Sings or plays instrument to demonstrate musical scales, tones, and rhythm. Instructs students in music theory, harmony, score and sight reading, composition, music appreciation, and provides individual or group vocal and instrumental lessons using technical knowledge, aesthetic appreciation, and prescribed teaching techniques. Conducts group rehearsals and instructs and coaches members in their individual parts, in fundamentals of musicianship, and ensemble performance. Critiques performance to identify errors and reinforce correct techniques. Leads orchestra and choral groups in regular and special performances for school program, community activities, concerts, and festivals. Meets with parents of student to resolve student problem. May accompany students on field trips to musical performances. May order, store, and inventory musical instruments, music, and supplies. May teach students with disabilities. May be required to have certification from state. May be designated Teacher, Instrumental (education); Teacher, Vocal (education). ● **GED:** R5, M3, L5 ● **SVP:** 2-4 yrs ● **Academic:** Ed=B, Eng=G ● **Work Field:** 296 ● **MPSMS:** 931 ● **Aptitudes:** G2, V2, N3, S3, P3, Q2, K2, F1, M2, E5, C5 ● **Temperaments:** D, F, P ● **Physical:** Stg=L; Freq: H, I, T, G, N Occas: S, R, E, F, D, A, V ● **Work Env:** Noise=L; ● **Salary:** 2 ● **Outlook:** 1

GOE: 01.04.02
Composing & Arranging

COPYIST (any industry) ● DOT #152.267-010 ● OES: 34050 ● Transcribes musical parts onto staff paper from score written by ARRANGER (profess. & kin.) or ORCHESTRATOR (profess. & kin.) for each instrument or voice, utilizing knowledge of music notation and experience and background in music. May transpose score to different key. ● **GED:** R5, M3, L5 ● **SVP:** 2-4 yrs ● **Academic:** Ed=H, Eng=G ● **Work Field:** 263 ● **MPSMS:** 756 ● **Aptitudes:** G2, V2, N3, S4, P3, Q3, K4, F3, M3, E5, C4 ● **Temperaments:** J, T ● **Physical:** Stg=S; Const: R, H, I, N ● **Work Env:** Noise=Q; ● **Salary:** 3 ● **Outlook:** 2

PROMPTER (amuse. & rec.) ● DOT #152.367-010 ● OES: 34050 ● Prompts performers in operatic productions: Marks copy of vocal score to note cues. Observes CONDUCTOR, ORCHESTRA (profess. & kin.) and follows vocal score to time cues accurately. Speaks or sings in language required by opera to prompt performers. ● **GED:** R4, M3, L4 ● **SVP:** 2-4 yrs ● **Academic:** Ed=H, Eng=G ● **Work Field:** 282 ● **MPSMS:** 754, 756 ● **Aptitudes:** G3, V2, N3, S5, P3, Q2, K4, F4, M4, E4, C5 ● **Temperaments:** J ● **Physical:** Stg=L; Freq: R, H, I, T, G, N, V ● **Work Env:** Noise=Q; ● **Salary:** 3 ● **Outlook:** 1

GOE: 01.04.03
Vocal Performing

SINGER (amuse. & rec.) ● DOT #152.047-022 ● OES: 34050 ● Sings as soloist or member of vocal ensemble: Interprets music, using knowledge of harmony, melody, rhythm, and voice production, to present characterization or to achieve individual style of vocal delivery. Sings, following printed text and musical notation, or memorizes score. May sing a cappella or with musical accompaniment. May watch CHORAL DIRECTOR (profess. & kin.) or CONDUCTOR, ORCHESTRA (profess. & kin.) for directions and cues. May be known according to voice range as soprano, contralto, tenor, baritone, or bass. May specialize in one type of music, such as opera, lieder, choral, gospel, folk, or country and western and be identified according to specialty. ● **GED:** R4, M3, L4 ● **SVP:** 4-10 yrs ● **Academic:** Ed=N, Eng=S ● **Work Field:** 297 ● **MPSMS:** 756, 919 ● **Aptitudes:** G2, V2, N3, S4, P4, Q3, K4, F4, M4, E5, C5 ● **Temperaments:** F, J ● **Physical:** Stg=L; Const: T, G Freq: N, A Occas: D ● **Work Env:** Noise=L; ● **Salary:** 4 ● **Outlook:** 1

GOE: 01.04.04
Instrumental Performing

MUSICIAN, INSTRUMENTAL (amuse. & rec.) ● DOT #152.041-010 ● OES: 34050 ● Plays musical instrument as soloist or as member of musical group, such as orchestra or band, to entertain audience: Studies and rehearses music to learn and interpret score. Plays from memory or by following score. May transpose music to play in alternate key. May improvise. May compose. May play instrument to signal activity, such as flag raising, post time, or arrival of dignitaries at sporting or other events. May be designated according to instrument played as Calliope Player (amuse. & rec.); Drummer (amuse. & rec.); Harpist (amuse. & rec.); Organist (amuse. & rec.); Pianist (amuse. & rec.); Violinist (amuse. & rec.). May accompany soloist or another MUSICIAN, INSTRUMENTAL (amuse. & rec.) and be designated Accompanist (amuse. & rec.). ● **GED:** R5, M3, L3 ● **SVP:** 4-10 yrs ● **Academic:** Ed=N, Eng=S ● **Work Field:** 297 ● **MPSMS:** 756 ● **Aptitudes:** G2, V2, N3, S4, P3, Q2, K2, F2, M2, E3, C4 ● **Temperaments:** F, J ● **Physical:** Stg=L; Const: R, H, I, T, G, N Freq: F ● **Work Env:** Noise=N; Occas: W ● **Salary:** 2 ● **Outlook:** 1

Artistic

01

01.05

Performing Arts: Dance

Workers in this group compose, perform, or teach dance routines or techniques. Performing dancers and composers (choreographers) work for motion picture and television studios, nightclubs and theaters, and other places where this kind of entertainment is regularly presented. Dance teachers are employed by schools and studios. Although some dancers work full-time as performers or teachers, most must audition for both chorus and solo work in theatrical productions of all kinds. Many dancers are self-employed as teachers who give private lessons to children and adults, specializing in ballroom or ballet instruction.

✓ What kind of work would you do?

Your work activities would depend upon your specific job. For example, you might:

- perform a dance routine as a member of a chorus line.
- create dance routines for a musical show.
- perform a solo dance in a variety show.
- teach people to dance.
- direct a troupe of dancers.

✓ What skills and abilities do you need for this kind of work?

To do this kind of work, you must be able to:

- memorize and follow instructions for dance routines.
- move with grace and rhythm, coordinating

your body movements to music, and with the movements of other dancers.

- keep in excellent physical condition by exercising and performing dance routines regularly.
- perform before an audience with poise and self-confidence.
- express emotions, such as joy, sorrow, or excitement, by the way you move your arms, legs, and body.
- understand all of the basic dance steps and the way they relate to various kinds of music, to devise routines for musical comedy dance sequences.

✓ How do you know if you would like or could learn to do this kind of work?

The following questions may give you clues about yourself as you consider this group of jobs.

- Have you participated in ballroom or social dancing? Do you like to learn new dances? Do you learn dance steps rapidly?
- Have you taken lessons in ballet or tap dancing? Were you able to learn different dance routines?
- Have you done free style or interpretive dancing? Do you like this kind of expression? Can you move your body and limbs gracefully?

✓ How can you prepare for and enter this kind of work?

Occupations in this group usually require education and/or training extending from one year to over ten years, depending upon the specific kind of work. Initial training in dance is often provided in physical education or music classes in elementary and high schools. However, instruction in a dance studio is usually needed to develop the skills. This instruction often starts at the preschool age and continues after employment as a dancer. Daily practice is a continuing requirement to develop and maintain the physical condition and techniques needed.

Liberal arts colleges, dance academies, and theater arts schools offer two- to four-year programs in dancing techniques, interpretation, and the history of dance. Many dance schools cooperate with professional ballet and interpretive dance companies to provide experience as well as instruction.

Some people find jobs as ballroom dancing instructors or part-time entertainers after taking dancing instructions. They usually have a natural aptitude and an attractive appearance. Intensive preparation is needed to be hired as a ballet or interpretive dancer, as a chorus dancer in musical comedies, or in television or other media. Dancers must audition for jobs with permanent resident or touring companies. Becoming a choreographer requires extensive performing experience as well as a thorough knowledge of dance.

Private dancing teachers must be able to demonstrate the techniques of many different types of dancing. Teachers in public schools and colleges are required to meet specific educational and licensing requirements.

✓ What else should you consider about these jobs?

Strong feet, ankles, and legs are essential for professional dancers. Most people cannot make dancing a lifetime occupation because of the strenuous physical demands of dancing. Teaching is too strenuous for some dancers nearing retirement age. Few dancers, other than well-known performers, are hired for show work after the age of thirty.

Performing jobs may be found in most metropolitan areas as well as areas where there are musical shows, nightclubs or other settings.

If you think you would like to do this kind of work, look at the job titles listed below.

■   ■   ■

GOE: 01.05.01
Instructing & Choreography, Dance

INSTRUCTOR, DANCING (education) ● DOT #151.027-014 ● OES: 31317 ● Alternate titles: PROFESSOR, DANCE; TEACHER, DANCING. Instructs pupils in ballet, ballroom, tap, and other forms of dancing: Observes students to determine physical and artistic qualifications and limitations and plans programs to meet students' needs and aspirations. Explains and demonstrates techniques and methods of regulating movements of body to musical or rhythmic accompaniment. Drills pupils in execution of dance steps. May teach history of dance. May teach theory and practice of dance notation. May choreograph and direct dance performance. May be designated according to style of dancing taught as Instructor, Ballroom Dancing (education); Instructor, Tap Dancing (education); Teacher, Ballet (education). May be employed by ballet company to train corps de ballet and be designated Ballet Master/Mistress (education). ● **GED:** R5, M2, L5 ● **SVP:** 1-2 yrs ● **Academic:** Ed=A, Eng=G ● **Work Field:** 296 ● **MPSMS:** 755 ● **Aptitudes:** G2, V2, N4, S2, P4, Q3, K2, F3, M3, E2, C5 ● **Temperaments:** D, F, P, T ● **Physical:** Stg=H; Freq: B, R, T, G, F, D, V Occas: H, I ● **Work Env:** Noise=Q; ● **Salary:** 4 ● **Outlook:** 3

GOE: 01.05.02
Performing, Dance

DANCER (amuse. & rec.) ● DOT #151.047-010 ● OES: 34053 ● Dances alone, with partner, or in group to entertain audience: Performs classical, modern, or acrobatic dances, coordinating body movements to musical accompaniment. Rehearses dance movements developed by CHOREOGRAPHER (amuse. & rec.). May choreograph own dance.

May sing and provide other forms of entertainment. May specialize in particular style of dancing and be designated according to specialty as Acrobatic Dancer (amuse. & rec.); Ballet Dancer (amuse. & rec.); Ballroom Dancer (amuse. & rec.); Belly Dancer (amuse. & rec.); Chorus Dancer (amuse. & rec.); Interpretative Dancer (amuse. & rec.); Strip-Tease Dancer (amuse. & rec.); Tap Dancer (amuse. & rec.). ● **GED:** R4, M2, L4 ● **SVP:** 2-4 yrs ● **Academic:** Ed=H, Eng=S ● **Work Field:** 297 ● **MPSMS:** 755, 919 ● **Aptitudes:** G2, V3, N3, S2, P3, Q4, K2, F3, M3, E1, C4 ● **Temperaments:** F, J ● **Physical:** Stg=H; Freq: C, B, R ● **Work Env:** Noise=Q; ● **Salary:** 3 ● **Outlook:** 1

Craft Arts

Workers in this group apply artistic techniques, fabricate, decorate or repair a variety of products, and reproduce photographs and graphics or printed materials. They use engraving and etching precision equipment, knives and chisels, paint brushes and power tools to work wood, stone, clay, metal, and gemstones, or embellish objects made from all these materials. They are employed by manufacturing firms, printing and publishing companies, and motion picture and television studios. They also work for advertising agencies and other firms which provide specialized services, museums, and retail stores. Some craft artists are self-employed, selling items they have made, or providing their services on a freelance basis to businesses and individuals.

✓ What kind of work would you do?

Your work activities would depend upon your specific job. For example, you might:

- carve designs and lettering on wooden blocks or rollers for printing greeting cards.
- engrave designs and names on athletic troph
- paint designs and letters on posters with an airbrush.
- retouch photographs to highlight features of subjects.
- hand letter documents, such as diplomas and charters, using pen and ink.
- use special tools and techniques to clean and prepare fossils for a museum display.

✓ What skills and abilities do you need for this kind of work?

To do this kind of work, you must be able to:

- apply artistic skills, such as painting, drawing, or modeling, in practical ways.
- select the tools, materials, and methods which are best for each purpose.
- picture the way the finished product should look from drawings prepared by a designer.
- take pride in turning out work that appears attractive and meets the standards set by a customer or your supervisor.
- use your eyes, hands, and fingers skillfully to guide knives, pens, brushes, and modeling tools precisely.
- look at an object and notice tiny flaws which should removed or repaired.

✓ How do you know if you would like or could learn to do this kind of work?

The following questions may give you clues about yourself as you consider this group of jobs.

- Have you made your own jewelry? Do you enjoy working with your hands and making things?
- Have you made or decorated clay pottery?
- Have you completed a paint-by-number picture? Did you have a steady hand?
- Have you used a wood-burning tool to etch a preprinted design? Do you like to use tools of this kind?
- Have you decorated a cake for a birthday or other event? Did you create your own designs?

✓ How can you prepare for and enter this kind of work?

Occupations in this group usually require education and/or training extending from one year to over ten years, depending upon the specific kind of work. Courses in industrial art, drafting, art, or craft work may provide initial preparation. More specific training is needed for some jobs depending on the industry, process, or product involved.

Vocational high schools, technical schools, and junior colleges offer training in lettering, engraving, or etching. Trade unions and employers sometimes cooperate to offer apprenticeship training.

Training in the conservation and restoration of art objects and artifacts is given at a number of colleges, and lasts from six months to two years. This is usually followed by a year or two of on-the-job training as an intern or assistant, working under the direction of a skilled craftsman in a museum or conservation laboratory.

Some employers hire workers on the basis of manual skill, experience, and learning ability. Workers are given on-the-job training to develop the knowledge and skills they need. Many of these jobs are specialized crafts, which require two or more years of training and experience.

Hand decorating jobs do not require formal training. Art courses, drafting, or mechanical drawing classes at the high school or junior college level are helpful. Most employers provide six months to one year of on-the-job training to teach the proper techniques.

✓ *What else should you consider about these jobs?*

Opportunities for workers to express their own creativity vary among the jobs in this group. People who are interested in art, but prefer working under specific instructions rather than strictly on their own, will find many job possibilities here. Although these workers use art and craft tools and materials, and produce work that is artistic in nature, they do not have to spend as much time or money in training as they would to prepare for other jobs in the visual arts.

Workers with skill and experience sometimes open their own businesses. Some do free-lance or contract work.

If you think you would like to do this kind of work, look at the job titles listed below.

■ ■ ■

GOE: 01.06.01
Graphic Arts & Related Crafts

ADVERTISING-SPACE CLERK (print. & pub.) ● DOT #247.387-018 ● OES: 53908 ● Alternate titles: SPACE CLERK. Measures and draws outlines of advertising space on dummy newspaper copy and compiles and records identifying data on dummy copy and other worksheets used as guides for production workers: Computes total inches of advertising and news copy for next day's edition, using adding machine, and reads chart to determine required number of newspaper pages. Measures and draws outlines of advertisements in sizes specified onto dummy copy sheets, using pencil and ruler and arranging advertisements on each sheet so that competitive ones do not appear on same page and balance is attained. Records name of advertiser and dimensions of advertisement within ruled outlines and date and page number on each sheet. Extracts data from dummy copy and other sources and records onto lineage breakdown sheets (production worksheets). Delivers dummy copy and lineage breakdown sheets to designated production and administrative personnnel for review and use. ● **GED:** R3, M3, L3 ● **SVP:** 6 mos-1 yr ● **Academic:** Ed=N, Eng=G ● **Work Field:** 231, 232, 242 ● **MPSMS:** 896 ● **Aptitudes:** G3, V3, N3, S4, P4, Q3, K3, F3, M3, E5, C4 ● **Temperaments:** T ● **Physical:** Stg=S; Freq: R, H, I, N Occas: X ● **Work Env:** Noise=N; ● **Salary:** 2 ● **Outlook:** 3

COMPUTER TYPESETTER-KEYLINER (print. & pub.) ● DOT #979.382-026 ● OES: 89716 ● Alternate titles: DESKTOP PUBLISHER. Lays out pages, selects size and style of type, and enters text and graphics into computer to produce printed materials, such as advertisements, brochures, newsletters, and forms, applying knowledge of graphic arts techniques and typesetting, and using computer: Reviews layout and customer order. Enters text into computer, using input device, such as mouse, keyboard, scanner, or modem. Scans artwork, using optical scanner which changes image into computer-readable form. Enters commands to position text and illustrations on page grid of computer monitor. Creates spaces between letters, columns, and lines, applying knowledge of typesetting, and enters commands, using input device. Arranges page according to aesthetic standards, layout specifications of GRAPHIC DESIGNER (profess. & kin.) 141.061-018, and applying knowledge of layout (keylining) and computer software. Prints paper or film copies of completed material. May alter illustration to enlarge, reduce, or clarify image. May operate stat camera to produce photostat. May operate automatic film developer to process photographs. May assemble art work into pasteup and perform keylining manually [PASTE-UP ARTIST (print. & pub.) 972.381-030]. ● **GED:** R4, M3, L4 ● **SVP:** 1-2 yrs ● **Academic:** Ed=H, Eng=G ● **Work Field:** 264 ● **MPSMS:** 896, 752 ● **Aptitudes:** G3, V3, N3, S3, P2, Q2, K3, F3, M3, E5, C4 ● **Temperaments:** T ● **Physical:** Stg=S; Const: N Freq: R, H, I, A Occas: G, X ● **Work Env:** Noise=Q; ● **Salary:** 2 ● **Outlook:** 3

ELECTRONIC MASKING SYSTEM OPERATOR (print. & pub.) ● DOT #972.282-018 ● OES: 89716 ● Alternate titles: ELECTRONIC PLOTTING SYSTEM OPERATOR. Operates computerized masking system to produce stripping masks used in production of offset lithographic printing plates: Positions artist's layout (comprehensive) on digitizing table of electronic masking system to prepare for data entry in system memory. Studies layout sheet to determine shapes of windows drawn on layout sheet. Selects options on menu of electronic masking system, such as shape, dimensions of designs to be drawn, register marks, and retrieval of stored designs. Touches symbol of option selected on menu with mouse (hand held input device) and presses button on mouse to activate option. Touches reference points of designs on layout sheet, using mouse, and presses button of mouse to enter coordinates of design in system memory. Views monitors for feedback and error prompts, for visual representations of work in progress, and for numerical information such as width of line and last point plotted. Presses button to transfer data from system memory to disk. Loads drafting unit with masking material to prepare for plotting and scoring of programmed figures or loads film into plotting drum to prepare for photographic mask exposure. Presses button to activate vacuum to hold masking material in place and to activate drafting unit that scores masking material with programmed figures or activates plotting drum to make photographic mask exposure. Removes scored masking material from drafting table, places material on light table and peels scored figures from masking material, using needle and tape, or removes film from plotting drum and puts film in automatic film processor, to create masks to be used by STRIPPER, LITHOGRAPHIC (print. & pub.) I 972.281-022. May operate electronic plotting system to draw artwork positions on pasteup. ● **GED:** R4, M3, L3 ● **SVP:** 4-10 yrs ● **Academic:** Ed=H, Eng=G ● **Work Field:** 241, 201 ● **MPSMS:** 752 ● **Aptitudes:** G3, V3, N3, S2, P2, Q3, K3, F3, M3, E5, C3 ● **Temperaments:** J, T ● **Physical:** Stg=L; Const: R, H, N Freq: S, I, X Occas: G, D, A ● **Work Env:** Noise=N; Freq: M Occas: V ● **Salary:** 3 ● **Outlook:** 3

ELECTRONIC PREPRESS SYSTEM OPERATOR (print. & pub.) ● DOT #979.282-010 ● OES: 89707 ● Alternate titles: CONSOLE OPERATOR; ELECTRONIC IMAGING SYSTEM OPERATOR; SYSTEM OPERATOR. Operates prepress system to electronically assemble images into pages and to retouch and make color corrections to page elements to be used in production of lithographic printing plates or gravure cylinders: Enters digitized data, such as artist's layout, color separations, text, page dimensions, and layout instructions, into electronic prepress system computer memory, using components of system such as scanner, camera, keyboard, or mouse, or loads floppy disks or tapes containing information into system. Studies layout or other instructions to determine work to be done and sequence of operations. Views monitors for visual representation of work in progress and for instructions and feedback throughout process. Activates options, such as masking or text processing; enters data, such as background color, shapes, and coordinates of images; and retrieves data from system memory to assemble elements on pages. Retrieves images from system memory; activates options, such as masking, pixel (picture element) editing, airbrushing, or image retouching; and enters data, such as co-ordinates of images and color specifications, into system to retouch and make color corrections. Saves completed work on floppy disks or magnetic tape. May create special effects, such as vignettes, mosaics, and image combining. May be designated according to area of special-ization and be known as Electronic Color Correction Operator (print. & pub.); Electronic Page Makeup System Operator (print. & pub.); Pagination System Operator (print. & pub.). ● **GED:** R4, M3, L3 ● **SVP:** 2-4 yrs ● **Academic:** Ed=N, Eng=S ● **Work Field:** 262, 241 ● **MPSMS:** 752 ● **Aptitudes:** G3, V3, N3, S2, P2, Q3, K2, F3, M3, E5, C2 ● **Temperaments:** J, R, T ● **Physical:** Stg=S; Const: R, I, N, A Freq: H, X ● **Work Env:** Noise=Q; ● **Salary:** 3 ● **Outlook:** 3

ENGRAVER, HAND, HARD METALS (engraving) ● DOT #704.381-026 ● OES: 89198 ● Lays out and cuts lettering and designs on surfaces of hard metal for hobs, dies, and molds or plates used to imprint designs on paper, metal, plastic, or porcelain products, follow-ing sketches and blueprints, and using engraving tools: Computes di-mensions of lettering and design, and marks or scribes layout lines on workpiece, using drawing tools, such as straightedge, compass, and scriber. Positions workpiece in vise and cuts designs in surface of workpiece or trims precut designs, using gravers, punches, files, ham-mer, and shaped chisels. Sharpens and forms cutting edge of gravers on cutter grinder [TOOL-GRINDER OPERATOR (machine shop)]. May sketch original design for customer. May enlarge or reduce repro-duction of pattern according to size of article to be made. May brush surface of metal with acidproof paint to prevent corrosion. May be designated according to type of imprinting device engraved as Stencil Maker (engraving). ● **GED:** R4, M3, L3 ● **SVP:** 4-10 yrs ● **Academic:** Ed=N, Eng=S ● **Work Field:** 183 ● **MPSMS:** 617 ● **Aptitudes:** G3, V3, N3, S2, P2, Q4, K2, F2, M2, E5, C5 ● **Temperaments:** J ● **Physi-cal:** Stg=M; Const: R, H, I Freq: N, D, A Occas: E ● **Work Env:** Noise=N; ● **Salary:** 3 ● **Outlook:** 2

ENGRAVER, HAND, SOFT METALS (engraving) ● DOT #704.381-030 ● OES: 89198 ● Alternate titles: CARVER; DECORA-TOR. Engraves lettering and ornamental designs on soft metal articles, such as silverware, trophies, aluminum or plastic eyeglass frames, and jewelry articles, according to sketches, diagrams, photographs, or sample workpieces, using engraver's handtools: Lays out design or lettering to be engraved by brushing chalklike powder or solution on object and sketching design in powder, locating reference points, and marking outline of design on item, using scribers or gravers, or by imprinting design on surface of item, using inked rubber stamp, and marking outline, using scribers. Mounts piece in chuck and affixes chuck in jeweler's ball (rotating vise) or mounts piece directly in jeweler's ball. Cuts design in workpiece, using chisel-like engraving tools. May sketch original designs. May be designated according to kind of prod-uct engraved as Engraver, Flatware (engraving); Engraver, Jewelry (en-graving); Engraver, Optical Frames (engraving); or according to specialty as Engraver, Lettering (engraving); Engraver, Ornamental Design (engraving). ● **GED:** R3, M2, L2 ● **SVP:** 2-4 yrs ● **Academic:** Ed=N, Eng=N ● **Work Field:** 183 ● **MPSMS:** 605, 611, 612 ● **Apti-tudes:** G3, V3, N4, S2, P2, Q4, K3, F2, M2, E5, C5 ● **Temperaments:** J, T ● **Physical:** Stg=S; Const: R, H Freq: I, N, D, A ● **Work Env:** Noise=N; ● **Salary:** 2 ● **Outlook:** 2

ETCHER (engraving) ● DOT #704.684-010 ● OES: 93998 ● Etches designs, lettering, and figures on processed plates of brass, steel, cop-per, zinc, magnesium, or plastic: Mixes acid solution according to for-mula, and pours mixture into etching tank. Places plate on rack in etching tank, sets tank timing controls, and starts machine that sprays plate with corrosive solution. Removes plate periodically, and measures depth to which metal has been etched, using gauge. Inspects plate to ensure that design is not undercut. Washes plate to remove etching powder and protective ink. May brush etching powder on surface of plate to prevent undercutting of reproduction. ● **GED:** R3, M2, L2 ● **SVP:** 1-2 yrs ● **Academic:** Ed=N, Eng=N ● **Work Field:** 182 ● **MPSMS:** 556 ● **Aptitudes:** G3, V4, N4, S3, P2, Q4, K4, F4, M3, E5, C5 ● **Tempera-ments:** J, T ● **Physical:** Stg=L; Freq: R, H, N Occas: I, D, A ● **Work Env:** Noise=N; Occas: T ● **Salary:** 2 ● **Outlook:** 2

PASTE-UP ARTIST (print. & pub.) ● DOT #972.381-030 ● OES: 89706 ● Alternate titles: KEYLINER; MECHANICAL ARTIST. As-sembles typeset copy and artwork into pasteup for printing reproduc-tion: Measures and marks board according to GRAPHIC DESIGNER (profess. & kin.) 141.061-018 or artist's layout to indicate position of artwork, typeset copy, page edges, folds, and colors, using ruler and drafting instruments. Measures artwork and layout space of artwork on pasteup and compares measurements, using ruler and proportion wheel to determine proportions needed to make reduced or enlarged photo-graphic prints for pasteup. Cuts and trims typeset copy and artwork to specified size, applies adhesive, and aligns artwork and typeset copy on board, following position marks, and removes excess adhesive from board, using scissors, artist's knife, and drafting instruments. Tapes transparent plastic overlay to board, positions and applies copy to plas-tic, and applies masking film to artwork layout space on overlay to create clear space on negative where artwork can be added later by STRIPPER, LITHOGRAPHIC (print. & pub.) I 972.281-022. Indi-cates crop marks and enlargement or reduction measurements on pho-tographs with grease pencil to prepare photographs for STRIPPER, LITHOGRAPHIC (print. & pub.) I and covers photographs with tissue paper to protect photographs. Tapes tracing paper to board to protect artwork and copy and writes specifications on tracing paper to provide information to PHOTOGRAPHER, LITHOGRAPHIC (print. & pub.) 972.382-014; STRIPPER, LITHOGRAPHIC (print. & pub.) I; and OFFSET-PRESS OPERATOR (print. & pub.) I 651.382-042. May make negatives or prints of artwork, using photographic equipment. May pre-pare artwork for pasteup. May operate electronic plotter to draw artwork positions on pasteup. ● **GED:** R4, M4, L3 ● **SVP:** 2-4 yrs ● **Aca-demic:** Ed=H, Eng=G ● **Work Field:** 241, 191 ● **MPSMS:** 752 ● **Aptitudes:** G3, V3, N3, S2, P2, Q2, K3, F3, M3, E5, C5 ● **Tempera-ments:** T ● **Physical:** Stg=L; Freq: R, H, N, A Occas: I, G ● **Work Env:** Noise=N; ● **Salary:** 3 ● **Outlook:** 4

PHOTOENGRAVER (print. & pub.) ● DOT #971.381-022 ● OES: 89712 ● Alternate titles: ENGRAVING OPERATOR; PHOTOLITH OPERATOR. Photographs copy, develops negatives, and prepares photosenitized metal plates, such as copper, zinc, aluminum, and mag-nesium for use in printing, using photography and developing equip-ment and engravers' handtools: Positions copy on copy board of darkroom camera and exposes film to copy. Fastens scoured metal plate to whirling machine table or suspension hooks, pours photosensitizing solution on plate, and starts machine which rotates plate to distribute and dry solution evenly over plate surface. Exposes negative and plate to bright light in vacuum type printing frame to transfer image onto plate. Rolls ink onto exposed plate and washes unexposed and unfixed emulsion from plate, using running water and cotton pad to expose bare metal. Places developed plate in acid bath or etching machine to erode unprotected metal to specified depth. Mounts etched plates on wood blocks, using hammer and nails or on metal base, using thermo-setting adhesive to raise printing surface type to specified height. Re-moves excess metal from nonprinting areas of cut, using routing machine [ROUTER (print. & pub.)]. Cuts mortises in mounted plates, using power drill and jigsaw, for insertion of type or other cuts. Modifies and repairs finished plates, using engravers' handtools, etching brush, and acid. May be designated according to type of plate made as Plate Maker, Zinc (print. & pub.). ● **GED:** R4, M3, L3 ● **SVP:** 4-10 yrs ● **Aca-demic:** Ed=H, Eng=S ● **Work Field:** 191 ● **MPSMS:** 752 ● **Apti-tudes:** G3, V3, N3, S3, P2, Q4, K3, F3, M3, E5, C3 ● **Temperaments:** J, T ● **Physical:** Stg=L; Freq: R, H, I, N, D, A Occas: X ● **Work Env:** Noise=N; Freq: A Occas: U, O ● **Salary:** 2 ● **Outlook:** 2

PHOTOGRAPHER, LITHOGRAPHIC (print. & pub.) ● DOT #972.382-014 ● OES: 89713 ● Alternate titles: LITHOGRAPHIC-CAMERA OPERATOR; PHOTOLITHOGRAPHER; PHOTOLITHO-GRAPHIC PROCESS WORKER; PROCESS-CAMERA OPERATOR. Sets up and operates horizontal or vertical process cam-era to photograph illustrations and printed material and produce film used in preparation of lithographic printing plates: Mounts material to be photographed on copyboard of camera and adjusts camera settings to enlarge or reduce size of copy to be reproduced. Selects and places screen over high contrast film in camera to reproduce image with dot pattern for halftone printing. Places color filters between lens and film to produce four-color separations. Performs exposure tests to deter-mine line, halftone and color reproduction exposure lengths for vari-ous photographic factors, such as type of camera, screens, films, and light intensity. Measures degrees of darkness (density) of continuous tone images to be photographed, using densitometer, and enters read-ings into exposure control system of process camera to set exposure time for halftone images. Adjusts lens and copyboard for reduction or enlargement of copy and focus, adjusts lights, and exposes high contrast film for predetermined period of time. Places film in automatic film processor that develops, fixes, washes, and dries film. May immerse film in series of chemical baths to develop image on film and hang film on rack to dry for manual method of processing film. May measure original layouts and determine proportions needed to make reduced or enlarged photographic prints for pasteup. ● **GED:** R4, M2, L3 ● **SVP:** 2-4 yrs ● **Academic:** Ed=H, Eng=S ● **Work Field:** 201, 202 ● **MPSMS:** 752 ● **Aptitudes:** G3, V3, N3, S3, P3, Q4, K3, F3, M3, E5, C3 ● **Temperaments:** J, T ● **Physical:** Stg=L; Freq: R, H, I, N, A Occas: X ● **Work Env:** Noise=N; ● **Salary:** 2 ● **Outlook:** 2

SILK-SCREEN CUTTER (any industry) ● DOT #979.681-022 ● OES: 89998 ● Alternate titles: FILM CUTTER; SILK-SCREEN MAKER; STENCIL CUTTER. Cuts stencils by hand for use in silk-screen printing: Superimposes transparent gelatinous film or shellacked onionskin paper on design or lettering to be reproduced, and cuts outline of design, using knife. Irons stencil on silk or fine copper mesh screen to transfer film or shellac onto screen. Cuts additional stencils for each color to be printed in design. May draw design directly on screen and fill in surfaces around design with glue, lacquer, or paper. May print designs [SCREEN PRINTER (any industry)]. May cut stencils for use in making computer circuit plug boards and be designated Silk-Screen-Layout Drafter (any industry). ● **GED:** R3, M1, L2 ● **SVP:** 6 mos-1 yr ● **Academic:** Ed=N, Eng=N ● **Work Field:** 191 ● **MPSMS:** 567 ● **Aptitudes:** G3, V3, N4, S3, P3, Q4, K3, F2, M3, E5, C4 ● **Temperaments:** J, T ● **Physical:** Stg=L; Freq: R, H, N, D, A Occas: I, X ● **Work Env:** Noise=N; ● **Salary:** 2 ● **Outlook:** 3

STRIPPER (print. & pub.) ● DOT #971.381-050 ● OES: 89717 ● Alternate titles: NEGATIVE ASSEMBLER; NEGATIVE TURNER. Strips photographic negative from film base and mounts negative on glass plate or platemaking flat to be used in preparing photoengraving plates, using art layout, blueprint, and handtools: Examines negative to detect defective areas, using lighted viewing table. Spots or blocks out defective areas, using opaque and brush. Pours rubber solution and collodion over film base to toughen negative. Dries base, using blotter, and cuts negative to size, using knife and straightedge. Immerses glass or film base in acid bath to loosen negative. Strips negative from base. Mounts and aligns negative on glass plate or platemaking flat, according to art layout, blueprint, and color register. Rubs negative to remove excess water and to ensure adhesion to plate, using blotter. May control equipment to produce photographic negatives preparatory to stripping. May be designated according to type of negative stripped as Stripper, Black And White (print. & pub.); Stripper, Color (print. & pub.). ● **GED:** R4, M2, L3 ● **SVP:** 4-10 yrs ● **Academic:** Ed=H, Eng=S ● **Work Field:** 191 ● **MPSMS:** 567, 897 ● **Aptitudes:** G3, V3, N3, S3, P2, Q4, K3, F2, M3, E4, C3 ● **Temperaments:** J, T ● **Physical:** Stg=S; Freq: R, H, I, N, D, A, X Occas: S, E ● **Work Env:** Noise=N; ● **Salary:** 2 ● **Outlook:** 3

STRIPPER, LITHOGRAPHIC I (print. & pub.) ● DOT #972.281-022 ● OES: 89717 ● Alternate titles: COLOR STRIPPER; COMMERCIAL STRIPPER; IMAGE ASSEMBLER; PROCESS STRIPPER. Plans composition of film flat according to customer's requirements, applying knowledge of film assembly; pieces together and positions negative or positive film on layout sheets; and makes composite film, using precision measuring instruments, artist's work aids and photographic equipment, to assemble multi- or single-color film flat used in production of lithographic printing plates: Examines materials received with order, such as pasteup, artwork, film, prints, or customer's instructions, to determine size and dimensions, number of colors on job, and camera work needed, such as number of base negatives, halftones, color separations (film for each primary color), and screen tints. Determines proportions needed to reduce or enlarge photographs and graphics to fit in designated areas of film flat and prevent color overlap, using calculator or proportion scale. Receives base negatives, halftones, and color separations from PHOTOGRAPHER, LITHOGRAPHIC (print. & pub.) 972.382-014 and SCANNER OPERATOR (print. & pub.) 972.282-010 to be used in composition of film flat. Touches up negatives to conceal pinholes and other imperfections, using artist's brush and opaque material, or examines positive film, using magnifier, and repairs broken lines and incomplete and missing half-tone dots, using needle and crayon pencil. Tapes layout sheet or grid to illuminated table and positions masking sheet and transparent plastic sheet over layout grid to prepare for positioning of film. Positions film negatives or positives on masking sheet or transparent plastic sheet according to predetermined reference marks on layout sheet and inserts illustrations, halftones, or four-color process negatives in windows of base negatives or complementary flats (flats that will be exposed onto same plate), using tape, triangles, straightedges, dividers, and magnifiers. Selects and inserts screen tints in film flat, using knowledge of dot percentages required to obtain specific colors. Cuts out masks, using razor blade, artist's knife, or mask cutting tool, and arranges negatives in order, to prepare for contact printing, plate exposure, or proof making. Aligns multiple negatives and masks over unexposed film in vacuum frame and activates light source to make negatives or positives for final film of each color. Determines or approves plans and page sequences to lay out job for specific printing press. Pieces together and aligns negatives or positives on masking sheet or transparent plastic sheet, applying knowledge acquired from experience in film assembly to assure register and fit with all units of color, to assemble film flat. Inverts assembled film flat on table and cuts windows behind image areas of negatives or positives, using razor blade or artist's knife, to allow exposure to plate or film. Routes completed negative or positive flat to proofing area for preparation of positive or negative proof. Examines proof returned by customer and makes corrections or remakes film to meet customer's specifications. Routes completed negative or positive flat to LITHOGRAPHIC PLATEMAKER (print. & pub.) 972.381-010 for preparation of positive or negative lithographic printing plate. May draw ruled lines and borders around negatives or positives, using scribing tools. May make proof from film flat to determine accuracy of flat. ● **GED:** R4, M3, L3 ● **SVP:** 4-10 yrs ● **Academic:** Ed=H, Eng=G ● **Work Field:** 241, 201 ● **MPSMS:** 752 ● **Aptitudes:** G3, V3, N3, S2, P2, Q3, K3, F3, M3, E5, C3 ● **Temperaments:** J, T, V ● **Physical:** Stg=L; Const: R, H, I Freq: N Occas: G, D, A, X ● **Work Env:** Noise=N; ● **Salary:** 2 ● **Outlook:** 2

SUPERVISOR, PREPRESS (print. & pub.) ● DOT #972.137-010 ● OES: 81000 ● Alternate titles: SUPERVISOR, PREP. Supervises and coordinates activities of workers engaged in photography, image assembly, platemaking, and other prepress activities in preparation for offset lithographic printing: Examines work to ensure conformity to job specifications and company standards. Maintains inventory of supplies and materials, such as film, layout sheets, and plates. Oversees maintenance and repair of machines and equipment. Performs other duties as described under SUPERVISOR (any industry) Master Title. May perform minor maintenance and repair of machines and equipment. May be designated according to department supervised as Camera Supervisor (print. & pub.); Scanner Supervisor (print. & pub.); Supervisor, Offset-Plate Preparation (print. & pub.); Supervisor, Stripping (print. & pub.); Systems Manager (print. & pub.). ● **GED:** R4, M4, L4 ● **SVP:** 4-10 yrs ● **Academic:** Ed=H, Eng=G ● **Work Field:** 191, 201, 202 ● **MPSMS:** 480 ● **Aptitudes:** G2, V3, N2, S3, P2, Q2, K3, F3, M3, E5, C3 ● **Temperaments:** D, J, P, T, V ● **Physical:** Stg=L; Freq: T, G, N Occas: R, H, I, F, D, A, X ● **Work Env:** Noise=N; ● **Salary:** 3 ● **Outlook:** 2

GOE: 01.06.02
Arts & Crafts

BOW MAKER, CUSTOM (toy-sport equip.) ● DOT #732.381-010 ● OES: 89998 ● Selects, laminates, shapes, and finishes woods, plastics, and metals to make archery bows: Selects materials from stock according to customer's specifications, and preshapes parts, using handtools and power tools. Applies specified adhesives between parts. Assembles parts and places assembled bows in glue press to cure. Heats bows in steam box until pliable and clamps bows on form to shape curves and recurves. Trims and smooths bows, using handtools and sandpaper. Stains, paints, and varnishes bows according to specifications. May apply decals to bows. May rework or repair damaged bow and be designated Bow Repairer, Custom (toy-sport equip.). May make arrows, using die cutter to cut feathers used on arrows. ● **GED:** R4, M2, L2 ● **SVP:** 2-4 yrs ● **Academic:** Ed=N, Eng=N ● **Work Field:** 102 ● **MPSMS:** 616 ● **Aptitudes:** G3, V4, N3, S2, P2, Q4, K3, F3, M3, E4, C4 ● **Temperaments:** J, T ● **Physical:** Stg=L; Freq: R, H, I, N Occas: E, X ● **Work Env:** Noise=L; Occas: H, A ● **Salary:** 4 ● **Outlook:** 3

CLAY MODELER (any industry) ● DOT #779.281-010 ● OES: 89998 ● Molds full-sized or scale models of products, such as automobiles, automobile parts, television sets, radios, washers, refrigerators, caskets, or boats from clay following artist's sketches or from verbal instructions: Builds rough lumber form to fit around model or centers preformed lath-covered wood frame on grid platform. Kneads clay into slots between laths so clay will adhere to frame. Molds clay by hand to approximate shape. Pulls sheet aluminum forming tool over surface of clay to shape areas that have constant cross sections. Shapes sculptured surfaces, using various types of sculptor's tools and scrapers. Verifies uniformity and smoothness of curved surfaces with splines and sweeps. Scrapes clay from high areas and builds up and smooths low areas to attain desired shape. Cuts cardboard templates for use as guides to shape symmetrical sections. Takes measurements from completed half of model and duplicates them on unfinished half to make both sides symmetrical. Covers bumpers, lights, door handles, and other parts with aluminum foil to simulate chrome or colored glass. ● **GED:** R4, M3, L4 ● **SVP:** 2-4 yrs ● **Academic:** Ed=N, Eng=S ● **Work Field:** 136 ● **MPSMS:** 539 ● **Aptitudes:** G2, V3, N3, S2, P2, Q4, K3, F2, M2, E5, C4 ● **Temperaments:** J, T, V ● **Physical:** Stg=L; Freq: R, H, I, E, N, D Occas: S, A, X ● **Work Env:** Noise=N; ● **Salary:** 2 ● **Outlook:** 2

CONSERVATOR, ARTIFACTS (profess. & kin.) ● DOT #055.381-010 ● OES: 27198 ● Alternate titles: PRESERVATIONIST. Cleans, restores, and preserves archeological specimens and historical artifacts according to accepted chemical and physical techniques and training in archeological science: Cleans and repairs or reinforces specimens, such as weapons, mummified remains, and pottery, using handtools and prescribed chemical agents. Restores artifacts by polishing, joining together broken fragments, or other procedures, using handtools, power tools, and acid, chemical, or electrolytic corrosion-removal baths. Treats specimens to prevent or minimize deterioriation, according to accepted procedures. Records treatment of each artifact. Prepares reports of activities. May plan and conduct research to improve methods of restoring and preserving specimen. ● **GED:** R4, M4, L4 ● **SVP:** 1-2 yrs ● **Academic:** Ed=H, Eng=S ● **Work Field:** 102, 031 ● **MPSMS:** 745 ● **Aptitudes:** G3, V3, N3, S2, P3, Q3, K3, F3, M3, E5, C4 ● **Temperaments:** J, V ● **Physical:** Stg=L; Freq: R, H, N Occas: I ● **Work Env:** Noise=Q; Occas: T ● **Salary:** 4 ● **Outlook:** 1

DECORATOR (any industry) ● DOT #298.381-010 ● OES: 39998 ● Alternate titles: COMMERCIAL DECORATOR. Prepares and installs decorations and displays from blueprints or drawings for trade and industrial shows, expositions, festivals, and other special events: Cuts out designs on cardboard, hard board, and plywood, according to motif of event. Constructs portable installations according to specifications, using woodworking power tools. Installs booths, exhibits, displays, carpets, and drapes, as guided by floor plan of building. Arranges installations, furniture, and other accessories in position shown in prepared sketch. Installs decorations, such as flags, banners, festive lights, and bunting, on or in building, street, exhibit halls, and booths, to achieve special effects [DECORATOR, STREET AND BUILDING (any industry)]. Assembles and installs prefabricated parts to reconstruct traveling exhibits from sketch submitted by client, using handtools. ● **GED:** R4, M4, L3 ● **SVP:** 2-4 yrs ● **Academic:** Ed=N, Eng=G ● **Work Field:** 102 ● **MPSMS:** 889 ● **Aptitudes:** G2, V3, N3, S2, P3, Q3, K3, F3, M3, E4, C3 ● **Temperaments:** J, T ● **Physical:** Stg=L; Freq: S, R, H, I, N, F, D, A, X, V Occas: K, O, E ● **Work Env:** Noise=N; ● **Salary:** 4 ● **Outlook:** 3

DISPLAY MAKER (fabrication, nec) ● DOT #739.361-010 ● OES: 89998 ● Designs, fabricates, assembles, or installs displays, exhibits, and models of point-of-sale displays: Designs displays or exhibits from pictures or sketches or according to verbal instructions from customer. Lays out, cuts, shapes, and finishes wood, plastic, plexiglass, sheet metal, and hardboard parts of displays, using woodworking machines, metal machines, and handtools, according to drawings or blueprints. Cuts glass to specified shape with glasscutter. Assembles parts with nails, screws, bolts, and glue, using handtools. Confers with designer, customer, or salesperson regarding refinements, additions, and adjustments. May disassemble display to make working drawings for production run and to produce estimates for accounting and sales departments. Reassembles display and sends it to prospective customer. May wire display for illumination, audio, or video. May travel and set up display on designated site. May specialize in making diorama models and be designated Diorama Model-Maker (fabrication, nec). ● **GED:** R4, M4, L3 ● **SVP:** 2-4 yrs ● **Academic:** Ed=N, Eng=S ● **Work Field:** 102 ● **MPSMS:** 896 ● **Aptitudes:** G3, V3, N4, S3, P2, Q4, K3, F3, M3, E5, C3 ● **Temperaments:** J ● **Physical:** Stg=M; Freq: R, H, I, N, F, D, A, X, V Occas: C, B, S, K, O, W, E, T, G ● **Work Env:** Noise=L; ● **Salary:** 4 ● **Outlook:** 3

EXHIBIT BUILDER (museums) ● DOT #739.261-010 ● OES: 89998 ● Alternate titles: EXHIBITION SPECIALIST; EXHIBIT TECHNICIAN; MUSEUM CRAFT WORKER; EXPERIMENTAL-DISPLAY BUILDER; MODEL MAKER. Constructs and installs museum exhibit structures, electric wiring, and fixtures of materials, such as wood, plywood, and fiberglass, using handtools and power tools: Studies sketches or scale drawings for temporary or permanent display or exhibit structures, such as framework, fixtures, booths, or cabinets to determine type, amount, and cost of material needed. Confers with exhibit planning and art personnel to discuss structural feasibility of plans and to suggest alternate methods of displaying objects in exhibit. Cuts, assembles, and fastens parts to construct framework, panels, shelves, and other exhibit components of specified materials, using handtools and power tools. Sprays or brushes paint, enamel, varnish, or other finish on structures, or creates special effects by applying finish with cloth, sponge, or fingers to prepare structure for addition of fittings. Mounts fittings and fixtures, such as shelves, panelboards, and shadowboxes to framework, using handtools or adhesives. Installs electrical wiring, fixtures, apparatus, audiovisual components, or control equipment in framework, according to design specifications. Installs or affixes murals, photographs, mounted legend materials, and graphics in framework or on fixtures. Assembles, installs, or arranges structures in exhibit galleries working with maintenance and installation personnel. Tests electrical, electronic, and mechanical components of exhibit structure to verify operation. May maintain inventory of building materials, tools, and equipment, and order supplies as needed for construction of exhibit fixtures. May assign duties to and supervise work of carpentry, electrical, and other craftworkers engaged in constructing and installing exhibit components. May assist in placement of display accessories and collection objects or specimens. May be designated according to speciality as Exhibit Carpenter (museums); Exhibit Electrician (museums); or job location as Planetarium Sky Show Technician (museums); Science Center Display Builder (museums). ● **GED:** R4, M4, L4 ● **SVP:** 2-4 yrs ● **Academic:** Ed=N, Eng=S ● **Work Field:** 102, 111 ● **MPSMS:** 360 ● **Aptitudes:** G3, V3, N3, S2, P2, Q4, K3, F3, M2, E5, C4 ● **Temperaments:** J, T, V ● **Physical:** Stg=M; Freq: R, H, I, N, D, A Occas: C, B, S, O, W, E, T, G, F, X ● **Work Env:** Noise=L; ● **Salary:** 4 ● **Outlook:** 3

JEWELER (jewelry-silver.) ● DOT #700.281-010 ● OES: 89123 ● Alternate titles: BENCH WORKER; JEWELRY JOBBER; JEWELRY REPAIRER. Fabricates and repairs jewelry articles, such as rings, brooches, pendants, bracelets, and lockets: Forms model of article from wax or metal, using carving tools. Places wax model in casting ring, and pours plaster into ring to form mold. Inserts plaster mold in furnace to melt wax. Casts metal model from plaster mold. Forms mold of sand or rubber from metal model for casting jewelry. Pours molten metal into mold, or operates centrifugal casting machine to cast article [CENTRIFUGAL-CASTING-MACHINE OPERATOR (jewelry-silver.)]. Cuts, saws, files, and polishes article, using handtools and polishing wheel. Solders pieces of jewelry together, using soldering torch or iron. Enlarges or reduces size of rings by sawing through band, adding or removing metal, and soldering ends together. Repairs broken clasps, pins, rings, and other jewelry by soldering or replacing broken parts. Reshapes and restyles old jewelry, following designs or instructions, using handtools and machines, such as jeweler's lathe and drill. Smooths soldered joints and rough spots, using hand file and emery paper. May be designated according to metals fashioned as Goldsmith (jewelry-silver.); Platinumsmith (jewelry-silver.); Silversmith (jewelry-silver.) I. ● **GED:** R4, M3, L3 ● **SVP:** 2-4 yrs ● **Academic:** Ed=H, Eng=S ● **Work Field:** 057 ● **MPSMS:** 611 ● **Aptitudes:** G3, V3, N3, S2, P2, Q4, K3, F2, M3, E5, C5 ● **Temperaments:** J, T, V ● **Physical:** Stg=S; Const: R, H, N, D, A Freq: I, E ● **Work Env:** Noise=N; Occas: H ● **Salary:** 5 ● **Outlook:** 3

MAKE-UP ARTIST (amuse. & rec.) ● DOT #333.071-010 ● OES: 68005 ● Studies production requirements, such as character, period, setting and situation, and applies makeup to performers to alter their appearance to accord with their roles: Examines sketches, photographs and plaster models in period files to obtain an image of character to be depicted. Confers with stage and motion picture officials and performer to determine alterations to be made and makeup to be used. Designs prostheses of rubber or plastic and requisitions cosmetics and makeup materials, such as wigs, beards, rouge, powder, and grease paint. Applies prostheses, cosmetics, and makeup to change such physical characteristics of performer as facial features, skin texture, bodily contours, and dimensions and to produce effect appropriate to depict character and situation. May make drawings or models based upon independent research to augment period files. ● **GED:** R4, M3, L3 ● **SVP:** 2-4 yrs ● **Academic:** Ed=N, Eng=S ● **Work Field:** 291, 264 ● **MPSMS:** 909 ● **Aptitudes:** G2, V2, N3, S3, P2, Q4, K3, F3, M3, E5, C2 ● **Temperaments:** F, J, P, V ● **Physical:** Stg=L; Const: R, H, I, E, N, A, X Freq: S, K, O Occas: T, G ● **Work Env:** Noise=Q; ● **Salary:** 4 ● **Outlook:** 1

MODEL MAKER I (any industry) ● DOT #777.261-010 ● OES: 89998 ● Constructs scale model of objects: Builds and molds models, using clay, metal, wood, fiberglass, other substance, depending on industry for which model is constructed, such as ship and boat building or automobile manufacturing. ● **GED:** R5, M3, L3 ● **SVP:** 2-4 yrs ● **Academic:** Ed=N, Eng=S ● **Work Field:** 102 ● **MPSMS:** 619 ● **Aptitudes:** G2, V3, N3, S2, P2, Q4, K3, F2, M2, E5, C4 ● **Temperaments:** F, J ● **Physical:** Stg=L; Freq: R, H, I, N, D Occas: A ● **Work Env:** Noise=N; ● **Salary:** 4 ● **Outlook:** 2

MOLD MAKER I (jewelry-silver.) ● DOT #700.381-034 ● OES: 89198 ● Alternate titles: CHASER. Finishes, alters, and repairs metal molds used to cast jewelry articles and trophy figurines, using hand carving and engraving tools: Cuts design in mold and files, grinds, and shapes points, surfaces, and contours. Fits halves of molds together to determine if they close tightly. Drills holes in mold to allow gases to escape during casting. Reshapes pouring funnels of molds to facilitate flow of molten metal. Drills holes in mold and attaches handles, using drill press and screwdriver. Forms sample castings in mold and measures casting to verify dimensions. May grind, sharpen, and make tools. ● **GED:** R4, M3, L3 ● **SVP:** 4-10 yrs ● **Academic:** Ed=N, Eng=S ● **Work Field:** 183 ● **MPSMS:** 611 ● **Aptitudes:** G3, V3, N3, S3, P3, Q4, K3, F3, M3, E5, C5 ● **Temperaments:** J, T, V ● **Physical:** Stg=L; Freq: R, H, I, N Occas: D, A ● **Work Env:** Noise=N; ● **Salary:** 5 ● **Outlook:** 2

MORTUARY BEAUTICIAN (personal ser.) ● DOT #339.361-010 ● OES: 68005 ● Alternate titles: EMBALMER ASSISTANT; FUNERAL-HOME ATTENDANT. Prepares embalmed bodies for interment: Manicures nails, using files and nail polish, and performs other grooming tasks, such as arching and plucking eyebrows and removing facial hair, using depilatory cream and tweezers. Shampoos, waves, presses, curls, brushes, and combs hair, and applies cosmetics on face to restore natural appearance, following photograph of deceased, or verbal or written description obtained from family. Dresses and arranges body in casket. May select casket or burial dress, arrange floral displays, and prepare obituary notices. May record personal effects delivered with body and information about deceased. May wash and dry bodies, using germicidal soap and towels or hot air drier. May reshape or reconstruct damaged or disfigured areas of body, using such materials as cotton or foam rubber. ● **GED:** R3, M2, L2 ● **SVP:** 1-2 yrs ● **Academic:** Ed=N, Eng=N ● **Work Field:** 291 ● **MPSMS:** 907, 904 ● **Aptitudes:** G3, V3, N4, S3, P3, Q4, K3, F3, M3, E5, C3 ● **Temperaments:** J, T, V ● **Physical:** Stg=M; Freq: R, H, N Occas: I, T, G, X ● **Work Env:** Noise=VQ; Occas: U ● **Salary:** 3 ● **Outlook:** 3

MUSEUM TECHNICIAN (museums) ● DOT #102.381-010 ● OES: 31511 ● Alternate titles: MUSEUM PREPARATOR. Prepares specimens for museum collections and exhibits: Cleans rock matrix from fossil specimens, using electric drills, awls, dental tools, chisels, and mallets. Brushes preservatives, such as plaster, resin, hardeners, and shellac on specimens. Molds and restores skeletal parts of fossil animals, using modeling clays and special molding and casting techniques. Constructs skeletal mounts of fossil animals, using tools, such as drill presses, pipe threaders, welding and soldering apparatus, and carpenter's tools. Constructs duplicate specimens, using plaster, glue, latex, and plastiflex-molding techniques. Reassembles fragmented artifacts, and fabricates substitute pieces. Maintains museum files. Cleans, catalogs, labels, and stores specimens. May install, arrange, and exhibit materials. ● **GED:** R4, M3, L4 ● **SVP:** 2-4 yrs ● **Academic:** Ed=H, Eng=G ● **Work Field:** 102 ● **MPSMS:** 933 ● **Aptitudes:** G3, V3, N4, S2, P2,

Q4, K4, F2, M2, E3, C3 ● **Temperaments:** J, V ● **Physical:** Stg=M; Freq: R, H, N Occas: C, B, S, K, F, D, A, X ● **Work Env:** Noise=L; Occas: O ● **Salary:** 3 ● **Outlook:** 3

PICTURE FRAMER (retail trade) ● DOT #739.684-146 ● OES: 93997 ● Alternate titles: FITTER. Frames pictures in custom-made or stock frames: Mounts picture on backing, using glue. Cuts mounted picture to fit frame, using papercutter or power saw. Cuts glass to fit frame, using glass-cutting tool. Cleans glass and places it in upturned frame. Places picture on top of glass. Cuts piece of cardboard to fit frame, and places it on back of picture. Pushes or taps brads into frame or uses stapler to staple picture in place. Glues paper cover to back of frame. Attaches screw eyes and wire to frame, using handtools or staple gun. May frame oil paintings that do not require glass fronts or paper covers. May repair and redecorate old or broken frames. ● **GED:** R3, M1, L1 ● **SVP:** 6 mos-1 yr ● **Academic:** Ed=N, Eng=N ● **Work Field:** 102 ● **MPSMS:** 457 ● **Aptitudes:** G3, V3, N4, S3, P4, Q4, K3, F3, M3, E5, C5 ● **Temperaments:** T, V ● **Physical:** Stg=L; Freq: S, R, H, I, N, D Occas: O, E, A ● **Work Env:** Noise=N; ● **Salary:** 1 ● **Outlook:** 4

PROP MAKER (amuse. & rec.) ● DOT #962.281-010 ● OES: 87110 ● Fabricates and assembles props, miniatures, and sets for motion pictures and theatrical productions from a variety of materials, using handtools and woodworking and metalworking machines and equipment: Analyzes sketches, blueprints, and verbal instructions to determine type props and other materials needed and equipment required. Measures and marks cutting lines on material, using work aids, such as jigs and fixtures, micrometers, calipers, and templates. Fabricates parts, using machinery, such as drill press, metal and wood lathes, power saws, router, and milling machine. Assembles parts into props, miniatures, and sets, using handtools and equipment, such as screwdrivers, wrenches, hammers, and welding apparatus. Rigs and controls moving or functioning elements of sets that depict action. ● **GED:** R4, M4, L4 ● **SVP:** 2-4 yrs ● **Academic:** Ed=N, Eng=S ● **Work Field:** 102, 121 ● **MPSMS:** 911, 754 ● **Aptitudes:** G3, V3, N3, S2, P2, Q4, K3, F2, M2, E4, C3 ● **Temperaments:** J, T, V ● **Physical:** Stg=M; Freq: R, H, I, E, N, F, D, A, X, V ● **Work Env:** Noise=N; Occas: W, M ● **Salary:** 1 ● **Outlook:** 2

REPAIRER, ART OBJECTS (any industry) ● DOT #779.381-018 ● OES: 85998 ● Repairs and restores objects of art, such as figurines and vases made of antique or fine porcelain, glass, or semiprecious stone: Fits together broken or otherwise marred pieces with wires and glue or other adhesive. Refinishes surfaces with lacquer or paint. Restores decorative patterns by repainting blemished lines or creating new designs. ● **GED:** R4, M3, L3 ● **SVP:** 2-4 yrs ● **Academic:** Ed=N, Eng=S ● **Work Field:** 102 ● **MPSMS:** 539 ● **Aptitudes:** G3, V3, N4, S2, P2, Q4, K4, F2, M2, E5, C3 ● **Temperaments:** J, T, V ● **Physical:** Stg=S; Freq: R, H, I, E, N, D, X Occas: A ● **Work Env:** Noise=Q; ● **Salary:** 4 ● **Outlook:** 2

SAMPLE MAKER I (jewelry-silver.) ● DOT #700.381-046 ● OES: 89123 ● Alternate titles: CRAFTER. Fabricates sample jewelry articles, according to drawings or instructions: Cuts and shapes metal into findings, using metal cutting and carving tools. Arranges metal findings into specified design, softens findings by heating with gas torch, and shapes findings, using hammer and die. Solders pieces together, and smooths rough surfaces, using wooden mallet, files, or polishing wheel. Attaches decorative trimmings, such as wax flowers, enamel motifs, and stones. ● **GED:** R3, M2, L2 ● **SVP:** 2-4 yrs ● **Academic:** Ed=N, Eng=N ● **Work Field:** 102 ● **MPSMS:** 611 ● **Aptitudes:** G3, V3, N4, S2, P2, Q4, K2, F2, M3, E5, C3 ● **Temperaments:** J, T, V ● **Physical:** Stg=L; Const: R, H, N Freq: I, X Occas: D ● **Work Env:** Noise=N; ● **Salary:** 2 ● **Outlook:** 2

SILVERSMITH II (jewelry-silver.) ● DOT #700.281-022 ● OES: 89123 ● Assembles and repairs silverware, such as coffee pots, tea sets, and trays: Anneals workpiece in gas oven for prescribed time to soften metal for reworking. Wires parts, such as legs, spouts, and handles, to body to prepare unit for soldering. Solders parts together and fills in holes and cracks with silver solder, using gas torch. Hammers out deformations and levels and sets bottoms, using dollies, hammers, and tracing punches. Shapes and straightens damaged legs, lids, and spouts with pliers. Restores dented embossing on articles, using hammers and punches. Pierces and cuts open design in ornamentation, using hand drill and scroll saw. Glues plastic separators to handles of coffee and teapots. May operate lathe to form articles of silverware out of silver or plated sheet, according to sketches. May hammer metal into shape and solder seams to make handles and spouts. May work with metals other than silver, such as pewter, brass, chromium, and nickel. ● **GED:** R4, M2, L3 ● **SVP:** 2-4 yrs ● **Academic:** Ed=N, Eng=S ● **Work Field:** 102 ● **MPSMS:** 612 ● **Aptitudes:** G3, V4, N4, S2, P2, Q4, K3, F2, M2, E5, C5 ● **Temperaments:** J, T, V ● **Physical:** Stg=L; Const: R, H, I, N, D, A Occas: E ● **Work Env:** Noise=N; Occas: H ● **Salary:** 3 ● **Outlook:** 2

SPECIAL EFFECTS SPECIALIST (amuse. & rec.) ● DOT #962.281-018 ● OES: 39998 ● Fabricates, installs, and activates equipment to produce special effects, such as rain, snow, explosions, and other mechanical and electrical effects as required by script for television, motion picture, and theatrical productions: Reads script to determine type of special effects required. Mixes chemicals to produce special effects, following standard formulas. Constructs towers and similar objects used in making effects, using handtools and machine tools. Fabricates parts for special effects from materials, such as wood, metal, plaster, and clay, using handtools and power tools. Installs special effects, using handtools. ● **GED:** R4, M3, L3 ● **SVP:** 1-2 yrs ● **Academic:** Ed=N, Eng=G ● **Work Field:** 121, 111 ● **MPSMS:** 910, 864 ● **Aptitudes:** G3, V3, N3, S3, P3, Q5, K3, F3, M3, E3, C3 ● **Temperaments:** J, T, V ● **Physical:** Stg=M; Freq: R, H, I, E, N, F, D, A, X, V Occas: C, B, S, K, O, W, G ● **Work Field:** Noise=L; Occas: W, A, X ● **Salary:** 4 ● **Outlook:** 3

STONE CARVER (stonework) ● DOT #771.281-014 ● OES: 89998 ● Alternate titles: HAND CARVER; SCULPTOR. Carves designs and figures in full and bas-relief on stone, employing knowledge of stone-carving techniques and sense of artistry to produce carving consistent with designer's plans: Analyzes artistic objects or graphic materials, such as models, sketches, or blueprints; visualizes finished product; and plans carving technique. Lays out figures or designs on stone surface by freehand sketching, marking over tracing paper, and transferring dimensions from sketches or blueprints, using rule, straightedge, square, compass, calipers, and chalk, or scriber. Selects chisels and pneumatic tools and determines sequence of their use according to intricacy of design or figure. Roughs out design freehand or by chipping along marks on stone, using mallet and chisel or pneumatic tool. Shapes, trims, or touches up roughed out design with appropriate tool to finish carving. Periodically compares carving with sketches, blueprints, or model and verifies dimensions of carving, using calipers, rule, straightedge, and square. Moves fingers over surface of carving to verify smoothness of finish. May smooth surface of carving with rubbing stone. May be designated according to type of work as Monument Carver (stonework); or according to kind of stone carved as Granite Carver (stonework); Marble Carver (stonework). ● **GED:** R4, M4, L4 ● **SVP:** 4-10 yrs ● **Academic:** Ed=N, Eng=S ● **Work Field:** 052, 264 ● **MPSMS:** 537, 539 ● **Aptitudes:** G2, V3, N2, S2, P2, Q3, K2, F2, M2, E5, C5 ● **Temperaments:** F, J ● **Physical:** Stg=M; Const: R, H, N, A Freq: E, D Occas: S, K, O, I ● **Work Env:** Noise=L; Const: A ● **Salary:** 2 ● **Outlook:** 1

TAXIDERMIST (profess. & kin.) ● DOT #199.261-010 ● OES: 39998 ● Prepares, stuffs, and mounts skins of birds or animals in lifelike form: Removes skin from dead body with special knives, scissors, and pliers, taking care to preserve hair and feathers in natural state. Rubs preservative solutions into skin. Forms body foundation by building up on wire foundation with papier mache and adhesive tape, to give natural attitude and show form and muscles of specimen. Covers foundation with skin, using specified adhesive or modeling clay. Affixes eyes, teeth, and claws; dresses feathers, and brushes fur to enhance lifelike appearance of specimen. May mount specimen in case with representations of natural surroundings. May make plaster cast of specimen to enhance physical details preparatory to making papier mache mold. May dress-out, preserve, or otherwise prepare animal carcasses preparatory to scientific or exhibition purposes. ● **GED:** R5, M3, L4 ● **SVP:** 2-4 yrs ● **Academic:** Ed=A, Eng=N ● **Work Field:** 136 ● **MPSMS:** 732 ● **Aptitudes:** G2, V2, N3, S2, P2, Q3, K2, F2, M2, E5, C1 ● **Temperaments:** J, T, V ● **Physical:** Stg=M; Freq: R, H, I, N, D, X Occas: E, A ● **Work Env:** Noise=N; Freq: A ● **Salary:** 3 ● **Outlook:** 3

WIG DRESSER (fabrication, nec) ● DOT #332.361-010 ● OES: 68005 ● Alternate titles: HAIRDRESSER. Dresses wigs and hair pieces according to instructions, samples, sketches, or photographs: Attaches

wig or hair piece onto model head, using hammer and tacks or pins. Combs and sets hair, using barber and beautician equipment. Arranges hair according to instructions, pictures, or photographs, using brush and comb. Sprays hair with lacquer to keep hair in place. May cut wigs and hair pieces to specified length and style, using scissors or razor. May wash and dry hair pieces. ● **GED:** R3, M2, L2 ● **SVP:** 1-2 yrs ● **Academic:** Ed=N, Eng=S ● **Work Field:** 264, 291 ● **MPSMS:** 904, 619 ● **Aptitudes:** G3, V3, N4, S3, P2, Q4, K3, F3, M3, E5, C3 ● **Temperaments:** J, P, T, V ● **Physical:** Stg=L; Freq: R, H, I, E, T, G, N Occas: A, X ● **Work Env:** Noise=Q; ● **Salary:** 2 ● **Outlook:** 3

GOE: 01.06.03
Hand Lettering, Painting & Decorating

GIFT WRAPPER (retail trade) ● DOT #299.364-014 ● OES: 49998 ● Alternate titles: WRAPPER. Wraps and decorates customer's purchases with gift-wrapping paper, ribbons, bows, and tape in retail store. May collect money and make change for gift-wrapping service. May assist customer to select appropriate wrapping materials. ● **GED:** R3, M2, L1 ● **SVP:** 1-3 mos ● **Academic:** Ed=N, Eng=N ● **Work Field:** 041, 292 ● **MPSMS:** 881 ● **Aptitudes:** G4, V4, N4, S3, P4, Q4, K4, F3, M4, E5, C4 ● **Temperaments:** P, R ● **Physical:** Stg=L; Freq: R, H, I, T, G, N, D Occas: S, X ● **Work Env:** Noise=N; ● **Salary:** 2 ● **Outlook:** 3

GILDER (any industry) ● DOT #749.381-010 ● OES: 89998 ● Alternate titles: GOLD CHARMER; GOLD-LEAF GILDER; METAL-LEAF GILDER; METAL-LEAF LAYER. Covers surfaces of items, such as books, furniture, harps, and signs, with metal leaf, such as aluminum, gold, or silver, to decorate them, using brushes, T-shaped handtool, and hands: Brushes sizing (thin glue) on sections of items which are to be covered with leaf (gilded), according to design. Transfers leaf from supply book onto pallet. Rubs camel-hair brush in hair to electrify brush and picks up leaf with brush, or picks up leaf with T-shaped, felt-edged tool, and lays leaf over sizing; or presses sheets or ribbons of leaf onto sizing by hand. Smooths leaf over surface and removes excess, using brush. Rubs leaf with polished burnishing agate, cotton pad, or gloved hand to polish leaf or simulate worn metal finish. May brush or spray protective lacquer coat over gilded surface. ● **GED:** R3, M1, L1 ● **SVP:** 1-2 yrs ● **Academic:** Ed=N, Eng=N ● **Work Field:** 092 ● **MPSMS:** 559 ● **Aptitudes:** G3, V4, N3, S3, P2, Q4, K3, F2, M2, E5, C2 ● **Temperaments:** J, T ● **Physical:** Stg=L; Freq: R, H, I, N, D, A, X Occas: E ● **Work Env:** Noise=N; Freq: A ● **Salary:** 2 ● **Outlook:** 2

PAINTER, AIRBRUSH (any industry) ● DOT #741.684-018 ● OES: 93947 ● Coats, decorates, glazes, retouches, or tints articles, such as fishing lures, toys, dolls, pottery, artificial flowers, greeting cards, and household appliances, using airbrush: Stirs or shakes coating liquid and thinner to mix solution to specified consistency. Pours solution into airbrush container, couples airbrush to airhose, and starts compressor or opens valve on compressed-air line. Turns adjusting sleeve on nozzle of airbrush to regulate spray pattern to size of workpiece or area to be sprayed. Presses button on airbrush to spray coating over workpiece, or to spray specified designs and decorations on workpiece, spraying freehand or using stencils, masks, screens, and tape. Cleans airbrush nozzle and hose with solvent. May be designated according to article sprayed as Bait Painter (toy-sport equip.). ● **GED:** R3, M1, L1 ● **SVP:** 6 mos-1 yr ● **Academic:** Ed=N, Eng=N ● **Work Field:** 262, 153 ● **MPSMS:** 610, 485, 535 ● **Aptitudes:** G3, V4, N4, S3, P3, Q4, K3, F3, M3, E5, C3 ● **Temperaments:** J, T ● **Physical:** Stg=L; Freq: R, H, I, N, D, A, X ● **Work Env:** Noise=N; ● **Salary:** 3 ● **Outlook:** 2

PAINTER, HAND (any industry) ● DOT #970.381-022 ● OES: 89998 ● Alternate titles: ARTIST; DECORATOR; FILLER-IN TINTER. Paints decorative freehand designs on objects, such as pottery, cigarette cases, and lampshades, using handbrushes: Sketches design, using pencil or permanent ink. Grinds colors on pottery tile, using palette knife, to mix colors and oils to desired consistency. Paints freehand or within sketched design, using mixed colors, or applies pure colors, one over another, to produce desired shade, allowing time for drying between applications. May stipple (create designs by dabbing dots on ware). May trace design prior to painting or sketch guidelines for decals and be designated Sketch Liner (pottery & porc.). ● **GED:** R4, M2, L3 ● **SVP:** 2-4 yrs ● **Academic:** Ed=N, Eng=G ● **Work Field:** 262 ● **MPSMS:** 889 ● **Aptitudes:** G3, V4, N4, S2, P2, Q5, K4, F2, M4, E5, C2 ● **Temperaments:** F, J, T ● **Physical:** Stg=S; Freq: R, H, I, N, D, A, X ● **Work Env:** Noise=N; ● **Salary:** 3 ● **Outlook:** 2

PAINTER, SIGN (any industry) ● DOT #970.381-026 ● OES: 89998 ● Alternate titles: LETTERER. Designs, lays out, and paints letters and designs to create signs, using measuring and drawing instruments, brushes, and handtools: Reads work orders to determine type of sign specified, work procedures, and materials required. Sketches design on paper, using drawing instruments, such as angles, rulers, and shading pencils. Lays out design on plastic, silk, or tin to prepare stencil, or on paper to draw pounce pattern, using measuring and drawing instruments. Sketches or follows pattern to draw design or lettering onto objects, such as billboards and trucks, using stencils and measuring and drawing instruments. Brushes paint, lacquer, enamel, or japan over stencil, or paints details, background, and shading to fill in outline or sketch of sign, using paintbrush or airbrush. When painting window signs, draws outline of sign on outside window, using chalk, or dusts pounce pattern to mark outline and paints inside of window following drawing or outline, using brush. When making gold or silver leaf signs, forms sign by either of following methods: (1) Paints sign, positions leaf over fresh paint, and removes excess leaf after sign has dried, using cotton swab and knife blade. (2) Paints inside of window with watersize (glue), applies leaf, and paints sign in reverse on back of leaf, using paintbrush or airbrush. May cut out letters and apply background coating to construct and prepare signs, using tinning shears. May project layout image on paper and trace outline of design, using projector and electric needle. May specialize in maintenance of signs along railroad right-of-way and be designated Painter, Sign, Maintenance (r.r. trans.). ● **GED:** R4, M3, L3 ● **SVP:** 2-4 yrs ● **Academic:** Ed=H, Eng=G ● **Work Field:** 262 ● **MPSMS:** 889 ● **Aptitudes:** G3, V3, N3, S3, P2, Q4, K3, F2, M2, E3, C2 ● **Temperaments:** J ● **Physical:** Stg=L; Const: R, H, I, N Freq: C, S, D, A, X ● **Work Env:** Noise=L; Occas: W, O ● **Salary:** 3 ● **Outlook:** 2

SIGN WRITER, HAND (any industry) ● DOT #970.281-022 ● OES: 89998 ● Alternate titles: CARD WRITER, HAND; SHOW-CARD WRITER. Writes, paints, or prints signs or showcards used for display or other purposes, using brushes. May cut out letters and signs for display purposes from wallboard or cardboard, by hand or machines, such as electrically powered jigsaw or bandsaw. ● **GED:** R4, M3, L3 ● **SVP:** 6 mos-1 yr ● **Academic:** Ed=N, Eng=G ● **MPSMS:** 889 ● **Aptitudes:** G3, V3, N4, S3, P3, Q3, K3, F3, M3, E5, C2 ● **Temperaments:** J, T ● **Physical:** Stg=S; Freq: R, H, I, N, D, A, X ● **Work Env:** Noise=L; ● **Salary:** 3 ● **Outlook:** 2

STRIPER, HAND (any industry) ● DOT #740.484-010 ● OES: 93947 ● Paints stripes, letters, or decorative edges on bicycle frames, motorcycle fenders and tanks, utensils, or other stamped products, using handbrushes and enamel or lacquer. Marks area to be stamped, lettered, or decorated, using rule or template. Mixes paint and matches colors according to specifications, or uses prepared paints. ● **GED:** R3, M2, L2 ● **SVP:** 1-2 yrs ● **Academic:** Ed=N, Eng=N ● **Work Field:** 262 ● **MPSMS:** 595, 556 ● **Aptitudes:** G3, V4, N4, S4, P3, Q4, K3, F3, M3, E5, C3 ● **Temperaments:** R, T ● **Physical:** Stg=L; Freq: R, H, I, N, D, X ● **Work Env:** Noise=N; ● **Salary:** 3 ● **Outlook:** 2

TYPE COPYIST (machinery mfg.) ● DOT #970.381-042 ● OES: 89998 ● Draws and cuts out type characters of plastic, such as letters, numbers, and logos for use in manufacturing phototypesetting type disks, using drawing and cutting instruments: Searches reference sources to determine availability of characters in type style specified on orders. Reproduces reference copies of new characters required to obtain working copies, using automatic film developer. Places tracing paper over working copies, and traces and draws new characters, using pencil and triangle. Measures width, thickness, and spacing of characters, using optical and other measuring instruments, and pencils in or erases markings of characters as necessary to arrive at specified size and spacing requirements. Places tracing paper with finalized characters in light box, positions plastic sheets over light box, and cuts plastic following character outlines on tracing paper to obtain plastic characters, using cutting tools and metal guides. Records identity of characters on card for filing with reference source and routes characters for further processing. ● **GED:** R4, M3, L3 ● **SVP:** 2-4 yrs ● **Academic:** Ed=H, Eng=G ● **Work Field:** 262 ● **MPSMS:** 752 ● **Aptitudes:** G3, V3, N3, S3, P2, Q2, K2, F2, M3, E5, C4 ● **Temperaments:** J, T ● **Physical:** Stg=S; Freq: R, H, I, N Occas: D, A, X ● **Work Env:** Noise=Q; ● **Salary:** 2 ● **Outlook:** 3

Elemental Arts

Workers in this group entertain or divert people by announcing features or performing acts at carnivals or amusement parks, or by conducting person-to-person consultations with people to predict their future or tell them other things about themselves. They work with traveling carnivals or circuses, or at permanently located amusement parks. Some are self-employed, conducting interviews in their homes or giving consultations by mail.

✓ What kind of work would you do?

Your work activities would depend upon your specific job. For example, you might:

■ introduce circus acts and signal the start and finish of each act.

■ shout show attractions to the passing public.

■ analyze handwriting to determine personal characteristics.

■ guess weight of people at an amusement park or carnival.

✓ What skills and abilities do you need for this kind of work?

To do this kind of work, you must be able to:

■ attract the attention of others by speaking, gesturing, or shouting.

■ be at ease when appearing before an audience.

■ speak clearly, using easily understood terms, and offering your information with sincerity when dealing with clients on a person-to-person basis.

■ learn and apply the specialized techniques needed for such feats as fire-eating, snake charming, or sword-swallowing.

✓ How do you know if you would like or could learn to do this kind of work?

The following questions may give you clues about yourself as you consider this group of jobs.

■ Have you played Santa Claus? Have you worn a costume as a mascot? Did you enjoy doing this type of activity?

- Have you played games involving reading the minds of others? Do you feel you have psychic powers?
- Have you performed card tricks for friends? Do you enjoy amusing others?
- Have you worked at a school or community fair or carnival? Were you able to get people to play the games or watch the shows?

✓ *How can you prepare for and enter this kind of work?*

Occupations in this group usually require education and/or training extending from a short demonstration to over six months, depending upon the specific kind of work. Many of these jobs require only brief training for workers to become familiar with the work setting and tasks. Greater training and practice in areas such as astrology, numerology, or graphology are necessary for some jobs. Other jobs, such as ring conductor in a circus, require related work experience. Some workers are hired if they fit a specific costume. Some people develop the necessary skills through practicing their hobbies such as snake handling or telling fortunes.

✓ *What else should you consider about these jobs?*

Many of these jobs are seasonal or temporary with few chances for promotion. Jobs with circuses and other amusement shows require frequent travel.

If you think you would like to do this kind of work, look at the job titles listed below.

GOE: 01.07.02
Announcing

ANNOUNCER (amuse. & rec.) ● DOT #159.347-010 ● OES: 39998 ● Alternate titles: PUBLIC-ADDRESS ANNOUNCER. Announces information of interest to patrons of sporting and other entertainment events, using public address system: Announces program and substitutions or other changes to patrons. Informs patrons of coming events or emergency calls. May observe sporting event to make running commentary, such as play-by-play description or explanation of official decisions. May speak extemporaneously to audience on items of interest, such as background and past record of players. May read prepared script to describe acts or tricks during performance. May furnish information concerning play to SCOREBOARD OPERATOR (amuse. & rec.). ● **GED:** R4, M2, L4 ● **SVP:** 1-2 yrs ● **Academic:** Ed=H, Eng=G ● **Work Field:** 297, 282 ● **MPSMS:** 919, 913 ● **Aptitudes:** G2, V2, N4, S3, P4, Q3, K4, F4, M4, E5, C4 ● **Temperaments:** J, P ● **Physical:** Stg=S; Const: T, G Freq: R, H, N ● **Work Env:** Noise=Q; ● **Salary:** 4 ● **Outlook:** 2

RING CONDUCTOR (amuse. & rec.) ● DOT #159.367-010 ● OES: 34056 ● Introduces circus acts, using presence and manner, to set style desired by circus management: Signals start and finish of individual acts, using knowledge of circus performance running order. Signals performers to coordinate smooth transition of acts and addresses audience to alleviate their concern in emergencies, such as accidents or equipment failure. ● **GED:** R4, M2, L4 ● **SVP:** 1-2 yrs ● **Academic:** Ed=N, Eng=G ● **Work Field:** 297 ● **MPSMS:** 919 ● **Aptitudes:** G3, V2, N3, S3, P3, Q5, K4, F4, M4, E5, C5 ● **Temperaments:** I, J, P, T ● **Physical:** Stg=L; Freq: T, G, N ● **Work Env:** Noise=N; ● **Salary:** 4 ● **Outlook:** 1

GOE: 01.07.03
Entertaining

AMUSEMENT PARK ENTERTAINER(amuse. & rec.) ● DOT #159.647-010 ● OES: 34056 ● Entertains audience in amusement park by exhibiting special skills. Designated according to specialty act performed as Fire Eater (amuse. & rec.); Hypnotist (amuse. & rec.); Organ Grinder (amuse. & rec.); Phrenologist (amuse. & rec.); Physiognomist (amuse. & rec.); Snake Charmer (amuse. & rec.); Sword Swallower (amuse. & rec.). May be designated Side-Show Entertainer (amuse. & rec.). May entertain in nightclubs and similar establishments. May entertain for live variety show or for television production. ● **GED:** R2, M2, L2 ● **SVP:** 2-30 days ● **Academic:** Ed=N, Eng=G ● **Work Field:** 297 ● **MPSMS:** 919 ● **Aptitudes:** G3, V3, N4, S4, P4, Q5, K4, F4, M4, E5, C5 ● **Temperaments:** F, P ● **Physical:** Stg=L; Freq: R, H, T, G Occas: I ● **Work Env:** Noise=N; Freq: W ● **Salary:** 3 ● **Outlook:** 1

Modeling

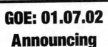

Workers in this group appear before a camera or live audience in nonspeaking capacities. They stand in for actors and take part in crowd scenes in television or motion picture productions. They show clothing, hair styles, and other products, appear in fashion shows and other public or private product exhibitions, and pose for artists and photographers. They work for manufacturers or wholesale and retail establishments. Some are employed by motion picture and television studios, nightclubs, and other entertainment facilities. Modeling instructors work for public or private schools. Many of these workers are self-employed, or obtain job assignments through model agencies or unions which represent persons in the entertainment industry.

✓ *What kind of work would you do?*

Your work activities would depend upon your specific job. For example, you might:

- model clothing for a designer or department store.
- pose for a photographer or an artist.
- stand in place for a movie star so cameras can be adjusted.
- parade across a stage to display costumes as background for a chorus line.

✓ *What skills and abilities do you need for this kind of work?*

To do this kind of work, you must be able to:

- follow directions for movements and poses to express certain emotions or convey various visual impressions.
- appear before an audience with poise and self-assurance.
- stand, sit, walk, or pose in front of an audience, photographer, or artist for long periods of time.

✓ *How do you know if you would like or could learn to do this kind of work?*

The following questions may give you clues about yourself as you consider this group of jobs.

- Have you modeled for an artist or photographer? Can you hold a pose for a half-hour or longer?

- Have you modeled clothes in a fashion show? Do you enjoy appearing before groups?

✓ *How can you prepare for and enter this kind of work?*

Occupations in this group usually require education and/or training extending from a short demonstration to over six months, depending upon the specific kind of work. Training for many of these jobs is usually brief and given on the job. Modeling schools offer courses in graceful movement and personal grooming.

Workers are often hired because of their appearance or size. Workers may be under contract to a booking agency or may obtain work on their own.

Models may work only part-time until the quality of their work is recognized. Workers in this group often hold other jobs.

✓ *What else should you consider about these jobs?*

Many of these jobs are short-term or seasonal and offer little opportunity for advancement. A few models may be in constant demand and earn large salaries.

If you think you would like to do this kind of work, look at the job title listed below.

■   ■   ■

GOE: 01.08.01
Personal Appearance

EXTRA (amuse. & rec.) ● DOT #159.647-014 ● OES: 34056 ● Performs as nonspeaking member of scene in stage, motion picture, or television productions: Stands, walks, or sits in scenes as background for stars actions, or performs actions requiring special skills, such as dancing, swimming, skating, riding, or handling livestock. Rehearses and performs pantomime, portraying points essential in staging of scene. Workers may be designated according to registration in union as General Extra (amuse. & rec.; motion picture; radio-tv broad.); Special Ability Extra (amuse. & rec.; motion picture; radio-tv broad.); Silent Bit Extra (amuse. & rec.; motion picture; radio-tv broad.). ● **GED:** R2, M2, L2 ● **SVP:** 2-30 days ● **Academic:** Ed=N, Eng=S ● **Work Field:** 297 ● **MPSMS:** 911, 912, 864 ● **Aptitudes:** G3, V3, N4, S4, P4, Q5, K4, F4, M4, E5, C5 ● **Temperaments:** R ● **Physical:** Stg=L; Freq: R, H ● **Work Env:** Noise=N; Occas: W ● **Salary:** 2 ● **Outlook:** 1

MODEL, ARTISTS' (any industry) ● DOT #961.667-010 ● OES: 49998 ● Poses as subject for paintings, sculptures, and other types of art for translation into plastic or pictorial values by PAINTER (profess. & kin.) or SCULPTOR (profess. & kin.). ● **GED:** R3, M1, L1 ● **SVP:** 1-3 mos ● **Academic:** Ed=N, Eng=N ● **Work Field:** 291 ● **MPSMS:** 750 ● **Aptitudes:** G3, V4, N5, S4, P5, Q5, K4, F4, M4, E4, C4 ● **Temperaments:** F, P ● **Physical:** Stg=L; Occas: S, R, H, G ● **Work Env:** Noise=N; ● **Salary:** 1 ● **Outlook:** 1

Scientific 02

An interest in discovering, collecting, and analyzing information about the natural world and applying scientific research findings to problems in medicine, the life sciences, and the natural sciences.

You can satisfy this interest by working with the knowledge and prcesses of the sciences. You may enjoy researching and developing new knowledge in mathematics. Perhaps solving problems in the physical or life sciences would appeal to you. You may wish to study medicine and help humans or animals. You could work as a practitioner in the health field. You may want to work with scientific equipment and procedures. You could seek a job in research or testing laboratories.

Physical Sciences

Workers in this group are concerned mostly with nonliving things, such as chemicals, rocks, metals, mathematics, movements of the earth and the stars, etc. They conduct scientific studies and perform other activities requiring a knowledge of math, physics, or chemistry. Some workers investigate, discover, and test new theories. Some look for ways to develop new or improved materials or processes for use in production and construction. Others do research in such fields as geology, astronomy, oceanography, and computer science. Workers base their conclusions on information that can be measured or proved. Industries, government agencies, or large universities employ most of these workers in their research facilities.

✓ What kind of work would you do?

Your work activities would depend upon your specific job. For example, you might:

- study (aerial) photographs for indications of possible oil or gas deposits.
- examine rock formations to develop theories about the earth and its history.
- use information about wind, temperature, humidity, and land formations to predict weather.
- help solve environmental problems such as pollution.
- develop chemical formulas for making fine perfumes.
- conduct experiments to develop new metals.
- gather and interpret information about movements in the earth.
- use advanced math to solve very complex problems.

✓ What skills and abilities do you need for this kind of work?

To do this kind of work, you must be able to:

- use logic or scientific thinking to deal with many different kinds of problems.
- make decisions based on information that can be measured or verified.
- understand and express complex, technical, and scientific information.
- recognize textures, colors, shapes, and sizes.
- make decisions using your own judgments.
- gather and interpret data about earth movements.
- use nonverbal symbols (such as numbers) to express ideas or solve problems.

The above statements may not apply to every job in this group.

✓ How do you know if you would like or could learn to do this kind of work?

The following questions may give you clues about yourself as you consider this group of jobs.

- Have you taken courses in earth science or space science?
- Have you read articles or stories about scientific expeditions? Do you understand scientific terminology?
- Have you collected rocks or minerals as a hobby? Can you recognize differences in ores or mineral deposits?
- Have you watched television weather shows? Do you understand the terms and symbols used?
- Have you owned a chemistry set or microscope? Do you enjoy testing new ideas with this type of equipment?

✓ *How can you prepare for and enter this kind of work?*

Occupations in this group usually require education and/or training extending from four years to over ten years, depending upon the specific kind of work. A bachelor's degree with a major in mathematics or a specific physical science is the minimum requirement for entrance into this type of work. Graduate degrees are needed for most research work or college teaching. A master's degree may qualify an individual for work in laboratory teaching or applied research in a college, university, or industrial setting. Advanced studies or a Ph.D. are usually required for work in basic research. Important courses include algebra, geometry, advanced math, physics, and earth and space

science. Chemistry and technical writing courses are helpful and in some cases required.

✓ *What else should you consider about these jobs?*

Physical scientists may be required to work irregular hours to meet research deadlines or to study phenomena. Frequent relocation or travel to remote areas may be required. Workers should keep informed of developments in their field by attending seminars, reading professional journals, and being active in professional organizations.

If you think you would like to do this kind of work, look at the job titles listed below.

■   ■   ■

GOE: 02.01.01
Theoretical Research

CHEMIST (profess. & kin.) ● DOT #022.061-010 ● OES: 24105 ● Conducts research, analysis, synthesis, and experimentation on substances, for such purposes as product and process development and application, quantitative and qualitative analysis, and improvement of analytical methodologies: Devises new equipment, and develops formulas, processes, and methods for solution of technical problems. Analyzes organic and inorganic compounds to determine chemical and physical properties, utilizing such techniques as chromatography, spectroscopy, and spectrophotometry. Induces changes in composition of substances by introduction of heat, light, energy, and chemical catalysts. Conducts research on manufactured products to develop and improve products. Conducts research into composition, structure, properties, relationships, and reactions of matter. Confers with scientists and engineers regarding research, and prepares technical papers and reports. Prepares standards and specifications for processes, facilities, products, and tests. May be designated according to chemistry specialty as CHEMIST, ANALYTICAL (profess. & kin.); CHEMIST, INORGANIC (profess. & kin.); CHEMIST, ORGANIC (profess. & kin.); CHEMIST, PHYSICAL (profess. & kin.). ● **GED:** R6, M6, L5 ● **SVP:** 4-10 yrs ● **Academic:** Ed=M, Eng=S ● **Work Field:** 211, 251, 147 ● **MPSMS:** 723 ● **Aptitudes:** G1, V1, N1, S2, P2, Q2, K3, F3, M3, E5, C2 ● **Temperaments:** J, T, V ● **Physical:** Stg=L; Freq: R, H, I, N, D, A, X Occas: E, T, G, M ● **Work Env:** Noise=N; Occas: A, T ● **Salary:** 4 ● **Outlook:** 3

GEOGRAPHER (profess. & kin.) ● DOT #029.067-010 ● OES: 24198 ● Studies nature and use of areas of earth's surface, relating and interpreting interactions of physical and cultural phenomena: Conducts research on physical and climatic aspects of area or region, making direct observation of landforms, climates, soils, plants, and animals within area under study and incorporating available knowledge from related scientific fields, such as physics, geology, oceanography, meteorology, and biology. Studies human activities within given area, such as ethnic distribution, economic activity, and political organization. Acts as adviser or consultant to governments and international organizations on subjects, such as economic exploitation of regions and determination of ethnic and natural boundaries between nations or administrative areas. May use surveying equipment or meteorological instruments. May construct and interpret maps, graphs, and diagrams. May specialize in particular branch of cultural geography, such as economic, political, urban, social, or historical geography. ● **GED:** R6, M6, L6 ● **SVP:** 2-4 yrs ● **Academic:** Ed=M, Eng=G ● **Work Field:** 251 ● **MPSMS:** 729 ● **Aptitudes:** G1, V1, N2, S3, P3, Q4, K4, F4, M4, E5, C4 ● **Temperaments:** D, J, V ● **Physical:** Stg=L; Freq: N, A Occas: R, H, I, T, G, F, D, X ● **Work Env:** Noise=N; Occas: W ● **Salary:** 5 ● **Outlook:** 2

GEOGRAPHER, PHYSICAL (profess. & kin.) ● DOT #029.067-014 ● OES: 24198 ● Studies origins, nature, and distribution of features of earth's surface, including landforms, climates, soils, plants, and animals: Makes surveys of physical characteristics of specific regions, conducting studies of features, such as elevations, drainage, geological formations, climate, vegetation, and access to other regions. May conduct environmental studies and prepare environmental impact reports. ● **GED:** R6, M6, L6 ● **SVP:** 2-4 yrs ● **Academic:** Ed=M, Eng=G ● **Work Field:** 251 ● **MPSMS:** 729 S3, P3, Q4, K4, F4, M4, E4, C3 ● **Temperaments:** D, J, V ● **Physical:** Stg=L; Freq: T, G, N, A Occas: R, H, I, F, D, X ● **Work Env:** Noise=N; Occas: W ● **Salary:** 4 ● **Outlook:** 2

GEOLOGIST (profess. & kin.) ● DOT #024.061-018 ● OES: 24111 ● Studies composition, structure, and history of earth's crust: Examines rocks, minerals, and fossil remains to identify and determine sequence of processes affecting development of earth. Applies knowledge of chemistry, physics, biology, and mathematics to explain these phenomena and to help locate mineral, geothermal, and petroleum deposits and underground water resources. Studies ocean bottom. Applies geological knowledge to engineering problems encountered in construction projects, such as dams, tunnels, and large buildings. Studies fossil plants and animals to determine their evolutionary sequence and age. Prepares geologic reports and maps, interprets research data, and recommends further study or action. May specialize in area of study and be designated Geomorphologist (profess. & kin.); Oceanographer, Geological (profess. & kin.); Photogeologist (profess. & kin.). May conduct or participate in environmental studies and prepare environmental reports. Workers applying principles of rock and soil mechanics for engineering projects may be designated Geological Engineer (profess. & kin.). Workers applying all branches of geologic knowledge to conditions that affect planning, design, construction, operation and safety to engineering projects may be designated Engineering Geologist (profess. & kin.). ● **GED:** R6, M6, L6 ● **SVP:** 4-10 yrs ● **Academic:** Ed=M, Eng=G ● **Work Field:** 251 ● **MPSMS:** 725 ● **Aptitudes:** G1, V1, N1, S2, P2, Q3, K3, F4, M3, E4, C3 ● **Temperaments:** J, T, V ● **Physical:** Stg=L; Freq: R, H, I, N, D, A, X Occas: C, B, S, K ● **Work Env:** Noise=N; Occas: W ● **Salary:** 5 ● **Outlook:** 3

GEOPHYSICIST (profess. & kin.) ● DOT #024.061-030 ● OES: 24111 ● Studies physical aspects of earth, including its atmosphere and hydrosphere: Investigates and measures seismic, gravitational, electrical, thermal, and magnetic forces affecting earth, utilizing principles of physics, mathematics, and chemistry. Analyzes data obtained to compute shape of earth, estimate composition and structure of earth's interior, determine flow pattern of ocean tides and currents, study physical properties of atmosphere, and help locate petroleum and mineral deposits. Investigates origin and activity of glaciers, volcanoes, and earthquakes. Compiles data to prepare navigational charts and maps, predict atmospheric conditions, prepare environmental reports, and establish water supply and flood-control programs. May study specific aspect of geophysics and be designated Geomagnetician (profess. & kin.); Glaciologist (profess. & kin.); Oceanographer, Physical (profess. & kin.); Tectonophysicist (profess. & kin.); Volcanologist (profess. & kin.). ● **GED:** R6, M5, L5 ● **SVP:** 4-10 yrs ● **Academic:** Ed=M, Eng=G ● **Work Field:** 251 ● **MPSMS:** 725 ● **Aptitudes:** G1, V1, N1, S2, P2, Q3, K3, F4, M3, E4, C4 ● **Temperaments:** D, J, T, V ● **Physical:** Stg=L; Freq: R, H, T, G, N, F, D, A, X Occas: I, V ● **Work Env:** Noise=N; Occas: W ● **Salary:** 5 ● **Outlook:** 2

HYDROLOGIST (profess. & kin.) ● DOT #024.061-034 ● OES: 24111 ● Studies distribution, disposition, and development of waters of land areas, including form and intensity of precipitation, and modes of return to ocean and atmosphere: Maps and charts water flow and disposition of sediment. Measures changes in water volume due to evaporation and melting of snow. Studies storm occurrences and nature and movement of glaciers, and determines rate of ground absorption and ultimate disposition of water. Evaluates data obtained in reference to such problems as flood and drought forecasting, soil and water conservation programs, and planning water supply, water power, flood control, drainage, irrigation, crop production, and inland navigation projects. ● **GED:** R6, M6, L6 ● **SVP:** 4-10 yrs ● **Academic:** Ed=M, Eng=G ● **Work Field:** 251 ● **MPSMS:** 725 ● **Aptitudes:** G1, V1, N1, S2, P3, Q3, K3, F3, M3, E4, C4 ● **Temperaments:** D, J, T, V ● **Physical:** Stg=L; Freq: R, H, I, T, G, N Occas: D, A, X ● **Work Env:** Noise=N; Occas: W ● **Salary:** 5 ● **Outlook:** 2

MATHEMATICIAN (profess. & kin.) ● DOT #020.067-014 ● OES: 25317 ● Conducts research in fundamental mathematics and in application of mathematical techniques to science, management, and other fields, and solves or directs solutions to problems in various fields by mathematical methods: Conducts research in such branches of mathematics as algebra, geometry, number theory, logic, and topology, and studies and tests hypotheses and alternative theories. Conceives and develops ideas for application of mathematics to wide variety of fields, including science, engineering, military planning, electronic data processing, and management. Applies mathematics or mathematical methods to solution of problems in research, development, production, logistics, and other functional areas, utilizing knowledge of subject or field to which applied, such as physics, engineering, astronomy, biology, economics, business and industrial management, or cryptography. Performs computations, applies methods of numerical analysis, and operates or directs operation of desk calculators and mechanical and electronic computation machines, analyzers, and plotters in solving problems in support of mathematical, scientific, or industrial research activity. Acts as advisor or consultant to research personnel concerning mathematical methods and applications. May be designated according to function as Mathematician, Applied (profess. & kin.); Mathematician, Research (profess. & kin.). ● **GED:** R6, M6, L6 ● **SVP:** 4-10 yrs ● **Academic:** Ed=M, Eng=S ● **Work Field:** 251 ● **MPSMS:** 721 ● **Aptitudes:** G1, V2, N1, S1, P4, Q4, K4, F4, M4, E5, C5 ● **Temperaments:** D, J, T ● **Physical:** Stg=S; Freq: R, H, I, N Occas: T, G, A ● **Work Env:** Noise=N; ● **Salary:** 4 ● **Outlook:** 3

METEOROLOGIST (profess. & kin.) ● DOT #025.062-010 ● OES: 24108 ● Alternate titles: WEATHER FORECASTER. Analyzes and interprets meteorological data gathered by surface and upper-air stations, satellites, and radar to prepare reports and forecasts for public and other users: Studies and interprets synoptic reports, maps, photographs, and prognostic charts to predict long and short range weather conditions. Operates computer graphic equipment to produce weather reports and maps for analysis, distribution to users, or for use in televised weather broadcast. Issues hurricane and other severe weather warnings. May broadcast weather forecast over television or radio. May prepare special forecasts and briefings for particular audiences, such as those involved in air and sea transportation, agriculture, fire prevention, air-pollution control, and school groups. May direct forecasting services at weather station, or at radio or television broadcasting facility. May conduct basic or applied research in meteorology. May establish and staff weather observation stations. ● **GED:** R5, M5, L5 ● **SVP:** 2-4 yrs ● **Academic:** Ed=M, Eng=G ● **Work Field:** 251, 282 ● **MPSMS:** 725, 864 ● **Aptitudes:** G2, V2, N2, S2, P2, Q2, K4, F3, M4, E3, C4 ● **Temperaments:** J, P, T ● **Physical:** Stg=L; Freq: H Occas: R, I, T, G, N, A, X ● **Work Env:** Noise=N; ● **Salary:** 5 ● **Outlook:** 3

MINERALOGIST (profess. & kin.) ● DOT #024.061-038 ● OES: 24111 ● Examines, analyzes, and classifies minerals, gems, and precious stones: Isolates specimen from ore, rocks, or matrices. Makes microscopic examination to determine shape, surface markings, and other physical characteristics. Performs physical and chemical tests and makes x-ray examinations to determine composition of specimen and type of crystalline structure. Identifies and classifies samples. Develops data and theories on mode of origin, occurrence, and possible uses of minerals. ● **GED:** R6, M6, L6 ● **SVP:** 4-10 yrs ● **Academic:** Ed=M, Eng=G ● **Work Field:** 251 ● **MPSMS:** 725 ● **Aptitudes:** G1, V1, N2, S2, P3, Q3, K3, F3, M3, E4, C3 ● **Temperaments:** D, J, T ● **Physical:** Stg=L; Freq: R, H, I, N, D, A, X Occas: S, K, O, E, T, G ● **Work Env:** Noise=N; Occas: W ● **Salary:** 5 ● **Outlook:** 2

PETROLOGIST (profess. & kin.) ● DOT #024.061-046 ● OES: 24111 ● Investigates composition, structure, and history of rock masses forming earth's crust. Applies findings to such fields of investigation as causes of formations, breaking down and weathering, chemical composition and forms of deposition of sedimentary rocks, methods of eruption, and origin and causes of metamorphosis. ● **GED:** R6, M6, L5 ● **SVP:** 4-10 yrs ● **Academic:** Ed=M, Eng=G ● **Work Field:** 251 ● **MPSMS:** 725 ● **Aptitudes:** G1, V1, N2, S2, P3, Q3, K3, F3, M3, E4, C3 ● **Temperaments:** D, J, T ● **Physical:** Stg=L; Freq: R, H, I, N, D, A, X Occas: S, K, O, E, T, G ● **Work Env:** Noise=N; Occas: W ● **Salary:** 5 ● **Outlook:** 3

PHYSICIST (profess. & kin.) ● DOT #023.061-014 ● OES: 24102 ● Conducts research into phases of physical phenomena, develops theories and laws on basis of observation and experiments, and devises methods to apply laws and theories of physics to industry, medicine, and other fields: Performs experiments with masers, lasers, cyclotrons, betatrons, telescopes, mass spectrometers, electron microscopes, and other equipment to observe structure and properties of matter, transformation and propagation of energy, relationships between matter and energy, and other physical phenomena. Describes and expresses observations and conclusions in mathematical terms. Devises procedures for physical testing of materials. Conducts instrumental analyses to determine physical properties of materials. May specialize in one or more branches of physics and be designated Physicist, Acoustics (profess. & kin.); Physicist, Astrophysics (profess. & kin.); Physicist, Atomic, Electronic And Molecular (profess. & kin.); Physicist, Cryogenics (profess. & kin.); Physicist, Electricity And Magnetism (profess. & kin.); Physicist, Fluids (profess. & kin.). May be designated: Physicist, Light And Optics (profess. & kin.); Physicist, Nuclear (profess. & kin.); Physicist, Plasma (profess. & kin.); Physicist, Solid Earth (profess. & kin.); Physicist, Solid State (profess. & kin.); Physicist, Thermodynamics (profess. & kin.). ● **GED:** R6, M6, L6 ● **SVP:** 4-10 yrs ● **Academic:** Ed=M, Eng=S ● **Work Field:** 251 ● **MPSMS:** 724 ● **Aptitudes:** G1, V1, N1, S1, P1, Q3, K3, F3, M3, E5, C2 ● **Temperaments:** J ● **Physical:** Stg=L; Freq: N, D, A, X Occas: R, H, I ● **Work Env:** Noise=Q; ● **Salary:** 5 ● **Outlook:** 2

SEISMOLOGIST (profess. & kin.) ● DOT #024.061-050 ● OES: 24111 ● Studies and interprets seismic data to locate earthquakes and earthquake faults: Reviews, analyzes, and interprets data from seismographs and geophysical instruments. Establishes existence and activity of faults, and direction, motion, and stress of earth movements before, during, and after earthquakes. Conducts research on seismic forces affecting deformative movements of earth. May issue maps or reports indicating areas of seismic risk to existing or proposed construction or development. ● **GED:** R6, M6, L6 ● **SVP:** 4-10 yrs ● **Academic:** Ed=M, Eng=G ● **Work Field:** 251 ● **MPSMS:** 725 ● **Aptitudes:** G1, V1, N1, S2, P3, Q3, K3, F3, M3, E4, C3 ● **Temperaments:** D, J, T, V ● **Physical:** Stg=L; Freq: R, H, N, F, D, A, X, V Occas: I ● **Work Env:** Noise=N; Occas: W ● **Salary:** 4 ● **Outlook:** 2

GOE: 02.01.02
Technology

CHEMICAL LABORATORY CHIEF (profess. & kin.) ● DOT #022.161-010 ● OES: 13017 ● Alternate titles: CHIEF CHEMIST; DIRECTOR, CHEMICAL LABORATORY. Plans and directs activities of chemical laboratory in industrial, research, governmental, or other organization: Plans, coordinates, and directs programs for research, product development, improvement of manufacturing processes; or for analysis and testing of substances to support criminal investigations, to detect toxins, or to verify composition of manufactured and agricultural products, and natural resources, such as air, soil, and water. Coordinates research and analysis activities according to applicable government regulations, manufacturing processes, or other considerations, and approves modification of formulas, standards, specifications, and processes. Reviews research, testing, quality control, and other operational reports to ensure that quality standards, efficiency, and schedules are met. Interprets results of laboratory activities to laboratory personnel, management, and professional and technical societies, and prepares reports and technical papers. May prepare and administer budgets. May advise and assist in obtaining patents for products, processes, or equipment. ● **GED:** R6, M6, L6 ● **SVP:** 4-10 yrs ● **Academic:** Ed=B, Eng=G ● **Work Field:** 295, 211, 251 ● **MPSMS:** 490, 723 ● **Aptitudes:** G1, V1, N1, S3, P3, Q3, K3, F3, M3, E5, C2 ● **Temperaments:** D, J, P, T ● **Physical:** Stg=L; Freq: R, H, I, T, G, N Occas: E, M, D, A, X ● **Work Env:** Noise=N; Occas: A ● **Salary:** 5 ● **Outlook:** 2

GEOLOGIST, PETROLEUM (petrol. & gas) ● DOT #024.061-022 ● OES: 24111 ● Explores and charts stratigraphic arrangement and structure of earth to locate gas and oil deposits: Studies well logs, analyzes cores and cuttings from well drillings, and interprets data obtained by electrical or radioactive well logging and other subsurface surveys to identify earth strata. Examines aerial photographs, evaluates results of geophysical prospecting, and prepares surface and subsurface maps and diagrams depicting stratigraphic arrangement and composition of earth and probable deposits of gas and oil. Recommends acquisition, retention, or release of property leases or contracts. Estimates oil reserves in proven or prospective fields, and consults with PETROLEUM ENGINEERS (petrol. & gas) concerning drilling and production methods. May direct drilling of shallow exploratory wells. ● **GED:** R6, M6, L5 ● **SVP:** 4-10 yrs ● **Academic:** Ed=M, Eng=G ● **Work Field:** 251 ● **MPSMS:** 725 ● **Aptitudes:** G1, V1, N2, S1, P2, Q3, K4, F3, M4, E5, C5 ● **Temperaments:** J, P, T, V ● **Physical:** Stg=L; Freq: T, G, N, F, D, A Occas: R, H, I, X ● **Work Env:** Noise=N; Occas: W ● **Salary:** 5 ● **Outlook:** 3

ENVIRONMENTAL ANALYST (profess. & kin.) ● DOT #029.081-010 ● OES: 24198 ● Alternate titles: ENVIRONMENTAL SCIENTIST. Conducts research studies to develop theories or methods of abating or controlling sources of environmental pollutants, utilizing knowledge of principles and concepts of various scientific and engineering disciplines: Determines data collection methods to be employed in research projects and surveys. Plans and develops research models, using knowledge of mathematical, statistical, and physical science concepts and approaches. Identifies and analyzes sources of pollution to determine their effects. Collects and synthesizes data derived from pollution emission measurements, atmospheric monitoring, meteorological and minerological information, and soil or water samples. Prepares graphs, charts, and statistical models from synthesized data, using knowledge of mathematical, statistical, and engineering analysis techniques. Analyzes data to assess pollution problems, establish standards,

and develop approaches for control of pollution. May be designated according to aspect of environment in which engaged as Air Pollution Analyst (profess. & kin.); Soils Analyst (profess. & kin.); Water Quality Analyst (profess. & kin.). ● **GED:** R6, M6, L6 ● **SVP:** 4-10 yrs ● **Academic:** Ed=M, Eng=G ● **Work Field:** 251, 244 ● **MPSMS:** 719 ● **Aptitudes:** G1, V1, N1, S2, P2, Q3, K3, F3, M3, E4, C4 ● **Temperaments:** D, J, T ● **Physical:** Stg=L; Freq: R, H, I, N Occas: C, B, S, K, O, W, T, G, F, A, X ● **Work Env:** Noise=N; Occas: W ● **Salary:** 5 ● **Outlook:** 3

MATERIALS SCIENTIST (profess. & kin.) ● DOT #029.081-014 ● OES: 24198 ● Conducts scientific studies for understanding, characterizing and developing materials leading to potential uses for the benefit of science and emerging technologies: Conducts programs for studying structures and properties of various materials, such as metals, alloys, ceramics, semiconductors and polymers to obtain research data. Plans experimental laboratory production of materials having special characteristics to confirm feasibility of processes and techniques for potential users. Prepares reports of materials studies for information of other scientists and requestors. May guide technical staff engaged in developing materials for specific use in projected product or device. ● **GED:** R6, M6, L5 ● **SVP:** 2-4 yrs ● **Academic:** Ed=M, Eng=S ● **Work Field:** 251 ● **MPSMS:** 720 ● **Aptitudes:** G1, V1, N1, S1, P1, Q2, K3, F3, M3, E4, C3 ● **Temperaments:** J ● **Physical:** Stg=S; Freq: R, H, I, N, X Occas: A ● **Work Env:** Noise=N; ● **Salary:** 3 ● **Outlook:** 4

PROJECT MANAGER, ENVIRONMENTAL RESEARCH (profess. & kin.) ● DOT #029.167-014 ● OES: 13017 ● Plans, directs, and coordinates activities of staff involved in developing procedures, equipment, and techniques to solve pollution problems, using scientific research methods: Schedules and assigns duties to staff research scientists and engineers based on evaluation of their knowledge of specific disciplines. Confers with project scientists and research engineers to formulate research plan, coordinate project activities, and establish reporting procedures. Prepares environmental research project feasibility and progress reports. Coordinates activities of research personnel conducting successive phases of problem analysis, solution proposals, and testing. Reviews technical aspects of project to assist staff and assess productivity of lines of research. Reviews project operations to ensure coordination of efforts and timely submission of reports. Analyzes reports to evaluate program effectiveness and budgetary needs. Approves expenditures necessary for completion of project. Coordinates planning, testing, and operating phases to complete project. Confers with local regulatory agencies to discover local environmental quality standards, industrial practices, and new developments in pollution abatement. May provide technical assistance to agencies conducting related environmental studies. ● **GED:** R5, M5, L5 ● **SVP:** 4-10 yrs ● **Academic:** Ed=M, Eng=S ● **Work Field:** 251, 244 ● **MPSMS:** 729, 719 ● **Aptitudes:** G2, V2, N2, S3, P3, Q3, K4, F4, M4, E5, C5 ● **Temperaments:** D, J ● **Physical:** Stg=L; Freq: R, H, T, G, N Occas: I, A, X ● **Work Env:** Noise=N; ● **Salary:** 5 ● **Outlook:** 4

Scientific   02

Life Sciences

02.02

Workers in this group are concerned mostly with living things such as plants and animals. They conduct research and do experiments to expand man's knowledge of living things. Some may work on problems related to how the environment affects plant and animal life. Others may study causes of disease and ways to control disease. These workers are usually employed in the research facilities of hospitals, government agencies, industries, or universities.

✓ What kind of work would you do?

Your work activities would depend upon your specific job. For example, you might:

- prepare slides and use microscopes to study cells and cell structure.
- examine animals and specimens to study the effect of drugs on living tissue.
- study the origin and classification of plants or animals.
- conduct research to develop improved ways to process food.

- conduct experiments with growing bacteria to develop new information about diseases.
- conduct experiments by breeding animals or plants to study characteristics passed from parents to offspring.

✓ What skills and abilities do you need for this kind of work?

To do this kind of work, you must be able to:

- use logic and scientific methods to study living things.
- understand and use instructions that use numbers, diagrams, or chemical formulas.
- learn and use knowledge about how living things function, how plants and animals are classified, and how to use laboratory and scientific equipment.
- recognize differences in size, form, shape, color, and textures.
- use eyes, hands, and fingers easily and accurately.
- do a lot of different things and change what you are doing frequently.
- make decisions using your own judgment.
- make decisions based on information that can be measured or verified.
- do things which require you to be very careful and accurate.

✓ How do you know if you would like or could learn to do this kind of work?

The following questions may give you clues about yourself as you consider this group of jobs.

- Have you studied plants in a garden, forest, or laboratory setting? Can you recognize and identify different types of plants?
- Have you been a member of a scouting or environmental protection group? Do you take part in efforts to preserve forests, parks, or campgrounds?

- Have you taken courses in biology or zoology? Do you enjoy conducting experiments which involve plants and animals?
- Have you participated in a project or hobby which involved breeding, caring for, or studying plant life?

✓ How can you prepare for and enter this kind of work?

Occupations in this group usually require education and/or training extending from four years to over ten years, depending upon the specific kind of work. Important academic courses include algebra, geometry, advanced math, chemistry, biological sciences. Technical writing or composition courses are helpful. A bachelor's degree with a major in biology or another life science is generally required. Graduate degrees are needed for most research work or for college teaching. A master's degree may qualify an individual for laboratory teaching. Advanced studies or a Ph.D. are usually required for work in basic research.

✓ What else should you consider about these jobs?

Some courses and some jobs require workers to cut up or handle tissue and waste products of humans and animals. Some jobs require living or working in remote areas such as forests or deserts.

It is important that life scientists keep informed of developments in their field by attending seminars, reading professional books and magazines, or being active in professional organizations.

If you think you would like to do this kind of work, look at the job titles listed below.

■ ■ ■

GOE: 02.02.01
Animal Specialization

BIOMEDICAL ENGINEER (profess. & kin.) ● DOT #019.061-010 ● OES: 22198 ● Conducts research into biological aspects of humans or other animals to develop new theories and facts, or test, prove, or modify known theories of life systems, and to design life-support apparatus, utilizing principles of engineering and bio-behavioral sciences: Plans and conducts research concerning behavioral, biological, psychological, or other life systems. Studies engineering aspects of bio-behavioral systems of humans, utilizing knowledge of electrical, mechanical, chemical, or other engineering principles and knowledge of human anatomy and physiology. Develops mathematical models to simulate human bio-behavioral systems in order to obtain data for measuring or controlling life processes, utilizing knowledge of computer, graphics, and other related technologies. Designs and develops instruments and devices, such as artificial organs, cardiac pacemakers, or ultrasonic imaging devices, capable of assisting medical or other health-care personnel in observing, repairing, or treating physical ailments or deformities, using knowledge of materials compatible with body tissues, energy exchanges within the body, and instrumentation capable of measuring and controlling body functions. May specialize in design and development of biomedical equipment used by medical facilities and be known as Clinical Engineer (profess. & kin.). ● **GED:** R6, M6, L5 ● **SVP:** 4-10 yrs ● **Academic:** Ed=B, Eng=S ● **Work Field:** 244, 251 ● **MPSMS:** 700 ● **Aptitudes:** G1, V1, N1, S1, P2, Q2, K3, F3, M3, E5, C3 ● **Temperaments:** D, J, T ● **Physical:** Stg=S; Freq: R, H, I, T, G, N, X Occas: F, D, A ● **Work Env:** Noise=N; ● **Salary:** 5 ● **Outlook:** 3

ANIMAL SCIENTIST (profess. & kin.) ● DOT #040.061-014 ● OES: 24305 ● Conducts research in selection, breeding, feeding, management, and marketing of beef and dual-purpose cattle, horses, mules, sheep, dogs, goats, and pet animals: Develops improved practices in feeding, housing, sanitation, and parasite and disease control. Controls breeding practices to improve strains of animals. May specialize in animal nutritional research and be designated Animal Nutritionist (profess. & kin.). May be designated according to animal specialty. ● **GED:** R6, M6, L6 ● **SVP:** 4-10 yrs ● **Academic:** Ed=M, Eng=S ● **Work Field:** 251 ● **MPSMS:** 731 ● **Aptitudes:** G1, V1, N2, S2, P2, Q3, K3, F2, M2, E5, C4 ● **Temperaments:** D, J, T, V ● **Physical:** Stg=M; Freq: R, H, I, N Occas: E, D, A, X ● **Work Env:** Noise=N; Freq: W ● **Salary:** 4 ● **Outlook:** 3

ENVIRONMENTAL EPIDEMIOLOGIST (government ser.) ● DOT #041.167-010 ● OES: 24398 ● Plans, directs, and conducts studies concerned with incidence of disease in industrial settings and effects of industrial chemicals on health: Confers with industry representatives to select occupational groups for study and to arrange for collection of data concerning work history of individuals and disease concentration and mortality rates among groups. Plans methods of conducting epidemiological studies and provides detailed specifications for collecting data to personnel participating in studies. Develops codes to facilitate computer input of demographic and epidemiological data for use by data processing personnel engaged in programming epidemiological statistics. Compares statistics on causes of death among members of selected working populations with those among general population, using life-table analyses. Analyzes data collected to determine probable effects of work settings and activities on disease and mortality rates, using valid statistical techniques and knowledge of epidemiology. Presents data in designated statistical format to illustrate common patterns among workers in selected occupations. Initiates and maintains contacts with statistical and data processing managers in other agencies to maintain access to epidemiological source materials. Evaluates materials from all sources for addition to or amendment of epidemiological data bank. Plans and directs activities of clerical and statistical personnel engaged in tabulation and analysis of epidemiological information to ensure accomplishment of objectives. ● **GED:** R6, M6, L5 ● **SVP:** 4-10 yrs ● **Academic:** Ed=B, Eng=S ● **Work Field:** 251 ● **MPSMS:** 732, 925 ● **Aptitudes:** G1, V2, N1, S2, P2, Q1, K3, F3, M3, E5, C2 ● **Temperaments:** D, J, T ● **Physical:** Stg=L; Freq: R, H, I, T, G, N, X Occas: A, V ● **Work Env:** Noise=N; ● **Salary:** 5 ● **Outlook:** 4

HISTOPATHOLOGIST (medical ser.) ● DOT #041.061-054 ● OES: 24311 ● Alternate titles: HISTOLOGIST. Studies human or animal tissue to provide data to delineate cause and progress of disease that impairs body function: Trains and oversees laboratory personnel in preparing tissue sections or prepares tissue sections from surgical and diagnostic cases and autopsies. Examines tissue under microscope to detect characteristics of cell structure indicative of disease and writes diagnostic reports. Devises and directs use of special stains and methods for isolating, identifying, and studying function, morphology, and pathology of obscure or difficult-to-identify cells, tissues, and connecting fibers. May conduct autopsies to select tissue specimens for study. May engage in research to develop techniques for diagnosing and identifying pathological conditions. May study anatomy of body tissues, formation of organs, and related problems to obtain data on body functions. ● **GED:** R6, M6, L6 ● **SVP:** 4-10 yrs ● **Academic:** Ed=M, Eng=G ● **Work Field:** 211, 251 ● **MPSMS:** 732, 925 ● **Aptitudes:** G1, V1, N2, S1, P1, Q2, K3, F2, M2, E5, C2 ● **Temperaments:** D, J, T ● **Physical:** Stg=L; Freq: R, H, I, E, N, D, A, X Occas: S, T, G ● **Work Env:** Noise=Q; Const: O ● **Salary:** 5 ● **Outlook:** 3

MEDICAL PHYSICIST (profess. & kin.) ● DOT #079.021-014 ● OES: 24311 ● Applies knowledge and methodology of science of physics to all aspects of medicine, to address problems related to diagnosis and treatment of human disease: Advises and consults with physicians in such applications as use of ionizing radiation in diagnosis, therapy, treatment planning with externally delivered radiation as well as use of internally implanted radioactive sources; complete subject of x-ray equipment, calibration, and dosimetry; medical uses of ultrasound and infrared; bioelectrical investigation of brain and heart; mathematical analysis and applications of computers in medicine; formulation of radiation protection guides and procedures specific to hospital environment; development of instrumentation for improved patient care and clinical service. Plans, directs, conducts, and participates in supporting programs to ensure effective and safe use of radiation and radionuclides in human beings by physician specialist. Teaches principles of medical physics to physicians, residents, graduate students, medical students, and technologists by means of lectures, problem solving, and

laboratory sessions. Directs and participates in investigations of biophysical techniques associated with any branch of medicine. Conducts research in development of diagnostic and remedial procedures and develops instrumentation for specific medical applications. Acts as consultant to education, medical research, and other professional groups and organizations. ● **GED:** R6, M6, L6 ● **SVP:** 4-10 yrs ● **Academic:** Ed=M, Eng=G ● **Work Field:** 293, 251 ● **MPSMS:** 725, 732 ● **Aptitudes:** G1, V1, N2, S2, P4, Q4, K4, F4, M4, E5, C5 ● **Temperaments:** D, J, P ● **Physical:** Stg=L; Freq: R, H, I, T, G, N, A ● **Work Env:** Noise=N; ● **Salary:** 5 ● **Outlook:** 3

PARASITOLOGIST (profess. & kin.) ● DOT #041.061-070 ● OES: 24311 ● Studies characteristics, habits, and life cycles of animal parasites, such as protozoans, tapeworms, roundworms, flukes, and other parasitic organisms, to determine manner in which they attack human beings and animals and effects produced: Investigates modes of transmission from host to host. Develops methods and agents to combat parasites. May specialize in study of one variety of parasite, such as animal parasites that attack man, and be designated Medical Parasitologist (profess. & kin.); of parasitic worms and be designated Helminthologist (profess. & kin.); of one celled free living and parasitic organisms and be designated Protozoologist (profess. & kin.). ● **GED:** R6, M6, L6 ● **SVP:** 4-10 yrs ● **Academic:** Ed=B, Eng=S ● **Work Field:** 251 ● **MPSMS:** 732 ● **Aptitudes:** G1, V1, N2, S2, P2, Q3, K4, F3, M3, E5, C4 ● **Temperaments:** D, J, T ● **Physical:** Stg=L; Freq: R, H, N, D, A, X Occas: I ● **Work Env:** Noise=N; ● **Salary:** 5 ● **Outlook:** 3

PHARMACOLOGIST (profess. & kin.) ● DOT #041.061-074 ● OES: 24311 ● Studies effects of drugs, gases, dusts, and other materials on tissue and physiological processes of animals and human beings: Experiments with animals, such as rats, guinea pigs, and mice, to determine reactions of drugs and other substances on functioning of organs and tissues, noting effects on circulation, respiration, digestion, or other vital processes. Standardizes drug dosages or methods of immunizing against industrial diseases by correlating results of animal experiments with results obtained from clinical experimentation on human beings. Investigates preventative methods and remedies for diseases, such as silicosis and lead, mercury, and ammonia poisoning. Analyzes food preservatives and colorings, vermin poisons, and other materials to determine toxic or nontoxic properties. Standardizes procedures for manufacture of drugs and medicinal compounds. ● **GED:** R6, M6, L6 ● **SVP:** 4-10 yrs ● **Academic:** Ed=B, Eng=S ● **Work Field:** 251 ● **MPSMS:** 732 ● **Aptitudes:** G1, V2, N1, S1, P2, Q3, K3, F2, M3, E5, C3 ● **Temperaments:** J, T ● **Physical:** Stg=L; Freq: R, H, I, N Occas: E, D, A, X ● **Work Env:** Noise=N; ● **Salary:** 5 ● **Outlook:** 4

ZOOLOGIST (profess. & kin.) ● DOT #041.061-090 ● OES: 24308 ● Studies origin, interrelationships, classification, life histories, habits, life processes, diseases, relation to environment, growth and development, genetics, and distribution of animals: Studies animals in natural habitat and collects specimens for laboratory study. Dissects and examines specimens under microscope and uses chemicals and various types of scientific equipment to carry out experimental studies. Prepares collections of preserved specimens or microscopic slides for such purposes as identification of species, study of species development, and study of animal diseases. May raise specimens for experimental purposes. May specialize in one aspect of animal study, such as functioning of animal as an organism, or development of organism from egg to embryo stage. May specialize in study of reptiles, frogs, and salamanders and be designated Herpetologist (profess. & kin.); of fish and fishlike forms and be designated Ichthyologist (profess. & kin.); of sponges, jellyfish, and protozoa and be designated Invertebrate Zoologist (profess. & kin.); of birds and be designated Ornithologist (profess. & kin.); of mammals and be designated Mammalogist (profess. & kin.). May study animals for purposes of identification and classification and be designated Animal Taxonomist (profess. & kin.); or study effects of environment on animals and be designated Animal Ecologist (profess. & kin.). ● **GED:** R6, M6, L6 ● **SVP:** 4-10 yrs ● **Academic:** Ed=B, Eng=S ● **Work Field:** 251 ● **MPSMS:** 732 ● **Aptitudes:** G1, V1, N2, S2, P2, Q4, K2, F2, M2, E5, C3 ● **Temperaments:** J, V ● **Physical:** Stg=L; Freq: R, H, I, N Occas: C, B, S, K, O, W, E, T, G, F, D, A, X, V ● **Work Env:** Noise=N; Freq: W ● **Salary:** 5 ● **Outlook:** 3

GOE: 02.02.02
Plant Specialization

AGRONOMIST (profess. & kin.) ● DOT #040.061-010 ● OES: 24305 ● Alte2 rnate titles: CROP-RESEARCH SCIENTIST; CROP SCIENTIST. Conducts experiments or investigations in field-crop problems and develops new methods of growing crops to secure more efficient production, higher yield, and improved quality: Plans and carries out breeding studies at experiment stations or farms to develop and improve varieties of field crops, such as cotton, tobacco, or cereal with respect to characteristics, such as yield, quality, adaptation to specific soils or climates, and resistance to diseases and pests [PLANT BREEDER (profess. & kin.)]. Studies crop production to discover best methods of planting, cultivation, harvesting, and effects of various climatic conditions on crops. Develops methods for control of noxious weeds, crop diseases, and insect pests [PLANT PATHOLOGIST (profess. & kin.)]. May specialize in specific field crop, group of field crops, or specific agronomic problem. ● **GED:** R6, M6, L6 ● **SVP:** 4-10 yrs ● **Academic:** Ed=M, Eng=S ● **Work Field:** 251 ● **MPSMS:** 731 ● **Aptitudes:** G1, V1, N2, S4, P4, Q3, K4, F3, M3, E4, C4 ● **Temperaments:** D, J ● **Physical:** Stg=L; Freq: R, H, I, E, N, D, A, X ● **Work Env:** Noise=N; Freq: W ● **Salary:** 4 ● **Outlook:** 2

BOTANIST (profess. & kin.) ● DOT #041.061-038 ● OES: 24308 ● Studies development and life processes, physiology, heredity, environment, distribution, anatomy, morphology, and economic value of plants for application in such fields as agronomy, forestry, horticulture, and pharmacology: Studies behavior of chromosomes and reproduction, internal and external structures, and examines mechanics and biochemistry of plants and plant cells, using microscopes, staining techniques, and scientific equipment. Investigates environment and plant communities and effect of rainfall, temperature, climate, soil, and elevation on plant growth from seed to mature plants. Identifies and classifies plants. May conduct environmental studies and prepare reports. May be designated according to field of specialization as Plant Ecologist (profess. & kin.); Plant Taxonomist (profess. & kin.). ● **GED:** R6, M6, L6 ● **SVP:** 4-10 yrs ● **Academic:** Ed=B, Eng=S ● **Work Field:** 251 ● **MPSMS:** 732 ● **Aptitudes:** G1, V1, N2, S1, P1, Q3, K3, F3, M4, E4, C3 ● **Temperaments:** D, J, T ● **Physical:** Stg=L; Freq: N, D, A, X Occas: S, K, O, R, H, I, E ● **Work Env:** Noise=N; ● **Salary:** 5 ● **Outlook:** 3

FOREST ECOLOGIST (profess. & kin.) ● DOT #040.061-030 ● OES: 24302 ● Conducts research in environmental factors affecting forests: Carries out studies to determine what conditions account for prevalence of different varieties of trees. Studies classification, life history, light and soil requirements, and resistance to disease and insects of different species. Investigates adaptability of different species to new environmental conditions, such as changes in soil type, climate, and altitude. ● **GED:** R6, M6, L6 ● **SVP:** 4-10 yrs ● **Academic:** Ed=B, Eng=S ● **Work Field:** 251 ● **MPSMS:** 731, 319 ● **Aptitudes:** G1, V1, N2, S3, P3, Q4, K4, F3, M3, E5, C4 ● **Temperaments:** D, J, T ● **Physical:** Stg=L; Occas: R, H, I, E, N, F, D, A, X, V ● **Work Env:** Noise=N; Freq: W ● **Salary:** 4 ● **Outlook:** 3

HORTICULTURIST (profess. & kin.) ● DOT #040.061-038 ● OES: 24305 ● Conducts experiments and investigations to determine methods of breeding, producing, storing, processing, and transporting of fruits, nuts, berries, vegetables, flowers, bushes, and trees: Experiments to develop new or improved varieties having higher yield, quality, nutritional value, resistance to disease, or adaptability to climates, soils, uses, or processes. Determines best methods of planting, spraying, cultivating, and harvesting. May specialize in research, breeding, production, or shipping and storage of fruits, nuts, berries, vegetables, ornamental plants, or other horticultural products and be identified according to specialty. May prepare articles and give lectures on horticultural specialty. ● **GED:** R6, M6, L6 ● **SVP:** 4-10 yrs ● **Academic:** Ed=B, Eng=S ● **Work Field:** 251 ● **MPSMS:** 731 ● **Aptitudes:** G1, V1, N2, S3, P3, Q3, K4, F3, M3, E5, C4 ● **Temperaments:** D, J, T ● **Physical:** Stg=M; Freq: R, H, I, T, G, N, D, A, X Occas: S, K, O, E ● **Work Env:** Noise=N; Occas: W ● **Salary:** 4 ● **Outlook:** 2

PLANT PATHOLOGIST (profess. & kin.) ● DOT #041.061-086 ● OES: 24308 ● Conducts research in nature, cause, and control of plant diseases and decay of plant products: Studies and compares healthy and diseased plants to determine symptoms of diseased condition. Inoculates healthy plants with culture of suspected agents taken from diseased plants and studies effects to determine agents responsible for disease. Isolates disease-causing agent, studies habits and life cycle, and devises methods of destroying or controlling agent [MICROBIOLOGIST (profess. & kin.)]. Tests possible control measures under laboratory and field conditions for comparative effectiveness, practicality, and economy. Investigates comparative susceptibility of different varieties of plants and develops varieties immune to disease [PLANT BREEDER (profess. & kin.)]. Studies rates of spread and intensity of disease under different conditions of soil, climate, and geography, and predicts outbreaks of plant diseases. Determines kinds of plants and insects that harbor or transmit disease. Studies losses from deterioration of perishable plant products in transit or storage and develops practices to prevent or reduce losses. Determines presence of disease producing agents in seed stocks to reduce losses from seed borne diseases. May specialize in type of plant affected, such as cereal crops, fruit, or forest trees, or by type of disease, such as bacterial, virus, fungus, mycoplasma, or nematode. May inspect flower and vegetable seeds and flowering bulbs for diseases, infections, and insect injuries. ● **GED:** R6, M6, L6 ● **SVP:** 4-10 yrs ● **Academic:** Ed=B, Eng=S ● **Work Field:** 251 ● **MPSMS:** 732 ● **Aptitudes:** G1, V1, N2, S2, P2, Q3, K4, F2, M2, E5, C3 ● **Temperaments:** D, J, T ● **Physical:** Stg=L; Freq: R, H, I, N, D, A, X Occas: S, K, O ● **Work Env:** Noise=N; Freq: W Occas: A ● **Salary:** 5 ● **Outlook:** 3

RANGE MANAGER (profess. & kin.) ● DOT #040.061-046 ● OES: 24302 ● Alternate titles: RANGE-MANAGEMENT SPECIALIST. Conducts research in range problems to provide sustained production of forage, livestock, and wildlife: Studies range lands to determine best grazing seasons and number and kind of livestock that can be most profitably grazed. Plans and directs construction and maintenance of range improvements, such as fencing, corrals, reservoirs for stock watering, and structures for soil-erosion control. Develops improved practices for range reseeding. Studies forage plants and their growth requirements to determine varieties best suited to particular range. Develops methods for controlling poisonous plants, and for protecting range from fire and rodent damage. May specialize in particular area and be designated Range Conservationist (profess. & kin.). ● **GED:** R6, M6, L6 ● **SVP:** 4-10 yrs ● **Academic:** Ed=B, Eng=S ● **Work Field:** 251 ● **MPSMS:** 310, 731 ● **Aptitudes:** G1, V1, N2, S2, P2, Q3, K3, F3, M3, E4, C4 ● **Temperaments:** J, T, V ● **Physical:** Stg=L; Freq: F, A, V Occas: R, H, I, E, T, G, N, D, X ● **Work Env:** Noise=N; Occas: W ● **Salary:** 3 ● **Outlook:** 3

SILVICULTURIST (profess. & kin.) ● DOT #040.061-050 ● OES: 24302 ● Establishes and cares for forest stands: Manages tree nurseries and thins forests to encourage natural growth of sprouts or seedlings of desired varieties. Conducts research in such problems of forest propagation and culture as tree growth rate, effects of thinning on forest yield, duration of seed viability, and effects of fire and animal grazing on growth, seed production, and germination of different species. Develops techniques for measuring and identifying trees. ● **GED:** R5, M5, L5 ● **SVP:** 2-4 yrs ● **Academic:** Ed=A, Eng=S ● **Work Field:** 251 ● **MPSMS:** 731, 310 ● **Aptitudes:** G1, V1, N2, S3, P3, Q4, K3, F2, M2, E5, C4 ● **Temperaments:** D, J, T ● **Physical:** Stg=L; Freq: S, K, O, R, H, I, T, G, N, D, X ● **Work Env:** Noise=N; Freq: W ● **Salary:** 3 ● **Outlook:** 3

SOIL CONSERVATIONIST (profess. & kin.) ● DOT #040.061-054 ● OES: 24302 ● Plans and develops coordinated practices for soil erosion control, moisture conservation, and sound land use: Conducts surveys and investigations on rural or urban planning, agriculture, construction, forestry, or mining on measures needed to maintain or restore proper soil management. Plans soil management practices, such as crop rotation, reforestation, permanent vegetation, contour plowing, or terracing as related to soil and water conservation. Prepares soil conservation plans in cooperation with state, county, or local government, farmers, foresters, miners, or urban planners to provide for use and treatment of land according to needs and capability. Applies principles of two or more specialized fields of science, such as agronomy, soil science, forestry, or agriculture to achieve objectives of conservation. May develop or participate in environmental studies. ● **GED:** R6, M6, L6 ● **SVP:** 4-10 yrs ● **Academic:** Ed=B, Eng=S ● **Work Field:** 251 ● **MPSMS:** 731 ● **Aptitudes:** G1, V1, N2, S2, P2, Q4, K3, F3,

M3, E5, C4 ● **Temperaments:** D, J, P ● **Physical:** Stg=L; Freq: R, H, I, N Occas: S, K, O, T, G, F, D, A, X, V ● **Work Env:** Noise=N; Freq: W ● **Salary:** 4 ● **Outlook:** 3

SOIL-CONSERVATION TECHNICIAN (profess. & kin.) ● DOT #040.261-010 ● OES: 24302 ● Provides technical assistance to land users in planning and applying soil and water conservation practices, utilizing basic engineering and surveying tools, instruments, and techniques and knowledge of agricultural and related sciences, such as agronomy, soil conservation, and hydrology: Analyzes conservation problems of land and discusses alternative solutions to problems with land users. Advises land users in developing plans for conservation practices, such as conservation cropping systems, woodlands management, pasture planning, and engineering systems, based on cost estimates of different practices, needs of land users, maintenance requirements, and life expectancy of practices. Computes design specification for particular practices to be installed, using survey and field information technical guides, engineering field manuals, and calculator. Submits copy of engineering design specifications to land users for implementation by land user or contractor. Surveys property to mark locations and measurements, using surveying instruments. Monitors projects during and after construction to ensure projects conform to design specifications. Periodically revisits land users to view implemented land use practices and plans. ● **GED:** R5, M4, L4 ● **SVP:** 2-4 yrs ● **Academic:** Ed=A, Eng=G ● **Work Field:** 243, 244 ● **MPSMS:** 731, 716 ● **Aptitudes:** G2, V2, N2, S2, P2, Q2, K2, F3, M3, E3, C4 ● **Temperaments:** J, P, T, V ● **Physical:** Stg=L; Freq: R, H, T, G, N, F Occas: S, K, O, I, D, A, X ● **Work Env:** Noise=L; Occas: U, T ● **Salary:** 4 ● **Outlook:** 3

SOIL SCIENTIST (profess. & kin.) ● DOT #040.061-058 ● OES: 24305 ● Studies soil characteristics and maps soil types, and investigates responses of soils to known management practices to determine use capabilities of soils and effects of alternative practices on soil productivity: Classifies soils according to standard types. Conducts experiments on farms or experimental stations to determine best soil types for different plants. Performs chemical analysis on micro-organism content of soil to determine microbial reactions and chemical and mineralogical relationship to plant growth. Investigates responses of specific soil types to tillage, fertilization, nutrient transformations, crop rotation, environmental consequences, water, gas or heat flow, industrial waste control and other soil management practices. Advises interested persons on rural or urban land use. May specialize in one or more types of activities relative to soil management and productivity and be designated Soil Fertility Expert (profess. & kin.). ● **GED:** R6, M6, L6 ● **SVP:** 4-10 yrs ● **Academic:** Ed=B, Eng=S ● **Work Field:** 251 ● **MPSMS:** 731 ● **Aptitudes:** G1, V1, N2, S3, P3, Q4, K4, F3, M3, E5, C3 ● **Temperaments:** D, J, T ● **Physical:** Stg=L; Freq: R, H, I, N Occas: S, K, O, W, E, T, G, D, A, X ● **Work Env:** Noise=N; Freq: W ● **Salary:** 4 ● **Outlook:** 3

WOOD TECHNOLOGIST (profess. & kin.) ● DOT #040.061-062 ● OES: 24302 ● Conducts research to determine composition, properties, behavior, utilization, development, treatments, and processing methods of wood and wood products: Analyzes physical, chemical, and biological properties of wood. Studies methods of curing wood to determine best and most economical procedure. Develops and improves methods of seasoning, preservation, and treating wood with substances to increase resistance to wear, fire, fungi, insects, and marine borers. Conducts tests to determine ability of wood adhesives to withstand water, oil penetration, temperature extremes, and stability, strength, hardness and crystallinity of wood under variety of conditions. Evaluates and improves effectiveness of industrial equipment and production processes. Investigates processes for converting wood into commodities, such as alcohol, veneer, plywood, wood plastics, and other uses. Determines best type of wood for specific application, and investigates methods of turning waste wood materials into useful products. May specialize in research, quality control, marketing and sales, materials engineering, management or administration, manufacturing, production, or process development. ● **GED:** R6, M5, L5 ● **SVP:** 4-10 yrs ● **Academic:** Ed=B, Eng=S ● **Work Field:** 251 ● **MPSMS:** 459, 739 ● **Aptitudes:** G1, V1, N2, S3, P3, Q4, K4, F3, M3, E4, C4 ● **Temperaments:** D, J, T ● **Physical:** Stg=L; Freq: R, H, N Occas: I, D, A, X ● **Work Env:** Noise=L; ● **Salary:** 3 ● **Outlook:** 2

GOE: 02.02.03
Plant & Animal Specialization

AQUATIC BIOLOGIST (profess. & kin.) ● DOT #041.061-022 ● OES: 24308 ● Alternate titles: AQUATIC ECOLOGIST. Studies plants and animals living in water, and environmental conditions affecting them: Investigates salinity, temperature, acidity, light, oxygen content, and other physical conditions of water to determine their relationship to aquatic life. Examines various types of water life, such as plankton, worms, clams, mussels, and snails. May specialize in study of salt water aquatic life and be designated Marine Biologist (profess. & kin.); or fresh water aquatic life and be designated Limnologist (profess. & kin.). May specialize in culture, breeding, and raising of aquatic life, such as shrimp, lobsters, clams, oysters, or fish, and commercial fish farm operations and be designated Aquaculturist (profess. & kin.). ● **GED:** R6, M6, L6 ● **SVP:** 4-10 yrs ● **Academic:** Ed=B, Eng=S ● **Work Field:** 251 ● **MPSMS:** 732 ● **Aptitudes:** G1, V2, N1, S1, P2, Q3, K3, F3, M3, E4, C3 ● **Temperaments:** D, J, T, V ● **Physical:** Stg=L; Freq: R, H, I, N Occas: E, D, A, X ● **Work Env:** Noise=N; Freq: W Occas: U ● **Salary:** 5 ● **Outlook:** 2

BIOCHEMIST (profess. & kin.) ● DOT #041.061-026 ● OES: 24308 ● Alternate titles: CHEMIST, BIOLOGICAL. Studies chemical processes of living organisms: Conducts research to determine action of foods, drugs, serums, hormones, and other substances on tissues and vital processes of living organisms. Isolates, analyzes, and identifies hormones, vitamins, allergens, minerals, and enzymes and determines effects on body functions. Examines chemical aspects of formation of antibodies, and conducts research into chemistry of cells and blood corpuscles. Studies chemistry of living processes, such as mechanisims of development of normal and abnormal cells, breathing and digestion, and of living energy changes, such as growth, aging, and death. May specialize in particular area or field of work and be designated Chemist, Clinical (profess. & kin.); Chemist, Enzymes (profess. & kin.); Chemist, Proteins (profess. & kin.); Chemist, Steroids (profess. & kin.). May clean, purify, refine, and otherwise prepare pharmaceutical compounds for commercial distribution and develop new drugs and medications and be designated Chemist, Pharmaceutical (profess. & kin.). ● **GED:** R6, M6, L6 ● **SVP:** 4-10 yrs ● **Academic:** Ed=B, Eng=S ● **Work Field:** 251 ● **MPSMS:** 732 ● **Aptitudes:** G1, V2, N1, S2, P2, Q2, K3, F3, M3, E5, C3 ● **Temperaments:** J, T ● **Physical:** Stg=L; Freq: R, H, I, N, D, A, X ● **Work Env:** Noise=N; ● **Salary:** 5 ● **Outlook:** 4

BIOLOGIST (profess. & kin.) ● DOT #041.061-030 ● OES: 24308 ● Studies basic principles of plant and animal life, such as origin, relationship, development, anatomy, and functions: May collect and analyze biological data to determine environmental effects of present and potential use of land and water areas, record data, and inform public, state, and federal representatives regarding test results. May prepare environmental impact reports. May specialize in research centering around particular plant, animal, or aspect of biology. May teach. May specialize in wildlife research and management and be designated Wildlife Biologist (profess. & kin.). ● **GED:** R6, M6, L6 ● **SVP:** 4-10 yrs ● **Academic:** Ed=B, Eng=S ● **Work Field:** 251 ● **MPSMS:** 732 ● **Aptitudes:** G1, V1, N1, S1, P2, Q3, K3, F3, M3, E4, C3 ● **Temperaments:** J, T ● **Physical:** Stg=L; Freq: R, H, I, N, D, A, X Occas: S, K, O, E, T, G ● **Work Env:** Noise=N; Occas: W ● **Salary:** 4 ● **Outlook:** 3

BIOPHYSICIST (profess. & kin.) ● DOT #041.061-034 ● OES: 24308 ● Studies physical principles of living cells and organisms, their electrical and mechanical energy, and related phenomena: Conducts research to investigate dynamics in such areas as seeing and hearing; the transmission of electrical impulses along nerves and muscles, and damage to cells and tissues caused by x rays and nuclear particles; manner in which characteristics of plants and animals are carried forward through successive generations; and absorption of light by chlorophyll in photosynthesis or by pigments of eye involved in vision. Analyzes functions of electronic and human brains, such as transfer of information into brain from outside (learning), transfer and manipulation of information within brain (thinking), and storage of information (memory). Studies spatial configuration of submicroscopic molecules, such as proteins, using x ray and electron microscope. May specialize in one activity, such as use of radiation and nuclear particles for treating cancer or use of atomic isotopes to discover transformation of substances in cells. ● **GED:** R6, M6, L6 ● **SVP:** 4-10 yrs ● **Academic:** Ed=B, Eng=S ● **Work Field:** 251 ● **MPSMS:** 732 ● **Aptitudes:** G1, V1, N1, S1, P1, Q3, K3, F3, M3, E5, C2 ● **Temperaments:** J ● **Physical:** Stg=L; Freq: R, H, N Occas: I, D, A, X ● **Work Env:** Noise=N; ● **Salary:** 5 ● **Outlook:** 4

MICROBIOLOGIST (profess. & kin.) ● DOT #041.061-058 ● OES: 24308 ● Alternate titles: BACTERIOLOGIST. Studies growth, structure, development, and general characteristics of bacteria and other micro-organisms: Isolates and makes cultures of significant bacteria or other micro-organisms in prescribed or standard inhibitory media, controlling factors, such as moisture, aeration, temperature, and nutrition. Identifies micro-organisms by microscopic examination of physiological, morphological, and cultural characteristics. Observes action of micro-organisms upon living tissues of plants, higher animals, and other micro-organisms and on dead organic matter. Makes chemical analyses of substances, such as acids, alcohols, and enzymes, produced by bacteria and other micro-organisms on organic matter. May specialize in study of viruses and rickettsiae and be designated Virologist (profess. & kin.). May specialize in particular material or product field and be designated Bacteriologist, Dairy (profess. & kin.); Bacteriologist, Fishery (profess. & kin.); Bacteriologist, Food (profess. & kin.); Bacteriologist, Industrial (profess. & kin.); Bacteriologist, Medical (profess. & kin.); Bacteriologist, Pharmaceutical (profess. & kin.); or Bacteriologist, Soil (profess. & kin.). ● **GED:** R6, M6, L6 ● **SVP:** 4-10 yrs ● **Academic:** Ed=B, Eng=S ● **Work Field:** 251 ● **MPSMS:** 732 ● **Aptitudes:** G1, V1, N2, S2, P2, Q3, K4, F3, M3, E5, C4 ● **Temperaments:** D, J, T ● **Physical:** Stg=L; Freq: R, H, N, D, A, X Occas: I ● **Work Env:** Noise=N; ● **Salary:** 5 ● **Outlook:** 4

PHYSIOLOGIST (profess. & kin.) ● DOT #041.061-078 ● OES: 24308 ● Conducts research on cellular structure and organ-system functions of plants and animals: Studies growth, respiration, circulation, excretion, movement, reproduction, and other functions of plants and animals under normal and abnormal conditions. Performs experiments to determine effects of internal and external environmental factors on life processes and functions, using microscope, x-ray equipment, spectroscope, and other equipment. Studies glands and their relationship to bodily functions. May specialize in physiology of particular body area, function, or system. May specialize in physiology of animals and be designated Animal Physiologist (profess. & kin.); of plants and be designated Plant Physiologist (profess. & kin.); of human organisms and be designated Medical Physiologist (medical ser.). ● **GED:** R6, M6, L6 ● **SVP:** 4-10 yrs ● **Academic:** Ed=B, Eng=S ● **Work Field:** 251 ● **MPSMS:** 732 ● **Aptitudes:** G1, V2, N1, S1, P1, Q3, K2, F2, M2, E5, C3 ● **Temperaments:** D, J, T ● **Physical:** Stg=L; Freq: R, H, I, N, D, A, X Occas: E ● **Work Env:** Noise=N; ● **Salary:** 4 ● **Outlook:** 2

GOE: 02.02.04
Food Research

CHEMIST, FOOD (profess. & kin.) ● DOT #022.061-014 ● OES: 24105 ● Conducts research and analysis concerning chemistry of foods to develop and improve foods and beverages: Experiments with natural and synthetic materials or byproducts to develop new foods, additives, preservatives, anti-adulteration agents, and related products. Studies effects of various methods of processing, preservation, and packaging on composition and properties of foods, such as color, texture, aroma, taste, shelf life, and nutritive content. Tests food and beverage samples, such as starch, sugar, cereals, beer, canned and dehydrated food products, meats, vegetables, dairy foods, and other products to ensure compliance with food laws, and standards of quality and purity. May perform, or supervise workers performing, quality control tests in food processing, canning, freezing, brewing or distilling. May specialize in particular food or process. ● **GED:** R6, M5, L5 ● **SVP:** 2-4 yrs ● **Academic:** Ed=M, Eng=S ● **Work Field:** 251, 211 ● **MPSMS:** 732 ● **Aptitudes:** G1, V2, N1, S3, P2, Q3, K3, F3, M3, E5, C3 ● **Temperaments:** D, J ● **Physical:** Stg=L; Freq: R, H, I, N, A, X Occas: E, T, G, M ● **Work Env:** Noise=N; ● **Salary:** 4 ● **Outlook:** 3

DAIRY TECHNOLOGIST (profess. & kin.) ● DOT #040.061-022 ● OES: 24501 ● Alternate titles: DAIRY-MANUFACTURING TECHNOLOGIST; DAIRY-PRODUCTS TECHNOLOGIST. Applies principles of bacteriology, chemistry, physics, engineering, and economics to develop new and improved methods in production, preservation, and utilization of milk, cheese, ice cream, and other dairy products: Conducts experiments in such problems as preventing bacterial increase in milk during handling and processing, improving pasteurization methods, and designing better packaging materials, dairy equipment, or supplies. May specialize according to product, as ice cream or cheese, or according to functional activity, as sanitation research or storage problems. ● **GED:** R6, M6, L6 ● **SVP:** 4-10 yrs ● **Academic:** Ed=B, Eng=S ● **Work Field:** 251 ● **MPSMS:** 383 ● **Aptitudes:** G1, V1, N2, S3, P3, Q3, K4, F2, M2, E4, C3 ● **Temperaments:** D, J ● **Physical:** Stg=L; Freq: R, H, N, A Occas: I, E, D, X ● **Work Env:** Noise=N; ● **Salary:** 4 ● **Outlook:** 2

FOOD TECHNOLOGIST (profess. & kin.) ● DOT #041.081-010 ● OES: 24305 ● Alternate titles: FOOD SCIENTIST. Applies scientific and engineering principles in research, development, production technology, quality control, packaging, processing, and utilization of foods: Conducts basic research, and new product research and development of foods. Develops new and improved methods and systems for food processing, production, quality control, packaging, and distribution. Studies methods to improve quality of foods, such as flavor, color, texture, nutritional value, convenience, or physical, chemical, and microbiological composition of foods. Develops food standards, safety and sanitary regulations, and waste management and water supply specifications. Tests new products in test kitchen and develops specific processing methods in laboratory pilot plant, and confers with process engineers, flavor experts, and packaging and marketing specialists to resolve problems. May specialize in one phase of food technology, such as product development, quality control, or production inspection, technical writing, teaching, or consulting. May specialize in particular branch of food technology, such as cereal grains, meat and poultry, fats and oils, seafood, animal foods, beverages, dairy products, flavors, sugars and starches, stabilizers, preservatives, colors, and nutritional additives, and be identified according to branch of food technology. ● **GED:** R6, M5, L4 ● **SVP:** 2-4 yrs ● **Academic:** Ed=B, Eng=S ● **Work Field:** 251, 212 ● **MPSMS:** 380, 390 ● **Aptitudes:** G1, V2, N2, S2, P2, Q2, K3, F2, M3, E5, C3 ● **Temperaments:** J, T ● **Physical:** Stg=L; Freq: R, H, I, N, X Occas: A ● **Work Env:** Noise=N; ● **Salary:** 3 ● **Outlook:** 3

Scientific   02

Medical Sciences   02.03

Workers in this group are involved in the prevention, diagnosis, and treatment of human and animal diseases, disorders, or injuries. It is common to specialize in specific kinds of illnesses, or special areas or organs of the body. Workers who prefer to be more general may become general practitioners, family practitioners, or may learn to deal with groups of related medical problems. A wide variety of work environments is available to medical workers ranging from large city hospitals and clinics, to home offices in rural areas, to field clinics in the military or in underdeveloped countries.

✓ What kind of work would you do?

Your work activities would depend upon your specific job. For example, you might:

- perform surgery to correct deformities, repair injuries, or remove diseased organs.
- diagnose and treat diseases of the ear, nose, and throat.
- examine patients to determine causes of speech defects.
- remove teeth and perform other mouth surgery.
- diagnose and treat mental illnesses.
- oversee all medical activities of a hospital.
- examine and treat patients for all physical problems, referring them to specialists when necessary.

✓ What skills and abilities do you need for this kind of work?

To do this kind of work, you must be able to:

- use logic and scientific thinking to diagnose and treat human or animal injuries and illnesses.
- deal with people or animals when they are in pain or under stress.
- stay calm and keep your head in emergencies.
- use eyes, hands, and fingers with great skill and accuracy.
- deal both with things that are known and obvious and with things which frequently are not easy to recognize or understand.
- make important decisions using your own judgment.
- make decisions based on information you can measure or verify.

✓ How do you know if you would like or could learn to do this kind of work?

The following questions may give you clues about yourself as you consider this group of jobs.

- Have you taken courses in biology, physiology, or anatomy? Can you understand scientific concepts?

- Have you had any training in first-aid techniques? Have you treated an accident victim? Can you work well with people in emotionally upsetting situations?
- Have you dissected an animal? Can you skillfully handle small instruments such as scalpels, syringes, or tweezers?
- Have you watched medical shows on television? Do you enjoy these programs? Can you understand the technical terms used?
- Have you been a medical corpsman in the armed services? Did you learn techniques and terminology that would be helpful in medical school?

✓ How can you prepare for and enter this kind of work?

Occupations in this group usually require education and/or training extending from four years to over ten years, depending upon the specific kind of work. Academic courses helpful in preparing for the medical sciences are: algebra, geometry, advanced math, chemistry, biological sciences, English, and Latin. Two to four years of undergraduate study followed by four years of advanced study is considered the minimum preparation. Most doctors serve a one- or two-year internship in an approved hospital after graduation from medical school.

Some physicians spend several additional years in study and training as a resident or intern to specialize. Dentists who specialize, teach, or perform research must have post-graduate courses or complete a residency in a hospital or clinic. Medical doctors, dentists, and veterinarians must have a license to practice.

✓ What else should you consider about these jobs?

The training time and cost involved are significant. Workers must adjust to irregular hours, weekend and holiday work, and 24-hour on-call duties.

Workers should update their knowledge and professional skills through periodic courses and continuous study.

If you think you would like to do this kind of work, look at the job titles listed below.

■ ■ ■

GOE: 02.03.01
Medicine & Surgery

ANESTHESIOLOGIST (medical ser.) ● DOT #070.101-010 ● OES: 32102 ● Administers anesthetics to render patients insensible to pain during surgical, obstetrical, and other medical procedures: Examines patient to determine degree of surgical risk, and type of anesthetic and sedation to administer, and discusses findings with medical practitioner concerned with case. Positions patient on operating table and administers local, intravenous, spinal, caudal, or other anesthetic according to prescribed medical standards. Institutes remedial measures to counteract adverse reactions or complications. Records type and amount of anesthetic and sedation administered and condition of patient before, during, and after anesthesia. May instruct medical students and other personnel in characteristics and methods of administering various types of anesthetics, signs and symptoms of reactions and complications, and emergency measures to employ. ● **GED:** R6, M5, L6 ● **SVP:** 4-10 yrs ● **Academic:** Ed=M, Eng=G ● **Work Field:** 294 ● **MPSMS:** 921 ● **Aptitudes:** G1, V2, N2, S2, P1, Q2, K2, F2, M2, E5, C3 ● **Temperaments:** J, P, S ● **Physical:** Stg=L; Freq: R, H, I, T, G, N, A, X Occas: D ● **Work Env:** Noise=Q; ● **Salary:** 5 ● **Outlook:** 4

CARDIOLOGIST(medical ser.) ● DOT #070.101-014 ● OES: 32102 ● Alternate titles: HEART SPECIALIST. Diagnoses and treats diseases of heart and its functions: Examines patient for symptoms indicative of heart disorders, using medical instruments and equipment. Studies diagnostic images and electrocardiograph recordings to aid in making diagnoses. Prescribes medications, and recommends dietary and activity program, as indicated. Refers patient to SURGEON (medical ser.) 070.101-094 specializing in cardiac cases when need for corrective surgery is indicated. May engage in research to study anatomy of and diseases peculiar to heart. ● **GED:** R6, M5, L6 ● **SVP:** Over 10 yrs ● **Academic:** Ed=M, Eng=G ● **Work Field:** 294 ● **MPSMS:** 921 ● **Aptitudes:** G1, V1, N2, S1, P1, Q2, K2, F1, M2, E4, C3 ● **Temperaments:** J, P, S ● **Physical:** Stg=L; Const: N Freq: H, I, E, T, G, A Occas: R, X ● **Work Env:** Noise=Q; ● **Salary:** 5 ● **Outlook:** 4

DERMATOLOGIST (medical ser.) ● DOT #070.101-018 ● OES: 32102 ● Alternate titles: SKIN SPECIALIST. Diagnoses and treats diseases of human skin: Examines skin to determine nature of disease, taking blood samples and smears from affected areas, and performing other laboratory procedures. Examines specimens under microscope, and makes various chemical and biological analyses and performs other tests to identify disease-causing organisms or pathological conditions. Prescribes and administers medications, and applies superficial radiotherapy and other localized treatments. Treats abscesses, skin injuries, and other skin infections, and surgically excises cutaneous malignancies, cysts, birthmarks, and other growths. Treats scars, using dermabrasion. ● **GED:** R6, M5, L6 ● **SVP:** 4-10 yrs ● **Academic:** Ed=M, Eng=G ● **Work Field:** 294 ● **MPSMS:** 921 ● **Aptitudes:** G1, V1, N2, S2, P1, Q2, K3, F1, M2, E4, C3 ● **Temperaments:** J, P, S ● **Physical:** Stg=L; Const: I, N Freq: H, E, T, G, A, X Occas: R ● **Work Env:** Noise=Q; ● **Salary:** 5 ● **Outlook:** 3

GENERAL PRACTITIONER (medical ser.) ● DOT #070.101-022 ● OES: 32102 ● Alternate titles: PHYSICIAN, GENERAL PRACTICE. Diagnoses and treats variety of diseases and injuries in general practice: Examines patients, using medical instruments and equipment. Orders or executes various tests, analyses, and diagnostic images to provide information on patient's condition. Analyzes reports and findings of tests and of examination, and diagnoses condition. Administers or prescribes treatments and drugs. Inoculates and vaccinates patients to immunize patients from communicable diseases. Advises patients concerning diet, hygiene, and methods for prevention of disease. Provides prenatal care to pregnant women, delivers babies, and provides postnatal care to mother and infant [OBSTETRICIAN (medical ser.) 070.101-054]. Reports births, deaths, and outbreak of contagious diseases to governmental authorities. Refers patients to medical specialist or other practitioner for specialized treatment. Performs minor surgery. May make house and emergency calls to attend to patients unable to visit office or clinic. May conduct physical examinations to provide information needed for admission to school, consideration for jobs, or eligibility for insurance coverage. May provide care for passengers and crew aboard ship and be designated Ship's Doctor (medical ser.). ● **GED:** R6, M5, L6 ● **SVP:** 4-10 yrs ● **Academic:** Ed=M, Eng=G ● **Work Field:** 294 ● **MPSMS:** 921 ● **Aptitudes:** G1, V1, N2, S1, P2, Q2, K2, F1, M2, E4, C3 ● **Temperaments:** D, J, P, S ● **Physical:** Stg=L; Freq: R, H, I, T, G, N, A Occas: E, M, X ● **Work Env:** Noise=Q; ● **Salary:** 5 ● **Outlook:** 3

INTERNIST (medical ser.) ● DOT #070.101-042 ● OES: 32102 ● Alternate titles: INTERNAL MEDICINE SPECIALIST. Diagnoses and treats diseases and injuries of human internal organ systems: Examines patient for symptoms of organic or congenital disorders and determines nature and extent of injury or disorder, referring to diagnostic images and tests, and using medical instruments and equipment. Prescribes medication and recommends dietary and activity program, as indicated by diagnosis. Refers patient to medical specialist when indicated. ● **GED:** R6, M5, L6 ● **SVP:** 4-10 yrs ● **Academic:** Ed=M, Eng=G ● **Work Field:** 294 ● **MPSMS:** 921 ● **Aptitudes:** G1, V1, N2, S1, P1, Q2, K2, F1, M1, E4, C3 ● **Temperaments:** D, J, P, S ● **Physical:** Stg=L; Const: N Freq: H, I, E, T, G, A Occas: R, X ● **Work Env:** Noise=Q; ● **Salary:** 5 ● **Outlook:** 4

OBSTETRICIAN (medical ser.) ● DOT #070.101-054 ● OES: 32102 ● Treats women during prenatal, natal, and postnatal periods: Examines patient to ascertain condition, utilizing physical findings, laboratory results, and patient's statements as diagnostic aids. Determines need for modified diet and physical activities, and recommends plan. Periodically examines patient, prescribing medication or surgery, if indicated. Delivers infant, and cares for mother for prescribed period of time following childbirth. Performs cesarean section or other surgical procedure as needed to preserve patient's health and deliver infant safely. May treat patients for diseases of generative organs [GYNECOLOGIST (medical ser.) 070.101-034]. ● **GED:** R6, M5, L6 ● **SVP:** 4-10 yrs ● **Academic:** Ed=M, Eng=G ● **Work Field:** 294 ● **MPSMS:** 921 ● **Aptitudes:** G1, V1, N2, S1, P1, Q2, K3, F1, M1, E4, C3 ● **Temperaments:** D, J, P, S ● **Physical:** Stg=L; Const: N Freq: H, I, E, T, G, A Occas: R, X ● **Work Env:** Noise=Q; ● **Salary:** 5 ● **Outlook:** 4

OPHTHALMOLOGIST (medical ser.) ● DOT #070.101-058 ● OES: 32102 ● Alternate titles: EYE SPECIALIST; OCULIST. Diagnoses and treats diseases and injuries of eyes: Examines patient for symptoms indicative of organic or congenital ocular disorders, and determines nature and extent of injury or disorder. Performs various tests to determine vision loss. Prescribes and administers medications, and performs surgery, if indicated. Directs remedial activities to aid in regaining vision, or to utilize sight remaining, by writing prescriptions for corrective glasses, and instructing patient in eye exercises. ● **GED:** R6, M5, L6 ● **SVP:** 4-10 yrs ● **Academic:** Ed=M, Eng=G ● **Work Field:** 294 ● **MPSMS:** 921 ● **Aptitudes:** G1, V1, N2, S1, P1, Q2, K2, F1, M2, E4, C2 ● **Temperaments:** D, J, P, S ● **Physical:** Stg=L; Const: N Freq: H, I, T, G, A, X Occas: R, E ● **Work Env:** Noise=Q; ● **Salary:** 5 ● **Outlook:** 3

PEDIATRICIAN (medical ser.) ● DOT #070.101-066 ● OES: 32102 ● Plans and carries out medical care program for children from birth through adolescence to aid in mental and physical growth and development: Examines patients to determine presence of disease and to establish preventive health practices. Determines nature and extent of disease or injury, prescribes and administers medications and immunizations, and performs variety of medical duties. ● **GED:** R6, M5, L6 ● **SVP:** 4-10 yrs ● **Academic:** Ed=M, Eng=G ● **Work Field:** 294 ● **MPSMS:** 921 ● **Aptitudes:** G1, V1, N2, S1, P1, Q2, K2, F1, M1, E5, C3 ● **Temperaments:** D, J, P, S ● **Physical:** Stg=L; Freq: H, I, E, T, G, N, A Occas: R, X ● **Work Env:** Noise=Q; ● **Salary:** 5 ● **Outlook:** 4

PODIATRIST (medical ser.) ● DOT #079.101-022 ● OES: 32111 ● Diagnoses and treats diseases and deformities of human foot: Diagnoses foot ailments, such as tumors, ulcers, fractures, skin or nail diseases, and congenital or acquired deformities, utilizing diagnostic aids, such as urinalysis, blood tests, and x-ray analysis. Treats deformities, such as flat or weak feet and foot imbalance, by mechanical and electrical methods, such as whirlpool or paraffin baths and short wave and low voltage currents. Treats conditions, such as corns, calluses, ingrowing nails, tumors, shortened tendons, bunions, cysts, and abscesses by surgical methods, including suturing, medications, and administration of local anesthetics. Prescribes drugs. Does not perform foot amputations. Corrects deformities by means of plaster casts and strappings. Makes and fits prosthetic appliances. Prescribes corrective footwear. Advises patients concerning continued treatment of disorders and proper foot care to prevent recurrence. Refers patients to physician when symptoms observed in feet and legs indicate systemic disorders, such as arthritis, heart disease, diabetes, or kidney trouble. May treat bone, muscle, and joint disorders and be disignated Podiatrist, Orthopedic (medical ser.); childrens' foot diseases and be designated Popopediatrician (medical ser.), or perform surgery and be designated Podiatric Surgeon (medical ser.). ● **GED:** R5, M4, L5 ● **SVP:** 2-4 yrs ● **Academic:** Ed=B, Eng=G ● **Work Field:** 294 ● **MPSMS:** 929 ● **Aptitudes:** G2, V3, N3, S3, P3, Q4, K4, F3, M3, E5, C5 ● **Temperaments:** J, P ● **Physical:** Stg=L; Freq: R, H, I, T, G, N Occas: D, A, X ● **Work Env:** Noise=N; ● **Salary:** 5 ● **Outlook:** 4

PSYCHIATRIST (medical ser.) ● DOT #070.107-014 ● OES: 32102 ● Diagnoses and treats patients with mental, emotional, and behavioral disorders: Organizes data concerning patient's family, medical history, and onset of symptoms obtained from patient, relatives, and other sources, such as NURSE, GENERAL DUTY (medical ser.) 075.364-010 and SOCIAL WORKER, PSYCHIATRIC (profess. & kin.) 195.107-034. Examines patient to determine general physical condition, following standard medical procedures. Orders laboratory and other special diagnostic tests and evaluates data obtained. Determines nature and extent of mental disorder, and formulates treatment program. Treats or directs treatment of patient, utilizing variety of psychotherapeutic methods and medications. ● **GED:** R6, M5, L6 ● **SVP:** 4-10 yrs ● **Academic:** Ed=M, Eng=G ● **Work Field:** 294 ● **MPSMS:** 921 ● **Aptitudes:** G1, V1, N2, S1, P2, Q3, K4, F4, M4, E5, C4 ● **Temperaments:** D, J, P, S ● **Physical:** Stg=L; Freq: T, G, N Occas: R, H, I, X ● **Work Env:** Noise=Q; ● **Salary:** 5 ● **Outlook:** 3

PUBLIC HEALTH PHYSICIAN (medical ser.) ● DOT #070.101-046 ● OES: 32102 ● Plans and participates in medical care or research program in hospital, clinic, or other public medical facility: Provides medical care for eligible persons, and institutes program of preventive health care in county, city, or other government or civic division. Gives vaccinations, imposes quarantines, and establishes standards for hospitals, restaurants, and other areas of possible danger. May conduct research in particular areas of medicine to aid in cure and control of disease. May be designated Medical Officer (government ser.). ● **GED:** R6, M5, L6 ● **SVP:** 4-10 yrs ● **Academic:** Ed=M, Eng=G ● **Work Field:** 294 ● **MPSMS:** 921, 953 ● **Aptitudes:** G1, V1, N2, S1, P2, Q2, K3, F2, M2, E5, C3 ● **Temperaments:** D, J, P ● **Physical:** Stg=L; Freq: R, H, I, T, G, N Occas: E, A, X ● **Work Env:** Noise=Q; ● **Salary:** 5 ● **Outlook:** 3

RADIOLOGIST (medical ser.) ● DOT #070.101-090 ● OES: 32102 ● Diagnoses and treats diseases of human body, using x-ray and radioactive substances: Examines internal structures and functions of organ systems, making diagnoses after correlation of x-ray findings with other examinations and tests. Treats benign and malignant internal and external growths by exposure to radiation from x-rays, high energy sources, and natural and manmade radioisotopes directed at or implanted in affected areas of body. Administers radiopaque substances by injection, orally, or as enemas to render internal structures and organs visible on x-ray films or fluoroscopic screens. May specialize in diagnostic radiology or radiation oncology. May diagnose and treat diseases of human body, using radioactive substances, and be certified in Nuclear Radiology or Nuclear Medicine. ● **GED:** R6, M5, L6 ● **SVP:** 4-10 yrs ● **Academic:** Ed=M, Eng=G ● **Work Field:** 294 ● **MPSMS:** 921 ● **Aptitudes:** G1, V1, N2, S1, P1, Q2, K2, F1, M1, E4, C3 ● **Temperaments:** D, J, P, S ● **Physical:** Stg=L; Const: N Freq: H, I, T, G Occas: R, E, A, X ● **Work Env:** Noise=Q; Occas: R ● **Salary:** 5 ● **Outlook:** 4

SURGEON (medical ser.) ● DOT #070.101-094 ● OES: 32102 ● Performs surgery to correct deformities, repair injuries, prevent diseases, and improve function in patients: Examines patient to verify necessity of operation, estimate possible risk to patient, and determine best operational procedure. Reviews reports of patient's general physical condition, reactions to medications, and medical history. Examines instruments, equipment, and surgical setup to ensure that antiseptic and aseptic methods have been followed. Performs operations, using variety of surgical instruments and employing established surgical techniques appropriate for specific procedures. May specialize in particular type of operation, as on nervous system, and be designated Neurosurgeon (medical ser). May specialize in repair, restoration, or improvement of lost, injured, defective, or misshapen body parts and be designated Plastic Surgeon (medical ser.). May specialize in correction or prevention of skeletal abnormalities, utilizing surgical, medical, and physical methodologies, and be designated Orthopedic Surgeon (medical ser.). ● **GED:** R6, M5, L6 ● **SVP:** Over 10 yrs ● **Academic:** Ed=M, Eng=G ● **Work Field:** 294 ● **MPSMS:** 921 ● **Aptitudes:** G1, V1, N2, S1, P1, Q2, K2, F1, M1, E4, C3 ● **Temperaments:** D, J, P, S ● **Physical:** Stg=L; Const: N Freq: H, I, E, T, G, A, X Occas: R ● **Work Env:** Noise=Q; Const: O ● **Salary:** 5 ● **Outlook:** 4

GOE: 02.03.02
Dentistry

DENTIST (medical ser.) ● DOT #072.101-010 ● OES: 32105 ● Diagnoses and treats diseases, injuries, and malformations of teeth and gums, and related oral structures: Examines patient to determine nature of condition, utilizing x rays, dental instruments, and other diagnostic

procedures. Cleans, fills, extracts, and replaces teeth, using rotary and hand instruments, dental appliances, medications, and surgical implements. Provides preventive dental services to patient, such as applications of fluoride and sealants to teeth, and education in oral and dental hygiene. ● **GED:** R6, M5, L5 ● **SVP:** 4-10 yrs ● **Academic:** Ed=M, Eng=G ● **Work Field:** 294 ● **MPSMS:** 922 ● **Aptitudes:** G1, V1, N2, S1, P2, Q2, K2, F1, M2, E4, C3 ● **Temperaments:** J, P, S, T ● **Physical:** Stg=L; Freq: R, H, I, E, T, G, N, D, A Occas: X ● **Work Env:** Noise=Q; ● **Salary:** 5 ● **Outlook:** 4

GOE: 02.03.03
Veterinary Medicine

VETERINARIAN (medical ser.) ● DOT #073.101-010 ● OES: 32114 ● Diagnoses, and treats diseases and injuries of pets, such as dogs and cats, and farm animals, such as cattle or sheep: Examines animal to determine nature of disease or injury and treats animal surgically or medically. Tests dairy herds, horses, sheep, and other animals for diseases and inoculates animals against rabies, brucellosis, and other disorders. Advises animal owners about sanitary measures, feeding, and general care to promote health of animals. May engage in research, teaching, or production of commercial products. May specialize in prevention and control of communicable animal diseases and be designated Veterinarian, Public Health (medical ser.). May specialize in diagnosis and treatment of animal diseases, using roentgen rays and radioactive substances, and be designated Veterinary Radiologist (medical ser.). ● **GED:** R5, M4, L5 ● **SVP:** 4-10 yrs ● **Academic:** Ed=M, Eng=G ● **Work Field:** 294 ● **MPSMS:** 929 ● **Aptitudes:** G1, V1, N2, S1, P1, Q3, K2, F1, M2, E5, C2 ● **Temperaments:** J, P, T, V ● **Physical:** Stg=M; Freq: R, H, I, T, G, N, D, A, X Occas: S, K, O, E, M, V ● **Work Env:** Noise=N; Freq: O ● **Salary:** 5 ● **Outlook:** 4

VETERINARY TECHNICIAN (medical ser.) ● DOT #079.361-014 ● OES: 32998 ● Alternate titles: ANIMAL HEALTH TECHNICIAN; ANIMAL TECHNICIAN; VETERINARY ASSISTANT. Performs variety of animal health care duties to assist VETERINARIAN (medical ser.) 073.101-010 in settings such as veterinarians' clinics, zoos, research laboratories, kennels, and commercial facilities: Prepares treatment room for examination of animals, and holds or restrains animals during examination, treatment, or innoculation. Administers injections, performs venipunctures, applies wound dressings, cleans teeth, and takes vital signs of animal, under supervision of veterinarian. Prepares patient, medications, and equipment for surgery, and hands instruments and materials to veterinarian during surgical procedures. Peforms routine laboratory tests, cares for and feeds laboratory animals, and assists professional personnel with research projects in commercial, public health, or research laboratories. Inspects products or carcasses when employed in food processing plants to ensure compliance with health standards. May assist veterinarian to artificially inseminate animals. May bathe and groom small animals. ● **GED:** R4, M3, L4 ● **SVP:** 1-2 yrs ● **Academic:** Ed=H, Eng=S ● **Work Field:** 294 ● **MPSMS:** 929 ● **Aptitudes:** G3, V3, N3, S3, P3, Q2, K3, F3, M3, E4, C3 ● **Temperaments:** J, S, T ● **Physical:** Stg=M; Freq: R, H, I, T, G, N Occas: S, O, E, M, A, X ● **Work Env:** Noise=N; ● **Salary:** 3 ● **Outlook:** 4

GOE: 02.03.04
Health Specialties

ACUPUNCTURIST (medical ser.) ● DOT #079.271-010 ● OES: 32998 ● Administers specific theraputic treatment of symptoms and disorders amenable to acupuncture procedures, as specifically indicated by supervising physician: Reviews patient's medical history, physical findings, and diagnosis made by physician to ascertain symptoms or disorder to be treated. Selects needles of various lengths, according to location of insertion. Inserts needles at locations of body known to be efficacious to certain disorders, utilizing knowledge of acupuncture points and their functions. Leaves needles in patient for specific length of time, according to symptom or disorder treated, and removes needles. Burns bark of mugwort tree in small strainer to administer moxibustion treatment. Covers insertion area with cloth and rubs strainer over cloth to impart heat and assist in relieving patient's symptoms. ● **GED:** R5, M4, L5 ● **SVP:** 1-2 yrs ● **Academic:** Ed=B, Eng=G ● **Work Field:** 294 ● **MPSMS:** 921 ● **Aptitudes:** G2, V2, N3, S2, P2, Q3, K2, F3, M3, E5, C3 ● **Temperaments:** J ● **Physical:** Stg=L; Freq: R, H, I, T, G, N, X Occas: D, A ● **Work Env:** Noise=Q; ● **Salary:** 3 ● **Outlook:** 3

AUDIOLOGIST (medical ser.) ● DOT #076.101-010 ● OES: 32314 ● Determines type and degree of hearing impairment and implements habilitation and rehabilitation services for patient: Administers and interprets variety of tests, such as air and bone conduction, and speech reception and discrimination tests, to determine type and degree of hearing impairment, site of damage, and effects on comprehension and speech. Evaluates test results in relation to behavioral, social, educational, and medical information obtained from patients, families, teachers, SPEECH PATHOLOGISTS (profess. & kin.) 076.107-010 and other professionals to determine communication problems related to hearing disability. Plans and implements prevention, habilitation, or rehabilitation services, including hearing aid selection and orientation, counseling, auditory training, lip reading, language habilitation, speech conservation, and other treatment programs developed in consultation with SPEECH PATHOLOGIST (profess. & kin.) and other professionals. May refer patient to physician or surgeon if medical treatment is determined necessary. May conduct research in physiology, pathology, biophysics, or psychophysics of auditory systems, or design and develop clinical and research procedures and apparatus. May act as consultant to educational, medical, legal, and other professional groups. May teach art and science of audiology and direct scientific projects. ● **GED:** R5, M4, L5 ● **SVP:** 2-4 yrs ● **Academic:** Ed=M, Eng=G ● **Work Field:** 294 ● **MPSMS:** 929 ● **Aptitudes:** G2, V2, N2, S2, P2, Q3, K3, F3, M3, E5, C4 ● **Temperaments:** D, J, P ● **Physical:** Stg=L; Freq: H, I, T, G, N Occas: R, A, X, V ● **Work Env:** Noise=Q; ● **Salary:** 4 ● **Outlook:** 4

CHIROPRACTOR (medical ser.) ● DOT #079.101-010 ● OES: 32113 ● Alternate titles: CHIROPRACTIC; DOCTOR, CHIROPRACTIC. Diagnoses and treats musculoskeletal conditions of spinal column and extremities to prevent disease and correct abnormalities of body believed to be caused by interference with nervous system: Examines patient to determine nature and extent of disorder. Performs diagnostic procedures including physical, neurologic, and orthopedic examinations, laboratory tests, and other procedures, using x-ray machine, proctoscope, electrocardiograph, otoscope, and other instruments and equipment. Manipulates spinal column and other extremities to adjust, align, or correct abnormalities caused by neurologic and kinetic articular dysfunction. Utilizes supplementary measures, such as exercise, rest, water, light, heat, and nutritional therapy. ● **GED:** R5, M4, L5 ● **SVP:** 4-10 yrs ● **Academic:** Ed=B, Eng=G ● **Work Field:** 294 ● **MPSMS:** 923 ● **Aptitudes:** G2, V2, N3, S2, P2, Q4, K2, F2, M2, E4, C4 ● **Temperaments:** J, P ● **Physical:** Stg=M; Freq: S, R, H, I, E, T, G, N Occas: D, X ● **Work Env:** Noise=Q; Occas: R ● **Salary:** 5 ● **Outlook:** 3

OPTOMETRIST (medical ser.) ● DOT #079.101-018 ● OES: 32108 ● Examines eyes to determine nature and degree of vision problem or eye disease and prescribes corrective lenses or procedures: Examines eyes and performs various tests to determine visual acuity and perception and to diagnose diseases and other abnormalities, such as glaucoma and color blindness. Prescribes eyeglasses, contact lenses, and other vision aids or therapeutic procedures to correct or conserve vision. Consults with and refers patients to OPHTHALMOLOGIST (medical ser.) 070.101-058 or other health care practitioner if additional medical treatment is determined necessary. May prescribe medications to treat eye diseases if state laws permit. May specialize in type of services provided, such as contact lenses, low vision aids or vision therapy, or in treatment of specific groups, such as children or elderly

patients. May conduct research, instruct in college or university, act as consultant, or work in public health field. ● **GED:** R5, M4, L5 ● **SVP:** 2-4 yrs ● **Academic:** Ed=B, Eng=G ● **Work Field:** 294 ● **MPSMS:** 923 ● **Aptitudes:** G2, V2, N2, S1, P2, Q2, K3, F3, M3, E5, C3 ● **Temperaments:** J, P, T ● **Physical:** Stg=L; Const: R, H Freq: I, T, G, N, D, A Occas: S, X ● **Work Env:** Noise=Q; ● **Salary:** 5 ● **Outlook:** 4

SPEECH PATHOLOGIST (profess. & kin.) ● DOT #076.107-010 ● OES: 32314 ● Alternate titles: SPEECH CLINICIAN; SPEECH THERAPIST. Specializes in diagnosis and treatment of speech and language problems, and engages in scientific study of human communication: Diagnoses and evaluates speech and language skills as related to educational, medical, social, and psychological factors. Plans, directs, or conducts habilitative and rehabilitative treatment programs to restore communicative efficiency of individuals with communication problems of organic and nonorganic etiology. Provides counseling and guidance and language development therapy to handicapped individuals. Reviews individual file to obtain background information prior to evaluation to determine appropriate tests and to ensure that adequate information is available. Administers, scores, and interprets specialized hearing and speech tests. Develops and implements individualized plans for assigned clients to meet individual needs, interests, and abilities. Evaluates and monitors individuals, using audio-visual equipment, such as tape recorders, overhead projectors, filmstrips, and demonstrative materials. Reviews treatment plan, and assesses individual performance to modify, change, or write new programs. Maintains records as required by law, establishment's policy, and administrative regulations. Attends meetings and conferences and participates in other activities to promote professional growth. Instructs individuals to monitor their own speech and provides ways to practice new skills. May act as consultant to educational, medical, and other professional groups. May conduct research to develop diagnostic and remedial techniques. May serve as consultant to classroom teachers to incorporate speech and language development activities into daily schedule. May teach manual sign language to student incapable of speaking. May instruct staff in use of special equipment designed to serve handicapped. See AUDIOLOGIST (medical ser.) 076.101-010 for one who specializes in diagnosis of, and provision of rehabilitative services for, auditory problems. ● **GED:** R5, M5, L5 ● **SVP:** 2-4 yrs ● **Academic:** Ed=M, Eng=G ● **Work Field:** 294, 296 ● **MPSMS:** 924, 931 ● **Aptitudes:** G2, V2, N3, S3, P2, Q3, K3, F3, M3, E5, C5 ● **Temperaments:** D, J, P ● **Physical:** Stg=L; Freq: R, H, I, E, T, G, N ● **Work Env:** Noise=N; ● **Salary:** 4 ● **Outlook:** 4

VOICE PATHOLOGIST (profess. & kin.) ● DOT #076.104-010 ● OES: 32314 ● Diagnoses and treats voice disorders, such as those associated with professional use of voice: Develops and implements perceptual evaluation procedures and psychophysical methods for voice assessment. Collects diagnostic data on individuals, such as output pressures, airflow, chestwall movements, and articular and laryngeal displacement, using scopes and other measuring instruments. Analyzes and interprets diagnostic data and consults with OTOLARYNGOLOGIST (medical ser.) 070.101-062 and other professionals to determine method of treatment, such as surgery, vocal modification, or voice therapy. Plans and conducts voice therapy sessions, applying auditory, visual, kinematic, and biofeedback techniques. Plans and conducts voice hygiene workshops. Calibrates equipment. May teach voice science to associates and direct research in area of voice. May establish procedures and direct operation of laboratory specializing in diagnosing and treating voice disorders and be designated Director, Bio-Communications Laboratory (medical ser.). ● **GED:** R5, M5, L5 ● **SVP:** 4-10 yrs ● **Academic:** Ed=B, Eng=G ● **Work Field:** 294 ● **MPSMS:** 920 ● **Aptitudes:** G1, V1, N2, S1, P2, Q2, K3, F3, M3, E5, C5 ● **Temperaments:** D, J, P ● **Physical:** Stg=L; Freq: R, H, I, T, G, N ● **Work Env:** Noise=N; ● **Salary:** 4 ● **Outlook:** 4

Laboratory Technology

Workers in this group use special laboratory techniques and equipment to perform tests in the fields of chemistry, biology, or physics. They record information that results from their experiments and tests. They help scientists, medical doctors, researchers, and engineers in their work. Hospitals, government agencies, universities, and private industries employ these workers in their laboratories and research facilities.

✓ **What kind of work would you do?**

Your work activities would depend upon your specific job. For example, you might:

- set up and operate laboratory equipment to conduct chemical and physical tests on metal ores.
- prepare slides and use microscopes to identify diseases in an organ removed by surgery.
- measure rainfall and riverflow, record findings, and prepare a summary report of conditions.
- set up equipment to testfire a gun to gather evidence for a criminal investigation.
- prepare compounds and package prescription drugs.
- conduct tests on samples from oil drilling operations.

✓ **What skills and abilities do you need for this kind of work?**

To do this kind of work, you must be able to:

- understand and use scientific and technical language and symbols.
- recognize slight differences in the shape, color, or texture of things.
- follow technical instructions which may be verbal, in writing, or in the form of charts or drawings.
- do work that requires being very precise or accurate.
- use eyes, hands, and fingers to operate delicate and sensitive equipment.
- use measurable and verifiable information for making decisions or judgments.

✓ **How do you know if you would like or could learn to do this kind of work?**

The following questions may give you clues about yourself as you consider this group of jobs.

- Have you used test tubes, microscopes, or other laboratory instruments? Do you enjoy working with scientific equipment?
- Have you read scientific or technical manuals or journals? Can you understand the language and symbols used?
- Have you collected rocks? Can you recognize different minerals that are present?
- Have you had algebra or geometry courses? Can you read and understand charts and graphs?
- Have you repaired or assembled a precision device such as a radio or clock? Did it work properly afterwards?
- Have you had military experience collecting water samples or conducting blood tests? Do you enjoy this type of work?

✓ **How can you prepare for and enter this kind of work?**

Occupations in this group usually require education and/or training extending from one year to over ten years, depending upon the specific kind of work. Most of these jobs are entry-level positions requiring workers to have a two-to four-year degree. Some workers may move into laboratory or testing work from production areas. On-the-job training is sometimes available to applicants who have appropriate skills or work related experience. Some jobs are offered to those who have taken scientific or technical courses in high school or a post-high school program. Courses in chemistry, physical science, or life science will be helpful.

✓ **What else should you consider about these jobs?**

Many medical and technical facilities operate on a 24-hour schedule. Some employees must work at night or at varying hours throughout the week.

If you think you would like to do this kind of work, look at the job titles listed below.

■■ ■■ ■

GOE: 02.04.01
Physical Sciences

ASSAYER (profess. & kin.) ● DOT #022.281-010 ● OES: 24501 ● Tests ores and minerals and analyzes results to determine value and properties of components, using spectrographic analysis, chemical solutions, and chemical or laboratory equipment, such as furnaces, beakers, graduates, pipettes, and crucibles: Separates metals or other components from dross materials by solution, flotation, or other liquid processes, or by dry methods, such as application of heat to form slags of lead, borax, and other impurities. Weighs residues on balance scale to determine proportion of pure gold, silver, platinum, or other metals or components. May specialize in testing and analyzing precious metals and be designated Gold-And-Silver Assayer (profess. & kin.). ● **GED:** R5, M5, L4 ● **SVP:** 2-4 yrs ● **Academic:** Ed=A, Eng=S ● **Work Field:** 211 ● **MPSMS:** 350 ● **Aptitudes:** G2, V2, N3, S2, P3, Q3, K3, F3, M3, E5, C3 ● **Temperaments:** J, T ● **Physical:** Stg=L; Freq: R, H, N, X Occas: I ● **Work Env:** Noise=N; ● **Salary:** 5 ● **Outlook:** 2

BALLISTICS EXPERT, FORENSIC (government ser.) ● DOT #199.267-010 ● OES: 24501 ● Alternate titles: FIREARMS EXPERT. Examines and tests firearms, spent bullets, and related evidence in criminal cases to develop facts useful in apprehension and prosecution of suspects: Examines bullets, bullet fragments, cartridge clips, firearms, and related evidence found at scene of crime or in possession of suspect to identify make and caliber of weapon. Test-fires weapons allegedly used to facilitate microscopic comparison of bullets from test weapon with those discovered at scene of crime. Determines, from knowledge of ballistics theory and standard test procedures, probable angle and distance from which crime weapon was fired, revealing origin of shot. Prepares reports of findings and testifies at inquests, trials, and other hearings to facilitate prosecution or exoneration of suspects on basis of determinations. May perform standardized tests on other articles of evidence, using chemical agents, physical-testing equipment, measuring instruments, and prescribed procedure, to determine relationship of evidence to suspect and to crime. May order and maintain departmental weapons and related equipment. May be designated by rank as Lieutenant, Ballistics (government ser.). ● **GED:** R5, M5, L5 ● **SVP:** 2-4 yrs ● **Academic:** Ed=A, Eng=G ● **Work Field:** 211 ● **MPSMS:** 373 ● **Aptitudes:** G2, V2, N2, S2, P2, Q3, K3, F3, M3, E5, C3 ● **Temperaments:** J ● **Physical:** Stg=L; Freq: R, H, I, T, G, N, F, D, A ● **Work Env:** Noise=V; ● **Salary:** 4 ● **Outlook:** 2

CALIBRATION LABORATORY TECHNICIAN (aircraft mfg.) ● DOT #019.281-010 ● OES: 22505 ● Alternate titles: ENGINEERING LABORATORY TECHNICIAN; QUALITY ASSURANCE CALIBRATOR; STANDARDS LABORATORY TECHNICIAN; TEST EQUIPMENT CERTIFICATION TECHNICIAN. Tests, calibrates, and repairs electrical, mechanical, electromechanical, and electronic measuring, recording, and indicating instruments and equipment for conformance to established standards, and assists in formulating calibration standards: Plans sequence of testing and calibration procedures for instruments and equipment, according to blueprints, schematics, technical manuals, and other specifications. Sets up standard and special purpose laboratory equipment to test, evaluate, and calibrate other instruments and test equipment. Disassembles instruments and equipment, using handtools, and inspects components for defects. Measures parts for conformity with specifications, using micrometers, calipers, and other precision instruments. Aligns, repairs, replaces, and balances component parts and circuitry. Reassembles and calibrates instruments and equipment. Devises formulas to solve problems in measurements and calibrations. Assists engineers in formulating test, calibration, repair, and evaluation plans and procedures to maintain precision accuracy of measuring, recording, and indicating instruments and equipment. ● **GED:** R5, M5, L4 ● **SVP:** 2-4 yrs ● **Academic:** Ed=A, Eng=S ● **Work Field:** 212, 111, 121 ● **MPSMS:** 601, 602 ● **Aptitudes:** G2, V3, N2, S2, P2, Q4, K3, F2, M2, E5, C4 ● **Temperaments:** J, T, V ● **Physical:** Stg=L; Freq: R, H, I, N, D Occas: S, O, E, A, X ● **Work Env:** Noise=N; Occas: E, T ● **Salary:** 3 ● **Outlook:** 4

CHEMICAL LABORATORY TECHNICIAN (profess. & kin.) ● DOT #022.261-010 ● OES: 24501 ● Conducts chemical and physical laboratory tests of solid materials, liquids, and gases, and analyzes test data for variety of purposes, such as research, product development, quality control, criminal investigation, and establishing standards, involving experimental, theoretical, or practical application of chemistry and related sciences: Sets up laboratory equipment and instrumentation required for tests, research, or process control. Tests and analyzes products, such as food, drugs, fertilizers, plastics, paints, detergents, paper, petroleum, and cement, to determine strength, stability, purity, chemical content, and other characteristics. Tests and analyzes materials and substances, such as ores, minerals, gases, soil, water, and pollutants. Documents results of tests and analyses. May prepare chemical solutions for use in processing materials, following standardized formulas or experimental procedures. May test and analyze radioactive and biological materials, applying knowledge of radiochemical procedures, emission spectrometry, and related techniques. ● **GED:** R5, M4, L4 ● **SVP:** 2-4 yrs ● **Academic:** Ed=A, Eng=S ● **Work Field:** 147, 211 ● **MPSMS:** 720 ● **Aptitudes:** G2, V2, N2, S3, P3, Q2, K3, F3, M3, E5, C4 ● **Temperaments:** J, T ● **Physical:** Stg=L; Freq: R, H, I, N Occas: E, T, G, D, A, X ● **Work Env:** Noise=N; Occas: A, T ● **Salary:** 4 ● **Outlook:** 3

CRIMINALIST (profess. & kin.) ● DOT #029.261-026 ● OES: 24501 ● Alternate titles: CRIME LABORATORY ANALYST; POLICE CHEMIST. Applies scientific principles to analysis, identification, and classification of mechanical devices, chemical and physical substances, materials, liquids, or other physical evidence related to criminology, law enforcement, or investigative work: Searches for, collects, photographs, and preserves evidence. Performs variety of analytical examinations, utilizing chemistry, physics, mechanics, and other sciences. Analyzes items, such as paint, glass, printed matter, paper, ink, fabric, dust, dirt, gases, or other substances, using spectroscope, microscope, infrared and ultraviolet light, microphotography, gas chromatograph, or other recording, measuring, or testing instruments. Identifies hair, skin, tissue, blood, bones, or human organs. Examines and classifies explosives, firearms, bullets, shells, and other weapons. Interprets laboratory findings relative to drugs, poisons, narcotics, alcohol, or other compounds ingested or injected into body. Reconstructs crime scene, preserving marks or impressions made by shoes, tires, or other objects by plaster or moulage casts. Prepares reports or presentations of findings, methods, and techniques used to support conclusions, and prepares results for court or other formal hearings. May testify as expert witness on evidence or crime laboratory techniques. Confers with experts in such specialties as ballistics, fingerprinting, handwriting, documents, electronics, metallurgy, biochemistry, medicine, or others. ● **GED:** R5, M5, L5 ● **SVP:** 2-4 yrs ● **Academic:** Ed=A, Eng=G ● **Work Field:** 271, 251 ● **MPSMS:** 739, 723, 951 ● **Aptitudes:** G1, V1, N1, S2, P2, Q2, K4, F4, M4, E5, C2 ● **Temperaments:** J, P, T, V ● **Physical:** Stg=L; Freq: R, H, I, T, G, N, D, A, X Occas: E, F, V ● **Work Env:** Noise=N; Occas: W, R ● **Salary:** 3 ● **Outlook:** 3

DECONTAMINATOR (any industry) ● DOT #199.384-010 ● OES: 39998 ● Decontaminates radioactive materials and equipment, using chemical solutions, and sandblasting machine: Reads contamination level, using radiation meter, and sorts contaminated items by size and radiation level, following specifications. Weighs out and mixes chemical solutions in tank according to prescribed formula, and heats solution, using steam hose. Immerses objects, such as pipes, motors, valves, hose, and containers, in solution for specified time, using hoist. Places smaller objects in sandblasting machine, using manipulators or protective gloves, and starts machine to remove greater proportion of contamination and reduce immersion time. Places hot (radioactive) waste, such as sweepings and broken sample bottles, into disposal containers to be processed for land or sea burial. Cleans objects having radiation count under specified amount, using cloth, soap, solvents, wire brush, and buffing wheel. Records type of material and equipment decontaminated and method used. May accompany coffins of waste to disposal area. May monitor radiation-exposed equipment, plant and hospital areas, and materials, using radiation-detector measuring instruments, such as portable gamma survey meter, Geiger counter, and alpha-beta-gamma survey meter. May determine method of decontamination according to size and nature of equipment, and degree of contamination. ● **GED:** R3, M3, L3 ● **SVP:** 1-2 yrs ● **Academic:** Ed=N, Eng=G ● **Work Field:** 031, 212 ● **MPSMS:** 920 ● **Aptitudes:** G3, V3, N4, S4, P4, Q4, K4, F4, M3, E5, C5 ● **Temperaments:** J, V ● **Physical:** Stg=M; Freq: R, H, I, N, D, A ● **Work Env:** Noise=L; Freq: U, V, A ● **Salary:** 4 ● **Outlook:** 3

EXAMINER, QUESTIONED DOCUMENTS (government ser.) ● DOT #199.267-022 ● OES: 39998 ● Alternate titles: HANDWRITING EXPERT. Examines handwritten material or other questioned documents to identify author, detect forgery, or determine method used to alter documents: Confers with laboratory specialists, such as chemists and photographers, to determine which scientific processes are necessary to effect analysis. Examines hand or typewritten sample to detect characteristics, such as open loop, quaver, or t-cross peculiar to an individual, using microscope. Measures angle or slant to estimate degree to which letters and lines vary from perpendicular, using protractor. Compares paper specimen with manufacturer's samples to ascertain type and source. Compares photographic blowup of written or typed specimen obtained from separate sources to ascertain similarity or differences. Works in consultative capacity to various agencies or organizations, including police force, and testifies in legal proceedings. ● **GED:** R5, M2, L4 ● **SVP:** 1-2 yrs ● **Academic:** Ed=A, Eng=G ● **Work Field:** 271, 211 ● **MPSMS:** 959 ● **Aptitudes:** G2, V2, N3, S2, P2, Q2, K4, F4, M4, E5, C4 ● **Temperaments:** J ● **Physical:** Stg=L; Freq: T, G, N, A Occas: R, H, I ● **Work Env:** Noise=N; ● **Salary:** 4 ● **Outlook:** 2

FILM LABORATORY TECHNICIAN I (motion picture) ● DOT #976.381-010 ● OES: 89914 ● Evaluates motion picture film to determine characteristics, such as sensitivity to light, density, and exposure time required for printing, using sensitometer, densitometer, and timer lights: Threads film strip through sensitometer, exposes film to light, and reads gauges to determine film's sensitivity to light. Threads film strip through densitometer and exposes film to light to determine density of film. Computes amount of light intensity needed to compensate for density of film, using standardized formulas. Exposes film strip to progressively timed lights to compare effects of various exposure times. Examines developed film strip to determine optimal exposure time and light intensity required for printing. Records test data and routes to FILM DEVELOPER (motion picture; photofinishing) and FILM PRINTER (motion picture). May be designated according to specialty as Densitometrist (motion picture); Sensitometrist (motion picture); Timer (motion picture). ● **GED:** R4, M4, L4 ● **SVP:** 2-4 yrs ● **Academic:** Ed=N, Eng=S ● **Work Field:** 212, 202, 232 ● **MPSMS:** 911 ● **Aptitudes:** G2, V3, N2, S3, P2, Q3, K3, F3, M3, E5, C2 ● **Temperaments:** J ● **Physical:** Stg=L; Freq: R, H, I, N, D, A, X ● **Work Env:** Noise=N; ● **Salary:** 3 ● **Outlook:** 4

FINGERPRINT CLASSIFIER (government ser.) ● DOT #375.387-010 ● OES: 39998 ● Alternate titles: FINGERPRINT EXPERT. Classifies fingerprints and compares fingerprints of unknown persons or suspects with fingerprint records to determine if prints were involved in previous crimes: Classifies record cards containing fingerprints of crime suspects according to specified grouping, and compares fingerprints with others in file to determine if prisoner has criminal record or is wanted for other crimes. Examines fingerprint evidence left at scene of crime, classifies prints, and endeavors to identify person. May fingerprint prisoner, using ink pad. May transfer residual fingerprints from objects, such as weapons or drinking glasses, to record cards, using standard technique. May keep files of criminals and suspects, containing such information as photographs, habits, and modus operandi of crimes with which individual has been connected. ● **GED:** R4, M2, L3 ● **SVP:** 1-2 yrs ● **Academic:** Ed=H, Eng=G ● **Work Field:** 271, 231 ● **MPSMS:** 951 ● **Aptitudes:** G3, V4, N4, S2, P2, Q3, K4, F4, M4, E5, C5 ● **Temperaments:** J, T ● **Physical:** Stg=L; Freq: N, D, A, V Occas: R, H, I ● **Work Env:** Noise=N; ● **Salary:** 4 ● **Outlook:** 3

GEOLOGICAL AIDE (petrol. & gas) ● DOT #024.267-010 ● OES: 24501 ● Examines and compiles geological information to provide technical data to GEOLOGIST, PETROLEUM (petrol. & gas) 024.061-022, using surface and subsurface maps, oil and gas well activity reports, and sand and core analysis studies: Studies geological reports to extract well data and posts data to maps and logs. Draws subsurface formation contours on charts to lay out and prepare geological cross section charts. Compiles information regarding well tests, completions,

and formation tops to prepare oil or gas well records. Records net sand and sand percentage counts and calculates isopachous values to compile sand analysis data. Studies directional logs and surveys to calculate and plot formation tops. Reads well activity reports and records key well locations in drilling activity book. Assembles and distributes prepared charts, maps, and reports to geologist requesting material. Maintains file record systems and geological library. Attends SCOUT (petrol. & gas) 010.267-010 meeting to compile information on well activity. Contacts competitors to acquire oil and gas samples from wells. Operates computer terminal for input and retrieval of geological data. ● **GED:** R5, M5, L5 ● **SVP:** 4-10 yrs ● **Academic:** Ed=A, Eng=S ● **Work Field:** 251 ● **MPSMS:** 725 ● **Aptitudes:** G2, V2, N1, S2, P2, Q2, K3, F3, M4, E5, C5 ● **Temperaments:** I, P, V ● **Physical:** Stg=L; Freq: R, H, T, G, N, D, A Occas: I ● **Work Env:** Noise=N; ● **Salary:** 2 ● **Outlook:** 2

GRAPHOLOGIST (profess. & kin.) ● DOT #199.267-038 ● OES: 39998 ● Analyzes handwriting to appraise personal characteristics: Obtains handwriting specimen to observe overall appearance of writing and detailed formation of letters. Measures height of letters and slant of writing, using calibrated templates. Observes individual writing strokes to determine unique or distinguishing characteristics, using ruler and low-power magnifying glass or microscope. Evaluates handwriting sample and interprets findings, according to theories of handwriting analysis. May use diagram to plot writing characteristics. ● **GED:** R4, M3, L3 ● **SVP:** 1-2 yrs ● **Academic:** Ed=N, Eng=G ● **Work Field:** 271 ● **MPSMS:** 949 ● **Aptitudes:** G3, V3, N4, S4, P2, Q2, K4, F4, M4, E5, C5 ● **Temperaments:** I, J, P ● **Physical:** Stg=S; Const: N Freq: T, G Occas: R, H, I ● **Work Env:** Noise=Q; ● **Salary:** 3 ● **Outlook:** 1

HOT-CELL TECHNICIAN (profess. & kin.) ● DOT #015.362-018 ● OES: 24501 ● Alternate titles: IRRADIATION TECHNICIAN. Operates remote-controlled equipment in hot cell to conduct metallurgical and chemical tests on radioactive materials: Controls slave manipulators from outside cell to remove metal or chemical materials from shielded containers inside hot cell and places on bench or equipment work station. Tests chemical or metallurgical properties of materials according to standardized procedures, and observes reaction through cell window. Sets up and operates machines to cut, lap, and polish test pieces, following blueprints, x-ray negatives, and sketches. Tests physical properties, using equipment, such as tensile tester, hardness tester, metallographic unit, micrometer, and gauges. Immerses test sample in chemical compound to prepare for testing. Places irradiated nuclear fuel materials in environmental chamber to test reaction to temperature changes. Records results of tests for further analysis by engineers, scientists, or customers. Places specimen in shielded container for removal from cell, using manipulators. Participates in cleaning and decontamination of cell during maintenance shutdown. May devise adapters and fixtures for use in hot cell operations. ● **GED:** R4, M3, L4 ● **SVP:** 2-4 yrs ● **Academic:** Ed=H, Eng=S ● **Work Field:** 211, 244 ● **MPSMS:** 725 ● **Aptitudes:** G3, V3, N3, S2, P2, Q4, K2, F2, M2, E4, C4 ● **Temperaments:** J, T, V ● **Physical:** Stg=L; Const: R, H Freq: N, F, D, A, V Occas: I, T, G, X ● **Work Env:** Noise=N; Occas: R ● **Salary:** 5 ● **Outlook:** 2

HYDROGRAPHER (waterworks) ● DOT #025.264-010 ● OES: 24501 ● Analyzes hydrographic data to determine trends in movement and utilization of water: Reads meters and gauges to measure waterflow and pressure in streams, conduits, and pipelines, and records data. Measures water level in lakes, reservoirs, and tanks. Calculates seepage and evaporation rates for dams and reservoirs. Measures depth of water in wells and test holes to determine ground water level. Measures snow characteristics to evaluate water yield from snow runoff. Prepares graphs and charts to illustrate water patterns. Positions sluice gates to direct water onto spreading grounds. Installs, calibrates, and maintains metering instruments. Recommends locations for metering stations and instrument placement. ● **GED:** R4, M4, L4 ● **SVP:** 1-2 yrs ● **Academic:** Ed=A, Eng=S ● **Work Field:** 232, 251 ● **MPSMS:** 725 ● **Aptitudes:** G3, V3, N2, S3, P2, Q2, K5, F3, M3, E3, C5 ● **Temperaments:** J ● **Physical:** Stg=M; Freq: N, A Occas: R, H, I ● **Work Env:** Noise=N; Freq: W ● **Salary:** 4 ● **Outlook:** 3

LABORATORY ASSISTANT (petrol. & gas) ● DOT #024.381-010 ● OES: 24501 ● Alternate titles: ANALYST, GEOCHEMICAL PROSPECTING; CORE ANALYST; LABORATORY TESTER. Tests sand, shale, and other earth materials to determine petroleum and mineral content and physical characteristics: Performs routine chemical or physical tests of earth samples in field or laboratory to determine content of hydrocarbon or other minerals indicating presence of petroleum and mineral deposits. Tests core samples brought up during well drilling to determine permeability and porosity of sample, fluid content of sand and shale, salinity of drilling mud, and other conditions affecting oil well drilling operations. ● **GED:** R4, M4, L3 ● **SVP:** 6 mos-1 yr ● **Academic:** Ed=H, Eng=S ● **Work Field:** 211 ● **MPSMS:** 340 ● **Aptitudes:** G2, V2, N2, S3, P3, Q4, K3, F2, M3, E5, C5 ● **Temperaments:** J, T ● **Physical:** Stg=L; Freq: R, H, N, A Occas: I, G ● **Work Env:** Noise=N; ● **Salary:** 2 ● **Outlook:** 3

LABORATORY ASSISTANT (textile) ● DOT #029.381-014 ● OES: 24501 ● Alternate titles: LABORATORY TESTER. Performs standardized laboratory tests to verify chemical characteristics or composition of textile fibers, yarns, and products, and materials used in processing textiles: Tests oil and soap products to determine fitness for use in cloth and yarn finishing processes. Tests dyed goods for stripping (removing dye). Tests greige goods to determine if goods are of specified quality for dyeing, printing, and finishing. Verifies dye formulas used to develop or match colors by dyeing samples of cloth, yarn or textile fibers, and determines fastness of dyes, using laboratory equipment. Tests raw stock for moisture content with meter-equipped probe. Verifies efficiency of scouring process by testing wool samples to determine percentage of natural greases removed, using scales, solvents, and ovens. Measures tear strength and wet and dry tensile strength, using tensile-testing equipment. Determines color value by subjecting material to lights. Visually inspects yarns and finished material. May classify finished product according to quality and estimate amount of mending required. ● **GED:** R3, M3, L3 ● **SVP:** 3-6 mos ● **Academic:** Ed=H, Eng=S ● **Work Field:** 152, 211 ● **MPSMS:** 410, 420 ● **Aptitudes:** G3, V3, N3, S3, P2, Q3, K3, F4, M3, E5, C2 ● **Temperaments:** J, T ● **Physical:** Stg=L; Freq: R, H, I, N, A, X Occas: E, G ● **Work Env:** Noise=N; ● **Salary:** 2 ● **Outlook:** 3

LABORATORY ASSISTANT (utilities) ● DOT #029.361-018 ● OES: 24501 ● Alternate titles: LABORATORY TECHNICIAN. Performs standardized physical and chemical tests on materials and supplies used throughout power system to ensure compliance with specifications: Tests water used in boilers of steam generating plant for alkalinity and silica and phosphate content, using colorimeter and spectrophotometer. Notifies POWER-PLANT OPERATOR (utilities) or AUXILIARY-EQUIPMENT OPERATOR (utilities) of amount of chemical additives required to bring water to prescribed level of purity. Tests coal to determine Btu content by burning coal samples in colorimeter. Tests oil used in circuit breakers for dielectric strength by placing sample of oil in ceramic cup positioned between two electrodes, and measuring current conducted by oil, using ohmmeter. Ascertains heat resisting qualities of insulating paints and varnishes by coating pieces of sheet metal with paint and varnish and subjecting them to high temperatures. May determine viscosity index of lubricating oils, using viscosimeter. May inspect rubber protective equipment, such as aprons, gloves, and blankets for flaws. ● **GED:** R5, M5, L5 ● **SVP:** 1-2 yrs ● **Academic:** Ed=A, Eng=S ● **Work Field:** 211 ● **MPSMS:** 720 ● **Aptitudes:** G2, V2, N3, S3, P2, Q4, K3, F2, M3, E4, C3 ● **Temperaments:** J, T, V ● **Physical:** Stg=L; Freq: R, H, I, N, X Occas: T, G, D, A ● **Work Env:** Noise=N; ● **Salary:** 2 ● **Outlook:** 3

LABORATORY ASSISTANT, METALLURGICAL (steel & rel.) ● DOT #011.261-022 ● OES: 35199 ● Alternate titles: METALLURGICAL ANALYST; METALLURGICAL INSPECTOR. Analyzes data obtained from investigation of physical and chemical properties of metals, or processes used in recovering metals from their ores to select method, standards, and procedures of examination and testing and conducts tests: Analyzes operating records and test reports, or by personal observation and investigation, determines conformance to established procedures, methods, and standards. Conducts physical, chemical, and process examinations, using metallurgical equipment and instruments for routine, special, and experimental investigations. Writes report indicating deviations from specifications and recommends corrective measures for approval. ● **GED:** R4, M4, L4 ● **SVP:** 2-4 yrs ● **Academic:** Ed=A, Eng=S ● **Work Field:** 211, 244 ● **MPSMS:** 540 ● **Aptitudes:** G3, V3, N3, S3, P4, Q3, K4, F3, M3, E5, C4 ● **Temperaments:** J, T, V ● **Physical:** Stg=L; Freq: R, H, T, G, N, A, X Occas: I ● **Work Env:** Noise=N; ● **Salary:** 2 ● **Outlook:** 4

LABORATORY SUPERVISOR (profess. & kin.) ● DOT #022.137-010 ● OES: 24105 ● Supervises and coordinates activities of personnel engaged in performing chemical and physical tests required for quality control of processes and products: Directs and advises personnel in special test procedures to analyze components and physical properties of materials. Compiles and analyzes test information to determine operating efficiency of process or equipment and to diagnose malfunctions. Confers with scientists or engineers to conduct analyses, interpret test results, or develop nonstandard tests. Performs other duties as described under SUPERVISOR (any industry) Master Title. May adjust formulas and processes based on test results. May test and analyze sample products. May prepare test solutions, compounds, and reagents for use by laboratory personnel in conducting tests. May conduct research to develop custom products and investigate complaints on existing products. ● **GED:** R5, M5, L4 ● **SVP:** 2-4 yrs ● **Academic:** Ed=B, Eng=G ● **Work Field:** 211 ● **MPSMS:** 723 ● **Aptitudes:** G2, V2, N2, S3, P3, Q3, K4, F4, M4, E5, C4 ● **Temperaments:** D, J, P, T, V ● **Physical:** Stg=L; Freq: R, H, I, T, G, N Occas: E, D, A, X ● **Work Env:** Noise=N; Occas: A, T ● **Salary:** 4 ● **Outlook:** 3

LABORATORY TECHNICIAN (auto. mfg.) ● DOT #019.261-030 ● OES: 24501 ● Tests chemical and physical properties of materials used in manufacturing or assembling motor vehicles: Performs standard chemical and physical tests on parts, solutions, and materials used in producing motor vehicles, using conventional and computerized machines and work aids. Conducts quantitative and qualitative analyses to determine chemical and physical properties of experimental and developmental materials [LABORATORY TESTER (any industry) 029.261-010]. ● **GED:** R4, M4, L4 ● **SVP:** 6 mos-1 yr ● **Academic:** Ed=A, Eng=S ● **Work Field:** 212 ● **MPSMS:** 591 ● **Aptitudes:** G3, V3, N3, S3, P5, Q3, K3, F4, M3, E5, C5 ● **Temperaments:** J, T ● **Physical:** Stg=L; Freq: R, H, I, N, D, A Occas: T, G ● **Work Env:** Noise=N; ● **Salary:** 3 ● **Outlook:** 4

LABORATORY TESTER (any industry) ● DOT #029.261-010 ● OES: 24501 ● Performs laboratory tests according to prescribed standards to determine chemical and physical characteristics or composition of solid, liquid, or gaseous materials for such purposes as quality control, process control, or product development: Sets up, adjusts and operates laboratory equipment and instruments, such as microscopes, centrifuge, agitators, viscosimeter, chemical balance scales, spectrophotometer, gas chromatograph, colorimeter, and other equipment. Tests materials used as ingredients in adhesives, cement, propellants, lubricants, refractories, synthetic rubber, plastics, paint, paper, cloth, and other products for such qualities as purity, stability, viscosity, density, absorption, burning rate, and melting or flash point. Tests solutions used in processes, such as anodizing, waterproofing, cleaning, bleaching, and pickling for chemical concentration, specific gravity, or other characteristics. Tests materials for presence and content of elements or substances, such as hydrocarbons, manganese, natural grease, tungsten, sulfur, cyanide, ash, dust, or impurities. Tests samples of manufactured products to verify conformity to specifications. Records test results on standardized forms and writes test reports describing procedures used. Cleans and sterilizes laboratory equipment. May prepare graphs and charts. May prepare chemical solutions according to standard formulas. May add chemicals or raw materials to process solutions or product batches to correct or establish formulation required to meet specifications. May calibrate laboratory instruments. May be designated according to product or material tested. For testing of food products see FOOD TESTER (any industry) 029.361-014. ● **GED:** R4, M4, L4 ● **SVP:** 1-2 yrs ● **Academic:** Ed=A, Eng=S ● **Work Field:** 211, 212 ● **MPSMS:** 720 ● **Aptitudes:** G3, V3, N3, S3, P3, Q3, K3, F3, M3, E5, C3 ● **Temperaments:** J, T ● **Physical:** Stg=L; Freq: R, H, I, N, A, X Occas: T, G ● **Work Env:** Noise=N; ● **Salary:** 4 ● **Outlook:** 4

LABORATORY TESTER (plastic-synth.) ● DOT #022.281-018 ● OES: 24501 ● Examines, measures, photographs, and tests synthetic fiber samples to facilitate quality control of forming, treating, and texturing processes, performing any combination of following tasks: Dips several twisted threads in melted wax and directs stream of cold water over threads to congeal wax. Slices threads crosswise, using microtome. Dissolves wax, using solvent, and positions thread sample on microscope slide. Inserts slide in microscope and photographs sample, using standard microphotographic equipment and techniques. Develops, prints, and labels photographs. Analyzes photographs to determine whether structure and other characteristics of thread meet plant standards. Determines tensile strength of thread samples, using device that draws material between two jaws until breakage occurs. Measures cross-sectional area of thread samples, using planimeter. Immerses samples in water, corrosives, or cleaning agents to detect shrinkage or damage. Places thread samples in dye bath to evaluate permeability of dye and exposes samples to controlled light source to ascertain fade resistance. Prepares and submits reports of findings to production personnel to facilitate quality control of product. ● **GED:** R4, M3, L3 ● **SVP:** 1-2 yrs ● **Academic:** Ed=H, Eng=S ● **Work Field:** 211 ● **MPSMS:** 414 ● **Aptitudes:** G2, V2, N2, S2, P2, Q3, K4, F3, M3, E5, C2 ● **Temperaments:** J, T ● **Physical:** Stg=L; Freq: R, H, I, N, X Occas: D, A ● **Work Env:** Noise=Q; ● **Salary:** 4 ● **Outlook:** 4

METALLURGICAL TECHNICIAN (profess. & kin.) ● DOT #011.261-010 ● OES: 35199 ● Alternate titles: METALLURGICAL-LABORATORY ASSISTANT; METALLURGICAL TESTER; PHYSICAL-LABORATORY ASSISTANT. Examines and tests metal samples to determine their physical properties, under direction of METALLOGRAPHER (profess. & kin.): Conducts routine microscopic examinations of metals and alloys to determine their crystal structure, porosity, homogeneity, and other characteristics. Polishes or etches metal specimens and photographs samples, using photomicroscope, or directs photography technical personnel to take, develop, and mount photomicrographs. Examines metal and alloy samples with x-ray, gamma-ray, and magnetic-flux equipment to detect internal fractures, impurities, and similar defects in metals. Tests samples in pressure devices, hot-acid baths, and other apparatus to determine strength, hardness, elasticity, toughness, or other properties of metal. ● **GED:** R4, M4, L4 ● **SVP:** 1-2 yrs ● **Academic:** Ed=A, Eng=S ● **Work Field:** 211, 244 ● **MPSMS:** 350, 540 ● **Aptitudes:** G3, V3, N3, S3, P3, Q3, K3, F3, M3, E4, C3 ● **Temperaments:** J, T ● **Physical:** Stg=L; Freq: R, H, I, N, A Occas: T, G, X ● **Work Env:** Noise=N; Occas: T ● **Salary:** 5 ● **Outlook:** 4

PHARMACIST (medical ser.) ● DOT #074.161-010 ● OES: 32517 ● Alternate titles: DRUGGIST. Compounds and dispenses prescribed medications, drugs, and other pharmaceuticals for patient care, according to professional standards and state and federal legal requirements: Reviews prescriptions issued by physician, or other authorized prescriber to assure accuracy and determine formulas and ingredients needed. Compounds medications, using standard formulas and processes, such as weighing, measuring, and mixing ingredients. Directs pharmacy workers engaged in mixing, packaging, and labeling pharmaceuticals. Answers questions and provides information to pharmacy customers on drug interactions, side effects, dosage and storage of pharmaceuticals. Maintains established procedures concerning quality assurance, security of controlled substances, and disposal of hazardous waste drugs. Enters data, such as patient name, prescribed medication and cost, to maintain pharmacy files, charge system, and inventory. May assay medications to determine identity, purity, and strength. May instruct interns and other medical personnel on matters pertaining to pharmacy, or teach in college of pharmacy. May work in hospital pharmacy and be designated Pharmacist, Hospital (medical ser.). ● **GED:** R5, M5, L5 ● **SVP:** 2-4 yrs ● **Academic:** Ed=M, Eng=G ● **Work Field:** 147, 294 ● **MPSMS:** 493, 920 ● **Aptitudes:** G1, V2, N2, S4, P2, Q2, K3, F2, M3, E5, C3 ● **Temperaments:** J, T, V ● **Physical:** Stg=L; Freq: R, H, I, T, G, N, A, X ● **Work Env:** Noise=N; Occas: T, O ● **Salary:** 5 ● **Outlook:** 3

PHARMACIST ASSISTANT (military ser.) ● DOT #074.381-010 ● OES: 32998 ● Mixes and dispenses prescribed medicines and pharmaceutical preparations in absence of or under supervision of PHARMACIST (medical ser.): Compounds preparations according to prescriptions issued by medical, dental, or veterinary officers. Pours, weighs, or measures dosages and grinds, heats, filters, or dissolves and mixes liquid or soluble drugs and chemicals. Procures, stores, and issues pharmaceutical materials and supplies. Maintains files and records and submits required pharmacy reports. ● **GED:** R4, M4, L3 ● **SVP:** 1-2 yrs ● **Academic:** Ed=H, Eng=S ● **Work Field:** 143, 221, 142 ● **MPSMS:** 493 ● **Aptitudes:** G2, V2, N3, S4, P3, Q4, K3, F3, M4, E5, C3 ● **Temperaments:** J, T ● **Physical:** Stg=L; Freq: R, H, I, T, G, N, X Occas: E, A ● **Work Env:** Noise=N; ● **Salary:** 4 ● **Outlook:** 4

PHOTOGRAPHER, SCIENTIFIC (profess. & kin.) ● DOT #143.062-026 ● OES: 34023 ● Photographs variety of subject material to illustrate or record scientific data or phenomena, utilizing knowledge of scientific procedures and photographic technology and techniques: Plans methods and procedures for photographing subject material and setup of equipment required, such as microscopes, telescopes, infrared or ultraviolet lighting, and x ray. Sets up and positions camera for photographing material or subject. Trips shutter to expose film. May prepare microscope slides. May make photographic copies of fragile documents and other material. May engage in research to develop new photographic procedures, methods, and materials. May process film and photographic paper to produce transparencies, prints, slides, and motion picture film. Usually specializes in specific field, such as chemistry, biology, medicine, metallurgy, physiology, astronomy, aerodynamics, ballistics, or engineering and is designated accordingly. ● **GED:** R4, M3, L4 ● **SVP:** 2-4 yrs ● **Academic:** Ed=H, Eng=S ● **Work Field:** 201 ● **MPSMS:** 720 ● **Aptitudes:** G2, V3, N3, S2, P2, Q4, K3, F3, M3, E5, C2 ● **Temperaments:** J, T, V ● **Physical:** Stg=L; Freq: R, H, I, N, F, D, A, X, V ● **Work Env:** Noise=Q; Occas: R ● **Salary:** 4 ● **Outlook:** 3

PHOTO-OPTICS TECHNICIAN (profess. & kin.) ● DOT #029.280-010 ● OES: 24501 ● Sets up and operates photo-optical instrumentation to record and photograph data for scientific and engineering projects: Operates and calibrates photo-optical equipment according to formalized procedures, maintenance manuals, and schematic diagrams. Operates test equipment and performs analysis of data for engineering and scientific personnel. May install and calibrate optical and photographic data collection equipment in missiles, aircraft, weaponry, weather or communication satelites, underwater devices, or other installations. May evaluate adequacy of data obtained to determine need for future changes in instrumentation. May modify existing equipment and participate in planning and testing modified equipment and instrumentation procedures. ● **GED:** R5, M4, L3 ● **SVP:** 1-2 yrs ● **Academic:** Ed=A, Eng=S ● **Work Field:** 201 ● **MPSMS:** 600 ● **Aptitudes:** G2, V2, N3, S2, P2, Q4, K3, F3, M3, E5, C4 ● **Temperaments:** J, T ● **Physical:** Stg=L; Freq: R, H, N, A Occas: I, F, D, X, V ● **Work Env:** Noise=L; ● **Salary:** 1 ● **Outlook:** 3

PROOF TECHNICIAN (ordnance) ● DOT #199.171-010 ● OES: 39998 ● Test-fires small arms, artillery weapons, ammunition, and bombs to evaluate mechanical performance and ballistic qualities, such as range, accuracy, bursting effect, and armor-piercing ability: Erects heavy weapons and connects electrical fire-control apparatus according to diagrams and written instructions. Positions small arms in holding fixtures and rigs trigger-pulling device. Loads, aims, and fires weapons. Measures gun barrel pressures and computes velocities of projectile. Examines and measures targets to verify accuracy of weapons and ammunition. Refrigerates, heats, or immerses ammunition in water before firing to verify performance under severe temperature and moisture conditions. Keeps records of observations. Prepares aerial bombs for test-dropping and loads bombs into aircraft. May prepare experimental ammunition and bombs and devise firing methods. May direct helpers. May specialize in testing of specific ordnance and be designated according to type of item involved. ● **GED:** R4, M4, L4 ● **SVP:** 1-2 yrs ● **Academic:** Ed=N, Eng=G ● **Work Field:** 211 ● **MPSMS:** 370 ● **Aptitudes:** G2, V3, N2, S3, P2, Q3, K3, F3, M3, E5, C4 ● **Temperaments:** J, T, V ● **Physical:** Stg=L; Freq: R, H, I, N, A Occas: F, D ● **Work Env:** Noise=V; Freq: O ● **Salary:** 4 ● **Outlook:** 1

QUALITY CONTROL TECHNICIAN (profess. & kin.) ● DOT #012.261-014 ● OES: 35199 ● Tests and inspects products at various stages of production process and compiles and evaluates statistical data to determine and maintain quality and reliability of products: Interprets engineering drawings, schematic diagrams, or formulas and confers with management or engineering staff to determine quality and reliability standards. Selects products for tests at specified stages in production process, and tests products for variety of qualities, such as dimensions, performance, and mechanical, electrical, or chemical characteristics. Records test data, applying statistical quality control procedures. Evaluates data and writes reports to validate or indicate deviations from existing standards. Recommends modifications of existing quality or production standards to achieve optimum quality within limits of equipment capability. May set up and perform destructive and nondestructive tests on materials, parts, or products to measure performance, life, or material characteristics. May prepare graphs or charts of data or enter data into computer for analysis. May specialize in particular area of quality control engineering, such as design, incoming material, process control, product evaluation, inventory control, product reliability, research and development, and administrative application. ● **GED:** R5, M5, L4 ● **SVP:** 2-4 yrs ● **Academic:** Ed=A, Eng=G ● **Work Field:** 211, 244 ● **MPSMS:** 712 ● **Aptitudes:** G2, V2, N2, S2, P2, Q3, K3, F3, M3, E5, C4 ● **Temperaments:** J, T, V ● **Physical:** Stg=L; Freq: R, H, I, N, D, A, X Occas: E, T, G ● **Work Env:** Noise=N; Occas: A ● **Salary:** 4 ● **Outlook:** 4

RADIOISOTOPE-PRODUCTION OPERATOR (profess. & kin.) ● DOT #015.362-022 ● OES: 24501 ● Alternate titles: ISOTOPE-PRO-DUCTION TECHNICIAN. Controls laboratory compounding equipment enclosed in protective hot cell to prepare radioisotopes and other radioactive materials for use as tracers for biological, biomedical, physiological, and industrial purposes according to written procedures: Places specified amounts of chemicals into container to be irradiated at nuclear reactor or with other irradiation equipment. Secures vacuum pump head to outlet valve on special container to replace air with inert gas, and routes container to irradiation facility. Receives irradiated chemicals delivered in shielded cell. Moves manipulator to open container and transfer irradiated contents into glass vessel. Opens pneumatic valves or uses manipulators to add specified types and quantities of chemical reagents into glass vessel to produce radioactive product. Controls manipulators to pour liquids required to perform standard chemical analyses involving titration and filtration. Withdraws radioactive sample for transport to chemical laboratory for analysis. Fills shipping container inside cell with prescribed quantity of radioisotope material for shipment pending sample approval. ● **GED:** R4, M3, L4 ● **SVP:** 1-2 yrs ● **Academic:** Ed=H, Eng=S ● **Work Field:** 147 ● **MPSMS:** 490, 725 ● **Aptitudes:** G3, V3, N3, S3, P3, Q4, K3, F3, M3, E3, C4 ● **Temperaments:** J, T ● **Physical:** Stg=L; Const: R, H Freq: I, N, F, D, A Occas: X, V ● **Work Env:** Noise=N; Occas: R ● **Salary:** 4 ● **Outlook:** 2

RADIOPHARMACIST (medical ser.) ● DOT #074.161-014 ● OES: 32517 ● Prepares and dispenses radioactive pharmaceuticals used for patient diagnosis and therapy, applying principles and practices of pharmacy and radiochemistry: Receives radiopharmaceutical prescription from physician and reviews prescription to determine suitability of radiopharmaceutical for intended use. Verifies that specified radioactive substance and reagent will give desired results in examination or treatment procedures, utilizing knowledge of radiopharmaceutical preparation and principles of drug biodistribution. Calculates volume of radioactive pharmaceutical required to provide patient with desired level of radioactivity at prescribed time, according to established rates of radioisotope decay. Compounds radioactive substances and reagents to prepare radiopharmaceutical, following radiopharmacy laboratory procedures. Assays prepared radiopharmaceutical, using measuring and analysis instruments and equipment, such as ionization chamber, pulse-height analyzer, and radioisotope dose calibrator, to verify rate of drug disintegration and to ensure that patient receives required dose. Consults with physician following patient treatment or procedure to review and evaluate quality and effectiveness of radiopharmaceutical. Conducts research to develop or improve radiopharmaceuticals. Prepares reports for regulatory agencies to obtain approval for testing and use of new radiopharmaceuticals. Maintains control records for receipt, storage, preparation, and disposal of radioactive nuclei. Occasionally conducts training for students and medical professionals concerning radiopharmacy use, characteristics, and compounding procedures. ● **GED:** R6, M5, L5 ● **SVP:** 2-4 yrs ● **Academic:** Ed=M, Eng=G ● **Work Field:** 147 ● **MPSMS:** 732, 484 ● **Aptitudes:** G1, V1, N2, S2, P1, Q2, K2, F2, M3, E5, C4 ● **Temperaments:** J, T ● **Physical:** Stg=L; Freq: R, H, I, N, A Occas: T, G, X ● **Work Env:** Noise=N; Occas: R ● **Salary:** 5 ● **Outlook:** 3

REACTOR OPERATOR, TEST-AND-RESEARCH (profess. & kin.) ● DOT #015.362-026 ● OES: 24501 ● Controls operation of nuclear reactor to create fissionable materials used for research purposes, study structure of atoms, and determine properties of materials: Positions fuel elements (uranium) and object to be irradiated in position in reactor core, using slave manipulators. Installs instrumentation leads in core to measure operating temperature and pressure in reactor working from mockups, blueprints, and wiring and instrumentation diagrams. Activates reactor and inserts object to be irradiated into rabbit (pneumatic) tube, beam hole, or irradiation tunnel according to size of object and nature of experiment. Monitors instruments at console and reactor panels to control chain reaction, following directions of nuclear experimenters. Calculates applicable limits of operating fac-

tors, such as temperature and pressure, using standard formulas, and adjusts controls to maintain operating conditions, such as power level, airflow and waterflow, temperature, and radiation and neutron levels in reactor within operating limits. Records data, such as type of material irradiated, exposure time, pile atmospheric conditions, and position of control rods in core. Disassembles reactor parts, such as core plug (shield) and control rods, using crane and handtools. Lifts spent fuel elements and irradiated objects from core, using extension tool, and drops them through chute into canal for recovery of fissionable material. May work as member of team and alternate between operating reactor controls and monitoring instruments, gauges, and other recording devices in control room. ● **GED:** R4, M4, L4 ● **SVP:** 2-4 yrs ● **Academic:** Ed=H, Eng=S ● **Work Field:** 251 ● **MPSMS:** 725 ● **Aptitudes:** G3, V3, N3, S3, P3, Q3, K3, F3, M3, E4, C4 ● **Temperaments:** J, T, V ● **Physical:** Stg=L; Freq: R, H, T, G, N ● **Work Env:** Noise=N; Const: R ● **Salary:** 5 ● **Outlook:** 2

SAMPLER (mine & quarry) ● DOT #579.484-010 ● OES: 83000 ● Alternate titles: BUCKER; COAL INSPECTOR; HARDNESS TESTER; MATERIALS INSPECTOR; ORE SAMPLER; TESTER. Collects samples of coal, ore, crushed stone, aggregate, sand or gravel from railroad cars, conveyors, stockpiles or mines and tests materials for conformance to specifications: Gathers samples from specified locations and transports samples to laboratory. Dumps material into sample divider to reduce volume of sample. Weighs material, using balance scale, and dumps sample into grinding machine to grind and blend sample or into screen testing machine to separate particles by size. Weighs segregated particles collected on each screen and computes percentage of each in total sample. Examines samples for presence of foreign matter and variation from color standard. Compiles reports indicating percentages of materials of specified size. Notifies management when materials do not meet specifications. May weigh, dry, and reweigh samples to determine moisture content of samples. May bag samples for testing at other locations. May perform chemical sedimentation or magnetic separation tests. May perform hardness test on pellets. May plot origin of samples on mine map. ● **GED:** R3, M2, L1 ● **SVP:** 3-6 mos ● **Academic:** Ed=N, Eng=N ● **Work Field:** 212 ● **MPSMS:** 340, 350 ● **Aptitudes:** G3, V4, N3, S4, P4, Q3, K3, F3, M4, E4, C4 ● **Temperaments:** J, T ● **Physical:** Stg=M; Freq: R, H, N Occas: C, I, D, A, X ● **Work Env:** Noise=L; Occas: W ● **Salary:** 2 ● **Outlook:** 3

SCANNER (profess. & kin.) ● DOT #015.384-010 ● OES: 24501 ● Compiles lists of events (collisions of atomic nuclei) from photographs of bubble chamber, cloud chamber, or other particle detector, and operates machine to record characteristics of events into computers: Observes projected photographs to locate particle tracks, locate and count events indicated by tracks, and identify nature of observed events. Receives instructions from scientist directing project as to specific events that are important in experiment, and identifies such events from other events. Turns cranks to move projector and locates point on track under crosshairs of eyepiece. Enters data into computer to record coordinates of particles. Repeats process to record successive stages of tracks resulting from each event to provide information for scientists to identify particles. May use microscope fitted with scales and protractors to scan photographic emulsions previously exposed to direct radiation and to compute direction, angle, length, curvature, density, and depth of tracks from standard formulas. ● **GED:** R4, M3, L4 ● **SVP:** 1-2 yrs ● **Academic:** Ed=H, Eng=G ● **Work Field:** 232, 212 ● **MPSMS:** 715 ● **Aptitudes:** G3, V3, N3, S2, P2, Q3, K3, F4, M4, E5, C5 ● **Temperaments:** J, T ● **Physical:** Stg=S; Const: R, H, I, N Occas: A ● **Work Env:** Noise=N; ● **Salary:** 5 ● **Outlook:** 2

SPECTROSCOPIST (profess. & kin.) ● DOT #011.281-014 ● OES: 35199 ● Alternate titles: SPECTROGRAPHER; SPECTROGRAPHIC ANALYST. Conducts spectrographic examinations of metal and mineral samples under established procedures, using spectrograph, spectrometer, densitometer, and other measuring instruments: Analyzes densitometer or spectrometer readings to measure density ratio of specific elements in sample. Computes percentage composition of sample by comparing intensity ratio with standard charts. Investigates deviations from standard, performing further examinations by other spectrographic procedures and methods to establish degree of conformance to standard. Records quantitative determination, procedure, and standard applied for each sample examined. ● **GED:** R4, M4, L4 ● **SVP:** 2-4 yrs ● **Academic:** Ed=A, Eng=S ● **Work Field:** 211 ● **MPSMS:**

711 ● **Aptitudes:** G2, V3, N2, S2, P3, Q4, K3, F3, M3, E5, C3 ●
Temperaments: J, T ● **Physical:** Stg=L; Freq: R, H, N Occas: F, D, A
● **Work Env:** Noise=N; ● **Salary:** 5 ● **Outlook:** 3

TESTER (petrol. refin.) ● DOT #029.261-022 ● OES: 24501 ● Alternate titles: CRUDE TESTER; GAS ANALYST; LABORATORY INSPECTOR; LABORATORY TECHNICIAN; LABORATORY TESTER; OIL TESTER. Tests and analyzes samples of crude oil and petroleum products during processing stages, using laboratory apparatus, testing equipment, and following standard test procedures to determine physical and chemical properties and ensure products meet quality control standards: Tests samples of crude and blended oils, gases, asphalts, and pressure distillates to determine characteristics, such as boiling, vapor, freeze, condensation, flash and aniline points, viscosity, specific gravity, penetration, doctor solution, distillation, and corrosion, using test and laboratory equipment, such as hydrometers, fractionators, distillation apparatus, and analytical scales. Analyzes content of products to determine presence of gases, such as propane, iso-butane, butane, iso-pentane, and ethene. Determines hydrocarbon composition of gasolines, blending stocks and gases, using fractional distillation equipment, gas chromatography, and mass spectrometer. Operates fractionation column to separate crude oil into oils with different boiling points to determine their properties. Analyzes composition of products to determine quantitative presence of gum, sulfur, aromatics, olefins, water, and sediment. Compares color of liquid product with charts to determine processing factors measurable by color. May test air and water samples to detect industrial pollutants. ● **GED:** R4, M4, L3 ● **SVP:** 1-2 yrs ● **Academic:** Ed=H, Eng=S ● **Work Field:** 211 ● **MPSMS:** 501 ● **Aptitudes:** G2, V3, N2, S3, P3, Q4, K4, F3, M3, E4, C3 ● **Temperaments:** J, T ● **Physical:** Stg=L; Freq: R, H, I, N, D, A, X ● **Work Env:** Noise=L; Occas: A, O ● **Salary:** 2 ● **Outlook:** 3

TESTER (profess. & kin.) ● DOT #011.361-010 ● OES: 35199 ● Alternate titles: PHYSICAL TESTER; TESTING-MACHINE OPERATOR. Measures tensile strength, hardness, ductility, or other physical properties of metal specimens, using following prescribed series of operations: Determines tensile strength on tension-testing machines. Measures dimensions of specimen with scales and micrometers and records measurements. Screws or clamps specimen in holders on machine. Clamps extensometer onto specimen and connects wire from extensometer to automatic stress-strain recorder. Turns handwheels or moves levers to apply tension to specimen at specified rate. Notes reading of indicator dial on control panel of machine or observes stress-strain curve (curve obtained by plotting applied tension against resultant elongation) being drawn by recorder to determine yield point and tensile strength of specimen. Removes pieces of broken specimen from machine, fits them together, and measures amount of elongation. Makes simple calculations of values, such as unit tensile strength and percentage elongation, using tables. Records readings and calculations on special forms. Measures hardness of specimens [HARDNESS INSPECTOR (heat treating) 504.387-010]. Measures ductility of sheet metal specimens in sheet metal testing machine. May test specimens for plasticity and compression. May specialize in testing iron or steel sheets for ductility and be designated Sheet Tester (steel & rel.). ● **GED:** R4, M4, L3 ● **SVP:** 6 mos-1 yr ● **Academic:** Ed=A, Eng=S ● **Work Field:** 211 ● **MPSMS:** 540 ● **Aptitudes:** G3, V3, N3, S3, P3, Q3, K3, F3, M3, E4, C4 ● **Temperaments:** J, T ● **Physical:** Stg=L; Freq: R, H, I, N, A Occas: X ● **Work Env:** Noise=N; ● **Salary:** 2 ● **Outlook:** 3

ULTRASOUND TECHNOLOGIST (medical ser.) ● DOT #078.364-010 ● OES: 32998 ● Alternate titles: DIAGNOSTIC MEDICAL SONOGRAPHER. Produces two-dimensional ultrasonic recordings of internal organs, using ultrasound equipment, for use by physician in diagnosis of disease and study of malfunction of organs: Selects equipment for use in ultrasound setup according to specifications of examination. Explains process to patient, and instructs and assists patient in assuming physical position for examination. Selects transducer and adjusts equipment controls according to organ to be examined, depth of field, and other specifications of test. Keys test data and patient information into computer of ultrasound equipment to maintain record of test results. Moves transducer, by hand, over specified area of body and observes sound wave display screen to monitor quality of ultrasonic pattern produced. Starts equipment which produces images of internal organs and records diagnostic data on magnetic tape, computer disk, strip printout, or film. Photographs images of organs shown

on display module, or removes strip printout from equipment, to obtain permanent record of internal examination. Discusses test results with supervisor or attending physician. ● **GED:** R5, M4, L4 ● **SVP:** 2-4 yrs ● **Academic:** Ed=A, Eng=G ● **Work Field:** 294 ● **MPSMS:** 925 ● **Aptitudes:** G3, V3, N3, S2, P2, Q3, K3, F3, M3, E5, C4 ● **Temperaments:** J, P, T ● **Physical:** Stg=L; Freq: R, H, I, T, G, N, D, A Occas: S, E, X ● **Work Env:** Noise=Q; ● **Salary:** 4 ● **Outlook:** 4

WEATHER OBSERVER (profess. & kin.) ● DOT #025.267-014 ● OES: 24501 ● Alternate titles: METEOROLOGICAL TECHNICIAN. Observes and records weather conditions for use in forecasting: Periodically observes general weather, sky and visibility conditions, and reads weather instruments including thermometers, barometers, and hygrometers to ascertain elements, such as temperature, barometric pressure, humidity, wind velocity, and precipitation. Transmits and receives weather data from other stations over teletype machine. May collect upper-air data on temperature, humidity, and winds, using weather balloon and radiosonde equipment. May conduct pilot briefings. ● **GED:** R4, M4, L4 ● **SVP:** 1-2 yrs ● **Academic:** Ed=H, Eng=S ● **Work Field:** 232, 251 ● **MPSMS:** 725 ● **Aptitudes:** G3, V3, N2, S3, P2, Q2, K5, F4, M5, E5, C5 ● **Temperaments:** J ● **Physical:** Stg=L; Freq: N, A Occas: R, H, I ● **Work Env:** Noise=N; ● **Salary:** 4 ● **Outlook:** 1

GOE: 02.04.02
Life Sciences

AEROSPACE PHYSIOLOGICAL TECHNICIAN (military ser.) ● DOT #199.682-010 ● OES: 39998 ● Operates physiological training devices, such as pressure suits, pressure chamber, parasail equipment, and ejection seats, that simulate flying conditions, to indoctrinate flying personnel to physical and physiological stresses encountered in flight: Interviews trainees to obtain physiological and medical histories to detect evidence of disqualifying conditions, prior to simulated flight. Moves levers, turns knobs, and presses buttons on control panel to regulate gas and airflow, temperature, and barometric pressure in pressure chamber to simulate flying conditions at varying altitudes and speeds. Operates altitude pressure suit control console which adjusts pressure inside flying suits and helmets. Operates parasail training equipment, such as tow reel, tow truck, radio equipment, and meteorological devices. Adjusts seat, harness, and headrest of ejection tower for safety of personnel. Places ammunition in catapult chamber to load catapult for firing. Fires catapult that ejects seat to simulate ejection from aircraft. ● **GED:** R4, M3, L3 ● **SVP:** 1-2 yrs ● **Academic:** Ed=H, Eng=G ● **Work Field:** 281, 296 ● **MPSMS:** 732, 601 ● **Aptitudes:** G3, V4, N4, S3, P3, Q4, K3, F3, M3, E5, C4 ● **Temperaments:** J, T ● **Physical:** Stg=S; Freq: R, H, I, N, D Occas: C, B, T, G, X ● **Work Env:** Noise=N; ● **Salary:** 4 ● **Outlook:** 3

BIOCHEMISTRY TECHNOLOGIST (medical ser.) ● DOT #078.261-010 ● OES: 32910 ● Alternate titles: MEDICAL TECHNOLOGIST, CHEMISTRY; TECHNOLOGIST, BIOCHEMISTRY. Performs qualitative and quantitative chemical analyses of body fluids and exudates, following instructions, to provide information used in diagnosis and treatment of diseases: Tests specimens, such as urine, blood, spinal fluid, and gastric juices, for presence and quantity of sugar, albumin, drugs, toxins, and blood gases such as oxygen. Prepares solutions used in chemical analysis. Calibrates and maintains manual and computer-controlled analyzers, spectrophotometers, colorimeters, flame photometers, and other equipment used in quantitative and qualitative analysis. May take blood samples. ● **GED:** R5, M4, L5 ● **SVP:** 2-4 yrs ● **Academic:** Ed=B, Eng=G ● **Work Field:** 294, 211 ● **MPSMS:** 925 ● **Aptitudes:** G2, V2, N2, S3, P2, Q3, K3, F2, M3, E5, C3 ● **Temperaments:** J, T, V ● **Physical:** Stg=L; Freq: R, H, I, N Occas: S, E, T, G, A, X ● **Work Env:** Noise=Q; Occas: T, O ● **Salary:** 4 ● **Outlook:** 3

BIOLOGICAL AIDE (agriculture) ● DOT #049.364-018 ● OES: 24501 ● Assists research workers in experiments in biology, bacteriology, plant pathology, mycology, and related agricultural sciences: Sets up laboratory and field equipment, performs routine tests, and keeps records of plant growth, experimental plots, greenhouse activity, use of insecticides, bee hives, and other agricultural experimentation. Cleans and maintains field and laboratory equipment. ● **GED:** R3, M3, L3 ●

SVP: 1-2 yrs ● **Academic:** Ed=H, Eng=S ● **Work Field:** 251, 003 ● **MPSMS:** 300, 310 ● **Aptitudes:** G3, V3, N4, S3, P3, Q4, K3, F4, M3, E4, C4 ● **Temperaments:** R ● **Physical:** Stg=M; Occas: S, K, O, W, R, H, I, E, T, G, N, D, A, X, V ● **Work Env:** Noise=N; Freq: W Occas: C, H, U, A ● **Salary:** 1 ● **Outlook:** 3

BIOLOGY SPECIMEN TECHNICIAN (profess. & kin.) ● DOT #041.381-010 ● OES: 24501 ● Prepares and embeds in plastic, biological specimens of plant and animal life for use as instructional aids: Selects plant or animal specimen in preserved or dried state. Dissects animal and cleans all matter from skeletal structures. Prepares slices or cross sections of small animals, embryos, or cross sections of animal organs, such as glands, kidneys, hearts, or eyes. Selects, trims, and stains a variety of stalks, flowers, and leaves to show plant structure and systems. Selects different stains to clearly indicate support structure, circulatory system, or other feature of plant or animal. Assembles and positions components of specimen in mold, using pins and holding devices. Mixes polylite plastic or other material and completes embedding by varied molding techniques. Works with plants, animals, mollusks, insects, and other classes of plants and animals. Identifies type and age of specimen, date of preparation, and type of embedding material used. May operate incubator to grow chicken eggs for embryo specimens. May prepare ecological kits which demonstrate polluting conditions in water, soil, or air. ● **GED:** R4, M3, L3 ● **SVP:** 2-4 yrs ● **Academic:** Ed=A, Eng=S ● **Work Field:** 136, 152 ● **MPSMS:** 732 ● **Aptitudes:** G3, V3, N4, S2, P2, Q4, K2, F2, M2, E5, C3 ● **Temperaments:** J ● **Physical:** Stg=S; Freq: R, H, I, N, A, X ● **Work Env:** Noise=N; ● **Salary:** 4 ● **Outlook:** 3

BIOMEDICAL EQUIPMENT TECHNICIAN (profess. & kin.) ● DOT #019.261-010 ● OES: 85908 ● Alternate titles: BIOMEDICAL ELECTRONICS TECHNICIAN; BIOMEDICAL ENGINEERING TECHNICIAN. Repairs, calibrates, and maintains medical equipment and instrumentation used in health-care delivery field: Inspects and installs medical and related technical equipment in medical and research facilities for use by physicians, nurses, scientists, or engineers involved in researching, monitoring, diagnosing, and treating physical ailments or dysfunctions. Services various equipment and apparatus, such as patient monitors, electrocardiographs, blood-gas analyzers, x-ray units, defibrillators, electrosurgical units, anesthesia apparatus, pacemakers, blood-pressure transducers, spirometers, sterilizers, diathermy equipment, in-house television systems, patient-care computers, and other related technical paraphernalia. Repairs, calibrates, and maintains equipment, using handtools, power tools, measuring devices, and knowledge of manufacturers' manuals, troubleshooting techniques, and preventive-maintenance schedules. Safety-tests medical equipment and health-care facility's structural environment to ensure patient and staff safety from electrical or mechanical hazards. Consults with medical or research staff to ascertain that equipment functions properly and safely, utilizing knowledge of electronics, medical terminology, human anatomy and physiology, chemistry, and physics. May demonstrate and explain correct operation of equipment to medical personnel. May modify or develop instruments or devices, under supervision of medical or engineering staff. May work as salesperson or service technician for equipment manufacturers or their sales representatives. ● **GED:** R4, M4, L4 ● **SVP:** 1-2 yrs ● **Academic:** Ed=A, Eng=S ● **Work Field:** 111 ● **MPSMS:** 580 ● **Aptitudes:** G3, V3, N3, S2, P2, Q3, K3, F3, M3, E5, C3 ● **Temperaments:** J, T ● **Physical:** Stg=L; Freq: R, H, I, N, A, X Occas: S, O ● **Work Env:** Noise=N; ● **Salary:** 3 ● **Outlook:** 3

CEPHALOMETRIC ANALYST (medical ser.) ● DOT #078.384-010 ● OES: 32998 ● Alternate titles: CEPHALOMETRIC TECHNICIAN; CEPHALOMETRIC TRACER; TRACER. Traces head x rays and illustrates cosmetic result of proposed orthodontic treatment: Traces frontal and lateral head x rays onto transparent paper, using template, compass, protractor, and knowledge of cranial-facial skeletal structure. Traces lower teeth from occlusal x ray or photograph to locate key points defining true curve of lower dental arch. Records cephalometric measurements to prepare data for computer analysis, using electronic data recording equipment. Compiles data from tracings and computer plot sheets to illustrate results of proposed surgery or other orthodontic treatment. ● **GED:** R4, M4, L4 ● **SVP:** 1-2 yrs ● **Academic:** Ed=H, Eng=S ● **Work Field:** 242, 282 ● **MPSMS:** 922 ● **Aptitudes:** G3, V3, N3, S3, P3, Q4, K3, F3, M3, E5, C4 ● **Temperaments:** J, T ● **Physical:** Stg=S; Freq: N Occas: R, H, A, X ● **Work Env:** Noise=N; ● **Salary:** 4 ● **Outlook:** 3

CHIEF TECHNOLOGIST, NUCLEAR MEDICINE (medical ser.) ● DOT #078.131-010 ● OES: 32914 ● Alternate titles: CHIEF, NUCLEAR MEDICINE TECHNOLOGIST. Supervises and coordinates activities of NUCLEAR MEDICINE TECHNOLOGISTS (medical ser.) 078.361-018 engaged in preparing, administering, and measuring radioactive isotopes in therapeutic, diagnostic, and tracer studies: Assigns workers to prepare radiopharmaceuticals, perform nuclear medicine studies, and conduct laboratory tests, and monitors activities to ensure efficiency and accuracy of procedures. Writes computer protocols for diagnostic studies. Develops protocols for new and revised procedures and trains department workers in overall operation of department and use of equipment. Administers radiopharmaceuticals under direction of physician or other qualified medical personnel. Implements and supervises radiation safety policies and procedures to ensure safety of personnel and legal requirements are met for handling and disposing of radioactive materials. Assists in coordinating activities with other departments and in resolving operating problems. Performs duties of NUCLEAR MEDICINE TECHNOLOGIST (medical ser.) as needed. ● **GED:** R5, M4, L5 ● **SVP:** 4-10 yrs ● **Academic:** Ed=M, Eng=G ● **Work Field:** 201, 294 ● **MPSMS:** 925 ● **Aptitudes:** G2, V2, N2, S2, P2, Q2, K3, F3, M3, E5, C3 ● **Temperaments:** D, J, P, T ● **Physical:** Stg=L; Freq: R, H, I, T, G, N, A Occas: X ● **Work Env:** Noise=Q; Freq: R Occas: O ● **Salary:** 5 ● **Outlook:** 1

CYTOGENETIC TECHNOLOGIST (medical ser.) ● DOT #078.261-026 ● OES: 32910 ● Prepares, examines, and analyzes chromosomes found in biological specimens, such as amniotic fluids, bone marrow, and blood, to aid in diagnosis and treatment of genetic diseases: Selects and prepares specimen and media for cell culture, using aseptic technique, knowledge of medium components, and cell nutritional requirements. Harvests cell culture at optimum time sequence based on knowledge of cell cycle differences and culture conditions. Prepares slide of cell culture, selects banding technique, and stains slide to make chromosomes visible under microscope, following standard laboratory procedures. Views slide through photomicroscope to count and identify chromosome number and presence of structural abnormality. Photographs slide and prints picture. Cuts images of chromosomes from photograph, identifies number and types of chromosomes, and arranges and attaches chromosomes in numbered pairs on karyotype chart, using standard genetics laboratory practices and nomenclature to identify normal or abnormal chromosomes. Communicates with physicians, family members, and researchers requesting technical information or test results. May supervise subordinate laboratory personnel and be known as Supervisor, Cytogenetic Laboratory (medical ser.). ● **GED:** R5, M4, L5 ● **SVP:** 2-4 yrs ● **Academic:** Ed=A, Eng=S ● **Work Field:** 211 ● **MPSMS:** 925 ● **Aptitudes:** G2, V2, N2, S2, P2, Q3, K3, F2, M2, E5, C3 ● **Temperaments:** J, T ● **Physical:** Stg=S; Freq: R, H, I, N Occas: T, G, A, X ● **Work Env:** Noise=Q; Occas: T, O ● **Salary:** 4 ● **Outlook:** 3

CYTOTECHNOLOGIST (medical ser.) ● DOT #078.281-010 ● OES: 32910 ● Stains, mounts, and studies cells of human body to detect evidence of cancer, hormonal abnormalities, and other pathological conditions, following established standards and practices: Prepares microscopic slides from specimens of blood, scrappings, or other bodily exudates, and fixes and stains slide to preserve specimen and enhance visibility of cells under microscope. Examines slide under microscope to identify abnormalities in cell structure. Reports abnormalities to PATHOLOGIST (medical ser.) 070.061-010. May supervise and coordinate activities of staff of cytology laboratory and be known as Supervisor, Cytology (medical ser.). ● **GED:** R5, M4, L5 ● **SVP:** 1-2 yrs ● **Academic:** Ed=A, Eng=S ● **Work Field:** 211 ● **MPSMS:** 925 ● **Aptitudes:** G2, V2, N3, S1, P1, Q3, K4, F1, M2, E4, C3 ● **Temperaments:** J, T ● **Physical:** Stg=S; Freq: R, H, I, N, X Occas: A ● **Work Env:** Noise=Q; Occas: O ● **Salary:** 4 ● **Outlook:** 4

EMBALMER (personal ser.) ● DOT #338.371-014 ● OES: 39099 ● Prepares bodies for interment in conformity with legal requirements: Washes and dries body, using germicidal soap and towels or hot air drier. Inserts convex celluloid or cotton between eyeball and eyelid to prevent slipping and sinking of eyelid. Presses diaphragm to evacuate air from lungs. May join lips, using needle and thread or wire. Packs body orifices with cotton saturated with embalming fluid to prevent escape of gases or waste matter. Makes incision in arm or thigh, using scalpel, inserts pump tubes into artery, and starts pump that drains blood from circulatory system and replaces blood with embalming fluid. Incises stomach and abdominal walls and probes internal organs, such as bladder and liver, using trocar to withdraw blood and waste matter from organs. Attaches trocar to pump-tube, starts pump, and repeats probing to force embalming fluid into organs. Closes incisions, using needle and suture. Reshapes or reconstructs disfigured or maimed bodies, using materials, such as clay, cotton, plaster of paris, and wax. Applies cosmetics to impart lifelike appearance. Dresses body and places body in casket. May arrange funeral details, such as type of casket or burial dress and place of interment [DIRECTOR, FUNERAL (personal ser.)]. May maintain records, such as itemized list of clothing or valuables delivered with body and names of persons embalmed. ● **GED:** R4, M4, L4 ● **SVP:** 2-4 yrs ● **Academic:** Ed=H, Eng=S ● **Work Field:** 291 ● **Aptitudes:** G2, V3, N3, S3, P2, Q4, K3, F2, M3, E5, C3 ● **Temperaments:** J, T, V ● **Physical:** Stg=H; Freq: R, H, N Occas: S, I, A, X ● **Work Env:** Noise=VQ; Freq: T, O ● **Salary:** 4 ● **Outlook:** 3

FOOD TESTER (any industry) ● DOT #029.361-014 ● OES: 24501 ● Performs standardized qualitative and quantitative tests to determine physical or chemical properties of food or beverage products, or to ensure compliance with company or government quality standards: Conducts standardized tests of food, beverages, additives, and preservatives for flavor, color, texture, nutritional value, or other factors, using incubator, autoclave, ovens, balance scales, refractometer, or other equipment. Tests flavoring and spices for moisture, oil content, coloring, and pungency, using spectrophotometer, stereomicroscope, and ovens. Tests production samples of food for compliance with standards, using spectrometer, pH meter, distillation equipment, balance scales, and other equipment. Refers to tables or computes such factors as moisture, salt content, sediment, or solubility. Smells samples of food for odors or tastes for prescribed flavor. Observes sample smear, sediment disk, or agar sample through microscope to identify bacterial or extraneous matter. Compares test results with standards and records results. Cleans laboratory equipment. May mix ingredients to make reagents. May operate calculating machine to compute percentages of ingredients in finished product. May be identified according to quality or product tested. ● **GED:** R4, M3, L3 ● **SVP:** 6 mos-1 yr ● **Academic:** Ed=A, Eng=S ● **Work Field:** 211, 212 ● **MPSMS:** 380, 390 ● **Aptitudes:** G3, V3, N3, S3, P3, Q3, K3, F3, M3, E5, C3 ● **Temperaments:** J, T ● **Physical:** Stg=L; Freq: R, H, I, N, A Occas: T, G, M, X ● **Work Env:** Noise=N; ● **Salary:** 1 ● **Outlook:** 2

HERBARIUM WORKER (profess. & kin.) ● DOT #041.384-010 ● OES: 24501 ● Fumigates, presses, and mounts plant specimens, and maintains collection records of herbarium maintained by botanical garden, museum, or other institution: Records identification information concerning incoming plants. Places specimens in fumigation cabinet and turns valves to release toxic fumes that destroy insects, fungus, or parasites adhering to specimens. Arranges specimens between sheets of unsized paper so that upper and under portions of leaves, blossoms, and other components are visible, and pads paper with layers of felt and newsprint to protect specimens and form stacks. Places specified number of stacks in pressing frame and writes identification information on top layer of paper on each stack. Secures frame around stacks by tightening frame section with screws, fastening with leather straps, or tying with twine, to compress stacks and press and dry specimens in desired configuration. Mounts dried specimens on heavy paper, using glue, adhesive strips, or needle and thread, taking care to prevent distortion or breakage of specimens. Writes identification information on papers and inserts mounted specimens in labeled envelopes or folders. Files folders in drawers or cabinets according to standard botanical classification system. Maintains card files of specimens in herbarium collection and records of acquisitions, loans, exchanges, or sales of specimens. ● **GED:** R4, M3, L4 ● **SVP:** 6 mos-1 yr ● **Academic:** Ed=H, Eng=S ● **Work Field:** 031, 063, 231 ● **MPSMS:** 310, 732, 969 ● **Aptitudes:** G3, V3, N4, S3, P2, Q3, K3, F3, M3, E5, C4 ● **Temperaments:** J, T, V ● **Physical:** Stg=L; Freq: R, H, I, N Occas: S, O, E, T, G, D, A, X ● **Work Env:** Noise=N; Occas: T ● **Salary:** 3 ● **Outlook:** 2

HISTOTECHNOLOGIST (medical ser.) ● DOT #078.261-030 ● OES: 32910 ● Alternate titles: HISTOLOGIC TECHNOLOGIST; TISSUE TECHNOLOGIST. Prepares histologic slides from tissue sections for microscopic examination and diagnosis by PATHOLOGIST (medical ser.) 070.061-010: Prepares sections of human or animal tissue for immediate examination, using rapid tissue processing and frozen section technique to freeze, cut, mount and stain tissue specimen

received from surgery. Operates computerized laboratory equipment to fix, dehydrate, and infiltrate with wax, tissue specimens to be preserved for study by PATHOLOGIST (medical ser.). Prepares slides of specimens, using specified stain, to enhance visibility under microscope. Examines slides under microscope to ensure tissue preparation meets laboratory requirements. May study slides under microscope to detect deviations from norm and report abnormalities for further study. May supervise activities of laboratory personnel and be known as Supervisor, Histology (medical ser.). ● **GED:** R5, M4, L5 ● **SVP:** 1-2 yrs ● **Academic:** Ed=A, Eng=S ● **Work Field:** 211, 294 ● **MPSMS:** 925 ● **Aptitudes:** G2, V2, N2, S3, P2, Q3, K3, F1, M1, E4, C2 ● **Temperaments:** J, T ● **Physical:** Stg=L; Freq: R, H, I, N, D, A, X Occas: E, T, G ● **Work Env:** Noise=Q; Occas: O ● **Salary:** 3 ● **Outlook:** 4

IMMUNOHEMATOLOGIST (medical ser.) ● DOT #078.261-046 ● OES: 32998 ● Performs immunohematology tests, recommends blood problem solutions to doctors, and serves as consultant to blood bank and community: Visually inspects blood in specimen tubes for hemolysis. Centrifuges blood specimen to separate red cells from serum and tests separated serum to detect presence of antibodies. Interprets reactions observed to devise experiments and suggest techniques that will resolve patient's blood problems. Combines known and unknown cells with serum in test tubes and selects reagents, such as albumin, protolytic enzymes, and anti-human globutin, for individual tests to enhance and make visible reactions of agglutination and hemolysis. Processes various combinations in centrifuge and examines resulting samples under microscope to identify evidence of agglutination or hemolysis. Repeats and varies tests until normal suspension of reagents, serum, and red cells is attained. Interprets results obtained and identifies specific antibodies. Writes blood specifications to meet patient's need, on basis of test results, and applies knowledge of blood classification system to locate donor's blood. Performs immunohematology tests on donor's blood to confirm matching blood types. Requisitions and sends blood to supply patient's need, and prepares written report to inform physician of test results and of required volume of blood to administer. Evaluates completeness of immunohematology tests. May advise MEDICAL TECHNOLOGISTS (medical ser.) 078.261-038 in techniques of microscopic identification of precipitation, agglutination, or hemolysis in blood that leads to resolution of problems. ● **GED:** R5, M3, L5 ● **SVP:** 4-10 yrs ● **Academic:** Ed=B, Eng=G ● **Work Field:** 211, 294 ● **MPSMS:** 925 ● **Aptitudes:** G2, V2, N3, S1, P1, Q3, K2, F2, M2, E5, C2 ● **Temperaments:** J, P, T ● **Physical:** Stg=L; Const: H, I, N, X Freq: A Occas: R, T, G ● **Work Env:** Noise=Q; ● **Salary:** 5 ● **Outlook:** 4

LABORATORY ASSISTANT, BLOOD AND PLASMA (medical ser.) ● DOT #078.687-010 ● OES: 66099 ● Performs routine laboratory tasks related to processing whole blood and blood components: Centrifuges whole blood to produce various components including packed red cells, platelet concentrate, washed red cells, and plasma. Examines blood stock at designated intervals to confirm that all units are in satisfactory condition. Observes thermostats on storage units to confirm that temperature remains constant at designated temperature. Inspects blood units returned from hospitals to determine whether plasma can be salvaged and if so refers to plasma salvage unit. Confirms that sedimentation has occurred, that color is normal, and that containers are in satisfactory condition. Cleans and maintains laboratory equipment, supplies, and laboratory. Performs related clerical duties including updating statistical records, labeling tubes, and scheduling processing runs. ● **GED:** R3, M3, L3 ● **SVP:** 1-2 yrs ● **Academic:** Ed=H, Eng=S ● **Work Field:** 211 ● **MPSMS:** 493 ● **Aptitudes:** G3, V3, N3, S4, P4, Q3, K3, F3, M3, E4, C4 ● **Temperaments:** J, R, T ● **Physical:** Stg=L; Const: N Freq: R, H, I Occas: X ● **Work Env:** Noise=N; ● **Salary:** 3 ● **Outlook:** 3

LABORATORY ASSISTANT, CULTURE MEDIA (pharmaceut.) ● DOT #559.384-010 ● OES: 24501 ● Alternate titles: LABORATORY AIDE; TECHNICAL ASSISTANT. Prepares culture media used to develop vaccines and toxoids or to conduct chemical, microscopic, and bacteriologic tests: Measures and weighs ingredients, such as food source, chemicals, preservatives, and vitamins, to prepare growth medium, using scales, graduated flasks, syringes, pipettes, and standard formulas. Adjusts controls of equipment, such as pumps, filters, steam kettles, and autoclaves, to obtain uniform consistency of sterile medium. Removes sample of medium from batch and tests sample for consistency, potency, and sterility, according to standardized procedures. Pours medium or adjusts controls on automatic equipment that dispenses medium into containers, such as petri dishes, test tubes, or storage drums. Seals containers and prepares and affixes identification labels to containers. Maintains production and test records. May order supplies. May mix ingredients to prepare stains used in tests. ● **GED:** R3, M3, L3 ● **SVP:** 6 mos-1 yr ● **Academic:** Ed=N, Eng=S ● **Work Field:** 147 ● **MPSMS:** 493 ● **Aptitudes:** G3, V3, N3, S3, P3, Q3, K3, F3, M3, E5, C4 ● **Temperaments:** J, T, V ● **Physical:** Stg=L; Freq: R, H, I, N Occas: S, T, G ● **Work Env:** Noise=L; Freq: T ● **Salary:** 2 ● **Outlook:** 4

LABORATORY TECHNICIAN, PHARMACEUTICAL (pharmaceut.) ● DOT #559.361-010 ● OES: 32910 ● Prepares vaccines, biologicals, and serums for prevention of animal diseases: Inoculates fertilized eggs, broths, or other bacteriological media with organisms. Incubates bacteria for specified period and prepares vaccines and serums by standard laboratory methods. Tests vaccines for sterility and virus inactivity. Prepares standard volumetric solutions and reagents used in testing. ● **GED:** R5, M4, L4 ● **SVP:** 1-2 yrs ● **Academic:** Ed=A, Eng=S ● **Work Field:** 147 ● **MPSMS:** 493 ● **Aptitudes:** G3, V3, N3, S3, P3, Q4, K3, F2, M3, E5, C4 ● **Temperaments:** J, T, V ● **Physical:** Stg=L; Freq: R, H, I, N, D, A Occas: E, X ● **Work Env:** Noise=Q; ● **Salary:** 3 ● **Outlook:** 3

MEDICAL-LABORATORY TECHNICIAN (medical ser.) ● DOT #078.381-014 ● OES: 32910 ● Alternate titles: LABORATORY ASSISTANT; MEDICAL TECHNICIAN. Performs routine tests in medical laboratory to provide data for use in diagnosis and treatment of disease: Conducts quantitative and qualitative chemical analyses of body fluids, such as blood, urine, and spinal fluid, under supervision of MEDICAL TECHNOLOGIST (medical ser.) 078.261-038. Performs blood counts, using microscope. Conducts blood tests for transfusion purposes. May draw blood from patient's finger, ear lobe, or vein, observing principles of asepsis to obtain blood samples. May specialize in hematology, blood bank, cytology, histology, or chemistry. ● **GED:** R4, M4, L4 ● **SVP:** 6 mos-1 yr ● **Academic:** Ed=A, Eng=S ● **Work Field:** 211 ● **MPSMS:** 925 ● **Aptitudes:** G3, V3, N3, S3, P3, Q4, K3, F3, M3, E5, C3 ● **Temperaments:** J, T ● **Physical:** Stg=L; Freq: R, H, I, N, A, X Occas: D ● **Work Env:** Noise=N; Occas: O ● **Salary:** 3 ● **Outlook:** 4

MEDICAL TECHNOLOGIST (medical ser.) ● DOT #078.261-038 ● OES: 32910 ● Performs medical laboratory tests, procedures, experiments, and analyses to provide data for diagnosis, treatment, and prevention of disease: Conducts chemical analyses of body fluids, such as blood, urine, and spinal fluid, to determine presence of normal and abnormal components. Studies blood cells, their numbers, and morphology, using microscopic technique. Performs blood group, type, and compatibility tests for transfusion purposes. Analyzes test results and enters findings in computer. Engages in medical research under direction of MEDICAL TECHNOLOGIST, CHIEF (medical ser.) 078.161-010. May train and supervise students. May specialize in area such as hematology, blood-bank, serology, immunohematology, bacteriology, histology, or chemistry. ● **GED:** R5, M4, L5 ● **SVP:** 2-4 yrs ● **Academic:** Ed=B, Eng=S ● **Work Field:** 211, 294 ● **MPSMS:** 925 ● **Aptitudes:** G2, V2, N2, S3, P1, Q2, K2, F2, M3, E5, C3 ● **Temperaments:** J, T ● **Physical:** Stg=L; Freq: R, H, I, T, G, N, A Occas: E, X ● **Work Env:** Noise=N; ● **Salary:** 4 ● **Outlook:** 4

MEDICAL TECHNOLOGIST, CHIEF (medical ser.) ● DOT #078.161-010 ● OES: 32910 ● Alternate titles: MEDICAL LABORATORY MANAGER. Directs and coordinates activities of workers engaged in performing chemical, microscopic, and bacteriologic tests to obtain data for use in diagnosis and treatment of diseases: Assigns workers to duties and oversees performance of tests in fields of microbiology, chemistry, histology, hematology, immunohematology, and serology. Purchases or directs purchase of laboratory equipment and supplies. Reviews test results to ensure quality control. Coordinates and conducts education and training programs for medical technology students and personnel. ● **GED:** R5, M4, L5 ● **SVP:** 4-10 yrs ● **Academic:** Ed=A, Eng=G ● **Work Field:** 211, 294, 295 ● **MPSMS:** 925 ● **Aptitudes:** G1, V2, N2, S2, P1, Q2, K2, F2, M3, E4, C2 ● **Temperaments:** D, J, P, T ● **Physical:** Stg=L; Const: N Freq: R, H, I, T, G, X Occas: S, A ● **Work Env:** Noise=Q; ● **Salary:** 5 ● **Outlook:** 1

MICROBIOLOGY TECHNOLOGIST (medical ser.) ● DOT #078.261-014 ● OES: 32910 ● Alternate titles: MEDICAL TECH-

NOLOGIST, MICROBIOLOGY. Cultivates, isolates, and assists in identifying bacteria and other microbial organisms, and performs various bacteriological, mycological, virological, mycobacteriological, and parasitological tests: Receives human or animal body materials from autopsy or diagnostic cases, or collects specimens directly from patients, under supervision of laboratory director. Examines materials for evidence of microbial organisms. Makes parasitological tests of specimens. May instruct medical laboratory students and other medical personnel in laboratory procedures. May supervise other technologists and be known as Supervisor, Microbiology Technologists (medical ser.). ● **GED:** R5, M4, L5 ● **SVP:** 2-4 yrs ● **Academic:** Ed=B, Eng=G ● **Work Field:** 211, 294 ● **MPSMS:** 925 ● **Aptitudes:** G2, V2, N2, S3, P1, Q2, K2, F2, M3, E5, C3 ● **Temperaments:** J, T ● **Physical:** Stg=L; Const: N, X Freq: H, I, T, G, A Occas: R ● **Work Env:** Noise=Q; ● **Salary:** 4 ● **Outlook:** 4

MORGUE ATTENDANT (medical ser.) ● DOT #355.667-010 ● OES: 66005 ● Prepares bodies, specimens of human organs, and morgue room to assist PATHOLOGIST (medical ser.) in postmortem examinations: Places body in compartment tray of refrigerator or on autopsy table, using portable hoist and stretcher. Lays out surgical instruments and laboratory supplies for postmortem examinations. Washes table, storage trays, and instruments, sharpens knives, and replaces soiled linens. Records identifying information for morgue file. Releases body to authorized person. May close post mortem incisions, using surgical needle and cord. May fill cranium with plaster. May feed, water, and clean quarters for animals used in medical research. May prepare preserving solutions according to formulas. May preserve specimens and stain slides. May photograph specimens. ● **GED:** R3, M2, L2 ● **SVP:** 3-6 mos ● **Academic:** Ed=N, Eng=N ● **Work Field:** 291, 031 ● **MPSMS:** 929 ● **Aptitudes:** G3, V4, N4, S4, P3, Q4, K3, F3, M3, E4, C5 ● **Temperaments:** R ● **Physical:** Stg=M; Freq: R, H Occas: S, I, N ● **Work Env:** Noise=Q; Occas: T, O ● **Salary:** 2 ● **Outlook:** 3

OPHTHALMIC PHOTOGRAPHER (medical ser.) ● DOT #143.362-014 ● OES: 34023 ● Photographs medical phenomena of eye to document diseases, surgeries, treatments, and congenital problems, to aid OPHTHALMOLOGIST (medical ser.) 070.101-058 in diagnosis and treatment of eye disorders: Focuses specialized microscope and cameras to take two- and three-dimensional photographs of external, anterior, and posterior segments of eye. Monitors patient's gaze through lens of microscope and camera to ensure that patient complies with instructions to obtain desired results. Selects filters to modify light. Injects contrast medium into vein of patient and photographs fluorescent dye as it flows through retina or iris vessels to obtain angiogram of eye. Develops exposed film, and mounts and labels slides for inclusion on patient's medical chart. May photograph eye to document research studies. ● **GED:** R4, M4, L4 ● **SVP:** 1-2 yrs ● **Academic:** Ed=A, Eng=G ● **Work Field:** 201, 294 ● **MPSMS:** 753, 925 ● **Aptitudes:** G3, V3, N3, S3, P2, Q3, K3, F3, M3, E4, C3 ● **Temperaments:** P, T ● **Physical:** Stg=L; Const: N Freq: H, I, G, F, A Occas: R, E, T, X ● **Work Env:** Noise=Q; Freq: T ● **Salary:** 5 ● **Outlook:** 3

PHLEBOTOMIST (medical ser.) ● DOT #079.364-022 ● OES: 66099 ● Draws blood from patients or donors in hospital, blood bank, or similar facility for analysis or other medical purposes: Assembles equipment, such as tourniquet, needles, disposable containers for needles, blood collection devices, gauze, cotton, and alcohol on work tray, according to requirements for specified tests or procedures. Verifies or records identity of patient or donor and converses with patient or donor to allay fear of procedure. Applies tourniquet to arm, locates accessible vein, swabs puncture area with antiseptic, and inserts needle into vein to draw blood into collection tube or bag. Withdraws needle, applies treatment to puncture site, and labels and stores blood container for subsequent processing. May prick finger to draw blood. May conduct interviews, take vital signs, and draw and test blood samples to screen donors at blood bank. ● **GED:** R3, M2, L3 ● **SVP:** 1-3 mos ● **Academic:** Ed=H, Eng=G ● **Work Field:** 294 ● **MPSMS:** 925 ● **Aptitudes:** G3, V3, N4, S3, P3, Q3, K2, F2, M2, E5, C4 ● **Temperaments:** J, P ● **Physical:** Stg=L; Freq: R, H, I, E, T, G, N Occas: S, A, X ● **Work Env:** Noise=Q; ● **Salary:** 4 ● **Outlook:** 4

POLYGRAPH EXAMINER (profess. & kin.) ● DOT #199.267-026 ● OES: 39998 ● Alternate titles: LIE-DETECTION EXAMINER. Interrogates and screens individuals to detect deception or to verify truthfulness, using polygraph equipment and standard polygraph techniques: Attaches apparatus to individual to measure and record changes in respiration, blood pressure, and electrical resistance of skin as result of perspiration changes. Evaluates reactions to questions of a non-emotional nature. Interprets and diagnoses individual's emotional responses to key questions recorded on graph. Visits morgues, examines scene of crime, or contacts other sources, when assigned to criminal case, to gather information for use in interrogating suspects, witnesses, and other persons. Appears in court as witness on matters relating to polygraph examinations, according to formalized procedures. Prepares reports and keeps records on polygraph examinations. May instruct classes in polygraph interrogation techniques, methods, and uses. When analyzing voice stress charted on moving tape by needle of recording device for deception or truthfulness verification, may be designated Psychological Stress Evaluator (profess. & kin.). ● **GED:** R5, M3, L5 ● **SVP:** 6 mos-1 yr ● **Academic:** Ed=H, Eng=G ● **Work Field:** 211, 271 ● **MPSMS:** 951 ● **Aptitudes:** G2, V1, N4, S3, P2, Q2, K3, F4, M3, E5, C4 ● **Temperaments:** J ● **Physical:** Stg=L; Freq: R, H, I, T, G, N, A ● **Work Env:** Noise=N; ● **Salary:** 4 ● **Outlook:** 2

PUBLIC-HEALTH MICROBIOLOGIST (government ser.) ● DOT #041.261-010 ● OES: 24311 ● Conducts experiments to detect presence of harmful or pathogenic bacteria in water, food supply, or general environment of community and to control or eliminate sources of possible pollution or contagion: Makes periodic laboratory counts of bacteria in water supply. Analyzes samples of sewage for harmful micro-organisms and for rate of sludge purification by aerobic bacteria. Examines milk, shellfish, and other food items for micro-organisms constituting menace to public health. Cooperates with hospitals and clinical laboratories in identifying micro-organisms taken from diseased persons to determine presence of bacteria causing contagious or epidemic diseases. May inoculate members of community against contagious diseases. ● **GED:** R6, M6, L6 ● **SVP:** 2-4 yrs ● **Academic:** Ed=B, Eng=S ● **Work Field:** 211 ● **MPSMS:** 732, 920 ● **Aptitudes:** G1, V1, N2, S2, P2, Q3, K3, F2, M2, E5, C4 ● **Temperaments:** J, P, T ● **Physical:** Stg=L; Freq: R, H Occas: I, T, G, D, A, X ● **Work Env:** Noise=N; Occas: T ● **Salary:** 4 ● **Outlook:** 4

SEED ANALYST (profess. & kin.) ● DOT #040.361-014 ● OES: 24501 ● Alternate titles: FARM-SEED SPECIALIST. Tests seed for germination, purity, and weed content: Plants definite number of seeds in box of pure soil and counts number of plants that grow to calculate percentage of germination. Inspects seed with magnifying glass or microscope for chaff, bits of wood, and weed content (any seed other than the one under consideration). ● **GED:** R4, M4, L4 ● **SVP:** 2-4 yrs ● **Academic:** Ed=A, Eng=S ● **Work Field:** 211 ● **MPSMS:** 311 ● **Aptitudes:** G3, V3, N3, S3, P2, Q4, K4, F3, M4, E5, C3 ● **Temperaments:** J, T ● **Physical:** Stg=L; Occas: R, H, I, E, N, A, X ● **Work Env:** Noise=N; Occas: W ● **Salary:** 3 ● **Outlook:** 2

TOXICOLOGIST (pharmaceut.) ● DOT #022.081-010 ● OES: 24398 ● Conducts research on toxic effects of cosmetic products and ingredients on laboratory animals for manufacturer of cosmetics: Applies cosmetic ingredient or cosmetic being developed to exposed shaved skin area of test animal and observes and examines skin periodically for possible development of abnormalities, inflammation, or irritation. Injects ingredient into test animal, using hypodermic needle and syringe, and periodically observes animal for signs of toxicity. Injects antidotes to determine which antidote best neutralizes toxic effects. Tests and analyzes blood samples for presence of toxic conditions, using microscope and laboratory test equipment. Dissects dead animals, using surgical instruments, and examines organs to determine effects of cosmetic ingredients being tested. Prepares formal reports of test results. ● **GED:** R5, M4, L5 ● **SVP:** 4-10 yrs ● **Academic:** Ed=M, Eng=S ● **Work Field:** 251 ● **MPSMS:** 732 ● **Aptitudes:** G2, V2, N3, S3, P2, Q3, K3, F3, M3, E5, C4 ● **Temperaments:** J, T ● **Physical:** Stg=L; Freq: R, H, I, N Occas: X ● **Work Env:** Noise=N; Occas: O ● **Salary:** 5 ● **Outlook:** 2

VECTOR CONTROL ASSISTANT (government ser.) ● DOT #049.364-014 ● OES: 24501 ● Assists public health staff in activities concerned with identification, prevention, and control of vectors (disease-carrying insects and rodents): Carries and sets up field equipment to be used in surveys of number and type of vectors in area. Sets traps and cuts through brush and weeds to obtain specimens of vector population for use in laboratory tests, using sweep. Prepares, mounts, and stores specimens, following instructions of supervisor. Prepares reports of field surveys and laboratory tests based upon information obtained from personnel involved in specific activities, for use in planning and carrying out projects for prevention and control of vectors. ● **GED:** R4, M2, L3 ● **SVP:** 6 mos-1 yr ● **Academic:** Ed=H, Eng=S ● **Work Field:** 211 ● **MPSMS:** 920 ● **Aptitudes:** G3, V3, N3, S3, P3, Q3, K4, F3, M3, E3, C4 ● **Temperaments:** J ● **Physical:** Stg=L; Freq: R, H, I, N Occas: S, K, O, T, G, X ● **Work Env:** Noise=N; Occas: W, U ● **Salary:** 2 ● **Outlook:** 3

Plants and Animals 03

An interest in activities to do with plants and animals, usually in an outdoor setting.

You can satisfy this interest by working in farming, forestry, fishing, and related fields. You may like doing physical work outdoors, such as working on a farm. You may enjoy animals. Perhaps training or taking care of animals would appeal to you. You may have management ability. You could own, operate, or manage farms or related businesses or services.

Managerial Work: Plants and Animals   03.01

Workers in this group operate or manage farming, fishing, forestry, and horticultural service business of many kinds. Some of them breed specialty plants and animals. Others provide services to increase production or beautify land areas. Many of them work in rural or woodland areas, on farms, ranches, and forest preserves. Others find employment with commercial nurseries, landscaping firms, business services, or government agencies located in large and small communities all over the country. Many are self-employed, operating their own large or small businesses.

✓ What kind of work would you do?

Your work activities would depend upon your specific job. For example, you might:

- plan and oversee the sales and shipment of farm crops or animals.
- arrange for the purchase of seed, livestock, fertilizer, feed, and other supplies.
- advise poultry farmers on ways to improve the quality of their products.
- breed earthworms and sell them as bait, or to companies that produce fish food or soil conditioners.
- study market trends to plan the type and quantity of crops to plant.
- plan and direct projects for cutting timber and replanting forests.

✓ What skills and abilities do you need for this kind of work?

To do this kind of work, you must be able to:

- understand and apply procedures related to a particular kind of activity in a practical way, such as rotating crops so that farm soil will stay fertile, treating trees with the right

chemicals to prevent the spread of disease, or feeding cattle to produce beef of prime quality.
- plan an entire activity and see that it is carried out.
- keep accurate financial and production records.
- get along well with other people in many different work situations, such as overseeing their activities or negotiating with them for the purchase of materials or the sale of products.
- spend much of your time outdoors in all kinds of weather, overseeing or participating in the work being done.

✓ How do you know if you would like or could learn to do this kind of work?

The following questions may give you clues about yourself as you consider this group of jobs.

- Have you raised plants or animals as a hobby? Would you like to take courses to help you expand your hobby?
- Have you been a leader in scouting or any other outdoor group? Do you enjoy planning and directing activities?
- Have you been a member of FFA or 4-H? Did you complete any projects which required planning, budgeting, and record keeping?

✓ How can you prepare for and enter this kind of work?

Occupations in this group usually require education and/or training extending from one year to over ten years, depending upon the specific kind of work. Most of the jobs in this group are open only to people with work experience. Growing up on a farm is good initial preparation for many of these jobs. Formal training for management jobs is available at the high school and post-high school levels. For example, vocational agriculture courses are offered in many high schools with similar courses available to adults at night and on weekends. Programs such as agribusiness, animal husbandry, forest management, and small business management are provided by many colleges and technical schools. Each state has at least one college which offers four or five year programs in related fields.

Workers with training in management and farm experience qualify for jobs with cooperative groups, corporations, and large farm owners. Some workers form companies which contract to provide farm services.

Courses in horticulture, gardening, or turf management provide preparation for jobs in nurseries, tree services, and landscaping firms.

✓ What else should you consider about these jobs?

Federal loans are available to qualified people who wish to start their own businesses. Most of these businesses are small and hire few people.

If you think you would like to do this kind of work, look at the job titles listed below.

■ ■ ■

GOE: 03.01.01
Farming

FARMER, FIELD CROP (agriculture) ● DOT #404.161-010 ● OES: 79998 ● Plants, cultivates, and harvests specialty crops, such as alfalfa, cotton, hops, peanuts, mint, sugarcane, and tobacco, applying knowledge of growth characteristics of individual crop, and soil, climate, and market conditions: Determines number and kind of employees to be hired, acreage to be tilled, and varieties and quantities of plants to be grown. Selects and purchases plant stock and farm machinery, implements, and supplies. Decides when and how to plant, cultivate, and irrigate plants and harvest crops, applying knowledge of plant culture. Attaches farm implements, such as plow, disc, and seed drill to tractor and drives tractor in fields to till soil and plant and cultivate crops. Drives and operates farm machinery to spray fertilizers, herbicides, and pesticides and haul harvested crops. Hires, assigns duties to, and oversees activities of farm workers. Demonstrates and explains farm work techniques and safety regulations to new workers. Maintains employee and financial records. Arranges with buyers for sale and shipment of crop. May install irrigation system(s) and irrigate fields. May set poles and string wires and twine on poles to form trellises. May lubricate, adjust, and make minor repairs on farm machinery, implements, and equipment, using mechanic's handtools and work aids. May plant seeds in cold-frame bed and cover bed with cloth or glass to protect seedlings from weather. May transplant seedlings in rows, by hand or using transplanter machine. May grade and package crop for marketing. May be designated according to crop grown as Cotton Grower (agriculture); Ginseng Farmer (agriculture); Hay Farmer (agriculture); Hop Grower (agriculture); Peanut Farmer (agriculture); Sugarcane Planter (agriculture); Tobacco Grower (agriculture). ● **GED:** R4, M4, L4 ● **SVP:** 2-4 yrs ● **Academic:** Ed=H, Eng=N ● **Work Field:** 003 ● **MPSMS:** 300 ● **Aptitudes:** G2, V3, N3, S2, P3, Q3, K4, F4, M4, E4, C4 ● **Temperaments:** D, J ● **Physical:** Stg=M; Freq: R, H, T, G, F, D, V Occas: C, S, K, O, W, I, N, X ● **Work Env:** Noise=L; Freq: O ● **Salary:** 4 ● **Outlook:** 1

FARMER, FRUIT CROPS, BUSH AND VINE (agriculture) ● DOT #403.161-014 ● OES: 79998 ● Alternate titles: BERRY GROWER. Plants and cultivates fruit bushes and vines and harvests crops, such as grapes, cranberries, and strawberries, applying knowledge of growth characteristics of specific varieties and soil, climate, and market conditions: Determines varieties and quantities of plants to be grown, acreage to be tilled, and employees to be hired. Selects and purchases plant stock and farm machines, implements, and supplies. Decides when and how to plant, bud, graft, prune, sucker, cultivate and irrigate plants, and harvest crop, based on knowledge of vine-crop culture. Attaches farm implements, such as harrow and ditcher, to tractor and drives tractor in fields to till soil. Drives and operates farm machinery to spray fertilizers, herbicides, and pesticides and haul fruit boxes. Hires, as-

signs duties to, and oversees activities of seasonal workers engaged in tilling and irrigating soil, pruning plants, and harvesting and marketing crop. Demonstrates and explains farm work techniques and safety regulations. Maintains employee and financial records. Makes arrangements with buyers for sale and shipment of crop. May make arrangements with AIRPLANE PILOT (agriculture) 196.263-010 to spray and dust fertilizers and pesticides on planted acreage. May install irrigation system(s) and irrigate fields. May set poles, string wires on poles to form trellises, and tie vines and canes to trellis wires. May prune vines and canes to size and shape growth. May lubricate, adjust, and make minor repairs on farm machinery, implements, and equipment, using oilcan, grease gun, and handtools, such as hammer and wrench. May be designated according to crop grown as Blueberry Grower (agriculture); Cranberry Grower (agriculture); Grape Grower (agriculture); Raspberry Grower (agriculture); Strawberry Grower (agriculture). ● **GED:** R4, M4, L4 ● **SVP:** 2-4 yrs ● **Academic:** Ed=H, Eng=N ● **Work Field:** 003 ● **MPSMS:** 303, 305 ● **Aptitudes:** G3, V3, N3, S3, P3, Q4, K3, F4, M3, E4, C4 ● **Temperaments:** D, J, V ● **Physical:** Stg=H; Freq: R, H, T, G Occas: C, S, K, O, N, F, D, X, V ● **Work Env:** Noise=L; Freq: O Occas: W, U, A ● **Salary:** 4 ● **Outlook:** 3

FARMER, GENERAL (agriculture) ● DOT #421.161-010 ● OES: 79998 ● Raises both crops and livestock: Determines kinds and amounts of crops to be grown and livestock to be bred, according to market conditions, weather, and size and location of farm. Selects and purchases seed, fertilizer, farm machinery, livestock, and feed, and assumes responsibility for sale of crop and livestock products. Hires and directs workers engaged in planting, cultivating, and harvesting crops, such as corn, peas, potatoes, strawberries, apples, peanuts, and tobacco, and to raise livestock, such as cattle, sheep, swine, horses, and poultry. Performs various duties of farm workers, depending on size and nature of farm, including setting up and operating farm machinery. ● **GED:** R4, M4, L4 ● **SVP:** 2-4 yrs ● **Academic:** Ed=H, Eng=S ● **Work Field:** 003, 002 ● **MPSMS:** 300, 320 ● **Aptitudes:** G2, V3, N3, S2, P3, Q3, K4, F4, M4, E4, C4 ● **Temperaments:** D, J, V ● **Physical:** Stg=H; Freq: R, H, D Occas: C, S, K, O, I, E, T, G, N, A, X ● **Work Env:** Noise=N; Freq: W, O ● **Salary:** 3 ● **Outlook:** 1

GENERAL MANAGER, FARM (agriculture) ● DOT #180.167-018 ● OES: 71005 ● Alternate titles: RANCH MANAGER. Manages farm concerned with raising, harvesting, packing, and marketing farm products for corporations, cooperatives, and other owners: Analyzes market conditions to determine acreage allocations. Negotiates with bank officials to obtain credit from bank. Purchases farm machinery and equipment and supplies, such as tractors, seed, fertilizer, and chemicals. Hires and discharges personnel. Prepares financial and other management reports. Supervises office personnel engaged in preparing payrolls and keeping records. Visits orchards and fields to inspect and estimate maturity dates of crops and potential crop damage due to harsh weather conditions. Confers with purchasers, and determines when and under what conditions to sell crops, marine life, or forest products. May be designated according to type of crop. ● **GED:** R5, M4, L4 ● **SVP:** 4-10 yrs ● **Academic:** Ed=A, Eng=S ● **Work Field:** 295, 003 ●

MPSMS: 300, 310, 320 ● **Aptitudes:** G2, V2, N2, S3, P3, Q3, K4, F4, M4, E4, C4 ● **Temperaments:** D, I, J, P, V ● **Physical:** Stg=L; Freq: T, G Occas: S, K, R, H, I, N, F, A, X, V ● **Work Env:** Noise=N; Freq: W ● **Salary:** 4 ● **Outlook:** 3

GROUP LEADER (agriculture) ● DOT #180.167-022 ● OES: 72000 ● Alternate titles: CREW BOSS; CREW LEADER; ROW BOSS. Co-ordinates activities of group of FARMWORKERS, GENERAL (agriculture) I engaged in planting, cultivating, and harvesting diversified crops: Recruits members for group. Locates jobs for group and accompanies group on job. May be required to hold state registration certificate. Performs other duties as described under SUPERVISOR (any industry) Master Title. ● **GED:** R3, M2, L2 ● **SVP:** 2-4 yrs ● **Academic:** Ed=N, Eng=N ● **Work Field:** 003 ● **MPSMS:** 300 ● **Aptitudes:** G3, V3, N4, S4, P4, Q4, K4, F4, M3, E4, C4 ● **Temperaments:** D, J, P, V ● **Physical:** Stg=L; Freq: T, G Occas: S, K, O, R, H, I, N, F, D, X ● **Work Field:** 003 ● **Salary:** 1 ● **Outlook:** 4

MANAGER, CHRISTMAS-TREE FARM (forestry) ● DOT #180.117-010 ● OES: 71005 ● Plans, directs, and coordinates district operations of Christmas tree farm: Plans activities of district according to executive directives, budget, projected sales volume, and other guidelines. Negotiates contracts for lease of private lands for farming, and purchase of wild (uncultivated) trees for harvesting. Issues instructions to supervisors pertaining to variety and density of tree planting, cultural practices to apply, harvesting dates and locations, and shipping schedules. Contracts for trucks to haul trees from cutting areas to sorting yard. Hires workers and coordinates planting and cultivating of seedlings, and pruning, harvesting, grading, and shipping of trees. Directs office activities, such as compilation of production reports, preparation of payroll, and maintenance of office records. ● **GED:** R5, M3, L4 ● **SVP:** 2-4 yrs ● **Academic:** Ed=N, Eng=G ● **Work Field:** 295 ● **MPSMS:** 319 ● **Aptitudes:** G2, V2, N3, S4, P4, Q4, K5, F5, M5, E5, C5 ● **Temperaments:** D, J, P, V ● **Physical:** Stg=L; Freq: R, H, I, T, G, N ● **Work Env:** Noise=N; ● **Salary:** 4 ● **Outlook:** 2

MANAGER, DAIRY FARM (agriculture) ● DOT #180.167-026 ● OES: 71005 ● Manages dairy farm: Plans, develops, and implements policies, procedures, and practices for operation of dairy farm to ensure compliance with company's or owner's standards for farm production, propagation of herd, and regulations of regulatory agencies. Directs and coordinates, through subordinate supervisory personnel, farm activities, such as breeding and rearing livestock, feeding and milking of cows, storage of milk, and sterilizing and maintaining facilities and equipment. Reviews breeding and milk production records to determine bulls and cows that are unproductive and should be sold. Inspects facilities and equipment to ensure compliance with sanitation standards, and to determine maintenance and repair requirements. Authorizes, requisitions, or purchases supplies and equipment, such as feed, disinfective and sanitation chemicals, and replacements for defective equipment. Secures services of VETERINARIAN (medical ser.) for treatment of herd or when cows are calving. Prepares farm activity reports for evaluation by management or owner. May direct and coordinate activities concerned with planting, growing, harvesting, and storage of feed forage crops. May directly supervise dairy workers on small farms. ● **GED:** R4, M3, L3 ● **SVP:** 4-10 yrs ● **Academic:** Ed=H, Eng=S ● **Work Field:** 295 ● **MPSMS:** 383 ● **Aptitudes:** G2, V3, N3, S3, P3, Q3, K4, F4, M4, E4, C4 ● **Temperaments:** D, J, P ● **Physical:** Stg=L; Freq: R, H, T, G, N Occas: S, O, I, E, F, A, X, V ● **Work Env:** Noise=N; Occas: W ● **Salary:** 4 ● **Outlook:** 3

MIGRANT LEADER (agriculture) ● DOT #180.167-050 ● OES: 72000 ● Alternate titles: CREW LEADER; FARM-CREW LEADER. Contracts seasonal farm employment of MIGRANT WORKERS (agriculture): Consults employment agencies to locate work and confers with FARMERS (agriculture) to obtain suitable contracts for crew. Recruits and organizes crew and furnishes transportation to work site. Schedules en-route rest stops that afford shelters, benches or beds, cooking facilities, fuel and water, and adequate toilet and sanitary provisions. Confers with employer and community officials at site of employment to ensure availability of living quarters for families and single individuals, educational and recreational facilities, medical care, and day care for children. Supplies farm implements and machinery to crew and directs them in methods of cultivation, harvesting, and packaging of crop. Prepares payroll and production records. May provide initial financing of trips and advance funds to workers during idle peri-

ods. May be required to hold state registration certificate. Performs other duties as described under SUPERVISOR (any industry) Master Title. ● **GED:** R3, M2, L2 ● **SVP:** 2-4 yrs ● **Academic:** Ed=N, Eng=N ● **Work Field:** 003 ● **MPSMS:** 300 ● **Aptitudes:** G3, V3, N3, S4, P4, Q3, K4, F4, M4, E4, C4 ● **Temperaments:** D, J, P, V ● **Physical:** Stg=L; Freq: R, H, I, T, G, N Occas: S, K, O, F, D, A, X, V ● **Work Env:** Noise=L; Const: W ● **Salary:** 1 ● **Outlook:** 3

GOE: 03.01.02
Specialty Breeding

BEEKEEPER (agriculture) ● DOT #413.161-010 ● OES: 79998 ● Alternate titles: APIARIST; BEE FARMER; BEE RAISER; BEE RANCHER; HONEY PRODUCER. Raises bees to produce honey and pollinate crops: Assembles beehives, using handtools. Arranges with sellers for purchases of honeybee colonies. Inserts honeycomb of bees into beehive or inducts wild swarming bees into hive of prepared honeycomb frames. Places screen plug in hive entrance to confine bees and sets hive in orchard, clover field, or near other source of nectar and pollen. Forces bees from hive, using smoke pot or by placing carbolic acid soaked pad over hive to inspect hive and to harvest honeycombs. Scrapes out parasites, such as wax moth larvae, and removes vermin, such as birds and mice. Collects royal jelly from queen bee cells for sale as base for cosmetics and as health food. Destroys superfluous queen bee cells to prevent division of colony by swarming. Destroys diseased bee colonies, using cyanide gas. Burns hive of diseased bee colony or sterilizes hive, using caustic soda solution. Uncaps harvested honeycombs and extracts honey. Arranges with buyers for sale of honey. May cultivate bees to produce bee colonies and queen bees for sale and be designated Bee Producer (agriculture); Queen Producer (agriculture). ● **GED:** R3, M3, L3 ● **SVP:** 2-4 yrs ● **Academic:** Ed=N, Eng=S ● **Work Field:** 002 ● **MPSMS:** 329, 399 ● **Aptitudes:** G3, V3, N3, S3, P3, Q3, K4, F4, M3, E4, C4 ● **Temperaments:** J, V ● **Physical:** Stg=H; Freq: S, K, O, R, H, I, N, A Occas: T, G, D, X ● **Work Env:** Noise=N; Freq: O Occas: W ● **Salary:** 2 ● **Outlook:** 2

FISH FARMER (fishing & hunt.) ● DOT #446.161-010 ● OES: 79998 ● Spawns and raises fish for commercial purposes: Strips eggs from female fish and places eggs in moist pans. Adds milt stripped from male fish to fertilize eggs. Fills hatchery trays with fertilized eggs and places trays in incubation troughs. Turns valves and places baffles in troughs to adjust volume, depth, velocity, and temperature of water. Transfers fingerlings to rearing ponds. Feeds high protein foods or cereal with vitamins and minerals to fingerlings to induce growth to size desired for commercial use. Arranges with buyers for sale of fish. Removes fish from pond, using dip net. Counts and weighs fish. Loads fish into tank truck, or dresses and packs in ice for shipment. May perform standard tests on water samples to determine oxygen content. May be designated according to kind of fish raised as Trout Farmer (fishing & hunt.). ● **GED:** R4, M1, L2 ● **SVP:** 1-2 yrs ● **Academic:** Ed=H, Eng=N ● **Work Field:** 002 ● **MPSMS:** 331 ● **Aptitudes:** G3, V3, N4, S4, P3, Q4, K4, F3, M3, E4, C4 ● **Temperaments:** D, J ● **Physical:** Stg=M; Freq: S, O, R, H, N Occas: C, B, K, I, E, T, G, F, D, X, V ● **Work Env:** Noise=N; Freq: W, U Occas: C ● **Salary:** 2 ● **Outlook:** 2

MANAGER, FISH HATCHERY (fishing & hunt.) l DOT #180.167-030 l OES: 71005 l Alternate titles: FISH CULTURIST; SUPERINTENDENT, FISH HATCHERY. Manages public or private fish hatchery, applying knowledge of management and fish culturing techniques: Determines, administers, and executes policies relating to administration, standards of hatchery operations, and maintenance of facilities. Confers with BIOLOGISTS (profess. & kin.) and other fishery personnel to obtain data concerning fish habits; food and environmental requirements; and techniques for collecting, fertilizing, incubating spawn, and treatment of spawn and fry. Oversees trapping and spawning of fish; incubating of eggs; rearing of fry; and movement of fish to lakes, ponds, and streams or commercial tanks. Prepares reports required by state and federal laws. Prepares budget reports, and receives, accounts for, and dispenses funds. May approve employment and discharge of employees, sign payrolls, and perform similar personnel duties. May manage hatchery concerned with culturing shellfish and other marine life and be designated Manager, Marine Life

Hatchery (fishing & hunt.); Manager, Shellfish Hatchery (fishing & hunt.). ● **GED:** R5, M3, L4 ● **SVP:** 2-4 yrs ● **Academic:** Ed=N, Eng=G ● **Work Field:** 295 ● **MPSMS:** 330 ● **Aptitudes:** G2, V2, N3, S3, P4, Q3, K4, F4, M4, E4, C4 ● **Temperaments:** D, J, P, V ● **Physical:** Stg=L; Freq: T, G, N Occas: R, H, I, E, D, A, X ● **Work Env:** Noise=N; Freq: W ● **Salary:** 4 ● **Outlook:** 2

SHELLFISH GROWER (fishing & hunt.) ● DOT #446.161-014 ● OES: 79998 ● Alternate titles: OYSTER CULTURIST. Cultivates and harvests beds of shellfish, such as clams and oysters: Lays out and stakes tide flats (ground beneath shallow water near shoreline). Piles up stone, poles, and mud, using farm tractor and hand implements to make dikes to control water drainage at low tide. Removes debris by hand and levels soil with tractor and harrow. Sows spat by hand or with shovel or sets out strings or baskets of shells onto which spat attaches. Covers seeded area with mixture of sand and broken shells or transfers seeded strings or baskets to growing area. Rigs net or star mop (mop of heavy rope yarn) and drags it over bed behind power boat to entangle and remove shellfish predators, such as crabs and starfish. Walks about bed at low tide, and scoops or digs shellfish and piles them onto barge or mud sled, using pitchfork or shovel. Packs shellfish, according to market specifications, in containers and returns small ones to bed. Poles barge to wharf at high tide or pulls it, using boat. Drags mud sled from bed, using tractor. May pour oil around bed and spread oil-treated sand over bed with shovel to form chemical barrier to shellfish predators. May reach from boat with rake-tongs and grope for shellfish by moving handles to open and close tongs. May supervise workers who cultivate and harvest bed. May negotiate with buyers for sale of crop. May be designated according to type of shellfish grown as Clam Grower (fishing & hunt.); Oyster Grower (fishing & hunt.). ● **GED:** R4, M1, L2 ● **SVP:** 1-2 yrs ● **Academic:** Ed=H, Eng=N ● **Work Field:** 002 ● **MPSMS:** 332 ● **Aptitudes:** G3, V3, N4, S4, P4, Q4, K3, F3, M3, E3, C5 ● **Temperaments:** D, V ● **Physical:** Stg=M; Freq: S, O, R, H, I Occas: B, T, G, N, D ● **Work Env:** Noise=L; Const: W Freq: U ● **Salary:** 2 ● **Outlook:** 2

GOE: 03.01.03
Specialty Cropping

HORTICULTURAL-SPECIALTY GROWER, FIELD (agriculture) ● DOT #405.161-014 ● OES: 79998 ● Propagates and grows horticultural-specialty products and crops, such as seeds, bulbs, rootstocks, sod, ornamental plants, and cut flowers: Plans acreage utilization and work schedules, according to knowledge of crop culture, climate and market conditions, seed, bulb, or rootstock availability, and employable work force and machinery. Attaches farm implements, such as disc and fertilizer spreader, to tractor and drives tractor in fields to till soil and plant and cultivate crop. Inspects fields periodically to ascertain nutrient deficiencies, detect insect, disease, and pest infestations, and identify foreign-plant growth, and selects, purchases, and schedules materials, such as fertilizers and herbicides, to ensure quality control. Hires field workers; assigns their duties according to scheduled activities, such as planting, irrigating, weeding, and harvesting; and oversees their activities. Maintains personnel and production records. Arranges with customers for sale of crop. May oversee activities, such as product cleaning, grading, and packaging. May provide customer services, such as planning and building planters, walls, and patios, and planting and caring for landscape and display arrangements. May bud or graft scion stock on plantings to alter growth characteristics. May develop new variations of species specialty to produce crops with specialized market-appeal, such as disease resistance or color brilliance. May cultivate out-of-season seedlings and crops, using greenhouse. May cultivate cover crop, such as hay or rye, in rotation with horticultural specialty to rejuvenate soil. May drive and operate self-propelled harvesting machine. May lubricate, adjust, and make minor repairs on farm machinery and equipment. May build, remove, and repair farm structures, such as fences and sheds. May be designated according to crop as Bulb Grower (agriculture); Flower Grower (agriculture); Grass Farmer (agriculture); Rose Grower (agriculture); Seed Grower (agriculture); Shrub Grower (agriculture). ● **GED:** R4, M3, L3 ● **SVP:** 2-4 yrs ● **Academic:** Ed=N, Eng=N ● **Work Field:** 003 ● **MPSMS:** 310 ● **Aptitudes:** G3, V3, N3, S3, P3, Q4, K3, F4, M3, E3, C3 ● **Tempera-**

ments: D, J ● **Physical:** Stg=M; Freq: R, H, T, G, N, F, D, V Occas: C, S, O, I, A, X ● **Work Env:** Noise=L; ● **Salary:** 4 ● **Outlook:** 2

LANDSCAPE CONTRACTOR (construction) ● DOT #182.167-014 ● OES: 15017 ● Contracts to landscape grounds of houses, industrial plants, other buildings, or areas around highways: Confers with prospective client, studies landscape designs or drawings, and bills of materials to ascertain scope of landscaping work required, such as installation of lighting or sprinkler systems, erection of fences, concrete work, and types of trees, shrubs, or ornamental plants specified. Inspects grounds or area to determine equipment requirements for grading, tilling, or replacing top soil, and labor requirements to install sprinkler or lighting system, build fences, or perform concreting and planting work. Calculates labor, equipment, material, and overhead costs to determine minimum estimate or bid which will provide for margin of profit. Prepares and submits estimate for client or bid to industrial concern or governmental agency. Prepares contract for client to sign or signs contract if successful bidder. Plans landscaping functions and sequences of work at various sites to obtain optimum utilization of work force and equipment. Directs and coordinates, through subordinate supervisory personnel, activities of workers engaged in performing landscaping functions in contractual agreement. Purchases and ensures that materials are on-site as needed. Inspects work at sites for compliance with terms and specifications of contract. May personally supervise workers. May participate in performing landscaping functions. May be required to possess state license as landscape contractor. May subcontract electrical installation or concrete work if not equipped to provide those services. ● **GED:** R4, M4, L4 ● **SVP:** 4-10 yrs ● **Academic:** Ed=H, Eng=S ● **Work Field:** 295 ● **MPSMS:** 719 ● **Aptitudes:** G3, V3, N2, S3, P3, Q3, K4, F4, M4, E5, C3 ● **Temperaments:** D, J, P, V ● **Physical:** Stg=L; Freq: R, H, T, G, N, X Occas: F ● **Work Env:** Noise=L; Freq: W ● **Salary:** 4 ● **Outlook:** 3

LANDSCAPE GARDENER (agriculture) ● DOT #408.161-010 ● OES: 79014 ● Alternate titles: LANDSCAPER. Plans and executes small scale landscaping operations and maintains grounds and landscape of private and business residences: Participates with LABORER, LANDSCAPE (agriculture) in preparing and grading terrain, applying fertilizers, seeding and sodding lawns, and transplanting shrubs and plants, using manual and power-operated equipment. Plans lawns, and plants and cultivates them, using gardening implements and power-operated equipment. Plants new and repairs established lawns, using seed mixtures and fertilizers recommended for particular soil type and lawn location. Locates and plants shrubs, trees, and flowers selected by property owner or those recommended for particular landscape effect. Mows and trims lawns, using hand mower or power mower. Trims shrubs and cultivates gardens. Cleans grounds, using rakes, brooms, and hose. Sprays trees and shrubs, and applies supplemental liquid and dry nutrients to lawn and trees. May dig trenches and install drain tiles. May make repairs to concrete and asphalt walks and driveways. ● **GED:** R4, M4, L4 ● **SVP:** 2-4 yrs ● **Academic:** Ed=N, Eng=S ● **Work Field:** 003 ● **MPSMS:** 969 ● **Aptitudes:** G3, V3, N3, S3, P4, Q4, K3, F3, M3, E4, C4 ● **Temperaments:** D, J, V ● **Physical:** Stg=H; Freq: S, K, R, H, I, D Occas: O, T, G, N, X ● **Work Env:** Noise=L; Const: W Freq: O ● **Salary:** 3 ● **Outlook:** 4

MANAGER, NURSERY (agriculture) ● DOT #180.167-042 ● OES: 71005 ● Manages nursery to grow horticultural plants, such as trees, shrubs, flowers, ornamental plants, or vegetables for sale to trade or retail customers: Determines type and quantity of horticultural plants to be grown, considering such factors as whether plants will be grown under controlled conditions in hothouse or greenhouse or under natural weather conditions in field, and market demand or conditions, utilizing knowledge of plant germination, growing habits of plants, soil conditions, plant nutrients, and disease control requirements. Selects and purchases seed, plant nutrients, and disease control chemicals according to type of horticultural plants and conditions under which plants will be grown. Tours work areas to observe quality and quantity of work being done, to inspect crops and to evaluate horticultural conditions, such as plant disease and soil conditions. Directs and coordinates, through subordinate supervisory personnel, activities of workers engaged in planting of seed, raising, feeding, and controlling growth and disease of plants, and transplanting, potting, or cutting plants for marketing. Coordinates clerical, record keeping, accounting, and marketing activities. May purchase nursery stock for resale and sell gardening accessories, such as sprays, garden implements, and plant nutrients and be known as Manager, Retail Nursery (agriculture; retail trade). May grow horticultural plants under controlled conditions hydroponically and be known as Manager, Hydroponics Nursery (agriculture). ● **GED:** R5, M4, L5 ● **SVP:** 4-10 yrs ● **Academic:** Ed=H, Eng=S ● **Work Field:** 295, 003, 292 ● **MPSMS:** 310 ● **Aptitudes:** G2, V2, N3, S3, P3, Q3, K3, F3, M3, E4, C4 ● **Temperaments:** D, J, P, V ● **Physical:** Stg=L; Freq: R, H, T, G, N, F Occas: S, O, I, E, D, A, X, V ● **Work Env:** Noise=N; Freq: W ● **Salary:** 2 ● **Outlook:** 3

TREE SURGEON (agriculture) ● DOT #408.181-010 ● OES: 24501 ● Prunes and treats ornamental and shade trees and shrubs in yards and parks to improve their appearance, health, and value: Cuts out dead and undesirable limbs and trims trees to enhance beauty and growth. Scrapes decayed matter from cavities in trees, and fills holes with cement to promote healing and prevent further deterioration. Sprays and dusts pesticides on shrubs and trees to control pests and disease or sprays foliar fertilizers to increase plant growth, using hand or machine dusters and sprayers. Tops trees to control growth characteristics and to prevent interference with utility wires. May apply herbicides to kill brush and weeds. May fell and remove trees and bushes. May plant trees and shrubs. ● **GED:** R4, M2, L2 ● **SVP:** 1-2 yrs ● **Academic:** Ed=H, Eng=S ● **Work Field:** 003 ● **MPSMS:** 310 ● **Aptitudes:** G2, V3, N4, S3, P3, Q3, K4, F4, M2, E2, C3 ● **Temperaments:** J, T, V ● **Physical:** Stg=M; Freq: C, B, S, K, O, R, H, F, D, V Occas: W, I, E, N, X ● **Work Env:** Noise=L; Const: W Freq: U, A, O ● **Salary:** 3 ● **Outlook:** 3

GOE: 03.01.04
Forestry & Logging

FORESTER (profess. & kin.) ● DOT #040.167-010 ● OES: 24302 ● Manages and develops forest lands and resources for economic and recreational purposes: Plans and directs forestation and reforestation projects. Maps forest areas, estimates standing timber and future growth, and manages timber sales. Plans cutting programs to assure continuous production of timber or to assist timber companies achieve production goals. Determines methods of cutting and removing timber with minimum waste and environmental damage and suggests methods of processing wood for various uses. Directs suppression of forest fires and conducts fire-prevention programs. Plans and directs construction and maintenance of recreation facilities, fire towers, trails, roads, and fire breaks. Assists in planning and implementing projects for control of floods, soil erosion, tree diseases, and insect pests in forests [ENTOMOLOGIST (profess. & kin.) 041.061-046; PLANT PATHOLOGIST (profess. & kin.) 041.061-086; SOIL CONSERVATIONIST (profess. & kin.) 040.061-054]. Advises landowners on forestry management techniques and conducts public educational programs on forest care and conservation. May participate in environmental studies and prepare environmental reports. May supervise activities of other forestry workers [SUPERVISOR (any industry) Master Title]. May patrol forests, enforce laws, and fight forest fires. May administer budgets. May conduct research to improve knowledge of forest management. May specialize in one aspect of forest management. May be designated Forestry Supervisor (profess. & kin.); Woods Manager (profess. & kin.). ● **GED:** R5, M5, L5 ● **SVP:** 4-10 yrs ● **Academic:** Ed=B, Eng=S ● **Work Field:** 251, 293, 295 ● **MPSMS:** 310, 731, 951 ● **Aptitudes:** G2, V2, N2, S3, P3, Q3, K4, F4, M4, E4, C4 ● **Temperaments:** D, J, P, V ● **Physical:** Stg=L; Freq: T, G Occas: C, B, S, K, O, R, H, I, E, N, F, D, A, X, V ● **Work Env:** Noise=N; Occas: W, A, T, O ● **Salary:** 4 ● **Outlook:** 1

LOGGING-OPERATIONS INSPECTOR (forestry) ● DOT #168.267-070 ● OES: 21911 ● Inspects contract logging operations to ensure adherence to contract provisions and safety laws and to prevent loss of timber through breakage and damage to residual stand: Examines logging area for utilization practices, slash disposal, sanitation, observance of boundaries, and safety precautions. Issues remedial instructions for violations of contract agreement and fire and safety regulations, and prepares report of logging method, efficiency, and progress. May initiate bid requests and negotiate terms of contracts with logging contractors. ● **GED:** R5, M3, L4 ● **SVP:** 2-4 yrs ● **Academic:** Ed=A, Eng=S ● **Work Field:** 212 ● **MPSMS:** 712 ● **Aptitudes:** G2, V2, N3, S3, P4, Q3, K4, F4, M4, E5, C5 ● **Temperaments:** J, P ● **Physical:** Stg=L; Freq: T, G Occas: C, B, R, H, I, N, F, D ● **Work Env:** Noise=N; ● **Salary:** 2 ● **Outlook:** 3

Plants and Animals   03

General Supervision: Plants and Animals   03.02

Workers in this group supervise others, and often work right along with them, on farms or ranches, fish hatcheries or forests, plant nurseries or parks. Most of them work in rural or forest locations, but some jobs are located in city or suburban areas. Some of these workers travel throughout an area to inspect or treat croplands for insects or disease, or supervise workers performing agricultural or lawn care services.

✓ *What kind of work would you do?*

Your work activities would depend upon your specific job. For example, you might:

- supervise workers in planting, cultivating, and harvesting all farm crops.
- supervise workers in milking, breeding, and caring for dairy cows.
- supervise workers in planting, cultivating, harvesting, and packing seedling forest trees.
- supervise workers in incubating eggs and caring for fish in a state hatchery.

- inspect fields for presence of insects or plant disease.
- coordinate activities of crew of workers engaged in caring for park grounds.

✓ *What skills and abilities do you need for this kind of work?*

To do this kind of work, you must be able to:

- get a clear picture of the work to be done during a specific time period, as explained to you by the manager of the business, and pass this information along clearly to the workers you supervise.
- assign duties to workers according to your judgment of their capabilities, and the amount of work to be done.
- demonstrate the use of tools and equipment to other workers and show them ways of doing their jobs more efficiently.
- organize details and use basic arithmetic to keep time and production records for the workers you supervise or prepare reports of areas you inspect.

■ work outdoors in all kinds of weather, sometimes performing tasks that require strenuous activities.

✓ *How do you know if you would like or could learn to do this kind of work?*

The following questions may give you clues about yourself as you consider this group of jobs.

■ Have you been in charge of a scout troop or other group during a clean-up campaign? Did the members follow your directions?

■ Have you been a member of FFA or 4-H? Did you have a project related to farming, fishing, or forestry?

■ Have you worked a whole day mowing lawns, cutting weeds, or picking fruit? Could you do this type of work every day? Are you interested in supervising this type of work?

■ Have you had military experience as a work detail leader? Did you like being responsible for getting the work done?

✓ *How can you prepare for and enter this kind of work?*

Occupations in this group usually require education and/or training extending from one year to over ten years, depending upon the specific kind of work. Most workers must have related work experience. They must know about the tools, processes, and methods used by the workers they supervise. This involves having practical knowledge of wide variety of tasks.

Almost all workers in this group start out in routine jobs in the same or similar work location. They are promoted to these jobs after showing that they have leadership ability and are thoroughly familiar with the work.

Vocational and technical courses in agriculture, forestry, or related fields provide a helpful background for some of these jobs.

✓ *What else should you consider about these jobs?*

Workers in this group may help to do many of the physical tasks they supervise. These workers are exposed to all types of weather conditions as well as natural hazards as storms, fires, and extremes of temperatures.

If you think you would like to do this kind of work, look at the job title listed below.

■ ■ ■

GOE: 03.02.02
Forestry & Logging

FORESTER AIDE (forestry) ● DOT #452.364-010 ● OES: 79002 ● Alternate titles: FOREST TECHNICIAN. Compiles data pertaining to size, content, condition, and other characteristics of forest tracts, under direction of FORESTER (profess. & kin.) 040.061-034; and leads workers in forest propagation, fire prevention and suppression, and facilities maintenance: Traverses forest in designated pattern to gather basic forest data, such as topographical features, species and population of trees, wood units available for harvest, disease and insect damage, tree seedling mortality, and conditions constituting fire danger. Marks trees of specified specie, condition, and size for thinning or logging. Collects and records data from instruments, such as rain gauge, thermometer, streamflow recorder, and soil moisture gauge. Holds stadia rod, clears survey line, measures distances, records survey data, and performs related duties to assist in surveying property lines, timber sale boundaries, and road and recreation sites. Trains and leads conservation workers in seasonal activities, such as planting tree seedlings, collecting seed cones, suppressing fires, cleaning and maintaining recreational facilities, and clearing fire breaks and access roads. Gives instructions to visitors of forest, and enforces camping, vehicle use, fire building, sanitation, and other forest regulations. ● **GED:** R4, M3, L3 ● **SVP:** 1-2 yrs ● **Academic:** Ed=H, Eng=S ● **Work Field:** 293, 243 ● **MPSMS:** 313 ● **Aptitudes:** G3, V3, N3, S3, P3, Q3, K3, F3, M3, E3, C3 ● **Temperaments:** J, P, V ● **Physical:** Stg=M; Freq: R, H, T, G, F, D Occas: C, B, S, K, O, W, I, E, M, N, X, V ● **Work Env:** Noise=L; Freq: W, H, O ● **Salary:** 4 ● **Outlook:** 2

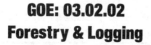

Animal Training and Service   03.03

Workers in this group take care of animals of many kinds and train them for a variety of purposes. They work in pet shops, testing laboratories, animal shelters, and veterinarians' offices. Some are employed by zoos, aquariums, circuses, and at other places where animals are exhibited or used in entertainment acts. Others work for animal training or obedience schools, or in stables or kennels maintained by individuals or such facilities as race tracks or riding academies. These workers are not employed on farms, ranches, or other places where animals are raised as crops.

✓ *What kind of work would you do?*

Your work activities would depend upon your specific job. For example, you might:

■ train and condition horses for racing.

■ train animals to obey commands, compete in

shows, or perform tricks.

- feed, water, and care for mice, guinea pigs, monkeys, and other animals in a hospital or research laboratory.
- feed, exercise, and groom horses to protect their health and improve their appearance.
- bathe and groom pets for their owners.
- control aquarium water temperature and acidity and meet other needs of aquatic life.

✓ What skills and abilities do you need for this kind of work?

To do this kind of work, you must be able to:

- understand the habits and physical needs of the animals you care for, and think of each of them on an individual basis.
- keep calm during emergencies.
- observe the animals you care for to notice changes in their appearance, appetite, or behavior, which might mean that they are sick.
- stay very patient while going over and over the same routines with animals, to train them to perform or to respond to commands.
- use your hands and fingers skillfully to perform such tasks as trimming the nails of dogs and cats without hurting them, fastening shoes to horses' hooves, or helping a veterinarian give shots to sick animals.
- do the hard physical work needed to keep stables and other animal quarters clean, using equipment such as shovels, pitchforks, rakes, mops, and high-pressure hoses.

✓ How do you know if you would like or could learn to do this kind of work?

The following questions may give you clues about yourself as you consider this group of jobs.

- Have you raised or cared for an animal? Do you enjoy the responsibility of caring for an animal?
- Have you had military experience training animals? Were you patient with the animal

when you had to repeat commands many times? Did the animals learn what you were teaching?

- Have you taken care of a sick or an injured animal? Can you tell if an animal is getting sick or getting better by the way it looks or acts?
- Have you had a hobby raising small animals or fish? Did you use eyedroppers, strainers or other tools to feed, treat, or care for them?

✓ How can you prepare for and enter this kind of work?

Occupations in this group usually require education and/or training extending from a short demonstration to over four years, depending upon the specific kind of work. Most beginning workers are given a few simple duties. More responsibility is added as these workers gain experience. Some high schools, vocational schools, and junior colleges have courses in animal care. These courses cover the housing and feeding of animals, basic zoology and anatomy, and methods of treating sick or injured animals.

Some of these jobs require special skills. For instance, workers who train or exercise horses must know how to ride, and those who work for aquariums must know how to swim.

Jobs that involve training guide dogs, saddle horses, or animal performers are given to workers who have at least six months experience in the care of animals.

✓ What else should you consider about these jobs?

Expansion in testing of food and drugs by government agencies will increase the need for people to care for laboratory animals. An increase in the number of household pets will create jobs for animal groomers, veterinary hospital helpers, and other pet-care workers.

If you think you would like to do this kind of work, look at the job titles listed below.

■ ■ ■

GOE: 03.03.01
Animal Training

ANIMAL TRAINER (amuse. & rec.) ● DOT #159.224-010 ● OES: 79998 ● Trains animals to obey commands, compete in shows, or perform tricks to entertain audience: Evaluates animal to determine temperament, ability, and aptitude for training. Conducts training program to develop desired behavior. May organize format of show. May conduct show. May cue or signal animal during performance. May rehearse animal according to script for motion picture or television film or stage or circus program. May train guard dog to protect property.

May teach guide dog and master to function as team. May feed, exercise, and give general care to animal. May observe animal's physical condition to detect illness or unhealthy condition requiring medical care. May be designated according to specific animal trained. May be designated Head Animal Trainer (amuse. & rec.) or Senior Animal Trainer (amuse. & rec.) when directing activities of other workers. ● **GED:** R4, M3, L3 ● **SVP:** 1-2 yrs ● **Academic:** Ed=N, Eng=N ● **Work Field:** 296, 297 ● **MPSMS:** 919 ● **Aptitudes:** G2, V3, N4, S3, P4, Q4, K3, F4, M3, E3, C4 ● **Temperaments:** D, J, S ● **Physical:** Stg=L; Freq: R, H, T, G, F, V Occas: S, K, O, I, N, D, X ● **Work Env:** Noise=N; Occas: W, O ● **Salary:** 3 ● **Outlook:** 2

EXERCISER, HORSE (amuse. & rec.) ● DOT #153.674-010 ● OES: 34058 ● Rides racehorses to exercise and condition them for racing:

Rides racehorse during workout and training races, following specific instructions of training personnel. Informs training personnel of horses' temperament, peculiarities, and physical condition as demonstrated during exercise so that training plans can be modified to prepare horse for racing. ● **GED:** R2, M1, L1 ● **SVP:** 1-3 mos ● **Academic:** Ed=N, Eng=N ● **Work Field:** 291 ● **MPSMS:** 327 ● **Aptitudes:** G4, V4, N4, S4, P4, Q5, K3, F4, M3, E4, C4 ● **Temperaments:** F, J ● **Physical:** Stg=M; Const: B, R, H Freq: F, D, A, V Occas: O ● **Work Env:** Noise=N; Freq: W Occas: O ● **Salary:** 2 ● **Outlook:** 5

GOE: 03.03.02
Animal Service

ANIMAL CARETAKER (any industry) ● DOT #410.674-010 ● OES: 79017 ● Alternate titles: ANIMAL ATTENDANT; FARMWORKER, ANIMAL. Performs any combination of following duties to attend animals, such as mice, canaries, guinea pigs, mink, dogs, and monkeys, on farms and in facilities, such as kennels, pounds, hospitals, and laboratories: Feeds and waters animals according to schedules. Cleans and disinfects cages, pens, and yards and sterilizes laboratory equipment and surgical instruments. Examines animals for signs of illness and treats them according to instructions. Transfers animals between quarters. Adjusts controls to regulate temperature and humidity of animals' quarters. Records information according to instructions, such as genealogy, diet, weight, medications, food intake, and license number. Anesthetizes, innoculates, shaves, bathes, clips, and grooms animals. Repairs cages, pens, or fenced yards. May kill and skin animals, such as fox and rabbit, and pack pelts in crates. May be designated according to place worked such as Dog-Pound Attendant (government ser.); Farmworker, Fur (agriculture); Helper, Animal Laboratory (pharmaceut.); Kennel Attendant (agriculture); Pet Shop Attendant (retail trade); Veterinary-Hospital Attendant (medical ser.). ● **GED:** R2, M1, L1 ● **SVP:** 3-6 mos ● **Academic:** Ed=N, Eng=N ● **Work Field:** 002, 291, 294 ● **MPSMS:** 329 ● **Aptitudes:** G3, V4, N4, S4, P4, Q4, K3, F3, M3, E5, C4 ● **Temperaments:** T, V ● **Physical:** Stg=M; Freq: R, H, I, T, G, N Occas: S, O, E, A, X ● **Work Env:** Noise=N; Freq: O ● **Salary:** 1 ● **Outlook:** 3

ANIMAL KEEPER (amuse. & rec.) ● DOT #412.674-010 ● OES: 79017 ● Alternate titles: ANIMAL CARETAKER; MENAGERIE CARETAKER; ZOO CARETAKER. Feeds, waters, and cleans quarters of animals and birds in zoo, circus, or menagerie: Prepares food for charges by chopping or grinding meat, fish, fruit, or vegetables; mixing prepared, dry, or liquid commercial feeds; or unbaling forage grasses. Adds vitamins or medication to food as prescribed by VETERINARIAN (medical ser.) 073.101-010. Fills water containers and places food in cages as specified. Cleans animals' quarters, using rake, water hose, and disinfectant. Observes animals to detect illnesses and injuries and notifies ANIMAL KEEPER, HEAD (amuse. & rec.) 412.137-010 or VETERINARIAN (medical ser.) of findings. Transfers animals from one enclosure to another for purposes such as breeding, giving birth, rearrangement of exhibits, or shipping. Sets temperature and humidity controls of quarters as specified. Answers visitors' questions concerning animals' habits or zoo operations. Bathes and grooms animals as required. May assist VETERINARIAN (medical ser.) in treatment of animals for illnesses and injuries. May assist ANIMAL TRAINER (amuse. & rec.) 159.224-010 or instructor in presentation of programs, shows, or lectures. May assist maintenance staff in cleaning zoo facilities. May be designated according to animal cared for as Bear Keeper (amuse. & rec.); Elephant Keeper (amuse. & rec.); Monkey Keeper (amuse. & rec.); or according to species as Bird Keeper (amuse. & rec.); Mammal Keeper (amuse. & rec.). May direct activities of other workers. ● **GED:** R3, M2, L2 ● **SVP:** 3-6 mos ● **Academic:** Ed=N, Eng=S ● **Work Field:** 291 ● **MPSMS:** 329 ● **Aptitudes:** G3, V4, N4, S4, P4, Q5, K3, F3, M3, E4, C4 ● **Temperaments:** J, V ● **Physical:** Stg=M; Freq: S, K, O, R, H, I, T, G, N Occas: C, E, F, A, X ● **Work Env:** Noise=N; Freq: W Occas: U, O ● **Salary:** 1 ● **Outlook:** 3

ANIMAL KEEPER, HEAD (amuse. & rec.) ● DOT #412.137-010 ● OES: 72000 ● Alternate titles: KEEPER, HEAD; SUPERINTENDENT, MENAGERIE. Supervises and coordinates activities of workers engaged in care and exhibition of birds and animals at establishments, such as zoos or circuses. Observes animals to detect signs of illness and consults with VETERINARIAN (medical ser.) to determine type of medication or treatment required. Inspects cages, grottos, and pens for cleanliness and structural defects. Assigns workers to various tasks, and oversees treatment, preparation of food, feeding of animals, and maintenance and repair of animal quarters. Specifies type of animal to exhibit in zoo and location of exhibit, according to weather, animal behavior characteristics, and physical condition. Performs other duties as described under SUPERVISOR (any industry) Master Title. May hire, train, and discharge workers. May keep time records and prepare supply requisitions and reports. May coordinate training of animals for circus performance. May give lectures to public to stimulate interest in animals. ● **GED:** R4, M3, L3 ● **SVP:** 2-4 yrs ● **Academic:** Ed=H, Eng=S ● **Work Field:** 291 ● **MPSMS:** 329 ● **Aptitudes:** G3, V3, N3, S3, P3, Q3, K4, F4, M4, E5, C4 ● **Temperaments:** D, J, P, V ● **Physical:** Stg=M; Freq: R, H, T, G, N Occas: S, K, O, I, E, F, A, X ● **Work Env:** Noise=N; Freq: W Occas: O ● **Salary:** 3 ● **Outlook:** 3

AQUARIST (amuse. & rec.) ● DOT #449.674-010 ● OES: 79017 ● Alternate titles: AQUARIUM TANK ATTENDANT. Attends fish and other aquatic life in aquarium exhibits: Prepares food and feeds fish according to schedule. Cleans tanks and removes algae from tank windows. Attends to aquatic plants and decorations in displays. Collects and compares water samples to color-coded chart for acid analysis and monitors thermometers to ascertain water temperature. Adjusts thermostat and adds chemicals to water to maintain specified water conditions. Observes fish to detect disease and injuries, reports condition to supervisor, and treats fish according to instructions. May fire sedation gun and assist crew expedition members in collection of aquatic life. ● **GED:** R3, M2, L2 ● **SVP:** 3-6 mos ● **Academic:** Ed=N, Eng=S ● **Work Field:** 291, 031 ● **MPSMS:** 330 ● **Aptitudes:** G3, V3, N4, S3, P3, Q4, K3, F3, M3, E4, C4 ● **Temperaments:** J, V ● **Physical:** Stg=L; Freq: R, H, I, N, X Occas: S, O, T, G, D, A ● **Work Env:** Noise=N; Freq: W, U ● **Salary:** 2 ● **Outlook:** 2

DOG BATHER (personal ser.) ● DOT #418.677-010 ● OES: 79017 ● Bathes dogs in preparation for grooming: Combs and cuts out heavy mats from dog's coat, using barber shears and steel comb. Brushes fur to remove dead skin, using dog brush. Draws bath water and regulates temperature. Washes dog, using perfumed soap or shampoo and handbrush and repeats process until dog is clean. Dries dog, using towel and electric drier. Cleans animals' quarters. May trim and shape dog's coat and clip toenails, using scissors and clippers. ● **GED:** R3, M2, L2 ● **SVP:** 2-30 days ● **Academic:** Ed=N, Eng=N ● **Work Field:** 291 ● **MPSMS:** 329 ● **Aptitudes:** G3, V4, N4, S3, P3, Q4, K3, F3, M3, E4, C4 ● **Temperaments:** P, T ● **Physical:** Stg=L; Freq: R, H, I, E, N Occas: D, A, X ● **Work Env:** Noise=N; Freq: U ● **Salary:** 1 ● **Outlook:** 2

DOG GROOMER (personal ser.) ● DOT #418.674-010 ● OES: 79017 ● Alternate titles: DOG BEAUTICIAN; DOG-HAIR CLIPPER. Combs, clips, trims, and shapes dogs' coats to groom dogs, using knowledge of canine characteristics and grooming techniques and styles: Reads written or receives oral instructions to determine clipping pattern desired. Places dog on grooming table and fits grooming collar on dog to hold animal to table. Studies proportions of dog to determine most appropriate cutting pattern to achieve desired style. Clips dog's hair according to determined pattern, using electric clippers, comb, and barber's shears. Combs and shapes dog's coat. Talks to dog or uses other techniques to calm animal. ● **GED:** R3, M2, L3 ● **SVP:** 3-6 mos ● **Academic:** Ed=N, Eng=S ● **Work Field:** 291 ● **MPSMS:** 329, 904 ● **Aptitudes:** G3, V4, N4, S3, P3, Q4, K2, F3, M3, E4, C4 ● **Temperaments:** J, P ● **Physical:** Stg=M; Freq: R, H, I, N, D Occas: S, G, X ● **Work Env:** Noise=L; Occas: O ● **Salary:** 2 ● **Outlook:** 1

HORSESHOER (agriculture) ● DOT #418.381-010 ● OES: 79017 ● Alternate titles: PLATER. Selects aluminum and steel shoes (plates) and fits, shapes, and nails shoes to animals' hooves: Removes worn or defective shoe from hoof, using nail snippers and pincers. Examines hoof to detect bruises and cracks and to determine trimming required. Trims and shapes hoof, using knife and snippers. Measures hoof, using calipers and steel tape. Selects aluminum or steel shoe from stock, according to hoof measurements and animal usage. Places leather pad, sponge, or oakum-pine tar mixture on bruised or cracked hoof for protection. Shapes shoe to fit hoof, using swage, forge, and hammer. Nails shoe to hoof and files hoof flush with shoe. May forge steel bar into shoe. May drive shop truck to work site. ● **GED:** R3, M2, L2 ● **SVP:** 1-2 yrs ● **Academic:** Ed=N, Eng=N ● **Work Field:** 291 ● **MPSMS:**

969 ● **Aptitudes:** G3, V4, N4, S3, P3, Q5, K3, F3, M2, E5, C4 ●
Temperaments: J, T ● **Physical:** Stg=M; Freq: S, R, H, I, N, A Occas:
D, X ● **Work Env:** Noise=N; Occas: O ● **Salary:** 3 ● **Outlook:** 2

STABLE ATTENDANT (any industry) ● DOT #410.674-022 ● OES:
79017 ● Alternate titles: BARNWORKER, GROOM. Cares for horses
and mules to protect their health and improve their appearance: Waters
animals and measures, mixes and apportions feed and feed supplements according to feeding instructions. Washes, brushes, trims and
curries animals' coats to clean and improve their appearance. Inspects
animals for disease, illness, and injury and treats animals according to
instructions. Cleans animals' quarters and replenishes bedding. Exercises animals. Unloads and stores feed and supplies. May whitewash
stables, using brush. May clean saddles and bridles. May saddle animals. May shoe animals. May be designated according to animal cared
for as Horse Tender (any industry); Mule Tender (any industry); Stal-
lion Keeper (agriculture). ● **GED:** R2, M1, L1 ● **SVP:** 2-30 days ●
Academic: Ed=N, Eng=N ● **Work Field:** 002, 291 ● **MPSMS:** 327 ●
Aptitudes: G4, V4, N4, S4, P4, Q4, K4, F4, M3, E4, C5 ● **Temperaments:** J, V ● **Physical:** Stg=H; Freq: R, H, N Occas: S, K, O, A, X ●
Work Env: Noise=N; Occas: U, O ● **Salary:** 1 ● **Outlook:** 2

Plants and Animals   03

Elemental Work: Plants and Animals   **03.04**

*Workers in this group perform active physi-
cal tasks, usually in an outdoor, nonindus-
trial setting. They work with their hands, use
various kinds of tools and equipment, or
operate machinery. They find employment on
farms or ranches, at logging camps or fish
hatcheries, in forests or game preserves, or
with commercial fishing businesses where
they may work onshore or in fishing boats. In
urban areas, they work in parks, gardens, or
nurseries, or for businesses that provide
horticultural or agricultural services.*

✓ What kind of work would you do?

Your work activities would depend upon your
specific job. For example, you might:

- operate farm machinery to plant, cultivate,
  harvest, and store grain crops.
- use shovels, hoes, and shears to plant,
  cultivate, and prune fruit trees.
- walk, stoop, crawl, or sit between rows of
  hops, peanuts, or tobacco to harvest the crop.
- use an auger or ax to cut a tap in trees to
  collect sap.
- use an ax and chainsaw to clear a path for
  trees to be felled.
- set and haul in large commercial fishing nets
  by hand or using a winch.

✓ What skills and abilities do you need for this kind of work?

To do this kind of work, you must be able to:

- work outside for long periods of time and in
  all kinds of weather, performing tasks that
  require physical strength and endurance.
- work quickly and skillfully with your hands,
  to do such things as picking fruit or vegetables, sawing or sorting logs, or operating
  tractors or lawn mowers.
- follow instructions exactly.
- adjust to doing the same kind of work all day
  long, with little opportunity for diversion, or

perform a variety of different tasks on the
same day, as they are needed to carry out the
activities of the business.

✓ How do you know if you would like or could learn to do this kind of work?

The following questions may give you clues about
yourself as you consider this group of jobs.

- Have you worked a whole day mowing
  lawns, cutting weeds, or picking fruit? Could
  you do this type of work every day?
- Have you used rakes, shovels, saws, or other
  tools? Do you like to work with your hands?
- Have you been a member of FFA or 4-H?
  Did you have a project related to farming,
  fishing, or forestry?
- Do you like to camp, fish, or hunt? Would
  you like a full-time job doing these activities?

✓ How can you prepare for and enter this kind of work?

Occupations in this group usually require education
and/or training extending from a short demonstration to over three months, depending upon the
specific kind of work. Prior training is not required
for most jobs in this group. Training is usually
given by the employer when workers are hired or
when their duties are changed. Most employers
require job applicants to be in good physical
condition, and commercial fisheries hire only
persons who can swim for jobs on fishing boats. To
be eligible for jobs in local, state, or national parks,
or with other government agencies, applicants must
take and pass Civil Service examinations. Some
vocational high schools offer courses in general
farming, farm animal care, and equipment operation, and a few participate in work/study projects.
This kind of training can help you get jobs of this
kind, since employers don't have to spend as much
time training you after employment.

Many vocational schools and training programs
offer related courses.

✓ *What else should you consider about these jobs?*

Jobs in this group may involve frequent bending and crouching. Machines and equipment may reduce the amount of heavy physical work. However, these labor-savers may also lead to fewer job openings.

Many of these jobs require long hours of hard work at certain times of the year, such as when planting or harvesting crops. Sometimes extra workers are hired for a short period of time to help in these busy seasons. Persons wanting full-time work need to look for other jobs in the off-season. Some workers in this group must face hazards such as storms, forest fires, and extreme temperatures.

If you think you would like to do this kind of work, look at the job titles listed below.

■ ■ ■

GOE: 03.04.01
Farming

CHRISTMAS-TREE FARM WORKER (forestry) ● DOT #451.687-010 ● OES: 79002 ● Plants, cultivates, and harvests evergreen trees on Christmas-tree farm: Removes brush, ferns, and other growth from planting area, using mattock and brush-hook. Plants seedlings, using mattock or dibble [TREE PLANTER (forestry)]. Scatters fertilizer pellets over planted areas by hand. Shears tops and limb tips from trees, using machete and pruning shears, to control growth, increase limb density, and improve shape. Selects trees for cutting according to markings or size, specie, and grade, and fells trees, using ax or chain saw. Drags cut trees from cutting area, and loads trees onto trucks. May be designated according to seasonal task performed. ● **GED:** R1, M1, L1 ● **SVP:** 2-30 days ● **Academic:** Ed=N, Eng=N ● **Work Field:** 003 ● **MPSMS:** 312 ● **Aptitudes:** G4, V5, N5, S4, P4, Q5, K4, F4, M3, E3, C5 ● **Temperaments:** R ● **Physical:** Stg=H; Freq: S, K, O, R, H, D Occas: I ● **Work Env:** Noise=L; Freq: U, A ● **Salary:** 2 ● **Outlook:** 2

FARM-MACHINE OPERATOR (agriculture) ● DOT #409.683-010 ● OES: 79998 ● Drives and operates one or more farm machines, such as tractors, trucks, and harvesters to perform specified farm activity as cutting hay, picking cranberries, and harvesting wheat: Hitches soil conditioning implement, such as plow or harrow to tractor, and operates tractor and towed implement to furrow and grade soil. Drives tractor and operates designated towed machine, such as seed drill or manure spreader, to plant, fertilize, dust, and spray crops. Prepares harvesting machine by adjusting speeds of cutters, blowers, and conveyors and height of cutting head or depth of digging blades according to type, height, weight, and condition of crop being harvested, and contour of terrain. Attaches towed- or mounted-type harvesting machine to tractor, using handtools, or drives self-propelled harvesting machine to cut, pull up, dig, thresh, clean, chop, bag, or bundle crops, such as sod, vine fruits, or livestock feed. Moves switches, pulls levers, and turns knobs and wheels to activate and regulate mechanisms. Refuels engine, lubricates machine parts, and monitors machine operations to ensure optimum performance. Drives truck to haul materials, supplies, or harvested crops to designated locations. May load and unload containers of materials and products on trucks, trailers, or railcars by hand or driving forklift truck. May mix specified materials and dump solutions, powders, or seeds into planter or sprayer machinery. May oversee activities of field crews. May drive horses or mules to tow farm machinery. May be identified with crop, such as hay, onions, and cranberries, or machine, such as baler, chopper, and digger. ● **GED:** R3, M2, L2 ● **SVP:** 1-3 mos ● **Academic:** Ed=N, Eng=N ● **Work Field:** 003 ● **MPSMS:** 300, 310 ● **Aptitudes:** G3, V4, N3, S3, P3, Q5, K3, F4, M3, E3, C5 ● **Temperaments:** J, T, V ● **Physical:** Stg=H; Freq: S, R, H, F, D, V Occas: C, K, O, I, N ● **Work Env:** Noise=L; Freq: W, A, O ● **Salary:** 1 ● **Outlook:** 3

FARMWORKER, DIVERSIFIED CROPS I (agriculture) ● DOT #407.663-010 ● OES: 79998 ● Drives and operates farm machines to grow and harvest combination of kinds of crops, such as grain, fruit, and vegetable: Attaches farm implements, such as plow, seed drill, and manure spreader to tractor, and drives tractor and operates implements in fields to till soil and plant, cultivate, and fertilize crops, such as sugar beets, asparagus, wheat, onions, and mint. Thins and weeds plants, such as field corn, lima beans, fresh peas, and dry beans, using handtools, such as hoes and shovels or power-drawn implement. Irrigates fields to provide moisture for crop growth, according to irrigation method appropriate for crops or locality. May mix chemical solutions, such as pesticides, herbicides, and fertilizers, and spray crops. May oversee activities of seasonal workers, and keep workers' time records. May adjust and maintain farm machines. ● **GED:** R3, M2, L3 ● **SVP:** 3-6 mos ● **Academic:** Ed=N, Eng=N ● **Work Field:** 003 ● **MPSMS:** 300 ● **Aptitudes:** G3, V4, N4, S3, P4, Q4, K3, F3, M3, E3, C4 ● **Temperaments:** T, V ● **Physical:** Stg=M; Freq: S, R, H, F, D, V Occas: C, K, O, I, T, G, N, X ● **Work Env:** Noise=L; Const: W Freq: A, O ● **Salary:** 1 ● **Outlook:** 2

FARMWORKER, FRUIT I (agriculture) ● DOT #403.683-010 ● OES: 79998 ● Drives and operates farm machinery to plant, cultivate, spray, and harvest fruit and nut crops, such as apples, oranges, strawberries, and pecans: Attaches farm implements, such as plow, planter, fertilizer applicator, and harvester to tractor and drives tractor in fields to prepare soil, and plant, fertilize, and harvest crops. Mixes chemical ingredients and sprays trees, vines, and grounds with solutions to control insects, fungus and weed growth, and diseases. Removes excess growth from trees and vines to improve fruit quality, using pruning saws and clippers. Irrigates soil, using portable-pipe or ditch system. Picks fruit during harvest. Drives truck or tractor to transport materials, supplies, workers, and products. Makes adjustments and minor repairs to farm machinery. May thin blossoms, runners, and immature fruit to obtain better-quality fruit. May select, cut, and graft stock-wood (scion) onto tree stem or trunk to propagate fruit and nut trees. May spray trees in spring to loosen and remove surplus fruit, and in fall to prevent early dropping and discoloration of fruit. May prop limbs to prevent them from breaking under weight of fruit. May start fans that circulate air or light smudge pots or torches to prevent frost damage. May be identified with work being performed, such as picking, plowing, and spraying; or according to crop worked such as cherries, cranberries, lemons, or walnuts. ● **GED:** R3, M2, L3 ● **SVP:** 6 mos-1 yr ● **Academic:** Ed=N, Eng=N ● **Work Field:** 003 ● **MPSMS:** 304, 305, 306 ● **Aptitudes:** G3, V4, N4, S3, P3, Q5, K3, F4, M3, E3, C4 ● **Temperaments:** T, V ● **Physical:** Stg=M; Freq: R, H, F, D, V Occas: C, B, S, O, T, G, N, X ● **Work Env:** Noise=L; Freq: W, A, O ● **Salary:** 1 ● **Outlook:** 4

FARMWORKER, GENERAL II (agriculture) ● DOT #421.687-010 ● OES: 74002 ● Alternate titles: CHORE TENDER; FARM LABORER. Performs variety of manual, animal-and-crop-raising tasks on general farm under close supervision: Feeds and waters cattle, poultry, and pets. Cleans barns, stables, pens, and kennels, using rake, shovel, water, and other cleaning materials. Digs seedlings, such as tobacco plants, strawberries, tomatoes, and orchard trees, using hoe, and transplants them by hand. Shovels earth to clear irrigation ditches and opens sluice gates to irrigate crops. Cleans plows, combines, and tractors, using scraper and broom. Picks, cuts, or pulls fruits and vegetables to harvest crop. Stacks loose hay, using pitchfork, or pitches hay into automatic baling machine. Stacks bales of hay and bucks them onto wagon or truck, using handhook. ● **GED:** R2, M1, L1 ● **SVP:** 2-30 days ● **Academic:** Ed=N, Eng=N ● **Work Field:** 003, 002 ● **MPSMS:** 300, 320 ● **Aptitudes:** G4, V5, N5, S4, P4, Q5, K4, F4, M3, E4, C5 ●

Temperaments: R ● **Physical:** Stg=H; Freq: R, H Occas: C, B, S, K, O ● **Work Env:** Noise=N; Freq: W ● **Salary:** 1 ● **Outlook:** 5

FARMWORKER, LIVESTOCK (agriculture) ● DOT #410.664-010 ● OES: 79998 ● Alternate titles: LABORER, LIVESTOCK; RANCH HAND, LIVESTOCK. Performs any combination of following tasks to attend livestock, such as cattle, sheep, swine, and goats on farm or ranch: Mixes feed and additives, fills feed troughs with feed, and waters livestock. Herds livestock to pasture for grazing. Examines animals to detect diseases and injuries. Vaccinates animals by placing vaccine in drinking water or feed or using syringes and hypodermic needles. Applies medications to cuts and bruises, sprays livestock with insecticide, and herds them into insecticide bath. Confines livestock in stalls, washes and clips them to prepare them for calving, and assists VETERINARIAN (medical ser.) 073.101-010 in delivery of offspring. Binds or clamps testes or surgically removes testes to castrate livestock. Clips identifying notches or symbols on animal or brands animal, using branding iron, to indicate ownership. Clamps metal rings into nostrils of livestock to permit easier handling and prevent rooting. Docks lambs, using hand snips. Cleans livestock stalls and sheds, using disinfectant solutions, brushes, and shovels. Grooms, clips, and trims animals for exhibition. May maintain ranch buildings and equipment. May plant, cultivate, and harvest feed grain for stock. May maintain breeding, feeding, and cost records. May shear sheep. ● **GED:** R3, M3, L3 ● **SVP:** 3-6 mos ● **Academic:** Ed=N, Eng=S ● **Work Field:** 002 ● **MPSMS:** 320 ● **Aptitudes:** G4, V4, N4, S4, P4, Q4, K3, F4, M3, E5, C4 ● **Temperaments:** J, V ● **Physical:** Stg=H; Freq: R, H Occas: C, S, K, O, I, N, D, X ● **Work Env:** Noise=N; Freq: W, A, O ● **Salary:** 1 ● **Outlook:** 5

FARMWORKER, VEGETABLE II (agriculture) ● DOT #402.687-010 ● OES: 79998 ● Alternate titles: GARDEN WORKER; LABORER, VEGETABLE FARM; VEGETABLE WORKER. Plants, cultivates, and harvests vegetables, working as crewmember: Dumps seed into hopper of planter towed by tractor. Rides on planter and brushes debris from seed spouts that discharge seeds into plowed furrow. Plants roots and bulbs, using hoe or trowel. Covers plants with sheet or caps of treated cloth or paper to protect plants from weather. Weeds and thins blocks of plants, using hoe or spoon-shaped tool. Transplants seedlings, using hand transplanter or by placing seedlings in rotating planting wheel while riding on power-drawn transplanter. Sets bean poles and strings them with wire or twine. Closes and ties leaves over heads of cauliflower and other cabbage and cabbagelike plants. Picks, cuts, pulls, or lifts crops to harvest them. Ties vegetables in bunches and removes tops from root crops. Pitches vine crops into viner (pea or bean shelling machine), using pitchfork or electric fork and boom, and cleans up spilled vines. May participate in irrigation activities. May be identified with work assigned, such as blocking, cutting, and stringing, or with crop raised, such as asparagus, beans, and celery. ● **GED:** R1, M1, L1 ● **SVP:** 2-30 days ● **Academic:** Ed=N, Eng=N ● **Work Field:** 003 ● **MPSMS:** 303 ● **Aptitudes:** G4, V4, N4, S4, P4, Q4, K3, F3, M3, E4, C4 ● **Temperaments:** R ● **Physical:** Stg=M; Freq: S, O, R, H, D Occas: C, B, K, I, X ● **Work Env:** Noise=L; Freq: W, A ● **Salary:** 1 ● **Outlook:** 3

LIVESTOCK-YARD ATTENDANT (any industry) ● DOT #410.674-018 ● OES: 79998 ● Performs any combination of the following tasks to bed, feed, water, load, weigh, mark, and segregate livestock: Feeds grains, hay, and prepared feed and waters livestock according to schedule. Opens gates and drives livestock to scales, pens, trucks, railcars, and holding and slaughtering areas according to instructions, using electric prod and whip. Weighs animals and records weight. Segregates animals according to weight, age, color, and physical condition. Marks livestock to identify ownership and grade, using brands, tags, paint, or tattoos. Cleans ramps, scales, trucks, railcars, and pens, using hose, fork, shovel, and rake. Scatters new bedding material, such as sawdust and straw, in pens, railcars, and trucks. May vaccinate, apply liniment, drench, isolate, and mark animals to effect disease control program. May make routine repairs and perform general maintenance duties in stockyard. ● **GED:** R3, M2, L2 ● **SVP:** 2-30 days ● **Academic:** Ed=N, Eng=N ● **Work Field:** 002, 291 ● **MPSMS:** 320 ● **Aptitudes:** G3, V4, N3, S4, P3, Q4, K3, F4, M3, E4, C4 ● **Temperaments:** R, S ● **Physical:** Stg=H; Freq: R, H, I, N Occas: C, B, S, O, F, D, X, V ● **Work Env:** Noise=L; Freq: W, A, O ● **Salary:** 1 ● **Outlook:** 2

PACKER, AGRICULTURAL PRODUCE (agriculture) ● DOT #920.687-134 ● OES: 98902 ● Alternate titles: PACKER. Packs agricultural produce, such as bulbs, fruits, nuts, eggs, and vegetables, for storage or shipment, performing any combination of following duties: Lines box, barrel, basket, carton, or crate with treated paper, cardboard, excelsior, or prepared padding, or inserts paper trays or separators in container. Places rows of produce in layers in containers, and inserts excelsior, shredded cellophane, or paper trays after each layer and over top layer of produce, or scoops produce into container. Wraps produce in treated paper, foil, or plastic film wrap before placing produce in container. Packs exposed top layer of produce, arranging produce in successive rows in container. Positions basket liner upside down over ring of produce on pallet and fills basket liner with specified amount of produce. Places basket upside down over filled liner on pallet. Pushes basket and pallet over conveyor rollers onto table of turning frame, clamps basket and pallet in place, and moves lever to turn basket upright. Fits lid on container and nails, wires, or tapes in place. Stamps grade, brand, and date of packing on container. Washes and trims produce, such as lettuce and carrots, preparatory to packing, working in warehouse or on harvesting machine in field. Sorts produce according to size, color, and grade before packing. May weigh packed produce and add or remove produce from container to obtain specified weight. May be designated Apple Packer (agriculture; wholesale tr.); Basket Turner (agriculture); Face-And-Fill Packer (agriculture); Lettuce Trimmer (agriculture); Ring Packer (agriculture; wholesale tr.); Topper Packer (agriculture); Apricot Packer (agriculture; wholesale tr.); Avocado Packer (agriculture; wholesale tr.); Boxer (agriculture); Capper (agriculture); Cherry Packer (agriculture; wholesale tr.); Citrus-Fruit Packer (agriculture; wholesale tr.); Crater (agriculture); Crate Tier (agriculture; wholesale tr.); Culled-Fruit Packer (agriculture); Egg Packer (agriculture; wholesale tr.); Fruit Packer, Face-And-Fill (agriculture; wholesale tr.); Fruit Packer, Wrap-And-Place (agriculture; wholesale tr.); Header (agriculture; wholesale tr.); Lider (agriculture; wholesale tr.); Make-Up Market Worker, Truck Garden (agriculture); Melon Packer (agriculture); Mushroom Packer (agriculture); Pear Packer (agriculture; wholesale tr.); Plant Packer (agriculture); Plant Wrapper (agriculture); Plum Packer (agriculture; wholesale tr.); Ring Facer (agriculture); Seed Packer (agriculture); Tobacco Packer (agriculture); Tree Wrapper (agriculture). ● **GED:** R2, M1, L1 ● **SVP:** 2-30 days ● **Academic:** Ed=N, Eng=N ● **Work Field:** 041 ● **MPSMS:** 300, 310 ● **Aptitudes:** G4, V4, N4, S4, P4, Q4, K3, F4, M3, E5, C3 ● **Temperaments:** R ● **Physical:** Stg=M; Freq: S, O, R, H Occas: I, N, D, X ● **Work Env:** Noise=N; ● **Salary:** 1 ● **Outlook:** 4

GOE: 03.04.02
Forestry & Logging

CHAIN SAW OPERATOR (chemical) ● DOT #454.687-010 ● OES: 73002 ● Trims limbs, tops, and roots from trees, and saws logs to predetermined lengths, using chain saw, preparatory to removal from forest or processing into wood products. May measure and mark logs for sawing. May be designated according to activity performed as LIMBER (logging). For related classifications involving judgment in determining cutting techniques, see BUCKER (logging); FALLER (logging) II; and TREE CUTTER (agriculture; logging). ● **GED:** R2, M1, L1 ● **SVP:** 2-30 days ● **Academic:** Ed=N, Eng=N ● **Work Field:** 056 ● **MPSMS:** 451 ● **Aptitudes:** G4, V4, N4, S3, P4, Q5, K4, F4, M3, E4, C5 ● **Temperaments:** R ● **Physical:** Stg=H; Freq: C, S, O, R, H, I, N, D, V Occas: B, K ● **Work Env:** Noise=L; Const: W Freq: A, O ● **Salary:** 2 ● **Outlook:** 4

FOREST-FIRE FIGHTER (forestry) ● DOT #452.687-014 ● OES: 63008 ● Alternate titles: FIRE CREW WORKER; SMOKE EATER. Suppresses forest fires, working alone or as member of crew: Fells trees, cuts and clears brush, digs trenches, and extinguishes flames and embers to contain or suppress fire, using ax, chain saw, shovel, and hand- or engine-driven water pumps. Patrols burned area after fire to watch for hot spots that may restart fire. When leading and directing fire-fighting activities of a crew of workers, may be designated Suppression-Crew Leader (forestry). ● **GED:** R2, M1, L1 ● **SVP:** 2-30 days ● **Academic:** Ed=N, Eng=N ● **Work Field:** 293 ● **MPSMS:** 313, 951 ● **Aptitudes:** G4, V4, N5, S3, P3, Q5, K3, F4, M3, E3, C4 ● **Temperaments:** R, S ● **Physical:** Stg=H; Freq: C, B, S, K, O, W, R, H Occas: X ● **Work Env:** Noise=L; Const: W Freq: H, A, O ● **Salary:** 3 ● **Outlook:** 3

FOREST WORKER (forestry) ● DOT #452.687-010 ● OES: 79002 ● Performs variety of tasks to reforest and protect timber tracts and maintain forest facilities, such as roads and campsites: Plants tree seedlings in specified pattern, using mattock, planting hoe, or dibble. Cuts out diseased, weak, or undesirable trees, and prunes limbs of young trees to deter knot growth, using handsaw, powersaw, and pruning tools. Fells trees, clears brush from fire breaks, and extinguishes flames and embers to suppress forest fires, using chain saw, shovel, and engine-driven or hand pumps. Clears and piles brush, limbs, and other debris from roadsides, fire trails, and camping areas, using ax, mattock, or brush hook. Sprays or injects trees, brush, and weeds with herbicides, using hand or powered sprayers or tree injector tool. Erects signs and fences, using posthole digger, shovel, tamper, or other handtools. Replenishes firewood and other supplies, and cleans kitchens, rest rooms, and campsites or recreational facilities. Holds measuring tape or survey rod, carries and sets stakes, clears brush from sighting line, and performs related tasks to assist forest survey crew. ● **GED:** R2, M1, L1 ● **SVP:** 2-30 days ● **Academic:** Ed=N, Eng=N ● **Work Field:** 003, 293 ● **MPSMS:** 313 ● **Aptitudes:** G4, V4, N4, S3, P4, Q5, K3, F4, M3, E4, C4 ● **Temperaments:** V ● **Physical:** Stg=H; Freq: C, B, S, K, O, R, H, I, N, D, X ● **Work Env:** Noise=L; Const: W Freq: O ● **Salary:** 3 ● **Outlook:** 3

LOGGER, ALL-ROUND (logging) ● DOT #454.684-018 ● OES: 73002 ● Harvests timber trees, performing combination of following tasks: Fells trees in specified direction, removes limbs and top, and measures and cuts tree into log lengths, using chain saw, wedges, and ax. Secures cables to logs and drives tractor or horses to skid logs to landing. Loads logs onto trucks by hand or using winch. May drive truck to haul logs to mill. ● **GED:** R2, M2, L1 ● **SVP:** 3-6 mos ● **Academic:** Ed=N, Eng=N ● **Work Field:** 004 ● **MPSMS:** 451 ● **Aptitudes:** G4, V4, N4, S3, P4, Q4, K3, F4, M3, E4, C5 ● **Temperaments:** J, R ● **Physical:** Stg=H; Freq: C, S, O, R, H, N, F, D, V Occas: B, K, I, G ● **Work Env:** Noise=L; Const: W Freq: A, O ● **Salary:** 3 ● **Outlook:** 4

LOGGING-TRACTOR OPERATOR (forestry) ● DOT #929.663-010 ● OES: 73008 ● Drives straight or articulated tractor equipped with one or more accessories, such as bulldozer blade, grapple, logging arch, cable winches, hoisting rack, and crane boom, to skid, load, unload, or stack logs, pull stumps, or clear brush. Gives or receives signals from coworkers regarding moving logs. May build or repair logging and skid roads. May drive logging tractor equipped with crawler treads. May saw felled trees into lengths [BUCKER (logging) 454.684-010]. May be designated according to accessory equipment operated as Logging-Arch Operator (logging); Logging-Tractor Operator, Swamp (logging); Log-Stacker Operator (logging; saw. & plan.); Skid-Grapple Operator (logging); Skidder Operator (forestry; logging). ● **GED:** R3, M1, L1 ● **SVP:** 3-6 mos ● **Academic:** Ed=N, Eng=N ● **Work Field:** 011 ● **MPSMS:** 451 ● **Aptitudes:** G3, V4, N4, S3, P4, Q5, K3, F4, M3, E3, C4 ● **Temperaments:** R, T ● **Physical:** Stg=M; Const: R, H, F, D, V Occas: C, S, K, O, I, T, G, N, X ● **Work Env:** Noise=L; Const: W Freq: O ● **Salary:** 4 ● **Outlook:** 2

GOE: 03.04.03
Hunting & Fishing

DECKHAND, FISHING VESSEL (fishing & hunt.) ● DOT #449.667-010 ● OES: 77005 ● Performs any combination of following duties aboard fishing vessel: Stands lookout, steering, and engine-room watches. Attaches nets, slings, hooks, and other lifting devices to cables, booms, and hoists. Loads equipment and supplies aboard vessel by hand or using hoisting equipment. Signals other workers to move, hoist, and position loads. Rows boats and dinghies and operates skiffs to transport fishers, divers, and sponge hookers and to tow and position nets. Attaches accessories, such as floats, weights, and markers to nets and lines. Pulls and guides nets and lines onto vessel. Removes fish from nets and hooks. Sorts and cleans marine life and returns undesirable and illegal catch to sea. Places catch in containers and stows in hold and covers with salt and ice. Washes deck, conveyors, knives and other equipment, using brush, detergent, and water. Lubricates, adjusts, and makes minor repairs to engines and equipment. Secures and removes vessel's docking lines to and from docks and other vessels. May be designated according to type of vessel worked as Deckhand, Clam

Dredge (fishing & hunt.); Deckhand, Crab Boat (fishing & hunt.); Deckhand, Oyster Dredge (fishing & hunt.); Deckhand, Shrimp Boat (fishing & hunt.); Deckhand, Sponge Boat (fishing & hunt.); Deckhand, Tuna Boat (fishing & hunt.). ● **GED:** R2, M1, L1 ● **SVP:** 1-3 mos ● **Academic:** Ed=N, Eng=N ● **Work Field:** 001 ● **MPSMS:** 330 ● **Aptitudes:** G4, V4, N4, S3, P4, Q5, K3, F4, M3, E3, C4 ● **Temperaments:** T, V ● **Physical:** Stg=H; Const: R, H, F, D Occas: S, T, G, X ● **Work Env:** Noise=L; Const: W Freq: U, A, O Occas: C ● **Salary:** 2 ● **Outlook:** 2

FISHER, DIVING (fishing & hunt.) ● DOT #443.664-010 ● OES: 77005 ● Gathers or harvests marine life, such as sponges, abalone, pearl oysters, and geoducks from sea bottom, wearing wet suit and scuba gear, or diving suit with air line extending to surface: Climbs overboard or is lowered into water from boat by lifeline. Picks up pearl oysters; tears sponges from sea bottom; pries abalone from rocks, using bar; and flushes geoducks from sand, using air gun connected to air compressor on boat. Places catch in bag or basket and tugs on line to have catch pulled to boat, or surfaces and empties catch on boat or in container. Signals other workers to extend or retract air lines. May monitor air lines and operate air compressor as alternating member of diving crew. May be designated according to quarry sought as Abalone Diver (fishing & hunt.); Geoduck Diver (fishing & hunt.); Pearl Diver (fishing & hunt.); Sponge Diver (fishing & hunt.). ● **GED:** R3, M2, L2 ● **SVP:** 3-6 mos ● **Academic:** Ed=N, Eng=N ● **Work Field:** 001 ● **MPSMS:** 332, 339 ● **Aptitudes:** G3, V4, N4, S3, P3, Q4, K4, F4, M3, E3, C4 ● **Temperaments:** J, S ● **Physical:** Stg=H; Const: O Freq: B, S, R, H, F, D, V Occas: C, T, G, X ● **Work Env:** Noise=N; Const: W Freq: U, O ● **Salary:** 2 ● **Outlook:** 2

FISHER, LINE (fishing & hunt.) ● DOT #442.684-010 ● OES: 77005 ● Alternate titles: FISHER. Catches fish and other marine life with hooks and lines, working alone or as member of crew: Lays out line and attaches hooks, bait, sinkers, and various anchors, floats, and swivels, depending on quarry sought. Puts line in water, and holds, anchors, or trolls (tows) line to catch fish. Hauls line onto boat deck or ashore by hand, reel, or winch, and removes catch. Stows catch in hold or boxes and packs catch in ice. May hit fish with club to stun it before removing it from hook. May fish with gaff to assist in hauling fish from water. May slit fish, remove viscera, and wash cavity to clean fish for storage. May steer vessel in fishing area. When fishing with line held in hand, is designated Fisher, Hand Line (fishing & hunt.). When fishing with fixed line equipped with hooks hung at intervals on line, is designated according to whether line is trawl (anchored in water at both ends) as Fisher, Trawl Line (fishing & hunt.); or trot (reaching across stream or from one bank) as Fisher, Trot Line (fishing & hunt.). When fishing with line that is trolled, is designated Fisher, Troll Line (fishing & hunt.). ● **GED:** R2, M1, L1 ● **SVP:** 1-3 mos ● **Academic:** Ed=N, Eng=N ● **Work Field:** 001 ● **MPSMS:** 330 ● **Aptitudes:** G4, V4, N4, S4, P4, Q5, K3, F4, M3, E4, C5 ● **Temperaments:** R ● **Physical:** Stg=M; Freq: B, S, R, H Occas: C, K, O, I ● **Work Env:** Noise=N; Const: W Freq: U, O Occas: C ● **Salary:** 2 ● **Outlook:** 2

SHELLFISH DREDGE OPERATOR (fishing & hunt.) ● DOT #446.663-010 ● OES: 77005 ● Alternate titles: SHELLFISH HARVESTER. Drives and operates mechanical or hydraulic dredge to cultivate, transplant, and harvest marine life, such as oysters, clams, and sea grass: Steers dredge to designated area, using navigational aids, such as compass and landmarks, and knowledge of tides, or is towed by other vessel. Fastens water pressure hoses, lifting and towing cables, and dredge baskets to dredge, using handtools. Primes pumps and adjusts angle of water jets and conveyor, to prepare for dredging. Activates dredge engine and lowers dredge baskets or hydraulic dredger to sea bottom, using hoisting boom and winch. Activates hydraulic dredge impeller pumps and conveyor and drags hydraulic dredger or dredge baskets along sea bottom to scoop or flush shellfish from beds. Inspects contents dumped from dredges onto deck to determine depth of cut into sea bottom, and adjusts water pressure or angle of basket blade to attain depth of cut desired. Observes flow of shellfish on conveyor and stops conveyor to prevent or clear jamming. Observes and listens to operation of equipment to detect malfunction and makes adjustments and minor repairs to correct operational defects. Attaches cutting blades or harrows to dredge and lowers to specified distance above or on sea bottom and steers dredge in diminishing circles to cultivate shellfish beds or cut sea grass. May record date, harvest area, and yield in logbook. May direct helpers in sorting of clams. May be designated according to type of dredge operated as Hydraulic Dredge Operator (fishing & hunt.); Self-Propelled Dredge Operator (fishing & hunt.); or kind of shellfish harvested as Clam Dredge Operator (fishing & hunt.); Oyster Dredge Operator (fishing & hunt.). ● **GED:** R3, M2, L2 ● **SVP:** 6 mos-1 yr ● **Academic:** Ed=N, Eng=N ● **Work Field:** 002 ● **MPSMS:** 332 ● **Aptitudes:** G3, V4, N4, S3, P3, Q5, K3, F4, M3, E4, C5 ● **Temperaments:** J, R, T ● **Physical:** Stg=H; Freq: B, R, H, F, D, V Occas: C, S, N ● **Work Env:** Noise=L; Freq: W, U, O ● **Salary:** 2 ● **Outlook:** 2

SKIFF OPERATOR (fishing & hunt.) ● DOT #441.683-010 ● OES: 77005 ● Operates seiner skiff to hold one end of purse seine in place while purse seiner circles school of fish to set net. Holds purse seine away from ship during pursing and brailing operations. May splash water with pole, on opposite side of school away from purse seiner, to prevent fish from escaping as fish are encircled by purse seine. May locate schools of fish sighted by other fishers. ● **GED:** R3, M1, L2 ● **SVP:** 3-6 mos ● **Academic:** Ed=N, Eng=N ● **Work Field:** 001 ● **MPSMS:** 331 ● **Aptitudes:** G3, V4, N4, S3, P4, Q5, K4, F4, M3, E3, C5 ● **Temperaments:** S ● **Physical:** Stg=H; Freq: C, B, R, H, F, D, V Occas: S, K, O ● **Work Env:** Noise=L; Freq: W, U, O ● **Salary:** 2 ● **Outlook:** 2

GOE: 03.04.04
Nursery & Groundskeeping

CEMETERY WORKER (real estate) ● DOT #406.684-010 ● OES: 79014 ● Alternate titles: GRAVEDIGGER. Prepares graves and maintains cemetery grounds: Locates grave site according to section, lot, and plot numbers, and marks area to be excavated. Removes sod from gravesite, using shovel. Digs grave to specified depth, using pick and shovel or backhoe. Places concrete slabs on bottom and around grave to line it. Mixes and pours concrete to construct foundation for grave marker, using premixed concrete, wheelbarrow, and handtools. Positions casket-lowering device on grave, covers dirt pile and sod with artificial grass carpet, erects canopy, and arranges folding chairs to prepare site for burial service. Builds wooden forms for concrete slabs, using hammer, saw, and nails. Sets grave marker in concrete on gravesite, using shovel and trowel. Mows grass, using hand or power mower. Prunes shrubs, trims trees, and plants flowers and shrubs on grave, using handtools. Removes leaves and other debris from graves, using leaf blowers and weed eaters. May drive vehicles, such as backhoe, trucks, and tractors. May repair and maintain tools and equipment, using handtools and power tools and applying mechanical knowledge. May open and close mausoleum vaults, using handtools. ● **GED:** R3, M1, L2 ● **SVP:** 6 mos-1 yr ● **Academic:** Ed=N, Eng=N ● **Work Field:** 003, 102 ● **MPSMS:** 969 ● **Aptitudes:** G3, V4, N4, S4, P4, Q4, K4, F4, M3, E4, C5 ● **Temperaments:** T, V ● **Physical:** Stg=H; Freq: R, H Freq: S, O Occas: I, T, G, N ● **Work Env:** Noise=N; Const: W ● **Salary:** 1 ● **Outlook:** 2

GROUNDSKEEPER, INDUSTRIAL-COMMERCIAL (any industry) ● DOT #406.684-014 ● OES: 79014 ● Alternate titles: CARETAKER, GROUNDS; GARDENER. Maintains grounds of industrial, commercial, or public property, performing any combination of following tasks: Cuts lawns, using hand mower or power mower. Trims and edges around walks, flower beds, and walls, using clippers, weed cutters, and edging tools. Prunes shrubs and trees to shape and improve growth or remove damaged leaves, branches, or twigs, using shears, pruners, or chain saw. Sprays lawn, shrubs, and trees with fertilizer, herbicides, and insecticides, using hand or automatic sprayer. Rakes and bags or burns leaves, using rake. Cleans grounds and removes litter, using spiked stick or broom. Shovels snow from walks and driveways. Spreads salt on public passage ways to prevent ice buildup. Plants grass, flowers, trees, and shrubs, using gardening tools. Waters lawn and shrubs, using hose or by activating fixed or portable sprinkler system. May repair fences, gates, walls, and walks, using carpentry and masonry tools. May paint fences and outbuildings. May clean out drainage ditches and culverts, using shovel and rake. May perform ground maintenance duties, using tractor equipped with attachments, such as mowers, lime or fertilizer spreaders, lawn roller, and snow removal equipment. May sharpen tools, such as weed cutters, edging tools, and shears, using file or knife sharpener. May make minor repairs on equip-

ment, such as lawn mower, spreader, and snow removal equipment, using handtools and power tools. May perform variety of laboring duties, common to type of employing establishment. ● **GED:** R3, M2, L2 ● **SVP:** 1-3 mos ● **Academic:** Ed=N, Eng=N ● **Work Field:** 003, 031 ● **MPSMS:** 969 ● **Aptitudes:** G4, V4, N4, S4, P4, Q4, K4, F4, M3, E4, C5 ● **Temperaments:** V ● **Physical:** Stg=M; Freq: R, H Occas: C, B, S, K, O, I, N, F, D, A, V ● **Work Env:** Noise=L; Const: W Occas: T ● **Salary:** 2 ● **Outlook:** 3

GREENSKEEPER I (any industry) ● DOT #406.137-010 ● OES: 72000 ● Alternate titles: GREENSKEEPER, HEAD. Supervises and coordinates activities of workers engaged in preserving grounds and turf of golf course in playing condition: Confers with SUPERINTENDENT, GREENS (amuse. & rec.) 406.137-014 to plan and review work projects. Determines work priority and assigns workers to specific tasks, such as fertilizing, irrigating, seeding, mowing, raking, and spraying. Mixes and prepares recommended spray and dust solutions. Performs other duties as desribed under SUPERVISOR (any industry) Master Title. May direct and assist workers engaged in maintenance and repair of mechanical equipment. May assist workers to perform more critical duties. ● **GED:** R4, M3, L3 ● **SVP:** 1-2 yrs ● **Academic:** Ed=H, Eng=N ● **Work Field:** 003 ● **MPSMS:** 311, 969 ● **Aptitudes:** G3, V3, N3, S3, P3, Q4, K4, F4, M4, E4, C4 ● **Temperaments:** D, P, V ● **Physical:** Stg=M; Freq: R, H, T, G Occas: S, I, F, D, X, V ● **Work Env:** Noise=N; Freq: W ● **Salary:** 1 ● **Outlook:** 3

GREENSKEEPER II (any industry) ● DOT #406.683-010 ● OES: 79014 ● Alternate titles: LABORER, GOLF COURSE. Performs any combination of following duties, as directed by GREENSKEEPER (any industry) I, to maintain grounds and turf of golf course in playing condition: Operates tractor, using specific attachments, to till, cultivate, and grade new turf areas, to apply prescribed amounts of lime, fertilizer, insecticide, and fungicide, and to mow rough and fairway areas at designated cut, exercising care not to injure turf or shrubs. Cuts turf on green and tee areas, using hand mower and power mower. Connects hose and sprinkler systems at designated points on course to irrigate turf. Digs and rakes ground to prepare new greens, grades and cleans traps, and repairs roadbeds, using shovels, rakes, spades, and other tools. May plant, trim, and spray trees and shrubs. ● **GED:** R2, M1, L2 ● **SVP:** 1-3 mos ● **Academic:** Ed=N, Eng=N ● **Work Field:** 003 ● **MPSMS:** 310 ● **Aptitudes:** G4, V4, N4, S3, P4, Q5, K3, F4, M3, E3, C4 ● **Temperaments:** R, T ● **Physical:** Stg=M; Freq: R, H Occas: C, B, S, K, O, D, X ● **Work Env:** Noise=L; Const: W Freq: O ● **Salary:** 1 ● **Outlook:** 4

HORTICULTURAL WORKER I (agriculture) ● DOT #405.684-014 ● OES: 79005 ● Plants, cultivates, and harvests horticultural specialties, such as flowers and shrubs, and performs related duties in environmentally controlled structure, applying knowledge of environmental systems: Ascertains growing schedules and deviations from established procedures from grower or manager. Sows seed and plants cuttings. Looks at and feels leaf texture, bloom development, and soil condition to determine nutrient and moisture requirements and to detect and identify germ and pest infestations. Sets fertilizer timing and metering devices that control frequency and amount of nutrients to be introduced into irrigation system. Applies herbicides, fungicides, and pesticides to destroy undesirable growth and pests, using spray wand connected to solution tank. Reads and interprets sensing indicators and regulates humidity, ventilation, and carbon dioxide systems to control environmental conditions. Grafts scions to seedling stock. Pollinates, prunes, transplants, and pinches plants, and culls flowers, branches, fruit, and plants to ensure development of marketable products. Harvests, packs, and stores crop, using techniques appropriate for individual horticultural specialty. May maintain and repair hydroponic and environmental control systems. May mix planting soil, following prescribed procedures. May record information, such as chemicals used, grafting performed, and environmental conditions, to maintain required records. May maintain and repair structures, using materials, such as corrugated fiberglass panels, lath, glass panes, and putty, and tools, such as hammer, saw, and putty knife. May be designated according to work location as Greenhouse Worker (agriculture); according to techniques employed as Hydroponics Worker (agriculture); or according to horticultural specialty as Orchid Worker (agriculture). ● **GED:** R3, M2, L3 ● **SVP:** 1-3 mos ● **Academic:** Ed=N, Eng=S ● **Work Field:** 003 ● **MPSMS:** 310, 300 ● **Aptitudes:** G3, V4, N4, S3, P3, Q4, K4, F4, M3, E4, C4 ● **Temperaments:** J, T, V ● **Physical:** Stg=H; Freq: R,

H Occas: C, B, S, K, O, I, E, T, G, N, F, D, X • **Work Env:** Noise=N; Freq: U Occas: A • **Salary:** 2 • **Outlook:** 3

HORTICULTURAL WORKER II (agriculture) • DOT #405.687-014 • OES: 79005 • Performs any combination of following duties concerned with preparing soil and growth media, cultivating, and otherwise participating in horticultural activities under close supervision on acreage, in nursery, or in environmentally controlled structure, such as greenhouse and shed: Hauls and spreads topsoil, fertilizer, peat moss, and other materials to condition land. Digs, rakes, and screens soil, and fills cold frames and hot beds to prepare them for planting. Fills growing tanks with water. Plants, sprays, weeds, and waters plants, shrubs, and trees. Sows grass seed and plants plugs of sod and cuts, rolls, and stacks sod. Prepares scion and ties buds to assist worker budding roses. Traps and poisons pests, such as moles, gophers, and mice. Plants shrubs and plants in containers. Ties, bunches, wraps, and packs flowers, plants, shrubs, and trees to fill orders. Moves containerized shrubs and trees, using wheelbarrow. Digs up shrubs and trees, and wraps their roots with burlap. May dip rose cuttings into vat to disinfect cuttings prior to storage. May fold and staple corrugated forms to make boxes used for packing horticultural products. May be designated according to employing establishment as Grass-Farm Laborer (agriculture); Greenhouse Laborer (agriculture); Nursery Laborer (agriculture); Rose-Farm Laborer (agriculture); or according to horticultural specialty as Bean-Sprout Laborer (agriculture); Mushroom Laborer (agriculture). • **GED:** R2, M1, L1 • **SVP:** 2-30 days • **Academic:** Ed=N, Eng=N • **Work Field:** 003 • **MPSMS:** 310 • **Aptitudes:** G4, V4, N5, S4, P4, Q5, K4, F4, M3, E4, C4 • **Temperaments:** R • **Physical:** Stg=H; Freq: S, K, R, H, D Occas: O, I, E, T, G, N, X • **Work Env:** Noise=N; Occas: W • **Salary:** 1 • **Outlook:** 3

LABORER, LANDSCAPE (agriculture) • DOT #408.687-014 • OES: 79014 • Moves soil, equipment, and materials, digs holes, and performs related duties to assist LANDSCAPE GARDENER (agriculture) 408.161-010 in landscaping grounds: Digs holes for plants and trees, using pick and shovel. Mixes fertilizer or lime with dirt in bottom of holes to enrich soil, places plants or trees in holes, and adds dirt to fill holes. Attaches wires from planted trees to stakes to support trees. Hauls or spreads topsoil, using wheelbarrow and rake. Waters lawns, trees, and plants, using portable sprinkler system, hose, or watering can. Spreads straw over seeded soil to prevent movement of seed and soil. Builds forms for concrete borders, using lumber, hammer, and nails. Mixes and pours cement for garden borders. Places decorative stones and plants flowers in garden areas. Mows lawns, using power mower. • **GED:** R2, M2, L2 • **SVP:** 2-30 days • **Academic:** Ed=N, Eng=N • **Work Field:** 003 • **MPSMS:** 969 • **Aptitudes:** G4, V4, N4, S4, P4, Q5, K4, F4, M3, E4, C4 • **Temperaments:** T, V • **Physical:** Stg=H; Freq: S, K, R, H, I Occas: O, T, G, X • **Work Env:** Noise=L; Freq: W, O • **Salary:** 1 • **Outlook:** 3

LAWN-SERVICE WORKER (agriculture) • DOT #408.684-010 • OES: 79014 • Cultivates lawns, using power aerator and thatcher and chemicals according to specifications: Lifts dead leaves and grass from between growing grass and soil, using thatcher. Pierces soil to make holes for fertilizer and water, using aerator. Presses aerator fork into soil and pulls rake through grass to cultivate areas not accessible to machines. Distributes granulated fertilizers, pesticides, and fungicides on lawn, using spreader. Records services rendered, materials used, and charges assessed on specified form. Transports thatcher, aerator, tools, and materials to and from job site, using truck with hydraulic lift-gate. May care for athletic field turf and be designated Athletic Turf Worker (amuse. & rec.). • **GED:** R3, M2, L2 • **SVP:** 3-6 mos • **Academic:** Ed=N, Eng=N • **Work Field:** 003 • **MPSMS:** 969 • **Aptitudes:** G3, V4, N4, S3, P4, Q4, K3, F4, M3, E4, C4 • **Temperaments:** T • **Physical:** Stg=H; Freq: R, H, I Occas: S, O, N, F, D, X • **Work Env:** Noise=L; Const: W • **Salary:** 1 • **Outlook:** 2

GOE: 03.04.05
Services

DOG CATCHER (government ser.) • DOT #379.673-010 • OES: 63099 • Alternate titles: DOG WARDEN. Captures and impounds unlicensed, stray, and uncontrolled animals: Snares animal with net, rope, or device. Cages or secures animal in truck. Drives truck to shelter. Removes animal from truck to shelter cage or other enclosure. Supplies food, water, and personal care to detained animals. Investigates complaints of animal bite cases. Destroys rabid animals as directed. Examines dog licenses for validity and issues warnings or summonses to delinquent owners. May destroy unclaimed animals, using gun, or by gas or electrocution. May examine captured animals for injuries and deliver injured animals to VETERINARIAN (medical ser.) for medical treatment. May maintain file of number of animals impounded and disposition of each. May enforce regulations concerning treatment of domestic animals and be designated Humane Officer (government ser.). • **GED:** R3, M1, L2 • **SVP:** 1-3 mos • **Academic:** Ed=N, Eng=G • **Work Field:** 291, 293 • **MPSMS:** 329, 969 • **Aptitudes:** G4, V4, N4, S4, P4, Q4, K3, F4, M3, E3, C5 • **Temperaments:** P, S, V • **Physical:** Stg=M; Freq: R, H, T, G, F, D, V Occas: I, N • **Work Env:** Noise=N; Freq: W • **Salary:** 3 • **Outlook:** 2

IRRIGATOR, SPRINKLING SYSTEM (agriculture) • DOT #409.685-014 • OES: 79998 • Alternate titles: IRRIGATOR, OVERHEAD. Tends sprinkler system that irrigates land: Lays out strings (pipe) along designated pipeline settings in field. Connects pipe, using snap lock or wrench to tighten collar clamp. Attaches revolving sprinkler heads to vertical pipes at designated points along pipeline. Starts gasoline engine and adjusts controls that move self-propelled wheel line sprinkler system across field or pushes on switch that activates circle sprinkler system, and starts pump that forces water through system to irrigate crops. Observes revolving sprinklers to ensure uniform distribution of water to all areas. Lubricates, adjusts, and repairs or replaces parts, such as sprinkler heads and drive chains to maintain system, using handtools. Disassembles system and moves it to next location after specified time intervals. • **GED:** R2, M1, L2 • **SVP:** 2-30 days • **Academic:** Ed=N, Eng=N • **Work Field:** 003 • **MPSMS:** 300, 310 • **Aptitudes:** G4, V4, N4, S3, P4, Q5, K4, F4, M4, E4, C5 • **Temperaments:** T • **Physical:** Stg=M; Freq: S, K, O, R, H, N, F Occas: C • **Work Env:** Noise=N; Freq: W, U • **Salary:** 1 • **Outlook:** 3

PLANT-CARE WORKER (agriculture) • DOT #408.364-010 • OES: 79005 • Alternate titles: INTERIOR HORTICULTURIST; PLANT TENDER. Cares for ornamental plants on various customer premises, applying knowledge of horticultural requirements, and using items such as insecticides, fertilizers, and gardening tools: Reads work orders and supply requisitions to determine job requirements, and confers with supervisor to clarify work procedures. Loads plants and supplies onto truck in order of scheduled stops, using handtruck. Drives truck to premises and carries needed supplies to work area. Examines plants and soil to determine moisture level, using water sensor gauge, and waters plants according to requirements of species, using hose and watering can. Sponges plant leaves to apply moisture and remove dust. Observes plants under magnifying glass to detect insects and disease, and consults plant care books or confers with supervisor to identify problems and determine treatments. Selects and applies specified chemical solutions to feed plants, kill insects, and treat diseases, using hose or mist-sprayer. Transplants root-bound plants into larger containers. Pinches and prunes stems and leaves to remove dead and diseased leaves, to shape plants, and to induce growth, using shears. Removes diseased and dying plants from premises and replaces them with healthy plants. Informs customer of plant care needs. Enters record of actions taken at each stop in route book and prepares requisitions for materials needed on subsequent visit. Returns diseased, dying, and unused plants and supplies to employer premises. • **GED:** R3, M2, L3 • **SVP:** 1-3 mos • **Academic:** Ed=N, Eng=S • **Work Field:** 003 • **MPSMS:** 310 • **Aptitudes:** G3, V3, N4, S4, P3, Q3, K4, F3, M3, E4, C3 • **Temperaments:** J, T • **Physical:** Stg=M; Freq: C, R, H, I, E, N, A, X Occas: S, K, O, T, G • **Work Env:** Noise=N; Freq: U Occas: T • **Salary:** 1 • **Outlook:** 3

TREE PRUNER (agriculture) • DOT #408.684-018 • OES: 79998 • Cuts away dead and excess branches from fruit, nut, and shade trees, using handsaws, pruning hooks and shears, and long-handled clippers. Applies tar or other protective substances to cut surfaces to seal surfaces against insects. May use truck-mounted hydraulic lifts and pruners and power pruners. May climb trees, using climbing hooks and belts, or climb ladders to gain access to work area. May specialize in pruning fruit trees and be designated Orchard Pruner (agriculture). May prune, cut down, fertilize, and spray trees as directed by TREE SURGEON (agriculture) and be designated Tree-Surgeon Helper (agriculture) I. ● **GED:** R3, M2, L3 ● **SVP:** 3-6 mos ● **Academic:** Ed=N, Eng=S ● **Work Field:** 054, 056, 293 ● **MPSMS:** 300, 310 ● **Aptitudes:** G3, V3, N4, S3, P4, Q4, K4, F4, M3, E3, C4 ● **Temperaments:** T ● **Physical:** Stg=M; Freq: C, B, R, H, D Occas: S, O, X ● **Work Env:** Noise=N; Freq: O Occas: D ● **Salary:** 1 ● **Outlook:** 3

TREE TRIMMER (tel. & tel.) ● DOT #408.664-010 ● OES: 73098 ● Alternate titles: TREE TRIMMER, LINE CLEARANCE; TREE-TRIMMING-LINE TECHNICIAN. Trims trees to clear right-of-way for communications lines and electric power lines to minimize storm and short-circuit hazards: Climbs trees to reach branches interfering with wires and transmission towers, using climbing equipment. Prunes treetops, using saws or pruning shears. Repairs trees damaged by storm or lightning by trimming jagged stumps and painting them to prevent bleeding of sap. Removes broken limbs from wires, using hooked extension pole. Fells trees interfering with power service, using chain saw (portable power saw). May work from bucket of extended truck boom to reach limbs. ● **GED:** R3, M2, L2 ● **SVP:** 3-6 mos ● **Academic:** Ed=N, Eng=N ● **Work Field:** 056, 054 ● **MPSMS:** 312 ● **Aptitudes:** G3, V4, N5, S3, P4, Q5, K4, F4, M3, E2, C5 ● **Temperaments:** R, S ● **Physical:** Stg=H; Freq: C, B, R, H, I, N, D ● **Work Env:** Noise=L; Const: W Freq: D, O Occas: E ● **Salary:** 3 ● **Outlook:** 3

Protective 04

An interest in using authority to protect people and property. You can satisfy this interest by working in law enforcement, fire fighting, and related fields. You may enjoy mental challenge and intrigue. You could investigate crimes or fires. You may prefer to fight fires and respond to other emergencies. Or you may want more routine work. Perhaps a job in guarding or patrolling would appeal to you. You may have management ability. You could seek a leadership position in law enforcement and the protective services.

Workers in this group are in charge of enforcing laws and regulations. Some investigate crimes, while others supervise workers who stop or arrest lawbreakers. Others make inspections to be sure that the laws are not broken. Most jobs are found in the federal, state, or local governments, such as the police and fire departments. Some are found in private businesses, such as factories, stores, and similar places.

✓ What kind of work would you do?

Your work activities would depend upon your specific job. For example, you might:

- set procedures, prepare work schedules, and assign duties for jailers.
- direct and coordinate daily activities of a police force.
- direct and coordinate activities of a fire department.
- hire, assign, and supervise store detectives.
- investigate and arrest persons suspected of the illegal sale or use of drugs.
- patrol an assigned area in a vehicle or on foot and issue tickets, investigate disturbances, render first aid, and arrest suspects.
- patrol an assigned area to observe hunting and fishing activities and warn or arrest persons violating fish and game laws.

✓ What skills and abilities do you need for this kind of work?

To do this kind of work, you must be able to:

- work with laws and regulations, sometimes written in legal language.
- use practical thinking to conduct or supervise investigations.

- supervise other workers.
- plan the work of a department or activity.
- deal with various kinds of people.
- work under pressure or in the face of danger.
- patrol an assigned area to observe hunting and fishing activities and warn or arrest persons violating fish and game laws.
- keep physically fit.
- use guns, fire-fighting equipment, and other safety devices.

✓ How do you know if you would like or could learn to do this kind of work?

The following questions may give you clues about yourself as you consider this group of jobs.

- Have you had courses in government, civics, or criminology? Did you find these subjects interesting?
- Have you been a member of a volunteer fire department or emergency rescue squad? Were you given training for this work?
- Have you watched detective television shows? Do you read detective stories? Do you try to solve mysteries?
- Have you been an officer of a school safety patrol? Do you like being responsible for the work of others?
- Have you used a gun for hunting or in target practice? Are you a good shot?
- Have you spoken at a civic or community organization? Do you like work that requires frequent public speaking?
- Have you been a military officer?

✓ How can you prepare for and enter this kind of work?

Occupations in this group usually require education and/or training extending from one to over ten years, depending upon the specific kind of work.

Local civil service regulations usually control the selection of police officers. People who want to do this kind of work must meet certain requirements. They must be U. S. citizens and be within certain height and weight ranges. In addition, they may be required to take written, oral, and physical examinations. The physical examinations often include tests of physical strength and the ability to move quickly and easily. To work in these jobs, persons should have the physical condition to use firearms or work on dangerous missions. Personal investigations are made of all applicants.

Most police departments prefer to hire people who have a high school education or its equal. However, some departments hire people if they have worked in related activities, such as guarding or volunteer police work.

Jobs with federal law enforcement agencies usually require a college degree. For example, to be hired as customs enforcement officer, a degree or three years of related work experience is required. FBI Special Agents are required to have a degree in law or accounting. Accounting degrees should be coupled with at least one year of related work experience.

Most management or supervisory jobs in this group are filled from within the ranks. Promotions are usually based on written examinations and job performance and are usually subject to civil service laws.

✓ What else should you consider about these jobs?

Most workers in these jobs are on call any time their services are needed. They may work overtime during emergencies. Many of these jobs expose workers to great physical danger.

If you think you would like to do this kind of work, look at the job titles listed below.

■ ■ ■

GOE: 04.01.01
Managing

DEPUTY, COURT (government ser.) ● DOT #377.137-018 ● OES: 61005 ● Supervises and coordinates activities of court peace officers engaged in providing security and maintaining order within individual courtrooms and throughout courthouse: Tours and inspects duty stations of BAILIFF (government ser.) to ensure compliance with regulation job duties and correct appearance. Patrols courthouse to quell disturbances and to keep order. Trains newly appointed officers in performance of job duties. Communicates with COURT CLERKS (government ser.) to identify day's court calendar. Prepares and schedules work assignments of court officers, and issues daily duty assignments. Prepares jury's meal vouchers for court official assigned to escort jurors to restaurant. Secures lodging facilities and transportation for jurors deliberating lengthy trials. Prepares and submits activity and time reports to DEPUTY SHERIFF, CHIEF (government ser.). May witness name selection list of prospective jurors to ensure impartiality. May perform duties of BAILIFF (government ser.). ● GED: R3, M2, L3 ● SVP: 1-2 yrs ● Academic: Ed=H, Eng=G ● Work Field: 293, 295 ● MPSMS: 951 ● Aptitudes: G3, V3, N4, S4, P4, Q4, K3, F4, M4, E5, C5 ● Temperaments: D, P, V ● Physical: Stg=L; Freq: R, H, I, T, G, N ● Work Env: Noise=N; ● Salary: 3 ● Outlook: 3

DESK OFFICER (government ser.) ● DOT #375.137-014 ● OES: 61005 ● Alternate titles: OPERATIONS OFFICER. Supervises and coordinates activities of personnel assigned to police precinct station: Assumes responsibility for safekeeping of money and valuables taken from prisoners, lost or stolen articles, and property held as evidence. Supervises work of POLICE OFFICER (government ser.) II 375.367-010 or POLICE OFFICER (government ser.) I 375.263-014 who search suspects. Supervises TELEPHONE OPERATOR (clerical) 235.662-022 engaged in sending and receiving police communication by telephone and radio systems. Receives notification and informs commanding officer of calls and orders received over police communication systems. Records information, such as name of arresting officer and prisoner's name, address, and charge, to complete precinct activity reports for commanding officer. Commands subordinate officers and subordinate personnel on assigned duty and assumes responsibility for efficiency and discipline of workers under command. Assumes command of station house in absence of commanding officer. May make inspection tour of police beats in precinct area [TRAFFIC LIEUTENANT (government ser.) 375.167-046]. May supervise and coordinate activities of police clerical staff [SECRETARY OF POLICE (government ser.) 375.137-022]. May be designated according to rank as Desk Captain (government ser.); Desk Lieutenant (government ser.); Desk Sergeant (government ser.). ● GED: R4, M2, L3 ● SVP: 2-4 yrs ● Academic: Ed=H, Eng=G ● Work Field: 293 ● MPSMS: 951 ● Aptitudes: G3, V3, N3, S4, P4, Q3, K4, F4, M4, E5, C5 ● Temperaments: D, P, V ● Physical: Stg=S; Freq: T, G, N, A Occas: R, H, I, F, X ● Work Env: Noise=N; ● Salary: 4 ● Outlook: 3

FIRE CAPTAIN (government ser.) ● DOT #373.134-010 ● OES: 61002 ● Supervises and coordinates activities of company of FIRE FIGHTERS (any industry) assigned to specific firehouse: Inspects station house, buildings, grounds, and facilities, and examines firetrucks and equipment, such as ladders and hoses, to ensure compliance with departmental maintenance standards. Responds to fire alarms and determines from observation nature and extent of fire, condition of building, danger to adjacent buildings, and source of water supply, and directs firefighting crews accordingly. Trains subordinates in use of equipment and methods of extinguishing all types of fires. Evaluates efficiency of personnel. Inspects commercial establishments in assigned district and reports fire hazards or safety violations to FIRE INSPECTOR (government ser.). Compiles report of each fire call, listing location, type, probable cause, estimated damage, and disposition. May respond to emergency calls to render first aid. May recommend corrective measures for fire hazards or safety violations to building owners. May conduct fire drills for occupants of buildings. May supervise and coordinate activities of fire companies fighting multiple alarm fire until relieved by superiors. May write and submit proposal for new equipment or modification of existing equipment to superiors. May be designated Fire Lieutenant (government ser.) in larger organizations. May be designated according to specialty as Fire Captain, Marine (government ser.); Fire Lieutenant, Marine (government ser.). ● GED: R4, M3, L4 ● SVP: 2-4 yrs ● Academic: Ed=H, Eng=G ● Work Field: 293, 295 ● MPSMS: 951 ● Aptitudes: G2, V3, N3, S2, P4, Q3, K4, F4, M4, E3, C3 ● Temperaments: D, J, P, S, V ● Physical: Stg=M; Freq: R, H, T, G, N, A Occas: C, B, S, K, O, I, F, D, X, V ● Work Env: Noise=L; Freq: W Occas: H, U, A, E, D, X, O ● Salary: 4 ● Outlook: 2

FIRE CHIEF (government ser.) ● DOT #373.117-010 ● OES: 19005 ● Alternate titles: CHIEF ENGINEER. Directs activities of municipal fire department: Directs training of personnel and administers laws and regulations affecting department. Evaluates fire prevention and fire control policies by keeping abreast of new methods and conducting studies of departmental operations. Assumes personal command at multiple-alarm fires. Supervises firefighters engaged in operation and maintenance of fire stations and equipment. Coordinates mutual fire protection plans with surrounding municipalities. Surveys buildings, grounds, and equipment to estimate needs of department and prepare departmental budget. Confers with officials and community groups and conducts public relations campaigns to present need for changes in laws and policies and to encourage fire prevention. May investigate causes of fires and inspect buildings for fire hazards. May control issue of occupancy permits and similar licenses. May perform duties of BATTALION CHIEF (government ser.) 373.167-010 in smaller communities. May be designated Chief Of Field Operations (government ser.); District Fire Chief (government ser.); or Fire Chief, Deputy (government ser.) in larger organizations. ● **GED:** R5, M4, L5 ● **SVP:** 4-10 yrs ● **Academic:** Ed=H, Eng=G ● **Work Field:** 295, 293 ● **MPSMS:** 951 ● **Aptitudes:** G2, V2, N3, S3, P3, Q3, K4, F4, M4, E5, C3 ● **Temperaments:** D, I, J, P, V ● **Physical:** Stg=L; Freq: T, G, N Occas: R, H, I, F, D, A, X, V ● **Work Env:** Noise=L; Freq: W Occas: H, U, A, E, D, X, O ● **Salary:** 5 ● **Outlook:** 3

FIRE MARSHAL (any industry) ● DOT #373.167-018 ● OES: 61002 ● Supervises and coordinates activities of firefighting personnel of industrial establishment and inspects equipment and premises to ensure adherence to fire regulations: Inspects and orders replacement or servicing of firefighting equipment, such as sprinklers and extinguishers. Issues permits for storage and use of hazardous or flammable materials. Inspects premises to detect combustion hazards [FIRE INSPECTOR (any industry) 373.367-010]. Orders and directs fire drills. Directs firefighting and rescue activities according to knowledge of accepted procedures. May be designated according to employing establishment as Fire Chief (saw. & plan.); Fire Marshal, Refinery (petrol. refin.). ● **GED:** R4, M3, L3 ● **SVP:** 2-4 yrs ● **Academic:** Ed=H, Eng=G ● **Work Field:** 293, 212 ● **MPSMS:** 951 ● **Aptitudes:** G3, V3, N3, S2, P4, Q3, K4, F4, M2, E3, C4 ● **Temperaments:** D, J, P, S ● **Physical:** Stg=M; Freq: R, H, N, A Occas: C, B, S, K, O, W, T, G, F, D, X, V ● **Work Env:** Noise=N; Occas: W, C, H, U, A, E, D, X, O ● **Salary:** 5 ● **Outlook:** 1

GUARD, CHIEF (any industry) ● DOT #372.167-014 ● OES: 69998 ● Supervises and coordinates activities of guard force of establishment, such as industrial plant, department store, or museum: Assigns personnel to posts or patrol, according to size and nature of establishment and protection requirements. Interprets security rules and directs subordinates in enforcing compliance, such as issuance of security badges, photographing of employees, and safekeeping of forbidden articles carried by visitors. Responds to calls from subordinates to direct activities during fires, storms, riots, or other emergencies. Inspects or directs inspection of premises to test alarm systems, detect safety hazards, and to ensure that safety rules are posted and enforced. Examines fire extinguishers and other safety equipment for serviceability. Reports irregularities and hazards to appropriate personnel. Cooperates with police, fire, and civil defense authorities in problems affecting establishment. May select and train subordinates in protective procedures, first aid, fire safety, and other duties. May be designated according to rank as Guard, Captain (any industry); Guard, Lieutenant (any industry); Guard, Sergeant (any industry); or according to establishment served as Plant-Protection Supervisor (any industry); Security Chief, Museum (museums). ● **GED:** R3, M2, L3 ● **SVP:** 1-2 yrs ● **Academic:** Ed=N, Eng=G ● **Work Field:** 293 ● **MPSMS:** 899 ● **Aptitudes:** G3, V3, N4, S3, P3, Q4, K4, F4, M4, E5, C4 ● **Temperaments:** D, P ● **Physical:** Stg=L; Freq: T, G, F, V Occas: R, H, I, N, D, A, X ● **Work Env:** Noise=N; Occas: W ● **Salary:** 4 ● **Outlook:** 3

MANAGER, INTERNAL SECURITY (business ser.) ● DOT #376.137-010 ● OES: 63035 ● Supervises and coordinates activities of STORE DETECTIVES (retail trade), conducts private investigations, and sells internal protective service to wholesale and retail businesses: Assigns STORE DETECTIVES (retail trade) to shifts at various locations according to job requirements and worker's abilities, skills, and experience. Observes workers in performance of duties to evaluate efficiency and to detect and correct inefficient work practices. Interviews and hires workers to fill vacant positions. Demonstrates and explains methods of detecting and apprehending shoplifters. Explains state laws concerning arrest and detention to employees. Conducts private investigation to obtain information concerning such matters as

divorce evidence, juvenile runaways, and background data on persons applying for employment, insurance, or bonding. Acts as undercover agent in retail stores to detect employee incompetency and dishonesty. Prepares detailed reports concerning matters investigated. Contacts business establishments to promote sales of security services. Analyzes security needs, estimates costs, and presents proposal to prospective customer. ● **GED:** R4, M3, L4 ● **SVP:** 2-4 yrs ● **Academic:** Ed=H, Eng=G ● **Work Field:** 293, 271 ● **MPSMS:** 969 ● **Aptitudes:** G2, V2, N3, S4, P3, Q3, K4, F4, M4, E5, C4 ● **Temperaments:** D, I, J, P, V ● **Physical:** Stg=L; Freq: R, H, T, G, N, F, X, V Occas: C, S, K, O, W, I, D, A ● **Work Env:** Noise=L; Occas: W, O ● **Salary:** 4 ● **Outlook:** 2

PARK SUPERINTENDENT (government ser.) ● DOT #188.167-062 ● OES: 19005 ● Alternate titles: SUPERVISORY PARK RANGER. Coordinates activities of PARK RANGERS (government ser.) and other workers engaged in development, protection, and utilization of national, state, or regional park: Tours areas to assess development possibilities and determine maintenance needs. Prepares estimates of costs to plan and provide or improve fish and wildlife protection, recreation, and visitor safety. Selects, trains, and supervises PARK RANGERS (government ser.). Directs workers engaged in rescue activities and fire suppression in park area. Investigates accidents, vandalism, theft, poaching, and other violations and presents evidence before court or designated legal authority. Answers letters of inquiry and addresses visitors and civic organizations to inform public of park regulations and available recreational facilities, and to point out historical, and scenic features of park. Prepares reports of area activities. May maintain records of attendance, permits issued, and monies received. ● **GED:** R5, M4, L4 ● **SVP:** 2-4 yrs ● **Academic:** Ed=A, Eng=G ● **Work Field:** 295, 282, 293 ● **MPSMS:** 959, 919 ● **Aptitudes:** G2, V2, N3, S4, P4, Q3, K4, F4, M4, E3, C4 ● **Temperaments:** D, I, J, P, V ● **Physical:** Stg=L; Freq: R, H, T, G, N Occas: C, B, S, K, O, W, I, F, D, A, X, V ● **Work Env:** Noise=N; Occas: W, C, H, U, O ● **Salary:** 4 ● **Outlook:** 1

POLICE CHIEF (government ser.) ● DOT #375.117-010 ● OES: 19005 ● Alternate titles: POLICE INSPECTOR, CHIEF; SUPERINTENDENT, POLICE. Directs and coordinates activities of governmental police department in accordance with authority delegated by Board of Police: Promulgates rules and regulations for department as delegated by regulating code. Coordinates and administers daily police activities through subordinates. Coordinates internal investigation of members of department for alleged wrong doing. Suspends or demotes members of force for infractions of rules or inefficiency. Directs activities of personnel engaged in preparing budget proposals, maintaining police records, and recruiting staff. Approves police budget and negotiates with municipal officials for appropriation of funds. May command force during emergencies, such as fires and riots. May make inspection visits to precincts. May address various groups to inform public of goals and operations of department. May prepare requests for government agencies to obtain funds for special operations or for purchasing equipment for department. In smaller communities, may assist one or more subordinates in investigation or apprehension of offenders. In communities having no Board of Police, may be designated Police Commissioner (government ser.) II. ● **GED:** R5, M3, L4 ● **SVP:** Over 10 yrs ● **Academic:** Ed=A, Eng=G ● **Work Field:** 295, 293 ● **MPSMS:** 951 ● **Aptitudes:** G2, V2, N3, S4, P4, Q3, K4, F4, M4, E5, C5 ● **Temperaments:** D, J, P, V ● **Physical:** Stg=S; Freq: T, G, N ● **Work Env:** Noise=N; ● **Salary:** 5 ● **Outlook:** 3

GOE: 04.01.02
Investigating

CUSTOMS PATROL OFFICER (government ser.) ● DOT #168.167-010 ● OES: 63009 ● Conducts surveillance, inspection, and patrol by foot, vehicle, boat, or aircraft at assigned points of entry into the United States to prohibit smuggled merchandise and contraband and to detect violations of Customs and related laws: Inspects vessels, aircraft, and vehicles at docking, landing, crossing, and entry points. Establishes working rapport with local residents, law enforcement agencies, and businesses. Observes activity and regularity of vessels, planes, cargo, and storage arrangements in assigned area. Gathers and evaluates information from informers and other sources. Locates and apprehends customs violators. Assists in developing and testing new enforcement techniques and equipment. Develops intelligence information and forwards data for use by U.S. Customs Service. Testifies in courts of law against customs violators. ● **GED:** R5, M3, L4 ● **SVP:** 4-10 yrs ● **Academic:** Ed=A, Eng=G ● **Work Field:** 271 ● **MPSMS:** 953 ● **Aptitudes:** G3, V3, N3, S3, P3, Q3, K3, F4, M3, E3, C4 ● **Temperaments:** J, P, S, V ● **Physical:** Stg=L; Freq: R, H, I, T, G, N, F, D, A, V Occas: C, B, S, K, O, W, X ● **Work Env:** Noise=N; Freq: W Occas: O ● **Salary:** 4 ● **Outlook:** 1

FIRE MARSHAL (government ser.) ● DOT #373.267-014 ● OES: 61002 ● Investigates and gathers facts to determine cause of fires and explosions and enforces fire laws: Investigates case when either arson or criminal negligence is suspected; multialarm fire results in serious injury or death; or fire takes place in commercial establishment of public building. Examines fire site to determine burn pattern and detect presence of flammable materials and gases and incendiary devices, using various detectors. Performs match test to determine flash point of suspicious material at fire site. Subpoenas and interviews witnesses, building owners, and occupants to obtain sworn testimony of observed facts. Prepares reports on each investigation and submits data indicating arson to DISTRICT ATTORNEY (government ser.) 110.117-010. Arrests, logs, fingerprints, and detains arson suspect. Testifies in court, citing evidence obtained from investigation. Conducts inquiries into departmental employees delinquency in performance of duties and violation of laws or regulations. ● **GED:** R4, M3, L4 ● **SVP:** 2-4 yrs ● **Academic:** Ed=H, Eng=G ● **Work Field:** 271, 293 ● **MPSMS:** 951 ● **Aptitudes:** G3, V3, N3, S3, P3, Q3, K4, F4, M3, E4, C3 ● **Temperaments:** J, P, V ● **Physical:** Stg=L; Freq: R, H, I, T, G, N Occas: C, B, S, K, O, W, F, D, X, V ● **Work Env:** Noise=N; Freq: O Occas: U, A, T ● **Salary:** 5 ● **Outlook:** 1

FISH AND GAME WARDEN (government ser.) ● DOT #379.167-010 ● OES: 63033 ● Alternate titles: CONSERVATION OFFICER; GAME AND FISH PROTECTOR; GAME WARDEN; GUARD, RANGE. Patrols assigned area to prevent game law violations, investigate reports of damage to crops and property by wildlife, and compile biological data: Travels through area by car, boat, airplane, horse, and on foot to observe persons engaged in taking fish and game, to ensure method and equipment used are lawful, and to apprehend violators. Investigates reports of fish and game law violations and issues warnings or citations. Serves warrants, makes arrests, and prepares and presents evidence in court actions. Seizes equipment used in fish and game law violations and arranges for disposition of fish and game illegally taken or possessed. Collects and reports information on condition of fish and wildlife in their habitat, availability of game food and cover, and suspected pollution of waterways. Investigates hunting accidents and files reports of findings. Addresses schools and civic groups to disseminate information and promote public relations. May enlist aid of sporting groups in such programs as lake and stream rehabilitation, and game habitat improvement. May assist in promoting hunter safety training by arranging for materials and instructors. May be designated according to specialty as Fish Protector (government ser.); Game Protector (government ser.); or according to assigned patrol as Fish-And-Game Warden, Marine Patrol (government ser.). ● **GED:** R4, M3, L4 ● **SVP:** 1-2 yrs ● **Academic:** Ed=H, Eng=G ● **Work Field:** 293 ● **MPSMS:** 959 ● **Aptitudes:** G2, V2, N3, S4, P4, Q4, K4, F4, M4, E4, C4 ● **Temperaments:** J, P, S ● **Physical:** Stg=M; Freq: R, H, T, G, N, F Occas: S, K, O, W, I, D, A, X, V ● **Work Env:** Noise=N; Freq: W Occas: O ● **Salary:** 4 ● **Outlook:** 2

FIRE WARDEN (forestry) ● DOT #452.167-010 ● OES: 63008 ● Administers fire prevention programs and enforces governmental fire regulations throughout assigned forest and logging areas: Inspects logging areas and forest tracts for fire hazards, such as accumulated wastes, hazardous storage or mishandling of fuels and solvents, defective engine exhaust systems, and unshielded electrical equipment. Examines and inventories water supplies and firefighting equipment, such as axes, firehoses, pumps, buckets, and chemical fire extinguishers to determine condition, amount, adequacy, and placement of materials with respect to governmental regulations and company rules. Prepares reports of conditions observed, issues directives and instructions for correcting violations, and reinspects areas to verify compliance. Directs maintenance and repair of firefighting tools and equipment and requisitions new equipment and materials to replace expended, lost, and broken items or add to inventory as required. Restricts public access

and recreational use of forest lands during critical fire season. Gives directions to crew section on fireline during forest fire. May direct FIRE RANGERS (forestry). ● **GED:** R5, M3, L3 ● **SVP:** 2-4 yrs ● **Academic:** Ed=A, Eng=G ● **Work Field:** 293 ● **MPSMS:** 313 ● **Aptitudes:** G2, V2, N3, S4, P4, Q4, K4, F4, M4, E4, C4 ● **Temperaments:** D, J, P, V ● **Physical:** Stg=L; Freq: S, K, O, R, H, T, G, F, D, V Occas: C, B, I, M, N, X ● **Work Env:** Noise=L; Freq: W, H, A, O ● **Salary:** 4 ● **Outlook:** 3

INVESTIGATOR (utilities) ● DOT #376.367-022 ● OES: 63035 ● Investigates persons suspected of securing services through fraud or error: Makes personal calls on individuals in question and tactfully attempts to secure evidence or personal admission that individual being investigated owes for previous service, or obtains pertinent data to show that suspicion was unwarranted. ● **GED:** R3, M2, L3 ● **SVP:** 1-2 yrs ● **Academic:** Ed=N, Eng=G ● **Work Field:** 271 ● **MPSMS:** 969 ● **Aptitudes:** G3, V3, N4, S4, P4, Q4, K4, F4, M4, E5, C5 ● **Temperaments:** J, P ● **Physical:** Stg=L; Freq: T, G ● **Work Env:** Noise=N; ● **Salary:** 3 ● **Outlook:** 3

INVESTIGATOR, PRIVATE (business ser.) ● DOT #376.267-018 ● OES: 63035 ● Alternate titles: DETECTIVE, PRIVATE EYE; UNDERCOVER AGENT; UNDERCOVER OPERATOR. Conducts private investigations to locate missing persons, obtain confidential information, and solve crimes: Questions individuals to locate missing persons. Conducts surveillance of suspects using binoculars and cameras. Conducts background investigation of individual to obtain data on character, financial status, and personal history. Examines scene of crime for clues and submits fingerprints and findings to laboratory for identification and analysis. Writes reports of investigations for clients. Reports criminal information to police and testifies in court. May investigate activities of individuals in divorce and child custody cases. May arrange lie detector tests for employees of clients or witnesses. May escort valuables to protect client's property. May be employed in commercial or industrial establishments for undercover work [DETECTIVE (any industry) I] or be assigned to guard persons [BODYGUARD (personal ser.)]. ● **GED:** R4, M3, L4 ● **SVP:** 6 mos-1 yr ● **Academic:** Ed=H, Eng=G ● **Work Field:** 271 ● **MPSMS:** 969 ● **Aptitudes:** G3, V3, N3, S4, P3, Q3, K4, F4, M4, E5, C4 ● **Temperaments:** J, P, S, V ● **Physical:** Stg=L; Freq: T, G, N, A Occas: S, K, O, R, H, I, F, D, X, V ● **Work Env:** Noise=N; Freq: W Occas: O ● **Salary:** 3 ● **Outlook:** 2

POLICE OFFICER I (government ser.) ● DOT #375.263-014 ● OES: 63014 ● Alternate titles: PATROL OFFICER; TRAFFIC OFFICER. Patrols assigned beat on foot, on motorcycle, in patrol car, or on horseback to control traffic, prevent crime or disturbance of peace, and arrest violators: Familiarizes self with beat and with persons living in area. Notes suspicious persons and establishments and reports to superior officer. Reports hazards. Disperses unruly crowds at public gatherings. Renders first aid at accidents, and investigates causes and results of accident. Directs and reroutes traffic around fire or other disruption. Inspects public establishments requiring licenses to ensure compliance with rules and regulations. Warns or arrests persons violating animal ordinances. Issues tickets to traffic violators. Registers at police call boxes at specified interval or time. Writes and files daily activity report with superior officer. May drive patrol wagon or police ambulance. May notify public works department of location of abandoned vehicles to tow away. May accompany parking meter personnel to protect money collected. May be designated according to assigned duty as Airport Safety And Security Officer (government ser.); Dance-Hall Inspector (government ser.); Traffic Police Officer (government ser.); or according to equipment used as Ambulance Driver (government ser.); Motorcycle Police Officer (government ser.); Mounted Police Officer (government ser.). May be designated: Emergency-Detail Driver (government ser.); Patrol Driver (government ser.); Pool-Hall Inspector (government ser.); Radio Police Officer (government ser.); Show Inspector (government ser.). ● **GED:** R4, M2, L3 ● **SVP:** 1-2 yrs ● **Academic:** Ed=H, Eng=G ● **Work Field:** 271, 293 ● **MPSMS:** 951 ● **Aptitudes:** G3, V3, N4, S3, P3, Q3, K3, F4, M3, E3, C4 ● **Temperaments:** J, P, S, V ● **Physical:** Stg=M; Freq: T, G, N, F, D, A, X, V Occas: C, B, S, K, O, W, R, H, I ● **Work Env:** Noise=N; Occas: W, O ● **Salary:** 4 ● **Outlook:** 2

POLICE OFFICER III (government ser.) ● DOT #375.267-038 ● OES: 63014 ● Conducts investigations to locate, arrest, and return fugitives and persons wanted for nonpayment of support payments and unemployment insurance compensation fraud, and to locate missing persons: Reviews files and criminal records to develop possible leads, such as previous addresses and aliases. Contacts employers, neighbors, relatives, law enforcement agencies, and other persons to locate person sought. Obtains necessary legal documents, such as warrants or extradition papers, to bring about return of fugitive. Serves warrants and makes arrests to return persons sought. Examines medical and dental x rays, fingerprints, and other information to identify bodies held in morgue. Completes reports to document information acquired and actions taken. Testifies in court to present evidence regarding cases. ● **GED:** R4, M2, L3 ● **SVP:** 2-4 yrs ● **Academic:** Ed=H, Eng=G ● **Work Field:** 271, 293 ● **MPSMS:** 951 ● **Aptitudes:** G3, V3, N4, S4, P4, Q3, K3, F3, M3, E5, C5 ● **Temperaments:** J, P, S ● **Physical:** Stg=M; Freq: R, H, I, T, G, N ● **Work Env:** Noise=N; ● **Salary:** 5 ● **Outlook:** 3

PUBLIC-SAFETY OFFICER (government ser.) ● DOT #379.263-014 ● OES: 63014 ● Patrols assigned beat and responds to emergency calls to protect persons or property from crimes, fires, or other hazards: Patrols assigned area on foot or horseback or using vehicle to regulate traffic, control crowds, prevent crime, or arrest violators. Responds to crimes in progress, initiating actions such as aid to victims and interrogation of suspects. Attends public gatherings to maintain order. Responds to fire alarms or other emergency calls. Forces openings in buildings for ventilation of fire or for entry, using ax or crowbar. Controls and extinguishes fires, using water and chemicals. Administers first aid and artificial respiration to injured persons. Participates in drills and emergency precautionary demonstrations. May inspect establishments for compliance with local regulations. May drive and operate firefighting and other emergency equipment. ● **GED:** R4, M3, L3 ● **SVP:** 2-4 yrs ● **Academic:** Ed=H, Eng=G ● **Work Field:** 293 ● **MPSMS:** 951, 962 ● **Aptitudes:** G3, V3, N4, S3, P4, Q4, K4, F4, M4, E3, C4 ● **Temperaments:** P, S, V ● **Physical:** Stg=V; Freq: T, G, N, F, D, A, V Occas: C, B, R, H, X ● **Work Env:** Noise=N; Freq: W, O ● **Salary:** 4 ● **Outlook:** 4

SHERIFF, DEPUTY (government ser.) ● DOT #377.263-010 ● OES: 63032 ● Maintains law and order and serves legal processes of courts: Patrols assigned area to enforce laws, investigate crimes, and arrest violators. Drives vehicle through assigned area, observing traffic violations and issuing citations. Assumes control at traffic accidents to maintain traffic flow, assist accident victims, and investigate causes of accidents. Investigates illegal or suspicious activities of persons, quells disturbances, and arrests law violators. Locates and takes persons into custody on arrest warrants. Transports or escorts prisoners between courtrooms, prison, and medical facilities. Serves subpoenas and summonses [PROCESS SERVER (business ser.)] and keeps record of dispositions. Keeps order in courtroom [BAILIFF (government ser.)]. May operate radio to deliver instructions to patrol units. May assist in dragging river to locate bodies. ● **GED:** R3, M2, L3 ● **SVP:** 6 mos-1 yr ● **Academic:** Ed=H, Eng=G ● **Work Field:** 293, 271 ● **MPSMS:** 951 ● **Aptitudes:** G3, V3, N4, S4, P3, Q3, K3, F4, M3, E3, C5 ● **Temperaments:** J, P, S ● **Physical:** Stg=M; Freq: R, H, T, G, N, F, D, A, X, V Occas: C, B, S, K, O, W, I ● **Work Env:** Noise=N; Occas: W, O ● **Salary:** 3 ● **Outlook:** 3

SPECIAL AGENT (government ser.) ● DOT #375.167-042 ● OES: 63009 ● Alternate titles: CRIMINAL INVESTIGATOR. Investigates alleged or suspected criminal violations of federal, state, or local laws to determine if evidence is sufficient to recommend prosecution: Analyzes charge, complaint, or allegation of law violation to identify issues involved and types of evidence needed. Assists in determining scope, timing, and direction of investigation. Develops and uses informants to get leads to information. Obtains evidence or establishes facts by interviewing, observing, and interrogating suspects and witnesses and analyzing records. Examines records to detect links in chain of evidence or information. Uses cameras and photostatic machines to record evidence and documents. Verifies information obtained to es-

tablish accuracy and authenticity of facts and evidence. Maintains surveillances and performs undercover assignments. Presents findings in clear, logical, impartial, and properly documented reports. Reports critical information to and coordinates activities with other offices or agencies when applicable. Testifies before grand juries. Serves subpoenas or other official papers. May lead or coordinate work of other SPECIAL AGENTS. May obtain and use search and arrest warrants. May serve on full-time, detail, or rotational protection assignments. May carry firearms and make arrests. May be designated according to agency worked for as Special Agent, FBI (government ser.); Special Agent, IRS (government ser.); Special Agent, Secret Service (government ser.). ● **GED:** R5, M5, L5 ● **SVP:** 2-4 yrs ● **Academic:** Ed=A, Eng=G ● **Work Field:** 271, 293 ● **MPSMS:** 951, 959 ● **Aptitudes:** G2, V2, N2, S2, P3, Q3, K3, F4, M4, E3, C4 ● **Temperaments:** J, P, S, V ● **Physical:** Stg=M; Freq: R, H, I, E, T, G, N, F, D, A, X, V Occas: C, B, S, K, O, W ● **Work Env:** Noise=N; Freq: W, O ● **Salary:** 4 ● **Outlook:** 2

STATE-HIGHWAY POLICE OFFICER (government ser.) ● DOT #375.263-018 ● OES: 63014 ● Alternate titles: STATE TROOPER. Patrols state highways within assigned area, in vehicle equipped with two-way radio, to enforce motor vehicle and criminal laws: Arrests or warns persons guilty of violating motor vehicle regulations and safe driving practices. Monitors passing traffic to detect stolen vehicles and arrests drivers where ownership is not apparent. Provides road information and assistance to motorists. Directs activities in accident or disaster area, rendering first aid and restoring traffic to normal. Investigates conditions and causes of accident. Directs traffic in congested areas and serves as escort for funeral processions, military convoys, and parades. Performs general police work by keeping order and apprehending criminals. Appears in court as witness in traffic violation and criminal cases. Keeps records and makes reports regarding activities. May assist law enforcement officers not under state jurisdiction. May serve as DISPATCHER, RADIO (government ser.) 379.362-010 at patrol substation. May supervise activities of station equipped to inspect automobiles for safe operating conditions. ● **GED:** R4, M2, L3 ● **SVP:** 1-2 yrs ● **Academic:** Ed=H, Eng=G ● **Work Field:** 293, 271 ● **MPSMS:** 951 ● **Aptitudes:** G3, V3, N4, S3, P3, Q4, K3, F4, M3, E4, C4 ● **Temperaments:** J, P, S, V ● **Physical:** Stg=M; Freq: R, H, I, T, G, N, F, D, A, V Occas: C, B, S, K, O, W, X ● **Work Env:** Noise=N; Freq: W, O ● **Salary:** 4 ● **Outlook:** 3

WILDLIFE AGENT, REGIONAL (government ser.) ● DOT #379.137-018 ● OES: 19005 ● Supervises and coordinates activities of FISH AND GAME WARDENS (government ser.) engaged in enforcing fish and game laws, reporting crops and property damage by wildlife, and compiling biological data: Studies and surveys assigned region to learn topography and available cover and feed for wildlife. Subdivides region into geographical districts and submits request for FISH AND GAME WARDENS (government ser.) to patrol districts. Plans location of access roads, trails, sanitary facilities, boat launching sites, and parking areas, based on number of people using area. Trains and assists subordinates to solve work problems and to interpret directives and regulations. Observes issuance of citations, apprehension of game law violators, and seizure of equipment to verify compliance with laws and regulations. Evaluates and submits efficiency reports on subordinates, and initiates personnel actions such as reprimand, disciplinary action, transfer, or discharge. Addresses school, civic, and sports groups on wildlife and recreational activities. Arranges for witnesses and evidence to be used at court trials of game law violators. Compiles consolidated report of region activities and approves requests for new equipment. ● **GED:** R5, M4, L4 ● **SVP:** 2-4 yrs ● **Academic:** Ed=B, Eng=G ● **Work Field:** 293 ● **MPSMS:** 326, 959 ● **Aptitudes:** G2, V2, N3, S4, P4, Q3, K4, F4, M4, E4, C4 ● **Temperaments:** D, J, P, V ● **Physical:** Stg=L; Freq: R, H, I, T, G, N, F Occas: S, K, O, W, X ● **Work Env:** Noise=N; Freq: W Occas: O ● **Salary:** 5 ● **Outlook:** 3

Security Services

Workers in this group protect people and animals from injury or danger. They enforce laws, investigate suspicious persons or acts, prevent crime, and fight fires. Some of the jobs are found in federal, state, or local governments. Some workers are hired by railroads, hotels, lumber yards, industrial plants, and amusement establishments. Some work on their own, acting as bodyguards or private detectives.

✓ What kind of work would you do?

Your work activities would depend upon your specific job. For example, you might:

- guard money and valuables being transported by an armored car.
- patrol a section of an international border to detect persons attempting to enter the country illegally.
- move among customers in a place of entertainment to preserve order and protect property.
- guard inmates and direct their activities in a penal institution.
- respond to alarms to fight fires, render first aid, and protect property.

✓ What skills and abilities do you need for this kind of work?

To do this kind of work, you must be able to:

- learn and apply rules and procedures which are sometimes hard to understand.
- use reason and judgment in dealing with all kinds of people in different ways.
- think clearly and react quickly in emergencies.
- keep physically fit.
- use guns and safety equipment skillfully.
- make conclusions based on facts and also on your personal judgment.

✓ How do you know if you would like or could learn to do this kind of work?

The following questions may give you clues about yourself as you consider this group of jobs.

- Have you been a member of a school safety patrol? Did you like enforcing safety rules?
- Have you used a gun for hunting or target practice? Are you a good shot?
- Have you worked as a camp counselor or other group leader? Do you like helping people?
- Have you been a member of a volunteer fire or rescue squad? Can you stay calm in emergencies?
- Have you taken a first aid course? Can you treat injuries quickly and skillfully?
- Have you been a member of a military police force or rescue team?

✓ How can you prepare for and enter this kind of work?

Occupations in this group usually require education and/or training extending from thirty days to over two years, depending upon the specific kind of work. People with experience in the military, local, or state police are often preferred. Some employers want people with a high school education or its equal.

People interested in these jobs must have character references and no police record. Some employers require a demonstration of skill in using firearms. Written and physical tests also may be required.

✓ What else should you consider about these jobs?

Some of these jobs involve night work. People often work alone, with no help nearby in case of accident or injury. In some jobs, they take turns working daytime, weekend, and holiday hours. There is always a danger of bodily injury by lawbreakers.

Workers are often required to have special insurance to protect the employer against dishonesty. They may also be fingerprinted.

If you think you would like to do this kind of work, look at the following job titles.

GOE: 04.02.01
Detention

CORRECTION OFFICER (government ser.) ● DOT #372.667-018 ● OES: 63017 ● Alternate titles: GUARD. Guards inmates in penal institution in accordance with established policies, regulations, and procedures: Observes conduct and behavior of inmates to prevent disturbances and escapes. Inspects locks, window bars, grills, doors, and gates for tampering. Searches inmates and cells for contraband articles. Guards and directs inmates during work assignments. Patrols assigned areas for evidence of forbidden activities, infraction of rules, and unsatisfactory attitude or adjustment of prisoners. Reports observations to superior. Employs weapons or force to maintain discipline and order among prisoners, if necessary. May escort inmates to and from visiting room, medical office, and religious services. May guard entrance of jail to screen visitors. May prepare written report concerning incidences of inmate disturbances or injuries. May be designated according to institution as Correction Officer, City or County Jail (government ser.); Correction Officer, Penitentiary (government ser.); Correction Officer, Reformatory (government ser.). May guard prisoners in transit between jail, courtroom, prison, or other point, traveling by automobile or public transportation and be designated Guard, Deputy (government ser.). ● **GED:** R3, M2, L2 ● **SVP:** 3-6 mos ● **Academic:** Ed=H, Eng=G ● **Work Field:** 293 ● **MPSMS:** 951 ● **Aptitudes:** G3, V3, N4, S4, P3, Q4, K3, F4, M3, E5, C5 ● **Temperaments:** J, P, S ● **Physical:** Stg=M; Freq: R, H, N, F, V Occas: T, G ● **Work Env:** Noise=N; Freq: O Occas: X ● **Salary:** 3 ● **Outlook:** 3

GUARD, IMMIGRATION (government ser.) ● DOT #372.567-014 ● OES: 63017 ● Guards aliens held by immigration service pending further investigation before being released or deported: Takes into custody and delivers aliens to designated jail, juvenile detention facility, hospital, court, claim's office, immigration facility, or other areas to transact business. Escorts aliens departing or arriving by airplane, train, car, ship, or bus. Prepares and maintains records relating to detention, release, transportation of alien, and completes application for travel documents. May prepare related correspondence. May be required to travel throughout nation and foreign countries. ● **GED:** R3, M2, L3 ● **SVP:** 3-6 mos ● **Academic:** Ed=N, Eng=G ● **Work Field:** 293, 231 ● **MPSMS:** 959 ● **Aptitudes:** G3, V3, N4, S4, P4, Q4, K3, F4, M3, E4, C5 ● **Temperaments:** P, S ● **Physical:** Stg=M; Freq: R, H, T, G Occas: N ● **Work Env:** Noise=N; Freq: O Occas: W ● **Salary:** 4 ● **Outlook:** 3

JAILER (government ser.) ● DOT #372.367-014 ● OES: 63017 ● Alternate titles: JAIL KEEPER; TURNKEY. Guards prisoners in precinct station house or municipal jail, assuming responsibility for all needs of prisoners during detention: Locks prisoner in cell after searching for weapons, valuables, or drugs. Serves meals to prisoner and provides or obtains medical aid if needed. May prepare arrest records identifying prisoner and charge assigned. May question prisoner to elicit information helpful in solving crime. May prepare meals for self and prisoner. May distribute commissary items purchased by inmates, such as candy, snacks, cigarettes, and toilet articles, and record payment on voucher. In small communities, may perform duties of SHERIFF, DEPUTY (government ser.) 377.263-010 or POLICE OFFICER (government ser.) I 375.263-014 when not engaged in guard duties. ● **GED:** R3, M2, L2 ● **SVP:** 3-6 mos ● **Academic:** Ed=N, Eng=G ● **Work Field:** 293 ● **MPSMS:** 959, 951 ● **Aptitudes:** G3, V3, N4, S4, P3, Q4, K3, F4, M3, E5, C5 ● **Temperaments:** J, P, S ● **Physical:** Stg=L; Freq: R, H, T, G, A, V Occas: I, N, F ● **Work Env:** Noise=Q; Occas: O ● **Salary:** 3 ● **Outlook:** 2

GOE: 04.02.02
Property & People

AIRLINE SECURITY REPRESENTATIVE (air trans.) ● DOT #372.667-010 ● OES: 63047 ● Alternate titles: CUSTOMER SECURITY CLERK; FLIGHT SECURITY SPECIALIST; SCREENING REPRESENTATIVE. Screens passengers and visitors for weapons, explosives, or other forbidden articles to prevent articles from being carried into restricted area of air terminal, performing any combination of following tasks: Greets individuals desiring to enter restricted area and informs them that they must be screened prior to entry. Asks individual to empty contents of pockets into tray. Examines contents of tray for forbidden articles and directs individual to pass through metal-detecting device. Asks individual to remove metal articles from person if metal detector signals presence of metal, or uses hand held metal detector to locate metal item on person. Places carry-on baggage or other containers onto x-ray device, actuates device controls, and monitors screen to detect forbidden articles. Requests owner to open baggage or containers when x ray shows questionable contents. Returns baggage and tray contents to individual if no forbidden articles are detected. Notifies GUARD, SECURITY (any industry) if forbidden articles are discovered or detector equipment indicates further search is needed. May turn on power and make adjustments to equipment. May perform duties of GUARD, SECURITY (any industry). May screen boarding passengers against Federal Aviation Administration approved profile of aircraft hijackers. May make reports. ● **GED:** R2, M1, L2 ● **SVP:** 2-30 days ● **Academic:** Ed=N, Eng=G ● **Work Field:** 293 ● **MPSMS:** 855 ● **Aptitudes:** G4, V4, N4, S3, P3, Q4, K4, F4, M4, E5, C5 ● **Temperaments:** P, R ● **Physical:** Stg=L; Freq: R, H, I, T, G, N ● **Work Env:** Noise=N; Occas: O ● **Salary:** 4 ● **Outlook:** 3

ARMORED-CAR GUARD AND DRIVER (business ser.) ● DOT #372.563-010 ● OES: 63047 ● Alternate titles: ARMORED-CAR MESSENGER. Drives armored van to transport money and valuables, and guards money and valuables during transit: Loads and carries bags of cash, coin, and other valuables into and from armored van at protective service building, bank, or customer establishment. Drives armored van along established routes to transport valuables to destination. Guards bags of money and valuables during receipt and transfer to ensure safe delivery. Issues and receives receipts from customers to verify transfer of valuables. May drive truck along established route and collect coins from parking meters. ● **GED:** R3, M2, L2 ● **SVP:** 1-3 mos ● **Academic:** Ed=N, Eng=S ● **Work Field:** 293, 013, 011 ● **MPSMS:** 899 ● **Aptitudes:** G3, V4, N3, S3, P4, Q3, K3, F4, M3, E3, C5 ● **Temperaments:** P, R, S ● **Physical:** Stg=M; Freq: R, H, N, F, D, V Occas: C, S, I, T, G ● **Work Env:** Noise=L; Occas: W, O ● **Salary:** 1 ● **Outlook:** 3

ARMORED-CAR GUARD (business ser.) ● DOT #372.567-010 ● OES: 63047 ● Alternate titles: ARMORED-CAR MESSENGER. Guards armored car enroute to business establishments to pick up or deliver money and valuables: Collects moneybags, receipts, daily guide sheet, and schedule from VAULT WORKER (business ser.). Guards money and valuables in transit to prevent theft. Records information, such as number of items received, destination, contents of packages, and delivery time at scheduled stops, on daily guide sheet. Deposits moneybags, receipts, daily guide sheet, change box, and money with cashiering department. ● **GED:** R3, M2, L2 ● **SVP:** 1-3 mos ● **Academic:** Ed=N, Eng=S ● **Work Field:** 293 ● **MPSMS:** 899 ● **Aptitudes:** G3, V3, N3, S4, P3, Q3, K3, F4, M4, E5, C5 ● **Temperaments:** P, R, S ● **Physical:** Stg=M; Freq: R, H, N, V Occas: I, T, G ● **Work Env:** Noise=N; Occas: O ● **Salary:** 1 ● **Outlook:** 3

BODYGUARD (personal ser.) ● DOT #372.667-014 ● OES: 63047 ● Escorts individuals to protect them from bodily injury, kidnapping, or invasion of privacy. May perform other duties, such as receiving and transcribing dictation or driving motor vehicle to transport individuals to disguise purpose of employment. ● **GED:** R2, M1, L2 ● **SVP:** 1-3 mos ● **Academic:** Ed=N, Eng=S ● **Work Field:** 293 ● **MPSMS:** 909 ● **Aptitudes:** G3, V3, N4, S4, P4, Q4, K3, F4, M3, E4, C5 ● **Temperaments:** J, P, S ● **Physical:** Stg=L; Freq: N, F, V Occas: R, H, I, T, G, D, A ● **Work Env:** Noise=N; Freq: W ● **Salary:** 2 ● **Outlook:** 2

DETECTIVE I (any industry) ● DOT #376.367-014 ● OES: 63035 ● Alternate titles: INVESTIGATOR. Protects property of business establishment by detecting vandalism, thievery, shoplifting, or dishonesty among employees or patrons, performing any combination of following duties: Conducts investigations on own initiative or on request of management. Stakes out company grounds to apprehend suspects in illegal acts. Questions suspects and apprehends culprits. Files complaints against suspects and testifies in court as witness. Writes case reports. Alerts other retail establishments when person of known criminal character is observed in store. May be designated according to type of establishment as Store Detective (retail trade). ● **GED:** R3, M2, L3 ● **SVP:** 3-6 mos ● **Academic:** Ed=N, Eng=G ● **Work Field:** 271, 293 ● **MPSMS:** 969 ● **Aptitudes:** G3, V3, N4, S4, P4, Q4, K4,

F4, M4, E5, C5 ● **Temperaments:** J, P, S ● **Physical:** Stg=L; Freq: R, H, T, G, N, F, V Occas: S, K, O, I ● **Work Env:** Noise=N; Occas: O ● **Salary:** 5 ● **Outlook:** 2

FIRE INSPECTOR (any industry) ● DOT #373.367-010 ● OES: 63008 ● Alternate titles: FIRE WATCHER. Inspects premises of industrial plant to detect and eliminate fire hazards: Inspects fire-extinguishing and fire-protection equipment to ensure equipment is operable and prepares reports listing repairs and replacements needed. Patrols plant areas and notes and investigates unsafe conditions and practices which might cause or increase fire hazards. Reports findings to FIRE MARSHAL (any industry) with recommendations for eliminating or counteracting hazards. Renders first aid in emergencies. Patrols plant areas in which raw and combustible materials are stored, takes temperature and pressure readings from instruments, and reports undesirable conditions or takes steps to correct such conditions. May instruct employees in fire safety practices. May perform tests on fire-prevention equipment in plants where explosive or flammable materials are processed. May participate in fighting fires [FIRE FIGHTER (any industry)]. ● **GED:** R3, M3, L3 ● **SVP:** 6 mos-1 yr ● **Academic:** Ed=H, Eng=S ● **Work Field:** 293 ● **MPSMS:** 951 ● **Aptitudes:** G3, V3, N3, S3, P3, Q3, K4, F4, M3, E3, C4 ● **Temperaments:** J, T ● **Physical:** Stg=M; Freq: R, H, N, F Occas: I, T, G, X ● **Work Env:** Noise=N; Occas: W ● **Salary:** 5 ● **Outlook:** 4

FIRE RANGER (forestry) ● DOT #452.367-014 ● OES: 63008 ● Patrols assigned area of forest to locate and report fires and hazardous conditions and to ensure compliance with fire regulations by travelers and campers: Hikes or drives to vista points to scan for fires and unusual or dangerous conditions. Reports findings and receives and relays emergency calls, using telephone or two-way radio. Visits camping sites to inspect activities of campers and ensure compliance with forest use and fire regulations. Gives instructions regarding sanitation, fire, and related forest regulations. Extinguishes smaller fires with portable extinguisher, shovel, and ax. Serves as crew leader for larger fires. Renders assistance or first aid to lost or injured persons. Participates in search for lost travelers or campers. ● **GED:** R3, M2, L3 ● **SVP:** 3-6 mos ● **Academic:** Ed=N, Eng=G ● **Work Field:** 293 ● **MPSMS:** 313 ● **Aptitudes:** G3, V3, N4, S3, P4, Q4, K4, F4, M4, E3, C4 ● **Temperaments:** J, P, S, V ● **Physical:** Stg=M; Freq: S, K, O, R, H, I, T, G, F, D Occas: C, B, M, N, X ● **Work Env:** Noise=L; Freq: W ● **Salary:** 5 ● **Outlook:** 3

GATE GUARD (any industry) ● DOT #372.667-030 ● OES: 63047 ● Alternate titles: GATEKEEPER; GUARD; WATCH GUARD, GATE. Guards entrance gate of industrial plant and grounds, warehouse, or other property to control traffic to and from buildings and grounds: Opens gate to allow entrance or exit of employees, truckers, and authorized visitors. Checks credentials or approved roster before admitting anyone. Issues passes at own discretion or on instructions from superiors. Directs visitors and truckers to various parts of grounds or buildings. Inspects outgoing traffic to prevent unauthorized removal of company property or products. May record number of trucks or other carriers entering and leaving. May perform maintenance duties, such as mowing lawns and sweeping gate areas. May require permits from employees for tools or materials taken from premises. May supervise use of time clocks for recording arrival and departure of employees [TIMEKEEPER (clerical) 215.362-022]. May answer telephone and transfer calls when switchboard is closed. When stationed at entrance to restricted area, such as explosives shed or research laboratory, may be designated Controlled-Area Checker (any industry). ● **GED:** R3, M2, L2 ● **SVP:** 1-3 mos ● **Academic:** Ed=N, Eng=S ● **Work Field:** 293 ● **MPSMS:** 361, 951, 969 ● **Aptitudes:** G3, V3, N4, S4, P4, Q4, K4, F4, M4, E5, C5 ● **Temperaments:** P, R ● **Physical:** Stg=L; Freq: T, G, N, F Occas: R, H, V ● **Work Env:** Noise=N; Freq: W, O ● **Salary:** 1 ● **Outlook:** 2

GUARD, SECURITY (any industry) ● DOT #372.667-034 ● OES: 63047 ● Alternate titles: PATROL GUARD; SPECIAL POLICE OFFICER; WATCHGUARD. Guards industrial or commercial property against fire, theft, vandalism, and illegal entry, performing any combination of following duties: Patrols, periodically, buildings and grounds of industrial plant or commercial establishment, docks, logging camp area, or work site. Examines doors, windows, and gates to determine that they are secure. Warns violators of rule infractions, such as loitering, smoking, or carrying forbidden articles, and apprehends or expels

miscreants. Inspects equipment and machinery to ascertain if tampering has occurred. Watches for and reports irregularities, such as fire hazards, leaking water pipes, and security doors left unlocked. Observes departing personnel to guard against theft of company property. Sounds alarm or calls police or fire department by telephone in case of fire or presence of unauthorized persons. Permits authorized persons to enter property. May register at watch stations to record time of inspection trips. May record data, such as property damage, unusual occurrences, and malfunctioning of machinery or equipment, for use of supervisory staff. May perform janitorial duties and set thermostatic controls to maintain specified temperature in buildings or cold storage rooms. May tend furnace or boiler. May be deputized to arrest trespassers. May regulate vehicle and pedestrian traffic at plant entrance to maintain orderly flow. May patrol site with guard dog on leash. May watch for fires and be designated Fire Patroller (logging). May be designated according to shift worked as Day Guard (any industry); area guarded as Dock Guard (any industry); Warehouse Guard (any industry); or property guarded as Powder Guard (construction). May be designated according to establishment guarded as Grounds Guard, Arboretum (any industry); Guard, Museum (museums); Watchguard, Racetrack (amuse. & rec.); or duty station as Coin-Vault Guard (any industry). May be designated Guard, Convoy (any industry) when accompanying or leading truck convoy carrying valuable shipments. May be designated: Armed Guard (r.r. trans.); Camp Guard (any industry); Deck Guard (fishing & hunt.; water trans.); Night Guard (any industry); Park Guard (amuse. & rec.). ● **GED:** R3, M1, L2 ● **SVP:** 1-3 mos ● **Academic:** Ed=N, Eng=S ● **Work Field:** 293 ● **MPSMS:** 905, 951 ● **Aptitudes:** G3, V4, N3, S4, P4, Q4, K4, F4, M4, E5, C4 ● **Temperaments:** P, R, S ● **Physical:** Stg=L; Freq: R, H, F, V Occas: T, G, N, D, A, X ● **Work Env:** Noise=Q; Freq: W Occas: O ● **Salary:** 2 ● **Outlook:** 2

PARKING ENFORCEMENT OFFICER (government ser.) ● DOT #375.587-010 ● OES: 63033 ● Alternate titles: PARKING ENFORCEMENT AGENT. Patrols assigned area, such as public parking lot or section of city, to issue tickets to overtime parking violators. Winds parking meter clocks. Surrenders ticket book at end of shift to supervisor to facilitate preparation of violation records. May report missing traffic signals or signs to superior at end of shift. May chalk tires of vehicles parked in unmetered spaces, record time, and return at specified intervals to ticket vehicles remaining in spaces illegally. May collect coins deposited in meters. When patrolling metered spaces, may be known as Meter Attendant (government ser.). ● **GED:** R2, M1, L2 ● **SVP:** 2-30 days ● **Academic:** Ed=N, Eng=N ● **Work Field:** 231, 293 ● **MPSMS:** 959 ● **Aptitudes:** G4, V4, N4, S4, P4, Q4, K4, F4, M4, E5, C4 ● **Temperaments:** P, R ● **Physical:** Stg=L; Freq: R, H, I Occas: N, X ● **Work Env:** Noise=N; Const: W ● **Salary:** 1 ● **Outlook:** 3

SECURITY CONSULTANT (business ser.) ● DOT #189.167-054 ● OES: 63035 ● Plans, directs, and oversees implementation of comprehensive security systems for protection of individuals and homes, and business, commercial, and industrial organizations, and investigates various crimes against client: Inspects premises to determine security needs. Studies physical conditions, observes activities, and confers with client's staff to obtain data regarding internal operations. Analyzes compiled data and plans and directs installation of electronic security systems, such as closed circuit surveillance, entry controls, burglar alarms, ultrasonic motion detectors, electric eyes, and outdoor perimeter and microwave alarms. Directs installation and checks operation of electronic security equipment. Plans and directs personal security and safety of individual, family, or group for contracted period. Provides bulletproof limousine and bodyguards to ensure client protection during trips and outings. Suggests wearing bulletproof vest when appropriate. Plans and reviews client travel itinerary, mode of transportation, and accommodations. Travels with client and directs security operations. Investigates crimes committed against client, such as fraud, robbery, arson, and patent infringement. Reviews personnel records of client staff and conducts background investigation of selected members to obtain personal histories, character references, and financial status. Conducts or directs surveillance of suspects and premises to apprehend culprits. Notifies client of security weaknesses and implements procedures for handling, storing, safekeeping, and destroying classified materials. Reports criminal information to authorities and testifies in court. ● **GED:** R5, M3, L5 ● **SVP:** 2-4 yrs ● **Academic:** Ed=A, Eng=G ● **Work Field:**

293, 271 ● **MPSMS:** 951 ● **Aptitudes:** G2, V3, N3, S2, P4, Q3, K4, F4, M4, E5, C5 ● **Temperaments:** D, I, P, S, V ● **Physical:** Stg=L; Freq: T, G, N, F, V Occas: R, H ● **Work Env:** Noise=N; Occas: O ● **Salary:** 5 ● **Outlook:** 3

GOE: 04.02.03
Law & Order

BAILIFF (government ser.) ● DOT #377.667-010 ● OES: 63033 ● Alternate titles: COURT OFFICER. Maintains order in courtroom during trial and guards jury from outside contact: Checks courtroom for security and cleanliness. Assures availability of sundry supplies for use of JUDGE (government ser.). Enforces courtroom rules of behavior and warns persons not to smoke or disturb court procedure. Collects and retains unauthorized firearms from persons entering courtroom. Stops people from entering courtroom while JUDGE (government ser.) charges jury. Provides jury escort to restaurant and other areas outside of courtroom to prevent jury contact with public. Guards lodging of sequestered jury. Reports need for police or medical assistance to sheriff's office. May advise attorneys of dress required of witnesses. May announce entrance of JUDGE (government ser.). ● **GED:** R2, M1, L2 ● **SVP:** 1-3 mos ● **Academic:** Ed=H, Eng=G ● **Work Field:** 293, 291 ● **MPSMS:** 951 ● **Aptitudes:** G3, V3, N4, S4, P4, Q4, K4, F4, M4, E5, C5 ● **Temperaments:** P, S, V ● **Physical:** Stg=L; Freq: T, G Occas: R, H, I, N, F, V ● **Work Env:** Noise=Q; ● **Salary:** 3 ● **Outlook:** 2

BEACH LIFEGUARD (amuse. & rec.) ● DOT #379.364-014 ● OES: 63099 ● Patrols public beach area to monitor activities of swimmers and prevent illegal conduct: Observes activities in assigned area on foot, in vehicle, or from tower or headquarters building with binoculars to detect hazardous conditions, such as swimmers in distress, disturbances, or safety infractions. Cautions people against use of unsafe beach areas or illegal conduct, such as drinking or fighting, using megaphone. Rescues distressed persons from ocean or adjacent cliffs, using rescue techniques and equipment. Examines injured individuals, administers first aid, and monitors vital signs, utilizing training, antiseptics, bandages, and instruments, such as stethoscope and sphygmomanometer. Administers artificial respiration, utilizing cardiopulmonary or mouth-to-mouth methods, or provides oxygen to revive persons. Compiles emergency and medical treatment report forms and maintains daily information on weather and beach conditions. Occasionally operates switchboard or two-way radio system to maintain contact and coordinate activities between emergency rescue units. ● **GED:** R3, M2, L2 ● **SVP:** 3-6 mos ● **Academic:** Ed=N, Eng=S ● **Work Field:** 293 ● **MPSMS:** 919 ● **Aptitudes:** G3, V3, N4, S3, P4, Q4, K3, F3, M3, E3, C4 ● **Temperaments:** J, P, S ● **Physical:** Stg=V; Freq: R, H, I, E, T, G, N, F, D, A, V Occas: X ● **Work Env:** Noise=N; Freq: W Occas: O ● **Salary:** 1 ● **Outlook:** 3

BORDER GUARD (government ser.) ● DOT #375.363-010 ● OES: 63014 ● Alternate titles: BORDER PATROL AGENT. Patrols on foot, by motor vehicle, power boat, or aircraft along border or seacoast of United States to detect persons attempting to enter country illegally. Apprehends and detains illegal entrants for subsequent action by immigration authorities. May question agricultural workers near border to identify and apprehend illegal aliens. May report evidence of smuggling observed on patrol to customs authorities. ● **GED:** R3, M2, L3 ● **SVP:** 6 mos-1 yr ● **Academic:** Ed=N, Eng=G ● **Work Field:** 293 ● **MPSMS:** 959 ● **Aptitudes:** G3, V3, N4, S4, P3, Q4, K3, F4, M4, E4, C5 ● **Temperaments:** J, P, S ● **Physical:** Stg=M; Freq: T, G Occas: C, B, S, K, O, W, R, H, I, N, F, D ● **Work Env:** Noise=N; Freq: W Occas: T ● **Salary:** 4 ● **Outlook:** 3

BOUNCER (amuse. & rec.) ● DOT #376.667-010 ● OES: 63047 ● Alternate titles: HOUSE DETECTIVE. Patrols place of entertainment to preserve order among patrons and protect property: Circulates among patrons to prevent improper dancing, skating, or similar activities, and to detect persons annoying other patrons or damaging furnishings of establishment. Warns patrons guilty of infractions and evicts them tactfully from premises if they become unruly or ejects them by force if necessary. Calls police if unable to quell disturbance. May be desig-

nated according to type of establishment patrolled as Fun-House Attendant (amuse. & rec.); Guard, Dance Hall (amuse. & rec.); Ice Guard, Skating Rink (amuse. & rec.). ● **GED:** R2, M1, L2 ● **SVP:** 1-3 mos ● **Academic:** Ed=N, Eng=S ● **Work Field:** 293 ● **MPSMS:** 910 ● **Aptitudes:** G3, V3, N4, S4, P4, Q5, K4, F4, M4, E4, C5 ● **Temperaments:** J, P, S ● **Physical:** Stg=L; Freq: T, G ● **Work Env:** Noise=N; ● **Salary:** 1 ● **Outlook:** 3

CHAPERON (personal ser.) ● DOT #359.667-010 ● OES: 69998 ● Accompanies minors on trips to educational institutions, public functions, or recreational activities such as dances, concerts, or sports events, to provide adult supervision in absence of parents. Follows parents' instructions regarding minors' activities and imposes limitations and restrictions to ensure their safety, well-being, and conformance to specified behavior standards. May plan free-time activities. May arrange for transportation, tickets, and meals. ● **GED:** R3, M2, L2 ● **SVP:** 2-30 days ● **Academic:** Ed=N, Eng=S ● **Work Field:** 291 ● **MPSMS:** 942 ● **Aptitudes:** G3, V3, N4, S4, P4, Q4, K4, F4, M4, E5, C5 ● **Temperaments:** P, V ● **Physical:** Stg=L; Freq: T, G, F, V Occas: N ● **Work Env:** Noise=N; ● **Salary:** 1 ● **Outlook:** 2

HOUSE OFFICER (hotel & rest.) ● DOT #376.367-018 ● OES: 63035 ● Alternate titles: HOUSE DETECTIVE; SECURITY OFFICER; SPECIAL OFFICER. Patrols hotel or motel premises to maintain order, enforce regulations, and ensure observance of applicable laws: Patrols lobbies, corridors, and public rooms, confers with management, interviews guests and employees, and interrogates persons to detect infringements and investigate disturbances, complaints, thefts, vandalisms, and accidents. Patrols public areas to detect fires, unsafe conditions, and missing or inoperative safety equipment. Warns or ejects troublemakers, and cautions careless persons. Obtains assistance for accident victims and writes accident reports. Notifies staff of presence of persons with questionable reputations. Assists management and enforcement officers in emergency situations. Usually is not armed. May enter and check rooms of guests suspected of leaving without paying bill to confirm suspicions and to seize any remaining personal property. ● **GED:** R3, M1, L2 ● **SVP:** 3-6 mos ● **Academic:** Ed=N, Eng=G ● **Work Field:** 293, 271 ● **MPSMS:** 969 ● **Aptitudes:** G3, V3, N4, S4, P4, Q4, K4, F4, M4, E5, C4 ● **Temperaments:** P, S ● **Physical:** Stg=L; Freq: T, G, N, F, V Occas: R, H, I ● **Work Env:** Noise=N; ● **Salary:** 3 ● **Outlook:** 2

LIFEGUARD (amuse. & rec.) ● DOT #379.667-014 ● OES: 63099 ● Monitors activities in swimming areas to prevent accidents and provide assistance to swimmers: Cautions swimmers regarding unsafe areas. Rescues swimmers in danger of drowning and administers first aid. Maintains order in swimming areas. Inspects facilities for cleanliness. May clean and refill swimming pool. May determine chlorine content and pH value of water, using water testing kit. May conduct or officiate at swimming meets. May give swimming instructions. ● **GED:** R3, M1, L2 ● **SVP:** 3-6 mos ● **Academic:** Ed=N, Eng=G ● **Work Field:** 293, 294 ● **MPSMS:** 913 ● **Aptitudes:** G3, V3, N4, S3, P4, Q4, K3, F4, M3, E3, C4 ● **Temperaments:** J, P, S ● **Physical:** Stg=M; Freq: T, G, F, D, V Occas: C, S, K, R, H, X ● **Work Env:** Noise=N; Const: W Freq: U ● **Salary:** 1 ● **Outlook:** 3

PARK RANGER (government ser.) ● DOT #169.167-042 ● OES: 21911 ● Alternate titles: RANGER. Enforces laws, regulations, and policies in state or national park: Registers vehicles and visitors, collects fees, and issues parking and use permits. Provides information pertaining to park use, safety requirements, and points of interest. Directs traffic, investigates accidents, and patrols area to prevent fires, vandalism, and theft. Cautions, evicts, or apprehends violators of laws and regulations. Directs or participates in first aid and rescue activities. May supervise workers engaged in construction and maintenance of park facilities and enforces standards of cleanliness and sanitation. May compile specified park-use statistics, keep records, and prepare reports of area activities. May train and supervise park workers and concession attendants. May specialize in snow safety and avalanche control and be designated Snow Ranger (government ser.). ● **GED:** R4, M3, L4 ● **SVP:** 2-4 yrs ● **Academic:** Ed=B, Eng=G ● **Work Field:** 293, 282 ● **MPSMS:** 951 ● **Aptitudes:** G3, V3, N3, S3, P2, Q4, K3, F4, M3, E2, C4 ● **Temperaments:** J, P, S, V ● **Physical:** Stg=L; Freq: R, H, I, T, G, N Occas: C, B, S, K, O, W, F, D, A, X, V ● **Work Env:** Noise=L; Freq: W Occas: O ● **Salary:** 4 ● **Outlook:** 1

REPOSSESSOR (clerical) ● DOT #241.367-022 ● OES: 53508 ● Locates debtors and solicits payment for delinquent accounts and removes merchandise for nonpayment of account. May initiate repossession proceedings. May drive truck to return merchandise to creditor. May locate, enter, and start vehicle being repossessed, using special tools, if key cannot be obtained from debtor, and return vehicle to creditor. May be designated according to merchandise repossessed as Automobile Repossessor (clerical). ● **GED:** R3, M2, L2 ● **SVP:** 1-3 mos ● **Academic:** Ed=N, Eng=G ● **Work Field:** 271 ● **MPSMS:** 894 ● **Aptitudes:** G3, V4, N4, S4, P3, Q4, K4, F4, M4, E3, C4 ● **Temperaments:** P ● **Physical:** Stg=M; Freq: R, H, T, G Occas: I, N, X ● **Work Env:** Noise=Q; Freq: W ● **Salary:** 3 ● **Outlook:** 4

SKI PATROLLER (amuse. & rec.) ● DOT #379.664-010 ● OES: 63099 ● Patrols ski trails and slope areas to provide assistance and protection to skiers and report condition of trails, ski lifts, and snow cover on slopes: Patrols assigned areas, using skis or snowshoes. Rescues injured skiers and renders first aid or transfers them to waiting ambulance, using toboggan. Notifies medical personnel in case of serious injury where moving skier might prove dangerous. Ensures that no skiers remain on slopes or trails at end of day or during inclement weather. Inspects ski lifts, such as rope tows, T-bar, J-bar, and chair lifts, to report safety hazards and evidence of damage or wear. May pack snow on slopes. May give ski instruction. May participate in skiing demonstrations for entertainment of resort guests. May assist demolition crew to blast for avalanche control. ● **GED:** R3, M2, L3 ● **SVP:** 1-2 yrs ● **Academic:** Ed=N, Eng=G ● **Work Field:** 293 ● **MPSMS:** 913 ● **Aptitudes:** G3, V3, N4, S3, P4, Q5, K3, F3, M3, E1, C5 ● **Temperaments:** J, P, S, V ● **Physical:** Stg=H; Freq: F, D, V Occas: C, B, S, K, O, R, H, I, E, T, G, N ● **Work Env:** Noise=N; Const: W Freq: O ● **Salary:** 1 ● **Outlook:** 3

SURVEILLANCE-SYSTEM MONITOR (government ser.) ● DOT #379.367-010 ● OES: 63099 ● Monitors premises of public transportation terminals to detect crimes or disturbances, using closed circuit television monitors, and notifies authorities by telephone of need for corrective action: Observes television screens that transmit in sequence views of transportation facility sites. Pushes hold button to maintain surveillance of location where incident is developing, and telephones police or other designated agency to notify authorities of location of disruptive activity. Adjusts monitor controls when required to improve reception, and notifies repair service of equipment malfunctions. ● **GED:** R3, M1, L3 ● **SVP:** 2-30 days ● **Academic:** Ed=N, Eng=S ● **Work Field:** 293, 281 ● **MPSMS:** 951 ● **Aptitudes:** G3, V3, N4, S4, P4, Q4, K4, F4, M4, E5, C5 ● **Temperaments:** P, R ● **Physical:** Stg=S; Freq: T, G, N ● **Work Env:** Noise=Q; ● **Salary:** 1 ● **Outlook:** 3

GOE: 04.02.04
Emergency Responding

ALARM INVESTIGATOR (business ser.) ● DOT #376.367-010 ● OES: 63035 ● Alternate titles: ARMED GUARD; INVESTIGATOR OPERATOR; SECURITY AGENT. Investigates source of alarm and trouble signals on subscribers' premises, as recorded in central station of electrical protective signaling system: Drives radio-equipped car to subscriber's establishment, and locates source of alarm. Investigates disturbances, such as unlawful intrusion, fires, and property damage. Apprehends unauthorized persons found on property, using armed force if necessary, and releases them to custody of authorities. Contacts supervisor by radio or telephone to report irregularities and obtain further instructions. Adjusts and repairs subscriber's signaling equipment to restore service, using handtools. Coordinates activities with police and fire departments during alarms. Writes investigation and automobile usage reports. ● **GED:** R3, M1, L3 ● **SVP:** 1-3 mos ● **Academic:** Ed=N, Eng=G ● **Work Field:** 293 ● **MPSMS:** 969 ● **Aptitudes:** G3, V3, N4, S3, P3, Q4, K3, F4, M3, E4, C4 ● **Temperaments:** P, S ● **Physical:** Stg=L; Freq: T, G, N Occas: R, H, I, F, A, X, V ● **Work Env:** Noise=N; Occas: O ● **Salary:** 3 ● **Outlook:** 3

FIRE FIGHTER (any industry) ● DOT #373.364-010 ● OES: 63008 ● Controls and extinguishes fires, protects life and property, and maintains equipment as volunteer or employee of city, township, or industrial plant: Responds to fire alarms and other emergency calls. Selects hose nozzle, depending on type of fire, and directs stream of water or chemicals onto fire. Positions and climbs ladders to gain access to upper levels of buildings or to assist individuals from burning structures. Creates openings in buildings for ventilation or entrance, using ax, chisel, crowbar, electric saw, core cutter, and other power equipment. Protects property from water and smoke by use of waterproof salvage covers, smoke ejectors, and deodorants. Administers first aid and artificial respiration to injured persons and those overcome by fire and smoke. Communicates with superior during fire, using portable two-way radio. Inspects buildings for fire hazards and compliance with fire prevention ordinances. Performs assigned duties in maintaining apparatus, quarters, buildings, equipment, grounds, and hydrants. Participates in drills, demonstrations, and courses in hydraulics, pump operation and maintenance, and firefighting techniques. May fill fire extinguishers in institutions or industrial plants. May issue forms to building owners, listing fire regulation violations to be corrected. May drive and operate firefighting vehicles and equipment. May be assigned duty in marine division of fire department and be designated Firefighter, Marine (any industry). ● **GED:** R4, M2, L3 ● **SVP:** 1-2 yrs ● **Academic:** Ed=H, Eng=G ● **Work Field:** 293 ● **MPSMS:** 951 ● **Aptitudes:** G3, V3, N4, S2, P4, Q4, K3, F4, M2, E2, C3 ● **Temperaments:** J, S, V ● **Physical:** Stg=V; Freq: R, H, T, G, N, F, D, X, V Occas: C, B, S, K, O, W, I, E, A ● **Work Env:** Noise=L; Freq: H, U, A, D, X, T, O Occas: W, E ● **Salary:** 3 ● **Outlook:** 2

Mechanical 05

An interest in applying mechanical principles to practical situations using machine, hand tools, or techniques. You can satisfy this interest in a variety of jobs ranging from routine to complex professional positions. You may enjoy working with ideas about things (objects). You could seek a job in engineering or in a related technical field. You may prefer to deal directly with things. You could find a job in the crafts or trades, building, making, or repairing objects. You may like to drive or operate vehicles and special equipment. You may prefer routine or physical work in settings other than factories. Perhaps work in mining or construction would appeal to you.

Engineering

Workers in this group plan, design, and direct the construction or development of buildings, bridges, roads, airports, dams, sewage systems, air-conditioning systems, mining machinery, and other structures and equipment. They also develop processes and/ or techniques for generating and transmitting electrical power, manufacturing chemicals, extracting metals from ore, and controlling the quality of products being made. Workers specialize in one or more kinds of engineering, such as civil, electrical, mechanical, mining, and safety. Some are hired by industrial plants, petroleum and mining companies, research laboratories, and construction companies. Others find employment with federal, state, and local governments. Some have their own engineering firms and accept work from various individuals or companies.

✓ What kind of work would you do?

Your work activities would depend upon your specific job. For example, you might:

- establish computational methods and computer input data to analyze problems in aircraft design.
- apply knowledge of properties of various materials to the development of electronic and electrical circuits.
- design facilities and equipment for an electrical distribution system.
- use computers to conduct technical research to solve construction problems in designing airport structures.
- conduct research to develop new and improved chemical manufacturing processes.

- analyze technical and cost factors to plan methods to recover oil and gas.
- apply knowledge of the properties of metals to develop improved welding techniques, procedures, and equipment.
- analyze manpower and equipment usage to improve efficiency of industrial operations.

✓ What skills and abilities do you need for this kind of work?

To do this kind of work, you must be able to:

- use high level mathematics.
- understand principles of chemistry, geology, physics, and related sciences.
- solve problems, using facts and personal judgment.
- work on different projects and with changing situations.
- deal with various kinds of people.

✓ How do you know if you would like or could learn to do this kind of work?

The following questions may give you clues about yourself as you consider this group of jobs.

- Have you read mechanical or automotive design magazines? Do you enjoy and understand the technical articles?
- Have you taken courses in algebra, geometry, and advanced math? Can you solve practical problems using math?
- Have you built a model airplane, automobile, or bridge? Can you look at a blueprint or drawing and visualize the final structure?
- Have you taken physics courses? Do you like to study energy and matter?
- Have you built or repaired a radio, television, or amplifier? Do you understand electrical or electronic terms and drawings?

■ Have you served in an engineering section of the armed forces?

✓ How can you prepare for and enter this kind of work?

Occupations in this group usually require education and/or training extending from four years to over ten years, depending upon the specific kind of work. Engineers whose work affects life, health, or property, or who serve the public must be licensed. A degree from an accredited engineering school, four years of related experience, and the passing of a state examination are common requirements for a license.

A bachelor's degree in engineering is usually required for entering this type of work. College graduates trained in one of the natural sciences or mathematics may qualify for a few beginning jobs. Experienced technicians with some engineering education may be advanced to engineering jobs.

Most engineering schools require an average or above average high school record in mathematics, physics, chemistry, and English for admission. Other courses such as history and social studies are helpful in gaining an understanding of fields related to engineering.

A typical four-year curriculum includes two years of study in the basic sciences, such as mathematics, physics, chemistry, introductory engineering, social sciences, and English. The last two years are devoted to specialized engineering courses.

Several engineering schools have agreements with liberal arts colleges to allow students to spend three years in the college and two years in the engineering school. A bachelor's degree is then granted by each. Some engineering schools offer a five or six year cooperative work-study program in which the students alternate periods in school with employment in related jobs. This permits students to earn a part of their tuition costs and get on-the-job experience as they learn.

✓ What else should you consider about these jobs?

Many engineers work under quiet conditions in modern offices and research laboratories. Others work in mines, factories, at construction sites, or at outdoor locations.

If you think you would like to do this kind of work, look at the job titles listed below.

■ ■ ■

GOE: 05.01.01
Research

AERODYNAMICIST (aircraft mfg.) ● DOT #002.061-010 ● OES: 22102 ● Alternate titles: AERODYNAMICS ENGINEER; AEROPHYSICS ENGINEER. Plans and conducts analysis of aerodynamic, thermodynamic, aerothermodynamic, and aerophysics concepts, systems, and designs to resolve problems and determine suitability and application to aircraft and aerospace products: Establishes computational methods and computer input data for analyzing problems. Analyzes designs and develops configurations to ensure satisfactory static and dynamic stability and control characteristics for completed vehicle. Initiates and assists in formulating and evaluating laboratory, flight, and wind tunnel test programs, and prepares reports and conclusions for other engineering and design personnel. Coordinates activities of model design group and model shop to assure required configuration of wind tunnel models. Prepares air load data on vehicle to conform to aerodynamic requirements. May prepare reports on results of analyses, such as flight performance validation, aircraft configuration, trade studies, and aircraft certification. May confer with customer on performance problems during operational life of vehicle. May specialize in analysis of thermodynamic effects and be designated Thermodynamics Engineer (aircraft mfg.). ● **GED:** R6, M6, L6 ● **SVP:** 4-10 yrs ● **Academic:** Ed=M, Eng=S ● **Work Field:** 244 ● **MPSMS:** 702 ● **Aptitudes:** G1, V1, N1, S1, P2, Q3, K3, F3, M3, E5, C4 ● **Temperaments:** D, J, T, V ● **Physical:** Stg=L; Freq: R, H, I, N Occas: C, B, S, K, O, T, G, F, A, X ● **Work Env:** Noise=N; ● **Salary:** 5 ● **Outlook:** 3

AERONAUTICAL-RESEARCH ENGINEER (aircraft mfg.) ● DOT #002.061-026 ● OES: 22102 ● Conducts research in field of aeronautics, performing duties as described under RESEARCH ENGINEER (profess. & kin.) Master Title. ● **GED:** R6, M6, L6 ● **SVP:** 4-10 yrs ● **Academic:** Ed=M, Eng=G ● **Work Field:** 244, 251 ● **MPSMS:** 702 ●

Aptitudes: G1, V1, N1, S1, P3, Q3, K3, F3, M3, E5, C4 ● **Temperaments:** D, J, T, V ● **Physical:** Stg=L; Freq: I, N Occas: R, H, T, G, A, X ● **Work Env:** Noise=Q; ● **Salary:** 5 ● **Outlook:** 4

CHEMICAL RESEARCH ENGINEER (profess. & kin.) ● DOT #008.061-022 ● OES: 22114 ● Conducts research on chemical processes and equipment, performing duties as described under RESEARCH ENGINEER (profess. & kin.) Master Title. ● **GED:** R5, M5, L5 ● **SVP:** 4-10 yrs ● **Academic:** Ed=B, Eng=G ● **Work Field:** 251, 244 ● **MPSMS:** 707 ● **Aptitudes:** G2, V2, N2, S2, P2, Q3, K4, F4, M4, E4, C4 ● **Temperaments:** D, J ● **Physical:** Stg=L; Freq: R, H, T, G, N, A Occas: I, D, X ● **Work Env:** Noise=N; ● **Salary:** 4 ● **Outlook:** 4

DIRECTOR, RESEARCH AND DEVELOPMENT (any industry) ● DOT #189.117-014 ● OES: 13017 ● Alternate titles: MANAGER, PRODUCT DEVELOPMENT; MANAGER, RESEARCH AND DEVELOPMENT; MANUFACTURING ENGINEER, CHIEF. Directs and coordinates research and development activities for organizational products, services, or ideologies: Plans and formulates aspects of research and development proposals, such as objective or purpose of project, applications that can be utilized from findings, costs of project, and equipment and human resource requirements. Reviews and analyzes proposals submitted to determine if benefits derived and possible applications justify expenditures. Approves and submits proposals considered feasible to management for consideration and allocation of funds or allocates funds from department budget. Develops and implements methods and procedures for monitoring projects, such as preparation of records of expenditures and research findings, progress reports, and staff conferences, in order to inform management of current status of each project. May recruit, hire, and train department staff, evaluate staff performance, and develop goals and objectives for staff. May negotiate contracts with consulting firms to perform research studies. May specialize in one type of research and be designated Director, Marketing Research and Analysis (profess. & kin); Director, Product Research and Development (profess. & kin.). ● **GED:** R5, M5, L5 ● **SVP:** 4-10 yrs ● **Academic:** Ed=B, Eng=G ● **Work Field:** 295, 251 ● **MPSMS:** 700, 880 ● **Aptitudes:** G2, V2, N2, S2, P3, Q4, K4, F4, M4, E5, C4 ● **Temperaments:** D, J, P, V ● **Physical:** Stg=S; Freq: T, G, N Occas: R, H, I, X ● **Work Env:** Noise=N; ● **Salary:** 5 ● **Outlook:** 2

ELECTRICAL-RESEARCH ENGINEER (profess. & kin.) ● DOT #003.061-026 ● OES: 22126 ● Conducts research in various fields of electrical phenomena performing duties as described under RESEARCH ENGINEER (profess. & kin.) Master Title. ● **GED:** R5, M5, L5 ● **SVP:** 4-10 yrs ● **Academic:** Ed=B, Eng=G ● **Work Field:** 244, 251 ● **MPSMS:** 703, 700 ● **Aptitudes:** G2, V2, N2, S2, P2, Q3, K3, F3, M3, E4, C3 ● **Temperaments:** J, T, V ● **Physical:** Stg=L; Freq: R, H, T, G, N, A Occas: X ● **Work Env:** Noise=N; ● **Salary:** 5 ● **Outlook:** 4

ELECTRICAL TECHNICIAN (profess. & kin.) ● DOT #003.161-010 ● OES: 22505 ● Alternate titles: ELECTRICAL-LABORATORY TECHNICIAN. Applies electrical theory and related knowledge to test and modify developmental or operational electrical machinery and electrical control equipment and circuitry in industrial or commercial plants and laboratories: Assembles and tests experimental motor-control devices, switch panels, transformers, generator windings, solenoids, and other electrical equipment and components according to engineering data and knowledge of electrical principles. Modifies electrical prototypes to correct functional deviations under direction of ELECTRICAL ENGINEER (profess. & kin.). Diagnoses cause of electrical or mechanical malfunction or failure of operational equipment and performs preventative and corrective maintenance. Develops wiring diagrams, layout drawings, and engineering specifications for system or equipment modifications or expansion, and directs personnel performing routine installation and maintenance duties. Plans, directs, and records periodic electrical testing, and recommends or initiates modification or replacement of equipment which fails to meet acceptable operating standards. ● **GED:** R4, M4, L4 ● **SVP:** 2-4 yrs ● **Academic:** Ed=A, Eng=S ● **Work Field:** 244, 111 ● **MPSMS:** 703, 580 ● **Aptitudes:** G2, V2, N2, S2, P2, Q3, K2, F2, M2, E4, C4 ● **Temperaments:** J, T, V ● **Physical:** Stg=L; Freq: R, H, I, N, A, X ● **Work Env:** Noise=N; ● **Salary:** 2 ● **Outlook:** 3

ELECTRONICS TECHNICIAN (profess. & kin.) ● DOT #003.161-014 ● OES: 22505 ● Lays out, builds, tests, troubleshoots, repairs and modifies developmental and production electronic components, parts, equipment, and systems, such as computer equipment, missile control instrumentation, electron tubes, test equipment, and machine tool numerical controls, applying principles and theories of electronics, electrical circuitry, engineering mathematics, electronic and electrical testing, and physics: Discusses layout and assembly procedures and problems with ELECTRONICS ENGINEER (profess. & kin.) 003.061-030 and draws sketches to clarify design details and functional criteria of electronic units. Assembles experimental circuitry (breadboard) or complete prototype model according to engineering instructions, technical manuals, and knowledge of electronic systems and components. Recommends changes in circuitry or installation specifications to simplify assembly and maintenance. Sets up standard test apparatus or devises test equipment and circuitry to conduct functional, operational, environmental, and life tests to evaluate performance and reliability of prototype or production model. Analyzes and interprets test data. Adjusts, calibrates, aligns, and modifies circuitry and components and records effects on unit performance. Writes technical reports and develops charts, graphs, and schematics to describe and illustrate system's operating characteristics, malfunctions, deviations from design specifications, and functional limitations for consideration by engineers in broader determinations affecting system design and laboratory procedures. May operate bench lathes, drills, or other machine tools to fabricate parts, such as coils, terminal boards, and chassis. May check functioning of newly installed equipment in aircraft, ships, and structures to evaluate system performance under actual operating conditions. May instruct and supervise other technical personnel. May be designated according to specialization in electronic applications as Computer-Laboratory Technician (profess. & kin.); Development-Instrumentation Technician (profess. & kin.); Electronic-Communications Technician (profess. & kin.); Electronics Technician, Nuclear Reactor (profess. & kin); Experimental Electronics Developer (aircraft mfg.); Systems-Testing Laboratory Technician (profess. & kin.). ● **GED:** R5, M5, L4 ● **SVP:** 2-4 yrs ● **Academic:** Ed=A, Eng=S ● **Work Field:** 111, 211, 244 ● **MPSMS:** 703, 587, 590 ● **Aptitudes:** G2, V2, N2, S2, P2, Q3, K2, F2, M2, E4, C4 ● **Temperaments:** J, T, V ● **Physical:** Stg=L; Freq: R, H,

I, N, A, X Occas: E, T, G, D ● **Work Env:** Noise=N; Occas: E ● **Salary:** 4 ● **Outlook:** 5

INSTRUMENTATION TECHNICIAN (profess. & kin.) ● DOT #003.261-010 ● OES: 22505 ● Devises, selects, sets up, and operates electronic instrumentation and related electromechanical or electrohydraulic apparatus used for operational and environmental testing of mechanical, structural, or electrical equipment, and translates test data for engineering personnel to formulate engineering design and evaluation decisions: Selects, installs, calibrates, and checks sensing, telemetering, and recording instrumentation and circuitry, and develops specifications for nonstandard apparatus according to engineering data, characteristics of equipment under test, and capabilities of procurable test apparatus. Sketches and builds or modifies jigs, fixtures, and instruments and related apparatus, and verifies dimensional and functional acceptability of devices fabricated by craft or technical personnel. Performs preventive and corrective maintenance of test apparatus and peripheral equipment. Installs or directs technical personnel in installation of unit in test chamber or other test facility. Operates test apparatus during test cycle to produce, regulate, and record effects of actual or simulated conditions, such as vibration, stress, temperature, humidity, pressure, altitude, and acceleration. Analyzes and converts test data to usable form, using mathematical formulas, and prepares graphs and written reports to translate test results. May plan test program. May use computerized equipment and software to perform testing functions and produce graphs. May be designated according to equipment tested as Rocket-Control Technician (profess. & kin.); or according to nature of test as Environmental-Research Test Technician (profess. & kin.); Vibration Technician (profess. & kin.). ● **GED:** R5, M5, L4 ● **SVP:** 2-4 yrs ● **Academic:** Ed=B, Eng=S ● **Work Field:** 211, 244, 251 ● **MPSMS:** 700, 580, 600 ● **Aptitudes:** G2, V2, N2, S2, P2, Q3, K2, F2, M2, E4, C4 ● **Temperaments:** J, T, V ● **Physical:** Stg=L; Freq: R, H, I, N Occas: T, G, D, A, X ● **Work Env:** Noise=L; ● **Salary:** 3 ● **Outlook:** 4

MECHANICAL-ENGINEERING TECHNICIAN (profess. & kin.) ● DOT #007.161-026 ● OES: 35199 ● Alternate titles: ENGINEERING TECHNICIAN; EXPERIMENTAL TECHNICIAN; LABORATORY-DEVELOPMENT TECHNICIAN; TECHANICAL TECHNICIAN. Develops and tests machinery and equipment, applying knowledge of mechanical engineering technology, under direction of engineering and scientific staff: Reviews project instructions and blueprints to ascertain test specifications, procedures, objectives, test equipment, nature of technical problem, and possible solutions, such as part redesign, substitution of material or parts, or rearrangement of parts or subassemblies. Drafts detail drawing or sketch for drafting room completion or to request parts fabrication by machine, sheet metal or wood shops. Devises, fabricates, and assembles new or modified mechanical components or assemblies for products, such as industrial equipment and machinery, power equipment, servosystems, machine tools, and measuring instruments. Sets up and conducts tests of complete units and components under operational conditions to investigate design proposals for improving equipment performance or other factors, or to obtain data for development, standardization, and quality control. Analyzes indicated and calculated test results in relation to design or rated specifications and test objectives, and modifies or adjusts equipment to meet specifications. Records test procedures and results, numerical and graphical data, and recommendations for changes in product or test method. ● **GED:** R5, M4, L4 ● **SVP:** 2-4 yrs ● **Academic:** Ed=A, Eng=S ● **Work Field:** 121, 244 ● **MPSMS:** 590, 567 ● **Aptitudes:** G2, V2, N3, S2, P2, Q4, K3, F3, M3, E5, C4 ● **Temperaments:** J, T ● **Physical:** Stg=L; Freq: R, H, I, N, A Occas: X ● **Work Env:** Noise=N; ● **Salary:** 4 ● **Outlook:** 4

MECHANICAL RESEARCH ENGINEER (profess. & kin.) ● DOT #007.161-022 ● OES: 22135 ● Conducts research to develop mechanical equipment and machinery, performing duties as described under RESEARCH ENGINEER (profess. & kin.) Master Title. ● **GED:** R5, M5, L5 ● **SVP:** 4-10 yrs ● **Academic:** Ed=B, Eng=G ● **Work Field:** 251, 244 ● **MPSMS:** 560, 567 ● **Aptitudes:** G2, V2, N2, S2, P2, Q3, K3, F3, M3, E4, C4 ● **Temperaments:** D, J, P ● **Physical:** Stg=L; Freq: R, H, T, G, N, D Occas: I, A ● **Work Env:** Noise=N; ● **Salary:** 5 ● **Outlook:** 3

OPTOMECHANICAL TECHNICIAN (optical goods) ● DOT #007.161-030 ● OES: 35199 ● Applies engineering theory and practical knowledge, under direction of engineering staff, to build and test prototype optomechanical devices to be used in such equipment as aerial cameras, gun sights, and telescopes: Reviews project instructions, and preliminary specifications to identify and plan requirements for parts fabrication, purchase, assembly, and test. Prepares sketches and writes work orders and purchase requests for items to be furnished by others, and follows up delivery. Designs, builds, or modifies fixtures used to assemble parts. Lays out cutting lines for machining, using drafting tools. Assembles and adjusts parts and related electrical units of prototype to prepare for test. Sets up prototype and test apparatus, such as control console, collimator, recording equipment, and cables in accordance with specifications. Operates controls of test apparatus and prototype to observe and record test results. Computes test data on laboratory forms for engineers. Confers in technical meetings, recommending design and material changes to reduce cost and lead time. May be assigned as group leader to coordinate work of technicians, model makers, and others assigned to assist. ● **GED:** R5, M4, L4 ● **SVP:** 4-10 yrs ● **Academic:** Ed=A, Eng=S ● **Work Field:** 121, 211, 244 ● **MPSMS:** 603, 606 ● **Aptitudes:** G2, V2, N2, S2, P2, Q3, K3, F2, M2, E4, C4 ● **Temperaments:** J ● **Physical:** Stg=L; Freq: R, H, I, T, G, N, D Occas: A ● **Work Env:** Noise=N; ● **Salary:** 3 ● **Outlook:** 3

TECHNICIAN, SEMICONDUCTOR DEVELOPMENT (profess. & kin.) ● DOT #003.161-018 ● OES: 22505 ● Tests developmental semiconductor devices or sample production units, and evaluates test equipment to develop data for engineering evaluation of new designs or special production yield study, applying knowledge of electronic theory and test equipment operating principles: Designs basic circuitry and prepares rough sketches for design documentation as directed by engineers, using drafting instruments and computer-assisted design/drafting equipment. Evaluates, calibrates, and tests new equipment circuits and fixtures, using testing equipment, such as oscilloscopes, logic and test probes, and calibrators. Builds and modifies electronic components, using handtools and power tools. Assists engineers in development of testing techniques and laboratory equipment. Assists with equipment maintenance. Liaises between test project sites to ensure orderly flow of information and materials. May supervise other technicians in unit. ● **GED:** R5, M5, L4 ● **SVP:** 4-10 yrs ● **Academic:** Ed=A, Eng=S ● **Work Field:** 244, 211 ● **MPSMS:** 587, 703 ● **Aptitudes:** G2, V2, N2, S2, P2, Q3, K2, F2, M2, E4, C4 ● **Temperaments:** J, T, V ● **Physical:** Stg=L; Freq: R, H, I, T, G, N Occas: D, A, X ● **Work Env:** Noise=N; Occas: A, E, T ● **Salary:** 4 ● **Outlook:** 4

WELDING TECHNICIAN (profess. & kin.) ● DOT #011.261-014 ● OES: 35199 ● Conducts experiments and tests and evaluates data to assist welding engineering personnel in development and application of new or improved welding equipment; welding techniques, procedures, and practices; and specifications for material heat treating: Assists engineering personnel in testing and evaluating welding equipment, metals, and alloys. Evaluates data and conducts experiments to develop application of new equipment or improved techniques, procedures, or practices. Recommends adoption of new developments and applications to engineering personnel and demonstrates practicability of recommendations. Inspects welded joints and conducts tests to ensure welds meet company standards, national code requirements, and customer job specifications. Records inspection and test results and prepares and submits reports to welding engineering personnel. Conducts certification tests for qualification of personnel with national code requirements. ● **GED:** R4, M3, L3 ● **SVP:** 4-10 yrs ● **Academic:** Ed=A, Eng=S ● **Work Field:** 244, 212 ● **MPSMS:** 871 ● **Aptitudes:** G3, V3, N3, S3, P2, Q3, K2, F3, M3, E5, C4 ● **Temperaments:** J, T ● **Physical:** Stg=L; Freq: R, H, I, T, G, N Occas: X ● **Work Env:** Noise=N; ● **Salary:** 3 ● **Outlook:** 4

GOE: 05.01.02
Environmental Protection

FIRE-PROTECTION ENGINEER (profess. & kin.) ● DOT #012.167-026 ● OES: 22198 ● Alternate titles: FIRE-LOSS-PREVENTION ENGINEER. Advises and assists private and public organizations and military services for purposes of safeguarding life and property against fire, explosion, and related hazards: Makes studies of industrial, mercantile, and public buildings, homes, and other property before and after construction, considering factors, such as fire resistance of construction, usage or contents of buildings, water supplies and water delivery, and egress facilities. Designs or recommends materials or equipment, such as structural components protection, fire-detection equipment, alarm systems, fire extinguishing devices and systems, and advises on location, handling, installation, and maintenance. Recommends materials, equipment, or methods for alleviation of conditions conducive to fire. Devises fire protection programs, and organizes and trains personnel to carry out such programs. May evaluate fire departments and adequacy of laws, ordinances, and regulations affecting fire prevention or firesafety. Conducts research and tests on fire retardants and firesafety of materials and devices and to determine fire causes and methods of fire prevention. May determine fire causes and methods of fire prevention. May teach courses on fire prevention and protection at accredited educational institutions. May advise and plan for prevention of destruction by fire, wind, water, or other causes of damage. ● **GED:** R5, M5, L5 ● **SVP:** 2-4 yrs ● **Academic:** Ed=A, Eng=G ● **Work Field:** 244, 251 ● **MPSMS:** 712 ● **Aptitudes:** G1, V1, N1, S2, P2, Q3, K3, F3, M3, E3, C4 ● **Temperaments:** D, J, P ● **Physical:** Stg=L; Const: N Freq: R, H, I, T, G, F Occas: A, X, V ● **Work Env:** Noise=N; Occas: W ● **Salary:** 4 ● **Outlook:** 3

HEALTH PHYSICIST (profess. & kin.) ● DOT #015.021-010 ● OES: 24102 ● Devises and directs research, training, and monitoring programs to protect plant and laboratory personnel from radiation hazards: Conducts research to develop inspection standards, radiation exposure limits for personnel, safe work methods, and decontamination procedures, and tests surrounding areas to ensure that radiation is not in excess of permissible standards. Develops criteria for design and modification of health physics equipment, such as detectors and counters, to improve radiation protection. Assists in developing standards of permissible concentrations of radioisotopes in liquids and gases. Directs testing and monitoring of equipment and recording of personnel and plant area radiation exposure data. Requests bioassay samples from individuals believed to be exposed. Consults with scientific personnel regarding new experiments to determine that equipment or plant design conforms to health physics standards for protection of personnel. Conducts research pertaining to potential environmental impact of proposed atomic energy related industrial development to determine qualifications for licensing. Requisitions and maintains inventory of instruments. Instructs personnel in principles and regulations related to radiation hazards. Assigns film badges and dosimeters to personnel, and recommends changes in assignment for health reasons. Advises public authorities on methods of dealing with radiation hazards, and procedures to be followed in radiation incidents, and assists in civil defense planning. May specialize in research concerning decontamination of radioactive equipment and work areas in nuclear plants, laboratories, and other facilities and be designated Nuclear-Decontamination Research Specialist (profess. & kin.). ● **GED:** R6, M5, L5 ● **SVP:** 4-10 yrs ● **Academic:** Ed=M, Eng=G ● **Work Field:** 293, 251 ● **MPSMS:** 732 ● **Aptitudes:** G1, V1, N2, S2, P2, Q2, K4, F4, M4, E5, C4 ● **Temperaments:** D, J, P ● **Physical:** Stg=L; Freq: R, H, T, G, N, A Occas: I, X ● **Work Env:** Noise=N; Occas: W, R ● **Salary:** 5 ● **Outlook:** 3

INDUSTRIAL-HEALTH ENGINEER (profess. & kin.) ● DOT #012.167-034 ● OES: 22198 ● Alternate titles: INDUSTRIAL HYGIENE ENGINEER. Plans and coordinates private or government industrial health program requiring application of engineering principles and technology to analyze and control conditions contributing to occupational hazards and diseases: Conducts plant or area surveys to determine safe limits of exposure to materials or conditions, such as temperatures, noise, dusts, fumes, vapors, mists, gases, solvents, and radiation which are known or suspected of being real or potential detriments to health, and implements or recommends control measures. Directs workers engaged in field and laboratory verification of compliance with health regulations. Provides technical guidance to management, labor organizations, government agencies, and civic groups regarding health-related problems, such as stream and air pollution and correct use of protective clothing or accessories. ● **GED:** R5, M5, L5 ● **SVP:** 2-4 yrs ● **Academic:** Ed=B, Eng=G ● **Work Field:** 244, 295 ● **MPSMS:** 712 ● **Aptitudes:** G1, V1, N1, S2, P3, Q3, K4, F4, M4, E5, C3 ● **Temperaments:** D, J, P ● **Physical:** Stg=S; Freq: T, G, N Occas: R, H, I, X ● **Work Env:** Noise=N; Occas: W ● **Salary:** 4 ● **Outlook:** 4

NUCLEAR-CRITICALITY SAFETY ENGINEER (profess. & kin.) ● DOT #015.067-010 ● OES: 22117 ● Conducts research and analyzes and evaluates proposed and existing methods of transportation, handling, and storage of nuclear fuel to preclude accidental nuclear reaction at nuclear facilities: Reviews and evaluates fuel transfer and storage plans received from nuclear plants. Studies reports of nuclear fuel characteristics to determine potential or inherent problems. Reads blueprints of proposed storage facilities and visits storage sites to determine adequacy of storage plans. Forecasts nuclear fuel criticality (point at which nuclear chain reaction becomes self-sustaining), given various factors which may exist in fuel handling and storage, using knowledge of nuclear physics, calculator, and computer terminal. Determines potential hazards and accident conditions which may exist in fuel handling and storage and recommends preventive measures. Summarizes findings and writes reports. Confers with project officials to resolve situations where hazard is beyond acceptable levels. Prepares proposal reports for handling and storage of fuels to be submitted to government review board. Studies existing procedures and recommends changes or additions to guidelines and controls to ensure prevention of self-sustaining nuclear chain reaction. ● **GED:** R6, M6, L5 ● **SVP:** 4-10 yrs ● **Academic:** Ed=B, Eng=G ● **Work Field:** 244, 251 ● **MPSMS:** 715 ● **Aptitudes:** G1, V1, N1, S1, P2, Q2, K3, F3, M4, E5, C5 ● **Temperaments:** J, T, V ● **Physical:** Stg=L; Freq: R, H, I, T, G, N, A Occas: S, K, O ● **Work Env:** Noise=L; Occas: R ● **Salary:** 5 ● **Outlook:** 2

POLLUTION-CONTROL ENGINEER (profess. & kin.) ● DOT #019.081-018 ● OES: 22198 ● Plans and conducts engineering studies to analyze and evaluate pollution problems, methods of pollution control, and methods of testing pollution sources to determine physiochemical nature and concentration of contaminants: Reviews data collected by POLLUTION-CONTROL TECHNICIAN (profess. & kin.) from pollution emission sources. Performs engineering calculations to determine pollution emissions from various industrial sources and to evaluate effectiveness of pollution control equipment. Reviews compliance schedules and inspection reports to ensure compliance with pollution control regulations. Recommends issuance or denial of permits for industries to construct or operate facilities. Advises enforcement personnel of noncompliance or unsatisfactory compliance with regulations. Develops or modifies techniques for monitoring pollution. Calibrates and adjusts pollution control monitors to ensure accurate functioning of instruments. May be designated according to specialty as Air-Pollution Engineer (profess. & kin.); Noise-Abatement Engineer (profess. & kin.); Water Quality-Control Engineer (profess. & kin.). ● **GED:** R6, M6, L6 ● **SVP:** 4-10 yrs ● **Academic:** Ed=B, Eng=S ● **Work Field:** 244, 212 ● **MPSMS:** 707, 706 ● **Aptitudes:** G1, V1, N1, S2, P2, Q4, K4, F4, M2, E5, C4 ● **Temperaments:** D, J, T ● **Physical:** Stg=L; Freq: R, H, I, N Occas: S, K, T, G, A, X ● **Work Env:** Noise=N; Occas: W, A ● **Salary:** 4 ● **Outlook:** 3

PRODUCT-SAFETY ENGINEER (profess. & kin.) ● DOT #012.061-010 ● OES: 22198 ● Develops and conducts tests to evaluate product safety levels and recommends measures to reduce or eliminate hazards: Establishes procedures for detection and elimination of physical and chemical hazards and avoidance of potential toxic effects and other product hazards. Investigates causes of accidents, injuries, and illnesses resulting from product usage and develops solutions. Evaluates potential health hazards or damage which could result from misuse of products and applies engineering principles and product standards to improve safety. May participate in preparation of product usage and precautionary label instructions. ● **GED:** R6, M6, L6 ● **SVP:** 4-10 yrs ● **Academic:** Ed=B, Eng=G ● **Work Field:** 244 ● **MPSMS:** 712 ● **Aptitudes:** G2, V2, N2, S2, P3, Q3, K3, F3, M3, E3, C3 ● **Temperaments:** D, J, P, V ● **Physical:** Stg=S; Freq: R, H, I, T, G, N, X ● **Work Env:** Noise=N; ● **Salary:** 5 ● **Outlook:** 4

RADIATION-PROTECTION ENGINEER (profess. & kin.) ● DOT #015.137-010 ● OES: 22117 ● Supervises and coordinates activities of workers engaged in monitoring radiation levels and condition of equipment used to generate nuclear energy to ensure safe operation of plant facilities: Evaluates water chemical analysis data in primary and supportive plant systems to determine compliance with radiation content and corrosion control regulations. Investigates problems, such as radioactive leaks in reactors and auxiliary systems, or excessive radiation or corrosion of equipment, applying knowledge of radiation protection techniques and principles of chemistry and engineering to correct conditions. Confers with departmental supervisors, manufacturing rep-

resentatives, and regulatory agency staff to discuss problems, to develop tests to detect radioactive leaks, and to design plans to monitor equipment and safety programs. Directs workers in testing and analyzing water samples and monitoring processing system. Prepares reports, such as environmental monitoring operation report, radioactive waste releases, and shipping reports, for review by administrative personnel and submission to regulatory agency. May prepare employee performance reviews and related reports. ● **GED:** R5, M4, L5 ● **SVP:** 4-10 yrs ● **Academic:** Ed=B, Eng=G ● **Work Field:** 211, 244 ● **MPSMS:** 715, 871 ● **Aptitudes:** G2, V2, N2, S2, P2, Q2, K3, F4, M4, E5, C5 ● **Temperaments:** D, J, P, V ● **Physical:** Stg=L; Freq: T, G, N Occas: R, H, I ● **Work Env:** Noise=N; Occas: R ● **Salary:** 5 ● **Outlook:** 2

RESOURCE-RECOVERY ENGINEER (government ser.) ● DOT #019.167-018 ● OES: 22121 ● Plans and participates in activities concerned with study, development, and inspection of solid-waste resource recovery systems and marketability of solid-waste recovery products: Conducts studies of chemical and mechanical solid-waste recovery processes and system designs to evaluate efficiency and cost-effectiveness of proposed operations. Inspects solid-waste resource recovery facilities to determine compliance with regulations governing construction and use. Collects data on resource recovery systems and analyzes alternate plans to determine most feasible systems for specific solid-waste recovery purposes. Prepares recommendations for development of resource recovery programs, based on analysis of alternate plans and knowledge of physical properties of various solid-waste materials. Confers with design engineers, management personnel, and others concerned with recovery of solid-waste resources to discuss problems and provide technical advice. Coordinates activities of workers engaged in study of potential markets for reclaimable materials. Lectures civic and professional organizations and provides information about practices to media representatives to promote interest and participation in solid-waste recovery practices. ● **GED:** R6, M6, L5 ● **SVP:** 4-10 yrs ● **Academic:** Ed=B, Eng=S ● **Work Field:** 271, 244 ● **MPSMS:** 719 ● **Aptitudes:** G1, V2, N1, S1, P2, Q1, K3, F3, M3, E5, C4 ● **Temperaments:** J, P, T ● **Physical:** Stg=S; Freq: R, H, I, T, G, N Occas: F, A, X ● **Work Env:** Noise=N; ● **Salary:** 5 ● **Outlook:** 4

SAFETY ENGINEER (profess. & kin.) ● DOT #012.061-014 ● OES: 22198 ● Develops and implements safety program to prevent or correct unsafe environmental working conditions, utilizing knowledge of industrial processes, mechanics, chemistry, psychology, and industrial health and safety laws: Examines plans and specifications for new machinery or equipment to determine if all safety precautions have been included. Determines amount of weight that can be safely placed on plant floor. Tours plant to inspect fire and safety equipment, machinery, and facilities to identify and correct potential hazards and ensure compliance with safety regulations. Determines requirements for safety clothing and devices, and designs, builds, and installs, or directs installation of safety devices on machinery. Conducts or coordinates safety and first aid training to educate workers about safety policies, laws, and practices. Investigates industrial accidents to minimize recurrence and prepares accident reports. May conduct air quality tests for presence of harmful gases and vapors. ● **GED:** R6, M6, L6 ● **SVP:** 4-10 yrs ● **Academic:** Ed=B, Eng=G ● **Work Field:** 244 ● **MPSMS:** 712 ● **Aptitudes:** G2, V2, N2, S2, P3, Q3, K3, F3, M3, E5, C4 ● **Temperaments:** D, J, P, V ● **Physical:** Stg=L; Freq: H, T, G Occas: R, I, N, F, D, A, X ● **Work Env:** Noise=N; ● **Salary:** 5 ● **Outlook:** 4

SAFETY MANAGER (profess. & kin.) ● DOT #012.167-058 ● OES: 13017 ● Plans, implements, and coordinates program to reduce or eliminate occupational injuries, illnesses, deaths, and financial losses: Identifies and appraises conditions which could produce accidents and financial losses and evaluates potential extent of injuries resulting from accidents. Conducts or directs research studies to identify hazards and evaluate loss producing potential of given system, operation or process. Develops accident-prevention and loss-control systems and programs for incorporation into operational policies of organization. Coordinates safety activities of unit managers to ensure implementation of safety activities throughout organization. Compiles, analyzes, and interprets statistical data related to exposure factors concerning occupational illnesses and accidents and prepares reports for information of personnel concerned. Maintains liaison with outside organizations, such as fire departments, mutual aid societies, and rescue teams to assure information exchange and mutual assistance. Devises methods to evaluate safety program and conducts or directs evaluations.

Evaluates technical and scientific publications concerned with safety management and participates in activities of related professional organizations to update knowledge of safety program developments. May store and retrieve statistical data, using computer. ● **GED:** R6, M6, L6 ● **SVP:** 4-10 yrs ● **Academic:** Ed=B, Eng=G ● **Work Field:** 244, 295 ● **MPSMS:** 712 ● **Aptitudes:** G2, V2, N2, S3, P3, Q3, K3, F3, M3, E4, C4 ● **Temperaments:** D, J, P, V ● **Physical:** Stg=S; Freq: T, G Occas: S, O, R, H, I, N, F, D, A, X ● **Work Env:** Noise=N; ● **Salary:** 4 ● **Outlook:** 3

GOE: 05.01.03
Systems Design

CABLE ENGINEER, OUTSIDE PLANT (tel. & tel.) ● DOT #003.167-010 ● OES: 22126 ● Plans, directs, and coordinates activities concerned with laying and repairing submarine telecommunication cables: Devises plans for laying cable lines, taking into consideration ocean currents and ocean depths. Determines where and how cables should be laid and decides such matters as where to place buoys, where to cut cable, what grapnel to use, what length of rope to use for a given depth, what type of cable to use, and what route to follow. Keeps charts and records to show depth and location of all cables laid. Analyzes test figures made when cable fault occurs to determine exact location of cable break. Oversees work of locating and repairing damaged cables. ● **GED:** R5, M5, L5 ● **SVP:** 4-10 yrs ● **Academic:** Ed=B, Eng=G ● **Work Field:** 244 ● **MPSMS:** 586, 703 ● **Aptitudes:** G2, V2, N2, P2, Q3, K3, F3, M3, E4, C3 ● **Temperaments:** D, J, T, V ● **Physical:** Stg=L; Freq: R, H, T, G, N, D Occas: I, A, X ● **Work Env:** Noise=N; Freq: W ● **Salary:** 5 ● **Outlook:** 4

CENTRAL-OFFICE EQUIPMENT ENGINEER (tel. & tel.) ● DOT #003.187-010 ● OES: 22126 ● Directs implementation of planning schedule for installation of central office toll or local switching facilities, or interoffice transmission facilities equipment, such as radio, TV, camera, and repeaters: Reviews planning schedule or equipment request and data on projected traffic to determine quantities of specific types of equipment required. Plans arrangement of equipment, prepares cost estimates for equipment and installation, and submits data to management for authorization approval. Prepares drawings and equipment specifications for installation. Monitors installation activities to solve any problems concerning arrangement or specifications. Assigns equipment and installation expenditures to specific program or project accounts. Closes out installation authorization when equipment has been tested and put in service. ● **GED:** R6, M6, L6 ● **SVP:** 4-10 yrs ● **Academic:** Ed=B, Eng=G ● **Work Field:** 244 ● **MPSMS:** 586 ● **Aptitudes:** G1, V1, N1, S2, P3, Q3, K4, F4, M4, E5, C5 ● **Temperaments:** J, T, V ● **Physical:** Stg=S; Freq: R, H, N, A Occas: I, X ● **Work Env:** Noise=N; ● **Salary:** 4 ● **Outlook:** 4

CHIEF ENGINEER, WATERWORKS (waterworks) ● DOT #005.167-010 ● OES: 13017 ● Plans and directs activities concerned with water utility systems installation, operation, maintenance, and service: Directs activities of engineers engaged in preparing designs and plans to construct, enlarge, and modify such facilities as water treatment plants, watersheds, and dams, hydroelectric stations, pumping stations, and to install water mains, and other appurtenances. Provides engineering and technical direction for planning and design of water utility projects. Reviews plans and specifications prior to instituting project to determine whether they meet organizational requirements. Analyzes and compiles data received from engineers to prepare budget estimates. Directs and coordinates engineers in conducting studies, such as economics of systems operation, water distribution, and water treatment plants or relative equipment performance to determine most feasible approach to meeting organizational and technical problems. Confers with municipal authorities concerning budget requirements, changes in organizational policy, regulation of water rates, and plumbing requirements, or other problems affecting community. ● **GED:** R5, M5, L5 ● **SVP:** Over 10 yrs ● **Academic:** Ed=A, Eng=G ● **Work Field:** 244 ● **MPSMS:** 873 ● **Aptitudes:** G2, V1, N1, S1, P2, Q2, K4, F4, M4, E5, C5 ● **Temperaments:** D, J, P, T ● **Physical:** Stg=L; Freq: R, H, T, G, N Occas: I, D ● **Work Env:** Noise=N; ● **Salary:** 5 ● **Outlook:** 2

COMMERCIAL ENGINEER (radio-tv broad.) ● DOT #003.187-014 ● OES: 22126 ● Alternate titles: TRAFFIC ENGINEER. Plans use of wire facilities connecting stations comprising a network to cover changing conditions and requirements: Evaluates technical capabilities of wire facilities, according to availability and range, to obtain most effective method of transmission. Reviews network program schedule to be linked to network stations, and projects use of wire facilities. Subdivides wire facilities linking network stations for simultaneous broadcasting of different programs to stations. Tests facilities prior to broadcast time to determine readiness of transmission line. May prepare engineering estimates of equipment installations or modification of existing equipment. ● **GED:** R5, M5, L5 ● **SVP:** 2-4 yrs ● **Academic:** Ed=B, Eng=S ● **Work Field:** 244 ● **MPSMS:** 863, 864 ● **Aptitudes:** G2, V2, N1, S2, P2, Q3, K4, F4, M4, E5, C5 ● **Temperaments:** J, T ● **Physical:** Stg=S; Freq: R, H, N Occas: I, A ● **Work Env:** Noise=N; ● **Salary:** 4 ● **Outlook:** 4

COMPUTER SYSTEMS HARDWARE ANALYST (profess. & kin.) ● DOT #033.167-010 ● OES: 25198 ● Alternate titles: COMPUTER SYSTEMS ENGINEER; INFORMATION PROCESSING ENGINEER; METHODS ANALYST, DATA PROCESSING. Analyzes data processing requirements to plan data processing system that will provide system capabilities required for projected work loads, and plans layout and installation of new system or modification of existing system: Confers with data processing and project managers to obtain information on limitations and capabilities of existing system and capabilities required for data processing projects and projected work load. Evaluates factors such as number of departments serviced by data processing equipment, reporting formats required, volume of transactions, time requirements and cost constraints, and need for security and access restrictions to determine hardware configurations. Analyzes information to determine, recommend, and plan layout for type of computers and peripheral equipment, or modifications to existing equipment and system, that will provide capability for proposed project or work load, efficient operation, and effective use of allotted space. May enter data into computer terminal to store, retrieve, and manipulate data for analysis of system capabilities and requirements. May specify power supply requirements and configuration. May recommend purchase of equipment to control dust, temperature, and humidity in area of system installation. May specialize in one area of system application or in one type or make of equipment. May train users to use new or modified equipment. May monitor functioning of equipment to ensure system operates in conformance with specifications. ● **GED:** R5, M5, L5 ● **SVP:** 2-4 yrs ● **Academic:** Ed=A, Eng=S ● **Work Field:** 244 ● **MPSMS:** 893 ● **Aptitudes:** G1, V2, N2, S2, P3, Q3, K4, F4, M4, E5, C5 ● **Temperaments:** D, J, P ● **Physical:** Stg=S; Freq: R, H, T, G, N Occas: I, A ● **Work Env:** Noise=N; ● **Salary:** 4 ● **Outlook:** 5

ELECTRICAL ENGINEER, POWER SYSTEM (utilities) ● DOT #003.167-018 ● OES: 22126 ● Alternate titles: POWER ENGINEER. Designs power system facilities and equipment and coordinates construction, operation, and maintenance of electric power generating, receiving, and distribution stations, transmission lines, and distribution systems and equipment: Designs and plans layout of generating plants, transmission and distribution lines, and receiving and distribution stations. Directs preparation of, or prepares drawings and specific type of equipment and materials to be used, in construction and equipment installation. Estimates labor, material, construction, and equipment costs. Inspects completed installations for conformance with design and equipment specifications and safety standards. Observes operation of installation for conformance with operational standards. Coordinates operation and maintenance activities to ensure opitimum utilization of power system facilities and meet customer demands for electrical energy. May compile power rates and direct others in evaluating properties and developing utilities in new territories. May be designated according to type of engineering functions as Engineer, Design-And-Construction (utilities); Engineer, Operations-And-Maintenance (utilities). ● **GED:** R6, M6, L6 ● **SVP:** 4-10 yrs ● **Academic:** Ed=B, Eng=G ● **Work Field:** 244 ● **MPSMS:** 871 ● **Aptitudes:** G1, V1, N1, S1, P2, Q3, K3, F3, M3, E4, C4 ● **Temperaments:** D, J, P, V ● **Physical:** Stg=L; Freq: R, H, I, N, D Occas: T, G, X ● **Work Env:** Noise=Q; ● **Salary:** 4 ● **Outlook:** 4

HYDRAULIC ENGINEER (profess. & kin.) ● DOT #005.061-018 ● OES: 22121 ● Alternate titles: HYDROLOGIC ENGINEER. Designs and directs construction of power and other hydraulic engineering projects for control and use of water: Computes and estimates rates of waterflow. Specifies type and size of equipment, such as conduits, pumps, turbines, pressure valves, and surge tanks, used in transporting water and converting water power into electricity. Directs, through subordinate supervisors, activities of workers engaged in dredging, digging cutoffs, placing jetties, and constructing levees to stabilize streams or open water ways. Designs and coordinates construction of artificial canals, conduits, and mains to transport and distribute water; and plans reservoirs, pressure valves, and booster stations to obtain proper water pressure at all levels. Frequently builds laboratory models to study construction and flow problems. ● **GED:** R5, M5, L5 ● **SVP:** 2-4 yrs ● **Academic:** Ed=B, Eng=G ● **Work Field:** 244 ● **MPSMS:** 704, 725 ● **Aptitudes:** G2, V2, N2, S2, P2, Q2, K3, F3, M3, E5, C4 ● **Temperaments:** D, J, T, V ● **Physical:** Stg=L; Freq: T, G, N Occas: R, H, F ● **Work Env:** Noise=N; Freq: W ● **Salary:** 5 ● **Outlook:** 4

ILLUMINATING ENGINEER (profess. & kin.) ● DOT #003.061-046 ● OES: 22126 ● Designs and directs installation of illuminating equipment and systems for buildings, plants, streets, stadia, tunnels, and outdoor displays: Studies lighting requirements of client to determine lighting equipment and arrangement of lamps that will provide optimum illumination with economy of installation and operation. Designs lamps of required light intensity and output, light control reflectors and lenses, and lamp arrangement required to meet illuminating standards. Plans and prepares drawings for installation of lighting system in accordance with client's specifications and municipal codes. Directs installation of system to ensure conformance with engineering specifications and compliance with electrical codes. May be designated according to type or location of illumination system designed and installed as Building-Illuminating Engineer (profess. & kin.); Industrial-Illuminating Engineer (profess. & kin.); Outdoor-Illuminating Engineer (profess. & kin.). ● **GED:** R5, M5, L5 ● **SVP:** 4-10 yrs ● **Academic:** Ed=B, Eng=G ● **Work Field:** 244 ● **MPSMS:** 871, 703 ● **Aptitudes:** G1, V1, N1, S2, P2, Q3, K3, F3, M3, E5, C4 ● **Temperaments:** D, J, T ● **Physical:** Stg=S; Freq: R, H, T, G, N Occas: I, D, X ● **Work Env:** Noise=N; ● **Salary:** 4 ● **Outlook:** 4

IRRIGATION ENGINEER (profess. & kin.) ● DOT #005.061-022 ● OES: 22121 ● Plans, designs, and oversees construction of irrigation projects for transporting and distributing water to agricultural lands: Plans and designs irrigation fixtures and installation of fixtures to requirements and specifications. Directs, through subordinate supervisors, construction of such irrigation systems as dams, canals, and ditches, according to type of soil, climatic characteristics, water supply, return flow, and other factors affecting irrigation requirements. Conducts research on problems of soil drainage and conservation, applying knowledge of civil engineering [RESEARCH ENGINEER (profess. & kin.)]. ● **GED:** R5, M5, L4 ● **SVP:** 4-10 yrs ● **Academic:** Ed=A, Eng=G ● **Work Field:** 244 ● **MPSMS:** 704, 367 ● **Aptitudes:** G2, V2, N2, S2, P2, Q2, K3, F3, M3, E3, C3 ● **Temperaments:** D, J, T, V ● **Physical:** Stg=L; Freq: R, H, T, G, N Occas: I, E, F, X ● **Work Env:** Noise=N; Occas: W ● **Salary:** 5 ● **Outlook:** 3

MARINE ENGINEER (profess. & kin.) ● DOT #014.061-014 ● OES: 22198 ● Designs and oversees installation and repair of marine powerplants, propulsion systems, heating and ventilating systems, and other mechanical and electrical equipment in ships, docks, and marine facilities: Studies drawings and specifications and performs complex calculations to conceive equipment and systems designed to meet requirements of marine craft or facility. Oversees and evaluates operation of equipment during acceptance testing and shakedown cruises. May specialize in design of equipment, such as boilers, steam-driven reciprocating engines, heat exchangers, fire-control and communication systems, electric power systems, or piping and related fittings and valves. ● **GED:** R6, M5, L5 ● **SVP:** 4-10 yrs ● **Academic:** Ed=B, Eng=G ● **Work Field:** 244 ● **MPSMS:** 714 ● **Aptitudes:** G1, V1, N1, S1, P2, Q3, K4, F3, M3, E4, C3 ● **Temperaments:** D, J, T, V ● **Physical:** Stg=L; Freq: R, H, T, G, N Occas: I, D, A ● **Work Env:** Noise=N; Occas: W ● **Salary:** 4 ● **Outlook:** 3

NUCLEAR ENGINEER (profess. & kin.) ● DOT #015.061-014 ● OES: 22117 ● Conducts research into problems of nuclear energy systems; designs and develops nuclear equipment; and monitors testing, operation, and maintenance of nuclear reactors: Plans and conducts nuclear research to discover facts or to test, prove, or modify known nuclear theories concerning release, control, and utilization of nuclear energy. Evaluates findings to develop new concepts of thermonuclear

analysis and new uses of radioactive processes. Plans, designs, and develops nuclear equipment such as reactor cores, radiation shielding, and associated instrumentation and control mechanisms. Studies nuclear fuel cycle to define most economical uses of nuclear material and safest means of waste products disposal. Monitors nuclear tests and examines operations of facilities which process or utilize radioactive or fissionable material to ensure efficient functioning and conformance with safety specifications, regulations, and laws. Prepares technical reports, utilizing knowledge obtained during research and development activities and inspectional functions. May direct operating and maintenance activities of operational nuclear facility. ● **GED:** R6, M6, L5 ● **SVP:** 4-10 yrs ● **Academic:** Ed=B, Eng=S ● **Work Field:** 244, 251 ● **MPSMS:** 725 ● **Aptitudes:** G1, V1, N1, S2, P3, Q3, K3, F3, M3, E5, C5 ● **Temperaments:** D, J, T ● **Physical:** Stg=S; Freq: R, H, I, T, G, N, F, D, A ● **Work Env:** Noise=N; Freq: R ● **Salary:** 5 ● **Outlook:** 2

NUCLEAR-FUELS RECLAMATION ENGINEER (profess. & kin.) ● DOT #015.061-026 ● OES: 22117 ● Plans, designs, and oversees construction and operation of nuclear fuels reprocessing systems: Performs research and experiments to determine acceptable methods of reclaiming various types of nuclear fuels. Designs nuclear fuel reclamation systems and equipment for pilot plants. Communicates with vendors and contractors, and computes cost estimates of reclamation systems. Writes project proposals and submits them to company review board. Studies safety procedures, guidelines, and controls, and confers with safety officials to ensure that safety limits are not violated in design, construction, or operation of systems and equipment. Oversees nuclear fuels reprocessing system construction and operation, conferring with construction supervisory and operating personnel. Tests system equipment and approves equipment for operation. Monitors operations to detect potential or inherent problems. Initiates corrective actions and orders plant shutdown in emergency situations. Identifies operational and processing problems and recommends solutions. Maintains log of plant operations, and prepares reports for review by plant officials. ● **GED:** R6, M5, L5 ● **SVP:** 2-4 yrs ● **Academic:** Ed=B, Eng=G ● **Work Field:** 244, 251 ● **MPSMS:** 715 ● **Aptitudes:** G1, V1, N1, S1, P2, Q3, K3, F3, M3, E5, C5 ● **Temperaments:** D, J, T, V ● **Physical:** Stg=L; Freq: R, H, I, T, G, N, D Occas: S, K, O ● **Work Env:** Noise=N; Occas: R ● **Salary:** 5 ● **Outlook:** 3

POWER-DISTRIBUTION ENGINEER (utilities) ● DOT #003.167-046 ● OES: 22126 ● Alternate titles: ELECTRIC-DISTRIBUTION ENGINEER. Plans construction and coordinates operation of facilities for transmitting power from distribution points to consumers: Lays out substations and overhead and underground lines in urban and rural areas. Prepares specifications and estimates costs. Makes complex electrical computations to determine type and arrangement of circuits and size, type and number of pieces of equipment, such as transformers, circuit breakers, switches, and lightning arresters. Computes sag and stress for specifications on wire and cable. Plans layout of pole lines and underground cable and solves problems, such as determining height, location, spacing, guying, and insulating of poles. May be designated according to specialization as Overhead-Distribution Engineer (utilities); Rural-Service Engineer (utilities); Substation Engineer (utilities); Underground-Distribution Engineer (utilities). ● **GED:** R5, M5, L5 ● **SVP:** 4-10 yrs ● **Academic:** Ed=B, Eng=G ● **Work Field:** 244 ● **MPSMS:** 871 ● **Aptitudes:** G1, V1, N1, S1, P2, Q3, K2, F2, M3, E5, C5 ● **Temperaments:** J, T ● **Physical:** Stg=S; Freq: R, H, N, D Occas: I, A ● **Work Env:** Noise=Q; ● **Salary:** 5 ● **Outlook:** 4

POWER-TRANSMISSION ENGINEER (utilities) ● DOT #003.167-050 ● OES: 22126 ● Alternate titles: ELECTRICAL-TRANSMISSION ENGINEER; TRANSMISSION-AND-COORDINATION ENGINEER; TRANSMISSION-LINE ENGINEER. Lays out plans and estimates costs for constructing transmission lines (high-tension facilities for carrying power from source to distributing points): Visits proposed construction site and selects best and shortest route to avoid interference with telephone or other lines. Submits data on proposed route to right-of-way department for obtaining necessary easements. Arranges for aerial, topographical, and other surveys to be made to obtain pertinent data for planning lines. Devises steel and wood supporting structures for cables and draws sketch showing their location. Performs detailed engineering calculations to draw up construction specifications, such as cable sag, pole strength, and necessary grounding. Estimates labor, material, and construction costs, and draws up specifications for purchase of materials and equipment. Keeps informed on new developments in electric power transmission. Assists various departments of power company on problems involving transmission-line operation and maintenance. Inspects completed installation. Does not usually plan facilities for distributing power to consumers [POWER-DISTRIBUTION ENGINEER (utilities)]. ● **GED:** R5, M5, L5 ● **SVP:** 4-10 yrs ● **Academic:** Ed=B, Eng=G ● **Work Field:** 244 ● **MPSMS:** 871, 703 ● **Aptitudes:** G1, V1, N1, S2, P2, Q3, K3, F3, M3, E4, C4 ● **Temperaments:** D, J, P, V ● **Physical:** Stg=L; Freq: R, H, I, T, G, N Occas: A, X ● **Work Env:** Noise=N; ● **Salary:** 4 ● **Outlook:** 4

SANITARY ENGINEER (profess. & kin.) ● DOT #005.061-030 ● OES: 22121 ● Alternate titles: PUBLIC-HEALTH ENGINEER. Designs and directs construction and operation of hygienic projects such as waterworks, sewage, garbage and trash disposal plants, drainage systems, and insect and rodent control projects: Plans development of watersheds and directs building of aqueducts, filtration plants, and storage and distribution systems for water supply. Directs swamp drainage, insect spraying, and design of insect-proof buildings. Plans and directs workers in building and operation of sewage-disposal plants. Designs and controls operation of incinerators, sanitary fills, and garbage-reduction plants to dispose of garbage and other refuse. Advises industrial plants in disposal of obnoxious gases, oils, greases, and other chemicals. Inspects and regulates sanitary condition of public places, such as markets, parks, and camps. May plan and direct operation of water treatment plant to soften and purify water for human consumption or industrial use and be known as Water-Treatment-Plant Engineer (profess. & kin.). ● **GED:** R5, M5, L5 ● **SVP:** 4-10 yrs ● **Academic:** Ed=B, Eng=G ● **Work Field:** 244 ● **MPSMS:** 704 ● **Aptitudes:** G1, V1, N1, S2, P2, Q2, K4, F3, M3, E4, C4 ● **Temperaments:** D, J, T, V ● **Physical:** Stg=L; Freq: R, H, T, G, N Occas: I, F, D, A, X, V ● **Work Env:** Noise=N; Occas: W ● **Salary:** 4 ● **Outlook:** 3

WASTE-MANAGEMENT ENGINEER, RADIOACTIVE MATERIALS (profess. & kin.) ● DOT #005.061-042 ● OES: 22117 ● Designs, implements, and tests systems and procedures to reduce volume and dispose of nuclear waste materials and contaminated objects: Identifies objects contaminated by exposure to radiation, such as trash, workers' clothing, and discarded tools and equipment. Analyzes samples of sludge and liquid effluents resulting from operation of nuclear reactors to determine level of radioactivity in substances and potential for retention of radioactivity, using radioactivity counters and chemical and electronic analyzers. Refers to state and federal regulations and technical manuals to determine disposal method recommended for prevention of leakage or absorption of radioactive waste. Compares costs of transporting waste to designated nuclear waste disposal sites and reducing volume of waste and storing waste on plant site. Confers with equipment manufacturers' representatives and plant technical and management personnel to discuss alternatives and to choose most suitable plan on basis of safety, efficiency, and cost-effectiveness. Designs and draws plans for systems to reduce volume of waste by solidification, compaction, or incineration. Oversees construction, testing, and implementation of waste disposal systems, and resolves operational problems. Develops plans for modification of operating procedures to reduce volume and radioactive level of effluents, and writes manuals to instruct workers in changes in work procedures. Advises management on selection of lands suitable for use as nuclear waste disposal sites and on establishment of effective safety, operating, and closure procedures. ● **GED:** R5, M5, L5 ● **SVP:** 4-10 yrs ● **Academic:** Ed=B, Eng=G ● **Work Field:** 244, 251 ● **MPSMS:** 723, 704 ● **Aptitudes:** G1, V2, N1, S1, P2, Q3, K3, F3, M3, E5, C4 ● **Temperaments:** D, J, T ● **Physical:** Stg=L; Freq: R, H, I, T, G, N, D Occas: X ● **Work Env:** Noise=N; Occas: R ● **Salary:** 4 ● **Outlook:** 3

GOE: 05.01.04
Testing & Quality Control

AERONAUTICAL TEST ENGINEER (aircraft mfg.) ● DOT #002.061-018 ● OES: 22102 ● Conducts testing activities on aerospace and aircraft products, performing duties as described under TEST ENGINEER (profess. & kin.) Master Title. ● **GED:** R5, M5, L5 ● **SVP:** 4-10 yrs ● **Academic:** Ed=B, Eng=G ● **Work Field:** 244 ● **MPSMS:** 702 ● **Aptitudes:** G2, V2, N2, S2, P3, Q3, K3, F3, M3, E5, C4 ● **Temperaments:** D, J, T, V ● **Physical:** Stg=L; Freq: R, H, N

Occas: C, S, O, I, T, G, F, D, X ● **Work Env:** Noise=N; ● **Salary:** 5 ● **Outlook:** 4

AIR ANALYST (profess. & kin.) ● DOT #012.261-010 ● OES: 24501 ● Alternate titles: AIR TESTER. Analyzes samples of air in industrial establishments or other work areas to determine amount of suspended foreign particles and effectiveness of control methods, using dust collectors: Starts dust collector apparatus that draws air through machine and precipitates dust on tubes, plates, electrodes, or in flasks. Weighs or otherwise determines amount of collected particles, such as lead, rock, or coal dust. Compares weight or count of particles with volume of air passed through machine, and computes percentage of concentration per cubic foot of air tested, using mathematical and chemical formulas. Prepares summary of findings for submission to appropriate department. May recommend remedial measures. ● **GED:** R5, M5, L4 ● **SVP:** 6 mos-1 yr ● **Academic:** Ed=A, Eng=S ● **Work Field:** 211 ● **MPSMS:** 706 ● **Aptitudes:** G2, V3, N2, S3, P3, Q3, K3, F3, M3, E4, C3 ● **Temperaments:** J, T ● **Physical:** Stg=L; Freq: R, H, N Occas: I ● **Work Env:** Noise=N; ● **Salary:** 4 ● **Outlook:** 4

CHEMICAL-TEST ENGINEER (profess. & kin.) ● DOT #008.061-026 ● OES: 22114 ● Conducts tests on chemicals, fuels, and processes performing, duties as described under TEST ENGINEER (profess. & kin.) Master Title. ● **GED:** R5, M5, L5 ● **SVP:** 4-10 yrs ● **Academic:** Ed=A, Eng=G ● **Work Field:** 244, 211 ● **MPSMS:** 500, 510 ● **Aptitudes:** G2, V2, N2, S2, P3, Q3, K3, F3, M3, E5, C4 ● **Temperaments:** D, J, T, V ● **Physical:** Stg=L; Freq: R, H, N, A Occas: I, D, X ● **Work Env:** Noise=N; ● **Salary:** 4 ● **Outlook:** 3

ELECTRICAL TEST ENGINEER (profess. & kin.) ● DOT #003.061-014 ● OES: 22126 ● Conducts tests on electrical equipment and systems, performing duties as described under TEST ENGINEER (profess. & kin.) Master Title. ● **GED:** R5, M5, L5 ● **SVP:** 4-10 yrs ● **Academic:** Ed=B, Eng=S ● **Work Field:** 211, 244 ● **MPSMS:** 580, 703 ● **Aptitudes:** G2, V2, N2, S2, P3, Q3, K3, F3, M3, E4, C3 ● **Temperaments:** D, J, T, V ● **Physical:** Stg=L; Freq: R, H, I, T, G, N, A Occas: X ● **Work Env:** Noise=N; ● **Salary:** 5 ● **Outlook:** 4

ELECTRONICS-TEST ENGINEER (profess. & kin.) ● DOT #003.061-042 ● OES: 22126 ● Plans, develops, and conducts tests on electronic components, products, and systems, applying knowledge and principles of electronic theory, testing methodology and procedures, and electronic engineering. Performs duties described under TEST ENGINEER (profess. & kin.) Master Title. May develop or use computer software and hardware to conduct tests on electronic products and systems. ● **GED:** R5, M5, L5 ● **SVP:** 4-10 yrs ● **Academic:** Ed=A, Eng=G ● **Work Field:** 244, 211 ● **MPSMS:** 703, 580 ● **Aptitudes:** G1, V2, N2, S1, P3, Q3, K3, F3, M3, E4, C4 ● **Temperaments:** D, J, T, V ● **Physical:** Stg=L; Freq: H, N Occas: R, I, T, G, D, A, X ● **Work Env:** Noise=N; ● **Salary:** 5 ● **Outlook:** 4

FIELD-SERVICE ENGINEER (aircraft mfg.) ● DOT #002.167-014 ● OES: 22102 ● Plans and coordinates activities concerned with investigating and resolving customer reports of technical problems with aircraft or aerospace vehicles and eliminating future operational or service difficulties: Reviews performance reports and documentation from customers and field representives, and inspects malfunctioning or damaged product to determine nature and scope of problem. Analyzes review and inspection findings to determine source of problem, and recommends repair, replacement, or other corrective action. Coordinates problem resolution with engineering, customer service, and other personnel to expedite repairs. Maintains records of performance reports. Analyzes reports of technical problems to determine trends affecting future design, production, service, and maintenance processes, and recommends modifications to eliminate future problems. May prepare service handbooks and bulletins based on field investigations, engineering changes, and overall knowledge of product. May provide on-site technical assistance to oversee repairs. ● **GED:** R5, M5, L5 ● **SVP:** 4-10 yrs ● **Academic:** Ed=B, Eng=G ● **Work Field:** 244 ● **MPSMS:** 702 ● **Aptitudes:** G1, V1, N1, S1, P3, Q3, K3, F3, M3, E5, C4 ● **Temperaments:** J, T, V ● **Physical:** Stg=L; Freq: R, H, T, G, N Occas: I, F, X ● **Work Env:** Noise=Q; ● **Salary:** 5 ● **Outlook:** 4

METALLOGRAPHER (profess. & kin.) ● DOT #011.061-014 ● OES: 22105 ● Conducts microscopic, macroscopic, and other tests and investigations on samples of metals and alloys for purposes as metallurgical control over products or use in developing new or improved grades and types of metals, alloys, or production methods: Directs laboratory personnel in preparing of samples, such as polishing or etching, and designates area of sample where microscopic or macroscopic examination is to be made. Studies photomicrographs and performs microscopic examinations on samples to determine metal characteristics, such as crystal structure, porosity, and homogeneity. Interprets findings and prepares drawings, charts, and graphs for inclusion in reports for reference or instruction purposes, and writes reports regarding findings, conclusions, and recommendations. Coordinates and participates in performing special tests, such as end-quench hardenability, bend and tensile, and grain size tests. ● **GED:** R5, M5, L5 ● **SVP:** 4-10 yrs ● **Academic:** Ed=B, Eng=G ● **Work Field:** 211, 244 ● **MPSMS:** 723, 711 ● **Aptitudes:** G1, V1, N1, S2, P3, Q3, K3, F3, M3, E4, C3 ● **Temperaments:** D, J, T, V ● **Physical:** Stg=S; Freq: R, H, N, X Occas: I, T, G ● **Work Env:** Noise=N; ● **Salary:** 5 ● **Outlook:** 4

METROLOGIST (profess. & kin.) ● DOT #012.067-010 ● OES: 22128 ● Develops and evaluates calibration systems that measure characteristics of objects, substances, or phenomena, such as length, mass, time, temperature, electric current, luminous intensity, and derived units of physical or chemical measure: Identifies magnitude of error sources contributing to uncertainty of results to determine reliability of measurement process in quantitative terms. Redesigns or adjusts measurement capability to minimize errors. Develops calibration methods and techniques based on principles of measurement science, technical analysis of measurement problems, and accuracy and precision requirements. Directs engineering, quality, and laboratory personnel in design, manufacture, evaluation, and calibration of measurement standards, instruments, and test systems to ensure selection of approved instrumentation. Advises others on methods of resolving measurement problems and exchanges information with other metrology personnel through participation in government and industrial standardization committees and professional societies. ● **GED:** R6, M6, L6 ● **SVP:** 4-10 yrs ● **Academic:** Ed=M, Eng=G ● **Work Field:** 244 ● **MPSMS:** 719 ● **Aptitudes:** G2, V2, N1, S2, P2, Q2, K3, F3, M3, E5, C3 ● **Temperaments:** D, J, T ● **Physical:** Stg=S; Freq: R, H, I, T, G, N, X Occas: A ● **Work Env:** Noise=N; ● **Salary:** 5 ● **Outlook:** 4

QUALITY CONTROL ENGINEER (profess. & kin.) ● DOT #012.167-054 ● OES: 22128 ● Plans and directs activities concerned with development, application, and maintenance of quality standards for industrial processes, materials, and products: Develops and initiates standards and methods for inspection, testing, and evaluation, utilizing knowledge in engineering fields such as chemical, electrical, or mechanical. Devises sampling procedures and designs and develops forms and instructions for recording, evaluating, and reporting quality and reliability data. Establishes program to evaluate precision and accuracy of production equipment and testing, measurement, and analytical equipment and facilities. Develops and implements methods and procedures for disposition of discrepant material and devises methods to assess cost and responsibility. Directs workers engaged in measuring and testing product and tabulating data concerning materials, product, or process quality and reliability. Compiles and writes training material and conducts training sessions on quality control activities. May specialize in areas of quality control engineering, such as design, incoming material, process control, product evaluation, product reliability, inventory control, metrology, automated testing, software, research and development, and administrative application. May manage quality control program [MANAGER, QUALITY CONTROL (profess. & kin.) 012.167-014]. ● **GED:** R6, M6, L6 ● **SVP:** 4-10 yrs ● **Academic:** Ed=B, Eng=S ● **Work Field:** 211, 244 ● **MPSMS:** 712 ● **Aptitudes:** G1, V1, N1, S2, P2, Q3, K3, F3, M3, E5, C4 ● **Temperaments:** D, J, P, T ● **Physical:** Stg=L; Freq: H, I, T, G Occas: R, N, A, X ● **Work Env:** Noise=N; ● **Salary:** 5 ● **Outlook:** 5

RELIABILITY ENGINEER (profess. & kin.) ● DOT #019.061-026 ● OES: 22198 ● Analyzes preliminary engineering-design concepts of major product, such as aircraft, naval vessel, or electronic communication or control system to recommend design or test methods for attaining customer-specified operational reliability, using knowledge of reliability engineering and other technologies: Analyzes preliminary plans and develops reliability engineering program to achieve customer reliability objectives. Analyzes projected product utilization and calculates cumulative effect on final system reliability of individual part reliabilities. Drafts failure mode and effect analysis sheets or formu-

lates mathematical models, using computer-aided engineering equipment, to identify units posing excessive failure risks and support proposed changes in design. Enters data to simulate electrical inputs, transient conditions, temperature, stress, and other factors to develop computer models, and analyzes and adjusts design to predict and improve system reliability. Advises and confers with engineers in design review meetings to give reliability findings and recommendations. Determines units requiring environmental testing and specifies minimum number of samples to obtain statistically valid data. Reviews subcontractors' proposals for reliability program and submits evaluation for decision. Reviews engineering specifications and drawings, proposing design modifications to improve reliability within cost and other performance requirements. Observes conduct of tests at supplier, plant, or field locations to evaluate reliability factors, such as numbers and causes of unit failures. Monitors failure data generated by customer using product to ascertain potential requirement for product improvement. ● **GED:** R6, M6, L5 ● **SVP:** 4-10 yrs ● **Academic:** Ed=B, Eng=S ● **Work Field:** 244 ● **MPSMS:** 719 ● **Aptitudes:** G1, V1, N1, S2, P2, Q3, K3, F3, M3, E5, C4 ● **Temperaments:** D, J, T, V ● **Physical:** Stg=S; Freq: R, H, I, N Occas: T, G, A, X ● **Work Env:** Noise=N; ● **Salary:** 5 ● **Outlook:** 4

RESEARCH MECHANIC (aircraft mfg.) ● DOT #002.261-014 ● OES: 35199 ● Alternate titles: LABORATORY TEST MECHANIC. Lays out, fabricates, assembles, and tests mechanical, electromechanical, structural, hydraulic, and pneumatic aircraft parts, assemblies, and mechanisms to assist engineers in determining faulty design or fabrication procedures: Lays out, fabricates, and assembles parts, assemblies, and mechanisms to be tested, according to blueprints, specifications, sketches, templates, or verbal instructions. Installs test specimens, such as rib assemblies, struts, landing gears, valves, ducts, fuselage sections, and control surfaces, in test equipment, and connects wiring, tubing, couplings, and power sources, using handtools and power tools. Operates test equipment to gather data on performance of parts, assemblies, and mechanisms under simulated flight and operational conditions. Measures induced variations from normal, using precision instruments, such as micrometers, verniers, calipers, pressure gauges, flowmeters, strain gauges, and dynamometers. Records and interprets test data. Confers with engineering personnel regarding test procedures and test results. Fabricates and assembles test equipment, tooling, shop aids, or other devices for experimental test projects. ● **GED:** R4, M4, L4 ● **SVP:** 2-4 yrs ● **Academic:** Ed=H, Eng=G ● **Work Field:** 102, 121, 211 ● **MPSMS:** 592 ● **Aptitudes:** G2, V3, N2, S2, P2, Q3, K3, F3, M3, E5, C4 ● **Temperaments:** J, T, V ● **Physical:** Stg=M; Freq: R, H, I, N Occas: C, B, S, K, O, W, E, T, G, F, D, X ● **Work Env:** Noise=L; Freq: M Occas: W, D, X, T ● **Salary:** 4 ● **Outlook:** 4

STRESS ANALYST (aircraft mfg.) ● DOT #002.061-030 ● OES: 22102 ● Conducts stress analyses on designs of experimental, prototype, or production aircraft, space vehicles, surface effect vehicles, missiles, and related components to evaluate ability to withstand stresses imposed during flight or ground operations: Analyzes ability of structural components to withstand stresses imposed by static, dynamic, or thermal loads, due to operational or test conditions. Studies preliminary specifications and design requirements to determine strength and bending characteristics of parts, assemblies, and total airframe. Consults with design personnel regarding results of analyses and need for additional analysis, testing, or design modifications. Formulates mathematical model of stress problem or devises other methods of computer analysis or simulation to assist in stress analysis. ● **GED:** R5, M5, L5 ● **SVP:** 4-10 yrs ● **Academic:** Ed=M, Eng=S ● **Work Field:** 244 ● **MPSMS:** 702 ● **Aptitudes:** G1, V1, N1, S2, P2, Q3, K2, F2, M3, E5, C4 ● **Temperaments:** J, T, V ● **Physical:** Stg=S; Freq: R, H, I, N, A Occas: T, G, X ● **Work Env:** Noise=Q; ● **Salary:** 4 ● **Outlook:** 3

STRESS ANALYST (profess. & kin.) ● DOT #007.061-042 ● OES: 22135 ● Conducts stress analyses on engineering designs for electronic components, systems, and products, using mathematical formulas and computer-aided engineering (CAE) systems: Analyzes engineering designs, schematics, and customer specifications to determine stress requirements on product. Formulates mathematical model or three-dimensional computer graphic model of product, using calculator or CAE system. Analyzes ability of product to withstand stress imposed by conditions such as temperature, loads, motion, and vibration, using mathematical formulas and computer simulation. Builds product model of wood or other material, performs physical stress tests on model, and evaluates test results. Consults with ELECTRONICS-DESIGN ENGINEER (profess. & kin.) 003.061-034 to recommend design modifications of product based on results of stress analysis. Prepares stress analysis reports. ● **GED:** R6, M6, L5 ● **SVP:** 4-10 yrs ● **Academic:** Ed=B, Eng=S ● **Work Field:** 244, 233 ● **MPSMS:** 703 ● **Aptitudes:** G1, V1, N1, S1, P2, Q1, K4, F3, M4, E5, C5 ● **Temperaments:** J, P, T ● **Physical:** Stg=S; Const: N Freq: I Occas: R, H, T, G, D, A ● **Work Env:** Noise=N; ● **Salary:** 5 ● **Outlook:** 4

TEST-ENGINE EVALUATOR (petrol. refin.) ● DOT #010.261-026 ● OES: 35199 ● Alternate titles: RESEARCH-TEST-ENGINE EVALUATOR. Collects and assists in evaluation of data obtained in testing petroleum fuels and lubricants under simulated operating conditions: Inspects engines after test runs have been made by TEST-ENGINE OPERATOR (petrol. refin.), for wear, deposits, and defective parts, using microscope and precision weighing and measuring devices to obtain accurate data. Records findings and assists in analyzing data. Assists in dismantling and reassembling engines during test runs. May obtain and analyze samples of engine-exhaust gas. ● **GED:** R4, M4, L4 ● **SVP:** 2-4 yrs ● **Academic:** Ed=H, Eng=S ● **Work Field:** 211 ● **MPSMS:** 501 ● **Aptitudes:** G3, V3, N3, S3, P2, Q4, K3, F3, M3, E4, C4 ● **Temperaments:** J, T ● **Physical:** Stg=M; Freq: R, H, I, E, N, D, A Occas: T, G, X ● **Work Env:** Noise=N; ● **Salary:** 3 ● **Outlook:** 4

TEST ENGINEER, NUCLEAR EQUIPMENT (profess. & kin.) ● DOT #015.061-022 ● OES: 22117 ● Conducts tests on nuclear machinery and equipment, performing duties as described under TEST ENGINEER (profess. & kin.) Master Title. ● **GED:** R5, M5, L5 ● **SVP:** 4-10 yrs ● **Academic:** Ed=B, Eng=S ● **Work Field:** 212, 244 ● **MPSMS:** 725 ● **Aptitudes:** G2, V2, N2, S2, P3, Q3, K3, F3, M3, E4, C4 ● **Temperaments:** D, J, P ● **Physical:** Stg=L; Freq: R, H, I, T, G, N Occas: A, X ● **Work Env:** Noise=N; ● **Salary:** 5 ● **Outlook:** 3

TEST TECHNICIAN (profess. & kin.) ● DOT #019.161-014 ● OES: 35199 ● Prepares specifications for fabrication, assembly, and installation of apparatus and control instrumentation used to test experimental or prototype mechanical, electrical, electromechanical, hydromechanical, or structural products, and conducts tests and records results, utilizing engineering principles and test technology: Confers with engineering personnel to resolve fabrication problems relating to specifications and to review test plans, such as types and cycles of tests, conditions under which tests are to be conducted, and duration of tests. Fabricates precision parts for test apparatus, using metalworking machines such as lathes, milling machines, and welding equipment, or interprets specifications for workers fabricating parts. Examines parts for conformance with dimensional specifications, using precision measuring instruments. Coordinates and participates in installing unit or system to be tested in test fixtures, connecting valves, pumps, hydraulic, mechanical or electrical controls, cabling, tubing, power source, and indicating instruments. Activates controls to apply electrical, hydraulic, pneumatic, or mechanical power and subject test item to successive steps in test cycle. Monitors controls and instruments and records test data for engineer's use. May recommend changes in test methods or equipment for engineering review. Workers are classified according to engineering specialty or type of product tested. ● **GED:** R5, M4, L4 ● **SVP:** 2-4 yrs ● **Academic:** Ed=A, Eng=S ● **Work Field:** 244, 111, 211 ● **MPSMS:** 560, 580, 590 ● **Aptitudes:** G2, V2, N2, S2, P2, Q3, K2, F2, M2, E4, C4 ● **Temperaments:** J, T, V ● **Physical:** Stg=L; Freq: R, H, T, G, N Occas: I, D, Λ, X ● **Work Env:** Noise=N; ● **Salary:** 3 ● **Outlook:** 3

GOE: 05.01.05
Sales Engineering

SALES ENGINEER, AERONAUTICAL PRODUCTS (aircraft mfg.) ● DOT #002.151-010 ● OES: 49998 ● Sells aeronautical products and provides customers with technical engineering services as described under SALES ENGINEER (profess. & kin.) Master Title. ● **GED:** R5, M5, L5 ● **SVP:** 4-10 yrs ● **Academic:** Ed=B, Eng=G ● **Work Field:** 244, 292 ● **MPSMS:** 702, 885 ● **Aptitudes:** G2, V2, N3, S2, P3, Q2, K3, F3, M3, E5, C4 ● **Temperaments:** D, I, J, P ● **Physical:** Stg=L; Freq: T, G, N Occas: R, H, I, X ● **Work Env:** Noise=N; ● **Salary:** 5 ● **Outlook:** 4

SALES-ENGINEER, ELECTRONICS PRODUCTS AND SYSTEMS (profess. & kin.) ● DOT #003.151-014 ● OES: 49998 ● Sells electronic products and systems and provides technical services to clients, performing duties as described under SALES ENGINEER (profess. & kin.) Master Title. ● **GED:** R5, M5, L5 ● **SVP:** 4-10 yrs ● **Academic:** Ed=A, Eng=G ● **Work Field:** 244, 292 ● **MPSMS:** 585, 586, 587 ● **Aptitudes:** G2, V2, N2, S3, P3, Q3, K4, F4, M4, E4, C3 ● **Temperaments:** D, I, J, T ● **Physical:** Stg=L; Freq: T, G, N Occas: R, H, A ● **Work Env:** Noise=Q; Occas: W ● **Salary:** 5 ● **Outlook:** 4

GOE: 05.01.06
Work Planning & Utilization

CONFIGURATION MANAGEMENT ANALYST (profess. & kin.) ● DOT #012.167-010 ● OES: 22128 ● Analyzes proposed changes of product design to determine effect on overall system, and coordinates recording of modifications for management control: Confers with manufacturer or customer representatives to establish change-reporting procedure, and prepares directives for change authorization and documentation by company and subcontractor personnel. Analyzes proposed part-design changes and exhibits to prepare report of effect on overall product for management action, using knowledge of engineering, manufacturing, and procurement activities. Confers with department managers to obtain additional information or to interpret policies and procedures for reporting changes in product design. Audits subcontractor's inspection or technical documents preparation procedure to verify compliance with contract requirements. Coordinates activities of personnel preparing manual or automated records of part-design change documents and first-article configuration inspection. ● **GED:** R5, M4, L5 ● **SVP:** 4-10 yrs ● **Academic:** Ed=B, Eng=G ● **Work Field:** 212, 282 ● **MPSMS:** 700 ● **Aptitudes:** G2, V2, N2, S3, P3, Q2, K4, F4, M4, E5, C5 ● **Temperaments:** D, J, T, V ● **Physical:** Stg=L; Freq: R, H, I, T, G, N ● **Work Env:** Noise=N; ● **Salary:** 5 ● **Outlook:** 4

DOCUMENTATION ENGINEER (profess. & kin.) ● DOT #012.167-078 ● OES: 22128 ● Plans, directs, and coordinates preparation of project documentation, such as engineering drawings, production specifications and schedules, and contract modifications, to ensure customer contract requirements are met: Reviews contract to determine documentation required for each phase of project, applying knowledge of engineering and manufacturing processes. Schedules due dates for drawings, specifications, software, technical manuals, and other documents. Monitors status of project to ensure documentation is submitted according to schedule. Reviews and verifies project documents for completeness, format, and compliance with contract requirements. Submits project documentation to management for approval, and transmits approved documents to customer. Confers with engineers, managers, customers, and others to discuss project, prepare documents, or modify contract schedules. ● **GED:** R5, M5, L5 ● **SVP:** 4-10 yrs ● **Academic:** Ed=A, Eng=G ● **Work Field:** 244 ● **MPSMS:** 712 ● **Aptitudes:** G1, V1, N1, S1, P2, Q1, K4, F4, M4, E5, C5 ● **Temperaments:** J, P, T ● **Physical:** Stg=L; Freq: T, G, N Occas: R, H, I, A ● **Work Env:** Noise=N; ● **Salary:** 4 ● **Outlook:** 5

FACILITIES PLANNER (any industry) ● DOT #019.261-018 ● OES: 35199 ● Alternate titles: OFFICE-PLANNING REPRESENTATIVE. Plans utilization of space and facilities for government agency or unit or business establishment consistent with requirements of organizational efficiency and available facilities and funds: Inspects buildings and office areas to evaluate suitability for occupancy, considering such factors as air circulation, lighting, location, and size. Measures or directs workers engaged in measurement of facilities to determine total square footage available for occupancy. Computes square footage available for each member of staff to determine whether minimum space restrictions can be met. Draws design layout, showing location of furniture, equipment, doorways, electrical and telephone outlets, and other facilities. May review real estate contracts for compliance with government specifications and suitability for occupancy of employing agency. May direct workers engaged in moving furniture and equipment and preparing facilities for occupancy. ● **GED:** R5, M5, L5 ● **SVP:** 2-4 yrs ● **Academic:** Ed=A, Eng=G ● **Work Field:** 211, 242 ● **MPSMS:** 719 ● **Aptitudes:** G2, V2, N2, S2, P3, Q3, K3, F2, M3, E5, C3 ● **Tempera-**

ments: D, J ● **Physical:** Stg=L; Const: N, F, D, A, X Freq: R, H, I, T, G ● **Work Env:** Noise=N; ● **Salary:** 4 ● **Outlook:** 3

FACTORY LAY-OUT ENGINEER (profess. & kin.) ● DOT #012.167-018 ● OES: 22128 ● Alternate titles: PLANNING ENGINEER. Plans layout of complete departments of industrial plant or commercial establishment to provide maximum possible operating efficiency: Measures and studies available floor space and draws plan of floor space to scale, using drafting tools. Studies sequence of operations to be performed and flow of materials. Studies and measures machines, conveyors, benches, furnaces, and other equipment. Coordinates all available knowledge and information into finished scale drawing, showing most efficient location for each piece of equipment and necessary working area around each. May use computer-assisted design/drafting equipment. ● **GED:** R5, M5, L5 ● **SVP:** 4-10 yrs ● **Academic:** Ed=B, Eng=G ● **Work Field:** 244 ● **MPSMS:** 712 ● **Aptitudes:** G2, V2, N2, S2, P2, Q3, K3, F3, M3, E5, C5 ● **Temperaments:** D, J, T ● **Physical:** Stg=L; Freq: R, H, N Occas: K, O, I, T, G, D, A ● **Work Env:** Noise=N; ● **Salary:** 4 ● **Outlook:** 4

INDUSTRIAL ENGINEER (profess. & kin.) ● DOT #012.167-030 ● OES: 22128 ● Plans utilization of facilities, equipment, materials, and personnel to improve efficiency of operations: Studies functional statements, organization charts, and project information to determine functions and responsibilities of workers and work units and to identify areas of duplication. Establishes work measurement programs and analyzes work samples to develop standards for labor utilization. Analyzes work force utilization, facility layout, and operational data, such as production costs, process flow charts, and production schedules, to determine efficient utilization of workers and equipment. Recommends methods for improving worker efficiency and reducing waste of materials and utilities, such as restructuring job duties, reorganizing work flow, relocating work stations and equipment, and purchase of equipment. Confers with management and engineering staff to implement plans and recommendations. May develop management systems for cost analysis, financial planning, wage and salary administration, and job evaluation. ● **GED:** R5, M5, L5 ● **SVP:** 2-4 yrs ● **Academic:** Ed=B, Eng=G ● **Work Field:** 244 ● **MPSMS:** 712 ● **Aptitudes:** G1, V1, N1, S2, P3, Q3, K4, F4, M4, E5, C5 ● **Temperaments:** D, J, P, V ● **Physical:** Stg=S; Freq: R, H, T, G, N Occas: I, A ● **Work Env:** Noise=Q; ● **Salary:** 5 ● **Outlook:** 4

LAND SURVEYOR (profess. & kin.) ● DOT #018.167-018 ● OES: 22310 ● Plans, organizes, and directs work of one or more survey parties engaged in surveying earth's surface to determine precise location and measurements of points, elevations, lines, areas, and contours for construction, mapmaking, land division, titles, mining or other purposes: Researches previous survey evidence, maps, deeds, physical evidence, and other records to obtain data needed for surveys. Develops new data from photogrammetric records. Determines methods and procedures for establishing or reestablishing survey control. Keeps accurate notes, records, and sketches to describe and certify work performed. Coordinates findings with work of engineering and architectural personnel, clients, and others concerned with project. Assumes legal responsibility for work and is licensed by state. ● **GED:** R5, M5, L4 ● **SVP:** 2-4 yrs ● **Academic:** Ed=A, Eng=S ● **Work Field:** 243 ● **MPSMS:** 716 ● **Aptitudes:** G2, V3, N2, S2, P2, Q3, K3, F3, M3, E3, C3 ● **Temperaments:** D, J, T ● **Physical:** Stg=L; Freq: R, H, I, T, G, N, F, D Occas: C, S, K, X ● **Work Env:** Noise=N; Freq: W ● **Salary:** 4 ● **Outlook:** 4

LIAISON ENGINEER (aircraft mfg.) ● DOT #012.167-038 ● OES: 22128 ● Coordinates activities to evaluate and resolve engineering-related production problems encountered in assigned area of aircraft manufacturing facility: Reviews production schedules, engineering specifications, orders, and related information to maintain current knowledge of manufacturing methods, procedures, and activities in assigned area. Confers with quality control, material, manufacturing, and other department personnel to provide technical support. Interprets engineering drawings and facilitates correction of errors on drawings and documents identified during manufacturing operations. Investigates reports of defective, damaged, or malfunctioning parts, assemblies, equipment, or systems to determine nature and scope of problem. Examines, measures, inspects, or tests defective part for conformance to engineering design drawings or blueprint specifications, using precision measuring and testing instruments, devices, and equipment. Consults with project

engineers to obtain specialized information. Evaluates findings to formulate corrective action plan and coordinates implementation of plan. Maintains records or oversees recording of information by others to ensure engineering drawings and documents are current and that engineering-related production problems and resolutions are documented. Serves as member of material review board to determine disposition of defective or damaged parts. May specialize in investigating and resolving tooling problems and be designated Tool Liaison (aircraft mfg.). ● **GED:** R5, M5, L4 ● **SVP:** 2-4 yrs ● **Academic:** Ed=B, Eng=G ● **Work Field:** 244 ● **MPSMS:** 712 ● **Aptitudes:** G2, V2, N2, S2, P2, Q3, K3, F3, M3, E5, C5 ● **Temperaments:** D, J, P, T, V ● **Physical:** Stg=L; Freq: I, T, G, N Occas: C, S, K, O, R, H, E, A ● **Work Env:** Noise=L; ● **Salary:** 4 ● **Outlook:** 3

MANAGEMENT ANALYST (profess. & kin.) ● DOT #161.167-010 ● OES: 21905 ● Alternate titles: SYSTEMS ANALYST. Analyzes business or operating procedures to devise most efficient methods of accomplishing work: Plans study of work problems and procedures, such as organizational change, communications, information flow, integrated production methods, inventory control, or cost analysis. Gathers and organizes information on problem or procedures including present operating procedures. Analyzes data gathered, develops information and considers available solutions or alternate methods of proceeding. Organizes and documents findings of studies and prepares recommendations for implementation of new systems, procedures or organizational changes. Confers with personnel concerned to assure smooth functioning of newly implemented systems or procedure. May install new systems and train personnel in application. May conduct operational effectiveness reviews to ensure functional or project systems are applied and functioning as designed. May develop or update functional or operational manuals outlining established methods of performing work in accordance with organizational policy. ● **GED:** R5, M5, L5 ● **SVP:** 2-4 yrs ● **Academic:** Ed=B, Eng=G ● **Work Field:** 232 ● **MPSMS:** 890 ● **Aptitudes:** G2, V2, N2, S3, P3, Q2, K4, F4, M4, E5, C5 ● **Temperaments:** J, P, V ● **Physical:** Stg=S; Freq: T, G Occas: R, H, I, N, A ● **Work Env:** Noise=N; ● **Salary:** 4 ● **Outlook:** 3

MANUFACTURING ENGINEER (profess. & kin.) ● DOT #012.167-042 ● OES: 22128 ● Plans, directs, and coordinates manufacturing processes in industrial plant: Develops, evaluates, and improves manufacturing methods, utilizing knowledge of product design, materials and parts, fabrication processes, tooling and production equipment capabilities, assembly methods, and quality control standards. Analyzes and plans work force utilization, space requirements, and workflow, and designs layout of equipment and workspace for maximum efficiency [INDUSTRIAL ENGINEER (profess. & kin.) 012.167-030]. Confers with planning and design staff concerning product design and tooling to ensure efficient production methods. Confers with vendors to determine product specifications and arrange for purchase of equipment, materials, or parts, and evaluates products according to specifications and quality standards. Estimates production times, staffing requirements, and related costs to provide information for management decisions. Confers with management, engineering, and other staff regarding manufacturing capabilities, production schedules, and other considerations to facilitate production processes. Applies statistical methods to estimate future manufacturing requirements and potential. ● **GED:** R5, M5, L5 ● **SVP:** 4-10 yrs ● **Academic:** Ed=B, Eng=S ● **Work Field:** 244 ● **MPSMS:** 712, 706 ● **Aptitudes:** G1, V1, N2, S1, P2, Q2, K4, F4, M4, E5, C5 ● **Temperaments:** D, J, P, T, V ● **Physical:** Stg=L; Freq: R, H, T, G, N Occas: I, A ● **Work Env:** Noise=N; ● **Salary:** 5 ● **Outlook:** 4

MATERIALS ENGINEER (profess. & kin.) ● DOT #019.061-014 ● OES: 22105 ● Evaluates technical and economic factors, recommending engineering and manufacturing actions for attainment of design objectives of process or product by applying knowledge of material science and related technologies: Reviews plans for new product and factors, such as strength, weight, and cost to submit material selection recommendations ensuring attainment of design objectives. Plans and implements laboratory operations to develop material and fabrication procedures for new materials to fulfill product cost and performance standards. Confers with producers of materials, such as metals, ceramics, or polymers, during investigation and evaluation of materials suitable for specific product applications. Reviews product failure data and interprets laboratory tests and analyses to establish or rule out material and process causes. ● **GED:** R5, M5, L5 ● **SVP:** 4-10 yrs ● **Aca-**

demic: Ed=B, Eng=S ● **Work Field:** 244 ● **MPSMS:** 700 ● **Aptitudes:** G2, V2, N2, S2, P2, Q3, K3, F3, M3, E5, C4 ● **Temperaments:** D, J, T, V ● **Physical:** Stg=S; Freq: R, H, T, G, N ● **Work Env:** Noise=N; ● **Salary:** 4 ● **Outlook:** 3

METALLURGIST, EXTRACTIVE (profess. & kin.) ● DOT #011.061-018 ● OES: 22105 ● Alternate titles: METALLURGIST, PROCESS. Originates, controls, and develops flotation, smelting, electrolytic, and other processes used in winning metals from their ores, for producing iron and steel, or for refining gold, silver, zinc, copper, and other metals: Studies ore reduction problems to determine most efficient methods of producing metals commercially. Controls temperature adjustments, charge mixtures, and other variables in blast-furnace operations and steel-melting furnaces to obtain pig iron and steel of specified metallurgical characteristics and qualities. Investigates methods of improving metallurgical processes, as in the reduction of alumina by electrolytic methods to produce aluminum, the distillation of molten ore to purify zinc, or selective oxidation methods to extract lead, nickel, mercury, and other nonferrous metals from their ores. ● **GED:** R6, M6, L6 ● **SVP:** 4-10 yrs ● **Academic:** Ed=M, Eng=G ● **Work Field:** 244, 251 ● **MPSMS:** 723, 711 ● **Aptitudes:** G1, V1, N1, S2, P3, Q3, K3, F3, M3, E4, C3 ● **Temperaments:** D, J, T, V ● **Physical:** Stg=L; Freq: R, H, N Occas: I, A, X ● **Work Env:** Noise=N; Occas: H ● **Salary:** 5 ● **Outlook:** 4

MINING ENGINEER (mine & quarry) ● DOT #010.061-014 ● OES: 22108 ● Conducts research to determine location and methods of extracting minerals, such as metallic ores and nonmetallic substances, such as coal, stone, and gravel: Conducts or collaborates in geological exploration, and reviews maps and drilling logs to determine location, size, accessibility, and estimated value of mineral deposit. Determines methods to extract minerals, considering factors such as safety, operational costs, deposit characteristics, overburden depth, and surrounding strata. Plans, recommends, and coordinates mining process, type and capacity of haulage equipment, such as power shovels and trucks, and labor utilization. Lays out and directs mine construction operations, such as location and development of shafts, tunnels, chambers, position of excavation benches (levels), and access roads. Designs, implements, and monitors facility projects, such as water and power supply, ventilation system, rock-dust and radon gas control, drainage, rail and conveyor systems, and material cleaning, grading, and reduction systems. May devise methods and locations to store and replace excavated soil to reclaim mine sites. May analyze labor requirements, equipment needs, and operational costs to compute and prepare annual budget reports. May apply knowledge of mining engineering to solve problems concerned with environment. ● **GED:** R5, M5, L5 ● **SVP:** 2-4 yrs ● **Academic:** Ed=B, Eng=G ● **Work Field:** 244 ● **MPSMS:** 708 ● **Aptitudes:** G1, V2, N1, S1, P2, Q2, K3, F3, M3, E5, C5 ● **Temperaments:** D, J, T, V ● **Physical:** Stg=L; Freq: T, G, N Occas: S, K, O, R, H, I, F, D ● **Work Env:** Noise=N; Occas: W, A, O ● **Salary:** 5 ● **Outlook:** 2

PREVENTIVE MAINTENANCE COORDINATOR (any industry) ● DOT #169.167-074 ● OES: 21905 ● Plans and coordinates schedule of preventive maintenance for equipment, machinery, tools, or buildings: Reviews manufacturers' service manuals, own establishment's usage schedules, and records of maintenance problems to determine optimum frequency of preventive maintenance. Studies production and operation schedules and confers with other staff and with maintenance supervisors to determine when planned maintenance will least interfere with operation of establishment. Estimates costs of personnel, parts, and supplies to be used during scheduled maintenance. Maintains records of planned and completed maintenance. May develop and coordinate plans for reconstruction or installation of new equipment, machinery, or buildings. May direct and coordinate activities of subordinate staff, such as MAINTENANCE DATA ANALYST (military ser.) 221.367-038. May direct and coordinate activities of maintenance workers. ● **GED:** R4, M3, L3 ● **SVP:** 2-4 yrs ● **Academic:** Ed=H, Eng=S ● **Work Field:** 271, 295 ● **MPSMS:** 893 ● **Aptitudes:** G2, V2, N2, S3, P3, Q3, K5, F5, M4, E5, C5 ● **Temperaments:** D, J, T, V ● **Physical:** Stg=L; Freq: T, G, N ● **Work Env:** Noise=N; ● **Salary:** 4 ● **Outlook:** 3

PRODUCTION ENGINEER (profess. & kin.) ● DOT #012.167-046 ● OES: 22128 ● Plans and coordinates production procedures in industrial plant: Directs production departments. Regulates and coordinates functions of office and shop. Introduces efficient production line

methods. Initiates and directs procedures to increase company output. ● **GED:** R5, M5, L5 ● **SVP:** 4-10 yrs ● **Academic:** Ed=B, Eng=S ● **Work Field:** 244 ● **MPSMS:** 712 ● **Aptitudes:** G2, V2, N2, S2, P2, Q3, K3, F3, M3, E5, C5 ● **Temperaments:** D, J, P, V ● **Physical:** Stg=L; Freq: H, T, G, N Occas: R, I ● **Work Env:** Noise=N; ● **Salary:** 5 ● **Outlook:** 4

PRODUCTION PLANNER (profess. & kin.) ● DOT #012.167-050 ● OES: 22128 ● Alternate titles: PLANNER, CHIEF; PLANNING SUPERVISOR; PROCESS PLANNER; PRODUCTION-PLANNING SUPERVISOR; PRODUCTION SCHEDULER; SCHEDULER; TOOL-AND-PRODUCTION PLANNER. Plans and prepares production schedules for manufacture of industrial or commercial products: Draws up master schedule to establish sequence and lead time of each operation to meet shipping dates according to sales forecasts or customer orders. Analyzes production specifications and plant capacity data and performs mathematical calculations to determine manufacturing processes, tools, and human resource requirements. Plans and schedules workflow for each department and operation according to previously established manufacturing sequences and lead times. Plans sequence of fabrication, assembly, installation, and other manufacturing operations for guidance of production workers. Confers with department supervisors to determine status of assigned projects. Expedites operations that delay schedules and alters schedules to meet unforeseen conditions. Prepares production reports. May prepare lists of required materials, tools, and equipment. May prepare purchase orders to obtain materials, tools, and equipment. ● **GED:** R5, M4, L4 ● **SVP:** 2-4 yrs ● **Academic:** Ed=B, Eng=G ● **Work Field:** 244 ● **MPSMS:** 712 ● **Aptitudes:** G2, V2, N2, S2, P3, Q3, K4, F4, M4, E5, C5 ● **Temperaments:** D, J, V ● **Physical:** Stg=L; Freq: H, T, G Occas: R, I, N ● **Work Env:** Noise=N; ● **Salary:** 3 ● **Outlook:** 4

STANDARDS ENGINEER (profess. & kin.) ● DOT #012.061-018 ● OES: 22128 ● Establishes engineering and technical limitations and applications for items, materials, processes, methods, designs, and engineering practices for use by designers of machines and equipment, such as aircraft, automobiles, and space vehicles: Communicates with management of industrial organization to maintain knowledge of current and proposed projects in order to develop appropriate standards for design and production of new items. Evaluates data in scientific journals, suppliers' catalogs, government standards documents, and other sources of information on materials, processes, and parts to update knowledge of available resources. Prepares specification sheets and standard drawings designating parts and materials acceptable for specific uses, using knowledge of primary engineering discipline and related disciplines. Examines all factors involved to confirm that standards will result in most economic use of material and labor consistent with safety and durability of final product. Reviews standards prepared with other departmental specialists to assure consistency with existing standards and those in other specialized disciplines. Communicates with user personnel to confirm knowledge of standards and cooperation of various project groups. Follows established procedures for retention of data developed to assure optimum storage and retrieval by manual or automated methods. ● **GED:** R5, M5, L5 ● **SVP:** 4-10 yrs ● **Academic:** Ed=B, Eng=G ● **Work Field:** 244 ● **MPSMS:** 719 ● **Aptitudes:** G1, V1, N1, S1, P2, Q3, K3, F4, M4, E5, C3 ● **Temperaments:** J, T, V ● **Physical:** Stg=S; Freq: R, H, T, G, N, X Occas: I ● **Work Env:** Noise=N; ● **Salary:** 5 ● **Outlook:** 4

TIME-STUDY ENGINEER (profess. & kin.) ● DOT #012.167-070 ● OES: 22128 ● Alternate titles: EFFICIENCY EXPERT; MANAGER, PRODUCTION; METHODS-AND-PROCEDURES ANALYST; PRODUCTION ENGINEER; PRODUCTION EXPERT; TIME-STUDY ANALYST; WORK-MEASUREMENT ENGINEER. Develops work measurement procedures and directs time-and-motion studies to promote efficient and economical utilization of personnel and facilities: Directs or conducts observation and analysis of personnel and work procedures to determine time-and-motion requirements of job duties. Analyzes work study data and equipment specifications to establish time and production standards. Applies mathematical analysis to determine validity and reliability of sampling and work study statistics. Applies principles of industrial engineering and applied psychology to evaluate work methods proposals and to develop recommendations to management affecting work methods, wage rates, and budget decisions. Trains INDUSTRIAL ENGINEERING TECHNICIAN (profess. & kin.) in time-and-motion study principles and techniques. ● **GED:** R5, M5, L5 ● **SVP:** 4-10 yrs ● **Academic:** Ed=B, Eng=G ● **Work Field:** 244 ● **MPSMS:** 712 ● **Aptitudes:** G1, V1, N1, S2, P2, Q3, K4, F4, M4, E5, C4 ● **Temperaments:** D, J ● **Physical:** Stg=L; Const: N Freq: R, H, I, T, G, A Occas: F ● **Work Env:** Noise=N; ● **Salary:** 4 ● **Outlook:** 3

TOOL PLANNER (any industry) ● DOT #012.167-074 ● OES: 22128 ● Alternate titles: PROCESSOR. Analyzes blueprints or prototype parts to determine tools, fixtures, and equipment needed for manufacture and plans sequence of operations for fabrication and assembly of products, such as aircraft assemblies, automobile parts, cutting tools, or ball bearings: Studies engineering blueprints, drawings, models, and other specifications to obtain data on proposed part. Applies knowledge of functions and processes of various departments and capacities of machines and equipment to determine tool requirements and establish sequence of operations to fabricate and assemble parts. Lists operations to be performed on routing card or paper, indicates machines, cutting tools, fixtures, and other equipment to be used, and estimates times needed to perform each operation. May prepare reports for PRODUCTION PLANNER (profess. & kin.) in scheduling work for entire plant. May plan tool and operation sequences for only one department. May specify type of material to be used in construction of tools. ● **GED:** R5, M5, L5 ● **SVP:** 4-10 yrs ● **Academic:** Ed=A, Eng=S ● **Work Field:** 244 ● **MPSMS:** 712 ● **Aptitudes:** G2, V2, N2, S2, P3, Q3, K4, F4, M4, E5, C5 ● **Temperaments:** D, J ● **Physical:** Stg=S; Freq: R, H, T, G, N, D Occas: I ● **Work Env:** Noise=N; ● **Salary:** 4 ● **Outlook:** 4

TOOL PROGRAMMER, NUMERICAL CONTROL (any industry) ● DOT #007.167-018 ● OES: 25111 ● Alternate titles: COMPUTER-PROGRAMMER, NUMERICAL CONTROL; PROGRAMMER, NUMERICAL CONTROL; TOOL PROGRAMMER. Plans numerical control program to control contour-path machining of metal parts on automatic machine tools: Analyzes drawings, sketches, and design data of part to determine dimension and configuration of cuts, selection of cutting tools, and machine speeds and feed rates, according to knowledge of machine shop processes, part specifications, and machine capabilities. Determines reference points and direction of machine cutting paths. Computes angular and linear dimensions, radii, and curvatures, and outlines sequence of operations required to machine part. Prepares geometric layout on graph paper or using computer-assisted drafting software to show location of reference points and direction of cutting paths, using drafting instruments or computer. Writes instruction sheets and cutter lists to guide setup and operation of machine. Writes program of machine instructions in symbolic language to encode numerical control tape or direct numerical control data base to regulate movement of machine along cutting path. Compares encoded tape or computer printout with original program sheet to assure accuracy of machine instructions. Revises program to eliminate instruction errors or omissions. Observes operation of machine on trial run to prove taped or programmed instructions. ● **GED:** R5, M4, L4 ● **SVP:** 2-4 yrs ● **Academic:** Ed=A, Eng=S ● **Work Field:** 241, 244 ● **MPSMS:** 566, 706 ● **Aptitudes:** G2, V3, N2, S2, P2, Q3, K4, F4, M4, E5, C4 ● **Temperaments:** J, T ● **Physical:** Stg=S; Freq: R, H, I, N, X Occas: T, G, D, A ● **Work Env:** Noise=L; ● **Salary:** 5 ● **Outlook:** 4

TOOL PROGRAMMER, NUMERICAL CONTROL (electron. comp.) ● DOT #609.262-010 ● OES: 25111 ● Alternate titles: PROGRAMMER OPERATOR, NUMERICAL CONTROL; SOFT TOOLING TECHNICIAN. Operates optical programming (digitizing) equipment to generate numerical control (NC) tape program used to control NC machine tools that drill, mill, rout, or notch printed circuit boards (PCB's): Analyzes drawings, specifications, and phototool (photographic film copy of printed circuit pattern) to determine program input data, such as hole sizes, tool sizes, reference points, and direction of machine cutting paths, and calculates data, such as starting point coordinates (location), size of panels or boards, and number of boards per panel. Draws machine tool paths on phototool, using colored markers and following guidelines for tool speed and efficiency, to prepare phototool for use as tool programming aid. Aligns and secures phototool on reference table of optical programmer. Observes enlarger scope of programmer that projects image of circuit board pattern from phototool. Moves reference table, following previously marked paths, to align phototool circuit pattern holes with reference marks on enlarger scope. Depresses pedal or pushes button of programmer to enter coordinates of hole locations into program memory. Repeats process for each hole

location on phototool to enter NC machine instructions, such as hole locations, machine paths, and reference points. Keys in additional instructions, such as tool size, machine feed and speed rates, and starting point coordinates, basing entries on specifications, calculations, and knowledge of machine capabilities and programming techniques. Types commands on keyboard to generate NC tape. Observes trial run of NC machine to verify tape program accuracy. Revises NC tape program to eliminate instruction errors. May operate NC machine tools on production basis. ● **GED:** R3, M3, L3 ● **SVP:** 6 mos-1 yr ● **Academic:** Ed=A, Eng=S ● **Work Field:** 233, 111 ● **MPSMS:** 706 ● **Aptitudes:** G3, V3, N3, S2, P2, Q2, K3, F3, M3, E4, C4 ● **Temperaments:** J, T, V ● **Physical:** Stg=S; Const: H, I Freq: R, N, X Occas: T, G ● **Work Env:** Noise=N; ● **Salary:** 4 ● **Outlook:** 4

UTILIZATION ENGINEER (utilities) ● DOT #007.061-034 ● OES: 22135 ● Solves engineering problems concerned with industrial utilization of gas as source of power: Studies industrial processes to determine where and how application of gas fuel-consuming equipment can be made. Designs equipment to meet process requirements. Examines gas-powered equipment after installation to ensure proper functioning. Investigates equipment failures and difficulties and diagnoses faulty operation. Corrects or makes recommendations to maintenance crew to correct faults. Conducts safety, breakdown, and other engineering tests on gas fuel-consuming equipment to ascertain efficiency and safety of design and construction. May solve problems concerned with other gas-consuming equipment, such as air-conditioning and heating. ● **GED:** R5, M5, L5 ● **SVP:** 4-10 yrs ● **Academic:** Ed=B, Eng=S ● **Work Field:** 244 ● **MPSMS:** 706 ● **Aptitudes:** G2, V2, N2, S2, P2, Q3, K4, F4, M4, E5, C4 ● **Temperaments:** D, J, T, V ● **Physical:** Stg=S; Freq: T, G, N Occas: A ● **Work Env:** Noise=N; ● **Salary:** 4 ● **Outlook:** 3

VALUE ENGINEER (aircraft mfg.) ● DOT #002.167-010 ● OES: 22102 ● Alternate titles: COST DEVELOPMENT ENGINEER; DESIGN SPECIALIST, PRODUCIBILITY, COST AND COMPONENT TECHNOLOGY. Plans and coordinates engineering activities to develop and apply standardized design criteria and production requirements for parts and equipment used in aircraft and aerospace vehicles: Establishes and maintains liaison between engineering and other departments to formulate and apply design criteria and production requirements for proposed products. Analyzes product design data to determine conformance to established design selection criteria, use of standardized parts and equipment, and design-to-cost ratio. Approves initial design or recommends modifications based on producibility, cost, and component technology factors. Coordinates testing of new parts and equipment, evaluates test results, and approves or rejects usage of parts and equipment based on test results. Evaluates and approves selection of vendors. Initiates and provides technical direction for research and development programs to enhance production methods, improve parts and equipment technology, and reduce costs. Develops methods and programs to predict, track, and report production costs during design development. ● **GED:** R6, M5, L6 ● **SVP:** 4-10 yrs ● **Academic:** Ed=B, Eng=G ● **Work Field:** 244 ● **MPSMS:** 700 ● **Aptitudes:** G2, V2, N2, S2, P2, Q2, K4, F4, M4, E5, C4 ● **Temperaments:** D, J, P ● **Physical:** Stg=S; Freq: N Occas: R, H, I, T, G, A, X ● **Work Env:** Noise=Q; ● **Salary:** 4 ● **Outlook:** 4

GOE: 05.01.07
Design

AERONAUTICAL-DESIGN ENGINEER (aircraft mfg.) ● DOT #002.061-022 ● OES: 22102 ● Develops basic design concepts used in design, development, and production of aeronautical and aerospace products and systems, performing duties as described under DESIGN ENGINEER, PRODUCTS (profess. & kin.) Master Title. ● **GED:** R5, M5, L5 ● **SVP:** 4-10 yrs ● **Academic:** Ed=B, Eng=G ● **Work Field:** 244, 251 ● **MPSMS:** 702 ● **Aptitudes:** G2, V2, N2, S2, P2, Q2, K3, F3, M3, E5, C4 ● **Temperaments:** J, T, V ● **Physical:** Stg=S; Freq: R, H, I, T, G, N Occas: A, X ● **Work Env:** Noise=N; ● **Salary:** 5 ● **Outlook:** 4

AERONAUTICAL ENGINEER (aircraft mfg.) ● DOT #002.061-014 ● OES: 22102 ● Designs, develops, and tests aircraft, space vehicles, surface effect vehicles, missiles, and related component systems, applying engineering principles and techniques: Designs and develops commercial, military, executive, general aviation, or special purpose aircraft, space vehicles, satellites, missiles, or related hardware or systems. Tests models, prototypes, subassemblies, or production vehicles to study and evaluate operational characteristics and effects of stress imposed during actual or simulated flight conditions. May specialize in design and development of structural components, such as wings, fuselage, rib assemblies, landing gear, or operational control systems. May specialize in analytical programs concerned with ground or flight testing, or development of acoustic, thermodynamic, or propulsion systems. May assist in planning technical phases of air transportation systems or other aspects of flight operations, maintenance, or logistics. ● **GED:** R6, M6, L6 ● **SVP:** 4-10 yrs ● **Academic:** Ed=M, Eng=G ● **Work Field:** 244 ● **MPSMS:** 702 ● **Aptitudes:** G1, V2, N1, S1, P3, Q2, K3, F3, M3, E5, C5 ● **Temperaments:** D, J, T, V ● **Physical:** Stg=L; Freq: R, H, I, N Occas: T, G, F, D ● **Work Env:** Noise=N; ● **Salary:** 5 ● **Outlook:** 4

AGRICULTURAL-ENGINEERING TECHNICIAN (profess. & kin.) ● DOT #013.161-010 ● OES: 35199 ● Prepares original layout and completes detailed drawings of agricultural machinery and equipment, such as farm machinery, irrigation, power, and electrification systems, soil and water conservation equipment and agricultural harvesting and processing equipment: Applies biological and engineering knowledge, design principles, and theories to ensure compliance with company policy, and an end product which will perform as required. Maintains working knowledge of functions, operations, and maintenance of various types of equipment and materials used in the industry to assure appropriate utilization. ● **GED:** R5, M5, L4 ● **SVP:** 2-4 yrs ● **Academic:** Ed=A, Eng=S ● **Work Field:** 244 ● **MPSMS:** 713 ● **Aptitudes:** G2, V3, N2, S2, P2, Q3, K3, F3, M3, E5, C4 ● **Temperaments:** J, T ● **Physical:** Stg=S; Freq: R, H, N, A Occas: I, D ● **Work Env:** Noise=N; ● **Salary:** 3 ● **Outlook:** 3

AIRPORT ENGINEER (profess. & kin.) ● DOT #005.061-010 ● OES: 22121 ● Plans and lays out airports and landing fields and directs construction work involved in leveling fields, laying out and surfacing runways, and providing drainage: Designs runways based on weight and size of aircraft and prepares material and construction specifications. Directs or participates in surveying to lay out installations and establish reference points, grades, and elevations to guide construction. Estimates costs to provide basis for payments to contractor. Observes progress of construction to ensure workmanship is in conformity with specifications and advises SUPERINTENDENT, CONSTRUCTION (construction) regarding necessary corrections. May serve as agent or employee of contractor and study plans and specifications to recommend special equipment or procedures to reduce time and cost of construction. May schedule delivery of materials, analyze costs, and provide technical advice in solution of construction problems. ● **GED:** R5, M5, L5 ● **SVP:** 4-10 yrs ● **Academic:** Ed=B, Eng=G ● **Work Field:** 244 ● **MPSMS:** 704 ● **Aptitudes:** G2, V2, N2, S2, P2, Q2, K3, F3, M3, E4, C3 ● **Temperaments:** D, J, T, V ● **Physical:** Stg=L; Freq: R, H, T, G, N, D Occas: I, F ● **Work Env:** Noise=N; Freq: W ● **Salary:** 4 ● **Outlook:** 4

ARCHITECT (profess. & kin.) ● DOT #001.061-010 ● OES: 22302 ● Researches, plans, designs, and administers building projects for clients, applying knowledge of design, construction procedures, zoning and building codes, and building materials: Consults with client to determine functional and spatial requirements of new structure or renovation, and prepares information regarding design, specifications, materials, color, equipment, estimated costs, and construction time. Plans layout of project and integrates engineering elements into unified design for client review and approval. Prepares scale drawings and contract documents for building contractors. Represents client in obtaining bids and awarding construction contracts. Administers construction contracts and conducts periodic on-site observation of work during construction to monitor compliance with plans. May prepare operating and maintenance manuals, studies, and reports. May use computer-assisted design software and equipment to prepare project designs and plans. May direct activities of workers engaged in preparing drawings and specification documents. ● **GED:** R6, M6, L6 ● **SVP:** 4-10 yrs ● **Academic:** Ed=M, Eng=G ● **Work Field:** 244, 264 ● **MPSMS:** 701 ● **Aptitudes:** G1, V2, N1, S1, P1, Q3, K4, F3, M4, E5, C3 ● **Temperaments:** D, I, J, T, V ● **Physical:** Stg=L; Freq: T, G, N, D Occas: R, H, I, F, A, X ● **Work Env:** Noise=N; ● **Salary:** 5 ● **Outlook:** 2

ARCHITECT, MARINE (profess. & kin.) ● DOT #001.061-014 ● OES: 22198 ● Alternate titles: ARCHITECT, NAVAL; NAVAL DESIGNER. Designs and oversees construction and repair of marine craft and floating structures, such as ships, barges, tugs, dredges, submarines, torpedoes, floats, and buoys: Studies design proposals and specifications to establish basic characteristics of craft, such as size, weight, speed, propulsion, armament, cargo, displacement, draft, crew and passenger complements, and fresh or salt water service. Oversees construction and testing of prototype in model basin and develops sectional and waterline curves of hull to establish center of gravity, ideal hull form, and buoyancy and stability data. Designs complete hull and superstructure according to specifications and test data, in conformity with standards of safety, efficiency, and economy. Designs layout of craft interior including cargo space, passenger compartments, ladder wells, and elevators. Confers with MARINE ENGINEERS (profess. & kin.) to establish arrangement of boiler room equipment and propulsion machinery, heating and ventilating systems, refrigeration equipment, piping, and other functional equipment. Evaluates performance of craft during dock and sea trials to determine design changes and conformance with national and international standards. ● **GED:** R6, M6, L6 ● **SVP:** Over 10 yrs ● **Academic:** Ed=M, Eng=G ● **Work Field:** 244 ● **MPSMS:** 714 ● **Aptitudes:** G1, V1, N1, S1, P2, Q2, K2, F3, M3, E5, C4 ● **Temperaments:** D, J, T, V ● **Physical:** Stg=L; Freq: R, H, T, G, N, D Occas: X ● **Work Env:** Noise=N; ● **Salary:** 5 ● **Outlook:** 2

CERAMIC ENGINEER (profess. & kin.) ● DOT #006.061-014 ● OES: 22105 ● Conducts research, designs machinery, develops processing techniques, and directs technical work concerned with manufacture of ceramic products: Directs testing of physical, chemical, and heat-resisting properties of materials, such as clays and silicas. Analyzes results of test to determine combinations of materials which will improve quality of products. Conducts research into methods of processing, forming, and firing of clays to develop new ceramic products, such as ceramic machine tools, refractories for space vehicles, and for use in glass and steel furnaces. Designs equipment and apparatus for forming, firing, and handling products. Coordinates testing activities of finished products for characteristics, such as texture, color, durability, glazing, and refractory properties. May specialize in one branch of ceramic production, such as brick, glass, crockery, tile, pipe, or refractories. May specialize in developing heat-resistant and corrosion-resistant materials for use in aerospace, electronics, and nuclear energy fields. nuclear energy field. ● **GED:** R6, M6, L6 ● **SVP:** 4-10 yrs ● **Academic:** Ed=B, Eng=G ● **Work Field:** 244, 251 ● **MPSMS:** 705 ● **Aptitudes:** G1, V1, N1, S1, P2, Q1, K4, F3, M4, E5, C3 ● **Temperaments:** D, J, T, V ● **Physical:** Stg=L; Freq: R, H, I, E, T, G, N Occas: D, X ● **Work Env:** Noise=N; Occas: H ● **Salary:** 5 ● **Outlook:** 4

CHEMICAL DESIGN ENGINEER, PROCESSES (profess. & kin.) ● DOT #008.061-014 ● OES: 22114 ● Designs equipment and processes to produce chemical changes in elements and compounds, performing duties as described under DESIGN ENGINEER, FACILITIES (profess. & kin.) Master Title. ● **GED:** R5, M5, L5 ● **SVP:** 4-10 yrs ● **Academic:** Ed=B, Eng=G ● **Work Field:** 147, 244 ● **MPSMS:** 707 ● **Aptitudes:** G2, V2, N2, S2, P3, Q3, K3, F3, M3, E5, C4 ● **Temperaments:** D, J, T ● **Physical:** Stg=S; Freq: R, H, I, N, D, A, X ● **Work Env:** Noise=N; ● **Salary:** 4 ● **Outlook:** 4

CHEMICAL ENGINEER (profess. & kin.) ● DOT #008.061-018 ● OES: 22114 ● Designs equipment and develops processes for manufacturing chemicals and related products utilizing principles and technology of chemistry, physics, mathematics, engineering and related physical and natural sciences: Conducts research to develop new and improved chemical manufacturing processes. Designs, plans layout, and oversees workers engaged in constructing, controlling, and improving equipment to carry out chemical processes on commercial scale. Analyzes operating procedures and equipment and machinery functions to reduce processing time and cost. Designs equipment to control movement, storage, and packaging of solids, liquids, and gases. Designs and plans measurement and control systems for chemical plants based on data collected in laboratory experiments and pilot plant operations. Determines most effective arrangement of unit operations such as mixing, grinding, crushing, heat transfer, size reduction, hydrogenation, distillation, purification, oxidation, polymerization, evaporation, and fermentation, exercising judgement to compromise between process requirements, economic evaluation, operator effectiveness, and physical and health hazards. Directs activities of workers who operate and control such equipment as condensers, absorption and evaporation towers, kilns, pumps, stills, valves, tanks, boilers, compressors, grinders, pipelines, electro-magnets, and centrifuges to effect required chemical or physical change. Performs tests and takes measurements throughout stages of production to determine degree of control over variables such as temperature, density, specific gravity, and pressure. May apply principles of chemical engineering to solve environmental problems. May apply principles of chemical engineering to solve biomedical problems. May develop electro-chemical processes to generate electric currents, using controlled chemical reactions or to produce chemical changes, using electric currents. May specialize in heat transfer and energy conversion, petrochemicals and fuels, materials handling, pharmaceuticals, foods, forest products, or products such as plastics, detergents, rubber, or synthetic textiles. May be designated according to area of specialization. ● **GED:** R6, M6, L6 ● **SVP:** 4-10 yrs ● **Academic:** Ed=B, Eng=G ● **Work Field:** 244, 251 ● **MPSMS:** 707 ● **Aptitudes:** G1, V1, N1, S2, P3, Q3, K3, F3, M3, E5, C4 ● **Temperaments:** D, J, T, V ● **Physical:** Stg=L; Freq: R, H, N, A Occas: I, D, X ● **Work Env:** Noise=N; Occas: W ● **Salary:** 5 ● **Outlook:** 4

CIVIL ENGINEER (profess. & kin.) ● DOT #005.061-014 ● OES: 22121 ● Plans, designs, and directs civil engineering projects, such as roads, railroads, airports, bridges, harbors, channels, dams, irrigation systems, pipelines, and powerplants: Analyzes reports, maps, drawings, blueprints, tests, and aerial photographs on soil composition, terrain, hydrological characteristics, and other topographical and geologic data to plan and design project. Calculates cost and determines feasibility of project based on analysis of collected data, applying knowledge and techniques of engineering, and advanced mathematics. Prepares or directs preparation and modification of reports, specifications, plans, construction schedules, environmental impact studies, and designs for project. Inspects construction site to monitor progress and ensure conformance to engineering plans, specifications, and construction and safety standards. May direct construction and maintenance activities at project site. May use computer-assisted engineering and design software and equipment to prepare engineering and design documents. May be designated according to specialty or product. ● **GED:** R5, M5, L5 ● **SVP:** 4-10 yrs ● **Academic:** Ed=B, Eng=G ● **Work Field:** 244 ● **MPSMS:** 704 ● **Aptitudes:** G2, V2, N1, S1, P2, Q2, K3, F3, M3, E4, C4 ● **Temperaments:** D, J, P, T, V ● **Physical:** Stg=L; Freq: N Occas: R, H, I, T, G, F, D, A, X ● **Work Env:** Noise=N; Occas: W ● **Salary:** 5 ● **Outlook:** 4

ELECTRICAL-DESIGN ENGINEER (profess. & kin.) ● DOT #003.061-018 ● OES: 22126 ● Designs electrical equipment and products, performing duties as described under DESIGN ENGINEER, FACILITIES (profess. & kin.) Master Title; DESIGN ENGINEER, PRODUCTS (profess. & kin.) Master Title. ● **GED:** R5, M5, L5 ● **SVP:** 4-10 yrs ● **Academic:** Ed=B, Eng=S ● **Work Field:** 244 ● **MPSMS:** 871 ● **Aptitudes:** G2, V2, N2, S2, P2, Q3, K3, F3, M3, E4, C4 ● **Temperaments:** J, P, T, V ● **Physical:** Stg=L; Freq: R, H, T, G, N, D Occas: I, A, X ● **Work Env:** Noise=Q; ● **Salary:** 4 ● **Outlook:** 4

ELECTRONICS-DESIGN ENGINEER (profess. & kin.) ● DOT #003.061-034 ● OES: 22126 ● Designs and develops electronic components, equipment, systems, and products, applying knowledge and principles of electronic theory, design, and engineering. Performs duties as described under DESIGN ENGINEER, PRODUCTS (profess. & kin.) Master Title. May use computer-assisted engineering and design software and equipment to formulate and test electronic designs. ● **GED:** R5, M5, L5 ● **SVP:** 4-10 yrs ● **Academic:** Ed=M, Eng=S ● **Work Field:** 244, 251 ● **MPSMS:** 703, 580 ● **Aptitudes:** G1, V1, N1, S1, P2, Q2, K3, F3, M3, E5, C3 ● **Temperaments:** J, T, V ● **Physical:** Stg=L; Freq: I, N Occas: R, H, T, G, A, X ● **Work Env:** Noise=N; ● **Salary:** 5 ● **Outlook:** 4

ELECTRO-OPTICAL ENGINEER (profess. & kin.) ● DOT #023.061-010 ● OES: 24102 ● Conducts research and plans development and design of gas and solid state lasers, masers, infrared, and other light emitting and light sensitive devices: Designs electronic circuitry and optical components with specific characteristics to fit within specified mechanical limits and to perform according to specifications. Designs suitable mounts for optics and power supply systems. Incorporates methods for maintenance and repair of components and designs, and develops test instrumentation and test procedures. Confers with engineering and technical personnel regarding fabrication and test-

ing of prototype systems, and modifies design as required. May conduct application analysis to determine commercial, industrial, scientific, medical, military, or other use for electro-optical devices. May assist with development of manufacturing, assembly, and fabrication processes. ● **GED:** R6, M6, L6 ● **SVP:** 4-10 yrs ● **Academic:** Ed=M, Eng=S ● **Work Field:** 244 ● **MPSMS:** 587, 703, 600 ● **Aptitudes:** G1, V1, N1, S1, P2, Q2, K4, F4, M4, E5, C4 ● **Temperaments:** D, J, T ● **Physical:** Stg=S; Freq: R, H, N Occas: I, X ● **Work Env:** Noise=N; ● **Salary:** 4 ● **Outlook:** 4

LANDSCAPE ARCHITECT (profess. & kin.) ● DOT #001.061-018 ● OES: 22308 ● Alternate titles: COMMUNITY PLANNER; ENVIRONMENTAL PLANNER; LAND PLANNER; SITE PLANNER. Plans and designs development of land areas for projects, such as parks and other recreational facilities, airports, highways, and parkways, hospitals, schools, land subdivisions, and commercial, industrial, and residential sites: Confers with clients, engineering personnel, and ARCHITECTS (profess. & kin.) on overall program. Compiles and analyzes data on such site conditions as geographic location; soil, vegetation, and rock features; drainage; and location of structures for preparation of environmental impact report and development of landscaping plans. Prepares site plans, working drawings, specifications, and cost estimates for land development, showing ground contours, vegetation, locations of structures, and such facilities as roads, walks, parking areas, fences, walls, and utilities, coordinating arrangement of existing and proposed land features and structures. Inspects construction work in progress to ensure compliance with landscape specifications, to approve quality of materials and work, and to advise client and construction personnel on landscape features. May be designated according to project as Highway-Landscape Architect (profess. & kin.); Park-Landscape Architect (profess. & kin.). ● **GED:** R5, M5, L5 ● **SVP:** 4-10 yrs ● **Academic:** Ed=B, Eng=G ● **Work Field:** 264 ● **MPSMS:** 719 ● **Aptitudes:** G1, V1, N2, S1, P2, Q2, K3, F3, M3, E4, C3 ● **Temperaments:** D, F, J ● **Physical:** Stg=L; Freq: R, H, T, G, N, D, A Occas: C, B, S, K, O, I, X ● **Work Env:** Noise=Q; Occas: W ● **Salary:** 5 ● **Outlook:** 2

MECHANICAL-DESIGN ENGINEER, FACILITIES (profess. & kin.) ● DOT #007.061-018 ● OES: 22135 ● Designs and directs installation of plant systems or product lines performing duties as described under DESIGN ENGINEER, FACILITIES (profess. & kin.) Master Title. ● **GED:** R5, M5, L5 ● **SVP:** 4-10 yrs ● **Academic:** Ed=A, Eng=G ● **Work Field:** 244 ● **MPSMS:** 706 ● **Aptitudes:** G1, V1, N2, S1, P2, Q3, K3, F3, M3, E5, C5 ● **Temperaments:** D, J ● **Physical:** Stg=S; Freq: R, H, T, G, N, D Occas: I ● **Work Env:** Noise=N; ● **Salary:** 5 ● **Outlook:** 3

OPTICAL ENGINEER (profess. & kin.) ● DOT #019.061-018 ● OES: 22198 ● Alternate titles: OPTICAL DESIGNER. Designs optical systems with specific characteristics to fit within specified physical limits of precision optical instruments, such as still- and motion-picture cameras, lens systems, telescopes, and viewing and display devices: Determines specifications for operations and makes adjustments to calibrate and obtain specified operational performance. Determines proper operation of optical system and makes adjustments to perfect system. Designs mounts for components to hold them in proper planes in relation to each other and instrument in which they will be used. Designs inspection instruments to test optical systems for defects, such as abberations and deviations. May work with electrical and mechanical engineering staff to develop overall design of optical system. ● **GED:** R6, M5, L5 ● **SVP:** 4-10 yrs ● **Academic:** Ed=B, Eng=S ● **Work Field:** 244 ● **MPSMS:** 606 ● **Aptitudes:** G2, V2, N2, S1, P2, Q2, K4, F4, M4, E5, C5 ● **Temperaments:** D, J ● **Physical:** Stg=S; Freq: R, H, I, T, G, N, D, A ● **Work Env:** Noise=Q; ● **Salary:** 5 ● **Outlook:** 3

RAILROAD ENGINEER (profess. & kin.) ● DOT #005.061-026 ● OES: 22121 ● Designs railroad and street railway tracks, terminals, yards, and other facilities and directs and coordinates construction and relocation of facilities: Plans roadbed, rail size, and curves to meet train speed and load requirements. Directs, through subordinate supervisors, construction of bridges, culverts, buildings, and other structures. Directs track and roadway maintenance. Surveys traffic problems related to street railway system and recommends grade revisions, additional trackage, use of heavier power, and other changes to relieve congestion and reduce hazards. ● **GED:** R5, M5, L5 ● **SVP:** 4-10 yrs ● **Academic:** Ed=A, Eng=G ● **Work Field:** 244 ● **MPSMS:** 704 ●

Aptitudes: G2, V2, N2, S2, P2, Q2, K3, F3, M3, E3, C3 ● **Temperaments:** D, T, V ● **Physical:** Stg=L; Freq: R, H, T, G, N, F, D Occas: I, X ● **Work Env:** Noise=N; Freq: W ● **Salary:** 5 ● **Outlook:** 2

TOOL DESIGN CHECKER (aircraft mfg.) ● DOT #007.267-014 ● OES: 35199 ● Alternate titles: TOOL DRAWING CHECKER. Examines tool drawings prepared by TOOL DESIGNER (profess. & kin.) 007.061-026 for inaccuracies of detail and evaluates overall tool design for fit, form, and function, utilizing knowledge of engineering principles, tool design methods, and manufacturing processes: Measures drawing dimensions, and compares figures with dimensions on original layout, specifications, or sample part to verify measurements conform to scale. Marks verified or out-of-scale dimensions on drawings. Inspects lines and figures on drawings for clarity. Evaluates overall tool design for functionality, conformance to drawing standards and design specifications, and manufacturing feasibility. Reviews material requirements for standardization and conformance to industry specification manuals. Discusses design, manufacturing, and related issues with engineering, production, or other personnel. Approves or rejects design. May operate computer to examine and evaluate computer-generated tool designs. ● **GED:** R5, M5, L5 ● **SVP:** 4-10 yrs ● **Academic:** Ed=A, Eng=S ● **Work Field:** 211, 242, 244 ● **MPSMS:** 706 ● **Aptitudes:** G2, V2, N2, S2, P2, Q3, K4, F4, M4, E5, C4 ● **Temperaments:** J, T ● **Physical:** Stg=S; Freq: R, H, I, N Occas: T, G, A, X ● **Work Env:** Noise=Q; ● **Salary:** 3 ● **Outlook:** 3

TOOL DESIGNER (profess. & kin.) ● DOT #007.061-026 ● OES: 22135 ● Designs single- or multiple-edged machine cutting tools, such as broaches, milling-machine cutters, and drills, and related jigs, dies, and fixtures: Studies specifications, engineering blueprints, tool orders, and shop data and confers with engineering and shop personnel to resolve design problems related to material characteristics, dimensional tolerances, service requirements, manufacturing procedures, and cost. Applies algebraic and geometric formulas and standard tool engineering data to develop tool configuration. Selects standard items, such as bushings and tool bits, to incorporate into tool design. Draws preliminary sketches and prepares layout and detail drawings, using standard drafting tools and equipment or computer-assisted design/drafting equipment and software. Modifies tool designs according to trial or production service data to improve tool life or performance. ● **GED:** R5, M5, L5 ● **SVP:** 4-10 yrs ● **Academic:** Ed=A, Eng=S ● **Work Field:** 244 ● **MPSMS:** 706 ● **Aptitudes:** G2, V2, N2, S2, P2, Q3, K3, F3, M3, E5, C4 ● **Temperaments:** J, T ● **Physical:** Stg=L; Freq: R, H, I, N, A Occas: T, G, X ● **Work Env:** Noise=L; ● **Salary:** 5 ● **Outlook:** 3

GOE: 05.01.08
General Engineering

AGRICULTURAL ENGINEER (profess. & kin.) ● DOT #013.061-010 ● OES: 22198 ● Applies engineering technology and knowledge of biological sciences to agricultural problems concerned with power and machinery, electrification, structures, soil and water conservation, and processing of agricultural products: Develops criteria for design, manufacture, or construction of equipment, structures, and facilities. Designs and uses sensing, measuring, and recording devices and instrumentation to study such problems as effects of temperature, humidity, and light, on plants or animals, or relative effectiveness of different methods of applying insecticides. Designs and directs manufacture of equipment for land tillage and fertilization, plant and animal disease and insect control, and for harvesting or moving commodities. Designs and supervises erection of structures for crop storage, animal shelter, and human dwelling, including light, heat, air-conditioning, water supply, and waste disposal. Plans and directs construction of rural electric-power distribution systems, and irrigation, drainage, and flood-control systems for soil and water conservation. Designs and supervises installation of equipment and instruments used to evaluate and process farm products, and to automate agricultural operations. May conduct radio and television educational programs to provide assistance to farmers, local groups, and related farm cooperatives. Workers are usually designated according to area of specialty or product. ● **GED:** R5, M5, L5 ● **SVP:** 4-10 yrs ● **Academic:** Ed=B, Eng=G ● **Work Field:** 244 ● **MPSMS:** 713 ● **Aptitudes:** G1, V1, N1, S2, P3, Q3, K3, F3, M3, E3, C3 ● **Temperaments:** D, J, V ● **Physical:** Stg=L;

Freq: R, H, N Occas: D, A, X ● **Work Env:** Noise=N; Freq: W ● **Salary:** 5 ● **Outlook:** 3

AUTOMOTIVE ENGINEER (auto. mfg.) ● DOT #007.061-010 ● OES: 22135 ● Develops improved or new designs for automotive structural members, engines, transmissions, and associated automotive equipment or modifies existing equipment on production vehicles, and directs building, modification, and testing of vehicle, using computerized work aids: Conducts experiments and tests on existing designs and equipment to obtain data on function of and performance of equipment. Analyzes data to develop new designs for motors, chassis, and other related mechanical, hydraulic, and electromechanical components and systems in automotive equipment. Designs components and systems to provide maximum customer value and vehicle function, including improved economy and safety of operation, control of emissions, and operational performance, at optimum costs. Directs and coordinates building, or modification of, automotive equipment or vehicle to ensure conformance with engineering design. Directs testing activities on components and equipment under designated conditions to ensure operational performance meets design specifications. Alters or modifies design to obtain specified functional and operational performance. May assist DRAFTER, AUTOMOTIVE DESIGN (auto. mfg.) 017.261-042 in developing structural design for auto body. May conduct research studies to develop new concepts in automotive engineering field. ● **GED:** R5, M5, L5 ● **SVP:** 4-10 yrs ● **Academic:** Ed=B, Eng=S ● **Work Field:** 244 ● **MPSMS:** 706 ● **Aptitudes:** G2, V2, N2, S2, P2, Q3, K3, F3, M3, E5, C3 ● **Temperaments:** D, J, T ● **Physical:** Stg=L; Freq: R, H, I, T, G, N, A Occas: D, X ● **Work Env:** Noise=Q; ● **Salary:** 5 ● **Outlook:** 3

CHEMICAL-ENGINEERING TECHNICIAN (profess. & kin.) ● DOT #008.261-010 ● OES: 35199 ● Applies chemical engineering principles and technical skills to assist CHEMICAL ENGINEER (profess. & kin.) in developing, improving, and testing chemical-plant processes, products, and equipment: Prepares charts, sketches, diagrams, flow charts, and compiles and records engineering data to clarify design details or functional criteria of chemical processing and physical operation units. Participates in fabricating, installing, and modifying equipment to ensure that critical standards are met. Tests developmental equipment and formulates standard operating procedures. Tests processing equipment and instruments to observe and record operating characteristics and performance of specified design or process. Observes chemical or physical operation processes and recommends modification or change. Observes and confers with equipment operators to ensure specified techniques are used. Writes technical reports and submits finding to CHEMICAL ENGINEER (profess. & kin.). Performs preventive and corrective maintenance of chemical processing equipment. May prepare chemical solutions for use in processing materials, such as synthetic textiles, detergents, and fertilizers following formula. May set up test apparatus. May instruct or direct activities of technical personnel. May assist in developing and testing prototype processing systems and be designated Chemical-Engineering Technician, Prototype-Development (profess. & kin.). May assist in development of pilot-plant units and be designated Pilot-Plant Research-Technician (petrol. refin.). ● **GED:** R5, M5, L5 ● **SVP:** 4-10 yrs ● **Academic:** Ed=A, Eng=S ● **Work Field:** 244 ● **MPSMS:** 707 ● **Aptitudes:** G2, V2, N2, S2, P2, Q3, K2, F2, M2, E3, C4 ● **Temperaments:** J, T ● **Physical:** Stg=L; Freq: R, H, N, A Occas: I, T, G, D, X ● **Work Env:** Noise=L; Occas: W ● **Salary:** 4 ● **Outlook:** 3

CUSTOMER-EQUIPMENT ENGINEER (tel. & tel.) ● DOT #003.187-018 ● OES: 22126 ● Alternate titles: SERVICES ENGINEER. Directs activities concerned with selection and installation of telephone facilities and special equipment on customer's premises to meet customer's communication requirements: Reviews sales order to ascertain extent of telephone facilities and equipment required. Inspects customer premises to ascertain space available for installation of equipment and to determine type and quantity of designated equipment that can be installed to provide specific communication facilities. Prepares floor plan of equipment arrangement for customer or architect approval. Prepares cost estimate for equipment and installation and submits data to management for authorization to proceed with job. Orders equipment, prepares installation specifications, and monitors progress of installation to ensure facilities are ready on specified date. Prepares all job-related paper work and closes out work authorization when equipment is in service. ● **GED:** R5, M5, L5 ● **SVP:** 4-10 yrs ● **Academic:**

Ed=B, Eng=G ● **Work Field:** 244 ● **MPSMS:** 861 ● **Aptitudes:** G2, V2, N2, S2, P2, Q4, K4, F4, M4, E5, C5 ● **Temperaments:** D, J, V ● **Physical:** Stg=L; Freq: R, H, T, G, N, D Occas: I, A, X ● **Work Env:** Noise=N; ● **Salary:** 4 ● **Outlook:** 4

ELECTRICAL ENGINEER (profess. & kin.) ● DOT #003.061-010 ● OES: 22126 ● Researches, develops, designs, and tests electrical components, equipment, and systems, applying principles and techniques of electrical engineering: Designs electrical equipment, facilities, components, products, and systems for commercial, industrial, and domestic purposes [DESIGN ENGINEER, FACILITIES (profess. & kin.) Master Title; DESIGN ENGINEER, PRODUCTS (profess. & kin.) Master Title]. Designs and directs engineering personnel in fabrication of test control apparatus and equipment, and determines methods, procedures, and conditions for testing products [TEST ENGINEER (profess. & kin.) Master Title]. Develops applications of controls, instruments, and systems for new commercial, domestic, and industrial uses. Directs activities to ensure that manufacturing, construction, installation, and operational testing conform to functional specifications and customer requirements. May direct and coordinate operation, maintenance, and repair of equipment and systems in field installations. May specialize in specific area of discipline, such as electrical energy generation, transmission, and distribution systems; products, such as appliances, generators, transformers, control devices, and relays; or area of work, such as manufacturing, applications, or installation. May use computer-assisted engineering and design software and equipment to perform engineering tasks. ● **GED:** R5, M5, L5 ● **SVP:** 4-10 yrs ● **Academic:** Ed=B, Eng=G ● **Work Field:** 244, 251 ● **MPSMS:** 703, 871, 580 ● **Aptitudes:** G2, V2, N2, S2, P2, Q3, K3, F3, M3, E4, C4 ● **Temperaments:** D, J, T, V ● **Physical:** Stg=L; Freq: I, N Occas: R, H, T, G, A, X ● **Work Env:** Noise=N; ● **Salary:** 5 ● **Outlook:** 5

ELECTRONICS ENGINEER (profess. & kin.) ● DOT #003.061-030 ● OES: 22126 ● Researches, develops, designs, and tests electronic components, products, and systems for commercial, industrial, medical, military, and scientific applications, applying principles and techniques of electronic engineering: Designs electronic circuits, components and integrated systems, utilizing ferroelectric, nonlinear, dielectric, phosphorescent, photo-conductive, and thermoelectric properties of materials [DESIGN ENGINEER, PRODUCTS (profess. & kin.) Master Title]. Designs test control apparatus and equipment, determines procedures for testing products [TEST ENGINEER (profess. & kin.) Master Title], and directs engineering personnel in fabrication of test control apparatus and equipment. Develops new applications of conductive properties of metallic and nonmetallic materials used in components, and in application of components to products or systems. May direct field operations and maintenance of electronic installations. May evaluate operational systems and recommend design modifications to eliminate causes of malfunctions or changes in system requirements. May specialize in development of electronic principles and technology in fields, such as telecommunications, telemetry, aerospace guidance, missile propulsion control, countermeasures, acoustics, nucleonic instrumentation, industrial controls and measurements, high-frequency heating, computers, radiation detection, encephalography, electron optics, and biomedical research. May use computer-assisted engineering and design software and equipment to perform engineering tasks. ● **GED:** R5, M5, L5 ● **SVP:** 4-10 yrs ● **Academic:** Ed=B, Eng=G ● **Work Field:** 244, 251 ● **MPSMS:** 703, 580, 600 ● **Aptitudes:** G2, V2, N2, S2, P2, Q3, K3, F3, M3, E4, C3 ● **Temperaments:** J, T, V ● **Physical:** Stg=L; Freq: R, H, I, N, X Occas: T, G, D, A ● **Work Env:** Noise=N; ● **Salary:** 5 ● **Outlook:** 5

ENGINEERING MANAGER, ELECTRONICS (profess. & kin.) ● DOT #003.167-070 ● OES: 13017 ● Directs and coordinates activities of engineering department to design, manufacture, and test electronic components, products, and systems: Directs department activities, through subordinates, to design new products, modify existing designs, improve production techniques, and develop test procedures. Analyzes technology trends, human resource needs, and market demand to plan projects. Confers with management, production, and marketing staff to determine engineering feasibility, cost effectiveness, and customer demand for new and existing products. Forecasts operating costs of department and directs preparation of budget requests. Directs personnel activities of department, such as recruitment, hiring, performance evaluations, and salary adjustments. May direct field testing of products and systems performed by field staff. ● **GED:** R6, M6, L5 ● **SVP:** Over 10

yrs ● **Academic:** Ed=B, Eng=G ● **Work Field:** 295, 244 ● **MPSMS:** 703 ● **Aptitudes:** G1, V1, N1, S1, P2, Q1, K4, F5, M4, E5, C5 ● **Temperaments:** D, J, P ● **Physical:** Stg=S; Freq: T, G Occas: R, H, N ● **Work Env:** Noise=N; ● **Salary:** 5 ● **Outlook:** 3

ENGINEER, SOILS (profess. & kin.) ● DOT #024.161-010 ● OES: 24111 ● Studies and analyzes surface and subsurface soils to determine characteristics for construction, development, or land planning: Inspects proposed construction site, and sets up test equipment and drilling machinery to obtain data and soil and rock samples. Analyzes data and soil samples through field and laboratory analysis, to determine type, classification, characteristics, and stability of soil. Computes bearing weights, prepares maps, charts, and reports of test results. May make recommendations regarding foundation design, slope angles, grading or building heights. May participate in environmental studies and prepare environmental impact reports. ● **GED:** R6, M5, L6 ● **SVP:** 2-4 yrs ● **Academic:** Ed=B, Eng=G ● **Work Field:** 244 ● **MPSMS:** 704 ● **Aptitudes:** G1, V1, N1, S2, P3, Q3, K3, F3, M3, E3, C3 ● **Temperaments:** D, J, T, V ● **Physical:** Stg=L; Freq: N, A Occas: R, H, I, E, F, D, X, V ● **Work Env:** Noise=N; Occas: W ● **Salary:** 4 ● **Outlook:** 3

FIBER TECHNOLOGIST (profess. & kin.) ● DOT #040.061-026 ● OES: 24501 ● Studies nature, origin, use, improvement, and processing methods of plant, animal, and synthetic fibers: Analyzes wool, mohair, cashmere, camel's hair, alpaca, bristles, feathers, and similar animal and fowl fibers, plant fibers, such as cotton, linen, and jute, and synthetic fibers and products made from these fibers. Applies principles of science to improve growth and quality of fibers. Conducts experiments in blending fibers and develops improved manufacturing methods for converting fibers into articles, such as cloth, felts, rugs, mattresses, and brushes. Conducts tests on fibrous structures for quality control, such as tensile strength and stability to heat, light, and chemicals. May be identified according to fibers studied. ● **GED:** R6, M6, L6 ● **SVP:** 4-10 yrs ● **Academic:** Ed=M, Eng=S ● **Work Field:** 251 ● **MPSMS:** 731 ● **Aptitudes:** G1, V1, N3, S2, P2, Q4, K3, F3, M4, E4, C4 ● **Temperaments:** D, J, T ● **Physical:** Stg=L; Freq: R, H, N Occas: I, E, D, A, X ● **Work Env:** Noise=N; ● **Salary:** 3 ● **Outlook:** 2

MAINTAINABILITY ENGINEER (profess. & kin.) ● DOT #019.081-010 ● OES: 22198 ● Analyzes engineering design of proposed product, such as aircraft, naval vessel, or electronic control or navigation system, and submits specifications for maintenance requirements, utilizing knowledge of maintainability engineering and related technologies: Analyzes customer's initial proposal for product utilization and recommends basic product specifications and techniques for satisfying customer requirements. Reviews engineering specifications and drawings during development and proposes design refinements to improve ratio of operational time to maintenance time. Participates in engineering discussions concerning design alternatives effecting product maintainability. Determines crew makeup, training requirements, and maintenance time by evaluating data from tests and maintainability programs of related products. Reviews subcontractor's technical practices for assuring maintainability of equipment and parts and submits evaluation for managment decision. Specifies standardized tests or drafts new test programs for demonstrating product maintainability in company or supplier test. Observes maintainability tests at supplier and plant locations to verify operations are conducted according to standards. ● **GED:** R5, M4, L5 ● **SVP:** 4-10 yrs ● **Academic:** Ed=B, Eng=S ● **Work Field:** 244 ● **MPSMS:** 700 ● **Aptitudes:** G2, V2, N2, S2, P2, Q3, K3, F3, M3, E5, C4 ● **Temperaments:** D, J, T ● **Physical:** Stg=S; Freq: R, H, I, T, G, N Occas: X ● **Work Env:** Noise=N; ● **Salary:** 4 ● **Outlook:** 4

MECHANICAL ENGINEER (profess. & kin.) ● DOT #007.061-014 ● OES: 22135 ● Researches, plans, and designs mechanical and electromechanical products and systems, and directs and coordinates activities involved in fabrication, operation, application, installation, and repair of mechanical or electromechanical products and systems: Researches and analyzes data, such as customer design proposal, specifications, and manuals to determine feasibility of design or application. Designs products or systems, such as instruments, controls, robots, engines, machines, and mechanical, thermal, hydraulic, or heat transfer systems, applying knowledge of engineering principles [DESIGN ENGINEER, PRODUCTS (profess. & kin.) Master Title]. Plans and directs engineering personnel in fabrication of test control apparatus and equipment, and development of methods and procedures for testing products or systems [TEST ENGINEER (profess. & kin.) Master Title]. Directs and coordinates fabrication and installation activities to ensure products and systems conform to engineering design and customer specifications. Coordinates operation, maintenance, and repair activities to obtain optimum utilization of machines and equipment. May design products and systems to interface machines, hardware, and software. May evaluate field installations and recommend design modifications to eliminate machine or system malfunctions. May specialize in specific field of mechanical engineering, such as heat transfer, hydraulics, electromechanics, controls and instrumentation, robotics, nuclear systems, tooling, air-conditioning and refrigeration; or in type of product, such as propulsion systems or machinery and mechanical equipment; or in type of work, such as steam or gas generation and distribution, steam plant engineering, or system planning. ● **GED:** R5, M5, L5 ● **SVP:** 4-10 yrs ● **Academic:** Ed=B, Eng=S ● **Work Field:** 244 ● **MPSMS:** 706 ● **Aptitudes:** G2, V2, N1, S2, P3, Q3, K3, F3, M3, E5, C5 ● **Temperaments:** D, J, T, V ● **Physical:** Stg=L; Freq: R, H, I, T, G, N Occas: D, A ● **Work Env:** Noise=N; ● **Salary:** 5 ● **Outlook:** 4

PETROLEUM ENGINEER (petrol. & gas) ● DOT #010.061-018 ● OES: 22111 ● Analyzes technical and cost factors to plan methods to recover maximum oil and gas in oil-field operations, utilizing knowledge of petroleum engineering and related technologies: Examines map of subsurface oil and gas reservoir locations to recommend placement of wells to maximize economical production from reservoir. Evaluates probable well production rate during natural or stimulated-flow production phases. Recommends supplementary processes to enhance recovery involving stimulation of flow by use of processes, such as pressurizing or heating in subsurface regions. Analyzes recommendations of reservoir engineering specialist for placement of well in oil field. Develops well drilling plan for management approval, specifying factors including drilling time, number of special operations, such as directional drilling, and testing, and material requirements and costs including well casing and drilling muds. Provides technical consultation during drilling operations to resolve problems such as bore directional change, unsatisfactory drilling rate or invasion of subsurface water in well bore. Advises substitution of drilling mud compounds or tool bits to improve drilling conditions. Inspects well to determine that final casing and tubing installations are completed. Plans oil and gas field recovery containers, piping, and treatment vessels to receive, remove contaminants, and separate oil and gas products flowing from well. Monitors production rate of gas or oil from established wells and plans rework process to correct well production, such as repacking of well bore and additional perforation of subsurface sands adjacent to well bottom. May apply knowledge of petroleum engineering to solve problems concerned with environment [ENVIRONMENTAL ENGINEER (profess. & kin.)]. May be designated according to specialty as Development Engineer, Geothermal Operations (profess. & kin.); Drilling Engineer (petrol. & gas); Production Engineer (petrol. & gas); Reservoir Engineer (petrol. & gas). ● **GED:** R5, M5, L5 ● **SVP:** 4-10 yrs ● **Academic:** Ed=B, Eng=G ● **Work Field:** 244 ● **MPSMS:** 708 ● **Aptitudes:** G1, V1, N1, S1, P2, Q3, K3, F3, M3, E5, C5 ● **Temperaments:** D, J, T, V ● **Physical:** Stg=L; Freq: R, H, T, G, N, A Occas: I, F, D ● **Work Env:** Noise=V; ● **Salary:** 5 ● **Outlook:** 4

PLANT ENGINEER (profess. & kin.) ● DOT #007.167-014 ● OES: 13017 ● Alternate titles: FACTORY ENGINEER; SUPERINTENDENT, MECHANICAL. Plans, directs, and coordinates activities concerned with design, construction, modification, and maintenance of equipment and machinery in industrial plant: Establishes standards and policies for pollution control, installation, modification, quality control, testing, operating procedure, inspection, and maintenance of equipment, according to engineering principles and safety regulations. Directs maintenance of plant buildings and coordinates requirements for new designs, surveys, and maintenance schedules for equipment and machinery. Prepares bid sheets and contracts for construction and facilities acquisition. Tests newly installed machines and equipment to ensure fulfillment of contract specifications. ● **GED:** R5, M5, L5 ● **SVP:** 4-10 yrs ● **Academic:** Ed=B, Eng=G ● **Work Field:** 244 ● **MPSMS:** 706, 712 ● **Aptitudes:** G2, V2, N2, S2, P2, Q3, K4, F4, M4, E5, C5 ● **Temperaments:** D, J, P, T ● **Physical:** Stg=L; Freq: T, G Occas: R, H, I, N, D ● **Work Env:** Noise=N; ● **Salary:** 5 ● **Outlook:** 4

PROJECT ENGINEER (profess. & kin.) ● DOT #019.167-014 ● OES: 13017 ● Alternate titles: CHIEF ENGINEER. Directs, coordi-

nates, and exercises functional authority for planning, organization, control, integration, and completion of engineering project within area of assigned responsibility: Plans and formulates engineering program and organizes project staff according to project requirements. Assigns project personnel to specific phases or aspects of project, such as technical studies, product design, preparation of specifications and technical plans, and product testing, in accordance with engineering disciplines of staff. Reviews product design for compliance with engineering principles, company standards, customer contract requirements, and related specifications. Coordinates activities concerned with technical developments, scheduling, and resolving engineering design and test problems. Directs integration of technical activities and products. Evaluates and approves design changes, specifications, and drawing releases. Controls expenditures within limitations of project budget. Prepares interim and completion project reports. ● **GED:** R5, M5, L5 ● **SVP:** 4-10 yrs ● **Academic:** Ed=A, Eng=S ● **Work Field:** 244, 295 ● **MPSMS:** 700 ● **Aptitudes:** G2, V2, N2, S2, P3, Q3, K3, F3, M3, E5, C5 ● **Temperaments:** D, J, P, V ● **Physical:** Stg=L; Freq: H, T, G, N Occas: R, I, A ● **Work Env:** Noise=N; ● **Salary:** 5 ● **Outlook:** 4

SCHOOL-PLANT CONSULTANT (education) ● DOT #001.167-010 ● OES: 22302 ● Formulates and enforces standards for construction and alteration of public school facilities throughout state: Develops legislation relative to school building sites and school design and construction. Guides school districts in development of long range comprehensive master plans, including such factors as site selection and expected population growth and mobility, and school finance and specifications. Coordinates activities, jurisdictions, and responsibilities of adjacent school districts and evaluates entire systems of schools. Provides technical information and advice to local school authorities considering construction or renovation of school plant. Inspects proposed sites and schools under construction or undergoing alteration to enforce applicable standards. Prepares suggested classroom plans and layouts, taking into consideration such factors as climate, construction costs, availability of materials, and accepted principles of institutional construction. Reviews plans for construction and renovation of school buildings and approves or disapproves plans in accordance with standards and policies of department. Confers with representatives of school boards, educators, and architects to explain and reach agreement on design concepts and construction standards. Arbitrates difficult and unusual construction disputes. Conducts special research studies concerned with lighting, heating, ventilation, air-conditioning, and acoustics. Prepares reports for state education department and state legislature. ● **GED:** R5, M5, L5 ● **SVP:** 1-2 yrs ● **Academic:** Ed=B, Eng=G ● **Work Field:** 244, 242 ● **MPSMS:** 701 ● **Aptitudes:** G2, V2, N2, S2, P2, Q3, K4, F4, M4, E5, C4 ● **Temperaments:** J, P ● **Physical:** Stg=S; Freq: T, G, N Occas: R, H, D, X ● **Work Env:** Noise=N; ● **Salary:** 4 ● **Outlook:** 1

STRUCTURAL ENGINEER (construction) ● DOT #005.061-034 ● OES: 22121 ● Directs or participates in planning, designing, or reviewing plans for erection of structures requiring stress analysis: Designs structure to meet estimated load requirements, computing size, shape, strength, and type of structural members, or performs structural analysis of plans and structures prepared by private engineers. May inspect existing projects and recommend repair and replacement of defective members or rebuilding of entire structure. ● **GED:** R5, M5, L5 ● **SVP:** 4-10 yrs ● **Academic:** Ed=B, Eng=G ● **Work Field:** 244 ● **MPSMS:** 704, 361 ● **Aptitudes:** G2, V2, N2, S2, P2, Q2, K3, F3, M3, E3, C3 ● **Temperaments:** J, T, V ● **Physical:** Stg=L; Freq: R, H, N ● **Work Env:** Noise=N; Freq: W ● **Salary:** 5 ● **Outlook:** 4

TRANSPORTATION ENGINEER (profess. & kin.) ● DOT #005.061-038 ● OES: 22121 ● Develops plans for surface transportation projects according to established engineering standards and state or federal construction policy: Prepares plans, estimates, and specifications to design transportation facilities. Plans alterations and modifications of existing streets, highways, and freeways to improve traffic flow. Prepares deeds, property descriptions, and right-of-way maps. Performs field engineering calculations to compensate for change orders and contract estimates. May prepare and present public reports of environmental analysis statements and other transportation information. May specialize in particular phase of work, such as making surveys, improving signs or lighting, preparing plans, or directing and coordinating construction or maintenance activities. May be designated Highway Engineer (government ser.). May specialize in studying vehicular and pedestrian traffic conditions and be designated Traffic Engineer (government ser.). May plan, organize, and direct work in transportation studies to plan surface systems and be designated Transportation Planning Engineer (government ser.). ● **GED:** R5, M5, L5 ● **SVP:** 4-10 yrs ● **Academic:** Ed=B, Eng=G ● **Work Field:** 244 ● **MPSMS:** 704 ● **Aptitudes:** G2, V2, N2, S2, P2, Q2, K3, F3, M3, E5, C3 ● **Temperaments:** D, J, T, V ● **Physical:** Stg=L; Freq: N Occas: R, H, I ● **Work Env:** Noise=N; Occas: W ● **Salary:** 4 ● **Outlook:** 4

WELDING ENGINEER (profess. & kin.) ● DOT #011.061-026 ● OES: 22105 ● Develops welding techniques, procedures, and application of welding equipment to problems involving fabrication of metals, utilizing knowledge of production specifications, properties and characteristics of metals and metal alloys, and engineering principles: Conducts research and development investigations to develop and test new fabrication processes and procedures, improve existing or develop new welding equipment, develop new or modify current welding methods, techniques, and procedures, discover new patterns of welding phenomena, or to correlate and substanitate hypotheses. Prepares technical reports as result of research and development and preventive maintenance investigations. Establishes welding procedures to guide production and welding personnel relating to specification restrictions, material processes, pre- and post-heating requirements which involve use of complex alloys, unusual fabrication methods, welding of critical joints, and complex postheating requirements. Evaluates new developments in welding field for possible application to current welding problems or production processes. Directs and coordinates technical personnel in performing inspections to ensure workers' compliance with established welding procedures, restrictions, and standards; in testing welds for conformance with national code requirements; or testing welding personnel for certification. Contacts personnel of other agencies, engineering personnel, or clients to exchange ideas, information, or offer technical advice concerning welding matters. May perform experimental welding to evaluate new equipment, techniques, and materials. ● **GED:** R5, M5, L5 ● **SVP:** 4-10 yrs ● **Academic:** Ed=B, Eng=G ● **Work Field:** 244, 251 ● **MPSMS:** 566, 711 ● **Aptitudes:** G1, V1, N1, S2, P2, Q3, K3, F3, M3, E5, C4 ● **Temperaments:** D, J, T, V ● **Physical:** Stg=L; Freq: R, H, I, T, G, N Occas: A ● **Work Env:** Noise=N; ● **Salary:** 4 ● **Outlook:** 3

Mechanical   05

Managerial Works: Mechanical   **05.02**

Workers in this group manage industrial plants or systems where technical work is being performed. Jobs are found in oil fields, power plants, transportation companies, radio and television networks, and telephone and related communications systems.

✓ What kind of work would you do?

Your work activities would depend upon your specific job. For example, you might:

- direct operations of a major generating plant of an electrical power system.
- coordinate engineering, construction, operation, and maintenance activities of a cross-country pipeline.
- direct studies of an existing communications system for a transportation firm and analyze results to plan equipment replacement.
- direct workers who repair and maintain motor transportation equipment to ensure safe and efficient operation.
- analyze machine and tool requisitions to determine whether to make tools in the plant or purchase them.
- inspect landfill sites and operations to plan with supervisory personnel the most efficient way to utilize available space.

✓ What skills and abilities do you need for this kind of work?

To do this kind of work, you must be able to:

- understand technologies required in the work you are directing.
- plan and direct the work of others, either directly or through lower level supervisors.
- work with a variety of situations.
- solve problems, using facts and personal judgment.
- react quickly in emergency situations and make decisions that may involve a great amount of money or the safety of others.
- work with different kinds of people.

✓ How do you know if you would like or could learn to do this kind of work?

The following questions may give you clues about yourself as you consider this group of jobs.

- Have you taken courses in advanced mathematics? Can you understand and work with mathematical concepts?
- Have you taken a physics course? Can you understand and work with the principles of matter and energy?
- Have you collected rocks or minerals as a hobby? Can you identify them?
- Have you owned a chemistry set or microscope? Do you enjoy testing new ideas?
- Have you served in an engineering section of the armed forces?

✓ How can you prepare for and enter this kind of work?

Occupations in this group usually require education and/or training extending from two years to over ten years, depending upon the specific kind of work. College level courses in both management and technical fields are usually required. Most jobs require supervisory experience. Some industries, such as public utilities, offer on-the-job training in management techniques. Seminars in principles of electronic data processing are often a part of this training.

✓ *What else should you consider about these jobs?*

Workers in these jobs must make policy decisions as well as operational decisions. These decisions must conform to the overall company policy and must be made quickly. These workers may have to work overtime without additional pay. However, they often receive benefits such as bonuses, stock options, and profit sharing plans.

Although they spend much of their time in an office doing paper work, they frequently tour work sites. While visiting these sites they observe operation, monitor progress, detect possible problems, and give directions to workers.

These workers are usually specialists and can transfer only to another firm in the same or a related industry.

If you think you would like to do this kind of work, look at the job titles listed below.

■ ■ ■

GOE: 05.02.02
Maintenance & Construction

SUPERINTENDENT, BUILDING (any industry) ● DOT #187.167-190 ● OES: 15011 ● Alternate titles: BUILDING-SERVICE SUPERVISOR; MANAGER, BUILDING. Directs activities of workers engaged in operating and maintaining facilities and equipment in buildings such as apartment houses or office buildings: Inspects facilities and equipment to determine need and extent of service, equipment required, and type and number of operation and maintenance personnel needed. Hires, trains, and supervises building service personnel. Assigns workers to duties such as maintenance, repair, or renovation and obtains bids for additional work from outside contractors. Directs contracted projects to ensure adherence to specifications. Purchases building and maintenance supplies, machinery, equipment, and furniture. Plans and administers building department budget. Compiles records of labor and material cost for operating building and issues cost reports to owner or managing agents. May prepare construction specifications or plans, obtaining advice from engineering consultants, assemble and analyze contract bids, and submit bids and recommendations to superiors for action. ● **GED:** R4, M4, L4 ● **SVP:** 2-4 yrs ● **Academic:** Ed=N, Eng=S ● **Work Field:** 295 ● **MPSMS:** 900 ● **Aptitudes:** G2, V3, N2, S2, P3, Q3, K4, F4, M4, E5, C4 ● **Temperaments:** D, J, P, V ● **Physical:** Stg=L; Freq: R, H, I, T, G, N Occas: F, D, A, X ● **Work Env:** Noise=N; ● **Salary:** 4 ● **Outlook:** 2

SUPERINTENDENT, CONSTRUCTION (construction) ● DOT #182.167-026 ● OES: 15017 ● Alternate titles: SUPERINTENDENT, JOB. Directs activities of workers concerned with construction of buildings, dams, highways, pipelines, or other construction projects: Studies specifications to plan procedures for construction on basis of starting and completion times and staffing requirements for each phase of construction, based on knowledge of available tools and equipment and various building methods. Assembles members of organization (supervisory, clerical, engineering, and other workers) at start of project. Orders procurement of tools and materials to be delivered at specified times to conform to work schedules. Confers with and directs supervisory personnel and subcontractors engaged in planning and executing work procedures, interpreting specifications, and coordinating various phases of construction to prevent delays. Confers with supervisory personnel and labor representatives to resolve complaints and grievances within work force. Confers with supervisory and engineering personnel and inspectors and suppliers of tools and materials to resolve construction problems and improve construction methods. Inspects work in progress to ensure that work conforms to specifications and that construction schedules are adhered to. Prepares, or receives from subordinates, reports on progress, materials used and costs, and adjusts work schedules as indicated by reports. May direct workers concerned with major maintenance or reconditioning projects for existing installations. Workers are usually designated according to type of project, work, or construction activity directed. ● **GED:** R5, M5, L4 ● **SVP:** 2-4 yrs ● **Academic:** Ed=N, Eng=S ● **Work Field:** 295, 102 ● **MPSMS:** 360 ● **Aptitudes:** G2, V3, N2, S2, P3, Q3, K4, F4, M4, E4, C5 ●

Temperaments: D, P, V ● **Physical:** Stg=L; Freq: R, H, I, T, G, N, A Occas: F ● **Work Env:** Noise=N; Freq: W ● **Salary:** 4 ● **Outlook:** 1

GOE: 05.02.03
Processing & Manufacturing

BREWING DIRECTOR (beverage) ● DOT #183.167-010 ● OES: 15014 ● Alternate titles: BREWING SUPERINTENDENT. Develops new or modifies existing brewing formulas and processing techniques and coordinates, through subordinate supervisors, brewing, fermenting, lagering, and malting departments of a brewery: Devises brewing formulas and processes or works in conjunction with research personnel to develop or modify formulas and processes. Directs and coordinates activities of departments to control processing, according to formula specifications. Confers with technical and administrative personnel to resolve formula and process problems. Reviews and analyzes production orders to determine brewing schedules and human resource requirements. Tests and inspects beer, grain, malt, wort, and yeast, using saccharimeter, hydrometer, and other test equipment and correlates results with quality control analyses. Advises and recommends to management methods and procedures for selecting, installing, and maintaining equipment. Reviews and resolves personnel actions. Prepares and submits production reports. May confer with worker's representatives to resolve grievances. ● **GED:** R5, M4, L4 ● **SVP:** 4-10 yrs ● **Academic:** Ed=A, Eng=S ● **Work Field:** 146 ● **MPSMS:** 395 ● **Aptitudes:** G2, V2, N2, S3, P3, Q3, K4, F4, M4, E5, C3 ● **Temperaments:** D, J, P, T ● **Physical:** Stg=L; Freq: R, H, T, G, N, X Occas: I, E, A ● **Work Env:** Noise=N; ● **Salary:** 3 ● **Outlook:** 1

BREWING DIRECTOR (beverage) ● DOT #183.167-010 ● OES: 15014 ● Alternate titles: BREWING SUPERINTENDENT. Develops new or modifies existing brewing formulas and processing techniques and coordinates, through subordinate supervisors, brewing, fermenting, lagering, and malting departments of a brewery: Devises brewing formulas and processes or works in conjunction with research personnel to develop or modify formulas and processes. Directs and coordinates activities of departments to control processing, according to formula specifications. Confers with technical and administrative personnel to resolve formula and process problems. Reviews and analyzes production orders to determine brewing schedules and human resource requirements. Tests and inspects beer, grain, malt, wort, and yeast, using saccharimeter, hydrometer, and other test equipment and correlates results with quality control analyses. Advises and recommends to management methods and procedures for selecting, installing, and maintaining equipment. Reviews and resolves personnel actions. Prepares and submits production reports. May confer with worker's representatives to resolve grievances. ● **GED:** R5, M4, L4 ● **SVP:** 4-10 yrs ● **Academic:** Ed=A, Eng=S ● **Work Field:** 146 ● **MPSMS:** 395 ● **Aptitudes:** G2, V2, N2, S3, P3, Q3, K4, F4, M4, E5, C3 ● **Temperaments:** D, J, P, T ● **Physical:** Stg=L; Freq: R, H, T, G, N, X Occas: I, E, A ● **Work Env:** Noise=N; ● **Salary:** 3 ● **Outlook:** 1

MANAGER, FOOD PROCESSING PLANT (can. & preserv.) ● DOT #183.167-026 ● OES: 15014 ● Directs and coordinates activities of food processing plant: Contacts buyers or growers to arrange for purchasing or harvesting and delivery of agricultural products, seafoods, meat, or other raw materials to plant for processing. Directs, through subordinate supervisory personnel, workers engaged in processing, canning, freezing, storing, and shipping food products. Directs and coordinates activities concerned with dismantling, moving, installing, or repairing of machines and equipment. Approves plant payroll and payments for purchased materials or products. Estimates quantities of foods for processing required and orders foods, materials, supplies, and equipment needed. Hires, transfers, and discharges employees. May provide suppliers with transportation to expedite delivery of purchased products or supplies to plant. May arrange for freezing of packaged products by other food processing plants. May negotiate with suppliers or growers prices to be paid for purchases. ● **GED:** R5, M4, L4 ● **SVP:** 4-10 yrs ● **Academic:** Ed=A, Eng=S ● **Work Field:** 295 ● **MPSMS:** 300, 320, 330 ● **Aptitudes:** G2, V2, N3, S3, P3, Q3, K4, F4, M4, E5, C4 ● **Temperaments:** D, J, P, V ● **Physical:** Stg=L; Freq: R, H, T, G, N Occas: I ● **Work Env:** Noise=N; ● **Salary:** 3 ● **Outlook:** 1

MANAGER, QUALITY CONTROL (profess. & kin.) ● DOT #012.167-014 ● OES: 22128 ● Plans, coordinates, and directs quality control program designed to ensure continuous production of products consistent with established standards: Develops and analyzes statistical data and product specifications to determine present standards and establish proposed quality and reliability expectancy of finished product. Formulates and maintains quality control objectives and coordinates objectives with production procedures in cooperation with other plant managers to maximize product reliability and minimize costs. Directs, through intermediate personnel, workers engaged in inspection and testing activities to ensure continuous control over materials, facilities, and products. Plans, promotes, and organizes training activities related to product quality and reliability. May investigate and adjust customer complaints regarding quality. ● **GED:** R5, M5, L5 ● **SVP:** 4-10 yrs ● **Academic:** Ed=B, Eng=S ● **Work Field:** 211, 244, 295 ● **MPSMS:** 712 ● **Aptitudes:** G1, V1, N2, S2, P3, Q3, K4, F4, M4, E5, C4 ● **Temperaments:** D, J, P, T ● **Physical:** Stg=L; Freq: T, G, N Occas: R, H, I, A, X ● **Work Env:** Noise=L; ● **Salary:** 5 ● **Outlook:** 4

PRODUCTION SUPERINTENDENT (any industry) ● DOT #183.117-014 ● OES: 15014 ● Alternate titles: MANAGER, FACTORY; MANAGER, GENERAL; MANAGER, PLANT; MANAGER, PRODUCTION; PLANT SUPERVISOR; SUPERINTENDENT, FACTORY; SUPERINTENDENT, GENERAL; SUPERINTENDENT, MILL; SUPERINTENDENT, PLANT. Directs and coordinates, through subordinate supervisory personnel, activities concerned with production of company product(s), utilizing knowledge of product technology, production methods and procedures, and capabilities of machines and equipment: Confers with management personnel to establish production and quality control standards, develop budget and cost controls, and to obtain data regarding types, quantities, specifications, and delivery dates of products ordered. Plans and directs production activities and establishes production priorities for products in keeping with effective operations and cost factors. Coordinates production activities with procurement, maintenance, and quality control activities to obtain optimum production and utilization of human resources, machines, and equipment. Reviews and analyzes production, quality control, maintenance, and operational reports to determine causes of nonconformity with product specifications, and operating or production problems. Develops and implements operating methods and procedures designed to eliminate operating problems and improve product quality. Revises production schedules and priorities as result of equipment failure or operating problems. Consults with engineering personnel relative to modification of machines and equipment in order to improve production and quality of products. Conducts hearings to resolve or effect settlement of grievances and refers unresolved grievances for management-union negotiations. Supervises subordinates directly in plants having no GENERAL SUPERVISOR (any industry) 183.167-018. PRODUCTION SUPERINTENDENTS (any industry) 183.117-014 are usually designated according to product produced or by type of plant, industry, or activity. May compile, store, and retrieve production data, using computer. ● **GED:** R5, M4, L4 ● **SVP:** 4-10 yrs ● **Academic:** Ed=H, Eng=S ● **Work Field:** 295 ● **MPSMS:** 712, 893 ● **Aptitudes:** G2, V2, N3, S3, P3, Q3, K4, F4, M4, E5, C5 ● **Tempera-**

ments: D, J, P, V ● **Physical:** Stg=L; Freq: R, H, T, G, N Occas: I, A ● **Work Env:** Noise=N; ● **Salary:** 4 ● **Outlook:** 1

QUALITY-CONTROL COORDINATOR (pharmaceut.) ● DOT #168.167-066 ● OES: 21911 ● Coordinates activities of workers engaged in testing and evaluating ethical and proprietary pharmaceuticals in order to control quality of manufacture and to ensure compliance with legal standards: Participates with management personnel in establishing procedures for testing drugs and related products, applying knowledge of controlled production, sampling techniques, testing procedures, and statistical analysis. Assigns subordinates to specific testing functions. Reviews laboratory reports of test batches. Recommends full-scale production of batches meeting company or consumer specifications and complying with federal purity standards. Orders destruction of substandard batches, as authorized by supervisor. Directs and coordinates investigation of complaints concerning defective products. Recommends response to complaints, considering test reports, production records, legal standards, and complaint validity. Reviews legislative developments to determine changes in legal requirements and probable effects on company's manufacturing activities. Directs retention of data and preparation of documents for use by self or other company personnel during inquiries concerning suspect products. ● **GED:** R4, M4, L4 ● **SVP:** 1-2 yrs ● **Academic:** Ed=A, Eng=S ● **Work Field:** 295, 211 ● **MPSMS:** 493 ● **Aptitudes:** G2, V2, N2, S3, P4, Q3, K4, F4, M4, E5, C4 ● **Temperaments:** D, J, P, T ● **Physical:** Stg=S; Freq: R, H, T, G, N, D, A, X Occas: I ● **Work Env:** Noise=N; ● **Salary:** 4 ● **Outlook:** 3

WINE MAKER (beverage) ● DOT #183.161-014 ● OES: 15014 ● Alternate titles: ENOLOGIST. Directs and coordinates all activities of winery concerned with production of wine: Contracts with growers to provide fruit for processing or cooperates with HORTICULTURIST (profess. & kin.) of company vineyard in grape production. Examines grape samples to ascertain presence and extent of such factors as sugar and acid content, and ripeness. Orders grapes picked when analysis indicates they are at degree of ripeness desired. Coordinates processes and directs workers concerned with testing and crushing grapes, fermenting juice, fortifying, clarifying, aging, and finishing of wine, including cooling, filtering, and bottling. Blends wines according to formulas or knowledge and experience in wine making. May develop new processes to improve product. When processing champagne, may be designated Champagne Maker (beverage). When processing wine into vinegar, is designated Vinegar Maker (beverage). ● **GED:** R5, M3, L4 ● **SVP:** 4-10 yrs ● **Academic:** Ed=A, Eng=S ● **Work Field:** 146 ● **MPSMS:** 395 ● **Aptitudes:** G2, V3, N2, S2, P2, Q3, K3, F3, M3, E4, C3 ● **Temperaments:** D, J, P ● **Physical:** Stg=L; Freq: T, G, N, X Occas: R, H ● **Work Env:** Noise=N; Occas: U ● **Salary:** 4 ● **Outlook:** 1

GOE: 05.02.04
Communications

PROGRAM DIRECTOR, CABLE TELEVISION (radio-tv broad.) ● DOT #194.162-010 ● OES: 15023 ● Alternate titles: PRODUCTION SUPERVISOR. Directs and coordinates activities of workers engaged in selection and production of cable television programs, and operates equipment to film events, and to copy/edit graphics, voice, and music onto videotape: Interviews and hires workers. Instructs workers in operation and maintenance of equipment, such as cameras and microphones, or directs instruction of workers through subordinate personnel. Gives work directives, resolves problems, interprets policies and procedures and prepares work schedules. Initiates disciplinary action for rules infractions and terminates workers. Contacts talent (entertainers) and companies to determine interest in program(s) and interest in supplying prizes to audience participants. Writes script and rehearses script with talent. Coordinates audio work, music, camera work and script to produce show. Operates equipment, such as camera, sound mixer, and videotape deck, to film events, and to edit/copy graphics, voice and music onto videotape. Performs public relations duties, such as contacting school personnel to discuss company's internship program for students, and prepares press releases for newspapers, indicating company trends and direction. Prepares and monitors budget to verify expenditures stay within budgetary restrictions. Prepares forms for government agencies and contract renewal. Prepares invoices and bills customers for services rendered. May operate broadcast equipment to transmit program to viewing audience. ● **GED:** R5, M3, L5 ● **SVP:** 4-10 yrs ● **Academic:** Ed=H, Eng=G ● **Work Field:** 281, 295 ● **MPSMS:** 869 ● **Aptitudes:** G2, V2, N3, S3, P3, Q3, K3, F3, M3, E5, C3 ● **Temperaments:** D, J, P, T, V ● **Physical:** Stg=H; Freq: I, T, G Occas: S, O, R, H, N, F, D, A, X, V ● **Work Env:** Noise=N; ● **Salary:** 3 ● **Outlook:** 2

GOE: 05.02.06
Services

APPLIANCE-SERVICE SUPERVISOR (utilities) ● DOT #187.167-010 ● OES: 81000 ● Alternate titles: ELECTRICAL-APPLIANCE SERVICE SUPERVISOR; MERCHANDISE SUPERVISOR; UTILIZATION SUPERVISOR. Coordinates activities of merchandise-servicing department of gas or electric appliance distributors: Supervises, trains, and assigns duties to workers engaged in servicing appliances, pricing, and disposition of returned merchandise and excess repair parts. Develops company policies and procedures regarding servicing of appliances and disposition of defective parts. Consults manufacturers to obtain advice on unusual service problems and to obtain service instructions and parts catalogs. May write instructions on care and use of appliances for distribution to public. ● **GED:** R4, M4, L4 ● **SVP:** 2-4 yrs ● **Academic:** Ed=H, Eng=S ● **Work Field:** 295 ● **MPSMS:** 880 ● **Aptitudes:** G2, V2, N3, S2, P3, Q3, K4, F4, M4, E5, C4 ● **Temperaments:** D, J, P ● **Physical:** Stg=L; Freq: T, G, N Occas: R, H, I ● **Work Env:** Noise=N; ● **Salary:** 3 ● **Outlook:** 2

MANAGER, LAND SURVEYING (profess. & kin.) ● DOT #018.167-022 ● OES: 13017 ● Plans, directs, and coordinates work of survey parties, and related staff, engaged in surveying earth's surface and preparing reports and legal descriptions of land: Develops organization policy or interprets it to staff. Prepares or approves budget for unit or organization within assigned area of responsibility. Coordinates work of LAND SURVEYOR (profess. & kin.) with that of legal, engineering, architectural, and other staff on project. Directs survey parties and projects, and reviews and certifies completed work to satisfy legal requirements. Writes or directs the writing of descriptions of land to satisfy legal requirements according to standard surveying practices. Appears as expert witness in court in cases involving land or boundary disputes. Monitors new technology, and evaluates and purchases or authorizes purchase of new equipment and supplies. Selects new staff for employment and takes disciplinary action when necessary. Assumes legal responsibility for work performed and is licensed by state. ● **GED:** R5, M5, L4 ● **SVP:** 4-10 yrs ● **Academic:** Ed=A, Eng=G ● **Work Field:** 295, 243 ● **MPSMS:** 716 ● **Aptitudes:** G2, V2, N2, S2, P2, Q3, K3, F3, M3, E3, C3 ● **Temperaments:** D, I, J ● **Physical:** Stg=L; Freq: R, H, I, T, G, N Occas: F, D, X ● **Work Env:** Noise=N; Occas: W ● **Salary:** 5 ● **Outlook:** 2

GOE: 05.02.07
Materials Handling

MANAGER, MARINA DRY DOCK (amuse. & rec.) ● DOT #187.167-226 ● OES: 19998 ● Directs and coordinates dry docking activities at marina: Administers affairs of department, such as planning and coordinating work schedules, assigning storage crib for each boat, and maintaining department budget. Directs workers in maintenance of boats and trailers, such as painting or washing boats, lubricating and repairing motors, and retrofitting trailers and cars with lights and turn signals. Monitors fuel dock operation to ensure services to patrons. Operates, or supervises workers operating, equipment to lift boats from water and transport and dry dock boats, using crane or forklift. Hires, orients, and trains personnel in job duties, safety practices, employer policy, and performance requirements. ● **GED:** R4, M3, L3 ● **SVP:** 1-2 yrs ● **Academic:** Ed=H, Eng=G ● **Work Field:** 295 ● **MPSMS:** 854, 593 ● **Aptitudes:** G2, V2, N3, S3, P4, Q3, K3, F4, M2, E3, C5 ● **Temperaments:** D, J, P, V ● **Physical:** Stg=H; Freq: R, H, I, T, G, N ● **Work Env:** Noise=N; ● **Salary:** 3 ● **Outlook:** 3

Mechanical   05

Engineering Technology   05.03

Workers in this group collect, record, and coordinate technical information in such activities as surveying, drafting, petroleum production, communications control, and materials scheduling. Workers find jobs in construction, factories, engineering and architectural firms, airports, and research laboratories.

✓ *What kind of work would you do?*

Your work activities would depend upon your specific job. For example, you might:

■ use astronomical observations, complex computations, and other techniques to compile data for preparing geodetic maps and charts.

■ organize and direct the work of surveying parties to determine precise location and measurement points.

■ use drafting instruments to prepare detailed drawings and blueprints for manufacturing electronic equipment.

■ prepare detailed working drawings of mechanical devices showing dimensions, tolerances, and other engineering data.

■ analyze survey data, source maps, and other records to draw detailed maps to scale.

■ provide meteorological, navigational, and other technical information to pilots.

■ direct activities of workers who set up seismographic recording instruments and gather data about oil-bearing rock layers.

✓ *What skills and abilities do you need for this kind of work?*

To do this kind of work, you must be able to:

■ use geometry and other kinds of higher mathematics.

■ use clear language to write technical reports.

■ perform detail work with great accuracy.

■ use fingers skillfully when making drawings.

■ make finger and hand movements correspond with seeing to operate equipment, adjust instruments, use pen to make sketches, or use measuring tools.

- make decisions quickly according to both personal judgment and facts.
- direct activities of workers who set up seismographic recording instruments and gather data about oil-bearing rock layers.
- perform under stress in emergency situations.

✓ How do you know if you would like or could learn to do this kind of work?

The following questions may give you clues about yourself as you consider this group of jobs.

- Have you taken courses in mechanical drawing? Do you enjoy this type of activity?
- Have you taken courses in geometry and advanced math? Do you like math studies?
- Have you made models of airplanes or cars following detailed plans? Can you follow such instructions easily?
- Have you taken courses in physics or chemistry? Can you work with formulas?
- Have you served in an engineering unit in the armed forces? Did you like the work involved?

✓ How can you prepare for and enter this kind of work?

Occupations in this group usually require education and/or training extending from two years to over ten years, depending upon the specific kind of work. The most common way of preparing for this kind of work is through related post high school courses, on-the-job training, and work experience.

Many technical and vocational schools, and community colleges offer programs in surveying. With some classroom instruction in surveying, beginners can start as instrument workers. After gaining experience, they may advance to supervisory positions, and may later apply for positions as registered surveyors. Advancement may be based on written examinations as well as experience. High school graduates with no formal training usually start by assisting instrument workers.

Basic preparation for jobs in drafting include high school level courses in mathematics, physical sciences, industrial arts, and mechanical drawing. Technical school courses in structural design and layout provide the knowledge and skills needed for advanced drafting jobs. A three- to four-year apprenticeship program is another method for entering drafting work. This program offers workers the advantages of classroom instruction and on-the-job training while they earn regular wages.

College courses in business administration or industrial engineering provide the most common preparation for jobs in production and material coordination. People with a high school education and work experience in a production firm may be admitted to on-the-job training programs. High school studies should include commercial courses, industrial arts, and bookkeeping or accounting. English courses are also important because they develop oral and written communications skills.

Technicians usually begin work as trainees in routine jobs under close supervision of an experienced technician or engineer. As they gain experience, they move up to jobs requiring less supervision. With additional training and experience, technicians may advance to supervisory or professional engineering positions.

✓ What else should you consider about these jobs?

Surveyors usually have a 40-hour work week. They sometimes work longer hours during the summer months. Most surveying work is done outdoors in all types of weather. However, workers usually prepare reports and draw maps in an office setting. Surveyors are exposed to hazards from moving machinery and falling objects on construction projects. There is danger from passing cars when surveying on or near highways. Some surveying work requires traveling to distant job sites or camping out at the site.

Drafters may have to buy some of their own equipment. However, most companies supply them with the equipment they need. They generally work in comfortable, well-lighted, air conditioned offices. They sometimes visit work sites such as factories or construction projects. At times they may work under pressure to meet deadlines.

If you think you would like this kind of work, look at the job titles listed below.

■ ■ ■

GOE: 05.03.01
Surveying

NAVIGATOR (air trans.) ● DOT #196.167-014 ● OES: 97702 ● Alternate titles: AERIAL NAVIGATOR; AIRPLANE NAVIGATOR. Locates position and directs course of airplane on international flights, using navigational aids, such as charts, maps, sextant, and slide rule:

Establishes position of airplane by use of navigation instruments and charts, celestial observation, or dead reckoning. Directs deviations from course required by weather conditions, such as wind drifts and forecasted atmospheric changes. Utilizes navigation aids, such as radio beams and beacons, when available. Keeps log of flight. Must be licensed by Federal Aviation Administration. ● **GED:** R5, M5, L4 ● **SVP:** 1-2 yrs ● **Academic:** Ed=A, Eng=G ● **Work Field:** 243 ● **MPSMS:** 719 ● **Aptitudes:** G2, V3, N2, S2, P2, Q2, K3, F4, M3, E4, C4 ● **Temperaments:** J, S, T, V ● **Physical:** Stg=S; Freq: R, H, I, N, A Occas: X ● **Work Env:** Noise=L; ● **Salary:** 4 ● **Outlook:** 3

PHOTOGRAMMETRIC ENGINEER (profess. & kin.) ● DOT #018.167-026 ● OES: 22310 ● Plans, coordinates, and directs activities of workers concerned with conducting aerial surveys and preparing topographic materials from aerial photographs and other data: Analyzes survey objectives and specifications, utilizing knowledge of survey uses, such as municipal and ecological planning, property and utility mapping, and petroleum and mineral exploration. Selects most appropriate and economical survey methods, using knowledge of capabilities of aerial photography and applications of remote sensing (imagery through electronic scanning). Estimates cost of survey. Advises customers and department supervisors regarding flights for aerial photography and plans for ground surveys designed to establish base lines, elevations, and other geodetic measurements. Prepares charts and tables for aerial navigation, to specify flight path, altitude, and airspeed of camera-carrying aircraft. Computes geodetic measurements and interprets survey data from ground or aerial photographs or remote-sensing images to determine position, shape, and elevation of geomorphic and topographic features. Conducts research in surveying and mapping methods and procedures, using knowledge of techniques of photogrammetric map compilation, electronic data processing, and flight and control planning. May direct one or more phases of technical operations concerned with preparing survey proposals, negotiating with clients, scheduling activities, conducting surveys, processing data, reviewing work quality, and training and assigning personnel. ● GED: R6, M6, L5 ● SVP: 4-10 yrs ● Academic: Ed=B, Eng=S ● Work Field: 243, 244 ● MPSMS: 716, 719 ● Aptitudes: G2, V2, N2, S1, P1, Q2, K3, F3, M3, E5, C3 ● Temperaments: D, J, P, V ● Physical: Stg=S; Const: H, I, N Freq: R, T, G, D, A Occas: X ● Work Env: Noise=Q; ● Salary: 4 ● Outlook: 4

SURVEYOR ASSISTANT, INSTRUMENTS (profess. & kin.) ● DOT #018.167-034 ● OES: 22310 ● Obtains data pertaining to angles, elevations, points, and coutours used for construction, map making, mining, or other purposes, using alidade, level, transit, plane table, Theodolite, electronic distance measuring equipment, and other surveying instruments. Compiles notes, sketches, and records of data obtained and work performed. Directs work of subordinate members of survey team. Performs other duties relating to surveying work as directed by CHIEF OF PARTY (profess. & kin.). ● GED: R5, M5, L4 ● SVP: 2-4 yrs ● Academic: Ed=A, Eng=S ● Work Field: 243 ● MPSMS: 716 ● Aptitudes: G2, V3, N2, S2, P2, Q3, K3, F3, M3, E3, C3 ● Temperaments: D, J, T ● Physical: Stg=L; Freq: R, H, I, T, G, N, F, D ● Work Env: Noise=N; Freq: W ● Salary: 3 ● Outlook: 3

GOE: 05.03.02
Drafting

AUTO-DESIGN CHECKER (auto. mfg.) ● DOT #017.261-010 ● OES: 35199 ● Alternate titles: CHECKER, PRODUCT DESIGN. Examines detail, layout, and master drawings of either auto-body or chassis parts, assemblies, and systems, for practicality of design, accuracy of mathematical calculations, dimensional accuracy, projection, and conformity to specifications and standards, using computerized work aids. Applies knowlege of auto-body and chassis design, methods of manufacture and assembly, and drafting techniques and procedures. Discusses necessary changes with staff members and coordinates corrections. ● GED: R5, M4, L4 ● SVP: 4-10 yrs ● Academic: Ed=A, Eng=S ● Work Field: 242 ● MPSMS: 706 ● Aptitudes: G2, V2, N2, S1, P2, Q2, K2, F3, M3, E5, C4 ● Temperaments: J, T ● Physical: Stg=L; Freq: R, H, I, N, A, X Occas: T, G ● Work Env: Noise=Q; ● Salary: 4 ● Outlook: 3

AUTO-DESIGN DETAILER (auto. mfg.) ● DOT #017.281-010 ● OES: 22512 ● Drafts full-size or scale detail drawings of either auto-body or chassis parts and assemblies from specifications, master drawings, layouts, models, prototypes, sketches, or verbal instructions, for engineering and manufacturing purposes [DRAFTER (profess. & kin.) Master Title], applying knowledge of auto-body or chassis structure and methods of manufacture and assembly. ● GED: R4, M4, L3 ● SVP: 1-2 yrs ● Academic: Ed=A, Eng=S ● Work Field: 242 ● MPSMS: 706 ● Aptitudes: G2, V2, N2, S1, P2, Q2, K2, F3, M3, E5, C4 ● Temperaments: J, T ● Physical: Stg=L; Freq: R, H, I, N, A Occas: X ● Work Env: Noise=Q; ● Salary: 3 ● Outlook: 3

CIVIL ENGINEERING TECHNICIAN (profess. & kin.) ● DOT #005.261-014 ● OES: 35199 ● Assists CIVIL ENGINEER (profess. & kin.) 005.061-014 in application of principles, methods, and techniques of civil engineering technology: Reviews project specifications and confers with CIVIL ENGINEER (profess. & kin.) concerning assistance required, such as plan preparation, acceptance testing, evaluation of field conditions, design changes, and reports. Conducts materials testing and analysis, using tools and equipment and applying engineering knowledge necessary to conduct tests. Prepares reports detailing tests conducted and results. Surveys project sites to obtain and analyze topographical details of sites, using maps and surveying equipment. Drafts detailed dimensional drawings, such as those needed for highway plans, structural steel fabrication, and water control projects, performing duties as described under DRAFTER (profess. & kin.) Master Title. Calculates dimensions, profile specifications, and quantities of materials such as steel, concrete, and asphalt, using calculator. Inspects construction site to determine conformance of site to design specifications. May assist engineers to ensure that construction and repair of water and wastewater treatment systems meet pollution control requirements. ● GED: R4, M4, L4 ● SVP: 2-4 yrs ● Academic: Ed=A, Eng=S ● Work Field: 242, 244, 243 ● MPSMS: 704 ● Aptitudes: G2, V2, N2, S2, P2, Q2, K2, F2, M3, E5, C4 ● Temperaments: J, T, V ● Physical: Stg=L; Freq: R, H, I, T, G, N, A Occas: D, X ● Work Env: Noise=N; ● Salary: 4 ● Outlook: 4

CONTROLS DESIGNER (profess. & kin.) ● DOT #003.261-014 ● OES: 22512 ● Alternate titles: CONTROLS PROJECT ENGINEER. Designs and drafts systems of electrical, hydraulic, and pneumatic controls for machines and equipment, such as arc welders, robots, conveyors, and programmable controllers, applying knowledge of electricity, electronics, hydraulics, and pneumatics: Discusses project with SUPERVISOR (any industry) Master Title and APPLICATIONS ENGINEER, MANUFACTURING (profess. & kin.) 007.061-038 to review functions of machines and equipment. Designs and drafts arrangement of linkage of conductors, relays, and other components of electrical, electronic, hydraulic, pneumatic, and lubrication devices, using drafting tools, and applying knowledge of electrical engineering and drafting [DRAFTER (profess. & kin.) Master Title]. Diagrams logic system for functions such as sequence and timing control. Designs and drafts diagrams of cable connection for robots, robot end-of-arm tool, robot controller, and other machines. Illustrates and describes installation and maintenance details, such as where bearings should be lubricated, types of lubrication, and which parts are lubricated automatically and manually. Confers with ASSEMBLER AND WIRER, INDUSTRIAL EQUIPMENT (elec. equip.; machinery mfg.) 826.361-010 to resolve problems regarding building of controls systems. Reviews schematics with customer's representatives to answer questions during installation of robot systems. Observes gauges during trial run of programmed machine and equipment operation to verify that electrical signals in system conform to specifications. May design controls for energy conversion or other industrial plant monitoring systems. May use computer and software programs to produce design drawings and be designated Controls Designer, Computer-Assisted (profess. & kin.). ● GED: R5, M4, L4 ● SVP: 4-10 yrs ● Academic: Ed=B, Eng=S ● Work Field: 242, 244, 264 ● MPSMS: 719 ● Aptitudes: G2, V2, N2, S2, P2, Q1, K2, F3, M3, E5, C5 ● Temperaments: J, T ● Physical: Stg=S; Freq: R, H, N Occas: I, T, G, F, D ● Work Env: Noise=N; ● Salary: 5 ● Outlook: 4

DESIGN TECHNICIAN, COMPUTER-AIDED (electron. comp.) ● DOT #003.362-010 ● OES: 35199 ● Alternate titles: DIGITIZER. Operates computer-aided design (CAD) system and peripheral equipment to resize or modify integrated circuit designs (artwork) and to generate computer tape of artwork for use in producing mask plates used in manufacturing integrated circuits: Reviews work order and procedural manuals to determine critical dimensions of design. Calculates figures to convert design dimensions to resizing dimensions specified for subsequent production processes, using conversion chart and calculator. Locates file relating to specified design projection data base library and loads program into computer. Enters specified commands into computer, using keyboard, to retrieve design information from file and display design on CAD equipment display screen. Types commands on keyboard to enter resizing specifications into computer. Confers with engineering and design staff to determine design modifications and enters editing information into computer. Keys in specified information, using keyboard connected to on-line or off-line peripheral equipment (plotter), to produce graphic representation (hard copy) of design for review and approval by engineering and design staff. Enters specified information into computer, using keyboard, to generate computer tape of approved design. ● **GED:** R3, M3, L3 ● **SVP:** 6 mos-1 yr ● **Academic:** Ed=H, Eng=S ● **Work Field:** 233, 264 ● **MPSMS:** 703 ● **Aptitudes:** G2, V3, N3, S2, P2, Q2, K2, F3, M3, E5, C5 ● **Temperaments:** J, T ● **Physical:** Stg=L; Freq: R, I, N Occas: H, T, G, D ● **Work Env:** Noise=L; ● **Salary:** 3 ● **Outlook:** 4

DESIGN DRAFTER, ELECTROMECHANISMS (profess. & kin.) ● DOT #017.261-014 ● OES: 22512 ● Drafts designs of electromechanical equipment such as aircraft engine subassemblies, electronic optical-character-recognition and related data processing systems, gyroscopes, rocket engine control systems, automatic materials handling and processing machinery, or bio-medical equipment: Confers with engineers and other drafters to interpret design concepts, determine nature and type of required detailed working drawings, and coordinate work with others. Drafts detail and assembly drawings performing duties described under DRAFTER (profess. & kin.) Master Title. Compiles data, computes quantities, determines materials needed, and prepares cost estimates. ● **GED:** R5, M5, L4 ● **SVP:** 2-4 yrs ● **Academic:** Ed=A, Eng=S ● **Work Field:** 244, 242 ● **MPSMS:** 703, 706 ● **Aptitudes:** G2, V3, N2, S2, P2, Q3, K2, F2, M3, E5, C4 ● **Temperaments:** J, T ● **Physical:** Stg=S; Const: H, I, N Freq: R, T, G, A Occas: D, X ● **Work Env:** Noise=Q; ● **Salary:** 4 ● **Outlook:** 3

DETAILER (profess. & kin.) ● DOT #017.261-018 ● OES: 22512 ● Drafts detailed drawings of parts of machines or structures from rough or general design drawings: Shows dimensions, material to be used, and other information necessary to make detailed drawing clear and complete. Makes tracing of finished drawing on semitransparent paper from which blueprints can be made. Performs other duties as described under DRAFTER (profess. & kin.) Master Title. May specialize in preparing detail drawings for specific type of machine, structure, or product. ● **GED:** R4, M4, L4 ● **SVP:** 2-4 yrs ● **Academic:** Ed=A, Eng=S ● **Work Field:** 242 ● **MPSMS:** 700 ● **Aptitudes:** G2, V2, N2, S2, P2, Q3, K3, F2, M2, E5, C5 ● **Temperaments:** J, V ● **Physical:** Stg=S; Const: H, I, N Freq: R, A Occas: D, X ● **Work Env:** Noise=Q; ● **Salary:** 4 ● **Outlook:** 3

DRAFTER, AERONAUTICAL (aircraft mfg.) ● DOT #002.261-010 ● OES: 22512 ● Drafts engineering drawings of developmental or production airplanes, missiles, and component and ancillary equipment, including launch mechanisms and scale models of prototype aircraft, as planned by AERONAUTICAL ENGINEER (aircraft mfg.) 002.061-014. Performs other duties as described under DRAFTER (profess. & kin.) Master Title. ● **GED:** R5, M5, L4 ● **SVP:** 2-4 yrs ● **Academic:** Ed=A, Eng=S ● **Work Field:** 242, 244 ● **MPSMS:** 702 ● **Aptitudes:** G2, V3, N2, S2, P2, Q2, K2, F3, M3, E5, C4 ● **Temperaments:** T ● **Physical:** Stg=S; Freq: R, I, N, A, X Occas: H, T, G ● **Work Env:** Noise=Q; ● **Salary:** 4 ● **Outlook:** 3

DRAFTER, ARCHITECTURAL (profess. & kin.) ● DOT #001.261-010 ● OES: 22512 ● Prepares detailed drawings of architectural designs and plans for buildings, according to specifications, sketches, and rough drafts provided by ARCHITECT (profess. & kin.) 001.061-010: Draws rough and detailed sketches, drawings, and plans to scale [DRAFTER (profess. & kin.) Master Title]. ● **GED:** R4, M4, L4 ● **SVP:** 2-4 yrs ● **Academic:** Ed=A, Eng=S ● **Work Field:** 242 ● **MPSMS:** 701 ● **Aptitudes:** G2, V3, N2, S2, P2, Q2, K2, F2, M3, E5, C4 ● **Temperaments:** J, T ● **Physical:** Stg=S; Const: R, H, I, N Freq: D Occas: T, G, X ● **Work Env:** Noise=Q; ● **Salary:** 4 ● **Outlook:** 3

DRAFTER, ASSISTANT (profess. & kin.) ● DOT #017.281-018 ● OES: 22512 ● Copies plans and drawings prepared by DRAFTER (profess. & kin.) Master Title by tracing them with ink and pencil on transparent paper or cloth spread over drawings, using triangle, T-square, compass, pens, and other drafting instruments. Makes simple sketches or drawings under close supervision. ● **GED:** R4, M4, L3 ● **SVP:** 2-4 yrs ● **Academic:** Ed=H, Eng=S ● **Work Field:** 242 ● **MPSMS:** 700 ● **Aptitudes:** G3, V4, N3, S3, P3, Q3, K3, F3, M3, E5, C4 ● **Temperaments:** J, T ● **Physical:** Stg=S; Const: N, A Freq: R, H, I ● **Work Env:** Noise=Q; ● **Salary:** 3 ● **Outlook:** 2

DRAFTER, AUTOMOTIVE DESIGN (auto. mfg.) ● DOT #017.261-042 ● OES: 22512 ● Designs and drafts working layouts and master drawings of automotive vehicle components, assemblies, and systems from specifications, sketches, models, prototype or verbal instructions, applying knowledge of automotive vehicle design, engineering principles, manufacturing processes and limitations, and conventional and computer drafting techniques and procedures, using drafting instruments and computerized work aids: Analyzes specifications, sketches, engineering drawings, ideas and related design data to determine critical factors affecting design of components based on knowledge of previous designs and manufacturing processes and limitations. Draws rough sketches and performs mathematical computations to develop design and work out detailed specifications of components. Applies knowledge of mathematical formulas and physical laws and uses conventional and computerized work aids to make calculations. Performs preliminary and advanced work in development of working layouts and final master drawings adequate for detailing parts and units of design. Makes revisions to size, shape and arrangement of parts to create practical design. Confers with AUTOMOTIVE ENGINEER (auto. mfg.) 007.061-010 and others on staff to resolve design problems. Specializes in design of specific type of body or chassis components, assemblies or systems, such as door panels, chassis frame and supports, or braking system. ● **GED:** R5, M4, L4 ● **SVP:** 2-4 yrs ● **Academic:** Ed=A, Eng=S ● **Work Field:** 242, 244 ● **MPSMS:** 706 ● **Aptitudes:** G2, V2, N2, S1, P2, Q2, K2, F3, M3, E5, C4 ● **Temperaments:** J, T ● **Physical:** Stg=L; Freq: R, H, I, N, A Occas: T, G, X ● **Work Env:** Noise=Q; ● **Salary:** 4 ● **Outlook:** 3

DRAFTER, AUTOMOTIVE DESIGN LAYOUT (auto. mfg.) ● DOT #017.281-026 ● OES: 22512 ● Prepares working layouts and master drawings of automotive vehicle components, assemblies, or systems from specifications, prior layouts, well-defined sketches, models or verbal instructions sufficient for detailing, applying knowledge of conventional and computerized drafting techniques and procedures, automotive vehicle design, manufacturing processes and limitations, using conventional drafting instruments and computerized work aids: Studies specifications, sketches, notes, and other design data and measures prior layouts, using scales and dividers, to determine details and dimensions of components being laid out from superimposed views and sections of parts on layouts. Lays out on vellum major or minor components, assemblies, or systems in full-scale working layouts. Performs mathematical calculations to work out detailed additions to specifications, applying knowledge of mathematical formulas, using slide rule or digital calculators. Develops design of details not completely defined. Projects sections and auxiliary views of components on layouts. Makes corrections, revisions, and changes to layouts as directed by AUTO-DESIGN CHECKER (auto. mfg.) 017.261-010 or DRAFTER, AUTOMOTIVE DESIGN (auto. mfg.) 017.261-042. Drafts master drawing of approved design on mylar, aluminum, or other materials. Specializes in laying out specific type of body or chassis components, assemblies, or systems. Coordinates and works in conjunction with other workers designing, laying out, or detailing same or related structures. May direct activities of detailers. ● **GED:** R4, M4, L3 ● **SVP:** 2-4 yrs ● **Academic:** Ed=A, Eng=G ● **Work Field:** 244, 242 ● **MPSMS:** 706 ● **Aptitudes:** G2, V2, N2, S1, P1, Q3, K2, F2, M2, E5, C4 ● **Temperaments:** J, T ● **Physical:** Stg=L; Freq: R, H, I, N, A, X ● **Work Env:** Noise=Q; ● **Salary:** 4 ● **Outlook:** 3

DRAFTER, CARTOGRAPHIC (profess. & kin.) ● DOT #018.261-010 ● OES: 22310 ● Alternate titles: MAP MAKER; MAPPER. Draws maps of geographical areas to show natural and constructed features, political boundaries, and other features, performing duties described under DRAFTER (profess. & kin.) Master Title: Analyzes survey data, source maps and photographs, computer or automated mapping products, and other records to determine location and names of features. Studies legal records to establish boundries of properties, and local, national, and international areas of political, economic, social, or other significance. Geological maps are drawn by DRAFTER, GEOLOGICAL (petrol. & gas). ● **GED:** R4, M4, L3 ● **SVP:** 2-4 yrs ● **Academic:** Ed=A, Eng=S ● **Work Field:** 242 ● **MPSMS:** 716 ● **Aptitudes:** G2, V3, N2, S2, P2, Q2, K2, F2, M3, E5, C3 ● **Temperaments:** J, T ● **Physical:** Stg=S; Const: N, F, D, A Freq: R, H, I, X ● **Work Env:** Noise=Q; ● **Salary:** 3 ● **Outlook:** 3

DRAFTER, COMMERCIAL (profess. & kin.) ● DOT #017.261-026 ● OES: 22512 ● Performs general duties of DRAFTER (profess. & kin.) Master Title in all-round drafting, such as laying out location of buildings, planning of arrangements in offices, large rooms, store buildings, and factories, and drawing of charts, forms, and records.

Paints and washes colored drawings when required. ● **GED:** R5, M5, L4 ● **SVP:** 1-2 yrs ● **Academic:** Ed=A, Eng=S ● **Work Field:** 242 ● **MPSMS:** 700 ● **Aptitudes:** G2, V3, N2, S2, P2, Q3, K2, F2, M3, E5, C3 ● **Temperaments:** J, T ● **Physical:** Stg=S; Freq: R, H, I, N, F, D, A, X ● **Work Env:** Noise=N; ● **Salary:** 3 ● **Outlook:** 3

DRAFTER, CIVIL (profess. & kin.) ● DOT #005.281-010 ● OES: 22512 ● Alternate titles: DRAFTER, CIVIL ENGINEERING; DRAFTER, CONSTRUCTION; DRAFTER, ENGINEERING. Drafts detailed construction drawings, topographical profiles, and related maps and specifications used in planning and construction of civil engineering projects, such as highways, river and harbor improvements, flood control, and drainage: Reviews rough sketches, drawings, specifications, and other engineering data received from CIVIL ENGINEER (profess. & kin.) \$I20005.061-014. Plots maps and charts showing profiles and cross-sections, indicating relation of topographical contours and elevations to buildings, retaining walls, tunnels, overhead power lines, and other structures. Drafts detailed drawings of structures and installations, such as roads, culverts, fresh water supply, sewage disposal systems, dikes, wharfs, and breakwaters. Computes volume of tonnage of excavations and fills and prepares graphs and hauling diagrams used in earthmoving operations. Performs other duties as described under DRAFTER (profess. & kin.) Master Title. May accompany survey crew in field to locate grading markers or to collect data required for revision of construction drawings. May specialize in drafting and modifying topographical maps from surveying notes and aerial photographs and be designated Drafter, Topographical (profess. & kin.). May use computer-assisted drafting (CAD) equipment and software and be designated Drafter, Civil (CAD) (profess. & kin.). ● **GED:** R4, M4, L4 ● **SVP:** 2-4 yrs ● **Academic:** Ed=A, Eng=S ● **Work Field:** 242 ● **MPSMS:** 704, 716 ● **Aptitudes:** G2, V3, N2, S2, P2, Q3, K3, F3, M3, E5, C4 ● **Temperaments:** J, T ● **Physical:** Stg=S; Freq: H, I, N Occas: R, D, A, X ● **Work Env:** Noise=Q; ● **Salary:** 4 ● **Outlook:** 3

DRAFTER, ELECTRICAL (profess. & kin.) ● DOT #003.281-010 ● OES: 22512 ● Drafts electrical equipment working drawings and wiring diagrams used by construction crews and repairers who erect, install, and repair electrical equipment and wiring in communications centers, power plants, industrial establishments, commercial or domestic buildings, or electrical distribution systems, performing duties as described under DRAFTER (profess. & kin.) Master Title. May use computer-assisted drafting (CAD) equipment and software and be designated Drafter (CAD), Electrical (profess. & kin.). May prepare detail cable layout and diagrams for cable installation and be designated Electric-Cable Diagrammer (elec. equip.). ● **GED:** R5, M5, L4 ● **SVP:** 2-4 yrs ● **Academic:** Ed=A, Eng=S ● **Work Field:** 242 ● **MPSMS:** 703 ● **Aptitudes:** G2, V3, N2, S2, P2, Q2, K4, F3, M4, E5, C4 ● **Temperaments:** J, T ● **Physical:** Stg=S; Freq: R, H, I, N Occas: T, G, X ● **Work Env:** Noise=N; ● **Salary:** 4 ● **Outlook:** 4

DRAFTER, ELECTRONIC (profess. & kin.) ● DOT #003.281-014 ● OES: 22512 ● Alternate titles: DRAFTER, ELECTROMECHANI-CAL. Drafts detailed drawings, such as wiring diagrams, layout drawings, mechanical detail drawings, and drawings of intermediate and final assemblies, used in manufacture, assembly, installation, and repair of electronic components, printed circuit boards, and equipment. Examines electronic schematics and supporting documents received from design engineering department to develop, compute, and verify specifications drafting data, such as configuration of parts, dimensions, and tolerances. Performs duties as described under DRAFTER (profess. & kin.) Master Title. May use computer-assisted drafting (CAD) equipment and software and be designated Drafter (CAD), Electronic (profess. & kin.). ● **GED:** R5, M5, L4 ● **SVP:** 2-4 yrs ● **Academic:** Ed=A, Eng=S ● **Work Field:** 242 ● **MPSMS:** 703 ● **Aptitudes:** G2, V3, N2, S2, P2, Q2, K4, F3, M4, E5, C4 ● **Temperaments:** J, T ● **Physical:** Stg=S; Const: N Freq: R, H, I, D, A, X ● **Work Env:** Noise=Q; ● **Salary:** 4 ● **Outlook:** 4

DRAFTER, GEOLOGICAL (petrol. & gas) ● DOT #010.281-014 ● OES: 22512 ● Draws maps, diagrams, profiles, cross sections, directional surveys, and subsurface formations to represent geological or geophysical stratigraphy and locations of gas and oil deposits, performing duties as described under DRAFTER (profess. & kin.) Master Title: Correlates and interprets data obtained from topographical surveys, well logs, or geophysical prospecting reports, utilizing special symbols to denote geological and geophysical formations or oil field

installations. May finish drawings in mediums and according to specifications required for reproduction by blueprinting, photographing, or other duplication methods. ● **GED:** R5, M5, L4 ● **SVP:** 1-2 yrs ● **Academic:** Ed=A, Eng=S ● **Work Field:** 242 ● **MPSMS:** 708 ● **Aptitudes:** G2, V3, N2, S1, P2, Q2, K2, F3, M3, E5, C5 ● **Temperaments:** J, T, V ● **Physical:** Stg=S; Freq: R, H, I, N ● **Work Env:** Noise=N; ● **Salary:** 3 ● **Outlook:** 2

DRAFTER, GEOPHYSICAL (petrol. & gas) ● DOT #010.281-018 ● OES: 22512 ● Draws subsurface contours in rock formations from data obtained by geophysical prospecting party. Plots maps and diagrams from computations based on recordings of seismograph, gravity meter, magnetometer, and other petroleum prospecting instruments and from prospecting and surveying field notes. Performs other duties as described under DRAFTER (profess. & kin.) Master Title. May be designated according to method of prospecting as Drafter, Seismograph (petrol. & gas). ● **GED:** R5, M5, L5 ● **SVP:** 2-4 yrs ● **Academic:** Ed=A, Eng=S ● **Work Field:** 242 ● **MPSMS:** 708 ● **Aptitudes:** G2, V3, N2, S1, P2, Q3, K2, F3, M2, E5, C5 ● **Temperaments:** J, T, V ● **Physical:** Stg=L; Freq: R, H, I, N ● **Work Env:** Noise=N; ● **Salary:** 4 ● **Outlook:** 4

DRAFTER, LANDSCAPE (profess. & kin.) ● DOT #001.261-014 ● OES: 22512 ● Prepares detailed scale drawings and tracings from rough sketches or other data provided by LANDSCAPE ARCHITECT (profess. & kin.), performing duties described under DRAFTER (profess. & kin.) Master Title. May prepare separate detailed site plan, grading and drainage plan, lighting plan, paving plan, irrigation plan, planting plan, and drawings and detail of garden structures. May build models of proposed landscape construction and prepare colored drawings for presentation to client. ● **GED:** R4, M4, L3 ● **SVP:** 2-4 yrs ● **Academic:** Ed=A, Eng=S ● **Work Field:** 242 ● **MPSMS:** 719 ● **Aptitudes:** G2, V3, N2, S2, P2, Q2, K2, F2, M3, E5, C3 ● **Temperaments:** J, T ● **Physical:** Stg=S; Const: R, H, I, N Freq: D, A Occas: X ● **Work Env:** Noise=Q; ● **Salary:** 3 ● **Outlook:** 3

DRAFTER, MARINE (profess. & kin.) ● DOT #014.281-010 ● OES: 22512 ● Draws structural and mechanical features of ships, docks, and other marine structures and equipment, performing duties of DRAFTER (profess. & kin.) Master Title. Works from general design drawings and notes made by ARCHITECT, MARINE (profess. & kin.) or MARINE ENGINEER (profess. & kin.). ● **GED:** R5, M5, L4 ● **SVP:** 2-4 yrs ● **Academic:** Ed=A, Eng=S ● **Work Field:** 242 ● **MPSMS:** 714 ● **Aptitudes:** G2, V3, N2, S2, P2, Q3, K2, F2, M3, E5, C4 ● **Temperaments:** J, T ● **Physical:** Stg=S; Freq: R, H, N, D ● **Work Env:** Noise=N; ● **Salary:** 4 ● **Outlook:** 2

DRAFTER, MECHANICAL (profess. & kin.) ● DOT #007.281-010 ● OES: 22512 ● Alternate titles: DRAFTER, ENGINEERING. Drafts detailed drawings of machinery and mechanical devices, indicating dimensions and tolerances, fasteners and joining requirements, and other engineering data: Reviews rough sketches and engineering specifications received from engineer or architect. Drafts multiple-view assembly, subassembly, and layout drawings as required for manufacture and repair of machines and equipment. Performs other duties as described under DRAFTER (profess. & kin.) Master Title. ● **GED:** R5, M5, L5 ● **SVP:** 2-4 yrs ● **Academic:** Ed=A, Eng=S ● **Work Field:** 242 ● **MPSMS:** 706 ● **Aptitudes:** G2, V3, N2, S2, P2, Q3, K2, F2, M3, E5, C4 ● **Temperaments:** J, T ● **Physical:** Stg=S; Freq: R, H, I, N Occas: D, A, X ● **Work Env:** Noise=N; ● **Salary:** 4 ● **Outlook:** 3

DRAFTER, STRUCTURAL (profess. & kin.) ● DOT #005.281-014 ● OES: 22512 ● Performs duties of DRAFTER (profess. & kin.) Master Title by drawing plans and details for structures employing structural reinforcing steel, concrete, masonry, wood, and other structural materials. Produces plans and details of foundations, building frame, floor and roof framing, and other structural elements. ● **GED:** R5, M5, L4 ● **SVP:** 2-4 yrs ● **Academic:** Ed=A, Eng=S ● **Work Field:** 242 ● **MPSMS:** 704 ● **Aptitudes:** G2, V3, N2, S2, P2, Q2, K2, F2, M3, E5, C4 ● **Temperaments:** J, T ● **Physical:** Stg=S; Const: R, H, I, N Freq: D, A Occas: X ● **Work Env:** Noise=Q; ● **Salary:** 4 ● **Outlook:** 3

DRAWINGS CHECKER, ENGINEERING (profess. & kin.) ● DOT #007.267-010 ● OES: 22135 ● Alternate titles: STANDARDS ANALYST. Examines engineering drawings of military and commercial parts, assemblies, and installations to detect errors in design documents: Compares figures and lines on production drawing or diagram with production layout, examining angles, dimensions, bend allowances, and tolerances for accuracy. Determines practicality of design, material selection, available tooling, and fabrication process, applying knowledge of drafting and manufacturing methods. Confers with design personnel to resolve drawing and design discrepancies. May specialize in checking specific types of designs, such as mechanical assemblies, microelectronic circuitry, or fluid-flow systems. May operate copier equipment to make duplicates of designs. ● **GED:** R4, M4, L4 ● **SVP:** 1-2 yrs ● **Academic:** Ed=A, Eng=S ● **Work Field:** 244 ● **MPSMS:** 559, 580, 592 ● **Aptitudes:** G2, V2, N2, S1, P2, Q2, K2, F2, M3, E5, C4 ● **Temperaments:** J, T ● **Physical:** Stg=S; Const: N Freq: A Occas: R, H, I, T, G, X ● **Work Env:** Noise=N; ● **Salary:** 3 ● **Outlook:** 3

EDITOR, MAP (profess. & kin.) ● DOT #018.261-018 ● OES: 22310 ● Verifies accuracy and completeness of topographical maps from aerial photographs and specifications: Views photographs and other reference materials, such as old maps and records and examines corresponding area of map to verify correct identification of specified topographical features and accuracy of contour lines. Verifies correct location and accuracy of scaled distances between control points and reference lines. Examines reference materials to detect omission of topographical features, poor register, or other defects in photography or draftsmanship. Marks errors and makes corrections, such as numbering grid lines or lettering names of rivers or towns. ● **GED:** R4, M4, L4 ● **SVP:** 2-4 yrs ● **Academic:** Ed=A, Eng=S ● **Work Field:** 242, 211 ● **MPSMS:** 716 ● **Aptitudes:** G2, V2, N2, S2, P2, Q3, K3, F3, M3, E5, C3 ● **Temperaments:** J, T ● **Physical:** Stg=L; Const: N Freq: R, H, I, D, A Occas: X ● **Work Env:** Noise=N; ● **Salary:** 4 ● **Outlook:** 4

ENGINEERING ASSISTANT, MECHANICAL EQUIPMENT (profess. & kin.) ● DOT #007.161-018 ● OES: 22512 ● Alternate titles: MECHANICAL DESIGN TECHNICIAN. Develops detailed design drawings and related specifications of mechanical equipment, according to engineering sketches and design proposal specifications: Analyzes engineering sketches, specifications, and related data and drawings to determine design factors, such as size, shape, and arrangement of parts. Sketches rough layout of machine and computes angles, weights, surface areas, dimensions, radii, clearances, tolerances, leverages, and location of holes. Computes magnitude, direction, and point of application of tension, compression, and bending forces, and develops geometric shape of machine parts to accommodate operating loads. Drafts detailed multiview drawings of machine and subassemblies, including specifications for gear ratios, bearing loads, and direction of moving parts, using engineering data and standard references. Compiles and analyzes test data to determine effect of machine design on various factors, such as temperature, pressures, speed, horsepower, and fuel consumption. Modifies machine design to correct operating deficiencies or to reduce production problems. May measure machine and parts during production to ensure compliance with design specifications, using precision measuring instruments. May specialize in specific type of machine, such as air-cooled internal combustion engines, diesel engines, or machine tools. May use computer-assisted design/drafting equipment and software to develop designs. ● **GED:** R5, M5, L5 ● **SVP:** 2-4 yrs ● **Academic:** Ed=A, Eng=S ● **Work Field:** 242, 244 ● **MPSMS:** 706 ● **Aptitudes:** G2, V2, N2, S2, P2, Q2, K2, F2, M2, E5, C4 ● **Temperaments:** J, T ● **Physical:** Stg=S; Freq: R, H, I, N, D, A Occas: T, G, X ● **Work Env:** Noise=N; ● **Salary:** 3 ● **Outlook:** 3

ESTIMATOR (profess. & kin.) ● DOT #169.267-038 ● OES: 21902 ● Alternate titles: COST ESTIMATOR; PRODUCTION ESTIMATOR. Analyzes blueprints, specifications, proposals, and other documentation to prepare time, cost, and labor estimates for products, projects, or services, applying knowledge of specialized methodologies, techniques, principles, or processes: Reviews data to determine material and labor requirements and prepares itemized lists. Computes cost factors and prepares estimates used for management purposes, such as planning, organizing, and scheduling work, preparing bids, selecting vendors or subcontractors, and determining cost effectiveness. Conducts special studies to develop and establish standard hour and related cost data or effect cost reductions. Consults with clients, vendors, or other individuals to discuss and formulate estimates and resolve issues. May specialize according to particular service performed, type of product manufactured, or phase of work involved, such as tool and fixture costs, production costs, construction costs, or material costs. ● **GED:** R4, M4, L4 ● **SVP:** 2-4 yrs ● **Academic:** Ed=A, Eng=G ● **Work Field:** 232 ● **MPSMS:** 899 ● **Aptitudes:** G2, V3, N2, S3, P3, Q3, K4, F4,

M4, E5, C5 ● **Temperaments:** J, T ● **Physical:** Stg=S; Freq: R, H, N Occas: I, T, G, A ● **Work Env:** Noise=N; ● **Salary:** 4 ● **Outlook:** 4

ESTIMATOR AND DRAFTER (utilities) ● DOT #019.261-014 ● OES: 22512 ● Alternate titles: DETAIL AND LAY-OUT DRAFTER; DISTRIBUTION ESTIMATOR; LAY-OUT AND DETAIL DRAFTER. Draws up specifications and instructions for installation of voltage transformers, overhead or underground cables, and related electrical equipment used to conduct electrical energy from transmission lines or high-voltage distribution lines to consumers: Studies work order request to determine type of service, such as lighting or power, demanded by installation. Visits site of proposed installation and draws rough sketch of location. Takes measurements, such as street dimensions, distances to be spanned by wire and cable, or space available in existing buildings and underground vaults which affect installation and arrangement of equipment. Estimates materials, equipment, and incidentals needed for installation. Draws master sketch showing relation of proposed installation to existing facilities. Makes other drawings, such as pertaining to wiring connections or cross sections of underground cables, as required for instructions to installation crew. Consults POWER-DISTRIBUTION ENGINEER (utilities) 003.167-046 on difficulties encountered. May draft sketches to scale [DRAFTER, ELECTRICAL (profess. & kin.) 003.281-010]. May estimate labor and material costs, using pricelists and records on previous projects. May inspect completed installation of electrical equipment and related building circuitry to verify conformance with specifications. May perform duties of LAND SURVEYOR (profess. & kin.) 018.167-018 and prepare specifications and diagrams for installation of gas distribution pipes owned by gas-electric utility. ● **GED:** R5, M5, L5 ● **SVP:** 2-4 yrs ● **Academic:** Ed=A, Eng=S ● **Work Field:** 242, 244 ● **MPSMS:** 581 ● **Aptitudes:** G2, V2, N2, S2, P2, Q3, K3, F3, M3, E5, C4 ● **Temperaments:** J, T ● **Physical:** Stg=L; Freq: R, H, I, T, G, N Occas: D, A, X ● **Work Env:** Noise=N; Freq: W ● **Salary:** 5 ● **Outlook:** 4

FIRE-PROTECTION ENGINEERING TECHNICIAN (profess. & kin.) ● DOT #019.261-026 ● OES: 35199 ● Designs and drafts plans and estimates costs for installation of fire protection systems for facilities and structures, applying knowledge of drafting, physical science, engineering principles, and fire protection codes: Analyzes blueprints and specifications prepared by ARCHITECT (profess. & kin.) 001.061-010 to determine dimensions of system to meet fire protection codes. Determines design and size of system components, using calculator or computer. Drafts detailed drawing of system to ensure conformance to specifications and applicable codes. May negotiate relocation of system components with SUPERINTENDENT, CONSTRUCTION (construction) 182.167-026 to resolve conflicts of co-location with other systems. May inspect fire-damaged structures to detect malfunctions. May specialize in one type of fire protection system, such as foam, water, dry chemical, or vaporous gas or specialize in one type of establishment, such as construction, insurance, or government. ● **GED:** R4, M4, L4 ● **SVP:** 2-4 yrs ● **Academic:** Ed=A, Eng=S ● **Work Field:** 244, 242 ● **MPSMS:** 719 ● **Aptitudes:** G2, V2, N2, S2, P2, Q2, K2, F3, M3, E3, C4 ● **Temperaments:** J, T ● **Physical:** Stg=L; Const: R, H, I, N Occas: C, T, G, F, D, X, V ● **Work Env:** Noise=N; Occas: W ● **Salary:** 4 ● **Outlook:** 3

INTEGRATED CIRCUIT LAYOUT DESIGNER (profess. & kin.) ● DOT #003.261-018 ● OES: 22512 ● Alternate titles: MASK DESIGNER. Designs layout for integrated circuits (IC), according to engineering specifications, using computer-assisted design (CAD) equipment and software, and utilizing knowledge of electronics, drafting, and IC design rules (standard IC manufacturing process requirements): Reviews and analyzes engineering design schematics and supporting documents, such as logic diagrams and design rules to plan layout of IC. Confers with engineering staff to resolve design details or problems. Enters engineering specifications into computer memory of CAD equipment and composes configurations on equipment display screen of IC logic elements (basic components of integrated circuit, such as resistors and transistors) for all IC layers, using keyboard, digitizing work aids (light pen or digitizing tablet), and engineering design schematics, and applying knowledge of design rules, programmed CAD functions, and electronics. Compares logic element configuration on equipment display screen with engineering schematics and redesigns or modifies logic elements, as needed, using digitizing work aids (light pen or digitizing tablet), keyboard, and programmed CAD functions. Lays out, redesigns, and modifies arrangement and interconnections of logic elements for each layer of integrated circuit, using digitizing work aids (light pen or digitizing tablet), keyboard and programmed CAD functions listed on display screen. Keys in specified commands, using CAD equipment keyboard, to test final IC layout for errors in design rules, using design rule software package. May generate copy of logic element design, using plotter to verify that logic element design copy meets design requirements and for use in laying out IC layer design for Very Large Scale (VLS) integrated circuits. May generate tape of final layout design for use in producing photo masks for each layer of IC, using CAD equipment. May program CAD equipment to change CAD functions listed on display screen, using keyboard. May be designated according to complexity of IC designed as IC Designer, Custom (profess. & kin.); IC Designer, Gate Arrays (profess. & kin.); IC Designer, Standard Cells (profess. & kin.). ● **GED:** R4, M4, L4 ● **SVP:** 4-10 yrs ● **Academic:** Ed=A, Eng=S ● **Work Field:** 242, 244, 264 ● **MPSMS:** 703 ● **Aptitudes:** G2, V2, N2, S2, P2, Q2, K2, F3, M3, E5, C4 ● **Temperaments:** J, T ● **Physical:** Stg=S; Freq: R, H, I, N, D, A, X Occas: T, G ● **Work Env:** Noise=N; ● **Salary:** 4 ● **Outlook:** 4

PATTERNMAKER (furniture) ● DOT #781.361-014 ● OES: 89502 ● Draws and cuts out sets of master patterns for articles, such as garments, parachutes, and upholstery, following sketches, sample articles and design specifications: Examines sketches or sample articles and design specifications to ascertain number, shape, and size of pattern parts and quantity of cloth required to make finished article, using knowledge of manufacturing processes and characteristics of fabrics. Discusses design specifications with designer, when necessary. Draws outlines of parts on paper, using drafting instruments, such as calipers, squares, straight and curved rules, and pencils. Draws details on outlined parts to indicate position of pleats, pockets, buttonholes, and other items. Marks outlined garment parts with lines and notches that serve as guides in joining parts of garment. Cuts out master patterns, using scissors and knife, and marks size and style information on patterns. May draw and cut out sets of patterns of different sizes, following master patterns [PATTERN GRADER-CUTTER (garment) 781.381-022]. May fabricate template from plywood, trace around template with chalk to outline pattern on material, and cut off parts, using power shears [DEVELOPER PROVER, INTERIOR ASSEMBLIES (aircraft mfg.) 693.261-010]. ● **GED:** R4, M3, L3 ● **SVP:** 1-2 yrs ● **Academic:** Ed=H, Eng=S ● **Work Field:** 241, 054 ● **MPSMS:** 489 ● **Aptitudes:** G3, V3, N3, S2, P2, Q3, K3, F2, M3, E5, C4 ● **Temperaments:** J, T ● **Physical:** Stg=L; Freq: R, H, I, N, A Occas: S, T, G, D, X ● **Work Env:** Noise=N; ● **Salary:** 4 ● **Outlook:** 3

PHOTOGRAMMETRIST (profess. & kin.) ● DOT #018.261-026 ● OES: 22310 ● Alternate titles: CARTOGRAPHIC TECHNICIAN. Analyzes source data and prepares mosaic prints, contour maps, profile sheets, and related cartographic materials requiring technical mastery of photogrammetric techniques and principles: Prepares original maps, charts, and drawings, from aerial photographs, and survey data and applies standard mathematical formulas and photogrammetric techniques to identify, scale, and orient geodetic points, elevations, and other planimetric or topographic features and cartographic detail. Graphically delineates aerial photographic detail, such as control points, hydrography, topography, and cultural features, using precision stereoplotting apparatus or drafting instruments. Revises existing maps and charts and corrects maps in various stages of compilation. May prepare rubber, plastic, or plaster three-dimensional relief models. ● **GED:** R4, M4, L4 ● **SVP:** 2-4 yrs ● **Academic:** Ed=A, Eng=S ● **Work Field:** 242, 243 ● **MPSMS:** 716 ● **Aptitudes:** G2, V3, N2, S2, P2, Q2, K2, F2, M2, E3, C3 ● **Temperaments:** J, T ● **Physical:** Stg=S; Const: N Freq: R, H, I, D, A Occas: X ● **Work Env:** Noise=Q; ● **Salary:** 3 ● **Outlook:** 3

PRINTED CIRCUIT DESIGNER (profess. & kin.) ● DOT #003.261-022 ● OES: 22512 ● Designs and drafts layout for printed circuit boards (PCB's) according to engineering specifications, utilizing knowledge of electronics, drafting, and PCB design: Reviews and analyzes engineering design schematics and supporting documents to plan layout of PCB components and printed circuitry. Confers with engineering staff to resolve design details and problems. Drafts detailed drawings [DRAFTER (profess. & kin.) Master Title] and composes master layout of design components and circuitry. Examines and verifies master layout for electrical and mechanical accuracy. May verify accuracy of film reproductions of master layout. May prepare copies of drawings for use in PCB fabrication, using blueprint or diazo print machine.

May generate computer tape for use in photo plotting design onto film, using digitizing equipment. ● **GED:** R4, M4, L4 ● **SVP:** 2-4 yrs ● **Academic:** Ed=A, Eng=S ● **Work Field:** 242, 244, 264 ● **MPSMS:** 703 ● **Aptitudes:** G2, V2, N2, S2, P2, Q2, K2, F2, M3, E5, C4 ● **Temperaments:** J, T, V ● **Physical:** Stg=S; Freq: R, H, I, N, D, A, X Occas: T, G ● **Work Env:** Noise=N; ● **Salary:** 4 ● **Outlook:** 4

SPECIFICATION WRITER (profess. & kin.) ● DOT #019.267-010 ● OES: 35199 ● Interprets architectural or engineering plans and prepares material lists and specifications to be used as standards by plant employees or contracting personnel in material processing or in manufacturing or construction activities: Analyzes plans and diagrams, or observes and makes notes on material processing, to determine material and material processing specifications, or specifications for manufacturing or construction activities. Writes technical descriptions specifying material qualities and properties, utilizing knowledge of material standards, industrial processes, and manufacturing procedures. May draw rough sketches or arrange for finished drawings or photographs to illustrate specified materials or assembly sequence. Workers usually specialize and are designated according to engineering specialization, product, or process. ● **GED:** R5, M4, L4 ● **SVP:** 2-4 yrs ● **Academic:** Ed=A, Eng=G ● **Work Field:** 244 ● **MPSMS:** 700 ● **Aptitudes:** G2, V2, N2, S2, P2, Q2, K5, F5, M5, E5, C5 ● **Temperaments:** J, T ● **Physical:** Stg=S; Freq: N Occas: R, H, I, F, D ● **Work Env:** Noise=Q; ● **Salary:** 3 ● **Outlook:** 4

STEREO-PLOTTER OPERATOR (profess. & kin.) ● DOT #018.281-010 ● OES: 22310 ● Alternate titles: STEREO OPERATOR; STEREOPTIC PROJECTION TOPOGRAPHER. Draws topographical maps from aerial photographs, using instruments that produce simultaneous projections of two photographs, taken from different positions, in manner that permits steroscopic viewing for delineation of planimetric detail and drawing of contours: Orients plotting instruments to form three dimensional stereo image. Orients plotting instruments to form three dimensional stereo image. Views stereoscopic image by using anaglyphic, binocular, or image alternator techniques. Determines contour interval and vertical scale of image, using mathematical table. Traces contours and topographical details to produce map. ● **GED:** R4, M4, L4 ● **SVP:** 2-4 yrs ● **Academic:** Ed=H, Eng=S ● **Work Field:** 242 ● **MPSMS:** 716 ● **Aptitudes:** G2, V3, N3, S2, P2, Q3, K2, F2, M3, E5, C3 ● **Temperaments:** J, R, T ● **Physical:** Stg=L; Const: H, I, N, D Freq: R, A, X ● **Work Env:** Noise=Q; ● **Salary:** 5 ● **Outlook:** 4

TECHNICAL ILLUSTRATOR (profess. & kin.) ● DOT #017.281-034 ● OES: 22512 ● Alternate titles: ENGINEERING ILLUSTRATOR; PRODUCTION ILLUSTRATOR. Lays out and draws illustrations for reproduction in reference works, brochures, and technical manuals dealing with assembly, installation, operation, maintenance, and repair of machines, tools, and equipment: Prepares drawings from blueprints, designs, mockups, and photoprints by methods and techniques suited to specified reproduction process or final use, such as blueprint, photo-offset, and projection transparencies, using drafting and optical equipment. Lays out and draws schematic, perspective, orthographic, or oblique-angle views to depict function, relationship, and assembly-sequence of parts and assemblies, such as gears, engines, and instruments. Shades or colors drawing to emphasize details or to eliminate undesired background, using ink, crayon, airbrush, and overlays. Pastes instructions and comments in position on drawing. May draw cartoons and caricatures to illustrate operation, maintenance, and safety manuals and posters. ● **GED:** R5, M5, L4 ● **SVP:** 2-4 yrs ● **Academic:** Ed=A, Eng=S ● **Work Field:** 242 ● **MPSMS:** 752 ● **Aptitudes:** G2, V3, N2, S2, P2, Q3, K3, F2, M3, E5, C3 ● **Temperaments:** J, T ● **Physical:** Stg=S; Const: H, I, N, D Freq: R, A Occas: X ● **Work Env:** Noise=Q; ● **Salary:** 4 ● **Outlook:** 2

GOE: 05.03.03
Expediting & Coordinating

AIR-TRAFFIC-CONTROL SPECIALIST, STATION (government ser.) ● DOT #193.162-014 ● OES: 39002 ● Receives and transmits flight plans, meteorological, navigational, and other information in air traffic control station to perform preflight and emergency service for airplane pilots: Accepts flight plans from pilots in person or by telephone and reviews them for completeness. Routes plans for operating under instrument flight rules to control center and for operating under visual flight rules to station in vicinity of destination airport, using radio, teletype, radiotelephone, radiotelegraph, telephone, or interphone. Provides meteorological, navigational, and other information to pilots during flight, using radio. Relays traffic control and other instructions concerned with aircraft safety to pilots. Radios such information as identifying landmarks, beacons, and available landing fields to pilots in flight. Maintains file of plans for operating under visual flight rules until completion of flight, and contacts facilities along route of flight to secure information on overdue aircraft. Reports lost aircraft to control center for rescue or local emergency services. Monitors such radio aids to navigation as range stations, fan markers, and voice communication facilities, and notifies air personnel of availability of these facilities. Maintains written records of messages transmitted and received. ● **GED:** R4, M3, L4 ● **SVP:** 4-10 yrs ● **Academic:** Ed=H, Eng=G ● **Work Field:** 281, 282 ● **MPSMS:** 855 ● **Aptitudes:** G2, V3, N3, S4, P4, Q3, K4, F3, M3, E5, C4 ● **Temperaments:** J, P, S, T, V ● **Physical:** Stg=L; Freq: R, H, I, T, G, N, A, X ● **Work Env:** Noise=N; ● **Salary:** 4 ● **Outlook:** 3

AIR-TRAFFIC-CONTROL SPECIALIST, TOWER (government ser.) ● DOT #193.162-018 ● OES: 39002 ● Alternate titles: AIRPORT-CONTROL OPERATOR; CONTROL-TOWER-RADIO OPERATOR; FLIGHT-CONTROL-TOWER OPERATOR. Controls air traffic on and within vicinity of airport according to established procedures and policies to prevent collisions and to minimize delays arising from traffic congestion: Answers radio calls from arriving and departing aircraft and issues landing and take-off instructions and information, such as runway to use, wind velocity and direction, visibility, taxiing instructions, and pertinent data on other aircraft operating in vicinity. Transfers control of departing flights to and accepts control of arriving flights from air traffic control center, using telephone or interphone. Alerts airport emergency crew and other designated personnel by radio or telephone when airplanes are having flight difficulties. Pushes buttons or pulls switches to control airport floodlights and boundary, runway, and hazard lights. Scans control panel to ascertain that lights are functioning. Operates radio and monitors radarscope to control aircraft operating in vicinity of airport. Receives cross-country flight plans and transmits them to air traffic control center. Signals aircraft flying under visual flight rules, using electric signal light or flags. May control cross-runway traffic by radio directions to guards or maintenance vehicles. May keep written record of messages received from aircraft. May control traffic within designated sector of airspace between centers and beyond airport control tower area and be designated Air-Traffic-Control Specialist, Center (government ser.). ● **GED:** R4, M3, L4 ● **SVP:** 4-10 yrs ● **Academic:** Ed=H, Eng=G ● **Work Field:** 281, 282 ● **MPSMS:** 855 ● **Aptitudes:** G2, V3, N3, S2, P3, Q3, K4, F3, M3, E5, C3 ● **Temperaments:** J, P, S, T, V ● **Physical:** Stg=L; Const: T, G Freq: R, H, I, N, F, D, X Occas: V ● **Work Env:** Noise=N; ● **Salary:** 4 ● **Outlook:** 4

DISPATCHER (air trans.) ● DOT #912.167-010 ● OES: 39002 ● Alternate titles: AIRPLANE DISPATCHER; HELICOPTER DISPATCHER. Authorizes, regulates, and controls commercial airline flights according to government and company regulations to expedite and ensure safety of flight: Analyzes and evaluates meteorological information, such as speed and direction of winds, visibility, and presence of storms, to determine potential safety of flight and desirable route. Computes amount of fuel needed according to type of aircraft, distance of flight, weather conditions, and fuel regulations prescribed by Federal Aviation Agency. Prepares flight plan containing information, such as maximum allowable gross takeoff and landing weights, weather, and landing field conditions. Signs authorization to release flight for takeoff. Delays or cancels flight if unsafe conditions prevail. Studies weather and pilot's position reports and terrain maps to evaluate progress of flight. Recommends flight plan alterations, such as changing course or altitude, canceling stops, or taking extra fuel. Prepares log of flights, delays, and cancellations, and lists reasons for changes in schedules or flight plans. Must be licensed by Federal Aviation Administration. ● **GED:** R5, M4, L4 ● **SVP:** 4-10 yrs ● **Academic:** Ed=N, Eng=G ● **Work Field:** 211, 281, 231 ● **MPSMS:** 855 ● **Aptitudes:** G2, V2, N2, S4, P3, Q2, K4, F4, M4, E5, C3 ● **Temperaments:** D, J, P, S ● **Physical:** Stg=S; Freq: R, H, T, G, N, A Occas: I, X ● **Work Env:** Noise=N; ● **Salary:** 3 ● **Outlook:** 3

MATERIAL SCHEDULER (aircraft mfg.) ● DOT #012.167-082 ● OES: 22128 ● Alternate titles: COMMODITIES REQUIREMENTS ANALYST; MATERIAL PLANNING AND ACQUISITION ANALYST; PRODUCTION CONTROL SCHEDULER. Develops and analyzes lists of raw materials, purchased parts, equipment, and other items required to manufacture aircraft and aerospace products: Reviews and evaluates engineering drawings and blueprints to estimate quantity and type of materials, parts, or other items required. Converts requirements to orders of conventional sizes and quantities, considering factors such as existing inventories, unavoidable waste, and kind of material to be used. Reviews material lists for conformance to company standard practices in regard to parts and materials used. Schedules deliveries based on production forecasts, material substitutions, storage and handling facilities, and maintenance requirements. Prepares or authorizes preparation of purchase requisitions. Estimates need to reorder supplies due to rejections and engineering changes during manufacturing cycle. Confers with purchasing, engineering, planning, and other personnel to exchange information regarding inventories, schedules, and related issues. ● **GED:** R5, M5, L5 ● **SVP:** 2-4 yrs ● **Academic:** Ed=A, Eng=G ● **Work Field:** 232 ● **MPSMS:** 898 ● **Aptitudes:** G2, V2, N2, S3, P3, Q3, K4, F4, M4, E5, C5 ● **Temperaments:** J, T ● **Physical:** Stg=S; Freq: R, H, N, A Occas: I, T, G ● **Work Env:** Noise=N; ● **Salary:** 2 ● **Outlook:** 4

PRODUCTION CLERK (clerical) ● DOT #221.382-018 ● OES: 58008 ● Alternate titles: PLANT CLERK; PRODUCTION CHECKER; PRODUCTION-CONTROL CLERK; PRODUCTION-POSTING CLERK. Compiles and records production data for industrial establishment to prepare records and reports on volume of production, consumption of raw material, quality control, and other aspects of production, performing any combination of following duties: Compiles and records production data from such documents as customer orders, work tickets, product specifications, and individual-worker production sheets, following prescribed recordkeeping procedures, using typewriter, computer terminal, and writing instruments. Calculates factors, such as types and quantities of items produced, materials used, amount of scrap, frequency of defects, and worker and department production rates, using adding machine or calculator. Writes production reports based on data compiled, tabulated, and computed, following prescribed formats. Maintains files of documents used and prepared. Compiles from customer orders and other specifications detailed production sheet or work tickets for use by production workers as guides in assembly or manufacture of product [ORDER DETAILER (clerical) 221.387-046]. Prepares written work schedules based on established guidelines and priorities. Compiles material inventory records and prepares requisitions for procurement of materials and supplies [MATERIAL CLERK (clerical) 222.387-034]. Charts production, using wall chart, graph, or pegboard, based on statistics compiled, for reference by production and management personnel. Sorts and distributes work tickets or material to workers. May compute wages from employee timecards and post wage data on records used for preparation of payroll [PAYROLL CLERK (clerical) 215.382-014]. May be designated according to type of data recorded as Machine-Load Clerk (woodworking); department or division of establishment to which data pertains as Production Clerk, Lace Tearing (tex. prod., nec); Mill Recorder (nonfer. metal); or work aids used as Production Control Pegboard Clerk (garment). ● **GED:** R3, M3, L3 ● **SVP:** 3-6 mos ● **Academic:** Ed=H, Eng=G ● **Work Field:** 232, 231 ● **MPSMS:** 898 ● **Aptitudes:** G3, V3, N3, S4, P3, Q2, K3, F3, M3, E5, C5 ● **Temperaments:** R, T ● **Physical:** Stg=S; Const: R, H, I Freq: T, G, N, A ● **Work Env:** Noise=Q; ● **Salary:** 2 ● **Outlook:** 3

GOE: 05.03.04
Petroleum

FIELD ENGINEER, SPECIALIST (petrol. & gas) ● DOT #010.261-010 ● OES: 35199 ● Collects fluid samples from oil-or gas-bearing formations and analyzes sample to determine potential productivity of formation: Moves controls on panel to fire charge into formation and to operate hydraulic mechanism which thrusts and seals probe into perforation. Analyzes fluid in sample to determine potential productivity of formation. ● **GED:** R4, M4, L4 ● **SVP:** 2-4 yrs ● **Academic:** Ed=A, Eng=G ● **Work Field:** 244 ● **MPSMS:** 708 ● **Aptitudes:** G2,

V3, N2, S3, P2, Q3, K4, F3, M4, E5, C4 ● **Temperaments:** J, T ● **Physical:** Stg=L; Freq: R, H, I, T, G, N ● **Work Env:** Noise=N; Freq: W Occas: M ● **Salary:** 5 ● **Outlook:** 2

PROSPECTOR (any industry) ● DOT #024.284-010 ● OES: 39998 ● Explores likely regions to discover valuable mineral deposits, using topographical maps, surveys, reports, and knowledge of geology and mineralogy: Examines outcrops, placer, and stream channels for mineral content. Drills, dynamites, or digs trenches or pits along rock formations or creek beds to obtain rock samples. Breaks off samples and tests them for presence of minerals with heat, acid, magnifying glass, or by pulverizing and washing or panning. Assays samples for preliminary quantitative estimate. Collects data on rock formations, using geophysical instruments and devices, such as geiger counters and electronic sounding equipment, and determines feasibility of staking and developing claim. Stakes claim according to federal or state legal requirements. Develops mineral deposits by means of placer or hard rock mining. May sell interests in discovered areas. ● **GED:** R4, M4, L4 ● **SVP:** 2-4 yrs ● **Academic:** Ed=N, Eng=N ● **Work Field:** 211, 005 ● **MPSMS:** 350 ● **Aptitudes:** G3, V3, N3, S3, P3, Q4, K4, F4, M4, E4, C3 ● **Temperaments:** J ● **Physical:** Stg=H; Freq: R, H Occas: S, K, O, I, N, F, A, X ● **Work Env:** Noise=L; Freq: W Occas: U, T ● **Salary:** 4 ● **Outlook:** 1

GOE: 05.03.05
Electrical - Electronic

ACCESS COORDINATOR, CABLE TELEVISION (radio-tv broad.) ● DOT #194.122-010 ● OES: 34028 ● Instructs trainees in use of equipment; and operates equipment, such as camera, sound mixer, and videotape deck, to film events, to copy/edit graphics, voice, and music onto videotape, for broadcast on cable television: Determines time and day of class and plans outline of material to be covered. Distributes manuals, and instructs and demonstrates to trainees, care, setup and operation of equipment, such as tripods, microphones and portable camera. Prepares and administers written and practical tests to test trainees' knowledge. Determines equipment required to film event, and sets up and operates equipment, such as lights and portable camera to film event. Prepares script of filmed event. Loads videotape deck with videotape and instructs assistant to read script. Sets recording level, and records verbal description of event onto videotape, using videotaping equipment. Reviews videotape of filmed event, using videotaping equipment, to determine quality of video and color. Observes scales in video and color monitors and operates controls to adjust video and color levels. Enters written information about filmed event into graphic equipment. Plays musical selection, using stereo equipment, and adjusts controls to improve clarity and balance music. Sets inpoints and outpoints for graphics, voice, and music. Records graphics, voice, and music onto videotape, using audio/video equipment. Observes monitors to verify that video, voice, and music are synchronized during editing/copying process. Reviews assembled videotape, using videotaping equipment, to discern quality of video and audio signals, and operates controls to clarify and adjust video and audio signals. Edits manuals and schedules programs. May prepare report outlining past programs and future programs to be aired, and contents of programs. ● **GED:** R4, M3, L4 ● **SVP:** 2-4 yrs ● **Academic:** Ed=H, Eng=G ● **Work Field:** 281, 296 ● **MPSMS:** 869 ● **Aptitudes:** G2, V2, N3, S3, P3, Q4, K3, F3, M3, E5, C3 ● **Temperaments:** D, J, P, T, V ● **Physical:** Stg=H; Freq: R, H, I Occas: S, O, T, G, N, D, A, X, V ● **Work Env:** Noise=N; ● **Salary:** 3 ● **Outlook:** 2

COMMUNICATIONS COORDINATOR (medical ser.) ● DOT #239.167-010 ● OES: 39998 ● Coordinates telephone communications services in hospital: Confers with administrative personnel to determine hospital requirements for communications equipment, such as switchboards, public-address paging systems, and extension telephones. Determines equipment to be installed, based on anticipated volume of calls, and knowledge of available equipment. Writes instruction and procedure manuals for switchboard operation and training, applying knowledge of hospital procedures, departmental functions, and equipment. Determines methods of improving telephone service from discussions with supervisory personnel, observation of switchboard operations, and analysis of service complaints. Arranges with telephone company personnel for special training of workers, as necessary. May estimate telephone services costs for use in preparing hospital budget. May prepare records and reports for management, concerning telephone services. ● **GED:** R4, M3, L3 ● **SVP:** 2-4 yrs ● **Academic:** Ed=N, Eng=G ● **Work Field:** 295 ● **MPSMS:** 860 ● **Aptitudes:** G2, V3, N3, S4, P4, Q3, K4, F4, M4, E5, C5 ● **Temperaments:** D, P, V ● **Physical:** Stg=S; Freq: R, H, T, G, N Occas: I ● **Work Env:** Noise=N; ● **Salary:** 4 ● **Outlook:** 2

FIELD ENGINEER (radio-tv broad.) ● DOT #193.262-018 ● OES: 34028 ● Alternate titles: FIELD TECHNICIAN. Installs and operates portable field transmission equipment to broadcast programs or events originating at points distant from studio: Determines availability of telephone wire facilities for use in making connections between microphones, amplifier, telephone line, and auxiliary power supply to relay broadcast to master control. Sets up, tests, and operates microwave transmitter to broadcast program in absence of telephone wire system. Conducts broadcast from field. Must be licensed by Federal Communications Commission. May perform duties of RECORDING ENGINEER (recording; radio-tv broad.) 194.362-010; ANNOUNCER (radio-tv broad.) 159.147-010. May be designated Microwave Engineer (radio-tv broad.) when restricted to operating microwave transmitter. ● **GED:** R5, M4, L5 ● **SVP:** 2-4 yrs ● **Academic:** Ed=A, Eng=S ● **Work Field:** 281 ● **MPSMS:** 860 ● **Aptitudes:** G2, V2, N3, S3, P2, Q3, K3, F3, M3, E5, C3 ● **Temperaments:** J, T, V ● **Physical:** Stg=L; Freq: R, H, I Occas: T, G, X ● **Work Env:** Noise=N; Occas: W ● **Salary:** 5 ● **Outlook:** 4

FLIGHT-TEST DATA ACQUISITION TECHNICIAN (aircraft mfg.) ● DOT #002.262-010 ● OES: 35199 ● Alternate titles: DATA ACQUISITION LABORATORY TECHNICIAN; TECHNICAL AIDE, FLIGHT TEST DATA. Sets up, operates, monitors, modifies, calibrates, and maintains computer systems and devices for acquisition and analysis of flight test data, utilizing knowledge of electronic theory and operation of computer systems: Reviews engineering notification of flight test to determine data required for post-flight analysis. Plans method and sequence of operations to acquire data, and sets up required electronic data acquisition, test, and measurement equipment and accessories. Inputs flight test data and program information into computer console for specific test requested. Enters commands to modify program to accommodate additional or revised test requirements. Calculates calibration values used as model for comparison and measurement of test data. Monitors lights, displays, and other operating features of computer equipment, such as console, receivers, and printers, to detect malfunctions and ensure integrity of processed data. Diagnoses cause of equipment malfunctioning, and adjusts, repairs, or replaces faulty components. Enters information to update flight test data base and to maintain records, such as electronic parts inventory and manuals for equipment maintenance and calibrations. Discusses flight test requirements and results with engineers and other personnel. ● **GED:** R5, M4, L4 ● **SVP:** 2-4 yrs ● **Academic:** Ed=A, Eng=G ● **Work Field:** 233, 244, 111 ● **MPSMS:** 702, 703 ● **Aptitudes:** G2, V3, N2, S3, P2, Q3, K3, F2, M3, E5, C4 ● **Temperaments:** J, T, V ● **Physical:** Stg=L; Freq: R, H, I, N, A Occas: T, G, D, X ● **Work Env:** Noise=N; Occas: M, E ● **Salary:** 4 ● **Outlook:** 3

LASER TECHNICIAN (electron. comp.) ● DOT #019.261-034 ● OES: 35199 ● Constructs and tests prototype gas or solid-state laser devices, applying theory and principles of laser engineering and electronic circuits: Reviews project instructions, such as assembly layout, blueprints, and sketches, and confers with engineering personnel to clarify laser device specifications. Interprets production details, such as dimensions and functional requirements, for workers engaged in grinding mirror blanks, coating mirror surfaces, and machining metal parts. Installs and aligns optical parts, such as mirrors and waveplates, in laser body, using precision instruments. Turns controls of vacuum pump and gas transfer equipment to purge, evacuate, and fill laser body with specified volume and pressure of gases, such as helium, neon, or carbon dioxide, to test laser beam. Assembles completed laser body in chassis, and installs and aligns electronic components, tubing, and wiring to connect controls, such as valves, regulators, dials, and switches. Sets up precision electronic and optical instruments to test laser device, using specified electrical or optical inputs. Tests laser for gas leaks, using leak detector. Analyzes test data and reports results to engineering personnel. May prepare and write technical reports to recommend solutions to technical problems. ● **GED:** R5, M4, L4 ● **SVP:** 2-4 yrs ●

Academic: Ed=A, Eng=S • **Work Field:** 111, 211, 244 • **MPSMS:** 580, 600, 703 • **Aptitudes:** G2, V2, N2, S2, P2, Q3, K2, F2, M2, E5, C4 • **Temperaments:** J, T, V • **Physical:** Stg=M; Const: R Freq: H, I, N, D Occas: S, K, O, T, G, M, A, X • **Work Env:** Noise=N; Freq: E, R • **Salary:** 3 • **Outlook:** 4

MASTER CONTROL OPERATOR (radio-tv broad.) • DOT #194.262-022 • OES: 34028 • Alternate titles: MASTER CONTROL ENGINEER. Sets up, controls and monitors television broadcasting equipment to transmit television programs and station breaks to viewing audience: Reads television programming log to ascertain name of program or station break, and at what time program or station break is scheduled to air. Verifies voice-over recording, using tape equipment, and informs supervisor of inconsistencies. Loads videotape equipment with videotapes containing program or station break or presses button on switching equipment to access videotape equipment. Subtracts preroll time from on-air time to determine at what time to begin preroll. Turns video and color monitors on and presses button to start videotape equipment. Observes scales in video and color monitors and turns knobs to set video and color levels to specifications. Turns knob to set audio level to specification. Observes clock, and presses buttons on switching equipment to begin preroll and to transmit program or station break to viewing audience. Observes on-air monitor to ascertain problems with transmission, such as loss of audio or video signals, and presses buttons to access and transmit technical difficulties sign or station identification to viewing audience. Presses buttons to access voice-over recording indicating nature of problem, name of station or name of next scheduled program. Troubleshoots equipment and observes lights on transmitter control panel to determine cause and area of problem and informs engineering personnel of transmission problems. Records onto television programming log actual time program or station break was aired. Prepares report describing problems encountered during transmission of program or station break and reason for problems. May control transmitting equipment to route television program to affiliated station. May take and record transmitter readings onto transmitter log. May be required to hold license issued by Federal Communications Commission. • **GED:** R4, M3, L4 • **SVP:** 4-10 yrs • **Academic:** Ed=H, Eng=G • **Work Field:** 281 • **MPSMS:** 864, 869 • **Aptitudes:** G2, V2, N3, S4, P4, Q3, K3, F3, M3, E5, C3 • **Temperaments:** J, T • **Physical:** Stg=S; Const: G, A, V Freq: R, H, I, X Occas: S, O, T, N • **Work Env:** Noise=N; • **Salary:** 5 • **Outlook:** 2

RADIOGRAPHER (any industry) • DOT #199.361-010 • OES: 39998 • Alternate titles: INDUSTRIAL X-RAY OPERATOR. Radiographs metal, plastics, concrete, or other materials, such as castings, sample parts, pipes, and structural members for flaws, cracks, or presence of foreign materials, utilizing knowledge of radiography equipment, techniques, and procedures: Aligns object on stand between source of x rays and film or plate; or aligns source of gamma rays, such as cobalt or iridium isotope and film or plate on opposite sides of object, manually or using hand or electric truck, chain hoist, or crane. Masks peripheral areas with lead shields. Selects type of radiation source and type of film, and applies standard mathematical formulas to determine exposure distance and time, considering size, mobility, and strength of radiation sources in relation to density and mobility of object. Verifies radiation intensities, using radiation meters. Adjusts controls of x-ray equipment on console or exposes source of radioactivity to take radiograph. Removes and develops film or plate. Monitors working area, using survey meters, to protect personnel area. May replace radioactive isotope source in containers by manipulating tongs from behind protective lead shield. Marks defects appearing on film and assists in analyzing findings. May specialize in x-ray work and be designated X-Ray Technician (any industry). • **GED:** R4, M4, L4 • **SVP:** 6 mos-1 yr • **Academic:** Ed=A, Eng=G • **Work Field:** 201, 211 • **MPSMS:** 540, 360 • **Aptitudes:** G3, V3, N3, S3, P3, Q4, K3, F3, M3, E4, C3 • **Temperaments:** J, T • **Physical:** Stg=L; Freq: R, H, I, N, A Occas: F, D, X • **Work Env:** Noise=N; Freq: O • **Salary:** 4 • **Outlook:** 4

RADIOTELEPHONE OPERATOR (any industry) • DOT #193.262-034 • OES: 39099 • Alternate titles: PHONE-CIRCUIT OPERATOR; RADIOPHONE OPERATOR; RADIOTELEPHONE-TECHNICAL OPERATOR. Operates and keeps in repair radiotelephone transmitter and receiving equipment for commercial communication: Throws switches to cut in power to stages of transmitter. Cuts in antennas and connects transmitting and receiving equipment into telephone system. Turns controls to adjust voice volume and modulation, and to set trans-

mitter on specified frequency. Conducts routine tests and repairs transmitting equipment, using electronic testing equipment, handtools, and power tools, to maintain communication system in operative condition. Must hold Radiotelephone Operator's License issued by Federal Communications Commission. • **GED:** R4, M3, L4 • **SVP:** 2-4 yrs • **Academic:** Ed=H, Eng=G • **Work Field:** 281 • **MPSMS:** 860 • **Aptitudes:** G3, V3, N3, S2, P2, Q3, K3, F3, M3, E5, C5 • **Temperaments:** P, T, V • **Physical:** Stg=L; Freq: R, H, T, G, N Occas: I • **Work Env:** Noise=L; • **Salary:** 4 • **Outlook:** 3

TECHNICIAN, NEWS GATHERING (radio-tv broad.) • DOT #194.362-022 • OES: 34028 • Alternate titles: TECHNICIAN-PHOTOGRAPHER/EDITOR. Locates news events, and sets up and controls field transmission equipment to record or transmit news events to television station: Drives vehicle to locate news events, such as fire or public rally, or receives information over two-way radio and scanner about location of news events. Turns power supply and monitors on, and activates air compressor to raise mast. Selects channel for transmission of audio and video signals. Converses with station operator, using two-way radio, while controlling lever to align antennae with receiving dish to obtain clearest signal for transmission of news event to station. Lays electrical cord and audio and video cables between vehicle, microphone, camera, and REPORTER (print. & pub.; radio-tv broad.) 131.262-018, or person being interviewed, to allow for receiving of off-air signal and transmission of audio and video signals to station. Observes scale in video monitor and sets video level to specifications. Sets audio level to specifications. Observes monitor and transmission light, and converses with station operator, using two-way radio, to verify transmission of news event to station, and makes adjustments to equipment. Records news event onto videotape, using recording equipment, during transmission of news event to studio, or receives videotape from CAMERA OPERATOR (motion picture; radio-tv broad.) 143.062-022 and makes dub, using recording equipment. Records information, such as location and news events recorded or transmitted to station, onto log. Is required to hold license issued by Federal Communications Commission. • **GED:** R4, M3, L3 • **SVP:** 4-10 yrs • **Academic:** Ed=H, Eng=G • **Work Field:** 281 • **MPSMS:** 864 • **Aptitudes:** G2, V3, N3, S4, P3, Q4, K4, F4, M4, E3, C3 • **Temperaments:** J, T • **Physical:** Stg=M; Const: G, V Freq: N, F, A Occas: R, H, I, T, D, X • **Work Env:** Noise=N; Occas: W • **Salary:** 4 • **Outlook:** 2

TRANSMITTER OPERATOR (radio-tv broad.) • DOT #193.262-038 • OES: 34028 • Alternate titles: TRANSMITTER ENGINEER. Operates and maintains radio transmitter to broadcast radio and television programs: Moves switches to cut in power to units and stages of transmitter. Monitors lights on console panel to ascertain that components are operative and that transmitter is ready to emit signal. Turns controls to set transmitter on FM, AM, or TV frequency assigned by Federal Communications Commission. Monitors signal emission and spurious radiations outside of licensed transmission frequency to ensure signal is not infringing on frequencies assigned other stations. Notifies broadcast studio when ready to transmit. Observes indicators and adjusts controls to maintain constant sound modulation and ensure that transmitted signal is sharp and clear. Maintains log of programs transmitted as required by Federal Communications Commission. Tests components of malfunctioning transmitter to diagnose trouble, using test equipment, such as oscilloscope, voltmeters, and ammeters. Disassembles and repairs equipment, using handtools [RADIO MECHANIC (any industry) 823.261-018]. May converse with studio personnel to determine cause of equipment failure and to solve problem. May operate microwave transmitter and receiver to receive or send programs to or from other broadcast stations. Must possess license issued by Federal Communications Commission. • **GED:** R4, M4, L4 • **SVP:** 2-4 yrs • **Academic:** Ed=A, Eng=G • **Work Field:** 281 • **MPSMS:** 860 • **Aptitudes:** G2, V2, N3, S3, P2, Q4, K3, F2, M3, E5, C3 • **Temperaments:** J, T • **Physical:** Stg=M; Const: A, V Freq: X Occas: C, R, H, I, T, G, N, D • **Work Env:** Noise=N; • **Salary:** 2 • **Outlook:** 1

VIDEO OPERATOR (radio-tv broad.) • DOT #194.282-010 • OES: 34028 • Alternate titles: CAMERA CONTROL OPERATOR; COLOR-TELEVISION CONSOLE MONITOR; VIDEO ENGINEER. Controls video console to regulate transmission of television scenes, including test patterns and filmed and live black-and-white or color telecast: Views action on television monitor and sets switches and observes dials on console to control framing, contrast, brilliance, color balance, and fidelity of image being transmitted. Monitors on-air programs to ensure technical quality of broadcast. Previews upcoming program to determine that signal is functioning and that program will be ready for transmission at required time. May maintain log on studio-to-transmitter microwave link. ● **GED:** R4, M4, L3 ● **SVP:** 2-4 yrs ● **Academic:** Ed=H, Eng=G ● **Work Field:** 281 ● **MPSMS:** 864 ● **Aptitudes:** G2, V2, N3, S3, P2, Q3, K3, F3, M3, E5, C2 ● **Temperaments:** J, T ● **Physical:** Stg=S; Const: A Freq: I, G, N, D, X Occas: R ● **Work Env:** Noise=N; ● **Salary:** 2 ● **Outlook:** 1

VIDEOTAPE OPERATOR (radio-tv broad.) ● DOT #194.382-018 ● OES: 34028 ● Alternate titles: STUDIO TECHNICIAN-VIDEO OPERATOR; VIDEOTAPE ENGINEER. Sets up and operates videotaping equipment to record and play back television programs, applying knowledge of videotaping equipment operation: Reads television programming log to ascertain program to be recorded or program to be aired. Selects source, such as satellite or studio, from which program will be recorded, and selects videotaping equipment on which program will be recorded. Observes monitor to verify that station is on-air, and informs supervisor if station not on-air. Cleans videotape path to remove contaminants that would affect quality of recording or playback, and mounts videotape onto videotaping equipment. Sets audio level, and records test pattern and program onto videotape, using videotaping equipment. Verifies quality of recording, using videotape equipment, and informs designated personnel of quality of recording. Inspects tape for defective ends, removes defective end, using cutting tool, and mounts videotape onto videotaping equipment to play back program. Starts videotaping equipment and turns video and color monitors on to verify setting of video and color levels. Observes scales in video and color monitors and operates controls to adjust video and color levels. Cues program, using videotaping equipment, and places videotaping equipment in remote control mode for use by other operator. May operate videotaping equipment to dub and edit tapes. May wire audio and video patch bays (socketed equipment that allows for transfer of audio and video signals between different pieces of equipment, via cables). May set up videotaping equipment to play station breaks. May set up film equipment to play program. May make minor repairs to equipment. ● **GED:** R4, M2, L3 ● **SVP:** 4-10 yrs ● **Academic:** Ed=H, Eng=G ● **Work Field:** 281 ● **MPSMS:** 864 ● **Aptitudes:** G3, V4, N4, S4, P3, Q4, K4, F3, M3, E5, C3 ● **Temperaments:** J, T ● **Physical:** Stg=L; Freq: R, H, I Occas: T, G, N, D, A, X ● **Work Env:** Noise=N; ● **Salary:** 3 ● **Outlook:** 3

GOE: 05.03.06
Industrial & Safety

BUILDING INSPECTOR (insurance) ● DOT #168.267-010 ● OES: 21908 ● Inspects buildings to determine fire insurance rates: Examines building for type of construction, condition of roof, and fireproofing. Determines risk represented by adjoining buildings, by nature of business, and building contents. Determines availability of fireplugs and firefighting equipment. Completes inspection report. May compute insurance rate. ● **GED:** R4, M3, L4 ● **SVP:** 2-4 yrs ● **Academic:** Ed=A, Eng=G ● **Work Field:** 211 ● **MPSMS:** 361, 895 ● **Aptitudes:** G2, V2, N3, S3, P4, Q2, K4, F4, M4, E4, C4 ● **Temperaments:** J ● **Physical:** Stg=L; Freq: C, N Occas: B, S, R, H, I, T, G, X ● **Work Env:** Noise=N; Freq: W ● **Salary:** 3 ● **Outlook:** 1

CODE INSPECTOR (government ser.) ● DOT #168.367-018 ● OES: 21911 ● Inspects existing residential buildings and dwelling units, visually, to determine compliance with city ordinance standards and explains ordinance requirements to concerned personnel: Obtains permission from owners and tenants to enter dwellings. Visually examines all areas to determine compliance with ordinance standards for heating, lighting, ventilating, and plumbing installations. Measures dwelling units and rooms to determine compliance with ordinance space requirements, using tape measure. Inspects premises for overall cleanliness, adequate disposal of garbage and rubbish, and for signs of vermin infestation. Prepares forms and letters advising property owners and tenants of possible violations and time allowed for correcting deficiencies. Consults file of violation reports and revisits dwellings at periodic intervals to verify correction of violations by property owners and tenants. Explains requirements of housing standards ordinance to

property owners, building contractors, and other interested parties. ● **GED:** R3, M2, L3 ● **SVP:** 6 mos-1 yr ● **Academic:** Ed=N, Eng=G ● **Work Field:** 211 ● **MPSMS:** 953 ● **Aptitudes:** G3, V3, N4, S3, P2, Q3, K4, F4, M4, E5, C5 ● **Temperaments:** P, T ● **Physical:** Stg=L; Freq: T, G, N, F Occas: S, K, R, H, A ● **Work Env:** Noise=N; ● **Salary:** 3 ● **Outlook:** 2

CONSTRUCTION INSPECTOR (construction) ● DOT #182.267-010 ● OES: 21908 ● Inspects and oversees construction of bridges, buildings, dams, highways, and other types of construction work to ensure that procedures and materials comply with plans and specifications: Measures distances to verify accuracy of dimensions of structural installations and layouts. Verifies levels, alignment, and elevation of installations, using surveyor's level and transit. Observes work in progress to ensure that procedures followed and materials used conform to specifications. Prepares samples of unapproved materials for laboratory testing. Examines workmanship of finished installations for conformity to standard and approves installation. Interprets blueprints and specifications for CONTRACTOR (construction) and discusses deviations from specified construction procedures to ensure compliance with regulations governing construction. Records quantities of materials received or used during specified periods. Maintains daily log of construction and inspection activities and compares progress reports. Computes monthly estimates of work completed and approves payment for contractors. Prepares sketches of construction installations that deviate from blueprints and reports such changes for incorporation on master blueprints. May be designated according to structure or material inspected as Building-Construction Inspector (construction); Ditch Inspector (construction); Highway Inspector (construction); Masonry Inspector (construction); Reinforced-Concrete Inspector (construction); Rod Inspector (construction). May be designated: Pipeline Inspector (construction); Structural-Steel Inspector (construction); Tunnel-Heading Inspector (construction). ● **GED:** R4, M4, L3 ● **SVP:** 1-2 yrs ● **Academic:** Ed=H, Eng=S ● **Work Field:** 243, 211 ● **MPSMS:** 360 ● **Aptitudes:** G2, V3, N2, S2, P3, Q4, K4, F4, M4, E2, C5 ● **Temperaments:** J, T, V ● **Physical:** Stg=L; Freq: R, H, I, T, G, N Occas: C, B, S, K, O, W, D, A ● **Work Env:** Noise=L; Freq: W ● **Salary:** 4 ● **Outlook:** 3

FLIGHT ENGINEER (air trans.) ● DOT #621.261-018 ● OES: 97702 ● Alternate titles: FLIGHT MECHANIC. Makes preflight, inflight, and postflight inspections, adjustments, and minor repairs to ensure safe and efficient operation of aircraft: Inspects aircraft prior to takeoff for defects, such as fuel or oil leaks and malfunctions in electrical, hydraulic, or pressurization systems, according to preflight checklist. Verifies passenger and cargo distribution and amount of fuel to ensure that weight and balance specifications are met. Monitors control panel to verify aircraft performance, and regulates engine speed according to instructions of AIRPLANE PILOT, COMMERCIAL (air trans.). Makes inflight repairs, such as replacing fuses, adjusting instruments, and freeing jammed flight control cables, using handtools, or takes emergency measures to compensate for failure of equipment, such as autopilot, wing heaters, and electrical and hydraulic systems. Monitors fuel gauges and computes rate of fuel consumption. Keeps log of fuel consumption and engine performance. Records malfunctions which were not corrected during flight and reports needed repairs to ground maintenance personnel. May perform repairs upon completion of flight. Must be licensed by Federal Aviation Administration. May be required to be licensed AIRFRAME-AND-POWER-PLANT MECHANIC (air trans.; aircraft mfg.) or AIRPLANE PILOT, COMMERCIAL (air trans.). ● **GED:** R4, M4, L4 ● **SVP:** 2-4 yrs ● **Academic:** Ed=H, Eng=G ● **Work Field:** 121, 111 ● **MPSMS:** 592 ● **Aptitudes:** G2, V2, N2, S3, P3, Q2, K3, F3, M3, E4, C4 ● **Temperaments:** J, S, T, V ● **Physical:** Stg=L; Freq: R, H, I, T, G, N, A, X Occas: S, K ● **Work Env:** Noise=V; Occas: W, M ● **Salary:** 5 ● **Outlook:** 3

INDUSTRIAL ENGINEERING TECHNICIAN (profess. & kin.) ● DOT #012.267-010 ● OES: 35199 ● Studies and records time, motion, methods, and speed involved in performance of maintenance, production, clerical, and other worker operations to establish standard production rate and to improve efficiency: Prepares charts, graphs, and diagrams to illustrate workflow, routing, floor layouts, material handling, and machine utilization. Observes workers operating equipment or performing tasks to determine time involved and fatigue rate, using stop watch, motion-picture camera, electrical recorder, and similar equipment. Recommends revision of methods of operation or material handling, alterations in equipment layout, or other changes to increase production or improve standards. Aids in planning work assignments in accordance with worker performance, machine capacity, production schedules, and anticipated delays. May be designated according to type of studies analyzed as Methods-Study Analyst (profess. & kin.); Motion-Study Analyst (profess. & kin.); Pace Analyst (profess. & kin.); Time-Study Analyst (profess. & kin.). ● **GED:** R5, M5, L4 ● **SVP:** 2-4 yrs ● **Academic:** Ed=A, Eng=G ● **Work Field:** 244 ● **MPSMS:** 712 ● **Aptitudes:** G2, V2, N2, S2, P2, Q3, K4, F3, M4, E5, C4 ● **Temperaments:** D, J ● **Physical:** Stg=L; Freq: R, H, I, T, G, N, F, A Occas: X ● **Work Env:** Noise=L; Occas: O ● **Salary:** 4 ● **Outlook:** 3

INSPECTOR, AIR-CARRIER (government ser.) ● DOT #168.264-010 ● OES: 21911 ● Alternate titles: AVIATION-SAFETY OFFICER; OPERATIONS INSPECTOR. Inspects aircraft and maintenance base facilities to assure conformance with federal safety and qualifications standards: Examines aircraft maintenance record and flight log to determine if service checks, maintenance checks, and overhauls were performed at intervals prescribed. Inspects landing gear, tires, and exterior of fuselage, wings, and engine for evidence of damage or corrosion and recommends repair. Examines access plates and doors for security. Inspects new, repaired, or modified aircraft, according to checklist, to determine structural and mechanical airworthiness, using handtools and test instruments. Starts aircraft and observes gauges, meters, and other instruments to detect evidence of malfunction. Examines electrical systems and accompanies flight crew on proving flight to test instruments. Inventories spare parts to determine whether stock meets requirements. Analyzes training programs to assure competency of persons operating, installing, and repairing equipment. Informs airline officials of deficiencies. Prepares report of inspection to document findings. Approves or disapproves issuance of certificate of airworthiness. Conducts examinations to test theoretical and practical knowledge of construction, maintenance, repair, and trouble diagnosis for aircraft mechanics license candidates. Investigates air accidents to determine whether cause was due to structural or mechanical malfunction. Required to have federal aviation rating for type of aircraft inspected and pass federal aviation medical certification. May be designated according to specialty as Air-Carrier Electronics Inspector (government ser.); Air-Carrier Maintenance Inspector (government ser.). ● **GED:** R5, M5, L4 ● **SVP:** 2-4 yrs ● **Academic:** Ed=A, Eng=S ● **Work Field:** 211 ● **MPSMS:** 592, 953, 586 ● **Aptitudes:** G2, V3, N2, S2, P2, Q3, K3, F3, M2, E4, C4 ● **Temperaments:** J ● **Physical:** Stg=L; Freq: R, H, I, T, G, N, D Occas: S, K, O, A, X, V ● **Work Env:** Noise=V; Occas: O ● **Salary:** 4 ● **Outlook:** 3

INSPECTOR, BUILDING (government ser.) ● DOT #168.167-030 ● OES: 21908 ● Inspects new and existing buildings and structures to enforce conformance to building, grading, and zoning laws and approved plans, specifications, and standards: Inspects residential, commercial, industrial, and other buildings during and after construction to ensure that components, such as footings, floor framing, completed framing, chimneys, and stairways meet provisions of building, grading, zoning, and safety laws and approved plans, specifications, and standards. Observes conditions and issues notices for corrections to persons responsible for conformance. Obtains evidence and prepares report concerning violations which have not been corrected. Interprets legal requirements and recommends compliance procedures to contractors, craftworkers, and owners. Keeps inspection records and prepares reports for use by administrative or judicial authorities. May conduct surveys of existing buildings to determine lack of prescribed maintenance, housing violations, or hazardous conditions. May review request for and issue building permits. May specialize in inspecting multifamily residences, temporary structures, buildings to be moved, or building appendages, such as chimneys, signs, swimming pools, retaining walls, and excavations and fills. May specialize in inspecting single-family residences for enforcement of full range of building, zoning, grading, and mechanical codes, including electrical, plumbing, heating and refrigeration, ventilating, and air-conditioning regulations and be designated Residential Building Inspector (government ser.). ● **GED:** R4, M4, L4 ● **SVP:** 2-4 yrs ● **Academic:** Ed=N, Eng=G ● **Work Field:** 211, 271 ● **MPSMS:** 953 ● **Aptitudes:** G2, V2, N3, S2, P3, Q3, K4, F4, M4, E4, C5 ● **Temperaments:** J, P, T ● **Physical:** Stg=L; Freq: R, H, T, G Occas: C, B, S, K, O, I, N, F, D, A, V ● **Work Env:** Noise=N; Occas: W, O ● **Salary:** 3 ● **Outlook:** 3

INSPECTOR, INDUSTRIAL WASTE (government ser.) ● DOT #168.267-054 ● OES: 21911 ● Inspects industrial and commercial waste disposal facilities and investigates source of pollutants in municipal sewage and storm-drainage system to ensure conformance with ordinance and permit requirements: Visits establishments to determine possession of industrial waste permits and to inspect waste treatment facilities, such as floor drains, sand traps, settling and neutralizing tanks, and grease removal equipment for conformance with regulations. Extracts samples of waste from sewers, storm drains, and water courses for laboratory tests. Conducts field tests for acidity, alkalinity, and other characteristics to determine if discharged wastes will cause water pollution or deterioration of sewerage facilities. Inspects sewers and storm drains to determine presence of explosive gases, using gas-analysis equipment. Reviews plans of proposed waste-treatment facilities and inspects construction to ensure conformance with ordinances. Issues citations to apparent violators of sanitation code or water-quality regulations. Compiles written reports of investigations and findings, and actions taken or recommended. May enforce ordinances concerned with commercial hauling and disposal of contents from cesspools and septic tanks into sewers. May inspect water wells for contamination and conformance with legal construction standards, and order closing of unsanitary or unsafe wells. May inspect solid waste disposal facilities, such as sanitary landfills and chemical disposal sites. ● **GED:** R5, M4, L5 ● **SVP:** 1-2 yrs ● **Academic:** Ed=A, Eng=S ● **Work Field:** 211 ● **MPSMS:** 874 ● **Aptitudes:** G2, V2, N3, S3, P3, Q3, K4, F4, M3, E4, C3 ● **Temperaments:** J, P, V ● **Physical:** Stg=M; Freq: R, H, I, T, G, N, A, X Occas: C, S, O, D, V ● **Work Env:** Noise=N; Freq: W, O Occas: V, A, D ● **Salary:** 4 ● **Outlook:** 3

INSPECTOR, PLUMBING (government ser.) ● DOT #168.167-050 ● OES: 21908 ● Inspects plumbing installations for conformance to governmental codes, sanitation standards, and construction specifications: Inspects commercial and industrial plumbing systems for conformance to plumbing laws and codes and approved plans and specifications. Inspects water-supply systems, drainage and sewer systems, water heater installations, fire sprinkler systems, and air and gas piping systems for approved materials, specified pipe sizes and connections, required grade and fitting, approved back-flow prevention devices, required bracing, ventilation, and air- and- water-tightness. Inspects building sites for soil type to determine fill conditions, water table level, site layout, seepage rate, and other conditions. Advises owners and contractors on acceptable locations for septic tanks, cesspools, and seepage pits. Interviews PLUMBER (construction) working in jurisdiction to determine possession of valid occupational licenses. Reviews plumbing permit applications and verifies payment of fees. Reviews complaints concerning alleged violations of plumbing code, gathers evidence, and appears in court as witness. Keeps records of inspections performed, actions taken, and corrections recommended and secured. ● **GED:** R5, M4, L4 ● **SVP:** 2-4 yrs ● **Academic:** Ed=A, Eng=G ● **Work Field:** 211, 271 ● **MPSMS:** 364, 959 ● **Aptitudes:** G2, V2, N2, S2, P3, Q3, K4, F4, M4, E3, C4 ● **Temperaments:** J, P, T ● **Physical:** Stg=L; Freq: R, H, I, T, G, N, D Occas: C, B, S, K, O, W, A, X ● **Work Env:** Noise=N; Occas: W ● **Salary:** 4 ● **Outlook:** 3

INSPECTOR, QUALITY ASSURANCE (government ser.) ● DOT #168.287-014 ● OES: 21911 ● Alternate titles: PROCUREMENT INSPECTOR. Inspects products manufactured or processed by private companies for government use to ensure compliance with contract specifications: Examines company's records to secure such information as size and weight of product and results of quality tests. Inspects product to determine compliance with order specifications, company's quality control system for compliance with legal requirements, and shipping and packing facilities for conformity to specified standards. Submits samples of product to government laboratory for testing as indicated by department procedures. Stamps mark of approval or rejection on product and writes report of examinations. May specialize in lumber, machinery, petroleum products, paper products, electronic equipment, furniture, or other specific product or group of related products. ● **GED:** R5, M5, L5 ● **SVP:** 2-4 yrs ● **Academic:** Ed=A, Eng=S ● **Work Field:** 211 ● **MPSMS:** 959 ● **Aptitudes:** G2, V2, N2, S3, P2, Q3, K4, F4, M4, E5, C3 ● **Temperaments:** J ● **Physical:** Stg=L; Freq: R, H, I, T, G, N Occas: D, A ● **Work Env:** Noise=L; ● **Salary:** 3 ● **Outlook:** 3

INSPECTOR, RAILROAD (government ser.) ● DOT #168.287-018 ● OES: 21911 ● Examines railroad equipment and systems to verify compliance with Federal safety regulations: Inspects railroad locomotives, engines, and cars to ensure adherence to safety standards governing condition of mechanical, structural, electrical, pneumatic, and hydraulic elements or systems, using blueprints, schematic diagrams, gauges, handtools, and test equipment. Tests railroad signals to determine warning light responses to commands from dispatcher or tripswitches, using simulator. Inspects roadbeds to detect damaged, worn, or defective equipment, such as rails, ties, bolts, fishplates, or switches. Inspects condition and movement of railroad cars containing flammable or explosive materials to ensure safe loading, switching, and transport. Reviews records, operating practices, and accident history to verify compliance with safety regulations. Issues citations to railroad employees of condition or equipment found in violation of standards. Investigates accidents and inspects wreckage to determine causes. Prepares inspection reports for use by administrative or judicial authorities. ● **GED:** R4, M3, L4 ● **SVP:** 2-4 yrs ● **Academic:** Ed=H, Eng=S ● **Work Field:** 211, 121 ● **MPSMS:** 594, 851 ● **Aptitudes:** G3, V3, N3, S2, P3, Q3, K3, F3, M3, E3, C3 ● **Temperaments:** J, T ● **Physical:** Stg=M; Freq: R, H, I, N, A Occas: C, B, S, K, O, X ● **Work Env:** Noise=L; Freq: W Occas: O ● **Salary:** 5 ● **Outlook:** 3

MARINE SURVEYOR (profess. & kin.) ● DOT #014.167-010 ● OES: 22198 ● Alternate titles: SHIP SURVEYOR. Surveys marine vessels and watercraft, such as ships, boats, tankers, and dredges, to ascertain condition of hull, machinery, equipment, and equipage, and to determine repairs required for vessel to meet requirements for insuring: Examines underwater section of hull while ship is drydocked to ascertain conditions that indicate repairs are required. Takes readings on tailshaft and tailshaft bearings. Inspects condition of propellers, rudders, and sea valves. Inspects above waterline section of ship, such as hatchways, freeing ports, ventilators, bulkheads, fittings, and attachments, for compliance with operating standards, and compliance with standards for protection of crew. Observes operating tests on machinery and equipment and inspects opened up machinery for interior condition. Observes testing of cargo gear for compliance with testing standards and issues or endorses certificate for gear tested. Prepares reports on types of surveys conducted, recommended actions and repairs, or conditions remedied. Submits report to client. ● **GED:** R5, M4, L4 ● **SVP:** 4-10 yrs ● **Academic:** Ed=A, Eng=G ● **Work Field:** 212 ● **MPSMS:** 593 ● **Aptitudes:** G2, V2, N2, S3, P3, Q4, K4, F4, M3, E4, C5 ● **Temperaments:** J ● **Physical:** Stg=L; Freq: C, R, H, T, G, N, D Occas: B, S, K, O, W, I ● **Work Env:** Noise=N; Freq: W ● **Salary:** 3 ● **Outlook:** 2

PLAN CHECKER (government ser.) ● DOT #168.267-102 ● OES: 21908 ● Examines commercial and private building plans and inspects construction sites to ensure compliance with building code regulations: Reviews building plans for completeness and accuracy. Examines individual plan components to ensure that all code mandated items are included. Calculates footage between building components, such as doors, windows, and parking areas and amount of area occupied by components to ensure compliance with code. Notes instances of noncompliance on plans and correction sheet and suggests modifications to bring plans into compliance. Approves and signs plans meeting code requirements. Inspects building sites and buildings to ensure construction follows plans. Submits reports detailing items of noncompliance to builder for correction. Provides code information to individuals planning buildings. Issues occupancy certificates to building owners when completed buildings are in compliance with codes. Tours jurisdictional area to detect unapproved or noncompliance construction. Proposes studies to improve or update building codes. Testifies at appeal hearings regarding buildings alleged to be not in compliance with codes. ● **GED:** R4, M4, L4 ● **SVP:** 2-4 yrs ● **Academic:** Ed=H, Eng=G ● **Work Field:** 211, 271 ● **MPSMS:** 953 ● **Aptitudes:** G3, V2, N2, S2, P2, Q2, K4, F4, M4, E4, C5 ● **Temperaments:** P, T ● **Physical:** Stg=L; Const: T, G Freq: R, H, N Occas: C, B, S, K, F, A ● **Work Env:** Noise=N; ● **Salary:** 4 ● **Outlook:** 2

SUPERVISOR, VENDOR QUALITY (any industry) ● DOT #012.167-062 ● OES: 13017 ● Alternate titles: CHIEF, VENDOR QUALITY. Directs and coordinates quality inspection of parts, components, and materials produced by subcontractors and vendors, and surveillance of subcontractors' manufacturing processes: Directs sampling inspection, and testing of received parts, components, and materials to determine conformance to standards. Conducts periodic and special surveys of subcontractors' facilities and manufacturing processes to determine adequacy and capability of quality control and ability

to comply with complete quality specifications. Reviews quality problems with engineering personnel and directs action required to correct defects. Prepares periodic and special reports concerning departmental activities, problems, subcontractor's quality system, schedules, and rejected items. Aids in organizational planning by participating in departmental conferences. ● **GED:** R5, M5, L5 ● **SVP:** 2-4 yrs ● **Academic:** Ed=A, Eng=S ● **Work Field:** 211 ● **MPSMS:** 580, 560, 470 ● **Aptitudes:** G2, V2, N2, S3, P4, Q4, K3, F3, M3, E5, C5 ● **Temperaments:** D, J, P ● **Physical:** Stg=S; Freq: R, H, T, G, N Occas: I, D, A ● **Work Env:** Noise=N; ● **Salary:** 4 ● **Outlook:** 4

GOE: 05.03.07
Mechanical

HEAT-TRANSFER TECHNICIAN (profess. & kin.) ● DOT #007.181-010 ● OES: 35199 ● Plans requirements for fabricating, installing, testing, and servicing climate control and heat transfer assemblies and systems to assist engineering personnel, utilizing knowledge of heat transfer technology and engineering methods: Calculates required capacities for equipment units of proposed system to obtain specified performance and submits data to engineering personnel for approval. Studies supplier catalogs and technical data to recommend equipment unit selections for system. Prepares unit design layouts and detail drawings for fabricating parts and assembling system. Estimates cost factors, such as labor and material for purchased and fabricated parts, and costs for assembling, testing and installing in customer's premises. Fabricates nonstandard parts for system, using metalworking machinery and assembles system, using handtools and power tools. Installs test fixtures, apparatus, and controls and conducts operational tests under specified conditions. Analyzes test data and prepares report for evaluation by engineering personnel. Installs system in customer premises and tests operational performance for compliance with contract specifications and applicable codes. Diagnoses special service problems of systems under service contract and writes instructions for service or repair personnel. May be designated according to specialty as Air-Conditioning Technician (profess. & kin.); Heating Technician (profess. & kin.); Refrigerating Technician (profess. & kin.). ● **GED:** R5, M5, L5 ● **SVP:** 2-4 yrs ● **Academic:** Ed=A, Eng=S ● **Work Field:** 212, 244 ● **MPSMS:** 706, 573, 553 ● **Aptitudes:** G2, V2, N2, S2, P2, Q3, K2, F2, M2, E4, C5 ● **Temperaments:** J, T, V ● **Physical:** Stg=L; Freq: R, H, I, N Occas: T, G, D, A ● **Work Env:** Noise=N; Occas: W ● **Salary:** 2 ● **Outlook:** 3

SOLAR-ENERGY-SYSTEMS DESIGNER (profess. & kin.) ● DOT #007.161-038 ● OES: 22135 ● Designs solar domestic hot water and space heating systems for new and existing structures, applying knowledge of energy requirements of structure, local climatological conditions, solar technology, and thermodynamics: Estimates energy requirements of new or existing structures, based on analysis of utility bills of structure, calculations of thermal efficiency of structure, and prevailing climatological conditions. Determines type of solar system, such as water, glycol, or silicone, which functions most efficiently under prevailing climatological conditions. Calculates on-site heat generating capacity of different solar panels to determine optimum size and type of panels which meet structure's energy requirements. Arranges location of solar system components, such as panel, pumps, and storage tanks, to minimize length and number of direction changes in pipes and reconstruction of existing structures. Studies engineering tables to determine size of pipes and pumps required to maintain specified flow rate through solar panels. Specifies types of electrical controls, such as differential thermostat, temperature sensors, and solenoid valves, compatible with other system components, using knowledge of control systems. Completes parts list, specifying components of system. Draws wiring, piping, and other diagrams, using drafting tools. May inspect structures to compile data used in solar system design, such as structure's angle of alignment with sun and temperature of incoming cold water. May inspect construction of system to ensure adherence to design specifications. ● **GED:** R5, M4, L4 ● **SVP:** 6 mos-1 yr ● **Academic:** Ed=A, Eng=G ● **Work Field:** 244, 242 ● **MPSMS:** 553, 706 ● **Aptitudes:** G2, V2, N2, S2, P2, Q2, K2, F3, M4, E5, C4 ● **Temperaments:** J, T, V ● **Physical:** Stg=L; Freq: R, H, I, N Occas: D, A, X ● **Work Env:** Noise=N; ● **Salary:** 4 ● **Outlook:** 3

TEST TECHNICIAN (agric. equip.) ● DOT #019.261-022 ● OES: 35199 ● Tests experimental and production agricultural equipment, such as tractors and power mowers and components to evaluate their performance, using test equipment and recording instruments: Reads data sheet denoting operating specification for unit or component and type of evaluation required. Tests unit for conformance with operating requirements, such as resistance to vibration, specified horsepower, and tensile strength and hardness of parts, using test equipment, such as bend-fatigue machine, dynamometer, strength tester, hardness tester, analytical balance, and electronic recorder. Records data from dial readings and graphs and computes values, such as horse-power and tensile strength, using algebraic formulas. Operates unit to evaluate attachment performance, such as depth of tillage or harvesting capabilities for different types of crops. Draws sketches and describes test procedures and results in test data log. ● **GED:** R4, M4, L4 ● **SVP:** 1-2 yrs ● **Academic:** Ed=A, Eng=S ● **Work Field:** 211 ● **MPSMS:** 562 ● **Aptitudes:** G3, V3, N3, S3, P3, Q3, K3, F3, M3, E5, C4 ● **Temperaments:** J, T ● **Physical:** Stg=L; Freq: R, H, N Occas: I, D, A, V ● **Work Env:** Noise=N; Occas: W, M ● **Salary:** 3 ● **Outlook:** 4

GOE: 05.03.08
Environmental Control

ENERGY-CONTROL OFFICER (education) ● DOT #199.167-018 ● OES: 39998 ● Monitors energy use and develops, promotes, implements, and coordinates energy conservation program in county school district facilities: Compiles monthly energy report on consumption of electricity, fuel, oil, coal, LP gas, and water in school facilities, listing units consumed and costs. Sets up energy monitoring devices in school facilities that graphically plot energy usage and temperature changes during extended periods of time. Visits school facilities on regular basis to inspect monitoring devices and utilities usage. Determines areas in which energy conservation measures are needed, and compiles needs-assessment report of all school facilities. Monitors energy usage of extracurricular activities in school facilities. Coordinates energy conservation activities in areas with those of local, state, and federal conservation groups. Recommends energy conservation policies to board of education. Presents lectures on resource conservation at teachers' meetings and to civic groups. ● **GED:** R4, M4, L4 ● **SVP:** 2-4 yrs ● **Academic:** Ed=H, Eng=G ● **Work Field:** 282, 211 ● **MPSMS:** 870 ● **Aptitudes:** G3, V3, N3, S4, P3, Q3, K3, F4, M4, E5, C5 ● **Temperaments:** I, P, T ● **Physical:** Stg=L; Freq: R, H, T, G, N Occas: I, A ● **Work Env:** Noise=N; ● **Salary:** 4 ● **Outlook:** 3

POLLUTION-CONTROL TECHNICIAN (profess. & kin.) ● DOT #029.261-014 ● OES: 24501 ● Alternate titles: ENVIRONMENTAL TECHNICIAN. Conducts tests and field investigations to obtain data for use by environmental, engineering, and scientific personnel in determining sources and methods of controlling pollutants in air, water, and soil, utilizing knowledge of agriculture, chemistry, meteorology, and engineering principles and applied technologies: Conducts chemical and physical laboratory and field tests according to prescribed standards to determine characteristics or composition of solid, liquid, or gaseous materials and substances, using pH meter, chemicals, autoclaves, centrifuge, spectrophotometer, microscope, analytical instrumentation, and chemical laboratory equipment. Collects samples of gases from smokestacks, and collects other air samples and meteorological data to assist in evaluation of atmospheric pollutants. Collects water samples from streams and lakes, or raw, semiprocessed or processed water, industrial waste water, or water from other sources to assess pollution problem. Collects soil, silt, or mud to determine chemical composition and nature of pollutants. Prepares sample for testing, records data, and prepares summaries and charts for review. Sets monitoring equipment to provide flow of information. Installs, operates, and performs routine maintenance on gas and fluid flow systems, chemical reaction systems, mechanical equipment, and other test instrumentation. May operate fixed or mobile monitoring or data collection station. May conduct bacteriological or other tests related to research in environmental or pollution control activity. May collect and analyze engine exhaust emissions to determine type and amount of pollutants and be designated Engine Emission Technician (profess. & kin.). May specialize in one phase or type of environmental pollution or protection and be identified according to specialty. ● **GED:** R4, M4, L4 ● **SVP:**

1-2 yrs ● **Academic:** Ed=A, Eng=S ● **Work Field:** 212, 251 ● **MPSMS:** 723, 729 ● **Aptitudes:** G3, V3, N3, S4, P3, Q3, K4, F4, M4, E5, C3 ● **Temperaments:** J, T ● **Physical:** Stg=L; Freq: R, H, I, T, G, N, D, X Occas: C, B, S, K, O, W, E, F, A, V ● **Work Env:** Noise=N; Occas: W, A, O ● **Salary:** 3 ● **Outlook:** 4

RADIATION MONITOR (profess. & kin.) ● DOT #199.167-010 ● OES: 24501 ● Alternate titles: HEALTH-PHYSICS TECHNICIAN; PERSONNEL MONITOR. Monitors personnel, plant facilities, and work environment to detect radio-active contamination, using radiation detectors and other instruments: Measures intensity and identifies type of radiation in working areas, using devices, such as beta-gamma survey meter, gamma-background monitor, and alphabeta-gamma counter. Collects air samples to determine airborne concentration of radioactivity, and collects and analyzes monitoring equipment worn by personnel, such as film badges and pocket detection chambers, to measure individual exposure to radiation. Takes smear test of suspected contaminated area by wiping floor with filter paper and placing paper in scaler to obtain contamination count. Informs supervisors when individual exposures and area radiation levels approach maximum permissible limits. Recommends work stoppage in unsafe areas, posts warning signs, and ropes off contaminated areas. Calculates amount of time personnel may be exposed safely to radiation in area, taking into account contamination count and HEALTH PHYSICIST'S (profess. & kin.) determinations concerning exposure limits of personnel. Instructs personnel in radiation safety procedures and demonstrates use of protective clothing and equipment. Monitors time and intensity of exposure of personnel working in radiation-waste disposal areas. Inspects shipments for contamination, using counter, and tags shipments in which radiation count exceeds specifications. May make periodic urinalyses of personnel and notify supervisors when overexposure to radiation is indicated. Logs data, such as status of areas being decontaminated, rate of radiation exposure to personnel, and location and intensity of radioactivity in contaminated areas. Tests detection instruments against standards to ensure their accuracy. May recommend decontamination procedures. ● **GED:** R4, M4, L4 ● **SVP:** 1-2 yrs ● **Academic:** Ed=H, Eng=G ● **Work Field:** 211 ● **MPSMS:** 715 ● **Aptitudes:** G3, V3, N3, S4, P4, Q3, K4, F4, M4, E5, C5 ● **Temperaments:** J, P, T ● **Physical:** Stg=L; Freq: R, H, I, T, G, N, A ● **Work Env:** Noise=N; Freq: R ● **Salary:** 4 ● **Outlook:** 2

GOE: 05.03.09
Packaging & Storing

FINE ARTS PACKER (museums) ● DOT #102.367-010 ● OES: 39998 ● Alternate titles: ART PREPARATOR. Specifies types of packing materials, crating, containerization, and special handling procedures for shipping or storing art objects, scientific specimens, and historical artifacts to minimize damage and deterioration: Confers with curatorial personnel regarding status of museum projects and proposed shipping or transfer dates of exhibitions. Develops methods and procedures for packing or containerization of art objects, according to weight and characteristics of shipment. Selects protective or preservative materials, such as excelsior, chemical agents, or moistureproof wrapping, to protect shipment against vibration, moisture, impact, or other hazards. Designs special crates, modules, brackets, and traveling frames to meet insurance and museum shipping specifications. Shapes and contours internal support modules, based on size and type of paintings, sculptures, bronzes, glass, and other art objects. Directs workers engaged in moving art objects from receiving or storage areas to galleries of museum, in packing shipments, or in rigging sculptures for installation of exhibition. Inspects incoming shipment to detect damages for insurance purposes. Keeps records and documents of incoming and outgoing shipments, or location of traveling exhibitions and loan materials. Prepares and attaches written or pictorial instructions for unpacking, storage, or for exhibition of contents of shipment. May specify type of carrier, such as barge, train, or messenger according to cost considerations and nature of shipment. ● **GED:** R4, M3, L3 ● **SVP:** 2-4 yrs ● **Academic:** Ed=H, Eng=S ● **Work Field:** 041 ● **MPSMS:** 969 ● **Aptitudes:** G2, V2, N3, S2, P4, Q4, K4, F4, M5, E5, C4 ● **Temperaments:** D, J ● **Physical:** Stg=M; Freq: R, H, I, T, G, N, D Occas: S, O, A ● **Work Env:** Noise=N; ● **Salary:** 5 ● **Outlook:** 3

PACKAGING ENGINEER (profess. & kin.) ● DOT #019.187-010 ● OES: 22198 ● Plans and directs activities concerned with design and development of protective packaging containers: Analyzes engineering drawings and specifications of product to determine physical characteristics of item, special-handling and safety requirements, and type of materials required for container. Consults with establishment's purchasing and production departments to determine costs and feasibility of producing proposed packaging. Develops or directs development of sketches, specifications, samples, and written analyses of proposed packaging in order to present design for approval. May confer with customers or sales representatives to draw up contracts. May advise employer or customers on efficient packing procedures, innovations in packaging materials, and utilization of sealing and fastening devices. ● **GED:** R5, M4, L5 ● **SVP:** 2-4 yrs ● **Academic:** Ed=B, Eng=S ● **Work Field:** 244 ● **MPSMS:** 475, 559, 492 ● **Aptitudes:** G3, V3, N3, S2, P2, Q3, K3, F3, M3, E5, C3 ● **Temperaments:** D, J, P ● **Physical:** Stg=S; Freq: R, H, I, T, G, N, X Occas: A ● **Work Env:** Noise=Q; ● **Salary:** 5 ● **Outlook:** 4

Mechanical

05

Air and Water Vehicle Operation

05.04

Workers in this group pilot airplanes or ships, or supervise others who do. Some instruct other persons in flying. Most of these workers are hired by shipping companies and commercial airlines. Some find jobs piloting planes or ships for private companies or individuals.

✓ **What kind of work would you do?**

Your work activities would depend upon your specific job. For example, you might:

- study load weight, fuel supply, weather conditions, and flight route to plan for a safe commercial plane flight.
- pilot a new airplane through stalls, dives, glides, rolls, and turns to test design and safety factors.
- use knowledge of local winds, weather, tides, and currents to pilot a ship through a harbor or strait.
- use charts, plotting sheets, compass, and sextant to plan and direct course of a ship.

✓ **What skills and abilities do you need for this kind of work?**

To do this kind of work, you must be able to:

- understand and use techniques and procedures for controlling the airplane or vessel.
- use judgment and make decisions that affect the lives of passengers on board.
- react quickly in emergencies.
- direct the crew on board.
- see readings on instrument panels clearly.
- use hand, feet, and eyes at the same time to control the ship or airplane.
- deal with different kinds of people.

✓ **How do you know if you would like or could learn to do this kind of work?**

The following questions may give you clues about yourself as you consider this group of jobs.

- Have you read airplane or boat magazines? Do you understand and enjoy technical articles?
- Have you built or operated a model airplane? Could you read and follow the instructions?
- Have you been a member of a Civil Air Patrol unit? Have you had flight or ground training?
- Have you operated a citizen's band radio? Do you understand and use the common code words?
- Have you driven in a bicycle rodeo, car rally, or other vehicle obstacle course? Did you receive a good score?
- Have you owned or operated a pleasure boat? Have you taken a Coast Guard safety training course?

✓ **How can you prepare for and enter this kind of work?**

Occupations in this group usually require education and/or training extending from two years to over ten years, depending upon the specific kind of work. Flight training may be obtained in the military or in FAA approved civilian flight schools. A high school education or its equal is the minimum requirement for acceptance.

Most major airlines have their own programs to provide additional specialized training before assigning pilots to service. Some airlines require a pilot to have two years of college. Many prefer college graduates. Before becoming an airline pilot, a person must have 1,500 hours of flying time.

Ship captains advance through several officer ranks. The beginning rank is that of third mate. Most third mate positions are earned by completing a training course at a marine academy.

Some marine trade unions offer programs to train seamen to become third mates. These trainees must be U.S. citizens and be approved by the U.S. Public Health Service for vision and general health. They must also pass Coast Guard tests on navigation, freight handling, and deck operations.

✓ **What else should you consider about these jobs?**

Pilots are often under mental stress and must always be alert and ready to make decisions quickly. Airlines have flights at all hours of the day and night. Pilots may be away from home frequently. Ship officers are usually away from home for long periods. Workers in this group face the possibility of injury through fires, collisions, and other disasters.

If you think you would like to do this kind of work, look at the job titles listed below.

■ ■ ■

GOE: 05.04.01
Air

AIRPLANE PILOT (agriculture) ● DOT #196.263-010 ● OES: 97702 ● Alternate titles: AERIAL-APPLICATOR PILOT; AGRICULTURAL-AIRCRAFT PILOT; AIRCRAFT PILOT; AIRPLANE PILOT, CROP DUSTING. Pilots airplane or helicopter, at low altitudes, over agricultural fields to dust or spray fields with seeds, fertilizers, or pesticides: Pilots aircraft over field, or drives to field, or studies maps to become acquainted with obstacles or hazards, such as air turbulence, hedgerows, and hills, peculiar to particular field. Arranges for warning signals to be posted. Notifies livestock owners to move livestock from property over which harmful material may drift. Signals AIRPLANE-PILOT HELPER (agriculture) 409.667-010 to load aircraft. Pilots aircraft to dust or spray fields with seeds, fertilizers, or pesticides, and observes field markers and flag waved by AIRPLANE-PILOT HELPER (agriculture) on ground to prevent overlaps of application and to ensure coverage of field. May be accompanied by property owner when piloting aircraft to survey field. May specialize in application of pesticides and be designated Pest-Control Pilot (agriculture). ● **GED:** R4, M4, L4 ● **SVP:** 1-2 yrs ● **Academic:** Ed=A, Eng=S ● **Work Field:** 003, 293 ● **MPSMS:** 300 ● **Aptitudes:** G2, V3, N2, S2, P2, Q3, K2, F3, M3, E2, C3 ● **Temperaments:** J, S, T ● **Physical:** Stg=L; Const: V Freq: R, H, T, G, N, F, D, A, X Occas: C, I ● **Work Env:** Noise=L; Const: T, O Occas: W ● **Salary:** 3 ● **Outlook:** 1

AIRPLANE PILOT, COMMERCIAL (air trans.) ● DOT #196.263-014 ● OES: 97702 ● Alternate titles: COMMERCIAL PILOT; PILOT. Pilots airplane to transport passengers, mail, or freight, or for other commercial purposes: Reviews ship's papers to ascertain factors, such as load weight, fuel supply, weather conditions, and flight route and schedule. Orders changes in fuel supply, load, route, or schedule to ensure safety of flight. Reads gauges to verify that oil, hydraulic fluid, fuel quantities, and cabin pressure are at prescribed levels prior to starting engines. Starts engines and taxies airplane to runway. Sets brakes, and accelerates engines to verify operational readiness of components, such as superchargers, carburetor-heaters, and controls. Contacts control tower by radio to obtain takeoff clearance and instructions. Releases brakes and moves throttles and hand and foot controls to take off and control airplane in flight. Pilots airplane to destination adhering to flight plan and regulations and procedures of federal government, company, and airport. Logs information, such as time in flight, altitude flown, and fuel consumed. Must hold commercial pilot's certificate issued by Federal Aviation Administration. May instruct students or pilots in operation of aircraft. May be designated according to federal license held as Transport Pilot (air trans.), or type of commercial activity engaged in as Airplane Pilot (air trans.) or Corporate Pilot (air trans.). May be designated Airplane-Patrol Pilot (business ser.) when piloting airplane over pipelines, train tracks, and communications systems to detect and radio location and nature of damage. May be designated Airplane Captain (air trans.) when in command of aircraft and crew or Airplane First-Officer (air trans.) or Copilot (air trans.) when second in command. ● **GED:** R5, M4, L4 ● **SVP:** 4-10 yrs ● **Academic:** Ed=A, Eng=G ● **Work Field:** 013 ● **MPSMS:** 855 ● **Aptitudes:** G2, V2, N2, S2, P3, Q3, K2, F4, M3, E3, C4 ● **Temperaments:** J, S, T, V ● **Physical:** Stg=L; Freq: R, H, T, G, N, F, D, A, X, V Occas: I ● **Work Env:** Noise=N; ● **Salary:** 5 ● **Outlook:** 3

INSTRUCTOR, FLYING I (education) ● DOT #196.223-010 ● OES: 97702 ● Instructs student pilots in flight procedures and techniques: Accompanies students on training flights and demonstrates techniques for controlling aircraft during taxiing, takeoff, spins, stalls, turns, and landings. Explains operation of aircraft components, such as rudder, flaps, ailerons, compass, altimeter, and tachometer. May give student proficiency tests at termination of training. Is required to hold Commercial Pilot's Certificate, with Instructor's Rating, issued by Federal Aviation Administration. ● **GED:** R5, M4, L5 ● **SVP:** 2-4 yrs ● **Academic:** Ed=A, Eng=G ● **Work Field:** 296 ● **MPSMS:** 931 ● **Aptitudes:** G2, V2, N2, S2, P2, Q2, K3, F4, M3, E2, C4 ● **Temperaments:** J, P, S, T, V ● **Physical:** Stg=L; Freq: R, H, I, T, G, N, F, D, A, X, V ● **Work Env:** Noise=L; Freq: O ● **Salary:** 3 ● **Outlook:** 3

INSTRUCTOR, FLYING II (education) ● DOT #097.227-010 ● OES: 31317 ● Instructs student pilots in flight procedures and techniques and in ground school courses: Develops and prepares course outlines, study materials, and instructional procedures for students enrolled in basic, advanced, or instrument ground school. Lectures on various subjects, such as aircraft construction, federal aviation regulations, and radio navigation. Demonstrates operation of various aircraft components and instruments, and techniques for controlling aircraft during maneuvers, such as taxiing, takeoff, and landing, using synthetic instrument trainers. Observes student's actions during training flights to ensure assimilation of classroom instruction and to comply with federal aviation regulations. Tests and evaluates students' progress, using written and performance tests and oral interviews. May teach advanced, basic, or instrument courses and be designated Ground Instructor, Advanced (education); Ground Instructor, Basic (education); Ground Instructor, Instrument (education). Must be certified by Federal Aviation Administration. ● **GED:** R4, M4, L3 ● **SVP:** 1-2 yrs ● **Academic:** Ed=A, Eng=G ● **Work Field:** 296 ● **MPSMS:** 855 ● **Aptitudes:** G2, V3, N3, S2, P2, Q2, K4, F4, M3, E3, C4 ● **Temperaments:** D, I, J ● **Physical:** Stg=L; Freq: R, H, I, T, G, N, D, A, X ● **Work Env:** Noise=N; ● **Salary:** 4 ● **Outlook:** 2

INSTRUCTOR, PILOT (air trans.) ● DOT #196.223-014 ● OES: 97702 ● Trains new and experienced company AIRLINE PILOTS (air trans.) in policy and in use of equipment: Instructs new pilots in company regulations and procedures and trains pilots in operation of types of aircraft used by company. Conducts courses for experienced company pilots to familiarize them with new equipment. May conduct review courses in navigation and meteorology. May make flights to observe performance of pilots [CHECK PILOT (air trans.)]. Must hold Commercial Pilot's Certificate, with Instructor's Rating, issued by Federal Aviation Administration. ● **GED:** R5, M4, L5 ● **SVP:** 4-10 yrs ● **Academic:** Ed=N, Eng=G ● **Work Field:** 296 ● **MPSMS:** 855 ● **Aptitudes:** G2, V2, N2, S2, P2, Q3, K3, F4, M3, E2, C4 ● **Temperaments:** J, P, S, T, V ● **Physical:** Stg=L; Freq: R, H, I, T, G, M, N, A Occas: F, D, X, V ● **Work Env:** Noise=V; Freq: O ● **Salary:** 5 ● **Outlook:** 3

GOE: 05.04.02
Water

CAPTAIN, FISHING VESSEL (fishing & hunt.) ● DOT #197.133-010 ● OES: 77002 ● Alternate titles: SKIPPER. Commands fishing vessel crew engaged in catching fish and other marine life: Interviews, hires, and gives instructions to crew, and assigns crew to watches and quarters. Plots courses on navigation charts and computes positions, using standard navigation aids, such as compass, sextant, clock, radio fix, and navigation tables. Steers vessel and operates electronic equipment, such as radio, sonic depth finder, and radar. Directs fishing operations, using knowledge of fishing grounds and work load capacities of vessel and crew. Records daily activities in ship's log. May purchase supplies and equipment for boat, such as food, fuel, webbing, rope, and cable. May tow and maneuver fish barges at cannery wharf. May contact buyers and make arrangements for sale of catch. May buy fish for resale and be designated Buy-Boat Operator (fishing & hunt.), or haul fish from other fishing vessels to cannery and be designated Captain, Cannery Tender (fishing & hunt.). ● **GED:** R4, M4, L4 ● **SVP:** 2-4 yrs ● **Academic:** Ed=H, Eng=G ● **Work Field:** 001 ● **MPSMS:** 330 ● **Aptitudes:** G3, V3, N3, S2, P2, Q2, K3, F4, M3, E3, C4 ● **Temperaments:** D, J, P, S, T ● **Physical:** Stg=L; Freq: C, B, R, H, I, T, G, N, F, D, A, X, V ● **Work Env:** Noise=L; Freq: W, U, O ● **Salary:** 5 ● **Outlook:** 1

MATE, SHIP (water trans.) ● DOT #197.133-022 ● OES: 97505 ● Alternate titles: SHIP OFFICER. Supervises and coordinates activities of crew aboard ship: Inspects holds of ship during loading to ensure that cargo is stowed according to specifications. Examines cargo-handling gear and lifesaving equipment and orders crew to repair or replace defective gear and equipment. Supervises crew engaged in cleaning and maintaining decks, superstructure, and bridge of ship. Stands watch during specified periods and determines geographical position of ship, upon request of MASTER, SHIP (water trans.), using loran and azimuths of celestial bodies. Assumes command of ship in event MASTER, SHIP (water trans.) becomes incapacitated. May be required to hold license issued by U.S. Coast Guard, depending on waters navigated and tonnage of ship. When more than one MATE, SHIP (water trans.) is required, may be designated Mate, Chief (water trans.) (usually on vessels inspected by U.S. Coast Guard); Mate, First (water trans.) (usually on uninspected vessels); Mate, Fourth (water trans.); Mate, Second (water trans.); Mate, Third (water trans.). May remain in port to relieve another MATE, SHIP (water trans.) who desires to go ashore while ship is in port and be designated Mate, Relief (water trans.). ● **GED:** R4, M4, L4 ● **SVP:** 2-4 yrs ● **Academic:** Ed=A, Eng=G ● **Work Field:** 013 ● **MPSMS:** 854 ● **Aptitudes:** G3, V3, N3, S2, P2, Q3, K3, F2, M3, E3, C4 ● **Temperaments:** D, J, P ● **Physical:** Stg=L; Freq: R, H, I, T, G, N Occas: C, B, S, K, O, F, D, A, X, V ● **Work Env:** Noise=L; Freq: O ● **Salary:** 2 ● **Outlook:** 3

PILOT, SHIP (water trans.) ● DOT #197.133-026 ● OES: 97510 ● Commands ships to steer them into and out of harbors, estuaries, straits, and sounds, and on rivers, lakes, and bays: Directs course and speed of ship on basis of specialized knowledge of local winds, weather, tides, and current. Orders worker at helm to steer ship, and navigates ship to avoid reefs, outlying shoals, and other hazards to shipping, utilizing aids to navigation, such as lighthouses and buoys. Signals TUGBOAT CAPTAIN (water trans.) to berth and unberth ship. Must be licensed by U.S. Coast Guard with limitations indicating class and tonnage of vessels for which license is valid and route and waters that may be piloted. May be designated according to vessel commanded as Pilot, Steam Yacht (water trans.); Pilot, Tank Vessel (water trans.). ● **GED:** R4, M4, L3 ● **SVP:** 4-10 yrs ● **Academic:** Ed=H, Eng=S ● **Work Field:** 013 ● **MPSMS:** 854 ● **Aptitudes:** G2, V1, N2, S2, P4, Q3, K3, F4, M3, E3, C4 ● **Temperaments:** D, J, P, S ● **Physical:** Stg=L; Freq: R, H, T, G, N, F, D, A, X, V Occas: C, B, I ● **Work Env:** Noise=L; Occas: W, U, O ● **Salary:** 5 ● **Outlook:** 1

Craft Technology

Workers in this group perform highly skilled hand and/or machine work requiring special techniques, training, and experience. Work occurs in a variety of nonfactory settings. Some workers own their own shops.

✓ What kind of work would you do?

Your work activities would depend upon your specific job. For example, you might:

- study blueprints and specifications for setting up a machine that shapes metal bolts and screws.
- lay out, drill, turn, grind, and fit metal castings to make patterns for use in a foundry.
- use knowledge of tool design, shop mathematics, metal properties, and machining procedures to make or repair machine tools.
- use handtools, precision-measuring instruments, and machine tools to repair diesel engines.
- use grinders, planers, millers, and handtools to repair or modify rifles and handguns.
- follow blueprints and use handtools and power tools to assemble or repair boilers and tanks in an industrial plant.
- lay brick or cement blocks to build a wall.
- follow blueprints and plans to measure, cut, fit, and nail wooden parts for a structure.
- set up and operate a variety of woodworking machines to make or repair cabinets and fine furniture.

- repair and maintain generators, alternators, motors, and communications systems aboard a ship.
- set up, adjust, and operate a printing press in a publishing company.
- adjust pipes and mechanisms in an organ to correct tone, pitch, or mechanical problems.
- make casts and prepare and fit artificial limbs.
- cut, shape, and polish precious gems and stones.
- develop designs and make tailored suits and coats for men.
- plan menus, order supplies, and oversee food preparation for a large motel.

✓ What skills and abilities do you need for this kind of work?

To do this kind of work, you must be able to:

- skillfully use handtools or machines needed for your work.
- read blueprints and drawings of items to be made or repaired.
- measure, cut, or otherwise work on materials or objects with great preciseness.
- use arithmetic and shop geometry to figure amounts of materials needed, dimensions to be followed, and cost of materials.
- picture what the finished product will look like.

■ accept responsibility for the accuracy of the work as it is turned out.

✓ *How do you know if you would like or could learn to do this kind of work?*

The following questions may give you clues about yourself as you consider this group of jobs.

- ■ Have you had hobbies such as model building which required assembling parts in a certain manner? Are you able to follow detailed instructions accurately?
- ■ Have you read magazines or trade papers about mechanics? Are you able to understand mechanical details?
- ■ Have you repaired an extension cord or lamp? Can you figure out how things work without looking at directions?
- ■ Have you made minor repairs to a house? Do you enjoy working with your hands?

✓ *How can you prepare for and enter this kind of work?*

Occupations in this group usually require education and/or training extending from two years to over ten years, depending upon the specific kind of work. A four-year formal apprenticeship is the best way to become a general machinist. Training includes the learning of proper machine speeds and feeds, and the operation of various machine tools. Apprentices are also trained in the use of handtools and assembly procedures. They study blueprint reading, shop mathematics, shop practices, and mechanical drawing. High school or vocational school courses in industrial mathematics, physics, machine shop, and mechanical drawing are very useful. Some machinists learn their trade without serving an apprenticeship.

Many mechanics and repairers acquire their skills by working with experienced workers for several years or through apprenticeship training. Some get basic training or increase their skills in vocational and technical schools or by taking correspondence courses. Experience in the armed forces may also help workers gain entry into occupations in this group.

Many high schools and vocational schools offer basic mechanics courses in cooperation with local employers. The programs last from two to three years. Courses in mathematics, physics, electronics, blueprint reading, and machine shop are helpful.

Most automobile mechanics learn their skills on the job. They usually start as helpers, lubrication workers, or gasoline station attendants. However, there are formal training programs available. Three to four years experience is required to become a general automobile mechanic. Experienced mechanics may advance to shop supervisors or service managers. Many mechanics open their own repair shops or gasoline service stations.

Formal apprenticeship training lasting three to four years is the best way to acquire the skills required in the construction trades. Apprentices generally must be at least 18 years of age, and in good physical condition. A high school or a vocational school education is desirable and should include courses in mathematics, mechanical drawing, carpentry, and electricity.

Although apprenticeship is the best way to train for these occupations, many people acquire construction skills by working as laborers and helpers and observing skilled workers. Some acquire skills by attending vocational or trade schools or by taking correspondence school courses.

Craft workers, such as electricians, are required to have a license to work in some localities. They must pass an examination to demonstrate a broad knowledge of the job and of state and local regulations.

✓ *What else should you consider about these jobs?*

Many of these workers are required to follow strict safety regulations. Machine workers must wear safety glasses and other protective devices. Construction workers are usually required to wear hard hats and sometimes safety straps and shoes.

Many people prefer construction work because it permits them to be outdoors. However, the weather and seasons sometimes affect the availability of work.

Many workers are required to furnish their own handtools.

If you think you would like to do this kind of work, look at the job titles listed below.

■ ■ ■

GOE: 05.05.01
Masonry, Stone & Brick Work

BRICKLAYER (construction) ● DOT #861.381-018 ● OES: 87310 ● Lays building materials, such as brick, structural tile, and concrete cinder, glass, gypsum, and terra cotta block (except stone) to construct or repair walls, partitions, arches, sewers, and other structures: Measures distance from reference points and marks guidelines on working surface to lay out work. Spreads soft bed (layer) of mortar that serves as base and binder for block, using trowel. Applies mortar to end of block and positions block in mortar bed. Taps block with trowel to level, align, and embed in mortar, allowing specified thickness of joint. Removes excess mortar from face of block, using trowel. Finishes mortar between brick with pointing tool or trowel. Breaks bricks to fit spaces too small for whole brick, using edge of trowel or brick hammer. Determines vertical and horizontal alignment of courses, using plumb bob, gaugeline (tightly stretched cord), and level. Fastens brick or terra cotta veneer to face of structures, with tie wires embedded in mortar between bricks, or in anchor holes in veneer brick. May weld metal parts to steel structural members. May apply plaster to walls and ceiling, using trowel, to complete repair work [PLASTERER (construction)]. May be designated according to material used as Cinder-Block Mason (construction); Concrete-Block Mason (construction); Terra-Cotta Mason (construction); or work performed as Bricklayer, Maintenance (any industry). When specializing in construction of specified structures, is designated according to specialty as Bricklayer, Sewer (construction); Chimney Builder, Brick (construction). May be designated: Block Setter, Gypsum (construction); Hollow-Tile-Partition Erector (construction); Plaster-Block Layer (construction); Silo Erector (construction). ● **GED:** R4, M3, L3 ● **SVP:** 4-10 yrs ● **Academic:** Ed=H, Eng=S ● **Work Field:** 091 ● **MPSMS:** 360 ● **Aptitudes:** G3, V3, N3, S3, P3, Q4, K3, F3, M3, E3, C4 ● **Temperaments:** J, T ● **Physical:** Stg=H; Freq: C, S, K, O, R, H, N Occas: B, I, F, D, A, X ● **Work Env:** Noise=L; Freq: W, D Occas: A ● **Salary:** 4 ● **Outlook:** 4

CEMENT MASON (construction) ● DOT #844.364-010 ● OES: 87311 ● Alternate titles: CEMENT FINISHER; CEMENT PAVER; CONCRETE FINISHER; CONCRETE FLOATER. Smooths and finishes surfaces of poured concrete floors, walls, sidewalks, or curbs to specified textures, using handtools or power tools, including floats, trowels, and screeds: Signals concrete deliverer to position truck to facilitate pouring concrete. Moves discharge chute of truck to direct concrete into forms. Spreads concrete into inaccessible sections of forms, using rake or shovel. Levels concrete to specified depth and workable consistency, using hand held screed and floats to bring water to surface and produce soft topping. Smooths, and shapes surfaces of freshly poured concrete, using straightedge and float or power screed. Finishes concrete surfaces, using power trowel, or wets and rubs concrete with abrasive stone to impart finish. Removes rough or defective spots from concrete surfaces, using power grinder or chisel and hammer, and patches holes with fresh concrete or epoxy compound. Molds expansion joints and edges, using edging tools, jointers, and straightedge. May sprinkle colored stone chips, powdered steel, or coloring powder on concrete to produce prescribed finish. May produce rough concrete surface, using broom. May mix cement, using hoe or concrete-mixing machine. May direct subgrade work, mixing of concrete, and setting of forms. May specialize in finishing steps and stairways and be designated Step Finisher (construction). May break up and repair old concrete surfaces, using pneumatic tools, and be designated Cement Mason, Maintenance (any industry). May spread premixed cement over deck, inner surfaces, joints, and crevices of ships and be designated Cementer (ship-boat mfg.). ● **GED:** R3, M3, L2 ● **SVP:** 2-4 yrs ● **Academic:** Ed=A, Eng=S ● **Work Field:** 102 ● **MPSMS:** 360, 536 ● **Aptitudes:** G3, V4, N4, S3, P3, Q4, K3, F4, M3, E4, C4 ● **Temperaments:** R, T ● **Physical:** Stg=H; Const: R, H, I Freq: S, K, O, N, D Occas: C, B, T, G, A, X ● **Work Env:** Noise=N; Freq: W, U Occas: O ● **Salary:** 2 ● **Outlook:** 3

MARBLE FINISHER (construction) ● DOT #861.664-010 ● OES: 98310 ● Alternate titles: MARBLE HELPER; MARBLE MASON HELPER; MARBLE MECHANIC HELPER; MARBLE SETTER HELPER. Supplies and mixes construction materials for MARBLE SETTER (construction) 861.381-030, applies grout, and cleans installed marble: Moves marble installation materials, tools, machines, and work devices to work areas. Mixes mortar, plaster, and grout, as required, following standard formulas and using manual or machine mixing methods. Moves mixed mortar or plaster to installation area, manually or using wheelbarrow. Selects marble slab for installation, following numbered sequence or drawings. Drills holes and chisels channels in edges of marble slabs to install metal wall anchors, using power drill and chisel. Bends wires to form metal anchors, using pliers, inserts anchors into drilled holes of marble slab, and secures anchors in place with wooden stake and plaster. Moves marble slabs to installation site, using dolly, hoist, or portable crane. Fills marble joints and surface imperfections with grout, using grouting trowel or spatula, and removes excess grout, using wet sponge. Grinds and polishes marble, using abrasives, chemicals, and manual or machine grinding and polishing techniques. Cleans installed marble surfaces, work and storage areas, installation tools, machinery, and work aids, using water and cleaning

agents. Stores marble, installation materials, tools, machinery, and related items. May modify mixing, material moving, grouting, polishing, and cleaning methods and procedures, according to type of installation or materials. May repair and fill chipped, cracked, or broken marble pieces, using torch, spatula, and heat sensitive adhesive and filler. May secure marble anchors to studding, using pliers, and cover ends of anchors with plaster to secure anchors in place. May assist MARBLE SETTER (construction) to saw and position marble. May erect scaffolding and related installation structures. ● **GED:** R2, M1, L1 ● **SVP:** 6 mos-1 yr ● **Academic:** Ed=N, Eng=N ● **Work Field:** 011, 143, 102 ● **MPSMS:** 361 ● **Aptitudes:** G4, V4, N4, S3, P3, Q4, K3, F3, M3, E4, C4 ● **Temperaments:** J, R ● **Physical:** Stg=V; Const: I, V Freq: S, K, O, W, R, H, E, D Occas: C, B, T, G, N, F, A, X ● **Work Env:** Noise=L; Freq: W Occas: U, M, X, O ● **Salary:** 2 ● **Outlook:** 1

SOFT-TILE SETTER (construction) ● DOT #861.381-034 ● OES: 87898 ● Alternate titles: TILE SETTER. Applies decorative steel, aluminum, and plastic tile (known as soft tile to distinguish from ceramic tile) to walls and cabinets of bathrooms and kitchens: Measures surface to locate center points and draws horizontal and vertical guidelines through them. Brushes waterproof compound over plaster surfaces to seal pores. Spreads adhesive cement over wall, using trowel or broad knife. Positions tile on cement, following specified pattern. Presses tile into cement. Removes excess cement from joints between tile to clean finished surface, using damp cloth or cleaning compound. Rolls sheet wall covering with hand roller to press into cement. May wipe grout into joints of tile to seal them. May be designated according to type of tile applied as Metal-Tile Setter (construction; retail trade); Plastic-Tile Layer (construction; retail trade). ● **GED:** R4, M2, L3 ● **SVP:** 2-4 yrs ● **Academic:** Ed=H, Eng=S ● **Work Field:** 092 ● **MPSMS:** 361 ● **Aptitudes:** G3, V4, N4, S3, P3, Q4, K3, F3, M3, E4, C4 ● **Temperaments:** J, T ● **Physical:** Stg=L; Freq: S, K, O, R, H, I, E, N, D, X Occas: C, B ● **Work Env:** Noise=N; ● **Salary:** 4 ● **Outlook:** 3

STONECUTTER, HAND (stonework) ● DOT #771.381-014 ● OES: 89998 ● Alternate titles: CHISEL WORKER; STONE DRESSER; STONEWORKER. Cuts, shapes, and finishes rough blocks of building or monumental stone according to diagrams or patterns: Traces around pattern or transfers dimensions from diagrams to stone, using rule, straightedge, compass, square, and chalk or scriber. Selects surfacing tools according to finish specified or step in finishing process. Chips fragments of stone away from marks on stone, working surface of stone down to specified finish. Verifies progress of finishing to ensure adherence to specifications, using straightedge, level, plumb, and square. May dress surface of stone with bushhammer. May cut decorative designs in stone surface. May cut moldings or grooves in stone that cannot be reached by machine. May drill holes in stone. May be designated according to product as Building Stonecutter (stonework); Curbing Stonecutter (stonework); Monument Stonecutter (stonework). ● **GED:** R4, M3, L3 ● **SVP:** 2-4 yrs ● **Academic:** Ed=N, Eng=S ● **Work Field:** 052 ● **MPSMS:** 537 ● **Aptitudes:** G3, V4, N4, S2, P2, Q4, K3, F3, M2, E5, C5 ● **Temperaments:** J ● **Physical:** Stg=M; Const: R, H, N Freq: I, E, D Occas: S, K, O, A ● **Work Env:** Noise=L; Freq: A Occas: W, M ● **Salary:** 2 ● **Outlook:** 1

STONEMASON (construction) ● DOT #861.381-038 ● OES: 87310 ● Sets stone to build stone structures, such as piers, walls, and abutments, or lays walks, curbstones, or special types of masonry, such as alberene (acid-resistant soapstone for vats, tanks, and floors), using mason's tools: Shapes stone preparatory to setting, using chisel, hammer, and other shaping tools. Spreads mortar over stone and foundation with trowel and sets stone in place by hand or with aid of crane. Aligns stone with plumbline and finishes joints between stone with pointing trowel. May spread mortar along mortar guides to ensure joints of uniform thickness. May clean surface of finished wall to remove mortar, using muriatic acid and brush. May be designated according to masonry work performed as Alberene-Stone Setter (construction); Artificial-Stone Setter (construction); Curb Setter (construction); Flagsetter (construction); Granite Setter (construction); Gutter-Mouth Cutter (construction). May set cut and dressed ornamental and structural stone in buildings and be designated Stone Setter (construction). ● **GED:** R4, M3, L3 ● **SVP:** 2-4 yrs ● **Academic:** Ed=H, Eng=S ● **Work Field:** 091 ● **MPSMS:** 360 ● **Aptitudes:** G3, V4, N4, S3, P3, Q4, K3, F3, M3, E3, C4 ● **Temperaments:** J, T ● **Physical:** Stg=M; Freq: S, K, O, R, H, I, N, D Occas: C, B, X ● **Work Env:** Noise=L; Freq: W, O ● **Salary:** 4 ● **Outlook:** 2

TERRAZZO FINISHER (construction) ● DOT #861.664-014 ● OES: 98310 ● Alternate titles: TERRAZZO HELPER; TERRAZZO ME-CHANIC HELPER; TERRAZZO WORKER HELPER. Supplies and mixes construction materials for TERRAZZO WORKER (construction) 861.381-046, applies grout, and finishes surface of installed terrazzo: Moves terrazzo installation materials, tools, machines, and work devices to work areas, manually or using wheelbarrow. Measures designated amounts of ingredients for terrazzo or grout, using graduated containers and scale, following standard formulas and specifications, and loads portable mixer, using shovel. Mixes materials according to experience and requests from TERRAZZO WORKER (construction) 861.381-046, and dumps mixed materials that form base or top surface of terrazzo into prepared installation site, using wheelbarrow. Applies curing agent to installed terrazzo to promote even curing, using brush or sprayer. Grinds surface of cured terrazzo, using power grinders, to smooth terrazzo and prepare for grouting. Spreads grout across terrazzo to fill surface imperfections, using trowel. Fine grinds and polishes surface of terrazzo, when grout has set, using power grinders. Washes surface of polished terrazzo, using cleaner and water, and applies sealer, according to manufacturer's specifications, using brush. Installs grinding stones in power grinders, using handtools. Cleans installation site, mixing and storage areas, tools, machines, and equipment, using water and various cleaning devices. Stores terrazzo installation materials, machines, tools, and equipment. May modify mixing, grouting, grinding, and cleaning procedures according to type of installation or material used. May assist TERRAZZO WORKER (construction) 861.381-046 to position and secure moisture membrane and wire mesh prior to pouring base materials for terrazzo installation. May spread marble chips or other material over fresh terrazzo surface and press into terrazzo, using roller. May cut divider and joint strips to size as directed. May assist TERRAZZO WORKER (construction) 861.381-046 to lay terrazzo. May cut grooves in terrazzo stairs, using power grinder, and fill grooves with nonskid material. ● GED: R2, M1, L2 ● SVP: 6 mos-1 yr ● Academic: Ed=N, Eng=N ● Work Field: 011, 102, 143 ● MPSMS: 361 ● Aptitudes: G4, V4, N4, S4, P3, Q4, K3, F4, M3, E3, C4 ● Temperaments: J, R ● Physical: Stg=V; Const: R, H Freq: S, K, O, N, D, X Occas: C, B, W, I, E, T, G, F, A, V ● Work Env: Noise=L; Occas: W, U, M, E, T ● Salary: 2 ● Outlook: 1

TERRAZZO WORKER (construction) ● DOT #861.381-046 ● OES: 87311 ● Alternate titles: ARTIFICIAL-MARBLE WORKER; FLOOR GRINDER. Applies cement, sand, pigment, and marble chips to floors, stairways, and cabinet fixtures to attain durable and decorative surfacing according to specifications and drawings: Spreads roofing paper on surface of foundation. Spreads mixture of sand, cement, and water over surface with trowel to form terrazzo base. Cuts metal division strips and presses them into terrazzo base so that top edges form desired design or pattern and define level of finished floor surface. Spreads mixture of marble chips, cement, pigment, and water over terrazzo base to form finished surface, using float and trowel. Scatters marble chips over finished surface. Pushes roller over surface to imbed chips. Allows surface to dry, and pushes electric-powered surfacing machine over floor to grind and polish terrazzo surface. Grinds curved surfaces and areas inaccessible to surfacing machine, such as stairways and cabinet tops, with portable hand grinder. May precast terrazzo blocks in wooden forms. May perform finishing operations only and be designated Terrazzo Polisher (construction). ● GED: R4, M2, L3 ● SVP: 2-4 yrs ● Academic: Ed=H, Eng=S ● Work Field: 091 ● MPSMS: 361 ● Aptitudes: G3, V4, N4, S3, P3, Q4, K3, F3, M3, E4, C4 ● Temperaments: J, T, V ● Physical: Stg=M; Freq: S, K, O, R, H, N, D Occas: I, A, X ● Work Env: Noise=L; Freq: U Occas: W, O ● Salary: 2 ● Outlook: 1

TILE FINISHER (construction) ● DOT #861.664-018 ● OES: 98310 ● Alternate titles: TILE MECHANIC HELPER; TILE SETTER HELPER. Supplies and mixes construction materials for TILE SETTER (construction) 861.381-054, applies grout, and cleans installed tile: Moves tiles, tilesetting tools, and work devices from storage area to installation site manually or using wheelbarrow. Mixes mortar and grout according to standard formulas and request from TILE SETTER (construction), using bucket, water hose, spatula, and portable mixer. Supplies TILE SETTER (construction) with mortar, using wheelbarrow and shovel. Applies grout between joints of installed tile, using grouting trowel. Removes excess grout from tile joints with wet sponge and scrapes corners and crevices with trowel. Wipes surface of tile after grout has set to remove grout residue and polish tile, using non-

abrasive materials. Cleans installation site, mixing and storage areas, and installation machines, tools, and equipment, using water and various cleaning tools. Stores tile setting materials, machines, tools, and equipment. May apply caulk, sealers, acid, steam, or related agents to caulk, seal, or clean installed tile, using various application devices and equipment. May modify mixing, grouting, grinding, and cleaning procedures according to type of installation or material used. May assist TILE SETTER (construction) to position and secure metal lath, wire mesh, or felt paper prior to installation of tile. May cut marked tiles to size, using power saw or tile cutter. ● GED: R2, M1, L2 ● SVP: 6 mos-1 yr ● Academic: Ed=N, Eng=N ● Work Field: 102, 143 ● MPSMS: 361 ● Aptitudes: G4, V4, N4, S4, P4, Q4, K3, F4, M3, E4, C4 ● Temperaments: R, T ● Physical: Stg=V; Const: R, H Freq: S, O, N, D Occas: C, B, K, I, T, G, F, A, X, V ● Work Env: Noise=L; Occas: U, M, T ● Salary: 2 ● Outlook: 3

TILE SETTER (construction) ● DOT #861.381-054 ● OES: 87308 ● Alternate titles: TILE FITTER; TILE LAYER; TILE MASON. Applies tile to walls, floors, ceilings, and promenade roof decks, following design specifications: Examines blueprints, measures and marks surfaces to be covered, and lays out work. Measures and cuts metal lath to size for walls and ceilings with tin snips. Tacks lath to wall and ceiling surfaces with staple gun or hammer. Spreads plaster base over lath with trowel and levels plaster to specified thickness, using screed. Spreads concrete on subfloor with trowel and levels it with screed. Spreads mastic or other adhesive base on roof deck, using serrated spreader to form base for promenade tile. Cuts and shapes tile with tile cutters and biters. Positions tile and taps it with trowel handle to affix tile to plaster or adhesive base. May be designated according to type of work done as Roof-Promenade-Tile Setter (construction). ● GED: R4, M3, L3 ● SVP: 2-4 yrs ● Academic: Ed=H, Eng=S ● Work Field: 092 ● MPSMS: 361 ● Aptitudes: G3, V4, N4, S3, P3, Q4, K3, F3, M3, E5, C4 ● Temperaments: J, T ● Physical: Stg=M; Const: R, H Freq: S, K, O, I, N, D Occas: C, A, X ● Work Env: Noise=L; Occas: W, O ● Salary: 2 ● Outlook: 2

GOE: 05.05.02
Construction & Maintenance

ACOUSTICAL CARPENTER (construction) ● DOT #860.381-010 ● OES: 87105 ● Alternate titles: ACOUSTICAL-MATERIAL WORKER; METAL-TILE LATHER. Mounts acoustical tile to walls and ceilings of buildings to reduce reflection of sound and to decorate rooms: Measures and marks surface to lay out work, according to blueprints and drawings. Inspects furrings, mechanical mountings, and masonry surface for plumbness and level, using spirit or water level. Nails or screws molding to wall to support and seal joint between ceiling tile and wall. Scribes and cuts edges of tile to fit wall where wall molding is not specified. Mounts tiles, using any of following methods: (1) Applies cement to back of tile and presses tile into place, aligning with layout marks and joints of previously laid tile. (2) Nails channels or wood furring stips to surfaces to provide mounting for tile. Places building paper between tile and furring strip preparatory to application of butt-edge tile. Nails, screws, or staples tile to wooden furring strips. (3) Hangs dry lines (stretched string) to wall molding to guide positioning of main runners. Drives hanger inserts into reinforced concrete ceiling, using power fastening tool, and suspends and bends hanger wires at points touching dry lines. Threads wires through holes in main runners, and cuts and attaches cross supports to suspended runners and wall molding, using snips, clips, and rivet gun. Cuts tiles for fixtures and borders, using keyhole saw, and inserts tiles into supporting framework. May wash concrete surfaces with washing soda and zinc sulfate solution before mounting tile to increase adhesive qualities of surfaces. ● GED: R4, M3, L2 ● SVP: 2-4 yrs ● Academic: Ed=A, Eng=N ● Work Field: 102 ● MPSMS: 361 ● Aptitudes: G3, V3, N3, S3, P3, Q4, K3, F3, M3, E4, C5 ● Temperaments: J, T, V ● Physical: Stg=M; Freq: C, R, H, I, N, D Occas: S, K, O, G ● Work Env: Noise=N; Occas: A, O ● Salary: 4 ● Outlook: 2

BOATBUILDER, WOOD (ship-boat mfg.) ● DOT #860.361-010 ● OES: 87110 ● Fabricates, repairs, or modifies wooden boats, life rafts, and pontoons, according to blueprints, using handtools, power tools, and measuring instruments: Lays out full-scale outline of boat on mold-loft floor, using crayon, scales, and protractor, following blueprints and table of offsets. Establishes dimensional reference points on layout and makes templates of parts. Scribes dimensional lines on lumber, following templates. Cuts and forms parts, such as keel, ribs, and sidings, using carpenter's handtools and power tools [MACHINIST, WOOD (woodworking) 669.380-014]. Attaches overhead hoist to precut sections of boat hull and signals coworker to position timbers according to layout of boat, using hoist. Secures timbers together following specified procedure, using adhesive, hardware, and handtools or power tools. Assembles shell of boat by forming steam-softened sidings on mold, removing mold, and securing sidings to keel, or by securing ribs to keel and covering ribs with planking. Builds and installs structures, such as pilot house, cabin, rudder, and foundations for machinery, shafting, and propeller's supports, and installs preformed decking, masts, booms, and ladders, according to blueprints, using handtools, power tools, scale, calipers, and gauges. Work is usually performed with other workers. May caulk seams [WOOD CAULKER (ship-boat mfg.) 843.384-010]. May specialize in fabricating particular part of boat and be designated Bulkhead Carpenter (ship-boat mfg.); Bulwark Carpenter (ship-boat mfg.); Hull Builder (ship-boat mfg.); Keel Assembler (ship-boat mfg.). ● **GED:** R3, M3, L2 ● **SVP:** 1-2 yrs ● **Academic:** Ed=A, Eng=S ● **Work Field:** 102 ● **MPSMS:** 593 ● **Aptitudes:** G3, V4, N3, S3, P3, Q4, K3, F3, M3, E4, C5 ● **Temperaments:** J, T ● **Physical:** Stg=M; Freq: R, H, I, N, D Occas: C, B, S, K, O, T, G ● **Work Env:** Noise=L; Occas: A, O ● **Salary:** 2 ● **Outlook:** 3

BOAT REPAIRER (ship-boat mfg.) ● DOT #807.361-014 ● OES: 85998 ● Repairs wooden and fiberglass boats according to blueprints and customer specifications, using handtools and power tools: Confers with customer or supervisory personnel and reads blueprints to determine repairs needed and plan sequence of operations. Examines boat to determine location and extent of defect. Cuts out defective area, using power saw, drills, and handtools. Measures and records dimensions of defective area and lays out dimension lines and reference points on materials, using rules, straightedge, squares, and scribing instruments. Sets up and operates saws, joiners, planers, and shapers to fabricate repair parts. Positions and fits repair part in boat and secures part to boat, using caulking gun, adhesive, or carpenter's handtools. Cuts fiberglass material to specified size and patches defective surfaces [BOAT PATCHER, PLASTIC (ship-boat mfg.)]. Smooths repaired surfaces, using power sander. Installs fittings and equipment according to customer specifications, using handtools and portable power tools. Hand brushes or sprays paint or other finishing solution on repaired areas and waxes and buffs area to specified finish. ● **GED:** R4, M3, L3 ● **SVP:** 2-4 yrs ● **Academic:** Ed=N, Eng=S ● **Work Field:** 102 ● **MPSMS:** 593 ● **Aptitudes:** G3, V3, N3, S3, P2, Q4, K3, F3, M3, E4, C4 ● **Temperaments:** J ● **Physical:** Stg=M; Freq: S, K, O, R, H, I, E, N, D, A Occas: C, B, W, T, G, X ● **Work Env:** Noise=L; Occas: W, O ● **Salary:** 3 ● **Outlook:** 3

CARPENTER (construction) ● DOT #860.381-022 ● OES: 87110 ● Constructs, erects, installs, and repairs structures and fixtures of wood, plywood, and wallboard, using carpenter's handtools and power tools, and conforming to local building codes: Studies blueprints, sketches, or building plans for information pertaining to type of material required, such as lumber or fiberboard, and dimensions of structure or fixture to be fabricated. Selects specified type of lumber or other materials. Prepares layout, using rule, framing square, and calipers. Marks cutting and assembly lines on materials, using pencil, chalk, and marking gauge. Shapes materials to prescribed measurements, using saws, chisels, and planes. Assembles cut and shaped materials and fastens them together with nails, dowel pins, or glue. Verifies trueness of structure with plumb bob and carpenter's level. Erects framework for structures and lays subflooring. Builds stairs and lays out and installs partitions and cabinet work. Covers subfloor with building paper to keep out moisture and lays hardwood, parquet, and wood-strip-block floors by nailing floors to subfloor or cementing them to mastic or asphalt base. Applies shock-absorbing, sound-deadening, and decorative paneling to ceilings and walls. Fits and installs prefabricated window frames, doors, doorframes, weather stripping, interior and exterior trim, and finish hardware, such as locks, letterdrops, and kick plates. Constructs forms and chutes for pouring concrete. Erects scaffolding and ladders for assembling structures above ground level. May weld metal parts to steel structural members. When specializing in particular phase of carpentry, is designated according to specialty as Combination-Window

Installer (construction); Lay-Out Carpenter (construction). When specializing in finish carpentry, such as installing interior and exterior trim, building stairs, and laying hardwood floors, is designated Finish Carpenter (construction). When erecting frame buildings and performing general carpentry work in residential construction, is designated House Carpenter (construction). May remove and replace sections of structures prior to and after installation of insulating materials and be designated Building-Insulating Carpenter (construction; retail trade). May perform carpentry work in construction of walk-in freezers and environmental test chambers and be designated Carpenter, Refrigerator (svc. ind. mach.). May be designated: Door Hanger (construction); Finished-Hardware Erector (construction); Garage-Door Hanger (construction); Hardwood-Floor Installer (construction); Jalousie Installer (construction); Stair Builder (construction); Trim Setter (construction); Weather Stripper (construction); Wood-Sash-And-Frame Carpenter (construction); Wood-Strip-Block Floor Installer (construction). ● **GED:** R4, M3, L3 ● **SVP:** 2-4 yrs ● **Academic:** Ed=A, Eng=S ● **Work Field:** 102 ● **MPSMS:** 360, 450 ● **Aptitudes:** G3, V3, N3, S3, P3, Q4, K3, F3, M3, E4, C4 ● **Temperaments:** J, T, V ● **Physical:** Stg=M; Freq: R, H, I, N, D Occas: C, B, S, K, O, E, G, F, A, X ● **Work Env:** Noise=L; Occas: W, A, D, O ● **Salary:** 4 ● **Outlook:** 3

CARPENTER APPRENTICE (construction) ● DOT #860.381-026 ● OES: 87110 ● Performs duties as described under APPRENTICE (any industry) Master Title. ● **GED:** R4, M3, L3 ● **SVP:** 2-4 yrs ● **Academic:** Ed=H, Eng=G ● **Work Field:** 102 ● **MPSMS:** 360, 450 ● **Aptitudes:** G3, V3, N3, S3, P3, Q4, K3, F3, M3, E4, C4 ● **Temperaments:** J, T, V ● **Physical:** Stg=M; Freq: R, H, I, N, D Occas: C, B, S, K, O, E, G, F, A, X ● **Work Env:** Noise=L; Occas: W, A, D, O ● **Salary:** 4 ● **Outlook:** 3

CARPENTER, MAINTENANCE (any industry) ● DOT #860.281-010 ● OES: 87110 ● Alternate titles: CARPENTER, REPAIR. Constructs and repairs structural woodwork and equipment in establishment, working from blueprints, drawings, or oral instructions: Builds, repairs, and installs counters, cabinets, benches, partitions, floors, doors, building framework, and trim, using carpenter's handtools and power tools. Installs glass in windows, doors, and partitions. Replaces damaged ceiling tile, floor tile, and wall coverings. May build cabinets and other wooden equipment in carpenter shop, using woodworking machines, such as saws, shaper, and jointer [CABINETMAKER (woodworking) 660.280-010]. May install items, such as window shades, venetian blinds, and curtain rods, wall fans, and door locks for tenants. May be designated according to place at which work is performed as Carpenter, Mine (mine & quarry); or according to specific items made or maintained as Flume Maker (mine & quarry); Frame Maker (leather mfg.); Meat-Cutting-Block Repairer (any industry). ● **GED:** R4, M4, L3 ● **SVP:** 2-4 yrs ● **Academic:** Ed=A, Eng=S ● **Work Field:** 102 ● **MPSMS:** 361, 450 ● **Aptitudes:** G3, V3, N3, S2, P3, Q4, K3, F3, M3, E4, C4 ● **Temperaments:** J, T, V ● **Physical:** Stg=M; Freq: C, B, S, R, H, I, N Occas: K, G, F, D, A, X, V ● **Work Env:** Noise=L; Freq: M Occas: W, A, D ● **Salary:** 3 ● **Outlook:** 3

CARPENTER, ROUGH (construction) ● DOT #860.381-042 ● OES: 87110 ● Alternate titles: BRACER. Builds rough wooden structures, such as concrete forms, scaffolds, tunnel and sewer supports, and temporary frame shelters, according to sketches, blueprints, or oral instructions: Examines specifications to determine dimensions of structure. Measures boards, timbers, or plywood, using square, measuring tape, and ruler, and marks cutting lines on materials, using pencil and scriber. Saws boards and plywood panels to required sizes. Nails cleats (braces) across boards to construct concrete-supporting forms. Braces forms in place with timbers, tie rods, and anchor bolts, for use in building concrete piers, footings, and walls. Erects chutes for pouring concrete. Cuts and assembles timbers to build trestles and cofferdams. Builds falsework to temporarily strengthen, protect, or disguise buildings undergoing construction. Erects scaffolding for buildings and ship structures and installs ladders, handrails, walkways, platforms, and gangways. Installs door and window bucks (rough frames in which finished frames are inserted) in designated positions in building framework, and braces them with boards nailed to framework. Installs subflooring in buildings. Nails plaster grounds (wood or metal strips) to studding to provide guide for PLASTERER (construction). Fits and nails sheathing (first covering of boards) on outer walls and roofs of buildings. Builds sleds from logs and timbers for use in hauling camp buildings and machinery through wooded areas. When specializing in particular phase of rough carpentry, is designated according to specialty as Carpenter, Cradle And Dolly (ship-boat mfg.); Dock Builder (construction); Falsework Builder (construction); Scaffold Builder (construction; ship-boat mfg.); Sheather (construction); Timber Setter (construction). When building and repairing timber structures which support sawmill machinery, is designated Construction Millwright (saw. & plan.). When performing rough carpentry work above ground on sewer or tunnel projects, is designated Surface Carpenter (construction). ● GED: R4, M4, L2 ● SVP: 2-4 yrs ● Academic: Ed=H, Eng=N ● Work Field: 102 ● MPSMS: 360 ● Aptitudes: G3, V4, N3, S3, P3, Q4, K3, F3, M3, E3, C5 ● Temperaments: J, T ● Physical: Stg=H; Freq: S, K, O, R, H, I, N, D Occas: C, B, G, A ● Work Env: Noise=L; Freq: W, O ● Salary: 4 ● Outlook: 3

CUSTOM VAN CONVERTER (auto. mfg.) ● DOT #806.381-070 ● OES: 85998 ● Performs any combination of following duties to customize vans according to specifications and work orders, using handtools, power tools and welding equipment: Measures interior of van to determine area to be modified. Fabricates and installs walls, cabinets, and supports. Cuts wall and floor sections of vehicle body for installation of customized interior components and specialized equipment, according to specifications. Installs new top on vehicle body to increase headroom. Installs electrical systems, such as wire harnesses, electrical outlets, and electrical/electronic controls for specialized equipment. Tests electrical systems, using ohmmeter and voltmeter. Positions and installs appliances in vehicle according to specifications. Installs customized interior components, such as carpet, linoleum, wall covering and preassembled windows, according to customer orders. Prepares and paints vehicle surfaces and parts, using spray paint equipment. Installs specialized equipment, such as wheelchair lift, steering and braking systems, for use by handicapped persons. ● GED: R4, M3, L3 ● SVP: 6 mos-1 yr ● Academic: Ed=H, Eng=S ● Work Field: 102, 111 ● MPSMS: 591 ● Aptitudes: G3, V3, N3, S3, P3, Q4, K3, F3, M3, E4, C4 ● Temperaments: J, T ● Physical: Stg=M; Freq: R, H, I, N Occas: S, K, O, D, A, X ● Work Env: Noise=N ● Salary: 2 ● Outlook: 4

FORM BUILDER (construction) ● DOT #860.381-046 ● OES: 87110 ● Alternate titles: CARPENTER, FORM; WOOD-FORM BUILDER. Constructs built-in-place or prefabricated wooden forms, according to specifications, for molding concrete structures: Studies blueprints and diagrams to determine type and dimension of forms to be constructed. Saws lumber to blueprint dimensions, using handsaw or power saw, and nails lumber together to make form panels. Erects built-in-place forms or assembles and installs prefabricated forms on construction site according to blueprint specifications, using handtools, plumb rule, and level. Inserts spreaders and tie rods between opposite faces of form to maintain specified dimensions. Anchors and braces forms to fixed objects, using nails, bolts, anchor rods, steel cables, planks, and timbers. ● GED: R4, M3, L2 ● SVP: 2-4 yrs ● Academic: Ed=A, Eng=N ● Work Field: 102 ● MPSMS: 369 ● Aptitudes: G3, V3, N3, S3, P3, Q4, K3, F3, M3, E4, C5 ● Temperaments: J, T ● Physical: Stg=H; Freq: S, R, H, I, N, F, D Occas: C, B, K, O ● Work Env: Noise=L; Freq: W Occas: O ● Salary: 3 ● Outlook: 3

MARINE-SERVICES TECHNICIAN (ship-boat mfg.) ● DOT #806.261-026 ● OES: 85109 ● Repairs and maintains boats and similar vessels in marine service facility: Examines repair or installation orders, drawings, and vessel, utilizing knowledge based on past experience to determine extent of repairs required or modifications necessary for installation of equipment, accessories, and hardware. Consults with supervisor regarding installation or repair problems, sequence of operations, and time required to complete repair or installation. Removes vessels from water, using movable lift crane or marine railway. Positions and secures blocking at bottom and sides of vessels according to size, weight, and weight distribution of vessels, using fasteners, handtools, and power tools. Removes flaked paint, barnacles, and encrusted debris from hulls of vessel, using scrapers, scrubbers, power washers, and sandblast equipment. Removes damaged or rotted sections from wooden or fiberglass vessels, using drill, saw, and handtools. Fabricates and installs wooden replacement parts, using drawings, measuring instruments, work aids, handtools, power tools, and woodworking machines and equipment, such as saws, drill press, shaper, planer, and steam cabinet. Caulks wooden hulls with cotton to prevent leaks. Grinds and sands edges around removed fiberglass sections. Mixes fiberglass bonding resin and catalyst, cuts fiberglass cloth to size, and

impregnates cloth with mixture. Positions layers of impregnated cloth over damaged area, and smooths area to match contour of hull, using rollers, squeegee, and power sander. Mixes and applies paint or gel coat to boats with hand and spray equipment, utilizing knowledge of color mixing, matching techniques, and application procedures. Tests engine, transmission, rigging, propeller, navigational, and related systems to diagnose malfunctions, using various measuring instruments. Replaces or repairs defective components, or fabricates new components. Installs and tests steering gear, sanitation and refrigeration systems, cabinetry, electrical systems and accessories, hardware, trim, and related components, following manufacturer's instructions and drawings. ● GED: R4, M3, L3 ● SVP: 2-4 yrs ● Academic: Ed=H, Eng=S ● Work Field: 121, 102 ● MPSMS: 593 ● Aptitudes: G3, V3, N3, S2, P3, Q4, K3, F3, M2, E2, C2 ● Temperaments: J, T, V ● Physical: Stg=H; Freq: R, H, I, T, G, N, X Occas: C, B, S, K, O, A ● Work Env: Noise=L; Freq: W Occas: A, M ● Salary: 3 ● Outlook: 3

SHIPWRIGHT (ship-boat mfg.) ● DOT #860.381-058 ● OES: 87110 ● Alternate titles: CARPENTER, SHIP; WOODWORKER. Constructs or repairs ships, following blueprints or ship's plans: Sights, plots, and marks reference points and lines on building dock or shipway to maintain alignment of vessel during construction or repair, using transit, plumb bob, tapes, and levels. Builds keel and bilge blocks, cradles, and shoring for supporting ships in drydock, marine railways, shipways, or building docks, using woodworking handtools and power tools. Positions and secures blocking and other structures on dock platform, according to ship's blueprints. Aligns vessel over blocks [DOCK HAND (ship-boat mfg.)]. Establishes reference points and lines on ship's hull for locating machinery and other equipment, in accordance with ship's alignment and shape. Fabricates and installs furring pieces, aprons, uprights, and other wood framing in ship. Shapes, finishes, and installs wooden spars, masts, and cargo and boat booms. Trims wooden frames and other timbers, using broadax and adz. Spikes or bolts metal fittings, plates, and bulkheads to wooden parts of ship, using brace and bits, augers, mauls, and wrenches. ● GED: R4, M4, L3 ● SVP: 4-10 yrs ● Academic: Ed=A, Eng=S ● Work Field: 102 ● MPSMS: 593 ● Aptitudes: G3, V3, N3, S3, P3, Q4, K3, F3, M2, E3, C4 ● Temperaments: J, T, V ● Physical: Stg=M; Freq: R, H, I, N, F, D Occas: C, B, S, K, O, W, A, X ● Work Env: Noise=L; Freq: W, O Occas: D ● Salary: 2 ● Outlook: 2

SUPERINTENDENT, MAINTENANCE (any industry) ● DOT #189.167-046 ● OES: 15014 ● Directs and coordinates, through subordinate supervisory personnel, activities of workers engaged in repair, maintenance, and installation of machines, tools and equipment, and in maintenance of buildings, grounds, and utility systems of mill, industrial plant, or other establishment: Reviews job orders to determine work priorities. Schedules repair, maintenance, and installation of machines, tools, and equipment to ensure continuous production operations. Coordinates activities of workers fabricating or modifying machines, tools, or equipment to manufacture new products or improve existing products. Directs maintenance activities on utility systems to provide continuous supply of heat, steam, electric power, gas, or air required for operations. Develops preventive maintenance program in conjunction with engineering and maintenance staff. Reviews production, quality control, and maintenance reports and statistics to plan and modify maintenance activities. Inspects operating machines and equipment for conformance with operational standards. Plans, develops, and implements new methods and procedures designed to improve operations, minimize operating costs, and effect greater utilization of labor and materials. Reviews new product plans and discusses equipment needs and modifications with design engineers. Requisitions tools, equipment, and supplies required for operations. Directs training and indoctrination of workers to improve work performance and acquaint workers with company policies and procedures. Confers with management, engineering, and quality control personnel to resolve maintenance problems and recommend measures to improve operations and conditions of machines and equipment. May confer with workers' representatives to resolve grievances. May perform supervisory functions in establishments where subordinate supervisory personnel are not utilized. May prepare department budget and monitor expenditure of funds in budget. ● GED: R5, M5, L5 ● SVP: 4-10 yrs ● Academic: Ed=H, Eng=G ● Work Field: 295 ● MPSMS: 893 ● Aptitudes: G2, V2, N2, S2, P2, Q2, K4, F4, M4, E4, C4 ● Temperaments: D, J, P, V ● Physical: Stg=L; Freq: T, G, N Occas: R, H, I, X ● Work Env: Noise=N; ● Salary: 4 ● Outlook: 1

GOE: 05.05.03
Plumbing & Pipefitting

GAS-MAIN FITTER (utilities) ● DOT #862.361-014 ● OES: 87510 ● Alternate titles: PIPE FITTER. Lays pipe to repair and extend nonwelded gas mains and to install or repair service pipes between mains and residences: Drills hole in section of main to which new pipe will be fitted and inserts inflated rubber bag to seal off flow of gas. Removes faulty pipe by unscrewing bolts at joint with hand wrench. Lays gas mains by fitting spigot end of one pipe section into bell end of another. Bolts joints together. Places wooden blocks under pipe to adjust pipe to line and grade, testing gradient with carpenter's level. Fastens steel cap over free end of gas-main extensions. Drills hole or installs reducing fitting in main where service pipes begin. Bolts saddle clamp around main, preparatory to welding. Drills hole through welded saddle clamp into main, using power drill. Cuts, threads, and screws together sections of pipe forming service line, and lays service line in trench. Bolts end of service line to saddle clamp, using special compression coupling to produce gas-tight connection. Removes rubber expanding bag to resume flow of gas and caps holes with screw plugs. Installs various gas-main attachments, such as drips, ells, and tees. Tests pipe for weak joints by forcing air into pipe with air compressor and coating joints with soap and water, and notes formation of bubbles, indicating leak. Tightens bolts or repairs leaky joints. May install gas meters. May install pipes beneath roads, lawns, or locations where not feasible to dig trenches, by forcing pipe through earth with special pipe jack. May direct crew in excavating trench and positioning pipe. May fuse bonds to pipe joints, using holder and flash chemicals (cad-weld), to concentrate high temperatures at point of fusion. May install and repair service lines only and be designated Pipe Fitter, Street Service (utilities). ● **GED:** R4, M2, L3 ● **SVP:** 2-4 yrs ● **Academic:** Ed=A, Eng=N ● **Work Field:** 102 ● **MPSMS:** 364 ● **Aptitudes:** G3, V3, N3, S3, P3, Q4, K3, F3, M3, E4, C5 ● **Temperaments:** J, T ● **Physical:** Stg=M; Freq: S, K, O, R, H, I, N, D Occas: T, G ● **Work Env:** Noise=L; Const: W Freq: A, O ● **Salary:** 3 ● **Outlook:** 3

PIPE FITTER (construction) ● DOT #862.281-022 ● OES: 87502 ● Alternate titles: PLUMBER, PIPE FITTING. Lays out, assembles, installs, and maintains pipe systems, pipe supports, and related hydraulic and pneumatic equipment for steam, hot water, heating, cooling, lubricating, sprinkling, and industrial production and processing systems, applying knowledge of system operation, and following blueprints: Selects type and size of pipe, and related materials and equipment, such as supports, hangers, and hydraulic cylinders, according to specifications. Inspects work site to determine presence of obstructions and to ascertain that holes cut for pipe will not cause structural weakness. Plans installation or repair to avoid obstructions and to avoid interfering with activities of other workers. Cuts pipe, using saws, pipe cutter, hammer and chisel, cutting torch, and pipe cutting machine. Threads pipe, using pipe threading machine. Bends pipe, using pipe bending tools and pipe bending machine. Assembles and installs variety of metal and nonmetal pipes, tubes, and fittings, including iron, steel, copper, and plastic. Connects pipes, using threaded, caulked, soldered, brazed, fused, or cemented joints, and handtools. Secures pipes to structure with brackets, clamps, and hangers, using handtools and power tools. Installs and maintains hydraulic and pneumatic components of machines and equipment, such as pumps and cylinders, using handtools. Installs and maintains refrigeration and air-conditioning systems, including compressors, pumps, meters, pneumatic and hydraulic controls, and piping, using handtools and power tools, and following specifications and blueprints. Increases pressure in pipe system and observes connected pressure gauge to test system for leaks. May weld pipe supports to structural steel members. May observe production machines in assigned area of manufacturing facility to detect machinery malfunctions. May operate machinery to verify repair. May modify programs of automated machinery, such as robots and conveyors, to change motion and speed of machine, using teach pendant, control panel, or keyboard and display screen of robot controller and programmable controller. May be designated Steam Fitter (construction) when installing piping systems that must withstand high pressure. May be designated according to type of system installed as Pipe Fitter, Ammonia (construction); Pipe Fitter, Fire-Sprinkler Systems (construction); Pipe Fitter, Gas Pipe (construction); or type of piping used as Pipe

Fitter, Plastic Pipe (construction); Pipe Fitter, Soft Copper (construction). May be designated: Airdox Fitter (mine & quarry); Freight-Air-Brake Fitter (railroad equip.); Instrument Fitter (construction); Maintainer, Sewer-And-Waterworks (construction); Pipe Fitter, Maintenance (any industry); Pipe Fitter, Welding (construction); Pneumatic-Tube Fitter (construction); Sprinkler-And-Irrigation-System Installer (construction); Tuyere Fitter (steel & rel.). ● **GED:** R4, M3, L3 ● **SVP:** 2-4 yrs ● **Academic:** Ed=A, Eng=S ● **Work Field:** 102, 121 ● **MPSMS:** 364, 559 ● **Aptitudes:** G3, V3, N3, S3, P3, Q4, K3, F3, M3, E4, C5 ● **Temperaments:** J, T ● **Physical:** Stg=H; Freq: R, H, N, D, A Occas: C, B, S, K, O, I, G ● **Work Env:** Noise=N; Occas: M, O ● **Salary:** 4 ● **Outlook:** 4

PLUMBER (construction) ● DOT #862.381-030 ● OES: 87502 ● Assembles, installs, and repairs pipes, fittings, and fixtures of heating, water, and drainage systems, according to specifications and plumbing codes: Studies building plans and working drawings to determine work aids required and sequence of installations. Inspects structure to ascertain obstructions to be avoided to prevent weakening of structure resulting from installation of pipe. Locates and marks position of pipe and pipe connections and passage holes for pipes in walls and floors, using ruler, spirit level, and plumb bob. Cuts openings in walls and floors to accommodate pipe and pipe fittings, using handtools and power tools. Cuts and threads pipe, using pipe cutters, cutting torch, and pipe-threading machine. Bends pipe to required angle by use of pipe-bending machine or by placing pipe over block and bending it by hand. Assembles and installs valves, pipe fittings, and pipes composed of metals, such as iron, steel, brass, and lead, and nonmetals, such as glass, vitrified clay, and plastic, using handtools and power tools. Joins pipes by use of screws, bolts, fittings, solder, plastic solvent, and caulks joints. Fills pipe system with water or air and reads pressure gauges to determine whether system is leaking. Installs and repairs plumbing fixtures, such as sinks, commodes, bathtubs, water heaters, hot water tanks, garbage disposal units, dishwashers, and water softeners. Repairs and maintains plumbing by replacing washers in leaky faucets, mending burst pipes, and opening clogged drains. May weld holding fixtures to steel structural members. When specializing in maintenance and repair of heating, water, and drainage systems in industrial or commercial establishments, is designated Plumber, Maintenance (any industry). ● **GED:** R4, M3, L3 ● **SVP:** 2-4 yrs ● **Academic:** Ed=H, Eng=S ● **Work Field:** 102 ● **MPSMS:** 364, 369 ● **Aptitudes:** G3, V3, N3, S3, P3, Q4, K3, F3, M2, E4, C4 ● **Temperaments:** J, T, V ● **Physical:** Stg=H; Freq: R, H, N, D Occas: C, B, S, K, O, I, A, X ● **Work Env:** Noise=L; Occas: W, A, O ● **Salary:** 4 ● **Outlook:** 4

GOE: 05.05.04
Painting, Plastering & Paperhanging

DRY-WALL APPLICATOR (construction) ● DOT #842.361-030 ● OES: 87120 ● Alternate titles: DRY-WALL INSTALLATIONS MECHANIC; DRY-WALL INSTALLER; GYPSUM DRY-WALL SYSTEMS INSTALLER. Plans gypsum drywall installations, erects metal framing and furring channels for fastening drywalls, and installs drywall to cover walls, ceilings, soffits, shafts, and movable partitions in residential, commercial, and industrial buildings: Reads blueprints and other specifications to determine method of installation, work procedures, and material, tool, and work aid requirements. Lays out reference lines and points for use in computing location and position of metal framing and furring channels and marks position for erecting metalwork, using chalkline. Measures, marks, and cuts metal runners, studs, and furring channels to specified size, using tape measure, straightedge and hand-and portable power-cutting tools. Secures metal framing to walls and furring channels to ceilings, using hand and portable power tools. Measures and marks cutting lines on drywall, using square, tape measure, and marking devices. Scribes cutting lines on drywall, using straightedge and utility knife and breaks board along cut lines. Fits and fastens board into specified position on wall, using screws, hand or portable power tools, or adhesive. Cuts openings into board for electrical outlets, vents or fixtures, using keyhole saw or other cutting tools. Measures, cuts, assembles and installs metal framing and decorative trim for windows, doorways, and vents. Fits, aligns, and hangs doors and installs hardware, such as locks and kickplates [CARPEN-

TER (construction)] 860.381-022]. Worker is usually assisted by other workers. ● **GED:** R3, M3, L3 ● **SVP:** 2-4 yrs ● **Academic:** Ed=N, Eng=N ● **Work Field:** 102, 241 ● **MPSMS:** 361, 536, 550 ● **Aptitudes:** G3, V4, N3, S3, P3, Q4, K3, F3, M3, E3, C3 ● **Temperaments:** D, J, T ● **Physical:** Stg=V; Freq: R, H, I, G, N, D Occas: C, B, S, K, O, W, T, A, X ● **Work Env:** Noise=L; Freq: A, O Occas: D ● **Salary:** 3 ● **Outlook:** 3

PAPERHANGER (construction) ● DOT #841.381-010 ● OES: 87402 ● Covers interior walls and ceilings of rooms with decorative wallpaper or fabric, using handtools: Measures walls and ceiling to compute number and length of strips required to cover surface. Sets up pasteboard and erects scaffolding. Marks vertical guideline on wall to align first strip, using plumb bob and chalkline. Smooths rough spots on walls and ceilings, using sandpaper. Fills holes and cracks with plaster, using trowel. Removes paint, varnish, and grease from surfaces, using paint remover and water soda solution. Applies acetic acid to damp plaster to prevent lime from bleeding through paper. Applies sizing (thin glue) to waterproof porous surfaces, using brush, roller, or pasting machine. Measures and cuts strips from roll of wallpaper or fabric, using shears or razor. Mixes paste to desired consistency and brushes paste on back of wallpaper or fabric, using paste brush. Trims selvage (rough edge) from strips, using straightedge and trimming knife. Places paste-coated strips on wall or ceiling to match adjacent edges of figured strips, and smooths strips with dry brush or felt-covered roller to remove wrinkles and bubbles. Smooths joints with seam roller and trims excess material at ceiling and baseboard, using knife. Removes old paper, using water, steam machine, or chemical remover and scraper. May apply paint to interior or exterior surface of buildings [PAINTER (construction)]. ● **GED:** R4, M2, L2 ● **SVP:** 2-4 yrs ● **Academic:** Ed=H, Eng=N ● **Work Field:** 102 ● **MPSMS:** 361 ● **Aptitudes:** G3, V3, N3, S3, P3, Q4, K3, F3, M2, E4, C3 ● **Temperaments:** J ● **Physical:** Stg=M; Const: N Freq: R, H, I, D, X Occas: C, B, S, K, O, E, A ● **Work Env:** Noise=N; ● **Salary:** 2 ● **Outlook:** 2

PLASTERER (construction) ● DOT #842.361-018 ● OES: 87317 ● Applies coats of plaster to interior walls, ceilings, and partitions of buildings, to produce finished surface, according to blueprints, architect's drawings, or oral instructions, using handtools and portable power tools: Directs workers to mix plaster to desired consistency and to erect scaffolds. Spreads plaster over lath or masonry base, using trowel, and smooths plaster with darby and float to attain uniform thickness. Applies scratch, brown, or finish coats of plaster to wood, metal, or board lath successively. Roughens undercoat with scratcher (wire or metal scraper) to provide bond for succeeding coats of plaster. Creates decorative textures in finish coat by marking surface of coat with brush and trowel or by spattering surface with pebbles [STUCCO MASON (construction) 842.381-014]. May install lathing [LATHER (construction) 842.361-010]. May mix mortar. May install guide wires on exterior surface of buildings to indicate thickness of plaster to be applied. May install precast ornamental plaster pieces by applying mortar to back of pieces and pressing pieces into place on wall or ceiling and be designated Ornamental-Plaster Sticker (construction). May specialize in applying finish or rough coats of plaster and be desigated Plasterer, Finish (construction); Plasterer, Rough (construction). May apply plaster with spray gun and be designated Plasterer, Spray Gun (construction). May perform maintenance work only and be designated Plasterer, Maintenance (construction). ● **GED:** R3, M2, L2 ● **SVP:** 2-4 yrs ● **Academic:** Ed=H, Eng=S ● **Work Field:** 091 ● **MPSMS:** 361, 536 ● **Aptitudes:** G3, V3, N4, S4, P3, Q4, K3, F4, M3, E3, C4 ● **Temperaments:** J, T ● **Physical:** Stg=M; Freq: S, K, O, R, H, I, N, D Occas: C, B, T, G, F, X, V ● **Work Env:** Noise=N; Freq: U Occas: W, D, O ● **Salary:** 2 ● **Outlook:** 2

GOE: 05.05.05
Elect.-Electronic Systems Installation & Repair

ANTENNA INSTALLER, SATELLITE COMMUNICATIONS (any industry) ● DOT #823.261-022 ● OES: 85598 ● Installs, tests, and repairs antennas and related equipment that receive communication satellite signals, following specifications and using handtools and test instruments: Reviews installation specifications, building permit,

manufacturer's instructions, and government ordinances to determine installation site for antenna. Measures distance from landmarks to identify exact site location. Visually inspects installation site to identify obstructions, such as trees or buildings, that could distort or block microwave signals from satellite. Discusses site location and construction requirements with customer. Digs hole for footing to support antenna base, using gasoline-powered auger, posthole digger, or shovel. Assembles and installs prefabricated form in hole to cast concrete base, using handtools, plumb rule, and level, following specifications. Mixes, pours, and finishes concrete, using concrete mixer, trowel, and float. Inserts pedestal mounting bolts in wet concrete. Digs trench and lays underground cable to connect antenna base to source of power in customer's building. Attaches antenna base to footing after concrete dries, using handtools. Assembles and attaches electronic and structural components of antenna, with co-worker, applying knowledge of electronics and electricity, following installation guidelines, and using handtools. Attaches antenna to base, using nuts, bolts, and handtools. Climbs ladder to install antenna when area is inaccessible from ground. Orients antenna to direction and altitude of communication satellite, using surveying instruments and following charts of satellite position. Solders connections to electronic controls, using soldering gun and wire cutters. Connects antenna and television set to signal converter control box, using handtools. Tests installed system for conformance to specifications, using test equipment, such as multimeters and oscilloscope. Observes picture on television screen to evaluate reception. Instructs customer in use of equipment. Replaces or repairs defective parts, using handtools and test equipment. May construct pole or roof mounts for antenna base, using carpenter's tools. May reinforce roof of building to provide secure installation site, using carpenter's tools. May install antennas and related equipment to receive satellite signals for such purposes as telephone, telex, facsimile, data, or radio communication. ● **GED:** R3, M3, L3 ● **SVP:** 1-2 yrs ● **Academic:** Ed=A, Eng=S ● **Work Field:** 111, 091 ● **MPSMS:** 587 ● **Aptitudes:** G3, V3, N3, S2, P3, Q3, K3, F3, M3, E3, C5 ● **Temperaments:** J, T, V ● **Physical:** Stg=M; Const: R, H, I Freq: S, K, O, N, F, D Occas: C, B, T, G ● **Work Env:** Noise=N; Freq: W Occas: D ● **Salary:** 3 ● **Outlook:** 4

AUTOMATED EQUIPMENT ENGINEER-TECHNICIAN (machinery mfg.) ● DOT #638.261-010 ● OES: 85123 ● Alternate titles: ENGINEER, AUTOMATED EQUIPMENT; TECHNICIAN, AUTOMATED EQUIPMENT. Installs machinery and equipment used to emboss, die-cut, score, fold, and transfer paper or cardboard stock to form box blanks, knock-down advertising displays, and similar products: Confers with customer's engineering staff to determine layout of equipment, to resolve problems of machine design, and to avoid construction problems in plant. Arranges machine parts according to sequence of assembly and effective use of floor space. Directs workers in positioning equipment, following floor plans and manufacturer's instructions. Assembles and installs electrical and electromechanical components and systems, using handtools, electrical testing instruments, soldering irons, and wiring diagrams. Operates equipment through trial run to verify setup. Adjusts controls and setup of machine for specified type, thickness, and size of stock to be processed, for prescribed sequence of operating stages, and to ensure maximum efficiency. Instructs equipment operators and engineering and maintenance personnel regarding setup, operation, and maintenance of equipment. Repairs and services equipment, following preventive maintenance schedule or upon customer's request. May modify previously installed equipment to ensure compatibility with new units, or install safety devices or attachments to old equipment. May confer with customer's engineers to determine effective methods of programming work for machine processing. ● **GED:** R4, M4, L4 ● **SVP:** 2-4 yrs ● **Academic:** Ed=H, Eng=S ● **Work Field:** 111 ● **MPSMS:** 567 ● **Aptitudes:** G2, V3, N2, S3, P2, Q3, K2, F2, M3, E4, C3 ● **Temperaments:** J, P, T, V ● **Physical:** Stg=M; Freq: R, H, I, N, D Occas: S, K, O, T, G, X ● **Work Env:** Noise=N; ● **Salary:** 4 ● **Outlook:** 3

CABLE INSTALLER-REPAIRER (utilities) ● DOT #821.361-010 ● OES: 85723 ● Alternate titles: ELECTRICIAN, UNDERGROUND. Installs and repairs underground conduit and cable systems used to conduct electrical energy between substations and consumers: Installs and repairs conduits following blueprints. Pulls cables through ducts [CABLE PULLER (construction; utilities)]. Splices cables together or to overhead transmission line, customer service line, or street light line [CABLE SPLICER (construction; tel. & tel.; utilities)]. Installs and repairs transformers, fuse boxes, bus bars, relays, and other electrical equipment in manhole and underground substations [UNDERGROUND REPAIRER (utilities)] according to wiring diagrams and specifications. Reinsulates or replaces worn cables and wires. Tests electric cables and equipment wiring to detect broken circuits or incorrect connections, using test lamp, voltmeter, ammeter, and thermocouple indicator. ● **GED:** R4, M4, L3 ● **SVP:** 4-10 yrs ● **Academic:** Ed=H, Eng=S ● **Work Field:** 111 ● **MPSMS:** 581, 585 ● **Aptitudes:** G3, V3, N3, S2, P2, Q2, K3, F3, M3, E3, C4 ● **Temperaments:** J, S, T, V ● **Physical:** Stg=M; Freq: C, S, K, O, W, R, H, I, E, N, D, A, X Occas: B, T, G ● **Work Env:** Noise=L; Freq: W, E ● **Salary:** 2 ● **Outlook:** 3

CABLE SPLICER (construction) ● DOT #829.361-010 ● OES: 85723 ● Alternate titles: ELECTRICIAN, CABLE-SPLICING; SPLICER. Splices overhead, underground, or submarine multiple-conductor cables used in telephone and telegraph communication and electric-power transmission systems: Climbs utility poles or towers, utilizes truck-mounted lift bucket, or descends into sewers and underground vaults where cables are located. Cuts lead sheath from installed cable to gain access to defective cable connections, using hacksaw. Cuts and peels lead sheath and insulation from newly installed cables and conductors preparatory to splicing. Tests (traces or phases-out) each conductor to identify corresponding conductors in adjoining cable sections, according to electrical diagrams and specifications, to prevent incorrect connections between individual communication circuits or electric power circuits, using test lamp or bell system. Cleans, tins, and splices corresponding conductors by twisting ends together or by joining ends with metal clips and soldering each connection. Covers conductors with insulating or fireproofing materials. Fits lead sleeve around cable joint and wipes molten lead into joints between sleeve and cable sheath to produce moistureproof joint. Fills completed sleeve with insulating oil. May work on energized circuits to avoid interruption of service. May locate and repair leaks in pressurized cable. May work on board marine craft when splicing underwater cable and be designated Jointer, Submarine Cable (tel. & tel.; utilities). ● **GED:** R4, M3, L3 ● **SVP:** 2-4 yrs ● **Academic:** Ed=N, Eng=S ● **Work Field:** 111 ● **MPSMS:** 580 ● **Aptitudes:** G3, V3, N3, S3, P2, Q3, K3, F2, M3, E3, C3 ● **Temperaments:** J, T ● **Physical:** Stg=L; Freq: C, B, R, H, I, N, A Occas: S, K, O, T, G, D, X ● **Work Env:** Noise=N; Freq: W Occas: E ● **Salary:** 1 ● **Outlook:** 3

CABLE SUPERVISOR (tel. & tel.) ● DOT #184.161-010 ● OES: 15023 ● Directs and coordinates, through subordinate supervisory personnel, activities of workers engaged in installation, maintenance, and repair of underground, buried, aerial, or submarine telephone carrier cables in plant district: Reviews proposed construction plans and schematic drawings to ensure that proposals are compatible with existing equipment and that plans adhere to specifications. Inspects construction sites and installations to ensure service deadlines are being met. Directs and coordinates testing and inspecting of plant equipment for operational performance. Prepares budget, determines work force requirements, and establishes production schedules to meet service loads. ● **GED:** R4, M2, L4 ● **SVP:** 4-10 yrs ● **Academic:** Ed=H, Eng=S ● **Work Field:** 111, 211 ● **MPSMS:** 586 ● **Aptitudes:** G2, V3, N3, S3, P3, Q4, K4, F4, M4, E5, C4 ● **Temperaments:** D, J, P ● **Physical:** Stg=L; Freq: R, H, T, G, N Occas: I, A, X ● **Work Env:** Noise=N; Occas: W ● **Salary:** 3 ● **Outlook:** 2

CABLE TESTER (tel. & tel.) ● DOT #822.361-010 ● OES: 83000 ● Tests insulated wires in aerial, underground, or submarine multiple-conductor cables to determine continuity, insulation, and correctness of cable loading, using standard testing procedures and impedance, resistance, and frequency oscillating meters. Listens for sound of escaping insulating gas from hole in cable sheathing to locate defects in cable. Determines continuity, insulation, capacity imbalance, and cable loading, using meters, such as capacity and resistance bridges. Prepares report identifying location and cause of malfunctions. May drive motor vehicle along route of cable, climb poles, and ride in cable car from pole to pole on cable strand to perform tests. May direct CABLE SPLICER (construction; tel. & tel.; utilities) in correction of malfunction. ● **GED:** R4, M3, L3 ● **SVP:** 2-4 yrs ● **Academic:** Ed=H, Eng=S ● **Work Field:** 111 ● **MPSMS:** 586 ● **Aptitudes:** G3, V3, N3, S3, P3, Q4, K4, F3, M4, E3, C4 ● **Temperaments:** J, T, V ● **Physical:** Stg=M; Freq: R, H, I, G, N Occas: C, B, S, K, O, W, X ● **Work Env:** Noise=N; Freq: W Occas: A, T ● **Salary:** 3 ● **Outlook:** 3

CENTRAL-OFFICE REPAIRER (tel. & tel.) ● DOT #822.281-014 ● OES: 85502 ● Alternate titles: CENTRAL-OFFICE MAINTAINER.

Tests, analyzes defects, and repairs telephone circuits and equipment in central office of telephone company, using test meters and handtools: Locates electrical, electronic, and mechanical failures in telephone switching equipment, using milliammeter boxes, schematic drawings, computer printouts, or trouble tickets. Installs, repairs, and adjusts equipment, such as switches, relays, and amplifiers, using handtools. Removes connections on wire distributing frames and solders or splices wires to terminal lugs, following diagrams [FRAME WIRER (tel. & tel.)]. May maintain telephone switching equipment at private establishments, such as hotels and office buildings [PRIVATE-BRANCH-EXCHANGE REPAIRER (tel. & tel.)]. May diagnose, isolate, and clear electrical faults in circuit [TROUBLE LOCATOR, TEST DESK (tel. & tel.)]. When servicing equipment for intercommunity telephone lines, may be designated Toll Repairer, Central Office (tel. & tel.). ● **GED:** R4, M3, L3 ● **SVP:** 2-4 yrs ● **Academic:** Ed=H, Eng=S ● **Work Field:** 111 ● **MPSMS:** 586 ● **Aptitudes:** G3, V3, N3, S3, P3, Q3, K3, F2, M2, E3, C4 ● **Temperaments:** J, T, V ● **Physical:** Stg=L; Freq: C, B, S, K, O, R, H, I, N, D Occas: A, X ● **Work Env:** Noise=L; ● **Salary:** 5 ● **Outlook:** 3

COMPUTERIZED ENVIRONMENTAL CONTROL INSTALLER (electron. comp.) ● DOT #828.281-026 ● OES: 85998 ● Installs and repairs programmable, computer-based control systems for regulating residential and commercial environmental energy equipment, such as heating, ventilating and air-conditioning (HVAC) systems, heat pumps, boilers, and chillers, applying knowledge of computer control systems and environmental energy equipment: Reads specifications, diagrams, and schematics detailing computer control installation requirements and existing environmental energy equipment design and layout. Installs, mounts, and connects specified computer hardware, such as central processing unit, keyboard, CRT display, temperature sensor, analog to digital converter, and interconnect wiring to interface with environmental energy equipment control circuits, using handtools and power tools. Types commands on input keyboard or inserts disk into disk drive to start and run computerized environmental control system through operating sequence. Tests control circuits to verify system operation or diagnose malfunctions, using voltmeter and oscilloscope. Isolates faults to computer controls or environmental energy units based on test results, specification data, and symptoms. Tests circuitry of faulty computer controls, using voltmeter, oscilloscope, and logic analyzer to isolate malfunctions to circuit board. Replaces faulty circuit boards, using handtools. Maintains records of installation, test results, and repairs. ● **GED:** R4, M4, L4 ● **SVP:** 2-4 yrs ● **Academic:** Ed=H, Eng=S ● **Work Field:** 111 ● **MPSMS:** 589 ● **Aptitudes:** G2, V3, N2, S2, P2, Q3, K2, F3, M2, E5, C4 ● **Temperaments:** J, T, V ● **Physical:** Stg=L; Const: R, H, I Freq: N, A Occas: S, K, O, T, G, X ● **Work Env:** Noise=N; ● **Salary:** 4 ● **Outlook:** 4

DATA COMMUNICATIONS TECHNICIAN (any industry) ● DOT #823.261-030 ● OES: 85598 ● Installs and repairs data communications lines and equipment for computer system, using handtools and test instruments: Reviews work orders to move, change, install, repair, or remove data communications equipment, such as modems, cables, and wires. Reads technical manuals to learn correct settings for equipment. Measures, cuts, and installs wires and cables. Splices wires or cables, using handtools or soldering iron. Connects microcomputer or terminal to data communication lines, using handtools and following diagrams and manuals. Disassembles equipment and inspects and tests wiring to locate and repair problem. Modifies equipment in accordance with user request. Tests communication lines to ensure that specifications are met, using testing instruments such as voltmeter and data scope. Enters commands into computer to test equipment. Reads messages on computer screen to verify that data is being transmitted between locations according to specifications. May plan layout and installation of data communications equipment. May demonstrate use of equipment. ● **GED:** R4, M3, L4 ● **SVP:** 2-4 yrs ● **Academic:** Ed=H, Eng=G ● **Work Field:** 111 ● **MPSMS:** 586 ● **Aptitudes:** G2, V3, N3, S3, P3, Q3, K2, F3, M3, E5, C4 ● **Temperaments:** J, T ● **Physical:** Stg=M; Freq: R, H, I, N Occas: C, S, K, O, E, T, G, F, D, X ● **Work Env:** Noise=N; ● **Salary:** 4 ● **Outlook:** 4

ELECTRIC-METER INSTALLER I (utilities) ● DOT #821.361-014 ● OES: 85911 ● Installs, disconnects, removes, and reconnects electric power meters used to record current consumption of residential, commercial, and industrial customers: Splices and connects covered insulated cable to bus bar in pull box or on switchboard. Mounts meter, and other electric equipment for high load installations, such as time clocks, transformers, and circuit breakers, on racks or wall, using electrician handtools. Installs and connects cable from pull box to meter socket or transformer. Attaches color-coded wires from current transformer to test blocks and from test blocks to meter terminals for testing purposes. Tests meter for current flow and recording of current consumption. Disconnects and seals meter on cut-off order or removes seal and reconnects meter on cut-in orders. Removes, replaces, and reconnects meters when current consumption is too high for existing installation. Installs temporary service meter for recording current consumption during construction. Splices and connects jumper cables from current transformer onto bus bar on switchboard to provide temporary power for customer during change of meter and cables or when customer's service equipment is defective. Records meter and installation data on meter cards, work orders, and field service orders. Locates, diagnoses, and clears electrical trouble on customers' premises. Performs minor repairs and changes faulty or incorrect wiring on customers' premises. May be designated according to specialty as Meter Installer-And-Remover (utilities). ● **GED:** R4, M4, L3 ● **SVP:** 2-4 yrs ● **Academic:** Ed=N, Eng=S ● **Work Field:** 111 ● **MPSMS:** 581 ● **Aptitudes:** G3, V3, N3, S3, P3, Q3, K3, F3, M3, E4, C4 ● **Temperaments:** J ● **Physical:** Stg=L; Freq: C, B, R, H, I, N, D, X Occas: T, G, A ● **Work Env:** Noise=N; Freq: W ● **Salary:** 3 ● **Outlook:** 3

ELECTRICIAN (construction) ● DOT #824.261-010 ● OES: 87202 ● Alternate titles: WIRER. Plans layout, installs, and repairs wiring, electrical fixtures, apparatus, and control equipment: Plans new or modified installations to minimize waste of materials, provide access for future maintenance, and avoid unsightly, hazardous, and unreliable wiring, consistent with specifications and local electrical codes. Prepares sketches showing location of wiring and equipment, or follows diagrams or blueprints, ensuring that concealed wiring is installed before completion of future walls, ceilings, and flooring. Measures, cuts, bends, threads, assembles, and installs electrical conduit, using tools, such as hacksaw, pipe threader, and conduit bender. Pulls wiring through conduit, assisted by ELECTRICIAN HELPER (any industry) 829.684-022. Splices wires by stripping insulation from terminal leads, using knife or pliers, twisting or soldering wires together, and applying tape or terminal caps. Connects wiring to lighting fixtures and power equipment, using handtools. Installs control and distribution apparatus, such as switches, relays, and circuit-breaker panels, fastening in place with screws or bolts, using handtools and power tools. Connects power cables to equipment, such as electric range or motor, and installs grounding leads. Tests continuity of circuit to ensure electrical compatibility and safety of components, using testing instruments, such as ohmmeter, battery and buzzer, and oscilloscope. Observes functioning of installed equipment or system to detect hazards and need for adjustments, relocation, or replacement. May repair faulty equipment or systems [ELECTRICIAN, MAINTENANCE (any industry) 829.261-018]. May be required to hold license. May cut and weld steel structural members, using flame-cutting and welding equipment. May be designated according to work location as Mine Electrician (mine & quarry). ● **GED:** R4, M4, L3 ● **SVP:** 2-4 yrs ● **Academic:** Ed=H, Eng=S ● **Work Field:** 111 ● **MPSMS:** 580 ● **Aptitudes:** G2, V3, N2, S2, P3, Q4, K3, F3, M3, E4, C4 ● **Temperaments:** J, T, V ● **Physical:** Stg=M; Freq: R, H, N, A, X Occas: C, B, S, K, O, W, I, T, G, D ● **Work Env:** Noise=L; Freq: E ● **Salary:** 5 ● **Outlook:** 4

ELECTRICIAN, AIRCRAFT (aircraft mfg.) ● DOT #825.261-018 ● OES: 85720 ● Alternate titles: AIRCRAFT AND ENGINE ELECTRICIAN, FIELD AND HANGAR; AIRCRAFT MECHANIC, ELECTRICAL. Installs, adjusts, tests, modifies, repairs, and maintains electrical and electronic parts, assemblies, systems, and equipment in prototype, developmental, or production aircraft, engines, and components: Installs electrical and electronic parts, assemblies, systems, and equipment in aircraft, according to blueprints, wiring diagrams, and other specifications, using handtools and power tools. Sets up and operates ground support and test equipment, such as test carts, panels, ground power unit, and ground servicing cart, to perform functional and continuity test of electrical and electronic systems. Interprets test results to diagnose malfunctions, and adjusts, repairs, or replaces defective parts. Modifies components according to blueprint specifications and engineering drawings. Fabricates parts and test aids as required. May accompany aircraft on test flight to perform functional tests or to make in-flight adjustments. ● **GED:** R4, M3, L3 ● **SVP:** 2-4 yrs ● **Academic:** Ed=H, Eng=G ● **Work Field:** 111, 211 ● **MPSMS:** 592 ●

Aptitudes: G3, V2, N3, S3, P3, Q4, K4, F3, M2, E5, C4 ● **Temperaments:** J, T ● **Physical:** Stg=M; Freq: R, H, I, N, D Occas: C, B, S, K, O, W, E, T, G, M, A, X ● **Work Env:** Noise=V; Occas: W, E, D ● **Salary:** 4 ● **Outlook:** 3

ELECTRICIAN, MAINTENANCE (any industry) ● DOT #829.261-018 ● OES: 87202 ● Alternate titles: ELECTRICAL REPAIRER. Installs and repairs electrical systems, apparatus, and electrical and electronic components of industrial machinery and equipment, following electrical code, manuals, schematic diagrams, blueprints, and other specifications, using handtools, power tools, and electrical and electronic test equipment: Installs power supply wiring and conduit for newly installed machines and equipment, such as robots, conveyors, and programmable controllers, following electrical code and blueprints, using handtools and voltage tester. Connects power supply wires to machines and equipment, and connects cables and wires between machines and equipment, following manuals, schematic diagrams, and blueprints, using handtools and test equipment. Diagnoses malfunctioning apparatus, such as transformers, motors, and lighting fixtures, using test equipment, and replaces damaged or broken wires and cables, using handtools. Tests malfunctioning machinery, using test equipment, and discusses malfunction with other maintenance workers, such as MACHINE REPAIRER, MAINTENANCE (any industry) 638.261-030 and TOOL MAKER, MAINTENANCE (machine shop) 601.280-042, to diagnose malfunction. Replaces faulty electrical components of machine, such as relays, switches, and motors, and positions sensing devices, using handtools. Diagnoses and repairs or replaces faulty electronic components, such as printed circuit boards [ELECTRONICS TESTER (any industry) 726.261-018], using electronic test equipment and handtools. Replaces electric motor bearings and rewires motors. May push buttons and press keys on robot controller, teach pendant, and programmable controller to program automated machinery, such as robots, to operate automated machinery, to test for malfunctions, and to verify repairs. May plan layout of wiring and install wiring, conduit, and electrical apparatus in buildings [ELECTRICIAN (construction) 824.261-010]. May diagnose and replace faulty mechanical, hydraulic, and pneumatic components of machines and equipment. May be required to hold electrician's license. May be designated according to equipment repaired as Circuit-Breaker Mechanic (utilities); Electrician, Crane Maintenance (any industry); Electrician, Rectifier Maintenance (utilities); Salvage Repairer (utilities) I; Time Clock Repairer (elec. equip.); Transformer-Coil Winder (utilities); or according to work location as Electrician, Machine Shop (machine shop); Electrician Refinery (petrol. refin.); Underground Repairer (utilities). May be designated: Watch Electrician (tel. & tel.); Wirer, Maintenance (utilities). ● **GED:** R4, M4, L4 ● **SVP:** 4-10 yrs ● **Academic:** Ed=H, Eng=S ● **Work Field:** 111 ● **MPSMS:** 560, 580 ● **Aptitudes:** G2, V3, N2, S2, P2, Q3, K3, F3, M2, E3, C4 ● **Temperaments:** J, T ● **Physical:** Stg=M; Freq: R, H, I, N Occas: C, B, S, K, O, W, E, T, G, M, D, A, X ● **Work Env:** Noise=L; Occas: M, E, D ● **Salary:** 4 ● **Outlook:** 4

ELECTRICIAN, POWERHOUSE (utilities) ● DOT #820.261-014 ● OES: 85998 ● Repairs and maintains electrical equipment in generating station or powerhouse: Tests defective equipment to determine cause of malfunction or failure, using voltmeters, ammeters, and related electrical testing apparatus. Notifies plant personnel of necessary equipment downtime requiring changes from normal generating and transmission equipment operation to maintain uninterrupted service. Repairs and replaces equipment, such as relays, switches, supervisory controls, and indicating and recording instruments. Tests and repairs switchboard and equipment circuitry, interpreting wiring diagrams to trace and connect numerous wires carrying current for independent functions. Cleans and repairs brushes, commutators, windings, and bearings of generators, motors, and converters. May test and maintain transmission equipment, performing such duties as oiling circuit breakers and transformers [ELECTRICIAN, SUBSTATION (utilities)]. ● **GED:** R4, M4, L3 ● **SVP:** 4-10 yrs ● **Academic:** Ed=A, Eng=S ● **Work Field:** 111 ● **MPSMS:** 580 ● **Aptitudes:** G2, V3, N3, S2, P2, Q4, K3, F3, M2, E3, C4 ● **Temperaments:** J, T, V ● **Physical:** Stg=M; Freq: R, H, I, N, D, X Occas: C, B, S, K, O, W, T, G ● **Work Env:** Noise=L; Freq: E Occas: W, M, D ● **Salary:** 4 ● **Outlook:** 2

ELECTRONIC-SALES-AND-SERVICE TECHNICIAN (profess. & kin.) ● DOT #828.251-010 ● OES: 85717 ● Analyzes technical requirements of customer desiring to utilize electronic equipment, and performs installation and maintenance duties. Determines feasibility of using standardized equipment, and develops specifications for equipment required to perform additional functions. Installs, maintains, and repairs equipment. ● **GED:** R4, M3, L3 ● **SVP:** 2-4 yrs ● **Academic:** Ed=H, Eng=S ● **Work Field:** 244, 111 ● **MPSMS:** 703 ● **Aptitudes:** G2, V2, N2, S2, P2, Q3, K2, F2, M2, E4, C4 ● **Temperaments:** J, T, V ● **Physical:** Stg=M; Freq: R, H, I, N Occas: T, G, D, A, X ● **Work Env:** Noise=N; ● **Salary:** 4 ● **Outlook:** 4

ELECTRONICS ASSEMBLER, DEVELOPMENTAL (any industry) ● DOT #726.261-010 ● OES: 22505 ● Alternate titles: DEVELOPER-PROVER, ELECTRICAL; ELECTRICAL AND ELECTRONICS DEVELOPMENT MECHANIC; PROTOTYPE ASSEMBLER, ELECTRONICS. Assembles, tests, and modifies prototype or custom electronic parts, systems, and apparatus to develop assembly methods and techniques for use by production workers, applying knowledge of electronic theory and assembly techniques: Reads blueprints, wiring diagrams, process sheets, and assembly and schematic drawings, and receives verbal instructions regarding work assignment. Aligns and assembles parts, such as leads, coils, wires, tabs, and terminals into housing, using handtools, power tools, soldering iron, brazing fixture, and welding head. Routes and laces cables [CABLE MAKER (elec. equip.; electron. comp.) 728.684-010]. Installs components and parts, such as switches, coils, transformers, relays, transistors, and semiconductor circuits on chassis, circuit boards, panels, and other units, using handtools, power tools, soldering and welding equipment, and thermocompression bonding, wave soldering, or resistance welding techniques. Routes and attaches wires and connectors to form circuitry and connects assembly to power supply sources, switch panels, or junction boxes. Attaches hardware and seals assembly, using rivets, screws, handtools, power tools, resistance welder or thermocompression bonding. Examines parts for defects, such as pinholes or chips. Test-operates unit to locate defects, measure performance, determine need for adjustment, and verify specified operation, using ohmmeter, oscilloscope, signal generator, and other electronic test instruments. Replaces defective components and wiring, using handtools and soldering iron. Calibrates unit according to specifications. Enters information on production records, logs, and other report forms. May assemble prototype microelectronic units, using binocular microscope. May repair defective units rejected by inspection or test personnel [ELECTRONIC EQUIPMENT REPAIRER (comm. equip.; electron. comp.) 726.381-014]. ● **GED:** R4, M4, L4 ● **SVP:** 2-4 yrs ● **Academic:** Ed=N, Eng=S ● **Work Field:** 111 ● **MPSMS:** 580, 571, 602 ● **Aptitudes:** G2, V3, N3, S2, P2, Q3, K2, F2, M2, E5, C3 ● **Temperaments:** J, T ● **Physical:** Stg=L; Freq: R, H, I, N, D, X Occas: T, G, A ● **Work Env:** Noise=N; ● **Salary:** 4 ● **Outlook:** 3

ELEVATOR REPAIRER (any industry) ● DOT #825.281-030 ● OES: 85932 ● Alternate titles: ELECTRICIAN, ELEVATOR-MAINTENANCE; ELEVATOR MECHANIC; ELEVATOR-REPAIR MECHANIC; MAINTENANCE MECHANIC, ELEVATORS. Repairs and maintains elevators, escalators, and dumb-waiters to meet safety regulations and building codes, using handtools, power tools, test lamps, ammeters, voltmeters, and other testing devices: Locates and determines causes of trouble in brakes, motors, switches, and signal and control systems, using test lamps, ammeters, and voltmeters. Disassembles defective units and repairs or replaces parts, such as locks, gears, cables, electric wiring, and faulty safety devices, using handtools. Installs push-button controls and other devices to modernize elevators. Lubricates bearings and other parts to minimize friction. ● **GED:** R4, M3, L3 ● **SVP:** 2-4 yrs ● **Academic:** Ed=A, Eng=S ● **Work Field:** 111, 121 ● **MPSMS:** 565 ● **Aptitudes:** G3, V3, N3, S2, P3, Q4, K4, F3, M2, E4, C4 ● **Temperaments:** J, T ● **Physical:** Stg=M; Freq: C, B, S, K, O, R, H, I, N, D Occas: G, A, X ● **Work Env:** Noise=N; Occas: E, O ● **Salary:** 4 ● **Outlook:** 5

FIELD SERVICE ENGINEER (profess. & kin.) ● DOT #828.261-014 ● OES: 85717 ● Alternate titles: FIELD SERVICE REPRESENTATIVE; FIELD TECHNICAL ASSISTANT. Installs and repairs electronic equipment, such as computer, radar, missile-control, avionics, and communication systems, in field installations: Consults with customer or supervisor to plan layout of equipment. Studies blueprints, schematics, manuals, and other specifications to determine installation procedures. Installs or oversees installation of equipment according to manufacturer's specifications. Operates system to demonstrate equipment and to analyze malfunctions. Interprets maintenance manuals, schematics, and wiring diagrams, and repairs equipment, utilizing

knowledge of electronics and using standard test instruments and handtools. Instructs and directs workers in servicing and repairing equipment. Consults with engineering personnel to resolve unusual problems in system operation and maintenance. May instruct workers in electronic theory. May supervise workers in testing, tuning, and adjusting equipment to obtain optimum operating performance. May advise management regarding customer satisfaction, product performance, and suggestions for product improvements. ● **GED:** R4, M4, L4 ● **SVP:** 2-4 yrs ● **Academic:** Ed=H, Eng=S ● **Work Field:** 111, 211 ● **MPSMS:** 571, 586, 601 ● **Aptitudes:** G2, V2, N2, S2, P2, Q3, K3, F3, M3, E4, C4 ● **Temperaments:** D, J, P, T, V ● **Physical:** Stg=L; Freq: I, T, G, N Occas: C, B, S, K, O, W, R, H, F, D, A, X ● **Work Env:** Noise=N; Occas: W, D ● **Salary:** 4 ● **Outlook:** 4

FURNACE INSTALLER (utilities) ● DOT #862.361-010 ● OES: 85902 ● Installs and regulates gas-burner units in building-heating furnaces to convert furnaces from wood, coal, or oil to gas: Directs helper to prepare furnace for installation of gas burner unit. Lays brick foundation [BRICKLAYER (construction)] in furnace ashpit and positions heating unit on foundation. Draws sketch of pipes and fittings required to connect gas burner to gas supply. Measures, cuts, threads, bends, and installs pipe between burner and gas supply with assistance of helper, using pipefitters' tools. Installs thermostat in heated area and makes wiring connections between building terminal box, switchbox, burner motor, and thermostat [ELECTRICIAN (construction)]. Ignites gas burner and adjusts gas-flow and air-supply control valves until observation of gas flame indicates correct combustion. ● **GED:** R4, M2, L3 ● **SVP:** 2-4 yrs ● **Academic:** Ed=A, Eng=S ● **Work Field:** 102, 111 ● **MPSMS:** 553, 602 ● **Aptitudes:** G3, V3, N3, S3, P3, Q4, K3, F3, M2, E5, C4 ● **Temperaments:** J, T, V ● **Physical:** Stg=M; Freq: S, K, O, R, H, I, N, D Occas: T, G, X ● **Work Env:** Noise=N; Freq: O ● **Salary:** 3 ● **Outlook:** 4

LINE ERECTOR (construction) ● DOT #821.361-018 ● OES: 85723 ● Erects, maintains, and repairs wood poles and prefabricated light-duty metal towers, cable, and related equipment to construct transmission and distribution power lines used to conduct electrical energy between generating stations, substations, and consumers: Directs and assists GROUND HELPERS (tel. & tel.; utilities) in attaching crossarms, insulators, lightning arresters, switches, wire conductors, and auxiliary equipment to poles preparatory to erection, as instructed by LINE SUPERVISOR (utilities), and assists in erection of poles or towers and adjustment of guy wires. Climbs erected poles or towers and installs equipment, such as transformers, which are ordinarily installed after poles are erected. Strings wire conductors between erected poles with assistance of GROUND HELPERS (tel. & tel.; utilities) and adjusts slack in conductors to compensate for contraction and elongation of conductors due to temperature variations, using winch. Splices, solders, and insulates conductors and related wiring to join sections of power line, and to connect transformers and electrical accessories. May trim trees and brush prior to new construction, during repair of damaged lines, or as part of routine maintenance [TREE TRIMMER (tel. & tel.; utilities)]. ● **GED:** R4, M3, L3 ● **SVP:** 2-4 yrs ● **Academic:** Ed=N, Eng=S ● **Work Field:** 102, 111 ● **MPSMS:** 581 ● **Aptitudes:** G3, V3, N4, S3, P3, Q4, K2, F3, M2, E2, C4 ● **Temperaments:** J, S, T ● **Physical:** Stg=H; Freq: C, B, S, K, O, R, H, I, N, F, D Occas: T, G, X ● **Work Env:** Noise=L; Const: W Freq: E, D, O ● **Salary:** 3 ● **Outlook:** 3

LINE INSTALLER-REPAIRER (tel. & tel.) ● DOT #822.381-014 ● OES: 85702 ● Installs and repairs telephone and telegraph lines, poles, and related equipment, according to diagrams, and using electrician's handtools: Digs holes, using power auger or shovel, hoists poles upright in holes, using truck-mounted winch, and fills and tamps holes, using cement, earth, and tamping device. Ascends poles or enters tunnels and sewers to cut in feeder lines, attach appliances, such as terminal boxes and repeaters, and repair or replace defective lines and auxiliary equipment. Unreels and strings lines from pole to pole and from pole to building, installs hardware, such as conduits and insulators, and attaches appliances on lines. Pulls lines through ducts by hand or with use of winch. When assisting in installation and removal of plant equipment, such as callboxes and clocks, in city locations, may be designated Line Installer-Repairer, City (tel. & tel.). When patrolling telephone lines between communities, may be designated Toll-Line Repairer (tel. & tel.). When patrolling telephone or telegraph lines between two established points or in designated areas, may be designated Line Maintainer, Section (tel. & tel.). ● **GED:** R4, M3, L3 ● **SVP:** 2-4 yrs ● **Academic:** Ed=H, Eng=S ● **Work Field:** 111 ● **MPSMS:** 586 ● **Aptitudes:** G3, V3, N3, S4, P3, Q4, K4, F4, M3, E4, C4 ● **Temperaments:** J, T, V ● **Physical:** Stg=H; Freq: C, B, S, K, O, R, H, I, N, D, X ● **Work Env:** Noise=L; ● **Salary:** 3 ● **Outlook:** 1

LINE MAINTAINER (any industry) ● DOT #821.261-014 ● OES: 85723 ● Installs, maintains, and repairs telephone and telegraph and electrical power lines between installations of industrial plant: Directs workers in setting poles. Climbs poles and installs hardware, lightning arresters, telephone repeaters, telephone and telegraph wires, and other equipment [LINE INSTALLER-REPAIRER (tel. & tel.)]. Installs electrical power cables and auxiliary equipment [LINE ERECTOR (construction; utilities)]. Makes repairs and replacements to maintain lines. May be designated according to area of operations as Line Maintainer, District (any industry). ● **GED:** R4, M4, L3 ● **SVP:** 2-4 yrs ● **Academic:** Ed=N, Eng=S ● **Work Field:** 111 ● **MPSMS:** 586 ● **Aptitudes:** G3, V3, N4, S3, P3, Q4, K3, F3, M3, E3, C4 ● **Temperaments:** J, T ● **Physical:** Stg=M; Freq: R, H, I, N, D Occas: T, G, X ● **Work Env:** Noise=N; Freq: W, E ● **Salary:** 3 ● **Outlook:** 3

LINE REPAIRER (utilities) ● DOT #821.361-026 ● OES: 85723 ● Alternate titles: HIKER; LINE SERVICER. Repairs and replaces transmission and distribution power lines between generating stations, substations, and consumers, requiring use of precautionary work methods and safety equipment due to electrical hazards present when working on or near energized conductors and electrical accessories: Opens switches or clamps grounding device to energized equipment to deenergize lines or accessories as directed by LINE SUPERVISOR (utilities). Climbs poles or rides in bucket attached to truck-mounted boom to remove broken or defective wires. Secures new wires to crossarm insulators and splices wire to adjoining sections of line to complete circuit. Transfers wires from defective poles to poles erected by GROUND HELPERS (tel. & tel.; utilities). Installs pole hardware and such auxiliary equipment as transformers, lightning arresters, switches, fuses, and insulators, using handtools. Suspends insulated ladders and platforms from pole crossarms and covers energized lines with rubber mats to facilitate safe handling of high-voltage lines without interrupting service by power shutoff, and uses long insulated poles (hot sticks) fitted with mechanically or hydraulically operated grasping and crimping tools. May service streetlight systems [STREET-LIGHT SERVICER (utilities)]. May patrol power lines [ELECTRIC POWER LINE EXAMINER (utilities)]. Qualifications of workers in this classification include work experience in terms of maximum voltage of power lines repaired, such as 120-240 volt secondary circuits, 2,300-4,000 volt distribution lines, or 138 kilovolt transmission lines. Power line repairers experienced in repair of energized or deenergized conductors suspended from electrically conductive metal towers, commonly one-hundred feet or more above ground, may be designated Line Repairer, Tower (utilities). ● **GED:** R4, M4, L4 ● **SVP:** 2-4 yrs ● **Academic:** Ed=H, Eng=S ● **Work Field:** 102, 111 ● **MPSMS:** 581 ● **Aptitudes:** G3, V3, N4, S3, P3, Q4, K2, F3, M2, E2, C4 ● **Temperaments:** J, S, T, V ● **Physical:** Stg=H; Freq: C, B, S, K, O, R, H, I, T, G, N, F, D Occas: X ● **Work Env:** Noise=L; Const: W Freq: E, D ● **Salary:** 3 ● **Outlook:** 3

MAINTENANCE MECHANIC, TELEPHONE (any industry) ● DOT #822.281-018 ● OES: 85726 ● Alternate titles: ELECTRICIAN, TELEPHONE. Installs, tests, and repairs communication equipment, such as public address and intercommunication systems, wired burglar alarms, switchboards, telegraphs, telephones, and related apparatus, including coin collectors, telephone booths, and switching keys, using schematic diagrams, testing devices, and handtools: Installs equipment according to layout plans and connects units with inside and outside service wires. Maintains equipment and analyzes operational malfunctioning with testing devices, such as oscilloscopes, generators, meters, and electric bridges, to locate and diagnose nature of defect and ascertain repairs to be made. Examines mechanism and disassembles components to replace, clean, adjust or repair parts, wires, switches, relays, circuits, or signaling units, using handtools. Operates and tests equipment to ensure elimination of malfunction. May climb poles to install or repair outside service lines. May repair cables, lay out plans for new equipment, and estimate material required. ● **GED:** R4, M4, L3 ● **SVP:** 2-4 yrs ● **Academic:** Ed=H, Eng=S ● **Work Field:** 111 ● **MPSMS:** 586 ● **Aptitudes:** G3, V3, N3, S3, P2, Q4, K3, F3, M3, E3, C3 ● **Temperaments:** J, T ● **Physical:** Stg=L; Freq: R, H, I, G, N, D, X

Occas: A ● **Work Env:** Noise=L; ● **Salary:** 3 ● **Outlook:** 4

MICROCOMPUTER SUPPORT SPECIALIST (profess. & kin.) ● DOT #039.264-010 ● OES: 25104 ● Installs, modifies, and makes minor repairs to microcomputer hardware and software systems and provides technical assistance and training to system users: Inspects microcomputer equipment and reads order sheet listing user requirements to prepare microcomputer for delivery. Installs or assists service personnel in installation of hardware and peripheral components, such as monitors, keyboards, printers, and disk drives on user's premises, following design or installation specifications. Loads specified software packages, such as operating systems, word processing, or spreadsheet programs into computer. Enters commands and observes system functions to verify correct system operation. Instructs user in use of equipment, software, and manuals. Answers client's inquiries in person and via telephone concerning systems operation; diagnoses system hardware, software, and operator problems; and recommends or performs minor remedial actions to correct problems based on knowledge of system operation. Replaces defective or inadequate software packages. Refers major hardware problems to service personnel for correction. Attends technical conferences and seminars to keep abreast of new software and hardware product developments. ● **GED:** R4, M3, L4 ● **SVP:** 2-4 yrs ● **Academic:** Ed=H, Eng=G ● **Work Field:** 233, 296, 111 ● **MPSMS:** 571 ● **Aptitudes:** G2, V3, N3, S3, P3, Q3, K2, F3, M3, E5, C4 ● **Temperaments:** J, P, T, V ● **Physical:** Stg=M; Freq: S, K, O, R, H, I, T, G, N Occas: C, W, F, X ● **Work Env:** Noise=N; ● **Salary:** 4 ● **Outlook:** 5

PROTECTIVE-SIGNAL INSTALLER (business ser.) ● DOT #822.361-018 ● OES: 87202 ● Alternate titles: BURGLAR-ALARM INSTALLER; INSTALLER. Installs electrical protective signaling systems used to notify central office of fire, burglary, or other irregularities on subscribers' premises: Installs wires, conduits, and signaling units, following blueprints of electrical layouts and building plans and using handtools, power tools and soldering iron. May repair signaling systems [PROTECTIVE-SIGNAL REPAIRER (business ser.)]. Usually is required to possess identification card issued by local authorities. ● **GED:** R4, M3, L2 ● **SVP:** 2-4 yrs ● **Academic:** Ed=H, Eng=S ● **Work Field:** 111 ● **MPSMS:** 586 ● **Aptitudes:** G3, V3, N3, S3, P2, Q3, K4, F3, M3, E4, C4 ● **Temperaments:** J, T ● **Physical:** Stg=M; Freq: S, K, O, R, H, I, T, G, N Occas: C, B, D, A, X ● **Work Env:** Noise=N; Occas: E ● **Salary:** 3 ● **Outlook:** 4

PROTECTIVE-SIGNAL REPAIRER (business ser.) ● DOT #822.361-022 ● OES: 87202 ● Alternate titles: BURGLAR-ALARM INSTALLER AND SERVICER. Inspects, repairs, and replaces electrical protective-signaling systems, such as burglar alarms: Examines signaling installation to ensure sound connections and unbroken insulation. Tests circuits, following wiring specifications, using electrical testing devices, such as ohmmeter or voltmeter. Tightens loose connections and disconnects and replaces defective parts and wiring, using electrician's handtools. Adjusts controls to test operation of signaling units on subscriber premises and transmission of signals to central station and police and fire departments. Recommends new installation or modification of existing equipment to meet subscriber needs. May install equipment [PROTECTIVE-SIGNAL INSTALLER (business ser.) 822.361-018]. Usually is required to possess identification card issued by local authorities. ● **GED:** R4, M3, L3 ● **SVP:** 2-4 yrs ● **Academic:** Ed=H, Eng=S ● **Work Field:** 111 ● **MPSMS:** 586 ● **Aptitudes:** G3, V3, N3, S3, P2, Q4, K4, F3, M2, E4, C4 ● **Temperaments:** J, T, V ● **Physical:** Stg=M; Freq: S, K, O, R, H, N, D Occas: C, B, I, T, G, A, X ● **Work Env:** Noise=N; Freq: E Occas: W ● **Salary:** 3 ● **Outlook:** 4

STATION INSTALLER-AND-REPAIRER (tel. & tel.) ● DOT #822.261-022 ● OES: 85726 ● Installs, maintains, and repairs telephone station equipment, such as telephones, coin collectors, telephone booths, and switching-key equipment: Inspects subscriber premises to determine method of installation. Climbs pole to attach outside (drop) wires. Assembles telephone equipment, mounts brackets, and connects wire leads, using handtools and following installation diagrams or work order. Tests newly installed equipment and repairs or replaces faulty equipment, using test telephone and other testing devices. May be designated according to specific task performed as Station Installer (tel. & tel.); Station Repairer (tel. & tel.). May maintain telephones, lines, and equipment in primarily small rural areas and be designated Section Maintainer (tel. & tel.). ● **GED:** R4, M4, L3 ● **SVP:** 2-4 yrs ● **Aca-**

demic: Ed=H, Eng=S ● **Work Field:** 111 ● **MPSMS:** 586 ● **Aptitudes:** G3, V3, N3, S3, P3, Q4, K3, F3, M3, E3, C4 ● **Temperaments:** J, P, T, V ● **Physical:** Stg=L; Freq: S, K, O, R, H, I, N, D, X Occas: C, B, T, G ● **Work Env:** Noise=N; Occas: W ● **Salary:** 5 ● **Outlook:** 3

STREET-LIGHT SERVICER (utilities) ● DOT #824.381-010 ● OES: 87202 ● Alternate titles: STREET-LIGHT REPAIRER. Maintains and repairs mercury-vapor, fluorescent, electric-arc, or incandescent street lights and traffic signals: Climbs ladder or stands in tower-truck bucket to reach lamp. Tests circuits and electric components to locate grounded wires, broken connections, or defective current-control mechanisms, using electrical testing instruments. Replaces blown fuses and bulbs, faulty transformers, photoelectric timers, electrodes, and wires, using electricians' handtools. See LINE REPAIRER (utilities) and TROUBLE SHOOTER (utilities) II for classification of workers also qualified to work on high-voltage power lines. May install and repair traffic signals only and be designated Traffic-Signal Repairer (utilities). ● **GED:** R4, M3, L3 ● **SVP:** 2-4 yrs ● **Academic:** Ed=N, Eng=S ● **Work Field:** 111 ● **MPSMS:** 584 ● **Aptitudes:** G3, V3, N4, S3, P3, Q4, K3, F3, M3, E3, C4 ● **Temperaments:** J, T ● **Physical:** Stg=M; Freq: C, B, R, H, I, N Occas: D, X ● **Work Env:** Noise=N; Freq: W, E, D ● **Salary:** 2 ● **Outlook:** 2

TOWER ERECTOR (construction) ● DOT #821.361-038 ● OES: 85723 ● Erects structural steel, wood, or aluminum transmission towers and installs electric cables and auxiliary equipment to construct transmission and high-voltage distribution power lines between generating stations and substations: Repairs and performs scheduled maintenance on towers, cables, and auxiliary equipment. Frequently works more than one hundred feet above ground when erecting upper portion of towers, and when installing insulators, cables, and electrical accessories on completed towers. May trim trees and remove brush along right-of-way [TREE TRIMMER (tel. & tel.; utilities)]. ● **GED:** R4, M3, L2 ● **SVP:** 2-4 yrs ● **Academic:** Ed=H, Eng=N ● **Work Field:** 102, 111 ● **MPSMS:** 581, 554 ● **Aptitudes:** G3, V3, N4, S3, P3, Q4, K2, F3, M2, E2, C4 ● **Temperaments:** J, S, T ● **Physical:** Stg=H; Freq: C, B, S, K, O, R, H, I, N, F, D Occas: T, G, X ● **Work Env:** Noise=L; Const: W Freq: E, D ● **Salary:** 4 ● **Outlook:** 3

WIND-GENERATING-ELECTRIC-POWER INSTALLER (construction) ● DOT #821.381-018 ● OES: 85720 ● Assembles, installs, and maintains electrical and mechanical parts, such as alternators, generators, and rotors of electric power generating windmills, according to production specifications, using tools and equipment: Assembles and adjusts alternator components according to production specifications, using handtools, drill presses, grinders, and micrometers. Welds steel supports to alternator for mounting on windmill tower, using welding equipment. Crates alternator for shipment to installation site. Attaches cables to alternator and pulls lever to activate truck-mounted hoist to position alternator on windmill tower. Secures alternator to tower structure, using bolts and wrenches. Attaches electric cables, windmill motor, and rotor to alternator, according to schematic, using handtools. Replaces bent or defective parts of windmill and lubricates machinery to service equipment, using handtools, oilcan, and grease gun. ● **GED:** R4, M3, L3 ● **SVP:** 4-10 yrs ● **Academic:** Ed=N, Eng=S ● **Work Field:** 111 ● **MPSMS:** 871 ● **Aptitudes:** G3, V3, N3, S2, P3, Q4, K3, F3, M3, E5, C4 ● **Temperaments:** S, T ● **Physical:** Stg=H; Freq: C, B, S, K, R, H, I, N Occas: O, X ● **Work Env:** Noise=N; Occas: W, U, O ● **Salary:** 5 ● **Outlook:** 3

GOE: 05.05.06
Metal Fabrication & Repair

AIRCRAFT BODY REPAIRER (air trans.) ● DOT #807.261-010 ● OES: 85323 ● Repairs sheet and extruded metal structural parts of aircraft and missiles according to design specifications, using handtools and power tools and metalworking machinery: Reads design specifications or examines sample parts to determine fabrication procedures and machines and tools required. Removes rivets and other fasteners to facilitate removal of defective part, using power drill and punch, or cuts out defective part, using power shears, hacksaw, and file. Locates and marks dimension and reference lines on defective or replacement part, using templates, scribes, compass, and steel rule. Sets up and op-

erates metal fabricating machines, such as saws, brakes, shears, drill press, and grinders, to repair defective part or fabricate new part. Reinstalls repaired or replacement parts for subsequent riveting or welding, using clamps and wrenches. Confers with other workers to expedite heat treating, anodizing, or other specified processing of repair parts. May signal crane operator to fit and align heavy parts. May stretch skin and panel sheets to remove surface tension, using sheet metal hand forming tools. ● **GED:** R4, M3, L3 ● **SVP:** 2-4 yrs ● **Academic:** Ed=N, Eng=S ● **Work Field:** 572, 375 ● **Aptitudes:** G3, V3, N3, S2, P2, Q4, K3, F4, M3, E4, C5 ● **Temperaments:** J, T ● **Physical:** Stg=M; Freq: R, H, T, G, N, D Occas: C, S, K, O, I ● **Work Env:** Noise=L; Freq: M Occas: A ● **Salary:** 4 ● **Outlook:** 3

ARC CUTTER (welding) ● DOT #816.364-010 ● OES: 93914 ● Alternate titles: ARC-AIR OPERATOR; BURN-OUT-SCARFING OPERATOR. Cuts, trims, or scarfs metal objects to dimensions, contour, or bevel specified by blueprints, work order, or layout, using arc-cutting equipment: Positions workpiece onto table or into fixture or with jib or crane. Selects carbon or metal-coated carbon electrode, gas nozzle, electric current, and gas pressure, according to thickness and type of metal, data on charts, or record of previous runs. Inserts electrode and gas nozzle into holder and connects hose from holder to compressed gas supply. Connects cables from power source to electrode and workpiece or fixture, to obtain desired polarity. Turns knobs to select amperage. Turns lever to adjust jet of gas to blow away molten metal. Strikes arc and guides electrode along lines to cut (melt) through metal. May cut off chips or sprues and burn out cracks and holes. May use holder having two electrodes. May cut without using gas jet. May use nonconsumable tungsten electrode and gases, such as helium or carbon dioxide, and be designated Arc Cutter, Gas-Tungsten Arc (welding). May use plasma-arc cutting torch and gases, such as nitrogen and carbon dioxide, and be designated Arc Cutter, Plasma Arc (welding). ● **GED:** R3, M3, L3 ● **SVP:** 6 mos-1 yr ● **Academic:** Ed=N, Eng=S ● **Work Field:** 082 ● **MPSMS:** 540 ● **Aptitudes:** G4, V4, N4, S3, P3, Q4, K3, F3, M3, E5, C3 ● **Temperaments:** J, T ● **Physical:** Stg=M; Freq: S, K, R, H, I, N, D Occas: O, T, G, X ● **Work Env:** Noise=L; Freq: A, O ● **Salary:** 2 ● **Outlook:** 3

AUTOMOBILE-BODY REPAIRER (automobile ser.) ● DOT #807.381-010 ● OES: 85305 ● Alternate titles: AUTOMOBILE-BODY WORKER; BODY-LINE FINISHER; BODY REPAIRER, BUS; DENT REMOVER; DOOR REPAIRER, BUS; METAL BUMPER; METAL SHRINKER; METAL WORKER; TOUCH-UP FINISHER, METAL. Repairs damaged bodies and body parts of automotive vehicles, such as automobiles, buses, and light trucks according to repair manuals, using handtools and power tools: Examines damaged vehicles and estimates cost of repairs [SHOP ESTIMATOR (automotive ser.) 807.267-010]. Removes upholstery, accessories, electrical and hydraulic window-and-seat-operating equipment, and trim to gain access to vehicle body and fenders. Positions dolly block against surface of dented area and beats opposite surface to remove dents, using hammer. Fills depressions with body filler, using putty knife. Removes damaged fenders, panels, and grills, using wrenches and cutting torch, and bolts or welds replacement parts in position, using wrenches or welding equipment. Straightens bent automobile frames, using pneumatic frame straightening machine. Files, grinds, and sands repaired surfaces, using power tools and handtools. Refinishes repaired surface, using paint spray gun and sander. Aims headlights, aligns wheels, and bleeds hydraulic brake system. May paint surfaces after performing body repairs and be designated Automobile-Body Repairer, Combination (automotive ser.). May repair or replace defective mechanical parts [AUTOMOBILE MECHANIC (automotive ser.) 620.261-010]. ● **GED:** R3, M3, L3 ● **SVP:** 2-4 yrs ● **Academic:** Ed=H, Eng=S ● **Work Field:** 102 ● **MPSMS:** 591 ● **Aptitudes:** G3, V4, N4, S3, P3, Q4, K3, F3, M3, E5, C4 ● **Temperaments:** J, T, V ● **Physical:** Stg=M; Freq: S, K, O, R, H, I, N, D Occas: W, E, G, X ● **Work Env:** Noise=L; ● **Salary:** 4 ● **Outlook:** 3

BLACKSMITH (forging) ● DOT #610.381-010 ● OES: 85998 ● Alternate titles: ANVIL SMITH. Forges and repairs variety of metal articles, such as tongs, edged tools, hooks, chains, machine and structural components, and agricultural implements as specified by work orders, diagrams, or sample parts: Heats metal stock in blacksmith's forge or furnace [HEATER (forging)]. Hammers stock into specified size and shape on blacksmith's anvil or positions stock on anvil of power hammer and depresses pedal to hammer stock with varying force and rapidity. Forge-welds metal parts by heating and hammering them together. Devises jigs and fixtures, forges special handtools, such as hammers or chisels, and sets up form blocks. Tempers or anneals forged articles [HEAT TREATER (heat treating) I]. May record type of repair or fabrication of tools or machine components performed during work shift to maintain daily activity report and records. May cut, assemble, and weld metal parts, using arc or acetylene welding equipment [WELDER, COMBINATION (welding)]. May repair farm machinery and be designated Blacksmith, Farm (agriculture). May be designated according to articles forged as Special-Trackwork Blacksmith (r.r. trans.); Tool-Dresser (forging). ● **GED:** R4, M3, L2 ● **SVP:** 2-4 yrs ● **Academic:** Ed=H, Eng=N ● **Work Field:** 134 ● **MPSMS:** 556, 567 ● **Aptitudes:** G3, V3, N3, S2, P3, Q4, K3, F3, M3, E4, C3 ● **Temperaments:** J, T, V ● **Physical:** Stg=H; Freq: R, H, I, N, D, X Occas: S, K, O, E ● **Work Env:** Noise=V; Freq: H, O ● **Salary:** 2 ● **Outlook:** 2

BOILERHOUSE MECHANIC (any industry) ● DOT #805.361-010 ● OES: 89135 ● Alternate titles: BOILER MECHANIC; HEATING-EQUIPMENT REPAIRER; STATION MECHANIC. Maintains and repairs stationary steam boilers and boiler house auxiliaries, using handtools and portable power tools: Cleans or directs other workers to clean boilers and auxiliary equipment, using scrapers, wire brush and cleaning solvent. Inspects and repairs boiler fittings, such as safety valves, regulators, automatic-control mechanisms, and water columns, and auxiliary machines, such as pumps, draft fans, stokers, and burners. Replaces damaged boiler tubes and plates [BOILERMAKER (struct. metal) I]. Repairs or replaces high-pressure piping, using power saw, gas torch, threading die, and welding equipment. May patch boiler insulation with cement. May paint surface of equipment, using brush. May perform water pressure test by pumping water into system to determine location of leaks. May remove and replace defective firebrick, using hammer and chisel. May operate lathe and milling machine to repair or make parts, such as valve stems and pump shafts. ● **GED:** R4, M3, L3 ● **SVP:** 2-4 yrs ● **Academic:** Ed=N, Eng=S ● **Work Field:** 102, 121 ● **MPSMS:** 554 ● **Aptitudes:** G3, V3, N3, S3, P3, Q4, K3, F3, M2, E5, C5 ● **Temperaments:** J, T, V ● **Physical:** Stg=M; Freq: K, R, H, N, D Occas: C, S, W, T, G, F ● **Work Env:** Noise=L; Occas: H ● **Salary:** 3 ● **Outlook:** 2

BOILERMAKER I (struct. metal) ● DOT #805.261-014 ● OES: 89135 ● Alternate titles: BOILERMAKER, ASSEMBLY AND ERECTION. Assembles, analyzes defects in, and repairs boilers, pressure vessels, tanks, and vats in field, following blueprints and using handtools and portable power tools and equipment: Locates and marks reference points for columns or plates on foundation, using master straightedge, squares, transit, and measuring tape, and applying knowledge of geometry. Attaches rigging or signals crane operator to lift parts to specified position. Aligns structures or plate sections to assemble boiler frame, tanks, or vats, using plumb bobs, levels, wedges, dogs, or turnbuckles. Hammers, flame-cuts, files, or grinds irregular edges of sections or structural parts to facilitate fitting edges together. Bolts or arc-welds structures and sections together. Positions drums and headers into supports and bolts or welds supports to frame. Aligns water tubes and connects and expands ends to drums and headers, using tube expander. Bells, beads with power hammer, or welds tube ends to ensure leakproof joints. Bolts or welds casing sections, uptakes, stacks, baffles, and such fabricated parts as chutes, air heaters, fan stands, feeding tube, catwalks, ladders, coal hoppers, and safety hatch to frame, using wrench. Installs manholes, handholes, valves, gauges, and feedwater connection in drums to complete assembly of water tube boilers. Assists in testing assembled vessels by pumping water or gas under specified pressure into vessel and observing instruments for evidence of leakage. Repairs boilers or tanks in field by unbolting or flame cutting defective sections or tubes, straightening plates, using torch or jacks, installing new tubes, fitting and welding new sections and replacing worn lugs on bolts. May rivet and caulk sections of vessels, using pneumatic riveting and caulking hammers. May line firebox with refractory brick and asbestos rope and blocks [BRICKLAYER, FIREBRICK AND REFRACTORY TILE (construction)]. May fabricate such parts as stacks, uptakes, and chutes to adapt boiler to premises in which it is installed [BOILERMAKER (struct. metal) II]. ● **GED:** R4, M4, L3 ● **SVP:** 2-4 yrs ● **Academic:** Ed=H, Eng=S ● **Work Field:** 102 ● **MPSMS:** 554 ● **Aptitudes:** G3, V3, N3, S2, P3, Q4, K3, F3, M3, E5, C5 ● **Temperaments:** J, T, V ● **Physical:** Stg=H; Freq: S, K, O, R, H, T, G, N, D Occas: C, B, I, E, A ● **Work Env:** Noise=L; Freq: W, O Occas: D ● **Salary:** 3 ● **Outlook:** 2

CONDUIT MECHANIC (construction) ● DOT #869.361-010 ● OES: 87898 ● Alternate titles: DUCT LAYER. Builds and repairs concrete underground vaults and manholes, and installs ducts to provide installation and maintenance facilities for underground power cables: Installs sheeting, shoring, and bracing for excavation. Builds wooden forms and erects steel reinforcing for concrete vaults and manholes. Directs workers engaged in pouring concrete into forms, and removes forms after concrete has set. Installs brackets and braces, and cuts apertures required for installation of electric equipment and ducts. Lays drainpipe and connects it to sewer system. Forces air through ducts to test for obstructions, using air compressor. Demolishes or trims vaults and manholes, using pneumatic tools, working in proximity to high-voltage electric cables and equipment. Cuts and lays tile or fiber ducts, using portable power saw and grinder and brickmason's handtools. Cuts, threads, bends, and installs metal conduit. May lay precast concrete ducts. ● **GED:** R3, M3, L3 ● **SVP:** 2-4 yrs ● **Academic:** Ed=N, Eng=S ● **Work Field:** 102 ● **MPSMS:** 369 ● **Aptitudes:** G3, V3, N3, S3, P3, Q4, K3, F3, M3, E4, C5 ● **Temperaments:** J, T ● **Physical:** Stg=H; Freq: R, H, I, T, G, N, D Occas: C, B, S, K, O, W, A ● **Work Env:** Noise=L; Const: W Freq: O ● **Salary:** 2 ● **Outlook:** 3

ELEVATOR CONSTRUCTOR (construction) ● DOT #825.361-010 ● OES: 85932 ● Alternate titles: ELEVATOR BUILDER; ELEVATOR ERECTOR; ELEVATOR INSTALLER; ELEVATOR MECHANIC. Assembles and installs electric and hydraulic freight and passenger elevators, escalators, and dumbwaiters, determining layout and electrical connections from blueprints: Studies blueprints and lays out location of framework, counterbalance rails, motor pump, cylinder, and plunger foundations. Drills holes in concrete or structural steel members with portable electric drill. Secures anchor bolts or welds brackets to support rails and framework, and verifies alignment with plumb bob and level. Cuts prefabricated sections of framework, rails, and other elevator components to specified dimensions, using acetylene torch, power saw, and disc grinder. Installs cables, counterweights, pumps, motor foundations, escalator drives, guide rails, elevator cars, and control panels, using handtools. Connects electrical wiring to control panels and electric motors. Installs safety and control devices. Positions electric motor and equipment on top of elevator shaft, using hoists and cable slings. May be designated according to type of equipment installed as Elevator Constructor, Electric (construction); Elevator Constructor, Hydraulic (construction); Escalator Constructor (construction). ● **GED:** R4, M3, L3 ● **SVP:** 2-4 yrs ● **Academic:** Ed=H, Eng=S ● **Work Field:** 111 ● **MPSMS:** 565 ● **Aptitudes:** G3, V3, N3, S2, P3, Q4, K3, F3, M3, E4, C4 ● **Temperaments:** J, T, V ● **Physical:** Stg=H; Freq: S, K, O, R, H, I, N, D Occas: C, B, F, X ● **Work Env:** Noise=N; Occas: D, O ● **Salary:** 4 ● **Outlook:** 5

FITTER I (any industry) ● DOT #801.261-014 ● OES: 93108 ● Alternate titles: JIG FITTER. Lays out, positions, aligns, and fits together fabricated parts of structural metal products in shop, according to blueprint and layout specifications, preparatory to welding or riveting: Plans sequence of operation, applying knowledge of geometry, effects of heat, and allowances for weld shrinkage, machining, and thickness of metal. Sets up face block, jigs and fixtures. Locates and marks centerlines and reference points onto floor or face block and transposes them to workpiece, using tape, chains, plumb bob, and squares. Moves parts into position, manually or by hoist or crane. Aligns parts, using jack, turnbuckles, wedges, drift pins, pry bars, and hammer. Removes high spots and cuts bevels, using hand files, portable grinders, and cutting torch. Gives directions to WELDER, ARC (welding) to build up low spots or short pieces with weld. Straightens warped or bent parts, using sledge, hand torch, straightening press, or bulldozer. Positions or tightens braces, jacks, clamps, ropes, or bolt straps, or bolts parts in positions for welding or riveting. May use transit to locate reference points and erect ladders and scaffolding to fit together large assemblies. May tack weld and be designated Fitter-Tacker (any industry). ● **GED:** R4, M4, L2 ● **SVP:** 2-4 yrs ● **Academic:** Ed=N, Eng=N ● **Work Field:** 102 ● **MPSMS:** 594, 554 ● **Aptitudes:** G3, V3, N3, S2, P3, Q4, K4, F4, M3, E3, C4 ● **Temperaments:** J, T ● **Physical:** Stg=H; Const: R, H Freq: N, D Occas: C, B, S, K, O, I, T, G, F, A, X ● **Work Env:** Noise=L; Freq: A, O ● **Salary:** 2 ● **Outlook:** 2

FORMER, HAND (any industry) ● DOT #619.361-010 ● OES: 89198 ● Bends and straightens cold and hot metal plates, bars, structural shapes, and weldments to angles, curves, or flanges as specified by drawings, layouts, and templates, using form blocks, fixtures forming bars, sledge, power hammer and portable grinders: Lays out reference points onto workpiece and form blocks, using tape, compass, radius bar and applying knowledge of geometry, effects of heat, and physical properties of metal. Sets up and bolts or clamps fixtures, dies, and forming bars to form block to outline specified contour. Heats metal, using furnace or hand torch. Lifts, positions, aligns, and clamps or bolts workpiece to form block of fixture, using tongs or hoist. Bends workpiece, using bar or by hammering with sledge or mallet. Straightens out warps or bumps by hammering against face block or by heating with hand torch. Chips, trims, and grinds edges to specified contour, using chipping hammer and portable and stand grinder. Verifies size of workpiece, using ruler or template. May operate hand-powered machines, such as roll, brake, or bender. May be designated by product formed as Tool Bender, Hand (any industry). ● **GED:** R4, M3, L3 ● **SVP:** 2-4 yrs ● **Academic:** Ed=N, Eng=S ● **Work Field:** 134 ● **MPSMS:** 554 ● **Aptitudes:** G3, V4, N3, S3, P3, Q4, K4, F4, M3, E5, C5 ● **Temperaments:** J, T, V ● **Physical:** Stg=M; Freq: R, H, N Occas: B, O, D, A ● **Work Env:** Noise=L; Occas: H, U, A ● **Salary:** 3 ● **Outlook:** 2

METAL FABRICATOR (any industry) ● DOT #619.361-014 ● OES: 91714 ● Fabricates and assembles structural metal products, such as framework or shells for machinery, ovens, tanks, stacks, and metal parts for buildings and bridges according to job order, verbal instructions, and blueprints: Develops layout and plans sequence of operations, applying knowledge of trigonometry, stock allowances for thickness, machine and welding shrinkage, and physical properties of metal. Locates and marks bending and cutting lines onto workpiece. Sets up and operates fabricating machines, such as brakes, rolls, shears, flame cutters, and drill presses [MACHINE OPERATOR (any industry) I 616.380-018]. Hammers, chips, and grinds workpiece to cut, bend, and straighten metal. Preheats workpieces, using hand torch or furnace. Positions, aligns, fits, and welds together parts [WELDER-FITTER (welding) 819.361-010]. Designs and constructs templates and fixtures. Verifies conformance of workpiece to specifications, using square, ruler, and measuring tape. May fabricate and assemble sheet metal products. May set up and operate machine tools associated with fabricating shops, such as radial drill press, end mill, and edge planer. ● **GED:** R4, M4, L3 ● **SVP:** 2-4 yrs ● **Academic:** Ed=H, Eng=S ● **Work Field:** 102 ● **MPSMS:** 554, 594 ● **Aptitudes:** G3, V3, N3, S2, P3, Q4, K3, F3, M2, E4, C4 ● **Temperaments:** J, T, V ● **Physical:** Stg=H; Freq: R, H, I, N, A Occas: B, O, T, G, D, X ● **Work Env:** Noise=L; Occas: O ● **Salary:** 3 ● **Outlook:** 3

MILLWRIGHT (any industry) ● DOT #638.281-018 ● OES: 85123 ● Installs machinery and equipment according to layout plans, blueprints, and other drawings in industrial establishment, using hoists, lift trucks, handtools, and power tools: Reads blueprints and schematic drawings to determine work procedures. Dismantles machines, using hammers, wrenches, crowbars, and other handtools. Moves machinery and equipment, using hoists, dollies, rollers, and trucks. Assembles and installs equipment, such as shafting, conveyors, and tram rails, using handtools and power tools. Constructs foundation for machines, using handtools and building materials, such as wood, cement, and steel. Aligns machines and equipment, using hoists, jacks, handtools, squares, rules, micrometers, and plumb bobs. Assembles machines, and bolts, welds, rivets, or otherwise fastens them to foundation or other structures, using handtools and power tools. May operate engine lathe to grind, file, and turn machine parts to dimensional specifications. May repair and lubricate machines and equipment. May install robot and modify its program, using teach pendant. May perform installation and maintenance work as part of team of skilled trades workers. ● **GED:** R4, M3, L3 ● **SVP:** 2-4 yrs ● **Academic:** Ed=A, Eng=S ● **Work Field:** 102, 121 ● **MPSMS:** 550, 560, 580 ● **Aptitudes:** G2, V3, N3, S2, P3, Q4, K3, F3, M2, E3, C5 ● **Temperaments:** J, T, V ● **Physical:** Stg=H; Freq: O, R, H, I, N Occas: C, S, K, T, G, D, A ● **Work Env:** Noise=L; Occas: O ● **Salary:** 4 ● **Outlook:** 3

ORNAMENTAL-IRON WORKER (construction) ● DOT #809.381-022 ● OES: 87898 ● Alternate titles: HOUSESMITH; METAL-TRIM ERECTOR; ORNAMENTAL-IRON ERECTOR. Installs prefabricated ornamental ironwork, other than structural ironwork, such as metal window and door frames, motor-driven and automatic power doors, metal trim and paneling, and aluminum curtain-wall frames: Measures and marks layout for installation, according to blueprints, using rule, template, square, and compass. Welds brackets to lintels, sills, columns, and other structural framework. Drills holes in metal, concrete, and

masonry structure, using portable power drills, airhammer, and handtools. Cuts, miters, and bevels metal trim and cover plates to size, using handsaws or portable power saws. Bolts, clips, welds, or solders ironwork together and to brackets or anchors. Verifies level and plumbness, using level or plumb bob. Bolts newell posts, balusters, and other parts of stairways and stair rails to supports or embeds them in sockets. Fastens cover plates and molding in place with metal screws to finish and trim work. Installs equipment, such as motor-driven or automatic doors, following procedures provided by manufacturer. May locate and mark reference points, dig postholes, mix concrete, and erect ornamental fences, using transit, posthole digger, and handtools. When working with bronze, is designated ORNAMENTAL-BRONZE WORKER (construction). May fabricate frames for mounting glass in ornamental cast stonework. May be designated according to equipment installed as Metal-Sash Setter (construction); Ornamental-Rail Installer (construction); Steel-Door Setter (construction); Steel-Sash Erector (construction). ● **GED:** R4, M3, L3 ● **SVP:** 2-4 yrs ● **Academic:** Ed=H, Eng=G ● **Work Field:** 102 ● **MPSMS:** 554 ● **Aptitudes:** G3, V3, N3, S3, P3, Q4, K3, F3, M2, E3, C5 ● **Temperaments:** J, T, V ● **Physical:** Stg=H; Freq: C, K, O, W, H, I, E, N, F, D Occas: B ● **Work Env:** Noise=L; Freq: W Occas: A, M, D ● **Salary:** 4 ● **Outlook:** 3

ORNAMENTAL-METAL WORKER (metal prod., nec) ● DOT #619.260-014 ● OES: 89198 ● Alternate titles: ART-METAL WORKER. Sets up and operates variety of machines and equipment to fabricate ornamental metal products, such as light fixtures, church statuary, lamps, plaques, and metal artwork, following sketches, artistic and architectural drawings, models, written descriptions, and photographs: Interprets data to select materials, lay out reference points, and develop sequence of operations. Operates metal fabricating machines, such as shears, saws, brakes, bending machines, and punch and forming presses, to cut stock to size and bend stock to shape. Heats pieces in forge to working temperature, as indicated by color. Bends, twists, and hammers hot or cold workpieces to achieve specified shape and ornamental imprints, using jigs, scroll iron, twisting fork, vise, and selected peening hammers. Operates machine tools to turn, drill, and mill metal to specified dimensions. Hammers and peens sheets of metal to form designs, such as flowers or leaves. Chases castings to finish metal statuary and plaques. Welds, forge welds, brazes, solders, rivets, or bolts components together to assemble workpiece. Grinds, buffs, and polishes surface to desired finish. Fabricates or forges special jigs, tools, and peening hammers. May sculpture plaster patterns for ornamental castings. May hand paint finished items. May install finished product. May specialize in fabricating religious artwork and be known as Ecclesiastical-Art-Metal Worker (jewelry-silver.; metal prod., nec). ● **GED:** R4, M3, L3 ● **SVP:** 4-10 yrs ● **Academic:** Ed=N, Eng=S ● **Work Field:** 102 ● **MPSMS:** 554 ● **Aptitudes:** G3, V3, N3, S2, P2, Q4, K3, F3, M2, E5, C4 ● **Temperaments:** J, T, V ● **Physical:** Stg=M; Freq: R, H, N Occas: B, O, I, A ● **Work Env:** Noise=L; Occas: O ● **Salary:** 3 ● **Outlook:** 2

SAFE-AND-VAULT SERVICE MECHANIC (business ser.) ● DOT #869.381-022 ● OES: 85923 ● Alternate titles: SAFE REPAIRER; VAULT MECHANIC. Installs and repairs safes and vault doors in banks and other establishments: Installs vault doors and deposit boxes in banks, according to blueprints, using equipment, such as powered drills, taps and dies, and truck crane and dolly. Removes, repairs, adjusts, and reinstalls safes, vault doors, vault compartments, hinges, and other vault and safe equipment, using handtools and other machines and equipment, such as lathes, drill presses, and welding and acetylene cutting apparatus. Tests and repairs locks and locking devices [LOCKSMITH (any industry)]. Removes interior and exterior finishes and sprays on new finishes. ● **GED:** R3, M3, L3 ● **SVP:** 2-4 yrs ● **Academic:** Ed=A, Eng=S ● **Work Field:** 102, 082 ● **MPSMS:** 559 ● **Aptitudes:** G3, V3, N3, S3, P3, Q4, K3, F3, M3, E4, C5 ● **Temperaments:** J, T, V ● **Physical:** Stg=H; Freq: S, K, O, R, H, I, N, D Occas: C, A ● **Work Env:** Noise=L; Occas: W ● **Salary:** 2 ● **Outlook:** 3

SHEET-METAL WORKER (any industry) ● DOT #804.281-010 ● OES: 87823 ● Alternate titles: SHEET-METAL MECHANIC. Plans, lays out, fabricates, assembles, installs, and repairs sheet metal parts, equipment, and products, utilizing knowledge of working characteristics of metallic and nonmetallic materials, machining, and layout techniques, using handtools, power tools, machines, and equipment: Reads and interprets blueprints, sketches, or product specifications to determine sequence and methods of fabricating, assembling, and installing sheet metal products. Selects gauge and type of sheet metal, such as galvanized iron, copper, steel, or aluminum, or nonmetallic material, such as plastics or fiberglass, according to product specifications. Lays out and marks dimensions and reference lines on material, using scribers, dividers, squares, and rulers, applying knowledge of shop mathematics and layout techniques to develop and trace patterns of product or parts [SHEET-METAL LAY-OUT WORKER (any industry) 809.281-010] or using templates. Sets up and operates fabricating machines, such as shears, brakes, presses, forming rolls, and routers, to cut, bend, block and form, or straighten materials. Shapes metal material over anvil, block, or other form, using handtools. Trims, files, grinds, deburrs, buffs, and smooths surfaces, using handtools and portable power tools. Welds, solders, bolts, rivets, screws, clips, caulks, or bonds component parts to assemble products, using handtools, power tools, and equipment. Installs assemblies in supportive framework according to blueprints, using handtools, power tools, and lifting and handling devices. Inspects assemblies and installation for conformance to specifications, using measuring instruments, such as calipers, scales, dial indicators, gauges, and micrometers. Repairs and maintains sheet metal products. May operate computer-aided-drafting (CAD) equipment to develop scale drawings of product or system. May operate laser-beam cutter [LASER-BEAM-MACHINE OPERATOR (welding) 815.682-010] or plasma arc cutter [ARC CUTTER, PLASMA ARC (welding) 816.364-010] to cut patterns from sheet metal. May be designated by type of metal as Coppersmith (any industry); Tinsmith (any industry); or according to type of activity as Fabricator, Special Items (any industry); Model Maker, Sheet-Metal (any industry); Product-Development Worker (any industry); Roofer, Metal (construction); Sheet-Metal Installer (any industry); Sheet-Metal Worker, Maintenance (any industry); Shop Mechanic (any industry). ● **GED:** R4, M4, L3 ● **SVP:** 2-4 yrs ● **Academic:** Ed=H, Eng=S ● **Work Field:** 102 ● **MPSMS:** 554 ● **Aptitudes:** G3, V3, N3, S2, P3, Q4, K3, F3, M3, E4, C5 ● **Temperaments:** J, T, V ● **Physical:** Stg=M; Freq: S, R, H, N, D Occas: I, E, G, A ● **Work Env:** Noise=L; Occas: M, O ● **Salary:** 2 ● **Outlook:** 3

SHIPFITTER (ship-boat mfg.) ● DOT #806.381-046 ● OES: 89121 ● Alternate titles: FITTER. Lays out and fabricates metal structural parts, such as plates, bulkheads, and frames, and braces them in position within hull of ship for riveting or welding: Lays out position of parts on metal, working from blueprints or templates and using scribe and handtools. Locates and marks reference lines, such as center, buttock, and frame lines. Positions parts in hull of ship, assisted by RIGGER (ship-boat mfg.). Aligns parts in relation to each other, using jacks, turnbuckles, clips, wedges, and mauls. Marks location of holes to be drilled and installs temporary fasteners to hold part in place for welding or riveting. Installs packing, gaskets, liners, and structural accessories and members, such as doors, hatches, brackets, and clips. May prepare molds and templates for fabrication of nonstandard parts. May tack weld clips and brackets in place prior to permanent welding. May roll, bend, flange, cut, and shape plates, beams, and other heavy metal parts, using shop machinery, such as plate rolls, presses, bending brakes, and joggle machines. ● **GED:** R4, M3, L2 ● **SVP:** 4-10 yrs ● **Academic:** Ed=A, Eng=N ● **Work Field:** 102 ● **MPSMS:** 593 ● **Aptitudes:** G3, V3, N3, S2, P3, Q4, K2, F3, M2, E3, C5 ● **Temperaments:** J, T ● **Physical:** Stg=H; Freq: C, B, S, K, R, H, N D Occas: O, W, I, E ● **Work Env:** Noise=L; Freq: W, O ● **Salary:** 2 ● **Outlook:** 1

SIGN ERECTOR I (fabrication, nec) ● DOT #869.381-026 ● OES: 89998 ● Alternate titles: SIGN HANGER. Erects preassembled illuminated signs on buildings or other structures, according to sketches, drawings, or blueprints: Measures location for sign and marks points where holes for expansion shields are to be drilled, using measuring tape and chalk. Drills holes, using star drill. Drives expansion shield into hole with hammer, and secures lag bolts in shield, using wrench. Attaches hanging pole for sign to building front with lag bolts, and secures pole with guy wires attached from pole to lag bolts. Secures cornice hook on roof, rigs block and tackle, and hoists sign into position, or operates hydraulic boom to position sign. Secures sign to hanging pole with hooks. Makes electrical connections to power source and tests sign for correct operation. May prewire sign before installing. May use welding equipment when installing sign. May mount plastic signs with adhesives. May fabricate signs according to specifications and be designated Sign Maker (fabrication, nec). ● **GED:** R4, M2, L3 ● **SVP:** 2-4 yrs ● **Academic:** Ed=N, Eng=G ● **Work Field:** 102 ● **MPSMS:** 559 ● **Aptitudes:** G3, V4, N3, S3, P4, Q3, K4, F4, M3,

E3, C5 ● **Temperaments:** J, V ● **Physical:** Stg=M; Freq: C, B, R, H, I, N, F, D Occas: A ● **Work Env:** Noise=L; Freq: W, O ● **Salary:** 2 ● **Outlook:** 3

STRUCTURAL-STEEL WORKER (construction) ● DOT #801.361-014 ● OES: 87320 ● Alternate titles: BRIDGE WORKER; HOUSESMITH; IRON ERECTOR; IRONWORKER; STEEL ERECTOR; STRUCTURAL-IRON ERECTOR; STRUCTURAL-IRON WORKER; STRUCTURAL-STEEL ERECTOR. Performs any combination of following duties to raise, place, and unite girders, columns, and other structural-steel members to form completed structures or structure frameworks, working as member of crew: Sets up hoisting equipment for raising and placing structural-steel members. Fastens steel members to cable of hoist, using chain, cable, or rope. Signals worker operating hoisting equipment to lift and place steel member. Guides member, using tab line (rope) or rides on member in order to guide it into position. Pulls, pushes, or pries steel members into approximate position while member is supported by hoisting device. Forces members into final position, using turnbuckles, crowbars, jacks, and handtools. Aligns rivet holes in member with corresponding holes in previously placed member by driving drift pins or handle of wrench through holes. Verifies vertical and horizontal alignment of members, using plumb bob and level. Bolts aligned members to keep them in position until they can be permanently riveted, bolted, or welded in place. Catches hot rivets tosssd by RIVET HEATER (heat treating) in bucket and inserts rivets in holes, using tongs. Bucks (holds) rivets while RIVETER, PNEUMATIC (any industry) uses airhammer to form heads on rivets. Cuts and welds steel members to make alterations, using oxyacetylene welding equipment. May specialize in erecting or repairing specific types of structures and be designated Bridge-Maintenance Worker (construction); Chimney Builder, Reinforced Concrete (construction); Scaffold Builder, Metal (construction); Structural-Steel-Equipment Erector (construction). ● **GED:** R3, M2, L3 ● **SVP:** 2-4 yrs ● **Academic:** Ed=N, Eng=S ● **Work Field:** 102 ● **MPSMS:** 360 ● **Aptitudes:** G3, V3, N3, S2, P3, Q4, K3, F3, M3, E2, C5 ● **Temperaments:** J, S, T ● **Physical:** Stg=H; Freq: C, B, S, K, O, W, R, H, T, G, N, D Occas: I, E, F, A, V ● **Work Env:** Noise=L; Const: W Freq: A, O ● **Salary:** 3 ● **Outlook:** 4

SUPERVISOR, AUTOMOBILE BODY REPAIR (automotive ser.) ● DOT #807.137-010 ● OES: 81000 ● Alternate titles: AUTOMOBILE-BODY REPAIR CHIEF. Supervises and coordinates activities of workers engaged in repairing and painting damaged bodies and body parts of automotive vehicles: May examine damaged vehicle and estimate cost of repairs [SHOP ESTIMATOR (automotive ser.)]. Performs other duties as described under SUPERVISOR (any industry) Master Title. ● **GED:** R4, M3, L3 ● **SVP:** 2-4 yrs ● **Academic:** Ed=H, Eng=G ● **Work Field:** 102 ● **MPSMS:** 591 ● **Aptitudes:** G3, V3, N3, S3, P2, Q3, K4, F4, M4, E5, C4 ● **Temperaments:** D, P, T, V ● **Physical:** Stg=L; Freq: R, H, T, G, N, D Occas: I, A, X ● **Work Env:** Noise=L; ● **Salary:** 4 ● **Outlook:** 2

WELDER, ARC (welding) ● DOT #810.384-014 ● OES: 93914 ● Welds together metal components of products, such as pipelines, automobiles, boilers, ships, aircraft, and mobile homes, as specified by layout, blueprints, diagram, work order, welding procedures, or oral instructions, using electric arc-welding equipment: Obtains specified electrode and inserts electrode into portable holder or threads consumable electrode wire through portable welding gun. Connects cables from welding unit to obtain amperage, voltage, slope, and pulse, as specified by WELDING ENGINEER (profess. & kin.) 011.061-026 or WELDING TECHNICIAN (profess. & kin.) 011.261-014. Starts power supply to produce electric current. Strikes (forms) arc which generates heat to melt and deposit metal from electrode to workpiece and join edges of workpiece. Manually guides electrode or gun along weld line, maintaining length of arc and speed of movement to form specified depth of fusion and bead, as judged from color of metal, sound of weld, and size of molten puddle. Welds in flat, horizontal, vertical, or overhead positions. Examines weld for bead size and other specifications. May manually apply filler rod to supply weld metal. May clean or degrease weld joint or workpiece, using wire brush, portable grinder, or chemical bath. May repair broken or cracked parts and fill holes. May prepare broken parts for welding by grooving or scarfing surfaces. May chip off excess weld, slag, and spatter, using hand scraper or power chipper. May preheat workpiece, using hand torch or heating furnace. May position and clamp workpieces together or assemble them in jig or fixture. May tack assemblies together. May cut metal plates or structural shapes [ARC CUTTER (welding) 816.364-010]. May be designated according to type of equipment used as Welder, Carbon Arc (welding); Welder, Flux-Cored Arc (welding); Welder, Gas-Metal Arc (welding); Welder, Gas-Tungsten Arc (welding); Welder, Hand, Submerged Arc (welding); Welder, Plasma Arc (welding); Welder, Shielded-Metal Arc (welding). May operate other machine shop equipment to prepare components for welding. May be designated according to product welded as Welder, Boilermaker (struct. metal). Important variations include types of metals welded, subprocesses used, trade name of equipment used, work site (in-plant, job shop, construction site, shipyard), method of application (manual, semiautomatic), high-production or custom, level of ambidexterity required, type of joints welded (seam, spot, butt). May be required to pass employer performance tests or standard tests to meet certification standards of governmental agencies or professional and technical associations. ● **GED:** R4, M4, L3 ● **SVP:** 6 mos-1 yr ● **Academic:** Ed=H, Eng=S ● **Work Field:** 081, 082 ● **MPSMS:** 540, 554, 591 ● **Aptitudes:** G3, V4, N4, S3, P3, Q4, K3, F3, M3, E5, C4 ● **Temperaments:** J, T ● **Physical:** Stg=H; Const: R, H Freq: I, G, N, D, A, X Occas: C, B, S, K, O, W ● **Work Env:** Noise=L; Freq: A, O ● **Salary:** 3 ● **Outlook:** 4

WELDER-ASSEMBLER (machinery mfg.) ● DOT #819.381-010 ● OES: 93914 ● Assembles and tack-welds steel frames and other component parts of machinery and equipment in preparation for final welding: Measures and marks locations for metal components on assembly table, following blueprints. Lifts and positions components on assembly table, using electric crane, jacks, and shims. Verifies position of metal components in assembly, using straightedge, combination square, calipers, and rule. Clamps metal components to assembly table for welding. Removes rough spots from castings, using portable powered grinder and hand file, to fit and assemble parts. Tack-welds parts in preparation for final welding. Moves assembly to storage area, using electric crane. ● **GED:** R3, M3, L2 ● **SVP:** 1-2 yrs ● **Academic:** Ed=N, Eng=N ● **Work Field:** 102, 081 ● **MPSMS:** 564 ● **Aptitudes:** G3, V4, N3, S3, P3, Q4, K3, F4, M3, E5, C5 ● **Temperaments:** J, T ● **Physical:** Stg=M; Freq: S, K, O, R, H, I, N, D Occas: C, B ● **Work Env:** Noise=L; Freq: O ● **Salary:** 4 ● **Outlook:** 3

WELDER, COMBINATION (welding) ● DOT #819.384-010 ● OES: 93914 ● Welds metal components together to fabricate or repair products, such as machine parts, plant equipment, mobile homes, motors, and generators, according to layouts, blueprints, or work orders, using brazing and variety of arc and gas welding equipment: Welds metal parts together, using both gas welding [WELDER, GAS (welding)] or brazing [BRAZER, ASSEMBLER (welding)] and any combination of arc welding processes [WELDER, ARC (welding)]. Performs related tasks, such as thermal cutting and grinding. Repairs broken or cracked parts, fills holes, and increases size of metal parts. Positions and clamps together components of fabricated metal products preparatory to welding. May locate and repair cracks in industrial engine cylinder heads, using inspection equipment and gas torch, and be designated Repairer, Cylinder Heads (welding). May perform repairs only and be designated Welder, Repair (welding). May be required to pass employer performance tests or standard tests to meet certification standards of governmental agencies or professional and technical associations. ● **GED:** R4, M3, L3 ● **SVP:** 1-2 yrs ● **Academic:** Ed=H, Eng=S ● **Work Field:** 081, 102 ● **MPSMS:** 550 ● **Aptitudes:** G3, V4, N3, S3, P3, Q4, K3, F3, M3, E5, C4 ● **Temperaments:** J, T ● **Physical:** Stg=M; Freq: R, H, I, N, D Occas: S, O, X ● **Work Env:** Noise=L; Freq: H Occas: W, O ● **Salary:** 3 ● **Outlook:** 4

WELDER, EXPERIMENTAL (welding) ● DOT #819.281-022 ● OES: 93914 ● Analyzes engineering data and welds experimental parts and assemblies to determine most effective welding processes, using various welding techniques and equipment: Analyzes engineering drawings and specifications to plan welding operations where procedural information is unavailable. Lays out parts and assemblies according to specifications. Develops templates and other work aids to hold and align parts. Determines type of welding to be used, such as metallic arc, inert gas, electrode, and oven treatment, applying knowledge of metals to be joined, contours and angles to be formed, and specified

stress tolerances. Welds components in flat, vertical, or overhead positions, and adjusts amperage, voltage, and speed during joining to assure required weld deposit. Inspects grooves, angles, gap allowances, and related aspects of assembly to ensure conformance to specifications, using micrometer, caliper, and related precision measuring instruments. Observes hydrostatic, x ray, dimension tolerance, and other tests on welded surfaces to evaluate quality of weld and conformance to production requirements. ● **GED:** R4, M4, L3 ● **SVP:** 4-10 yrs ● **Academic:** Ed=N, Eng=S ● **Work Field:** 081, 241 ● **MPSMS:** 379 ● **Aptitudes:** G3, V3, N3, S3, P2, Q4, K3, F3, M3, E4, C4 ● **Temperaments:** J ● **Physical:** Stg=L; Freq: R, H, I, N, D, A Occas: S, K, O, X ● **Work Env:** Noise=N; Freq: A, O ● **Salary:** 4 ● **Outlook:** 3

WELDER-FITTER (welding) ● DOT #819.361-010 ● OES: 93914 ● Lays out, fits, and welds fabricated, cast, and forged components to assemble structural forms, such as machinery frames, tanks, pressure vessels, furnace shells, and building and bridge parts, according to blueprints and knowledge of welding and metallurgy: Selects equipment and plans layout, assembly, and welding, applying knowledge of geometry, physical properties of metal machining weld skrinkage, and welding techniques. Lays out, positions, aligns, and fits components together. Bolts, clamps, and tack-welds parts to secure in position for welding [WELDER, TACK (welding)]. Sets up equipment and welds parts, using arc, gas-shielded arc, submerged arc, or gas welding equipment [WELDER, COMBINATION (welding)]. May assemble parts by bolting and riveting. May repair products by dismantling, straightening, reshaping, and reassembling parts, using cutting torch, straightening press, and handtools, and be designated Welder, Structural Repair (welding). May specialize in using one welding process and be designated Welder-Fitter, Arc (welding); Welder-Fitter, Gas (welding). May specialize in fitting and welding components of metal tools, dies, and fixtures and be designated Welder, Tool And Die (welding). ● **GED:** R4, M3, L3 ● **SVP:** 2-4 yrs ● **Academic:** Ed=H, Eng=S ● **Work Field:** 081, 102 ● **MPSMS:** 550 ● **Aptitudes:** G3, V3, N3, S2, P2, Q4, K3, F3, M2, E4, C4 ● **Temperaments:** J, T ● **Physical:** Stg=M; Freq: S, O, R, H, I, N, D Occas: C, B, K, T, G, F, X ● **Work Env:** Noise=L; Freq: A, O Occas: W ● **Salary:** 4 ● **Outlook:** 4

WELDER, GAS (welding) ● DOT #811.684-014 ● OES: 93914 ● Welds metal parts, using gas welding equipment as specified by layout, welding diagram, or work order: Positions parts in jigs or fixtures on bench or floor, or clamps parts together along layout marks. Selects torch, torch tip, filler rod and flux, according to welding chart specifications or type and thickness of metal. Connects regulator valves and hoses to oxygen and fuel gas cylinders, and welding torch. Turns regulator valves to activate flow of gases, lights torch and adjusts gas mixture and pressure, to obtain desired flame, based on knowledge of gas-welding techniques. Holds torch at proper angle to metal and guides along weld joint, applying filler rod to molten area to form weld. Examines weld for bead size and other specifications. Repairs broken or cracked metal objects, fills holes, and builds up metal parts. May apply flux to workpiece instead of filler rod. May preheat workpiece in furnace or with torch. May layout, position and tack weld workpieces. May weld along vertical or overhead weld lines. May scarf or groove weld prior to applying filler metal, using gas welding equipment. May chip or grind off excess weld, slag, or spatter [GRINDER-CHIPPER (any industry) II]. May clean or degrease parts, using wire brush, portable grinder, or chemical bath. May cut metal plates or structural shapes using gas torch. May be designated according to type of gases used such as Welder, Acetylene (welding); Welder, Oxyacetylene (welding); Welder, Oxyhydrogen (welding). Important variations include type of metal welded, products, subprocesses, trade name of equipment, worksite (inplant), job shop, construction site, shipyard), high-production or custom, level of ambidexterity required or type of joints welded (seam, spot, butt). May be required to pass employer performance tests or standard tests to meet certification standards of governmental agencies or professional and technical associations. ● **GED:** R3, M3, L3 ● **SVP:** 6 mos-1 yr ● **Academic:** Ed=N, Eng=S ● **Work Field:** 081 ● **MPSMS:** 550, 591 ● **Aptitudes:** G3, V4, N3, S3, P3, Q4, K3, F3, M3, E5, C4 ● **Temperaments:** J, T ● **Physical:** Stg=M; Freq: R, H, I, N Occas: S, K, O, A, X ● **Work Env:** Noise=L; Freq: A, M ● **Salary:** 4 ● **Outlook:** 3

GOE: 05.05.07
Machining

DIE MAKER (jewelry-silver.) ● DOT #601.381-014 ● OES: 89102 ● Alternate titles: DIE CUTTER; HUB CUTTER. Fabricates set of dies for use in forming and shaping metal jewelry blanks, following drawings or blueprints and using variety of metalworking machines and engraver's handtools: Brushes blue dye on surface of steel block workpiece. Measures, locates, and marks center of block with crosslines, using divider and drafter's pencil. Copies design, freehand, from sample drawing or blueprint, maintaining size specifications. Scribes along drawn line, using scribe. Measures finished design for conformance to specifications, using calipers and gauges. Positions workpiece in vise and cuts out lines of design. Chips and cuts away excess metal to complete design, using metalworking machines and handtools. Verifies dimensions of workpiece, using calipers and gauges. Hardens and tempers steel block and drives it into another block of soft steel or plastic to form sunken design, using press, or sends it to machine shop for processing. Engraves other half of die by pounding thin sheets of metal into completed half. May engrave lettering and designs into dies, using pantograph machine. May cut out, shape, and harden upper steel die (forcer) used to stamp out jewelry articles and be known as Forcer Maker (jewelry-silver.). ● **GED:** R4, M3, L3 ● **SVP:** 2-4 yrs ● **Academic:** Ed=H, Eng=S ● **Work Field:** 057, 183, 241 ● **MPSMS:** 566 ● **Aptitudes:** G3, V3, N3, S2, P2, Q4, K3, F2, M2, E5, C5 ● **Temperaments:** J, T, V ● **Physical:** Stg=M; Freq: R, H, I, N, D, A Occas: E ● **Work Env:** Noise=N; ● **Salary:** 4 ● **Outlook:** 4

DIE SINKER (machine shop) ● DOT #601.280-022 ● OES: 89102 ● Alternate titles: FORGING-DIE SINKER. Lays out, machines, and finishes impression cavities in die blocks to produce forging dies, following blueprints and applying knowledge of diesinking: Analyzes blueprint of part or die and plans sequence of operations. Measures and marks die block to lay out designs of cavities. Sets up and operates variety of machine tools, such as shaper, vertical turret lathe, and engine lathe to machine cavities in die block [TOOL-MACHINE SET-UP OPERATOR (machine shop)]. Obtains specified dimensions, contours, and finish of die cavities, using tools, such as power grinder, scrapers, files, and emery cloth. Inspects die cavities, using templates and measuring instruments, such as calipers, micrometers, and height gauges to verify conformance to specifications. May develop die design from blueprint of part, using knowledge of machining and forging processes. May make templates to verify dimensions of cavities [TEMPLATE MAKER, EXTRUSION DIE (machine shop)]. May make and inspect sample lead or plaster cast of part to verify fit of die members and basic shape of part. May repair forging dies and be designated Die Repairer, Forging (machine shop). May set up and operate machines to plane surfaces and edges of forging dies and be known as Edger Machine Setter (machine shop). ● **GED:** R4, M3, L3 ● **SVP:** 2-4 yrs ● **Academic:** Ed=H, Eng=S ● **Work Field:** 057, 241 ● **MPSMS:** 566 ● **Aptitudes:** G3, V3, N3, S2, P3, Q4, K3, F3, M3, E5, C5 ● **Temperaments:** J, T ● **Physical:** Stg=M; Freq: R, H, I, N, D, A Occas: S, K, O, E ● **Work Env:** Noise=L; ● **Salary:** 3 ● **Outlook:** 4

FLUID-POWER MECHANIC (any industry) ● DOT #600.281-010 ● OES: 89108 ● Fabricates, assembles, services, maintains, repairs, and tests fluid power equipment, such as power steering units, and components, following blueprints, schematics, or drawings, using handtools, power tools, and testing devices and applying knowledge of hydraulic, pneumatic, and electrical principles: Analyzes blueprints, schematics, diagrams, and drawings to determine fabrication specifications. Sets up and operates milling machines, lathes, shapers, grinders, drill presses, and welders to make precision parts. Verifies conformance to specifications, using instruments, such as micrometers, verniers, and calipers. Assembles fluid power components, such as pumps, cylinders, valves, reservoirs, motors, accumulators, filters, and controls, using handtools and holding devices. Connects unit to test equipment, and analyzes and records data, such as fluid pressure, flow measure, and power loss due to friction and parts wear. Recommends modifications in unit and in test procedures, instrumentation, or setup, based on analysis of test results. ● **GED:** R4, M4, L3 ● **SVP:** 2-4 yrs ● **Academic:** Ed=H, Eng=S ● **Work Field:** 057 ● **MPSMS:** 568 ● **Aptitudes:** G2, V3, N2, S2, P2, Q3, K3, F3, M3, E3, C3 ● **Tempera-

ments: J, T ● **Physical:** Stg=L; Freq: R, H, I, N, D, X Occas: S, T, G, A ● **Work Env:** Noise=N; ● **Salary:** 4 ● **Outlook:** 4

GUNSMITH (any industry) ● DOT #632.281-010 ● OES: 85998 ● Alternate titles: REPAIRER. Repairs and modifies firearms to blueprint and customer specifications, using handtools and machines, such as grinders, planers, and millers: Fits action and barrel into stock and aligns parts. Installs parts, such as metallic or optical sights, pistol grips, recoil pads, and decorative pieces of firearms, using screws and handtools. Rebores barrels on boring machine to enlarge caliber of bore. Operates broaching machine to cut rifling in barrel of small arms. Installs choke device on shotguns to control shot pattern. Operates machine to grind and polish metal parts. Immerses metal parts in bluing salt bath to impart rust resistant surface and blue color to metal. Fires firearms with proof loads to determine strength characteristics, correct alignment, and assembly of piece. Fabricates wooden stock for guns according to customer specifications. Refinishes wooden stocks for rifles and shotguns by hand sanding and rubbing with special finishing oil and quick-drying lacquer. May lay out plans on paper and calculate bullet-flight arcs, sight positions, and other details to design new guns. ● **GED:** R4, M3, L3 ● **SVP:** 4-10 yrs ● **Academic:** Ed=N, Eng=S ● **Work Field:** 121 ● **MPSMS:** 373 ● **Aptitudes:** G2, V3, N3, S2, P2, Q4, K3, F2, M2, E5, C3 ● **Temperaments:** J, T, V ● **Physical:** Stg=L; Freq: R, H, I, N, D, A Occas: X ● **Work Env:** Noise=L; ● **Salary:** 1 ● **Outlook:** 2

LAY-OUT WORKER (machine shop) ● DOT #600.281-018 ● OES: 89198 ● Lays out metal stock or workpieces, such as castings, plates, or machine parts, to indicate location, dimensions, and tolerances necessary for further processing, such as machining, welding, or assembly, analyzing specifications and computing dimensions according to knowledge of product, subsequent processing, shop mathematics, and layout procedures: Studies blueprint, sketch, model, or other specifications and plans layout. Examines workpiece and verifies such requirements as dimensions and squareness, using rule, square, and straightedge. Lifts and positions workpiece in relation to surface plate manually or with hoist, using work aids as shims, parallel blocks, and angle plates. Verifies position with measuring instruments, such as gauge blocks, height gauges, and dial indicators. Determines reference points and computes layout dimensions. Sets indicators on height gauge, protractor, or layout machine to computed dimensions, or projects dimensions by setting indicators to specified locations on model and moving instrument or machine so that indicators bear on corresponding locations on workpiece. Indents layout points, using prick punch, center punch, and hammer. Marks or scribes layout lines, using handtools and work aids, such as surface gauge, straightedge, compasses, templates, and scriber. Marks such data as dimensions, instructions, and part identification on workpiece. Works to tolerances as close as plus 0.001 inch. May position model in parallel relationship to workpiece. May apply pigment to layout surfaces, using paint brush. May inspect machined parts to verify conformance to specifications. May add dimensional details to blueprints or prepare dimensional drawings to be followed by other workers. May layout sheet metal or plate steel, applying specialized knowledge of sheet metal layout geometry [SHEET-METAL LAY-OUT WORKER (any industry)]. ● **GED:** R4, M4, L3 ● **SVP:** 2-4 yrs ● **Academic:** Ed=H, Eng=S ● **Work Field:** 241 ● **MPSMS:** 540, 567 ● **Aptitudes:** G2, V3, N3, S2, P2, Q4, K3, F3, M3, E5, C5 ● **Temperaments:** J, T ● **Physical:** Stg=M; Freq: R, H, I, N, D, A Occas: T, G ● **Work Env:** Noise=L; ● **Salary:** 2 ● **Outlook:** 3

MACHINIST (machine shop) ● DOT #600.280-022 ● OES: 89108 ● Alternate titles: MACHINIST, FIRST-CLASS; MACHINIST, GENERAL. Sets up and operates conventional, special-purpose, and numerical control (NC) machines and machining centers to fabricate metallic and nonmetallic parts, and fits and assembles machined parts into complete units, applying knowledge of machine shop theory and procedures, shop mathematics, machinability of materials, and layout techniques: Studies blueprints, sketches, drawings, manuals, specifications, or sample part to determine dimensions and tolerances of finished workpiece, sequence of operations, and setup requirements. Measures, marks, and scribes dimensions and reference points on material or workpiece as guides for subsequent machining [LAY-OUT WORKER (machine shop) 600.281-018]. Selects, aligns, and secures holding fixtures, cutting tools, attachments, accessories, and materials on machines, such as mills, lathes, jig borers, grinders, and shapers.

Calculates and sets controls to regulate machining factors, such as speed, feed, coolant flow, and depth and angle of cut, or enters commands to retrieve, input, or edit computerized machine control media. Starts and observes machine operation to detect malfunctions or out-of-tolerance machining, and adjusts machine controls or control media as required. Verifies conformance of finished workpiece to specifications, using precision measuring instruments. Sets up and operates machine on trial run to verify accuracy of machine settings or programmed control data. Fits and assembles parts into complete assembly, using jigs, fixtures, surface plate, surface table, handtools, and power tools. Verifies dimensions and alignment of assembly, using measuring instruments, such as micrometers, height gauges, and gauge blocks. May install machined replacement parts in mechanisms, machines, and equipment, and test operation of unit to ensure functionality and performance. May operate welding equipment to cut or weld parts. May develop specifications from general description and draw sketch of part or product to be fabricated. May confer with engineers, production personnel, programmers, or others to resolve machining or assembly problems. May specialize in setting up and operating NC machines and machining centers and be designated Numerical Control Machine Machinist (machine shop); or set up and operate NC machines linked to automated storage, retrieval, and moving devices and be designated Flexible Machining System Machinist (machine shop). ● **GED:** R4, M4, L4 ● **SVP:** 2-4 yrs ● **Academic:** Ed=A, Eng=S ● **Work Field:** 057, 121, 241 ● **MPSMS:** 550, 560 ● **Aptitudes:** G2, V3, N3, S2, P2, Q4, K3, F2, M2, E5, C4 ● **Temperaments:** J, T, V ● **Physical:** Stg=M; Freq: R, H, I, N, D Occas: S, K, O, E, G, A, X ● **Work Env:** Noise=L; Freq: M Occas: A ● **Salary:** 4 ● **Outlook:** 3

MACHINIST, EXPERIMENTAL (machine shop) ● DOT #600.260-022 ● OES: 89108 ● Alternate titles: PROTOTYPE MACHINIST. Sets up and operates machine tools, and fits and assembles parts to fabricate tools, mechanisms, and machines for experimental purposes, such as solving problems relative to materials, tools, work-holding arrangements, machine settings, product specifications, and fabrication methods for production process, applying knowledge of mechanics, shop mathematics, metal properties, layout, and machining procedures: Consults with engineer and other personnel regarding product information, such as design, capacity and purpose, and types of material to be used to fabricate product. Analyzes written specifications, drawings, rough sketches, and verbal instructions to plan layout and determine sequence of operations. Selects metal stock and lays out design according to dimensions computed from scale drawings [LAY-OUT WORKER (any industry) I 809.281-010]. Designs fixtures, tooling, and experimental parts to meet special engineering needs. Sets up and operates metalworking machine tools, such as lathe, milling machine, shaper, or grinder to machine parts to specifications, and verifies conformance of parts to specifications, using measuring instruments [TOOL-MACHINE SET-UP OPERATOR (machine shop) 601.280-054]. Tests experimental models under simulated operating conditions for such purposes as development, standardization, and feasibility of design. Installs parts and materials, such as sheet metal covering, hydraulic systems, electrical wiring, lubricants, and batteries into machines and mechanisms. Evaluates experimental procedures and recommends changes or modifications for efficiency and adaptability to setup and production. May establish work procedures for fabricating new structural products, using variety of metalworking machines. May fabricate molds and power press dies to produce plastic parts and stamp metal parts. May perform heat-treating and heliarc welding. May train workers in setup and operation of machine tools. ● **GED:** R4, M4, L3 ● **SVP:** 4-10 yrs ● **Academic:** Ed=H, Eng=S ● **Work Field:** 057, 121, 241 ● **MPSMS:** 566, 580 ● **Aptitudes:** G2, V3, N3, S2, P2, Q3, K3, F3, M2, E5, C4 ● **Temperaments:** J, T, V ● **Physical:** Stg=H; Freq: R, H, I, N, D Occas: S, K, O, E, T, G, A, X ● **Work Env:** Noise=L; Occas: M, E ● **Salary:** 4 ● **Outlook:** 4

MAINTENANCE MACHINIST (machine shop) ● DOT #600.280-042 ● OES: 89108 ● Alternate titles: MACHINE REPAIRER; MACHINIST, GENERAL MAINTENANCE; SHOP MECHANIC. Sets up and operates variety of machine tools, and fits and assembles parts to fabricate or repair machine tools and maintain industrial machines, applying knowledge of mechanics, shop mathematics, metal properties, layout, and machining procedures: Observes and listens to operating machines or equipment to diagnose machine malfunction and determine need for adjustment or repair. Studies blueprints, sketches, machine parts or specifications to determine type and dimensions of

metal stock required. Measures, marks, and scribes dimensions and reference points on metal stock surfaces, using such measuring and marking devices as calibrated ruler, micrometer, caliper, and scriber [LAY-OUT WORKER (machine shop) 600.281-018]. Dismantles machine or equipment, using handtools or power tools, to examine parts for defect or to remove defective part. Replaces defective part with new part or repairs or reproduces part from various kinds of metal stock, using handtools, such as scraper, file, and drill, and machine tools, such as lathe, milling machine, shaper, borer, and grinder [MACHINIST (machine shop) 600.280-022]. Assembles and test operates machine to verify correction of malfunction. Maintains and lubricates machine tools and equipment. May weld parts, using arc or gas welding equipment. May repair or replace faulty wiring, switches, or relays. ● **GED:** R4, M4, L3 ● **SVP:** 2-4 yrs ● **Academic:** Ed=H, Eng=S ● **Work Field:** 057, 121, 241 ● **MPSMS:** 560, 580 ● **Aptitudes:** G3, V3, N3, S2, P3, Q3, K3, F3, M3, E4, C4 ● **Temperaments:** J, T, V ● **Physical:** Stg=M; Freq: R, H, I, N, D Occas: C, B, S, K, O, W, E, G, A, X ● **Work Env:** Noise=L; Occas: M ● **Salary:** 3 ● **Outlook:** 4

PATTERNMAKER, METAL (foundry) ● DOT #600.280-050 ● OES: 89198 ● Lays out, mills, drills, turns, grinds, fits, and assembles castings and parts to make metal foundry patterns, core boxes, and match plates, using handtools and machine tools, and analyzing specifications, according to knowledge of patternmaking methods: Studies blueprint of part to be cast, computes dimensions, and plans sequence of operations. Measures, marks, and scribes layout on castings [LAY-OUT WORKER (machine shop)]. Sets up and operates machine tools, such as milling machines, lathes, drill presses, and grinders, to machine castings to specifications [TOOL-MACHINE SET-UP OPERATOR (machine shop)]. Assembles pattern, using handtools, and bolts, screws, or other fasteners. Cleans and hand finishes workpiece, using emery cloth, files, scrapers, and powered hand grinders. Verifies conformance of machined pattern to blueprint specifications, using templates and measuring instruments, such as scale, calipers, and micrometers. May make templates for layout and inspection [TEMPLATE MAKER (any industry)]. May operate welding equipment in assembling pattern [WELDER, COMBINATION (welding)]. ● **GED:** R4, M4, L3 ● **SVP:** 4-10 yrs ● **Academic:** Ed=A, Eng=S ● **Work Field:** 057 ● **MPSMS:** 540, 567 ● **Aptitudes:** G3, V3, N3, S2, P2, Q4, K3, F3, M3, E5, C4 ● **Temperaments:** J, T, V ● **Physical:** Stg=M; Freq: R, H, I, N, A Occas: E, D, X ● **Work Env:** Noise=L; ● **Salary:** 3 ● **Outlook:** 4

ROCKET-MOTOR MECHANIC (aircraft mfg.) ● DOT #693.261-022 ● OES: 89108 ● Fabricates, assembles, and tests experimental solid fuel rocket motor parts and assemblies according to specifications, using handtools, precision instruments, machines, and test equipment: Reads and interprets blueprints, drawings, and engineering information to determine methods and sequence of operations to fabricate experimental units. Sets up and operates machines, such as milling machines, lathes, drill presses, and power saws, to machine parts. Measures parts for conformance to specifications, using calipers and micrometers. Assembles parts into completed units, such as valves and pressure vessels, using handtools. Operates vacuum pressure testing equipment to test assembled units for air leaks. Confers with engineering, supervisory, and manufacturing personnel to exchange technical information. May mix chemicals used in fabrication of composite materials. May operate winding machine to fabricate composite parts for solid fuel rocket motor. May specialize in fabricating, assembling, and testing experimental liquid fuel rocket engines and be designated Rocket-Engine Mechanic, Liquid (aircraft mfg.). ● **GED:** R4, M4, L4 ● **SVP:** 2-4 yrs ● **Academic:** Ed=H, Eng=G ● **Work Field:** 121 ● **MPSMS:** 596 ● **Aptitudes:** G3, V3, N2, S2, P3, Q4, K3, F3, M3, E5, C5 ● **Temperaments:** J, T ● **Physical:** Stg=M; Freq: R, H, I, N Occas: C, S, T, G, M, D ● **Work Env:** Noise=L; Occas: A, M, E, D, T ● **Salary:** 5 ● **Outlook:** 2

SAW FILER (any industry) ● DOT #701.381-014 ● OES: 89198 ● Alternate titles: FILER. Repairs bandsaw, handsaw, and circular saw blades according to customer's or manufacturer's specifications, using handtools, machine tools, and welding equipment: Examines saw for defects. Cuts broken teeth from saw, using power shear [SHEAR OPERATOR (any industry) I]. Forms teeth on saw blade by beveling joints on grinder and welding or brazing them together. Brazes or welds cracks in saw blades. Straightens twists and kinks in blades, using straightening press, and hammers out dents in blade on metal table. Adjusts cutting width of teeth, using swage or special pliers. Computes number and angle of teeth to produce specified cut. Clamps blade in saw-filing machine and turns handwheel to adjust distance between teeth, angle of bevel, and depth of cut of file or abrasive wheel. Starts machine that automatically grinds and files saw teeth. May be designated according to type of saw sharpened as Band-Saw Filer (any industry); Circular-Saw Filer (any industry). ● **GED:** R3, M3, L3 ● **SVP:** 1-2 yrs ● **Academic:** Ed=N, Eng=S ● **Work Field:** 121 ● **MPSMS:** 552 ● **Aptitudes:** G3, V3, N3, S3, P3, Q4, K3, F3, M3, E4, C5 ● **Temperaments:** J, T ● **Physical:** Stg=M; Freq: R, H, I, N, D Occas: S ● **Work Env:** Noise=L; Occas: A, M ● **Salary:** 3 ● **Outlook:** 1

TOOL-AND-DIE MAKER (machine shop) ● DOT #601.260-010 ● OES: 89102 ● Analyzes specifications, lays out metal stock, sets up and operates machine tools, and fits and assembles parts to fabricate and repair metalworking dies, cutting tools, jigs and fixtures, gauges, and machinists' handtools, applying knowledge of tool and die design and construction, shop mathematics, metal properties, and layout, machining, and assembly procedures: Studies specifications, such as blueprints, sketches, models, or descriptions, and visualizes product to determine materials required and machines to be used to fabricate parts. Computes dimensions, plans layout, and determines assembly method and sequence of operations. Measures, marks, and scribes metal stock for machining [LAY-OUT WORKER (machine shop) 600.281-018]. Sets up and operates machine tools, such as lathes, milling machine, shaper, and grinder, to machine parts, and verifies conformance of machined parts to specifications [TOOL-MACHINE SET-UP OPERATOR (machine shop) 601.280-054]. Lifts machined parts manually or using hoist, and positions and secures parts on surface plate or worktable, using devices, such as vises, V-blocks, and angle plates. Smooths flat and contoured surfaces, using scrapers, abrasive stones, and power grinders, and fits and assembles parts together and into assemblies and mechanisms, using handtools. Verifies dimensions, alignments, and clearances, using measuring instruments, such as dial indicators, gauge blocks, thickness gauges, and micrometers. Heat-treats tools or parts [HEAT TREATER (heat treating) II 504.682-018]. May connect wiring and hydraulic lines to install electrical and hydraulic components. May examine standard or previously used dies, tools, and jigs and fixtures, and recommend design modifications regarding construction and function of part. May develop specifications from general descriptions for specialty tools and draw or sketch design of product. May specialize in repair work and be designated Tool-And-Die Repairer (machine shop). ● **GED:** R4, M4, L4 ● **SVP:** 4-10 yrs ● **Academic:** Ed=A, Eng=S ● **Work Field:** 057, 121, 241 ● **MPSMS:** 566 ● **Aptitudes:** G2, V3, N3, S2, P2, Q3, K3, F2, M2, E5, C4 ● **Temperaments:** J, T, V ● **Physical:** Stg=M; Freq: R, H, I, N, D Occas: S, K, O, E, G, A, X ● **Work Env:** Noise=L; Freq: M Occas: A ● **Salary:** 4 ● **Outlook:** 4

TOOL GRINDER I (any industry) ● DOT #701.381-018 ● OES: 89198 ● Alternate titles: CUTLERY GRINDER; TOOL SHARPENER. Sharpens shears, scissors, hair clippers, surgical instruments, cleavers, and other fine-edged cutting tools, using whetstone and grinding and polishing wheels: Holds cutting edge of tool against rotating wheel or clamps tool in holder or carriage to steady it during sharpening process. Sharpens surgical instruments and razors, using fine-grained grinding wheels, and hones them on whetstone. May sharpen handsaws. May brush heated mixture of glue and grit onto worn grinding wheels to rebuild them. May specialize in sharpening barbers' tools and be designated Barber-Tool Sharpener (any industry). May specialize in sharpening shears and scissors and be designated Scissors Grinder (any industry). May specialize in sharpening tools and implements in homes and business establishments and be designated Grinder (any industry) III. ● **GED:** R3, M2, L2 ● **SVP:** 1-2 yrs ● **Academic:** Ed=N, Eng=N ● **Work Field:** 051 ● **MPSMS:** 552 ● **Aptitudes:** G3, V4, N4, S3, P3, Q4, K3, F3, M3, E5, C5 ● **Temperaments:** J, T ● **Physical:** Stg=L; Freq: R, H, I, N Occas: D, A ● **Work Env:** Noise=L; ● **Salary:** 3 ● **Outlook:** 2

TOOL-MACHINE SET-UP OPERATOR (machine shop) ● DOT #601.280-054 ● OES: 91510 ● Alternate titles: MACHINE-TOOL OPERATOR, GENERAL; MACHINIST; SET-UP-OPERATOR, TOOL. Sets up and operates variety of machine tools, such as radial drill press, lathes, milling machines, shapers, and grinders, to machine metal workpieces, such as patterns and machine, tool, or die parts, usually on custom basis. Analyzes specifications and determines tooling, applying knowledge of metal properties, machining, and shop mathematics: Studies blueprint or layout on workpiece to visualize machin-

ing required, and plans sequence of operations. Selects method of holding workpiece. Lifts workpiece manually or using hoist, and positions and secures it to holding device, such as machine table, chuck, centers, or fixture, using wrenches and aids, such as shims, parallel blocks, planter gauges, and clamps. Verifies workpiece position, using instruments, such as surface gauges, height gauges, and dial indicator. Selects feed rate, cutting speed, depth of cut, and cutting tool (bar tool, rotary cutter, or abrasive wheel) for each operation, according to knowledge of metal properties, machining, and shop mathematics. Positions and secures tool in toolholder (chuck, collet, or toolpost). Moves controls to position tool and workpiece in relation to each other, and to set feeds, speeds, and depth of cut. Starts machine, turns handwheel to feed tool in workpiece or vice versa, and engages automatic feeding device. Turns valve handle to start flow of coolant against tool and workpiece. Observes operation and regulates tool position and action. Verifies conformance of machined workpiece to specifications, using instruments, such as micrometers, gauges, and gauge blocks. May measure, mark, and scribe workpiece to lay out for machining [LAY-OUT WORKER (machine shop) 600.281-018]. May devise ways of clamping workpieces and make special jigs and fixtures as needed. May work on nonmetallic materials. May operate bench grinder or cutter grinding machine to sharpen tools [TOOL-GRINDER OPERATOR (machine shop) 603.280-038]. ● **GED:** R4, M4, L3 ● **SVP:** 2-4 yrs ● **Academic:** Ed=H, Eng=S ● **Work Field:** 057, 121 ● **MPSMS:** 540, 566 ● **Aptitudes:** G3, V3, N3, S2, P2, Q4, K3, F3, M3, E5, C5 ● **Temperaments:** J, T ● **Physical:** Stg=M; Freq: R, H, I, N, D, A Occas: E, V ● **Work Env:** Noise=L; Occas: M ● **Salary:** 4 ● **Outlook:** 3

GOE: 05.05.08
Woodworking

CABINETMAKER (woodworking) ● DOT #660.280-010 ● OES: 89311 ● Sets up and operates variety of woodworking machines and uses various handtools to fabricate and repair wooden cabinets and high-grade furniture: Studies blueprints or drawings of articles to be constructed or repaired, and plans sequence of cutting or shaping operations to be performed. Marks outline or dimensions of parts on paper or lumber stock, according to blueprint or drawing specifications. Matches materials for color, grain, or texture. Sets up and operates woodworking machines, such as power saws, jointer, mortiser, tenoner, molder, and shaper, to cut and shape parts from woodstock. Trims component parts of joints to ensure snug fit, using handtools, such as planes, chisels, or wood files. Bores holes for insertion of screws or dowels by hand or using boring machine. Glues, fits, and clamps parts and subassemblies together to form complete unit, using clamps or clamping machine. Drives nails or other fasteners into joints at designated places to reinforce joints. Sands and scrapes surfaces and joints of articles to prepare articles for finishing. May repair high-grade articles of furniture. May dip, brush, or spray assembled articles with protective or decorative materials, such as stain, varnish, or paint. May install hardware, such as hinges, catches, and drawer pulls. May repair furniture, equipment, and fixtures and be designated Cabinetmaker, Maintenance (woodworking). May be designated according to products made as Piano-Case Maker (musical inst.). May cut, shape, and assemble wooden parts to construct frames for refrigeration equipment and be designated Refrigerator Cabinetmaker (svc. ind. mach.). ● **GED:** R4, M4, L3 ● **SVP:** 1-2 yrs ● **Academic:** Ed=H, Eng=S ● **Work Field:** 102 ● **MPSMS:** 450, 460 ● **Aptitudes:** G3, V3, N3, S3, P3, Q3, K3, F3, M3, E4, C4 ● **Temperaments:** J, T, V ● **Physical:** Stg=M; Freq: R, H, I, N, D Occas: A, X ● **Work Env:** Noise=L; ● **Salary:** 4 ● **Outlook:** 3

FURNITURE FINISHER (woodworking) ● DOT #763.381-010 ● OES: 89314 ● Alternate titles: FURNITURE REFINISHER; RECOATER; REFINISHER; WOOD FINISHER. Finishes or refinishes damaged, worn, or used furniture or new high-grade furniture to specified color or finish, utilizing knowledge of wood properties, finishes, and furniture styling: Disassembles article, masks areas adjacent to areas being finished, or removes accessories such as knobs and hinges, using handtools, to prepare article for finishing. Removes old finish from surfaces, using steel wool, sandpaper, or solvent and putty knife. Removes excess solvent with cloth immersed in paint thinner or sal soda. Applies plastic-putty, wood putty, or lacquer-stick to surface, using spatula or knife, to fill nicks, depressions, holes, and cracks. Smooths surface for finishing, using sandpaper or power sander. Selects finish ingredients and mixes them by hand or machine to obtain specified color or shade or to match existing finish. Brushes or sprays successive coats of stain, varnish, shellac, lacquer, or paint on workpiece. Grains wood or paints wood trim, using graining roller, comb, sponge, or brush. Polishes and waxes finished surfaces. May restore wood to natural color, using bleaching acid and neutralizer. May spread graining ink over metal portions of surfaces with cheesecloth to simulate wood-grainlike finish. May finish piano and organ cases and be designated Piano-And-Organ Refinisher (woodworking). May finish mirror and picture frames and be designated according to type of finish applied as Powder Gilder (wood prod., nec); Whitener (wood prod., nec). May finish television receiver cabinets and be designated Television-Cabinet Finisher (woodworking). May finish wooden parts of custom-made firearms and be designated Finisher, Special Stocks (ordnance). May stain and finish surfaces of new furniture pieces to simulate antiques, bringing out highlights and shadings by rubbing surfaces with abrasives or cloth, and be designated Antiquer (furniture). ● **GED:** R4, M2, L2 ● **SVP:** 2-4 yrs ● **Academic:** Ed=H, Eng=N ● **Work Field:** 051, 153 ● **MPSMS:** 460 ● **Aptitudes:** G3, V4, N4, S4, P2, Q4, K3, F4, M3, E5, C3 ● **Temperaments:** J, T ● **Physical:** Stg=L; Freq: R, H, N, A, X Occas: S, K, I, E ● **Work Env:** Noise=L; Occas: A ● **Salary:** 2 ● **Outlook:** 2

FURNITURE RESTORER (museums) ● DOT #763.380-010 ● OES: 89314 ● Alternate titles: FURNISHINGS CONSERVATOR; COATER. Restores and preserves historical furniture in collection of museum or similar institution, using variety of handtools and power tools and applying knowledge of antique fabrics and wood furniture: Examines furnishings to determine type of material, extent of deterioration or damage, or date of construction to verify authenticity and plan restoration. Sets up and operates variety of woodworking machines to fabricate, repair, reinforce, and replace parts of furniture. Cuts, shapes, and attaches parts according to blueprints or drawings, using handtools. Matches materials for color, grain, and texture. Strips old finish from furnishings, using solvents and abrasives. Fills cracks, depressions, and other blemishes, using plastic wood or lacquer stick. Treats warped or stained surfaces to restore original contour and color. Glues or replaces veneer sections. Smooths surfaces, using power sander or abrasive material. Washes or bleaches furniture surfaces to prepare surface for application of finish. Selects coatings, such as stain, lacquer, or varnish according to type wood, and brushes or sprays material onto surface to protect surface and produce desired appearance. Polishes, sprays, or waxes finished pieces. Removes damaged or deteriorated coverings from upholstered furniture. Repairs, reinforces, or replaces components, such as springs, webbing, and padding. Selects fabric for new covering, using knowledge of period and style of furniture or following instructions of CURATOR (museums) 102.017-010. Tacks, sews, glues, or staples covering to furniture frame to attach upholstery. Refurbishes leather coverings of furnishings, using softeners, solvents, adhesives, stains, or polishes. Replaces damaged coverings with leather pieces of appropriate color, grain, and weight. Stencils, gilds, embosses, or paints designs or borders on restored pieces to reproduce original appearance. May advise curatorial staff on environmental conditions necessary for preservation of furnishings in exhibit and storage areas. May fabricate replicas of period furniture for use in exhibits. May be designated according to specialty as Finish Specialist (museums); Upholstery Restorer (museums). ● **GED:** R4, M3, L4 ● **SVP:** 1-2 yrs ● **Academic:** Ed=N, Eng=S ● **Work Field:** 102, 153 ● **MPSMS:** 460 ● **Aptitudes:** G3, V3, N3, S3, P3, Q4, K3, F3, M2, E5, C3 ● **Temperaments:** J, T, V ● **Physical:** Stg=L; Freq: R, H, I, N, A, X Occas: S, O, T, G, D ● **Work Env:** Noise=L; ● **Salary:** 2 ● **Outlook:** 2

LOFT WORKER (ship-boat mfg.) ● DOT #661.281-010 ● OES: 89398 ● Alternate titles: MOLD LOFT WORKER. Lays out lines of ship to full scale on mold-loft floor and constructs templates and molds to be used as patterns and guides for layout and fabrication of various structural parts of ships: Lays out full-scale portions of ship's plan, working from blueprints and tables of offsets. Marks frame lines and other reference lines on loft floor with marking instrument. Measures dimensions between lines and prepares table of offsets. Compares prepared tables with tables on blueprints. Constructs template, using knowledge of geometric construction, and handtools and woodworking machines, such as crosscut, rip, and bandsaws. Marks templates with identifying data and instructions, such as number of pieces to be made, type, and weight of stock, and location for installation. Constructs full scale wood mockups of ship's parts and sections for use as guide in shaping or positioning parts. May construct wooden plug mold parts, such as hulls, decks, and cabins of fiberglass boats, and be designated Plug Builder (ship-boat mfg.). ● **GED:** R4, M4, L3 ● **SVP:** 2-4 yrs ● **Academic:** Ed=N, Eng=S ● **Work Field:** 241, 102 ● **MPSMS:** 593 ● **Aptitudes:** G3, V3, N3, S2, P3, Q4, K3, F3, M3, E5, C5 ● **Temperaments:** J, T ● **Physical:** Stg=L; Freq: R, H, I, N Occas: S, O, D, A ● **Work Env:** Noise=N; ● **Salary:** 1 ● **Outlook:** 2

MACHINIST, WOOD (woodworking) ● DOT #669.380-014 ● OES: 89308 ● Alternate titles: WOODWORKING-MACHINE OPERATOR. Sets up and operates variety of woodworking machines to surface, cut, and shape lumber, and to fabricate parts for wood products, such as doors, door and window frames, furniture, and sashes, according to specifications: Selects, installs, and adjusts saw blades, cutterheads, boring bits, and sanding belts in respective machines, using handtools and rule. Starts machine and makes trial cut. Operates machines to saw [CUT-OFF-SAW OPERATOR (woodworking) I 667.682-022; RIP-SAW OPERATOR (woodworking) 667.682-066; VARIETY-SAW OPERATOR (woodworking) 667.682-086]; to smooth and shape lumber and wood parts [PLANER OPERATOR (woodworking) 665.682-022; SHAPER OPERATOR (woodworking) 665.682-034]; to cut tenons and mortises in woodstock [TENONER OPERATOR (woodworking) 669.382-018; MORTISING-MACHINE OPERATOR (woodworking) 665.482-014]; to bore holes [BORING-MACHINE OPERATOR (woodworking) 666.382-010]; to cut slots, grooves, and designs in woodstock [ROUTER OPERATOR (woodworking) 665.682-030]; and to sand lumber, woodstock, and parts [MOLDING SANDER (woodworking) 662.682-010; CYLINDER-SANDER OPERATOR (woodworking) 662.685-014; SANDER, MACHINE (woodworking) 761.682-014]. Periodically verifies dimensions of parts for adherence to specifications, using gauges and templates. May assemble fabricated parts to make millwork products, such as doors, sashes, and door and window frames. May sharpen machine cutting heads, using handtools and grinder. May be designated according to products as Door Maker (saw. & plan.); Frame Maker (saw. & plan.); Sash Maker (saw. & plan.). ● **GED:** R3, M3, L3 ● **SVP:** 1-2 yrs ● **Academic:** Ed=N, Eng=S ● **Work Field:** 057 ● **MPSMS:** 450, 460 ● **Aptitudes:** G3, V4, N3, S3, P3, Q4, K3, F3, M3, E4, C4 ● **Temperaments:** J, T, V ● **Physical:** Stg=M; Freq: S, O, R, H, I, N Occas: K, E, G, D, A, X ● **Work Env:** Noise=L; Freq: A, M Occas: T, O ● **Salary:** 4 ● **Outlook:** 3

GOE: 05.05.09
Mechanical Work

AIR-CONDITIONING INSTALLER-SERVICER, WINDOW UNIT (construction) ● DOT #637.261-010 ● OES: 85710 ● Installs, services, and repairs window air-conditioning units, ranging from 1/2 to 2 tons capacity, in private residences and small establishments: Inspects existing wiring, fuses, or circuit-breaker panels on customer's premises to ensure adequate power supply for operating air-conditioner. Measures window, transom, or other existing openings for air-conditioning unit, using measuring tape or rule, or cuts opening through wall, using mallet and cold chisel. Assembles and positions support brackets in place, using screws, clamps, or other braces, and power tools and handtools. Fills space between window support and edge of opening with caulking compound and filler board. Places air-conditioner on support frame and secures unit in position, leveling unit, using screws, clips, and bolts. Starts unit, adjusts controls, and listens for excessive noise or sounds indicating malfunction. Examines malfunctioning unit for defective parts, utilizing knowledge of mechanical, electrical, and refrigeration theory, to determine cause of malfunction. Dismantles whole or part of unit, as indicated by type of malfunction, and repairs or replaces such parts as switches, relays, fan motors, thermostats, and other components, using handtools and power tools. Replaces filters, lubricates unit, and adjusts controls. Reassembles unit, making necessary adjustments to ensure efficient operation. May give instructions to customer regarding operation and care of unit. May estimate cost of repairs or adjustments. May remove unit from customer's premises for major repairs or overhaul in shop, or for return to manufacturer for extensive repairs. May repair sealed refrigeration units of machines. For installation, service, and repair of central air-conditioning units, see HEATING-AND-AIR-CONDITIONING INSTALLER-SERVICER (construction) 637.261-014. ● **GED:** R4, M3, L3 ● **SVP:** 4-10 yrs ● **Academic:** Ed=H, Eng=S ● **Work Field:** 111, 121 ● **MPSMS:** 573 ● **Aptitudes:** G3, V3, N3, S2, P3, Q4, K3, F3, M3, E4, C5 ● **Temperaments:** J, T ● **Physical:** Stg=H; Freq: R, H, I, T, G, N, D, A Occas: C, S, K, O, X ● **Work Env:** Noise=N; Occas: W ● **Salary:** 4 ● **Outlook:** 3

AIR-CONDITIONING MECHANIC (automotive ser.) ● DOT #620.281-010 ● OES: 85302 ● Alternate titles: AUTOMOBILE-REFRIGERATION MECHANIC. Installs and repairs automotive air-conditioning units: Bolts compressor to engine block and installs driving pulley on front end of crankshaft. Places fan belt on pulleys, adjusts tension, and tightens bolts. Bolts evaporator unit under dashboard or in trunk. Welds or bolts mounting brackets to automobile frame. Drills holes through interior panels, threads hoses through holes and connects hoses to compressor, evaporator, and cool-air outlet. Fills compressor with refrigerant and starts unit. Measures compressor pressure to determine efficiency of compressor, using gauge. Listens to operating unit for indications of malfunction. Removes faulty units from vehicles, disassembles them, and replaces worn and broken parts and fluid in unit. Makes electrical connections as required. May specialize in installation of automotive air-conditioning units and be designated Automotive Air-Conditioner Installer (automotive ser.). ● **GED:** R3, M2, L3 ● **SVP:** 1-2 yrs ● **Academic:** Ed=N, Eng=N ● **Work Field:** 121 ● **MPSMS:** 591 ● **Aptitudes:** G3, V3, N3, S2, P3, Q4, K3, F3, M3, E5, C5 ● **Temperaments:** J, T, V ● **Physical:** Stg=M; Freq: R, H, I, N, D Occas: S, K, O, A ● **Work Env:** Noise=N; ● **Salary:** 3 ● **Outlook:** 4

AIRFRAME-AND-POWER-PLANT MECHANIC (aircraft mfg.) ● DOT #621.281-014 ● OES: 85323 ● Alternate titles: AIRCRAFT MECHANIC; AIRPLANE MECHANIC. Services, repairs, and overhauls aircraft and aircraft engines to ensure airworthiness: Repairs, replaces, and rebuilds aircraft structures, such as wings and fuselage, and functional components including rigging, surface controls, and plumbing and hydraulic units, using handtools, power tools, machines, and equipment such as shears, sheet metal brakes, welding equipment, rivet gun, and drills. Reads and interprets manufacturers' and airline's maintenance manuals, service bulletins, and other specifications to determine feasibility and method of repairing or replacing malfunctioning or damaged components. Examines engines for cracked cylinders and oil leaks, and listens to operating engine to detect and diagnose malfunctions, such as sticking or burned valves. Inspects turbine blades to detect cracks or breaks. Tests engine operation, using testing equipment such as ignition analyzer, compression checker, distributor timer, and ammeter, to locate source of malfunction. Replaces or repairs worn or damaged components, such as carburetors, alternators, and magnetos, using handtools, gauges, and testing equipment. Removes engine from aircraft, using hoist or forklift truck. Disassembles and inspects parts for wear, warping, or other defects. Repairs or replaces defective engine parts and reassembles and installs engine in aircraft. Adjusts, repairs, or replaces electrical wiring system and aircraft accessories. Performs miscellaneous duties to service aircraft, including flushing crankcase, cleaning screens, greasing moving parts, and checking brakes. May be required to be licensed by Federal Aviation Administration. May service engines and airframe components at line station making repairs, short of overhaul, required to keep aircraft in safe operating condition and be designated Airframe-And-Power-Plant Mechanic, Line Service (air trans.). May service and repair aircraft and engines prior to, during, or after flight to ensure airworthiness, working on flight line of aircraft manufacturing facility, and be designated Aircraft-And-Engine Mechanic, Field-And-Hangar (aircraft mfg.); Flight-Line Mechanic (aircraft mfg.); Mechanic, Field-Service (aircraft mfg.). May specialize in rework, repair, and modification of structural, precision, and functional spare parts and assemblies at manufacturing facility and be designated Spares Rework Mechanic (aircraft mfg.). May specialize in engine repair and be designated Aircraft-Engine Assembler (air trans.); Aircraft-Engine-Cylinder Mechanic (air trans.); Aircraft-Engine Dismantler (air trans.); Aircraft-Engine Installer (air trans.); Aircraft-Engine Mechanic (air trans.); Aircraft-Engine Mechanic, Overhaul (air trans.). May be designated: Carburetor Mechanic (air trans.); Helicopter Mechanic (air trans.); Hydraulic Tester (air trans.); Ignition Specialist (air trans.); Overhaul And Repair Mechanic (aircraft mfg.); Supercharger Mechanic (air trans.). ● **GED:** R4, M4, L4 ● **SVP:** 2-4 yrs ● **Academic:** Ed=A, Eng=S ● **Work Field:** 102, 111,

121 ● **MPSMS:** 592 ● **Aptitudes:** G3, V3, N3, S2, P2, Q4, K3, F3, M2, E4, C4 ● **Temperaments:** J, T, V ● **Physical:** Stg=M; Freq: R, H, I, D Occas: C, B, S, K, O, W, E, G, M, N, A, X ● **Work Env:** Noise=L; Occas: W, A, M, E, D, T, O ● **Salary:** 4 ● **Outlook:** 2

AIRFRAME-AND-POWER-PLANT-MECHANIC APPRENTICE (air trans.) ● DOT #621.281-018 ● OES: 85323 ● Alternate titles: AIRPLANE-MECHANIC APPRENTICE. Performs duties as described under APPRENTICE (any industry) Master Title. ● **GED:** R4, M4, L4 ● **SVP:** 2-4 yrs ● **Academic:** Ed=H, Eng=G ● **Work Field:** 102, 111, 121 ● **MPSMS:** 592 ● **Aptitudes:** G3, V3, N3, S2, P2, Q4, K3, F3, M2, E4, C4 ● **Temperaments:** J, T, V ● **Physical:** Stg=M; Freq: R, H, I, D Occas: C, B, S, K, O, W, E, G, M, N, A, X ● **Work Env:** Noise=L; Occas: W, A, M, E, D, T, O ● **Salary:** 4 ● **Outlook:** 4

AUTOMOBILE MECHANIC (automotive ser.) ● DOT #620.261-010 ● OES: 85302 ● Alternate titles: GARAGE MECHANIC. Repairs and overhauls automobiles, buses, trucks, and other automotive vehicles: Examines vehicle and discusses with customer or AUTOMOBILE-REPAIR-SERVICE ESTIMATOR (automotive ser.); AUTOMOBILE TESTER (automotive ser.); or BUS INSPECTOR (automotive ser.) nature and extent of damage or malfunction. Plans work procedure, using charts, technical manuals, and experience. Raises vehicle, using hydraulic jack or hoist, to gain access to mechanical units bolted to underside of vehicle. Removes unit, such as engine, transmission, or differential, using wrenches and hoist. Disassembles unit and inspects parts for wear, using micrometers, calipers, and thickness gauges. Repairs or replaces parts, such as pistons, rods, gears, valves, and bearings, using mechanic's handtools. Overhauls or replaces carburetors, blowers, generators, distributors, starters, and pumps. Rebuilds parts, such as crankshafts and cylinder blocks, using lathes, shapers, drill presses, and welding equipment. Rewires ignition system, lights, and instrument panel. Relines and adjusts brakes, aligns front end, repairs or replaces shock absorbers, and solders leaks in radiator. Mends damaged body and fenders by hammering out or filling in dents and welding broken parts. Replaces and adjusts headlights, and installs and repairs accessories, such as radios, heaters, mirrors, and windshield wipers. May be designated according to specialty as Automobile Mechanic, Motor (automotive ser.); Bus Mechanic (automotive ser.); Differential Repairer (automotive ser.); Engine-Repair Mechanic, Bus (automotive ser.); Foreign-Car Mechanic (automotive ser.); Truck Mechanic (automotive ser.). May be designated: Compressor Mechanic, Bus (automotive ser.); Drive-Shaft-And-Steering-Post Repairer (automotive ser.); Engine-Head Repairer (automotive ser.); Motor Assembler (automotive ser.). ● **GED:** R4, M3, L3 ● **SVP:** 2-4 yrs ● **Academic:** Ed=H, Eng=S ● **Work Field:** 111, 121 ● **MPSMS:** 591 ● **Aptitudes:** G3, V3, N4, S2, P3, Q4, K3, F3, M2, E4, C4 ● **Temperaments:** J, T, V ● **Physical:** Stg=M; Freq: R, H, I, N, D Occas: S, K, O, W, T, G, A, X ● **Work Env:** Noise=L; Freq: A ● **Salary:** 3 ● **Outlook:** 4

AUTOMOBILE-SERVICE-STATION MECHANIC (automotive ser.) ● DOT #620.261-030 ● OES: 85302 ● Repairs and services vehicles of service station customers through performance of any of following tasks: Examines vehicles and confers with customers to determine malfunction and repairs desired. Refers customer with major vehicle repairs to garage. Removes and replaces parts of ignition system, such as spark plugs, points, coil, or alternator to complete tune-up or replace malfunctioning part of system, using mechanic's handtools, gauges, and test meters. Turns adjustment screws of carburetor to set idle speed of engine, using screwdriver. Replaces defective chassis parts, such as shock absorbers, balljoint suspension, brakeshoes, and wheel bearings. Services vehicles [AUTOMOBILE-SERVICE-STATION ATTENDANT (automotive ser.) 915.467-010]. ● **GED:** R3, M2, L3 ● **SVP:** 6 mos-1 yr ● **Academic:** Ed=N, Eng=S ● **Work Field:** 121, 292 ● **MPSMS:** 591, 961 ● **Aptitudes:** G3, V3, N3, S2, P3, Q4, K3, F3, M3, E5, C5 ● **Temperaments:** J, T ● **Physical:** Stg=M; Freq: S, K, O, R, H, I, T, G, N, A ● **Work Env:** Noise=N; Occas: T ● **Salary:** 4 ● **Outlook:** 4

AUTOMOTIVE-COOLING-SYSTEM DIAGNOSTIC TECHNICIAN (automotive ser.) ● DOT #620.261-034 ● OES: 85302 ● Inspects and tests automotive cooling systems to diagnose malfunctions and estimates cost of repairs: Questions customer and examines cooling system, hoses, and connections to determine nature and extent of malfunctions. Tests and analyzes electrical, vacuum, pressure, and related functions of system components to locate cause of malfunctions, using vacuum tester, pressure tester, voltmeter, and other specialized test equipment and handtools. Compiles estimate of system repair costs and secures customer approval to perform repairs. Occasionally assists AUTOMOBILE-RADIATOR MECHANIC (automotive ser.) 620.381-010 in repair of cooling system components, using mechanic's handtools. Computes parts and labor charges and routes customer bill to office. ● **GED:** R4, M3, L3 ● **SVP:** 2-4 yrs ● **Academic:** Ed=N, Eng=N ● **Work Field:** 121, 212 ● **MPSMS:** 591 ● **Aptitudes:** G2, V3, N3, S3, P3, Q3, K3, F4, M3, E5, C4 ● **Temperaments:** J, T ● **Physical:** Stg=M; Freq: R, H, I, N, A Occas: S, O, E, T, G, D, X ● **Work Env:** Noise=N; ● **Salary:** 3 ● **Outlook:** 4

AUTOMOTIVE-MAINTENANCE-EQUIPMENT SERVICER (any industry) ● DOT #620.281-018 ● OES: 85109 ● Alternate titles: AUTOMOTIVE-MAINTENANCE-EQUIPMENT REPAIRER; EQUIPMENT-SERVICE ENGINEER; PUMP-AND-TANK SERVICER. Adjusts and repairs automotive repairing, servicing, and testing equipment, using handtools and power tools: Disassembles defective equipment, such as gasoline pumps, air compressors, and dynamometers. Replaces defective parts, using pipe fitting and welding tools. Reassembles, adjusts, and tests repaired equipment. May be required to register with government agency to adjust meters and gauges of fuel and oil pumps serving public. May install new equipment. May specialize in repairing gasoline pumps, lubrication equipment, air compressors, or other type of automotive service equipment. ● **GED:** R4, M3, L3 ● **SVP:** 2-4 yrs ● **Academic:** Ed=H, Eng=S ● **Work Field:** 121, 111 ● **MPSMS:** 568 ● **Aptitudes:** G3, V3, N3, S2, P3, Q4, K3, F3, M2, E5, C4 ● **Temperaments:** J, T, V ● **Physical:** Stg=M; Freq: S, K, O, R, H, N Occas: I, E, D, A ● **Work Env:** Noise=L; ● **Salary:** 3 ● **Outlook:** 3

CASH-REGISTER SERVICER (any industry) ● DOT #633.281-010 ● OES: 85926 ● Alternate titles: CASH-REGISTER REPAIRER. Tests and repairs cash registers, using handtools, power tools, and circuit test meters: Examines mechanical assemblies, such as printing mechanisms, counters, and keyboards, for worn or damaged parts, using precision gauges. Replaces defective parts, or reshapes parts on bench lathe or grinder. Tests electrical control units, wiring, and motors, using circuit test equipment. Replaces defective electrical parts, using handtools and welding and soldering equipment. Cleans and oils moving parts. May service adding machines [OFFICE-MACHINE SERVICER (any industry)]. ● **GED:** R4, M3, L3 ● **SVP:** 2-4 yrs ● **Academic:** Ed=N, Eng=S ● **Work Field:** 111, 121 ● **MPSMS:** 571 ● **Aptitudes:** G3, V3, N3, S3, P3, Q3, K3, F3, M2, E5, C5 ● **Temperaments:** J, T, V ● **Physical:** Stg=M; Freq: R, H, I, N ● **Work Env:** Noise=L; ● **Salary:** 1 ● **Outlook:** 2

CONSTRUCTION-EQUIPMENT MECHANIC (construction) ● DOT #620.261-022 ● OES: 85314 ● Alternate titles: HEAVY-EQUIPMENT MECHANIC. Analyzes malfunctions and repairs, rebuilds, and maintains construction equipment, such as cranes, power shovels, scrapers, paving machines, motor graders, trench-digging machines, conveyors, bulldozers, dredges, pumps, compressors and pneumatic tools: Operates and inspects machines or equipment to diagnose defects. Dismantles and reassembles equipment, using hoists and handtools. Examines parts for damage or excessive wear, using micrometers and gauges. Replaces defective engines and subassemblies, such as transmissions. Tests overhauled equipment to ensure operating efficiency. Welds broken parts and structural members. May direct workers engaged in cleaning parts and assisting with assembly and disassembly of equipment. May repair, adjust, and maintain mining machinery, such as stripping and loading shovels, drilling and cutting machines, and continuous mining machines, and be designated Mine-Machinery Mechanic (mine & quarry). ● **GED:** R3, M2, L3 ● **SVP:** 2-4 yrs ● **Academic:** Ed=N, Eng=S ● **Work Field:** 121 ● **MPSMS:** 563 ● **Aptitudes:** G3, V3, N3, S3, P3, Q4, K3, F3, M3, E4, C5 ● **Temperaments:** J, T, V ● **Physical:** Stg=M; Freq: S, K, O, R, H, I, N, D, A ● **Work Env:** Noise=L; Const: W Freq: A, M Occas: O ● **Salary:** 4 ● **Outlook:** 4

DIESEL MECHANIC (any industry) ● DOT #625.281-010 ● OES: 85311 ● Repairs and maintains diesel engines used to power machines, such as buses, ships, trucks, railroad trains, electric generators, and construction machinery, using handtools, precision measuring instruments, and machine tools: Diagnoses trouble, disassembles engines, and examines parts for defects and excessive wear. Reconditions and replaces parts, such as pistons, bearings, gears, valves, and bushings, using engine lathes, boring machines, handtools, and precision mea-

suring instruments. May weld and cut parts, using arc-welding and flame cutting equipment. May be designated according to type of diesel engine or equipment repaired as Diesel-Engine Mechanic, Automobile (automotive ser.); Diesel-Engine Mechanic, Bus (automotive ser.); Diesel-Engine Mechanic, Marine (ship-boat mfg.); Diesel-Engine Mechanic, Truck (automotive ser.); Diesel-Mechanic, Construction (construction); Diesel-Mechanic, Farm (agric. equip.); Locomotive Repairer, Diesel (railroad equip.). ● **GED:** R4, M3, L3 ● **SVP:** 2-4 yrs ● **Academic:** Ed=H, Eng=S ● **Work Field:** 121 ● **MPSMS:** 560 ● **Aptitudes:** G3, V3, N3, S3, P3, Q4, K3, F3, M2, E4, C4 ● **Temperaments:** J, T, V ● **Physical:** Stg=H; Freq: S, K, O, R, H, N, F, D, A Occas: C, I, G, X ● **Work Env:** Noise=L; Occas: W, H, A, T, O ● **Salary:** 4 ● **Outlook:** 4

EXPERIMENTAL AIRCRAFT MECHANIC (aircraft mfg.) ● DOT #621.261-022 ● OES: 85326 ● Alternate titles: EXPERIMENTAL AIRCRAFT AND ENGINE MECHANIC, FIELD AND HANGAR; EXPERIMENTAL FLIGHT TEST MECHANIC; EXPERIMENTAL PREFLIGHT MECHANIC. Inspects, tests, repairs, maintains, services, and modifies experimental and prototype aircraft, engines, accessories, and components according to governmental, company, and customer requirements: Assembles and installs aircraft electrical, plumbing, mechanical, and structural accessories and components, such as ejection seats, hatch mechanisms, and safety belts, using handtools and power tools. Installs, operates, and adjusts test apparatus, such as recorders, oscillographs, limit switches, inverters, thermocouples, instruments, cameras, timing devices, and photo recorders. Operates aircraft engines and systems, such as hydraulic, air-conditioning, pressurization, fuel, controls, and landing gear, to diagnose malfunctions, using test equipment, such as hydraulic test bench, pressure ratio bench, water injection test cart, and ground power unit. Repairs, adjusts, aligns, and calibrates aircraft systems. Modifies aircraft structure or components following drawings, engineering orders, and other technical publications, as required. Services and maintains gaseous, liquid oxygen, pneumatic, and hydraulic systems on aircraft. May specialize in testing and modifying spacecraft systems and be designated Experimental Mechanic, Spacecraft (aircraft mfg.). ● **GED:** R4, M3, L4 ● **SVP:** 2-4 yrs ● **Academic:** Ed=A, Eng=S ● **Work Field:** 111, 121, 211 ● **MPSMS:** 592 ● **Aptitudes:** G2, V3, N3, S2, P2, Q3, K3, F3, M3, E4, C4 ● **Temperaments:** J, T, V ● **Physical:** Stg=M; Freq: R, H, I, N, F Occas: C, B, S, K, O, W, E, T, G, D, A, X, V ● **Work Env:** Noise=V; Occas: W, A, M, E, D, T ● **Salary:** 5 ● **Outlook:** 3

FARM-EQUIPMENT MECHANIC I (agric. equip.) ● DOT #624.281-010 ● OES: 85321 ● Alternate titles: FARM MECHANIC. Maintains, repairs, and overhauls farm machinery, equipment, and vehicles, such as tractors, harvesters, pumps, tilling equipment, trucks, and other mechanized, electrically powered, or motor-driven equipment, on farms or in farm-equipment repair shops: Examines and listens to machines, motors, gasoline and diesel engines, and equipment for operational defects and dismantles defective units, using handtools. Repairs or replaces defective parts, using handtools and machine tools, such as drill press, lathe, milling machine, woodworking machines, welding equipment, grinders, and saws. Reassembles, adjusts, and lubricates machines and equipment to ensure efficient operation. May install and repair wiring and motors to maintain farm electrical system. May install and repair plumbing systems on farm. May construct and repair buildings and other farm structures. May assemble and erect new farm machinery and equipment. May be designated according to equipment maintained as Viner Mechanic (agric. equip.). ● **GED:** R4, M3, L3 ● **SVP:** 2-4 yrs ● **Academic:** Ed=H, Eng=S ● **Work Field:** 121 ● **MPSMS:** 562 ● **Aptitudes:** G3, V3, N3, S3, P3, Q4, K3, F3, M2, E4, C4 ● **Temperaments:** J, T, V ● **Physical:** Stg=M; Freq: R, H, I, N Occas: C, S, K, O, W, G, D, A, X ● **Work Env:** Noise=L; Occas: W, M ● **Salary:** 2 ● **Outlook:** 3

FIELD SERVICE TECHNICIAN (machinery mfg.) ● DOT #638.261-026 ● OES: 85123 ● Alternate titles: ROBOT TECHNICIAN. Installs, programs, and repairs robots and related equipment, such as programmable controllers, robot controllers, end-of-arm tools, conveyors, and parts orienters, applying knowledge of electronics, electrical circuits, mechanics, pneumatics, hydraulics, and programming, using power tools, handtools, and testing instruments and following manuals, schematic diagrams, and blueprints: Reviews work order and related manuals, blueprints, and schematic diagrams to determine tasks to be performed and tools, equipment, and parts needed for installation of repair assignment. Discusses assignment with customer's representative and inspects installation site to verify that electrical supply wires, conduit, switches, and circuit breakers are installed according to specifications. Positions and secures robot and related equipment to floor, assisted by customer's staff, using crane, handtools, and power tools and following manuals and blueprints, or inspects installation site to ensure that robot has been installed according to specifications. Attaches electrical wires to robot controller and programmable controller and connects cables between robot, robot controller, programmable controller, and hydraulic power unit, using handtools. Connects hoses between hydraulic power unit and robot, using handtools. Verifies that electrical power is reaching robot and that voltage is as specified, using testing instruments. Pushes buttons, flips switches, and moves levers to start robot and related equipment to verify that operation is as specified. Programs robot to perform specified tasks, applying knowledge of programming language, using teach pendant and keyboard or control panel on robot controller. Modifies program to refine movement of robot, using teach pendant. Observes and listens to robot and related equipment to detect malfunction and repairs or replaces defective parts, using handtools and power tools [MAINTENANCE MECHANIC (any industry) 638.281-014]. Tests electrical components, such as wiring, switches, and relays, using testing instruments, and replaces faulty components, using handtools. Locates and replaces faulty printed circuit boards in robot controller, applying knowledge of circuit board function, using computer display screen on robot controller and following schematic diagram. May train customer's staff in operation of robot and related equipment. May install electric or pneumatic end-of-arm tools on robot. May repair faulty printed circuit boards. ● **GED:** R4, M4, L4 ● **SVP:** 2-4 yrs ● **Academic:** Ed=A, Eng=G ● **Work Field:** 111, 121 ● **MPSMS:** 560, 580 ● **Aptitudes:** G2, V2, N2, S2, P2, Q2, K3, F3, M2, E5, C4 ● **Temperaments:** J, P, T ● **Physical:** Stg=H; Freq: R, H, I, G, N, D, A, X, V Occas: C, B, S, K, O, E, T, M, F ● **Work Env:** Noise=L; Occas: H, M, E ● **Salary:** 3 ● **Outlook:** 2

FUEL-INJECTION SERVICER (any industry) ● DOT #625.281-022 ● OES: 85302 ● Rebuilds, tests, and calibrates fuel injection units as used on diesel engines, railroad locomotives, trucks, construction equipment, tractors, and power plants: Studies repair order and disassembles unit to determine cause of malfunction. Refinishes defective parts, using lapping machine to grind and smooth nozzle point and seat. Replaces parts which cannot be refinished. Assembles and calibrates injection pumps, using test equipment. Assembles and tests nozzle assemblies, using test equipment. ● **GED:** R4, M4, L4 ● **SVP:** 1-2 yrs ● **Academic:** Ed=N, Eng=S ● **Work Field:** 121 ● **MPSMS:** 567 ● **Aptitudes:** G3, V4, N4, S3, P3, Q4, K4, F3, M3, E5, C5 ● **Temperaments:** J ● **Physical:** Stg=M; Freq: R, H, I, N Occas: S, T, G, A ● **Work Env:** Noise=L; ● **Salary:** 3 ● **Outlook:** 3

FURNACE INSTALLER-AND-REPAIRER, HOT AIR (any industry) ● DOT #869.281-010 ● OES: 85902 ● Alternate titles: FURNACE WORKER; HEATING WORKER. Installs and repairs hot-air furnaces, stoves, and similar equipment in accordance with diagrams and other specifications, using handtools and pipe-threading tools: Constructs foundation of concrete or other noncombustible material. Assembles and positions heating units in accordance with diagrams, using handtools. Cuts holes in floors and walls to form air duct outlets. Installs air ducts, smoke pipes, blowers, and stokers, following blueprints of building and using handtools. Installs fuel pipes, using dies, pipe cutters, and pipe wrenches. Wraps insulating asbestos around air ducts. Connects and adjusts timers and thermostats. Inspects inoperative heating units to locate causes of trouble. Disassembles heating unit and replaces or repairs defective parts, using handtools. Cuts, bends, and crimps sheet metal to repair furnace and stove casing and pipes, using crimpers, files, snips, handbrakes, and sheet metal hammers. Reassembles and starts heating unit to test operation. ● **GED:** R3, M3, L3 ● **SVP:** 2-4 yrs ● **Academic:** Ed=H, Eng=S ● **Work Field:** 102 ● **MPSMS:** 553 ● **Aptitudes:** G3, V3, N3, S3, P3, Q4, K3, F3, M3, E4, C4 ● **Temperaments:** J, T, V ● **Physical:** Stg=M; Freq: S, K, O, R, H, I, N, D Occas: A, X ● **Work Env:** Noise=N; ● **Salary:** 3 ● **Outlook:** 3

GAS-ENGINE REPAIRER (any industry) ● DOT #625.281-026 ● OES: 85328 ● Repairs and maintains gas-driven, internal-combustion engines that power electric generators, compressors, and similar equipment, using handtools and precision-measuring devices: Reads operating reports and diagnoses causes of trouble. Disassembles engines and adjusts or replaces parts, using handtools. Verifies clearances and ad-

justments, using precision-measuring devices. Reassembles engines and listens to engines in action to detect operational difficulties. May repair air or gas compressors. ● **GED:** R3, M3, L3 ● **SVP:** 1-2 yrs ● **Academic:** Ed=N, Eng=S ● **Work Field:** 121 ● **MPSMS:** 561 ● **Aptitudes:** G3, V3, N3, S3, P3, Q4, K3, F3, M2, E5, C5 ● **Temperaments:** J, T ● **Physical:** Stg=M; Freq: R, H, I, N Occas: D, A ● **Work Env:** Noise=L; ● **Salary:** 3 ● **Outlook:** 3

GAS-WELDING-EQUIPMENT MECHANIC (any industry) ● DOT #626.381-014 ● OES: 85109 ● Alternate titles: APPARATUS-REPAIR MECHANIC. Repairs acetylene gas welding equipment, using handtools and metalworking machines: Disassembles parts, such as worn hose, torch tips, torch valves, pressure gauges and regulators. Examines parts and repairs usable ones, using hand files and metalworking machines, such as lathes, drill presses, and grinding wheels. Replaces defective parts with new or rebuilt ones, using handtools. ● **GED:** R3, M3, L3 ● **SVP:** 2-4 yrs ● **Academic:** Ed=N, Eng=S ● **Work Field:** 121 ● **MPSMS:** 566 ● **Aptitudes:** G3, V3, N3, S3, P3, Q4, K4, F3, M2, E5, C5 ● **Temperaments:** J, T, V ● **Physical:** Stg=L; Freq: R, H, I, N, D, A ● **Work Env:** Noise=L; ● **Salary:** 3 ● **Outlook:** 3

HEATING-AND-AIR-CONDITIONING INSTALLER-SERVICER (construction) ● DOT #637.261-014 ● OES: 85902 ● Alternate titles: AIR-CONDITIONING MECHANIC; ENVIRONMENTAL-CONTROL-SYSTEM INSTALLER-SERVICER; HEATING-AND-AIR-CONDITIONING MECHANIC; HEATING MECHANIC. Installs, services, and repairs environmental control systems in residences, department stores, office buildings, and commercial establishments, utilizing knowledge of refrigeration theory, pipefitting, and structural layout: Mounts compressor and condenser units on platform or floor, using handtools, following blueprints or engineering specifications. Fabricates, assembles, and installs ductwork and chassis parts, using portable metalworking tools and welding equipment [DUCT INSTALLER (construction; mfd. bldgs.) 869.664-014]. Installs evaporator unit in chassis or in air duct system, using handtools. Cuts and bends tubing to correct length and shape, using cutting and bending equipment and tools. Cuts and threads pipe, using machine-threading or hand-threading equipment. Joins tubing or pipe to various refrigerating units by means of sleeves, couplings, or unions, and solders joints, using torch, forming complete circuit for refrigerant [PIPE FITTER (construction) 862.281-018]. Installs expansion and discharge valves in circuit. Connects motors, compressors, temperature controls, humidity controls, and circulating-ventilation fans to control panels and connects control panels to power source [ELECTRICIAN (construction) 824.261-010]. Installs air and water filters in completed installation. Injects small amount of refrigerant into compressor to test systems, and adds freon gas to build up prescribed operating pressure. Observes pressure and vacuum gauges and adjusts controls to ensure efficient operation. Tests joints and connections for gas leaks, using gauges or soap-and-water solution. Wraps pipes in insulation batting and secures them in place with cement or wire bands. Replaces defective breaker controls, thermostats, switches, fuses, and electrical wiring to repair installed units, using electrician's handtools and test equipment. May install, repair, and service air-conditioners, ranging from fifteen to twenty tons cooling capacity, in warehouses and factory buildings and be designated Air-Conditioning Mechanic, Industrial (any industry). ● **GED:** R4, M3, L3 ● **SVP:** 2-4 yrs ● **Academic:** Ed=H, Eng=S ● **Work Field:** 111, 121 ● **MPSMS:** 573 ● **Aptitudes:** G3, V3, N3, S2, P3, Q4, K3, F3, M3, E4, C5 ● **Temperaments:** J, T, V ● **Physical:** Stg=M; Freq: D, A Occas: C, S, K, O, R, H, I, T, G, N ● **Work Env:** Noise=L; Occas: W, A ● **Salary:** 4 ● **Outlook:** 3

HYDRAULIC REPAIRER (any industry) ● DOT #638.281-034 ● OES: 85109 ● Maintains and repairs hydraulic systems of machinery and equipment, such as robots, applying knowledge of hydraulics and mechanics and using handtools: Observes and listens to operating machinery to detect malfunctions. Visually inspects hydraulic lines and components to detect leaks, damage, and wear. Reads pressure gauges to detect abnormal oil pressure and smells to detect overheated oil. Depresses buttons and switches to turn off machinery. Turns valve to release pressure from hydraulic system and disconnects hydraulic supply and return lines, using handtools. Removes and replaces defective accumulator, using handtools. Connects charging assembly to accumulator and fills accumulator bladder with nitrogen gas to recharge accumulator, following manufacturer's specifications. Replaces worn or damaged hydraulic components, such as oil lines, fittings, cylinders, servo-valves, pressure release valves, gaskets, and seals, using handtools. Disassembles hydraulic system and removes and replaces defective actuator, pump bearings, and pump motor, using handtools and hoist. Observes operation of machinery and equipment to verify repair. Performs routine maintenance, such as changing filters, following schedule, using handtools. May observe readout on display screen of robot controller to determine nature of system malfunction. May disassemble defective hydraulic components, such as pumps and accumulator, at workbench and rebuilds or repairs components. May install hydraulic oil lines on new machinery and equipment. ● **GED:** R3, M3, L3 ● **SVP:** 2-4 yrs ● **Academic:** Ed=H, Eng=S ● **Work Field:** 121 ● **MPSMS:** 560, 582 ● **Aptitudes:** G3, V3, N3, S4, P4, Q4, K3, F3, M3, E5, C5 ● **Temperaments:** J, T ● **Physical:** Stg=H; Freq: R, H, I, D Occas: C, B, S, K, O, G, N, A ● **Work Env:** Noise=L; Occas: M, E ● **Salary:** 3 ● **Outlook:** 4

LOCKSMITH (any industry) ● DOT #709.281-010 ● OES: 85923 ● Alternate titles: LOCK EXPERT. Installs, repairs, rebuilds, and services mechanical or electrical locking devices, using handtools and special equipment: Disassembles locks, such as padlocks, safe locks, and door locks, and repairs or replaces worn tumblers, springs, and other parts. Inserts new or repaired tumblers into lock to change combination. Cuts new or duplicate keys, using keycutting machine. Moves lockpick in cylinder to open door locks without keys. Opens safe locks by drilling. May keep records of company locks and keys. ● **GED:** R4, M3, L3 ● **SVP:** 1-2 yrs ● **Academic:** Ed=A, Eng=S ● **Work Field:** 121 ● **MPSMS:** 552 ● **Aptitudes:** G3, V3, N3, S3, P2, Q4, K3, F3, M2, E5, C5 ● **Temperaments:** J, T ● **Physical:** Stg=L; Freq: R, H, I, N, D Occas: K, O, G ● **Work Env:** Noise=N; ● **Salary:** 4 ● **Outlook:** 3

MACHINE BUILDER (machinery mfg.) ● DOT #600.281-022 ● OES: 93105 ● Alternate titles: ASSEMBLER, SPECIAL MACHINE; BENCH HAND; FITTER; MACHINIST, BENCH; VISE HAND. Fits and assembles components according to assembly blueprints, manuals, engineering memos, sketches, and knowledge of machine construction to construct, rebuild, and repair machines and equipment, using handtools and power tools: Analyzes assembly blueprint and specifications manual, and plans machine building operations. Verifies conformance of parts to stock list and blueprints, using measuring instruments, such as calipers, gauges, and micrometers. Lays out hole locations and drills and taps holes on parts for assembly. Aligns components for assembly, manually or with hoist, and bolts, screws, dowels, welds, or rivets parts together, using handtools, rivet gun, and welding equipment, or arranges for assembly by welder and electrician. Brushes blue pigment on parts and mates them to detect high spots on surfaces. Removes high spots, and smooths surfaces, using chisels, scrapers, files, and powered hand grinder [SCRAPER, HAND (machine shop)]. Verifies alignment and tolerances of moving parts, using measuring instruments, such as dial indicators and thickness gauges. Tests operation of assembly by hand. Assembles, sets up, and operates machine to verify functioning, machine capabilities, and conformance to customer's specifications. May form and fasten piping, fixtures, and attachments required to service machine with air, water, and oil. May install wiring and electrical components to specifications. May work as member of team on limited part of fabrication process. May set up and operate metalworking machines to shape parts [TOOL-MACHINE SET-UP OPERATOR (machine shop)]. May be designated according to type of machine or machine component as Fixture Builder (machinery mfg.). ● **GED:** R4, M4, L3 ● **SVP:** 2-4 yrs ● **Academic:** Ed=H, Eng=S ● **Work Field:** 121 ● **MPSMS:** 566 ● **Aptitudes:** G3, V3, N3, S2, P3, Q4, K3, F3, M3, E5, C5 ● **Temperaments:** J, T, V ● **Physical:** Stg=M; Freq: R, H, I, N Occas: S, K, O, D, A ● **Work Env:** Noise=L; ● **Salary:** 3 ● **Outlook:** 3

MACHINERY ERECTOR (engine-turbine) ● DOT #638.261-014 ● OES: 85123 ● Alternate titles: ERECTOR; HEAVY-MACHINERY ASSEMBLER. Erects and tests machinery and heavy equipment, such as hydraulic turbines, turbine wheels, jaw stone crushers, industrial surface condensers, flaking machines, valves, and mine hoists, according to blueprints and specifications, using handtools, heating equipment, and measuring instruments: Positions steel beams to support bedplates of machines and equipment. Levels bedplate and establishes centerline, using straightedge, levels, and transit. Signals OVERHEAD CRANE OPERATOR (any industry) 921.663-010 to lower basic assembly unit, such as shaft, shaft casing, frame, or housing unit, to bedplate and aligns unit to centerline. Lays out mounting holes, using

measuring instruments and drills holes with power drill. Bolts parts, such as side and deck plates, jaw plates, and journals, to basic assembly unit. Attaches moving parts and subassemblies, such as shafts, rollers, flywheels, runners (water wheels), valves, gates, bearings, and bearing supports, to basic assembly unit, using handtools and power tools. Shrink-fits bushings, sleeves, rings, liners, gears, and wheels to specified items, using portable gas heating equipment. Inserts shims, adjusts tension on nuts and bolts, or positions parts, using handtools and measuring instruments to set specified clearances between moving and stationary parts. Connects power unit to machines, or steam piping to equipment, and tests unit to evaluate its mechanical operation. Replaces defective parts of machine or adjusts clearances and alignment of moving parts. Dismantles machinery and equipment for shipment to installation site. ● **GED:** R4, M4, L4 ● **SVP:** 4-10 yrs ● **Academic:** Ed=N, Eng=S ● **Work Field:** 121 ● **MPSMS:** 561, 564 ● **Aptitudes:** G3, V3, N3, S2, P3, Q4, K3, F3, M2, E4, C5 ● **Temperaments:** D, J, T, V ● **Physical:** Stg=H; Const: R, H, I Freq: S, K, O Occas: C, B, T, G, N, D, A ● **Work Env:** Noise=L; Occas: M ● **Salary:** 3 ● **Outlook:** 3

MACHINE REPAIRER, MAINTENANCE (any industry) ● DOT #638.261-030 ● OES: 85109 ● Repairs and maintains mechanical and hydraulic components of production machines and equipment, such as metal fabricating machine tools, material handling system, and automated lubrication system, following blueprints and specifications and using handtools, power tools, and precision measuring instruments: Visually inspects and listens to machines and equipment to locate causes of malfunctions. Dismantles machines and equipment to gain access to problem area, using handtools and power tools. Inspects and measures parts to detect wear, misalignment, or other problems. Removes and replaces worn or defective parts of drive mechanism or hydraulic system, using handtools and power tools, and following blueprints, diagrams, and service manuals. Realigns and adjusts components, such as spindles and clutches, using handtools and following diagrams. Locates damaged air and hydraulic pipes on machine, and measures, cuts, threads, and installs new pipe. Starts machines and equipment to test operation following repair. Repairs broken parts, using brazing, soldering, and welding equipment and handtools. May modify computer-controlled motion of robot, applying knowledge of program commands and using robot controller and teach pendant. May set up and operate metalworking tools, such as lathe, drill press, or grinder, to make or repair parts. May assist MECHANICAL ENGINEER (profess. & kin.) 007.061-014 to modify sketches or computer-generated designs of machine components, such as hydraulic system and drive mechanism, applying knowledge of shop mathematics, hydraulics, and mechanics, and using computer keyboard and software programs. May work as part of team including such workers as ELECTRICIAN, MAINTENANCE (any industry) 829.261-018; MILLWRIGHT (any industry) 638.281-018; PIPE FITTER (construction) 862.281-022; TOOL MAKER (machine shop) 601.280-042. May be designated according to type of machine repaired as Broaching-Machine Repairer (machine tools); Centerless-Grinding-Machine Adjuster (ordnance); Screw-Machine Adjuster, Automatic (ordnance); Screw-Machine Repairer (machine shop). ● **GED:** R4, M4, L4 ● **SVP:** 2-4 yrs ● **Academic:** Ed=H, Eng=S ● **Work Field:** 121 ● **MPSMS:** 560, 580 ● **Aptitudes:** G2, V3, N2, S2, P2, Q4, K3, F3, M2, E5, C4 ● **Temperaments:** J, T ● **Physical:** Stg=H; Freq: S, K, O, R, H, I, N, A Occas: C, T, G, D, X ● **Work Env:** Noise=L; Occas: M ● **Salary:** 4 ● **Outlook:** 3

MAINTENANCE MECHANIC (any industry) ● DOT #638.281-014 ● OES: 85109 ● Alternate titles: FIXER; MACHINE-MAINTENANCE SERVICER; MACHINE OVERHAULER; MACHINE REPAIRER; MECHANICAL ADJUSTER; REPAIR MECHANIC; TOOL-AND-MACHINE MAINTAINER. Repairs and maintains, in accordance with diagrams, sketches, operation manuals, and manufacturer's specifications, machinery and mechanical equipment, such as engines, motors, pneumatic tools, conveyor systems, and production machines and equipment, using handtools, power tools, and precision-measuring and testing instruments: Observes mechanical devices in operation and listens to their sounds to locate causes of trouble. Dismantles devices to gain access to and remove defective parts, using hoists, cranes, handtools, and power tools. Examines form and texture of parts to detect imperfections. Inspects used parts to determine changes in dimensional requirements, using rules, calipers, micrometers, and other measuring instruments. Adjusts functional parts of devices and control instruments, using handtools, levels, plumb bobs, and straightedges. Repairs or replaces defective parts, using handtools and power tools. Installs special functional and structural parts in devices, using handtools. Starts devices to test their performance. Lubricates and cleans parts. May set up and operate lathe, drill press, grinder, and other metalworking tools to make and repair parts. May initiate purchase order for parts and machines. May repair electrical equipment. May be designated according to machine repaired as Carton-Forming-Machine Adjuster (any industry); Machine Adjuster (tobacco); Maintenance Mechanic, Record Processing Equipment (recording). ● **GED:** R4, M4, L3 ● **SVP:** 2-4 yrs ● **Academic:** Ed=H, Eng=S ● **Work Field:** 121 ● **MPSMS:** 567, 560 ● **Aptitudes:** G3, V3, N3, S2, P2, Q4, K2, F3, M2, E4, C4 ● **Temperaments:** J, T, V ● **Physical:** Stg=H; Freq: R, H, N, D Occas: C, B, S, K, O, W, I, E, T, G, X ● **Work Env:** Noise=L; Freq: U, A Occas: W, M, T ● **Salary:** 3 ● **Outlook:** 4

MAINTENANCE MECHANIC (construction) ● DOT #620.281-046 ● OES: 85311 ● Alternate titles: SERVICE ENGINEER; SHOP MECHANIC. Inspects, repairs, and maintains functional parts of automotive and mechanical equipment and machinery, such as pumps, compressors, pipe-laying machines, ditchdiggers, trucks, and tractors used in petroleum exploration, on oil fields, in pipeline construction, and in airfield maintenance and pipeline operations, using hoists, handtools, gauges, drills, grinding wheels, and testing devices: Inspects defective equipment and diagnoses malfunctions, using motor analyzers, pressure gauges, chassis charts, and factory manuals. Disassembles and overhauls internal combustion engines, pumps, pump power units, generators, transmissions, clutches, and rear ends, using handtools and hoist. Grinds and reseats valves, using valve-grinding machine. Adjusts brakes, aligns wheels, tightens bolts and screws, and reassembles equipment. Operates equipment to test its functioning. Changes oil, checks batteries, repairs tires and tubes, and lubricates equipment and machinery. ● **GED:** R4, M3, L3 ● **SVP:** 2-4 yrs ● **Academic:** Ed=H, Eng=N ● **Work Field:** 121, 102 ● **MPSMS:** 568, 591, 564 ● **Aptitudes:** G3, V3, N3, S3, P3, Q4, K3, F3, M2, E4, C4 ● **Temperaments:** J, T ● **Physical:** Stg=M; Freq: R, H, I, N Occas: S, K, O, E, D, A ● **Work Env:** Noise=L; ● **Salary:** 3 ● **Outlook:** 4

MAINTENANCE REPAIRER, INDUSTRIAL (any industry) ● DOT #899.261-014 ● OES: 85132 ● Alternate titles: MAINTENANCE ASSOCIATE; PLANT-MAINTENANCE WORKER; UTILITY REPAIRER. Installs, maintains, and repairs machinery, equipment, physical structures, and pipe and electrical systems in commercial or industrial establishments, following specifications, blueprints, manuals, and schematic drawings, using handtools, power tools, hoist, crane, and measuring and testing instruments: Visually inspects and tests machinery and equipment, using electrical and electronic test equipment. Listens for unusual sounds from machines or equipment to detect malfunction and discusses machine operation variations with supervisors or other maintenance workers to diagnose problem or repair machine. Dismantles defective machines and equipment and installs new or repaired parts, following specifications and blueprints, using precision measuring instruments and handtools [MACHINE REPAIRER, MAINTENANCE (any industry) 638.261-030]. Cleans and lubricates shafts, bearings, gears, and other parts of machinery, using rags, brushes, and grease gun. Installs and repairs electrical apparatus, such as transformers and wiring, and electrical and electronic components of machinery and equipment [ELECTRICIAN, MAINTENANCE (any industry) 829.261-018]. Lays out, assembles, installs, and maintains pipe systems and related hydraulic and pneumatic equipment, and repairs and replaces gauges, valves, pressure regulators, and related equipment [PIPE FITTER (construction) 862.281-022]. Repairs and maintains physical structure of establishment [MAINTENANCE REPAIRER, BUILDING (any industry) 899.381-010]. May install machinery and equipment according to blueprints and other specifications [MILLWRIGHT (any industry) 638.281-018]. May install, program, or repair automated machinery and equipment, such as robots or programmable controllers. May set up and operate machine tools, such as lathe, grinder, drill, and milling machine to repair or fabricate machine parts, jigs and fixtures, and tools. May operate cutting torch or welding equipment to cut or join metal parts. May fabricate and repair counters, benches, partitions, and other wooden structures. ● **GED:** R4, M4, L3 ● **SVP:** 4-10 yrs ● **Academic:** Ed=N, Eng=S ● **Work Field:** 102, 111, 121 ● **MPSMS:** 560, 580, 590 ● **Aptitudes:** G3, V3, N3, S2, P2, Q4, K3, F3, M2, E4, C4 ● **Temperaments:** J, T, V ● **Physical:** Stg=H; Freq: R, H, I, N, D Occas: C, B, S, K, O, W, E, T, G, A, X ● **Work Env:** Noise=L; Occas: M, E, D ● **Salary:** 3 ● **Outlook:** 4

MANAGER, MARINE SERVICE (ship-boat mfg.) ● DOT #187.167-130 ● OES: 81000 ● Directs activities of boat-repair service, according to knowledge of maintenance needs of small craft and marine safety requirements: Confers with owner or crew of vessel to obtain maintenance history and details concerning condition of craft. Observes and listens to vessel in operation to detect unsafe or malfunctioning equipment and leaks or other flaws in hull and superstructure. Performs tests on vessel and equipment, using gauges and other standard testing devices. Estimates cost of repairs according to familiarity with labor and materials requirements or fee schedule. Directs and coordinates activities of workers engaged in repairing, painting, and otherwise restoring vessels to seaworthy condition. May repair vessels, assisted by other workers. ● **GED:** R4, M3, L3 ● **SVP:** 4-10 yrs ● **Academic:** Ed=H, Eng=S ● **Work Field:** 102, 121 ● **MPSMS:** 593 ● **Aptitudes:** G2, V3, N3, S2, P2, Q4, K4, F4, M3, E4, C4 ● **Temperaments:** D, J, P, V ● **Physical:** Stg=L; Freq: R, H, I, T, G, N Occas: C, B, S, K, O, W, E, F, D, A, X, V ● **Work Env:** Noise=L; Freq: W Occas: U ● **Salary:** 5 ● **Outlook:** 2

MECHANIC, INDUSTRIAL TRUCK (any industry) ● DOT #620.281-050 ● OES: 85311 ● Alternate titles: TRUCK REPAIRER. Repairs and maintains electric, diesel, and gasoline industrial trucks, following manuals, and using handtools, power tools, and knowledge of electrical, power transmission, brake, and other automotive systems: Reads job order and observes and listens to truck in operation to determine malfunction and to plan work procedures. Installs new ignition systems, aligns front wheels, changes or recharges batteries, and replaces transmissions and other parts, using handtools. Overhauls gas or diesel engines, using mechanic's handtools, welding equipment, standard charts, and hoists. Examines protective guards, loose bolts, and specified safety devices on trucks, and makes adjustments, using handtools. Lubricates moving parts and drives repaired truck to verify conformance to specifications. May fabricate special lifting or towing attachments, hydraulic systems, shields, or other devices according to blueprints or schematic drawings. ● **GED:** R4, M3, L3 ● **SVP:** 2-4 yrs ● **Academic:** Ed=N, Eng=S ● **Work Field:** 121 ● **MPSMS:** 565 ● **Aptitudes:** G3, V3, N3, S3, P3, Q4, K3, F3, M2, E4, C4 ● **Temperaments:** J, T, V ● **Physical:** Stg=M; Freq: R, H, I, N, D Occas: S, K, O, G, A, X ● **Work Env:** Noise=L; Freq: A, M, T, O Occas: W ● **Salary:** 4 ● **Outlook:** 4

MOTORBOAT MECHANIC (engine-turbine) ● DOT #623.281-038 ● OES: 85328 ● Alternate titles: BOAT MECHANIC. Repairs and adjusts electrical and mechanical equipment of gasoline- or diesel-powered inboard or inboard-outboard boat engines, using handtools, power tools, and electrical testing meters: Starts motor and listens to its sound to determine causes of trouble. Tests motor for conformance to manufacturer's specifications, using electrical testing meters. Dismantles motors, using handtools, and examines parts for defects. Adjusts generator and replaces faulty wiring, using handtools and soldering iron. Installs piston rings, adjusts carburetor, grinds valves, and repairs or replaces reduction gears, and other parts, using lathe, drill press, handtools, and power tools. Examines propeller and propeller shafts and repairs defective parts. Aligns engine to propeller shaft. May operate boat on water to test repairs. May repair only mechanical equipment of engines, such as power-tilt, bilge pumps, or power take-offs. May be designated according to type of engine repaired as Motorboat Mechanic, Inboard (ship-boat mfg.); Motorboat Mechanic, Inboard/Outboard (ship-boat mfg.). ● **GED:** R4, M3, L3 ● **SVP:** 2-4 yrs ● **Academic:** Ed=N, Eng=N ● **Work Field:** 111, 121 ● **MPSMS:** 593 ● **Aptitudes:** G3, V3, N3, S2, P3, Q4, K3, F3, M2, E5, C5 ● **Temperaments:** J, T, V ● **Physical:** Stg=M; Freq: S, O, R, H, I, N, A Occas: C, B ● **Work Env:** Noise=L; Occas: W ● **Salary:** 3 ● **Outlook:** 3

MOTORCYCLE REPAIRER (automotive ser.) ● DOT #620.281-054 ● OES: 85308 ● Alternate titles: MOTORCYCLE MECHANIC. Repairs and overhauls motorcycles, motor scooters, and similar motor vehicles: Listens to engine, examines vehicle's frame, and confers with customer to determine nature and extent of malfunction or damage. Connects test panel to engine and measures generator output, ignition timing, and other engine performance indicators. Dismantles engine and repairs or replaces defective parts, such as magneto, carburetor, and generator. Removes cylinder heads, grinds valves, and scrapes off carbon, and replaces defective valves, pistons, cylinders, and rings, using handtools and power tools. Hammers out dents and bends in frame, welds tears and breaks, and reassembles and reinstalls engine. Repairs and adjusts clutch, brakes, and drive chain. Repairs or replaces other motorcycle and motor scooter parts, such as spring fork, headlight, horn, handlebar controls, valve release, gear lever, gasoline and oil tanks, starter, brake lever, and muffler. May specialize in repair of motor scooters and be designated Motor-Scooter Repairer (automotive ser.). ● **GED:** R3, M3, L3 ● **SVP:** 1-2 yrs ● **Academic:** Ed=N, Eng=S ● **Work Field:** 121 ● **MPSMS:** 595 ● **Aptitudes:** G3, V3, N4, S3, P2, Q4, K3, F3, M2, E4, C4 ● **Temperaments:** J, T, V ● **Physical:** Stg=H; Freq: R, H, G, N Occas: S, O, I, D, A, X ● **Work Env:** Noise=L; ● **Salary:** 2 ● **Outlook:** 4

OFFICE-MACHINE SERVICER (any industry) ● DOT #633.281-018 ● OES: 85926 ● Alternate titles: BUSINESS-MACHINE MECHANIC; OFFICE-EQUIPMENT MECHANIC; OFFICE-MACHINE INSPECTOR. Repairs and services office machines, such as adding, accounting, and calculating machines, and typewriters, using handtools, power tools, micrometers, and welding equipment: Operates machines to test moving parts and to listen to sounds of machines to locate causes of trouble. Disassembles machine and examines parts, such as gears, guides, rollers, and pinions for wear and defects, using micrometers. Repairs, adjusts, or replaces parts, using handtools, power tools, and soldering and welding equipment. Cleans and oils moving parts. May give instructions in operation and care of machines to machine operators. May assemble new machines. May be designated according to machine repaired or serviced as Accounting-Machine Servicer (any industry); Adding-Machine Servicer (any industry); Calculating-Machine Servicer (any industry); Duplicating-Machine Servicer (any industry); Typewriter Servicer (any industry). ● **GED:** R4, M3, L3 ● **SVP:** 2-4 yrs ● **Academic:** Ed=H, Eng=S ● **Work Field:** 121, 111 ● **MPSMS:** 571 ● **Aptitudes:** G3, V3, N3, S2, P3, Q4, K3, F3, M2, E5, C5 ● **Temperaments:** J, T ● **Physical:** Stg=L; Freq: R, H, I, G, N Occas: D, A ● **Work Env:** Noise=N; ● **Salary:** 2 ● **Outlook:** 4

PARTS SALVAGER (any industry) ● DOT #638.281-026 ● OES: 85998 ● Repairs salvable mechanical parts of machines and equipment: Dismantles machinery, equipment, and parts, using handtools, such as hacksaws, files, reamers, wrenches and screwdrivers. Inspects parts to determine salvageability or method of repairing or reworking parts. Sets up and operates metalworking tools, such as engine lathes, milling, drilling, grinding, polishing, and buffing machines to repair parts. Files, taps, reams, bends, and straightens, or uses other methods to recondition parts, using handtools. Verifies dimensions and tolerances, using blueprints, scale, and precision-measuring instruments. May reassemble parts, using handtools and power tools. May direct cleaning, storing, and issuing of reclaimed parts, and packing of usable materials, such as metal sweepings. May arrange for sale of scrap. ● **GED:** R4, M3, L3 ● **SVP:** 2-4 yrs ● **Academic:** Ed=N, Eng=S ● **Work Field:** 121 ● **MPSMS:** 567 ● **Aptitudes:** G3, V3, N3, S3, P3, Q4, K3, F3, M2, E5, C5 ● **Temperaments:** J, T, V ● **Physical:** Stg=M; Freq: R, H, I, N, D, A ● **Work Env:** Noise=L; ● **Salary:** 1 ● **Outlook:** 3

PNEUMATIC-TOOL REPAIRER (any industry) ● DOT #630.281-010 ● OES: 85109 ● Alternate titles: AIR-MOTOR REPAIRER; DRILL DOCTOR. Repairs pneumatic tools and air motors, such as pneumatic hammers, chisels, and reamers, using mechanic's tools: Starts motor or tool and listens to sound to locate cause of trouble. Disassembles motor and repairs or replaces defective gears, pistons, connecting rods, and other parts, using taps, files, reamers, wrenches, and other handtools. ● **GED:** R4, M3, L3 ● **SVP:** 2-4 yrs ● **Academic:** Ed=N, Eng=S ● **Work Field:** 121 ● **MPSMS:** 566 ● **Aptitudes:** G3, V3, N3, S3, P3, Q4, K3, F3, M2, E4, C5 ● **Temperaments:** J, T ● **Physical:** Stg=M; Freq: S, K, R, H, I, E, N, D ● **Work Env:** Noise=L; Occas: A ● **Salary:** 2 ● **Outlook:** 3

POWERHOUSE MECHANIC (utilities) ● DOT #631.261-014 ● OES: 85109 ● Alternate titles: STATION MECHANIC. Installs, adjusts, maintains, and repairs electrical and mechanical equipment and parts in power-generating station: Installs equipment. Dismantles and overhauls equipment [MILLWRIGHT (any industry) 638.281-018; BOILERMAKER (struct. metal) I 805.261-014]. Dismantles and repairs auxiliary equipment, such as pumps, compressors, and pipe systems [MAINTENANCE REPAIRER, INDUSTRIAL (any industry) 899.261-014]. Assists in conducting acceptance and performance tests on new or existing equipment. Fabricates special tools, rigging equipment, and replacement parts for equipment. May install wiring between machinery, switchboards, and control panels [ELECTRICIAN, MAIN-

TENANCE (any industry) 829.261-018]. May be designated according to type of plant in which maintenance is performed as Diesel-Powerplant Mechanic (utilities); Gas-Turbine-Powerplant Mechanic (utilities); Geothermal-Powerplant Mechanic (utilities); Nuclear-Powerplant Mechanic (utilities); Steam-Generating-Powerplant Mechanic (utilities). ● **GED:** R4, M3, L3 ● **SVP:** 4-10 yrs ● **Academic:** Ed=H, Eng=S ● **Work Field:** 121, 111 ● **MPSMS:** 560 ● **Aptitudes:** G2, V3, N3, S2, P2, Q3, K3, F3, M3, E3, C4 ● **Temperaments:** J, T, V ● **Physical:** Stg=H; Freq: S, R, H, I, T, G, N, D, A Occas: C, B, K, O, W, X ● **Work Env:** Noise=L; Freq: A, M, E, D Occas: W, V ● **Salary:** 4 ● **Outlook:** 2

PUMP SERVICER (any industry) ● DOT #630.281-018 ● OES: 85109 ● Alternate titles: PUMP REPAIRER. Repairs pumps and pump power units, such as centrifugal and plunger-type pumps, and diesel-engine, gasoline-engine, and electric-motor power units, using hoists and handtools: Diagnoses trouble in pumps. Dismantles pumps and repairs or replaces defective parts, using handtools. Reseats and grinds valves. Tests performances of repaired pumps. May wire motor to switchboard and install fuse box. May be designated according to type of pump repaired as Water-Pump Servicer (any industry). ● **GED:** R3, M3, L3 ● **SVP:** 2-4 yrs ● **Academic:** Ed=N, Eng=S ● **Work Field:** 121, 111 ● **MPSMS:** 568 ● **Aptitudes:** G3, V3, N3, S3, P3, Q4, K3, F3, M2, E5, C4 ● **Temperaments:** J, T ● **Physical:** Stg=M; Freq: R, H Occas: S, K, O, W, N, D, X ● **Work Env:** Noise=L; Freq: W Occas: A ● **Salary:** 2 ● **Outlook:** 2

REFRIGERATION MECHANIC (any industry) ● DOT #637.261-026 ● OES: 85902 ● Installs and repairs industrial and commercial refrigerating systems according to blueprints and engineering specifications, using knowledge of refrigeration, structural layout, and function and design of components: Lays out reference points for installation of structural and functional components, using measuring instruments, such as tape, transit, plumb bob, levels, and square. Drills holes and installs mounting brackets and hangers into floor and walls of building. Lifts and aligns components into position, using hoist or block and tackle. Screws, bolts, rivets, welds, and brazes parts to assemble structural and functional components, such as motors, controls, switches, gauges, wiring harnesses, valves, pumps, compressors, condensors, cores, and pipes. Cuts, threads, and connects pipe to functional components and water or power system of premises [PIPE FITTER (construction) 862.281-018]. Pumps specified gas or fluid into system. Starts system, observes operation, reads gauges and instruments, and adjusts mechanisms, such as valves, controls, and pumps to control level of fluid, pressure, and temperature in system. Dismantles malfunctioning systems and tests components, using electrical, mechanical, and pneumatic testing equipment. Replaces or adjusts defective or worn parts to repair systems. May insulate shells and cabinets of systems. May install wiring to connect components to electric power source. May specialize in installing systems and be designated Refrigeration-System Installer (any industry). ● **GED:** R4, M3, L3 ● **SVP:** 4-10 yrs ● **Academic:** Ed=H, Eng=S ● **Work Field:** 102, 121 ● **MPSMS:** 573 ● **Aptitudes:** G3, V3, N3, S2, P3, Q4, K3, F3, M3, E4, C4 ● **Temperaments:** J, T ● **Physical:** Stg=H; Freq: R, H, N, A Occas: C, S, I, T, G, M, D, X, V ● **Work Env:** Noise=L; Freq: W, C, U, A, T ● **Salary:** 3 ● **Outlook:** 3

REFRIGERATION MECHANIC (svc. ind. mach.) ● DOT #827.361-014 ● OES: 85902 ● Fabricates and assembles components of refrigeration systems for environmental test equipment according to blueprints or schematic drawings and knowledge of refrigeration systems, using handtools, powered tools and welding equipment: Reads blueprints or schematic drawings to determine location, size, capacity, and type of components, such as compressor, condenser, expansion tank, valves, and tubing or piping needed to build refrigeration system. Mounts compressor, condenser, and other components in specified locations on frame, using handtools and arc or acetylene welding equipment. Cuts, bends, and brazes specified tubing to inlets and outlets of components to form liquid and suction lines of refrigeration system, using knowledge of metal properties. Installs expansion and control valves, using acetylene torch and wrenches. Adjusts valves according to specifications. Removes air from system and charges system with specified amount and type of refrigerant [GAS CHARGER (svc. ind. mach.)]. Tests lines, components, and connections for leaks with leak detector which indicates presence of refrigerant [GAS-LEAK TESTER (svc. ind. mach.)]. Attaches thermocouples to various points of refrigeration system and test-operates equipment to evaluate functioning and cooling capacity of system. Records pressure and temperature readings from gauges and temperature potentiometer during test run. Compares reading with specifications to evaluate performance of system, and adjusts or replaces parts as indicated. May fabricate and assemble structural portions of test equipment. May assemble and mount electrical wiring circuits, controls, and recording devices. May fabricate and assemble cascade and multiple stage refrigeration systems. ● **GED:** R4, M3, L3 ● **SVP:** 2-4 yrs ● **Academic:** Ed=A, Eng=S ● **Work Field:** 121, 111 ● **MPSMS:** 573 ● **Aptitudes:** G3, V3, N3, S3, P3, Q4, K3, F3, M3, E5, C5 ● **Temperaments:** J, T, V ● **Physical:** Stg=H; Freq: R, H, I, N, D Occas: C, B, S, K, O, T, G, A ● **Work Env:** Noise=N; ● **Salary:** 4 ● **Outlook:** 3

ROCKET-ENGINE-COMPONENT MECHANIC (aircraft mfg.) ● DOT #621.281-030 ● OES: 85998 ● Assembles, tests, and repairs pneumatic, hydraulic, and mechanical components of rocket motors or rocket engines, according to specifications, using handtools, power tools, and precision measuring and testing instruments: Positions parts in jigs and holding fixtures to facilitate assembly. Fits and assembles interrelating precision parts, using handtools. Inspects configuration and dimensions of assemblies, using instruments, such as optical flats, micrometers, calipers, dial indicators, and monolight instruments. Tests assemblies to determine conditions, such as internal leakage, pressure differentials, and cycles of operation, using gauges, meters, and chemicals. Conducts functional tests to determine mechanical performance. Analyzes malfunctions to determine causes, and repairs, adjusts, synchronizes, and calibrates assemblies. May perform welding and acid etching on various materials. May operate computer to record, analyze, and interpret test data. ● **GED:** R4, M4, L4 ● **SVP:** 2-4 yrs ● **Academic:** Ed=A, Eng=S ● **Work Field:** 121, 211 ● **MPSMS:** 592 ● **Aptitudes:** G3, V3, N3, S2, P2, Q4, K3, F3, M3, E5, C4 ● **Temperaments:** J, T ● **Physical:** Stg=M; Freq: R, H, N, D Occas: C, S, O, I, E, X ● **Work Env:** Noise=L; Occas: M, D, T ● **Salary:** 4 ● **Outlook:** 3

SMALL-ENGINE MECHANIC (any industry) ● DOT #625.281-034 ● OES: 85328 ● Repairs fractional-horsepower gasoline engines used to power lawnmowers, garden tractors, and similar machines, using handtools: Locates causes of trouble, dismantles engines, using handtools, and examines parts for defects. Replaces or repairs parts, such as rings and bearings, using handtools. Cleans and adjusts carburetor and magneto. Starts repaired engines and listens to sounds to test performance. Replaces engines on machine. May be designated according to type of engine repaired as Lawnmower Mechanic (any industry). ● **GED:** R3, M3, L3 ● **SVP:** 1-2 yrs ● **Academic:** Ed=N, Eng=S ● **Work Field:** 121 ● **MPSMS:** 561 ● **Aptitudes:** G3, V3, N4, S3, P3, Q4, K3, F4, M2, E5, C5 ● **Temperaments:** J, R, T ● **Physical:** Stg=M; Freq: R, H, G, N, D, A Occas: S, K, I, T ● **Work Env:** Noise=L; Occas: W ● **Salary:** 3 ● **Outlook:** 3

SOLAR-ENERGY-SYSTEM INSTALLER (any industry) ● DOT #637.261-030 ● OES: 85902 ● Installs and repairs solar-energy systems designed to collect, store, and circulate solar-heated water or other medium for residential, commercial, or industrial use: Locates and marks position of collectors, holding tank, and distribution system on structure, according to specifications and blueprints. Cuts holes in roof, walls, and ceiling to install equipment and plumbing, using power saws and drills. Installs supports and brackets to anchor solar collectors and holding tank, using carpenter's handtools. Cuts, threads, and fits plumbing according to specifications for connecting circulation system, using plumber's handtools. Lays out and connects electrical wiring between controls and pumps according to wiring diagram and knowledge of standard industry practice, using electrician's handtools. Tests electrical circuits and components for continuity, using electrical test equipment. Tests plumbing for leaks, using pressure gauge. Pushes control buttons to activate pumps and observes system to detect malfunctions. Repairs or replaces defective equipment. ● **GED:** R4, M4, L4 ● **SVP:** 2-4 yrs ● **Academic:** Ed=N, Eng=S ● **Work Field:** 102, 111 ● **MPSMS:** 364 ● **Aptitudes:** G3, V4, N3, S2, P2, Q3, K3, F3, M3, E4, C5 ● **Temperaments:** J, T ● **Physical:** Stg=H; Freq: K, R, H, I, N Occas: C, B, S, O, F, A, X ● **Work Env:** Noise=L; Freq: W Occas: M, E ● **Salary:** 3 ● **Outlook:** 3

TRACTOR MECHANIC (automotive ser.) ● DOT #620.281-058 ● OES: 85311 ● Diagnoses mechanical failures and repairs tractors and tractor components according to manuals, factory specifications, and knowledge of engine performances, using handtools, power tools, and testing instruments: Attaches compression, ignition, and timing test instruments to certain parts of tractor, using clamps and handtools. Starts engine dials and reads meters and gauges of testing equipment to diagnose engine malfunction. Removes and disassembles engine, transmission, and clutches, using hoists, jacks, and mechanic's handtools. Inspects parts for damage, and verifies dimensions and clearances of parts for conformance to factory specifications, using gauges, such as calipers, and micrometers. Replaces or repairs worn or damaged parts. Grinds valves, relines and adjusts brakes, tightens body bolts, aligns wheels, and tunes engine. May weld defective body or frame parts. ● **GED:** R4, M3, L3 ● **SVP:** 2-4 yrs ● **Academic:** Ed=H, Eng=S ● **Work Field:** 121 ● **MPSMS:** 565 ● **Aptitudes:** G3, V3, N3, S2, P3, Q4, K3, F3, M2, E4, C4 ● **Temperaments:** J, T, V ● **Physical:** Stg=M; Freq: S, K, O, W, R, H, I, G, N Occas: C, E, T, D, A, X ● **Work Env:** Noise=N; ● **Salary:** 4 ● **Outlook:** 3

TUNE-UP MECHANIC (automotive ser.) ● DOT #620.281-066 ● OES: 85302 ● Tunes automotive vehicle engines to ensure efficient operation: Removes spark plugs, using socket wrench, and tests them, using spark-plug tester. Cleans electrodes in sandblasting machine, sets spark gap with feeler gauge, and replaces or installs new plugs. Inspects distributor breaker points for wear and pits, using feeler gauge, and replaces or resets points. Observes ignition timing, using timing light, and adjusts timing, using handtools. Adjusts carburetor needle setting, using handtools, and verifies adjustment, using instruments, such as fuel analyzer, vacuum gauge, oscilloscope, and tachometer. Sets valve tappets, using feeler gauge or dial indicator. Replaces defective coils, condensers, and electrical connection. Removes and cleans carburetor and fuel pump. Examines battery and connections and electrical charging and starting circuit. Adjusts, and repairs fan belt, and fuel and water pumps. May tune engine while vehicle runs on rollers connected to dynamometer and be designated Dynamometer Tuner (automotive ser.). ● **GED:** R4, M3, L3 ● **SVP:** 2-4 yrs ● **Academic:** Ed=H, Eng=N ● **Work Field:** 121 ● **MPSMS:** 591 ● **Aptitudes:** G3, V3, N3, S2, P2, Q4, K3, F2, M3, E5, C4 ● **Temperaments:** J, T, V ● **Physical:** Stg=L; Freq: R, H, I, G, N Occas: S, O, T, D, A, X ● **Work Env:** Noise=L; ● **Salary:** 3 ● **Outlook:** 3

GOE: 05.05.10
Elect.-Electronic Equipment Repair

AUDIO-VIDEO REPAIRER (any industry) ● DOT #729.281-010 ● OES: 85708 ● Alternate titles: AUDIOVISUAL-AIDS TECHNICIAN. Installs and repairs audio-video equipment, such as tape recorders, public address systems, slide and motion picture projectors, and record players, using handtools, soldering iron, and special testing equipment. Inspects equipment for defects and repairs or replaces parts. Returns equipment to shop for more complicated repairs. ● **GED:** R4, M3, L3 ● **SVP:** 1-2 yrs ● **Academic:** Ed=H, Eng=S ● **Work Field:** 111 ● **MPSMS:** 585 ● **Aptitudes:** G3, V4, N4, S3, P3, Q4, K4, F3, M3, E5, C4 ● **Temperaments:** J, T ● **Physical:** Stg=L; Freq: R, H, I, N, D, A, X ● **Work Env:** Noise=N; ● **Salary:** 2 ● **Outlook:** 4

AVIONICS TECHNICIAN (aircraft mfg.) ● DOT #823.261-026 ● OES: 85717 ● Alternate titles: AVIONICS AND RADAR TECHNICIAN; AVIONICS MECHANIC; RADIO AND RADAR TECHNICIAN. Inspects, tests, adjusts, and repairs avionics equipment, such as radar, radio, pulse, navigation, auto pilot, and compass systems, installed in aircraft and space vehicles, using handtools and test equipment: Inspects components of avionics equipment for defects, such as loose connections and frayed wire, and for accuracy of assembly and installation. Tests avionics equipment under simulated or actual operating conditions to determine performance and airworthiness, using test equipment, such as oscilloscopes, digital meters and counters, and circuit analyzers. Adjusts, repairs, or replaces defective components based on analysis of test results, following blueprints, schematics, handbooks, and other technical documents, using handtools. Calibrates installed or repaired equipment to prescribed specifications. Adjusts frequencies of radio sets by signaling ground station and turning set-screws. Must possess Radiotelephone License issued by Federal Communications Commission. May accompany flight crew to perform in-flight adjustments and to determine and record required post-flight repair work. May sign overhaul documents for equipment replaced or repaired. May operate ground station for air-to-station check of radar or other equipment. ● **GED:** R4, M4, L4 ● **SVP:** 1-2 yrs ● **Academic:** Ed=A, Eng=S ● **Work Field:** 111, 211 ● **MPSMS:** 592, 596 ● **Aptitudes:** G2, V3, N3, S2, P2, Q4, K3, F3, M2, E4, C4 ● **Temperaments:** J, T, V ● **Physical:** Stg=L; Freq: R, H, I, N Occas: C, B, S, K, O, W, E, T, G, D, A, X ● **Work Env:** Noise=L; Occas: E, D, O ● **Salary:** 5 ● **Outlook:** 4

ELECTRIC-METER REPAIRER (utilities) ● DOT #729.281-014 ● OES: 85911 ● Alternate titles: METER REPAIRER. Inspects, adjusts, and repairs electric meters used for recording electric current consumption: Disassembles defective meters, using handtools. Examines parts of meter for wear and detects warped or bent parts, using straightedge. Soaks electric parts in chemical solutions to clean parts. Removes dirt from other parts, using brushes, sandpaper, and soap and water. Reassembles meter, using new or repaired parts. Turns setscrews or makes other adjustments required to bring meter accuracy within prescribed limits. May test meters for accuracy [ELECTRIC-METER TESTER (utilities)] or for correctness of assembly and dielectric strength, using testing apparatus. May repair demand register mechanism of demand meters. May repair such electric components as instrument transformers and relays. May install meters. ● **GED:** R4, M2, L3 ● **SVP:** 2-4 yrs ● **Academic:** Ed=N, Eng=S ● **Work Field:** 111 ● **MPSMS:** 581 ● **Aptitudes:** G3, V3, N3, S3, P2, Q4, K3, F2, M3, E5, C4 ● **Temperaments:** J, T ● **Physical:** Stg=L; Freq: R, H, I, N, D, A Occas: E, X ● **Work Env:** Noise=N; ● **Salary:** 3 ● **Outlook:** 4

ELECTRIC-METER TESTER (utilities) ● DOT #821.381-010 ● OES: 83000 ● Alternate titles: METER TESTER. Tests accuracy of meters used for recording electric current consumption and makes necessary adjustments, using following methods: (1) Connects meter to standard (specially calibrated electric meter mechanism) and adjusts standard's dials to meter being tested. Pushes switch and allows needle on standard to revolve specified number of turns or for clocked period. Compares meter and standard calibrated dials to ascertain accuracy of meter. (2) Connects testing instruments, such as wattmeter, voltmeter, and ammeter, across coils of meter and allows load to pass through meter for clocked period. Computes watt-hours of current consumed, using instrument readings and time factor. Compares watt-hour computations with dial on tested meter to determine meter accuracy. Adjusts meters by loosening or tightening screws, using screwdriver. Inspects wiring of installed meters for improper connections or diversions of current. May make minor repairs and recommend meter removal for major repair. May clean mechanism with solution and small brush. May calculate inaccurate meter variations from standard. May set up auxiliary equipment to route current around installed meter during testing to avoid interruption to service. Does not perform tests on inaccurate meters to diagnose malfunctioning if inaccuracy cannot be corrected by screw adjustment [INSIDE-METER TESTER (utilities) 729.281-034].May be designated according to types of meters tested as Tester, Demand Meters (utilities); Meter Tester, Polyphase (utilities); Meter Tester, Primary (utilities); Meter Tester, Single Phase (utilities). ● **GED:** R4, M4, L3 ● **SVP:** 2-4 yrs ● **Academic:** Ed=N, Eng=S ● **Work Field:** 111 ● **MPSMS:** 581 ● **Aptitudes:** G3, V3, N3, S3, P2, Q3, K3, F3, M3, E4, C4 ● **Temperaments:** J, T ● **Physical:** Stg=L; Freq: C, B, R, H, I, N, A Occas: G, X ● **Work Env:** Noise=N; ● **Salary:** 3 ● **Outlook:** 3

ELECTRIC-MOTOR REPAIRER (any industry) ● DOT #721.281-018 ● OES: 85720 ● Repairs electric motors, generators, and equipment, such as starting devices and switches, following schematic drawings, and using handtools, coil-winding machines, power tools, and test equipment: Disassembles and removes armature, stator, or rotor from housing. Examines coil connections for broken or defective wiring. Tests coils, armatures, stator, rotor, and field coils for continuity, shorts, and grounds and insulation resistance, using test lamp, ammeter, and ohmmeter. Cuts out or removes defective coils and removes insulation from core slots. Cuts and forms insulation and inserts insulation into armature, rotor, or stator slots. Rewinds coils on core while in slots manually or makes replacement coils, using coil-winding machine. Installs and aligns prewound coils in slots, using hammer, drift, or mallet. Replaces defective coil leads and solders connections of coils in specified sequence. Examines bearings, shafts, and other moving parts for excessive wear or defects. Refaces commutators and machines parts to specified tolerances, using machine tools. Assembles and tests motor for specified performance. May be designated according to size

of motor repaired as Fractional-Horsepower Motor Repairer (any industry); equipment repaired as Dynamotor Repairer (any industry); or part repaired as Armature Straightener (elec. equip.); Coil-Connector Repairer (elec. equip.); Commutator Repairer (any industry); Field-Coil Repairer (elec. equip.); Stator Repairer (any industry). ● **GED:** R4, M3, L3 ● **SVP:** 2-4 yrs ● **Academic:** Ed=H, Eng=S ● **Work Field:** 111 ● **MPSMS:** 582 ● **Aptitudes:** G3, V3, N3, S3, P2, Q4, K3, F3, M2, E5, C4 ● **Temperaments:** J, T ● **Physical:** Stg=M; Freq: R, H, I, N, D, A Occas: E, X ● **Work Env:** Noise=N; ● **Salary:** 3 ● **Outlook:** 3

ELECTRICAL-APPLIANCE SERVICER (any industry) ● DOT #827.261-010 ● OES: 85710 ● Alternate titles: APPLIANCE-SERVICE REPRESENTATIVE. Installs, services, and repairs stoves, refrigerators, dishwashing machines, and other electrical household or commercial appliances, using handtools, test equipment, and following wiring diagrams and manufacturer's specifications: Connects appliance to power source and test meters, such as wattmeter, ammeter, or voltmeter. Observes readings on meters and graphic recorders. Examines appliance during operating cycle to detect excess vibration, overheating, fluid leaks, and loose parts. Disassembles appliance and examines mechanical and electrical parts. Traces electrical circuits, following diagram, and locates shorts and grounds, using ohmmeter. Calibrates timers, thermostats, and adjusts contact points. Cleans and washes parts, using wire brush, buffer, and solvent, to remove carbon, grease, and dust. Replaces worn or defective parts, such as switches, pumps, bearings, transmissions, belts, gears, blowers, and defective wiring. Repairs and adjusts appliance motors. Reassembles appliance, adjusts pulleys, and lubricates moving parts, using handtools and lubricating equipment. May be known according to appliance repaired as Clothes-Drier Repairer (any industry); Coffee-Maker Servicer (any industry); Dishwashing-Machine Repairer (any industry); Electric-Range Servicer (any industry); Electric-Refrigerator Servicer (any industry); Washing-Machine Servicer (any industry). ● **GED:** R4, M3, L3 ● **SVP:** 2-4 yrs ● **Academic:** Ed=N, Eng=S ● **Work Field:** 111 ● **MPSMS:** 583 ● **Aptitudes:** G3, V3, N3, S3, P3, Q4, K3, F3, M2, E5, C4 ● **Temperaments:** J, T, V ● **Physical:** Stg=M; Freq: S, K, O, R, H, I, N Occas: W, T, G, F, D, A, X ● **Work Env:** Noise=N; ● **Salary:** 3 ● **Outlook:** 3

ELECTRICIAN, AUTOMOTIVE (automotive ser.) ● DOT #825.281-022 ● OES: 85720 ● Repairs and overhauls electrical systems in automotive vehicles, such as automobiles, buses, and trucks: Confers with customer to determine nature of electrical malfunction. Determines malfunction of electrical system by visual inspection and by use of testing devices, such as oscilloscope, voltmeter, and ammeter. Adjusts ignition timing and measures and adjusts distributor breaker-point gaps, using dwell meter or thickness gauge. Tests and repairs starters, generators, and distributors. Repairs or replaces defective wiring in ignition, lighting, air-conditioning, and safety control systems, using electrician's handtools. Rebuilds electrical units, such as starters, generators, and door controls. May estimate cost of repairs based on parts and labor charges. May be designated according to specialty as Electrical Repairer, Internal Combustion Engines (automotive ser.; engine-turbine); Electrical-Unit Rebuilder (automotive ser.); Electrician, Bus (automotive ser.); Ignition-And-Carburetor Mechanic (automotive ser.); Windshield-Wiper Repairer (automotive ser.). ● **GED:** R4, M3, L3 ● **SVP:** 2-4 yrs ● **Academic:** Ed=H, Eng=S ● **Work Field:** 111 ● **MPSMS:** 591 ● **Aptitudes:** G3, V3, N3, S3, P2, Q5, K3, F3, M3, E5, C4 ● **Temperaments:** J, T, V ● **Physical:** Stg=L; Freq: S, K, O, R, H, I, N, D Occas: E, A, X ● **Work Env:** Noise=N; Occas: A ● **Salary:** 4 ● **Outlook:** 4

ELECTRICAL-INSTRUMENT REPAIRER (any industry) ● DOT #729.281-026 ● OES: 85905 ● Alternate titles: INSTRUMENT MAKER; INSTRUMENT REPAIRER. Repairs, calibrates, and tests instruments, such as voltmeters, ammeters, resistance bridges, galvanometers, temperature bridges, and temperature controlling and recording gauges and instruments, using jewelers' tools, electricians' tools, handtools, and measuring instruments: Tests instruments for resistance, voltage, and other characteristics, using potentiometer, voltage divider, and other testing devices. Disassembles instruments, using handtools, and examines parts for defects. Measures, cuts, and fits glass for meters and instruments, using glass cutter. Repairs or replaces defective parts of instruments, using handtools, soldering equipment, grinders, calipers, micrometers, and dividers. Reassembles instruments, following circuit diagrams and using jewelers' tools. Tests new and repaired instruments, using test board. May operate lathe and drill press to make replacement parts. May plan, construct, and assemble test panels for experimental and production testing. May keep records on repair and calibration of instruments. May rebuild induction cores for electric furnaces. May install, repair, and adjust electronically controlled dynamometers and be known as Dynamometer Repairer (elec. equip.). ● **GED:** R4, M3, L3 ● **SVP:** 1-2 yrs ● **Academic:** Ed=N, Eng=S ● **Work Field:** 111 ● **MPSMS:** 581, 602 ● **Aptitudes:** G2, V3, N2, S2, P2, Q3, K3, F3, M2, E5, C3 ● **Temperaments:** J, T ● **Physical:** Stg=L; Freq: R, H, N Occas: I, D, A, X ● **Work Env:** Noise=N; ● **Salary:** 3 ● **Outlook:** 3

ELECTRONICS MECHANIC (any industry) ● DOT #828.261-022 ● OES: 85705 ● Alternate titles: COMMUNICATION TECHNICIAN; ELECTRONICS-EQUIPMENT MECHANIC; ELECTRONICS SPECIALIST; ELECTRONICS-SYSTEM MECHANIC; ELECTRONICS TECHNICIAN; MAINTENANCE ENGINEER. Repairs electronic equipment, such as computers, industrial controls, audio and video systems, radar systems, telemetering and missile control systems, transmitters, antennas, and servomechanisms, following blueprints and manufacturers' specifications, and using handtools and test instruments: Converses with equipment operators to ascertain problems with equipment before breakdown, and to determine if breakdown is due to human error or mechanical problems. Tests faulty equipment and applies knowledge of functional operation of electronic units and systems to diagnose cause of malfunction. Tests electronic components and circuits to locate defects, using oscilloscopes, signal generators, ammeters, and voltmeters. Replaces defective components and wiring and adjusts mechanical parts, using handtools and soldering iron. Aligns, adjusts, and calibrates equipment according to specifications. Calibrates testing instruments. Maintains records of repairs, calibrations, and tests. May enter information into computer to copy program from one electronic component to another, or to draw, modify or to store schematics, applying knowledge of software package used. May install equipment in industrial or military establishments and in aircraft and missiles. May operate equipment, such as communication equipment or missile control systems in ground and flight test, and be required to hold license from governmental agency. May be designated according to type of equipment repaired as Customer-Engineering Specialist (office machines); Electronics Mechanic, Computer (any industry); Radar Mechanic (any industry); Voting-Machine Repairer (government ser.). ● **GED:** R4, M4, L4 ● **SVP:** 2-4 yrs ● **Academic:** Ed=H, Eng=G ● **Work Field:** 111 ● **MPSMS:** 580 ● **Aptitudes:** G2, V3, N3, S2, P2, Q4, K3, F2, M2, E5, C3 ● **Temperaments:** J, T, V ● **Physical:** Stg=M; Freq: R, H, I, N, D, X Occas: C, S, K, O, T, G, A ● **Work Env:** Noise=N; Occas: W ● **Salary:** 4 ● **Outlook:** 5

INSTRUMENT-MAKER AND REPAIRER (petrol. & gas) ● DOT #600.280-014 ● OES: 89198 ● Sets up and operates machine tools to remodel electrical and electronic instruments used in electrical logging, gun perforating, sub-surface surveying, and other oil, gas, or borehole prospecting, testing and servicing operations, following engineering orders and specifications and applying knowledge of electronics, mechanics, metal properties, shop mathematics, and machining procedures: Measures, marks, and scribes dimensions of parts to be made on metal or plastic stock, using layout tools, such as rule, square, or scribe [LAYOUT WORKER (machine shop)]. Machines parts to specifications, using machine tools, such as lathes, drill presses, and grinders [MACHINIST (machine shop)]. Assembles fabricated mechanical parts and such purchased parts as pulleys, springs, and dials, using bolts, screws, tweezers, wrenches, and screwdrivers [INSTRUMENT MAKER (any industry)]. Installs electrical and electronic parts, such as sockets, switches, and rheostats, in chassis. Connects circuit components, such as tubes, coils, and switches, using wire strippers and soldering iron and following circuit diagrams. Tests instruments to determine conformance to specifications, using equipment, such as voltmeters and ohmmeters. May be designated according to product remodeled or repaired. ● **GED:** R4, M4, L2 ● **SVP:** 2-4 yrs ● **Academic:** Ed=H, Eng=N ● **Work Field:** 111, 121, 057 ● **MPSMS:** 580, 602 ● **Aptitudes:** G3, V3, N3, S2, P3, Q4, K3, F2, M3, E5, C5 ● **Temperaments:** J, T, V ● **Physical:** Stg=L; Const: R, H, I Freq: N, D, A Occas: S, K, O ● **Work Env:** Noise=N; ● **Salary:** 4 ● **Outlook:** 3

INSTRUMENT MECHANIC (any industry) ● DOT #710.281-026 ● OES: 85905 ● Alternate titles: INSTRUMENT REPAIRER. Installs, repairs, maintains, and adjusts indicating, recording, telemetering, and controlling instruments and test equipment, used to control and mea-

sure variables, such as pressure, flow, temperature, motion, force, and chemical composition, using precision instruments, and handtools: Disassembles malfunctioning instruments or test equipment, such as bargraphs, electrical ovens, multimeters, environmental cabinets, and weatherometers, and examines and tests mechanisms and circuitry for defects. Replaces or repairs defective parts, using handtools. Reassembles instrument or test equipment, and tests assembly for conformance to specifications, using instruments, such as potentiometer, resistance bridge, manometer, and pressure gauge. Inspects instruments and test equipment periodically and adjusts calibration to ensure functioning within specified standards. May calibrate instruments or test equipment according to established standards. May be designated according to type of instrument repaired as Aircraft Instrument Repairer (air trans.); Panel-Instrument Repairer (any industry); X-Ray-Control-Equipment Repairer (any industry). ● **GED:** R4, M3, L4 ● **SVP:** 2-4 yrs ● **Academic:** Ed=A, Eng=S ● **Work Field:** 111, 121 ● **MPSMS:** 602 ● **Aptitudes:** G3, V3, N3, S3, P3, Q3, K2, F3, M2, E5, C4 ● **Temperaments:** J, T ● **Physical:** Stg=M; Freq: R, H, I, N, D, A Occas: S, K, O, E, X ● **Work Env:** Noise=N; ● **Salary:** 4 ● **Outlook:** 3

METEOROLOGICAL-EQUIPMENT REPAIRER (any industry) ● DOT #823.281-018 ● OES: 85905 ● Alternate titles: ELECTRONICS TECHNICIAN. Installs, maintains, and repairs electronic, mercurial, aneroid, and other types of weather-station equipment, using handtools and electronic testing instruments: Tests meteorological instruments for compliance with printed specifications and schematic diagrams, using voltmeters, oscilloscopes, tube testers, and other test instruments. Replaces defective parts, using handtools and soldering iron. Inspects barometers, thermographs, and hydrographs, including recording mechanisms, and repairs, adjusts, or replaces defective parts. Calibrates graphs and other recording devices. Installs radar and two-way radio systems to detect and communicate weather signals. Adjusts and repairs masts, supporting structures, clearance lights, control panels, control cabling and wiring, and other electrical and mechanical devices and equipment, using handtools. ● **GED:** R4, M3, L3 ● **SVP:** 2-4 yrs ● **Academic:** Ed=H, Eng=S ● **Work Field:** 111, 121 ● **MPSMS:** 602, 586 ● **Aptitudes:** G3, V3, N2, S2, P2, Q3, K3, F3, M2, E5, C3 ● **Temperaments:** J, T, V ● **Physical:** Stg=M; Freq: R, H, I, N, D, X Occas: A ● **Work Env:** Noise=N; Freq: W ● **Salary:** 4 ● **Outlook:** 2

PINSETTER ADJUSTER, AUTOMATIC (toy-sport equip.) ● DOT #829.381-010 ● OES: 85998 ● Inspects and adjusts automatic pinsetters, following blueprints, using handtools and gauges: Inspects pinsetter for defects and missing components following blueprint parts list. Mounts components or returns machine to assembly department for reworking. Rolls pinsetter to test bay and connects drive mechanism and power source. Adjusts microswitches, spring tension, traverse or circuit stops, cams, and other control mechanisms to specified settings, using handtools. Operates pinsetters to detect malfunctioning. Measures and regulates height and sweep of rake, using fixed gauge and handtools. Runs machine through complete cycle and inspects for pinsetting accuracy. Tests automatic shutoffs by running undersized pins through mechanism. Examines and adjusts each pin and pickup scissor to correct malfunctions. ● **GED:** R4, M3, L3 ● **SVP:** 1-2 yrs ● **Academic:** Ed=N, Eng=S ● **Work Field:** 111 ● **MPSMS:** 616 ● **Aptitudes:** G3, V3, N3, S3, P4, Q4, K4, F3, M3, E4, C5 ● **Temperaments:** J, T ● **Physical:** Stg=M; Freq: R, H, I, N, D, A Occas: S, O ● **Work Env:** Noise=N; ● **Salary:** 3 ● **Outlook:** 3

PUBLIC-ADDRESS SERVICER (any industry) ● DOT #823.261-010 ● OES: 85598 ● Alternate titles: ELECTRONIC-SOUND TECHNICIAN; PUBLIC-ADDRESS-SYSTEM OPERATOR. Installs and repairs sound-amplifying systems used at public and private assemblages, using handtools and electronic test meters: Positions loudspeakers on posts or other supports. Strings cable from loudspeakers to amplifiers. Places microphones in position near speaker, orchestra, or other attraction, and plugs microphone wires into amplifiers. Switches on installation. Listens to sound output and adjusts volume controls or repositions microphones. Tests and repairs equipment in shop, using handtools, soldering iron, and electronic test meters. May test and repair sound recorders, radio and television receivers, and other electronic equipment. May drive sound truck. May install and repair mobile sound-amplifying system in truck and be designated Sound-Truck Operator (any industry). ● **GED:** R4, M3, L2 ● **SVP:** 2-4 yrs ● **Academic:** Ed=N, Eng=G ● **Work Field:** 111 ● **MPSMS:** 585 ● **Aptitudes:** G3, V3, N3, S3, P3, Q4, K3, F3, M3, E4, C3 ● **Temperaments:**

J ● **Physical:** Stg=M; Freq: C, B, R, H, I, G, N, D Occas: S, K, O, A, X ● **Work Env:** Noise=N; Freq: W ● **Salary:** 4 ● **Outlook:** 2

RADIO MECHANIC (any industry) ● DOT #823.261-018 ● OES: 85514 ● Tests and repairs radio transmitting and receiving equipment in accordance with diagrams and manufacturer's specifications, using electrical measuring instruments, wiring diagrams, and handtools: Examines equipment for damaged components and loose or broken connections and wires. Attaches test leads or plugs in test equipment to unit being tested, turns knobs on equipment to specified settings, and observes dial readings to test radio circuitry for defects. Tests equipment for factors such as power output, frequency power, noise level, audio quality, and dial calibration, using oscilloscopes, radio frequency and wattmeter, ammeters, and voltmeters. Replaces defective components and parts, such as transistors, coils, and integrated circuits, using soldering iron, wire cutters, and handtools. Removes and replaces defective units that are not repairable. Inserts plugs into receptacles and bolts or screws leads to terminals to connect radios and equipment to power source, using handtools. Turns setscrews to adjust receivers for sensitivity and transmitters for maximum output. Tests batteries with hydrometer and ammeter and charges batteries. Required to have Federal Communications Commission Radiotelephone Operator's license. May install, test, adjust, modify, and repair intercommunication systems. May specialize in testing and repairing radio transmitting and receiving equipment in motor vehicles and commercial and government establishments. ● **GED:** R4, M3, L3 ● **SVP:** 1-2 yrs ● **Academic:** Ed=H, Eng=S ● **Work Field:** 111 ● **MPSMS:** 586 ● **Aptitudes:** G3, V3, N3, S2, P2, Q3, K3, F3, M2, E4, C4 ● **Temperaments:** J, T, V ● **Physical:** Stg=M; Freq: R, H, I, N, D, A, X Occas: C, S, K, O, W, T, G ● **Work Env:** Noise=N; Occas: W, D ● **Salary:** 4 ● **Outlook:** 2

GOE: 05.05.11
Sci., Med., & Tech. Equip.
Fabrication & Repair

DENTAL CERAMIST (protective dev.) ● DOT #712.381-042 ● OES: 89921 ● Alternate titles: CERAMICS TECHNICIAN. Applies layers of porcelain or acrylic paste over metal framework to form dental prostheses, such as crowns, bridges, and tooth facings, according to prescription of DENTIST (medical ser.) 072.101-010: Mixes porcelain or acrylic paste according to prescription to match color of natural teeth. Applies layers of mixture over metal framework, using brushes and spatula. Brushes excess mixture from denture and places denture in furnace to harden. Removes denture from furnace, brushes on additional layer of mixture, and shapes mixture to contour of denture, using spatula. Repeats mixture-application process and baking until denture conforms to specifications. Verifies accuracy of tooth dimensions and occlusion of teeth, using micrometer and articulator. Cleans and polishes dental prostheses, using ultrasonic machine and polishing machine. ● **GED:** R4, M3, L4 ● **SVP:** 2-4 yrs ● **Academic:** Ed=N, Eng=S ● **Work Field:** 136, 133 ● **MPSMS:** 604, 925 ● **Aptitudes:** G3, V3, N3, S2, P3, Q3, K3, F2, M3, E4, C3 ● **Temperaments:** J, T ● **Physical:** Stg=S; Freq: R, H, I, N, D, X ● **Work Env:** Noise=N; ● **Salary:** 3 ● **Outlook:** 2

DENTAL CERAMIST ASSISTANT (protective dev.) ● DOT #712.664-010 ● OES: 89921 ● Alternate titles: PORCELAIN FINISHER; PORCELAIN WAXER. Performs any combination of following tasks to assist DENTAL CERAMIST (protective dev.) 712.381-042 in molding dental prostheses, such as crowns, bridges, and tooth facings: Brushes liquid separating solution on tip of tooth die and covers die with wax sheet. Invests wax impressions in plaster molds, and inserts mold in furnace to melt wax. Positions mold in casting machine to cast metal framework. Removes metal framework from mold, using sandblasting equipment or hammer. Smooths rough spots from framework, using abrasive grinding wheel. Mixes porcelain or acrylic resin solution to match color of natural teeth, under direction of DENTAL CERAMIST (protective dev.). Fills wax impression of tooth with graphite solution, plates impression in electroplating machine, removes die (plated impression) from electroplating machine, and applies acrylic resin to base of die, using spatula, to fabricate copper dies for dentures. ● **GED:** R3, M2, L3 ● **SVP:** 1-2 yrs ● **Academic:** Ed=N, Eng=S ●

Work Field: 102 ● **MPSMS:** 925, 604 ● **Aptitudes:** G3, V3, N4, S3, P3, Q4, K3, F3, M3, E5, C2 ● **Temperaments:** J, T ● **Physical:** Stg=S; Freq: R, H, I, N, D, A Occas: E, T, G, X ● **Work Env:** Noise=N; ● **Salary:** 2 ● **Outlook:** 3

DENTAL-LABORATORY TECHNICIAN (protective dev.) ● DOT #712.381-018 ● OES: 89921 ● Alternate titles: DENTAL TECHNICIAN. Performs any combination of following tasks to fabricate and repair dental appliances, according to DENTIST'S (medical ser.) 072.101-010 prescription, using handtools, molding equipment, and bench fabricating machines: Reads prescription and examines dental models and impressions to determine type of denture to be made or repaired applying knowledge of dental laboratory techniques. Fabricates full or partial dentures, using wax, plastic, and plaster models, articulators, grinders, and polishers. Casts plastic or plaster models of dentures to be repaired [DENTURE-MODEL MAKER (protective dev.) 712.684-046]. Selects and mounts replacement teeth in model to match color and shape of natural or adjacent teeth, using tooth color scales and tooth illustrations. Molds wax over denture setup to form contours of gums, using knives and spatula [DENTURE WAXER (protective dev.) 712.381-046]. Removes excess plastic and polishes surfaces of cast dentures, using grinding and polishing tools and ultrasonic equipment [FINISHER, DENTURE (protective dev.) 712.381-050]. Rebuilds denture linings to duplicate original thickness, contour, and color according to specifications. Tests repaired dentures for accuracy of occlusion, using articulator. Bends and solders gold and platinum wire to construct wire frames for dentures, using soldering gun and handtools [CONTOUR WIRE SPECIALIST, DENTURE (protective dev.) 712.381-014]. May confer with DENTIST (medical ser.) to resolve problems in design and setup of dentures. May be designated according to type of denture fabricated as Dental Technician, Crown And Bridge (protective dev.); Dental Technician, Metal (protective dev.). ● **GED:** R4, M3, L4 ● **SVP:** 2-4 yrs ● **Academic:** Ed=H, Eng=S ● **Work Field:** 102 ● **MPSMS:** 604, 925 ● **Aptitudes:** G3, V3, N3, S2, P2, Q4, K3, F2, M3, E4, C3 ● **Temperaments:** J, T ● **Physical:** Stg=L; Freq: R, H, I, N, D, X Occas: E, A ● **Work Env:** Noise=N; ● **Salary:** 3 ● **Outlook:** 4

DENTAL-LABORATORY-TECHNICIAN APPRENTICE (protective dev.) ● DOT #712.381-022 ● OES: 89921 ● Alternate titles: DENTAL-TECHNICIAN APPRENTICE. Performs tasks as described under APPRENTICE (any industry) Master Title. ● **GED:** R4, M3, L4 ● **SVP:** 2-4 yrs ● **Academic:** Ed=H, Eng=S ● **Work Field:** 102 ● **MPSMS:** 604, 925 ● **Aptitudes:** G3, V3, N3, S2, P2, Q4, K3, F2, M3, E4, C3 ● **Temperaments:** J, T ● **Physical:** Stg=L; Freq: R, H, I, N, D, X Occas: E, A ● **Work Env:** Noise=N; ● **Salary:** 3 ● **Outlook:** 3

DENTURE-MODEL MAKER (protective dev.) ● DOT #712.684-046 ● OES: 93997 ● Forms plaster, metal, plastic, or rubber models and molds from dental impressions and wax models of dentures and dental appliances, using casting equipment and handtools: Mixes specified amounts of special plaster and water or other model-making ingredients, by hand or electric mixer-vibrator, to form compound used for models and molds. Pours mixture into impressions to form models for upper and lower dentures. Melts pieces of gold, silver, or other metal, using gas torch, and casts inlays, crowns, and pontics for fixed bridges, using centrifugal casting machine. Packs plasttic mixture or composition rubber strips in molds to cast orthodontic appliances, such as tooth positioners, mouthguards, and retainers. Positions models in articulator and verifies occlusions. Packs plaster or other denture-making ingredient around wax model of denture to form model or matrix for casting denture. Places mold in boiling water to melt wax from cast model. Scrapes remaining wax from model, using knife, and washes model in soapy solution to remove dirt and foreign matter. ● **GED:** R3, M2, L3 ● **SVP:** 6 mos-1 yr ● **Academic:** Ed=N, Eng=S ● **Work Field:** 132 ● **MPSMS:** 925, 604 ● **Aptitudes:** G3, V3, N4, S3, P3, Q4, K3, F3, M3, E5, C4 ● **Temperaments:** J, T ● **Physical:** Stg=L; Freq: R, H, N, D Occas: I, X ● **Work Env:** Noise=N; Occas: U ● **Salary:** 4 ● **Outlook:** 2

ELECTROMECHANICAL TECHNICIAN (inst. & app.) ● DOT #710.281-018 ● OES: 93111 ● Fabricates, tests, analyzes, and adjusts precision electromechanical instruments, such as accelerometers, altimeters, electromedical instruments, gyroscopes, temperature probes, and x-ray inspection systems, according to blueprints and other specifications, using handtools, metalworking machines, and precision measuring and testing instruments: Operates metalworking machines, such as bench lathe, milling machine, punch press, and drill press to fabricate housings, fittings, jigs, and fixtures, and verifies dimensions, using precision measuring instruments. Assembles wires, insulation, and electrical components, such as resistors and capacitors, following method layouts, using fixtures, binocular microscope, soldering equipment, tweezers, and handtools. Installs electrical assemblies and hardware in housing, using handtools and soldering equipment. Tests assembled instruments for circuit continuity and operational reliability, using test instruments, such as multimeter, oscilloscope, oscillator, electronic voltmeter, and bridge. Analyzes test results and repairs or adjusts instruments according to analysis. Records test results and writes report on fabrication techniques used. May calibrate instruments according to specifications. May specialize in assembly of prototype or production instruments and be designated Development Technician (inst. & app.). ● **GED:** R4, M4, L4 ● **SVP:** 2-4 yrs ● **Academic:** Ed=H, Eng=S ● **Work Field:** 111, 121, 211 ● **MPSMS:** 589, 600 ● **Aptitudes:** G2, V3, N2, S2, P3, Q3, K3, F3, M2, E5, C4 ● **Temperaments:** J, T, V ● **Physical:** Stg=L; Freq: R, H, I, N, D, A Occas: E, G, X ● **Work Env:** Noise=L; Occas: M, E ● **Salary:** 3 ● **Outlook:** 4

EXPERIMENTAL ASSEMBLER (any industry) ● DOT #739.381-026 ● OES: 83000 ● Assembles, inspects, tests, and adjusts variety of optical, electrical, and mechanical devices on pilot run basis to improve assembly methods and to discover and correct deficiencies in materials, specifications, and equipment prior to production runs: Reads and interprets blueprints, diagrams, schematics, and narrative instructions to determine required parts and tools and lays out workbench to provide assembly arrangement. Assembles up to 100 units or components of optical, electrical, or mechanical devices, such as slide projectors, plastic tape dispensers, duplicating machines, and ribbon-bow-making machines, using power tools and handtools. Inspects, tests, and adjusts assembled devices for specified functioning, using light meter, ammeter, voltmeter, stopwatch, rulers, feeler gauges, spring tension tester, torque tester, and depth micrometer. ● **GED:** R4, M4, L4 ● **SVP:** 1-2 yrs ● **Academic:** Ed=N, Eng=S ● **Work Field:** 111 ● **MPSMS:** 600 ● **Aptitudes:** G3, V3, N3, S3, P2, Q4, K3, F3, M3, E4, C4 ● **Temperaments:** J, T, V ● **Physical:** Stg=M; Freq: R, H, I, N, D Occas: E, A, X ● **Work Env:** Noise=L; Occas: O ● **Salary:** 3 ● **Outlook:** 3

FINISHER, DENTURE (protective dev.) ● DOT #712.381-050 ● OES: 89921 ● Alternate titles: DENTURE FINISHER; FINISHER; FINISHER-POLISHER. Polishes, cleans, and adjusts dentures and dental appliances to obtain specified finish, using handtools, polishing wheels, and cleaning equipment: Removes mold from frame, using ejector press, and chips molding material from denture, using hammer and chisel. Smooths and polishes denture and denture frames to remove excess material, using polishing machine. Removes excess plastic from teeth, using sharp pointed tool. Fills chipped or low spots in surfaces of plastic areas with acrylic resins, using brush. Repairs and adjusts metal framework of dentures, using soldering torch and handtools. Verifies occlusion of dentures, using articulator. ● **GED:** R3, M2, L3 ● **SVP:** 6 mos-1 yr ● **Academic:** Ed=N, Eng=S ● **Work Field:** 102 ● **MPSMS:** 604 ● **Aptitudes:** G3, V3, N3, S3, P3, Q4, K3, F3, M3, E5, C5 ● **Temperaments:** J, T ● **Physical:** Stg=L; Freq: R, H, I, N Occas: E ● **Work Env:** Noise=N; ● **Salary:** 2 ● **Outlook:** 2

INSTRUMENT MAKER (any industry) ● DOT #600.280-010 ● OES: 89198 ● Alternate titles: MECHANICAL TECHNICIAN; PARTS MECHANIC; PRECISION-INSTRUMENT AND TOOL MAKER; PRECISION-MECHANICAL-INSTRUMENT MAKER. Fabricates, modifies, or repairs mechanical instruments or mechanical assemblies of electrical or electronic instruments, such as chronometric timing devices, barographs, thermostats, seismographs, and servomechanisms, applying knowledge of mechanics, metal properties, shop mathematics, and machining procedures and using machine tools, welding and heat-treating equipment, precision measuring instruments, and handtools: Measures, marks, and scribes stock, such as silver, nickel, platinum, steel, ivory, and plastic, following blueprints and engineering sketches, and using square, rule, and scribe to lay out workpiece for machining [LAY-OUT WORKER (machine shop)]. Sets up and operates machine tools, such as lathes, drill presses, punch presses, milling machines, grinders, brakes, and lapping and polishing machines, to machine parts to specifications [MACHINIST (machine shop)]. Anneals and tempers metal parts [HEAT TREATER (heat treating) I]. Assembles parts in jig and brazes or welds. Fits and installs precision

components, such as timing devices, springs, balance mechanisms, and gear trains, in housing, using jeweler's lathe, tweezers, loupe, and handtools. Verifies dimensions of parts and installation of components, using measuring instruments, such as micrometer, calipers, and electronic gauges. Coats assembled instrument with protective finish, such as lacquer or enamel, using spray gun. May install wiring and electrical components to specifications. May set up and operate machines to fabricate dies for punch presses [DIE MAKER, BENCH, STAMPING (machine shop)]. May be designated according to product assembled. ● **GED:** R4, M4, L3 ● **SVP:** 2-4 yrs ● **Academic:** Ed=H, Eng=S ● **Work Field:** 121, 057 ● **MPSMS:** 580, 566, 600 ● **Aptitudes:** G3, V3, N3, S2, P2, Q4, K3, F3, M2, E5, C5 ● **Temperaments:** J, T, V ● **Physical:** Stg=M; Freq: R, H, I, N Occas: D, A ● **Work Env:** Noise=N; ● **Salary:** 4 ● **Outlook:** 3

INSTRUMENT REPAIRER (any industry) ● DOT #710.261-010 ● OES: 85905 ● Repairs and calibrates speedometers and other automotive gauges and meters, using handtools and test equipment: Confers with customer to determine nature of malfunction. Inspects components, connections, and drive mechanisms to detect defects. Removes instrument from vehicle and disassembles, cleans, and inspects instrument to determine which parts are defective. Replaces worn and defective parts, using handtools. Tests and calibrates instruments, using mechanical and electronic devices, such as voltmeters, pressure generators, and speedometer tester. Installs instruments in vehicle, using handtools. Computes speedometer drive ratio changes for modified vehicles. Maintains stock and parts inventory. May operate jeweler's lathe and other machines to fabricate instrument parts. May repair automotive clocks [WATCH REPAIRER (clock & watch)]. ● **GED:** R4, M3, L4 ● **SVP:** 4-10 yrs ● **Academic:** Ed=N, Eng=S ● **Work Field:** 121, 111 ● **MPSMS:** 602 ● **Aptitudes:** G3, V3, N3, S2, P2, Q3, K3, F2, M2, E5, C4 ● **Temperaments:** J ● **Physical:** Stg=L; Freq: R, H, I, N Occas: S, K, O, W, T, G, D, A, X ● **Work Env:** Noise=N; Occas: W ● **Salary:** 4 ● **Outlook:** 3

INSTRUMENT TECHNICIAN (utilities) ● DOT #710.281-030 ● OES: 85905 ● Alternate titles: OSCILLOGRAPH TECHNICIAN. Inspects, tests, adjusts, and repairs electric, electronic, mechanical, and pneumatic instruments and systems used to indicate, record, and control generating operations in conventional or nuclear power electric generating plant: Inspects meters, indicators, and gauges to detect abnormal fluctuations. Tests accuracy of flowmeters, pressure gauges, temperature indicators, controllers, radiation counters or detectors, and other recording, indicating or controlling instruments to locate defective components in system, using test equipment, such as pressure gauges, mercury manometers, potentiometers, pulse and signal generators, oscilloscopes, transistor curve tracers, and ammeters, voltmeters, and wattmeters. Traces out and tests electronic solid state and vacuum tube circuitry and components to locate defective parts in analog and digital, protection, or radiation monitoring systems, using test equipment, schematics, and maintenance manuals. Removes defective instruments from system, decontaminates, disassembles, and cleans instruments, and replaces defective parts, using handtools. Reassembles instruments and replaces instruments in system, using handtools. Lubricates instruments and replaces defective wiring and tubing. Calibrates readings on instruments according to standards and adjusts phasing and aligns stages to ensure accuracy of recording and indicating function. Records calibrations made, parts and components used, and inventory of parts on hand. Prepares schematic drawings, sketches, and reports to reflect changes or alterations made in instruments, circuits, and sytems. May be designated according to type power plant as Nuclear-Plant-Instrument Technician (utilities); Instrument Repairer, Steam Plant (utilities). ● **GED:** R4, M3, L3 ● **SVP:** 4-10 yrs ● **Academic:** Ed=H, Eng=S ● **Work Field:** 121, 111 ● **MPSMS:** 602 ● **Aptitudes:** G3, V3, N3, S3, P2, Q4, K2, F2, M2, E5, C3 ● **Temperaments:** J, T ● **Physical:** Stg=L; Freq: S, K, O, R, H, I, N, X Occas: C, W, D, A ● **Work Env:** Noise=L; Freq: O Occas: R ● **Salary:** 4 ● **Outlook:** 4

LENS MOUNTER II (optical goods) ● DOT #713.681-010 ● OES: 89917 ● Mounts prescription eyeglass lenses in metal, plastic, or combination frames, using handtools: Examines eyeglass prescription to determine style, color, and size of frame. Inspects lenses to detect flaws, such as pits, chips, and scratches. Holds and turns lenses against grinding wheel to remove flaws. Assembles eyeglass frame and attaches ornaments, shields, nose pads, and temple pieces, using pliers and screwdrivers. Drills holes in lenses for mounting on rimless frames, using diamond drill. Immerses plastic frame rims in hot salt solution to soften rims or stretches rims, using hot, metal cone. Inserts and aligns lenses in frame. Verifies frame dimensions and alignment of lenses, using protractor, ruler, and straightedge. Turns lenses in frame to correct alignment, using padded pliers. Immerses plastic frames in cold water to set plastic around lenses. Tightens screws to hold lenses in metal frames. Examines lenses under polarized light to detect stress caused by over-tightening screws and adjusts screws as necessary. Heats plastic frame bridge and bends frame according to prescription specifications, using fingers and handtools. Immerses plastic frames in dye for specified period to color frames. Solders broken metal bridges and replaces damaged temples to repair frames, using soldering iron and handtools. Cleans and polishes finished eyeglasses, using cloth and solvent. May be designated according to type frame mounted as Metal-Frame Inserter (optical goods); Plastic-Frame Inserter (optical goods); or according to part assembled as Trim Mounter (optical goods) II. ● **GED:** R3, M2, L3 ● **SVP:** 1-2 yrs ● **Academic:** Ed=N, Eng=S ● **Work Field:** 102 ● **MPSMS:** 605 ● **Aptitudes:** G3, V4, N4, S3, P3, Q4, K3, F3, M3, E5, C4 ● **Temperaments:** J, T ● **Physical:** Stg=M; Const: R, H, I, N Freq: D, A Occas: E, X ● **Work Env:** Noise=N; ● **Salary:** 2 ● **Outlook:** 3

OPTICIAN (optical goods) ● DOT #716.280-014 ● OES: 89917 ● Alternate titles: OPTICAL MECHANIC. Sets up and operates machines to grind eyeglass lenses to prescription specifications and assembles lenses in frames: Reads lens and frame specifications from prescription. Selects lens blanks from stock. Sets up and operates machines, such as generator, polisher, edger, and hardener, to fabricate lenses to specifications. Mounts lenses in metal, plastic, or rimless frames. Inspects mounted lenses for conformance to specifications [INSPECTOR, EYEGLASS (optical goods)]. Examines broken lenses to identify original lens prescription, using power determining and optical centering instruments. ● **GED:** R4, M4, L4 ● **SVP:** 4-10 yrs ● **Academic:** Ed=A, Eng=S ● **Work Field:** 102 ● **MPSMS:** 605 ● **Aptitudes:** G3, V3, N3, S2, P2, Q4, K3, F3, M2, E5, C4 ● **Temperaments:** J, T, V ● **Physical:** Stg=L; Freq: R, H, I, N Occas: E, D, A, X ● **Work Env:** Noise=N; ● **Salary:** 5 ● **Outlook:** 3

ORTHODONTIC TECHNICIAN (protective dev.) ● DOT #712.381-030 ● OES: 89921 ● Constructs and repairs appliances for straightening teeth according to ORTHODONTIST'S (medical ser.) 072.101-022 prescription: Shapes, grinds, polishes, carves, and assembles metal and plastic appliances, such as retainers, tooth bands, and positioners, using spatula, pliers, soldering torch, and electric grinders and polishers. Tests appliance for conformance to specifications, using articulator. ● **GED:** R4, M3, L4 ● **SVP:** 1-2 yrs ● **Academic:** Ed=H, Eng=S ● **Work Field:** 102 ● **MPSMS:** 925, 604 ● **Aptitudes:** G3, V3, N3, S2, P2, Q4, K3, F2, M3, E5, C4 ● **Temperaments:** J, T ● **Physical:** Stg=S; Freq: R, H, I, E, N, D Occas: X ● **Work Env:** Noise=N; ● **Salary:** 4 ● **Outlook:** 3

ORTHOTICS ASSISTANT (medical ser.) ● DOT #078.361-022 ● OES: 32998 ● Assists ORTHOTIST (medical ser.) 078.261-018 in providing care and fabricating and fitting orthopedic braces to patients with disabling conditions of limbs and spine: Under guidance of and in consultation with ORTHOTIST (medical ser.), makes assigned casts, measurements, model modifications, and layouts. Performs fitting, including static and dynamic alignments. Evaluates orthopedic braces on patient to ensure fit, function, and workmanship. Repairs and maintains orthopedic braces. May be responsible for performance of other personnel. May also perform functions of PROSTHETICS ASSISTANT (medical ser.) 078.361-026 and be designated Orthotics-Prosthetics Assistant (medical ser.). ● **GED:** R4, M4, L4 ● **SVP:** 2-4 yrs ● **Academic:** Ed=H, Eng=S ● **Work Field:** 294, 102 ● **MPSMS:** 604 ● **Aptitudes:** G2, V3, N3, S2, P2, Q4, K4, F3, M3, E4, C4 ● **Temperaments:** J, P, T ● **Physical:** Stg=M; Freq: R, H, I, E, N, D, A Occas: S, K, O, T, G, X ● **Work Env:** Noise=N; ● **Salary:** 4 ● **Outlook:** 3

ORTHOTICS TECHNICIAN (protective dev.) ● DOT #712.381-034 ● OES: 89998 ● Fabricates, fits, repairs, and maintains orthotic devices, such as braces and surgical supports, according to specifications and under guidance of ORTHOTIST (medical ser.) 078.261-018 or ORTHOTICS ASSISTANT (medical ser.) 078.361-022: Bends, forms, welds, and saws metal brace structural components to conform to measurements, using hammers, anvils, welding equipment, and saws. Drills and taps holes for rivets, and rivets components together. Shapes plastic and metal around cast of patient's torso or limbs. Covers and pads

metal or plastic brace structures, using layers of rubber, felt, plastic, and leather. May also perform functions of PROSTHETICS TECHNICIAN (protective dev.) 712.381-038 and be designated Orthotics-Prosthetics Technician (protective dev.). ● **GED:** R4, M3, L4 ● **SVP:** 1-2 yrs ● **Academic:** Ed=H, Eng=S ● **Work Field:** 102 ● **MPSMS:** 604 ● **Aptitudes:** G3, V3, N3, S3, P3, Q3, K3, F2, M2, E4, C4 ● **Temperaments:** J, T ● **Physical:** Stg=M; Freq: R, H, I, N, D, A Occas: X ● **Work Env:** Noise=L; Occas: A, M ● **Salary:** 4 ● **Outlook:** 3

ORTHOTIST (medical ser.) ● DOT #078.261-018 ● OES: 32998 ● Provides care to patients with disabling conditions of limbs and spine by fitting and preparing orthopedic braces, under direction of and in consultation with physician: Assists in formulation of specifications for braces. Examines and evaluates patient's needs in relation to disease and functional loss. Formulates design of orthopedic brace. Selects materials, making cast measurements, model modifications, and layouts. Performs fitting, including static and dynamic alignments. Evaluates brace on patient and makes adjustments to assure fit, function, and quality of work. Instructs patient in use of orthopedic brace. Maintains patient records. May supervise ORTHOTICS ASSISTANTS (medical ser.) 078.361-022 and other support personnel. May supervise laboratory activities relating to development of orthopedic braces. May lecture and demonstrate to colleagues and other professionals concerned with orthotics. May participate in research. May perform functions of PROSTHETIST (medical ser.) 078.261-022 and be designated Orthotist-Prosthetist (medical ser.). ● **GED:** R5, M4, L4 ● **SVP:** 4-10 yrs ● **Academic:** Ed=B, Eng=G ● **Work Field:** 294, 102 ● **MPSMS:** 604 ● **Aptitudes:** G2, V3, N3, S2, P2, Q4, K4, F3, M3, E4, C4 ● **Temperaments:** J, P, T ● **Physical:** Stg=M; Freq: R, H, T, G, N, D Occas: S, K, O, I, A, X ● **Work Env:** Noise=N; ● **Salary:** 3 ● **Outlook:** 4

PACKER, DENTURE (protective dev.) ● DOT #712.684-034 ● OES: 93997 ● Alternate titles: MOLDER. Packs plastic material in molds to form base for full or partial dentures: Mixes specified amounts of plastic powder and chemical solution, using spatula. Packs mixture around base of exposed artificial teeth and into cavities of mold sections. Positions sheet of plastic or wax paper or foil over bottom of mold to permit separation of mold from denture. Fits top section of mold over bottom and places assembly in press. Starts press that forces sections together and compresses mixture around teeth to form reproduction of gums. Removes model from press and trims excess plastic from mold, using knife. Submerges mold in hot water for specified time to cure plastic. ● **GED:** R3, M2, L3 ● **SVP:** 6 mos-1 yr ● **Academic:** Ed=N, Eng=S ● **Work Field:** 132 ● **MPSMS:** 925, 604 ● **Aptitudes:** G3, V4, N4, S3, P3, Q5, K4, F3, M3, E5, C4 ● **Temperaments:** J, T ● **Physical:** Stg=L; Freq: R, H, I, N, D, X ● **Work Env:** Noise=N; ● **Salary:** 2 ● **Outlook:** 2

PROSTHETICS ASSISTANT (medical ser.) ● DOT #078.361-026 ● OES: 32998 ● Assists PROSTHETIST (medical ser.) 078.261-022 in providing care to and fabricating and fitting prostheses for patients with partial or total absence of limb: Under direction of PROSTHETIST (medical ser.), makes assigned casts, measurements, and model modifications. Performs fitting, including static and dynamic alignments. Evaluates prosthesis on patient to ensure fit, function, and quality of work. Repairs and maintains prostheses. May be responsible for performance of other personnel. May also perform functions of ORTHOTICS ASSISTANT (medical ser.) 078.361-022. ● **GED:** R4, M4, L4 ● **SVP:** 2-4 yrs ● **Academic:** Ed=H, Eng=S ● **Work Field:** 294, 102 ● **MPSMS:** 604 ● **Aptitudes:** G2, V3, N3, S2, P2, Q4, K4, F3, M3, E4, C4 ● **Temperaments:** J, P, T ● **Physical:** Stg=M; Freq: R, H, I, T, G, N Occas: S, K, O, D, A, X ● **Work Env:** Noise=N; ● **Salary:** 3 ● **Outlook:** 3

PROSTHETICS TECHNICIAN (protective dev.) ● DOT #712.381-038 ● OES: 89998 ● Alternate titles: RESTORATION TECHNICIAN. Fabricates, fits, maintains, and repairs artificial limbs, plastic cosmetic appliances, and other prosthetic devices, according to prescription specifications and under guidance of PROSTHETIST (medical ser.) 078.261-022 or PROSTHETICS ASSISTANT (medical ser.) 078.361-026: Reads specifications to determine type of prosthesis to be fabricated and materials and tools required. Lays out and marks dimensions of parts, using precision measuring instruments and templates. Saws, carves, cuts, and grinds wood, plastic, metal, or fabric to fabricate parts, using rotary sawing and cutting machines and hand cutting tools. Drills and taps holes for rivets and screws, using drill press. Glues, welds, bolts, sews, and rivets parts together to form prostheses, such as artificial limbs. Makes wax or plastic impression of patient's amputated area, prepares mold from impression, and pours molten plastic into mold to form cosmetic appliances, such as artificial ear, nose, or hand. Assembles layers of padding over prosthesis and fits and attaches outer covering, such as leather, sheet plastic, or fiberglass, over device, using sewing machine, rivet gun, and handtools. Mixes pigments according to formula to duplicate skin coloring of patient and applies pigments to outer covering of prosthesis. Polishes finished device, using grinding and buffing wheels. Tests prostheses for freedom of movement, alignment of parts, and biomechanical stability, using plumbline, goniometer, and alignment fixtures. May harness prosthesis to patient's stump, applying knowledge of functional anatomy. May instruct patient in use of prosthesis. May also perform functions of ORTHOTICS TECHNICIAN (protective dev.) 712.381-034. ● **GED:** R4, M4, L4 ● **SVP:** 1-2 yrs ● **Academic:** Ed=H, Eng=S ● **Work Field:** 121, 102 ● **MPSMS:** 604 ● **Aptitudes:** G2, V3, N3, S2, P2, Q4, K3, F2, M2, E4, C3 ● **Temperaments:** J, T, V ● **Physical:** Stg=M; Const: R, H, I, N, D, A Freq: E Occas: X ● **Work Env:** Noise=N; ● **Salary:** 4 ● **Outlook:** 3

PROSTHETIST (medical ser.) ● DOT #078.261-022 ● OES: 32998 ● Provides care to patients with partial or total absence of limb by planning fabrication of, writing specifications for, and fitting prothesis under guidance of and in consultation with physician: Assists physician in formulation of prescription. Examines and evaluates patient's prosthetic needs in relation to disease entity and functional loss. Formulates design of prosthesis and selects materials and components. Makes casts, measurements, and model modifications. Performs fitting, including static and dynamic alignments. Evaluates prosthesis on patient and makes adjustments to assure fit, function, comfort, and workmanship. Instructs patient in prosthesis use. Maintains patient records. May supervise PROSTHETICS ASSISTANTS (medical ser.) 078.361-026 and other personnel. May supervise laboratory activities relating to development of prosthesis. May lecture and demonstrate to colleagues and other professionals concerned with practice of prosthetics. May participate in research. May also perform functions of ORTHOTIST (medical ser.) 078.261-018. ● **GED:** R5, M4, L4 ● **SVP:** 4-10 yrs ● **Academic:** Ed=B, Eng=G ● **Work Field:** 294, 102 ● **MPSMS:** 604 ● **Aptitudes:** G2, V3, N3, S2, P2, Q4, K4, F3, M3, E4, C4 ● **Temperaments:** J, P, T ● **Physical:** Stg=M; Freq: R, H, I, T, G, N, D, A, X ● **Work Env:** Noise=N; ● **Salary:** 3 ● **Outlook:** 4

RADIOLOGICAL-EQUIPMENT SPECIALIST (inst. & app.) ● DOT #719.261-014 ● OES: 85908 ● Alternate titles: RADIOLOGIC ELECTRONIC SPECIALIST. Tests, repairs, calibrates, and assists in installation of radiological and related equipment used in medical diagnosis or therapy, applying technical knowledge of electronic, radiological, and mechanical systems, and user knowledge of computers, and using manuals, test equipment, measuring instruments, handtools, and power tools: Confers with supervisor, manufacturers' representatives, equipment operators, and other workers to discuss and establish work priorities, resolve equipment related problems, and plan installation, preventive maintenance, and repair procedures. Inspects and tests malfunctioning equipment to determine cause of malfunction, following learned procedures and repair manual instructions, using specialized test and analysis instruments and manufacturers' specifications. Disassembles malfunctioning equipment and removes, replaces, or repairs defective components, and readjusts components to manufacturers' specifications, using handtools, power tools, and measuring instruments. Removes old equipment, prepares space for installation of new equipment, and oversees installation of new equipment by manufacturer. Tests and calibrates equipment at regular or required intervals, using test and measuring instruments and handtools to maintain manufacturers' operational specifications. Selects, devises, designs, and installs mechanical or structural hardware, using tools and utilizing knowledge of mechanics and structures to resolve special equipment operation problems. Maintains records of maintenance and repair work and approved updates of equipment as required by manufacturer. Demonstrates operational procedures for equipment to users. May fabricate hardware, using machine and power tools, handtools, and related equipment. May work for manufacturer and specialize in particular line of equipment. ● **GED:** R5, M5, L5 ● **SVP:** 2-4 yrs ● **Academic:** Ed=A, Eng=S ● **Work Field:** 111 ● **MPSMS:** 589 ● **Aptitudes:** G2, V2, N2, S2, P2, Q3, K2, F2, M2, E3, C3 ● **Temperaments:** J, P, S, T ● **Physical:** Stg=M; Const: R, H, I, N Freq: S, O, E, T, G, A, X Occas: C, B, K, M, D ● **Work Env:** Noise=N; Freq: E, R ● **Salary:** 5 ● **Outlook:** 4

SCIENTIFIC GLASS BLOWER (glass products) ● DOT #006.261-010 ● OES: 35199 ● Alternate titles: GLASS TECHNICIAN; GLASS TECHNOLOGIST. Fabricates, modifies, and repairs experimental and laboratory glass products, using variety of machines and tools, and provides technical advice to scientific and engineering staff on function, properties, and proposed design of products, applying knowledge of glass technology: Confers with scientific or engineering personnel to exchange information and suggest design modifications regarding proposed glass apparatus, such as distillation and high-vacuum systems. Cuts glass tubing of specified type, using cutting tools, such as glass saw and hot-wire cutter. Heats glass tubing until pliable, using gas torch, and blows, bends, and shapes tubing to specified form, using blowhose, handtools, and manual pressure. Performs finishing operations to fabricate glass product or section, using machines and equipment, such as lapping and polishing wheels, spot-welding and sandblasting machines, internal-plating equipment, and drill press. Measures products to verify dimensions, using optical scanner, micrometers, and calipers, and examines glass coloration for degree of internal stress, using polariscope, to determine annealing requirements. Anneals products, using annealing oven. Joins and seals subassemblies to assemble finished product, using gas torch, handtools, and vacuum pump. May operate special equipment, such as radio-frequency-fusing machine, to bond glass to metal, quartz, and ceramic materials. May identify glass of unknown composition by heating with gas torch and evaluating curvature, bondability, and color characteristics. May direct and train GLASS BLOWERS, LABORATORY APPARATUS (glass products; inst. & app.). May design fixtures for use in production of prototype glass products and prepare sketches for machine-shop personnel. May prepare cost estimates for prototype glass products. May requisition or recommend purchase of materials, tools, and equipment. May specialize in specific types of glass scientific apparatus and have knowledge of effects of special environments on glass, such as radioactivity, vacuums, gases, chemicals, and electricity. ● **GED:** R4, M4, L4 ● **SVP:** 4-10 yrs ● **Academic:** Ed=H, Eng=S ● **Work Field:** 102, 133 ● **MPSMS:** 531, 532 ● **Aptitudes:** G2, V2, N2, S2, P2, Q3, K2, F2, M2, E5, C2 ● **Temperaments:** J ● **Physical:** Stg=L; Freq: R, H, I, N, A, X Occas: T, G ● **Work Env:** Noise=N; Occas: A, O ● **Salary:** 3 ● **Outlook:** 3

GOE: 05.05.12
Musical Instrument Fabrication & Repair

ELECTRIC-ORGAN INSPECTOR AND REPAIRER (musical inst.) ● DOT #730.281-018 ● OES: 85708 ● Inspects and repairs electric and electronic organs: Plays organ to determine nature of malfunction. Studies circuit diagrams and performs standard tests to locate mechanical, electrical, or electronic difficulties. Replaces defective components and wiring and adjusts mechanical parts, using soldering equipment and handtools. Aligns, adjusts, and calibrates equipment according to specifications, following circuit diagrams and using alignment tools, handtools, and test equipment. ● **GED:** R4, M3, L4 ● **SVP:** 1-2 yrs ● **Academic:** Ed=N, Eng=S ● **Work Field:** 212, 111 ● **MPSMS:** 614 ● **Aptitudes:** G3, V4, N3, S4, P4, Q4, K4, F3, M3, E3, C4 ● **Temperaments:** J, T ● **Physical:** Stg=L; Freq: R, H, I, N Occas: S, K, O, G, A, X ● **Work Env:** Noise=N; ● **Salary:** 3 ● **Outlook:** 1

ELECTRONIC-ORGAN TECHNICIAN (any industry) ● DOT #828.261-010 ● OES: 85708 ● Alternate titles: ELECTRIC-ORGAN TECHNICIANC;. Installs, tests, adjusts, and repairs electronic organs, pianos, or related musical instruments, using circuit diagrams, service manuals, and standard test equipment: Places speakers along wall or in sound chambers, or mounts speakers on wall. Wires speakers to console. Tunes or adjusts instruments and amplification systems, using electronic test equipment and handtools. May be designated according to specialized function as Electronic-Organ Installer (any industry); Electronic-Piano Installer (any industry); Organ Tuner, Electronic (any industry). ● **GED:** R4, M3, L3 ● **SVP:** 1-2 yrs ● **Academic:** Ed=A, Eng=S ● **Work Field:** 111 ● **MPSMS:** 614 ● **Aptitudes:** G2, V3, N3, S2, P3, Q4, K4, F3, M3, E4, C4 ● **Temperaments:** J ● **Physical:** Stg=L; Freq: S, R, H, I, G, N, A Occas: O, X ● **Work Env:** Noise=N; ● **Salary:** 4 ● **Outlook:** 3

FRETTED-INSTRUMENT MAKER, HAND (musical inst.) ● DOT #730.281-022 ● OES: 93196 ● Constructs fretted musical instruments, such as banjos, guitars, and mandolins, by hand, applying knowledge of wood properties and instrument design and construction. May construct bowed instruments [VIOLIN MAKER, HAND (musical inst.)]. May repair bowed instruments [VIOLIN REPAIRER (any industry)]. May repair fretted instruments [FRETTED-INSTRUMENT REPAIRER (any industry)]. May be designated according to instrument made as Guitar Maker, Hand (musical inst.). ● **GED:** R4, M3, L4 ● **SVP:** 4-10 yrs ● **Academic:** Ed=N, Eng=S ● **Work Field:** 102 ● **MPSMS:** 614 ● **Aptitudes:** G3, V3, N3, S2, P2, Q4, K3, F2, M2, E5, C4 ● **Temperaments:** J ● **Physical:** Stg=L; Freq: R, H, I, N Occas: E, G, A, X ● **Work Env:** Noise=N; ● **Salary:** 3 ● **Outlook:** 1

VIOLIN MAKER, HAND (musical inst.) ● DOT #730.281-046 ● OES: 93196 ● Constructs bowed musical instruments, such as violins, cellos, and violas, using handtools: Selects wood according to type, grain, and seasoning. Lays out parts to be cut, using templates. Saws, carves, and shapes instrument parts, using handtools. Glues parts together, using jigs, forms, and clamps. Finishes surface with stain and varnish. Strings instrument. Plays instrument to evaluate tonal quality. Relocates bridge and sounding post, or shaves wood from bottom of instrument to improve tone. May repair bowed instruments [VIOLIN REPAIRER (any industry)]. May construct fretted instruments [FRETTED-INSTRUMENT MAKER, HAND (musical inst.)]. May repair fretted instruments [FRETTED-INSTRUMENT REPAIRER (any industry)]. May rebuild and restore bowed instruments and be designated Violin Restorer (musical inst.). ● **GED:** R4, M3, L3 ● **SVP:** 4-10 yrs ● **Academic:** Ed=N, Eng=S ● **Work Field:** 102 ● **MPSMS:** 614 ● **Aptitudes:** G3, V3, N3, S2, P2, Q4, K3, F2, M2, E5, C3 ● **Temperaments:** J ● **Physical:** Stg=L; Const: I, E Freq: R, H, G, N Occas: A, X ● **Work Env:** Noise=N; ● **Salary:** 3 ● **Outlook:** 1

GOE: 05.05.13
Printing

ASSISTANT-PRESS OPERATOR (print. & pub.) ● DOT #651.585-010 ● OES: 92542 ● Alternate titles: FLEXOGRAPHIC-PRESS HELPER; WEB-PRESS-OPERATOR ASSISTANT. Performs any combination of following duties to assist printing press operator to make ready, operate, and maintain roll-fed (web) or sheet-fed, single-or-multicolor flatbed, cylinder, offset, flexographic, or web press: Assists press operator to install paper packing sheets on impression (back-up) cylinder, fasten reinforcing bars to metal printing plates and offset blankets, and install plates and blankets on press cylinders, using moves excess metal from nonprinting areas of plate surface, using radial or cylindrical routing machine. May operate proof press to obtain proof of plate reproduction and registration. May revise plates to customer's specifications. May be known according to task performed as Electrotype Caster (print. & pub.); Electrotype Molder (print. & pub.). ● **GED:** R4, M3, L3 ● **SVP:** 4-10 yrs ● **Academic:** Ed=N, Eng=S ● **Work Field:** 191 ● **MPSMS:** 567 ● **Aptitudes:** G3, V3, N3, S3, P2, Q4, K3, F3, M3, E4, C3 ● **Temperaments:** J, T ● **Physical:** Stg=M; Freq: R, H, I, N, D, A, X Occas: S ● **Work Env:** Noise=L; Freq: O Occas: A ● **Salary:** 5 ● **Outlook:** 2

CYLINDER-PRESS OPERATOR (print. & pub.) ● DOT #651.362-010 ● OES: 92515 ● Alternate titles: FLATBED-PRESS OPERATOR; PRESS OPERATOR. Makes ready and operates cylinder-type printing press: Verifies size, color, and type of paper and color of ink from job order. Cleans inking rollers with solvent and replaces them in press, using handtools. Adjusts controls to regulate volume of ink. Packs impression cylinder with tissue or folio. Adjusts delivery tapes, and positions and locks form (type setup or plate) on bed or cylinder of press. Directs CYLINDER-PRESS FEEDER (print. & pub.) in adjustment of feed guides, grippers, and elevator, or hand-feeding press. Starts press and runs off proofsheet. Examines proof to determine off-level areas, variation in ink volume, register slippage, indications of offsetting, and color register. Adjusts press controls, inking fountains, and automatic feeders, and repacks cylinder with overlay to equalize off-level areas as required. May register forms and mix colors. May make overlay for half-tone shades. May operate cylinder press equipped with cutting attachment or may replace type dies with cutting dies to cut or

shape paper or paperboard. May operate more than one press. May be designated according to kind of material printed as Check Imprinter (print. & pub.); Envelope-Press Operator (print. & pub.) I; Label-Press Operator (print. & pub.) I; size of press as Pony-Cylinder-Press Operator (print. & pub.). Important variations may be indicated by trade names of machine used. ● **GED:** R4, M3, L3 ● **SVP:** 2-4 yrs ● **Academic:** Ed=N, Eng=S ● **Work Field:** 191 ● **MPSMS:** 567 ● **Aptitudes:** G3, V3, N3, S3, P2, Q4, K3, F3, M3, E5, C3 ● **Temperaments:** J, T ● **Physical:** Stg=M; Freq: R, H, I, N, X Occas: S, K, O, D, A ● **Work Env:** Noise=L; Freq: O ● **Salary:** 3 ● **Outlook:** 2

OFFSET-PRESS OPERATOR I (print. & pub.) ● DOT #651.382-042 ● OES: 92512 ● Alternate titles: FIRST PRESS OPERATOR; LITHOGRAPHIC-PRESS OPERATOR. Makes ready and operates web or sheet-fed offset printing press to print single and multicolor copy from lithographic plates: Examines job order to determine quantity to be printed, stock specifications, colors, and special printing instructions. Measures plate thickness and inserts packing sheets on plate cylinder to build up plate to printing height and installs and locks plate into position, using handtools, to achieve pressure required for printing. Washes plate to remove protective gum coating. Measures paper thickness and adjusts space between blanket and impression cylinders according to thickness of paper stock. Fills ink and dampening solution fountains and adjusts controls to regulate flow of ink and dampening solution to plate cylinder. Starts press, examines printed copy for ink density, position on paper, and registration, and makes adjustments to press throughout production run to maintain specific registration and color density. Removes and cleans plate and cylinders. May apply packing sheets to blanket cylinder to build up blanket thickness to diameter of plate cylinder. May load paper into feeder or install rolls of paper, make adjustments to feeder and delivery mechanisms, and unload printed material from delivery mechanism. May lead, give directions to, and monitor work of ASSISTANT PRESS OPERATOR, OFFSET (print. & pub.) 651.685-026; FEEDER (print. & pub.) 651.686-014; JOGGER (print. & pub.) 651.686-018; or ROLL TENDER (print. & pub.) 651.686-022. ● **GED:** R4, M2, L3 ● **SVP:** 4-10 yrs ● **Academic:** Ed=N, Eng=S ● **Work Field:** 191 ● **MPSMS:** 480 ● **Aptitudes:** G3, V3, N3, S3, P2, Q3, K3, F3, M3, E5, C3 ● **Temperaments:** T, V ● **Physical:** Stg=L; Freq: R, H, I, N, F, D Occas: S, G, A, X ● **Work Env:** Noise=V; Freq: A, M Occas: U, V ● **Salary:** 3 ● **Outlook:** 2

ROTOGRAVURE-PRESS OPERATOR (print. & pub.) ● DOT #651.362-026 ● OES: 92519 ● Makes ready and operates rotary-type press that prints illustrative and other subject matter by rotogravure process: Installs engraved copper printing cylinder in press, using handtools. Adjusts doctor (wiper) blade to remove excess ink from surface of printing cylinder. Threads web (roll) of paper or other printing stock through press, adjusting guides and tension bars. Sets focus of electronic scanners on guideline of paper (for multicolor printing) to automatically control color registration. Regulates temperature in web-drying chambers and adjusts automatic cutter at discharge end of press. Inspects material being printed, during production run, and adjusts press as required to produce printed matter to specifications. Directs workers in feeding and unloading press, replenishing ink supply in fountains, cleaning equipment, and other press operations. May operate press equipped to print, cut, and crease paper goods. ● **GED:** R3, M2, L2 ● **SVP:** 2-4 yrs ● **Academic:** Ed=N, Eng=N ● **Work Field:** 191 ● **MPSMS:** 567 ● **Aptitudes:** G3, V3, N3, S3, P2, Q4, K3, F3, M3, E5, C3 ● **Temperaments:** J, T, V ● **Physical:** Stg=M; Freq: R, H, I, N, D, X Occas: A ● **Work Env:** Noise=L; Occas: O ● **Salary:** 2 ● **Outlook:** 2

STEREOTYPER (print. & pub.) ● DOT #974.382-014 ● OES: 89716 ● Operates machines to press face of composed type and plates into wood-fiber mat to form stereotype casting mold, pour molten metal into mold, and finish castings by cutting, shaving, and trimming to form plates for printing: Drills matching holes in series of mounted color plates to be duplicated and inserts pilot pins in base to register all plates to key plate for mat molding. Lays sheet of mat paper on form or plates, covers assembly with molding blanket and protective sheet, and pushes assembly to self-feeding rollers of mat-rolling machine or into cavity of hydraulic press. Adjusts time, temperature, and pressure controls to form and dry mold. Cuts and pastes pieces of paper felt or cardboard in large nonprinting areas of mat to prevent collapse during casting of plate. Aligns and notches mats of series with key color mat (mold), using matching machine with monocolor magnifier attachment.

Aligns notches with pins of trimming machine and pushes lever to trim three edges of mat simultaneously. Lays mat on casting box platen and arranges steel bars on three sides of mat to confine molten type metal. Pours metal into casting box by hand or by operating automatic stereotype plate-casting machine. Trims plates to specified size [PLATE FINISHER (print. & pub.)]. Coats curved plates with nickel [PLATER (electroplating)]. May register series of color plates and mats by transparent acetate overlay process. May be designated according to task performed as Stereotype Caster (print. & pub.); Stereotype Molder (print. & pub.). ● **GED:** R4, M2, L2 ● **SVP:** 4-10 yrs ● **Academic:** Ed=N, Eng=S ● **Work Field:** 191 ● **MPSMS:** 567 ● **Aptitudes:** G3, V3, N3, S3, P3, Q4, K3, F3, M2, E5, C4 ● **Temperaments:** J, T ● **Physical:** Stg=M; Freq: R, H, I, N, D, A Occas: X ● **Work Env:** Noise=L; Freq: O ● **Salary:** 5 ● **Outlook:** 2

WEB-PRESS OPERATOR (print. & pub.) ● DOT #651.362-030 ● OES: 92515 ● Makes ready and operates multiunit, web-fed rotary press to print newspapers, books, and periodicals according to written specifications: Locks printing plates on printing cylinder and threads loose end of paper supply roll (web) through and around rollers to cutter and folder. Adjusts compensators to guide paper over rollers and cylinders. Inspects printed sheets visually after registration or position printing and readjusts guides and controls to rectify spacing errors. Adjusts feed controls to rotate cylinder into position where plate locking mechanism is accessible. Unlocks plates and replaces with makeover plates according to directions marked on plate regarding location and time of printing. Rethreads paper through press if web breaks (press stops automatically if web breaks) and readjusts tension rollers. Operates pasting device to splice end of new paper roll to depleted roll. Inspects printed material visually during production and readjusts controls to correct irregular ink distribution, faulty cuts or folds. Replaces cutting blades, worn or damaged ink rolls, and fills ink wells. Cleans, inspects, and lubricates moving parts of press. May supervise and instruct apprentices. May load supply rolls of paper in press at beginning and during run. May be designated Tension Regulator (print. & pub.) when installing paper rolls in press and adjusting controls to regulate tension of paper; or Color-Control Operator (print. & pub.) when adjusting ink controls to secure specified color registration. May operate press from central control console. ● **GED:** R4, M3, L3 ● **SVP:** 2-4 yrs ● **Academic:** Ed=N, Eng=S ● **Work Field:** 191 ● **MPSMS:** 567 ● **Aptitudes:** G3, V3, N3, S3, P3, Q4, K4, F3, M3, E4, C4 ● **Temperaments:** J, T ● **Physical:** Stg=M; Freq: R, H, I, N, D Occas: S, K, O, T, G, A, X ● **Work Env:** Noise=L; Occas: O ● **Salary:** 3 ● **Outlook:** 2

GOE: 05.05.14
Gem Cutting & Finishing

GEM CUTTER (jewelry-silver.) ● DOT #770.281-014 ● OES: 89998 ● Alternate titles: CUTTER; LAPIDARY; STONECUTTER. Cuts, shapes, and polishes precious and synthetic gems: Positions rough stone in holder and holds stone against edge of revolving saw or lapidary slitter impregnated with diamond dust to cut and slit stone. Removes cut stone and places it in lapidary stick. Selects shaping wheel and applies abrasive compound. Holds lapidary stick against revolving shaping wheel and lapidary disk to further shape stone and grind facets. Examines stone for accuracy of cut, using magnifying glass. Polishes stone, using felt or canvas-covered polishing wheel, and polishing compounds, such as tripoli or rouge. May use mechanical facet-cutting device. May cut and polish diamonds for industrial purposes and be designated Industrial-Diamond Polisher (jewelry-silver.). ● **GED:** R4, M3, L3 ● **SVP:** 1-2 yrs ● **Academic:** Ed=H, Eng=N ● **Work Field:** 051 ● **MPSMS:** 613 ● **Aptitudes:** G3, V4, N3, S2, P2, Q4, K3, F3, M2, E5, C3 ● **Temperaments:** J, T, V ● **Physical:** Stg=S; Const: R, H Freq: I, E, N, X Occas: D, A ● **Work Env:** Noise=N; ● **Salary:** 5 ● **Outlook:** 3

GEMOLOGIST (jewelry-silver.) ● DOT #199.281-010 ● OES: 39998 ● Alternate titles: GEM EXPERT. Examines gemstones, such as jade, sapphires, and rubies, to evaluate their genuineness, quality, and value, utilizing knowledge of gems and market valuations: Examines gem surfaces and internal structure, using polariscope, refractometer, microscope, and other optical instruments, to differentiate between stones, identify rare specimens, or to detect flaws, defects, or peculiarities affecting gem values. Immerses stones in prescribed chemical solutions to determine specific gravities and key properties of gemstones or substitutes, which indicate physical characteristics of stone for gem identification, quality determination, and for appraisal. Grades stones for color, perfection, and quality of cut. Estimates wholesale and retail value of gems, following pricing guides, market fluctuations, and various economic changes that affect distribution of precious stones. May advise customers and others in use of gems to create attractive jewelry items. ● **GED:** R4, M3, L4 ● **SVP:** 2-4 yrs ● **Academic:** Ed=H, Eng=G ● **Work Field:** 211 ● **MPSMS:** 611 ● **Aptitudes:** G2, V2, N3, S2, P2, Q4, K3, F3, M3, E5, C3 ● **Temperaments:** J, T ● **Physical:** Stg=L; Freq: R, H, I, N, D, A, X ● **Work Env:** Noise=N; ● **Salary:** 5 ● **Outlook:** 3

STONE SETTER (jewelry-silver.) ● DOT #700.381-054 ● OES: 89198 ● Alternate titles: JEWELRY SETTER. Sets precious, semiprecious, or ornamental stones in rings, earrings, bracelets, brooches, metal optical frames, and other jeweled items, using handtools: Places item in vise. Cuts and files setting to accommodate stones, using files, chisels, and hand or electric drills. Positions stone in setting and fixes in place by pressing prongs around stone, by raising retaining metal ridge around stone, or by tapping edges of setting with setting tool and hammer, forcing metal against stone. Smooths edges, using emery file and pointed steel tool. Examines union of stone and setting, using magnifying glass. May drill holes in settings preparatory to setting stones in piece. May replace stones in rings. May be designated according to stone set as Diamond Setter (jewelry-silver.) or according to item worked on as Stone Setter, Metal Optical Frames (optical goods). ● **GED:** R3, M2, L2 ● **SVP:** 2-4 yrs ● **Academic:** Ed=N, Eng=N ● **Work Field:** 061 ● **MPSMS:** 605, 611 ● **Aptitudes:** G3, V3, N3, S2, P2, Q4, K2, F2, M3, E5, C5 ● **Temperaments:** J, T, V ● **Physical:** Stg=L; Const: R, H, N, D, A Occas: I, E ● **Work Env:** Noise=N; ● **Salary:** 2 ● **Outlook:** 2

GOE: 05.05.15
Custom Sewing, Tailoring & Upholstering

ALTERATION TAILOR (garment) ● DOT #785.261-010 ● OES: 89505 ● Alternate titles: ALTERER; BUSHELER. Alters clothing to fit individual customers or repairs defective garments, following alteration or repair tags or marks on garments: Examines tag or garment to ascertain necessary alterations. Removes stitches from garment, using ripper or razor blade. Shortens or lengthens sleeves and legs, expands or narrows waist and chest, raises or lowers collar, and inserts or eliminates padding in shoulders while maintaining drape and proportions of garment. Trims excess material, using scissors. Resews garment, using needle and thread or sewing machine. Repairs or replaces defective garment parts, such as pockets, pocket flaps, and coat linings. May fit garments on customer to determine required alterations [GARMENT FITTER (retail trade) 785.361-014]. May press garment, using hand iron [PRESSER, HAND (any industry) 363.684-018] or pressing machine [PRESSER, MACHINE (any industry) 363.682-018]. May be designated according to type of garment altered or repaired as Tailor, Men's Ready-To-Wear (retail trade); Tailor, Women's-Garment Alteration (retail trade); or according to garment part altered or repaired as Pants Busheler (Retail trade); Vest Busheler (retail trade). ● **GED:** R4, M3, L3 ● **SVP:** 2-4 yrs ● **Academic:** Ed=N, Eng=S ● **Work Field:** 171 ● **MPSMS:** 440 ● **Aptitudes:** G3, V3, N3, S2, P3, Q4, K3, F2, M3, E4, C3 ● **Temperaments:** J, T ● **Physical:** Stg=L; Const: I, N Freq: R, H, D Occas: E, A, X ● **Work Env:** Noise=N; ● **Salary:** 4 ● **Outlook:** 3

AUTOMOBILE UPHOLSTERER (automotive ser.) ● DOT #780.381-010 ● OES: 89508 ● Repairs or replaces upholstery in automobiles, buses, and trucks: Removes old upholstery from seats and door panels of vehicle. Measures new padding and covering materials, and cuts them to required dimensions, using knife or shears. Adjusts or replaces seat springs and ties them in place. Sews covering material together, using sewing machine. Fits covering to seat frame and secures it with glue and tacks. Repairs or replaces convertible tops. Refurbishes interiors of streetcars and buses by replacing cushions, drapes, and floor coverings. May be designated according to specialty as Body Trimmer (automotive ser.); Bus Upholsterer (automotive ser.); Top Installer (automotive ser.). ● **GED:** R3, M2, L3 ● **SVP:** 1-2 yrs ● **Academic:** Ed=N, Eng=S ● **Work Field:** 101 ● **MPSMS:** 591 ● **Aptitudes:** G3, V3, N3, S3, P3, Q4, K3, F3, M3, E4, C4 ● **Temperaments:** J, T ● **Physical:** Stg=M; Freq: S, K, O, R, H, I, N, D Occas: E, A, X ● **Work Env:** Noise=N; ● **Salary:** 3 ● **Outlook:** 2

BOOKBINDER (print. & pub.) ● DOT #977.381-010 ● OES: 89721 ● Alternate titles: BOOKMAKER. Cuts, assembles, glues, and sews components to bind books, according to specification, using automatic and manually operated machines, handtools, and equipment: Folds printed sheets to form signatures (pages) and assembles signatures in numerical order to form book body. Attaches endpapers to top and bottom of book body. Sews signatures and endpapers together along spine of book body, using sewing machine, or glues endpapers and signatures together along spine, using brush or glue machine. Compresses sewed or glued signatures to reduce book to required thickness, using handpress or smashing machine. Trims edges of book to size, using cutting or book trimming machine or hand cutter. Inserts book body in device that forms back edge of book into convex shape and produces grooves to facilitate attachment of cover. Applies glue to back of book, using brush or glue machine, and attaches cloth backing and headband. Applies color to edges of signatures, using brush, pad, or atomizer. Cuts binder board to specified dimension, using board shears, hand cutter, or cutting machine. Cuts cover material, such as leather or cloth, to specified dimensions and fits and glues material to binder board manually or by machine. Glues outside endpapers to cover. Places bound book in press that exerts pressure on cover until glue dries. May imprint and emboss lettering, designs, or numbers on cover, using gold, silver, or colored foil and stamping machine. May pack, weigh, and stack books on pallet for shipment. May specialize in repairing and rebinding damaged or worn books for resale or reuse. ● **GED:** R3, M2, L2 ● **SVP:** 2-4 yrs ● **Academic:** Ed=N, Eng=N ● **Work Field:** 102, 192 ● **MPSMS:** 480 ● **Aptitudes:** G3, V3, N4, S3, P3, Q4, K3, F3, M3, E4, C3 ● **Temperaments:** T, V ● **Physical:** Stg=M; Freq: R, H, I, N, D, A, X Occas: S, G ● **Work Env:** Noise=N; Freq: M Occas: V ● **Salary:** 2 ● **Outlook:** 2

CUSTOM TAILOR (garment) ● DOT #785.261-014 ● OES: 89505 ● Alternate titles: MADE-TO-MEASURE TAILOR; TAILOR. Develops designs and makes tailored garments, such as suits, topcoats, overcoats, and other dress clothing, applying principles of garment design, construc- tion, and styling: Confers with customer to determine type of material and garment style desired. Measures customer for size and records measurements for use in preparing patterns and making garment. Develops designs for garments or copies existing designs. Draws individual pattern for garment or alters standard pattern to fit customer's measurements. Outlines patterns of garment parts on fabric and cuts fabric along outlines, using scissors. Assembles garments, sewing padding to coat fronts, lapels, and collars to give them shape and joining garment parts with basting stitches, using needle and thread or sewing machine. Fits basted garment on customer and marks areas requiring alterations. Alters garment and joins parts, using needle and thread or sewing machine. Sews buttons and buttonholes to finish garment. May press garment [PRESSER, HAND (any industry); PRESSER, MACHINE (any industry)]. May supervise activities of other workers in tailoring shop. May specialize in making garments and be designated Coat Tailor (garment). May perform specific tasks in tailor shop and be designated Coat Fitter (garment); Try-On Baster (garment). ● **GED:** R4, M3, L3 ● **SVP:** 4-10 yrs ● **Academic:** Ed=N, Eng=S ● **Work Field:** 171, 264 ● **MPSMS:** 440 ● **Aptitudes:** G2, V2, N3, S2, P3, Q4, K2, F2, M3, E4, C3 ● **Temperaments:** J ● **Physical:** Stg=L; Const: I, N Freq: R, H, T, G, D Occas: E, A, X ● **Work Env:** Noise=L; ● **Salary:** 4 ● **Outlook:** 4

DRESSMAKER (any industry) ● DOT #785.361-010 ● OES: 89505 ● Makes women's garments, such as dresses, coats, and suits, according to customer specifications and measurements: Discusses with customer type of material, pattern, or style to be used in making garment. Measures customer to determine modification from pattern, using tape measure. Positions and pins pattern sections, such as collar, sleeve, or waist, on fabric, and cuts fabric with scissors following pattern edge. Pins or bastes together fabric parts in preparation for final sewing. Sews fabric parts by hand or operates single-needle sewing machine that joins fabric parts to form garment. Sews felling stitch in hem of garment by hand to conceal thread. Presses garment, using hand iron, to smooth seams and remove wrinkles [PRESSER, HAND (any indus-

try)]. May draft standard pattern according to measurements of customer and adapt pattern to obtain specified style. May make garment according to picture furnished by customer. ● **SVP:** 2-4 yrs ● **Academic:** Ed=N, Eng=S ● **Work Field:** 171 ● **MPSMS:** 443, 909 ● **Aptitudes:** G3, V3, N4, S3, P3, Q4, K3, F3, M3, E4, C3 ● **Temperaments:** J, T, V ● **Physical:** Stg=L; Freq: R, H, I, N, D Occas: S, K, O, E, T, G, A, X ● **Work Env:** Noise=N; ● **Salary:** 1 ● **Outlook:** 3

FURNITURE UPHOLSTERER (any industry) ● DOT #780.381-018 ● OES: 89508 ● Alternate titles: UPHOLSTERER. Repairs and rebuilds upholstered furniture, using handtools and knowledge of fabrics and upholstery methods: Removes covering, webbing, and padding from seat, arms, back, and sides of workpiece, using tack puller, chisel, and mallet. Removes defective springs by cutting cords or wires that hold them in place. Replaces webbing and springs or reties springs [SPRINGER (furniture) 780.684-106]. Measures and cuts new covering material [CUTTER, MACHINE (any industry) I 781.684-014]. Installs material on inside of arms, back, and seat, and over outside back and arms of wooden frame. Tacks or sews ornamental trim, such as braid and buttons, to cover or frame [UPHOLSTERY TRIMMER (furniture) 780.684-126]. May operate sewing machine to seam cushions and join various sections of covering material. May repair wooden frame of workpiece. May refinish wooden surfaces [FURNITURE FINISHER (woodworking) 763.381-010]. May upholster cornices and be designated Cornice Upholsterer (any industry). May repair seats, carpets, curtains, mattresses, and window shades of railroad coaches and sleeping cars and be designated Upholsterer (r.r. trans.). ● **GED:** R4, M3, L3 ● **SVP:** 2-4 yrs ● **Academic:** Ed=N, Eng=S ● **Work Field:** 101 ● **MPSMS:** 460 ● **Aptitudes:** G3, V3, N3, S2, P2, Q4, K3, F3, M2, E5, C3 ● **Temperaments:** J, T ● **Physical:** Stg=M; Freq: S, R, H, I, E, N, D, A, X Occas: K, O ● **Work Env:** Noise=L; ● **Salary:** 2 ● **Outlook:** 3

RUG REPAIRER (laundry & rel.) ● DOT #782.381-018 ● OES: 89598 ● Repairs and remodels rugs and carpets: Cuts patch from corner or edge of defective rug, or from carpet material or another rug of similar color and pattern for use in repair of damaged rug. Darns holes in rug-backing by hand, using cross-stitch to sew fibers together. Selects matching rug fibers and stitches them to rug-backing with needle and thread to reburl (reweave) damaged area and restore nap (pile). Patches rug by stitching edges of rug and patch together with carpet stitch. Remodels rugs by cutting to required size and shape, using hand shears. Binds edges of rugs by operating serging machine, or sews edges of rug or carpet, using needle and thread. ● **GED:** R3, M2, L3 ● **SVP:** 1-2 yrs ● **Academic:** Ed=N, Eng=S ● **MPSMS:** 431 ● **Aptitudes:** G3, V4, N3, S3, P3, Q4, K3, F2, M3, E4, C3 ● **Temperaments:** J, T, V ● **Physical:** Stg=M; Freq: R, H, I, N, D, X Occas: S ● **Work Env:** Noise=L; ● **Salary:** 1 ● **Outlook:** 2

SHOE REPAIRER (personal ser.) ● DOT #365.361-014 ● OES: 89511 ● Alternate titles: COBBLER; SHOEMAKER. Repairs or refinishes shoes, following customer specifications, or according to nature of damage, or type of shoe: Positions shoe on last and pulls and cuts off sole or heel with pincers and knife. Starts machine, and holds welt against rotating sanding wheel or rubs with sandpaper to bevel and roughen welt for attachment of new sole. Selects blank or cuts sole or heel piece to approximate size from material, using knife. Brushes cement on new sole or heel piece and on shoe welt and shoe heel. Positions sole over shoe welt or heel piece on shoe heel and pounds piece, using machine or hammer, so piece adheres to shoe; drives nails around sole or heel edge into shoe; or guides shoe and sole under needle of sewing machine to fasten sole to shoe. Trims sole or heel edge to shape of shoe with knife. Holds and turns shoe sole or heel against revolving abrasive wheel to smooth edge and remove excess material. Brushes edge with stain or polish and holds against revolving buffing wheels to polish edge. Nails heel and toe cleats to shoe. Restitches ripped portions or sews patches over holes in shoe uppers by hand or machine. Dampens portion of shoe and inserts and twists adjustable stretcher in shoes or pull portion of moistened shoe back and forth over warm iron to stretch shoe. May build up portions of shoes by nailing, stapling, or stitching additional material to shoe sole to add height or make other specified alterations to orthopedic shoes. May repair belts, luggage, purses, and other products made of materials, such as canvas, leather, and plastic. May quote charges, receive articles, and collect payment for repairs [SERVICE-ESTABLISHMENT ATTENDANT (laundry & rel.; personal ser.) 369.477-014]. ● **GED:** R3, M2, L1 ● **SVP:** 1-2 yrs ● **Academic:** Ed=N, Eng=N ● **Work Field:** 102 ● **MPSMS:** 906 ● **Aptitudes:** G3, V3, N4, S3, P3, Q4, K3, F3, M2, E3, C4 ● **Temperaments:** J, R, T ● **Physical:** Stg=L; Freq: R, H, I, N, A Occas: E, D, X ● **Work Env:** Noise=Q; ● **Salary:** 2 ● **Outlook:** 3

SHOP TAILOR (garment) ● DOT #785.361-022 ● OES: 89505 ● Performs specialized hand and machine sewing operations in manufacture of made-to-measure or ready-to-wear clothing, applying knowledge of garment construction and fabrics: Trims and shapes edges of garment parts preparatory to sewing and cuts excess material from seam edges, using shears or knife. Fits collar facing to underfacing, trims edge of undercollar with shears, and sews undercollar to collar. Bastes collar or sleeves to coat body and sews collar or sleeves to coat with permanent stitches. Stitches shoulder padding, coat facing, and lining together at armhole. Bastes and sews canvas material in various coat parts, such as undercollar, shoulder, and front edge. Joins shoulder padding to coat with basting stitches. May sew on buttons and make buttonholes to finish suits. May be designated according to tasks performed or garments sewn as Coat Baster (garment; retail trade); Coat Padder (garment; retail trade); Collar Setter (garment; retail trade); Lapel Padder (garment; retail trade); Sleeve Tailor (garment; retail trade); Suit Finisher (garment; retail trade). May be designated: Top-Collar Maker (garment; retail trade); Undercollar Baster (garment; retail trade); Undercollar Maker (garment; retail trade); Vest Tailor (garment; retail trade). ● **GED:** R4, M3, L3 ● **SVP:** 2-4 yrs ● **Academic:** Ed=N, Eng=S ● **Work Field:** 171 ● **MPSMS:** 440 ● **Aptitudes:** G3, V3, N3, S3, P3, Q4, K3, F3, M3, E4, C3 ● **Temperaments:** J, T ● **Physical:** Stg=L; Freq: R, H, I, N, D Occas: S, E, T, G, A, X ● **Work Env:** Noise=N; ● **Salary:** 2 ● **Outlook:** 3

UPHOLSTERY REPAIRER (furniture) ● DOT #780.684-122 ● OES: 89508 ● Repairs or replaces damaged or defective upholstery on chairs or sofas: Examines upholstery to locate defects. Sews tears or rips with needle and thread. Pulls tacks or staples from defective upholstery, using hammer or pliers, and removes upholstery from frame. Tacks, sews, or staples replacement upholstery to frame. May cut covering from bolt of cloth, using part removed as pattern, or may carry defective parts to cutters to have replacement parts cut to specifications. ● **GED:** R3, M1, L1 ● **SVP:** 1-2 yrs ● **Academic:** Ed=N, Eng=N ● **Work Field:** 101 ● **MPSMS:** 460 ● **Aptitudes:** G3, V4, N4, S3, P3, Q4, K3, F3, M3, E5, C4 ● **Temperaments:** R, T ● **Physical:** Stg=M; Const: N Freq: R, H, I, E, D Occas: S, K, O, X ● **Work Env:** Noise=N; ● **Salary:** 4 ● **Outlook:** 3

GOE: 05.05.17
Food Preparation

ANALYST, FOOD AND BEVERAGE (hotel & rest.) ● DOT #310.267-010 ● OES: 21905 ● Alternate titles: RESEARCH WORKER, KITCHEN. Examines food samples and food service records and other data to determine sales appeal and cost of preparing and serving meals and beverages in establishments, such as restaurants and cafeterias or for chain of food establishments: Tastes food samples to determine palatability and customer appeal. Estimates number of servings obtainable from standard and original recipes and unit cost of preparation. Converts recipes for use in quantity preparation. Studies reservation lists and previous records and forecasts customer traffic and number of servings required for specified period of time. May investigate complaints relative to faulty cooking or quality of ingredients. May plan menus. May specialize in industrial-employee food service or cafeteria food service. May supervise FOOD-AND-BEVERAGE CONTROLLER (hotel & rest.) and kitchen employees. ● **GED:** R5, M4, L4 ● **SVP:** 4-10 yrs ● **Academic:** Ed=A, Eng=G ● **Work Field:** 212, 251 ● **MPSMS:** 903 ● **Aptitudes:** G2, V2, N2, S3, P3, Q3, K3, F3, M3, E5, C3 ● **Temperaments:** D, J, P, T ● **Physical:** Stg=L; Freq: R, H, I, N, A Occas: T, G, X ● **Work Env:** Noise=N; ● **Salary:** 2 ● **Outlook:** 3

CAKE DECORATOR (bakery products) ● DOT #524.381-010 ● OES: 89898 ● Alternate titles: PASTRY DECORATOR. Decorates cakes and pastries with designs, using icing bag or handmade paper cone: Trims uneven surfaces of cake or cuts and shapes cake to re-quired size, using knife. Spreads icing between layers and on surfaces of cake, using spatula. Tints white icing with food coloring. Inserts die of specific design into tip of bag or paper cone and fills bag or cone with colored icing. Squeezes bag to eject icing while moving bag with free-arm writing motions to form design on cake. Forms decorations on flower nail and transfers decorations to cake, using spatula. May mix icing. ● **GED:** R3, M2, L2 ● **SVP:** 1-2 yrs ● **Academic:** Ed=N, Eng=N ● **Work Field:** 146 ● **MPSMS:** 384 ● **Aptitudes:** G3, V4, N4, S4, P3, Q4, K3, F3, M3, E5, C3 ● **Temperaments:** F, J ● **Physical:** Stg=L; Freq: R, H, I, N, X Occas: A ● **Work Env:** Noise=Q; ● **Salary:** 1 ● **Outlook:** 2

CHEF (hotel & rest.) ● DOT #313.131-014 ● OES: 69998 ● Alternate titles: COOK, CHIEF; KITCHEN CHEF. Supervises, coordinates, and participates in activities of cooks and other kitchen personnel engaged in preparing and cooking foods in hotel, restaurant, cafeteria, or other establishment: Estimates food consumption, and requisitions or purchases foodstuffs. Receives and examines foodstuffs and supplies to ensure quality and quantity meet established standards and specifications. Selects and develops recipes based on type of food to be prepared and applying personal knowledge and experience in food preparation. Supervises personnel engaged in preparing, cooking, and serving meats, sauces, vegetables, soups, and other foods. Cooks or otherwise prepares food according to recipe [COOK (hotel & rest.) 313.361-014]. Cuts, trims, and bones meats and poultry for cooking. Portions cooked foods, or gives instructions to workers as to size of portions and methods of garnishing. Carves meats. May employ, train, and discharge workers. May maintain time and payroll records. May plan menus. May supervise kitchen staff, plan menus, purchase foodstuffs, and not prepare and cook foods [EXECUTIVE CHEF (hotel & rest.) 187.167-010]. May be designated according to cuisine specialty as Chef, French (hotel & rest.); Chef, German (hotel & rest.); Chef, Italian (hotel & rest.); or according to food specialty as Chef, Broiler Or Fry (hotel & rest.); Chef, Saucier (hotel & rest.). May supervise worker preparing food for banquet and be designated Banquet Chef (hotel & rest.). ● **GED:** R4, M3, L3 ● **SVP:** 2-4 yrs ● **Academic:** Ed=H, Eng=S ● **Work Field:** 146 ● **MPSMS:** 903 ● **Aptitudes:** G3, V3, N3, S4, P3, Q3, K3, F4, M3, E5, C4 ● **Temperaments:** D, J, P, V ● **Physical:** Stg=L; Freq: R, H, T, G, N Occas: I, M, D, X ● **Work Env:** Noise=N; Occas: O ● **Salary:** 3 ● **Outlook:** 4

CHEF DE FROID (hotel & rest.) ● DOT #313.281-010 ● OES: 65026 ● Designs and prepares decorated foods and artistic food arrangements for buffets in formal restaurants: Confers with EXECUTIVE CHEF (hotel & rest.) and SOUS CHEF (hotel & rest.) and reviews advance menus to determine amount and type of food to be served and decor to be carried out. Prepares foods, such as hors d'oeuvres, cold whole salmon, roast suckling pig, casseroles, and fancy aspics, according to recipe, and decorates them following customer's specifications, designated color scheme, or theme, using colorful fruit, vegetables, and relishes. Molds butter into artistic forms, such as dancing girls or animals. Sculptures blocks of ice, using chisels and ice picks. Carves meats in patron's presence, employing showmanship. May prepare cold meats, casseroles, and other foods during slack periods [GARDE MANGER (hotel & rest.)]. ● **GED:** R4, M3, L3 ● **SVP:** 2-4 yrs ● **Academic:** Ed=N, Eng=S ● **Work Field:** 146 ● **MPSMS:** 903 ● **Aptitudes:** G3, V3, N3, S2, P2, Q3, K2, F2, M3, E5, C3 ● **Temperaments:** F, J, V ● **Physical:** Stg=M; Freq: R, H, T, G, N Occas: I, A, X ● **Work Env:** Noise=V; ● **Salary:** 3 ● **Outlook:** 4

COOK (hotel & rest.) ● DOT #313.361-014 ● OES: 65026 ● Alternate titles: COOK, RESTAURANT. Prepares, seasons, and cooks soups, meats, vegetables, desserts, and other foodstuffs for consumption in eating establishments: Reads menu to estimate food requirements and orders food from supplier or procures food from storage. Adjusts thermostat controls to regulate temperature of ovens, broilers, grills, roasters, and steam kettles. Measures and mixes ingredients according to recipe, using variety of kitchen utensils and equipment, such as blenders, mixers, grinders, slicers, and tenderizers, to prepare soups, salads, gravies, desserts, sauces, and casseroles. Bakes, roasts, broils, and steams meats, fish, vegetables, and other foods. Adds seasoning to foods during mixing or cooking, according to personal judgment and experience. Observes and tests foods being cooked by tasting, smelling, and piercing with fork to determine that it is cooked. Carves meats, portions food on serving plates, adds gravies and sauces, and garnishes servings to fill orders. May supervise other cooks and kitchen employees. May wash, peel, cut, and shred vegetables and fruits to prepare them for use. May butcher chickens, fish, and shellfish. May cut, trim, and bone meat prior to cooking. May bake bread, rolls, cakes, and pastry [BAKER (hotel & rest.) 313.381-010]. May price items on menu. May be designated according to meal cooked or shift worked as Cook, Dinner (hotel & rest.); Cook, Morning (hotel & rest.); or according to food item prepared as Cook, Roast (hotel & rest.); or according to method of cooking as Cook, Broiler (hotel & rest.). May substitute for and relieve or assist other cooks during emergencies or rush periods and be designated Cook, Relief (hotel & rest.). May prepare and cook meals for institutionalized patients requiring special diets and be designated Food-Service Worker (hotel & rest.). May be designated: Cook, Dessert (hotel & rest.); Cook, Fry (hotel & rest.); Cook, Night (hotel & rest.); Cook, Sauce (hotel & rest.); Cook, Soup (hotel & rest.); Cook, Special Diet (hotel & rest.); Cook, Vegetable (hotel & rest.). May oversee work of patients assigned to kitchen for work therapy purposes ● **GED:** R3, M3, L3 ● **SVP:** 2-4 yrs ● **Academic:** Ed=H, Eng=S ● **Work Field:** 146 ● **MPSMS:** 903 ● **Aptitudes:** G3, V3, N3, S4, P3, Q3, K3, F3, M3, E5, C4 ● **Temperaments:** J, T, V ● **Physical:** Stg=M; Freq: R, H, I, N Occas: T, G, M, X ● **Work Env:** Noise=N; Freq: H, O ● **Salary:** 1 ● **Outlook:** 4

DIETITIAN, CLINICAL (profess. & kin.) ● DOT #077.127-014 ● OES: 32521 ● Alternate titles: DIETITIAN, THERAPEUTIC. Plans therapeutic diets and implements preparation and service of meals for patients in hospital, clinic, or other health care facility: Consults with physician and other health care personnel to determine nutritional needs and diet restrictions, such as low fat or salt free, of patients. Formulates menus for therapeutic diets based on medical and physical condition of patients and integrates patient's menus with basic institutional menus. Inspects meals served for conformance to prescribed diets and for standards of palatability and appearance. Instructs patients and their families in nutritional principles, dietary plans, food selection, and preparation. May supervise activities of workers engaged in food preparation and service. May engage in research [DIETITIAN, RESEARCH (profess. & kin.) 077.061-010]. May teach nutrition and diet therapy to medical students and hospital personnel [DIETITIAN, TEACHING (profess. & kin.) 077.127-022]. ● **GED:** R5, M4, L5 ● **SVP:** 2-4 yrs ● **Academic:** Ed=B, Eng=G ● **Work Field:** 295 ● **MPSMS:** 924 ● **Aptitudes:** G2, V2, N3, S4, P4, Q3, K4, F4, M4, E5, C4 ● **Temperaments:** D, J, P ● **Physical:** Stg=L; Freq: R, H, T, G, N Occas: I, M, X ● **Work Env:** Noise=Q; ● **Salary:** 3 ● **Outlook:** 4

DIETETIC TECHNICIAN (profess. & kin.) ● DOT #077.124-010 ● OES: 32998 ● Provides services in assigned areas of food service management, teaches principles of food and nutrition, and provides dietary consultation, under direction of DIETITIAN, CLINICAL (profess. & kin.) 077.127-014: Plans menus based on established guidelines. Standardizes recipes and tests new products for use in facility. Supervises food production and service. Obtains and evaluates dietary histories of individuals to plan nutritional programs. Guides individuals and families in food selection, preparation, and menu planning, based upon nutritional needs. Assists in referrals for continuity of patient care. May select, schedule, and conduct orientation and in-service education programs. May develop job specifications, job descriptions, and work schedules. May assist in implementing established cost control procedures. ● **GED:** R5, M4, L5 ● **SVP:** 2-4 yrs ● **Academic:** Ed=A, Eng=G ● **Work Field:** 296, 282 ● **MPSMS:** 924, 903 ● **Aptitudes:** G2, V3, N3, S3, P3, Q3, K4, F4, M3, E5, C4 ● **Temperaments:** D, J, P, V ● **Physical:** Stg=L; Freq: R, H, T, G, N, A Occas: I, M, X ● **Work Env:** Noise=N; ● **Salary:** 3 ● **Outlook:** 3

SOUS CHEF (hotel & rest.) ● DOT #313.131-026 ● OES: 69998 ● Alternate titles: CHEF ASSISTANT; CHEF, UNDER; EXECUTIVE-CHEF ASSISTANT; SUPERVISING-CHEF ASSISTANT. Supervises and coordinates activities of COOKS (hotel & rest.) and other workers engaged in preparing and cooking foodstuffs: Observes workers engaged in preparing, portioning, and garnishing foods to ensure that methods of cooking and garnishing and sizes of portions are as prescribed. Gives instructions to cooking personnel in fine points of cooking. Cooks and carves meats, and prepares dishes, such as sauces, during rush periods and for banquets and other social functions. Assumes responsibility for kitchen in absence of EXECUTIVE CHEF (hotel & rest.). In establishments not employing EXECUTIVE CHEF (hotel & rest.), may be designated Supervising Chef (hotel & rest.). ● **GED:** R4, M3, L3 ● **SVP:** 4-10 yrs ● **Academic:** Ed=N, Eng=S ● **Work Field:** 146, 295 ● **MPSMS:** 903 ● **Aptitudes:** G3, V3, N3, S4, P3, Q3, K3, F4, M3, E5, C4 ● **Temperaments:** D, J, P, V ● **Physical:** Stg=M; Freq: R, H, I, T, G, N Occas: E, D, X ● **Work Env:** Noise=N; Freq: H ● **Salary:** 2 ● **Outlook:** 4

TESTER, FOOD PRODUCTS (any industry) ● DOT #199.251-010 ● OES: 39998 ● Alternate titles: CONSULTANT; DIRECTOR OF CONSUMER SERVICES; NUTRITION CONSULTANT. Develops, tests, and promotes various types of food products: Selects recipes from conventional cookbooks, or develops new recipes for company food products. Prepares and cooks food according to recipe to test quality and standardize procedures and ingredients. Evaluates prepared item as to texture, appearance, flavor, and nutritional value. Records amount and kinds of ingredients and various test results. Suggests new products, product improvements, and promotions for company use or for resale to dealers, manufacturers, or other users. Presents food items at demonstration functions to promote desired qualities, nutritional values, and related characteristics. Samples shipments to verify weights, measures, coding data, and other evaluations for product control. Answers consumer mail. ● **GED:** R4, M3, L4 ● **SVP:** 1-2 yrs ● **Academic:** Ed=H, Eng=S ● **Work Field:** 146, 211, 292 ● **MPSMS:** 380, 390 ● **Aptitudes:** G3, V2, N3, S4, P3, Q3, K4, F4, M2, E5, C4 ● **Temperaments:** I, J, P ● **Physical:** Stg=L; Freq: R, H, I, T, G, N, D, A, X ● **Work Env:** Noise=N; ● **Salary:** 3 ● **Outlook:** 2

Mechanical   05

Systems Operation   05.06

Workers in this group operate and maintain equipment in an overall system, or a section of a system, for such purposes as generating and distributing electricity; treating and providing water to customers; pumping oil from oilfields to storage tanks; making ice in an ice plant; and providing telephone service to users. These jobs are found in utility companies, refineries, construction projects, large apartment houses, industrial establishments, and with city and county governments.

✓ *What kind of work would you do?*

Your work activities would depend upon your specific job. For example, you might:

■ coordinate activities of power-line crews and workers in generating stations and substations to ensure adequate production and distribution of power.

■ watch panelboard and adjust throttle and valves to regulate turbines which generate electricity.

■ operate and maintain steam engines, air compressors, generators, motors, and steam boilers to provide heat and power to a building complex.

- study gas supplies and customer demands to coordinate flow of natural gas through pipes.

✓ What skills and abilities do you need for this kind of work?

To do this kind of work, you must be able to:

- learn the functioning of the overall system, as well as the part you are involved in.
- use judgment and make decisions to keep the system operating.
- remain calm in the face of emergencies.
- use arithmetic.
- direct the work of others.
- use eyes, hands, and fingers to operate or adjust equipment.

✓ How do you know if you would like or could learn to do this kind of work?

The following questions may give you clues about yourself as you consider this group of jobs.

- Have you taken shop or mechanical drawing courses? Do you enjoy working with machines?
- Have you taken courses that required you to solve problems by using mathematical formulas?
- Have you taken physics courses? Do you understand the principles of electricity?
- Have you operated a model train layout? Can you spot and correct malfunctions?
- Have you subscribed to or read on a regular basis magazines about mechanics?
- Have you worked in electricity, electronics, or mechanics in the armed forces?

✓ How can you prepare for and enter this kind of work?

Occupations in this group usually require education and/or training extending from one year to over ten years, depending upon the specific kind of work.

Operators of systems which transmit oil or natural gas usually start as helpers. High school and vocational school courses in machine shop, mechanical drawing, mathematics, and physics are helpful.

Water and sewage treatment plants are usually government operated and jobs usually require civil service examinations.

Workers who operate boilers usually enter through apprenticeship programs lasting up to four years. It is also possible to become an operator after several years of experience as an assistant. However, this type of preparation usually takes longer. Some states require operators of various types of equipment to have licenses.

Operators of generating or distributing systems for electricity usually start as manual workers. They advance as they become experienced. One to four years of experience is usually required to develop the necessary knowledge and skills. Some cities and states require licenses for these workers.

Workers in atomic-powered plants must have special training. Some of them must be licensed by appropriate nuclear regulatory commissions or authorities.

✓ What else should you consider about these jobs?

Many systems are operated 24 hours a day and require one or more operators to be on duty at all times. Work hours often include weekends and holidays. Sometimes shift work is required.

Operators of boilers are sometimes exposed to high temperatures, dust, dirt, and fumes. They may have to crawl inside boilers and work in cramped spaces to inspect, clean, or repair interiors.

If you think you would like to do this kind of work, look at the job titles listed below.

■ ■ ■

GOE: 05.06.01
Electricity Generation & Transmission

CABLE MAINTAINER (utilities) ● DOT #952.464-010 ● OES: 85998 ● Maintains pressure in oil-filled and gas-filled cables used to transmit high-voltage electricity: Computes amount of oil or gas required for given section of cable, using standard specifications. Pumps oil or gas into cable until specified pressure is attained. Installs relay (regulating devices) used to control pressure inside cables. Attaches temporary reservoirs to ends of cable to maintain pressure during installation of cable. Tests cables with manual pressure gauges. Reports cable sheath defects and joint failure for repair. ● **GED:** R3, M3, L3 ● **SVP:** 6 mos-1 yr ● **Academic:** Ed=N, Eng=S ● **Work Field:** 111, 014 ● **MPSMS:** 871 ● **Aptitudes:** G3, V3, N3, S3, P4, Q4, K4, F3, M3, E4, C4 ● **Temperaments:** J, T ● **Physical:** Stg=L; Freq: C, B, S, K, O, W, R, H, I, N, D Occas: X ● **Work Env:** Noise=L; Const: W Freq: U, E ● **Salary:** 2 ● **Outlook:** 3

GAS-ENGINE OPERATOR (any industry) ● DOT #950.382-018 ● OES: 95032 ● Operates stationary internal-combustion engines, using natural gas for fuel, to supply power for equipment, such as electrical generators and air or gas compressors: Starts auxiliary air compressor and turns compressed air and fuel valves to start engine. Observes gauges and meters and adjusts controls to regulate ignition, governor, lubrication and cooling systems, and load distribution between engines. Observes operation of equipment, such as generators or compressors to detect malfunctions. May specialize in engines designed for specific processes and be designated Gas-Engine Operator, Compressors (any industry); Gas-Engine Operator, Generators (any industry). ● **GED:** R3, M2, L2 ● **SVP:** 1-2 yrs ● **Academic:** Ed=N, Eng=N ● **Work Field:** 021 ● **MPSMS:** 871 ● **Aptitudes:** G3, V3, N3, S4, P4, Q3, K4, F4, M3, E5, C5 ● **Temperaments:** J, T ● **Physical:** Stg=M; Freq: R, H, I, N, D, A Occas: C, S, K, O ● **Work Env:** Noise=L; ● **Salary:** 3 ● **Outlook:** 3

HYDROELECTRIC-STATION OPERATOR (utilities) ● DOT #952.362-018 ● OES: 95200 ● Controls electrical generating units and related mechanical and hydraulic equipment at hydroelectric-generating station: Operates switchboard and manually operated controls to control water wheels, generators, and auxiliary hydroelectric-generating station equipment and distribute power output among generating units, according to power demands [SWITCHBOARD OPERATOR (utilities)]. Operates feeder switchboard to control distribution of electric power over feeder circuits between generating station and substations [FEEDER-SWITCHBOARD OPERATOR (utilities)]. Records control-board meter and gauge readings, inspects operating equipment, and notifies HYDROELECTRIC-STATION OPERATOR, CHIEF (utilities) of conditions indicating abnormal equipment operation. May perform minor maintenance on equipment, such as replacing generator brushes, cleaning insulators, and lubricating machines. ● **GED:** R4, M3, L3 ● **SVP:** 2-4 yrs ● **Academic:** Ed=H, Eng=S ● **Work Field:** 021 ● **MPSMS:** 871 ● **Aptitudes:** G3, V3, N3, S4, P4, Q3, K4, F3, M3, E5, C4 ● **Temperaments:** J ● **Physical:** Stg=L; Freq: C, B, R, H, I, N, F, D, A, X, V Occas: T, G ● **Work Env:** Noise=L; Occas: E, T ● **Salary:** 2 ● **Outlook:** 3

POWER-REACTOR OPERATOR (utilities) ● DOT #952.362-022 ● OES: 95200 ● Alternate titles: NUCLEAR PLANT CONTROL OPERATOR; REACTOR OPERATOR. Controls nuclear reactor that produces steam for generation of electric power and coordinates operation of auxiliary equipment: Adjusts controls, under supervision, to start and shut down reactor and to regulate flux level, reactor period, coolant temperature, and rate of flow, control rod positions, and other control elements that affect power level within reactor, following standard instructions and prescribed practices. Dispatches orders and instructions to plant personnel through radiotelephone or intercommunication system to coordinate operation of such auxiliary equipment as pumps, compressors, switchgears, and water-treatment systems. May assist in preparing, transferring, loading, and unloading nuclear fuel elements. May be required to hold Nuclear Reactor Operator's license. May be required to hold Radiotelephone Operator's license. May control dual purpose reactors that produce plutonium and steam. May control operation of auxiliary equipment, such as turbines and generators [SWITCHBOARD OPERATOR (utilities); TURBINE OPERATOR (utilities)]. ● **GED:** R4, M3, L3 ● **SVP:** 2-4 yrs ● **Academic:** Ed=H, Eng=S ● **Work Field:** 021 ● **MPSMS:** 871 ● **Aptitudes:** G2, V2, N3, S3, P3, Q3, K3, F4, M3, E4, C4 ● **Temperaments:** J, S, T, V ● **Physical:** Stg=M; Freq: R, H, T, G, N, X Occas: I, D, A ● **Work Env:** Noise=N; Occas: R ● **Salary:** 5 ● **Outlook:** 2

SUBSTATION OPERATOR (utilities) ● DOT #952.362-026 ● OES: 95028 ● Alternate titles: POWER-SWITCHBOARD OPERATOR; RECEIVING-DISTRIBUTION-STATION OPERATOR. Controls equipment, such as current converters, voltage transformers, and circuit breakers, that regulate flow of electricity through substation of electric power system and over distribution lines to consumers: Records readings of switchboard instruments to compile data concerning quantities of electric power used for substation operation and amounts distributed from station. Communicates with LOAD DISPATCHER (utilities) to report amount of electricity received into substation, and to receive switching instructions. Observes switchboard instruments to detect indications of line disturbances, such as grounded, shorted, or open circuits. Pulls circuit breaker switch or pushes buttons to interrupt flow of current in disturbed line preparatory to repair, and to connect alternate circuit to carry load of deenergized lines. Records temperature of transformers at specified intervals. May inspect equipment, such as transformers, pumps, fans, batteries, and circuit breakers to detect defects. May calculate average and peak load conditions from electric recording instrument data and compile periodic report of load variations for system planning purposes. May locate and replace defective fuses and switches, using test lamp and handtools. May be designated according to primary function of substation as Substation Operator, Conversion (utilities); Substation Operator, Distribution (r.r. trans.; utilities); Substation Operator, Transforming (utilities). May operate auxiliary generators and be designated Substation Operator, Generation (utilities). May control several remote-controlled substations from central station switchboard and be designated Substation Operator, Automatic (utilities). ● **GED:** R4, M3, L3 ● **SVP:** 2-4 yrs ● **Academic:** Ed=H, Eng=S ● **Work Field:** 021 ● **MPSMS:** 871 ● **Aptitudes:** G3, V3, N3, S4, P3, Q3, K4, F4, M3, E4, C4 ● **Temperaments:** J, T ● **Physical:** Stg=L; Freq: R, H, N Occas: I, T, G, A, X ● **Work Env:** Noise=L; Occas: E ● **Salary:** 4 ● **Outlook:** 3

AIR-COMPRESSOR OPERATOR (any industry) ● DOT #950.685-010 ● OES: 92999 ● Alternate titles: COMPRESSOR ENGINEER; COMPRESSOR OPERATOR. Tends air compressors driven by steam, electric, or gasoline powered units, to generate and supply compressed air for operation of pneumatic tools, hoists, and air lances: Starts power unit to build up specified pressure in compressor. Adjusts controls or sets automatic controls to maintain continuous air supply to pneumatic tools or equipment. Observes temperature and pressure gauges and adjusts controls accordingly. Lubricates and cleans equipment. May connect pipelines from compressor to pneumatic tools or equipment. May repair low pressure steam boilers that furnish power for air compressor units by disassembling unit of boiler and replacing damaged parts, using handtools. May be designated according to type of equipment operated as Air-Compressor Operator, Stationary (any industry); Compressor Operator, Portable (any industry). ● **GED:** R3, M2, L2 ● **SVP:** 6 mos-1 yr ● **Academic:** Ed=N, Eng=N ● **Work Field:** 021 ● **MPSMS:** 875 ● **Aptitudes:** G3, V4, N4, S4, P4, Q4, K4, F4, M3, E5, C5 ● **Temperaments:** J, T ● **Physical:** Stg=M; Freq: R, H, N, F, D Occas: S, O ● **Work Env:** Noise=L; ● **Salary:** 2 ● **Outlook:** 3

BOILER OPERATOR (any industry) ● DOT #950.382-010 ● OES: 95032 ● Alternate titles: BOILER HOUSE OPERATOR; CONTROL-ROOM OPERATOR; FIRER, BOILER; STEAM-POWER-PLANT OPERATOR. Operates automatically fired boilers to generate steam that supplies heat or power for buildings or industrial processes: Lights gas- or oil-fed burners, using torch. Starts pulverizer and stoker to grind and feed coal into furnace of boiler. Observes pressure, temperature, and draft meters on panel to verify specified operation of automatic combustion control systems, feed water regulators, stoker, pulverizer, and burners. Turns valves and adjusts controls to set specified fuel feed, draft openings, water level, and steam pressure of boiler. Observes boiler and auxiliary units to detect malfunctions and makes repairs, such as changing burners and tightening pipes and fittings. May test and treat boiler feed water, using specified chemicals. May maintain log of meter and gauge readings and record data, such as water test results and quantity of fuel consumed. May be designated according to fuel burned, type of boilers, or class of license required. ● **GED:** R4, M3, L3 ● **SVP:** 2-4 yrs ● **Academic:** Ed=N, Eng=S ● **Work Field:** 021 ● **MPSMS:** 875 ● **Aptitudes:** G3, V3, N3, S3, P4, Q3, K4, F4, M3, E5, C4 ● **Temperaments:** J, T ● **Physical:** Stg=M; Freq: R, H, N, A Occas: C, B, S, K, O, I, G, D, X ● **Work Env:** Noise=L; Const: H Freq: O ● **Salary:** 3 ● **Outlook:** 3

ENGINEER (water trans.) ● DOT #197.130-010 ● OES: 97521 ● Alternate titles: MARINE ENGINEER; MECHANIC, MARINE ENGINE. Supervises and coordinates activities of crew engaged in operating and maintaining propulsion engines and other engines, boilers, deck machinery, and electrical, refrigeration, and sanitary equipment aboard ship: Inspects engines and other equipment and orders crew to repair or replace defective parts. Starts engines to propel ship and regulates engines and power transmission to control speed of ship. Stands engine-room watch during specified periods, observing that required water levels are maintained in boilers, condensers, and evaporators, load on generators is within acceptable limits, and oil and grease cups are kept full. Repairs machinery, using handtools and power tools. Maintains engineering log and bell book (orders for changes in speed and direction of ship). May be required to hold appropriate U.S. Coast Guard license, depending upon tonnage of ship, type of engines, and means of transmitting power to propeller shaft. When more than one ENGINEER (water trans.) is required, may be designated Engineer, Chief (water trans.); Engineer, First Assistant (water trans.); Engineer, Second Assistant (water trans.); Engineer, Third Assistant (water trans.). May be designated according to ship assigned as Barge Engineer (water trans.); Cannery-Tender Engineer (water trans.); Engineer, Fishing Vessel (water trans.); Tugboat Engineer (water trans.). May be designated Cadet Engineer (water trans.) when in training. ● **GED:** R4, M3, L3 ● **SVP:** 4-10 yrs ● **Academic:** Ed=H, Eng=G ● **Work Field:** 021 ● **MPSMS:** 870 ● **Aptitudes:** G3, V3, N3, S2, P3, Q3, K3, F4, M3, E4,

C4 ● **Temperaments:** D, J ● **Physical:** Stg=M; Freq: R, H, I, T, G, N, F, D, A, X, V Occas: C, B, S, K, O, W ● **Work Env:** Noise=L; Freq: H, O ● **Salary:** 5 ● **Outlook:** 2

FUEL ATTENDANT (any industry) ● DOT #953.362-010 ● OES: 95010 ● Controls equipment to regulate flow and pressure of gas from mains to fuel feedlines of gas-fired boilers, furnaces, kilns, soaking pits, smelters, and related steam-generating or heating equipment in such establishments as power plants, steel mills, pottery works, chemical plants, and petroleum refining facilities: Opens valve on feedlines to supply adequate gas for fuel when boilers are to be put in operation and to maintain standard pressure on gaslines. Closes valve to reduce gas pressure when increase in gas consumption by boilers causes pressure to rise. Observes, records, and reports flow and pressure gauge readings on gas mains and fuel feedlines. ● **GED:** R3, M2, L2 ● **SVP:** 6 mos-1 yr ● **Academic:** Ed=N, Eng=N ● **Work Field:** 021 ● **MPSMS:** 872 ● **Aptitudes:** G3, V4, N4, S4, P3, Q3, K3, F4, M4, E4, C4 ● **Temperaments:** J, T ● **Physical:** Stg=L; Freq: R, H, N, D, A Occas: I, T, G, X ● **Work Env:** Noise=L; Occas: H ● **Salary:** 2 ● **Outlook:** 3

GAS-COMPRESSOR OPERATOR (any industry) ● DOT #950.382-014 ● OES: 97910 ● Alternate titles: GAS-LIFT ENGINEER. Operates steam or internal combustion engines to transmit, compress, or recover gases, such as butane, nitrogen, hydrogen, and natural gas in various production processes: Moves controls and turns valves to start compressor engines, pumps, and auxiliary equipment. Monitors meters, gauges, and recording instrument charts to ensure specified temperature, pressure, and flow of gas through system. Observes operation of equipment to detect malfunctions. Records instrument readings and operational changes in operating log. May operate purification tanks (scrubbers) to purify air or byproduct gases. May tend pumps to mix specified amounts of acids and caustics with water for use in purifying gases. May perform minor repairs on equipment, using handtools. May conduct chemical tests to determine sulfur or moisture content in gas. May be designated according to type of gas compressed or recovered as Butadiene-Compressor Operator (chemical); Butane-Compressor Operator (petrol. refin.); Ethylene-Compressor Operator (chemical). May operate equipment to control transmission of natural gas through pipelines and be designated Compressor-Station Engineer (pipe lines). ● **GED:** R4, M3, L3 ● **SVP:** 2-4 yrs ● **Academic:** Ed=N, Eng=S ● **Work Field:** 021 ● **MPSMS:** 872 ● **Aptitudes:** G3, V3, N3, S4, P4, Q3, K4, F4, M3, E5, C5 ● **Temperaments:** J, T ● **Physical:** Stg=M; Freq: R, H, N, D, A Occas: C, S, K, O, I ● **Work Env:** Noise=L; Freq: A, O ● **Salary:** 3 ● **Outlook:** 3

REFRIGERATING ENGINEER (any industry) ● DOT #950.362-014 ● OES: 95032 ● Alternate titles: COOLING-SYSTEM OPERATOR; OPERATING ENGINEER; STATIONARY ENGINEER, REFRIGERATION. Operates freon, carbon-dioxide, or ammonia gas-cooling systems to refrigerate rooms in establishments, such as slaughtering and meat packing plants and dairies, to air-condition buildings, or to provide refrigeration for industrial processes: Opens valves on equipment, such as compressors, pumps, and condensers to prepare system for operation and starts equipment and auxiliary machinery. Observes temperature, pressure and ampere readings for system and equipment and adjusts controls or overrides automatic controls to obtain specified operation of equipment. Records temperature, pressure, and other readings on logsheet at specified intervals. Measures density of brine, using hydrometer, and adds calcium chloride to lower temperature to specified degree. Connects hose from supply tank to compressor to replace coolant. Makes periodic inspection of equipment and system to observe operating condition and need for repair or adjustment. Adjusts controls to isolate and clear broken lines for repair or shuts down equipment. May repack pumps and compressors, clean condensers, and replace worn or defective parts using hand and power tools. When operating refrigeration or air-conditioning equipment aboard ship, may be known as Reefer Engineer (water trans.) and must have endorsement on Merchant Mariner's document as Refrigerating Engineer. ● **GED:** R4, M3, L3 ● **SVP:** 2-4 yrs ● **Academic:** Ed=A, Eng=S ● **Work Field:** 021 ● **MPSMS:** 875 ● **Aptitudes:** G3, V3, N3, S3, P4, Q3, K4, F4, M3, E4, C4 ● **Temperaments:** J, T ● **Physical:** Stg=M; Freq: C, R, H, N Occas: B, S, K, O, W, I, X ● **Work Env:** Noise=L; Freq: U, T ● **Salary:** 4 ● **Outlook:** 3

STATIONARY ENGINEER (any industry) ● DOT #950.382-026 ● OES: 95032 ● Alternate titles: MAINTENANCE ENGINEER; OPERATING ENGINEER; POWER-PLANT OPERATOR; WATCH ENGINEER. Operates and maintains stationary engines and mechanical equipment, such as steam engines, air compressors, generators, motors, turbines, and steam boilers to provide utilities, such as light, heat, or power for buildings and industrial processes: Reads meters and gauges or automatic recording devices at specified intervals to verify operating conditions. Records data, such as temperature of equipment, hours of operation, fuel consumed, temperature or pressure, water levels, analysis of flue gases, voltage load and generator balance. Adjusts manual controls or overrides automatic controls to bring equipment into recommended or prescribed operating ranges, switch to backup equipment or systems, or to shut down equipment. Visually inspects equipment at periodic intervals to detect malfunctions or need for repair, adjustment or lubrication. Maintains equipment by tightening fittings, repacking bearings, replacing packing glands, gaskets, valves, recorders, and gauges, and cleaning or replacing burners or other components, using handtools and power tools. May be required to hold license issued by state or municipality, restricting equipment operated to specified types and sizes. May oil and lubricate equipment [OILER (any industry) 950.685-014]. May perform water titration tests and pour chemical additives, such as water softener, into treatment tank to prevent scale buildup and to clean boiler lines. May record operation and maintenance actions taken during shift in operators logbook. May specialize in equipment designed for industrial processes and be designated Acid-Concentration-Plant-Equipment Engineer (any industry); Air-Compressor-Station Engineer (any industry); Diesel-Engine Operator, Stationary (any industry); Water-Pumping-Station Engineer (any industry). ● **GED:** R4, M4, L3 ● **SVP:** 2-4 yrs ● **Academic:** Ed=H, Eng=S ● **Work Field:** 021 ● **MPSMS:** 870 ● **Aptitudes:** G3, V3, N3, S3, P4, Q3, K4, F4, M3, E5, C5 ● **Temperaments:** J, T, V ● **Physical:** Stg=M; Freq: R, H, N Occas: C, S, O, I, G ● **Work Env:** Noise=L; Freq: A Occas: H, U ● **Salary:** 4 ● **Outlook:** 2

VENTILATION EQUIPMENT TENDER (any industry) ● DOT #950.585-010 ● OES: 95098 ● Alternate titles: AIR-CONTROL TENDER; BLOWER-ROOM ATTENDANT; EXHAUST TENDER; HEATING-AND-VENTILATING TENDER; SCRUBBER-SYSTEM ATTENDANT; VENTILATION MECHANIC. Tends ventilating and heating equipment, such as fans, vacuum pumps, air compressors, vents and ducts, and lubrication-oil coolers used in buildings or industrial processes: Adjusts valves to regulate temperature of lubrication oil and flow of water through system. Moves controls to regulate speed of fans and to adjust vents and ducts. Records gauge readings, repairs completed, and time lost because of inoperative equipment. Writes repair work order tickets and out-of-order tags preparatory to equipment repair. Inspects equipment to detect excessive noise and heat. Replaces gauges and tightens and caulks leaky fittings, using wrenches, hammers, and caulking tool. Cleans carbon deposits, pitch, and grease from fans, vents, and ducts, using scrapers, hammer, and compressed air or steam. ● **GED:** R3, M2, L3 ● **SVP:** 3-6 mos ● **Academic:** Ed=N, Eng=S ● **Work Field:** 021, 121 ● **MPSMS:** 870 ● **Aptitudes:** G3, V4, N4, S3, P3, Q4, K4, F4, M3, E4, C5 ● **Temperaments:** J, T ● **Physical:** Stg=L; Freq: R, H, N, D Occas: S, O, I, A ● **Work Env:** Noise=L; Occas: A ● **Salary:** 3 ● **Outlook:** 3

GOE: 05.06.03
Oil, Gas & Water Distribution

PUMPER (any industry) ● DOT #914.682-010 ● OES: 97910 ● Alternate titles: CIRCULATOR; PUMP-MACHINE OPERATOR; PUMP OPERATOR; PUMP RUNNER; PUMP TENDER; SIPHONER. Operates power-driven pumps that transfer liquids, semiliquids, gases, or powdered materials, performing any combination of following duties: Observes pressure gauges and flowmeters, and adjusts valves to regulate speed of pumps and control pressure and rate of flow of materials. Transfers materials to and from storage tanks, processing tanks, trucks, railroad cars, ships, canals, and mines. Pumps crude oil from wells. Maintains pumps and lines by replacing filters and gaskets, tightening connections, and adjusting pumps, using handtools. May transfer liquids by siphoning. May connect pipelines between pumps and containers or storage tanks being filled or emptied. May collect samples of materials for laboratory analysis. May determine density of liquids, using hydrometer. May record quantity of item pumped. May inventory contents of storage tank, using calibrated rod, or by reading mercury gauge and tank charts. Usually receives verbal or written orders from superior as to amount to be pumped and is not responsible for mixing or processing. May be designated according to material pumped or area of work as Acid Pumper (chemical); Glycol-Service Operator (plastic-synth.); Irrigating-Pump Operator (agriculture); Tailings-Dam Pumper (smelt. & refin.); Yard Pumper (any industry). ● **GED:** R3, M2, L3 ● **SVP:** 6 mos-1 yr ● **Academic:** Ed=N, Eng=S ● **Work Field:** 014 ● **MPSMS:** 568 ● **Aptitudes:** G3, V3, N3, S3, P4, Q4, K3, F4, M3, E5, C5 ● **Temperaments:** J, T ● **Physical:** Stg=M; Freq: S, R, H, N Occas: C, B, K, O, D ● **Work Env:** Noise=N; Freq: W Occas: U ● **Salary:** 2 ● **Outlook:** 3

PUMP-STATION OPERATOR, WATERWORKS (waterworks) ● DOT #954.382-010 ● OES: 95002 ● Alternate titles: PUMPING-PLANT OPERATOR; WATER-PLANT-PUMP OPERATOR. Operates pumping equipment to transfer raw water to treatment plant, or distribute processed water to residential, commercial, and industrial establishments: Turns valves, pulls levers, and flips switches to operate and control turbine- or motor-driven pumps that transfer water from reservoir to treatment plant, or to transfer processed water to consumer establishments. Reads flowmeters and gauges to regulate equipment according to water consumption and demand. Inspects equipment to detect malfunctions, such as pump leaks or worn bearings. Repairs and lubricates equipment, using handtools. Records data, such as utilization of equipment, power consumption, and water output in log. May operate equipment to treat and process raw water [WATER-TREATMENT-PLANT OPERATOR (waterworks)]. May test water for chlorine content, alkalinity, acidity, or turbidity to determine potability of water, following color analysis standards. May operate hydroelectric equipment to generate power. ● **GED:** R3, M2, L3 ● **SVP:** 6 mos-1 yr ● **Academic:** Ed=N, Eng=S ● **Work Field:** 014 ● **MPSMS:** 873 ● **Aptitudes:** G3, V4, N4, S3, P3, Q4, K4, F3, M3, E5, C4 ● **Temperaments:** J, T ● **Physical:** Stg=L; Freq: R, H, I, N Occas: C, B, S, K, E, F, D, A, X, V ● **Work Env:** Noise=L; Occas: W ● **Salary:** 4 ● **Outlook:** 3

GOE: 05.06.04
Processing

WATER-TREATMENT-PLANT OPERATOR (waterworks) ● DOT #954.382-014 ● OES: 95002 ● Alternate titles: FILTER OPERATOR; PURIFYING-PLANT OPERATOR; WATER-CONTROL-STATION ENGINEER; WATER FILTERER; WATER PURIFIER. Controls treatment plant machines and equipment to purify and clarify water for human consumption and for industrial use: Operates and controls electric motors, pumps, and valves to regulate flow of raw water into treating plant. Dumps specified amounts of chemicals, such as chlorine, ammonia, and lime into water or adjusts automatic devices that admit specified amounts of chemicals into tanks to disinfect, deodorize, and clarify water. Starts agitators to mix chemicals and allows impurities to settle to bottom of tank. Turns valves to regulate water through filter beds to remove impurities. Pumps purified water into water mains. Monitors panelboard and adjusts controls to regulate flow rates, loss of head pressure and water elevation, and distribution of water. Cleans tanks and filter beds, using backwashing (reverse flow of water). Repairs and lubricates machines and equipment, using handtools and power tools. Tests water samples to determine acidity, color, and impurities, using colorimeter, turbidimeter, and conductivity meter. Adds chemicals such, as alum into tanks to coagulate impurities and to reduce acidity. Records data, such as residual content of chemicals, water turbidity, and water pressure. May operate portable water-purification plant to supply drinking water. ● **GED:** R3, M3, L3 ● **SVP:** 6 mos-1 yr ● **Academic:** Ed=H, Eng=S ● **Work Field:** 147, 014 ● **MPSMS:** 873 ● **Aptitudes:** G3, V4, N3, S4, P3, Q3, K4, F4, M3, E5, C4 ● **Temperaments:** J, T ● **Physical:** Stg=M; Freq: R, H, N Occas: S, K, O, I, G, D, A, X ● **Work Env:** Noise=L; Occas: W, U, A ● **Salary:** 4 ● **Outlook:** 2

Mechanical

05

Quality Control

05.07

Workers in this group inspect and/or test materials and products to be sure they meet standards. The work is carried out in a non-factory setting, and includes such activities as grading logs at a lumber yard, inspecting bridges to be sure they are safe, inspecting gas lines for leaks, and grading gravel for use in building roads. Jobs may be found with construction companies, sawmills, petroleum refineries, and utility companies.

✓ What kind of work would you do?

Your work activities would depend upon your specific job. For example, you might:

- inspect automobiles to see that they meet state safety laws.
- patrol oil or gas pipeline to locate and repair leaks.
- inspect boilers and pipes to locate leaks and identify needed repairs.
- check pressures, gauges, and structures to certify the readiness of an airplane for flight.
- inspect crude and refined petroleum before and after transfer from terminal tanks to ship tanks.

- measure and examine logs to determine grade according to specifications.

✓ What skills and abilities do you need for this kind of work?

To do this kind of work, you must be able to:

- learn about the product, materials, or structure you are inspecting or testing.
- keep records and make reports.
- use measuring and testing equipment.
- use specifications, blueprints, and written directions to make decisions about the quality of the object or material you are inspecting.

✓ How do you know if you would like or could learn to do this kind of work?

The following questions may give you clues about yourself as you consider this group of jobs.

- Have you had courses in mechanical drawing or drafting? Can you read blueprints and diagrams?
- Have you inspected cars, appliances, or furniture for surface defects? Do you notice small details?

- Have you taken industrial arts or vocational courses? Can you use rulers, micrometers, scales, and other measuring devices?
- Have you had military experience inspecting equipment or materials? Did you like the work?

✓ How can you prepare for and enter this kind of work?

Occupations in this group usually require education and/or training extending from six months to over ten years, depending upon the specific kind of work. Some jobs in this group are open only to those who are familiar with the materials, processes, or products involved. These workers often get the necessary experience as unskilled workers in the same setting. Other jobs require the ability to read blueprints or specifications. High school or vocational courses in machine shop, mechanical drawing, or blueprint reading are helpful in developing these skills. A few jobs require experience as a skilled worker to develop the knowledge needed to judge quality. Most workers receive on-the-job training in order to learn procedures or to learn how to use measuring or testing equipment.

✓ What else should you consider about these jobs?

Working conditions for inspectors are similar to those for other workers at the site.

If you think you would like to do this kind of work, look at the job titles listed below.

GOE: 05.07.01
Structural

FIRE-EXTINGUISHER-SPRINKLER INSPECTOR (any industry) ● DOT #379.687-010 ● OES: 63008 ● Alternate titles: FIRE-APPARATUS SPRINKLER INSPECTOR. Inspects and tests sprinkler valves. Inspects pipes, hoses, and hose houses of fire apparatus in plants, offices, apartment buildings, and similar structures. Fills out inspection report on condition of valves, pipes, tanks, pumps, and alarms for superiors and customers. ● GED: R3, M2, L2 ● SVP: 3-6 mos ● Academic: Ed=N, Eng=S ● Work Field: 212 ● MPSMS: 969 ● Aptitudes: G3, V4, N4, S3, P4, Q4, K4, F4, M3, E5, C5 ● Temperaments: R, T ● Physical: Stg=L; Freq: N, A Occas: C, S, K, O, R, H, I ● Work Env: Noise=N; Occas: W ● Salary: 3 ● Outlook: 4

INSPECTOR, TOOL (machine shop) ● DOT #601.281-022 ● OES: 83000 ● Alternate titles: PRECISION INSPECTOR; SURFACE-PLATE INSPECTOR; TOOL-AND-DIE INSPECTOR; TOOL-AND-GAUGE INSPECTOR; TOOLING INSPECTOR. Inspects, tests, and adjusts new and reworked tools, dies, gauges, jigs, and fixtures, for conformance to specifications, such as dimensions, tolerances, and hardness, applying knowledge of tool and die design, shop mathematics, and machining and testing procedures, using precision measuring instruments, testing equipment, and handtools: Computes angles, radii, and other unspecified dimensions of workpiece, using algebra, geometry, and trigonometry. Positions workpiece on surface plate and lays out reference points and center lines on parts [LAY-OUT WORKER (machine shop) 600.281-018]. Measures angular dimensions, radii, contours, clearances, thread lead, and other specifications, using precision measuring instruments, such as micrometer, gauge blocks, dial indicators, height gauges, level protractors, and optical comparators. Tests units for fit of moving parts and mechanical functioning. Tests parts for hardness, using hardness testing equipment [HARDNESS INSPECTOR (heat treating) 504.387-010]. Inspects, adjusts, and verifies accuracy of gauges and measuring instruments for conformance to specifications [INSPECTOR, GAUGE AND INSTRUMENT (machine shop) 601.281-018]. Examines defective parts to determine cause of defect and recommends changes or modifications. Determines salvageability of defective items, utilizing knowledge of material and machining costs. Measures surface finish of part, using profilometer. Inspects first run parts and assemblies. Writes report regarding inspection and testing results. May draw enlarged part details for use on optical comparator. May use laser-equipped measuring instruments. May inspect parts for flaws or internal fissures, using ultrasonic equipment or fluorescent lights. May test gauges used in manufacture and assembly of watches, using measuring devices and microscope, and be designated Gauge Controller (clock & watch). ● GED: R4, M4, L4 ● SVP: 4-10 yrs ● Academic: Ed=H, Eng=S ● Work Field: 211, 241, 121 ● MPSMS: 566, 590, 602 ● Aptitudes: G2, V3, N2, S2, P2, Q3, K3, F3, M3, E5, C4 ● Temperaments: J, T, V ● Physical: Stg=M; Freq: R, H, I, N, D, A Occas: E, X ● Work Env: Noise=N; ● Salary: 3 ● Outlook: 3

LINE WALKER (petrol. & gas) ● DOT #869.564-010 ● OES: 83000 ● Alternate titles: LINE RIDER. Patrols oil and gas pipelines and communication systems on foot, horseback, or in automobile to locate and repair leaks, breaks, washouts, and damaged utility wires and poles: Inspects pipelines to detect evidence of leaks, such as oil stains, odors, and dead vegetation. Repairs small leaks, using caulking tools, hammers, clamps, and wrenches. Reports large leaks and washouts to district office. Inspects telephone and telegraph wires to locate broken insulators, wires and fallen poles, and reports findings. Inspects operation of automatic drip bleeder on gaslines to detect malfunctions, such as clogged valves, and adjusts or repairs valves, using handtools. Installs and replaces warning signs along road and water crossings. Prepares inspection reports. ● GED: R3, M2, L3 ● SVP: 3-6 mos ● Academic: Ed=N, Eng=S ● Work Field: 293, 121 ● MPSMS: 364 ● Aptitudes: G3, V4, N4, S4, P3, Q4, K3, F4, M3, E4, C4 ● Temperaments: R, T ● Physical: Stg=L; Freq: S, O, R, H, N, F, D, V Occas: I, T, G, M, X ● Work Env: Noise=L; Freq: W Occas: A, D ● Salary: 3 ● Outlook: 3

NONDESTRUCTIVE TESTER (profess. & kin.) ● DOT #011.261-018 ● OES: 35199 ● Conducts radiographic, penetrant, ultrasonic, and magnetic particle tests on metal parts to determine if parts meet nondestructive specifications: Reviews test orders to determine type of test requested, test procedures to follow, and part acceptability criteria. Applies agents, such as cleaners, penetrants, and developers, and couplant (light oil which acts as medium), to parts, or heats parts in oven, to prepare parts for testing. Determines test equipment settings according to type of metal, thickness, distance from test equipment, and related variables, using standard formulas. Calibrates test equipment, such as magnetic particle, x-ray, and ultrasonic contact machines, to standard settings, following manual instructions. Sets up equipment to perform tests, and conducts tests on parts, following procedures established for specified tests performed. Examines surface-treated materials during penetrant and magnetic particle tests to locate and identify cracks or other defects, using black light. Moves transducer probe across part when conducting ultrasonic tests and observes CRT (cathode ray tube) screen to detect and locate discontinuities in metal structure [ULTRASONIC TESTER (any industry) 739.281-014]. Examines film when conducting radiographic tests to locate structural or welding flaws. Marks tested parts to indicate defective areas. Evaluates test results against designated standards, utilizing knowledge of metals and testing experience. Prepares reports outlining findings and conclusions. May perform similar tests on nonmetallic parts or structures. ● **GED:** R4, M3, L3 ● **SVP:** 1-2 yrs ● **Academic:** Ed=A, Eng=S ● **Work Field:** 211 ● **MPSMS:** 592, 969 ● **Aptitudes:** G3, V3, N3, S3, P3, Q3, K3, F3, M4, E4, C3 ● **Temperaments:** J, T, V ● **Physical:** Stg=M; Freq: R, H, N, X Occas: S, K, O, I, T, G, A ● **Work Env:** Noise=L; Occas: H, U, A, R, T ● **Salary:** 2 ● **Outlook:** 5

SEWER-LINE PHOTO-INSPECTOR (sanitary ser.) ● DOT #851.362-010 ● OES: 34023 ● Operates camera to photograph inside of sewer lines to conduct inspection and determine need for repairs: Locates line sections to be photographed, using map. Determines setup procedures. Floats rope used to pull camera to adjacent manhole to thread sewer lines. Directs workers in setting up cable stands over manholes. Loads camera with film and inspects battery of camera. Depresses button on camera to photograph small blackboard giving location of manhole, manhole number, data, and weather conditions for future reference. Attaches pulling cable to camera and instructs workers to position camera in sewer line and to turn cable stand handles that enable camera to move inside pipe. Snaps pictures at designated intervals until camera reaches downstream manhole. Detaches camera from cable, rewinds cable into reel, and disassembles equipment. Removes film and batteries from camera and sends film to be developed. Confers with supervisor to discuss condition of sewer lines as indicated in developed photographs. Drives pickup truck to haul crew and equipment. Services, adjusts, and makes minor repairs to camera, equipment, and attachments. Communicates with supervisor, using radio telephone. Gives directions to workers in efficient and safe use of camera and equipment, work methods, and safety precautions. Prepares daily report listing lines photographed. ● **GED:** R3, M2, L2 ● **SVP:** 6 mos-1 yr ● **Academic:** Ed=N, Eng=N ● **Work Field:** 211, 201 ● **MPSMS:** 364 ● **Aptitudes:** G3, V3, N4, S3, P3, Q4, K4, F3, M3, E4, C4 ● **Temperaments:** J, T ● **Physical:** Stg=M; Freq: C, S, K, O, H, I, T, G, N, D, A Occas: X ● **Work Env:** Noise=L; Occas: W, O ● **Salary:** 3 ● **Outlook:** 3

SHOP ESTIMATOR (automotive ser.) ● DOT #807.267-010 ● OES: 85305 ● Estimates cost of repairing damaged automobile and truck bodies, on basis of visual inspection of vehicle and familiarity with standard parts, costs, and labor rates: Examines damaged vehicle for dents, scratches, broken glass, and other areas requiring repair, replacement, or repainting. Sights along fenders to detect frame damage, or positions vehicle in frame-aligning rig that indicates location and extent of misalignment. Examines interior for evidence of fire or water damage to upholstery and appointments. Determines feasibility of repair or replacement of parts, such as bumpers, fenders, and doors, according to familiarity with relative costs and extent of damage. Computes cost of replacement parts and labor to restore vehicle to condition specified by customer, using standard labor and parts cost manuals. Enters itemized estimate on job order card or estimate form and explains estimate to customer. May estimate cost of mechanical, electrical, or other repairs where shop performs both body work and mechanical servicing of vehicles [AUTOMOBILE-REPAIR-SERVICE ESTIMATOR (automotive ser.) 620.261-018]. May estimate cost of repainting, converting vehicles to special purposes, or customizing undamaged vehicles, depending on specialty of shop. ● **GED:** R4, M3, L3 ● **SVP:** 1-2 yrs ● **Academic:** Ed=H, Eng=S ● **Work Field:** 212 ● **MPSMS:** 591 ● **Aptitudes:** G3, V3, N3, S3, P3, Q3, K4, F4, M4, E5, C4 ● **Temperaments:** J, P ● **Physical:** Stg=L; Freq: R, H, I, T, G, N, D Occas: S, K, O, E, A, X ● **Work Env:** Noise=L; ● **Salary:** 4 ● **Outlook:** 3

ULTRASONIC TESTER (any industry) ● DOT #739.281-014 ● OES: 83000 ● Conducts ultrasonic tests on fabricated metallic and nonmetallic parts and products to identify discontinuities: Reviews work orders, test procedure sheets, and product acceptance criteria to determine test specifications. Attaches specified crystal probe transducer to ultrasound test device and moves switch to actuate device. Calibrates and adjusts ultrasonic test equipment to required standards and settings, applying knowledge of ultrasonic testing procedures. Sprays couplant (light oil which acts as medium) or other liquid over part to be tested, moves transducer over part to be tested, and observes CRT (cathode ray tube) screen to detect patterns of discontinuity, such as cracks, inclusions, bonding defects, or porosity. Marks defective areas of part or product and prepares report of test findings. May set up and operate

computerized inspection equipment. ● **GED:** R4, M3, L3 ● **SVP:** 1-2 yrs ● **Academic:** Ed=N, Eng=S ● **Work Field:** 211 ● **MPSMS:** 560, 590, 899 ● **Aptitudes:** G3, V3, N3, S3, P3, Q3, K3, F3, M4, E5, C5 ● **Temperaments:** J, T ● **Physical:** Stg=M; Freq: R, H, N Occas: I, D, A ● **Work Env:** Noise=N; ● **Salary:** 4 ● **Outlook:** 4

GOE: 05.07.02
Mechanical

AIRPLANE INSPECTOR (air trans.) ● DOT #621.261-010 ● OES: 83000 ● Alternate titles: AIRPLANE-AND-ENGINE INSPECTOR. Examines airframe, engines, and operating equipment to ensure that repairs are made according to specifications, and certifies airworthiness of aircraft: Tests tightness of airframe connections with handtools and employs flashlight and mirror to inspect fit of parts. Signals AIRFRAME-AND-POWER-PLANT MECHANIC (air trans.; aircraft mfg.) to start engine and manipulate aircraft controls. Collects data, such as engine revolutions per minute and fuel and oil pressures, to evaluate engine performance, using tachometer and pressure gauges. Examines assembly, installation, and adjustment of ailerons and rudders to ensure that workmanship and materials conform with Civil Air Regulations, company specifications, and manual procedures. Determines accuracy of installation of components in power plant and hydraulic system with protractor, micrometer, calipers, and gauge to ensure that specified tolerances are met. Signs inspection tag to approve unit, or records reasons for rejecting unit. Logs inspections performed on aircraft. Must hold Airframe and Power Plant Mechanic's License and Inspection Authorization, issued by Federal Aviation Administration. May prepare dismantling schedules for airplanes to be overhauled. May service, repair, and replace airframe components, engines, and operating equipment [AIRFRAME-AND-POWER-PLANT MECHANIC (air trans.; aircraft mfg.)]. ● **GED:** R4, M4, L4 ● **SVP:** 4-10 yrs ● **Academic:** Ed=H, Eng=S ● **Work Field:** 121 ● **MPSMS:** 592 ● **Aptitudes:** G2, V3, N3, S2, P2, Q4, K3, F3, M3, E4, C4 ● **Temperaments:** J ● **Physical:** Stg=L; Freq: C, B, R, H, I, N, D, A Occas: S, K, O, W ● **Work Env:** Noise=V; Occas: W, M, D ● **Salary:** 5 ● **Outlook:** 3

AUTOMOBILE-REPAIR-SERVICE ESTIMATOR (automotive ser.) ● DOT #620.261-018 ● OES: 83000 ● Alternate titles: AUTOMOBILE INSPECTOR; COLLISION ESTIMATOR; MANAGER, SERVICE; MECHANIC, TROUBLE-SHOOTING; SALES ASSOCIATE, GARAGE SERVICE; SERVICE WRITER. Inspects and tests automobiles and trucks to determine need for and cost of repairs: Determines need for repairs by road test [AUTOMOBILE TESTER (automotive ser.) 620.261-014], by use of mechanical testing devices [BRAKE REPAIRER (automotive ser.) 620.281-026; FRONT-END MECHANIC (automotive ser.) 620.281-038], by questioning customer about vehicle's performance, or by visual inspection of vehicle. Estimates cost of repair and prepares itemized work order, listing costs of parts and labor. May make minor adjustments or repairs, such as brake adjustment, battery cable replacement, or hinge lubrication. May supervise AUTOMOBILE-BODY REPAIRER (automotive ser.) 807.381-010; AUTOMOBILE MECHANIC (automotive ser.) 620.261-010; PAINTER, TRANSPORTATION EQUIPMENT (aircraft mfg.; air trans.; automotive ser.) 845.381-014; and other garage workers. May be designated according to specialty as Truck-Repair-Service Estimator (automotive ser.). ● **GED:** R4, M3, L3 ● **SVP:** 2-4 yrs ● **Academic:** Ed=H, Eng=S ● **Work Field:** 211, 212, 121 ● **MPSMS:** 591 ● **Aptitudes:** G3, V3, N3, S3, P4, Q3, K4, F4, M3, E4, C5 ● **Temperaments:** J, V ● **Physical:** Stg=L; Freq: R, H, T, G, N, D, A Occas: S, K, O, I, F ● **Work Env:** Noise=N; Occas: W, A, M ● **Salary:** 4 ● **Outlook:** 4

AUTOMOBILE TESTER (automotive ser.) ● DOT #620.261-014 ● OES: 83000 ● Tests and examines automotive vehicles, such as automobiles, buses, and trucks, to determine repairs required: Starts engine of automotive vehicle and listens for sounds indicative of malfunctions. Drives vehicle, noting performance of parts, such as clutch, gears, and brakes. Tests motor timing, cylinder compression, fuel consumption, wheel alignment, and steering, using testing devices. Examines body and fenders of vehicle for scratches and dents. Reports findings to supervisor or customer and recommends repairs required. May examine disassembled engine, differential, or other parts during repair.

May be designated according to specialty as Motor Analyst (automotive ser.). ● **GED:** R4, M3, L3 ● **SVP:** 2-4 yrs ● **Academic:** Ed=H, Eng=S ● **Work Field:** 121 ● **MPSMS:** 591 ● **Aptitudes:** G3, V3, N4, S3, P3, Q4, K4, F3, M3, E3, C4 ● **Temperaments:** J, V ● **Physical:** Stg=L; Freq: R, H, T, G, N Occas: S, K, O, I, A, X ● **Work Env:** Noise=N; ● **Salary:** 4 ● **Outlook:** 3

INSPECTOR, HEATING AND REFRIGERATION (government ser.) ● DOT #168.167-046 ● OES: 21908 ● Inspects heating, ventilating, air-conditioning, and refrigeration installations for conformance to safety laws and regulations and approved plans and specifications: Inspects heating, ventilating, air-conditioning, and refrigeration equipment and installations in residential, commercial, and industrial buildings and facilities for conformance to safety laws and ordinances designed to prevent use of faulty equipment. Issues notices for correction of defective installations and issues citations to violators of safety code. Inspects gas heating appliances in retail stores and notifies dealers to remove unapproved appliances. Confers with property owners or agents to discuss and approve alteration plans to heating, ventilating, air-conditioning, and refrigeration equipment that comply with safety regulations. Investigates complaints regarding installation of heating and refrigeration equipment by unlicensed contractors. Keeps records and prepares reports of inspections and investigations for use by administrative or judicial authorities. May investigate installations where fire or death has occurred. May determine percentage and acceptability of contract work completed for purposes of progress payments. ● **GED:** R5, M4, L4 ● **SVP:** 2-4 yrs ● **Academic:** Ed=A, Eng=G ● **Work Field:** 212, 111 ● **MPSMS:** 553, 573 ● **Aptitudes:** G2, V2, N2, S2, P3, Q3, K5, F5, M5, E3, C4 ● **Temperaments:** J, P, T ● **Physical:** Stg=L; Freq: R, H, N, D, A Occas: C, S, K, O, I, T, G, X ● **Work Env:** Noise=L; ● **Salary:** 4 ● **Outlook:** 3

GOE: 05.07.03
Electrical

ELEVATOR EXAMINER-AND-ADJUSTER (any industry) ● DOT #825.261-014 ● OES: 85932 ● Alternate titles: ELEVATOR INSPECTOR. Inspects and adjusts installed freight and passenger elevators and escalators to meet factory specifications and safety codes, using handtools and measuring instruments: Inspects door installations for plumbness, lap, and working action. Adjusts mechanism of doors, using handtools. Inspects car hoistway and mechanical installations for alignment and clearance. Tests power consumption and line voltage changes of motors and motor-generator sets under no-load and full-load conditions to detect overload factors, using tachometer, voltmeter, and ammeter. Adjusts counterweights and regulates controls to compensate for power overload. Inspects wiring connections and control panel hookups, and adjusts switches to meet specifications for gap and timing. Tests and adjusts safety controls, such as brakes and governors. Turns valve or pushes switches to adjust pump pressures, fluid levels, and power supply on hydraulic units of elevators. Operates elevator to determine power demands at various car speeds. May compile service reports to verify conformance of each unit to prescribed standards. ● **GED:** R4, M3, L3 ● **SVP:** 4-10 yrs ● **Academic:** Ed=A, Eng=S ● **Work Field:** 212, 121 ● **MPSMS:** 565 ● **Aptitudes:** G2, V3, N3, S2, P2, Q4, K3, F3, M2, E3, C4 ● **Temperaments:** J, T, V ● **Physical:** Stg=L; Freq: S, K, O, R, H, I, N, D Occas: C, A, X ● **Work Env:** Noise=N; Freq: E, O ● **Salary:** 5 ● **Outlook:** 3

Mechanical

Land and Water Vehicle Operation

Workers in this group drive large or small trucks, delivery vans, or locomotives, to move materials or deliver products. Some drive ambulances; others operate small boats. Most of these jobs are found with trucking companies, railroads, and water transportation companies. Wholesale and retail companies hire delivery drivers; ambulance drivers are hired by hospitals, fire departments, and other establishments concerned with moving the sick or injured.

✓ What kind of work would you do?

Your work activities would depend upon your specific job. For example, you might:

- drive a truck to pick up and deliver materials or products.
- drive a bus or locomotive engine to designated stations within a garage or storage yard.
- inspect a truck to see that it is loaded properly and in good running condition.
- operate a locomotive engine for a freight train.
- complete trip logs and other reports to show materials hauled and deliveries made.
- obtain signed receipts from customers for freight delivered.

- operate and maintain a motorboat to deliver passengers or supplies.

✓ What skills and abilities do you need for this kind of work?

To do this kind of work, you must be able to:

- understand traffic laws.
- move eyes, hands, and feet together to control the movement of the vehicle.
- use arithmetic to collect money, make change, and total receipts.
- drive vehicle for long periods with few stops.

✓ How do you know if you would like or could learn to do this kind of work?

The following questions may give you clues about yourself as you consider this group of jobs.

- Have you read automotive, trucking, or railroad magazines regularly? Do you enjoy reading this type of material?
- Have you driven in heavy traffic? Does it bother you to do so?

✓ How can you prepare for and enter this kind of work?

Occupations in this group usually require education and/or training extending from thirty days to over one year, depending on the specific kind of work.

High school driver education courses and private driving schools are helpful. Truck driving courses offered by some private vocational employers may require drivers to pass a physical. A good driving record is also necessary.

Requirements for local drivers vary with the type of vehicle driven and the employer's business. New drivers may train by riding with an experienced driver, but more training may be offered if a special type of truck is used. Requirements are similar for long-haul truckers. Some firms give classes on general duties, operating and loading procedures, and company rules and records.

The U.S. Department of Transportation sets standards for interstate trucking. Long-distance truckers must pass a written exam on the Motor Carrier Safety Regulations. They will drive on the job. Many firms have height and weight limits for their drivers. Others only hire those with long-distance experience.

Railroads prefer that engineer helpers have a high school education or equivalency. Eligibility for promotion is based on knowledge of locomotive equipment and operations and passing tests.

✓ What else should you consider about these jobs?

Some jobs require you to work evenings, nights, on-call, weekends, and holidays. In addition, long-distance haulers often spend many nights away from home. Some truck drivers must load and unload their own trucks. Although advancement in trucking is limited, some drivers become supervisors or managers and many of these workers are self-employed.

If you think you would like to do this kind of work, look at the job titles listed below.

■ ■ ■

GOE: 05.08.01
Truck Driving

DUMP-TRUCK DRIVER (any industry) ● DOT #902.683-010 ● OES: 97001 ● Drives truck equipped with dump body to transport and dump loose materials, such as sand, gravel, crushed rock, coal, or bituminous paving materials: Pulls levers or turns crank to tilt body and dump contents. Moves hand and foot controls to jerk truck forward and backward to loosen and dump material adhering to body. May load truck by hand or by operating mechanical loader. May be designated according to type of material hauled as Coal Hauler (any industry); Dust-Truck Driver (any industry); Mud Trucker (steel & rel.). May be designated according to type of equipment driven for off-highway projects as Dump-Truck Driver, Off-Highway (any industry). ● **GED:** R3, M1, L1 ● **SVP:** 2-30 days ● **Academic:** Ed=N, Eng=N ● **Work Field:** 013, 011 ● **MPSMS:** 853 ● **Aptitudes:** G3, V4, N4, S3, P4, Q4, K3, F4, M3, E3, C4 ● **Temperaments:** R ● **Physical:** Stg=M; Freq: R, H, N, F, D, X, V Occas: I, G ● **Work Env:** Noise=L; Occas: W ● **Salary:** 3 ● **Outlook:** 4

MILK DRIVER (dairy products) ● DOT #905.483-010 ● OES: 97001 ● Alternate titles: MILK HAULER. Drives insulated tank truck to transport bulk milk between farms, dairies, and commercial establishments: Examines milk to detect sediment or stale odor, and takes sample for laboratory analysis. Observes level gauge of storage tank and computes and records weight of milk in tank. Connects hose and turns valves to pump milk into truck. Washes truck. May clean and sterilize tank. May load and drive refrigerated van to haul cans of milk. ● **GED:** R3, M2, L2 ● **SVP:** 1-3 mos ● **Academic:** Ed=N, Eng=S ● **Work Field:** 013, 231 ● **MPSMS:** 383 ● **Aptitudes:** G3, V4, N3, S3, P3, Q4, K3, F4, M3, E3, C4 ● **Temperaments:** R ● **Physical:** Stg=M; Freq: R, H, I, N, F, D, X, V Occas: C, B, S, M ● **Work Env:** Noise=L; Occas: W, A ● **Salary:** 2 ● **Outlook:** 3

TRACTOR-TRAILER-TRUCK DRIVER (any industry) ● DOT #904.383-010 ● OES: 97001 ● Alternate titles: SEMI-TRUCK DRIVER; TRAILER-TRUCK DRIVER. Drives gasoline or diesel-powered tractor-trailer combination, usually long distances, to transport and deliver products, livestock, or materials in liquid, loose, or packaged form: Drives truck to destination, applying knowledge of commercial driving regulations and skill in maneuvering vehicle in difficult situations, such as narrow passageways. Inspects truck for defects before and after trips and submits report indicating truck condition. Maintains driver log according to I.C.C. regulations. May assist workers in loading and unloading truck. May transport new automobiles or trucks from manufacturers or rail terminals to dealers and be designated Transport Driver (motor trans.). May drive tractor with two trailers hitched in tandem and be designated Double-Bottom Driver (any industry). May drive tractor-trailer combination to deliver poles for utility and construction companies and be designated Pole-Truck Driver (construction; tel. & tel.; utilities). May work as member of two-person team driving tractor with sleeper bunk behind cab and be designated Long-Haul-Sleeper Driver (any industry). May drive tractor-trailer combination to deliver or spray water and be designated Water-Truck Driver (construction; petrol. & gas) I. ● **GED:** R3, M2, L3 ● **SVP:** 3-6 mos ● **Academic:** Ed=N, Eng=S ● **Work Field:** 013 ● **MPSMS:** 853 ● **Aptitudes:** G3, V4, N4, S2, P3, Q3, K3, F4, M3, E3, C4 ● **Temperaments:** J ● **Physical:** Stg=M; Freq: R, H, I, N, F, D, X, V Occas: C, B, S, O, G ● **Work Env:** Noise=L; Occas: W, O ● **Salary:** 4 ● **Outlook:** 3

TRUCK DRIVER, HEAVY (any industry) ● DOT #905.663-014 ● OES: 97001 ● Drives truck with capacity of more than 3 tons, to transport materials to and from specified destinations: Drives truck to destination, applying knowledge of commercial driving regulations and area roads. Prepares receipts for load picked up. Collects payment for goods delivered and for delivery charges. May maintain truck log, according to state and federal regulations. May maintain telephone or radio contact with supervisor to receive delivery instructions. May load and unload truck. May inspect truck equipment and supplies, such as tires, lights, brakes, gas, oil, and water. May perform emergency roadside repairs, such as changing tires, installing light bulbs, tire chains, and spark plugs. May position blocks and tie rope around items to secure cargo during transit. When driving truck equipped for specific purposes, such as fighting fires, digging holes, and installing and repairing utility company lines, may be designated Fire-Truck Driver (petrol. & gas); Hole-Digger-Truck Driver (construction; tel. & tel.; utilities). When specializing in making deliveries, may be designated Delivery-Truck Driver, Heavy (any industry). May be designated according to type of truck driven as Truck Driver, Flatbed (logging). May be designated according to kind of cargo transported as Water Hauler (logging). ● **GED:** R3, M2, L2 ● **SVP:** 3-6 mos ● **Academic:** Ed=N, Eng=S ● **Work Field:** 013 ● **MPSMS:** 853, 536 ● **Aptitudes:** G3, V4, N4, S3, P4, Q4, K3, F4, M3, E3, C4 ● **Temperaments:** R ● **Physical:** Stg=M; Freq: R, H, I, N, F, D, X, V Occas: C, S, O, T, G ● **Work Env:** Noise=L; Occas: W ● **Salary:** 3 ● **Outlook:** 4

TRUCK DRIVER, LIGHT (any industry) ● DOT #906.683-022 ● OES: 97001 ● Drives truck with capacity under 3 tons to transport materials in liquid or packaged form and personnel to and from specified destinations, such as railroad stations, plants, residences, offices, or within industrial yards: Verifies load against shipping papers. Drives truck to destination, applying knowledge of commercial driving regulations and roads in area. Prepares receipts for load picked up. Collects payment for goods delivered and for delivery charges. May maintain truck log according to state and federal regulations. May maintain telephone or radio contact with supervisor to receive delivery instructions. May drive truck equipped with public address system through city streets to broadcast announcements over system for advertising or publicity purposes. May load and unload truck. May inspect truck equipment and supplies, such as tires, lights, brakes, gas, oil, and water. May perform emergency roadside repairs, such as changing tires, installing light bulbs, fuses, tire chains, and spark plugs. May be known in establishment according to type of activity as Crew-Truck Driver (any industry); Insect Sprayer, Mobile Unit (government ser.); Mail-Truck Driver (any industry); Motor-Vehicle-Escort Driver (business ser.); Pick-Up Driver (motor trans.); Service-Parts Driver (automotive ser.); Sprinkler-Truck Driver (any industry). ● **GED:** R3, M2, L2 ● **SVP:** 1-3 mos ● **Academic:** Ed=N, Eng=N ● **Work Field:** 013 ● **MPSMS:** 853 ● **Aptitudes:** G3, V4, N4, S3, P4, Q5, K3, F4, M3, E3, C4 ● **Temperaments:** R ● **Physical:** Stg=M; Freq: R, H, I, N, F, D, X, V Occas: C, S, K, O, G ● **Work Env:** Noise=L; Occas: W ● **Salary:** 3 ● **Outlook:** 3

GOE: 05.08.02
Rail Vehicle Operation

LOCOMOTIVE ENGINEER (r.r. trans.) ● DOT #910.363-014 ● OES: 97305 ● Drives electric, diesel-electric, or gas-turbine-electric locomotive, interpreting train orders, train signals, and railroad rules and regulations, to transport passengers or freight: Inspects locomotive before run to verify specified fuel, sand, water, and other supplies. Syncronizes watch with that of CONDUCTOR, PASSENGER CAR (r.r. trans.) or CONDUCTOR, ROAD FREIGHT (r.r. trans.) to ensure departure time from station or terminal is in accordance with time schedule. Receives starting signal from CONDUCTOR, PASSENGER CAR (r.r. trans.) or CONDUCTOR, ROAD FREIGHT (r.r. trans.) and moves controls, such as throttle and airbrakes to drive locomotive. Interprets train orders, train signals, and railroad rules and regulations to drive locomotive, following safety regulations and time schedule. Calls out train signals to FIRER, LOCOMOTIVE (r.r. trans.) for verification of meaning to avoid errors in interpretation. Confers with CONDUCTOR, ROAD FREIGHT (r.r. trans.) or traffic control center personnel via radiophone to issue or receive information or instructions concerning stops, delays, or oncoming trains. Observes track to detect obstructions. Inspects locomotive after run to detect damaged or defective equipment. Prepares reports to explain accidents, unscheduled stops, or delays. May lubricate moving parts of locomotive. May drive diesel-electric rail-detector car to transport rail-flaw-detecting machine over railroad and be designated Rail-Flaw-Detector-Car Operator (r.r. trans.). May be designated according to type of locomotive driven as Locomotive Engineer, Diesel (r.r. trans.); Locomotive Engineer, Electric (r.r. trans.); or according to type of traffic assigned as Road Engineer, Freight (r.r. trans.); Road Engineer, Passenger (r.r. trans.). ● **GED:** R4, M2, L3 ● **SVP:** 2-4 yrs ● **Academic:** Ed=H, Eng=G ● **Work Field:** 013 ● **MPSMS:** 851, 594 ● **Aptitudes:** G3, V3, N4, S3, P3, Q3, K3, F4, M3, E4, C4 ● **Temperaments:** D, J, V ● **Physical:** Stg=L; Freq: F, V Occas: C, B, S, K, O, R, H, I, T, G, N, X ● **Work Env:** Noise=L; ● **Salary:** 5 ● **Outlook:** 1

GOE: 05.08.03
Services Requiring Driving

AMBULANCE DRIVER (medical ser.) ● DOT #913.683-010 ● OES: 66023 ● Drives ambulance to transport sick, injured, or convalescent persons: Places patients on stretcher and loads stretcher into ambulance, usually with help of AMBULANCE ATTENDANT (medical ser.). Takes sick or injured persons to hospital, or convalescents to des-

tination, using knowledge and skill in driving to avoid sudden motions deterimental to patients. Changes soiled linen on stretcher. Administers first aid as needed. May shackle violent patients. May report facts concerning accident or emergency to hospital personnel or law enforcement officials. ● **GED:** R3, M2, L2 ● **SVP:** 3-6 mos ● **Academic:** Ed=N, Eng=S ● **Work Field:** 013, 294 ● **MPSMS:** 929 ● **Aptitudes:** G3, V4, N4, S3, P4, Q4, K3, F4, M3, E3, C4 ● **Temperaments:** P, S ● **Physical:** Stg=V; Freq: R, H, I, N, F, D, X, V Occas: C, B, T, G ● **Work Env:** Noise=L; ● **Salary:** 3 ● **Outlook:** 3

CHAUFFEUR, FUNERAL CAR (personal ser.) ● DOT #359.673-014 ● OES: 97114 ● Alternate titles: FUNERAL DRIVER. Drives mortuary vehicles, such as hearses and limousines: Drives hearse to transport bodies to mortuary for embalming and from mortuary to place of funeral service or interment. Helps PALLBEARERS (personal ser.) to move casket from mortuary into hearse and from hearse to destination. Arranges flowers in hearse. Drives limousine in funeral procession, following prearranged schedule, to transport mourners. Assists passengers entering or leaving limousine. May clean vehicles prior to funeral. May dust furniture and sweep floors in mortuary. May be designated according to type of vehicle driven as Funeral-Limousine Driver (personal ser.); Hearse Driver (personal ser.). ● **GED:** R2, M1, L2 ● **SVP:** 3-6 mos ● **Academic:** Ed=N, Eng=N ● **Work Field:** 013 ● **MPSMS:** 907 ● **Aptitudes:** G3, V4, N4, S3, P4, Q5, K3, F4, M3, E3, C3 ● **Temperaments:** R, T ● **Physical:** Stg=V; Freq: R, H, N, F, D, A, X, V Occas: S ● **Work Env:** Noise=Q; ● **Salary:** 2 ● **Outlook:** 2

COIN COLLECTOR (business ser.) ● DOT #292.483-010 ● OES: 97117 ● Alternate titles: ROUTE DRIVER, COIN MACHINES; SERVICER, COIN MACHINES. Drives truck over established route to collect money from and refill coin-operated amusement-game machines, jukeboxes, and vending machines that dispense merchandise, such as cigarettes, coffee, food, beverages, and candy: Loads truck with supplies according to written or verbal instructions. Drives truck to establishment, collects coins, refills machine, cleans inside of machines that dispense food or beverages, and records amount of money collected. Turns in money to cashiering department at completion of route and unloads truck. Reports malfunctioning machines to maintenance department for repair. May perform minor repairs or adjustments on machines, using handtools, to correct malfunctions. May promote installation of new or additional coin-operated machines at locations of customers or potential customers. May be designated according to type of machine serviced as Amusement-Game Machine Coin Collector (business ser.); Jukebox Coin Collector (business ser.); Vending-Machine Coin Collector (business ser.). ● **GED:** R3, M2, L3 ● **SVP:** 1-3 mos ● **Academic:** Ed=N, Eng=N ● **Work Field:** 013, 221 ● **MPSMS:** 883 ● **Aptitudes:** G3, V4, N4, S4, P4, Q4, K3, F4, M3, E3, C4 ● **Temperaments:** R ● **Physical:** Stg=M; Freq: S, R, H, I, N, F, D, X, V ● **Work Env:** Noise=N; Occas: W ● **Salary:** 3 ● **Outlook:** 3

CONCRETE-MIXING-TRUCK DRIVER (construction) ● DOT #900.683-010 ● OES: 97001 ● Alternate titles: BATCH-MIXING-TRUCK DRIVER; MOTO-MIX OPERATOR; READY-MIX-TRUCK DRIVER; TRANSIT-MIX OPERATOR. Drives truck equipped with auxiliary concrete mixer to deliver concrete mix to job sites: Drives truck under loading hopper to receive sand, gravel, cement, and water and starts mixer. Drives truck to location for unloading. Moves levers on truck to release concrete down truck chute into wheelbarrow or other conveying container or directly into area to be poured with concrete. Cleans truck after delivery to prevent concrete from hardening in mixer and on truck, using water hose and hoe. May spray surfaces of truck with protective compound to prevent adhering of concrete. May assemble cement chute. ● **GED:** R3, M1, L1 ● **SVP:** 1-3 mos ● **Academic:** Ed=N, Eng=N ● **Work Field:** 013, 143 ● **MPSMS:** 536 ● **Aptitudes:** G3, V4, N4, S3, P4, Q4, K3, F4, M3, E3, C4 ● **Temperaments:** R ● **Physical:** Stg=M; Freq: R, H, N, F, D, V Occas: I, X ● **Work Env:** Noise=N; Occas: U ● **Salary:** 4 ● **Outlook:** 2

DELIVERER, CAR RENTAL (automotive ser.) ● DOT #919.663-010 ● OES: 97114 ● Alternate titles: WASHER DRIVER. Delivers rental cars to customers, and services them prior to delivery: Sweeps out and vacuum cleans interior of rental automobile. Washes windows and exterior of automobile, using water and other cleansing compounds and cloth. Regulates tire pressure and adds gasoline and oil. Adds water to battery and radiator. Delivers automobile to customer at specified pickup point. Collects rental payment and deposit from customer; and observes that customer reads and signs rental contract. May deliver new or used automobiles to customer from automobile dealership. ● **GED:** R2, M2, L2 ● **SVP:** 1-3 mos ● **Academic:** Ed=N, Eng=S ● **Work Field:** 013, 031 ● **MPSMS:** 859 ● **Aptitudes:** G4, V4, N4, S3, P4, Q4, K3, F4, M3, E3, C4 ● **Temperaments:** R ● **Physical:** Stg=L; Freq: R, H Occas: S, K, O, I, E, T, G, N, D, X ● **Work Env:** Noise=N; Freq: W Occas: U ● **Salary:** 2 ● **Outlook:** 3

ESCORT-VEHICLE DRIVER (motor trans.) ● DOT #919.663-022 ● OES: 97001 ● Drives vehicle equipped with warning lights and signs to escort trucks hauling mobile homes on public thoroughfares: Precedes escort and maintains specified distance between pilot vehicle and escort to provide warning to other motorists and to clear traffic at locations. Communicates by two-way radio with truck and other pilot vehicle drivers to coordinate changes in speed and route, emergencies, or traffic congestion. ● **GED:** R2, M1, L2 ● **SVP:** 2-30 days ● **Academic:** Ed=N, Eng=N ● **Work Field:** 013 ● **MPSMS:** 859 ● **Aptitudes:** G4, V4, N4, S4, P4, Q4, K3, F4, M3, E3, C4 ● **Temperaments:** R ● **Physical:** Stg=S; Freq: R, H, N, F, D, A, X, V ● **Work Env:** Noise=N; ● **Salary:** 2 ● **Outlook:** 3

FOOD-SERVICE DRIVER (hotel & rest.) ● DOT #906.683-010 ● OES: 97001 ● Alternate titles: FOOD-SERVICE AGENT. Drives truck to deliver refrigerated and electric-warming cabinets containing previously prepared meals to airports, and unloads cabinets into airplanes: Loads cabinets into truck and drives truck to flight field. Maneuvers truck beneath airplane to be loaded and moves truck levers to elevate truck bed to level of airplane door. Unloads cabinets into airplane and connects electrical cords of cabinets to electrical outlets of airplane. Presents billing form to designated airline representative and collects receipt. Loads empty cabinets onto truck and returns them to commissary kitchen. ● **GED:** R2, M1, L1 ● **SVP:** 1-3 mos ● **Academic:** Ed=N, Eng=N ● **Work Field:** 013, 011 ● **MPSMS:** 853, 903 ● **Aptitudes:** G4, V4, N4, S3, P4, Q4, K3, F4, M3, E3, C4 ● **Temperaments:** R ● **Physical:** Stg=M; Freq: R, H, N, F, D, X, V Occas: C, B, I ● **Work Env:** Noise=L; Occas: W ● **Salary:** 3 ● **Outlook:** 3

GARBAGE COLLECTOR DRIVER (motor trans.) ● DOT #905.663-010 ● OES: 97001 ● Drives packer-type truck, dump truck, or truck equipped with hydraulic lifting device to collect garbage and trash, and transports load to disposal area. Records mileage and fuel consumption. ● **GED:** R3, M1, L1 ● **SVP:** 1-3 mos ● **Academic:** Ed=N, Eng=N ● **Work Field:** 013, 011 ● **MPSMS:** 874 ● **Aptitudes:** G3, V4, N4, S3, P4, Q4, K3, F4, M3, E3, C4 ● **Temperaments:** R ● **Physical:** Stg=M; Freq: R, H, I, N, F, D, X, V Occas: S, T, G ● **Work Env:** Noise=L; Occas: W ● **Salary:** 4 ● **Outlook:** 4

GARBAGE-COLLECTION SUPERVISOR (motor trans.) ● DOT #909.137-014 ● OES: 81000 ● Alternate titles: RUBBISH-COLLECTION SUPERVISOR; TRASH-COLLECTION SUPERVISOR. Supervises and coordinates activities of workers engaged in collecting garbage and other refuse and transporting refuse to disposal plants or areas. Assigns routes and trucks to workers. Performs other duties as described under SUPERVISOR (any industry) Master Title. ● **GED:** R4, M3, L3 ● **SVP:** 1-2 yrs ● **Academic:** Ed=N, Eng=G ● **Work Field:** 011, 013 ● **MPSMS:** 859 ● **Aptitudes:** G3, V3, N4, S3, P4, Q3, K3, F4, M3, E3, C4 ● **Temperaments:** D, P, V ● **Physical:** Stg=L; Freq: R, H, I, T, G, N, D Occas: F, X, V ● **Work Env:** Noise=L; Freq: W ● **Salary:** 4 ● **Outlook:** 2

HEALTH-EQUIPMENT SERVICER (medical ser.) ● DOT #359.363-010 ● OES: 66099 ● Delivers, installs, demonstrates, and maintains rental medical equipment, such as respirator, oxygen equipment, hospital beds, and wheelchairs, for use in private residences: Loads medical equipment on truck and delivers equipment to renter's or patient's residence. Unloads, installs, and sets up equipment, using handtools. Inspects and maintains rental oxygen equipment, performing such tasks as inspecting hoses and water traps to detect leaks and condensation; observing gauges of oxygen analyzer, pressure gauges, and other monitoring equipment to determine pressure and oxygen content of air output of compressors and concentrators; and changing filters. Maintains record on oxygen equipment by hours of usage to determine need for maintenance. ● **GED:** R3, M2, L3 ● **SVP:** 6 mos-1 yr ● **Academic:** Ed=N, Eng=S ● **Work Field:** 013, 121 ● **MPSMS:** 929 ● **Aptitudes:** G3, V3, N4, S4, P4, Q4, K3, F3, M3, E4, C4 ● **Temperaments:** J, T ● **Physical:** Stg=V; Freq: R, H, I, T, G, N Occas: A, X, V ● **Work Env:** Noise=N; ● **Salary:** 4 ● **Outlook:** 3

LOT ATTENDANT (retail trade) ● DOT #915.583-010 ● OES: 97808 ● Verifies receipt of new cars delivered to dealer and parks cars in new car lot in orderly manner: Compares serial numbers of incoming cars against invoice. Inspects cars to detect damage and to verify presence of accessories listed on invoice, such as spare tires and radio and stereo equipment. Records description of damages and lists missing items on delivery receipt. Parks new cars in assigned area according to model. Assigns stock control numbers to cars, and catalogs and stores keys. Reparks cars, following sales, to maximize use of space and maintain lot in order. Delivers sold cars to new car preparation department. Services cars in storage to protect tires, battery, and finish against deterioration. ● **GED:** R3, M2, L3 ● **SVP:** 1-3 mos ● **Academic:** Ed=N, Eng=S ● **Work Field:** 231, 013 ● **MPSMS:** 961 ● **Aptitudes:** G3, V3, N4, S4, P3, Q3, K3, F4, M3, E3, C4 ● **Temperaments:** R, T ● **Physical:** Stg=L; Freq: R, H, N, V Occas: I, F, A, X ● **Work Env:** Noise=N; Freq: W ● **Salary:** 1 ● **Outlook:** 3

NEWSPAPER-DELIVERY DRIVER (wholesale tr.) ● DOT #292.363-010 ● OES: 97117 ● Drives truck or automobile over prescribed route to deliver newspapers to wholesale or retail newspaper dealers, or to bus, airline, or express stations for shipment: Loads newspapers onto vehicle. Reviews list of dealers, customers, or station drops for change in deliveries. Drives truck or automobile over prescribed route on city streets or rural roads. Delivers newspapers to dealers or individual subscribers at their homes or place of business, or to bus, airline, or express station for shipment. Keeps records of deliveries made. Collects receipts for deliveries to newsdealers. May pick up unsold newspapers and credit newsdealer's account. May collect payment for newspaper deliveries from customers. May keep records pertaining to driving expenses, such as mileage, oil, and gasoline. May stock newspapers in street sales rack, and collect coins from rack coin boxes. May distribute sales promotion material to customers with newspaper deliveries. May be designated according to publication delivered as Magazine-Delivery Driver (wholesale tr.). ● **GED:** R3, M2, L2 ● **SVP:** 3-6 mos ● **Academic:** Ed=N, Eng=S ● **Work Field:** 013, 292 ● **MPSMS:** 883 ● **Aptitudes:** G3, V4, N4, S4, P4, Q3, K4, F4, M4, E3, C5 ● **Temperaments:** P ● **Physical:** Stg=M; Freq: R, H, I, T, G, N, F, D, V ● **Work Env:** Noise=N; Occas: W ● **Salary:** 1 ● **Outlook:** 3

TELEPHONE-DIRECTORY-DISTRIBUTOR DRIVER (business ser.) ● DOT #906.683-018 ● OES: 97001 ● Drives automobile or truck to transport telephone directories from central storage facilities to distribution area: Loads vehicle with assigned number of books and drives to distribution district, parking vehicle in convenient or centralized location. Distributes books to TELEPHONE-DIRECTORY DELIVERERS (business ser.) for delivery to residences and business establishments indicated on address lists. May transport TELEPHONE-DIRECTORY DELIVERERS (business ser.) to distribution area. May deliver telephone directories, on foot, after parking vehicle. ● **GED:** R2, M1, L2 ● **SVP:** 1-3 mos ● **Academic:** Ed=N, Eng=N ● **Work Field:** 013, 011 ● **MPSMS:** 859 ● **Aptitudes:** G4, V4, N4, S3, P4, Q4, K3, F4, M3, E3, C4 ● **Temperaments:** R ● **Physical:** Stg=L; Freq: R, H, N, F, D, X, V Occas: S, K, O, I ● **Work Env:** Noise=L; Freq: W ● **Salary:** 1 ● **Outlook:** 4

TOW-TRUCK OPERATOR (automotive ser.) ● DOT #919.663-026 ● OES: 97001 ● Alternate titles: TOW-CAR DRIVER; WRECKER OPERATOR. Drives tow-truck to move motor vehicles damaged by accident, stalled, or ticketed by police for traffic violation: Receives call or is dispatched to location by repair garage, automobile association, or police department by radio or telephone. Attaches antisway bar to vehicle by means of cable, chains, or other grappling devices, and hoists one end of vehicle, using hand or powered winch, to tow vehicle to repair garage or to police department's impounding area. May make minor repairs to vehicles along highway, such as replacing spark plugs, batteries, and light bulbs, and connecting loose wires. May perform other duties when not engaged in towing, such as AUTOMOBILE-SERVICE-STATION ATTENDANT (automotive ser.); TIRE REPAIRER (automotive ser.). May dismantle vehicles to salvage parts, using such handtools as wrenches, pry bar, and hacksaws [AUTOMOBILE WRECKER (wholesale tr.)]. May remove, bend, or cut parts of damaged vehicles preparatory to towing. ● **GED:** R2, M1, L2 ● **SVP:** 1-3 mos ● **Academic:** Ed=N, Eng=S ● **Work Field:** 011, 013 ● **MPSMS:** 961 ● **Aptitudes:** G3, V4, N4, S3, P4, Q4, K3, F4, M3, E3, C4 ● **Temperaments:** J ● **Physical:** Stg=M; Freq: S, K, O, R, H, F, D, X, V Occas: W, I, T, G, N ● **Work Env:** Noise=L; Freq: W ● **Salary:** 3 ● **Outlook:** 3

VAN DRIVER (motor trans.) ● DOT #905.663-018 ● OES: 97001 ● Alternate titles: FURNITURE-MOVER DRIVER. Loads furniture into van, drives truck to specified destination, and unloads furniture: Drives van to loading point and consults householder on furniture to be moved. Gives directions to VAN-DRIVER HELPER (motor trans.) in moving articles to van. Wraps furniture with blankets to prevent damage. Wraps dishes and fragile items in packing paper and packs them into containers. Loads truck, using dollies and handtruck, distributing weight evenly, forming compact load, and utilizing space. Drives van to destination and unloads cargo. Obtains customers signature or collects payment for services. May service van [GAS-AND-OIL SERVICER (motor trans.)]. May remove window frames and erect block and tackle on house to remove bulky items. May move delicate equipment or instruments for industrial firms. May deliver items such as furniture and large appliances to department store customers and be designated Bulk Driver (motor trans.). ● **GED:** R3, M2, L3 ● **SVP:** 3-6 mos ● **Academic:** Ed=N, Eng=S ● **Work Field:** 011, 013 ● **MPSMS:** 853 ● **Aptitudes:** G3, V3, N4, S3, P4, Q4, K3, F3, M3, E3, C4 ● **Temperaments:** J, P ● **Physical:** Stg=V; Freq: S, O, R, H, N, F, D, X, V Occas: I, T, G ● **Work Env:** Noise=L; Occas: W ● **Salary:** 2 ● **Outlook:** 3

GOE: 05.08.04
Boat Operation

MOTORBOAT OPERATOR (any industry) ● DOT #911.663-010 ● OES: 97898 ● Operates motor-driven boat to carry passengers and freight, take depth soundings in turning basin, serve as liaison between ships, ship to shore, harbor and beach area patrol, or tow, push, or guide other boats, barges, logs, or rafts: Casts off securing lines and starts motor. Starts boat and steers boat with helm or tiller. Maintains equipment, such as range markers, fire extinguishers, boat fenders, lines, pumps, and fittings. Services motor by changing oil and lubricating parts. Cleans boat and repairs hull and superstructure, using handtools, paint, and brushes. May tune up, overhaul, or replace engine. May give directions for loading and seating in boat. May be designated according to type of boat operated as Boat Tender (logging); Boomboat Operator (logging); Charter-Boat Operator (amuse. & rec.); Sightseeing-Boat Operator (water trans.); Water-Taxi Driver (water trans.); or operate motor-driven boat to haul fish or other marine life from offshore fishing vessel to buyer and be designated Run-Boat Operator (water trans.). ● **GED:** R3, M2, L3 ● **SVP:** 6 mos-1 yr ● **Academic:** Ed=N, Eng=S ● **Work Field:** 013 ● **MPSMS:** 854 ● **Aptitudes:** G3, V4, N4, S3, P3, Q4, K3, F4, M3, E3, C4 ● **Temperaments:** J ● **Physical:** Stg=M; Freq: R, H, I, T, G, F, D, A, X, V Occas: N ● **Work Env:** Noise=N; ● **Salary:** 2 ● **Outlook:** 2

DECKHAND (water trans.) ● DOT #911.687-022 ● OES: 97504 ● Performs any combination of following duties aboard watercraft, such as dredges, ferryboats, scows, and river boats: Handles lines to moor vessel to wharves, tie up vessel to another vessel, or rig towing lines. Sweeps and washes decks, using broom, brushes, mops, and firehose. Lowers and mans lifeboat in case of emergencies. Stands steering watches or lookout watches while underway. Moves controls or turns handwheels to raise or lower passenger or vehicle landing ramps or kelp-cutter mechanism. Inserts blocks under wheels of vehicles to prevent them from moving on ferryboats. Loads or unloads material from barges, scows, and dredges. Paints lifeboats, decks, and superstructure of vessel, using brush. Lubricates machinery and equipment. Splices and repairs cables and ropes, using handtools. Examines cables that holds vessels in tow and tightens cables to ensure vessels are snug. May tour decks during watch to caution passengers engaged in unsafe practices, and ensures departure of passengers at end of voyage. Deckhands are designated according to type of craft as Barge Hand (water trans.); Dredge Deckhand (water trans.); Ferryboat Deckhand (water trans.); Pilot-Boat Deckhand (water trans.); Scow Deckhand (water trans.); Tugboat Deckhand (water trans.). ● **GED:** R2, M1, L1 ● **SVP:** 3-6 mos ● **Academic:** Ed=N, Eng=N ● **Work Field:** 013, 031, 153 ● **MPSMS:** 854 ● **Aptitudes:** G3, V3, N4, S3, P4, Q5, K4, F4, M3, E3, C4 ● **Temperaments:** J ● **Physical:** Stg=H; Freq: S, O, R, H, F Occas: C, B, X ● **Work Env:** Noise=L; Freq: W, U Occas: O ● **Salary:** 1 ● **Outlook:** 2

DOCK HAND (air trans.) ● DOT #919.683-010 ● OES: 97898 ● Operates motorboat to transport passengers or cargo to and from anchored amphibious airplanes and operates tractor to remove planes from water: Loads cargo or directs passengers aboard motorboat. Pilots boat to plane or dock and discharges cargo or passengers. Positions wheeled beaching gear at end of ramp in water and, standing in water, pushes and pulls plane over ramping gear. Drives tractor to draw plane and gear up ramp onto shore for removal to hangar. Cleans plane interiors and exteriors. ● **GED:** R2, M2, L2 ● **SVP:** 3-6 mos ● **Academic:** Ed=N, Eng=N ● **Work Field:** 013, 011 ● **MPSMS:** 855, 854 ● **Aptitudes:** G3, V3, N4, S3, P4, Q4, K3, F4, M3, E3, C5 ● **Temperaments:** P ● **Physical:** Stg=H; Freq: B, R, H, F, D Occas: S, K, N ● **Work Env:** Noise=L; Freq: W, U, M Occas: O ● **Salary:** 3 ● **Outlook:** 3

Mechanical   05

Material Control   05.09

Workers in this group receive, store, and/or ship materials and products. Some estimate and order the quantities and kinds of materials needed. Others regulate and control the flow of materials to places in the plant where they are to be used. Most have to keep records. Jobs are found in institutions, industrial plants, and government agencies.

✓ **What kind of work would you do?**

Your work activities would depend upon your specific job. For example, you might:

- weigh truck loaded with cotton and compute weight and gin charges.
- count, sort, or weigh articles in a shipment to check accuracy of invoices or requisitions.
- verify inventory records of a department store against the actual count of items.
- fill out receiving tickets on incoming items or complete delivery tickets on outgoing items.
- receive, store, and issue tools, dies, and equipment in a factory.
- store and issue sports equipment for a professional athletic team.
- check the progress of an order in a factory and write a report.

✓ **What skills and abilities do you need for this kind of work?**

To do this kind of work, you must be able to:

- use arithmetic to keep records, take inventory, estimate quantities, or schedule the flow of materials through the plant.
- avoid errors in recordkeeping.
- use hands and fingers to measure, handle, store, or move large and small items.

- reach to place materials on shelves higher than your head.
- see small print and figures in catalogs, on shipping tickets, and on invoices.

✓ How do you know if you would like or could learn to do this kind of work?

The following questions may give you clues about yourself as you consider this group of jobs.

- Have you taken industrial arts or vocational courses? Did you learn how to issue, store, and care for tools?
- Have you been an equipment manager for a sports team? Were you responsible for issuing and maintaining the equipment?
- Have you mailed or sent packages by freight? Can you compute freight or postal rates accurately?
- Have you been a stock clerk in the military service? Did you enjoy this type of work?

✓ How can you prepare for and enter this kind of work?

Occupations in this group usually require education and/or training extending from a short demonstra-tion to over two years, depending upon the specific kind of work. Evidence of basic reading, writing, and mathematics skills are usually required by employers. On-the-job training is provided to teach workers the procedures involved in each particular job. Complex tasks involving judgment or responsi-bility are assigned as workers become experienced.

Jobs involving tools and machines often require a knowledge of the use and care of such equipment. One year of shop experience is sometimes required.

✓ What else should you consider about these jobs?

Many jobs in this group require workers to be on their feet most of the workday. Most of the work is done indoors. However, different working condi-tions are sometimes present on loading platforms, storage yards, or cold storage rooms.

Workers who move heavy objects have to use care to avoid body strain or injury.

If you think you would like to do this kind of work, look at the job titles listed on the following pages.

■ ■ ■

GOE: 05.09.01
Shipping, Receiving, & Stock Checking

BOOKMOBILE DRIVER (library) ● DOT #249.363-010 ● OES: 53902 ● Drives bookmobile or light truck that pulls book trailer, and assists in providing library services in mobile library: Drives vehicle to specified locations on predetermined schedule. Places books and peri-odicals on shelves according to such groupings as subject matter, reader's age grouping, or reading level. Stamps dates on library cards, files cards, and collects fines. Compiles reports of mileage, number of books is-sued, and amount of fines collected. Drives vehicle to garage for re-pairs, such as motor or transmission overhauls, and for preventive maintenance, such as chassis lubrication and oil change. May operate microfilm camera to photograph library cards [PHOTOGRAPHIC-MACHINE OPERATOR (clerical) 207.685-018]. ● **GED:** R3, M2, L2 ● **SVP:** 1-3 mos ● **Academic:** Ed=N, Eng=S ● **Work Field:** 013, 221 ● **MPSMS:** 933 ● **Aptitudes:** G3, V3, N3, S4, P4, Q3, K3, F4, M3, E3, C4 ● **Temperaments:** P, V ● **Physical:** Stg=L; Freq: R, H, I, T, G, N, A Occas: F, D, X, V ● **Work Env:** Noise=N; ● **Salary:** 2 ● **Outlook:** 2

CARGO AGENT (air trans.) ● DOT #248.367-018 ● OES: 58098 ● Alternate titles: AIR-FREIGHT AGENT; CUSTOMER SERVICE AGENT. Routes inbound and outbound air freight shipments to their destinations: Takes telephone orders from customers and arranges for pickup of freight and delivery to loading platform. Assembles cargo according to destination. Weighs items and determines cost, using rate book. Itemizes charges, prepares freight bills, accepts payments and issues refunds. Prepares manifest to accompany shipments. Notifies shippers of delays in departure of shipment. Unloads inbound freight and notifies consignees on arrival of shipments and arranges for deliv-ery to consignees. May force conditioned air into interior of plane for passenger comfort prior to departure, using mobile aircraft-air-condi-tioning-unit. ● **GED:** R3, M3, L3 ● **SVP:** 6 mos-1 yr ● **Academic:** Ed=N, Eng=G ● **Work Field:** 013, 221 ● **MPSMS:** 855 ● **Aptitudes:** G3, V3, N3, S3, P4, Q3, K3, F3, M3, E4, C4 ● **Temperaments:** J ● **Physical:** Stg=M; Freq: R, H, I, T, G, N Occas: D ● **Work Env:** Noise=N; ● **Salary:** 2 ● **Outlook:** 3

CHECKER (motor trans.) ● DOT #919.687-010 ● OES: 58028 ● Counts and herds cattle, hogs, or sheep as they are unloaded from ship-ping trucks in stockyard and verifies information on ticket, such as number of head, identifying markings on livestock, and designated commission agency: Marks time of arrival on ticket and gives it to shipper as receipt. Herds livestock into separate pens according to mark-ings which identify commission agency to which stock is assigned. May mark identification on stock, using shears or chalk. ● **GED:** R1, M1, L1 ● **SVP:** 2-30 days ● **Academic:** Ed=N, Eng=N ● **Work Field:** 221 ● **MPSMS:** 859 ● **Aptitudes:** G4, V4, N4, S4, P4, Q4, K4, F4, M3, E5, C5 ● **Temperaments:** R ● **Physical:** Stg=L; Freq: R, H, N, D Occas: I ● **Work Env:** Noise=L; Freq: O ● **Salary:** 2 ● **Outlook:** 3

CHECKER, BAKERY PRODUCTS (bakery products) ● DOT #222.487-010 ● OES: 58097 ● Alternate titles: ORDER FILLER, BAKERY PRODUCTS. Loads racks with bakery products to prepare orders for shipping, according to products available and following or-der slips: Adjusts amount of products going to routes according to sup-ply and route-return records of DRIVER, SALES ROUTE (retail trade; wholesale tr.) 292.353-010. Loads products onto tiered racks and pushes racks to loading area. Records adjustments on route slips. ● **GED:** R2, M2, L2 ● **SVP:** 2-30 days ● **Academic:** Ed=N, Eng=S ● **Work Field:** 221 ● **MPSMS:** 384, 898 ● **Aptitudes:** G4, V4, N4, S4, P4, Q3, K4, F4, M4, E4, C4 ● **Temperaments:** R ● **Physical:** Stg=H; Const: R, H Occas: S, I, N, F, D, A, X ● **Work Env:** Noise=N; ● **Salary:** 1 ● **Outlook:** 3

CUSTODIAN, ATHLETIC EQUIPMENT (amuse. & rec.) ● DOT #969.367-010 ● OES: 58097 ● Alternate titles: MANAGER, EQUIP-MENT. Keeps stock of new and used athletic supplies, such as balls, gloves, bats, shoes, and uniforms, and issues supplies to players: Keeps record of supplies in stock and supplies issued to players. Informs offi-cials when additional supplies are needed. Inspects supplies in stock to detect those requiring repair or cleaning. Repairs torn or damaged sup-plies or sends supplies out for repair. Issues new or clean supplies to players in exchange for supplies that are worn or dirty. Packs and unpacks supplies for road trips and ensures that arrangements are made for transportation. Accompanies players on trips. Modifies protective supplies, such as adding additional arch supports to shoes, padding uniforms and helmets, or preparing slings for injured players, under specific directions from INSTRUCTOR, SPORTS (amuse. & rec.; education) or ATHLETIC TRAINER (amuse. & rec.; education). May prepare budget estimate for supplies. May purchase supplies. May wash soiled uniforms and other supplies in automatic washing machine or may arrange to have supplies laundered. ● **GED:** R3, M2, L2 ● **SVP:** 6 mos-1 yr ● **Academic:** Ed=N, Eng=S ● **Work Field:** 221 ● **MPSMS:** 913 ● **Aptitudes:** G3, V3, N3, S4, P4, Q3, K3, F3, M3, E5, C4 ● **Temperaments:** P, T, V ● **Physical:** Stg=M; Freq: R, H, I, E, T, G, N Occas: D, A, X ● **Work Env:** Noise=N; ● **Salary:** 1 ● **Outlook:** 2

DISPATCHER (construction) ● DOT #849.137-010 ● OES: 81000 ● Supervises and coordinates activities of workers engaged in weighing, mixing, and shipping concrete and concrete aggregates. Performs duties as described under SUPERVISOR (any industry) Master Title. ● **GED:** R4, M3, L3 ● **SVP:** 1-2 yrs ● **Academic:** Ed=N, Eng=G ● **Work Field:** 013, 143 ● **MPSMS:** 536 ● **Aptitudes:** G3, V3, N3, S4, P4, Q3, K4, F4, M4, E5, C5 ● **Temperaments:** D, J, P, T ● **Physical:** Stg=L; Freq: R, H, T, G, N Occas: I ● **Work Env:** Noise=L; ● **Salary:** 4 ● **Outlook:** 3

DISTRIBUTION SUPERVISOR (pipe lines) ● DOT #914.137-010 ● OES: 81000 ● Supervises and coordinates activities of workers engaged in loading petroleum products, such as oils, kerosene, and gasoline into tank trucks, and schedules delivery of products to retail service stations or distributors: Reviews written or telephone shipping orders specifying type and volume of product to be loaded, shipping priorities, and delivery dates to prepare delivery schedules for truckdrivers, employing knowledge of routes, time required for loading, and average customer demands. Compiles and submits reports to regional office. Develops and implements preventive maintenance program for tank trucks. Performs other duties as described under SUPERVISOR (any industry) Master Title. ● **GED:** R4, M3, L4 ● **SVP:** 1-2 yrs ● **Academic:** Ed=H, Eng=G ● **Work Field:** 232, 014 ● **MPSMS:** 850 ● **Aptitudes:** G2, V3, N3, S4, P3, Q3, K4, F4, M4, E5, C5 ● **Temperaments:** D, J, P, T ● **Physical:** Stg=S; Freq: R, H, T, G, N Occas: I ● **Work Env:** Noise=N; ● **Salary:** 3 ● **Outlook:** 2

INVENTORY CLERK (clerical) ● DOT #222.387-026 ● OES: 58097 ● Compiles and maintains records of quantity, type, and value of material, equipment, merchandise, or supplies stocked in establishment: Counts material, equipment, merchandise, or supplies in stock and posts totals to inventory records, manually or using computer. Compares inventories to office records or computes figures from records, such as sales orders, production records, or purchase invoices to obtain current inventory. Verifies clerical computations against physical count of stock and adjusts errors in computation or count, or investigates and reports reasons for discrepancies. Compiles information on receipt or disbursement of material, equipment, merchandise, or supplies, and computes inventory balance, price, and cost. Prepares reports, such as inventory balance, price lists, and shortages. Prepares list of depleted items and recommends survey of defective or unusable items. May operate office machines, such as typewriter or calculator. May stock and issue materials or merchandise. May be designated according to item inventoried as Property-And-Equipment Clerk (petrol. & gas); or type of inventory as Inventory Clerk, Physical (clerical). ● **GED:** R3, M3, L3 ● **SVP:** 3-6 mos ● **Academic:** Ed=N, Eng=S ● **Work Field:** 221 ● **MPSMS:** 898 ● **Aptitudes:** G3, V3, N3, S4, P4, Q2, K4, F4, M4, E5, C4 ● **Temperaments:** R, T ● **Physical:** Stg=M; Freq: R, H, I, N Occas: C, S, K, O, F, A, X ● **Work Env:** Noise=N; ● **Salary:** 2 ● **Outlook:** 3

LABORER, STORES (any industry) ● DOT #922.687-058 ● OES: 98998 ● Alternate titles: ORDER PICKER; PARTS PICKER; STOCK SELECTOR; WAREHOUSE WORKER. Performs any combination of following tasks to receive, store, and distribute material, tools, equipment, and products within establishments: Reads production schedule, customer order, work order, shipping order, or requisition to determine items to be moved, gathered, or distributed. Conveys materials and items from receiving or production areas to storage or to other designated areas by hand, handtruck, or electric handtruck. Sorts and places materials or items on racks, shelves, or in bins according to predetermined sequence, such as size, type, style, color, or product code. Sorts and stores perishable goods in refrigerated rooms. Fills requisitions, work orders, or requests for materials, tools, or other stock items and distributes items to production workers or assembly line. Assembles customer orders from stock and places orders on pallets or shelves, or conveys orders to packing station or shipping department. Marks materials with identifying information, using stencil, crayon, or other marking device. Opens bales, crates, and other containers, using handtools. Records amounts of materials or items received or distributed. Weighs or counts items for distribution within plant to ensure conformance to company standards. Arranges stock parts in specified sequence for assembly by other workers. May use computer to enter records. May compile worksheets or tickets from customer specifications [ORDER DETAILER (clerical) 221.387-046]. May drive vehicle to transport stored items from warehouse to plant or to pick up items from several locations for shipment. May complete requisition forms to order supplies from other plant departments. May prepare parcels for mailing. May maintain inventory records. May restock aircraft commissary supplies, such as linens, glasses, emergency kits, and beverages, and be designated Commissary Agent (air trans.). May be known according to specific duty performed as Cloth-Bin Packer (textile); Cooler Worker (dairy products); Order Filler (any industry); Produce Clerk (retail trade) II; Tool Chaser (any industry). ● **GED:** R2, M1, L1 ● **SVP:** 2-30 days ● **Academic:** Ed=N, Eng=N ● **Work Field:** 221 ● **MPSMS:** 898 ● **Aptitudes:** G4, V4, N4, S4, P4, Q4, K4, F4, M4, E4, C4 ● **Temperaments:** R ● **Physical:** Stg=M; Freq: S, O, R, H, I, N, D Occas: C, K, G, A, X ● **Work Env:** Noise=N; ● **Salary:** 2 ● **Outlook:** 3

LABORATORY CLERK (clerical) ● DOT #222.587-026 ● OES: 58098 ● Keeps records of chemicals, apparatus, and samples, such as coal, ash, and oil, received for testing in control laboratory. Weighs and prepares for shipment chemical supplies furnished by laboratory. Cleans glassware and other laboratory apparatus, and salvages sample bottles or containers for reuse. Returns unused chemicals to designated cabinets and cleans work area, using mop. ● **GED:** R3, M2, L2 ● **SVP:** 1-3 mos ● **Academic:** Ed=N, Eng=S ● **Work Field:** 221, 212 ● **MPSMS:** 891 ● **Aptitudes:** G3, V3, N3, S4, P4, Q3, K4, F4, M4, E5, C5 ● **Temperaments:** R ● **Physical:** Stg=L; Freq: R, H Occas: I, N ● **Work Env:** Noise=Q; ● **Salary:** 3 ● **Outlook:** 3

LINEN-ROOM ATTENDANT (hotel & rest.) ● DOT #222.387-030 ● OES: 58097 ● Alternate titles: LINEN CHECKER; LINEN CLERK; LINEN-EXCHANGE ATTENDANT; LINEN-ROOM HOUSEPERSON; UNIFORM ATTENDANT. Stores, inventories, and issues or distributes bed and table linen and uniforms in establishments, such as hotels, hospitals, and clinics: Collects or receives, and segregates, counts, and records number of items of soiled linen and uniforms for repair or laundry, and places items in containers. Examines laundered items to ensure cleanliness and serviceability. Stamps items with identifying marks. Stores laundered items on shelves, after verifying numbers and types of items. Counts and assembles laundered items on cart or linen truck, records amounts of linens and uniforms to fill requisitions, and transports carts to floors. Conducts monthly and yearly inventories to identify items for replacement. Keeps linen room in clean and orderly condition. May mend torn articles with needle and thread or sewing machine or send articles to SEWER, LINEN ROOM (hotel & rest.) 787.682-030. ● **GED:** R3, M2, L2 ● **SVP:** 2-30 days ● **Academic:** Ed=N, Eng=N ● **Work Field:** 221 ● **MPSMS:** 898, 906 ● **Aptitudes:** G4, V4, N4, S4, P4, Q3, K4, F4, M3, E5, C4 ● **Temperaments:** J, R ● **Physical:** Stg=M; Freq: R, H Occas: S, I, N, X ● **Work Env:** Noise=Q; ● **Salary:** 1 ● **Outlook:** 3

LINEN-ROOM SUPERVISOR (laundry & rel.) ● DOT #222.137-014 ● OES: 51002 ● Alternate titles: SUPERVISOR, INDUSTRIAL GARMENT. Supervises and coordinates activites of workers engaged in storing linens and wearing apparel, assembling loads for DRIVER, SALES ROUTE (retail trade; wholesale tr.), and maintaining stock in linen supply establishments: Assigns duties to workers. Inventories articles in stock, such as table linens, bed sheets, towels, and uniforms, and confers with SUPERINTENDENT, LAUNDRY (laundry & rel.) to request replacement of articles in short supply. Counts articles in loads for DRIVER, SALES ROUTE (retail trade; wholesale tr.) to ensure agreement with quantity specified on load sheet. Confers with DRIVER, SALES ROUTE (retail trade; wholesale tr.) and with customers to resolve complaints, and to modify orders according to size, color, and type of articles specified. Interviews employees to resolve complaints and grievances. May supervise workers engaged in attaching labels and emblems, repairing, and altering linens and wearing apparel. May purchase linen supplies. Performs other duties as described under SUPERVISOR (clerical) Master Title. ● **GED:** R4, M3, L3 ● **SVP:** 1-2 yrs ● **Academic:** Ed=N, Eng=G ● **Work Field:** 221 ● **MPSMS:** 906 ● **Aptitudes:** G3, V3, N3, S3, P3, Q3, K4, F4, M4, E5, C5 ● **Temperaments:** D, P, V ● **Physical:** Stg=L; Freq: R, H, T, G, N Occas: I ● **Work Env:** Noise=Q; ● **Salary:** 4 ● **Outlook:** 2

MAILER (print. & pub.) ● DOT #222.587-030 ● OES: 57302 ● Mails or dispatches newspapers, periodicals, envelopes, cartons, or other bulk printed matter by performing any combination of following duties: Wraps or bundles printed matter by hand or using tying machine. Addresses bundle or wrapped printed matter by hand or stamps, tags, or labels them according to mailing lists and dispatching orders, using stencils and stamping machine. Sorts bundles according to zip code and places bundles to be mailed in specified mail bags. Stacks bundles for shipment and loads and unloads bundles onto and from trucks and conveyors. Files and corrects stencils. Counts and records number of bundles and copies handled. May keep card record distribution file of units mailed or dispatched to subscribers and dealers. ● **GED:** R2, M2, L2 ● **SVP:** 1-3 mos ● **Academic:** Ed=N, Eng=S ● **Work Field:** 231 ● **MPSMS:** 899 ● **Aptitudes:** G3, V4, N3, S4, P4, Q3, K3, F3, M3, E5, C5 ● **Temperaments:** R ● **Physical:** Stg=L; Freq: R, H, I, N Occas: A ● **Work Env:** Noise=N; ● **Salary:** 1 ● **Outlook:** 3

MEAT CLERK (retail trade) ● DOT #222.684-010 ● OES: 58097 ● Receives, stores, and grinds meats in retail establishment: Unloads fresh, cured, and boxed meats and poultry from delivery truck and transports them to storage room on conveyor and with handtruck. Counts and weighs incoming articles and compares results against invoice. Examines meats in storage and rotates meats to avoid aging. Cuts meat into small pieces suitable for grinding, and grinds for use as hamburgers, meat loaf, and sausage, using powered grinding machine. Cleans grinder, meat containers, and storage room with water hose and broom. May take meat orders from customers. ● **GED:** R2, M1, L1 ● **SVP:** 2-30 days ● **Academic:** Ed=N, Eng=G ● **Work Field:** 146, 221 ● **MPSMS:** 382 ● **Aptitudes:** G4, V4, N4, S4, P4, Q4, K3, F3, M3, E5, C4 ● **Temperaments:** R, T ● **Physical:** Stg=M; Freq: R, H, I Occas: N, D, A, X ● **Work Env:** Noise=Q; ● **Salary:** 3 ● **Outlook:** 4

ORDER FILLER (retail trade) ● DOT #222.487-014 ● OES: 58026 ● Fills customers' mail and telephone orders and marks price of merchandise on order form: Reads order to ascertain catalog number, size, color, and quantity of merchandise. Obtains merchandise from bins or shelves. Computes price of each group of items. Places merchandise on conveyor leading to wrapping area. ● **GED:** R3, M2, L2 ● **SVP:** 1-3 mos ● **Academic:** Ed=N, Eng=N ● **Work Field:** 221 ● **MPSMS:** 880 ● **Aptitudes:** G3, V3, N3, S5, P3, Q3, K4, F4, M3, E5, C4 ● **Temperaments:** R ● **Physical:** Stg=L; Freq: R, H, I, N Occas: X ● **Work Env:** Noise=Q; ● **Salary:** 2 ● **Outlook:** 4

PARTS CLERK (clerical) ● DOT #222.367-042 ● OES: 58097 ● Alternate titles: SHOP CLERK; SPARE-PARTS CLERK. Receives, stores, and issues spare and replacement parts, equipment, and expendable items used in repair or maintenance shop. Takes inventory of parts and equipment and maintains inventory records. May drive truck to pick up incoming stock or to pick up and deliver parts to units in other buildings or locations. May sell auto parts to customers. May be designated according to type of parts issued as Parts Clerk, Automobile Repair (clerical); Parts Clerk, Plant Maintenance (clerical). ● **GED:** R3, M3, L3 ● **SVP:** 1-3 mos ● **Academic:** Ed=N, Eng=S ● **Work Field:** 221 ● **MPSMS:** 898 ● **Aptitudes:** G3, V3, N3, S4, P4, Q3, K4, F3, M3, E5, C5 ● **Temperaments:** R, T ● **Physical:** Stg=H; Freq: R, H, I, T, G, N Occas: C, B, S ● **Work Env:** Noise=N; ● **Salary:** 1 ● **Outlook:** 3

PARTS-ORDER-AND-STOCK CLERK (clerical) ● DOT #249.367-058 ● OES: 58097 ● Alternate titles: PURCHASER, AUTOMOTIVE PARTS. Purchases, stores, and issues spare parts for motor vehicles or industrial equipment: Obtains purchase order number from purchasing department and assigns identifying number. Reads shop manuals to ascertain type and specification of part. Visits, telephones, telegraphs, or contacts vendors by mail to order parts. Compares invoices against requisitions to verify quality and quantity of merchandise received. Stores purchased parts in storeroom bins and issues parts to workers upon request. Keeps records of parts received and issued, and inventories parts in storeroom periodically. May record repair time expended by mechanics. May requisition parts from central parts department for

national organization. ● **GED:** R3, M2, L2 ● **SVP:** 6 mos-1 yr ● **Academic:** Ed=N, Eng=S ● **Work Field:** 221 ● **MPSMS:** 898 ● **Aptitudes:** G3, V3, N3, S4, P4, Q3, K4, F4, M4, E5, C5 ● **Temperaments:** R, T ● **Physical:** Stg=L; Freq: S, K, R, H, I, T, G, N Occas: D, A ● **Work Env:** Noise=Q; ● **Salary:** 2 ● **Outlook:** 3

PHARMACY TECHNICIAN (medical ser.) ● DOT #074.382-010 ● OES: 32998 ● Alternate titles: PHARMACY CLERK. Performs any combination of following duties to assist PHARMACIST (medical ser.) 074.161-010 in hospital pharmacy or retail establishment: Mixes pharmaceutical preparations, fills bottles with prescribed tablets and capsules, and types labels for bottles. Assists PHARMACIST (medical ser.) to prepare and dispense medication. Receives and stores incoming supplies. Counts stock and enters data in computer to maintain inventory records. Processes records of medication and equipment dispensed to hospital patient, computes charges, and enters data in computer. Prepares intravenous (IV) packs, using sterile technique, under supervision of hospital pharmacist. Cleans equipment and sterilizes glassware according to prescribed methods. ● **GED:** R3, M3, L3 ● **SVP:** 1-3 mos ● **Academic:** Ed=H, Eng=S ● **Work Field:** 147, 221 ● **MPSMS:** 493 ● **Aptitudes:** G3, V3, N3, S4, P3, Q3, K4, F3, M3, E5, C3 ● **Temperaments:** T, V ● **Physical:** Stg=L; Freq: R, H, I, N Occas: S, G, A, X ● **Work Env:** Noise=Q; ● **Salary:** 4 ● **Outlook:** 3

PRODUCTION TECHNICIAN, SEMICONDUCTOR PROCESSING EQUIPMENT (electron. comp.) ● DOT #590.384-014 ● OES: 85109 ● Cleans and maintains wafer processing machines and equipment and mixes chemical solutions, following production specifications: Reads work orders and specifications to determine machines and equipment requiring replenishment of chemical solutions. Measures and mixes chemical solutions, using graduated beakers and funnels. Pours chemical solutions into wafer processing machine tanks to replenish machine supplies. Cleans furnace accessories, such as quartz tubes and stainless steel tubing, using chemical solutions. Removes broken quartzware and wafers from furnace and vacuums interior of furnace. Cleans processing machines and equipment, using cleaning solvent and cloth. Removes and replaces empty machine and equipment gas tanks. Measures furnace temperatures, using thermal rod or thermocouple, and turns knobs on furnace control panel to adjust temperature. May re-stock storage shelves and work station with supplies, such as chemicals, alcohol, and rubber gloves. May maintain log records of machine and equipment processing readings. ● **GED:** R3, M2, L2 ● **SVP:** 6 mos-1 yr ● **Academic:** Ed=N, Eng=N ● **Work Field:** 031, 143, 221 ● **MPSMS:** 567, 491 ● **Aptitudes:** G3, V3, N3, S4, P3, Q3, K3, F4, M3, E5, C5 ● **Temperaments:** T, V ● **Physical:** Stg=V; Freq: R, H, I, N Occas: C, S, M, D, A ● **Work Env:** Noise=L; Occas: H, T ● **Salary:** 3 ● **Outlook:** 4

SHIPPING AND RECEIVING CLERK (clerical) ● DOT #222.387-050 ● OES: 58028 ● Verifies and keeps records on incoming and outgoing shipments and prepares items for shipment: Compares identifying information and counts, weighs, or measures items of incoming and outgoing shipments to verify information against bills of lading, invoices, orders, or other records. Determines method of shipment, utilizing knowledge of shipping procedures, routes, and rates. Affixes shipping labels on packed cartons or stencils identifying shipping information on cartons, using stenciling equipment. Assembles wooden or cardboard containers or selects preassembled containers. Inserts items into containers, using spacers, fillers, and protective padding. Nails covers on wooden crates and binds containers with metal tape, using strapping machine. Stamps, stencils, or glues identifying information and shipping instructions onto crates or containers. Posts weights and shipping charges, and affixes postage. Unpacks and examines incoming shipments, rejects damaged items, records shortages, and corresponds with shipper to rectify damages and shortages. Routes items to departments. Examines outgoing shipments to ensure shipments meet specifications. Maintains inventory of shipping materials and supplies. May operate tier-lift truck or use handtruck to move, convey, or hoist shipments from shipping-and-receiving platform to storage or work area. May direct others in preparing outgoing and receiving incoming shipments. May perform only shipping or receiving activities and be known as Shipping Clerk (clerical) or Receiving Clerk (clerical). May be designated according to specialty as Freight Clerk (clerical); Reshipping Clerk (clerical). May receive damaged or defective goods returned to establishment and be designated Returned-Goods Receiving Clerk (clerical). May receive unsold products returned by DRIVER,

SALES ROUTE (retail trade; wholesale tr.) 292.353-010 and be designated Route Returner (clerical). ● **GED:** R3, M3, L2 ● **SVP:** 6 mos-1 yr ● **Academic:** Ed=N, Eng=S ● **Work Field:** 221 ● **MPSMS:** 898 ● **Aptitudes:** G3, V3, N3, S3, P3, Q3, K4, F4, M3, E5, C5 ● **Temperaments:** J, V ● **Physical:** Stg=M; Freq: R, H, T, G, N Occas: I, A ● **Work Env:** Noise=N; ● **Salary:** 2 ● **Outlook:** 3

SHIPPING-AND-RECEIVING WEIGHER (clerical) ● DOT #222.387-074 ● OES: 58017 ● Alternate titles: WEIGHT RECORDER. Weighs and records weight of filled containers, cargo of loaded vehicles, or rolls of materials, such as cotton, sugarcane, paper, cloth, plastic, and tobacco, to keep receiving and shipping records: Reads scale dial to ascertain weight and records weight on ticket, product, or material; or subtracts tare from gross weight to obtain net weight of product or material; or inserts ticket into automatic scale recorder that prints weight on ticket. May convey objects to scale, using handtruck, and lift objects onto scale. May record information on weight ticket, such as grade and yardage. May be designated according to item weighed as Cloth Weigher (knitting); Garment Weigher (knitting); Roll Weigher (paper & pulp; paper goods; plastics-synth.); Tobacco Weigher (clerical). May signal YARD ENGINEER (r.r. trans.) 910.363-018 to move cars on and off scale and be designated Scaler (r.r. trans.). May weigh only incoming or outgoing materials or products and be designated Receiving Weigher (clerical); Shipping Weigher (cerical). ● **GED:** R3, M2, L2 ● **SVP:** 2-30 days ● **Academic:** Ed=N, Eng=S ● **Work Field:** 212 ● **MPSMS:** 898 ● **Aptitudes:** G3, V4, N4, S4, P4, Q3, K4, F4, M4, E5, C5 ● **Temperaments:** T ● **Physical:** Stg=L; Freq: H, N Occas: R, I, G ● **Work Env:** Noise=N; ● **Salary:** 2 ● **Outlook:** 3

SHIPPING CHECKER (clerical) ● DOT #222.687-030 ● OES: 58028 ● Alternate titles: LOADING CHECKER; ORDER CHECKER; PACKING CHECKER. Verifies quantity, quality, labeling, and addressing of products and items of merchandise ready for shipment at manufacturing or commercial establishment: Counts, weighs, measures, or examines packaging and contents of items for conformance to company specifications. Affixes postage on packages, using postal meter. Compares items packed with customer's order and other identifying data. May keep records on number of baskets of tobacco sold and removed from auction warehouse and be designated Tobacco-Checkout Clerk (wholesale tr.). May oversee crew of workers engaged in loading and bracing material in railroad cars or trucks. ● **GED:** R3, M3, L2 ● **SVP:** 3-6 mos ● **Academic:** Ed=N, Eng=S ● **Work Field:** 221 ● **MPSMS:** 898 ● **Aptitudes:** G3, V3, N3, S3, P3, Q3, K3, F4, M4, E5, C4 ● **Temperaments:** J, T ● **Physical:** Stg=L; Freq: R, H, I, N, A Occas: S, X ● **Work Env:** Noise=N; ● **Salary:** 2 ● **Outlook:** 3

STOCK CLERK (clerical) ● DOT #222.387-058 ● OES: 58097 ● Alternate titles: STOCK CHECKER; STOCKROOM CLERK; STOREKEEPER; STOREROOM CLERK; STOREROOM KEEPER; STORES CLERK; SUPPLY CLERK; SUPPLY-ROOM CLERK. Receives, stores, and issues equipment, material, supplies, merchandise, foodstuffs, or tools, and compiles stock records in stockroom, warehouse, or storage yard: Counts, sorts, or weighs incoming articles to verify receipt of items on requisition or invoices. Examines stock to verify conformance to specifications. Stores articles in bins, on floor, or on shelves, according to identifying information, such as style, size, or type of material. Fills orders or issues supplies from stock. Prepares periodic, special, or perpetual inventory of stock. Requisitions articles to fill incoming orders. Compiles reports on use of stock handling equipment, adjustments of inventory counts and stock records, spoilage of or damage to stock, location changes, and refusal of shipments. May mark identifying codes, figures, or letters on articles, using labeling equipment. May distribute stock among production workers, keeping records of material issued. May make adjustments or repairs to articles carried in stock. May determine methods of storage, identification, and stock location, considering temperature, humidity, height and weight limits, turnover, floor loading capacities, and required space. May cut stock to size to fill order. May move or transport material or supplies to other departments, using hand or industrial truck. May maintain inventory and other stock records, using computer terminal. May be designated according to material, equipment, or product stored as Camera-Storeroom Clerk (motion picture); Oil-House Attendant (clerical); Wire Stockkeeper (steel & rel.); or work location as Wine-Cellar Stock Clerk (hotel & rest.); or stage in manufacture of material or goods as Finished-Goods Stock Clerk (clerical); or container in which goods are stored as Drum-Stock Clerk (clerical). May receive and store in-

coming shipments of yarn, thread, or jute stock and verify color standards of shipment and be known as Color Standards Clerk (clerical). May be designated: Custodian, Blood Bank (medical ser.); Food Storeroom Clerk (hotel & rest.); Hogshead-Stock Clerk (tobacco); Material Stockkeeper, Yard (petrol. & gas); Mold Picker (rubber goods); Paint Stocker (aircraft mfg.); Pattern-Room Attendant (foundry); Printing-Plate (clerical); Refrigerator-Room Clerk (clerical). May receive, store, and sort unserviceable equipment and supplies for sale, disposal, or reclamation and be known as Salvage Clerk (clerical). ● **GED:** R3, M3, L2 ● **SVP:** 3-6 mos ● **Academic:** Ed=N, Eng=S ● **Work Field:** 221 ● **MPSMS:** 898 ● **Aptitudes:** G3, V3, N3, S3, P3, Q2, K4, F4, M3, E5, C4 ● **Temperaments:** J, T, V ● **Physical:** Stg=H; Freq: R, H, N Occas: S, K, O, I, X ● **Work Env:** Noise=Q; ● **Salary:** 3 ● **Outlook:** 3

STOCK CLERK (retail trade) ● DOT #299.367-014 ● OES: 58097 ● Alternate titles: STOCK CLERK, SELF-SERVICE STORE. Inventories, stores, prices, and restocks merchandise displays in retail store: Takes inventory or examines merchandise to identify items to be reordered or replenished. Requisitions merchandise from supplier based on available space, merchandise on hand, customer demand, or advertised specials. Receives, opens, and unpacks cartons or crates of merchandise, checking invoice against items received. Stamps, attaches, or changes price tags on merchandise, referring to price list. Stocks storage areas and displays with new or transferred merchandise. Sets up advertising signs and displays merchandise on shelves, counters, or tables to attract customers and promote sales. Cleans display cases, shelves, and aisles. May itemize and total customer merchandise selection at check out counter, using cash register, and accept cash or charge card for purchases. May pack customer purchases in bags or cartons. May transport packages to specified vehicle for customer. May be designated according to type of merchandise handled as Baked-Goods Stock Clerk (retail trade); Delicatessen-Goods Stock Clerk (retail trade); Discount-Variety-Store Clerk (retail trade); Liquor-Store Stock Clerk (retail trade); Meat Stock Clerk (retail trade); Pharmacy Stock Clerk (retail trade); Produce Stock Clerk (retail trade); or type of store worked in as Supermarket Stock Clerk (retail trade). ● **GED:** R3, M2, L2 ● **SVP:** 3-6 mos ● **Academic:** Ed=N, Eng=S ● **Work Field:** 221 ● **MPSMS:** 881 ● **Aptitudes:** G3, V3, N4, S4, P4, Q3, K3, F4, M3, E5, C5 ● **Temperaments:** R ● **Physical:** Stg=H; Freq: R, H Occas: S, O, I, T, G, N ● **Work Env:** Noise=N; ● **Salary:** 1 ● **Outlook:** 3

STOCK SUPERVISOR (clerical) ● DOT #222.137-034 ● OES: 51002 ● Alternate titles: MANAGER, STOCKROOM; STOCKROOM SUPERVISOR; STOREROOM SUPERVISOR; WAREHOUSE SUPERVISOR. Supervises and coordinates activities of workers concerned with ordering, receiving, storing, inventorying, issuing, and shipping materials, supplies, tools, equipment, and parts, in stockroom, warehouse, or yard: Plans layout of stockroom, warehouse, and other storage areas, considering turnover, size, weight, and related factors of items stored. Advises employees on care and preservation of items received, stored, and shipped, methods and use of equipment in handling, storing, maintaining, and shipping stock, and related problems. Studies records and recommends remedial actions for reported nonusable, slow-moving, and excess stock. Reviews records for accuracy of information and compliance with established procedures, and to determine adequacy of stock levels. Schedules work for special and periodic inventories. Traces history of items to determine reasons for discrepancies between inventory and stock-control records and recommends remedial actions to resolve discrepancies. Performs other duties as described under SUPERVISOR (clerical) Master Title. May supervise and coordinate activities of workers engaged in handling of merchandise in stockroom or warehouse of retail store and be known as Head of Stock (retail trade). ● **GED:** R4, M3, L3 ● **SVP:** 1-2 yrs ● **Academic:** Ed=H, Eng=G ● **Work Field:** 221 ● **MPSMS:** 898 ● **Aptitudes:** G3, V3, N3, S3, P4, Q3, K4, F4, M4, E5, C5 ● **Temperaments:** D, J, P, V ● **Physical:** Stg=L; Freq: R, H, I, T, G, N Occas: S, K, O, V ● **Work Env:** Noise=N; ● **Salary:** 3 ● **Outlook:** 3

SUPPLY CLERK (personal ser.) ● DOT #339.687-010 ● OES: 58097 ● Alternate titles: DISPENSARY ATTENDANT; STOREKEEPER. Dispenses supplies in beauty parlor or barber shop: Counts, sorts, issues, and collects articles, such as towels, drapes, combs, brushes, curlers, and nets. Washes combs and brushes in antiseptic soap solution and places them in sterilizing cabinet. Dilutes concentrated shampoo, rinses, and waving solutions with water according to instructions. Dissolves cake soap in water to make shampoo. Assembles materials, solutions, and equipment specified for individual treatment, such as facial, permanent wave, and manicure. Maintains perpetual supply inventory and lists items needed to replace stock. Sweeps floor and tidies rooms. ● **GED:** R2, M2, L1 ● **SVP:** 1-3 mos ● **Academic:** Ed=N, Eng=N ● **Work Field:** 031, 221 ● **MPSMS:** 904 ● **Aptitudes:** G4, V4, N4, S4, P4, Q4, K4, F4, M4, E5, C4 ● **Temperaments:** V ● **Physical:** Stg=L; Freq: S, R, H, I Occas: N, X ● **Work Env:** Noise=Q; Freq: U ● **Salary:** 2 ● **Outlook:** 3

TIRE ADJUSTER (retail trade) ● DOT #241.367-034 ● OES: 53123 ● Examines defective tires and tubes returned by customers to determine allowance due on replacement: Visually and tactually examines tire to determine if defect resulted from faulty construction or curing. Measures tread depth, using tread depth gauge, to determine remaining tire life. Prorates allowances based on tread wear, warranty provisions, and knowledge of tire characteristics. Explains basis for allowance to customer, sales representative, or distributor. May train new workers. ● **GED:** R3, M3, L2 ● **SVP:** 1-3 mos ● **Academic:** Ed=N, Eng=G ● **Work Field:** 292, 212 ● **MPSMS:** 511 ● **Aptitudes:** G3, V3, N3, S3, P3, Q4, K4, F4, M4, E5, C5 ● **Temperaments:** J, P ● **Physical:** Stg=M; Freq: S, O, R, H, T, G, N, A Occas: I, E ● **Work Env:** Noise=Q; ● **Salary:** 4 ● **Outlook:** 3

TOOL-CRIB ATTENDANT (clerical) ● DOT #222.367-062 ● OES: 58097 ● Alternate titles: TOOL CLERK. Receives, stores, and issues handtools, machine tools, dies, materials, and equipment in industrial establishment: Issues tools and equipment to workers and maintains records of tools and equipment issued and returned, manually or using computer. Locates lost or misplaced tools and equipment. Prepares periodic inventory or maintains perpetual inventory of tools and equipment, manually or using computer. Receives, unpacks, and stores incoming tools and equipment, and requisitions stock to replenish inventory. Inspects and measures tools and equipment for defects and wear, visually or using micrometer, and reports damage or wear to supervisors. Repairs, services, and lubricates tools and equipment, using handtools, spray gun, or pressurized spray can. May deliver tools or equipment to workers, manually or using handtruck. May mark and identify tools and equipment, using identification tag, stamp, or electric marking tool. ● **GED:** R3, M2, L2 ● **SVP:** 6 mos-1 yr ● **Academic:** Ed=N, Eng=S ● **Work Field:** 221 ● **MPSMS:** 898 ● **Aptitudes:** G3, V3, N3, S4, P3, Q3, K4, F4, M3, E5, C4 ● **Temperaments:** T ● **Physical:** Stg=M; Freq: R, H, I, T, G, N Occas: S, K, O, D, A, X ● **Work Env:** Noise=L; ● **Salary:** 3 ● **Outlook:** 3

GOE: 05.09.02
Estimating, Scheduling & Record Keeping

CONTROL CLERK (clock & watch) ● DOT #221.387-018 ● OES: 58008 ● Alternate titles: PRODUCTION-CONTROL CLERK. Keeps record of clock and watch parts being worked on and completed, and distributes material and parts to workers: Requisitions parts, based on production orders, and distributes parts to designated work stations. Moves completed work to next operation to keep workers supplied with material. Keeps records of quantity and type of material received, completed, and being worked on. Determines number of hours worked by employees in department, and collects work tickets from which pay is calculated. May be designated according to section of plant as Control Clerk, Repairs (clock & watch); Control Clerk, Subassembly (clock & watch); Control Clerk, Training And Mechanism (clock & watch). ● **GED:** R3, M3, L3 ● **SVP:** 1-2 yrs ● **Academic:** Ed=H, Eng=G ● **Work Field:** 221 ● **MPSMS:** 898 ● **Aptitudes:** G3, V3, N3, S4, P3, Q2, K4, F4, M3, E5, C5 ● **Temperaments:** T, V ● **Physical:** Stg=L; Freq: R, H, N Occas: I ● **Work Env:** Noise=Q; ● **Salary:** 2 ● **Outlook:** 3

CUSTOMER SERVICES COORDINATOR (print. & pub.) ● DOT #221.167-026 ● OES: 58008 ● Coordinates production of printed materials, prepress or printing services with customers' requirements: Confers with customers throughout production to keep them informed of status of job, to solicit and resolve inquiries and complaints, to obtain approval of materials, such as artwork, color separations (film for each primary color), ink samples, and proofs, and to procure informa-

tion and materials needed by establishment personnel to process order. Determines supplies, materials, and equipment needed for job order, plans and draws layout of job, and routes supplies and materials, such as paste-ups, artwork, copy, film, or prints, to work areas to put job order into production. Monitors progress of job order throughout production, confers with establishment personnel, orders supplies, contracts services with outside vendors, and alters production schedule and job order to expedite timely processing of job in accordance with customers' requirements and company standards. ● **GED:** R5, M4, L4 ● **SVP:** 1-2 yrs ● **Academic:** Ed=H, Eng=G ● **Work Field:** 295 ● **MPSMS:** 899 ● **Aptitudes:** G2, V2, N3, S3, P3, Q3, K4, F4, M4, E5, C2 ● **Temperaments:** D, J, P ● **Physical:** Stg=L; Const: T, G Occas: R, H, I, N, D, A, X ● **Work Env:** Noise=N; Occas: A, T ● **Salary:** 4 ● **Outlook:** 4

DRAPERY AND UPHOLSTERY ESTIMATOR (retail trade) ● DOT #299.387-010 ● OES: 49998 ● Estimates price of making and installing household accessories, such as draperies, slipcovers, window shades, and furniture upholstery: Computes cost of fabric and hardware, according to measurements, work specifications, and type of fabric to be used, using calculator. Itemizes cost of labor in making and installing goods. Records total price on sales check or contract. May contact customer to obtain additional information about order. May confer with ARCHITECTS (profess. & kin.) and interior decorators to obtain additional information when computing estimates for commercial orders. May take measurements for draperies, upholstery, slip covers, or shades in customer's home [DRAPERY AND UPHOLSTERY MEASURER (retail trade)]. May specialize in estimating price of specific type of household accessory and be designated Drapery Estimator (retail trade); Upholstery Estimator (retail trade). ● **GED:** R3, M3, L2 ● **SVP:** 6 mos-1 yr ● **Academic:** Ed=N, Eng=N ● **Work Field:** 212, 292 ● **MPSMS:** 435, 881 ● **Aptitudes:** G3, V3, N3, S3, P3, Q3, K4, F4, M4, E5, C4 ● **Temperaments:** J, T ● **Physical:** Stg=S; Freq: R, H, I, N, A Occas: X ● **Work Env:** Noise=N; ● **Salary:** 3 ● **Outlook:** 3

ESTIMATOR, PRINTING (print. & pub.) ● DOT #221.367-014 ● OES: 58008 ● Estimates labor and material costs of printing and binding books, pamphlets, periodicals, and other printed matter, based on specifications outlined on sales order or submitted by prospective customer: Examines specifications, sketches, and sample layouts, and calculates unit and production costs, using labor and material pricing schedules, and considering factors such as size and number of sheets or pages, paper stock requirements, binding operations, halftones, number and units of colors, and quality of finished product, to determine cost effective and competitive price. Confers with department heads or production personnel to develop or confirm information regarding various cost elements. May estimate cost of mailing finished printed matter if specified on order. May estimate labor and material cost of specific phase of printing, such as plate making or binding, and be designated according to specialty as Estimator, Printing-Plate-Making (print. & pub.) or Estimator, Binding (print. & pub.). ● **GED:** R4, M3, L3 ● **SVP:** 1-2 yrs ● **Academic:** Ed=H, Eng=G ● **Work Field:** 232 ● **MPSMS:** 898, 897 ● **Aptitudes:** G2, V3, N2, S3, P3, Q2, K4, F4, M4, E5, C4 ● **Temperaments:** J, P, T ● **Physical:** Stg=L; Freq: R, H, I, N Occas: T, G, A, X ● **Work Env:** Noise=L; Occas: A, T ● **Salary:** 4 ● **Outlook:** 3

EVALUATOR (nonprofit org.) ● DOT #249.367-034 ● OES: 55344 ● Estimates market value of items donated to vocational rehabilitation organization and prepares and mails tax receipts to donors: Sorts collection receipts by type of items donated. Estimates market value of items, using standard formula, and totals amount donated. Prepares tax receipt and mails to donor. ● **GED:** R4, M2, L2 ● **SVP:** 3-6 mos ● **Academic:** Ed=H, Eng=G ● **Work Field:** 212, 232 ● **MPSMS:** 891 ● **Aptitudes:** G3, V3, N3, S5, P5, Q2, K4, F4, M4, E5, C5 ● **Temperaments:** J ● **Physical:** Stg=L; Freq: R, H, N Occas: I ● **Work Env:** Noise=N; ● **Salary:** 3 ● **Outlook:** 3

FIELD RECORDER (utilities) ● DOT #229.367-010 ● OES: 58097 ● Alternate titles: FIELD CLERK. Maintains records of equipment, materials, and supplies used in construction, installation, and maintenance of electric-power distribution lines and facilities: Observes operations of field crew, and records data, such as equipment installed or replaced, materials and supplies used, and labor costs. Prepares sketches or enters on drawing type of equipment installed and location of equipment in order that circuit maps and blueprints can be corrected. Prepares and attaches identification tags to equipment, such as transformers and switches removed from service for repair or storage. Prepares and nails metal tags on pole indicating circuit and station in transmission or distribution line. Maintains inventory of equipment in field truck and prepares requisitions for replacement parts, materials, and supplies. ● **GED:** R3, M3, L3 ● **SVP:** 3-6 mos ● **Academic:** Ed=N, Eng=S ● **Work Field:** 221 ● **MPSMS:** 891 ● **Aptitudes:** G3, V4, N3, S4, P4, Q3, K4, F3, M4, E5, C5 ● **Temperaments:** R ● **Physical:** Stg=L; Freq: R, H, I, N Occas: T, G ● **Work Env:** Noise=N; ● **Outlook:** 3

JOB TRACER (clerical) ● DOT #221.387-034 ● OES: 58008 ● Alternate titles: JOB CHECKER; JOB SPOTTER; PROGRESS CLERK. Locates and determines progress of job orders in various stages of production, such as fabrication, assembly, and inspection, and compiles reports used by scheduling and production personnel. ● **GED:** R3, M2, L3 ● **SVP:** 3-6 mos ● **Academic:** Ed=N, Eng=S ● **Work Field:** 231 ● **MPSMS:** 898 ● **Aptitudes:** G3, V3, N3, S4, P4, Q3, K4, F4, M4, E5, C4 ● **Temperaments:** R ● **Physical:** Stg=L; Freq: R, H, N Occas: I, X ● **Work Env:** Noise=Q; ● **Salary:** 4 ● **Outlook:** 3

LAUNDRY CLERK (clerical) ● DOT #221.387-038 ● OES: 58098 ● Alternate titles: FLOOR CLERK. Compiles and maintains work-production records of each employee for use in payroll and efficiency records. Frequently performs other clerical duties, such as recording weights of laundry bundles. May convert count of each type of garment to production points achieved, following prepared charts or verbal instructions. ● **GED:** R3, M2, L3 ● **SVP:** 1-3 mos ● **Academic:** Ed=N, Eng=S ● **Work Field:** 231 ● **MPSMS:** 898 ● **Aptitudes:** G3, V4, N3, S4, P4, Q3, K4, F4, M4, E5, C4 ● **Temperaments:** R, T ● **Physical:** Stg=L; Freq: R, H, N Occas: I, X ● **Work Env:** Noise=N; ● **Salary:** 1 ● **Outlook:** 3

MATERIAL COORDINATOR (clerical) ● DOT #221.167-014 ● OES: 58008 ● Alternate titles: MATERIAL CONTROL EXPEDITER; PRODUCTION CONTROL SCHEDULER. Coordinates and expedites flow of materials, parts, and assemblies between sections or departments, according to production and shipping schedules or department priorities, and compiles and maintains manual or computerized records: Reviews production schedules and related information and confers with department supervisors to determine material requirements to identify overdue materials and to track material. Requisitions material and establishes sequential delivery dates to departments, according to job order priorities and material availability. Examines material delivered to production departments to verify conformance to specifications. Arranges in-plant transfer of materials to meet production schedules. Computes amount of material required to complete job orders, applying knowledge of product and manufacturing processes. Compiles and maintains manual or computerized records, such as material inventory, in-process production reports, and status and location of materials. May move or transport materials from one department to another, manually or using material handling equipment. May arrange for repair and assembly of material or part. May monitor and control movement of material and parts on automated conveyor system. ● **GED:** R4, M3, L4 ● **SVP:** 1-2 yrs ● **Academic:** Ed=H, Eng=G ● **Work Field:** 221 ● **MPSMS:** 898 ● **Aptitudes:** G3, V3, N3, S4, P3, Q3, K4, F4, M4, E5, C4 ● **Temperaments:** J, P, T, V ● **Physical:** Stg=L; Freq: R, H, I, T, G, N Occas: S, A, X ● **Work Env:** Noise=N; ● **Salary:** 3 ● **Outlook:** 3

MATERIAL EXPEDITER (clerical) ● DOT #221.367-042 ● OES: 58008 ● Alternate titles: EXPEDITER; STOCK CHASER. Compiles and maintains material and parts inventory and status information to expedite movement of material and parts between production areas, according to predetermined production schedules and order priorities: Reads production schedules, inventory reports, and work orders to determine type and quantity of materials required, availability of stock, and order priority. Confers with department supervisors to determine overdue material and parts and to inform supervisors of material status. Locates and distributes materials to specified production areas, manually or using handcart, handtruck, or forklift. Records and maintains perpetual inventory of quantity and type of materials and parts received, stocked, and distributed, manually or using computer. Compiles and maintains records, such as material inventory records, production records, and timecards, manually or using computer. May direct INDUSTRIAL-TRUCK OPERATOR (any industry) 921.683-050 or MATERIAL HANDLER (any industry) 929.687-030 to expedite trans-

fer of materials from stock area to production areas. May examine material received, verify part numbers, and check discrepancies, such as damaged or unmarked parts. May compare work ticket specifications to material used at work stations to verify appropriate assignment. May drive truck to outlying work areas to check status of orders or to deliver materials. ● **GED:** R3, M3, L3 ● **SVP:** 3-6 mos ● **Academic:** Ed=N, Eng=G ● **Work Field:** 221 ● **MPSMS:** 898 ● **Aptitudes:** G3, V3, N3, S4, P4, Q3, K4, F4, M4, E4, C4 ● **Temperaments:** P, T, V ● **Physical:** Stg=M; Freq: R, H, I, T, G, N Occas: S, K, F, D, A, X, V ● **Work Env:** Noise=L; Occas: W, M ● **Salary:** 3 ● **Outlook:** 3

ORDER DETAILER (clerical) ● DOT #221.387-046 ● OES: 58008 ● Alternate titles: JOB-ORDER CLERK; TICKETER; WORK-ORDER DETAILER. Compiles purchase orders and product specifications to prepare worksheets used in assembly or manufacture of products: Compares customer purchase order with specifications to determine method of assembly or manufacture and materials needed. Records data, such as quantity, quality, type, and size of material, and expected completion date, on worksheet. Obtains documents, such as assembly instructions and blueprints, from files and attaches to worksheet. Routes worksheet and other assembly documents to specified department. May keep inventory of stock on hand and requisition needed material and supplies. May compile purchase order data, maintain stock and production records, and prepare production worksheets, using computer. May prepare worksheets pertaining to cloth printing and mixing of printing colors and be designated Formula Checker (tex. prod., nec; textile). May prepare worksheets and order steel stock for rolling mill and be designated Provider (steel & rel.). May prepare work order and allocate silicon crystal ingots that meet customer specifications for use in manufacturing semiconductor wafers and be designated Allocations Clerk (electronics). May compile process specification sheets and prepare and issue materials for use in semiconductor crystal growing and be designated Production Material Coordinator (electron. comp.). ● **GED:** R3, M3, L3 ● **SVP:** 3-6 mos ● **Academic:** Ed=N, Eng=S ● **Work Field:** 231 ● **MPSMS:** 898 ● **Aptitudes:** G3, V3, N4, S4, P4, Q3, K4, F3, M3, E5, C4 ● **Temperaments:** R, T ● **Physical:** Stg=L; Freq: R, H, I, N Occas: A, X ● **Work Env:** Noise=N; ● **Salary:** 2 ● **Outlook:** 3

PRESCRIPTION CLERK, LENS-AND-FRAMES (optical goods) ● DOT #222.367-050 ● OES: 58097 ● Selects lens blanks and frames for production of eyeglasses, according to prescription specifications, and keeps stock inventory at specified level: Reads prescription to determine specifications, such as lens power and base curve and frame style and color. Selects lens blanks and frames from stock and routes them with prescription to production section. Requisitions lens blanks and eyeglass frames and communicates by letter and telephone with suppliers to keep stock at specified level. May work with only lenses or frames and be designated Prescription Clerk, Frames (optical goods); Prescription Clerk, Lenses (optical goods). ● **GED:** R3, M2, L3 ● **SVP:** 6 mos-1 yr ● **Academic:** Ed=N, Eng=G ● **Work Field:** 221 ● **MPSMS:** 605, 898 ● **Aptitudes:** G3, V3, N3, S4, P3, Q3, K4, F4, M3, E5, C4 ● **Temperaments:** J, T ● **Physical:** Stg=L; Freq: R, H, I, N, X Occas: T, G, A ● **Work Env:** Noise=Q; ● **Salary:** 1 ● **Outlook:** 3

PRODUCTION COORDINATOR (clerical) ● DOT #221.167-018 ● OES: 58008 ● Alternate titles: PRODUCTION CONTROLLER; PRODUCTION EXPEDITER; PRODUCTION SCHEDULER; PROGRESS CLERK; SCHEDULE CLERK; SCHEDULER. Schedules and coordinates flow of work within or between departments of manufacturing plant to expedite production: Reviews master production schedule and work orders, establishes priorities for specific customer orders, and revises schedule according to work order specifications, established priorities, and availability or capability of workers, parts, material, machines, and equipment. Reschedules identical processes to eliminate duplicate machine setups. Distributes work orders to departments, denoting number, type, and proposed completion date of units to be produced. Confers with department supervisors to determine progress of work and to provide information on changes in processing methods received from methods or engineering departments. Compiles reports concerning progress of work and downtime due to failures of machines and equipment to apprise production planning personnel of production delays. Maintains inventory of materials and parts needed to complete production. May expedite material [MATERIAL COORDINATOR (clerical) 221.167-014]. May expedite production of spare parts and establish delivery dates for spare parts orders and be designated Spares Scheduler (clerical). May coordinate and expedite work in automobile repair and service establishment from control tower, using public address system, and be designated Work Coordinator, Tower Control (automotive ser.). May use computer system to track and locate production units. ● **GED:** R4, M3, L4 ● **SVP:** 1-2 yrs ● **Academic:** Ed=H, Eng=G ● **Work Field:** 231, 221 ● **MPSMS:** 898 ● **Aptitudes:** G3, V3, N3, S4, P3, Q3, K4, F4, M4, E5, C5 ● **Temperaments:** D, J, P, T ● **Physical:** Stg=S; Freq: R, H, T, G Occas: I, N ● **Work Env:** Noise=N; ● **Salary:** 4 ● **Outlook:** 3

RUG MEASURER (laundry & rel.) ● DOT #369.367-014 ● OES: 49017 ● Alternate titles: RUG-RECEIVING CLERK. Determines type of rug received for cleaning, measures it, calculates area, and records information for use in case rug is lost and to facilitate proper billing to customer. Affixes identifying tag to rug which indicates type of work to be performed. May examine rugs for stains and holes, and determine from its condition if rug will withstand cleaning. May determine repairs which should be made and contact customer concerning repairs. ● **GED:** R3, M2, L2 ● **SVP:** 3-6 mos ● **Academic:** Ed=N, Eng=N ● **Work Field:** 231 ● **MPSMS:** 906 ● **Aptitudes:** G3, V4, N3, S4, P3, Q4, K4, F4, M4, E5, C3 ● **Temperaments:** J, R ● **Physical:** Stg=L; Freq: R, H Occas: B, I, N, X ● **Work Env:** Noise=N; ● **Salary:** 3 ● **Outlook:** 3

SALES CORRESPONDENT (clerical) ● DOT #221.367-062 ● OES: 55317 ● Compiles data pertinent to manufacture of special products for customers: Reads correspondence from customers to determine needs of customer not met by standard products. Confers with engineering department to ascertain feasibility of designing special equipment. Confers with production personnel to determine feasibility of fabrication and to obtain estimate of cost and production time. Corresponds with customer to inform of production progress and costs. May specialize in correspondence dealing with customer service agreements and be designated Service Correspondent (clerical). ● **GED:** R4, M2, L4 ● **SVP:** 1-2 yrs ● **Academic:** Ed=H, Eng=G ● **Work Field:** 231, 244 ● **MPSMS:** 898 ● **Aptitudes:** G2, V2, N3, S3, P3, Q3, K4, F4, M4, E5, C5 ● **Temperaments:** J, P, V ● **Physical:** Stg=L; Freq: R, H, T, G, N Occas: I ● **Work Env:** Noise=N; ● **Salary:** 3 ● **Outlook:** 3

SUPERVISOR, LAUNDRY (laundry & rel.) ● DOT #361.137-010 ● OES: 81000 ● Supervises and coordinates activities of workers engaged in receiving, marking, washing, and ironing clothes or linen in laundry: Determines sequence in which flatwork, one-day service, and white and colored work are to be scheduled through laundry to provide quick and efficient service to customers and to regulate work loads. Inspects articles to determine methods of specific cleaning requirements. Inspects finished laundered articles to ensure conformance to standards. Observes operation of machines and equipment to detect possible malfunctions. Investigates and resolves customer complaints of unsatisfactory work or bundle shortage. Studies literature of launderers' and dry cleaners' associations, and confers with salespersons to obtain information on new or improved work methods and equipment. Performs other duties as described under SUPERVISOR (any industry) Master Title. May be designated according to activity supervised as Flatwork Supervisor (laundry & rel.); Laundry-Marker Supervisor (laundry & rel.); Receiving, Marking, And Washing Supervisor (laundry & rel.); Shirt-Ironer Supervisor (laundry & rel.); Sorting-And-Folding Supervisor (laundry & rel.); Washroom Supervisor (laundry & rel.). ● **GED:** R3, M3, L3 ● **SVP:** 1-2 yrs ● **Academic:** Ed=N, Eng=G ● **Work Field:** 031, 032, 221 ● **MPSMS:** 906 ● **Aptitudes:** G3, V3, N4, S4, P4, Q3, K4, F4, M4, E5, C4 ● **Temperaments:** D, J, P ● **Physical:** Stg=L; Freq: R, H, I, T, G, N, A, X ● **Work Env:** Noise=N; Const: U Freq: H ● **Salary:** 4 ● **Outlook:** 2

GOE: 05.09.03
Verifying, Recording & Marking

CHECKER, DUMP GROUNDS (business ser.) ● DOT #219.367-010 ● OES: 58017 ● Estimates size of load on truck entering dump grounds. Collects fees based on size of load and type of material dumped. Keeps record of truckloads and money received. Directs truck drivers to designated dumping areas. May weigh truck, using scale, to determine amount of load. ● **GED:** R3, M3, L2 ● **SVP:** 1-3 mos ● **Aca-**

demic: Ed=N, Eng=S ● **Work Field:** 212, 232 ● **MPSMS:** 874, 899 ● **Aptitudes:** G4, V4, N3, S3, P4, Q3, K4, F4, M4, E5, C5 ● **Temperaments:** J, T ● **Physical:** Stg=L; Freq: R, H, I Occas: T, G, N ● **Work Env:** Noise=N; Occas: W ● **Salary:** 1 ● **Outlook:** 2

FOOD ORDER EXPEDITER (hotel & rest.) ● DOT #319.467-010 ● OES: 65300 ● Calls out and verifies food orders in drive-in restaurant or restaurant specializing in fast service: Removes order placed on device, such as wheel or nail board, at kitchen service counter. Calls out food orders to cooks and pantry and fountain workers. Examines portioning and garnishing of completed food order. Reviews order for accuracy and tabulates check. Notifies serving personnel when order is ready. May record count of items, such as entrees drawn from supply or entrees served, to accumulate food control data. May prepare and cook foods that can be completed in short time [COOK, FAST FOOD (hotel & rest.) 313.374-010]. ● **GED:** R3, M2, L2 ● **SVP:** 1-3 mos ● **Academic:** Ed=N, Eng=S ● **Work Field:** 231, 232 ● **MPSMS:** 903 ● **Aptitudes:** G3, V3, N3, S4, P4, Q3, K4, F3, M3, E4, C4 ● **Temperaments:** J, P ● **Physical:** Stg=L; Freq: R, H, I, T, G, N, A Occas: X ● **Work Env:** Noise=Q; ● **Salary:** 1 ● **Outlook:** 5

INDUSTRIAL-ORDER CLERK (clerical) ● DOT #221.367-022 ● OES: 58028 ● Verifies completion of industrial orders and conformance of product to specifications: Compares blueprints with contract or order to ascertain that product meets engineering specifications. Communicates with customer and delivery personnel to verify delivery of product. Fills out completion slip after order is filled. May route products not meeting specifications to production units for correction. ● **GED:** R4, M3, L4 ● **SVP:** 3-6 mos ● **Academic:** Ed=N, Eng=S ● **Work Field:** 221 ● **MPSMS:** 898 ● **Aptitudes:** G3, V3, N3, S3, P3, Q3, K3, F3, M3, E5, C5 ● **Temperaments:** P, T ● **Physical:** Stg=S; Freq: R, H, N Occas: I, T, G ● **Work Env:** Noise=Q; ● **Salary:** 2 ● **Outlook:** 3

MARKER (retail trade) ● DOT #209.587-034 ● OES: 58098 ● Alternate titles: MARKING CLERK; MERCHANDISE MARKER; PRICE MARKER; TICKET MAKER. Marks and attaches price tickets to articles of merchandise to record price and identifying information: Marks selling price by hand on boxes containing merchandise, or on price tickets. Ties, glues, sews, or staples price ticket to each article. Presses lever or plunger of mechanism that pins, pastes, ties, or staples ticket to article. May record number and types of articles marked and pack them in boxes. May compare printed price tickets with entries on purchase order to verify accuracy and notify supervisor of discrepancies. May print information on tickets, using ticket-printing machine [TICKETER (any industry)]; [TICKET PRINTER AND TAGGER (garment)]. ● **GED:** R2, M1, L1 ● **SVP:** 2-30 days ● **Academic:** Ed=N, Eng=N ● **Work Field:** 231 ● **MPSMS:** 881, 882 ● **Aptitudes:** G4, V4, N4, S4, P4, Q3, K4, F3, M4, E5, C5 ● **Temperaments:** R, T ● **Physical:** Stg=L; Freq: R, H, I, N ● **Work Env:** Noise=N; ● **Salary:** 2 ● **Outlook:** 3

MATERIAL CLERK (clerical) ● DOT #222.387-034 ● OES: 58097 ● Alternate titles: STOCK-RECORD CLERK. Compiles and maintains records of quantity, cost, and type of material received, stocked, and issued, and prepares material requisitions: Compares information on requisitions, invoices, and shipping notices to material received or issued to verify accuracy of order. Compiles and maintains inventory of material received, stocked, and issued [INVENTORY CLERK (clerical) 222.387-026]. Prepares requests for procurement of material. May inspect, accept or reject material received. May mark identifying information on material. May be designated according to location of goods as Warehouse-Record Clerk (clerical). ● **GED:** R3, M3, L3 ● **SVP:** 6 mos-1 yr ● **Academic:** Ed=N, Eng=N ● **Work Field:** 221 ● **MPSMS:** 898 ● **Aptitudes:** G3, V3, N3, S4, P4, Q3, K4, F3, M3, E5, C5 ● **Temperaments:** R ● **Physical:** Stg=L; Freq: R, H, I, N Occas: S, K, O, E, A ● **Work Env:** Noise=N; ● **Salary:** 2 ● **Outlook:** 3

METER READER (utilities) ● DOT #209.567-010 ● OES: 58014 ● Reads electric, gas, water, or steam consumption meters and records volume used by residential and commercial consumers: Walks or drives truck over established route and takes readings of meter dials. Inspects meters and connections for defects, damage, and unauthorized connections. Indicates irregularities on forms for necessary action by servicing department. Verifies readings to locate abnormal consumption and records reasons for fluctuations. Turns service off for nonpayment of charges in vacant premises, or on for new occupants. Collects bills in arrears. Returns route book to business office for billing purposes. May be designated according to type of meter read as Electric-Meter Reader (utilities); Gas-Meter Reader (utilities); Steam-Meter Reader (utilities); Water-Meter Reader (waterworks). ● **GED:** R3, M2, L2 ● **SVP:** 1-3 mos ● **Academic:** Ed=N, Eng=N ● **Work Field:** 231, 232 ● **MPSMS:** 871 ● **Aptitudes:** G3, V3, N3, S4, P4, Q3, K5, F4, M5, E5, C4 ● **Temperaments:** R, T ● **Physical:** Stg=L; Freq: R, H, N, V Occas: S, K, O, I, M, D, A, X ● **Work Env:** Noise=N; Const: W Occas: O ● **Salary:** 1 ● **Outlook:** 3

ORDER CALLER (clerical) ● DOT #209.667-014 ● OES: 58098 ● Alternate titles: CALLER; CALL-OUT CLERK; ORDER-DESK CALLER. Reads items listed on order sheets to LABORER, STORES (any industry) who gathers and assembles items or to BILLING TYPIST (clerical) who prepares bills for items. Indicates on order sheets items located and items that are not available. May read items to CHECKER (clerical) I who examines articles prior to shipping. May be designated by kind of data called out to other worker as Weight Caller (clerical); Yardage Caller (textile). ● **GED:** R2, M1, L2 ● **SVP:** 2-30 days ● **Academic:** Ed=N, Eng=G ● **Work Field:** 221 ● **MPSMS:** 880, 898 ● **Aptitudes:** G4, V4, N4, S4, P4, Q4, K4, F4, M4, E5, C5 ● **Temperaments:** R ● **Physical:** Stg=L; Const: N Freq: R, H, I, T, G ● **Work Env:** Noise=N; ● **Salary:** 2 ● **Outlook:** 3

RECEIVING CHECKER (clerical) ● DOT #222.687-018 ● OES: 58017 ● Alternate titles: CHECKING CLERK; ORDER CHECKER; RECEIVING INSPECTOR; UNLOADING CHECKER. Counts, measures, or weighs articles to verify contents of shipments against bills of lading, invoices, or storage receipts. May examine articles for defects and sort articles according to extent of defect. May attach identification data onto article. May record factors causing goods to be returned.

May unload and unpack incoming shipments. ● **GED:** R3, M2, L2 ● **SVP:** 1-3 mos ● **Academic:** Ed=N, Eng=S ● **Work Field:** 221 ● **MPSMS:** 898 ● **Aptitudes:** G3, V4, N4, S4, P4, Q3, K4, F4, M3, E5, C5 ● **Temperaments:** R, T ● **Physical:** Stg=M; Freq: R, H, I, N Occas: S ● **Work Env:** Noise=N; ● **Salary:** 1 ● **Outlook:** 3

SORTER-PRICER (nonprofit org.) ● DOT #222.387-054 ● OES: 58028 ● Alternate titles: PRICER-SORTER. Sorts used merchandise received from donors and appraises, prices, wraps, packs, and allocates merchandise for resale in retail outlets of nonprofit organization and maintains related records. Discards unsalable items or sets them aside for salvage or repair. May make minor repairs on damaged merchandise. May be designated according to merchandise sorted as Book Sorter (nonprofit org.); Clothing Sorter (nonprofit org.); Jewelry Sorter (nonprofit org.); Wares Sorter (nonprofit org.). ● **GED:** R3, M2, L2 ● **SVP:** 6 mos-1 yr ● **Academic:** Ed=N, Eng=S ● **Work Field:** 221 ● **MPSMS:** 898 ● **Aptitudes:** G3, V3, N3, S4, P4, Q3, K4, F4, M4, E5, C5 ● **Temperaments:** J, V ● **Physical:** Stg=L; Freq: R, H, I, N Occas: A ● **Work Env:** Noise=Q; ● **Salary:** 2 ● **Outlook:** 3

TURBINE ATTENDANT (utilities) ● DOT #952.567-010 ● OES: 83000 ● Records meter and instrument readings, such as oil and steam temperature and pressure of hydro-electric turbines and related generators that produce electricity. Notifies STATIONARY-ENGINEER SUPERVISOR (any industry) when recording instruments indicate machine malfunctions. Cleans and lubricates equipment. ● **GED:** R3, M2, L3 ● **SVP:** 3-6 mos ● **Academic:** Ed=N, Eng=S ● **Work Field:** 231 ● **MPSMS:** 871 ● **Aptitudes:** G3, V4, N3, S4, P3, Q3, K4, F4, M3, E5, C4 ● **Temperaments:** J, T ● **Physical:** Stg=L; Freq: R, H, I, N Occas: T, G, X ● **Work Env:** Noise=L; ● **Salary:** 3 ● **Outlook:** 3

Mechanical   05

Crafts   **05.10**

Workers in this group use hands and handtools skillfully to fabricate, process, install, and/or repair materials, products, and/or structural parts. They follow established procedures and techniques. The jobs are not found in factories, but are in repair shops, garages, wholesale and retail stores, and hotels. Some are found on construction projects, and others with utilities, such as telephone and power systems.

✓ What kind of work would you do?

Your work activities would depend upon your specific job. For example, you might:

- take apart household appliances to replace defective parts.
- repair and adjust gas or electric appliances in homes.
- install venetian blinds in commercial establishments.
- repair and adjust radios and television sets.
- plan, set, and shoot explosive charges in mining or oil well drilling.
- operate equipment to regulate volume and quality of sound recordings in a motion picture studio.
- repair, adjust, or replace parts in office machines.

- prepare and cook soups, meats, vegetables, desserts, and other foods in a restaurant.
- install mufflers on automobiles and trucks.
- install air conditioning units in homes.

✓ What skills and abilities do you need for this kind of work?

To do this kind of work, you must be able to:

- understand and use blueprints, sketches, drawings, and other kinds of specifications.
- use hands, arms, and fingers.
- work to precise measurements.
- visualize how finished product will look, or how a system operates.
- use arithmetic to measure, compute amount of materials to use, and to inspect product to be sure it conforms to requirements.
- lift and move materials and products.
- climb and balance self.
- work outdoors in all kinds of weather.
- stay calm in face of emergency or danger.

✓ How do you know if you would like or could learn to do this kind of work?

The following questions may give you clues about yourself as you consider this group of jobs.

- Have you repaired things that were broken? Can you locate and fix the defective parts?

- Have you cooked or baked? Can you measure and mix ingredients according to recipes?
- Have you repaired or installed parts on an automobile? Can you work skillfully with handtools?
- Have you taken courses in industrial arts or electronics? Can you understand repair instructions and schematic diagrams?
- Have you had military experience involving repair of mechanical or electrical equipment?

✓ How can you prepare for and enter this kind of work?

Occupations in this group usually require education and/or training extending from three months to over four years, depending upon the specific kind of work. The education and training required for jobs involving equipment repair varies according to the type of equipment. Some jobs only require on-the-job training. However, repairers of electronic equipment and business machines must have special training and experience. High schools and vocational schools offer courses in electricity, electronics, mathematics, or blueprint reading.

A few companies provide extensive training to prepare workers for some repair jobs. Correspondence courses in such fields as electricity and electronics are often helpful. Apprenticeships are available.

Many cooks begin as kitchen helpers to get the needed experience and on-the-job training. High school or post-high school training in food preparation is helpful. Training programs are also offered by the armed services, private schools, and some large hotels and restaurants. Apprenticeships are available. It takes several years of training and experience to become a head cook or chef in a large restaurant.

✓ What else should you consider about these jobs?

Working conditions for equipment repairers vary according to the type of equipment. Some jobs require repairs and adjustments to be made in the customer's office or home. Others require that repairs be made in a repair shop setting. Sometimes workers must work in narrow spaces and in uncomfortable positions. Dirt, dust, and grease sometimes create unpleasant conditions.

Working conditions for cooks depend upon the size of the establishment. Many kitchens are well-lighted, well-equipped, and properly ventilated. However, heavy lifting, oven and range heat, and long hours of standing and walking are common to these jobs.

If you think you would like to do this kind of work, look at the job titles listed below.

■ ■ ■

GOE: 05.10.01
Structural

ARCH-SUPPORT TECHNICIAN (protective dev.) • DOT #712.381-010 • OES: 89998 • Fabricates steel arch support to fit patient's foot, according to medical prescription: Receives plaster cast of foot from PROSTHETIST (medical ser.) or PODIATRIST (medical ser.). Places protection cloth into cast and fills cast with plaster to mold model of patient's foot. Removes hardened model from cast and traces model outline on paper to use as pattern in cutting support. Selects stainless steel sheet of prescribed thickness and cuts sheet to specified dimensions, using shears, guided by pattern. Hammers steel into prescribed contours to form support and places support against plaster model to determine accuracy of fit. Splits support into front and back pieces when indicated according to prescription, using shears. Polishes support, using abrasive wheel. Glues leather to bottom of arch support to protect shoe, and rivets additional leather across top edge for foot comfort, using riveting tool. • **GED:** R3, M2, L2 • **SVP:** 6 mos-1 yr • **Academic:** Ed=N, Eng=N • **Work Field:** 102 • **MPSMS:** 604 • **Aptitudes:** G3, V4, N4, S3, P3, Q4, K3, F3, M3, E5, C5 • **Temperaments:** J, T • **Physical:** Stg=L; Freq: R, H, I, N Occas: D • **Work Env:** Noise=N; • **Salary:** 2 • **Outlook:** 2

ASBESTOS REMOVAL WORKER (construction) • DOT #869.684-082 • OES: 87898 • Removes asbestos from ceilings, walls, beams, boilers, and other structures, following hazardous waste handling guidelines: Assembles scaffolding and seals off work area, using plastic sheeting and duct tape. Positions mobile decontamination unit or portable showers at entrance of work area. Builds connecting walkway between mobile unit or portable showers and work area, using handtools, lim-

ber, nails, plastic sheeting, and duct tape. Positions portable air evacuation and filtration system inside work area. Sprays chemical solution over asbestos covered surfaces, using tank with attached hose and nozzle, to soften asbestos. Cuts and scrapes asbestos from surfaces, using knife and scraper. Shovels asbestos into plastic disposal bags and seals bags, using duct tape. Cleans work area of loose asbestos, using vacuum, broom, and dust pan. Places asbestos in disposal bags and seals bags, using duct tape. Dismantles scaffolding and temporary walkway, using handtools, and places plastic sheeting and disposal bags into transport bags. Seals bags, using duct tape, and loads bags into truck. • **GED:** R3, M2, L2 • **SVP:** 2-30 days • **Academic:** Ed=N, Eng=N • **Work Field:** 031 • **MPSMS:** 360 • **Aptitudes:** G3, V3, N4, S4, P4, Q4, K3, F4, M3, E2, C5 • **Temperaments:** S, T • **Physical:** Stg=H; Freq: C, B, R, H Occas: S, K, O, W, I, N • **Work Env:** Noise=L; Occas: W, A, D, T • **Salary:** 2 • **Outlook:** 5

BOAT RIGGER (retail trade) • DOT #806.464-010 • OES: 93997 • Alternate titles: BOAT ACCESSORIES INSTALLER; OUTBOARD-MOTORBOAT RIGGER. Installs accessories in outboard or inboard motorboats: Drills holes, attaches brackets, and installs accessories, such as lights, batteries, ignition switches, fuel tanks, and guide pulleys, using handtools and power tools. May change propellors and adjust motors to obtain maximum performance. May install outboard and inboard motors and controls, using handtools. May load boats on trailers and make deliveries to customers. • **GED:** R3, M2, L1 • **SVP:** 3-6 mos • **Academic:** Ed=N, Eng=N • **Work Field:** 102 • **MPSMS:** 593 • **Aptitudes:** G3, V4, N4, S3, P4, Q4, K4, F4, M3, E5, C4 • **Temperaments:** J, T • **Physical:** Stg=M; Freq: R, H, I, D Occas: C, S, K, O, W, T, G, N, X • **Work Env:** Noise=L; Occas: W • **Salary:** 3 • **Outlook:** 1

BUILDING CLEANER (any industry) • DOT #891.684-022 • OES: 87898 • Cleans brick, stone, or metal exterior of structures, using cleaning agents, such as sand, acid solution, and steam: Cleans limited section of surface to determine strength of cleaning agents needed to prepare desired surface finish. Erects swinging scaffold, positions ladders, or assembles metal scaffolding to facilitate cleaning of structures. Pours specified portions and type of cleaning agents into hoppers or tanks of truck-mounted pumping equipment, and turns valves of equipment to produce steam and pump cleaning agents through hoses. Presses levers of spray nozzles to regulate flow of cleaning agent over structure surface. Cleans excessively stained surface areas, using brushes and cleaning compound. Sprays concrete floor to etch surface for cleaning and applies filler compound to seal floor surface. Cleans exterior surfaces of vehicles, using high pressure hoses and cleaning solutions. Cleans rugs on premise of customer, using chemicals, handbrushes, or portable scrubbing machine. Replaces worn parts of cleaning equipment and maintains equipment, using handtools. ● **GED:** R3, M2, L2 ● **SVP:** 3-6 mos ● **Academic:** Ed=N, Eng=N ● **Work Field:** 031 ● **MPSMS:** 360 ● **Aptitudes:** G3, V4, N4, S3, P3, Q4, K3, F3, M3, E4, C5 ● **Temperaments:** R, T ● **Physical:** Stg=H; Freq: C, B, K, O, W, R, H, I, N, D ● **Work Env:** Noise=N; Freq: W, A, D Occas: U, T ● **Salary:** 2 ● **Outlook:** 3

CARPET CUTTER (retail trade) ● DOT #929.381-010 ● OES: 93998 ● Measures, marks, and cuts carpeting and linoleum, using measuring and marking devices and knife, or cutting machine, to get maximum number of usable pieces from standard sized rolls, following floor dimensions or diagrams. May be designated according to type of floor covering cut as Linoleum Cutter (retail trade). ● **GED:** R3, M2, L2 ● **SVP:** 6 mos-1 yr ● **Academic:** Ed=N, Eng=N ● **Work Field:** 054, 241 ● **MPSMS:** 431 ● **Aptitudes:** G3, V4, N3, S3, P3, Q4, K3, F3, M3, E5, C3 ● **Temperaments:** J, T ● **Physical:** Stg=H; Freq: S, K, O, W, R, H, I, N, D, A, X ● **Work Env:** Noise=N; ● **Salary:** 2 ● **Outlook:** 3

CARPET LAYER (retail trade) ● DOT #864.381-010 ● OES: 87602 ● Lays carpet and rugs: Measures and cuts carpeting to size according to floor sketches, using carpet knife. Sews sections of carpeting together by hand. Cuts and trims carpet to fit along wall edges, openings, and projections. May lay linoleum. ● **GED:** R3, M2, L2 ● **SVP:** 2-4 yrs ● **Academic:** Ed=N, Eng=S ● **Work Field:** 092 ● **MPSMS:** 431 ● **Aptitudes:** G3, V3, N3, S3, P3, Q4, K3, F3, M3, E5, C3 ● **Temperaments:** J, T ● **Physical:** Stg=H; Freq: S, K, O, W, R, H, I, E Occas: N, D, A, X ● **Work Env:** Noise=N; ● **Salary:** 2 ● **Outlook:** 3

CASTING REPAIRER (any industry) ● DOT #619.281-010 ● OES: 85998 ● Repairs broken or cracked castings and forgings, using special cold process requiring no welding: Calculates factors, such as size, depth, and position of fracture, and tensile strength and distribution of stress and strain in material. Employs combination of holding and locking devices to make repair, using airhammers, air drills, air grinders, punches, and strippers to insert holding and locking devices in casting and to smooth finish. May fabricate special angle heads for airhammer, air grinder, and air drill, using blacksmith tools and anvil. ● **GED:** R3, M3, L3 ● **SVP:** 1-2 yrs ● **Academic:** Ed=N, Eng=S ● **Work Field:** 102 ● **MPSMS:** 542, 556 ● **Aptitudes:** G3, V3, N3, S3, P3, Q4, K4, F4, M3, E5, C5 ● **Temperaments:** J, T, V ● **Physical:** Stg=M; Freq: R, H, I, N, D, A ● **Work Env:** Noise=N; ● **Salary:** 4 ● **Outlook:** 2

CONSTRUCTION WORKER I (construction) ● DOT #869.664-014 ● OES: 87898 ● Performs any combination of following duties on construction projects, usually working in utility capacity, by transferring from one task to another where demands require worker with varied experience and ability to work without close supervision: Measures distances from grade stakes, drives stakes, and stretches tight line. Bolts, nails, aligns, and blocks up under forms. Signals operators of construction equipment to facilitate alignment, movement, and adjustment of machinery to conform to grade specifications. Levels earth to fine grade specifications, using pick and shovel. Mixes concrete, using portable mixer. Smooths and finishes freshly poured cement or concrete, using float, trowel, or screed. Positions, joins, aligns, and seals pipe sections. Erects scaffolding, shoring, and braces. Mops, brushes, or spreads paints or bituminous compounds over surfaces for protection. Sprays materials such as water, sand, steam, vinyl, paint, or stucco through hose to clean, coat, or seal surfaces. Applies caulking compounds by hand or with caulking gun to seal crevices. Grinds, sands, or polishes surfaces, such as concrete, marble, terrazzo, or wood flooring, using abrasive tools or machines. Performs variety of tasks involving dextrous use of hands and tools, such as demolishing buildings, sawing lumber, dismantling forms, removing projections from concrete, mounting pipe

hangers, and cutting and attaching insulating material. Work is usually performed with other workers. May be designated according to duties performed as Batterboard Setter (construction); Billboard-Erector Helper (construction); Bricklayer, Paving Brick (construction); Caulker (construction). May be designated: Carpenter Helper, Maintenance (construction); Cement Mason, Highways And Streets (construction); Cement Sprayer, Nozzle (concrete prod.; construction); Concrete-Wall-Grinder Operator (construction); Corrugated-Sheet-Material Sheeter (construction); Cradle Placer (construction); Dampproofer (construction); Drain Layer (construction); Duct Installer (construction; mfd. bldgs.); Fine Grader (construction); Fitter (construction; pipe lines); Floor Finisher (construction); Floor-Sanding-Machine Operator (construction); Form-Builder Helper (construction); Form Setter, Metal-Road Forms (construction); Form Setter, Steel Forms (construction); Form Setter, Steel-Pan Forms (construction); Foundation-Drill-Operator Helper (construction); Glazier Helper (construction); Ground Wirer (construction); Holder, Pile Driving (construction); Hydrant-And-Valve Setter (construction); Insulation Installer (construction); Joist Setter, Adjustable Steel (construction); Laborer, Adjustable Steel Joist (construction); Laborer, Carpentry, Dock (construction); Layer-Out, Plate Glass (construction); Lightning-Rod Erector (construction); Ornamental-Iron-Worker Helper (construction); Painter, Rough (construction); Painter, Structural Steel (construction); Paint-Striping-Machine Operator (construction); Permastone Dresser (construction); Pile-Driving Setter (construction); Pipe Caulker (construction); Pipe Layer (construction); Pipeline Worker (construction); Plumber Helper (construction); Pointer, Caulker, And Cleaner (construction); Pump-Erector Helper (construction); Receiver Setter (construction); Roofer, Vinyl Coating (construction); Seat Installer (construction); Septic-Tank Servicer (construction); Sewer Tapper (construction); Shorer (construction); Stone Polisher (construction); Tapping-Machine Operator (construction); Tuck Pointer (construction); Waterproofer (construction); Well-Drill-Operator Helper, Cable Tool (construction); Well-Drill-Operator Helper, Rotary Drill (construction); Wrecker (construction). ● **GED:** R3, M3, L3 ● **SVP:** 3-6 mos ● **Academic:** Ed=N, Eng=S ● **Work Field:** 102 ● **MPSMS:** 360 ● **Aptitudes:** G3, V4, N4, S3, P3, Q4, K3, F3, M3, E4, C4 ● **Temperaments:** R, T ● **Physical:** Stg=H; Freq: C, S, K, O, R, H, I, N, D Occas: B, T, G, F, X ● **Work Env:** Noise=L; Const: W Freq: A Occas: O ● **Salary:** 1 ● **Outlook:** 3

DIVER (any industry) ● DOT #899.261-010 ● OES: 85998 ● Alternate titles: SUBMARINE WORKER. Works below surface of water, using scuba gear (self-contained underwater breathing apparatus) or in diving suit with air line extending to surface to inspect, repair, remove, and install equipment and structures: Descends into water with aid of DIVER HELPER (any industry), and communicates with surface by signal line or telephone. Inspects docks and bottoms and propellers of ships. Repairs vessels below water line, replacing missing or leaking rivets with bolts. Caulks leaks in ships or caissons. Guides placement of pilings for structures, such as docks, bridges, cofferdams, and oil drilling platforms. Lays, inspects, and repairs underwater pipelines, cables, and sewers, using handtools. Cuts and welds steel, using oxyycetylene cutting torch and arc-welding equipment, utilizing air balloon device for working underwater. Cleans debris from intake and discharge strainers. Removes obstructions from marine railway or launching ways with pneumatic and power handtools. Levels rails by driving wedges beneath track with maul or sledgehammer. Removes launching cradles and sliding ways from keels of newly launched vessels, using power and handtools. Places rigging around sunken objects and hooks rigging to crane lines. Rigs explosives for underwater demolitions. Searches for lost, missing, or sunken objects, such as bodies, torpedoes, sunken vessels, and equipment. Places recording instruments below surface of water preparatory to underwater tests or experiments. May set sheet pilings for cofferdams. May drill holes in rock for blasting purposes at bottom of lake or harbor and be designated Marine Driller (construction). May work in flooded mines. May use armored diving equipment for dangerous missions. May photograph underwater structures or marine life. May place sandbags around pipelines or base of cofferdam to provide structural support. ● **GED:** R4, M3, L3 ● **SVP:** 2-4 yrs ● **Academic:** Ed=N, Eng=S ● **Work Field:** 102, 005 ● **MPSMS:** 365, 593 ● **Aptitudes:** G3, V3, N3, S2, P3, Q4, K3, F3, M3, E2, C5 ● **Temperaments:** S, T, V ● **Physical:** Stg=H; Freq: S, K, O, R, H, I, E, T, G, N, D Occas: W, A ● **Work Env:** Noise=N; Const: W Freq: C, U, O ● **Salary:** 2 ● **Outlook:** 2

DRAPERY HANGER (retail trade) ● DOT #869.484-014 ● OES: 87898 ● Alternate titles: INSTALLATION WORKER, DRAPERIES; INSTALLER. Installs draperies in customers' homes: Measures area to be covered, and delivers finished draperies to customers' homes. Screws and bolts brackets and hangers onto wall, using handtools. Hangs and arranges draperies to enhance appearance of room. May install window shades and venetian blinds. ● **GED:** R3, M2, L2 ● **SVP:** 6 mos-1 yr ● **Academic:** Ed=N, Eng=S ● **Work Field:** 102 ● **MPSMS:** 435, 881 ● **Aptitudes:** G3, V4, N3, S3, P4, Q4, K3, F4, M3, E5, C5 ● **Temperaments:** R, T ● **Physical:** Stg=M; Freq: R, H, I Occas: C, B, S, K, O, N, D ● **Work Env:** Noise=Q; ● **Salary:** 2 ● **Outlook:** 3

DRY-WALL APPLICATOR (construction) ● DOT #842.684-014 ● OES: 87120 ● Alternate titles: DRY-WALL NAILER; SHEETROCK INSTALLER. Installs plasterboard or other wallboard to ceiling and interior walls of building, using handtools and portable power tools: Installs horizontal and vertical metal or wooden studs for attachment of wallboard on interior walls, using handtools. Cuts angle iron and channel iron to specified size, using hacksaw, and suspends angle iron grid and channel iron from ceiling, using wire. Scribes measurements on wallboard, using straightedge and tape measure, and cuts wallboard to size, using knife or saw. Cuts out openings for electrical and other outlets, using knife or saw. Attaches wallboard to wall and ceiling supports, using glue, nails, screws, hammer, or powered screwdriver. Trims rough edges from wallboard to maintain even joints, using knife. Nails prefabricated metal pieces around windows and doors and between dissimilar materials to protect drywall edges. Work is usually performed with other workers. May remove plaster, drywall, or paneling during renovation project, using crowbar and hammer. ● **GED:** R2, M2, L2 ● **SVP:** 1-2 yrs ● **Academic:** Ed=N, Eng=N ● **Work Field:** 102 ● **MPSMS:** 361, 455, 536 ● **Aptitudes:** G3, V4, N4, S3, P4, Q4, K3, F3, M3, E4, C5 ● **Temperaments:** J, T ● **Physical:** Stg=M; Freq: S, K, O, R, H, I, N, D Occas: C, B, G, A ● **Work Env:** Noise=N; ● **Salary:** 3 ● **Outlook:** 3

FENCE ERECTOR (construction) ● DOT #869.684-022 ● OES: 87898 ● Alternate titles: IRONWORKER, WIRE-FENCE ERECTOR; WIRE-FENCE BUILDER. Erects and repairs metal and wooden fences and fence gates around industrial establishments, residences, or farms, using power tools and handtools: Lays out fence line, using tape measure, and marks positions for postholes. Digs postholes with spade, posthole digger, or power-driven auger. Blasts rock formations with dynamite to facilitate digging of postholes. Sets metal or wooden post in upright position in posthole. Mixes concrete by hand or by use of cement mixer. Pours concrete around base of post or tamps soil into posthole to embed post. Aligns posts, using line or by sighting along edges of posts. Verifies vertical alignment of posts with plumb bob or spirit level. Attaches fence-rail support to post, using hammer and pliers. Cuts metal tubing, using pipe cutter and inserts tubing through rail supports. Completes top fence rail of metal fence by connecting tube sections by use of metal sleeves. Attaches rails or tension wire along bottoms of posts to form fencing frame. Stretches wire, wire mesh, or chain link fencing between posts and attaches fencing to frame. Assembles gate and fastens it in position, using handtools. Saws required lengths of lumber to make rails for wooden fence. Nails top and bottom rails to fence posts, or inserts them in slots on posts. Nails pointed slats to rails to construct picket fence. Erects alternate panel, basket weave, and louvered fences. May weld metal parts together, using portable gas welding equipment. May be designated according to material used as Metal-Fence Erector (construction); Wire-Fence Erector (construction); Wooden-Fence Erector (construction); or according to specific duty performed as Fence-Gate Assembler (construction); Fence Setter (construction); Fence Stretcher (construction). ● **GED:** R3, M2, L2 ● **SVP:** 6 mos-1 yr ● **Academic:** Ed=N, Eng=N ● **Work Field:** 102 ● **MPSMS:** 369 ● **Aptitudes:** G3, V4, N4, S3, P3, Q4, K3, F3, M3, E4, C4 ● **Temperaments:** R, T ● **Physical:** Stg=H; Freq: S, K, O, R, H, I, N, D Occas: F, X ● **Work Env:** Noise=L; Freq: W Occas: O ● **Salary:** 2 ● **Outlook:** 3

FIXTURE REPAIRER-FABRICATOR (any industry) ● DOT #630.384-010 ● OES: 85109 ● Fabricates and repairs fixtures, rods, baskets, and hooks used to suspend articles in plating, cleansing, and painting vats, using handtools and portable power tools: Cuts metal stock to size, using handsaws or power saws and forming machines and following working sketches. Bends metal, using vise or hammer. Drills and taps holes, using portable power drill. Bolts or screws parts

together, using wrenches and screwdrivers. May braze, solder, or weld parts together. ● **GED:** R3, M2, L2 ● **SVP:** 6 mos-1 yr ● **Academic:** Ed=N, Eng=N ● **Work Field:** 102 ● **MPSMS:** 550 ● **Aptitudes:** G3, V3, N4, S3, P3, Q4, K4, F3, M3, E5, C5 ● **Temperaments:** J, T ● **Physical:** Stg=M; Freq: R, H, I, N Occas: S, T, G, D ● **Work Env:** Noise=L; Occas: H, A ● **Salary:** 3 ● **Outlook:** 2

FLOOR LAYER (construction) ● DOT #864.481-010 ● OES: 87898 ● Alternate titles: FLOOR COVERER; FLOOR-COVERING-TILE LAYER. Applies blocks, strips, or sheets of shock-absorbing, sound-deadening, or decorative covering to floors, walls, and cabinets: Disconnects and removes obstacles, such as appliances and light fixtures. Sweeps, scrapes, sands, or chips dirt and irregularities from base surfaces, and fills cracks with putty, plaster, or cement grout to form smooth, clean foundation. Measures and cuts covering materials, such as rubber, linoleum or cork tile, and foundation material, such as felt, according to blueprints and sketches, using rule, straightedge, linoleum knife, and snips. Spreads adhesive cement over floor to cement foundation material to floor for sound-deadening, and to prevent covering from wearing at board joints. Lays out centerlines, guidelines, and borderlines on foundation with chalkline and dividers. Spreads cement on foundation material with serrated trowel. Lays covering on cement, following guidelines, to keep tile courses straight and butts edges of blocks to match patterns and execute designs. Joins sections of sheet covering by overlapping adjoining edges and cutting through both layers with knife to form tight joint. Rolls finished floor to smooth it and press cement into base and covering. May soften area of floor covering with butane torch to fit materials around irregular surfaces. May lay carpet [CARPET LAYER (retail trade)]. May be designated according to type of floor laid as Asphalt-Tile-Floor Layer (construction; retail trade); Cork-Tile-Floor Layer (construction; retail trade); Linoleum-Floor Layer (construction; retail trade); Linoleum Layer (construction; retail trade); Linoleum-Tile-Floor Layer (construction; retail trade); Rubber-Tile-Floor Layer (construction; retail trade). ● **GED:** R3, M2, L2 ● **SVP:** 1-2 yrs ● **Academic:** Ed=N, Eng=S ● **Work Field:** 092 ● **MPSMS:** 361 ● **Aptitudes:** G3, V3, N3, S3, P3, Q4, K3, F3, M3, E4, C4 ● **Temperaments:** T, V ● **Physical:** Stg=M; Freq: S, K, O, R, H, I, N, D Occas: C, B, W, A, X ● **Work Env:** Noise=N; Occas: O ● **Salary:** 2 ● **Outlook:** 3

FRONT-END MECHANIC (automotive ser.) ● DOT #620.281-038 ● OES: 85302 ● Alternate titles: ALIGNMENT MECHANIC; AXLE-AND-FRAME MECHANIC; CHASSIS MECHANIC; WHEEL-ALIGNMENT MECHANIC. Aligns wheels, axles, frames, torsion bars, and steering mechanisms of automotive vehicles, such as automobiles, buses, and trucks: Drives automotive vehicle onto wheel alignment rack and tests vehicle for faulty wheel alignment, bent axle, worn ball joints, and bent steering rods, using alignment-testing machine. Straightens axle and steering rods and adjusts shims, tie rods, and joining pins to align wheels, or installs new parts, using handtools. Places wheel on balancing machine to determine where counterweights must be added to balance wheel. Hammers counterweights onto rim of wheel. Installs shock absorbers. Straightens frame, using hydraulic jack, chassis aligner, and acetylene torch. ● **GED:** R3, M3, L3 ● **SVP:** 1-2 yrs ● **Academic:** Ed=N, Eng=N ● **Work Field:** 121 ● **MPSMS:** 591 ● **Aptitudes:** G3, V3, N4, S3, P3, Q4, K3, F3, M3, E4, C5 ● **Temperaments:** J, T, V ● **Physical:** Stg=M; Freq: S, K, O, R, H, N, D Occas: I, G, A ● **Work Env:** Noise=N; Freq: A, M ● **Salary:** 4 ● **Outlook:** 4

FURNITURE ASSEMBLER-AND-INSTALLER (retail trade) ● DOT #739.684-082 ● OES: 93998 ● Uncrates, assembles, installs, and repairs furniture and office equipment in customers' homes or offices: Uncrates and assembles items, using handtools. Repairs and paints dents and scratches in metal or wood. Cleans, repairs, and replaces safe and file drawers, locks, catches, and slides. May repair or replace damaged vinyl or fabric upholstery material, using handtools, patching, needle, and thread. ● **GED:** R3, M2, L1 ● **SVP:** 3-6 mos ● **Academic:** Ed=N, Eng=N ● **Work Field:** 102 ● **MPSMS:** 460 ● **Aptitudes:** G3, V4, N4, S3, P3, Q4, K3, F4, M3, E4, C4 ● **Temperaments:** J, T, V ● **Physical:** Stg=H; Freq: S, R, H, I, N, D Occas: O, E, A, X ● **Work Env:** Noise=N; ● **Salary:** 4 ● **Outlook:** 2

GLASS INSTALLER (automotive ser.) ● DOT #865.684-010 ● OES: 85305 ● Alternate titles: AUTO-GLASS WORKER; GLAZIER; WINDSHIELD INSTALLER. Replaces broken or pitted windshields and window glass in motor vehicles: Removes broken glass by unscrewing frame, using handtools. Cuts flat safety glass according to specified pattern, using glasscutter. Smooths cut edge of glass by holding against abrasive belt. Applies moistureproofing compound along cut edges and installs glass in vehicle. Weatherproofs window or windshield and prevents it from rattling by installing rubber channeling strips around sides of glass. Installs precut replacement glass to replace curved windows. May replace or adjust parts in window-raising mechanism. ● **GED:** R3, M1, L2 ● **SVP:** 3-6 mos ● **Academic:** Ed=N, Eng=S ● **Work Field:** 102 ● **MPSMS:** 531 ● **Aptitudes:** G3, V4, N4, S3, P3, Q4, K3, F3, M3, E5, C5 ● **Temperaments:** R, T ● **Physical:** Stg=M; Freq: R, H, I, N, D Occas: S, K, O, E ● **Work Env:** Noise=N; ● **Salary:** 3 ● **Outlook:** 3

GLAZIER (construction) ● DOT #865.381-010 ● OES: 87811 ● Alternate titles: GLASS SETTER; GLASSWORKER; GLAZIER, PLATE GLASS. Installs glass in windows, skylights, store fronts, and display cases, or on surfaces, such as building fronts, interior walls, ceilings, and tabletops: Marks outline or pattern on glass, and cuts glass, using glasscutter. Breaks off excess glass by hand or with notched tool. Fastens glass panes into wood sash with glazier's points, and spreads and smooths putty around edge of panes with knife to seal joints. Installs mirrors or structural glass on building fronts, walls, ceilings, or tables, using mastic, screws, or decorative molding. Bolts metal hinges, handles, locks, and other hardware to prefabricated glass doors. Sets glass doors into frame and fits hinges. May install metal window and door frames into which glass panels are to be fitted. May press plastic adhesive film to glass or spray glass with tinting solution to prevent light glare. May install stained glass windows. May assemble and install metal-framed glass enclosures for showers and be designated Shower-Enclosure Installer (construction). May be designated according to type of glass installed as Glazier, Structural Glass (construction); Plate-Glass Installer (construction). ● **GED:** R3, M2, L2 ● **SVP:** 2-4 yrs ● **Academic:** Ed=N, Eng=N ● **Work Field:** 102 ● **MPSMS:** 360, 460 ● **Aptitudes:** G3, V4, N4, S3, P3, Q4, K3, F3, M3, E4, C5 ● **Temperaments:** J, T, V ● **Physical:** Stg=M; Freq: C, B, S, R, H, I, N, D Occas: K, O ● **Work Env:** Noise=L; Freq: W, O ● **Salary:** 3 ● **Outlook:** 3

GRIP (amuse. & rec.) ● DOT #962.684-014 ● OES: 85998 ● Erects sets and moves scenery on stage for theatrical productions on stage and television studio, using handtools and power tools and equipment: Ties sets upright with lash lines. Hooks stage brace onto set and adjusts brace to straighten and support set. Connects lines to overhead steel work to support hanging units, using handtools and power tools. Fits and hangs painted backdrops and curtains. Inserts weights as specified to counter balance hanging units. Changes scenery between acts or scenes according to script. ● **GED:** R3, M2, L2 ● **SVP:** 6 mos-1 yr ● **Academic:** Ed=N, Eng=N ● **Work Field:** 102 ● **MPSMS:** 864, 912 ● **Aptitudes:** G3, V4, N4, S2, P4, Q4, K3, F4, M3, E2, C5 ● **Temperaments:** T, V ● **Physical:** Stg=V; Freq: C, B, S, O, R, H, I, D ● **Work Env:** Noise=N; Freq: D ● **Salary:** 1 ● **Outlook:** 2

INSULATION WORKER (construction) ● DOT #863.364-014 ● OES: 87802 ● Applies insulating material to exposed surfaces of structures, such as air ducts, hot and cold pipes, storage tanks, and cold storage rooms: Reads blueprints and selects required insulation material (in sheet, tubular, or roll form), such as fiberglass, foam rubber, styrofoam, cork, or urethane, based on material's heat retaining or excluding characteristics. Brushes adhesives on or attaches metal adhesive-backed pins to flat surfaces as necessary to facilitate application of insulation material. Measures and cuts insulation material to specified size and shape for covering flat or round surfaces, using tape measure, knife, or scissors. Fits, wraps, or attaches required insulation material around or to structure, following blueprint specifications. Covers or seals insulation with preformed plastic covers, canvas strips, sealant, or tape to secure insulation to structure, according to type of insulation used and structure covered, using staple gun, trowel, paintbrush, or caulking gun. ● **GED:** R3, M2, L3 ● **SVP:** 1-2 yrs ● **Academic:** Ed=N, Eng=S ● **Work Field:** 092 ● **MPSMS:** 361 ● **Aptitudes:** G3, V4, N4, S3, P3, Q4, K3, F3, M3, E4, C5 ● **Temperaments:** J ● **Physical:** Stg=M; Const: R, H Freq: I, N, D Occas: S, K, O ● **Work Env:** Noise=N; Freq: W Occas: A, D ● **Salary:** 2 ● **Outlook:** 3

JIG BUILDER (wood. container) ● DOT #761.381-014 ● OES: 89398 ● Alternate titles: SETTER. Builds jigs used as guides for assembling oversized or special type box shooks, following blueprints: Measures

and marks position of stops on worktable, according to blueprint, using tape measure and chalk. Nails stops to worktable as indicated by layout. May build first shook on layout as demonstration. ● **GED:** R3, M2, L2 ● **SVP:** 1-2 yrs ● **Academic:** Ed=N, Eng=N ● **Work Field:** 102 ● **MPSMS:** 450 ● **Aptitudes:** G3, V4, N4, S3, P3, Q4, K3, F4, M3, E5, C5 ● **Temperaments:** J, T ● **Physical:** Stg=M; Freq: W, R, H, I, N, D, A, V ● **Work Env:** Noise=L; Occas: A, M ● **Salary:** 4 ● **Outlook:** 3

LAWN-SPRINKLER INSTALLER (construction) ● DOT #869.684-030 ● OES: 87898 ● Installs underground lawn sprinkler systems: Lays out plastic or copper tubing, according to sketch or blueprint. Digs trenches with shovel or by use of ditching machine. Cuts tubing to desired length, using handtools. Connects lengths of tubing, using paintbrush and solvent to fuse ends of plastic tubing, and handtorch and solder to join metal piping and connections. Makes connection to water main, using handtools. Turns valve to start water flow and observes operation to detect leaks. Installs electrical and mechanical control mechanisms for automatic operation. Fills trench with dirt after installation, using shovel. ● **GED:** R3, M2, L2 ● **SVP:** 6 mos-1 yr ● **Academic:** Ed=N, Eng=S ● **Work Field:** 102 ● **MPSMS:** 369 ● **Aptitudes:** G3, V4, N4, S3, P3, Q5, K4, F4, M3, E4, C5 ● **Temperaments:** J, T ● **Physical:** Stg=M; Freq: S, K, O, R, H, N, D Occas: I ● **Work Env:** Noise=L; Const: W Occas: O ● **Salary:** 2 ● **Outlook:** 4

LUGGAGE REPAIRER (any industry) ● DOT #365.361-010 ● OES: 89511 ● Alternate titles: HAND LUGGAGE REPAIRER. Repairs and renovates worn or damaged luggage made of leather, fiber, and other materials: Sews rips by hand or machine, inserts and repairs linings, and replaces locks, catches, straps, buckles, corner protectors, and other parts to repair all types of hand luggage. Repairs and reconditions trunks and other heavy luggage, constructing and gluing together frame, cutting and bending fiberboard pieces together, and riveting on locks, catches, corner protectors, and other parts. May construct leather articles, such as purses, wallets, and briefcases, ordered specially by customers. May specialize in repairing trunks and other heavy luggage and be designated Trunk Repairer (any industry). ● **GED:** R3, M2, L2 ● **SVP:** 1-2 yrs ● **Academic:** Ed=N, Eng=N ● **Work Field:** 102, 171 ● **MPSMS:** 524 ● **Aptitudes:** G3, V4, N4, S3, P3, Q4, K3, F3, M3, E4, C4 ● **Temperaments:** J, T ● **Physical:** Stg=M; Freq: R, H, I, E, N, A, X ● **Work Env:** Noise=N; ● **Salary:** 2 ● **Outlook:** 3

MAINTENANCE REPAIRER, BUILDING (any industry) ● DOT #899.381-010 ● OES: 85132 ● Alternate titles: BUILDING REPAIRER. Repairs and maintains physical structures of commercial and industrial establishments, such as factories, office buildings, apartment houses, and logging and mining constructions, using handtools and power tools: Replaces defective electrical switches and other fixtures. Paints structures, and repairs woodwork with carpenter's tools. Repairs plumbing fixtures. Repairs plaster and lays brick. Builds sheds and other outbuildings. ● **GED:** R4, M3, L3 ● **SVP:** 2-4 yrs ● **Academic:** Ed=H, Eng=S ● **Work Field:** 102 ● **MPSMS:** 360 ● **Aptitudes:** G3, V3, N3, S2, P2, Q4, K3, F3, M2, E4, C4 ● **Temperaments:** T, V ● **Physical:** Stg=M; Freq: R, H, N, D Occas: C, B, S, K, O, I, X ● **Work Env:** Noise=L; Freq: W ● **Salary:** 3 ● **Outlook:** 3

MUFFLER INSTALLER (automotive ser.) ● DOT #807.664-010 ● OES: 85302 ● Replaces defective mufflers and pipes on automobiles, buses, trucks, and other automotive vehicles according to factory or customer specifications, using handtools and power tools: Removes defective muffler, using hacksaw, wrenches, air-powered tools, or acetylene torch. Selects replacement muffler according to automotive vehicle model and customer's preference. Bolts or tack welds new muffler in place. Bends and shapes tailpipe sections according to customer specifications, using pipe-bending machine. Welds tailpipe sections to muffler or exhaust pipe, using arc welding equipment. Aligns muffler and tailpipe within frame and bolts hangers to frame to secure muffler. ● **GED:** R3, M2, L2 ● **SVP:** 3-6 mos ● **Academic:** Ed=N, Eng=N ● **Work Field:** 102 ● **MPSMS:** 591 ● **Aptitudes:** G3, V4, N4, S3, P3, Q4, K3, F3, M3, E5, C5 ● **Temperaments:** J, T ● **Physical:** Stg=M; Freq: R, H, I, N, D Occas: S, K, O, T, G ● **Work Env:** Noise=L; ● **Salary:** 3 ● **Outlook:** 3

OPTICIAN, DISPENSING (optical goods) ● DOT #299.361-010 ● OES: 32514 ● Fills ophthalmic eyeglass prescriptions and fits and adapts lenses and frames, utilizing written optical prescription: Evaluates prescription in conjunction with client's vocational and avocational visual requirements. Determines client's current lens prescription, when necessary, using lensometer or lens analyzer and client's eyeglasses. Recommends specific lenses, lens coatings, and frames to suit client needs. Assists client in selecting frames according to style and color, coordinating frames with facial and eye measurements and optical prescription. Measures client's bridge and eye size, temple length, vertex distance, pupillary distance, and optical centers of eyes, using millimeter rule and light reflex pupillometer. Prepares work order and instructions for grinding lenses and fabricating eyeglasses. Verifies finished lenses are ground to specification. Heats, shapes, or bends plastic or metal frames to adjust eyeglasses to fit client, using pliers and hands. Instructs clients in adapting to, wearing, and caring for eyeglasses. Sells optical goods, such as binoculars, plano sunglasses, magnifying glasses, and low vision aids. Repairs damaged frames. May be required to hold license issued by governing state. May fabricate lenses to prescription specifications. May select and order frames for display. May grind lens edges or apply coating to lenses. May manage one or more optical shops. May compute amount of sale and collect payment for services. May fit contact lenses only and be designated Optician, Contact-Lens Dispensing (optical goods; retail trade). ● **GED:** R4, M3, L4 ● **SVP:** 2-4 yrs ● **Academic:** Ed=A, Eng=G ● **Work Field:** 292, 061 ● **MPSMS:** 605, 881 ● **Aptitudes:** G3, V3, N3, S2, P2, Q4, K3, F3, M3, E5, C4 ● **Temperaments:** J, P, T ● **Physical:** Stg=L; Freq: R, H, I, T, G, N, D, A Occas: E, X ● **Work Env:** Noise=Q; ● **Salary:** 5 ● **Outlook:** 3

PUMP INSTALLER (any industry) ● DOT #630.684-018 ● OES: 85998 ● Installs and adjusts electric, gasoline, and diesel-driven pumps and blowers, using handtools, power tools, and diagrams: Cuts and threads pipes, ducts, and fittings, using handtools and power tools. Levels and bolts down pump. Connects ducts and drive couplings, and aligns them to minimize friction, using handtools and gauges. Oils and greases moving parts, and adjusts valves to prevent overloading. May recommend repair or adjustment of driving mechanism to improve operation of pumps. ● **GED:** R3, M2, L3 ● **SVP:** 6 mos-1 yr ● **Academic:** Ed=N, Eng=S ● **Work Field:** 121 ● **MPSMS:** 568 ● **Aptitudes:** G3, V3, N3, S3, P3, Q4, K3, F3, M3, E5, C5 ● **Temperaments:** R, T ● **Physical:** Stg=H; Freq: S, O, R, H, I, N ● **Work Env:** Noise=N; Occas: W ● **Salary:** 2 ● **Outlook:** 3

REPAIRER (furniture) ● DOT #709.684-062 ● OES: 85998 ● Alternate titles: SALVAGE WORKER. Repairs or replaces damaged metal furniture parts, using handtools and power tools: Welds cracks, using acetylene torch. Files, scrapes, or sands parts to remove dirt, paint, or rust. Melts solder into holes and cracks. Grinds solder until smooth and flush with surrounding metal, using portable grinder. Bends or hammers dented or twisted parts to original shape. Replaces inoperative furniture parts. May reassemble metal furniture. ● **GED:** R3, M1, L2 ● **SVP:** 6 mos-1 yr ● **Academic:** Ed=N, Eng=N ● **Work Field:** 102 ● **MPSMS:** 466 ● **Aptitudes:** G3, V4, N4, S3, P3, Q5, K3, F3, M3, E5, C5 ● **Temperaments:** R, T ● **Physical:** Stg=L; Freq: R, H, I, N Occas: S ● **Work Env:** Noise=N; Occas: O ● **Salary:** 2 ● **Outlook:** 3

REPAIRER, RECREATIONAL VEHICLE (vehicles, nec) ● DOT #869.261-022 ● OES: 85998 ● Repairs recreational vehicles, such as campers, travel trailers, and motor homes according to customer service request or work order: Confers with customer or reads work order to determine nature and extent of damage to vehicle. Inspects, examines, or tests parts or item to be repaired or replaced. Lists parts needed, estimates costs, and plans work procedure, using parts list, technical manuals, diagrams, and personal knowledge. Removes damaged exterior panels of vehicle, using handtools. Repairs and replaces structural frame members, seals leaks, and replaces or repairs malfunctioning items, such as heaters, stoves, refrigerators, or water pumps, using equipment and tools, such as drill press, wrenches, and saws. Repairs electrical wiring, plumbing, and gaslines (propane), using items such as caulking compounds, electrical wiring and tape, and plastic or copper pipe. Refinishes wood surfaces on cabinets, doors, moldings, and walls, using woodworking tools, spray equipment, paints, and varnishes. Inspects, examines, and tests functional parts of vehicle, using pressure gauges, ohmmeter, and other test equipment, according to work order, to verify completeness of work performed on new or repaired units before delivery to customer. ● **GED:** R4, M3, L3 ● **SVP:** 1-2 yrs ● **Academic:** Ed=H, Eng=S ● **Work Field:** 102, 111, 121 ● **MPSMS:** 591 ● **Aptitudes:** G3, V3, N3, S3, P3, Q3, K4, F3, M4, E4, C4 ●

Temperaments: J, T ● **Physical:** Stg=M; Freq: S, K, O, R, H, I, T, G, N, A Occas: D, X ● **Work Env:** Noise=N; ● **Salary:** 3 ● **Outlook:** 4

ROOFER (construction) ● DOT #866.381-010 ● OES: 87808 ● Covers roofs with roofing materials other than sheet metal, such as composition shingles or sheets, wood shingles, or asphalt and gravel, to waterproof roofs: Cuts roofing paper to size, using knife, and nails or staples it to roof in overlapping strips to form base for roofing materials. Aligns roofing material with edge of roof, and overlaps successive layers, gauging distance of overlap with chalkline, gauge on shingling hatchet, or by lines on shingles. Fastens composition shingles or sheets to roof with asphalt, cement, or nails. Punches holes in slate, tile, terra cotta, or wooden shingles, using punch and hammer. Cuts strips of flashing and fits them into angles formed by walls, vents, and intersecting roof surfaces. When applying asphalt or tar and gravel to roof, mops or pours hot asphalt or tar onto roof base. Applies alternate layers of hot asphalt or tar and roofing paper until roof covering is as specified. Applies gravel or pebbles over top layer, using rake or stiff-bristled broom. May construct and attach prefabricated roof sections to rafters [CARPENTER (construction)]. May attach shingles to exterior walls and apply roofing paper and tar to shower pans, decks, and promenades to waterproof surfaces. When specializing in one type of roofing materials, is designated according to specialty as Aluminum-Shingle Roofer (construction); Asbestos-Shingle Roofer (construction); Asphalt, Tar, And Gravel Roofer (construction); Composition Roofer (construction); Roofer, Gypsum (construction); Slate Roofer (construction); Tile-And-Terra-Cotta Roofer (construction); Wood-Shingle Roofer (construction). ● **GED:** R3, M2, L2 ● **SVP:** 2-4 yrs ● **Academic:** Ed=N, Eng=N ● **Work Field:** 092 ● **MPSMS:** 361 ● **Aptitudes:** G3, V4, N3, S3, P3, Q4, K3, F3, M3, E3, C5 ● **Temperaments:** J, T ● **Physical:** Stg=M; Freq: B, S, K, O, R, H, I, N, D Occas: C, F ● **Work Env:** Noise=L; Const: W Freq: H, A, D, O ● **Salary:** 2 ● **Outlook:** 3

ROUSTABOUT (petrol. & gas) ● DOT #869.684-046 ● OES: 87921 ● Alternate titles: CONNECTION WORKER; GANG WORKER; ROUGHNECK. Assembles and repairs oil field machinery and equipment, using handtools and power tools: Digs holes, sets forms, and mixes and pours concrete into forms, to make foundations for wood or steel derricks, using posthole digger, handtools, and wheelbarrow. Bolts or nails together wood or steel framework to erect derrick. Dismantles and assembles boilers and steam engine parts, using handtools and power tools. Bolts together pump and engine parts. Connects tanks and flow lines, using wrenches. Unscrews or tightens pipe, casing, tubing, and pump rods, using hand and power wrenches and tongs. ● **GED:** R3, M1, L2 ● **SVP:** 6 mos-1 yr ● **Academic:** Ed=N, Eng=N ● **Work Field:** 102 ● **MPSMS:** 564 ● **Aptitudes:** G3, V4, N4, S3, P4, Q4, K3, F3, M3, E5, C5 ● **Temperaments:** R, T ● **Physical:** Stg=H; Freq: R, H, I, N, D Occas: S, K, O ● **Work Env:** Noise=L; Freq: W Occas: O ● **Salary:** 4 ● **Outlook:** 2

SERVICE REPRESENTATIVE (utilities) ● DOT #959.574-010 ● OES: 85998 ● Discontinues or connects service to consumer's establishment, following written or oral instructions: Locates curb cock (valve) at customer's establishment and turns valve to shut off or to permit flow of gas or water, using handtools. Records meter readings [METER READER (utilities; waterworks)]. Investigates consumer complaints of high service cost. Inspects meters, valves, and pipes to detect defects, such as leaks or malfunctioning meters, using testing equipment. Tightens pipe connections to prevent leaks, using wrench. Recommends necessary repairs to consumer. May collect delinquent accounts. May install meters [WATER-METER INSTALLER (waterworks); GAS-METER INSTALLER (utilities)]. ● **GED:** R3, M2, L2 ● **SVP:** 1-3 mos ● **Academic:** Ed=N, Eng=G ● **Work Field:** 014 ● **MPSMS:** 870 ● **Aptitudes:** G3, V4, N4, S4, P3, Q4, K4, F4, M3, E5, C5 ● **Temperaments:** J, T ● **Physical:** Const: R, H Freq: S, N, F, D, V Occas: K, O, I, T, G, A ● **Work Env:** Noise=L; Freq: W Occas: U ● **Salary:** 2 ● **Outlook:** 3

SEWER-LINE REPAIRER, TELE-GROUT (sanitary ser.) ● DOT #851.262-010 ● OES: 83000 ● Operates mobile television and chemical sealing units to conduct internal inspection of sewer lines and to seal defects for prevention of water infiltration: Locates line sections to be inspected, using map, and determines setup procedures. Turns knobs to activate television equipment for video viewing. Adjusts TV camera and monitors controls for optimal clarity and contrast. Locates and identifies infiltration points and sewer defects to determine extent of sewer line damage. Prepares description of each sewer defect, and records pertinent data, including exact location of defect. Photographs screen picture of serious or unusual irregularities, using camera. Determines chemical composition of sealing compound based on type of sealing activity necessary to seal defects, and oversees preparation of compound. Turns control knobs of sealing unit to inflate packer to desired pressure, to air test infiltration point, to determine volume of needed sealing compound, and to pump correct amount of sealing chemicals. Turns air release valve to deflate packer after allowing specified time for sealing compound to set. Communicates with workers, using intercom system, and confers with supervisors to discuss condition of sewer lines, based on television inspection. Services, adjusts, and makes minor repairs to equipment and attachments. Gives directions to workers in efficient and safe use of television and grout, in work methods, and safety precautions. Drives television and grout unit truck. ● **GED:** R4, M3, L2 ● **SVP:** 2-4 yrs ● **Academic:** Ed=N, Eng=N ● **Work Field:** 211, 094 ● **MPSMS:** 364 ● **Aptitudes:** G3, V3, N3, S3, P3, Q4, K4, F3, M3, E5, C4 ● **Temperaments:** D, J ● **Physical:** Stg=L; Freq: C, S, K, O, R, H, I, T, G, N, D, A Occas: F, X ● **Work Env:** Noise=N; Occas: W ● **Salary:** 3 ● **Outlook:** 3

SWIMMING POOL INSTALLER-AND-SERVICER (construction) ● DOT #869.463-010 ● OES: 87898 ● Performs any combination of following tasks in constructing, installing, and servicing swimming pools at commercial and residential sites: Plots length and width of pool site, according to specifications, and marks corners of site, using stakes and sledgehammer. Confers with customer to ensure that pool location and dimensions meet customer's demands. Operates backhoe to dig, shape, and grade walls of in-ground pool. Assembles and aligns wall panel sections, using nuts, bolts, electric air gun, and transit. Pours premixed concrete mixture between dirt wall and wall panels to establish footing (foundation base) to anchor bottoms of wall panels and cross braces. Dumps and spreads gravel into hollow foundation to form drain field, using wheelbarrow, shovel, and rake. Digs trenches, spreads gravel, and lays drain tiles uphill of pool site to divert ground water. Lays out and connects pipelines for water inlets, return valves, and filters, using handtools. Snaps coping section to inside upper edge of wall panels around pool circumference to secure liner edge and protect pool users. Mixes prescribed amounts of cement, sand, and water, and pours mixture into foundation. Spreads and smooths mixture evenly throughout foundation, using trowel, and allows mixture to set. Assembles heater parts, connects gas, oil, or electric lines, and starts heater to verify working order of unit. Installs liner into pool, starts pump to fill pool with water, and installs return valves. Builds concrete deck around pool. Lays out and assembles prefabricated parts of above-ground pool, installs liner, connects plumbing lines, starts pump, and checks pool for leaks. Maintains and repairs pool and equipment, advises customers, and sells chemicals to prevent pool water problems. ● **GED:** R4, M4, L4 ● **SVP:** 4-10 yrs ● **Academic:** Ed=N, Eng=S ● **Work Field:** 007, 102 ● **MPSMS:** 369 ● **Aptitudes:** G3, V3, N3, S3, P2, Q4, K3, F4, M3, E3, C5 ● **Temperaments:** T, V ● **Physical:** Stg=V; Freq: S, K, O, R, H, N, D ● **Work Env:** Noise=N; Freq: W Occas: U ● **Salary:** 4 ● **Outlook:** 3

TAPER (construction) ● DOT #842.664-010 ● OES: 87120 ● Alternate titles: DRY-WALL FINISHER; FINISHER, WALLBOARD AND PLASTERBOARD; SHEETROCK TAPER; TAPER AND BEDDER; TAPER AND FLOATER. Seals joints between plasterboard or other wallboards to prepare wall surface for painting or papering: Mixes sealing compound by hand or with portable electric mixer, and spreads compound over joints between boards, using trowel, broadknife, or spatula. Presses paper tape over joint to embed tape into compound and seal joint, or tapes joint, using mechanical applicator that spreads compound and embeds tape in one operation. Spreads and smooths cementing material over tape, using trowel or floating machine to blend joint with wall surface. Sands rough spots after cement has dried. Fills cracks and holes in walls and ceiling with sealing compound. Installs metal molding at corners in lieu of sealant and tape. Usually works as member of crew. May apply texturing compound and primer to walls and ceiling preparatory to final finishing, using brushes, roller, or spray gun. May countersink nails or screws below surface of wall prior to applying sealing compound, using hammer or screwdriver. ● **GED:** R3, M2, L2 ● **SVP:** 6 mos-1 yr ● **Academic:** Ed=N, Eng=N ● **Work Field:** 102, 143 ● **MPSMS:** 361, 455, 536 ● **Aptitudes:** G3, V4, N4, S4, P3, Q4, K3, F3, M3, E4, C4 ● **Temperaments:** R, T ●

Physical: Stg=M; Const: R, H Freq: N Occas: C, B, S, K, O, W, I, E, T, G, A, X, V ● **Work Env:** Noise=L; Freq: A Occas: D, O ● **Salary:** 1 ● **Outlook:** 3

TEMPLATE MAKER, TRACK (any industry) ● DOT #809.484-014 ● OES: 93998 ● Fabricates and assembles track templates for flame-cutting machines from aluminum bar stock and precut plywood board, using handtools and measuring instruments: Positions and tacks or staples template layout onto specified template board, using hammer or staple gun, or draws specified radial shapes onto board, using compass. Measures and cuts aluminum bars to specified length, using hand shears or saw. Bends bar to contour of template design, using hand roll and handtools. Tacks bent bars to template board along layout lines or pattern, using hammer. Changes track sections of template on flame-cutting machine when used for more than one job. Dismantles track templates and straightens bar for reuse, using straightening roll [STRAIGHTENING-ROLL OPERATOR (any industry)]. ● **GED:** R3, M2, L1 ● **SVP:** 1-3 mos ● **Academic:** Ed=N, Eng=N ● **Work Field:** 102 ● **MPSMS:** 554 ● **Aptitudes:** G3, V4, N4, S3, P4, Q4, K3, F4, M3, E5, C5 ● **Temperaments:** J, T ● **Physical:** Stg=L; Freq: R, H, I, N, D ● **Work Env:** Noise=L; Freq: O ● **Salary:** 3 ● **Outlook:** 2

TORCH-STRAIGHTENER-AND HEATER (any industry) ● DOT #709.684-086 ● OES: 93914 ● Alternate titles: STRAIGHTENER, TORCH. Straightens metal plates, weldments, and structural shapes or preheats them preparatory to welding or bending, using torch: Selects torch tip from data charts according to thickness, area, and temperature of metal to heat. Screws tip on torch and connects hoses from torch to tanks of oxygen and fuel gas, such as acetylene. Turns levers to activate flow of gas, lights flame, and adjusts mixture to obtain desired size and color of flame. Holds or guides flame along surface of workpiece to heat and expand metal, to achieve specified straightness, or until color indicates sufficient heating for welding or machine straightening or bending. Measures workpiece with straightedge or template to ensure conformance with specifications. May hammer out bulges and bends. May place workpiece into heating furnace for specified period of time, using jib of crane. ● **GED:** R3, M2, L2 ● **SVP:** 3-6 mos ● **Academic:** Ed=N, Eng=N ● **Work Field:** 102, 133 ● **MPSMS:** 540, 550 ● **Aptitudes:** G4, V4, N4, S4, P3, Q5, K4, F4, M4, E5, C3 ● **Temperaments:** J, T ● **Physical:** Stg=H; Freq: R, H, N, X Occas: C, S, K, O, I, A ● **Work Env:** Noise=L; Occas: H, A, O ● **Salary:** 3 ● **Outlook:** 2

WATER-SOFTENER SERVICER-AND-INSTALLER (business ser.) ● DOT #862.684-034 ● OES: 87502 ● Installs and services water-softener tanks: Tests water quality for acidity, iron content, and hardness, using test kit. Examines plumbing system to determine connections, pipes, and pipe fittings required. Cuts, threads, and installs pipes, control valves, and couplings, using wrenches, pipe cutters, pipe threaders, and gas soldering equipment. Installs tank and attaches pipes and hoses to tank, fills tank with water, and inspects tank and pipes for leaks or other defects. Connects hoses of portable regenerating equipment to water-softener tank, and operates equipment to regenerate tank with chemicals to restore water-softener qualities at specified time intervals. Replaces sodium chloride in brine holding tank of automatic soft water conditioning system on specified schedule. ● **GED:** R3, M2, L2 ● **SVP:** 3-6 mos ● **Academic:** Ed=N, Eng=S ● **Work Field:** 102 ● **MPSMS:** 969 ● **Aptitudes:** G3, V3, N4, S3, P4, Q4, K3, F3, M3, E5, C5 ● **Temperaments:** T ● **Physical:** Stg=H; Freq: R, H, N, D Occas: S, O, I, A ● **Work Env:** Noise=N; Occas: U ● **Salary:** 4 ● **Outlook:** 3

WELDER, TACK (welding) ● DOT #810.684-010 ● OES: 93914 ● Alternate titles: TACKER. Welds short beads at points specified by layout, welding diagram, or by FITTER (any industry) I 801.261-014, along overlapping edges of metal parts to hold parts in place for final welding. Performs tasks of FITTER HELPER (any industry) 801.687-014. May tack-weld, using hand, submerged, or gas-shielded arc welding equipment. May tack-weld, using portable spotwelding gun [WELDER, GUN (welding) 810.664-010]. ● **GED:** R3, M2, L2 ● **SVP:** 6 mos-1 yr ● **Academic:** Ed=N, Eng=N ● **Work Field:** 081 ● **MPSMS:** 540, 554, 591 ● **Aptitudes:** G3, V4, N4, S4, P4, Q4, K3, F3, M3, E5, C4 ● **Temperaments:** R, T ● **Physical:** Stg=H; Freq: S, O, R, H, G, N, D Occas: C, B, K, W, I, F, X ● **Work Env:** Noise=L; Freq: W, A, E ● **Salary:** 3 ● **Outlook:** 3

GOE: 05.10.02
Mechanical

AUTOMOBILE-ACCESSORIES INSTALLER (automotive ser.) ● DOT #806.684-038 ● OES: 85302 ● Installs automobile accessories, such as heaters, radios, antennas, safety seat belts, seat covers, or special clamps, and mirrors: Drills and taps holes, assembles and fits accessories to automobile, and tightens bolts and clamps. May be designated according to specialty as Radio Installer, Automobile (automotive ser.). ● **GED:** R2, M1, L2 ● **SVP:** 3-6 mos ● **Academic:** Ed=N, Eng=N ● **Work Field:** 102, 121 ● **MPSMS:** 591 ● **Aptitudes:** G3, V4, N4, S3, P3, Q4, K3, F3, M3, E5, C4 ● **Temperaments:** J, T, V ● **Physical:** Stg=M; Freq: S, O, R, H, I, D Occas: W, N, X ● **Work Env:** Noise=N; ● **Salary:** 3 ● **Outlook:** 3

AUTOMOBILE-RADIATOR MECHANIC (automotive ser.) ● DOT #620.381-010 ● OES: 85302 ● Alternate titles: AUTOMOBILE MECHANIC, RADIATOR; RADIATOR REPAIRER. Repairs cooling systems and fuel tanks in automobiles, buses, trucks, and other automotive vehicles: Pumps water or compressed air through radiator to test it for obstructions or leaks. Flushes radiator with cleaning compound to remove obstructions, such as rust or mineral deposits. Removes radiator core from automobile and cleans it, using rods or boiling water and solvent, or combination of boil out and rod out. Solders leaks in core or tanks, using soldering iron or acetylene torch. Disassembles, repairs, or replaces defective water pump. Replaces faulty thermostats and leaky head gaskets. Installs new cores, hoses, and pumps. Cleans, tests, and repairs fuel tanks. ● **GED:** R3, M2, L3 ● **SVP:** 1-2 yrs ● **Academic:** Ed=N, Eng=N ● **Work Field:** 121, 031 ● **MPSMS:** 591 ● **Aptitudes:** G4, V4, N4, S2, P3, Q4, K3, F3, M3, E5, C5 ● **Temperaments:** J, T, V ● **Physical:** Stg=M; Freq: R, H, I, N, D Occas: S, K, O, E, T, G, A ● **Work Env:** Noise=N; Occas: U ● **Salary:** 4 ● **Outlook:** 3

AUTOMOBILE-SERVICE-STATION ATTENDANT (automotive ser.) ● DOT #915.467-010 ● OES: 97805 ● Alternate titles: FILLING-STATION ATTENDANT; GAS-STATION ATTENDANT; GAS TENDER; SERVICE-STATION ATTENDANT. Services automobiles, buses, trucks, and other automotive vehicles with fuel, lubricants, and accessories: Fills fuel tank of vehicles with gasoline or diesel fuel to level specified by customer. Observes level of oil in crankcase and amount of water in radiator, and adds required amounts of oil and water. Adds necessary amount of water to battery, and washes windshield of vehicle. Lubricates vehicle and changes motor oil [LUBRICATION SERVICER (automotive ser.) 915.687-018]. Replaces accessories, such as oil filter, air filter, windshield wiper blades, and fan belt. Installs antifreeze and changes spark plugs. Repairs or replaces tires [TIRE REPAIRER (automotive ser.) 915.684-010]. Replaces lights, and washes and waxes vehicle. Collects cash from customer for purchases and makes change or charges purchases, using customer's credit card. May adjust brakes [BRAKE ADJUSTER (automotive ser.) 620.684-018]. May sell batteries and automobile accessories usually found in service stations. May assist in arranging displays, taking inventories, and making daily reports. ● **GED:** R3, M2, L2 ● **SVP:** 1-3 mos ● **Academic:** Ed=N, Eng=S ● **Work Field:** 292, 014 ● **MPSMS:** 591, 881, 961 ● **Aptitudes:** G3, V3, N3, S4, P3, Q4, K4, F4, M3, E5, C5 ● **Temperaments:** P, V ● **Physical:** Stg=M; Const: T, G, N Freq: R, H, I Occas: S, K, O ● **Work Env:** Noise=L; Freq: W Occas: U, V, O ● **Salary:** 1 ● **Outlook:** 3

BICYCLE REPAIRER (any industry) ● DOT #639.681-010 ● OES: 85951 ● Alternate titles: BICYCLE MECHANIC; CYCLE REPAIRER. Repairs and services bicycles, using power tools and handtools: Tightens and loosens spokes to align wheels. Disassembles axle to repair coaster brakes and to adjust and replace defective parts, using handtools. Adjusts cables or replaces worn or damaged parts to repair handbrakes. Installs and adjusts speed and gear mechanisms. Shapes replacement parts, using bench grinder. Installs, repairs, and replaces equipment or accessories, such as handle bars, stands, lights, and seats. Paints bicycle frame, using spray gun or brush. Rubs tubes with scraper and places patch over hole to repair tube. May weld broken or cracked frame together, using oxyacetylene torch and welding rods. May assemble and sell new bicycles and accessories. ● **GED:** R3, M2, L3 ● **SVP:** 3-6 mos ● **Academic:** Ed=N, Eng=S ● **Work Field:** 121 ●

MPSMS: 595 ● **Aptitudes:** G3, V4, N4, S3, P3, Q4, K3, F3, M3, E5, C3 ● **Temperaments:** R, T ● **Physical:** Stg=M; Freq: R, H, I, N Occas: D, X ● **Work Env:** Noise=N; ● **Salary:** 2 ● **Outlook:** 4

BRAKE REPAIRER (automotive ser.) ● DOT #620.281-026 ● OES: 85302 ● Alternate titles: BRAKE MECHANIC; BRAKE-REPAIR MECHANIC; BRAKESHOE REPAIRER. Repairs and overhauls brake systems in automobiles, buses, trucks, and other automotive vehicles: Pushes handle of hydraulic jack or pushes hoist control to raise vehicle axle. Removes wheels, using wrenches, wheel puller, and sledgehammer. Replaces defective brakeshoe units or attaches new linings to brakeshoes. Measures brakedrum to determine amount of wear, using feeler gauge. Inserts vacuum gauge into power-brake cylinder, starts engine, and reads gauge to detect brake-line leaks. Repairs or replaces leaky brake cylinders. Repairs or replaces defective air compressor in airbrake systems. Replaces wheel on axle and adjusts drumshoe clearance, using wrench. Fills master brake cylinder with brake fluid, pumps brake pedal, or uses pressure tank, and opens valves on hydraulic brake system to bleed air from brake lines. Closes valves and refills master brake cylinder. May be designated according to specialty as Brake Repairer, Air (automotive ser.); Brake Repairer, Bus (automotive ser.); Brake Repairer, Hydraulic (automotive ser.). ● **GED:** R3, M3, L3 ● **SVP:** 1-2 yrs ● **Academic:** Ed=N, Eng=N ● **Work Field:** 121 ● **MPSMS:** 591 ● **Aptitudes:** G3, V3, N3, S3, P3, Q4, K3, F3, M3, E5, C5 ● **Temperaments:** J, T, V ● **Physical:** Stg=M; Freq: R, H, I, N, D Occas: S, K, O, E ● **Work Env:** Noise=L; ● **Salary:** 4 ● **Outlook:** 3

CARBURETOR MECHANIC (automotive ser.) ● DOT #620.281-034 ● OES: 85302 ● Alternate titles: CARBURETOR REPAIRER. Repairs and adjusts motor vehicle carburetors: Disassembles carburetors and gasoline filter units, using handtools. Examines parts for defects and tests needle valves with wire gauges and flowmeter. Cleans parts in solvents to remove dirt and gum deposits. Repairs or replaces defective parts. Reassembles carburetor and gasoline filter, and installs them in vehicle. Starts engine and turns adjustment screw to regulate flow of air and gasoline through carburetor, using testing equipment. May operate drill press, lathe, and other power tools to retap jets, ream throttle bodies and chokes, and machine seating surfaces of carburetor housings. May install and repair mechanical devices that convert conventional systems to use of other fuels [VEHICLE-FUEL-SYSTEMS CONVERTER (automotive ser.)]. ● **GED:** R3, M2, L3 ● **SVP:** 2-4 yrs ● **Academic:** Ed=N, Eng=N ● **Work Field:** 121 ● **MPSMS:** 591 ● **Aptitudes:** G3, V4, N4, S3, P2, Q4, K4, F3, M3, E5, C5 ● **Temperaments:** J, T ● **Physical:** Stg=L; Freq: R, H, I, N Occas: A ● **Work Env:** Noise=N; ● **Salary:** 4 ● **Outlook:** 4

COIN-MACHINE-SERVICE REPAIRER (svc. ind. mach.) ● DOT #639.281-014 ● OES: 85947 ● Alternate titles: VENDING-MACHINE REPAIRER. Installs, services, adjusts, and repairs vending, amusement, and other coin-operated machines placed in establishments on concession basis: Assembles machines following specifications, using handtools and power tools. Fills machines with ingredients or products and tests ice making, refrigeration, carbonation, evaporation, dispensing, electrical, and coin-handling systems. Examines defective machines to determine causes of malfunctions. Adjusts and repairs machines, replacing worn or defective electrical or mechanical parts, using handtools, such as screwdrivers, hammers, and pliers. May collect coins from machine and make settlements with concessionaires. May replenish vending machines with gum, candy, or other articles. May be designated according to type of machine serviced as Juke-Box Servicer (business ser.); Pinball-Machine Repairer (business ser.). ● **GED:** R3, M3, L3 ● **SVP:** 6 mos-1 yr ● **Academic:** Ed=N, Eng=S ● **Work Field:** 111 ● **MPSMS:** 572, 579 ● **Aptitudes:** G3, V4, N3, S2, P2, Q3, K2, F3, M3, E5, C4 ● **Temperaments:** J, T, V ● **Physical:** Stg=M; Freq: S, K, O, R, H, I, N, D, A, X Occas: G ● **Work Env:** Noise=N; Occas: H, U, A, M, E ● **Salary:** 1 ● **Outlook:** 4

CONVEYOR-MAINTENANCE MECHANIC (any industry) ● DOT #630.381-010 ● OES: 85109 ● Repairs and adjusts conveyor systems, using handtools: Installs belts in machinery, tightens bolts, adjusts tension rolls, straightens parts, aligns rollers, and replaces defective parts. May install conveyor systems. ● **GED:** R3, M3, L3 ● **SVP:** 1-2 yrs ● **Academic:** Ed=N, Eng=S ● **Work Field:** 121 ● **MPSMS:** 565 ● **Aptitudes:** G3, V4, N4, S3, P3, Q5, K4, F4, M2, E4, C5 ● **Temperaments:** J, T ● **Physical:** Stg=M; Freq: R, H, N Occas: C, B, S, K, O, I, F, D, A ● **Work Env:** Noise=L; Occas: M, E ● **Salary:** 3 ● **Outlook:** 2

DOOR-CLOSER MECHANIC (any industry) ● DOT #630.381-014 ● OES: 85998 ● Repairs, services, and installs hydraulic door closers, using machines and handtools: Disassembles closers, using handtools and vise. Immerses parts in solution of caustic soda and water to clean parts. Removes encrusted dirt and rust, using electric rotary wire brush and grinding wheel. Replaces worn or broken parts. Fabricates parts, using lathes, drill presses, shaping and milling machines, and precision measuring instruments, such as micrometers, calipers, and scales. Welds cracked closer casings, using acetylene torch. Fills oil chamber and packs spindle with leather washers. Paints finished door closer. ● **GED:** R3, M3, L3 ● **SVP:** 2-4 yrs ● **Academic:** Ed=M, Eng=S ● **Work Field:** 121 ● **MPSMS:** 559 ● **Aptitudes:** G3, V3, N3, S3, P2, Q4, K3, F3, M3, E4, C4 ● **Temperaments:** J, T, V ● **Physical:** Stg=L; Freq: R, H, N Occas: I, D, A, X ● **Work Env:** Noise=L; Occas: U, T ● **Salary:** 3 ● **Outlook:** 2

GAS-APPLIANCE SERVICER (any industry) ● DOT #637.261-018 ● OES: 85710 ● Alternate titles: APPLIANCE SERVICER; CUSTOMER SERVICER. Installs and repairs gas meters, regulators, ranges, heaters, and refrigerators in customer's establishment, using manometer, voltmeter, handtools, and pipe-threading tools: Measures, cuts, and threads pipe and connects it to feeder line and equipment or appliance, using rule, pipe cutter, threader, and wrench. Tests and examines pipelines and equipment to locate leaks and faulty pipe connections and to determine pressure and flow of gas, using manometer, voltmeter, combustible gas indicator, and soap lather. Dismantles meters and regulators, and replaces defective pipes, thermocouples, thermostats, valves, and indicator spindles, using handtools. May assemble new or reconditioned appliances. May collect for monthly bills or overdue payments. May be designated according to appliance serviced as Gas-Refrigerator Servicer (any industry); Gas-Stove Servicer (any industry). ● **GED:** R4, M3, L3 ● **SVP:** 2-4 yrs ● **Academic:** Ed=N, Eng=S ● **Work Field:** 121 ● **MPSMS:** 553, 602 ● **Aptitudes:** G3, V3, N3, S3, P3, Q4, K4, F3, M3, E4, C4 ● **Temperaments:** J, T, V ● **Physical:** Stg=M; Freq: R, H, I, N Occas: C, S, K, O, E, T, D, A, X ● **Work Env:** Noise=N; Occas: W, A ● **Salary:** 2 ● **Outlook:** 2

LUBRICATION-EQUIPMENT SERVICER (any industry) ● DOT #630.381-022 ● OES: 85109 ● Repairs and adjusts hand-or power-operated equipment used to lubricate automobiles, trucks, and industrial equipment, using handtools: Dismantles equipment, such as grease guns, air lines, and lubricating pumps. Examines parts for breaks, wear, and dirt. Replaces defective parts. Cleans and assembles equipment. ● **GED:** R3, M2, L2 ● **SVP:** 1-2 yrs ● **Academic:** Ed=N, Eng=N ● **Work Field:** 121 ● **MPSMS:** 568 ● **Aptitudes:** G3, V4, N4, S3, P3, Q4, K3, F4, M3, E4, C5 ● **Temperaments:** J, T ● **Physical:** Stg=M; Freq: R, H, I, E, N ● **Work Env:** Noise=N; ● **Salary:** 3 ● **Outlook:** 2

MAINTENANCE MECHANIC HELPER (construction) ● DOT #620.664-014 ● OES: 98998 ● Alternate titles: MECHANIC HELPER; SHOP-MECHANIC HELPER. Assists MAINTENANCE MECHANIC (construction; petrol. & gas; pipe lines) in repairing and maintaining automotive and mechanical machinery and equipment, such as pumps, compressors, pipelaying machines, ditch-diggers, trucks, and tractors, using jacks, hoists, and handtools: Installs jacks and hoists to raise equipment. Disassembles and assembles equipment, using handtools. Cleans tools and parts with naphtha, gasoline, and other cleaning compounds. Performs other duties as described under HELPER (any industry) Master Title. ● **GED:** R3, M2, L2 ● **SVP:** 6 mos-1 yr ● **Academic:** Ed=N, Eng=N ● **Work Field:** 121 ● **MPSMS:** 560, 567 ● **Aptitudes:** G3, V4, N4, S3, P3, Q4, K3, F4, M3, E5, C5 ● **Temperaments:** R, T ● **Physical:** Stg=H; Freq: R, H, N Occas: S, K, O, I ● **Work Env:** Noise=N; ● **Salary:** 3 ● **Outlook:** 3

MANAGER, CUSTOMER SERVICES (business ser.) ● DOT #187.167-082 ● OES: 19998 ● Directs and coordinates customer service activities of establishment to install, service, maintain, and repair durable goods, such as machines, equipment, major appliances, or other items sold, leased, or rented with service contract or warranty: Reviews customer requests for service to ascertain cause for service request, type of malfunction, and customer address. Determines staff hours, number of personnel, and parts and equipment required for service call, utilizing knowledge of product, typical malfunctions, and service procedures and practices. Prepares schedules for service personnel, assigns personnel to routes or to specific repair and maintenance work according to workers' knowledge, experience, and repair capabilities on specific types of products. Arranges for transportation

of machines and equipment to customer's location for installation or from customer's location to shop for repairs that cannot be performed on premises. Keeps records of work hours and parts utilized, and work performed for each service call. Requisitions replacement parts and supplies. May contact service personnel over radio-telephone to obtain or give information and directions regarding service or installation activities. ● **GED:** R4, M4, L4 ● **SVP:** 4-10 yrs ● **Academic:** Ed=H, Eng=S ● **Work Field:** 111, 121 ● **MPSMS:** 560, 580, 884 ● **Aptitudes:** G3, V3, N3, S3, P3, Q3, K4, F4, M4, E5, C5 ● **Temperaments:** D, J, P ● **Physical:** Stg=L; Freq: R, H, I, T, G, N Occas: F, D, A, V ● **Work Env:** Noise=L; Occas: U ● **Salary:** 5 ● **Outlook:** 3

MEDICAL-EQUIPMENT REPAIRER (protective dev.) ● DOT #639.281-022 ● OES: 85998 ● Alternate titles: DURABLE MEDICAL EQUIPMENT REPAIRER; WHEELCHAIR REPAIRER. Repairs medical equipment, such as manual or powered wheelchairs, hospital beds, and suction equipment, using knowledge of equipment function and handtools: Test operates and examines malfunctioning equipment to determine cause of malfunction. Disassembles and inspects equipment to locate defective components, such as motors, valves, and electrical controls, using test instruments and handtools. Replaces defective parts, and solders, tightens, and aligns parts which have become loose or out of adjustment, using handtools and soldering iron. Cleans, lubricates, and polishes equipment components to restore surface, using solvent, polish, rags, and grease gun. Test operates unit to ensure equipment functions according to manufacturer's specifications. Occasionally installs modified parts, such as respirator equipment or foot rest, onto wheelchairs, according to customer specification, and fills parts orders from customers. ● **GED:** R3, M2, L3 ● **SVP:** 6 mos-1 yr ● **Academic:** Ed=N, Eng=S ● **Work Field:** 121, 111 ● **MPSMS:** 604 ● **Aptitudes:** G3, V4, N4, S3, P4, Q4, K4, F3, M3, E5, C5 ● **Temperaments:** J, T ● **Physical:** Stg=H; Freq: R, H, I, N, A Occas: S, O ● **Work Env:** Noise=N; Occas: O ● **Salary:** 3 ● **Outlook:** 3

METER REPAIRER (any industry) ● DOT #710.281-034 ● OES: 85998 ● Disassembles, cleans, adjusts, repairs, and tests oil, gas, and water meters, using handtools and testing equipment: Connects meter to testing apparatus. Turns valve to permit specified quantity of oil, gas, or water to pass through meter under varying pressure to test meter for leaks and accuracy of recording. Disassembles meter, removing gear train and disk assembly, using handtools. Removes plant growth, rust, and scale from internal housing and parts, using wire brush, electric buffer, and acid. Repairs or replaces warped or broken disks and gears, and grinds and straightens parts to specified tolerance to fit parts to meter, using grinding machine and hydraulic press. Reassembles and tests meter. Tests large capacity meters in industrial plants to determine accuracy of operation. Records materials used and meters repaired. May install meters [WATER-METER INSTALLER (waterworks)]. May read meters [METER READER (utilities; waterworks)]. ● **GED:** R4, M2, L3 ● **SVP:** 6 mos-1 yr ● **Academic:** Ed=N, Eng=S ● **Work Field:** 121 ● **MPSMS:** 602 ● **Aptitudes:** G3, V3, N3, S3, P3, Q4, K3, F3, M3, E5, C5 ● **Temperaments:** J, T ● **Physical:** Stg=M; Freq: R, H, I, N Occas: S, K, O, D, A ● **Work Env:** Noise=L; Occas: W, U, O ● **Salary:** 3 ● **Outlook:** 3

NEW-CAR GET-READY MECHANIC (automotive ser.) ● DOT #806.361-026 ● OES: 85302 ● Alternate titles: CAR CHECKER; MAKE-READY MECHANIC. Inspects and services new automobiles on delivery to dealer or customer, and makes minor repairs or adjustments to place vehicle in salable condition, using handtools, portable power tools, and specification sheets: Inspects vehicle for obvious damage and missing major components. Records discrepancies and signs acceptance slip for each vehicle delivered. Inspects vehicle for loose or misaligned items, such as trim, doors, and hardware, and positions defective items according to specifications, using handtools. Starts engine and drives automobile to test steering, brakes, transmission, and engine operation. Activates power equipment, such as electric windows, seats, radio, horn, lights, and directional signals to ensure specified operating standards. Washes car and vacuums interior. Inspects surfaces to detect minor chips and scratches in paint and touches up imperfections, using brush applicator and factory-supplied matching paint. Installs optional equipment specified by customer or dealer, such as outside mirrors, rugs, and seat covers, using handtools. Installs standard components, such as hubcaps and wiper blades, using handtools. Pours antifreeze into radiator according to seasonal requirements. Polishes car to remove preservative coating and road film accumulated during transit. May spray undercoating material on vehicle, using spray gun. May tune engine, using mechanic's tools and test equipment. May install or repair major mechanical, hydraulic, or electromechanical equipment, such as radios, air-conditioners, power steering units, and power brakes, using mechanic's handtools. ● **GED:** R3, M2, L2 ● **SVP:** 1-2 yrs ● **Academic:** Ed=N, Eng=N ● **Work Field:** 121, 111, 031 ● **MPSMS:** 591 ● **Aptitudes:** G3, V3, N4, S3, P3, Q4, K3, F4, M3, E3, C4 ● **Temperaments:** J, T ● **Physical:** Stg=M; Freq: R, H, I, N, D Occas: S, K, O, E, T, G, A, X, V ● **Work Env:** Noise=L; Occas: W ● **Salary:** 4 ● **Outlook:** 3

PARKING-METER SERVICER (government ser.) ● DOT #710.384-026 ● OES: 85998 ● Inspects, repairs, and maintains parking meters on designated route: Winds meters according to schedule, adjusts mechanisms, and repairs or replaces worn parts, using handtools. Straightens meter standards, using wrenches, and replaces broken glass. Disassembles meter and cleans and oils parts with gasoline and carbon tetrachloride. Keeps records of machine service histories to facilitate preventive maintenance or replacement of meters. ● **GED:** R3, M2, L2 ● **SVP:** 3-6 mos ● **Academic:** Ed=H, Eng=S ● **Work Field:** 121 ● **MPSMS:** 602 ● **Aptitudes:** G3, V4, N4, S3, P3, Q4, K3, F3, M3, E5, C5 ● **Temperaments:** J, T ● **Physical:** Stg=M; Freq: S, R, H, I, N Occas: O, A ● **Work Env:** Noise=N; Occas: W ● **Salary:** 2 ● **Outlook:** 3

RIDE OPERATOR (amuse. & rec.) ● DOT #342.663-010 ● OES: 68014 ● Alternate titles: AMUSEMENT-EQUIPMENT OPERATOR. Operates or informs patrons how to operate mechanical riding devices furnished by amusement parks, carnivals, or similar places of entertainment: Informs patron to fasten belt, bar, or other safety device. Moves controls to start and stop equipment, such as roller coaster, merry-go-round, and ferris wheel. Gives directions to patrons, usually over microphone, regarding safety and operation of such rides as midget autos and speedboats. Turns on current to permit operation of ride by patron and turns off current after allotted time. Drives vehicles, such as trains, on which persons ride, guiding and controlling their speed. Adds to or removes equipment, according to amount of patronage. Oils, refuels, adjusts, and repairs device. Tests equipment daily before opening ride to patrons. May notify patron of expiration of period for which fee was paid to use device. May observe patrons boarding vehicle to ensure they are safely seated without being overcrowded and safety belts or bars are secure. May collect tickets or cash fares from patrons. May space rides operated in cars or sections to avoid danger of collisions. May be designated according to equipment operated as Auto-Speedway Operator (amuse. & rec.); Ferris-Wheel Operator (amuse. & rec.); Flume-Ride Operator (amuse. & rec.); Merry-Go-Round Operator (amuse. & rec.); Monorail Operator (amuse. & rec.); Railroad Operator (amuse. & rec.); Roller-Coaster Operator (amuse. & rec.); Speedboat Operator (amuse. & rec.); Swing-Ride Operator (amuse. & rec.); Train Operator (amuse. & rec.); Whip Operator (amuse. & rec.). ● **GED:** R2, M2, L2 ● **SVP:** 1-3 mos ● **Academic:** Ed=N, Eng=S ● **Work Field:** 291 ● **MPSMS:** 919 ● **Aptitudes:** G4, V4, N4, S4, P4, Q4, K3, F4, M3, E4, C5 ● **Temperaments:** P, R ● **Physical:** Stg=L; Occas: C, R, H, I, T, G, F, V ● **Work Env:** Noise=L; Occas: M, E ● **Salary:** 1 ● **Outlook:** 3

SERVICE MANAGER (retail trade) ● DOT #185.164-010 ● OES: 81000 ● Coordinates activities of service department in lawnmower sales and service establishment: Directs activities of workers through supervisory staff. Discusses with supervisory staff methods of assembling and repairing lawnmowers to ensure compliance with prescribed procedures. Interviews and hires workers. Maintains time and production records. Answers questions and discusses complaints with customers regarding services as specified in equipment warranty agreement. Assembles and tests operation of new lawnmowers to prepare mowers for sales floor, following assembly and test procedures and using handtools. ● **GED:** R4, M3, L3 ● **SVP:** 2-4 yrs ● **Academic:** Ed=H, Eng=S ● **Work Field:** 121, 295 ● **MPSMS:** 552 ● **Aptitudes:** G3, V3, N3, S3, P3, Q4, K3, F3, M3, E4, C5 ● **Temperaments:** D, P, T, V ● **Physical:** Stg=H; Freq: R, H, T, G, N Occas: S, K, O, I ● **Work Env:** Noise=L; ● **Salary:** 3 ● **Outlook:** 1

SERVICE MANAGER (automotive ser.) ● DOT #185.167-058 ● OES: 81000 ● Coordinates activities of workers in one or more service departments of automotive accessories sales-service establishment: Directs activities of workers, such as TIRE REPAIRER (automotive ser.) and BRAKE REPAIRER (automotive ser.). Assists sales personnel in adjusting customers' service complaints. Hires, transfers, and discharges workers. Directs activities of workers engaged in testing new equipment and recommends purchase or rejection of equipment. Determines work standards and evaluates workers' performance. May handle claims regarding defective factory work quality. May determine need and cost of automobile repair [AUTOMOBILE-REPAIR-SERVICE ESTIMATOR (automotive ser.)]. ● **GED:** R4, M3, L4 ● **SVP:** 1-2 yrs ● **Academic:** Ed=H, Eng=G ● **Work Field:** 111, 121 ● **MPSMS:** 590 ● **Aptitudes:** G2, V2, N3, S4, P4, Q3, K4, F4, M4, E5, C5 ● **Temperaments:** D, J, P, V ● **Physical:** Stg=L; Freq: R, H, I, T, G, N, A ● **Work Env:** Noise=L; ● **Salary:** 4 ● **Outlook:** 2

SEWING-MACHINE REPAIRER (any industry) ● DOT #639.281-018 ● OES: 85109 ● Alternate titles: SEWING-MACHINE ADJUSTER. Repairs and adjusts sewing machines in homes and sewing departments of industrial establishments, using handtools: Turns screws and nuts to adjust machine parts. Regulates length of stroke of needle and horizontal movement of feeding mechanism under needle. Dismantles machines and replaces or repairs broken or worn parts, using handtools. Inspects machines, shafts, and belts. Repairs broken transmission belts. Installs attachments on machines. Initiates orders for new machines or parts. May operate machine tools, such as lathes and drill presses, to make new parts. May be designated according to location in which employed as Fitting-Room Maintenance Mechanic (boot & shoe). ● **GED:** R3, M3, L3 ● **SVP:** 2-4 yrs ● **Academic:** Ed=N, Eng=S ● **Work Field:** 121 ● **MPSMS:** 583 ● **Aptitudes:** G3, V3, N3, S3, P3, Q4, K3, F3, M2, E5, C4 ● **Temperaments:** J, T ● **Physical:** Stg=M; Freq: R, H, I, M, N, D Occas: S, K, O, G, A, X, V ● **Work Env:** Noise=L; Occas: A, O ● **Salary:** 1 ● **Outlook:** 2

THERMOSTAT REPAIRER (inst. & app.) ● DOT #710.381-050 ● OES: 85998 ● Alternate titles: FIELD RETURN REPAIRER; PRODUCTION REPAIRER. Repairs defective thermostats used in refrigeration, air-conditioning, and heating equipment, following blueprints and other specifications: Disassembles and examines thermostats to locate and remove defective parts, using handtools. Replaces defective parts, such as bellows, range spring, and toggle switch, and reassembles thermostat according to blueprint specifications, using cam press and handtools. Measures tolerances of assembled parts, using micrometer and calipers. Repairs leaks in valve seats or bellows of automotive heater thermostats, using soft solder, flux, and acetylene torch. Examines thermostat for defects, such as loose screws and dents. Writes repair ticket to identify thermostat and places repaired thermostats in tote boxes. Calibrates thermostat for specified temperature or pressure settings [CALIBRATOR (inst. & app.) 710.381-034]. ● **GED:** R3, M3, L3 ● **SVP:** 6 mos-1 yr ● **Academic:** Ed=N, Eng=N ● **Work Field:** 121 ● **MPSMS:** 602 ● **Aptitudes:** G3, V3, N4, S3, P3, Q3, K3, F3, M3, E5, C5 ● **Temperaments:** T ● **Physical:** Stg=M; Freq: R, H, I, N, D Occas: E, A ● **Work Env:** Noise=N; ● **Salary:** 2 ● **Outlook:** 3

TRANSMISSION MECHANIC (automotive ser.) ● DOT #620.281-062 ● OES: 85302 ● Repairs manual and automatic transmissions in automobiles, buses, trucks, and other automotive vehicles: Raises automotive vehicle, using jacks or hoists, and removes transmission, using mechanic's handtools. Disassembles transmission unit and replaces broken or worn parts, such as bands, gears, seals, and valves. Adjusts pumps, bands, and gears as required, using wrenches. Installs repaired transmission and fills it with specified fluid. Adjusts operating linkage and tests operation on road. May adjust carburetor. May verify idle speed of motor, using equipment, such as tachometer, making required adjustments. May specialize in repair of automatic transmissions and be designated Automatic-Transmission Mechanic (automotive ser.). ● **GED:** R3, M3, L3 ● **SVP:** 2-4 yrs ● **Academic:** Ed=H, Eng=N ● **Work Field:** 121 ● **MPSMS:** 591 ● **Aptitudes:** G3, V4, N4, S2, P3, Q4, K3, F3, M2, E4, C4 ● **Temperaments:** J, T ● **Physical:** Stg=M; Freq: R, H, I, G, N, D Occas: S, K, O, E, T, A ● **Work Env:** Noise=N; ● **Salary:** 4 ● **Outlook:** 4

GOE: 05.10.03
Electrical-Electronic

APPLIANCE REPAIRER (house. appl.) ● DOT #723.584-010 ● OES: 85710 ● Alternate titles: REPAIRER. Repairs portable, household electrical appliances, such as fans, heaters, vacuum cleaners, toasters, and flatirons, on assembly line: Refers to inspector's checklist, or defect-symbol marked on appliance, to identify defective or malfunctioning part. Disassembles appliance to remove defective part, using power screwdrivers, soldering iron, and handtools. Installs new part, and reassembles appliance. Records nature of repair in log or on mechanical counting device. Maintains stock of replacement parts. May determine repair requirements by connecting appliance to power source or examining parts for defects while disassembling. May file or bend parts to remove burrs or to improve alignment and fit. May hold appliance against buffing or polishing wheel to remove scratches from metal surfaces. May touch up paint defects, using brush or spray gun. May be designated according to part repaired as Heating-Element Repairer (house. appl.); or appliance repaired as Electric-Frying-Pan Repairer (house. appl.); Food-Mixer Repairer (house. appl.); Toaster-Element Repairer (house. appl.); Vacuum-Cleaner Repairer (house. appl.). ● **GED:** R3, M2, L2 ● **SVP:** 1-3 mos ● **Academic:** Ed=N, Eng=N ● **Work Field:** 111 ● **MPSMS:** 583 ● **Aptitudes:** G3, V4, N4, S3, P3, Q4, K3, F4, M3, E5, C4 ● **Temperaments:** J ● **Physical:** Stg=M; Freq: R, H, I, N, X Occas: E, D, A ● **Work Env:** Noise=N; ● **Salary:** 3 ● **Outlook:** 3

AUTOMATIC-DOOR MECHANIC (construction) ● DOT #829.281-010 ● OES: 85998 ● Installs, services, and repairs opening and closing mechanisms of automatic doors used in self-service grocery stores and similar establishments: Bores and cuts holes in flooring, using handtools and power tools. Sets in and secures floor treadle for activating mechanism and connects hydraulic powerpack and electrical panelboard to treadle. Covers treadle with carpeting and screws or nails down chrome strips around edges. Tests system by stepping on treadle. Repairs nonoperating systems, using handtools, blueprints, and schematic diagrams. May install frames and door units, using cutting tools and handtools. May install systems actuated by electronic-eye mechanism. ● **GED:** R3, M2, L2 ● **SVP:** 1-2 yrs ● **Academic:** Ed=N, Eng=N ● **Work Field:** 111 ● **MPSMS:** 580 ● **Aptitudes:** G3, V3, N2, S2, P3, Q4, K3, F3, M3, E4, C5 ● **Temperaments:** J, T, V ● **Physical:** Stg=M; Freq: S, K, O, R, H, I, N Occas: C, B, D, A ● **Work Env:** Noise=N; Occas: W ● **Salary:** 3 ● **Outlook:** 3

CABLE TELEVISION INSTALLER (radio-tv broad.) ● DOT #821.281-010 ● OES: 85702 ● Installs cable television cables and equipment on customer's premise, using electrician's tools and test equipment: Measures television signal strength at utility pole, using electronic test equipment. Computes impedance of wire from pole to house to determine additional resistance needed for reducing signal to desired level. Installs terminal boxes and strings lead-in wires, using electrician's tools. Connects television set to cable system and evaluates incoming signal. Adjusts and repairs cable system to ensure optimum reception. May collect installation fees and explain cable service operation to subscriber. May communicate with COMMUNICATIONS ELECTRICIAN SUPERVISOR (any industry) 823.131-010, using two-way radio or telephone, to receive instructions or technical advice and to report problems to be repaired by CABLE TELEVISION LINE TECHNICIAN (radio-tv broad.) 821.261-010. May report unauthorized use of cable system to COMMUNICATIONS ELECTRICIAN SUPERVISOR (any industry). May clean and maintain tools, test equipment, and motor vehicle. ● **GED:** R4, M4, L3 ● **SVP:** 6 mos-1 yr ● **Academic:** Ed=N, Eng=S ● **Work Field:** 111 ● **MPSMS:** 586, 869 ● **Aptitudes:** G3, V3, N3, S2, P3, Q4, K3, F3, M3, E4, C4 ● **Temperaments:** J, T ● **Physical:** Stg=H; Freq: R, H Occas: C, B, S, K, O, I, G, N, F, D, A, X, V ● **Work Env:** Noise=N; Freq: W, D ● **Salary:** 2 ● **Outlook:** 4

ELECTRIC-GOLF-CART REPAIRER (amuse. & rec.) ● DOT #620.261-026 ● OES: 85720 ● Alternate titles: GOLF-CART MECHANIC. Repairs and maintains electric golf carts at golf course or in automotive repair shop, using handtools and electrical testing devices: Determines type of repairs required by reading work orders, talking to cart operator, or test-driving cart. Tests operational performance of motor, using voltmeter, ammeter, and wattmeter. Dismantles motor and repairs or replaces defective parts, such as brushes, armatures, and commutator, using wrenches, pliers, and screwdrivers. Rewires electrical systems, and repairs or replaces electrical accessories, such as horn and headlights. Tests and recharges or replaces batteries. Lubricates moving parts and adjusts brakes and belts. May perform structural repairs to body of cart, seats, and fabric tops. May record parts used and labor

time on work order. ● **GED:** R3, M2, L3 ● **SVP:** 6 mos-1 yr ● **Academic:** Ed=N, Eng=S ● **Work Field:** 111, 121 ● **MPSMS:** 582 ● **Aptitudes:** G3, V3, N3, S3, P2, Q4, K3, F3, M2, E5, C4 ● **Temperaments:** J, T, V ● **Physical:** Stg=M; Freq: R, H, I, N Occas: S, K, O, D, A, X ● **Work Env:** Noise=N; ● **Salary:** 3 ● **Outlook:** 4

ELECTRIC-TOOL REPAIRER (any industry) ● DOT #729.281-022 ● OES: 85710 ● Alternate titles: POWER-TOOL REPAIRER. Repairs electrical handtools and bench tools, such as drills, saws, grinders, and sanders, using lathe, circuit testers, handtools, and power tools: Tests motors, switches, and wiring for grounds, shorts, and loose connections, using electrical circuit testers. Turns motor commutators, using bench lathe. Repairs or replaces defective electrical parts, using handtools, power tools, and soldering and welding equipment. Inspects parts, such as mechanical gears, bearings, and bushings, for wear and damage, and repairs or replaces parts. ● **GED:** R4, M3, L3 ● **SVP:** 1-2 yrs ● **Academic:** Ed=N, Eng=S ● **Work Field:** 111 ● **MPSMS:** 566, 567 ● **Aptitudes:** G3, V3, N3, S3, P3, Q4, K3, F3, M2, E5, C4 ● **Temperaments:** J, T ● **Physical:** Stg=L; Freq: R, H, I, N Occas: X ● **Work Env:** Noise=N; ● **Salary:** 2 ● **Outlook:** 3

ELECTRICAL-APPLIANCE REPAIRER (any industry) ● DOT #723.381-010 ● OES: 85710 ● Alternate titles: APPLIANCE-SERVICE REPRESENTATIVE; SMALL-APPLIANCE REPAIRER. Repairs electrical appliances, such as toasters, cookers, percolators, lamps, and irons, using handtools and electrical testing instruments: Examines appliance for mechanical defects and disassembles appliance. Tests wiring for broken or short circuits, using voltmeters, ohmmeters, and other circuit testers. Replaces defective wiring and parts, such as toaster elements and percolator coils, using handtools, soldering iron, and spot-welding equipment. May compute charges for labor and materials. May assist ELECTRICAL-APPLIANCE SERVICER (any industry) in repairing such appliances as refrigerators and stoves. ● **GED:** R4, M2, L3 ● **SVP:** 1-2 yrs ● **Academic:** Ed=N, Eng=S ● **Work Field:** 111 ● **MPSMS:** 583 ● **Aptitudes:** G3, V4, N4, S3, P3, Q4, K3, F3, M3, E5, C4 ● **Temperaments:** J, T ● **Physical:** Stg=L; Freq: R, H, I, N, X Occas: D, A ● **Work Env:** Noise=N; ● **Salary:** 4 ● **Outlook:** 4

ELECTRONIC EQUIPMENT REPAIRER (comm. equip.) ● DOT #726.381-014 ● OES: 85514 ● Alternate titles: PRODUCTION REPAIRER. Repairs electronic equipment, such as radio and television receivers, radio transmitters, speakers, amplifiers, and related antenna and cable assemblies, according to product specifications, manufacturing instructions and diagrams, using test equipment, handtools, and soldering iron: Reads inspection tag and examines unit to locate defects, such as broken wires, burned-out components, or scratches on cabinet, using model schematics and electronic test equipment. Inspects wiring and removes broken wires from units, using soldering iron and pliers. Cuts new wires to specified lengths, using wire cutters, or obtains precut wires and re-routes and solders wires to specified terminals, following wiring diagram. Repairs defective soldering, using soldering iron. Removes, repairs, or replaces defective components, such as resistors, transformers, and capacitors, using soldering iron and handtools. May brush touch-up paint on cabinet or case, and varnish on exposed wiring. ● **GED:** R3, M3, L3 ● **SVP:** 1-2 yrs ● **Academic:** Ed=N, Eng=N ● **Work Field:** 111 ● **MPSMS:** 585, 586 ● **Aptitudes:** G3, V3, N3, S3, P3, Q3, K3, F3, M3, E5, C3 ● **Temperaments:** J, T ● **Physical:** Stg=H; Freq: R, H, I, N, D, X Occas: A ● **Work Env:** Noise=N; Occas: E ● **Salary:** 4 ● **Outlook:** 3

LIGHT TECHNICIAN (motion picture) ● DOT #962.362-014 ● OES: 39998 ● Alternate titles: OPERATOR, LIGHTS; SET ELECTRICIAN, ASSISTANT CHIEF. Sets up and controls lighting equipment for television broadcast or motion picture production: Confers with directors and studies script to determine lighting effects required. Sets up spot, flood, incandescent, and mercury vapor lights, reflectors, and other equipment. Switches lights on during broadcast, following script or instructions from directors. Makes minor repairs, such as replacing broken cables on equipment. May lead and give directions to workers while performing same duties. ● **GED:** R4, M2, L3 ● **SVP:** 2-4 yrs ● **Academic:** Ed=A, Eng=S ● **Work Field:** 111 ● **MPSMS:** 864, 911 ● **Aptitudes:** G3, V3, N3, S3, P3, Q4, K3, F3, M3, E5, C3 ● **Temperaments:** J, T ● **Physical:** Stg=L; Freq: I, T, G, X Occas: C, R, H ● **Work Env:** Noise=N; ● **Salary:** 1 ● **Outlook:** 2

SIGHT-EFFECTS SPECIALIST (amuse. & rec.) ● DOT #962.267-010 ● OES: 39998 ● Alternate titles: ELECTRICIAN, MASTER. Provides special stage lighting and sight effects for theatrical performances and directs electrical crew engaged in installing and arranging lighting and wiring equipment: Studies work drawings of stage sets showing light details. Confers with producing personnel and studies continuity script to determine lighting of sets and special sight effects desired. Suggests changes and orders special mechanical stage contrivances to obtain mobile or stationary sight effects, such as forests burning, oceans rolling, or other scenic effects. Attaches stereopticon lens on lamp and operates lamp from rear of stage to project pictures of desired effects on scrim (transparent curtain), following cue sheet. Directs crew in setting up and arranging electrical equipment and lights for use on stage and in theater. May originate designs for artistic lighting of sets. ● **GED:** R4, M3, L3 ● **SVP:** 4-10 yrs ● **Academic:** Ed=N, Eng=S ● **Work Field:** 111 ● **MPSMS:** 912 ● **Aptitudes:** G3, V3, N3, S2, P3, Q3, K4, F4, M4, E5, C3 ● **Temperaments:** D, F, J, P ● **Physical:** Stg=L; Freq: R, H, T, G, N, D, X Occas: I ● **Work Env:** Noise=L; ● **Salary:** 5 ● **Outlook:** 2

SOUND CONTROLLER (amuse. & rec.) ● DOT #194.262-014 ● OES: 35199 ● Operates sound-mixing board to control output of voices, music, and previously taped sound effects during stage performances: Analyzes script of dialog, music, and sound effects as applied to particular scene to determine sound requirements. Confers with producing personnel concerning microphone placement, special sound effects, cues, and acoustical characteristics of theater. Locates sound-mixing board backstage or in theater control room. Arranges microphones in theater to achieve best sound pickup. Moves control to turn microphones on or off and adjusts volume, fader, and mixer controls to blend output of individual microphones. Listens to overall effect on monitor loudspeaker and observes dials on control panel to verify suitability of sounds. May modify design of sound equipment used. May operate record and electrical transcription turntables to supply musical selections and other sound material. ● **GED:** R4, M4, L3 ● **SVP:** 2-4 yrs ● **Academic:** Ed=H, Eng=G ● **Work Field:** 281 ● **MPSMS:** 586 ● **Aptitudes:** G2, V2, N3, S3, P3, Q3, K3, F3, M3, E4, C5 ● **Temperaments:** J ● **Physical:** Stg=L; Freq: R, H, I, T, G, N ● **Work Env:** Noise=L; ● **Salary:** 3 ● **Outlook:** 2

TAPE-RECORDER REPAIRER (any industry) ● DOT #720.281-014 ● OES: 85708 ● Tests, repairs, and adjusts tape-recording machines, following schematic diagrams and manufacturer's specifications, using handtools and electronic testing instruments: Disassembles machine and replaces worn parts, such as sprocket wheels, drive belts, electrical switches, and guide rollers, using handtools. Records voice and listens to playbacks to detect distortion in sound. Tests circuits, using instruments, such as voltmeters, oscilloscopes, audiogenerators, and distortion meters. Replaces defective resistors, condensers, and tubes. Solders loose connections. Tests operation of repaired recorder. ● **GED:** R4, M3, L2 ● **SVP:** 2-4 yrs ● **Academic:** Ed=N, Eng=N ● **Work Field:** 111 ● **MPSMS:** 585 ● **Aptitudes:** G3, V3, N3, S2, P2, Q4, K3, F3, M2, E5, C3 ● **Temperaments:** J, T ● **Physical:** Stg=M; Freq: R, H, I, E, G, N, D, X Occas: A ● **Work Env:** Noise=N; ● **Salary:** 3 ● **Outlook:** 4

TELEVISION-AND-RADIO REPAIRER (any industry) ● DOT #720.281-018 ● OES: 85708 ● Alternate titles: TELEVISION REPAIRER. Repairs and adjusts radios and television receivers, using handtools and electronic testing instruments: Tunes receiver on all channels and observes audio and video characteristics to locate source of trouble. Adjusts controls to obtain desired density, linearity, focus, and size of picture. Examines chassis for defects. Tests voltages and resistances of circuits to isolate defect, following schematic diagram and using voltmeter, oscilloscope, signal generator, and other electronic testing instruments. Tests and changes tubes. Solders loose connections and repairs or replaces defective parts, using handtools and soldering iron. Repairs radios and other audio equipment [RADIO REPAIRER (any industry)]. May install television sets [TELEVISION INSTALLER (any industry)]. ● **GED:** R4, M3, L2 ● **SVP:** 2-4 yrs ● **Academic:** Ed=H, Eng=N ● **Work Field:** 111 ● **MPSMS:** 585 ● **Aptitudes:** G3, V3, N3, S2, P2, Q4, K3, F3, M2, E4, C5 ● **Temperaments:** J, T, V ● **Physical:** Stg=M; Const: R, H Freq: I, N, X Occas: A ● **Work Env:** Noise=N; Occas: E ● **Salary:** 3 ● **Outlook:** 3

TELEVISION INSTALLER (any industry) ● DOT #823.361-010 ● OES: 85708 ● Installs and adjusts television receivers and antennas, using handtools: Selects antenna according to type of set and location of transmitting station. Bolts crossarms and dipole elements in posi-

tion to assemble antenna. Secures antenna in place with bracket and guy wires, observing insurance codes and local ordinances to protect installation from lightning and other hazards. Drills and waterproofs holes in building to make passages for transmission line. Connects line between receiver and antenna and fastens line in place. Tunes receiver on all channels and adjusts screws to obtain desired density, linearity, focus, and size of picture. Orients antenna and installs reflector to obtain optimum signal reception. ● **GED:** R3, M3, L3 ● **SVP:** 1-2 yrs ● **Academic:** Ed=N, Eng=S ● **Work Field:** 111 ● **MPSMS:** 585 ● **Aptitudes:** G3, V3, N4, S3, P3, Q4, K4, F3, M3, E4, C5 ● **Temperaments:** J, R, T ● **Physical:** Stg=M; Freq: S, K, O, R, H, I, N, D Occas: C, B, T, G ● **Work Env:** Noise=N; Freq: W, E ● **Salary:** 2 ● **Outlook:** 2

TRANSFORMER REPAIRER (any industry) ● DOT #724.381-018 ● OES: 85720 ● Alternate titles: TRANSFORMER ASSEMBLER; TRANSFORMER REBUILDER. Cleans and repairs distribution, streetlight, and instrument transformers: Disassembles transformers, using handtools, and opens valve to drain oil. Boils metal transformer case and cover in chemical solution to remove grease, rinses with hose, and dries with cloth to remove dirt and oil. Reassembles transformer, replacing worn or defective parts, using handtools. Solders input and output wires in position and pours compound in transformer-case terminal openings to seal out moisture. Pours oil into transformer until coils are submerged. ● **GED:** R3, M2, L2 ● **SVP:** 2-4 yrs ● **Academic:** Ed=N, Eng=N ● **Work Field:** 111 ● **MPSMS:** 581 ● **Aptitudes:** G3, V3, N3, S3, P3, Q4, K3, F4, M3, E5, C4 ● **Temperaments:** J, T ● **Physical:** Stg=M; Freq: R, H, N Occas: I, D, X ● **Work Env:** Noise=N; ● **Salary:** 4 ● **Outlook:** 3

VACUUM CLEANER REPAIRER (any industry) ● DOT #723.381-014 ● OES: 85710 ● Repairs and adjusts vacuum cleaners, using handtools: Observes ammeter reading and listens to sound of cleaner motor to detect cause of faulty operation. Repairs, adjusts, or replaces defective brushes, belts, fans, control switches, extension cords, electric motors, or other mechanical or electrical parts, using handtools. Lubricates cleaner parts, using grease gun. May sell and demonstrate vacuum cleaners. ● **GED:** R3, M2, L2 ● **SVP:** 1-2 yrs ● **Academic:** Ed=N, Eng=N ● **Work Field:** 111, 121 ● **MPSMS:** 583 ● **Aptitudes:** G3, V3, N3, S3, P3, Q4, K3, F3, M2, E5, C4 ● **Temperaments:** J ● **Physical:** Stg=M; Freq: R, H, I, G, N, D, A Occas: S ● **Work Env:** Noise=N; ● **Salary:** 2 ● **Outlook:** 3

WIRER, CABLE (comm. equip.) ● DOT #729.381-022 ● OES: 93114 ● Installs cables and solders wires to connect electrical instruments mounted on control apparatus, such as panelboards and telephone crossbar frames, according to diagrams and blueprints: Pulls assembled crossbar frame or unit to work area, using monorail chain hoist or handtruck. Ties preformed wiring cable to brackets. Positions arms of cable (groups of wires tied off from trunk of cable) and spreads wires to facilitate wiring. May strip insulation from ends of wires with pliers to prepare for connections. Connects color-coded wires to terminals, using soldering iron or pneumatic wire-wrapping tool. Examines and feels wires to detect loose connections. Writes and ties tickets to wires or terminals in apparatus to identify surplus or missing wires. May secure parts, such as diodes and resistors to specified locations on equipment, using soldering iron or screwdriver. Tapes insulating sleeves over auxiliary lead wires of cable. Pulls or carries wired apparatus to storage area. May be designated according to equipment wired as Crossbar-Frame Wirer (elec. equip.); Crossbar-Unit Wirer (elec. equip.); Switchboard Assembler (comm. equip.). ● **GED:** R3, M2, L2 ● **SVP:** 1-2 yrs ● **Academic:** Ed=N, Eng=N ● **Work Field:** 111 ● **MPSMS:** 586 ● **Aptitudes:** G3, V4, N5, S3, P3, Q4, K3, F3, M3, E5, C4 ● **Temperaments:** J, T ● **Physical:** Stg=M; Freq: R, H, I, N, D, A Occas: E, X ● **Work Env:** Noise=N; ● **Salary:** 2 ● **Outlook:** 3

GOE: 05.10.04
Structural-Mechanical-Electrical-Electronic

AIRPORT ATTENDANT (air trans.) ● DOT #912.364-010 ● OES: 69998 ● Performs any combination of following duties in maintenance of small airports and in servicing aircraft: Periodically inspects buildings and hangars to detect fire hazards and violations of airport regulations. Examines firefighting equipment to detect malfunctions and fills depleted fire extinguishers. Performs necessary minor repairs to fire trucks and tractors. Fills light bombs with kerosene and positions bombs on landing field to illuminate danger areas. Cleans, fills, and lights smokepots used to indicate wind direction, and repairs or replaces windsock and other wind indicating devices. Replaces defective bulbs or burnt-out fuses in lighting equipment, such as landing lights and boundary lights. Fills holes and levels low places and bumps in runways and taxiing areas. Cuts grass on airport grounds [LABORER, AIRPORT MAINTENANCE (air trans.)]. Patrols airfield to ensure security of aircraft and facilities. Verifies and reports specified amount of gasoline and oil supplies. Blocks and stakes down airplanes. Records airport data, such as number of planes stored in hangars, plane landings and departures, and number of passengers carried on planes. May wash and clean cabins and exterior surfaces of airplanes. May fill airplane tanks with gasoline and oil [LINE-SERVICE ATTENDANT (air trans.)]. May be required to possess Red Cross first-aid certificate to render emergency treatment to victims. ● **GED:** R3, M2, L3 ● **SVP:** 6 mos-1 yr ● **Academic:** Ed=N, Eng=S ● **Work Field:** 111 ● **MPSMS:** 855 ● **Aptitudes:** G3, V3, N4, S3, P3, Q3, K3, F4, M3, E4, C4 ● **Temperaments:** J, V ● **Physical:** Stg=M; Freq: R, H Occas: C, B, S, K, O, I, T, G, N, A, X ● **Work Env:** Noise=V; Freq: W ● **Salary:** 3 ● **Outlook:** 3

DOLL REPAIRER (any industry) ● DOT #731.684-014 ● OES: 85998 ● Repairs damaged dolls: Examines doll to determine extent of damage and repairs needed. Disassembles doll to remove damaged parts. Repairs or replaces parts and reassembles doll. Repaints dolls, retouches lips, and cheeks, using paint and brush. Replaces eyelashes and hair, using glue. May package or otherwise prepare repaired doll for shipment or storage. ● **GED:** R2, M1, L1 ● **SVP:** 1-3 mos ● **Academic:** Ed=N, Eng=N ● **Work Field:** 102 ● **MPSMS:** 615 ● **Aptitudes:** G4, V4, N4, S3, P3, Q4, K4, F3, M3, E5, C3 ● **Temperaments:** R, T ● **Physical:** Stg=L; Freq: H, I, N, D, A, X Occas: R ● **Work Env:** Noise=N; ● **Salary:** 3 ● **Outlook:** 2

EQUIPMENT INSTALLER (any industry) ● DOT #828.381-010 ● OES: 85720 ● Installs electronic control panels and related mechanical or electrical equipment, such as motor generator units, battery chargers, utility reels, and darkroom equipment, in panel trucks following blueprint specifications: Measures distances with rule to lay out work in body of truck. Drills holes and bolts metal framework and supports in place, using electric drill and wrenches. Cuts, drills, and fits brackets, supports, covers, and fixtures from metal sheet, strap or bar stock, using metal cutting saws, drill press, grinders, and files. Bolts and screws control panels and assembled operating units to framework. Connects electrical wiring and cables, using electricians' handtools. Installs lighting fixtures, outlets, switches, wall boxes, and terminal boards. ● **GED:** R4, M3, L3 ● **SVP:** 2-4 yrs ● **Academic:** Ed=N, Eng=S ● **Work Field:** 111, 121 ● **MPSMS:** 596 ● **Aptitudes:** G3, V3, N3, S3, P3, Q4, K4, F3, M3, E4, C4 ● **Temperaments:** J, T, V ● **Physical:** Stg=M; Freq: R, H, I, N, D Occas: S, K, O, A, X ● **Work Env:** Noise=N; Freq: W Occas: E ● **Salary:** 3 ● **Outlook:** 3

EVAPORATIVE-COOLER INSTALLER (any industry) ● DOT #637.381-010 ● OES: 85902 ● Repairs and installs cooling units to draw air over moistened pads, using handtools and portable power tools: Disassembles, cleans, and oils parts. Replaces motor bearings, aligns pulleys on motor and blower shafts, and tightens slack in drive belts. Replaces defective wiring. Holds tachometer against revolving centers of blowers and motors to verify specified revolutions per minute. Bolts cooler to window or platform adjacent to window, following layout lines. Cuts and installs plywood or building board to fit vacant window space. Installs electrical outlets and thermostat or humidistat controls. Cuts and connects tubing to cooler and water source. Adjusts rate of water flow. May install cooler on roof and assemble prefabricated sheet metal ducts in attic. ● **GED:** R3, M3, L3 ● **SVP:** 1-2 yrs ● **Academic:** Ed=N, Eng=S ● **Work Field:** 111, 102 ● **MPSMS:** 568 ● **Aptitudes:** G3, V3, N4, S3, P3, Q4, K3, F3, M2, E3, C5 ● **Temperaments:** R, T ● **Physical:** Stg=M; Freq: R, H, I, N Occas: C ● **Work Env:** Noise=N; Occas: W ● **Salary:** 4 ● **Outlook:** 3

FIRE-EXTINGUISHER REPAIRER (any industry) ● DOT #709.384-010 ● OES: 85998 ● Repairs and tests fire extinguishers in repair shops and in establishments, such as factories, homes, garages, and office buildings, using handtools and hydrostatic test equipment: Dismantles extinguisher and examines tubings, horns, head gaskets, cutter discs, and other parts for defects. Replaces worn or damaged parts, using handtools. Cleans extinguishers and recharges them with materials, such as soda water and sulfuric acid, carbon tetrachloride, nitrogen, or patented solutions. Tests extinguishers for conformity with legal specifications, using hydrostatic test equipment. May install cabinets and brackets to hold extinguishers. May sell fire extinguishers. ● **GED:** R3, M2, L2 ● **SVP:** 1-3 mos ● **Academic:** Ed=N, Eng=N ● **Work Field:** 121 ● **MPSMS:** 969 ● **Aptitudes:** G3, V3, N4, S3, P3, Q4, K4, F4, M3, E5, C5 ● **Temperaments:** T ● **Physical:** Stg=M; Freq: R, H, N Occas: S, O, I ● **Work Env:** Noise=N; Occas: A, O ● **Salary:** 1 ● **Outlook:** 3

HOUSEHOLD-APPLIANCE INSTALLER (any industry) ● DOT #827.661-010 ● OES: 85710 ● Installs household appliances, such as refrigerators, washing machines, stoves, and related appliances, in mobile homes or customers' homes, using handtools: Levels refrigerators and adjusts doors. Connects water pipes to washing machines, using plumbing tools. Observes complete cycle of automatic washers and dryers and makes adjustments. Lights and adjusts pilot lights on gas stoves and examines valves and burners for gas leakage and specified flame. May assemble and install prefabricated kitchen cabinets in conjunction with appliances. May stain or finish cabinets. ● **GED:** R3, M3, L3 ● **SVP:** 1-2 yrs ● **Academic:** Ed=N, Eng=S ● **Work Field:** 121 ● **MPSMS:** 583 ● **Aptitudes:** G3, V4, N4, S3, P4, Q4, K3, F4, M3, E4, C4 ● **Temperaments:** R, T ● **Physical:** Stg=H; Freq: R, H, I Occas: C, B, S, K, O, N, X ● **Work Env:** Noise=N; ● **Salary:** 4 ● **Outlook:** 3

HOUSE REPAIRER (construction) ● DOT #869.381-010 ● OES: 87110 ● Repairs and remodels houses and small buildings, according to blueprints or oral instructions: Measures distances and marks reference points on existing structure to lay out work. Removes defective members, existing siding, sheathing, and trim, using pinch bar, portable power saw, hammer, and other carpenter's handtools. Cuts lumber to size and shape, using hand or portable power saw. Nails and screws new framework, sheathing, and trim in place. Fills cracks and other defects in plaster or plasterboard with patching plaster, using trowel. Sands plaster patch after drying to match existing surface. Paints interior and exterior surfaces to specified color and texture. Replaces or installs new electrical fixtures, plumbing hardware, and brickwork, using pliers, screwdrivers, wrenches, and trowel. ● **GED:** R4, M3, L3 ● **SVP:** 2-4 yrs ● **Academic:** Ed=A, Eng=S ● **Work Field:** 102 ● **MPSMS:** 361 ● **Aptitudes:** G3, V3, N3, S3, P2, Q4, K3, F3, M3, E4, C4 ● **Temperaments:** J, T, V ● **Physical:** Stg=M; Freq: C, B, S, K, O, W, R, H, I, E, N, F, D Occas: G, A, X ● **Work Env:** Noise=L; Freq: W, O ● **Salary:** 4 ● **Outlook:** 3

MANAGER, CAMP (construction) ● DOT #187.167-066 ● OES: 15026 ● Directs and coordinates activities of workers concerned with preparing and maintaining buildings and facilities in residential construction or logging camp: Coordinates through subordinate personnel or personally directs workers engaged in preparing and maintaining such camp facilities as dining halls and barracks used by resident laborers. Directs activities of food service workers. Schedules purchase and delivery of food supplies. Enforces safety and sanitation regulations. ● **GED:** R4, M3, L3 ● **SVP:** 1-2 yrs ● **Academic:** Ed=H, Eng=S ● **Work Field:** 291 ● **MPSMS:** 900 ● **Aptitudes:** G3, V3, N3, S3, P3, Q3, K4, F4, M4, E4, C5 ● **Temperaments:** D, J, V ● **Physical:** Stg=L; Freq: T, G, N Occas: R, H, I ● **Work Env:** Noise=L; Occas: W ● **Salary:** 4 ● **Outlook:** 3

PINSETTER MECHANIC, AUTOMATIC (any industry) ● DOT #638.261-022 ● OES: 85998 ● Alternate titles: BOWLING-PIN-MACHINE MECHANIC. Adjusts and repairs automatic pinsetting bowling machines, following maintenance manuals, schematics, and knowledge of equipment, using handtools, power tools, and testing equipment: Observes operation of machine to determine nature and cause of malfunction. Tests relays, solenoids, transformers, electric motors, and wiring for defects, using continuity tester, ammeter, and voltmeter. Disassembles and replaces or repairs mechanical and electrical components or parts, such as bearings, coils, armatures, and wiring, using handtools. Cleans and lubricates machine. Instructs assistants in locating and repairing minor defects. Directs workers or participates in reconditioning and painting bowling pins. Maintains perpetual inventory of and orders replacements for spare parts. ● **GED:** R3, M2, L2 ● **SVP:** 3-6 mos ● **Academic:** Ed=N, Eng=N ● **Work Field:** 111,

121 ● **MPSMS:** 616 ● **Aptitudes:** G3, V3, N4, S3, P3, Q4, K3, F3, M3, E4, C4 ● **Temperaments:** J, T, V ● **Physical:** Stg=M; Freq: C, B, S, K, O, R, H, I Occas: T, G, N, F, X ● **Work Env:** Noise=N; ● **Salary:** 3 ● **Outlook:** 3

SPORTS-EQUIPMENT REPAIRER (any industry) ● DOT #732.684-122 ● OES: 85998 ● Repairs and replaces sporting and athletic equipment, such as fishing tackle, tennis rackets, or archery equipment: Restrings tennis rackets with animal gut or synthetic string. Replaces defective parts of fishing tackle, such as reels and rods. Replaces metal points on arrow shafts. Refinishes surfaces of sporting and athletic equipment with lacquer or paint. May carve wooden parts for sporting and athletic equipment, using handtools and powered woodworking tools. May make new gun stocks and pistol grips. May reglue and rewind bamboo sections of fly rods. May rewind shafts of bows and arrows. May be designated according to type of sporting or athletic equipment repaired as Archery-Equipment Repairer (any industry); Fishing-Tackle Repairer (any industry); Football-Pad Repairer (any industry); Tennis-Racket Repairer (any industry). ● **GED:** R3, M2, L2 ● **SVP:** 3-6 mos ● **Academic:** Ed=N, Eng=N ● **Work Field:** 102 ● **MPSMS:** 616 ● **Aptitudes:** G3, V4, N4, S3, P3, Q4, K3, F3, M3, E5, C5 ● **Temperaments:** R, T ● **Physical:** Stg=L; Freq: H, I, N, D, A Occas: R, E ● **Work Env:** Noise=N; ● **Salary:** 3 ● **Outlook:** 3

STAGE TECHNICIAN (amuse. & rec.) ● DOT #962.261-014 ● OES: 39998 ● Installs rigging, lighting, sound equipment, and scenery, and erects stages for theatrical, musical, and other entertainment events in arenas, stadiums, theaters, studios, and other amusement places: Reads stage layout specifications and blueprints and confers with MANAGER, STAGE (amuse. & rec.) 159.167-018 to determine type and location of sets, props, scenery, lighting, and sound equipment required for specific event. Assembles props provided by production company, constructs additional props, scenery, or stages, and attaches braces that support scenery frames in upright position, using carpenter's handtools and power tools. Climbs ladder or scaffolding to ceiling grid, crawls and balances on beams, inserts ends of cables or ropes through ceiling grid, and attaches cables to scenery, curtains, equipment, support pipes, and counterbalance weights [GRIP (amuse. & rec.; radio-tv broad.) 962.684-014]. Positions lighting fixtures on and around stage area, clamps light fixtures to supports, connects electrical wiring from fixtures to power source and control panel [LIGHTING-EQUIPMENT OPERATOR (amuse. & rec.) 962.381-014], positions sound equipment, such as microphones, speakers, and amplifiers, on and around stage area, and connects electrical lines to power source and mixing console [PUBLIC-ADDRESS SERVICER (any industry) 823.261-010], utilizing knowledge of electrical codes and use of electrician's handtools and power tools. Pulls cables that raise and lower scenery, curtains, and equipment [FLYER (amuse. & rec.; radio-tv broad.) 962.687-018] and operates lighting and sound equipment during rehearsals and performances, following audio or visual cues. ● **GED:** R4, M3, L4 ● **SVP:** 2-4 yrs ● **Academic:** Ed=N, Eng=S ● **Work Field:** 111, 102 ● **MPSMS:** 919 ● **Aptitudes:** G2, V3, N3, S2, P3, Q3, K2, F3, M3, E2, C4 ● **Temperaments:** J, T, V ● **Physical:** Stg=H; Freq: R, H, I Occas: C, B, S, K, O, W, T, G, N, F, D, A, X ● **Work Env:** Noise=L; Occas: D ● **Salary:** 4 ● **Outlook:** 2

SWIMMING-POOL SERVICER (any industry) ● DOT #891.684-018 ● OES: 85998 ● Alternate titles: MAINTENANCE WORKER, SWIMMING POOL; POOL SERVICER. Cleans, adjusts, and performs minor repairs to swimming pools and auxiliary equipment: Removes leaves and other debris from surface of water, using net. Cleans bottom and sides of pool, using such aids as underwater vacuum cleaner, hose, brush, detergent, acid solution, and sander. Inspects and replaces loose or damaged tile. Cleans and repairs filter system. Adjusts and performs minor repairs to heating and pumping equipment, using mechanic's handtools. Dumps chemicals, in prescribed amounts, to purify water in pool. Prepares service report of materials used and work performed. ● **GED:** R3, M1, L2 ● **SVP:** 3-6 mos ● **Academic:** Ed=N, Eng=S ● **Work Field:** 031, 121 ● **MPSMS:** 369, 568 ● **Aptitudes:** G3, V4, N4, S3, P3, Q4, K3, F4, M3, E4, C4 ● **Temperaments:** R, T ● **Physical:** Stg=M; Freq: S, K, O, R, H, I, N, D Occas: C, X ● **Work Env:** Noise=N; Freq: W, U ● **Salary:** 3 ● **Outlook:** 3

USED-CAR RENOVATOR (retail trade) ● DOT #620.684-034 ● OES: 85305 ● Alternate titles: USED-CAR CONDITIONER. Renovates used cars for resale at used car lot: Inspects cars for noticeable defects, such as dents, scratches, torn upholstery, and poor mechanical

operation. Hammers out dents. Polishes scratches and retouches with enamel. Sews rips and tears in upholstery. Cleans and vacuums interiors. Washes and polishes exteriors. Replaces missing or defective small parts. Performs minor mechanical repairs and adjustments. May inspect cars for compliance with state safety regulations. ● **GED:** R3, M2, L2 ● **SVP:** 3-6 mos ● **Academic:** Ed=N, Eng=N ● **Work Field:** 121 ● **MPSMS:** 591 ● **Aptitudes:** G3, V4, N4, S3, P3, Q4, K4, F3, M3, E4, C4 ● **Temperaments:** J, T, V ● **Physical:** Stg=M; Freq: R, H, I, N Occas: S, O, A, X ● **Work Env:** Noise=N; Freq: W ● **Salary:** 4 ● **Outlook:** 3

WIND TUNNEL MECHANIC (aircraft mfg.) ● DOT #869.261-026 ● OES: 35199 ● Constructs, modifies, maintains, and services wind and propulsion tunnel research facilities used to test models of aircraft components, utilizing knowledge of engineering test methods and procedures, using handtools, power tools, machines, and equipment: Installs and aligns mechanical, hydraulic, and pneumatic test equipment and models on support structures, using handtools, power tools, and precision instruments. Installs instrumentation, such as thermocouples and pressure taps, on model and test equipment. Inspects test setup and operates equipment to detect and correct malfunctions. Maintains instrumentation equipment and accessories, such as pressure valves, icing indicators, drive units, spray units, and pumps. Confers with engineering and other personnel during testing and modifies model, test support structure, or test equipment as directed. ● **GED:** R4, M4, L4 ● **SVP:** 2-4 yrs ● **Academic:** Ed=H, Eng=G ● **Work Field:** 102, 121, 244 ● **MPSMS:** 601, 602 ● **Aptitudes:** G2, V3, N2, S2, P3, Q4, K3, F3, M3, E4, C4 ● **Temperaments:** J, T, V ● **Physical:** Stg=M; Freq: R, H, I, N Occas: C, B, S, K, O, W, E, T, G, D, A, X ● **Work Env:** Noise=V; Occas: A, M, E, D ● **Salary:** 5 ● **Outlook:** 3

GOE: 05.10.05
Reproduction

AUDIO OPERATOR (radio-tv broad.) ● DOT #194.262-010 ● OES: 34028 ● Alternate titles: AUDIO ENGINEER; AUDIO TECHNICIAN; SOUND ENGINEER, AUDIO CONTROL. Controls audio equipment to regulate volume level and quality of sound during television broadcasts, according to script and instructions of DIRECTOR, TECHNICAL (radio-tv broad.) 962.162-010: Places microphones or directs worker in placing microphones in locations that ensure quality of sound reproduction. Cuts microphones in, and blends output of individual microphones by adjusting volume, fader, and mixer controls. Monitors audio signals by earphone, loudspeaker, and by observing dials on control panel to verify quality of sound reproduction. Sets keys, switches, and dials to synchronize sound with picture presentation. Obtains tapes, records, and themes from library according to program schedule. Operates turntables and tape recording machines to reproduce music and audio sounds for specific programs. May direct adjustment of acoustical curtains and blinds within studio. ● **GED:** R4, M4, L3 ● **SVP:** 2-4 yrs ● **Academic:** Ed=H, Eng=S ● **Work Field:** 281 ● **MPSMS:** 864 ● **Aptitudes:** G3, V3, N3, S3, P3, Q4, K2, F3, M3, E5, C5 ● **Temperaments:** J, T ● **Physical:** Stg=L; Freq: I, G, N Occas: R, H, T ● **Work Env:** Noise=N; ● **Salary:** 3 ● **Outlook:** 3

AUDIOVISUAL TECHNICIAN (any industry) ● DOT #960.382-010 ● OES: 92905 ● Alternate titles: AUDIOVISUAL-EQUIPMENT OPERATOR; PROJECTIONIST. Operates audiovisual or sound-reproducing equipment to provide or complement educational or public service programs offered by institutions, such as museums, zoos, or libraries: Operates motion picture projecting equipment to show films in auditorium or lecture hall for entertainment or enlightenment of visitors to institution. Operates film, slide, video, audio tape, or turntable equipment to project or produce still or moving pictures, background music, oral commentary, or sound effects to illustrate, clarify, or enhance impact of presentation by TEACHER (museums) 099.227-038. Coordinates equipment operation with material presented, according to notations in script or instructions of speaker. Maintains equipment in working condition. Makes minor adjustments and repairs to equipment, and notifies maintenance personnel when correction of major malfunction is required. Positions, installs, and connects equipment, such as microphones, amplifiers, and lights. ● **GED:** R4, M3, L3 ● **SVP:** 1-3 mos ● **Academic:** Ed=A, Eng=G ● **Work Field:** 281 ●

MPSMS: 939, 910 ● **Aptitudes:** G3, V3, N4, S3, P3, Q4, K3, F3, M3, E5, C4 ● **Temperaments:** J, T ● **Physical:** Stg=M; Freq: R, H, I, G, N Occas: S, O, F, X ● **Work Env:** Noise=N; ● **Salary:** 1 ● **Outlook:** 3

COLOR-PRINTER OPERATOR (photofinishing) ● DOT #976.382-014 ● OES: 92908 ● Controls equipment to produce color prints from negatives: Reads customer instructions to determine processing requirement. Loads roll or magazine of printing paper into color printing equipment. Examines color negative to determine equipment control settings for production of prints meeting acceptable color-fidelity standards. Sets controls in accordance with examination, loads negative into machine, and starts machine to produce specified number of prints. Removes printed photographic paper from machine and places paper in film bag for further processing or in developing machine. Inspects finished prints for defects, such as dust and smudges, and removes defects, using brush, cloth, and cleaning fluid. Inserts processed negatives and prints into envelope for return to customer. ● **GED:** R3, M2, L2 ● **SVP:** 1-3 mos ● **Academic:** Ed=N, Eng=N ● **Work Field:** 202 ● **MPSMS:** 897 ● **Aptitudes:** G3, V3, N3, S3, P3, Q4, K4, F4, M3, E5, C2 ● **Temperaments:** J, T ● **Physical:** Stg=L; Const: R, H, I Freq: N, D, A, X Occas: T, G ● **Work Env:** Noise=N; ● **Salary:** 2 ● **Outlook:** 4

CONTACT WORKER, LITHOGRAPHY (print. & pub.) ● DOT #976.684-038 ● OES: 92908 ● Combines multiple photographic film images onto single film to assist in film assembly (stripping) process for lithographic printing: Aligns negative or positive film image over unexposed film (duplicating or contact) and places film assembly into or on top of vacuum frame. Lowers top of frame or places vinyl sheeting over film and activates vacuum to maintain contact between original and unexposed film. Sets time controls and activates high intensity light source that exposes film to specified amount of time and light. Removes negative or positive and places exposed film in automatic processor that develops image on film. ● **GED:** R3, M2, L2 ● **SVP:** 1-2 yrs ● **Academic:** Ed=N, Eng=N ● **Work Field:** 201, 202 ● **MPSMS:** 753 ● **Aptitudes:** G3, V3, N4, S3, P3, Q3, K3, F3, M3, E5, C5 ● **Temperaments:** R, T ● **Physical:** Stg=L; Freq: R, H, N Occas: I, G, A ● **Work Env:** Noise=L; Freq: R ● **Salary:** 2 ● **Outlook:** 3

DEVELOPER (photofinishing) ● DOT #976.681-010 ● OES: 89914 ● Alternate titles: DARKROOM WORKER; DOPER; HAND DEVELOPER. Develops exposed photographic film or sensitized paper in series of chemical and water baths to produce negative or positive prints: Mixes developing and fixing solutions, following formula. Immerses exposed film or photographic paper in developer solution to bring out latent image. Immerses negative or paper in stop-bath to arrest developer action, in hyposolution to fix image, and in water to remove chemicals. Dries prints or negatives, using sponge or squeegee, or places them in mechanical air drier. May produce color photographs, negatives, and slides, using color reproduction processes, and be designated Color-Laboratory Technician (photofinishing). May perform duties as described under GROUP LEADER (any industry). ● **GED:** R3, M2, L2 ● **SVP:** 3-6 mos ● **Academic:** Ed=N, Eng=N ● **Work Field:** 202 ● **MPSMS:** 897 ● **Aptitudes:** G3, V4, N3, S3, P3, Q4, K3, F3, M3, E5, C4 ● **Temperaments:** J ● **Physical:** Stg=L; Freq: S, R, H, I, E, N, D, A, X ● **Work Env:** Noise=N; Freq: U Occas: A, O ● **Salary:** 3 ● **Outlook:** 4

DUPLICATING-MACHINE OPERATOR I (clerical) ● DOT #207.682-010 ● OES: 56200 ● Operates machine to reproduce data or ruled forms on paper from type in flat impression bed or plates on revolving cylinder: Selects type or embossed plate and positions type or plate on cylinder or flat bed of machine. Loads paper in feed tray and makes adjustments to parts, such as inking rolls or ribbon and feeding mechanism. Starts machine which automatically pushes sheets under revolving cylinder or against flat impression bed of type where paper is printed. May keep record of number of copies made. Important variations may be indicated by trade name of machines used. ● **GED:** R3, M2, L1 ● **SVP:** 3-6 mos ● **Academic:** Ed=N, Eng=N ● **Work Field:** 191 ● **MPSMS:** 891 ● **Aptitudes:** G3, V3, N4, S3, P3, Q3, K3, F3, M3, E5, C5 ● **Temperaments:** J, T ● **Physical:** Stg=L; Freq: R, H Occas: N ● **Work Env:** Noise=L; ● **Salary:** 2 ● **Outlook:** 2

ENGRAVER, MACHINE (print. & pub.) ● DOT #979.382-014 ● OES: 92599 ● Sets up and operates engraving machine to transfer designs from mills to copper printing rollers used in color-printing cloth: Lifts printing roller into position on machine with aid of another worker. Places truing I roller in fixture on head of machine and lowers machine

head until truing roller rests on surface of printing roller. Starts machine to rotate truing roller against printing roller and turns setscrews until truing roller rotates without horizontal motion to align head of machine with printing roller. Divides register wheel on machine into divisions, according to number of times design is to be repeated around printing roller, and marks divisions on wheel, using chalk. Inserts stud in specified slot on register wheel, replaces truing roller with mill, and moves pitch finger against stop on head of machine to set mill in register for engraving. Lowers mill to surface of printing roller, releases catch on weight lever to apply pressure on mill, and rotates mill one revolution to transfer one repeat of pattern to roller. Repeats procedure until design has been repeated around circumference of printing roller. Examines impression of design on roller to detect repeats of pattern that are out of register. Replaces mill with burnishing roller and works burnishing roller against printing roller to erase defective impressions. Increases pressure on mill if design is in register and starts machine that works mill against printing roller to increase depth of impression. Measures depth of engraving, using depth gauge. Measures width of embossed design on mill, using divider, and converts measurement into number of teeth on side-shift gear, using conversion tables. Releases pressure on mill and turns gear specified number of teeth to move mill into position for engraving design adjacent to first impression and repeats procedure as above until design has been engraved across length of roller. Engages dog in teeth of gear and pitches design in register. Repeats procedure until design has been engraved across length of roller. Mounts engraved roller on mandrel of polishing lathe and operates lathe to remove burrs and smooth roller [PRINTING-ROLLER POLISHER (machine shop)]. ● **GED:** R4, M2, L2 ● **SVP:** 4-10 yrs ● **Academic:** Ed=H, Eng=S ● **Work Field:** 192 ● **MPSMS:** 567 ● **Aptitudes:** G3, V3, N3, S2, P2, Q5, K3, F3, M3, E4, C5 ● **Temperaments:** J, T ● **Physical:** Stg=V; Freq: R, H, I, N, D, A Occas: S, O ● **Work Env:** Noise=L; ● **Salary:** 5 ● **Outlook:** 2

ENGRAVER, MACHINE I (engraving) ● DOT #704.682-010 ● OES: 93998 ● Operates pantograph engraving machine to engrave letters and figures on products, such as badges, fraternal emblems, pendants, and thermometers: Inserts specified letters and figures into pattern frame. Positions and secures workpiece in machine holding fixture and sets stylus at beginning of pattern. Depresses pedal to lower cutting tool onto workpiece. Engraves designs on workpiece by moving stylus around pattern, causing cutting tool to duplicate motion on workpiece. Removes workpiece and places in tray. ● **GED:** R3, M2, L2 ● **SVP:** 1-3 mos ● **Academic:** Ed=N, Eng=N ● **Work Field:** 183 ● **MPSMS:** 610, 556 ● **Aptitudes:** G4, V4, N4, S4, P3, Q4, K3, F3, M3, E5, C5 ● **Temperaments:** R ● **Physical:** Stg=S; Freq: R, H, I, N Occas: T, G, A ● **Work Env:** Noise=N; ● **Salary:** 2 ● **Outlook:** 2

ENGRAVING-PRESS OPERATOR (print. & pub.) ● DOT #651.382-010 ● OES: 92519 ● Alternate titles: DIE-STAMPING-PRESS OPERATOR. Makes ready and operates press to engrave decorative designs or lettering on announcements, greeting and business cards, letterheads, and related items, following operating procedures outlined on job order: Installs appropriate die and inking rollers on ram, using wrench. Cuts out and fastens paper template to bed of press to maintain flatness of finished cards or sheets. Inserts and adjusts roll of wiping paper that automatically cleans die between impressions. Thins ink to desired consistency and fills ink fountain. Starts press to obtain proof copy. Examines proof and adjusts press and ink fountain to obtain uniform indentation and color registration. Starts press and feeds cards or sheets to be engraved onto bed of press. ● **GED:** R4, M2, L3 ● **SVP:** 2-4 yrs ● **Academic:** Ed=N, Eng=S ● **Work Field:** 192 ● **MPSMS:** 567 ● **Aptitudes:** G3, V3, N4, S3, P3, Q3, K3, F3, M3, E4, C3 ● **Temperaments:** J, R, T ● **Physical:** Stg=L; Freq: R, H, I, N, X Occas: D, A ● **Work Env:** Noise=N; Occas: O ● **Salary:** 2 ● **Outlook:** 2

EQUIPMENT MONITOR, PHOTOTYPESETTING (print. & pub.) ● DOT #650.682-010 ● OES: 92541 ● Monitors and controls electronic computer system used in phototypesetting: Sets control switches on optical character reader, computer, or phototypesetter. Inserts command codes to integrate and operate equipment according to data requirements specified in mark-up instructions. Selects and loads input and output units with materials for operating equipment. Moves switches to clear system and start operation of equipment. Observes equipment and control panels on consoles for error lights, messages, and machine stoppage or faulty output. Notifies superior of errors or equipment stoppage. ● **GED:** R3, M1, L2 ● **SVP:** 3-6 mos ● **Academic:** Ed=N, Eng=N

● **Work Field:** 191 ● **MPSMS:** 567 ● **Aptitudes:** G3, V4, N4, S4, P4, Q3, K3, F3, M4, E5, C5 ● **Temperaments:** J, T ● **Physical:** Stg=L; Freq: R, H, I, N ● **Work Env:** Noise=N; ● **Salary:** 2 ● **Outlook:** 2

FILM DEVELOPER (motion picture) ● DOT #976.382-018 ● OES: 92908 ● Alternate titles: DEVELOPER OPERATOR. Operates machine to develop still or motion-picture film: Pulls reel of motion-picture film or rack of film strips through trapdoor into darkroom. Examines film to determine type processing required, utilizing knowledge of film developing techniques. Feels edges of film to detect tears and repairs film, using hand stapler. Mounts film in guide slot of developing machine according to length of time required for processing and pulls lever to lower film into processing position. Flips switch to start machine that transports film through series of solutions and into drying cabinet to develop and dry film. Observes film passing through machine to determine density of image and adjusts machine controls to shorten or lengthen path of film through solutions according to observation. May be designated according to type film developed as Negative Developer (motion picture; photofinishing); Positive Developer (motion picture; photofinishing). ● **GED:** R3, M1, L1 ● **SVP:** 1-2 yrs ● **Academic:** Ed=N, Eng=N ● **Work Field:** 202 ● **MPSMS:** 911, 897 ● **Aptitudes:** G3, V4, N4, S4, P3, Q4, K3, F3, M3, E5, C5 ● **Temperaments:** J, T ● **Physical:** Stg=L; Freq: R, H, I, E, N, D ● **Work Env:** Noise=L; Freq: O Occas: U ● **Salary:** 3 ● **Outlook:** 4

FILM INSPECTOR (photofinishing) ● DOT #976.362-010 ● OES: 83000 ● Alternate titles: QUALITY-CONTROL PROJECTIONIST; REEL-FILM INSPECTOR. Operates motion picture projector to inspect home movie film and visually examines slides for defects to determine need for reprocessing and repair: Randomly selects specified number of home movie reels and inserts reels in magazine of projector. Threads film through projector onto take-up reel. Starts projector and adjusts lens to focus image on screen. Examines projected image to detect defective exposure or color density and presence of scratches or foreign matter. Records findings on quality control sheet and notifies processing department personnel regarding need for machine adjustments or customer regarding defective camera lens. Measures width of film to determine accuracy of slitting, using precision measuring instrument, and notifies slitting department personnel when width is not within specified tolerances. Examines specified number of randomly selected photographic slides to detect scratches or defects in color density, accuracy, and exposure. Records type defect and reprocessing required on quality control form and routes form and defective slides to processing department. Conveys acceptable reels and slides to packaging department. Collects daily reports from production personnel, totals production figures, and calculates production averages to determine whether quotas have been met. ● **GED:** R4, M2, L2 ● **SVP:** 6 mos-1 yr ● **Academic:** Ed=N, Eng=N ● **Work Field:** 212 ● **MPSMS:** 897 ● **Aptitudes:** G3, V3, N3, S3, P2, Q3, K3, F3, M3, E5, C2 ● **Temperaments:** J ● **Physical:** Stg=L; Freq: R, H, I, E, N, F, D, A, X Occas: T, G ● **Work Env:** Noise=N; ● **Salary:** 3 ● **Outlook:** 3

FILM LABORATORY TECHNICIAN (motion picture) ● DOT #976.684-014 ● OES: 92908 ● Performs any combination of following tasks to process motion picture film: Mixes specified chemicals according to formula to prepare solutions for use in processing film. Cuts and arranges film and splices film together according to written instructions or edited test print, using splicer. Compares film with edited print to detect irregularities in detail and color. Projects film on screen to detect defects in printing and developing, such as blurs, scratches, and perforations, using motion picture projector. Approves film for release, rejects defective film, or routes film to specified department for further processing. May be designated according to specialty as Film Inspector (motion picture); Film Splicer (motion picture). ● **GED:** R3, M2, L2 ● **SVP:** 1-3 mos ● **Academic:** Ed=N, Eng=N ● **Work Field:** 054, 062, 143 ● **MPSMS:** 911 ● **Aptitudes:** G3, V4, N4, S4, P3, Q4, K4, F3, M3, E5, C4 ● **Temperaments:** J ● **Physical:** Stg=L; Freq: R, H, I, N, F, D, A, X ● **Work Env:** Noise=N; Occas: O ● **Salary:** 3 ● **Outlook:** 2

INSTANT PRINT OPERATOR (print. & pub.) ● DOT #979.362-010 ● OES: 92542 ● Alternate titles: OFFSET-DUPLICATING MACHINE OPERATOR, INSTANT PRINT; PRESS OPERATOR, INSTANT PRINT SHOP; QUICK PRINT OPERATOR. Operates offset-duplicating machine, photocopier, and related machines and equipment to produce copies of original materials for customers in instant print shop: Accepts printing orders from customers and computes and quotes prices to customers. Reads job orders to determine quantity of materials to be printed, and stock and ink specifications. Adjusts settings and operates camera plate maker to produce plastic or paper plates for use in offset duplicating. Operates offset duplicating machine to reproduce single or multicolor copies of text, drawings, graphs, or similar materials [OFFSET-DUPLICATING-MACHINE OPERATOR (print. & pub.) 651.682-014]. Operates copier to produce photocopies of single color or small run jobs [PHOTOCOPYING-MACHINE OPERATOR (clerical) 207.685-014]. Examines proof copy to assure accurate reproduction of color, centering of print, and conformance of copy to layout specifications. Operates auxiliary machines such as collator, pad and tablet making machine, stapler, and paper punching, folding, cutting, and perforating machines to assemble materials. May operate computerized typesetting machine to set type for printing. May assemble typeset copy and artwork into pasteup for printing reproduction. May receive payment from customers and box or wrap printed materials. ● **GED:** R3, M2, L3 ● **SVP:** 1-2 yrs ● **Academic:** Ed=N, Eng=S ● **Work Field:** 191, 201 ● **MPSMS:** 480, 897 ● **Aptitudes:** G3, V3, N3, S3, P3, Q3, K3, F3, M3, E5, C4 ● **Temperaments:** P, T, V ● **Physical:** Stg=M; Freq: R, H Occas: S, I, T, G, N, A, X ● **Work Env:** Noise=L; Freq: V, A, M ● **Salary:** 3 ● **Outlook:** 4

MICROFILM PROCESSOR (business ser.) ● DOT #976.385-010 ● OES: 92908 ● Tends machine that automatically processes microfilm and examines processed film to ensure that quality of microfiche meets established standards: Loads film into magazine of camera under darkroom conditions, attaches magazine to camera, and splices end of film to leader in machine to facilitate threading film, using splicing tape. Flips switches and turns valves to activate machine components and functions, such as blower, squeegee, water flow into processor, and rate of processing chemical replenishment. Monitors machine warning lights to detect processing malfunctions, such as break in film or leader, and takes action to correct malfunction, using knowledge of machine operation. Records film processing information, such as film type, developing speed, and rate of chemical replenishment to maintain film log. Examines processed film to ensure numerical order and clarity of microfiche, using film winder, light table, and magnifier. Marks defective microfiche section of film and lists identifying number of sections on identification sheet to indicate refilming required. Measures optical density of random film section to ensure standard processing, using densitometer. Places film on cutter, aligns markings on cutter and film, and moves cutting instrument across film to separate individual microfiche sections of film. Discards defective microfiche and places acceptable microfiche in envelope for further processing. Mixes processing chemicals to maintain supply, following specified formula, using mixing machine. Processes sample film and measures density of film to enable MICROFILM-CAMERA OPERATOR (business ser.) 976.682-022 to determine exposure settings for new batches of film. ● **GED:** R3, M2, L2 ● **SVP:** 2-30 days ● **Academic:** Ed=N, Eng=N ● **Work Field:** 202, 212 ● **MPSMS:** 897 ● **Aptitudes:** G3, V4, N3, S3, P3, Q4, K4, F3, M3, E5, C5 ● **Temperaments:** T ● **Physical:** Stg=L; Freq: R, H, I, N, A ● **Work Env:** Noise=Q; ● **Salary:** 1 ● **Outlook:** 2

MOTION-PICTURE PROJECTIONIST (amuse. & rec.) ● DOT #960.362-010 ● OES: 92905 ● Alternate titles: AUDIOVISUAL EQUIPMENT OPERATOR; PROCESS PROJECTIONIST; PROJECTIONIST; THEATER PROJECTIONIST. Sets up and operates motion picture projection and sound-reproducing equipment to produce coordinated effects on screen: Inserts film into top magazine reel of projector. Threads film through picture aperture of projector, around pressure rollers, sprocket wheels, and sound drum or magnetic sound pickup on film, and onto spool that automatically takes up film slack. Regulates projection light and adjusts sound-reproducing equipment. Monitors operation of machines and transfers operation from one machine to another without interrupting flow of action on screen. Rewinds broken end of film onto reels by hand to minimize loss of time. Inspects and rewinds projected films for another showing. Repairs faulty sections of film. Operates stereopticon (magic lantern) or other special-effects equipment to project picture slides on screen. Cleans lenses, oils equipment, and makes minor repairs and adjustments. ● **GED:** R4, M2, L2 ● **SVP:** 1-2 yrs ● **Academic:** Ed=N, Eng=N ● **Work Field:** 281 ● **MPSMS:** 921 ● **Aptitudes:** G3, V3, N3, S3, P3, Q4, K3, F3, M3, E5, C3 ● **Temperaments:** J, T ● **Physical:** Stg=L; Freq: R, H, I, E, F, X Occas: G, N ● **Work Env:** Noise=L; Occas: O ● **Salary:** 1 ● **Outlook:** 1

OFFSET-DUPLICATING-MACHINE OPERATOR (clerical) ● DOT #207.682-018 ● OES: 56200 ● Operates offset-duplicating machine to reproduce single or multicolor copies of charts, schedules, bulletins, and related matter, according to oral instructions or layout and stock specifications on job order: Installs sensitized metal printing plate or master copy of plastic-coated paper around press cylinder of machine and locks plate or master copy into position, using handtools. Turns handwheel and ink fountain screws to regulate ink flow. Selects paper stock to be printed according to color, size, thickness, and quantity specified, stacks paper on feed table, and positions spring guide on side of paper stack. Turns elevator crank to raise feed table to paper height. Sets dial controls to adjust speed and feed of machine according to weight of paper. Starts machine that automatically reproduces copy by offset process. Cleans and files master copy or plate. Cleans and oils machine. May prepare printing plates. May operate stencil-process or spirit-duplicating machines and photocopy equipment. Important variations may be indicated by trade names of machines used. ● **GED:** R3, M2, L1 ● **SVP:** 6 mos-1 yr ● **Academic:** Ed=N, Eng=N ● **Work Field:** 191 ● **MPSMS:** 891 ● **Aptitudes:** G3, V4, N3, S4, P3, Q4, K3, F3, M3, E5, C4 ● **Temperaments:** R, T ● **Physical:** Stg=M; Freq: R, H, I, T, G, N, D, A, X ● **Work Env:** Noise=L; ● **Salary:** 2 ● **Outlook:** 2

PHOTOCOMPOSING-MACHINE OPERATOR (print. & pub.) ● DOT #650.582-018 ● OES: 92541 ● Alternate titles: TYPESETTER. Sets up and operates photocomposing machine to transfer data from perforated or magnetic tape into print on film or photographic paper, using either of following methods: (1) Loads roll of film or paper in machine magazine. Secures roll of perforated tape on machine reel and threads end of tape through machine feed rollers. Selects type font according to size and face of type specified and positions it on photographic unit. Turns dials to adjust line spacing and light intensity according to size and face of type. Starts machine that automatically prints type onto film or paper according to coded signal on tape. Removes finished copy from magazine for development. (2) Places reel of magnetic tape onto feed spindle of phototypesetting unit. Depresses keys to enter command codes, such as size and style of type, width and length of column, and to activate computer to produce phototypesetting film, phototypesetting paper, or copy of tape. Removes and stacks finished copies from photocopy printing unit. Removes printing unit from machine, drains chemical solution, washes unit, and refills unit with specified developing solution. ● **GED:** R3, M1, L1 ● **SVP:** 1-2 yrs ● **Academic:** Ed=N, Eng=N ● **Work Field:** 191, 202 ● **MPSMS:** 897 ● **Aptitudes:** G3, V3, N4, S3, P3, Q4, K3, F3, M3, E5, C4 ● **Temperaments:** R, T ● **Physical:** Stg=L; Freq: R, H, I, N, D Occas: X ● **Work Env:** Noise=N; ● **Salary:** 3 ● **Outlook:** 2

PHOTOGRAPHER, FINISH (amuse. & rec.) ● DOT #143.382-014 ● OES: 34023 ● Alternate titles: PHOTO-FINISH PHOTOGRAPHER. Operates photographic equipment to photograph finish of horse race: Loads film into camera and advances to picture taking position. Sights camera on finish line and adjusts exposure controls and focus. Observes race and starts camera as horses approach finish line. Stops camera after last horse has crossed finish line. Removes exposed film from camera and places it into film-developing machine that automatically develops film. Prints and enlarges photographs used to determine winner of race when finish is close. ● **GED:** R4, M2, L3 ● **SVP:** 1-2 yrs ● **Academic:** Ed=N, Eng=G ● **Work Field:** 201, 202 ● **MPSMS:** 753 ● **Aptitudes:** G3, V4, N3, S4, P3, Q4, K4, F3, M3, E5, C5 ● **Temperaments:** T ● **Physical:** Stg=L; Freq: R, H, I, N, A ● **Work Env:** Noise=N; ● **Salary:** 4 ● **Outlook:** 3

PHOTOGRAPH FINISHER (photofinishing) ● DOT #976.487-010 ● OES: 93998 ● Alternate titles: PRINT FINISHER. Performs any combination of following tasks to dry, trim, and mount photographic prints: Places washed print on conveyor leading to heated rotating cylinder that dries and flattens print. Trims print edges, using paper cutter or scissors. Inserts print in specified frame or mounts print on material, such as paper, cardboard, or fabric, using cement or hand-operated press. Inserts print and corresponding negative in customer envelope. Computes price of order, according to size and number of prints, and marks price on customer envelope. May cut film lengthwise to separate individual print rolls, using slitting machine. ● **GED:** R2, M1, L1 ● **SVP:** 2-30 days ● **Academic:** Ed=N, Eng=N ● **Work Field:** 054, 063, 061 ● **MPSMS:** 897 ● **Aptitudes:** G4, V4, N3, S4, P4, Q4, K4, F3, M3, E5, C4 ● **Temperaments:** R ● **Physical:** Stg=L; Freq: R, H, I, N, D Occas: X ● **Work Env:** Noise=N; ● **Salary:** 3 ● **Outlook:** 4

PHOTOGRAPHIC-PLATE MAKER (electron. comp.) ● DOT #714.381-018 ● OES: 89718 ● Alternate titles: PHOTOGRAPHIC-PROCESS ATTENDANT. Prepares photographic plates used to print pattern of aperture masks on sensitized steel: Examines unexposed plate to detect foreign particles or emulsion flaws. Transfers image from master plate to unexposed plate by means of contact exposure and immerses plate in series of chemical and water baths to develop image on plate [DEVELOPER (photofinishing)]. Examines plate over light box in darkroom to detect flaws and verify conformity of pattern with master plate. Measures dot size and center distance, using calibrated microscope, and examines master and production plates for dot damage. Repairs defective plates by filling in missing dots, using photographic touch-up tool and ink. Installs and alignes plates in printing case for DISPLAY-SCREEN FABRICATOR (electron. comp.). Prepares developing solutions, following formula. ● **GED:** R4, M3, L3 ● **SVP:** 1-2 yrs ● **Academic:** Ed=H, Eng=S ● **Work Field:** 202 ● **MPSMS:** 567 ● **Aptitudes:** G3, V3, N3, S3, P2, Q5, K4, F3, M3, E5, C4 ● **Temperaments:** J, T ● **Physical:** Stg=L; Freq: R, H, I, N, A Occas: D, X ● **Work Env:** Noise=N; ● **Salary:** 3 ● **Outlook:** 3

PHOTO MASK TECHNICIAN, ELECTRON-BEAM (electron. comp.) ● DOT #972.382-022 ● OES: 25104 ● Generates computer tape or disk of processing instructions for use in electron-beam fabrication of photo masks used in integrated circuit (IC) manufacture, using computer graphics system and software and applying knowledge of photo mask layout: Reviews work order and specification manuals to determine data required to lay out array (arrangement of integrated circuit layer patterns) for reproduction onto photo mask. Enters commands into computer, using keyboard, to retrieve from data file and display on display screen existing array format information. Calculates additional array information required, such as array center and coordinates, number of rows and columns in array, and location of test patterns in array, following specification manual and work order instructions. Locates file (computer tape) relating to specified IC layer and loads tape into computer tape drive. Enters specified commands into computer, using keyboard to retrieve IC layer pattern from file and display pattern on array format on computer display screen. Positions IC layer patterns and test patterns within array format on display screen, using knowledge of photo mask layout and computer graphics. Enters electron-beam exposure instructions into computer and keys in commands to transfer array data and exposure instructions onto computer disk or tape for use by PHOTO MASK MAKER, ELECTRON-BEAM (electron. comp.) 972.382-018. May enter commands into computer, using keyboard, to transfer IC layer patterns onto hard copy (plots), using plotter peripheral equipment. May inspect plots of IC layer patterns for layout errors. ● **GED:** R3, M3, L3 ● **SVP:** 1-2 yrs ● **Academic:** Ed=N, Eng=S ● **Work Field:** 233, 242, 201 ● **MPSMS:** 587 ● **Aptitudes:** G3, V3, N3, S3, P2, Q2, K2, F2, M3, E5, C5 ● **Temperaments:** J, T ● **Physical:** Stg=L; Const: N, A Freq: R, I Occas: H ● **Work Env:** Noise=N; ● **Salary:** 3 ● **Outlook:** 4

PLANETARIUM TECHNICIAN (museums) ● DOT #962.261-010 ● OES: 39998 ● Alternate titles: ASTRO-TECHNICIAN; TECHNICAL SPECIALIST. Installs, modifies, operates, and maintains sound and projection equipment used in presentation of planetarium classes and shows: Consults with personnel who plan classes and shows to determine feasibility of achieving specified effects, modifications in equipment necessary to create desired effects, and additional equipment or properties to be incorporated into technical equipment layout. Modifies projectors, electro-optic equipment, console controls, and auxiliary instruments, following script or lecture outline, to adjust equipment for producing desired visual effects, basing modifications on knowledge of equipment capabilities, and using handtools, precision instruments, and circuitry diagrams. Selects tapes of musical compositions from planetarium files and records portions of each, as designated in script, to produce tape recording with musical background. Modifies sound system to permit synchronization of recorded commentary and background music with visual presentation. Installs special effect properties, such as models of space ships or slides of ancient interpretations of constellations, in designated positions in dome of theater, and secures properties to control wires or machinery to facilitate manipulation of properties according to script or lecture outline, using handtools. Operates electro-optic, audio, and auxiliary equipment to present show or to complement presentation of class lectures. Repairs and maintains equipment, using handtools and precision calibrating and testing instruments, applying knowledge of electronic circuitry and electro-optics, and following manufacturer's maintenance instructions and diagrams. Constructs and installs permanent or temporary displays, incorporating electromechanical or electronic components, in planetarium's exhibit area. ● **GED:** R4, M4, L4 ● **SVP:** 2-4 yrs ● **Academic:** Ed=H, Eng=G ● **Work Field:** 111, 121, 281 ● **MPSMS:** 606, 939 ● **Aptitudes:** G2, V3, N2, S2, P2, Q3, K2, F2, M3, E3, C3 ● **Temperaments:** J, T ● **Physical:** Stg=M; Freq: R, H, I, N, X Occas: C, B, S, O, T, G, A ● **Work Env:** Noise=N; ● **Salary:** 4 ● **Outlook:** 2

PROOFER, PREPRESS (print. & pub.) ● DOT #972.381-034 ● OES: 89716 ● Makes single or multicolored prepress proofs of text and graphics, performing any combination of following duties: Places base material and color coated sheet or light sensitive film into laminating machine that transfers pigment from sheet or laminates light sensitive film to base. Exposes base to corresponding color-separated negative or positive film, using vacuum frame, and places color coated base in automatic processor that develops and reveals color image on base, or places light sensitive base into corresponding color bin of automatic toner machine that deposits powdered ink pigment onto image. Registers succeeding color negatives or positives over base, using magnifier or register device system, and repeats process to produce multicolor proof. Exposes film to proofing paper to make single-color proof. Exposes film to colored base material to produce overlay of each color, and assembles and aligns individual overlays on top of one another to form multicolor overlay proof. Compares test exposures to quality control color guides to determine data for exposure settings. Measures density levels of colors or color guides on proofs, using densitometer, and compares readings to set standards. Mixes powdered ink pigments, using ink matching book and measuring and mixing tools, to create nonstandard colors, and applies ink pigments to base by hand. Immerses exposed materials in chemical baths to hand-develop proofing materials. Method used to make proof is determined by brand of equipment and quality of proof required. ● **GED:** R3, M2, L3 ● **SVP:** 6 mos-1 yr ● **Academic:** Ed=N, Eng=G ● **Work Field:** 201, 202, 063 ● **MPSMS:** 753 ● **Aptitudes:** G3, V3, N3, S3, P3, Q3, K3, F3, M3, E5, C3 ● **Temperaments:** T ● **Physical:** Stg=L; Const: R, H Freq: I, N, X Occas: G, D, A ● **Work Env:** Noise=L; Const: R ● **Salary:** 3 ● **Outlook:** 3

QUALITY-CONTROL TECHNICIAN (photofinishing) ● DOT #976.267-010 ● OES: 83000 ● Examines photographic prints, processed film, cameras and other photographic equipment for defects or faulty operation to determine course of action required to satisfy customer complaints: Reviews unresolved requests for adjustment of complaints and reads customer comments to determine basis of complaint and plan of action needed to resolve complaint. Spreads negatives and prints on illuminated worktable and uses magnifying glass to detect defects, such as incorrect coloring, shading, or cutting. Determines cause of defect and type correction required based on knowledge of photo processing and finishing techniques. Prepares memorandum to processing department and confers with SUPERVISOR, QUALITY CONTROL (photofinishing) to suggest remedies to prevent subsequent errors in processing. Contacts customer to explain causes for defects and confers with sales-service personnel to resolve technical questions and to demonstrate correct usage of photographic equipment. Prepares reports indicating complaints handled and dispositions made. ● **GED:** R4, M2, L3 ● **SVP:** 1-2 yrs ● **Academic:** Ed=N, Eng=G ● **Work Field:** 212 ● **MPSMS:** 606, 897 ● **Aptitudes:** G3, V3, N4, S3, P3, Q3, K4, F3, M3, E5, C3 ● **Temperaments:** J, P ● **Physical:** Stg=L; Freq: R, H, I, T, G, N, D, A, X Occas: E ● **Work Env:** Noise=N; ● **Salary:** 4 ● **Outlook:** 4

RECORDING ENGINEER (radio-tv broad.) ● DOT #194.362-010 ● OES: 35199 ● Alternate titles: SOUND RECORDING TECHNICIAN. Operates disk or tape recording machine to record music, dialog, or sound effects of phonograph recording sessions, radio broadcasts, television shows, training courses, or conferences, or to transfer transcribed material to sound-recording medium: Threads tape through recording device or places blank disk on turntable. Moves lever to regulate speed of turntable. Places cutting stylus on record. Examines grooves during cutting by stylus to determine if grooves are level, using microscope. Turns knobs on cutting arm to shift or adjust weight of stylus and cause grooves to be cut evenly. Starts recording machine and moves switches to open microphone and tune in live or recorded programs.

Listens through earphone to detect imperfections of recording machines or extraneous noises emanating from recording studio or production stage. Observes dials, mounted on machine, to ensure that volume level and intensity remain within specified limits. Removes filled reel or completed recordings from machine and attaches identifying labels. Keeps record of recordings in logbook. May service and repair recording machines and allied equipment. May be designated according to type of machine used as Disk-Recording-Machine Operator (radio-tv broad.; recording); Tape-Recording-Machine Operator (radio-tv broad.; recording). When transcribing to disk used in production of phonograph records, may be designated Dubbing-Machine Operator (recording). When recording live television programs in monochrome or color on magnetic tape is designated Videotape-Recording Engineer (radio-tv broad.). ● **GED:** R3, M3, L3 ● **SVP:** 2-4 yrs ● **Academic:** Ed=A, Eng=G ● **Work Field:** 281 ● **MPSMS:** 869 ● **Aptitudes:** G3, V3, N3, S3, P4, Q4, K3, F4, M3, E5, C5 ● **Temperaments:** J, T ● **Physical:** Stg=L; Freq: R, H, I, G, N Occas: A ● **Work Env:** Noise=L; ● **Salary:** 5 ● **Outlook:** 1

RECORDIST (motion picture) ● DOT #962.382-010 ● OES: 35199 ● Controls equipment to record sound originating on motion-picture set, using magnetic film, optical film, and acetate disk recording equipment: Tests and sets up recording mechanism according to specifications. Starts recorder and synchronizes sound with film. Observes operation to ensure that sound is properly recorded. May be designated according to equipment used as Disk Recordist (motion picture); Film Recordist (motion picture). ● **GED:** R3, M2, L2 ● **SVP:** 1-2 yrs ● **Academic:** Ed=A, Eng=G ● **Work Field:** 281 ● **MPSMS:** 911 ● **Aptitudes:** G3, V3, N3, S4, P3, Q4, K4, F3, M3, E5, C5 ● **Temperaments:** J ● **Physical:** Stg=L; Const: G Freq: R, H, I Occas: N, D, A ● **Work Env:** Noise=L; Occas: W ● **Salary:** 2 ● **Outlook:** 2

REPRODUCTION TECHNICIAN (any industry) ● DOT #976.361-010 ● OES: 89914 ● Alternate titles: COPY-CAMERA OPERATOR; PHOTOLITH OPERATOR; VACUUM-FRAME OPERATOR. Duplicates printed material on sensitized paper, cloth, or film according to customer specifications, using photographic equipment and handtools: Reads work order and confers with supervisor to determine processes, techniques, equipment, and materials required. Places original on sensitized material in vacuum frame. Mounts camera on tripod or stand and loads prescribed type and size film in camera. Sets camera controls to regulate exposure time according to line density of original and type of sensitized material. Activates camera to expose sensitized material, imprinting original on material. Develops exposed material [DEVELOPER (photofinishing) 976.681-010]. Examines developed reprint for defects, such as broken lines, spots, and blurs, and touches up defects, using chemicals, inks, brushes, and pens. May enlarge reprints [PROJECTION PRINTER (photofinishing) 976.381-018]. May reprint original in sections and piece sections together. ● **GED:** R4, M2, L2 ● **SVP:** 1-2 yrs ● **Academic:** Ed=N, Eng=N ● **Work Field:** 201, 202 ● **MPSMS:** 897 ● **Aptitudes:** G3, V3, N3, S2, P2, Q4, K3, F3, M3, E4, C2 ● **Temperaments:** J, T ● **Physical:** Stg=L; Freq: S, R, H, I, E, T, G, N, D, A, X ● **Work Env:** Noise=N; Freq: U, A, O ● **Salary:** 3 ● **Outlook:** 2

RERECORDING MIXER (motion picture) ● DOT #194.362-014 ● OES: 35199 ● Operates console to synchronize and equalize prerecorded dialog, music, and sound effects with action of motion picture or television production: Reads script and dupe sheets of film and tape or video tape to learn sequence of speaking parts, music, and sound effects to be synchronized and integrated in film or tape or video tape. Informs DUBBING-MACHINE OPERATOR (motion picture; radio-tv broad.) 962.665-010 to load sound tracks onto dubbing machine and MOTION-PICTURE PROJECTIONIST (amuse. & rec.; motion picture) 960.362-010 to place film in projector. Operates console to control starting and stopping of projector and dubbing machine. Observes film or video tape projected onto screen, listens to sound over loud speakers, and turns knobs on panel of console to balance intensity and volume. Informs MOTION-PICTURE PROJECTIONIST (amuse. & rec.; motion picture) to project film onto screen. Observes projection and listens to determine that sound is synchronized and equalized with action on film. ● **GED:** R4, M4, L4 ● **SVP:** 2-4 yrs ● **Academic:** Ed=H, Eng=G ● **Work Field:** 281 ● **MPSMS:** 911, 860 ● **Aptitudes:** G3, V3, N3, S3, P5, Q5, K3, F3, M3, E5, C5 ● **Temperaments:** J, T, V ● **Physical:** Stg=S; Freq: I, G Occas: R, H, T, N, F, D ● **Work Env:** Noise=N; ● **Salary:** 5 ● **Outlook:** 3

SOUND MIXER (motion picture) ● DOT #194.262-018 ● OES: 35199 ● Alternate titles: BOARD OPERATOR; MIXER OPERATOR; MUSIC MIXER; STUDIO ENGINEER; STUDIO TECHNICIAN. Operates console to regulate volume level and quality of sound during filming of motion picture, phonograph recording session, or television and radio productions: Determines acoustics of recording studio and adjusts controls to specified levels. Directs installation of microphones and amplifiers for use in sound pickup. Turns knobs and dials on console while recording to cut microphones in and out, and to blend output of individual microphones to obtain balance between music, dialog, and sound effects. Instructs performers to project voices for pickup by microphones. Copies and edits recordings, using recording and editing equipment. May test machines and equipment, using electronic testing equipment, such as ohm and voltage meters, to detect defects. May repair and replace audio amplifier parts. ● GED: R4, M4, L3 ● SVP: 2-4 yrs ● Academic: Ed=H, Eng=G ● Work Field: 281 ● MPSMS: 863, 864, 911 ● Aptitudes: G2, V2, N3, S3, P3, Q4, K3, F3, M3, E5, C5 ● Temperaments: J, T, V ● Physical: Stg=S; Const: H, G Freq: R, I, T, N ● Work Env: Noise=N; ● Salary: 3 ● Outlook: 2

TAKE-DOWN SORTER (photofinishing) ● DOT #976.665-010 ● OES: 92908 ● Sorts and examines processed photographic film, repairs defective film, and tends drying cabinet that dries film: Flips switch to activate exhaust fan of drier, reads temperature gauge, and adjusts heat controls to maintain specified temperature in drier. Notifies supervisor or darkroom personnel concerning need for machine adjustments or solution changes if excessive amounts of film damage occurs. Monitors drying operation to detect dirty, twisted, or torn film in drier and removes defective film from drier. Washes film in negative cleaner to clean, soften, and straighten film and mends torn film, using tape, sealing solution, and scissors. Feels surface of film in drier to determine dryness and removes film from drier when completely dry. Examines film for clearness of image to determine printability and matches numbered label attached to film with number on customer envelope to avoid missorts. Sorts film into bins or attaches film to hooks according to size and type processing required. May compute customer charges, using pricelist. ● GED: R3, M1, L1 ● SVP: 1-3 mos ● Academic: Ed=N, Eng=N ● Work Field: 212, 202 ● MPSMS: 897 ● Aptitudes: G3, V4, N4, S3, P3, Q3, K3, F3, M3, E5, C3 ● Temperaments: J, T ● Physical: Stg=L; Const: R, H Freq: S, I, E, N, D, X Occas: T, G ● Work Env: Noise=N; ● Salary: 1 ● Outlook: 2

TAPE TRANSFERRER (radio-tv broad.) ● DOT #194.382-014 ● OES: 35199 ● Alternate titles: TAPE DUPLICATOR. Operates machines to reproduce tape recordings from master tapes (original tape recording): Consults charts to determine amount of tape needed, considering running time of master tape. Positions master tape in master-reproducing machine and mounts blank tape on spindle of tape-recording machine. Threads tapes through machines. Interconnects and starts machines to record selection on blank tape. Stops machines and reverses tape in recording machine to record second selection on reverse side of tape. Operates recording machine to play back reproduced recording to test quality of reproduced sound. ● GED: R3, M3, L3 ● SVP: 6 mos-1 yr ● Academic: Ed=N, Eng=S ● Work Field: 281 ● MPSMS: 585, 869 ● Aptitudes: G3, V3, N4, S4, P3, Q3, K3, F3, M3, E5, C5 ● Temperaments: J, R, T ● Physical: Stg=L; Freq: R, H, I, N ● Work Env: Noise=N; ● Salary: 3 ● Outlook: 2

GOE: 05.10.06
Blasting

BLASTER (any industry) ● DOT #859.261-010 ● OES: 87988 ● Alternate titles: FIRER; SHOOTER. Assembles, plants, and detonates charges of industrial explosives to loosen earth, rock, stumps, or to demolish structures to facilitate removal: Examines mass, composition, structure, and location of object to be blasted, estimates amount and determines kind of explosive to be used, and marks location of charge holes for drilling. Assembles primer (blasting cap and fuse or electric squib and booster charge) and places primer with main charge in hole or near object to be blasted. Covers charge with mud, sand, clay, or other material and tamps firm to improve detonation and confine force of blast. Signals to clear area of personnel and equipment. Lights fuse or connects wires from charge to battery or detonator to detonate charge. May operate jackhammer, hand drill, or electric drill to bore holes for charges. May climb cliffs or banks to plant explosive charge, using ropes and safety harness, and be designated High Scaler (construction). May set and detonate explosive charges to improve flow of water into wells and be designated Shooter, Water Well (construction). ● GED: R4, M4, L4 ● SVP: 2-4 yrs ● Academic: Ed=A, Eng=S ● Work Field: 005 ● MPSMS: 360 ● Aptitudes: G3, V3, N3, S3, P3, Q4, K3, F3, M3, E3, C4 ● Temperaments: J, S ● Physical: Stg=H; Freq: S, R, H, I, N, F, D Occas: C, K, O, W, E, T, G, X ● Work Env: Noise=V; Const: O Freq: W Occas: A ● Salary: 3 ● Outlook: 3

FIREWORKS DISPLAY SPECIALIST (chemical) ● DOT #969.664-010 ● OES: 39998 ● Alternate titles: SETTER-OFF; SETTER-UP. Assembles and sets off fireworks displays at fairs, expositions, or celebrations, according to picture programs or diagrams: Advises committee as to distance audience should be from setoff site of display, according to wind direction and velocity, considering fallout of sparks and acid, and types of fireworks used. Lays out setoff arrangement. Directs workers to set mortars (pipes used to fire aerial shells) apart from ground display, and places barrier of sandbags, railroad ties, or boxes of gravel between mortars to avoid detonating shells from sparks. Assembles framework and affixes display to framework, using hammer, saw, nails, scissors, and twine. Ties fuses of components to lead fuse to create simultaneous fireworks display. Determines appropriate time for setting off of display, according to environmental conditions. ● GED: R4, M2, L2 ● SVP: 6 mos-1 yr ● Academic: Ed=N, Eng=N ● Work Field: 102, 297 ● MPSMS: 499 ● Aptitudes: G3, V3, N3, S3, P3, Q5, K3, F3, M3, E5, C4 ● Temperaments: J, T ● Physical: Stg=M; Freq: R, H, I, N, D, A Occas: S, K, O, W, T, G, X ● Work Env: Noise=L; Const: W Freq: X ● Salary: 2 ● Outlook: 2

GOE: 05.10.07
Painting, Dyeing & Coating

PAINTER (construction) ● DOT #840.381-010 ● OES: 87402 ● Applies coats of paint, varnish, stain, enamel, or lacquer to decorate and protect interior or exterior surfaces, trimmings, and fixtures of buildings and other structures: Reads work order or receives instructions from supervisor or homeowner regarding painting. Smooths surfaces, using sandpaper, brushes, or steel wool, and removes old paint from surfaces, using paint remover, scraper, wire brush, or blowtorch to prepare surfaces for painting. Fills nail holes, cracks, and joints with caulk, putty, plaster, or other filler, using caulking gun and putty knife. Selects premixed paints, or mixes required portions of pigment, oil, and thinning and drying substances to prepare paint that matches specified colors. Removes fixtures, such as pictures and electric switchcovers from walls prior to painting, using screwdriver. Spreads dropcloths over floors and room furnishings, and covers surfaces, such as baseboards, door frames, and windows with masking tape and paper to protect surfaces during painting. Paints surfaces, using brushes, spray gun, or paint rollers. Simulates wood grain, marble, brick, or tile effects. Applies paint with cloth, brush, sponge, or fingers to create special effects. Erects scaffolding or sets up ladders to perform tasks above ground level. May be designated according to type of work performed as Painter, Interior Finish (construction); Painter, Maintenance (any industry); or according to type of material used as Calciminer (construction); Varnisher (construction). May also hang wallpaper and fabrics [PAPERHANGER (construction) 841.381-010]. May wash surfaces prior to painting with mildew remover, using brush. ● GED: R3, M2, L2 ● SVP: 2-4 yrs ● Academic: Ed=N, Eng=N ● Work Field: 102 ● MPSMS: 360, 495 ● Aptitudes: G3, V4, N4, S4, P3, Q4, K3, F3, M3, E4, C3 ● Temperaments: J, T ● Physical: Stg=M; Freq: S, R, H, N, X Occas: C, B, K, O, I, E, T, G, F, D ● Work Env: Noise=N; Occas: W, A, D, T ● Salary: 2 ● Outlook: 3

PAINTER, TRANSPORTATION EQUIPMENT (aircraft mfg.) ● DOT #845.381-014 ● OES: 92947 ● Paints surfaces of transportation equipment, such as automobiles, buses, trucks, and aircraft, applying knowledge of surface preparation and painting techniques, using spray painting equipment, power tools, and work aids: Cleans, sands, and applies chemical solutions to prepare and condition surfaces prior to painting. Mixes and thins paint or other coating to specified color and consistency according to standard formulas or color charts, using spatula or mixing equipment and viscometer. Masks and covers surfaces not to be painted. Sprays specified amount or thickness of primer, protective, decorative, or finish coatings, such as paint, lacquer, sealer, or enamel, onto prepared surfaces, using spray equipment. Strips, sands, masks, and repaints surfaces, and blends and polishes finish to match surrounding areas, manually or using portable power tools. May apply or re-touch paint, using brush. May lay out and paint insignias, symbols, designs, or other markings on painted surfaces, according to blueprints or specifications, using stencils, patterns, measuring instruments, brushes, or spray equipment. May regulate controls on equipment to cure and dry paint or other coatings. May set up portable ventilators, exhaust units, ladders, and scaffolding prior to painting. May operate lifting and moving devices to move materials and equipment and access areas to be painted. May remove accessories from motor vehicles, such as chrome, mirrors, and windshield wipers, prior to repainting. May be designated according to vehicle painted as Auto-Body Painter (automotive ser.); Painter, Aircraft (aircraft mfg.; air trans.); Painter, Aircraft-Production (aircraft mfg.); Painter, Automotive (automotive ser.); Painter, Decorative-Commercial Aircraft (aircraft mfg.). ● **GED:** R3, M2, L3 ● **SVP:** 1-2 yrs ● **Academic:** Ed=N, Eng=N ● **Work Field:** 153 ● **MPSMS:** 591, 592 ● **Aptitudes:** G3, V3, N3, S3, P3, Q4, K3, F3, M3, E4, C2 ● **Temperaments:** J, T ● **Physical:** Stg=M; Freq: R, H, I, N, D, X Occas: C, B, S, K, O, W, E, A ● **Work Env:** Noise=N; Const: A Occas: W, D, T ● **Salary:** 4 ● **Outlook:** 2

GOE: 05.10.08
Food Preparation

BAKER (hotel & rest.) ● DOT #313.381-010 ● OES: 65021 ● Alternate titles: BAKER, BREAD; BREAD MAKER; OVEN TENDER. Prepares bread, rolls, muffins, and biscuits according to recipe: Checks production schedule to determine variety and quantity of goods to bake. Measures ingredients, using measuring cups and spoons. Mixes ingredients to form dough or batter by hand or using electric mixer. Cuts dough into uniform portions with knife or divider. Molds dough into loaves or desired shapes. Places shaped dough in greased or floured pans. Spreads or sprinkles topping, such as jelly, cinnamon, and poppy seeds on specialties. Places pans of dough in proof box to rise. Inserts pans of raised dough in oven to bake, using peel. Adjusts drafts or thermostatic controls to regulate oven temperature. Removes baked goods from oven and places goods on cooling rack. May bake pies, cakes, cookies, and other pastries [COOK, PASTRY (hotel & rest.)]. May be designated according to specialty baked as Baker, Biscuit (hotel & rest.); Hot-Bread Baker (hotel & rest.); Rolls Baker (hotel & rest.); or according to shift worked as Night Baker (hotel & rest.). ● **GED:** R3, M2, L2 ● **SVP:** 1-2 yrs ● **Academic:** Ed=N, Eng=N ● **Work Field:** 146 ● **MPSMS:** 384 ● **Aptitudes:** G3, V4, N4, S3, P3, Q4, K3, F4, M3, E5, C4 ● **Temperaments:** J, T ● **Physical:** Stg=M; Freq: R, H, I, N, D Occas: E, X ● **Work Env:** Noise=N; Freq: H Occas: O ● **Salary:** 2 ● **Outlook:** 4

BAKER, HEAD (hotel & rest.) ● DOT #313.131-010 ● OES: 69998 ● Alternate titles: BAKER, BREAD, CHIEF; BAKER CHEF. Supervises and coordinates activities of personnel in bread-baking department: Plans production according to daily requirements. Requisitions supplies and equipment. Maintains production records. ● **GED:** R4, M3, L3 ● **SVP:** 2-4 yrs ● **Academic:** Ed=N, Eng=S ● **Work Field:** 146 ● **MPSMS:** 384 ● **Aptitudes:** G3, V4, N3, S3, P3, Q3, K4, F4, M2, E5, C4 ● **Temperaments:** D, J, T ● **Physical:** Stg=L; Freq: R, H, I, T, G, N Occas: E, D, A, X, V ● **Work Env:** Noise=N; Freq: H ● **Salary:** 4 ● **Outlook:** 3

BAKER, PIZZA (hotel & rest.) ● DOT #313.381-014 ● OES: 65030 ● Prepares and bakes pizza pies: Measures ingredients, such as flour, water, and yeast, using measuring cup, spoon, and scale. Dumps specified ingredients into pan or bowl of mixing machine preparatory to mixing. Starts machine and observes operation until ingredients are mixed to desired consistency. Stops machine and dumps dough into proof box to allow dough to rise. Kneads fermented dough. Cuts out and weighs amount of dough required to produce pizza pies of desired thickness. Shapes dough sections into balls or mounds and sprinkles each section with flour to prevent crust forming until used. Greases pan. Stretches or spreads dough mixture to size of pan. Places dough in

pan and adds olive oil and tomato puree, tomato sauce, mozarella cheese, meat, or other garnish on surface of dough, according to kind of pizza ordered. Sets thermostatic controls and inserts pizza into heated oven to bake for specified time. Removes product from oven and observes color to determine when pizza is done. ● **GED:** R3, M2, L1 ● **SVP:** 6 mos-1 yr ● **Academic:** Ed=N, Eng=N ● **Work Field:** 146 ● **MPSMS:** 903 ● **Aptitudes:** G3, V4, N4, S4, P3, Q4, K4, F4, M3, E5, C4 ● **Temperaments:** J ● **Physical:** Stg=M; Freq: R, H, I, N Occas: S, E, A, X ● **Work Env:** Noise=N; ● **Salary:** 3 ● **Outlook:** 3

BUTCHER, CHICKEN AND FISH (hotel & rest.) ● DOT #316.684-010 ● OES: 65038 ● Alternate titles: CHICKEN-AND-FISH CLEANER; POULTRY-AND-FISH BUTCHER. Butchers and cleans fowl, fish, and shellfish preparatory to cooking: Cleans and prepares fowl, fish, and shellfish, using knife and fork. Discards inedible parts. Cuts up fowl, using knife and cleaver or bandsaw. Bones game fowl and fish, using boning knife. Reshapes boned fowl into natural form for cooking and serving. Cuts fillets and steaks from fish. May butcher poultry in retail establishment and be designated Sales Clerk, Fresh Poultry (retail trade). ● **GED:** R2, M2, L1 ● **SVP:** 1-3 mos ● **Academic:** Ed=N, Eng=N ● **Work Field:** 034 ● **MPSMS:** 324, 331 ● **Aptitudes:** G4, V4, N4, S3, P3, Q5, K3, F3, M2, E5, C4 ● **Temperaments:** R, T ● **Physical:** Stg=L; Freq: R, H, N Occas: C, I, D, X ● **Work Env:** Noise=Q; ● **Salary:** 3 ● **Outlook:** 4

BUTCHER, MEAT (hotel & rest.) ● DOT #316.681-010 ● OES: 89803 ● Alternate titles: BUTCHER; MEAT CUTTER. Cuts, trims, bones, ties, and grinds meats, using butcher's cutlery and powered equipment, such as electric grinder and bandsaw, to portion and prepare meat in cooking form: Cuts, trims, and bones carcass sections or prime cuts, using knives, meat saw, cleaver, and bandsaw, to reduce to cooking cuts, such as roasts, steaks, chops, stew cubes, and grinding meat. Cuts and weighs steaks and chops for individual servings. Tends electric grinder to grind meat. Shapes and ties roasts. May estimate requirements and requisition or order meat supply. May receive, inspect, and store meat upon delivery. May record quantity of meat received and issued to cooks. May clean fowl and fish [BUTCHER, CHICKEN AND FISH (hotel & rest.)]. May oversee other butchers and be designated Butcher, Head (hotel & rest.). ● **GED:** R3, M2, L2 ● **SVP:** 1-2 yrs ● **Academic:** Ed=N, Eng=N ● **Work Field:** 034 ● **MPSMS:** 382, 903 ● **Aptitudes:** G3, V4, N4, S3, P3, Q4, K3, F3, M2, E5, C4 ● **Temperaments:** J ● **Physical:** Stg=H; Const: N, D, A Freq: R, H Occas: C, I ● **Work Env:** Noise=Q; Occas: M, O ● **Salary:** 3 ● **Outlook:** 3

CARVER (hotel & rest.) ● DOT #316.661-010 ● OES: 65038 ● Alternate titles: DISPLAY CARVER; EXHIBITION CARVER; MEAT CARVER. Carves individual portions from roasts and poultry to obtain maximum number of meat portions, using carving knives and meat-slicing machines: Disjoints roasts and poultry. Slices uniform portions of meat and places sliced meat in steamtable container, or arranges individual portions on plate. Ladles gravy over food and garnishes plate. Removes shells from seafood and bones fish, using forks. May weigh sliced meat to ensure that portions are uniform. May serve food from steamtable. May serve customers [WAITER/WAITRESS, FORMAL (hotel & rest.)]. ● **GED:** R3, M2, L2 ● **SVP:** 3-6 mos ● **Academic:** Ed=N, Eng=N ● **Work Field:** 146 ● **MPSMS:** 903 ● **Aptitudes:** G3, V4, N4, S4, P3, Q4, K3, F4, M3, E5, C4 ● **Temperaments:** R, T ● **Physical:** Stg=L; Freq: R, H, I, N Occas: X ● **Work Env:** Noise=Q; Occas: O ● **Salary:** 2 ● **Outlook:** 3

COOK (any industry) ● DOT #315.361-010 ● OES: 65028 ● Alternate titles: COOK, MESS. Prepares and cooks family-style meals for crews or residents and employees of institutions: Cooks foodstuffs in quantities according to menu and number of persons to be served. Washes dishes. Bakes breads and pastry [BAKER (hotel & rest.)]. Cuts meat [BUTCHER, MEAT (hotel & rest.)]. Plans menu taking advantage of foods in season and local availability. May serve meals. May order supplies and keep records and accounts. May direct activities of one or more workers who assist in preparing and serving meals. May be designated according to work location as Cook, Camp (any industry); Cook, Institution (any industry); Cook, Ranch (agriculture); Cook, Ship (water trans.). ● **GED:** R3, M2, L2 ● **SVP:** 1-2 yrs ● **Academic:** Ed=N, Eng=N ● **Work Field:** 146 ● **MPSMS:** 903 ● **Aptitudes:** G3, V4, N3, S4, P3, Q3, K3, F4, M3, E5, C4 ● **Temperaments:** J, T, V ● **Physical:** Stg=M; Freq: R, H, I, N Occas: E, T, G, D, A, X ● **Work Env:** Noise=N; Freq: U, O ● **Salary:** 3 ● **Outlook:** 2

COOK (domestic ser.) ● DOT #305.281-010 ● OES: 62021 ● Plans menus and cooks meals, in private home, according to recipes or tastes of employer: Peels, washes, trims, and prepares vegetables and meats for cooking. Cooks vegetables and bakes breads and pastries. Boils, broils, fries, and roasts meats. Plans menus and orders foodstuffs. Cleans kitchen and cooking utensils. May serve meals. May perform seasonal cooking duties, such as preserving and canning fruits and vegetables, and making jellies. May prepare fancy dishes and pastries. May prepare food for special diets. May work closely with persons performing household or nursing duties. May specialize in preparing and serving dinner for employed, retired, or other persons and be designated Family-Dinner Service Specialist (domestic ser.). ● **GED:** R3, M2, L2 ● **SVP:** 1-2 yrs ● **Academic:** Ed=N, Eng=N ● **Work Field:** 146 ● **MPSMS:** 901 ● **Aptitudes:** G3, V3, N4, S4, P3, Q4, K4, F4, M3, E5, C4 ● **Temperaments:** J, V ● **Physical:** Stg=L; Freq: R, H, I, N, X Occas: S, G, M ● **Work Env:** Noise=N; Occas: U ● **Salary:** 1 ● **Outlook:** 4

COOK, BARBECUE (hotel & rest.) ● DOT #313.381-022 ● OES: 65026 ● Prepares, seasons, and barbecues pork, beef, chicken, and other types of meat: Builds fire in pit below spit, using hickory wood or other fuel to obtain bed of live coals, or regulates gas or electric heat. Secures meat on spit which is slowly turned by hand or electric motor to cook meat uniformly. Seasons meat and bastes it frequently during roasting. May kill and dress animals or fowls or purchase meat from vendors. When cooking whole pigs, may be designated Cook, Roast Pig (hotel & rest.). ● **GED:** R3, M2, L2 ● **SVP:** 6 mos-1 yr ● **Academic:** Ed=N, Eng=N ● **Work Field:** 146 ● **MPSMS:** 903 ● **Aptitudes:** G3, V4, N4, S4, P3, Q5, K4, F4, M3, E5, C4 ● **Temperaments:** J, V ● **Physical:** Stg=M; Freq: R, H, I, N Occas: S, E, X ● **Work Env:** Noise=N; ● **Salary:** 1 ● **Outlook:** 4

COOK, FAST FOOD (hotel & rest.) ● DOT #313.374-010 ● OES: 65030 ● Prepares and cooks to order foods requiring short preparation time: Reads food order slip or receives verbal instructions as to food required by patron, and prepares and cooks food according to instructions. Prepares sandwiches [SANDWICH MAKER (hotel & rest.) 317.664-010]. Prepares salads and slices meats and cheese, using slicing machine, [PANTRY GOODS MAKER (hotel & rest.) 317.684-014]. Cleans work area and food preparation equipment. May prepare beverages [COFFEE MAKER (hotel & rest.) 317.684-010]. May serve meals to patrons over counter. ● **GED:** R3, M2, L2 ● **SVP:** 6 mos-1 yr ● **Academic:** Ed=N, Eng=S ● **Work Field:** 146 ● **MPSMS:** 903 ● **Aptitudes:** G3, V4, N4, S4, P3, Q4, K3, F4, M3, E5, C4 ● **Temperaments:** J, R, T ● **Physical:** Stg=M; Freq: R, H, I, N Occas: G, M, D, X ● **Work Env:** Noise=N; Freq: H, O ● **Salary:** 1 ● **Outlook:** 4

COOK, PASTRY (hotel & rest.) ● DOT #313.381-026 ● OES: 65021 ● Alternate titles: BAKER, CAKE; BAKER, PASTRY; CAKE MAKER. Prepares and bakes cakes, cookies, pies, puddings, or desserts, according to recipe: Measures ingredients, using measuring cups and spoons. Mixes ingredients to form dough or batter, using electric mixer or beats and stirs ingredients by hand. Shapes dough for cookies, pies, and fancy pastries, using pie dough roller and cookie cutters or by hand. Places shaped dough portions in greased or floured pans and inserts them in oven, using long-handled paddle (peel). Adjusts drafts or thermostatic controls to regulate oven temperatures. Prepares and cooks ingredients for pie fillings, puddings, custards, or other desserts. Pours filling into pie shells and tops filling with meringue or cream. Mixes ingredients to make icings. Decorates cakes and pastries [CAKE DECORATOR (bakery products) 524.381-010]. Blends colors for icings and for shaped sugar ornaments and statuaries. May specialize in preparing one or more types of pastry or dessert when employed in large establishment. May oversee work of patients assigned to kitchen for work therapy purposes when working in psychiatric hospital. ● **GED:** R4, M3, L3 ● **SVP:** 2-4 yrs ● **Academic:** Ed=N, Eng=S ● **Work Field:** 146 ● **MPSMS:** 384 ● **Aptitudes:** G3, V3, N4, S3, P3, Q4, K3, F4, M2, E5, C4 ● **Temperaments:** F, J, T ● **Physical:** Stg=M; Freq: R, H, N Occas: I, E, A, X ● **Work Env:** Noise=N; Freq: H Occas: O ● **Salary:** 3 ● **Outlook:** 4

COOK, SCHOOL CAFETERIA (hotel & rest.) ● DOT #313.381-030 ● OES: 65028 ● Prepares soups, meats, vegetables, salads, dressings, and desserts for consumption in school cafeteria, utilizing cafeteria equipment and cooking experience. Specializes in providing lightly seasoned, nutritionally adequate, and varied diet. Inspects equipment for cleanliness and functional operation. Work is usually performed with other workers. May plan menus, order food supplies, and receive supplies delivered. ● **GED:** R3, M2, L2 ● **SVP:** 1-2 yrs ● **Academic:** Ed=N, Eng=N ● **Work Field:** 146 ● **MPSMS:** 903 ● **Aptitudes:** G3, V4, N4, S4, P4, Q3, K4, F4, M3, E5, C4 ● **Temperaments:** J, V ● **Physical:** Stg=M; Freq: R, H, I, N Occas: S, O, G, M, A, X ● **Work Env:** Noise=N; Occas: O ● **Salary:** 1 ● **Outlook:** 4

COOK, SHORT ORDER (hotel & rest.) ● DOT #313.374-014 ● OES: 65030 ● Prepares food and serves restaurant patrons at counters or tables: Takes order from customer and cooks foods requiring short preparation time, according to customer requirements. Completes order from steamtable and serves customer at table or counter. Accepts payment and makes change, or writes charge slip. Carves meats, makes sandwiches, and brews coffee. May clean food preparation equipment and work area. May clean counter or tables. ● **GED:** R3, M2, L2 ● **SVP:** 1-3 mos ● **Academic:** Ed=N, Eng=S ● **Work Field:** 146 ● **MPSMS:** 903 ● **Aptitudes:** G3, V3, N4, S4, P3, Q4, K4, F4, M3, E5, C4 ● **Temperaments:** P, R ● **Physical:** Stg=L; Freq: R, H, I, T, G, N Occas: D, X ● **Work Env:** Noise=N; Freq: H, O ● **Salary:** 1 ● **Outlook:** 4

COOK, SPECIALTY (hotel & rest.) ● DOT #313.361-026 ● OES: 65030 ● Prepares specialty foods, such as fish and chips, tacos, and pasties (Cornish meat pies) according to recipe and specific methods applicable to type of cookery. May serve orders to customers at window or counter. May prepare and serve beverages, such as coffee, clam nectar, and fountain drinks. May be required to exercise showmanship in preparation of food, such as flipping pancakes in air to turn or tossing pizza dough in air to lighten texture. May be designated according to food item prepared as Cook, Fish And Chips (hotel & rest.). ● **GED:** R3, M2, L2 ● **SVP:** 6 mos-1 yr ● **Academic:** Ed=N, Eng=N ● **Work Field:** 146 ● **MPSMS:** 903 ● **Aptitudes:** G3, V4, N4, S4, P3, Q4, K3, F3, M3, E5, C4 ● **Temperaments:** J, T ● **Physical:** Stg=M; Freq: R, H, I, G, N Occas: T, X ● **Work Env:** Noise=N; Freq: H ● **Salary:** 1 ● **Outlook:** 4

COOK, SPECIALTY, FOREIGN FOOD (hotel & rest.) ● DOT #313.361-030 ● OES: 65026 ● Plans menus and cooks foreign-style dishes, dinners, desserts, and other foods, according to recipes: Prepares meats, soups, sauces, vegetables, and other foods prior to cooking. Seasons and cooks food according to prescribed method. Portions and garnishes food. Serves food to waiters on order. Estimates food consumption and requisitions or purchases supplies. Usually employed in restaurant specializing in foreign cuisine, such as French, Scandinavian, German, Swiss, Italian, Spanish, Hungarian, and Cantonese. May be designated according to type of food specialty prepared as Cook, Chinese-Style Food (hotel & rest.); Cook, Italian-Style Food (hotel & rest.); Cook, Kosher-Style Food (hotel & rest.); Cook, Spanish-Style Food (hotel & rest.). ● **GED:** R3, M3, L2 ● **SVP:** 2-4 yrs ● **Academic:** Ed=N, Eng=N ● **Work Field:** 146 ● **MPSMS:** 903 ● **Aptitudes:** G3, V3, N3, S4, P3, Q3, K4, F4, M3, E5, C4 ● **Temperaments:** J, T, V ● **Physical:** Stg=M; Freq: R, H, I, N Occas: T, G, D, X ● **Work Env:** Noise=N; ● **Salary:** 1 ● **Outlook:** 5

FORMULA-ROOM WORKER (dairy products) ● DOT #520.487-014 ● OES: 66099 ● Prepares, bottles, and sterilizes infant formulas: Weighs or measures and mixes specified quantities of ingredients, such as evaporated, condensed, or powdered milk, food supplements, sugar product, soy product, and prepared meat base, using scales, graduated measures, spoons, and electric blender. Computes number of calories per fluid ounce of formula from information on labels of ingredients, and records information on gummed label and places on bottles. Pours formula into bottles, seals with nipple, protector cap, and collar, and places in autoclave for prescribed length of time to sterilize, or affixes hermetically sealed protector caps and places in commercial retort for sterilization and cooling. Removes sterilized bottles from autoclave and stores in refrigerator or removes bottles from retort after cooling process and packages for delivery. Washes and sterilizes empty bottles and unused nipples and caps. May be known according to specific duties performed as Formula Bottler (dairy products); Formula Maker (dairy products). ● **GED:** R2, M2, L2 ● **SVP:** 1-3 mos ● **Academic:** Ed=N, Eng=N ● **Work Field:** 146, 031 ● **MPSMS:** 903 ● **Aptitudes:** G4, V4, N3, S4, P4, Q4, K4, F4, M3, E5, C5 ● **Temperaments:** R, T ● **Physical:** Stg=L; Const: R, H, I Freq: N Occas: S ● **Work Env:** Noise=Q; ● **Salary:** 1 ● **Outlook:** 2

GARDE MANGER (hotel & rest.) ● DOT #313.361-034 ● OES: 65026 ● Alternate titles: COLD-MEAT CHEF; COOK, COLD MEAT.

Prepares such dishes as meat loaves and salads, utilizing leftover meats, seafoods, and poultry: Consults with supervisory staff to determine dishes that will use greatest amount of leftovers. Prepares appetizers, relishes, and hors d'oeuvres. Chops, dices, and grinds meats and vegetables. Slices cold meats and cheese. Arranges and garnishes cold meat dishes. Prepares cold meat sandwiches. Mixes and prepares cold sauces, meat glazes, jellies, salad dressings, and stuffings. May supervise pantry workers. May follow recipes to prepare foods. ● **GED:** R3, M2, L2 ● **SVP:** 2-4 yrs ● **Academic:** Ed=N, Eng=N ● **Work Field:** 146 ● **MPSMS:** 903 ● **Aptitudes:** G3, V4, N4, S4, P3, Q4, K3, F4, M3, E5, C4 ● **Temperaments:** J, P, V ● **Physical:** Stg=L; Freq: R, H, I, N Occas: T, G, D, X ● **Work Env:** Noise=N; ● **Salary:** 3 ● **Outlook:** 3

KITCHEN SUPERVISOR (hotel & rest.) ● DOT #319.137-030 ● OES: 69998 ● Alternate titles: DIETARY ASSISTANT; MANAGER, KITCHEN. Supervises and coordinates activities of food preparation, kitchen, pantry, and storeroom personnel and purchases or requisitions foodstuffs and kitchen supplies: Plans or participates in planning menus, preparing and apportioning foods, and utilizing food surpluses and leftovers. Specifies number of servings to be made from any vegetable, meat, beverage, and dessert to control portion costs. Supervises noncooking personnel, such as KITCHEN HELPER (hotel & rest.) 318.687-010, to ensure cleanliness of kitchen and equipment. Supervises COOK (hotel & rest.) 313.361-014 and tastes, smells, and observes food to ensure conformance with recipes and appearance standards. Supervises workers engaged in inventory, storage, and distribution of foodstuffs and supplies. Purchases foodstuffs, kitchen supplies, and equipment, or requisitions them from PURCHASING AGENT (profess. & kin.) 162.157-038. Hires and discharges employees. Trains new workers. Performs other duties as described under SUPERVISOR (any industry) Master Title. May set prices to be charged for food items. May meet with professional staff, customers, or client group to resolve menu inconsistencies or to plan menus for special occasions. May assist dietitian to plan, change, test, and standardize recipes to increase number of servings prepared. This job occurs typically in restaurants, cafeterias, and institutions as opposed to STEWARD/STEWARDESS (hotel & rest.) 310.137-018 which occurs typically in hotels. ● **GED:** R4, M3, L4 ● **SVP:** 2-4 yrs ● **Academic:** Ed=N, Eng=S ● **Work Field:** 146, 232 ● **MPSMS:** 903 ● **Aptitudes:** G3, V3, N3, S4, P4, Q3, K4, F4, M4, E5, C4 ● **Temperaments:** D, P, V ● **Physical:** Stg=M; Freq: T, G, N Occas: S, O, R, H, I, X ● **Work Env:** Noise=N; ● **Salary:** 4 ● **Outlook:** 2

MEAT CUTTER (retail trade) ● DOT #316.684-018 ● OES: 89803 ● Alternate titles: BUTCHER; SALESPERSON, MEATS. Cuts and trims meat to size for display or as ordered by customer, using handtools and power equipment, such as grinder, cubing machine, and power saw. Cleans and cuts fish and poultry. May shape, lace, and tie meat cuts by hand, using boning knife, skewer, and twine to form roasts. May place meat in containers to be wrapped by other workers. May place meat on trays in display counter. May clean work area. May unload meat from delivery truck and store meat into refrigerator. May wrap and weigh meat for customers and collect money for sales. May inspect and grade meats and be designated Meat Inspector (retail trade; wholesale tr.). ● **GED:** R3, M2, L3 ● **SVP:** 1-2 yrs ● **Academic:** Ed=N, Eng=S ● **Work Field:** 034 ● **MPSMS:** 382, 881, 882 ● **Aptitudes:** G3, V4, N4, S3, P3, Q4, K3, F3, M2, E5, C4 ● **Temperaments:** J, T ● **Physical:** Stg=H; Const: H Freq: R, I, N Occas: E, G, D, X ● **Work Env:** Noise=N; Freq: O Occas: C ● **Salary:** 3 ● **Outlook:** 3

PANTRY GOODS MAKER (hotel & rest.) ● DOT #317.684-014 ● OES: 65038 ● Prepares salads, appetizers, sandwich fillings, and other cold dishes: Washes, peels, slices, and mixes vegetables, fruits, or other ingredients for salads, cold plates, and garnishes. Carves and slices meats and cheese. Portions and arranges food on serving dishes. Prepares fruit or seafood cocktails and hors d'oeuvres. Measures and mixes ingredients to make salad dressings, cocktail sauces, gelatin salads, cold desserts, and waffles, following recipes. Makes sandwiches to order [SANDWICH MAKER (hotel & rest.) 317.664-010]. Brews tea and coffee [COFFEE MAKER (hotel & rest.) 317.684-010]. Prepares breakfast and dessert fruits, such as melons, grapefruit, and bananas. Portions fruit sauces and juices. Distributes food to waiters/waitresses to serve to customers. May serve food to customers. May be designated Salad Maker (hotel & rest.) when specializing in making salads. ● **GED:** R3, M2, L2 ● **SVP:** 3-6 mos ● **Academic:** Ed=N, Eng=S ● **Work Field:** 146 ● **MPSMS:** 903 ● **Aptitudes:** G3, V4, N4, S4, P4, Q4, K4,

F3, M3, E5, C4 ● **Temperaments:** R, T ● **Physical:** Stg=L; Const: I Freq: R, H Occas: E, N, X ● **Work Env:** Noise=N; Occas: O ● **Salary:** 1 ● **Outlook:** 3

PASTRY CHEF (hotel & rest.) ● DOT #313.131-022 ● OES: 69998 ● Supervises and coordinates activities of COOKS (hotel & rest.) engaged in preparation of desserts, pastries, confections, and ice cream: Plans production for pastry department, according to menu or special requirements. Supplies recipes for, and suggests methods and procedures to pastry workers. Fashions table and pastry decorations, such as statuaries and ornaments, from sugar paste and icings, using cream bag, spatula, and various decorating tools. Requisitions supplies and equipment. Maintains production records. May participate in preparing desserts. ● **GED:** R4, M3, L3 ● **SVP:** 4-10 yrs ● **Academic:** Ed=N, Eng=S ● **Work Field:** 146 ● **MPSMS:** 903 ● **Aptitudes:** G3, V3, N3, S3, P3, Q3, K3, F3, M2, E5, C3 ● **Temperaments:** D, F, J, P ● **Physical:** Stg=L; Freq: R, H, I, T, G, N, D, A, X Occas: E ● **Work Env:** Noise=N; Freq: H ● **Salary:** 1 ● **Outlook:** 4

PIE MAKER (hotel & rest.) ● DOT #313.361-038 ● OES: 65021 ● Alternate titles: BAKER, PIE; COOK, PASTRY; COOK, PIE; PIE CHEF. Mixes ingredients and bakes pies, tarts, and cobblers, according to recipes: Weighs and measures ingredients, using measuring cup and spoons. Mixes ingredients by hand or with electric mixer to form piecrust dough. Rolls and shapes dough, using rolling pin. Places portions of rolled dough in piepans and trims overlapping edges with knife. Cuts, peels, and prepares fruit for pie fillings. Mixes and cooks ingredients for fillings, such as creams and custards. Pours fillings into pie shells. Covers filling with top crust or spreads topping, such as cream or meringue, over filling. Places pie in oven to bake. Adjusts drafts or thermostatic controls to regulate oven temperatures. Usually found in restaurant or cafeteria where no COOK, PASTRY (hotel & rest.) is employed and need not be able to bake other desserts or pastries as opposed to COOK, PASTRY (hotel & rest.). ● **GED:** R3, M2, L2 ● **SVP:** 1-2 yrs ● **Academic:** Ed=N, Eng=N ● **Work Field:** 146 ● **MPSMS:** 903, 384 ● **Aptitudes:** G3, V4, N4, S4, P3, Q4, K3, F3, M2, E5, C4 ● **Temperaments:** J, T ● **Physical:** Stg=L; Freq: R, H, I, N Occas: E, D, X ● **Work Env:** Noise=N; Occas: O ● **Salary:** 2 ● **Outlook:** 2

SALAD MAKER (water trans.) ● DOT #317.384-010 ● OES: 65038 ● Prepares salads, fruits, melons, and gelatin desserts: Cleans vegetables, fruits, and berries for salads, relishes, and gelatin desserts. Mixes ingredients for green salads, fruit salads, and potato salad. Prepares relish plates of green onions, celery, radishes, and olives. Prepares dressings, such as Thousand Island, French, and Roquefort, to be served on green salads. Peels, cleans, and cuts fruits, to be served for breakfast or compotes. Prepares cold sandwiches and cheeses. Requisitions supplies daily. ● **GED:** R3, M2, L3 ● **SVP:** 6 mos-1 yr ● **Academic:** Ed=N, Eng=S ● **Work Field:** 146 ● **MPSMS:** 903 ● **Aptitudes:** G3, V4, N4, S4, P4, Q4, K3, F3, M3, E5, C4 ● **Temperaments:** R ● **Physical:** Stg=L; Freq: R, H, I, N Occas: X ● **Work Env:** Noise=Q; ● **Salary:** 1 ● **Outlook:** 3

GOE: 05.10.09
Environmental

EXTERMINATOR (business ser.) ● DOT #389.684-010 ● OES: 67008 ● Alternate titles: PEST CONTROL WORKER; VERMIN EXTERMINATOR. Sprays chemical solutions or toxic gases and sets mechanical traps to kill pests that infest buildings and surrounding areas: Fumigates rooms and buildings, using toxic gases. Sprays chemical solutions or dusts powders in rooms and work areas. Places poisonous paste or bait and mechanical traps where pests are present. May clean areas that harbor pests, using rakes, brooms, shovels, and mops, preparatory to fumigating. May be required to hold state license. May be designated according to type of pest eliminated as Rodent Exterminator (business ser.). ● **GED:** R3, M2, L2 ● **SVP:** 6 mos-1 yr ● **Academic:** Ed=N, Eng=N ● **Work Field:** 293 ● **MPSMS:** 962 ● **Aptitudes:** G4, V4, N4, S4, P4, Q4, K4, F4, M4, E5, C5 ● **Temperaments:** J, V ● **Physical:** Stg=L; Freq: S, K, O, R, H Occas: C, W, I, N, D, A ● **Work Env:** Noise=N; Freq: A Occas: T ● **Salary:** 2 ● **Outlook:** 3

EXTERMINATOR, TERMITE (business ser.) ● DOT #383.364-010 ● OES: 67008 ● Alternate titles: TERMITE TREATER. Treats termite-infested and fungus-damaged wood in buildings: Studies report and diagram of infested area prepared by SALES AGENT, PEST CONTROL SERVICE (business ser.) to determine sequence of operations. Examines building to determine means of reaching infested areas. Cuts openings in building to gain access to infested areas, using handtools and power tools, such as electric drills, pneumatic hammers, saws, and chisels. Inserts nozzle into holes and opens compressed air valve of treating unit to force termicide into holes. Sprays pesticide under and around building, using pressure spray gun. Bores holes in concrete around buildings and injects termicide to impregnate ground. Keeps record of work performed. May direct EXTERMINATOR HELPER, TERMITE (business ser.). May replace damaged wood in sills, flooring, or walls, using carpenter's tools. May pour concrete or lay concrete blocks to raise height of foundation or isolate wood from contact with earth to prevent reinfestation. ● **GED:** R3, M2, L2 ● **SVP:** 1-2 yrs ● **Academic:** Ed=N, Eng=N ● **Work Field:** 293 ● **MPSMS:** 962 ● **Aptitudes:** G3, V4, N3, S3, P3, Q3, K3, F3, M3, E4, C5 ● **Temperaments:** D, J, V ● **Physical:** Stg=H; Freq: S, K, O, W, R, H, I Occas: C, B, T, G, N, F, D ● **Work Env:** Noise=L; Freq: W, O ● **Salary:** 2 ● **Outlook:** 3

FUMIGATOR (business ser.) ● DOT #383.361-010 ● OES: 67008 ● Releases poisonous gas and sets traps in buildings to kill dry-wood termites, beetles, vermin, and other pests, using cylinders of compressed gas and mechanical traps: Inspects infested building to identify pests causing damage and to determine treatment necessary. Examines porosity of walls and roof, based on knowledge of construction techniques, to determine method of sealing house. Measures inside dimensions of rooms with rule, and calculates volume of fumigant required and cost to owner. Tapes vents. Climbs ladder, pulls tarpaulins over building, and fastens edges of tarpaulins with clamps to make building airtight. Posts warning signs and padlocks doors. Turns valve on cylinder to discharge gas into building through hose. Holds halide lamp near seams of tarpaulins and building vents to detect leaking fumigant. Sprays or dusts chemicals in rooms or work areas and sets mechanical traps to destroy pests. May fumigate clothing and house furnishing in vaults at business establishment. ● **GED:** R4, M3, L3 ● **SVP:** 6 mos-1 yr ● **Academic:** Ed=N, Eng=N ● **Work Field:** 293 ● **MPSMS:** 962 ● **Aptitudes:** G3, V3, N3, S3, P4, Q3, K4, F4, M3, E4, C4 ● **Temperaments:** J, P, V ● **Physical:** Stg=H; Freq: S, K, O, R, H, T, G Occas: C, W, I, N, D, A, X ● **Work Env:** Noise=N; Freq: O Occas: W ● **Salary:** 2 ● **Outlook:** 3

Mechanical | 05

Equipment Operation | 05.11

Workers in this group operate heavy machines and equipment to dig, dredge, hoist, or move substances and materials. They also operate machines to pave roads. These jobs are found at mining, logging, and construction sites; docks; receiving and shipping areas of industrial plants; and large storage buildings and warehouses.

✓ What kind of work would you do?

Your work activities would depend upon your specific job. For example, you might:

- set up and operate a horizontal earth-boring machine.
- operate a long-wall mining machine in a coal mine.
- operate a portable drilling rig to prospect for oil.
- pump cement through a pipeline to a construction site.
- drive an asphalt spreader on a highway construction site.
- operate a bulldozer to grade a lawn for a new home.
- operate a crane to hoist materials and equipment into place at a building construction site.

✓ What skills and abilities do you need for this kind of work?

To do this kind of work, you must be able to:

- operate equipment according to work orders, signals, and oral instructions.
- withstand the jolting and vibration of heavy equipment.
- work outdoors in all kinds of weather.
- move eyes, hands, and feet together to control movement of equipment.
- estimate distances.

✓ How do you know if you would like or could learn to do this kind of work?

The following questions may give you clues about yourself as you consider this group of jobs.

- Have you driven a car, motorcycle, or other motorized vehicle? Can you react quickly and safely to sudden dangerous situations?
- Have you taken shop classes or had a home workshop where you operated machines? Do you enjoy this type of activity?
- Have you operated a tractor on a farm?
- Have you operated construction equipment in the armed forces?

✓ How can you prepare for and enter this kind of work?

Occupations in this group usually require education and/or training extending from thirty days to over two years, depending upon the specific kind of work. Many workers learn to operate equipment by on-the-job training. However, the best way to prepare for these jobs is to complete a three-year apprenticeship. Apprentices are supervised by experienced workers. They progress from these simple tasks to mechanical operations, such as lifting light loads with a crane. They also receive classroom instruction, which may include engine operation and repair, cable splicing, hydraulics, welding, and safety.

To qualify for an apprenticeship program, workers must be U. S. citizens and have a high school or vocational school diploma, or its equal. Applicants must also pass a physical fitness examination.

Shorter training courses are offered by the manufacturers of heavy equipment and by the armed services. High school and vocational courses in driver education and automobile mechanics are especially helpful.

Workers with leadership abilities may advance to supervisors. Some workers start their own construction companies, equipment rental agencies, or equipment maintenance firms.

Some machine tenders are promoted from manual jobs within a company. Others with machine shop classes are hired immediately after high school graduation. Additional skills are learned on the job.

✓ *What else should you consider about these jobs?*

For most jobs in this group, work hours and pay rates are dependent upon local union scales.

Machinery and equipment operators and drivers often work outside under noisy and dusty conditions. They must be alert in order to keep machines under control. Those who drive machines on public streets and roads must have state motor vehicle operator licenses. Work in the construction industry is seasonal in some regions of the country.

Some workers operate one type of equipment and change employers from project to project. People who can operate a variety of machines and equipment or who have special skills usually have more job opportunities. Training in operating new machinery may be provided by employers or through union programs.

If you think you would like to do this kind of work, look at the job titles listed below.

■ ■ ■

GOE: 05.11.01
Construction

ASPHALT-PAVING-MACHINE OPERATOR (construction) ● DOT #853.663-010 ● OES: 87708 ● Alternate titles: ASPHALT-SPREADER OPERATOR; BITUMINOUS-PAVING-MACHINE OPERATOR; BLACKTOP-PAVER OPERATOR; BLACKTOP SPREADER; MECHANICAL-SPREADER OPERATOR; PAVING-MACHINE OPERATOR, ASPHALT OR BITUMINOUS. Operates machine that spreads and levels hot-mix bituminous paving material on subgrade of highways and streets: Bolts extensions to screed to adjust width, using wrenches. Lights burners to heat screed. Starts engine and controls paving machine to push dump truck and maintain constant flow of asphalt into hopper. Observes distribution of paving material along screed and controls direction of screed to eliminate voids at curbs and joints. Turns valves to regulate temperature of asphalt flowing from hopper when asphalt begins to harden on screed. ● **GED:** R3, M1, L1 ● **SVP:** 6 mos-1 yr ● **Academic:** Ed=A, Eng=N ● **Work Field:** 095 ● **MPSMS:** 362 ● **Aptitudes:** G3, V4, N5, S3, P3, Q5, K3, F4, M3, E3, C5 ● **Temperaments:** J, T ● **Physical:** Stg=M; Const: F, D, V Freq: R, H, I Occas: C, S, K, O, T, G, N ● **Work Env:** Noise=L; Const: W, A Occas: O ● **Salary:** 3 ● **Outlook:** 3

BULLDOZER OPERATOR I (any industry) ● DOT #850.683-010 ● OES: 97938 ● Alternate titles: GRADER OPERATOR. Operates tractor equipped with concave blade attached across front to gouge out, level, and distribute earth and to push trees and rocks from land preparatory to constructing roads and buildings or planting crops, or in mining, quarrying, and lumbering operations: Fastens attachments to tractor with clevis or wedge-pin hitches. Connects hydraulic hoses, belts, mechanical linkage, or power takeoff shaft to tractor to provide power to raise, lower, or tilt attachment. Moves levers to control tool bars, carriers, and disks. Moves levers and depresses pedals to maneuver tractor and raise, lower, and tilt attachment to clear right-of-way. Feels lever and listens for stalling action of engine to estimate depth of cut. Drives bulldozer in successive passes over terrain to raise or lower terrain to specified grade following markings on grade stakes or hand signals. Greases, oils, and performs minor repairs on tractor, using grease gun, oilcans, and handtools. When required to work to close tolerances, may be designated Fine-Grade-Bulldozer Operator (any industry). When operating bulldozer to loosen soil, may be designated Scarifier Operator (any industry). May be designated according to type of tractor op-

erated as Crawler-Tractor Operator (any industry); Forest Fire Equipment Operator (government ser.); or attachment added as Angledozer Operator (any industry). May operate bulldozer to scrape surface clay to determine existence and types of clay deposits or to gather clay into piles preparatory to removal to brick-and-tile manufacturing plant and be designated Scraper Operator (mine & quarry). ● **GED:** R3, M2, L2 ● **SVP:** 6 mos-1 yr ● **Academic:** Ed=N, Eng=N ● **Work Field:** 007, 011 ● **MPSMS:** 360, 340, 350 ● **Aptitudes:** G3, V4, N4, S3, P3, Q4, K3, F4, M3, E3, C5 ● **Temperaments:** J, T ● **Physical:** Stg=H; Const: R, H Freq: G, F, D, V Occas: C, S, O, I, N ● **Work Env:** Noise=N; Const: W, V Occas: O ● **Salary:** 4 ● **Outlook:** 4

CHERRY-PICKER OPERATOR (construction) ● DOT #921.663-014 ● OES: 97944 ● Alternate titles: CAR CHANGER. Operates cherry picker (pneumatic hoist attached to structural framework) which moves on rails along tunnel side to hoist loaded dinkey cars from mucking machine to front of train: Hooks hoist line into lift-hooks on dinkey car. Moves lever to activate pneumatic hoist that lifts car. Pushes hoist block and car to side of frame and signals DINKEY OPERATOR (any industry) to move train to position empty car at mucking machine. Pushes hoisting frame along rails to front of train and operates hoist to place car in position on rails. ● **GED:** R2, M1, L1 ● **SVP:** 1-3 mos ● **Academic:** Ed=N, Eng=N ● **Work Field:** 011 ● **MPSMS:** 565 ● **Aptitudes:** G4, V4, N4, S3, P4, Q4, K3, F4, M3, E4, C5 ● **Temperaments:** R, S ● **Physical:** Stg=M; Freq: R, H, D Occas: N ● **Work Env:** Noise=L; Freq: U, A, O ● **Salary:** 2 ● **Outlook:** 4

CONCRETE-PAVING-MACHINE OPERATOR (construction) ● DOT #853.663-014 ● OES: 87708 ● Operates concrete paving machine to spread and smooth freshly poured concrete surfaces for concrete roads and landing fields: Starts machine, engages clutch, and shifts gears to control machine's movement along rails on concrete forms. Moves levers and turns handwheels to lower attachment that spreads wet concrete within forms. Observes surface of concrete to point out low spots for workers to add concrete. Operates machine with attachments to successively vibrate, screed, strike-off (remove excess from), and float surface of concrete, to spray on curing compound, and cut expansion joints. When cutting expansion joints, places strips of material, such as cork, asphalt, or steel, in joints, or places roll of expansion-joint material on machine that automatically inserts material into joints. When operating machine to screed and float surface, may be designated Concrete-Finishing-Machine Operator (construction). May be designated according to specific function of machine attachment as Center-Line-Cutter Operator (construction); Curing-Machine Operator (construction); Gang-Vibrator Operator (construction); Joint-Machine Operator (construction); Longitudinal-Float Operator (construction). May be designated: Screed Operator (construction); Spreader Operator (construction); Strike-Off-Machine Operator (construction); Vibrating-Screed Operator (construction). ● **GED:** R3, M1, L1 ● **SVP:** 1-3 mos ● **Academic:** Ed=N, Eng=N ● **Work Field:** 095 ● **MPSMS:** 362 ● **Aptitudes:** G3, V4, N4, S3, P3, Q5, K3, F4, M3, E3, C5 ● **Temperaments:** R, T ● **Physical:** Stg=M; Freq: R, H, I, N, F, D Occas: C, S, K, O, T, G ● **Work Env:** Noise=L; Const: W ● **Salary:** 2 ● **Outlook:** 3

OPERATING ENGINEER (construction) ● DOT #859.683-010 ● OES: 97956 ● Alternate titles: HEAVY-EQUIPMENT OPERATOR. Operates several types of power construction equipment, such as compressors, pumps, hoists, derricks, cranes, shovels, tractors, scrapers, or motor graders, to excavate, move, and grade earth, erect structural and reinforcing steel, and pour concrete or other hard surface paving materials: Turns valves to control air and water output of compressors and pumps. Adjusts handwheels and depresses pedals to drive machines and control attachments, such as blades, buckets, scrapers, and swing booms. Repairs and maintains equipment. May operate machinery on sales lot or customer's property to demonstrate saleable features of construction equipment and be designated Demonstrator, Construction Equipment (wholesale tr.). ● **GED:** R3, M1, L2 ● **SVP:** 1-2 yrs ● **Academic:** Ed=H, Eng=G ● **Work Field:** 007, 011 ● **MPSMS:** 360, 340 ● **Aptitudes:** G3, V4, N4, S3, P3, Q4, K3, F4, M3, E3, C4 ● **Temperaments:** J, T, V ● **Physical:** Stg=M; Const: R, H Freq: F, D, V Occas: C, S, K, O, G, N, X ● **Work Env:** Noise=V; Freq: W Occas: A, O ● **Salary:** 5 ● **Outlook:** 3

PILE-DRIVER OPERATOR (construction) ● DOT #859.682-018 ● OES: 87898 ● Alternate titles: HOISTING ENGINEER, PILE DRIVING. Operates pile driver mounted on skids, barge, crawler treads, or locomotive crane to drive piling as foundations for structures, such as buildings, bridges, and piers: Moves hand and foot levers to control diesel-, electric-, gasoline-, or steam-powered hoisting equipment to position piling leads, hoist piling into leads, and position hammer over top of pile. Moves levers and turns valves to activate power-driven hammer, or raise and lower drophammer which drives piles to required depth. May be designated according to type of power used to activate pile driver as Compressed-Air-Pile-Driver Operator (construction); Diesel-Pile-Driver Operator (construction); or type of piles driven as Concrete-Pile-Driver Operator (construction); Sheet-Pile-Driver Operator (construction); Wood-Pile-Driver Operator (construction); or type of mounting used as Pile-Driver Operator, Barge Mounted (construction). May be designated: Drop-Hammer-Pile-Driver Operator (construction); Electric-Pile-Driver Operator (construction); Steam-Pile-Driver Operator (construction). ● **GED:** R3, M2, L2 ● **SVP:** 6 mos-1 yr ● **Academic:** Ed=A, Eng=S ● **Work Field:** 102 ● **MPSMS:** 360 ● **Aptitudes:** G3, V3, N4, S3, P4, Q5, K3, F4, M3, E3, C5 ● **Temperaments:** J, T ● **Physical:** Stg=M; Const: R, H Freq: F, D Occas: C ● **Work Env:** Noise=V; Const: W Freq: O ● **Salary:** 4 ● **Outlook:** 3

POWER-SHOVEL OPERATOR (any industry) ● DOT #850.683-030 ● OES: 97923 ● Operates power-driven machine, equipped with movable shovel, to excavate or move coal, dirt, rock, sand, and other materials: Receives written or oral instructions from supervisor regarding material to move or excavate. Pushes levers and depresses pedals to move machine, to lower and push shovel into stockpiled material, to lower and dig shovel into surface of ground, and to lift, swing, and dump contents of shovel into truck, car, or onto conveyor, hopper, or stockpile. Observes markings on ground, hand signals, or grade stakes to remove material, when operating machine at excavation site. May tend mining machinery, such as pulverizer. May be designated according to type of power unit as Diesel-Power-Shovel Operator (any industry); Electric-Power-Shovel Operator (any industry); Gasoline-Power-Shovel Operator (any industry). May operate power shovel equipped with duck-bill scoop and be designated Duck-Bill Operator (mine & quarry). May operate power shovel which digs by pulling dipper toward machine and be designated Back-Hoe Operator (any industry). May operate power shovel on which excavating bucket runs outward along horizontal boom to dig into materials and be designated Skimmer-Scoop Operator (any industry). May operate power shovel designed to be converted to crane, skimmer scoop, backhoe, or dragline and be designated Convertible-Power-Shovel Operator (any industry). ● **GED:** R3, M1, L1 ● **SVP:** 6 mos-1 yr ● **Academic:** Ed=A, Eng=N ● **Work Field:** 011, 007 ● **MPSMS:** 340, 350 ● **Aptitudes:**

G4, V4, N4, S3, P4, Q4, K3, F4, M3, E3, C4 ● **Temperaments:** R, T ● **Physical:** Stg=M; Const: R, H Freq: I, F, D, V Occas: C, G, N, X ● **Work Env:** Noise=L; Const: W Freq: V ● **Salary:** 3 ● **Outlook:** 4

PROJECT-CREW WORKER (any industry) ● DOT #891.687-018 ● OES: 67001 ● Cleans walls, floors, ceilings, and structural members of buildings, using steam-cleaning equipment, brooms, and scrapers, and removes spillage and overflow of materials being processed or manufactured, with shovel and rake. Applies sealer to tile and concrete floors to protect them against subsequent spillage, using mop or brush. Sprays insecticides and fumigants over cleaned areas to prevent insect and rodent infestation. ● **GED:** R2, M1, L1 ● **SVP:** 1-3 mos ● **Academic:** Ed=N, Eng=N ● **Work Field:** 031 ● **MPSMS:** 361 ● **Aptitudes:** G3, V4, N5, S4, P4, Q5, K4, F4, M3, E4, C5 ● **Temperaments:** R, T ● **Physical:** Stg=M; Freq: C, B, S, R, H ● **Work Env:** Noise=L; Freq: U, A, O Occas: W ● **Salary:** 2 ● **Outlook:** 3

ROAD-ROLLER OPERATOR (construction) ● DOT #859.683-030 ● OES: 87708 ● Alternate titles: ROLLER OPERATOR; ROLLER, PNEUMATIC; ROLL OPERATOR. Drives heavy rolling machine (road roller) to compact earth fills, subgrades, flexible base, and bituminous surface to grade specifications preparatory to construction of highways, streets, and runways: Moves levers, depresses pedals, turns handwheels, and pushes throttle to control and guide machine. Drives machine in successive overlapping passes over surface to be compacted. Determines speed and direction of machine, based on knowledge of compressibility of material under changing temperatures, so that ridges are not formed by excessive pressure. Pushes hand roller and pounds surfaces, using hand tamp, or guides portable power roller over areas not accessible to road roller. May be designated according to surface rolled as Road-Roller Operator, Hot Mix (construction); Subgrade-Roller Operator (construction); or according to source of power used as Diesel-Roller Operator (construction); Gas-Roller Operator (construction). ● **GED:** R2, M1, L1 ● **SVP:** 1-3 mos ● **Academic:** Ed=N, Eng=N ● **Work Field:** 095 ● **MPSMS:** 362 ● **Aptitudes:** G3, V4, N5, S4, P3, Q5, K3, F4, M3, E3, C5 ● **Temperaments:** J, T ● **Physical:** Stg=L; Const: R, H Freq: F, D, V Occas: C, S ● **Work Env:** Noise=L; Freq: W Occas: A ● **Salary:** 2 ● **Outlook:** 3

SANITARY LANDFILL OPERATOR (sanitary ser.) ● DOT #955.463-010 ● OES: 97938 ● Alternate titles: SOLID WASTE FACILITY OPERATOR. Performs any combination of following duties to dispose of solid waste materials at landfill site: Operates heavy equipment, such as bulldozer, front-end loader, and compactor, to excavate landfill site, transport solid waste materials, and to spread and compact layers of waste and earth cover. Directs incoming vehicles to dumping area. Examines cargo to prohibit disposal of caustic waste, according to government regulations. Sprays poisons and other specified chemicals over waste material to control disease carrying pests. Drives truck to distribute oil or water over landfill to control dust. Weighs vehicles entering and leaving site and collects dumping fees. ● **GED:** R2, M1, L1 ● **SVP:** 6 mos-1 yr ● **Academic:** Ed=N, Eng=S ● **Work Field:** 011 ● **MPSMS:** 874 ● **Aptitudes:** G3, V4, N4, S3, P4, Q4, K3, F4, M3, E4, C5 ● **Temperaments:** R ● **Physical:** Stg=M; Freq: R, H, I, F, D, V ● **Work Env:** Noise=L; Occas: W, A, T ● **Salary:** 2 ● **Outlook:** 3

SCRAPER OPERATOR (construction) ● DOT #850.683-038 ● OES: 97938 ● Operates tractor-drawn or self-propelled scraper to move, haul, and grade earth on construction sites, such as roadbeds, ditch banks, and water reservoirs: Moves switches, levers, and pedals to control loading gate on bucket (scraper), to adjust depth of cut, to raise and close filled bucket for hauling, and to spread or dump earth. ● **GED:** R3, M1, L2 ● **SVP:** 6 mos-1 yr ● **Academic:** Ed=N, Eng=N ● **Work Field:** 011 ● **MPSMS:** 360 ● **Aptitudes:** G3, V4, N4, S3, P3, Q5, K3, F4, M3, E3, C5 ● **Temperaments:** J, T ● **Physical:** Stg=M; Const: R, H Freq: F, D, V Occas: I ● **Work Env:** Noise=L; Const: W Occas: A ● **Salary:** 3 ● **Outlook:** 4

STREET-SWEEPER OPERATOR (government ser.) ● DOT #919.683-022 ● OES: 97199 ● Alternate titles: TRACTOR-SWEEPER DRIVER. Drives sweeping machine that cleans streets of trash and other accumulations: Fills water tank of machine from hydrant. Drives sweeper along street near curb. Moves controls to activate rotary brushes and water spray so that machine automatically picks up dust and trash from paved street and deposits it in dirt trap at rear of machine. Pulls lever to dump refuse in piles at curb for removal. May be employed by industrial plant, shopping center, or other establishment to drive modified sweeper through parking lots, factory aisles, or along private roads and be designated Power-Sweeper Operator (any industry). May drive machine that sucks leaves into vacuum chamber and be designated Leaf-Sucker Operator (government ser.). May drive vehicle equipped with rotating brushes to remove sand and litter from newly constructed highways and be designated Sweeper Operator, Highways (construction). ● **GED:** R2, M1, L1 ● **SVP:** 1-3 mos ● **Academic:** Ed=N, Eng=N ● **Work Field:** 031 ● **MPSMS:** 362 ● **Aptitudes:** G4, V4, N4, S3, P4, Q5, K3, F4, M4, E4, C5 ● **Temperaments:** R ● **Physical:** Stg=L; Const: R, H, N, F, D, V Occas: I ● **Work Env:** Noise=L; Occas: W, U ● **Salary:** 3 ● **Outlook:** 3

GOE: 05.11.02
Mining & Quarrying

CORE-DRILL OPERATOR (any industry) ● DOT #930.682-010 ● OES: 87988 ● Alternate titles: SHOT-CORE-DRILL OPERATOR; TEST BORER; TEST-HOLE DRILLER; WASH DRILLER. Sets up and operates drilling equipment to obtain solid core samples of strata for analyzing geological characteristics of ground, nature of ore, or strength of foundation material: Drives or guides truck-mounted drilling equipment onto metal or wood foundation, or assembles equipment in position. Connects power lines to equipment. Attaches diamond churn, alloy, or percussion bit to drill rod, and fastens rod in machine, using wrench or other handtools. Starts power unit. Moves clutch and throttle to control rotation and feed of drill bit into ground. Couples additional lengths of drill rod as bit advances. Withdraws drill rod from hole after specified depth has been reached and extracts core from hollow barrel located behind drilling bit. Records depths from which core samples are taken. Lubricates machine, using grease gun, and replaces parts, such as worn winch cables. May replace diamonds in bit as they become worn, chipped, or lost, where diamond drill is used [DIAMOND MOUNTER (machine tools)]. May operate water pump to pump water down borehole to cool drill bit. May be designated according to type of drill used as Diamond Driller (any industry). ● **GED:** R3, M2, L2 ● **SVP:** 1-2 yrs ● **Academic:** Ed=N, Eng=N ● **Work Field:** 005 ● **MPSMS:** 340, 350, 369 ● **Aptitudes:** G3, V4, N4, S4, P3, Q4, K3, F4, M3, E4, C5 ● **Temperaments:** R, T ● **Physical:** Stg=M; Freq: S, O, R, H, N, D Occas: K, I ● **Work Field:** Noise=L; Freq: W Occas: O ● **Salary:** 3 ● **Outlook:** 1

PLANT OPERATOR (concrete prod.) ● DOT #570.682-014 ● OES: 95098 ● Operates concrete, asphalt, or sand and gravel plant to batch, crush, or segregate materials used in construction: Moves controls on panelboard or control board to heat, dry, and mix ingredients, such as asphalt, sand, stone, and naphtha to produce asphalt paving material; to weigh and mix aggregate, cement, and water to produce concrete; or to control feeding, crushing, and sifting machinery in sand and gravel plant. Observes gauges, dials, and operation of machinery to ensure conformance to processing specifications. May repair machinery, using handtools, power tools, and welding equipment. May be designated according to type of plant operated as Asphalt-Plant Operator (construction); Concrete-Batch-Plant Operator (concrete prod.; construction); Sand-And-Gravel-Plant Operator (construction); or according to machine function as Crusher Operator (concrete prod.; construction). ● **GED:** R3, M2, L2 ● **SVP:** 3-6 mos ● **Academic:** Ed=N, Eng=N ● **Work Field:** 143, 142 ● **MPSMS:** 340, 502, 536 ● **Aptitudes:** G3, V4, N4, S4, P4, Q4, K3, F4, M3, E4, C5 ● **Temperaments:** J, T ● **Physical:** Stg=M; Freq: R, H, I, N Occas: C, S, T, G, D ● **Work Env:** Noise=L; Freq: W, A Occas: O ● **Salary:** 5 ● **Outlook:** 3

GOE: 05.11.03
Drilling & Oil Exploration

ROTARY DRILLER (petrol. & gas) ● DOT #930.382-026 ● OES: 87929 ● Alternate titles: CORE DRILLER; DRILLER; WELL DRILLER. Operates gasoline, diesel, electric, or steam draw works to drill oil or gas wells: Observes pressure gauge and moves throttles and levers to control speed of rotary table which rotates string of tools in borehole, and to regulate pressure of tools at bottom of borehole. Connects sections of drill pipe, using handtools and powered wrenches and tongs. Selects and changes drill bits according to nature of strata, using handtools. Pushes levers and brake pedals to control draw works which lowers and raises drill pipe and casing into and out of well. Examines operation of slush pumps to ensure circulation and consistency of mud (drilling fluid) in well. Examines drillings or core samples from bottom of well to determine nature of strata. Fishes for and recovers lost or broken bits, casing and drill pipes from well, using special tools attached to end of drill pipe or cable. Keeps record of footage drilled, location and nature of strata penetrated, and materials used. Caps well or turns valves to regulate outflow of oil from well. Repairs or replaces defective parts of machinery, using handtools. May lower and explode charge in borehole to start flow of oil from well. May specialize in drilling underwater wells from barge-mounted derricks or drilling platforms and be designated Rotary Driller, Marine Operations (petrol. & gas). ● **GED:** R3, M2, L2 ● **SVP:** 1-2 yrs ● **Academic:** Ed=A, Eng=S ● **Work Field:** 005 ● **MPSMS:** 342 ● **Aptitudes:** G3, V3, N3, S3, P3, Q4, K3, F3, M3, E3, C4 ● **Temperaments:** J, T ● **Physical:** Stg=M; Freq: R, H, I, N, D Occas: C, B, S, O, W, X, V ● **Work Env:** Noise=V; Const: W Freq: O ● **Salary:** 3 ● **Outlook:** 2

GOE: 05.11.04
Materials Handling

DRAGLINE OPERATOR (any industry) ● DOT #850.683-018 ● OES: 97910 ● Operates power-driven crane equipped with dragline bucket, suspended from boom by cable to excavate or move sand, gravel, clay, mud, coal, or other materials: Drives machine to work site. Moves hand levers and depresses pedals to rotate crane on chassis and position boom above excavation point, to raise and lower boom, to lower bucket to material, to drag bucket toward crane to excavate or move material, to place bucket over unloading point, and to tilt bucket to release material. May direct workers engaged in placing blocks and outriggers to prevent capsizing of machine when lifting heavy loads. May be designated according to type of chassis or power unit as Crawler-Dragline Operator (any industry); Diesel-Dragline Operator (any industry); Electric-Dragline Operator (any industry); Gasoline-Dragline Operator (any industry); or material excavated as Clay Hoister (cement); Walking-Dragline Operator (any industry). ● **GED:** R3, M2, L2 ● **SVP:** 6 mos-1 yr ● **Academic:** Ed=N, Eng=N ● **Work Field:** 011 ● **MPSMS:** 340, 360 ● **Aptitudes:** G3, V4, N4, S3, P4, Q5, K3, F4, M3, E3, C5 ● **Temperaments:** J, T ● **Physical:** Stg=M; Const: R, H, F, D, V Occas: C, S, K, O ● **Work Env:** Noise=L; Occas: W ● **Salary:** 3 ● **Outlook:** 4

DUMP OPERATOR (any industry) ● DOT #921.685-038 ● OES: 97910 ● Alternate titles: CAR-DUMPER OPERATOR; TIPPLE WORKER. Tends mechanical or electrical dumping equipment to dump materials, such as grain, raw materials, coal, or ore, from mine cars, railroad cars, or trucks into bins or onto conveyor for storage, reloading, or further processing, using either of following methods: (1) Observes that car or truck is spotted accurately on bed of rotary dump. Moves controls to secure clamps over couplings that hold car while being tipped. Starts motor or pulls lever that tips car and dumps contents. Releases clamps to remove car. (2) Opens bottom or side doors of car or truck spotted over gravity dump. Moves controls to lower car shakeout device into car and to start vibration that loosens remaining coal or ore. May hook winch cables to cars to draw them onto dumping bed. May couple and uncouple cars. May be required to maintain records of unloading operations. May be designated according to type of equipment tended as Car-Shakeout Operator (cement; mine & quarry); Rotary-Dump Operator (mine & quarry; steel & rel.); or according to material unloaded as Grain Unloader, Machine (grain-feed mills). ● **GED:** R2, M1, L1 ● **SVP:** 1-3 mos ● **Academic:** Ed=N, Eng=N ● **Work Field:** 011 ● **MPSMS:** 300, 350, 340 ● **Aptitudes:** G4, V4, N4, S3, P4, Q4, K3, F4, M3, E4, C5 ● **Temperaments:** R ● **Physical:** Stg=L; Freq: R, H, I, N, D ● **Work Env:** Noise=L; Occas: W ● **Salary:** 3 ● **Outlook:** 3

FRONT-END LOADER OPERATOR (any industry) ● DOT #921.683-042 ● OES: 97947 ● Alternate titles: LOADER OPERATOR; WHEEL LOADER OPERATOR. Operates straight or articulated rubber-tired tractor-type vehicle equipped with front-mounted hydraulically powered bucket or scoop to lift and transport bulk materials to and from storage or processing areas, to feed conveyors, hoppers, or chutes, and to load trucks or railcars: Starts engine, shifts gears, presses pedals, and turns steering wheel to operate loader. Moves levers to lower and tilt bucket and drives front-end loader forward to force bucket into bulk material. Moves levers to raise and tilt bucket when filled, drives vehicle to work site, and moves levers to dump material. Performs routine maintenance on loader, such as lubricating, fueling, and cleaning. ● **GED:** R2, M1, L1 ● **SVP:** 1-3 mos ● **Academic:** Ed=N, Eng=N ● **Work Field:** 011 ● **MPSMS:** 456, 459, 344 ● **Aptitudes:** G3, V4, N4, S3, P4, Q4, K3, F3, M3, E3, C5 ● **Temperaments:** R, T ● **Physical:** Stg=M; Const: R, H, V Freq: F, A Occas: C, I, G, N, D ● **Work Env:** Noise=L; Const: A Freq: W, V Occas: M ● **Salary:** 4 ● **Outlook:** 3

HOISTING ENGINEER (any industry) ● DOT #921.663-030 ● OES: 97941 ● Alternate titles: HOISTING-MACHINE OPERATOR. Operates compressed air, diesel, electric, gasoline, or steam drum hoists to control movement of cableways, cages, derricks, draglines, loaders, railcars, or skips to move workers and materials for construction, logging, mining, sawmill, and other industrial operations: Starts hoist engine and moves hand and foot levers to wind or unwind cable on drum. Moves brake lever and throttle to stop, start, and regulate speed of drum in response to hand, bell, telephone, loud-speaker, or whistle signals or by oobserving dial indicator or marks on cable. May fire boiler on steam hoist. May operate hoist with more than one drum. May repair, maintain, and adjust equipment. May be designated according to equipment controlled as Cableway Operator (any industry); Cage Operator (any industry); Gin-Pole Operator construction); Inclined-Railway Operator (any industry); Skip-Hoist Operator (any industry). May transfer logs from trucks to railroad cars and be designated Transfer Engineer (logging). ● **GED:** R3, M1, L1 ● **SVP:** 3-6 mos ● **Academic:** Ed=N, Eng=N ● **Work Field:** 011 ● **MPSMS:** 586 ● **Aptitudes:** G3, V4, N4, S3, P4, Q5, K3, F4, M3, E3, C4 ● **Temperaments:** R, T ● **Physical:** Stg=M; Freq: R, H, F, D, V Occas: C, S, K, I, T, G, N, X ● **Salary:** 4 ● **Outlook:** 3

OVERHEAD CRANE OPERATOR (any industry) ● DOT #921.663-010 ● OES: 97944 ● Alternate titles: CRANE OPERATOR, CAB; CRANE OPERATOR, GROUND CONTROL; TRAVELING-CRANE OPERATOR. Operates traveling or stationary overhead crane (cab- or ground controlled) to lift, move, and position loads, such as machinery, equipment, products, and solid or bulk materials, using hoisting attachments, such as hook, sling, electromagnet, or bucket: Observes load hookup and determines safety of load. Manipulates or depresses crane controls, such as pedals, levers, and buttons, to regulate speed and direction of crane and hoist movement according to written, verbal, or signal instructions. Cleans and maintains crane and hoisting mechanism. Inspects crane for defective parts and notifies supervisor of defects or malfunctions. May attach load to hook or other crane accessory prior to operating crane and be designated Crane Operator-Hooker (steel & rel.) or Crane Operator-Hooktender (aircraft mfg.). May be designated by type of crane operated or material handled as Bridge Crane Operator (any industry); Charging Crane Operator (foundry; steel & rel.); Cinder Crane Operator (foundry; steel & rel.) I; Gantry Crane Operator (any industry); Hot-Metal Crane Operator (foundry; nonfer. metal; steel & rel.) I; Ingot Stripper (steel & rel.) I; Scrap Crane Operator (steel & rel.) I; Tower Whirler Operator (any industry); Wall Crane Operator (foundry). ● **GED:** R3, M2, L2 ● **SVP:** 6 mos-1 yr ● **Academic:** Ed=N, Eng=N ● **Work Field:** 011 ● **MPSMS:** 969 ● **Aptitudes:** G3, V4, N4, S3, P4, Q5, K3, F4, M3, E3, C5 ● **Temperaments:** R, T ● **Physical:** Stg=L; Const: D Freq: R, H, F, V Occas: C, S, O, I, T, G ● **Work Env:** Noise=L; ● **Salary:** 4 ● **Outlook:** 3

RIGGER (any industry) ● DOT #921.260-010 ● OES: 85935 ● Alternate titles: CRANE RIGGER; HOOK TENDER; SLINGER; YARD RIGGER. Assembles rigging to lift and move equipment or material in manufacturing plant, shipyard, or on construction project: Selects cables, ropes, pulleys, winches, blocks, and sheaves, according to weight and size of load to be moved. Attaches pulley and blocks to fixed overhead structures, such as beams, ceilings, and gin pole booms, with bolts and clamps. Attaches load with grappling devices, such as loops, wires, ropes, and chains, to crane hook. Gives directions to OVERHEAD CRANE OPERATOR (any industry) 921.663-010 or HOISTING ENGINEER (any industry) engaged in hoisting and moving loads to ensure safety of workers and material handled, using hand signals, loud-speaker, or telephone. Sets up, braces, and rigs hoisting equipment, using handtools and power wrenches. Splices rope and wire cables to make or repair slings and tackle. May direct workers engaged in hoisting of machinery and equipment into ships and be designated Machinery Erector (ship-boat mfg.). When hoisting and moving construction machinery onto truck beds, may be designated Machine Mover (construction). ● **GED:** R4, M2, L2 ● **SVP:** 1-2 yrs ● **Academic:** Ed=N, Eng=N ● **Work Field:** 011 ● **MPSMS:** 565 ● **Aptitudes:** G3, V3, N4, S3, P3, Q4, K4, F3, M3, E4, C5 ● **Temperaments:** T, V ● **Physical:** Stg=H; Freq: C, S, K, R, H, N, F, D, V Occas: B, O, W, I, T, G, X ● **Work Env:** Noise=L; Freq: W, O ● **Salary:** 4 ● **Outlook:** 3

STEVEDORE I (water trans.) ● DOT #911.663-014 ● OES: 97910 ● Operates material-handling equipment, such as power winch, grain trimmer, crane, and lift truck, to transfer cargo into or from hold of ship and about dock area: Operates crane or winch to load or unload cargo, such as automobiles, crates, scrap, and steel beams, using hook, magnet, or sling attached in accordance with signals from other workers. Moves controls to start flow of grain from spouts of grain trimmer, stopping flow and repositioning spout over each hatch when previous hatch is filled. Drives lift truck along dock or aboard ship to transfer bulk items, such as lumber, pallet-mounted machinery, and crated products within range of winch. Drives tractor to transfer loaded trailers from warehouse to dockside. May position and fasten hose lines to ships' cargo tanks when loading or unloading liquid cargo, such as animal fats, vegetable oils, molasses, or chemicals. May perform variety of manual duties, such as lashing and shoring cargo aboard ship, attaching slings, hooks, or other lifting devices to winch for loading or unloading, and signaling other workers to move, raise, or lower cargo. May direct activities of cargo gang consisting of STEVEDORE (water trans.) II. May be designated according to equipment operated as Lift-Truck Operator (water trans.); Tractor Operator (water trans.); Winch Operator (water trans.). ● **GED:** R3, M2, L2 ● **SVP:** 6 mos-1 yr ● **Academic:** Ed=N, Eng=N ● **Work Field:** 011 ● **MPSMS:** 854 ● **Aptitudes:** G3, V4, N4, S3, P4, Q4, K3, F4, M3, E3, C5 ● **Temperaments:** J ● **Physical:** Stg=M; Freq: R, H, F Occas: C, S, K, O, I, N, D, V ● **Work Env:** Noise=N; Freq: W ● **Salary:** 4 ● **Outlook:** 2

TRACTOR OPERATOR (any industry) ● DOT #929.683-014 ● OES: 97947 ● Drives gasoline or diesel powered tractor to move materials, draw farm implements, tow trailers, pull out objects imbedded in ground, or pull cable of winch to raise, lower, or load heavy material or equipment: Fastens attachments, such as graders, plows, and rollers, to tractor with hitchpins. Releases brake, shifts gears, and depresses accelerator or moves throttle to control forward and backward movement of tractor. Steers tractor by turning steering wheel and depressing brake pedals. May lubricate and repair tractor and attachments. May be designated according to type of power utilized as Diesel-Tractor Operator (any industry); Gasoline-Tractor Operator (any industry); Tractor Operator, Battery (mine & quarry). May operate tractor mounted with wide spread pneumatic or metallic treads to transport materials over marshes or swamps and be designated Marsh-Buggy Operator (construction). May operate tractor equipped with laser leveling equipment to level large fields for farming or industrial purposes and be designated Tractor Operator, Laser Leveling (any industry). ● **GED:** R3, M2, L2 ● **SVP:** 1-3 mos ● **Academic:** Ed=N, Eng=N ● **Work Field:** 003, 011 ● **MPSMS:** 562 ● **Aptitudes:** G3, V4, N4, S3, P4, Q4, K3, F4, M3, E3, C5 ● **Temperaments:** R, T ● **Physical:** Stg=M; Freq: R, H, N, F, D, V Occas: C, S, K, O, I, G ● **Work Env:** Noise=L; Freq: W ● **Salary:** 4 ● **Outlook:** 2

Elemental Work: Mechanical   05.12

Workers in this group perform a variety of unskilled tasks, such as moving materials, cleaning work areas, operating simple machines, or helping skilled workers. These jobs are found in a variety of nonfactory settings.

✓ What kind of work would you do?

Your work activities would depend upon your specific job. For example, you might:

- dump barrels of oil into tanks and take samples to the refinery.
- position cables around logs in a logging camp and signal for winch to move them.
- clean filters, tanks, and wallways at a sewage-disposal plant.
- lubricate moving parts of vehicles such as automobiles, buses, and trucks.
- use a shovel to remove excess dirt from a ditch or excavation.
- use brooms, vacuums, and shovels to clean working areas in a factory.
- carry brick and mortar to masons constructing a wall.

✓ What skills and abilities do you need for this kind of work?

To do this kind of work, you must be able to:

- use hands to lift, carry, or pull objects that may be heavy.
- understand simple instructions.
- work outdoors in all kinds of weather.
- learn simple procedures and techniques.
- perform routine work or the same task over and over again.

✓ How do you know if you would like or could learn to do this kind of work?

The following questions may give you clues about yourself as you consider this group of jobs.

- Have you done work of a physical nature? Do you like to do this type of work?
- Have you been responsible for cleaning a house or garage? Do you take pride in maintaining an orderly work area?
- Have you helped someone move household goods? Can you lift and carry heavy objects?

✓ How can you prepare for and enter this kind of work?

Occupations in this group usually require education and/or training extending from a short demonstration to over three months, depending upon the specific kind of work. This kind of work requires only a brief explanation of job duties. The most important hiring consideration is usually the physical ability of the applicant. Many of these jobs are available through union hiring halls.

✓ What else should you consider about these jobs?

Weather conditions can cause periods of unemployment for construction workers. Others usually work a 40-hour week all year.

Workers are often required to wear safety clothing to protect themselves from common job hazards such as falling objects, extreme temperature levels, or exposure to dangerous chemicals. Employers often provide classes or on-the-job training about safety. Work locations are often checked by government inspectors to ensure that conditions are safe.

With additional training, workers in this group may qualify for machine tending or operating jobs. Workers with a high school education or its equal may qualify for apprenticeship programs leading to more skilled jobs, especially in construction. Those with leadership ability can advance to supervisory jobs.

If you think you would like to do this kind of work, look at the job titles listed below.

■   ■   ■

GOE: 05.12.01
Supervision

BARGE CAPTAIN (water trans.) ● DOT #911.137-010 ● OES: 97510 ● Alternate titles: SCOW CAPTAIN. Supervises and coordinates activities of workers on towed barge that transports cargo on lakes, bays, sounds, and rivers: Directs workers engaged in loading and unloading barge to ensure that cargo is loaded according to balancing specifications. Inspects barge to ensure that craft is seaworthy. Signals TUG-

BOAT CAPTAIN (water trans.) to tow barge to destination. Logs barge's movements and ports-of-call. Steers barge when it has steering equipment. ● **GED:** R4, M3, L3 ● **SVP:** 1-2 yrs ● **Academic:** Ed=N, Eng=S ● **Work Field:** 011, 013 ● **MPSMS:** 854 ● **Aptitudes:** G3, V3, N4, S3, P3, Q4, K4, F4, M3, E4, C5 ● **Temperaments:** D, J ● **Physical:** Stg=M; Freq: R, H, T, G, N Occas: I, F, D ● **Work Env:** Noise=N; Freq: W ● **Salary:** 5 ● **Outlook:** 2

HOUSEKEEPER (hotel & rest.) ● DOT #321.137-010 ● OES: 61008 ● Alternate titles: FLOOR HOUSEKEEPER. Supervises work activities of cleaning personnel to ensure clean, orderly attractive rooms in hotels, hospitals, and similar establishments: Obtains list of vacant rooms which need to be cleaned immediately and list of prospective check-outs or discharges in order to prepare work assignments. Assigns workers their duties, and inspects work for conformance to prescribed standards of cleanliness. Advises manager, desk clerk, or admitting personnel of rooms ready for occupancy. Inventories stock to ensure adequate supplies. Issues supplies and equipment to workers. Investigates complaints regarding housekeeping service and equipment, and takes corrective action. Examines rooms, halls, and lobbies to determine need for repairs or replacement of furniture or equipment, and makes recommendations to management. Screens job applicants, hires new employees, and recommends promotions, transfers, or dismissals. Conducts orientation training of new employees and in-service training of other employees to explain company policies, housekeeping work procedures, and to demonstrate use and maintenance of equipment. Attends training seminars to perfect housekeeping techniques and procedures, and enhance supervisory skills. Records data concerning work assignments, personnel actions, and time cards, and prepares periodic reports. Attends periodic staff meetings with other department heads to discuss company policies and patrons' complaints, and to make recommendations to improve service and ensure more efficient operation. May prepare reports concerning room occupancy, payroll expenses, and department expenses. ● **GED:** R3, M2, L3 ● **SVP:** 1-2 yrs ● **Academic:** Ed=N, Eng=S ● **Work Field:** 031 ● **MPSMS:** 905 ● **Aptitudes:** G3, V3, N4, S3, P3, Q3, K4, F4, M3, E5, C5 ● **Temperaments:** D, J, P, V ● **Physical:** Stg=L; Freq: R, H, I, T, G, N Occas: S ● **Work Env:** Noise=Q; ● **Salary:** 2 ● **Outlook:** 4

HOUSEKEEPER, HOME (domestic ser.) ● DOT #301.137-010 ● OES: 62031 ● Alternate titles: MANAGER, HOUSEHOLD. Supervises and coordinates activities of household employees in a private residence: Informs new employees of employer's desires and gives instructions in work methods and routines. Assigns duties, such as cooking and serving meals, cleaning, washing, and ironing, adjusting work activities to accommodate family members. Orders foodstuffs and cleaning supplies. Keeps record of expenditures. May hire and discharge employees. Works in residence employing large staff. ● **GED:** R4, M2, L3 ● **SVP:** 1-2 yrs ● **Academic:** Ed=N, Eng=S ● **Work Field:** 291 ● **MPSMS:** 900 ● **Aptitudes:** G3, V3, N3, S4, P3, Q4, K4, F4, M4, E5, C5 ● **Temperaments:** D, P, V ● **Physical:** Stg=L; Freq: R, H, I, T, G, N ● **Work Env:** Noise=N; ● **Salary:** 1 ● **Outlook:** 4

LABOR-CREW SUPERVISOR (construction) ● DOT #899.131-010 ● OES: 81000 ● Supervises and coordinates activities of workers engaged in constructing manholes, transformer vaults, and substation foundations, in installing street light poles, and in laying pipe and ductwork for telephone, electric, water and sewage systems, and gas and oil lines: Reads blueprints and interprets data, including angles required in bending pipe, mixture of concrete most suitable for soil conditions, locations for placement of pipe sections, and type and amount of insulating wrapping and adhesive compound required to protect pipe. Directs activities of workers engaged in inspecting pipe for deficiencies by use of x-ray equipment or by means of high-pressure air tests, of workers engaged in removing rust and applying protective coating to pipe, of workers engaged in laying pipe on land or underwater, of workers engaged in performing dredging, underwater blasting and backfilling activities, and of workers engaged in digging up and removing pipelines. Performs other duties as described under SUPERVISOR (any industry) Master Title. May be designated according to area of specialization as Duct-Layer Supervisor (construction; utilities); Fabrication Supervisor (construction); Lower-In Supervisor (construction); Pipe-And-Test Supervisor (construction); Pipe-Laying Supervisor (construction); River-Crossing Supervisor (construction); Take-Up Supervisor (construction). ● **GED:** R4, M3, L3 ● **SVP:** 4-10 yrs ● **Academic:** Ed=N, Eng=G ● **Work Field:** 102 ● **MPSMS:** 360, 364 ● **Aptitudes:** G3, V3, N3, S3, P3, Q3, K3, F3, M3, E4, C5 ● **Temperaments:** D, J, P, V ● **Physical:** Stg=L; Freq: C, S, O, R, H, I, T, G, N, F, D, A, V ● **Work Env:** Noise=L; Freq: W, O Occas: A ● **Salary:** 5 ● **Outlook:** 2

STEWARD/STEWARDESS (hotel & rest.) ● DOT #310.137-018 ● OES: 69998 ● Alternate titles: CHIEF STEWARD/STEWARDESS; EXECUTIVE STEWARD/STEWARDESS; HOUSE STEWARD/STEWARDESS. Supervises and coordinates activities of pantry, storeroom, and noncooking kitchen workers, and purchases or requisitions foodstuffs, kitchen supplies, and equipment: Inspects kitchens and storerooms to ensure that premises and equipment are clean and in order,

and that sufficient foodstuffs and supplies are on hand to ensure efficient service. Examines incoming purchases for quality and to ensure that purchases are as specified in order. Approves invoices or bills for payment. Coordinates work of noncooking kitchen and storeroom workers engaged in activities, such as dishwashing, silver cleaning, and storage and distribution of foodstuffs and supplies. Establishes controls to guard against theft and wastage. Confers with EXECUTIVE CHEF (hotel & rest.) or MANAGER, CATERING (hotel & rest.) concerning banquet arrangements for food service, equipment, and extra employees. May plan and price menus, keep cost records, and establish budget controls to ensure profitable food service operation. May perform duties for recreational or business clubs. This job occurs in hotels as opposed to KITCHEN SUPERVISOR (hotel & rest.) which occurs in restaurants and cafeterias. ● **GED:** R4, M3, L4 ● **SVP:** 2-4 yrs ● **Academic:** Ed=H, Eng=G ● **Work Field:** 221 ● **MPSMS:** 903 ● **Aptitudes:** G3, V3, N3, S4, P4, Q3, K4, F4, M4, E5, C4 ● **Temperaments:** D, J, P, V ● **Physical:** Stg=L; Freq: R, H, I, T, G, N, A Occas: E, X ● **Work Env:** Noise=L; ● **Salary:** 4 ● **Outlook:** 3

SUPERVISOR, CENTRAL SUPPLY (medical ser.) ● DOT #381.137-014 ● OES: 51002 ● Supervises and coordinates activities of personnel in medical central supply room engaged in furnishing sterile and nonsterile supplies and equipment for use in care and treatment of patients: Directs activities of workers engaged in cleaning, assembling, and packing of linens, gowns, dressings, gloves, treatment trays, instruments, and related items; preparation of solutions; arrangement of stock; and requisitioning, issuing, controlling, and charging of supplies and equipment. Instructs personnel in use of sterilizing equipment and water distillation apparatus, setting up standardized treatment trays, and maintaining equipment of central supply room. Establishes standards of work performance and methods of operation for department. Inspects work activities to ensure workers are following prescribed procedures to meet hospital standards. Ensures that aseptic techniques are employed by personnel in preparing and handling sterile items. Inspects daily inventory, maintains records of supply usage, and compiles periodic reports. ● **GED:** R4, M3, L4 ● **SVP:** 2-4 yrs ● **Academic:** Ed=H, Eng=S ● **Work Field:** 031, 041, 221 ● **MPSMS:** 929 ● **Aptitudes:** G3, V3, N3, S4, P4, Q3, K4, F4, M4, E5, C5 ● **Temperaments:** D, J, P, V ● **Physical:** Stg=L; Freq: R, H, I, T, G Occas: N ● **Work Env:** Noise=N; ● **Salary:** 2 ● **Outlook:** 4

GOE: 05.12.02
Mining, Quarrying, Drilling

HORIZONTAL-EARTH-BORING-MACHINE-OPERATOR HELPER (construction) ● DOT #850.684-014 ● OES: 98310 ● Alternate titles: BORING-MACHINE-OPERATOR HELPER. Performs any combination of following duties to aid in drilling of horizontal holes for installation of pipelines under highways, railroads, canals, and other obstructions: Lays foundation timbers for boring machine and places timber braces to hold machine in place. Couples auger sections together and bolts sections to drive shaft. Removes dirt from hole, using shovel. Removes seepage water from boring machine pit, using portable sump. May place props between hydraulic rams and end of casing pipe. May hammer steel wedges into shaft collar to lock auger drive to ram yoke. May weld sections of casing pipe together, using arc-welding equipment. ● **GED:** R2, M1, L1 ● **SVP:** 2-30 days ● **Academic:** Ed=N, Eng=N ● **Work Field:** 005 ● **MPSMS:** 369 ● **Aptitudes:** G3, V4, N5, S4, P4, Q5, K3, F4, M3, E4, C5 ● **Temperaments:** R, T ● **Physical:** Stg=H; Freq: R, H, I, N Occas: C, S, K, O ● **Work Env:** Noise=L; Const: W Freq: U ● **Salary:** 2 ● **Outlook:** 3

SURVEYOR HELPER (any industry) ● DOT #869.567-010 ● OES: 98310 ● Performs any of following duties to assist in surveying land: Holds level or stadia rod at designated points to assist in determining elevations and laying out stakes for mapmaking, construction, mining, land, and other surveys. Calls out reading or writes station number and reading in notebook. Marks points of measurement with elevation, station number, or other identifying mark. Measures distance between survey points, using steel or cloth tape or surveyor's chain. Marks measuring points with keel (marking crayon), paint sticks, scratches, tacks, or stakes. Places stakes at designated points and drives them into ground at specified elevation, using hammer or hatchet. Cuts and clears brush and trees from line of survey, using brush hook, knife, ax, or other cutting tools. May perform duties as directed by LAND SURVEYOR (profess. & kin.) or SURVEYOR ASSISTANT, INSTRUMENTS (profess. & kin.). May perform one operation and be designated Brush Clearer, Surveying (any industry); Staker, Surveying (any industry); Surveyor Helper, Chain (any industry); Surveyor Helper, Rod (any industry). ● **GED:** R3, M1, L2 ● **SVP:** 3-6 mos ● **Academic:** Ed=N, Eng=N ● **Work Field:** 243, 031 ● **MPSMS:** 310, 360 ● **Aptitudes:** G4, V4, N4, S4, P4, Q4, K4, F4, M3, E4, C5 ● **Temperaments:** R, T ● **Physical:** Stg=M; Freq: S, K, O, R, H, I, N, F, D, A Occas: X ● **Work Env:** Noise=N; ● **Salary:** 2 ● **Outlook:** 2

GOE: 05.12.03
Loading, Moving

ABLE SEAMAN (water trans.) ● DOT #911.364-010 ● OES: 97504 ● Alternate titles: ABLE-BODIED SEAMAN. Performs following tasks on board ship to watch for obstructions in vessel's path and to maintain equipment and structures: Stands watch at bow or on wing of bridge to look for obstructions in path of vessel. Measures depth of water in shallow or unfamiliar waters, using leadline, and telephones or shouts information to bridge. Turns wheel on bridge or uses emergency steering apparatus to steer vessel as directed by MATE, SHIP (water trans.). Breaks out, rigs, overhauls, and stows cargo-handling gear, stationary rigging, and running gear. Overhauls lifeboats and lifeboat gear and lowers or raises lifeboats with winch or falls. Paints and chips rust on deck or superstructure of ship. Must hold certificate issued by U.S. Government. When working aboard vessels carrying liquid cargoes, must hold tanker operator's certificate. May stow or remove cargo from ship's hold [STEVEDORE (water trans.) II]. May be concerned with only one phase of duties, as maintenance of ship's gear and decks or watch duties, and be known as Deckhand, Maintenance (water trans.); Watchstander (water trans.). ● **GED:** R3, M2, L2 ● **SVP:** 6 mos-1 yr ● **Academic:** Ed=N, Eng=N ● **Work Field:** 013 ● **MPSMS:** 854 ● **Aptitudes:** G3, V4, N4, S3, P3, Q4, K3, F3, M3, E2, C4 ● **Temperaments:** J, T ● **Physical:** Stg=H; Freq: C, B, R, H, F, D Occas: S, K, O, I, T, G, X ● **Work Env:** Noise=N; Freq: W, M Occas: O ● **Salary:** 4 ● **Outlook:** 2

BAGGAGE HANDLER (r.r. trans.) ● DOT #910.687-010 ● OES: 98998 ● Loads and stores baggage on passenger train: Inspects tags on baggage to ensure that baggage is routed to designated train. Loads baggage in car according to destination recorded on tags, placing baggage to be unloaded last in rear of car. Unloads baggage from train onto trailers at destination. ● **GED:** R2, M1, L1 ● **SVP:** 2-30 days ● **Academic:** Ed=N, Eng=N ● **Work Field:** 011 ● **MPSMS:** 851 ● **Aptitudes:** G4, V4, N4, S3, P4, Q4, K3, F4, M3, E3, C5 ● **Temperaments:** R ● **Physical:** Stg=H; Freq: S, K, O, R, H, I, N ● **Work Env:** Noise=N; ● **Salary:** 2 ● **Outlook:** 2

DUMPER (any industry) ● DOT #921.667-018 ● OES: 97910 ● Alternate titles: BULK LOADER. Dumps materials, such as coal, chemicals, flue dust, grain, ore, sugar, and salt, into and from railway cars, trucks, or other vehicles, according to specific instructions: Positions and blocks vehicles by signaling LOCOMOTIVE ENGINEER (r.r. trans.) 910.363-014 or TRUCK DRIVER, HEAVY (any industry) 905.663-014, or by using winch and car jack or powered tractor to spot cars and set brakes. Positions spout, chute, and conveyor over or into car, truck, bin, or storage pile and opens slide in spout or chute to start flow of material into or from vehicles. Positions vehicle over storage bin and opens air valve, side door, or car hopper door, starts conveyors, pneumatic conveyors, or elevators, and adjusts dampers to feed materials to specified bin. May use power scoop to pull grain from car into receiving chute. May collect grain sample, using probe. May drive truck onto ramp, secure it with blocks, and attach hook from electric hoist to front end of trailer or truck and push buttom to activate hoist or move lever of hydraulic lift to elevate front end of truck as tailgate is opened to dump material. May vibrate hopper to facilitate flow into slurry pit, using airhammer. May open solvent tank valve and start pump to wash and transfer residue of materials to saturator and other tanks. May observe pressure gauges and adjust valves to maintain specified pumping pressure. May record car identifying information, such as weight and volume of material loaded and number of cars dumped or filled. May

be designated according to kind of vehicle unloaded as Car Dumper (any industry); according to kind of material unloaded as Grain Unloader (grain-feed mils); or according to type of equipment used as Spout Positioner (any industry); Wincher (any industry). ● **GED:** R2, M1, L1 ● **SVP:** 2-30 days ● **Academic:** Ed=N, Eng=N ● **Work Field:** 011, 041 ● **MPSMS:** 859 ● **Aptitudes:** G4, V4, N4, S3, P4, Q5, K3, F4, M3, E4, C4 ● **Temperaments:** R ● **Physical:** Stg=H; Freq: C, S, O, R, H, N, F, D, V Occas: I, T, G, X ● **Work Env:** Noise=L; Freq: W, A, O ● **Salary:** 4 ● **Outlook:** 2

GARBAGE COLLECTOR (motor trans.) ● DOT #955.687-022 ● OES: 98705 ● Collects refuse on designated route within municipality and dumps refuse from containers onto truck. May be designated according to refuse collected as Trash Collector (motor trans.). May drive truck [GARBAGE COLLECTOR DRIVER (motor trans.)]. May start hoisting device that raises refuse bin attached to rear of truck and dumps contents into opening in enclosed truck body. ● **GED:** R1, M1, L1 ● **SVP:** 1 day ● **Academic:** Ed=N, Eng=N ● **Work Field:** 011 ● **MPSMS:** 874 ● **Aptitudes:** G4, V4, N5, S4, P4, Q5, K4, F4, M3, E4, C5 ● **Temperaments:** R ● **Physical:** Stg=V; Freq: C, S, O, R, H ● **Work Env:** Noise=L; Const: W Freq: A Occas: O ● **Salary:** 2 ● **Outlook:** 2

INSTALLER (museums) ● DOT #922.687-050 ● OES: 98710 ● Moves, installs, and stores paintings, statuary, and other art objects in art museum: Places protective pads on handtruck platform and lifts paintings, statuary, or other art objects onto handtruck and places protective pads between and around objects to ensure against damage. Pushes handtruck from shipping-receiving area to storage or display gallery as directed by supervisor. Places objects to be stored in designated sections of storage area. Removes objects to be displayed from handtruck, hangs paintings, and positions statuary and other objects in cabinets or on stands as directed. Dismantles exhibit components, as directed, and moves art objects, cabinets, and other display items to storage area. Moves designated objects from storage area to shipping room. ● **GED:** R2, M1, L1 ● **SVP:** 2-30 days ● **Academic:** Ed=N, Eng=N ● **Work Field:** 011 ● **MPSMS:** 969 ● **Aptitudes:** G4, V4, N5, S3, P4, Q5, K3, F4, M3, E4, C5 ● **Temperaments:** R ● **Physical:** Stg=H; Freq: R, H, N Occas: C, B, S, O, I ● **Work Env:** Noise=N; ● **Salary:** 2 ● **Outlook:** 3

LABORER, PETROLEUM REFINERY (petrol. refin.) ● DOT #549.687-018 ● OES: 98998 ● Alternate titles: PROCESS HELPER. Performs any combination of following tasks in refinery: Digs ditches, builds dikes and levees, and fills holes with earth, rock, sand, and asphalt gravels, using pick and shovel. Smooths ground surfaces and roadways, using hand tamper. Cleans refining equipment. Removes debris from roadways and work areas, and sprays and hoes weeds. Shovels sand and gravel off vehicles and dumps or shovels cement and sand into mixers. Mixes and pours cement and transports cement to forms with wheelbarrow. Unloads materials, such as tools, equipment, sacks of cement, sand, catalyst, salt, and lime, and oil barrels from freight cars and trucks, manually or with handtruck; and stacks barrels and sacks for storage. Uncrates equipment and parts, such as fractionating or treating towers and bubble trays, using pry bar and hammer; and installs bubble caps, using wrenches. Rips open sacks and dumps chemicals and catalysts into mixing, treating, or storage tanks. Dopes pipelines to prevent corrosion, using doping pot and tar. Changes hoist cables, and rigs chain hoists, rope blocks, power winches, and gin poles used to move or raise equipment. Skims oil from cooling water in water boxes. May be designated according to section of refinery in which work is performed as Laborer, Filter Plant (petrol. refin.). ● **GED:** R2, M1, L1 ● **SVP:** 1-3 mos ● **Academic:** Ed=N, Eng=N ● **Work Field:** 031, 011 ● **MPSMS:** 501 ● **Aptitudes:** G4, V4, N4, S4, P4, Q5, K4, F4, M3, E5, C5 ● **Temperaments:** R ● **Physical:** Stg=H; Freq: C, B, S, K, O, R, H ● **Work Env:** Noise=L; Const: W Freq: A, O ● **Salary:** 2 ● **Outlook:** 2

LABORER, SHIPYARD (ship-boat mfg.) ● DOT #809.687-022 ● OES: 98998 ● Performs following tasks in shipyards: Loads vehicles, using handtruck or dolly. Washes trucks and other vehicles. Cleans ships, piers, drydocks, and other working areas, using broom and water hose. Opens shipping crates, using hammer and pinchbar. Sorts lumber, metals, and other scrap materials. Collects and burns trash. Mixes and pours cement on inner bottoms of ships and around joints on decks to prepare surfaces for tile or to make joints watertight. Removes paint and scale from ships' metal surfaces, using hand or powered wire brushes. Conveys materials and tools to work site. ● **GED:**

R2, M1, L1 ● **SVP:** 2-30 days ● **Academic:** Ed=N, Eng=N ● **Work Field:** 011, 102 ● **MPSMS:** 593 ● **Aptitudes:** G4, V4, N5, S4, P4, Q5, K4, F4, M4, E5, C5 ● **Temperaments:** R ● **Physical:** Stg=H; Freq: R, H Occas: S, K, O, N, D ● **Work Env:** Noise=L; Freq: W, U ● **Salary:** 2 ● **Outlook:** 1

MATERIAL HANDLER (any industry) ● DOT #929.687-030 ● OES: 98710 ● Alternate titles: DISTRIBUTOR; FLOOR WORKER; LINE SUPPLY; LOADER AND UNLOADER; SERVICER; STACKER; UTILITY WORKER. Loads, unloads, and moves materials within or near plant, yard, or work site, performing any combination of following duties: Reads work order or follows oral instructions to ascertain materials or containers to be moved. Opens containers, using steel cutters, crowbar, clawhammer, or other handtools. Loads and unloads materials onto or from pallets, trays, racks, and shelves by hand. Loads materials into vehicles and installs strapping, bracing, or padding to prevent shifting or damage in transit, using handtools. Conveys materials from storage or work sites to designated area, using handtruck, electric dolly, wheelbarrow, or other device. Secures lifting attachments to materials and conveys load to destination, using hand-operated crane or hoist, or signals crane or hoisting operators to move load to destination [LABORER, HOISTING (any industry) 921.667-022]. Counts, weighs, and records number of units of materials moved or handled on daily production sheet. Attaches identifying tags or labels to materials or marks information on cases, bales, or other containers. Loads truck for INDUSTRIAL-TRUCK OPERATOR (any industry) 921.683-050. Stacks or assembles materials into bundles and bands bundles together, using banding machine and clincher. Clamps sections of portable conveyor together or places conveyor sections on blocks or boxes to facilitate movement of materials or products. Removes samples of materials, labels with identifying information, and takes samples to laboratory for analysis [LABORATORY-SAMPLE CARRIER (any industry) 922.687-054]. Lifts heavy objects by hand or using power hoist, and cleans work area, machines, and equipment, using broom, rags, and cleaning compounds, to assist machine operators. Makes simple adjustments or repairs, such as realigning belts or replacing rollers, using handtools. Assembles crates to contain products, such as machines or vehicles, using handtools and precut lumber. Shovels loose materials, such as sand, gravel, metals, plastics, or chemicals, into machine hoppers or into vehicles and containers, such as wheelbarrows, scrap truck, or barrels. May occasionally operate industrial truck or electric hoist to assist in loading or moving materials and products. May be designated according to material handled as Filling Hauler, Weaving (textile); according to method of conveying materials as Lugger (agriculture); according to machine or equipment loaded or unloaded as Blunger Loader (pottery & porc.); Vehicle Unloader (any industry); or according to work station as Outside Trucker (any industry); Platform Loader (any industry). May be designated: Bale Piler (textile); Batch Trucker (rubber tire); Bobbin Handler (textile); Car Loader (any industry); Cloth Hauler (textile); Coal Passer (any industry); Compress Trucker (agriculture); Hogshead Dumper (tobacco); Kiln Car Unloader (brick & tile); Laborer, Yard (any industry); Loader (any industry) II; Lumber-Yard Worker (woodworking); Merchandise Carrier (any industry); Mold Mover (toy-sport equip.); Oven Stripper (any industry); Oven Unloader (any industry); Packaging-Machine-Supplies Distributor (tobacco); Slab Picker (saw. & plan.); Powder Trucker (chemical; ordnance); Rack Carrier (paper goods); Racker (any industry); Retort Loader (chemical); Roper (agriculture); Roving Stock Handler (textile); Scrap Wheeler (machine shop); Segregator (agriculture; wholesale tr.); Sugar Trucker (grain-feed mills); Tire Trucker (rubber tire); Trucker, Hand (any industry). ● **GED:** R2, M1, L1 ● **SVP:** 1-3 mos ● **Academic:** Ed=N, Eng=N ● **Work Field:** 011 ● **MPSMS:** 898 ● **Aptitudes:** G4, V4, N4, S4, P4, Q4, K4, F4, M4, E4, C4 ● **Temperaments:** R ● **Physical:** Stg=H; Freq: R, H, I, N, D Occas: C, B, S, K, O, W, G, X ● **Work Env:** Noise=L; Freq: W Occas: C, H, U, A, O ● **Salary:** 4 ● **Outlook:** 2

PRESS BUCKER (any industry) ● DOT #920.686-042 ● OES: 98502 ● Removes pressed bales of material, such as cotton, hay, wastepaper, waste metals, and rags from baling machine, using hook. May push bales to storage area, using handtruck. When removing pressed bales of materials by shoving steel band through press platen, is designated Band Shover, Press (agriculture). ● **GED:** R1, M1, L1 ● **SVP:** 1 day ● **Academic:** Ed=N, Eng=N ● **Work Field:** 011 ● **MPSMS:** 414, 470, 549 ● **Aptitudes:** G4, V4, N5, S4, P4, Q5, K4, F4, M3, E5, C5 ● **Temperaments:** R ● **Physical:** Stg=H; Freq: R, H ● **Work Env:** Noise=L; ● **Salary:** 3 ● **Outlook:** 3

RECORDING STUDIO SET-UP WORKER (recording) ● DOT #962.664-014 ● OES: 98710 ● Arranges sound recording equipment in studio preparatory to recording session following work order specifications: Reads work order to determine position of equipment and arranges equipment, such as consoles, isolation booths, microphones, tape machines, amplifiers, music stands, and musical instruments, by hand or using handtrucks and dollies. Connects equipment electrical lines to outlets according to oral or written instructions. Dismantles equipment subsequent to recording session and returns items to storage. Maintains storage area and assists in maintaining tape library. ● **GED:** R3, M1, L1 ● **SVP:** 3-6 mos ● **Academic:** Ed=N, Eng=N ● **Work Field:** 011, 061 ● **MPSMS:** 869 ● **Aptitudes:** G3, V4, N4, S4, P4, Q3, K3, F4, M3, E5, C5 ● **Temperaments:** R, T ● **Physical:** Stg=M; Freq: S, R, H, N Occas: I, T, G, D, A ● **Work Env:** Noise=N; ● **Salary:** 1 ● **Outlook:** 2

WASTE-DISPOSAL ATTENDANT (any industry) ● DOT #955.383-010 ● OES: 97910 ● Disposes of radioactive equipment and wastes, performing any combination of following duties: Loads contaminated equipment and lead pigs of waste material onto truck, using forklift. Drives truck to storage area and removes load. Shovels specified quantities of ingredients into and tends concrete mixer. Pours or shovels concrete into forms to make disposal coffins (containers). Lifts contaminated equipment or wastes from lead pigs and places them in coffin, using stainless steel rods. Pours concrete into coffin to encase waste. Loads coffins onto truck, using forklift, and transports them to burial ground or arranges for burial at sea. Records amount and type of equipment and waste disposed. May accompany coffins for burial at sea. May clean contaminated equipment for reuse by operating sand blasters, filtering pumps, and steam cleaners or by scrubbing with detergents or solvents. Workers must follow prescribed safety procedures and federal laws regulating waste disposal. ● **GED:** R3, M2, L2 ● **SVP:** 6 mos-1 yr ● **Academic:** Ed=N, Eng=N ● **Work Field:** 011, 013 ● **MPSMS:** 520, 530, 491 ● **Aptitudes:** G3, V4, N4, S3, P3, Q4, K3, F4, M3, E3, C4 ● **Temperaments:** S, T, V ● **Physical:** Stg=H; Freq: R, H, N, F, D, X, V Occas: S, I ● **Work Env:** Noise=L; Freq: W, A, R ● **Salary:** 2 ● **Outlook:** 3

YARD LABORER (paper & pulp) ● DOT #922.687-102 ● OES: 98998 ● Moves and stores material and maintains yard and grounds of paper and pulp plant by performing any combination of following tasks: Shovels wood chips, pulpwood, sulfur, and limerock into trucks or onto conveyors. Cleans chips or bark from conveyors; bark, leaves, and twigs from water canal, and burns refuse. Removes driftwood from canal, using hoist. May load waste paper from paper machines into carts. May stack bundles of woodpulp and dump pulp and waste paper into beaters. May dig ditches and install pipelines from railroad tank cars to facilitate unloading of chemicals used in paper manufacture. ● **GED:** R1, M1, L1 ● **SVP:** 1 day ● **Academic:** Ed=N, Eng=N ● **Work Field:** 011, 031 ● **MPSMS:** 450, 471 ● **Aptitudes:** G4, V4, N5, S4, P4, Q5, K4, F4, M3, E5, C5 ● **Temperaments:** R ● **Physical:** Stg=H; Freq: R, H, D Occas: C, B, S ● **Work Env:** Noise=L; Occas: W, O ● **Salary:** 1 ● **Outlook:** 3

GOE: 05.12.04
Hoisting, Conveying

CHOKE SETTER (logging) ● DOT #921.687-014 ● OES: 73098 ● Fastens choker cables around logs for yarding from cutting area to landing: Pulls choker cables from tractor winch or main-line of yarding machine, passes ball (one end) under and around log, and secures end to bell (sliding fastener) to form noose. May clear brush and earth from under log, using ax and shovel. May assist RIGGING SLINGER (logging) in installing and dismantling rigging of high lead or similar yarding system. May be designated Cat Hooker (logging) in tractor yarding. ● **GED:** R1, M1, L1 ● **SVP:** 2-30 days ● **Academic:** Ed=N, Eng=N ● **Work Field:** 011 ● **MPSMS:** 451 ● **Aptitudes:** G4, V4, N5, S4, P4, Q5, K3, F4, M3, E3, C5 ● **Temperaments:** R, S ● **Physical:** Stg=V; Const: G Freq: C, B, S, K, O, W, R, H, D, V ● **Work Env:** Noise=L; Const: W, O ● **Salary:** 1 ● **Outlook:** 3

CONVEYOR-SYSTEM OPERATOR (any industry) ● DOT #921.662-018 ● OES: 97999 ● Alternate titles: CONVEYOR CONSOLE OPERATOR. Operates console to control automated conveyor system that receives, sorts, distributes, and conveys bulk or packaged materials or products to and from loading dock and storage area, and between departments or processes: Reads production and delivery schedules and confers with supervisor to determine sorting and routing procedures. Presses buttons and turns dials to start conveyor system and regulate speed of conveyors. Observes materials or products moving on conveyors, or observes lights on control panel to monitor flow and operation of system. Moves switches or pushes buttons to route order to designated areas and to raise, lower, and align conveyor with specific adjoining conveyors. Contacts work stations by telephone or intercom to request movement of order or to notify work stations of shipment enroute and approximate delivery time. Stops equipment and clears jams, using handtools. Observes operation to detect equipment malfunction and informs supervisor when malfunction occurs. May operate elevator system in conjunction with conveyor system. May weigh trucks and railroad cars before and after loading, or read scale that continually weighs product on conveyor to ascertain when specified tonnage has been loaded and record weight on loading ticket. May join sections of conveyor frames at temporary working areas and connect power units. May collect samples of materials for analysis. May lubricate moving parts of conveyors. May operate scoop to load materials onto conveyor. May record data, such as weight and type of material moved and condition of equipment. May be designated according to product moved as Bulk-Loader Operator (water trans.); Coal-Conveyor Operator (any industry); Grain Distributor (grain-feed mills); or according to type of equipment as Grain-Elevator Operator (grain-feed mills); Screen Operator (cement); Suction Operator (agriculture). ● **GED:** R3, M2, L2 ● **SVP:** 1-3 mos ● **Academic:** Ed=N, Eng=S ● **Work Field:** 011 ● **MPSMS:** 300, 350, 540 ● **Aptitudes:** G3, V3, N4, S4, P4, Q3, K3, F4, M4, E5, C5 ● **Temperaments:** R, T ● **Physical:** Stg=M; Freq: R, H, T, G, N Occas: I, F, V ● **Work Env:** Noise=L; ● **Salary:** 3 ● **Outlook:** 3

ELEVATOR OPERATOR, FREIGHT (any industry) ● DOT #921.683-038 ● OES: 67098 ● Alternate titles: ELEVATOR OPERATOR, SERVICE. Operates elevator to transport materials and equipment between floors of industrial or commercial establishment: Moves control levers, or pushes buttons to control movement of elevator. Opens and closes safety gate and door of elevator at each floor where stop is made. May load and unload elevator. May transport freight from elevator to designated area, using handtruck. May transport passengers. ● **GED:** R2, M1, L1 ● **SVP:** 2-30 days ● **Academic:** Ed=N, Eng=N ● **Work Field:** 011 ● **MPSMS:** 969 ● **Aptitudes:** G4, V4, N4, S4, P4, Q4, K4, F4, M4, E4, C5 ● **Temperaments:** R ● **Physical:** Stg=H; Const: R, H Freq: I, D Occas: S, N ● **Work Env:** Noise=L; ● **Salary:** 1 ● **Outlook:** 3

GRIP (motion picture) ● DOT #962.687-022 ● OES: 98710 ● Alternate titles: PROPERTY HANDLER. Performs any combination of following tasks in motion picture or television studio or set location: Moves control levers and wheels to guide cranes, booms, and dollies that move cameras and other equipment. Sews canvas and other materials to make and repair tents, tarps, scrims, and backings, using sewing machine. Erects canvas covers to protect camera from rain on location. Cuts gelatin and fiberglass light diffusers to fit metal frame of camera and inserts diffusers into frame. Rigs and dismantles frames, scaffolding, backdrops, prefabricated dressing rooms, camera platforms, and tents for set in studio or on location, using carpenter's handtools. May be designated according to department assigned as Construction Grip (motion picture); Production Grip (motion picture); Sewing Room Grip (motion picture). ● **GED:** R2, M1, L2 ● **SVP:** 6 mos-1 yr ● **Academic:** Ed=N, Eng=N ● **Work Field:** 011, 102, 171 ● **MPSMS:** 911 ● **Aptitudes:** G3, V3, N4, S3, P3, Q4, K3, F3, M3, E3, C4 ● **Temperaments:** V ● **Physical:** Stg=H; Freq: C, B, S, K, O, R, H, I, E, N, F, D, X, V Occas: A ● **Work Env:** Noise=L; Occas: W, D ● **Salary:** 1 ● **Outlook:** 2

LABORER, CONCRETE-MIXING PLANT (construction) ● DOT #579.665-014 ● OES: 98710 ● Alternate titles: CONCRETE-MIXER-OPERATOR HELPER; LABORER, MIXING PLANT; MACHINE HELPER; MIXER HELPER; MIXER TENDER; MIXING-PLANT DUMPER. Performs any combination of following duties in concrete mixing plant: Verifies amount of aggregate in storage bins by visual inspection, and turns swivel head to direct aggregate into specified bin. Tends electrically powered conveyor or pneumatic pump to hoist cement from feeder hopper, railroad car, or transport truck into storage container, such as cement silo. Loosens locking pin, using hammer, to dump cement from cars into storage hopper, prodding cement with pole through trapdoor in car until car is empty. Positions trucks, cars, or buckets under spouts of concrete mixers, batching plants, or hoppers, using hand signals, and moving levers or handwheels to discharge concrete into trucks, cars, or buckets. May haul cement from storage in bulk or bags, emptying, cleaning, and bundling empty bags. May be designated according to duties performed as Aggregate-Conveyor Operator (construction); Bag Shaker (construction); Cement Car Dumper (construction); Cement-Conveyor Operator (construction); Cement Handler (construction); Cement-Sack Breaker (construction). May be designated: Concrete-Bucket Loader (construction); Concrete-Bucket Unloader (construction); Concrete-Conveyor Operator (construction); Concrete-Hopper Operator (construction); Concrete-Mixer Loader, Truck Mounted (construction); Conveyor Tender, Concrete-Mixing Plant (construction); Dumper, Central-Concrete-Mixing Plant (construction); Loft Worker, Concrete-Mixing Plant (construction). ● **GED:** R2, M1, L1 ● **SVP:** 2-30 days ● **Academic:** Ed=N, Eng=N ● **Work Field:** 011 ● **MPSMS:** 536 ● **Aptitudes:** G4, V4, N5, S4, P4, Q5, K4, F4, M4, E4, C5 ● **Temperaments:** R ● **Physical:** Stg=H; Freq: C, B, R, H, I Occas: S, K, T, G ● **Work Env:** Noise=L; Freq: W ● **Salary:** 1 ● **Outlook:** 3

LABORER, POWERHOUSE (utilities) ● DOT #952.665-010 ● OES: 98998 ● Performs any combination of following duties in power plants, such as electrical power companies, industrial plants, and central heating plants: Assists in control and maintenance of coal conveying equipment, using handtools and lubricating equipment. Shovels coal spillage onto conveyors. Takes samples of coal and carries samples to laboratory for analysis. Loads trucks or railcars with fly ash from dust collectors, using suction hose. Starts and stops pumps, opens and closes floodgates, and adjusts valves of ash sluice system. Sweeps, washes, cleans, and paints buildings, floors, and equipment. Assists in inspection, maintenance, and repair of rail tracks, ties, and roadbeds, using shovels, picks, sledgehammers, jacks, and cutting torches. Maintains roads, lawns, shrubs, and flowers, using power mowers and gardener's handtools. Drives, loads, and unloads trucks to transport personnel and equipment. Keeps logs on equipment and materials and submits production reports to supervisor. ● **GED:** R2, M1, L1 ● **SVP:** 1-3 mos ● **Academic:** Ed=N, Eng=N ● **Work Field:** 021, 031 ● **MPSMS:** 870 ● **Aptitudes:** G4, V4, N4, S4, P4, Q4, K4, F4, M3, E4, C5 ● **Temperaments:** V ● **Physical:** Stg=H; Const: R, H Freq: C, S, K Occas: B, T, G, N, F, D, A ● **Work Env:** Noise=L; Freq: W, A, M, D ● **Salary:** 4 ● **Outlook:** 3

GOE: 05.12.05
Braking, Switching, & Coupling

SWITCH TENDER (r.r. trans.) ● DOT #910.667-026 ● OES: 97317 ● Throws track switches within yard of railroad, industrial plant, quarry, construction project, or similar location to switch cars for loading, unloading, making up, and breaking up of trains: Receives oral or written instructions from CONDUCTOR, YARD (r.r. trans.), YARD COUPLER (r.r. trans.) or YARD MANAGER (r.r. trans.). Observes arm or lantern signal from YARD COUPLER (r.r. trans.) and relays information to HOSTLER (r.r. trans.) or throws track switch to facilitate shunting of cars to different locations in yard. May couple and uncouple cars for makeup and breakup of trains. May ride atop cars that have been shunted and turn handwheel to control speed of car or stop it at specified position. May wave arm or lantern to signal YARD ENGINEER (r.r. trans.) to start or stop engine. ● **GED:** R2, M1, L2 ● **SVP:** 2-30 days ● **Academic:** Ed=N, Eng=S ● **Work Field:** 013 ● **MPSMS:** 851 ● **Aptitudes:** G4, V4, N4, S4, P4, Q4, K3, F4, M3, E4, C4 ● **Temperaments:** J ● **Physical:** Stg=M; Freq: R, H, N, F, D, V Occas: T, G, X ● **Work Env:** Noise=L; Const: W ● **Salary:** 3 ● **Outlook:** 1

GOE: 05.12.06
Pumping

AIRPORT UTILITY WORKER (air trans.) ● DOT #912.663-010 ● OES: 97898 ● Services aircraft, working as member of crew, performing any combination of following tasks: Directs incoming and outgoing aircraft near terminal area to assist pilot's maneuvering of aircraft, using visual hand or light signals. Operates service vehicles to replenish fuel, water, and waste system chemicals and to remove liquid waste. Cleans exterior or interior of aircraft, using portable platform, ladders, brushes, rags, waterhose, and vacuum. Positions and removes boarding platform to unload or load aircraft passengers. Unloads and loads luggage and cargo from aircraft, using tow truck with luggage carts. Traces lost baggage for customers and prepares lost baggage claims. ● **GED:** R3, M2, L3 ● **SVP:** 3-6 mos ● **Academic:** Ed=N, Eng=S ● **Work Field:** 013, 031, 014 ● **MPSMS:** 855 ● **Aptitudes:** G3, V3, N3, S2, P3, Q3, K3, F4, M3, E3, C4 ● **Temperaments:** T, V ● **Physical:** Stg=H; Freq: C, B, R, H, G, N, F Occas: S, K, O, T, X, V ● **Work Env:** Noise=V; Freq: W Occas: M ● **Salary:** 3 ● **Outlook:** 3

BOAT LOADER I (water trans.) ● DOT #911.364-014 ● OES: 97910 ● Alternate titles: DOCK HAND; PIER HAND; WHARF HAND; WHARF OPERATOR; WHARF TENDER. Connects hose couplings to enable liquid cargo, such as petroleum, gasoline, heating oil, sulfuric acid, and alum liquor, to be pumped from and into barges and tankers: Reads timetable to determine name of ship, location of pier, and number and types of hoses to be connected. Climbs aboard ship and lowers measuring tape and thermometer into each tank to measure depth and temperature of liquid cargo to be unloaded. Positions coupling of pier hose next to valve of ship, using winch and boom, and connects coupling to valve, using wrench. Attaches ground wire to hose to prevent explosion caused by static electricity generated when liquid cargo flows through hose. Opens valve to allow flow of cargo through hose and signals worker aboard ship to start pumps to unload cargo. Signals worker aboard ship to pump ballast from cargo tanks in order to prepare transfer of cargo onto ship. Signals worker on shore to pump liquid cargo onto ship. May be designated according to water vessel loaded as Barge Loader (water trans.). ● **GED:** R2, M2, L2 ● **SVP:** 1-3 mos ● **Academic:** Ed=N, Eng=N ● **Work Field:** 014 ● **MPSMS:** 854 ● **Aptitudes:** G3, V4, N3, S3, P3, Q4, K3, F3, M3, E4, C5 ● **Temperaments:** J ● **Physical:** Stg=M; Freq: R, H, I, N Occas: B, S, K, O, F ● **Work Env:** Noise=N; Freq: W, M Occas: O ● **Salary:** 2 ● **Outlook:** 2

LOADER HELPER (any industry) ● DOT #914.687-014 ● OES: 98710 ● Assists LOADER (any industry) I in pumping liquid chemicals, petroleum products, and other liquids into or from tank cars, trucks, or barges, performing any combination of following duties: Cleans tanks, using brooms, hose, and cleaning compound. Removes and replaces dome caps, using wrenches. Attaches ground cable to truck to prevent sparks due to static electricity when flammable or volatile material is to be loaded or unloaded. Connects hose to outlet plugs at bottom of tank to prepare car for unloading. Disconnects hose and replaces plugs after unloading, using wrenches. Performs other duties as described under HELPER (any industry) Master Title. ● **GED:** R2, M1, L1 ● **SVP:** 1-3 mos ● **Academic:** Ed=N, Eng=N ● **Work Field:** 014, 031 ● **MPSMS:** 490, 500 ● **Aptitudes:** G4, V4, N4, S4, P4, Q5, K4, F4, M3, E4, C5 ● **Temperaments:** R, T ● **Physical:** Stg=M; Freq: C, B, S, K, O, R, H ● **Work Env:** Noise=L; Const: W Freq: A, O ● **Salary:** 1 ● **Outlook:** 4

WATER TENDER (any industry) ● DOT #599.685-122 ● OES: 92999 ● Tends pumps that maintain level of water in boilers: Reads boiler gauges to ascertain need for water. Opens valves and starts boiler-feed water pumps to supply water, or adjusts controls to start pumps automatically when water level reaches specified point. Observes operation of pumps to detect malfunctions. Tests water to determine suitability for boiler use or obtains sample for laboratory analysis. Adds specified chemical to condition boiler water. May clean boilers. May tend evaporator to purify water. ● **GED:** R2, M2, L2 ● **SVP:** 3-6 mos ● **Academic:** Ed=N, Eng=N ● **Work Field:** 014 ● **MPSMS:** 875 ● **Aptitudes:** G4, V4, N4, S4, P3, Q3, K4, F4, M3, E5, C5 ● **Temperaments:** R ● **Physical:** Stg=L; Freq: R, H, N Occas: C, B, S, K, W ● **Work Env:** Noise=L; Occas: U, A, T ● **Salary:** 3 ● **Outlook:** 2

GOE: 05.12.08
Lubricating

GARAGE SERVICER, INDUSTRIAL (any industry) ● DOT #915.687-014 ● OES: 97805 ● Services trucks, buses, automobiles, and other automotive equipment used in industrial or commericial establishments: Inspects equipment to ascertain gasoline, oil, and water requirements. Tests batteries and tires. Changes oil and lubricates automotive equipment [LUBRICATION SERVICER (automotive ser.) 915.687-018]. May keep record of gas and oil supplied to each vehicle and gasoline and oil supplies in storage tanks. ● **GED:** R2, M1, L1 ● **SVP:** 1-3 mos ● **Academic:** Ed=N, Eng=N ● **Work Field:** 033 ● **MPSMS:** 591 ● **Aptitudes:** G3, V4, N4, S4, P4, Q4, K4, F4, M3, E5, C5 ● **Temperaments:** R ● **Physical:** Stg=M; Freq: R, H, N Occas: S, K, O, I, A ● **Work Env:** Noise=L; ● **Salary:** 1 ● **Outlook:** 3

LUBRICATION SERVICER (automotive ser.) ● DOT #915.687-018 ● OES: 97805 ● Alternate titles: GREASER; LUBRICATION TECHNICIAN; OILER. Lubricates moving parts of automotive vehicles, such as automobiles, buses, and trucks: Injects grease into units, such as springs, universal joints, and steering knuckles, using hand or compressed-air powered grease gun. Inspects fluid level of steering gear, power steering reservoir, transmission, differential, rear axle housings, and shackles. Checks air pressure of tires. Lubricates moving parts with specified lubricants. Drains oil from crankcase and refills crankcase with required amount of oil. Sprays leaf springs with lubricant, using spray gun. Adds water to radiator and battery. Replaces oil and air filters. May sell lubrication and safety inspection services and maintain related records on regular customers, following up periodically with telephone, mail, or personal reminders. ● **GED:** R2, M1, L1 ● **SVP:** 3-6 mos ● **Academic:** Ed=N, Eng=N ● **Work Field:** 033 ● **MPSMS:** 961 ● **Aptitudes:** G3, V4, N4, S4, P4, Q4, K3, F4, M3, E5, C5 ● **Temperaments:** J, T ● **Physical:** Stg=M; Freq: R, H Occas: S, K, O, N, D ● **Work Env:** Noise=L; ● **Salary:** 3 ● **Outlook:** 3

OILER (any industry) ● DOT #699.687-018 ● OES: 85109 ● Alternate titles: BOILER-ROOM HELPER; GREASER AND OILER; GREASER; HOSTLER; LUBRICATOR; MACHINE HOSTLER; OILER AND GREASER. Oils and greases moving parts of friction surfaces of mechanical equipment, such as shaft and motor bearings, sprockets, drive chains, gears, and pulleys, according to specified procedures and oral instructions: Fills container, such as oilcan, grease gun, or tank of lubrication truck with specified lubricant. Squirts or pours oil on moving parts and friction surfaces, or into holes, oil cups, or reservoirs. Turns oil cup valves to regulate flow of oil to moving parts. Forces grease into bearings with grease-gun, smears grease on friction surfaces, or packs grease cups by hand. Fills wells and sumps of lubricating systems with oil. Reports machinery defects or malfunctions to supervisor. May clean machines, sweep floors, and transport stock. May be specified according to type of machine or equipment lubricated. May tend machine that automatically oils parts. ● **GED:** R2, M1, L1 ● **SVP:** 1-3 mos ● **Academic:** Ed=N, Eng=N ● **Work Field:** 033 ● **MPSMS:** 560, 567 ● **Aptitudes:** G4, V4, N5, S4, P4, Q5, K4, F3, M3, E5, C5 ● **Temperaments:** R ● **Physical:** Stg=M; Freq: R, H, I, N Occas: S, K, O, T, G ● **Work Env:** Noise=L; Occas: W ● **Salary:** 3 ● **Outlook:** 3

GOE: 05.12.10
Heating & Melting

RIVET HEATER (heat treating) ● DOT #504.485-010 ● OES: 92923 ● Tends furnace that heats rivets to specified temperature: Places specified rivets in gas, oil, or coke furnace, or between electrodes in electric furnace. Turns knobs to regulate heat or current of furnace. Removes rivets from furnace when color indicates rivets are heated to specified temperature and throws rivets to RIVETER HELPER (any industry), using tongs. May tend portable coke furnace to heat rivets in field. May be designated according to type of furnace tended as Rivet Heater, Electric (heat treating); Rivet Heater, Gas (heat treating). ● **GED:** R3, M2, L2 ● **SVP:** 3-6 mos ● **Academic:** Ed=N, Eng=N ● **Work Field:**

133 ● **MPSMS:** 555 ● **Aptitudes:** G3, V4, N4, S4, P4, Q4, K3, F4, M3, E5, C3 ● **Temperaments:** R, T ● **Physical:** Stg=M; Freq: R, H, I, D, X Occas: C, N ● **Work Env:** Noise=L; Freq: H, O Occas: W ● **Salary:** 3 ● **Outlook:** 3

GOE: 05.12.12
Structural Work

AIR-CONDITIONING INSTALLER-SERVICER HELPER, WINDOW UNIT (construction) ● DOT #637.687-010 ● OES: 98998 ● Assists AIR-CONDITIONING INSTALLER-SERVICER, WINDOW UNIT (any industry) in repairing, servicing, or installing window-mounted air-conditioning units, performing any combination of following duties: Carries unit from delivery vehicle to work site. Assembles window-support brackets, using handtools. Cuts opening through wall for insertion of unit, using hammer and chisel. Applies caulking compound to excess space between air-conditioner and wall opening. Performs other duties as described under HELPER (any industry) Master Title. ● **GED:** R2, M1, L2 ● **SVP:** 1-3 mos ● **Academic:** Ed=N, Eng=N ● **Work Field:** 102 ● **MPSMS:** 573 ● **Aptitudes:** G4, V4, N4, S4, P4, Q4, K4, F4, M4, E5, C5 ● **Temperaments:** J, T ● **Physical:** Stg=H; Freq: R, H, N Occas: C, S, K, O, I, D ● **Work Env:** Noise=N; Freq: W ● **Salary:** 2 ● **Outlook:** 4

AUTOMOBILE-BODY-REPAIRER HELPER (automotive ser.) ● DOT #807.687-010 ● OES: 98998 ● Performs duties as described under HELPER (any industry) Master Title. ● **GED:** R2, M1, L1 ● **SVP:** 2-30 days ● **Academic:** Ed=N, Eng=N ● **Work Field:** 102 ● **MPSMS:** 591 ● **Aptitudes:** G4, V4, N5, S4, P3, Q5, K4, F4, M3, E5, C5 ● **Temperaments:** R ● **Physical:** Stg=M; Freq: R, H Occas: S, O, I, N, D ● **Work Env:** Noise=L; ● **Salary:** 2 ● **Outlook:** 3

BILLPOSTER (any industry) ● DOT #299.667-010 ● OES: 98998 ● Alternate titles: SIGN POSTER. Places posters and banners in prominent places to advertise entertainment, political event, or product: Secures permission from owner to place posters and banners on private property. Displays posters in windows of stores, restaurants, and other public places. Fastens banners and posters to fences, poles, and sides of buildings, using paste, twine, tacks and hammer, hand staplers, and ladders. ● **GED:** R2, M1, L2 ● **SVP:** 2-30 days ● **Academic:** Ed=N, Eng=N ● **Work Field:** 062, 063, 072 ● **MPSMS:** 896 ● **Aptitudes:** G4, V4, N4, S4, P4, Q5, K4, F4, M3, E4, C5 ● **Temperaments:** R ● **Physical:** Stg=M; Freq: C, B, R, H, T, G, D Occas: S, O ● **Work Env:** Noise=N; Freq: W ● **Salary:** 1 ● **Outlook:** 3

DECORATOR, STREET AND BUILDING (any industry) ● DOT #899.687-010 ● OES: 87898 ● Installs decorations, such as flags, lights, and bunting, on streets, on or in buildings, halls, and booths for events, such as parades, conventions, and festivals: Strings and connects electric wiring and lights. Hangs decorations in streets and in or on buildings and structures, using wire, rope, and handtools, working from ladders or elevated truck platforms. Constructs framework to support displays, using woodworking machines and handtools. May build and decorate parade floats and be designated Float Builder (any industry). ● **GED:** R2, M1, L1 ● **SVP:** 3-6 mos ● **Academic:** Ed=N, Eng=N ● **Work Field:** 102 ● **MPSMS:** 360 ● **Aptitudes:** G4, V4, N4, S4, P4, Q4, K3, F3, M3, E5, C4 ● **Temperaments:** R, T ● **Physical:** Stg=V; Freq: C, B, S, K, O, R, H, I, N, D Occas: F, X ● **Work Env:** Noise=N; Freq: W, D, O ● **Salary:** 2 ● **Outlook:** 3

HIGHWAY-MAINTENANCE WORKER (government ser.) ● DOT #899.684-014 ● OES: 87711 ● Alternate titles: HIGHWAY WORKER. Maintains highways, municipal and rural roads, and rights-of-way in safe condition, performing combination of following duties: Erects and repairs guardrails, highway markers, and snow fences, using handtools and nails, and power tools. Dumps, spreads, and tamps asphalt, using pneumatic tamper to patch broken or eroded pavement. Drives truck [TRUCK DRIVER, HEAVY (any industry)] to transport crew and equipment to work site. May drive snow-removal equipment, consisting of truck or tractor equipped with adjustable snowplow and blower unit, and be designated Snow-Plow Operator, Truck (government ser.); Snow-Plow Tractor Operator (government ser.). May drive tractor with mower attachment to cut grass around airfield runways. ● **GED:** R3,

M1, L2 ● **SVP:** 1-3 mos ● **Academic:** Ed=N, Eng=N ● **Work Field:** 102, 095 ● **MPSMS:** 362 ● **Aptitudes:** G3, V4, N4, S4, P4, Q4, K4, F4, M4, E4, C5 ● **Temperaments:** R, T ● **Physical:** Stg=M; Freq: S, K, R, H, I, N, D ● **Work Env:** Noise=N; Freq: W Occas: O ● **Salary:** 3 ● **Outlook:** 2

PIPE-FITTER HELPER (construction) ● DOT #862.684-022 ● OES: 98310 ● Alternate titles: FITTER HELPER. Assists PIPE FITTER (construction) to assemble and install piping for air, ammonia, gas, and water systems: Cuts or drills holes in walls to permit passage of pipes, using pneumatic drill. Selects specified type and size of pipe. Mounts pipe hangers and brackets on walls and ceiling to hold pipe. Assists PIPE FITTER (construction) to install valves, couplings, and other fittings. May disassemble and remove damaged or worn pipe. Performs other duties as described under HELPER (any industry) Master Title. May assist in installation of high-pressure piping and be designated Steam-Fitter Helper (construction). May assist in installation of gas burner to convert furnaces from wood, coal, or oil and be designated Furnace Installer Helper (utilities). ● **GED:** R2, M1, L2 ● **SVP:** 1-3 mos ● **Academic:** Ed=N, Eng=N ● **Work Field:** 102 ● **MPSMS:** 364 ● **Aptitudes:** G4, V4, N4, S3, P3, Q4, K4, F4, M3, E4, C5 ● **Temperaments:** R, T ● **Physical:** Stg=H; Freq: C, R, H, N, D Occas: S, K, O ● **Work Env:** Noise=L; Occas: W, O ● **Salary:** 1 ● **Outlook:** 2

SEWER-LINE REPAIRER (sanitary ser.) ● DOT #869.664-018 ● OES: 87898 ● Repairs and maintains municipal storm and sanitary sewer lines, performing any combination of following tasks: Inspects manholes to locate stoppage. Runs cleaning rods through rod guide, fits front end of rod with auger, using wrench, and lowers guide into position. Thrusts rods into invert and advances them until auger reaches obstruction. Rotates rods manually with turning pin, or attaches end of rod to portable power rodder to rotate rods. Pulls lever and depresses pedal of machine to advance cleaning tool to encounter obstruction and to rotate cable or rods until obstacle is broken. Retracts rods to drag out obstructions, such as roots, grease, and other deposits. Cleans and repairs catch basins, manholes, culverts, and storm drains, using handtools. Lays brick to raise manhole walls to prescribed street level, using masonry tools. Measures distance of excavation site, using tape measure, and marks outline of area to be trenched according to direction of supervisor. Breaks asphalt and other pavement, using airhammer, pick, and shovel. Cuts damaged section of pipe with cutters and removes broken section from ditch. Replaces broken pipes and reconnects pipe sections, using pipe sleeve. Inspects joints to ensure tightness and seal before backfilling. Packs backfilled excavation, using air and gasoline tamper. Taps mainline sewers to install sewer saddles. Replaces manhole covers. Updates sewer maps and manhole charting. Drives pickup trucks to haul crew, materials, and equipment. Services, adjusts, and makes minor repairs to equipment, machines, and attachments. Communicates with supervisor and other workers, using radio telephone. Prepares records showing actions taken, human resource and equipment utilization, and disposition of material. Requisitions tools and equipment. Operates sewer cleaning equipment including power rodder, high velocity water jet, sewer flusher, bucket machine, wayne ball, and vac-all. Cleans and disinfects domestic basements and other areas flooded as a result of sewer stoppages. May lead workers in large repair and construction crew and direct other workers in efficient and safe use of machines, work methods, and safety procedures. ● **GED:** R3, M2, L2 ● **SVP:** 1-2 yrs ● **Academic:** Ed=N, Eng=N ● **Work Field:** 102, 031 ● **MPSMS:** 369 ● **Aptitudes:** G3, V3, N3, S2, P3, Q4, K3, F3, M3, E4, C4 ● **Temperaments:** R, T, V ● **Physical:** Stg=H; Freq: C, S, K, O, W, R, H, I, T, G, N, D, A Occas: F, X ● **Work Env:** Noise=L; Const: W Occas: U, A, T ● **Salary:** 2 ● **Outlook:** 3

SEWER-PIPE CLEANER (business ser.) ● DOT #899.664-014 ● OES: 87898 ● Alternate titles: ELECTRIC-SEWER-CLEANING-MACHINE OPERATOR. Removes roots, debris, and other refuse from clogged sewer lines and drains, using portable electric sewer cleaning machine, and repairs breaks in underground piping: Positions or disassembles sewer trap machine at sewer or drain outlet. Removes drain cover, using wrench. Installs rotary knives on flexible cable, mounted on reel of machine, according to diameter of pipe to be cleaned. Starts machine to feed revolving cable into opening, stopping machine and changing knives as necessary to conform to diameter or contour of pipe. Withdraws cable to deposit accumulated residue removed from pipe in containers for disposal. Observes residue for evidence of mud, indicating broken sewer line. Measures distance from sewer opening to suspected break, using plumbers' snake, tapeline, or by estimating position of cutting head within sewer. Notifies coworkers to dig out ruptured line or digs out shallow sewers, using shovel. Removes and replaces broken tile section or pipe, using caulking compound and cement to form watertight joint. Replaces or directs replacement of earth. Replaces dull knives and performs repairs on machine, using handtools. May estimate cost of service to customer. May clean sewage collection points and sanitary lines in streets and sewage plants. ● **GED:** R3, M1, L2 ● **SVP:** 1-3 mos ● **Academic:** Ed=N, Eng=N ● **Work Field:** 102, 031 ● **MPSMS:** 364 ● **Aptitudes:** G3, V4, N4, S2, P3, Q4, K3, F4, M3, E5, C5 ● **Temperaments:** R, T ● **Physical:** Stg=M; Freq: R, H, I, D Occas: C, B, S, K, O, T, G, N, F ● **Work Env:** Noise=N; Freq: W, A Occas: O ● **Salary:** 2 ● **Outlook:** 3

WINDOW REPAIRER (any industry) ● DOT #899.684-042 ● OES: 85998 ● Repairs and adjusts metal and wooden casement windows, storm windows and doors, and jalousies, using handtools and portable power tools: Repairs or replaces locks, hinges, and cranks. Realigns windows and screens to fit casements. Oils moving parts of sections. May cut and install glass. May paint windows, using brush or spray equipment. ● **GED:** R2, M1, L1 ● **SVP:** 3-6 mos ● **Academic:** Ed=N, Eng=N ● **Work Field:** 102 ● **MPSMS:** 554, 452 ● **Aptitudes:** G3, V4, N4, S4, P3, Q4, K4, F4, M3, E5, C5 ● **Temperaments:** R, T ● **Physical:** Stg=M; Freq: S, O, R, H, I, N, D Occas: K ● **Work Env:** Noise=N; ● **Salary:** 1 ● **Outlook:** 3

GOE: 05.12.13
Cutting & Finishing

BLOCK MAKER (protective dev.) ● DOT #719.381-018 ● OES: 93997 ● Molds lead blocks to be used as shields in radiation therapy treatments: Lays out x-ray film taken of patient in treatment position and tapes film over grid on lighted table. Sets distances on mold cutting machine, duplicating distances from which x ray was taken. Calculates required thickness of block, based upon equipment to be used in treatment and applying knowledge of geometry. Aligns template and styrofoam piece in blocking tray over x-ray film. Guides hand held stylus along lines drawn on x-ray film or print showing area to be treated, simultaneously cutting styrofoam piece with hot wire to form styrofoam mold used in making block. Sets mold in vise and tightens metal clamps to hold mold securely in position. Pours heated lead alloy into mold to form block. Mounts cooled block on lucite board, using screws. Installs finished block in tray of machine and views superimposed outline of block on x-ray film to verify accuracy of block and adherence to standards. Records patient information on finished block. May transport patients to and from treatment area. ● **GED:** R3, M3, L3 ● **SVP:** 1-3 mos ● **Academic:** Ed=H, Eng=S ● **Work Field:** 241, 131, 132 ● **MPSMS:** 604 ● **Aptitudes:** G3, V3, N3, S3, P3, Q4, K2, F3, M3, E5, C5 ● **Temperaments:** J, T ● **Physical:** Stg=M; Freq: R, H, I, N, A Occas: S ● **Work Env:** Noise=Q; ● **Salary:** 2 ● **Outlook:** 3

KEY CUTTER (any industry) ● DOT #709.684-050 ● OES: 92100 ● Alternate titles: KEY MAKER; KEYSMITH; KEY WORKER. Cuts notches in key blanks to duplicate notches of original key, using key-duplicating machine: Selects key blank according to size, shape, or code number of original key. Positions original key and blank in vises on carriage of machine and against guides. Turns thumbscrews to secure key and blank in vises. Starts cutting disk of machine. Pushes and pulls horizontally moving carriage of machine to slide notched edge of original key against stationary guide on machine and to move key blank against cutting disk, duplicating notches of original key in bit of blank. Turns thumbscrews and removes keys from vises. Presses and holds duplicated key against revolving wire wheel to remove burrs from key. Positions one key atop other to compare notches of keys. May collect payment from customer and make change. May sell key holders or related novelty items. ● **GED:** R2, M2, L2 ● **SVP:** 2-30 days ● **Academic:** Ed=N, Eng=S ● **Work Field:** 055 ● **MPSMS:** 552 ● **Aptitudes:** G4, V4, N4, S3, P3, Q4, K3, F4, M3, E5, C5 ● **Temperaments:** R, T ● **Physical:** Stg=L; Freq: R, H, N Occas: I ● **Work Env:** Noise=L; ● **Salary:** 1 ● **Outlook:** 3

GOE: 05.12.14
Painting, Caulking & Coating

ASPHALT-DISTRIBUTOR TENDER (construction) ● DOT #853.665-010 ● OES: 87708 ● Alternate titles: OIL-DISTRIBUTOR TENDER. Tends bituminous distributor on rear of road-oiling truck that sprays tar, asphalt, road oils, and emulsions over highways, streets, and parking areas: Snaps or screws on spray bars to attain required width of spray. Turns valve to regulate flow of material at specified rate. Moves levers to adjust height of spray bar from road surfaces. Signals ROAD-OILING-TRUCK DRIVER (construction) or AS-PHALT-PAVING-MACHINE OPERATOR (construction) to start and stop truck or paving machine. Observes distribution of material over road surface to ensure uniform distribution. Turns handwheels to set angle and depth of screed. Verifies depth specifications of compacted asphalt, using depth gauge. Monitors flow gauges, tachometer, and temperature gauge. Oils and lubricates equipment. ● **GED:** R2, M2, L1 ● **SVP:** 2-30 days ● **Academic:** Ed=N, Eng=N ● **Work Field:** 095 ● **MPSMS:** 362 ● **Aptitudes:** G4, V4, N4, S4, P3, Q4, K3, F4, M3, E5, C5 ● **Temperaments:** R, T ● **Physical:** Stg=L; Const: R, H Freq: C, B, T, G, N, F, D, V Occas: S, O ● **Work Env:** Noise=L; Const: W, A Freq: O ● **Salary:** 2 ● **Outlook:** 3

WOOD CAULKER (ship-boat mfg.) ● DOT #843.384-010 ● OES: 93998 ● Caulks seams between planking in hull or deck of wooden ships or boats to make them watertight by either of following methods: (1) Guides caulking tool that automatically forces caulking material into seam. Hammers material into seam, using tamping tool. Heats marine glue in melting pot. Fills glue runner (funnel) with glue and guides runner along seam to fill seam with glue. Removes excess glue, using scraper. (2) Pushes cotton line and hemp rope into seam and hammers them in place, using caulking iron and mallet. Smears hot pitch over seam, using mop, or spreads putty in seam. May hammer old caulking from seams, using reaming iron and mallet. ● **GED:** R2, M1, L1 ● **SVP:** 1-3 mos ● **Academic:** Ed=N, Eng=N ● **Work Field:** 094 ● **MPSMS:** 593, 495 ● **Aptitudes:** G3, V4, N4, S4, P3, Q5, K3, F3, M3, E4, C5 ● **Temperaments:** J, T ● **Physical:** Stg=M; Freq: C, B, R, H, I, N, D Occas: S, K, O ● **Work Env:** Noise=N; Occas: W ● **Salary:** 2 ● **Outlook:** 2

GOE: 05.12.15
Mechanical Work

AUTOMOBILE WRECKER (wholesale tr.) ● DOT #620.684-010 ● OES: 85998 ● Alternate titles: WRECKING MECHANIC. Salvages usable parts from wrecked cars and trucks in auto salvage yard: Dismantles vehicles, using handtools, bolt cutters, and oxyacetylene torch. Cleans parts, using solvents and brush, or vapor-degreasing machine, and stores parts in bins according to condition and part number. Sorts, piles, and loads scrap on railroad cars or trucks. May drive tow-truck. May sell automobile glass, tires, and parts. ● **GED:** R3, M2, L2 ● **SVP:** 3-6 mos ● **Academic:** Ed=N, Eng=N ● **Work Field:** 121, 212 ● **MPSMS:** 591 ● **Aptitudes:** G4, V4, N4, S4, P4, Q4, K3, F3, M3, E5, C5 ● **Temperaments:** V ● **Physical:** Stg=H; Freq: R, H, I Occas: C, S, K, O ● **Work Env:** Noise=N; Freq: W ● **Salary:** 2 ● **Outlook:** 3

BELT REPAIRER (any industry) ● DOT #630.684-014 ● OES: 85109 ● Repairs and replaces canvas, leather, or rubber belts used to drive machinery and convey materials: Examines belts for defects and cuts out defective sections, using knife. Cuts strip of unused belting material, using knife. Clamps metal fasteners to ends of belt, using pincers, or splices ends of belt, using splicing machine. Positions repaired belt on pulleys. Applies dressing compound to belt to prevent slippage. May patch and sew defective areas of belts, using needle and thread. May specialize in repairing conveyor belts and be designated Conveyor-Belt Repairer (any industry). ● **GED:** R2, M1, L1 ● **SVP:** 3-6 mos ● **Academic:** Ed=N, Eng=N ● **Work Field:** 121 ● **MPSMS:** 560 ● **Aptitudes:** G4, V4, N4, S4, P4, Q4, K4, F4, M3, E5, C5 ● **Temperaments:** R, T ● **Physical:** Stg=L; Freq: R, H, N Occas: I ● **Work Env:** Noise=L; ● **Salary:** 4 ● **Outlook:** 2

CONSTRUCTION-EQUIPMENT-MECHANIC HELPER (construction) ● DOT #620.664-010 ● OES: 98998 ● Assists CONSTRUCTION-EQUIPMENT MECHANIC (construction) in repairing, assembling, and adjusting construction equipment, such as internal combustion engines, lighting plants, pumps, air compressors, concrete and mortar mixers, concrete vibrators, generators, pneumatic tools, and portable winches. Disassembles and assembles equipment, using mechanic's handtools. Washes parts and tools with cleaning fluids, such as gasoline or naptha. Performs other duties as described under HELPER (any industry) Master Title. ● **GED:** R2, M1, L2 ● **SVP:** 1-3 mos ● **Academic:** Ed=N, Eng=N ● **Work Field:** 121, 102 ● **MPSMS:** 563 ● **Aptitudes:** G3, V4, N4, S4, P4, Q4, K3, F3, M3, E5, C5 ● **Temperaments:** V ● **Physical:** Stg=M; Freq: S, K, O, R, H, N Occas: C, B, I, D ● **Work Env:** Noise=L; Freq: W Occas: U, A ● **Salary:** 2 ● **Outlook:** 3

ROLLER-SKATE REPAIRER (any industry) ● DOT #732.684-102 ● OES: 85998 ● Repairs roller skates by disassembling skates, and cleaning and replacing bearings, wheels, and other worn parts, using handtools and power tools. May repair attached shoes and leather straps. ● **GED:** R2, M2, L1 ● **SVP:** 3-6 mos ● **Academic:** Ed=N, Eng=N ● **Work Field:** 121 ● **MPSMS:** 616 ● **Aptitudes:** G4, V4, N4, S4, P4, Q4, K4, F3, M3, E5, C5 ● **Temperaments:** R, T ● **Physical:** Stg=L; Freq: R, H, I ● **Work Env:** Noise=N; ● **Salary:** 1 ● **Outlook:** 2

TIRE REPAIRER (automotive ser.) ● DOT #915.684-010 ● OES: 85953 ● Alternate titles: TIRE-AND-TUBE REPAIRER; TIRE-AND-TUBE SERVICER; TIRE FIXER; TIRE SERVICER. Repairs damaged tires of automobiles, buses, trucks, and other automotive vehicles: Raises vehicle, using hydraulic jack, and unbolts wheel, using lug wrench. Removes wheel from vehicle by hand or, when repairing giant tires of heavy equipment, by use of power hoist. Locates puncture in tubeless tire by visual inspection or by immersing inflated tire in water bath and observing air bubbles emerging from puncture. Seals puncture in tubeless tire by inserting adhesive material and expanding rubber plug into puncture, using handtools. Separates tubed tire from wheel, using rubber mallet and metal bar or mechanical tire changer. Removes inner tube from tire and inspects tire casing for defects, such as holes and tears. Glues boot (tire patch) over rupture in tire casing, using rubber cement. Inflates inner tube and immerses it in water to locate leak. Buffs defective area of inner tube, using scraper, and patches tube with adhesive rubber patch or seals rubber patch to tube, using hot vulcanizing plate. Reassembles tire onto wheel, and places wheel on balancing machine to determine counterweights required to balance wheel. Hammers required counterweights onto rim of wheel. Cleans sides of white wall tires and remounts wheel onto vehicle. Responds to emergency calls to make repairs or replacements of damaged tires at customer's home or on road. May be designated according to specialty as Giant-Tire Repairer (automotive ser.); Tire Changer (automotive ser.); Tire Changer, Aircraft (air trans.); Tire Changer, Road Service (automotive ser.). May rotate tires to different positions on vehicle, using tire changing machine, handtools, and tire balancing machine. ● **GED:** R2, M1, L1 ● **SVP:** 1-3 mos ● **Academic:** Ed=N, Eng=N ● **Work Field:** 121 ● **MPSMS:** 511 ● **Aptitudes:** G4, V4, N4, S3, P3, Q4, K3, F4, M3, E4, C5 ● **Temperaments:** R, T ● **Physical:** Stg=H; Freq: S, K, O, R, H, I, E, N, D, A Occas: G ● **Work Env:** Noise=L; Freq: W, M ● **Salary:** 4 ● **Outlook:** 3

GOE: 05.12.16
Electrical Work

CABLE PULLER (construction) ● DOT #829.684-018 ● OES: 93998 ● Alternate titles: CABLE PLACER; CABLE RIGGER. Pulls lead-sheathed electrical cables for electric power systems through ducts: Pushes long, flexible, steel ribbon (fish tape) or rods through duct. Attaches wire to rod or fish tape and pulls wire through duct. Attaches wire to cable and pulls cable through duct by hand or using winch. May pull ball or mandrel through duct to ensure clear passage for cable. ● **GED:** R2, M1, L1 ● **SVP:** 3-6 mos ● **Academic:** Ed=N, Eng=N ● **Work Field:** 111, 011 ● **MPSMS:** 871 ● **Aptitudes:** G4, V4, N5, S4, P4, Q5, K4, F4, M3, E3, C5 ● **Temperaments:** R ● **Physical:** Stg=H; Freq: C, B, S, K, O, W, R, H, I ● **Work Env:** Noise=N; Freq: W ● **Salary:** 1 ● **Outlook:** 3

ELECTRICAL-APPLIANCE PREPARER (any industry) ● DOT #827.584-010 ● OES: 93997 ● Alternate titles: UNCRATER. Assembles and tests electrical appliances, such as ranges, refrigerators, and washing machines, to prepare appliance for delivery and installation, using handtools and test lamp: Uncrates appliances, using pry bar, wire cutters, and nail puller. Assembles appliance parts, using screws and handtools. Connects appliance to electric current to test performance. Locates faulty circuits with test lamp. Solders and wraps wires with friction tape to repair insulation. Washes and polishes appliances. Examines exterior of appliance for chips, scratches, and dents. Keeps records of appliances received, assembled, and delivered. May be designated according to type of appliance assembled and tested as Dishwasher Preparer (any industry); Electric-Range Preparer (any industry); Electric-Refrigerator Preparer (any industry); Washer-Drier Preparer (any industry). ● **GED:** R2, M2, L2 ● **SVP:** 1-3 mos ● **Academic:** Ed=N, Eng=N ● **Work Field:** 061, 111 ● **MPSMS:** 583 ● **Aptitudes:** G3, V4, N4, S4, P4, Q4, K4, F4, M3, E5, C4 ● **Temperaments:** R, T ● **Physical:** Stg=H; Freq: R, H, I, N Occas: S, K, O, D, A, X ● **Work Env:** Noise=N; ● **Salary:** 4 ● **Outlook:** 3

LIGHTING-EQUIPMENT OPERATOR (amuse. & rec.) ● DOT #962.381-014 ● OES: 39998 ● Alternate titles: ELECTRICIAN, FRONT. Controls lighting equipment, such as floodlamps, strip lights, and spotlights from projection room and front or backstage areas of theater to cast spotlight on stage performers: Places spotlights in specified locations in theater and connects wiring for lighting. Moves spotlight to follow movements of performers with beam of light, according to instructions on prepared cue sheet. Turns color wheel, causing light to be diffused through varicolored gelatin disks to change color of light. Cleans and adjusts light, replacing carbons or bulbs as needed. May insert varicolored gelatin sheets in frame to assemble color wheel. ● **GED:** R4, M2, L3 ● **SVP:** 1-2 yrs ● **Academic:** Ed=N, Eng=S ● **Work Field:** 111 ● **MPSMS:** 912 ● **Aptitudes:** G3, V3, N4, S3, P3, Q4, K3, F3, M3, E4, C3 ● **Temperaments:** J, T ● **Physical:** Stg=L; Freq: R, H, I, N, F, D, X, V Occas: S ● **Work Env:** Noise=N; ● **Salary:** 1 ● **Outlook:** 2

PROP ATTENDANT (amuse. & rec.) ● DOT #962.684-022 ● OES: 39998 ● Readies stage, equipment, and seating area of theater prior to performances, and produces special lighting and sound effects during performances, using various equipment and devices: Lifts, places, and repositions special effect props, such as breakaway walls, dry ice in smoke/fog generator, and stage elevators, for use by performers during show. Starts, connects, and tests light and sound equipment, such as microphones, magnetic tape players, amplifiers, and stage lighting system, prior to show. Cleans and prepares stage, seating, and dressing areas prior to show [CLEANER, COMMERCIAL OR INSTITUTIONAL (any industry) 381.687-014]. Pushes buttons, presses and flips switches, and turns valves to achieve special sound and lighting effects and to raise and lower scenery and stage curtain during performance, following sight or sound cues. Hands props to performers and assists performers with costume changes during show. May order makeup supplies and props to replace those used or damaged during shows. Prior to show may test equipment and during show may tend equipment that activates and controls animated characters. ● **GED:** R3, M2, L3 ● **SVP:** 2-30 days ● **Academic:** Ed=N, Eng=S ● **Work Field:** 111, 031 ● **MPSMS:** 912 ● **Aptitudes:** G3, V4, N4, S3, P4, Q4, K4, F4, M4, E4, C4 ● **Temperaments:** R, T ● **Physical:** Stg=M; Freq: C, S, K, O, R, H, I, T, G, N, F, D, V Occas: X ● **Work Env:** Noise=L; ● **Salary:** 2 ● **Outlook:** 2

GOE: 05.12.17
Food Preparation

BAKER HELPER (hotel & rest.) ● DOT #313.684-010 ● OES: 65038 ● Assists BAKER (hotel & rest.) by performing any combination of following duties in bread-baking department: Carries and distributes supplies, such as flour, shortening, and baking pans. Mixes, kneads, or shapes dough for bread, rolls, muffins, or biscuits. Cuts dough into uniform portions. Greases pans used to mold or bake breads and lines pans with waxed paper. Places pans of dough into oven to bake. Removes baked products from oven. Cleans bakery utensils, equipment, and work area. Performs other duties as described under HELPER (any industry) Master Title. ● **GED:** R2, M1, L1 ● **SVP:** 1-3 mos ● **Academic:** Ed=N, Eng=N ● **Work Field:** 146 ● **MPSMS:** 384 ● **Aptitudes:** G4, V4, N4, S4, P4, Q5, K4, F4, M3, E5, C4 ● **Temperaments:** J, R ● **Physical:** Stg=M; Freq: R, H, I Occas: E, N, X ● **Work Env:** Noise=N; Freq: O ● **Salary:** 1 ● **Outlook:** 4

COFFEE MAKER (hotel & rest.) ● DOT #317.684-010 ● OES: 65038 ● Alternate titles: COFFEE-URN ATTENDANT. Brews coffee, tea, and chocolate, using coffee urns, drip or vacuum coffee makers, teapots, drink mixers, and other kitchen equipment. Performs various duties to assist in filling customers' orders, such as cooking hot cakes and waffles, boiling eggs, and making toast [PANTRY GOODS MAKER (hotel & rest.)]. Cleans and polishes utensils and equipment used in food and beverage preparation. May serve coffee. May prepare and issue iced beverages, such as coffee, tea, and fountain or bottled drinks, to be served by COUNTER ATTENDANT, LUNCHROOM OR COFFEE SHOP (hotel & rest.). ● **GED:** R2, M1, L1 ● **SVP:** 2-30 days ● **Academic:** Ed=N, Eng=N ● **Work Field:** 146 ● **MPSMS:** 903 ● **Aptitudes:** G4, V4, N4, S4, P4, Q4, K3, F4, M3, E5, C4 ● **Temperaments:** R, T ● **Physical:** Stg=M; Freq: R, H, N Occas: I, X ● **Work Env:** Noise=Q; Occas: O ● **Salary:** 1 ● **Outlook:** 3

COOK HELPER (hotel & rest.) ● DOT #317.687-010 ● OES: 65038 ● Assists workers engaged in preparing foods for hotels, restaurants, or ready-to-serve packages by performing any combination of following duties: Washes, peels, cuts, and seeds vegetables and fruits. Cleans, cuts, and grinds meats, poultry, and seafood. Dips food items in crumbs, flour, and batter to bread them. Stirs and strains soups and sauces. Weighs and measures designated ingredients. Carries pans, kettles, and trays of food to and from work stations, stove, and refrigerator. Stores foods in designated areas, utilizing knowledge of temperature requirements and food spoilage. Cleans work areas, equipment and utensils, segregates and removes garbage, and steam-cleans or hoses garbage containers [KITCHEN HELPER (hotel & rest.) 318.687-010]. Distributes supplies, utensils, and portable equipment, using handtruck. May be designated according to worker assisted as Cook Helper, Broiler or Fry (hotel & rest.); Cook Helper, Dessert (hotel & rest.); Cook Helper, Vegetable (hotel & rest.); Pantry Goods Maker Helper (hotel & rest.). Performs other duties as described under HELPER (any industry) Master Title. ● **GED:** R2, M1, L1 ● **SVP:** 2-30 days ● **Academic:** Ed=N, Eng=N ● **Work Field:** 146, 031 ● **MPSMS:** 903 ● **Aptitudes:** G4, V4, N4, S4, P4, Q4, K4, F3, M3, E5, C5 ● **Temperaments:** R ● **Physical:** Stg=M; Const: H Freq: R, I Occas: S, E, G, M, N, D ● **Work Env:** Noise=N; Occas: H, O ● **Salary:** 1 ● **Outlook:** 4

DELI CUTTER-SLICER (retail trade) ● DOT #316.684-014 ● OES: 65038 ● Cuts delicatessen meats and cheeses, using slicing machine, knives, or other cutters: Places meat or cheese on cutting board and cuts slices to designated thickness, using knives or other hand cutters. Positions and clamps meat or cheese on carriage of slicing machine. Adjusts knob to set machine for desired thickness. Presses button to start motor that moves carriage past rotary blade that slices meats and cheeses. Stacks cut pieces on tray or platter, separating portions with paper. May weigh and wrap sliced foods and affix sticker showing price and weight. ● **GED:** R2, M2, L1 ● **SVP:** 2-30 days ● **Academic:** Ed=N, Eng=N ● **Work Field:** 054 ● **MPSMS:** 382, 383, 881 ● **Aptitudes:** G4, V4, N4, S4, P3, Q4, K3, F3, M3, E5, C4 ● **Temperaments:** R, T ● **Physical:** Stg=L; Freq: R, H, N, A Occas: I, D, X ● **Work Env:** Noise=Q; Freq: O ● **Salary:** 1 ● **Outlook:** 4

FOOD ASSEMBLER, KITCHEN (hotel & rest.) ● DOT #319.484-010 ● OES: 65038 ● Alternate titles: DINING-SERVICE WORKER; FOOD ASSEMBLER, COMMISSARY KITCHEN; FOOD-TRAY ASSEMBLER; SUPPLY SERVICE WORKER; TRAY SETTER. Prepares meal trays in commissary kitchen for inflight service of airlines, multiunit restaurant chains, industrial caterers, or educational, and similar institutions, performing any combination of following duties: Reads charts to determine amount and kind of foods and supplies to be packaged. Fills individual serving cartons with portions of various foods and condiments, such as cream, jams, and sauces, by hand or using automatic filling machine. Portions and garnishes hot cooked foods, such as meat and vegetables, into individual serving dishes. Stores dishes of hot food on shelves of portable electric warming cabinet or food cart for stowing aboard airplane or transfer to restaurant or cafeteria dining unit. Removes pans of portioned salads, desserts, rolls, cream, and other cold food items from refrigerator or pantry, and places at appropriate stations of tray assembly counter to facilitate loading meal trays. Places food items, silverware, and dishes in depression of compartmented food tray passing on conveyor belt. Examines filled tray for completeness and appearance, and stores completed trays in refrigerated storage cabinets to be transported to airplane, dining room, or cafeteria. May be designated according to type of food assembled as Appetizer Packer (hotel & rest.); Casserole Preparer (hotel & rest.); Cold-Food Packer (hotel & rest.); Hot-Food Packer (hotel & rest.). ● **GED:** R2, M2, L1 ● **SVP:** 1-3 mos ● **Academic:** Ed=N, Eng=N ● **Work Field:** 146 ● **MPSMS:** 903 ● **Aptitudes:** G4, V4, N4, S4, P3, Q4, K3, F3, M3, E5, C4 ● **Temperaments:** R, T ● **Physical:** Stg=L; Freq: R, H, I Occas: S, N, X ● **Work Env:** Noise=Q; ● **Salary:** 1 ● **Outlook:** 4

SANDWICH MAKER (hotel & rest.) ● DOT #317.664-010 ● OES: 65038 ● Alternate titles: SANDWICH-COUNTER ATTENDANT. Prepares sandwiches to individual order of customers: Receives sandwich orders from customers. Slices cold meats and cheese by hand or machine. Selects and cuts bread, such as white, whole wheat, or rye, and toasts or grills bread, according to order. Places meat or filling and garnish, such as chopped or sliced onion and lettuce, between bread slices. Prepares garnishes for sandwiches, such as sliced tomatoes and pickles. May cook, mix, and season ingredients to make dressings, fillings, and spreads. May fry hamburgers, bacon, steaks, and eggs for hot sandwiches. May butter bread slices, using knife. ● **GED:** R2, M1, L1 ● **SVP:** 2-30 days ● **Academic:** Ed=N, Eng=N ● **Work Field:** 146 ● **MPSMS:** 903 ● **Aptitudes:** G4, V4, N4, S4, P4, Q4, K3, F3, M3, E5, C5 ● **Temperaments:** R, T ● **Physical:** Stg=M; Const: R, H, I, N, A Freq: T, G ● **Work Env:** Noise=N; ● **Salary:** 1 ● **Outlook:** 4

GOE: 05.12.18
Cleaning & Maintenance

ATTENDANT, CAMPGROUND (amuse. & rec.) ● DOT #329.683-010 ● OES: 67098 ● Alternate titles: CAMPGROUND HAND;. Performs general maintenance on facilities and grounds at recreational camp or park: Operates riding lawn mower to mow grass. Checks buildings and furnishings, repairs minor damage, using handtools, and reports major repair needs to DIRECTOR, CAMP (social ser.). Replaces light bulbs. Carries and places supplies in storage areas. Cleans swimming pool, using vacuum cleaner and scrub brushes. Measures and pours chemicals into pool water to maintain chemical balance. Performs minor repairs to dock, and keeps lakefront swimming area clean and free from hazards. Drives truck to pick up trash and garbage for delivery to central area. ● **GED:** R2, M1, L1 ● **SVP:** 2-30 days ● **Academic:** Ed=N, Eng=N ● **Work Field:** 003, 031, 013 ● **MPSMS:** 969 ● **Aptitudes:** G4, V4, N4, S4, P4, Q5, K4, F4, M3, E4, C5 ● **Temperaments:** V ● **Physical:** Stg=M; Occas: C, B, S, K, O, R, H, N, D ● **Work Env:** Noise=L; Const: W ● **Salary:** 2 ● **Outlook:** 2

AUTOMOBILE DETAILER (automotive ser.) ● DOT #915.687-034 ● OES: 98905 ● Cleans and refurbishes new and used automobiles, performing any combination of following duties: Washes vehicle exterior to clean cars, using cleaning solution, water, cloths, and brushes. Applies wax to auto body, and wipes or buffs surfaces to protect surfaces and preserve shine, using cloth or buffing machine. Vacuums interiors of vehicles to remove loose dirt and debris, using vacuum cleaner. Cleans upholstery, rugs, and other surfaces, using cleaning agents, applicators, and cleaning devices. Applies revitalizers and preservatives to vinyl or leather surfaces, and treats fabrics with spot and stain resistant chemicals to preserve and protect interior components. Cleans engine and engine compartment with steam cleaning equipment and various cleaning agents to remove grease and grime. Applies special purpose cleaners to remove foreign materials which do not respond to normal cleaning procedures, utilizing experience and following recommendations of product manufacturer. Paints engine components and related parts, using spray gun or aerosol can and masking material. Applies paint to chipped body surfaces of vehicle, using container of touchup paint. Applies dyes and reconditioning chemical to vinyl tops of vehicle to restore color and condition. ● **GED:** R2, M1, L1 ● **SVP:** 2-30 days ● **Academic:** Ed=N, Eng=N ● **Work Field:** 031 ● **MPSMS:** 960 ● **Aptitudes:** G4, V4, N4, S5, P4, Q5, K4, F4, M4, E5, C4 ● **Temperaments:** R ● **Physical:** Stg=M; Freq: S, O, R, H, I,

N, D, A Occs: K, X ● **Work Env:** Noise=L; Occas: W, U, A ● **Salary:** 4 ● **Outlook:** 4

BARTENDER HELPER (hotel & rest.) ● DOT #312.687-010 ● OES: 65014 ● Alternate titles: BAR PORTER; BAR RUNNER. Cleans bar and equipment, and replenishes bar supplies, such as liquor, fruit, ice, and dishes: Stocks refrigerating units with wines and bottled beer. Replaces empty beer kegs with full ones. Slices and pits fruit used to garnish drinks. Washes glasses, bar, and equipment, and polishes bar fixtures. Mops floors. Removes empty bottles and trash. May mix and prepare flavors for mixed drinks. ● **GED:** R2, M1, L1 ● **SVP:** 2-30 days ● **Academic:** Ed=N, Eng=N ● **Work Field:** 031, 011 ● **MPSMS:** 903 ● **Aptitudes:** G4, V4, N4, S4, P4, Q4, K4, F4, M4, E4, C5 ● **Temperaments:** R ● **Physical:** Stg=M; Freq: S, O, R, H ● **Work Env:** Noise=N; Occas: C, U ● **Salary:** 1 ● **Outlook:** 4

CARETAKER (domestic ser.) ● DOT #301.687-010 ● OES: 62061 ● Alternate titles: ODD-JOB WORKER. Performs any combination of following duties in keeping private home clean and in good condition: Cleans and dusts furnishings, hallways, and lavatories. Beats and vacuums rugs and scrubs them with cleaning solutions. Washes windows and waxes and polishes floors. Removes and hangs draperies. Cleans and oils furnace. Shovels coal into furnace and removes ashes. Replaces light switches and repairs broken screens, latches, or doors. Paints exterior structures, such as fences, garages, and sheds. May drive family car. May mow and rake lawn. May groom and exercise pets. When duties are confined to upkeep of house, may be designated House Worker (domestic ser.). ● **GED:** R2, M1, L2 ● **SVP:** 2-30 days ● **Academic:** Ed=N, Eng=N ● **Work Field:** 031 ● **MPSMS:** 901, 909 ● **Aptitudes:** G4, V4, N4, S4, P4, Q5, K4, F4, M3, E4, C5 ● **Temperaments:** V ● **Physical:** Stg=M; Freq: S, K, R, H Occas: C, B ● **Work Env:** Noise=N; Occas: W ● **Salary:** 1 ● **Outlook:** 3

CENTRAL-SUPPLY WORKER (medical ser.) ● DOT #381.687-010 ● OES: 58097 ● Alternate titles: CENTRAL-SERVICE TECHNICIAN. Performs any combination of following duties: Scrubs and washes surgical instruments, containers, and equipment, such as aspirators and suction units. Sterilizes instruments, equipment, surgical linens, and supplies, such as surgical packs and treatment trays, using autoclave, sterilizer, or antiseptic solutions. Prepares packs of supplies, instruments, and dressing and treatment trays, according to designated lists or codes, and wraps, labels, and seals packs. Stores prepared articles and supplies in designated areas. Fills requisitions, writes charges, and inventories supplies. May be assigned to hospital areas, such as surgery and delivery rooms. ● **GED:** R3, M2, L2 ● **SVP:** 3-6 mos ● **Academic:** Ed=H, Eng=N ● **Work Field:** 031, 221 ● **MPSMS:** 604, 929 ● **Aptitudes:** G3, V3, N4, S4, P4, Q4, K4, F3, M3, E5, C4 ● **Temperaments:** T, V ● **Physical:** Stg=L; Freq: R, H, I, N Occas: S, X ● **Work Env:** Noise=Q; Occas: U ● **Salary:** 2 ● **Outlook:** 3

CHIMNEY SWEEP (any industry) ● DOT #891.687-010 ● OES: 67001 ● Alternate titles: CHIMNEY CLEANER; CLEANING OPERATOR. Cleans soot from chimneys: Removes pipe connecting furnace to flue, using handtools. Cleans soot from chimney pit, using vacuum cleaner that automatically discharges into receptacle mounted on truck. Cleans connecting pipes with brush, replaces pipe, and seals joints with cement. Closes fireplace openings and other outlets to clean chimney from above. Lowers weighted bag down flue, withdraws bag which expands and scrapes soot from lining of chimney. Empties bag and inspects interior of chimney to ensure completion of cleaning process, using reflecting light of mirror. May make oral or written reports to request services of CHIMNEY REPAIRER (business ser.). May brush interior of chimney, boilers, and furnaces. ● **GED:** R2, M1, L1 ● **SVP:** 1-3 mos ● **Academic:** Ed=N, Eng=N ● **Work Field:** 031 ● **MPSMS:** 553 ● **Aptitudes:** G3, V4, N4, S3, P3, Q4, K3, F3, M3, E5, C5 ● **Temperaments:** R ● **Physical:** Stg=M; Freq: C, S, K, R, H, D Occas: N ● **Work Env:** Noise=N; Freq: W, A, O ● **Salary:** 1 ● **Outlook:** 3

CLEANER II (any industry) ● DOT #919.687-014 ● OES: 98905 ● Cleans interiors and exteriors of transportation vehicles, such as airplanes, automobiles, buses, railroad cars, and streetcars: Cleans interior of vehicle, using broom, cloth, mop, vacuum cleaner, and whisk broom. Cleans windows with water, cleansing compounds, and cloth or chamois. Replenishes sanitary supplies in vehicle compartments. Removes dust, grease, and oil from exterior surfaces of vehicles, using steam-cleaning equipment, or by spraying or washing vehicles, using spraying equipment, brush or sponge. May polish exterior of vehicle.

May fumigate interior of vehicle, using fumigating gases or sprays. May be designated according to type of vehicle cleaned as Airplane Cleaner (air trans.); Automobile Washer (automotive ser.); Bus Cleaner (automotive ser.); Car Cleaner (r.r. trans.); Coach Cleaner (r.r. trans.); Truck Washer (dairy products). When cleaning aircraft interiors may be designated Cabin-Service Agent (air trans.). ● **GED:** R2, M1, L1 ● **SVP:** 1 day ● **Academic:** Ed=N, Eng=N ● **Work Field:** 031 ● **MPSMS:** 960 ● **Aptitudes:** G4, V4, N4, S4, P4, Q5, K4, F4, M3, E5, C5 ● **Temperaments:** R ● **Physical:** Stg=M; Const: R, H Occas: C, S, K ● **Work Env:** Noise=L; Const: U Freq: W ● **Salary:** 1 ● **Outlook:** 3

CLEANER, COMMERCIAL OR INSTITUTIONAL (any industry) ● DOT #381.687-014 ● OES: 67001 ● Alternate titles: CLEAN-UP WORKER; HOUSEKEEPER; JANITOR; LABORER, BUILDING MAINTENANCE; MOPPER; PORTER; SCRUBBER; SWEEPER. Keeps premises of office building, apartment house, or other commercial or institutional building in clean and orderly condition: Cleans and polishes lighting fixtures, marble surfaces, and trim, and performs duties described in CLEANER (any industry) I Master Title. May cut and trim grass, and shovel snow, using power equipment or handtools. May deliver messages. May transport small equipment or tools between departments. May setup tables and chairs in auditorium or hall. May be designated according to duties performed as Hall Cleaner (hotel & rest.); Light-Fixture Cleaner (any industry); Marble Cleaner (any industry); Metal Polisher (any industry); Paint Cleaner (any industry); or according to equipment used as Scrubbing-Machine Operator (any industry). ● **GED:** R1, M1, L1 ● **SVP:** 2-30 days ● **Academic:** Ed=N, Eng=N ● **Work Field:** 031 ● **MPSMS:** 905 ● **Aptitudes:** G4, V4, N5, S4, P4, Q5, K4, F4, M3, E4, C5 ● **Temperaments:** R ● **Physical:** Stg=H; Freq: S, K, O, R, H Occas: C, T, G, N ● **Work Env:** Noise=N; ● **Salary:** 1 ● **Outlook:** 3

CLEANER, HOSPITAL (medical ser.) ● DOT #323.687-010 ● OES: 67001 ● Alternate titles: HOUSEKEEPER, HOSPITAL. Cleans hospital patient rooms, baths, laboratories, offices, halls, and other areas: Washes beds and mattresses, and remakes beds after dismissal of patients. Keeps utility and storage rooms in clean and orderly condition. Distributes laundered articles and linens. Replaces soiled drapes and cubicle curtains. Performs other duties as described under CLEANER (any industry) I Master Title. May disinfect and sterilize equipment and supplies, using germicides and sterilizing equipment. ● **GED:** R2, M1, L2 ● **SVP:** 2-30 days ● **Academic:** Ed=N, Eng=N ● **Work Field:** 031 ● **MPSMS:** 905 ● **Aptitudes:** G4, V4, N5, S4, P4, Q4, K4, F4, M3, E4, C5 ● **Temperaments:** R ● **Physical:** Stg=M; Freq: S, R, H Occas: C, O, I ● **Work Env:** Noise=Q; Freq: U ● **Salary:** 2 ● **Outlook:** 4

CLEANER, HOUSEKEEPING (any industry) ● DOT #323.687-014 ● OES: 67001 ● Alternate titles: MAID. Cleans rooms and halls in commercial establishments, such as hotels, restaurants, clubs, beauty parlors, and dormitories, performing any combination of following duties: Sorts, counts, folds, marks, or carries linens. Makes beds. Replenishes supplies, such as drinking glasses and writing supplies. Checks wraps and renders personal assistance to patrons. Moves furniture, hangs drapes, and rolls carpets. Performs other duties as described under CLEANER (any industry) I Master Title. May be designated according to type of establishment cleaned as Beauty Parlor Cleaner (personal ser.); Motel Cleaner (hotel & rest.); or according to area cleaned as Sleeping Room Cleaner (hotel & rest.). ● **GED:** R1, M1, L1 ● **SVP:** 2-30 days ● **Academic:** Ed=N, Eng=N ● **Work Field:** 031 ● **MPSMS:** 902 ● **Aptitudes:** G4, V4, N4, S4, P4, Q4, K4, F4, M4, E5, C5 ● **Temperaments:** R ● **Physical:** Stg=L; Freq: R, H Occas: S, K, O, I ● **Work Env:** Noise=N; ● **Salary:** 1 ● **Outlook:** 3

CLEANER, INDUSTRIAL (any industry) ● DOT #381.687-018 ● OES: 67001 ● Alternate titles: CLEAN-UP WORKER; JANITOR; SANITOR; SCRUBBER; SWEEPER; TRASH COLLECTOR; VACUUM CLEANER; WASTE COLLECTOR. Keeps working areas in production departments of industrial establishment in clean and orderly condition, performing any combination of following duties: Transports raw materials and semifinished products or supplies between departments or buildings to supply machine tenders or operators with materials for processing, using handtruck. Arranges boxes, material, and handtrucks or other industrial equipment in neat and orderly manner. Cleans lint, dust, oil, and grease from machines, overhead pipes, and conveyors, using brushes, airhoses, or steam cleaner. Cleans screens and filters. Scrubs processing tanks and vats. Cleans floors, using water hose, and applies floor drier. Picks up reusable scrap for salvage and stores in containers. Performs other duties as described under CLEANER (any industry) I Master Title. May burn waste and clean incinerator. May pick up refuse from plant grounds and maintain area by cutting grass or shoveling snow. May operate industrial truck to transport materials within plant. May start pumps to force cleaning solution through production machinery, piping, or vats. May start pumps to lubricate machines. May be designated according to area cleaned as Alley Cleaner (textile); Can-Filling-Room Sweeper (beverage); Casting-And-Locker-Room Servicer (plastic-synth.); Ceiling Cleaner (any industry); Engine-Room Cleaner (any industry); Floor Cleaner (any industry); Overhead Cleaner (any industry). ● **GED:** R2, M1, L2 ● **SVP:** 2-30 days ● **Academic:** Ed=N, Eng=N ● **Work Field:** 031 ● **MPSMS:** 905 ● **Aptitudes:** G4, V4, N5, S4, P4, Q5, K4, F4, M3, E4, C5 ● **Temperaments:** R ● **Physical:** Stg=M; Freq: S, O, R, H Occas: C, B, K, I, N ● **Work Env:** Noise=N; Occas: U ● **Salary:** 1 ● **Outlook:** 3

CLEANER, LABORATORY EQUIPMENT (any industry) ● DOT #381.687-022 ● OES: 67001 ● Alternate titles: EQUIPMENT WASHER; LABORATORY AIDE; LABORATORY ASSISTANT; LABORATORY HELPER; LABORER, LABORATORY; TESTER HELPER. Cleans laboratory equipment, such as glassware, metal instruments, sinks, tables, and test panels, using solvents, brushes, and rags: Mixes water and detergents or acids in container to prepare cleaning solution according to specifications. Washes, rinses, and dries glassware and instruments, using water, acetone bath, and cloth or hot-air drier. Scrubs walls, floors, shelves, tables, and sinks, using cleaning solution and brush. May sterilize glassware and instruments, using autoclave. May fill tubes and bottles with specified solutions and apply identification labels. May label and file microscope slides. May arrange specimens and samples on trays to be placed in incubators and refrigerators. May deliver supplies and laboratory specimens to designated work areas, using handtruck. May tend still that supplies laboratory with distilled water. May be designated Glass Washer, Laboratory (any industry) when cleaning glassware. May maintain inventory reports and logs. ● **GED:** R2, M2, L1 ● **SVP:** 2-30 days ● **Academic:** Ed=N, Eng=N ● **Work Field:** 031 ● **MPSMS:** 601 ● **Aptitudes:** G4, V4, N4, S4, P4, Q4, K4, F4, M3, E5, C3 ● **Temperaments:** R ● **Physical:** Stg=M; Const: H Freq: R Occas: S, K, O, I, G, N, X ● **Work Env:** Noise=N; Freq: U Occas: T ● **Salary:** 1 ● **Outlook:** 3

CLEANER, WINDOW (any industry) ● DOT #389.687-014 ● OES: 67001 ● Alternate titles: WINDOW WASHER. Cleans windows, glass partitions, mirrors, and other glass surfaces of building interior or exterior, using pail of soapy water or other cleaner, sponge, and squeegee. Crawls through window from inside and hooks safety belt to brackets for support, sets and climbs ladder to reach second or third story, or uses bosun's chair, swing stage, or other scaffolding lowered from roof to reach outside windows, or stands to reach first floor or inside windows. ● **GED:** R1, M1, L1 ● **SVP:** 2-30 days ● **Academic:** Ed=N, Eng=N ● **Work Field:** 031 ● **MPSMS:** 905 ● **Aptitudes:** G4, V4, N4, S4, P4, Q5, K3, F4, M3, E3, C5 ● **Temperaments:** R, S ● **Physical:** Stg=M; Freq: C, B, S, R, H, D Occas: K, O, W ● **Work Env:** Noise=N; Freq: W, U, D, O ● **Salary:** 1 ● **Outlook:** 4

DAY WORKER (domestic ser.) ● DOT #301.687-014 ● OES: 62061 ● Performs any combination of following domestic duties: Cleans and dusts furnishings, hallways, and lavatories. Changes and makes beds. Washes and irons clothings by hand or machine. Vacuums carpets, using vacuum cleaner. May watch children to keep them out of mischief. May wash windows and wax and polish floors. ● **GED:** R2, M1, L1 ● **SVP:** 2-30 days ● **Academic:** Ed=N, Eng=N ● **Work Field:** 031, 032 ● **MPSMS:** 901 ● **Aptitudes:** G4, V4, N4, S4, P4, Q5, K4, F4, M3, E5, C5 ● **Temperaments:** V ● **Physical:** Stg=M; Freq: R, H Occas: S, K, O, I, G, N, D ● **Work Env:** Noise=N; ● **Salary:** 1 ● **Outlook:** 4

FURNACE CLEANER (any industry) ● DOT #891.687-014 ● OES: 98905 ● Cleans fire pots, ducts, vents, registers, air chambers, and filter screens of domestic furnaces: Scrapes soot and ash from fire pot and smoke chambers, using scraper and wire brush. Cleans filter screens, using solvent. Removes dust-clogged air filters and places clean filters into brackets. Brushes and washes dust from air chamber and ducts, using wire or fiber brush. Removes loose soot, ash, and dust, using hand scoop and portable vacuum cleaner. Examines seams of furnace section for defects, such as cracks, and reports defects to customer or furnace repairer. May extract dust from ducts and jackets, using vacuum equipment. May tighten nuts, bolts, and screws on furnace, using handtools. ● **GED:** R2, M1, L1 ● **SVP:** 2-30 days ● **Academic:** Ed=N, Eng=N ● **Work Field:** 031 ● **MPSMS:** 553 ● **Aptitudes:** G4, V4, N4, S4, P4, Q5, K4, F4, M4, E4, C5 ● **Temperaments:** R ● **Physical:** Stg=M; Freq: S, K, O, R, H, I Occas: C, B, W, N ● **Work Env:** Noise=L; Freq: A Occas: W ● **Salary:** 2 ● **Outlook:** 2

GOLF-RANGE ATTENDANT (amuse. & rec.) ● DOT #341.683-010 ● OES: 68014 ● Performs combination of following duties at golf driving range: Picks up golf balls by hand or drives vehicle equipped with trailer that automatically picks up balls as vehicle moves over fairway. Starts revolving tumbler filled with soapy water and immerses golf balls to remove dirt, grass stain, and club marks. Removes and rinses washed balls. Applies liquid cleaner to head and shank of golf clubs and buffs with steel wool. Replaces golf balls and clubs in racks for use by driving range patrons. May perform minor maintenance on benches, using handtools. ● **GED:** R2, M1, L2 ● **SVP:** 2-30 days ● **Academic:** Ed=N, Eng=N ● **Work Field:** 031, 013 ● **MPSMS:** 616, 913 ● **Aptitudes:** G4, V4, N5, S4, P4, Q5, K3, F4, M3, E4, C5 ● **Temperaments:** R ● **Physical:** Stg=M; Freq: R, H, I, N Occas: S, F ● **Work Env:** Noise=Q; Freq: W ● **Salary:** 2 ● **Outlook:** 2

HOUSECLEANER (hotel & rest.) ● DOT #323.687-018 ● OES: 67001 ● Alternate titles: HALL CLEANER; MOVER; NIGHT CLEANER. Performs any combination of following duties to maintain hotel premises in clean and orderly manner: Moves and arranges furniture. Turns mattresses. Hangs draperies. Dusts venetian blinds. Polishes metalwork. Prepares sample rooms for sales meetings. Arranges decorations, apparatus, or furniture for banquets and social functions. Collects soiled linens for laundering, and receives and stores linen supplies in linen closet. Performs other duties as described under CLEANER (any industry) I Master Title. May deliver television sets, ironing boards, baby cribs, and rollaway beds to guests rooms. May clean swimming pool with vacuum. May clean and remove debris from driveway and garage areas. May be designated according to specialization as Curtain Cleaner (hotel & rest.); Housecleaner, Floor (hotel & rest.); Linen-Room Worker (hotel & rest.); Porter, Lobby (hotel & rest.); Vacuum Worker (hotel & rest.). ● **GED:** R2, M1, L1 ● **SVP:** 2-30 days ● **Academic:** Ed=B, Eng=N ● **Work Field:** 011, 031 ● **MPSMS:** 902, 905 ● **Aptitudes:** G4, V4, N4, S4, P4, Q4, K4, F4, M4, E4, C5 ● **Temperaments:** R ● **Physical:** Stg=H; Freq: H Occas: C, S, K, O, R, I, G ● **Work Env:** Noise=N; ● **Salary:** 1 ● **Outlook:** 4

JANITOR (any industry) ● DOT #382.664-010 ● OES: 67001 ● Alternate titles: MAINTENANCE ENGINEER; SUPERINTENDENT, BUILDING. Keeps hotel, office building, apartment house, or similar building in clean and orderly condition and tends furnace, air-conditioner, and boiler to provide heat, cool air, and hot water for tenants, performing any combination of following duties: Sweeps, mops, scrubs, and vacuums hallways, stairs and office space. Regulates flow of fuel into automatic furnace or shovels coal into hand-fired furnace. Empties tenants' trash and garbage containers. Maintains building, performing minor and routine painting, plumbing, electrical wiring, and other related maintenance activities, using handtools. Replaces air-conditioner filters. Cautions tenants regarding complaints about excessive noise, disorderly conduct, or misuse of property. Notifies management concerning need for major repairs or additions to lighting, heating, and ventilating equipment. Cleans snow and debris from sidewalk. Mows lawn, trims shrubbery, and cultivates flowers, using handtools and power tools. Posts signs to advertise vacancies and shows empty apartments to prospective tenants. May reside on property and be designated Manager, Resident (any industry). ● **GED:** R3, M2, L3 ● **SVP:** 1-3 mos ● **Academic:** Ed=N, Eng=N ● **Work Field:** 021, 031 ● **MPSMS:** 905 ● **Aptitudes:** G3, V4, N3, S3, P4, Q4, K3, F4, M3, E4, C4 ● **Temperaments:** T, V ● **Physical:** Stg=M; Freq: R, H, I Occas: C, B, S, K, O, T, G, N, D, X ● **Work Env:** Noise=N; Occas: W, H ● **Salary:** 1 ● **Outlook:** 3

KITCHEN HELPER (hotel & rest.) ● DOT #318.687-010 ● OES: 65038 ● Alternate titles: COOKEE; COOK HELPER; KITCHEN HAND; KITCHEN PORTER; KITCHEN RUNNER. Performs any combination of following duties to maintain kitchen work areas and restaurant equipment and utensils in clean and orderly condition: Sweeps and mops floors. Washes worktables, walls, refrigerators, and meat blocks. Segregates and removes trash and garbage and places it in designated containers. Steam-cleans or hoses-out garbage cans. Sorts bottles, and breaks disposable ones in bottle-crushing machine. Washes pots, pans, and trays by hand. Scrapes food from dirty dishes and washes them by hand or places them in racks or on conveyor to dishwashing machine. Polishes silver, using burnishing-machine tumbler, chemical dip, buffing wheel, and hand cloth. Holds inverted glasses over revolving brushes to clean inside surfaces. Transfers supplies and equipment between storage and work areas by hand or by use of handtruck. Sets up banquet tables. Washes and peels vegetables, using knife or peeling machine. Loads or unloads trucks picking up or delivering supplies and food. ● **GED:** R2, M1, L1 ● **SVP:** 2-30 days ● **Academic:** Ed=N, Eng=N ● **Work Field:** 031 ● **MPSMS:** 903 ● **Aptitudes:** G4, V4, N5, S4, P4, Q5, K4, F4, M4, E4, C4 ● **Temperaments:** R ● **Physical:** Stg=M; Const: R, H Freq: S, O Occas: I, G, X ● **Work Env:** Noise=L; Freq: H, U, O Occas: C ● **Salary:** 1 ● **Outlook:** 4

LABORER, GENERAL (motor trans.) ● DOT #909.687-014 ● OES: 98998 ● Performs variety of manual tasks around dock area of motor freight transportation company as directed: Sweeps dock area and cleans truck yard, using broom, shovel, and wheelbarrow. May clean interior and exterior of trucks [CLEANER (any industry) II]. ● **GED:** R1, M1, L1 ● **SVP:** 2-30 days ● **Academic:** Ed=N, Eng=N ● **Work Field:** 031, 011 ● **MPSMS:** 859 ● **Aptitudes:** G4, V4, N5, S4, P4, Q5, K4, F4, M4, E5, C5 ● **Temperaments:** R ● **Physical:** Stg=H; Freq: B, S, K, O, R, H ● **Work Env:** Noise=L; Freq: W ● **Salary:** 2 ● **Outlook:** 3

LAUNDRY WORKER I (any industry) ● DOT #361.684-014 ● OES: 92726 ● Alternate titles: CAMP-LAUNDRY OPERATOR; COMPANY LAUNDRY WORKER. Washes and irons wearing apparel, sheets, blankets, and other linens and clothes used by employees of logging, construction, mining, or other camp, or washes uniforms, aprons, and towels in establishments supplying employees with these linens. Uses equipment usually found in household or in small laundry. ● **GED:** R2, M1, L1 ● **SVP:** 2-30 days ● **Academic:** Ed=N, Eng=N ● **Work Field:** 031, 032 ● **MPSMS:** 420, 440 ● **Aptitudes:** G4, V4, N4, S4, P4, Q4, K3, F3, M3, E4, C4 ● **Temperaments:** J, V ● **Physical:** Stg=M; Freq: R, H, I Occas: X ● **Work Env:** Noise=N; Occas: U ● **Salary:** 1 ● **Outlook:** 2

LIGHT-FIXTURE SERVICER (any industry) ● DOT #389.687-018 ● OES: 67098 ● Alternate titles: FIXTURE RELAMPER; FLUORESCENT LAMP REPLACER; LIGHT-BULB REPLACER; LIGHT CLEANER. Replaces electric light fixture parts, such as bulbs, fluorescent tubes, and starters. Repairs fixture parts, such as switches and sockets, using handtools. Cleans fixtures and lamps, using soap, water and rags. Requisitions and keeps supply of bulbs, tubes, and replacement parts. ● **GED:** R1, M1, L1 ● **SVP:** 2-30 days ● **Academic:** Ed=N, Eng=N ● **Work Field:** 111, 031 ● **MPSMS:** 909 ● **Aptitudes:** G4, V4, N5, S4, P4, Q5, K4, F4, M4, E3, C5 ● **Temperaments:** R ● **Physical:** Stg=M; Freq: C, B, R, H, I ● **Work Env:** Noise=L; Freq: O ● **Salary:** 2 ● **Outlook:** 2

SANDBLASTER (any industry) ● DOT #503.687-010 ● OES: 98905 ● Alternate titles: ABRASIVE-BLASTING EQUIPMENT OPERATOR. Abrades surfaces of metal or hard-composition objects to remove adhering scale, sand, paint, grease, tar, rust, and dirt, and to impart specified finish, using abrasive-blasting equipment: Shovels or pours abrasives, such as sand, grit, or shot of specified grade into machine hopper. Masks specified areas of object to protect from abrading action. Loads parts on racks in enclosed rooms, into tumbling barrels, or into cabinets. Turns valves on equipment to regulate pressure and composition of abrasive mixture flowing through nozzle or into tumbling barrel. Starts equipment that directs blast or flow of abrasive-laden compressed air, gas, or liquid over surface of parts. Manually directs nozzle over surface of large parts or inserts arms through glove-fitted cabinet openings and manipulates small parts under nozzle for specified interval. May examine finished parts to ensure conformance to specifications. May be designated by type of equipment or abrasive used as Cabinet-Abrasive Sandblaster (any industry); Shotblaster (any industry). ● **GED:** R2, M2, L1 ● **SVP:** 2-30 days ● **Academic:** Ed=N, Eng=N ● **Work Field:** 051 ● **MPSMS:** 530, 540, 590 ● **Aptitudes:** G4, V4, N4, S4, P4, Q5, K3, F4, M3, E4, C5 ● **Temperaments:** R, T ● **Physical:** Stg=M; Freq: R, H, I, N, D Occas: S, K, E ● **Work Env:** Noise=L; Freq: A ● **Salary:** 2 ● **Outlook:** 3

SILVER WRAPPER (hotel & rest.) ● DOT #318.687-018 ● OES: 65038 ● Spreads silverware on absorbent cloth to remove moisture. Wraps individual place settings in napkins or inserts them with prescribed accessory condiments in plastic bag and closes bag with electric sealer. May immerse silverware in cleaning solution to remove soap stains before wrapping. May place tarnished and bent eating utensils aside. ● **GED:** R2, M1, L1 ● **SVP:** 1 day ● **Academic:** Ed=N, Eng=N ● **Work Field:** 041 ● **MPSMS:** 903 ● **Aptitudes:** G4, V4, N4, S4, P4, Q4, K4, F4, M3, E5, C5 ● **Temperaments:** R ● **Physical:** Stg=L; Const: R, H, I ● **Work Env:** Noise=Q; ● **Salary:** 1 ● **Outlook:** 2

STEAM CLEANER (automotive ser.) ● DOT #915.687-026 ● OES: 98905 ● Alternate titles: AUTOMOBILE WASHER, STEAM. Cleans engines, bodies, and chassis of automotive vehicles, using high pressure steam hose and detergent solution: Starts boiler to generate steam. Sprays steam and detergent solution over vehicle chassis, engine, or parts, to remove dirt and grease. Lowers engine or chassis parts into tank of detergent solution, by hand or by use of hoist, to clean inaccessible surfaces. Scrapes off adherent grime and grease, using wire brush or putty knife. May spray vehicle body with steam and caustic compound to remove paint. May clean forging dies and be designated Steam-Clean-Machine Operator (forging). ● **GED:** R2, M1, L1 ● **SVP:** 2-30 days ● **Academic:** Ed=N, Eng=N ● **Work Field:** 031 ● **MPSMS:** 961 ● **Aptitudes:** G4, V4, N4, S4, P4, Q4, K4, F4, M3, E5, C5 ● **Temperaments:** R ● **Physical:** Stg=M; Freq: S, K, O, R, H Occas: N, D ● **Work Env:** Noise=N; Occas: W, U ● **Salary:** 2 ● **Outlook:** 3

STREET CLEANER (government ser.) ● DOT #955.687-018 ● OES: 98998 ● Alternate titles: STREET SWEEPER. Sweeps refuse from municipal streets, gutters, and sidewalks into pile and shovels refuse into movable container that is pushed from place to place. May pick up paper and similar rubbish from lawns, flower beds, or highway median strips, using spike-tipped stick. ● **GED:** R1, M1, L1 ● **SVP:** 1 day ● **Academic:** Ed=N, Eng=N ● **Work Field:** 031 ● **MPSMS:** 959 ● **Aptitudes:** G4, V4, N5, S4, P4, Q5, K4, F4, M4, E4, C5 ● **Temperaments:** R ● **Physical:** Stg=L; Const: R, H Freq: S, D Occas: K, O ● **Work Env:** Noise=N; Const: W Occas: O ● **Salary:** 1 ● **Outlook:** 2

SWEEPER-CLEANER, INDUSTRIAL (any industry) ● DOT #389.683-010 ● OES: 67001 ● Alternate titles: CLEANER OPERATOR; POWER-CLEANER OPERATOR; VACUUM-CLEANER OPERATOR. Drives industrial vacuum cleaner through designated areas, such as factory aisles and warehouses, to collect scrap, dirt, and other refuse. Empties trash collecting box or bag at end of each shift. May sift refuse to recover usable materials, such as screws, metal scrap, or machine parts. May clean machine, using rags and vacuum cleaner. May refuel machine and lubricate parts. May hand sweep areas inaccessible to machine and pick up scrap. ● **GED:** R1, M1, L1 ● **SVP:** 2-30 days ● **Academic:** Ed=N, Eng=N ● **Work Field:** 031 ● **MPSMS:** 905 ● **Aptitudes:** G4, V4, N5, S3, P4, Q5, K3, F4, M3, E3, C5 ● **Temperaments:** R ● **Physical:** Stg=M; Freq: R, H, D, V Occas: S, K, O, I ● **Work Env:** Noise=L; ● **Salary:** 2 ● **Outlook:** 2

TANK CLEANER (any industry) ● DOT #891.687-022 ● OES: 98905 ● Cleans interiors of boilers, storage tanks, industrial processing tanks, kilns, and tank and refrigerator railroad cars to remove emulsion and incrustations, using shovels, squeegees, brooms, scrapers, hoses, water, and solvents: Drains tank, connects hose to water or steam lines, and sprays walls, roof, and bottom of tank to flush residue, such as oil, acid, grease, and sludge through tank openings. Scrapes and scrubs walls, using detergents, solvents, scrapers, and brushes to remove incrustations, scale, or deposits of coke or catalyst. Sweeps up debris and shovels sludge into buckets or wheelbarrows or down chutes. Removes chemical residues and other liquids from tank bottoms with squeegees or pump and suction hoses. May dry tanks with wood shavings or portable air-drying equipment. May test gas content of tanks. May add specified chemicals to industrial tanks to maintain and replenish tank processing solutions. May be designated according to type of tank cleaned as Acid-Tank Cleaner (petrol. refin.); Boiler Cleaner (any industry); Plating-Tank Cleaner (electron. comp.); Tank-Car Cleaner (petrol. refin.). ● **GED:** R2, M1, L1 ● **SVP:** 1-3 mos ● **Academic:** Ed=N, Eng=N ● **Work Field:** 031 ● **MPSMS:** 568 ● **Aptitudes:** G4, V4, N4, S4, P3, Q5, K4, F4, M3, E5, C5 ● **Temperaments:** R ● **Physical:** Stg=H; Freq: R, H, N Occas: C, S, I ● **Work Env:** Noise=N; Occas: W, U, A, T ● **Salary:** 2 ● **Outlook:** 3

TUBE CLEANER (any industry) ● DOT #891.687-030 ● OES: 98905 ● Cleans scale from inside of tubes that are used in boilers, kilns, and stills to circulate hot air or water: Removes plugs or assemblies from tube ends, using handtools. Pushes compressed-air rotary scraper or wire brush through tubes to scrape scales from interior surfaces. Flushes or blows out loosened deposits, using water or airhose. May inspect tubes by drawing electric light through them. May be designated according to type of tube cleaned as Boiler-Tube Reamer (any industry); Evaporator Repairer (chemical); Flue Cleaner (any industry); Still Cleaner, Tube (petrol. refin.); Tar Heat-Exchanger Cleaner (petrol. refin.). May steam clean outside of boiler tubes and be designated Boiler-Tube Blower (any industry). ● **GED:** R2, M1, L1 ● **SVP:** 2-30 days ● **Academic:** Ed=N, Eng=N ● **Work Field:** 031 ● **MPSMS:** 550 ● **Aptitudes:** G4, V4, N5, S4, P4, Q5, K3, F4, M3, E5, C5 ● **Temperaments:** R ● **Physical:** Stg=M; Freq: S, K, O, R, H, N, D Occas: C, B ● **Work Env:** Noise=L; Freq: H, U, A, O Occas: W ● **Salary:** 2 ● **Outlook:** 3

WAXER, FLOOR (any industry) ● DOT #381.687-034 ● OES: 67001 ● Cleans, waxes, and polishes floors by hand or machine: Removes dirt and blemishes from floor, using various cleaning solvents and compounds, according to composition of floor. Applies paste or liquid wax to floor with rags or machine. Polishes floor with electric polishing machine or weighted brush. ● **GED:** R1, M1, L1 ● **SVP:** 2-30 days ● **Academic:** Ed=N, Eng=N ● **Work Field:** 031 ● **MPSMS:** 905 ● **Aptitudes:** G4, V4, N5, S4, P4, Q5, K3, F4, M4, E4, C4 ● **Temperaments:** J, R ● **Physical:** Stg=M; Freq: S, K, R, H, X ● **Work Env:** Noise=N; Freq: O ● **Salary:** 1 ● **Outlook:** 3

GOE: 05.12.19
Reproduction Services

ADDRESSING-MACHINE OPERATOR (clerical) ● DOT #208.582-010 ● OES: 56200 ● Operates machine to print addresses, code numbers, and similar information on items, such as envelopes, accounting forms, packages, and advertising literature: Positions plates, stencils, or tapes in machine magazine and places articles to be addressed into loading rack. Starts machine that automatically feeds plates, stencils, or tapes through mechanism. Adjusts flow of ink and guides to fit size of paper and sets stops and selectors so that only certain plates will be printed, using wrench and pliers. Maintains plate file and operates embossing machine or typewriter to make corrections, additions, and changes on plates. May type statistical lists of plate files and correspondence concerning addressing jobs. ● **GED:** R3, M2, L2 ● **SVP:** 3-6 mos ● **Academic:** Ed=N, Eng=N ● **Work Field:** 191 ● **MPSMS:** 891 ● **Aptitudes:** G3, V3, N4, S3, P4, Q4, K4, F4, M4, E5, C5 ● **Temperaments:** R ● **Physical:** Stg=L; Freq: R, H Occas: I, N ● **Work Env:** Noise=N; ● **Salary:** 2 ● **Outlook:** 2

BRAILLE-DUPLICATING-MACHINE OPERATOR (print. & pub.) ● DOT #207.685-010 ● OES: 56200 ● Alternate titles: BRAILLE-THERMOFORM OPERATOR. Tends equipment to reproduce braille-embossed pages, using one of following methods: (1) Places master page on screen bed. Places roll of treated paper on stand. Threads paper through equipment and locks paper in clamping frame. Pulls heat unit over clamping frame. Depresses pedal or handle to lower clamping frame onto screen bed and to create vacuum that forms braille impressions. Pushes heat unit from bed. Releases pedal or handle to raise clamping frame, and releases catch on frame to draw reproduced copy through equipment. Repeats process to make required number of copies. Cuts copies apart, using scissors. Writes identifying information, such as page number or title, on each copy. (2) Positions master page on screen bed. Places sheet of heat-sensitive plastic paper over page and lowers clamping frame to lock page into position on bed. Pulls heat unit over clamping frame to activate vacuum pump trip-lever. Holds heat unit over frame to form braille impressions. Pushes heat unit from bed to release vacuum. Raises frame to release individual copy. Repeats process to make required number of copies. Most workers in this occupation are blind. ● **GED:** R2, M1, L2 ● **SVP:** 2-30 days ● **Academic:** Ed=N, Eng=N ● **Work Field:** 192 ● **MPSMS:** 567 ● **Aptitudes:** G4, V4, N4, S4, P4, Q4, K4, F4, M3, E5, C5 ● **Temperaments:** R ● **Physical:** Stg=M; Freq: R, H, I, E ● **Work Env:** Noise=N; ● **Salary:** 2 ● **Outlook:** 2

COIN-COUNTER-AND-WRAPPER (clerical) ● DOT #217.585-010 ● OES: 56200 ● Alternate titles: COIN-MACHINE OPERATOR; COIN TELLER. Sorts, counts, and wraps coins, using various machines: Sorts coins according to denomination, using coin-separating machine. Removes counterfeit and mutilated coins. Feeds coins into hopper of counting machine that counts and bags them. Removes, seals, and weighs bags of counted coins. Wraps coins, using coin-wrapping machine, and places rolls of coins into bags or boxes for distribution. Records machine totals, shortages or overages, and kind and value of coins removed from circulation. Verifies totals against deposit slips or other documents and prepares coins for shipment. May sort, count, and wrap paper money by hand or machine [CURRENCY SORTER (financial) 217.485-010]. ● **GED:** R3, M2, L2 ● **SVP:** 1-3 mos ● **Academic:** Ed=N, Eng=N ● **Work Field:** 232, 041, 212 ● **MPSMS:** 894 ● **Aptitudes:** G3, V4, N3, S4, P4, Q3, K3, F3, M3, E5, C5 ● **Temperaments:** T ● **Physical:** Stg=M; Const: H, I, N Freq: R Occas: S, O, G, A ● **Work Env:** Noise=L; ● **Salary:** 3 ● **Outlook:** 3

COLLATOR OPERATOR (clerical) ● DOT #208.685-010 ● OES: 56200 ● Tends machine that assembles pages of printed material in numerical sequence: Adjusts control that regulates stroke of paper pusher, according to size of paper. Places pages to be assembled in holding trays. Starts machine. Removes assembled pages from machine. ● **GED:** R2, M1, L1 ● **SVP:** 2-30 days ● **Academic:** Ed=N, Eng=N ● **Work Field:** 231 ● **MPSMS:** 898 ● **Aptitudes:** G4, V4, N4, S4, P4, Q3, K4, F4, M3, E5, C5 ● **Temperaments:** R ● **Physical:** Stg=L; Freq: R, H, I ● **Work Env:** Noise=N; ● **Salary:** 2 ● **Outlook:** 2

CURRENCY COUNTER (financial) ● DOT #217.485-010 ● OES: 56200 ● Alternate titles: CURRENCY-MACHINE OPERATOR. Sorts and counts paper money, using automatic currency-counting machine: Examines money to detect and remove counterfeit, mutilated, and worn bills. Requisitions replacements. Sorts bills according to denomination or federal reserve district number, and inserts bills into slot or hopper of machine to be automatically counted. Verifies totals registered on machine against amount of deposit reported by member bank or depositor, using calculator, and posts shortage or overage to account. Bundles and wraps counted money to be placed in vault. May sort, count, and wrap coins [COIN-COUNTER-AND-WRAPPER (financial) 217.585-010]. ● **GED:** R3, M2, L2 ● **SVP:** 1-3 mos ● **Academic:** Ed=N, Eng=N ● **Work Field:** 232, 041, 212 ● **MPSMS:** 894 ● **Aptitudes:** G3, V4, N3, S4, P3, Q3, K3, F3, M3, E5, C5 ● **Temperaments:** T ● **Physical:** Stg=L; Const: H, I, N Freq: R Occas: S, O, G, A ● **Work Env:** Noise=N; ● **Salary:** 3 ● **Outlook:** 3

FEEDER (print. & pub.) ● DOT #651.686-014 ● OES: 98502 ● Stacks sheets of paper into loading tray of sheet-fed offset press or preloading stand adjacent to press: Compares identifying information on paper stock with specifications on work order to verify delivery of specified paper stock. Flexes stack of paper with hands to prevent paper from jamming in press and places stack into loading tray of sheet-fed offset press or preloading stand adjacent to press. Adjusts feeder mechanism on press to correspond with size of paper. May operate mechanical truck to transport boxes of paper to press area. May fill ink fountains and clean press and press components to maintain press in working order. ● **GED:** R2, M1, L1 ● **SVP:** 1-3 mos ● **Academic:** Ed=N, Eng=N ● **Work Field:** 191 ● **MPSMS:** 472 ● **Aptitudes:** G4, V4, N4, S3, P4, Q4, K3, F3, M3, E5, C5 ● **Temperaments:** R ● **Physical:** Stg=H; Const: R, H, N, D Freq: S, I Occas: G ● **Work Env:** Noise=V; Const: A Freq: V, M ● **Salary:** 1 ● **Outlook:** 2

FOLDING-MACHINE OPERATOR (clerical) ● DOT #208.685-014 ● OES: 56200 ● Alternate titles: FOLDER OPERATOR. Tends machine that folds advertising literature, forms, letters, or other paper sheets: Turns indicator knobs to adjust folding rollers, side guides, and stops, according to specified size and number of folds. Starts machine and feeds paper sheets between folding rollers. Removes folded sheets. May place folded sheets into envelopes preparatory to mailing. ● **GED:** R2, M1, L1 ● **SVP:** 2-30 days ● **Academic:** Ed=N, Eng=N ● **Work Field:** 062 ● **MPSMS:** 891 ● **Aptitudes:** G4, V4, N4, S4, P4, Q4, K3, F4, M3, E5, C5 ● **Temperaments:** R ● **Physical:** Stg=L; Freq: R, H Occas: I, N ● **Work Env:** Noise=N; ● **Salary:** 1 ● **Outlook:** 2

INSERTING-MACHINE OPERATOR (clerical) ● DOT #208.685-018 ● OES: 56200 ● Tends machine that inserts printed matter, such as letters or booklets into folders or envelopes: Stacks quantities of inserts and covers into machine feedboxes and turns setscrews to adjust feeder mechanisms, according to thickness of material. Starts machine and replenishes feedboxes with inserts and covers. ● **GED:** R2, M1, L2 ● **SVP:** 2-30 days ● **Academic:** Ed=N, Eng=N ● **Work Field:** 062 ● **MPSMS:** 891 ● **Aptitudes:** G4, V4, N4, S4, P4, Q4, K3, F4, M3, E5, C5 ● **Temperaments:** R ● **Physical:** Stg=L; Freq: R, H Occas: I, N ● **Work Env:** Noise=N; ● **Salary:** 1 ● **Outlook:** 2

MICROFILM MOUNTER (clerical) ● DOT #208.685-022 ● OES: 56200 ● Tends machine that automatically mounts developed microfilm onto cards for filing purposes: Inserts roll of microfilm into machine. Fills hopper with presorted cards. Pours specified amount of adhesive solution into hopper to coat cards. Starts machine and observes coating of cards with adhesive solution and mounting of film onto cards. ● **GED:** R2, M1, L1 ● **SVP:** 2-30 days ● **Academic:** Ed=N, Eng=N ● **Work Field:** 063 ● **MPSMS:** 891 ● **Aptitudes:** G4, V4, N4, S4, P4, Q4, K4, F4, M4, E5, C4 ● **Temperaments:** R, T ● **Physical:** Stg=L; Freq: R, H, I, N ● **Work Env:** Noise=N; ● **Salary:** 2 ● **Outlook:** 2

PHOTOCOPYING-MACHINE OPERATOR (clerical) ● DOT #207.685-014 ● OES: 56200 ● Tends duplicating machine to reproduce handwritten or typewritten matter: Places original copy on glass plate in machine. Places blank paper on loading tray. Sets control switch for number of copies. Presses button to start machine which transfers image of original copy onto blank paper by photographic and static electricity process. May clean and repair machine. May receive payment for duplicate copies. Important variables may be indicated by trade name of machine tended. ● **GED:** R2, M1, L1 ● **SVP:** 2-30 days ● **Academic:** Ed=N, Eng=N ● **Work Field:** 201 ● **MPSMS:** 891 ● **Aptitudes:** G4, V4, N4, S4, P3, Q4, K3, F4, M3, E5, C5 ● **Temperaments:** R ● **Physical:** Stg=L; Freq: R, H, I Occas: N ● **Work Env:** Noise=N; ● **Salary:** 3 ● **Outlook:** 2

PHOTOGRAPHIC-MACHINE OPERATOR (clerical) ● DOT #207.685-018 ● OES: 56200 ● Tends machine that photographs original documents, such as bills, statements, receipts, and checks: Loads machine with film. Feeds records to be photographed into feed rolls that carry material to be photographed past camera lens, or positions records on table beneath camera lens. May adjust camera distance from document, focus, and exposure settings to accommodate size of record and ensure clarity and resolution of image. May tend equipment which encases roll film in cartridges or mounts microfiche (sheet of micro-

film) on aperture card. ● **GED:** R3, M2, L2 ● **SVP:** 2-30 days ● **Academic:** Ed=N, Eng=N ● **Work Field:** 201 ● **MPSMS:** 899 ● **Aptitudes:** G4, V4, N4, S4, P4, Q4, K4, F4, M4, E4, C5 ● **Temperaments:** R ● **Physical:** Stg=L; Const: R, H Freq: I, N Occas: S, O, G, A ● **Work Env:** Noise=N; ● **Salary:** 2 ● **Outlook:** 2

ROLL TENDER (print. & pub.) ● DOT #651.686-022 ● OES: 98502 ● Alternate titles: ROLL SETTER. Loads rolls of paper onto automatic splicing unit of web offset printing press: Inspects rolls of paper for blemishes or tears and cuts away damaged area with knife. Rolls paper into loading position on automatic splicer, inserts shaft of automatic splicer through roll core, secures holding chucks of automatic splicer to shaft ends, and threads paper through press components to prepare press for printing. Applies adhesive strip to backup roll and inserts backup roll onto automatic splicing unit of press to prepare paper for automatic splicing. Removes roll of leftover paper from press after automatic splicing. May operate mechanical truck to transport rolls of paper to press area. May clean press and clean and install press components to maintain press in working order. ● **GED:** R2, M1, L1 ● **SVP:** 6 mos-1 yr ● **Academic:** Ed=N, Eng=N ● **Work Field:** 191 ● **MPSMS:** 472 ● **Aptitudes:** G4, V4, N4, S4, P4, Q4, K3, F4, M4, E5, C5 ● **Temperaments:** R ● **Physical:** Stg=V; Const: R, H Freq: S, I Occas: G, F, D, A, V ● **Work Env:** Noise=V; Const: A Freq: V, M ● **Salary:** 1 ● **Outlook:** 2

GOE: 05.12.20
Signalling

CROSSING TENDER (any industry) ● DOT #371.667-010 ● OES: 63044 ● Guards railroad crossing to warn motorists and pedestrians of approaching trains: Consults train schedules and listens for approaching trains from watchtower. Presses button to flash warning signal lights. Presses control button to lower crossing gates until train passes, and raises gate when crossing is clear. May wave flags, signs, or lanterns in emergencies. ● **GED:** R2, M2, L2 ● **SVP:** 1-3 mos ● **Academic:** Ed=N, Eng=N ● **Work Field:** 293 ● **MPSMS:** 851 ● **Aptitudes:** G3, V4, N4, S3, P3, Q4, K4, F4, M4, E5, C4 ● **Temperaments:** R ● **Physical:** Stg=L; Freq: R, H, T, G, N, F, V Occas: I, D, A, X ● **Work Env:** Noise=N; ● **Salary:** 1 ● **Outlook:** 2

Industrial 06

An interest in repetitive, concrete, organized activities in a factory setting. You can satisfy this interest by working in one of many industries that manufacture goods on a mass production basis. You may enjoy manual work — using your hands or handtools. Perhaps you prefer to operate or take care of machines. You may like to inspect, sort, count, or weigh products. Using your training and experience to set up machines or supervise other workers may appeal to you.

Production Technology

Workers in this group use their skill and knowledge of machines and processes to perform one or more demanding or complex activities. Some set up machines for others to operate or set up and perform a variety of machine operations on their own. Some do precision handwork; some supervise or instruct others in the use of machines, processes to be carried out, and the techniques to be used.

✓ What kind of work would you do?

Your work activities would depend upon your specific job. For example, you might:

- set up a textile weaving loom to produce specified patterns in cloth.
- use precision measuring devices to inspect watch parts to determine defects in the production process.
- set up a group of production machines and check them to ensure they are operating correctly.
- supervise salvage operations in a factory.
- assemble precision optical instruments.
- inspect electronic systems by following blueprints and diagrams.

✓ What skills and abilities do you need for this kind of work?

To do this kind of work, you must be able to:

- read and understand blueprints and diagrams in order to set up and adjust machines and equipment.
- use eyes, hands, and fingers to do precision assembly work or to operate precision instruments.
- use math skills to plan schedules and keep production records.

- detect small differences in shape, size, and texture of products.
- explain how to operate a machine to other workers.
- direct and organize the work of others.
- inspect electronic systems by following blueprints and diagrams.
- pay strict attention to set standards and guidelines.

The above statements may not apply to every job in this group.

✓ How do you know if you would like or could learn to do this kind of work?

The following questions may give you clues about yourself as you consider this group of jobs.

- Have you taken industrial arts or machine shop courses? Do you like to set up machines according to written standards?
- Have you taken general or applied maintenance courses? Do you like projects which use math skills such as measuring?
- Have you assembled a bicycle or toy by following drawings or written instructions? Did you have a fairly easy time doing it?
- Have you held a summer or part-time job where mechanical equipment was used? Do you enjoy working in this type of surroundings?
- Have you been in charge of a group project? Do you like to assume the responsibility for getting a project completed?

✓ How can you prepare for and enter this kind of work?

Occupations in this group usually require education and/or training extending from one year to over ten years, depending upon the specific kind of work. Many of the jobs in this group require shop courses.

Some may require math classes. Some jobs have formal apprenticeship programs. Others require on-the-job training.

Supervisory positions are usually filled by promoting workers with seniority and skill. Other jobs, such as inspecting, may be advancement positions for machine operators.

✓ What else should you consider about these jobs?

Overtime or night and shift work may be required on some jobs. Some workers are paid hourly wages.

Other workers are paid according to the number of pieces they produce.

Workers are exposed to different types of factory conditions. Most plants are well-lighted and ventilated. However, working around machinery may be hazardous or noisy, and safety procedures must be followed.

If you think you would like to do this kind of work, look at the job titles listed on the following pages.

■ ■ ■

GOE: 06.01.01
Supervision & Instruction

COOK, MEXICAN FOOD (food prep., nec) ● DOT #526.134-010 ● OES: 81000 ● Supervises and coordinates activities of workers engaged in preparing, cooking, portioning, and packaging ready-to-serve Mexican food specialties, such as chili, tamales, enchiladas, and tacos (seasoned chili beans wrapped in tortillas): Requisitions ingredients, such as meat, olives, chili, garlic, and spices from storeroom. Directs activities of workers engaged in feeding and tending grinding and mixing machines, rolling, cutting, and baking tortillas, and stirring and tending food in cooking vessels. Tastes foods to determine that they meet seasoning specifications. Supervises workers engaged in portioning and packaging foods. Frequently performs duties of workers supervised. May be designated according to food cooked as Cook, Chili (food prep., nec); Cook, Enchilada (food prep., nec); Cook, Taco (food prep., nec); Cook, Tamale (food prep., nec); Cook, Tortilla (food prep., nec). ● **GED:** R4, M2, L3 ● **SVP:** 2-4 yrs ● **Academic:** Ed=N, Eng=S ● **Work Field:** 146 ● **MPSMS:** 399 ● **Aptitudes:** G3, V3, N4, S4, P4, Q4, K3, F3, M3, E5, C5 ● **Temperaments:** D, J, T, V ● **Physical:** Stg=M; Freq: R, H, I, E, T, G, N Occas: A ● **Work Env:** Noise=N; ● **Salary:** 1 ● **Outlook:** 3

SUPERVISOR, FILM PROCESSING (motion picture) ● DOT #976.131-014 ● OES: 81000 ● Alternate titles: FILM TECHNICIAN; LABORATORY CONTACT SUPERVISOR. Supervises and coordinates activities of workers engaged in developing exposed black-and-white and color motion picture film. Examines samples of developed film for defects, such as scratches, cracks, and contours. Directs workers to make machine adjustments to correct defects. Monitors gauges of developing solution tanks to ensure adherence to specifications. Sets up or corrects set-up of photographic processing machines. Collects and submits film strips and processing solutions to quality control department for analysis. Mends film breaks, replaces film reels, and performs minor repair work on machines, using handtools. Notifies maintenance supervisor when major repair is required. Performs other duties as described under SUPERVISOR (any industry) Master Title. ● **GED:** R4, M3, L3 ● **SVP:** 2-4 yrs ● **Academic:** Ed=N, Eng=G ● **Work Field:** 202 ● **MPSMS:** 911, 864, 897 ● **Aptitudes:** G3, V3, N3, S4, P3, Q3, K4, F3, M3, E5, C3 ● **Temperaments:** D, J, P, V ● **Physical:** Stg=L; Freq: R, H, I, T, G, N, D, A, X ● **Work Env:** Noise=N; ● **Salary:** 4 ● **Outlook:** 3

QUALITY ASSURANCE SUPERVISOR (auto. mfg.) ● DOT #806.137-022 ● OES: 81000 ● Supervises and coordinates activities of workers engaged in inspecting and testing assembled motor vehicles, components, and parts, as vehicles and subassemblies proceed through stages of assembly process, applying knowledge of quality assurance standards and procedures: Reviews quality assurance instructions, assembly specifications, and production schedules to determine method of conducting inspections and tests, sequence of operations, and work assignments. Directs workers in quality assurance inspection and testing, to assure that establishment and regulatory standards are met. Assigns training of new workers to qualified workers. Reviews reports and confers with quality assurance, production, management, and engineering personnel to solve work-related problems. Performs other duties as described under SUPERVISOR (any industry) Master Title. May be designated according to stage of assembly as Quality Assurance Supervisor, Body (auto. mfg.); Quality Assurance Supervisor, Trim (auto. mfg.); Quality Assurance Supervisor, Chassis (auto. mfg.); Quality Assurance Supervisor, Final (auto. mfg.). ● **GED:** R4, M3, L4 ● **SVP:** 2-4 yrs ● **Academic:** Ed=H, Eng=G ● **Work Field:** 212 ● **MPSMS:** 591 ● **Aptitudes:** G2, V2, N3, S2, P2, Q3, K4, F4, M4, E5, C4 ● **Temperaments:** D, J, P, T ● **Physical:** Stg=L; Freq: R, H, I, T, G, N, F, D, A Occas: X ● **Work Env:** Noise=N; ● **Salary:** 3 ● **Outlook:** 4

GOE: 06.01.02
Machine Set-up

DIE SETTER (forging) ● DOT #612.360-010 ● OES: 91399 ● Sets up forging machines, such as forging presses, coining presses, drophammers, forging rolls, and upsetters, following blueprint, work order, and data-chart specifications, and using handtools and measuring instruments, such as rules, squares, and gauges: Aligns and bolts specified dies to ram and anvil of presses and hammers. Installs impression and gripping dies and synchronizing cams on upsetting machines. Sets and bolts roll dies into self-positioning slots or dogs on roll shafts of forging rolls. Aligns and bolts positioning fixtures and stops, and turns handles or knobs to synchronize conveyor speed with forging-machining action and heating cycle of furnace. Starts machine and inspects work to verify conformance of die setup to specifications. May be designated according to machine set up as Drophammer Setter-Up (forging); Forging Press Setter-Up (forging); Upsetter Setter-Up (forging). ● **GED:** R4, M3, L3 ● **SVP:** 2-4 yrs ● **Academic:** Ed=H, Eng=S ● **Work Field:** 134 ● **MPSMS:** 556 ● **Aptitudes:** G3, V3, N3, S2, P2, Q4, K3, F2, M2, E5, C5 ● **Temperaments:** J, T ● **Physical:** Stg=M; Freq: R, H, I, N, D Occas: S, K, O, A ● **Work Env:** Noise=L; Freq: H, O ● **Salary:** 4 ● **Outlook:** 3

KNITTER MECHANIC (knitting) ● DOT #685.360-010 ● OES: 92702 ● Alternate titles: PATTERN-AND-CHAIN MAKER. Builds metal chains, consisting of multisize pattern plates, or installs pattern tapes that control operation of jacquard loom and link-and-link flat knitting machines and sets up machines to produce specified design in knitted fabric: Obtains specifications for new knitting pattern from supervisor. Studies number, type, and arrangement of stitches in sample and determines arrangement of pattern plates on chains, employing knowledge of machine operation. Connects plates to form chain. Studies sample to determine which perforations in pattern plates are to be covered to produce specified knit and informs JACQUARD-PLATE MAKER (knitting). Installs chains and pattern plates in machine and makes trial run to determine if knitting meets specifications. May make minor repairs to knitting machines. ● **GED:** R4, M3, L3 ● **SVP:** 2-4 yrs ● **Academic:** Ed=N, Eng=S ● **Work Field:** 165, 061 ● **MPSMS:** 424, 567 ● **Aptitudes:** G3, V3, N3, S2, P2, Q4, K3, F3, M2, E5, C4 ● **Temperaments:** J, T ● **Physical:** Stg=M; Freq: R, H, I, N, A Occas: X ● **Work Env:** Noise=N; ● **Salary:** 1 ● **Outlook:** 2

KNITTING-MACHINE FIXER (knitting) ● DOT #689.260-026 ● OES: 92702 ● Sets up, adjusts, and repairs knitting machines to knit hose, garments, and cloth according to specifications, using knowledge of machine function: Reads work order and confers with supervisor or engineer to determine knitting machine setup. Inserts cams, links, buttons, or needle jacks in pattern chain to set up machine to knit hose, garment, or cloth according to pattern design chart. Observes operation of machine and examines knitted material to detect defects. Turns setscrews and handwheels to adjust machine parts, such as gears and cams, and to synchronize yarn carriers, needles, dividers, and sinkers. Repairs and replaces machine parts, using handtools. Aligns and straightens needles, sinkers, and dividers, using pliers. Cleans and oils machines. May only repair and adjust knitting machines and be designated Line Fixer (knitting). ● **GED:** R4, M3, L3 ● **SVP:** 2-4 yrs ● **Academic:** Ed=N, Eng=S ● **Work Field:** 121, 165 ● **MPSMS:** 420, 567 ● **Aptitudes:** G3, V3, N4, S2, P2, Q3, K3, F3, M3, E5, C4 ● **Temperaments:** J, T, V ● **Physical:** Stg=L; Freq: S, R, H, I, N, D, A Occas: K, O, E, T, G, X ● **Work Env:** Noise=L; ● **Salary:** 2 ● **Outlook:** 2

LOOM FIXER (narrow fabrics) ● DOT #683.260-018 ● OES: 92702 ● Alternate titles: FIXER; LOOM REPAIRER. Sets up, adjusts, and repairs looms to weave cloth of specified quality and design, using knowledge of loom function and weaving, diagrams, and manuals: Inspects loom or woven cloth to determine adjustments or repairs needed. Repairs or replaces defective parts, such as harness straps and shuttles, and adjusts tension and timing of parts, using handtools. Levels and aligns parts, such as shuttle boxes, race plates, and reeds, to prevent excessive wear, using straightedge, level, and square. May change setup of loom to weave different pattern or different type yarn [LOOM CHANGER (textile) 683.360-010]. May be designated according to type of loom serviced as Dobby-Loom Fixer (textile); Jacquard-Loom Fixer (textile); Narrow-Fabric-Loom Fixer (narrow fabrics); Rapier-Insertion Loom Fixer (textile); Water-Jet Loom Fixer (textile). ● **GED:** R4, M3, L3 ● **SVP:** 2-4 yrs ● **Academic:** Ed=N, Eng=S ● **Work Field:** 121, 164 ● **MPSMS:** 567, 420 ● **Aptitudes:** G3, V4, N4, S3, P3, Q4, K3, F3, M3, E5, C4 ● **Temperaments:** J, T ● **Physical:** Stg=M; Freq: S, K, O, R, H, I, N, F, D, A Occas: C, W, E, T, G, X ● **Work Env:** Noise=L; Occas: A, M ● **Salary:** 3 ● **Outlook:** 2

MACHINE SETTER (any industry) ● DOT #616.360-022 ● OES: 91510 ● Sets up various metal fabricating machines, such as brakes, shears, punch presses, bending and straightening machines, to cut, bend, and straighten metal as specified by layout, work order blueprints, and templates: Positions, aligns, and bolts dies, blades, bedplates, cushion pins, and stops, using shims and measuring tools, such as squares, straightedges, rules, micrometers, gauges, feelers, templates, and handtools. Adjusts flow of lubricants, pressure and depth of stroke, or feed of material, applying knowledge of thickness and properties of metal or according to standard specifications. Makes trial runs and measures workpiece for conformance to specifications. Instructs operator in special handling techniques. Clears jams and corrects malfunction of machines. Reports need for machine repairs to supervisor. Dismantles setups. May sharpen shear blades, drills, on cutting tools. May set up drill presses, flame cutting, and welding machines. May set up automatic or multipurpose machines. May specialize in setup of single type of machine and be designated accordingly as Brake Machine Setter (any industry). May set up machines common to sheet metal operations and be designated Machine Setter, Sheet Metal (any industry). ● **GED:** R4, M3, L3 ● **SVP:** 1-2 yrs ● **Academic:** Ed=N, Eng=S ● **Work Field:** 054, 102 ● **MPSMS:** 554 ● **Aptitudes:** G3, V3, N3, S2, P3, Q4, K3, F3, M2, E4, C5 ● **Temperaments:** J, T, V ● **Physical:** Stg=M; Freq: S, R, H, I, N, D Occas: K, O, E, T, G, A ● **Work Env:** Noise=L; Freq: A, O ● **Salary:** 3 ● **Outlook:** 2

MACHINE SETTER (machine shop) ● DOT #600.360-014 ● OES: 91510 ● Alternate titles: MACHINIST, JOB SETTER. Sets up and adjusts machine tools, such as lathes, milling machines, boring machines, drills and punch presses, grinders, gear hobbers, and plastic molding machines for other workers, such as PRODUCTION-MA-

CHINE TENDERS (machine shop) 609.685-018, according to specifications, applying knowledge of machining methods: Reads blueprint or job order for product specifications, such as dimensions and tolerances, and tooling instructions, such as feed rate, cutting speed, depth of cut, fixtures, and cutting tools to be used. Installs and adjusts holding device and fastens specified cutting and shaping tools in position to enable operator to produce finished workpiece to specifications, using handtools, such as wrenches, screwdrivers, and pliers. Selects and sets speed and feed of machine according to type of operation and specified material and finish. Starts machine to obtain first-run workpiece and verifies dimensional tolerances, using micrometers, gauges, and templates. Changes worn cutting tools and adjusts operation of machine, such as cutting speed, feed rate, or depth of cut, when required. May replace parts on machines, such as bearings, filters, wiring, and switches, using handtools. May instruct operators or other workers in machine setup and operation. May set up machines and equipment other than machine tools, such as welding machine and flame cutting equipment. ● **GED:** R4, M4, L3 ● **SVP:** 2-4 yrs ● **Academic:** Ed=N, Eng=S ● **Work Field:** 057 ● **MPSMS:** 560, 580 ● **Aptitudes:** G3, V3, N3, S2, P2, Q3, K3, F3, M3, E5, C5 ● **Temperaments:** J, T, V ● **Physical:** Stg=M; Freq: R, H, I, N, D, A Occas: E, T, G ● **Work Env:** Noise=L; Occas: M ● **Salary:** 3 ● **Outlook:** 3

MACHINE SET-UP OPERATOR, PAPER GOODS (paper goods) ● DOT #649.380-010 ● OES: 92914 ● Sets up and adjusts machines that convert, saw, corrugate, band, wrap, box, stitch, form, or seal paper or paperboard sheets into products, such as toilet tissue, towels, napkins, bags, envelopes, tubing, cartons, wax rolls, and containers, according to specifications, by any combination of following tasks: Adjusts rolls, guides, and chutes to accommodate type of paper or paperboard fed from parent rolls or flat stock from automatic feedracks, using handtools. Measures, spaces, and sets saw blades, cutters, and perforators, according to product specifications, using rule, thumbscrews, and wrenches. Installs printing attachment to machine and makes adjustment for clarity of print. Threads wire through stitching head and synchronizes speed for spacing stitches. Installs or resets cutting dies according to work orders, using handtools. Operates machine for test run to verify adjustments and observes functioning of machine parts, such as gauges, elevator, belts, slip clutches, oil injectors, glue feeders, and electrical devices. Repairs or replaces defective parts. May be designated according to type of machine adjusted as Bag-Machine Set-Up Operator (paper goods); Gluing-Machine Adjuster (paper goods); Stitcher Set-Up Operator, Automatic (paper goods). ● **GED:** R3, M2, L2 ● **SVP:** 2-4 yrs ● **Academic:** Ed=N, Eng=N ● **Work Field:** 121, 102 ● **MPSMS:** 474, 475 ● **Aptitudes:** G3, V3, N4, S3, P3, Q4, K3, F3, M3, E4, C4 ● **Temperaments:** J, T ● **Physical:** Stg=M; Freq: S, R, H, N Occas: C, K, O, I, G, F, D, A, X ● **Work Env:** Noise=L; Occas: H, U, A, M, O ● **Salary:** 2 ● **Outlook:** 2

PRINT CONTROLLER (photofinishing) ● DOT #976.360-010 ● OES: 92999 ● Sets up and adjusts photographic print developing equipment according to density, color, and size of prints: Positions film in densitometer, reads dials, and records findings on plot sheet to locate defects in density and color balance. Confers with SUPERVISOR, QUALITY CONTROL (photofinishing) to determine adjustments required to bring print machine into balance. Runs test film strip through print machine to evaluate machine exposure. Removes cover from control panel of print machine to gain access to control shafts and adjustment knobs, using wrench. Plugs electric timer into printer to determine time elapsed during printing operation. Starts equipment, observes timer, and adjusts shafts and knobs to attain specified process settings, using handtools. Locks control shafts of printer into position subsequent to final adjustment to prevent shifting in color or density balance during printing. Keeps record of adjustments made for departmental use. ● **GED:** R4, M3, L2 ● **SVP:** 1-2 yrs ● **Academic:** Ed=A, Eng=N ● **Work Field:** 202, 212 ● **MPSMS:** 897 ● **Aptitudes:** G3, V3, N3, S3, P3, Q3, K3, F3, M3, E5, C3 ● **Temperaments:** J, T ● **Physical:** Stg=L; Freq: R, H, I, N, D, X Occas: S, K, O, T, G ● **Work Env:** Noise=L; ● **Salary:** 1 ● **Outlook:** 2

SCREEN-PRINTING-EQUIPMENT SETTER (paper goods) ● DOT #979.360-010 ● OES: 92524 ● Sets up and adjusts silk-screen printing equipment used to hand print multicolored designs on wallpaper: Adjusts feed rollers and spindle reel to specified tension, using wrench. Compares ink prepared for printing run with master color swatch to confirm accuracy of match. Examines printing screen for sharpness of stencil design and feels screen to verify specified tension on frame. Measures distance between printing guide marker on table and center of screen and adjusts distance as required to ensure specified color print registration. Starts drying oven and sets thermostat to temperature specified for printing run. Observes test run or manipulates equipment to produce test print. Examines print for defects and adjusts equipment to correct defective printing as required. Monitors production activities to ensure standard quality of printing. Trains workers in use of printing equipment. ● **GED:** R4, M2, L3 ● **SVP:** 2-4 yrs ● **Academic:** Ed=H, Eng=S ● **Work Field:** 191 ● **MPSMS:** 567, 474 ● **Aptitudes:** G3, V3, N3, S3, P2, Q4, K2, F3, M3, E5, C2 ● **Temperaments:** J ● **Physical:** Stg=L; Freq: R, H, I, E, N, D, A, X Occas: T, G ● **Work Env:** Noise=L; ● **Salary:** 3 ● **Outlook:** 4

SETTER, AUTOMATIC-SPINNING LATHE (any industry) ● DOT #604.360-010 ● OES: 91105 ● Sets up automatic spinning lathe to spin (form) shaped articles from sheet or plate metal as specified by blueprints and computed from data charts: Bolts specified spinning chuck to headstock spindle and follow block to tailstock, using handtools or power tools. Positions, aligns, and bolts specified circular forming tool on hydraulic carriage according to diameter and thickness of metal disk, using such measuring tools as calipers, micrometers, and verniers. Turns control knobs to set speed of lathe and feed speed of carriage according to chart. Makes trial run and measures dimensions of first piece for conformance to blueprint specifications. May set up automatic spinning lathe equipped with special forming tools to shape, trim, or form knurls or beads on workpiece and be designated Setter, Automatic-Spinning-And-Beading-Lathe (any industry). ● **GED:** R4, M3, L3 ● **SVP:** 1-2 yrs ● **Academic:** Ed=N, Eng=S ● **Work Field:** 055, 057 ● **MPSMS:** 550, 554 ● **Aptitudes:** G3, V3, N3, S2, P3, Q4, K3, F3, M3, E5, C5 ● **Temperaments:** J, T ● **Physical:** Stg=M; Freq: R, H, I, N, D, A ● **Work Env:** Noise=L; ● **Salary:** 3 ● **Outlook:** 3

GOE: 06.01.03
Machine Set-up & Operation

CHIEF OPERATOR (chemical) ● DOT #558.260-010 ● OES: 95008 ● Controls chemical process equipment from instrumented control board or other control station: Monitors recording instruments, flowmeters, panel lights, and other indicators, and listens for warning signals to verify conformity of process conditions to plant standards of safety and efficiency. Moves control settings or notifies CHEMICAL OPERATOR (chemical) III 559.382-018 or other workers to make control adjustments on equipment units affecting speed of chemical reactions and quality and yield of product, using telephone or intercommunications system. Notifies maintenance, stationary-engineering, and other auxiliary personnel to correct equipment malfunctions and adjust power, steam, water, or air supply as indicated. Confers with technical and supervisory personnel to report or resolve conditions affecting safety, efficiency, and product quality. Interprets chemical reactions visible through sight glasses or on television monitor and reviews laboratory test reports to determine need for process adjustments. Inspects equipment for potential and actual hazards, wear, leaks, and other conditions requiring maintenance or shutdown. Records instrument readings, process conditions, and other operating data in shift log, calculating material requirements or product yield as necessary from standard formulas. Manually regulates or shuts down equipment during emergency situations, as directed by supervisory personnel. May be designated according to product produced as Chief Operator, Ammonium Sulfate (chemical); according to equipment used as Chief Operator, Reformer (chemical); or according to chemical process as Chief Operator, Purification And Reaction (chemical); Chief Operator, Synthesis (chemical). ● **GED:** R4, M3, L4 ● **SVP:** 2-4 yrs ● **Academic:** Ed=H, Eng=S ● **Work Field:** 147 ● **MPSMS:** 490 ● **Aptitudes:** G3, V3, N3, S3, P3, Q3, K4, F4, M3, E5, C4 ● **Temperaments:** J, T ● **Physical:** Stg=L; Freq: R, H, I, T, G, N, X, V Occas: F, A ● **Work Env:** Noise=L; Occas: A, O ● **Salary:** 4 ● **Outlook:** 1

DRILL-PRESS SET-UP OPERATOR, MULTIPLE SPINDLE (machine shop) ● DOT #606.380-010 ● OES: 91108 ● Alternate titles: GANG-DRILL-PRESS OPERATOR; MULTIPLE-SPINDLE-DRILLING-MACHINE OPERATOR. Sets up and operates multiple-spindle drilling machine to perform simultaneously or in sequence machining

operations, such as drilling, reaming, countersinking, spot-facing, and tapping of holes in metal workpieces, according to specifications, tooling instructions, standard charts, and knowledge of machining procedures: Reads blueprint or job order for product specifications, such as hole locations and dimensions, and tooling instructions, such as drilling jigs, holding fixtures, feed rates, cutting speeds, and cutting tools to be used. Places workpiece in fixture or positions it on machine table, and secures it with clamps. Mounts cutting tools in spindles. Positions and secures specified drilling jig and moves controls and positions spindles to align tools with guide bushings in jig. Sets stops to control depth of cut. Moves controls to set cutting speeds and feed rates, and regulate flow of coolant. Engages power feed and observes machine operation. Periodically verifies conformance of machined work to specifications, using such measuring instruments as calipers, micrometers, and fixed gauges. May machine plastics or other nonmetallic materials. May tilt table or spindles to machine holes at specified angles. ● **GED:** R4, M4, L3 ● **SVP:** 1-2 yrs ● **Academic:** Ed=H, Eng=N ● **Work Field:** 053 ● **MPSMS:** 540 ● **Aptitudes:** G3, V3, N3, S3, P3, Q4, K3, F3, M3, E5, C5 ● **Temperaments:** J, T ● **Physical:** Stg=M; Freq: R, H, I, N, D, A Occas: S, O ● **Work Env:** Noise=L; ● **Salary:** 3 ● **Outlook:** 3

ENGINE-LATHE SET-UP OPERATOR (machine shop) ● DOT #604.380-018 ● OES: 91105 ● Alternate titles: BENCH-LATHE OPERATOR. Sets up and operates engine lathes to machine metallic and nonmetallic workpieces according to specifications, tooling instructions, and standard charts, applying knowledge of machining methods: Reads blueprint or job order for specifications, such as dimensions and tolerances, tooling instructions on holding devices, feed rates, cutting speeds, depth of cuts, and cutting tools. Positions and secures tools in holders, using wrenches. Lifts workpiece manually or with hoist, and positions and secures workpiece in holding device, machine table, chuck, centers, or fixture, using clamps and wrenches. Sets specified rotation speed, feed rate, and depth of cut, and positions tool in relation to workpiece. Starts machine, turns handwheels to feed tool to workpiece, and engages feed. Turns valve handle to direct flow of coolant against tool and workpiece. Observes cutting action of machine to detect excessive wear or malfunction. Verifies conformance of machined workpiece to specifications, using micrometers, calipers, and fixed gauges. May scribe reference lines on workpiece, using scale, or template and scriber, to lay out interrelated surfaces, lengths, and depths of cut. May compute unspecified dimensions and machine settings, using knowledge of metal properties and shop mathematics. May set up tracing attachment that guides cutting tool to follow movement of tracing stylus along template to duplicate template profile on turned workpiece and be designated Tracing-Lathe Set-Up Operator (machine shop). May be required to have experience with custom or production work, or with particular material, product, level of precision, or size, type, or trade name of machine. ● **GED:** R4, M4, L3 ● **SVP:** 1-2 yrs ● **Academic:** Ed=H, Eng=N ● **Work Field:** 055 ● **MPSMS:** 540, 591, 592 ● **Aptitudes:** G3, V3, N3, S3, P3, Q3, K3, F3, M3, E4, C5 ● **Temperaments:** J, T ● **Physical:** Stg=M; Freq: R, H, I, N, D Occas: A ● **Work Env:** Noise=L; Freq: M Occas: A ● **Salary:** 3 ● **Outlook:** 3

EXHAUST EQUIPMENT OPERATOR (electron. comp.) ● DOT #599.382-014 ● OES: 92999 ● Alternate titles: EXHAUST OPERATOR. Sets up and controls exhaust equipment to remove gases and impurities from electron and cathode ray tubes, following procedure manuals, work orders, and specifications: Reads production schedules and procedure manuals to determine tube specifications and operational sequence. Calculates equipment control settings, applying standard formulas to determine power, temperature, and vacuum, according to tube size and type. Sets controls on power supplies, ovens, and pumps according to calculations. Observes meters, gauges, and recording instruments during operation, and adjusts controls to ensure tubes are exhausted as specified. Troubleshoots exhaust equipment to locate malfunction when tubes fail to exhaust. Repairs faulty exhaust equipment, or notifies maintenance department of faulty equipment. May test and inspect tubes for leaks, using leak detection equipment. May set up and operate aging equipment to stabilize electrical properties of tube. May be designated according to type of equipment operated as Rotary Pump Operator (electron. comp.). ● **GED:** R4, M4, L4 ● **SVP:** 1-2 yrs ● **Academic:** Ed=N, Eng=S ● **Work Field:** 111 ● **MPSMS:** 586, 587, 589 ● **Aptitudes:** G3, V3, N3, S3, P3, Q4, K4, F4, M3, E5, C4 ● **Temperaments:** T ● **Physical:** Stg=M; Freq: R, H, N Occas: I, G, D, X ● **Work Env:** Noise=N; ● **Salary:** 3 ● **Outlook:** 3

FIRESETTER (elec. equip.) ● DOT #692.360-018 ● OES: 92999 ● Sets up, adjusts, and maintains machines to make flares and stems, seal stems to bulbs, or seal exhaust tubing to bulbs in manufacture of electron tubes and light bulbs: Installs and adjusts specified types and sizes of machine parts, such as cutter, revolving heads, bulb loader, tubing loader, burners, and etching stamp, using handtools. Lights burners and adjusts gas, air, oxygen and hydrogen valves to attain specified cone, color, and density of flames. Starts machine and deposits bulbs, tubing, or other glass parts into hoppers that automatically feed parts into heads of rotating turret, or inserts bulbs and glass parts into sockets of conveyor or molds of rotating turret. Operates machine through trial run and adjusts machine to ensure accuracy of setup. Observes processing operations and inspects sample items for conformance to specifications. Readjusts valves and machine parts to achieve specified standard of product. Maintains machines and replaces faulty parts, using handtools. May operate machine to manufacture production parts. ● GED: R4, M3, L3 ● SVP: 1-2 yrs ● Academic: Ed=N, Eng=S ● Work Field: 111, 082 ● MPSMS: 587 ● Aptitudes: G3, V3, N3, S3, P3, Q4, K3, F3, M3, E5, C4 ● Temperaments: J, T ● Physical: Stg=M; Freq: R, H, I, N, A, X Occas: D ● Work Env: Noise=N; Freq: H Occas: M ● Salary: 3 ● Outlook: 2

LATHE OPERATOR, NUMERICAL CONTROL (machine shop) ● DOT #604.362-010 ● OES: 91502 ● Sets up and operates numerically controlled horizontal lathe to perform machining operations, such as turning, boring, facing, and threading parts, such as castings, forgings, and bar stock: Reads process sheets, blueprints, and sketches of part to determine machining to be done, dimensional specifications, set up, and operating requirements. Inserts beginning point of tape in reading head of control unit. Mounts workpiece between centers, in chuck, or to faceplate, manually or using hoist. Selects and installs preset tooling in tool posts, turrets or indexing heads, and automatic-tool-change magazine, in sequence specified on process sheet. Depresses buttons, toggles, or sets tape and starts machining operation. Observes numerical displays on control panel and compares with data on process sheet to verify dimensional adjustments, feed rates, and speeds of machining cuts. Turns dials and switches to override tape control and correct machine performance, applying practical knowledge of lathe operation. Inspects first-run piece and spot-checks succeeding pieces for conformance to specifications, using micrometers and precision dial gauges. Studies job packet and organizes materials for next run during automatic tape-controlled cycles to shorten changeover time. May set tools before positioning them in lathe, using precision gauges and instruments. May set up and operate another machine tool during tape-controlled machining cycles. May machine nonmetallic materials. May be designated by type of lathe operated as Engine Lathe Operator, Numerical Control (machine shop); Turret Lathe Operator, Numerical Control (machine shop). ● GED: R4, M3, L3 ● SVP: 1-2 yrs ● Academic: Ed=H, Eng=S ● Work Field: 053, 055, 057 ● MPSMS: 540 ● Aptitudes: G3, V3, N3, S2, P2, Q4, K3, F3, M3, E5, C5 ● Temperaments: J, T ● Physical: Stg=M; Freq: R, H, I, N, D, A ● Work Env: Noise=L; ● Salary: 3 ● Outlook: 4

MACHINE OPERATOR I (any industry) ● DOT #616.380-018 ● OES: 91510 ● Alternate titles: FABRICATING-MACHINE OPERATOR. Sets up and operates metal fabricating machines, such as brakes, rolls, shears, saws, and presses, to cut, bend, straighten, and form metal plates, sheets, and structural shapes according to blueprints and specifications: Reads and interprets blueprints, engineering specifications, and shop orders to determine machine setup, production methods, and sequence of operation. Selects, positions, and secures dies, blades, cutters, and fixtures onto machine, using rule, square, shims, templates, handtools, and built-in gauges. Positions and clamps stops, guides, and turntables. Adjusts controls to set and regulate machining factors, such as pressure and depth of ram stroke, adjustment rolls, blade angle, and machine speed. Locates and marks bending or cutting lines and reference points on workpiece, using instruments, such as rule and compass, or by tracing from templates. Positions workpiece against stops and guides or aligns layout marks with dies or cutting blades manually or using hoist. Starts machine and observes machine operation to reposition workpiece, change dies, or adjust machine settings for multiple or successive passes. Inspects or measures work, using rule, gauges, and templates. May operate machines to fabricate nonmetallic materials, such as composites or plastics. May set up and operate sheet-metal fabricating machines only and be designated Sheet-Metal-Fabricating-Machine Operator (any industry). ● GED: R3, M3, L3 ● SVP: 1-2

yrs ● Academic: Ed=H, Eng=N ● Work Field: 057, 134, 135 ● MPSMS: 550, 560, 590 ● Aptitudes: G3, V4, N3, S3, P3, Q4, K3, F3, M3, E4, C5 ● Temperaments: J, T ● Physical: Stg=M; Freq: R, H, I, N, D, A Occas: E ● Work Env: Noise=L; Occas: A, M ● Salary: 3 ● Outlook: 3

MACHINE SET-UP OPERATOR (machine shop) ● DOT #600.380-018 ● OES: 91510 ● Alternate titles: MACHINE OPERATOR, ALL AROUND; MACHINE OPERATOR, GENERAL; MACHINE SPECIALIST; MACHINIST. Sets up and operates machine tools, such as lathes, milling machines, boring machines, and grinders, to machine metallic and nonmetallic workpieces according to specifications, tooling instructions, and standard charts, applying knowledge of machining methods: Reads blueprint or job order for product specifications, such as dimensions and tolerances, and tooling instructions, such as fixtures, feed rates, cutting speeds, depth of cut, and determines sequence of operations. Selects, positions, and secures tool in toolholder (chuck, collet, or toolpost). Positions and secures workpiece in holding device, machine table, chuck, centers, or fixtures, using clamps and wrenches. Moves controls to position tool and workpiece in relation to each other, and to set specified feeds, speeds, and depth of cut. Sets up fixture or feeding device, starts machine, and turns handwheel to feed tool to workpiece or vice versa, and engages feed. Turns valve handle to direct flow of coolant or cutting oil against tool and workpiece. Observes operation of machine and verifies conformance of machined workpiece to specifications, using measuring instruments, such as fixed gauges, calipers, and micrometers. Operates bench grinder to sharpen tools. May set up and operate machines and equipment other than machine tools, such as welding machines and flame-cutting equipment. ● GED: R4, M4, L3 ● SVP: 1-2 yrs ● Academic: Ed=H, Eng=S ● Work Field: 057 ● MPSMS: 540, 560, 580 ● Aptitudes: G3, V3, N3, S3, P3, Q3, K3, F3, M3, E5, C4 ● Temperaments: J, T ● Physical: Stg=M; Freq: R, H, I, N, D Occas: S, K, O, E, G, A, X ● Work Env: Noise=L; Freq: M Occas: A ● Salary: 3 ● Outlook: 3

MICROELECTRONICS TECHNICIAN (electron. comp.) ● DOT #590.362-022 ● OES: 92902 ● Operates variety of semiconductor processing, testing, and assembly equipment to assist engineering staff in development and fabrication of prototype, custom-designed, electronic circuitry chips in research laboratory, using knowledge of microelectronic processing equipment, procedures, and specifications: Operates equipment to convert integrated circuit layout designs into working photo masks; clean, coat, bake, align, expose, develop, and cure photoresist on wafers; grow layers of dielectric, metal, and semiconductor material on masked areas of wafers; clean, etch, or remove materials on areas not covered by photoresist; and implant chemicals to selective areas of wafer substrate to alter substrate electrical characteristics. Operates various test equipment to verify product conformance to processing and company specifications. Operates equipment to assemble, dice, clean, mount, bond, and package integrated circuit devices. May perform some assembly and packaging operations manually. May assist in interpretation and evaluation of processing data and in preparation of related reports. May assist in technical writing of semiconductor processing specifications. ● GED: R4, M4, L3 ● SVP: 1-2 yrs ● Academic: Ed=H, Eng=S ● Work Field: 147, 182, 212 ● MPSMS: 587 ● Aptitudes: G3, V3, N3, S3, P3, Q2, K3, F3, M3, E4, C4 ● Temperaments: J, T, V ● Physical: Stg=L; Freq: R, H, I, N, D, A Occas: T, G, X ● Work Env: Noise=N; Freq: T Occas: H ● Salary: 4 ● Outlook: 4

MILLING-MACHINE SET-UP OPERATOR I (machine shop) ● DOT #605.280-010 ● OES: 91399 ● Sets up and operates variety of milling machines to mill flat or curved surfaces on metal workpieces, such as machine, tool, or die parts, analyzing specifications and selecting tooling, according to knowledge of milling procedures: Studies blueprints or layout on workpiece to determine sequence of operations and finished dimensions of workpiece. Lifts and positions workpiece on machine table manually or with hoist, and secures it, using clamps, bolts, or fixtures. Selects feed rate, cutting speed, depth of cut, and milling cutter, applying knowledge of metal properties and shop mathematics. Mounts milling cutter in spindle, and positions cutter and workpiece in relation to each other. Verifies alignment of workpiece, using measuring instruments, such as dial indicator and thickness gauge. Turns handwheel to feed workpiece to cutter or vice versa. Turns valve handle to start flow of coolant or lubricant on work area, starts machine, and engages automatic feed. May compute indexing ratios and set up and operate dividing head to index workpiece for such operations as milling helical cuts. May mount different tool in place of cutter and perform other operations, such as drilling and boring. May set up and operate attachments, such as pantograph mechanism to duplicate contours from models or profiles from templates, or universal head to mill at angles. May mill nonmetallic materials. ● **GED:** R4, M4, L3 ● **SVP:** 2-4 yrs ● **Academic:** Ed=H, Eng=N ● **Work Field:** 055 ● **MPSMS:** 540 ● **Aptitudes:** G2, V3, N3, S2, P3, Q4, K3, F3, M3, E5, C5 ● **Temperaments:** J, T ● **Physical:** Stg=M; Freq: R, H, I, N Occas: S, D, A ● **Work Env:** Noise=L; ● **Salary:** 3 ● **Outlook:** 3

NUMERICAL CONTROL MACHINE SET-UP OPERATOR (machine shop) ● DOT #609.360-010 ● OES: 91502 ● Sets up and operates numerical control machines or machining centers to perform various machine functions, such as cutting, drilling, milling, reaming, boring, and broaching of metallic and nonmetallic workpieces, utilizing knowledge of machine tool capabilities, machinability of materials, and shop math: Reads and interprets blueprints, planning sheets, sketches, and related technical data to determine tooling requirements, setup procedures, control settings, and machining methods and sequences. Mounts, aligns, and secures tooling, attachments, and workpiece on machine. Selects and installs cutting tools in machine spindle. Loads control media, such as tape, card, or disk, in machine controller or enters commands to retrieve preprogrammed instructions from data base. Calculates and sets machine controls to position spindle in relationship to workpiece and to regulate factors, such as cutting depth, speed, feed, and coolant flow. Starts machine and monitors displays and machine operation to detect malfunctions. Stops machine to change cutting tools and setup according to required machining sequence or to measure parts for conformance to blueprint specifications, using precision measuring instruments. Enters commands or manually adjusts machine controls to correct malfunctions or out-of-tolerance machining. Operates machine manually to perform nonautomated functions and when automatic programming is faulty or machine malfunctions. Discusses control media errors with supervisor or programming personnel to resolve problems. May clean machine, tooling, and parts. May perform machine maintenance. ● **GED:** R4, M4, L3 ● **SVP:** 1-2 yrs ● **Academic:** Ed=A, Eng=S ● **Work Field:** 057 ● **MPSMS:** 540, 550, 590 ● **Aptitudes:** G3, V3, N3, S3, P3, Q4, K3, F3, M3, E5, C5 ● **Temperaments:** J, T ● **Physical:** Stg=M; Freq: R, H, N, D Occas: S, K, O, I, E, T, G, A ● **Work Env:** Noise=L; Occas: A, M, T ● **Salary:** 3 ● **Outlook:** 4

REFINERY OPERATOR (petrol. refin.) ● DOT #549.260-010 ● OES: 95010 ● Analyzes specifications and controls continuous operation of petroleum refining and processing units to produce products, such as gasoline, kerosene, and fuel and lubricating oils, by such methods as distillation, absorption, extraction, adsorption, thermal and catalytic cracking and reforming, polymerization, isomerization, coking, visbreaking, and alkylation: Reads processing schedules, operating logs, test results of oil samples, and laboratory recommendations to determine changes in equipment controls required to produce specified quantity and quality of product. Moves and sets controls, such as knobs, valves, switches, levers, and index arms, on control panels to control process variables, such as flows, temperatures, pressures, vacuum, time, catalyst, and chemicals, by automatic regulation and remote control of processing units, such as heaters, furnaces, compressors, exchangers, reactors, quenchers, stabilizers, fractionators, rechargers, absorbers, strippers, debutanizers, stills, and towers [CONTROL-PANEL OPERATOR (petrol. refin.)]. Moves controls to regulate valves, pumps, compressors, and auxiliary equipment to direct flow of product. Reads temperature and pressure gauges and flowmeters, records readings, and compiles operating records. Determines malfunctioning units by observing control instruments, such as meters and gauges, or by automatic warning signals, such as lights and sounding of horns. Inspects equipment to determine location and nature of malfunction, such as leaks, breakages, and faulty valves. Determines need for schedules and performs repair and maintenance of equipment. Patrols unit to verify safe and efficient operating conditions. May sample liquids and gases [SAMPLER (petrol. refin.)] and test products for chemical characteristics and color [TESTER (petrol. refin.)]. May inspect and adjust furnaces, heaters, and damper controls. May lubricate equipment. May clean interior of processing units by circulating chemicals and solvents through them. May treat products [TREATER (petrol. refin.)]. May control activities of several processing units operated in conjunction. May be designated according to process involved or plant operated as Absorption Plant Operator (petrol. refin.); Purification Operator (petrol.

refin.); Refinery Operator, Cracking Unit (petrol. refin.); Refinery Operator, Polymerization Plant (petrol. refin.); Refinery Operator, Reforming Unit (petrol. refin.); Refinery Operator, Visbreaking (petrol. refin.). May be designated: Refinery Operator, Alkylation (petrol. refin.); Refinery Operator, Coking (petrol. refin.); Refinery Operator, Crude Unit (petrol. refin.); Refinery Operator, Gas Plant (petrol. refin.); Refinery Operator, Light-Ends Recovery (petrol. refin.); Refinery Operator, Vapor Recovery Unit (petrol. refin.). ● **GED:** R4, M3, L3 ● **SVP:** 4-10 yrs ● **Academic:** Ed=H, Eng=S ● **Work Field:** 147 ● **MPSMS:** 500 ● **Aptitudes:** G2, V3, N3, S3, P3, Q4, K4, F4, M3, E5, C4 ● **Temperaments:** J, S, T, V ● **Physical:** Stg=L; Freq: I, T, G, N, D, A, X Occas: C, B, S, O, R, H ● **Work Env:** Noise=L; Freq: W Occas: H, M ● **Salary:** 5 ● **Outlook:** 2

RIVETING MACHINE OPERATOR, AUTOMATIC (aircraft mfg.) ● DOT #806.380-010 ● OES: 92100 ● Sets up and operates riveting machines that automatically drill, countersink, and rivet aircraft assemblies, such as wing panels and fuselage sections: Reads and interprets blueprints, engineering drawings, and specifications to determine setup and operating procedures. Positions, aligns, and levels parts to be assembled in machine locating tools, or loads part in automatic work positioner installed on machine, using hoist or overhead crane. Selects and installs tools, such as drills, countersinks, rams, rivet injector, and chamfer tools in machine spindles, using handtools. Loads control media, such as tape or disk, in machine. Adjusts controls to synchronize control media, parts, and machine, and to regulate depth of countersink, air pressure, and ram stroke. Fills hopper with rivets or other fasteners. Starts machine, observes operation, monitors displays, and readjusts machine to ensure riveted assemblies conform to specifications. Operates machine manually or from automatic settings. Replaces defective cutting tools. May assemble parts prior to loading parts on machine, using rivet gun and bucking bar. May be designated by type of media controlling machine as Riveting Machine Operator, Programmed Control (aircraft mfg.); Riveting Machine Operator, Tape Control (aircraft mfg.). ● **GED:** R4, M3, L3 ● **SVP:** 1-2 yrs ● **Academic:** Ed=H, Eng=S ● **Work Field:** 102 ● **MPSMS:** 592 ● **Aptitudes:** G3, V3, N3, S3, P3, Q4, K3, F3, M3, E5, C5 ● **Temperaments:** T ● **Physical:** Stg=M; Freq: R, H, I, N, D, A Occas: C, S, E ● **Work Env:** Noise=V; Occas: M ● **Salary:** 3 ● **Outlook:** 2

ROLLING ATTENDANT (steel & rel.) ● DOT #613.662-010 ● OES: 95098 ● Controls equipment from central console to operate rolling mill which reduces steel into products of specified size, shape, and gauge: Selects prepunched schedule cards for section to be rolled according to specifications and feeds into card reader. Activates card reader memory bank (push-button) which reads and interprets schedule card information and stores data in storage unit for response to electronic signal in rolling cycle. Sets selector switches of console for automatic operation of electronic equipment, roll stands, and auxiliary equipment. Moves console controls to advance steel from approach table to mill entry table and through complete rolling cycle automatically, to reduce steel products to specified shape, size, and gauge. Observes, from control pulpit, rolling irregularities in ingot, such as pipe, split end, or heat loss, and notifies other worker through intercom system to shear defective parts. Observes rolling operations, dial and colored light indicators, and other gauges, and manipulates control levers and switches to adjust roll draft, alignment, or mill speed to correct rolling and tolerance deviations or drift. Stops automated mill and chages to manual control operations on breakdown or failure of electronic or mill equipment. Assists mill crew in setup, roll change, maintenance, and adjustment of mill and auxiliary equipment during manual operation of rolling mill. May make adjustments or minor repairs to electronic control equipment or devices. May move electrical control levers in pulpit to operate mill tables, scale breakers, and broadsiding mill screwdown when mill operates under manual control. ● **GED:** R4, M3, L3 ● **SVP:** 1-2 yrs ● **Academic:** Ed=N, Eng=N ● **Work Field:** 135 ● **MPSMS:** 541 ● **Aptitudes:** G3, V3, N3, S3, P3, Q3, K2, F2, M3, E4, C4 ● **Temperaments:** J, T, V ● **Physical:** Stg=L; Freq: R, H, I, N, F, D Occas: X ● **Work Env:** Noise=L; Freq: H, O ● **Salary:** 3 ● **Outlook:** 2

SCREW-MACHINE SET-UP OPERATOR, MULTIPLE SPINDLE (machine shop) ● DOT #604.280-014 ● OES: 91105 ● Alternate titles: AUTOMATIC-SCREW-MACHINE OPERATOR; BAR-MACHINE OPERATOR, MULTIPLE SPINDLE; SCREW-MACHINE OPERATOR; SCREW-MACHINE SETTER. Sets up and operates one or more multiple-spindle lathe-type screw machines equipped with automatic indexing and feeding mechanisms to perform turning, boring, threading, and facing operations on metal bar stock on custom basis, analyzing specifications and deciding on tooling according to knowledge of screw-machine operations: Studies blueprint, visualizes machining to be done, dimensions of parts and permissible tolerances, and plans sequence of operations. Visualizes movements of machine parts, workpieces, and tools in each operation in relation to others, and decides on station and timing of each operation to assure efficient use of tools and time. Selects cutting speeds, feed rates, depth of cuts, and cutting tools to be used on basis of experience and knowledge of metal properties and shop mathematics. Installs collets, bushings, and stock pushers in stock-feeding mechanism, using wrenches and screwdrivers. Installs and adjusts cams, gears, and stops to control stock and tool movements at each station. Positions and secures tools in tool holders, verifying positions with gauges and other measuring instruments. Moves controls to set cutting speeds and feed rates. Cranks machine through cycle, stopping machine and adjusting tool positions and machine controls to allow for such factors as timing, clearance between moving parts, and chip removal. Starts machine, observes operation, and verifies conformance to specifications of first-run and sample workpieces, using such instruments as plug and ring gauges, calipers, and micrometers. Replaces worn tools. May operate bench grinder or cutter-grinding machine to sharpen tools. May machine plastics or other nonmetallic materials. May set up and operate single-spindle screw machine. May be required to have experience with particular material or product or machine of particular size, type, or trade name. May set up machines for other workers. ● **GED:** R4, M3, L3 ● **SVP:** 4-10 yrs ● **Academic:** Ed=H, Eng=N ● **Work Field:** 057 ● **MPSMS:** 541, 568, 566 ● **Aptitudes:** G3, V3, N3, S2, P3, Q4, K3, F3, M3, E5, C5 ● **Temperaments:** J ● **Physical:** Stg=M; Freq: R, H, I, N, D, A ● **Work Env:** Noise=L; ● **Salary:** 3 ● **Outlook:** 3

GOE: 06.01.04
Precision Hand Work

ASSEMBLER, ELECTROMECHANICAL (aircraft mfg.) ● DOT #828.381-018 ● OES: 93111 ● Assembles, tests, and repairs precision electromechanical parts, assemblies, and equipment, such as gyros, servomechanisms, electronic instruments, radar, and missile controls, according to blueprints, diagrams, and specifications, using handtools, power tools, precision instruments, and test equipment: Reads blueprints, schematics, and technical orders to determine methods and sequence of assembly operations. Examines parts for surface defects. Aligns, fits, and assembles component parts into completed units, using handtools, power tools, fixtures, and templates. Verifies dimensions and clearances of parts to ensure conformance to blueprint specifications, using instruments, such as micrometers, calipers, and height gauges. Solders and bolts electrical and electronic components in specified location on assembly [ELECTRONICS ASSEMBLER (comm. equip.; electron. comp.; inst. & app.) 726.684-018]. Tests functional performance of completed electromechanical assemblies, using test equipment. Repairs, reworks, and calibrates assemblies to meet operational tolerances. May fabricate parts, using shop equipment. ● **GED:** R4, M3, L3 ● **SVP:** 2-4 yrs ● **Academic:** Ed=H, Eng=S ● **Work Field:** 111, 121, 212 ● **MPSMS:** 580, 590, 600 ● **Aptitudes:** G3, V3, N3, S2, P2, Q4, K4, F3, M3, E4, C4 ● **Temperaments:** T ● **Physical:** Stg=M; Freq: R, H, I, N, D Occas: S, K, O, E, A, X ● **Work Env:** Noise=L; Occas: M, E ● **Salary:** 3 ● **Outlook:** 4

BENCH HAND (jewelry-silver.) ● DOT #735.381-010 ● OES: 89198 ● Alternate titles: BENCH WORKER. Cuts out, files, and solders parts for jewelry articles, such as bracelets, brooches, emblems, and rings, performing any combination of following tasks: Cuts out parts, using power saw or handsaw. Shapes, trims, and smooths parts, using files. Joins parts together, using solder and torch. May bend ring settings and brooch clasps, using pliers. May assemble finished parts of jewelry articles. ● **GED:** R3, M2, L1 ● **SVP:** 1-2 yrs ● **Academic:** Ed=N, Eng=N ● **Work Field:** 102 ● **MPSMS:** 611 ● **Aptitudes:** G3, V4, N4, S3, P2, Q4, K3, F3, M3, E5, C5 ● **Temperaments:** J, T, V ● **Physical:** Stg=L; Freq: R, H, I, N, D Occas: E, A ● **Work Env:** Noise=N; ● **Salary:** 2 ● **Outlook:** 3

CALIBRATOR (inst. & app.) ● DOT #710.381-034 ● OES: 83000 ● Alternate titles: CALIBRATION TECHNICIAN. Tests and calibrates controlling, indicating, and measuring instruments and devices, such as monochromators, pressure regulators, tachometers, temperature controls, and thermometers, to ensure specified operating performance, using handtools, testing and calibrating instruments and equipment, and precision measuring instruments: Reads quality control manual and testing specifications to obtain data to test or calibrate specific devices. Selects and installs accessories, such as adapters, indicating gauges, or holding devices on test or calibration fixture, and connects instrument or device to fixture, according to specifications, using handtools. Sets controls to regulate factors, such as current flow, timing cycle, pressure, temperature, or vacuum, according to specifications, and activates test or calibration equipment. Observes readings on meters and gauges, and other displays and performance of device or instrument to identify functional defects and determine calibration requirements. Adjusts calibration mechanisms to obtain specified operational performance of device or in- strument, using handtools and precision measuring and calibrating instruments and equipment. Applies sealing compound on calibration mechanism to prevent readjustment of settings and loss of calibration. Rejects malfunctioning devices and routes devices to specified department for rework or salvaging of parts. May disassemble instrument or device to determine cause of defective operation and notify supervisory personnel of findings. ● **GED:** R4, M3, L3 ● **SVP:** 1-2 yrs ● **Academic:** Ed=H, Eng=S ● **Work Field:** 111, 121, 211 ● **MPSMS:** 600, 589 ● **Aptitudes:** G3, V3, N3, S3, P3, Q3, K3, F2, M2, E5, C4 ● **Temperaments:** J, T ● **Physical:** Stg=L; Freq: R, H, I, N, D, A Occas: X ● **Work Env:** Noise=N; ● **Salary:** 2 ● **Outlook:** 3

CANVAS WORKER (ship-boat mfg.) ● DOT #739.381-010 ● OES: 89598 ● Lays out canvas, plastic, rubber, and other materials and fabricates and assembles material into sails, awnings, tents, and tarpaulins: Lays out full scale drawings on sail loft floor, according to blueprints or sketches, using chalk. Cuts pattern from paper according to full scale drawing. Marks outline on material with crayon. Cuts material with shears or power cutter. Sews sections of material together on power sewing machine. Installs grommets, metal fittings, and fasteners by machine. When hand-sewing grommets, measures and marks off grommet holes on material, punches holes, using mallet, punch, and hardwood block, and sews galvanized iron ring to edge of hole, using sailmaker's palm and sail twine. Splices, inserts, and hems manila or wire rope in edges to relieve strain or sews rope at points where sail is attached to boom or mast. Secures rope or cable to finished article. Wraps and sews parts of rope or wire that are subject to chafing. Installs and adjusts completed product on shipboard. Examines completed sails for conformance to specifications. May make awning frames [AWNING-FRAME MAKER (tex. prod., nec)]. May be designated according to type of product made as Awning Maker (tex. prod., nec); Sailmaker (ship-boat mfg.; tex. prod., nec); Tentmaker (tex. prod., nec). ● **GED:** R4, M3, L2 ● **SVP:** 2-4 yrs ● **Academic:** Ed=N, Eng=N ● **Work Field:** 171 ● **MPSMS:** 436 ● **Aptitudes:** G3, V4, N3, S3, P3, Q4, K3, F3, M3, E5, C5 ● **Temperaments:** J, T, V ● **Physical:** Stg=M; Freq: R, H, I, N, D Occas: C, B, S, K, O, E, F, A, V ● **Work Env:** Noise=L; Occas: W, O ● **Salary:** 4 ● **Outlook:** 2

CHEESEMAKER (dairy products) ● DOT #529.361-018 ● OES: 89898 ● Alternate titles: CHEESE COOKER. Cooks milk and specified ingredients to make cheese, according to formula: Pasteurizes and separates milk to obtain prescribed butterfat content. Turns valves to fill vat with milk and heat milk to specified temperature. Dumps measured amounts of dye and starter into milk. Starts agitator to mix ingredients. Tests sample of milk for acidity and allows agitator to mix ingredients until specified level of acidity is reached. Dumps and mixes measured amount of rennet into milk. Stops agitator to allow milk to coagulate into curd. Pulls curd knives through curd or separates curd with hand scoop to release whey. Observes thermometer, adjusts steam valve, and starts agitator to stir and cook curd at prescribed temperature for specified time. Squeezes and stretches sample of curd with fingers and extends cooking time to achieve desired firmness or texture. Gives directions to CHEESEMAKER HELPER (dairy products) or other workers to make curd, drain whey from curd, add ingredients, such as seasonings, or mold, pack, cut, pile, mill, dump, and press curd into specified shapes. Directs other workers who immerse cheese in brine or roll cheese in dry salt, pierce or smear cheese with cultured wash to develop mold growth, and place or turn cheese blocks on shelves to cure cheese. Tastes, smells, feels, and observes sample plug of cheese for quality. Records amounts of ingredients used, test results, and time cycles. Makes variations in time cycles and ingredients used for succeeding batches. Dumps specified culture into milk or whey in pasteurizer to make bulk starter. May be required to hold state cheesemaker's license. ● **GED:** R4, M3, L4 ● **SVP:** 2-4 yrs ● **Academic:** Ed=H, Eng=S ● **Work Field:** 146 ● **MPSMS:** 383 ● **Aptitudes:** G3, V3, N3, S4, P3, Q4, K4, F4, M3, E5, C4 ● **Temperaments:** D, J ● **Physical:** Stg=L; Freq: R, H, M, N, D Occas: I, E, X ● **Work Env:** Noise=L; ● **Salary:** 2 ● **Outlook:** 3

COREMAKER (foundry) ● DOT #518.381-014 ● OES: 89998 ● Alternate titles: COREMAKER, EXPERIMENTAL. Makes sand cores used in molds to form holes or hollows in metal castings: Cleans core box with blast of compressed air. Dusts parting sand over inside of core box to facilitate removal of finished core. Partially fills core box with sand by pulling cord that releases sand from overhead chute or by using hands or shovel. Compacts sand in core box, using hands, hand rammer, and air rammer. Bends reinforcing wires by hand, and inserts them in sand. Fills core box and rams sand in tightly. Inverts core box onto metal plate, and lifts box from sand core. Patches cracked or chipped places on core and smooths core surfaces, using spoon and trowel. May bake cores to harden them. May assemble cores. May work at bench making small cores and be designated Coremaker, Bench (foundry); or make large cores on floor of foundry and be designated Coremaker, Floor (foundry). ● **GED:** R3, M2, L2 ● **SVP:** 6 mos-1 yr ● **Academic:** Ed=N, Eng=N ● **Work Field:** 136 ● **MPSMS:** 566 ● **Aptitudes:** G3, V3, N4, S3, P3, Q4, K3, F3, M3, E5, C5 ● **Temperaments:** J, R, T ● **Physical:** Stg=M; Freq: S, O, R, H, N, D Occas: E ● **Work Env:** Noise=L; ● **Salary:** 4 ● **Outlook:** 2

DEVELOPMENT MECHANIC (aircraft mfg.) ● DOT #693.261-014 ● OES: 93102 ● Alternate titles: EXPERIMENTAL MECHANIC. Lays out, fabricates, and assembles developmental or experimental structural and mechanical parts and assemblies, and installs parts and assemblies in prototype aircraft or spacecraft, following engineering information, using precision instruments, handtools, power tools, and shop equipment: Reads and interprets blueprints, sketches, loft information, and related engineering data to plan sequence of operations and methods for fabricating, assembling, and installing parts and assemblies. Lays out radii, angle, and dimensions of parts on assorted materials, using precision measuring and marking instruments, such as gauges, calipers, scale, and scriber, applying trigonometric calculations to solve layout problems. Sets up and operates shop equipment, such as bandsaw, lathe, table saw, drill press, shear, and brake, to shape and form parts. Verifies dimensions of parts, using precision measuring instruments. Drills, countersinks, and reams holes in parts and assemblies for bolts, rivets, and other fasteners, using power tools. Aligns and joins structural assemblies, using transit, sight level, handtools, power tools, clamps, and fasteners. Installs experimental parts and assemblies in prototype structure to verify accuracy of layout and assembly. Tests functional performance of installed parts. Confers with engineers to resolve fabrication and installation problems. May fabricate or modify tooling, such as jigs, fixtures, templates, and form blocks. May fabricate and assemble reduced-scale mockups of parts and assemblies. May be designated by type of part or assembly developed as Controls Development Mechanic (aircraft mfg.); Developer-Prover, Mechanical (aircraft mfg.); Fabrication And Structures Development Mechanic (aircraft mfg.); Hydraulic And Plumbing Development Mechanic (aircraft mfg.); Mechanic, Experimental Structural Assembly (aircraft mfg.). ● **GED:** R4, M4, L4 ● **SVP:** 2-4 yrs ● **Academic:** Ed=H, Eng=G ● **Work Field:** 102, 121, 241 ● **MPSMS:** 592, 596 ● **Aptitudes:** G2, V3, N2, S2, P2, Q4, K3, F3, M3, E4, C4 ● **Temperaments:** J, T ● **Physical:** Stg=M; Freq: R, H, I, N, D Occas: C, B, S, K, O, E, T, G, A, X ● **Work Env:** Noise=L; Freq: M Occas: D ● **Salary:** 5 ● **Outlook:** 2

ELECTRIC-MOTOR-CONTROL ASSEMBLER (elec. equip.) ● DOT #721.381-014 ● OES: 93114 ● Alternate titles: CONTROL-PANEL ASSEMBLER; PANELBOARD ASSEMBLER; POWER-PANEL ASSEMBLER. Assembles electric-motor control units, such as transmitters, relays, switches, voltage controls, and starters and mounts unit on panel according to drawings and specifications, using handtools and power tools: Cleans parts, using liquid cleaner, airhose, and cloth. Assembles units, using handtools, pneumatic nut runners, power press, and torque wrenches. Lays out and drills mounting holes and mounts units to panel, using scribers, rule, dividers, drill press,

portable power drill, reamer, screwdrivers, and wrenches. Adjusts and aligns parts to maintain specified airgap, contact wipe, dimensions, and part movement, using feeler gauges and micrometers. Solders electric wire connections and secures spring guides, setscrews, and spring post to units, using soldering iron and acetylene torch. Tests electrical circuits for resistance, current, and potential difference, using instruments, such as ohmmeter, ammeter, and voltmeter. May be designated according to control assembled as Transmitter Assembler (elec. equip.); Voltage-Regulator Assembler (elec. equip.). May also operate sheet metal forming machines to fabricate housing for synchro-units and be designated Synchro-Unit Assembler (elec. equip.). ● **GED:** R4, M3, L2 ● **SVP:** 1-2 yrs ● **Academic:** Ed=H, Eng=N ● **Work Field:** 111 ● **MPSMS:** 581, 582 ● **Aptitudes:** G3, V4, N3, S3, P2, Q4, K3, F3, M3, E4, C4 ● **Temperaments:** J, T ● **Physical:** Stg=M; Freq: R, H, I, N, X Occas: C, B, S, K, O, D, A ● **Work Env:** Noise=L; ● **Salary:** 3 ● **Outlook:** 3

FINAL ASSEMBLER (office machines) ● DOT #706.381-018 ● OES: 93111 ● Assembles, installs, and adjusts variety of electromechanical units, such as feed drives, control key assemblies, and printing units, on new and rebuilt punched card office machines according to blueprints and written specifications, using handtools, assembly fixtures, and test devices: Reads blueprints to determine position of unit and component parts. Positions components in assembly fixture. Assembles unit and mounts it on office machine frame, using screwdrivers and wrenches. Starts machine and adjusts unit for specified clearances and time cycles, using fixed gauges, test lights, and handtools. Inspects machine to verify that optional equipment changes have been made according to customer order. May operate electric hoist to position unit on office machine frame. ● **GED:** R3, M2, L3 ● **SVP:** 1-2 yrs ● **Academic:** Ed=N, Eng=S ● **Work Field:** 121 ● **MPSMS:** 571 ● **Aptitudes:** G3, V3, N3, S3, P3, Q4, K3, F3, M3, E5, C4 ● **Temperaments:** J, T ● **Physical:** Stg=M; Freq: R, H, I, N, D Occas: S, K, O, E, X ● **Work Env:** Noise=N; ● **Salary:** 2 ● **Outlook:** 2

GLASS BLOWER (glass mfg.) ● DOT #772.381-022 ● OES: 89998 ● Alternate titles: BLOWER; GAFFER. Shapes gather (gob of molten glass) into glassware by blowing through blowpipe: Receives blowpipe from GATHERER (glass mfg.) 575.684-026 and examines gather on blowpipe for imperfections, utilizing knowledge of molten glass characteristics. Blows through pipe to inflate gather while rotating pipe to prevent sagging and to obtain desired shape, or blows and rotates gather in mold or on board to obtain final shape. May dip end of blowpipe into molten glass to collect gather on head of pipe. May strike neck of finished article to separate article from blow pipe. May pull gather with tongs to aid in shaping. May use compressed air to inflate gather. May be designated according to article blown as Bottle Blower (glass mfg.). ● **GED:** R3, M2, L2 ● **SVP:** 2-4 yrs ● **Academic:** Ed=N, Eng=N ● **Work Field:** 136 ● **MPSMS:** 531 ● **Aptitudes:** G3, V4, N4, S3, P3, Q4, K3, F3, M3, E4, C4 ● **Temperaments:** J, T ● **Physical:** Stg=L; Const: R, H, I Freq: N, D, A Occas: S, X, V ● **Work Env:** Noise=L; Freq: H, O ● **Salary:** 2 ● **Outlook:** 1

INSTALLER, INTERIOR ASSEMBLIES (aircraft mfg.) ● DOT #806.381-078 ● OES: 93196 ● Alternate titles: CABIN FURNISHINGS INSTALLER. Installs aircraft interior furnishings, trim, and accessories, such as carpeting, sidewalls, doors, windows, seats, partitions, galleys, and passenger service units, according to specifications, using handtools and power tools: Reads and interprets blueprints, drawings, and production procedures to determine measurements and installation procedures. Measures and marks installation areas in aircraft interior, using measuring and marking instruments and templates. Drills, reams, countersinks, rivets, trims, and files parts and assemblies, using handtools and power tools. Fits and installs items in aircraft, using handtools, power tools, and fasteners, such as screws, rivets, bolts, and speednuts. Fabricates and installs supporting structural devices, such as clips, brackets, angles, gussets, and doublers, using shop equipment. Tests functional performance of installed items. Reworks installations as required. ● **GED:** R4, M3, L3 ● **SVP:** 1-2 yrs ● **Academic:** Ed=H, Eng=S ● **Work Field:** 102 ● **MPSMS:** 592 ● **Aptitudes:** G3, V4, N4, S3, P3, Q4, K4, F3, M3, E4, C4 ● **Temperaments:** J, T ● **Physical:** Stg=M; Freq: R, H, I, N, D Occas: C, S, K, O, W, E, A, X ● **Work Env:** Noise=L; Occas: M, E ● **Salary:** 3 ● **Outlook:** 2

MOLDER (aircraft mfg.) ● DOT #518.361-010 ● OES: 89998 ● Alternate titles: SAND MOLDER. Forms sand molds to fabricate metal castings, using patterns or match plates, flasks, handtools and power tools, following instructions and applying knowledge of variables, such as metal characteristics, molding sand, pattern contours, and pouring procedures: Places flask and drag onto molding board and positions pattern inside drag. Sprinkles or sprays parting agent onto pattern and flask, to facilitate removal of pattern from mold, and positions reinforcing wire in flask. Sifts sand over pattern, using riddle, and compacts sand around pattern contours. Shovels and packs sand into flask, using hand or pneumatic ramming tools. Inverts drag, positions cope half of pattern and flask onto drag, and repeats sand molding operation to imbed pattern into cope. Lifts cope from drag and removes pattern. Cuts runner and sprue hole into mold and repairs damaged impressions, using handtools, such as slick, trowel, spoon, and sprue cutter. Positions specified cores into drag and reassembles cope and drag. Moves and positions workpieces, such as flasks, patterns, and bottom boards, using overhead crane, or signals OVERHEAD CRANE OPERATOR (any industry) 921.663-010 to move and position workpieces. Pours molten metal into mold, manually or using crane ladle, or directs POURER, METAL (foundry) 514.684-022 to fill mold. May form and assemble slab cores around pattern to reinforce mold, using handtools and glue. May operate ovens or furnaces to melt, skim, and flux metal. May form molds at bench and be designated Molder, Bench (concrete prod.; foundry) or form molds on floor and be designated Molder, Floor (foundry). ● **GED:** R4, M3, L3 ● **SVP:** 1-2 yrs ● **Academic:** Ed=N, Eng=N ● **Work Field:** 132, 136 ● **MPSMS:** 542, 567 ● **Aptitudes:** G3, V3, N3, S3, P3, Q4, K3, F3, M3, E5, C5 ● **Temperaments:** J, T ● **Physical:** Stg=M; Freq: R, H, N, D Occas: S, K, O, I, E, T, G, F, A, V ● **Work Env:** Noise=L; Occas: H, V, A, O ● **Salary:** 4 ● **Outlook:** 2

PLASTICS FABRICATOR (aircraft mfg.) ● DOT #754.381-018 ● OES: 89998 ● Alternate titles: PLASTICS BENCH MECHANIC; PLASTICS FABRICATOR AND ASSEMBLER. Fabricates, assembles, reworks, and repairs plastic products, applying knowledge of working characteristics of plastics and bonding techniques, using precision instruments, handtools, power tools, machines, and equipment: Reads and interprets blueprints, work orders, and related documentation to determine methods and sequence of operations and dimensional and finish specifications. Lays out cutting lines on plastic materials, such as sheet stock and fiberglass or graphite cloth, following template pattern, blueprints, sketches, or sample part, using measuring and marking instruments. Cuts material to size, using shears, knives, cutters, scissors, router, or saw. Mixes ingredients, such as resins, catalysts, fillers, accelerators, and colors, according to formulas, manually or using mixer. Sets up and operates forming machines and presses, or laminates plastic cloth and resins or preimpregnated cloth onto layup mold or bonding fixture, to shape parts. Wraps bonding fixture or mold in vacuum bagging materials, attaches fittings to mold or fixture, such as vacuum connections, thermocouples, and probes, and exhausts air from vacuum bag to prepare lamination for curing or bonding. Operates oven to cure parts. Trims, drills, reams, countersinks, grinds, and finishes parts to specifications, using templates, handtools, and power tools. Verifies dimensions of parts, using precision instruments, such as dial indicators, micrometers, and calipers. Fits and assembles parts and attaches hardware and fittings, such as brackets and hinges, using clamps, jigs, fixtures, power tools, and fasteners. Applies tape, foam, or other type of adhesives to assembly for subsequent bonding in autoclave. Repairs and reworks damaged or defective parts and assemblies by lay up, foaming, cementing, molding, potting, casting, or similar methods. May heat parts or materials to facilitate shaping, using oven or heat gun. May fabricate and assemble parts from fiber reinforced plastics (composites) and assorted materials, such as metal and honeycomb, and be designated Bonding And Composite Fabricator (aircraft mfg.); Composites Fabricator And Assembler (aircraft mfg.). May press, smooth, trim, measure, and adjust composite tape during automatic application of tape onto mold or fixture by numerical-control tape laying machine, using scale, knife, and scraper. May wind fiberglass, graphite, nylon, or other natural or synthetic fiber or filament around parts, using filament winding machine, manually applying layers of resinous materials to part at specified intervals during winding process. May be designated by type of part or activity involved as Experimental Plastics Fabricator (aircraft mfg.); Filament-Wound Parts Fab- ricator (aircraft mfg.); Plastic Parts Fabricator (aircraft mfg.); Plastic-Sign Fabricator (plastic prod.); Plastics Rework And Repair Mechanic (aircraft mfg.). ● **GED:** R4, M4, L4 ● **SVP:** 2-4 yrs ● **Academic:** Ed=N, Eng=N ● **Work Field:** 102 ● **MPSMS:** 510, 560, 590 ● **Aptitudes:** G3, V3, N3, S3, P3, Q4, K3, F3, M3, E4, C4 ● **Temperaments:** J, T ● **Physical:** Stg=M; Freq: R, H, I, N, D Occas: S, K, O, E, A, X ● **Work Env:** Noise=L; Occas: A, M, T ● **Salary:** 3 ● **Outlook:** 3

RING MAKER (jewelry-silver.) ● DOT #700.381-042 ● OES: 89123 ● Fabricates rings by any of following methods: (1) Casts rings, using molds of rubber, plaster, wax, sand, and metal. (2) Cuts out ring blanks from flat metal and shapes blanks into ring bands. (3) Ties or twists gold or silver wires together and bends to form rings. Removes gates, solders ends, and files rings to remove excess metal. Cleans and polishes rings by immersing them in metal cleaning or acid solution. May set stones in rings. ● **GED:** R3, M2, L2 ● **SVP:** 2-4 yrs ● **Academic:** Ed=N, Eng=N ● **Work Field:** 132, 102 ● **MPSMS:** 611 ● **Aptitudes:** G3, V3, N4, S3, P3, Q4, K3, F3, M3, E5, C4 ● **Temperaments:** J, T, V ● **Physical:** Stg=L; Const: R, H Freq: N Occas: I, X ● **Work Env:** Noise=N; ● **Salary:** 4 ● **Outlook:** 2

SOLDERER (jewelry-silver.) ● DOT #700.381-050 ● OES: 89198 ● Solders together parts of new or broken jewelry, using gas torch and solder: Selects type of solder to be used and lays parts on asbestos board. Lights torch and applies solder and flux to article as needed. Immerses article in water to cool. ● **GED:** R3, M2, L3 ● **SVP:** 6 mos-1 yr ● **Academic:** Ed=N, Eng=S ● **Work Field:** 083 ● **MPSMS:** 611 ● **Aptitudes:** G3, V4, N4, S3, P3, Q4, K3, F3, M3, E5, C4 ● **Temperaments:** J, T ● **Physical:** Stg=S; Freq: R, H, I, N, A ● **Work Env:** Noise=N; Occas: A ● **Salary:** 3 ● **Outlook:** 2

TEMPLATE MAKER (any industry) ● DOT #601.381-038 ● OES: 89198 ● Designs and fabricates templates of assorted materials, such as metal, fiberglass, wood, and plastic, for laying out reference points and dimensions on metal plates, sheets, tubes, and structural shapes used for fabricating, welding, and assembling structural metal products or dies: Plans and develops layout according to blueprints, work orders, tool planning orders, mockups, or sample parts, applying knowledge of trigonometry, product design, and properties of metal. Lays out design onto template material, using instruments, such as compass, protractor, dividers, and ruler, and marks shape and reference points, using scriber, pencil, chalk, and punch. Cuts, trims, drills, reams, files, shapes, and forms templates, using handtools, power tools, and fabricating machines, such as bandsaw, drill press, jointer, punch press, and shear. Nails, glues, screws, bolts, solders, or welds component parts to assemble templates. Marks job numbers, file codes, dimensions, layout, and fabricating instructions on templates. Repairs and reworks templates. May construct jigs and fixtures for fabricating machine operations [TOOL MAKER, BENCH (machine shop) 601.281-026]. ● **GED:** R4, M4, L3 ● **SVP:** 2-4 yrs ● **Academic:** Ed=H, Eng=S ● **Work Field:** 102, 241 ● **MPSMS:** 566 ● **Aptitudes:** G3, V3, N3, S2, P3, Q4, K3, F3, M3, E4, C5 ● **Temperaments:** J, T ● **Physical:** Stg=M; Freq: R, H, I, N, D, A Occas: S, O, E ● **Work Env:** Noise=L; Occas: M, T ● **Salary:** 3 ● **Outlook:** 4

TEST EQUIPMENT MECHANIC (aircraft mfg.) ● DOT #710.361-014 ● OES: 89998 ● Alternate titles: ENGINEERING TEST MECHANIC; STRUCTURAL TEST MECHANIC. Plans, lays out, constructs, modifies, tests, and maintains laboratory test equipment and related structural assemblies used to test experimental aircraft and space vehicle parts and assemblies, using precision instruments, handtools, power tools, and shop equipment: Reads and interprets blueprints, engineering drawings, and sketches, or receives verbal instructions, to determine methods and sequence of operations to lay out and construct mechanical, electrical, electronic, pneumatic, or hydraulic test equipment and related structures. Lays out and fabricates parts from assorted materials, such as aluminum, steel, wood, plastic, and graphite composites, using measuring instruments and shop equipment, such as saws, shears, drill presses, lathes, and routers. Fits, aligns, and assembles parts, equipment, specialized test devices, and structural framework to build test units, using precision measuring instruments, such as transit and level, power tools, rivets, bolts, clamps, pins, and other fasteners. Installs, or assists other workers in installing, test specimens in test equipment, using hoist, overhead crane, or related equipment. Assists engineers in operating test equipment to obtain research data on performance of experimental parts and assemblies under varying operational conditions. Diagnoses test equipment malfunctions and services and repairs equipment as required. May repair test specimens damaged during testing to prepare item for retesting. May specialize in constructing mechanical, electrical, electronic, pneumatic, hydraulic, or structural test equipment. ● **GED:** R4, M4, L4 ● **SVP:** 2-4 yrs ● **Academic:** Ed=H, Eng=S ● **Work Field:** 102, 111, 121 ● **MPSMS:** 601 ● **Aptitudes:** G3, V3, N3, S2, P3, Q4, K3, F3, M3, E4, C4 ● **Temperaments:** J, T, V ● **Physical:** Stg=M; Freq: R, H, I, N, D Occas: C, B, S,

K, O, W, E, T, G, F, A, X, V ● **Work Env:** Noise=L; Occas: M, E, D ● **Salary:** 4 ● **Outlook:** 3

TOOL BUILDER (aircraft mfg.) ● DOT #693.281-030 ● OES: 89998 ● Lays out, fabricates, assembles, and repairs jigs, fixtures, forms, templates, and related tooling used in manufacturing aircraft parts and assemblies, following blueprints, sketches, and specifications, using handtools, power tools, machines, and equipment: Reviews engineering information, tool design drawings, and other specifications to determine methods and sequence of operations to fabricate tools. Examines blueprint of part for which template, jig, fixture, or other tooling is to be built. Calculates unspecified dimensions, and lays out design on assorted materials to establish and coordinate reference points and tooling holes, using measuring instruments, such as dividers and straightedges. Sets up and operates variety of machines and shop equipment to cut, shape, and finish materials to specified dimensions. Fits, aligns, and assembles tooling components, and measures tooling assembly for conformance to specifications, using precision measuring and checking instruments. Joins assembly components, using bolts, pins, clamps, screws, rivets, or other method. Repairs or reworks tools. May draw sketches and prepare detailed instructions for fabricating or machining to be performed by other workers. May specialize in building specific type tool and be designated Form Block Maker (aircraft mfg.); Jig And Fixture Builder (aircraft mfg.); Machine Tool Fixture Builder (aircraft mfg.); Wood-Tool Maker (aircraft mfg.). ● **GED:** R4, M4, L4 ● **SVP:** 2-4 yrs ● **Academic:** Ed=H, Eng=G ● **Work Field:** 102, 241 ● **MPSMS:** 566 ● **Aptitudes:** G2, V3, N3, S2, P2, Q3, K3, F3, M2, E5, C4 ● **Temperaments:** T ● **Physical:** Stg=M; Freq: R, H, I, N, D Occas: C, B, S, K, O, E, A, X ● **Work Env:** Noise=L; Occas: A, M ● **Salary:** 3 ● **Outlook:** 3

GOE: 06.01.05
Inspection

ELECTRONICS INSPECTOR (comm. equip.) ● DOT #726.381-010 ● OES: 83000 ● Alternate titles: QUALITY CONTROL INSPECTOR; SYSTEMS INSPECTOR. Performs any combination of following tasks to inspect electronic systems, assemblies, subassemblies, components, and parts for conformance to specifications, following blueprints, drawings, and production and assembly manuals: Examines layout and installation of wiring, cables, subassemblies, hardware, and components to detect assembly errors. Compares assembly with parts list to detect missing hardware. Examines joints, using magnifying glass and mirror, and pulls wires and cables to locate soldering defects. Examines alignment of parts and measures parts for conformance to specified dimensions, using precision measuring instruments, such as micrometers, vernier calipers, and gauges. Twists dials, knobs, shafts, and gears to verify freedom of movement. Traces cables and harness assemblies, following cable wiring diagram, to verify routing of wires to specified connections and conformance of cable lacing and insulation to manufacturing standards. Measures plated areas for uniformity and thickness, using micrometers or dial indicators. Verifies location of bolt and rivet holes, using templates, check fixtures, and precision measuring instruments. Examines parts for surface defects, such as chips, scratches, and pinholes. Examines production documents to ensure that all assembly, inspecting, and testing steps were performed according to specifications. Calculates percentage of defective parts, using calculator. Records inspection data, such as serial number, type and percent of defects, and rework required. Resolders broken connections on components and parts. Performs functional and operational tests, using electronic test equipment such as frequency meter, oscilloscope, and signal generator [ELECTRONICS TESTER (any industry) 726.261-018], or performs destructive tests to determine tensile strength of product or part. May inspect and lay out optic axis of raw quartz crystals, using optical inspection equipment, and be designated Inspector, Raw Quartz (electron. comp.). May inspect parts at random and be designated Check Inspector (electron. comp.). May inspect units on assembly line and be designated In-Process Inspector (electron. comp.) or final product and be designated Final Inspector (electron. comp.). May be designated according to type of unit inspected as Inspector, Subassemblies (electron. comp.); Inspector, Tubes (electron. comp.). ● **GED:** R4, M4, L4 ● **SVP:** 1-2 yrs ● **Academic:** Ed=H, Eng=S ●

Work Field: 211 ● **MPSMS:** 580 ● **Aptitudes:** G3, V3, N3, S3, P3, Q3, K3, F2, M2, E5, C4 ● **Temperaments:** J, T ● **Physical:** Stg=L; Freq: R, H, I, N, A, X Occas: E ● **Work Env:** Noise=N; ● **Salary:** 3 ● **Outlook:** 4

ELECTRONICS TESTER (any industry) ● DOT #726.261-018 ● OES: 83000 ● Alternate titles: QUALITY-CONTROL-ASSEMBLY-TEST TECHNICIAN; TECHNICIAN, TEST SYSTEMS; TESTER, SYSTEMS; TEST TECHNICIAN; TROUBLE SHOOTER. Performs variety of electronic, mechanical, and electromechanical tests on electronic systems, subassemblies, and parts to ensure unit functions according to specifications or to determine cause of unit failure, using electronic test instruments: Reads test schedule, work orders, test manuals, performance specifications, wiring diagrams, and schematics to determine testing procedure and equipment to be used. Tests functional performance of systems, subassemblies, and parts under specified environmental conditions, such as temperature change, vibration, pressure, and humidity, using testing devices, such as temperature cabinets, shake-test machines, and centrifuges. Calibrates test instruments according to specifications. Connects unit to be tested to test equipment, such as signal generator, frequency meter, or spectrum analyzer. Reads dials or digital displays that indicate electronic characteristics, such as voltage, frequency, distortion, inductance, and capacitance. Compares results with specifications and records test data or plots test results on graph. Analyzes test results on defective units to determine cause of failure, applying knowledge of electronic theory and using electronic test equipment. Replaces defective wiring and components, using handtools and soldering iron, or records defects on tag attached to unit and returns unit to production department for repair. Confers with engineers, technicians, production personnel, and others regarding testing procedures and results and to resolve problems. May write computer programs to control semiconductor device and electronic component test equipment prior to testing, utilizing knowledge of programming techniques, electronics, test equipment, and testing specifications. May explain and demonstrate testing procedures to other workers. May verify dimensions of pins, shafts, and other mechanical parts, using calipers, vernier gauges, and micrometers. May operate x-ray equipment to verify internal assembly and alignment of parts according to specifications. May devise test equipment setup to evaluate performance and operation of nonstandard or customer returned units. May be designated according to unit tested as Memory-Unit Test Technician (electron. comp.); Television-Receiver Analyzer (electron. comp.); Transmitter Tester (electron. comp.); Tube-Test Technician (electron. comp.). ● **GED:** R4, M4, L3 ● **SVP:** 2-4 yrs ● **Academic:** Ed=H, Eng=S ● **Work Field:** 211, 111 ● **MPSMS:** 580, 600 ● **Aptitudes:** G2, V3, N3, S2, P3, Q3, K3, F3, M3, E5, C4 ● **Temperaments:** J, T ● **Physical:** Stg=M; Freq: R, H, I, N, A Occas: T, G, X ● **Work Env:** Noise=N; ● **Salary:** 4 ● **Outlook:** 4

INSPECTOR, ASSEMBLIES AND INSTALLATIONS (aircraft mfg.) ● DOT #806.261-030 ● OES: 83000 ● Alternate titles: INSPECTOR, ASSEMBLY. Inspects assemblies, such as fuselage, tail, and wings, joining of assemblies into major structure, installation of parts, equipment, and accessories, or complete aircraft for conformance to specifications and quality standards: Reads and interprets blueprints, engineering documents, and inspection manuals and procedures to determine methods and sequence of inspection. Examines parts and assemblies for physical characteristics, such as surface finish, color, and texture, and for defects, such as cracks, scratches, and loose connections. Measures parts and assemblies for dimensional accuracy and adherence to blueprint specifications. Inspects assembly, mating, and installation of parts, assemblies, and equipment for alignment, fit, clearance, tension, throw limits, torque, and related factors, using fixtures, jigs, and precision measuring and checking instruments, such as scales, protractor, tensiometer, and gauges. Conducts or witnesses functional or operational tests of partial or completed units, such as landing gear, auto pilot, engine controls, and rudders, to verify conformance to specifications, using test equipment. Accepts or rejects assemblies or installations, and recommends repair, rework, or replacement of component parts. Confers with engineering, production, and inspection personnel to exchange inspection information. May be designated according to assembly or installation inspected as Inspector, Subassembly (aircraft mfg.); Inspector, Final Assembly (aircraft mfg.); Inspector, Final Assembly, Electrical (aircraft mfg.); Inspector, Final Assembly, Mechanical (aircraft mfg.); Inspector, Structures (aircraft mfg.); Inspector, Engines And Components Assembly (aircraft mfg.); Inspector, Experimental Assembly (aircraft mfg.); Inspector, Electrical And Electronic Installations (aircraft mfg.). ● **GED:** R4, M4, L4 ● **SVP:** 2-4 yrs ● **Academic:** Ed=H, Eng=N ● **Work Field:** 102, 121, 211 ● **MPSMS:** 592 ● **Aptitudes:** G2, V3, N3, S2, P2, Q3, K3, F3, M3, E4, C4 ● **Temperaments:** J, T ● **Physical:** Stg=M; Freq: R, H, N Occas: C, B, S, K, O, W, I, E, T, G, F, D, A, X, V ● **Work Env:** Noise=L; Occas: M, E, D ● **Salary:** 3 ● **Outlook:** 4

INSPECTOR, ELECTROMECHANICAL (inst. & app.) ● DOT #729.361-010 ● OES: 83000 ● Inspects and tests components, housings, and finished assemblies of electromechanical instruments and equipment, such as oceanographic instruments, navigational systems, medical diagnostic equipment, and measuring, indicating, and controlling instruments, for conformance to specifications, using magnifying devices, test equipment, and precision measuring instruments: Reviews work orders, blueprints, or other specifications and confers with supervisor, engineer, and other personnel to determine product dimensions and specifications. Examines electrical, structural, and mechanical components and housings for defects in assembly, soldering, bonding, and finish. Measures dimensions and verifies locations of parts, holes, grooves, and other points, using precision measuring instruments, such as calipers, micrometers, gauges, dial indicators, and optical comparators. Tests electrical components and finished devices for electrical functioning, using electrical test equipment, such as oscilloscope, multimeter, voltmeter, and computerized test equipment. Tests functional characteristics, such as freedom of movement, leaks, and torque, and tests performance of device under simulated operating conditions, using specialized test equipment. Maintains records of inspection and test results and presents results to other staff for corrective action. May inspect and calibrate precision measuring instruments used to measure electromechanical instruments and equipment, using calibrating equipment. May inspect and test purchased parts and materials and be designated Receiving Inspector (inst. & app.). ● **GED:** R4, M3, L4 ● **SVP:** 2-4 yrs ● **Academic:** Ed=N, Eng=N ● **Work Field:** 111, 121, 212 ● **MPSMS:** 587, 589, 600 ● **Aptitudes:** G3, V3, N3, S2, P2, Q3, K3, F3, M3, E5, C4 ● **Temperaments:** J, T ● **Physical:** Stg=M; Freq: R, H, I, N Occas: E, T, G, D, A, X ● **Work Env:** Noise=N; ● **Salary:** 5 ● **Outlook:** 4

INSPECTOR, MATERIAL DISPOSITION (aircraft mfg.) ● DOT #806.261-034 ● OES: 83000 ● Inspects rejected or obsolete aircraft parts, assemblies, or materials to determine disposition, utilizing knowledge of production processes, repair methods, and cost, using precision measuring instruments: Reviews rejection slips to determine method of inspection required. Inspects and measures parts to determine nature and extent of defect, using surface plate or table and precision measuring instruments, such as calipers, gauges, and micrometers. Compares inspection results with specifications and consults with manufacturing, engineering, and other personnel to determine possibility and practicability of salvaging rejected parts, assemblies, or materials. Evaluates inspection data, considering value, costs involved, production delays, quality, appearance, and related factors, and recommends final disposition, such as scrap, return to vendor, salvage, or rework. Records inspection results and recommendations for disposition of parts, assemblies, or materials. May investigate rejections of parts and assemblies to determine corrective action to prevent recurrence and be designated Material Review Board Representative, Quality Control (aircraft mfg.). ● **GED:** R4, M4, L4 ● **SVP:** 2-4 yrs ● **Academic:** Ed=H, Eng=S ● **Work Field:** 211 ● **MPSMS:** 592 ● **Aptitudes:** G2, V3, N2, S3, P2, Q4, K4, F3, M3, E5, C4 ● **Temperaments:** J, T ● **Physical:** Stg=M; Freq: R, H, I, N Occas: C, B, S, K, O, E, T, G, D, A, X ● **Work Env:** Noise=L; Occas: M, D ● **Salary:** 4 ● **Outlook:** 3

INSPECTOR, METAL FABRICATING (any industry) ● DOT #619.261-010 ● OES: 83000 ● Alternate titles: PLATE-AND-WELD INSPECTOR; PLATE-SHOP INSPECTOR; STRUCTURAL INSPECTOR. Inspects materials received, finished products, and work in process of fabrication into metal products to ensure conformance with work orders and diagrammatic and template specifications: Measures centerlines and reference points to verify initial and assembly layout and machine setup, using layout plate, templates, squares, straightedge, feelers, tape, transit, and plumblines. Verifies physical properties and size of materials, such as plates, sheets, structural shapes, castings, forgings, dies, fixtures, and work produced by fabricating machines, using magnaflux machine, surface plate, hardness testing equipment, gauges, and micrometers. Verifies hole size, using plug gauge. Examines finished products for rough edges, cracks, and ap-

pearance. Marks parts for acceptance or rejection. Makes reports to suggest changes in dies, fixtures, and materials used. Reports inspection results. Makes sketches and recommends procedure for special salvage or scrapping operations. May inspect material for internal defects, using x-ray and ultrasonic test equipment. May specialize in single phase of inspection and be designated Lay-Out Inspector (any industry); Machine-Operations Inspector (any industry); Template Inspector (any industry). ● **GED:** R4, M4, L4 ● **SVP:** 2-4 yrs ● **Academic:** Ed=N, Eng=S ● **Work Field:** 102, 212 ● **MPSMS:** 550 ● **Aptitudes:** G3, V3, N3, S3, P3, Q3, K3, F3, M3, E4, C5 ● **Temperaments:** J, T ● **Physical:** Stg=L; Const: R, H, N Freq: C, B, S, I, A Occas: T, G ● **Work Env:** Noise=L; Freq: A Occas: O ● **Salary:** 4 ● **Outlook:** 2

INSPECTOR, OUTSIDE PRODUCTION (aircraft mfg.) ● DOT #806.261-042 ● OES: 83000 ● Inspects and tests aircraft, space capsule, and missile parts, assemblies, and materials at subcontractor's plant or airline maintenance base for conformance to engineering requirements and specifications, using blueprints, test equipment, and precision measuring instruments: Sets up and adjusts hardness testers to test metal parts for specified hardness. Inspects dimensions, alignment, and assembly of machined parts and tools, such as landing gears, brakes, gear boxes, jigs, and fixtures, using measuring instruments and devices, such as surface plate, height gauges, calipers, and micrometers. Approves or rejects parts, assemblies, and materials, and prepares inspection reports. Consults with vendors and subcontractors regarding interpretation of specifications, rejection, rework, salvage or other disposition of parts, and related issues. May inspect surfaces of metal parts and assemblies subsequent to or following chemical milling, heat treating, and micro-particle cleaning for defects or surface contaminants, using inspection devices. May examine and test ordnance devices and pyrotechnic apparatus, such as ejection seats, under simulated operating conditions to ensure specified operational characteristics. May specialize according to parts inspected, such as machined parts, plastics, sheet metal, and precision assemblies, or according to process involved, such as welding or electroplating. ● **GED:** R4, M4, L4 ● **SVP:** 2-4 yrs ● **Academic:** Ed=H, Eng=S ● **Work Field:** 211 ● **MPSMS:** 592 ● **Aptitudes:** G2, V3, N3, S2, P2, Q3, K3, F3, M3, E5, C5 ● **Temperaments:** J, T ● **Physical:** Stg=L; Freq: R, H, N Occas: C, B, S, K, O, W, I, T, G, D, A ● **Work Env:** Noise=N; Occas: W, D ● **Salary:** 3 ● **Outlook:** 3

INSPECTOR, PLASTICS AND COMPOSITES (aircraft mfg.) ● DOT #806.261-046 ● OES: 83000 ● Inspects and tests plastic and composite aircraft and aerospace parts, assemblies, and structures for work quality, dimensional accuracy, and conformance to engineering drawings and specifications, using precision measuring and testing instruments and equipment: Reads inspection logs and operation sheets to determine nature and sequence of inspection. Reviews blueprints and production diagrams to visualize layout and assembly procedures, locate critical references, determine parts and materials requirements, dimensions, and finish specifications. Inspects laminated and molded structures during all phases of fabrication and assembly to ensure adherence to specifications. Visually inspects parts and assemblies for fissures, porosity, delaminations, contour, and other physical characteristics. Measures parts and assemblies for dimensional accuracy, using precision measuring instruments, templates, jigs, and fixtures. Verifies location of installed fasteners and hardware. Reads pyrometers, timers, and pressure instruments to verify that operation of curing ovens and other equipment conforms to specifications. Examines assembly surfaces subsequent to curing to ensure specified smoothness and evenness of finish. Sets up and operates test equipment to perform pressure and functional testing of parts and assemblies, and to measure physical properties, such as thickness and hardness. Calculates and records test results. Accepts or rejects parts and assemblies, and prepares documentation to record inspection results, rework required, and disposition of unacceptable products. Confers with production, liaison, inspection, and other personnel to coordinate inspection process and to discuss inspection results. May inspect and test bonding of parts from metal and nonmetallic materials, such as graphite and fiberglass, and be designated Metal Bond Inspector (aircraft mfg.). May be designated by material or process as Inspector, Advanced Composite (aircraft mfg.); Inspector, Plastics Fabrication-Developmental (aircraft mfg.); Inspector, Production Plastic Parts (aircraft mfg.); Inspector, Structural Bonding (aircrraft mfg.). ● **GED:** R4, M4, L4 ● **SVP:** 2-4 yrs ● **Academic:** Ed=H, Eng=S ● **Work Field:** 211, 102 ● **MPSMS:** 592 ● **Aptitudes:** G2, V3, N3, S2, P2, Q4, K4, F3, M3, E5, C4 ●

Temperaments: J, T • **Physical:** Stg=L; Freq: R, H, I, N Occas: S, K, O, E, T, G, D, A, X • **Work Env:** Noise=L; Occas: A • **Salary:** 3 • **Outlook:** 3

INSPECTOR, PROCESSING (aircraft mfg.) • DOT #806.381-074 • OES: 83000 • Inspects aircraft and space vehicle parts, assemblies, and materials for results or effects of manufacturing processes or operations, such as anodizing, painting, etching, passivating, sandblasting, and chemical milling, for conformance to specifications, using precision measuring instruments and equipment: Examines surfaces of processed parts, assemblies, and materials for uniformity of finish, color, and area covered, and to detect defects, such as corrosion, blistering, pinholes, and dents. Measures dimensions of parts, assemblies, and materials before, during, and after processing cycles for conformance to blueprints, engineering data, shop orders, and other specifications, using precision measuring instruments, such as micrometers and gauges, and equipment. Verifies that temperature ranges and density of processing mixtures and solutions adhere to specifications. Approves or rejects parts, assemblies, and materials, and prepares documentation indicating reason for rejection, rework required, and disposition of parts. May inspect parts and materials for soundness, hardness [HARDNESS INSPECTOR (heat treating) 504.387-010], and for effects of heat-treating [HEAT-TREAT INSPECTOR (heat treating) 504.281-010], using testing equipment. • **GED:** R3, M3, L3 • **SVP:** 6 mos-1 yr • **Academic:** Ed=N, Eng=S • **Work Field:** 211 • **MPSMS:** 592 • **Aptitudes:** G3, V3, N3, S3, P2, Q4, K4, F3, M3, E5, C3 • **Temperaments:** J, T • **Physical:** Stg=L; Freq: R, H, I, N Occas: S, K, O, E, D, A, X • **Work Env:** Noise=N; Occas: A, T • **Salary:** 3 • **Outlook:** 3

OPERATIONAL TEST MECHANIC (aircraft mfg.) • DOT #806.261-050 • OES: 83000 • Alternate titles: SYSTEMS CHECK-OUT MECHANIC. Conducts final operational testing and troubleshooting of entire electrical, hydraulic, oxygen, pneumatic, fuel, surface control and rigging systems, and component parts installed in aircraft, under simulated flight conditions, according to blueprints, diagrams, engineering documents, and specifications, using precision instruments and test equipment: Locates and disassembles structural, mechanical, electrical, or other parts and assemblies to facilitate testing, using blueprints, diagrams, handtools, and power tools. Attaches fittings, clamps, lines, and hoses to test equipment, such as hydraulic test bench, pressure or vacuum test cart, and fuel quantity calibration equipment, and connects test equipment to system components to be tested. Operates test consoles, test equipment, and aircraft controls, or observes operation of system components, such as control surfaces and landing gear, being operated by other workers to determine system performance under simulated flight conditions. Communicates with other workers during system checkout, using radio headset or other communication device.

Operates steering cart or aircraft controls to move aircraft. Interprets and analyzes test results to diagnose malfunctions. Adjusts, replaces, or repairs defective components, or documents rework to be completed by others. Records operational test and rework information. Fabricates test aids as required. May perform operational testing of specific electrical, mechanical, or other aircraft system and be designated Checkout Mechanic, Hydraulic And Rigging (aircraft mfg.); Electrical Checkout Mechanic (aircraft mfg.); Mechanic, Electrical Operational Test (aircraft mfg.); Mechanic, General Operational Test (aircraft mfg.). • **GED:** R4, M3, L3 • **SVP:** 4-10 yrs • **Academic:** Ed=A, Eng=S • **Work Field:** 211, 121, 111 • **MPSMS:** 592 • **Aptitudes:** G3, V3, N3, S3, P2, Q4, K3, F3, M3, E4, C4 • **Temperaments:** J, T, V • **Physical:** Stg=M; Freq: R, H, I, N, D Occas: C, B, S, K, O, W, E, T, G, F, A, X, V • **Work Env:** Noise=V; Occas: M, E, D • **Salary:** 5 • **Outlook:** 3

ROADABILITY-MACHINE OPERATOR (auto. mfg.) • DOT #806.383-010 • OES: 83000 • Drives completed motor vehicle onto roller drums of computerized roadability machine that tests mechanical and electrical systems of vehicle: Drives vehicle onto roller drums of test machine, and connects computer cables of machine to terminals of vehicle instrument control panel. Moves shift lever through range of gears, to run rear wheels of rear-wheel drive vehicles and front wheels of front-wheel drive vehicles at specified speeds for computer testing of vehicle components, such as transmission, cruise control, and brake system. Observes computer video display screen of test machine to verify that vehicle performance conforms to specifications. Attaches computer printout of test results to inspection document in vehicle. Disconnects test cables, and drives vehicle to repair or shipping area. • **GED:** R3, M2, L3 • **SVP:** 3-6 mos • **Academic:** Ed=N, Eng=S • **Work Field:** 212 • **MPSMS:** 591 • **Aptitudes:** G3, V3, N4, S3, P3, Q4, K3, F4, M3, E4, C5 • **Temperaments:** T • **Physical:** Stg=L; Freq: R, H, I, N, D, A, V • **Work Env:** Noise=L; • **Salary:** 4 • **Outlook:** 2

X-RAY-EQUIPMENT TESTER (any industry) • DOT #729.281-046 • OES: 83000 • Alternate titles: X-RAY CONSULTANT; X-RAY EQUIPMENT SERVICER; X-RAY SERVICE ENGINEER. Tests x-ray machines and accessory equipment to locate defects, using voltmeter and laboratory testing instruments: Compares readings on x-ray control meter and timer with measurements taken with standard instruments during machine operation to verify or adjust meter and timer calibration. Tests performance of transformer and measures voltages, using voltmeter, and compares results with standard graphs. May plan layouts of x-ray departments and install equipment. • **GED:** R4, M3, L3 • **SVP:** 1-2 yrs • **Academic:** Ed=N, Eng=S • **Work Field:** 212 • **MPSMS:** 589 • **Aptitudes:** G2, V3, N2, S3, P2, Q3, K4, F3, M3, E5, C4 • **Temperaments:** J, V • **Physical:** Stg=L; Freq: R, H, I, N, D, A, X • **Work Env:** Noise=N; Freq: R • **Salary:** 3 • **Outlook:** 3

Industrial   06

Production Work   06.02

Workers in this group perform skilled hand and/or machine work to make products in a factory setting.

✓ What kind of work would you do?

Your work activities would depend upon your specific job. For example, you might:

- control vacuum pan boilers to crystallize liquid sugar.
- set up and operate machines that make paper products.
- thread nuts and bolts by operating a tapping machine.
- tend a series of coating machines to make artificial leather or oilcloth.
- split animal hides into layers by operating a machine which rolls and cuts leather to specified thicknesses.
- determine amount of fabric to be used for garment patterns and supervise marking and cutting activities.
- use power screw drivers to install automobile doors.

✓ What skills and abilities do you need for this kind of work?

To do this kind of work, you must be able to:

- read and follow instructions to set up and adjust machines and equipment.

- use eyes, hands, and fingers to adjust controls on machines, manipulate hand tools, or assemble products.
- use math skills for measuring, computing, or recordkeeping.
- detect differences in the shape, size, and texture of various items.
- pay strict attention to set standards and guidelines.
- direct the work of others.

The above statements may not apply to every job in this group.

✓ How do you know if you would like or could learn to do this kind of work?

The following questions may give you clues about yourself as you consider this group of jobs.

- Have you taken industrial arts or machine shop courses? Do you like to operate machines?
- Have you taken general or applied mathematics courses? Do you like projects which use math skills such as measuring?
- Have you assembled a bicycle or toy by following drawings or written instructions? Was it fairly easy for you to do?
- Have you held a summer or part-time job where mechanical equipment was used? Do you enjoy working around mechanical equipment?

✓ How can you prepare for and enter this kind of work?

Occupations in this group usually require education and/or training extending from three months to over four years, depending upon the specific kind of work. Machine shop courses are helpful for most jobs in this group. General or applied mathematics courses may also be helpful for some jobs. Apprenticeship programs are available for some jobs. However, most workers are trained on the job. Several jobs in this group can be attained by promotion from a helper's position.

Supervisory jobs are usually given to workers with seniority and skill.

✓ What else should you consider about these jobs?

Workers in this group usually follow established work procedures and their activities seldom change from day to day.

Overtime or night and shift work may be required. Workers may advance to higher level jobs as supervisors and inspectors.

Workers are exposed to different types of factory conditions. Most plants are well-lighted and ventilated. However, working around machinery may be hazardous or noisy, and safety procedures must be followed.

If you think you would like to do this kind of work, look at the job titles listed on the following pages.

■ ■ ■

GOE: 06.02.01
Supervision

SUPERVISOR (office machines) ● DOT #706.131-014 ● OES: 81000 ● Supervises and coordinates activities of workers engaged in fabrication of standard and electric typewriters: Examines defective parts to determine whether to stop or continue assembly process, using job knowledge of acceptable quality and manufacturing standards, such as process sheets, blueprints, and sketches. May verify dimensions of parts, using precision measuring instruments. Performs tasks as described under SUPERVISOR (any industry) Master Title. May be designated according to activities of workers supervised as Supervisor, Assembly (office machines) II; Supervisor, Fabrication (office machines); Supervisor, Inspection (office machines); Supervisor, Soldering (office machines); Supervisor, Type-Bar-And-Segment (office machines). ● **GED:** R4, M3, L4 ● **SVP:** 2-4 yrs ● **Academic:** Ed=N, Eng=G ● **Work Field:** 121 ● **MPSMS:** 571 ● **Aptitudes:** G3, V3, N3, S2, P2, Q3, K3, F2, M3, E5, C5 ● **Temperaments:** D, J, P, T, V ● **Physical:** Stg=L; Freq: R, H, I, T, G, N, F Occas: E ● **Work Env:** Noise=L; Occas: M ● **Salary:** 4 ● **Outlook:** 2

SUPERVISOR I (rubber goods) ● DOT #759.137-010 ● OES: 81000 ● Supervises and coordinates activities of workers engaged in testing, printing, and assembling dipped latex products, such as balloons, gloves, and prophylactics: Trains new workers in production methods. Inspects quality of work. Performs other duties as described under SUPERVISOR (any industry) Master Title. May be designated according to area supervised as Supervisor, Assembling (rubber goods); Supervisor, Printing (rubber goods); Supervisor, Testing (rubber goods). ● **GED:** R4, M3, L3 ● **SVP:** 2-4 yrs ● **Academic:** Ed=N, Eng=G ● **Work Field:** 191, 212 ● **MPSMS:** 510 ● **Aptitudes:** G3, V3, N3, S4, P3, Q3, K3, F2, M2, E4, C4 ● **Temperaments:** D, J, P, V ● **Physical:** Stg=L; Freq: R, H, I, T, G, N, D Occas: S, O, E, A, X ● **Work Env:** Noise=N; ● **Salary:** 4 ● **Outlook:** 2

TOOL GRINDER II (any industry) ● DOT #603.664-010 ● OES: 91117 ● Alternate titles: TOOL SHARPENER. Sharpens and smooths cutting edge of tools, such as axes, chisels, drills, picks, and straight cutting blades, using abrasive wheel: Presses button to start abrasive wheel. Positions and holds cutting edge of tool against machine guide and abrasive wheel to sharpen and smooth tool edge. Immerses tool in oil to cool edge. Repositions and holds tool edge against guide and abrasive wheel to further sharpen and smooth edge. May heat tools and immerse them in brine, oil, or water to harden them. May remove burrs from ground edges of tools, using whetstone. May sharpen and reduce diameter of circular cutting blades. May be designated according to kind of tool sharpened as Ax Sharpener (any industry); Chisel Grinder (any industry); Knife And Spur Grinder (saw. & plan.); Knife Grinder (any industry). ● **GED:** R2, M1, L1 ● **SVP:** 1-3 mos ● **Academic:** Ed=N, Eng=N ● **Work Field:** 051 ● **MPSMS:** 552 ● **Aptitudes:** G4, V4, N5, S4, P3, Q5, K4, F4, M3, E5, C5 ● **Temperaments:** R, T ● **Physical:** Stg=M; Freq: R, H, I, N Occas: A ● **Work Env:** Noise=L; ● **Salary:** 1 ● **Outlook:** 3

GOE: 06.02.02
Machine Work, Metal & Plastics

BRAKE OPERATOR II (any industry) ● DOT #619.685-026 ● OES: 91321 ● Alternate titles: PRESS-BRAKE OPERATOR. Tends power brake that bends, punches, forms, rolls, arcs, or straightens metal sheets, plates, and bars: Positions work manually or with crane against stops, or aligns layout marks to dies. Brushes oil on dies and workpiece. Starts machine to lower ram and shape workpiece. Tightens die nuts to prevent movement of die, using wrenches. Inspects work for conformance to specifications, using rule, square, or templates. Cleans scale or scrap from die with airhose or brush. May depress pedal to lower ram and shape workpiece. May tend furnace to preheat metal to specified temperatures before bending. May be designated according to material shaped as Brake Operator, Sheet Metal (any industry) II. ● GED: R3, M2, L2 ● SVP: 3-6 mos ● Academic: Ed=N, Eng=N ● Work Field: 134 ● MPSMS: 554 ● Aptitudes: G3, V4, N4, S3, P4, Q5, K3, F4, M3, E4, C5 ● Temperaments: R, T ● Physical: Stg=M; Freq: R, H, N, A Occas: I, D ● Work Env: Noise=L; ● Salary: 3 ● Outlook: 2

CRIMPING-MACHINE OPERATOR (any industry) ● DOT #616.682-022 ● OES: 92100 ● Sets up and operates machine to crimp wire to specified shape: Bolts specified crimping wheels into machine jaws, using wrench. Threads end of coiled wire through straightening and feed rollers into wire shaping machine. Starts machine and crimps sample wire of specified type. Measures sample, using micrometers and gauges, and changes crimping wheels or adjusts tension of machine until crimp meets specifications. May place shaped wire in rack. May be designated according to product worked on as Zig-Zag-Spring-Machine Operator (metal prod., nec). ● GED: R3, M2, L2 ● SVP: 6 mos-1 yr ● Academic: Ed=N, Eng=N ● Work Field: 134 ● MPSMS: 557 ● Aptitudes: G3, V4, N4, S4, P3, Q4, K3, F4, M3, E5, C5 ● Temperaments: J, T ● Physical: Stg=L; Freq: R, H, I, N, D Occas: S ● Work Env: Noise=V; ● Salary: 3 ● Outlook: 2

DRILL-PRESS OPERATOR (machine shop) ● DOT #606.682-014 ● OES: 91117 ● Alternate titles: PRODUCTION-DRILLING-MACHINE OPERATOR. Operates previously set up drilling machines, such as single- or multiple-spindle drill presses to drill, ream, countersink, spot face, or tap holes in metal or nonmetal workpieces according to specifications: Lifts workpiece manually or with hoist, and positions and secures it on machine table in drilling jig or holding fixture. Moves machine controls to feed tools into workpiece, and engages automatic feed. Observes machine operation, and verifies conformance of drilled workpiece to specifications, using fixed gauges, calipers, and micrometers. Changes worn cutting tools, using wrenches. Moves controls to adjust cutting speeds, feed rates, and depth of cut. May assist MACHINE SETTER (machine shop) 600.360-014 in setting up machine. May sharpen cutting tools, using bench grinder. May perform minor assembly, such as fastening parts with nuts, bolts, and screws, using power tools and handtools. May be designated according to product as Barrel Reamer (ordnance); or function of machine as Reamer Operator (machine shop); Tapper Operator (machine shop). ● GED: R3, M2, L2 ● SVP: 1-3 mos ● Academic: Ed=N, Eng=N ● Work Field: 053 ● MPSMS: 540 ● Aptitudes: G4, V4, N4, S4, P4, Q4, K3, F3, M3, E5, C5 ● Temperaments: R, T ● Physical: Stg=M; Freq: R, H, I, N, D, A Occas: S, O ● Work Env: Noise=L; Occas: O ● Salary: 3 ● Outlook: 3

DROPHAMMER OPERATOR (aircraft mfg.) ● DOT #610.362-010 ● OES: 91399 ● Alternate titles: BLACKSMITH, HAMMER OPERATOR. Sets up and operates closed-die drophammer to forge metal parts according to specifications, using measuring instruments and handtools: Informs HEATER (forging) 619.682-022 of forging specifications, such as specified quantity and temperature setting. Aligns and bolts specified dies to machine ram and anvil, using scale, rule, square, feeler gauges, shims, and handtools. Positions workpiece onto lower die and depresses pedal to activate ram that repeatedly strikes and forces metal workpiece into die impression. Moves workpiece through series of dies to attain specified detail. May plan work procedures, select tooling, and operate drophammer to form experimental or developmental parts. May turn knobs to regulate conveyor speed and feed that automatically carries heated stock from furnace, places stock on anvil, and removes finished workpiece. May forge unheated metal. May set stops or turn

handles to set specified striking force of ram. May trim flash from finished forging. May operate hammer to compress finished forgings to specified tolerances and be designated Restrike Hammer Operator (forging). May be designated according to type of hammer operated as Board Drophammer Operator (forging); Impact Hammer Operator (forging); Steam Hammer Operator (forging). ● GED: R3, M3, L3 ● SVP: 1-2 yrs ● Academic: Ed=N, Eng=N ● Work Field: 134 ● MPSMS: 542, 556, 592 ● Aptitudes: G3, V4, N4, S3, P3, Q4, K3, F4, M3, E4, C5 ● Temperaments: J, T ● Physical: Stg=H; Const: R, H, D Occas: I, N ● Work Env: Noise=V; Const: M Freq: H, V Occas: O ● Salary: 2 ● Outlook: 2

GRINDER SET-UP OPERATOR (machine shop) ● DOT #603.382-034 ● OES: 91114 ● Sets up and operates grinding machines to grind threads on metal objects, such as screws, bolts, and micrometer spindles, and to grind internal and external surfaces of metal workpieces to specifications, following tooling instructions, standard charts, blueprints, and job orders, applying knowledge of grinding procedures: Reads blueprint and job order for product specifications, such as dimensions, tolerances, and number of parts to be ground, and tooling instructions, such as grinding speeds, feed rates, holding fixtures, and grinding wheel to be used. Mounts wheel on spindle, using wrenches. Dresses wheel to specifications, using dressing device. Sets machine controls to specified grinding speeds, feed rates, and angle of wheel. Positions and tightens cams and stops to control depth of cut and length of stroke. Lifts and positions workpiece, manually or using hoist, and secures workpiece on faceplate or magnetic chuck, in fixture or chuck, or directly to machine table. Starts machine and activates controls to feed wheel against workpiece or vice versa, or engages automatic feeding device. Verifies dimensions of finished workpiece for conformance to specifications, using measuring instruments, such as micrometers, calipers, preset gauges, load test equipment, thread measuring wires, and thread gauges. Changes worn grinding wheel, using wrenches. May place workpiece in hopper or fixture of automatic feeding device. May grind nonmetallic materials. May be required to have experience with custom or production work or with specific type of machine, material, product, or precision level and be designated Grinder Set-Up Operator, External (machine shop); Grinder Set-Up Operator, Internal (machine shop); Grinder Set-Up Operator, Surface (machine shop); Grinder Set-Up Operator, Thread (machine shop). ● GED: R3, M3, L3 ● SVP: 1-2 yrs ● Academic: Ed=N, Eng=S ● Work Field: 051 ● MPSMS: 540, 560, 590 ● Aptitudes: G3, V3, N3, S3, P3, Q3, K3, F3, M3, E5, C5 ● Temperaments: T ● Physical: Stg=M; Freq: R, H, I, N, D, A Occas: E ● Work Env: Noise=L; Freq: M Occas: A ● Salary: 4 ● Outlook: 3

LASER-BEAM-TRIM OPERATOR (electron. comp.) ● DOT #726.682-010 ● OES: 91502 ● Operates computer-controlled laser machine to trim excess material from electronic components: Reads production sheet to determine specified operation code and enters commands, using control console, to retrieve programmed instructions. Inserts electronic component into holding fixture of laser machine, using tweezers, and presses console buttons to actuate laser beam that automatically trims excess metal and glass from component. Observes light indicator on control panel or monitor to determine if component meets specifications. Removes trimmed component from holding fixture and examines component for defects and completeness of trim, using microscope. May repair holding fixture on laser machine, using handtools, such as allen wrench, wire strippers, hand drill, and soldering iron. ● GED: R3, M3, L3 ● SVP: 3-6 mos ● Academic: Ed=N, Eng=S ● Work Field: 082 ● MPSMS: 587 ● Aptitudes: G3, V3, N4, S3, P4, Q4, K3, F2, M2, E4, C4 ● Temperaments: R, T ● Physical: Stg=L; Freq: R, H, I, N, D, A Occas: X ● Work Env: Noise=N; Occas: R ● Salary: 3 ● Outlook: 3

NUMERICAL CONTROL MACHINE OPERATOR (machine shop) ● DOT #609.362-010 ● OES: 91502 ● Sets up and operates numerical control machine to cut, shape, or form metal workpieces to specifications: Reviews setup sheet and specifications to determine setup procedure, machining sequence, and dimensions of finished workpiece. Attaches fixture to machine bed and positions and secures workpiece in fixture according to setup instructions, using clamps, bolts, handtools, power tools, and measuring instruments, such as rule and calipers. Assembles cutting tools in toolholders and positions toolholders in machine spindles as specified, using handtools, or inserts cutting tools in specified machine magazines. Loads control media, such as disk, tape, or punch card, in machine control console or enters commands to retrieve preprogrammed machine instructions from data base. Manipulates controls and enters commands to index cutting tool to specified set point and to start machine. Observes and listens to machine operation to detect malfunctions, such as worn or damaged cutting tools. Changes cutting tools and location of workpiece during machining process as specified in setup instructions. Measures workpiece for conformance to specifications, using measuring instruments, such as micrometers, dial indicators, and gauges. Notifies supervisor of discrepancies. May adjust machine feed and speed and change cutters to machine parts according to specifications when automatic programming is faulty or machine malfunctions. May machine materials other than metal, such as composites, plastic, and rubber. ● **GED:** R3, M3, L3 ● **SVP:** 6 mos-1 yr ● **Academic:** Ed=A, Eng=S ● **Work Field:** 057 ● **MPSMS:** 540, 550 ● **Aptitudes:** G3, V3, N3, S3, P3, Q4, K3, F3, M4, E5, C5 ● **Temperaments:** T ● **Physical:** Stg=M; Freq: R, H, N, D Occas: I, E, T, G ● **Work Env:** Noise=L; Occas: M ● **Salary:** 3 ● **Outlook:** 4

POLISHING-MACHINE OPERATOR (any industry) ● DOT #603.682-026 ● OES: 91114 ● Sets up and operates belt sanding machine to polish flat metal surfaces, such as small arms parts and metal strips: Pushes button to lower drive wheel and installs abrasive belt of specified grit, using wrenches. Places metal part on conveyor belt and turns knobs to raise conveyor and bring workpiece into contact with polishing belt. Turns valves to regulate flow of coolant onto polishing belt and starts machine. Examines first run part to determine conformance of finish to specifications and adjusts height of conveyor as indicated to achieve specified finish. Replaces worn polishing belts, fills coolant tank, and cleans collection tank, using handtools, to maintain machine in operating condition. ● **GED:** R3, M2, L2 ● **SVP:** 3-6 mos ● **Academic:** Ed=N, Eng=N ● **Work Field:** 051 ● **MPSMS:** 373, 601, 581 ● **Aptitudes:** G3, V4, N4, S4, P3, Q5, K4, F4, M3, E5, C5 ● **Temperaments:** R, T ● **Physical:** Stg=M; Freq: R, H Occas: I, E, N, D ● **Work Env:** Noise=L; ● **Salary:** 2 ● **Outlook:** 3

PRESS OPERATOR, HEAVY DUTY (any industry) ● DOT #617.260-010 ● OES: 91399 ● Alternate titles: BENDING-PRESS OPERATOR; HYDRAULIC-PRESS OPERATOR; TOGGLE-PRESS OPERATOR. Sets up and operates heavy-duty power press to bend, form, stretch, and straighten metal plates, metal extrusions, formed sheet metal, structural shapes, forgings, and weldments as specified by blueprints, layout, and templates: Plans sequence of operations, applying knowledge of physical properties of metal. Measures and sights along workpiece, using tape, rule, straightedge, and transit, to mark reference lines. Selects and positions flat, V-block, radius, or special purpose die sets into ram and bed of machine, using jib or crane. Aligns and bolts dies to ram and bed of machine, using gauges, templates, feelers, shims, and wrenches. Turns handwheel or levers to set depth and pressure of ram stroke. Preheats workpiece in furnace, using hand torch. Lifts and positions workpiece between dies of machine, using jib or crane and sledge. Starts machine to lower ram which bends or straightens workpiece between dies. Repositions workpiece and changes dies when making multiple or successive passes. Hand forms or finishes workpiece, using hand sledge and anvil. Grinds out burrs and sharp edges, using portable grinder. Inspects and marks job number on finished workpiece. May bend or straighten cold metal. May set dies to punch and blank heavy metal. May operate horizontal power press to bend or straighten long pieces of bar stock or structural shapes. May operate press equipped with two or more rams to bend angles or flanges or bend to radius by successive passes; or operate multiple acting hydraulic press to perform deep progressive and reverse draw operations of sheet metal. May be designated according to type press operated as Bulldozer Operator (any industry) II; Stretch-Press Operator (any industry); or according to shape product produced as Dishing-Machine Operator (any industry). ● **GED:** R3, M2, L2 ● **SVP:** 2-4 yrs ● **Academic:** Ed=N, Eng=N ● **Work Field:** 134, 133 ● **MPSMS:** 554, 566, 594 ● **Aptitudes:** G3, V4, N3, S3, P3, Q4, K4, F4, M3, E4, C3 ● **Temperaments:** J, T ● **Physical:** Stg=H; Freq: R, H, I, N, A Occas: S, O, F, D, X ● **Work Env:** Noise=L; Const: O Occas: H ● **Salary:** 3 ● **Outlook:** 2

PUNCH-PRESS OPERATOR I (any industry) ● DOT #615.382-010 ● OES: 91302 ● Sets up and operates power press to trim, punch, shape, notch, draw, or crimp metal, composite, or plastic stock: Assembles, installs, and aligns dies in press according to specifications, using feelers, shims, templates, bolts, clamps, and wrenches. Adjusts ram stroke to specified length. Positions workpiece against fixtures or stops on machine bed or on die. Starts press and observes operation to detect misalignment or malfunction. Inspects workpieces for conformance to specifications, visually or using gauges or templates, and adjusts machine to correct errors. May clean and lubricate machines. May be designated according to type of machine as Multiple-Punch-Press Operator (any industry) I; or by function of machine as Draw-Press Operator (any industry); Forming-Press Operator (any industry) I; Straightening-Press Operator (any industry) I; Stretching-Press Operator (any industry). ● **GED:** R3, M2, L2 ● **SVP:** 6 mos-1 yr ● **Academic:** Ed=N, Eng=N ● **Work Field:** 134 ● **MPSMS:** 540, 550, 560 ● **Aptitudes:** G3, V4, N3, S3, P4, Q4, K3, F4, M3, E4, C5 ● **Temperaments:** R, T ● **Physical:** Stg=M; Freq: R, H, I, N, D Occas: E, A ● **Work Env:** Noise=L; Freq: V, M ● **Salary:** 3 ● **Outlook:** 2

PUNCH-PRESS OPERATOR III (any industry) ● DOT #615.682-014 ● OES: 91321 ● Operates power press equipped with punch to notch or punch metal or plastic plates, sheets, or structural shapes: Positions, aligns, and clamps specified punch and die set into ram and bed of machine, using feelers, gauges, shims, rule, or template. Turns handwheel or installs shims to set depth of stroke. Lifts workpiece onto machine bed or roller table, manually or by using jib or crane. Positions layout marks on workpiece between punch and die. Positions and clamps guide stops to run successive pieces. Starts ram to drive punch through workpiece. May operate machine equipped with two or more punch and die sets. May trace layout marks or workpiece from template. May be designated according to function of machine as Notching-Press Operator (any industry). ● **GED:** R3, M2, L2 ● **SVP:** 3-6 mos ● **Academic:** Ed=N, Eng=N ● **Work Field:** 134 ● **MPSMS:** 541, 554 ● **Aptitudes:** G3, V4, N4, S3, P3, Q4, K4, F4, M3, E4, C5 ● **Temperaments:** J, R, T ● **Physical:** Stg=H; Freq: R, H, I, N, D, A Occas: S, O, E ● **Work Env:** Noise=L; Freq: M, O ● **Salary:** 3 ● **Outlook:** 2

RIVETING-MACHINE OPERATOR I (any industry) ● DOT #699.482-010 ● OES: 92100 ● Sets up and operates riveting machine to rivet together parts fabricated from materials, such as sheet metal and plastic, according to work orders and specifications: Positions, aligns, and bolts specified dies over anvil and ram of machine and positions fixtures in machine bed, using micrometer, rule, gauge, shims, and wrenches. Installs cam and spring in anvil to synchronize action or clinching post of lower die with action of ram and with rivet feed agitator or lever when setting up semiautomatic machines which position rivets over anvil. Turns knobs and sets screws to adjust depth and pressure limit of ram stroke. Aligns holes of workpieces and inserts shanks of rivets into holes or onto anvil of machine. Positions rivets or holes in workpieces over anvil or against fixtures. Depresses pedal to lower ram that spreads rivet shank to clinch workpieces. Fills hopper with rivets when operating semiautomatic machines. May set up machines equipped with several rams, or with turret to punch and dimple rivet holes and to reposition workpiece after each operation. ● **GED:** R3, M2, L3 ● **SVP:** 6 mos-1 yr ● **Academic:** Ed=N, Eng=S ● **Work Field:** 073 ● **MPSMS:** 580, 590 ● **Aptitudes:** G3, V3, N3, S3, P3, Q4, K4, F3, M3, E4, C5 ● **Temperaments:** J, R, T ● **Physical:** Stg=M; Freq: R, H, I, N, D Occas: S, O ● **Work Env:** Noise=N; ● **Salary:** 3 ● **Outlook:** 2

SAWYER (plastic prod.) ● DOT #690.482-010 ● OES: 91399 ● Sets up and operates power-driven circular and abrasive saws and bandsaw to cut plastic sheets, rods, or tubes to specified dimensions: Installs blade in saw and sets guide bars and stops. Positions plastic material on saw table. Starts saw and feeds material to blade. Verifies dimensions of pieces, using micrometer, gauges, and rule. Examines pieces for defects, such as chipped edges and marred surfaces, and sorts defective pieces according to defect. May mark cutting lines on material. May sharpen blade, using abrasive wheel. ● **GED:** R3, M2, L2 ● **SVP:** 6 mos-1 yr ● **Academic:** Ed=N, Eng=N ● **Work Field:** 056 ● **MPSMS:** 510, 492 ● **Aptitudes:** G4, V4, N4, S4, P3, Q4, K3, F4, M3, E5, C5 ● **Temperaments:** R, T ● **Physical:** Stg=M; Freq: R, H, N Occas: S, I, A ● **Work Env:** Noise=L; Freq: A, O ● **Salary:** 3 ● **Outlook:** 2

SCREW-MACHINE OPERATOR, MULTIPLE SPINDLE (machine shop) ● DOT #604.382-010 ● OES: 91117 ● Alternate titles: BAR-MACHINE OPERATOR, MULTIPLE SPINDLE. Operates one or more previously set up multiple-spindle screw machines equipped with automatic indexing and feeding mechanism to perform series of machining operations on metal bar stock, following specifications:

Reads blueprint and job order for such information as dimensions, tolerances, and number of workpieces to be machined. Examines machine to become familiar with tooling setup. Loads stock into feeding mechanism. Starts machine and observes operation. Verifies conformance of sample workpieces to specifications, using preset gauges, micrometers and dial indicators. Replaces worn tools. Adjusts machine controls and changes tool settings to keep dimensions within specified tolerances. May operate bench grinder or cutter-grinding machine to sharpen tools [TOOL-GRINDER OPERATOR (machine shop)]. May machine plastics or other nonmetallic materials. May operate single-spindle screw machine [SCREW-MACHINE OPERATOR, SINGLE SPINDLE (machine shop)]. May be required to have experience with particular material or product or machine of particular size, type, or trade name. ● **GED:** R3, M2, L2 ● **SVP:** 1-2 yrs ● **Academic:** Ed=H, Eng=N ● **Work Field:** 057, 053 ● **MPSMS:** 541, 566 ● **Aptitudes:** G3, V4, N3, S3, P3, Q4, K3, F3, M3, E5, C5 ● **Temperaments:** J, T ● **Physical:** Stg=M; Freq: R, H, I, N, D, A Occas: S, O, E ● **Work Env:** Noise=N; ● **Salary:** 2 ● **Outlook:** 3

SHEAR OPERATOR I (any industry) ● DOT #615.682-018 ● OES: 91399 ● Alternate titles: PLATE-SHEAR OPERATOR; POWER-SHEAR OPERATOR. Sets up and operates power shear to cut metal objects, such as plates, sheets, slabs, billets, or bars to specified dimensions and angle: Turns handwheels to adjust rake (angle) and pressure of blade. Positions and clamps stops and side guides to set length and angle of cut, using rule, built-in gauges, or template. Lifts workpiece manually or by hoist or crane to machine bed or roller table and positions it against side guide and end stops. Starts machine which clamps workpiece and lowers blade to cut metal. Lays out cutting lines on metal, using rule, square, or template when shearing single pieces. May tilt bed, blade, or install fixtures to shear, bevel, or trim fabricated items. May set up and operate shear on production line in which shear is fed by conveyor, such as automobile frame line or rolling mill. May operate portable shear to cut sheet metal. May inspect work, using tape, compass, gauge, template, or micrometer to verify dimensions. May be designated by type of shear as Gate-Shear Operator (any industry) II; or by application of shear as Square-Shear Operator (any industry) I; Staple-Shear Operator (steel & rel.). May operate shear that automatically shears to uniform length metal sheets, plates, or structural shapes fed into machine by continuous coil or conveyor and be designated Shear Operator, Automatic (any industry) I. ● **GED:** R3, M2, L2 ● **SVP:** 3-6 mos ● **Academic:** Ed=N, Eng=N ● **Work Field:** 054 ● **MPSMS:** 554, 594, 541 ● **Aptitudes:** G3, V4, N4, S3, P3, Q4, K3, F4, M3, E4, C5 ● **Temperaments:** R, T ● **Physical:** Stg=H; Freq: R, H, I, N, D, A ● **Work Env:** Noise=L; Freq: H, A, M, O ● **Salary:** 3 ● **Outlook:** 3

SPINNER, HAND (any industry) ● DOT #619.362-018 ● OES: 91105 ● Alternate titles: SPINNING-LATHE OPERATOR. Sets up and operates spinning lathe to spin (form) shaped articles from sheet or plate metal, using blueprints and knowledge of physical properties of metal: Bolts specified spinning chuck to headstock spindle and follow block to tailstock, using handtools or power tools. Clamps metal disk to chuck by turning handwheel that forces follow block against disk. Secures steady rest fixture on cross-slide. Starts machine and coats outside of rotating disk with spinning compound. Positions, holds, and moves long-handled compound lever tool against disk, using steady rest as fulcrum point, to apply required pressure to form disk over and into shape of spinning chuck. Varies amount and location of pressure on disk according to type of metal, shape of spinning chuck, speed of lathe, and temperature and thickness of metal disk. Replaces steady rest with bar tool attachment, turns handwheel to set bar tool and cut off excess metal from workpiece. Verifies dimension of finished article with steel rule and diameter tape. May form wood spinning chucks by turning on lathe. ● **GED:** R4, M3, L3 ● **SVP:** 2-4 yrs ● **Academic:** Ed=N, Eng=S ● **Work Field:** 134 ● **MPSMS:** 550 ● **Aptitudes:** G3, V3, N3, S2, P2, Q4, K3, F4, M3, E4, C4 ● **Temperaments:** J, T ● **Physical:** Stg=M; Freq: R, H, N, A ● **Work Env:** Noise=L; ● **Salary:** 3 ● **Outlook:** 2

STRAIGHTENING-PRESS OPERATOR II (any industry) ● DOT #617.482-026 ● OES: 91321 ● Alternate titles: STRAIGHTENER. Operates power press equipped with pressure blocks or dies to straighten warped or bent metal objects, such as plates, structural castings, shapes, forgings, and shafts to specified dimensions: Examines workpiece to locate defects, using such devices as straightedge, deflection gauge,

template, and square. Positions and locks specified pressure blocks, or die, into ram of machine, or positions shims under high spots of workpiece. Lifts and positions workpiece into bed of machine manually or using jib or crane. Starts ram which presses out bent or high spots of workpiece. Reexamines and repositions workpiece, changing shims for each pass until workpiece conforms with specifications. May turn levers or handwheels to adjust depth and pressure of ram. May preheat metal, using heating furnace or hand torch and clean dies between pressings, using compressed air, oil, and brush. May tend machine equipped with preset dies to bend metal to specified shapes. May grind rough edges from finished workpiece, using portable hand grinder. May be designated according to part straightened as Barrel Straightener (ordnance) II; Crankshaft Straightener (auto. mfg.); Gear Straightener (auto. mfg.); or according to type press operated as Gag-Press Straightener (steel & rel.). ● **GED:** R3, M2, L1 ● **SVP:** 6 mos-1 yr ● **Academic:** Ed=N, Eng=N ● **Work Field:** 134 ● **MPSMS:** 554, 594 ● **Aptitudes:** G3, V4, N4, S3, P3, Q5, K3, F3, M3, E4, C5 ● **Temperaments:** J, T ● **Physical:** Stg=M; Freq: S, R, H, N, D, A Occas: I ● **Work Env:** Noise=L; Occas: O ● **Salary:** 3 ● **Outlook:** 2

STRAIGHTENING-ROLL OPERATOR (any industry) ● DOT #613.662-022 ● OES: 91321 ● Alternate titles: STRAIGHTENING-MACHINE OPERATOR. Operates rolling machine to straighten warped or bent metal plates, bars, or sheets: Threads workpiece between rolls of machine manually or with crane. Turns handwheels or nuts to adjust tension between one or more sets of aligned drive and adjustment rolls. Pulls lever to move workpiece through rolls of machine. Hammers or pries workpiece into alignment, using hammer or pry bar. Examines work for straightness, using straightedge and plumb bob. Inserts shims under bulges and repeats process to straighten workpiece to specifications. May be designated by product straightened as Bar-Straightening-Machine Operator (any industry); Plate Roller (any industry); Wire-Straightening-Machine Operator (any industry). ● **GED:** R3, M1, L1 ● **SVP:** 3-6 mos ● **Academic:** Ed=N, Eng=N ● **Work Field:** 135 ● **MPSMS:** 554, 541 ● **Aptitudes:** G3, V4, N4, S3, P3, Q4, K3, F3, M3, E4, C5 ● **Temperaments:** J, T ● **Physical:** Stg=M; Freq: S, R, H, N, F, D Occas: K, I ● **Work Env:** Noise=L; Freq: H Occas: O ● **Salary:** 3 ● **Outlook:** 2

WIRE DRAWING MACHINE OPERATOR (inst. & app.) ● DOT #614.382-018 ● OES: 91321 ● Operates wire drawing machine to shape or emboss wire used in dental work and costume jewelry: Reviews work orders and selects shaping, reducing, or embossing roller dies according to specifications. Positions roller die in machine that shapes, reduces, or embosses wire, such as gold, silver, or copper, to form dental or jewelry wire. Turns setscrews to secure roller die in machine. Inserts wire into machine feed mechanism, starts machine, and monitors machine operation. Measures wire thickness to verify conformance to specifications, using micrometer. Installs progressively smaller dies in machine and repeats operation until wire diameter meets specifications. May measure physical properties of wire, such as tensile strength and bend set, and calculate elongation data, using test instruments and calculator. May record production information, manually or using computer. ● **GED:** R3, M2, L2 ● **SVP:** 3-6 mos ● **Academic:** Ed=N, Eng=N ● **Work Field:** 135 ● **MPSMS:** 544, 604, 613 ● **Aptitudes:** G3, V4, N4, S4, P3, Q4, K4, F4, M3, E5, C5 ● **Temperaments:** J, T ● **Physical:** Stg=M; Freq: R, H, I, E, N Occas: D, A ● **Work Env:** Noise=L; ● **Salary:** 3 ● **Outlook:** 2

GOE: 06.02.03
Machine Work, Wood

CUT-OFF-SAW OPERATOR I (woodworking) ● DOT #667.682-022 ● OES: 92305 ● Alternate titles: CROSS-CUT-SAW OPERATOR; TRIMMER OPERATOR. Operates one or more single- or multiple-blade circular saws to cut wood and wood products to specified lengths: Adjusts and secures ends and backstops on saw table, using wrench, or bolts saws to shaft and turns handwheels to space saws and stops, according to specified length of stock. Starts saw and places material to be cut on conveyor belt, drums, or feed chain that feeds stock into saws, or positions workpiece against end stop and under saw, syncronizing action with automatically descending blade, or pushes material on table and cuts wood, depending on type saw, utilizing one of following methods: (1) Pulls lever to swing saw through material. (2) Pushes moveable table past saw. (3) Depresses treadle to raise saw through slot in machine table. (4) Tilts table for angle cut and presses pedal to move saw through workpiece to cut stock. Replaces dull or damaged saw blades and lubricates machine, using wrench and grease gun. May examine material prior to cutting to determine what cuts will remove defects and produce maximum footage. May verify dimensions of stock cut and accuracy of cuts, using rule and square. May be designated according to type of saw used as Double-Cut-Off-Saw Operator (woodworking); Drum-Saw Operator (saw. & plan.); Swinging-Cut-Off-Saw Operator (woodworking); Table-Cut-Off-Saw Operator (woodworking); Tilting-Saw Operator (woodworking); Treadle-Cut-Off-Saw Operator (woodworking). May be designated: Equalizing-Saw Operator (woodworking); Multiple-Cut-Off-Saw Operator (millwork-plywood; wood. container); Timber Cutter (mine & quarry). ● **GED:** R3, M2, L2 ● **SVP:** 3-6 mos ● **Academic:** Ed=N, Eng=N ● **Work Field:** 056 ● **MPSMS:** 450 ● **Aptitudes:** G3, V4, N4, S3, P3, Q4, K3, F4, M3, E4, C5 ● **Temperaments:** R, T ● **Physical:** Stg=M; Freq: R, H, N, D Occas: S, O, I, G, A ● **Work Env:** Noise=L; Freq: V, A Occas: T ● **Salary:** 3 ● **Outlook:** 2

HEAD SAWYER (saw. & plan.) ● DOT #667.662-010 ● OES: 92305 ● Alternate titles: BAND-LOG-MILL-AND-CARRIAGE OPERATOR; BAND-SAWMILL OPERATOR. Operates head saw and feed carriage to saw logs into cants or boards: Starts mechanical loader arms that place log on carriage. Sets dogs and adjusts carriage blocks to align log for sawing. Activates carriage that moves log against saw blade. Starts saw to cut log. Observes exposed face of log after first cut to determine grade and size of next cut and adjusts setting of carriage blocks. Starts mechanical log turner that turns log over on carriage for subsequent cuts. May change saw blades. May be designated according to type of saw operated as Band-Head-Saw Operator (saw. & plan.); Circular-Head-Saw Operator (saw. & plan.). ● **GED:** R3, M2, L1 ● **SVP:** 2-4 yrs ● **Academic:** Ed=N, Eng=N ● **Work Field:** 056 ● **MPSMS:** 452 ● **Aptitudes:** G3, V4, N4, S3, P3, Q5, K2, F3, M3, E3, C3 ● **Temperaments:** J ● **Physical:** Stg=L; Freq: R, H, I, N Occas: S ● **Work Env:** Noise=L; Occas: M ● **Salary:** 4 ● **Outlook:** 2

LOG-CHIPPER OPERATOR (logging) ● DOT #564.662-010 ● OES: 92965 ● Alternate titles: CHIPPER. Operates trailer-mounted grapple-loader and chipping machine to reduce logs and logging waste to wood chips: Controls loading boom and power-grapple attachment to pick up logs and place them on feed conveyor. Adjusts speed and opening of feed rolls according to log diameter, and activates feed rolls that pushes log through chipper unit. Monitors gauges and adjusts speed and opening of feed rolls to prevent equipment strain. Replaces defective chipping knives, using wrenches and feeler gauges. May control opening of debarking spuds (tined rotating drums) that remove bark from log before chipping. ● **GED:** R3, M1, L2 ● **SVP:** 3-6 mos ● **Academic:** Ed=N, Eng=N ● **Work Field:** 142, 011 ● **MPSMS:** 459 ● **Aptitudes:** G3, V4, N4, S3, P4, Q4, K3, F4, M3, E3, C5 ● **Temperaments:** R, T ● **Physical:** Stg=M; Freq: R, H, N Occas: S, K, O, I ● **Work Env:** Noise=L; ● **Salary:** 2 ● **Outlook:** 3

NAILING-MACHINE OPERATOR (any industry) ● DOT #669.682-058 ● OES: 92310 ● Alternate titles: BOX MAKER; NAILER, MACHINE. Sets up and operates machines to drive nails into boards to fasten wood assemblies, such as boxes, furniture frames, crates, and pallets, and to nail lids on boxes: Spaces nail chucks and rails according to specifications and turns setscrews to fasten chucks to rails. Turns wheel to raise or lower table according to size of pieces to be nailed. Fills hopper with nails. Fastens or adjusts stops and jigs on machine table to facilitate positioning of material to be nailed. Starts machine, positions boards on table under chucks, and depresses pedal to drive nails into boards. May move levers to control nail feed and turn knobs to position nail setting heads. May be designated according to part nailed as Bottom Nailer (wood. container); Cleat Nailer (wood. container); Frame Nailer (wood. container); Strap Nailer (wood. container); or according to type of machine as Lidding-Machine Operator (any industry). ● **GED:** R2, M1, L1 ● **SVP:** 3-6 mos ● **Academic:** Ed=N, Eng=N ● **Work Field:** 072 ● **MPSMS:** 450 ● **Aptitudes:** G4, V4, N4, S4, P3, Q5, K3, F4, M3, E4, C5 ● **Temperaments:** R, T ● **Physical:** Stg=M; Freq: R, H Occas: I ● **Work Env:** Noise=L; Occas: M ● **Salary:** 2 ● **Outlook:** 2

ROUTER OPERATOR (woodworking) ● DOT #665.682-030 ● OES: 92310 ● Alternate titles: ROUTING-MACHINE OPERATOR. Sets up and operates single- or multiple-spindle routing machine to cut slots, grooves, designs, or recesses in woodstock: Studies blueprints, drawings, or samples and written specifications to ascertain size, depth, and location of cuts to be made. Selects and installs router bits in spindle chucks according to specifications, using chuck key. Spaces spindles on shaft at specified intervals, using wrenches, and turns handwheels or sets stops to regulate depth of cut. Clamps stock to jig, inserts pin in guidehole of machine table, and places jig over guide pin, or clamps part to movable table of machine. Starts machine and presses pedal to raise table and feed stock into rotating bits. Moves stock under bits, following guides, lines, or slots in jig, to cut specified slots, designs, grooves, or recesses in stock. Measures dimensions of processed woodstock to verify conformance to specifications, using ruler, gauges, or calipers. May be designated according to machine operated as Multiple-Spindle-Router Operator (woodworking); or according to cut made as Handhole-Machine Operator (wood. container). ● **GED:** R3, M2, L2 ● **SVP:** 3-6 mos ● **Academic:** Ed=N, Eng=N ● **Work Field:** 055 ● **MPSMS:** 452, 460 ● **Aptitudes:** G3, V4, N4, S3, P3, Q4, K3, F4, M3, E4, C5 ● **Temperaments:** J, T ● **Physical:** Stg=M; Const: R, H Freq: S, N, D, A Occas: I, G ● **Work Env:** Noise=L; Occas: A, M ● **Salary:** 3 ● **Outlook:** 3

TIMBER-SIZER OPERATOR (saw. & plan.) ● DOT #665.482-018 ● OES: 92310 ● Alternate titles: PLANER OPERATOR. Operates planing machine to surface planks and timbers and reduce stock to specified dimensions: Installs cutting heads on machine drive spindles and adjusts blade exposure according to specified depth of cut, using wrenches and gauges. Adjusts feed roll tension and positions fences that guide stock between cutterheads. Starts machine, exhaust blower, and conveyors, and slides timber against guide to align timber on feed rolls. Verifies dimensions of sized stock, using gauge or rule. ● **GED:** R3, M2, L1 ● **SVP:** 3-6 mos ● **Academic:** Ed=N, Eng=N ● **Work Field:** 055 ● **MPSMS:** 452 ● **Aptitudes:** G3, V4, N3, S3, P3, Q4, K3, F4, M3, E4, C5 ● **Temperaments:** J, T ● **Physical:** Stg=M; Freq: R, H, N Occas: S, O, I, T, G ● **Work Env:** Noise=L; Occas: W, A, M ● **Salary:** 3 ● **Outlook:** 2

GOE: 06.02.05
Machine Work, Leather & Fabrics

BINDER (any industry) ● DOT #787.682-010 ● OES: 92721 ● Alternate titles: BINDING-END STITCHER; BINDING-MACHINE OPERATOR; TAPER. Operates sewing machine equipped with folding attachment to sew binding material over edges or seams of articles, such as camping equipment, linens, parachutes, gloves and mittens, or hats and caps, to reinforce, prevent raveling, and give finished appearance: Places roll of binding on holder and draws end through folding attachment. Positions edge of article between folds of binding material and guides article and material under needle. Performs duties as described under SEWING-MACHINE OPERATOR, REGULAR EQUIPMENT (any industry) Master Title. When binding blankets, folds binding material at end of seam to form corners and sews over folded corner. When binding fitted sheets, matches curved edges of sheet and guides edges under needle to form sheet corners. May operate sewing machine equipped with shirring mechanism to gather binding as binding is attached to article. May be designated according to article or part bound as Band-Lining Bander (hat & cap); Blanket Binder (tex. prod., nec); Ear-Flap Binder (hat & cap); Fitted Sheet Binder (tex. prod., nec); Flap-Lining Binder (hat & cap); Helmet Binder (hat & cap). May be designated: Parachute Taper (tex. prod., nec); Pot-Holder Binder (tex. prod., nec); Screen-Vent Binder (hat & cap); Soft-Hat Binder (hat & cap). May bind rug samples and be designated Sample Processor (carpet & rug). ● **GED:** R3, M1, L1 ● **SVP:** 3-6 mos ● **Academic:** Ed=N, Eng=N ● **Work Field:** 171 ● **MPSMS:** 420, 435, 445 ● **Aptitudes:** G3, V4, N4, S4, P3, Q4, K3, F3, M3, E4, C4 ● **Temperaments:** R, T ● **Physical:** Stg=L; Const: A Freq: R, H, I, E, N, D, X ● **Work Env:** Noise=L; Occas: M ● **Salary:** 1 ● **Outlook:** 3

CARPET SEWER (carpet & rug) ● DOT #787.682-014 ● OES: 92721 ● Alternate titles: FRINGE-BINDER OPERATOR; LENO SEWER; SEWING-MACHINE OPERATOR, CARPET AND RUGS. Operates sewing machine to join carpet sections or braided yarn strips to form rug and finish edges, performing any combination of following duties: Joins sections of carpeting to form rug of desired size or continuous length (runner). Sews decorative trimmings on rugs, borders on runners, or binding to prevent edges from raveling. Operates sewing machine that loops yarn into fringe and stitches fringe to edge of rug. Joins braided strips of yarn to form round or oval rug of desired size. Joins widths of leno cloth used on backing of rugs. May join sections of carpet together, using seaming tape and liquid cement. Performs other duties as described under SEWING-MACHINE OPERATOR, REGULAR EQUIPMENT (any industry) Master Title. ● **GED:** R3, M2, L2 ● **SVP:** 1-3 mos ● **Academic:** Ed=N, Eng=N ● **Work Field:** 171 ● **MPSMS:** 431, 439 ● **Aptitudes:** G3, V4, N4, S4, P3, Q4, K3, F3, M3, E4, C4 ● **Temperaments:** R, T ● **Physical:** Stg=M; Const: R, H Freq: I, N, D, X Occas: A ● **Work Env:** Noise=L; Freq: M ● **Salary:** 3 ● **Outlook:** 2

HEMMER (any industry) ● DOT #787.682-026 ● OES: 92721 ● Alternate titles: PLAIN-GOODS HEMMER. Operates sewing machine equipped with folding attachment to hem articles, such as curtains and draperies, gloves and mittens, sheets, towels, and pillowcases: Guides edge of material through folding attachment and under machine needle. Inserts and sews labels into hem. May reinforce hem by backstitching at ends of seam. May fold hem manually. When operating machine to hem curtains and draperies to form rod inserts, is designated HEADER (tex. prod., nec). May be designated according to article or part hemmed as Pillowcase Sewer (tex. prod., nec); Sheet Sewer (tex. prod., nec); Towel Sewer (tex. prod., nec); Window-Shade-Cloth Sewer (furniture); Wrist Hemmer (glove & mit.). Performs duties as described under SEWING-MACHINE OPERATOR, REGULAR EQUIPMENT (any industry) Master Title. ● **GED:** R3, M1, L1 ● **SVP:** 3-6 mos ● **Academic:** Ed=N, Eng=N ● **Work Field:** 171 ● **MPSMS:** 435, 449 ● **Aptitudes:** G4, V4, N4, S4, P3, Q5, K3, F3, M3, E4, C4 ● **Temperaments:** R, T ● **Physical:** Stg=L; Freq: R, H, I, N, D, A Occas: X ● **Work Env:** Noise=L; ● **Salary:** 1 ● **Outlook:** 2

MENDER (any industry) ● DOT #787.682-030 ● OES: 85998 ● Operates sewing machine to repair defects, such as tears and holes in garments, linens, curtains, draperies, and blankets: Patches, darns, or reweaves holes or tears in garments, curtains, or linens, and resews ripped seams. Sews fringe, tassels, and ruffles onto drapes and curtains. Sews buttons and trimming on garments after they have been cleaned. Operates sewing machine to restitch or replace binding ribbon on edge of blankets. May cut curtains to specified measurements and hem edges. May shorten or lengthen hems to alter size of garments. May replace pockets in coats or trousers. May sew identifying labels and emblems on uniforms, linens, or diapers for linen supply or diaper service. May repair defective stitching on articles. May be designated according to type of article sewn as Sewer, Linen Room (hotel & rest.) or machine used as Darning-Machine Operator (any industry). May examine lace webbing for defects and be designated Examiner-Mender (tex. prod., nec). Performs duties as described under SEWING-MACHINE OPERATOR, REGULAR EQUIPMENT (any industry) Master Title. ● **GED:** R3, M1, L2 ● **SVP:** 3-6 mos ● **Academic:** Ed=N, Eng=N ● **Work Field:** 171 ● **MPSMS:** 420, 440 ● **Aptitudes:** G3, V4, N4, S4, P3, Q5, K3, F3, M3, E4, C4 ● **Temperaments:** R, T ● **Physical:** Stg=L; Const: H, I, N, X Freq: R, E, A Occas: G ● **Work Env:** Noise=L; Occas: M ● **Salary:** 1 ● **Outlook:** 2

SEWING MACHINE OPERATOR (leather prod.) ● DOT #783.682-014 ● OES: 92721 ● Operates sewing machine to join parts of leather products, such as suitcases, handbags, and wallets. May operate machine equipped with shirring attachment. May operate machine equipped with wrapping and folding attachment to join parts of handbag handles and be designated Handle Sewer (leather prod.). May cut thread, using blade attached to machine or scissors. May oil machine and change needles. When joining or decorating handbag parts with decorative stitches, is designated Fancy Sewer (leather prod.). May be designated according to parts joined as Applique Sewer (leather prod.); Lining-Parts Sewer (leather prod.); or according to article assembled and sewed as Briefcase Sewer (leather prod.); Handbag Finisher (leather prod.). Performs duties as described under SEWING MACHINE OPERATOR, REGULAR EQUIPMENT (any industry) Master Title. ● **GED:** R3, M1, L1 ● **SVP:** 1-3 mos ● **Academic:** Ed=N, Eng=N ● **Work Field:** 171 ● **MPSMS:** 524, 525 ● **Aptitudes:** G3, V4, N4, S3, P3, Q4, K3, F3, M3, E4, C4 ● **Temperaments:** R, T ● **Physical:** Stg=L; Const: R, H, I, N, A Freq: X, V ● **Work Env:** Noise=L; Freq: M ● **Salary:** 1 ● **Outlook:** 3

STITCHER, STANDARD MACHINE (boot & shoe) ● DOT #690.682-082 ● OES: 92723 ● Alternate titles: CLOSER; FITTER; JOINER; MAKER; SEAMER; SEWER; STAYER; STITCHER; STITCHING-MACHINE OPERATOR. Operates single, double, or multiple-needle stitching machine to join or decorate shoe parts, or to reinforce edges: Selects spool of thread or prewound bobbin, places spool or bobbin on spindle or looper, and draws thread through guides and needles. Aligns parts and presses knee control or pedal to raise presser foot or roller. Positions parts under needle and lowers presser foot or roller. Presses foot or knee control to start machine and guides parts under needle, following seams, edges, or markings, or moves edges of part against guide. Cuts excess thread or material from shoe parts, using scissors or knife. When operating double or multiple-needle machine, may turn setscrew on needle bar and position one or more needles as specified. May be designated according to shoe parts stitched as Back-Seam Stitcher (boot & shoe); Box-Toe Stitcher (boot & shoe). May be designated according to machine operated as Flatbed Stitcher (boot & shoe); Zig-Zag Stitcher (boot & shoe). May be designated according to number of needles in machine operated as Double-Needle Stitcher (boot & shoe); Multiple-Needle Stitcher (boot & shoe); Single-Needle Stitcher (boot & shoe). May be designated: Backstay Stitcher (boot & shoe); Barrer And Tacker (boot & shoe); Binding Stitcher (boot & shoe); Buckle Sewer, Machine (boot & shoe); California Seamer (boot & shoe); Counter-Pocket Sewer (boot & shoe); Cover Maker (boot & shoe); Cut-Out Stitcher (boot & shoe); Edge Stitcher (boot & shoe); Fancy Stitcher (boot & shoe); Flare Stitcher (boot & shoe); Gore Inserter (boot & shoe); Insole Tape Stitcher, UCO (boot & shoe); Label Stitcher (boot & shoe); Lining Closer (boot & shoe); Lining Stitcher (boot & shoe); Lining-Strap Closer (boot & shoe); Lining Vamper (boot & shoe); Neverslip Stitcher (boot & shoe); Postbed Stitcher (boot & shoe); Quarter-Lining Stitcher (boot & shoe); Rand Sewer (boot & shoe); Saddle Stitcher (boot & shoe); Saddle-Lining Stitcher (boot & shoe); Seam-Stay Stitcher (boot & shoe); Shank Stitcher (boot & shoe); Sock-Lining Stitcher (boot & shoe); Stitcher, Utility (boot & shoe); Strap Stitcher (boot & shoe); Tape Stitcher (boot & shoe); Tip Stitcher (boot & shoe); Toe-Lining Closer (boot & shoe); Tongue And Quarter Stitcher (boot & shoe); Tongue-Lining Stitcher (boot & shoe); Tongue Stitcher (boot & shoe); Top Stitcher (boot & shoe); Underlay Stitcher (boot & shoe); Upper Stitcher (boot & shoe); Vamp Stitcher (boot & shoe); Welting Stitcher, Front (boot & shoe); Wrapper Stitcher (boot & shoe). ● **GED:** R3, M2, L2 ● **SVP:** 3-6 mos ● **Academic:** Ed=N, Eng=N ● **Work Field:** 171 ● **MPSMS:** 522 ● **Aptitudes:** G4, V4, N4, S3, P3, Q4, K3, F3, M3, E4, C4 ● **Temperaments:** R, T ● **Physical:** Stg=L; Const: R, H, N, A Freq: I Occas: G, D, X ● **Work Env:** Noise=L; ● **Salary:** 1 ● **Outlook:** 4

TRIMMER, MACHINE (garment) ● DOT #781.682-010 ● OES: 92710 ● Operates sewing machine equipped with cutting blade attachment to trim excess fabric from material or article. Depresses pedal to start machine, moves hand and foot controls, and guides material or articles under blade to trim excess fabric and facilitate subsequent operation. May be designated by type of article or material trimmed as Collar Trimmer (garment; knitting); Brassiere-Cup-Mold Cutter (garment). ● **GED:** R2, M1, L1 ● **SVP:** 2-30 days ● **Academic:** Ed=N, Eng=N ● **Work Field:** 054 ● **MPSMS:** 420 ● **Aptitudes:** G4, V4, N4, S4, P3, Q5, K3, F4, M3, E4, C5 ● **Temperaments:** R, T ● **Physical:** Stg=L; Const: R, H Freq: I, N, A ● **Work Env:** Noise=L; ● **Salary:** 1 ● **Outlook:** 3

ZIPPER SETTER (any industry) ● DOT #787.682-086 ● OES: 92721 ● Operates sewing machine equipped with guides that prevent needle from contacting metal to sew slide fasteners in openings or on parts of articles, such as mattresses, blankets, cushions, upholsteries, sleeping bags and other camping equipment, and quilt covers: Places roll of zippers on holder, or selects zipper of specified length, and draws end of zipper through guides. Cuts zippers from roll after sewing, using scissors. Attaches zipper slide to zipper and opens zipper before sewing stops on each end of zipper opening. When sewing zippers on plastic material, operates machine equipped with folding attachment to sew binding material over seam. Performs duties as described under SEWING-MACHINE OPERATOR, REGULAR EQUIPMENT (any industry) Master Title. ● **GED:** R3, M1, L1 ● **SVP:** 3-6 mos ● **Academic:** Ed=N, Eng=N ● **Work Field:** 171 ● **MPSMS:** 435, 439 ● **Aptitudes:** G4, V4, N4, S4, P3, Q5, K3, F3, M3, E4, C5 ● **Temperaments:** R, T ● **Physical:** Stg=L; Const: R, H, I, N, A Freq: D ● **Work Env:** Noise=L; ● **Salary:** 3 ● **Outlook:** 2

GOE: 06.02.06
Machine Work, Textiles

WEAVER (nonmet. min.) ● DOT #683.682-038 ● OES: 92710 ● Alternate titles: LOOM OPERATOR; WEAVER, BROADLOOM. Operates battery of looms to weave yarn into cloth: Observes cloth being woven to detect weaving defects. Removes defects in cloth by cutting and pulling out filling. Adjusts pattern chain to resume weaving. Examines looms to determine cause of loom stoppage, such as warp, filling, harness breaks, or mechanical defects. Ties piece of yarn to broken end and threads yarn through drop wires, heddle eyes, and reed dents to repair warp breaks, using reed hook. Pulls out broken filling and pushes shuttle through shed to insert new pick and repair filling breaks. Notifies LOOM FIXER (narrow fabrics; nonmet. min.; textile) 683.260-018 of mechanical defects. Marks or cuts cloth when sufficient yardage has been woven and notifies CLOTH DOFFER (textile) 689.686-058. May place quills or bobbins in battery or magazine of loom [BATTERY LOADER (textile) 683.686-010]. May replace empty bobbins in shuttle with full ones on nonautomatic looms [SHUTTLE HAND (textile) 689.686-038]. May tend winding units attached to looms that wind filling onto quills [LOOM-WINDER TENDER (textile) 681.685-062]. May be designated according to type of loom operated as Weaver, Dobby Loom (textile). When weaving samples, is known as Sample Weaver (textile). ● **GED:** R3, M1, L2 ● **SVP:** 3-6 mos ● **Academic:** Ed=N, Eng=N ● **Work Field:** 164 ● **MPSMS:** 420 ● **Aptitudes:** G3, V4, N4, S3, P3, Q4, K3, F3, M3, E5, C4 ● **Temperaments:** R, T ● **Physical:** Stg=L; Const: R, H, I Freq: N Occas: S, K, O, E, G, A, X ● **Work Env:** Noise=L; Const: A ● **Salary:** 1 ● **Outlook:** 2

GOE: 06.02.08
Machine Work, Stone, Glass & Clay

EYEGLASS-LENS CUTTER (optical goods) ● DOT #716.682-010 ● OES: 92940 ● Alternate titles: LENS CUTTER. Sets up and operates bench-mounted cutting machine to cut eyeglass lenses to specified size and shape: Selects metal pattern according to prescription specifications and mounts pattern in spring clamp of cutting machine. Sets control dial for specified lens diameter plus allowance for edge grinding. Aligns center and axis marks on lens with markings on pad of cutting machine and lowers cushioned pressure arm of machine which holds lens in position. Lowers cutting arm over lens and turns crank which rotates lens under cutting wheel to determine if machine settings are correct. Presses cutting arm down to hold cutting wheel against lens and turns crank to cut lens. Removes lens from machine and chips excess material from lens edges, using chipping pliers. Routes cut lenses to edging department. ● **GED:** R3, M2, L2 ● **SVP:** 1-3 mos ● **Academic:** Ed=N, Eng=N ● **Work Field:** 054 ● **MPSMS:** 605 ● **Aptitudes:** G3, V4, N4, S3, P3, Q5, K3, F3, M3, E5, C5 ● **Temperaments:** R, T ● **Physical:** Stg=L; Freq: R, H, I, N Occas: D, A ● **Work Env:** Noise=N; ● **Salary:** 2 ● **Outlook:** 3

PRECISION-LENS GRINDER (optical goods) ● DOT #716.382-018 ● OES: 89917 ● Alternate titles: LENS GRINDER; OPTICAL TECHNICIAN. Sets up and operates grinding and polishing machines to make lenses, optical flats, and other precision optical elements for optical instruments and ophthalmic goods, such as telescopes, aerial cameras, military optical systems, and eyeglasses: Operates machine to rough-grind blanks of optical glass to approximate size and shape or manually positions and turns blanks against grinding wheel or lap I. Blocks optical element in plaster or other compound. Mounts blocked element in machine and operates machine to oscillate and rotate element against abrasive to fine-grind element to final size and shape. Periodically stops machine to inspect and measure elements for accuracy and degree of completion. Polishes surfaces, using lens-polishing machine [PRECISION-LENS POLISHER (optical goods) 716.682-018]. May cement lens elements together to obtain corrected lens assemblies. May mount optical elements in holders or adapters for use in instruments. May be designated according to type of lens ground as Eyeglass-Lens Grinder (optical goods); Instrument-Lens Grinder (optical goods); Multifocal-Button Grinder (optical goods). ● **GED:** R4, M3, L4 ● **SVP:** 2-4 yrs ● **Academic:** Ed=N, Eng=S ● **Work Field:** 051 ● **MPSMS:** 603, 605 ● **Aptitudes:** G3, V3, N3, S2, P3, Q4, K2, F3, M3, E5, C5 ● **Temperaments:** J, T ● **Physical:** Stg=L; Const: H, I Freq: N, D Occas: R ● **Work Env:** Noise=N; ● **Salary:** 3 ● **Outlook:** 3

GOE: 06.02.09
Machine Work, Assorted Materials

AUTOMATED CUTTING MACHINE OPERATOR (aircraft mfg.) ● DOT #699.362-010 ● OES: 91502 ● Sets up and operates automated cutting machine to cut assorted materials, such as graphite, bleeder and breather cloth, and fiberglass, used in manufacturing composite (fiber reinforced plastic) aircraft parts and assemblies: Reads cutting requests to determine job specifications, such as part identification number, type and quantity of material required, and cutting instructions. Mounts material onto machine fixture or dispensing device, manually or using overhead crane and handtools. Pulls specified length of material over machine cutting table and cuts material, using knife. Positions material on machine cutting table, following blueprints, sketches, and other specifications, using measuring instruments. Pulls and positions additional plies of material onto cutting table. Positions cutter above material plies in specified location. Loads machine control media or enters commands in computer control console to retrieve preprogrammed cutting instructions. Enters commands to activate vacuum that secures materials to table, identify cutter location coordinates, and start machine. Monitors operation of cutting machine to detect malfunctions and informs supervisor or programmer of problem. Removes cut plies from table, marks part identification on plies, and bags and labels cut material for subsequent production use. Sets up and operates machine to cut test pattern from sample material, and obtains approval of test pattern by quality control, programming, or other authorized personnel prior to cutting production materials. Removes and replaces broken or worn blades, using handtools. ● **GED:** R3, M2, L3 ● **SVP:** 3-6 mos ● **Academic:** Ed=N, Eng=S ● **Work Field:** 054 ● **MPSMS:** 592 ● **Aptitudes:** G3, V3, N4, S3, P3, Q4, K4, F4, M4, E5, C5 ● **Temperaments:** T ● **Physical:** Stg=L; Freq: R, H, N, D Occas: I, T, G ● **Work Env:** Noise=N; ● **Salary:** 3 ● **Outlook:** 3

CLOTH PRINTER (any industry) ● DOT #652.382-010 ● OES: 92599 ● Alternate titles: PRINTER; PRINTING-MACHINE OPERATOR. Sets up and operates machine to print designs on materials, such as cloth, fiberglass, plastic sheeting, coated felt, or oilcloth: Turns handwheel to set pressure on printing rollers, according to specifications. Turns screws to align register marks on printing rollers with register marks on machine, using allen wrench. Sharpens doctor blade, using file and oilstone, and verifies evenness of blade, using straightedge. Aligns doctor blade against printing roller, using handtools. Dips color from tubs into color boxes to supply printing rollers. Scans cloth leaving machine for printing defects, such as smudges, variations in color shades, and designs that are out of register (alignment). Realigns printing rollers and adjusts position of blanket or back gray cloth to absorb excess color from printing rollers. Records yardage of cloth printed. Coordinates printing activities with activities of workers who feed and doff machine and aid in setting up and cleaning machine. May notify COLORIST (profess. & kin.) 022.161-014 when color shade varies from specifications. May mix own colors. May mount printing rollers on machine for change of pattern [PRINTING-ROLLER HANDLER (textile) 652.385-010]. May position knives specified distance from edge of plastic material to trim excess material from edges. When printing samples of new patterns and novelty designs, is designated Novelty-Printing-Machine Operator (textile) or Proofing-Machine Operator (print. & pub.). May set up and operate cloth printing machine utilizing caustic soda paste instead of color paste to print designs on cloth which shrink to form plisse and be designated Plisse-Machine Operator (textile). ● **GED:** R4, M1, L3 ● **SVP:** 2-4 yrs ● **Academic:** Ed=N, Eng=S ● **Work Field:** 191 ● **MPSMS:** 420, 434 ● **Aptitudes:** G3, V4, N4, S3, P2, Q4, K3, F3, M3, E5, C2 ● **Temperaments:** J, T ● **Physical:** Stg=M; Freq: R, H, I, N, F, X Occas: S, K, O, E, G, D, A ● **Work Env:** Noise=L; Freq: H, A ● **Salary:** 2 ● **Outlook:** 2

CUTTER OPERATOR (any industry) ● DOT #699.682-018 ● OES: 92940 ● Alternate titles: SHEETER OPERATOR; SLITTER SHEETER OPERATOR. Sets up and operates cutting machine equipped with rotary or reciprocating blades to cut rolls of material, such as cloth, paper, paperboard, cellophane, or plastic into sheets, according to specifications: Reads work order to determine dimensions of sheets to be cut. Inserts shaft into core of one or more rolls and raises and positions roll or rolls on cutter rack, using hoist. Threads ends of material through feed rollers, under or across cutting blades, and aligns material against machine guides. Turns rheostat or handwheel to adjust tension of material and to synchronize timing of cutting blades with rate of material feed to regulate length and width of cut. Starts machine and verifies size of cut material, using rule, or notes accuracy of knife cut on spots of premarked paper. Readjusts machine to ensure specified dimensions of sheet. Starts counting device, conveyor belt, or automatic take off table, or raises platform (bearing pallet) on machines equipped with these devices. Observes operation of machine to detect malfunctions, such as jamming, wrinkling, or tearing of material. Stops machine to make required adjustments. Replaces worn cutting blades, using handtools. May oversee duties of assistant operator. May operate machine equipped with electronic eye to control timing of cutting blades and be designated Spot Cutter (any industry). May be designated according to material cut as Cellophane Sheeter (any industry); Foil Cutter (electron. comp.); Paperboard Sheeter (paper products); Paper Sheeter (any industry); or according to purpose for which material is cut as Envelope Cutter (paper products); Liner Sheeter (any industry); Tag-And-Label Cutter (print. & pub.); Wrapper Sheeter (any industry). ● **GED:** R3, M2, L2 ● **SVP:** 6 mos-1 yr ● **Academic:** Ed=N, Eng=N ● **Work Field:** 054 ● **MPSMS:** 420, 470, 492 ● **Aptitudes:** G3, V4, N4, S4, P4, Q4, K4, F4, M3, E4, C5 ● **Temperaments:** T ● **Physical:** Stg=M; Freq: R, H, I, N, D, A Occas: S ● **Work Env:** Noise=L; Freq: M ● **Salary:** 3 ● **Outlook:** 2

DIE CUTTER (any industry) ● DOT #699.682-022 ● OES: 92940 ● Alternate titles: BEAM-MACHINE OPERATOR; CLICKER; CLICKER OPERATOR; CLICKING-MACHINE OPERATOR; DIE-PRESS OPERATOR; DINKING-MACHINE OPERATOR; POWER-PRESS OPERATOR. Operates machine to cut out parts of specified size and shape from materials, such as cardboard, cloth, leather, mica, paper, plastic, or rubber: Places single or multiple layers of material on bed of machine. Turns handwheel to raise or lower head of machine (ram) according to thickness of material or depth of die. Positions one or more cutting dies on material or clamps dies to head of machine and positions material under dies to ensure maximum utilization of material. Depresses pedal or moves lever to activate ram that forces die through material. Removes cut parts from die or bed of machine. Measures parts with rule or compares parts with standard to verify conformance to specifications. Stacks parts in storage area according to size and shape. May sharpen cutting edges of dies, using file or hone. When operating machine to trim hat brims, is designated Rounding-Machine Operator (hat & cap). May be designated according to type of die used as Adjustable-Die Cutter (paper goods); Solid-Die Cutter (paper goods); or according to part cut as Sole-Leather-Cutting-Machine Operator (boot & shoe); Toppiece Cutter (boot & shoe); Trimming Cutter (garment). May be designated: Beam-Press Operator (rubber goods); Box-Toe Cutter (boot & shoe); Brim Cutter (hat & cap); Buckram Cutter (boot & shoe; hat & cap; leather prod.); Cap-Parts Cutter (hat & cap); Double Cutter (boot & shoe); Glove-Parts Cutter (glove & mit.); Handbag-Parts Cutter (leather prod.); Hat-Parts Cutter (leather prod.); Heel-Lift-Beam Cutter (boot & shoe); Helmet-Hat-Brim Cutter (hat & cap); Insole Cutter, Machine (boot & shoe); Label Cutter (garment); Leather-Novelty-Parts Cutter (leather prod.); Lining Cutter, Machine (boot & shoe); Outsole Cutter, Machine (boot & shoe); Shoe-Parts Cutter (boot & shoe); Silk-Lining Cutter, Machine (boot & shoe; hat & cap; leather prod.); Single-Beam Clicker (boot & shoe; hat & cap; leather prod.); Sole-Cutting-Machine Operator (boot & shoe); Top-Lift Cutter (boot & shoe); Trimming Cutter, Machine (boot & shoe); Twin-Beam Clicker (boot & shoe; hat & cap; leather prod.); Upper Cutter, Machine (boot & shoe). ● **GED:** R3, M2, L3 ● **SVP:** 3-6 mos ● **Academic:** Ed=N, Eng=S ● **Work Field:** 134, 054 ● **MPSMS:** 420, 470, 519 ● **Aptitudes:** G3, V4, N4, S4, P3, Q4, K3, F4, M3, E4, C4 ● **Temperaments:** R, T ● **Physical:** Stg=M; Freq: R, H, I, N, D Occas: O, E, X ● **Work Env:** Noise=L; ● **Salary:** 3 ● **Outlook:** 2

DYNAMITE-PACKING-MACHINE OPERATOR (chemical) ● DOT #692.662-010 ● OES: 92999 ● Sets up and operates machine to pack dynamite into paper cartridge shells to form sticks: Installs and adjusts tamping sticks and nipple plates in packing machine according to diameter and length of cartridges to be packed, using nonsparking handtools. Starts machine, directs DYNAMITE-PACKING-MACHINE FEEDER (chemical) to fill powder hopper with dynamite, and fills shuttle board (cartridge forming block) with paper cartridge shells. Secures shuttle board in filling position on machine, and scoops dynamite from hopper into box above tamping sticks. Lifts shuttle board of filled cartridges from machine and tends crimping press to finish ends, or passes filled cartridges to DYNAMITE-CARTRIDGE CRIMPER (chemical). ● **GED:** R3, M2, L3 ● **SVP:** 6 mos-1 yr ● **Academic:** Ed=N, Eng=S ● **Work Field:** 041 ● **MPSMS:** 499 ● **Aptitudes:** G3, V4, N4, S3, P3, Q4, K3, F4, M3, E5, C4 ● **Temperaments:** J, S, T ● **Physical:** Stg=M; Freq: S, O, R, H, I, E, D, A Occas: T, G, N, X ● **Work Env:** Noise=L; Occas: A, M, T ● **Salary:** 4 ● **Outlook:** 2

FLUID JET CUTTER OPERATOR (aircraft mfg.) ● DOT #699.382-010 ● OES: 92940 ● Sets up and operates high-speed water jet cutter to cut and trim parts and materials from assorted materials according to specifications: Reads work order, blueprints, and specifications to determine machine setup, type of material or part, quantity, and finish dimensions. Measures and marks cutting and trimming lines on material or part, using measuring instruments, scriber, or marking pen, or mounts material or part in cutting or trimming fixture. Installs and aligns machine accessories, such as cutting tips, work positioner, plates, fixtures, and shields, using handtools and measuring instruments, or enters coordinate information into computer control panel, using teach pendant. Manipulates machine controls, such as buttons, switches, dials, levers, and pedals, to regulate and adjust cutting speed and flow of fluid. Cuts and trims parts by manually moving part or material under stream of fluid along cutting lines, controlling movement of part secured in fixture or on work positioner, or entering commands to retrieve and start preprogrammed cutting or trimming instructions to cut materials mounted on machine bed. Observes displays, cutting or trimming process, and listens to sound of machines to detect malfunctions. Replaces worn or damaged machine parts, such as nozzles, tips, and washers. Measures dimensions of finished part, using measuring instruments, such as micrometers, calipers, and dial indicators, or check fixture. Cleans machines and work area. May scoop or pour abrasive particles into hopper of machine. May trim, sand, and drill parts, using shop equipment. May operate automated cutter and be designated Abrasive Water Jet Cutter Operator (aircraft mfg.); or operate manual cutter and be designated Water Router Operator (aircraft mfg.). ● **GED:** R3, M2, L3 ● **SVP:** 6 mos-1 yr ● **Academic:** Ed=N, Eng=S ● **Work Field:** 051 ● **MPSMS:** 592 ● **Aptitudes:** G3, V3, N4, S3, P3, Q4, K3, F3, M3, E4, C5 ● **Temperaments:** T ● **Physical:** Stg=M; Freq: R, H, I, N, D Occas: S, E, G, A ● **Work Env:** Noise=L; Freq: M ● **Salary:** 3 ● **Outlook:** 3

NUMERICAL-CONTROL DRILL OPERATOR, PRINTED CIRCUIT BOARDS (electron. comp.) ● DOT #606.382-018 ● OES: 91502 ● Sets up and operates numerical-control drilling machine to drill holes into printed circuit boards (PCB's): Reviews setup instructions and specifications. Loads control media containing programmed commands into control console of machine or enters commands to retrieve programmed control data. Attaches depth collars to drill bits and measures bit depth, using depth gauge, to verify specified drill bit cutting depth. Measures drill bit sizes, using micrometer, and installs specified drill bits in tool magazine of machine. Positions and secures PCB's to indexing table of machine. Enters commands to activate machine that automatically aligns indexing table and printed circuit boards under spindle, selects drill bit, and drills holes of specified dimension, location, and sequence into PCB's. Monitors machine operation and display readouts to detect malfunctions. Compares display data to specifications and notifies supervisor of machine malfunctions. Inspects and measures drilled PCB's to verify conformance to specifications, using measuring devices, such as micrometer, plug gauges, and test board. Performs machine adjustments and maintenance, such as setting speed and feed rates, cleaning machine parts, and replacing worn or damaged drill bits, using handtools. ● **GED:** R3, M3, L3 ● **SVP:** 3-6 mos ● **Academic:** Ed=H, Eng=G ● **Work Field:** 053 ● **MPSMS:** 587 ● **Aptitudes:** G3, V3, N3, S3, P3, Q4, K4, F3, M3, E5, C5 ● **Temperaments:** J, T ● **Physical:** Stg=L; Freq: R, H, I, N, D Occas: E, A ● **Work Env:** Noise=L; ● **Salary:** 3 ● **Outlook:** 4

NUMERICAL-CONTROL ROUTER OPERATOR (aircraft mfg.) ● DOT #605.382-046 ● OES: 91502 ● Sets up and operates numerical control router machine to rout (cut) parts, such as individual printed circuit boards (PCB's) from printed circuit panels or metal workpieces from sheet metal stock: Reviews setup instructions and specifications. Loads control media into computer console or enters commands to retrieve programmed control data. Selects and installs specified cutting tools into machine spindle or magazine. Positions and secures materials onto indexing table of machine. Enters commands to activate machine that automatically aligns indexing table and panels or metal stock under tool spindle and routs or notches materials, according to programmed instructions. Monitors machine operation and display readouts to detect malfunction. Measures dimensions of finished parts to verify conformance to specifications, using precision measuring instruments. Notifies supervisor of machine malfunction or when parts do not conform to specifications. Cleans machine, using solvent, rag, and airhose. May perform maintenance and replace worn or damaged cutting tools, using handtools. ● **GED:** R3, M2, L2 ● **SVP:** 3-6 mos ● **Academic:** Ed=N, Eng=S ● **Work Field:** 055 ● **MPSMS:** 587, 592 ● **Aptitudes:** G3, V3, N4, S3, P4, Q4, K4, F3, M4, E5, C5 ● **Temperaments:** J, T ● **Physical:** Stg=M; Freq: R, H, I, N, D Occas: A ● **Work Env:** Noise=L; ● **Salary:** 3 ● **Outlook:** 4

ROBOTIC MACHINE OPERATOR (aircraft mfg.) ● DOT #606.382-026 ● OES: 91502 ● Alternate titles: INDUSTRIAL ROBOT OPERATOR. Sets up and operates industrial robot to drill, countersink, and counterbore metallic and nonmetallic workpieces used to manufacture aircraft parts or tooling, according to specifications and preprogrammed machine control instructions: Reads work order and specifications to determine prescribed setup and operation. Mounts and positions workpiece on locating pins of holding fixture adjacent to robot, manually or using hoist, and aligns and secures workpiece on holding fixture, using template, bolts, handtools, and power tools. Installs specified type and size drill bits in end effectors and places end effectors in holding station adjacent to robot. Loads cassette tape of machine instructions into machine controller or enters commands to retrieve preprogrammed instructions from mainframe computer. Pushes button or enters commands to activate robot that automatically retrieves and secures designated end effector on robot arm and positions arm for drilling. Operates robot to drill holes in test specimen and measures holes for conformance to specifications, using measuring instruments. Obtains written approval of test specimen from quality control inspector. Enters commands to start robot, observes robotic operation, and monitors screen of machine controller for malfunctions and error messages. Changes worn drill bits or adjusts machine according to error message instructions. Inspects finished workpiece for conformance to specifications. Notifies supervisor of numerical control programming problems. Cleans parts, tools, and fixtures, using solvents and rags. May drill holes in parts manually, using drill motor. May perform machine maintenance. May set up and operate robot to perform additional machine operations, such as sealing and fastener installation, to join component parts into complete assembly and be designated Assembly Line Robot Operator (aircraft mfg.). ● **GED:** R3, M2, L3 ● **SVP:** 6 mos-1 yr ● **Academic:** Ed=N, Eng=G ● **Work Field:** 053 ● **MPSMS:** 592 ● **Aptitudes:** G3, V3, N4, S3, P3, Q4, K4, F3, M3, E5, C5 ● **Temperaments:** T ● **Physical:** Stg=M; Freq: R, H, N, D Occas: C, S, O, I, E, G ● **Work Env:** Noise=L; Occas: A, M, T ● **Salary:** 5 ● **Outlook:** 4

WIRE-WRAPPING-MACHINE OPERATOR (electron. comp.) ● DOT #726.682-014 ● OES: 93908 ● Operates computer-controlled semiautomatic machine that wraps wires around electronic-pin connectors: Mounts connector panel on machine pallet that moves panel along programmed path, using wrench and screwdriver. Depresses specified button to start automatic programmed tape for pin sequence and observes panel lights that indicate size of wire prescribed in program. Selects and mounts specified wire on machine spindle. Threads wire through bit of wire-wrap gun, positions gun in support to align gun with pins on connector panel, and depresses trigger of wire-wrap gun to wrap wire on pins. Observes directional lights of machine to determine movement of pallet and gun support. Inspects wire-wrap of completed panels for tightness, neatness of fold, or broken wire. ● **GED:** R3, M3, L3 ● **SVP:** 2-30 days ● **Academic:** Ed=N, Eng=S ● **Work Field:** 163 ● **MPSMS:** 587 ● **Aptitudes:** G4, V4, N5, S3, P4, Q4, K4, F2, M3, E5, C5 ● **Temperaments:** R, T ● **Physical:** Stg=L; Freq: R, H, I, N, A ● **Work Env:** Noise=N; ● **Salary:** 3 ● **Outlook:** 3

GOE: 06.02.10
Equipment Operation, Metal Processing

COLD-MILL OPERATOR (steel & rel.) ● DOT #613.662-018 ● OES: 91399 ● Sets up and operates rolling mill to flatten, temper, and reduce gauge of steel strip, following rolling orders and using measuring instruments: Reads rolling order to determine setup and work sequence. Calculates draft (space between rolls) and roll speed for each mill stand to roll strip to specified dimensions and temper. Turns controls to adjust roll speed, draft, and tension of strip between reels of coiling mechanism. Installs guides, guards, and cooling equipment in stands, using handtools. Starts mill to roll test strip and adjusts roll screws, hydraulic sprays, and mill speeds. Moves controls to start production rolling of steel strip. Examines steel for surface defects, such as cracks and scratches. Verifies dimensions of steel for conformance to specifications, using micrometers, thickness gauges, and measuring tape. Directs other workers in changing rolls, operating mill equipment, removing coils, and banding and loading strip steel. May be designated according to type of mill operated as Reversing-Mill Roller (steel & rel.); Tandem-Mill Roller (steel & rel.). May operate mill to temper steel strip and be designated Temper-Mill Roller (steel & rel.). ● **GED:** R4, M3, L3 ● **SVP:** 2-4 yrs ● **Academic:** Ed=N, Eng=N ● **Work Field:** 135 ● **MPSMS:** 541 ● **Aptitudes:** G3, V3, N3, S3, P3, Q4, K3, F3, M3, E5, C5 ● **Temperaments:** J, T ● **Physical:** Stg=M; Freq: R, H, I, N, D Occas: T, G, A ● **Work Env:** Noise=L; Freq: U, O ● **Salary:** 3 ● **Outlook:** 2

HEAT TREATER I (heat treating) ● DOT #504.382-014 ● OES: 91932 ● Controls heat-treating furnaces, baths and quenching equipment to alter physical and chemical properties of metal objects, using specifications and methods of controlled heating and cooling, such as hardening, tempering, annealing, case-hardening, and normalizing: Determines temperature and time of heating cycle, and type and temperature of baths and quenching medium to attain specified hardness, toughness, and ductility of parts, using standard heat-treating charts, and utilizing knowledge of heat-treating methods, equipment, and properties of metals. Adjusts furnace controls and observes pyrometer to bring furnace to prescribed temperature. Loads parts into furnace. Removes parts after prescribed time and quenches parts in water, oil, brine, or other bath, or allows parts to cool in air. May test hardness of parts [HARDNESS INSPECTOR (heat treating)]. May set up and operate die-quenching machine to prevent parts from warping. May set up and operate electronic induction equipment to heat objects [INDUCTION-MACHINE SETTER (heat treating)]. May align warped fuel elements, containing radioactive uranium, using hydraulic ram straightener. ● **GED:** R4, M3, L3 ● **SVP:** 2-4 yrs ● **Academic:** Ed=N, Eng=S ● **Work Field:** 133 ● **MPSMS:** 540 ● **Aptitudes:** G3, V3, N3, S4, P3, Q4, K3, F4, M3, E5, C3 ● **Temperaments:** J, T, V ● **Physical:** Stg=M; Freq: R, H, I, N, D, X ● **Work Env:** Noise=L; Freq: H, A, O ● **Salary:** 2 ● **Outlook:** 3

SAND MIXER, MACHINE (foundry) ● DOT #570.682-018 ● OES: 92965 ● Alternate titles: SAND CONDITIONER, MACHINE; SAND MILL OPERATOR; SAND-SYSTEM OPERATOR. Operates machine to mix or recondition molding sand: Weighs out specified amounts of ingredients, such as sand, sea coal, and bonding agents, and shovels them into machine or automatic hopper. Sets dials for specified amounts of water, core oil, and other ingredients that are automatically measured and fed into machine. Turns dials to time mixing cycle of machine. Removes sample of sand and feels sand for consistency. Adjusts controls and adds ingredients to vary mixture according to sampling. May be designated according to purpose for which sand is to be used as Sand-Mill Operator, Core-Sand (foundry); Sand-Mill Operator, Facing-Sand (foundry); Sand-Mill Operator, Molding-Sand (foundry). ● **GED:** R3, M1, L1 ● **SVP:** 3-6 mos ● **Academic:** Ed=N, Eng=N ● **Work Field:** 143 ● **MPSMS:** 345 ● **Aptitudes:** G3, V4, N4, S4, P3, Q4, K4, F4, M3, E5, C5 ● **Temperaments:** J, T ● **Physical:** Stg=M; Freq: R, H Occas: S, I, E, N, D, A ● **Work Env:** Noise=L; ● **Salary:** 3 ● **Outlook:** 2

TEMPERER (heat treating) ● DOT #504.682-026 ● OES: 91932 ● Controls furnace to reheat previously quenched and hardened metal objects, and quenches them in brine, water, oil, or molten lead to remove quenching strains and brittleness and to impart toughness to metal. ● **GED:** R3, M3, L2 ● **SVP:** 3-6 mos ● **Academic:** Ed=N, Eng=N ● **Work Field:** 133 ● **MPSMS:** 540 ● **Aptitudes:** G3, V4, N4, S4, P3, Q4, K3, F4, M3, E5, C3 ● **Temperaments:** J, R, T ● **Physical:** Stg=M; Freq: R, H, N Occas: I ● **Work Env:** Noise=L; Freq: H, A, O ● **Salary:** 2 ● **Outlook:** 3

GOE: 06.02.11
Equipment Operation, Chemical Processing

WASTE-TREATMENT OPERATOR (chemical) ● DOT #955.382-014 ● OES: 95002 ● Controls heat exchange unit, pumps, compressors, and related equipment to decontaminate, neutralize, and dispose of radioactive waste liquids collected from chemical processing operations: Removes sample of liquid from collection tank, using pipette. Pours sample into dish and bakes dish under heat lamp to evaporate water, leaving radioactive residue. Tests residue with Geiger counter and compares reading with chart to determine whether radioactivity level is within prescribed safety limits. Determines degree of acidity or alkalinity in liquid, using pH meter, and adds acid or alkali to neutralize liquid. Starts pump and admits waste liquid into sewer for disposal or into storage tanks for evaporation, according to degree of radioactivity. Transfers radioactive waste liquid from storage tanks to heat exchange unit. Operates heat evaporation system to reduce volume of liquid, and observes gauges and adjusts controls during process to maintain steam pressure, temperature, and liquid at specified levels. Starts compressed-air pump to blow slurry on bottom of evaporator into lead container for permanent storage. Records data, such as number of gallons of waste pumped into sewer system or storage tanks, or reduced by heat exchange unit, and radioactivity levels. May monitor panelboard to control operation of recovery systems that store or dispose of radioactive waste and be designated Nuclear-Waste-Process Operator (any industry). ● **GED:** R4, M4, L4 ● **SVP:** 1-2 yrs ● **Academic:** Ed=H, Eng=S ● **Work Field:** 147, 014 ● **MPSMS:** 499, 870 ● **Aptitudes:** G3, V3, N3, S4, P3, Q3, K3, F4, M3, E4, C4 ● **Temperaments:** J, T ● **Physical:** Stg=L; Freq: R, H, I, N Occas: S, K, O, D, X ● **Work Env:** Noise=L; Freq: O ● **Salary:** 4 ● **Outlook:** 3

GOE: 06.02.13
Equipment Operation, Rubber, Plastics & Glass Processing

BLANKMAKER (glass mfg.) ● DOT #579.382-022 ● OES: 92999 ● Operates glass lathe to form glass tubes into glass blanks used in fabrication of laser light conductors: Reads work orders and technical manuals to determine lathe setup procedures, and pushes buttons and turns knobs to adjust lathe gas-injection and temperature controls. Locks glass tube into spindle chuck, using wrench. Trues and flares glass tube, using lathe carriage burner, ruler, and calipers. Attaches chemical spray nozzle to glass tube to coat interior of tube with gases, and inserts auger into tube to remove chemical residue. Lowers and locks spindle shield to form dust-free chamber. Presses keys on keyboard to transmit production specifications to computer and to transfer lathe operation from manual to automatic control for duration of blankmaking process. Observes lathe dials and gauges, computer display panel, and color of flame on lathe carriage burner to verify adherence to manufacturing specifications. Calculates data, such as blank weights, diameters, and densities, using calculator, and enters data on record sheet. Repairs lathe, using wrenches, pliers, and screwdrivers to correct malfunctions. ● **GED:** R3, M3, L3 ● **SVP:** 1-2 yrs ● **Academic:** Ed=N, Eng=N ● **Work Field:** 147 ● **MPSMS:** 532 ● **Aptitudes:** G3, V3, N3, S3, P2, Q2, K3, F4, M4, E5, C3 ● **Temperaments:** T ● **Physical:** Stg=L; Freq: N Occas: S, R, H, I, A, X ● **Work Env:** Noise=N; ● **Salary:** 4 ● **Outlook:** 2

EXTRUDER OPERATOR (plastic prod.) ● DOT #557.382-010 ● OES: 91399 ● Alternate titles: STUFFER, VERTICAL HYDRAULIC; TUBER OPERATOR. Sets up and operates machine to extrude thermoplastic materials to form tubes, rods, and film according to specifications: Installs dies, machine screws, and sizing rings, using handtools. Couples hose to die holder to circulate steam, water, air, or oil to die. Weighs and mixes pelletized, granular, or powdered thermoplastic materials and coloring pigments in tumbling machine according to formula. Fills machine hopper with mixed materials, using conveyor auger, or stuffs rolls of plastic dough into machine cylinders. Starts machine and sets controls to regulate vacuum, air pressure, sizing rings, and temperature; and synchronizes speed of extrusion with pulling rolls. Examines extruded product for defects, such as wrinkles, bubbles, and splits. Measures extruded articles for conformance to specifications, using micrometers, calipers, and gauges; and adjusts speed and weight controls or turns hot and cold water, air, oil, or steam valves to obtain product of specified dimensions. Tests physical properties of product with acid-bath tester, burst tester, and impact tester. May reel extruded product into rolls of specified length and weight [EXTRUDER-OPERATOR HELPER (plastic prod.; plastic-synth.)]. ● **GED:** R3, M2, L2 ● **SVP:** 6 mos-1 yr ● **Academic:** Ed=N, Eng=N ● **Work Field:** 135 ● **MPSMS:** 492 ● **Aptitudes:** G3, V4, N4, S3, P3, Q4, K3, F3, M3, E5, C4 ● **Temperaments:** J, T ● **Physical:** Stg=M; Freq: R, H, N Occas: I, E, X ● **Work Env:** Noise=L; Occas: H, U ● **Salary:** 3 ● **Outlook:** 2

MIXING-MACHINE OPERATOR (any industry) ● DOT #550.382-022 ● OES: 92965 ● Operates mixing machine to blend ingredients into compounds for processing: Loads ingredients into mixing machine hopper from conveyor, scales, or handtrucks, or directs other workers in performing this task. Starts machine and adjusts valves to admit steam or cooling fluids to steam jacket or devices in mixing chamber to aid in blending and densifying mixture. Operates machine until mixture reaches desired consistency, and turns lever to unload mixture into container, conveyor, or mill for sheeting. May operate auxiliary equipment to break up, grind, dry mix, or otherwise prepare mixture for final processing. May tend automatic mixing machine. May be designated according to trade name of machine. ● **GED:** R3, M2, L2 ● **SVP:** 3-6 mos ● **Academic:** Ed=N, Eng=N ● **Work Field:** 143 ● **MPSMS:** 492, 510 ● **Aptitudes:** G3, V3, N4, S4, P3, Q4, K4, F4, M3, E5, C5 ● **Temperaments:** J ● **Physical:** Stg=H; Freq: R, H Occas: I, G, N ● **Work Env:** Noise=L; Freq: A ● **Salary:** 2 ● **Outlook:** 2

GOE: 06.02.15
Equipment Operation, Food Processing

BAKER (bakery products) ● DOT #526.381-010 ● OES: 89805 ● Mixes and bakes ingredients according to recipes to produce breads, pastries, and other baked goods: Measures flour, sugar, shortening, and other ingredients to prepare batters, doughs, fillings, and icings, using scale and graduated containers [DOUGH MIXER (bakery products) 520.685-234]. Dumps ingredients into mixing-machine bowl or steam kettle to mix or cook ingredients according to specifications. Rolls, cuts, and shapes dough to form sweet rolls, piecrust, tarts, cookies, and related products preparatory to baking. Places dough in pans, molds, or on sheets and bakes in oven or on grill. Observes color of products being baked and turns thermostat or other controls to adjust oven temperature. Applies glaze, icing, or other topping to baked goods, using spatula or brush. May specialize in baking one type of product, such as breads, rolls, pies, or cakes. May decorate cakes [CAKE DECORATOR (bakery products) 524.381-010]. May develop new recipes for cakes and icings. ● **GED:** R3, M2, L2 ● **SVP:** 2-4 yrs ● **Academic:** Ed=N, Eng=N ● **Work Field:** 146 ● **MPSMS:** 384 ● **Aptitudes:** G3, V3, N3, S4, P3, Q4, K3, F3, M3, E5, C3 ● **Temperaments:** J, T, V ● **Physical:** Stg=H; Freq: R, H, I, E, N Occas: S, M, A, X ● **Work Env:** Noise=Q; ● **Salary:** 2 ● **Outlook:** 3

BUTTERMAKER (dairy products) ● DOT #529.362-010 ● OES: 92962 ● Controls equipment to make grades of butter by either of following methods: (1) Butter churn method: Connects sanitary pipe between cream storage vat and churn. Starts pump to convey sterile solution through equipment and to admit measured amount of pasteurized cream into churn, and starts churn. Observes separation of buttermilk from butter and pumps buttermilk from churn. Opens churn and sprays butter with chlorinated water to remove residue buttermilk. Compares butter with color chart and adds coloring to meet specifications. Tests butter for moisture, salt content, and consistency, using testing apparatus, and achieves specified consistency by adding or removing water. Examines, smells, and tastes butter to grade it according to prescribed standard. (2) Butter chilling method: Pasteurizes and separates cream to obtain butter oil, and tests butter oil in standardizing vat for butter fat, moisture, salt content, and acidity, using testing apparatus. Adds water, alkali, and coloring to butter oil to achieve specified grade, and starts agitator to mix ingredients. Turns valves and observes gauges to regulate temperature and flow of water, refrigerant, and butter oil through chilling vat. Smells, tastes, and feels sample to grade butter emerging from chilling vat. May be designated according to equipment operated as Butter-Chilling Equipment Operator (dairy products); Butter Churner (dairy products). ● **GED:** R3, M3, L2 ● **SVP:** 1-2 yrs ● **Academic:** Ed=N, Eng=N ● **Work Field:** 146 ● **MPSMS:** 383 ● **Aptitudes:** G3, V3, N3, S4, P4, Q4, K3, F3, M3, E5, C3 ● **Temperaments:** J ● **Physical:** Stg=H; Freq: S, O, R, H, I, E, M, N, D, A, X ● **Work Env:** Noise=L; Occas: C, U ● **Salary:** 3 ● **Outlook:** 2

CENTER-MACHINE OPERATOR (sugar & conf.) ● DOT #520.682-014 ● OES: 92970 ● Alternate titles: CASTING-MACHINE OPERATOR; EXTRUDING-MACHINE OPERATOR. Sets up and operates machine that extrudes soft candy, such as fondant, to form centers of specified size and shape for bonbons and chocolates: Inserts die plate in machine and tightens thumbscrews to secure plate. Examines and feels candy for specified consistency. Dumps candy into machine hopper. Starts machine that automatically feeds candy through openings in die plate and cuts off and deposits formed pieces on conveyor, or moves control to force candy through openings in die plate and moves wires that cut extruded candy to specified thickness. Weighs formed pieces at random to determine adherence to specifications. Adjusts wire or knife that cuts extruded candy to specified dimensions. When making cream centers to be coated with chocolate, may synchronize speed of center machine with enrobing machine. May be designated by product formed as Fondant-Puff Maker (sugar & conf.); Marshmallow Runner (sugar & conf.). ● **GED:** R3, M2, L2 ● **SVP:** 6 mos-1 yr ● **Academic:** Ed=N, Eng=N ● **Work Field:** 135 ● **MPSMS:** 393 ● **Aptitudes:** G3, V3, N3, S3, P3, Q4, K3, F4, M3, E5, C5 ● **Temperaments:** J, T ● **Physical:** Stg=M; Freq: R, H, I, E, N, D ● **Work Env:** Noise=N; ● **Salary:** 2 ● **Outlook:** 2

CHOCOLATE-PRODUCTION-MACHINE OPERATOR (sugar & conf.) ● DOT #529.382-014 ● OES: 92999 ● Alternate titles: GENERAL UTILITY MACHINE OPERATOR. Operates any of following machines and equipment to relieve regular operators engaged in processing cocoa beans into chocolate liquor and in producing cocoa powder and sweet chocolate, according to formula: Controls roaster that roasts cocoa beans to develop specified color and flavor and reduces moisture content of beans [COCOA-BEAN ROASTER (sugar & conf.) I; COCOA-BEAN ROASTER (sugar & conf.) II]. Tends mill to grind nibs (cracked cocoa beans) into liquid chocolate of specified fineness [LIQUOR-GRINDING-MILL OPERATOR (sugar & conf.)]. Tends hydraulic press to extract cocoa butter from chocolate liquor, and operates cocoa room machinery and equipment to grind and pulverize cocoa cakes into cocoa powder [COCOA-PRESS OPERATOR (sugar & conf.); COCOA-ROOM OPERATOR (sugar & conf.)]. Mixes ingredients, such as chocolate liquor, sugar, and powdered milk to make sweet chocolate [MIXER OPERATOR (sugar & conf.)]. Operates refining machine to grind chocolate paste to specified consistency [REFINING-MACHINE OPERATOR (sugar & conf.)]. Operates tempering equipment to control temperature of chocolate in cooling process before molding [CHOCOLATE TEMPERER (bakery products; grain-feed mills)]. May tend molding machines, pressure cookers, and dryers. May assist in supervising and training production line workers. ● **GED:** R4, M3, L3 ● **SVP:** 1-2 yrs ● **Academic:** Ed=N, Eng=S ● **Work Field:** 146 ● **MPSMS:** 393 ● **Aptitudes:** G3, V3, N3, S4, P4, Q4, K3, F4, M3, E5, C4 ● **Temperaments:** T, V ● **Physical:** Stg=H; Freq: R, H Occas: S, O, N, A, X ● **Work Env:** Noise=L; Occas: H ● **Salary:** 2 ● **Outlook:** 2

COFFEE ROASTER (food prep., nec) ● DOT #523.682-014 ● OES: 92910 ● Controls gas fired roasters to remove moisture from coffee beans: Weighs batch of coffee beans in scale-hopper, and opens chute to allow beans to flow into roasting oven. Observes thermometer and adjusts controls to maintain required temperature. Compares color of roasting beans in oven with standard to estimate roasting time. Opens discharge gate to dump roasted beans into cooling tray. Starts machine

that blows air through beans to cool them. Records amounts, types, and blends of coffee beans roasted. ● **GED:** R3, M2, L2 ● **SVP:** 6 mos-1 yr ● **Academic:** Ed=N, Eng=N ● **Work Field:** 141, 212 ● **MPSMS:** 391 ● **Aptitudes:** G3, V3, N4, S4, P4, Q4, K3, F4, M4, E4, C3 ● **Temperaments:** J ● **Physical:** Stg=L; Freq: R, H, I, N, X ● **Work Env:** Noise=L; ● **Salary:** 1 ● **Outlook:** 3

CRACKER-AND-COOKIE-MACHINE OPERATOR (bakery products) ● DOT #520.682-034 ● OES: 92970 ● Alternate titles: MACHINE CAPTAIN. Operates machine to roll dough into sheets and to form crackers or cookies, preparatory to baking: Turns crank to adjust space between rollers. Selects and installs stamping or extruding die unit in machine, using wrench. Pushes trough of dough to machine and shovels dough into hopper or dumps it into hopper, using hoist. Starts machine and inserts end of dough from hopper into roller. Observes operation and removes malformed cookies or crackers. Verifies weight of samples against standards, using balance scale. Scoops such ingredients as salt, sugar, and nuts into hoppers located along conveyor belt. May be designated according to machine operated as Bar-Machine Operator (bakery products); Drop-Machine Operator (bakery products); Rotary-Machine Operator (bakery products); or according to product formed as Fig-Bar-Machine Operator (bakery products); Matzo-Forming-Machine Operator (bakery products). ● **GED:** R3, M2, L2 ● **SVP:** 6 mos-1 yr ● **Academic:** Ed=N, Eng=N ● **Work Field:** 146 ● **MPSMS:** 384 ● **Aptitudes:** G3, V4, N4, S3, P3, Q4, K3, F3, M3, E5, C5 ● **Temperaments:** J, T ● **Physical:** Stg=M; Freq: R, H, I, N, D Occas: E ● **Work Env:** Noise=L; ● **Salary:** 3 ● **Outlook:** 2

DAIRY-PROCESSING-EQUIPMENT OPERATOR (dairy products) ● DOT #529.382-018 ● OES: 92932 ● Operates continuous flow or vat-type equipment to process milk, cream, and other dairy products, following specified methods and formulas: Connects pipes between vats and processing equipment. Assembles fittings, valves, bowls, plates, disks, impeller shaft, and other parts to equipment with wrench to prepare for operation. Turns valves to pump sterilizing solution and rinse water through pipes and equipment and spray vats with atomizer. Starts pumps and equipment, observes temperature and pressure gauges, and opens valves on continuous flow equipment to force milk through centrifuge to separate cream from milk, through homogenizer to produce specified emulsion, and through filter to remove sediment. Turns valves to admit steam and water into pipes to pasteurize milk and to circulate refrigerant through coils to cool milk. Starts pump and agitator, observes pressure and temperature gauges, and opens valves on vat equipment to fill, stir, and steam-heat milk in vat. Pumps or pours specified amounts of liquid or powder ingredients, such as skim milk, lactic culture, stabilizer, neutralizer, and vitamins into vat to make dairy products, such as buttermilk, chocolate milk, or ice cream mix. Tests product for acidity at various stages of processing. Records specified time, temperature, pressure, and volume readings. May be designated according to process performed as Byproducts Maker (dairy products); Clarifier Operator (dairy products); Cooler Operator (dairy products); Homogenizer Operator (dairy products); Mix Maker (dairy products); Pasteurizer Operator (dairy products); Separator Operator (dairy products). May be required to hold license from State Board of Health or local government unit. ● **GED:** R4, M2, L3 ● **SVP:** 6 mos-1 yr ● **Academic:** Ed=N, Eng=S ● **Work Field:** 146 ● **MPSMS:** 383 ● **Aptitudes:** G3, V3, N4, S3, P3, Q4, K3, F3, M3, E5, C4 ● **Temperaments:** J, T ● **Physical:** Stg=H; Freq: R, H Occas: C, B, S, O, N ● **Work Env:** Noise=L; Occas: U, A, M ● **Salary:** 3 ● **Outlook:** 2

DOUGH MIXER (bakery products) ● DOT #520.685-234 ● OES: 92965 ● Alternate titles: MIXING-MACHINE ATTENDANT. Tends machines and equipment that automatically mix ingredients to make straight and sponge (yeast) doughs according to formula: Moves controls and turns valves to adjust metering devices that weigh, measure, sift, and convey water, flour, and shortening into mixer, and that measure and dump yeast, vitamins, yeast food, sugar, salt, and other ingredients into mixing machine. Turns knobs or dials to set mixing cycle time and maintain temperature of dough. Starts machine. Feels dough for desired consistency. Positions wheeled dough trough in front of mixer, opens mixer door, and starts mixer to rotate blades and dumps dough into trough. Pushes troughs of sponge dough into room to ferment for specified time. Dumps raised sponge dough into mixer, using hoist, and adds ingredients to complete mixture. Records number of batches mixed. May weigh and measure ingredients which are manually fed into mixer. May dump all ingredients into mixer by hand. May be designated according to type of dough mixed as Bread-Dough Mixer (bakery products); Cookie Mixer (bakery products); Dog-Food Dough Mixer (bakery products); Doughnut-Dough Mixer (bakery products); Pastry Mixer (bakery products); Pie-Crust Mixer (bakery products). May be designated: Cracker-Dough Mixer (bakery products); Pretzel-Dough Mixer (bakery products); Sweet-Dough Mixer (bakery products). ● **GED:** R3, M3, L3 ● **SVP:** 6 mos-1 yr ● **Academic:** Ed=N, Eng=S ● **Work Field:** 143, 146 ● **MPSMS:** 384 ● **Aptitudes:** G3, V4, N3, S4, P4, Q3, K3, F4, M3, E5, C4 ● **Temperaments:** J, T ● **Physical:** Stg=H; Freq: R, H, I, E, N, D Occas: X ● **Work Env:** Noise=L; ● **Salary:** 3 ● **Outlook:** 2

DOUGHNUT-MACHINE OPERATOR (bakery products) ● DOT #526.682-022 ● OES: 92999 ● Alternate titles: CRULLER MAKER, MACHINE; DOUGHNUT-COOKING-MACHINE OPERATOR; FRIED-CAKE MAKER. Operates machine that shapes and fries doughnuts: Slides block of ejectors (cutters) into machine and tightens them, using wingnuts. Turns switch to heat frying tank to desired temperature. Mixes prepared ingredients with specified amount of water in mixing machine to form batter. Dumps batter into doughnut machine hopper, using chain hoist. Turns and adjusts valves to control air pressure for ejecting batter into frying tank and to regulate size of doughnuts, temperature and feed of grease, and speed of conveyor. Starts machine and observes color and verifies weight of doughnuts to ensure conformity to standards. Dismantles doughnut ejectors for cleaning. May melt and temper chocolate [CHOCOLATE TEMPERER (bakery products; grain-feed mills)]. ● **GED:** R3, M2, L3 ● **SVP:** 3-6 mos ● **Academic:** Ed=N, Eng=S ● **Work Field:** 146 ● **MPSMS:** 384 ● **Aptitudes:** G3, V4, N4, S4, P4, Q4, K4, F3, M3, E5, C4 ● **Temperaments:** J ● **Physical:** Stg=L; Freq: R, H Occas: I, N, A, X ● **Work Env:** Noise=Q; ● **Salary:** 2 ● **Outlook:** 3

DRIER OPERATOR (food prep., nec) ● DOT #523.362-014 ● OES: 92910 ● Controls equipment that dries macaroni according to laboratory specifications: Turns dials and opens steam valves on panelboard to regulate temperature, humidity, and drying time in preliminary, secondary, and final drying chambers, according to outside atmospheric conditions, specific product requirements, and drying stage. Enters chambers and feels macaroni to determine if product is drying according to specifications, relying upon knowledge and experience. Opens chamber hatch to admit cold air and adjusts controls to change drying speed at particular drying stages to comply with laboratory recommendation or to meet changing atmospheric conditions. Regulates temperature and humidity in pressroom to maintain required atmospheric conditions. Evaluates quality of dried macaroni on basis of color. ● **GED:** R4, M2, L3 ● **SVP:** 2-4 yrs ● **Academic:** Ed=N, Eng=S ● **Work Field:** 141 ● **MPSMS:** 397 ● **Aptitudes:** G3, V3, N3, S4, P4, Q4, K3, F4, M3, E5, C2 ● **Temperaments:** J, T ● **Physical:** Stg=L; Freq: R, H, I, E, X Occas: N ● **Work Env:** Noise=N; Freq: H, U ● **Salary:** 3 ● **Outlook:** 1

EXTRUDER OPERATOR (grain-feed mills) ● DOT #520.682-018 ● OES: 92999 ● Operates dough-mixing and -extruding press to produce cereal products in form of letters, pellets, or other shapes: Cleans and installs perforated metal disk, containing openings of various shapes, in mixer. Attaches blade, using wrench, that sweeps around disk, shearing off extruded dough as it is forced through holes. Moves controls to set temperature of water, start flow of flour, water, and other ingredients into mixer, and regulate pressure forcing dough through extrusion die to maintain specified moisture content, color, and consistency of dough. May operate extruding press only, when mixing is performed by another worker. May be designated by form of extruded product as Pellet Operator (grain-feed mills). ● **GED:** R3, M2, L2 ● **SVP:** 6 mos-1 yr ● **Academic:** Ed=N, Eng=N ● **Work Field:** 135, 143 ● **MPSMS:** 381 ● **Aptitudes:** G3, V4, N4, S3, P3, Q4, K4, F4, M3, E5, C4 ● **Temperaments:** J, T ● **Physical:** Stg=L; Freq: R, H, N, D, X Occas: I, E ● **Work Env:** Noise=V; ● **Salary:** 3 ● **Outlook:** 3

FREEZER OPERATOR (dairy products) ● DOT #529.482-010 ● OES: 92999 ● Alternate titles: FREEZER; ICE-CREAM FREEZER. Operates one or more continuous freezers and other equipment to freeze ice cream mix into semisolid consistency: Weighs or measures powder and liquid ingredients, such as color, flavoring, or fruit puree, using graduate, and dumps ingredients into flavor vat. Starts agitator to blend contents. Starts pumps and turns valves to force mix into freezer barrels, admit refrigerant into freezer coils, and inject air into mix. Starts beater, scraper, and expeller blades to mix contents with air and pre-

vent adherence of mixture to barrel walls. Observes ammeter and pressure gauge and adjusts controls to obtain specified freezing temperature, air pressure, and machine speed. Fills hopper of fruit feeder with candy bits, fruit, and nuts, using scoop, or pours syrups into holder of rippling pump. Sets controls according to freezer speed to feed or ripple ingredients evenly into ice cream expelled from freezer. Opens valve to transfer contents to filling machine that pumps ice cream into cartons, cups, and cones, or molds for pies, rolls, and tarts. Places novelty dies in filler head that separates flavors and forms center designs or rosettes in packaged product. Weighs package and adjusts freezer air valve or switch on filler head to obtain specified amount of product in each container. Assembles pipes, fittings, and equipment for operation, using wrench. Sprays equipment with sterilizing solution. ● **GED:** R3, M2, L2 ● **SVP:** 6 mos-1 yr ● **Academic:** Ed=N, Eng=N ● **Work Field:** 146 ● **MPSMS:** 383 ● **Aptitudes:** G3, V4, N4, S4, P4, Q4, K4, F4, M3, E4, C5 ● **Temperaments:** J, T ● **Physical:** Stg=L; Freq: R, H, N Occas: I ● **Work Env:** Noise=N; Occas: C ● **Salary:** 2 ● **Outlook:** 2

GRINDER OPERATOR (grain-feed mills) ● DOT #521.682-026 ● OES: 92965 ● Alternate titles: FEED MILLER; GRISTMILLER; MILL OPERATOR; ROLLER-MILL OPERATOR. Operates bank of roll grinders to grind grain into meal or flour: Opens and closes slides in spouts to route grain to various grinders and sifters. Turns wheels to adjust pressure of grinding rollers for each break (passage of grain between rollers), according to grain size and hardness, and adjusts feed chutes to regulate flow of grain to rollers. Inspects product and sifts out chaff to determine percentage of yield. Adjusts rollers to maintain maximum yield. Replaces worn grinding rollers, using handtools. May sift and bolt meal or flour. May clean and temper grain prior to grinding. May direct workers who drain and temper grain and bolt meal or flour. May be designated according to grain milled as Corn Miller (grain-feed mills). May operate burr mills instead of roll grinders to grind grain and be designated Burr-Mill Operator (grain-feed mills). ● **GED:** R3, M1, L2 ● **SVP:** 2-4 yrs ● **Academic:** Ed=N, Eng=N ● **Work Field:** 142 ● **MPSMS:** 381 ● **Aptitudes:** G3, V3, N4, S4, P3, Q4, K4, F4, M3, E5, C4 ● **Temperaments:** J, T ● **Physical:** Stg=M; Freq: R, H, N Occas: I, X ● **Work Env:** Noise=L; Freq: A ● **Salary:** 4 ● **Outlook:** 2

SYRUP MAKER (beverage) ● DOT #520.485-026 ● OES: 92965 ● Alternate titles: COOKER, SYRUP; SAUCE MAKER. Tends equipment to mix ingredients that produce syrups used in canned fruits and preserves, flavorings, frozen novelty confections, or non-alcoholic beverages: Determines amounts of ingredients, such as sugar, water, and flavoring, required for specified quantity of syrup of designated specific gravity, using sugar concentration and dilution charts. Opens valve to admit liquid sugar and water into mixer, or dumps crystalline sugar into mixer and admits water. Adds flavoring ingredients and starts mixer to make syrup. Opens valve to admit steam into jacket of mixer to invert sugar, eliminate air, and sterilize syrup. Tests syrup for sugar content, using hydrometer or refractometer. Pumps syrup to storage tank. May filter syrup to remove impurities and be designated Syrup Filterer (beverage). May blend raw syrups and be designated Syrup Blender (beverage). ● **GED:** R3, M2, L3 ● **SVP:** 3-6 mos ● **Academic:** Ed=N, Eng=S ● **Work Field:** 143 ● **MPSMS:** 394 ● **Aptitudes:** G3, V4, N3, S4, P3, Q4, K4, F4, M3, E5, C4 ● **Temperaments:** J, T ● **Physical:** Stg=M; Freq: R, H, I Occas: C, B, N, X ● **Work Env:** Noise=N; Const: U ● **Salary:** 1 ● **Outlook:** 2

GOE: 06.02.16
Equipment Operation, Textile, Fabric, and Leather Processing

DRY CLEANER (laundry & rel.) ● DOT #362.382-014 ● OES: 92726 ● Alternate titles: DRY-CLEANING-MACHINE OPERATOR. Operates dry cleaning machine to clean garments, drapes, and other materials, utilizing knowledge of cleaning processes, fabrics, and colors: Sorts articles, places lot of sorted articles in drum of dry cleaning machine. Fastens cover and starts drum rotating. Turns or pushes valves, levers, and switches to admit cleaning solvent into drum. Adds liquid soap or chemicals to facilitate cleaning process. Tends extractor that removes excess cleaning solvent from articles [EXTRACTOR OPERATOR (any industry) 581.685-038]. Tends tumbler that dries articles and removes odor of solvent from articles [TUMBLER OPERATOR (laundry & rel.) 369.685-034]. Opens valves of dry cleaning machine to drain dirty solvent into filter tank. Adds chemicals to solvent to facilitate filtration, and starts electric pumps, forcing solvent through filters to screen lint, dirt, and other impurities. Pulls sludge box from bottom of tank to remove sludge. Starts electric pumps and turns valves to operate distilling system that reclaims dirty solvent. May operate dry cleaning machine that automatically extracts excess cleaning solvent from articles. May clean by hand articles that cannot be cleaned by machine because of amount of soil on article or delicacy of fabric [DRY CLEANER, HAND (laundry & rel.) 362.684-010]. May add chemicals to dry cleaning machine to render garments water repellant. May spot articles [SPOTTER (laundry & rel.) II 362.381-010]. ● **GED:** R3, M2, L2 ● **SVP:** 6 mos-1 yr ● **Academic:** Ed=N, Eng=N ● **Work Field:** 031 ● **MPSMS:** 906 ● **Aptitudes:** G3, V4, N4, S4, P3, Q4, K4, F4, M3, E5, C3 ● **Temperaments:** J, T, V ● **Physical:** Stg=M; Freq: R, H Occas: S, I, N, A, X ● **Work Env:** Noise=N; Freq: H Occas: A ● **Salary:** 1 ● **Outlook:** 2

GOE: 06.02.17
Equipment Operation, Clay, & Coke Processing

BRIQUETTE-MACHINE OPERATOR (fabrication, nec) ● DOT #549.662-010 ● OES: 92999 ● Alternate titles: BRIQUETTE MOLDER; MOLDING-MACHINE OPERATOR. Operates machines and equipment to dehydrate, pulverize, mix, and mold ingredients to produce fuel briquettes: Shovels or empties sacks of materials into hoppers or bins, or starts elevator-conveyors. Turns valves, handwheels, or rheostats to move and control flow of fuels, water, and dry or liquid binders to machines. Starts conveyors, rotary drier, mixers, pulverizer, mixing augers, and compressing machines. Inspects briquettes and adjusts flow of materials to produce briquettes of specified dimensions. Removes and replaces broken bolts and worn shafts, using handtools. Lubricates machinery or directs oiling of equipment. May be designated according to type of briquette produced as Barbecue-Briquette-Machine Operator (fabrication, nec); Charcoal-Briquette-Machine Operator (fabrication, nec); Coal-Briquette-Machine Operator (fabrication, nec). ● **GED:** R3, M2, L2 ● **SVP:** 3-6 mos ● **Academic:** Ed=N, Eng=N ● **Work Field:** 147, 132 ● **MPSMS:** 504 ● **Aptitudes:** G3, V4, N4, S4, P4, Q4, K4, F4, M3, E5, C5 ● **Temperaments:** R, T ● **Physical:** Stg=M; Freq: S, O, R, H, I, E, N Occas: C ● **Work Env:** Noise=L; Freq: A, O ● **Salary:** 2 ● **Outlook:** 3

GOE: 06.02.18
Equipment Operation, Assorted Materials Processing

AUTOCLAVE OPERATOR (aircraft mfg.) ● DOT #553.362-014 ● OES: 92923 ● Alternate titles: BONDING EQUIPMENT OPERATOR. Sets up and operates autoclaves and auxiliary equipment to cure and bond metallic and nonmetallic aircraft parts and assemblies according to specifications: Reads and interprets shop orders and authorization documents to determine bonding process specifications. Selects parts and assemblies for simultaneous bonding, based on similarity of processing requirements and autoclave capacity. Arranges jigs and fixtures containing parts and assemblies on bonding racks and positions racks in autoclave, manually or using equipment, such as hoist, forklift, or tow. Inspects general condition of parts and assemblies, examines positioning of parts and assemblies in jigs and fixtures, and verifies that vacuum bag installation conforms to specifications prior to bonding. Connects thermocouples and vacuum lines to fittings on jigs and fixtures and inside autoclave. Adjusts manual controls or enters commands in computerized control panel to regulate and activate autoclave power supply, cooling system, vacuum, heat, and pressure gauges and recorders, and to close interlocking autoclave doors. Monitors instruments, switches, and recorders and listens for warning signals during autoclave operation to ensure conformance to specifications, and modifies or aborts process as required. Maintains manual or computerized autoclave processing records. Operates curing ovens and presses with heated platens [METAL-BONDING PRESS OPERATOR (aircraft mfg.) 553.382-026] to cure and bond parts. Suggests methods or procedures for improved operations to supervision or liaison personnel. Discusses loading, unloading, and operation of autoclaves and auxiliary equipment with other operators and workers to ensure safety of individuals working in and around high-pressure autoclaves. May calibrate autoclave system components. ● **GED:** R4, M3, L3 ● **SVP:** 1-2 yrs ● **Academic:** Ed=N, Eng=S ● **Work Field:** 063 ● **MPSMS:** 592 ● **Aptitudes:** G3, V3, N3, S3, P3, Q3, K4, F4, M4, E4, C4 ● **Temperaments:** J, T ● **Physical:** Stg=M; Freq: R, I, G, N, A Occas: C, S, K, O, H, E, T, M, D, X ● **Work Env:** Noise=N; Occas: M, O ● **Salary:** 3 ● **Outlook:** 3

ROOFING-MACHINE OPERATOR (build. mat., nec) ● DOT #554.682-022 ● OES: 92960 ● Operates machine to coat continuous rolls of roofing felt with asphalt, colored slate granules, powdered mica, or tar, to make roll roofing or shingles: Threads felt through or around series of coating rollers. Pulls felt through rollers and adjusts tension. Sets machine controls to gradually increase speed of rollers to specified operating speeds, or pulls levers and turns valves and wheels to synchronize machine speed and flow of coating material. Observes gauge and adjusts rheostat to regulate temperature of coating material in reservoir. Examines felt as it emerges from rollers to ensure that coating material is applied according to specifications. May feel moving felt to determine whether granules are being deposited uniformly and are adhering as specified. May be designated according to type of coating applied as Coater, Asphalt (nonmet. min.); Coater, Slate (nonmet. min.). ● **GED:** R3, M1, L2 ● **SVP:** 3-6 mos ● **Academic:** Ed=N, Eng=N ● **Work Field:** 151 ● **MPSMS:** 503 ● **Aptitudes:** G3, V4, N4, S3, P3, Q4, K3, F4, M3, E5, C5 ● **Temperaments:** J, T ● **Physical:** Stg=L; Freq: S, R, D Occas: H, I, N, A ● **Work Env:** Noise=L; Occas: A, T ● **Salary:** 1 ● **Outlook:** 2

RUG CLEANER, MACHINE (laundry & rel.) ● DOT #361.682-010 ● OES: 92726 ● Operates machine that washes, rinses, and partially dries rugs and carpets: Starts machine, and turns valves to admit cleaning solutions and water. Feels rug to determine end to be fed into machine to retain natural lay of pile. Fastens edge of rug to pins on conveyor bar and guides rug into machine. Sprinkles chemical solutions on stained area to dissolve stains. Moves levers or turns handwheels to regulate roller clearance, sprayer, water force, and speed of machine to avoid damage to rugs. May soap and scrub rugs requiring special attention, using portable scrubber prior to cleaning in machine. May sort rugs according to pile before cleaning. May turn valve handle to regulate heat when machine is drier equipped. May sew rugs end-to-end, using rail-mounted sewing machine and portable sewing machine to obtain continuous rug lengths for processing through machine. May load and push handtruck to transport rugs within plant. ● **GED:** R3, M1, L1 ● **SVP:** 3-6 mos ● **Academic:** Ed=N, Eng=N ● **Work Field:** 031 ● **MPSMS:** 906 ● **Aptitudes:** G4, V4, N5, S4, P3, Q5, K4, F4, M3, E5, C4 ● **Temperaments:** R, T ● **Physical:** Stg=M; Freq: R, H Occas: S, I, E, D, X, V ● **Work Env:** Noise=N; Freq: U ● **Salary:** 3 ● **Outlook:** 3

SOAP MAKER (soap & rel.) ● DOT #559.382-054 ● OES: 92965 ● Alternate titles: SOAP BOILER. Controls equipment that produces soap according to formula: Opens valves to charge kettle with prescribed amounts of ingredients. Turns valve to admit steam through bottom of tank to boil and agitate mixture. Observes mixture through opening in top of tank to detect variations of color, consistency, and homogeneity of boiling ingredients. Adds soda or water to mixture as directed by laboratory; or determines degree of alkalinity of caustic soda in mixture, using meter, and adds soda or water as required. Observes color, consistency, and homogeneity of product to determine when boiling and agitating cycle are completed, and allows batch to cool and settle for specified period of time. Raises or lowers pumpline to locate separation level of neat (pure soap) and nigre (residue). Starts pump to transfer neat to designated department. Lowers pump line to bottom of tank to transfer residue to reclaiming tank. May calculate amount of ingredients needed to make various soaps, using formula. ● **GED:** R3, M2, L3 ● **SVP:** 2-4 yrs ● **Academic:** Ed=N, Eng=N ● **Work Field:** 147 ● **MPSMS:** 494 ● **Aptitudes:** G3, V3, N4, S4, P3, Q4, K4, F4, M3, E5, C3 ● **Temperaments:** J, T ● **Physical:** Stg=L; Freq: R, H, N, X ● **Work Env:** Noise=L; Freq: A Occas: U, T ● **Salary:** 2 ● **Outlook:** 2

GOE: 06.02.19
Equipment Operation, Welding, Brazing, & Soldering

LASER-BEAM-MACHINE OPERATOR (welding) • DOT #815.682-010 • OES: 91750 • Operates laser-beam machine, which produces heat from concentrated light beam, to weld metal components: Pushes button to open safety enclosure at rear of laser cavity. Positions metal components in fixture and places components on fixture-holding table inside cavity. Pushes button to close safety enclosure. Aligns rear mirror of laser cavity, using micrometer screws, according to chart specifications. Types instructions, using teletype machine, to computer that automatically places fixture-holding table in operative position. Sights reference mark through microscope and turns controls to move fixture to welding position. Teletypes instructions to initiate weld cycle and to return fixture-holding table to unload position. Pushes button to open safety enclosure and removes fixtures containing welded components. Cleans optics, using brush, and replaces used flash tubes. May cut metal components, using laser-beam machine, and be designated Laser-Beam Cutter (welding). • **GED:** R3, M3, L3 • **SVP:** 3-6 mos • **Academic:** Ed=N, Eng=S • **Work Field:** 081 • **MPSMS:** 566 • **Aptitudes:** G3, V3, N3, S3, P3, Q3, K3, F3, M4, E5, C5 • **Temperaments:** T • **Physical:** Stg=L; Freq: R, H, I, N, D, A • **Work Env:** Noise=L; • **Salary:** 3 • **Outlook:** 3

WELDING-MACHINE OPERATOR, ARC (welding) • DOT #810.382-010 • OES: 91750 • Sets up and operates arc welding machine that welds together parts of fabricated metal products, as specified by blueprints, layouts, welding procedures, and operating charts: Welds flat, cylindrical, or irregular parts that may be clamped, tack-welded, or otherwise positioned. May position weld line parallel to carriage. Turns cranks or pushes buttons to align electrode on welding head over weld joint to weld linear joints, or adjust length of radial arm to position electrode over weld joint when welding radial joints. Clamps cylindrical workpieces onto turning rolls under stationary head to weld circular joints. Threads specified electrode wire from reel through feed rolls and welding head. Turns welding head to set specified angle of electrode. May fill hopper with specified flux and direct nozzle or gravity feed over weld line, or adjust shielding gas or gas mixture flow rate. Turns knobs to set current, voltage, and slope, and synchronize feed of wire and flux with speed of welding action. May set limit switch which automatically stops machine at end of weld. Starts machine and observes meters and gauges, or observes welding action for compliance with procedures. Visually examines welds for adherence to specifications. May grind welded surfaces for penetrant test. Adjusts machine setup to vary size, location, and penetration of bead. May install track template to weld irregularly shaped seams. May make trial run before welding and record setup and operating data. May layout, fit, and tack workpieces together. May preheat workpiece, using hand torch or heating furnace. May reweld defective joints, using hand-welding equipment. May remove surplus slag, flux, and spatter, using brush, portable grinder, and hand scraper. May operate machine equipped with two or more heads. May be designated according to type of welding machine operated as Welding-Machine Operator, Electro-Gas (welding); Welding-Machine Operator, Gas-Metal Arc (welding); Welding-Machine Operator, Gas-Tungsten Arc (welding); Welding-Machine Operator, Plasma Arc (welding); Welding-Machine Operator, Submerged Arc (welding). • **GED:** R4, M4, L3 • **SVP:** 1-2 yrs • **Academic:** Ed=N, Eng=S • **Work Field:** 081 • **MPSMS:** 554, 540 • **Aptitudes:** G3, V4, N3, S4, P3, Q4, K3, F4, M4, E5, C4 • **Temperaments:** J, T • **Physical:** Stg=M; Freq: R, H, N, D Occas: S, X • **Work Env:** Noise=L; Freq: O • **Salary:** 3 • **Outlook:** 3

WELDING-MACHINE OPERATOR, GAS (welding) • DOT #811.482-010 • OES: 91750 • Alternate titles: WELDER, GAS, AUTOMATIC. Sets up and operates oxy-fuel-gas-welding machine to weld metal parts, according to work order, blueprints, layout, and operating charts: Clamps workpieces into holding fixture on machine bed, movable carriage, or turntable. Positions and clamps or bolts welding torch onto overhead carriage, radial arm, or into stationary fixture at specified angle and distance from workpiece. Turns cranks to align torch with weld line. Selects torch tip, filler wire, and flux, according

to charts or thickness and type of metal. Fills hoppers with flux and positions spout over weld line. Places reel of filler wire onto spindle and threads end through feed rolls to welding seam. Connects hoses from torch to regulator valves and cylinders of oxygen and fuel gas. Turns regulator valves to start flow of gases, lights torch, and adjusts gas mixture and pressure to obtain flame of desired size and color. Turns knobs to synchronize movement of torch or workpiece, feed of flux and filler with welding action, and sets switch to stop machine at end of weld. Starts machine, observes welding action, and examines weld for defects. Adjusts machine setup to vary bead size and other weld characteristics. May record setup and operating data. May reweld defective joints, using handtorch. May preheat workpiece in furnace. May lay out, fit, and tack-weld workpieces together. May operate machine equipped with two or more welding torches. May remove surplus flux, slag, and splatter, using wirebrush, portable grinder, and hand scraper. • **GED:** R3, M3, L2 • **SVP:** 1-2 yrs • **Academic:** Ed=N, Eng=N • **Work Field:** 081 • **MPSMS:** 540 • **Aptitudes:** G3, V4, N3, S3, P3, Q4, K3, F3, M3, E5, C4 • **Temperaments:** J, T • **Physical:** Stg=M; Freq: R, H, I, N, D Occas: S, X • **Work Env:** Noise=L; Freq: A, O • **Salary:** 3 • **Outlook:** 3

GOE: 06.02.20
Machine Assembling

KICK-PRESS OPERATOR I (any industry) • DOT #616.682-026 • OES: 91399 • Alternate titles: ASSEMBLER, PRESS OPERATOR; BENCH-PRESS OPERATOR. Sets up and operates power press to assemble metal, plastic, rubber, or glass products by crimping, shaping, locking, staking, or press fitting: Installs specified dies on machine bed and ram, using measuring instruments and handtools. Positions and clamps holding fixtures to machine bed, using sample workpiece, template, rule, and gauge. Adjusts setscrews to regulate stroke of ram. Aligns parts between dies or positions them against fixtures on machine. Moves controls to lower ram that bends, clinches, or forces parts together. May operate machine to separate parts. May set up and operate machine to punch, cut, face, chamfer, or compress parts preparatory to assembly. May install gears and cams to synchronize action of multiple ram, feed, and positioning action of automatic presses. • **GED:** R3, M2, L2 • **SVP:** 3-6 mos • **Academic:** Ed=N, Eng=N • **Work Field:** 134 • **MPSMS:** 610 • **Aptitudes:** G3, V4, N4, S3, P3, Q4, K4, F3, M3, E4, C5 • **Temperaments:** J, T • **Physical:** Stg=L; Freq: R, H, I, N, D Occas: S, O • **Work Env:** Noise=V; Occas: O • **Salary:** 2 • **Outlook:** 2

STACKING-MACHINE OPERATOR I (any industry) • DOT #692.682-054 • OES: 92999 • Alternate titles: LAMINATION STACKER, MACHINE; PLATE STACKER, MACHINE. Operates machine to stack plates or sheets of material, such as metal or plastic, to assemble laminated products, such as rotor cores and storage battery elements or to form bundles for shipment: Places specified material into one or more feed magazines or holding devices. Moves lever to set automatic feed for number of items specified for stack. Turns screws to adjust opening in feed mechanism to size of item, using measuring instruments or built-in scale and handtools. Starts machine that automatically measures or counts and stacks specified number of pieces in desired arrangement. Clears jams and adjusts machine to correct malfunction, using handtools. Removes finished stack from machine and places stack into basket or into magazine of machine performing subsequent operation. May insert spacers between bundles to form continuous stack. • **GED:** R3, M2, L3 • **SVP:** 3-6 mos • **Academic:** Ed=N, Eng=S • **Work Field:** 061 • **MPSMS:** 554 • **Aptitudes:** G3, V4, N4, S3, P4, Q4, K3, F4, M4, E5, C5 • **Temperaments:** J, R, T • **Physical:** Stg=L; Freq: S, O, R, H, I, N Occas: D • **Work Env:** Noise=L; • **Salary:** 3 • **Outlook:** 2

GOE: 06.02.21
Coating & Plating

ANODIZER (any industry) • DOT #500.682-010 • OES: 91920 • Alternate titles: WHITE-METAL CORROSION PROOFER. Controls anodizing equipment to provide corrosion resistant surface to aluminum objects: Selects holding rack according to size, shape, and number of objects to be anodized. Wires or clips objects to anodizing rack and immerses rack in series of cleaning, etching, and rinsing baths. Positions objects in anodizing tank by suspending them from anode. Estimates amount of electric current and time required to anodize material. Turns rheostat to regulate flow of current. Removes objects from tank after specified time, rinses objects, and immerses them in bath of hot water or dichromate solution to seal oxide coating. Hangs objects on racks to air-dry. May immerse objects in dye bath to color them for decorative or identification purposes. May anodize workpiece with corrosion resistant material, using automated equipment that automatically cleans, rinses, and coats. ● **GED:** R3, M2, L3 ● **SVP:** 3-6 mos ● **Academic:** Ed=N, Eng=S ● **Work Field:** 154 ● **MPSMS:** 550 ● **Aptitudes:** G3, V4, N4, S3, P3, Q4, K4, F4, M3, E5, C4 ● **Temperaments:** R, T ● **Physical:** Stg=H; Freq: R, H, N, D Occas: I, X ● **Work Env:** Noise=L; Freq: H, U, A Occas: W ● **Salary:** 3 ● **Outlook:** 3

OPTICAL-ELEMENT COATER (optical goods) ● DOT #716.382-014 ● OES: 89917 ● Controls vacuum coating equipment to coat optical elements with chemical or metal film to alter reflective properties of elements: Reads work order to ascertain thickness of optical element and type coating material specified. Installs heating filament in coating machine according to type coating applied, using screwdriver. Fills crucible with coating material and positions crucible under heating filament. Secures optical element in jig and centers jig in vacuum chamber of machine to ensure uniform coating of optical surface. Places dome-shaped lid (vacuum bell) over jig or lowers lid equipped with window depending upon machine used. Starts machine that creates vacuum and releases chemicals or metal to form coating on optical element by process of sublimation or atomization. Observes changing colors of element through vacuum bell or through window in lid to determine when element is coated to specifications, or reads exposure meter to determine coating thickness. Applies and removes strip of cellophane to test adherence of coating to optical element. May immerse elements in chemical solution to clean elements. May operate ultrasonic vibrator to clean element. May inspect optical elements prior to coating to detect defects, such as blemishes, abrasions, and rough edges, using microscope. May cement optical elements together to form multiple laminated elements [CEMENTER (optical goods)]. May spray emulsion on lens preparatory to coating. ● **GED:** R3, M2, L2 ● **SVP:** 6 mos-1 yr ● **Academic:** Ed=N, Eng=N ● **Work Field:** 151, 154 ● **MPSMS:** 603 ● **Aptitudes:** G3, V3, N4, S4, P3, Q4, K4, F3, M3, E5, C3 ● **Temperaments:** J, T ● **Physical:** Stg=L; Freq: R, H, I, N Occas: A, X ● **Work Env:** Noise=N; ● **Salary:** 4 ● **Outlook:** 3

PAINT-SPRAYER OPERATOR, AUTOMATIC (any industry) ● DOT #599.382-010 ● OES: 92960 ● Alternate titles: SPRAY-MACHINE OPERATOR. Sets up and operates painting and drying units along conveyor line to coat metal, plastic, ceramic, and wood products with lacquer, paint, varnish, enamel, oil, or rustproofing material: Places or racks workpieces on conveyor. Turns valve to regulate water shield spray. Starts pumps to mix chemicals and paints, to fill tanks, and to control viscosity, adding prescribed amounts or proportions of paints, thinner, and chemicals to mixture. Screws specified nozzles into spray guns and positions nozzles to direct spray onto workpiece. Lights ovens, turns knobs, and observes gauges on control panel to set specified temperature and air circulation in oven, to synchronize speed of conveyor with action of spray guns and ovens, and to regulate air pressure in spray guns that atomize spray. Determines flow and viscosity of paints and quality of coating visually or by use of viscometer. May spray coated product with salt solution for prescribed time to determine resistance to corrosion. May be designated according to coating applied as Bonderite Operator (any industry); Control Operator, Flow Coat (elec. equip.); or according to article coated as Gunstock-Spray-Unit Adjuster (ordnance). ● **GED:** R3, M2, L3 ● **SVP:** 6 mos-1 yr ● **Academic:** Ed=N, Eng=S ● **Work Field:** 153, 141 ● **MPSMS:** 495, 550 ● **Aptitudes:** G3, V4, N3, S4, P3, Q4, K3, F4, M3, E5, C4 ● **Temperaments:** J, T ● **Physical:** Stg=M; Freq: R, H Occas: I, N, X ● **Work Env:** Noise=L; Occas: A ● **Salary:** 3 ● **Outlook:** 3

PLATER (electroplating) ● DOT #500.380-010 ● OES: 91920 ● Alternate titles: ELECTROPLATER; PLATING-TANK OPERATOR. Sets up and controls plating equipment to coat metal objects electrolytically with chromium, copper, cadmium, or other metal to provide protective or decorative surfaces or to build up worn surfaces according to specifications: Reads work order to determine size and composi-

tion of object to be plated; type concentration and temperature of plating solution; type and thickness and location of specified plating metal; and amount of electrical current and time required to complete plating process. Immerses object in cleaning and rinsing baths [METAL-CLEANER, IMMERSION (any industry)]. Suspends object, such as part or mold, from cathode rod (negative terminal) and immerses object in plating solution. Suspends stick or piece of plating metal from anode (positive terminal) and immerses metal in plating solution. Moves controls on rectifier to adjust flow of current through plating solution from anode to cathode and to permit electrodeposition of metal on object. Removes plated object from solution at periodic intervals and observes object to ensure conformance to specifications. Adjusts voltage and amperage based on observation. Examines object visually at end of process to determine thickness of metal deposit or measures thickness, using instruments, such as micrometers or calipers. Grinds, polishes or rinses object in water and dries object to maintain clean even surface. May mix, and test strength of plating solution, using instruments and chemical tests. May measure, mark, and mask areas excluded from plating. May plate small objects, such as nuts or bolts, using motor-driven barrel. May direct other workers performing variety of duties, such as racking, cleaning, or plating objects. May operate electroplating equipment with reverse polarity and be known as Plating Stripper (electroplating). May be designated according to plating materials used as Brass Plater (electroplating); Bronze Plater (electroplating); Cadmium Plater (electroplating); Chromium Plater (electroplating); Copper Plater (electroplating); Gold Plater (electroplating). May be designated: Nickel Plater (electroplating); Plastics Plater (plastic prod.); Silver Plater (electroplating); Tin Plater (electroplating). ● **GED:** R4, M3, L3 ● **SVP:** 2-4 yrs ● **Academic:** Ed=H, Eng=S ● **Work Field:** 154 ● **MPSMS:** 540 ● **Aptitudes:** G3, V3, N3, S3, P3, Q4, K4, F3, M3, E5, C4 ● **Temperaments:** J, T ● **Physical:** Stg=M; Freq: R, H, I, N, D, A Occas: E, X ● **Work Env:** Noise=L; Freq: U, A ● **Salary:** 3 ● **Outlook:** 3

PLATER, PRINTED CIRCUIT BOARD PANELS (electron. comp.) ● DOT #500.684-026 ● OES: 91920 ● Electroplates printed circuit board (PCB) panels with metals, such as copper, tin, gold, nickel, or solder, to resist corrosion, improve electrical conductivity, and facilitate solder connections: Dips panels in cleaning solutions or wipes panels with cloth to clean panels. Clamps panels or rack of panels to overhead bar above tanks to complete electrolytic current. Immerses panels in plating solution. Sets timer for specified plating time and turns on electrical current. Observes meter and turns dial to maintain specified current in plating solution. Removes plated panels and immerses panels in rinsing tank. Examines plated panels for defects. May test thickness of plating, using gauge or test equipment. May tape areas to be excluded from plating, using tape machine. May trim excess material from PCB panels, using shearing machine. May calculate amperage setting, following specified formula. May be designated according to plating material used as Gold Plater (electron. comp.); Nickel Plater (electron. comp.). ● **GED:** R2, M1, L2 ● **SVP:** 1-3 mos ● **Academic:** Ed=N, Eng=N ● **Work Field:** 154 ● **MPSMS:** 587 ● **Aptitudes:** G4, V4, N4, S4, P4, Q4, K4, F4, M3, E5, C5 ● **Temperaments:** T ● **Physical:** Stg=H; Const: R, H Freq: N, D Occas: I ● **Work Env:** Noise=L; Occas: T ● **Salary:** 3 ● **Outlook:** 3

GOE: 06.02.22
Manual Work, Assembly Large Parts

ASSEMBLER, INTERNAL COMBUSTION ENGINE (engine-turbine) ● DOT #806.481-014 ● OES: 93105 ● Alternate titles: ENGINE ASSEMBLER. Assembles internal combustion engines according to standard procedures, using handtools, power wrenches, and gauges, performing any of following operations on assembly line: Positions and bolts crankcase, block, and trunion support together to form basic unit of engine, using wrenches, hammer, and power hoist. Mounts crankshaft and camshaft to bearings and tightens bearing caps, using power wrench. Presses gears, sheave, flywheel, or sprocket to shafts, using hand or hydraulic press, and locks them with keys and pins. Inserts cylinder sleeves into engine block or casing and fits piston and connecting rod assembly into cylinder and bolts it to crankshaft. Aligns engine parts, such as camshaft and crankshaft gears, and sets timing and clearances between fixed or moving parts, using aligning gauges, dial indicator, feeler gauges, and timing light. Examines parts or observes movement of completed assemblies to detect malfunction, and discards or replaces defective parts or assemblies. Bolts subassemblies, such as cylinder head, camshaft assembly, fuel pump, carburetor, governor, and water pump, to engine, using torque wrench and other handtools. Flares and connects copper or brass tubing for lubricating and cooling systems, using flaring tools and wrenches. May cut and bend tubing to conform to curvature of engine, using bending fixtures and tubing cutters. May lap cylinder counterbore and valve seats to seat cylinder sleeves and valves, using hand lapping tool and compound. May disassemble, polish, buff, and reassemble motors for demonstration purposes and be designated Assembler, Show Motor (engine-turbine). May be designated according to type of engine assembled as Diesel-Engine Assembler (engine-turbine); Gasoline-Engine Assembler (engine-turbine); Motorcycle-Engine Assembler (engine-turbine); Outboard-Motor Assembler (engine-turbine). ● **GED:** R4, M3, L3 ● **SVP:** 1-2 yrs ● **Academic:** Ed=N, Eng=S ● **Work Field:** 121 ● **MPSMS:** 561 ● **Aptitudes:** G3, V3, N3, S3, P4, Q4, K3, F3, M2, E5, C5 ● **Temperaments:** J, T ● **Physical:** Stg=M; Freq: S, K, O, R, H, I, N, D Occas: C, E ● **Work Env:** Noise=L; ● **Salary:** 3 ● **Outlook:** 3

ASSEMBLER, SUBASSEMBLY (aircraft mfg.) ● DOT #806.384-034 ● OES: 93997 ● Alternate titles: DETAIL ASSEMBLER; SHEET METAL ASSEMBLER. Assembles parts, such as spars, ribs, and braces, to form structural subassemblies of aircraft, such as airfoils, control surfaces, fuselage tops and bulkheads, doors, and windows, according to specifications, using handtools and power tools: Reads and interprets blueprints and specifications to determine assembly sequence, tooling requirements, measurements, and allowable tolerances. Marks reference lines and points on parts, using templates, or by measuring from blueprint index points and station lines, using rule, protractor, and divider. Cuts, trims, files, and deburrs parts, using handtools or power tools. Measures parts to verify dimensions, using precision instruments, such as micrometers and calipers. Fits and assembles parts and fittings, such as braces, hinges, brackets, keyways, and nut plates, in jigs and fixtures, using clamps. Drills, reams, and countersinks holes, using power tools. Deburrs keyways, holes, and cable grooves, using burring tool. Marks reference symbols on parts for subsequent riveting. Installs bolts, screws, rivets, and other fasteners to join parts, using power tools. Cements, tapes, and glues parts as required. May install electric and hydraulic components. May bend tubing. May make temporary assembly fixtures. May buck rivets. ● **GED:** R3, M2, L3 ● **SVP:** 6 mos-1 yr ● **Academic:** Ed=N, Eng=N ● **Work Field:** 102 ● **MPSMS:** 592 ● **Aptitudes:** G3, V3, N4, S3, P4, Q4, K4, F3, M3, E5, C4 ● **Temperaments:** J, T ● **Physical:** Stg=M; Freq: R, H, I, N, D Occas: S, K, O, E, A, X ● **Work Env:** Noise=V; Occas: V, M ● **Salary:** 3 ● **Outlook:** 3

CABINET ASSEMBLER (furniture) ● DOT #763.684-014 ● OES: 93997 ● Assembles radio, television, and phonograph cabinets, using handtools: Fits prefabricated wooden parts together. Trims and smooths parts to fit, using handtools and sandpaper. Inserts screws or dowels in predrilled holes, and fastens parts together with screwdriver, glue, and clamps. Installs hardware, such as hinges, catches, and knobs, on assembled cabinet. May cut baffle cloths and plastic screens to specified size and install them in cabinets, using hand or machine cutters, screwdriver, and stapling gun. ● **GED:** R3, M2, L3 ● **SVP:** 1-3 mos ● **Academic:** Ed=N, Eng=S ● **Work Field:** 102 ● **MPSMS:** 461 ● **Aptitudes:** G3, V4, N4, S3, P4, Q4, K3, F3, M3, E5, C5 ● **Temperaments:** R, T ● **Physical:** Stg=L; Freq: R, H, I, N, D ● **Work Env:** Noise=L; ● **Salary:** 4 ● **Outlook:** 3

CASKET ASSEMBLER (fabrication, nec) ● DOT #739.684-190 ● OES: 93997 ● Alternate titles: FITTER. Assembles wooden caskets from preformed panels and moldings and attaches supplemental hardware: Nails and glues side, end, and bottom sections together to form casket body. Assembles preformed sections of top frame, using hammer, glue, clamping nails, and bar clamps. Locates and marks midpoint of top frame, using ruler and pencil. Glues and nails panelboard and brace block between sides at midpoint for reinforcement. Positions template over top edge of body or measures body with ruler to locate position of hinges and catches, and recesses positions, using hammer and chisel or portable router. Drills holes at specified locations, using portable power drill. Installs hardware, such as corners,

handles, hinges, and catches, using hand or power screwdriver. Sands and planes edges between body, top frame, and top panel to form tight joint, using planer or portable sander. Attaches top panel to top frame, using hand or powered screwdriver. Measures, cuts, and attaches ornamental molding or beading to casket body, using saw, hammer, miter box, and ruler. Sets nailheads, using hammer and nail set. Fills cracks and nail holes with wood filler or plaster of paris by hand or with putty knife. Smooths joints and edges, using sandpaper and handtools. May cut or trim wood to specified size for use in assembly of casket, using cutoff saw. May be designated according to part of casket assembled as Body Maker (fabrication, nec); Cap Maker (fabrication, nec); Molding Fitter (fabrication, nec); Panel Fitter (fabrication, nec); Top-Frame Fitter (fabrication, nec); Top-Frame Maker (fabrication, nec). ● **GED:** R3, M2, L2 ● **SVP:** 1-3 mos ● **Academic:** Ed=N, Eng=N ● **Work Field:** 102 ● **MPSMS:** 619 ● **Aptitudes:** G3, V4, N3, S3, P3, Q4, K3, F3, M3, E5, C5 ● **Temperaments:** T ● **Physical:** Stg=M; Freq: S, R, H, I, E, N, D, A ● **Work Env:** Noise=L; Occas: A, M ● **Salary:** 2 ● **Outlook:** 3

ELECTRIC-SIGN ASSEMBLER (fabrication, nec) ● DOT #729.684-022 ● OES: 93905 ● Assembles electric signs, mounts tubing, and connects electrical equipment to sign box: Fastens back of sign to precut metal frame to form sign box, using screws and screwdriver. Fits precut glass, plexiglass, or plastic pane into bottom channel of metal frame. Crimps frame channel to secure pane, using pliers. Attaches tubing support brackets to sign box with self-tapping screws, using screwdriver. Screws or clamps glass elevation posts to brackets. Binds neon sign scroll to posts with wire. Connects wires between tubing electrodes and secondary-winding terminals of transformer. Attaches animation mechanism to back of sign, and connects part to be animated. May assemble fiberboard or cardboard cutout parts for animated window display signs. ● **GED:** R3, M2, L2 ● **SVP:** 1-3 mos ● **Academic:** Ed=N, Eng=N ● **Work Field:** 111 ● **MPSMS:** 584 ● **Aptitudes:** G3, V4, N4, S3, P3, Q4, K3, F3, M3, E5, C4 ● **Temperaments:** R, T ● **Physical:** Stg=M; Freq: R, H, I, N Occas: X ● **Work Env:** Noise=N; ● **Salary:** 3 ● **Outlook:** 2

LAMINATOR (rubber goods) ● DOT #899.684-018 ● OES: 93997 ● Glues rubberized fabric and foam to form sections of inflatable buildings: Measures and cuts strips of fabric to specified length, using tape measure and knife. Cleans edges of fabric with solvent and glues strips of fabric together, overlapping edges for specified size. Cleans strip of joined fabric with solvent, and applies glue to strip of foam and fabric, working as member of crew. Fits glued sections together, and repeats process until fabric is covered with foam. Applies glue to other side of foam and to other strip of fabric. Attaches fabric to foam by hand or uses hand roller while crewmember holds and guides fabric. Trims rubberized fabric to specified size, and cuts openings for doors and windows, using template and knife. Inserts metal framed doors and windows in openings. Cleans and attaches edges of frame and fabric, using solvent and tape. ● **GED:** R2, M1, L2 ● **SVP:** 1-3 mos ● **Academic:** Ed=N, Eng=N ● **Work Field:** 063 ● **MPSMS:** 519 ● **Aptitudes:** G3, V4, N4, S4, P3, Q4, K3, F3, M3, E5, C5 ● **Temperaments:** R, T ● **Physical:** Stg=M; Freq: R, H, I, N, D ● **Work Env:** Noise=L; ● **Salary:** 2 ● **Outlook:** 3

MACHINE ASSEMBLER (machinery mfg.) ● DOT #638.361-010 ● OES: 93105 ● Assembles machines, equipment, and their subassemblies, such as baling presses, stokers, blowers, compression pumps, and food wrapping machines, according to customer's needs, following blueprints and other written and verbal specifications: Plans assembly procedures, following specifications and using knowledge gained by experience. Removes small quantities of metal, using hand files or portable grinders, to clean parts or to produce close fit between parts. Drills, taps, or reams holes, using drill press or portable drill. Aligns components, and bolts, screws, or rivets them together, using handtools or portable powered tools. Installs moving parts, such as shafts, levers, or bearings, and works them to test free movement. May bend and install pipe for hydraulic systems. May align and mesh gears in gearbox to assemble system of gears. May test or assist in testing operation of completed product. ● **GED:** R3, M3, L3 ● **SVP:** 1-2 yrs ● **Academic:** Ed=N, Eng=S ● **Work Field:** 121 ● **MPSMS:** 567 ● **Aptitudes:** G3, V3, N3, S3, P4, Q4, K3, F3, M2, E5, C5 ● **Temperaments:** J, T ● **Physical:** Stg=M; Freq: R, H, I, N, D Occas: C, S, K, O ● **Work Env:** Noise=L; Occas: M ● **Salary:** 4 ● **Outlook:** 3

MOTORCYCLE ASSEMBLER (motor-bicycles) ● DOT #806.684-090 ● OES: 93997 ● Assembles complete motorcycles, performing any combination of following tasks: Positions and clamps frame in fixture on conveyor line. Bolts fork, motor, transmission, rear and front wheels, chain drives, handlebars, lights, seats, and other parts to frame, using handtools or power tools. Turns gas or spark handle controls, and adjustment screws on distributor and carburetor to set spark and gas feed. Turns screws to adjust chain drive and clutch to specified tension. Focuses headlight on testing board and turns adjustment screws to align beam of light. Lubricates motorcycle with grease gun. Records motor and sales numbers. May relieve assemblers and be known as Utility Assembler (motor-bicycles). ● **GED:** R3, M1, L1 ● **SVP:** 6 mos-1 yr ● **Academic:** Ed=N, Eng=N ● **Work Field:** 102, 121 ● **MPSMS:** 595 ● **Aptitudes:** G3, V4, N4, S3, P3, Q4, K3, F3, M3, E4, C5 ● **Temperaments:** T ● **Physical:** Stg=H; Freq: S, R, H, I, N, D Occas: E ● **Work Env:** Noise=L; ● **Salary:** 3 ● **Outlook:** 3

TRANSFORMER ASSEMBLER II (elec. equip.) ● DOT #820.684-010 ● OES: 93905 ● Assembles transformers according to specifications, performing any combination of following tasks: Reads work order to determine assembly procedure specified by customer. Cleans coils to remove materials accumulated during production processing. Removes accessories from coils, using screwdriver, and wraps coils with paper and tape, leaving ends of wire leads exposed. Inserts ends of wire leads of cores and coils into wire stripping machine to remove coating from wires. Inspects and twists stripped wires together by hand to join designated colored wires. Disassembles cores to facilitate attachment of coils and attaches cores to coils, using cloth tape and glue. Secures core/coils, using metal strapping, metal cutters, and band clippers. Positions wooden wedges that facilitate further processing of units in designated openings of core/coils, using rubber hammer. Turns knobs to set controls of test machine to verify that core/coils operate within specified range, attaches clips to wire leads of core/coils, and observes machine dials to determine test results. Routes defective core/coils for rework. Places component parts of terminals in press, activates press to join parts; or positions parts in fixture and joins parts, using solder and soldering iron, to fabricate terminals. Attaches terminals to core/coils, according to work order, using handtools, spacers, and soldering iron. Applies adhesive to inside of transformer case side sections. Positions and aligns wires and terminals of core/coils with openings in sections. Positions core/coil and side sections in welding machine, aligns seams of sections for welding, and presses buttons to activate welding machine to weld seams. Attaches clip probes to transformer terminals, and activates test equipment to determine whether units meet specifications. Positions, inserts, and attaches transformer parts, such as insulation panels, front and back metal covers, and base plates to complete assembly of transformers, using handtools. Stamps identification numbers on base of transformer, using metal dies and hammer. Repairs transformers with minor defects. ● **GED:** R3, M1, L2 ● **SVP:** 1-3 mos ● **Academic:** Ed=N, Eng=N ● **Work Field:** 111 ● **MPSMS:** 581 ● **Aptitudes:** G3, V4, N4, S3, P3, Q4, K3, F2, M2, E4, C4 ● **Temperaments:** R, T ● **Physical:** Stg=H; Freq: R, H, I, N, D Occas: E, G, X ● **Work Env:** Noise=L; Occas: A ● **Salary:** 4 ● **Outlook:** 2

UTILITY WORKER (mfd. bldgs.) ● DOT #869.684-074 ● OES: 93998 ● Performs any combination of following tasks in manufacture of mobile homes and travel trailers: Tends woodworking and metalworking machines to cut and shape wood and metal parts. Cuts, shapes, and assembles parts, using handtools and power tools. Installs parts, household appliances, furnishings, and fixtures, using handtools and power tools. Trains inexperienced workers. Assists, relieves, or substitutes for INSTALLER (mfd. bldgs.; vehicles, nec); ASSEMBLER (mfd. bldgs.; vehicles, nec); and PLUMBER (mfd. bldgs.). ● **GED:** R3, M2, L2 ● **SVP:** 6 mos-1 yr ● **Academic:** Ed=N, Eng=S ● **Work Field:** 102 ● **MPSMS:** 361, 597 ● **Aptitudes:** G3, V4, N3, S3, P4, Q4, K3, F4, M3, E4, C4 ● **Temperaments:** T, V ● **Physical:** Stg=M; Freq: R, H, I, N, D Occas: C, S, K, O, E, X, V ● **Work Env:** Noise=L; Occas: O ● **Salary:** 3 ● **Outlook:** 3

GOE: 06.02.23
Manual Work, Assembly Small Parts

ASSEMBLER I (office machines) ● DOT #706.684-014 ● OES: 93902 ● Alternate titles: ASSEMBLER-ADJUSTER. Assembles and adjusts typewriters and office machine assemblies and subassemblies, using blueprints, gauges, handtools, and holding devices: Screws and bolts parts together, using screwdrivers, wrenches, and other handtools. Tests operation of machines and typewriters to detect loose and binding parts and to determine synchronization of related parts. Bends and taps parts into alignment, using pliers and mallets. Turns compensating screws to set parts at specified tensions and clearances. Verifies tensions and clearances of parts, using tension scales and space and feeler gauges. May ream and tap holes and file and fit carriages and covers of equipment, using hand reamer, tap, and file. ● **GED:** R3, M2, L2 ● **SVP:** 3-6 mos ● **Academic:** Ed=N, Eng=N ● **Work Field:** 121 ● **MPSMS:** 571 ● **Aptitudes:** G3, V3, N3, S3, P3, Q4, K3, F3, M3, E5, C5 ● **Temperaments:** J, T ● **Physical:** Stg=M; Freq: R, H, I, N, D Occas: S, K, O, G, A ● **Work Env:** Noise=L; ● **Salary:** 2 ● **Outlook:** 3

ASSEMBLER, MUSICAL INSTRUMENTS (musical inst.) ● DOT #730.684-010 ● OES: 93997 ● Performs any combination of following tasks to assemble and fasten together parts to form subassemblies or complete musical instruments, such as drums, keyed brass, woodwind, or stringed instruments according to specified instructions or diagrams: Drills, taps, or reams holes to prepare parts for assembly, using drill press or bench-mounted drill. Bends tubing and laps parts by hand to form or join parts. Applies abrasive solvents to sliding joints to cause parts to move freely. Fits or faces parts, using hand file or bench grinder to trim parts to fit. Aligns metal brass-wind parts, such as valves, knobs, keys, and bars by sight, by placing them in jigs and clamping them on instrument, or by positioning parts, using rulers or gauges. Screws, clips, solders, and glues parts, such as drum hardware, corks, violin necks, wooden bridges, and metal snares, using handtools, portable powered tools, or hand torches. Removes excess solder, using scraping tool. Winds and bends spring wire around valve keys by hand to install valves on brass-wind instruments. Inserts steel bars and squeezes or separates bars to adjust tube spacing on brass-wind instruments. Cleans inside of tubes of brass-wind instruments with swab and cleaning solvent. Installs electric pick-ups in electrically operated instruments, using screwdriver and soldering gun. May polish or buff exterior of instruments, using rotating buffing wheel. May cut tubing, using power saw. May inspect instruments for defects and reject instruments not meeting specifications. May be designated according to instrument assembled as Final Assembler, Brass-Wind Instruments (musical inst.); Mounter, Brass-Wind Instruments (musical inst.); Stringed-Instrument Assembler (musical inst.); or by part assembled as Bridge Fitter (musical inst.); Knobber (musical inst.); Neck Fitter (musical inst.). May be designated: Mounter, Clarinets (musical inst.); Mounter, Flutes And Piccolos (musical inst.); Mounter, Keyed Instruments (musical inst.); Mounter, Saxophones (musical inst.); Mounter, Sousaphones (musical inst.); Mounter, Trombones (musical inst.); Mounter, Trumpets And Cornets (musical inst.). ● **GED:** R3, M2, L2 ● **SVP:** 1-3 mos ● **Academic:** Ed=N, Eng=N ● **Work Field:** 102 ● **MPSMS:** 614 ● **Aptitudes:** G3, V4, N4, S3, P3, Q4, K3, F3, M3, E5, C5 ● **Temperaments:** R, T ● **Physical:** Stg=L; Const: R, H, I Freq: N Occas: D, A ● **Work Env:** Noise=N; ● **Salary:** 3 ● **Outlook:** 2

ASSEMBLER, PRODUCT (machine shop) ● DOT #706.684-018 ● OES: 93997 ● Alternate titles: ASSEMBLER; ERECTOR. Assembles metal products, such as vacuum cleaners, valves, or hydraulic cylinders, partially or completely, working at bench or on shop floor: Positions parts according to knowledge of unit being assembled or following blueprints. Fastens parts together with bolts, screws, speed clips, rivets, or other fasteners, using handtools and portable powered tools. May remove small quantities of metal with hand files and scrapers to produce close fit between parts. May operate drill presses, punch presses, or riveting machines to assist in assembly operation. May disassemble power brake boosters, air-brake compressors, and valves for salvage of parts and be designated Disassembler, Product (machine shop). May assemble and test patient lifting devices and be designated Assembler, Patient Lifting Device (protective dev.). Usually specializes in assembly of one type of product. ● **GED:** R3, M2, L2 ● **SVP:** 1-3 mos ● **Academic:** Ed=N, Eng=N ● **Work Field:** 121 ● **MPSMS:** 560, 590 ● **Aptitudes:** G3, V4, N4, S3, P3, Q4, K3, F3, M3, E5, C4 ● **Temperaments:** J, R, T ● **Physical:** Stg=M; Freq: R, H, I, N Occas: S, K, O, E, T, G, D, X ● **Work Env:** Noise=N; Occas: O ● **Salary:** 2 ● **Outlook:** 3

ASSEMBLER, SEMICONDUCTOR (electron. comp.) ● DOT #726.684-034 ● OES: 93905 ● Alternate titles: MICROELECTRONICS PROCESSOR. Assembles microelectronic semiconductor devices, components, and subassemblies according to drawings and specifications, using microscope, bonding machines, and handtools, performing any combination of following duties: Reads work orders and studies assembly drawings to determine operation to be performed. Observes processed semiconductor wafer under scribing machine microscope and aligns scribing tool with markings on wafer. Adjusts scribing machine controls, according to work order specifications, and presses switch to start scribing. Removes scribed wafer and breaks wafer into dice (chips), using probe. Places dice under microscope, visually examines dice for defects, according to procedures, and rejects defective dice. Positions mounting device on holder under bonding machine microscope, and adjusts bonding machine controls according to work order specifications. Positions die (chip) on mounting surface according to diagram. Presses switch on bonding machine to bond die to mounting surface. Places mounted die into holding fixture under microscope of lead bonding machine. Adjusts bonding machine controls according to work order specifications. Views die and moves controls to align and position bonding head for lead bonding according to diagram. Presses switch to bond lead and moves bonding head to points indicated in bonding diagram to attach and route leads as illustrated. Inserts and seals unprotected assembly into designated assembly container device, using welding machine and epoxy syringe, to protect microelectronic assembly and complete device, component, or subassembly package. Examines and tests assembly at various stages of production, using microscope, go-not-go test equipment, measuring instruments, pressure-vacuum tanks, and related devices, according to standard procedures, to detect nonstandard or defective assemblies. Rejects or routes nonstandard components for rework. Cleans parts and assemblies at various stages of production, using cleaning devices and equipment. Maintains records of production and defects. Bonds multiple dice to headers or other mounting devices. Important variations are kinds of equipment used, such as thermal compression, wedge, wire ball, and wobble bonders, items assembled, or procedure performed. ● **GED:** R3, M2, L2 ● **SVP:** 1-3 mos ● **Academic:** Ed=N, Eng=N ● **Work Field:** 111 ● **MPSMS:** 587 ● **Aptitudes:** G3, V3, N4, S3, P2, Q3, K3, F2, M3, E4, C4 ● **Temperaments:** J, R, T ● **Physical:** Stg=S; Freq: R, H, I, N, F, A Occas: D, X ● **Work Env:** Noise=N; ● **Salary:** 2 ● **Outlook:** 4

CHAIN MAKER, MACHINE (jewelry-silver.) ● DOT #700.684-022 ● OES: 93997 ● Forms chains for watches and other jewelry articles: Feeds wire into machine. Hooks together ends of chain formed by machine, using pliers, and solders on trimming. May be designated according to type of chain as Novelty-Chain Maker (jewelry-silver.). ● **GED:** R3, M2, L2 ● **SVP:** 1-3 mos ● **Academic:** Ed=N, Eng=N ● **Work Field:** 102 ● **MPSMS:** 611 ● **Aptitudes:** G3, V4, N4, S4, P4, Q5, K4, F4, M3, E4, C5 ● **Temperaments:** R, T ● **Physical:** Stg=L; Freq: W, R, H, N ● **Work Env:** Noise=N; ● **Salary:** 3 ● **Outlook:** 2

ELECTRICAL ASSEMBLER (aircraft mfg.) ● DOT #729.384-026 ● OES: 93905 ● Alternate titles: ASSEMBLER, RADIO AND ELECTRICAL; ASSEMBLER, WIRE GROUP; BENCH ASSEMBLER, ELECTRICAL. Routes, wires, assembles, and installs electrical and electronic components in aircraft and missile units, such as main junction and terminal boxes, main control switch panels, and instrument and radio panels, according to specifications, using jig boards, handtools, and equipment: Reads work orders, blueprints, and specifications to determine established assembly methods. Cuts wire to specified lengths, using wire cutters. Cuts plastic sleeves and slips sleeves over wire ends to insulate connections. Crimps terminal eyelets and lugs to wire ends, using hand or machine crimping device. Routes, combs, twists, wraps, ties, and attaches wire to terminal points, according to jig board layout, using soldering gun and handtools. Connects wiring to accessories, such as relays, circuit breakers, plugs, condensors, switches, and solenoids, and installs accessory assemblies in electrical or electronic units, using soldering gun and handtools. Conducts functional and continuity tests of electrical assemblies, components, wire harness, and plugs, using ohmmeter, test lights, and other electrical testing instruments. Pots or encapsulates electrical and electronic details [ENCAPSULATOR (elec. equip.; electron. comp.) 726.687-022]. May attach eyelets, terminals, and mounting studs to etched circuit boards. ● **GED:** R3, M2, L3 ● **SVP:** 1-3 mos ● **Academic:** Ed=N, Eng=S ● **Work Field:** 111 ● **MPSMS:** 592 ● **Aptitudes:** G3, V3, N4, S3, P3, Q4, K3, F3, M3, E5, C4 ● **Temperaments:** T ● **Physical:** Stg=L; Freq: R, H, I, N, D Occas: S, A, X ● **Work Env:** Noise=N; ● **Salary:** 3 ● **Outlook:** 3

ELECTRONICS ASSEMBLER (comm. equip.) ● DOT #726.684-018 ● OES: 93905 ● Performs any combination of following tasks to assemble electronic components, subassemblies, products, or systems: Reads work orders, follows production drawings and sample assemblies, or receives verbal instructions regarding duties to be performed. Positions and aligns parts in specified relationship to each other in jig, fixture, or other holding device. Crimps, stakes, screws, bolts, rivets, welds, solders, cements, press fits, or performs similar operations to join or secure parts in place, using handtools, power tools, machines, and equipment. Mounts assembled components, such as transformers, resistors, transistors, capacitors, integrated circuits, and sockets, on chassis panel. Connects component lead wires to printed circuit or routes and connects wires between individual component leads and other components, connectors, terminals, and contact points, using soldering, welding, thermocompression, or related bonding procedures and equipment. Installs finished assemblies or subassemblies in cases and cabinets. Assembles and attaches hardware, such as caps, clamps, knobs, and switches, to assemblies. Performs intermediate assembly tasks, such as potting, encapsulating, sanding, cleaning, epoxy bonding, curing, stamping, etching, impregnating, and color coding parts and assemblies. Tends machines that press, shape, or wind component parts. Adjusts or trims materials from components to achieve specified electrical or dimensional characteristics. Performs on-line go-not-go testing and inspection, using magnifying devices, measuring instruments, and electronic test equipment, to ensure parts and assemblies meet production specifications and standards. May perform assembly operations under microscope or other magnifying device. Occupations related to assembly of printed circuit boards and fabrication of integrated circuit chips are defined under separate definitions. ● **GED:** R2, M1, L2 ● **SVP:** 3-6 mos ● **Academic:** Ed=N, Eng=N ● **Work Field:** 102, 111, 134 ● **MPSMS:** 580, 600 ● **Aptitudes:** G4, V4, N4, S3, P3, Q4, K3, F2, M2, E5, C4 ● **Temperaments:** R ● **Physical:** Stg=L; Freq: R, H, I, N, D Occas: G, A, X ● **Work Env:** Noise=N; ● **Salary:** 1 ● **Outlook:** 4

INSTRUMENT ASSEMBLER (inst. & app.) ● DOT #710.684-046 ● OES: 93997 ● Assembles instruments and devices, such as barometers, control valves, gyroscopes, hygrometers, speedometers, tachometers, and thermostats, using handtools, power tools, and measuring instruments: Visually examines parts for defects. Fits, aligns, and secures internal and external component parts to assemble finished unit, using handtools, power tools, soldering iron, and measuring instruments. May inspect assembled unit for conformance to specifications, using measuring and testing equipment. May test functional performance of unit, using test equipment. May be designated according to product assembled as Regulator Assembler (inst. & app.); Thermostat Assembler (inst. & app.); Valve Assembler (inst. & app.). ● **GED:** R3, M2, L2 ● **SVP:** 3-6 mos ● **Academic:** Ed=N, Eng=N ● **Work Field:** 111, 121 ● **MPSMS:** 600 ● **Aptitudes:** G3, V4, N4, S3, P3, Q4, K3, F3, M3, E5, C4 ● **Temperaments:** T ● **Physical:** Stg=L; Freq: R, H, I, N, D Occas: E, A, X ● **Work Env:** Noise=N; ● **Salary:** 2 ● **Outlook:** 3

LAMINATION ASSEMBLER (elec. equip.) ● DOT #729.684-066 ● OES: 93997 ● Alternate titles: STACKING ASSEMBLER. Stacks, aligns, and secures metal laminations and insulating separators, to assemble laminated cores for electrical parts, such as commutators, coils, armatures, and stators, according to specifications, using either of following methods: (1) Places core laminations and separators into holding device of machine. Starts machine that automatically measures and stacks specified quantity of laminations for each core and inserts separators between laminations. Unloads laminations from machine, and secures laminations using tape or other material. (2) Stacks specified quantity of laminations in holding fixture. Squeezes stack, manually, or presses laminations together in vise or press to reduce kinks or bulges. Measures stack, using rule, and adds or removes laminations and separators to obtain specified dimensions. Aligns edges of laminations, using hammer, and secures laminations, using rubber wrapping material. May place stack of lamination cores into machine that automatically welds laminations into individual cores. May be designated according to method used or type of core assembled as Lamination Stacker, Hand (elec. equip.; electron. comp.); Lamination Stacker, Machine (elec. equip.; electron. comp.); Transformer-Core Assembler (elec. equip.). ● **GED:** R2, M1, L2 ● **SVP:** 1-3 mos ● **Academic:** Ed=N, Eng=N ● **Work Field:** 063, 111 ● **MPSMS:** 580 ● **Aptitudes:** G4, V4, N4, S4, P4, Q4, K3, F4, M3, E5, C5 ● **Temperaments:** R, T ● **Physical:** Stg=L; Freq: R, H, I, N, D, A ● **Work Env:** Noise=N; ● **Salary:** 2 ● **Outlook:** 3

PRINTED CIRCUIT BOARD ASSEMBLER, HAND (comm. equip.) ● DOT #726.684-070 ● OES: 93905 ● Performs any combination of following duties in assembly of electronic components onto printed circuit boards (PCB's) according to specifications, using handtools: Reads worksheets and wiring diagrams, receives verbal instructions, or follows sample board to determine assembly duties, and selects components, such as transistors, resistors, relays, capacitors, and integrated circuits. Twists, bends, trims, strips, or files wire leads of components or reams holes in boards to insert wire leads, using handtools. Inserts color-coded wires in designated holes and clinches wire ends, using pliers. Press-fits (mounts) component leads onto board. Places plastic insulating sleeves around specified wire leads of components and shrinks sleeves into place, using heat gun. Crimps wire leads on underside of board, using handtools or press. Applies sealer or masking compound to selected parts of board to protect parts from effects of wave solder process. Solders wire leads and joints on underside of board, using soldering iron, to route and connect lead wires to board and between individual components. Installs heat sinks, sockets, faceplates, and accessories on boards, using handtools. May be designated according to unit installed as Socket Assembler (electron. comp.) or stage of production as Post-Wave Assembler (electron. comp.); Pre-Wave Assembler (electron. comp.). May assist other workers in wave-soldering PCB's. ● **GED:** R3, M1, L2 ● **SVP:** 3-6 mos ● **Academic:** Ed=N, Eng=N ● **Work Field:** 111 ● **MPSMS:** 587 ● **Aptitudes:** G4, V4, N4, S3, P3, Q4, K3, F2, M3, E5, C4 ● **Temperaments:** R, T ● **Physical:** Stg=L; Freq: R, H, I, N, D, A, X ● **Work Env:** Noise=N; ● **Salary:** 2 ● **Outlook:** 4

TUBE ASSEMBLER, CATHODE RAY (electron. comp.) ● DOT #725.684-022 ● OES: 93997 ● Performs any combination of following tasks to assemble cathode-ray tubes used in television and display equipment: Removes funnel from rack and places funnel onto conveyorized washing, rinsing, and drying equipment. Positions funnel in rotatable holding chuck to secure funnel for painting. Inserts brush into rotating funnel and paints dag (conductive graphite) coating as indicated by chuck guide to provide electric conductivity. Verifies that aperture mask and display screen fit together according to corresponding numbers. Examines aperture mask and screen in light box to detect misaligned color dots, using microscope. Positions funnel in rotatable chuck equipped with automatic frit dispenser. Moves controls that index frit dispenser around edge of funnel mouth to dispense sealant. Removes frit-coated funnel from chuck and secures funnel in jig for joining display screen assembly onto funnel. Positions display screen assembly on funnel edge and aligns screen with reference points on funnel. Pushes jig onto conveyor leading into oven to fuse funnel and display screen assembly into bulb. Places bulb on holding fixture of sprayer to coat interior surface of bulb with protective layer of lacquer. Places bulb onto holding fixture of evaporation equipment to apply aluminized coating to interior surface of bulb. Places bulb onto conveyor that carries bulb through processing stations to preheat bulb, insert and fuse gun to neck of bulb to form tube, and anneals and cools tube assembly. Places tube onto cart or conveyor for further processing. Inspects tube for imperfections, such as blemishes, coating defects, scratches, bubbles, or stains, using magnifier, ultraviolet light, inspection booth, or unaided vision. May be designated according to duties performed as Aluminizer (electron. comp.); Bulb Assembler (electron. comp.); Dag Coater (electron. comp.); Frit Coater (electron. comp.); Funnel Coater (electron comp.); Gun-Sealing-Machine Operator (electron. comp.); Lacquer Sprayer (electron. comp.). ● **GED:** R2, M1, L1 ● **SVP:** 1-3 mos ● **Academic:** Ed=N, Eng=N ● **Work Field:** 111, 153, 141 ● **MPSMS:** 587 ● **Aptitudes:** G3, V4, N4, S4, P3, Q4, K3, F3, M3, E5, C4 ● **Temperaments:** R ● **Physical:** Stg=M; Freq: R, H Occas: I, N, D, A, X ● **Work Env:** Noise=N; ● **Salary:** 3 ● **Outlook:** 3

TUBE ASSEMBLER, ELECTRON (electron. comp.) ● DOT #725.384-010 ● OES: 93997 ● Performs any combination of following tasks to fabricate parts and assemble custom or production electron tubes: Reads work orders, receives verbal instructions, and follows drawings and sample assemblies to fabricate and assemble parts. Winds wire around grid core or mandrel to form filaments, grids, and heaters, using manual or automatic winding machines. Stretches and presses wound grid cores to designated shape, and cuts cores to specified size, using manual or power tools. Forms parts, such as grids, stems, and leads, using special purpose automatic machines. Coats designated parts with specified materials to change conductive properties of parts or provide electrostatic shield for tube elements, using spray equipment, paint brush, pressurized needle, or other coating method. Positions parts, such as grids, spacers, plates, caps, shields, stems, heaters, and radiators, in specified relationship to one another. Mounts parts in holding fixtures and bonds parts together, using welding and brazing techniques and equipment. Fills bases or top caps of designated tubes with adhesive and attaches bases or caps to glass bulbs and metal shells. Places assembled tube in equipment to remove impurities, create vacuum, and seal tube. Stamps and etches identifying information on tube and tube parts, using printing or etching equipment. Polishes designated parts and assemblies, using buffing wheel. Tends ovens that cure adhesives, inks, and coatings. Assembles parts for cathodes, using microscope. Tests and inspects parts and assemblies for conformance to specifications, using test equipment, precision measuring instruments, and microscope. Tends electronic ageing equipment that stabilize electrical characteristics of tubes. May be designated by duties performed as Electron Gun Assembler (electron. comp.); Stem-Lead Former (electron. comp.); Tube-Component Assembler (electron comp.); Tube Fitter (electron. comp.). ● **GED:** R2, M2, L2 ● **SVP:** 2-30 days ● **Academic:** Ed=N, Eng=N ● **Work Field:** 111 ● **MPSMS:** 587 ● **Aptitudes:** G4, V4, N4, S4, P4, Q4, K3, F3, M3, E5, C4 ● **Temperaments:** J, T ● **Physical:** Stg=L; Freq: R, H, I, N Occas: D, A, X ● **Work Env:** Noise=N; ● **Salary:** 3 ● **Outlook:** 2

WHEEL LACER AND TRUER (motor-bicycles) ● DOT #706.684-106 ● OES: 93997 ● Alternate titles: WHEEL ASSEMBLER; WHEEL TRUER. Laces and trues-up (aligns) motorcycle and bicycle wheels according to specifications, using gauges and handtools or power tools: Hooks wire spokes onto perforated hubs and screws nipples of spokes onto rim to lace (assemble) wheel, using special hand wrench. Measures diameter of wheel, using fixed gauge. Grinds protruding end of spokes from inside surface of rim, using portable hand grinder. Mounts tires on wheels [TIRE MOUNTER (fabrication, nec)] and clamps wheel in fixture. Positions dial indicator against tire and rim, turns wheel, and notes points at which wheel needs alignment as indicated by needle deflection on indicator. Turns spoke nipples with wrench to adjust tension of spokes at indicated points to align wheel. ● **GED:** R2, M1, L2 ● **SVP:** 3-6 mos ● **Academic:** Ed=N, Eng=N ● **Work Field:** 061 ● **MPSMS:** 595 ● **Aptitudes:** G4, V4, N4, S4, P3, Q4, K4, F3, M3, E5, C5 ● **Temperaments:** J, R, T ● **Physical:** Stg=M; Freq: R, H, I, N, D Occas: S ● **Work Env:** Noise=N; ● **Salary:** 1 ● **Outlook:** 3

GOE: 06.02.24
Manual Work, Metal & Plastics

ASSEMBLER, METAL BONDING (aircraft mfg.) ● DOT #806.384-030 ● OES: 93997 ● Alternate titles: ASSEMBLER, BONDING. Bonds aircraft and space vehicle parts and assemblies, such as sheet metal skins to honeycomb core, according to blueprints and specifications, using handtools, power tools, and equipment: Reads process charts, work orders, and specifications to determine sequence of bonding operations, amount of bonding agent to be applied, and areas to be bonded. Examines parts to verify that prior processes have been completed and that identifying information corresponds with specifications. Measures, trims, fits, forms, and shapes mating surfaces of parts to ensure required contact can be accomplished, using measuring instruments, handtools, and power tools. Cleans dust, dirt, oil, and other foreign matter from contact surfaces, using cleaning solutions and rags. Positions, aligns, fits, and assembles parts, materials, and incidental functional items on jigs, fixtures, platen or project plates, using handtools, power tools, and fasteners. Applies primer and metal bonding film, foam, or other adhesives to bonding surfaces. Dries and cures parts and assemblies, using vacuum fixtures or presses with heated platens. Adjusts curing oven controls to regulate pressure, time, and heating temperature. Loads and unloads assemblies from oven, manually or using equipment. May mix adhesives. ● **GED:** R3, M2, L3 ● **SVP:** 6 mos-1 yr ● **Academic:** Ed=N, Eng=N ● **Work Field:** 102 ● **MPSMS:** 592 ● **Aptitudes:** G3, V3, N4, S3, P3, Q4, K3, F3, M3, E5, C5 ● **Temperaments:** T ● **Physical:** Stg=M; Freq: R, H, I, N, D Occas: S, K, O, E ● **Work Env:** Noise=L; Occas: A, M, T ● **Salary:** 2 ● **Outlook:** 3

BRIGHT CUTTER (jewelry-silver.) ● DOT #700.684-018 ● OES: 93926 ● Cuts layer of metal from walls of settings and other surfaces of jewelry articles to reveal bright inner metals: Clamps article in chuck preparatory to cutting. Lubricates cutting tool and pushes tool over surface to remove specified layer of metal. ● **GED:** R3, M2, L2 ● **SVP:** 1-3 mos ● **Academic:** Ed=N, Eng=N ● **Work Field:** 054 ● **MPSMS:** 611 ● **Aptitudes:** G3, V4, N4, S4, P3, Q5, K3, F4, M3, E5, C4 ● **Temperaments:** R, T ● **Physical:** Stg=S; Const: R, H Freq: I, N, A Occas: X ● **Work Env:** Noise=N; ● **Salary:** 3 ● **Outlook:** 2

BOAT PATCHER, PLASTIC (ship-boat mfg.) ● DOT #807.684-014 ● OES: 85998 ● Alternate titles: ASSEMBLY DETAILER; PATCHER, PLASTIC BOAT. Repairs and repaints defects in fiberglass boat hulls, decks, and cabins, using handtools and power tools: Examines parts for defects, such as cracks and holes. Drills out defective areas or smooths rough edges, using portable electric drill and grinder. Cuts out patch of fiberglass material, using shears. Mixes resin and catalyst, dips patch in solution, and places patch over defect. Shapes and smooths edges to match contour of patched area. Fills holes with plastic filler material. Smooths repaired surfaces, using sandpaper or power disk sander. Mixes plastic paint with catalyst and sprays repaired surfaces, using spray gun. Cuts out damaged wood bracing strips, using portable electric saw. Replaces and bonds strips in place with saturated fiberglass mat. Touches up flaws, using paintbrush. May polish repainted sections. ● **GED:** R3, M1, L1 ● **SVP:** 3-6 mos ● **Academic:** Ed=N, Eng=N ● **Work Field:** 102 ● **MPSMS:** 593 ● **Aptitudes:** G3, V4, N4, S4, P3, Q4, K3, F3, M3, E5, C3 ● **Temperaments:** T ● **Physical:** Stg=M; Freq: S, K, O, R, H, I, N, D ● **Work Env:** Noise=L; Occas: W ● **Salary:** 3 ● **Outlook:** 3

CASTER (jewelry-silver.) ● DOT #502.381-010 ● OES: 89198 ● Alternate titles: MOLDER; SLUSH CASTER. Casts jewelry pieces and ornamental figures for trophies and placques from molten lead or zinc: Melts zinc or lead alloy bars in kettle. Assembles sections of mold and secures mold with C-clamp. Pours molten metal into mold, using hand ladle. Disassembles mold after specified time and knocks sand from casting, using mallet. Places jewelry piece or figure in tray to cool. ● **GED:** R3, M2, L2 ● **SVP:** 1-2 yrs ● **Academic:** Ed=N, Eng=N ● **Work Field:** 132 ● **MPSMS:** 611 ● **Aptitudes:** G3, V4, N4, S3, P3, Q5, K3, F3, M3, E5, C5 ● **Temperaments:** R, T ● **Physical:** Stg=M; Freq: R, H, D Occas: I ● **Work Env:** Noise=N; Freq: O ● **Salary:** 3 ● **Outlook:** 3

FABRICATOR-ASSEMBLER, METAL PRODUCTS (any industry) ● DOT #809.381-010 ● OES: 93196 ● Fabricates and assembles metal products, such as window sashes, casements, doors, awning frames, shells, cases, and tubular products, such as golf carts or furniture, as specified by work orders, diagrams, and templates, using handtools, power tools, and metalworking machinery: Lays out and marks reference points onto components, using template, rule, square, compass, and scale [LAY-OUT WORKER (any industry) II 809.381-014]. Operates machines, such as shears, cutoff saws, brakes, punch press, form roll and drill press, to cut and shape components to specified dimensions [MACHINE OPERATOR (any industry) II 619.685-062]. Fits [FITTER (any industry) II 706.684-054] and assembles components, using fixtures, handtools, and portable power tools, such as grinders, drills, power wrenches, and riveters. Operates machines, such as arbor presses, riveting press, brazing machine, and resistance-welding machines, to complete assembly. May weld components together. May be designated by specialty as Awning-Frame Maker (fabrication, nec); Metal Screen, Storm Door, And Window Builder (struct. metal); Tubular-Products Fabricator (any industry). ● **GED:** R3, M2, L2 ● **SVP:** 6 mos-1 yr ● **Academic:** Ed=N, Eng=N ● **Work Field:** 102 ● **MPSMS:** 550 ● **Aptitudes:** G3, V3, N3, S3, P3, Q4, K3, F3, M3, E4, C5 ● **Temperaments:** J, T ● **Physical:** Stg=M; Freq: R, H, I, E, N, D, A Occas: S, G ● **Work Env:** Noise=L; ● **Salary:** 3 ● **Outlook:** 3

GREASE BUFFER (jewelry-silver.) ● DOT #705.684-022 ● OES: 93953 ● Holds and turns silverware, such as bowls, tea sets, trays, or flatware, against grease-coated cloth wheel or leather belt to impart specified finish. May remove scratches, spots, or blemishes with pumice stone. May bolt layers of precut cloth onto spindle and form into buff of desired shape by holding rakelike handtool against rotating cloth. May buff silverware to specified final finish, using soft cloth buffing wheel and fine grained rouge or buffing compound and be designated Finisher (jewelry-silver.). ● **GED:** R3, M1, L2 ● **SVP:** 3-6 mos ● **Academic:** Ed=N, Eng=N ● **Work Field:** 051 ● **MPSMS:** 612 ● **Aptitudes:** G3, V4, N4, S4, P3, Q4, K3, F3, M3, E5, C4 ● **Temperaments:** J, R, T ● **Physical:** Stg=L; Freq: R, H, I, N Occas: S, X ● **Work Env:** Noise=L; Occas: A, M ● **Salary:** 2 ● **Outlook:** 2

PRESSURE SEALER-AND-TESTER (aircraft mfg.) ● DOT #806.384-038 ● OES: 85323 ● Alternate titles: SEALER, AIRCRAFT. Cleans, seals, and tests aircraft pressurized sections and cavities, according to blueprints and specifications, using handtools, power tools, and pressure testing equipment: Reads and interprets blueprints and process specifications to determine area to be sealed, volume of pressure to be applied, and allowable tolerances. Applies cleaning solvent or other solution to interior and exterior surfaces of section to be sealed, such as fuel and water tanks, integral wings, and fuselage, using brushes, rags, spray guns, liquid vacuum cleaners, and air hoses. Applies sealing compounds to surfaces, using fillet guns, brushes, and similar equipment. Dries sealant, using heat lamps and compressed hot air. Bolts access doors and hatches, disconnects plumbing lines, electrical cable and rigging, and caps connections with plugs and threaded fixtures to make section airtight. Sets up and operates pressure-testing equipment to detect leakage. Visually and audibly checks for leakage of areas under pressure, and applies sealing tape, cement, liquid rubber, grommets, and other aids to eliminate leakage. Reinstalls accessories disconnected prior to test. May repair structural defects, using tools and equipment. May seal and test integral wing sections serving as fuel cells, working within closed or difficult areas to access, and be designated Fuel Tank Sealer And Tester (aircraft mfg.) or Integral Tank Sealer (aircraft mfg.). May seal and pressurize aircraft fuselage sections and be designated Pressurization Mechanic (aircraft mfg.) or Pressurizer (aircraft mfg.). May set up and operate air pressure cabinet located outside section being tested by others to maintain constant internal pressure and be designated Pressurization Mechanic, Air Control (aircraft mfg.). ● **GED:** R3, M2, L3 ● **SVP:** 3-6 mos ● **Academic:** Ed=N, Eng=N ● **Work Field:** 102 ● **MPSMS:** 592 ● **Aptitudes:** G3, V3, N4, S3, P3, Q4, K3, F3, M3, E4, C4 ● **Temperaments:** T ● **Physical:** Stg=L; Freq: R, H, I, D Occas: C, B, S, K, O, W, E, G, N, X ● **Work Env:** Noise=L; Freq: A, T Occas: D ● **Salary:** 2 ● **Outlook:** 3

REPAIRER, FINISHED METAL (any industry) ● DOT #809.684-034 ● OES: 85998 ● Repairs surface defects, such as dings, dents, and buckles, in finished metal items, such as automobile bodies, refrigerators, or other appliances, using dolly blocks, ding and pick hammers, and other handtools: Visually examines and feels surface of workpiece to determine extent of defect. Holds dolly block against defect and hammers opposite side to smooth surface, being careful not to stretch surface or mar finish. Cleans and polishes repaired area, using buffer and cloth. May file dings to remove burrs and rough spots. Polishes working surfaces of dolly blocks and hammers, using naphtha-soaked emery cloth to prevent scratching or gouging of workpiece. ● **GED:** R3, M1, L1 ● **SVP:** 6 mos-1 yr ● **Academic:** Ed=N, Eng=N ● **Work Field:** 102 ● **MPSMS:** 583, 591 ● **Aptitudes:** G3, V4, N4, S4, P3, Q4, K3, F4, M3, E4, C5 ● **Temperaments:** J, T ● **Physical:** Stg=H; Const: H, N Freq: R, D Occas: S, E, T, G ● **Work Env:** Noise=L; Freq: A, M ● **Salary:** 3 ● **Outlook:** 2

REPAIRER, TYPEWRITER (office machines) ● DOT #706.381-030 ● OES: 85926 ● Repairs and adjusts defective typewriters removed from production line, using handtools, power tools, and gauges: Operates typewriter to test functioning of parts and mechanisms to determine repairs required. Disassembles machines to repair or replace defective components, using handtools and holding devices. Bends, taps, turns parts, such as screws, nuts, and type bar, to eliminate binding, looseness, and misalignment, using special handtools. Verifies specified clearance between parts, using spacebars, tension scales, dial indicators, and feeler gauges. Measures rotation of motor drive-wheel to determine speed of drive, using tachometer. May adjust interrelated typewriter parts to synchronize machine operation and be designated Adjuster (office machines). ● **GED:** R3, M2, L3 ● **SVP:** 1-2 yrs ● **Academic:** Ed=N, Eng=S ● **Work Field:** 121 ● **MPSMS:** 571 ● **Aptitudes:** G3, V3, N3, S3, P3, Q4, K3, F3, M3, E5, C5 ● **Temperaments:** J, T ● **Physical:** Stg=M; Freq: R, H, I, N, D Occas: E, A ● **Work Env:** Noise=N; ● **Salary:** 4 ● **Outlook:** 2

ROUTER OPERATOR, HAND (aircraft mfg.) ● DOT #806.684-150 ● OES: 93926 ● Routs and trims metallic and nonmetallic parts and materials to provide cutouts for windows, air vents, and tubing runs, used in manufacturing transportation equipment, such as aircraft and railroad cars, using portable router and handtools: Selects and installs specified type and size bit and collar combinations in hand router, guided by template, jig, or fixture markings or information obtained from blueprints and specifications. Positions and secures parts or materials to be routed, template, and router guide on router board, jig, or fixture, using bolts, screws, clamps, handtools, and power tools. Moves router along guide to cut openings in parts and materials or to trim excess material. Grinds, smooths, or deburrs parts, using handtools or power tools. May drill coordinating holes in parts or materials, using drill motor. ● **GED:** R3, M1, L2 ● **SVP:** 3-6 mos ● **Academic:** Ed=N, Eng=N ● **Work Field:** 055 ● **MPSMS:** 592, 594 ● **Aptitudes:** G3, V4, N4, S4, P3, Q4, K3, F4, M3, E5, C5 ● **Temperaments:** R, T ● **Physical:** Stg=M; Freq: S, O, R, H, N, D Occas: K, I, E, A ● **Work Env:** Noise=L; Const: M Occas: A ● **Salary:** 3 ● **Outlook:** 2

SKI REPAIRER, PRODUCTION (toy-sport equip.) ● DOT #732.684-118 ● OES: 93998 ● Repairs defects in skis damaged in production or defective in material, using handtools and power tools: Examines designated defects and markings on ski to determine type repair required. Selects specified fiberglass mat patch and positions patch over defect. Pours epoxy resin on patch to cause patch to adhere to ski. Places patched area into heated mold press to shape and dry patch. Removes ski from mold press and trims patched area with knife. Drills holes and trims damaged area to provide access to defect for skis having defects in plastic base layer, using portable drill and knife. Aligns polyethylene-plastic sliver with defect in base layer and rubs soldering iron over sliver to melt plastic into defect. Smooths repaired ski to remove excess patching, using belt sander. May repair and refinish user-damaged skis in ski manufacturer's service shop. ● **GED:** R2, M1, L1 ● **SVP:** 6 mos-1 yr ● **Academic:** Ed=N, Eng=N ● **Work Field:** 102 ● **MPSMS:** 616 ● **Aptitudes:** G4, V4, N4, S4, P3, Q4, K3, F4, M3, E5, C4 ● **Temperaments:** J, T ● **Physical:** Stg=L; Freq: R, H, N Occas: I, E, D, A, X ● **Work Env:** Noise=L; ● **Salary:** 1 ● **Outlook:** 3

SOLAR-FABRICATION TECHNICIAN (machine shop) ● DOT #809.381-034 ● OES: 93196 ● Fabricates and assembles metal solar collectors according to job order specifications, using machine shop tools and equipment: Lays out and marks reference points on metal tubing and sheets according to job order specifications, using rule and scriber. Aligns, cuts, and drills copper tubing to form pipe sections, using jig, bandsaw, and drill press. Smooths edges of pipe sections, using file and T-bar. Inserts other precut pipes into drilled holes of pipe sections according to job order specifications, and brazes joints to form manifold unit. Aligns and bends copper sheeting to form absorber plate, using power brake. Aligns manifold unit with grooves of absorber plate, squirts liquid solder into grooves, and bakes assembly to permanently bond joints, using oven. Sprays black paint on assembly to facilitate solar heat absorption, using paint sprayer. Aligns and bends galvanized sheeting to form enclosure frame parts of solar collector, using power brake. Drills holes into frame parts and screws or rivets parts together, using pneumatic drill and rivet gun. Inserts absorber plate and manifold assembly into enclosure frame, and rivets sections together. Caulks assembly corners to prevent water leaks, using caulk gun. Cuts and inserts insulation into enclosure frame to provide heat retention. Aligns and rivets frame end to assembly. Rivets covering to unit to complete solar collector assembly. Packs solar collectors into cardboard boxes for shipment, using tape, strapping, and crimper. Records product identification information on packed boxes. ● **GED:** R3, M3, L2 ● **SVP:** 3-6 mos ● **Academic:** Ed=A, Eng=N ● **Work Field:** 102 ● **MPSMS:** 553 ● **Aptitudes:** G3, V4, N3, S2, P2, Q3, K3, F3, M2, E4, C4 ● **Temperaments:** T, V ● **Physical:** Stg=H; Freq: R, H, I, N, D, A Occas: S, O, X ● **Work Env:** Noise=L; ● **Salary:** 2 ● **Outlook:** 3

SPINNER (jewelry-silver.) ● DOT #700.684-074 ● OES: 93998 ● Stretches and shapes metal into symmetrical forms, using handtools and bench lathe, for use in making jewelry: Mounts work in lathe chuck. Starts lathe and forces handtools against metal to bend and stretch it as specified. ● **GED:** R3, M2, L2 ● **SVP:** 6 mos-1 yr ● **Academic:** Ed=N, Eng=N ● **Work Field:** 134 ● **MPSMS:** 611 ● **Aptitudes:** G3, V4, N4, S3, P3, Q4, K3, F3, M3, E5, C5 ● **Temperaments:** J, T ● **Physical:** Stg=L; Freq: R, H, I, N ● **Work Env:** Noise=N; ● **Salary:** 3 ● **Outlook:** 2

STRAIGHTENER, HAND (any industry) ● DOT #709.484-014 ● OES: 93998 ● Straightens metal workpieces to blueprint specifications, using handtools and knowledge of metal properties: Rolls workpiece on flat surface or mounts and rotates it between centers to ascertain irregularities visually or with dial indicator. Positions workpiece on surface plate or anvil and hammers workpiece at points of irregularity to straighten it. Hammers mandrel through cylindrical objects, such as pipes or tubing to remove dents or kinks. Measures straightened workpiece for conformance with specifications, using straightedge, micrometers, and calipers. May straighten workpiece in straightening press. May heat workpiece in furnace or with heating torch to straighten it. May be designated according to parts straightened as Tool Straightener (any industry); Straightener, Gun Parts (ordnance). ● **GED:** R3, M2, L2 ● **SVP:** 6 mos-1 yr ● **Academic:** Ed=N, Eng=N ● **Work Field:** 134 ● **MPSMS:** 540 ● **Aptitudes:** G3, V3, N3, S3, P3, Q4, K3, F3, M3, E5, C4 ● **Temperaments:** R, T ● **Physical:** Stg=M; Freq: S, R, H, I, N Occas: D ● **Work Env:** Noise=L; Occas: O ● **Salary:** 1 ● **Outlook:** 3

TROPHY ASSEMBLER (jewelry-silver.) ● DOT #735.684-018 ● OES: 93997 ● Assembles trophies to customer's specifications, using drill press and handtools: Selects parts, such as base, tubing, metal plates, figures, and hardware from stock. Drills holes in base or plaque, using electric drill or drill press. Glues felt to bottom of base, or screws in metal feet. Staples or tapes metal plate to base. Bolts parts together, using screwdriver and socket wrench. Touches up scratch marks with scratch remover and polishes assembled trophy. May attach marble or onyx decoration to formed column with adhesive tape. May wrap trophy in tissue paper preparatory to shipping. ● **GED:** R3, M2, L2 ● **SVP:** 6 mos-1 yr ● **Academic:** Ed=N, Eng=N ● **Work Field:** 102 ● **MPSMS:** 612 ● **Aptitudes:** G3, V4, N4, S3, P3, Q4, K3, F3, M3, E5, C4 ● **Temperaments:** R, T ● **Physical:** Stg=L; Freq: R, H, I, N, D Occas: E, X ● **Work Env:** Noise=N; ● **Salary:** 2 ● **Outlook:** 3

GOE: 06.02.27
Manual Work, Textile, Fabric, & Leather

CUTTER, HAND I (any industry) ● DOT #781.684-074 ● OES: 93926 ● Cuts out, shapes, or trims material or articles, such as canvas goods, garment parts, hats and caps, house furnishings, or knit goods, to facilitate subsequent operations, using scissors or knife: Unrolls and lays out material along calibrated scale on cutting table or measures material with ruler and cuts material into lengths, using scissors or knife. Positions pattern or template on material or marks around pattern or template, using chalk or pencil, and cuts out parts, using scissors or knife. Cuts notches in edges of parts to mark them for assembly. Shapes or trims excess material from parts. May match materials for color or shade. May cut or trim knit goods, using hot-wire device. May mark identification numbers on parts. May spread cloth on table in single or multiple lays prior to cutting. May assemble and fold articles after cutting. May be designated according to type of material or article cut as Applique Cutter, Hand (tex. prod., nec); Bedspread Cutter, Hand (tex. prod., nec); Blanket Cutter, Hand (tex. prod., nec); Canvas Cutter, Hand (tex. prod., nec); Curtain Cutter, Hand (tex. prod., nec); Drapery Cutter, Hand (tex. prod., nec); Garment-Parts Cutter, Hand (garment). May be designated: Hat-And-Cap-Parts Cutter, Hand (hat & cap); Knit-Goods Cutter, Hand (knitting); Terry-Cloth Cutter, Hand (tex. prod., nec). ● **GED:** R3, M1, L2 ● **SVP:** 3-6 mos ● **Academic:** Ed=N, Eng=N ● **Work Field:** 054, 241 ● **MPSMS:** 420, 430, 440 ● **Aptitudes:** G4, V4, N4, S3, P3, Q4, K3, F3, M3, E5, C4 ● **Temperaments:** R, T ● **Physical:** Stg=L; Const: R, H Freq: I, N, D, A, X Occas: S ● **Work Env:** Noise=N; ● **Salary:** 3 ● **Outlook:** 2

LEATHER CUTTER (leather prod.) ● DOT #783.684-022 ● OES: 93926 ● Lays out, marks, and cuts leather or skins into parts for articles, such as holsters, belts, gun cases, garments and garment trim, surgical appliances, and paint roller covers, using leather knife or shears: Lays leather or skins on cutting table and positions pattern pieces on leather or skins to determine number of cuts. Marks outline of pattern on leather or skins, using pencil. Cuts around outline, using leather knife or shears. Turns screws on strap knife to adjust width of cut when cutting leather for rifle slings and gun case handles. Lays leather side on table, positions dies on leather to obtain maximum number of cuts from side, and strikes die with mallet to cut out part. May stack and tie cut pieces together. May cut parts with guillotine cutter. May punch holes in parts, using kick press. ● **GED:** R3, M2, L2 ● **SVP:** 3-6 mos ● **Academic:** Ed=N, Eng=N ● **Work Field:** 054, 241 ● **MPSMS:** 529 ● **Aptitudes:** G3, V4, N4, S3, P3, Q4, K3, F3, M3, E5, C5 ● **Temperaments:** J, T ● **Physical:** Stg=L; Const: R, H, N Freq: I, D, A Occas: S, O ● **Work Env:** Noise=L; ● **Salary:** 2 ● **Outlook:** 3

LEATHER WORKER (leather prod.) ● DOT #783.684-026 ● OES: 93997 ● Punches holes, installs rivets, and finishes edges of leather products, such as holsters, rifle cases, and belts, using handtools: Marks holes in article, using template and marking pencil. Punches holes for rivets, snaps, or buttons, using hand punch. Fastens parts together, using rivets, stitching machine, needle and thread, or adhesive. Attaches eyelets and metal decorations to article, using hammer and punch. Cuts around edge of article to smooth edge, using knife. Brushes stain on cut edge to match color of article. Rubs finished article with damp cloth to clean leather and rubs paste wax on surface, using cloth, to produce shine. May emboss designs on leather surface. May be designated according to article fabricated or repaired as Holster Maker (leather prod.); Rifle-Case Repairer (leather prod.). ● GED: R3, M2, L2 ● SVP: 6 mos-1 yr ● Academic: Ed=N, Eng=N ● Work Field: 102 ● MPSMS: 529 ● Aptitudes: G4, V4, N4, S3, P3, Q4, K3, F3, M3, E4, C4 ● Temperaments: T, V ● Physical: Stg=M; Freq: R, H, I, E, N, D Occas: X ● Work Env: Noise=L; ● Salary: 2 ● Outlook: 3

RUG CLEANER, HAND (laundry & rel.) ● DOT #369.384-014 ● OES: 93998 ● Alternate titles: CARPET CLEANER; RUG RENOVATOR; RUG SCRUBBER; RUG SHAMPOOER; RUG WASHER. Cleans rugs with chemical solutions in plant or on customer's premises, using handbrushes or portable scrubbing machine, determining washing method according to condition of rug: Vacuums rugs to remove loose dirt. Guides scrubbing machine over rug surface or sprays rug with cleaning solution under pressure to agitate nap and loosen embedded dirt. Removes excess suds and water from rug during scrubbing operation, using vacuum nozzle or squeegee. Identifies persistent stains and selects spotting agent to remove stain according to type of fiber, dye, and stain. Rubs chemical solution into rug with handbrush until stain disappears. Rinses rug, using water hose, and hangs rug on rack to dry. Pushes pilating (pile lifting) machine over surface of dried rug to raise and fluff nap or brushes pile, using broom. Removes excess water by feeding rugs between rollers of mechanical wringer, putting rugs in extractor, or going over surface with squeegee or vacuum nozzle. Brushes, sprays, or sprinkles sizing solutions on the backs of rugs, using handbrush, spray gun, or sprinkling can. May scrub fragile or oriental rugs, using handbrush, soap, and water. May spray acetic acid or salt solution over washed rugs to prevent colors from running. May measure rugs to determine cleaning fee. May clean upholstered furniture, using sponge, brush, and cleaning solutions. May trim frayed edges of carpet and rebind carpet edges, using scissors, knife, needle, and thread. May perform rug cleaning duties as employee of establishment, such as hotel. ● GED: R3, M1, L2 ● SVP: 6 mos-1 yr ● Academic: Ed=N, Eng=N ● Work Field: 031 ● MPSMS: 906 ● Aptitudes: G4, V4, N4, S4, P4, Q4, K4, F4, M3, E4, C4 ● Temperaments: R, T ● Physical: Stg=M; Freq: R, H, N Occas: S, K, I, A, X ● Work Env: Noise=Q; Occas: U ● Salary: 3 ● Outlook: 2

SPOTTER I (laundry & rel.) ● DOT #361.684-018 ● OES: 93998 ● Identifies stains in washable cotton and synthetic garments or household linens prior to laundering and applies chemicals until stain dissolves, using brush, sponge, or bone spatula: Sorts stained articles to segregate items stained with oil, grease or blood. Applies and rubs chemicals into garment, using bone spatula, sponge or brush, until stain dissolves. Places spotted articles in net bags for return to washroom. Bleaches and washes some articles in small washing machine. ● GED: R3, M1, L1 ● SVP: 1-3 mos ● Academic: Ed=N, Eng=N ● Work Field: 031 ● MPSMS: 420, 440, 906 ● Aptitudes: G4, V4, N5, S4, P3, Q5, K3, F4, M3, E5, C3 ● Temperaments: J ● Physical: Stg=L; Freq: R, H, N Occas: I, E, A, X ● Work Env: Noise=N; ● Salary: 1 ● Outlook: 2

GOE: 06.02.28
Manual Work, Food Processing

BENCH HAND (bakery products) ● DOT #520.384-010 ● OES: 93998 ● Alternate titles: BAKER, BENCH; DOUGH MOLDER, HAND. Forms dough for bread, buns, and other bakery products: Rolls dough to desired thickness with rolling pin or guides dough through rolling machine. Sprinkles flour on dough and workbench to prevent dough from sticking. Kneads dough to eliminate gases formed by yeast. Cuts dough into pieces with knife or handcutter. Adds spices, fruits, or seeds when making special rolls or breads. Weighs pieces on scales and keeps record of production. Places dough in baking pans. May cut dough into bun divisions by machine. May form dough into special shapes and add fillings or flavorings. ● GED: R3, M2, L2 ● SVP: 1-2 yrs ● Academic: Ed=N, Eng=N ● Work Field: 146 ● MPSMS: 384 ● Aptitudes: G3, V4, N3, S3, P3, Q4, K3, F3, M3, E5, C4 ● Temperaments: J, T ● Physical: Stg=M; Freq: R, H, I, N, D Occas: E, X ● Work Env: Noise=N; ● Salary: 1 ● Outlook: 2

BUTCHER, ALL-ROUND (meat products) ● DOT #525.381-014 ● OES: 89803 ● Performs slaughtering and butchering tasks in small slaughtering and meat packing establishment, using cutting tools, such as cleaver, knife, and saw: Stuns animals prior to slaughtering [STUNNER, ANIMAL (meat products)]. Shackles hind legs of animals, such as cattle, sheep, and hogs, to raise them for slaughtering or skinning [SHACKLER (meat products)]. Severs jugular vein to drain blood and facilitate slaughtering [STICKER, ANIMAL (meat products)]. Trims head meat and otherwise severs or removes parts of animal heads or skulls [HEAD TRIMMER (meat products)]. Saws, splits, or scribes slaughtered animals to reduce carcass [CARCASS SPLITTER (meat products)]. Slits open, eviscerates, and trims carcasses of slaughtered animals. Cuts, trims, skins, sorts, and washes viscera of slaughtered animals to separate edible portions from offal [OFFAL SEPARATOR (meat products)]. Washes carcasses [WASHER, CARCASS (meat products)]. Wraps muslin cloth about dressed animal carcasses or sides to enhance appearance and protect meat [SHROUDER (meat products)]. Shaves hog carcasses [SHAVER (meat products)]. Trims and cleans animal hides, using knife [HIDE TRIMMER (meat products; oils & grease)]. Cuts bones from standard cuts of meat, such as chucks, hams, loins, plates, rounds, and shanks, to prepare meat for marketing [BONER, MEAT (meat products)]. Examines, weighs, and sorts fresh pork cuts [GRADER, GREEN MEAT (meat products)]. Skins sections of animals or whole animals, such as cattle, sheep, and hogs [SKINNER (meat products)]. Works in small slaughtering and meat packing establishment. May prepare meats for smoking [SMOKED MEAT PREPARER (meat products)]. May cut and wrap meat. May salt (cure) and trim hides [HIDE HANDLER (meat products; oils & grease)]. ● GED: R3, M2, L2 ● SVP: 1-2 yrs ● Academic: Ed=N, Eng=N ● Work Field: 034 ● MPSMS: 382 ● Aptitudes: G3, V3, N4, S4, P3, Q4, K3, F3, M3, E5, C4 ● Temperaments: T, V ● Physical: Stg=H; Const: R, H, I, E, N Freq: A, X Occas: S, K, O, D ● Work Env: Noise=Q; Const: U ● Salary: 2 ● Outlook: 3

CANDY MAKER (sugar & conf.) ● DOT #529.361-014 ● OES: 89898 ● Alternate titles: BATCH MAKER; BOILER; CONFECTIONER; COOK, CANDY. Mixes and cooks candy ingredients by following, modifying, or formulating recipes to produce product of specified flavor, texture, and color: Cooks ingredients [CONFECTIONERY COOKER (sugar & conf.)] at specified temperatures in open-fire or steam-jacketed kettles or in batch or continuous pressure cookers. Casts candy by hand, using molds and funnel, or tends machine that casts candy in starch or rubber molds [DEPOSITING-MACHINE OPERATOR (sugar & conf.)]. Spreads candy onto cooling and heating slabs. Kneads and machine-pulls candy [CANDY PULLER (sugar & conf.)]. Spins or rolls candy into strips ready for cutting [SPINNER (sugar & conf.)]. Examines, feels, and tastes product to evaluate color, texture, and flavor. Adds ingredients or modifies cooking and forming operations as needed. May direct CANDY-MAKER HELPERS (sugar & conf.). May be designated according to type of candy produced as Caramel-Candy Maker (sugar & conf.); Coconut-Candy Maker (sugar & conf.); Fudge-Candy Maker (sugar & conf.); Hard-Candy Maker (sugar & conf.); Nougat-Candy Maker (sugar & conf.); Taffy-Candy Maker (sugar & conf.). ● GED: R4, M3, L4 ● SVP: 2-4 yrs ● Academic: Ed=N, Eng=S ● Work Field: 146 ● MPSMS: 393 ● Aptitudes: G3, V3, N3, S3, P3, Q4, K3, F3, M3, E5, C3 ● Temperaments: J, T, V ● Physical: Stg=M; Freq: R, H, T, G, N, X Occas: S, I, E, M ● Work Env: Noise=L; Occas: H ● Salary: 2 ● Outlook: 3

DOUGHNUT MAKER (bakery products) ● DOT #526.684-010 ● OES: 93998 ● Alternate titles: BAKER, DOUGHNUT; CRULLER MAKER. Mixes, forms, and fries dough to produce doughnuts, according to work order: Dumps prepared doughnut mix into mixing-machine bowl, adds water and dehydrated eggs, and starts mixer. Turns switch on heating unit of frying tank and sets thermostat at specified temperature. Dumps dough from mixing bowl into hopper of doughnut cutter. Sets lever to control amount of dough that doughnut cutter will portion to frying tank. Moves cutter machine back and forth over frying tank and depresses trigger to eject individual doughnuts into hot cooking oil. Turns doughnuts over in tank, using stick. Lifts wire tray of fried doughnuts from tank and places it in glazing tank. Slides trough containing glazing syrup over doughnuts. May glaze doughnuts, using hand dipper. May roll dough with rolling pin and form doughnuts with hand cutter. May lower wire tray of uncooked doughnuts into fryer, using hooks. May tend automatic equipment that mixes, cuts, and fries doughnuts. May weigh cut dough and fried doughnuts to verify weight specifications, and adjust controls of equipment accordingly when weights vary from standards. ● **GED:** R3, M1, L1 ● **SVP:** 3-6 mos ● **Academic:** Ed=N, Eng=N ● **Work Field:** 146 ● **MPSMS:** 384 ● **Aptitudes:** G3, V4, N4, S4, P3, Q4, K4, F4, M3, E5, C4 ● **Temperaments:** J, T ● **Physical:** Stg=M; Freq: R, H, I, N Occas: S, A, X ● **Work Env:** Noise=N; Const: H Occas: U ● **Salary:** 2 ● **Outlook:** 4

GOE: 06.02.29
Manual Work, Rubber

RUBBER-GOODS REPAIRER (any industry) ● DOT #759.684-054 ● OES: 85998 ● Repairs rubber products, such as life rafts and vests, gas-tank linings, inner tubes, and rubber vent systems, using oven or autoclave and steam curing iron: Cements rubber patch to torn or damaged areas and vulcanizes patch, using steam curing iron. Cuts rubber into pieces, covers metal and other surfaces with pieces, and places rubber article in oven or autoclave to bond surfaces. May make gaskets, washers, and hose, using molds and dies. ● **GED:** R3, M1, L1 ● **SVP:** 3-6 mos ● **Academic:** Ed=N, Eng=N ● **Work Field:** 063 ● **MPSMS:** 519 ● **Aptitudes:** G3, V4, N4, S4, P3, Q5, K4, F4, M3, E5, C5 ● **Temperaments:** R, T ● **Physical:** Stg=L; Freq: R, H, N Occas: I, E, D ● **Work Env:** Noise=L; Freq: U ● **Salary:** 4 ● **Outlook:** 2

GOE: 06.02.30
Manual Work, Stone, Glass & Clay

CASTER (nonmet. min.) ● DOT #575.684-018 ● OES: 93997 ● Casts plaster of paris objects, such as ashtrays, piggybanks, lamps, figurines, and statuary, using prepared molds: Assembles sections of prepared mold and secures them together with cord, clamps, or bolts, and nuts. Dumps plaster of paris into container, adds specified amount of water, and stirs mixture to required consistency to make casting, using spatula. Inserts wires and tubing into mold to reinforce casting when necessary. Pours plaster of paris into mold, shakes mold to distribute layer of plaster of paris on inside of mold and pours off excess mixture. Repeats process after each layer hardens until specified thickness of casting is attained. Disassembles mold, fills holes and defects in casting with plaster of paris, and smooths surface of casting, using scraping tool and sandpaper. ● **GED:** R2, M1, L1 ● **SVP:** 3-6 mos ● **Academic:** Ed=N, Eng=N ● **Work Field:** 132 ● **MPSMS:** 530 ● **Aptitudes:** G3, V4, N4, S3, P3, Q4, K3, F3, M3, E5, C5 ● **Temperaments:** J, T ● **Physical:** Stg=H; Freq: R, H, N ● **Work Env:** Noise=N; Freq: U ● **Salary:** 2 ● **Outlook:** 3

CEMENTER (optical goods) ● DOT #711.684-014 ● OES: 93997 ● Cements optical elements together to form units which have specific optical properties: Cleans elements, using solvent, tissue, brush, and compressed air device. Holds elements together to verify fit. Applies cement to element surfaces, using glass rod. Presses and rotates elements together to remove air pockets and distribute cement evenly over joined surfaces. Centers and clamps elements together. Places elements in curing oven for specified period. ● **GED:** R2, M2, L2 ● **SVP:** 6 mos-1 yr ● **Academic:** Ed=N, Eng=N ● **Work Field:** 063 ● **MPSMS:** 603 ● **Aptitudes:** G3, V4, N4, S3, P3, Q4, K4, F3, M4, E5, C4 ● **Temperaments:** R, T ● **Physical:** Stg=S; Freq: R, H, I, N Occas: X ● **Work Env:** Noise=N; ● **Salary:** 2 ● **Outlook:** 4

GLASS CUTTER (any industry) ● DOT #775.684-022 ● OES: 93926 ● Alternate titles: CUTTER; PATTERN CUTTER; STRAIGHT CUTTER. Cuts flat glass and mirrors to specified size and shape, using patterns, straightedge, tape measure, and glass cutting tools: Positions pattern on glass or measures dimensions and marks cutting lines, using glass cutting tool. Scribes around pattern or along straightedge, using cutting tool. Breaks away excess glass by hand or with notched tool or glass pinchers. May smooth rough edges, using belt sander. ● **GED:** R3, M1, L1 ● **SVP:** 3-6 mos ● **Academic:** Ed=N, Eng=N ● **Work Field:** 054 ● **MPSMS:** 531, 532 ● **Aptitudes:** G3, V4, N4, S4, P3, Q4, K3, F3, M3, E5, C5 ● **Temperaments:** R, T ● **Physical:** Stg=H; Const: R, H, N Freq: I, D, A Occas: S, G, V ● **Work Env:** Noise=N; Occas: O ● **Salary:** 4 ● **Outlook:** 2

MOLDER (optical goods) ● DOT #575.381-010 ● OES: 89998 ● Molds optical glass into various shaped blanks: Reads work order to determine type and quantity of optical glass to be molded. Changes dies and adjusts length of stroke and pressure of press, and regulates temperature of ovens and die heater according to type of glass to be processed. Places glass pieces in preheating oven to prepare glass for molding. Spreads refractory powder on oven floor to prevent glass from sticking and places preheated glass in oven. Presses glass pieces with paddles to determine readiness for molding and to shape glass to approximate shape of spoon die. Slides glass into spoon die, positions die in press, and depresses pedal to lower ram of press to mold glass blank. Removes spoon die from press and drops molded blank onto floor of cooling oven. ● **GED:** R3, M2, L2 ● **SVP:** 1-2 yrs ● **Academic:** Ed=N, Eng=N ● **Work Field:** 136 ● **MPSMS:** 603 ● **Aptitudes:** G3, V4, N4, S3, P3, Q5, K3, F4, M3, E4, C4 ● **Temperaments:** J, T ● **Physical:** Stg=M; Freq: R, H, I, N, A Occas: D, X ● **Work Env:** Noise=N; Const: H, O ● **Salary:** 3 ● **Outlook:** 2

PLASTER-DIE MAKER (pottery & porc.) ● DOT #774.684-026 ● OES: 93997 ● Alternate titles: RAM-DIE MAKER. Casts plaster dies for hydraulic ram press that forms pottery ware: Places wire mesh over die face of master model and presses or taps mesh with wooden mallet to contour of model. Wires nonmetallic conduit to wire mesh. Removes wire mesh assembly and sponges soap solution on model surface to separate die halves after casting. Lowers steel die rings over outside rim of each half of model and places wire mesh assembly over model face. Wires assembly to die rings. Mixes hydrostone (powdered plaster) with water and pours mixture into each half of model to top of die ring. Separates die from model and attaches airhose to die to remove water from dies. Sponges remaining moisture from dies. Places finished dies in storage rack. ● **GED:** R3, M1, L1 ● **SVP:** 6 mos-1 yr ● **Academic:** Ed=N, Eng=N ● **Work Field:** 132, 143 ● **MPSMS:** 536 ● **Aptitudes:** G3, V4, N4, S4, P3, Q4, K3, F3, M3, E5, C5 ● **Temperaments:** R, T ● **Physical:** Stg=H; Freq: R, H, I, E, N, D Occas: S ● **Work Env:** Noise=N; Freq: U ● **Salary:** 2 ● **Outlook:** 2

PLASTER MAKER (nonmet. min.) ● DOT #779.684-046 ● OES: 93997 ● Alternate titles: CASTER. Casts plaster art objects, such as statuary and plaques, using flexible molds: Assembles mold that consists of inner shell and outer casing. Mixes specified proportions of water and plaster, by hand or using mechanical mixer, and pours mixture into rubber mold. Shakes and squeezes mold to eliminate air bubbles, and smooths plaster mixture at mouth of mold, with spatula. Flexes mold to remove casting, when plaster has set. Places casting in oven to dry. May be designated according to object cast as Plaque Maker (nonmet. min.). ● **GED:** R3, M1, L2 ● **SVP:** 6 mos-1 yr ● **Academic:** Ed=N, Eng=N ● **Work Field:** 132 ● **MPSMS:** 538 ● **Aptitudes:** G3, V4, N4, S4, P3, Q5, K3, F4, M3, E5, C4 ● **Temperaments:** J, R, T ● **Physical:** Stg=M; Freq: R, H Occas: S, O, I, E, N, D, X ● **Work Env:** Noise=N; Freq: U Occas: O ● **Salary:** 2 ● **Outlook:** 2

THROWER (pottery & porc.) ● DOT #774.381-010 ● OES: 89998 ● Alternate titles: CLAY THROWER; POT MAKER. Molds plastic clay into such ware as vases, urns, saggers, and pitchers, as clay revolves on potter's wheel: Positions ball of clay in center of potter's wheel and starts motor, or pumps treadle with foot to revolve wheel. Presses thumbs down into center of revolving clay to form hollow. Presses on inside and outside of emerging clay cylinder with hands and fingers, gradually raising and shaping clay to desired form and size. Constantly adjusts speed of wheel to conform with changing tenacity (firmness) of clay as piece enlarges and walls become thinner, judging degrees of change by feel. Smooths surfaces of finished piece, using rubber scrapers and wet sponge. Verifies size and form, using calipers and templates. Pulls wire held taut between both hands through base of article and wheel to separate finished piece, or removes piece from wheel to dry. May form saggers only and be known as Sagger Former (pottery

& porc.). ● **GED:** R3, M2, L3 ● **SVP:** 2-4 yrs ● **Academic:** Ed=N, Eng=S ● **Work Field:** 136 ● **MPSMS:** 535 ● **Aptitudes:** G3, V4, N4, S2, P2, Q5, K2, F2, M2, E2, C4 ● **Temperaments:** J, R, T ● **Physical:** Stg=M; Freq: R, H, I, N, D Occas: E, X ● **Work Env:** Noise=N; Freq: U ● **Salary:** 3 ● **Outlook:** 2

GOE: 06.02.31
Manual Work, Laying Out & Marking

LAY-OUT WORKER II (any industry) ● DOT #809.381-014 ● OES: 89198 ● Alternate titles: DUPLICATOR; LAY-OUT MAKER. Traces patterns and marks specifications for fabricating operations onto sheet metal, metal plates, and structural shapes, using templates, measuring instruments, and handtools: Measures stock, using rule to locate center line for positioning template. Tapes, clamps, bolts, or holds template on workpiece. Marks bending and cutting lines, using scribe, and punches or spot drills location of holes, using center punch or hand drill. May lay out straight lines and location of holes detailed on blueprints. ● **GED:** R3, M3, L2 ● **SVP:** 6 mos-1 yr ● **Academic:** Ed=N, Eng=N ● **Work Field:** 241 ● **MPSMS:** 554 ● **Aptitudes:** G3, V4, N3, S3, P3, Q4, K3, F3, M3, E5, C5 ● **Temperaments:** J, T ● **Physical:** Stg=M; Const: R, H, I Freq: N, D Occas: S ● **Work Env:** Noise=L; ● **Salary:** 3 ● **Outlook:** 3

GOE: 06.02.32
Manual Work, Assorted Materials

BONDED STRUCTURES REPAIRER (aircraft mfg.) ● DOT #807.381-014 ● OES: 85323 ● Alternate titles: BONDER, REWORK AND REPAIR. Repairs aircraft and space vehicle bonded structures according to blueprints and specifications, using handtools, power tools, and equipment: Reads inspection reports, rework instructions, and blueprints to determine type of repair, tools required, and to plan sequence of operations. Positions and secures bonded structure in fixture or bonding form, or attaches fixture to structure, using clamps and handtools. Examines structure to determine location, nature, and extent of defect or damage. Spreads plastic film over area to be repaired to prevent damage to surrounding area. Drills holes in structure to gain access to internal defect or damage. Scribes around repair area and cuts out defective or damaged section, using power tools and equipment. Laminates variety of metallic and nonmetallic materials, such as aluminum, fiberglass, plastic, and honeycomb, to fabricate replacement section. Trims and shapes replacement section to specified size, using handtools and power tools. Injects adhesive into cutout areas, using injection gun. Fits replacement section into cutout area and secures section in place, using adhesive tape and tack iron. Cures bonded structure, using portable or stationary curing equipment. Cleans, strips, primes, and sands structural surfaces and materials prior to bonding. ● **GED:** R3, M2, L3 ● **SVP:** 1-2 yrs ● **Academic:** Ed=N, Eng=N ● **Work Field:** 102 ● **MPSMS:** 592, 596 ● **Aptitudes:** G3, V3, N3, S3, P2, Q4, K4, F3, M3, E4, C5 ● **Temperaments:** J, T ● **Physical:** Stg=M; Freq: R, H, I, N, D Occas: C, B, S, K, O, E, A ● **Work Env:** Noise=L; Occas: H, A, M, D, T, O ● **Salary:** 4 ● **Outlook:** 3

CATHODE RAY TUBE SALVAGE PROCESSOR (electron. comp.) ● DOT #725.684-026 ● OES: 93997 ● Performs any combination of following duties to disassemble salvaged cathode ray tubes for reprocessing: Removes vacuum and electron gun from bulb of salvaged cathode ray tube, using portable air drill. Places bulb on fixture of deband machine and activates machine that cuts metal band that surrounds joint between funnel and viewing screen of bulb. Places debanded bulb on conveyor that carries bulb through series of acid and water baths to loosen and dissolve frit that bonds funnel to viewing screen. Positions bulb on chuck of machine and presses pedal on machine that pneumatically separates funnel from viewing screen. Places funnel and screen in vats of acid and water to remove remaining frit from parts. Examines funnel and screen to ensure all frit was removed during acid processing. Places funnel and screen on cart for further processing. ● **GED:** R2, M1, L1 ● **SVP:** 1-3 mos ● **Academic:** Ed=N, Eng=N ● **Work**

Field: 111, 147, 031 ● **MPSMS:** 587 ● **Aptitudes:** G4, V4, N4, S4, P4, Q4, K3, F4, M3, E5, C5 ● **Temperaments:** ● **Physical:** Stg=H; Freq: R, H Occas: I, N, D ● **Work Env:** Noise=L; Occas: A, X, T ● **Salary:** 2 ● **Outlook:** 2

COIL WINDER, REPAIR (any industry) ● DOT #724.381-014 ● OES: 93908 ● Winds coils for repair of electric motor and generator parts, such as rotors, stators, and armatures, using original winding as guide to determine number of turns and size of wire: Winds coil on machine or directly into slots of rotors, stators, and armatures or pounds heavy copper over template to form coils. Operates coil spreading machine to shape rigid coils for placement into slots. Tends coil taping machine or winds tape around coils by hand to insulate coils. Cuts and forms sheet insulation to fit slots, using paper cutter and forming fixture. Inserts coils into slots and pounds, using mallet and block, to compress and shape windings. Twists coil leads together to form groups of coils according to original winding and solders connections, using soldering iron. May paint coils with insulating varnish or enamel. May be designated according to coil wound as Field-Coil Winder (any industry). ● **GED:** R3, M2, L2 ● **SVP:** 6 mos-1 yr ● **Academic:** Ed=N, Eng=N ● **Work Field:** 163 ● **MPSMS:** 582 ● **Aptitudes:** G3, V4, N3, S3, P3, Q4, K3, F3, M3, E4, C4 ● **Temperaments:** R, T ● **Physical:** Stg=L; Freq: R, H, I, N, D, A Occas: X ● **Work Env:** Noise=L; ● **Salary:** 3 ● **Outlook:** 3

DENTURE WAXER (protective dev.) ● DOT #712.381-046 ● OES: 89921 ● Alternate titles: WAXER. Molds wax over denture setup to form contour molds of gums, palates, bridges, and other denture surfaces for use in casting plaster models or metal framework of dentures, using molding equipment and handtools: Applies softened wax to base of denture setup and fills spaces between adjacent teeth, using spatula and fingers. Carves and shapes wax, using scraper, knife, and heated spatula to form natural-appearing denture contours. Verifies occlusion of teeth, using articulator. May mix plaster or melt metals and pour plaster or molten metal in contour molds to form model for duplicate casting [DENTURE-MODEL MAKER (protective dev.) 712.684-046]. May construct wax bite blocks and plastic trays [BITE-BLOCK MAKER (protective dev.) 712.684-014]. ● **GED:** R3, M3, L3 ● **SVP:** 1-2 yrs ● **Academic:** Ed=N, Eng=S ● **Work Field:** 136 ● **MPSMS:** 925, 604 ● **Aptitudes:** G3, V3, N3, S3, P3, Q4, K3, F3, M4, E5, C4 ● **Temperaments:** J, T ● **Physical:** Stg=S; Freq: R, H, I, N, D, A Occas: X ● **Work Env:** Noise=N; ● **Salary:** 3 ● **Outlook:** 2

ETCHED-CIRCUIT PROCESSOR (electron. comp.) ● DOT #590.684-018 ● OES: 93998 ● Performs any combination of following tasks to print and etch conductive patterns on copper-faced plastic, fiberglass, or epoxy board to fabricate printed circuit boards (PCB's): Cuts board to designated size, using sheet metal shears, following written or verbal instructions. Sands board and either places board in vapor degreaser or immerses board in chemical solution to clean and remove oxides and other contaminants. Sprays or brushes light-sensitive enamel on copper surface and places board in whirler machine to spread enamel evenly, or tends machine that flows light-sensitive resist over board. Laminates light-sensitive dry film to board, using heat and pressure equipment. Exposes board and circuit negative to light in contact printer for specified period of time to transfer image of circuit to board. Immerses exposed board in solution to develop acid-resistant circuit pattern on surface. Compares board to sample to verify development of pattern. Applies acid resist over sections of pattern not developed, using brush. Immerses board in acid or tends etching machine to etch conductive pattern on copper surface. Immerses board in solution to dissolve enamel. Drills holes in board, using drill press, following work sample, drawing, and diagrams. Installs hardware, such as brackets, eyelets, and terminals, using eyelet machine and hand arbors. Reduces circuit artwork prior to printing onto board, using reduction camera. Prints conductive pattern onto board, using silk-screen printing device. Fabricates PCB used as prototype of production model. ● **GED:** R3, M3, L3 ● **SVP:** 3-6 mos ● **Academic:** Ed=N, Eng=S ● **Work Field:** 111, 182, 191 ● **MPSMS:** 587 ● **Aptitudes:** G3, V4, N4, S3, P2, Q5, K4, F3, M3, E5, C4 ● **Temperaments:** T ● **Physical:** Stg=L; Const: D Freq: R, H, I, N Occas: A, X ● **Work Env:** Noise=L; Occas: A ● **Salary:** 3 ● **Outlook:** 4

OPAQUER (protective dev.) ● DOT #712.684-030 ● OES: 93947 ● Alternate titles: PORCELAIN-BUILDUP ASSISTANT. Applies coating of opaque procelain over cast metal tooth cap, using brush: Mixes porcelain of specified color and water to required consistency. Brushes porcelain mixture over surfaces of metal cap. Places cap in electric oven for specified time to dry and harden porcelain. Removes cap and examines cap to ensure even application and smoothness of coating. Routes workpiece to specified department for application of finish porcelain. May grind and shape dried porcelain to contours of metal cap, using abrasive wheels. May measure dimensions of tooth cap and verify occlusion, using gauges and articulator. ● **GED:** R3, M2, L2 ● **SVP:** 3-6 mos ● **Academic:** Ed=N, Eng=N ● **Work Field:** 153, 141 ● **MPSMS:** 925, 604 ● **Aptitudes:** G3, V4, N4, S4, P3, Q4, K3, F3, M3, E5, C3 ● **Temperaments:** J, T ● **Physical:** Stg=S; Freq: R, H, I, E, N, D, X Occas: T, G ● **Work Env:** Noise=N; ● **Salary:** 3 ● **Outlook:** 2

RACKET STRINGER (toy-sport equip.) ● DOT #732.684-094 ● OES: 93997 ● Strings tennis and badminton rackets with synthetic fiber or animal gut strings: Clamps racket in stand and threads warp (main strings) through holes in bow. Clamps ends of strings in jaws of tensioner arms, depresses pedal to tighten strings to prescribed tension, and locks strings in place by wedging awl in hole with string until next set of holes are strung, or string is tied. Threads weave (cross strings) through holes in bow, weaves them through main strings, applies tension, and secures them similarly to main strings. May wrap bow at intervals with bands of colored thread to strengthen and decorate it.

May varnish wooden parts of racket. May replace leather or plastic grips on racket handle. ● **GED:** R3, M2, L2 ● **SVP:** 6 mos-1 yr ● **Academic:** Ed=N, Eng=N ● **Work Field:** 164 ● **MPSMS:** 616 ● **Aptitudes:** G3, V4, N4, S3, P3, Q4, K3, F3, M3, E3, C4 ● **Temperaments:** R, T ● **Physical:** Stg=L; Const: R, H, I Freq: N, D Occas: X ● **Work Env:** Noise=N; ● **Salary:** 3 ● **Outlook:** 3

SKI MOLDER (toy-sport equip.) ● DOT #732.684-114 ● OES: 93998 ● Fabricates sock (inner-construction, ski-component) and aligns sock with other ski parts in die press that molds components into partially fabricated ski: Places fiberglass lay-up (mat of specified size) on worktable, pours epoxy resin over lay-up, and spreads resin with paddle to facilitate saturation. Positions ski core on lay-up, places foot-pad on top of core, and pours resin over core and foot-pad. Folds lay-up around core and foot-pad to form sock, cuts sock to contour of ski toe (front) with scissors and template, and aligns sock assembly in specified manner within mold press. Places ski base layer in press with sock assembly in specified alignment and activates press to shape and mold layers. ● **GED:** R3, M1, L2 ● **SVP:** 1-3 mos ● **Academic:** Ed=N, Eng=N ● **Work Field:** 102 ● **MPSMS:** 616 ● **Aptitudes:** G4, V4, N4, S3, P3, Q5, K3, F4, M3, E4, C5 ● **Temperaments:** J, T ● **Physical:** Stg=L; Freq: R, H, I, E, N, D Occas: A ● **Work Env:** Noise=L; ● **Salary:** 2 ● **Outlook:** 2

Industrial

Quality Control

Workers in this group check the quality and quantity of products and materials being manufactured. They inspect, test, weigh, sort, and grade specific items to be sure that they meet certain standards. Some may also keep inspection records of the number or kind of defects and flaws they find. They work in factories and other large plants that process materials and manufacture products.

✓ What kind of work would you do?

Your work activities would depend upon your specific job. For example, you might:

- examine unground optical lenses for flaws and sort them according to defects.
- inspect watch dials and hands for flaws and proper alignment.
- inspect the dimensions of fountain pen nibs by using measuring instruments such as calipers.
- examine rejected rubber footwear and sort according to whether pairs should be salvaged or scrapped.

✓ What skills and abilities do you need for this kind of work?

To do this kind of work, you must be able to:

- do the same thing over and over according to a set procedure.
- use eyes, hands, and fingers to handle gauges and measuring tools.
- use math skills to count, measure, or keep inspection records.

- make decisions based on standards that can be measured or checked.

The above statements may not apply to every job in this group.

✓ How do you know if you would like or could learn to do this kind of work?

The following questions may give you clues about yourself as you consider this group of jobs.

- Have you had industrial arts or machine shop courses? Did you learn how to use measuring devices such as gauges, calipers, and micrometers?
- Have you sorted paper, metal, or glass for recycling? Were you able to tell the difference between similar types of materials?
- Have you had general or applied mathematics courses? Do you like to keep tallies or other simple records?

✓ How can you prepare for and enter this kind of work?

Occupations in this group usually require education and/or training extending from thirty days to over one year, depending upon the specific kind of work. Most jobs in this group have no specific educational requirements. However, vocational shop courses are helpful.

Employers usually train workers through on-the-job training programs.

✓ *What else should you consider about these jobs?*

Overtime or night and shift work may be required. Many of these jobs are available to persons without any training. After gaining skill and experience in these jobs, workers often move up to better paying jobs.

Workers are exposed to different types of factory conditions. However, these jobs usually do not require working near machinery.

If you think you would like to do this kind of work, look at the job titles listed below.

■ ■ ■

GOE: 06.03.01
Inspecting, Testing & Repairing

COMPARATOR OPERATOR (any industry) ● DOT #699.384-010 ● OES: 83000 ● Alternate titles: SHADOWGRAPH OPERATOR. Inspects parts for defects in finish and dimensions, using machine that projects magnified shadows of parts on screen: Reads specifications of part to ascertain form and degree to be magnified. Draws enlarged outline of part to scale on chart (celluloid disk), using scribers, dividers, and straightedge. Places chart over translucent glass disk of comparator (shadowgraph) machine. Inserts specified lens into machine and adjusts mirrors to magnify parts. Positions and secures parts on machine table. Turns light on and moves levers of machine to bring shadows of parts into focus with chart outline. Inspects shadows for imperfections of finish and incorrect dimensions. Prepares reports of findings. May rotate part in holding fixture to examine surfaces and to verify concentricity of parts. ● **GED:** R3, M3, L3 ● **SVP:** 3-6 mos ● **Academic:** Ed=N, Eng=S ● **Work Field:** 121, 212 ● **MPSMS:** 587, 607 ● **Aptitudes:** G3, V3, N4, S3, P2, Q3, K3, F3, M4, E5, C5 ● **Temperaments:** J, T ● **Physical:** Stg=L; Freq: R, H, I, N, D, A ● **Work Env:** Noise=N; ● **Salary:** 3 ● **Outlook:** 2

GRADER, MEAT (meat products) ● DOT #525.387-010 ● OES: 83000 ● Examines animal carcasses to determine grade in terms of sales value: Examines carcasses suspended from stationary hooks or hooks attached to overhead conveyor to determine grade based on age, sex, shape, thickness of meat, quantity and distribution of fat, color, texture, and marbling of lean meat. Attaches grade identification tag to carcass. May estimate weight of carcass or observe dial of automatic weighing scale to determine weight of carcass. May be designated according to carcass graded as Beef Grader (meat products); Hog Grader (meat products); Sheep Or Calf Grader (meat products). ● **GED:** R3, M2, L1 ● **SVP:** 6 mos-1 yr ● **Academic:** Ed=H, Eng=N ● **Work Field:** 212 ● **MPSMS:** 382 ● **Aptitudes:** G3, V4, N4, S3, P3, Q4, K4, F4, M4, E5, C2 ● **Temperaments:** J, T ● **Physical:** Stg=L; Const: R, H, N, A, X Occas: I ● **Work Env:** Noise=Q; Freq: C, U ● **Salary:** 2 ● **Outlook:** 3

INSPECTOR (office machines) ● DOT #710.384-014 ● OES: 83000 ● Inspects and tests parts, subassemblies, and finished scales and balances for conformance to quality standards, using written specifications, precision measuring instruments, and handtools: Inspects purchased or in-plant-fabricated parts for observable defects and tests specific components for hardness, dimensions and tolerances, using blueprints, hardness testing machine, and precision measuring instruments, such as micrometers, calipers, and thread gauges. Inspects and tests assembled scales and balances for appearance, allowable tolerances, reliability (repeated use), and accuracy (calibration), using master weights. Rejects unacceptable parts, subassemblies, and completed scales and prepares reports indicating defects and suspected cause. ● **GED:** R4, M3, L3 ● **SVP:** 2-4 yrs ● **Academic:** Ed=H, Eng=S ● **Work Field:** 212 ● **MPSMS:** 571 ● **Aptitudes:** G3, V3, N3, S3, P3, Q3, K3, F3, M3, E5, C5 ● **Temperaments:** J ● **Physical:** Stg=L; Freq: R, H, I, N, A Occas: S ● **Work Env:** Noise=N; ● **Salary:** 3 ● **Outlook:** 3

INSPECTOR (plastic prod.) ● DOT #559.381-010 ● OES: 83000 ● Alternate titles: CUSTOMER-RETURN INSPECTOR; PROCESS INSPECTOR. Inspects and tests plastic sheets, rods, tubes, powders, or fabricated articles for uniformity of color, surface defects, hardness, and dimensional accuracy, following plant specifications or blueprints and using measuring instruments and test equipment: Examines surface of product for defects, such as scratches, burns, and discolorations. Positions transparent sheet between light and calibrated screen and observes shadow pattern of sheet projected on screen to determine optical distortion. Verifies weight and dimensions of product, using scales, gauges, calipers, micrometers, and templates. Compares color of product with color standard. Determines hardness and structural strength of product, using acid bath, burst tester, and hardness tester. Records test data, and grades and labels product according to type of defect. May investigate cause of recurring defects and recommend changes in production procedures. May file, buff, or sand product to remove defects. ● **GED:** R3, M3, L3 ● **SVP:** 6 mos-1 yr ● **Academic:** Ed=N, Eng=S ● **Work Field:** 212, 231 ● **MPSMS:** 510 ● **Aptitudes:** G3, V3, N3, S3, P3, Q3, K4, F4, M3, E5, C3 ● **Physical:** Stg=L; Freq: R, H, I, N, X Occas: E ● **Work Env:** Noise=L; Freq: A ● **Salary:** 3 ● **Outlook:** 2

INSPECTOR II (pottery & porc.) ● DOT #774.384-010 ● OES: 83000 ● Examines ceramic and porcelain products at various stages of manufacture for defects and adherence to standards: Examines ware surfaces for defects, such as pin marks, glaze runs, chips, cracks, mold marks, and deformities. Marks correctable defects with pencil, or finishes ware, using trimming tools, abrasives, and sponges. Feels edges (rims) and surfaces of ware with finger tips to detect rough spots. Smooths rough spots, using pumice stone or wet sponge and abrasive powder. Mixes ceramic and porcelain ingredients and examines mixture for foreign matter. May verify measurements of metal dies for machine forming presses, using calipers, gauges, and micrometers. Maintains records of test results, and prepares analysis of defect causes based on test results. May measure viscosity and specific gravity of mixed ceramic, porcelain, and glaze batches, using viscometer and volume device. May test durability of ware at prescribed temperatures, using electric oven. May conduct chipping test, using impact tester. ● **GED:** R2, M1, L1 ● **SVP:** 6 mos-1 yr ● **Academic:** Ed=N, Eng=N ● **Work Field:** 212 ● **MPSMS:** 535 ● **Aptitudes:** G3, V3, N3, S3, P2, Q3, K3, F3, M3, E5, C3 ● **Temperaments:** J, T ● **Physical:** Stg=L; Freq: S, R, H, I, E, N, D, X Occas: A ● **Work Env:** Noise=L; Occas: U ● **Salary:** 3 ● **Outlook:** 3

INSPECTOR, PRINTED CIRCUIT BOARDS (electron. comp.) ● DOT #726.684-062 ● OES: 83000 ● Alternate titles: CIRCUIT BOARD INSPECTOR; TOUCH-UP INSPECTOR, PRINTED CIRCUIT BOARDS. Performs any combination of following tasks to inspect and repair printed circuit boards (PCB's): Inserts plug gauges into drilled holes of PCB panels to verify conformance to specified dimensions. Measures thickness and dimensions of plating on PCB panels to verify that plating meets specifications, using micrometers, dial indicators, calipers, rulers, eye loupes, and electronic measuring devices. Examines PCB circuitry to detect defects, such as shorts, breaks, excess or missing solder, scratches, cracks, and incorrect layout, using light table, eye loupe, magnifier, or microscope. Brushes solder mask ink on PCB's to repair defects in screen printing. Scrapes excess plating, or solder mask ink from PCB's, using utility knife. Repairs broken circuitry, using soldering iron or circuit bonding equipment. Records type and quantity of defective PCB's. Tests adherence of solder mask ink to PCB's, using tape. Tests continuity of PCB circuits, using bare board tester. May inspect inner layers of multilayer PCB's to verify that internal alignment and location of drilled holes meet specifications and be designated X-Ray Technician, Printed Circuit Boards (electron. comp.). ● **GED:** R3, M2, L2 ● **SVP:** 1-3 mos ● **Academic:** Ed=N, Eng=S ● **Work Field:** 212 ● **MPSMS:** 587 ● **Aptitudes:** G3, V3, N4, S4, P3, Q4, K3, F3, M3, E5, C5 ● **Temperaments:** T ● **Physical:** Stg=L; Freq: R, H, I, N, D Occas: A ● **Work Env:** Noise=N; ● **Salary:** 4 ● **Outlook:** 5

INSPECTOR, RECEIVING (aircraft mfg.) ● DOT #222.384-010 ● OES: 83000 ● Inspects purchased parts, assemblies, accessories, and materials for conformance to specifications, using precision measuring instruments and devices: Examines items for defects in materials, workmanship, and damage occurring in transit. Compares quantity and part number of items received with procurement data and other specifications to ensure completeness and accuracy of order. Inspects and measures items for dimensional accuracy, fit, alignment, and functional operation, according to blueprints, parts manuals, company or military standards, and other specifications, using precision measuring instruments and devices. Approves or rejects items, and records inspection and disposition information. May test hardness of metals, using testing equipment. May examine x rays of welded parts to determine that welds conform to established standards. May inspect outgoing and production line parts and materials. May prepare inspection procedure outlines for reference use in subsequent inspections, using data obtained from blueprints, customer specifications, and catalogs. ● **GED:** R3, M2, L3 ● **SVP:** 6 mos-1 yr ● **Academic:** Ed=N, Eng=G ● **Work Field:** 212 ● **MPSMS:** 580, 590 ● **Aptitudes:** G3, V3, N3, S3, P3, Q4, K3, F3, M3, E5, C4 ● **Temperaments:** T ● **Physical:** Stg=M; Freq: R, H, I, N, A Occas: S, K, O, E, D, X ● **Work Env:** Noise=L; ● **Salary:** 3 ● **Outlook:** 3

MACHINE TESTER (office machines) ● DOT #706.387-014 ● OES: 83000 ● Tests machines, such as calculating or adding machines, manually or automatically to detect malfunctions, using handtools, alignment gauge, and tester: Sets machine on ball swivel mount to facilitate turning in all directions when examining parts. Plugs cord of machine into electrical outlet. Presses keys on keyboard and moves levers in prescribed sequence to test alignment of printing, repeat latch, ribbon and paper feed, correction release, noise, and clearance of type bars, according to checklist. Test-runs battery of machines through fixed computation cycle automatically, using auto typist or tester. Reads arithmetic results recorded on paper tapes of machines and compares them with test chart to verify accuracy. Indicates defects on inspection worksheet and gives worksheet and machine to repairer. May disassemble machine to determine cause of defect. May be designated according to type of inspection done as Clearing Inspector (office machines); Final Inspector (office machines); Sampling Inspector (office machines); Utility Inspector (office machines). ● **GED:** R3, M2, L2 ● **SVP:** 3-6 mos ● **Academic:** Ed=N, Eng=N ● **Work Field:** 212 ● **MPSMS:** 571 ● **Aptitudes:** G3, V3, N4, S4, P3, Q3, K3, F3, M3, E5, C5 ● **Temperaments:** J, R, T ● **Physical:** Stg=L; Freq: R, H, I, N, A Occas: G ● **Work Env:** Noise=N; ● **Salary:** 2 ● **Outlook:** 2

MOTORCYCLE TESTER (motor-bicycles) ● DOT #620.384-010 ● OES: 83000 ● Inspects and tests motorcycles, performing any combination of following tasks according to standard procedures, using handtools and testing instruments: Mounts motorcycle on test stand. Attaches lead wires of test panel to ignition system of motor and runs motor at various speeds to measure generator output, oil pressure, revolution per minute, and other specified operating characteristics. Compares test instrument readings with operational charts to detect malfunctions. Engages clutch and transmission of motorcycle and listens for sounds denoting malfunction. Records findings on worksheet. Turns adjustment screw on carburetor to regulate idling speed of motor, using screwdriver. Inspects frame and fenders for dents and scratches. Tightens frame nuts and bolts, using handtools. Tests operation of horn and lights. Verifies identification number and optional equipment against data on work order. ● **GED:** R3, M3, L3 ● **SVP:** 6 mos-1 yr ● **Academic:** Ed=N, Eng=S ● **Work Field:** 121 ● **MPSMS:** 595 ● **Aptitudes:** G3, V3, N3, S3, P3, Q4, K3, F3, M3, E4, C4 ● **Temperaments:** R, T ● **Physical:** Stg=M; Freq: R, H, I, G, N, A Occas: S, O, T, D, X ● **Work Env:** Noise=N; ● **Salary:** 2 ● **Outlook:** 3

QUALITY-CONTROL INSPECTOR (recording) ● DOT #194.387-010 ● OES: 83000 ● Alternate titles: MATRIX INSPECTOR; MOTHER TESTER. Inspects metal phonograph record mothers for surface defects, using optical and sound-reproducing equipment: Places

matrix on turntable and measures grooved surface and width of grooves in matrix, using ruler and calibrated microscope. Places tone arm on matrix and starts sound-reproducing machine. Listens for defects in matrix, such as pops and ticks, and observes meter that indicates surface noise and sound level. Stops machine and locates defects in matrix, using microscope and magnifying glass. Marks location of defects with bar soap and returns matrix for repair. Notes reasons for rejection on worksheet. Listens to repaired matrices to ensure that defects have been eliminated. ● **GED:** R3, M2, L2 ● **SVP:** 3-6 mos ● **Academic:** Ed=H, Eng=S ● **Work Field:** 212 ● **MPSMS:** 585 ● **Aptitudes:** G3, V4, N3, S4, P2, Q4, K4, F4, M4, E5, C5 ● **Temperaments:** J ● **Physical:** Stg=S; Freq: R, H, I, G, N, A Occas: D ● **Work Env:** Noise=L; ● **Salary:** 3 ● **Outlook:** 3

SPECIAL TESTER (tobacco) ● DOT #529.487-010 ● OES: 83000 ● Tests tobacco samples from various stages of processing to determine conformance to quality standards: Obtains tobacco samples from various processing areas to ensure representative sampling. Conducts tests to determine characteristics of tobacco batch, such as stem length, percentage of lamina, stem, and foreign matter content, using scales, laboratory equipment, and calculator. ● **GED:** R3, M3, L3 ● **SVP:** 1-3 mos ● **Academic:** Ed=N, Eng=S ● **Work Field:** 212 ● **MPSMS:** 403 ● **Aptitudes:** G3, V3, N3, S4, P4, Q3, K4, F4, M4, E5, C5 ● **Temperaments:** J, T ● **Physical:** Stg=L; Freq: R, H, N Occas: I ● **Work Env:** Noise=N; ● **Salary:** 3 ● **Outlook:** 2

TEST DRIVER I (auto. mfg.) ● DOT #806.283-014 ● OES: 83000 ● Alternate titles: CAR TESTER; CHASSIS DRIVER; OVERLAND DRIVER; ROAD TESTER. Drives completed motor vehicle, as vehicle comes from assembly line, on proving ground under simulated road conditions, and observes performance to detect mechanical and structural defects: Examines vehicle before road testing to ensure that equipment, such as electrical wiring, hydraulic lines, and fan belts are installed as specified, and verifies that vehicle has been serviced with oil, gas, and water. Drives vehicle to simulate actual driving conditions. Listens for rattles and excessive mechanical noise, and moves controls to test functioning of equipment, such as horn, heater, wipers, and power windows. Writes inspection report on standardized form indicating defects or malfunctions. ● **GED:** R3, M2, L3 ● **SVP:** 1-2 yrs ● **Academic:** Ed=N, Eng=S ● **Work Field:** 212 ● **MPSMS:** 591 ● **Aptitudes:** G3, V3, N4, S3, P3, Q4, K3, F4, M3, E3, C4 ● **Temperaments:** J, T ● **Physical:** Stg=L; Freq: R, H, G, N, F, D, A, X, V Occas: I ● **Work Env:** Noise=N; ● **Salary:** 4 ● **Outlook:** 3

GOE: 06.03.02
Inspecting, Grading, Sorting, Weighing & Recording

ELECTRONICS INSPECTOR (electron. comp.) ● DOT #726.684-022 ● OES: 83000 ● Alternate titles: CHECKER; INSPECTOR, COMPONENT PARTS; LINE INSPECTOR. Inspects electronic assemblies, subassemblies, parts, and components for defects, following samples, production illustrations, or using comparator: Examines unit for physical defects, such as broken or missing leads, excess solder, holes in sealing material, unevenly wound coil, coating and plating blemishes, oil leaks, faulty welds, scratches, cracks, and chips. Compares hardware on assemblies, subassemblies, and parts to parts list to verify installation. Examines hardware for specified contact with conductor area. Rejects faulty assembly, part, or component and records type and quantity of defects. May measure parts to verify accuracy of dimensions, using precision measuring instruments. May sort defective components and parts for salvage or scrap. May inspect parts, using microscope or magnifier. May be designated according to item inspected, as Capacitor Inspector (electron. comp.); Electron Gun Inspector (electron. comp.); Filter Inspector (electron. comp.); Resistor Inspector (electron. comp.); Tube Inspector (electron. comp.). ● **GED:** R3, M2, L2 ● **SVP:** 1-3 mos ● **Academic:** Ed=N, Eng=N ● **Work Field:** 212 ● **MPSMS:** 587 ● **Aptitudes:** G3, V4, N4, S4, P3, Q4, K4, F3, M3, E5, C4 ● **Temperaments:** R, T ● **Physical:** Stg=L; Const: N Freq: R, H, I, D, A Occas: X ● **Work Env:** Noise=N; ● **Salary:** 5 ● **Outlook:** 4

ELECTRONICS TESTER (comm. equip.) ● DOT #726.684-026 ● OES: 83000 ● Tests function of electronic assemblies, components, and parts according to established procedures, using computerized or standard test equipment: Connects electronic assembly, component, or part to test instrument, such as ohmmeter, voltmeter, ammeter, resistance bridge, or oscilloscope, or to automatic or computerized test equipment, and turns switch to actuate test equipment. Reads instrument dial or scope, or observes viewing screen, that indicates resistance, capacitance, continuity, and wave pattern or defect, such as short circuit or current leakage. Compares instrument reading or monitor display with standard and rejects defective units. Records type and quantity of defect. May verify dimensions of parts, using standard gauges. May examine assembly, component, or part for defects, such as short leads, bent plate, or cracked seal. May tend equipment that subjects unit to stress prior to testing. May replace defective components or repair defective wiring after testing. May operate burn-in oven to elevate printed circuit board temperature prior to testing. May adjust circuits in radios and televisions for maximum signal response. May be designated according to unit tested or test equipment used as Auto-Test Equipment Operator (electron. comp.); Solid State Tester (electron. comp.); Tester, Printed Circuit Boards (electron. comp.); Tube Tester (electron. comp.). ● **GED:** R3, M3, L3 ● **SVP:** 1-3 mos ● **Academic:** Ed=N, Eng=S ● **Work Field:** 212 ● **MPSMS:** 580 ● **Aptitudes:** G3, V4, N4, S4, P4, Q4, K4, F4, M4, E5, C4 ● **Temperaments:** R, T ● **Physical:** Stg=L; Freq: R, H, I, N, D, A Occas: X ● **Work Env:** Noise=N; ● **Salary:** 2 ● **Outlook:** 4

FILM FLAT INSPECTOR (print. & pub.) ● DOT #972.284-010 ● OES: 83000 ● Inspects film flats for quality, content, and positioning of elements at printing establishment: Places film flats and companion materials, such as artwork, pasteups, layouts, film, and corrected proofs, on light table and examines materials, using magnifying glass to view details in materials. Examines film flat label for identifying information, such as date and job number. Compares film flat to companion materials, using knowledge of film assembly, and measures film flat with ruler to verify conformance to specifications, such as positioning of pages in rotation for folding, trim marks, colors on pages, window sizes, and size, colors, and positioning of elements, such as halftones, screen tints, and type. Examines film flats for defects, such as holes or scratches on film, overlapping or unaligned elements, and incorrect dot percentages in halftones. Returns film flat to STRIPPER, LITHOGRAPHIC (print. & pub.) I 972.281-022 for corrections, or repairs defects, such as pinholes or incomplete and missing halftone dots, with opaque material or needle and crayon pencil. ● **GED:** R4, M3, L3 ● **SVP:** 2-4 yrs ● **Academic:** Ed=H, Eng=G ● **Work Field:** 212 ● **MPSMS:** 752 ● **Aptitudes:** G3, V3, N3, S2, P2, Q3, K3, F3, M3, E5, C3 ● **Temperaments:** J, T ● **Physical:** Stg=L; Const: R, H, I Freq: N Occas: D, A, X ● **Work Env:** Noise=Q; ● **Salary:** 3 ● **Outlook:** 2

GARMENT INSPECTOR (any industry) ● DOT #789.687-070 ● OES: 83000 ● Alternate titles: TRIMMER. Inspects garments for defects in sewing, knitting, or finishing: Spreads garment on table or draws garment over inspection form. Scans garment to detect defects, such as faulty seaming, incorrect sleeve or collar setting, misaligned fasteners or trim, and variations in color of fabric. Examines fabric for mispicks, slubs, runs, dropped stitches, holes, or stains. Marks defects, using chalk, thread, tags, tape, or pins. Measures garment at designated places, using tape measure or following markings on table, to determine that garments conform to standard size. Trims excess material and thread ends from garment, using scissors, or tends trimming machine to remove excess material and loose threads [THREAD CUTTER (any industry) 789.684-050]. Folds garment or hangs it on hanger or rack. May remove spots and stains from garments [SPOT CLEANER (garment; knitting) 582.684-014]. May inspect surgical garments and appliances, such as belts, hosiery, or knee and ankle braces, and be designated Inspector (protective dev.).May examine cut garment parts to detect inaccuracies in cutting and be designated Cutting Inspector (garment). May be designated according to production stage as Finished-Garment Inspector (garment; knitting); Greige-Goods Inspector (knitting); Seconds Inspector (garment; knitting). ● **GED:** R2, M1, L2 ● **SVP:** 1-3 mos ● **Academic:** Ed=N, Eng=N ● **Work Field:** 212, 054 ● **MPSMS:** 424, 440 ● **Aptitudes:** G4, V4, N4, S4, P3, Q4, K4, F3, M3, E5, C4 ● **Temperaments:** R, T ● **Physical:** Stg=L; Freq: S, R, H, I, N, D, A, X Occas: G ● **Work Env:** Noise=L; ● **Salary:** 2 ● **Outlook:** 3

GLASS INSPECTOR (any industry) ● DOT #579.687-022 ● OES: 83000 ● Visually inspects plate glass or glass products, including fiberglass, for defects, such as scratches, cracks, chips, holes, or bubbles: Places workpiece on inspection stand or table for examination. Examines workpiece and marks defects. Rejects or classifies pieces for potential use, such as mirrors, glass pane, or furniture tops. Scrapes or washes foreign material from surface, using scraper, sponge, or brush. May clean or polish glass by washing with water or solvent and drying with cloth. May place straightedge over glass plates to determine if plates are warped. May attach identifying label to glassware. ● **GED:** R2, M1, L2 ● **SVP:** 1-3 mos ● **Academic:** Ed=N, Eng=N ● **Work Field:** 212, 031 ● **MPSMS:** 531 ● **Aptitudes:** G4, V4, N4, S4, P3, Q4, K4, F4, M3, E5, C4 ● **Temperaments:** R, T ● **Physical:** Stg=L; Const: N, D, A, X Freq: R, H, I ● **Work Env:** Noise=N; ● **Salary:** 3 ● **Outlook:** 2

GAS-LEAK TESTER (svc. ind. mach.) ● DOT #827.584-014 ● OES: 83000 ● Performs one or more of following tasks to test assembled and charged refrigeration units for refrigerant leaks: Adjusts controls to set balance and range of electronic leak tester. Moves nozzle of tester along refrigerant lines, condenser, and compressor and listens for buzzer indicating presence of gas. Narrows range of tester and probes area to pinpoint exact location of leak. Turns valve of gas tester to adjust flow of gas to copper flame-ring and ignites gas. Moves suction hose, joined to flame-ring, along surfaces of refrigeration unit and observes flame for change in color denoting presence of leaking refrigerant gas. Wraps wet litmus paper around joints of refrigeration unit and observes paper for color change indicating refrigerant leak. Marks number of defective part or joint on inspection tag, according to blueprint numbering chart, and attaches tag to unit. Records number and location of leaks on inspection chart. ● **GED:** R2, M1, L1 ● **SVP:** 2-30 days ● **Academic:** Ed=N, Eng=N ● **Work Field:** 211 ● **MPSMS:** 583, 573 ● **Aptitudes:** G4, V4, N4, S4, P4, Q4, K4, F4, M4, E5, C4 ● **Temperaments:** J, R ● **Physical:** Stg=L; Freq: R, H, N Occas: I, X ● **Work Env:** Noise=N; ● **Salary:** 2 ● **Outlook:** 3

GRADER (woodworking) ● DOT #669.687-030 ● OES: 83000 ● Alternate titles: LUMBER INSPECTOR; SIZER GRADER. Inspects and grades milled, rough-sawed, or dimensional stock lumber according to standards: Examines lumber on table, moving belt, chain conveyor, or in racks for defects, such as knots, stains, decay, splits, faulty edges, pitch pockets, wormholes, and defective milling. Grades lumber, using caliper rule, to ensure specified dimensions. Marks lumber to indicate grade and processing instructions, using marker. Tallies pieces of lumber according to grade and board footage. May determine cuts to be made to obtain highest marketable value from material. May remove unsatisfactory pieces from conveyor or table and place pieces on stacks, in bins, or on carts. May scale board footage, using calibrated scale on lumber ruler, and record results. May be designated according to lumber graded as Flooring Grader (saw. & plan.); Green-Lumber Grader (woodworking); or according to location of work as Dock Grader (woodworking); Green-Chain Marker (saw. & plan.); Planer-Mill Grader (saw. & plan.). May review work of other graders and be designated Check Grader (woodworking). May be designated: Dry-Lumber Grader (woodworking); Milled-Lumber Grader (woodworking); Puncher (saw. & plan.); Rough-Lumber Grader (woodworking). ● **GED:** R3, M2, L2 ● **SVP:** 3-6 mos ● **Academic:** Ed=N, Eng=N ● **Work Field:** 212 ● **MPSMS:** 450 ● **Aptitudes:** G3, V4, N3, S3, P3, Q4, K3, F4, M3, E4, C4 ● **Temperaments:** J, T ● **Physical:** Stg=L; Const: R, H, N, F, A Freq: I, D, X Occas: G ● **Work Env:** Noise=L; Occas: A, M ● **Salary:** 2 ● **Outlook:** 2

HYDRO-PNEUMATIC TESTER (any industry) ● DOT #862.687-018 ● OES: 83000 ● Tests boilers, tanks, fittings, pipes, and similar objects to detect and locate leaks, using compressed air or water pressure: Installs fittings on object to seal outlets and connects object to high-pressure air or water line, using handtools. Activates air compressor or water pump until gauge registers specified internal pressure. Observes gauge for loss of pressure indicative of leaks, and examines object for escaping air or water to detect leaks. Marks object at source of leaks for subsequent repair. May apply soap solution to surface of object or immerse object to facilitate location of air leaks. May test object under high pressure to ensure compliance with product safety ratings. May be designated according to type of test used as Hydrostatic Tester (any industry); Pneumatic Tester (any industry). ● **GED:** R3, M2, L2 ● **SVP:** 3-6 mos ● **Academic:** Ed=N, Eng=N ● **Work**

Field: 212 ● **MPSMS:** 550 ● **Aptitudes:** G3, V4, N4, S4, P4, Q4, K4, F4, M3, E5, C5 ● **Temperaments:** J, T ● **Physical:** Stg=L; Freq: R, H, I, N, D Occas: S, O, G ● **Work Env:** Noise=L; Freq: U Occas: W ● **Salary:** 3 ● **Outlook:** 3

INKER (print. & pub.) ● DOT #659.667-010 ● OES: 83000 ● Compares color of printing ink with sample to ensure adherence to formula or customer specifications: Determines ink viscosity by timing flow from test cup and adds desired amount of solvent to meet viscosity requirements for kind of ink and application. Fills ink reservoirs in presses and adds more solvent to thin ink or uncovers reservoirs to allow evaporation of excess solvent during press run. May fill lubricating cups with oil and grease. May assist press operator to set up printing press. ● **GED:** R3, M2, L2 ● **SVP:** 3-6 mos ● **Academic:** Ed=N, Eng=N ● **Work Field:** 191 ● **MPSMS:** 499 ● **Aptitudes:** G3, V4, N3, S4, P3, Q3, K4, F4, M4, E5, C2 ● **Temperaments:** J, R, T ● **Physical:** Stg=L; Freq: R, H, N, X Occas: C, S, I ● **Work Env:** Noise=L; ● **Salary:** 2 ● **Outlook:** 2

INSPECTOR (pharmaceut.) ● DOT #559.387-014 ● OES: 83000 ● Inspects pharmaceutical ingredients and products to detect deviations from manufacturing standards: Selects samples of in-process pharmaceutical ingredients, capsules, tablets, and related products for testing, according to prescribed procedures. Weighs samples, using scales, and measures samples, using micrometer. Places specified samples in disintegration baths and observes and times rate of dissolution. Records inspection results on designated forms. Checks incoming purchased pharmaceutical ingredients against invoice to verify conformity of product name, count, and labeling. Carries samples of incoming products to analytical laboratory for quality assurance testing. ● **GED:** R3, M2, L3 ● **SVP:** 3-6 mos ● **Academic:** Ed=N, Eng=S ● **Work Field:** 211, 212 ● **MPSMS:** 493 ● **Aptitudes:** G3, V3, N4, S4, P3, Q3, K4, F4, M4, E5, C4 ● **Temperaments:** T ● **Physical:** Stg=L; Freq: R, H, N, A Occas: S, O, I, X ● **Work Env:** Noise=N; ● **Salary:** 3 ● **Outlook:** 3

INSPECTOR, INTEGRATED CIRCUITS (electron. comp.) ● DOT #726.684-058 ● OES: 83000 ● Inspects integrated circuit (IC) assemblies, semiconductor wafers, and IC dies for conformance to company standards, using microscope: Reads work order to determine inspection criteria. Places group of items in trays on microscope stage, or positions items individually on stage for inspection, using vacuum pencil or tweezers. Turns knobs on microscope to adjust focus and magnification as required to view items for inspection. Views and inspects items according to company standards to detect defects, such as broken circuit lines, bridged circuits, misalignments, symbol errors, and missing solder. Discards defective items. May remove contaminants from items, using brush or airhose. May use magnifying glass to inspect electronic items. ● **GED:** R2, M2, L2 ● **SVP:** 1-3 mos ● **Academic:** Ed=N, Eng=S ● **Work Field:** 212 ● **MPSMS:** 587 ● **Aptitudes:** G4, V4, N4, S3, P3, Q4, K4, F3, M4, E5, C5 ● **Temperaments:** R, T ● **Physical:** Stg=L; Const: H, I, N, A Freq: R Occas: D ● **Work Env:** Noise=N; ● **Salary:** 4 ● **Outlook:** 4

INSPECTOR, SEMICONDUCTOR WAFER (electron. comp.) ● DOT #726.684-066 ● OES: 83000 ● Performs any of following duties to inspect, measure, and test semiconductor wafers for conformance to specifications: Inspects wafers under high intensity lamp to detect surface defects, such as scratches, chips, stains, burns, or haze. Measures thickness and resistivity of wafers, using electronic gauges or automated sorting machine. Measures diameter and flat of wafers, using calipers. Inspects bow or flatness of wafers, using electronic gauges, or examines surface of wafers under high intensity lamp. Tests for positive or negative conductivity of wafers, using electronic probe and gauge. Determines crystal orientation of wafers, using x-ray equipment. Encloses containers of inspected wafers in plastic bags for protection, using heat sealer. Records inspection data on production records or in computer, using computer terminal. May tend equipment that cleans surface of wafers [WAFER CLEANER (electron. comp.) 590.685-102]. ● **GED:** R3, M2, L2 ● **SVP:** 1-3 mos ● **Academic:** Ed=N, Eng=S ● **Work Field:** 212 ● **MPSMS:** 587 ● **Aptitudes:** G3, V4, N4, S3, Q4, K3, F3, M4, E5, C5 ● **Temperaments:** T ● **Physical:** Stg=L; Const: H Freq: R, I, N, D ● **Work Env:** Noise=N; ● **Salary:** 4 ● **Outlook:** 5

INSTRUMENT INSPECTOR (inst. & app.) ● DOT #710.684-050 ● OES: 83000 ● Inspects measuring, indicating, and controlling instruments, such as speedometers, sequence timers, and thermostats, and component parts, for conformance to specifications: Examines com-

ponents and housings for specified characteristics, such as smoothness and centering of holes, or defects, such as scratches and chips. Measures instrument parts to verify conformance to blueprint specifications, using measuring devices, such as ruler, thread gauge, micrometer, and dial indicator. May use microscope to inspect bearings or other component parts. May test functional performance of instrument, using test equipment. May write inspection reports concerning defective parts and assemblies. ● **GED:** R3, M2, L2 ● **SVP:** 3-6 mos ● **Academic:** Ed=N, Eng=N ● **Work Field:** 212 ● **MPSMS:** 602 ● **Aptitudes:** G3, V4, N4, S3, P3, Q4, K3, F3, M3, E5, C5 ● **Temperaments:** T ● **Physical:** Stg=L; Freq: R, H, I, N, A Occas: E, D ● **Work Env:** Noise=N; ● **Salary:** 2 ● **Outlook:** 3

METAL-FINISH INSPECTOR (any industry) ● DOT #703.687-014 ● OES: 83000 ● Inspects surfaces of sheet metal articles, such as refrigerator and freezer cabinets, or automobile bodies for burrs, dings, scratches, laminated metal, or other surface defects prior to painting or porcelainizing: Rubs gloved hand over surfaces and examines workpiece. Marks defects for repair, using knowledge of acceptable metal finish standards and specifications. Records recurring defects on inspection report and submits report to quality control department for action. Records and submits daily inspection report. ● **GED:** R3, M2, L2 ● **SVP:** 6 mos-1 yr ● **Academic:** Ed=N, Eng=N ● **Work Field:** 212 ● **MPSMS:** 556, 583 ● **Aptitudes:** G3, V3, N4, S4, P3, Q4, K4, F4, M3, E5, C5 ● **Temperaments:** R, T ● **Physical:** Stg=L; Freq: R, H, N, A Occas: S, I ● **Work Env:** Noise=N; ● **Salary:** 3 ● **Outlook:** 2

PHOTO CHECKER AND ASSEMBLER (photofinishing) ● DOT #976.687-014 ● OES: 83000 ● Alternate titles: CHECKER; INSPECTOR. Inspects, assembles, and packs mounted or unmounted negatives, color film transparencies, and photographic prints: Examines items for natural color shading, density, sharpness of image, or identifying numbers, using lighted viewing screen. Marks defective prints, using grease pencil and standardized symbols to indicate nature of defect and corrective action required in reprinting. Removes defects, such as dust and smudges from prints, using brush, cloth, and cleaning fluid. Packages and labels satisfactory prints and negatives. Maintains daily production records. May cut negatives and prints from roll, using cutting machine. May be designated according to type of print inspected as Color-Print Inspector (photofinishing); Full-Roll Inspector (photofinishing); Mounting Inspector (photofinishing); Reversal-Print Inspector (photofinishing); May inspect prints for tears, dirt, scum, or other surface defects preparatory to mounting and be designated Take-Down Inspector (photofinishing). ● **GED:** R3, M1, L1 ● **SVP:** 3-6 mos ● **Academic:** Ed=N, Eng=N ● **Work Field:** 212, 041, 221 ● **MPSMS:** 897 ● **Aptitudes:** G3, V4, N4, S3, P3, Q4, K4, F3, M3, E4, C2 ● **Temperaments:** J, T ● **Physical:** Stg=L; Freq: R, H, I, N, D, A, X Occas: S ● **Work Env:** Noise=N; ● **Salary:** 3 ● **Outlook:** 2

PHOTOFINISHING LABORATORY WORKER (photofinishing) ● DOT #976.687-018 ● OES: 58028 ● Alternate titles: FILM NUMBERER; FILM SORTER; PRICER-BAGGER; PROOF SORTER; RACKER; REPRINT SORTER; SORTER-PACKER. Performs any combination of following tasks to prepare and disseminate negatives, positives, and prints in photofinishing laboratory: Reads instructions written on orders, and examines contents of orders to ascertain size, type, and number of pieces. Sorts orders according to size and type processing required. Pastes identifying label on customer order envelopes and transfer bags to ensure matching of orders subsequent to processing. Removes finished work from transfer bags subsequent to processing and computes customer charges according to pricelist. Inserts order in bag or envelope, and staples bag together or seals envelope. Pastes address label on bag or envelope. Conveys orders between departments. Distributes supplies to other photofinishing workers. Maintains records of orders sorted and packaged. ● **GED:** R2, M2, L2 ● **SVP:** 1-3 mos ● **Academic:** Ed=N, Eng=N ● **Work Field:** 221, 041 ● **MPSMS:** 897, 753 ● **Aptitudes:** G4, V4, N4, S4, P4, Q3, K4, F3, M3, E5, C4 ● **Temperaments:** J, R ● **Physical:** Stg=L; Freq: R, H, I, N, X Occas: S ● **Work Env:** Noise=N; ● **Salary:** 2 ● **Outlook:** 4

PLATE INSPECTOR (print. & pub.) ● DOT #972.687-010 ● OES: 83000 ● Inspects offset lithographic printing plates for quality and content at printing establishment: Visually examines plates for defects, such as spaces, spots, broken type, and crooked or overlapping halftones, and views film and film flat used to produce plates to determine cause of defect. Compares halftones and screen tints on plates to film flat, using magnifier, to detect overdevelopment or underdevelopment of plates. Measures plates with ruler and compares measurements and appearance of plates to prepress proofs to verify accuracy of positioning and presence of artwork and type for each color. Applies correcting solutions to plates or notifies supervisor of defects and suspected causes. Delivers plates meeting establishment criteria and companion materials, such as artwork, proofs, pasteups, film, and film flats, to press for printing. ● **GED:** R3, M2, L2 ● **SVP:** 6 mos-1 yr ● **Academic:** Ed=N, Eng=N ● **Work Field:** 212 ● **MPSMS:** 567 ● **Aptitudes:** G3, V3, N4, S3, P2, Q3, K4, F4, M4, E5, C3 ● **Temperaments:** R, T ● **Physical:** Stg=L; Const: N Freq: R, H Occas: I, G, D, A, X ● **Work Env:** Noise=N; ● **Salary:** 4 ● **Outlook:** 3

PRINT INSPECTOR (pottery & porc.) ● DOT #774.687-018 ● OES: 83000 ● Alternate titles: DECORATOR INSPECTOR. Inspects printed decoration on pottery and porcelain ware: Compares printed decoration and quality of workmanship of ware with sample and discards misprinted ware. Returns salvageable pieces for rework. Rubs ware with abrasive stone or wet sponge to remove paint spots. ● **GED:** R3, M1, L1 ● **SVP:** 3-6 mos ● **Academic:** Ed=N, Eng=N ● **Work Field:** 212 ● **MPSMS:** 535 ● **Aptitudes:** G3, V4, N3, S3, P3, Q4, K3, F4, M3, E5, C3 ● **Temperaments:** J, R, T ● **Physical:** Stg=L; Freq: R, H, I, N, D, X ● **Work Env:** Noise=N; Occas: U ● **Salary:** 1 ● **Outlook:** 2

QUALITY ASSURANCE GROUP LEADER (auto. mfg.) ● DOT #806.367-014 ● OES: 83000 ● Alternate titles: TEAM COORDINATOR; TEAM LEADER. Assists QUALITY ASSURANCE SUPERVISOR (auto. mfg.) 806.137-022 in coordinating and monitoring activities of workers engaged in inspecting and testing assembled motor vehicles, components, and parts, as vehicles and subassemblies proceed through stages of assembly process, applying knowledge of quality assurance standards and procedures: Confers with supervisor and reviews assembly specifications and production schedules. Assigns workers to work stations and monitors department activities. Interprets standards and procedures, and assists workers in resolving technical problems. Reports unresolved problems to supervisor. Demonstrates tools, equipment, and work aids used in performing quality assurance tasks. May attend management meetings to represent work group and record minutes of meeting. May conduct work group (team) meetings to relay management information to workers, and solicit response to work-related problems. May perform duties of absent workers to maintain work schedules. ● **GED:** R3, M2, L3 ● **SVP:** 6 mos-1 yr ● **Academic:** Ed=N, Eng=G ● **Work Field:** 212 ● **MPSMS:** 591 ● **Aptitudes:** G3, V3, N4, S3, P3, Q3, K4, F4, M4, E5, C4 ● **Temperaments:** J, P, T, V ● **Physical:** Stg=L; Freq: R, H, T, G, N, F, D, A, X, V Occas: I ● **Work Env:** Noise=N; ● **Salary:** 5 ● **Outlook:** 4

QUALITY ASSURANCE MONITOR (auto. mfg.) ● DOT #806.367-018 ● OES: 83000 ● Inspects and tests assembled motor vehicle, components, and parts as vehicle and subassemblies proceed through stages of assembly process, performing any combination of following tasks, to assure that assembly work and materials meet establishment and regulatory standards, using conventional and electronic test equipment and machines: Pries welded surfaces of vehicle body apart to observe welded seams and compare characteristics of spot welds with standards. Conducts nondestructive ultrasonic tests on unpainted vehicle body to assure that production welding standards have been met. Inspects vehicle subassemblies and parts received from suppliers to detect substandard materials prior to distribution to assembly line. Inspects painted vehicle to detect defects in painted surfaces. Measures gaps between vehicle doors, deck lid, hood, and body, and flushness of parts to vehicle body. Measures force required to close vehicle doors and deck lids, operate door-opening buttons, and turn key in doors and deck lid locks. Verifies predetermined torque settings on bolts and nuts

used to assemble parts, subassemblies and vehicle body. Verifies and calibrates setting of pneumatic powered and hand torque wrenches. Inspects trim parts and components of vehicle body, such as molding, instrument control panel, wire harnesses, and seat belts. Inspects and tests chassis parts and components, such as engine and transmission, and suspension, brake, and exhaust systems. Functionally tests electrical and mechanical systems of completed motor vehicle. Drives completed vehicle on test track to determine origin of wind noise, squeaks, and rattles. Records results of individual observations and tests, using printed graphic and written forms, electronic data collecting equipment, or keyboard of central computer system. Reviews overall quality of vehicle leaving one stage of production prior to entering next or final stage. Observes assembly and quality assurance process to trace cause of production defects, and confers with production and quality assurance workers and supervisors, and engineering personnel to resolve problems. Attends meetings to obtain and discuss report of production defects observed and recorded by quality audit personnel (centralized auditing unit), for later discussion with department workers and supervisor. Corrects substandard work or replaces defective parts, using handtools and power tools. May work as member of quality assurance group (team) and be assigned different work stations as monitoring needs require. May be designated according to stage of assembly process as Quality Assurance Monitor, Body (auto. mfg.); Quality Assurance Monitor, Chassis (auto. mfg.); Quality Assurance Monitor, Final (auto. mfg.); Quality Assurance Monitor, Trim (auto. mfg.). ● **GED:** R3, M2, L3 ● **SVP:** 6 mos-1 yr ● **Academic:** Ed=N, Eng=S ● **Work Field:** 212 ● **MPSMS:** 591 ● **Aptitudes:** G3, V4, N4, S4, P3, Q3, K4, F4, M4, E4, C4 ● **Temperaments:** J, P, T, V ● **Physical:** Stg=L; Freq: R, H, N, F, D, A Occas: I, T, G, X, V ● **Work Env:** Noise=N; ● **Salary:** 5 ● **Outlook:** 4

SELECTOR (glass mfg.) ● DOT #579.687-030 ● OES: 83000 ● Alternate titles: GLASS-PRODUCTS INSPECTOR; INSPECTOR, MACHINE-CUT GLASS; INSPECTOR-PACKER, GLASS CONTAINER. Inspects finished glassware for conformance to quality standards: Examines glassware for defects, such as cracks, chips, reams (wavy distortions), discolorations, and blisters. Verifies weight and dimensions of glassware, such as height, circumference, thickness, and bottle throat openings, using templates, jigs, micrometers, and fixed gauges; or monitors automatic gauging equipment that measures glassware. Examines glass for annealing defects, using polariscope. Removes glassware to unjam automatic equipment. Throws rejects in cullet (waste glass) bin. May record production, number of rejects, and lehr temperatures. May pack acceptable glassware in cartons, close and seal cartons, and stencil information on carton, using brush and ink. May turn controls to synchronize automatic gauging equipment with conveyor speed. ● **GED:** R2, M2, L1 ● **SVP:** 1-3 mos ● **Academic:** Ed=N, Eng=N ● **Work Field:** 212 ● **MPSMS:** 531 ● **Aptitudes:** G4, V4, N4, S4, P3, Q4, K3, F3, M3, E5, C4 ● **Temperaments:** J, R, T ● **Physical:** Stg=L; Freq: R, H, N, A Occas: I, X ● **Work Env:** Noise=N; ● **Salary:** 4 ● **Outlook:** 3

WATER LEAK REPAIRER (auto. mfg.) ● DOT #807.684-034 ● OES: 83000 ● Detects and seals areas of water leaks on motor vehicle bodies, using ultraviolet light, caulking gun, and handtools: Illuminates areas of inner compartments of vehicle bodies, using ultraviolet light (black light) to detect water inside compartments. Seals areas suspected of water leaks, using caulking gun. Aligns parts, such as hoods, doors, and deck lids (trunks) to fit body contours to correct cause of water leaks, using handtools. May work as part of team. ● **GED:** R2, M1, L2 ● **SVP:** 1-3 mos ● **Academic:** Ed=N, Eng=N ● **Work Field:** 102, 212 ● **MPSMS:** 591 ● **Aptitudes:** G4, V4, N4, S4, P4, Q4, K3, F4, M3, E5, C5 ● **Temperaments:** J, R, T ● **Physical:** Stg=L; Freq: R, H, I, N Occas: S ● **Work Env:** Noise=L; Occas: R ● **Salary:** 3 ● **Outlook:** 2

Elemental Work: Industrial

Workers in this group feed, off bear, tend machines and equipment, or do manual work. They perform routine, uncomplicated work that requires little training or experience. They also assist other, more skilled workers. They work in a factory setting.

✓ What kind of work would you do?

Your work activities would depend upon your specific job. For example, you might:

- use a handtruck to move supplies to workers on an assembly line.
- smooth wooden furniture posts using sandpaper and steel wool.
- tend a machine that seals paper cartons.
- carry containers and materials and wash mixing vats to assist syrup-mixer in making table syrup.
- tend machine that cuts continuous strips of zipper into certain lengths.
- clean and polish plated products with a cloth and liquid cleanser.
- tend a machine that rivets metal furniture parts together.
- sort and bag scrap leather to salvage usable pieces.

✓ What skills and abilities do you need for this kind of work?

To do this kind of work, you must be able to:

- follow instructions carefully.
- adjust to doing the same thing over and over.
- move or lift heavy objects.
- pay attention to safety rules when working around machinery.

✓ How do you know if you would like or could learn to do this kind of work?

The following questions may give you clues about yourself as you consider this group of jobs.

- Have you taken an industrial arts course? Would you like to work in an industrial setting?
- Have you helped a worker install, repair, or build something in your home? Can you follow directions?
- Have you helped a custodian at school or church?

✓ How can you prepare for and enter this kind of work?

Occupations in this group usually require education and/or training extending from a short demonstration to over three months, depending upon the specific kind of work. Most jobs in this group do not require specific training before employment. Brief on-the-job training is often provided at the time of employment or as work assignments are changed. Industrial arts or shop courses provide useful background for jobs in this group.

✓ What else should you consider about these jobs?

Many people accept jobs in this group as their first full-time employment. As they develop experience and skills, they may advance to other jobs in the work setting.

Work activities change very little from day to day because workers must follow set procedures. It is important that workers follow strict safety rules when working around machines.

If you think you would like to do this kind of work, look at the job titles listed on the following pages.

■   ■   ■

GOE: 06.04.02
Machine Work, Metal & Plastics

BENDING-MACHINE OPERATOR II (any industry) ● DOT #617.685-010 ● OES: 91321 ● Tends machine that bends metal structural shapes, such as bars, strips, rods, angles, and tubes to specified angle or contour: Positions workpiece against end stops. Locks holding clamp and guide clamp onto workpiece. Lubricates workpiece with oil. Pulls lever or depresses pedal to activate turntable which draws workpiece through guide clamp and around die block until stopped by plug stops. May slide mandrel into tubing instead of using guide clamp. May use hand-powered bending machine. May perform such fabricat-ing tasks as flaring tube ends, using tube flarer, or cutting metal stock to length, using power shears or saws. May attach specified die to machine, using wrench. May be designated according to type of stock bent as Rod-Bending-Machine Operator (any industry) II; Tube-Bending-Machine Operator (any industry) II; or type of machine tended as Two-Stage, Steel-Bender Annealer (toy-sport equip.). ● **GED:** R2, M1, L1 ● **SVP:** 1-3 mos ● **Academic:** Ed=N, Eng=N ● **Work Field:** 134 ● **MPSMS:** 554 ● **Aptitudes:** G4, V4, N4, S4, P4, Q5, K3, F4, M3, E4, C5 ● **Temperaments:** R, T ● **Physical:** Stg=M; Const: R, H Freq: N, A Occas: I, G, D ● **Work Env:** Noise=L; Freq: M ● **Salary:** 2 ● **Outlook:** 2

BUFFING-MACHINE TENDER (any industry) ● DOT #603.665-010 ● OES: 91117 ● Tends automatic buffing machine that buffs parts, such as automobile hardware or trim: Loads parts on holding fixture of revolving table that is preset for regular indexing and starts machine.

Removes buffed parts and examines them for surface defects. Places buffed parts into shallow tray and covers them with cardboard separators. Informs BUFFER (any industry) I or BUFFING-LINE SET-UP WORKER (any industry) of buffing defects. May maintain count of buffed parts and parts which do not meet specifications. ● **GED:** R2, M1, L1 ● **SVP:** 2-30 days ● **Academic:** Ed=N, Eng=N ● **Work Field:** 051 ● **MPSMS:** 550 ● **Aptitudes:** G4, V4, N4, S4, P4, Q4, K4, F4, M3, E5, C5 ● **Temperaments:** R, T ● **Physical:** Stg=L; Const: R, H, N, A Occas: I ● **Work Env:** Noise=L; ● **Salary:** 1 ● **Outlook:** 2

DRILL PRESS TENDER (machine shop) ● DOT #606.685-026 ● OES: 91117 ● Tends single- or multiple-spindle drill presses that drill, tap, ream, or countersink holes in metal workpieces according to specifications: Lifts workpiece manually, or using hoist, and positions and secures workpiece in drilling jig or fixture on machine table, using clamps and wrenches. Starts machine and feeds workpiece to cutter or vice versa, or engages automatic feeding mechanism. Turns valve to direct flow of coolant and cutting oils over cutting area. Observes operation and releases lever or turns handwheel to raise cutting tool from workpiece when machining is completed. Inspects or measures machined workpiece for conformance to specifications and shop standards, using instruments, such as fixed, plug, depth, and thread gauges, calipers, micrometers, and templates. Changes worn cutting tools, using wrenches. May machine plastics or other nonmetallic materials. ● **GED:** R2, M2, L2 ● **SVP:** 1-3 mos ● **Academic:** Ed=N, Eng=N ● **Work Field:** 053 ● **MPSMS:** 540 ● **Aptitudes:** G4, V4, N4, S4, P4, Q4, K4, F4, M4, E5, C5 ● **Temperaments:** T ● **Physical:** Stg=M; Const: R, H, I, N Freq: D Occas: S, E, A ● **Work Env:** Noise=L; Const: M Occas: A ● **Salary:** 3 ● **Outlook:** 3

ELECTRIC-SEALING-MACHINE OPERATOR (any industry) ● DOT #690.685-154 ● OES: 92100 ● Alternate titles: BONDING-MACHINE OPERATOR; DIELECTRIC-HEAT-SEALING-MACHINE OPERATOR; HEAT-SEAL OPERATOR; PLASTIC-WELDING-MACHINE OPERATOR. Tends machine that heats and seals precut or predesigned plastic material or film to form book covers, eyeglass cases, baby pants, tubing, and other plastic-coated products: Moves controls on machine to adjust temperature, pressure, and time cycle. Loads feeding mechanism with rolls of plastic material. Aligns edges of continuous plastic strips and guides them into position under electrode. Starts machine and depresses pedal to lower electrode that heats and seals edges of material. Removes product from machine and stacks it in rack or on table. May position plastic strip over article preparatory to heat sealing article. ● **GED:** R2, M1, L2 ● **SVP:** 2-30 days ● **Academic:** Ed=N, Eng=N ● **Work Field:** 063 ● **MPSMS:** 492 ● **Aptitudes:** G4, V4, N4, S4, P4, Q4, K3, F4, M3, E4, C5 ● **Temperaments:** R, T ● **Physical:** Stg=L; Freq: R, H, N Occas: I ● **Work Env:** Noise=L; ● **Salary:** 3 ● **Outlook:** 3

EMBOSSER (any industry) ● DOT #583.685-030 ● OES: 92999 ● Alternate titles: EMBOSSING-CALENDER OPERATOR; EMBOSSING-MACHINE OPERATOR; ROLLER EMBOSSER. Tends machine that imparts raised design or finish on cloth, coated fabrics, or plastic sheeting, by means of heat and pressure from engraved steel rollers: Adjusts automatic device that regulates heat, or turns valve to admit steam to rollers. Slides bar through center of material roll and lifts it onto machine feed brackets. Threads material between rollers and laps end onto takeup tube. Starts machine and moves controls to adjust speed, pressure of rollers, and tension of material. Observes material as it passes through machine to prevent seams, rolled selvages, or trash from damaging rollers. May guide material by hand. May verify temperature of roller, using pyrometer. May sew cuts of cloth together, using portable sewing machine. May be designated according to material embossed as Silk-Crepe-Machine Operator (textile). May tend machine that imparts artificial graining, size, trademark, or other designs to sweatbands and be designated Sweatband-Decorating-Machine Operator (hat & cap). Important variables may be indicated by trade names of machine used. ● **GED:** R2, M1, L2 ● **SVP:** 1-3 mos ● **Academic:** Ed=N, Eng=N ● **Work Field:** 192, 032 ● **MPSMS:** 420 ● **Aptitudes:** G4, V4, N4, S4, P4, Q4, K4, F4, M3, E4, C5 ● **Temperaments:** R, T ● **Physical:** Stg=M; Freq: R, H, N, F, V Occas: I, E, D ● **Work Env:** Noise=L; ● **Salary:** 3 ● **Outlook:** 2

GRAINER, MACHINE (any industry) ● DOT #652.686-014 ● OES: 98502 ● Feeds metal or simulated wood panels, sheets, or strips into machine that prints lines resembling natural wood grain. Holds or moves

irregularly shaped pieces against printing roller to impart grainlike appearance. Stacks grained pieces for further processing or assembly into articles, such as television cabinets, automobile dashboards, and office furniture. ● **GED:** R2, M1, L1 ● **SVP:** 2-30 days ● **Academic:** Ed=N, Eng=N ● **Work Field:** 191 ● **MPSMS:** 456, 459 ● **Aptitudes:** G3, V4, N3, S3, P3, Q5, K3, F3, M3, E5, C4 ● **Temperaments:** R ● **Physical:** Stg=M; Freq: R, H, I, N, D Occas: S, X ● **Work Env:** Noise=N; ● **Salary:** 2 ● **Outlook:** 2

GRINDER (plastic prod.) ● DOT #555.685-026 ● OES: 92965 ● Alternate titles: CUTTER OPERATOR; PULVERIZER. Tends machine that grinds particles of solid plastics materials to specified size: Starts machine and dumps or shovels plastics into hopper. Observes equipment to detect stoppages. May clean equipment with airhose, scrapers, or brushes. May tend machine that grinds scrap material for reuse and be designated Regrinder Operator (plastic prod.). ● **GED:** R2, M1, L1 ● **SVP:** 2-30 days ● **Academic:** Ed=N, Eng=N ● **Work Field:** 142 ● **MPSMS:** 492 ● **Aptitudes:** G4, V4, N5, S4, P4, Q5, K4, F4, M4, E5, C5 ● **Temperaments:** R ● **Physical:** Stg=H; Freq: S, R, H Occas: I, D ● **Work Env:** Noise=L; Occas: A ● **Salary:** 2 ● **Outlook:** 2

MACHINE OPERATOR II (any industry) ● DOT #619.685-062 ● OES: 91510 ● Tends fabricating machines, such as cutoff saws, shears, rolls, brakes, presses, forming machines, spinning machines, and punch, that cut, shape, and bend metal plates, sheets, tubes, and structures: Reads job specifications to determine machine adjustments and material requirements. Sets stops or guides to specified length as indicated by scale, rule, or template. Positions workpiece against stops, manually or using hoist, or aligns layout marks with die or blade. Pushes button or depresses pedal to activate machine. Observes machine operation to detect workpiece defects or machine malfunction. Measures workpiece dimensions, using rule, template, or other measuring instruments to determine accuracy of machine operation. Removes burrs, sharp edges, rust, or scale from workpiece, using file, hand grinder, or wire brush. Performs minor machine maintenance, such as oiling machines, dies, or workpieces. Assists machine operators to set up machine, and stack, mark, pack, and transport finished workpieces. May rivet and spot-weld workpieces. May tend machines that fabricate and assemble sheet metal products and be designated Sheet-Metal Production Worker (any industry). ● **GED:** R2, M1, L2 ● **SVP:** 1-3 mos ● **Academic:** Ed=N, Eng=N ● **Work Field:** 054, 134 ● **MPSMS:** 554, 619 ● **Aptitudes:** G4, V4, N4, S3, P4, Q4, K4, F4, M3, E4, C5 ● **Temperaments:** R, T ● **Physical:** Stg=M; Const: R, H Freq: I, N, D Occas: S ● **Work Env:** Noise=L; Occas: M ● **Salary:** 3 ● **Outlook:** 3

NIBBLER OPERATOR (any industry) ● DOT #615.685-026 ● OES: 91321 ● Tends machine that cuts metal plates, sheets, or structural shapes into specified radial or irregular shapes by action of reciprocating cutting knives or punches: Positions and clamps specified cutter or punch into ram and bed of machine. Turns thumbscrews to adjust depth of stroke to thickness of metal. Turns handwheel to set specified distance between cutter or punch and center point of turntable or fixtures, using built-in scale or rule. Clamps guide and drive rollers over workpiece. Depresses pedal which activates ram and feed rollers to cut or punch along radius. Guides workpiece manually along cutting lines or template to cut irregular shapes. May lay out guidelines onto workpiece by tracing from template. Mat drill center hole into workpiece, using portable drill. May bevel edges of steel plates, using portable pneumatic nibbler. ● **GED:** R2, M2, L2 ● **SVP:** 1-3 mos ● **Academic:** Ed=N, Eng=N ● **Work Field:** 054 ● **MPSMS:** 554 ● **Aptitudes:** G3, V4, N4, S3, P4, Q5, K4, F4, M3, E4, C5 ● **Temperaments:** R, T ● **Physical:** Stg=M; Freq: S, R, H, N Occas: I, D ● **Work Env:** Noise=V; Freq: A, O ● **Salary:** 3 ● **Outlook:** 2

POWER-PRESS TENDER (any industry) ● DOT #617.685-026 ● OES: 91321 ● Tends power press that cuts, punches, or stamps various size articles from sheets or blocks of materials: Bolts or clamps specified die to machine. Positions or clamps sheet or block of material on machine bed or in holding fixture to obtain maximum cuts from each sheet. Starts machine and depresses pedal or moves lever that rotates or forces cutting die through sheet or block to obtain article of specified size and shape. May tend machine that automatically feeds and positions material under die for cutting. May examine parts for defects, visually or using measuring gauges, and discards parts not meeting specifications. May be designated according to type of machine tended as Blanking-Machine Operator (any industry); Punch-Press Operator (any industry) IV; Stamping-Press Operator (any industry). ● **GED:**

R2, M1, L2 ● **SVP:** 1-3 mos ● **Academic:** Ed=N, Eng=N ● **Work Field:** 134 ● **MPSMS:** 556, 587 ● **Aptitudes:** G4, V4, N4, S4, P4, Q4, K3, F4, M3, E4, C5 ● **Temperaments:** R ● **Physical:** Stg=M; Freq: R, H, N, D Occas: I ● **Work Env:** Noise=V; Occas: M ● **Salary:** 3 ● **Outlook:** 2

PUNCH-PRESS OPERATOR II (any industry) ● DOT #615.685-030 ● OES: 91321 ● Tends one or more power presses that trim, punch, shape, notch, draw, or crimp metal, composite materials, or plastic stock between preset dies: Places workpiece against fixtures or stops on machine bed and under machine die, or threads roll of metal into jig. Starts press and monitors machine operation to detect misalignment or malfunction. Inspects parts visually, or with fixed gauges to verify conformance to specifications or to detect fabrication defects. May be designated according to product machined as Sprue-Cutting-Press Operator (foundry); or function of machine as Forming-Press Operator (any industry) II; Trimming-Press Operator (forging); or according to type of press operated as Multiple-Punch-Press Operator (any industry) II. ● **GED:** R2, M1, L2 ● **SVP:** 1-3 mos ● **Academic:** Ed=N, Eng=N ● **Work Field:** 134 ● **MPSMS:** 540, 550, 587 ● **Aptitudes:** G4, V4, N4, S4, P4, Q5, K4, F4, M3, E4, C5 ● **Temperaments:** R, T ● **Physical:** Stg=M; Freq: R, H, I, N, D Occas: G ● **Work Env:** Noise=L; Freq: M ● **Salary:** 3 ● **Outlook:** 4

SCROLL-MACHINE OPERATOR (struct. metal) ● DOT #616.685-062 ● OES: 92100 ● Tends machine that forms metal stock, such as bars, rods, squares, tubing, and wire, into coils or ornamental scrolls: Positions and clamps specified scroll (die) into bed of machine. Threads workpiece through drag roll and clamps roll to center of die. Starts machine that turns die to draw workpiece along contour of die as vertical rod pushes workpiece into center of die, forming scroll or coil. May tend power shear or cutoff saw to cut stock to specified length. May insert leather strip along edge of die to protect finish of workpiece. May bend workpieces along edge of die manually. ● **GED:** R2, M1, L1 ● **SVP:** 2-30 days ● **Academic:** Ed=N, Eng=N ● **Work Field:** 135 ● **MPSMS:** 554 ● **Aptitudes:** G4, V4, N4, S4, P4, Q5, K4, F4, M4, E5, C5 ● **Temperaments:** R, T ● **Physical:** Stg=M; Freq: R, H Occas: S, K, O, I ● **Work Env:** Noise=L; ● **Salary:** 3 ● **Outlook:** 3

TOOL DRESSER (any industry) ● DOT #601.682-010 ● OES: 92100 ● Alternate titles: DRILL-SHARPENER OPERATOR. Operates compressed-air or steam-driven machine to sharpen large drills, such as rock drills, used in construction, mining, quarrying, and well-drilling: Places cutting end of drill in forge to heat cutting edge to increase malleability. Inserts heated drill into die space on machine. Starts hammering action of die to shape cutting edge of drill. Stops machine and removes edged drill. Tempers drill by heating it in forge and quenching it in water, brine, or oil. ● **GED:** R3, M2, L2 ● **SVP:** 6 mos-1 yr ● **Academic:** Ed=N, Eng=N ● **Work Field:** 134 ● **MPSMS:** 552 ● **Aptitudes:** G3, V4, N4, S4, P3, Q4, K3, F4, M3, E5, C4 ● **Temperaments:** J, T ● **Physical:** Stg=M; Freq: R, H, N, D, A Occas: I ● **Work Env:** Noise=L; ● **Salary:** 4 ● **Outlook:** 2

TURRET-PUNCH-PRESS OPERATOR, TAPE-CONTROL (any industry) ● DOT #615.685-042 ● OES: 91321 ● Tends tape-controlled turret or hydraulic-powered punch press that automatically positions indexing table, selects punch, and punches holes, or layout marks in metal sheets, plates, strips, or bars: Positions and clamps workpiece against fixtures or to specified point on built-in scale. Threads tape through electronic reader to specified position. Starts machine and observes operation. May verify first piece, using rule and plug gauges. May open chucks, using wrench to replace worn or broken punches and dies. ● **GED:** R2, M2, L2 ● **SVP:** 1-3 mos ● **Academic:** Ed=N, Eng=N ● **Work Field:** 134 ● **MPSMS:** 554 ● **Aptitudes:** G4, V4, N4, S4, P4, Q5, K4, F3, M4, E5, C5 ● **Temperaments:** R, T ● **Physical:** Stg=H; Freq: S, R, H, I, N Occas: D, A ● **Work Env:** Noise=L; Freq: O ● **Salary:** 3 ● **Outlook:** 4

GOE: 06.04.03
Machine Work, Wood

BUZZSAW OPERATOR (any industry) ● DOT #667.685-026 ● OES: 92305 ● Tends circular cutoff saw that custom cuts fireplace and stove

fuel wood from random lengths of wood: Places wood on carriage and adjusts guides to specified length. Starts saw and moves carriage past saw to cut wood to length. Advances wood to carriage guides and repeats moving carriage past saw. ● **GED:** R2, M1, L1 ● **SVP:** 1-3 mos ● **Academic:** Ed=N, Eng=N ● **Work Field:** 056 ● **MPSMS:** 452 ● **Aptitudes:** G4, V4, N4, S4, P4, Q5, K3, F4, M3, E4, C5 ● **Temperaments:** R, T ● **Physical:** Stg=H; Freq: R, H Occas: I, N ● **Work Env:** Noise=L; Freq: W Occas: M ● **Salary:** 2 ● **Outlook:** 2

CHAIN OFFBEARER (saw. & plan.) ● DOT #669.686-018 ● OES: 98502 ● Pulls lumber from moving conveyor coming from ripsaw, resaw, planer, trimmer, and grading tables, and slides and stacks lumber on piles, according to grade marked on each piece. May push buttons to start and stop conveyor and deposit waste material onto slasher conveyor for waste recovery. May band stacked lumber to facilitate moving, using banding machine. May be designated according to condition of lumber removed from conveyor as Dry-Chain Offbearer (saw. & plan.); Green-Chain Offbearer (saw. & plan.); or may be designated according to machine from which lumber is conveyed as Planer-Chain Offbearer (saw. & plan.). ● **GED:** R2, M1, L1 ● **SVP:** 2-30 days ● **Academic:** Ed=N, Eng=N ● **Work Field:** 011 ● **MPSMS:** 452 ● **Aptitudes:** G4, V4, N5, S4, P4, Q5, K4, F4, M3, E4, C5 ● **Temperaments:** R ● **Physical:** Stg=H; Const: R, H, D Occas: I ● **Work Env:** Noise=L; Occas: W, M ● **Salary:** 2 ● **Outlook:** 2

GLUING-MACHINE OPERATOR (woodworking) ● DOT #569.685-046 ● OES: 92970 ● Tends machine that utilizes pressure and heat to bond preglued boards into panels of specified size: Regulates speed and pressure of rollers and temperature of heating unit, according to type of glue, thickness of wood parts, and density and moisture content of wood. Starts machine, and places preglued boards of combined specified length edge to edge on feed rolls or chain that carry them through machine and curing tunnel. May tend machine with saw attachment that bonds preglued boards into continuous panel and automatically cuts panel into specified lengths and be designated Plycor Operator (woodworking). ● **GED:** R2, M2, L2 ● **SVP:** 1-3 mos ● **Academic:** Ed=N, Eng=N ● **Work Field:** 063 ● **MPSMS:** 451, 460 ● **Aptitudes:** G4, V4, N4, S3, P4, Q5, K3, F4, M3, E4, C5 ● **Temperaments:** R, T ● **Physical:** Stg=H; Freq: S, R, H Occas: I, D, A ● **Work Env:** Noise=L; ● **Salary:** 3 ● **Outlook:** 3

LATHE SPOTTER (millwork-plywood) ● DOT #663.686-022 ● OES: 97941 ● Positions veneer blocks (logs cut to length) between spindles of veneer lathe, using electric hoist: Measures diameter of block to locate and mark center, using ruler. Examines end of log to detect rot, cracks, and splits. Selects chuck of minimum diameter according to size and conditon of block, and places block on lathe spindle. Secures hooks to ends of block, activates hoist to suspend block between lathe chucks, and signals VENEER-LATHE OPERATOR (millwork-plywood; wood. container) to press chucks into block. Removes knots, dirt, and other foreign matter, using ax, steam hose, and pick. May assist in chaining lathe knives. May operate lathe-charging-machine from console to position logs for automatic loading into rotary veneer lathe. May be designated according to type of log peeled as Flitch Hanger (millwork-plywood). ● **GED:** R2, M1, L1 ● **SVP:** 1-3 mos ● **Academic:** Ed=N, Eng=N ● **Work Field:** 054 ● **MPSMS:** 453 ● **Aptitudes:** G4, V4, N4, S3, P4, Q4, K3, F4, M3, E5, C5 ● **Temperaments:** R ● **Physical:** Stg=H; Freq: R, H Occas: S, I, N, D ● **Work Env:** Noise=L; ● **Salary:** 3 ● **Outlook:** 2

GOE: 06.04.04
Machine Work, Paper

BAG-MACHINE OPERATOR (paper goods) ● DOT #649.685-014 ● OES: 92999 ● Alternate titles: BAG-MAKING-MACHINE OPERATOR. Tends machine that automatically measures, prints, cuts, folds, and glues, or seals plain or wax papers, polyethylene film, or cellophane to form bags: Threads materials from parent roll through guides and rollers to cutters, gluer, printer, folding device, or electric sealer. Starts machine, observes operation, and adjusts machine to ensure uniform shearing, printing, folding, gluing, or sealing of continuous roll of material into finished bags. May insert shaft into core of parent roll and secure with steel collars, using handtools, and mount roll onto machine, using hoist. May be designated according to material processed as Cellophane-Bag-Machine Operator (paper goods); Polyethylene-Bag-Machine Operator (paper goods); Waxed-Bag-Machine Operator (paper goods). ● **GED:** R2, M1, L1 ● **SVP:** 1-3 mos ● **Academic:** Ed=N, Eng=N ● **Work Field:** 102 ● **MPSMS:** 474 ● **Aptitudes:** G4, V4, N4, S3, P4, Q5, K4, F4, M3, E5, C4 ● **Temperaments:** J, T ● **Physical:** Stg=M; Freq: S, R, H, I, N, D Occas: K, O, X ● **Work Env:** Noise=L; Occas: O ● **Salary:** 2 ● **Outlook:** 1

BINDERY WORKER (print. & pub.) ● DOT #653.685-010 ● OES: 92540 ● Alternate titles: BINDERY OPERATOR; TABLE WORKER. Tends various machines and equipment and performs any combination of following tasks involved in binding books, periodicals, and pamphlets, and assembling related printed materials in accordance with work order specifications: Punches holes in paper sheets, manually or by machine. Creases and compresses signatures prior to affixing covers, using press or by hand. Fastens sheets, signatures, or other printed materials together, using hand or machine stapler, or adjusts or tends machine that inserts wire or plastic binding strips into punched holes to fasten pages and covers together. Feeds covers, signatures, and sheets into various machines for collating, stitching, trimming, folding, ruling, stapling, roughing, indexing, gluing, and perforating operations. Removes, stacks, and packs printed material in various stages of completion on pallets as it accumulates on delivery table of machines. Examines stitched, collated, bound, and unbound publications to ascertain that pages are bound in numerical or folio order according to sample copy, and for such defects as imperfect bindings, ink spots, torn, loose, and uneven pages, and loose and uncut threads. Inserts illustrated pages, extra sheets, and collated sets into catalogs, periodicals, directories, pocket portfolios, or looseleaf binders, and inserts sheets and applies labels to envelopes or periodicals by hand or machine. Places paper jackets on acceptable books. Applies gold leaf, silver leaf, or metallic foil lettering or designs on covers, using stamping machine. Applies adhesive tape, mylar strips, and index tabs to sheets by machine. Wraps product in plastic, using shrink-wrapping machine, packs products in boxes, and tapes lids of boxes shut. Records daily production. Cleans work area around machine. May make ready bindery equipment and work stations. May lead, train, and monitor work of less experienced workers. ● **GED:** R2, M2, L2 ● **SVP:** 3-6 mos ● **Academic:** Ed=N, Eng=N ● **Work Field:** 062, 063, 134 ● **MPSMS:** 480 ● **Aptitudes:** G4, V4, N4, S4, P3, Q4, K3, F3, M3, E4, C4 ● **Temperaments:** R, T ● **Physical:** Stg=L; Freq: R, H, I Occas: N, D, A, X, V ● **Work Env:** Noise=L; Freq: M ● **Salary:** 2 ● **Outlook:** 2

BOOK TRIMMER (print. & pub.) ● DOT #640.685-010 ● OES: 92940 ● Alternate titles: BINDERY OPERATOR; MULTIPLE-KNIFE-EDGE-TRIMMER OPERATOR; SHEARING-MACHINE OPERATOR; TRIMMER OPERATOR, THREE KNIFE. Tends paper-cutting machine that cuts edges of bound and unbound books, periodicals, catalogs, and directories to specified size for binding and rebinding: Reads instructions on worksheet to ascertain machine setting requirements. Inserts or replaces knives in trimmer and adjusts guides to trim head (top), tail (bottom), and fore (front) edges of book to specified dimensions, and locks sections in place. Starts machine for test run, and examines finished book body to ensure finished sample meets job order specifications and book body sample. Loads book bodies into feed receptacle of machine. Starts machine and observes operation. Examines book bodies to ensure specifications are met. Observes operation of machine during production run. Stops machine when machine malfunctions and adjusts knives and guides as required. Replenishes supply of book bodies periodically. May tend manually operated trimmer, jogging book bodies to align edges and placing book body against three sections of guide in turn to trim three edges of book. Depresses treadle or lever to clamp cut edges at each position. May be required to watch for colored markers between pages that indicate narrow margins and foldouts when positioning edges of book bodies against guides. May stack books as they are trimmed. May operate cutter to cut cardboard, paper, or book covers to specified size. May push cart stacked with books to next work station. ● **GED:** R2, M1, L1 ● **SVP:** 1-3 mos ● **Academic:** Ed=N, Eng=S ● **Work Field:** 054 ● **MPSMS:** 480 ● **Aptitudes:** G4, V4, N4, S4, P4, Q4, K4, F3, M3, E4, C4 ● **Temperaments:** R, T ● **Physical:** Stg=M; Freq: R, H, N Occas: S, I, G, D, X ● **Work Env:** Noise=L; Freq: V, M ● **Salary:** 3 ● **Outlook:** 3

CARTON-FORMING-MACHINE OPERATOR (any industry) ● DOT #641.685-022 ● OES: 92999 ● Tends machine that forms and glues flat blanks or continuous roll of paperboard into finished cartons for packing merchandise: Adjusts forming bars to accommodate size of box to be shaped, using handtools. Fills glue pots with adhesive and positions rollers to dispense glue onto paperboard. Loads feeding magazine with blanks, or mounts roll of paper on machine standard and threads paper to feeding mechanism and starts machine. Observes machine operation to detect malfunction. May load machine with roll of waxed, parchment, or other paper used to line cartons. May mount roll of metal strip to form cutting edge on cartons. May stamp data with handstamp or attach automatic stamping device. ● **GED:** R2, M1, L1 ● **SVP:** 2-30 days ● **Academic:** Ed=N, Eng=N ● **Work Field:** 062, 063, 041 ● **MPSMS:** 475 ● **Aptitudes:** G4, V4, N4, S4, P4, Q4, K4, F4, M4, E5, C5 ● **Temperaments:** R, T ● **Physical:** Stg=M; Freq: R, H, I, N, D Occas: A ● **Work Env:** Noise=L; Occas: O ● **Salary:** 3 ● **Outlook:** 1

CARTON-FORMING-MACHINE TENDER (paper goods) ● DOT #641.685-026 ● OES: 92999 ● Tends one or more machines that automatically cut, glue, and form cartons or caddies from pasteboard rolls for kitchen, penny, and book matches: Rolls pasteboard to machine, positions on letoff rack, and threads end of pasteboard strip into machine. Starts and observes machine operation and corrects malfunctions, such as improper forming, glue flow, or pasteboard tension, using handtools. Observes finished cartons as they drop from forming machine into rotating hopper, then into gravity feed chute, to prevent jamming. May lift tote box of finished cartons and dump cartons into feed hopper. ● **GED:** R2, M1, L1 ● **SVP:** 2-30 days ● **Academic:** Ed=N, Eng=N ● **Work Field:** 102 ● **MPSMS:** 475 ● **Aptitudes:** G4, V4, N4, S4, P4, Q4, K4, F4, M3, E5, C5 ● **Temperaments:** R ● **Physical:** Stg=H; Freq: R, H, N, D Occas: S, I ● **Work Env:** Noise=L; ● **Salary:** 3 ● **Outlook:** 1

GOE: 06.04.05
Machine Work, Fabric & Leather

BUTTONHOLE-AND-BUTTON-SEWING-MACHINE OPERATOR (garment) ● DOT #786.685-042 ● OES: 92717 ● Tends semiautomatic sewing machines that cut and stitch buttonholes and sew buttons and other fasteners to garments: Pours buttons into hopper for automatic feeding into holding clamp of sewing machine or places buttons and fasteners in clamp. Turns knobs to adjust stitching and cutting mechanisms of machine to set size of buttonholes according to garment styles. Positions garment, garment parts, buttons, or fasteners under needle, and starts short-cycle sewing machine that cuts and stitches buttonholes in garment or parts or sews buttons and fasteners to garment. Cuts threads, using scissors. ● **GED:** R2, M1, L2 ● **SVP:** 2-30 days ● **Academic:** Ed=N, Eng=N ● **Work Field:** 171 ● **MPSMS:** 440 ● **Aptitudes:** G4, V4, N4, S4, P3, Q5, K4, F4, M3, E4, C4 ● **Temperaments:** R, T ● **Physical:** Stg=L; Freq: R, H, I, N Occas: A, X ● **Work Env:** Noise=L; ● **Salary:** 2 ● **Outlook:** 2

PRESSER, MACHINE (any industry) ● DOT #363.682-018 ● OES: 92728 ● Alternate titles: BUCK PRESSER; FINISHER, MACHINE; FLATTENING-MACHINE OPERATOR; IRONER, MACHINE; PRESSING MACHINE OPERATOR; STEAM FLATTENER; STEAM PRESSER; STEAM-PRESS OPERATOR. Operates pressing machine to smooth surfaces, flatten seams, or shape articles, such as garments, drapes, slipcovers, and hose, in manufacturing or dry cleaning establishments, using either of following methods: (1) Spreads articles to be pressed on buck (padded table) of machine. Pulls pressing head onto article and depresses pedals or presses buttons to admit steam from buck through garments to press them and to exhaust steam from presser. Rearranges articles on buck and repeats process until pressing is complete. (2) Positions garment on buck and depresses pedal to lower jump iron onto garment and to apply pressure. Pushes lever to release steam from iron. Pushes iron attached to movable arm back and forth over garment and shifts garment under iron until garment is pressed. Hangs pressed articles on wire hangers. May operate two presses simultaneously, positioning articles on one press while another article is steamed on other press. May finish pressed articles, using hand or puff irons. May tend machine that presses and shapes articles, such as shirts, blouses, and sweaters [PRESSER, FORM (any industry) 363.685-018]. May be designated according to article pressed as Coat Presser (any industry); Pants Presser (any industry); or according to fabric pressed as Silk Presser (garment) II; or according to part of garment pressed as Armhole-And-Shoulder Off-Presser (garment); Lining Presser (laundry & rel.); or according to type of machine used as Jump-Iron-Machine Presser (garment). May be designated according to article, part, type of fabric, or machine used as Band Presser (garment); Collar Fuser (garment); Form-Press Operator (laundry & rel.); Legger-Press Operator (laundry & rel.); Mushroom-Press Operator (laundry & rel.); Puff-Iron Operator (laundry & rel.) II; Shirt Finisher (garment); Topper-Press Operator (laundry & rel.); Topper-Press Operator, Automatic (laundry & rel.); Vest-Front Presser (garment); Wash-Clothes Presser (laundry & rel.); Wool Presser (laundry & rel.). ● **GED:** R2, M1, L1 ● **SVP:** 2-30 days ● **Academic:** Ed=N, Eng=N ● **Work Field:** 032 ● **MPSMS:** 906, 420 ● **Aptitudes:** G4, V4, N5, S4, P4, Q5, K3, F3, M3, E4, C5 ● **Temperaments:** R ● **Physical:** Stg=M; Freq: R, H, I, N ● **Work Env:** Noise=N; Freq: H, U, O ● **Salary:** 2 ● **Outlook:** 2

SEWING-MACHINE OPERATOR, SEMIAUTOMATIC (garment) ● **DOT** #786.685-030 ● OES: 92717 ● Tends one or more semiautomatic sewing machines that attach, join, reinforce, or decorate garments or garment parts, or perform other preset cycle operations, such as buttonhole making: Threads machine and adjusts thread tensions. Positions fabric layers, garment, or garment part in holding device on machine bed or according to guides, edges, or markings, and starts machine. Notifies SUPERVISOR, GARMENT MANUFACTURING (garment) 786.132-010 if machine malfunctions. May select supplies, such as fasteners and thread, according to specifications or color of fabric. May change needles and oil machine. ● **GED:** R2, M1, L2 ● **SVP:** 2-30 days ● **Academic:** Ed=N, Eng=N ● **Work Field:** 440 ● **MPSMS:** 440 ● **Aptitudes:** G4, V4, N4, S4, P3, Q4, K4, F4, M3, E4, C4 ● **Temperaments:** R, T ● **Physical:** Stg=L; Const: R, H, I Freq: N, D Occas: X ● **Work Env:** Noise=L; Occas: M ● **Salary:** 2 ● **Outlook:** 1

SPREADER, MACHINE (any industry) ● DOT #781.685-010 ● OES: 92999 ● Alternate titles: LAYER UP. Tends machine that spreads cloth in successive layers on table to prepare cloth for cutting: Positions bolt of cloth on carriage of machine, turns handle to align edge of cloth with marks on table, threads cloth end through feed rollers, and clamps cloth to end of table. Starts machine that automatically spreads cloth in even layers as it moves back and forth over table, or pushes machine along track over cutting table. Inspects cloth as it is spread to detect defects, such as dye shadings and holes. Cuts out defects with hand shears. Laps ends of cloth at points marked on table. Straightens edges and smooths layers of cloth with hands. Turns handwheel to adjust feeding mechanism of machine according to weight of cloth. Cuts cloth from roll, using hand shears. May mark pattern outlines on top ply of cloth [MARKER (any industry) I 781.384-014]. May cut spread cloth [CUTTER, MACHINE (any industry) I 781.684-014]. ● **GED:** R3, M2, L2 ● **SVP:** 1-3 mos ● **Academic:** Ed=N, Eng=N ● **Work Field:** 062, 054 ● **MPSMS:** 420 ● **Aptitudes:** G3, V4, N4, S4, P3, Q4, K3, F3, M3, E5, C3 ● **Temperaments:** R, T ● **Physical:** Stg=H; Freq: S, R, H, N, D, X, V Occas: I ● **Work Env:** Noise=N; ● **Salary:** 1 ● **Outlook:** 2

STRIP-CUTTING-MACHINE OPERATOR (textile) ● DOT #686.685-066 ● OES: 92710 ● Alternate titles: SLICER; SLITTER. Tends machine that cuts rolls of textile material into narrow rolls of specified width: Lifts roll of material onto machine bar and hammers wedge into core of roll to secure roll to bar. Turns handwheel to move rotary blade into cutting position, following markings on calibrated scale to obtain specified cutting width. Starts machine that rotates blade and roll in opposite directions. Presses lever to move rotating blade forward and cut through roll of material. Releases lever and positions blade for subsequent cut. Removes narrow rolls of material from machine and stacks rolls on shelf according to width. When cutting rolls of bias material into narrow widths, is designated Bias-Binding Cutter (tex. prod., nec). May be designated according to product cut as Band-Cutting-Machine Operator (garment; knitting); Binding Cutter (garment; textile); Facing-Cutting-Machine Operator (garment); Handkerchief Cutter (textile); Piping-Cutting-Machine Operator (garment); Suspender Cutter (garment); Tape-Cutting-Machine Operator (garment; tex. prod., nec). ● **GED:** R2, M1, L1 ● **SVP:** 2-30 days ● **Academic:** Ed=N, Eng=N ● **Work Field:** 054 ● **MPSMS:** 420 ● **Aptitudes:** G4, V4, N4, S4, P4, Q4, K3, F4, M3, E5, C4 ● **Temperaments:** R, T ● **Physical:** Stg=H; Freq: R, H, N, D Occas: S, O, I, E, A, X ● **Work Env:** Noise=L; ● **Salary:** 3 ● **Outlook:** 2

SURGICAL-DRESSING MAKER (protective dev.) ● DOT #689.685-130 ● OES: 92999 ● Alternate titles: PAD MAKER. Tends machine that automatically cuts and folds gauze backing around absorbent cotton to form surgical dressings: Starts machine that cuts gauze and absorbent cotton to size, folds gauze around cotton in prescribed manner to form surgical pad, and ejects pad. Examines ejected pads for size, folding of gauze and defects in absorbent cotton. May pack specified quantity of pads in bags or cartons. ● **GED:** R2, M1, L1 ● **SVP:** 2-30 days ● **Academic:** Ed=N, Eng=N ● **Work Field:** 054, 062 ● **MPSMS:** 604 ● **Aptitudes:** G4, V4, N4, S4, P4, Q4, K4, F4, M4, E4, C4 ● **Temperaments:** R, T ● **Physical:** Stg=L; Freq: R, H Occas: I, N, A, X ● **Work Env:** Noise=N; ● **Salary:** 2 ● **Outlook:** 2

GOE: 06.04.06
Machine Work, Textiles

BEAM-WARPER TENDER, AUTOMATIC (knitting) ● DOT #681.685-018 ● OES: 92710 ● Alternate titles: BEAM WARPER; SECTION BEAMER; SECTION WARPER; TRICOT- WARPER TENDER; WARPER TENDER. Tends high-speed warpers that automatically wind yarn in parallel sheets onto beams preparatory to dyeing, weaving, or knitting: Examines yarn in creel to ensure that yarn corresponds to warp pattern sheet specifications, for number of yarn ends, arrangement of yarn in creel, yarn size, and color. Requests CREELER (any industry) 689.687-030 to alter creel setup to correspond with warp pattern sheet. Pulls yarn ends from packages mounted on creel, through drop wires, and tension, measuring, and spreading devices, and fastens ends to empty warp beam to thread machine. Sets yardage counter to record amount of yarn wound and starts machine. Observes operation to detect yarn breaks which cause machine to stop. Turns beam back to point of break, locates and ties broken ends, and cuts excess yarn, using scissors. Stops machine when specified yardage is wound on beam, cuts yarn, and places gummed tape over ends or loops ends together to secure ends. Doffs full beams and sets in empties [BEAM RACKER (textile) 681.686-010]. May wrap beam with paper. May replace empty yarn packages [CREELER (any industry) 689.687- 030]. ● **GED:** R2, M1, L1 ● **SVP:** 3-6 mos ● **Academic:** Ed=N, Eng=N ● **Work Field:** 163 ● **MPSMS:** 411 ● **Aptitudes:** G4, V4, N4, S4, P3, Q4, K3, F3, M3, E5, C4 ● **Temperaments:** R, T ● **Physical:** Stg=L; Freq: R, H, I, F, D Occas: S, K, E, N, X, V ● **Work Env:** Noise=L; ● **Salary:** 1 ● **Outlook:** 2

CLOTH DOFFER (textile) ● DOT #689.686-058 ● OES: 98502 ● Alternate titles: CLOTH HANDLER; LOOM DOFFER; SHORT PIECE HANDLER. Removes rolls of cloth from looms or knitting machines and trucks cloth to storage: Pulls lever or presses button to stop machine when roll has sufficient yardage as indicated by yardage clock, mark on cloth, or color-coded card flag. Turns handle to lower roll of cloth, cuts cloth, using scissors, and places cloth roll on handtruck. Places empty takeup beam on bracket of machine, attaches cloth to beam, and restarts machine. Writes identifying information, such as lot and style number, on ticket and attaches ticket to cloth roll. Trucks cloth to storage or inspection department. May weigh and keep record of cloth beams doffed. ● **GED:** R2, M1, L2 ● **SVP:** 2-30 days ● **Academic:** Ed=N, Eng=N ● **Work Field:** 011, 164, 165 ● **MPSMS:** 420 ● **Aptitudes:** G4, V4, N4, S4, P4, Q4, K4, F4, M3, E4, C4 ● **Temperaments:** R ● **Physical:** Stg=H; Freq: S, K, O, R, H, I, X Occas: N ● **Work Env:** Noise=L; Const: A ● **Salary:** 2 ● **Outlook:** 2

KNITTING-MACHINE OPERATOR (knitting) ● DOT #685.665-014 ● OES: 92710 ● Alternate titles: KNITTER; KNITTER, MACHINE. Tends one or more machines that knit fabrics, garment parts, or other articles from yarn: Creels machine and ties end of yarn to yarn in machine or threads yarn through guides, tension springs, stop-motion devices, and yarn carrier or needles, using hook. Starts machine and laps end of tubular or flat knitted goods around takeup roller. Observes knitting to detect yarn breaks, exhausted yarn packages, and knitting defects. Ties broken yarn ends, replaces exhausted yarn packages, and notifies KNITTING-MACHINE FIXER (knitting) 689.260-026 of mechanical defects. Cuts knitted fabric, using scissors, and doffs roll of cloth from machine. May mark ticket to indicate number of holes in knitted goods. May replace defective needles, using needle pliers or wrench. May weigh roll of knitted goods and record weight.

May oil machine. May be designated according to type of machine tended as Circular Knitter (knitting); Flat Knitter (knitting). May be designated according to type of fabric knitted as Jersey Knitter (knitting); Pile-Fabric Knitter (knitting); Rib-Cloth Knitter (knitting), or garment part as Collar Knitter (knitting); Cuff Knitter (knitting). ● **GED:** R3, M1, L1 ● **SVP:** 1-3 mos ● **Academic:** Ed=N, Eng=N ● **Work Field:** 165 ● **MPSMS:** 424 ● **Aptitudes:** G4, V4, N4, S4, P3, Q4, K4, F3, M3, E5, C4 ● **Temperaments:** R, T ● **Physical:** Stg=M; Freq: R, H, I, N, A, V Occas: S, O, E, G, X ● **Work Env:** Noise=L; ● **Salary:** 2 ● **Outlook:** 2

PICKING-MACHINE OPERATOR (any industry) ● DOT #680.685-082 ● OES: 92999 ● Alternate titles: BLENDER OPERATOR; SHREDDER; WILLOWER. Tends picking machine that opens or shreds and fluffs raw or used materials, such as wool, kapok, foam rubber, or hair to facilitate further processing: Cuts open bales of raw materials. Starts machine and deposits handfuls of raw material on feeding apron that conveys material into picking or shredding rollers. Observes machine to detect clogged rollers. Stops machine, and strips fiber from rollers, using knife, scissors, or hands. May spray raw material with oil emulsion. May be designated according to material processed as Hair-Picking-Machine Operator (furniture; tex. prod., nec); Tow-Picker Operator (furniture); Wool-Picker Operator (textile). ● **GED:** R2, M1, L1 ● **SVP:** 2-30 days ● **Academic:** Ed=N, Eng=N ● **Work Field:** 161 ● **MPSMS:** 410 ● **Aptitudes:** G4, V4, N5, S4, P4, Q5, K4, F4, M4, E5, C5 ● **Temperaments:** R ● **Physical:** Stg=M; Freq: R, H, N Occas: I, F ● **Work Env:** Noise=L; Occas: A ● **Salary:** 1 ● **Outlook:** 3

SEAMLESS-HOSIERY KNITTER (knitting) ● DOT #684.685-010 ● OES: 92710 ● Alternate titles: KNITTER; KNITTING-MACHINE OPERATOR, AUTOMATIC; KNITTING-MACHINE OPERATOR, SEAMLESS HOSIERY; SOCK-KNITTING-MACHINE OPERATOR. Tends circular knitting machines with automatic pattern controls that knit seamless hose: Places yarn spools on creel; threads and starts machine. Observes operation of machines and notifies KNITTING-MACHINE FIXER (knitting) 689.260-026 of any malfunction. Removes knitted hose from machines. Pulls hose over inspection form or over hand to examine for defects, such as holes, runs, or picks. Classifies hose according to specifications into grades, such as first quality, rejects, and mends. Counts, bundles, ties, and labels each grade of hose. Clips loose or connecting threads on or joining socks, using scissors. May measure overall length of hose, using scale on inspection form. May mark defective portion of hose for HOSIERY MENDER (knitting) 782.684-030, using crayon. May be designated according to type of hose knitted as Sock Knitter (knitting). ● **GED:** R2, M1, L1 ● **SVP:** 1-3 mos ● **Academic:** Ed=N, Eng=N ● **Work Field:** 165 ● **MPSMS:** 446 ● **Aptitudes:** G4, V4, N4, S4, P3, Q4, K3, F3, M3, E5, C4 ● **Temperaments:** R, T ● **Physical:** Stg=L; Const: R, H Freq: S, I, N Occas: G, X ● **Work Env:** Noise=N; ● **Salary:** 3 ● **Outlook:** 2

YARN WINDER (tex. prod., nec) ● DOT #681.685-154 ● OES: 92710 ● Alternate titles: BACK WINDER; PACKAGE WINDER; REWINDER; SPOOLER; WINDER; WINDING-MACHINE OPERATOR. Tends machine that winds strands of yarn from bobbins, cakes, pirns, and other yarn packages into packages specified for further processing, shipment, or storage: Places supply packages on spindles or holders. Threads ends of yarn from each package through guides and tension device and attaches them to takeup package. Moves lever, depresses pedal, or flips switch to start machine. Observes winding units to detect breaks in yarn and ties broken ends by hand or with knotter. Stops machine or winding unit and doffs packages. Inspects yarn for defects. Reports malfunction of machine to MACHINE FIXER (textile) 689.260-010. May weigh yarn package or keep production records. May tend machine that winds yarn through emulsion-filled trough or against paraffin disk to soften or strengthen yarn. May be designated according to package wound or supply package used as Bobbin Winder (textile); Cake Winder (textile); or according to material wound as Worsted Winder (textile). When winding continuous filament yarn to or from packages used in throwing processes, is known as Redraw Operator (textile). When rewinding tangled or short lengths of yarn, is known as Salvage Winder (textile). Important variables may be indicated by trade names or machines used. May be designated Brass-Bobbin Winder (tex. prod., nec); Cone Spooler (any industry); Cone Winder (textile); Cop Winder (textile); Muff Winder (textile); Piece Hand (textile); Pirn Winder (textile); Quill Winder (narrow fabrics); Spool Winder (textile); Tailing-Machine Operator (textile); Tube Winder (any industry); Twine Winder (tex. prod., nec). ● **GED:** R2, M1, L2 ● **SVP:** 1-3 mos ● **Academic:** Ed=N, Eng=N ● **Work Field:** 163 ● **MPSMS:** 411 ● **Aptitudes:** G4, V4, N4, S4, P4, Q4, K4, F3, M3, E5, C4 ● **Temperaments:** R, T ● **Physical:** Stg=M; Freq: R, H, I, N, D Occas: S, O, E, G, F, A, X ● **Work Env:** Noise=L; ● **Salary:** 2 ● **Outlook:** 2

GOE: 06.04.07
Machine Work, Rubber

DESIGN PRINTER, BALLOON (rubber goods) ● DOT #651.685-014 ● OES: 92542 ● Tends cylinder press that prints designs and lettering on balloons: Rolls preinflated balloon against printing plate on revolving cylinder press that prints design. Pours ink and solvent in trough of cylinder press and adjusts ink flow. Cleans machine rollers, plates, and troughs with solvent and rag when color changes are specified. May inflate balloon on air nozzle, align and press one or more inked block dies against balloon, deflate balloon, and place balloon in box. ● **GED:** R2, M1, L1 ● **SVP:** 2-30 days ● **Academic:** Ed=N, Eng=N ● **Work Field:** 191 ● **MPSMS:** 519 ● **Aptitudes:** G4, V4, N4, S4, P3, Q4, K3, F3, M3, E5, C4 ● **Temperaments:** R ● **Physical:** Stg=L; Freq: R, H, I Occas: N, X ● **Work Env:** Noise=N; ● **Salary:** 4 ● **Outlook:** 2

RUBBER CUTTER (rubber goods) ● DOT #559.685-158 ● OES: 92940 ● Tends machine that cuts bales of crude rubber into pieces: Removes wired wooden wrapping or metal straps, using cutters. Loads bale into machine bed, using electric hoist or pulls bale from chute, using hook. Moves lever to release hydraulic ram that pushes bale through stationary knives. May remove burlap covering from bales and truck them to machine. May push bales onto bed of cutting machine. May pull layers of smoked or crepe rubber apart, using hook. ● **GED:** R1, M1, L1 ● **SVP:** 2-30 days ● **Academic:** Ed=N, Eng=N ● **Work Field:** 054 ● **MPSMS:** 519 ● **Aptitudes:** G4, V4, N5, S4, P4, Q5, K4, F4, M3, E5, C5 ● **Temperaments:** R ● **Physical:** Stg=H; Freq: S, R, H ● **Work Env:** Noise=L; Freq: A ● **Salary:** 2 ● **Outlook:** 2

GOE: 06.04.08
Machine Work, Stone, Glass, & Clay

CERAMIC CAPACITOR PROCESSOR (electron. comp.) ● DOT #590.684-010 ● OES: 92999 ● Performs any combination of following tasks to process substrate, electrode, and termination materials to form monolithic ceramic capacitors: Reviews work orders and production schedules to determine processing specifications. Deposits layer of dielectric ceramic material on thermoplastic sheets, using tape casting equipment. Cuts cast sheets into ceramic wafers. Verifies and sorts wafers according to thickness and quality, using thickness gauge and magnifying device. Deposits electrode material onto wafers, using silk screen printing machine. Heats and compresses stacks of imprinted, ceramic wafers to form laminates, using laminating press. Cuts laminate into chips, using bench-mounted cutting equipment or automatic cutter. Loads chips onto boat and fires chips in kiln to fuse laminated material. Applies conductive termination material to specified edges of ceramic chips, manually or using automatic dipping equipment. Fuses conductive termination material to ceramic chip, using automatic oven. Polishes fused chip, using tumbler. Solders lead wires to ceramic chip, manually or using automatic soldering machine. Encases capacitors in epoxy material. ● **GED:** R2, M2, L2 ● **SVP:** 1-3 mos ● **Academic:** Ed=N, Eng=N ● **Work Field:** 147, 121, 111 ● **MPSMS:** 587 ● **Aptitudes:** G4, V4, N4, S4, P3, Q4, K3, F3, M3, E5, C4 ● **Temperaments:** T ● **Physical:** Stg=L; Const: R, H, I, N Occas: D, X ● **Work Env:** Noise=N; Occas: H, M ● **Salary:** 3 ● **Outlook:** 4

COREMAKER, MACHINE I (foundry) ● DOT #518.685-014 ● OES: 91910 ● Alternate titles: CORE STRIPPER. Tends turnover draw-type coremaking machine that makes sand cores for use in casting metal: Clamps core box over die on front table of machine, and partly fills core box with sand from overhead chute, or by using hands or shovel. Depresses pedal to open compressed-air valve that causes table to rise and fall with series of jolts, to compress sand in box. Positions reinforcing wires in sand, fills box with sand, and repeats jolting. Tamps sand into core box with hand or pneumatic tool. Removes excess sand from top of core box with hands or straightedge and clamps metal plate to top of box. Pulls lever to roll front table over and deposit box top down on rear table. Pushes rear table down to withdraw core from core box and lifts core from machine. ● **GED:** R2, M1, L2 ● **SVP:** 1-3 mos ● **Academic:** Ed=N, Eng=N ● **Work Field:** 132 ● **MPSMS:** 566 ● **Aptitudes:** G4, V4, N5, S4, P3, Q5, K3, F4, M3, E4, C5 ● **Temperaments:** R, T ● **Physical:** Stg=M; Freq: R, H, I, D ● **Work Env:** Noise=L; Freq: A ● **Salary:** 3 ● **Outlook:** 2

CRUSHER TENDER (any industry) ● DOT #570.685-022 ● OES: 92965 ● Alternate titles: CRUSHER OPERATOR; PRIMARY-CRUSHER OPERATOR; ROLL ATTENDANT. Tends any of several types of crushers that size materials, such as coal, rock, salt, clay and shale, or ore for industrial use or for further processing: Moves levers to regulate flow of materials to and from conveyors, chutes, pumps, or storage bins. Starts crusher, and prods, breaks, or discards lumps to prevent plugging, using bar, sledgehammer, or jackhammer. Adjusts equipment, such as screens, conveyors, and fans, to control or vary size or grade of product, or to maintain uniform flow of materials. Cleans and lubricates equipment. May keep record of materials processed. ● **GED:** R2, M2, L1 ● **SVP:** 1-3 mos ● **Academic:** Ed=N, Eng=N ● **Work Field:** 142 ● **MPSMS:** 340, 350 ● **Aptitudes:** G4, V4, N4, S4, P3, Q4, K4, F4, M3, E5, C4 ● **Temperaments:** R ● **Physical:** Stg=M; Freq: R, H Occas: C, S, K, O, I, N, D, X ● **Work Env:** Noise=L; Freq: A Occas: M ● **Salary:** 1 ● **Outlook:** 3

LENS-FABRICATING-MACHINE TENDER (optical goods) ● DOT #716.685-022 ● OES: 92965 ● Tends one or more bench machines that generate, grind, edge, or polish ophthalmic lenses and precision optical elements: Mounts blocked element in machine holding device. Verifies machine settings or adjusts machines for variables, such as speed, machining time, and flow rate of abrasive or coolant. Starts machine that automatically generates, grinds, polishes, or edges optical element. Removes element after specified machining time, rinses element in water, and measures to verify specified dimensions of element, using micrometer, caliper, dial gauge, and shadowgraph. May deblock and clean element in degreasing tank. May be designated according to fabricating process or type lens fabricated as Contact-Lens-Curve Grinder (optical goods); Contact-Lens-Edge Buffer (optical goods); Fusion-Juncture Grinder (optical goods); Lens-Edge Grinder, Machine (optical goods); Lens-Generating-Machine Tender (optical goods); Multifocal-Button Countersink Grinder (optical goods). ● **GED:** R2, M2, L2 ● **SVP:** 3-6 mos ● **Academic:** Ed=N, Eng=N ● **Work Field:** 051 ● **MPSMS:** 603, 605 ● **Aptitudes:** G4, V4, N4, S4, P3, Q4, K4, F4, M3, E5, C5 ● **Temperaments:** R, T ● **Physical:** Stg=L; Freq: R, H, N Occas: I, A ● **Work Env:** Noise=N; ● **Salary:** 2 ● **Outlook:** 3

MILLER (cement) ● DOT #570.685-046 ● OES: 92965 ● Alternate titles: GRINDER OPERATOR. Tends machines that crush, mix, or pulverize materials, such as limestone, shale, oyster shells, clay, iron ore, silica, gypsum, and cement clinkers, used in making cement: Starts mill and conveyors. Observes conveyor system to ensure continuous flow of material. Stops conveyor and removes clogged material, using bar. Opens chute over conveyor to add materials, such as iron, silica, or gypsum, according to specifications. Observes operation of auxiliary equipment, such as cement pumps, air or screen separators, air slides, cement coolers, and dust collectors. Turns valves to regulate water, air, and oil lines on machine, according to laboratory specifications. May regulate feeder mechanism on machines not equipped with automatic regulators. May add moisture to materials to facilitate flow into machine. May be designated according to type of mill tended as Ball-Mill Operator (cement); Finish-Mill Operator (cement); Hammer-Mill Operator (cement); Miller, Rod-Mill (cement); Pug-Mill Operator (cement); Raw-Finish-Mill Operator (cement); Tube-Mill Operator (cement); Vertical-Mill Operator (cement). ● **GED:** R2, M1, L1 ● **SVP:** 1-3 mos ● **Academic:** Ed=N, Eng=N ● **Work Field:** 142, 143 ● **MPSMS:** 533 ● **Aptitudes:** G4, V4, N5, S4, P4, Q4, K4, F4, M3, E5, C4 ● **Temperaments:** R, T ● **Physical:** Stg=M; Freq: R, H, I Occas: G, D, A, X ● **Work Env:** Noise=L; Occas: A, M ● **Salary:** 3 ● **Outlook:** 3

GOE: 06.04.09
Machine Work, Assorted Materials

CUTTER, MACHINE II (any industry) ● DOT #699.685-014 ● OES: 92940 ● Alternate titles: SHEARER; STRAIGHT CUTTER. Tends machine that cuts materials, such as braid, cardboard, cloth, felt, leather, ribbon, roofing paper, strands of wire, or tape to specified dimensions, by any of following methods: (1) Spaces guide or stop gauge along calibrated scale of cutting table according to length of cut specified and tightens setscrew to secure guide or gauge in position. Stacks single or multiple layers of material on cutting table with edges against stop gauge or pulls material across cutting table to guide. Lowers lever-type blade by hand to cut material. (2) Spaces stop gauge along calibrated scale, according to length of cut specified, and tightens setscrew to secure gauge in position. Places single or multiple layers of material on bed of machine with edges against stop gauge or moves lever to advance material in bed of machine against stop gauge. Depresses pedal to activate lever-type-blade that lowers and cuts material. May tend machine that trims excess material or irregular edges from variety of materials or garment and shoe parts. (3) Mounts roll of material on shaft or positions container of flat folded material at feed end of machine. Threads end of material through guides and automatic feeding device. Turns setscrew to regulate feeding device according to length of cut specified. Starts machine that automatically feeds material under lever-type blade and cuts material into lengths. Stacks lengths of material on table or in handtruck. May change blade, using handtools. When cutting materials for use in making rubber stamp pads, is designated Guillotine Operator (pen & pencil). When trimming feathers for use in making shuttlecocks, is designated Shuttlecock-Feather Trimmer (toy-sport equip.). May be designated according to material or article cut or trimmed as Belt-Loop Cutter (garment); Collar Trimmer (garment); Sample Cutter (garment; textile). May be designated: Band Cutter (garment); Belt Cutter (garment); Braid Cutter (rubber goods); Elastic Cutter (garment); Foil Cutter (any industry); Hose-Suspender Cutter (garment); Label Cutter (garment; knitting); Piping Blocker (boot & shoe); Ribbon Cutter (garment; Sheet Cutter (tex. prod., nec) I; Strap Cutter (garment); Tape Cutter (garment); Toppiece Chopper (boot & shoe). ● **GED:** R2, M1, L2 ● **SVP:** 2-30 days ● **Academic:** Ed=N, Eng=N ● **Work Field:** 054 ● **MPSMS:** 420, 520 ● **Aptitudes:** G4, V4, N4, S4, P3, Q4, K4, F4, M3, E4, C4 ● **Temperaments:** R, T ● **Physical:** Stg=L; Freq: R, H, N, D Occas: I, X ● **Work Env:** Noise=N; ● **Salary:** 3 ● **Outlook:** 2

CUTTER (photofinishing) ● DOT #976.685-010 ● OES: 92940 ● Alternate titles: FILM CUTTER; PRINT CUTTER. Tends automatic or semiautomatic machines that cut processed film or prints into single or multiple units: Examines film or print roll to determine size, number of cuts required, and type machine to use. Turns setscrews to adjust machine guides to roll width and sets density meter on automatic machine to coincide with sensitized marks on roll that control release of cutting blade. Threads roll through machine guides and starts machine that automatically cuts roll into individual or multiple units or depresses pedal of semiautomatic machine to cut roll. Cuts rolls of nonstandard width, using scissors or hand operated paper cutter. Inserts units in customer envelope. Keeps production records. ● **GED:** R2, M1, L1 ● **SVP:** 2-30 days ● **Academic:** Ed=N, Eng=N ● **Work Field:** 054 ● **MPSMS:** 897 ● **Aptitudes:** G4, V4, N4, S4, P4, Q4, K4, F3, M3, E5, C4 ● **Temperaments:** R, T ● **Physical:** Stg=L; Freq: R, H, I, N, D Occas: X ● **Work Env:** Noise=L; Occas: O ● **Salary:** 1 ● **Outlook:** 2

MACHINE FEEDER (any industry) ● DOT #699.686-010 ● OES: 98502 ● Feeds or removes metal, plastic, or other stock and material from automatic fabricating machines: Places stock into hoppers, onto conveyors of self-centering machine bed, or lifts coils of sheet metal or wire onto feedrack. Removes stock from conveyor and piles it into boxes, truck, or on feed conveyor for next operation. May push dual control buttons to activate machine. May work in pairs to feed or remove pieces from machine. May thread sheet metal or wire through machine. May be designated by machine fed as Shear Operator, Automatic (any industry) II; or by task performed as Punch-Press Feeder (any industry); Punch-Press Offbearer (any industry); Straightening-Machine Feeder (any industry). ● **GED:** R1, M1, L1 ● **SVP:** 2-30 days ● **Academic:** Ed=N, Eng=N ● **Work Field:** 054, 134 ● **MPSMS:**

492, 540, 582 ● **Aptitudes:** G4, V4, N5, S4, P4, Q5, K4, F4, M4, E5, C5 ● **Temperaments:** R ● **Physical:** Stg=M; Freq: R, H Occas: I ● **Work Env:** Noise=L; ● **Salary:** 2 ● **Outlook:** 3

PHOTORESIST LAMINATOR, PRINTED CIRCUIT BOARD (electron. comp.) ● DOT #554.685-034 ● OES: 92999 ● Alternate titles: HOT ROLL LAMINATOR; LAMINATING MACHINE TENDER. Tends machine that laminates dry photoresist film to surfaces of panels used in manufacturing printed circuit boards (PCB's): Mounts rolls of photoresist film and plastic protective film on machine spindles. Threads film through machine rollers and secures film to takeup spindles. Presses button to activate machine. Adjusts controls to regulate speed, temperature, and pressure of laminating rollers. Moves levers and adjusts controls to align panels with edge of film. Feeds panels into roller, or positions panels on conveyor that feeds panels into laminating machine. Observes lamination process, monitors speed and temperature gauges, and adjusts controls to ensure compliance with standards. Removes laminated panels from machine. Cuts excess photoresist and protective plastic film from panel edges, using knife. May tend machine that scrubs, cleans, and dries PCB panels prior to laminating process [SCRUBBER MACHINE TENDER (electron. comp.) 599.685-134]. May examine laminated panels for defects. ● **GED:** R2, M1, L2 ● **SVP:** 2-30 days ● **Academic:** Ed=N, Eng=N ● **Work Field:** 063 ● **MPSMS:** 587 ● **Aptitudes:** G4, V4, N4, S4, P4, Q4, K4, F4, M4, E5, C5 ● **Temperaments:** R ● **Physical:** Stg=M; Const: R, H Freq: I, N Occas: D ● **Work Env:** Noise=N; Occas: M ● **Salary:** 1 ● **Outlook:** 2

SANDER (toy-sport equip.) ● DOT #690.685-346 ● OES: 92965 ● Tends machine that sands and smooths golf club grips, skis, and other sports equipment: Inserts article to be sanded in roller carriage brackets or grip in holding device of machine. Starts machine that automatically feeds article to sanding belt or rotates article against moving abrasive wheel to remove excess stock, paint, and blemishes from article. ● **GED:** R2, M1, L1 ● **SVP:** 2-30 days ● **Academic:** Ed=N, Eng=N ● **Work Field:** 051 ● **MPSMS:** 616 ● **Aptitudes:** G4, V4, N4, S4, P3, Q4, K3, F4, M3, E4, C5 ● **Temperaments:** R, T ● **Physical:** Stg=L; Const: R, H Freq: N, D Occas: A ● **Work Env:** Noise=L; ● **Salary:** 2 ● **Outlook:** 3

SCRAP HANDLER (any industry) ● DOT #509.685-050 ● OES: 92962 ● Tends machines, such as baling machine, centrifugal separator, and oil purifier to salvage metal parts and cutting oil: Loads and moves barrels or crates of metal chips, shavings, or clippings from machining operations, using handtruck. Dumps metal scrap into baling machine and activates machine to compress scrap into bales. Binds bales of metal scrap with wire or metal strapping. Shovels scrap in spinner bucket. Clamps covers, sets timer, adjusts sump pump and oil line valves, and flips switches to start automatic cycle of centrifugal machine that spins metal scrap to separate cutting oil from scrap. Starts centrifugal oil purifier that filters foreign matter from used cutting oil to make oil reusable. Disassembles rejected devices and materials, such as thermostats, valves, conduit, and connectors, using handtools, arbor press, vises, and power hacksaw. Sorts parts according to type of metal or part. Weighs bales and barrels of scrap metal and ties identification tags on scrap. May oversee and demonstrate salvaging procedures to other SCRAP HANDLERS (any industry). ● **GED:** R3, M2, L2 ● **SVP:** 1-3 mos ● **Academic:** Ed=N, Eng=N ● **Work Field:** 145, 041, 011 ● **MPSMS:** 549 ● **Aptitudes:** G3, V4, N4, S4, P4, Q4, K3, F4, M3, E5, C5 ● **Temperaments:** R ● **Physical:** Stg=H; Freq: R, H Occas: I ● **Work Env:** Noise=L; ● **Salary:** 4 ● **Outlook:** 3

SILK-SCREEN PRINTER, MACHINE (any industry) ● DOT #979.685-010 ● OES: 92542 ● Alternate titles: SCREEN PRINTER. Tends silk screen machine that prints designs, patterns, lettering, or other images on assorted materials and products, such as glassware, ceramics, metal, plastic, or electronic components: Bolts framed silk screen onto machine, and installs and adjusts workpiece holding fixture, stops, and guides, using handtools, ruler, and workpiece pattern. Attaches squeegee to pneumatic drive mechanism, using wrench, and connects air line to mechanism. Regulates air pressure and manipulates squeegee to adjust pressure and angle of sweep. Applies printing compound to screen, using spatula or brush. Places workpiece in or on holding fixture, presses button to lower screen, and depresses pedal or pushes button to activate squeegee. Observes silk screen and workpiece to detect printing defects caused by ripped screen and applies glue to rip to repair screen. Cleans silk screen, using brush and solvent. May

thin printing compound, using specified thinner. May tend firing oven to dry printed workpiece. May sharpen squeegee on sanding machine. May transfer image of original artwork to screen, using vacuum printer. May be designated according to type of machine tended as Decorating-Machine Tender (glass mfg.); Squeegee-Machine Tender (glass mfg.); or Stenciling-Machine Tender (glass mfg.; glass products). May tend machine that screen-prints circuit pattern and nomenclature on printed circuit board (PCB) panels used in fabricating PCB's and be designated Screen-Printing-Machine Tender, Printed Circuit Boards (electron. comp.). ● **GED:** R2, M1, L2 ● **SVP:** 1-3 mos ● **Academic:** Ed=N, Eng=N ● **Work Field:** 191 ● **MPSMS:** 540, 560, 580 ● **Aptitudes:** G4, V4, N4, S4, P3, Q4, K3, F4, M3, E4, C4 ● **Temperaments:** R, T ● **Physical:** Stg=L; Freq: R, H, I, N Occas: G, D, A, X ● **Work Env:** Noise=N; ● **Salary:** 2 ● **Outlook:** 3

STAMPING-PRESS OPERATOR (any industry) ● DOT #652.682-030 ● OES: 92542 ● Alternate titles: GOLD-LEAF PRINTER; GOLD MARKER; GOLD STAMPER; HOT STAMPER; LEAF STAMPER; LETTERING-MACHINE OPERATOR; STAMPER. Operates machine to emboss and imprint designs, lettering, numbers, or product information onto surfaces of material, such as paper, cloth, leather, or plastic, using foil, gold-leaf, coated ribbon, or plastic tape, following specifications: Receives verbal instructions, reads work order sheet, or inserts disk in drive of computer and depresses keys to retrieve job order slip with printing instructions on computer screen. Sets heat, pressure, and time controls, according to material to be stamped. Installs and locks character wheel, embossing die, or stamping die in heated chase of machine. Turns on heating element. Inserts reel of specified material, such as foil, gold-leaf, coated ribbon, or plastic tape in holder or on spindle, and threads end through rollers which feed and guide material under die mounted on ram of machine or places sheet of foil over impression. Positions and aligns workpiece under holding arm in bed of hand fed machine or feed hopper of automatically fed machine in position specified on work order or in illuminated window on computerized machine. Starts machine which lowers ram to heated die or character wheel and ribbon to emboss and imprint workpiece and automatically moves coated ribbon with each stroke of machine. May operate machine to imprint trade names, brand, and grade onto leather sweatbands and be designated Sweatband Printer (hat & cap). When printing titles and designs on book covers, is designated Embosser (print. & pub.). When imprinting identifying information on battery lids or encasements, is designated Embossing-Press Operator (elec. equip.). ● **GED:** R2, M1, L1 ● **SVP:** 1-3 mos ● **Academic:** Ed=N, Eng=N ● **Work Field:** 191, 192 ● **MPSMS:** 470, 480, 510 ● **Aptitudes:** G4, V4, N4, S3, P3, Q4, K3, F3, M3, E4, C4 ● **Temperaments:** R, T ● **Physical:** Stg=L; Freq: R, H, I, N, D, A, X Occas: S, O, T, G ● **Work Env:** Noise=L; Freq: M Occas: H, V ● **Salary:** 3 ● **Outlook:** 2

TRACK LAMINATING MACHINE TENDER (inst. & app.) ● DOT #692.685-290 ● OES: 92999 ● Tends machine that laminates and trims vinyl from aluminum track used in drafting machines: Loads spool of vinyl onto laminating machine wheel, starts machine, and feeds track into machine that automatically laminates vinyl onto track and trims vinyl. Monitors track conveyance and visually examines track to detect lamination and trimming flaws, such as excess vinyl, air bubbles, and oil or adhesive accumulation on edge of track. Smooths air bubbles from lamination and trims excess vinyl, using handtools. Cleans excess oil and adhesive from edge of track, using rag and brush. Rejects defective track. May cut vinyl at joint to separate track sections, using knife or saw. ● **GED:** R1, M1, L1 ● **SVP:** 2-30 days ● **Academic:** Ed=N, Eng=N ● **Work Field:** 054, 063 ● **MPSMS:** 601 ● **Aptitudes:** G4, V4, N4, S4, P4, Q4, K4, F4, M3, E5, C4 ● **Temperaments:** R ● **Physical:** Stg=M; Freq: R, H, I, E, N, D, X Occas: S ● **Work Env:** Noise=N; Occas: A, M, T ● **Salary:** 4 ● **Outlook:** 2

WAX MOLDER (foundry) ● DOT #549.685-038 ● OES: 92970 ● Tends semiautomatic wax-molding machine that produces wax patterns used in lost-wax casting process: Sprays interior surface of die with parting agent. Places die against stops in bed of machine and starts machine that forces melted wax into die by injection or centrifugal process. Loosens pattern from die, using airhose. Removes pattern from die and inspects it for defects. Cleans excess wax from pattern, using knife. May pour melted wax into holding cup of machine. May be designated according to molding process used as Centrifugal-Wax Molder (foundry; jewelry-silver.); Injection-Wax Molder (foundry; jewelry-silver.). ● **GED:** R2, M1, L2 ● **SVP:** 2-30 days ● **Academic:**

Ed=N, Eng=N ● **Work Field:** 132 ● **MPSMS:** 568, 566 ● **Aptitudes:** G4, V4, N4, S4, P3, Q5, K3, F3, M3, E5, C5 ● **Temperaments:** R, T ● **Physical:** Stg=L; Freq: R, H, I, N Occas: E ● **Work Env:** Noise=N; ● **Salary:** 3 ● **Outlook:** 2

GOE: 06.04.10
Equipment Operation, Metal Processing

ANNEALER (jewelry-silver.) ● DOT #504.687-010 ● OES: 91932 ● Alternate titles: HEAT TREATER. Heat treats jewelry fittings to soften fittings for further processing, using electric or gas furnace: Sets automatic controls to specified temperature. Fills steel tray with fittings and places fittings in oven, using tongs. Removes tray after specified time and immerses fittings in water. May clean oxide and scale from fittings by immersing fittings in chemical and water baths. May heat treat ingots, using Bunsen burner or torch, and immerse ingots in alcohol to restore ingot malleability. May open and close gas valves, ignite and extinguish gas flames, and set time clock alarm for heating and cooling periods. ● **GED:** R2, M1, L1 ● **SVP:** 2-30 days ● **Academic:** Ed=N, Eng=N ● **Work Field:** 133 ● **MPSMS:** 611 ● **Aptitudes:** G4, V4, N4, S4, P4, Q4, K3, F3, M3, E5, C5 ● **Temperaments:** R, T ● **Physical:** Stg=L; Freq: R, H, I, N, D ● **Work Env:** Noise=L; Freq: H ● **Salary:** 3 ● **Outlook:** 3

INJECTION-MOLDING-MACHINE TENDER (plastic prod.) ● DOT #556.685-038 ● OES: 91950 ● Tends injection-molding machines that form plastic or rubber products, such as typewriter keys, phonograph records, and luggage handles: Dumps plastic powder, preformed plastic pellets, or preformed rubber slugs into hopper of molding machine. Starts machine that automatically liquefies pellets, slugs, or powder in heating chamber, injects liquefied material into mold, and ejects molded product. Observes gauges to ensure specified molding temperature and pressure are maintained. Examines molded product for surface defects, such as dents and cracks. May heat plastic material over steamtable or in oven to prepare material for molding. May remove product from mold, using handtools. May trim flash from product, using shears or knife. May place product in cold water or position it on cooling fixture to prevent distortion. ● **GED:** R2, M1, L1 ● **SVP:** 2-30 days ● **Academic:** Ed=N, Eng=N ● **Work Field:** 132 ● **MPSMS:** 519 ● **Aptitudes:** G4, V4, N4, S4, P4, Q5, K4, F4, M4, E5, C5 ● **Temperaments:** R, T ● **Physical:** Stg=L; Freq: R, H, I, E, N Occas: T, G ● **Work Env:** Noise=L; ● **Salary:** 3 ● **Outlook:** 2

GOE: 06.04.11
Equipment Operation, Chemical Processing

CHEMICAL OPERATOR II (chemical) ● DOT #558.685-062 ● OES: 92930 ● Alternate titles: REACTOR OPERATOR. Tends equipment units or semiautomatic system that processes chemical substances into industrial or consumer products, such as detergents, emulsifiers, salts, bleaching agents, acids, and synthetic resins: Dumps specified amounts of solid materials into heating vessels or blending tanks; and turns valves to feed liquid and gaseous materials through equipment units, or sets controls in specified sequence on control panel to start automatic feed. Turns valves or moves controls to maintain system at specified temperature, pressure, and vacuum levels. Observes chemical reactions; monitors gauges, signals, and recorders; and receives notification from control laboratory, supervisor, or other workers to make specified operating adjustments. Draws samples of products for laboratory analysis. Maintains log of gauge readings and shift production. May perform chemical tests on product to ensure conformance with specifications, using standard test equipment, materials, and procedure. May be designated according to substance processed as Low-Chloride Soda Operator (chemical); Salt-Plant Operator (chemical); Sodium-Methylate Operator (chemical); equipment tended as Styrene-Dehydration-Reactor Operator (chemical); Tower Operator (chemical) II; or reaction produced as Emulsification Operator (oils & grease); Precipitation Equipment Tender (chemical). ● **GED:** R3, M2, L2 ● **SVP:** 3-6 mos ● **Academic:** Ed=N, Eng=N ● **Work Field:** 147 ● **MPSMS:** 490

● **Aptitudes:** G3, V4, N3, S4, P4, Q4, K4, F4, M3, E5, C4 ● **Temperaments:** J, T ● **Physical:** Stg=M; Freq: R, H, I, N Occas: C, S, O, G, D, X ● **Work Env:** Noise=L; Freq: A, O ● **Salary:** 4 ● **Outlook:** 2

CHEMICAL PREPARER (chemical) ● DOT #550.685-030 ● OES: 92965 ● Tends equipment that compounds ingredients into chemical solutions used as adhesive or conductive coatings for electron tubes: Weighs and measures specified type and quantity of liquid and powdered ingredients. Pours, dumps, or pumps ingredients into mixing equipment. Starts equipment that compounds chemical ingredients and deionized water into chemical solutions, such as frit or conductive graphite. Tests mixture for conformance to prescribed standards, using testing devices, such as pH meter, resistivity meter, titration apparatus, colorimeter, thermometer, and viscometer. Pours compounded product into containers for application to tube seams, funnel, or ceramic parts by other workers. ● **GED:** R3, M3, L3 ● **SVP:** 3-6 mos ● **Academic:** Ed=N, Eng=S ● **Work Field:** 143 ● **MPSMS:** 490 ● **Aptitudes:** G3, V3, N3, S4, P3, Q3, K3, F3, M3, E5, C4 ● **Temperaments:** T ● **Physical:** Stg=L; Freq: R, H Occas: I, N, A, X ● **Work Env:** Noise=N; Freq: A, T ● **Salary:** 4 ● **Outlook:** 2

DRIER OPERATOR (chemical) ● DOT #553.685-042 ● OES: 92923 ● Alternate titles: DRUM-DRIER OPERATOR; VACUUM-DRUM-DRIER OPERATOR. Tends vacuum drum driers that heat liquid compounds to form caked or powdered chemical products: Connects tube from feed inlet to drum containing liquid to be dried. Turns steam and coolant valves and observes thermometer to regulate temperature of steam-jacketed drum enclosed in vacuum chamber, according to specifications. Starts pump and observes vacuum gauge to maintain prescribed vacuum in chamber. Starts revolving drum that dries liquid as it splashes against heated drum, forming caked or powdered product that is removed from surface of drum by scraper blade. Observes and feels dried product, periodically submits sample for laboratory moisture analysis, and adjusts drying temperature and vacuum if product does not meet plant standards. Records drying time of batch, gauge readings, and amount or weight of materials dried. May set scraper blade at specified distance from drum, using handtools. May fill containers with dried materials, weigh containers, and tag containers for shipment or storage. ● **GED:** R3, M2, L2 ● **SVP:** 1-3 mos ● **Academic:** Ed=N, Eng=N ● **Work Field:** 141 ● **MPSMS:** 490 ● **Aptitudes:** G3, V4, N4, S4, P4, Q4, K3, F4, M3, E5, C5 ● **Temperaments:** J, T ● **Physical:** Stg=M; Freq: R, H, E Occas: S, O, I, N, D ● **Work Env:** Noise=L; Occas: H, A ● **Salary:** 4 ● **Outlook:** 2

MIXER (paint & varnish) ● DOT #550.685-078 ● OES: 92965 ● Alternate titles: BATCH MIXER; BLENDER; DISPERSION MIXER. Tends mixing machines that blend solid and liquid ingredients to make products, such as paints, lacquers, putty, paint pigments, and binders, following formula: Turns valves or sets pump meters to admit specified amounts of liquids, such as oils, solvents, and water into mixer. Weighs and dumps specified amounts of dry ingredients, such as plastic flash, color concentrates, and resins into mixer, as indicated on batch ticket, or dumps preweighed ingredients into tank. Pushes or pulls tank to dispersion mixing machine. Depresses pedal to lower mixing blades into tank and presses button to start blades revolving to mix and disperse ingredients. Turns valves to drain batch through hoses into pebble or ball mill or into holding tank. Draws sample from batch for laboratory test and adds ingredients to mixture as specified by laboratory. May clean equipment, using rags, solvent, and scraper. May be designated according to product mixed as Glass Enamel Mixer (paint & varnish); Lacquer Blender (paint & varnish); Paint Maker (paint & varnish); Paste Mixer (paint & varnish); Pigment Mixer (paint & varnish); Putty Maker (paint & varnish). ● **GED:** R3, M1, L2 ● **SVP:** 1-3 mos ● **Academic:** Ed=N, Eng=N ● **Work Field:** 143 ● **MPSMS:** 495 ● **Aptitudes:** G4, V4, N4, S4, P4, Q4, K3, F4, M3, E5, C4 ● **Temperaments:** J, R, T ● **Physical:** Stg=H; Freq: R, H, I, N, D, A, X ● **Work Env:** Noise=L; Freq: A ● **Salary:** 2 ● **Outlook:** 2

PAINT MIXER, MACHINE (any industry) ● DOT #550.485-018 ● OES: 92965 ● Tends paint-mixing machines that mix paint, lacquer, and stain: Attaches powered mixer to barrels of unmixed paint and starts mixer to stir paint for specified time to obtain specified consistency. Computes amounts and weights of paint, lacquer, solvent, or thinner required from standard formula, and pours specified amounts into mixing machine. Starts mixer and allows it to run for prescribed time to attain specified viscosity and color. Measures viscosity, using viscosimeter and stop watch. May pump paint from central pumping station to spray booths. May filter paint or pyroxylin to remove impurities. May maintain record of paint issued and inventory of supplies on hand. ● **GED:** R2, M1, L1 ● **SVP:** 1-3 mos ● **Academic:** Ed=N, Eng=N ● **Work Field:** 143 ● **MPSMS:** 495 ● **Aptitudes:** G3, V4, N4, S4, P4, Q4, K3, F4, M3, E5, C3 ● **Temperaments:** R, T ● **Physical:** Stg=H; Freq: S, R, H, I, N, X Occas: D ● **Work Env:** Noise=L; Freq: A ● **Salary:** 3 ● **Outlook:** 2

GOE: 06.04.12
Equipment Operation, Petroleum, Gas, & Coal Processing

CYLINDER FILLER (chemical) ● DOT #559.565-010 ● OES: 92974 ● Alternate titles: CHARGING OPERATOR; CYLINDER LOADER; DRUM FILLER; FILLER; GAS WORKER; MANIFOLD OPERATOR; PUMPER. Tends equipment to fill cylinders and other containers with liquefied or compressed gases: Changes cylinder valves with wrench, or adjusts them to prescribed tension, using torque wrench. Rolls cylinders onto platform scale, or positions cylinders in manifold racks manually or with chain hoist. Connects lines from manifold to cylinders, using wrench. Fills cylinders by any of following methods: (1) Sets pressure gauge to specified reading and listens for buzzer indicating completion of filling. (2) Adjusts valves and observes gauge to fill cylinders to specified pressure. (3) Observes scale indicator to fill cylinders to specified weight. (4) Fills cylinder to excess, rolls cylinder onto scale, and connects exhaust line to release excess gas and attain prescribed gross weight. Sprays or brushes chemical solution onto cylinder valve to test for leaks. Fills out and attaches warning and identification tags or decals, specifying tare and gross weight, cylinder number, type of gas, and date filled, and records data. May test gas for purity, using burette or other testing equipment. May inspect or test empty cylinder [CYLINDER INSPECTOR-AND-TESTER (chemical)]. May evacuate residual gases from cylinders. May test filled cylinders for specified gas pressure by connecting gauge and comparing reading with chart. May tend and maintain generator or compressor in filling process. May be designated according to type of container filled as Ton-Container Filler (chemical); Tube-Trailer Filler (chemical). ● **GED:** R3, M2, L2 ● **SVP:** 1-3 mos ● **Academic:** Ed=N, Eng=N ● **Work Field:** 014 ● **MPSMS:** 491 ● **Aptitudes:** G4, V4, N4, S4, P3, Q4, K3, F4, M3, E5, C5 ● **Temperaments:** T ● **Physical:** Stg=H; Freq: S, O, R, H, I, N Occas: G ● **Work Env:** Noise=N; Freq: A, O ● **Salary:** 3 ● **Outlook:** 3

GOE: 06.04.13
Equipment Operation, Rubber, Plastics, & Glass Processing

BLOW-MOLDING-MACHINE TENDER (toy-sport equip.) ● DOT #556.685-086 ● OES: 91950 ● Tends blow molding machine that automatically forms plastic toy parts: Observes continuous operation of automatic molding machine, adjusts plastic flow, and notifies supervisor of machine malfunctions. Removes molded part from conveyor or mold and trims flash from part, using knife, hammer, and file. Examines part for defects, such as bubbles, splits, or thin areas, and weighs part on scale to ensure specifications are maintained. Stacks molded parts in boxes for subsequent processing. Throws flash and rejected parts into regrinder machine to be recycled. ● **GED:** R2, M1, L1 ● **SVP:** 2-30 days ● **Academic:** Ed=N, Eng=N ● **Work Field:** 132 ● **MPSMS:** 615 ● **Aptitudes:** G4, V4, N5, S4, P4, Q4, K5, F5, M4, E5, C5 ● **Temperaments:** R ● **Physical:** Stg=L; Freq: R, H, N Occas: I ● **Work Env:** Noise=L; ● **Salary:** 3 ● **Outlook:** 2

COMPRESSION-MOLDING-MACHINE TENDER (plastic prod.) ● DOT #556.685-022 ● OES: 91950 ● Alternate titles: MOLDER; PLASTIC-PRESS MOLDER. Tends compression-molding machines that mold thermosetting plastics into products, such as automobile heater housings, ashtrays, buttons, electronic parts, plastic panels, and dishes:

Dumps specified amount of plastic powders or pellets into hopper of machine, or positions pellets or sausage-shaped plastics in mold installed on machine. Starts machine that compresses plastic into mold under heat and pressure, and allows plastic to set for specified time. Removes product from mold and cleans mold, hopper, and bed of machine, using airhose and handtools. May place plastics material on hot grid or in oven to soften it prior to molding. May weigh prescribed amount of material for molding. May place plastic sheet into machine fixture to fabricate buttons. ● **GED:** R2, M1, L1 ● **SVP:** 2-30 days ● **Academic:** Ed=N, Eng=N ● **Work Field:** 132 ● **MPSMS:** 519 ● **Aptitudes:** G4, V4, N5, S4, P4, Q5, K3, F4, M3, E5, C5 ● **Temperaments:** R, T ● **Physical:** Stg=L; Freq: R, H, I, N, D ● **Work Env:** Noise=L; ● **Salary:** 3 ● **Outlook:** 2

FUSING-FURNACE LOADER (optical goods) ● DOT #573.686-014 ● OES: 98502 ● Alternate titles: FURNACE CLERK; PICKER. Loads and unloads conveyor of furnace that fuses multifocal lens parts: Positions multifocal lens blank and button assemblies, or assembled button parts, on emery disks, places disks on trays, and places filled trays on conveyor that passes through fusing furnace. Removes trays of fused items from end of conveyor and places them in rack to cool. Records production count. May mark identification number on lenses, using marking pen. May observe temperature indicators and inform supervisor of furnace malfunction. ● **GED:** R2, M1, L1 ● **SVP:** 2-30 days ● **Academic:** Ed=N, Eng=N ● **Work Field:** 131 ● **MPSMS:** 605 ● **Aptitudes:** G4, V4, N4, S4, P4, Q4, K3, F3, M3, E5, C5 ● **Temperaments:** R ● **Physical:** Stg=L; Freq: R, H Occas: I, N ● **Work Env:** Noise=L; Occas: H, A ● **Salary:** 2 ● **Outlook:** 2

TIRE MOLDER (rubber tire) ● DOT #553.685-102 ● OES: 92999 ● Alternate titles: CURING FINISHER; RETREAD-MOLD OPERATOR. Tends retreading mold that vulcanizes camelback (raw rubber tread) onto tire casing and molds tread design: Places air bag of specified size inside tire, using tire-spreading device, and clamps tire into mold. Inflates air bag to specified pressure and heats mold to specified temperature to cook and mold tread. Removes tire after predetermined time and trims loose ends from molded tread, using knife. ● **GED:** R2, M1, L1 ● **SVP:** 1-3 mos ● **Academic:** Ed=N, Eng=N ● **Work Field:** 132, 136 ● **MPSMS:** 511 ● **Aptitudes:** G4, V4, N5, S4, P4, Q5, K4, F4, M3, E5, C5 ● **Temperaments:** R, T ● **Physical:** Stg=H; Freq: R, H ● **Work Env:** Noise=L; Occas: H ● **Salary:** 4 ● **Outlook:** 2

GOE: 06.04.15
Equipment Operation, Food Processing

BAKER HELPER (bakery products) ● DOT #526.686-010 ● OES: 98998 ● Performs any combination of following tasks in production of baked goods: Moves and distributes bakery supplies and products in and around production area of bakery, using handtrucks, dollies, troughs, and rack trucks. Weighs and measures ingredients, such as sugar, flour, yeast, syrup, and dough. Lifts and dumps containers of materials to help load and unload machines, bins, hoppers, racks, and ovens. Feeds lumps or sheets of dough into hopper or between rolls of machine. Cleans equipment, using brushes, cleanser, and water. Greases, lines, or dusts pans or boards preparatory to receiving product for baking. May cut, turn, or twist dough into specified products and fill baking pans with dough. May observe and rearrange baked products on conveyor before products enter slicing machine. May tend equipment that dumps baked bread from pans onto conveyor for further processing. May push racks of bakery products into designated areas to await further processing. May be designated according to worker assisted as Batter-Mixer Helper (bakery products); or according to machine operator assisted as Cracker-And-Cookie-Machine Operator Helper (bakery products); Doughnut-Machine-Operator Helper (bakery products); Cookie-Mixer Helper (bakery products); Dividing-Machine-Operator Helper (bakery products); Dough-Mixer Helper (bakery products); Ingredient-Scaler Helper (bakery products). ● **GED:** R2, M1, L1 ● **SVP:** 2-30 days ● **Academic:** Ed=N, Eng=N ● **Work Field:** 011, 146 ● **MPSMS:** 384 ● **Aptitudes:** G4, V4, N4, S4, P4, Q4, K4, F4, M4, E4, C5 ● **Temperaments:** R, T ● **Physical:** Stg=H; Freq: S, R, H, D Occas: I, T, G, N, X ● **Work Env:** Noise=N; Occas: H, A, M ● **Salary:** 1 ● **Outlook:** 4

BATTER MIXER (bakery products) ● DOT #520.685-010 ● OES: 92965 ● Alternate titles: MIXING-MACHINE ATTENDANT. Tends machine that mixes ingredients to produce batter for cakes and other bakery products: Positions mixing bowl under mixer and attaches water hose. Selects and installs beater in mixer, according to type of batter being produced. Observes meter and moves lever to admit specified amount of water into bowl. Dumps preweighed ingredients into bowl. Starts machine, turns cranks, and sets dials to regulate speed and mixing time. Feels texture of batter to judge desired consistency. Weighs batch of batter to ensure conformance to weight specifications. May mix dough. May be designated according to type of batter mixed as Cake-Batter Mixer (bakery products); Doughnut-Batter Mixer (bakery products); Wafer-Batter-Mixer (bakery products). ● **GED:** R3, M2, L2 ● **SVP:** 3-6 mos ● **Academic:** Ed=N, Eng=N ● **Work Field:** 143 ● **MPSMS:** 384 ● **Aptitudes:** G3, V4, N4, S4, P4, Q4, K4, F4, M3, E5, C4 ● **Temperaments:** J, T ● **Physical:** Stg=L; Freq: S, R, H, I, E, N, D, X ● **Work Env:** Noise=L; ● **Salary:** 2 ● **Outlook:** 3

BREWERY CELLAR WORKER (beverage) ● DOT #522.685-014 ● OES: 92999 ● Tends equipment that cools and adds yeast to wort to produce beer: Starts pumps and turns valves to control flow of refrigerant through cooler coils, to regulate flow of hot wort from tank through cooler into starting tank, and to admit specified amounts of air into wort [COOLING-MACHINE OPERATOR (beverage)]. Turns valves to add yeast to wort and to transfer wort to fermenting tanks [RECEIVER, FERMENTING CELLARS (beverage)]. ● **GED:** R2, M1, L1 ● **SVP:** 2-30 days ● **Academic:** Ed=N, Eng=N ● **Work Field:** 146 ● **MPSMS:** 395 ● **Aptitudes:** G4, V4, N4, S4, P4, Q4, K4, F4, M3, E5, C5 ● **Temperaments:** R, T ● **Physical:** Stg=M; Freq: R, H, N Occas: S, O ● **Work Env:** Noise=N; Const: C Freq: U ● **Salary:** 1 ● **Outlook:** 2

CANNERY WORKER (can. & preserv.) ● DOT #529.686-014 ● OES: 93935 ● Performs any combination of following duties to can, freeze, preserve, or pack food products: Dumps or places food products in hopper, on sorting table, or on conveyor. Sorts or grades products according to size, color, or quality. Feeds products into processing equipment, such as washing, refrigerating, peeling, coring, pitting, trimming, grinding, dicing, cooking, or slicing machines. Trims, peels, and slices products with knife or paring tool. Feeds empty containers onto conveyor or forming machines. Fills containers, using scoop or filling form, or packs by hand [PACKAGER, HAND (any industry) 920.587-018]. Counts, weighs, or tallies processed items according to specifications. Inspects and weighs filled containers to ensure product conforms to quality and weight standards. Places filled containers on trays, racks, or into boxes. Loads, moves, or stacks containers by hand or handtruck, and cleans glass jar containers, using airhose. May be designated according to work performed as Dumper (can. & preserv.); Peeler (can. & preserv.); Sorter (can & preserv.); Trimmer (can & preserv.). ● **GED:** R2, M2, L2 ● **SVP:** 2-30 days ● **Academic:** Ed=N, Eng=N ● **Work Field:** 146, 041, 212 ● **MPSMS:** 380 ● **Aptitudes:** G4, V4, N4, S4, P4, Q4, K3, F3, M3, E5, C4 ● **Temperaments:** R, T ● **Physical:** Stg=L; Const: R, H, I, E Freq: N, D, A Occas: S, X ● **Work Env:** Noise=L; Occas: U, A, M ● **Salary:** 2 ● **Outlook:** 2

CENTRIFUGE OPERATOR (dairy products) ● DOT #521.685-042 ● OES: 92962 ● Tends centrifuge machines that refine liquid wort for use in making malted milk: Assembles and attaches bowl, rings, and cover onto centrifuge, using hoist and handtools. Starts machine, observes tachometer, and adjusts controls to regulate speed. Starts pumps, turns valves, and observes gauges to convey wort through machine at specified pressure. Regulates clarity of wort by observing color and turning valves to alter pressure flow. Removes solids from machine with wooden paddle. Cleans machine with water. ● **GED:** R2, M2, L2 ● **SVP:** 2-30 days ● **Academic:** Ed=N, Eng=N ● **Work Field:** 145 ● **MPSMS:** 383 ● **Aptitudes:** G4, V4, N4, S4, P4, Q4, K4, F4, M3, E5, C3 ● **Temperaments:** R, T ● **Physical:** Stg=H; Freq: R, H, N Occas: I, A, X ● **Work Env:** Noise=L; Occas: U ● **Salary:** 4 ● **Outlook:** 3

CHEESE CUTTER (dairy products) ● DOT #529.585-010 ● OES: 92940 ● Tends machine that cuts blocks of cheese into pieces of specified shape and size: Examines cheese for defects in color, texture, and body. Bolts specified cutting head to machine, using wrench, adjusts stops on cutting table, and turns wheels to position cutting wires. Places block on table, and moves lever to lower cutting head or raise table to cut cheese. Weighs cut cheese, places pieces on conveyor, and records

amount cut. May measure cheese with ruler and cut with hand cutter. May trim rind, mold, or sediment from cheese, using knife. ● **GED:** R2, M1, L1 ● **SVP:** 2-30 days ● **Academic:** Ed=N, Eng=N ● **Work Field:** 054, 212 ● **MPSMS:** 383 ● **Aptitudes:** G4, V4, N4, S4, P3, Q4, K3, F4, M3, E5, C3 ● **Temperaments:** J, R, T ● **Physical:** Stg=M; Const: R, H Freq: I, N, D, A Occas: S, X ● **Work Env:** Noise=L; ● **Salary:** 2 ● **Outlook:** 2

CHOCOLATE MOLDER, MACHINE (sugar & conf.) ● DOT #529.685-054 ● OES: 92970 ● Tends machine and equipment that deposit tempered chocolate into molds to form bars, blocks, and assorted figures: Opens valves to draw chocolate from tempering kettle or automatic tempering equipment into water-jacketed depositor of molding machine. Observes thermometer and turns valves to admit and circulate water in jacket to maintain specified temperature of chocolate in depositor. Adjusts piston stroke of depositor that forces measured amounts of chocolate into conveyorized molds, using handtools. Turns handwheel to adjust speed of conveyor. Starts machine. Weighs filled molds to ensure that weight of chocolate casts meet specifications. Observes thermometer and turns thermostat and valve to control temperature in cooling tunnel. Observes action of machine to ensure that molds do not jam. May temper chocolate [CHOCOLATE TEMPERER (bakery products; grain-feed mills)]. ● **GED:** R3, M2, L2 ● **SVP:** 3-6 mos ● **Academic:** Ed=N, Eng=N ● **Work Field:** 132 ● **MPSMS:** 393 ● **Aptitudes:** G3, V4, N4, S4, P4, Q4, K4, F4, M3, E5, C4 ● **Temperaments:** J, T ● **Physical:** Stg=L; Const: R, H Freq: N Occas: X ● **Work Env:** Noise=L; ● **Salary:** 2 ● **Outlook:** 3

COFFEE GRINDER (food prep., nec) ● DOT #521.685-078 ● OES: 92965 ● Alternate titles: GRANULIZING-MACHINE OPERATOR. Tends machines that grind coffee beans to specified fineness: Pulls lever or adjusts control to regulate flow of coffee beans into grinding machines. Starts machines and turns dials or moves levers to adjust grinding rollers. May control conveyors that carry ground coffee to storage bins. ● **GED:** R1, M1, L1 ● **SVP:** 2-30 days ● **Academic:** Ed=N, Eng=N ● **Work Field:** 142 ● **MPSMS:** 391 ● **Aptitudes:** G4, V4, N4, S4, P4, Q4, K4, F4, M4, E5, C5 ● **Temperaments:** R, T ● **Physical:** Stg=L; Freq: R, H Occas: N ● **Work Env:** Noise=L; ● **Salary:** 1 ● **Outlook:** 3

COOK, FRY, DEEP FAT (can. & preserv.) ● DOT #526.685-014 ● OES: 92910 ● Tends deep-fat cookers to fry meats, vegetables, or fish in cooking oil: Empties containers or opens valves to fill cookers with oil. Sets thermostat to heat oil to specified temperature. Empties containers of meat, vegetable, or fish into metal basket and immerses basket into vat manually or by hoist. Sets timer. Observes color at end of frying time to determine conformity to standards and extends frying time accordingly. Removes basket from cooker, drains it, and dumps contents onto tray. May dip foods into batter or dye before frying. May specialize in a particular food product for canning or freezing or may fry variety of foods for immediate consumption. ● **GED:** R2, M1, L1 ● **SVP:** 2-30 days ● **Academic:** Ed=N, Eng=N ● **Work Field:** 146 ● **MPSMS:** 386, 387 ● **Aptitudes:** G4, V4, N4, S4, P4, Q5, K4, F4, M3, E5, C4 ● **Temperaments:** R, T ● **Physical:** Stg=M; Freq: R, H Occas: I, N, A, X ● **Work Env:** Noise=N; ● **Salary:** 1 ● **Outlook:** 3

FLOUR BLENDER (grain-feed mills) ● DOT #520.685-106 ● OES: 92965 ● Alternate titles: BLENDER. Tends machines that blend and sift flour, and conveyors that carry flour between machines: Starts screw conveyors or turns valves on feed chutes to transfer flour from storage bins to mixing machine, or dumps designated bags of flour into hopper of machine. Starts machine to mix flour and pulls lever to open gate and allow blended flour to flow from machine. Starts separator that sifts mixed flour to remove lumps. Starts conveyors that transfer blended and sifted flour to packing machine. ● **GED:** R2, M1, L1 ● **SVP:** 1-3 mos ● **Academic:** Ed=N, Eng=N ● **Work Field:** 143 ● **MPSMS:** 381 ● **Aptitudes:** G4, V4, N4, S4, P4, Q4, K4, F4, M3, E5, C5 ● **Temperaments:** R ● **Physical:** Stg=H; Freq: R, H ● **Work Env:** Noise=L; Freq: A ● **Salary:** 2 ● **Outlook:** 2

HONEY PROCESSOR (food prep., nec) ● DOT #522.685-070 ● OES: 92962 ● Alternate titles: PASTEURIZER. Tends equipment that pasteurizes and filters liquid honey, and seeds honey with crystals to make crystallized honey for use as food spread: Turns valve to admit honey from blending tanks to pasteurizer, and to adjust and control pasteurizing temperature. Installs pads in filter press and turns handcrank to tighten pads. Starts pumps and adjusts pressure to force honey through filter and transfer honey to bottling machine or cooling vats. Pours container of honey crystals into vat of liquid honey and mixes it with paddle or electric stirring rod to induce controlled crystallization. May bottle honey. ● **GED:** R2, M1, L1 ● **SVP:** 1-3 mos ● **Academic:** Ed=N, Eng=N ● **Work Field:** 146 ● **MPSMS:** 399 ● **Aptitudes:** G3, V4, N4, S4, P3, Q4, K3, F3, M3, E4, C4 ● **Temperaments:** R, T ● **Physical:** Stg=L; Freq: C, R, H, I, N, D Occas: S, X ● **Work Env:** Noise=L; Freq: U ● **Salary:** 3 ● **Outlook:** 2

MEAT GRINDER (meat products) ● DOT #521.685-214 ● OES: 92965 ● Tends machine that grinds meat for use in making such products as bologna, meat loaves, and sausages: Pushes truck of cut meat from cooler room to grinding machine. Selects and inserts grinding plate in machine for specified particle size. Shovels meat into machine hopper, using fork, and positions truck under discharge spout. Starts machine. May cut chunks of meat into smaller pieces, using power operated cleaver or slicer. May select and weigh meat in cooler room for grinding. ● **GED:** R1, M1, L1 ● **SVP:** 2-30 days ● **Academic:** Ed=N, Eng=N ● **Work Field:** 142 ● **MPSMS:** 382 ● **Aptitudes:** G4, V4, N5, S4, P4, Q5, K4, F4, M3, E5, C5 ● **Temperaments:** R ● **Physical:** Stg=H; Freq: S, R, H, D ● **Work Env:** Noise=L; ● **Salary:** 3 ● **Outlook:** 3

MIXING-MACHINE OPERATOR (food prep., nec) ● DOT #520.665-014 ● OES: 92965 ● Tends machine that mixes compressed yeast with oils and whiteners preparatory to extrusion and packing: Signals worker to fill mixer with specified amount of compressed yeast. Pours specified quantity of cutting oils and whitening agents into yeast and starts agitators to mix ingredients for specified time. Observes and feels mixed yeast to determine its consistency and pours specified amount of water into yeast to achieve required consistency. Starts screw conveyor to transfer yeast to extruders. ● **GED:** R2, M1, L1 ● **SVP:** 2-30 days ● **Academic:** Ed=N, Eng=N ● **Work Field:** 143 ● **MPSMS:** 399 ● **Aptitudes:** G3, V4, N4, S3, P4, Q4, K4, F4, M4, E5, C5 ● **Temperaments:** J, T ● **Physical:** Stg=M; Freq: R, H, E Occas: C, T, G, N ● **Work Env:** Noise=L; Occas: U ● **Salary:** 2 ● **Outlook:** 2

OVEN OPERATOR, AUTOMATIC (bakery products) ● DOT #526.685-070 ● OES: 92910 ● Alternate titles: BAKER OPERATOR, AUTOMATIC. Tends automatic reel or conveyor type oven that bakes bread, pastries, and other bakery products: Reads work order to determine quantity and type products to be baked. Turns dials and valves to set operation speed of conveyor, baking time, and temperature controls of baking unit. Presses buttons to start equipment, and observes gauges to maintain heat according to specifications. Observes filled baking pans entering oven to determine whether pans are filled to standard, spacing between pans is sufficient to prevent pans jamming together, and speed of pans entering oven is specified speed to control baking time of product in oven. Observes color of baking product to detect burning or over baking and to verify uniformity of finished products. Adjusts controls according to procedure or notifies supervisor when conditions require equipment adjustments. May load and unload ovens. May be designated according to type of oven controlled as Conveyorized Oven Tender (bakery products); Reel Oven Tender (bakery products). May tend mixing machine and auxiliary equipment that automatically mixes, shapes, and bakes batter to form fortune cookies and be designated Fortune Cookie Maker (bakery products). ● **GED:** R3, M2, L2 ● **SVP:** 1-3 mos ● **Academic:** Ed=N, Eng=N ● **Work Field:** 146 ● **MPSMS:** 384 ● **Aptitudes:** G4, V4, N4, S4, P4, Q4, K4, F4, M3, E5, C4 ● **Temperaments:** J, T ● **Physical:** Stg=L; Freq: R, H, I, N Occas: E, A, X ● **Work Env:** Noise=N; Const: H ● **Salary:** 2 ● **Outlook:** 2

PRESS OPERATOR, MEAT (meat products) ● DOT #520.685-182 ● OES: 92970 ● Tends machine that presses such meats as bacon slabs, beef cuts, hams, and hog butts, into shape to facilitate slicing or packing: Positions meat on table of pressing machine and depresses pedal or pulls lever to lower ram onto meat that compresses meat into shape. Removes meat from machine and places in container, or on conveyor for transfer to slicing machine. May tend slicing machine [SLICING-MACHINE OPERATOR (dairy products; meat products)]. May be designated according to cut of meat pressed as Butt Presser (meat products); Ham Molder (meat products). ● **GED:** R1, M1, L1 ● **SVP:** 2-30 days ● **Academic:** Ed=N, Eng=N ● **Work Field:** 034, 134 ● **MPSMS:** 382 ● **Aptitudes:** G4, V4, N5, S4, P4, Q5, K4, F4, M3, E5, C5 ● **Temperaments:** R ● **Physical:** Stg=M; Freq: S, R, H, D ● **Work Env:** Noise=L; ● **Salary:** 3 ● **Outlook:** 2

GOE: 06.04.16
Equipment Operation, Textile, Fabric and Leather Processing

MACHINE FEEDER, RAW STOCK (tex. prod., nec) ● DOT #680.686-018 ● OES: 98502 ● Alternate titles: FEEDER TENDER; GUILLOTINE OPERATOR; HOPPER FEEDER; SHREDDER PICKER. Feeds raw fiber stock into machines that loosen, shred, separate, clean, form nubs, or straighten fibers: Reads work ticket to determine amount and type of stock to be processed. Records amount of materials processed, during work shift. Places fibers on conveyor belt or into machine hopper for processing by machine. Opens and closes gates of belt and pneumatic conveyors on machines fed directly from preceding machines. Loosens material before dumping material into hoppers by pulling fibers apart. Moves stock from storage or other departments to machine, using industrial truck or handtruck. May tend automatic machines and equipment that process fiber stock. May feed polyurethane foam into machines. May feed fiber stock into drum to apply oil to stock prior to further processing. May be designated according to type of machine fed as Carding-Machine Feeder (textile); Garnett Feeder (tex. prod., nec); Nub-Card Tender (textile); Picker Feeder (tex. prod., nec; textile). ● **GED:** R1, M1, L1 ● **SVP:** 2-30 days ● **Academic:** Ed=N, Eng=N ● **Work Field:** 161 ● **MPSMS:** 410 ● **Aptitudes:** G4, V4, N4, S4, P4, Q4, K4, F4, M4, E5, C5 ● **Temperaments:** R ● **Physical:** Stg=H; Const: R, H Freq: S, O Occas: I, G, N, D ● **Work Env:** Noise=L; Occas: A ● **Salary:** 2 ● **Outlook:** 3

SLASHER TENDER (textile) ● DOT #582.562-010 ● OES: 92999 ● Alternate titles: SIZER. Operates machine to saturate warp yarn with size and wind sized yarn onto loom beam: Positions section beams onto creel with aid of another worker, using hoist. Gathers ends of warp together and ties warp to corresponding leaders left in machine from previous run, or when machine is empty, bunches ends together and threads yarn through size pot, around drying cylinders, and onto loom beams. Inserts lease rods between alternate strands of yarn to prevent yarn from sticking together. Lays individual warp ends between teeth of expansion comb for even distribution across loom beam. Turns valves to admit size into vat and steam into drying cylinders. Sets yardage clock to indicate yardage to be wound on loom beam. Starts machine and observes flow of warp through machine to detect breaks and tangles in yarn. Disentangles yarn and ties broken ends with fingers. Feels yarn to verify adherence of size to yarn and ensure that yarn is dry but not burned. Inserts lease string in warp yarn and secures yarn ends with tape. Doffs loom beam onto handtruck and replaces with empty beam, using hoist. Records style number, yardage beamed, yarn breaks, and machine stops. May change temperature control chart on control panel. May clean machine. May process yarn for use on narrow fabric looms and be designated Warp-Spool Slasher (narrow fabrics). ● **GED:** R3, M2, L3 ● **SVP:** 1-2 yrs ● **Academic:** Ed=N, Eng=S ● **Work Field:** 152 ● **MPSMS:** 411 ● **Aptitudes:** G3, V4, N4, S3, P3, Q4, K3, F3, M3, E5, C4 ● **Temperaments:** R, T ● **Physical:** Stg=H; Freq: S, O, R, H, I, N, F, D, X Occas: E, T, G ● **Work Env:** Noise=L; Freq: H, U ● **Salary:** 1 ● **Outlook:** 2

GOE: 06.04.17
Equipment Operation, Clay Processing

KILN WORKER (pottery & porc.) ● DOT #573.687-022 ● OES: 98998 ● Alternate titles: KILN MAINTENANCE LABORER. Performs routine tasks concerned with maintenance and repair of kilns under direction of such workers as KILN PLACERS (pottery & porc.) or BRICKLAYERS (brick & tile). ● **GED:** R1, M1, L1 ● **SVP:** 2-30 days ● **Academic:** Ed=N, Eng=N ● **Work Field:** 102 ● **MPSMS:** 568 ● **Aptitudes:** G4, V4, N5, S4, P3, Q5, K4, F4, M3, E4, C5 ● **Temperaments:** R ● **Physical:** Stg=M; Const: R, H Occas: S ● **Work Env:** Noise=L; ● **Salary:** 3 ● **Outlook:** 2

SHELL MOLDER (foundry) ● DOT #518.685-026 ● OES: 91910 ● Tends machine that makes shell molds used to produce metal castings:

Starts machine that automatically forms and cures shell. Strips cured shell halves from machine and positions shell half on fixture of mold-closing machine. Brushes glue around edges of shell half. Positions remaining shell half on top of lower half and activates ram that exerts pressure on shell until glue has set. May glue and assemble shell halves by hand. May clamp, wire, or bolt shell halves together. May bolt pattern and core box to bed of machine. May produce cores on shell making machine and be designated Shell Coremaker (foundry). ● **GED:** R2, M1, L2 ● **SVP:** 2-30 days ● **Academic:** Ed=N, Eng=N ● **Work Field:** 136, 141 ● **MPSMS:** 566 ● **Aptitudes:** G4, V4, N4, S4, P3, Q4, K3, F3, M3, E4, C5 ● **Temperaments:** R, T ● **Physical:** Stg=H; Freq: R, H, I, N, D ● **Work Env:** Noise=L; Freq: A ● **Salary:** 3 ● **Outlook:** 2

GOE: 06.04.18
Equipment Operation, Wood Processing

DIGESTER-OPERATOR HELPER (paper & pulp) ● DOT #532.686-010 ● OES: 98502 ● Alternate titles: COOK HELPER; DIGESTER-COOK HELPER; PULP-MAKING-PLANT OPERATOR. Feeds wood chips and soda ash or acid into digester that processes wood chips into pulp: Unbolts and removes digester cover, using wrench and chain hoist. Lowers feed pipe into digester, using hoist, and pushes button or turns handwheel to load digester with wood chips. Pushes control panel button or turns valve to admit specified quantities of soda ash or acid into digester. Replaces and bolts cover. May remove cover and blow steam from digester at completion of cooking cycle. May tend conveyors that convey chips to hopper or cooked pulp to storage bins. May open valves to blow cooked pulp into pit. May pull lever to dump cooked pulp from rotary digester. May draw and deliver pulp sample to laboratory for analysis. ● **GED:** R2, M2, L1 ● **SVP:** 2-30 days ● **Academic:** Ed=N, Eng=N ● **Work Field:** 147 ● **MPSMS:** 471 ● **Aptitudes:** G4, V4, N4, S4, P4, Q5, K4, F4, M3, E5, C5 ● **Temperaments:** R ● **Physical:** Stg=L; Freq: R, H, D Occas: C, B, S, K, I ● **Work Env:** Noise=N; Freq: A Occas: T ● **Salary:** 2 ● **Outlook:** 2

TANKER (wood prod., nec) ● DOT #561.665-010 ● OES: 92999 ● Alternate titles: DIP TANKER; PLATFORM WORKER; SCAFFOLD WORKER. Tends open tank to impregnate wood products with preservatives: Signals OVERHEAD CRANE OPERATOR (any industry) 921.663-010 to lift load of material over tank and guides load into tank by hand or with rod, working from elevated platform. Chains tank loads of poles to high rack to prevent toppling. Observes gauges and turns valves to regulate heat and flow of preserving solution in tank. Impregnates sashes, doors, and other millwork products, using hand or power hoist to load and unload tank. May tend vacuum-type dip tank that impregnates wood by pressure. ● **GED:** R2, M1, L1 ● **SVP:** 1-3 mos ● **Academic:** Ed=N, Eng=N ● **Work Field:** 152 ● **MPSMS:** 452 ● **Aptitudes:** G4, V4, N4, S3, P4, Q4, K4, F4, M3, E4, C5 ● **Temperaments:** R, T ● **Physical:** Stg=M; Freq: R, H, I, D, A Occas: S, T, G ● **Work Env:** Noise=L; Occas: W, U ● **Salary:** 3 ● **Outlook:** 2

GOE: 06.04.19
Equipment Operation, Assorted Materials Processing

COATING EQUIPMENT OPERATOR, PRINTED CIRCUIT BOARDS (electron. comp.) ● DOT #590.685-066 ● OES: 92960 ● Tends automated equipment that applies photosensitive coating of masking ink to printed circuit board (PCB) panels to facilitate development of circuit design on boards in fabrication of PCBs: Pushes buttons and switches to start heater, conveyor, and coating equipment. Measures conveyor travel time of sample panel, using stopwatch, and weighs sample panel, using digital scale, to ensure that specifications are met. Turns dials to adjust conveyor speed and to add or delete masking ink in solution, as needed. Feeds panels onto conveyor of automated equipment that cleans, heats, and applies masking ink to panels. Removes panels from unloading rack upon completion of coating process and dries panels in oven. Records production data. ● **GED:** R2,

M2, L2 ● **SVP:** 1-3 mos ● **Academic:** Ed=N, Eng=N ● **Work Field:** 151 ● **MPSMS:** 587 ● **Aptitudes:** G3, V4, N4, S4, P4, Q4, K3, F4, M3, E5, C5 ● **Temperaments:** R ● **Physical:** Stg=M; Const: R, H Freq: I, N Occas: S, D ● **Work Env:** Noise=N; Occas: H ● **Salary:** 1 ● **Outlook:** 4

CREMATOR (personal ser.) ● DOT #359.685-010 ● OES: 69998 ● Tends retort furnace that cremates human bodies: Slides casket containing body into furnace. Starts furnace. Adjusts valves to attain extreme heat and to maintain temperature for specified time. Allows furnace to cool. Removes unburned metal casket parts from furnace. Scrapes ashes of casket and body from furnace, using handtools. Sifts ashes through fine screen and removes extraneous material. Places remains in canister and attaches metal identification tag to canister. Cleans furnace and sweeps and washes floors. May place rings and jewelry in temporary box for return to relatives. May clean building and fixtures. May care for lawns and shrubs. ● **GED:** R3, M2, L2 ● **SVP:** 1-3 mos ● **Academic:** Ed=N, Eng=N ● **Work Field:** 291 ● **MPSMS:** 907 ● **Aptitudes:** G3, V4, N4, S4, P4, Q4, K3, F4, M3, E5, C5 ● **Temperaments:** R, T ● **Physical:** Stg=H; Freq: R, H Occas: S, I, N ● **Work Env:** Noise=Q; Occas: H ● **Salary:** 4 ● **Outlook:** 2

DEVELOPER, AUTOMATIC (photofinishing) ● DOT #976.685-014 ● OES: 92908 ● Alternate titles: CONTINUOUS PROCESS MACHINE OPERATOR; FILM MACHINE OPERATOR. Tends machine that develops sheets, strips, or continuous roll of film preparatory to printing: Pulls film through trapdoor into darkroom. Strips paper backing from film and attaches identifying label. Feels edges of film to detect tears and repairs film, using stapler. Reads work order or feels film for size or notches to determine type of process and developing time required. Positions racks of film on machine chain links according to developing time required or threads leader of continuous roll through machine preparatory to processing. Activates machine that automatically transports film through series of chemical baths to develop, fix, harden, bleach, and wash film. Listens for sounds that indicate machine malfunctioning and notifies supervisor or maintenance personnel when repairs are needed. May run test strip through machine for inspection by supervisor and add chemicals to or adjust machine as directed. May tend equipment that develops, fixes image, and dries x-ray plates and be designated X-Ray-Developing-Machine Operator (medical ser.). ● **GED:** R2, M1, L1 ● **SVP:** 2-30 days ● **Academic:** Ed=N, Eng=N ● **Work Field:** 202 ● **MPSMS:** 897 ● **Aptitudes:** G3, V4, N4, S4, P3, Q4, K3, F3, M3, E5, C5 ● **Temperaments:** R, T ● **Physical:** Stg=L; Freq: R, H, I, E, T, G, N, D ● **Work Env:** Noise=L; Freq: O Occas: U ● **Salary:** 3 ● **Outlook:** 3

DISPLAY-SCREEN FABRICATOR (electron. comp.) ● DOT #725.685-010 ● OES: 92100 ● Tends equipment that forms and prepares aperture masks and display screens for oscilloscope and television picture tubes: Feeds specified sections of sensitized steel between plates in photographic printing chase to flatten sheet to specification. Sets timer for specified exposure and turns on heliarc lamp to imprint pattern of aperture mask from photographic plate onto steel. Verifies alignment of plates, using microscope. Tends furnace that blackens aperture masks and rings. Feeds mask through series of rollers that flatten mask. Positions mask on bed of forming press and lowers die to form mask. Tends processing equipment to clean, dry, and coat phosphor on inside face of display screen. Positions aperture mask and screen on fixture over time-cycled light source to print color-emitting dots on phosphor coating. Starts cycle to expose coating to light through mask aperture. Marks mating screen and aperture mask with matching numbers for future assembly. Fastens screen in holder on conveyor that carries screen through equipment that develops exposed phosphor, removes unexposed phosphor, and dries screen. May be designated according to process as Aperture-Mask Etcher (electron. comp.); Mask Former (electron. comp.); Screener (electron. comp.). ● **GED:** R2, M2, L2 ● **SVP:** 2-30 days ● **Academic:** Ed=N, Eng=N ● **Work Field:** 134, 141, 182 ● **MPSMS:** 587 ● **Aptitudes:** G4, V4, N4, S4, P4, Q5, K4, F3, M3, E5, C5 ● **Temperaments:** T ● **Physical:** Stg=M; Freq: R, H, I Occas: N, D ● **Work Env:** Noise=N; Occas: H, A ● **Salary:** 4 ● **Outlook:** 3

ELECTRONIC-COMPONENT PROCESSOR (electron. comp.) ● DOT #590.684-014 ● OES: 92902 ● Performs any combination of following tasks to process materials into finished or semifinished electronic components: Reads work orders, formulas, and processing charts, and receives verbal instructions to determine specifications and sequence of operations. Weighs or measures specified ingredients and binding agents, using scales and graduates. Mixes and grinds material, using manual or automatic machines and equipment. Loads, unloads, monitors operation, and adjusts controls of various processing machines and equipment that bake, diffuse, cast, x ray, cut, polish, coat, plate, silk-screen, and perform similar operations to prepare, combine, or change structure of materials to produce compositions with specific electronic properties. Cleans materials as required prior to processing operations, using solvents. Inspects, measures, and tests components according to specifications, using measuring instruments and test equipment. Encloses components in housings. Stamps or etches identifying information on finished component. Counts, sorts, and weighs processed items. Maintains manual or computerized records of production and inspection data. May be designated according to duties performed as Baker, Beads (electron. comp.); Firer (electron. comp.); Pellet-Preparation Operator (electron. comp.); Preforming-Machine Operator (electron. comp.); Vacuum-Evaporation Operator (electron. comp.); Weight-Count Operator (electron. comp.). Assembly of processed materials, parts, and components is covered under ELECTRONICS ASSEMBLER (electron. comp.) 726.684-018 and ELECTRONICS ASSEMBLER, DEVELOPMENTAL (electron. comp.) 726.261-010. ● **GED:** R2, M2, L2 ● **SVP:** 1-3 mos ● **Academic:** Ed=N, Eng=N ● **Work Field:** 147 ● **MPSMS:** 587 ● **Aptitudes:** G4, V4, N4, S4, P3, Q4, K3, F3, M3, E5, C4 ● **Temperaments:** R ● **Physical:** Stg=L; Freq: R, H, D Occas: I, N, A, X ● **Work Env:** Noise=N; ● **Salary:** 3 ● **Outlook:** 4

FILTER OPERATOR (any industry) ● DOT #551.685-078 ● OES: 92962 ● Alternate titles: SLUDGE-FILTER OPERATOR; VACUUM-FILTER OPERATOR. Tends rotary drum-filters that separate slurries into liquid and filter cake (insoluble material): Couples flexible hose or pipe to vat, starts pump, and turns valves to regulate flow of slurry to filter tanks. Adjusts controls to regulate rotation speed of drums. Turns valve to regulate pressure that forces slurry through filter, separating filter cake from liquid. Observes discharge to ensure that scrapers are removing filter cake from drum. May tend thickeners, washing sprays, settlers, or related equipment. May draw sample for laboratory analysis. May be known according to trade name of machine. ● **GED:** R2, M1, L1 ● **SVP:** 2-30 days ● **Academic:** Ed=N, Eng=N ● **Work Field:** 145 ● **MPSMS:** 490, 380 ● **Aptitudes:** G4, V4, N4, S4, P4, Q4, K4, F4, M3, E5, C4 ● **Temperaments:** R, T ● **Physical:** Stg=M; Const: C Freq: R, H, N Occas: S, K, O, X ● **Work Env:** Noise=L; Occas: T ● **Salary:** 2 ● **Outlook:** 2

LABORER (pharmaceut.) ● DOT #559.686-022 ● OES: 98502 ● Alternate titles: BATCHER. Performs any combination of following duties concerned with processing and packaging drug and toilet products: Transfers specified ingredients from storage to production area, using handtruck. Assembles specified ingredients for compounding. Feeds plants, roots, and herbs into machines, such as silage cutters, fanning mills, and washing machines. Loads botanicals into driers. Cuts animal tissue into strips, using saws. Feeds strips into meat grinders. Opens drums and scoops or dumps contents into kettles, tanks, or machine hopper. Removes filled cartons from packaging machine conveyor. ● **GED:** R2, M1, L2 ● **SVP:** 2-30 days ● **Academic:** Ed=N, Eng=N ● **Work Field:** 147 ● **MPSMS:** 493 ● **Aptitudes:** G4, V4, N4, S4, P4, Q5, K4, F4, M3, E5, C5 ● **Temperaments:** R ● **Physical:** Stg=H; Freq: S, O, R, H ● **Work Env:** Noise=N; ● **Salary:** 2 ● **Outlook:** 2

METALLIZATION EQUIPMENT TENDER, SEMICONDUCTORS (comm. equip.) ● DOT #590.685-086 ● OES: 92902 ● Tends equipment that deposits layer of metal on semiconductor surfaces to provide electrical contact between circuit components: Places semiconductors, such as silicon wafers, crystal units, or fiber optic microchannel plates, in container, using vacuum wand or tweezers. Cleans semiconductors to remove contaminants prior to metal deposition, using chemical baths or automatic cleaning equipment. Loads semiconductors into metallization equipment holders, using vacuum wand or tweezers. Places loaded holders and specified metals in chamber of equipment that deposits layer of metal, such as aluminum, gold, or platinum, on semiconductor surfaces, by sputtering or evaporation process. Manipulates equipment controls that start and adjust metallization process, following processing specifications. Measures electrical conductivity and thickness of metal layer on processed semiconductors, using test equipment. Maintains chemicals and met-

als for equipment. May tend equipment that deposits insulating layer of glass onto semiconductor wafer surfaces and be designated Glass Deposition Tender (electron. comp.). ● **GED:** R3, M2, L2 ● **SVP:** 1-3 mos ● **Academic:** Ed=N, Eng=S ● **Work Field:** 147 ● **MPSMS:** 587 ● **Aptitudes:** G3, V4, N4, S4, P4, Q4, K4, F3, M3, E5, C4 ● **Temperaments:** R, T ● **Physical:** Stg=L; Freq: R, H, I, N, D Occas: G, A, X ● **Work Env:** Noise=L; Occas: T ● **Salary:** 3 ● **Outlook:** 4

PLATER, SEMICONDUCTOR WAFERS AND COMPONENTS (electron. comp.) ● DOT #500.684-030 ● OES: 91920 ● Electroplates semiconductor wafers and electronic components, such as copper leads and rectifiers, with metals, such as gold, silver, and lead: Reads processing sheet to determine plating time and specifications. Places components or wafers in basket or fixture, using tweezers, and immerses components or wafers in chemical solution baths for specified time to clean and plate components or wafers. May measure thickness of photoresist and metal on wafer surface, using micrometer, and test electrical circuitry of individual die on wafer, using test probe equipment. May measure anode width on wafer surface, using microscope measuring equipment. ● **GED:** R3, M2, L2 ● **SVP:** 1-3 mos ● **Academic:** Ed=N, Eng=N ● **Work Field:** 154 ● **MPSMS:** 587 ● **Aptitudes:** G3, V4, N4, S3, P3, Q4, K4, F4, M4, E5, C3 ● **Temperaments:** T ● **Physical:** Stg=L; Freq: R, H, I Occas: N, D, A, X ● **Work Env:** Noise=L; Freq: T Occas: H ● **Salary:** 3 ● **Outlook:** 3

POLYSILICON PREPARATION WORKER (electron. comp.) ● DOT #590.684-038 ● OES: 92999 ● Performs any combination of following tasks to prepare polysilicon for crystal growing process: Operates drilling machine to remove core sample from polysilicon rod for evaluation. Breaks polysilicon rod into chunks, using hammer. Removes tungsten filament from chunks, using circular saw or drill. Immerses polysilicon chunks into series of vats containing chemical solutions to remove contaminants, using steel basket and hoist. Breaks chunks of polysilicon into pieces, using hammer, to prepare polysilicon for meltdown in crystal growing process. Records production information. ● **GED:** R2, M2, L2 ● **SVP:** 2-30 days ● **Academic:** Ed=N, Eng=N ● **Work Field:** 057, 031 ● **MPSMS:** 349 ● **Aptitudes:** G4, V4, N4, S3, P3, Q4, K3, F4, M3, E4, C4 ● **Temperaments:** R ● **Physical:** Stg=V; Freq: R, H, I, N, D, X Occas: G ● **Work Env:** Noise=L; Occas: M ● **Salary:** 3 ● **Outlook:** 4

PRINT DEVELOPER, AUTOMATIC (photofinishing) ● DOT #976.685-026 ● OES: 92908 ● Tends one or more machines that automatically develop, fix, wash, and dry photographic prints: Threads leaders (paper strips) around rollers, through processing tanks and dryer, around polished drum, and onto takeup reel. Turns valves to fill tanks with premixed solutions, such as developer, dyes, stop-baths, fixers, bleaches, and washes. Moves thermostatic control to keep steam-heated drum at specified temperature. Splices sensitized paper to leaders, using tape. Starts machine and throws switches to synchronize drive speeds of processing and drying units. Compares processed prints with color standard and reports variations to control department. Adds specified amounts of chemicals to renew solutions. Maintains production records. ● **GED:** R2, M1, L1 ● **SVP:** 3-6 mos ● **Academic:** Ed=N, Eng=N ● **Work Field:** 202 ● **MPSMS:** 897 ● **Aptitudes:** G4, V4, N4, S4, P4, Q4, K4, F3, M3, E5, C3 ● **Temperaments:** R, T ● **Physical:** Stg=L; Freq: R, H, I, N, D, X, V Occas: S, O ● **Work Env:** Noise=L; Freq: A, O ● **Salary:** 1 ● **Outlook:** 4

STERILIZER (medical ser.) ● DOT #599.585-010 ● OES: 92999 ● Alternate titles: AUTOCLAVE OPERATOR. Tends autoclave that sterilizes drug products, containers, supplies, instruments, and equipment: Places articles in autoclave manually or by use of electric hoist. Secures door or lid, turns dials to adjust temperature and pressure, and opens steam valve. Shuts off steam and removes sterilized articles after specified time. Records time and temperature setting and gauge readings. May wrap supplies and instruments in paper or cloth preparatory to sterilizing. ● **GED:** R3, M2, L3 ● **SVP:** 1-3 mos ● **Academic:** Ed=N, Eng=S ● **Work Field:** 141 ● **MPSMS:** 493 ● **Aptitudes:** G3, V3, N4, S4, P4, Q4, K4, F4, M3, E5, C5 ● **Temperaments:** R, T ● **Physical:** Stg=L; Freq: R, H, N Occas: I ● **Work Env:** Noise=L; ● **Salary:** 2 ● **Outlook:** 3

STILL TENDER (any industry) ● DOT #552.685-026 ● OES: 92962 ● Tends flash-type still that reclaims or separates liquids, such as solvents, through volatilization and condensation: Starts pump to draw liquid into tank and allows impurities to settle. Turns valve to transfer liquids into still. Observes temperature gauge and adjusts valve to heat liquid to specified temperature and vaporize liquid in tank. Turns valve to circulate water through tank jackets to condense vapors. Observes distillate for clarity, through pipeline viewer. May be designated according to liquid recovered as Solvent Recoverer (plastic-synth.). ● **GED:** R3, M2, L2 ● **SVP:** 1-3 mos ● **Academic:** Ed=N, Eng=N ● **Work Field:** 144 ● **MPSMS:** 490 ● **Aptitudes:** G4, V4, N4, S4, P4, Q4, K4, F4, M3, E5, C5 ● **Temperaments:** J, T ● **Physical:** Stg=L; Freq: R, H, F, A Occas: I, N ● **Work Env:** Noise=L; ● **Salary:** 4 ● **Outlook:** 2

STRIPPER-ETCHER, PRINTED CIRCUIT BOARDS (electron. comp.) ● DOT #590.685-082 ● OES: 92100 ● Tends equipment that strips photoresist film and etches layers of copper laminate from exposed surface of printed circuit board (PCB) panels leaving unexposed areas to form conductive circuitry pattern: Reads process specifications and adjusts equipment controls to regulate conveyor speed, spray intensity, and solution strengths and temperatures. Positions copper panels coated with photoresist on conveyor that carries panels through series of processing units, such as sprayers, rinsers, scrubbers, and dryers. Starts and monitors equipment that chemically strips photoresist and excess copper from exposed areas of PCB panels leaving unexposed copper to form circuitry pattern. Observes equipment operation, gauges, and meters to detect malfunctions or variance from specifications. Visually examines sample boards during and after processing for conformance to specifications. Notifies supervisor of equipment malfunction or substandard etching quality. Reroutes panels through processing units to complete stripping or etching process. May periodically change or adjust chemicals and solutions. May test acid solution, using pH meter. May manually immerse panels into processing tanks. May inspect circuitry pattern on panels, using microscope. May be identified according to process involved and be designated Etcher, Printed Circuit Boards (electron. comp.); Stripper, Printed Circuit Boards (electron. comp.). ● **GED:** R2, M2, L2 ● **SVP:** 1-3 mos ● **Academic:** Ed=N, Eng=N ● **Work Field:** 182 ● **MPSMS:** 587 ● **Aptitudes:** G4, V4, N4, S4, P4, Q4, K4, F4, M4, E5, C5 ● **Temperaments:** R, T ● **Physical:** Stg=M; Freq: R, H, N, D, A Occas: I ● **Work Env:** Noise=L; Freq: A, T ● **Salary:** 3 ● **Outlook:** 4

THERMOMETER PRODUCTION WORKER (inst. & app.) ● DOT #710.685-014 ● OES: 92999 ● Performs any combination of following tasks to fabricate and test clinical mercury thermometers: Reads work order to determine sequence of tasks and specifications. Tends machines that heat glass capillary tubes to form blister, constrict and adjust blister, fuse bulb to tube, form top chamber, seal end of tube, and fuse tops to form thermometer. Tends vacuum equipment that fills thermometer bores with mercury. Tends centrifuges, shakers, chill tanks, warming tanks, or related machines and equipment that disperse mercury in bore and remove excess mercury or air. Tends automated machines that grade and mark calibration reference points on thermometers. Tends equipment that prints scale on thermometer [SILK-SCREEN PRINTER, MACHINE (any industry) 979.685-010]. Tends heat tank that heats thermometer to standard temperature and reads thermometer scale to test accuracy. Inspects thermometers to detect defects, such as cracks, cloudiness, and screen printing errors. Records production information, such as number of thermometers processed, number rejected, and reason for rejection. ● **GED:** R2, M1, L1 ● **SVP:** 2-30 days ● **Academic:** Ed=N, Eng=N ● **Work Field:** 133, 145, 212 ● **MPSMS:** 609 ● **Aptitudes:** G4, V4, N4, S4, P4, Q4, K4, F3, M4, E5, C4 ● **Temperaments:** R ● **Physical:** Stg=L; Freq: R, H, I, N, D Occas: E, A, X ● **Work Env:** Noise=L; Occas: M, T ● **Salary:** 2 ● **Outlook:** 3

UTILITY WORKER, FILM PROCESSING (photofinishing) ● DOT #976.685-030 ● OES: 92908 ● Performs variety of tasks to assist or substitute for other workers in photofinishing laboratory: Sorts prints according to size and order number to facilitate handling. Tends automatic cutting machine that cuts roll into individual prints [CUTTER (photofinishing)]. Tends automatic film developing machine that develops and fixes image on film [DEVELOPER, AUTOMATIC (photofinishing)]. Removes prints from print developer rinse tray and tends drum-type drier that dries prints. Prepares daily production sheet, noting quantity and kind of work performed. ● **GED:** R3, M1, L2 ● **SVP:** 1-3 mos ● **Academic:** Ed=N, Eng=N ● **Work Field:** 202, 054, 221 ● **MPSMS:** 897 ● **Aptitudes:** G3, V3, N4, S4, P4, Q4, K3, F3, M3, E5, C4 ● **Temperaments:** V ● **Physical:** Stg=L; Freq: R, H, I, E, N, D Occas: X ● **Work Env:** Noise=L; Freq: O ● **Salary:** 1 ● **Outlook:** 2

GOE: 06.04.20
Machine Assembling

CORRUGATED-FASTENER DRIVER (woodworking) ● DOT #669.685-042 ● OES: 92310 ● Alternate titles: CORRUGATOR OPERATOR; SHOOK SPLICER; SPLICER-MACHINE OPERATOR; STITCHER OPERATOR. Tends machine that cuts metal fasteners from corrugated metal stripping and drives fasteners into boards across joints to fasten boards together: Positions spool of corrugated metal stripping onto machine spindles and threads end of stripping between clamps of automatic feed driver-head. Positions and tightens machine driver-head above workpiece joint, using wrench. Starts machine, positions workpiece against machine table stop, and depresses pedal to activate machine driver-head and force fastener into workpiece. May be designated according to parts fastened as Box-Top-Stitching-Machine Operator (wood. container); Door-Frame Assembler, Machine (woodworking). ● **GED:** R2, M1, L1 ● **SVP:** 2-30 days ● **Academic:** Ed=N, Eng=N ● **Work Field:** 072 ● **MPSMS:** 450 ● **Aptitudes:** G4, V4, N5, S4, P4, Q5, K3, F4, M3, E4, C5 ● **Temperaments:** R ● **Physical:** Stg=M; Freq: R, H Occas: S, O, I, N ● **Work Env:** Noise=L; ● **Salary:** 2 ● **Outlook:** 2

MOUNTER, AUTOMATIC (photofinishing) ● DOT #976.685-022 ● OES: 92908 ● Tends automatic-mounting press that cuts film into individual transparencies, and inserts and seals transparencies in mounting frames: Loads mounting frames into machine and depresses lever to lock frames into feed position. Compares identifying labels to ensure numbers on film reel and customer envelope match. Records customer charges on envelope according to standard price listing. Mounts film reel on machine spindle and trims rough edges of film, using scissors. Threads film through machine guides and activates machine that automatically cuts film and mounts transparencies. Observes movement of film through machine to detect jamming and adjusts machine guides, using screwdriver. Notifies supervisor of major machine malfunction. ● **GED:** R2, M1, L1 ● **SVP:** 2-30 days ● **Academic:** Ed=N, Eng=N ● **Work Field:** 054, 062 ● **MPSMS:** 897 ● **Aptitudes:** G4, V4, N4, S4, P3, Q4, K3, F3, M3, E5, C5 ● **Temperaments:** R ● **Physical:** Stg=L; Freq: R, H, I, N, D ● **Work Env:** Noise=N; ● **Salary:** 2 ● **Outlook:** 2

STAPLING-MACHINE OPERATOR (any industry) ● DOT #692.685-202 ● OES: 92999 ● Alternate titles: WIRE-STITCHER OPERATOR. Tends machine that staples together parts of products made from materials, such as plastic, paper, leather, felt, and canvas: Loads machine with wire staples or spool of wire, and positions material under head of machine. Steps on pedal to lower ram that cuts off wire staple and forces it through material to clinch it together. May adjust machine table to accommodate different sizes of materials being stapled. ● **GED:** R2, M1, L2 ● **SVP:** 2-30 days ● **Academic:** Ed=N, Eng=N ● **Work Field:** 062 ● **MPSMS:** 610 ● **Aptitudes:** G4, V4, N4, S4, P4, Q4, K3, F3, M3, E5, C5 ● **Temperaments:** R ● **Physical:** Stg=M; Freq: R, H, I, N Occas: S ● **Work Env:** Noise=L; ● **Salary:** 3 ● **Outlook:** 2

GOE: 06.04.21
Machine Work, Brushing, Spraying, & Coating

CERAMIC COATER, MACHINE (any industry) ● DOT #509.685-022 ● OES: 91930 ● Alternate titles: CERAMIC PLATER. Tends machine that coats metal objects with ceramic material: Places workpiece on rack, observing reflection in mirror below rack to determine when surface to be coated is exposed. Closes machine door and presses button to start rack revolving and initiate coating cycle. Observes gauges and turns valves to maintain specified flow through coating nozzle. Fills reservoir with ceramic material and turns valves on hydrogen supply tanks to maintain flow of gas to machine. Removes coated parts, blows away excess material with airhose, and places parts in container. ● **GED:** R2, M2, L1 ● **SVP:** 2-30 days ● **Academic:** Ed=N, Eng=N ●

Work Field: 153 ● **MPSMS:** 559 ● **Aptitudes:** G4, V4, N4, S3, P3, Q5, K3, F3, M3, E5, C4 ● **Temperaments:** R, T ● **Physical:** Stg=M; Freq: R, H, I, N, D Occas: X ● **Work Env:** Noise=N; Freq: H ● **Salary:** 3 ● **Outlook:** 3

DIPPER AND BAKER (any industry) ● DOT #599.685-030 ● OES: 92999 ● Alternate titles: IMPREGNATING-TANK OPERATOR. Dips assembled electrical equipment components into materials, such as varnish, enamel, or asphalt to insulate wires and coils and tends oven that dries dipped components: Pours dipping solution into vat and measures consistency with hydrometer, adding thinner to control density. Sets vat thermostat at prescribed temperature. Hangs or bolts components to be dipped, such as armatures or transformers, on racks, lifts them manually or by use of hand-operated hoist, and immerses them in vat for prescribed time. Removes components and places them on racks to drain. Sets oven temperature controls and places dipped units in oven to bake and dry for specified time. May clean and coat electrical leads by dipping them in molten solder. May paint armatures and field coils, using brush, or pour insulating compound over coils. May be designated according to unit impregnated as Armature Varnisher (any industry); Field-Coil Enameler (any industry). ● **GED:** R2, M1, L1 ● **SVP:** 2-30 days ● **Academic:** Ed=N, Eng=N ● **Work Field:** 151, 141 ● **MPSMS:** 582 ● **Aptitudes:** G4, V4, N4, S4, P4, Q4, K4, F4, M3, E4, C4 ● **Temperaments:** R, T ● **Physical:** Stg=M; Freq: R, H, N Occas: X ● **Work Env:** Noise=L; Occas: H ● **Salary:** 1 ● **Outlook:** 3

PLATING EQUIPMENT TENDER (electroplating) ● DOT #500.685-014 ● OES: 91920 ● Alternate titles: ELECTROPLATER, AUTOMATIC; PLATER PRODUCTION. Tends automatic equipment that conveys objects through series of cleaning, rinsing, and electrolytic plating solutions to plate objects with metallic coating: Starts equipment and regulates flow of electricity through plating solution and immersion time of objects in solutions, according to specifications. Monitors automatic plating process to ensure conformance to standards. Adds water or other materials to maintain specified mixture and level of cleaning, rinsing, and plating solutions. Observes temperature gauges and adjusts controls to maintain specified temperatures of cleaning and rinsing solutions. Lubricates moving parts of plating conveyor. Cleans plating and cleaning tanks. May test plating solution, using hydrometer and litmus paper, or obtain random sample of plating solutions for laboratory analysis. May replace anodes and cathodes in plating equipment. May fasten objects onto hooks or racks, or place objects into containers or onto conveyor attached to plating equipment. May start and monitor computerized plating process. May manually immerse objects into plating or rinsing solutions. ● **GED:** R2, M2, L2 ● **SVP:** 1-3 mos ● **Academic:** Ed=N, Eng=N ● **Work Field:** 154 ● **MPSMS:** 540, 587 ● **Aptitudes:** G3, V4, N4, S3, P4, Q4, K4, F4, M3, E5, C4 ● **Temperaments:** R, T ● **Physical:** Stg=M; Freq: R, H, N, D Occas: S, I, F, X ● **Work Env:** Noise=L; Const: A Occas: U, M, T ● **Salary:** 3 ● **Outlook:** 3

SEED PELLETER (agriculture) ● DOT #599.685-126 ● OES: 92960 ● Tends equipment that applies coating to agricultural seeds and separates coated seeds according to size specifications to allow for uniform planting: Dumps seeds into rotary drum and presses buttons to start drum rotation. Adds water, powder, and glue for specified period, using spray guns and scoop and following work order specifications. Stops drum and scoops coated seeds (pellets) from drum, dumps pellets into electric sizing mill or onto manual sizing screen to remove undersized pellets. Returns undersized pellets to drums for additional coating. Dumps and spreads pellets on trays in drying tunnel for drying. Repeats sizing procedure for dried pellets to ensure that pellets meet sizing specifications. Fills pails with pellets specified on shipping order, using scoop, covers pails with lids, and places pails on pallet for shipment. Cleans interior and exterior of drums and work area, using brushes, rags, mop, detergent, and water. ● **GED:** R2, M1, L2 ● **SVP:** 2-30 days ● **Academic:** Ed=N, Eng=N ● **Work Field:** 151, 145 ● **MPSMS:** 311 ● **Aptitudes:** G4, V4, N4, S4, P4, Q4, K4, F4, M3, E5, C5 ● **Temperaments:** R ● **Physical:** Stg=L; Freq: R, H, N Occas: I ● **Work Env:** Noise=N; Occas: U ● **Salary:** 3 ● **Outlook:** 3

SPRAY-UNIT FEEDER (any industry) ● DOT #599.686-014 ● OES: 98502 ● Alternate titles: MACHINE SPRAYER. Feeds manufactured articles or parts onto conveyor or feed mechanism that carries them through paint dipping and spraying operations. May be designated according to coating applied as Lacquerer (button & notion); or according to article sprayed as Gunstock-Spray-Unit Feeder (ordnance);

Sprayer, Light Bulbs (light. fix.); or according to mechanism fed as Hook Loader (toy-sport equip.). ● **GED:** R2, M1, L1 ● **SVP:** 2-30 days ● **Academic:** Ed=N, Eng=N ● **Work Field:** 153, 151 ● **MPSMS:** 495 ● **Aptitudes:** G4, V4, N4, S4, P4, Q4, K4, F4, M3, E5, C5 ● **Temperaments:** R ● **Physical:** Stg=L; Freq: R, H, F Occas: S, K, O, I ● **Work Env:** Noise=L; ● **Salary:** 3 ● **Outlook:** 2

GOE: 06.04.22
Manual Work, Assembly Large Parts

ASSEMBLER, BICYCLE II (motor-bicycles) ● DOT #806.687-010 ● OES: 93997 ● Assembles bicycles on assembly line, performing one or a combination of tasks as described under ASSEMBLER, BICYCLE (motor-bicycles) I, using handtools and portable power tools. May assemble and package bicycle subassemblies, such as shift levers, axles, and reflectors and be designated Bicycle Subassembler (motor-bicycles). ● **GED:** R1, M1, L1 ● **SVP:** 2-30 days ● **Academic:** Ed=N, Eng=N ● **Work Field:** 121 ● **MPSMS:** 595 ● **Aptitudes:** G4, V4, N4, S4, P4, Q5, K3, F4, M3, E5, C5 ● **Temperaments:** R ● **Physical:** Stg=L; Freq: R, H, I, N, D Occas: E ● **Work Env:** Noise=N; ● **Salary:** 2 ● **Outlook:** 3

ASSEMBLER, MOTOR VEHICLE (auto. mfg.) ● DOT #806.684-010 ● OES: 93997 ● Alternate titles: QUALITY WORKER; TEAM MEMBER. Assembles motor vehicles, such as automobiles, trucks, buses, or limousines, at assigned work stations on moving assembly line, performing any combination of following repetitive tasks according to specifications and using handtools, power tools, welding equipment, and production fixtures: Loads stamped metal body components into automated welding equipment that welds together components to form body subassemblies. Positions and fastens together body subassemblies, such as side frames, underbodies, doors, hoods, and trunk lids, to assemble vehicle bodies and truck cabs preparatory to body welding process. Bolts, screws, clips, or otherwise fastens together parts to form subassemblies, such as doors, seats, instrument control panels, steering columns, and axle units. Installs mechanical and electrical components and systems, such as engine, transmission, and axle units; pumps; wire harnesses; instrument control panels; and exhaust, brake, and air-conditioning systems. Fits and adjusts doors, hoods, and trunk lids. Seals joints and seams, using caulking gun. Fastens seats, door paneling, headliners, carpeting, molding, and other trim into position. Fills vehicle systems with brake and transmission fluids, engine coolant, and oil. May apply precut and adhesive coated vinyl tops and pads to vehicle roofs. May verify quality of own work and write description of defects observed on documents attached to vehicle bodies. May enter and retrieve production data, using computer terminals. May work as member of assembly group (team) and be assigned different work stations as production needs require or shift from one station to another to reduce fatigue factor. May participate in group meetings to exchange job related information. May be designated according to component assembled or installed as Assembler, Engine (auto. mfg.); Assembler, Seat (auto. mfg.); or stage of assembly as Assembler, Body (auto. mfg.); Assembler, Chassis (auto. mfg.); Assembler, Final (auto. mfg.); Assembler, Trim (auto. mfg.). ● **GED:** R2, M1, L2 ● **SVP:** 2-30 days ● **Academic:** Ed=N, Eng=N ● **Work Field:** 102, 111, 121 ● **MPSMS:** 591 ● **Aptitudes:** G4, V4, N4, S4, P4, Q4, K4, F4, M3, E5, C4 ● **Temperaments:** R, T ● **Physical:** Stg=M; Freq: R, H, I, N, D, A Occas: S, O, E, X ● **Work Env:** Noise=N; ● **Salary:** 3 ● **Outlook:** 2

ASSEMBLER, PRODUCTION (any industry) ● DOT #706.687-010 ● OES: 93997 ● Performs repetitive bench or line assembly operations to mass-produce products, such as automobile or tractor radiators, blower wheels, refrigerators, or gas stoves: Places parts in specified relationship to each other. Bolts, clips, screws, cements, or otherwise fastens parts together by hand, or using handtools or portable power tools. May tend machines, such as arbor presses or riveting machine, to perform force fitting or fastening operations on assembly line. May be assigned to different work stations as production needs require. May work on line where tasks vary as different model of same article moves along line. May be designated according to part or product produced. ● **GED:** R2, M1, L1 ● **SVP:** 2-30 days ● **Academic:** Ed=N, Eng=N ● **Work Field:** 102, 121 ● **MPSMS:** 550, 560 ● **Aptitudes:** G4, V4, N4, S4, P4, Q4, K3, F4, M3, E5, C5 ● **Temperaments:** R ● **Physical:**

Stg=L; Freq: R, H, I, N Occas: S, O, D, A ● **Work Env:** Noise=L; ● **Salary:** 2 ● **Outlook:** 2

LAMINATOR, HAND (furniture) ● DOT #763.684-050 ● OES: 93997 ● Cements precut laminated plastic covering materials to plywood panels to form furniture parts, such as cabinet tops, countertops, tabletops, and desktops: Applies cement to surface of plywood panels, using brush. Glues plastic laminated covering material to plywood panel to form furniture part and smooths surface with rollers. Wipes acetone on edges of covering and panel with rag and solvent to remove excess cement. Examines edges of laminated part to detect ridges, and removes excess material with file or electric hand trimmer. May attach metal molding trim to edges, using glue and handtools. May cut plastic laminated material and plywood to specified size and shape, using handtools and power tools. May clamp laminated plastic in place until glue sets, using clamps or vise. May install laminated plastic tops on furniture and be designated Plastic-Top Installer (furniture). May cover tops of kitchen and bathroom fixtures and be designated Cabinet Assembler (mfd. bldgs.). ● **GED:** R2, M1, L1 ● **SVP:** 1-3 mos ● **Academic:** Ed=N, Eng=N ● **Work Field:** 063 ● **MPSMS:** 460 ● **Aptitudes:** G3, V4, N4, S3, P4, Q5, K4, F4, M3, E5, C5 ● **Temperaments:** T ● **Physical:** Stg=M; Const: R, H, N ● **Work Env:** Noise=L; ● **Salary:** 2 ● **Outlook:** 2

NAILER, HAND (any industry) ● DOT #762.684-050 ● OES: 93997 ● Assembles wooden products, such as boxes, packing cases, kegs, pallets, furniture frames, door and window units, and hogshead subassemblies, using handtools: Positions workpiece on table, floor, easel, or jig, according to verbal instructions, and nails or staples materials together at designated points, using hammer, pneumatic gun, or staple gun. Drives nails in carvings, molding, and scroll work, using hammer, before attaching to furniture. Attaches metal cleats to bottoms of nail kegs to reinforce containers, using hammer and nails. Clinches exposed nail ends and places assembled unit aside for further processing or shipment. May insert bolts in predrilled holes and tighten bolts with wrench. May glue joints before nailing. May record production. May repair containers and be designated Box Repairer (any industry). May be designated according to product assembled as Box Maker, Wood (any industry); Panel Maker (woodworking). ● **GED:** R2, M1, L1 ● **SVP:** 1-3 mos ● **Academic:** Ed=N, Eng=N ● **Work Field:** 072 ● **MPSMS:** 450, 460 ● **Aptitudes:** G4, V4, N4, S4, P4, Q5, K3, F4, M3, E5, C5 ● **Temperaments:** R, T ● **Physical:** Stg=M; Freq: S, R, H, N, D, A Occas: O, I, G ● **Work Env:** Noise=L; ● **Salary:** 1 ● **Outlook:** 2

PLASTIC-TOP ASSEMBLER (furniture) ● DOT #763.684-062 ● OES: 93997 ● Stacks sheets of glue-coated plywood, fiberboard, and plastic, in specified sequence for pressing into laminated tops for furniture, such as dressers, tables, and desks. Builds tops for matched sets, by matching color, type of finish, and grain pattern of face sheets. May tend cold press to compress stack [HYDRAULIC-PRESS OPERATOR (millwork-plywood)]. ● **GED:** R2, M1, L1 ● **SVP:** 2-30 days ● **Academic:** Ed=N, Eng=N ● **Work Field:** 063 ● **MPSMS:** 460 ● **Aptitudes:** G4, V4, N4, S4, P3, Q4, K4, F4, M3, E5, C4 ● **Temperaments:** R, T ● **Physical:** Stg=H; Freq: S, R, H, I, N, X ● **Work Env:** Noise=L; ● **Salary:** 4 ● **Outlook:** 2

GOE: 06.04.23
Manual Work, Assembly Small Parts

ASSEMBLER, MOLDED FRAMES (optical goods) ● DOT #713.684-014 ● OES: 93997 ● Alternate titles: FRAME ASSEMBLER. Assembles plastic eyeglass frames, using drill press and rivet press: Positions frame parts in jig and drills holes in parts, using drill press. Inserts rivets through holes, positions clips and hinges on rivets, and depresses pedal of pneumatic press to set rivets. ● **GED:** R2, M1, L1 ● **SVP:** 2-30 days ● **Academic:** Ed=N, Eng=N ● **Work Field:** 073, 053 ● **MPSMS:** 605 ● **Aptitudes:** G4, V4, N4, S4, P4, Q4, K4, F3, M4, E4, C5 ● **Temperaments:** R ● **Physical:** Stg=L; Freq: R, H, I, N Occas: D ● **Work Env:** Noise=N; ● **Salary:** 2 ● **Outlook:** 3

ASSEMBLER, SMALL PRODUCTS I (any industry) ● DOT #706.684-022 ● OES: 93997 ● Alternate titles: BENCH ASSEMBLER. Performs any combination of following repetitive tasks on assembly line to mass produce small products, such as ball bearings, automobile door locking units, speedometers, condensers, distributors, ignition coils, drafting table subassemblies, or carburetors: Positions parts in specified relationship to each other, using hands, tweezers, or tongs. Bolts, screws, clips, cements, or otherwise fastens parts together by hand or using handtools or portable powered tools. Frequently works at bench as member of assembly group assembling one or two specific parts and passing unit to another worker. Loads and unloads previously setup machines, such as arbor presses, drill presses, taps, spot-welding machines, riveting machines, milling machines, or broaches, to perform fastening, force fitting, or light metal-cutting operation on assembly line. May be assigned to different work stations as production needs require or shift from one station to another to reduce fatigue factor. May be known according to product assembled. ● **GED:** R2, M1, L1 ● **SVP:** 2-30 days ● **Academic:** Ed=N, Eng=N ● **Work Field:** 061 ● **MPSMS:** 611, 560 ● **Aptitudes:** G4, V4, N5, S4, P3, Q4, K3, F3, M3, E5, C5 ● **Temperaments:** R ● **Physical:** Stg=L; Freq: R, H, I, N, D, A Occas: E, G ● **Work Env:** Noise=L; ● **Salary:** 2 ● **Outlook:** 3

BATTERY ASSEMBLER, DRY CELL (elec. equip.) ● DOT #727.664-010 ● OES: 93997 ● Performs any combination of following duties to assemble batteries for commercial use in products, such as photographic equipment, flashlights, and pagers: Fills electrolyte or mercury dispensing devices to specified levels. Pours partial battery assembly parts into respective conveyor line bowl feeders, places spools of metal strips and paper on holding brackets, or positions battery subassemblies in conveyor holding attachments. Observes automatic equipment that cuts blotter and cathode inserts, places inserts in subassembly, joins top and bottom subassembly of batteries, dispenses specified amounts of electrolyte or mercury, and spot welds metal strip to each battery; or tamps pellets into bottom sections of battery subassembly. Positions inserts, such as poly ring and anode ring, in subassembly before or after designated steps of assembly process. Notifies supervisor or setup personnel, or signals coworkers, to stop conveyor when malfunctions occur. Gathers batteries with metal strips attached, and places specified number of batteries in concave work aid that facilitates positioning metal strips over side of batteries in stack prior to spot welding. Positions each battery of stack under spot welder and depresses pedal to spot weld strips to successive batteries to join stacks of batteries. Spot welds battery top to joined batteries. Inserts battery stacks into battery sleeves with crimped tops, positions battery sleeves in crimping machine, and presses button to crimp bottom of sleeves to secure stacks in sleeves. Positions batteries in test equipment to determine whether batteries meet standard for acceptability. Tends equipment that automatically cuts out blotter and cathode battery inserts and places inserts in partial battery assemblies. Packs batteries meeting company standards for shipment. ● **GED:** R3, M2, L2 ● **SVP:** 3-6 mos ● **Academic:** Ed=N, Eng=N ● **Work Field:** 061 ● **MPSMS:** 589 ● **Aptitudes:** G3, V4, N4, S3, P3, Q4, K4, F3, M4, E4, C5 ● **Temperaments:** R, T ● **Physical:** Stg=M; Const: R, H, I, N, D Occas: S, T, G ● **Work Env:** Noise=L; Occas: M, T ● **Salary:** 2 ● **Outlook:** 2

COIL WINDER (elec. equip.) ● DOT #724.684-026 ● OES: 93908 ● Winds coils used in electrical equipment and instruments, or as electronic components, according to wiring diagrams, sample coil, or work order, using coil-winding machines and handtools: Reviews wiring diagrams and work order or examines sample coil to ascertain type and size of wire specified, and type, size, length, circumference, and primary and secondary windings of coil to be wound. Selects coil-forming device for specified coil and fastens device onto machine arbor, mandrel, or spindle or fastens device between chuck and tail stock. Threads end of wire from reel through tension device, guides, and spreader, bends wire ends to form lead, and attaches lead to coil core. Turns setscrews to adjust tension on wire and sets counter for number of turns specified. Starts machine and manually feeds wire over coil core or spreader to obtain even and uniform winding and shape of coil. Observes counter and stops machine at specified number of coils. Wraps insulation between layers and around wound coil or inserts plastic blocks between turns to form cooling ducts. Cuts wire to form leads, using wire or bolt cutters. Pounds coil with hammer or mallet to shape end windings or remove coil from fixtures. Winds asbestos, cotton, glass mica, paper, or tape around coil, and brushes varnish on coil or dips coil in varnish, epoxy, or wax to reinforce and seal coil. Strips insulation from end of lead wires, threads lead wires through insulating sleeves or slides sleeves over leads, and solders lead wires to terminals. May test coils for winding continuity, using test lamp. May cut and form insulating materials and be known as Insulator Cutter And Former (elec. equip.); or insert insulation in core slots and be known as Insulator (elec. equip.). May wind heavy ribbon, strap, or round wire over fixture to form coil and be designated Coil Former, Template (elec. equip.); Coil Winder, Open Slot (elec. equip.); Coil Winder, Strap (elec. equip.). May be designated according to type of coil wound or work station as Armature Coil Winder (elec. equip.); Audio-Coil Winder (electron. comp.); Bender, Armature Coil (elec. equip.); Bobbin-Coil Winder (electron. comp.); Coil Finisher (elec. equip.; electron. comp.); Coil Taper (elec. equip.). May be designated: Coil Winder, Hand (electron. comp.); Field-Coil Winder (elec. equip.); Filament-Coil Winder (electron. comp.); Helix-Coil Winder (elec. equip.; electron. comp.); Resistor Winder (elec. equip.; electron. comp.); Transformer-Coil Winder (elec. equip.; electron. comp.). ● **GED:** R2, M2, L2 ● **SVP:** 3-6 mos ● **Academic:** Ed=N, Eng=N ● **Work Field:** 163, 111 ● **MPSMS:** 580 ● **Aptitudes:** G4, V4, N4, S4, P3, Q4, K3, F3, M3, E4, C4 ● **Temperaments:** R, T ● **Physical:** Stg=L; Freq: R, H, I, N, D, A Occas: G, X ● **Work Env:** Noise=N; ● **Salary:** 3 ● **Outlook:** 2

EARRING MAKER (jewelry-silver.) ● DOT #700.684-030 ● OES: 93997 ● Assembles pearl earrings according to designs or instructions: Winds wire-threaded pearls, by hand, around metal-looped earring blanks. Cuts end of wire thread with cutter. Fastens pearls on loops by twisting wire with pliers. May paste loops of pearls and single pearls to facing of other loop blank. ● **GED:** R3, M2, L2 ● **SVP:** 1-3 mos ● **Academic:** Ed=N, Eng=N ● **Work Field:** 061 ● **MPSMS:** 611 ● **Aptitudes:** G3, V4, N4, S4, P3, Q5, K4, F3, M4, E5, C4 ● **Temperaments:** R, T ● **Physical:** Stg=S; Freq: R, H, I, N Occas: X ● **Work Env:** Noise=N; Occas: O ● **Salary:** 2 ● **Outlook:** 2

ELECTRIC-MOTOR ASSEMBLER (elec. equip.) ● DOT #721.684-022 ● OES: 93905 ● Alternate titles: ASSEMBLER; ASSEMBLY HAND. Assembles subassemblies and parts of dynamotors, converters, and electric motors used in instruments, appliances, and power tools, performing any combination of following tasks, using power tools and handtools: Bolts field windings and brush holders into motor housings, using wrenches, screwdrivers, and holding fixtures. Presses bushings and bearings into motor head, using arbor press. Secures fans and gears to armature shaft, using nuts and lock washers, and places armature shaft in bearings. Solders or screws electrical leads to brushes, and switch and cord assembly, using soldering iron. Assembles end brackets and base to housing and fastens assembly with screws. Lubricates gears and other moving parts, using oilcan, paddle, or grease gun. Turns shaft to ensure free movement of parts. May screw covers on motor ends to keep out dirt and moisture during shipment. When replacing defective parts in motors is designated Repairer, Electric Motor (elec. equip.). May be designated according to type motor assembled as Assembbler, Instrument Motors (elec. equip.) or part assembled as Brush-Holder Assembler (elec. equip.). ● **GED:** R2, M1, L2 ● **SVP:** 1-3 mos ● **Academic:** Ed=N, Eng=N ● **Work Field:** 111 ● **MPSMS:** 582 ● **Aptitudes:** G4, V4, N4, S4, P4, Q5, K3, F2, M3, E5, C4 ● **Temperaments:** R, T ● **Physical:** Stg=L; Freq: R, H, I, N Occas: S, O, E, D, A, X ● **Work Env:** Noise=L; ● **Salary:** 3 ● **Outlook:** 3

FISHING-REEL ASSEMBLER (toy-sport equip.) ● DOT #732.684-062 ● OES: 93997 ● Alternate titles: REEL ASSEMBLER. Assembles fishing reels, performing any combination of following tasks: Positions parts, such as washers, levers, springs, line spool, and retaining rings, in slots, holes, or over pins provided on frame of fishing reel. Inserts drive shaft through line spool and frame bearing. Positions side plate assembly containing gears and crankshaft on frame, aligns screw holes, and screws assembly to frame, using powered screwdriver. Places crank on crankshaft and tightens nut with wrench to fasten crank to shaft. Screws parts, such as control knobs and case covers, to frame. Tests and adjusts reel for unrestricted, positive movement of parts by performing such tasks as rotating reel crank, pulling fishline off spool, and turning adjustment screws or knobs located on reel. May disassemble reel, realign parts, and remove burrs to rework defective reels, using handtools. May operate arbor and kick presses to perform such tasks as forcing bushings into reel frames, riveting parts to subassemblies, and pressing or staking gears on shafts. ● **GED:** R2, M1, L1 ● **SVP:** 2-30 days ● **Academic:** Ed=N, Eng=N ● **Work Field:** 121 ● **MPSMS:** 616 ● **Aptitudes:** G4, V4, N4, S4, P4, Q4, K3, F3, M3, E5, C5 ● **Temperaments:** R, T ● **Physical:** Stg=S; Freq: R, H Occas: I ● **Work Env:** Noise=N; ● **Salary:** 2 ● **Outlook:** 3

LENS INSERTER (optical goods) ● DOT #713.687-026 ● OES: 93997 ● Alternate titles: ROLL-OVER LOADER. Fits lenses into plastic sunglass frames and places frames on conveyor belt that passes under heat lamps which soften frames preparatory to setting of lenses. ● **GED:** R1, M1, L1 ● **SVP:** 2-30 days ● **Academic:** Ed=N, Eng=N ● **Work Field:** 061 ● **MPSMS:** 605 ● **Aptitudes:** G4, V4, N4, S4, P4, Q4, K4, F3, M4, E5, C5 ● **Temperaments:** R ● **Physical:** Stg=S; Freq: R, H, I, N ● **Work Env:** Noise=N; ● **Salary:** 1 ● **Outlook:** 3

LOCK ASSEMBLER (cutlery-hrdwr.) ● DOT #706.684-074 ● OES: 93997 ● Fastens together parts of locks with screws, bolts, and rivets, using handtools and power tools: Files and fits parts to obtain smooth functioning of lock. Assembles inside lock parts in lock case and rivets side plate in place, using rivet tool. May pack locks in cartons and mark cartons to identify contents. ● **GED:** R2, M1, L2 ● **SVP:** 1-3 mos ● **Academic:** Ed=N, Eng=N ● **Work Field:** 073, 071 ● **MPSMS:** 552 ● **Aptitudes:** G4, V4, N5, S3, P4, Q5, K4, F3, M4, E4, C5 ● **Temperaments:** R, T ● **Physical:** Stg=S; Freq: R, H, I, N Occas: D ● **Work Env:** Noise=L; ● **Salary:** 2 ● **Outlook:** 2

RUBBER-GOODS ASSEMBLER (rubber goods) ● DOT #752.684-038 ● OES: 93997 ● Assembles rubber goods, such as water bottles, ice bags, swim fins, water goggles, rubber gloves, and ring cushions: Cements and stretches molded opening in goods to insert styrene eyepieces, closures, and ferrules. Clamps buckles and straps to fins and goggles, using air vise and handtools. Wraps fabric tape around inserted closures and ferrules to hold them in place and stretches band of rubber around tape. Brushes cement on valves and closures. May be designated according to product assembled as Bottle Assembler (rubber goods); Goggles Assembler (rubber goods); Graphite-Disk Assembler (rubber goods); Ice-Bag Assembler (rubber goods). ● **GED:** R2, M1, L1 ● **SVP:** 2-30 days ● **Academic:** Ed=N, Eng=N ● **Work Field:** 061, 063 ● **MPSMS:** 519 ● **Aptitudes:** G4, V4, N5, S4, P3, Q5, K4, F3, M3, E5, C5 ● **Temperaments:** R, T ● **Physical:** Stg=L; Const: R, H Freq: I, E ● **Work Env:** Noise=N; ● **Salary:** 2 ● **Outlook:** 3

SILK-SCREEN-FRAME ASSEMBLER (any industry) ● DOT #709.484-010 ● OES: 93997 ● Alternate titles: FRAME BUILDER, SILK-SCREEN; SETTER-UP, SILK-SCREEN FRAME. Builds frames for silk or metal screens used to stencil identifying or operational data on parts or products following blueprints: Bends bar stock to specified shape and dimensions to form frame, using vise and handtools. Solders joints, using soldering iron. Measures and marks location of holes on frame, using rule. Drills and threads holes, using drill press and handtap. Screws guides and stops in holes for use in positioning part in frame. ● **GED:** R3, M2, L2 ● **SVP:** 1-3 mos ● **Academic:** Ed=N, Eng=N ● **Work Field:** 102 ● **MPSMS:** 567 ● **Aptitudes:** G4, V4, N4, S4, P3, Q4, K3, F3, M3, E5, C5 ● **Temperaments:** R, T ● **Physical:** Stg=L; Freq: R, H, I, N ● **Work Env:** Noise=N; ● **Salary:** 2 ● **Outlook:** 3

TOY ASSEMBLER (toy-sport equip.) ● DOT #731.687-034 ● OES: 93997 ● Assembles parts of various materials, such as plastic, wood, metal, or fabric to mass produce toys, performing any combination of following tasks: Selects parts specified and positions parts in designated relationship to each other, using hands, tweezers, or pliers. Assembles and fastens parts of toys together, using clips, glue, jig, screws, dowels, nails, handtools, and portable powered tools. Inspects toys for specified color and operation of parts. May tend previously set up machines, such as drill press, reamer, welding machine, nailing machine, flanging press, and punch press to drill, cut, weld, trim, fit, or insert toy parts on assembly line. May be designated according to item assembled or material used as Assembler, Toy Voices (toy-sport equip.); Doll-Eye-Setter (toy-sport equip.); Stuffed-Toy Joiner (toy-sport equip.); Toy Assembler, Plastic (toy-sport equip.); Toy Assembler, Wood (toy-sport equip.); Wheel Assembler, Baby Carriage (toy-sport equip.). ● **GED:** R2, M1, L1 ● **SVP:** 2-30 days ● **Academic:** Ed=N, Eng=N ● **Work Field:** 102, 121 ● **MPSMS:** 615 ● **Aptitudes:** G4, V4, N5, S4, P4, Q5, K3, F3, M3, E4, C4 ● **Temperaments:** R, T ● **Physical:** Stg=L; Freq: R, H, I, N, A Occas: D, X ● **Work Env:** Noise=N; ● **Salary:** 1 ● **Outlook:** 3

TIRE MOUNTER (fabrication, nec) ● DOT #739.684-158 ● OES: 93997 ● Alternate titles: TIRE ASSEMBLER. Assembles hard rubber tires and wheel rims for articles, such as lawn mowers and baby carriages: Places rubber tire into jaws of spreading device and depresses pedal to close jaws and stretch tire. Positions wheel rim on spindle mandrel at center of tire. Pushes button to open jaws that release tire onto rim and removes wheel from spreading device. ● **GED:** R2, M1, L1 ● **SVP:** 2-30 days ● **Academic:** Ed=N, Eng=N ● **Work Field:** 061 ● **MPSMS:** 551 ● **Aptitudes:** G4, V4, N5, S4, P4, Q5, K3, F4, M3, E4, C5 ● **Temperaments:** R ● **Physical:** Stg=L; Freq: R, H, I ● **Work Env:** Noise=L; ● **Salary:** 4 ● **Outlook:** 3

GOE: 06.04.24
Manual Work, Metal & Plastics

ASSEMBLER, PLASTIC HOSPITAL PRODUCTS (inst. & app.) ● DOT #712.687-010 ● OES: 93997 ● Performs any combination of following tasks to assemble and package disposable plastic hospital products, such as hypodermic syringes, catheters, and intravenous apparatus: Reviews work order and selects component parts to assemble specified product. Fits and assembles parts together, using adhesives and handtools, or heats, bonds, and welds parts together, using automatic equipment. Visually inspects products for defects, verifies conformance to specifications, and rejects defective products. Packages assembled product into plastic bag or other container and seals package, using sealing machine. Packs sealed product and instructional information into cartons, and labels cartons with identifying information. May stack cartons in sterilization chamber, seal chamber, and turn valves to admit gas into chamber to sterilize product. ● **GED:** R2, M1, L1 ● **SVP:** 2-30 days ● **Academic:** Ed=N, Eng=N ● **Work Field:** 041, 102 ● **MPSMS:** 604 ● **Aptitudes:** G4, V4, N5, S4, P4, Q4, K3, F3, M4, E5, C4 ● **Temperaments:** R ● **Physical:** Stg=L; Freq: R, H, I, E, N, D Occas: X ● **Work Env:** Noise=N; Occas: A ● **Salary:** 3 ● **Outlook:** 2

BENCH WORKER (optical goods) ● DOT #713.684-018 ● OES: 93998 ● Performs any combination of following activities to prepare plastic eyeglass frames for assembly, using bench-mounted machines and handtools or power tools: Drills or punches holes in frame components, using drill or punch press. Inserts and tightens screws, nuts, and bolts to assemble parts, using handtools. Inserts and expands rivets to assemble parts, using rivet gun. Aligns and miters frame part edges, using mitering machine. Cuts grooves in parts for insertion of lenses, using grooving machine. May be designated according to activity as Groover (optical goods). ● **GED:** R2, M1, L1 ● **SVP:** 1-3 mos ● **Academic:** Ed=N, Eng=N ● **Work Field:** 102 ● **MPSMS:** 605 ● **Aptitudes:** G4, V4, N4, S3, P4, Q5, K3, F3, M4, E4, C5 ● **Temperaments:** R ● **Physical:** Stg=L; Freq: R, H, I, N Occas: D, A ● **Work Env:** Noise=N; ● **Salary:** 1 ● **Outlook:** 3

BUFFER I (any industry) ● DOT #705.684-014 ● OES: 91117 ● Alternate titles: COLOR BUFFER. Buffs items, such as automobile trim or accessories, hardware, or fabricated plastic parts with cloth buffing wheel: Holds and moves parts against wheel to smooth surfaces, produce specified finish, or cut down plating defects, such as burns or salt deposits, using knowledge of metals and buffing operations. Coats buffing wheel by holding buffing compound stick against revolving wheel. Pushes and manipulates workpiece against buffing wheel to remove scratches and defects and produce specified finish, using knowledge of buffing operations and finishes. Replaces worn buffs, using wrench. Uses care not to cut through plate when buffing plated surfaces. May be designated according to type of material buffed as Buffer, Chrome (any industry); Buffer, Copper (any industry); Buffer, Nickel (any industry). May polish articles [POLISHER (any industry)] and buff articles and be designated Polisher And Buffer (any industry) I. May polish brass eye castings used in fitting wooden shuttles and clean castings in series of chemical solutions and be designated Strapper And Buffer (woodworking). ● **GED:** R2, M1, L2 ● **SVP:** 3-6 mos ● **Academic:** Ed=N, Eng=N ● **Work Field:** 051 ● **MPSMS:** 542, 556 ● **Aptitudes:** G3, V4, N4, S4, P3, Q4, K3, F3, M3, E5, C4 ● **Temperaments:** J, R, T ● **Physical:** Stg=M; Freq: R, H, I, N, A Occas: S, X ● **Work Env:** Noise=N; Occas: O ● **Salary:** 1 ● **Outlook:** 2

FILER (jewelry-silver.) ● DOT #700.684-034 ● OES: 93953 ● Alternate titles: FITTER; SHAPER. Trims and smooths edges, surfaces, and impressed or raised designs of jewelry articles and jewelry findings, using files, chisels, and saws: Places article in holding device or against bench pin. Files or cuts excess metal from surfaces and ornamentations, such as filigree or relief designs. Miters joints and ends of formed ring blanks, using file. May smooth and polish edges and soldered areas of jewelry, using abrasive wheel. May operate motor-driven filing machine. ● **GED:** R3, M1, L2 ● **SVP:** 1-3 mos ● **Academic:** Ed=N, Eng=N ● **Work Field:** 051, 057 ● **MPSMS:** 611 ● **Aptitudes:** G4, V4, N5, S3, P3, Q5, K3, F3, M3, E5, C4 ● **Temperaments:** R, T ● **Physical:** Stg=L; Freq: R, H, I, N Occas: X ● **Work Env:** Noise=N; ● **Salary:** 1 ● **Outlook:** 2

JIGSAWYER (jewelry-silver.) ● DOT #700.684-046 ● OES: 91117 ● Alternate titles: JIGSAW OPERATOR. Cuts out metal jewelry findings according to pattern, using jigsaw: Receives metal sheets with patterns cemented to tops, or prints patterns on printing press and cements onto metal sheets. Assembles several sheets into laminated block with oiled paper between layers to produce multiple findings in one cutting operation. Drills holes for saw blade, using drill press. Mounts blade on jigsaw, starts saw, and guides metal sheet against blade to cut along lines of pattern. ● **GED:** R2, M1, L1 ● **SVP:** 3-6 mos ● **Academic:** Ed=N, Eng=N ● **Work Field:** 056 ● **MPSMS:** 611 ● **Aptitudes:** G3, V4, N4, S4, P3, Q5, K3, F3, M3, E5, C5 ● **Temperaments:** R, T ● **Physical:** Stg=L; Freq: R, H, I, N ● **Work Env:** Noise=N; ● **Salary:** 3 ● **Outlook:** 2

MELTER (jewelry-silver.) ● DOT #700.687-042 ● OES: 93941 ● Melts gold, or gold and silver alloys, using furnace, electric heating unit, or torch, and pours molten metal into ingot molds to prepare metal for use in making jewelry: Places metal in clay crucible. Places crucible in preheated oven or heats crucible with torch to melt metal. Observes color changes in metals to ensure that specified temperature is attained. Pours molten metal into ingot mold. Opens mold, lifts out ingot with tongs, and quenches ingot in water. May operate roller machine to roll ingots into metal strips for use in stamping out jewelry blanks [ROLLER (jewelry-silver.)]. ● **GED:** R2, M1, L2 ● **SVP:** 2-30 days ● **Academic:** Ed=N, Eng=N ● **Work Field:** 131, 132 ● **MPSMS:** 541 ● **Aptitudes:** G4, V4, N4, S4, P4, Q5, K4, F4, M4, E5, C4 ● **Temperaments:** J, R, T ● **Physical:** Stg=M; Freq: R, H, N, X Occas: I ● **Work Env:** Noise=N; Freq: H Occas: M ● **Salary:** 3 ● **Outlook:** 2

METAL FINISHER (any industry) ● DOT #705.684-034 ● OES: 93953 ● Grinds, files, or sands surfaces of metal items, such as automobile bodies and household appliances, using handtools, power tools, and knowledge of metal finishing techniques: Examines and feels surface of metal to detect defects, such as dents, scratches, or breaks in metal. Removes dents, using hammer and dolly block, and fills uneven surface with molten solder. Smooths surface of item to specified finish, using handtools and powered tools. May polish metal surface, using powered polishing wheel or belt [POLISHER (any industry)]. ● **GED:** R2, M1, L2 ● **SVP:** 3-6 mos ● **Academic:** Ed=N, Eng=N ● **Work Field:** 051 ● **MPSMS:** 556, 583 ● **Aptitudes:** G4, V4, N4, S3, P3, Q4, K3, F4, M3, E5, C5 ● **Temperaments:** R, T ● **Physical:** Stg=L; Freq: R, H, N Occas: I, E, A ● **Work Env:** Noise=L; ● **Salary:** 3 ● **Outlook:** 2

MOLD DRESSER (any industry) ● DOT #519.684-018 ● OES: 93953 ● Alternate titles: MOLD REPAIRER. Removes residue, blemishes, corrosion, and similar defects from interior of molds, using handtools and power tools: Inspects interior surfaces of molds to locate pits and holes. Positions molds for work, using hoist. Repairs defects, using hammers, drills, chisels, routers, or grinding wheel. Smooths interior of mold, using file, buffing wheel, emery paper, or steelwool. May add metal to or remove metal from plates, rings, and molds, using welding equipment and files. May reassemble molds after repairing. May be designated according to type of mold repaired as Glass-Mold Repairer (glass mfg.). ● **GED:** R2, M1, L1 ● **SVP:** 3-6 mos ● **Academic:** Ed=N, Eng=N ● **Work Field:** 031, 102 ● **MPSMS:** 566 ● **Aptitudes:** G4, V4, N4, S4, P3, Q4, K3, F3, M3, E5, C5 ● **Temperaments:** R, T ● **Physical:** Stg=M; Freq: R, H, I, E, N, D ● **Work Env:** Noise=L; Freq: A, O ● **Salary:** 4 ● **Outlook:** 2

POLISHER (any industry) ● DOT #705.684-058 ● OES: 91117 ● Removes excess metal and surface defects from such items as hardware, small arms barrels, automobile trim, or accessory parts prior to buffing, bluing, or plating, using revolving abrasive wheel or belt: Selects abrasive belt or wheel according to grain size, type of finish specified, product being polished, or amount of metal to be removed, using knowledge of polishing operations and abrasives. Attaches wheel or belt to drive mechanism. Starts polisher and manipulates workpiece against abrasive wheel or portable wheel against workpiece to remove metal and surface defects. Examines part for acceptability of finish. May be designated according to type of material polished as Polisher, Aluminum (any industry); Polisher, Brass (any industry); Polisher, Bronze (any industry); Polisher, Zinc (any industry). ● **GED:** R3, M2, L2 ● **SVP:** 1-2 yrs ● **Academic:** Ed=N, Eng=N ● **Work Field:** 051 ● **MPSMS:** 550 ● **Aptitudes:** G3, V4, N4, S3, P3, Q4, K3, F3, M3, E5, C5 ● **Temperaments:** R, T ● **Physical:** Stg=M; Freq: R, H, I, N Occas: A ● **Work Env:** Noise=L; Occas: A ● **Salary:** 2 ● **Outlook:** 2

PREPARER (jewelry-silver.) ● DOT #700.687-062 ● OES: 93998 ● Alternate titles: BENCH HAND. Performs any combination of following tasks in preparing cast jewelry findings for further processing: Cuts, saws, or breaks off gates from jewelry castings, using shears, jeweler's saw, pliers, or foot press equipped with cutting tool. Removes burrs and smooths rough edges of casting, using file or grinding wheel. Straightens distorted castings, using foot press equipped with shaping dies. May remove plaster from castings by dipping castings in water and acid solution. May count and separate jewelry casting into containers, according to type, and marks containers with identifying information. May specialize in breaking off gates from jewelry castings and be designated Breaker-Off (jewelry-silver.). ● **GED:** R2, M1, L1 ● **SVP:** 2-30 days ● **Academic:** Ed=N, Eng=N ● **Work Field:** 054 ● **MPSMS:** 611 ● **Aptitudes:** G4, V4, N5, S4, P4, Q5, K4, F4, M4, E4, C5 ● **Temperaments:** R ● **Physical:** Stg=S; Freq: R, H Occas: I ● **Work Env:** Noise=N; ● **Salary:** 3 ● **Outlook:** 2

REFINER (protective dev.) ● DOT #712.684-038 ● OES: 93998 ● Recovers precious metals, such as gold, platinum, and palladium from scrap dentures and extracted teeth, using furnace, retort, and laboratory equipment: Breaks scrap dentures, using hammer, and removes precious metals. Weighs each type metal and records weights. Places metal in retort and positions retort in furnace to melt metal particles. Turns valves to adjust temperature of furnace. Removes retort and pours molten metal solution into beaker, using tongs. Adds specified amounts of chemicals to molten metal solution to separate metal from solution. Pours solution through filter to recover precious dental metals. ● **GED:** R3, M2, L2 ● **SVP:** 3-6 mos ● **Academic:** Ed=N, Eng=N ● **Work Field:** 145 ● **MPSMS:** 549, 604 ● **Aptitudes:** G3, V4, N4, S4, P3, Q4, K4, F4, M3, E5, C5 ● **Temperaments:** J, T ● **Physical:** Stg=L; Freq: R, H, N, D Occas: I ● **Work Env:** Noise=N; Freq: U, A Occas: H ● **Salary:** 5 ● **Outlook:** 2

GOE: 06.04.25
Manual Work, Wood

CANER II (furniture) ● DOT #763.684-022 ● OES: 85998 ● Installs or replaces prewoven panels of cane, willow, or rattan in furniture frames: Cuts damaged panel from furniture frame, using knife. Pries wooden splines from grooves in frame, using chisel. Places frame in water to soften dried glue and adhering panel of cane or willow, and scrapes surfaces clean. Brushes glue into grooves around frame opening and stretches water-soaked panel over opening. Forces edges of panel into grooves, using wedge and mallet or pneumatic press. Brushes glue over panel edges in grooves, and forces splines into grooves flush with surface. Trims excess material, using knife. May cut prewoven panels to size, using pattern and scissors or cutting machine. ● **GED:** R2, M1, L1 ● **SVP:** 1-3 mos ● **Academic:** Ed=N, Eng=N ● **Work Field:** 102 ● **MPSMS:** 461, 462 ● **Aptitudes:** G4, V4, N4, S4, P4, Q4, K4, F4, M3, E5, C5 ● **Temperaments:** R, T ● **Physical:** Stg=L; Const: R, H, I Freq: N Occas: S, E, G ● **Work Env:** Noise=N; Occas: U ● **Salary:** 1 ● **Outlook:** 2

CROSSBAND LAYER (millwork-plywood) ● DOT #762.687-026 ● OES: 98998 ● Alternate titles: CORE LAYER, PLYWOOD; GLUE SPREADER HELPER. Stacks glued crossbands alternately with core stock to assemble plywood panels for bonding, working as member of team: Grasps glue-coated crossbands as they emerge from glue spreader and places them cross-grained between back sheet, core stock, and face sheet placed by VENEER-STOCK LAYER (millwork-plywood) 762.687-066 until specified ply is obtained. Discards broken crossbands. Pushes assembled panels down conveyor to hot-plate press for bonding into plywood. May assist GLUE SPREADER, VENEER (millwork-plywood; wood prod., nec) 569.685-042 to clean rollers of glue spreader. May brush glue on irregularly

shaped veneer sheets that will not fit in glue spreader. May assemble 3-ply panels alone, laying back sheet, glued core or inner sheet, and face sheet in sequence, and be designated Plywood Builder (millwork-plywood). ● **GED:** R2, M1, L1 ● **SVP:** 2-30 days ● **Academic:** Ed=N, Eng=N ● **Work Field:** 063 ● **MPSMS:** 453 ● **Aptitudes:** G4, V4, N4, S4, P4, Q5, K3, F4, M3, E5, C5 ● **Temperaments:** R ● **Physical:** Stg=M; Const: R, H Freq: S, N Occas: I, G, D ● **Work Env:** Noise=L; Freq: A ● **Salary:** 2 ● **Outlook:** 3

WOODWORKING-SHOP HAND (woodworking) ● DOT #769.687-054 ● OES: 98998 ● Alternate titles: MILL LABORER; WOODWORKING-SHOP LABORER. Performs any combination of following duties to facilitate cutting, finishing, storing, cleaning, and shipping wood products, and inspects products prior to shipment: Stacks lumber or wood products on floor or in bins to supply machine operators or assemblers, or in kiln cars, yard, or shed for storage or seasoning. Places sticks between lumber to permit air circulation, and binds stacks together during seasoning. Hammers shaped steel bands into timbers and railroad ties to prevent splitting during seasoning and inserts bolts or metal dowels through split timbers to hold parts together. Dismantles crates and removes nails and other metal from wooden parts to salvage material, using handtools. Applies filler, putty, or other material, using brush, putty knife, and fingers to fill wood pores, holes, cracks, or other indentations. Removes paint, lacquer, and other finishes from wood products, using solvent, steel wool, brush, and cloths, and sands rough spots, using sandpaper or sanding machine, to prepare surfaces for finishing. Traces patterns on lumber stock as guide for machine operator. Attaches articles to wires, cord, or hooks preparatory to dipping. Dips article into vats to coat them with paint, asphalt, or other ingredients. Marks furniture surfaces with crayon or rough-edged object to simulate antique finish. Brushes surfaces with glue preparatory to covering surfaces with leather, paper, or other materials. Nails together lumber for cutting, and places lumber on machine table. Examines materials and products for defects, finish, and grade, and accuracy of dimension and matching panels, using measuring instruments. Stamps grade on product and weighs and records units processed and inspected. Changes cutterheads and blades, adjusts belts, and performs other duties as instructed to facilitate setting up woodworking machines. Loads and unloads materials from railroad cars, trucks and barges by hand, using handtruck or industrial truck to move material to designated areas. Cleans cars and trucks and lines them with paper preparatory to loading. ● **GED:** R2, M1, L1 ● **SVP:** 2-30 days ● **Academic:** Ed=N, Eng=N ● **Work Field:** 102, 212 ● **MPSMS:** 460, 450 ● **Aptitudes:** G4, V4, N4, S4, P3, Q4, K4, F4, M3, E4, C4 ● **Temperaments:** R, T ● **Physical:** Stg=V; Freq: S, O, R, H, N, D, A Occas: I, G, X ● **Work Env:** Noise=L; Freq: A, M, T ● **Salary:** 1 ● **Outlook:** 3

GOE: 06.04.26
Manual Work, Paper

LABEL CODER (any industry) ● DOT #920.587-014 ● OES: 98998 ● Alternate titles: LABEL MARKER. Cuts notches in container or bottle labels to indicate data, such as type, batch, date, and destination of product, following predetermined code: Turns setscrews to space and lock blades of notching device according to coding guide, using ruler. Clamps stack of labels on bed of notching device and pushes bed forward to force labels against blades. Prepares label-coding report. May insert or remove symbols, using tweezers to set up carton-coding wheels. May wash defective labels from bottles. ● **GED:** R2, M1, L1 ● **SVP:** 2-30 days ● **Academic:** Ed=N, Eng=N ● **Work Field:** 054 ● **MPSMS:** 470 ● **Aptitudes:** G4, V4, N4, S4, P4, Q4, K4, F3, M4, E5, C5 ● **Temperaments:** R, T ● **Physical:** Stg=L; Freq: R, H, I, N, D Occas: C, S ● **Work Env:** Noise=L; ● **Salary:** 1 ● **Outlook:** 3

GOE: 06.04.27
Manual Work, Textile, Fabric, & Leather

BOW MAKER (any industry) ● DOT #789.684-010 ● OES: 93998 ● Forms ornamental bows for hair or dress wear, by hand: Winds length of ribbon on rack to form bows. Cuts ribbon into sections with scissors and ties folds together at middle with twine to form bow. Inserts bobby pin or safety pin through twine, and removes bows from rack. Arranges artificial flower or lace medallion on bow as specified, and ties them together with twine or ribbon. May sew comb attachment to middle section of underside of bow, using needle and thread. ● **GED:** R2, M1, L2 ● **SVP:** 1-3 mos ● **Academic:** Ed=N, Eng=N ● **Work Field:** 062 ● **MPSMS:** 618 ● **Aptitudes:** G4, V4, N4, S4, P4, Q5, K4, F3, M4, E5, C5 ● **Temperaments:** R, T ● **Physical:** Stg=L; Const: R, H, I Occas: N, D ● **Work Env:** Noise=N; ● **Salary:** 3 ● **Outlook:** 2

CANVAS REPAIRER (any industry) ● DOT #782.684-010 ● OES: 85998 ● Repairs damaged or worn tent, awning, or other canvas articles: Spreads canvas on worktable and examines it for holes, tears, and worn areas. Trims edges of damaged area, using scissors or knife. Patches holes, sews tears, or darns defective area, using needle and thread or sewing machine. Stamps grommets into edges of canvas, using mallet and punch or eyelet machine. May repair leatherette fabrics. May measure structures for canvas coverings, using tape measure. ● **GED:** R2, M1, L1 ● **SVP:** 3-6 mos ● **Academic:** Ed=N, Eng=N ● **Work Field:** 171 ● **MPSMS:** 436 ● **Aptitudes:** G4, V4, N4, S4, P3, Q5, K3, F3, M3, E4, C4 ● **Temperaments:** R, T ● **Physical:** Stg=H; Freq: R, H, I, N, D Occas: X ● **Work Env:** Noise=L; ● **Salary:** 2 ● **Outlook:** 2

CARPET CUTTER II (carpet & rug) ● DOT #585.687-014 ● OES: 93998 ● Cuts specified lengths from continuous roll of carpet, using power cut-off knife or long-handled cutting blade. May cut felt padding to specified lengths and be designated Felt-Pad Cutter (tex. prod., nec). ● **GED:** R2, M1, L1 ● **SVP:** 1-3 mos ● **Academic:** Ed=N, Eng=N ● **Work Field:** 054 ● **MPSMS:** 430 ● **Aptitudes:** G4, V4, N4, S4, P4, Q4, K4, F4, M3, E5, C5 ● **Temperaments:** R ● **Physical:** Stg=L; Freq: S, K, R, H, N, D ● **Work Env:** Noise=N; ● **Salary:** 2 ● **Outlook:** 2

SEWER, HAND (any industry) ● DOT #782.684-058 ● OES: 93923 ● Alternate titles: ASSEMBLER; BANDER; BAND SEWER; GARMENT FINISHER; GARMENT SEWER, HAND; HAND STITCHER; HAND TACKER; NEEDLEWORKER; TABLE WORKER, SEWING; TRIMMER. Joins and reinforces parts of articles, such as garments, curtains, parachutes, stuffed toys, or sews buttonholes and attaches fasteners to articles, or sews decorative trimmings to articles, using needle and thread: Selects thread, according to specifications or color of parts. Aligns parts, fasteners, or trimmings, following seams, edges, or markings on parts. Sews parts with various types of stitches, such as felling tacking, stitch and basting. Trims excess threads, using scissors or knife. May trim edges of parts, using scissors. When sewing fasteners or trimmings to articles, may be designated Finisher, Hand (garment). May be designated according to stitch sewn as Baster, Hand (garment); Feller, Hand (garment). May be designated according to article or part sewn as Armhole Baster, Hand (garment); Bow Attacher (garment); Bow Tacker (hat & cap) I; Buttonhole Maker, Hand (garment); Buttonhole Tacker (garment); Button Sewer, Hand (garment); Collar Feller (garment). May be designated: Collar Tacker (garment); Drapery Sewer, Hand (tex. prod., nec); Dressmaker (garment); Edge Maker (garment); Hook-And-Eye Attacher (garment); Label Sewer, Hand (any industry); Lapel Baster (garment); Lapel Padder (garment); Lining Finisher (garment); Neck Feller (garment); Sleeve Baster (garment); Sleeve-Bottom Feller (garment); Tacker (garment); Top-Collar Baster (garment); Trimming Finisher (garment). ● **GED:** R2, M1, L1 ● **SVP:** 1-3 mos ● **Academic:** Ed=N, Eng=N ● **Work Field:** 171 ● **MPSMS:** 440, 439, 435 ● **Aptitudes:** G4, V4, N4, S4, P4, Q5, K3, F2, M3, E5, C4 ● **Temperaments:** J, R, T ● **Physical:** Stg=L; Const: R, H, I, N Freq: A, X Occas: G ● **Work Env:** Noise=N; ● **Salary:** 2 ● **Outlook:** 3

THREAD CUTTER (any industry) ● DOT #789.684-050 ● OES: 93926 ● Alternate titles: TRIMMING-MACHINE OPERATOR. Trims loose threads from edges or seams of articles, such as garments, hats, linens, and surgical appliances, using either of following methods: (1) Moves edges or seams of article over stationary cutting head equipped with vacuum attachment that draws threads between reciprocal blades to cut threads. (2) Spreads article on table or pulls article over form and guides electric hand clippers equipped with vacuum hose along edges or seams of article to cut threads. When trimming knitted garments, pulls loose threads through several stitches with latch needle or ties

threads from converging seams to secure stitching. May cut short or thick threads unsuitable for machine cutting, using scissors. ● **GED:** R2, M1, L1 ● **SVP:** 2-30 days ● **Academic:** Ed=N, Eng=N ● **Work Field:** 054 ● **MPSMS:** 420, 440, 604 ● **Aptitudes:** G4, V4, N5, S4, P4, Q5, K4, F4, M3, E5, C4 ● **Temperaments:** R ● **Physical:** Stg=L; Freq: R, H, N Occas: S, I, E, X ● **Work Env:** Noise=L; ● **Salary:** 2 ● **Outlook:** 2

GOE: 06.04.28
Manual Work, Food Processing

BONER, MEAT (meat products) ● DOT #525.684-010 ● OES: 93938 ● Alternate titles: RIBBER. Cuts bones from standard cuts of meat, such as chucks, hams, loins, plates, rounds, and shanks to prepare meat for packing and marketing, using knife and meat hook: Inserts knife in meat around bones to separate meat, fat, or tissue. Pulls and twists bones loose from meat. Cuts and trims such meat cuts as butts, hams, flanks, and shoulders to shape meat and remove fat and defects. Trims meat from bones and ribs. May pull bones and skin from cooked pigs feet, and cut out toe bones and nails. May be designated according to cut of meat boned as Blade Boner (meat products); Chuck Boner (meat products); Ham Boner (meat products); or type of animal boned as Beef Boner (meat products); Hog Ribber (meat products); Sheep Boner (meat products). May be designated: Loin Boner (meat products); Plate Boner (meat products); Rib Boner (meat products); Round Boner (meat products); Shank Boner (meat products); Shoulder Boner (meat products). ● **GED:** R2, M1, L2 ● **SVP:** 3-6 mos ● **Academic:** Ed=N, Eng=N ● **Work Field:** 034 ● **MPSMS:** 382 ● **Aptitudes:** G4, V4, N5, S3, P3, Q5, K3, F3, M3, E5, C4 ● **Temperaments:** R, T ● **Physical:** Stg=M; Const: R, H Freq: I, N Occas: E, D, A, X ● **Work Env:** Noise=Q; Freq: C, U ● **Salary:** 2 ● **Outlook:** 3

BUTCHER, FISH (can. & preserv.) ● DOT #525.684-014 ● OES: 93938 ● Butchers eviscerated frozen, fresh, and salted fish for marketing or further processing: Dumps containers of fish into fresh water tank for cleaning. Places cleaned fish on table or bench. Trims off fins and tails, removes skin, and cuts fish into pieces of specified size, using knife or bandsaw. Sorts pieces according to color and texture. ● **GED:** R1, M1, L1 ● **SVP:** 2-30 days ● **Academic:** Ed=N, Eng=N ● **Work Field:** 034 ● **MPSMS:** 331 ● **Aptitudes:** G4, V4, N5, S4, P4, Q5, K3, F4, M3, E5, C3 ● **Temperaments:** R ● **Physical:** Stg=H; Const: R, H Freq: S, O, I, N, A Occas: D, X ● **Work Env:** Noise=Q; Freq: U, A ● **Salary:** 2 ● **Outlook:** 3

CANDY DIPPER, HAND (sugar & conf.) ● DOT #524.684-010 ● OES: 93947 ● Dips candy centers, fruit, or nuts into coatings to coat, decorate, and identify product: Scoops liquid coating material onto slab of heated dipping table and kneads material, such as chocolate, fondant, or icing to attain specified consistency. Drops candy into mass and swirls candy about until thoroughly coated, using fingers or fork. Removes candy and marks identifying design or symbol on top, using fingers or fork, to identify type of center or brand. May decorate top of candy with nuts, coconut, or other garnishment. May mix coating ingredients and dip candy into vat containing coating material, regulating vat temperature to maintain specified consistency. May pour liquid chocolate into molds to form figures [CANDY MOLDER, HAND (sugar & conf.)]. May be designated according to type of center dipped as Bonbon Dipper (sugar & conf.); Cherry Dipper (sugar & conf.); Cream Dipper (sugar & conf.); Pecan-Mallow Dipper (sugar & conf.); or according to type of coating as Chocolate Coater (sugar & conf.); Icing Coater (sugar & conf.). ● **GED:** R2, M1, L1 ● **SVP:** 3-6 mos ● **Academic:** Ed=N, Eng=N ● **Work Field:** 151 ● **MPSMS:** 393 ● **Aptitudes:** G4, V4, N5, S4, P3, Q5, K3, F3, M3, E5, C4 ● **Temperaments:** R, T ● **Physical:** Stg=L; Freq: R, H, N Occas: I, X ● **Work Env:** Noise=Q; ● **Salary:** 2 ● **Outlook:** 2

DECORATOR (bakery products) ● DOT #524.684-014 ● OES: 93947 ● Alternate titles: DECORATOR, HAND; ORNAMENTER. Decorates confectionery products with chocolate, colored icings, or pastry cream: Screws nozzle of specified size and shape into outlet of decorating bag. Fills bag with icing, chocolate, or pastry cream. Squeezes bag to force material through nozzle, forming decorations, such as lines, letters, figures, or flowers. May mix, cook, and color decorating material. May spread material with brush, fingers, pronged instrument, or spatula. May fill molds with icing to form decorations, such as bells, birds, and bootees. May be designated according to product decorated as Candy Decorator (sugar & conf.). ● **GED:** R2, M1, L1 ● **SVP:** 1-3 mos ● **Academic:** Ed=N, Eng=N ● **Work Field:** 146 ● **MPSMS:** 384, 393 ● **Aptitudes:** G4, V4, N4, S3, P3, Q4, K3, F3, M2, E5, C3 ● **Temperaments:** R, T ● **Physical:** Stg=L; Freq: R, H, I, N Occas: A, X ● **Work Env:** Noise=Q; ● **Salary:** 2 ● **Outlook:** 2

FISH CLEANER (can. & preserv.) ● DOT #525.684-030 ● OES: 93938 ● Alternate titles: DRESS-GANG WORKER; FISH CUTTER; FISH DRESSER. Cleans fish aboard ship or ashore, performing any combination of following tasks, alone or as member of crew: Scrapes scales from fish with knife. Cuts or rips fish from vent to throat with knife, and tears out viscera and gills. Cuts off head of fish with knife, drops head in tub, and slides fish along table to next worker. Washes blood from abdominal cavity by dropping fish in tub of water or by use of hose, and removes discolored membrane from abdomen lining with knife, spoon, scraper, glove, or piece of burlap. Cuts gashes along sides of fish to facilitate salt penetration during curing. Cuts fish behind gill slits, draws knife along backbone and ribs to free fillet (boneless portion of flesh), lays fillet skinside down on table, and draws knife laterally between skin and flesh to remove skin. Slices flesh from bones in fletches (longitudinal quarter sections) for further processing into boneless slices of fish. Unloads catch from fishing vessels [LABORER, WHARF (can. & preserv.) 922.687-062]. May pack fish in containers. May remove slime from fish preparatory to canning and be designated Slimer (can. & preserv.; fishing & hunt.). May clean, dress, wrap, label, and store fish for guests at resort establishments and be designated Fish Housekeeper (hotel & rest.). May fillet fish and be designated Fish Filleter (can. & preserv.; fishing & hunt.). ● **GED:** R1, M1, L1 ● **SVP:** 2-30 days ● **Academic:** Ed=N, Eng=N ● **Work Field:** 034 ● **MPSMS:** 331 ● **Aptitudes:** G4, V4, N4, S3, P4, Q5, K3, F3, M3, E5, C4 ● **Temperaments:** R ● **Physical:** Stg=M; Const: R, H, I, N Freq: S, D, X ● **Work Env:** Noise=Q; Const: U, A ● **Salary:** 1 ● **Outlook:** 2

POULTRY BONER (meat products) ● DOT #525.687-066 ● OES: 93938 ● Cuts, scrapes and pulls meat from cooked poultry carcasses, using fingers and boning knife: Pulls wings and drumsticks from carcasses. Cuts along each side of breast plate, using knife, and peels meat from breast, using hands. Pulls and scrapes meat from rest of carcass, using knife and hands. Segregates light and dark meat into separate piles. Discards wastes, such as skin, bones, and gristle, into waste containers. ● **GED:** R1, M1, L1 ● **SVP:** 2-30 days ● **Academic:** Ed=N, Eng=N ● **Work Field:** 034 ● **MPSMS:** 324 ● **Aptitudes:** G4, V4, N4, S4, P4, Q4, K4, F3, M3, E5, C4 ● **Temperaments:** R ● **Physical:** Stg=L; Const: R, H, I ● **Work Env:** Noise=N; ● **Salary:** 2 ● **Outlook:** 3

POULTRY DRESSER (agriculture) ● DOT #525.687-070 ● OES: 93938 ● Alternate titles: TIPPER. Slaughters and dresses fowl in preparation for marketing, performing any combination of following tasks: Chops off bird's head or slits bird's throat to slaughter bird, using knife. Hangs bird by feet to drain blood. Dips bird into scalding water to loosen feathers. Holds bird against projecting rubber fingers of rotating drum to remove feathers. Cuts bird open, removes viscera, and washes bird and giblets. May pluck chickens by hand. May be designated according to type of fowl dressed as Chicken Dresser (meat products); Turkey Dresser (meat products). May be known according to specific duties performed as Poultry Picker (meat products); Poultry Scalder (meat products). ● **GED:** R1, M1, L1 ● **SVP:** 2-30 days ● **Academic:** Ed=N, Eng=N ● **Work Field:** 034 ● **MPSMS:** 324 ● **Aptitudes:** G4, V4, N5, S4, P4, Q5, K4, F4, M3, E5, C5 ● **Temperaments:** R ● **Physical:** Stg=L; Const: R, H Freq: N ● **Work Env:** Noise=N; Const: U, A ● **Salary:** 2 ● **Outlook:** 3

TIER (meat products) ● DOT #525.687-118 ● OES: 98902 ● Alternate titles: ROAST TIER. Rolls and ties cuts of meat to form roasts: Places cut of meat on table and rolls meat into circular shape. Forces skewer threaded with twine through roll of meat at various points to hold roll in place. Knots and cuts twine. ● **GED:** R1, M1, L1 ● **SVP:** 2-30 days ● **Academic:** Ed=N, Eng=N ● **Work Field:** 146 ● **MPSMS:** 382 ● **Aptitudes:** G4, V4, N4, S4, P4, Q4, K4, F3, M3, E5, C5 ● **Temperaments:** R ● **Physical:** Stg=L; Freq: R, H ● **Work Env:** Noise=N; ● **Salary:** 2 ● **Outlook:** 3

TRIMMER, MEAT (meat products) ● DOT #525.684-054 ● OES: 93938 ● Trims fat, skin, tendons, tissues, and ragged edges from meat

cuts, such as loins, spareribs, butts, hams, rounds, sirloins, fillets, and chops, using meat-hook and knife: Trims meat and fat from bones and places trimmings and bones in separate containers. Trims fatback from hog bellies and cuts bellies into specified shapes, using knife. Feeds bacon bellies through rolls to flatten bellies to prescribed thickness. May wash or scrape dirt and blood from meat. May be designated according to section of meat trimmed as Belly Trimmer (meat products); Butt Trimmer (meat products); Fatback Trimmer (meat products); Loin Trimmer (meat products); Spareribs Trimmer (meat products). ● **GED:** R1, M1, L1 ● **SVP:** 2-30 days ● **Academic:** Ed=N, Eng=N ● **Work Field:** 034 ● **MPSMS:** 382 ● **Aptitudes:** G4, V4, N5, S4, P4, Q5, K3, F3, M3, E5, C4 ● **Temperaments:** R, T ● **Physical:** Stg=M; Const: R, H, N, A Freq: I Occas: D, X ● **Work Env:** Noise=N; Occas: C, U ● **Salary:** 2 ● **Outlook:** 3

GOE: 06.04.30
Manual Work, Stone, Glass & Clay

GLASS FINISHER (glass products) ● DOT #775.684-026 ● OES: 93926 ● Cuts and finishes plate glass to make variety of glass products: Lays out pattern on plate glass and cuts it, using glasscutter. Holds glass against series of rotating grinding and polishing wheels to bevel and polish edges. Sprays silver solution on glass to provide mirrored surface, using spray gun. Assembles glass pieces to make various novelties. May lay out design or monogram on glass and sandblast surface within guidelines, using sandblasting tool. ● **GED:** R3, M2, L2 ● **SVP:** 6 mos-1 yr ● **Academic:** Ed=N, Eng=N ● **Work Field:** 054, 051 ● **MPSMS:** 531 ● **Aptitudes:** G3, V4, N4, S3, P3, Q5, K3, F4, M3, E5, C5 ● **Temperaments:** R, T ● **Physical:** Stg=L; Freq: R, H, I, N, D Occas: E ● **Work Env:** Noise=N; Freq: O ● **Salary:** 3 ● **Outlook:** 2

GOE: 06.04.31
Manual Work, Welding & Flame Cutting

WELDER, GUN (welding) ● DOT #810.664-010 ● OES: 93914 ● Alternate titles: SPOT WELDER, LINE; SPOT WELDER, BODY ASSEMBLY. Welds or tack-welds overlapping edges of positioned components to fabricate sheet metal assemblies, such as panels, refrigerator shells, and automobile bodies, using portable spot-welding gun: Positions and clamps electrode under overlapping edges of workpiece. Presses electrode against workpiece at specified weld points to complete circuit between electrodes and heat metal to joining temperature. Removes electrode after specified period of time. May adjust equipment for automatic timing of current. May periodically attend group meetings to learn new or modified tasks. May position and clamp workpieces together. May examine welded components to detect defects. ● **GED:** R2, M2, L2 ● **SVP:** 2-30 days ● **Academic:** Ed=N, Eng=N ● **Work Field:** 081 ● **MPSMS:** 540, 554, 591 ● **Aptitudes:** G4, V4, N4, S4, P4, Q4, K3, F3, M3, E5, C4 ● **Temperaments:** R, T ● **Physical:** Stg=M; Freq: C, R, H, I, N, D, A Occas: S, O, T, G, X ● **Work Env:** Noise=L; Const: A Freq: M, E ● **Salary:** 3 ● **Outlook:** 3

GOE: 06.04.32
Manual Work, Casting & Molding

CANDLEMAKER (fabrication, nec) ● DOT #739.664-010 ● OES: 92999 ● Forms candles according to one of following methods: (1) Strings wicks through notches or rings of dipping frame, according to length of candle to be formed. Dips wicks manually or with aid of motorized mechanism into vat of molten wax mixture to build up candles to specified circumference. Cuts or trims candles to specified sizes, using knife or hand die. Grades candles according to type, color, and size. (2) Inserts wick through center of molds and attaches ends to racks. Pours molten wax mixture into molds, using container or opens valves to admit wax into molds. Adjusts steam and coolant valves to maintain prescribed thermometer reading in mold. Turns handcrank of ejection mechanism to release candles from molds into rack after specified time. Scrapes remaining wax from molds, using handtools. May record production data, such as name, color, and quantity of candles. May add color ingredients to molten wax, according to specifications. ● **GED:** R2, M1, L1 ● **SVP:** 3-6 mos ● **Academic:** Ed=N, Eng=N ● **Work Field:** 136, 054 ● **MPSMS:** 619 ● **Aptitudes:** G3, V4, N4, S4, P4, Q4, K3, F3, M3, E5, C3 ● **Temperaments:** R, T ● **Physical:** Stg=M; Freq: R, H, I, N, D, X Occas: E ● **Work Env:** Noise=N; ● **Salary:** 3 ● **Outlook:** 3

MOLD MAKER (smelt. & refin.) ● DOT #518.664-010 ● OES: 93941 ● Forms molds used in casting copper: Assembles metal casting frame on flat car, using wrench. Seals frame with fire clay, using trowel, and sprays interior of frame and core with bone ash to prevent adherence of molten metal to core. Pushes car under pouring spout of ladle. Moves lever to tilt ladle of molten copper and fill frame to indicated level. Pulls lever to lower core, attached to hydraulic press ram, to imbed core in molten copper. Turns valve to circulate water through core to solidify copper. Withdraws core when mold cools, dismantles frame, and removes mold. ● **GED:** R2, M1, L2 ● **SVP:** 3-6 mos ● **Academic:** Ed=N, Eng=N ● **Work Field:** 132 ● **MPSMS:** 541 ● **Aptitudes:** G4, V4, N4, S4, P4, Q5, K3, F4, M3, E5, C5 ● **Temperaments:** R, T ● **Physical:** Stg=M; Freq: R, H Occas: S, K, O, I, E ● **Work Env:** Noise=L; Freq: A, O ● **Salary:** 3 ● **Outlook:** 3

SEMICONDUCTOR PROCESSOR (electron. comp.) ● DOT #590.684-022 ● OES: 92902 ● Performs any combination of following tasks to process materials used in manufacture of electronic semiconductors: Saws, breaks, cleans, and weighs semiconductor materials to prepare materials for crystal growing. Forms seed crystal for crystal growing, using x-ray equipment, drill, and sanding machine. Loads semiconductor material, seed crystal, and dopant into crystal growing furnace and monitors furnace to grow crystal ingot of specified characteristics. Grinds ingot to attain specified diameter and cylindricity, using grinding machine. Locates crystal axis of ingot, using x-ray equipment, and grinds flat on ingot. Saws ingot into wafers, using power saw. Etches, laps, polishes, and heat treats wafers to produce wafers of specified thickness and finish, using etching equipment, lapping and polishing machines, and furnace. Cleans materials, seed crystals, ingots, and wafers, using cleaning, etching, and sandblasting equipment. Inspects materials, ingots, and wafers for surface defects. Measures dimensions of ingots and wafers, using precision measuring instruments. Tests electrical characteristics of materials, ingots, and wafers, using electrical test equipment. ● **GED:** R2, M2, L2 ● **SVP:** 1-3 mos ● **Academic:** Ed=N, Eng=N ● **Work Field:** 147, 057, 212 ● **MPSMS:** 587 ● **Aptitudes:** G3, V4, N4, S4, P3, Q4, K4, F4, M3, E5, C5 ● **Temperaments:** R, T ● **Physical:** Stg=M; Freq: R, H, I, N, D Occas: G ● **Work Env:** Noise=N; Occas: M, T ● **Salary:** 3 ● **Outlook:** 4

GOE: 06.04.33
Manual Work, Brushing, Spraying, & Coating

PAINTER, BRUSH (any industry) ● DOT #740.684-022 ● OES: 93947 ● Alternate titles: PAINTER, HAND. Brushes paint, lacquer, rustproofing agent, or other coating onto metal, woodstock, or fabricated items, using brush: Places workpiece on bench, stanchion, or floor. Cleans surfaces, using hand scraper, wire brush, sandpaper, or turpentine. Pours desired amount of thinner into paint. Paints articles, using brush. Cleans brushes and floor, using solvent or soap and water. May transfer items to and from work area, using hoist or handtruck. May be designated according to article painted as Last-Code Striper (wood prod., nec); Painter, Drum (any industry); Painter, Mannequin (fabrication, nec); Pipe Coater (steel & rel.); or according to coating applied as Japanner (any industry); Lacquerer (machine shop); Car Varnisher (railroad equip.). ● **GED:** R2, M1, L1 ● **SVP:** 2-30 days ● **Academic:** Ed=N, Eng=N ● **Work Field:** 153 ● **MPSMS:** 495 ● **Aptitudes:** G4, V4, N4, S4, P4, Q5, K4, F4, M3, E5, C4 ● **Temperaments:** R, T ● **Physical:** Stg=M; Freq: S, R, H, N, D Occas: K, O, X ● **Work Env:** Noise=L; ● **Salary:** 3 ● **Outlook:** 3

PUTTY GLAZER (any industry) ● DOT #749.684-042 ● OES: 93947 ● Applies coating of putty, mastic, or similar material to imperfections in manufactured articles, preparatory to application of paint or other final coating: Inspects surface of article for defects, such as holes, cracks, and indentations. Spreads material over flaws, using dauber or knife, and brushes or spreads thinned putty or sealer over surface to conceal blemish. May spray article with prescribed coating, using spray gun. May prepare surface for finishing coat, using wire brushes, sandpaper, power grinder, or sandblasting equipment. May tend oven to bake article before or after application of final coating. May be designated according to article coated as Wheel Filler (auto. mfg.). ● **GED:** R2, M1, L1 ● **SVP:** 1-3 mos ● **Academic:** Ed=N, Eng=N ● **Work Field:** 094 ● **MPSMS:** 495 ● **Aptitudes:** G4, V4, N5, S4, P3, Q5, K3, F4, M3, E5, C5 ● **Temperaments:** R, T ● **Physical:** Stg=M; Freq: R, H, I, N, D ● **Work Env:** Noise=N; ● **Salary:** 1 ● **Outlook:** 2

GOE: 06.04.34
Manual Work, Assorted Materials

ARTIFICIAL-FLOWER MAKER (button & notion) ● DOT #739.684-014 ● OES: 93997 ● Alternate titles: FLOWER ARRANGER; FOLIAGE ARRANGER. Cuts out and assembles materials, such as fabric, wood, and paper, performing any combination of following tasks to make artificial foliage, such as flowers, wreaths, and trees: Cuts out flower parts, such as leaves and petals from paper, fabric, or plastic, using handtools, such as scissors, knives, hammers, and dies. Stamps out flower parts with hand-operated or power-driven machine. Places roll of material on spindle of machine that automatically forms artificial-flower stems. Prints veining on artificial leaves, using stamps and handpress. Dips flowers into specified dye and squeezes out excess dye, using hands. Fastens twigs and buds to steel wire to form branches by hand or using twisting machine. Wires or glues flower parts to stem or branch. Fastens artificial flowers and foliage to wreath stand and inserts cones and grass decorations to form artificial wreath. May wrap stems with green and brown paper to effect natural appearance. May be designated according to product produced as Wreath And Garland Maker, Hand (button & notion); or shape artificial flower petals from fabric, using tweezers, heated metal ball, and wooden form, and be designated Petal Shaper, Hand (button & notion). ● **GED:** R2, M1, L1 ● **SVP:** 1-3 mos ● **Academic:** Ed=N, Eng=N ● **Work Field:** 102 ● **MPSMS:** 618 ● **Aptitudes:** G4, V4, N4, S3, P3, Q4, K3, F3, M3, E5, C3 ● **Temperaments:** R, T ● **Physical:** Stg=L; Freq: R, H, I, N, D, A, X Occas: S ● **Work Env:** Noise=L; ● **Salary:** 2 ● **Outlook:** 3

DRILLER, HAND (any industry) ● DOT #809.684-018 ● OES: 92100 ● Alternate titles: DRILLER, PORTABLE. Drills rivet or bolt holes in material, such as metal, wood, or plastic, following layout marks and using portable power drill: Punches indentations along layout marks to guide drill bit, using center punch and hammer. Fastens specified drill bit in chuck of drill. Drills holes, replaces drill bit with specified reamer, tap, or countersink and enlarges, threads, or countersinks holes. Sharpens cutting tools, using power grinder. May align offcenter holes in structural members, using drift pins, and bolt members together, using wrench. ● **GED:** R2, M1, L1 ● **SVP:** 2-30 days ● **Academic:** Ed=N, Eng=N ● **Work Field:** 053 ● **MPSMS:** 610, 594, 593 ● **Aptitudes:** G4, V4, N4, S4, P3, Q5, K4, F4, M3, E5, C5 ● **Temperaments:** J, T ● **Physical:** Stg=M; Freq: R, H, I, N, D Occas: C, S, K, O, A ● **Work Env:** Noise=L; Freq: M ● **Salary:** 4 ● **Outlook:** 2

ELECTRONICS UTILITY WORKER (comm. equip.) ● DOT #726.364-018 ● OES: 93905 ● Alternate titles: SETUP WORKER, ELECTRONICS. Arranges layout of work stations for workers engaged in fabricating, processing, or assembling electronic equipment and components, such as semiconductor devices, printed circuit boards (PCB's), chassis assemblies, and wire harnesses and cables: Reads specifications, such as process guide, bill of material, wiring diagram, mechanical print, and schematic diagram, to determine materials and equipment needed, such as component parts, chemicals and gases, tools, test instruments, and jigs and fixtures, for work stations. Prepares and submits requisitions for equipment, parts, or tools required to initially set up or resupply work stations. Positions materials and equipment in specified arrangement at work stations. May explain or demonstrate work procedures to other workers in fabricating, processing, and assembly functions. May perform fabricating, processing, or assembly work in absence of line worker. May set and adjust controls for processing, fabricating, and assembly line equipment, such as furnaces, process chambers, power supplies, timers, and multimeters. May test assemblies, using testing machines or instruments, such as meters, resistance bridges, and automatic component testers. May repair or rework assembled items by removing, adding, or replacing parts or resoldering or rebonding defective connections, using handtools or power tools. ● **GED:** R3, M2, L3 ● **SVP:** 6 mos-1 yr ● **Academic:** Ed=N, Eng=N ● **Work Field:** 111, 221 ● **MPSMS:** 587 ● **Aptitudes:** G3, V3, N3, S3, P3, Q3, K4, F4, M3, E5, C4 ● **Temperaments:** T ● **Physical:** Stg=L; Freq: R, H, N, D Occas: I, T, G, X ● **Work Env:** Noise=N; ● **Salary:** 3 ● **Outlook:** 3

ELECTRONICS WORKER (electron. comp.) ● DOT #726.687-010 ● OES: 93998 ● Performs any combination of following tasks to clean, trim, or prepare components or parts for assembly by other workers: Receives verbal or written instructions from supervisor regarding work assignment. Cleans and deglosses parts, using cleaning devices, solutions, and abrasives. Trims flash from molded or cast parts, using cutting tool or file. Applies primers, plastics, adhesives, and other coatings to designated surfaces, using applicators, such as spray guns, brushes, or rollers. Fills shells, caps, cases, and other cavities with plastic encapsulating fluid or dips parts in fluid to protect, coat, and seal parts. Prepares wires for assembly by measuring, cutting, stripping, twisting, tinning, and attaching contacts, lugs, and other terminal devices, using handtools, and power tools and equipment. Positions and fastens together parts, such as laminates, electron tube mounts and cages, variable capacitor rotors and stators, paper loudspeaker cones, faceplates, and shells and cases for various electronic components, using handtools and power tools. Prints identifying information on components and parts, using silk screen, transfer press, or electro-etch printing devices, or ink pad and stamp. Moves parts and finished components to designated areas of plant, such as assembly, shipping and receiving, or storage. Loads and unloads parts from ovens, baskets, pallets, and racks. Disassembles and reclaims parts, using heating equipment and handtools. ● **GED:** R2, M1, L2 ● **SVP:** 2-30 days ● **Academic:** Ed=N, Eng=N ● **Work Field:** 111 ● **MPSMS:** 580 ● **Aptitudes:** G4, V4, N4, S4, P4, Q4, K4, F3, M3, E5, C4 ● **Temperaments:** R ● **Physical:** Stg=L; Freq: R, H, I, N Occas: E, D, A, X ● **Work Env:** Noise=N; Occas: T ● **Salary:** 3 ● **Outlook:** 3

INTEGRATED CIRCUIT FABRICATOR (electron. comp.) ● DOT #590.684-042 ● OES: 92902 ● Alternate titles: WAFER FAB OPERATOR. Performs any combination of following tasks to fabricate integrated circuits on semiconductor wafers according to written specifications: Loads semiconductor wafers into processing containers for processing or into inspection equipment, using tweezers or vacuum wand. Cleans and dries photo masks and semiconductor wafers to remove contaminants, using cleaning and drying equipment. Inspects photo masks and wafers for defects, such as scratches, using microscope, magnifying lens, or computer-aided inspection equipment. Deposits layer of photoresist solution on wafers, using automated equipment. Aligns photo mask pattern on photoresist layer, exposes pattern to ultraviolet light, and develops pattern, using specialized equipment. Alters electrical nature of wafer layers according to photo mask patterns to form integrated circuits on wafers, using equipment, such as acid baths, diffusion furnaces, ion implant equipment, and metallization equipment. Removes photoresist from wafers, using stripping chemicals and equipment. Inspects and measures circuitry for conformance to pattern specifications, using microscope with measuring attachment. Tests functioning of circuitry, using electronic test equipment and standard procedures. ● **GED:** R3, M2, L2 ● **SVP:** 1-3 mos ● **Academic:** Ed=N, Eng=N ● **Work Field:** 147, 182, 202 ● **MPSMS:** 587 ● **Aptitudes:** G4, V4, N4, S3, P3, Q4, K4, F3, M3, E5, C4 ● **Temperaments:** R, T ● **Physical:** Stg=L; Freq: R, H, I, N Occas: D, A, X ● **Work Env:** Noise=N; Occas: R, T ● **Salary:** 4 ● **Outlook:** 3

LABORER, GRINDING AND POLISHING (any industry) ● DOT #705.687-014 ● OES: 93953 ● Alternate titles: FINISHER. Cleans, deburrs, polishes, or grinds items of metal, plastic, or rubber, using handtools or powered equipment, performing any combination of following tasks: Scrapes or rubs parts with file, wire brush, or buffing cloth. Holds part against buffing or grinding wheel. Deburrs or polishes parts, using portable grinder, chipping hammer, buffer, deburring tool, or hand pick. Mounts part on revolving spindle or chuck and holds or moves tools, such as file, abrasive stone, or cloth against workpiece to file, grind, polish, or buff surface. Cleans interior sur-

faces of holes, using reamer. Changes tools on powered equipment. Applies abrasive compound, wax, or other dressing to facilitate cleaning or polishing operation. May be known according to process performed as Buffer (any industry) II; Burrer (machine shop); Burrer-Marker, Axle (machine shop); Top-Edge Beveler (any industry); Wire Brusher (any industry). ● **GED:** R2, M2, L2 ● **SVP:** 2-30 days ● **Academic:** Ed=N, Eng=N ● **Work Field:** 051, 052 ● **MPSMS:** 540, 610 ● **Aptitudes:** G4, V4, N4, S4, P3, Q4, K3, F3, M3, E5, C5 ● **Temperaments:** R, T ● **Physical:** Stg=M; Freq: R, H, I, N, A Occas: S ● **Work Env:** Noise=L; Occas: A ● **Salary:** 2 ● **Outlook:** 3

MACHINE SNELLER (toy-sport equip.) ● DOT #732.685-026 ● OES: 92999 ● Tends machine that attaches snells (leaders) to fishhooks: Threads snell from spool through guides to machine chuck. Starts machine and inserts hook between chuck jaws. Depresses pedal to actuate chuck that spins and wraps snell around hook shank, and cuts snell to predetermined length. Removes snelled hook from machine, threads snell through eye of hook, and ties overhand loop knot in end to facilitate attaching to fishing line. May attach snelled hooks to display cards. May tie second hook above first to make special baiting hookup. ● **GED:** R2, M1, L1 ● **SVP:** 2-30 days ● **Academic:** Ed=N, Eng=N ● **Work Field:** 062 ● **MPSMS:** 616 ● **Aptitudes:** G4, V4, N4, S3, P3, Q5, K3, F2, M2, E4, C5 ● **Temperaments:** R ● **Physical:** Stg=L; Freq: R, H, I, N, D ● **Work Env:** Noise=N; ● **Salary:** 2 ● **Outlook:** 2

MASKER (any industry) ● DOT #749.687-018 ● OES: 93998 ● Alternate titles: BODY MASKER; TAPER. Covers specified areas of metal or wooden parts to be spray-painted, using masking tape, cardboard, or paper: Marks area to be masked on parts or articles, such as aircraft and automobile assemblies, lamp bases, or motorcycle fenders, using rule or template. Cuts or tears paper or cardboard to specified size. Secures masking in place with gummed tape to protect parts while surrounding areas are spray-painted. May smooth unmasked surface, using sandpaper. May dip or coat article with liquid wax instead of applying masking. May tape precut masks or stencils to article. ● **GED:** R2, M1, L1 ● **SVP:** 1-3 mos ● **Academic:** Ed=N, Eng=N ● **Work Field:** 062, 153 ● **MPSMS:** 495 ● **Aptitudes:** G4, V4, N4, S4, P4, Q5, K4, F4, M3, E5, C5 ● **Temperaments:** R ● **Physical:** Stg=L; Const: R, H Freq: N, D ● **Work Env:** Noise=L; ● **Salary:** 2 ● **Outlook:** 2

MAT CUTTER (wood prod., nec) ● DOT #739.684-126 ● OES: 93926 ● Cuts materials to form bordering frames (mats) for pictures: Measures and marks materials, such as matboards, fabrics, or paper according to size and width of picture. Inserts material in holding device and cuts with knife or razor blade to form bordering frame. May cut backing board to size, using knife or saw. ● **GED:** R2, M1, L1 ● **SVP:** 2-30 days ● **Academic:** Ed=N, Eng=N ● **Work Field:** 054 ● **MPSMS:** 457 ● **Aptitudes:** G4, V4, N4, S3, P3, Q5, K3, F4, M4, E4, C5 ● **Temperaments:** R, T ● **Physical:** Stg=L; Freq: R, H, I, N, A Occas: E ● **Work Env:** Noise=N; ● **Salary:** 1 ● **Outlook:** 2

PAINT MIXER, HAND (any industry) ● DOT #550.684-018 ● OES: 93998 ● Mixes stains, paints, and other coatings for use in painting according to formulas: Pours pigments, paint paste, vehicle, and thinner into can. Stirs mixture with paddle. Compares mixed liquid with desired color sample to ensure that it matches. May blend colors to obtain desired shades. May test specific gravity of mixture, using hydrometer. When mixing colors for spray painting, may be designated Spray Blender (any industry). ● **GED:** R2, M1, L1 ● **SVP:** 1-3 mos ● **Academic:** Ed=N, Eng=N ● **Work Field:** 143 ● **MPSMS:** 495 ● **Aptitudes:** G4, V4, N4, S4, P4, Q4, K4, F4, M3, E5, C3 ● **Temperaments:** J, R ● **Physical:** Stg=L; Freq: R, H, I, N, X ● **Work Env:** Noise=L; Freq: A ● **Salary:** 3 ● **Outlook:** 2

PHOTO MASK CLEANER (electron. comp.) ● DOT #590.684-034 ● OES: 98905 ● Performs any combination of following tasks to clean production photo mask plates used in fabrication of semiconductor devices: Reads specifications sheet to verify type of photo mask plate and number of production runs for each plate. Marks number of production runs on border of each photo mask plate, using diamond scribe. Immerses photo mask plates into series of chemical baths to strip photoresist from photo mask. Places photo mask plates in chamber of specified cleaning machine and starts machine that automatically cleans and dries photo mask plates. Places photo mask plates in chamber of coating machine and starts machine that automatically deposits specified coating onto photo mask. Monitors operation of machines. Inspects photo mask plates for defects or insufficient cleaning, using microscope. Records process and inspection information in logbook. ● **GED:** R2, M1, L2 ● **SVP:** 2-30 days ● **Academic:** Ed=N, Eng=N ● **Work Field:** 182, 031 ● **MPSMS:** 587 ● **Aptitudes:** G4, V4, N5, S4, P4, Q4, K4, F4, M4, E5, C5 ● **Temperaments:** T ● **Physical:** Stg=L; Freq: R, H Occas: I, N ● **Work Env:** Noise=N; ● **Salary:** 1 ● **Outlook:** 4

SCREEN PRINTER (any industry) ● DOT #979.684-034 ● OES: 93998 ● Alternate titles: DECORATOR; LETTERER; SCREENER; SILK-SCREEN OPERATOR; SILK-SCREEN PAINTER. Prints lettering and designs on objects, such as posters, targets, instrument dials, furniture, glass, and toys, using screen printing device: Positions object against guides on setup board or holding fixture of screening device and lowers screen. Pours paint into screen frame or dips squeegee in paint and draws squeegee across screen to transfer design to object. Cleans screen with solvent at end of run and when using different colors. May mix paints according to standard formulas. May affix decals to parts and assemblies, using roller. May examine printed object for defects. May fabricate silk-screen stencil, using photographic equipment. May be designated according to object printed as Target-Face Maker (toy-sport equip.). May tend semiautomatic machine that advances wallpaper under printing screen and be designated Wallpaper Printer (paper goods) II. May screen print electrode material onto substrate used in electronic components, such as ceramic capacitors and film resistors, and be known as Silk-Screen Printer (electron. comp.). May screen print solder mask or nomenclature on printed circuit boards and be designated Screen Printer, Printed Circuit Boards (electron. comp.). ● **GED:** R2, M1, L1 ● **SVP:** 1-3 mos ● **Academic:** Ed=N, Eng=N ● **Work Field:** 191 ● **MPSMS:** 480, 580 ● **Aptitudes:** G3, V4, N4, S3, P3, Q4, K3, F4, M3, E5, C3 ● **Temperaments:** R, T ● **Physical:** Stg=L; Const: R, H, I Freq: N, D, A, X Occas: S, T, G ● **Work Env:** Noise=N; Occas: T ● **Salary:** 3 ● **Outlook:** 3

STUFFER (toy-sport equip.) ● DOT #731.685-014 ● OES: 92974 ● Alternate titles: BLOWER; TOY STUFFER. Tends machine that blows filler into stuffed-toy shells: Inserts precut supporting wire into shell. Places shell opening over stuffing machine nozzle. Depresses pedal to blow cotton or chopped foam rubber filler into shell to impart shape to toy. Places stuffed toy in tote box. Records production. May stuff toys by hand. ● **GED:** R2, M1, L1 ● **SVP:** 2-30 days ● **Academic:** Ed=N, Eng=N ● **Work Field:** 102 ● **MPSMS:** 615 ● **Aptitudes:** G4, V4, N4, S4, P4, Q4, K4, F4, M3, E4, C5 ● **Temperaments:** R ● **Physical:** Stg=S; Freq: R, H Occas: I, N ● **Work Env:** Noise=N; ● **Salary:** 1 ● **Outlook:** 2

WIREWORKER (elec. equip.) ● DOT #728.684-022 ● OES: 93998 ● Alternate titles: WIRE-PREPARATION WORKER. Performs any combination of following tasks involved in cutting, stripping, taping, forming, and soldering wires or wire leads of components used in electrical and electronic units, such as communication equipment, ignition systems, electrical appliances, test equipment, or other electrical or electronic systems: Cuts wire to specified lengths, using wire cutters and ruler or measuring jig. Strips insulation from wire ends, using stripping tool. Twists wire ends and dips ends into pot of solder to prevent fraying. Solders wires to specified connectors and terminals, using soldering iron, or crimps connectors and terminals to wire ends, using handtools. Wraps numbered or colored identification tape around wires. Rolls wires of identical number or color together and attaches tag to roll. Inserts wires into plastic insulation tubing. Bends, cuts, and crimps component leads to prepare component for mounting onto printed circuit board or other assembly, using handtools. Inserts wires in automatic numbering or color-coding machine to imprint part numbers or color codes. Dips wire or component leads into paraffin solution to insulate wire and leads. Applies protective coatings onto wires, using brush. Tests wire and cable assemblies and repairs defective assemblies. May use automated equipment or bench-mounted devices to cut, strip, bend, or crimp wire. May be designated by type of wire worked as Component Lead Former (electron. comp.). ● **GED:** R2, M1, L2 ● **SVP:** 2-30 days ● **Academic:** Ed=N, Eng=N ● **Work Field:** 111 ● **MPSMS:** 587 ● **Aptitudes:** G4, V4, N4, S4, P3, Q4, K3, F3, M3, E5, C4 ● **Temperaments:** R, T ● **Physical:** Stg=L; Freq: R, H, I, N, D, A Occas: X ● **Work Env:** Noise=N; ● **Salary:** 2 ● **Outlook:** 3

GOE: 06.04.35
Laundering, Dry Cleaning

DRY CLEANER, HAND (laundry & rel.) ● DOT #362.684-010 ● OES: 93998 ● Cleans, by hand, articles, such as garments, drapes, lampshades, and leather goods that require individual treatment or are too delicate for machine cleaning: Determines whether article will be cleaned with water or drycleaning solvents. Determines work aids to use, such as cloths, brushes, or sponges. Immerses articles in water or cleaning solvent, or dips brush or sponge into liquid and rubs article until clean. Observes work methods to ensure that articles are not damaged. Rinses and dries cleaned article. May bleach articles, such as draperies and bedspreads, to strip articles of color or discoloration. ● **GED:** R2, M1, L1 ● **SVP:** 1-3 mos ● **Academic:** Ed=N, Eng=N ● **Work Field:** 031 ● **MPSMS:** 906 ● **Aptitudes:** G4, V4, N4, S4, P3, Q4, K3, F3, M3, E5, C3 ● **Temperaments:** V ● **Physical:** Stg=M; Const: S, R, H, I, E, N, A, X ● **Work Env:** Noise=N; Const: U Occas: A ● **Salary:** 2 ● **Outlook:** 3

FURNITURE CLEANER (laundry & rel.) ● DOT #362.684-022 ● OES: 93998 ● Alternate titles: DRY CLEANER, FURNITURE, HAND; FURNITURE SHAMPOOER. Cleans upholstered furniture in plant or on customer's premises, using vacuum cleaner, brush, sponge, drycleaning fluids, or detergent solutions: Cleans loose dust and dirt from furniture, using vacuum cleaner. Applies cleaning solutions selected according to stains and pats or rubs stained areas with brush or sponge to remove stains. Scrubs upholstery with brush and drycleaning solvents or detergent solutions and water to clean upholstery. Rubs leather or plastic surfaces with oiled cloth and buffs with cloth or hand buffer to restore softness and luster. May spray upholstery, using spray gun and solutions such as stain repellent or plastic fluid which reduces soil collection. May polish wooden parts of furniture. ● **GED:** R2, M1, L2 ● **SVP:** 1-3 mos ● **Academic:** Ed=N, Eng=N ● **Work Field:** 031 ● **MPSMS:** 906 ● **Aptitudes:** G4, V4, N4, S4, P3, Q4, K4, F4, M3, E5, C4 ● **Temperaments:** R ● **Physical:** Stg=M; Const: N, A, X Freq: S, R, H, I Occas: K, O, E ● **Work Env:** Noise=N; Freq: A Occas: U ● **Salary:** 2 ● **Outlook:** 2

LAUNDERER, HAND (laundry & rel.) ● DOT #361.684-010 ● OES: 92726 ● Washes, dries, and irons articles in hand-laundries and laundromats, using equipment, such as hand iron, and small washing and drying machines: Sorts articles on worktable or in baskets on floor to separate special washes, such as fugitives and starch work. Loads and unloads washing and drying machines, and adds detergent powder and bleach as required. Folds fluff-dry articles preparatory to wrapping. Presses wearing apparel, using hand iron [PRESSER, HAND (any industry)]. Assembles, wraps, or bags laundered articles for delivery to customer. Some hand laundries are machine-equipped and only touching-up is done by hand iron; in others, some articles, such as flatwork and shirts, are sent to larger machine-equipped plants. ● **GED:** R2, M1, L2 ● **SVP:** 2-30 days ● **Academic:** Ed=N, Eng=N ● **Work Field:** 031, 032 ● **MPSMS:** 906, 440 ● **Aptitudes:** G4, V4, N4, S4, P3, Q4, K3, F3, M3, E5, C4 ● **Temperaments:** J, V ● **Physical:** Stg=M; Freq: R, H, I, N ● **Work Env:** Noise=N; Const: U ● **Salary:** 2 ● **Outlook:** 2

LAUNDRY LABORER (laundry & rel.) ● DOT #361.687-018 ● OES: 98998 ● Alternate titles: BUNDLE CLERK. Prepares laundry for processing and distributes laundry, performing any combination of following duties: Opens bundles of soiled laundry. Places bundles onto conveyor belt or drops down chute for distribution to marking and classification sections. Weighs laundry on scales and records weight on tickets. Removes bundles from conveyor and distributes to workers, using handtruck. Fastens identification pins or clips onto laundry to facilitate subsequent assembly of customers' orders. Sorts net bags containing clean wash according to customers' identification tags. Sorts empty net bags according to color and size. Collects identification tags from lots of laundered articles for reuse. Moistens clean wash preparatory to ironing. Operates power hoist to load and unload washing machines and extractors. Stacks linen supplies on storage room shelves. Unloads soiled linen from trucks. May be designated according to duties performed as Bundle Weigher (laundry & rel.); Chute Worker (laundry & rel.); Clipper (laundry & rel.); Linen-Supply-Room Worker (laundry & rel.); Net Sorter (laundry & rel.). May be designated: Pin Sorter And Bagger (laundry & rel.); Pin Worker (laundry & rel.); Washing-Machine Loader (laundry & rel.) II. ● **GED:** R1, M1, L1 ● **SVP:** 2-30 days ● **Academic:** Ed=N, Eng=N ● **Work Field:** 011 ● **MPSMS:** 906 ● **Aptitudes:** G4, V4, N4, S4, P4, Q4, K4, F4, M4, E5, C4 ● **Temperaments:** R ● **Physical:** Stg=M; Freq: R, H Occas: S, I, N, X ● **Work Env:** Noise=N; Freq: U ● **Salary:** 2 ● **Outlook:** 3

LAUNDRY OPERATOR (laundry & rel.) ● DOT #369.684-014 ● OES: 92726 ● Receives, marks, washes, finishes, checks, and wraps articles in laundry, performing any combination of following tasks: Classifies and marks incoming laundry with identifying code number, by hand or using machine [MARKER (laundry & rel.)]. Tends washing machine, extractor, and tumbler to clean and dry laundry. Finishes laundered articles, using hand iron, pressing machine, or feeds and folds flatwork on flatwork ironing machine. Sorts laundry and verifies count on laundry ticket [ASSEMBLER (laundry & rel.); CHECKER (laundry & rel.)]. May perform related tasks, such as mending torn articles, using sewing machine or by affixing adhesive patches. May wrap articles. May specialize in receiving and washing, or in finishing and checking, and be designated according to unit in which work is performed as Laundry Operator, Finishing (laundry & rel.); Laundry Operator, Wash Room (laundry & rel.). ● **GED:** R2, M1, L2 ● **SVP:** 1-3 mos ● **Academic:** Ed=N, Eng=N ● **Work Field:** 031, 032 ● **MPSMS:** 906 ● **Aptitudes:** G4, V4, N4, S4, P4, Q4, K4, F4, M3, E4, C4 ● **Temperaments:** R ● **Physical:** Stg=M; Freq: R, H, N Occas: I, X ● **Work Env:** Noise=L; Occas: H, U ● **Salary:** 2 ● **Outlook:** 2

LEATHER CLEANER (laundry & rel.) ● DOT #362.684-026 ● OES: 92726 ● Cleans suede and leather garments, such as gloves, jackets, and coats: Sorts and classifies articles into lots according to color, degree of dirtiness, and work to be performed. Brushes or sponges stains with fatty liquors (leather oils extracted from hides) to spot garment preparatory to cleaning. Observes surface and modifies pressure on brush according to type of leather to avoid damage to garment. Loads sorted articles into drum of cleaning machine. Turns valve to admit cleaning fluid into drum. Loads cleaned garments into extractor and tumbler to dry and fluff garments. May hand clean articles that are too delicate or badly soiled for machine cleaning. ● **GED:** R3, M2, L2 ● **SVP:** 1-3 mos ● **Academic:** Ed=N, Eng=N ● **Work Field:** 031 ● **MPSMS:** 529, 906 ● **Aptitudes:** G3, V4, N4, S5, P4, Q4, K4, F4, M3, E5, C3 ● **Temperaments:** R, T ● **Physical:** Stg=L; Freq: S, R, H, I, E, N, A, X ● **Work Env:** Noise=L; Occas: U, A ● **Salary:** 2 ● **Outlook:** 2

PRESS OPERATOR (laundry & rel.) ● DOT #363.685-010 ● OES: 92728 ● Alternate titles: WEARING-APPAREL PRESSER. Tends pressing-machine (hot-head type) to press washed wearing apparel, such as uniforms, jackets, aprons, and shirts: Smooths section of garment on buck (table) of machine, and moistens dry portions of garment with wet cloth or water spray. Pushes buttons to lower pressing head of machine to press and dry garment. Rearranges garment on buck, repeating process until pressing is completed. May work as part of team and press only portion of garment. May tend two or three presses simultaneously, positioning garment on one press while other presses are closed. ● **GED:** R2, M1, L1 ● **SVP:** 2-30 days ● **Academic:** Ed=N, Eng=N ● **Work Field:** 032 ● **MPSMS:** 906 ● **Aptitudes:** G4, V4, N5, S4, P4, Q5, K4, F4, M3, E5, C5 ● **Temperaments:** R ● **Physical:** Stg=L; Freq: R, H, I Occas: S ● **Work Env:** Noise=N; Freq: H, U ● **Salary:** 3 ● **Outlook:** 3

PRESSER, ALL-AROUND (laundry & rel.) ● DOT #363.682-014 ● OES: 92728 ● Alternate titles: COMBINATION PRESSER. Operates steam pressing machine [PRESSER, MACHINE (any industry) 363.682-018] or uses hand iron [PRESSER, HAND (any industry) 363.684- 018] to press garments, such as trousers, sweaters, and dresses, usually in small cleaning establishment. Presses silk garments [SILK FINISHER (laundry & rel.) 363.681-010] and wool garments [WOOL PRESSER (laundry & rel.) 363.682-018]. ● **GED:** R2, M2, L1 ● **SVP:** 1-3 mos ● **Academic:** Ed=N, Eng=N ● **Work Field:** 032 ● **MPSMS:** 906 ● **Aptitudes:** G4, V4, N4, S4, P3, Q5, K3, F3, M3, E4, C5 ● **Temperaments:** R ● **Physical:** Stg=M; Freq: S, R, H, I, E, N, A, X Occas: D ● **Work Env:** Noise=L; Const: H, U, A, O ● **Salary:** 2 ● **Outlook:** 3

PRESSER, HAND (any industry) ● DOT #363.684-018 ● OES: 93921 ● Alternate titles: FINISHER, HAND; IRONER, HAND. Presses ar-

ticles, such as drapes, knit goods, millinery parts, parachutes, garments, and slip covers, or delicate textiles, such as lace, synthetics, and silks to remove wrinkles, flatten seams, and give shape to article, using hand iron: Places article in position on ironing board or worktable. Smooths and shapes fabric prior to pressing. Sprays water over fabric to soften fibers when not using steam iron. Adjusts temperature of iron, according to type of fabric, and uses covering cloths to prevent scorching or to avoid sheen on delicate fabrics. Pushes and pulls iron over surface of article, according to type of fabric. Fits odd-shaped pieces which cannot be pressed flat over puff iron. May pin, fold, and hang article after pressing. May be designated according to article or part pressed as Coat Ironer, Hand (garment); Lining Presser (garment; laundry & rel.); Seam Presser (garment); Vest Presser (garment); or according to type of cloth pressed as Cotton Presser (garment); Silk Presser (garment) I or part pressed as: Flatwork Finisher, Hand (laundry & rel.); Piece Presser (garment); Pocket Presser (garment); Underpresser, Hand (garment); Waist Presser (garment); Wearing-Apparel Finisher, Hand (laundry & rel.). ● **GED:** R2, M1, L1 ● **SVP:** 2-30 days ● **Academic:** Ed=N, Eng=N ● **Work Field:** 032 ● **MPSMS:** 906, 440 ● **Aptitudes:** G4, V4, N5, S4, P4, Q5, K3, F4, M3, E5, C4 ● **Temperaments:** R ● **Physical:** Stg=L; Freq: R, H, I, N, A, X ● **Work Env:** Noise=N; Freq: H Occas: U ● **Salary:** 3 ● **Outlook:** 3

SILK FINISHER (laundry & rel.) ● DOT #363.681-010 ● OES: 89598 ● Presses drycleaned and wet-cleaned silk and synthetic fiber garments, using hot-head press or steamtable, puff irons, and hand iron: Operates machine presses to finish those parts that can be pressed flat and completes other parts of garments by pressing with hand iron. Finishes parts difficult to reach, such as flounces, by fitting parts over puff irons. Finishes velvet garments by steaming on buck of hot-head press or steamtable, and brushing pile (nap) with handbrush. Finishes fancy garments, such as evening gowns and costumes, with hand iron, applying knowledge of fabrics and heats to produce high quality finishes which cannot be obtained on machine presses. Presses ties on small pressing machine or by inserting heated metal form into tie and touching up rough places with hand iron. Finishes pleated garments, determining size of pleat from evidence of old pleat or from work order (for new garments) and presses with machine press or hand iron. May press wool fabrics requiring precision finishing. In establishments where many SILK FINISHERS (laundry & rel.) are employed may be designated according to specialty as Finisher, Hand (laundry & rel.); Form-Finishing-Machine Operator (laundry & rel.); Hot-Head-Machine Operator (laundry & rel.); Pleat Presser (laundry & rel.); Puff-Iron Operator (laundry & rel.) I; Tie Presser (laundry & rel.); Velvet Steamer (laundry & rel.). ● **GED:** R3, M1, L2 ● **SVP:** 3-6 mos ● **Academic:** Ed=N, Eng=N ● **Work Field:** 032 ● **MPSMS:** 906 ● **Aptitudes:** G3, V4, N4, S4, P3, Q5, K3, F3, M3, E4, C4 ● **Temperaments:** R, T ● **Physical:** Stg=L; Freq: R, H, I, E, N, X Occas: D ● **Work Env:** Noise=L; Freq: U, A Occas: O ● **Salary:** 2 ● **Outlook:** 2

WASHER, HAND (laundry & rel.) ● DOT #361.687-030 ● OES: 98998 ● Washes articles, such as curtains, table linens, and lingerie by hand: Soaps and rubs articles, and rinses them in chemical solutions and clear water. Extracts excess moisture with hand wringer or tends small extractor [EXTRACTOR OPERATOR (any industry)]. Hangs articles on racks to dry. May immerse articles in tint or dye solutions to restore color. May operate small machines to wash articles. May wash and card blankets. ● **GED:** R2, M1, L1 ● **SVP:** 2-30 days ● **Academic:** Ed=N, Eng=N ● **Work Field:** 031 ● **MPSMS:** 906 ● **Aptitudes:** G4, V4, N4, S4, P4, Q5, K4, F4, M3, E5, C4 ● **Temperaments:** R ● **Physical:** Stg=L; Freq: S, R, H Occas: I, X ● **Work Env:** Noise=N; Freq: U ● **Salary:** 2 ● **Outlook:** 3

WASHER, MACHINE (laundry & rel.) ● DOT #361.665-010 ● OES: 92726 ● Alternate titles: STEAM CLEANER, MACHINE; WET CLEANER, MACHINE; WET WASHER, MACHINE. Tends one or more machines that wash commercial, industrial, or household articles, such as garments, blankets, curtains, draperies, fine linens, and rags: Loads, or directs workers engaged in loading, machine with articles requiring identical treatment. Starts machine and turns valves to admit specified amounts of soap, detergent, water, bluing, and bleach. Adds starch to loads of such articles as curtains or linens, when bell signal indicates that washing cycle is completed. Removes, or directs workers in removing, articles from washer and into handtrucks or extractors. May wash delicate fabrics by hand. May mix solutions, such as bleach, bluing, or starch, and apply them to articles before or after washing to remove color or improve appearance. May spot-clean articles, before washing, to remove heavy stains. May sterilize items. May hang curtains, draperies, or blankets on stretch-frames to dry. May brush blankets, or feed blankets into carding machine, to raise and fluff nap. May pull trousers over heated metal forms to dry and stretch legs. May load and remove articles from extractor or drier by hand or hoist, using metal basket or cord mesh bag. May tend semiautomatic or computer-controlled washing machines that automatically select water levels, temperature, cleaning additives, and wash cycle according to type of articles to be laundered. May tend machines that dry articles. When washing contaminated laundry from hospital isolation wards, may be designated Isolation-Washer (laundry & rel.). May be designated according to type of articles washed as Flatwork Washer (laundry & rel.); Overall Washer (laundry & rel.); Rag Washer (laundry & rel.); Washer, Blanket (laundry & rel.). ● **GED:** R3, M2, L2 ● **SVP:** 3-6 mos ● **Academic:** Ed=N, Eng=N ● **Work Field:** 031 ● **MPSMS:** 906 ● **Aptitudes:** G4, V4, N4, S4, P4, Q5, K4, F4, M3, E5, C5 ● **Temperaments:** R ● **Physical:** Stg=M; Freq: S, R, H, I, N ● **Work Env:** Noise=N; Freq: H, U ● **Salary:** 1 ● **Outlook:** 2

GOE: 06.04.37
Manual Work, Stamping, Marking, Labeling, & Ticketing

MARKER, SEMICONDUCTOR WAFERS (electron. comp.) ● DOT #920.587-026 ● OES: 92902 ● Scribes identifying information onto semiconductor wafer, using metal stylus (scribe): Obtains container loaded with semiconductor wafers and removes wafers from container, using tweezers. Marks lot number and description number in designated area of wafers, following specifications and using metal stylus. Records production data. Cleans containers, using soap and water. ● **GED:** R2, M1, L2 ● **SVP:** 2-30 days ● **Academic:** Ed=N, Eng=N ● **Work Field:** 183, 231 ● **MPSMS:** 587 ● **Aptitudes:** G4, V4, N5, S5, P4, Q3, K4, F3, M4, E5, C5 ● **Temperaments:** R ● **Physical:** Stg=L; Freq: R, H, I, N ● **Work Env:** Noise=N; ● **Salary:** 1 ● **Outlook:** 3

NAME-PLATE STAMPER (any industry) ● DOT #652.685-054 ● OES: 92542 ● Tends machine that stamps or embosses identifying data on nameplates for manufactured products, using one of following methods: (1) Assembles dies or aligns type in die block, using setscrews. Positions die block on press bed, lowers ram with handwheel, and feeds blank plates into powered machine or pulls lever to imprint data on blank. (2) Turns wheel to specified character and pulls lever to stamp character on blank. Repeats operation for each character until specified information is embossed on plate. May place nameplate in hinged forming block and close block manually to shape plate to specified curvature. ● **GED:** R2, M1, L1 ● **SVP:** 2-30 days ● **Academic:** Ed=N, Eng=N ● **Work Field:** 192 ● **MPSMS:** 567 ● **Aptitudes:** G4, V4, N4, S4, P3, Q3, K3, F4, M4, E4, C5 ● **Temperaments:** R ● **Physical:** Stg=L; Const: R, H Freq: N, D ● **Work Env:** Noise=N; ● **Salary:** 2 ● **Outlook:** 2

STENCILER (any industry) ● DOT #920.687-178 ● OES: 93947 ● Alternate titles: MARKER, SHIPMENTS. Marks size, lot number, contents, or other identifying information or symbols on containers or directly on article by placing stencil on container or article and rubbing ink or paint brush across open lettering, or by spraying paint on stencil. May mix paints or lacquers. May be designated according to type of container stenciled as Carton Stenciler (any industry); Drum Stenciler (beverage); Sack Stenciler (any industry). ● **GED:** R1, M1, L1 ● **SVP:** 2-30 days ● **Academic:** Ed=N, Eng=N ● **Work Field:** 191, 262 ● **MPSMS:** 898 ● **Aptitudes:** G4, V4, N4, S4, P4, Q5, K4, F4, M3, E5, C4 ● **Temperaments:** R ● **Physical:** Stg=L; Const: R, H Freq: N Occas: C, X ● **Work Env:** Noise=L; ● **Salary:** 2 ● **Outlook:** 2

GOE: 06.04.38
Wrapping & Packing

BANDER, HAND (any industry) ● DOT #929.687-058 ● OES: 98902 ● Alternate titles: BALER; LOAD CLERK; PACKAGER AND

STRAPPER. Fastens plastic or metal bands around stacks, bundles, or palletized articles prior to storage or shipment, using strapping tool and clamps: Counts number of articles to be banded to verify number specified on work order. Unwinds plastic or metal banding material from reel, wraps band around stack or bundle, inserts loose end of banding material into strapping tool, and cinches and crimps banding material and clamp with strapping tool to secure articles during storage or shipment. Counts and records number of banded bundles. May operate hydraulic jack lift or truck to move articles before or after bundling. May cut lumber or other reinforcing material, using handsaw or power saw, and include reinforcing material in bundle or nail lumber together to protect articles during storage or shipment. May stack bundled articles on pallet by hand. May band articles to pallet to secure articles for moving. May mark or stencil size of article, customer's name, order number, address, or other identifying data on visible portion of bundle or shipping ticket with markers, brushes, or paint. ● **GED:** R2, M2, L2 ● **SVP:** 2-30 days ● **Academic:** Ed=N, Eng=N ● **Work Field:** 041 ● **MPSMS:** 453, 474, 532 ● **Aptitudes:** G4, V4, N4, S4, P4, Q4, K4, F4, M4, E5, C5 ● **Temperaments:** R ● **Physical:** Stg=H; Const: R, H Freq: S, K, N, D, A Occas: O, I ● **Work Env:** Noise=L; Occas: A ● **Salary:** 2 ● **Outlook:** 2

CRATER (any industry) ● DOT #920.684-010 ● OES: 98902 ● Alternate titles: BOXER; CARPENTER, PACKING; CASE MAKER. Fabricates wooden crates or boxes, using woodworking handtools and powered tools, and packs such items as machinery, vehicles, or other large or odd-shaped products: Reads blueprints, shipping notices, and other specifications, and inspects product to determine size and shape of container, materials to be used, and types of supports and braces to be used. Lays out dimensions on materials with ruler, measuring tape, and pencil. Saws materials to size, using handsaws and powered saws. Assembles materials, using nailing or stapling machine, screws, bolts, glue, and handtools. Places product in container, manually or using hoist. Bolts heavy pieces to bottom of container or skid. Wraps and pads product with excelsior, paper or other packing material. Builds crate around large or odd-shaped articles. Nails cover on crate. Wraps and tightens metal bands around crate, using banding equipment. Attaches identification labels or stencils containing such information as shipping destination, weight, and type of product contained on crate. Repairs broken crates. May cover military tanks and other equipment with neoprene or other protective covering to protect them during shipment. May count items to be packed to ensure compliance with shipping orders. May weigh loaded crate. May move container to shipping area, and move lumber, paper, and other wrapping supplies to crating area, using hand or industrial truck. May sharpen saw blades, using file. May be designated according to item crated as Machinery Crater (machinery mfg.); Refrigerator Crater (svc. ind. mach.), or specific duty performed as Crate Repairer (any industry). ● **GED:** R3, M2, L2 ● **SVP:** 1-3 mos ● **Academic:** Ed=N, Eng=N ● **Work Field:** 041, 102 ● **MPSMS:** 454 ● **Aptitudes:** G3, V4, N4, S3, P3, Q4, K3, F3, M3, E5, C5 ● **Temperaments:** R, T ● **Physical:** Stg=M; Freq: O, R, H, N, D Occas: S, I ● **Work Env:** Noise=N; Occas: M ● **Salary:** 2 ● **Outlook:** 3

MAILING-MACHINE OPERATOR (print. & pub.) ● DOT #208.462-010 ● OES: 56200 ● Operates machine that automatically addresses, weighs, and ties into bundles printed publications, such as magazines, catalogs, and pamphlets, for mailing according to zip code: Reads production order to determine type and size of publication scheduled for mailing. Adjusts guides, rollers, loose card inserter, weighing machine, and tying arm, using rule and handtools. Fills paste reservoir. Mounts roll of subscriber address labels onto machine spindle and threads twine through tying arm. Starts machine and observes operation to detect evidence of malfunctions throughout production run. Stops machine to make adjustments or clear jams. Records production according to customer name and zip code, and machine down time due to malfunctions or lack of work. ● **GED:** R4, M2, L3 ● **SVP:** 6 mos-1 yr ● **Academic:** Ed=N, Eng=S ● **Work Field:** 041, 063 ● **MPSMS:** 899 ● **Aptitudes:** G3, V4, N3, S3, P3, Q4, K3, F3, M3, E5, C5 ● **Temperaments:** J, T ● **Physical:** Stg=M; Freq: R, H, N, D Occas: I, A ● **Work Env:** Noise=L; ● **Salary:** 2 ● **Outlook:** 2

PACKAGER, HAND (any industry) ● DOT #920.587-018 ● OES: 98902 ● Alternate titles: HAND PACKAGER. Packages materials and products manually, performing any combination of following duties: Cleans packaging containers. Lines and pads crates and assembles cartons. Obtains and sorts product. Wraps protective material around product. Starts, stops, and regulates speed of conveyor. Inserts or pours product into containers or fills containers from spout or chute. Weighs containers and adjusts quantity. Nails, glues, or closes and seals containers. Labels containers, container tags, or products. Sorts bundles or filled containers. Packs special arrangements or selections of product. Inspects materials, products, and containers at each step of packaging process. Records information, such as weight, time, and date packaged. May stack, separate, count, pack, wrap, and weigh bakery products and be designated Bakery Worker (bakery products). May apply preservative to aircraft and spaceship parts, package parts for shipment, and be designated Wrapper and Preserver (aircraft mfg.). May be designated according to whether high-production or small-lot packaging as Fancy Packer (retail trade; wholesale tr.); Packaging-Line Attendant (any industry); specific packaging duty performed as filling, wrapping, packing, labeling, and container cleaning as Sack Sewer, Hand (any industry); kinds of equipment used or product packaged as Candle Wrapper (fabrication, nec); Carton Stapler (any industry); or whether packager performs associated duties as final assembly before packaging product as Novelty-Balloon Assembler And Packer (rubber goods). May weigh and package meat in retail store and be designated Meat Wrapper (retail trade). May be designated: Bagger (any industry); Bow Maker, Gift Wrapping (any industry); Box Maker, Cardboard (any industry); Box Wrapper (any industry); Bundler (any industry); Candy Packer (sugar & conf.); Caser, Rolled Glass (glass mfg.); Coil Strapper (steel & rel.); Container Filler (any industry); Filler (any industry); Furniture Packer (retail trade); Grader, Sausage And Wiener (meat products); Guncotton Packer (chemical); Inserter, Promotional Item (any industry); Inspector-Packager (any industry); Lidder (any industry); Mattress Packer (furniture); Packager, Meat (meat products); Packer, Dried Beef (meat products); Packer, Foamed-In-Place (any industry); Packer, Sausage And Wiener (meat products); Piece-Goods Packer (textile); Scaler, Sliced Bacon (meat products); Sponge Packer (wholesale tr.); Stamper (any industry); Table Worker (any industry); Tube Packer (rubber tire); Wrapper (any industry); Wrapper, Hand (can. & preserv.); Wrapping Remover (any industry). Workers who tend packaging machines are classified under PACKAGER, MACHINE (any industry) 920.685-078. ● **GED:** R2, M1, L1 ● **SVP:** 2-30 days ● **Academic:** Ed=N, Eng=N ● **Work Field:** 041 ● **MPSMS:** 898 ● **Aptitudes:** G4, V4, N4, S4, P4, Q4, K3, F3, M3, E4, C4 ● **Temperaments:** R ● **Physical:** Stg=M; Const: R, H, I Occas: B, G, N, D, X ● **Work Env:** Noise=L; Freq: H, A ● **Salary:** 2 ● **Outlook:** 3

PACKAGER, MACHINE (any industry) ● DOT #920.685-078 ● OES: 92974 ● Alternate titles: MACHINE OPERATOR, PACKAGING. Tends machine that performs one or more packaging functions, such as filling, marking, labeling, banding, tying, packing, or wrapping containers: Starts machine and observes operation to detect malfunctions of machine. Stops machine and reports malfunction to supervisor. Makes minor adjustments or repairs, such as opening valves, changing forming and cutting dies, setting guides, or clearing away damaged product containers. Inspects filled container to ensure that product is packaged according to specifications. May feed product to conveyors, hoppers, or other feeding devices, and unload packaged product. May replenish packaging supplies, such as wrapping paper, plastic sheet, boxes, cartons, glue, ink, or labels. May mount supplies on spindles or place supplies in hopper or other feeding devices. May position and hold container in machine and depress pedal, press button, or move lever to clean, glue, label, sew, or staple container. May cut stencils and stencil information on container, such as lot number or shipping destination. May tally number of units of product packaged or record information, such as size, weight, and type of products packaged. May be designated according to specific function or functions performed by machine tended as Bottle Washer, Machine (any industry) II; Capping-Machine Operator (any industry); Container-Maker-Filler-Packer Operator (any industry); Filling-Machine Operator (any industry); Labeler, Machine (any industry); Wrapping-Machine Operator (any industry). May be designated: Aerosol-Line Operator (any industry); Bag Printer (chemical); Blister-Packing-Machine Tender (any industry); Bread-Wrapping-Machine Feeder (bakery products); Candy-Wrapping-Machine Operator (sugar & conf.); Carton-Gluing-Machine Operator (any industry); Cellophane Wrapper, Machine (any industry); Cover Marker (paint & varnish); Glassine-Machine Tender (any industry); Packing-Machine Tender (any industry); Palletizer Operator (any industry) II; Sack Sewer, Machine (any industry); Silk Screener (optical goods); Spring Crater (furniture); Stencil Cutter, Machine (any

industry); Tea-Bag-Machine Tender (food prep., nec); Tire Wrapper (automotive ser.; rubber tire); Tube-Filling Machine Operator (can. & preserv.; chemical); Tying-Machine Operator (any industry); Wrapping-And-Packing-Machine Operator (any industry). Workers who package products by hand are classified under PACKAGER, HAND (any industry) 920.587-018. May act as lead worker. ● **GED:** R2, M1, L1 ● **SVP:** 2-30 days ● **Academic:** Ed=N, Eng=N ● **Work Field:** 041 ● **MPSMS:** 551, 531, 475 ● **Aptitudes:** G4, V4, N4, S4, P4, Q4, K3, F3, M3, E4, C4 ● **Temperaments:** R ● **Physical:** Stg=M; Const: H Freq: R, I, N, D Occas: S, E, G, F, A, X ● **Work Env:** Noise=L; ● **Salary:** 1 ● **Outlook:** 3

PACKING-LINE WORKER (rubber goods) ● DOT #753.687-038 ● OES: 98902 ● Performs any combination of following tasks as member of conveyor line crew, to finish and pack plastic or rubber footwear: Sorts and mates pairs and places them on conveyor. Opens or closes buckles, snaps fasteners together, inserts laces in eyelets, and ties loops (frogs) around buttons. Counts and tallies production or records on counter. Wraps pair in tissue, places them in shoe box, and packs boxes in cartons. Places rejects in boxes or racks for repair or mating. ● **GED:** R2, M2, L1 ● **SVP:** 2-30 days ● **Academic:** Ed=N, Eng=N ● **Work Field:** 041 ● **MPSMS:** 512 ● **Aptitudes:** G4, V4, N4, S4, P4, Q4, K4, F3, M3, E5, C4 ● **Temperaments:** R ● **Physical:** Stg=L; Const: R, H Freq: I, N, D Occas: X ● **Work Env:** Noise=N; ● **Salary:** 2 ● **Outlook:** 3

GOE: 06.04.39
Cleaning

CLEANER (ordnance) ● DOT #503.684-010 ● OES: 93947 ● Cleans and prepares subassemblies of pistols, rifles, shotguns, and revolvers for bluing: Disassembles components, such as barrel and ratchet, trigger and hammer, trigger guard, and back strap. Blows out particles remaining after sand blasting, using airhose. Places parts in rack or wire basket and immerses parts in degreasing tank to remove oil and dirt. Mixes alcohol and whitening powder and rubs resultant paste onto gun parts to facilitate bluing. Wires parts together and attaches them to immersing rod. Blows excess solution from blued parts with airhose. Inspects parts for nicks, scratches, clearness of trademark, and cleanness. Reassembles subassemblies, using screwdriver. May pour specified amount of chemical solution (acid) into degreasing tanks. ● **GED:** R2, M1, L1 ● **SVP:** 1-3 mos ● **Academic:** Ed=N, Eng=N ● **Work Field:** 031 ● **MPSMS:** 373 ● **Aptitudes:** G4, V4, N4, S4, P3, Q4, K3, F3, M3, E5, C4 ● **Temperaments:** R ● **Physical:** Stg=L; Freq: R, H, I, N, D, X Occas: E ● **Work Env:** Noise=N; Freq: U, A ● **Salary:** 2 ● **Outlook:** 3

CLEANER AND POLISHER (any industry) ● DOT #709.687-010 ● OES: 98998 ● Cleans and polishes chromium or nickel plated articles with cloth and liquid cleanser. May remove paint or other foreign matter adhering to surface of article with solvent, knife, or steel wool. May be designated according to type of metal cleaned as Chrome Cleaner (any industry); Nickel Cleaner (any industry). ● **GED:** R1, M1, L1 ● **SVP:** 2-30 days ● **Academic:** Ed=N, Eng=N ● **Work Field:** 031 ● **MPSMS:** 550 ● **Aptitudes:** G4, V4, N5, S4, P4, Q5, K4, F3, M3, E5, C4 ● **Temperaments:** R ● **Physical:** Stg=L; Const: R, H, N Occas: I, X ● **Work Env:** Noise=N; ● **Salary:** 1 ● **Outlook:** 2

EQUIPMENT CLEANER (any industry) ● DOT #599.684-010 ● OES: 98905 ● Alternate titles: NIGHT CLEANER. Cleans and sterilizes machinery, utensils, and equipment used to process or store products, such as chemicals, paint, food, or beverages: Turns valves to drain machines or tanks and disconnects pipes, using wrenches. Sprays machines, tanks, and conveyors with water to loosen and remove dirt or other foreign matter. Scrubs machines, tanks, tables, pans, bowls, compartments, and conveyors, using brushes, rags, cleaning preparations, and diluted acids. Rinses articles with water, and dries them with compressed air. Scrubs floors and walls, using brushes, rags, and diluted acids. Connects hoses and lines to pump and starts pump to circulate cleaning and sterilizing solution through hoses and lines. Scrubs interior of disconnected pipes, valves, spigots, gauges, and meters, using spiral brushes. Mixes cleaning solutions and diluted acids, according to formula. Draws off samples of cleaning solutions from mixing tanks for laboratory analysis. May replace defective sections of metal coils and lines, using handtools, soldering iron, and pipe couplings. May lubricate machinery. May be designated according to equipment cleaned as Beer-Coil Cleaner (any industry); Lard-Tub Washer (meat products); Line Cleaner (beverage; dairy products); Pipe Washer (dairy products). May sterilize equipment and be designated Equipment Sterilizer (dairy products). ● **GED:** R2, M1, L2 ● **SVP:** 2-30 days ● **Academic:** Ed=N, Eng=N ● **Work Field:** 031 ● **MPSMS:** 550, 592, 567 ● **Aptitudes:** G4, V4, N4, S4, P3, Q4, K3, F4, M3, E4, C4 ● **Temperaments:** R ● **Physical:** Stg=H; Freq: R, H, N Occas: C, B, S, K, O, I, G, F, D, X ● **Work Env:** Noise=L; Freq: U Occas: A ● **Salary:** 2 ● **Outlook:** 3

MACHINE CLEANER (any industry) ● DOT #699.687-014 ● OES: 98905 ● Alternate titles: MACHINE BRUSHER; MACHINE RUBBER; WIPER. Cleans dust, dirt, grease, and lint from machines and auxiliary equipment, such as tanks and pipelines, in industrial plant or aboard ship, using cleaning solutions, waste, rags, waterhose, pumps, lint vacuum system, airhose, brushes, and scraping tools: Cleans screen on lint vacuum system and replaces worn screen. May clean plant sewage treatment system and water supply wells. May remove machine guards and accessories, using handtools. May paint exposed surfaces of machines to prevent rust. May oil moving parts or wearing surfaces. May clean floors around machine, using broom or vacuum cleaner. May be designated according to machine or part of machine cleaned as Bottle-Packing-Machine Cleaner (any industry); Creel Cleaner (textile); Opening-Machine Cleaner (textile); Pin Cleaner (textile); Rack Cleaner (textile); Shafting Cleaner (any industry). May be designated: Card Cleaner (textile); Guide-Rail Cleaner (textile); Loom Blower (textile). ● **GED:** R2, M1, L1 ● **SVP:** 2-30 days ● **Academic:** Ed=N, Eng=N ● **Work Field:** 031 ● **MPSMS:** 568 ● **Aptitudes:** G4, V4, N5, S4, P4, Q5, K4, F4, M3, E5, C5 ● **Temperaments:** R ● **Physical:** Stg=M; Freq: R, H, N Occas: C, S, K, O, W, I ● **Work Env:** Noise=L; Occas: U ● **Salary:** 2 ● **Outlook:** 3

SCRUBBER MACHINE TENDER (electron. comp.) ● DOT #599.685-134 ● OES: 92999 ● Tends machine that scrubs, cleans, and dries surface of printed circuit board (PCB) panels during manufacturing processes: Loads PCB panels onto conveyor that carries panels through scrubbing (abrading or sanding), cleaning, and drying cycles of machine. Adjusts machine controls to regulate pressure of scrubbing mechanisms, fluid levels, and conveyor speed. Observes gauges and examines processed panels to detect machine malfunctions and conformance to processing specifications. Removes and stacks cleaned PCBs from discharge end of machine. May clean and maintain scrubbing machine. May be designated by type of panels processed as Inner-Layer Scrubber Tender (electron. comp.). May be designated according to point in production when scrubbing occurs as Final Cleaner (electron. comp.). ● **GED:** R2, M1, L2 ● **SVP:** 2-30 days ● **Academic:** Ed=N, Eng=N ● **Work Field:** 031, 051 ● **MPSMS:** 587 ● **Aptitudes:** G4, V4, N5, S4, P4, Q5, K4, F4, M4, E5, C5 ● **Temperaments:** R ● **Physical:** Stg=M; Const: R, H Freq: N Occas: S, I ● **Work Env:** Noise=L; Occas: T ● **Salary:** 3 ● **Outlook:** 3

GOE: 06.04.40
Loading, Moving, Hoisting & Conveying

CHAR-CONVEYOR TENDER (sugar & conf.) ● DOT #529.685-050 ● OES: 97910 ● Tends conveyor-belt system to distribute wet char from filters to drying hoppers and dried char from driers or bins to filters: Starts conveyor system under filter being emptied, and positions gate on belt over designated hopper to divert char from belt into hopper. Rakes char from one hopper to another to keep hoppers full. Starts shaker machine that distributes dried char from hopper or bins onto conveyor for transmission to filters. Inspects and cleans drier screens and pots. Sweeps and weighs char dust from dust-cooler room. May be designated according to condition of char as Wet-Char Conveyor Tender (sugar & conf.); or location of job as Char Conveyor Tender, Cellar (sugar & conf.). ● **GED:** R2, M1, L1 ● **SVP:** 2-30 days ● **Academic:** Ed=N, Eng=N ● **Work Field:** 011 ● **MPSMS:** 499 ● **Aptitudes:** G4, V4, N4, S4, P4, Q5, K4, F4, M3, E5, C5 ● **Temperaments:** R, T ● **Physical:** Stg=M; Freq: R, H, N, D ● **Work Env:** Noise=L; Occas: H, U, A, M ● **Salary:** 2 ● **Outlook:** 2

COMPRESSED-GAS-PLANT WORKER (chemical) ● DOT #549.587-010 ● OES: 98998 ● Performs any combination of following tasks in establishment making compressed and liquefied gas: Loads cylinders or ton containers on vehicles, using handtruck or chain hoist, and records type and quantity of cylinders. Examines returned cylinders for surface defects, such as dents, cracks, and burns, and rolls cylinders to designated work area. Removes valves and installs reconditioned valves on cylinders, using wrenches. Connects exhaust manifold to cylinders and turns valve to draw off residual gas. Bounces or hammers cylinders to loosen rust and scale, and inserts water, steam, and air nozzles and turns valves to clean and dry cylinders. Tests filled cylinders for leaks by brushing or spraying chemical solution around valve. Weighs filled cylinders on platform scale and records weight. Screws protection cap over valve and ties warning and identification tags on cylinder. Wraps cakes of dry ice in paper and stores them in icehouse. May clean cylinder exteriors with wire brush. May place cylinders on heating rack to expand gas to ensure complete removal. May be known according to work performed as Blow-Off Worker (chemical); Cylinder Handler (chemical); Cylinder Valver (chemical); Hoist-Cylinder Loader (chemical); Ice Handler (chemical); Valve Steamer (chemical). May be designated: Cylinder Checker (chemical); Cylinder Devalver (chemical); Cylinder Steamer (chemical); Ton-Container Shipper (chemical). ● **GED:** R2, M2, L2 ● **SVP:** 2-30 days ● **Academic:** Ed=N, Eng=N ● **Work Field:** 011, 031 ● **MPSMS:** 551 ● **Aptitudes:** G4, V4, N4, S4, P3, Q4, K3, F3, M3, E4, C5 ● **Temperaments:** R ● **Physical:** Stg=M; Freq: R, H, I, N Occas: S, O ● **Work Env:** Noise=N; ● **Salary:** 3 ● **Outlook:** 2

CONVEYOR FEEDER-OFFBEARER (any industry) ● DOT #921.686-014 ● OES: 98502 ● Alternate titles: CARTON CATCHER; DUMPER-BULK SYSTEM. Feeds and off bears conveyor or conveyor system performing any of following tasks: Picks up materials or products from pallet, handtruck, or dolly, and places materials or products onto conveyor, or opens bins or chutes to dump bulk materials onto conveyor, or hangs products on chain or overhead conveyor, or transfers materials or products from one conveyor to another conveyor, and aligns materials or products on conveyor to prevent jams. Dislodges jams by hand or pole. Removes materials or products from discharge end of conveyor and stacks materials or products on trays, pallets, or handtrucks. May feed and off bear conveyor that conveys material or products through machines or equipment operated or tended by another worker. May inspect materials or products for damage or for conformity to specifications. May push material or products between machines or departments on roller conveyor. May move materials or products to or from conveyor, using handtruck, dolly, or electric handtruck. May start or stop conveyor. May open cartons or shipping containers and place contents on conveyor. May use hoist to load or unload conveyor. May stencil, tag, stamp, or write identifying information on packaged products. May record production. May keep work area clean and orderly. ● **GED:** R1, M1, L1 ● **SVP:** 2-30 days ● **Academic:** Ed=N, Eng=N ● **Work Field:** 011 ● **MPSMS:** 450, 460, 480 ● **Aptitudes:** G4, V4, N4, S4, P4, Q5, K4, F5, M2, E5, C5 ● **Temperaments:** R ● **Physical:** Stg=M; Const: H Freq: R Occas: S, D ● **Work Env:** Noise=L; ● **Salary:** 2 ● **Outlook:** 3

DISTILLERY WORKER, GENERAL (beverage) ● DOT #529.687-066 ● OES: 98998 ● Cleans, transports and applies identifying data on steel drums in liquor distilling plant, performing any combination of following duties: Cleans interior of metal drums, using steam-cleaning apparatus, or interiors of barrels by rinsing them with water and alcohol. Stencils identifying information on barrelheads, using paint brush or spray gun to paint over cut-out stencils, or cuts identifying information on barrelheads, using metal dies and mallet. Paints or scrapes heads of used barrels to remove identifying information. Removes bungs from drums, using wrench or chisel and hammer. Rolls barrels into position for filling. Empties barrels or drums filled with liquor into dumping trough. Stamps serial numbers on barrelheads, using hand-stamping machine. Empties cartons of empty whiskey bottles on conveyor belt for filling. Stacks cartons filled with whiskey bottles. Repairs damaged cartons, using adhesive tape to cover tears and rips in cartons. Removes metal sealing rings from improperly labeled whiskey bottles preparatory to removal of labels. May be known according to specific work performed as Barrel Cutter (beverage); Barrel Roller (beverage); Barrel Scraper (beverage); Bung Remover (beverage); Carton Repairer (beverage); Drum Cleaner (beverage); Drum Sealer (beverage); Dumper (beverage). ● **GED:** R2, M1, L1 ● **SVP:** 2-30 days ● **Academic:** Ed=N,

Eng=N ● **Work Field:** 011, 031 ● **MPSMS:** 454, 551 ● **Aptitudes:** G4, V4, N4, S4, P4, Q4, K3, F4, M4, E4, C5 ● **Temperaments:** R ● **Physical:** Stg=H; Freq: R, H, N Occas: S, K, O, W ● **Work Env:** Noise=L; Occas: U ● **Salary:** 2 ● **Outlook:** 2

FINISHER (plastic-synth.) ● DOT #554.586-010 ● OES: 98998 ● Performs any combination of following duties involved in final processing of plastics sheets: Removes plastics sheets from overhead monorail conveyor, weighs them, and replaces them on conveyor. Moves sheets to various locations, using handtruck. Cuts masking paper to size. Mixes adhesive and transfers it to reservoir of masking machine. Copies identification data, such as size, thickness, and weight on sheets or labels. ● **GED:** R2, M1, L1 ● **SVP:** 2-30 days ● **Academic:** Ed=N, Eng=N ● **Work Field:** 011, 212 ● **MPSMS:** 492 ● **Aptitudes:** G4, V4, N4, S4, P4, Q4, K4, F4, M3, E5, C5 ● **Temperaments:** R ● **Physical:** Stg=M; Freq: R, H Occas: S, I, N, D, A ● **Work Env:** Noise=L; Occas: M, O ● **Salary:** 2 ● **Outlook:** 2

INDUSTRIAL-TRUCK OPERATOR (any industry) ● DOT #921.683-050 ● OES: 97947 ● Drives gasoline-, liquefied gas-, or electric-powered industrial truck equipped with lifting devices, such as forklift, boom, scoop, lift beam and swivel-hook, fork-grapple, clamps, elevating platform, or trailer hitch, to push, pull, lift, stack, tier, or move products, equipment, or materials in warehouse, storage yard, or factory: Moves levers and presses pedals to drive truck and control movement of lifting apparatus. Positions forks, lifting platform, or other lifting device under, over, or around loaded pallets, skids, boxes, products, or materials or hooks tow trucks to trailer hitch, and transports load to designated area. Unloads and stacks material by raising and lowering lifting device. May inventory materials on work floor, and supply workers with materials as needed. May weigh materials or products and record weight on tags, labels, or production schedules. May load or unload materials onto or off of pallets, skids, or lifting device. May lubricate truck, recharge batteries, fill fuel tank, or replace liquefied-gas tank. May be designated according to article moved as Lead Loader (smelt. & refin.); process in which involved as Stripper Truck Operator (smelt. & refin.); or type of truck operated as Electric-Truck-Crane Operator (any industry); Fork-Lift-Truck Operator (any industry); Tier-Lift-Truck Operator (any industry). May be designated: Burnt-Lime Drawer (concrete prod.); Casting Trucker (foundry); Electric-Freight-Car Operator (r.r. trans.); Electric-Truck Operator (any industry); Gasoline-Truck Operator (any industry); Metal-Storage Worker (nonfer. metal); Package-Lift Operator (any industry). ● **GED:** R2, M1, L1 ● **SVP:** 1-3 mos ● **Academic:** Ed=N, Eng=N ● **Work Field:** 011, 013 ● **MPSMS:** 450, 460 ● **Aptitudes:** G4, V4, N4, S3, P4, Q4, K3, F4, M3, E3, C4 ● **Temperaments:** R, T ● **Physical:** Stg=M; Const: R, H Freq: I, F, D, V Occas: C, S, O, G, N, A, X ● **Work Env:** Noise=L; Freq: W Occas: O ● **Salary:** 4 ● **Outlook:** 2

LABORER, CHEMICAL PROCESSING (chemical) ● DOT #559.687-050 ● OES: 98998 ● Alternate titles: DRUM CARRIER. Performs any combination of following tasks in chemical manufacturing establishment: Fills or empties equipment and containers by pumping, opening valves, scooping, dumping, scraping, or shoveling liquid, gaseous, or solid materials. Weighs materials and writes or stencils identifying information on containers. Fastens caps or covers on container, or screws bungs in place. Transports materials, using handtruck. Cleans stills and other equipment, using detergents, brushes, or scrapers. Loads railroad cars or trucks. Delivers samples to laboratory. Cleans work areas. Prepares materials by pulverizing, milling, crushing, or liquefying. Paints containers, using spray gun. May be known according to task performed as Carboy Filler (chemical); Drum Filler (chemical); Kettle-Room Helper (chemical); Shipping Hand (chemical); Wheeler (chemical). ● **GED:** R2, M1, L1 ● **SVP:** 1-3 mos ● **Academic:** Ed=N, Eng=N ● **Work Field:** 031, 212, 041 ● **MPSMS:** 490 ● **Aptitudes:** G4, V4, N4, S4, P4, Q4, K4, F4, M3, E5, C5 ● **Temperaments:** R ● **Physical:** Stg=H; Freq: C, B, S, K, R, H Occas: D, A ● **Work Env:** Noise=L; Occas: U, A, T, O ● **Salary:** 2 ● **Outlook:** 2

LABORER, CONCRETE PLANT (concrete prod.) ● DOT #579.687-042 ● OES: 98998 ● Performs variety of tasks in establishment manufacturing concrete products: Ties strip of cloth around bell of freshly cast concrete pipe to maintain circular shape of bell during curing. Arranges pipe in storage yard and stacks pipe for shipment. Places rubber gaskets on pipe. Stacks concrete blocks on pallets for removal by forklift truck. Feeds concrete blocks into block-breaking machine

or abrasive saw to shape blocks. Immerses chimney flue liner sections in sealing compound. Brushes stone facings to remove loose material, applies acid solution, using brush to remove concrete around stones, and washes acid from stone, using water hose. Repairs defects in concrete surfaces, using mortar or grout and trowel, and smooths rough spots, using chisel and abrasive stone. Opens gates of railroad cars to allow materials to flow into storage chutes. Loads, unloads, and moves cement, sand, and gravel to work areas, using wheelbarrow, handtruck, or industrial truck. Cleans yard and plant, using shovel, broom, and water hose, and performs other duties as assigned. May be designated according to specific duties performed as Acid Cutter (concrete prod.); Bell Tier (concrete prod.); Block Breaker (concrete prod.); Block Cuber (concrete prod.); Flue-Lining Dipper (concrete prod.); Rough Patcher (concrete prod.); Yarder (concrete prod.). ● **GED:** R2, M1, L1 ● **SVP:** 2-30 days ● **Academic:** Ed=N, Eng=N ● **Work Field:** 011, 031 ● **MPSMS:** 536 ● **Aptitudes:** G4, V4, N4, S4, P4, Q5, K4, F4, M3, E5, C5 ● **Temperaments:** R ● **Physical:** Stg=H; Const: R, H Freq: S Occas: I, D, A ● **Work Env:** Noise=L; Occas: W, U, A ● **Salary:** 1 ● **Outlook:** 3

LABORER, GENERAL (plastic-synth.) ● DOT #559.667-014 ● OES: 98998 ● Performs any combination of following tasks involved in manufacturing plastics materials, synthetic resins, and synthetic rubber: Transports materials to workers and machines, using hoist or handtruck. Inserts metal core in rolls of plastics film. Tightens clamps on supply racks, using wrenches. Cleans machinery and work area, using vacuum cleaner, brushes, and cleaning solvents. Measures, weighs, and dumps ingredients into mills, kettles, or hoppers. Replaces spools or coils of materials on supply racks or reels. Delivers samples of materials to testing laboratory. Records weights, types, and amounts of materials used, stored, or shipped. ● **GED:** R2, M1, L1 ● **SVP:** 2-30 days ● **Academic:** Ed=N, Eng=N ● **Work Field:** 011, 031 ● **MPSMS:** 492 ● **Aptitudes:** G4, V4, N4, S4, P4, Q4, K4, F4, M3, E5, C5 ● **Temperaments:** R ● **Physical:** Stg=M; Freq: R, H Occas: C, S, I, T, G, D, A ● **Work Env:** Noise=L; Occas: H, A ● **Salary:** 2 ● **Outlook:** 3

LABORER, GENERAL (steel & rel.) ● DOT #509.687-026 ● OES: 98502 ● Performs any combination of following tasks to assist workers engaged in production of iron and steel: Feeds and off bears equipment, such as conveyors, pilers, and loaders, to charge furnaces, transport hot metal to rollers, and store finished products. Bundles and ties metal rods, sheets, and wire, using banding machine and handtools. Attaches crane hooks, slings, or cradles to material for moving by OVERHEAD CRANE OPERATOR (any industry) 921.663-010. Transports material to and from production stations, using handtruck. Feeds material, such as ganister, magnesite, and limestone into crushers to prepare additives for molten metal. Grinds defects, such as burrs, seams, and scratches from rolled steel, using portable grinder. Sweeps scale from work area and empties dust bins, using wheelbarrow, broom, and shovel. Breaks up manganese and scrap metal to facilitate handling, using sledge and pneumatic hammer. Marks identification numbers on steel billets, using chalk. Verifies dimension of products, using fixed gauge. Wipes grease and oil from machinery with rags and solvent. May be designated Conveyor Feeder (steel & rel.); Crusher Feeder (steel & rel.); Loading Checker (steel & rel.); Marker (steel & rel.); Racker (steel & rel.); Scrap Breaker (steel & rel.). ● **GED:** R2, M1, L1 ● **SVP:** 1-3 mos ● **Academic:** Ed=N, Eng=N ● **Work Field:** 011, 031 ● **MPSMS:** 540 ● **Aptitudes:** G4, V4, N4, S4, P4, Q5, K4, F4, M3, E5, C5 ● **Temperaments:** R ● **Physical:** Stg=H; Freq: R, H Occas: C, S, K, O, I ● **Work Env:** Noise=L; Freq: H, U, A, O Occas: W ● **Salary:** 2 ● **Outlook:** 3

LOADER I (any industry) ● DOT #914.667-010 ● OES: 97910 ● Alternate titles: CAR FILLER; LIQUID LOADER; TANK-CAR LOADER; TRUCK LOADER. Pumps liquid chemicals, liquid petroleum products, and other liquids into or from tank cars, trucks, or barges: Verifies tank car numbers with loading instructions to ensure accurate placement of cars by crew. Connects ground cable to carry off static electricity. Removes and replaces or gives directions to another worker to remove and replace dome caps, using wrenches. Inspects interior for cleanliness and exterior for leaks or damage. Swings loading spout over dome and turns valve to admit liquids to tank. Lowers gauge rod into tank or reads meter to verify specified volume of liquids loaded. Lowers sample bottle into tank for laboratory testing. Copies load specification on placard and tacks placard to tank. Seals outlet valves on car. When unloading cars, connects hose to outlet plugs on cars and attaches special dome, using wrenches. Starts pumps or turns valves to admit compressed air into tank car and force liquids into storage tanks. May test sample for specific gravity, using hydrometer, and record reading on loading slip. May clean interior of tank cars or tank trucks, using mechanical spray nozzle. May inspect rupture disc, vacuum relief valve, rubber gaskets on valves and cover plates, and replace defective parts, using wrenches. May pump nitrogen or compressed air into car to test for leaks. May be designated according to material loaded and unloaded as Acid Loader (chemical); Caustic Loader (chemical); Fats And Oils Loader (soap & rel.). ● **GED:** R3, M2, L2 ● **SVP:** 6 mos-1 yr ● **Academic:** Ed=N, Eng=N ● **Work Field:** 014 ● **MPSMS:** 380, 490, 501 ● **Aptitudes:** G3, V4, N4, S3, P3, Q3, K3, F4, M3, E4, C4 ● **Temperaments:** R, T ● **Physical:** Stg=M; Freq: R, H, I, N, D Occas: C, B, S, O, T, G, X ● **Work Env:** Noise=L; Freq: W, A, O ● **Salary:** 1 ● **Outlook:** 3

PALLETIZER OPERATOR I (any industry) ● DOT #921.682-014 ● OES: 97999 ● Operates console that controls automatic palletizing equipment to sort, transfer, and stack on pallets containers of finished products, such as sugar, canned vegetables, citrus juice, and cigarettes: Reads production and delivery schedules and stacking pattern to determine sorting and transfer procedures, arrangement of packages on pallet, and destination of loaded pallet. Observes packages moving along conveyor to identify packages and to detect defective packaging, and presses console buttons to deflect packages to predetermined accumulator or reject lines. Turns selector switch on palletizer to control stacking arrangement of packages on pallet and to transfer loaded pallet to storage or delivery platform. Supplies loading equipment with empty pallets. Stops equipment to clear jams. Informs supervisor of equipment malfunction. May keep record of production and equipment performance. May operate depalletizing equipment and be designated Depalletizer Operator (any industry). ● **GED:** R3, M1, L1 ● **SVP:** 3-6 mos ● **Academic:** Ed=N, Eng=N ● **Work Field:** 011, 145, 212 ● **MPSMS:** 565 ● **Aptitudes:** G3, V3, N4, S3, P3, Q4, K4, F4, M3, E5, C5 ● **Temperaments:** J, T ● **Physical:** Stg=L; Freq: R, H, I, N, D Occas: S ● **Work Env:** Noise=L; ● **Salary:** 4 ● **Outlook:** 4

SAWMILL WORKER (saw. & plan.) ● DOT #667.687-018 ● OES: 92305 ● Alternate titles: SWAMPER. Performs any combination of following duties in preparing logs for cutting into lumber and storing cut lumber in sawmill: Unloads logs from trucks or cars. Rolls logs onto sawmill deck. Examines logs for defects, such as embedded pieces of iron or stone, decayed wood from splits, and marks defects for removal by other workers. Rolls logs from deck onto log or carriage. Rides log carriage of head saw and adjusts position of logs on carriage to cut planks of required thickness. Sorts and guides planks emerging from saw onto roller tables or conveyors for trimming edges. Straightens lumber on moving conveyors. Straightens edges of rough lumber, using saw. Operates and maintains donkey engines. Sharpens and adjusts teeth of woodworking saws. Tends fires in donkey engine. May relieve designated workers engaged in preparing or cutting logs into lumber and be designated Sawmill-Relief Worker (saw. & plan.). ● **GED:** R3, M1, L1 ● **SVP:** 1-3 mos ● **Academic:** Ed=N, Eng=N ● **Work Field:** 056 ● **MPSMS:** 451 ● **Aptitudes:** G3, V4, N4, S3, P4, Q5, K3, F4, M3, E4, C5 ● **Temperaments:** R, T ● **Physical:** Stg=M; Freq: C, B, S, R, H, I, G, F ● **Work Env:** Noise=L; Occas: M, O ● **Salary:** 3 ● **Outlook:** 3

Business Detail 07

An interest in organized, clearly defined activities requiring accuracy and attention to details, primarily in an office setting. You can satisfy this interest in a variety of jobs in which you can attend to the details of a business operation. You may enjoy using your math skills. Perhaps a job in billing, computing, or financial recordkeeping would satisfy you. You may prefer to deal with people. You may want a job in which you meet the public, talk on the telephone, or supervise other workers. You may like to operate computer terminals, typewriters, or bookkeeping machines. Perhaps a job in recordkeeping, filing, or recording would satisfy you. You may wish to use your training and experience to manage offices and supervise other workers.

Administrative Detail   07.01

Workers in this group perform clerical work which requires special skills and knowledge. They perform management activities according to established regulations and procedures. Jobs in this group are found in the offices of businesses, industries, courts of law, and government agencies, as well as in offices of doctors, lawyers, and other professionals.

✓ What kind of work would you do?

Your work activities would depend upon your specific job. For example, you might:

- organize and oversee all clerical operations in a business office.
- prepare correspondence and keep records for a board of education.
- use knowledge of medical terms and procedures to prepare and maintain medical records and correspondence.
- search public records to identify title restrictions for a title insurance company.
- use knowledge of insurance underwriting to select and process routine policy applications.
- administer and score psychological, vocational, or educational tests.

✓ What skills and abilities do you need for this kind of work?

To do this kind of work, you must be able to:

- use logical thinking and personal judgment to perform a variety of office tasks that require special skills and knowledge.
- make decisions based on your own judgment and company policy.

- follow instructions without close supervision.
- speak and write clearly and accurately.
- plan your own work and sometimes the work of others.
- deal with people.
- change work activities frequently; for example, typing, interviewing, taking dictation, or supervising others.

✓ How do you know if you would like or could learn to do this kind of work?

The following questions may give you clues about yourself as you consider this group of jobs.

- Have you taken courses in typing or short hand? Can you type rapidly and accurately?
- Have you written a letter of inquiry to a business? Can you write concisely and to the point, using proper grammar and punctuation?
- Have you been a secretary of an organization or club? Did you keep minutes of the meet ings? Do you enjoy this type of activity?
- Have you had clerical work experience in the armed services?

✓ How can you prepare for and enter this kind of work?

Occupations in this group usually require education and/or training extending from six months to over four years, depending upon the specific kind of work. People who have a good working knowledge of English, grammar, and basic math can qualify for beginning jobs in this group. These workers will receive training on the job. Some workers will need special vocational training in a specific technology such as shorthand, stenotype, legal stenography, and business management.

✓ *What else should you consider about these jobs?*

Some positions require workers who can be trusted to handle confidential information. Workers in small offices often do a variety of tasks. They may serve as bookkeeper, clerk, and receptionist. Working conditions usually are pleasant, in a modern well-lighted office building.

If you think you would like to do this kind of work, look at the job titles listed on the following pages.

■ ■ ■

GOE: 07.01.01
Interviewing

CONTACT REPRESENTATIVE (government ser.) ● DOT #169.167-018 ● OES: 21911 ● Provides information and assistance to public on government agency programs and procedures: Explains regulations, agency policies, form completion procedures, and determinations of agency to advise individuals regarding obtainment of required documents and eligibility requirements for receiving benefits. Analyzes applications and information for benefits, privileges, or relief from obligations, using knowledge of rules, regulations, and precedent decisions to determine qualifications for benefits and privileges or liability for obligations. Investigates errors or delays in processing of applications for benefits and initiates corrective action. May be designated according to title of agency represented. ● **GED:** R5, M3, L5 ● **SVP:** 1-2 yrs ● **Academic:** Ed=A, Eng=G ● **Work Field:** 271, 298, 282 ● **MPSMS:** 941, 959 ● **Aptitudes:** G2, V2, N3, S4, P4, Q2, K4, F4, M4, E5, C5 ● **Temperaments:** I, J, P ● **Physical:** Stg=S; Freq: T, G Occas: R, H, I, N, D, A ● **Work Env:** Noise=N; ● **Salary:** 4 ● **Outlook:** 3

CREDIT COUNSELOR (profess. & kin.) ● DOT #160.207-010 ● OES: 21998 ● Provides financial counseling to individuals in debt: Confers with client to ascertain available monthly income after living expenses to meet credit obligations. Calculates amount of debt and funds available to plan method of payoff and estimate time for debt liquidation. Contacts creditors to explain client's financial situation and to arrange for payment adjustments so that payments are feasible for client and agreeable to creditors. Establishes payment priorities to reduce client's overall costs by liquidating high-interest, short-term loans or contracts first. Opens account for client and disburses funds from account to creditors as agent for client. Keeps records of account activity. May counsel client on personal and family financial problems, such as excessive spending and borrowing of funds, and be designated Budget Consultant (profess. & kin.). May be required to be licensed by state agency. ● **GED:** R5, M5, L5 ● **SVP:** 2-4 yrs ● **Academic:** Ed=A, Eng=G ● **Work Field:** 232, 271, 282 ● **MPSMS:** 890 ● **Aptitudes:** G2, V2, N1, S4, P4, Q2, K5, F5, M4, E5, C5 ● **Temperaments:** D, I, J, P ● **Physical:** Stg=S; Freq: R, H, I, T, G, N, A ● **Work Env:** Noise=N; ● **Salary:** 2 ● **Outlook:** 4

ELIGIBILITY-AND-OCCUPANCY INTERVIEWER (government ser.) ● DOT #168.267-038 ● OES: 53502 ● Interviews and investigates prospective tenants to determine eligibility for public low-rent housing: Receives and processes initial or reactivated applications for public housing. Interviews applicant to obtain additional information such as family composition, health and social problems, veteran status, rent paying ability, net assets, and need for housing assistance. Advises applicant on eligibility requirements, methods of selecting tenants, and housing opportunities. Contacts employers, and public and private health and welfare agencies to verify applicant information. Provides information to tenant or applicant on availability of community resources for financial or social welfare assistance. Determines applicant eligibility according to agency rules and policies. Selects and refers eligible applicant to MANAGER, HOUSING PROJECT (profess. & kin.). Notifies eligible applicant of vacancy and assignment procedures. Computes rent in proportion to applicant's income. Receives and records security deposit and advance rent from selected applicant. Conducts annual, interim, and special housing reviews with tenants. May assist in resolving tenant complaints on maintenance problems. May visit home to determine housekeeping habits, verify housing condition, and establish housing need. ● **GED:** R4, M3, L4 ● **SVP:** 6 mos-1 yr ● **Academic:** Ed=H, Eng=S ● **Work Field:** 271 ● **MPSMS:** 941 ● **Aptitudes:** G3, V3, N3, S5, P3, Q2, K4, F4, M4, E4, C4 ● **Temperaments:** J ● **Physical:** Stg=L; Freq: R, H, I, T, G, N Occas: X ● **Work Env:** Noise=N; ● **Salary:** 3 ● **Outlook:** 3

ELIGIBILITY WORKER (government ser.) ● DOT #195.267-010 ● OES: 53502 ● Interviews applicants or recipients to determine eligibility for public assistance: Interprets and explains rules and regulations governing eligibility and grants, methods of payment, and legal rights to applicant or recipient. Records and evaluates personal and financial data obtained from applicant or recipient to determine initial or continuing eligibility, according to departmental directives. Initiates procedures to grant, modify, deny, or terminate eligibility and grants for various aid programs, such as public welfare, employment, and medical assistance. Authorizes amount of grants, based on determination of eligibility for amount of money payments, food stamps, medical care, or other general assistance. Identifies need for social services, and makes referrals to various agencies and community resources available. Prepares regular and special reports as required, and submits individual recommendations for consideration by supervisor. Prepares and keeps records of assigned cases. ● **GED:** R4, M3, L4 ● **SVP:** 1-2 yrs ● **Academic:** Ed=H, Eng=G ● **Work Field:** 271 ● **MPSMS:** 941 ● **Aptitudes:** G2, V2, N3, S4, P4, Q2, K4, F4, M4, E5, C5 ● **Temperaments:** J ● **Physical:** Stg=S; Freq: R, H, T, G, N Occas: I ● **Work Env:** Noise=N; ● **Salary:** 3 ● **Outlook:** 3

FINANCIAL-AID COUNSELOR (education) ● DOT #169.267-018 ● OES: 21998 ● Interviews students applying for financial aid, such as loans, grants-in-aid, or scholarships, to determine eligibility for assistance in college or university: Confers with individuals and groups to disseminate information and answer questions relating to financial assistance available to students enrolled in college or university. Interviews students to obtain information needed to determine eligibility for aid. Compares data on students' applications, such as proposed budget, family income, or transcript of grades, with eligibility requirements of assistance program. Determines amount of aid, considering such factors as funds available, extent of demand, and needs of students. Authorizes release of funds to students and prepares required records and reports. May assist in selection of candidates for financial awards or aid granted by specific department. May specialize in specific aid program and be designated Loan Counselor (education); Scholarship Counselor (education). ● **GED:** R4, M4, L4 ● **SVP:** 6 mos-1 yr ● **Academic:** Ed=B, Eng=G ● **Work Field:** 271, 295 ● **MPSMS:** 894 ● **Aptitudes:** G3, V2, N3, S4, P3, Q2, K4, F4, M4, E5, C5 ● **Temperaments:** J ● **Physical:** Stg=S; Freq: T, G Occas: R, H, I, N ● **Work Env:** Noise=N; ● **Salary:** 4 ● **Outlook:** 3

MANAGEMENT AIDE (social ser.) ● DOT #195.367-014 ● OES: 27308 ● Aids residents of public and private housing projects and apartments in relocation and provides information concerning regulations, facilities, and services: Explains rules established by owner or management, such as sanitation and maintenance requirements, and parking regulations. Demonstrates use and care of equipment for tenant use. Informs tenants of facilities, such as laundries and playgrounds. Advises homemakers needing assistance in child care, food, money management, and housekeeping problems. Provides information on location and nature of available community services, such as clinics and recreation centers. Keeps records and prepares reports for owner or manangement. ● **GED:** R4, M3, L4 ● **SVP:** 6 mos-1 yr ● **Academic:** Ed=H, Eng=G ● **Work Field:** 282, 291 ● **MPSMS:** 941 ● **Aptitudes:** G3, V3, N4, S5, P4, Q4, K4, F4, M4, E5, C5 ● **Temperaments:** J, P ● **Physical:** Stg=L; Freq: T, G Occas: R, H, N ● **Work Env:** Noise=N; ● **Salary:** 3 ● **Outlook:** 3

RETIREMENT OFFICER (government ser.) ● DOT #166.267-030 ● OES: 21511 ● Provides information and advice concerning provisions and regulations of state-administered retirement program for public employees: Explains retirement annuity system to personnel officers of local or state governmental entities covered by system, utilizing knowledge of rules and policies of retirement plan. Explains retirement policies and regulations of retirement board to covered employee groups, utilizing knowledge of annuity payments, procedure manuals, and official interpretations. Audits retirement accounts and examines records of employing entities to ensure compliance with prescribed standards and regulations. Attends and addresses conferences and other meetings of employees concerned, as representative of retirement board. ● **GED:** R5, M5, L4 ● **SVP:** 2-4 yrs ● **Academic:** Ed=A, Eng=G ● **Work Field:** 282, 271 ● **MPSMS:** 894, 895 ● **Aptitudes:** G3, V2, N2, S5, P5, Q3, K5, F5, M5, E5, C5 ● **Temperaments:** J, P, T ● **Physical:** Stg=L; Freq: T, G Occas: R, H, I, N ● **Work Env:** Noise=N; ● **Salary:** 2 ● **Outlook:** 3

GOE: 07.01.02
Administration

ADMINISTRATIVE CLERK (clerical) ● DOT #219.362-010 ● OES: 55347 ● Alternate titles: CLERK, GENERAL OFFICE. Compiles and maintains records of business transactions and office activities of establishment, performing variety of following or similar clerical duties and utilizing knowledge of systems or procedures: Copies data and compiles records and reports. Tabulates and posts data in record books. Computes wages, taxes, premiums, commissions, and payments. Records orders for merchandise or service. Gives information to and interviews customers, claimants, employees, and sales personnel. Receives, counts, and pays out cash. Prepares, issues, and sends out receipts, bills, policies, invoices, statements, and checks. Prepares stock inventory. Adjusts complaints. Operates office machines, such as typewriter, adding, calculating, and duplicating machines. Opens and routes incoming mail, answers correspondence, and prepares outgoing mail. May take dictation. May greet and assist visitors. May prepare payroll. May keep books. May purchase supplies. May operate computer terminal to input and retrieve data. May be designated according to field of activity or according to location of employment as Adjustment Clerk (retail trade; tel. & tel.); Airport Clerk (air trans.); Colliery Clerk (mine & quarry); Death-Claim Clerk (insurance); Field Clerk (clerical). May be designated: Agency Clerk (insurance); Auction Clerk (clerical); Construction-Records Clerk (construction; utilities); Shop Clerk (clerical). ● **GED:** R4, M3, L3 ● **SVP:** 3-6 mos ● **Academic:** Ed=N, Eng=G ● **Work Field:** 231, 232, 282 ● **MPSMS:** 890 ● **Aptitudes:** G3, V3, N3, S4, P4, Q2, K3, F3, M4, E5, C5 ● **Temperaments:** J, P, V ● **Physical:** Stg=L; Freq: R, H, I, T, G, N, A ● **Work Env:** Noise=N; ● **Salary:** 2 ● **Outlook:** 3

ADMINISTRATIVE SECRETARY (any industry) ● DOT #169.167-014 ● OES: 21998 ● Alternate titles: EXECUTIVE SECRETARY. Keeps official corporation records and executes administrative policies determined by or in conjunction with other officials: Prepares memorandums outlining and explaining administrative procedures and policies to supervisory workers. Plans conferences. Directs preparation of records, such as notices, minutes, and resolutions for stockholders' and directors' meetings. Directs recording of company stock issues and transfers. Acts as custodian of corporate documents and records. Directs preparation and filing of corporate legal documents with government agencies to conform with statutes. In small organizations, such as trade, civic, or welfare associations, often performs publicity work. Depending on organization, works in line or staff capacity. ● **GED:** R5, M4, L5 ● **SVP:** 4-10 yrs ● **Academic:** Ed=A, Eng=G ● **Work Field:** 295, 231 ● **MPSMS:** 891 ● **Aptitudes:** G2, V2, N3, S4, P4, Q3, K4, F4, M4, E5, C5 ● **Temperaments:** D, J ● **Physical:** Stg=S; Freq: R, H, I, T, G, N, A ● **Work Env:** Noise=N; ● **Salary:** 3 ● **Outlook:** 4

AUTOMOBILE-CLUB-SAFETY-PROGRAM COORDINATOR (nonprofit org.) ● DOT #249.167-010 ● OES: 51002 ● Coordinates activities and gives information and advice regarding traffic-engineering and safety programs of automobile club: Develops and revises automobile-club procedures regarding traffic-engineering and safety programs. Arranges for speakers to address gatherings to promote and explain traffic-engineering and safety programs. Schedules, monitors, and keeps records on program activities. Advises club members about traffic summonses and violations and contacts courts to expedite processing or clarify disposition of summonses. Answers questions and gives information to callers or visitors about traffic-engineering and safety programs of automobile club. Prepares reports about road or traffic-control conditions based on information received from club members or other staff members. ● **GED:** R4, M3, L4 ● **SVP:** 1-2 yrs ● **Academic:** Ed=H, Eng=G ● **Work Field:** 282, 271, 231 ● **MPSMS:** 961, 891 ● **Aptitudes:** G3, V3, N3, S4, P4, Q3, K4, F4, M4, E5, C5 ● **Temperaments:** D, P, V ● **Physical:** Stg=S; Freq: T, G Occas: R, H ● **Work Env:** Noise=N; ● **Salary:** 4 ● **Outlook:** 3

COORDINATOR, SKILL-TRAINING PROGRAM (government ser.) ● DOT #169.167-062 ● OES: 21511 ● Plans and arranges for cooperation with and participation in skill training program by private industry, agencies, and concerned individuals: Organizes and coordinates recruiting, training, and placement of participants. Contacts various service agencies on behalf of trainees with social problems and refers trainees to appropriate agencies to ensure trainees receive maximum available assistance. Prepares periodic reports to monitor and evaluate progress of program. ● **GED:** R5, M4, L4 ● **SVP:** 1-2 yrs ● **Academic:** Ed=H, Eng=G ● **Work Field:** 295 ● **MPSMS:** 931 ● **Aptitudes:** G2, V2, N2, S3, P4, Q3, K4, F4, M3, E4, C4 ● **Temperaments:** D, I, J, P ● **Physical:** Stg=S; Freq: T, G, N Occas: R, H, I, A, X ● **Work Env:** Noise=N; ● **Salary:** 4 ● **Outlook:** 2

COURT CLERK (government ser.) ● DOT #243.362-010 ● OES: 53702 ● Performs clerical duties in court of law: Prepares docket or calendar of cases to be called, using typewriter. Examines legal documents submitted to court for adherence to law or court procedures, prepares case folders, and posts, files, or routes documents. Explains procedures or forms to parties in case. Secures information for judges, and contacts witnesses, attorneys, and litigants to obtain information for court, and instructs parties when to appear in court. Notifies district attorney's office of cases prosecuted by district attorney. Administers oath to witnesses. Records minutes of court proceedings, using stenotype machine or shorthand, and trsnscribes testimony, using typewriter. Records case disposition, court orders, and arrangement for payment of court fees. Collects court fees or fines and records amounts collected. ● **GED:** R4, M2, L4 ● **SVP:** 1-2 yrs ● **Academic:** Ed=H, Eng=G ● **Work Field:** 231, 282 ● **MPSMS:** 950 ● **Aptitudes:** G3, V3, N3, S4, P4, Q2, K3, F3, M3, E5, C5 ● **Temperaments:** P, V ● **Physical:** Stg=S; Freq: T, G Occas: R, H, I, N ● **Work Env:** Noise=Q; ● **Salary:** 4 ● **Outlook:** 3

DIRECTOR, NURSES' REGISTRY (medical ser.) ● DOT #187.167-034 ● OES: 19998 ● Alternate titles: REGISTRAR, NURSES' REGISTRY. Directs registry services for NURSES, PRIVATE DUTY (medical ser.) according to regulations established by state or district professional nurses' association: Maintains roster of nurses available for duty. Refers nurses in response to requests. Keeps record of number and type of calls received. Analyzes problems of registry to render more efficient service and operations. Informs registrants of new and revised requirements and regulations. May assist in recruiting nurses for emergencies. May be responsible for financial administration of registry. ● **GED:** R5, M4, L5 ● **SVP:** 1-2 yrs ● **Academic:** Ed=A, Eng=G ● **Work Field:** 295 ● **MPSMS:** 943, 924 ● **Aptitudes:** G2, V2, N3, S3, P4, Q2, K4, F4, M4, E5, C5 ● **Temperaments:** D, P ● **Physical:** Stg=S; Freq: T, G Occas: R, H, I, N ● **Work Env:** Noise=N; ● **Salary:** 4 ● **Outlook:** 4

LABOR EXPEDITER (construction) ● DOT #249.167-018 ● OES: 58008 ● Expedites movement of labor to construction locations: Contacts representatives of transportation, feeding, and housing facilities to arrange for servicing workers at transient points. Issues permits, identification cards, and tickets to workers for travel to specified areas. May contact labor union with jurisdiction, where project is located, to inform labor official of recruited workers and to determine union regulations in area. May direct workers to report to local union after arrival in area. May meet recruited workers at designated depot, airport, or dock. ● **GED:** R4, M3, L4 ● **SVP:** 6 mos-1 yr ● **Academic:** Ed=N, Eng=G ● **Work Field:** 291, 282 ● **MPSMS:** 850, 900 ● **Aptitudes:** G3, V3, N3, S5, P4, Q3, K4, F4, M4, E5, C5 ● **Temperaments:** D, P, V ● **Physical:** Stg=L; Freq: T, G Occas: R, H, I, N ● **Work Env:** Noise=Q; Occas: W ● **Salary:** 2 ● **Outlook:** 3

MANAGER, OFFICE (any industry) ● DOT #169.167-034 ● OES: 13014 ● Alternate titles: CHIEF CLERK; MANAGER, ADMINISTRATIVE SERVICES. Coordinates activities of clerical personnel in establishment or organization: Analyses and organizes office operations and procedures, such as typing, bookkeeping, preparation of payrolls, flow of correspondence, filing, requisition of supplies, and other clerical services. Evaluates office production, revises procedures, or devises new forms to improve efficiency of workflow. Establishes uniform correspondence procedures and style practices. Formulates procedures for systematic retention, protection, retrieval, transfer, and disposal of records. Plans office layouts and initiates cost reduction programs. Reviews clerical and personnel records to ensure completeness, accuracy, and timeliness. Prepares activities reports for guidance of management, using computer. Prepares employee ratings and conducts employee benefit and insurance programs, using computer. Coordinates activities of various clerical departments or workers within department. May prepare organizational budget and monthly financial reports. May hire, train, and supervise clerical staff. May compile, store, and retrieve managerial data, using computer. ● **GED:** R4, M3, L4 ● **SVP:** 2-4 yrs ● **Academic:** Ed=H, Eng=G ● **Work Field:** 231, 232, 295 ● **MPSMS:** 890 ● **Aptitudes:** G2, V2, N3, S4, P4, Q3, K4, F3, M4, E5, C5 ● **Temperaments:** D, J, P, V ● **Physical:** Stg=S; Freq: R, H, I, T, G, N, A ● **Work Env:** Noise=N; ● **Salary:** 3 ● **Outlook:** 4

MANAGER, TRAFFIC I (motor trans.) ● DOT #184.167-102 ● OES: 15023 ● Directs and coordinates activities concerned with documentation and routing of outgoing freight, and verification and reshipment of incoming freight, at motor-transportation company warehouse: Directs activities of workers engaged in assigning tariff classifications according to type and weight of freight or merchandise, routing and scheduling shipment by air, rail, or truck, and preparing billings from tariff and classification manuals. Reviews documents to ensure that assigned classifications and tariffs are in accordance with mode of transportation and destination of shipment. Investigates shipper or consignee complaints regarding lost or damaged merchandise or shortages in shipment to determine responsibility. Directs preparation of claims against carrier responsible and corresponds with shipper or consignee to effect settlement. Schedules shipments to ensure compliance with interstate traffic laws and regulations and company policies. ● **GED:** R5, M4, L5 ● **SVP:** 4-10 yrs ● **Academic:** Ed=A, Eng=G ● **Work Field:** 221 ● **MPSMS:** 853 ● **Aptitudes:** G2, V2, N2, S4, P4, Q2, K4, F4, M4, E5, C5 ● **Temperaments:** D, P ● **Physical:** Stg=S; Freq: T, G, N Occas: R, H, I, A ● **Work Env:** Noise=N; ● **Salary:** 5 ● **Outlook:** 2

MEMBERSHIP SECRETARY (nonprofit org.) ● DOT #201.362-018 ● OES: 55198 ● Compiles and maintains membership lists, records receipts of dues and contributions, and gives information to members of nonprofit organization: Compiles and maintains membership lists and contribution records. Welcomes new members and issues membership cards. Explains privileges and obligations of membership, discusses organization problems, adjusts complaints, and provides other information to members. Types and sends notices of dues. Collects and records receipts of dues and contributions. Sends newsletters, promotional materials, and other publications to persons on mailing list. May prepare and distribute monthly financial reports to department heads. May assign numbers and codes to new corporate and individual members and input billing schedule into computer. May revise existing membership records, compile list of delinquent dues, and forward information to president. ● **GED:** R4, M3, L4 ● **SVP:** 6 mos-1 yr ● **Academic:** Ed=H, Eng=G ● **Work Field:** 231, 232, 282 ● **MPSMS:** 891 ● **Aptitudes:** G3, V3, N4, S5, P3, Q2, K3, F3, M4, E5, C5 ● **Temperaments:** J, P, V ● **Physical:** Stg=S; Freq: R, H, I, T, G, N ● **Work Env:** Noise=N; ● **Salary:** 4 ● **Outlook:** 3

PROCUREMENT CLERK (clerical) ● DOT #249.367-066 ● OES: 55326 ● Alternate titles: AWARD CLERK; BID CLERK; BUYER, ASSISTANT; PURCHASE-REQUEST EDITOR; PURCHASING-AND-FISCAL CLERK; PURCHASING CLERK; PURCHASING-CONTRACTING CLERK. Compiles information and records to

prepare purchase orders for procurement of material for industrial firm, governmental agency, or other establishment: Verifies nomenclature and specifications of purchase requests. Searches inventory records or warehouse to determine if material on hand is in sufficient quantity. Consults catalogs and interviews suppliers to obtain prices and specifications. Types or writes invitation-of-bid forms and mails forms to supplier firms or for public posting. Writes or types purchase order and sends copy to supplier and department originating request. Compiles records of items purchased or transferred between departments, prices, deliveries, and inventories. Computes total cost of items purchased, using calculator. Confers with suppliers concerning late deliveries. May compare prices, specifications, and delivery dates and award contract to bidders or place orders with suppliers or mail order firms. May verify bills from suppliers with bids and purchase orders and approve bills for payment. May classify priority regulations. ● **GED:** R4, M3, L3 ● **SVP:** 3-6 mos ● **Academic:** Ed=N, Eng=S ● **Work Field:** 232, 221 ● **MPSMS:** 891, 898 ● **Aptitudes:** G3, V3, N3, S4, P3, Q2, K4, F3, M4, E5, C5 ● **Temperaments:** P, T, V ● **Physical:** Stg=S; Freq: R, H, I, T, G, N Occas: A ● **Work Env:** Noise=N; ● **Salary:** 3 ● **Outlook:** 3

SUPERVISOR, CUSTOMER SERVICES (motor trans.) ● DOT #248.137-018 ● OES: 51002 ● Supervises and coordinates activities of workers engaged in servicing and promoting shipper accounts for parcel-delivery firm: Reviews records indicating shipper parcel volume, claims for damaged and lost parcels, and deficiencies in parcel preparation for pickup and delivery. Discusses service to shippers with assigned representatives to develop plans of service. Meets with, or directs representatives to meet with, shippers to resolve problems in wrapping and handling of parcels and relationships between firm's employees and shippers. Assigns representatives to solicit prospective accounts. Evaluates performance and productivity of workers and reports to management. Performs other duties as described under SUPERVISOR (clerical) Master Title. ● **GED:** R4, M3, L4 ● **SVP:** 1-2 yrs ● **Academic:** Ed=H, Eng=G ● **Work Field:** 221, 292 ● **MPSMS:** 853 ● **Aptitudes:** G2, V3, N3, S3, P4, Q3, K4, F4, M4, E4, C5 ● **Temperaments:** D, I, J, P ● **Physical:** Stg=L; Freq: T, G Occas: R, H, N ● **Work Env:** Noise=N; ● **Salary:** 4 ● **Outlook:** 2

SUPERVISOR, LENDING ACTIVITIES (financial) ● DOT #249.137-034 ● OES: 51002 ● Supervises and coordinates activities of workers engaged in processing and recording commercial, residential, and consumer loans: Answers workers' and customers' questions regarding procedures. Reviews and authorizes corrections to loan records. Supervises MORTGAGE LOAN PROCESSOR (financial) 249.362-022; MORTGAGE LOAN CLOSER (financial) 249.362-018; CLERK-TYPIST (clerical) 203.362-010; and others. Performs other duties as described under SUPERVISOR (clerical) Master Title. Workers who supervise loan collection are classified under SUPERVISOR, CREDIT AND LOAN COLLECTIONS (clerical) 241.137-010. ● **GED:** R4, M3, L4 ● **SVP:** 4-10 yrs ● **Academic:** Ed=H, Eng=G ● **Work Field:** 231 ● **MPSMS:** 894 ● **Aptitudes:** G2, V2, N3, S4, P4, Q2, K4, F3, M4, E5, C5 ● **Temperaments:** D, J, P, T ● **Physical:** Stg=S; Const: T, G, N Occas: R, H, I, A ● **Work Env:** Noise=Q; ● **Salary:** 4 ● **Outlook:** 2

SUPERVISOR, NETWORK CONTROL OPERATORS (any industry) ● DOT #031.132-010 ● OES: 25198 ● Alternate titles: DATA COMMUNICATIONS TECHNICIAN SUPERVISOR. Supervises and coordinates activities of workers engaged in monitoring or installing data communication lines and resolving user data communication problems: Distributes work assignments and monitors daily logs of NETWORK CONTROL OPERATORS (any industry) 031.262-014, using microcomputer. Explains data communications diagnostic and monitoring procedures to operators, using computer terminal and following vendor's equipment and software instructions. Explains and demonstrates installation of data communication lines and equipment to operators, using handtools and following vendor manuals. Enters diagnostic commands into computer and determines nature of problem to assist operators to resolve data communication problems. Enters record of actions taken to resolve problem in daily log, using microcomputer. Attends staff meetings to report on and resolve recurrent data communications problems. Attends vendor seminars to learn about changes in data communications technology. Performs other duties as described under SUPERVISOR (any industry) Master Title. ● **GED:** R4, M4, L4 ● **SVP:** 2-4 yrs ● **Academic:** Ed=A, Eng=G ● **Work Field:** 233 ● **MPSMS:** 893 ● **Aptitudes:** G2, V2, N3, S3, P3, Q3, K4, F4,

M4, E5, C5 ● **Temperaments:** D, J, P, T ● **Physical:** Stg=L; Freq: R, H, I, T, G, N, A ● **Work Env:** Noise=N; ● **Salary:** 5 ● **Outlook:** 5

SUPERVISOR, SAFETY DEPOSIT (financial) ● DOT #295.137-010 ● OES: 51002 ● Alternate titles: SAFE DEPOSIT MANAGER. Supervises and coordinates activities of workers engaged in renting and maintaining safe-deposit boxes: Turns controls to set vault clock for reopening. Authorizes forcing, servicing, and repair of safe-deposit box locks. Approves or disapproves rentals and requests for admittance to safe-deposit boxes in accordance with bank regulations. Develops, implements, and evaluates improved procedures for safe deposit operations. Monitors prices charged by competitors, recommends rental fees for safe-deposit boxes, and develops marketing plan to advertise safe-deposit services. Prepares cost, expense, and budget reports. Keeps departmental records. Trains and assigns duties to new employees. May open and close vault. May admit customer to vault. Performs duties as described under SUPERVISOR (clerical) Master Title. ● **GED:** R4, M3, L3 ● **SVP:** 1-2 yrs ● **Academic:** Ed=N, Eng=G ● **Work Field:** 231, 232 ● **MPSMS:** 894 ● **Aptitudes:** G3, V3, N3, S4, P4, Q3, K4, F4, M4, E5, C5 ● **Temperaments:** D, P ● **Physical:** Stg=L; Const: T, G Freq: N Occas: S, O, R, H, I, F, A ● **Work Env:** Noise=N; ● **Salary:** 4 ● **Outlook:** 2

TEACHER AIDE II (education) ● DOT #249.367-074 ● OES: 53904 ● Alternate titles: TEACHER AIDE, CLERICAL. Performs any combination of following duties in classroom to assist teaching staff of public or private elementary or secondary school: Takes attendance. Grades homework and tests, using answer sheets, and records results. Distributes teaching materials to students, such as textbooks, workbooks, or paper and pencils. Maintains order within school and on school grounds. Operates learning aids, such as film and slide projectors and tape recorders. Prepares requisitions for library materials and stockroom supplies. Types material and operates duplicating equipment to reproduce instructional materials. ● **GED:** R3, M3, L3 ● **SVP:** 1-3 mos ● **Academic:** Ed=N, Eng=G ● **Work Field:** 296, 231 ● **MPSMS:** 931 ● **Aptitudes:** G3, V3, N3, S4, P4, Q3, K4, F3, M4, E5, C5 ● **Temperaments:** J, P, V ● **Physical:** Stg=L; Freq: R, H, I, T, G, N Occas: F ● **Work Env:** Noise=N; ● **Salary:** 1 ● **Outlook:** 3

TOWN CLERK (government ser.) ● DOT #243.367-018 ● OES: 53705 ● Performs variety of clerical and administrative duties required by municipal government: Prepares agendas and bylaws for town council; records minutes of council meetings; answers official correspondence; keeps fiscal records and accounts; and prepares reports on civic needs. ● **GED:** R4, M4, L3 ● **SVP:** 6 mos-1 yr ● **Academic:** Ed=N, Eng=G ● **Work Field:** 231, 232 ● **MPSMS:** 890 ● **Aptitudes:** G2, V2, N2, S4, P2, Q2, K4, F4, M5, E5, C5 ● **Temperaments:** J ● **Physical:** Stg=S; Freq: R, H, I, G, N Occas: T ● **Work Env:** Noise=N; ● **Salary:** 4 ● **Outlook:** 3

TRANSFER CLERK, HEAD (financial) ● DOT #216.137-014 ● OES: 51002 ● Supervises and coordinates activities of TRANSFER CLERKS (financial) 216.362-046 in transactions relating to stock certificates, applying knowledge of company policies and procedures, and commercial law: Explains company policies to stockholders with regard to stock transfers and payment of dividends. Examines certificates presented for transfer to verify legality of transactions. Answers inquiries concerning stock transfer requirements, dividend payments, and tax on certificates. Performs duties as described under SUPERVISOR (clerical) Master Title. May arrange meetings for bank-shareholders. ● **GED:** R4, M4, L4 ● **SVP:** 1-2 yrs ● **Academic:** Ed=H, Eng=G ● **Work Field:** 232 ● **MPSMS:** 894 ● **Aptitudes:** G3, V2, N3, S4, P3, Q2, K4, F3, M4, E5, C5 ● **Temperaments:** D, P ● **Physical:** Stg=S; Freq: R, H, T, G, N Occas: I, A ● **Work Env:** Noise=Q; ● **Salary:** 4 ● **Outlook:** 2

GOE: 07.01.03
Secretarial Work

LEGAL SECRETARY (clerical) ● DOT #201.362-010 ● OES: 55102 ● Prepares legal papers and correspondence of legal nature, such as summonses, complaints, motions, and subpoenas, using typewriter, word processor, or personal computer. May review law journals and other legal publications to identify court decisions pertinent to pending cases and submit articles to company officials. ● **GED:** R4, M2, L4 ● **SVP:** 1-2 yrs ● **Academic:** Ed=H, Eng=G ● **Work Field:** 231 ● **MPSMS:** 891 ● **Aptitudes:** G2, V2, N3, S4, P2, Q2, K2, F2, M3, E5, C4 ● **Temperaments:** J, P, T, V ● **Physical:** Stg=S; Freq: R, H, I, T, G, N, A Occas: X ● **Work Env:** Noise=N; ● **Salary:** 4 ● **Outlook:** 4

MEDICAL SECRETARY (medical ser.) ● DOT #201.362-014 ● OES: 55105 ● Performs secretarial duties, utilizing knowledge of medical terminology and hospital, clinic, or laboratory procedures: Takes dictation in shorthand or using dictaphone. Compiles and records medical charts, reports, and correspondence, using typewriter or word processor. Answers telephone, schedules appointments, and greets and directs visitors. Maintains files. ● **GED:** R4, M3, L4 ● **SVP:** 1-2 yrs ● **Academic:** Ed=H, Eng=G ● **Work Field:** 231 ● **MPSMS:** 891 ● **Aptitudes:** G2, V2, N3, S4, P2, Q2, K2, F2, M3, E5, C5 ● **Temperaments:** J, P, T ● **Physical:** Stg=S; Freq: R, H, I, T, G, N Occas: S, O, A ● **Work Env:** Noise=N; ● **Salary:** 3 ● **Outlook:** 4

SCHOOL SECRETARY (education) ● DOT #201.362-022 ● OES: 55198 ● Performs secretarial duties in public or private school: Composes, or transcribes from rough draft, correspondence, bulletins, memorandums, and other material, using typewriter or computer. Compiles and files student grade and attendance reports and other school records. Greets visitors to school, determines nature of business, and directs visitors to destination. Talks with student encountering problem and resolves problem or directs student to other worker. Answers telephone to provide information, take message, or transfer calls. May order and dispense school supplies. May accept and deposit funds for lunches, school supplies, and student activities. May disburse funds, record financial transactions, and audit and balance student-organization and other school-fund accounts. May take dictation in shorthand and transcribe notes, using typewriter or computer. May maintain calendar of school events. May oversee student playground activities and monitor classroom during temporary absence of teacher. ● **GED:** R4, M3, L3 ● **SVP:** 6 mos-1 yr ● **Academic:** Ed=H, Eng=G ● **Work Field:** 231, 282 ● **MPSMS:** 891 ● **Aptitudes:** G3, V3, N3, S4, P3, Q2, K2, F3, M3, E5, C5 ● **Temperaments:** P, T, V ● **Physical:** Stg=S; Freq: R, H, I, T, G, N Occas: A ● **Work Env:** Noise=N; ● **Salary:** 2 ● **Outlook:** 3

SECRETARY (clerical) ● DOT #201.362-030 ● OES: 55198 ● Alternate titles: SECRETARIAL STENOGRAPHER. Schedules appointments, gives information to callers, takes dictation, and otherwise relieves officials of clerical work and minor administrative and business detail: Reads and routes incoming mail. Locates and attaches appropriate file to correspondence to be answered by employer. Takes dictation in shorthand or by machine [STENOTYPE OPERATOR (clerical) 202.362-022] and transcribes notes on typewriter, or transcribes from voice recordings [TRANSCRIBING-MACHINE OPERATOR (clerical) 203.582-058]. Composes and types routine correspondence. Files correspondence and other records. Answers telephone and gives information to callers or routes call to appropriate official and places outgoing calls. Schedules appointments for employer. Greets visitors, ascertains nature of business, and conducts visitors to employer or appropriate person. May not take dictation. May arrange travel schedule and reservations. May compile and type statistical reports. May oversee clerical workers. May keep personnel records [PERSONNEL CLERK (clerical) 209.362-026]. May record minutes of staff meetings. May make copies of correspondence or other printed matter, using copying or duplicating machine. May prepare outgoing mail, using postage-metering machine. May prepare notes, correspondence, and reports, using word processor or computer terminal. ● **GED:** R4, M3, L4 ● **SVP:** 1-2 yrs ● **Academic:** Ed=H, Eng=G ● **Work Field:** 231, 282 ● **MPSMS:** 891 ● **Aptitudes:** G3, V2, N3, S4, P3, Q2, K2, F2, M3, E5, C5 ● **Temperaments:** J, P, V ● **Physical:** Stg=S; Freq: R, H, I, T, G, N, A ● **Work Env:** Noise=N; ● **Salary:** 3 ● **Outlook:** 4

SOCIAL SECRETARY (clerical) ● DOT #201.162-010 ● OES: 55198 ● Coordinates social, business, and personal affairs of employer. Confers with employer on contemplated social functions, sends invitations, and arranges for decorations and entertainment. Advises employer on etiquette, dress, and current events. Reads and answers routine correspondence, using typewriter or in own handwriting as situation demands. May manage financial affairs of entire house. ● **GED:** R4, M2, L4 ● **SVP:** 1-2 yrs ● **Academic:** Ed=N, Eng=G ● **Work Field:** 231, 291 ● **MPSMS:** 891, 909 ● **Aptitudes:** G2, V2, N3, S4, P3, Q3, K3,

F3, M3, E5, C4 ● **Temperaments:** J, P, V ● **Physical:** Stg=S; Freq: R, H, I, T, G, N, A Occas: X ● **Work Env:** Noise=N; ● **Salary:** 3 ● **Outlook:** 2

TRUST OPERATIONS ASSISTANT (financial) ● DOT #219.362-074 ● OES: 55198 ● Opens and closes trust accounts; arranges transfer of trust assets; updates trust account records; pays bills, dividends, and interest; and performs clerical duties in personal or corporate trust department: Compiles, records, and enters names and addresses, description of assets, and other information, or deletes information previously entered, to open or close trust account, using computer. Calls or writes holders of assets, trust customer, stock transfer company, and other parties, and transmits specified documents to arrange for transfer of securities and other trust assets to or from trust account. Documents funds received or disbursed and updates records. Prepares and mails checks, or enters commands to generate checks, to pay bills for personal trust customers, disburse loan proceeds, and remit dividends, interest, and other funds to recipients. Composes and types business letters, using computer or typewriter. Opens mail and answers telephone. May call investment department to obtain information on investments and market conditions requested by trust customer. May place customer order for purchase or sale of investment with establishment investment department. ● **GED:** R4, M3, L4 ● **SVP:** 1-2 yrs ● **Academic:** Ed=N, Eng=G ● **Work Field:** 231, 232 ● **MPSMS:** 894 ● **Aptitudes:** G3, V3, N3, S4, P4, Q2, K2, F4, M4, E5, C5 ● **Temperaments:** J, P, T ● **Physical:** Stg=L; Const: I, T, G, N Freq: R, H, A Occas: S, K, O ● **Work Env:** Noise=N; ● **Salary:** 4 ● **Outlook:** 3

GOE: 07.01.04
Financial Work

CLOSER (real estate) ● DOT #186.167-074 ● OES: 28499 ● Coordinates closing transactions in real estate company: Receives and deposits escrow monies in established accounts and disburses funds from each account. Reviews closing documents to determine accuracy of information and need for additional documents. Contacts courthouse personnel, buyer and seller, and other real estate personnel to obtain additional information. Confers with legal counsel regarding legal aspects of closing transactions. Calculates pro-rated balances on mortgages, taxes, and fire insurance premiums, as of closing date, and records balances on closing statement form to provide both parties with accurate and complete financial and legal information regarding property ownership transfer transaction. Reviews contract between buyer and seller to ensure seller can convey acceptable property title to prospective buyer. Prepares closing statement for purchase of property, using figures gathered in previous transactions and listing financial settlement between buyer and seller. Compiles figures to determine closing cost of final transaction, including loan, title, appraisal, and other fees included in sale of property. Schedules appointment to complete closing process and to answer any questions regarding procedures. Presides over closing meeting, reviews and explains contract documents and terms of transaction to buyer and seller, and obtains and notarizes signatures that ensure acceptance of agreement. Collects down payment from buyer for deposit in trust fund account. Disburses funds, based on final statement, to pay seller's debts against property, such as liens, taxes, and assessments. Reviews documents to determine that they have been executed according to regulations and are ready to be recorded. Disburses completed documents to concerned parties to effect transfer of property ownership. May prepare and type legal documents, contracts, warranty deeds, and deeds of trust. May notify contract inspection or pest control businesses to perform needed service. May prepare work assignments and complete closing work schedules to maintain efficient work flow. May compile statistical reports and keep daily log on closing activities. ● **GED:** R4, M3, L4 ● **SVP:** 2-4 yrs ● **Academic:** Ed=H, Eng=G ● **Work Field:** 232, 295 ● **MPSMS:** 895 ● **Aptitudes:** G2, V2, N2, S3, P3, Q2, K2, F3, M3, E5, C5 ● **Temperaments:** J, P, T, V ● **Physical:** Stg=S; Const: N Freq: R, H, I, T, G ● **Work Env:** Noise=N; ● **Salary:** 3 ● **Outlook:** 3

CREDIT ANALYST (clerical) ● DOT #241.267-022 ● OES: 21105 ● Analyzes paying habits of customers who are delinquent in payment of bills and recommends action: Reviews files to select delinquent accounts for collection efforts. Evaluates customer records and recommends that account be closed, credit limit reduced or extended, or collection attempted, based on earnings and savings data, payment history, and purchase activity of customer. Confers with representatives of credit associations and other businesses to exchange information concerning credit ratings and forwarding addresses. Interviews customers in person or by telephone to investigate complaints, verify accuracy of charges, or to correct errors in accounts [BILL ADJUSTER (clerical)]. ● **GED:** R4, M3, L4 ● **SVP:** 2-4 yrs ● **Academic:** Ed=H, Eng=G ● **Work Field:** 271, 282 ● **MPSMS:** 894 ● **Aptitudes:** G3, V3, N3, S4, P4, Q3, K4, F4, M4, E5, C5 ● **Temperaments:** J ● **Physical:** Stg=S; Freq: T, G, N Occas: R, H, I ● **Work Env:** Noise=N; ● **Salary:** 4 ● **Outlook:** 3

ESCROW OFFICER (profess. & kin.) ● DOT #119.367-010 ● OES: 28499 ● Holds in escrow, funds, legal papers, and other collateral posted by contracting parties to ensure fulfillment of contracts or trust agreements: Prepares escrow agreement. Executes terms of contract or trust agreement, such as holding money or legal papers, paying off mortgages, or paying sums to designated parties. Files and delivers deeds and other legal papers. May assist buyer to secure financing. ● **GED:** R4, M3, L3 ● **SVP:** 4-10 yrs ● **Academic:** Ed=H, Eng=G ● **Work Field:** 231, 272 ● **MPSMS:** 895, 932 ● **Aptitudes:** G2, V3, N2, S4, P4, Q2, K3, F3, M3, E4, C4 ● **Temperaments:** J, T ● **Physical:** Stg=S; Freq: R, H, I, T, G, N, A ● **Work Env:** Noise=N; ● **Salary:** 3 ● **Outlook:** 3

MORTGAGE CLERK (financial) ● DOT #249.362-014 ● OES: 53121 ● Performs any combination of following duties to process payments and maintain records of mortgage loans: Types letters, forms, checks, and other documents used for collecting, disbursing, and recording mortgage principal, interest, and escrow account payments, using computer. Answers customer questions regarding mortgage account and corrects records, using computer. Examines documents such as deeds, assignments, and mortgages, to ensure compliance with escrow instructions, institution policy, and legal requirements. Records disbursement of funds to pay insurance and tax. Types notices to government, specifying changes to loan documents, such as discharge of mortgage. Orders property insurance policies to ensure protection against loss on mortgaged property. Enters data in computer to generate tax and insurance premium payment notices to customers. Reviews printouts of allocations for interest, principal, insurance, or tax payments to locate errors. Corrects errors, using computer. May call or write loan applicants to obtain information for bank official. May be designated according to type of work assigned as Escrow Clerk (financial); Foreclosure Clerk (financial); Insurance Clerk (financial); Tax Clerk (financial). ● **GED:** R3, M3, L3 ● **SVP:** 6 mos-1 yr ● **Academic:** Ed=N, Eng=G ● **Work Field:** 231 ● **MPSMS:** 894 ● **Aptitudes:** G3, V3, N3, S4, P3, Q2, K4, F3, M3, E5, C5 ● **Temperaments:** P, T ● **Physical:** Stg=S; Const: N Freq: I, A Occas: R, H, T, G ● **Work Env:** Noise=N; ● **Salary:** 3 ● **Outlook:** 3

MORTGAGE LOAN CLOSER (financial) ● DOT #249.362-018 ● OES: 53121 ● Schedules loan closing and compiles and types closing documents: Reviews approved mortgage loan to determine conditions that must be met prior to closing, such as purchase of private mortgage insurance. Calls borrower, real estate broker, and title company to request specified documents, such as receipt for payment of outstanding tax bill. Verifies accuracy and consistency of specifications on documents, such as title abstract and insurance forms. Calls borrower, broker, and other specified individuals to arrange time and date for closing. Answers questions regarding closing requirements. Enters numbers and calculates loan interest and principal payment, and closing costs, using computer or factor table and calculator. Types closing documents. Assembles documents for delivery to title company, real estate broker, or lending officer for closing. Records loan information in log and on government reporting forms, using computer. May compile closed loan forms for delivery to marketing department for sale to investors. ● **GED:** R4, M3, L4 ● **SVP:** 6 mos-1 yr ● **Academic:** Ed=N, Eng=G ● **Work Field:** 231 ● **MPSMS:** 894 ● **Aptitudes:** G3, V3, N3, S5, P4, Q2, K3, F3, M4, E5, C5 ● **Temperaments:** P, T ● **Physical:** Stg=S; Const: N Freq: R, H, I, T, G Occas: A ● **Work Env:** Noise=N; ● **Salary:** 3 ● **Outlook:** 4

REAL-ESTATE CLERK (real estate) ● DOT #219.362-046 ● OES: 53914 ● Maintains records concerned with rental, sale, and management of real estate, performing any combination of following duties: Types copies of listings of real estate rentals and sales for distribution to trade publications, and for use as reference data by other departments. Computes interest owed, penalty payment, amount of principal, and taxes due on mortgage loans, using calculating machine. Holds in escrow collateral posted to ensure fulfillment of contracts in transferring real estate and property titles. Checks due notices on taxes and renewal dates of insurance and mortgage loans to take follow-up action. Sends out rent notices to tenants. Writes checks in payment of bills due, keeps record of disbursements, and examines cancelled returned checks for endorsement. Secures estimates from contractors for building repairs. May compile list of prospects from leads in newspapers and trade periodicals to locate prospective purchasers of real estate. May open, sort, and distribute mail. May submit photographs and descriptions of property to newspaper for publication. May maintain and balance bank accounts for sales transactions and operating expenses. May maintain log of sales and commissions received by SALES AGENT, REAL ESTATE (real estate) 250.357-018. May scan records and files to identify dates requiring administrative action, such as insurance premium due dates, tax due notices, and lease expiration dates. May compose and prepare routine correspondence, rental notices, letters, and material for advertisement. ● **GED:** R4, M3, L3 ● **SVP:** 6 mos-1 yr ● **Academic:** Ed=N, Eng=G ● **Work Field:** 232, 231 ● **MPSMS:** 895 ● **Aptitudes:** G3, V3, N2, S4, P4, Q2, K3, F3, M3, E5, C5 ● **Temperaments:** J, T, V ● **Physical:** Stg=S; Const: N Freq: R, H, I, T, G ● **Work Env:** Noise=N; ● **Salary:** 1 ● **Outlook:** 3

SECURITIES CLERK (financial) ● DOT #219.362-054 ● OES: 53128 ● Records security transactions, such as purchases and sales, stock dividends and splits, conversions, and redemptions: Issues receipts for securities received from customers. Prepares transmittal papers or endorsements for securities sold to ensure payment, transfer, and delivery. Issues vault withdrawal orders at customer request. Computes dividends to be disbursed to customers. Writes letters to customers to answer inquiries on security transactions. May prepare reports on individual customer accounts. ● **GED:** R4, M4, L3 ● **SVP:** 6 mos-1 yr ● **Academic:** Ed=H, Eng=G ● **Work Field:** 232 ● **MPSMS:** 894 ● **Aptitudes:** G3, V3, N2, S4, P4, Q2, K4, F4, M4, E5, C5 ● **Temperaments:** P, T ● **Physical:** Stg=S; Freq: R, H, I, N Occas: O, T, G, A ● **Work Env:** Noise=N; ● **Salary:** 4 ● **Outlook:** 3

SUPERVISOR, REAL-ESTATE OFFICE (real estate) ● DOT #249.137-030 ● OES: 51002 ● Supervises and coordinates activities of clerical personnel in real estate office: Interviews clerical applicants, gives performance tests, and evaluates applicant data to determine new hires. Verifies completeness, accuracy, and timeliness of clerical personnel production. Prepares or assists in preparaing papers for closings of real estate transactions, such as sales contracts and purchase agreements. Analyzes financial activities of establishment and prepares reports for review of SALES AGENT, REAL ESTATE (real estate) 250.357-018 or other personnel. Schedules government inspections of properties to ensure that offerings meet code regulations. Contacts mortgage companies to determine insurance status of properties. Notifies utility companies of transfer of property to new owners. Performs other duties as described under SUPERVISOR (clerical) Master Title. ● **GED:** R4, M3, L4 ● **SVP:** 2-4 yrs ● **Academic:** Ed=H, Eng=G ● **Work Field:** 232 ● **MPSMS:** 895 ● **Aptitudes:** G2, V2, N2, S4, P3, Q2, K3, F3, M3, E5, C5 ● **Temperaments:** D, J, P ● **Physical:** Stg=S; Freq: R, H, I, T, G, N ● **Work Env:** Noise=N; ● **Salary:** 4 ● **Outlook:** 2

SUPERVISOR, STATEMENT CLERKS (financial) ● DOT #214.137-014 ● OES: 51002 ● Supervises and coordinates activities of workers engaged in preparing customer bank statements for distribution, maintaining cancelled checks and customer signature files, and adjusting customer accounts: Coordinates assignments of workers preparing bank statements for delivery, reconciling account differences, and filing checks. Writes letters and makes telephone calls to recover checks returned in error and to adjust customer accounts and complaints. Assists customers in establishing depository arrangements for large accounts. Accepts stop-payment orders and directs workers in flagging customer accounts to prevent withdrawal of uncollected portions of deposits, or to prevent payment of protested checks. Performs other duties as described under SUPERVISOR (clerical) Master Title. ● **GED:** R4, M3, L4 ● **SVP:** 2-4 yrs ● **Academic:** Ed=H, Eng=G ● **Work Field:** 232 ● **MPSMS:** 894 ● **Aptitudes:** G3, V3, N3, S4, P4, Q2, K3, F3, M3, E5, C5 ● **Temperaments:** D, P, T ● **Physical:** Stg=L; Freq: H, I, T, G, N Occas: A ● **Work Env:** Noise=N; ● **Salary:** 4 ● **Outlook:** 2

UNDERWRITING CLERK (insurance) ● DOT #219.367-038 ● OES: 59998 ● Alternate titles: UNDERWRITING ANALYST. Compiles data and performs routine clerical tasks to relieve UNDERWRITER (insurance) of minor administrative detail, using knowledge of underwriting and policy issuing procedures: Reviews correspondence, records, and reports to select routine matters for processing. Routes risk-involved matters to UNDERWRITER (insurance) for evaluation. Prepares requisitions for and reviews credit and motor vehicle reports and results of investigations to compile and summarize pertinent data onto underwriting worksheets. Consults manuals to determine rate classifications and assigns rates to pending applications, using adding machine. Corresponds with or telephones field personnel to inform them of underwriting actions taken. Maintains related files. ● **GED:** R3, M3, L3 ● **SVP:** 3-6 mos ● **Academic:** Ed=H, Eng=S ● **Work Field:** 232 ● **MPSMS:** 895 ● **Aptitudes:** G3, V3, N3, S4, P4, Q3, K3, F3, M4, E5, C5 ● **Temperaments:** R, T ● **Physical:** Stg=L; Freq: R, H, I, N ● **Work Env:** Noise=N; ● **Salary:** 2 ● **Outlook:** 3

VAULT CASHIER (business ser.) ● DOT #222.137-050 ● OES: 51002 ● Alternate titles: VAULT SUPERVISOR. Supervises and coordinates activities of workers engaged in receiving, processing, routing, and shipping money and other valuables in armored car firm: Prepares route and work schedules. Oversees loading, unloading, and moving of money and other valuables to and from vault. Issues work and route sheets to workers and collects delivery and pickup receipts from guards. Supervises workers preparing payroll envelopes for customers. Observes workers to ensure that security regulations are followed. Performs other duties as described under SUPERVISOR (clerical) Master Title. ● **GED:** R4, M3, L3 ● **SVP:** 6 mos-1 yr ● **Academic:** Ed=N, Eng=G ● **Work Field:** 221, 293, 013 ● **MPSMS:** 899 ● **Aptitudes:** G3, V3, N3, S4, P3, Q3, K3, F4, M4, E5, C4 ● **Temperaments:** D, P, T ● **Physical:** Stg=L; Freq: T, G Occas: R, H, I, N, X ● **Work Env:** Noise=Q; ● **Salary:** 1 ● **Outlook:** 3

GOE: 07.01.05
Certifying

ADMISSIONS EVALUATOR (education) ● DOT #205.367-010 ● OES: 59998 ● Alternate titles: ADMINISTRATIVE ASSISTANT; DEGREE CLERK. Examines academic records of students to determine eligibility for graduation or for admission to college, university, or graduate school: Compares transcripts of courses with school entrance or degree requirements and prepares evaluation form listing courses for graduation. Studies course prerequisites, degree equivalents, and accreditation of schools, and computes grade-point averages to establish students' qualifications for admission, transfer, or graduation. Explains evaluations to students. Refers students with academic discrepancies to proper department heads for further action. Types list of accepted applicants or of degree candidates and submits it for approval. Issues registration permits and records acceptances and fees paid. Performs related duties, such as preparing commencement programs and computing student averages for honors. May advise students concerning their eligibility for teacher certificates. May specialize in evaluation of transfer students' records and be designated Evaluator, Transfer Students (education). ● **GED:** R4, M2, L4 ● **SVP:** 1-2 yrs ● **Academic:** Ed=H, Eng=G ● **Work Field:** 271, 282 ● **MPSMS:** 931 ● **Aptitudes:** G2, V2, N2, S4, P4, Q3, K4, F4, M4, E5, C5 ● **Temperaments:** J, P ● **Physical:** Stg=S; Freq: R, H, I, T, G, N ● **Work Env:** Noise=N; ● **Salary:** 4 ● **Outlook:** 4

AGENT-CONTRACT CLERK (insurance) ● DOT #241.267-010 ● OES: 55314 ● Alternate titles: CONTRACT ADMINISTRATOR. Evaluates character and ability of prospective agents, and approves their contracts to sell insurance for company: Reviews prospect's application for employment, inspection report, and recommendations to evaluate applicant's character and qualifications. Approves contract if applicant meets company requirements. Corresponds with agency to explain rejection of prospect. Sends application and fee for license to licensing agency. Notifies licensing agency of agent's contract termination. May prepare bulletins to inform insurance agency personnel of revisions in company practices and procedures. ● **GED:** R5, M1, L4 ● **SVP:** 6 mos-1 yr ● **Academic:** Ed=H, Eng=G ● **Work Field:** 271 ● **MPSMS:** 895 ● **Aptitudes:** G2, V2, N5, S5, P5, Q3, K4, F4, M5, E5,

C5 ● **Temperaments:** J ● **Physical:** Stg=S; Freq: R, H, I, N ● **Work Env:** Noise=N; ● **Salary:** 3 ● **Outlook:** 3

CONTRACT CLERK (profess. & kin.) ● DOT #119.267-018 ● OES: 28499 ● Alternate titles: CONTRACT CONSULTANT; CONTRACT TECHNICIAN. Reviews agreements or proposed agreements for conformity to company rates, rules, and regulations: Analyzes contracts and confers with various department heads to detect ambiguities, inaccurate statements, omissions of essential terms, and conflicts with possible legal prohibitions. Recommends modifications. Converts agreements into contract form or prepares amended agreement for approval by legal department. May initiate changes in standard form contracts. ● **GED:** R5, M2, L5 ● **SVP:** 2-4 yrs ● **Academic:** Ed=H, Eng=G ● **Work Field:** 272, 261 ● **MPSMS:** 932 ● **Aptitudes:** G2, V1, N3, S4, P4, Q3, K4, F4, M4, E5, C5 ● **Temperaments:** J ● **Physical:** Stg=S; Freq: R, H, T, G, N Occas: I ● **Work Env:** Noise=Q; ● **Salary:** 3 ● **Outlook:** 3

EXAMINER (government ser.) ● DOT #169.267-014 ● OES: 21911 ● Examines and evaluates data to determine persons' or organizations' eligibility for, conformity with, or liability under, government regulated activity or program: Examines data contained in application forms, agency reports, business records, public documents or other records to gather facts, verify correctness, or establish authenticity. Interviews persons, visits establishments, or confers with technical or professional specialists, to obtain information or clarify facts. Analyzes data obtained, utilizing knowledge of administrative policies, regulatory codes, legislative directives, precedent, or other guidelines. Determines eligibility for participation in activity, conformity to program requirements, or liability for damages or financial losses incurred, based on findings. Prepares correspondence to inform concerned parties of decision and rights to appeal. Prepares reports of examinations, evaluations, and decisions. May be classified according to job function, program involved, or agency concerned. ● **GED:** R4, M4, L4 ● **SVP:** 1-2 yrs ● **Academic:** Ed=H, Eng=G ● **Work Field:** 271, 211 ● **MPSMS:** 959 ● **Aptitudes:** G2, V2, N2, S3, P3, Q3, K4, F4, M5, E5, C5 ● **Temperaments:** J ● **Physical:** Stg=S; Freq: R, H, I, T, G, N ● **Work Env:** Noise=N; ● **Salary:** 4 ● **Outlook:** 3

HOSPITAL-INSURANCE REPRESENTATIVE (insurance) ● DOT #166.267-014 ● OES: 21511 ● Interprets hospital and medical insurance services and benefits to contracting hospital personnel: Discusses contract provisions and hospital claims forms with medical and hospital personnel. Instructs hospital clerical staff in resolving problems concerning billing and admitting procedures. Writes reports outlining hospital and contract benefits for incorporation into brochures and pamphlets. May travel from city to city. ● **GED:** R4, M3, L4 ● **SVP:** 1-2 yrs ● **Academic:** Ed=H, Eng=G ● **Work Field:** 282 ● **MPSMS:** 895 ● **Aptitudes:** G2, V2, N3, S4, P3, Q2, K4, F4, M4, E5, C5 ● **Temperaments:** J ● **Physical:** Stg=S; Freq: R, H, I, T, G, N ● **Work Env:** Noise=N; ● **Salary:** 2 ● **Outlook:** 4

PASSPORT-APPLICATION EXAMINER (government ser.) ● DOT #169.267-030 ● OES: 21911 ● Approves applications for United States passports and related privileges and services: Reviews information on applications, such as applicant's birthplace and birthplaces of applicant's parents, to determine eligibility according to nationality laws and governmental policies. Examines supporting documents, such as affidavits, records, newspaper files, and Bibles, to evaluate relevance and authenticity of documents. Queries applicants to obtain additional or clarifying data. Forwards approved applications to designated official, and prepares summaries for cases not approved, indicating points of law. Answers questions of individuals concerning passport applications and related services. ● **GED:** R4, M3, L4 ● **SVP:** 6 mos-1 yr ● **Academic:** Ed=H, Eng=S ● **Work Field:** 271 ● **MPSMS:** 959 ● **Aptitudes:** G2, V3, N3, S4, P3, Q3, K4, F4, M4, E5, C5 ● **Temperaments:** J, P ● **Physical:** Stg=L; Freq: T, G, N Occas: R, H, I ● **Work Env:** Noise=N; ● **Salary:** 3 ● **Outlook:** 3

TITLE CLERK (petrol. & gas) ● DOT #162.267-010 ● OES: 28499 ● Procures testimonial documents required to remove restrictions affecting title of landowners to property, and requisitions purchase orders and bank checks to satisfy requirements of contracts and agreements covering lease or purchase of land and gas, oil, and mineral rights: Examines leases, contracts, and purchase agreements to assure conformity to specified requirements. Examines abstract to assure complete title-coverage of land described, completeness of land description, and

to detect lapses of time in abstract coverage of landowner's title. Prepares correspondence and other records to transmit leases and abstracts. Reviews title opinion to determine nature of testimonial documents needed to meet legal objections and to assure accuracy in terms of trade. Confers with personnel of abstract company, landowners, and LEASE BUYERS (mine & quarry; petrol. & gas) to explain reasons for and to obtain testimonial documents needed to clear title. Prepares or requests deeds, affidavits, and other documents and transmits them to appropriate persons for execution to meet title requirements. Investigates whether delinquent taxes are due on land involved in agreements and confers or corresponds with landowner to assure payment. Verifies computations of fees, rentals, bonuses, brokerage commissions and other expenses and prepares records to initiate requests for payment. Prepares purchase data sheet for records unit covering each trade or exchange. Answers queries regarding leases and contracts by mail, telephone, or personal discussion. ● **GED:** R5, M4, L5 ● **SVP:** 1-2 yrs ● **Academic:** Ed=A, Eng=S ● **Work Field:** 271, 232 ● **MPSMS:** 891 ● **Aptitudes:** G3, V3, N3, S4, P4, Q2, K4, F4, M4, E4, C4 ● **Temperaments:** J, P, V ● **Physical:** Stg=S; Freq: R, H, I, T, G, N, A Occas: X ● **Work Env:** Noise=N; ● **Salary:** 2 ● **Outlook:** 4

TITLE EXAMINER (profess. & kin.) ● DOT #119.287-010 ● OES: 28306 ● Searches public records and examines titles to determine legal condition of property title: Examines copies of records, such as mortgages, liens, judgments, easements, vital statistics, and plat and map books to determine ownership and legal restrictions and to verify legal description of property. Copies or summarizes (abstracts) recorded documents, such as mortgages, trust deeds, and contracts affecting condition of title to property. Analyzes restrictions and prepares report outlining restrictions and actions required to clear title. When working in title-insurance company, prepares and issues policy that guarantees legality of title. ● **GED:** R5, M3, L5 ● **SVP:** 2-4 yrs ● **Academic:** Ed=A, Eng=G ● **Work Field:** 271, 231 ● **MPSMS:** 932 ● **Aptitudes:** G2, V2, N3, S4, P4, Q2, K4, F4, M4, E5, C5 ● **Temperaments:** J ● **Physical:** Stg=S; Freq: R, H, N Occas: I ● **Work Env:** Noise=Q; ● **Salary:** 3 ● **Outlook:** 4

TITLE SUPERVISOR (profess. & kin.) ● DOT #119.167-018 ● OES: 28306 ● Directs and coordinates activities of subordinates engaged in searching public records and examining titles to determine legal condition of property title. ● **GED:** R5, M3, L5 ● **SVP:** 4-10 yrs ● **Academic:** Ed=A, Eng=G ● **Work Field:** 271 ● **MPSMS:** 932 ● **Aptitudes:** G2, V1, N3, S3, P3, Q2, K4, F4, M4, E5, C5 ● **Temperaments:** D, J, P ● **Physical:** Stg=S; Freq: R, H, I, T, G ● **Work Env:** Noise=Q; ● **Salary:** 4 ● **Outlook:** 3

GOE: 07.01.06
Investigating

ATTENDANCE OFFICER (education) ● DOT #168.367-010 ● OES: 21911 ● Alternate titles: TRUANT OFFICER. Investigates continued absences of pupils from public schools to determine if such absences are lawful and known to parents. ● **GED:** R4, M2, L4 ● **SVP:** 2-4 yrs ● **Academic:** Ed=H, Eng=S ● **Work Field:** 271 ● **MPSMS:** 931, 932 ● **Aptitudes:** G2, V2, N4, S4, P4, Q3, K4, F4, M4, E4, C5 ● **Temperaments:** J, P ● **Physical:** Stg=L; Freq: R, H, I, T, G ● **Work Env:** Noise=N; Occas: W ● **Salary:** 2 ● **Outlook:** 3

CASEWORKER (government ser.) ● DOT #169.262-010 ● OES: 21998 ● Performs research into laws of United States and procedures of federal agencies and prepares correspondence in office of Member of Congress to resolve problems or complaints of constituents: Confers with individuals who have requested assistance to determine nature and extent of problems. Analyzes U.S. Code to become familiar with laws relating to specific complaints of constituents. Researches procedures and systems of governmental agencies and contacts representatives of federal agencies to obtain information on policies. Contacts Congressional Research Service to collect information relating to agency policies and laws. Contacts colleges and universities to obtain information relating to constituent problems. Determines action to facilitate resolution of constituent problems. Composes and types letters to Federal agencies and Congressional Committees concerning resolution of problems of constituents. Prepares memoranda to inform Member of Congress of problems which require legislative attention. Confers with personnel assisting Member of Congress to discuss introduction of legislation to solve constituent problems. Calculates social security benefits, veterans' benefits, tax assessments, and other data concerning constituent complaints, using desk calculator. ● **GED:** R5, M3, L4 ● **SVP:** 6 mos-1 yr ● **Academic:** Ed=A, Eng=G ● **Work Field:** 271, 231 ● **MPSMS:** 893, 891 ● **Aptitudes:** G2, V2, N3, S4, P4, Q2, K2, F3, M4, E5, C5 ● **Temperaments:** J, P ● **Physical:** Stg=S; Freq: R, H, I, T, G, N, A Occas: S, K ● **Work Env:** Noise=N; ● **Salary:** 1 ● **Outlook:** 4

IDENTIFICATION OFFICER (government ser.) ● DOT #377.264-010 ● OES: 63009 ● Collects, analyzes, classifies and photographs physical evidence and fingerprints to identify criminals: Searches for evidence and dusts surfaces to reveal latent fingerprints. Photographs crime site and fingerprints to obtain record of evidence. Lifts print on tape and transfers to permanent record cards. Vacuums site to collect physical evidence and submits to SUPERVISOR, IDENTIFICATION AND COMMUNICATIONS (government ser.) for verifications. Photographs, fingerprints, and measures height and weight of arrested suspects, noting physical characteristics, and posts data on record for filing. Prepares and photographs plastic moulage of footprints and tire tracks. Compares fingerprints obtained with suspect or unknown files to identify perpetrator [FINGERPRINT CLASSIFIER (government ser.)]. Manipulates mask mirror on specialized equipment to prepare montage of suspect according to description from witnesses. May fingerprint applicant for employment or federal clearance and forward prints to other law enforcement agencies. May testify in court as qualified fingerprint expert. ● **GED:** R4, M3, L4 ● **SVP:** 4-10 yrs ● **Academic:** Ed=H, Eng=G ● **Work Field:** 271, 231, 201 ● **MPSMS:** 951 ● **Aptitudes:** G2, V2, N3, S2, P2, Q3, K2, F3, M3, E4, C4 ● **Temperaments:** J ● **Physical:** Stg=L; Freq: R, H, I, N, A Occas: S, K, O, T, G, D, X ● **Work Env:** Noise=N; Occas: W ● **Salary:** 3 ● **Outlook:** 3

GOE: 07.01.07
Test Administration

DRIVER'S LICENSE EXAMINER (government ser.) ● DOT #168.267-034 ● OES: 21911 ● Gives written and visual acuity tests and conducts road performance tests to determine applicant's eligibil-ity for driver's license: Scores written and visual acuity tests and issues and collects fees for instruction permits. Conducts road tests and observes applicant's driving ability throughout specified maneuvers and compliance with traffic safety rules. Rates ability for each maneuver. Collects fees and issues licenses. Lectures to school and community groups concerning driver improvement program. May inspect brakes, stop and signal lights, and horn to determine if applicant's vehicle is safe to operate. ● **GED:** R3, M2, L3 ● **SVP:** 3-6 mos ● **Academic:** Ed=H, Eng=S ● **Work Field:** 211 ● **MPSMS:** 950 ● **Aptitudes:** G3, V3, N3, S3, P3, Q3, K3, F3, M3, E4, C4 ● **Temperaments:** J, P ● **Physical:** Stg=L; Freq: T, G, N, F, D, A, X, V Occas: R, H, I ● **Work Env:** Noise=Q; ● **Salary:** 3 ● **Outlook:** 3

EXAMINATION PROCTOR (government ser.) ● DOT #199.267-018 ● OES: 39998 ● Administers civil service qualifying examinations: Verifies admissions credentials of examinees, maintains order, distributes and collects examination materials, keeps time, and answers questions relative to examination procedures. May participate in oral interviews of candidates. May score examinations, using scoring template or answer sheet. ● **GED:** R4, M3, L4 ● **SVP:** 6 mos-1 yr ● **Academic:** Ed=H, Eng=G ● **Work Field:** 295 ● **MPSMS:** 211 ● **Aptitudes:** G3, V2, N3, S4, P3, Q3, K4, F4, M4, E5, C5 ● **Temperaments:** J, P ● **Physical:** Stg=L; Freq: R, H, T, G, N ● **Work Env:** Noise=N; ● **Salary:** 3 ● **Outlook:** 3

TEST TECHNICIAN (clerical) ● DOT #249.367-078 ● OES: 59998 ● Alternate titles: EVALUATION AIDE; TEST EXAMINER. Administers and scores psychological, vocational, or educational tests: Distributes test blanks or apparatus to individuals being tested. Reads directions orally from testing manual, or gives other standardized directions. Demonstrates use of test apparatus or discusses practice exercises to familiarize individuals with testing material. Monitors test group to ensure compliance with directions. Times test with stop watch or electric timer. Scores test with test-scoring key or machine. May schedule time and place for test to be administered. May administer test designed to measure work skills of mentally or physically handicapped individuals. Records results on test paper, work application, or test profile form. ● **GED:** R3, M2, L3 ● **SVP:** 3-6 mos ● **Academic:** Ed=H, Eng=G ● **Work Field:** 296 ● **MPSMS:** 940 ● **Aptitudes:** G3, V3, N3, S4, P3, Q2, K3, F3, M3, E5, C4 ● **Temperaments:** J, P, T ● **Physical:** Stg=L; Freq: R, H, I, T, G, N Occas: X ● **Work Env:** Noise=N; ● **Salary:** 2 ● **Outlook:** 3

Business Detail

Mathematical Detail

Workers in this group use clerical and math skills to gather, organize, compute, and record, with or without machines, the numerical information used in business or in financial transactions. Jobs in this group are found wherever numerical recordkeeping is important. Banks, finance companies, accounting firms, or the payroll and inventory control departments in business and government are typical of places where this work is done.

✓ *What kind of work would you do?*

Your work activities would depend upon your specific job. For example, you might:

■ use a calculator to compute wages for payroll records.
■ compute the cost of labor and materials for production records of a factory.
■ compute freight charges and prepare bills for a truck company.
■ compute or verify credit card data to keep customer accounts.
■ supervise statistical clerks or insurance underwriting clerks.

✓ *What skills and abilities do you need for this kind of work?*

To do this kind of work, you must be able to:

■ compute and record numbers correctly.
■ follow procedures for keeping records.
■ use eyes, hands, and fingers at the same time to enter figures in books and forms, or to operate a calculating machine.
■ perform work that is routine and detailed.
■ read and copy large amounts of numbers without error.

The above statements may not apply to every job in this group.

✓ How do you know if you would like or could learn to do this kind of work?

The following questions may give you clues about yourself as you consider this group of jobs.

- Have you had courses in arithmetic or business math? Are you accurate?
- Have you taken bookkeeping or accounting? Do you like working with numbers?
- Have you balanced a checking account or figured interest rates? Do you spot errors quickly?
- Have you had experience working with numbers while in the armed forces? Do you like routine work of this kind?

✓ How can you prepare for and enter this kind of work?

Occupations in this group usually require education and/or training extending from thirty days to over two years, depending upon the specific kind of work. People with basic math skills can enter many of the jobs in this group. They receive on-the-job training for specific tasks. To enter some jobs, training in bookkeeping or other business subjects is required. Business training is offered by high schools and business schools.

✓ What else should you consider about these jobs?

Workers in small offices may do a variety of tasks. Some may keep all records for a business or agency. Usually, experience is needed for some positions.

In large offices, workers may have only certain tasks to do, and may repeat these tasks every day. Most jobs of this nature are entry-level jobs requiring little or no experience.

If you think you would like to do this kind of work, look at the job titles listed on the following pages.

■ ■ ■

GOE: 07.02.01
Bookkeeping & Auditing

AUDIT CLERK (clerical) ● DOT #210.382-010 ● OES: 55338 ● Verifies accuracy of figures, calculations, and postings pertaining to business transactions recorded by other workers: Examines expense accounts, commissions paid to employees, loans made on insurance policies, interest and account payments, cash receipts, sales tickets, bank records, inventory and stock-record sheets, and similar items to verify accuracy of recorded data. Corrects errors or lists discrepancies for adjustment. Computes percentages and totals, using adding or calculating machines, and compares results with recorded entries. May be designated according to type of records audited as Cash-Sales-Audit Clerk (clerical); Charge-Accounts-Audit Clerk (clerical); C.O.D. Audit Clerk (clerical); Commission Auditor (insurance); Expense Clerk (clerical); Federal-Housing-Administration-Loan Auditor (insurance). May be designated: Inventory-Audit Clerk (clerical); Journal-Entry-Audit Clerk (clerical); Medical-Records Auditor (medical ser.); Remittance-On-Farm-Rental-And-Soil-Conservation Auditor (insurance). ● **GED:** R4, M4, L3 ● **SVP:** 2-4 yrs ● **Academic:** Ed=H, Eng=G ● **Work Field:** 232, 233 ● **MPSMS:** 892 ● **Aptitudes:** G3, V3, N2, S4, P4, Q2, K3, F3, M3, E5, C5 ● **Temperaments:** J, T ● **Physical:** Stg=S; Freq: R, H, I, N, A ● **Work Env:** Noise=N; ● **Salary:** 3 ● **Outlook:** 3

BOOKKEEPER (clerical) ● DOT #210.382-014 ● OES: 55338 ● Keeps records of financial transactions for establishment, using calculator and computer: Verifies, allocates, and posts details of business transactions to subsidiary accounts in journals or computer files from documents, such as sales slips, invoices, receipts, check stubs, and computer printouts. Summarizes details in separate ledgers or computer files and transfers data to general ledger, using calculator or computer. Reconciles and balances accounts. May compile reports to show statistics, such as cash receipts and expenditures, accounts payable and receivable, profit and loss, and other items pertinent to operation of business. May calculate employee wages from plant records or time cards and prepare checks for payment of wages. May prepare withholding, Social Security, and other tax reports. May compute, type, and mail monthly statements to customers. May be designated according to kind of records of financial transactions kept, such as Accounts-Receivable Bookkeeper (clerical), and Accounts-Payable Bookkeeper (clerical). May complete records to or through trial balance. ● **GED:** R4, M4, L3 ● **SVP:** 1-2 yrs ● **Academic:** Ed=H, Eng=S ● **Work Field:** 232 ● **MPSMS:** 892 ● **Aptitudes:** G3, V3, N2, S4, P3, Q2, K3, F3, M3, E5, C5 ● **Temperaments:** T ● **Physical:** Stg=S; Const: N Freq: R, H, I, A Occas: G ● **Work Env:** Noise=N; ● **Salary:** 2 ● **Outlook:** 3

ELECTRONIC FUNDS TRANSFER COORDINATOR (financial) ● DOT #216.362-038 ● OES: 55338 ● Compiles and reconciles data involving electronic transfer of funds to maintain accounting records: Examines electronic funds transaction entries on documents, such as bank statements and printouts, for completeness and accuracy. Adds debits and credits, using adding machine or calculator, to ensure that figures balance. Identifies and corrects errors or calls customers, other bank personnel, or personnel from other financial institutions, such as correspondent banks, Automated Clearing House, or Federal Reserve Bank, to obtain information needed to reconcile differences. Posts transaction data to specified accounts, using ledger sheets or computer. May prepare checks to deposit funds in specified accounts. May transmit funds between specified accounts by wire [WIRES-TRANSFER CLERK (financial) 203.562-010]. ● **GED:** R4, M4, L4 ● **SVP:** 2-4 yrs ● **Academic:** Ed=H, Eng=G ● **Work Field:** 232 ● **MPSMS:** 894 ● **Aptitudes:** G3, V3, N3, S5, P5, Q2, K2, F3, M4, E5, C5 ● **Temperaments:** P, T ● **Physical:** Stg=L; Freq: R, H, I, T, G, N, A ● **Work Env:** Noise=N; ● **Salary:** 1 ● **Outlook:** 3

FOREIGN-EXCHANGE-POSITION CLERK (financial) ● DOT #210.367-014 ● OES: 55338 ● Maintains current record of bank's funds on deposit (position) in foreign banks: Records bank's balances on deposit in foreign banks, outstanding (future) purchase and sales contracts, and undelivered items, to maintain record, using computer. Lists totals in holdover register and posts net balances to daily position reports to determine new position. Reviews records to determine when balances need replenishing. Computes net balances and informs trading personnel. May compare current and previous balance sheets to eliminate double-posting to transactions and verification of limits. May assist trading personnel in preparing monthly revaluation of foreign currency accounts. May answer inquiries regarding foreign exchange trading regulations. May quote established conversion rates for bank branch staff and customers. ● **GED:** R4, M4, L3 ● **SVP:** 6 mos-1 yr ● **Academic:** Ed=H, Eng=G ● **Work Field:** 232 ● **MPSMS:** 894 ●

Aptitudes: G3, V3, N2, S4, P4, Q2, K4, F3, M4, E5, C5 ● **Temperaments:** T ● **Physical:** Stg=S; Const: N Freq: I Occas: R, H, T, G, A ● **Work Env:** Noise=N; ● **Salary:** 4 ● **Outlook:** 3

GENERAL-LEDGER BOOKKEEPER (clerical) ● DOT #210.382-046 ● OES: 55338 ● Compiles and posts in general ledgers information or summaries concerning various business transactions that have been recorded in separate ledgers by other clerks, using calculating or adding machine. ● **GED:** R4, M4, L3 ● **SVP:** 6 mos-1 yr ● **Academic:** Ed=H, Eng=S ● **Work Field:** 232 ● **MPSMS:** 892 ● **Aptitudes:** G3, V3, N2, S4, P3, Q2, K3, F3, M3, E5, C5 ● **Temperaments:** R, T ● **Physical:** Stg=S; Const: R, H, I, N ● **Work Env:** Noise=Q; ● **Salary:** 2 ● **Outlook:** 2

RESERVES CLERK (financial) ● DOT #216.362-034 ● OES: 55338 ● Compiles records of fund reserves of bank and branches to ensure conformity with Federal Reserve requirements: Reviews cash orders from branches to determine that order follows established procedure and amount meets with bank limitations and requirements. Posts order to department record sheet, or computer files, using computer. Telephones order to Federal Reserve Bank, and prepares letter to Federal Reserve confirming order, using computer or typewriter. Charges or credits accounts, following bank regulations. Keeps records of bank balance with Federal Reserve Bank. ● **GED:** R4, M3, L3 ● **SVP:** 6 mos-1 yr ● **Academic:** Ed=N, Eng=G ● **Work Field:** 232 ● **MPSMS:** 892 ● **Aptitudes:** G3, V3, N3, S5, P4, Q2, K3, F3, M3, E5, C5 ● **Temperaments:** T ● **Physical:** Stg=S; Const: N Freq: I, T, G Occas: R, H, A ● **Work Env:** Noise=N; ● **Salary:** 1 ● **Outlook:** 3

GOE: 07.02.02
Accounting

ACCOUNTING CLERK (clerical) ● DOT #216.482-010 ● OES: 55338 ● Performs any combination of following calculating, posting, and verifying duties to obtain financial data for use in maintaining accounting records: Compiles and sorts documents, such as invoices and checks, substantiating business transactions. Verifies and posts details of business transactions, such as funds received and disbursed, and totals accounts, using calculator or computer. Computes and records charges, refunds, cost of lost or damaged goods, freight charges, rentals, and similar items. May type vouchers, invoices, checks, account statements, reports, and other records, using typewriter or computer. May reconcile bank statements. May be designated according to type of accounting performed, such as Accounts-Payable Clerk (clerical); Accounts-Receivable Clerk (clerical); Bill-Recapitulation Clerk (utilities); Rent and Miscellaneous Remittance Clerk (insurance); Tax-Record Clerk (utilities). ● **GED:** R4, M3, L3 ● **SVP:** 6 mos-1 yr ● **Academic:** Ed=H, Eng=S ● **Work Field:** 232 ● **MPSMS:** 892 ● **Aptitudes:** G3, V3, N3, S4, P3, Q2, K3, F3, M4, E5, C5 ● **Temperaments:** T ● **Physical:** Stg=S; Freq: R, H, I, N, A Occas: G ● **Work Env:** Noise=N; ● **Salary:** 2 ● **Outlook:** 1

BROKERAGE CLERK I (financial) ● DOT #219.482-010 ● OES: 53128 ● Records purchase and sale of securities, such as stocks and bonds, for investment firm: Computes federal and state transfer taxes and commissions, using calculator and rate tables. Verifies information, such as owners' names, transaction dates, and distribution instructions, on securities certificates to ensure accuracy and comformance with government regulations. Posts transaction data to accounting ledgers and certificate records. Types data on confirmation form to effect transfer of securities purchased and sold. Receives securities and cash and schedules delivery of customer securities. ● **GED:** R4, M4, L4 ● **SVP:** 6 mos-1 yr ● **Academic:** Ed=N, Eng=G ● **Work Field:** 232 ● **MPSMS:** 894 ● **Aptitudes:** G3, V3, N3, S4, P4, Q3, K4, F4, M4, E5, C5 ● **Temperaments:** T ● **Physical:** Stg=S; Const: N Freq: H, I Occas: R, G, A ● **Work Env:** Noise=Q; ● **Salary:** 1 ● **Outlook:** 3

BROKERAGE CLERK II (financial) ● DOT #219.362-018 ● OES: 53128 ● Compiles security purchases and sales made for client and records information in journal. Totals daily transactions, using calculator, and summarizes effects on customers' accounts and earnings of REGISTERED REPRESENTATIVE (financial) 250.257-018. Calls customers to inform them of market fluctuations and purchase and sale of securities affecting their accounts. ● **GED:** R3, M3, L3 ● **SVP:** 3-6

mos ● **Academic:** Ed=H, Eng=G ● **Work Field:** 232, 282 ● **MPSMS:** 892 ● **Aptitudes:** G3, V3, N3, S4, P4, Q2, K3, F3, M4, E5, C5 ● **Temperaments:** R, T ● **Physical:** Stg=L; Const: N Freq: H, I Occas: R, T, G, A ● **Work Env:** Noise=Q; ● **Salary:** 3 ● **Outlook:** 3

CALCULATING-MACHINE OPERATOR (clerical) ● DOT #216.482-022 ● OES: 56002 ● Alternate titles: CALCULATOR OPERATOR. Computes and records statistical, accounting and other numerical data, utilizing knowledge of mathematics and using machine that automatically performs mathematical processes, such as addition, subtraction, multiplication, division, and extraction of roots: Calculates statistical, accounting, and other numerical data, using calculating machine, and posts totals to records, such as inventories and summary sheets. May verify computations made by other workers. May be designated according to subject matter as Formula Figurer (paint & varnish); Premium-Note Interest-Calculator Clerk (insurance). May compute and record inventory data from audio transcription, using transcribing machine and calculator, and be designated Inventory Transcriber (business ser.). May be designated according to type of computations made as Weight Calculator (ship-boat mfg.). ● **GED:** R3, M3, L2 ● **SVP:** 1-3 mos ● **Academic:** Ed=N, Eng=S ● **Work Field:** 232 ● **MPSMS:** 892 ● **Aptitudes:** G3, V3, N3, S5, P4, Q2, K3, F3, M4, E5, C5 ● **Temperaments:** R, T ● **Physical:** Stg=S; Const: N Freq: R, H, I Occas: G, A ● **Work Env:** Noise=N; ● **Salary:** 2 ● **Outlook:** 2

CANCELLATION CLERK (insurance) ● DOT #203.382-014 ● OES: 53314 ● Alternate titles: MEMORANDUM-STATEMENT CLERK; POLICY-CANCELLATION CLERK; PREMIUM-CANCELLATION CLERK; PREMIUM-CARD-CANCELLATION CLERK; TERMINATION CLERK. Cancels insurance policies as requested by agents: Receives computer printout of cancellation data or retrieves expiration card from file. Checks number on card with number of policy. Computes refunds, using calculator, adding machine, and rate tables. Types cancellation correspondence and mails with canceled policy to policyholder. Types cancellation notice and routes to bookkeeping department for recording. Mails cancellation notice to agent. ● **GED:** R3, M3, L3 ● **SVP:** 6 mos-1 yr ● **Academic:** Ed=N, Eng=G ● **Work Field:** 231, 232 ● **MPSMS:** 895 ● **Aptitudes:** G3, V3, N3, S4, P3, Q2, K4, F3, M4, E5, C4 ● **Temperaments:** R, T ● **Physical:** Stg=S; Freq: R, H, I, N ● **Work Env:** Noise=N; ● **Salary:** 2 ● **Outlook:** 3

COLLECTION CLERK (financial) ● DOT #216.362-014 ● OES: 55338 ● Receives and processes collection items (negotiable instruments), such as checks, drafts, and coupons presented to bank by customers or corresponding banks: Reads letter of instructions accompanying negotiable instruments to determine disposition of items. Debits bank account and credits customer's account to liquidate outstanding collections. Computes interest on bills of exchange (drafts), using adding machine or computer terminal, and lists debits and credits on liability sheet, or enters information into computer system, to record customer's outstanding balance. Examines, calculates interest on, endorses, records, and issues receipts, and mails outgoing collections for payment. Traces unpaid items to determine reasons for nonpayment and notifies customer of disposition. May prove and balance daily transactions. May act as agent for collections payable in United States and possessions and be designated Out-of-Town-Collection Clerk (financial). May process collection items drawn on local bond and securities exchanges or transfers within a locality and be designated Local Collection Clerk (financial). May collect foreign bills of exchange and be designated Foreign-Collection Clerk (financial). May process matured bonds and coupons and be designated Coupon-and-Bond-Collection Clerk (financial); Coupon-Collection Clerk (financial). ● **GED:** R4, M4, L4 ● **SVP:** 6 mos-1 yr ● **Academic:** Ed=H, Eng=G ● **Work Field:** 232 ● **MPSMS:** 894 ● **Aptitudes:** G3, V3, N3, S4, P3, Q2, K2, F3, M4, E5, C5 ● **Temperaments:** T ● **Physical:** Stg=S; Freq: R, H, I, N, A Occas: T, G ● **Work Env:** Noise=N; ● **Salary:** 2 ● **Outlook:** 4

CONTRACT CLERK, AUTOMOBILE (retail trade) ● DOT #219.362-026 ● OES: 55347 ● Verifies accuracy of automobile sales contracts: Calculates tax, transfer and license fees, insurance premiums, and interest rates, using tables, schedules, and calculating machine. Verifies amount and number of payments, trade-in allowance, and total price of automobile. Interviews customer to obtain additional information and explain terms of contract. Corresponds with motor vehicle agencies to clear automobile titles. Obtains license, signs registration documents on cars traded in, and transfers titles on cars sold. Keeps file of sales contracts. ● **GED:** R4, M3, L3 ● **SVP:** 6 mos-1 yr ● **Academic:** Ed=N, Eng=G ● **Work Field:** 232, 231 ● **MPSMS:** 890 ● **Aptitudes:** G3, V3, N3, S4, P4, Q2, K3, F3, M3, E5, C5 ● **Temperaments:** T, V ● **Physical:** Stg=S; Freq: R, H, T, G, N Occas: I ● **Work Env:** Noise=Q; ● **Salary:** 3 ● **Outlook:** 3

COST CLERK (clerical) ● DOT #216.382-034 ● OES: 55344 ● Alternate titles: COST-ACCOUNTING CLERK; EXPENSE CLERK. Compiles production or sales cost reports on unit or total basis for department or working unit: Calculates individual items, such as labor, material, and time costs, relationship of sales or revenues to cost, and overhead expenditures, using calculating machine. Examines records, such as time and production sheets, payrolls, operations charts and schedules, to obtain data for calculations. Prepares reports showing total cost, selling prices, or rates profits. May be designated according to work performed as Cost-Estimating Clerk (utilities); Operating-Cost Clerk (clerical). ● **GED:** R3, M3, L3 ● **SVP:** 3-6 mos ● **Academic:** Ed=H, Eng=S ● **Work Field:** 232 ● **MPSMS:** 890 ● **Aptitudes:** G3, V3, N3, S4, P4, Q2, K3, F3, M3, E5, C5 ● **Temperaments:** J, T ● **Physical:** Stg=S; Freq: R, H, I, N, A Occas: G ● **Work Env:** Noise=N; ● **Salary:** 2 ● **Outlook:** 2

COUPON CLERK (financial) ● DOT #219.462-010 ● OES: 53102 ● Receives matured bond coupons from bank departments, local banks, and customers to effect collection on cash basis, or for payment when future collection is made: Examines coupons presented for payment to verify issue, payment date, and amount due. Enters credit in customer's passbook or into computer system, for coupons accepted for payment. Liquidates collection payment by debiting and crediting accounts. Issues checks to bond owners in settlement of transactions. Totals and proves daily transactions, using adding machine or calculator. Composes, types, and mails correspondence relating to discrepancies, errors, and outstanding unpaid items. Totals outstanding unpaid cash coupons, using adding machine or calculator, and records amounts in ledgers or into computer system. ● **GED:** R4, M3, L4 ● **SVP:** 6 mos-1 yr ● **Academic:** Ed=N, Eng=S ● **Work Field:** 232 ● **MPSMS:** 894 ● **Aptitudes:** G3, V3, N3, S4, P4, Q2, K3, F3, M3, E5, C5 ● **Temperaments:** T ● **Physical:** Stg=S; Freq: R, H, I, N, A Occas: T, G ● **Work Env:** Noise=N; ● **Salary:** 1 ● **Outlook:** 2

CREDIT-CARD CLERK (hotel & rest.) ● DOT #210.382-038 ● OES: 55338 ● Compiles and verifies credit-card data from vouchers and other records and computes charges and payments due to establishment to keep records of hotel credit-card transactions: Compares charges on vouchers with audit tape to detect errors and corrects faulty vouchers. Sorts and combines vouchers and other credit transaction records by individual card-issuing firm. Computes totals, discounts, net charges, and amounts due, using calculator and adding machine, and posts to account journals. Prepares invoices for payment by card-issuing firms. ● **GED:** R3, M3, L2 ● **SVP:** 1-3 mos ● **Academic:** Ed=N, Eng=G ● **Work Field:** 232 ● **MPSMS:** 892 ● **Aptitudes:** G3, V4, N3, S4, P3, Q2, K2, F3, M3, E5, C5 ● **Temperaments:** R, T ● **Physical:** Stg=S; Const: R, H, N, A Freq: I ● **Work Env:** Noise=N; ● **Salary:** 2 ● **Outlook:** 3

DIVIDEND CLERK (financial) ● DOT #216.482-034 ● OES: 53128 ● Alternate titles: OPERATIONS CLERK. Computes, records, and pays dividends to customers of brokerage firm: Reviews stock records and reports to determine customer stock ownership on record date. Totals stock owned by customers and computes dividends due, using calculator. Records dividends due, and enters information into customer accounts, using computer. Reviews customer accounts to obtain dividend payment instructions, and pays dividends and interest due to customers. Solves dividend related problems with customer accounts, applying knowledge of policies and procedures concerning payment of dividends and interest. May perform other clerical tasks such as filing, typing, and operating office machines. ● **GED:** R3, M3, L3 ● **SVP:** 6 mos-1 yr ● **Academic:** Ed=H, Eng=G ● **Work Field:** 232 ● **MPSMS:** 894 ● **Aptitudes:** G3, V3, N4, S4, P4, Q2, K3, F3, M4, E5, C5 ● **Temperaments:** T ● **Physical:** Stg=L; Freq: R, H, I, N Occas: O, G, A ● **Work Env:** Noise=Q; ● **Salary:** 2 ● **Outlook:** 3

MARGIN CLERK I (financial) ● DOT #216.362-042 ● OES: 55338 ● Compiles data, using computer, to determine customer margin (equity) in stock purchased: Totals customer accounts and computes difference between purchase price of stock and present market value, using

calculator, to show amount due for brokerage fees. Notifies REGISTERED REPRESENTATIVE (financial) 250.257-018 or other workers when customer margin is less than government regulations or brokerage firm requirements. May solve customer margin account problems, using customer account information and transaction records. ● **GED:** R3, M3, L3 ● **SVP:** 1-2 yrs ● **Academic:** Ed=H, Eng=G ● **Work Field:** 232 ● **MPSMS:** 894 ● **Aptitudes:** G3, V3, N3, S4, P4, Q2, K3, F3, M4, E5, C5 ● **Temperaments:** P, T ● **Physical:** Stg=S; Const: N Freq: H, I, T, G, A Occas: O, R ● **Work Env:** Noise=Q; ● **Salary:** 3 ● **Outlook:** 3

NIGHT AUDITOR (hotel & rest.) ● DOT #210.382-054 ● OES: 55338 ● Alternate titles: NIGHT-CLERK AUDITOR. Verifies and balances entries and records of financial transactions reported by various hotel departments during day, using adding, bookkeeping, and calculating machines. May perform duties of HOTEL CLERK (hotel & rest.) 238.367-038 in smaller establishment. ● **GED:** R4, M4, L3 ● **SVP:** 6 mos-1 yr ● **Academic:** Ed=N, Eng=S ● **Work Field:** 232 ● **MPSMS:** 892 ● **Aptitudes:** G3, V3, N2, S4, P3, Q2, K3, F3, M3, E5, C5 ● **Temperaments:** R, T ● **Physical:** Stg=S; Freq: R, H, I, N, A ● **Work Env:** Noise=Q; ● **Salary:** 2 ● **Outlook:** 3

POLICY-CHANGE CLERK (insurance) ● DOT #219.362-042 ● OES: 53314 ● Compiles data and records changes in insurance policies: Examines letter from insured or agent, original application, and other company documents to determine how to effect proposed changes, such as change in beneficiary or method of payment, increase in principal sum or type of insurance. Corresponds with insured or agent to obtain supplemental information or to explain how change would not conform to company regulations or state laws, or routes file to POLICYHOLDER-INFORMATION CLERK (insurance) 249.262-010. Calculates premium, commission adjustments, and new reserve requirements, using rate books, statistical tables, and calculator or computer, and knowledge of specific types of policies. Transcribes data to abstract (work sheet) or enters data into computer for use in preparing documents and adjusting accounts. May write abstract or enter data into computer to prepare new policy or rider to existing policy. May underwrite changes when increase in amount of risk occurs. ● **GED:** R4, M3, L4 ● **SVP:** 6 mos-1 yr ● **Academic:** Ed=N, Eng=G ● **Work Field:** 231, 232 ● **MPSMS:** 895 ● **Aptitudes:** G3, V3, N3, S4, P4, Q2, K4, F4, M4, E5, C5 ● **Temperaments:** J, T ● **Physical:** Stg=S; Const: N Freq: R, H Occas: I, T, G, A ● **Work Env:** Noise=N; ● **Salary:** 3 ● **Outlook:** 3

STATEMENT CLERK (financial) ● DOT #214.362-046 ● OES: 53126 ● Compares previously prepared bank statements with cancelled checks, prepares statements for distribution to customers, and reconciles discrepancies in records and accounts: Matches statement with batch of cancelled checks by account number. Inserts statements and cancelled checks in envelopes and affixes postage, or inserts statements and checks in feeder of machine which automatically stuffs envelopes and meters postage. Routes statements for mailing or over-the-counter delivery to customers. Keeps cancelled checks and customer signature files. May recover checks returned to customer in error, adjust customer account, and answer inquiries. May post stop-payment notices to prevent payment of protested checks. May encode and cancel checks, using machine. May take orders for imprinted checks. ● **GED:** R3, M2, L3 ● **SVP:** 3-6 mos ● **Academic:** Ed=N, Eng=G ● **Work Field:** 232, 231 ● **MPSMS:** 894 ● **Aptitudes:** G3, V3, N3, S4, P3, Q2, K3, F3, M4, E5, C5 ● **Temperaments:** R, T ● **Physical:** Stg=S; Freq: R, H, I, N, A Occas: T, G ● **Work Env:** Noise=N; ● **Salary:** 2 ● **Outlook:** 3

SUPERVISOR, MONEY-ROOM (amuse. & rec.) ● DOT #211.137-018 ● OES: 51002 ● Supervises and coordinates activities of money-room workers engaged in keeping account of money wagered on each race at racetrack: Keeps continuous balance sheet of cash transactions and verifies with cash on hand. Requisitions additional cash as needed. Determines workers needed each day and assigns their duties. Performs duties as described under SUPERVISOR (clerical) Master Title. ● **GED:** R4, M4, L3 ● **SVP:** 1-2 yrs ● **Academic:** Ed=H, Eng=G ● **Work Field:** 232 ● **MPSMS:** 892 ● **Aptitudes:** G3, V3, N3, S5, P3, Q2, K4, F3, M4, E5, C5 ● **Temperaments:** D, P, T ● **Physical:** Stg=L; Freq: R, H, I, T, G, N ● **Work Env:** Noise=Q; ● **Salary:** 4 ● **Outlook:** 2

SUPERVISOR, POLICY-CHANGE CLERKS (insurance) ● DOT #219.132-010 ● OES: 51002 ● Alternate titles: SUPERVISOR,

RECORDS CHANGE. Supervises and coordinates activities of workers engaged in compiling data on changes to insurance policies in force, changing provisions of policies to conform to insured's specifications, and computing premium rates based on changes to policies: Reviews correspondence from insured or agents requesting policy changes to determine work assignments based on types of changes requested. Assigns duties to POLICY-CHANGE CLERKS (insurance) 219.362-042; POLICY-VALUE CALCULATORS (insurance) 216.382-050; POLICYHOLDER-INFORMATION CLERKS (insurance) 249.262-010, and related clerical workers. Interprets policy provisions to workers, as needed, to assist workers in effecting changes according to company regulations. Assists workers in locating and changing policy information, using computer. Verifies accuracy of premium computations, using calculator. Performs other duties as described under SUPERVISOR (clerical) Master Title. ● **GED:** R4, M3, L4 ● **SVP:** 2-4 yrs ● **Academic:** Ed=H, Eng=G ● **Work Field:** 232, 231 ● **MPSMS:** 895 ● **Aptitudes:** G2, V3, N3, S5, P5, Q2, K4, F3, M4, E5, C5 ● **Temperaments:** D, J, P ● **Physical:** Stg=S; Const: N Freq: R, H, I, T, G Occas: A ● **Work Env:** Noise=N; ● **Salary:** 4 ● **Outlook:** 2

SUPERVISOR, TRUST ACCOUNTS (financial) ● DOT #219.132-014 ● OES: 51002 ● Supervises and coordinates activities of workers engaged in processing settlement of cash or securities transactions for trust-account customers in trust division of commercial bank: Reviews debit and credit entries to customer trust accounts pertaining to cash or securities transactions to determine whether funds were received or disbursed according to predetermined schedules, trust or investment-department instructions, or instructions on customer account records, using computer terminal and computer printouts. Assists workers with more difficult aspects of preparing records and transmittal documents for transactions involving purchase or sale of customer assets, recording interest and balance on contracts and notes, recording stock dividends, and placing insurance for customer property held in trust. Trains new workers. Performs other duties as described under SUPERVISOR (clerical) Master Title. May be designated according to specialized area of work as Securities Supervisor (financial). ● **GED:** R4, M3, L4 ● **SVP:** 2-4 yrs ● **Academic:** Ed=H, Eng=G ● **Work Field:** 232 ● **MPSMS:** 894 ● **Aptitudes:** G2, V2, N3, S4, P4, Q2, K4, F4, M4, E5, C5 ● **Temperaments:** D, J, P, T ● **Physical:** Stg=S; Const: T, G, N Freq: I Occas: R, H, A ● **Work Env:** Noise=N; ● **Salary:** 4 ● **Outlook:** 2

SUPERVISOR, UNDERWRITING CLERKS (insurance) ● DOT #219.132-022 ● OES: 51002 ● Alternate titles: POLICY-ISSUE SUPERVISOR. Supervises and coordinates activities of workers engaged in computing premiums, recording, and issuing insurance policies following acceptance of insurance applications by underwriting department. Performs duties as described under SUPERVISOR (clerical) Master Title. ● **GED:** R4, M3, L4 ● **SVP:** 2-4 yrs ● **Academic:** Ed=H, Eng=G ● **Work Field:** 232, 231 ● **MPSMS:** 895 ● **Aptitudes:** G2, V2, N3, S4, P4, Q2, K4, F3, M4, E5, C5 ● **Temperaments:** D, P, T ● **Physical:** Stg=L; Freq: R, H, I, T, G, N ● **Work Env:** Noise=N; ● **Salary:** 4 ● **Outlook:** 2

TRANSFER CLERK (financial) ● DOT #216.362-046 ● OES: 53128 ● Alternate titles: OPERATIONS CLERK; STOCK-TRANSFER CLERK; STOCK-TRANSFER TECHNICIAN. Records transfer of securities and corrects problems related to transfer: Enters information, such as type and amount of securities that client wishes to purchase or sell, into computer terminal. Reviews client instructions for transfer of securities. Examines securities certificates to verify that information is correct, and mails certificates to department or company specializing in transfer of securities certificates. Receives new certificates from department or company, and sends certificates to client to complete transfer. Talks with coworkers, including REGISTERED REPRESENTATIVES (financial) 250.257-018 to correct problems related to transfer of securities. ● **GED:** R3, M2, L3 ● **SVP:** 1-2 yrs ● **Academic:** Ed=H, Eng=G ● **Work Field:** 232 ● **MPSMS:** 894 ● **Aptitudes:** G3, V3, N4, S5, P5, Q2, K3, F3, M4, E5, C5 ● **Temperaments:** T ● **Physical:** Stg=L; Freq: R, H, I, N Occas: O, T, G, A ● **Work Env:** Noise=Q; ● **Salary:** 3 ● **Outlook:** 3

TAX PREPARER (business ser.) ● DOT #219.362-070 ● OES: 21998 ● Alternate titles: INCOME-TAX-RETURN PREPARER; TAX FORM PREPARER. Prepares income tax return forms for individuals and small businesses: Reviews financial records, such as prior tax return forms, income statements, and documentation of expenditures to determine forms needed to prepare return. Interviews client to obtain additional information on taxable income and deductible expenses and allowances. Computes taxes owed, using adding machine, and completes entries on forms, following tax form instructions and tax tables. Consults tax law handbooks or bulletins to determine procedure for preparation of atypical returns. Occasionally verifies totals on forms prepared by others to detect errors of arithmetic or procedure. Calculates form preparation fee according to complexity of return and amount of time required to prepare forms. ● **GED:** R4, M4, L3 ● **SVP:** 3-6 mos ● **Academic:** Ed=H, Eng=G ● **Work Field:** 232 ● **MPSMS:** 892 ● **Aptitudes:** G3, V3, N3, S4, P4, Q2, K4, F3, M4, E5, C5 ● **Temperaments:** J, P, T ● **Physical:** Stg=S; Const: N, A Freq: R, H, I, T, G ● **Work Env:** Noise=N; ● **Salary:** 3 ● **Outlook:** 3

GOE: 07.02.03
Statistical Reporting & Analysis

ACCOUNT-INFORMATION CLERK (utilities) ● DOT #210.367-010 ● OES: 55338 ● Keeps accounting records and compiles information requested by customer and others pertaining to customer accounts: Keeps records and prepares report of meters registering use of gas- or electric-power, showing results of investigations and amounts recovered or lost. Prepares lists and enters charges and payments to customers' accounts for losses, additional deposits, special and irregular charges. Keeps records of overpayments on customer accounts. Applies overpayments to charges on customers' account or prepares voucher for refund. Investigates incorrect billings due to charges or credits on customers' accounts and prepares written instructions for correction. Reviews accounts not billed and prepares bill from available information. Enters information in meter books which was received too late for billing, such as meter test reports and missed meter readings. Prepares lists of special billing instructions, incorporating charges shown on customers' account. Processes final bills that exceed amount of deposit to enter amount of net bill. Prepares and mails duplicate bills as requested. Interviews customers and others in person or by telephone to answer inquiries and complaints pertaining to bills, customer deposits, and accounts. May specialize in handling inquiries received by mail, compiling information from customer accounting records for replies dictated by others. ● **GED:** R4, M3, L3 ● **SVP:** 1-2 yrs ● **Academic:** Ed=H, Eng=G ● **Work Field:** 232 ● **MPSMS:** 892 ● **Aptitudes:** G3, V3, N3, S4, P4, Q2, K4, F3, M3, E5, C5 ● **Temperaments:** P, T, V ● **Physical:** Stg=S; Freq: R, H, I, T, G, N ● **Work Env:** Noise=N; ● **Salary:** 3 ● **Outlook:** 3

CLAIM EXAMINER (insurance) ● DOT #168.267-014 ● OES: 21921 ● Reviews settled insurance claims to determine that payments and settlements have been made in accordance with company practices and procedures: Analyzes data used in settling claim to determine its validity in payment of claims. Reports overpayments, underpayments, and other irregularities. Confers with legal counsel on claims requiring litigation. ● **GED:** R5, M3, L4 ● **SVP:** 2-4 yrs ● **Academic:** Ed=A, Eng=S ● **Work Field:** 271 ● **MPSMS:** 895 ● **Aptitudes:** G2, V2, N3, S4, P4, Q3, K4, F4, M4, E5, C5 ● **Temperaments:** J, V ● **Physical:** Stg=S; Freq: R, H, I, T, G, N, A ● **Work Env:** Noise=N; ● **Salary:** 3 ● **Outlook:** 3

GRADING CLERK (education) ● DOT #219.467-010 ● OES: 53904 ● Alternate titles: GRADE RECORDER; TEST CLERK. Scores objective-type examination papers and computes and records test grades and averages of students in school or college: Grades papers, using electric marking machine. Totals errors found and computes and records percentage grade on student's grade card. Averages test grades to compute student's grade for course. May use weight factors in computing test grades and arriving at final averages. ● **GED:** R4, M3, L3 ● **SVP:** 1-3 mos ● **Academic:** Ed=H, Eng=S ● **Work Field:** 232 ● **MPSMS:** 899 ● **Aptitudes:** G3, V3, N3, S4, P4, Q3, K4, F4, M4, E5, C5 ● **Temperaments:** R, T ● **Physical:** Stg=S; Freq: R, H, N Occas: I ● **Work Env:** Noise=Q; ● **Salary:** 1 ● **Outlook:** 3

POLICY-VALUE CALCULATOR (insurance) ● DOT #216.382-050 ● OES: 55344 ● Compiles and computes loan or surrender value of life insurance policy, using calculator, and rate books and tables: Computes amount payable to policyholder who drops insurance, allows insurance to lapse, or requests loan on policy, considering factors, such as unclaimed dividends, premiums paid in advance, length of time held, and principal sum (loan value), using calculator. Records values on sheet for preparation of correspondence to policyholder and entry onto master file. When working on dropped policies and policyholder requests full cash value, is known as Cash-Surrender Calculator (insurance). When working on dropped policies and policyholder does not request full cash value, prorates cash value to determine time policy may be kept in force and is known as Extended-Insurance Clerk (insurance). When working on policy loans, calculates repayments, using interest tables, and is known as Policy-Load Calculator (insurance). May specialize in data related to pension plans and life insurance, such as premiums, dividends, retirements, and death benefits, and be designated Calculation Clerk (insurance). May verify and recompute calculations made by other workers and be designated Calculation Reviewer (insurance). ● **GED:** R3, M2, L2 ● **SVP:** 6 mos-1 yr ● **Academic:** Ed=H, Eng=G ● **Work Field:** 232 ● **MPSMS:** 895 ● **Aptitudes:** G3, V3, N3, S5, P4, Q2, K3, F3, M4, E5, C5 ● **Temperaments:** J, T ● **Physical:** Stg=S; Freq: R, H, I, N ● **Work Env:** Noise=Q; ● **Salary:** 2 ● **Outlook:** 3

RECEIPT-AND-REPORT CLERK (water trans.) ● DOT #216.382-054 ● OES: 55344 ● Alternate titles: COST-REPORT CLERK. Prepares reports of labor and equipment costs incurred in loading and unloading ship cargoes: Compiles reports of tonnage and type of cargo handled, labor charges involved in loading and unloading cargo, and charges for equipment used, such as cranes, barges, and conveyors. Computes cost per ton for each type of cargo handled and prepares report of total costs for each ship. ● **GED:** R4, M3, L3 ● **SVP:** 6 mos-1 yr ● **Academic:** Ed=H, Eng=G ● **Work Field:** 232 ● **MPSMS:** 892 ● **Aptitudes:** G3, V3, N3, S4, P4, Q2, K3, F3, M4, E5, C5 ● **Temperaments:** J, R ● **Physical:** Stg=S; Freq: R, H, I, N ● **Work Env:** Noise=N; ● **Salary:** 1 ● **Outlook:** 3

STATISTICAL CLERK (clerical) ● DOT #216.382-062 ● OES: 55328 ● Alternate titles: RECORD CLERK; REPORT CLERK; TABULATING CLERK. Compiles data and computes statistics for use in statistical studies, using calculator and adding machine: Compiles statistics from source materials, such as production and sales records, quality control and test records, personnel records, timesheets, survey sheets, and questionnaires. Assembles and classifies statistics, following prescribed procedures. Computes statistical data according to formulas, using calculator. May compile and compute statistics, using computer. May verify authenticity of source material. May be designated according to type of statistics compiled as Census Clerk (government ser.); Mileage Clerk (r.r. trans.); Production-Statistical Clerk (clerical); Sales-Record Clerk (clerical); Steam-Plant Records Clerk (utilities); Time-Analysis Clerk (clerical); Traffic Enumerator (clerical). May compile actuarial statistics, charts, and graphs and be designated Actuarial Clerk (insurance). May compile data and statistics from media guides and team data for use during televised sporting event and be designated Statistician (radio-tv broad.). ● **GED:** R3, M3, L3 ● **SVP:** 3-6 mos ● **Academic:** Ed=H, Eng=S ● **Work Field:** 232 ● **MPSMS:** 891 ● **Aptitudes:** G3, V3, N3, S4, P3, Q2, K3, F3, M4, E5, C5 ● **Temperaments:** R, T ● **Physical:** Stg=S; Const: R, H, I Freq: N, A Occas: T, G ● **Work Env:** Noise=N; ● **Salary:** 2 ● **Outlook:** 3

GOE: 07.02.04
Billing & Rate Computation

ADVERTISING CLERK (business ser.) ● DOT #247.387-010 ● OES: 53908 ● Compiles advertising orders for submission to publishers and verifies conformance of published advertisements to specifications, for billing purposes: Reviews order received from advertising agency or client to determine specifications. Computes cost of advertisement, based on size, date, position, number of insertions, and other requirements, using rate charts. Posts cost data on order and worksheet. Types and mails order and specifications to designated publishers. Files order data pending receipt of publication. Scans publication to locate published advertisement. Measures advertisement, using ruler or transparent calibrated overlay, to verify conformance to size specifications [ADVERTISING-SPACE CLERK (print. & pub.)]. Compares advertisement with order to verify conformance to other specifications. Computes differ-

ence in cost when published advertisement varies from specifications and posts corrected costs on order controls. Separates tear sheet (page upon which advertisement appears) from publication, types and attaches identifying information to tear sheet; and routes with order and worksheet to billing department. ● **GED:** R3, M2, L2 ● **SVP:** 3-6 mos ● **Academic:** Ed=N, Eng=G ● **Work Field:** 232, 231 ● **MPSMS:** 896 ● **Aptitudes:** G3, V3, N3, S4, P3, Q2, K3, F3, M4, E5, C5 ● **Temperaments:** T ● **Physical:** Stg=S; Freq: R, H, I, N ● **Work Env:** Noise=N; ● **Salary:** 2 ● **Outlook:** 3

BILLING CLERK (clerical) ● DOT #214.362-042 ● OES: 55344 ● Operates calculator and typewriter to compile and prepare customer charges, such as labor and material costs: Reads computer printout to ascertain monthly costs, schedule of work completed, and type of work performed for customer, such as plumbing, sheet metal, and insulation. Computes costs and percentage of work completed, using calculator. Compiles data for billing personnel. Types invoices indicating total items for project and cost amounts. ● **GED:** R4, M3, L3 ● **SVP:** 3-6 mos ● **Academic:** Ed=H, Eng=S ● **Work Field:** 232 ● **MPSMS:** 899 ● **Aptitudes:** G3, V3, N3, S4, P4, Q2, K2, F3, M4, E5, C4 ● **Temperaments:** R, T ● **Physical:** Stg=S; Const: R, H, I, N, A Occas: X ● **Work Env:** Noise=N; ● **Salary:** 2 ● **Outlook:** 3

BILLING-CONTROL CLERK (utilities) ● DOT #214.387-010 ● OES: 55344 ● Reviews and posts data from meter books, computes charges for utility services, and marks special accounts for billing purposes: Marks accounts with fixed demands, combined bills for more than one meter connection, and those requiring use of constant multipliers to extend meter reading to actual consumption. Posts late and special meter readings and estimated readings. Examines meter-reading entries for evidence of irregular conditions, such as defective meters or use of service without contract, and prepares forms for corrective actions by others. Marks accounts for no bill when irregular conditions cannot be resolved before billing date. ● **GED:** R3, M3, L3 ● **SVP:** 6 mos-1 yr ● **Academic:** Ed=N, Eng=S ● **Work Field:** 231, 232 ● **MPSMS:** 892 ● **Aptitudes:** G3, V3, N3, S4, P4, Q2, K3, F3, M3, E5, C5 ● **Temperaments:** R, T ● **Physical:** Stg=S; Freq: R, H, I, N ● **Work Env:** Noise=N; ● **Salary:** 2 ● **Outlook:** 3

DEMURRAGE CLERK (r.r. trans.) ● DOT #214.362-010 ● OES: 55344 ● Alternate titles: CAR-RECORD CLERK. Compiles demurrage charges, using basic rates from rate tables: Communicates with consignee by telephone or letter to notify consignee of date and time of arrival of freight shipment, location, and allowable time for moving or unloading freight before demurrage charges are levied. Reviews bills of lading and other shipping documents to ascertain number of carloads of shipment and computes demurrage charges, using basic rates from rate table and adding or calculating machine. Prepares demurrage bill and forwards it to consignee or shipper. May reconsign or reroute cars on order from shippers. May prepare new waybills and bills of lading on receipt of notice of sale of carload of freight from shipper. ● **GED:** R3, M3, L3 ● **SVP:** 6 mos-1 yr ● **Academic:** Ed=N, Eng=G ● **Work Field:** 232 ● **MPSMS:** 892 ● **Aptitudes:** G3, V3, N3, S4, P4, Q3, K3, F3, M4, E5, C5 ● **Temperaments:** J, T ● **Physical:** Stg=S; Freq: R, H, T, G, N, A Occas: I ● **Work Env:** Noise=N; ● **Salary:** 2 ● **Outlook:** 3

INSURANCE CLERK (medical ser.) ● DOT #214.362-022 ● OES: 55344 ● Alternate titles: HOSPITAL-INSURANCE CLERK; PATIENT-INSURANCE CLERK. Verifies hospitalization insurance coverage, computes patients' benefits, and compiles itemized hospital bills: Types insurance assignment form with data, such as names of insurance company and policy holder, policy number, and physician's diagnosis. Telephones, writes, or wires insurance company to verify patient's coverage and to obtain information concerning extent of benefits. Computes total hospital bill showing amounts to be paid by insurance company and by patient, using adding and calculating machines. Answers patient's questions regarding statements and insurance coverage. Telephones or writes companies with unpaid insurance claims to obtain settlement of claim. Prepares forms outlining hospital expenses for governmental, welfare, and other agencies paying bill of specified patient. ● **GED:** R4, M3, L4 ● **SVP:** 6 mos-1 yr ● **Academic:** Ed=N, Eng=G ● **Work Field:** 232 ● **MPSMS:** 895, 899 ● **Aptitudes:** G3, V3, N3, S4, P4, Q3, K4, F4, M4, E5, C5 ● **Temperaments:** P, R, T ● **Physical:** Stg=S; Freq: R, H, I, T, G, N ● **Work Env:** Noise=N; ● **Salary:** 2 ● **Outlook:** 4

INVOICE-CONTROL CLERK (clerical) ● DOT #214.362-026 ● OES: 55344 ● Alternate titles: PURCHASE-ORDER CHECKER. Compiles data from vendor invoices and supporting documents to verify accuracy of billing data and to ensure receipt of items ordered, using calculator and computer: Compares invoices against purchase orders and shipping and receiving documents to verify receipt of items ordered. Reads computer files or computes figures to determine prices and discounts, following invoices and credit memorandums, and using calculator. Records data in control records. Contacts vendors or buyers regarding errors in partial or duplicate shipments, prices, and substitutions. Maintains file of returnable items received from or returned to vendors. Writes check or prepares voucher authorizing payment to vendors. ● **GED:** R4, M3, L3 ● **SVP:** 3-6 mos ● **Academic:** Ed=N, Eng=S ● **Work Field:** 232 ● **MPSMS:** 892 ● **Aptitudes:** G3, V3, N3, S4, P3, Q3, K4, F3, M4, E5, C5 ● **Temperaments:** T ● **Physical:** Stg=S; Freq: R, H, I, T, G, N, A ● **Work Env:** Noise=N; ● **Salary:** 2 ● **Outlook:** 3

MEDIA CLERK (business ser.) ● DOT #247.382-010 ● OES: 59998 ● Keeps record of clients' advertising schedules for advertising agency: Computes cost of space allotment and advertising program from standard rates and data. Records media used, such as newspapers and magazines, and expenses. Types contract after receiving client's approval. Determines cost of advertising space in various media in other areas considering factors, such as size and population of city, space rates, and kind and frequency of publication for comparison. ● **GED:** R4, M3, L3 ● **SVP:** 6 mos-1 yr ● **Academic:** Ed=H, Eng=G ● **Work Field:** 232, 231 ● **MPSMS:** 896 ● **Aptitudes:** G3, V3, N3, S4, P3, Q2, K4, F3, M4, E5, C5 ● **Temperaments:** J, T ● **Physical:** Stg=S; Const: I Freq: R, H, N ● **Work Env:** Noise=Q; ● **Salary:** 3 ● **Outlook:** 3

RATER (insurance) ● DOT #214.482-022 ● OES: 55344 ● Alternate titles: POLICY RATER; RATE INSERTER; RATING CLERK. Calculates amount of premium to be charged for various types of insurance, using rate book, calculator, and adding machine: Selects premium rate based on information in case record folder relating to type and amount of policy based on standard risk factors, such as use and age of automobile, location and value of property, or age of applicant. Adds premium rates of basic policy and endorsements to compute total annual premium. Records rates on abstract sheet (worksheet), from which policies will be typed. May calculate commissions. ● **GED:** R3, M3, L3 ● **SVP:** 3-6 mos ● **Academic:** Ed=N, Eng=S ● **Work Field:** 232 ● **MPSMS:** 895 ● **Aptitudes:** G3, V3, N3, S4, P2, Q2, K3, F3, M4, E5, C5 ● **Temperaments:** R, T ● **Physical:** Stg=S; Freq: R, H, I, N Occas: A ● **Work Env:** Noise=Q; ● **Salary:** 2 ● **Outlook:** 3

REINSURANCE CLERK (insurance) ● DOT #219.482-018 ● OES: 59998 ● Types reinsurance applications and contracts and calculates reinsurance liability, working for either prime insurer or reinsurer and by either of following methods: (1) Calculates reinsurance required on each risk, considering limit of liability. Selects reinsurers who may accept part of ceded liability. Types applications. Computes amount of each premium due, using calculating machine. Accepts reinsurers and their liability for cash values and dividends. Prepares abstract for typing of contracts. (2) Receives reinsurance application from prime insurer. Determines amount of insurance already held on risk from company records and calculates reinsurance that company can accept, based on limit of liability. Determines if reinsurance is automatic from treaty provisions and sends application to underwriting department when it is not automatic. Types notice of acceptance or rejection, based on limit of liability, and action of UNDERWRITER (insurance). Operates calculator to verify computations made by prime insurer. ● **GED:** R4, M3, L3 ● **SVP:** 6 mos-1 yr ● **Academic:** Ed=N, Eng=G ● **Work Field:** 232, 231 ● **MPSMS:** 895 ● **Aptitudes:** G3, V3, N3, S5, P4, Q2, K3, F3, M3, E5, C5 ● **Temperaments:** J, T ● **Physical:** Stg=S; Const: I Freq: R, H, N Occas: A ● **Work Env:** Noise=N; ● **Salary:** 3 ● **Outlook:** 3

TAX CLERK (clerical) ● DOT #219.487-010 ● OES: 55338 ● Alternate titles: REVENUE-STAMP CLERK. Computes state or federal taxes on sales transactions, production processes, or articles produced, and keeps record of amount due and paid. May affix revenue stamps to tax reports to cover amount of tax due. ● **GED:** R3, M2, L2 ● **SVP:** 1-3 mos ● **Academic:** Ed=N, Eng=G ● **Work Field:** 232 ● **MPSMS:** 892 ● **Aptitudes:** G3, V3, N3, S4, P4, Q3, K3, F3, M4, E5, C5 ● **Temperaments:** R, T ● **Physical:** Stg=S; Freq: R, H, I, N Occas: A ● **Work Env:** Noise=Q; ● **Salary:** 3 ● **Outlook:** 3

TICKETING CLERK (air trans.) ● DOT #248.382-010 ● OES: 53810 ● Alternate titles: TELETICKETING AGENT; TICKET AGENT. Compiles and records information to assemble airline tickets for transmittal or mailing to passengers: Reads coded data on booking card to ascertain destination, carrier, flight number, type of accommodation, and stopovers enroute. Selects ticket blank, invoice, and customer account card if applicable, and compiles, computes, and records identification and fare data, using tariff manuals, rate tables, flight schedules, and pen or ticket imprinter. Separates and files copies of completed tickets. Clips completed tickets and invoices to booking cards and routes to other workers for Teletype transmittal or mails tickets to customers. Computes total daily fares, using adding machine, to compile daily revenue report. ● **GED:** R3, M3, L3 ● **SVP:** 3-6 mos ● **Academic:** Ed=N, Eng=G ● **Work Field:** 232 ● **MPSMS:** 899 ● **Aptitudes:** G3, V3, N3, S4, P4, Q2, K4, F4, M4, E5, C5 ● **Temperaments:** R, T ● **Physical:** Stg=S; Freq: R, H, I, N ● **Work Env:** Noise=N; ● **Salary:** 3 ● **Outlook:** 3

TRAFFIC CLERK (clerical) ● DOT #214.587-014 ● OES: 58028 ● Records incoming and outgoing freight data, such as destination, weight, route-initiating department, and charges: Ensures accuracy of rate charges by comparing classification of materials with rate chart. May keep file of claims for overcharges and for damages to goods in transit. ● **GED:** R3, M3, L2 ● **SVP:** 3-6 mos ● **Academic:** Ed=N, Eng=S ● **Work Field:** 232 ● **MPSMS:** 892 ● **Aptitudes:** G3, V3, N4, S4, P4, Q3, K4, F3, M4, E5, C5 ● **Temperaments:** J, T ● **Physical:** Stg=S; Freq: R, H, I, N ● **Work Env:** Noise=Q; ● **Salary:** 2 ● **Outlook:** 3

GOE: 07.02.05
Payroll & Timekeeping

PAYROLL CLERK (clerical) ● DOT #215.382-014 ● OES: 55341 ● Compiles payroll data, and enters data or computes and posts wages, and reconciles errors, to maintain payroll records, using computer or calculator: Compiles payroll data, such as hours worked, sales or piecework, taxes, insurance, and union dues to be withheld, and employee identification number, from time sheets and other records. Prepares computer input forms, enters data into computer files, or computes wages and deductions, using calculator, and posts to payroll records. Reviews wages computed and corrects errors to ensure accuracy of payroll. Records changes affecting net wages, such as exemptions, insurance coverage, and loan payments for each employee to update master payroll records. Records data concerning transfer of employees between departments. May prorate expenses to be debited or credited to each department for cost accounting records. May prepare periodic reports of earnings, taxes, and deductions. May keep records of leave pay and nontaxable wages. May prepare and issue paychecks. ● **GED:** R4, M3, L3 ● **SVP:** 3-6 mos ● **Academic:** Ed=N, Eng=S ● **Work Field:** 232 ● **MPSMS:** 892 ● **Aptitudes:** G3, V3, N3, S4, P4, Q2, K3, F3, M4, E5, C5 ● **Temperaments:** T ● **Physical:** Stg=S; Const: N Freq: R, H, I Occas: G, A ● **Work Env:** Noise=N; ● **Salary:** 2 ● **Outlook:** 3

TIMEKEEPER (clerical) ● DOT #215.362-022 ● OES: 55341 ● Compiles employees' time and production records, using calculator or computer: Reviews timesheets, workcharts, and timecards for completeness. Computes total time worked by employees, using calculator or computer, posts time worked to master timesheet, and routes timesheet to payroll department. May pay employees. May calculate time worked and units produced by piece-work or bonus work employees, using calculator or computer, and be designated Time Checker (clerical) or Work Checker (clerical). May locate workers on jobs at various times to verify attendance of workers listed on daily spot sheet and be designated Spotter (any industry). May interview employees to discuss hours worked and pay adjustments to be made and be designated Pay Agent (clerical). ● **GED:** R3, M2, L2 ● **SVP:** 1-3 mos ● **Academic:** Ed=N, Eng=S ● **Work Field:** 232 ● **MPSMS:** 898 ● **Aptitudes:** G3, V3, N3, S4, P4, Q2, K3, F3, M3, E5, C5 ● **Temperaments:** T ● **Physical:** Stg=S; Freq: H, I, N Occas: T, G ● **Work Env:** Noise=N; ● **Salary:** 1 ● **Outlook:** 3

Workers in this group use basic math skills as they deal with the public. Keeping records, answering customers' questions, and supervising others is often part of the job. Jobs in this group are found where money is paid to or received from the public. Banks, grocery check-out counters, and ticket booths are typical places of employment.

✓ What kind of work would you do?

Your work activities would depend upon your specific job. For example, you might:

- receive money from customers and compute payments and interest for a loan company.
- operate a cash register, receive cash, and make change in a grocery store.
- cash winning tickets at a race track.
- record bids for items and collect deposits at an auction.
- keep records of the money you receive and pay out in a bank.

✓ What skills and abilities do you need for this kind of work?

To do this kind of work, you must be able to:

- use math to figure the cost of things and make change.
- use eyes, hands, and fingers at the same time to operate an adding machine, calculator, or cash register.
- deal with the public with tact and courtesy.
- perform work that is routine and organized.
- make decisions based on information that can be checked or verified.

✓ How do you know if you would like or could learn to do this kind of work?

The following questions may give you clues about yourself as you consider this group of jobs.

- Have you balanced a checking account? Did your balance agree with the bank statement?
- Have you used a calculator or adding machine? Do you like operating this type of equipment?
- Have you sold tickets, candy, or other items? Can you make change rapidly and accurately?
- Have you been the treasurer of a club or social group? Did your records balance at the end of your term in office?
- Have you worked as a cashier in a military PX? Do you like working with the public?

✓ How can you prepare for and enter this kind of work?

Occupations in this group usually require education and/or training extending from a short demonstration to over two years, depending upon the specific kind of work. Basic math skills are required for most of the jobs in this group. Workers usually receive on-the-job training for specific tasks. A few jobs may require experience or more formal business training. This training is offered by high schools, business schools, and government training programs. Jobs with the federal government usually require a civil service examination.

✓ What else should you consider about these jobs?

Workers who handle money may have to be bonded to protect the employer against dishonest activities. At the end of their shift, workers must make sure that their cash on hand balances with their records. Sometimes this may mean working after the firm or company closes to the public.

If you think you would like to do this kind of work, look at the job titles listed on the following pages.

■ ■ ■

GOE: 07.03.01
Paying & Receiving

AUCTION CLERK (retail trade) ● DOT #294.567-010 ● OES: 49023 ● Records amounts of final bids for merchandise at auction sales, and receives money from final bidders at auction: Locates lot and item number of article up for bidding on record sheet. Listens to amount of bids called for by AUCTIONEER (retail trade; wholesale tr.) and records final amount bid for article. Receives deposit money or full payment from final bidders. ● **GED:** R2, M2, L2 ● **SVP:** 1-3 mos ● **Academic:** Ed=N, Eng=G ● **Work Field:** 231 ● **MPSMS:** 881, 882 ● **Aptitudes:**

G3, V4, N3, S5, P5, Q3, K4, F4, M5, E5, C5 ● **Temperaments:** P, R ● **Physical:** Stg=S; Freq: R, H, I, T, G, N, A ● **Work Env:** Noise=L; ● **Salary:** 2 ● **Outlook:** 3

CASHIER I (clerical) ● DOT #211.362-010 ● OES: 49023 ● Alternate titles: CASH-ACCOUNTING CLERK. Receives funds from customers and employees, disburses funds, and records monetary transactions in business establishment or place of public accommodation: Receives cash or checks or completes credit-card charge transactions. Counts money to verify amounts and issues receipts for funds received. Issues change and cashes checks. Compares totals on cash register with amount of currency in register to verify balances. Endorses checks and lists and totals cash and checks for bank deposit. Prepares bank deposit slips. Withdraws cash from bank accounts and keeps custody of cash fund. Disburses cash and writes vouchers and checks in payment of company expenditures. Posts data and balances accounts. Compiles collection, disbursement, and bank-reconciliation reports. Operates office machines, such as typewriter, computer terminal, and adding, calculating, bookkeeping, and check-writing machines. May authorize various plant expenditures and purchases. May prepare payroll and paychecks. May issue itemized statement to customer. May be designated according to specialization as Agency Cashier (insurance); Cashier, Front Office (hotel & rest.). When disbursing money in payment of wages, materials, taxes, plant maintenance, and other company expenses, is designated Disbursement Clerk (clerical). ● **GED:** R4, M3, L3 ● **SVP:** 6 mos-1 yr ● **Academic:** Ed=H, Eng=G ● **Work Field:** 232 ● **MPSMS:** 899 ● **Aptitudes:** G3, V3, N3, S4, P3, Q2, K3, F3, M3, E5, C5 ● **Temperaments:** P, T, V ● **Physical:** Stg=S; Freq: R, H, I, T, G, N Occas: A ● **Work Env:** Noise=N; ● **Salary:** 5 ● **Outlook:** 3

CASHIER II (clerical) ● DOT #211.462-010 ● OES: 49023 ● Alternate titles: CASH CLERK; CASHIER, GENERAL; CASHIER, OFFICE; TICKET CLERK. Receives cash from customers or employees in payment for goods or services and records amounts received: Recomputes or computes bill, itemized lists, and tickets showing amount due, using adding machine or cash register. Makes change, cashes checks, and issues receipts or tickets to customers. Records amounts received and prepares reports of transactions. Reads and records totals shown on cash register tape and verifies against cash on hand. May be required to know value and features of items for which money is received. May give cash refunds or issue credit memorandums to customers for returned merchandise. May operate ticket-dispensing machine. May operate cash register with peripheral electronic data processing equipment by passing individual price coded items across electronic scanner to record price, compile printed list, and display cost of customer purchase, tax, and rebates on monitor screen. May sell candy, cigarettes, gum, and gift certificates, and issue trading stamps. May be designated according to nature of establishment as Cafeteria Cashier (hotel & rest.); Cashier, Parking Lot (automotive ser.); Dining-Room Cashier (hotel & rest.); Service-Bar Cashier (hotel & rest.); Store Cashier (clerical); or according to type of account as Cashier, Credit (clerical); Cashier, Payments Received (clerical). May press numeric keys of computer corresponding to gasoline pump to reset meter on pump and to record amount of sale and be designated Cashier, Self-Service Gasoline (automotive ser.). May receive money, make change, and cash checks for sales personnel on same floor and be designated Floor Cashier (clerical). May make change for patrons at places of amusement other than gambling establishments and be designated Change-Booth Cashier (amuse. & rec.). ● **GED:** R3, M2, L2 ● **SVP:** 2-30 days ● **Academic:** Ed=N, Eng=S ● **Work Field:** 232 ● **MPSMS:** 880 ● **Aptitudes:** G3, V3, N3, S4, P4, Q3, K3, F3, M4, E5, C5 ● **Temperaments:** P, T ● **Physical:** Stg=L; Freq: R, H, I, T, G, N ● **Work Env:** Noise=N; ● **Salary:** 1 ● **Outlook:** 3

CASHIER-CHECKER (retail trade) ● DOT #211.462-014 ● OES: 49023 ● Operates cash register to itemize and total customer's purchases in grocery, department, or other retail store: Reviews price sheets to note price changes and sale items. Records prices and departments, subtotals taxable items, and totals purchases on cash register. Collects cash, check, or charge payment from customer and makes change for cash transactions. Stocks shelves and marks prices on items. Counts money in cash drawer at beginning and end of work shift. May record daily transaction amounts from cash register to balance cash drawer. May weigh items, bag merchandise, issue trading stamps, and redeem food stamps and promotional coupons. May cash checks. May use electronic scanner to record price. May be designated according to items checked as Grocery Checker (retail trade). ● **GED:** R3, M2, L2 ● **SVP:** 1-3 mos ● **Academic:** Ed=N, Eng=S ● **Work Field:** 221, 232 ● **MPSMS:** 881 ● **Aptitudes:** G3, V3, N3, S4, P4, Q3, K2, F3, M3, E5, C5 ● **Temperaments:** P, R, T ● **Physical:** Stg=L; Const: R, H, I Freq: T, G, N Occas: S, K, O, A ● **Work Env:** Noise=N; ● **Salary:** 2 ● **Outlook:** 4

CASHIER, GAMBLING (amuse. & rec.) ● DOT #211.462-022 ● OES: 49023 ● Accepts and pays off bets placed by patrons of cardrooms, bookmaking, or other gambling establishments: Sells color-coded gambling chips or tickets to patrons or to other workers for resale to patrons. Records transaction, using cash register. Accepts cash or checks for chips or approves patrons' credit and charges individual accounts for amount issued. Reconciles daily summaries of transactions to bal-

ance books. May accept patrons' credit applications and verify credit references to obtain check-cashing authorization. May accept bets only and be designated Bet Taker (amuse. & rec.). ● **GED:** R3, M3, L2 ● **SVP:** 3-6 mos ● **Academic:** Ed=N, Eng=S ● **Work Field:** 232 ● **MPSMS:** 899 ● **Aptitudes:** G3, V3, N3, S4, P4, Q3, K3, F3, M4, E5, C3 ● **Temperaments:** P, R, T ● **Physical:** Stg=S; Freq: R, H, I, T, G, N, X ● **Work Env:** Noise=N; ● **Salary:** 3 ● **Outlook:** 3

CHANGE PERSON (amuse. & rec.) ● DOT #211.467-034 ● OES: 49023 ● Exchanges coins for customer's paper money in slot machine area of gambling establishment: Walks and carries money belt in assigned section to exchange size and value of coins desired by customers. Listens for jackpot alarm bell, issues payoffs, and obtains customer's signature on receipt when winnings exceed amount contained in machine. ● **GED:** R2, M2, L1 ● **SVP:** 2-30 days ● **Academic:** Ed=N, Eng=S ● **Work Field:** 232 ● **MPSMS:** 919 ● **Aptitudes:** G4, V4, N4, S5, P4, Q4, K4, F4, M4, E5, C5 ● **Temperaments:** P, T ● **Physical:** Stg=M; Freq: R, H, I, N Occas: T, G ● **Work Env:** Noise=N; ● **Salary:** 2 ● **Outlook:** 3

CHECK CASHIER (business ser.) ● DOT #211.462-026 ● OES: 49023 ● Alternate titles: CASHIER, CHECK-CASHING AGENCY. Cashes checks, prepares money orders, receives payment for utilities bills, and collects and records fees charged for check-cashing service. May receive payment and issue receipts for such items as license plates. ● **GED:** R3, M3, L2 ● **SVP:** 1-3 mos ● **Academic:** Ed=N, Eng=S ● **Work Field:** 232 ● **MPSMS:** 899 ● **Aptitudes:** G3, V3, N3, S4, P4, Q3, K4, F4, M4, E5, C5 ● **Temperaments:** P, R, T ● **Physical:** Stg=S; Freq: R, H, I, N Occas: T, G ● **Work Env:** Noise=Q; ● **Salary:** 1 ● **Outlook:** 3

COLLECTOR (clerical) ● DOT #241.367-010 ● OES: 53508 ● Alternate titles: BILL COLLECTOR; COLLECTION AGENT; OUTSIDE COLLECTOR. Locates customers to collect installments or overdue accounts, damage claims, or nonpayable checks: Visits or phones customer and attempts to persuade customer to pay amount due or arranges for payment at later date. Questions neighbors and postal workers at post office to determine new address of customers. May have service discontinued or merchandise repossessed. Keeps record of collections and status of accounts. May deliver bills. May sell insurance or other service. May be designated according to type of collection as Claims Collector (clerical); Insurance Collector (insurance); Utility-Bill Collector (clerical). ● **GED:** R3, M3, L3 ● **SVP:** 3-6 mos ● **Academic:** Ed=H, Eng=G ● **Work Field:** 271 ● **MPSMS:** 894 ● **Aptitudes:** G3, V3, N3, S5, P4, Q3, K4, F4, M4, E5, C5 ● **Temperaments:** I, P ● **Physical:** Stg=L; Freq: T, G, N Occas: R, H, I, A ● **Work Env:** Noise=N; Freq: W ● **Salary:** 2 ● **Outlook:** 4

COUPON-REDEMPTION CLERK (retail trade) ● DOT #290.477-010 ● OES: 49011 ● Redeems books of trading stamps or coupons in exchange for merchandise and vacation trips: Shows customer selection of merchandise in display catalog and aids customer to make selection. Counts books and verifies number of coupons required for requested articles, and cancels books exchanged for merchandise, using canceling machine. Collects sales tax on merchandise. Orders or obtains merchandise from stockroom. Fills out order form to request merchandise from warehouse when items requested by customer are not in stock. Talks to customers to resolve complaints or problems about merchandise and stamps. May keep record of books redeemed, taxes collected, and merchandise distributed. May take inventory of stock. May arrange merchandise for display on counters, racks, shelves, or stands. May wrap items. ● **GED:** R3, M2, L2 ● **SVP:** 2-30 days ● **Academic:** Ed=N, Eng=S ● **Work Field:** 221, 292 ● **MPSMS:** 899 ● **Aptitudes:** G3, V3, N3, S4, P4, Q3, K3, F3, M3, E5, C5 ● **Temperaments:** P, R ● **Physical:** Stg=L; Freq: R, H, I, T, G, N ● **Work Env:** Noise=N; ● **Salary:** 2 ● **Outlook:** 3

COUNTER CLERK (photofinishing) ● DOT #249.366-010 ● OES: 49017 ● Receives film for processing, loads film into equipment that automatically processes film for subsequent photo printing, and collects payment from customers of photofinishing establishment: Answers customer's questions regarding prices and services. Receives film to be processed from customer and enters identification data and printing instructions on service log and customer order envelope. Loads film into equipment that automatically processes film, and routes processed film for subsequent photo printing. Files processed film and photographic prints according to customer's name. Locates processed film and prints for customer. Totals charges, using cash register, collects payment, and returns prints and processed film to customer. Sells photo supplies, such as film, batteries, and flashcubes. ● **GED:** R2, M2, L2 ● **SVP:** 2-30 days ● **Academic:** Ed=N, Eng=S ● **Work Field:** 232, 202 ● **MPSMS:** 899 ● **Aptitudes:** G4, V4, N4, S4, P4, Q3, K4, F4, M4, E5, C5 ● **Temperaments:** P ● **Physical:** Stg=L; Freq: T, G, N Occas: R, H, I ● **Work Env:** Noise=N; ● **Salary:** 2 ● **Outlook:** 4

INFORMATION CLERK-CASHIER (amuse. & rec.) ● DOT #249.467-010 ● OES: 49023 ● Cashes checks for patrons and provides information concerning racetrack activities: Receives specified amounts of monies from money room for check-cashing funds. Examines patrons' credentials and cashes checks. Directs patrons to such facilities as betting and paying windows and food and beverage concessions. Resolves patrons' claims of winning tickets not honored by PARIMUTUEL-TICKET CASHIER (amuse. & rec.). Examines tickets under fluorescent light to verify watermark and establish validity. Confers with payment personnel to effect payment or refers disputed claims to supervisory personnel for resolution. Keeps records of customer complaints and suggestions regarding facilities and submits records to supervisory personnel. ● **GED:** R3, M2, L3 ● **SVP:** 6 mos-1 yr ● **Academic:** Ed=N, Eng=G ● **Work Field:** 232, 282 ● **MPSMS:** 899 ● **Aptitudes:** G3, V3, N3, S4, P4, Q2, K4, F4, M4, E5, C3 ● **Temperaments:** P, T ● **Physical:** Stg=L; Const: T, G Freq: R, H, N, X Occas: I ● **Work Env:** Noise=L; ● **Salary:** 3 ● **Outlook:** 2

LAYAWAY CLERK (retail trade) ● DOT #299.467-010 ● OES: 49011 ● Alternate titles: WILL-CALL CLERK. Stores and releases merchandise and receives payments for merchandise held in layaway department: Places ordered merchandise on shelves in storeroom. Receives payments on account and final payments for merchandise and issues receipts, using cash register. Keeps records of packages held, amount of each payment, and balance due. Contacts customer when specified period of time has passed without payment to determine if customer still wants merchandise. Releases merchandise to customer upon receipt of final payment, or when customer opens charge account, or routes merchandise for delivery to shipping or delivery department. Packs merchandise when picked up by or being delivered to customer. ● **GED:** R3, M3, L3 ● **SVP:** 1-3 mos ● **Academic:** Ed=N, Eng=G ● **Work Field:** 232, 221 ● **MPSMS:** 881 ● **Aptitudes:** G3, V4, N3, S4, P4, Q3, K4, F4, M4, E5, C5 ● **Temperaments:** P, T ● **Physical:** Stg=L; Freq: R, H, I, T, G, N ● **Work Env:** Noise=N; ● **Salary:** 1 ● **Outlook:** 3

PARIMUTUEL-TICKET CASHIER (amuse. & rec.) ● DOT #211.467-018 ● OES: 49023 ● Alternate titles: MUTUEL CASHIER; PARIMUTUEL CASHIER. Cashes winning parimutuel tickets for patrons at race track: Posts official race results and value of winning tickets on worksheet to compute payouts. Compares ticket submitted by patron with sample to determine validity. Pays winnings to patron. Summons security personnel to apprehend persons attempting to cash fraudulent tickets, or directs patron to INFORMATION CLERK-CASHIER (amuse. & rec.) or to supervisory personnel to resolve questions of ticket validity. Records number of tickets cashed and amount paid out after each race. Requisitions additional cash from MONEY COUNTER (amuse. & rec.) as required. Keeps daily balance sheet of amount and number of transactions. ● **GED:** R3, M2, L2 ● **SVP:** 2-30 days ● **Academic:** Ed=N, Eng=S ● **Work Field:** 232 ● **MPSMS:** 899 ● **Aptitudes:** G3, V3, N3, S5, P3, Q3, K4, F3, M4, E5, C3 ● **Temperaments:** P, R, T ● **Physical:** Stg=L; Freq: R, H, I, T, G, N, X ● **Work Env:** Noise=Q; ● **Salary:** 2 ● **Outlook:** 2

PARIMUTUEL-TICKET SELLER (amuse. & rec.) ● DOT #211.467-022 ● OES: 49023 ● Alternate titles: MUTUEL CLERK; PARIMUTUEL CLERK. Sells parimutuel tickets to patrons at racetrack: Reads entry sheets to ascertain entry number of specific horses in designated race and depresses corresponding numbered key of ticket-dispensing machine that automatically ejects ticket requested by patron. Accepts money and makes change. After start of race records totals of tickets sold and cash received and forwards to money room for counting and verification. ● **GED:** R3, M2, L2 ● **SVP:** 2-30 days ● **Academic:** Ed=N, Eng=S ● **Work Field:** 232 ● **MPSMS:** 899 ● **Aptitudes:** G3, V3, N3, S5, P4, Q3, K4, F3, M4, E5, C4 ● **Temperaments:** P, R, T ● **Physical:** Stg=L; Freq: R, H, I, T, G, N ● **Work Env:** Noise=Q; ● **Salary:** 1 ● **Outlook:** 3

POST-OFFICE CLERK (government ser.) ● DOT #243.367-014 ● OES: 57308 ● Alternate titles: POSTAL CLERK. Performs any combination of following tasks in post office: Sells postage stamps, postal cards, and stamped envelopes. Issues money orders. Registers and insures mail and computes mailing costs of letters and parcels. Places mail into pigeonholes of mail rack, or into bags, according to state, address, name of person, organization, or other scheme. Examines mail for correct postage and cancels mail, using rubber stamp or canceling machine. Weighs parcels and letters on scale and computes mailing cost based on weight and destination. Records daily transactions. Receives complaints concerning mail delivery, mail theft, and lost mail, completes and routes appropriate forms for investigation. Answers questions pertaining to mail regulations or procedures. Posts circulars on bulletin board for public information; distributes public announcements; and assists public in complying with other federal agency requirements, such as registration of aliens. May drive motorcycle or light truck to deliver special delivery letters. May be employed in remote retail store contracted by post office to provide postal services and be designated Contract-Post-Office Clerk (retail trade). ● **GED:** R3, M3, L3 ● **SVP:** 3-6 mos ● **Academic:** Ed=H, Eng=G ● **Work Field:** 221, 292 ● **MPSMS:** 954 ● **Aptitudes:** G3, V3, N3, S4, P3, Q2, K3, F3, M3, E5, C5 ● **Temperaments:** P, V ● **Physical:** Stg=L; Freq: R, H, I, T, G, N, A ● **Work Env:** Noise=Q; ● **Salary:** 4 ● **Outlook:** 1

SAFE-DEPOSIT-BOX RENTAL CLERK (financial) ● DOT #295.367-022 ● OES: 59998 ● Rents safe-deposit boxes to bank customers: Interviews customer to obtain information necessary to open account. Types rental contract and obtains customer signature. Collects initial rental fee from customer and writes receipt. Issues safe-deposit box key to customer. Files safe-deposit records, such as signature cards, rental contract, and access slips to vault. Admits customer to safe-deposit vault. Orders replacements for lost keys. Schedules repairs for safe-deposit box locks. Contacts vendor to forcibly open safe-deposit box when necessary, such as when customer loses key. Receives and records customer payment of yearly safe-deposit fee. May record box rental information, payment, and account changes, using computer terminal. May perform clerical duties. ● **GED:** R3, M3, L3 ● **SVP:** 3-6 mos ● **Academic:** Ed=H, Eng=G ● **Work Field:** 231, 232 ● **MPSMS:** 894 ● **Aptitudes:** G3, V3, N3, S4, P3, Q3, K3, F3, M3, E5, C5 ● **Temperaments:** P ● **Physical:** Stg=L; Freq: R, H, I, T, G, N Occas: S, K, O, F, A ● **Work Env:** Noise=N; ● **Salary:** 2 ● **Outlook:** 2

SUPERVISOR, CASHIERS (hotel & rest.) ● DOT #211.137-010 ● OES: 51002 ● Supervises and coordinates activities of workers engaged in receiving cash or credit-card payment for merchandise or services and keeping records of funds received in retail establishments or places of public accommodation: Performs cashiering and other clerical duties to relieve subordinates during peak work periods. Searches records to assist subordinates in locating and reconciling posting errors on customers' invoices, such as hotel bills or sales tickets, or compares cash register totals with receipts in register to verify accuracy of transactions. Withdraws monies from bank and keeps custody of operating funds, or retains next day's operating funds from daily receipts. Allocates operating funds to cashiering stations. Totals and summarizes funds received, endorses checks, and prepares bank deposit slip. Performs duties as described under SUPERVISOR (clerical) Master Title. ● **GED:** R4, M3, L3 ● **SVP:** 2-4 yrs ● **Academic:** Ed=H, Eng=G ● **Work Field:** 232 ● **MPSMS:** 899 ● **Aptitudes:** G2, V3, N3, S4, P4, Q3, K4, F3, M4, E5, C5 ● **Temperaments:** D, J, P ● **Physical:** Stg=L; Freq: R, H, I, T, G, N ● **Work Env:** Noise=N; ● **Salary:** 4 ● **Outlook:** 2

SUPERVISOR, FOOD CHECKERS AND CASHIERS (hotel & rest.) ● DOT #211.137-014 ● OES: 51002 ● Plans, supervises, and coordinates activities of FOOD-AND-BEVERAGE CHECKERS (hotel & rest.) and CASHIERS (clerical) II at multiple stations in large food-service establishment: Establishes food-checking and cashiering stations to support activities, such as dining rooms, bars, clubs, banquets, and social functions. Hires and trains workers. Observes food-checking, billing, and cashiering activities; counts cash; and reconciles charge sales and cash receipts with total sales to verify accuracy of transactions. Compiles reports, such as cash receipts, guest-bill charges, and sales for accounting and management purposes, or supervises clerical workers preparing reports. ● **GED:** R4, M4, L3 ● **SVP:** 2-4 yrs ● **Academic:** Ed=H, Eng=G ● **Work Field:** 232 ● **MPSMS:** 903, 899 ● **Aptitudes:** G2, V3, N2, S4, P4, Q3, K4, F4, M4, E5, C5 ● **Temperaments:** D, J, P, V ● **Physical:** Stg=L; Freq: R, H, I, T, G, N, D Occas: A ● **Work Env:** Noise=N; ● **Salary:** 4 ● **Outlook:** 2

TELLER (financial) ● DOT #211.362-018 ● OES: 53102 ● Alternate titles: GENERAL TELLER. Receives and pays out money, and keeps records of money and negotiable instruments involved in financial transactions: Receives checks and cash for deposit, verifies amount, and examines checks for endorsements. Cashes checks and pays out money after verification of signatures and customer balances. Enters customers' transactions into computer to record transactions, and issues computer-generated receipts. Places holds on accounts for uncollected funds. Orders daily supply of cash, and counts incoming cash. Balances currency, coin, and checks in cash drawer at end of shift, using calculator, and compares totaled amounts with data displayed on computer screen. Explains, promotes, or sells products or services, such as travelers checks, savings bonds, money orders, and cashier's checks. May open new accounts. May remove deposits from, and count and balance cash in, automated teller machines and night depository. May accept utility bill and loan payments. May use typewriter, photocopier, and check protector to prepare checks and financial documents. ● **GED:** R4, M3, L3 ● **SVP:** 6 mos-1 yr ● **Academic:** Ed=H, Eng=G ● **Work Field:** 232 ● **MPSMS:** 894 ● **Aptitudes:** G3, V3, N3, S4, P3, Q2, K2, F2, M3, E5, C4 ● **Temperaments:** P, T ● **Physical:** Stg=L; Const: R, H, I, N Freq: T, G, A Occas: S, O, E, X ● **Work Env:** Noise=N; ● **Salary:** 1 ● **Outlook:** 3

TELLER, HEAD (financial) ● DOT #211.132-010 ● OES: 51002 ● Supervises and coordinates activities of workers engaged in receiving and paying out money and keeping records of transactions in banks and similar financial institutions: Assigns duties and work schedules to workers to ensure efficient functioning of department. Trains employees in customer service and banking procedures. Approves checks for payment. Adjusts customer complaints. Examines TELLERS' (financial) 211.362-018 reports of daily transactions for accuracy. Consolidates and balances daily transactions, using adding machine and computer. Ensures supply of money for financial institution's needs based on legal requirements and business demand. May allow customers access to safe deposit boxes, following specified procedures. May monitor and review financial institution's security procedures and control access to vault. May count and record currency and coin in vault. Performs other duties as described under SUPERVISOR (clerical) Master Title. ● **GED:** R4, M3, L4 ● **SVP:** 4-10 yrs ● **Academic:** Ed=N, Eng=G ● **Work Field:** 232 ● **MPSMS:** 894 ● **Aptitudes:** G2, V2, N2, S4, P3, Q2, K4, F4, M4, E5, C4 ● **Temperaments:** D, J, P, T ● **Physical:** Stg=L; Const: T, G Freq: R, H, I, N, A Occas: S, O, E, X ● **Work Env:** Noise=N; ● **Salary:** 2 ● **Outlook:** 3

TELLER, VAULT (financial) ● DOT #211.382-010 ● OES: 53102 ● Fills orders for currency and coins, and counts and records cash deposits in vault of commercial bank: Counts currency, coins, and checks received for deposit in vault from business or branch bank, by hand and using currency-counting machine. Totals currency and checks, using computer or calculator, to verify amount on deposit slip or other form. Records deposit in customer account record. Removes specified amount of currency and coins from vault and places cash in bag for shipment to business or branch bank. Records amount of cash shipped. Counts and records large denomination bills, mutilated currency, and food stamps, by hand and using currency-counting machine, for shipment to Federal Reserve Bank. Balances transactions for day, using computer or calculator, and records results. ● **GED:** R4, M3, L3 ● **SVP:** 3-6 mos ● **Academic:** Ed=H, Eng=G ● **Work Field:** 232 ● **MPSMS:** 894 ● **Aptitudes:** G3, V3, N3, S4, P3, Q2, K2, F2, M3, E5, C5 ● **Temperaments:** T ● **Physical:** Stg=M; Const: R, H, I, N, A Occas: S, K, O, G ● **Work Env:** Noise=N; ● **Salary:** 1 ● **Outlook:** 3

TICKET SELLER (clerical) ● DOT #211.467-030 ● OES: 49023 ● Alternate titles: CASHIER, TICKET SELLING. Sells tickets for travel on ferryboats, street railroads, buses, and for admission to places of entertainment, such as skating rinks, baseball parks, stadiums, and amusement parks: Depresses key on ticket-dispensing machine that automatically ejects number of tickets requested by patron or tears tickets from roll and hands ticket to patron. Accepts payment and makes change. Answers questions concerning fares, routes, schedules, and reservations, and gives information concerning coming attractions. Keeps daily balance sheet of cash received and tickets sold. May fill reservations for seats by telephone or mail. May sell tickets from box office and be designated Cashier, Box Office (amuse. & rec.). May collect fares from repeat riders at amusement park and be designated Second-Ride-Fare Collector (amuse. & rec.). May collect fares from railroad passengers at station and sell commuter tickets and be designated Station Agent (r.r. trans.) II. ● **GED:** R3, M2, L2 ● **SVP:** 2-30 days ● **Academic:** Ed=N, Eng=S ● **Work Field:** 292, 282 ● **MPSMS:** 912, 919 ● **Aptitudes:** G3, V3, N3, S5, P4, Q3, K3, F3, M4, E5, C4 ● **Temperaments:** P, T ● **Physical:** Stg=L; Const: R, H, I, T, G Freq: N Occas: X ● **Work Env:** Noise=N; ● **Salary:** 2 ● **Outlook:** 3

TOLL COLLECTOR (government ser.) ● DOT #211.462-038 ● OES: 49023 ● Collects toll charged for use of bridges, highways, or tunnels by motor vehicles, or fare for vehicle and passengers on ferryboats: Collects money and gives customer change. Accepts toll and fare tickets previously purchased. At end of shift balances cash and records money and tickets received. May sell round-trip booklets. May be designated according to place of employment as Toll-Bridge Attendant (government ser.); or type of fare as Vehicle-Fare Collector (motor trans.; water trans.). May admit passengers through turnstile and be designated Turnstile Collector (water trans.). ● **GED:** R3, M2, L2 ● **SVP:** 2-30 days ● **Academic:** Ed=N, Eng=S ● **Work Field:** 232 ● **MPSMS:** 899 ● **Aptitudes:** G3, V3, N3, S4, P4, Q3, K3, F3, M4, E5, C4 ● **Temperaments:** R, T ● **Physical:** Stg=L; Freq: R, H Occas: I ● **Work Env:** Noise=Q; Occas: W ● **Salary:** 4 ● **Outlook:** 3

Business Detail

Oral Communications

Workers in this group give and receive information verbally. Workers may deal with people in person, by telephone, telegraph, or radio. Recording of information in an organized way is frequently required. Private businesses, institutions such as schools and hospitals, and government agencies hire these workers in their offices, reception areas, registration desks, and other areas of information exchange.

✓ What kind of work would you do?

Your work activities would depend upon your specific job. For example, you might:

- interview people and compile information for a survey or census.
- give information to bus or train travelers.
- operate a telephone switchboard.
- register hotel guests and assign rooms.
- prepare reports and insurance-claim forms for customers.
- receive callers at an office and direct them to the proper area.
- use a radio to receive trouble calls and dispatch repairers.
- register park visitors and explain rules and hazards.

✓ *What skills and abilities do you need for this kind of work?*

To do this kind of work, you must be able to:

■ speak clearly and listen carefully.
■ use personal judgment and specialized knowledge to give information to people orally.
■ communicate well with many different kinds of people.
■ change easily and frequently from one activity to another, such as from typing, to interviewing, to searching in a directory, to using a telephone or radio transmitter.
■ use eyes, hands, and fingers accurately while operating a switchboard or computer key board.

✓ *How do you know if you would like or could learn to do this kind of work?*

The following questions may give you clues about yourself as you consider this group of jobs.

■ Have you participated in a school or community survey? Do you enjoy meeting and interviewing people?
■ Have you given directions to others for finding your home? Were they able to follow your directions?
■ Have you had speech courses? Do you have a clear speaking voice? Do you use good grammar?
■ Have you operated a CB radio? Do you like to use the equipment?

■ Have you been involved in a communications unit of the armed forces? Would you like to continue doing this type of work?

✓ *How can you prepare for and enter this kind of work?*

Occupations in this group usually require education and/or training extending from thirty days to over four years, depending upon the specific kind of work. People with a good speaking vocabulary and who like contact with the public usually enter these jobs. Some jobs require typing or general clerical skills. On-the-job training ranging from one month to two years is usually provided. Many employers prefer workers with a high school education or its equal. Chances for promotion are improved with additional education and training. Jobs in the federal government usually require a civil service examination.

✓ *What else should you consider about these jobs?*

Often the worker may have to ask for information that is considered personal or confidential. People may have an unfavorable attitude about giving this information.

Workers may be assigned a wide range of duties, depending on the size of their company.

If you think you would like to do this kind of work, look at the job titles listed on the following pages.

■ ■ ■

GOE: 07.04.01
Interviewing

ADMITTING OFFICER (medical ser.) ● DOT #205.162-010 ● OES: 51002 ● Coordinates activities related to admission of patients in hospital or other medical facility: Confers with physicians, and nursing, housekeeping, transport, and other staff members to coordinate and schedule admission of patient. Assigns accommodations based on physician's admittance orders, patient's preference, nature of illness, availability of space, and other information, and enters bed assignment information into computer. Prepares records of admission, transfer, and other required data. Notifies departments of patient's admission. Reviews clerical work of interviewers and other personnel. Keeps records of admissions and discharges, and compiles occupancy-census data. May interview patient or patient's representative to obtain necessary personal and financial data to determine eligibility for admission. May perform duties described under SUPERVISOR (clerical) Master Title. ● **GED:** R4, M2, L3 ● **SVP:** 2-4 yrs ● **Academic:** Ed=H, Eng=G ● **Work Field:** 231, 282 ● **MPSMS:** 929 ● **Aptitudes:** G3, V3, N3, S4, P4, Q3, K4, F3, M4, E5, C5 ● **Temperaments:** D, J, P, V ● **Physical:** Stg=S; Freq: I, T, G, N Occas: R, H, A ● **Work Env:** Noise=Q; ● **Salary:** 3 ● **Outlook:** 4

BLOOD-DONOR-UNIT ASSISTANT (medical ser.) ● DOT #245.367-014 ● OES: 55347 ● Performs any combination of follow-ing supportive duties at blood-collection unit of blood bank: Schedules appointments over telephone for blood donors. Interviews blood donors and records identifying and blood-credit information on registration form. Notifies nurse if donor appears to be underweight or too old to give blood. Takes blood donor's temperature and pulse to assist during medical interview. Unpacks, labels, and stamps date on empty blood packs. Posts donor names, blood-control numbers, and donor-group numbers to unit logsheet. Seals filled blood packs and sample tubes, using handtools and heat-sealing machine. Serves refreshments, such as coffee, juice, cookies, and jelly beans, to donors to prevent or relieve adverse reactions and to begin replenishment of blood fluids. ● **GED:** R2, M1, L2 ● **SVP:** 2-30 days ● **Academic:** Ed=N, Eng=S ● **Work Field:** 231, 291, 041 ● **MPSMS:** 929, 903 ● **Aptitudes:** G4, V3, N4, S4, P3, Q3, K3, F4, M3, E5, C4 ● **Temperaments:** P, T, V ● **Physical:** Stg=L; Freq: R, H, I Occas: T, G ● **Work Env:** Noise=N; ● **Salary:** 4 ● **Outlook:** 2

BONDING AGENT (business ser.) ● DOT #186.267-010 ● OES: 21998 ● Alternate titles: BAIL BONDING AGENT. Investigates arrested person to determine bondability: Interviews bond applicant to ascertain character and financial status. Furnishes bond for prescribed fee upon determining intention of accused to appear in court. Posts and signs bond with court clerk to obtain release of client. Forfeits amount of bond if client fails to appear for trial. ● **GED:** R4, M3, L4 ● **SVP:** 1-2 yrs ● **Academic:** Ed=H, Eng=G ● **Work Field:** 271 ● **MPSMS:** 899 ● **Aptitudes:** G3, V3, N4, S5, P5, Q3, K4, F4, M4, E5, C5 ● **Temperaments:** J, P, V ● **Physical:** Stg=S; Freq: R, H, I, T, G, N ● **Work Env:** Noise=N; ● **Salary:** 5 ● **Outlook:** 2

CREDIT CLERK (clerical) ● DOT #205.367-022 ● OES: 53121 ● Alternate titles: LOAN CLERK. Processes applications of individuals applying for loans and credit: Interviews applicant to obtain personal and financial data and fills out application. Calls or writes to credit bureaus, employers, and personal references to check credit and personal references. Establishes credit limit, considering such factors as applicant's assets, credit experience, and personal references, based on predetermined standards. Notifies customer by mail, telephone, or in person of acceptance or rejection of application. May keep record or file of credit transactions, deposits, and payments, and sends letters or confers with customers having delinquent accounts to make payment [COLLECTION CLERK (clerical) 241.357-010]. May send form letters and brochures to solicit business from prospective customers. May adjust incorrect credit charges and grant extensions of credit on overdue accounts. May accept payment on accounts. May keep record of applications for loans and credit, using computer. May compute interest and payments, using calculator. May provide customer credit information or rating on request to retail stores, credit agencies, or banks. May check value of customer's collateral, such as securities, held as security for loan. May advise customer by phone or in writing about loan or credit information. May assist customer in filling out loan or credit application. ● **GED:** R4, M3, L4 ● **SVP:** 3-6 mos ● **Academic:** Ed=H, Eng=G ● **Work Field:** 231, 271 ● **MPSMS:** 894 ● **Aptitudes:** G3, V3, N3, S5, P5, Q2, K4, F4, M4, E5, C5 ● **Temperaments:** P, T ● **Physical:** Stg=S; Const: N Freq: R, H, I, T, G Occas: S ● **Work Env:** Noise=N; ● **Salary:** 2 ● **Outlook:** 4

CUSTOMER SERVICE REPRESENTATIVE (financial) ● DOT #205.362-026 ● OES: 53105 ● Opens accounts, explains and processes investments and other financial services, and corrects records: Interviews customers to obtain information and explain available financial services, such as savings and checking accounts, Individual Retirement Account, Certificates of Deposit, savings bonds, and securities. Rents safe deposit boxes. Types account information obtained from customer on record card or form, and enters into computer. Answers customer questions and investigates and corrects errors, following customer and establishment records, and using calculator or computer. Presents funds received from customer to TELLER (financial) 211.362-018 for deposit, and obtains receipt for customer. May help customer complete loan application. May obtain credit records from credit reporting agency. May admit customers to safe deposit vault. May execute wire transfers of funds. ● **GED:** R4, M3, L4 ● **SVP:** 1-2 yrs ● **Academic:** Ed=H, Eng=G ● **Work Field:** 231, 282 ● **MPSMS:** 894 ● **Aptitudes:** G3, V3, N3, S4, P4, Q2, K4, F4, M4, E5, C5 ● **Temperaments:** P, T ● **Physical:** Stg=L; Const: T, G Freq: R, H, I, N, A ● **Work Env:** Noise=N; ● **Salary:** 3 ● **Outlook:** 4

CUSTOMER SERVICE REPRESENTATIVE (radio-tv broad.) ● DOT #239.362-014 ● OES: 55335 ● alternates titles: adjustment clerk; application clerk; order clerk; outside contact clerk; service representative Interviews applicants and records interview information into computer for water, gas, electric, telephone, or cable television system service: Talks with customers by phone or in person and receives orders for installation, turn-on, discontinuance, or change in service. Fills out contract forms, determines charges for service requested, collects deposits, prepares change of address records, and issues discontinuance orders, using computer. May solicit sale of new or additional services. May adjust complaints concerning billing or service rendered, referring complaints of service failures, such as low voltage or low pressure, to designated departments for investigation. May visit customers at their place of residence to investigate conditions preventing completion of service-connection orders and to obtain contract and deposit when service is being used without contract. May discuss cable television equipment operation with customer over telephone to explain equipment usage and to troubleshoot equipment problems. ● **GED:** R3, M2, L3 ● **SVP:** 6 mos-1 yr ● **Academic:** Ed=H, Eng=G ● **Work Field:** 231, 282 ● **MPSMS:** 891 ● **Aptitudes:** G3, V3, N4, S4, P4, Q3, K4, F4, M4, E5, C5 ● **Temperaments:** P, V ● **Physical:** Stg=S; Const: T, G Freq: I, A Occas: R, H, N ● **Work Env:** Noise=N; ● **Salary:** 2 ● **Outlook:** 4

EMPLOYMENT CLERK (clerical) ● DOT #205.362-014 ● OES: 55314 ● Alternate titles: INTERVIEWER; RECEPTION INTERVIEWER. Interviews applicants for employment and processes application forms: Interviews applicants to obtain information, such as age, marital status, work experience, education, training, and occupational interest. Informs applicants of company employment policies. Refers qualified applicants to employing official. Types letters to references indicated on application, or telephones agencies, such as credit bureaus and finance companies. Files applications forms. Compiles and types reports for supervisors on applicants and employees from personnel records. May review credentials to establish eligibility of applicant in regard to identification and naturalization. May telephone or write applicant to inform applicant of acceptance or rejection for employment. May administer aptitude, personality, and interest tests. May compile personnel records [PERSONNEL CLERK (clerical)]. ● **GED:** R4, M2, L4 ● **SVP:** 6 mos-1 yr ● **Academic:** Ed=H, Eng=G ● **Work Field:** 231, 271 ● **MPSMS:** 943 ● **Aptitudes:** G2, V2, N3, S4, P4, Q2, K3, F3, M4, E5, C5 ● **Temperaments:** J, P, V ● **Physical:** Stg=S; Freq: R, H, I, T, G, N ● **Work Env:** Noise=N; ● **Salary:** 2 ● **Outlook:** 4

EMPLOYMENT-AND-CLAIMS AIDE (government ser.) ● DOT #169.367-010 ● OES: 21998 ● Assists applicants completing application forms for job referrals or unemployment compensation claims: Answers questions concerning registration for jobs or application for unemployment insurance benefits. Reviews data on job application to claim forms to ensure completeness. Refers applicants to job opening or interview with EMPLOYMENT INTERVIEWER (profess. & kin.), in accordance with administrative guidelines or office procedures. Schedules unemployment insurance claimants for interview by CLAIMS ADJUDICATOR (government ser.) when question of eligibility arises. Interviews claimants returning at specified intervals to certify claimants for continuing benefits. May assist applicants in filling out forms using knowledge of information required or native language of applicant. ● **GED:** R3, M3, L3 ● **SVP:** 6 mos-1 yr ● **Academic:** Ed=N, Eng=G ● **Work Field:** 282 ● **MPSMS:** 959 ● **Aptitudes:** G3, V3, N3, S3, P3, Q3, K4, F4, M4, E5, C3 ● **Temperaments:** P, R, V ● **Physical:** Stg=S; Freq: R, H, I, T, G, N ● **Work Env:** Noise=N; ● **Salary:** 4 ● **Outlook:** 4

HOSPITAL-ADMITTING CLERK (medical ser.) ● DOT #205.362-018 ● OES: 55332 ● Alternate titles: ADMISSIONS CLERK; CLINIC CLERK; HOSPITAL-RECEIVING CLERK; MEDICAL CLERK. Interviews incoming patient or representative and enters information required for admission into computer: Interviews patient or representative to obtain and record name, address, age, religion, persons to notify in case of emergency, attending physician, and individual or insurance company responsible for payment of bill. Explains hospital regulations, such as visiting hours, payment of accounts, and schedule of charges. Escorts patient or arranges for escort to assigned room or ward. Enters patient admitting information into computer and routes printed copy to designated department. Obtains signed statement from patient to protect hospital's interests. May assign patient to room or ward. May compile data for occupancy and census records. May store patient's valuables. May receive payments on account. ● **GED:** R3, M2, L3 ● **SVP:** 3-6 mos ● **Academic:** Ed=H, Eng=G ● **Work Field:** 231, 282 ● **MPSMS:** 890, 929 ● **Aptitudes:** G3, V3, N3, S4, P4, Q3, K3, F3, M4, E5, C5 ● **Temperaments:** P, V ● **Physical:** Stg=S; Freq: R, H, I, T, G, N ● **Work Env:** Noise=Q; ● **Salary:** 2 ● **Outlook:** 4

IDENTIFICATION CLERK (clerical) ● DOT #205.362-022 ● OES: 55314 ● Alternate titles: SECURITY CLERK. Compiles and records personal data about civilian workers, vendors, contractors, military personnel, and dependents of military personnel at defense installation and prepares badges, passes, and identification cards: Interviews applicants to obtain and verify information, such as name, date of birth, physical description, and type of security clearance held. Corresponds with law enforcement officials, previous employers, and other references to obtain applicant's social, moral, and political background for use by department in determining employment acceptability. Photographs new workers, using automatic identification camera. May fingerprint workers and keep other supplemental identification systems. May keep records of badges issued, lost, and reissued. May issue temporary identification badges to visitors. ● **GED:** R3, M1, L3 ● **SVP:** 1-3 mos ● **Academic:** Ed=H, Eng=G ● **Work Field:** 231 ● **MPSMS:** 891 ● **Aptitudes:** G3, V3, N4, S5, P4, Q3, K2, F3, M3, E5, C5 ● **Temperaments:** P, T, V ● **Physical:** Stg=S; Freq: R, H, I, T, G, N ● **Work Env:** Noise=N; ● **Salary:** 2 ● **Outlook:** 3

LOAN INTERVIEWER, MORTGAGE (financial) ● DOT #241.367-018 ● OES: 53111 ● Alternate titles: LOAN OFFICER. Interviews applicants applying for mortgage loans: Interviews loan applicants to document income, debt, and credit history. Requests documents, such as income tax return, bank account number, purchase agreement, and property description, for verification. Determines if applicant meets establishment standards for further consideration, following manual and using calculator. Informs applicant of closing costs, such as appraisal, credit report, and notary fees. Answers applicant's questions and asks for signature on information authorization forms. Submits application forms to MORTGAGE LOAN PROCESSOR (financial) 249.362-022 for verification of application information. Calls applicant or other persons to resolve discrepancies, such as credit report showing late payment history. Informs applicant of loan denial or acceptance. May visit establishments, such as branch banks, credit unions, real estate brokers, and builders, to promote mortgage service. May work on commission basis. ● **GED:** R4, M3, L3 ● **SVP:** 1-2 yrs ● **Academic:** Ed=H, Eng=G ● **Work Field:** 271 ● **MPSMS:** 894 ● **Aptitudes:** G3, V3, N3, S4, P5, Q3, K4, F4, M4, E5, C5 ● **Temperaments:** J, P ● **Physical:** Stg=S; Const: T, G, N Freq: R, H Occas: I ● **Work Env:** Noise=Q; ● **Salary:** 3 ● **Outlook:** 4

OUTPATIENT-ADMITTING CLERK (medical ser.) ● DOT #205.362-030 ● OES: 55332 ● Interviews new outpatients at hospital or clinic and records data on medical charts: Obtains specified information from patient, such as age, insurance coverage, and symptoms, and types information onto prescribed forms. Places records and blank history sheets in order and files them in folder. Schedules appointments for examinations in hospital clinics, according to nature of illness. Gives general information about outpatient care and answers telephone. May tally number of outpatients entering each day or week. May give first aid. ● **GED:** R3, M2, L3 ● **SVP:** 3-6 mos ● **Academic:** Ed=H, Eng=G ● **Work Field:** 231 ● **MPSMS:** 920 ● **Aptitudes:** G3, V3, N4, S4, P4, Q3, K3, F3, M3, E5, C5 ● **Temperaments:** P, V ● **Physical:** Stg=S; Freq: R, H, I, T, G, N, A ● **Work Env:** Noise=Q; ● **Salary:** 2 ● **Outlook:** 4

REGISTRATION CLERK (government ser.) ● DOT #205.367-042 ● OES: 55332 ● Interviews persons to compile information for legal or other records: Records answers to personal history queries, such as date of birth, length of residence in United States, and change of address to enroll persons for voting, citizenship applications, or other purposes. May record number of applicants registered. May fingerprint registrants [FINGERPRINT CLERK (government ser.) I]. May take affidavits concerning registrants' statement. ● **GED:** R3, M2, L3 ● **SVP:** 1-3 mos ● **Academic:** Ed=H, Eng=G ● **Work Field:** 271 ● **MPSMS:** 950 ● **Aptitudes:** G3, V3, N4, S5, P3, Q3, K4, F3, M3, E5, C5 ● **Temperaments:** P, R, T ● **Physical:** Stg=S; Freq: R, H, T, G, N Occas: I ● **Work Env:** Noise=Q; ● **Salary:** 1 ● **Outlook:** 3

REHABILITATION CLERK (nonprofit org.) ● DOT #205.367-046 ● OES: 53502 ● Compiles, verifies, and records client data in vocational rehabilitation facility: Interviews clients to obtain information, such as medical history and work limitations. Prepares and assists clients to complete routine intake and personnel forms. Gives and receives client information in person, by telephone, or mail to authorized persons. Prepares and types client attendance, training, and counseling reports from client records. Reviews training approval forms and payment vouchers for completeness and accuracy. ● **GED:** R3, M2, L2 ● **SVP:** 3-6 mos ● **Academic:** Ed=H, Eng=G ● **Work Field:** 231, 282 ● **MPSMS:** 733, 891 ● **Aptitudes:** G3, V3, N4, P3, Q2, K3, F3, M3, E5, C5 ● **Temperaments:** P, T ● **Physical:** Stg=S; Freq: R, H, I, T, G, N, A ● **Work Env:** Noise=N; ● **Salary:** 2 ● **Outlook:** 3

SKIP TRACER (clerical) ● DOT #241.367-026 ● OES: 53117 ● Alternate titles: DEBTOR; TRACER. Traces skips (debtors who change residence without notifying creditors to evade payment of bills) for creditors or other concerned parties: Searches city and telephone directories, and street listings, and inquires at post office. Interviews, telephones, or writes former neighbors, stores, friends, relatives, and former employers to elicit information pertaining to whereabouts of skips. Follows up each lead and prepares report of investigation to creditor. May trace individuals for purposes of serving legal papers. May contact debtors by mail or phone to attempt collection of money owed [COLLECTION CLERK (clerical)]. ● **GED:** R4, M2, L4 ● **SVP:** 3-6 mos ● **Academic:** Ed=N, Eng=G ● **Work Field:** 271, 231 ● **MPSMS:** 894 ● **Aptitudes:** G3, V3, N4, S5, P4, Q3, K4, F4, M4, E5, C5 ● **Temperaments:** P ● **Physical:** Stg=S; Freq: R, H, T, G, N Occas: I ● **Work Env:** Noise=Q; ● **Salary:** 3 ● **Outlook:** 3

SURVEY WORKER (clerical) ● DOT #205.367-054 ● OES: 55332 ● Alternate titles: INTERVIEWER; MERCHANDISING REPRESENTATIVE; PUBLIC INTERVIEWER. Interviews people and compiles statistical information on topics, such as public issues or consumer buying habits: Contacts people at home or place of business, or approaches persons at random on street, or contacts them by telephone, following specified sampling procedures. Asks questions following specified outline on questionnaire and records answers. Reviews, classifies, and sorts questionnaires following specified procedures and criteria. May participate in federal, state, or local population survey and be known as Census Enumerator (government ser.). ● **GED:** R3, M1, L2 ● **SVP:** 2-30 days ● **Academic:** Ed=N, Eng=G ● **Work Field:** 231, 271 ● **MPSMS:** 893, 896 ● **Aptitudes:** G3, V3, N4, S4, P4, Q3, K4, F4, M4, E5, C5 ● **Temperaments:** P, T ● **Physical:** Stg=L; Freq: R, H, I, T, G, N ● **Work Env:** Noise=Q; Occas: W ● **Salary:** 2 ● **Outlook:** 2

TRAFFIC CHECKER (government ser.) ● DOT #205.367-058 ● OES: 55332 ● Interviews motor vehicle drivers at specified road intersection or highway to secure information for use in highway planning: Places equipment, such as barricades, signs, and automatic vehicle counting devices. Signals driver to stop, presents identification credentials, and explains reason for halting vehicle. Questions driver to obtain data, such as itinerary and purpose of trip. Records results of interview, and permits driver to continue journey. May secure information on load (either passenger or cargo) carried and type and weight of vehicle. ● **GED:** R2, M2, L2 ● **SVP:** 2-30 days ● **Academic:** Ed=N, Eng=G ● **Work Field:** 231 ● **MPSMS:** 959 ● **Aptitudes:** G3, V3, N3, S3, P3, Q3, K3, F4, M4, E5, C5 ● **Temperaments:** P ● **Physical:** Stg=L; Const: T, G Freq: R, H, I, N ● **Work Env:** Noise=L; Const: W ● **Salary:** 2 ● **Outlook:** 2

GOE: 07.04.02
Order, Complaint & Claims Handling

CLAIMS CLERK II (insurance) ● DOT #205.367-018 ● OES: 53311 ● Alternate titles: LOSS-CLAIM CLERK. Prepares reports and insurance-claim forms for damage or loss against insurance companies: Obtains information from insured to prepare claim form. Forwards report of claim or claim form to insurance company. Acts as intermediary between company and insured. May assist in settling claims. ● **GED:** R3, M3, L3 ● **SVP:** 3-6 mos ● **Academic:** Ed=N, Eng=G ● **Work Field:** 231 ● **MPSMS:** 895 ● **Aptitudes:** G3, V3, N3, S5, P4, Q3, K4, F4, M4, E5, C5 ● **Temperaments:** J ● **Physical:** Stg=S; Freq: R, H, I, T, G, N ● **Work Env:** Noise=Q; ● **Salary:** 2 ● **Outlook:** 4

COLLECTION CLERK (clerical) ● DOT #241.357-010 ● OES: 53508 ● Alternate titles: DELINQUENT-ACCOUNT CLERK; PAST-DUE-ACCOUNTS CLERK. Notifies or locates customers with delinquent accounts and attempts to secure payment, using postal services, telephone, or personal visit: Mails form letters to customers to encourage payment of delinquent accounts. Confers with customer by telephone in attempt to determine reason for overdue payment, reviewing terms of sales, service, or credit contract with customer. Notifies credit department if customer fails to respond. Contacts delinquent account customers in person [COLLECTOR (clerical) 241.367-010]. Records information about financial status of customer and status of collection efforts. May order repossession or service disconnection, or turn over account to attorney. May sort and file correspondence. May receive payments and post amount paid to customer account. May grant extensions of credit. May use automated telephone dialing system to contact customers and computer to record customer account information. May void sales tickets for unclaimed c.o.d. and lay-away merchandise. May trace customer to new address by inquiring at post office or by questioning neighbors [SKIP TRACER (clerical) 241.367-026]. May attempt to repossess merchandise, such as automobile, furniture, and appliances when customer fails to make payment [REPOSSESSOR (clerical) 241.367-022]. May be designated according to type of establishment as Bank-Credit-Card-Collection Clerk (financial); Department-Store-Collection Clerk (retail trade); Hospital Collection Clerk (medical ser.); Utility-Bill-Collection Clerk (clerical). ● **GED:** R4, M3, L4 ● **SVP:** 6 mos-1 yr ● **Academic:** Ed=N, Eng=G ● **Work Field:** 271 ● **MPSMS:** 894 ● **Aptitudes:** G3, V3, N3, S5, P5, Q3, K4, F4, M4, E5, C5 ● **Temperaments:** I, P ● **Physical:** Stg=S; Const: T, G, N Freq: I Occas: R, H, A ● **Work Env:** Noise=N; ● **Salary:** 2 ● **Outlook:** 4

CORRESPONDENCE CLERK (clerical) ● DOT #209.362-034 ●
OES: 55317 ● Composes letters in reply to correspondence concerning such items as requests for merchandise, damage claims, credit information, delinquent accounts, incorrect billing, unsatisfactory service, or to request information: Reads incoming correspondence and gathers data to formulate reply. Operates typewriter to prepare correspondence or to complete form letters, or dictates reply. May route correspondence to other departments for reply. May keep files of correspondence sent, received, or requiring further action. May process orders, prepare order forms, and check progress of orders [ORDER CLERK (clerical) 249.362-026]. May be designated according to type of correspondence handled as Claim Clerk (clerical); Credit-Correspondence Clerk (clerical); Fan-Mail Clerk (amuse. & rec.); Sales-Correspondence Clerk (clerical). ● **GED:** R3, M2, L2 ● **SVP:** 1-2 yrs ● **Academic:** Ed=H, Eng=G ● **Work Field:** 231, 282 ● **MPSMS:** 891 ● **Aptitudes:** G3, V3, N4, S4, P4, Q3, K3, F3, M3, E5, C5 ● **Temperaments:** J, T ● **Physical:** Stg=S; Freq: R, H, N Occas: I, T, G ● **Work Env:** Noise=N; ● **Salary:** 2 ● **Outlook:** 2

ORDER CLERK, FOOD AND BEVERAGE (hotel & rest.) ● DOT #209.567-014 ● OES: 49023 ● Takes food and beverage orders over telephone or intercom system and records order on ticket: Records order and time received on ticket to ensure prompt service, using time-stamping device. Suggests menu items, and substitutions for items not available, and answers questions regarding food or service. Distributes order tickets or calls out order to kitchen employees. May collect charge vouchers and cash for service and keep record of transactions. May be designated according to type of order handled as Telephone-Order Clerk, Drive-In (hotel & rest.); Telephone-Order Clerk, Room Service (hotel & rest.). ● **GED:** R3, M1, L2 ● **SVP:** 2-30 days ● **Academic:** Ed=N, Eng=S ● **Work Field:** 231 ● **MPSMS:** 890, 903 ● **Aptitudes:** G3, V3, N4, S5, P4, Q3, K4, F4, M4, E5, C5 ● **Temperaments:** P, T ● **Physical:** Stg=S; Freq: R, H, I, T, G, N ● **Work Env:** Noise=Q; ● **Salary:** 1 ● **Outlook:** 4

REFERRAL-AND-INFORMATION AIDE (government ser.) ● DOT #237.367-042 ● OES: 55305 ● Receives callers and responds to complaints in person or by telephone for government agency: Questions callers to ascertain nature of complaints against government agency; records complaint on standard form; and routes form to appropriate department or office for action. Contacts department or office to which complaint was referred to determine disposition. Contacts complainant to verify data and follow-up on results of referral. Compiles complaint records, by category, department office, and disposition. Notifies supervisor of patterns of poor provision of service. Maintains up-to-date reference materials and files. ● **GED:** R3, M2, L3 ● **SVP:** 1-3 mos ● **Academic:** Ed=N, Eng=G ● **Work Field:** 282, 231 ● **MPSMS:** 959 ● **Aptitudes:** G3, V2, N4, S4, P4, Q3, K4, F4, M4, E5, C5 ● **Temperaments:** J, P ● **Physical:** Stg=S; Freq: R, H, T, G, N ● **Work Env:** Noise=N; ● **Salary:** 3 ● **Outlook:** 3

GOE: 07.04.03
Registration

ANIMAL-HOSPITAL CLERK (medical ser.) ● DOT #245.367-010 ● OES: 55347 ● Registers and admits animals brought to animal hospital; advises owners about condition of pets being treated; prepares case records of treated animals; and computes and records payment of fees: Questions animal owners to determine symptoms and to complete admission form. Answers questions by phone, letter, or in person about condition of animals treated, visiting hours, first aid, and discharge date. Prepares case record on each animal treated, including identifying information, diagnosis, and treatment. Computes treatment cost and records fees collected. ● **GED:** R3, M2, L3 ● **SVP:** 3-6 mos ● **Academic:** Ed=N, Eng=G ● **Work Field:** 232, 282 ● **MPSMS:** 929 ● **Aptitudes:** G3, V3, N3, S5, P4, Q3, K4, F4, M4, E5, C5 ● **Temperaments:** P ● **Physical:** Stg=S; Freq: R, H, T, G Occas: I ● **Work Env:** Noise=N; ● **Salary:** 3 ● **Outlook:** 2

ANIMAL-SHELTER CLERK (nonprofit org.) ● DOT #249.367-010 ● OES: 55347 ● Assists public to adopt animals in animal shelter and compiles records of impounded animals: Assists prospective owners in selection of animals for adoption and in preparation of adoption forms.

Advises new owners of pet-examination and neuterization services. Maintains list of prospective dog owners and contacts them when desired type of dog is available. Prepares dog-license forms and collects fees. Reviews shelter records of licensed-dog owners to identify owners of lost dogs; reviews other shelter records to help owners find lost pets. Compiles daily records required by animal shelter describing stray animals found by shelter workers and animals turned in by public. ● **GED:** R3, M2, L3 ● **SVP:** 1-3 mos ● **Academic:** Ed=N, Eng=G ● **Work Field:** 231, 282 ● **MPSMS:** 969 ● **Aptitudes:** G3, V3, N4, S5, P4, Q3, K4, F4, M4, E5, C5 ● **Temperaments:** P ● **Physical:** Stg=S; Freq: R, H, T, G Occas: I ● **Work Env:** Noise=N; ● **Salary:** 2 ● **Outlook:** 3

DOG LICENSER (nonprofit org.) ● DOT #249.367-030 ● OES: 53799 ● Canvasses assigned area to locate and advise dog owners of licensing law; to assist with license applications; and to collect license fees: Visits homes and questions dog owners to determine compliance with licensing law. Explains requirements to dog owners, fills out applications, and collects license fees or gives application to owners for mailing. Counts collected fees and applications. Submits fees and reports to department for record. ● **GED:** R3, M2, L3 ● **SVP:** 3-6 mos ● **Academic:** Ed=N, Eng=G ● **Work Field:** 271, 282, 231 ● **MPSMS:** 953 ● **Aptitudes:** G3, V3, N3, S4, P4, Q4, K5, F4, M4, E5, C5 ● **Temperaments:** P ● **Physical:** Stg=L; Freq: T, G Occas: C, S, R, H, I, N, A ● **Work Env:** Noise=N; Freq: W ● **Salary:** 3 ● **Outlook:** 3

ELECTION CLERK (government ser.) ● DOT #205.367-030 ● OES: 59998 ● Alternate titles: POLL CLERK; RETURNING OFFICER. Performs any combination of the following duties during elections: Compiles and verifies voter lists from official registration records. Requests identification of voters at polling place. Obtains signatures and records names of voters to prevent voting of unauthorized persons. Distributes ballots to voters and answers questions concerning voting procedure. Counts valid ballots and prepares official reports of election results. ● **GED:** R3, M2, L2 ● **SVP:** 2-30 days ● **Academic:** Ed=N, Eng=G ● **Work Field:** 231 ● **MPSMS:** 959 ● **Aptitudes:** G3, V3, N4, S5, P4, Q3, K4, F4, M4, E5, C5 ● **Temperaments:** J ● **Physical:** Stg=S; Freq: T, G, N Occas: R, H, I ● **Work Env:** Noise=Q; ● **Salary:** 3 ● **Outlook:** 1

HOTEL CLERK (hotel & rest.) ● DOT #238.367-038 ● OES: 53808 ● Alternate titles: MOTEL CLERK; MOTOR-LODGE CLERK. Performs any combination of following duties for guests of hotel or motel: Greets, registers, and assigns rooms to guests. Issues room key and escort instructions to BELLHOP (hotel & rest.) 324.677-010. Date-stamps, sorts, and racks incoming mail and messages. Transmits and receives messages, using telephone or telephone switchboard. Answers inquiries pertaining to hotel services; registration of guests; and shopping, dining, entertainment, and travel directions. Keeps records of room availability and guests' accounts, manually or using computer. Computes bill, collects payment, and makes change for guests [CASHIER (clerical) I 211.362-010]. Makes and confirms reservations. May post charges, such as room, food, liquor, or telephone, to ledger, manually or using computer [BOOKKEEPER (clerical) 210.382-014]. May make restaurant, transportation, or entertainment reservation, and arrange for tours. May deposit guests' valuables in hotel safe or safe-deposit box. May order complimentary flowers or champagne for guests. May rent dock space at marina-hotel. May work on one floor and be designated Floor Clerk (hotel & rest.). May be known as Key Clerk (hotel & rest.); Reservation Clerk (hotel & rest.); Room Clerk (hotel & rest.) or according to specific area in which employed as Front Desk Clerk (hotel & rest.). ● **GED:** R3, M3, L3 ● **SVP:** 3-6 mos ● **Academic:** Ed=N, Eng=G ● **Work Field:** 291, 282, 232 ● **MPSMS:** 902 ● **Aptitudes:** G3, V3, N3, S4, P4, Q3, K4, F3, M4, E5, C5 ● **Temperaments:** P, V ● **Physical:** Stg=L; Freq: I, T, G, N Occas: R, H ● **Work Env:** Noise=N; ● **Salary:** 2 ● **Outlook:** 3

LICENSE CLERK (government ser.) ● DOT #205.367-034 ● OES: 53799 ● Issues licenses or permits to qualified applicants: Questions applicant to obtain information, such as name, address, and age, and records data on prescribed forms. Evaluates information obtained to determine applicant qualification for licensure. Collects prescribed fee. Issues driver, automobile, marriage, or other license. May conduct oral, visual, written, or performance test to determine applicant qualifications. ● **GED:** R3, M2, L3 ● **SVP:** 1-3 mos ● **Academic:** Ed=H, Eng=G ● **Work Field:** 231, 271 ● **MPSMS:** 953 ● **Aptitudes:** G3, V3, N4, S4, P4, Q3, K4, F4, M4, E5, C5 ● **Temperaments:** J, P ● **Physical:**

Stg=L; Freq: R, H, I, T, G, N Occas: A ● **Work Env:** Noise=N; ● **Salary:** 3 ● **Outlook:** 3

PARK AIDE (government ser.) ● DOT #249.367-082 ● OES: 55305 ● Alternate titles: PARK TECHNICIAN; RANGER AIDE. Assists PARK RANGER (government ser.) 169.167-042 or PARK SUPERINTENDENT (government ser.) 188.167-062 in operation of state or national park, monument, historic site, or recreational area through performance of any combination of clerical and other duties: Greets visitors at facility entrance and explains regulations. Assigns campground or recreational vehicle sites, and collects fees at park offering camping facilities. Monitors campgrounds, cautions visitors against infractions of rules, and notifies PARK RANGER (government ser.) of problems. Replenishes firewood, and assists in maintaining camping and recreational areas in clean and orderly condition. Conducts tours of premises and answers visitors' questions when stationed at historic park, site, or monument. Operates projection and sound equipment and assists PARK RANGER (government ser.) in presentation of interpretive programs. Provides simple first-aid treatment to visitors injured on premises and assists persons with more serious injuries to obtain appropriate medical care. Participates in carrying out fire-fighting or conservation activities. Assists other workers in activities concerned with restoration of buildings and other facilities or excavation and preservation of artifacts when stationed at historic or archeological site. ● **GED:** R4, M3, L4 ● **SVP:** 1-3 mos ● **Academic:** Ed=H, Eng=G ● **Work Field:** 282, 293 ● **MPSMS:** 919, 959 ● **Aptitudes:** G3, V3, N4, S4, P3, Q3, K3, F4, M3, E5, C4 ● **Temperaments:** P, V ● **Physical:** Stg=L; Freq: T, G, F Occas: R, H, I, N, D, A, X ● **Work Env:** Noise=N; Freq: W ● **Salary:** 1 ● **Outlook:** 3

PUBLIC HEALTH REGISTRAR (government ser.) ● DOT #169.167-046 ● OES: 21998 ● Records and maintains birth and death certificates and communicable disease reports, and prepares statistical data and medical reports for city or county public health department: Registers birth, death, and communicable disease statistics from information supplied by physicians, hospital personnel, funeral directors, and representatives from other agencies. Analyzes cause of death statements and communicable disease reports for compliance with laws and local regulations, consistency, and completeness. Contacts information sources concerning vital statistics and disease reports to resolve discrepencies and obtain additional information. Makes certified copies of documents and issues permits to remove and bury bodies. Prepares reports, such as epidemiological case history and morbidity report and keeps file of communicable disease cases. Refers tuberculosis cases and contacts to appropriate health agencies for consultation, treatment referral, and assistance in disease control. Obtains medical, statistical, and sociological data for use by workers in various public health departments. Assists in maintaining statistical data file and medical information reference library. ● **GED:** R4, M3, L4 ● **SVP:** 2-4 yrs ● **Academic:** Ed=H, Eng=G ● **Work Field:** 231 ● **MPSMS:** 721, 920 ● **Aptitudes:** G3, V3, N3, S4, P4, Q3, K4, F4, M4, E4, C5 ● **Temperaments:** J ● **Physical:** Stg=L; Freq: R, H, T, G, N Occas: I ● **Work Env:** Noise=N; ● **Salary:** 4 ● **Outlook:** 3

RECREATION-FACILITY ATTENDANT (amuse. & rec.) ● DOT #341.367-010 ● OES: 68014 ● Schedules use of recreation facilities, such as golf courses, tennis courts, and softball and sandlot diamonds, in accordance with private club or public park rules: Makes reservations for use of facilities by players. Settles disputes between groups or individual players regarding use of facilities. Coordinates use of facilities to prevent players from interfering with one another. May collect fees from players. May inform players of rules concerning dress, conduct, or equipment and enforce rules or eject unruly player or unauthorized persons as necessary. May sell or rent golf and tennis balls, racquets, golf clubs, and other equipment. May render emergency first aid to injured or stricken players. May patrol facilities to detect damage to facilities and report damages to appropriate authority. May be designated according to facility tended as Golf-Course Starter (amuse. & rec.); Tennis-Court Attendant (amuse. & rec.). ● **GED:** R4, M2, L3 ● **SVP:** 1-3 mos ● **Academic:** Ed=N, Eng=S ● **Work Field:** 291, 282 ● **MPSMS:** 913 ● **Aptitudes:** G3, V3, N3, S4, P4, Q3, K4, F4, M4, E5, C5 ● **Temperaments:** P, V ● **Physical:** Stg=L; Freq: H, T, G Occas: R, I, N ● **Work Env:** Noise=N; ● **Salary:** 2 ● **Outlook:** 2

REGISTRAR (government ser.) ● DOT #205.367-038 ● OES: 55305 ● Alternate titles: ENTRANCE GUARD. Registers visitors to public facilities, such as national or state parks, military bases, and monu-

ments: Stops vehicles and pedestrians at gate and records name, nationality, home address, license plate number of vehicle, and time of entrance and departure. Cautions visitors about fires, wild animals, travel hazards, and domestic pets and informs them of laws and regulations pertaining to area. May issue information leaflets. May collect fees and issue entry and fire permits. May give talks describing historical, natural, or scenic points of area. ● **GED:** R3, M2, L3 ● **SVP:** 6 mos-1 yr ● **Academic:** Ed=H, Eng=G ● **Work Field:** 282 ● **MPSMS:** 959 ● **Aptitudes:** G3, V3, N4, S4, P4, Q3, K4, F4, M4, E5, C5 ● **Temperaments:** P, V ● **Physical:** Stg=L; Freq: R, H, T, G, N Occas: I ● **Work Env:** Noise=N; Occas: W ● **Salary:** 1 ● **Outlook:** 5

REGISTRATION CLERK (library) ● DOT #249.365-010 ● OES: 53902 ● Registers library patrons to permit them to borrow books, periodicals, and other library materials: Copies identifying data, such as name and address, from application onto registration list and borrowers' cards to register borrowers, and issues cards to borrowers. Records change of address or name onto registration list and borrowers' cards to amend records. Tends microfilm machine to record identification of borrower and materials issued [PHOTOGRAPHIC-MACHINE OPERATOR (clerical)]. Reviews records, such as microfilm and issue cards, to determine title of overdue materials and to identify borrower. Types notices to notify borrower of overdue material and amount of fine due. ● **GED:** R3, M1, L3 ● **SVP:** 6 mos-1 yr ● **Academic:** Ed=N, Eng=S ● **Work Field:** 221 ● **MPSMS:** 933 ● **Aptitudes:** G3, V3, N4, S4, P4, Q2, K3, F3, M3, E5, C5 ● **Temperaments:** P, T, V ● **Physical:** Stg=L; Freq: R, H, I, T, G, N, A ● **Work Env:** Noise=N; ● **Salary:** 2 ● **Outlook:** 4

RESERVATIONS AGENT (air trans.) ● DOT #238.367-018 ● OES: 53810 ● Alternate titles: TELEPHONE-SALES AGENT. Makes and confirms reservations for passengers on scheduled airline flights: Arranges reservations and routing for passengers at request of TICKET AGENT (any industry) 238.367-026 or customer, using timetables, airline manuals, reference guides, and tariff book. Types requested flight number on keyboard of on-line computer reservation system and scans screen to determine space availability. Telephones customer or TICKET AGENT (any industry) to advise of changes in flight plan or to cancel or confirm reservation. May maintain advance or current inventory of available passenger space on flights. May advise load control personnel and other stations of changes in passenger itinerary to control space and ensure utilization of seating capacity on flights. ● **GED:** R4, M3, L3 ● **SVP:** 3-6 mos ● **Academic:** Ed=H, Eng=G ● **Work Field:** 291, 282, 231 ● **MPSMS:** 855 ● **Aptitudes:** G3, V3, N3, S4, P4, Q3, K3, F3, M3, E5, C5 ● **Temperaments:** I, P, R ● **Physical:** Stg=S; Freq: R, H, I, T, G, N ● **Work Env:** Noise=N; ● **Salary:** 2 ● **Outlook:** 3

GOE: 07.04.04
Reception & Information Giving

CONGRESSIONAL-DISTRICT AIDE (government ser.) ● DOT #209.362-030 ● OES: 55347 ● Provides information and assistance to public and performs variety of clerical tasks in office of congressional legislator: Answers requests for information and assistance from constituents and other members of public, by phone or in person, using knowledge of governmental agencies and programs and source materials, such as agency listings and directories. Transcribes reports and types letters, using electric typewriter. Operates telecopier to receive and send messages, reports, and other documents. Opens and sorts mail according to addressee or type of assistance or information requested. Maintains record of telephone calls. Files correspondence, reports, and documents. Occasionally composes correspondence in response to written requests. Occasionally contacts other governmental or private agencies to act as liaison on behalf of constituents. ● **GED:** R4, M3, L4 ● **SVP:** 6 mos-1 yr ● **Academic:** Ed=H, Eng=G ● **Work Field:** 282, 231 ● **MPSMS:** 891 ● **Aptitudes:** G3, V3, N3, S4, P4, Q3, K4, F3, M3, E5, C5 ● **Temperaments:** P, V ● **Physical:** Stg=S; Freq: R, H, I, T, G, N Occas: A ● **Work Env:** Noise=N; ● **Salary:** 3 ● **Outlook:** 4

INFORMATION CLERK (clerical) ● DOT #237.367-022 ● OES: 55305 ● Answers inquiries from persons entering establishment: Provides information regarding activities conducted at establishment, and location of departments, offices, and employees within organization.

Informs customer of location of store merchandise in retail establishment. Provides information concerning services, such as laundry and valet services, in hotel. Receives and answers requests for information from company officials and employees. May call employees or officials to information desk to answer inquiries. May keep record of questions asked. ● **GED:** R4, M2, L3 ● **SVP:** 3-6 mos ● **Academic:** Ed=H, Eng=G ● **Work Field:** 282 ● **MPSMS:** 899 ● **Aptitudes:** G3, V3, N4, S4, P4, Q3, K4, F5, M4, E5, C5 ● **Temperaments:** J, P, V ● **Physical:** Stg=S; Freq: T, G, N Occas: R, H ● **Work Env:** Noise=N; ● **Salary:** 1 ● **Outlook:** 3

INFORMATION CLERK, AUTOMOBILE CLUB (nonprofit org.) ● DOT #237.267-010 ● OES: 55305 ● Provides telephone inquirers with information concerning activities and programs of automobile club: Provides information on matters, such as traffic engineering and motor-vehicle safety, applicable motor vehicle laws, licensing regulations, automobile insurance and financing, and legal actions. Receives and records complaints on road conditions. Participates in traffic surveys. May specialize in assisting members file insurance claims for motor vehicle property damage and be designated Claims And Insurance Information Clerk, Automobile Club (nonprofit org.). ● **GED:** R4, M3, L4 ● **SVP:** 6 mos-1 yr ● **Academic:** Ed=N, Eng=G ● **Work Field:** 282 ● **MPSMS:** 859 ● **Aptitudes:** G3, V2, N3, S4, P4, Q2, K4, F4, M4, E5, C5 ● **Temperaments:** J ● **Physical:** Stg=S; Freq: T, G, N Occas: R, H, I ● **Work Env:** Noise=N; ● **Salary:** 3 ● **Outlook:** 3

LAND-LEASING EXAMINER (government ser.) ● DOT #237.367-026 ● OES: 55305 ● Alternate titles: LAND-LEASE-INFORMATION CLERK. Furnishes information to public concerning status of state-owned lands for lease, and assists applicants to file documents required to lease land: Answers public inquiries concerning types of land leases available. Furnishes current information concerning land classification, withdrawals from market, or mineral reservations. Assists applicant in completing required documents. Examines applications, transfers, and supporting documents for conformance with agency specifications. Processes documents, collects fees, and maintains history ledgers of state-owned land. ● **GED:** R4, M3, L4 ● **SVP:** 2-4 yrs ● **Academic:** Ed=H, Eng=G ● **Work Field:** 282 ● **MPSMS:** 959 ● **Aptitudes:** G3, V3, N3, S4, P3, Q2, K5, F5, M4, E5, C5 ● **Temperaments:** J ● **Physical:** Stg=S; Freq: T, G, N Occas: R, H, I ● **Work Env:** Noise=N; ● **Salary:** 4 ● **Outlook:** 3

MUSEUM ATTENDANT (museums) ● DOT #109.367-010 ● OES: 31511 ● Conducts operation of museum and provides information about regulations, facilities, and exhibits to visitors: Opens museum at designated hours, greets visitors, and invites visitors to sign guest register. Monitors visitors viewing exhibits, cautions persons not complying with museum regulations, distributes promotional materials, and answers questions concerning exhibits, regulations, and facilities. Arranges tours of facility for schools or other groups, and schedules volunteers or other staff members to conduct tours. Examines exhibit facilities and collection objects periodically and notifies museum professional personnel or governing body when need for repair or replacement is observed. ● **GED:** R4, M3, L4 ● **SVP:** 1-3 mos ● **Academic:** Ed=H, Eng=G ● **Work Field:** 231, 282, 293 ● **MPSMS:** 933 ● **Aptitudes:** G3, V3, N4, S4, P3, Q3, K3, F4, M4, E5, C5 ● **Temperaments:** P, V ● **Physical:** Stg=L; Freq: T, G, F, V Occas: R, H, I, N, A ● **Work Env:** Noise=N; ● **Salary:** 1 ● **Outlook:** 2

POLICYHOLDER-INFORMATION CLERK (insurance) ● DOT #249.262-010 ● OES: 55305 ● Alternate titles: CORRESPONDENT; CUSTOMER-SERVICE CLERK. Analyzes and answers requests by mail, telephone, or in person from policyholders, beneficiaries, or others for information concerning insurance policies: Searches company records to obtain information requested by customer. Estimates loan or cash value of policy for policyholders, using rate books and calculating machine. Interprets policy provisions to determine methods of effecting desired changes, such as change of beneficiary or type of insurance, or change in method of payment. Mails or gives out specified forms and routes completed forms to various units for processing. Analyzes policy transactions and corrects company records to adjust errors. May compose formal synopses of company and competitor policies for use by sales force. May provide information for pensioners and be designated Pensionholder-Information Clerk (insurance). ● **GED:** R4, M2, L4 ● **SVP:** 1-2 yrs ● **Academic:** Ed=N, Eng=G ● **Work Field:** 282 ● **MPSMS:** 895 ● **Aptitudes:** G2, V2, N3, S5, P4, Q2, K4, F4, M4, E5, C5 ● **Temperaments:** J ● **Physical:** Stg=S; Freq: R, H, I, T, G, N ● **Work Env:** Noise=N; ● **Salary:** 3 ● **Outlook:** 3

RECEPTIONIST (clerical) ● DOT #237.367-038 ● OES: 55305 ● Alternate titles: RECEPTION CLERK. Receives callers at establishment, determines nature of business, and directs callers to destination: Obtains caller's name and arranges for appointment with person called upon. Directs caller to destination and records name, time of call, nature of business, and person called upon. May operate PBX telephone console to receive incoming messages. May type memos, correspondence, reports, and other documents. May work in office of medical practitioner or in other health care facility and be designated Outpatient Receptionist (medical ser.) or Receptionist, Doctor's Office (medical ser.). May issue visitor's pass when required. May make future appointments and answer inquiries [INFORMATION CLERK (clerical) 237.367-022]. May perform variety of clerical duties [ADMINISTRATIVE CLERK (clerical) 219.362-010] and other duties pertinent to type of establishment. May collect and distribute mail and messages. ● **GED:** R3, M2, L3 ● **SVP:** 3-6 mos ● **Academic:** Ed=N, Eng=G ● **Work Field:** 282, 231 ● **MPSMS:** 891 ● **Aptitudes:** G3, V3, N4, S4, P4, Q3, K4, F4, M4, E5, C5 ● **Temperaments:** P, R ● **Physical:** Stg=S; Freq: R, H, T, G Occas: I ● **Work Env:** Noise=Q; ● **Salary:** 1 ● **Outlook:** 3

TELEPHONE QUOTATION CLERK (financial) ● DOT #237.367-046 ● OES: 55305 ● Alternate titles: INFORMATION CLERK, BROKERAGE; QUOTE CLERK; TELEPHONE-INFORMATION CLERK. Answers telephone calls from customers requesting current stock quotations and provides information posted on electronic quote board. Relays calls to REGISTERED REPRESENTATIVE (financial) 250.257-018 as requested by customer. May call customers to inform them of stock quotations. ● **GED:** R3, M2, L3 ● **SVP:** 2-30 days ● **Academic:** Ed=N, Eng=G ● **Work Field:** 282 ● **MPSMS:** 894 ● **Aptitudes:** G3, V3, N4, S4, P3, Q3, K4, F4, M4, E5, C5 ● **Temperaments:** P, R ● **Physical:** Stg=S; Freq: R, H, I, T, G, N Occas: A ● **Work Env:** Noise=N; ● **Salary:** 2 ● **Outlook:** 3

TOURIST-INFORMATION ASSISTANT (government ser.) ● DOT #237.367-050 ● OES: 55305 ● Provides travel information and other services to tourists at State Information Center: Greets tourists, in person or by telephone, and answers questions and gives information on resorts, historical sites, scenic areas, and other tourist attractions. Assists tourists in planning itineraries and advises them of traffic regulations. Sells hunting and fishing licenses and provides information on fishing, hunting, and camping regulations. Composes letters in response to inquiries. Maintains personnel, license-sales, and other records. Contacts motel, hotel, and resort operators by mail or telephone to obtain advertising literature. ● **GED:** R4, M3, L4 ● **SVP:** 1-2 yrs ● **Academic:** Ed=H, Eng=G ● **Work Field:** 282, 292, 291 ● **MPSMS:** 959 ● **Aptitudes:** G3, V2, N3, S4, P4, Q4, K4, F4, M4, E5, C5 ● **Temperaments:** J, P, V ● **Physical:** Stg=S; Freq: T, G Occas: R, H, N ● **Work Env:** Noise=N; ● **Salary:** 3 ● **Outlook:** 5

TRAVEL CLERK (hotel & rest.) ● DOT #238.367-030 ● OES: 53810 ● Alternate titles: TRANSPORTATION CLERK. Provides travel information and arranges accommodations for tourists: Answers inquiries, offers suggestions, and provides descriptive literature pertaining to trips, excursions, sports events, concerts, and plays. Discusses routes, time schedules, rates, and types of accommodations with patrons to determine preferences and makes reservations. Verifies arrival and departure times, traces routes on maps, and arranges for baggage handling and other services requested by guests. May deliver tickets. May arrange for visas and other documents required by foreign travelers. May contact individuals and groups to inform them of package tours. ● **GED:** R3, M3, L3 ● **SVP:** 3-6 mos ● **Academic:** Ed=N, Eng=G ● **Work Field:** 282, 291 ● **MPSMS:** 859 ● **Aptitudes:** G3, V3, N3, S4, P3, Q2, K4, F4, M4, E5, C5 ● **Temperaments:** D, P, V ● **Physical:** Stg=S; Freq: T, G Occas: R, H, I, N ● **Work Env:** Noise=Q; ● **Salary:** 3 ● **Outlook:** 3

GOE: 07.04.05
Information Transmitting & Receiving

AIRLINE-RADIO OPERATOR (air trans.) ● DOT #193.262-010 ● OES: 39099 ● Transmits and receives messages between station and aircraft or other ground stations by radiotelephone: Sends meteorological data to aircraft by radiotelephone. Relays by telegraphic typewriter to DISPATCHER (air trans.) transmissions from aircraft, such as number of passengers aboard, estimated time of arrival, mechanical condition of plane, and requests for repairs. Relays instructions of air traffic control centers to airplane when communication fails. Makes connections between telephone and radio equipment to permit direct communication between DISPATCHER (air trans.) and airplane. Must be licensed by Federal Communications Commission. ● **GED:** R4, M4, L4 ● **SVP:** 2-4 yrs ● **Academic:** Ed=H, Eng=G ● **Work Field:** 281 ● **MPSMS:** 860 ● **Aptitudes:** G2, V2, N3, S4, P3, Q2, K3, F2, M2, E5, C4 ● **Temperaments:** J, P, V ● **Physical:** Stg=S; Freq: R, H, T, G, N Occas: I, X ● **Work Env:** Noise=N; ● **Salary:** 4 ● **Outlook:** 2

ALARM OPERATOR (government ser.) ● DOT #379.162-010 ● OES: 58002 ● Alternate titles: FIRE-ALARM DISPATCHER. Operates municipal fire alarm system, radio transmitter and receiver, and telephone switchboard: Receives incoming fire calls by telephone or through alarm system. Questions caller, observes alarm register that codes location of fire, and scans map of city to determine whether fire is located within area served by city fire department. Determines type and number of units to respond to emergency. Notifies fire station, using radio, and starts alarm system that automatically contacts all fire stations and indicates location of fire. Relays messages from scene of fire, such as requests for additional help and medical assistance. Records date, time, type of call and destination of messages received or transmitted. Maintains activity, code, and locator files. Tests various communications systems and reports malfunctions to maintenance units. May operate telegraph to relay code as back-up if transmitter fails. ● **GED:** R4, M3, L4 ● **SVP:** 1-2 yrs ● **Academic:** Ed=H, Eng=S ● **Work Field:** 281 ● **MPSMS:** 860, 951 ● **Aptitudes:** G3, V3, N3, S4, P4, Q3, K4, F3, M4, E5, C4 ● **Temperaments:** D, P ● **Physical:** Stg=S; Freq: R, H, T, G, N Occas: I, A, X, V ● **Work Env:** Noise=N; ● **Salary:** 3 ● **Outlook:** 2

DISPATCHER (government ser.) ● DOT #193.262-014 ● OES: 39099 ● Operates radio and telephone equipment to receive reports and requests from firefighting crews, fire-lookout stations, and mobile units, and relays information or orders to officials concerned. Maintains communications log and maps location of fires, men, and equipment from field reports. May organize and direct activities of firefighting crew. ● **GED:** R4, M3, L4 ● **SVP:** 1-2 yrs ● **Academic:** Ed=H, Eng=G ● **Work Field:** 281 ● **MPSMS:** 860, 951 ● **Aptitudes:** G3, V3, N4, S4, P4, Q3, K4, F4, M3, E5, C5 ● **Temperaments:** V ● **Physical:** Stg=S; Freq: T, G, N, A Occas: R, H, I ● **Work Env:** Noise=N; ● **Salary:** 3 ● **Outlook:** 3

DISPATCHER, MAINTENANCE SERVICE (clerical) ● DOT #239.367-014 ● OES: 58005 ● Alternate titles: DISPATCHER; MAINTENANCE CLERK. Receives telephone and written orders from plant departments for maintenance service, such as repair work, machine adjustments, and renewals or installation of other plant property, and relays requests to appropriate maintenance division. Keeps record of requests and services rendered. Requisitions supplies for maintenance and clerical workers. ● **GED:** R3, M2, L3 ● **SVP:** 1-3 mos ● **Academic:** Ed=N, Eng=G ● **Work Field:** 231 ● **MPSMS:** 891 ● **Aptitudes:** G3, V3, N3, S4, P4, Q3, K4, F4, M4, E5, C5 ● **Temperaments:** R ● **Physical:** Stg=S; Freq: R, H, T, G, N Occas: I ● **Work Env:** Noise=Q; ● **Salary:** 3 ● **Outlook:** 2

DISPATCHER, RADIO (government ser.) ● DOT #379.362-010 ● OES: 58002 ● Alternate titles: DISPATCHER; POLICE RADIO DISPATCHER; STATION OPERATOR. Receives complaints from public concerning crimes and police emergencies, broadcasts orders to police radio patrol units in vicinity to investigate complaint, and relays instructions or questions from remote units. Records calls broadcast and complaints received. In some municipalities coordinates all police, fire, ambulance, and other emergency requests, relaying instructions to radio unit concerned. May make operating adjustments to transmitting equipment where station is not automatic and be required to hold federal license. May transmit and receive messages between divisions of own agency and other law enforcement agencies. May monitor silent alarm system to detect illegal entry into business establishments. May contact POLICE OFFICERS (government ser.) I 375.263-014 and GUARDS, SCHOOL-CROSSING (government ser.) 371.567-010 to verify assignment locations. ● **GED:** R3, M2, L3 ● **SVP:** 3-6 mos ● **Academic:** Ed=H, Eng=G ● **Work Field:** 281 ● **MPSMS:** 863, 951 ● **Aptitudes:** G3, V3, N4, S4, P4, Q3, K3, F4, M4, E5, C5 ● **Temperaments:** P, R, S ● **Physical:** Stg=S; Freq: R, H, I, T, G Occas: N ● **Work Env:** Noise=N; ● **Salary:** 3 ● **Outlook:** 3

FIRE LOOKOUT (forestry) ● DOT #452.367-010 ● OES: 63008 ● Alternate titles: WATCHER, LOOKOUT TOWER. Locates and reports forest fires and weather phenomena from remote fire-lookout station: Maintains surveillance from station to detect evidence of fires and observe weather conditions. Locates fires on area map, using azimuth sighter and known landmarks, estimates size and characteristics of fire, and reports findings to base camp by radio or telephone. Observes instruments and reports daily meterological data, such as temperature, relative humidity, wind direction and velocity, and type of cloud formations. Relays messages from base camp, mobile units, and law enforcement and governmental agencies relating to weather forecasts, fire hazard conditions, emergencies, accidents, and location of crews and personnel. Explains state and federal laws, timber company policies, fire hazard conditions, and fire prevention methods to visitors of forest. Maintains records and logbooks. ● **GED:** R3, M2, L3 ● **SVP:** 6 mos-1 yr ● **Academic:** Ed=N, Eng=S ● **Work Field:** 293 ● **MPSMS:** 313 ● **Aptitudes:** G3, V3, N4, S3, P3, Q3, K4, F4, M4, E4, C3 ● **Temperaments:** J ● **Physical:** Stg=L; Freq: C, B, R, H, I, T, G, N, F, D, V Occas: X ● **Work Env:** Noise=N; Occas: W ● **Salary:** 2 ● **Outlook:** 3

FLIGHT-INFORMATION EXPEDITER (air trans.) ● DOT #912.367-010 ● OES: 58008 ● Determines flight times of airplanes and transmits information to flight operations and Air Traffic Command centers: Evaluates data, such as weather conditions, flight plans, ramp delays, and enroute stopovers, to determine arrival and departure times for each flight, using aids, such as weather charts, slide rule, and computer. Transmits identity and type of airplane, flight locations, time of arrival and departure, and names of crewmembers to Air Traffic Command to obtain clearance for flight over restricted areas. Notifies departments of airline of pending arrival of inbound flight to ensure that personnel are available to load or unload fuel, baggage, and cargo. ● **GED:** R4, M4, L4 ● **SVP:** 6 mos-1 yr ● **Academic:** Ed=N, Eng=G ● **Work Field:** 231, 281 ● **MPSMS:** 855 ● **Aptitudes:** G3, V3, N3, S4, P3, Q3, K4, F4, M4, E5, C4 ● **Temperaments:** J ● **Physical:** Stg=L; Freq: R, H, T, G, N Occas: I ● **Work Env:** Noise=N; ● **Salary:** 3 ● **Outlook:** 3

GAS-DISTRIBUTION-AND-EMERGENCY CLERK (utilities) ● DOT #249.367-042 ● OES: 55323 ● Receives and relays telephone reports of gas emergencies and control-panel readings for gas-distribution-control-center of public utility company: Answers telephone reports of gas emergencies, such as leaks and fires, from general public, police, and fire departments, and notifies company personnel responsible for dispatch of service crews and issuance of reports to governmental agencies. Files charts and records of gas pressure, volume, and flow, and posts by category in daily logbook. Calculates statistical data from recorded readings and prepares gas supply-and-demand charts for use by GAS DISPATCHER (pipe lines; utilities). ● **GED:** R4, M3, L3 ● **SVP:** 1-2 yrs ● **Academic:** Ed=H, Eng=G ● **Work Field:** 282, 232 ● **MPSMS:** 872, 898 ● **Aptitudes:** G3, V3, N3, S4, P3, Q2, K4, F4, M4, E5, C4 ● **Temperaments:** J ● **Physical:** Stg=S; Freq: R, H, I, T, G, N Occas: X ● **Work Env:** Noise=N; ● **Salary:** 2 ● **Outlook:** 2

POLICE AIDE (government ser.) ● DOT #243.362-014 ● OES: 55347 ● Performs any combination of following tasks in police department to relieve police officers of clerical duties: Types and files police forms, such as accident reports, arrest records, evidence cards, and attendance records and schedules. Posts information to police records, manually or using typewriter or computer. Gives information to public, over phone or in person, concerning arrests, missing persons, or other police related business. Operates telephone system to take or relay information. Receives and records physical evidence recovered from crime scenes by police officers. ● **GED:** R3, M2, L3 ● **SVP:** 1-3 mos ● **Academic:** Ed=H, Eng=G ● **Work Field:** 231, 282 ● **MPSMS:** 951 ● **Aptitudes:** G3, V3, N4, S4, P4, Q3, K3, F3, M3, E5, C5 ● **Temperaments:** J, P, T ● **Physical:** Stg=S; Freq: R, H, I, T, G, N, A ● **Work Env:** Noise=N; ● **Salary:** 3 ● **Outlook:** 3

PROTECTIVE-SIGNAL OPERATOR (any industry) ● DOT #379.362-014 ● OES: 57198 ● Alternate titles: ALARM-SIGNAL OPERATOR; DROP-BOARD OPERATOR; DX BOARD OPERATOR; OPERATOR, CIRCUIT; OPERATOR, DIRECT WIRE; SIGNAL TIMER. Reads and records coded signals received in central station of electrical protective signaling system: Interprets coded audible or visible signals received on alarm signal board by direct wire or register tape from subscribers' premises that indicate opening and closing of protected premises, progress of security guard, unlawful intrusions, or fire. Reports irregular signals for corrective action. Reports alarms to police or fire department. Posts changes of subscriber opening and closing schedules. Prepares daily alarm activity and subscriber service reports. May adjust central station equipment to ensure uninterrupted service. May dispatch security personnel to premises after receiving alarm. ● **GED:** R3, M2, L3 ● **SVP:** 6 mos-1 yr ● **Academic:** Ed=N, Eng=S ● **Work Field:** 281, 231, 293 ● **MPSMS:** 899 ● **Aptitudes:** G3, V3, N3, S3, P3, Q3, K3, F3, M4, E5, C3 ● **Temperaments:** P, S, V ● **Physical:** Stg=S; Freq: R, H, I, T, G, N, A, X ● **Work Env:** Noise=Q; ● **Salary:** 3 ● **Outlook:** 2

RECEIVER-DISPATCHER (nonprofit org.) ● DOT #239.367-022 ● OES: 58005 ● Alternate titles: SERVICE AIDE. Receives and records requests for emergency road service from automobile club members, and dispatches tow truck or service truck to stranded vehicle: Answers telephone and obtains and records on road service card such information as name of club member, location of disabled vehicle, and nature of vehicle malfunction. Routes card to dispatch station, or relays information to service station or tow truck in motorist's vicinity, using telephone or two-way radio. May locate site of stranded vehicle, using maps. May maintain file of road service cards. ● **GED:** R3, M2, L3 ● **SVP:** 3-6 mos ● **Academic:** Ed=H, Eng=G ● **Work Field:** 281, 282 ● **MPSMS:** 859 ● **Aptitudes:** G3, V3, N3, S5, P5, Q3, K4, F4, M4, E5, C5 ● **Temperaments:** P ● **Physical:** Stg=L; Freq: R, H, T, G, N Occas: I ● **Work Env:** Noise=N; ● **Salary:** 2 ● **Outlook:** 3

SCOREBOARD OPERATOR (amuse. & rec.) ● DOT #349.665-010 ● OES: 69998 ● Watches players and officials at athletic event and posts or moves indicators and buttons to record progress of game on scoreboard to inform spectators. Confers, by telephone, with AN-NOUNCER (amuse. & rec.) or sideline officials to verify observation of plays. ● **GED:** R3, M2, L3 ● **SVP:** 2-30 days ● **Academic:** Ed=N, Eng=G ● **Work Field:** 281 ● **MPSMS:** 913 ● **Aptitudes:** G3, V3, N4, S4, P3, Q4, K3, F5, M4, E5, C5 ● **Temperaments:** R, T ● **Physical:** Stg=S; Const: F, V Freq: R, H, I Occas: T, G ● **Work Env:** Noise=N; Freq: W ● **Salary:** 2 ● **Outlook:** 2

SERVICE CLERK (clerical) ● DOT #221.367-070 ● OES: 58005 ● Alternate titles: REPAIR-SERVICE CLERK; SERVICE-ORDER DISPATCHER. Receives, records, and distributes work orders to service crews upon customers' requests for service on articles or utilities purchased from wholesale or retail establishment or utility company: Records information, such as name, address, article to be repaired, or service to be rendered. Prepares work order and distributes to service crew. Schedules service call and dispatches service crew. Calls or writes customer to ensure satisfactory performance of service. Keeps record of service calls and work orders. May dispatch orders and relay messages and special instructions to mobile crews and other departments, using radio-telephone equipment. ● **GED:** R3, M2, L2 ● **SVP:** 3-6 mos ● **Academic:** Ed=N, Eng=G ● **Work Field:** 231 ● **MPSMS:** 898 ● **Aptitudes:** G3, V3, N4, S4, P4, Q3, K4, F4, M4, E5, C5 ● **Temperaments:** P, V ● **Physical:** Stg=S; Freq: R, H, I, T, G, N ● **Work Env:** Noise=Q; ● **Salary:** 3 ● **Outlook:** 3

SWITCHBOARD OPERATOR, POLICE DISTRICT (government ser.) ● DOT #235.562-014 ● OES: 57102 ● Operates switchboard to receive and transmit police communications: Talks to police officers reporting from callboxes and records messages on special forms. Enters time of call and callbox number. Telephones for ambulances or fire-fighting equipment when requested. Routes messages for radio broadcast to DISPATCHER, RADIO (government ser.). ● **GED:** R3, M1, L2 ● **SVP:** 3-6 mos ● **Academic:** Ed=N, Eng=G ● **Work Field:** 281 ● **MPSMS:** 861 ● **Aptitudes:** G3, V3, N4, S4, P4, Q4, K3, F3, M3, E5, C5 ● **Temperaments:** P, R ● **Physical:** Stg=L; Const: R, H, T, G Freq: I, N ● **Work Env:** Noise=Q; ● **Salary:** 2 ● **Outlook:** 3

TELECOMMUNICATOR (government ser.) ● DOT #379.362-018 ● OES: 58002 ● Alternate titles: DISPATCHER. Operates communication equipment to receive incoming calls for assistance and dispatches personnel and equipment to scene of emergency: Operates telephone console to receive incoming calls for assistance. Questions caller to determine nature of problem and type and number of personnel and equipment needed, following established guidelines. Scans status charts and computer screen to determine units available. Monitors alarm system signals that indicate location of fire or other emergency. Operates

two-way radio to dispatch police, fire, medical, and other personnel and equipment and to relay instructions or information to remove units. Types commands on computer keyboard to update files and maintain logs. Tests communications and alarm equipment and backup systems to ensure serviceability. May provide prearrival instructions to caller, utilizing knowledge of emergency medical techniques. May activate alarm system to notify fire stations. ● **GED:** R4, M2, L4 ● **SVP:** 6 mos-1 yr ● **Academic:** Ed=H, Eng=G ● **Work Field:** 281 ● **MPSMS:** 861 ● **Aptitudes:** G2, V2, N4, S3, P3, Q2, K3, F3, M3, E5, C5 ● **Temperaments:** J, P, S, V ● **Physical:** Stg=S; Const: T, G Freq: R, H, I, N, A ● **Work Env:** Noise=N; ● **Salary:** 3 ● **Outlook:** 2

TRAIN DISPATCHER (r.r. trans.) ● DOT #184.167-262 ● OES: 81000 ● Alternate titles: CTC OPERATOR; DISPATCHER; TRAFFIC-CONTROL OPERATOR. Coordinates railroad traffic on specified section of line from CTC (centralized-traffic-control) unit that electrically activates track switches and signals: Reads train orders and schedules to familiarize self with scheduled runs, destination of trains, times of arrivals and departures, and priority of trains. Monitors CTC panelboard that indicates location of trains by lights that illuminate as train passes specified positions on run. Operates controls to activate track switches and traffic signals. Reroutes trains or signals LOCOMOTIVE ENGINEER (r.r. trans.) to stop train or change speed according to traffic conditions. Talks by telephone with crewmembers to relay changes in train orders and schedules, and to receive notification of emergency stops, delays, or accidents. Records time each train reaches specified point, time messages are given or received, and name of person giving or receiving message. May chart train movements on graph to estimate arrival times at specified points. May operate teletypewriter to transmit messages to freight offices or other points along line. ● **GED:** R4, M3, L4 ● **SVP:** 2-4 yrs ● **Academic:** Ed=H, Eng=S ● **Work Field:** 013, 281 ● **MPSMS:** 851 ● **Aptitudes:** G2, V3, N3, S4, P3, Q3, K4, F4, M4, E5, C4 ● **Temperaments:** D, J, P ● **Physical:** Stg=S; Freq: R, H, I, T, G, N, A, X ● **Work Env:** Noise=L; ● **Salary:** 4 ● **Outlook:** 1

UTILITY CLERK (utilities) ● DOT #239.367-034 ● OES: 55335 ● Responds to telephone requests for information concerning location of underground utility distribution lines: Informs construction contractors and others excavating near company installations of buried line locations to prevent safety hazards and damage to company equipment, utilizing plat and distribution line maps. Updates maps to indicate extensions and revisions of utility distribution lines within specified jurisdiction. May relay telephone reports of gas emergencies to specified personnel [GAS-DISTRIBUTION-AND-EMERGENCY CLERK (utilities) 249.367-042] or radio customer service requests to mobile service crews, using two-way radio. May issue tools and parts used by company work crews [STOCK CLERK (clerical) 222.387-058]. ● **GED:** R4, M3, L3 ● **SVP:** 6 mos-1 yr ● **Academic:** Ed=H, Eng=G ● **Work Field:** 282 ● **MPSMS:** 870 ● **Aptitudes:** G3, V3, N3, S4, P4, Q2, K3, F4, M3, E5, C4 ● **Temperaments:** P, T ● **Physical:** Stg=L; Const: R, H Freq: I, T, G, N, A Occas: S, X ● **Work Env:** Noise=N; ● **Salary:** 1 ● **Outlook:** 3

GOE: 07.04.06
Switchboard Services

CENTRAL-OFFICE OPERATOR (tel. & tel.) ● DOT #235.462-010 ● OES: 57108 ● Alternate titles: SWITCHBOARD OPERATOR; TELEPHONE OPERATOR. Operates telephone switchboard to establish or assist customers in establishing local or long-distance telephone connections: Observes signal light on switchboard, plugs cords into trunk-jack, and dials or presses button to make connections. Inserts tickets in calculagraph (time-stamping device) to record time of toll calls. Consults charts to determine charges for pay-telephone calls, and requests coin deposits for calls. May give information regarding subscribers' telephone numbers [DIRECTORY-ASSISTANCE OPERATOR (tel. & tel.)]. Calculates and quotes charges on long-distance calls. May make long-distance connections and be designated Long-Distance Operator (tel. & tel.). ● **GED:** R3, M1, L3 ● **SVP:** 1-3 mos ● **Academic:** Ed=N, Eng=G ● **Work Field:** 281 ● **MPSMS:** 861 ● **Aptitudes:** G3, V3, N4, S4, P5, Q3, K3, F3, M3, E5, C5 ● **Temperaments:** P, R ● **Physical:** Stg=L; Const: R, H, T, G Freq: I, N ● **Work Env:** Noise=Q; ● **Salary:** 1 ● **Outlook:** 3

DIRECTORY-ASSISTANCE OPERATOR (tel. & tel.) • DOT #235.662-018 • OES: 57105 • Provides telephone information from cord or cordless central office switchboard: Plugs in headphones when signal light flashes on cord switchboard, or pushes switch keys on cordless switchboard to make connections. Refers to alphabetical or geographical reels or directories to answer questions and suggests alternate locations and spelling under which number could be listed. May type location and spelling of name on computer terminal keyboard, and scan directory or microfilm viewer to locate number. May keep record of calls received. May keep reels and directories up to date. • **GED:** R3, M2, L3 • **SVP:** 1-3 mos • **Academic:** Ed=N, Eng=G • **Work Field:** 282 • **MPSMS:** 861 • **Aptitudes:** G3, V3, N4, S4, P3, Q3, K3, F3, M3, E5, C5 • **Temperaments:** P, R • **Physical:** Stg=S; Const: R, H, T, G Freq: I, N • **Work Env:** Noise=Q; • **Salary:** 1 • **Outlook:** 3

TELEPHONE-ANSWERING-SERVICE OPERATOR (business ser.) • DOT #235.662-026 • OES: 57102 • Alternate titles: INTERCEPTOR OPERATOR; TELEPHONE-INTERCEPTOR OPERATOR. Operates cord or cordless switchboard to provide answering service for clients. Greets caller and announces name or phone number of client. Records and delivers messages, furnishes information, accepts orders, and relays calls. Places telephone calls at request of client and to locate client in emergencies. Date stamps and files messages. • **GED:** R3, M2, L3 • **SVP:** 1-3 mos • **Academic:** Ed=N, Eng=G • **Work Field:** 231, 281 • **MPSMS:** 861 • **Aptitudes:** G3, V3, N4, S4, P5, Q3, K3, F3, M3, E5, C5 • **Temperaments:** P, R • **Physical:** Stg=S; Const: R, H, I, T, G Freq: N • **Work Env:** Noise=Q; • **Salary:** 1 • **Outlook:** 3

TELEPHONE OPERATOR (clerical) • DOT #235.662-022 • OES: 57102 • Alternate titles: CONTROL-BOARD OPERATOR; PBX OPERATOR; PRIVATE-BRANCH-EXCHANGE OPERATOR; SWITCHBOARD OPERATOR; TELEPHONE-SWITCHBOARD OPERATOR. Operates cord or cordless switchboard to relay incoming, outgoing, and interoffice calls: Pushes switch keys on cordless switchboard to make connections and relay calls. Plugs cord of cord type equipment into switchboard jacks to make connections and relay calls. May supply information to callers and record messages. May keep record of calls placed and toll charges. May perform clerical duties, such as typing, proofreading, and sorting mail. May operate system of bells or buzzers to call individuals in establishment to phone. May receive visitors, obtain name and nature of business, and schedule appointments [RECEPTIONIST (clerical) 237.367-038]. • **GED:** R3, M2, L3 • **SVP:** 1-3 mos • **Academic:** Ed=N, Eng=G • **Work Field:** 281 • **MPSMS:** 861 • **Aptitudes:** G3, V3, N4, S4, P4, Q4, K3, F3, M3, E5, C5 • **Temperaments:** P, R • **Physical:** Stg=S; Const: H, T, G Freq: R, I, N, A • **Work Env:** Noise=N; • **Salary:** 1 • **Outlook:** 3

TELEPHONE OPERATOR, CHIEF (clerical) • DOT #235.137-010 • OES: 51002 • Supervises and coordinates activities of TELEPHONE OPERATORS (clerical) 235.662-022 in telephone or telegraph office or in industrial establishment: Notifies telephone company maintenance department of switchboard operational difficulties reported by operators. Prepares work schedules and assigns switchboard positions. Trains new employees and keeps attendance records. Maintains record of incoming and outgoing long-distance and tie line calls, noting duration and time of calls. Keeps record of employees' personal calls and forwards record to department head for collection. Compiles plant phone directory, arranges for distribution to designated personnel, and keeps record of directories distributed. Performs other duties as described under SUPERVISOR (clerical) Master Title. May relieve operators. May supervise operators of telephone answering and message service and be designated Supervisor, Telephone-Answering-Service (business ser.). • **GED:** R4, M3, L4 • **SVP:** 1-2 yrs • **Academic:** Ed=H, Eng=G • **Work Field:** 281 • **MPSMS:** 861 • **Aptitudes:** G3, V3, N3, S4, P4, Q3, K3, F3, M4, E5, C5 • **Temperaments:** D, J, P, V • **Physical:** Stg=S; Freq: H, T, G, N Occas: R, I • **Work Env:** Noise=N; • **Salary:** 4 • **Outlook:** 3

Business Detail 07

Records Processing 07.05

Workers in this group prepare, review, maintain, route, distribute, and coordinate recorded information. They check records and schedules for accuracy. They may schedule the activities of people or the use of equipment. Jobs in this group are found in most businesses, institutions, and government agencies.

✓ What kind of work would you do?

Your work activities would depend upon your specific job. For example, you might:

- issue route slips to drivers to pick up items.
- file correspondence, cards, invoices, receipts, and other records.
- sort and deliver mail in a city or rural mail route.
- open and inspect incoming correspondence and packages and route them to the proper person in an office.
- read typeset copy and mark errors for a publishing company.
- keep records of securities held as collateral by a bank.

- take dictation in shorthand and type letters or other documents from your notes.
- compile records showing cost and volume of advertising.
- compile, verify, and file medical records in a hospital.
- help to prepare duty rosters for crew members of scheduled airline flights.

✓ What skills and abilities do you need for this kind of work?

To do this kind of work, you must be able to:

- use specialized recordkeeping procedures.
- recognize errors in recorded information.
- plan the activities of others.
- perform work which may be routine or repetitive.

✓ How do you know if you would like or could learn to do this kind of work?

The following questions may give you clues about yourself as you consider this group of jobs.

- Have you taken business or office practice courses? Do you like to work with business forms and filing systems?
- Have you used the library card catalog to compile a report? Can you locate the information you need quickly and easily by using the library system?
- Have you collected stamps or coins? Do you have them classified and arranged according to a plan?
- Have you been in charge of records for a club or social group? Do you enjoy maintaining files?
- Have you have experience in the armed forces requiring processing or keeping information?

✓ How can you prepare for and enter this kind of work?

Occupations in this group usually require education and/or training extending from thirty days to over one year, depending upon the specific kind of work. A high school education or its equal is usually required. Special courses in language skills such as punctuation, grammar, and spelling, as well as basic math courses, are helpful. Some employers prefer workers who have completed general business or clerical courses. Training programs for many of these jobs are available through federal or state agencies.

On-the-job training, ranging from a short demonstration to a one-year program, may be provided. Through this training, workers become familiar with their duties.

Sometimes applicants are tested to determine their ability to do or to learn to do the tasks involved.

✓ What else should you consider about these jobs?

Many of these jobs offer advancement possibilities. Part-time or temporary work is usually available. Job duties are assigned to workers according to the size of the company.

If you think you would like to do this kind of work, look at the job titles listed on the following pages.

■ ■ ■

GOE: 07.05.01
Coordinating & Scheduling

ADVERTISING-DISPATCH CLERK (print. & pub.) ● DOT #247.387-014 ● OES: 58008 ● Alternate titles: SCHEDULE CLERK. Compiles and dispatches advertising schedule and material to composing room of daily or weekly publication: Reviews advertising order and prepares advertising schedule, listing size of ad, date(s) to appear, and page and position of ad. Searches advertising files and selects mat that corresponds to advertising layout. Dispatches mat, advertising layout and copy, and advertising schedule to composing department. Obtains advertising proofs from composing department and dispatches them to advertising department for proofreading. Maintains files of all advertising material. May proofread and correct advertising proofs. May read advertisement in first edition of publication for errors. ● **GED:** R3, M2, L3 ● **SVP:** 3-6 mos ● **Academic:** Ed=N, Eng=G ● **Work Field:** 231 ● **MPSMS:** 896 ● **Aptitudes:** G3, V3, N4, S4, P3, Q2, K4, F4, M4, E5, C5 ● **Temperaments:** R, T ● **Physical:** Stg=S; Freq: R, H, N Occas: I ● **Work Env:** Noise=Q; ● **Salary:** 2 ● **Outlook:** 3

CLERK, TELEVISION PRODUCTION (radio-tv broad.) ● DOT #221.367-086 ● OES: 58008 ● Schedules use of facility and equipment and compiles and maintains employee work schedules and equipment and facility usage records for public broadcasting station: Schedules personnel based on written or oral requisition for studio usage, equipment needed for television production, and availability of workers. Compiles leave and vacation schedules. Prepares daily and weekly charts that indicate worker assignment and usage of facilities and equipment. Duplicates charts for distribution to staff, using photocopy machine. Revises schedule charts to accommodate changing priorities and worker absences. Compiles and submits timesheet information to payroll office. ● **GED:** R4, M3, L3 ● **SVP:** 1-2 yrs ● **Academic:** Ed=H, Eng=G ● **Work Field:** 232, 282 ● **MPSMS:** 864, 898 ● **Aptitudes:** G3, V3, N4, S4, P3, Q3, K4, F4, M4, E5, C5 ● **Temperaments:** V ● **Physical:** Stg=S; Freq: R, H, I, T, G, N, A ● **Work Env:** Noise=N; ● **Salary:** 4 ● **Outlook:** 3

COMPUTER PROCESSING SCHEDULER (clerical) ● DOT #221.362-030 ● OES: 58008 ● Schedules work for computer processing and monitors execution of schedule, using software and computer terminal: Reviews computer processing job requests received from programmers and computer users, and talks with programmers and users to determine processing requirements, such as computer time and memory required, and priority. Develops processing schedule, using computer terminal and job scheduling software. Reviews completed schedule to detect conflicts and ensure availability of memory and other computer resources, using computer terminal. Talks with programmers and users to resolve conflicts in schedule. Enters commands to ensure that new processing jobs do not hinder computer operation, following programmers' specifications. Monitors computer terminal display to detect problem, and to ensure that data entered are correct and that jobs will run as scheduled. Corrects problem, such as failure of program to run, or program running incorrect sequence. May establish guidelines for scheduling work. May train other workers in use of scheduling software. ● **GED:** R4, M2, L4 ● **SVP:** 1-2 yrs ● **Academic:** Ed=H, Eng=G ● **Work Field:** 233 ● **MPSMS:** 893 ● **Aptitudes:** G3, V3, N3, S4, P4, Q2, K3, F3, M4, E5, C5 ● **Temperaments:** J, P, T ● **Physical:** Stg=S; Freq: I, T, G, N, A Occas: R, H ● **Work Env:** Noise=N; ● **Salary:** 4 ● **Outlook:** 4

CREW SCHEDULER (air trans.) ● DOT #215.362-010 ● OES: 58008 ● Compiles duty rosters of flight crews and maintains records of crewmembers' flying time for scheduled airline flights: Prepares flight register which crewmembers sign to indicate their preference and availability for flights and time they wish to be called prior to each flight. Types names of crewmembers onto flight schedule in order of seniority to indicate flights to which crewmembers are assigned. Posts names of extra crewmembers in order of seniority on reserve list. Selects replacements from reserve list and notifies replacement when needed. Computes and logs cumulative flight time for crewmembers and removes crewmember's name from flight schedule when flying time limit as prescribed by Federal Aviation Administration has been reached. Schedules vacations as requested by crewmembers. May notify crewmembers of assignments, using telephone. ● **GED:** R3, M3, L3 ● **SVP:** 6 mos-1 yr ● **Academic:** Ed=N, Eng=S ● **Work Field:** 232 ● **MPSMS:** 898 ● **Aptitudes:** G3, V3, N3, S4, P3, Q3, K4, F3, M4, E5,

C5 ● **Temperaments:** R, T ● **Physical:** Stg=S; Freq: R, H, I, N Occas: T, G ● **Work Env:** Noise=Q; ● **Salary:** 2 ● **Outlook:** 3

DISPATCHER, MOTOR VEHICLE (clerical) ● DOT #249.167-014 ● OES: 58005 ● Assigns motor vehicles and drivers for conveyance of freight or passengers: Compiles list of available vehicles. Assigns vehicles according to factors, such as length and purpose of trip, freight or passenger requirements, and preference of user. Issues keys, record sheets, and credentials to drivers. Records time of departure, destination, cargo, and expected time of return. Investigates overdue vehicles. Directs activities of drivers, using two-way radio. May confer with customers to expedite or locate missing, misrouted, delayed, or damaged merchandise. May maintain record of mileage, fuel used, repairs made, and other expenses. May establish service or delivery routes. May issue equipment to drivers, such as handtrucks, dollies, and blankets. May assign helpers to drivers. May be designated according to type of motor vehicle dispatched as Dispatcher, Automobile Rental (automotive ser.); Dispatcher, Tow Truck (automotive ser.). ● **GED:** R3, M2, L3 ● **SVP:** 6 mos-1 yr ● **Academic:** Ed=N, Eng=G ● **Work Field:** 231, 232, 281 ● **MPSMS:** 853, 852 ● **Aptitudes:** G3, V3, N4, S4, P4, Q3, K4, F4, M4, E5, C5 ● **Temperaments:** D, P ● **Physical:** Stg=S; Freq: R, T, G Occas: H, I, N ● **Work Env:** Noise=N; ● **Salary:** 3 ● **Outlook:** 3

EXPEDITER (clerical) ● DOT #222.367-018 ● OES: 58008 ● Contacts vendors and shippers to ensure that merchandise, supplies, and equipment are forwarded on specified shipping date: Contacts vendor by mail, phone, or visit to verify shipment of goods on specified date. Communicates with transportation company to preclude delays in transit. May arrange for distribution of materials upon arrival. May contact vendors to requisition materials. May inspect products for quality and quantity to ensure adherence to specifications. ● **GED:** R3, M3, L3 ● **SVP:** 1-2 yrs ● **Academic:** Ed=H, Eng=G ● **Work Field:** 232 ● **MPSMS:** 898 ● **Aptitudes:** G3, V3, N3, S4, P3, Q3, K4, F3, M4, E5, C5 ● **Temperaments:** P ● **Physical:** Stg=S; Freq: R, H, I, T, G, N Occas: S ● **Work Env:** Noise=N; ● **Salary:** 3 ● **Outlook:** 3

GUIDE, TRAVEL (personal ser.) ● DOT #353.167-010 ● OES: 69998 ● Alternate titles: GUIDE, EXCURSION; GUIDE, ITINERARY; GUIDE, TOUR. Arranges transportation and other accommodations for groups of tourists, following planned itinerary, and escorts groups during entire trip, within single area or at specified stopping points of tour: Makes reservations on ships, trains, and other modes of transportation, and arranges for other accommodations, such as baggage handling, dining and lodging facilities, and recreational activities, using communication media, such as cable, telegraph, or telephone. Accompanies tour group and describes points of interest. May assist tourists to plan itinerary, obtain travel certificates, such as visas, passports, and health certificates, and convert currency into travelers' checks or foreign moneys. May be designated according to method of transportation used as Guide, Cruise (personal ser.); or locality of tour as Guide, Domestic Tour (personal ser.); Guide, Foreign Tour (personal ser.). ● **GED:** R4, M3, L4 ● **SVP:** 1-2 yrs ● **Academic:** Ed=N, Eng=G ● **Work Field:** 291, 282 ● **MPSMS:** 859 ● **Aptitudes:** G2, V2, N3, S4, P4, Q3, K4, F4, M4, E5, C4 ● **Temperaments:** D, P, V ● **Physical:** Stg=L; Freq: T, G Occas: R, H, I, N, X ● **Work Env:** Noise=Q; ● **Salary:** 2 ● **Outlook:** 1

MANAGER, RESERVATIONS (hotel & rest.) ● DOT #238.137-010 ● OES: 51002 ● Supervises and coordinates activities of workers engaged in taking, recording, and canceling reservations in front office of hotel: Sorts reservations received by mail into current (up to 3 days) and future (over 3 days). Sends futures to reservation center in other hotel of chain. Gives current reservations to clerks for computerization. Receives contracts detailing room allotments for conventions from sales representative and feeds information into terminal. Corresponds with groups and travel agents to answer special requests for rooms and rates. Verifies that daily printouts listing guests' arrivals and individual guest folios are received by ROOM CLERKS (hotel & rest.). Maintains weekly attendance sheet and sends to payroll department. Delegates assistants to train clerks in taking telephone reservations and in operating computer terminals and printers to store and receive reservation data. Reschedules workers to accommodate arrivals of conventions and other groups. Recommmends promotion and discharge of workers to MANAGER, FRONT OFFICE (hotel & rest.). Performs other duties as described under SUPERVISOR (clerical) Master Title.

● **GED:** R4, M2, L3 ● **SVP:** 6 mos-1 yr ● **Academic:** Ed=H, Eng=G ● **Work Field:** 291, 231 ● **MPSMS:** 902 ● **Aptitudes:** G3, V3, N3, S4, P3, Q3, K4, F4, M4, E5, C5 ● **Temperaments:** D, J ● **Physical:** Stg=L; Freq: R, H, I, T, G, N ● **Work Env:** Noise=N; ● **Salary:** 3 ● **Outlook:** 2

PERSONNEL SCHEDULER (clerical) ● DOT #215.367-014 ● OES: 58008 ● Alternate titles: SCHEDULER AND PLANNER. Compiles weekly personnel assignment schedules for production department in manufacturing plant: Studies production schedules and staffing tables to ascertain personnel requirements. Determines and records work assignments according to worker availability, seniority, job classification, and preferences. Compiles and oversees in-plant distribution of work schedule. Adjusts schedules to meet emergencies caused by extended leave or increased production demands. Compiles annual seniority lists on which employees indicate vacation preferences and approves leave requests to prevent production losses. ● **GED:** R4, M3, L3 ● **SVP:** 3-6 mos ● **Academic:** Ed=N, Eng=S ● **Work Field:** 232 ● **MPSMS:** 898 ● **Aptitudes:** G3, V3, N3, S4, P4, Q2, K3, F3, M4, E5, C5 ● **Temperaments:** J, T ● **Physical:** Stg=S; Freq: R, H, I, N ● **Work Env:** Noise=N; ● **Salary:** 3 ● **Outlook:** 3

POLICE CLERK (government ser.) ● DOT #375.362-010 ● OES: 55347 ● Compiles daily duty roster and types and maintains various records and reports in municipal police department to document information, such as daily work assignments, equipment issued, vacation scheduled, training records, and personnel data: Prepares duty roster to indicate such personnel information as days on, days off, equipment assigned, and watch. Arranges schedule to most efficiently use personnel and equipment and ensure availability of personnel for court dates. Submits roster to superior for approval. Compiles and records data to maintian personnel folders. Reviews duty roster, personnel folders, and training schedules to schedule training for police personnel. Performs other duties as described under POLICE AIDE (government ser.) 243.362-014. ● **GED:** R4, M3, L3 ● **SVP:** 1-2 yrs ● **Academic:** Ed=H, Eng=G ● **Work Field:** 231, 293 ● **MPSMS:** 951 ● **Aptitudes:** G3, V3, N3, S4, P3, Q3, K2, F3, M4, E5, C5 ● **Temperaments:** T ● **Physical:** Stg=S; Freq: R, H, I, N Occas: T, G ● **Work Env:** Noise=N; ● **Salary:** 1 ● **Outlook:** 2

RESERVATION CLERK (clerical) ● DOT #238.362-014 ● OES: 53810 ● Alternate titles: CLERK, TRAVEL RESERVATIONS; TRAVEL CLERK. Obtains travel and hotel accommodations for guests and employees of industrial concern, issues tickets, types itineraries, and compiles reports of transactions: Obtains confirmation of travel and lodging space and rate information. Issues and validates airline tickets from stock or teleticketer and obtains rail and bus tickets from carriers. Prepares passenger travel booklet containing tickets, copy of itinerary, written lodging confirmations, pertinent credit cards, and travel suggestions. Keeps current directory of hotels, motels, and timetables, and answers inquiries concerning routes, fares, and accommodations. Reviews routine invoices of transportation charges, and types and submits reports to company and to transportation agencies. Prepares and types claim forms for refunds and adjustments and reports of transactions processed. ● **GED:** R3, M3, L3 ● **SVP:** 6 mos-1 yr ● **Academic:** Ed=H, Eng=G ● **Work Field:** 291, 282 ● **MPSMS:** 859 ● **Aptitudes:** G3, V3, N3, S4, P4, Q2, K2, F3, M3, E5, C5 ● **Temperaments:** P, T, V ● **Physical:** Stg=S; Freq: R, H, I, T, G, N ● **Work Env:** Noise=N; ● **Salary:** 1 ● **Outlook:** 2

RESERVATION CLERK (r.r. trans.) ● DOT #238.367-014 ● OES: 53810 ● Receives requests for and assigns space on trains to passengers on railroad passenger trains. Accepts requests for space assignments and examines diagram charts of each car on train to verify available space on specified train. Informs STATION AGENTS (r.r. trans.) I or INFORMATION CLERKS (clerical) of available space. Marks blocks on diagram to indicate that space is reserved. Prepares Teletype requests to other interline carriers to complete passage. Informs STATION AGENTS (r.r. trans.) I and INFORMATION CLERKS (clerical) upon completion of booking arrangements. Informs RESERVATION CLERKS (r.r. trans.) at other cities and towns of space reserved or space remaining available. ● **GED:** R3, M2, L3 ● **SVP:** 1-3 mos ● **Academic:** Ed=N, Eng=G ● **Work Field:** 231 ● **MPSMS:** 851 ● **Aptitudes:** G3, V3, N4, S4, P4, Q3, K4, F3, M3, E5, C5 ● **Temperaments:** J ● **Physical:** Stg=S; Freq: R, H, I, T, G, N ● **Work Env:** Noise=N; ● **Salary:** 2 ● **Outlook:** 3

SCHEDULER (museums) ● DOT #238.367-034 ● OES: 55305 ● Alternate titles: EDUCATION DEPARTMENT REGISTRAR; MUSEUM SERVICE SCHEDULER. Makes reservations and accepts payment for group tours, classes, field trips, and other educational activities offered by museum, zoo, or similar establishment: Provides information regarding tours for school, civic, or other groups, suggests tours on institution calendar, and contacts group leaders prior to scheduled dates to confirm reservations. Provides information regarding classes, workshops, field trips, and other educational programs designed for such special groups as school or college students, teachers, or handicapped persons. Registers groups and individuals for participation in programs, enters registration information in department records, and contacts participants prior to program dates to confirm registration and provide preparatory information. Prepares lists of groups scheduled for tours and persons registered for other activities for use of DIRECTOR, EDUCATION (museums) 099.117-030 or other personnel. Collects and records receipts of fees for tours, classes, and other activities. Maintains records of participating groups, fees received, and other data related to educational programs for use in preparation of department reports. May take reservations and sell advance tickets to exhibits, concerts, and other events sponsored by institution, prepare periodic summaries of department activities for review by administrative personnel, or arrange for various support services to facilitate presentation of special activities. ● **GED:** R3, M3, L3 ● **SVP:** 1-3 mos ● **Academic:** Ed=H, Eng=G ● **Work Field:** 232, 282 ● **MPSMS:** 939 ● **Aptitudes:** G3, V3, N3, S4, P4, Q2, K3, F3, M3, E5, C5 ● **Temperaments:** J, P, V ● **Physical:** Stg=S; Freq: R, H, I, T, G, N ● **Work Env:** Noise=N; ● **Salary:** 3 ● **Outlook:** 3

SCHEDULER, MAINTENANCE (clerical) ● DOT #221.367-066 ● OES: 58008 ● Alternate titles: DISPATCHER, MAINTENANCE. Schedules repairs and lubrication of motor vehicles for vehicle-maintenance concern or company automotive-service shop: Schedules vehicles for lubrication or repairs based on date of last lubrication and mileage traveled or urgency of repairs. Contacts garage to verify availability of facilities. Notifies parking garage workers to deliver specified vehicles. Maintains file of requests for services. ● **GED:** R3, M2, L3 ● **SVP:** 3-6 mos ● **Academic:** Ed=N, Eng=S ● **Work Field:** 231 ● **MPSMS:** 591 ● **Aptitudes:** G3, V3, N3, S4, P4, Q3, K4, F4, M4, E5, C5 ● **Temperaments:** P ● **Physical:** Stg=S; Freq: R, H, I, T, G Occas: N ● **Work Env:** Noise=Q; ● **Salary:** 4 ● **Outlook:** 3

SENIOR RESERVATIONS AGENT (air trans.) ● DOT #238.137-014 ● OES: 51002 ● Supervises and coordinates activities of workers engaged in reserving seat space for passengers on scheduled airline flights: Assigns workers to tasks in accordance with abilities and personnel requirements. Observes work procedures, monitors telephone calls, and reviews completed work to ensure adherence to quality and efficiency standards and to rules and regulations. Directs, explains, and demonstrates improved work practices and procedures to attain efficient utilization of personnel. Writes revisions to procedure guides and memoranda describing changes in reservations methods, flight schedules, and rates. Records teletypewriter messages and telephones passenger service personnel to obtain information regarding flight cancellations and schedule changes and to determine disposition of passengers holding reservations on cancelled or rescheduled flights. Posts flight schedule changes and passenger disposition information on bulletin board, and directs staff to telephone passengers to notify of schedule and reservation changes. Performs other duties as described under SUPERVISOR (clerical) Master Title. ● **GED:** R4, M3, L3 ● **SVP:** 1-2 yrs ● **Academic:** Ed=H, Eng=G ● **Work Field:** 013, 231 ● **MPSMS:** 855 ● **Aptitudes:** G2, V2, N3, S4, P4, Q3, K4, F4, M4, E5, C5 ● **Temperaments:** D, J ● **Physical:** Stg=L; Freq: R, H, I, T, G, N, D, A ● **Work Env:** Noise=N; ● **Salary:** 4 ● **Outlook:** 2

TELEVISION-SCHEDULE COORDINATOR (radio-tv broad.) ● DOT #199.382-010 ● OES: 58008 ● Alternate titles: LOG OPERATIONS COORDINATOR; MEDIA COORDINATOR; PROGRAM SCHEDULE CLERK. Enters data, such as program and commercial formats, into computer to prepare daily operations schedules and advance program log for newspapers, magazines, traffic or broadcast department: Provides for clearance and rotation of spot-commercial films and slides for television programs, and performs related clerical duties for DIRECTOR PROGRAM (radio-tv broad.) 184.167-030. May compose courtesy, apology, and stay-tuned announcements, using computer. May review overnight television ratings to determine number of viewers watching television programs containing station promotions. ● **GED:** R4, M3, L4 ● **SVP:** 3-6 mos ● **Academic:** Ed=H, Eng=S ● **Work Field:** 231, 232 ● **MPSMS:** 863, 864 ● **Aptitudes:** G3, V3, N3, S4, P4, Q2, K4, F3, M4, E5, C5 ● **Temperaments:** J, T ● **Physical:** Stg=L; Freq: I, A Occas: R, H, T, G, N ● **Work Env:** Noise=N; ● **Salary:** 3 ● **Outlook:** 3

TRAFFIC CLERK (business ser.) ● DOT #221.367-078 ● OES: 58008 ● Compiles schedules and control records on work in process in advertising agency to ensure completion of artwork, copy, and layouts prior to deadline and notifies staff and clients of schedule changes: Keeps schedules and records on work to ensure arrival of printing and artwork, as needed, and to ensure completion of copy. Contacts vendors and notifies agency personnel and clients of changes in schedules. ● **GED:** R4, M2, L3 ● **SVP:** 3-6 mos ● **Academic:** Ed=N, Eng=S ● **Work Field:** 231 ● **MPSMS:** 898, 896 ● **Aptitudes:** G3, V3, N4, S4, P4, Q3, K4, F4, M4, E5, C5 ● **Temperaments:** P, T ● **Physical:** Stg=S; Freq: R, H, N Occas: I, T, G ● **Work Env:** Noise=Q; ● **Salary:** 2 ● **Outlook:** 3

TRANSPORTATION AGENT (air trans.) ● DOT #912.367-014 ● OES: 58098 ● Alternate titles: DEPARTURE CLERK; OPERATIONS AGENT; SERVICE COORDINATOR. Expedites movement of freight, mail, baggage, and passengers through airline terminal by performing following tasks: Prepares airway bill of lading on freight from consignors and routes freight on first available flight. Telephones consignees to report arrival of air freight. Obtains flight number, airplane number, and names of crewmembers from teletyped message of DISPATCHER (air trans.), and records data on airplane's flight papers. Records baggage, mail, and freight weights, and number of passengers on airplane's papers and teletypes data to flight's destination. Positions ramp for loading of airplane. Verifies passengers' tickets as they board plane. Oversees or participates in loading cargo to ensure completeness of load and even distribution of weight. Removes ramp, and signals pilot that personnel and equipment are clear of plane. May load and unload freight and baggage by operating forklift truck. ● **GED:** R3, M3, L3 ● **SVP:** 6 mos-1 yr ● **Academic:** Ed=N, Eng=G ● **Work Field:** 281, 221 ● **MPSMS:** 855 ● **Aptitudes:** G3, V3, N3, S4, P4, Q3, K3, F3, M3, E4, C4 ● **Temperaments:** P, V ● **Physical:** Stg=L; Freq: R, H, I, T, G, N Occas: X ● **Work Env:** Noise=V; Occas: W ● **Salary:** 3 ● **Outlook:** 3

GOE: 07.05.02
Record Verification & Proofing

BRAILLE PROOFREADER (nonprofit org.) ● DOT #209.367-014 ● OES: 53911 ● Verifies proof copy of braille transcription against original script, such as pamphlet, book, or newspaper, to detect grammatical, typographical, or compositional errors and marks proof for correction: Reads original script to compare it with proof copy (if sighted); or listens to reading or recording of original and slides fingers over braille characters to feel discrepancies in proof (if blind). Consults reference books or secures aid of reader to check references to rules of grammar and composition. Marks proof with braille stylus or pencil to correct errors, using standard printers' marks. May direct workers in use of braille slates (printing devices). May select material for transcription. ● **GED:** R4, M1, L4 ● **SVP:** 6 mos-1 yr ● **Academic:** Ed=H, Eng=G ● **Work Field:** 261 ● **MPSMS:** 898 ● **Aptitudes:** G2, V2, N4, S3, P3, Q2, K4, F4, M4, E5, C5 ● **Temperaments:** J, T ● **Physical:** Stg=S; Freq: R, H, I, E, T, G, N ● **Work Env:** Noise=N; ● **Salary:** 3 ● **Outlook:** 3

CLASSIFIED-AD CLERK II (print. & pub.) ● DOT #247.387-022 ● OES: 53908 ● Alternate titles: CLASSIFIED-COPY-CONTROL CLERK. Examines and marks classified advertisements of newspaper according to copy sheet specifications to guide composing room in assembling type: Marks advertisements that have expired and indicates number of days others are to continue, using classified file copy and copy sheet for current day. Computes and records total number of lines expired and number of lines for new advertisements. ● **GED:** R3, M3, L2 ● **SVP:** 6 mos-1 yr ● **Academic:** Ed=N, Eng=G ● **Work Field:** 231 ● **MPSMS:** 898 ● **Aptitudes:** G3, V3, N3, S5, P4, Q2, K4, F4, M4, E5, C5 ● **Temperaments:** R, T ● **Physical:** Stg=S; Freq: R, H, I, N ● **Work Env:** Noise=N; ● **Salary:** 1 ● **Outlook:** 3

CREDIT AUTHORIZER (clerical) ● DOT #249.367-022 ● OES: 53114 ● Alternate titles: AUTHORIZER; CHARGE-ACCOUNT AUTHORIZER. Authorizes credit charges against customer's account: Receives charge slip or credit application by mail, or receives information from salespeople or merchants over telephone. Verifies credit standing of customer from information in files, and approves or disapproves credit, based on predetermined standards. May file sales slips in customer's ledger for billing purposes. May prepare credit cards or charge account plates. May keep record of customer's charges and payments and mail charge statement to customer. ● **GED:** R3, M2, L2 ● **SVP:** 1-3 mos ● **Academic:** Ed=N, Eng=G ● **Work Field:** 282, 231 ● **MPSMS:** 894 ● **Aptitudes:** G3, V3, N4, S5, P4, Q3, K3, F4, M4, E5, C5 ● **Temperaments:** J ● **Physical:** Stg=S; Freq: R, H, T, G, N Occas: I ● **Work Env:** Noise=N; ● **Salary:** 3 ● **Outlook:** 3

CREDIT REFERENCE CLERK (financial) ● DOT #209.362-018 ● OES: 53117 ● Telephones or writes to references listed on application form to investigate credit standing of applicant. Records information on previous employment, received from employers, using typewriter or computer. Reciprocates credit information with credit bureaus. ● **GED:** R3, M2, L3 ● **SVP:** 1-3 mos ● **Academic:** Ed=H, Eng=S ● **Work Field:** 271 ● **MPSMS:** 894, 891 ● **Aptitudes:** G3, V3, N4, S5, P5, Q3, K2, F2, M3, E5, C5 ● **Temperaments:** P, T ● **Physical:** Stg=S; Const: T, G, N Freq: R, H, I Occas: S, O, A ● **Work Env:** Noise=N; ● **Salary:** 2 ● **Outlook:** 4

CUSTOMER-COMPLAINT CLERK (clerical) ● DOT #241.367-014 ● OES: 53123 ● Alternate titles: ADJUSTMENT CLERK; CONSUMER-RELATIONS-COMPLAINT CLERK. Investigates customer complaints about merchandise, service, billing, or credit rating: Examines records, such as bills, computer printouts, microfilm, meter readings, bills of lading, and related documents and correspondence, and converses or corresponds with customer and other company personnel, such as billing, credit, sales, service, or shipping, to obtain facts regarding customer complaint. Examines pertinent information to determine accuracy of customer complaint and to determine responsibility for errors. Notifies customer and designated personnel of findings, adjustments, and recommendations, such as exchange of merchandise, refund of money, credit of customer's account, or adjustment of customer's bill. May recommend to management improvements in product, packaging, shipping methods, service, or billing methods and procedures to prevent future complaints of similar nature. May examine merchandise to determine accuracy of complaint. May follow up on recommended adjustments to ensure customer satisfaction. May key information into computer to obtain computerized records. May trace missing merchandise and be designated Tracer Clerk (clerical). May investigate overdue and damaged shipments or shortages in shipments for common carrier and be designated Over-Short-And-Damage Clerk (clerical). May be designated according to type of complaint adjusted as Bill Adjuster (clerical); Merchandise-Adjustment Clerk (retail trade); Service Investigator (utilities; tel. & tel.). ● **GED:** R4, M3, L4 ● **SVP:** 6 mos-1 yr ● **Academic:** Ed=H, Eng=G ● **Work Field:** 271, 282 ● **MPSMS:** 860, 880, 890 ● **Aptitudes:** G3, V3, N3, S4, P4, Q2, K4, F4, M4, E5, C5 ● **Temperaments:** J, P, V ● **Physical:** Stg=S; Freq: T, G Occas: R, H, I, N, A ● **Work Env:** Noise=N; ● **Salary:** 2 ● **Outlook:** 3

DATA-EXAMINATION CLERK (clerical) ● DOT #209.387-022 ● OES: 59998 ● Reviews computer input and output documents to ensure accuracy, completeness, and adherence to establishment standards: Reviews documents, such as surveys, to ensure completeness and appropriateness prior to data entry. Reads notes and instructions written on source documents and compares information with printouts to detect errors and ensure completeness and conformity with establishment policies and procedures. Notifies supervisor when errors and shortage of output are detected, and corrects errors or refers work to other workers for correction. Compares corrected input and output data with source documents, worksheets, and data displayed on screen of computer terminal to verify corrections. May review only computer input or output. May operate machines to separate and remove carbon paper from computer generated forms. May re-type mutilated forms, using typewriter. May sort printouts for distribution. ● **GED:** R3, M2, L3 ● **SVP:** 1-3 mos ● **Academic:** Ed=H, Eng=G ● **Work Field:** 231 ● **MPSMS:** 891 ● **Aptitudes:** G3, V3, N4, S4, P3, Q2, K4, F4, M4, E5, C5 ● **Temperaments:** T ● **Physical:** Stg=S; Freq: R, H, I, N, A Occas: S ● **Work Env:** Noise=N; ● **Salary:** 2 ● **Outlook:** 3

DISBURSEMENT CLERK (financial) ● DOT #219.367-046 ● OES: 53121 ● Verifies accuracy of consumer loan applications and records loan: Compares original application against credit report. Types checks for approved loans. Prepares loan work sheet, insurance record, credit report, and application copy for each loan. Records loan and types daily report of loan transactions, using computer. Prepares payment book and mails payment book to customer. Answers customer's question, such as current rates and date loan checks were issued. ● **GED:** R3, M3, L3 ● **SVP:** 3-6 mos ● **Academic:** Ed=N, Eng=G ● **Work Field:** 231 ● **MPSMS:** 894 ● **Aptitudes:** G3, V3, N3, S4, P3, Q2, K3, F3, M4, E5, C5 ● **Temperaments:** T ● **Physical:** Stg=S; Const: I, N Freq: R, H, A Occas: T, G ● **Work Env:** Noise=N; ● **Salary:** 2 ● **Outlook:** 3

INVESTIGATOR, UTILITY-BILL COMPLAINTS (utilities) ● DOT #241.267-034 ● OES: 53123 ● Alternate titles: CUSTOMER-SERVICE REPRESENTATIVE. Investigates customers' bill complaints for gas and electric-power service: Examines weather reports for weather conditions during billing period that might have contributed to increased use of service. Examines meter reading schedules to determine if early readings increased billing period. Reviews meter books, microfilm, computer printouts, and machine accounting records for errors causing high bill. Orders tests to detect meter malfunctions. Confers with customer in person, by telephone, or dictates correspondence to explain reasons for high bill. Prepares forms required for correction of meter reading or billing errors. ● **GED:** R4, M4, L4 ● **SVP:** 1-2 yrs ● **Academic:** Ed=H, Eng=G ● **Work Field:** 271 ● **MPSMS:** 891 ● **Aptitudes:** G3, V3, N2, S4, P4, Q2, K4, F4, M4, E5, C4 ● **Temperaments:** J ● **Physical:** Stg=L; Freq: T, G, N Occas: R, H, I, X ● **Work Env:** Noise=N; ● **Salary:** 2 ● **Outlook:** 4

LETTER-OF-CREDIT CLERK (financial) ● DOT #219.367-050 ● OES: 55338 ● Issues import and export letters of credit and accepts payments: Notifies exporters and importers of issuance of letters of credit covering shipment of merchandise. Reviews letter of credit documents to determine compliance with international standards. Verifies terms of credit, such as amount, insurance coverage, and shipping conditions to determine compliance with established standards. Coordinates customer credit information and collateral papers with LOAN OFFICER (financial) 186.267-018 to comply with bank credit standards. Types letters of credit and related documents, using typewriter or computer. Records payments and liabilities and other customer account information, using computer. May translate correspondence into English or foreign language. ● **GED:** R4, M3, L3 ● **SVP:** 6 mos-1 yr ● **Academic:** Ed=H, Eng=G ● **Work Field:** 232 ● **MPSMS:** 894 ● **Aptitudes:** G3, V3, N3, S5, P4, Q3, K3, F3, M4, E5, C5 ● **Temperaments:** T ● **Physical:** Stg=S; Const: N Freq: I Occas: R, H, T, G, A ● **Work Env:** Noise=N; ● **Salary:** 1 ● **Outlook:** 3

MORTGAGE-CLOSING CLERK (clerical) ● DOT #219.362-038 ● OES: 53121 ● Alternate titles: LOAN CLOSER. Completes mortgage transactions between loan establishment, sellers, and borrowers after loans have been approved: Verifies completeness of data on loan papers. Answers questions of buyers and sellers relating to details of transaction and obtains signatures of principal parties on necessary documents. Closes out seller's interest in property by presenting seller with check to cover seller's equity. Operates office machines to compute rebates or adjustments. Prepares and mails rebates and other papers to clients. ● **GED:** R4, M3, L4 ● **SVP:** 6 mos-1 yr ● **Academic:** Ed=H, Eng=G ● **Work Field:** 232, 282 ● **MPSMS:** 894 ● **Aptitudes:** G3, V3, N3, S5, P4, Q2, K4, F4, M4, E5, C5 ● **Temperaments:** P ● **Physical:** Stg=S; Freq: R, H, I, T, G, N Occas: A ● **Work Env:** Noise=Q; ● **Salary:** 3 ● **Outlook:** 4

MORTGAGE LOAN PROCESSOR (financial) ● DOT #249.362-022 ● OES: 53121 ● Verifies, compiles, and types application information for mortgage loans: Reviews residential loan application file to verify that application data is complete and meets establishment standards, including type and amount of mortgage, borrower assets, liabilities, and length of employment. Recommends that loan not meeting standards be denied. Calls or writes credit bureau and employer to verify accuracy of information. Types loan application forms, using computer. Calls specified companies to obtain property abstract, survey, and appraisal. Informs supervisor of discrepancies in title or survey. Submits mortgage loan application file for underwriting approval. Types and mails approval and denial letters to applicants. Submits approved mortgage loan file to MORTGAGE LOAN CLOSER (financial) 249.362-

018 for settlement. Records data on status of loans, including number of new applications and loans approved, canceled, or denied, using computer. ● **GED:** R3, M3, L3 ● **SVP:** 6 mos-1 yr ● **Academic:** Ed=N, Eng=G ● **Work Field:** 231 ● **MPSMS:** 894 ● **Aptitudes:** G3, V3, N3, S4, P4, Q2, K3, F3, M3, E5, C5 ● **Temperaments:** T ● **Physical:** Stg=S; Const: I, N Freq: R, H, A Occas: T, G ● **Work Env:** Noise=N; ● **Salary:** 3 ● **Outlook:** 3

PARIMUTUEL-TICKET CHECKER (amuse. & rec.) ● DOT #219.587-010 ● OES: 55338 ● Alternate titles: TICKET COUNTER. Counts and records number of parimutuel tickets cashed at race track to verify records of cashiers. Compares totals with entries on daily balance sheet. Compares each ticket with sample or examines tickets under fluorescent light to verify validity of tickets. Reports discrepancies. ● **GED:** R3, M3, L3 ● **SVP:** 2-30 days ● **Academic:** Ed=N, Eng=G ● **Work Field:** 231, 232 ● **MPSMS:** 891 ● **Aptitudes:** G3, V4, N3, S4, P3, Q3, K3, F4, M3, E5, C3 ● **Temperaments:** J, T ● **Physical:** Stg=S; Const: R, H, I, N, A Occas: X ● **Work Env:** Noise=N; ● **Salary:** 2 ● **Outlook:** 3

PRODUCTION PROOFREADER (print. & pub.) ● DOT #247.667-010 ● OES: 53911 ● Compares proofs of store advertisements with original copy to detect errors in printed material. Reads proofs and corrects errors in type, arrangement, grammar, punctuation, or spelling, using proofreader's marks. Routes proofs with corrections to be reprinted and reads corrected proofs. ● **GED:** R3, M2, L3 ● **SVP:** 3-6 mos ● **Academic:** Ed=N, Eng=G ● **Work Field:** 261 ● **MPSMS:** 896 ● **Aptitudes:** G3, V3, N4, S5, P4, Q1, K4, F4, M4, E5, C5 ● **Temperaments:** J, T ● **Physical:** Stg=S; Const: N, A Freq: R, H, I ● **Work Env:** Noise=N; ● **Salary:** 3 ● **Outlook:** 2

PROOFREADER (print. & pub.) ● DOT #209.387-030 ● OES: 53911 ● Reads typescript (original copy) or proof of type setup to detect and mark for correction any grammatical, typographical, or compositional errors, by either of following methods: (1) Places proof and copy side by side on reading board. Reads proof against copy, marking by standardized code, errors that appear in proof. Returns marked proof for correction and later checks corrected proof against copy. (2) Reads and corrects proof while COPY HOLDER (print. & pub.) reads aloud from original copy or reads proof aloud to COPY HOLDER (print. & pub.) who calls out discrepancies between proof and copy. May measure dimensions, spacing, and positioning of page elements (copy and illustrations) to verify conformance to specifications, using printer's ruler. ● **GED:** R4, M1, L4 ● **SVP:** 6 mos-1 yr ● **Academic:** Ed=H, Eng=G ● **Work Field:** 261 ● **MPSMS:** 891 ● **Aptitudes:** G2, V2, N4, S3, P3, Q2, K4, F4, M4, E5, C4 ● **Temperaments:** J, T ● **Physical:** Stg=L; Const: N, A Freq: R, H, I ● **Work Env:** Noise=N; ● **Salary:** 3 ● **Outlook:** 3

READER (business ser.) ● DOT #249.387-022 ● OES: 59998 ● Alternate titles: CLIPPING MARKER; PRESS READER; PRESS-SERVICE READER. Reads newspapers, magazines, and other periodicals for articles of prescribed subject matter, and marks items to be clipped, using colored pencils and customer code system. ● **GED:** R3, M1, L3 ● **SVP:** 3-6 mos ● **Academic:** Ed=N, Eng=G ● **Work Field:** 231 ● **MPSMS:** 899 ● **Aptitudes:** G3, V3, N4, S4, P4, Q3, K4, F4, M4, E5, C4 ● **Temperaments:** J, R ● **Physical:** Stg=S; Const: N Occas: R, H, I ● **Work Env:** Noise=Q; ● **Salary:** 1 ● **Outlook:** 2

REVIEWER (insurance) ● DOT #209.687-018 ● OES: 53314 ● Alternate titles: FINAL-APPLICATION REVIEWER; NEW-BUSINESS CLERK; SALES-REVIEW CLERK. Reviews insurance applications to ensure that all questions have been answered. Corresponds with sales personnel to inform them of status of application being processed, and to encourage prompt delivery of policies to policyholders. May collect initial premiums and issue receipts. May compile periodic reports on new business for management. ● **GED:** R3, M1, L3 ● **SVP:** 3-6 mos ● **Academic:** Ed=H, Eng=G ● **Work Field:** 231, 211 ● **MPSMS:** 895 ● **Aptitudes:** G3, V3, N4, S4, P4, Q3, K4, F4, M4, E5, C5 ● **Temperaments:** R ● **Physical:** Stg=S; Freq: R, H, I, N ● **Work Env:** Noise=N; ● **Salary:** 4 ● **Outlook:** 3

THROW-OUT CLERK (retail trade) ● DOT #241.367-030 ● OES: 53117 ● Alternate titles: CHARGE-ACCOUNT IDENTIFICATION CLERK. Processes records of department-store transactions which cannot be applied to customer's account by routine procedures in order that charges, cash payments, and refunds may be recorded, collected, or credited: Reviews and talks to sales-audit, charge-account-authori-

zation, and collection personnel to identify missing information or compare signatures on sales or credit slips. Telephones or writes to customers for additional information. Corrects or adds information to customer accounts as necessary. Mails dunning correspondence to customers in arrears on their charge accounts [COLLECTION CLERK (clerical)]. ● **GED:** R3, M3, L3 ● **SVP:** 3-6 mos ● **Academic:** Ed=N, Eng=G ● **Work Field:** 271, 232 ● **MPSMS:** 894 ● **Aptitudes:** G3, V3, N3, S5, P3, Q2, K4, F4, M4, E5, C5 ● **Temperaments:** P ● **Physical:** Stg=S; Freq: R, H, T, G, N Occas: I ● **Work Env:** Noise=N; ● **Salary:** 1 ● **Outlook:** 3

TITLE SEARCHER (real estate) ● DOT #209.367-046 ● OES: 28306 ● Alternate titles: ABSTRACTOR. Searches public and private records and indices to compile list of legal instruments pertaining to property titles, such as mortgages, deeds, and assessments, for insurance, real estate, or tax purposes: Reads search request to ascertain type of title evidence required, and to obtain legal description of property and names of involved parties. Compares legal description of property with legal description contained in records and indices, to verify such factors as deed of ownership, tax code and parcel number, and description of property's boundaries. Requisitions maps or drawings delineating property from company title plant, county surveyor, or assessor's office. Confers with realtors, lending institution personnel, buyers, sellers, contractors, surveyors, and courthouse personnel to obtain additional information. Compiles list of transactions pertaining to property, using legal description or name of owner to search lot books, geographic and general indices, or assessor's rolls. Examines title to determine if there are any restrictions which would limit use of property, prepares report listing restrictions, and indicates action needed to remove restrictions to clear title. Compiles information and documents required for title binder. Prepares title commitment and final policy of title insurance based on information compiled from title search. May specialize in searching tax records and be designated Tax Searcher (real estate). May use computerized system to retrieve additional documentation needed to complete real estate transaction. May retrieve and examine closing files to determine accuracy of information and to ensure that information included is recorded and executed according to regulations governing real estate industry. May prepare closing statement, utilizing knowledge of and expertise in real estate procedures. ● **GED:** R3, M1, L3 ● **SVP:** 6 mos-1 yr ● **Academic:** Ed=N, Eng=G ● **Work Field:** 231, 271 ● **MPSMS:** 895 ● **Aptitudes:** G3, V3, N3, S4, P4, Q2, K4, F4, M4, E5, C5 ● **Temperaments:** J, P, T ● **Physical:** Stg=L; Const: N Freq: R, H, I Occas: T, G ● **Work Env:** Noise=N; ● **Salary:** 3 ● **Outlook:** 3

GOE: 07.05.03
Record Preparation & Maintenance

ASSIGNMENT CLERK (clerical) ● DOT #249.367-090 ● OES: 55314 ● Compiles data to notify establishment personnel of position vacancies, and identifies and assigns qualified applicants, following specified guidelines and procedures: Scans reports to detect listings of vacancies or receives telephone notices of vacancies from establishment personnel. Types or writes information, such as position titles, shifts, days off, and application deadlines, on vacancy advertisement forms. Reviews bid slips or similar application forms submitted by employees in response to advertisement and verifies relevant data on application against data in personnel records. Selects applicants meeting specified criterion, such as seniority, and notifies concerned personnel of selection. Compiles and disperses position assignment notices to notify other establishment personnel of applicants selected to fill vacancies. Records data on specified forms to update personnel and employment records. ● **GED:** R3, M2, L2 ● **SVP:** 6 mos-1 yr ● **Academic:** Ed=N, Eng=G ● **Work Field:** 282, 231 ● **MPSMS:** 891 ● **Aptitudes:** G3, V3, N4, S4, P4, Q3, K3, F3, M4, E5, C5 ● **Temperaments:** J, P, V ● **Physical:** Stg=S; Freq: R, H, I, N Occas: S ● **Work Env:** Noise=N; ● **Salary:** 2 ● **Outlook:** 2

ATTENDANCE CLERK (education) ● DOT #219.362-014 ● OES: 59998 ● Compiles attendance records for school district, issues attendance permits, and answers inquiries: Obtains district attendance figures from each school daily, using telephone. Records figures by grade level and for special classes, such as mentally retarded or gifted, in workbook. Totals figures, using calculator. Collates data and prepares standard state reports, using typewriter. Computes average daily attendance figures and forwards to state for compensation and to school cafeteria for meal planning. Interviews applicants for interdistrict attendance permits to attend elementary and secondary schools in district and issues permits, if requirements are met. Sends copy of permit to applicable school and retains file copy. Maintains file of interdistrict attendance agreements, bills outside districts for attendance within district, and notifies supervisor of agreement expirations. Answers inquiries from parents and school officials, using state education code as guide. Prepares special reports, such as ethnic or racial-distribution surveys, requested by state or district education officials. ● **GED:** R4, M3, L4 ● **SVP:** 1-2 yrs ● **Academic:** Ed=N, Eng=G ● **Work Field:** 232, 282 ● **MPSMS:** 891, 931 ● **Aptitudes:** G3, V3, N3, S4, P4, Q2, K4, F3, M4, E5, C5 ● **Temperaments:** P, T, V ● **Physical:** Stg=S; Freq: R, H, I, T, G, N ● **Work Env:** Noise=N; ● **Salary:** 2 ● **Outlook:** 3

AUTOMOBILE LOCATOR (retail trade) ● DOT #296.367-010 ● OES: 49998 ● Phones other new or used automobile dealers to locate type of automobile desired by customer. Prepares papers for transfer of automobile. Keeps records of automobiles traded. ● **GED:** R3, M2, L3 ● **SVP:** 1-3 mos ● **Academic:** Ed=N, Eng=S ● **Work Field:** 231 ● **MPSMS:** 899 ● **Aptitudes:** G3, V3, N4, S4, P4, Q3, K4, F4, M4, E5, C5 ● **Temperaments:** P ● **Physical:** Stg=S; Freq: R, H, I, T, G, N ● **Work Env:** Noise=N; ● **Salary:** 3 ● **Outlook:** 3

BENEFITS CLERK II (clerical) ● DOT #205.567-010 ● OES: 55314 ● Alternate titles: INSURANCE AND BENEFITS CLERK. Answers employees' questions and records employee enrollment in benefits and group insurance programs: Explains and interprets company insurance program to employees and dependents. Answers questions regarding benefits, such as pension and retirement plan, and group insurance, such as life, hospitalization, and workers' compensation. Fills out application forms or verifies information on forms submitted by employees. Mails applications to insurance company. Files records of claims and fills out cancellation forms when employees leave company service. May correspond with or telephone physicians, hospitals, and employees regarding claims. ● **GED:** R3, M3, L3 ● **SVP:** 3-6 mos ● **Academic:** Ed=H, Eng=G ● **Work Field:** 231, 282 ● **MPSMS:** 891 ● **Aptitudes:** G3, V3, N3, S5, P5, Q2, K3, F3, M3, E5, C5 ● **Temperaments:** P, T ● **Physical:** Stg=S; Freq: R, H, I, T, G, N ● **Work Env:** Noise=N; ● **Salary:** 3 ● **Outlook:** 2

CALL-OUT OPERATOR (business ser.) ● DOT #237.367-014 ● OES: 53117 ● Compiles credit information, such as status of credit accounts, personal references, and bank accounts to fulfill subscribers' requests, using telephone. Copies information onto form to update information for credit record on file, or for computer input. Telephones subscriber to relay requested information or submits data obtained for typewritten report to subscriber. ● **GED:** R3, M2, L3 ● **SVP:** 2-30 days ● **Academic:** Ed=N, Eng=G ● **Work Field:** 282, 231 ● **MPSMS:** 894 ● **Aptitudes:** G3, V3, N4, S4, P5, Q3, K3, F3, M4, E5, C5 ● **Temperaments:** P, R, T ● **Physical:** Stg=S; Freq: T, G, N Occas: R, H, I ● **Work Env:** Noise=N; ● **Salary:** 3 ● **Outlook:** 3

CAPTION WRITER (motion picture) ● DOT #203.362-026 ● OES: 34001 ● Alternate titles: SUBTITLE WRITER. Operates computerized captioning system to provide captions for movies or taped television productions for hearing-impaired viewers, and to provide captions (subtitles) in English or foreign language: Listens to dialogue of production and writes caption phrases for dialogue. Watches production and reviews captions simultaneously to determine which caption phrases to leave in, which to revise, and where captions should be placed on screen. Enters commands to edit and place captions, and to synchronize captions with dialogue. May write captions to describe music and background noises. May discuss captions with DIRECTOR, MOTION PICTURE (motion picture) 159.067-010, DIRECTOR, TELEVISION (radio-tv broad.) 159.067-014, PRODUCER (motion picture) 187.167-174, or PRODUCER (radio-tv broad.) 159.117-010. May translate foreign language dialogue into English language captions, or translate English dialogue into foreign language captions. May oversee encoding of captions to master tape of television production. ● **GED:** R4, M2, L4 ● **SVP:** 1-2 yrs ● **Academic:** Ed=H, Eng=G ● **Work Field:** 231 ● **MPSMS:** 864, 911 ● **Aptitudes:** G3, V2, N4, S4, P2, Q1, K2, F2, M3, E3, C4 ● **Temperaments:** J, T ● **Physical:** Stg=L; Freq: I, G Occas: R, H, T, X ● **Work Env:** Noise=N; ● **Salary:** 2 ● **Outlook:** 3

CLASSIFICATION CLERK (clerical) ● DOT #206.387-010 ● OES: 55321 ● Alternate titles: CODING FILE CLERK. Classifies materials according to subject matter and assigns numbers or symbols from predetermined coding system to facilitate accurate filing and reference: Scans correspondence, reports, drawings, and other materials to be filed to determine subject matter. Ascertains specified number or symbol, using code book or chart, and marks or stamps code on material. Assigns cross-indexing numbers if subject matter should be classified and filed under more than one heading. May revise coding system to improve code usage. ● **GED:** R3, M2, L3 ● **SVP:** 6 mos-1 yr ● **Academic:** Ed=H, Eng=G ● **Work Field:** 231 ● **MPSMS:** 891 ● **Aptitudes:** G3, V3, N4, S4, P4, Q3, K4, F4, M4, E5, C5 ● **Temperaments:** R, T ● **Physical:** Stg=S; Freq: H, I, N Occas: R, G ● **Work Env:** Noise=N; ● **Salary:** 1 ● **Outlook:** 2

COMPILER (clerical) ● DOT #209.387-014 ● OES: 55328 ● Compiles directories, survey findings, opinion polls, and census reports from data obtained from surveys or census: Compiles names, addresses, vital statistics, and other facts or opinions from business subscribers or persons in communities or cities. Verifies information for completeness and accuracy. Records and arranges information in specified order or groupings, such as by name, location, sex, occupation, or affiliation. May use typewriter or other recording device to duplicate information for filing or distribution. May prepare graphs or charts to show survey results. May be designated according to type of information compiled as Directory Compiler (clerical); Survey Compiler (clerical). May compile lists of prospective customers and be designated Mailing-List Compiler (clerical). ● **GED:** R3, M2, L3 ● **SVP:** 3-6 mos ● **Academic:** Ed=N, Eng=G ● **Work Field:** 231 ● **MPSMS:** 890 ● **Aptitudes:** G3, V3, N4, S5, P4, Q3, K4, F4, M4, E5, C5 ● **Temperaments:** T ● **Physical:** Stg=S; Freq: R, H, I, N ● **Work Env:** Noise=N; ● **Salary:** 2 ● **Outlook:** 3

CONTINUITY CLERK (motion picture) ● DOT #209.382-010 ● OES: 55398 ● Types descriptive record of motion picture scenes, including dialog, and such details as wardrobe, hairdress, and on-scene entrances and exits of ACTORS (amuse. & rec.); ACTRESS (amuse. & rec.) to aid editorial personnel in editing and assembling complete film: Mounts film on spindle of film viewer and starts equipment. Observes film on screen to determine action being depicted and pertinent details. Types brief narrative description and identifying information for each scene. Keeps records of completed work. ● **GED:** R3, M1, L3 ● **SVP:** 6 mos-1 yr ● **Academic:** Ed=N, Eng=G ● **Work Field:** 231 ● **MPSMS:** 891 ● **Aptitudes:** G3, V3, N4, S3, P3, Q2, K3, F3, M3, E4, C3 ● **Temperaments:** J, T ● **Physical:** Stg=S; Freq: R, H, I, T, G, N ● **Work Env:** Noise=N; ● **Salary:** 2 ● **Outlook:** 1

CREDIT CARD CONTROL CLERK (financial) ● DOT #249.367-026 ● OES: 59998 ● Alternate titles: CARD PROCESSING CLERK. Compiles, verifies, and files records and forms to control issuing, blocking (withholding), or renewal of credit cards, performing any combination of following duties: Receives shipments of plastic credit card blanks and verifies totals received against invoices. Assigns consecutive batch numbers to blank cards and stores cards in vault. Issues blank cards for imprinting, on requisition, and keeps records of batch numbers issued. Receives new or reissued printed cards, verifies number sequence, and compares identifying data on cards with data on application files to detect errors. Compiles lists of cards containing errors and initiates correction forms. Places completed credit cards and establishment literature into envelopes for mailing. Receives returned cards and reviews correspondence or searches records to determine customer reasons for return. Receives blocking notices from officials and places designated cards in hold file until release is authorized. Destroys inaccurate, mutilated, undelivered, withheld, or expired cards, in presence of witnesses, using scissors. Compiles list of destroyed cards and records reasons for destruction, using computer. Occasionally verifies customers' account balances to expedite issuance or renewal of cards. Maintains related files and control records. Issues cards for automated teller machines. ● **GED:** R3, M2, L2 ● **SVP:** 1-3 mos ● **Academic:** Ed=N, Eng=G ● **Work Field:** 231 ● **MPSMS:** 891 ● **Aptitudes:** G4, V3, N3, S4, P4, Q2, K3, F3, M3, E5, C5 ● **Temperaments:** R, T ● **Physical:** Stg=S; Const: R, H, N Freq: I Occas: S, O, T, G, A ● **Work Env:** Noise=N; ● **Salary:** 3 ● **Outlook:** 3

DETAILER, SCHOOL PHOTOGRAPHS (photofinishing) ● DOT #976.564-010 ● OES: 58008 ● Performs variety of tasks to prepare and disseminate school photographs: Reads photographers' work orders and records information, such as number of prints and type finish specified as guide for processing film. Assigns control number to each order. Records customer charges on worksheet and submits to accounting department for billing. Sorts and bags film according to processing required. Cuts prints to prepare composite for group photographs, using chopping block, die, and mallet. Assembles composite and mails to picture service for processing of negative. Routes composite negative to printing section and records cost of composite service. Feeds specified photographs in gluing machine that automatically applies adhesive backing to photographs. Confers with photographers to discuss school programs available, costs, and shipping dates. Confers with customers to resolve complaints regarding missing or defective photographs. Cuts out, arranges, and pastes letters, numbers, and pictures to design advertising circulars. Maintains records indicating orders received, unit prices charged, and department earnings. ● **GED:** R3, M2, L2 ● **SVP:** 3-6 mos ● **Academic:** Ed=N, Eng=N ● **Work Field:** 282, 264 ● **MPSMS:** 897 ● **Aptitudes:** G3, V3, N3, S3, P3, Q3, K4, F3, M3, E5, C3 ● **Temperaments:** J, T, V ● **Physical:** Stg=L; Freq: R, H, I, T, G, N, D, X ● **Work Env:** Noise=N; ● **Salary:** 1 ● **Outlook:** 2

DIET CLERK (medical ser.) ● DOT #245.587-010 ● OES: 59998 ● Prepares dietary information for use by kitchen personnel in preparation of foods for hospital patients: Examines diet orders and menus received from hospital units and tallies portions and foods of general and soft diets. Tallies quantities of specific foods, such as vegetables and meats, to be prepared in kitchen. Marks tally on master menu to inform kitchen personnel of food requirements. Processes new diets and changes as required. May calculate diabetic diets, using calculator, and following standards established by DIETITIAN, CLINICAL (profess. & kin.) 077.127-014. May answer telephone and intercom calls and relay information to kitchen concerning meal changes, complaints, or patient discharge. May prepare and deliver formula and special nourishments to unit pantries. ● **GED:** R3, M3, L3 ● **SVP:** 1-3 mos ● **Academic:** Ed=N, Eng=G ● **Work Field:** 232 ● **MPSMS:** 903 ● **Aptitudes:** G3, V3, N3, S4, P4, Q3, K4, F4, M4, E5, C5 ● **Temperaments:** R ● **Physical:** Stg=S; Freq: R, H, I, N Occas: G ● **Work Env:** Noise=N; ● **Salary:** 1 ● **Outlook:** 2

DOCUMENT PREPARER, MICROFILMING (business ser.) ● DOT #249.587-018 ● OES: 58098 ● Prepares documents, such as brochures, pamphlets, and catalogs, for microfilming, using paper cutter, photocopying machine, rubber stamps, and other work devices: Cuts documents into individual pages of standard microfilming size and format when allowed by margin space, using paper cutter or razor knife. Reproduces document pages as necessary to improve clarity or to reduce one or more pages into single page of standard microfilming size, using photocopying machine. Stamps standard symbols on pages or inserts instruction cards between pages of material to notify MICRO-FILM-CAMERA OPERATOR (business ser.) 976.682-022 of special handling, such as manual repositioning, during microfilming. Prepares cover sheet and document folder for material and index card for company files indicating information, such as firm name and address, product category, and index code, to identify material. Inserts material to be filmed in document folder and files folder for processing according to index code and filming priority schedule. ● **GED:** R3, M1, L2 ● **SVP:** 2-30 days ● **Academic:** Ed=N, Eng=N ● **Work Field:** 231, 054, 201 ● **MPSMS:** 891 ● **Aptitudes:** G3, V4, N4, S3, P4, Q3, K4, F4, M4, E5, C4 ● **Temperaments:** T, V ● **Physical:** Stg=S; Freq: R, H, I, N Occas: X ● **Work Env:** Noise=N; ● **Salary:** 2 ● **Outlook:** 3

FILE CLERK II (clerical) ● DOT #206.367-014 ● OES: 55321 ● Files correspondence, cards, invoices, receipts, and other records in alphabetical or numerical order, or according to subject matter, or other system [FILE CLERK (clerical) I 206.387-034], searches for and investigates information contained in files, inserts additional data on file records, completes reports, keeps files current, and supplies information from file data. Classifies material when classification is not readily discernible [CLASSIFICATION CLERK (clerical) 206.387-010]. Disposes of obsolete files in accordance with established retirement schedule or legal requirements. May copy records on photocopying or microfilming machines. May type labels or reports. May make calculations or use calculating machine to keep files current. May be designated according to material filed. ● **GED:** R3, M2, L3 ● **SVP:** 1-3 mos ● **Academic:** Ed=H, Eng=S ● **Work Field:** 231 ● **MPSMS:** 891 ● **Aptitudes:** G3, V3, N4, S4, P3, Q2, K4, F3, M3, E5, C5 ● **Tempera-**

ments: J, T ● **Physical:** Stg=L; Freq: R, H, I, N Occas: S, O, T, G, A ● **Work Env:** Noise=N; ● **Salary:** 1 ● **Outlook:** 2

FINGERPRINT CLERK II (government ser.) ● DOT #206.387-014 ● OES: 55321 ● Examines fingerprint patterns and classifies prints according to standard system: Examines fingerprints, using magnifying glass, to determine pattern formations. Classifies fingerprints according to standard system and records classification on file cards. Files records, following prescribed sequence. Searches fingerprint identification files to provide information to authorized persons. ● **GED:** R4, M2, L3 ● **SVP:** 3-6 mos ● **Academic:** Ed=H, Eng=S ● **Work Field:** 231, 271 ● **MPSMS:** 959 ● **Aptitudes:** G3, V3, N4, S3, P2, Q3, K4, F4, M4, E5, C5 ● **Temperaments:** J, T ● **Physical:** Stg=S; Freq: R, H, I, N ● **Work Env:** Noise=Q; ● **Salary:** 3 ● **Outlook:** 2

IDENTIFICATION CLERK (government ser.) ● DOT #209.362-022 ● OES: 59998 ● Performs any combination of following duties to compile and transmit records, relay information, microfilm documents, and take and classify fingerprints in police agency: Retrieves and prints copies of police records and reports requested by public and police personnel, using computer and printer. Retrieves information on vehicles and persons requested by patrolling police officers, and provides information to officers over police radio communications system. Operates equipment to microfilm crime and accident reports. Files microfilm. Retrieves microfilmed information upon request of police officials or public, and operates equipment to copy requested information. Tends facsimile machine to transmit and receive photographs, fingerprints, and accompanying information. Fingerprints applicants for licenses and assists in preparation of applications. Classifies fingerprints and matches fingerprints with prints previously filed as evidence in unsolved crimes [FINGERPRINT CLASSIFIER (government ser.) 375.387-010]. Compiles and submits periodic reports pertaining to police department activities. ● **GED:** R3, M2, L3 ● **SVP:** 3-6 mos ● **Academic:** Ed=H, Eng=G ● **Work Field:** 201, 231, 281 ● **MPSMS:** 951 ● **Aptitudes:** G3, V3, N4, S4, P3, Q2, K3, F3, M3, E5, C4 ● **Temperaments:** P, T, V ● **Physical:** Stg=L; Freq: H, I, T, G, N Occas: R, A, X ● **Work Env:** Noise=N; ● **Salary:** 3 ● **Outlook:** 3

INSURANCE CLERK (clerical) ● DOT #219.387-014 ● OES: 59998 ● Compiles records of insurance policies covering risks to property and equipment of industrial organization: Files records of insurance transactions and keeps calendar of premiums due and expiration dates of policies. Prepares vouchers for payment of premiums and verifies that payments have been made. Fills in data on renewal policy applications and forwards applications to insurance company. Compiles statistical data for reports to insurance company and departments in organization. May notify insurance company of changes in property or equipment affecting insurance coverage. May type amortization schedules. ● **GED:** R4, M3, L3 ● **SVP:** 3-6 mos ● **Academic:** Ed=A, Eng=G ● **Work Field:** 232, 231 ● **MPSMS:** 891 ● **Aptitudes:** G3, V3, N3, S4, P4, Q3, K4, F4, M4, E5, C5 ● **Temperaments:** R, T ● **Physical:** Stg=S; Freq: R, H, I, N ● **Work Env:** Noise=Q; ● **Salary:** 2 ● **Outlook:** 3

MEDICAL-RECORD CLERK (medical ser.) ● DOT #245.362-010 ● OES: 55328 ● Compiles, verifies, types, and files medical records of hospital or other health care facility: Prepares folders and maintains records of newly admitted patients. Reviews medical records for completeness, assembles records into standard order, and files records in designated areas according to applicable alphabetic and numeric filing system. Locates, signs out, and delivers medical records requested by hospital departments. Compiles statistical data, such as admissions, discharges, deaths, births, and types of treatment given. Operates computer to enter and retrieve data and type correspondence and reports. May assist other workers with coding of records. May post results of laboratory tests to records and be designated Charting Clerk (medical ser.). ● **GED:** R4, M3, L3 ● **SVP:** 3-6 mos ● **Academic:** Ed=N, Eng=G ● **Work Field:** 231 ● **MPSMS:** 891 ● **Aptitudes:** G3, V3, N3, S4, P4, Q3, K2, F3, M4, E5, C5 ● **Temperaments:** T ● **Physical:** Stg=L; Freq: R, H, I, N Occas: T, G ● **Work Env:** Noise=Q; ● **Salary:** 3 ● **Outlook:** 3

MEDICAL RECORD TECHNICIAN (medical ser.) ● DOT #079.362-014 ● OES: 32911 ● Compiles and maintains medical records of patients of health care delivery system to document patient condition and treatment: Reviews medical records for completeness and to abstract and code clinical data, such as diseases, operations, procedures and therapies, using standard classification systems. Compiles medical care and census data for statistical reports on types of diseases treated, surgery performed, and use of hospital beds, in response to inquiries from law firms, insurance companies, and government agencies. Maintains and utilizes variety of health record indexes and storage and retrieval systems. Operates computer to process, store, and retrieve health information. Assists MEDICAL-RECORD ADMINISTRATOR (medical ser.) 079.167-014 in special studies or research, as needed. ● **GED:** R4, M3, L4 ● **SVP:** 1-2 yrs ● **Academic:** Ed=A, Eng=G ● **Work Field:** 231 ● **MPSMS:** 929 ● **Aptitudes:** G2, V2, N3, S4, P4, Q3, K4, F3, M4, E5, C5 ● **Temperaments:** J, T, V ● **Physical:** Stg=L; Freq: R, H, I, N Occas: S, T, G, A ● **Work Env:** Noise=Q; ● **Salary:** 4 ● **Outlook:** 4

MEDICAL-SERVICE TECHNICIAN (military ser.) ● DOT #079.367-018 ● OES: 32998 ● Administers medical aid to personnel aboard submarines, small ships, and isolated areas in absence of or under supervision of medical superior: Examines patients and diagnoses condition. Prescribes medication to treat condition of patient. Inoculates and vaccinates patients to immunize patients from communicable diseases. Treats cuts and burns, performs minor surgery and administers emergency medical care to patients during emergency situations in absence of superior. Inspects food and facilities to determine conformance to sanitary regulations. Recommends necessary measures to ensure sanitary conditions are maintained. Records, transcribes, and files medical case histories. Prepares requisitions for supplies, services, and equipment. ● **GED:** R4, M3, L3 ● **SVP:** 2-4 yrs ● **Academic:** Ed=A, Eng=S ● **Work Field:** 294, 231 ● **MPSMS:** 924, 921 ● **Aptitudes:** G2, V2, N3, S2, P3, Q3, K3, F3, M3, E4, C4 ● **Temperaments:** J, P, S, T ● **Physical:** Stg=L; Freq: R, H, I, T, G, N, X Occas: E, D, A ● **Work Env:** Noise=L; Freq: O ● **Salary:** 3 ● **Outlook:** 3

NEWS ASSISTANT (radio-tv broad.) ● DOT #209.367-038 ● OES: 59998 ● Alternate titles: DESK ASSISTANT. Compiles, dispenses, and files newsstories and related copy to assist editorial personnel in broadcasting newsroom: Telephones government agencies and sports facilities and monitors other stations to obtain weather, traffic, and sports information. Telephones people involved in news events to obtain further information or to arrange for on-air or background interviews by news broadcasting personnel. Files and retrieves news scripts, printouts, and recording tapes. May make written copies of newsstories called in from remote locations. May record, edit, and play back tapes of newsstories to assist COLUMNIST/COMMENTATOR (print. & pub.; radio-tv broad.), using recording and splicing machines and equipment. ● **GED:** R4, M2, L4 ● **SVP:** 1-3 mos ● **Academic:** Ed=H, Eng=G ● **Work Field:** 231 ● **MPSMS:** 863 ● **Aptitudes:** G3, V3, N4, S4, P4, Q3, K4, F4, M4, E5, C5 ● **Temperaments:** J, T ● **Physical:** Stg=L; Freq: R, H, T, G, N Occas: I ● **Work Env:** Noise=N; ● **Salary:** 2 ● **Outlook:** 2

ORDER CLERK (clerical) ● DOT #249.362-026 ● OES: 55323 ● Alternate titles: CUSTOMER-ORDER CLERK; ORDER FILLER; ORDER TAKER. Processes orders for material or merchandise received by mail, telephone, or personally from customer or company employee, manually or using computer or calculating machine: Edits orders received for price and nomenclature. Informs customer of unit prices, shipping date, anticipated delays, and any additional information needed by customer, using mail or telephone. Writes or types order form, or enters data into computer, to determine total cost for customer. Records or files copy of orders received according to expected delivery date. May ascertain credit rating of customer [CREDIT CLERK (clerical) 205.367-022]. May check inventory control and notify stock control departments of orders that would deplete stock. May initiate purchase requisitions. May route orders to departments for filling and follow up on orders to ensure delivery by specified dates and be designated Telephone-Order Dispatcher (clerical). May compute price, discount, sales representative's commission, and shipping charges. May prepare invoices and shipping documents, such as bill of lading [BILLING TYPIST (clerical) 214.382-014]. May recommend type of packing or labeling needed on order. May receive and check customer complaints [CUSTOMER-COMPLAINT CLERK (clerical) 241.367-014]. May confer with production, sales, shipping, warehouse, or common carrier personnel to expedite or trace missing or delayed shipments. May attempt to sell additional merchandise to customer [TELEPHONE SOLICITOR (any industry) 299.357-014]. May compile statistics and prepare various reports for management. May be designated according to method of receiving orders as Mail-Order Clerk (clerical); Telephone-Order Clerk (clerical). ● **GED:** R3, M3, L3 ● **SVP:** 3-6 mos ● **Academic:** Ed=N, Eng=S ● **Work Field:** 231, 282 ● **MPSMS:** 881, 882, 891 ● **Aptitudes:** G3, V3, N3, S4, P4, Q2, K4, F4, M4, E5, C5 ● **Temperaments:** P, T ● **Physical:** Stg=S; Freq: R, H, I, T, G, N Occas: A ● **Work Env:** Noise=N; ● **Salary:** 2 ● **Outlook:** 3

ORDER DEPARTMENT SUPERVISOR (any industry) ● DOT #169.167-038 ● OES: 21998 ● Coordinates activities of personnel of order-writing department: Plans and initiates order-writing procedures, using knowledge of company products, pricing methods, and discount classifications. Directs establishment and maintenance of customer order records, such as discount classifications, cost basis, special routing, and transportation information. Supervises workers writing master orders used by production, shipping, invoicing, advertising, cost, and estimating departments. ● **GED:** R4, M3, L4 ● **SVP:** 2-4 yrs ● **Academic:** Ed=H, Eng=S ● **Work Field:** 232 ● **MPSMS:** 892 ● **Aptitudes:** G2, V2, N3, S4, P4, Q3, K4, F4, M4, E5, C5 ● **Temperaments:** D, P ● **Physical:** Stg=S; Freq: T, G Occas: H, I, N ● **Work Env:** Noise=N; ● **Salary:** 3 ● **Outlook:** 3

PERSONNEL CLERK (clerical) ● DOT #209.362-026 ● OES: 55314 ● Alternate titles: HUMAN RESOURCES CLERK; PERSONNEL RECORDS CLERK. Compiles and maintains personnel records: Records employee information, such as personal data; compensation, benefits, and tax data; attendance; performance reviews or evaluations; and termination date and reason. Processes employment applications and assists in other employment activities. Updates employee files to document personnel actions and to provide information for payroll and other uses. Examines employee files to answer inquiries and provides information to authorized persons. Compiles data from personnel records and prepares reports using typewriter or computer. May administer and score aptitude, personality, and interest tests. May explain bonding procedure required by company, and assist in completion of bonding application. May compute wages and record data for use in payroll processing [PAYROLL CLERK (clerical) 215.382-014]. May compile and maintain records for use in employee benefits administration and be designated Benefits Clerk (clerical) I. May prepare and file reports of accidents and injuries at establishment and be designated Accident-Report Clerk (clerical). ● **GED:** R4, M2, L4 ● **SVP:** 3-6 mos ● **Academic:** Ed=H, Eng=G ● **Work Field:** 231 ● **MPSMS:** 890 ● **Aptitudes:** G3, V3, N3, S4, P4, Q2, K3, F3, M4, E5, C5 ● **Temperaments:** P, T, V ● **Physical:** Stg=S; Freq: R, H, I, T, G, N Occas: S, O, A ● **Work Env:** Noise=N; ● **Salary:** 3 ● **Outlook:** 3

PROPERTY CLERK (government ser.) ● DOT #222.367-054 ● OES: 59998 ● Alternate titles: PROPERTY CUSTODIAN. Receives, stores, records, and issues money, valuables, and other articles seized as evidence, removed from prisoner, or recovered, lost, or stolen property: Prepares record of articles and valuables received, including description of article, name of owner (if known), name of police officer from whom received, and reason for retention. Issues property being retained as evidence to officer at time of trial upon receipt of authorization. Telephones owners or mails letters to notify owners to claim property, and releases lost or stolen property to owners upon proof of ownership. Returns property to released prisoners. Prepares list of articles required by law to be destroyed and destroys narcotics and drugs (upon authorization) in presence of official witnesses. Sends alcoholic beverages to state liquor commission. Lists and sends unclaimed or confiscated money to auditor's office. Sends unclaimed and illegal weapons for official destruction. Prepares inventory of unclaimed articles for possible sale at auction or donation to charitable organization. ● **GED:** R3, M2, L3 ● **SVP:** 6 mos-1 yr ● **Academic:** Ed=N, Eng=G ● **Work Field:** 221 ● **MPSMS:** 959 ● **Aptitudes:** G3, V3, N4, S4, P4, Q3, K4, F4, M4, E5, C5 ● **Temperaments:** J, P, T ● **Physical:** Stg=L; Freq: R, H, N Occas: I, T, G ● **Work Env:** Noise=N; ● **Salary:** 2 ● **Outlook:** 3

QUALITY-CONTROL CLERK (pharmaceut.) ● DOT #229.587-014 ● OES: 58097 ● Stores samples of materials tested and records test result data for product stability study program: Files bottles of raw materials used in pharmaceutical compounding, samples of purchased and plant-processed intermediate products, lot control samples, and samples of finished pharmaceutical batches. Stores samples of finished products in cartons labeled with type of product (cream, liquid, tablet) and records identifying data in alphabetical index listing. Keeps tickler file for withdrawal of samples for testing. Withdraws samples on dates indicated and takes them to laboratory. Keeps file of product stability study control charts. Records on charts test result data, such as appearance, color, and melting point. ● **GED:** R3, M2, L3 ● **SVP:** 1-3 mos ● **Academic:** Ed=N, Eng=S ● **Work Field:** 221 ● **MPSMS:** 898 ● **Aptitudes:** G3, V3, N4, S4, P4, Q3, K4, F4, M4, E5, C4 ● **Temperaments:** R, T ● **Physical:** Stg=L; Freq: R, H, I, N Occas: S, A, X ● **Work Env:** Noise=Q; ● **Salary:** 2 ● **Outlook:** 3

REFERRAL CLERK, TEMPORARY HELP AGENCY (clerical) ● **DOT** #205.367-062 ● OES: 55314 ● Alternate titles: REFERRAL CLERK; STAFFING CLERK. Compiles and records information about temporary job openings and refers qualified applicants from register of temporary help agency: Answers call from hospital, business, or other type of organization requesting temporary workers and obtains and records job requirements. Reviews records to locate registered workers who match job requirements and are available for scheduled shift. Notifies selected workers of job availability and records referral information on agency records. Sorts mail, files records, and performs other clerical duties. May give employment applications to applicants, schedule interviews with agency registration interviewers, or administer skill tests. May refer workers in specific occupations, such as nursing. ● **GED:** R3, M3, L3 ● **SVP:** 1-3 mos ● **Academic:** Ed=H, Eng=G ● **Work Field:** 231, 282 ● **MPSMS:** 943 ● **Aptitudes:** G3, V3, N4, S4, P4, Q3, K4, F3, M4, E5, C5 ● **Temperaments:** P ● **Physical:** Stg=S; Freq: I, T, G, N Occas: R, H, A ● **Work Env:** Noise=N; ● **Salary:** 3 ● **Outlook:** 2

REPAIR-ORDER CLERK (clerical) ● DOT #221.382-022 ● OES: 58008 ● Alternate titles: WORK-ORDER CLERK. Receives interdepartmental work orders for construction or repairs, routes work orders to maintenance shop, and compiles cost reports: Files copy of each work order received, and routes original copy to maintenance shop. Receives and files cost reports of work accomplished, and prepares bills to be charged against department requesting construction or repairs. Types cost reports of work completed or in progress. ● **GED:** R3, M3, L3 ● **SVP:** 1-3 mos ● **Academic:** Ed=N, Eng=S ● **Work Field:** 232, 231 ● **MPSMS:** 898 ● **Aptitudes:** G3, V3, N3, S4, P4, Q3, K3, F3, M3, E5, C5 ● **Temperaments:** R, T ● **Physical:** Stg=S; Freq: R, H, I, N ● **Work Env:** Noise=Q; ● **Salary:** 2 ● **Outlook:** 3

REPRODUCTION ORDER PROCESSOR (clerical) ● DOT #221.367-058 ● OES: 58008 ● Reviews request orders for duplication of printed, typed, and handwritten materials and determines appropriate reproduction method, based on knowledge of cost factors and duplicating machines and processes: Reads duplication requests to ascertain number of copies to be made and completion date requested. Confers with order requestor when additional information is necessary to facilitate completion of order. Designates method of duplication, such as photocopying or offset, and routes request orders for processing. Examines completed reproduced material for adherence to order specifications. Keeps files on status of request orders. Keeps supply of standard forms and issues forms as requested. ● **GED:** R3, M2, L3 ● **SVP:** 6 mos-1 yr ● **Academic:** Ed=N, Eng=G ● **Work Field:** 191, 201 ● **MPSMS:** 898 ● **Aptitudes:** G3, V3, N3, S4, P3, Q3, K4, F4, M4, E5, C5 ● **Temperaments:** J, P ● **Physical:** Stg=S; Freq: R, H, T, G, N, A Occas: I ● **Work Env:** Noise=N; ● **Salary:** 2 ● **Outlook:** 3

SHORTHAND REPORTER (clerical) ● DOT #202.362-010 ● OES: 55302 ● Alternate titles: COURT REPORTER; LAW REPORTER. Records examination, testimony, judicial opinions, judge's charge to jury, judgment or sentence of court, or other proceedings in court of law by machine shorthand [STENOTYPE OPERATOR (clerical)], takes shorthand notes, or reports proceedings into steno-mask. Reads portions of transcript during trial on judge's request, and asks speakers to clarify inaudible statements. Operates typewriter to transcribe recorded material, or dictates material into recording machine. May record proceedings of quasi-judicial hearings and formal and informal meetings and be designated Hearings Reporter (clerical). May be self-employed, performing duties in court of law or at hearings and meetings, and be designated Freelance Reporter (clerical). ● **GED:** R3, M2, L3 ● **SVP:** 1-2 yrs ● **Academic:** Ed=H, Eng=G ● **Work Field:** 231 ● **MPSMS:** 932, 891 ● **Aptitudes:** G2, V2, N4, S4, P2, Q2, K2, F2, M3, E5, C5 ● **Temperaments:** P, T ● **Physical:** Stg=S; Freq: I, T, G, N Occas: R, H ● **Work Env:** Noise=N; ● **Salary:** 3 ● **Outlook:** 4

STENOCAPTIONER (radio-tv broad.) ● DOT #202.382-010 ● OES: 55302 ● Operates computerized stenographic captioning equipment to provide captions of live television broadcast for hearing-impaired viewers: Discusses program or news story content with broadcast's PRODUCER (radio-tv broad.) 159.117-010 to learn new words and terms which are not included in computer's stenographic glossary. Devises stenographic equivalents of new words or terms and adds them to stenographic glossary. Reviews glossary items before broadcast for words and terms that are likely to be used on-air. Listens to live program dialogue and types stenographic equivalents for words and phrases to provide on-screen captions. May type captions for movie or taped television program [CAPTION WRITER (motion picture; radio-tv broad.) 203.362-026]. ● **GED:** R4, M2, L4 ● **SVP:** 4-10 yrs ● **Academic:** Ed=H, Eng=G ● **Work Field:** 231 ● **MPSMS:** 864 ● **Aptitudes:** G2, V2, N4, S4, P3, Q1, K2, F1, M3, E5, C5 ● **Temperaments:** J, T ● **Physical:** Stg=S; Const: I Freq: G Occas: R, H ● **Work Env:** Noise=N; ● **Salary:** 3 ● **Outlook:** 3

STENOGRAPHER (clerical) ● DOT #202.362-014 ● OES: 55302 ● Alternate titles: CLERK-STENOGRAPHER. Takes dictation in shorthand of correspondence, reports, and other matter, and operates typewriter to transcribe dictated material. Performs variety of clerical duties [ADMINISTRATIVE CLERK (clerical) 219.362-010], except when working in stenographic pool. May transcribe material from sound recordings [TRANSCRIBING-MACHINE OPERATOR (clerical) 203.582-058]. May perform stenographic duties in professional office and be designated Legal Stenographer (clerical); Medical Stenographer (clerical); Technical Stenographer (clerical). May take dictation in foreign language and be known as Foreign-Language Stenographer (clerical). May be designated according to department in which employed as Police Stenographer (government ser.). May work for public stenographic service and be designated Public Stenographer (clerical). ● **GED:** R3, M2, L3 ● **SVP:** 6 mos-1 yr ● **Academic:** Ed=H, Eng=G ● **Work Field:** 231 ● **MPSMS:** 891 ● **Aptitudes:** G3, V2, N4, S4, P2, Q2, K2, F3, M3, E5, C5 ● **Temperaments:** T ● **Physical:** Stg=S; Freq: R, H, I, G, N, A Occas: T ● **Work Env:** Noise=N; ● **Salary:** 2 ● **Outlook:** 3

STENOTYPE OPERATOR (clerical) ● DOT #202.362-022 ● OES: 55302 ● Alternate titles: STENOTYPE-MACHINE OPERATOR; STENO-TYPIST. Takes dictation of correspondence, reports, and other matter on machine that writes contractions or symbols for full words on paper roll. Operates typewriter to transcribe notes. May dictate notes into recording machine for TRANSCRIBING-MACHINE OPERATOR (clerical) to transcribe. ● **GED:** R4, M2, L4 ● **SVP:** 6 mos-1 yr ● **Academic:** Ed=N, Eng=G ● **Work Field:** 231 ● **MPSMS:** 891 ● **Aptitudes:** G3, V3, N4, S4, P3, Q2, K2, F2, M3, E5, C5 ● **Temperaments:** R, T ● **Physical:** Stg=S; Const: R, I Freq: N Occas: H, T, G ● **Work Env:** Noise=N; ● **Salary:** 3 ● **Outlook:** 4

STOCK CONTROL CLERK (clerical) ● DOT #219.387-030 ● OES: 58097 ● Alternate titles: INVENTORY CLERK; INVENTORY CONTROL CLERK; STOCK ORDER LISTER. Performs any combination of following tasks to compile records concerned with ordering, receiving, storing, issuing, and shipping materials, supplies, and equipment: Compiles data from sources, such as contracts, purchase orders, invoices, requisitions, and accounting reports and writes, types, or enters information into computer to maintain inventory, purchasing, shipping, or other records. Keeps back order file in established sequence and releases back orders for issue or shipment as stock becomes available. Compiles stock control records and information, such as consumption rate, characteristics of items in storage, and current market conditions, to determine stock supply and need for replenishment. Prepares requisitions, orders, or other documents for purchasing or requisitioning new or additional stock items. Compares nomenclature, stock numbers, authorized substitutes, and other listed information with catalogs, manuals, parts lists, and similar references to verify accuracy of requisitions and shipping orders. Reviews files to determine unused items and recommends disposal of excess stock. ● **GED:** R4, M3, L3 ● **SVP:** 6 mos-1 yr ● **Academic:** Ed=N, Eng=S ● **Work Field:** 231, 232 ● **MPSMS:** 898 ● **Aptitudes:** G3, V3, N3, S4, P4, Q3, K4, F4, M3, E5, C4 ● **Temperaments:** T ● **Physical:** Stg=L; Freq: R, H, I, N Occas: T, G, A, X ● **Work Env:** Noise=N; ● **Salary:** 3 ● **Outlook:** 3

TAPE LIBRARIAN (clerical) ● DOT #206.367-018 ● OES: 55321 ● Classifies, catalogs, and maintains library of computer tapes: Classifies reels and cartridges of magnetic computer tape according to content, purpose, principal user, date generated, or other criteria. Assigns identification number, following standard system. Prepares catalog of tapes classified, using logbook and computer. Stores tapes according to classification and identification number. Issues tapes and maintains charge-out records. Inspects returned tapes and notifies supervisor when tapes are worn or damaged. Removes obsolete tapes from library, following data retention requirements. May send tapes to vendor for cleaning and to off-site location for secure storage. May maintain files of program developmental records and operating instructions. May work in computer room operations, performing tasks such as loading and removing paper and printouts and reels of tape. ● **GED:** R4, M2, L3 ● **SVP:** 3-6 mos ● **Academic:** Ed=H, Eng=S ● **Work Field:** 231, 221 ● **MPSMS:** 891 ● **Aptitudes:** G3, V3, N4, S4, P3, Q2, K3, F3, M4, E5, C5 ● **Temperaments:** T ● **Physical:** Stg=L; Freq: R, H, I, T, G, N, A Occas: S, O ● **Work Env:** Noise=L; ● **Salary:** 2 ● **Outlook:** 2

TAXICAB COORDINATOR (motor trans.) ● DOT #215.367-018 ● OES: 58005 ● Assigns taxicabs to TAXI DRIVERS (motor trans.) and maintains record of assignments and trip data. Reviews report of meter readings taken from incoming cabs for accuracy or takes and records taximeter readings. Compiles and maintains records of mileage traveled and fuel used. ● **GED:** R3, M2, L2 ● **SVP:** 6 mos-1 yr ● **Academic:** Ed=N, Eng=S ● **Work Field:** 232 ● **MPSMS:** 852, 898 ● **Aptitudes:** G4, V4, N4, S4, P4, Q3, K4, F4, M4, E5, C5 ● **Temperaments:** J, T ● **Physical:** Stg=S; Freq: R, H, N Occas: I ● **Work Env:** Noise=Q; ● **Salary:** 3 ● **Outlook:** 2

TECHNICAL COORDINATOR (government ser.) ● DOT #209.132-014 ● OES: 51002 ● Supervises and coordinates activities of workers engaged in processing applications and claims in water rights office: Prepares correspondence and takes dictation. Examines applications for errors. Prepares notices for owners to close, clean, deepen, repair, or replace wells. Prepares closing notices for publication. Plats descriptions on documents, using drafting tools. Answers telephone and personal inquiries. Performs other duties as described under SUPERVISOR (clerical) Master Title. ● **GED:** R4, M4, L4 ● **SVP:** 2-4 yrs ● **Academic:** Ed=H, Eng=G ● **Work Field:** 231 ● **MPSMS:** 959, 890 ● **Aptitudes:** G3, V2, N3, S3, P3, Q3, K3, F3, M3, E5, C4 ● **Temperaments:** J, P, V ● **Physical:** Stg=S; Freq: R, H, I, T, G, N Occas: D, A ● **Work Env:** Noise=N; ● **Salary:** 4 ● **Outlook:** 1

TUMOR REGISTRAR (medical ser.) ● DOT #079.362-018 ● OES: 32911 ● Compiles and maintains records of hospital patients treated for cancer to provide data for physicians and research studies, utilizing tumor registry data system: Reviews hospital records to identify and compile patient data for use in cancer managment program and to comply with government regulations. Reviews patient's medical record, abstracts and codes information, such as demographic characteristics, history and extent of disease, diagnostic procedures and treatment, and enters data into computer. Contacts discharged patients, their families, and physicians to maintain registry with follow-up information, such as quality of life and length of survival of cancer patients. Prepares statistical reports, narrative reports and graphic presentations of tumor registry data for use by hospital staff, researchers, and other users of registry data. May supervise subordinate tumor registry staff and be known as Manager, Tumor Registry (medical ser.). ● **GED:** R5, M4, L5 ● **SVP:** 2-4 yrs ● **Academic:** Ed=A, Eng=G ● **Work Field:** 231 ● **MPSMS:** 930 ● **Aptitudes:** G3, V2, N3, S4, P4, Q3, K4, F4, M4, E5, C5 ● **Temperaments:** J, T ● **Physical:** Stg=S; Freq: R, H, I, T, G, N ● **Work Env:** Noise=Q; ● **Salary:** 4 ● **Outlook:** 3

UNIT CLERK (medical ser.) ● DOT #245.362-014 ● OES: 55347 ● Alternate titles: HEALTH UNIT CLERK; WARD CLERK. Prepares and compiles records in nursing unit of hospital or medical facility: Records name of patient, address, and name of attending physician to prepare medical records on new patients. Copies information, such as patient's temperature, pulse rate, and blood pressure from nurses' records onto patient's medical records. Records information, such as physicians' orders and instructions, dietary requirements, and medication information, on patient charts and medical records. Keeps file of medical records on patients in unit. Prepares notice of patient's discharge to inform business office. Requisitions supplies designated by nursing staff. Answers telephone and intercom calls and provides information or relays messages to patients and medical staff. Directs visitors to patients' rooms. Distributes mail, newspapers, and flowers to patients. Compiles census of patients. May keep record of absences and hours worked by unit personnel. May transport patients in wheelchair or conveyance to locations within facility. May key patient information into computer. ● **GED:** R3, M3, L3 ● **SVP:** 1-3 mos ● **Academic:** Ed=N,

Eng=G ● **Work Field:** 231, 232 ● **MPSMS:** 891 ● **Aptitudes:** G3, V3, N3, S4, P3, Q3, K3, F3, M3, E5, C5 ● **Temperaments:** T, V ● **Physical:** Stg=L; Freq: R, H, I, T, G, N ● **Work Env:** Noise=Q; ● **Salary:** 2 ● **Outlook:** 3

YARD CLERK (r.r. trans.) ● DOT #209.367-054 ● OES: 58098 ● Alternate titles: CHECK CLERK. Prepares switching orders for railroad yard switching crew: Types or writes switching orders to inform switching crew of railroad yard, location, disposition, and number of railroad cars to be switched for loading, unloading, makeup, and breakup of trains, based on information received from YARD MANAGER (r.r. trans.) and other personnel or records. Keeps record of and reports movement and disposition of railroad cars for YARD MANAGER (r.r. trans.). May count and record number of cars remaining in yard each day. May telephone various personnel to verify location of railroad cars. ● **GED:** R3, M2, L2 ● **SVP:** 1-3 mos ● **Academic:** Ed=N, Eng=S ● **Work Field:** 231 ● **MPSMS:** 851 ● **Aptitudes:** G3, V3, N4, S5, P4, Q3, K3, F3, M4, E5, C5 ● **Temperaments:** R, T ● **Physical:** Stg=S; Freq: R, H, I, N Occas: T, G ● **Work Env:** Noise=N; ● **Salary:** 2 ● **Outlook:** 2

GOE: 07.05.04
Routing & Distribution

CORRESPONDENCE-REVIEW CLERK (clerical) ● DOT #209.367-018 ● OES: 55317 ● Reads and routes incoming correspondence to individual or department concerned: Reviews correspondence, determines appropriate routing, and requisitions records needed to process correspondence. Types acknowledgement letter to person sending correspondence. Reviews requested records for completeness and accuracy and attaches records to correspondence for reply by other workers. May maintain files and control records to show status of action in processing correspondence. May compile data from records to prepare periodic reports. May investigate discrepancies in reports and records and confer with personnel in affected departments to ensure accuracy and compliance with procedures. ● **GED:** R3, M1, L3 ● **SVP:** 6 mos-1 yr ● **Academic:** Ed=H, Eng=G ● **Work Field:** 231 ● **MPSMS:** 891 ● **Aptitudes:** G3, V3, N4, S4, P4, Q3, K4, F3, M3, E5, C5 ● **Temperaments:** T ● **Physical:** Stg=S; Freq: R, H, I, N ● **Work Env:** Noise=N; ● **Salary:** 2 ● **Outlook:** 3

MAIL CARRIER (government ser.) ● DOT #230.367-010 ● OES: 57305 ● Alternate titles: CITY CARRIER; LETTER CARRIER. Sorts mail for delivery and delivers mail on established route: Inserts mail into slots of mail rack to sort for delivery. Delivers mail to residences and business establishments along route. Completes delivery forms, collects charges, and obtains signature on receipts for delivery of specified types of mail. Enters changes of address in route book and re-addresses mail to be forwarded. May drive vehicle over established route. May deliver specialized types of mail and be designated Parcel-Post Carrier (government ser.); Special-Delivery Carrier (government ser.). ● **GED:** R3, M2, L3 ● **SVP:** 3-6 mos ● **Academic:** Ed=N, Eng=G ● **Work Field:** 221 ● **MPSMS:** 954 ● **Aptitudes:** G3, V3, N4, S4, P4, Q3, K3, F4, M3, E5, C4 ● **Temperaments:** R ● **Physical:** Stg=M; Freq: R, H, I, N Occas: T, G ● **Work Env:** Noise=N; Freq: W Occas: O ● **Salary:** 4 ● **Outlook:** 2

MAIL CLERK (clerical) ● DOT #209.687-026 ● OES: 57302 ● Alternate titles: MAILROOM CLERK; MAIL SORTER; POSTAL CLERK. Sorts incoming mail for distribution and dispatches outgoing mail: Opens envelopes by hand or machine. Stamps date and time of receipt on incoming mail. Sorts mail according to destination and type, such as returned letters, adjustments, bills, orders, and payments. Re-addresses undeliverable mail bearing incomplete or incorrect address. Examines outgoing mail for appearance and seals envelopes by hand or machine. Stamps outgoing mail by hand or with postage meter. May fold letters or circulars and insert in envelopes [FOLDING-MACHINE OPERATOR (clerical) 208.685-014]. May distribute and collect mail. May weigh mail to determine that postage is correct. May keep record of registered mail. May address mail, using addressing machine [AD-DRESSING-MACHINE OPERATOR (clerical) 208.582-010]. May be designated according to type of mail handled as Mail Clerk, Bills (clerical). ● **GED:** R3, M1, L2 ● **SVP:** 2-30 days ● **Academic:** Ed=N, Eng=N ● **Work Field:** 231, 221 ● **MPSMS:** 891 ● **Aptitudes:** G3, V3, N4, S4, P3, Q3, K4, F4, M4, E5, C5 ● **Temperaments:** R, T ● **Physical:** Stg=L; Freq: R, H, I, N Occas: G ● **Work Env:** Noise=N; ● **Salary:** 1 ● **Outlook:** 3

MAIL HANDLER (government ser.) ● DOT #209.687-014 ● OES: 57308 ● Alternate titles: DISTRIBUTION CLERK. Sorts and processes mail in post office: Sorts incoming or outgoing mail into mail rack pigeonholes or into mail sacks according to destination. May feed letters into electric canceling machine or hand-stamp mail with rubber stamp to cancel postage. May serve at public window or counter. May transport mail within post office [MATERIAL HANDLER (any industry)]. May sort mail in mobile post office and be designated Distribution Clerk, Railway Or Highway Post Office (government ser.). May sort mail which other workers have been unable to sort and be designated Speical-Distribution Clerk (government ser.). ● **GED:** R3, M2, L2 ● **SVP:** 3-6 mos ● **Academic:** Ed=N, Eng=N ● **Work Field:** 231 ● **MPSMS:** 954 ● **Aptitudes:** G3, V4, N4, S3, P4, Q2, K2, F4, M3, E5, C5 ● **Temperaments:** R ● **Physical:** Stg=L; Freq: R, H, I, N ● **Work Env:** Noise=Q; ● **Salary:** 1 ● **Outlook:** 2

MAILROOM SUPERVISOR (clerical) ● DOT #209.137-010 ● OES: 51002 ● Supervises and coordinates activities of clerks who open, sort, and route mail, and prepare outgoing material for mailing: Reads letters and determines department or official for whom mail is intended and informs MAIL CLERK (clerical) of routing. Computes amount of postage required for outgoing mail according to weight and classification. Computes cost of mail permits from postage meter readings. Performs other duties as described under SUPERVISOR (clerical) Master Title. May interview and recommend hiring of mailroom employees. May train new employees. May maintain personnel records [PERSONNEL CLERK (clerical)]. ● **GED:** R4, M3, L4 ● **SVP:** 1-2 yrs ● **Academic:** Ed=H, Eng=G ● **Work Field:** 231, 232 ● **MPSMS:** 891 ● **Aptitudes:** G3, V3, N3, S4, P4, Q3, K4, F4, M4, E5, C5 ● **Temperaments:** D, J, P, V ● **Physical:** Stg=L; Freq: R, H, T, G, N Occas: I ● **Work Env:** Noise=Q; ● **Salary:** 1 ● **Outlook:** 3

MERCHANDISE DISTRIBUTOR (retail trade) ● DOT #219.367-018 ● OES: 58097 ● Compiles reports of stock on hand and kind and amount sold: Dispatches inventory data to units of retail chain. Routes merchandise from one branch store to another on the basis of sales. Usually specializes in one type of merchandise, such as dresses, sportswear, or lingerie. May give directions to one or more workers. ● **GED:** R3, M2, L2 ● **SVP:** 1-3 mos ● **Academic:** Ed=N, Eng=N ● **Work Field:** 232 ● **MPSMS:** 891 ● **Aptitudes:** G3, V3, N3, S4, P4, Q3, K4, F4, M4, E5, C5 ● **Temperaments:** J, T ● **Physical:** Stg=L; Freq: R, H, I, N ● **Work Env:** Noise=Q; ● **Salary:** 5 ● **Outlook:** 4

PARCEL POST CLERK (clerical) ● DOT #222.387-038 ● OES: 57302 ● Alternate titles: PARCEL POST PACKER; PARCEL POST WEIGHER. Wraps, inspects, weighs, and affixes postage to parcel post packages, and records c.o.d. and insurance information: Wraps packages or inspects wrapping for conformance to company standards and postal regulations. Weighs packages and determines postage, using scale and parcel post zone book, and affixes postage stamps to packages. Records information, such as value, charges, and destination of insured and c.o.d. packages. Copies and attaches c.o.d. card to packages to indicate amount to be collected. Addresses packages or compares addresses with records to verify accuracy. May compute cost of merchandise, shipping fees, and other charges, and bill customer. May sort parcels for shipment, according to destination or other classification, and place parcels in mail bags or bins and be designated Mail-Order Sorter (retail trade). May process incoming and outgoing mail [MAIL CLERK (clerical) 209.687-026]. May fill orders from stock and be designated Parcel-Post Order-Clerk (clerical). ● **GED:** R3, M2, L3 ● **SVP:** 1-3 mos ● **Academic:** Ed=N, Eng=S ● **Work Field:** 232, 212 ● **MPSMS:** 898 ● **Aptitudes:** G3, V3, N3, S4, P3, Q3, K4, F4, M4, E5, C5 ● **Temperaments:** R, T ● **Physical:** Stg=H; Freq: S, R, H, I, N ● **Work Env:** Noise=N; ● **Salary:** 1 ● **Outlook:** 3

ROUTING CLERK (nonprofit org.) ● DOT #249.367-070 ● OES: 58005 ● Determines truck routes involved and issues route slips to drivers to pick up donated clothing, furniture, and general merchandise for vocational rehabilitation organization: Reviews presorted route slips and reviews street maps to determine appropriate route, based on type and quantity of merchandise pledged and location of donor. Issues route slips to drivers. Answers telephone and mail inquiries and complaints from donors concerning pickups; and advises drivers of problems or reschedules pickup. Occasionally takes pickup orders. Prepares daily truck-collection report based on information from drivers, and keeps attendance, safety, and maintenance records. ● **GED:** R3, M2, L3 ● **SVP:** 1-3 mos ● **Academic:** Ed=N, Eng=G ● **Work Field:** 231, 282 ● **MPSMS:** 853 ● **Aptitudes:** G3, V3, N4, S5, P3, Q3, K4, F4, M4, E5, C5 ● **Temperaments:** J ● **Physical:** Stg=S; Freq: R, H, I, T, G, N ● **Work Env:** Noise=N; ● **Salary:** 2 ● **Outlook:** 3

ROUTE-DELIVERY CLERK (clerical) ● DOT #222.587-034 ● OES: 58028 ● Prepares itemized delivery sheet for items of merchandise to be delivered by truck drivers, grouping and routing deliveries according to designated districts: Copies information, such as name, address of consignee, type of merchandise, number of pieces, and mailing designation, from records onto delivery sheet. Locates and selects merchandise and verifies against delivery sheet specifications. May arrange for unloading of merchandise from freight cars, transport trucks, or ships, into consignees' trucks. May keep records of and arrange for storage of undelivered merchandise. ● **GED:** R2, M2, L2 ● **SVP:** 1-3 mos ● **Academic:** Ed=N, Eng=S ● **Work Field:** 221 ● **MPSMS:** 853 ● **Aptitudes:** G3, V3, N4, S4, P4, Q3, K4, F4, M4, E5, C4 ● **Temperaments:** R, T ● **Physical:** Stg=L; Freq: R, H, I, N Occas: X ● **Work Env:** Noise=Q; Occas: W ● **Salary:** 2 ● **Outlook:** 3

RURAL MAIL CARRIER (government ser.) ● DOT #230.363-010 ● OES: 57305 ● Delivers mail along established route outside town or city corporate limits: Sorts mail for delivery according to location along route. Delivers mail over route by motor vehicle. Picks up outgoing mail, sells stamps, and issues money orders. ● **GED:** R3, M3, L2 ● **SVP:** 2-30 days ● **Academic:** Ed=N, Eng=S ● **Work Field:** 221, 013 ● **MPSMS:** 954 ● **Aptitudes:** G3, V3, N3, S4, P4, Q3, K4, F4, M4, E4, C4 ● **Temperaments:** R ● **Physical:** Stg=M; Freq: R, H, I, N, X ● **Work Env:** Noise=N; Occas: W ● **Salary:** 3 ● **Outlook:** 4

SHIPPING-ORDER CLERK (clerical) ● DOT #219.367-030 ● OES: 58028 ● Requisitions transportation from freight carriers to ship plant products: Reads shipping orders to determine quantity and type of transportation needed. Contacts carrier representative to make arrangements and to issue instructions for loading products. Annotates shipping orders to inform shipping department of loading location and time of arrival of transportation. May perform other clerical tasks, such as typing and mailing bills, typing correspondence, and keeping files. ● **GED:** R3, M2, L3 ● **SVP:** 3-6 mos ● **Academic:** Ed=N, Eng=S ● **Work Field:** 232, 282 ● **MPSMS:** 898, 850 ● **Aptitudes:** G3, V3, N3, S4, P4, Q3, K4, F4, M4, E5, C5 ● **Temperaments:** J ● **Physical:** Stg=L; Freq: R, H, T, G, N Occas: I ● **Work Env:** Noise=Q; ● **Salary:** 3 ● **Outlook:** 3

SUPERVISOR, MAIL CARRIERS (government ser.) ● DOT #230.137-018 ● OES: 51002 ● Supervises and coordinates activities of workers engaged in collecting, sorting, and delivering mail: Receives, investigates, and initiates action on patron's complaints. May analyze carrier routes and recommend changes of route boundaries to regulate amount of mail being delivered. Performs other duties as described under SUPERVISOR (clerical) Master Title. ● **GED:** R4, M3, L4 ● **SVP:** 1-2 yrs ● **Academic:** Ed=H, Eng=G ● **Work Field:** 221 ● **MPSMS:** 954 ● **Aptitudes:** G3, V3, N4, S4, P4, Q2, K4, F4, M4, E5, C5 ● **Temperaments:** D, J, P, V ● **Physical:** Stg=L; Freq: T, G Occas: R, H, I, N ● **Work Env:** Noise=Q; ● **Salary:** 4 ● **Outlook:** 1

VAULT WORKER (business ser.) ● DOT #222.587-058 ● OES: 58028 ● Keeps records of, sorts, and routes sealed money bags received at and dispatched from vault of armored car firm: Receives bags and signs routing slip to acknowledge receipt. Sorts bags according to delivery routes. Records data, such as origin, routing, and destination of bags. Delivers bags to ARMORED-CAR GUARD (business ser.) for loading onto truck and verifies that guard has signed routing slip. Submits logs and routing slips to VAULT CASHIER (business ser.) for review. ● **GED:** R3, M2, L2 ● **SVP:** 1-3 mos ● **Academic:** Ed=N, Eng=S ● **Work Field:** 221 ● **MPSMS:** 899 ● **Aptitudes:** G3, V3, N4, S4, P4, Q3, K4, F4, M4, E5, C4 ● **Temperaments:** J ● **Physical:** Stg=M; Freq: S, O, R, H, I Occas: N, A, X ● **Work Env:** Noise=Q; ● **Salary:** 1 ● **Outlook:** 3

Clerical Machine Operation

Workers in this group use business machines to record or process data. They operate machines that type, print, sort, compute, send, or receive information. Their jobs are found in businesses, industries, government agencies, or wherever large amounts of data are processed, sent, or received.

✓ What kind of work would you do?

Your work activities would depend upon your specific job. For example, you might:

- type letters, forms, lists, and other materials.
- operate a special typewriter which automatically adjusts margins to prepare copy for reproduction.
- operate checkwriting machine to imprint checks.
- monitor and control a computer terminal to process data according to instructions.
- operate a telegraphic typewriter to send and receive messages.
- operate a keypunch machine to transcribe data onto punch cards or magnetic tape.
- operate billing machine to prepare bills, statements, and invoices.

✓ What skills and abilities do you need for this kind of work?

To do this kind of work, you must be able to:

- use eyes, hands, and fingers to operate keyboard of a clerical machine quickly and accurately.
- perform repetitive tasks.
- follow set or routine procedures.
- work with speed and accuracy.

The above statements may not apply to every job in this group.

✓ How do you know if you would like or could learn to do this kind of work?

The following questions may give you clues about yourself as you consider this group of jobs.

- Have you taken courses in typing? Were your speed test scores average or above? Do you enjoy typing?

- Have you had a part-time job in an office setting? Do you enjoy work that follows a set routine?
- Have you used a calculator or adding machine regularly? Can you use these machines rapidly and accurately?
- Have you had clerical work experience in the armed forces?

✓ How can you prepare for and enter this kind of work?

Occupations in this group usually require education and/or training extending from three months to over two years, depending upon the specific kind of work. Most employers require an applicant to have a high school education or its equal. Spelling and grammar are important to prepare for jobs in this group. Basic arithmetic skills are required for some jobs.

Some employers provide machine instruction and on-the-job training. However, graduation from a business school can be an advantage. The ability to operate several office machines improves chances for employment. Specialized training on a particular machine is required for certain jobs.

Supervisory positions are usually assigned to experienced workers who have leadership ability.

✓ What else should you consider about these jobs?

Some workers operate one machine all day. They may report malfunctions or make minor repairs. Large company offices usually have enough work to keep machines operating constantly. In small firms, however, machine operators may also do a variety of other clerical tasks.

Workers in supervisory jobs should enjoy dealing with people because they often train new workers, interview job applicants, and assign workers to jobs.

If you think you would like to do this kind of work, look at the job titles listed on the following pages.

GOE: 07.06.01
Computer Operation

COMPUTER OPERATOR (clerical) ● DOT #213.362-010 ● OES: 56011 ● Operates computer and peripheral equipment to process business, scientific, engineering, or other data, according to operating instructions: Enters commands, using keyboard of computer terminal, and presses buttons and flips switches on computer and peripheral equipment, such as tape drive, printer, data communications equipment, and plotter, to integrate and operate equipment, following operating instructions and schedule. Loads peripheral equipment with selected materials, such as tapes and printer paper for operating runs, or oversees loading of peripheral equipment by peripheral equipment operators. Enters commands to clear computer system and start operation, using keyboard of computer terminal. Observes peripheral equipment and error messages displayed on monitor of terminal to detect faulty output or machine stoppage. Enters commands to correct error or stoppage and resume operations. Notifies supervisor of errors or equipment stoppage. Clears equipment at end of operating run and reviews schedule to determine next assignment. Records problems which occurred, such as down time, and actions taken. May answer telephone calls to assist computer users encountering problem. May assist workers in classifying, cataloging, and maintaining tapes [TAPE LIBRARIAN (clerical) 206.367-018]. ● **GED:** R4, M2, L3 ● **SVP:** 1-2 yrs ● **Academic:** Ed=H, Eng=S ● **Work Field:** 233 ● **MPSMS:** 893 ● **Aptitudes:** G3, V3, N3, S3, P3, Q2, K3, F3, M4, E5, C5 ● **Temperaments:** J, T ● **Physical:** Stg=L; Freq: R, H, I, T, G, N, A Occas: C, B, S, K, O ● **Work Env:** Noise=N; ● **Salary:** 3 ● **Outlook:** 4

COMPUTER PERIPHERAL EQUIPMENT OPERATOR (clerical) ● DOT #213.382-010 ● OES: 56014 ● Operates computer peripheral equipment, such as printer, plotter, computer output microfiche machine, and document reader-sorter to transfer data to and from computer and to convert data from one format to another: Reads instructions and schedule, such as schedule of documents to be printed, or receives instructions from supervisor orally, to determine work for shift. Mounts reels and cartridges of magnetic tape in tape drives, loads paper in printer, loads checks or other documents in magnetic ink reader-sorter or optical character reader, sets guides, keys, and switches, enters commands into computer, using computer terminal, and performs other tasks, to start and operate peripheral machines. Observes machine operation and error lights on machines to detect malfunction. Observes materials printed for defects, such as creases and tears. Removes faulty materials and notifies supervisor of error or machine stoppage. Unloads and labels magnetic tape for delivery to other worker or tape library. May separate, sort, and distribute output. May clean and supply equipment operated with paper, ink, film, developing solution, and other materials. ● **GED:** R3, M2, L3 ● **SVP:** 3-6 mos ● **Academic:** Ed=N, Eng=S ● **Work Field:** 233 ● **MPSMS:** 893 ● **Aptitudes:** G3, V3, N4, S3, P4, Q2, K3, F3, M3, E5, C5 ● **Temperaments:** T ● **Physical:** Stg=L; Freq: R, H, I Occas: S, G, N, A ● **Work Env:** Noise=N; ● **Salary:** 3 ● **Outlook:** 3

CREDIT REPORTING CLERK (business ser.) ● DOT #203.362-014 ● OES: 55305 ● Alternate titles: CRT OPERATOR. Compiles, posts, and retrieves credit information, using computer, and reports credit information to subscribers of credit reporting agency: Answers requests received by computer modem, mail, or telephone from subscribers for information about credit applicants. Identifies caller by code. Enters inquiry into computer to retrieve requested information. Transmits information to subscriber, using computer and modem, reads information to subscriber over telephone, or generates printout for mailing to subscriber. Compiles and enters credit information into computer. ● **GED:** R3, M2, L3 ● **SVP:** 3-6 mos ● **Academic:** Ed=N, Eng=G ● **Work Field:** 282, 281 ● **MPSMS:** 899 ● **Aptitudes:** G3, V3, N4, S4, P4, Q3, K3, F3, M4, E5, C5 ● **Temperaments:** P, R, T ● **Physical:** Stg=S; Freq: R, H, I, T, G, N, A ● **Work Env:** Noise=N; ● **Salary:** 2 ● **Outlook:** 4

DATA ENTRY CLERK (clerical) ● DOT #203.582-054 ● OES: 56017 ● Alternate titles: DATA ENTRY OPERATOR. Operates keyboard or other data entry device to enter data into computer or onto magnetic tape or disk for subsequent entry: Enters alphabetic, numeric, or symbolic data from source documents into computer, using data entry device, such as keyboard or optical scanner, and following format displayed on screen. Compares data entered with source documents, or re-enters data in verification format on screen to detect errors. Deletes incorrectly entered data, and re-enters correct data. May compile, sort, and verify accuracy of data to be entered. May keep record of work completed. ● **GED:** R3, M2, L3 ● **SVP:** 3-6 mos ● **Academic:** Ed=N, Eng=G ● **Work Field:** 231 ● **MPSMS:** 891 ● **Aptitudes:** G3, V3, N4, S4, P4, Q2, K3, F3, M4, E5, C5 ● **Temperaments:** R, T ● **Physical:** Stg=S; Const: I, N, A Freq: R, H Occas: G ● **Work Env:** Noise=N; ● **Salary:** 1 ● **Outlook:** 4

NETWORK CONTROL OPERATOR (any industry) ● DOT #031.262-014 ● OES: 25198 ● Monitors data communications network to ensure that network is available to all system users and resolves data communications problems: Receives telephone call from user with data communications problem, such as failure of data to be transmitted to another location. Reviews procedures user followed to determine if specified steps were taken. Explains user procedures necessary to transmit data. Monitors modems and display screen of terminal to mainframe computer to detect error messages that signal malfunction in communications software or hardware. Enters diagnostic commands into computer to determine nature of problem, and reads codes on screen to diagnose problem. Attaches diagnostic equipment to phone line to learn if line meets specification. Reads technical reference manuals for communications hardware and software to learn cause of problem. Instructs user to enter specified commands into computer to resolve problem. Calls service technician for service when problem cannot be resolved. Enters operating commands into computer to restart program. Records number of daily data communications transactions and number of problems and actions taken, using computer terminal. Updates documentation to record new equipment installed, new sites, and changes to computer configurations. May inspect communications wires and cables. May train staff and users to use equipment. May coordinate installation of or install communications lines. ● **GED:** R4, M3, L4 ● **SVP:** 1-2 yrs ● **Academic:** Ed=A, Eng=G ● **Work Field:** 233 ● **MPSMS:** 893 ● **Aptitudes:** G3, V3, N3, S3, P3, Q3, K4, F4, M4, E5, C4 ● **Temperaments:** J, P, T ● **Physical:** Stg=L; Freq: I, T, G, N Occas: S, K, R, H, A, X ● **Work Env:** Noise=N; ● **Salary:** 3 ● **Outlook:** 5

SUPERVISOR, COMPUTER OPERATIONS (clerical) ● DOT #213.132-010 ● OES: 51002 ● Alternate titles: CHIEF CONSOLE OPERATOR; SUPERVISOR, DATA PROCESSING. Supervises and coordinates activities of workers operating computers and peripheral equipment: Assigns staff and schedules work to facilitate production. Directs training or trains workers to operate computer and peripheral equipment. Confers with programmers and operates computer to test new and modified programs. Directs operation of computer to execute program, and observes operation to detect error or failure in progress of program. Reads monitor and enters commands to help computer operators identify and correct errors. Revises input data and program to continue operation of program, using computer terminal. Notifies programming and maintenance personnel if unable to locate and correct cause of processing error or failure. Revises operation schedule to adjust for delays, or notifies scheduling workers of need to adjust schedule. Prepares or reviews production, operating, and down time records and reports. Recommends changes in programs, routines, and quality control standards to improve computer operating efficiency. Consults with supervisor about problems, such as equipment performance, output quality, and maintenance schedule. Coordinates flow of work between shifts to ensure continuity. Performs other duties as described under SUPERVISOR (clerical) Master Title. ● **GED:** R5, M4, L4 ● **SVP:** 2-4 yrs ● **Academic:** Ed=H, Eng=G ● **Work Field:** 233 ● **MPSMS:** 893 ● **Aptitudes:** G2, V2, N2, S3, P3, Q2, K4, F4, M4, E5, C5 ● **Temperaments:** D, J, P, T ● **Physical:** Stg=L; Freq: T, G, N Occas: S, K, O, R, H, I, A ● **Work Env:** Noise=N; ● **Salary:** 4 ● **Outlook:** 3

TERMINAL-MAKEUP OPERATOR (print. & pub.) ● DOT #208.382-010 ● OES: 56021 ● Alternate titles: AD-TERMINAL-MAKEUP OPERATOR. Operates computer terminal and related equipment to transfer and typeset display advertising data from perforated tape onto computer tapes for subsequent reproduction as printed matter: Secures perforated tape roll on machine reel and presses button to feed perforated tape into terminal console. Presses button to activate video display screen. Reads work order to determine combination of type style, point size, line width, and spacing to be set. Pushes terminal controls and depresses keys to observe and arrange elements on screen according to specifications. Measures copy margins to verify margin specifications, using ruler. Presses buttons to transfer typeset copy onto computer tape and into computer for storage. ● **GED:** R3, M2, L3 ● **SVP:** 6 mos-1 yr ● **Academic:** Ed=N, Eng=S ● **Work Field:** 231, 281, 264 ● **MPSMS:** 567, 752 ● **Aptitudes:** G3, V3, N4, S4, P3, Q2, K2, F3, M4, E5, C5 ● **Temperaments:** J, T ● **Physical:** Stg=S; Freq: R, H, I, N Occas: A ● **Work Env:** Noise=N; ● **Salary:** 2 ● **Outlook:** 2

GOE: 07.06.02
Keyboard Machine Operation

BRAILLE OPERATOR (print. & pub.) ● DOT #203.582-010 ● OES: 56017 ● Operates machine, similar to typewriter, to impress dots in metal sheets for making braille books, transcribing from prepared copy or original script: Inserts metal sheet into machine carriage. Depresses one or combination of keys to form braille letter. Depresses pedal that forces punches to impress on metal sheet combinations of dots that distinguish braille letters. If worker is blind, transcribes from recorded rather than manuscript copy. ● **GED:** R3, M1, L3 ● **SVP:** 3-6 mos ● **Academic:** Ed=N, Eng=G ● **Work Field:** 192 ● **MPSMS:** 567 ● **Aptitudes:** G3, V3, N4, S4, P3, Q3, K3, F3, M3, E4, C5 ● **Temperaments:** R, T ● **Physical:** Stg=L; Freq: R, H, I, N ● **Work Env:** Noise=N; ● **Salary:** 3 ● **Outlook:** 3

BRAILLE TYPIST (education) ● DOT #203.582-014 ● OES: 56017 ● Alternate titles: BRAILLE CODER; BRAILLE TRANSCRIBER. Operates braille typewriter to transcribe reading matter for use by the blind: Reads copy and operates braille typewriter to emboss specially treated paper with various combinations of dots that characterize braille alphabet, using braille code form. ● **GED:** R4, M1, L3 ● **SVP:** 6 mos-1 yr ● **Academic:** Ed=H, Eng=G ● **Work Field:** 192 ● **MPSMS:** 567 ● **Aptitudes:** G3, V3, N4, S3, P3, Q2, K3, F2, M3, E5, C5 ● **Temperaments:** R, T ● **Physical:** Stg=S; Freq: R, H, I, N ● **Work Env:** Noise=N; ● **Salary:** 2 ● **Outlook:** 3

CHECK WRITER (retail trade) ● DOT #219.382-010 ● OES: 59998 ● Imprints payment data on checks, records payment details on check register, using checkwriting machine, and compiles summaries of daily disbursements: Receives checks and vouchers authorized for payment, selects specified check register form, and inserts form into checkwriting-machine slot. Depresses buttons to transcribe payment data from voucher into machine. Inserts blank check into additional slot and presses bar to imprint details on check register and check. Removes check and repeats procedure to process batch of checks. Turns key to release signature plate and removes plate when processing checks totalling more than designated amount and sets such checks aside for handwritten signature by authorized personnel. Pulls lever to clear machine and print total on individual register. Compares register total with total on adding-machine tape to verify accuracy of register totals. Corrects errors or returns vouchers to other personnel for correction. Compiles daily summary of payment amounts by bank, merchandise, and expense categories and totals amounts, using adding machine. ● **GED:** R4, M4, L2 ● **SVP:** 1-3 mos ● **Academic:** Ed=N, Eng=S ● **Work Field:** 232 ● **MPSMS:** 892 ● **Aptitudes:** G4, V4, N3, S4, P4, Q2, K3, F3, M4, E5, C5 ● **Temperaments:** J, T ● **Physical:** Stg=S; Freq: R, H, I, N ● **Work Env:** Noise=N; ● **Salary:** 1 ● **Outlook:** 4

CLERK-TYPIST (clerical) ● DOT #203.362-010 ● OES: 55398 ● Compiles data and operates typewriter or computer in performance of routine clerical duties to maintain business records and reports: Types reports, business correspondence, application forms, shipping tickets, and other material. Files records and reports, posts information to records, sorts and distributes mail, answers telephone, and performs similar duties. May compute amounts, using adding or calculating machine. May type on or from specialized forms and be designated Guest-History Clerk (hotel & rest.); Storage-Receipt Poster (clerical). May compile reports and type prescription data on labels in hospital pharmacy and be designated Dispensary Clerk (medical ser.). May be designated: Collection-Card Clerk (clerical); Motor-Pool Clerk (clerical); Order Clerk (utilities); Policy-Issue Clerk (insurance). May oper-

ate telex machine to produce records and reports. ● **GED:** R3, M3, L3 ● **SVP:** 3-6 mos ● **Academic:** Ed=N, Eng=G ● **Work Field:** 231, 232 ● **MPSMS:** 891 ● **Aptitudes:** G3, V3, N3, S4, P3, Q2, K3, F3, M3, E5, C5 ● **Temperaments:** R ● **Physical:** Stg=S; Freq: R, H, I, T, G, N, A ● **Work Env:** Noise=N; ● **Salary:** 2 ● **Outlook:** 4

CRYPTOGRAPHIC-MACHINE OPERATOR (clerical) ● DOT #203.582-018 ● OES: 56017 ● Alternate titles: CODE CLERK; CRYPTOGRAPHIC TECHNICIAN. Operates cryptographic equipment to code, transmit, and decode secret messages for units of armed forces, law enforcement agencies, or business organizations: Selects required code according to instructions, using code book. Inserts specified code card into machine station to program encoding machine. Types plain text data on keyboard of automatic machine which encrypts and transmits message, or on semiautomatic machine which converts plain text into taped code for transmission via teletype machine. Feeds incoming tape into decoder device on semiautomatic machine and distributes decoded messages. Resolves garbled or undecipherable messages, using cryptographic procedures and equipment or requests retransmission of message. May operate teletype or teleprinter equipment to transmit messages. May operate radio to send and receive data. ● **GED:** R4, M2, L3 ● **SVP:** 6 mos-1 yr ● **Academic:** Ed=H, Eng=G ● **Work Field:** 231 ● **MPSMS:** 869 ● **Aptitudes:** G3, V3, N3, S4, P3, Q2, K3, F3, M4, E5, C5 ● **Temperaments:** J, T ● **Physical:** Stg=S; Freq: R, H, I, N ● **Work Env:** Noise=N; ● **Salary:** 5 ● **Outlook:** 3

FOOD CHECKER (hotel & rest.) ● DOT #211.482-014 ● OES: 56002 ● Scans loaded trays carried by patrons in hotel or restaurant cafeteria to compute bill: Operates machine similar to cash register to compute bill and presents check to patron for payment to CASHIER (clerical) II. May operate adding machine and present tape rather than check to customer for payment. May act as CASHIER (clerical) II. ● **GED:** R3, M2, L1 ● **SVP:** 1-3 mos ● **Academic:** Ed=N, Eng=S ● **Work Field:** 232 ● **MPSMS:** 899 ● **Aptitudes:** G3, V3, N3, S4, P4, Q3, K4, F3, M4, E5, C4 ● **Temperaments:** R ● **Physical:** Stg=S; Freq: R, H, I, N Occas: X ● **Work Env:** Noise=Q; ● **Salary:** 3 ● **Outlook:** 4

MAGNETIC-TAPE-COMPOSER OPERATOR (print. & pub.) ● DOT #203.382-018 ● OES: 56021 ● Alternate titles: COMPOSING-MACHINE OPERATOR. Operates magnetic-tape recording and typographic composing machine to prepare copy used for offset printing of forms, documents, advertisements, and other matter, following copy and layout instructions and using knowledge of typesetting and typing techniques: Clips copy and instructions to copy holder. Inserts blank tape cartridges on tape-station hubs and starts recorder to thread tape. Selects and attaches specified type-font element to typewriter carrier. Adjusts margins and other spacing mechanisms to set line justification. Types from marked copy, using electric typewriter that simultaneously produces proof copy and master tape. Types in composer control codes according to program sequence to allow change of type font and format. Proofreads copy. Makes corrections by strikeover on proof copy, automatically correcting identical material on master tape, or retypes corrected portions only, generating correction tape. Reference codes correction tape to error location in original copy and tape. Removes tape cartridges from recorder and installs cartridges, with correction tape, if any, into composer-output printer. Installs specified type font and sets escapement and vertical spacing controls. Keys in layout and composing codes on control panel, following program sequence. Inserts coated paper and starts composer. Operates composer controls in response to function-light indicators and changes type font and format as work progresses. Removes copy from composer, examines copy for errors, and makes necessary corrections. May specialize in operation of recorder or composer units. May operate varitype machine to set headline copy [VARITYPE OPERATOR (clerical)]. May prepare final camera-ready copy and layout, using waxing machine and drafting tools and equipment. ● **GED:** R4, M3, L3 ● **SVP:** 6 mos-1 yr ● **Academic:** Ed=N, Eng=G ● **Work Field:** 191 ● **MPSMS:** 567 ● **Aptitudes:** G3, V3, N4, S3, P2, Q2, K2, F3, M3, E4, C4 ● **Temperaments:** J, T ● **Physical:** Stg=S; Const: N Freq: R, H, I, D, A Occas: X ● **Work Env:** Noise=L; ● **Salary:** 2 ● **Outlook:** 3

NOTEREADER (clerical) ● DOT #203.582-078 ● OES: 55398 ● Operates typewriter to transcribe stenotyped notes of court proceedings, following standard formats for type of material transcribed: Reads work order to obtain information, such as type of case, case number, number of copies required, and spelling of participants' names. Reviews form books to ascertain format required for specified document, and adjusts typewriter settings for indentation, line spacing, and other style requirements. Operates typewriter to transcribe contractions and symbols of stenotyped text into standard language form. Proofreads typed copy to identify and correct errors and to verify format specifications. Copies typed documents, using copying machines. May use automatic or manual stenotype noteholder. ● **GED:** R3, M1, L3 ● **SVP:** 6 mos-1 yr ● **Academic:** Ed=H, Eng=G ● **Work Field:** 231 ● **MPSMS:** 891 ● **Aptitudes:** G3, V2, N4, S4, P3, Q2, K2, F3, M3, E5, C5 ● **Temperaments:** T ● **Physical:** Stg=S; Const: N, A Freq: R, H, I ● **Work Env:** Noise=N; ● **Salary:** 2 ● **Outlook:** 1

PHOTOCOMPOSITION-KEYBOARD OPERATOR (print. & pub.) ● DOT #203.582-046 ● OES: 56021 ● Operates keyboard of computer terminal equipped with video display screen to record data from manuscript for storage and retrieval into and from computer system for subsequent reproduction as printed matter: Reads instructions on worksheet to obtain codes which direct specific computer activity and depresses command keys on terminal keyboard to store or retrieve data. Reads manuscript and types on keyboard to record and store data into computer memory. Reads corrected proof sheet and depresses keys to retrieve specified portions of text for display on video screen. Observes screen to locate text to be corrected and types corrections. Maintains log of activities. If worker operates similar equipment to perforate paper tape used to activate photocomposing machine, see PHOTO-COMPOSING-PERFORATOR-MACHINE OPERATOR (print. & pub.). ● **GED:** R3, M2, L3 ● **SVP:** 3-6 mos ● **Academic:** Ed=N, Eng=G ● **Work Field:** 231, 281 ● **MPSMS:** 567 ● **Aptitudes:** G3, V3, N3, S3, P3, Q3, K3, F3, M3, E5, C5 ● **Temperaments:** T ● **Physical:** Stg=S; Const: N Freq: R, H, I, A ● **Work Env:** Noise=N; ● **Salary:** 3 ● **Outlook:** 3

PHOTOTYPESETTER OPERATOR (print. & pub.) ● DOT #650.582-022 ● OES: 92541 ● Alternate titles: PHOTOTYPESETTER. Operates keyboard of automatic phototypesetting machine to photographically print type matter onto film or strips of photosensitive paper to prepare positives or paper flats for making printing plates: Loads roll of photosensitive paper or film into camera magazine, positions magazine on machine, and pulls lever to open exposure slot. Starts typesetting mechanism. Turns dial to select lens and regulate gear that controls size (magnification or reproduction) of matrix letter, exposure, and light intensity, or moves selector levers, depresses keys or control buttons to select style and size of type. Depresses keys of keyboard to select foto mats for printing onto photopaper or film. Cuts photopaper with knife to separate exposed portion. Removes exposed photopaper or film from magazine for developing. May perform routine maintenance and adjustments on machine, using handtools. ● **GED:** R4, M2, L3 ● **SVP:** 6 mos-1 yr ● **Academic:** Ed=N, Eng=G ● **Work Field:** 191 ● **MPSMS:** 567 ● **Aptitudes:** G3, V3, N3, S3, P3, Q2, K3, F3, M3, E5, C4 ● **Temperaments:** J, T ● **Physical:** Stg=L; Freq: R, H, I, N, D, X Occas: S, K ● **Work Env:** Noise=L; Occas: O ● **Salary:** 2 ● **Outlook:** 3

PROOF-MACHINE OPERATOR (financial) ● DOT #217.382-010 ● OES: 56200 ● Alternate titles: PROOF CLERK; TRANSIT CLERK. Operates machines to encode, add, cancel, photocopy, and sort checks, drafts, and money orders for collection and to prove records of transactions: Places checks into machine that encodes amounts in magnetic ink, adds amounts, and cancels check. Enters amount of each check, using keyboard. Places encoded checks in sorter and activates machine to automatically microfilm, sort, and total checks according to bank drawn on. Observes panel light to note check machine cannot read. Reads check and enters data, such as amount, bank, or account number, using keyboard. Compares machine totals to listing recorded with batch of checks and rechecks each item if totals differ. Encodes correct amount or prepares transaction correction record, if error is found. Bundles sorted check with tape listing each item to prepare checks, drawn on other banks, for collection. May enter commands to transfer data from machine to computer. May operate separate photocopying machine. May clean equipment and replace printer ribbons, film, and tape. May manually sort and list items for proof or collection. May record, sort, and prove other transaction documents, such as deposit and withdrawal slips, using proof machine. ● **GED:** R3, M3, L3 ● **SVP:** 3-6 mos ● **Academic:** Ed=N, Eng=S ● **Work Field:** 232 ● **MPSMS:** 892, 894 ● **Aptitudes:** G3, V3, N3, S4, P4, Q2, K3, F3, M3, E5, C5 ● **Temperaments:** R, T ● **Physical:** Stg=S; Const: R, H, N Freq: I Occas: G, A ● **Work Env:** Noise=N; ● **Salary:** 2 ● **Outlook:** 3

PROOF-MACHINE-OPERATOR SUPERVISOR (financial) ● DOT #217.132-010 ● OES: 51002 ● Supervises and coordinates activities of workers engaged in operating machines to encode, add, cancel, photocopy, and sort checks, drafts, and money orders for collection, and to prove records of transactions: Locates check copies and proof records to answer inquiries from staff or customers. Prepares journal voucher to correct account when error is found. Requests equipment maintenance and repair from vendors. Participates in work of subordinates. May compile check processing cost information for management use in determining service fees. May supervise retention and retrieval of microfilmed checks [SUPERVISOR, FILES (clerical) 206.137-010]. Performs duties as described under SUPERVISOR (clerical) Master Title. ● **GED:** R4, M3, L4 ● **SVP:** 1-2 yrs ● **Academic:** Ed=H, Eng=G ● **Work Field:** 232 ● **MPSMS:** 892, 894 ● **Aptitudes:** G2, V2, N3, S4, P4, Q2, K3, F3, M3, E5, C5 ● **Temperaments:** D, P, T ● **Physical:** Stg=S; Freq: R, H, T, G, N Occas: I, A ● **Work Env:** Noise=N; ● **Salary:** 4 ● **Outlook:** 2

TRANSCRIBING-MACHINE OPERATOR (clerical) ● DOT #203.582-058 ● OES: 55302 ● Alternate titles: DICTATING-MACHINE TRANSCRIBER; DICTATING-MACHINE TYPIST. Operates typewriter or word processor/computer to transcribe letters, reports, or other recorded data heard through earphones of transcribing machine: Inserts cassette tape into cassette player or positions tape on machine spindle and threads tape through machine. Positions earphones on ears and presses buttons on transcribing machine to listen to recorded data. Turns dials to control volume, tone, and speed of voice reproduction. Depresses pedal to pause tape. Types message heard through earphones. Reads chart prepared by dictator to determine length of message and corrections to be made. May type unrecorded information, such as name, address, and date. May keep file of records. May receive and route callers [RECEPTIONIST (clerical) 237.367-038]. May be designated by subject matter transcribed as Legal Transcriber (clerical); Medical Transcriber (clerical). ● **GED:** R3, M1, L3 ● **SVP:** 6 mos-1 yr ● **Academic:** Ed=N, Eng=G ● **Work Field:** 231 ● **MPSMS:** 891 ● **Aptitudes:** G3, V3, N4, S4, P4, Q2, K2, F2, M3, E4, C5 ● **Temperaments:** R, T ● **Physical:** Stg=S; Const: I, G Freq: R, H, N ● **Work Env:** Noise=N; ● **Salary:** 2 ● **Outlook:** 4

TYPIST (clerical) ● DOT #203.582-066 ● OES: 55398 ● Operates typewriter or computer to type and revise documents: Compiles material to be typed. Reads instructions accompanying material, or follows verbal instructions from supervisor or person requesting document, to determine format desired, number of copies needed, priority, and other requirements. Types and revises material such as correspondence, reports, statistical tables, addresses, and forms, from rough draft, corrected copy, recorded voice dictation, or previous version displayed on screen, using typewriter or computer and word processing software. May verify totals on report forms, requisitions, or bills. May operate duplicating machine to reproduce copy. May be designated according to material typed, as Address-Change Clerk (insurance); Endorsement Clerk (insurance); Policy Writer (insurance); Record Clerk (hotel & rest.); Statistical Typist (clerical). May be designated: Application-Register Clerk (insurance); Filing Writer (insurance); Master-Sheet Clerk (insurance); Mortgage-Papers-Assignment-and-Assembly Clerk (insurance); Stencil Cutter (clerical); Tabular Typist (clerical); Title Clerk, Automobile (clerical). ● **GED:** R3, M2, L3 ● **SVP:** 1-3 mos ● **Academic:** Ed=N, Eng=G ● **Work Field:** 231 ● **MPSMS:** 891 ● **Aptitudes:** G3, V3, N4, S4, P4, Q2, K2, F2, M3, E5, C5 ● **Temperaments:** T ● **Physical:** Stg=S; Const: I, N Freq: H, A Occas: R, G ● **Work Env:** Noise=N; ● **Salary:** 2 ● **Outlook:** 4

VARITYPE OPERATOR (clerical) ● DOT #203.382-026 ● OES: 56021 ● Operates one or variety of electrically powered typewriting machines equipped with changeable type fonts to typeset master copies, such as stencils, direct plates, photo-offsets, and tracings, for reproduction of copies having printed appearance: Plans layout of page elements (illustrations, headlines, and text) from rough draft or specifications, using knowledge of design. Pastes up preprinted type and reproduction proofs on master layout, using paste and brush. Determines size and style of type, horizontal and vertical spacing, and margins, using knowledge of typesetting. Calculates anticipated dimensions of photo-offset copy to be enlarged or reduced, using arithmetic percentages. Attaches fonts to type holder. Attaches gear to platen to control spacing between lines. Moves lever to control spacing between characters. Sets stops to control right margin. Changes style and size of type

by pressing type-change key and turning font from reserve to typing position. May draw decorative or illustrative designs on copy. May lay out and rule forms and charts, using drafting tools. ● **GED:** R3, M2, L3 ● **SVP:** 6 mos-1 yr ● **Academic:** Ed=N, Eng=G ● **Work Field:** 231, 264 ● **MPSMS:** 891, 752 ● **Aptitudes:** G3, V3, N4, S3, P2, Q2, K2, F2, M3, E5, C5 ● **Temperaments:** J ● **Physical:** Stg=S; Freq: R, H, I, N, D, A ● **Work Env:** Noise=N; ● **Salary:** 2 ● **Outlook:** 3

WIRE-TRANSFER CLERK (financial) ● DOT #203.562-010 ● OES: 57198 ● Alternate titles: FUNDS TRANSFER CLERK. Transfers funds or securities and maintains records of transactions, using computer: Types, transmits, and receives funds transfer messages on computer terminal to or from other banks and Federal Reserve Bank. Records funds or securities transferred and disposition, using computer. May maintain file of customers requiring daily transfer of funds or securities. May verify or assign code number to telecommunication messages. ● **GED:** R3, M3, L3 ● **SVP:** 3-6 mos ● **Academic:** Ed=N, Eng=G ● **Work Field:** 232, 281 ● **MPSMS:** 894 ● **Aptitudes:** G3, V3, N3, S4, P4, Q2, K3, F3, M4, E5, C5 ● **Temperaments:** T ● **Physical:** Stg=S; Const: N Freq: I Occas: R, H, T, G, A ● **Work Env:** Noise=N; ● **Salary:** 1 ● **Outlook:** 3

WORD PROCESSING MACHINE OPERATOR (clerical) ● DOT #203.382-030 ● OES: 55398 ● Operates word processing equipment to compile, type, revise, combine, edit, print, and store documents: Compiles material to be typed, following written or oral instructions.

Reads instructions accompanying material, or follows verbal instructions from supervisor or person requesting document, to determine format and content required. Enters commands, flips switches, and presses buttons to establish spacing, margins, type size, style, and color, and other parameters, using computer and word processing software or other word processing equipment. Types, revises, and combines material such as correspondence, reports, records, forms, minutes of meetings, scientific or technical material, numerical data, and tabular information, from rough draft, corrected copy, recorded voice dictation, or previous version displayed on screen. Checks completed document on screen for spelling errors, using software. Proofreads and edits document for grammar, spelling, punctuation, and format. Corrects errors. Stores completed document in machine memory or on data storage medium, such as disk. Enters commands to print document. May load paper in printer and change printer ribbon, print wheel, or fluid cartridges. May keep record of work performed. May input data for revision or editing, using data entry device other than keyboard, such as optical scanner. Variations in means by which tasks are accomplished result from brand of computer, printer, other word processing equipment, and software used. ● **GED:** R3, M2, L3 ● **SVP:** 6 mos-1 yr ● **Academic:** Ed=N, Eng=G ● **Work Field:** 231 ● **MPSMS:** 891 ● **Aptitudes:** G3, V3, N4, S4, P4, Q2, K2, F3, M3, E5, C5 ● **Temperaments:** T ● **Physical:** Stg=S; Const: I Freq: R, H, G, N, A Occas: S, O ● **Work Env:** Noise=N; ● **Salary:** 2 ● **Outlook:** 4

Business Detail

07

Clerical Handling

07.07

Workers in this group perform clerical duties that require little special training or skill. Workers routinely file, sort, copy, route, or deliver things like letters, packages, or messages. Most large businesses, industries, and government agencies employ these workers.

✓ What kind of work would you do?

Your work activities would depend upon your specific job. For example, you might:

- wrap, inspect, weigh, and affix postage to packages and record COD and insurance information.
- pick up and deliver messages in an office or office building.
- put printed pages together in sequence.
- keep office workers supplied with pencils, paper, and other materials.

✓ What skills and abilities do you need for this kind of work?

To do this kind of work, you must be able to:

- perform clerical tasks that do not require special skills.
- follow directions.
- perform work that is routine.
- read or copy information correctly.
- work well with others.

The above statements may not apply to every job in this group.

✓ How do you know if you would like or could learn to do this kind of work?

The following questions may give you clues about yourself as you consider this group of jobs.

- Have you kept attendance records for a class or club? Do you enjoy this type of work?
- Have you helped to address and stamp newsletters?
- Have you maintained a checkbook for yourself or a club? Can you copy and compute numbers accurately?

✓ How can you prepare for and enter this kind of work?

Occupations in this group usually require education and/or training extending from a short demonstration to over three months, depending upon the specific kind of work. Basic arithmetic and English skills are required for many of these jobs. On-the-job training is provided by most employers. However, high school commercial or business courses are helpful in getting beginning jobs. Workers entering federal government jobs usually are required to take civil service examinations.

✓ What else should you consider about these jobs?

Both full- and part-time jobs are usually available for workers in this group. There are often opportunities for advancement or transfer, both within a company or to other employers.

If you think you would like to do this kind of work, look at the job titles listed on the following pages.

GOE: 07.07.01
Filing

FILE CLERK I (clerical) ● DOT #206.387-034 ● OES: 55321 ● Files records in alphabetical or numerical order, or according to subject matter or other system: Reads incoming material and sorts according to file system. Places cards, forms, microfiche, or other material in storage receptacle, such as file cabinet, drawer, or box. Locates and removes files upon request. Keeps records of material removed, stamps material received, traces missing files, and types indexing information on folders. May verify accuracy of material to be filed. May enter information on records. May examine microfilm and microfiche for legibility, using microfilm and microfiche viewers. May color-code material to be filed to reduce filing errors. May be designated according to subject matter filed, such as Change-of-Address Clerk (clerical); or according to material filed, such as File Clerk, Correspondence (clerical). ● **GED:** R3, M1, L2 ● **SVP:** 1-3 mos ● **Academic:** Ed=N, Eng=S ● **Work Field:** 231 ● **MPSMS:** 891 ● **Aptitudes:** G3, V3, N4, S4, P4, Q2, K3, F3, M3, E5, C4 ● **Temperaments:** R, T ● **Physical:** Stg=L; Freq: R, H, I, N, A Occas: S, O, G, X ● **Work Env:** Noise=N; ● **Salary:** 1 ● **Outlook:** 4

GOE: 07.07.02
Sorting & Distribution

ADDRESSER (clerical) ● DOT #209.587-010 ● OES: 59998 ● Alternate titles: ADDRESSING CLERK; ENVELOPE ADDRESSER. Addresses by hand or typewriter, envelopes, cards, advertising literature, packages, and similar items for mailing. May sort mail. ● **GED:** R2, M1, L2 ● **SVP:** 2-30 days ● **Academic:** Ed=N, Eng=N ● **Work Field:** 231 ● **MPSMS:** 891 ● **Aptitudes:** G4, V4, N4, S4, P4, Q3, K4, F4, M3, E5, C5 ● **Temperaments:** R ● **Physical:** Stg=S; Const: N Freq: R, H, I ● **Work Env:** Noise=N; ● **Salary:** 1 ● **Outlook:** 2

AUCTION ASSISTANT (retail trade) ● DOT #294.667-010 ● OES: 59998 ● Alternate titles: LOT CALLER. Assists AUCTIONEER (retail trade; wholesale tr.) at auction by tagging and arranging articles for sale, calling out lot and item numbers, and holding or displaying articles being auctioned: Receives and stores incoming merchandise to be auctioned. Writes assigned record numbers on tags and wires tags to articles. Arranges articles into group lots, according to similarity of type of merchandise, such as household goods, art objects, jewelry, and furniture. Assigns lot and item numbers to grouped articles and records numbers on tags and in record book. Calls out lot and item numbers of article being auctioned and holds or otherwise displays article during bidding. Assists final bidders in locating purchased items. ● **GED:** R2, M1, L2 ● **SVP:** 2-30 days ● **Academic:** Ed=N, Eng=S ● **Work Field:** 221 ● **MPSMS:** 881, 882 ● **Aptitudes:** G4, V4, N4, S4, P4, Q4, K4, F4, M4, E5, C4 ● **Temperaments:** P, R ● **Physical:** Stg=L; Freq: R, H, I, T, G, N, A Occas: C, B, S, D, X ● **Work Env:** Noise=L; ● **Salary:** 2 ● **Outlook:** 3

CHECKER I (clerical) ● DOT #222.687-010 ● OES: 58017 ● Verifies quantities, quality, condition, value, and type of articles purchased, sold, or produced against records or reports. May sort data or items into predetermined sequence or groups. May record items verified. May be designated according to type of establishment as Warehouse Checker (clerical). ● **GED:** R2, M2, L2 ● **SVP:** 2-30 days ● **Academic:** Ed=N, Eng=S ● **Work Field:** 221 ● **MPSMS:** 898 ● **Aptitudes:** G3, V4, N3, S4, P4, Q3, K4, F4, M4, E5, C5 ● **Temperaments:** R, T ● **Physical:** Stg=L; Freq: R, H, I, N ● **Work Env:** Noise=N; ● **Salary:** 1 ● **Outlook:** 3

DELIVERER, OUTSIDE (clerical) ● DOT #230.663-010 ● OES: 57311 ● Alternate titles: COURIER; MESSENGER. Delivers messages, telegrams, documents, packages, and other items to business establishments and private homes, traveling on foot or by bicycle, motorcycle, automobile, or public conveyance. May keep log of items received and delivered. May obtain receipts or payment for articles delivered. May service vehicle driven, such as checking fluid levels and replenishing fuel. May be designated according to item delivered, as Telegram Messenger (tel. & tel.). ● **GED:** R2, M1, L2 ● **SVP:** 2-30 days ● **Academic:** Ed=N, Eng=S ● **Work Field:** 013 ● **MPSMS:** 899 ● **Aptitudes:** G4, V4, N4, S4, P4, Q4, K4, F4, M4, E4, C5 ● **Temperaments:** R ● **Physical:** Stg=L; Freq: R, H, F, D, V Occas: I, T, G, N, A ● **Work Env:** Noise=N; Freq: W ● **Salary:** 1 ● **Outlook:** 3

DIRECT-MAIL CLERK (clerical) ● DOT #209.587-018 ● OES: 57302 ● Mails letters, merchandise samples, and promotional literature to prospective customers. Receives requests for samples and prepares required shipping slips. Maintains files and records of customer transactions. ● **GED:** R3, M1, L2 ● **SVP:** 3-6 mos ● **Academic:** Ed=N, Eng=N ● **Work Field:** 231 ● **MPSMS:** 891 ● **Aptitudes:** G3, V3, N3, S5, P4, Q3, K4, F4, M4, E5, C5 ● **Temperaments:** R ● **Physical:** Stg=L; Freq: R, H, I, N ● **Work Env:** Noise=Q; ● **Salary:** 1 ● **Outlook:** 3

DISTRIBUTING CLERK (clerical) ● DOT #222.587-018 ● OES: 58028 ● Alternate titles: PACKING-AND-SHIPPING CLERK; PUBLICATIONS-DISTRIBUTION CLERK. Assembles and routes various types of printed material: Assembles specified number of forms, manuals, or circulars for each addressee as indicated by distribution tables or instructions. Wraps, ties, or places material in envelopes, boxes, or other containers. Stamps, types, or writes addresses on packaged materials. Forwards packages by mail, messenger, or through message center. Keeps records of materials sent. May requisition and store materials to maintain stock [STOCK CLERK (clerical)]. ● **GED:** R3, M2, L3 ● **SVP:** 1-3 mos ● **Academic:** Ed=N, Eng=S ● **Work Field:** 231 ● **MPSMS:** 896 ● **Aptitudes:** G3, V3, N4, S4, P3, Q3, K4, F3, M3, E5, C4 ● **Temperaments:** V ● **Physical:** Stg=L; Freq: R, H, I ● **Work Env:** Noise=Q; ● **Salary:** 3 ● **Outlook:** 3

MAILROOM SUPERVISOR (print. & pub.) ● DOT #222.137-022 ● OES: 51002 ● Supervises and coordinates activities of workers engaged in wrapping and addressing printed material, such as periodicals, books, and newspapers, for mailing and dispatching: Revises local, state, and out-of-state mailing lists. Inspects work stations to ensure that material is wrapped and addressed in time to meet scheduled departure of buses, trains, and airlines. Records distribution of material to subscribers and dealers in city, suburban, home, and country divisions, working from shipping and mailing reports. Maintains file of bus, train, and airline schedules and transfer points, and baggage, express, air, or postal mailing rates. Performs other duties as described under SUPERVISOR (clerical) Master Title. ● **GED:** R4, M2, L3 ● **SVP:** 2-4 yrs ● **Academic:** Ed=N, Eng=G ● **Work Field:** 221 ● **MPSMS:** 480, 859 ● **Aptitudes:** G3, V3, N3, S4, P3, Q3, K4, F4, M4, E5, C5 ● **Temperaments:** D, J, P, V ● **Physical:** Stg=L; Freq: R, H, T, G, N, A Occas: I ● **Work Env:** Noise=Q; ● **Salary:** 4 ● **Outlook:** 2

MONEY COUNTER (amuse. & rec.) ● DOT #211.467-014 ● OES: 49023 ● Alternate titles: MONEY-ROOM TELLER. Counts, sorts, and issues money to PARIMUTUEL-TICKET SELLERS (amuse. & rec.), and PARIMUTUEL-TICKET CASHIERS (amuse. & rec.) to conduct daily transactions at racetrack. Observes totaling board for official race results and issues money to cashiering stations to pay holders of winning tickets. Compares workers' reports of cash collected and paid out to verify accuracy of transactions. ● **GED:** R3, M3, L2 ● **SVP:** 1-3 mos ● **Academic:** Ed=N, Eng=S ● **Work Field:** 232 ● **MPSMS:** 899 ● **Aptitudes:** G3, V3, N3, S4, P3, Q2, K3, F3, M4, E5, C5 ● **Temperaments:** J, T ● **Physical:** Stg=L; Const: R, H, I, N Freq: F ● **Work Env:** Noise=Q; ● **Salary:** 2 ● **Outlook:** 3

PROCESS SERVER (business ser.) ● DOT #249.367-062 ● OES: 59998 ● Serves court orders and processes, such as summonses and subpoenas: Receives papers to be served from magistrate, court clerk, or attorney. Locates person to be served, using telephone directories, state, county, and city records, or public utility records, and delivers document. Records time and place of delivery. May deliver general messages and documents between courts and attorneys. ● **GED:** R3,

M2, L3 ● **SVP:** 1-3 mos ● **Academic:** Ed=N, Eng=G ● **Work Field:** 282 ● **MPSMS:** 959 ● **Aptitudes:** G3, V3, N4, S5, P4, Q3, K4, F4, M4, E5, C5 ● **Temperaments:** P ● **Physical:** Stg=L; Freq: R, H, I, T, G, N ● **Work Env:** Noise=N; Freq: W ● **Salary:** 4 ● **Outlook:** 3

ROUTER (clerical) ● DOT #222.587-038 ● OES: 58098 ● Alternate titles: DISPATCHER; MARKER, DELIVERY; ROUTING CLERK. Stamps, stencils, letters, or tags packages, boxes, or lots of merchandise to indicate delivery routes. Reads addresses on articles and determines route, using standard charts. ● **GED:** R2, M1, L2 ● **SVP:** 2-30 days ● **Academic:** Ed=N, Eng=S ● **Work Field:** 231 ● **MPSMS:** 898 ● **Aptitudes:** G4, V4, N4, S4, P3, Q3, K3, F3, M3, E5, C5 ● **Temperaments:** R ● **Physical:** Stg=L; Freq: R, H, N Occas: I ● **Work Env:** Noise=Q; ● **Salary:** 3 ● **Outlook:** 3

ROUTING CLERK (clerical) ● DOT #222.687-022 ● OES: 58028 ● Alternate titles: ROUTE CLERK; ROUTER. Sorts bundles, boxes, or lots of articles for delivery: Reads delivery or route numbers marked on articles or delivery slips, or determines locations of addresses indicated on delivery slips, using charts. Places or stacks articles in bins designated according to route, driver, or type. May be designated according to work station as Conveyor Belt Package Sorter (retail trade). May sort sacks of mail and be known as Mail Sorter (r.r. trans.). ● **GED:** R2, M2, L2 ● **SVP:** 2-30 days ● **Academic:** Ed=N, Eng=S ● **Work Field:** 221 ● **MPSMS:** 898 ● **Aptitudes:** G4, V4, N4, S4, P4, Q4, K3, F4, M3, E5, C5 ● **Temperaments:** R ● **Physical:** Stg=L; Freq: R, H, I, N Occas: A ● **Work Env:** Noise=Q; ● **Salary:** 2 ● **Outlook:** 3

SORTER (clerical) ● DOT #209.687-022 ● OES: 59998 ● Sorts data, such as forms, correspondence, checks, receipts, bills, and sales tickets, into specified sequence or grouping, such as by address, code, quantity, and class, for such purposes as filing, mailing, copying, or preparing records. May be designated according to work performed as Bill Sorter (clerical); Sales-Slip Sorter (clerical). ● **GED:** R2, M1, L2 ● **SVP:** 1-3 mos ● **Academic:** Ed=N, Eng=N ● **Work Field:** 231 ● **MPSMS:** 890 ● **Aptitudes:** G4, V4, N4, S4, P3, Q3, K4, F3, M3, E5, C4 ● **Temperaments:** R ● **Physical:** Stg=S; Freq: R, H, I, N ● **Work Env:** Noise=N; ● **Salary:** 2 ● **Outlook:** 3

SUPERVISOR, ADVERTISING-MATERIAL DISTRIBUTORS (business ser.) ● DOT #230.137-010 ● OES: 41002 ● Supervises and coordinates activities of crew of workers engaged in distributing sample merchandise, handbills, or coupons: Issues advertising material to ADVERTISING-MATERIAL DISTRIBUTORS (any industry) and instructs them in methods of distribution. Assigns workers to specified routes and tours area to ensure coverage of assigned territory. Records information, such as area covered, material distributed, and working hours. May hire crewmembers. Performs other duties as described under SUPERVISOR (clerical) Master Title. ● **GED:** R4, M2, L4 ● **SVP:** 1-2 yrs ● **Academic:** Ed=N, Eng=G ● **Work Field:** 011 ● **MPSMS:** 896 ● **Aptitudes:** G3, V3, N3, S4, P4, Q3, K4, F4, M4, E5, C5 ● **Temperaments:** D, P, V ● **Physical:** Stg=L; Freq: R, H, I, T, G, N ● **Work Env:** Noise=N; Occas: W ● **Salary:** 4 ● **Outlook:** 2

TELEPHONE-DIRECTORY DELIVERER (business ser.) ● DOT #230.667-014 ● OES: 98998 ● Alternate titles: PHONE-BOOK DELIVERER. Delivers telephone directories to residences and business establishments, on foot: Receives supply of directories from TELEPHONE-DIRECTORY-DISTRIBUTOR DRIVER (business ser.) or from other individual at central distribution point or from vehicle parked in distribution area, places books on handtruck or in sacks or other containers, and delivers books, following verbal instructions or address list. May pick up outdated directories for return for salvage purposes. ● **GED:** R1, M1, L1 ● **SVP:** 1 day ● **Academic:** Ed=N, Eng=N ● **Work Field:** 011 ● **MPSMS:** 899 ● **Aptitudes:** G4, V4, N5, S4, P5, Q4, K4, F4, M4, E5, C5 ● **Temperaments:** R ● **Physical:** Stg=H; Freq: C, S, R, H Occas: G, N ● **Work Env:** Noise=Q; Freq: W ● **Salary:** 1 ● **Outlook:** 3

GOE: 07.07.03
General Clerical Work

CLERK, GENERAL (clerical) ● DOT #209.562-010 ● OES: 55347 ● Alternate titles: OFFICE CLERK, ROUTINE. Performs any combination of following and similar clerical duties requiring limited knowledge of systems or procedures: Writes, types, or enters information into computer, using keyboard, to prepare correspondence, bills, statements, receipts, checks, or other documents, copying information from one record to another. Proofreads records or forms. Counts, weighs, or measures material. Sorts and files records. Receives money from customers and deposits money in bank. Addresses envelopes or packages by hand or with typewriter or addressograph machine. Stuffs envelopes by hand or with envelope stuffing machine. Answers telephone, conveys messages, and runs errands. Stamps, sorts, and distributes mail. Stamps or numbers forms by hand or machine. Photocopies documents, using photocopier. ● **GED:** R3, M2, L3 ● **SVP:** 1-3 mos ● **Academic:** Ed=N, Eng=G ● **Work Field:** 231 ● **MPSMS:** 891 ● **Aptitudes:** G3, V3, N3, S4, P4, Q3, K4, F3, M4, E5, C5 ● **Temperaments:** T ● **Physical:** Stg=L; Freq: R, H, I, N Occas: T, G, A ● **Work Env:** Noise=N; ● **Salary:** 2 ● **Outlook:** 3

COIN-MACHINE COLLECTOR (business ser.) ● DOT #292.687-010 ● OES: 59998 ● Alternate titles: COIN-BOX COLLECTOR; PAY-STATION COLLECTOR. Collects coins or coin boxes from parking meters or telephone pay stations: Unlocks telephone faceplate and removes box containing money. Inserts empty box and locks faceplate. Tags boxes to identify pay stations. Reports malfunctioning telephones or parking meters to repair department. Delivers boxes to central depot for machine counting, tabulating, and customer payment. May count coins and compute amount due subscriber, according to difference between minimum guaranteed rate and total cash in box. May pay subscriber percentage refund. May adjust or repair parking meters, using handtools. May keep records of collections, balances due, and refunds. May be designated according to type of equipment involved as Parking-Meter-Coin Collector (business ser.); Telephone Coin-Box Collector (tel. & tel.). ● **GED:** R2, M1, L2 ● **SVP:** 2-30 days ● **Academic:** Ed=N, Eng=N ● **Work Field:** 221 ● **MPSMS:** 899 ● **Aptitudes:** G3, V4, N4, S4, P4, Q4, K4, F4, M3, E3, C5 ● **Temperaments:** R ● **Physical:** Stg=L; Freq: R, H Occas: I, T, G, N ● **Work Env:** Noise=Q; Freq: W ● **Salary:** 2 ● **Outlook:** 3

OFFICE HELPER (clerical) ● DOT #239.567-010 ● OES: 57311 ● Performs any combination of following duties in business office of commercial or industrial establishment: Furnishes workers with clerical supplies. Opens, sorts, and distributes incoming mail, and collects, seals, and stamps outgoing mail. Delivers oral or written messages. Collects and distributes paperwork, such as records or timecards, from one department to another. Marks, tabulates, and files articles and records. May use office equipment, such as envelope-sealing machine, letter opener, record shaver, stamping machine, and transcribing machine. May deliver items to other business establishments [DELIVERER, OUTSIDE (clerical) 230.663-010]. May specialize in delivering mail, messages, documents, and packages between departments of establishment and be designated Messenger, Office (clerical). May deliver stock certificates and bonds within and between stock brokerage offices and be designated Runner (financial). ● **GED:** R2, M2, L2 ● **SVP:** 2-30 days ● **Academic:** Ed=N, Eng=G ● **Work Field:** 231, 011, 221 ● **MPSMS:** 890, 899 ● **Aptitudes:** G3, V4, N4, S4, P4, Q3, K4, F3, M3, E5, C5 ● **Temperaments:** V ● **Physical:** Stg=L; Freq: R, H, I, N Occas: S, T, G ● **Work Env:** Noise=N; ● **Salary:** 1 ● **Outlook:** 3

Selling 08

An interest in bringing others to a point of view by personal persuasion, using sales and promotional techniques. You can satisfy this interest in a variety of sales jobs. You may enjoy selling technical products or services. Perhaps you prefer a selling job requiring less background knowledge. You may work in stores, sales offices, or in customers' homes. You may wish to buy and sell products to make a profit. You can also satisfy this interest in legal work, business negotiations, advertising, and related fields found under other categories in the Guide.

Sales Technology

Workers in this group sell products such as industrial machinery, data processing equipment, and pharmaceuticals; services such as industrial shipping, insurance, and advertising. They advise customers of the capabilities, uses, and other important features of these products and services, and help them choose those best suited to their needs. They work for manufacturers, wholesalers, and insurance, financial, and business service institutions. Also included in this group are workers who buy products, materials, securities, and properties for resale. Some work for themselves.

✓ What kind of work would you do?

Your work activities would depend upon your specific job. For example, you might:

- call on oil companies to sell them oil field equipment.
- call on businesses to sell them radio and television time.
- call on businesses to sell them computers.
- advise people about the type and amount of insurance they should buy.
- buy clothing and accessories for stocking a department store.
- sell professional supplies and equipment to dentists, doctors, or engineers.
- buy the grain harvest from farmers for resale to processing plants.

✓ What skills and abilities do you need for this kind of work?

To do this kind of work, you must be able to:

- understand the principles of electronics, chemistry, economics, or communications, as they relate to the products you sell or buy.

- organize your own activities to make the best use of your time and effort.
- express yourself well when talking to potential buyers or sellers, to discuss features of the products or services involved and convince the other person of both your knowledge and integrity.
- use arithmetic in computing the mark-up on merchandise, cost of installing equipment or machinery in a plant, or quoting special rates for varying amounts of materials purchased.
- maintain enthusiasm and interest throughout all conferences with buyers or sellers.
- keep accurate records of contacts, sales, and purchases.

✓ How do you know if you would like or could learn to do this kind of work?

The following questions may give you clues about yourself as you consider this group of jobs.

- Have you taken business or sales related courses? Did you like the courses?
- Have you attended auctions? Can you estimate, in advance, the selling prices of the items?
- Have you bought items to sell? Did you make a profit on your sales? Do you enjoy doing this type of activity?
- Have you made speeches or been in debates? Do you enjoy presenting ideas to people?
- Have you worked as a salesperson in a store? Do you enjoy sales work?

✓ How can you prepare for and enter this kind of work?

Occupations in this group usually require education and/or training extending from six months to over ten years, depending upon the specific kind of work. A common way to prepare is to obtain a two-

or four-year degree with a major in business administration, marketing, or a similar field. For jobs involving technical sales, a degree in a field such as engineering, chemistry, or physics is helpful. Sometimes workers in other sales groups advance after obtaining related work experience.

Most employers give new employees formal and informal training. This training may last up to one year. Workers learn the policies, procedures, and details involved.

Jobs in real estate or insurance may require a state or local license. Workers usually must take a written test to obtain these licenses.

✓ *What else should you consider about these jobs?*

Most of these jobs require meeting new people. Some jobs involve frequent travel. Many workers are under pressure as they make decisions which affect sales or investments involving large sums of money.

Some workers receive a salary, others work on a commission. A commission is usually a percent of the selling price of an item. Sometimes a worker may receive a combination of salary and commission. Some workers in this group own their own businesses.

If you think you would like to do this kind of work, look at the job titles listed below.

■ ■ ■

GOE: 08.01.01
Technical Sales

PHARMACEUTICAL DETAILER (wholesale tr.) ● DOT #262.157-010 ● OES: 49998 ● Alternate titles: DETAILER, PHARMACEUTICALS. Promotes use of and sells ethical drugs and other pharmaceutical products to physicians, DENTISTS (medical ser.) 072.101-010, hospitals, and retail and wholesale drug establishments, utilizing knowledge of medical practices, drugs, and medicines: Calls on customers, informs customer of new drugs, and explains characteristics and clinical studies conducted with drug. Discusses dosage, use, and effect of new drugs and medicinal preparations. Gives samples of new drugs to customer. Promotes and sells other drugs and medicines manufactured by company. May sell and take orders for pharmaceutical supply items from persons contacted. ● **GED:** R5, M3, L5 ● **SVP:** 2-4 yrs ● **Academic:** Ed=B, Eng=G ● **Work Field:** 292 ● **MPSMS:** 493 ● **Aptitudes:** G2, V2, N3, S3, P3, Q3, K4, F4, M4, E5, C4 ● **Temperaments:** I, J, P ● **Physical:** Stg=L; Freq: R, H, T, G Occas: I, N, X ● **Work Env:** Noise=Q; ● **Salary:** 4 ● **Outlook:** 4

SALES REPRESENTATIVE, AIRCRAFT (retail trade) ● DOT #273.253-010 ● OES: 49998 ● Sells aircraft to individuals and to business and industrial establishments: Discusses suitability of different types of aircraft to meet customer's requirements. Demonstrates aircraft in flight, stressing maneuverability, safety factors, and ease of handling. Verifies customer's credit rating. Prepares contracts for plane storage and maintenance service. Performs other duties as described under SALES REPRESENTATIVE (retail trade; wholesale tr.) Master Title. May appraise aircraft traded-in on new plane. May rent aircraft to customers [AIRPLANE-CHARTER CLERK (air trans.)]. May pilot aircraft during demonstrations and be required to have private pilot's license issued by Federal Aviation Administration. ● **GED:** R5, M3, L4 ● **SVP:** 1-2 yrs ● **Academic:** Ed=N, Eng=G ● **Work Field:** 292 ● **MPSMS:** 592 ● **Aptitudes:** G2, V2, N3, S2, P3, Q3, K3, F4, M3, E3, C4 ● **Temperaments:** I, J, P ● **Physical:** Stg=L; Freq: R, H, T, G, N, F, D, A, X, V Occas: I ● **Work Env:** Noise=L; Occas: W ● **Salary:** 4 ● **Outlook:** 2

SALES REPRESENTATIVE, CHEMICALS AND DRUGS (wholesale tr.) ● DOT #262.357-010 ● OES: 49998 ● Sells chemical or pharmaceutical products, such as explosives, acids, industrial or agricultural chemicals, medicines, and drugs, performing duties as described under SALES REPRESENTATIVE (retail trade; wholesale tr.) Master Title. ● **GED:** R4, M3, L4 ● **SVP:** 6 mos-1 yr ● **Academic:** Ed=A, Eng=G ● **Work Field:** 292 ● **MPSMS:** 490 ● **Aptitudes:** G3, V3, N3, S4, P4, Q3, K4, F4, M4, E5, C5 ● **Temperaments:** I, J, P ● **Physical:** Stg=L; Freq: T, G Occas: R, H, I, N ● **Work Env:** Noise=N; ● **Salary:** 4 ● **Outlook:** 4

SALES REPRESENTATIVE, COMMUNICATION EQUIPMENT (wholesale tr.) ● DOT #271.257-010 ● OES: 49998 ● Sells communication equipment, such as telephone and telegraph apparatus, intercommunication equipment, and radio broadcasting equipment, utilizing knowledge of electronics. Analyzes customer's communication needs and recommends equipment needed. Performs other duties as described under SALES REPRESENTATIVE (retail trade; wholesale tr.) Master Title. May train personnel of business establishments in use of equipment. ● **GED:** R4, M4, L4 ● **SVP:** 1-2 yrs ● **Academic:** Ed=N, Eng=G ● **Work Field:** 292 ● **MPSMS:** 586 ● **Aptitudes:** G2, V2, N2, S2, P3, Q3, K4, F4, M4, E5, C4 ● **Temperaments:** I, J, P ● **Physical:** Stg=L; Freq: R, H, T, G, N Occas: I, X ● **Work Env:** Noise=N; ● **Salary:** 3 ● **Outlook:** 4

SALES REPRESENTATIVE, COMPUTERS AND EDP SYSTEMS (wholesale tr.) ● DOT #275.257-010 ● OES: 49998 ● Sells computers and electronic data processing systems to business or industrial establishments, performing duties as described under SALES REPRESENTATIVE (retail trade; wholesale tr.) Master Title. Analyzes customer's needs and recommends computer system that best meets customer's requirements. Emphasizes salable features, such as flexibility, cost, capacity, and economy of operation. Consults with staff engineers on highly technical problems. ● **GED:** R5, M4, L4 ● **SVP:** 1-2 yrs ● **Academic:** Ed=A, Eng=G ● **Work Field:** 292 ● **MPSMS:** 571 ● **Aptitudes:** G2, V2, N3, S3, P4, Q3, K4, F4, M4, E5, C5 ● **Temperaments:** I, J, P ● **Physical:** Stg=L; Freq: R, H, I, T, G, N ● **Work Env:** Noise=N; ● **Salary:** 4 ● **Outlook:** 4

SALES REPRESENTATIVE, DENTAL AND MEDICAL EQUIPMENT AND SUPPLIES (wholesale tr.) ● DOT #276.257-010 ● OES: 49998 ● Sells medical and dental equipment and supplies, except drugs and medicines, to doctors, dentists, hospitals, medical schools, and retail establishments: Studies data describing new products to develop sales approach. Compiles data on equipment and supplies preferred by customers. Advises customers of equipment for given need based on technical knowledge of products. Provides customers with advice in such areas as office layout, legal and insurance regulations, cost analysis, and collection methods to develop goodwill and promote sales. Performs other duties as described under SALES REPRESENTATIVE (retail trade; wholesale tr.) Master Title. May be designated according to type of equipment and supplies sold as Sales Representative, Dental Equipment And Supplies (wholesale tr.). May sell orthopedic appliances, trusses, and artificial limbs and be designated Sales Representative, Prosthetic And Orthotic Appliances (wholesale tr.). May sell services of dental laboratory and be designated Sales Representative, Dental Prosthetics (wholesale tr.). ● **GED:** R4, M3, L4 ● **SVP:** 1-2 yrs ● **Academic:** Ed=B, Eng=G ● **Work Field:** 292 ● **MPSMS:** 604 ● **Aptitudes:** G2, V2, N3, S3, P3, Q3, K4, F4, M4, E5, C4 ● **Temperaments:** I, J, P ● **Physical:** Stg=L; Freq: T, G Occas: R, H, I, N, X ● **Work Env:** Noise=Q; ● **Salary:** 4 ● **Outlook:** 4

SALES REPRESENTATIVE, ELECTRONICS PARTS (wholesale tr.) ● DOT #271.357-010 ● OES: 49998 ● Sells radio, television, and other electronics parts to establishments, such as appliance stores, dealers, and repair shops or electronics and aircraft manufacturing firms, performing duties as described under SALES REPRESENTATIVE (retail trade; wholesale tr.) Master Title. ● **GED:** R4, M3, L4 ● **SVP:** 1-2 yrs ● **Academic:** Ed=N, Eng=G ● **Work Field:** 292 ● **MPSMS:** 587 ● **Aptitudes:** G2, V2, N3, S3, P3, Q3, K4, F4, M4, E5, C5 ● **Temperaments:** I, J, P ● **Physical:** Stg=L; Freq: T, G Occas: R, H, I, N ● **Work Env:** Noise=N; ● **Salary:** 3 ● **Outlook:** 4

SALES REPRESENTATIVE, GRAPHIC ART (business ser.) ● DOT #254.251-010 ● OES: 49998 ● Sells graphic art, such as layout, illustration, and photography, to advertising agencies and industrial organizations for use in advertising and illustration: Plans and sketches layouts to meet customer needs. Advises customer in methods of composing layouts, utilizing knowledge of photographic and illustrative art and printing terminology. Informs customer of types of artwork available by providing samples. Computes job costs. Delivers advertising or illustration proofs to customer for approval. May write copy as part of layout. ● **GED:** R5, M3, L4 ● **SVP:** 2-4 yrs ● **Academic:** Ed=H, Eng=G ● **Work Field:** 292, 262 ● **MPSMS:** 752 ● **Aptitudes:** G2, V2, N3, S2, P3, Q3, K3, F3, M4, E5, C2 ● **Temperaments:** F, I, P, V ● **Physical:** Stg=L; Freq: R, H, T, G, N Occas: I, A, X ● **Work Env:** Noise=N; ● **Salary:** 3 ● **Outlook:** 3

SALES REPRESENTATIVE, SIGNS AND DISPLAYS (fabrication, nec) ● DOT #254.257-010 ● OES: 49998 ● Solicits and draws up contracts for signs and displays: Calls on advertisers and sales promotion people to obtain information concerning prospects for current advertising and sales promotion. Discusses advantages of and suggests ideas for signs and displays. Submits rendering or drawing of proposed sign or display to prospect. Draws up contract covering arrangements for designing, fabricating, erecting, and maintaining sign or display, depending on type of job and customer's wishes. May confer with architect in determining type of sign. May select and arrange for lease of site [SALES AGENT, REAL ESTATE (real estate)]. ● **GED:** R4, M3, L4 ● **SVP:** 1-2 yrs ● **Academic:** Ed=H, Eng=G ● **Work Field:** 292 ● **MPSMS:** 896 ● **Aptitudes:** G2, V2, N3, S2, P2, Q3, K4, F4, M4, E5, C3 ● **Temperaments:** I, J, P ● **Physical:** Stg=L; Freq: T, G, N, F, D, A, X, V Occas: R, H, I ● **Work Env:** Noise=N; ● **Salary:** 3 ● **Outlook:** 3

GOE: 08.01.02
Intangible Sales

ESTATE PLANNER (insurance) ● DOT #186.167-010 ● OES: 21998 ● Reviews assets and liabilities of estate to determine that insurance is adequate for financial protection of estate: Studies legal instruments, such as wills, trusts, business agreements, life insurance policies, and government benefits to estimate value and expenses of estate. Computes expenses, taxes, and debts to determine value of adjusted gross estate, using knowledge of accounting and tax laws. Prepares and discusses insurance program with client that will provide maximum financial security for family and protect investments. Suggests purchase of additional or new life insurance when analysis of estate indicates need for meeting cash demands at death. Discusses legal instruments with family attorney if study indicates need for change. May be required to hold state license. ● **GED:** R5, M4, L5 ● **SVP:** 2-4 yrs ● **Academic:** Ed=H, Eng=G ● **Work Field:** 292, 211 ● **MPSMS:** 895 ● **Aptitudes:** G1, V1, N2, S4, P4, Q3, K4, F4, M4, E5, C5 ● **Temperaments:** J, P ● **Physical:** Stg=S; Freq: R, H, I, T, G, N Occas: A ● **Work Env:** Noise=N; ● **Salary:** 4 ● **Outlook:** 3

PLACER (insurance) ● DOT #239.267-010 ● OES: 43002 ● Advises clients of broker (independent agent) in selecting casualty, life, or property insurance: Discusses advantages and disadvantages of various policies to help client make choice. Selects company that offers type of coverage requested by client to underwrite policy. Contacts underwriter and submits forms to obtain binder coverage. Contacts company to determine if policy was issued or rejected. ● **GED:** R4, M3, L4 ● **SVP:** 6 mos-1 yr ● **Academic:** Ed=N, Eng=G ● **Work Field:** 282 ● **MPSMS:** 895 ● **Aptitudes:** G3, V2, N3, S4, P4, Q2, K4, F4, M4, E5, C5 ●

Temperaments: J, T ● **Physical:** Stg=S; Freq: R, H, T, G, N Occas: I ● **Work Env:** Noise=Q; ● **Salary:** 4 ● **Outlook:** 4

SALES AGENT, INSURANCE (insurance) ● DOT #250.257-010 ● OES: 43002 ● Alternate titles: INSURANCE AGENT. Sells insurance to new and current clients: Compiles lists of prospective clients to provide leads for additional business. Contacts prospective clients and explains features and merits of policies offered, recommending amount and type of coverage based on analysis of prospect's circumstances, and utilizing persuasive sales techniques. Calculates and quotes premium rates for recommended policies, using calculator and rate books. Calls on policyholders to deliver and explain policy, to suggest additions or changes in insurance program, or to make changes in beneficiaries. May collect premiums from policyholders and keep record of payments. Must hold license issued by state. May be designated according to type of insurance sold as Sales Agent, Casualty Insurance (insurance); Sales Agent, Fire Insurance (insurance); Sales Agent, Life Insurance (insurance); Sales Agent, Marine Insurance (insurance). May work independently selling variety of insurance, such as life, fire, casualty, and marine, for many companies and be designated Insurance Broker (insurance). May work independently selling for one company and be designated General Agent (insurance). ● **GED:** R4, M3, L4 ● **SVP:** 1-2 yrs ● **Academic:** Ed=H, Eng=G ● **Work Field:** 292 ● **MPSMS:** 895 ● **Aptitudes:** G2, V2, N2, S5, P5, Q2, K4, F4, M4, E5, C5 ● **Temperaments:** I, J, P ● **Physical:** Stg=L; Const: T, G Freq: R, H, I, N ● **Work Env:** Noise=Q; ● **Salary:** 3 ● **Outlook:** 4

SALES REPRESENTATIVE, ADVERTISING (print. & pub.) ● DOT #254.357-014 ● OES: 49998 ● Alternate titles: ADVERTISING-SALES REPRESENTATIVE; ADVERTISING SOLICITOR. Sells classified and display advertising space for publication: Prepares list of prospects from leads in other papers and from old accounts. Obtains pertinent information concerning prospect's past and current advertising for use in sales presentation. Visits advertisers to point out advantages of own publication and exhibits prepared layouts with mats and copy with headings. May collect payments due. Usually designated by type of advertising sold as Sales Representative, Classified Advertising (print. & pub.); Sales Representative, Display Advertising (print. & pub.). ● **GED:** R4, M3, L4 ● **SVP:** 1-2 yrs ● **Academic:** Ed=H, Eng=G ● **Work Field:** 292 ● **MPSMS:** 882, 896 ● **Aptitudes:** G2, V2, N3, S2, P3, Q4, K4, F4, M4, E5, C4 ● **Temperaments:** I, J, P ● **Physical:** Stg=L; Freq: T, G, N Occas: R, H, I, X ● **Work Env:** Noise=N; ● **Salary:** 4 ● **Outlook:** 3

SALES REPRESENTATIVE, DATA PROCESSING SERVICES (business ser.) ● DOT #251.157-014 ● OES: 49998 ● Contacts representatives of government, business, and industrial organizations to solicit business for data processing establishment: Calls on prospective clients to explain types of services provided by establishment, such as inventory control, payroll processing, data conversion, sales analysis, and financial reporting. Analyzes data processing requirements of prospective client and draws up prospectus of data processing plan designed specifically to serve client's needs. Consults SYSTEMS ANALYST (profess. & kin.) 030.167-014 and COMPUTER SYSTEMS HARDWARE ANALYST (profess. & kin.) 033.167-010 employed by data processing establishment to secure information concerning methodology for solving unusual problems. Quotes prices for services outlined in prospectus. Revises or expands prospectus to meet client's needs. Writes order and schedules initiation of services. Periodically confers with clients and establishment personnel to verify satisfaction with service or to resolve complaints. ● **GED:** R5, M5, L5 ● **SVP:** 2-4 yrs ● **Academic:** Ed=A, Eng=G ● **Work Field:** 292 ● **MPSMS:** 893 ● **Aptitudes:** G2, V2, N2, S2, P3, Q2, K4, F4, M4, E5, C5 ● **Temperaments:** I, J, P ● **Physical:** Stg=L; Freq: T, G, N, A Occas: R, H ● **Work Env:** Noise=N; ● **Salary:** 4 ● **Outlook:** 4

SALES REPRESENTATIVE, EDUCATION COURSES (education) ● DOT #259.257-010 ● OES: 49998 ● Solicits applications for enrollment in technical, commercial, and industrial schools: Contacts prospects, explains courses offered by school, and quotes fees. Advises prospective students on selection of courses based on their education and vocational objectives. Compiles registration information. May accept registration fees or tuition payments. May be designated according to type of school as Sales Representative, Business Courses (education); Sales Representative, Correspondence Courses (education). ● **GED:** R4, M3, L4 ● **SVP:** 6 mos-1 yr ● **Academic:** Ed=H, Eng=G ● **Work Field:** 292, 282 ● **MPSMS:** 931 ● **Aptitudes:** G2, V2, N3,

S3, P4, Q3, K4, F4, M4, E5, C5 ● **Temperaments:** I, J, P ● **Physical:** Stg=L; Freq: T, G Occas: R, H, I, N ● **Work Env:** Noise=N; ● **Salary:** 3 ● **Outlook:** 2

SALES REPRESENTATIVE, FINANCIAL SERVICES (financial) ● DOT #250.257-022 ● OES: 43014 ● Sells financial services to customers of financial institution: Develops prospects from current commercial customers, referral leads, and other sources. Contacts prospective customers to present information on available services, such as deposit accounts, lines-of-credit, sales or inventory financing, cash management, or investment services. Determines customers' financial services needs and prepares proposals to sell services. Reviews business trends and advises customers regarding expected fluctuations. Attends sales and trade meetings to develop new business prospects. May make presentations on financial services to groups to attract new clients. May prepare forms or agreement to complete sale. May evaluate costs and revenue of agreements to determine if they are profitable to continue. May sell services, such as check processing and collecting, record keeping and reporting, trust, investment, or safekeeping services, or products such as travelers checks, to other financial institutions. May solicit businesses to participate in consumer credit card program. ● **GED:** R5, M4, L5 ● **SVP:** 2-4 yrs ● **Academic:** Ed=A, Eng=G ● **Work Field:** 292 ● **MPSMS:** 894 ● **Aptitudes:** G2, V2, N2, S4, P4, Q3, K4, F4, M4, E5, C5 ● **Temperaments:** I, J, P ● **Physical:** Stg=L; Const: T, G Freq: R, H, N Occas: I ● **Work Env:** Noise=Q; ● **Salary:** 4 ● **Outlook:** 4

SALES REPRESENTATIVE, HOTEL SERVICES (hotel & rest.) ● DOT #259.157-014 ● OES: 49998 ● Contacts representatives of government, business, associations, and social groups to solicit business for hotel, motel, or resort: Reviews information on sales meetings, conventions, training classes, overnight travel, and other functions held by organization members to select prospective customers for hotel services. Calls on prospects to solicit business, analyzes requirements of function, outlines available hotel facilities and services offered, and quotes prices. Verifies reservations by letter, or draws up contract and obtains signatures. Confers with customer and hotel department heads to plan function details, such as space requirements, publicity, time schedule, food service, and decorations. May serve as convention advisor or coordinator during function to minimize confusion and resolve problems, such as space adjustment and need for additional equipment. May select and release hotel publicity. May prepare and mail advance brochures to prospective customers. ● **GED:** R4, M3, L4 ● **SVP:** 2-4 yrs ● **Academic:** Ed=H, Eng=G ● **Work Field:** 292 ● **MPSMS:** 902 ● **Aptitudes:** G2, V2, N3, S4, P3, Q3, K4, F4, M4, E5, C5 ● **Temperaments:** D, I, J, P ● **Physical:** Stg=S; Freq: T, G Occas: R, H, I, N ● **Work Env:** Noise=N; ● **Salary:** 3 ● **Outlook:** 3

SALES REPRESENTATIVE, PRINTING (wholesale tr.) ● DOT #254.357-018 ● OES: 49998 ● Visits business establishments to solicit business for printing firm: Interviews purchasing personnel and quotes prices on printed material from schedule or secures price from ESTIMATOR, PRINTING (print. & pub.). Explains technical phases, such as type size and style, paper stock, binding materials, and various methods of reproduction. Contacts prospects, following leads submitted by management, established customers, or developed through other sources. May prepare sales promotional letters to be sent to prospective customers. May submit formal bids on large orders of printed matter. ● **GED:** R4, M3, L4 ● **SVP:** 6 mos-1 yr ● **Academic:** Ed=H, Eng=G ● **Work Field:** 292 ● **MPSMS:** 882 ● **Aptitudes:** G3, V3, N3, S4, P3, Q3, K4, F4, M4, E5, C4 ● **Temperaments:** I, J, P ● **Physical:** Stg=L; Freq: T, G Occas: R, H, I, N, X ● **Work Env:** Noise=N; ● **Salary:** 3 ● **Outlook:** 3

SALES REPRESENTATIVE, PUBLIC UTILITIES (tel. & tel.) ● DOT #253.357-010 ● OES: 49998 ● Alternate titles: COMMERCIAL SERVICE REPRESENTATIVE. Solicits prospective and existing commercial and residential clients to promote increased or economical use of public utilities, such as gas, electric power, telephone, and telegraph service: Inspects installations in existing establishments or reviews plans for new construction to determine potential need or necessity for extension of utility service. Advises customers in most economical use of utility to promote energy conservation and reduce cost. Quotes approximate rates, installation charges, and operating costs and explains company services. Writes construction requisitions and service applications, conforming to needs and requests of consumer. May investigate customers' complaints concerning bills. May be designated by type of utility sold as Sales Representative, Electric Service (utilities); Sales Representative, Gas Service (utilities); Sales Representative, Telephone and Telegraph Services (tel. & tel.) or by area in which utility is sold as Sales Representative, Rural Power (utilities). ● **GED:** R4, M3, L4 ● **SVP:** 1-2 yrs ● **Academic:** Ed=H, Eng=G ● **Work Field:** 292 ● **MPSMS:** 860, 870 ● **Aptitudes:** G2, V2, N3, S3, P3, Q3, K4, F4, M4, E5, C5 ● **Temperaments:** I, J, P ● **Physical:** Stg=L; Freq: R, H, T, G Occas: I, N, F, A ● **Work Env:** Noise=N; ● **Salary:** 4 ● **Outlook:** 3

SALES REPRESENTATIVE, RADIO AND TELEVISION TIME (radio-tv broad.) ● DOT #259.357-018 ● OES: 49998 ● Alternate titles: ACCOUNT EXECUTIVE. Contacts prospective customers to sell radio and television time or captioning services for broadcasting station, network, or cable television franchise: Calls on prospects and presents outlines of various programs or commercial announcements. Discusses current popularity of various types of programs, such as news, drama, and variety. Drives auto vehicle to prospective customer's location. May arrange for and accompany prospect to commercial taping sessions. May prepare promotional plans, sales literature, and sales contracts, using computer. ● **GED:** R4, M3, L4 ● **SVP:** 1-2 yrs ● **Academic:** Ed=H, Eng=G ● **Work Field:** 292 ● **MPSMS:** 863, 864, 869 ● **Aptitudes:** G2, V2, N3, S3, P3, Q3, K4, F4, M4, E5, C5 ● **Temperaments:** I, J, P ● **Physical:** Stg=L; Const: T, G Occas: R, H, I, N, F, D, A, V ● **Work Env:** Noise=N; ● **Salary:** 4 ● **Outlook:** 3

SALES REPRESENTATIVE, SECURITY SYSTEMS (business ser.) ● DOT #259.257-022 ● OES: 49998 ● Sells burglar, fire, and medical emergency alarm systems and security monitoring services to individuals and businesses: Contacts prospective customers to explain security monitoring services and to demonstrate alarm systems. Examines customer's home or business and analyzes customer's requirements to recommend security system to meet customer's needs. Explains operation of security system after installation. Performs other duties as described under SALES REPRESENTATIVE (retail trade; wholesale tr.) Master Title. ● **GED:** R4, M3, L4 ● **SVP:** 6 mos-1 yr ● **Academic:** Ed=H, Eng=G ● **Work Field:** 292, 211 ● **MPSMS:** 586, 951 ● **Aptitudes:** G2, V2, N3, S3, P5, Q3, K4, F4, M4, E5, C5 ● **Temperaments:** I, J, P ● **Physical:** Stg=M; Freq: T, G, N Occas: C, S, K, O, R, H ● **Work Env:** Noise=N; ● **Salary:** 2 ● **Outlook:** 3

SALES REPRESENTATIVE, SHIPPING SERVICES (motor trans.) ● DOT #252.357-014 ● OES: 49998 ● Solicits shipper's account for parcel-delivery firm: Visits management of new businesses and those with change of ownership to promote new business and obtain contracts for service. Explains shipping rates and regulations regarding wrapping, size, handling, and weight of parcels. Completes service contract form. Reviews shipper's accounts to identify problems, such as overdue accounts, proposed changes in pickup and delivery schedules, failure of shipper to follow parcel wrapping and handling requirements, and frequency and type of shipper's claims. Calls on shipper's representatives to discuss and resolve problems. ● **GED:** R3, M3, L3 ● **SVP:** 6 mos-1 yr ● **Academic:** Ed=N, Eng=G ● **Work Field:** 292 ● **MPSMS:** 853 ● **Aptitudes:** G3, V3, N3, S3, P4, Q3, K4, F4, M4, E4, C5 ● **Temperaments:** I, J, P ● **Physical:** Stg=L; Freq: R, H, T, G, N Occas: I ● **Work Env:** Noise=N; Occas: W ● **Salary:** 3 ● **Outlook:** 2

SALES REPRESENTATIVE, TELEPHONE SERVICES (tel. & tel.) ● DOT #253.257-010 ● OES: 49998 ● Alternate titles: COMMERCIAL REPRESENTATIVE. Sells telephone services to business accounts: Contacts and visits commercial customers to review telephone service. Analyzes communication needs of business establishments, using knowledge of type of business, available telephone equipment, and traffic studies. Recommends services, such as additional telephone instruments and lines, switchboard systems, dial- and key-telephone systems, private-branch exchanges, and speaker telephones. Quotes rates for equipment and writes up orders. Explains equipment usage, using brochures and demonstration equipment. May specialize in selling services to a particular industry. ● **GED:** R5, M3, L4 ● **SVP:** 1-2 yrs ● **Academic:** Ed=H, Eng=G ● **Work Field:** 292 ● **MPSMS:** 861 ● **Aptitudes:** G2, V2, N3, S3, P3, Q3, K4, F4, M4, E5, C5 ● **Temperaments:** I, J, P ● **Physical:** Stg=L; Freq: T, G Occas: R, H, I, N ● **Work Env:** Noise=N; ● **Salary:** 3 ● **Outlook:** 4

SPECIAL AGENT, GROUP INSURANCE (insurance) ● DOT #169.167-050 ● OES: 43002 ● Explains group insurance programs to promote sale of insurance to prospective clients and establishes bookkeeping system for insurance plan: Explains types of insurance coverage, such as health, accident, life, or liability, and accounting documentation required by company, as requested by SALES AGENT, INSURANCE (insurance). Plans and oversees incorporation of insurance program into a company's bookkeeping system. Establishes client's method of payment. May install accounting systems and resolve system problems. ● **GED:** R5, M3, L5 ● **SVP:** 2-4 yrs ● **Academic:** Ed=H, Eng=G ● **Work Field:** 292, 282 ● **MPSMS:** 895 ● **Aptitudes:** G2, V2, N3, S4, P3, Q2, K4, F4, M4, E5, C5 ● **Temperaments:** D, I, J, P ● **Physical:** Stg=S; Freq: R, H, I, T, G, N ● **Work Env:** Noise=N; ● **Salary:** 4 ● **Outlook:** 3

TRAFFIC AGENT (air trans.) ● DOT #252.257-010 ● OES: 49998 ● Alternate titles: SALES REPRESENTATIVE. Solicits freight business from industrial and commercial firms and passenger-travel business from travel agencies, schools, clubs, and other organizations: Calls on prospective shippers to explain advantages of using company facilities. Quotes tariffs, rates, and train schedules. Explains available routes, load limits, and special equipment available, and offers suggestions in method of loading, crating, and handling freight. Calls on travel agents, schools, clubs, and other organizations to explain available accommodations offered by company. Quotes fares, schedules, and available itineraries offered to groups by company. Speaks to members of groups and organizations and exhibits travel movies showing points of interest along routes to stimulate interest in travel. Distributes descriptive pamphlets. Acts as liaison between shipper and carrier to obtain information for settling complaints. May specialize in soliciting freight or passenger contracts or may travel from community to community to solicit freight and passenger patronage and be designated Freight-Traffic Agent (air trans.; motor trans.; r.r. trans.; water trans.); Passenger Traffic Agent (air trans.; motor trans.; r.r. trans.; water trans.); Traveling-Freight-And-Passenger Agent (air trans.; motor trans.; r.r. trans.; water trans.). ● **GED:** R5, M3, L4 ● **SVP:** 2-4 yrs ● **Academic:** Ed=N, Eng=G ● **Work Field:** 292 ● **MPSMS:** 850 ● **Aptitudes:** G2, V2, N3, S4, P3, Q2, K4, F4, M4, E5, C5 ● **Temperaments:** I, J, P ● **Physical:** Stg=L; Freq: T, G Occas: R, H, I, N ● **Work Env:** Noise=N; ● **Salary:** 2 ● **Outlook:** 3

GOE: 08.01.03
Purchasing & Sales

BUSINESS-OPPORTUNITY-AND-PROPERTY-INVESTMENT BROKER (business ser.) ● DOT #189.157-010 ● OES: 21998 ● Alternate titles: BUSINESS INVESTOR; PROPERTY INVESTOR. Buys and sells business enterprises or investment property on speculative or commission basis: Reviews trade journals, business opportunity advertisements, or other publications to ascertain business enterprises or investment property up for sale. Investigates financial rating of business, customer appeal for type of merchandise, and desirability of location for type of business, or condition and location of investment property. Estimates cost of improving business or property and potential market value to determine resale value. Purchases business or property on speculative basis or on commission basis for client. Repairs, remodels, or redecorates building; purchases competitive merchandise; and installs sound management practices to improve value of property or business acquisition. Contacts prospective clients through newspaper advertisements or mailing lists. Describes to client selling points of property or business, emphasizing such factors as improvements made and profit potential. Sells business or property to buyer and makes arrangements for escrow and title change. Must be licensed by state. ● **GED:** R5, M4, L4 ● **SVP:** 2-4 yrs ● **Academic:** Ed=N, Eng=G ● **Work Field:** 292 ● **MPSMS:** 890 ● **Aptitudes:** G2, V2, N3, S3, P4, Q3, K4, F4, M4, E5, C5 ● **Temperaments:** D, I, J, P ● **Physical:** Stg=L; Freq: T, G Occas: R, H, I, N ● **Work Env:** Noise=N; Occas: W ● **Salary:** 5 ● **Outlook:** 3

BUYER (profess. & kin.) ● DOT #162.157-018 ● OES: 21302 ● Alternate titles: BROKER. Purchases merchandise or commodities for resale: Inspects and grades or appraises agricultural commodities, durable goods, apparel, furniture, livestock, or other merchandise offered for sale to determine value and yield. Selects and orders merchandise from showings by manufacturing representatives, growers, or other sellers, or purchases merchandise on open market for cash, basing se-

lection on nature of clientele, or demand for specific commodity, merchandise, or other property, utilizing knowledge of various articles of commerce and experience as buyer. Transports purchases or contacts carriers to arrange transportation of purchases. Authorizes payment of invoices or return of merchandise. May negotiate contracts for severance of agricultural or forestry products from land. May conduct staff meetings with sales personnel to introduce new merchandise. May price items for resale. May be required to be licensed by state. May be identified according to type of commodities, merchandise, or goods purchased. ● **GED:** R4, M3, L4 ● **SVP:** 1-2 yrs ● **Academic:** Ed=H, Eng=G ● **Work Field:** 292, 211 ● **MPSMS:** 880 ● **Aptitudes:** G2, V2, N2, S4, P4, Q3, K4, F4, M4, E5, C5 ● **Temperaments:** D, I, J, P, V ● **Physical:** Stg=L; Freq: R, H, I, T, G, N Occas: E ● **Work Env:** Noise=N; ● **Salary:** 4 ● **Outlook:** 4

BUYER, ASSISTANT (retail trade) ● DOT #162.157-022 ● OES: 21302 ● Performs following duties in connection with purchase and sale of merchandise to aid BUYER (profess. & kin.): Verifies quantity and quality of stock received from manufacturer. Authorizes payment of invoices or return of shipment. Approves advertising copy for newspaper. Gives MARKERS (retail trade; wholesale tr.) information, such as price mark-ups or mark-downs, manufacturer number, season code, and style number to print on price tickets. Inspects exchanged or refunded merchandise. May sell merchandise to become familiar with customers' attitudes, preferences, and purchasing problems. ● **GED:** R4, M3, L3 ● **SVP:** 1-2 yrs ● **Academic:** Ed=H, Eng=S ● **Work Field:** 292 ● **MPSMS:** 881 ● **Aptitudes:** G2, V2, N3, S3, P3, Q3, K4, F4, M4, E5, C3 ● **Temperaments:** J, P ● **Physical:** Stg=L; Freq: R, H, I, T, G Occas: N, A ● **Work Env:** Noise=N; ● **Salary:** 3 ● **Outlook:** 3

COMMISSION AGENT, AGRICULTURAL PRODUCE (wholesale tr.) ● DOT #260.357-010 ● OES: 49998 ● Alternate titles: BROKER, AGRICULTURAL PRODUCE. Sells bulk shipments of agricultural produce on commission basis to WHOLESALERS (wholesale tr.) I or other buyers for growers or shippers. Deducts expenses and commission from payment received from sale of produce, and remits balance to shipper. May call on wholesalers' customers, such as restaurants and institutional food services, to promote sales and provide nutritional and other information about products. May be required to be licensed and bonded by state. ● **GED:** R4, M3, L4 ● **SVP:** 1-2 yrs ● **Academic:** Ed=N, Eng=G ● **Work Field:** 292 ● **MPSMS:** 300, 882 ● **Aptitudes:** G2, V2, N2, S4, P4, Q3, K4, F4, M4, E5, C5 ● **Temperaments:** I, J, P ● **Physical:** Stg=S; Const: T, G Occas: R, H, I, N ● **Work Env:** Noise=Q; ● **Salary:** 4 ● **Outlook:** 3

COMPARISON SHOPPER (retail trade) ● DOT #296.367-014 ● OES: 49998 ● Compares prices, packaging, physical characteristics, and styles of merchandise in competing stores: Visits stores to observe details of merchandise and gather information that will be valuable to employer in setting prices and determining buying policies. Verifies complaints of customers on price of merchandise by shopping at designated store to ascertain same quality and style for specified price. Prepares reports of findings. May check with BUYER (profess. & kin.) to verify that advertised merchandise will be available for customer purchase, and that merchandise, price, and sales dates are accurately described in advertising copy and illustration. May purchase merchandise in various locations for quality comparison tests. ● **GED:** R4, M2, L3 ● **SVP:** 1-3 mos ● **Academic:** Ed=N, Eng=G ● **Work Field:** 211, 292 ● **MPSMS:** 889 ● **Aptitudes:** G3, V3, N4, S5, P3, Q3, K5, F4, M4, E5, C3 ● **Temperaments:** J ● **Physical:** Stg=L; Freq: R, H, I, T, G, N, D, A, X ● **Work Env:** Noise=N; ● **Salary:** 3 ● **Outlook:** 3

FOREIGN BANKNOTE TELLER-TRADER (financial) ● DOT #211.362-014 ● OES: 53102 ● Buys and sells foreign currencies and drafts and sells travelers' checks, according to daily international exchange rates, working at counter in foreign exchange office: Questions patrons to determine type of currency or draft desired or offered for sale. Quotes unit exchange rate, following daily international rate sheet or computer display. Computes exchange value including fee for transaction, using calculator, and counts out currency. Sells foreign and domestic travelers' checks. Prepares sales slips and records transactions in daily log. Gives information to patrons about foreign currency regulations. Prepares daily inventory of currency, drafts, and travelers' checks. Computes amounts on logsheets and reconciles totals with inventory report. ● **GED:** R4, M4, L4 ● **SVP:** 6 mos-1 yr ● **Academic:** Ed=H, Eng=G ● **Work Field:** 232 ● **MPSMS:** 894 ● **Aptitudes:** G2, V3, N2, S4, P3, Q2, K2, F2, M3, E5, C4 ● **Temperaments:** P, T ●

Physical: Stg=S; Freq: R, H, I, T, G, N Occas: X ● **Work Env:** Noise=N; ● **Salary:** 5 ● **Outlook:** 3

PAWNBROKER (retail trade) ● DOT #191.157-010 ● OES: 49998 ● Estimates pawn or pledge value of articles, such as jewelry, cameras, and musical instruments, and lends money to customer: Examines article to determine condition and worth. Weighs gold or silver articles on coin scales or employs acid tests to determine carat content and purity to verify value of articles. Inspects diamonds and other gems for flaws and color, using loupe (magnifying glass). Assigns pledge value to article based on knowledge of values or listing of wholesale prices. Rejects articles in unsatisfactory condition or having no pledge value. Issues pledge tickets and keeps record of loans. Computes interest when pledges are redeemed or extended. Sells unredeemed pledged items. May examine customer's identification and record thumbprints for police reports. May testify in court proceedings involving stolen merchandise. ● **GED:** R4, M4, L4 ● **SVP:** 1-2 yrs ● **Academic:** Ed=N,

Eng=S ● **Work Field:** 211 ● **MPSMS:** 894 ● **Aptitudes:** G3, V3, N3, S4, P3, Q3, K4, F4, M4, E5, C3 ● **Temperaments:** J, P, V ● **Physical:** Stg=L; Freq: R, H, I, T, G, N, D, A Occas: E, X ● **Work Env:** Noise=N; Occas: T ● **Salary:** 4 ● **Outlook:** 1

SALES REPRESENTATIVE, LIVESTOCK (wholesale tr.) ● DOT #260.257-010 ● OES: 49998 ● Sells cattle, horses, hogs, and other livestock on commission to packing houses, farmers, or other purchasers: Contacts prospective buyers to persuade them to purchase livestock. Reviews current market information and inspects livestock to determine their value. Informs buyers of market conditions, care, and breeding of livestock. Attends livestock meetings to keep informed of livestock trends and developments. ● **GED:** R4, M3, L4 ● **SVP:** 6 mos-1 yr ● **Academic:** Ed=N, Eng=G ● **Work Field:** 292, 282 ● **MPSMS:** 320 ● **Aptitudes:** G2, V2, N3, S4, P4, Q3, K4, F4, M4, E5, C5 ● **Temperaments:** I, J, P ● **Physical:** Stg=L; Freq: T, G Occas: R, H, I, N ● **Work Env:** Noise=N; ● **Salary:** 3 ● **Outlook:** 2

Selling

08

General Sales

08.02

Workers in this group sell, demonstrate, and solicit orders for products and services of many kinds. They are employed by retail and wholesale firms, manufacturers and distributors, business services, and nonprofit organizations. Some spend all their time in a single location, such as a department store or automobile agency. Others call on businesses or individuals to sell products or services, or follow up on earlier sales.

✓ What kind of work would you do?

Your work activities would depend upon your specific job. For example, you might:

- demonstrate and sell radios and television sets in a department store.
- sell hardware supplies to stock stores.
- help customers find what they want in a jewelry store.
- sell pets and pet supplies in a pet store.
- call people on the telephone to sell them products.
- arrange and conduct demonstration parties in people's homes.
- drive a truck on a set route and sell products to people at their homes.
- call on people in their homes to sell pest control services.
- train or supervise workers in a sales department and keep records of merchandise on hand.

✓ What skills and abilities do you need for this kind of work?

To do this kind of work, you must be able to:

- understand and explain company policies about such things as deferred payment plans, financing charges, returned goods privileges, or service guarantees.

- use arithmetic to total costs of purchase, make change, compute percentages, fill out order and sales forms, and draw up time purchase contracts.
- treat customers with courtesy and respect, even in difficult situations.
- talk easily and persuasively to other people, using language that they'll understand.
- help customers to make up their minds about purchases by suggesting appropriate products.

✓ How do you know if you would like or could learn to do this kind of work?

The following questions may give you clues about yourself as you consider this group of jobs.

- Have you had courses in sales, bookkeeping, or business math? Did you like these courses? Do you have an ability to work with numbers?
- Have you sold items door-to-door? Have you collected money or items for a charity? Do you like to meet people this way?
- Have you given oral reports in front of a group? Do you express your ideas easily to strangers?
- Have you worked in a military PX or cafeteria? Do you enjoy selling items to people?

✓ How can you prepare for and enter this kind of work?

Occupations in this group usually require education and/or training extending from three months to over two years, depending upon the specific kind of work. Most employers require applicants to have a high school education or its equal. Courses in selling or retailing are helpful. Many high schools, junior colleges, and community colleges offer courses and programs in this field. Some schools provide work-study programs in which students work part-time as well as attend classes. Selling experience during vacations is also helpful in preparing for this kind of work.

Employers usually provide on-the-job training to teach new workers about the company policies and the products or services to be sold. These training programs may last from one week to three months. Some workers are required to have extra skills such as driving a truck or playing a musical instrument. Other workers are required to make minor repairs or adjustments on equipment they sell.

Some jobs in this group are supervisory or management positions to which workers with sales experience may be promoted.

✓ What else should you consider about these jobs?

Many retail sales jobs require workers to vary working hours. Some businesses are open to the public on Sundays, holidays, or evenings. Selling is usually done at the customer's convenience.

Some workers are paid by the hour. Others are paid according to how much they sell. However, some workers receive earnings from a combination of these ways.

If you think you would like to do this kind of work, look at the job titles listed on the following pages.

■ ■ ■

GOE: 08.02.01
Wholesale

MANUFACTURER'S REPRESENTATIVE (wholesale tr.) ● DOT #279.157-010 ● OES: 49998 ● Alternate titles: MANUFACTURER'S AGENT. Sells single, allied, diversified, or multiline products to WHOLESALERS (wholesale tr.) I 185.167-070 or other customers for one or more manufacturers on commission basis: Contacts manufacturers and arranges to sell their products. Calls on regular or prospective customers to solicit orders. Demonstrates products and points out salable features. Answers questions concerning products, such as price, credit terms, and durability. Completes sales contracts or forms to record required sales information. May forward orders to manufacturer. May promote products at trade shows and conferences. ● **GED:** R4, M3, L4 ● **SVP:** 1-2 yrs ● **Academic:** Ed=H, Eng=G ● **Work Field:** 292 ● **MPSMS:** 882 ● **Aptitudes:** G2, V2, N3, S4, P3, Q3, K4, F4, M4, E5, C4 ● **Temperaments:** I, J, P ● **Physical:** Stg=L; Freq: R, H, I, T, G, N Occas: F, D, A, X, V ● **Work Env:** Noise=N; ● **Salary:** 3 ● **Outlook:** 3

SALES-PROMOTION REPRESENTATIVE (wholesale tr.) ● DOT #269.357-018 ● OES: 49998 ● Persuades customers to use sales promotion display items of wholesale commodity distributor: Visits retail establishments, such as department stores, taverns, supermarkets, and clubs to persuade customers to use display items to promote sale of company products. Delivers promotion items, such as posters, glasses, napkins, and samples of product, and arranges display of items in customer's establishment. May take sales order from customer. ● **GED:** R4, M2, L3 ● **SVP:** 1-3 mos ● **Academic:** Ed=N, Eng=G ● **Work Field:** 292 ● **MPSMS:** 882 ● **Aptitudes:** G3, V3, N4, S4, P3, Q3, K3, F3, M3, E4, C4 ● **Temperaments:** I, J, P ● **Physical:** Stg=L; Freq: R, H, I, T, G Occas: N, X ● **Work Env:** Noise=N; ● **Salary:** 4 ● **Outlook:** 3

SALES REPRESENTATIVE, ANIMAL-FEED PRODUCTS (wholesale tr.) ● DOT #272.357-010 ● OES: 49998 ● Sells livestock- and poultry-feed products to farmers and retail establishments: Suggests feed changes to improve breeding of fowl and stock. Performs other duties as described under SALES REPRESENTATIVE (retail trade; wholesale tr.) Master Title. May specialize in selling feed supplements and be designated Sales Representative, Cattle-And-Poultry Feed Supplements (wholesale tr.). ● **GED:** R4, M3, L4 ● **SVP:** 1-2 yrs ● **Academic:** Ed=N, Eng=G ● **Work Field:** 292 ● **MPSMS:** 381 ● **Aptitudes:** G3, V3, N3, S4, P4, Q3, K4, F4, M4, E5, C5 ● **Temperaments:** I, J, P ● **Physical:** Stg=L; Freq: T, G Occas: R, H, I, N ● **Work Env:** Noise=N; ● **Salary:** 3 ● **Outlook:** 2

SALES REPRESENTATIVE, FARM AND GARDEN EQUIPMENT AND SUPPLIES (wholesale tr.) ● DOT #272.357-014 ● OES:

49998 ● Sells farm and garden machinery, equipment, and supplies, such as tractors, feed, fertilizer, seed, insecticide, and farm and garden implements, performing duties as described under SALES REPRESENTATIVE (retail trade; wholesale tr.) Master Title. May sell spare parts and service contracts for machinery and equipment. ● **GED:** R4, M3, L4 ● **SVP:** 6 mos-1 yr ● **Academic:** Ed=N, Eng=G ● **Work Field:** 292 ● **MPSMS:** 562 ● **Aptitudes:** G3, V3, N3, S3, P4, Q3, K4, F4, M4, E5, C5 ● **Temperaments:** I, J, P ● **Physical:** Stg=L; Freq: T, G Occas: R, H, I, N ● **Work Env:** Noise=N; ● **Salary:** 4 ● **Outlook:** 3

SALES REPRESENTATIVE, FOOD PRODUCTS (wholesale tr.) ● DOT #260.357-014 ● OES: 49998 ● Sells food products, such as bakery products, confectionery, canned goods, coffee, tea, spices, poultry, meats, and seafood, to retail food stores, wholesale grocers, restaurants, hotels, or institutions. Performs other duties as described under SALES REPRESENTATIVE (retail trade; wholesale tr.) Master Title. May be designated according to kind of food sold as Sales Representative, Flour And Cereals (wholesale tr.); Sales Representative, Groceries (wholesale tr.); Sales Representative, Meats (wholesale tr.). ● **GED:** R4, M3, L4 ● **SVP:** 6 mos-1 yr ● **Academic:** Ed=N, Eng=G ● **Work Field:** 292 ● **MPSMS:** 380, 390 ● **Aptitudes:** G3, V3, N3, S4, P4, Q3, K4, F4, M4, E5, C5 ● **Temperaments:** I, P ● **Physical:** Stg=L; Freq: R, H, T, G Occas: I, N ● **Work Env:** Noise=N; ● **Salary:** 4 ● **Outlook:** 3

SALES REPRESENTATIVE, FOOTWEAR (wholesale tr.) ● DOT #261.357-018 ● OES: 49011 ● Sells footwear, such as shoes, boots, overshoes, and slippers, performing duties as described under SALES REPRESENTATIVE (retail trade; wholesale tr.) Master Title. ● **GED:** R4, M3, L4 ● **SVP:** 1-2 yrs ● **Academic:** Ed=H, Eng=G ● **Work Field:** 292 ● **MPSMS:** 522, 512 ● **Aptitudes:** G3, V3, N3, S4, P3, Q3, K4, F4, M4, E5, C4 ● **Temperaments:** I, J, P ● **Physical:** Stg=L; Freq: T, G Occas: R, H, I, N, X ● **Work Env:** Noise=N; ● **Salary:** 3 ● **Outlook:** 4

SALES REPRESENTATIVE, HARDWARE SUPPLIES (wholesale tr.) ● DOT #274.357-034 ● OES: 49998 ● Sells hardware supplies, such as plumbing and electrical supplies, power tools and handtools, paints and varnishes, plate glass, and builder's hardware, performing duties as described under SALES REPRESENTATIVE (retail trade; wholesale tr.) Master Title. ● **GED:** R4, M3, L4 ● **SVP:** 6 mos-1 yr ● **Academic:** Ed=H, Eng=G ● **Work Field:** 292 ● **MPSMS:** 552 ● **Aptitudes:** G3, V3, N3, S4, P3, Q3, K4, F4, M4, E5, C4 ● **Temperaments:** I, J, P ● **Physical:** Stg=L; Freq: R, H, T, G Occas: I, N, X ● **Work Env:** Noise=N; ● **Salary:** 4 ● **Outlook:** 3

SALES REPRESENTATIVE, HOME FURNISHINGS (wholesale tr.) ● DOT #270.357-010 ● OES: 49011 ● Sells home furnishings, such as china, glassware, floor coverings, furniture, linens, brooms, and kitchen articles, performing duties as described under SALES REPRESENTATIVE (retail trade; wholesale tr.) Master Title. ● **GED:** R4, M3, L4 ● **SVP:** 6 mos-1 yr ● **Academic:** Ed=N, Eng=G ● **Work Field:**

292 ● **MPSMS:** 882 ● **Aptitudes:** G3, V3, N3, S3, P3, Q3, K4, F4, M4, E5, C4 ● **Temperaments:** I, J, P ● **Physical:** Stg=L; Freq: T, G Occas: R, H, I, N, X ● **Work Env:** Noise=Q; ● **Salary:** 3 ● **Outlook:** 4

SALES REPRESENTATIVE, HOUSEHOLD APPLIANCES (wholesale tr.) ● DOT #270.357-014 ● OES: 49011 ● Sells household appliances, such as refrigerators, ranges, laundry equipment, dishwashers, vacuum cleaners, and room air-conditioning units. Performs duties as described under SALES REPRESENTATIVE (retail trade; wholesale tr.) Master Title. May train dealers in operation and use of appliances. ● **GED:** R4, M3, L4 ● **SVP:** 6 mos-1 yr ● **Academic:** Ed=N, Eng=G ● **Work Field:** 292 ● **MPSMS:** 583 ● **Aptitudes:** G3, V3, N3, S4, P4, Q3, K4, F4, M4, E5, C5 ● **Temperaments:** I, J, P ● **Physical:** Stg=L; Freq: T, G Occas: R, H, I, N ● **Work Env:** Noise=N; ● **Salary:** 3 ● **Outlook:** 4

SALES REPRESENTATIVE, MALT LIQUORS (wholesale tr.) ● DOT #260.357-018 ● OES: 49998 ● Sells beer and other malt liquors to taverns, hotels, restaurants, cocktail lounges, bowling alleys, steamship companies, railroads, military establishments, delicatessens, and supermarkets for wholesale distributor. Performs other duties as described under SALES REPRESENTATIVE (retail trade; wholesale tr.) Master Title. Confers with SALES SUPERVISOR, MALT LIQUORS (wholesale tr.) to resolve customer problems. ● **GED:** R4, M3, L3 ● **SVP:** 3-6 mos ● **Academic:** Ed=N, Eng=G ● **Work Field:** 292 ● **MPSMS:** 882 ● **Aptitudes:** G3, V3, N3, S4, P4, Q3, K4, F4, M4, E5, C4 ● **Temperaments:** I, J, P ● **Physical:** Stg=L; Freq: R, H, I, T, G, N Occas: X ● **Work Env:** Noise=N; ● **Salary:** 4 ● **Outlook:** 3

SALES REPRESENTATIVE, MEN'S AND BOYS' APPAREL (wholesale tr.) ● DOT #261.357-022 ● OES: 49998 ● Sells men's and boys' clothing, such as suits, coats, sport jackets, and slacks, utilizing knowledge of garment construction, fabrics, and styles. Performs other duties as described under SALES REPRESENTATIVE (retail trade; wholesale tr.) Master Title. ● **GED:** R4, M3, L4 ● **SVP:** 1-2 yrs ● **Academic:** Ed=N, Eng=G ● **Work Field:** 292 ● **MPSMS:** 441 ● **Aptitudes:** G3, V3, N3, S3, P3, Q3, K4, F4, M4, E5, C4 ● **Temperaments:** I, J, P ● **Physical:** Stg=L; Freq: T, G Occas: R, H, I, N, X ● **Work Env:** Noise=Q; ● **Salary:** 3 ● **Outlook:** 3

SALES REPRESENTATIVE, NOVELTIES (wholesale tr.) ● DOT #277.357-018 ● OES: 49998 ● Sells novelties, such as souvenirs, toys, statuettes, glassware, and trinkets, to variety stores, toy stores, and carnivals, performing duties as described under SALES REPRESENTATIVE (retail trade; wholesale tr.) Master Title. ● **GED:** R4, M3, L4 ● **SVP:** 3-6 mos ● **Academic:** Ed=A, Eng=G ● **Work Field:** 292 ● **MPSMS:** 610 ● **Aptitudes:** G3, V3, N3, S4, P4, Q3, K4, F4, M4, E5, C5 ● **Temperaments:** I, J, P ● **Physical:** Stg=L; Freq: R, H, I, T, G, N ● **Work Env:** Noise=N; ● **Salary:** 3 ● **Outlook:** 3

SALES REPRESENTATIVE, PETROLEUM PRODUCTS (wholesale tr.) ● DOT #269.357-014 ● OES: 49998 ● Sells petroleum products, such as gasoline, oil, greases, and lubricants, performing duties as described under SALES REPRESENTATIVE (retail trade; wholesale tr.) Master Title. May be designated according to specific petroleum product sold as Sales Representative, Industrial Lubricants (wholesale tr.). ● **GED:** R4, M3, L4 ● **SVP:** 1-2 yrs ● **Academic:** Ed=N, Eng=G ● **Work Field:** 292 ● **MPSMS:** 500 ● **Aptitudes:** G3, V3, N3, S4, P4, Q3, K4, F4, M4, E5, C5 ● **Temperaments:** I, J, P ● **Physical:** Stg=L; Freq: T, G Occas: R, H, I, N ● **Work Env:** Noise=Q; ● **Salary:** 4 ● **Outlook:** 3

SALES REPRESENTATIVE, PRINTING SUPPLIES (wholesale tr.) ● DOT #274.357-062 ● OES: 49998 ● Sells printing supplies, such as ink, plates, rollers, and type, performing duties as described under SALES REPRESENTATIVE (retail trade; wholesale tr.) Master Title. ● **GED:** R4, M3, L4 ● **SVP:** 6 mos-1 yr ● **Academic:** Ed=H, Eng=G ● **Work Field:** 292 ● **MPSMS:** 567, 499 ● **Aptitudes:** G3, V2, N3, S3, P3, Q3, K4, F4, M4, E5, C4 ● **Temperaments:** I, J, P ● **Physical:** Stg=L; Freq: T, G Occas: R, H, I, N, X ● **Work Env:** Noise=Q; ● **Salary:** 4 ● **Outlook:** 3

SALES REPRESENTATIVE, RECREATION AND SPORTING GOODS (wholesale tr.) ● DOT #277.357-026 ● OES: 49998 ● Sells amusement and sporting goods, such as hunting and fishing equipment, camping equipment, athletic equipment, playground equipment, toys, and games: Performs duties as described under SALES REPRESENTATIVE (retail trade; wholesale tr.) Master Title. May be desig-

nated according to product sold as Sales Representative, Playground Equipment (wholesale tr.); Sales Representative, Sporting Goods (wholesale tr.); Sales Representative, Toys And Games (retail trade; wholesale tr.). ● **GED:** R4, M3, L4 ● **SVP:** 6 mos-1 yr ● **Academic:** Ed=N, Eng=G ● **Work Field:** 292 ● **MPSMS:** 610 ● **Aptitudes:** G3, V3, N3, S3, P3, Q3, K4, F4, M4, E5, C4 ● **Temperaments:** I, J, P ● **Physical:** Stg=L; Freq: T, G Occas: R, H, I, N, X ● **Work Env:** Noise=Q; ● **Salary:** 3 ● **Outlook:** 3

SALES REPRESENTATIVE, TOILET PREPARATIONS (wholesale tr.) ● DOT #262.357-014 ● OES: 49011 ● Sells toilet preparations, such as cosmetics, perfumes, soaps, bath oils, and facial and hair preparations, utilizing knowledge of promotion and display techniques. Performs other duties as described under SALES REPRESENTATIVE (retail trade; wholesale tr.) Master Title. ● **GED:** R4, M3, L4 ● **SVP:** 6 mos-1 yr ● **Academic:** Ed=H, Eng=G ● **Work Field:** 292 ● **MPSMS:** 494 ● **Aptitudes:** G3, V3, N3, S4, P3, Q3, K4, F4, M4, E5, C4 ● **Temperaments:** I, J, P ● **Physical:** Stg=L; Freq: R, H, T, G Occas: I, M, N, X ● **Work Env:** Noise=Q; ● **Salary:** 4 ● **Outlook:** 4

SALES REPRESENTATIVE, TEXTILES (wholesale tr.) ● DOT #261.357-030 ● OES: 49998 ● Sells textile fabrics, such as cottons, wools, synthetics, and combination blends, to garment manufacturers, retail stores, textile converters, and buying offices, utilizing knowledge of textile construction, fabrics, fashion, and textile products. Performs duties as described under SALES REPRESENTATIVE (retail trade; wholesale tr.) Master Title. May sell raw fibers to spinning mills and be designated Sales Representative, Raw Fibers (wholesale tr.). ● **GED:** R4, M3, L4 ● **SVP:** 1-2 yrs ● **Academic:** Ed=N, Eng=G ● **Work Field:** 292 ● **MPSMS:** 420, 410, 430 ● **Aptitudes:** G2, V2, N3, S4, P3, Q3, K4, F4, M4, E5, C3 ● **Temperaments:** I, J, P ● **Physical:** Stg=L; Const: T, G Freq: R, H, N Occas: I, E, F, D, A, X, V ● **Work Env:** Noise=N; ● **Salary:** 1 ● **Outlook:** 3

SALES REPRESENTATIVE, VIDEOTAPE (wholesale tr.) ● DOT #271.357-014 ● OES: 49011 ● Sells television tape, used to record programs for delayed play-back, performing duties as described under SALES REPRESENTATIVE (retail trade; wholesale tr.) Master Title. ● **GED:** R4, M3, L4 ● **SVP:** 1-3 mos ● **Academic:** Ed=N, Eng=S ● **Work Field:** 292 ● **MPSMS:** 586 ● **Aptitudes:** G3, V3, N3, S4, P4, Q3, K4, F4, M4, E5, C5 ● **Temperaments:** I, J, P ● **Physical:** Stg=L; Freq: T, G Occas: R, H, I, N ● **Work Env:** Noise=Q; ● **Salary:** 3 ● **Outlook:** 4

SALES REPRESENTATIVE, WOMEN'S AND GIRLS' APPAREL (wholesale tr.) ● DOT #261.357-038 ● OES: 49998 ● Sells women's and girls' apparel, such as coats, dresses, lingerie, and accessories, utilizing knowledge of fabrics, style, and prices. Performs other duties as described under SALES REPRESENTATIVE (retail trade; wholesale tr.) Master Title. May specialize according to price range of garment sold. May sell only girls' or women's apparel and be designated Sales Representative, Girls' Apparel (wholesale tr.); Sales Representative, Women's Apparel (wholesale tr.). ● **GED:** R4, M3, L4 ● **SVP:** 6 mos-1 yr ● **Academic:** Ed=N, Eng=G ● **Work Field:** 292 ● **MPSMS:** 440 ● **Aptitudes:** G3, V3, N3, S4, P3, Q3, K4, F4, M4, E5, C4 ● **Temperaments:** I, J, P ● **Physical:** Stg=L; Freq: T, G Occas: R, H, I, N, X ● **Work Env:** Noise=N; ● **Salary:** 3 ● **Outlook:** 3

GOE: 08.02.02
Retail

HEARING AID SPECIALIST (retail trade) ● DOT #276.354-010 ● OES: 49011 ● Alternate titles: HEARING INSTRUMENT SPECIALIST; SALESPERSON, HEARING AIDS. Fits and sells hearing amplification systems to individuals in retail establishment: Tests auditory system of hearing-impaired individuals, using test equipment and applying standardized evaluation procedures; or receives individuals referred by physician for fitting and purchasing of hearing amplification systems. Interprets and evaluates auditory test results and confers with hearing-impaired individuals to demonstrate, select, fit, adapt, and modify hearing amplification systems for individuals. Performs other duties as described under SALESPERSON (retail trade; wholesale tr.) Master Title. May replace defective parts or make repairs to hearing amplification systems returned by customers. May make impression of client's ear to facilitate shaping of hearing aid. May visit homes of confined individuals to administer auditory system tests. May assist individuals in aural rehabilitation methods. ● **GED:** R4, M3, L4 ● **SVP:** 1-2 yrs ● **Academic:** Ed=H, Eng=G ● **Work Field:** 292 ● **MPSMS:** 589 ● **Aptitudes:** G3, V3, N3, S3, P3, Q3, K3, F3, M3, E5, C5 ● **Temperaments:** I, J, P ● **Physical:** Stg=L; Freq: R, H, T, G, N Occas: I, D, A ● **Work Env:** Noise=Q; ● **Salary:** 4 ● **Outlook:** 3

SALESPERSON, ART OBJECTS (retail trade) ● DOT #277.457-010 ● OES: 49011 ● Sells paintings, art materials, curios, and mirror and picture frames, performing duties as described under SALESPERSON (retail trade; wholesale tr.) Master Title. ● **GED:** R3, M2, L3 ● **SVP:** 3-6 mos ● **Academic:** Ed=N, Eng=S ● **Work Field:** 292 ● **MPSMS:** 881 ● **Aptitudes:** G3, V3, N3, S4, P4, Q3, K4, F4, M4, E5, C4 ● **Temperaments:** I, J, P ● **Physical:** Stg=L; Freq: R, H, T, G Occas: N, X ● **Work Env:** Noise=N; ● **Salary:** 5 ● **Outlook:** 3

SALESPERSON, AUTOMOBILES (retail trade) ● DOT #273.353-010 ● OES: 49011 ● Sells new or used automobiles, trucks, and vans on premises of vehicle sales establishment: Explains features and demonstrates operation of car in showroom or on road. Suggests optional equipment for customer to purchase. Computes and quotes sales price, including tax, trade-in allowance, license fee, and discount, and requirements for financing payment of vehicle on credit. Performs other duties as described under SALESPERSON (retail trade; wholesale tr.) Master Title. May be designated Salesperson, New Cars (retail trade); Salesperson, Used Cars (retail trade). ● **GED:** R4, M3, L4 ● **SVP:** 1-2 yrs ● **Academic:** Ed=H, Eng=G ● **Work Field:** 292 ● **MPSMS:** 591, 881 ● **Aptitudes:** G3, V3, N3, S3, P3, Q3, K4, F4, M4, E3, C4 ● **Temperaments:** I, P ● **Physical:** Stg=L; Freq: R, H, T, G, N, F Occas: I, D, A, X, V ● **Work Env:** Noise=N; ● **Salary:** 4 ● **Outlook:** 3

SALESPERSON, BOOKS (retail trade) ● DOT #277.357-034 ● OES: 49011 ● Sells books in book or department store: Suggests selection of books, based on knowledge of current literature and familiarity with publishers' catalogs and book reviews. Arranges books on shelves and racks according to type, author, or subject matter. Performs other duties as described under SALESPERSON (retail trade; wholesale tr.) Master Title. May specialize in selling technical publications. ● **GED:** R4, M3, L4 ● **SVP:** 3-6 mos ● **Academic:** Ed=N, Eng=G ● **Work Field:** 292 ● **MPSMS:** 881, 483 ● **Aptitudes:** G3, V2, N3, S4, P4, Q3, K3, F3, M4, E5, C5 ● **Temperaments:** I, J, P ● **Physical:** Stg=L; Freq: R, H, I, T, G, N ● **Work Env:** Noise=N; ● **Salary:** 2 ● **Outlook:** 3

SALESPERSON, COSMETICS AND TOILETRIES (retail trade) ● DOT #262.357-018 ● OES: 49011 ● Sells cosmetics and toiletries, such as skin creams, hair preparations, face powder, lipstick, and perfume, to customers in department store or specialty shop: Demonstrates methods of application of various preparations to customer. Explains beneficial properties of preparations and suggests shades or varieties of makeup to suit customer's complexion. May weigh and mix facial powders, according to established formula, to obtain desired shade, using spatula and scale. Performs other duties as described under SALESPERSON (retail trade; wholesale tr.) Master Title. ● **GED:** R3, M3, L3 ● **SVP:** 3-6 mos ● **Academic:** Ed=N, Eng=G ● **Work Field:** 292 ● **MPSMS:** 494 ● **Aptitudes:** G3, V3, N3, S4, P3, Q3, K3, F3, M3, E5, C3 ● **Temperaments:** I, J, P ● **Physical:** Stg=L; Freq: R, H, T, G Occas: I, M, N, A, X ● **Work Env:** Noise=Q; ● **Salary:** 4 ● **Outlook:** 3

SALESPERSON, CURTAINS AND DRAPERIES (retail trade) ● DOT #270.357-022 ● OES: 49011 ● Sells curtains, draperies, slipcovers, bedspreads, and yard goods from which these may be made: Displays samples of fabric and advises customer regarding color and pattern of material or style that will complement furnishings in customer's home. Selects size or number of curtains or drapes required, based on customer's specifications or window measurements. May estimate cost of fabricating draperies, curtains, or slipcovers. May measure and cut fabric from bolt. May also sell curtain and drapery rods and window shades. Performs other duties as described under SALESPERSON (retail trade; wholesale tr.) Master Title. May sell custom-made draperies to customers in their homes and be designated Salesperson, Custom Draperies (retail trade). ● **GED:** R4, M3, L4 ● **SVP:** 3-6 mos ● **Academic:** Ed=N, Eng=S ● **Work Field:** 292 ● **MPSMS:** 435, 881 ● **Aptitudes:** G3, V3, N3, S3, P3, Q3, K4, F4, M4, E5, C3 ● **Temperaments:** I, J, P ● **Physical:** Stg=L; Freq: R, H, I, T, G, N, X Occas: D, A ● **Work Env:** Noise=Q; ● **Salary:** 3 ● **Outlook:** 4

SALESPERSON, FLOWERS (retail trade) ● DOT #260.357-026 ● OES: 49011 ● Sells natural and artificial flowers, potted plants, floral pieces, and accessories: Advises customer regarding type of flowers, floral arrangements, and decorations desirable for specific occasions, utilizing knowledge of social and religious customs. Arranges display of flowers and decorative accessories, such as vases and ceramics. Performs other duties as described under SALESPERSON (retail trade; wholesale tr.) Master Title. May contact florists in other communities by telegraph or telephone to place orders for out-of-town delivery. May design and make up corsages, wreaths, sprays, and other floral decorations. ● **GED:** R4, M3, L3 ● **SVP:** 3-6 mos ● **Academic:** Ed=N, Eng=S ● **Work Field:** 292 ● **MPSMS:** 311 ● **Aptitudes:** G3, V3, N3, S3, P3, Q3, K3, F3, M3, E5, C3 ● **Temperaments:** F, I, J, P ● **Physical:** Stg=L; Freq: R, H, I, T, G, D, X Occas: N ● **Work Env:** Noise=L; Const: U ● **Salary:** 2 ● **Outlook:** 4

SALES EXHIBITOR (nonprofit org.) ● DOT #279.357-010 ● OES: 49998 ● Sells variety of products made by the blind, such as wallets, mops, neckties, rugs, aprons, and babywear: Contacts businesses and civic establishments and arranges to exhibit and sell merchandise made by the blind on their premises. Sets up and displays merchandise to attract attention of prospective customers. Performs other duties as described under SALESPERSON (retail trade; wholesale tr.) Master Title. ● **GED:** R3, M2, L3 ● **SVP:** 1-3 mos ● **Academic:** Ed=N, Eng=G ● **Work Field:** 292 ● **MPSMS:** 885 ● **Aptitudes:** G3, V3, N3, S4, P4, Q4, K4, F4, M4, E5, C4 ● **Temperaments:** I, J, P ● **Physical:** Stg=L; Freq: R, H, I, T, G, N Occas: X ● **Work Env:** Noise=N; ● **Salary:** 2 ● **Outlook:** 3

SALESPERSON, FURNITURE (retail trade) ● DOT #270.357-030 ● OES: 49011 ● Sells furniture and bedding in furniture or department store: Suggests furniture size, period style, color, fabric, and wood that will complement customer's home and other furnishings. Discusses quality of fabric and finish, and type and quality of construction with customer. May resolve customer complaints regarding delivery of damaged or incorrect merchandise. Performs other duties as described under SALESPERSON (retail trade; wholesale tr.) Master Title. ● **GED:** R3, M3, L3 ● **SVP:** 3-6 mos ● **Academic:** Ed=N, Eng=S ● **Work Field:** 292 ● **MPSMS:** 460, 881 ● **Aptitudes:** G3, V3, N3, S3, P3, Q3, K4, F4, M4, E5, C3 ● **Temperaments:** I, P ● **Physical:** Stg=L; Freq: R, H, I, T, G, X Occas: S, O, E, N ● **Work Env:** Noise=N; ● **Salary:** 3 ● **Outlook:** 4

SALESPERSON, HOUSEHOLD APPLIANCES (retail trade) ● DOT #270.357-034 ● OES: 49011 ● Sells radios, television sets, and other household appliances to customers: Explains features of appliances, such as stoves, refrigerators, vacuum cleaners, and washing machines. Demonstrates television, radio, and phonograph sets. Performs other duties as described under SALESPERSON (retail trade; wholesale tr.) Master Title. May sell service contracts for appliances sold. May demonstrate appliances on display floor of utility company and refer interested customers to appliance dealers for purchase. ● **GED:** R4, M3, L4 ● **SVP:** 3-6 mos ● **Academic:** Ed=N, Eng=S ● **Work Field:** 292 ● **MPSMS:** 583, 585 ● **Aptitudes:** G3, V3, N3, S4, P4, Q3, K4, F3, M3, E5, C4 ● **Temperaments:** I, J, P ● **Physical:** Stg=L; Freq: R, H, T, G Occas: I, N, A, X ● **Work Env:** Noise=N; ● **Salary:** 3 ● **Outlook:** 4

SALESPERSON, INFANTS' AND CHILDREN'S WEAR (retail trade) ● DOT #261.357-046 ● OES: 49011 ● Sells infants' and children's wearing apparel, nursery furniture, and bedding: Advises customer on durability of merchandise and quantity to purchase for infants. Suggests gift items or sizes of infants' clothes. May sell infants' and children's shoes. Performs other duties as described under SALESPERSON (retail trade; wholesale tr.) Master Title. ● **GED:** R4, M3, L4 ● **SVP:** 1-3 mos ● **Academic:** Ed=N, Eng=S ● **Work Field:** 292 ● **MPSMS:** 881 ● **Aptitudes:** G3, V3, N3, S4, P3, Q4, K3, F3, M3, E5, C4 ● **Temperaments:** I, J, P ● **Physical:** Stg=L; Freq: S, R, H, T, G Occas: I, N, X ● **Work Env:** Noise=Q; ● **Salary:** 3 ● **Outlook:** 3

SALESPERSON, JEWELRY (retail trade) ● DOT #279.357-058 ● OES: 49011 ● Displays and sells jewelry and watches: Advises customer on quality, cuts, or value of jewelry and gems and in selecting mountings or settings for gems. Informs customer of various grades of watch movements and type of servicing offered by manufacturer. Performs other duties as described under SALESPERSON (retail trade; wholesale tr.) Master Title. May estimate cost of jewelry and watch repair. May suggest designs for custom jewelry. May sell flatware, hollowware, and tableware, and advise customer on quality, grades, and patterns. ● **GED:** R4, M3, L4 ● **SVP:** 6 mos-1 yr ● **Academic:** Ed=H, Eng=S ● **Work Field:** 292 ● **MPSMS:** 607, 611 ● **Aptitudes:** G3, V3, N3, S4, P3, Q3, K3, F3, M4, E5, C3 ● **Temperaments:** I, J, P ● **Physical:** Stg=L; Freq: R, H, I, E, T, G, N, D, A, X ● **Work Env:** Noise=Q; ● **Salary:** 5 ● **Outlook:** 3

SALESPERSON, MEN'S AND BOYS' CLOTHING (retail trade) ● DOT #261.357-050 ● OES: 49011 ● Sells men's and boys' outer garments, such as suits, pants, and coats: Advises customer about prevailing styles and appropriateness of garments for particular occasions. Answers questions about fabric, design, and quality of garment. Selects standard-size garments nearest customer's measurements. May measure customer to determine garment size required, using measuring tape. May mark garment for alterations. Performs other duties as described under SALESPERSON (retail trade; wholesale tr.) Master Title. ● **GED:** R3, M3, L3 ● **SVP:** 3-6 mos ● **Academic:** Ed=N, Eng=S ● **Work Field:** 292 ● **MPSMS:** 441, 881 ● **Aptitudes:** G3, V3, N3, S4, P3, Q3, K4, F4, M4, E5, C3 ● **Temperaments:** I, J, P ● **Physical:** Stg=L; Const: H Freq: R, I, T, G, N, X Occas: S, K ● **Work Env:** Noise=N; ● **Salary:** 3 ● **Outlook:** 3

SALESPERSON, MUSICAL INSTRUMENTS AND ACCESSORIES (retail trade) ● DOT #277.357-038 ● OES: 49011 ● Sells brass, percussion, stringed, and woodwind musical instruments, musical accessories, equipment, and supplies: Explains function, mechanisms, and care of musical instruments to customer. Demonstrates and discusses quality of tone and variations in instruments of different prices. Performs other duties as described under SALESPERSON (retail trade; wholesale tr.) Master Title. May make repairs. May solicit business of orchestras or other musical groups. May rent instruments to customers and prepare rental contracts. ● **GED:** R4, M3, L4 ● **SVP:** 1-2 yrs ● **Academic:** Ed=N, Eng=G ● **Work Field:** 292 ● **MPSMS:** 614 ● **Aptitudes:** G2, V3, N3, S3, P3, Q3, K3, F3, M3, E5, C4 ● **Temperaments:** I, J, P ● **Physical:** Stg=L; Freq: R, H, I, T, G, N Occas: A, X ● **Work Env:** Noise=Q; ● **Salary:** 2 ● **Outlook:** 2

SALESPERSON, ORTHOPEDIC SHOES (retail trade) ● DOT #276.257-018 ● OES: 49011 ● Alternate titles: ORTHOPEDIC-SHOE FITTER. Evaluates customers' foot conditions and fits and sells corrective shoes, using knowledge of orthopedics or following prescription: Examines malformed or injured joints and bone structure of customer's feet, or reads physician's prescription to determine type of corrective shoe required. Selects shoes from stock or draws outline and takes measurements of customer's feet to order custom-made shoes. Examines shoes on customer's feet to verify correctness of fit. Performs other duties as described under SALESPERSON (retail trade; wholesale tr.) Master Title. ● **GED:** R4, M3, L4 ● **SVP:** 1-2 yrs ● **Academic:** Ed=N, Eng=G ● **Work Field:** 292 ● **MPSMS:** 604 ● **Aptitudes:** G2, V3, N3, S2, P3, Q3, K3, F3, M3, E5, C4 ● **Temperaments:** I, J, P ● **Physical:** Stg=L; Freq: R, H, I, T, G, N, A Occas: O, E, D, X ● **Work Env:** Noise=Q; ● **Salary:** 4 ● **Outlook:** 3

SALESPERSON, PETS AND PET SUPPLIES (retail trade) ● DOT #277.357-042 ● OES: 49011 ● Sells pets and pet accessories, equipment, food, and remedies: Advises customer on care, training, feeding, living habits, and characteristics of pets, such as dogs, cats, birds, fish, and hamsters. Explains use of equipment, such as aquarium pumps and filters. Feeds and provides water for pets. Performs other duties as described under SALESPERSON (retail trade; wholesale tr.) Master Title. May clean cages and tanks. May suggest remedies for certain animal diseases or recommend services of VETERINARIAN (medical ser.). ● **GED:** R4, M3, L4 ● **SVP:** 3-6 mos ● **Academic:** Ed=N, Eng=G ● **Work Field:** 292 ● **MPSMS:** 320, 330 ● **Aptitudes:** G3, V3, N3, S4, P4, Q3, K3, F3, M3, E5, C4 ● **Temperaments:** I, J, P ● **Physical:** Stg=L; Freq: R, H, I, T, G, N Occas: F, A, X ● **Work Env:** Noise=N; ● **Salary:** 3 ● **Outlook:** 2

SALESPERSON, PHONOGRAPH RECORDS AND TAPE RECORDINGS (retail trade) ● DOT #277.357-046 ● OES: 49011 ● Sells phonograph records and tape recordings in music store, record shop, or department store, performing duties as described under SALESPERSON (retail trade; wholesale tr.) Master Title. Assists customers in selection of instrumental and vocal recordings in musical categories, such as popular, classical, folk, and religious, using knowledge of available releases, catalogs, and lists. May also sell recording maintenance

equipment and supplies. ● **GED:** R3, M3, L3 ● **SVP:** 1-3 mos ● **Academic:** Ed=N, Eng=S ● **Work Field:** 292 ● **MPSMS:** 881 ● **Aptitudes:** G3, V3, N3, S4, P4, Q3, K4, F4, M4, E5, C5 ● **Temperaments:** I, J, P ● **Physical:** Stg=L; Freq: R, H, T, G Occas: I, N ● **Work Env:** Noise=N; ● **Salary:** 2 ● **Outlook:** 3

SALESPERSON, PIANOS AND ORGANS (retail trade) ● DOT #277.354-010 ● OES: 49011 ● Sells pianos or organs: Plays instrument to demonstrate tonal qualities of piano or combinations of tones on organ. Discusses construction and operating techniques of organs, or construction of piano with effect on tone, quality, and limitations. Advises customer on style of organ or piano to harmonize with other furniture. May appraise used organs or pianos for trade-in allowance. May rent pianos or organs and prepare rental contracts. Performs duties as described under SALESPERSON (retail trade; wholesale tr.) Master Title. ● **GED:** R4, M3, L4 ● **SVP:** 1-2 yrs ● **Academic:** Ed=N, Eng=G ● **Work Field:** 292 ● **MPSMS:** 614 ● **Aptitudes:** G2, V3, N3, S4, P3, Q3, K3, F3, M3, E5, C4 ● **Temperaments:** I, J, P ● **Physical:** Stg=L; Freq: R, H, I, T, G Occas: N, A, X ● **Work Env:** Noise=Q; ● **Salary:** 4 ● **Outlook:** 3

SALESPERSON, SHEET MUSIC (retail trade) ● DOT #277.357-054 ● OES: 49011 ● Sells books and sheet music for instrumental and vocal groups or soloists, utilizing knowledge of composers, compositions, and types of music, such as classical, popular, and sacred. Performs duties as described under SALESPERSON (retail trade; wholesale tr.) Master Title. ● **GED:** R4, M3, L4 ● **SVP:** 6 mos-1 yr ● **Academic:** Ed=N, Eng=G ● **Work Field:** 292 ● **MPSMS:** 756 ● **Aptitudes:** G2, V3, N3, S4, P3, Q3, K4, F4, M4, E5, C5 ● **Temperaments:** I, J, P ● **Physical:** Stg=L; Freq: R, H, I, T, G, N ● **Work Env:** Noise=N; ● **Salary:** 3 ● **Outlook:** 2

SALESPERSON, SHOES (retail trade) ● DOT #261.357-062 ● OES: 49011 ● Fits and sells shoes, boots, and other footwear: Ascertains style and color of shoe customer wishes. Asks customer shoe size or measures customer's foot, using measuring device. Obtains footwear of specified style, color, and size from stock. Helps customer try on shoes, observes and questions customer about fit, and feels customer's feet through shoes to ensure fit. May stretch shoes, using hand stretcher, or insert insoles or instep pads to improve fit. May sell related products, such as handbags, hosiery, shoetrees, and shoe polish. Performs other duties as described under SALESPERSON (retail trade; wholesale tr.) Master Title. May be designated according to type of shoes sold as Salesperson, Children's Shoes (retail trade); Salesperson, Men's Shoes (retail trade); Salesperson, Women's Shoes (retail trade). ● **GED:** R3, M2, L3 ● **SVP:** 3-6 mos ● **Academic:** Ed=N, Eng=S ● **Work Field:** 292 ● **MPSMS:** 522, 881 ● **Aptitudes:** G3, V3, N3, S4, P4, Q3, K4, F3, M3, E5, C4 ● **Temperaments:** I, P ● **Physical:** Stg=L; Const: H Freq: S, O, R, I, T, G, N, X Occas: C, B, E ● **Work Env:** Noise=N; ● **Salary:** 3 ● **Outlook:** 3

SALESPERSON, SPORTING GOODS (retail trade) ● DOT #277.357-058 ● OES: 49011 ● Sells sporting goods and athletic equipment: Advises customer on type of equipment for specific purposes, such as length of golf club, size of grip on tennis racket, weight of bowling ball, length of skis and poles, and caliber and make of gun or rifle. Explains care of equipment, regulations of games, and fish and game laws. Informs customer of areas for hunting, fishing, or skiing, and cost of such outings. Performs other duties as described under SALESPERSON (retail trade; wholesale tr.) Master Title. May repair sporting goods. ● **GED:** R4, M3, L4 ● **SVP:** 6 mos-1 yr ● **Academic:** Ed=N, Eng=S ● **Work Field:** 292 ● **MPSMS:** 616 ● **Aptitudes:** G3, V3, N3, S4, P3, Q3, K3, F3, M3, E5, C4 ● **Temperaments:** I, J, P ● **Physical:** Stg=L; Freq: R, H, T, G Occas: I, N, X ● **Work Env:** Noise=Q; ● **Salary:** 4 ● **Outlook:** 3

SALESPERSON, STEREO EQUIPMENT (retail trade) ● DOT #270.357-038 ● OES: 49011 ● Sells home-entertainment electronic sound equipment and parts, such as stereophonic phonographs, recording equipment, radios, speakers, tuners, amplifiers, microphones, and record changers. Explains features of various brands, meaning of technical manufacturers' specifications, and method of installation, applying knowledge of electronics. Performs other duties as described under SALESPERSON (retail trade; wholesale tr.) Master Title. ● **GED:** R4, M3, L4 ● **SVP:** 3-6 mos ● **Academic:** Ed=N, Eng=S ● **Work Field:** 292 ● **MPSMS:** 585 ● **Aptitudes:** G3, V3, N3, S4, P3, Q3, K3, F3, M3, E5, C4 ● **Temperaments:** I, J, P ● **Physical:** Stg=M; Freq: T, G

Occas: S, K, R, H, I, N, A, X ● **Work Env:** Noise=N; ● **Salary:** 3 ● **Outlook:** 4

SALESPERSON, SURGICAL APPLIANCES (retail trade) ● DOT #276.257-022 ● OES: 49998 ● Alternate titles: FITTER; SURGICAL-APPLIANCE FITTER. Fits and sells surgical appliances, such as trusses, abdominal supports, braces, cervical collars, and artificial limbs, using knowledge of anatomy, orthopedics, orthotics, and prosthetics: Measures customer with tape measure or follows prescription from physician to determine type and size of appliance required. Selects appliance from stock and fits appliance on customer. Writes specifications for and orders custom-made appliances. Performs other duties as described under SALESPERSON (retail trade; wholesale tr.) Master Title. May design and fabricate, or direct fabrication of custom-made appliances. ● **GED:** R5, M3, L4 ● **SVP:** 1-2 yrs ● **Academic:** Ed=A, Eng=S ● **Work Field:** 292 ● **MPSMS:** 604 ● **Aptitudes:** G2, V2, N3, S2, P3, Q3, K4, F4, M4, E5, C4 ● **Temperaments:** I, J, P ● **Physical:** Stg=L; Freq: R, H, T, G, N Occas: S, O, I, D, A, X ● **Work Env:** Noise=Q; ● **Salary:** 3 ● **Outlook:** 2

SALESPERSON, TOY TRAINS AND ACCESSORIES (retail trade) ● DOT #277.357-066 ● OES: 49011 ● Sells toy trains, model train kits, and accessories, such as tracks, batteries, tunnels, and signal lights, performing duties as described under SALESPERSON (retail trade; wholesale tr.) Master Title. ● **GED:** R4, M3, L4 ● **SVP:** 1-3 mos ● **Academic:** Ed=N, Eng=G ● **Work Field:** 292 ● **MPSMS:** 881, 615 ● **Aptitudes:** G3, V3, N3, S4, P4, Q3, K4, F3, M4, E5, C4 ● **Temperaments:** I, J, P ● **Physical:** Stg=L; Freq: R, H, I, T, G, N Occas: X ● **Work Env:** Noise=N; ● **Salary:** 2 ● **Outlook:** 3

SALESPERSON, TRAILERS AND MOTOR HOMES (retail trade) ● DOT #273.357-034 ● OES: 49011 ● Alternate titles: SALESPERSON, RECREATIONAL VEHICLES. Sells travel and camping trailers, motor homes, and truck campers to individuals: Determines customer's needs and exhibits vehicle of particular type or model. Demonstrates use of equipment and furnishings. Performs other duties as described under SALESPERSON (retail trade; wholesale tr.) Master Title. May prepare sales contract. May arrange financing and insurance. May sell mobile homes, motorcycles, and snowmobiles. ● **GED:** R4, M3, L4 ● **SVP:** 6 mos-1 yr ● **Academic:** Ed=N, Eng=G ● **Work Field:** 292 ● **MPSMS:** 590 ● **Aptitudes:** G3, V3, N3, S4, P4, Q3, K4, F4, M4, E5, C5 ● **Temperaments:** I, J, P ● **Physical:** Stg=L; Freq: R, H, T, G Occas: I, N ● **Work Env:** Noise=Q; Freq: W ● **Salary:** 4 ● **Outlook:** 3

SALESPERSON, WIGS (personal ser.) ● DOT #261.351-010 ● OES: 49011 ● Sells wigs, wiglets, falls, and other hairpieces in salon, department store, specialty shop, or customer's home, performing duties as described under SALESPERSON (retail trade; wholesale tr.) Master Title: Observes customer's facial features and complexion and selects wig for customer's consideration. Fits and styles wig on customer, combing and brushing wig to achieve desired effect. Advises customer on care and homestyling of wig. Styles wigs and hairpieces for display purposes, using combs, brushes, hair sprays, and cleaning compounds. May clean, cut, and style hairpieces for customer and be designated Wig Stylist (personal ser.). ● **GED:** R3, M3, L3 ● **SVP:** 3-6 mos ● **Academic:** Ed=N, Eng=G ● **Work Field:** 292, 264 ● **MPSMS:** 881, 904 ● **Aptitudes:** G3, V3, N4, S2, P3, Q4, K3, F3, M3, E5, C2 ● **Temperaments:** I, J, P ● **Physical:** Stg=L; Freq: R, H, I, E, T, G, N, X Occas: S, D, A ● **Work Env:** Noise=N; ● **Salary:** 3 ● **Outlook:** 3

SALESPERSON, WOMEN'S APPAREL AND ACCESSORIES (retail trade) ● DOT #261.357-066 ● OES: 49011 ● Alternate titles: SALESPERSON, LADIES' WEAR. Sells women's clothing and accessories, such as coats, sportswear, suits, dresses, formal gowns, lingerie, hosiery, belts, gloves, costume jewelry, handbags, and scarfs: Advises customer on current fashion and coordinating accessories. Answers questions regarding washability, durability, and color fastness of fabrics. May mark garments for alterations. Performs other duties as described under SALESPERSON (retail trade; wholesale trade) Master Title. May be designated according to specific category or type of item sold as Salesperson, Fashion Accessories (retail trade); Salesperson, Handbags (retail trade); Salesperson, Hosiery (retail trade); Salesperson, Lingerie (retail trade); Salesperson, Women's Dresses (retail trade); Salesperson, Women's Sportswear (retail trade.). ● **GED:**

R3, M2, L3 ● **SVP:** 1-3 mos ● **Academic:** Ed=N, Eng=S ● **Work Field:** 292 ● **MPSMS:** 440, 881 ● **Aptitudes:** G3, V3, N3, S4, P4, Q4, K4, F3, M3, E5, C3 ● **Temperaments:** I, P ● **Physical:** Stg=L; Freq: R, H, T, G Occas: S, O, I, N, X ● **Work Env:** Noise=N; ● **Salary:** 3 ● **Outlook:** 3

SALESPERSON, YARD GOODS (retail trade) ● DOT #261.357-070 ● OES: 49011 ● Sells yard goods made from cotton, linen, wool, silk, synthetic fibers, and other materials: Unrolls bolts of cloth to display assortment of fabrics to customer. Advises customer as to kind and quantity of material required to make garments, bed clothes, curtains, and other articles. Discusses features and qualities of fabric, such as weave, texture, color, and washability. Suggests harmonizing or matching colors of fabrics. Measures and cuts length of fabric from bolt, using scissors and measuring machine or yardstick. Performs other duties as described under SALESPERSON (retail trade; wholesale tr.) Master Title. May sell sewing accessories and notions, such as dress patterns, needlecraft books, needles, thread, buttons, and zippers. ● **GED:** R4, M3, L4 ● **SVP:** 1-3 mos ● **Academic:** Ed=N, Eng=S ● **Work Field:** 292 ● **MPSMS:** 420 ● **Aptitudes:** G3, V3, N3, S3, P3, Q4, K3, F3, M3, E5, C3 ● **Temperaments:** I, J, P ● **Physical:** Stg=L; Freq: R, H, I, T, G, N, X Occas: A ● **Work Env:** Noise=Q; ● **Salary:** 1 ● **Outlook:** 3

SALES-SERVICE REPRESENTATIVE, MILKING MACHINES (retail trade) ● DOT #299.251-010 ● OES: 49998 ● Sells, installs, and repairs milking equipment: Calls on farmers to solicit repair business and to sell new milking equipment, such as vacuum pumps, buckets, pipelines, and replacement parts. Demonstrates milking machines. Cuts and threads pipe and attaches fittings, using plumber's tools, to install pipelines. Cleans and flushes pipelines, and repairs pulsators and vacuum pumps. ● **GED:** R4, M3, L4 ● **SVP:** 1-2 yrs ● **Academic:** Ed=H, Eng=S ● **Work Field:** 121, 292 ● **MPSMS:** 562 ● **Aptitudes:** G2, V3, N3, S2, P3, Q3, K3, F3, M3, E4, C5 ● **Temperaments:** I, J, P ● **Physical:** Stg=M; Freq: R, H, T, G, N Occas: S, O, I, D ● **Work Env:** Noise=N; Freq: W ● **Salary:** 4 ● **Outlook:** 3

GOE: 08.02.03
Wholesale & Retail

AUCTIONEER (retail trade) ● DOT #294.257-010 ● OES: 49998 ● Sells articles at auction to highest bidder: Appraises merchandise before sale and assembles merchandise in lots according to estimated value of individual pieces or type of article. Selects article to be auctioned at suggestion of bidders or by own choice. Appraises article and determines or asks for starting bid. Describes merchandise and gives information about article, such as history and ownership, in order to encourage bidding. Continues to ask for bids, attempting to stimulate buying desire of bidders. Closes sale to highest bidder. May write auction catalog and advertising copy for local or trade newspapers and periodicals. May be designated according to property auctioned as Auctioneer, Art (retail trade; wholesale tr.); Auctioneer, Automobile (wholesale tr.); Auctioneer, Furniture (retail trade; wholesale tr.); Auctioneer, Livestock (retail trade; wholesale tr.); Auctioneer, Real Estate (retail trade; wholesale tr.); Auctioneer, Tobacco (wholesale tr.). ● **GED:** R3, M2, L3 ● **SVP:** 1-2 yrs ● **Academic:** Ed=N, Eng=G ● **Work Field:** 211, 292 ● **MPSMS:** 881, 882 ● **Aptitudes:** G3, V2, N4, S5, P3, Q3, K4, F4, M4, E5, C4 ● **Temperaments:** F, I, J, P ● **Physical:** Stg=L; Freq: T, G, F, V Occas: R, H, I, N, D, A, X ● **Work Env:** Noise=L; ● **Salary:** 5 ● **Outlook:** 1

SALESPERSON, AUTOMOBILE ACCESSORIES (retail trade) ● DOT #273.357-030 ● OES: 49011 ● Sells automobile supplies and accessories, such as tires, batteries, seat covers, mufflers, and headlights: Ascertains make and year of automobile and reads catalog for stock number of item. Performs other duties as described under SALESPERSON (retail trade; wholesale tr.) Master Title. ● **GED:** R4, M3, L4 ● **SVP:** 3-6 mos ● **Academic:** Ed=H, Eng=S ● **Work Field:** 292 ● **MPSMS:** 591 ● **Aptitudes:** G3, V3, N3, S4, P4, Q3, K4, F4, M3, E5, C5 ● **Temperaments:** I, J, P ● **Physical:** Stg=L; Freq: R, H, T, G Occas: C, S, I, N ● **Work Env:** Noise=Q; ● **Salary:** 4 ● **Outlook:** 4

SALESPERSON, ELECTRIC MOTORS (retail trade) ● DOT #271.354-010 ● OES: 49011 ● Alternate titles: ELECTRIC-MOTOR-REPAIR CLERK. Sells new and used fractional horsepower electric motors and estimates costs of repairs in manufacturing, retail, or repair establishment: Determines malfunction of motors received for repair, using test equipment. Estimates repair cost, using pricelist for parts and labor. Receives motors in exchange for new or used motors. Keeps records of exchange or sales of new and used motors. Performs other duties as described under SALESPERSON (retail trade; wholesale tr.) Master Title. May repair motors [ELECTRIC-MOTOR REPAIRER (any industry)]. ● GED: R4, M3, L4 ● SVP: 1-2 yrs ● Academic: Ed=N, Eng=G ● Work Field: 292, 212 ● MPSMS: 582 ● Aptitudes: G3, V3, N3, S3, P3, Q3, K4, F3, M3, E5, C4 ● Temperaments: I, J, P ● Physical: Stg=L; Freq: R, H, I, T, G, N Occas: D, A, X ● Work Env: Noise=N; ● Salary: 4 ● Outlook: 2

SALESPERSON, FLOOR COVERINGS (retail trade) ● DOT #270.357-026 ● OES: 49011 ● Displays and sells floor coverings, such as carpets, rugs, and linoleum, in department store, specialty store, or showroom: Shows rugs or samples of carpets to customer. Explains qualities of various rugs and carpets, such as composition, method of fabrication, and wearing qualities. Estimates cost and amount of covering required, referring to customer's floor plans. Performs other duties as described under SALESPERSON (retail trade; wholesale tr.) Master Title. May measure floor and sell floor coverings in customer's home or place of business and be designated Floor-Coverings Estimator (retail trade; wholesale tr.); Salesperson, Terrazzo Tiles (retail trade; wholesale tr.). ● GED: R4, M3, L4 ● SVP: 3-6 mos ● Academic: Ed=N, Eng=S ● Work Field: 292 ● MPSMS: 431, 619 ● Aptitudes: G3, V3, N3, S4, P4, Q3, K3, F4, M4, E5, C3 ● Temperaments: I, J, P ● Physical: Stg=L; Freq: R, H, T, G, N Occas: S, K, I, X ● Work Env: Noise=N; ● Salary: 3 ● Outlook: 4

SALESPERSON, GENERAL HARDWARE (retail trade) ● DOT #279.357-050 ● OES: 49011 ● Sells hardware, such as nails, bolts, screws, hand-and-power tools, electrical equipment, plumbing supplies, garden tools, and paint: Advises customer on tools, hardware, and materials needed, and procedure to follow to complete task customer wishes to perform. Informs customer about quality of tools, hardware, and equipment, and demonstrates use. Performs related duties, such as estimating amount of paint required to cover given area, mixing paint, and cutting screen, glass, wire, or window shades to specified size. Performs other duties as described under SALESPERSON (retail trade; wholesale tr.) Master Title. May specialize in selling paint or wall coverings and be designated Salesperson, Paint (retail trade; wholesale tr.); Salesperson, Wall Coverings (retail trade; wholesale tr.). ● GED: R3, M2, L2 ● SVP: 3-6 mos ● Academic: Ed=N, Eng=S ● Work Field: 292 ● MPSMS: 550, 881, 882 ● Aptitudes: G3, V3, N3, S4, P4, Q3, K4, F4, M4, E5, C4 ● Temperaments: I, P ● Physical: Stg=L; Freq: R, H, I, T, G, N Occas: X ● Work Env: Noise=N; ● Salary: 4 ● Outlook: 3

SALESPERSON, GENERAL MERCHANDISE (retail trade) ● DOT #279.357-054 ● OES: 49011 ● Sells variety of commodities in sales establishment, performing duties as described under SALESPERSON (retail trade; wholesale tr.) Master Title. May demonstrate use of merchandise. May examine defective article returned by customer to determine if refund or replacement should be made. May estimate quantity of merchandise required to fill customer's need. ● GED: R3, M2, L2 ● SVP: 1-3 mos ● Academic: Ed=N, Eng=S ● Work Field: 292 ● MPSMS: 881, 882 ● Aptitudes: G3, V3, N3, S4, P4, Q3, K4, F4, M4, E5, C4 ● Temperaments: I, P ● Physical: Stg=L; Freq: R, H, T, G, N Occas: S, O, I, X ● Work Env: Noise=N; ● Salary: 2 ● Outlook: 3

SALESPERSON, HORTICULTURAL AND NURSERY PRODUCTS (retail trade) ● DOT #272.357-022 ● OES: 49011 ● Sells container-grown plants and garden supplies in nursery, greenhouse, or department store: Advises customer on selection of plants and methods of planting and cultivation. Suggests trees and shrubbery suitable for specified growing conditions. Performs other duties as described under SALESPERSON (retail trade; wholesale tr.) Master Title. May water and trim growing plants on sales floor. ● GED: R4, M3, L4 ● SVP: 3-6 mos ● Academic: Ed=N, Eng=G ● Work Field: 292 ● MPSMS: 310 ● Aptitudes: G3, V3, N3, S4, P4, Q4, K3, F3, M3, E5, C4 ● Temperaments: I, J, P ● Physical: Stg=L; Freq: H, T, G Occas: S, K, R, I, N, X ● Work Env: Noise=N; ● Salary: 3 ● Outlook: 3

SALESPERSON, PARTS (retail trade) ● DOT #279.357-062 ● OES: 49998 ● Alternate titles: COUNTER CLERK; PARTS CLERK. Sells automotive, appliance, electrical, and other parts and equipment in repair facility or parts store: Ascertains make, year, and type of part needed, inspects worn, damaged, or defective part to determine replacement required, or advises customer of part needed according to description of malfunction. Discusses use and features of various parts, based on knowledge of machine or equipment. Reads catalog, microfiche viewer, or computer for replacement part stock number and price. Advises customer on substitution or modification of part when replacement is not available. Examines returned part to determine if defective, and exchanges part or refunds money. Fills customer orders from stock. Marks and stores parts in stockroom according to prearranged system. Receives and fills telephone orders for parts. Performs other duties as described under SALESPERSON (retail trade; wholesale tr.) Master Title. May measure engine parts, using precision measuring instruments, to determine whether similar parts may be machined down or built up to required size. Usually specializes in selling parts for one type of machinery or equipment and is designated according to part sold, as Counter Clerk, Appliance Parts (retail trade; wholesale tr.); Counter Clerk, Automotive Parts (retail trade; wholesale tr.); Counter Clerk, Farm Equipment Parts (retail trade; wholesale tr.); Counter Clerk, Industrial Machinery and Equipment Parts (retail trade; wholesale tr.); Counter Clerk, Radio, Television, and Electronics Parts (retail trade; wholesale tr.); Counter Clerk, Tractor Parts (retail trade; wholesale tr.); Counter Clerk, Truck Parts (retail trade; wholesale tr.). ● GED: R4, M3, L3 ● SVP: 6 mos-1 yr ● Academic: Ed=N, Eng=S ● Work Field: 292 ● MPSMS: 881, 882 ● Aptitudes: G3, V3, N3, S4, P4, Q3, K4, F3, M4, E5, C4 ● Temperaments: I, J, P ● Physical: Stg=L; Freq: R, H, I, T, G, N, A Occas: S, O, X ● Work Env: Noise=N; ● Salary: 4 ● Outlook: 3

SALESPERSON, PHOTOGRAPHIC SUPPLIES AND EQUIPMENT (retail trade) ● DOT #277.357-050 ● OES: 49011 ● Sells photographic and optical equipment and supplies, such as cameras, projectors, film, and binoculars: Demonstrates equipment to customer and explains functioning of various cameras, filters, lenses, and other photographic accessories. Receives film for processing. Performs other duties as described under SALESPERSON (retail trade; wholesale tr.) Master Title. May repair photographic or optical equipment. ● GED: R4, M3, L4 ● SVP: 6 mos-1 yr ● Academic: Ed=H, Eng=S ● Work Field: 292 ● MPSMS: 603, 606 ● Aptitudes: G3, V3, N3, S3, P3, Q3, K3, F3, M3, E5, C4 ● Temperaments: I, J, P ● Physical: Stg=L; Freq: R, H, T, G, N Occas: I, A, X ● Work Env: Noise=Q; ● Salary: 2 ● Outlook: 3

SALESPERSON, STAMPS OR COINS (retail trade) ● DOT #277.357-062 ● OES: 49011 ● Sells stamps or coins, or both, to collectors: Locates stamp or coin desired by customer. Discusses value of items with customer. Performs other duties as described under SALESPERSON (retail trade; wholesale tr.) Master Title. May appraise and classify stamps or coins, using magnifier and catalogs. May buy coins or stamps from collectors and wholesalers for resale. ● GED: R4, M3, L4 ● SVP: 6 mos-1 yr ● Academic: Ed=N, Eng=G ● Work Field: 292 ● MPSMS: 880 ● Aptitudes: G3, V3, N3, S4, P2, Q3, K4, F3, M4, E5, C3 ● Temperaments: I, J, P ● Physical: Stg=L; Freq: R, H, I, T, G, N, A, X ● Work Env: Noise=N; ● Salary: 3 ● Outlook: 2

SALES REPRESENTATIVE, BOATS AND MARINE SUPPLIES (retail trade) ● DOT #273.357-018 ● OES: 49011 ● Sells boats and marine equipment and supplies, such as fixtures, pumps, instruments, cordage, paints, and motor parts: Shows boat on sales floor or shows catalog pictures and blueprints. Explains construction and performance of boat and differences between various types of marine equipment. Advises boat owners on selection of new equipment and problems pertaining to repairs. Performs other duties as described under SALES REPRESENTATIVE (retail trade; wholesale tr.) Master Title. May demonstrate boat in water. May arrange for delivery, registration, and inspection of boat. May sell water-sports equipment, such as water skis and scuba gear. May sell marine equipment and supplies, except boats, and be designated Sales Representative, Marine Supplies (retail trade; wholesale tr.). ● GED: R4, M3, L4 ● SVP: 6 mos-1 yr ● Academic: Ed=N, Eng=G ● Work Field: 292 ● MPSMS: 593, 882, 881 ● Aptitudes: G3, V3, N3, S3, P3, Q3, K4, F4, M3, E5, C4 ● Temperaments: I, J, P ● Physical: Stg=L; Freq: R, H, T, G Occas: I, N, X ● Work Env: Noise=Q; ● Salary: 4 ● Outlook: 3

SALES REPRESENTATIVE, OFFICE MACHINES (retail trade) ● DOT #275.357-034 ● OES: 49998 ● Sells office machines, such as typewriters and adding, calculating, and duplicating machines, to business establishments: Performs duties as described under SALES REPRESENTATIVE (retail trade; wholesale tr.) Master Title. May instruct employees or purchasers in use of machine. May make machine adjustments. May sell office supplies, such as paper, ribbons, ink, and tapes. May rent or lease office machines. May be designated according to type of machine sold as Sales Representative, Adding Machines (wholesale tr.); Sales Representative, Calculating Machines (wholesale tr.); Sales Representative, Cash Registers (wholesale tr.); Sales Representative, Dictating Machines (wholesale tr.); Sales Representative, Duplicating Machines (wholesale tr.); Sales Representative, Typewriters (wholesale tr.). May be designated: Sales Representative, Addressing Machines (wholesale tr.); Sales Representative, Bookkeeping-And-Accounting Machines (wholesale tr.); Sales Representative, Check-Endorsing-And-Signing Machines (wholesale tr.); Sales Representative, Stenographic Machines (wholesale tr.). ● GED: R4, M3, L4 ● SVP: 6 mos-1 yr ● Academic: Ed=N, Eng=G ● Work Field: 292 ● MPSMS: 881, 882 ● Aptitudes: G3, V2, N3, S3, P3, Q3, K3, F3, M3, E5, C5 ● Temperaments: I, J, P ● Physical: Stg=M; Freq: T, G Occas: R, H, I, N ● Work Env: Noise=Q; ● Salary: 4 ● Outlook: 4

GOE: 08.02.04
Real Estate

BUILDING CONSULTANT (wholesale tr.) ● DOT #250.357-010 ● OES: 43008 ● Sells new home construction to property owners: Displays and explains features of company house plans, using such visual aids as brochures, architectural drawings, samples of construction materials, and photographic slides. Secures construction financing with own firm or mortgage company. Contacts utility companies for service hookup to client's property. May appraise client's unimproved property to determine loan value. May investigate client's credit status. May search public records to ascertain that client has clear title to property. May contact utility companies for service hookup in customer's property. ● GED: R4, M3, L4 ● SVP: 6 mos-1 yr ● Academic: Ed=H, Eng=G ● Work Field: 292 ● MPSMS: 895 ● Aptitudes: G2, V2, N3, S3, P3, Q3, K4, F4, M4, E5, C5 ● Temperaments: I, J, P ● Physical: Stg=L; Freq: R, H, T, G, N Occas: I ● Work Env: Noise=N; ● Salary: 3 ● Outlook: 4

LEASING AGENT, RESIDENCE (real estate) ● DOT #250.357-014 ● OES: 43008 ● Alternate titles: RENTAL AGENT. Shows and leases apartments, condominiums, homes, or mobile home lots to prospective tenants: Interviews prospective tenants and records information to ascertain needs and qualifications. Accompanies prospects to model homes and apartments and discusses size and layout of rooms, available facilities, such as swimming pool and saunas, location of shopping centers, services available, and terms of lease. Completes lease form or agreement and collects rental deposit. May inspect condition of premises periodically and arrange for necessary maintenance. May compile listings of available rental property. May compose newspaper advertisements. May be required to have real estate agent's license. May contact credit bureau to obtain credit report on prospective tenant. ● GED: R4, M2, L4 ● SVP: 6 mos-1 yr ● Academic: Ed=N, Eng=G ● Work Field: 292 ● MPSMS: 895 ● Aptitudes: G2, V2, N3, S4, P4, Q3, K3, F4, M4, E5, C5 ● Temperaments: D, J, P ● Physical: Stg=L; Freq: R, H, I, T, G, N Occas: C, S, F, D, A, V ● Work Env: Noise=N; Occas: W ● Salary: 2 ● Outlook: 3

SALES AGENT, REAL ESTATE (real estate) ● DOT #250.357-018 ● OES: 43005 ● Alternate titles: REAL-ESTATE AGENT. Rents, buys, and sells property for clients on commission basis: Studies property listings to become familiar with properties for sale. Reviews trade journals and attends staff and association meetings to keep informed of marketing conditions, property values, and legislation which would affect real estate industry. Interviews prospective clients to solicit listings. Accompanies prospects to property sites, quotes purchase price, describes features, and discusses conditions of sale or terms of lease. Draws up real estate contracts, such as deeds, leases, and mortgages, and negotiates loans on property. Must have license issued by state. May hold broker's license and be designated Real-Estate Broker (real

estate). May assist buyer and seller in obtaining pertinent information or services, such as finance, maintenance, repair, or obtaining an appraisal. May obtain pictures and measurements of rooms, doors, windows, or any other specified areas for inclusion in newspaper advertisement and real estate booklets listing description of property. May inspect property to determine if repairs are needed and notify owner. May conduct seminars and training sessions for sales agents to improve sales techniques. May prepare closing statements, oversee signing of real estate documents, disburse funds, and coordinate closing activities. ● GED: R4, M3, L4 ● SVP: 6 mos-1 yr ● Academic: Ed=H, Eng=G ● Work Field: 292 ● MPSMS: 895 ● Aptitudes: G2, V2, N3, S3, P3, Q3, K4, F4, M4, E5, C5 ● Temperaments: I, J, P ● Physical: Stg=L; Freq: R, H, I, T, G, N Occas: C, F, D, A ● Work Env: Noise=N; Occas: W ● Salary: 3 ● Outlook: 4

GOE: 08.02.05
Demonstration & Sales

DEMONSTRATOR (retail trade) ● DOT #297.354-010 ● OES: 49998 ● Demonstrates merchandise and products to customers to promote sales: Displays product and explains features to customers. Answers customer's questions about product. Demonstrates use or production of product and simultaneously explains merits to persuade customers to buy product. May perform duties described under SALESPERSON (retail trade; wholesale tr.) Master Title. May suggest product improvements to employer. May use graphic aids, such as charts, slides, or films, to facilitate demonstration. May give product samples to customers. May conduct guided tours of plant where product is made. May train other demonstrators. May visit retail store or customer's home to demonstrate products. May be designated according to type merchandise demonstrated as Bakery Demonstrator (retail trade); Ceramic-Maker Demonstrator (retail trade); Cosmetics Demonstrator (retail trade); Food Demonstrator (retail trade; wholesale tr.); Glassware-Maker Demonstrator (retail trade); Housewares Demonstrator (retail trade; wholesale tr.). ● GED: R3, M3, L3 ● SVP: 1-3 mos ● Academic: Ed=N, Eng=G ● Work Field: 292 ● MPSMS: 885 ● Aptitudes: G3, V3, N3, S4, P4, Q4, K3, F3, M3, E4, C4 ● Temperaments: I, J, P ● Physical: Stg=L; Freq: R, H, I, T, G, N Occas: F, D, A, X, V ● Work Env: Noise=N; Occas: W ● Salary: 2 ● Outlook: 3

DEMONSTRATOR, ELECTRIC-GAS APPLIANCES (utilities) ● DOT #297.357-010 ● OES: 49998 ● Demonstrates and explains operation and care of electric or gas appliances to utility company customers to promote appliance sales, and advises customers on energy conservation methods: Visits community organizations and schools to demonstrate operating features and care of appliances, such as air-conditioners, driers, ranges, and washers. Explains how electricity or gas is produced and transmitted, reasons for electricity and gas rate increases, and methods of efficiently using appliances to conserve energy and reduce utility bills. Lectures to dealers, sales personnel, and employees of utility company on efficient use and care of appliances, as part of training program. Answers telephone and written requests from customers for information about appliance use. May advise customers on related homemaking problems, such as kitchen planning, home lighting, heating-fuel conservation, food preparation, and laundering with new fabrics. May write articles and pamphlets on appliance use. May represent utility company as guest on radio or television programs to discuss conservation of electrical or gas energy. ● GED: R5, M3, L5 ● SVP: 1-2 yrs ● Academic: Ed=N, Eng=G ● Work Field: 292, 282 ● MPSMS: 583, 931 ● Aptitudes: G2, V2, N3, S3, P3, Q3, K4, F3, M3, E5, C3 ● Temperaments: I, J, P, V ● Physical: Stg=L; Freq: R, H, T, G, N Occas: I, X ● Work Env: Noise=Q; ● Salary: 2 ● Outlook: 3

DEMONSTRATOR, KNITTING (retail trade) ● DOT #297.354-014 ● OES: 49998 ● Shows customers how to knit garments or accessories by hand: Demonstrates methods of holding needles and making various stitches. Interprets knitting terminology and how to read and follow knitting instructions for customer. Suggests yarn for use in particular style of garment and estimates amount to purchase. Takes customer's measurements for proposed garment and estimates number of stitches required for each part of garment. Sells customer yarn required for knitting specified garment or clothing accessory. ● GED: R4, M4, L4

● **SVP:** 6 mos-1 yr ● **Academic:** Ed=H, Eng=S ● **Work Field:** 292, 296, 165 ● **MPSMS:** 424 ● **Aptitudes:** G3, V3, N3, S3, P4, Q5, K3, F3, M3, E5, C5 ● **Temperaments:** J, P, T ● **Physical:** Stg=S; Freq: R, H, I, T, G, N, D, A Occas: E ● **Work Env:** Noise=N; ● **Salary:** 2 ● **Outlook:** 3

SALESPERSON-DEMONSTRATOR, PARTY PLAN (retail trade) ● DOT #279.357-038 ● OES: 49998 ● Displays and sells merchandise, such as clothes, household items, jewelry, toiletries, or toys, to guests attending house party: Confers with party sponsor to arrange date, time, and number of guests. Sets up display of sample merchandise. Meets guests and converses with them to establish rapport. Discusses items on display or demonstrates uses of product, and explains program to guests. Hands out catalogs or brochures that picture merchandise available. Writes orders for merchandise and arranges for payment. Delivers orders to sponsor or individual and collects monies due. May give small sample items to guests. May discuss program with guests to persuade them to sponsor house party by describing benefits derived from sponsorship. May assist sponsor to serve refreshments. ● **GED:** R4, M3, L4 ● **SVP:** 3-6 mos ● **Academic:** Ed=N, Eng=G ● **Work Field:** 292 ● **MPSMS:** 881 ● **Aptitudes:** G3, V3, N3, S4, P4, Q3, K4, F4, M4, E4, C4 ● **Temperaments:** I, J, P ● **Physical:** Stg=L; Freq: R, H, T, G Occas: N, X ● **Work Env:** Noise=N; ● **Salary:** 2 ● **Outlook:** 3

SALES REPRESENTATIVE, DANCING INSTRUCTIONS (education) ● DOT #259.357-014 ● OES: 49998 ● Sells dancing instructions to patrons at dance studio: Interviews patron to ascertain dancing background. Dances with patron to determine dancing ability and discusses ability with patron. Devises plan of instruction and persuades patron to purchase lessons. May prepare sales contracts and receive payments. May instruct patron in dancing [INSTRUCTOR, DANCING (education)]. ● **GED:** R3, M2, L3 ● **SVP:** 3-6 mos ● **Academic:** Ed=N, Eng=G ● **Work Field:** 292 ● **MPSMS:** 919, 931 ● **Aptitudes:** G3, V3, N4, S3, P4, Q3, K4, F4, M4, E3, C5 ● **Temperaments:** F, I, J, P ● **Physical:** Stg=L; Freq: T, G Occas: R, H, N, F, D, A, V ● **Work Env:** Noise=N; ● **Salary:** 3 ● **Outlook:** 2

GOE: 08.02.06
Services

CRATING-AND-MOVING ESTIMATOR (motor trans.) ● DOT #252.357-010 ● OES: 49998 ● Solicits freight or storage business from homeowners and business establishments and estimates packing, crating, moving, and storage costs: Develops lists of prospective customers from review of publications and contacts with business and real estate firms, providing such information as personnel transfers and home-sales listings. Calls on prospect at home or business establishment and describes services provided by company. Examines goods to be moved or stored, estimates cubic feet of storage or shipping space required, using comparison chart, and computes cost of packing, crating, moving, shipping, and delivering household goods, machinery, or other material. Records details on itemized sales contract, such as value and description of goods, packing instructions, and charge for each service. ● **GED:** R4, M3, L4 ● **SVP:** 6 mos-1 yr ● **Academic:** Ed=N, Eng=G ● **Work Field:** 292, 212 ● **MPSMS:** 850 ● **Aptitudes:** G2, V3, N2, S2, P3, Q3, K4, F4, M4, E5, C4 ● **Temperaments:** I, J, P ● **Physical:** Stg=L; Freq: R, H, T, G Occas: I, N, D, X ● **Work Env:** Noise=N; ● **Salary:** 3 ● **Outlook:** 2

LINEN CONTROLLER (laundry & rel.) ● DOT #299.357-010 ● OES: 49998 ● Contacts customers of linen rental service to discuss inventory control and usage of rented articles and to solicit new business: Examines rented articles and discusses with customers selection and use of articles to prevent abuse. Reviews customer inventory records to determine charges for replacement of damaged articles. Recommends account cancellation when customers continue to ruin articles. Solicits new business and estimates required inventory. May inspect plant equipment for defects that stain or tear articles during laundry process. ● **GED:** R4, M2, L3 ● **SVP:** 1-2 yrs ● **Academic:** Ed=N, Eng=G ● **Work Field:** 292 ● **MPSMS:** 906 ● **Aptitudes:** G3, V3, N3, S5, P4, Q3, K4, F4, M4, E4, C5 ● **Temperaments:** I, J, P ● **Physical:** Stg=L; Freq: R, H, I, T, G, N ● **Work Env:** Noise=N; ● **Salary:** 3 ● **Outlook:** 2

SALES AGENT, BUSINESS SERVICES (business ser.) ● DOT #251.357-010 ● OES: 49998 ● Sells business service, such as food-vending, trading stamps, detective, armored truck, telephone-answering, linen supply, and cleaning service: Develops list of prospective customers by studying business and telephone directories, consulting business associates, and observing business establishment while driving through sales territory. Reviews orders for ideas to expand services available to present customers. Calls on prospects to explain features of services, cost, and advantages. Writes orders and schedules initiation of services. Confers with customers and company officials to resolve complaints. May collect payments on accounts. May be designated according to service sold as Sales Agent, Food-Vending Service (wholesale tr.); Sales Agent, Protective Service (business ser.); Sales Agent, Trading Stamps (business ser.). ● **GED:** R4, M3, L4 ● **SVP:** 6 mos-1 yr ● **Academic:** Ed=H, Eng=G ● **Work Field:** 292 ● **MPSMS:** 899 ● **Aptitudes:** G3, V3, N3, S3, P4, Q3, K4, F4, M4, E5, C4 ● **Temperaments:** I, J, P ● **Physical:** Stg=L; Freq: T, G, N Occas: R, H, I, X ● **Work Env:** Noise=N; Occas: W ● **Salary:** 4 ● **Outlook:** 3

SALES REPRESENTATIVE (motor trans.) ● DOT #250.357-022 ● OES: 49998 ● Sells warehouse space and services to manufacturers and jobbers, performing duties as described under SALESPERSON (retail trade; wholesale tr.) Master Title. ● **GED:** R3, M3, L3 ● **SVP:** 6 mos-1 yr ● **Academic:** Ed=B, Eng=G ● **Work Field:** 292 ● **MPSMS:** 853 ● **Aptitudes:** G2, V2, N2, S3, P3, Q3, K4, F4, M4, E5, C5 ● **Temperaments:** I, J, P ● **Physical:** Stg=L; Freq: T, G Occas: R, H, I, N ● **Work Env:** Noise=Q; ● **Salary:** 4 ● **Outlook:** 4

SALES REPRESENTATIVE, AUTOMOTIVE-LEASING (business ser.) ● DOT #273.357-014 ● OES: 49998 ● Sells automotive-leasing services to businesses and individuals: Visits prospective customers to stimulate interest in establishing or expanding automotive-leasing programs. Explains advantages of leasing automotive equipment, such as tax savings and reduced capital expenditures. Recommends types and number of vehicles needed to satisfactorily perform job with minimal expense. Computes leasing charges, based on such factors as length of contract, anticipated mileage, and applicable taxes. Prepares and sends leasing contract to leasing agency. Performs other tasks to increase sales, such as evaluating advertising campaigns or revising administrative procedures. Performs other duties as described under SALES REPRESENTATIVE (retail trade; wholesale tr.) Master Title. ● **GED:** R4, M3, L4 ● **SVP:** 6 mos-1 yr ● **Academic:** Ed=N, Eng=G ● **Work Field:** 292 ● **MPSMS:** 889, 884 ● **Aptitudes:** G3, V3, N3, S4, P4, Q3, K4, F4, M4, E5, C5 ● **Temperaments:** I, J, P ● **Physical:** Stg=L; Freq: T, G Occas: R, H, N ● **Work Env:** Noise=N; ● **Salary:** 4 ● **Outlook:** 3

SALES REPRESENTATIVE, FRANCHISE (business ser.) ● DOT #251.357-022 ● OES: 49998 ● Solicits purchase of franchise operation by contacting persons who meet organization's standards: Visits prospects to explain advantages of franchised business, services to be rendered, costs, location, and financial arrangements. Performs other duties as described under SALES REPRESENTATIVE (retail trade; wholesale tr.) Master Title. May assist franchise purchaser in early stages of operating business. May confer with purchaser and company officials to resolve complaints. ● **GED:** R4, M3, L4 ● **SVP:** 6 mos-1 yr ● **Academic:** Ed=H, Eng=G ● **Work Field:** 292 ● **MPSMS:** 894 ● **Aptitudes:** G3, V3, N3, S4, P4, Q3, K4, F4, M4, E5, C5 ● **Temperaments:** I, J, P ● **Physical:** Stg=L; Freq: T, G, N Occas: R, H, I ● **Work Env:** Noise=N; ● **Salary:** 4 ● **Outlook:** 4

SALES REPRESENTATIVE, TELEVISION CABLE SERVICE (radio-tv broad.) ● DOT #259.357-022 ● OES: 49998 ● Contacts homeowners, apartment managers, and other prospects to sell cable television service: Compiles list of prospective customers from lists of homes that do not have cable television and lists of residential addresses with names of owners and occupants. Travels throughout assigned territory to call on prospective customers in their homes to solicit orders. Performs duties as described under SALES REPRESENTATIVE (retail trade; wholesale tr.) Master Title. ● **GED:** R4, M3, L4 ● **SVP:** 1-3 mos ● **Academic:** Ed=N, Eng=G ● **Work Field:** 292 ● **MPSMS:** 869 ● **Aptitudes:** G3, V3, N3, S3, P4, Q3, K4, F4, M4, E5, C4 ● **Temperaments:** I, J, P ● **Physical:** Stg=L; Const: T, G Freq: H Occas: R, I, N, X ● **Work Env:** Noise=N; ● **Salary:** 2 ● **Outlook:** 3

SALES REPRESENTATIVE, UPHOLSTERY AND FURNITURE REPAIR (retail trade) ● DOT #259.357-026 ● OES: 49998 ● Calls on prospective customers to sell and estimate cost of furniture repair and upholstery service, utilizing knowledge of upholstery and repair procedures and material and labor costs: Examines worn or damaged furniture to determine extent of repairs required. Estimates amount of material required based on style and dimensions of furniture. Advises customer on color and type of fabric. Completes estimate form and gives form to customer. Prepares sales contract for upholstery work. ● **GED:** R4, M3, L3 ● **SVP:** 6 mos-1 yr ● **Academic:** Ed=N, Eng=G ● **Work Field:** 292, 211 ● **MPSMS:** 462, 420 ● **Aptitudes:** G3, V3, N3, S3, P3, Q3, K4, F4, M4, E5, C3 ● **Temperaments:** I, J, P ● **Physical:** Stg=L; Freq: T, G, N Occas: R, H, I, A, X ● **Work Env:** Noise=N; ● **Salary:** 3 ● **Outlook:** 2

TRAVEL AGENT (business ser.) ● DOT #252.152-010 ● OES: 43021 ● Alternate titles: TRAVEL COUNSELOR. Plans itineraries, and arranges accommodations and other travel services for customers of travel agency: Converses with customer to determine destination, mode of transportation, travel dates, financial considerations, and accommodations required. Provides customer with brochures and publications containing travel information, such as local customs, points of interest, and special events occurring in various locations, or foreign country regulations, such as consular requirements and currency limitations. Computes cost of travel and accommodations, using calculator, computer, carrier tariff books, and hotel rate books, or quotes package tours' costs. Books transportation and hotel reservations, using computer terminal or telephone. Prints or requests transportation carrier tickets, using computer printer system or system link to travel carrier. Collects payment for transportation and accommodations from customer. Plans, describes, arranges, and sells itinerary tour packages and promotional travel incentives offered by various travel carriers, utilizing knowledge of available travel services and promotional techniques. May specialize in foreign or domestic travel, individual or group travel, specific geographic area, airplane charters, or package tours. May be located in transportation terminal and specialize in group and individual escorted tours and be designated Tour Agent (motor trans.). ● **GED:** R4, M3, L4 ● **SVP:** 6 mos-1 yr ● **Academic:** Ed=H, Eng=G ● **Work Field:** 282, 292 ● **MPSMS:** 850 ● **Aptitudes:** G3, V2, N3, S4, P4, Q2, K3, F3, M3, E5, C4 ● **Temperaments:** I, J, P, V ● **Physical:** Stg=S; Freq: R, H, I, T, G, N Occas: X ● **Work Env:** Noise=N; ● **Salary:** 4 ● **Outlook:** 3

WEDDING CONSULTANT (retail trade) ● DOT #299.357-018 ● OES: 49998 ● Advises prospective brides in all phases of wedding planning, such as etiquette, attire of wedding party, and selection of trousseau: Compiles list of prospective brides from newspaper announcements of engagements. Mails promotional material to offer own and store's services as consultant. Recommends trousseau for bride, and costumes and accessories for attendants. Advises bride on selection of silverware style and pattern, china, glassware, stationery, invitations, flowers, and catering service. May display and sell wedding trousseau to bride, and attire for attendants, and silverware, china, and glassware to brides and wedding gift purchasers, performing duties as described under SALESPERSON (retail trade; wholesale tr.) Master Title. May compile and maintain gift register. May arrange for photographers to take pictures of wedding party. May attend rehearsals and wedding ceremony to give advice on etiquette. May accompany bride when shopping in store or shop for her. ● **GED:** R4, M3, L4 ● **SVP:** 1-2 yrs ● **Academic:** Ed=H, Eng=S ● **Work Field:** 292 ● **MPSMS:** 881 ● **Aptitudes:** G3, V2, N3, S4, P3, Q3, K4, F4, M4, E5, C3 ● **Temperaments:** F, I, J, P, V ● **Physical:** Stg=L; Freq: R, H, I, T, G, N, F, D, A, X, V Occas: E ● **Work Env:** Noise=N; ● **Salary:** 2 ● **Outlook:** 2

GOE: 08.02.07
Driving-Selling

DRIVER, SALES ROUTE (retail trade) ● DOT #292.353-010 ● OES: 97117 ● Alternate titles: DELIVERY-ROUTE TRUCK DRIVER; ROUTE DRIVER; TRUCK DRIVER, SALES ROUTE. Drives truck or automobile over established route to deliver and sell products or render services, collects money from customers, and makes change: Drives truck to deliver such items as beer, soft drinks, bakery products, dry cleaning, laundry, specialty foods, and medical supplies to customer's home or place of business. Collects money from custom-

ers, makes change, and records transactions on customer receipt. Writes customer order and instructions. Records sales or deliveries information on daily sales or delivery record. Calls on prospective customers to solicit new business. Prepares order forms and sales contracts. Informs regular customers of new products or services. Listens to and resolves service complaints. May place stock on shelves or racks. May set up merchandise and sales promotion displays or issue sales promotion materials to customers. May collect or pick up empty containers or rejected or unsold merchandise. May load truck. May issue or obtain customer signature on receipt for pickup or delivery. May clean inside of truck. May perform routine maintenance on truck. May direct DRIVER HELPER, SALES ROUTE (retail trade; wholesale tr.) 292.667-010 to load and unload truck and carry merchandise. May be designated according to product delivered or service rendered. ● **GED:** R3, M2, L3 ● **SVP:** 1-3 mos ● **Academic:** Ed=N, Eng=S ● **Work Field:** 013, 292 ● **MPSMS:** 880 ● **Aptitudes:** G3, V3, N3, S4, P4, Q3, K3, F4, M3, E3, C4 ● **Temperaments:** I, P ● **Physical:** Stg=M; Freq: R, H, T, G, F, D, X, V Occas: S, I, N, A ● **Work Env:** Noise=L; Occas: W ● **Salary:** 3 ● **Outlook:** 3

GOE: 08.02.08
Soliciting-Selling

FUND RAISER II (nonprofit org.) ● DOT #293.357-014 ● OES: 49998 ● Alternate titles: CONTRIBUTION SOLICITOR. Contacts individuals and firms to solicit donations for charity or other causes: Confers with supervisor, or reads potential donor list, to determine which individuals or firms to approach. Contacts individuals and firms by telephone, in person, or by mail to solicit funds or gifts-in-kind. Takes pledges for amounts or gifts-in-kind to be contributed, or accepts immediate cash payments. May sell emblems or other tokens of organization represented. May write letter to express appreciation for donation. May arrange for pick-up of gifts-in-kind. ● **GED:** R3, M2, L3 ● **SVP:** 2-30 days ● **Academic:** Ed=N, Eng=G ● **Work Field:** 292 ● **MPSMS:** 880, 890 ● **Aptitudes:** G3, V3, N3, S4, P4, Q4, K4, F4, M4, E5, C5 ● **Temperaments:** I, J, P ● **Physical:** Stg=L; Freq: R, H, I, T, G Occas: N ● **Work Env:** Noise=N; ● **Salary:** 4 ● **Outlook:** 4

GROUP-SALES REPRESENTATIVE (amuse. & rec.) ● DOT #259.357-010 ● OES: 49998 ● Alternate titles: PROMOTOR, GROUP-TICKET SALES. Promotes sale of group or season tickets for sports or other entertainment events: Telephones, visits, or writes to organizations, such as chambers of commerce, corporate-employee-recreation clubs, social clubs, and professional groups, to persuade them to purchase group tickets or season tickets to sports or other entertainment events, such as baseball, horseracing, or stage plays. Quotes group-ticket rates, arranges for sale of tickets and seating for group on specific date(s), and obtains payment. May arrange for club to sponsor sports event, such as one of races at horseracing track. ● **GED:** R3, M2, L3 ● **SVP:** 1-3 mos ● **Academic:** Ed=N, Eng=G ● **Work Field:** 292 ● **MPSMS:** 910 ● **Aptitudes:** G3, V2, N3, S5, P4, Q3, K4, F4, M4, E5, C5 ● **Temperaments:** I, J, P ● **Physical:** Stg=L; Freq: T, G Occas: R, H, N ● **Work Env:** Noise=N; ● **Salary:** 2 ● **Outlook:** 2

MEMBERSHIP SOLICITOR (any industry) ● DOT #293.357-022 ● OES: 49998 ● Solicits membership for club or trade association: Visits or contacts prospective members to explain benefits and costs of membership and to describe organization and objectives of club or association. May collect dues and payments for publications from members. May solicit funds for club or association [FUND RAISER (nonprofit org.) II]. May speak to members at meetings about services available. ● **GED:** R4, M3, L4 ● **SVP:** 3-6 mos ● **Academic:** Ed=N, Eng=G ● **Work Field:** 292 ● **MPSMS:** 896 ● **Aptitudes:** G3, V3, N4, S5, P5, Q3, K5, F4, M5, E5, C5 ● **Temperaments:** I, P ● **Physical:** Stg=L; Freq: T, G Occas: R, H, I, N ● **Work Env:** Noise=N; ● **Salary:** 4 ● **Outlook:** 4

SALES REPRESENTATIVE, DOOR-TO-DOOR (retail trade) ● DOT #291.357-010 ● OES: 49998 ● Alternate titles: CANVASSER; PEDDLER; SOLICITOR. Sells merchandise or service, such as books, magazines, notions, brushes, and cosmetics, going from door to door without making appointments or following leads from management, other workers, or from listings in city and telephone directories: Displays sample products, explains desirable qualities of products, and leaves samples, or distributes advertising literature explaining service or products. Writes and submits orders to company. Delivers merchandise, collects money, and makes change. May contact individuals previously solicited in person, by telephone, or by mail to close sale. May travel from one area to another, or be assigned to specified territory. ● **GED:** R3, M2, L3 ● **SVP:** 2-30 days ● **Academic:** Ed=N, Eng=G ● **Work Field:** 292 ● **MPSMS:** 881 ● **Aptitudes:** G3, V3, N3, S4, P4, Q3, K4, F4, M4, E5, C4 ● **Temperaments:** I, P ● **Physical:** Stg=L; Freq: R, H, I, T, G, N Occas: F, D, A, X, V ● **Work Env:** Noise=N; Freq: W ● **Salary:** 3 ● **Outlook:** 4

TELEPHONE SOLICITOR (any industry) ● DOT #299.357-014 ● OES: 49998 ● Alternate titles: TELEMARKETER; TELEPHONE

SALES REPRESENTATIVE. Solicits orders for merchandise or services over telephone: Calls prospective customers to explain type of service or merchandise offered. Quotes prices and tries to persuade customer to buy, using prepared sales talk. Records names, addresses, purchases, and reactions of prospects solicited. Refers orders to other workers for filling. Keys data from order card into computer, using keyboard. May develop lists of prospects from city and telephone directories. May type report on sales activities. May contact DRIVER, SALES ROUTE (retail trade; wholesale tr.) 292.353-010 to arrange delivery of merchandise. ● **GED:** R3, M3, L3 ● **SVP:** 1-3 mos ● **Academic:** Ed=N, Eng=G ● **Work Field:** 292 ● **MPSMS:** 885 ● **Aptitudes:** G3, V3, N3, S4, P4, Q3, K4, F4, M4, E5, C5 ● **Temperaments:** I, J, P ● **Physical:** Stg=S; Freq: I, T, G, A Occas: R, H, N ● **Work Env:** Noise=N; ● **Salary:** 1 ● **Outlook:** 4

Selling

Vending

08

08.03

Workers in this group sell novelties, snacks and other inexpensive items. They work at stadiums and street fairs, in night clubs or restaurants or wherever crowds gather for entertainment or recreation. Some of them sell products on the street, staying in one location, or moving through commercial and residential areas.

✓ What kind of work would you do?

Your work activities would depend upon your specific job. For example, you might:

- walk around a football stadium or baseball park calling out items to be sold.
- walk among guests in a nightclub, restaurant, or hotel selling cigars, cigarettes, or corsages.
- take pictures of people in restaurants and try to sell them the finished prints.
- sell merchandise such as flowers, fruit, or ice cream from a pushcart or truck.

✓ What skills and abilities do you need for this kind of work?

To do this kind of work, you must be able to:

- speak clearly, shout, sing, or call out to attract customers.
- accept payment and make change quickly and accurately.
- stand or walk for long periods of time, often climbing stairs or pushing through crowds while carrying heavy containers or pushing a cart.
- be very persuasive in getting people to buy your products.

The above statements may not apply to every job in this group.

✓ How do you know if you would like or could learn to do this kind of work?

The following questions may give you clues about yourself as you consider this group of jobs.

- Have you worked at a carnival or fair? Do you enjoy shouting or gesturing to get the attention of a crowd?
- Have you sold things to raise money for a school or civic project? Do you enjoy this type of activity?
- Have you sold magazines or candy door-to-door? Do you like work in which you persuade others to buy products?
- Have you worked as a cashier in a store? Can you figure the cost of several items and make change accurately?

✓ How can you prepare for and enter this kind of work?

Occupations in this group usually require education and/or training extending from a short demonstration to over three months, depending upon the specific kind of work. Most jobs in this group are open to almost anyone. Formal training, experience, or education is seldom required.

✓ What else should you consider about these jobs?

Jobs in this group are usually short-term and opportunities for advancement are few. In many cases, payment is based only on how many items are sold, so workers must use all possible means to convince customers to buy. However, some jobs provide permanent employment. These jobs provide experience that can be applied to other saleswork. Some jobs in this group require the worker to be outside in all kinds of weather. Some workers own their own carts and are in business for themselves.

If you think you would like to do this kind of work, look at the job titles listed on the next page.

GOE: 08.03.01
Peddling & Hawking

CIGARETTE VENDOR (hotel & rest.) ● DOT #291.457-010 ● OES: 49998 ● Sells cigars, cigarettes, corsages, and novelties to patrons in hotels, restaurants, and nightclubs: Walks among guests carrying tray of articles and persuades patrons to make purchases. May order supplies. May wire flowers and attach ribbons to form corsages. ● **GED:** R2, M2, L2 ● **SVP:** 2-30 days ● **Academic:** Ed=N, Eng=S ● **Work Field:** 292 ● **MPSMS:** 884 ● **Aptitudes:** G4, V4, N4, S4, P4, Q4, K4, F4, M4, E4, C4 ● **Temperaments:** P ● **Physical:** Stg=L; Freq: R, H, I, T, G, N Occas: X ● **Work Env:** Noise=N; ● **Salary:** 2 ● **Outlook:** 2

LOUNGE-CAR ATTENDANT (r.r. trans.) ● DOT #291.457-014 ● OES: 49998 ● Alternate titles: SANDWICH SELLER; VENDOR. Sells beverages, cakes, candies, cigarettes, and sandwiches to passengers in railroad passenger coaches: Walks down aisle of car, with basket or cart containing items for sale, and calls out offerings. Serves items to passengers. Accepts money for items purchased and returns change. May sell newspapers, magazines, postcards, playing cards, and similar nonfood items only and be designated News Agent (r.r. trans.). ● **GED:** R2, M2, L2 ● **SVP:** 2-30 days ● **Academic:** Ed=N, Eng=S ● **Work Field:** 292 ● **MPSMS:** 903 ● **Aptitudes:** G4, V4, N3, S5, P4, Q4, K4, F3, M3, E3, C5 ● **Temperaments:** P, R ● **Physical:** Stg=M; Freq: B, R, H, I, T, G, N ● **Work Env:** Noise=N; ● **Salary:** 2 ● **Outlook:** 3

PHOTOGRAPHER (amuse. & rec.) ● DOT #143.457-010 ● OES: 34023 ● Persuades nightclub and restaurant patrons to pose for pictures and operates camera to photograph them: Carries camera and flashbulb equipment to tables and solicits customers' patronage. Adjusts camera and photographs customers. Takes exposed film to darkroom on premises for immediate processing by DEVELOPER (photofinishing). Returns to customers with finished photographs or proofs and writes orders for additional prints selected. Receives payment for photographs. May use camera which produces instant picture. ● **GED:** R3, M1, L3 ● **SVP:** 1-3 mos ● **Academic:** Ed=N, Eng=S ● **Work Field:** 292 ● **MPSMS:** 753 ● **Aptitudes:** G3, V2, N3, S5, P4, Q4, K4, F4, M4, E5, C5 ● **Temperaments:** I, P ● **Physical:** Stg=L; Freq: R, H, I, T, G, N, F, D ● **Work Env:** Noise=Q; ● **Salary:** 4 ● **Outlook:** 1

VENDOR (amuse. & rec.) ● DOT #291.457-022 ● OES: 49998 ● Alternate titles: PEDDLER. Sells refreshments, programs, novelties, or cushions at sports events, parades, or other entertainments: Circulates among patrons or spectators, calling out items for sale. Hands, passes, or throws item to purchaser, receives payment, and makes change as required. Checks out items to replenish stock and turns in monies from sales. ● **GED:** R2, M2, L2 ● **SVP:** 2-30 days ● **Academic:** Ed=N, Eng=S ● **Work Field:** 292 ● **MPSMS:** 884 ● **Aptitudes:** G4, V4, N4, S4, P4, Q4, K4, F4, M4, E5, C5 ● **Temperaments:** P ● **Physical:** Stg=M; Freq: R, H, I, T, G, N ● **Work Env:** Noise=L; Freq: W ● **Salary:** 1 ● **Outlook:** 3

Accommodating 09

An interest in catering to the wishes and needs of others, usually on a one-to-one basis. You can satisfy this interest by providing services for the convenience of others, such as hospitality services in hotels, restaurants, airplanes, etc. You may enjoy improving the appearance of others. Perhaps working in the hair and beauty care field would satisfy you. You may wish to provide personal services, such as taking tickets, baggage, or ushering.

Hospitality Services   09.01

Workers in this group help persons, such as visitors, travelers, and customers, get acquainted with and feel at ease in an unfamiliar setting; provide escort and guide services; and plan and direct social activities. They may also be concerned with the safety and comfort of people when they are traveling or vacationing. These workers find employment with air-, rail-, and water transportation companies; radio and television broadcasting stations; hotels and restaurants; museums; retirement homes; and related establishments.

✓ What kind of work would you do?

Your work activities would depend upon your specific job. For example you might:

- greet guests and answer questions concerning social and recreational activities in a hotel.
- greet and seat customers in a restaurant.
- provide personal services to airplane passengers, such as answering questions and serving meals.
- escort a group of people through an industrial plant and explain what is taking place.
- take people on a tour of model homes and explain their features.
- conduct visitors on tour of television studios.

✓ What skills and abilities do you need for this kind of work?

To do this kind of work, you must be able to:

- speak clearly.
- talk easily with all kinds of people to put them at ease.

- use judgment and reasoning to cope with emergencies, such as sudden illness, accident, or interrupted service.
- perform a variety of activities and change activities frequently and sometimes without notice.
- plan and carry out an activity, such as a card party or dance.

✓ How do you know if you would like or could learn to do this kind of work?

The following questions may give you clues about yourself as you consider this group of jobs.

- Have you been a member of a community or civil group? Do you like socializing with others?
- Have you had courses in speech? Do you like to speak to groups?
- Have you planned or organized a party? Can you lead others in games and group activities?
- Have you taught friends to dance? Did they enjoy the lessons?
- Have you been a treasurer or secretary for an organization? Can you keep accurate records?

✓ How can you prepare for and enter this kind of work?

Occupations in this group usually require education and/or training extending from thirty days to over two years, depending upon the specific kind of work. The methods of entry for these jobs vary. For example, guides in public buildings receive on-the-job training after they are hired. Airplane flight attendants are usually trained by employers. Dude wranglers and stewards enter through experience in lower level jobs. Hostesses, chaperones, and escorts are hired because of their manners and charming personalities.

✓ *What else should you consider about these jobs?*

Workers in this group may have to travel and live in hotels or resorts instead of at home. Night or holiday work may be required. Some workers must wear uniforms.

If you think you would like to do this kind of work, look at the job titles listed on the following pages.

■ ■ ■

GOE: 09.01.01
Social & Recreational Activities

AMUSEMENT PARK WORKER (amuse. & rec.) ● DOT #349.664-010 ● OES: 68014 ● Performs any combination of following duties in amusement park: Escorts patrons on tours of park's points of interest. Takes pictures of patrons to impart pictures onto T-shirts, using camera, automatic printing equipment, and heating press. Maintains and distributes uniforms worn by park employees. Cleans park grounds, office facilities, and rest room areas, using broom, dust pan, or vacuum cleaner. Distributes literature, such as maps, show schedules, and pass information, to acquaint visitors with park facilities. Monitors activities of children using park playground area to ensure safe use of equipment. Directs patrons to seats for park attractions and opens doors to assist patrons' entry and exit from attractions. Receives cash for tickets or items sold to patrons and records sales, using cash register. ● **GED:** R2, M2, L2 ● **SVP:** 2-30 days ● **Academic:** Ed=N, Eng=S ● **Work Field:** 281, 282 ● **MPSMS:** 919 ● **Aptitudes:** G3, V3, N4, S4, P4, Q4, K3, F4, M3, E5, C4 ● **Temperaments:** P ● **Physical:** Stg=M; Freq: T, G Occas: R, H, N, F, X ● **Work Env:** Noise=N; ● **Salary:** 1 ● **Outlook:** 4

COUNSELOR, CAMP (amuse. & rec.) ● DOT #159.124-010 ● OES: 27311 ● Directs activities of children at vacation camp: Plans activities, such as hikes, cookouts, and campfires, to provide wide variety of camping experiences. Demonstrates use of camping equipment and explains principles and techniques of activities, such as backpacking, nature study, and outdoor cooking, to increase campers' knowledge and competence. Plans and arranges competition in activities, such as team sports or housekeeping, to stimulate campers interest and participation. Demonstrates use of materials and tools to instruct children in arts and crafts. Instructs campers in skills, such as canoeing, sailing, swimming, archery, horseback riding, and animal care, explaining and demonstrating procedures and safety techniques. Organizes, leads, instructs, and referees games. Enforces camp rules and regulations to guide conduct, maintain discipline, and safeguard health of campers. May be identified according to type of camp activity. ● **GED:** R4, M2, L4 ● **SVP:** 6 mos-1 yr ● **Academic:** Ed=N, Eng=G ● **Work Field:** 296 ● **MPSMS:** 919 ● **Aptitudes:** G2, V2, N4, S3, P4, Q4, K3, F3, M3, E3, C4 ● **Temperaments:** D, P, V ● **Physical:** Stg=M; Freq: T, G Occas: C, B, S, K, O, W, R, H, I, E, N, F, D, A, X, V ● **Work Env:** Noise=N; Freq: W ● **Salary:** 3 ● **Outlook:** 3

DIRECTOR, SOCIAL (hotel & rest.) ● DOT #352.167-010 ● OES: 27311 ● Alternate titles: DIRECTOR, RECREATION. Plans and organizes recreational activities and creates friendly atmosphere for guests in hotels and resorts or for passengers on board ship: Greets new arrivals, introduces them to other guests, acquaints them with recreation facilities, and encourages them to participate in group activities. Ascertains interests of group and evaluates available equipment and facilities to plan activities, such as card parties, games, tournaments, dances, musicals, and field trips. Arranges for activity requirements, such as setting up equipment, transportation, decorations, refreshments, and entertainment. Associates with lonely guests and visits those who are ill. May greet and seat guests in dining room. May assist management in resolving guests' complaints. ● **GED:** R4, M3, L4 ● **SVP:** 1-2 yrs ● **Academic:** Ed=N, Eng=G ● **Work Field:** 291, 295 ● **MPSMS:** 919 ● **Aptitudes:** G3, V2, N3, S4, P4, Q3, K4, F4, M4, E4, C5 ● **Temperaments:** D, J, P, V ● **Physical:** Stg=L; Freq: T, G Occas: R, H, I, N ● **Work Env:** Noise=N; Occas: W ● **Salary:** 3 ● **Outlook:** 3

GROUP WORKER (social ser.) ● DOT #195.164-010 ● OES: 27310 ● Organizes and leads groups, such as senior citizens, children, and street gangs, in activities that meet interests of individual members: Develops recreational, physical education, and cultural programs for various age groups. Demonstrates and instructs participants in activities, such as active sports, group dances and games, arts, crafts, and dramatics. Organizes current-events discussion groups, conducts consumer problem surveys, and performs similar activities to stimulate interest in civic responsibility. Promotes group work concept of enabling members to develop their own program activities through encouragement and leadership of membership discussions. Consults with other community resources regarding specific individuals, and makes referral when indicated. Keeps records. May recruit, train, and supervise paid staff and volunteers. Employed in settings, such as community center, neighborhood or settlement house, hospital, institution for children or aged, youth centers, and housing projects. ● **GED:** R5, M4, L5 ● **SVP:** 2-4 yrs ● **Academic:** Ed=A, Eng=G ● **Work Field:** 298 ● **MPSMS:** 941 ● **Aptitudes:** G2, V2, N3, S3, P3, Q4, K3, F3, M3, E3, C3 ● **Temperaments:** D, I, J, P, V ● **Physical:** Stg=L; Freq: T, G Occas: R, H, I, N, F, D, A, X, V ● **Work Env:** Noise=L; Occas: W ● **Salary:** 3 ● **Outlook:** 2

GUIDE, HUNTING AND FISHING (amuse. & rec.) ● DOT #353.161-010 ● OES: 69998 ● Plans, organizes and conducts hunting and fishing trips for individuals and groups: Plans itinerary for hunting and fishing trips applying knowledge of countryside to determine best route and sites. Arranges for transporting sportsman, equipment and supplies to hunting or fishing area using horses, land vehicles, motorboat, or airplane. Explains hunting and fishing laws to ensure compliance. Instructs members of party in use of hunting or fishing gear. Prepares meals for members of party. Administers first aid to injured sportsmen. May care for animals. May sell or rent equipment, clothing and supplies. May pilot airplane or drive land and water vehicles. ● **GED:** R4, M3, L3 ● **SVP:** 2-4 yrs ● **Academic:** Ed=N, Eng=G ● **Work Field:** 291, 282, 146 ● **MPSMS:** 913 ● **Aptitudes:** G3, V3, N3, S3, P4, Q4, K3, F3, M2, E3, C4 ● **Temperaments:** D, J, P, V ● **Physical:** Stg=H; Freq: R, H, I, E, T, G, F, D, V Occas: C, B, S, K, O, N, X ● **Work Env:** Noise=N; Const: W ● **Salary:** 1 ● **Outlook:** 1

HOST/HOSTESS (any industry) ● DOT #352.667-010 ● OES: 69998 ● Alternate titles: RECEPTIONIST. Greets guests arriving at country club, catered social function, or other gathering place. Introduces guests and suggests planned activities, such as dancing or games. Gives directions to personnel engaged in serving of refreshments. May plan menus and supervise activities of food-service workers. May plan and participate in social activities, games, and sports, depending on nature of establishment or function. May deposit or pick up guests at railway station, home, or other location as directed. ● **GED:** R3, M2, L3 ● **SVP:** 1-3 mos ● **Academic:** Ed=N, Eng=G ● **Work Field:** 291 ● **MPSMS:** 909 ● **Aptitudes:** G3, V3, N4, S4, P4, Q4, K4, F4, M4, E5, C5 ● **Temperaments:** D, V ● **Physical:** Stg=L; Freq: R, H, T, G ● **Work Env:** Noise=N; ● **Salary:** 1 ● **Outlook:** 3

RECREATION AIDE (social ser.) ● DOT #195.367-030 ● OES: 68014 ● Assists RECREATION LEADER (social ser.) 195.227-014 in conducting recreation activities in community center or other voluntary recreation facility: Arranges chairs, tables, and sporting or exercise equipment in designated rooms or other areas for scheduled group activities, such as banquets, wedding receptions, parties, group meetings, or sports events. Welcomes visitors and answers incoming telephone calls. Notifies patrons of activity schedules and registration requirements. Monitors spectators and participants at sports events to ensure orderly conduct. Receives, stores, and issues sports equipment and supplies. May keep attendance records or scores at sporting events, operate audiovisual equipment, monitor activities of children during recreational trips or tours, or perform other duties as directed by RECREATION LEADER (social ser.) 195.227-014. ● **GED:** R3, M2, L3 ●

SVP: 2-30 days ● **Academic:** Ed=N, Eng=G ● **Work Field:** 291 ● **MPSMS:** 941 ● **Aptitudes:** G3, V3, N3, S4, P4, Q4, K4, F4, M4, E5, C5 ● **Temperaments:** P, V ● **Physical:** Stg=L; Freq: R, H, T, G Occas: I ● **Work Env:** Noise=N; ● **Salary:** 2 ● **Outlook:** 2

RECREATION LEADER (social ser.) ● DOT #195.227-014 ● OES: 27311 ● Conducts recreation activities with assigned groups in public department of voluntary agency: Organizes, promotes, and develops interest in activities, such as arts and crafts, sports, games, music, dramatics, social recreation, camping, and hobbies. Cooperates with other staff members in conducting community wide events and works with neighborhood groups to determine recreation interests and needs of persons of all ages. Works under close supervision of RECREATION SUPERVISOR (profess. & kin.) 187.167-238. Cooperates with recreation and nonrecreation personnel when in agency setting, such as settlement house, institution for children or aged, hospital, armed services, or penal institution. ● **GED:** R4, M3, L4 ● **SVP:** 1-2 yrs ● **Academic:** Ed=A, Eng=G ● **Work Field:** 291, 296 ● **MPSMS:** 941, 910 ● **Aptitudes:** G2, V2, N4, S3, P3, Q4, K3, F3, M3, E3, C4 ● **Temperaments:** D, P ● **Physical:** Stg=L; Freq: R, H, I, T, G Occas: S, N, F, X, V ● **Work Env:** Noise=N; Occas: W ● **Salary:** 3 ● **Outlook:** 3

GOE: 09.01.02
Guide Services

CRAFT DEMONSTRATOR (museums) ● DOT #109.364-010 ● OES: 31511 ● Demonstrates and explains techniques and purposes of handicraft or other activity, such as candle dipping, horseshoeing, or soap making, as part of display in history or folk museum, or restored or refurbished farm, village, or neighborhood: Studies historical and technical literature to acquire information about time period and lifestyle depicted in display and craft techniques associated with time and area, to devise plan for authentic presentation of craft. Drafts outline of talk, assisted by research personnel, to acquaint visitors with customs and crafts associated with folk life depicted. Practices techniques involved in handicraft to ensure accurate and skillful demonstrations. Molds candles, shoes horses, operates looms, or engages in other crafts or activities, working in appropriate period setting, to demonstrate craft to visitors. Explains techniques of craft, and points out relationship of craft to lifestyle depicted to assist visitors to comprehend traditional techniques of work and play peculiar to time and area. Answers visitor questions or refers visitor to other sources for information. ● **GED:** R4, M2, L4 ● **SVP:** 3-6 mos ● **Academic:** Ed=H, Eng=G ● **Work Field:** 282 ● **MPSMS:** 919, 931, 939 ● **Aptitudes:** G3, V3, N3, S3, P3, Q4, K3, F3, M3, E5, C3 ● **Temperaments:** F, J, P, T ● **Physical:** Stg=L; Freq: R, H, I, T, G, N, X ● **Work Env:** Noise=N; Occas: W ● **Salary:** 4 ● **Outlook:** 3

EXHIBIT-DISPLAY REPRESENTATIVE (any industry) ● DOT #297.367-010 ● OES: 49998 ● Attends trade, traveling, promotional, educational, or amusement exhibit to answer visitors' questions, explain or describe exhibit, and to protect it against theft or damage. May set up or arrange display. May demonstrate use of displayed items. May lecture and show slides. May collect fees or accept donations. May solicit patronage. May distribute brochures. May obtain names and addresses of prospective customers. May drive truck and trailer to transport exhibit. May be designated Trade-Show Representative (any industry). ● **GED:** R4, M2, L4 ● **SVP:** 6 mos-1 yr ● **Academic:** Ed=N, Eng=G ● **Work Field:** 293, 282 ● **MPSMS:** 960 ● **Aptitudes:** G3, V3, N4, S4, P3, Q4, K4, F4, M4, E5, C5 ● **Temperaments:** P ● **Physical:** Stg=L; Freq: T, G Occas: R, H, I, N ● **Work Env:** Noise=N; ● **Salary:** 2 ● **Outlook:** 3

GUIDE (personal ser.) ● DOT #353.367-010 ● OES: 69998 ● Alternate titles: GUIDE, VISITOR. Escorts visitors around city or town: Advises visitors, such as convention delegates, foreign government personnel, or salesmen, as to location of buildings, points of interest, and other sites, or escorts visitors to designated locations, using private or public transportation. May carry equipment, luggage, or sample cases for visitors. May be required to speak foreign language when communicating with foreign visitors. May be designated according to type of visitor directed or escorted as Guide, Delegate (personal ser.). ● **GED:** R3, M1, L2 ● **SVP:** 1-3 mos ● **Academic:** Ed=N, Eng=G ● **Work**

Field: 282, 291 ● **MPSMS:** 909 ● **Aptitudes:** G3, V3, N4, S4, P4, Q4, K4, F4, M4, E5, C5 ● **Temperaments:** P, V ● **Physical:** Stg=L; Freq: T, G Occas: R, H, I, N ● **Work Env:** Noise=N; Freq: W ● **Salary:** 1 ● **Outlook:** 2

GUIDE, ESTABLISHMENT (any industry) ● DOT #353.367-014 ● OES: 69998 ● Alternate titles: GUIDE, TOUR. Escorts group of people through establishment, such as museum, aquarium, or public or historical building, or through historic or scenic outdoor site, such as battlefield, park, or cave, usually following specified route: Lectures concerning size, value, and history of establishment, points out features of interest, and gives other information peculiar to establishment. Answers questions of group. Assumes responsibility for safety of group. May collect fees from members of group. May solicit patronage. May distribute brochures on establishment or historical site to visitors. May be designated Airport Guide (air trans.). ● **GED:** R3, M1, L3 ● **SVP:** 1-3 mos ● **Academic:** Ed=H, Eng=G ● **Work Field:** 282 ● **MPSMS:** 919 ● **Aptitudes:** G3, V3, N4, S4, P4, Q3, K4, F4, M4, E4, C5 ● **Temperaments:** I, P, R ● **Physical:** Stg=L; Const: T, G Freq: R, H, N, F Occas: C, B, S, O, I ● **Work Env:** Noise=N; Occas: W ● **Salary:** 2 ● **Outlook:** 3

GUIDE, PLANT (any industry) ● DOT #353.367-018 ● OES: 69998 ● Alternate titles: PLANT TOUR GUIDE. Escorts group of people through industrial establishment, and describes features of interest: Leads way along specified route and explains various processes and operation of machines. Answers questions and supplies information on work of department or departments visited. ● **GED:** R3, M2, L3 ● **SVP:** 1-3 mos ● **Academic:** Ed=N, Eng=G ● **Work Field:** 282 ● **MPSMS:** 931 ● **Aptitudes:** G3, V3, N4, S4, P4, Q4, K4, F4, M4, E5, C4 ● **Temperaments:** P, V ● **Physical:** Stg=L; Freq: T, G Occas: R, H, I, N, X ● **Work Env:** Noise=N; Occas: W ● **Salary:** 2 ● **Outlook:** 2

GUIDE, SIGHTSEEING (amuse. & rec.) ● DOT #353.363-010 ● OES: 69998 ● Alternate titles: BARKER; CICERONE; SPIELER. Drives motor vehicle to transport sightseers and lectures group concerning points of interest during sightseeing tour: Drives limousine or sightseeing bus, stopping vehicle at establishments or locations, such as art gallery, museum, battlefield, and cave, to permit group to be escorted through buildings by GUIDE, ESTABLISHMENT (any industry) 353.367-014. Describes points of interest along route of tour, using public address system or megaphone. May collect fees or tickets, and plan refreshment and rest stops. May escort group through establishment and describe points of interest. May operate tram to transport patrons through amusement park and be designated Tram Operator (amuse. & rec.). ● **GED:** R3, M2, L3 ● **SVP:** 3-6 mos ● **Academic:** Ed=N, Eng=G ● **Work Field:** 282, 013 ● **MPSMS:** 919 ● **Aptitudes:** G3, V3, N4, S3, P4, Q4, K3, F4, M3, E3, C4 ● **Temperaments:** P, V ● **Physical:** Stg=L; Freq: R, H, T, G, F, D, X, V Occas: S, K, O, I, N, A ● **Work Env:** Noise=N; Occas: W ● **Salary:** 2 ● **Outlook:** 3

GOE: 09.01.03
Food Services

BUTLER (domestic ser.) ● DOT #309.137-010 ● OES: 62031 ● Supervises and coordinates activities of household employees engaged in cooking, cleaning, and related domestic duties: Oversees serving of luncheon and dinner, sets table, directs workers in serving meals, or personally serves them. Performs other services as requested, such as mixing and serving cocktails and tea. Answers telephone and delivers messages. Receives and announces guests. May prepare salads. May keep silver service clean and intact. May employ and discharge other household employees. ● **GED:** R4, M2, L3 ● **SVP:** 1-2 yrs ● **Academic:** Ed=B, Eng=S ● **Work Field:** 291 ● **MPSMS:** 900 ● **Aptitudes:** G3, V3, N3, S4, P3, Q3, K4, F4, M3, E4, C5 ● **Temperaments:** D, P, V ● **Physical:** Stg=L; Freq: R, H, I, T, G Occas: N ● **Work Env:** Noise=N; ● **Salary:** 1 ● **Outlook:** 4

HOST/HOSTESS, RESTAURANT (hotel & rest.) ● DOT #310.137-010 ● OES: 65002 ● Alternate titles: DINING-ROOM MANAGER; WAITER/WAITRESS, HEAD. Supervises and coordinates activities of dining room personnel to provide fast and courteous service to patrons: Schedules dining reservations and arranges parties or special services for diners. Greets guests, escorts them to tables, and provides menus. Adjusts complaints of patrons. Assigns work tasks and coordinates activities of dining room personnel to ensure prompt and courteous service to patrons. Inspects dining room serving stations for neatness and cleanliness, and requisitions table linens and other dining room supplies for tables and serving stations. May interview, hire, and discharge dining room personnel. May train dining room employees. May schedule work hours and keep time records of dining room workers. May assist in planning menus. May prepare beverages and expedite food orders. May total receipts, at end of shift, to verify sales and clear cash register. May collect payment from customers [CASHIER (clerical) II 211.462-010]. ● **GED:** R4, M3, L4 ● **SVP:** 1-2 yrs ● **Academic:** Ed=N, Eng=S ● **Work Field:** 291 ● **MPSMS:** 903 ● **Aptitudes:** G3, V3, N3, S4, P3, Q3, K3, F4, M4, E5, C5 ● **Temperaments:** D, P, V ● **Physical:** Stg=L; Freq: R, H, T, G Occas: I, N ● **Work Env:** Noise=N; ● **Salary:** 1 ● **Outlook:** 4

WAITER/WAITRESS, CAPTAIN (hotel & rest.) ● DOT #311.137-018 ● OES: 69998 ● Alternate titles: CAPTAIN. Supervises activities of workers in section of dining room: Receives guests and conducts them to tables. Describes or suggests food courses and appropriate wines. When serving banquets, may be designated Banquet Captain (hotel & rest.). ● **GED:** R4, M2, L3 ● **SVP:** 1-2 yrs ● **Academic:** Ed=H, Eng=S ● **Work Field:** 291 ● **MPSMS:** 903 ● **Aptitudes:** G3, V3, N4, S4, P4, Q3, K4, F4, M4, E5, C5 ● **Temperaments:** D, P ● **Physical:** Stg=L; Freq: R, H, T, G Occas: I, N ● **Work Env:** Noise=N; ● **Salary:** 2 ● **Outlook:** 4

WAITER/WAITRESS, HEAD (hotel & rest.) ● DOT #311.137-022 ● OES: 69998 ● Supervises and coordinates activities of dining-room employees engaged in providing courteous and rapid service to diners: Greets guests and escorts them to tables. Schedules dining reservations. Arranges parties for patrons. Adjusts complaints regarding food or service. Hires and trains dining-room employees. Notifies payroll department regarding work schedules and time records. May assist in preparing menus. May plan and execute details for banquets [STEWARD/STEWARDESS, BANQUET (hotel & rest.); MANAGER, CATERING (hotel & rest.)]. May supervise WAITERS/WAITRESSES, ROOM SERVICE (hotel & rest.) and be designated Captain, Room Service (hotel & rest.). ● **GED:** R4, M3, L4 ● **SVP:** 1-2 yrs ● **Academic:** Ed=N, Eng=S ● **Work Field:** 291 ● **MPSMS:** 903 ● **Aptitudes:** G3, V3, N3, S4, P4, Q4, K4, F4, M4, E4, C4 ● **Temperaments:** D, P, V ● **Physical:** Stg=L; Freq: R, H, I, T, G, N Occas: X ● **Work Env:** Noise=N; ● **Salary:** 4 ● **Outlook:** 2

GOE: 09.01.04
Safety & Comfort Services

AIRPLANE-FLIGHT ATTENDANT (air trans.) ● DOT #352.367-010 ● OES: 68026 ● Alternate titles: AIRPLANE-CABIN ATTENDANT. Performs variety of personal services conducive to safety and comfort of airline passengers during flight: Greets passengers, verifies tickets, records destinations, and directs passengers to assigned seats. Assists passengers to store carry-on luggage in overhead, garment, or under seat storage. Explains use of safety equipment, such as seat belts, oxygen masks, and life jackets. Walks aisle of plane to verify that passengers have complied with federal regulations prior to take off. Serves previously prepared meals and beverages. Observes passengers to detect signs of discomfort, and issues palliatives to relieve passenger ailments, such as airsickness and insomnia. Administers first aid according to passenger distress when needed. Answers questions regarding performance of aircraft, stopovers, and flight schedules. Performs other personal services, such as distributing reading material and pointing out places of interest. Prepares reports showing place of departure and destination, passenger ticket numbers, meal and beverage inventories, palliatives issued, and lost and found articles. May collect money for meals and beverages. ● **GED:** R4, M3, L3 ● **SVP:** 1-3 mos ● **Academic:** Ed=H, Eng=G ● **Work Field:** 291, 282 ● **MPSMS:** 855 ● **Aptitudes:** G3, V3, N3, S4, P4, Q3, K3, F4, M3, E3, C4 ● **Temperaments:** P, S, V ● **Physical:** Stg=M; Freq: B, R, H, T, G, N Occas: S, I, X ● **Work Env:** Noise=L; Occas: O ● **Salary:** 3 ● **Outlook:** 1

FUNERAL ATTENDANT (personal ser.) ● DOT #359.677-014 ● OES: 69998 ● Alternate titles: UNDERTAKER ASSISTANT; USHER. Performs variety of tasks during funeral: Places casket in parlor or chapel prior to wake or funeral service and arranges floral offerings and lights around casket, following instructions of DIRECTOR, FUNERAL (personal ser.) or EMBALMER (personal ser.). Directs or escorts mourners to parlor or chapel in which wake or funeral is held. Assists DIRECTOR, FUNERAL (personal ser.) to close coffin. Carries flowers to hearse or limousine for transportation to place of interment. Assists mourners into and out of limousines. Issues and stores funeral equipment, such as casket lowering devices and grass mats used at place of interment. May carry casket [PALLBEARER (personal ser.)]. ● **GED:** R2, M1, L2 ● **SVP:** 1-3 mos ● **Academic:** Ed=N, Eng=N ● **Work Field:** 291 ● **MPSMS:** 907 ● **Aptitudes:** G4, V4, N4, S4, P4, Q4, K4, F4, M4, E5, C4 ● **Temperaments:** P ● **Physical:** Stg=M; Freq: T, G Occas: S, R, H, X ● **Work Env:** Noise=Q; ● **Salary:** 2 ● **Outlook:** 2

PASSENGER SERVICE REPRESENTATIVE I (r.r. trans.) ● DOT #352.677-010 ● OES: 69998 ● Alternate titles: HOST/HOSTESS, RAILWAY. Renders personal services to railroad passengers to make their trip pleasant and comfortable: Straightens seat cushions and window shades to prepare cars for passengers. Greets passengers boarding trains and introduces passengers to each other. Answers questions about train schedules, travel routes, and railway services. Assists in feeding and caring for children during transit. Assists ill passengers. ● **GED:** R3, M2, L3 ● **SVP:** 1-3 mos ● **Academic:** Ed=N, Eng=G ● **Work Field:** 291, 282 ● **MPSMS:** 851 ● **Aptitudes:** G3, V3, N4, S4, P4, Q4, K4, F4, M3, E4, C5 ● **Temperaments:** P, V ● **Physical:** Stg=L; Freq: R, H, T, G Occas: B, S, I, N ● **Work Env:** Noise=L; ● **Salary:** 2 ● **Outlook:** 2

Accommodating   09

Barber and Beauty Services

09.02

Workers in this group provide people with a variety of barbering and beauty services. These services involve care of the hair, skin, and nails. These workers find employment in barber and beauty shops, department stores, hotel, and retirement homes. A few workers find jobs on passenger ships. Some are self-employed and work in their own homes or go to the customer.

✓ *What kind of work would you do?*

Your work activities would depend upon your specific job. For example, you might:

- cut, trim, shampoo, curl, or style hair.
- lather and shave facial hair.
- remove unwanted facial hair by using an electrically-charged needle.
- give hair and scalp-conditioning treatments.

✓ *What skills and abilities do you need for this kind of work?*

To do this kind of work, you must be able to:

- understand written and diagram instructions for applying hair coloring and permanent waving solutions.
- adapt a procedure to an individual customer's physical features.
- use a variety of tools, such as scissors, tweezers, combs, curlers, and hair blowers.
- add and subtract to mix solutions in proper proportions.
- see differences in shapes, widths, and lengths of lines when cutting hair and shaping eyebrows.
- deal pleasantly with all kinds of people.
- use hands and fingers skillfully to wrap hair around rollers.

✓ *How do you know if you would like or could learn to do this kind of work?*

The following questions may give you clues about yourself as you consider this group of jobs.

- Have you cut someone's hair? Do you style your own hair? Do you like to try new and different hairstyles?
- Have you read health and beauty magazines? Can you recognize various skin tones or hair textures?
- Have you applied theatrical make-up? Do you enjoy changing the appearance of others?
- Have you worked at a health spa or athletic club? Do you enjoy helping others?

✓ *How can you prepare for and enter this kind of work?*

Occupations in this group usually require education and/or training extending from six months to over two years, depending upon the specific kind of work. Both public and private vocational schools offer courses in cosmetology and barbering. In a few areas, apprenticeships in cosmetology are available. Manufacturers of barbering and cosmetology equipment and materials offer training courses about the use of their products.

Formal training requirements vary according to the occupation and state. Studies usually include anatomy, bacteriology, dermatology, and physiology. Techniques such as hair cutting, permanent waving, electrolysis, and hair and scalp analysis are also included.

Students of cosmetology or barbering schools get supervised practical experience. Trainees and workers develop further expertise by attending and participating in seminars and contests sponsored by schools, trade associations, and manufacturers.

✓ *What else should you consider about these jobs?*

Workers may be required to furnish and wear uniforms. Irregular hours may be required, including evening and weekends. Standing for varying lengths of time is typical of this work but it is not a requirement.

Many workers use stools with rolling casters to move around the customer's chair. Changing hair styles and the development of new products and techniques make it necessary for workers to attend training and demonstration classes frequently.

Workers usually are paid on the basis of how many customers they serve. They rarely receive a straight salary. Most employers set the prices for the services offered and the worker receives a part of these prices. The amount a worker is paid may vary and may depend on the supplies and tools provided by the employer. For example, some employers provide the needed towels, shampoo, or lotions and keep a larger share of the money collected. Workers may or may not be allowed to accept tips. They may be expected to join a union and pay membership dues.

If you think you would like to do this kind of work, look at the job titles listed below.

■   ■   ■

GOE: 09.02.01
Cosmetology

COSMETOLOGIST (personal ser.) ● DOT #332.271-010 ● OES: 68005 ● Alternate titles: BEAUTICIAN; BEAUTY CULTURIST; BEAUTY OPERATOR; COSMETICIAN. Provides beauty services for customers: Analyzes hair to ascertain condition of hair. Applies bleach, dye, or tint, using applicator or brush, to color customer's hair, first applying solution to portion of customer's skin to determine if customer is allergic to solution. Shampoos hair and scalp with water, liquid soap, dry powder, or egg, and rinses hair with vinegar, water, lemon, or prepared rinses. Massages scalp and gives other hair and scalp-conditioning treatments for hygienic or remedial purposes

[SCALP-TREATMENT OPERATOR (personal ser.) 339.371-014]. Styles hair by blowing, cutting, trimming, and tapering, using clippers, scissors, razors, and blow-wave gun. Suggests coiffure according to physical features of patron and current styles, or determines coiffure from instructions of patron. Applies water or waving solutions to hair and winds hair around rollers, or pin curls and finger-waves hair. Sets hair by blow-dry or natural-set, or presses hair with straightening comb. Suggests cosmetics for conditions, such as dry or oily skin. Applies lotions and creams to customer's face and neck to soften skin and lubricate tissues. Performs other beauty services, such as massaging face or neck, shaping and coloring eyebrows or eyelashes, removing unwanted hair, applying solutions that straighten hair or retain curls or waves in hair, and waving or curling hair. Cleans, shapes, and polishes fingernails and toenails [MANICURIST (personal ser.) 331.674-010]. May be designated according to beauty service provided as Facial Operator (personal ser.); Finger Waver (personal ser.); Hair Colorist (personal ser.); Hair Tinter (personal ser.); Marceller (personal ser.); Permanent Waver (personal ser.); Shampooer (personal ser.). ● **GED:** R4, M3, L3 ● **SVP:** 1-2 yrs ● **Academic:** Ed=H, Eng=S ● **Work Field:** 291, 264 ● **MPSMS:** 904 ● **Aptitudes:** G3, V3, N4, S3, P2, Q4, K3, F3, M3, E5, C2 ● **Temperaments:** J, P, V ● **Physical:** Stg=L; Freq: R, H, I, T, G, N Occas: E, D, X ● **Work Env:** Noise=N; Freq: A Occas: U ● **Salary:** 2 ● **Outlook:** 3

HAIR STYLIST (personal ser.) ● DOT #332.271-018 ● OES: 68005 ● Alternate titles: HAIRDRESSER. Specializes in dressing hair according to latest style, period, or character portrayal, following instructions of patron, MAKE-UP ARTIST (amuse. & rec.; motion picture; radio-tv broad.), or script: Questions patron or reads instructions of MAKE-UP ARTIST (amuse. & rec.; motion picture; radio-tv broad.) or script to determine hairdressing requirements. Studies facial features of patron or performing artist and arranges, shapes, and trims hair to achieve desired effect, using fingers, combs, barber scissors, hair-waving solutions, hairpins, and other accessories. Dyes, tints, bleaches, or curls or waves hair as required. May create new style especially for patron. May clean and style wigs. May style hairpieces and be designated Hairpiece Stylist (fabrication, nec). ● **GED:** R4, M3, L3 ● **SVP:** 1-2 yrs ● **Academic:** Ed=N, Eng=S ● **Work Field:** 291, 264 ● **MPSMS:** 904 ● **Aptitudes:** G3, V3, N4, S3, P3, Q4, K2, F3, M3, E5, C3 ● **Temperaments:** J, P, V ● **Physical:** Stg=L; Freq: R, H, I, E, T, G, N, A, X ● **Work Env:** Noise=Q; ● **Salary:** 2 ● **Outlook:** 3

SCALP-TREATMENT OPERATOR (personal ser.) ● DOT #339.371-014 ● OES: 68011 ● Alternate titles: HAIR-AND-SCALP SPECIALIST; SCALP SPECIALIST; TRICHOLOGIST. Gives hair and scalp conditioning treatments for hygienic or remedial purposes: Massages, shampoos, and steams hair and scalp of patron to clean and remove excess oil, using liquid soap, rinses, and hot towels. Applies medication to and massages scalp to increase blood circulation, stimu-late glandular activity, and promote growth of hair, using hands and fingers or vibrating equipment. Administers other remedial treatments to relieve such conditions as dandruff or itching scalp, using such therapeutic equipment as infrared or ultraviolet lamps. Advises patrons with chronic or potentially contagious scalp conditions to seek medical treatment. May maintain treatment records. ● **GED:** R3, M2, L3 ● **SVP:** 6 mos-1 yr ● **Academic:** Ed=N, Eng=S ● **Work Field:** 294 ● **MPSMS:** 904 ● **Aptitudes:** G3, V3, N4, S3, P3, Q4, K3, F3, M3, E5, C4 ● **Temperaments:** J, P, V ● **Physical:** Stg=L; Freq: R, H, I, E, T, G, N Occas: X ● **Work Env:** Noise=Q; Occas: R ● **Salary:** 1 ● **Outlook:** 3

GOE: 09.02.02
Barbering

BARBER (personal ser.) ● DOT #330.371-010 ● OES: 68002 ● Alternate titles: HAIRCUTTER; TONSORIAL ARTIST. Provides customers with barbering services: Cuts, shapes, trims, and tapers hair, using clippers, comb, blow-out gun, and scissors. Applies lather and shaves beard or shapes hair contour (outline) on temple and neck, using razor. Performs other tonsorial services, such as applying hairdressings or lotions, dyeing, shampooing, singeing, or styling hair, and massaging face, neck, or scalp. Records service charge on ticket or receives payment. Cleans work area and work tools. Orders supplies. May sell lotions, tonics, or other cosmetic supplies. ● **GED:** R3, M2, L3 ● **SVP:** 1-2 yrs ● **Academic:** Ed=H, Eng=S ● **Work Field:** 291 ● **MPSMS:** 904 ● **Aptitudes:** G3, V3, N4, S3, P2, Q4, K2, F3, M3, E5, C4 ● **Temperaments:** J, P, T ● **Physical:** Stg=L; Const: H Freq: R, I, N Occas: E, T, G, D, X ● **Work Env:** Noise=N; ● **Salary:** 1 ● **Outlook:** 2

Passenger Services

Workers in this group drive buses, taxis, limousines, or other vehicles to transport people. Workers who teach driving are also included in this group. Taxi, bus, and street railway companies hire most of the workers in this group but they can also find employment with government agencies.

✓ What kind of work would you do?

Your work activities would depend upon your specific job. For example, you might:

- drive a taxi and pick up customers who signal and assist them with baggage.
- drive a bus on a regular route in a city.
- give directions and other information to passengers of your bus or taxi.
- record taxi fares and destinations in a log.
- drive a bus from city to city.
- enforce safety rules when loading or unloading your passengers.
- work as a chauffeur for an individual or company.

✓ What skills and abilities do you need for this kind of work?

To do this kind of work, you must be able to:

- follow written and oral instructions and use time schedules, meters, and traffic regulations.
- think, reason, and act quickly to cope with traffic situations.
- read maps to locate addresses and select the best routes.
- memorize routes and established passenger pick-up locations.
- speak clearly to give information to passengers.
- deal courteously with all kinds of people.
- judge distances and speeds to avoid accidents.
- move eyes, hands and feet easily and together to brake, steer, and use other vehicle controls, such as directional signals and windshield wipers.
- read street and traffic signs at a distance and identify colors of traffic lights.

✓ How do you know if you would like or could learn to do this kind of work?

The following questions may give you clues about yourself as you consider this group of jobs.

- Have you completed a driver's education course? Do you have a driver's or chauffeur's license?

- Have you driven a vehicle in heavy traffic? Did you stay calm?
- Have you driven in a bicycle rodeo, car rally, or other vehicle obstacle course? Did you receive a good score?
- Have you driven a church or school bus? Can you drive a vehicle loaded with passengers without being distracted?
- Have you had military experience driving a motor vehicle?

✓ How can you prepare for and enter this type of work?

Occupations in this group usually require education and/or training extending from thirty days to over six months, depending upon the specific kind of work. Many employers want workers with a high school education or its equal. The U.S. Department of Transportation requires intercity bus drivers to be able to communicate with passengers and prepare reports. These drivers must meet specific physical requirements. They must take a written test on motor vehicle regulations. They must pass a test in the type of bus they will drive. Many intercity bus lines want workers with driving experience. Most of these firms have their own training programs for new drivers.

Local bus drivers are usually required to have a chauffeur's license. Many employers require applicants to take a written test. Workers also need to be of normal adult height and weight and have good eyesight and health. They are usually required to have one or two years of experience driving a large vehicle. Most local transit companies hold

training courses and behind-the-wheel sessions. Each state has special rules for drivers of school buses. These rules are set by the State Department of Education.

Taxi drivers also must have a chauffeur's license. They are required to have a special taxi operator's license issued by the local police department, state safety department, or the public utilities commission. Most large cities require an applicant for a taxi driver's license to pass a written test on traffic laws and street locations. Some cities also require workers to have a good driving record and no criminal history. Workers often need an eighth grade education or its equal to complete the required forms.

✓ What else should you consider about these jobs?

Workers in these jobs may have to work nights and weekends or report for work on short notice. Heavy traffic and long trips can cause nervous tension in drivers. Steering and controlling the larger vehicles will require free shoulder movements and more strength than is used in driving private passenger automobiles.

Chances for promotion in these jobs are limited. However, experienced drivers may be assigned preferred routes or may get more pay. A few drivers may become dispatchers or terminal managers. Some taxi drivers buy and drive their own cabs.

If you think you would like to do this kind of work, look at the job titles listed below.

■ ■ ■

GOE: 09.03.01
Group Transportation

BUS DRIVER (motor trans.) ● DOT #913.463-010 ● OES: 97108 ● Alternate titles: CHAUFFEUR, MOTORBUS; COACH OPERATOR. Drives bus to transport passengers over specified routes to local or distant points according to time schedule: Assists passengers with baggage and collects tickets or cash fares. Regulates heating, lighting, and ventilating systems for passenger comfort. Complies with local traffic regulations. Reports delays or accidents. Records cash receipts and ticket fares. May make repairs and change tires. May inspect bus and check gas, oil, and water before departure. May load or unload baggage or express checked by passengers in baggage compartment. May transport pupils between pickup points and school and be designated Bus Driver, School (motor trans.). May drive diesel or electric powered transit bus to transport passengers over established city route and be designated Motor-Coach Driver (motor trans.); Trolley-Coach Driver (motor trans.). ● **GED:** R3, M2, L2 ● **SVP:** 3-6 mos ● **Academic:** Ed=N, Eng=S ● **Work Field:** 013 ● **MPSMS:** 852 ● **Aptitudes:** G3, V3, N4, S3, P4, Q3, K3, F4, M3, E3, C4 ● **Temperaments:** J, P ● **Physical:** Stg=M; Const: R, H, F, D, V Freq: T, G, N, A, X Occas: I ● **Work Env:** Noise=L; ● **Salary:** 2 ● **Outlook:** 2

DRIVER (motor trans.) ● DOT #913.663-018 ● OES: 97001 ● Alternate titles: SHUTTLE-BUS DRIVER; VAN DRIVER. Drives minibus, van, or lightweight truck to transport clients, trainees, or company personnel: Drives vehicle from individual or central loading area to social services or rehabilitation center, training location, job site, or other destination according to assigned schedule. May assist disabled passengers into and out of vehicle. May secure passengers' wheelchairs to restraining devices to stabilize wheelchairs during trip. May operate radio or similar device to communicate with base station or other vehicles to report disruption of service. May clean and service vehicle with fuel, lubricants, and accessories. May keep records of trips and behavior of passengers. May perform other duties when not driving, such as custodial and building maintenance tasks. ● **GED:** R2, M2, L2 ● **SVP:** 1-3 mos ● **Academic:** Ed=N, Eng=S ● **Work Field:** 013 ● **MPSMS:** 852 ● **Aptitudes:** G3, V4, N4, S3, P3, Q4, K3, F4, M3, E3, C5 ● **Temperaments:** P, R ● **Physical:** Stg=M; Const: R, H, F, D, V Freq: N Occas: S, I, T, G ● **Work Env:** Noise=L; ● **Salary:** 3 ● **Outlook:** 3

STREETCAR OPERATOR (r.r. trans.) ● DOT #913.463-014 ● OES: 97314 ● Alternate titles: TROLLEY-CAR OPERATOR. Drives electric-powered streetcar to transport passengers, collects fares, and gives information to passengers: Drives streetcar in accordance with traffic regulations and observes traffic lights and other vehicles on street to avoid accidents. Opens and closes doors and starts and stops streetcar to allow passengers to enter or leave vehicle. Collects fares from passengers and issues change and transfers. Answers questions from passengers concerning fare, schedules, and routings. Records readings of coin receptor at beginning and end of shift to verify amount of money received during shift. ● **GED:** R3, M2, L2 ● **SVP:** 1-3 mos ● **Academic:** Ed=N, Eng=S ● **Work Field:** 013 ● **MPSMS:** 852 ● **Aptitudes:** G3, V3, N3, S3, P4, Q4, K3, F4, M3, E3, C4 ● **Temperaments:** J, P ● **Physical:** Stg=L; Const: R, H, F, D, V Freq: T, G, X Occas: I, N ● **Work Env:** Noise=N; ● **Salary:** 2 ● **Outlook:** 4

GOE: 09.03.02
Individual Transportation

CHAUFFEUR (any industry) ● DOT #913.663-010 ● OES: 97114 ● Drives automobile to transport office personnel and visitors of commercial or industrial establishment. Performs miscellaneous errands, such as carrying mail to and from post office. May make overnight drives and extended trips requiring irregular hours. May be required to have chauffeurs license. May clean vehicle and make minor repairs or adjustments. ● **GED:** R3, M2, L2 ● **SVP:** 1-3 mos ● **Academic:** Ed=N, Eng=S ● **Work Field:** 013 ● **MPSMS:** 852 ● **Aptitudes:** G3, V4, N4, S3, P4, Q4, K3, F4, M3, E3, C4 ● **Temperaments:** J, P ● **Physical:** Stg=L; Freq: R, H, N, F, D, V Occas: S, O, I, T, G, X ● **Work Env:** Noise=L; Occas: W ● **Salary:** 4 ● **Outlook:** 3

CHAUFFEUR (domestic ser.) ● DOT #359.673-010 ● OES: 97114 ● Alternate titles: DRIVER. Drives private car as ordered by owner or other passenger and performs other miscellaneous duties: Assists passengers to enter and leave car and holds umbrellas in wet weather. Keeps car clean, polished, and in operating condition. May make minor repairs, such as fixing punctures, cleaning spark plugs, or adjusting carburetor. May assist CARETAKER (domestic ser.) with heavy work. May groom and exercise pets. ● **GED:** R2, M1, L2 ● **SVP:** 1-3 mos ● **Academic:** Ed=N, Eng=S ● **Work Field:** 013, 291 ● **MPSMS:** 850, 859 ● **Aptitudes:** G3, V4, N4, S3, P4, Q4, K3, F4, M4, E3, C4 ● **Temperaments:** V ● **Physical:** Stg=L; Freq: R, H, N, F, D, A, X, V Occas: S, K ● **Work Env:** Noise=N; ● **Salary:** 2 ● **Outlook:** 3

TAXI DRIVER (motor trans.) ● DOT #913.463-018 ● OES: 97114 ● Alternate titles: CAB DRIVER. Drives taxicab to transport passengers for fee: Picks up passengers in response to radio or telephone relayed request for service. Collects fee recorded on taximeter based on mileage or time factor and records transaction on log. Reports by radio or telephone to TAXICAB STARTER (motor trans.) 913.367-010 on completion of trip. May drive limousine or custom-built sedan to pick up and discharge airport passengers arriving or leaving on scheduled flights and be designated Chauffeur, Airport Limousine (motor trans.) ● **GED:** R3, M2, L2 ● **SVP:** 1-3 mos ● **Academic:** Ed=N, Eng=S ● **Work Field:** 013 ● **MPSMS:** 852 ● **Aptitudes:** G3, V3, N3, S3, P4, Q4, K3, F4, M3, E3, C4 ● **Temperaments:** J, P ● **Physical:** Stg=M; Const: R, H Freq: T, G, N, F, D, A, X, V Occas: S, I ● **Work Env:** Noise=N; Freq: W, O ● **Salary:** 2 ● **Outlook:** 2

09.03.03
Instruction & Supervision

INSTRUCTOR, DRIVING (education) ● DOT #099.223-010 ● OES: 31317 ● Instructs individuals and groups in theory and application of automobile driving skills: Demonstrates and explains handling of automobile in emergencies, driving techniques, and mechanical operation of automobile, using blackboard diagrams, audiovisual aids, and driving simulators. Observes individual's driving habits and reactions under various driving conditions to ensure conformance with vehicle operational standards and state vehicle code. May test hearing and vision of individuals, using lettered charts and colored lights. May teach motor vehicle regulations and insurance laws. May teach operation of vehicles other than automobile and be identified according to type of vehicle. ● **GED:** R4, M2, L3 ● **SVP:** 3-6 mos ● **Academic:** Ed=H, Eng=G ● **Work Field:** 296 ● **MPSMS:** 931 ● **Aptitudes:** G3, V3, N4, S3, P3, Q3, K2, F3, M3, E2, C4 ● **Temperaments:** I, J, S ● **Physical:** Stg=L; Freq: R, H, T, G, N, F, D, X, V Occas: I ● **Work Env:** Noise=L; Occas: O ● **Salary:** 3 ● **Outlook:** 3

Accommodating   09

Customer Services   09.04

Workers in this group provide customers in commercial settings with various services ranging from delivering newspapers to serving food. Their duties usually include receiving payment and making change. Most of these workers find employment in hotels, restaurants, stores, and concessions. However, some do work on board trains and ships and at amusement parks and resorts.

✓ What kind of work would you do?

Your work activities would depend upon your specific job. For example, you might:

- sell sandwiches, drinks, and other food from a truck or cart.
- rent bicycles to patrons at recreational areas.
- collect fees and issue equipment in a bowling center.
- mix and sell drinks to patrons of a bar.
- rent canoes, rowboats, motorboats, or fishing equipment to people at a resort.
- total bills, receive money, and make change for drug store customers.

- write special orders for services and merchandise, and perform personal services for customers, such as gift wrapping or monogramming.
- fill out forms and receive payments for auto rental customers.
- serve meals in a diner or formal dining room.

✓ What skills and abilities do you need for this kind of work?

To do this kind of work, you must be able to:

- use arithmetic to total costs and make change
- talk with different kinds of people to find out what services they want and to give them information.
- stand or walk for varying lengths of time, sometimes for long periods.
- move fingers and hands easily and quickly to handle things like dishes, money, and merchandise.
- lift and carry things like heavy trays, sports equipment, and bundles of newspapers.

✓ *How do you know if you would like or could learn to do this kind of work?*

The following questions may give you clues about yourself as you consider this group of jobs.

- Have you sold things to raise money for clubs or local organizations? Did you collect money and keep records of sales?
- Have you given directions to anyone who was lost? Did you make the directions clear?
- Have you served food or beverages at a party or reception? Can you do so without dropping or spilling food or drink?

✓ *How can you prepare for and enter this kind of work?*

Occupations in this group usually require education and/or training extending from a short demonstration to over three months, depending upon the specific kind of work. People can learn most of the jobs in this group after being hired. However, some restaurants hire only persons with experience. Workers may get the training and experience they need by starting in a related job. For example, a person may start as a dining room attendant and become a waiter or waitress. Some schools offer classes in food service work.

✓ *What else should you consider about these jobs?*

Night and holiday work, changing work hours, and weekend work are often required. Uniforms may be required, especially for food service work.

Income for these workers is often a combination of wages and tips. Some jobs in this group require the worker to adapt to specific demands. For example, a newspaper carrier may have to be out very early in the morning regardless of weather. An attendant at a lodging facility may have to live on the premises.

If you think you would like to do this kind of work, look at the job titles listed on the following pages.

GOE: 09.04.01
Food Services

BARTENDER (hotel & rest.) ● DOT #312.474-010 ● OES: 65005 ● Alternate titles: BAR ATTENDANT; BARKEEPER. Mixes and serves alcoholic and nonalcoholic drinks to patrons of bar, following standard recipes: Mixes ingredients, such as liquor, soda, water, sugar, and bitters, to prepare cocktails and other drinks. Serves wine and draught or bottled beer. Collects money for drinks served. Orders or requisitions liquors and supplies. Arranges bottles and glasses to make attractive display. May slice and pit fruit for garnishing drinks. May prepare appetizers, such as pickles, cheese, and cold meats. May tend service bar and be designated Service Bartender (hotel & rest.). ● **GED:** R3, M2, L3 ● **SVP:** 1-3 mos ● **Academic:** Ed=N, Eng=S ● **Work Field:** 291, 143 ● **MPSMS:** 903 ● **Aptitudes:** G3, V3, N3, S4, P4, Q3, K3, F4, M4, E5, C5 ● **Temperaments:** P, R ● **Physical:** Stg=L; Freq: R, H, T, G, N, D Occas: S, I ● **Work Env:** Noise=N; ● **Salary:** 2 ● **Outlook:** 4

CANTEEN OPERATOR (any industry) ● DOT #311.674-010 ● OES: 65040 ● Serves sandwiches, salads, beverages, desserts, candies, and tobacco to employees in industrial establishment. May collect money for purchases. May order items to replace stocks. May serve hot dishes, such as soups. May serve employees from mobile canteen. ● **GED:** R2, M1, L2 ● **SVP:** 1-3 mos ● **Academic:** Ed=N, Eng=S ● **Work Field:** 291 ● **MPSMS:** 903 ● **Aptitudes:** G4, V4, N4, S4, P4, Q4, K4, F4, M4, E5, C5 ● **Temperaments:** P ● **Physical:** Stg=L; Freq: R, H, T, G ● **Work Env:** Noise=N; ● **Salary:** 1 ● **Outlook:** 4

CAR HOP (hotel & rest.) ● DOT #311.477-010 ● OES: 65040 ● Alternate titles: DRIVE-IN WAITER/WAITRESS. Serves food and refreshments to patrons in cars: Takes order and relays order to kitchen or serving counter to be filled. Places filled order on tray and fastens tray to car door. Totals and presents check to customer and accepts payment for service. Removes tray and stacks dishes for return to kitchen. Sweeps service area with broom. May prepare fountain drinks, such as sodas, milkshakes, and malted milks. May restock service counter with items, such as ice, napkins, and straws. ● **GED:** R2, M2, L2 ● **SVP:** 2-30 days ● **Academic:** Ed=N, Eng=S ● **Work Field:** 291 ● **MPSMS:** 903 ● **Aptitudes:** G4, V4, N4, S4, P4, Q4, K3, F4, M3,

E4, C4 ● **Temperaments:** P ● **Physical:** Stg=L; Freq: R, H, I, T, G, N Occas: X ● **Work Env:** Noise=N; Freq: W ● **Salary:** 1 ● **Outlook:** 3

COUNTER ATTENDANT, LUNCHROOM OR COFFEE SHOP (hotel & rest.) ● DOT #311.477-014 ● OES: 65040 ● Alternate titles: WAITER/WAITRESS, COUNTER. Serves food or beverages to customers seated at counter: Calls order to kitchen and picks up and serves order when it is ready. Itemizes and totals check for service or totals takeout transaction on cash register and accepts payment. May prepare sandwiches, salads, and other short order items [COOK, SHORT ORDER (hotel & rest.) 313.374-014]. May perform other duties, such as cleaning counters, washing dishes, and selling cigars and cigarettes. ● **GED:** R2, M2, L2 ● **SVP:** 2-30 days ● **Academic:** Ed=N, Eng=S ● **Work Field:** 291 ● **MPSMS:** 903 ● **Aptitudes:** G4, V3, N3, S4, P4, Q4, K4, F4, M3, E4, C5 ● **Temperaments:** P, R ● **Physical:** Stg=L; Freq: R, H, T, G Occas: S, O, I, N ● **Work Env:** Noise=N; Occas: O ● **Salary:** 4 ● **Outlook:** 4

FAST-FOODS WORKER (hotel & rest.) ● DOT #311.472-010 ● OES: 65040 ● Alternate titles: CASHIER, FAST FOODS RESTAURANT. Serves customer of fast food restaurant: Requests customer order and depresses keys of multicounting machine to simultaneously record order and compute bill. Selects requested food items from serving or storage areas and assembles items on serving tray or in takeout bag. Notifies kitchen personnel of shortages or special orders. Serves cold drinks, using drink-dispensing machine, or frozen milk drinks or desserts, using milkshake or frozen custard machine. Makes and serves hot beverages, using automatic water heater or coffeemaker. Presses lids onto beverages and places beverages on serving tray or in takeout container. Receives payment. May cook or apportion french fries or perform other minor duties to prepare food, serve customers, or maintain orderly eating or serving areas. ● **GED:** R2, M2, L2 ● **SVP:** 2-30 days ● **Academic:** Ed=N, Eng=S ● **Work Field:** 291, 292 ● **MPSMS:** 903 ● **Aptitudes:** G4, V4, N4, S4, P4, Q3, K3, F3, M3, E5, C5 ● **Temperaments:** P, T ● **Physical:** Stg=L; Const: R, H Freq: I, T, G, N Occas: S, M, X ● **Work Env:** Noise=N; ● **Salary:** 1 ● **Outlook:** 4

FOUNTAIN SERVER (hotel & rest.) ● DOT #319.474-010 ● OES: 65040 ● Alternate titles: FOUNTAIN DISPENSER; ICE CREAM DISPENSER; SODA CLERK; SODA DISPENSER; SODA JERKER. Prepares and serves soft drinks and ice cream dishes, such as ice cream sundaes, malted milks, sodas, and fruitades, using memorized formulas and methods or following directions. Cleans glasses, dishes, and fountain equipment and polishes metalwork on fountain. May prepare and serve sandwiches [SANDWICH MAKER (hotel & rest.) 317.664-010] or other foods [COUNTER ATTENDANT, LUNCHROOM OR COFFEE SHOP (hotel & rest.) 311.477-014]. May verify and total customer's bill, accept cash, and make change. ● **GED:** R2, M2, L2 ● **SVP:** 2-30 days ● **Academic:** Ed=N, Eng=S ● **Work Field:** 146, 291 ● **MPSMS:** 903 ● **Aptitudes:** G4, V4, N3, S4, P4, Q4, K4, F4, M3, E5, C5 ● **Temperaments:** P, R ● **Physical:** Stg=L; Freq: R, H, I, G Occas: T, N ● **Work Env:** Noise=N; ● **Salary:** 1 ● **Outlook:** 4

LUNCH-TRUCK DRIVER (hotel & rest.) ● DOT #292.463-010 ● OES: 97117 ● Alternate titles: CATERING-TRUCK OPERATOR; LUNCH-TRUCK OPERATOR. Drives lunch truck over regular scheduled route, and sells miscellaneous food specialties, such as sandwiches, box lunches, and beverages, to industrial and office workers, students, and to patrons of sports and public events. Loads and unloads truck. Maintains truck and food-despensing equipment in sanitary condition and good working order. May prepare and wrap sandwiches for delivery. May push lunch-cart through departments of industrial establishment or office building to sell merchandise and be known as Lunch-Wagon Operator (hotel & rest.). ● **GED:** R2, M2, L2 ● **SVP:** 2-30 days ● **Academic:** Ed=N, Eng=S ● **Work Field:** 013, 292 ● **MPSMS:** 903 ● **Aptitudes:** G3, V3, N3, S3, P4, Q4, K3, F4, M3, E3, C4 ● **Temperaments:** P ● **Physical:** Stg=M; Freq: R, H, I, T, G, N, F, D, X, V ● **Work Env:** Noise=N; Occas: W ● **Salary:** 1 ● **Outlook:** 3

MANAGER, FOOD CONCESSION (hotel & rest.) ● DOT #185.167-022 ● OES: 41002 ● Manages refreshment stand or other food concession at public gatherings, sports events, amusement park, or similar facility: Purchases refreshments, according to anticipated demand and familiarity with public taste in food and beverages. Directs storage, preparation, and serving of refreshments by other workers at refreshment stand or circulating throughout audience. Assigns VENDORS (amuse. & rec.) to locations. Tabulates receipts and balances accounts. Inventories supplies on hand at end of each day or other designated period. ● **GED:** R3, M3, L3 ● **SVP:** 1-2 yrs ● **Academic:** Ed=N, Eng=S ● **Work Field:** 295 ● **MPSMS:** 903 ● **Aptitudes:** G3, V3, N3, S4, P4, Q2, K4, F4, M4, E5, C5 ● **Temperaments:** D, J, P ● **Physical:** Stg=L; Freq: R, H, I, T, G, N ● **Work Env:** Noise=L; ● **Salary:** 3 ● **Outlook:** 3

VENDING-MACHINE ATTENDANT (hotel & rest.) ● DOT #319.464-014 ● OES: 85947 ● Stocks machines and assists customers in facility where food is dispensed from coin-operated machines: Places food or drink items on shelves of vending machines and changes shelf labels as required to indicate selections. Makes change for customers and answers questions regarding selections. Adjusts temperature gauges to maintain food items at specified temperatures. Performs minor repairs or adjustments on machines to correct jams or similar malfunctions, using handtools. Prepares requisitions for food and drink supplies. Cleans interior and exterior of machines, using damp cloth. Maintains eating area in orderly condition. May remove money from vending machines and keep records of receipts. ● **GED:** R2, M2, L2 ● **SVP:** 2-30 days ● **Academic:** Ed=N, Eng=N ● **Work Field:** 291, 221 ● **MPSMS:** 903 ● **Aptitudes:** G3, V4, N4, S4, P4, Q4, K4, F4, M3, E5, C4 ● **Temperaments:** P ● **Physical:** Stg=L; Freq: R, H, N Occas: I, T, G, X ● **Work Env:** Noise=N; ● **Salary:** 1 ● **Outlook:** 4

VENDING-STAND SUPERVISOR (government ser.) ● DOT #185.167-066 ● OES: 41002 ● Alternate titles: OPERATIONS SUPERVISOR; VENDING-ENTERPRISES SUPERVISOR. Coordinates activities of persons engaged in vending-stand operations of state program for rehabilitation of the blind: Observes stand operation and advises blind vendor on merchandise purchase and display, improved methods of operation, personal appearance, and sanitation. Inspects condition of stock and fixtures to ascertain adherence to regulations and to determine need for maintenance and repairs. Examines invoices and receipts to determine equity of charges and to prepare monthly profit and loss statement. Investigates and resolves problems varying from nuisance complaints to breach-of-contract. May address civic groups to promote public relations. May collect cash, invoices, receipts, and specified assessments as determined by state program requirements. May plan, locate, and arrange for installation of stands, train vendors,

and negotiate contracts with building managers for stand operation [BUSINESS-ENTERPRISE OFFICER (government ser.)]. ● **GED:** R5, M4, L4 ● **SVP:** 2-4 yrs ● **Academic:** Ed=A, Eng=S ● **Work Field:** 295, 292 ● **MPSMS:** 881, 940 ● **Aptitudes:** G2, V2, N3, S3, P3, Q3, K4, F4, M4, E5, C4 ● **Temperaments:** D, J, P, V ● **Physical:** Stg=L; Freq: R, H, I, T, G, N Occas: A ● **Work Env:** Noise=N; ● **Salary:** 4 ● **Outlook:** 2

WAITER/WAITRESS, BAR (hotel & rest.) ● DOT #311.477-018 ● OES: 65008 ● Alternate titles: WAITER/WAITRESS, COCKTAIL LOUNGE. Serves beverages to patrons seated at tables in bar or cocktail lounge. Computes bill and accepts payment. May take orders for and serve light meals and hors d'oeuvres. May request identification from customers when legal age is questioned. When working in establishment serving only beer and wine, is designated Waiter/Waitress, Tavern (hotel & rest.). ● **GED:** R3, M2, L2 ● **SVP:** 1-3 mos ● **Academic:** Ed=N, Eng=S ● **Work Field:** 291 ● **MPSMS:** 903 ● **Aptitudes:** G3, V3, N4, S4, P4, Q4, K3, F4, M3, E4, C4 ● **Temperaments:** P ● **Physical:** Stg=L; Freq: R, H, I, T, G, N Occas: X ● **Work Env:** Noise=L; ● **Salary:** 1 ● **Outlook:** 4

WAITER/WAITRESS, FORMAL (hotel & rest.) ● DOT #311.477-026 ● OES: 65008 ● Alternate titles: SERVER. Serves meals to patrons according to established rules of etiquette, working in formal setting: Presents menu to diner, suggesting dinner courses, appropriate wines, and answering questions regarding food preparation. Writes order on check or memorizes it. Relays order to kitchen and serves courses from kitchen and service bars. Garnishes and decorates dishes preparatory to serving. Serves patrons from chafing dish at table. Observes diners to respond to any additional requests and to determine when meal has been completed. Totals bill and accepts payment or refers patron to CASHIER (clerical) II 211.462-010. May carve meats, bone fish and fowl, and prepare flaming dishes and desserts at patron's table. May be designated Waiter/Waitress, Banquet (hotel & rest.) when serving at banquets. ● **GED:** R3, M2, L2 ● **SVP:** 3-6 mos ● **Academic:** Ed=N, Eng=S ● **Work Field:** 291 ● **MPSMS:** 903 ● **Aptitudes:** G3, V3, N4, S4, P3, Q4, K3, F4, M3, E4, C4 ● **Temperaments:** P, R ● **Physical:** Stg=L; Freq: R, H, I, T, G, N Occas: F, X ● **Work Env:** Noise=N; Occas: O ● **Salary:** 2 ● **Outlook:** 4

WAITER/WAITRESS, INFORMAL (hotel & rest.) ● DOT #311.477-030 ● OES: 65008 ● Alternate titles: SERVER. Serves food to patrons at counters and tables of coffeeshops, lunchrooms, and other dining establishments where food service is informal: Presents menu, answers questions, and makes suggestions regarding food and service. Writes order on check or memorizes it. Relays order to kitchen and serves courses from kitchen and service bars. Observes guests to respond to additional requests and to determine when meal has been completed. Totals bill and accepts payment or refers patron to CASHIER (clerical) II 211.462-010. May ladle soup, toss salads, portion pies and desserts, brew coffee, and perform other services as determined by establishment's size and practices. May clear and reset counters or tables at conclusion of each course [DINING ROOM ATTENDANT (hotel & rest.) 311.677-018]. ● **GED:** R3, M2, L2 ● **SVP:** 1-3 mos ● **Academic:** Ed=N, Eng=S ● **Work Field:** 291 ● **MPSMS:** 903 ● **Aptitudes:** G3, V3, N4, S4, P4, Q4, K4, F4, M3, E4, C5 ● **Temperaments:** P, R ● **Physical:** Stg=L; Freq: R, H, T, G, N Occas: I, F ● **Work Env:** Noise=N; Occas: O ● **Salary:** 1 ● **Outlook:** 4

WAITER/WAITRESS, TAKE OUT (hotel & rest.) ● DOT #311.477-038 ● OES: 65040 ● Serves customers at take out counter of restaurant or lunchroom: Writes items ordered on order tickets, totals orders, passes orders to cook, and gives ticket stubs to customers to identify filled orders. Wraps menu items, such as sandwiches, hot entrees, and desserts. Fills containers with requested beverages, such as coffee, tea, or carbonated drink. Receives payment for orders and makes change. May prepare fountain drinks, such as sodas and milkshakes. May record orders and compute bill simultaneously, using cash register. ● **GED:** R2, M2, L2 ● **SVP:** 1-3 mos ● **Academic:** Ed=N, Eng=S ● **Work Field:** 291 ● **MPSMS:** 903 ● **Aptitudes:** G4, V4, N4, S4, P4, Q3, K4, F4, M4, E5, C5 ● **Temperaments:** P ● **Physical:** Stg=L; Freq: R, H, I, T, G, N ● **Work Env:** Noise=N; ● **Salary:** 1 ● **Outlook:** 4

GOE: 09.04.02
Sales Services

ATTENDANT, ARCADE (amuse. & rec.) ● DOT #342.667-014 ● OES: 68014 ● Assists patrons of amusement facility, and performs minor repairs on game machines: Explains operation of game machines to patrons and exchanges coins for paper currency. Listens to patron complaints regarding malfunction of machines. Removes coin accepter mechanism of machines, using key, and observes mechanism to detect causes of malfunctions, such as bent coins, slugs, or foreign material. Removes obstructions, repositions mechanism, inserts coins, and observes machine operation to determine whether malfunctions are still present. Places out-of-order signs on defective machines and returns money lost in defective machines to patrons. Notifies maintenance department of defective machines, and records times of machine malfunctions and repairs to maintain required records. Observes conduct of patrons in facility to ensure orderliness, and asks disruptive patrons to leave. ● **GED:** R2, M2, L2 ● **SVP:** 2-30 days ● **Academic:** Ed=N, Eng=S ● **Work Field:** 282 ● **MPSMS:** 919 ● **Aptitudes:** G3, V3, N3, S4, P4, Q4, K4, F4, M3, E5, C5 ● **Temperaments:** P ● **Physical:** Stg=L; Freq: R, H, T, G Occas: N ● **Work Env:** Noise=N; ● **Salary:** 1 ● **Outlook:** 2

AUTOMOBILE RENTAL CLERK (automotive ser.) ● DOT #295.467-026 ● OES: 49017 ● Alternate titles: AUTOMOBILE RENTAL AGENT; AUTOMOBILE RENTAL REPRESENTATIVE; CAR RENTAL CLERK. Rents automobiles to customers: Talks with customer to determine type of automobile and accessories desired, such as power steering and air-conditioning, location for pick up and return of automobile, and number of days needed for rental. Quotes cost of rental, based on type of automobile, daily rates, estimated mileage, insurance coverages requested, and amount of deposit required. Examines customer's driver's license and credit card, to determine validity of identification and eligibility for rental. Completes rental contract, explains rental policies and procedures, verifies credit, and obtains customer signature and deposit. Calls storage or service area to determine automobile availability and request delivery, and to check automobile upon return for damage and to record mileage and fuel level reading. Accepts automobiles returned by customer and computes rental charges based on type of automobile, length of time, distance traveled, taxes, and other expenses, such as late charges or damage fees incurred during rental. May reconcile cash or credit card slips with rental agreements and send to management. May inspect automobile fluid levels and add fluids, such as fuel, oil, and engine coolant to maintain automobile. May deliver automobile to customer. May keep log to track location of rented automobiles. May be designated according to type of automobile rented as Limousine Rental Clerk (automotive ser.). ● **GED:** R3, M3, L3 ● **SVP:** 3-6 mos ● **Academic:** Ed=N, Eng=G ● **Work Field:** 292 ● **MPSMS:** 884 ● **Aptitudes:** G3, V3, N3, S4, P4, Q3, K4, F4, M4, E5, C5 ● **Temperaments:** J, P ● **Physical:** Stg=L; Freq: R, H, I, T, G Occas: N, F, V ● **Work Env:** Noise=N; Occas: W ● **Salary:** 3 ● **Outlook:** 3

BICYCLE-RENTAL CLERK (retail trade) ● DOT #295.467-010 ● OES: 49017 ● Rents bicycles to patrons at beach, resort, or retail bicycle-rental store: Explains bicycle-rental rates and conditions to customer. Issues bicycle to customer and records time of transaction. Receives returned bicycles and examines them for abuse or breakage. Computes rental charge according to elapsed time and accepts payment, imposing specified fee for damage to bicycle. Records time bicycle was returned. Prepares cash report at end of shift. Tags bicycles needing repair or service. May adjust bicycle seat to suit customer. May receive money deposit or identification, such as driver's license, as security toward return of bicycle. May explain operation of bicycle and features of certain bicycles, such as gear shifting and hand brakes to customers. ● **GED:** R2, M2, L2 ● **SVP:** 2-30 days ● **Academic:** Ed=N, Eng=S ● **Work Field:** 292 ● **MPSMS:** 881 ● **Aptitudes:** G4, V4, N3, S4, P4, Q3, K4, F4, M4, E5, C5 ● **Temperaments:** J, P ● **Physical:** Stg=L; Freq: R, H, I, T, G, N ● **Work Env:** Noise=N; Freq: W ● **Salary:** 1 ● **Outlook:** 3

BOAT-RENTAL CLERK (amuse. & rec.) ● DOT #295.467-014 ● OES: 49017 ● Rents canoes, motorboats, rowboats, sailboats, and fish-ing equipment: Explains rental rates and operation of boats and equipment to customer. Assists customers in and out of boats. Launches and moors boats. Tows disabled boats to shore, using motorboat. Calculates rental payment and collects payment from customer. May make minor adjustments and repairs on motors of motorboats, such as replacing battery, using handtools. May pump water out of boats, using mechanical pump. ● **GED:** R3, M3, L3 ● **SVP:** 2-30 days ● **Academic:** Ed=N, Eng=G ● **Work Field:** 292 ● **MPSMS:** 919 ● **Aptitudes:** G4, V3, N3, S4, P4, Q4, K4, F4, M4, E4, C5 ● **Temperaments:** P ● **Physical:** Stg=L; Occas: S, O, R, H, I, T, G, N, D ● **Work Env:** Noise=N; Freq: W ● **Salary:** 2 ● **Outlook:** 3

CASHIER, COURTESY BOOTH (retail trade) ● DOT #211.467-010 ● OES: 49023 ● Cashes checks for customers and monitors checkout stations in self-service store: Cashes personal and payroll checks. Provides information to customers. Receives customer's complaints and resolves complaints when possible. Monitors checkout stations to reduce customer delay. Calls additional workers to stations when situation warrants. Issues cash to stations and removes excess cash. Audits cash register tapes. May compile reports, verify employee time records, and prepare payroll. ● **GED:** R3, M3, L3 ● **SVP:** 3-6 mos ● **Academic:** Ed=N, Eng=S ● **Work Field:** 232, 282 ● **MPSMS:** 892 ● **Aptitudes:** G3, V3, N3, S4, P3, Q3, K4, F4, M4, E5, C5 ● **Temperaments:** P, T, V ● **Physical:** Stg=L; Freq: R, H, I, T, G, N ● **Work Env:** Noise=Q; ● **Salary:** 2 ● **Outlook:** 4

CASHIER-WRAPPER (retail trade) ● DOT #211.462-018 ● OES: 49023 ● Operates cash register to compute and record total sale and wraps merchandise for customers in department, variety, and specialty stores: Receives sales slip, money, and merchandise from salesperson or customer. Records amount of sale on cash register and makes change. Obtains credit authorization on charge purchases in excess of floor limit from designated official, using telephone or pneumatic tube carrier. Inspects merchandise prior to wrapping to see that it is in satisfactory condition and verifies sales slip with price tickets on merchandise. Places merchandise in bags or boxes and gives change and packages to selling personnel. Wraps packages for shipment and routes to delivery department. Balances cash received with cash sales daily. May gift wrap merchandise. ● **GED:** R3, M2, L2 ● **SVP:** 1-3 mos ● **Academic:** Ed=N, Eng=S ● **Work Field:** 232, 041 ● **MPSMS:** 899 ● **Aptitudes:** G3, V3, N3, S4, P4, Q3, K3, F3, M3, E5, C3 ● **Temperaments:** P, R, T ● **Physical:** Stg=L; Freq: R, H, N Occas: I, T, G ● **Work Env:** Noise=N; ● **Salary:** 1 ● **Outlook:** 4

CURB ATTENDANT (laundry & rel.) ● DOT #369.477-010 ● OES: 49017 ● Gives curb service to customers: Receives and delivers articles to customers remaining in cars outside store or plant. Writes tickets to identify and to indicate work to be done. Receives amount due for servicing articles. Opens doors for customers entering or leaving store. May perform other duties, such as sweeping and dusting store, placing garments in paper bags, and running errands. ● **GED:** R2, M2, L2 ● **SVP:** 2-30 days ● **Academic:** Ed=N, Eng=S ● **Work Field:** 291 ● **MPSMS:** 906 ● **Aptitudes:** G4, V4, N4, S5, P4, Q3, K4, F4, M4, E5, C5 ● **Temperaments:** P, R ● **Physical:** Stg=M; Freq: R, H, I, T, G, N ● **Work Env:** Noise=Q; Occas: W ● **Salary:** 2 ● **Outlook:** 3

CUSTOMER-SERVICE CLERK (retail trade) ● DOT #299.367-010 ● OES: 49998 ● Alternate titles: CUSTOMER-SERVICE SPECIALIST, POST EXCHANGE. Performs any combination of following tasks in post exchange: Arranges for gift wrapping, monogramming, printing, and fabrication of such items as desk nameplates and rubber stamps, and repair or replacement of defective items covered by warranty. Takes orders for such items as decorated cakes, cut flowers, personalized greeting cards and stationery, and merchandise rentals and repairs. Prepares special order worksheet. Keeps record of services in progress. Notifies customer when service is completed and accepts payment. Acts as WEDDING CONSULTANT (retail trade). Assists customers to select and purchase specified merchandise [PERSONAL SHOPPER (retail trade)]. Keeps records of items in layaway, receives and posts customer payments, and prepares and forwards delinquent notices [LAYAWAY CLERK (retail trade)]. Issues temporary identification cards from information on military records. Approves customer's checks and provides check cashing service according to exchange policy. Answers customer's telephone, mail, and in-person inquiries and directs customers to appropriate sales area [INFORMATION CLERK (clerical)]. Resolves customer complaints and requests for refunds, exchanges, and adjustments. Provides customers with catalogs and information concerning prices, shipping time, and costs. ● **GED:** R3, M3, L3 ● **SVP:** 3-6 mos ● **Academic:** Ed=N, Eng=G ● **Work Field:** 291, 292, 231 ● **MPSMS:** 881 ● **Aptitudes:** G3, V3, N3, S4, P3, Q3, K4, F3, M4, E5, C3 ● **Temperaments:** P, V ● **Physical:** Stg=L; Freq: R, H, I, T, G, N Occas: X ● **Work Env:** Noise=N; ● **Salary:** 2 ● **Outlook:** 3

DELIVERER, MERCHANDISE (retail trade) ● DOT #299.477-010 ● OES: 49998 ● Delivers merchandise from retail store to customers on foot, bicycle, or public conveyance: Unpacks incoming merchandise, marks prices on articles, and stacks them on counters and shelves [STOCK CLERK (retail trade) 299.367-014]. Walks, rides bicycle, or uses public conveyances to deliver merchandise to customer's home or place of business. Collects money from customers or signature from charge-account customers. Sweeps floors, runs errands, and waits on customers [SALES CLERK (retail trade) 290.477-014]. May drive light truck to deliver orders. May be designated according to merchandise delivered as Deliverer, Food (retail trade); Deliverer, Pharmacy (retail trade). ● **GED:** R2, M2, L2 ● **SVP:** 2-30 days ● **Academic:** Ed=N, Eng=S ● **Work Field:** 221, 291 ● **MPSMS:** 881 ● **Aptitudes:** G4, V4, N3, S4, P4, Q4, K4, F4, M4, E4, C5 ● **Temperaments:** P ● **Physical:** Stg=M; Freq: R, H, I, N Occas: B, S, O ● **Work Env:** Noise=N; Freq: W ● **Salary:** 1 ● **Outlook:** 3

FLOOR ATTENDANT (amuse. & rec.) ● DOT #343.467-014 ● OES: 68014 ● Verifies winning bingo cards to award prize or pay prize money to players holding winning cards: Collects money (fee) for participation in game and issues game cards to players. Listens for shouts or looks for waving arms from players who have winning cards. Compares numbers on card with numbers called and displayed on board to verify winning cards. Gives prize or pays money to players holding winning cards. ● **GED:** R2, M1, L1 ● **SVP:** 2-30 days ● **Academic:** Ed=N, Eng=S ● **Work Field:** 232 ● **MPSMS:** 919 ● **Aptitudes:** G4, V4, N4, S4, P3, Q3, K4, F4, M4, E5, C5 ● **Temperaments:** P, R ● **Physical:** Stg=L; Freq: R, H, T, G, N Occas: I ● **Work Env:** Noise=N; ● **Salary:** 1 ● **Outlook:** 3

FURNITURE-RENTAL CONSULTANT (retail trade) ● DOT #295.357-018 ● OES: 49017 ● Alternate titles: DECORATOR CONSULTANT; RENTAL CLERK, FURNITURE. Rents furniture and accessories to customers: Talks to customer to determine furniture preferences and requirements. Guides or accompanies customer through showroom, answers questions, and advises customer on compatibility of various styles and colors of furniture items. Compiles list of customer-selected items. Computes rental fee, explains rental terms, and presents list to customer for approval. Prepares order form and lease agreement, explains terms of lease to customer, and obtains customer signature. Obtains credit information from customer. Forwards forms to credit office for verification of customer credit status and approval of order. Collects initial payment from customer. Contacts customers to encourage followup transactions. May visit commercial customer site to solicit rental contracts, or review floor plans of new construction and suggest suitable furnishings. May sell furniture or accessories [SALESPERSON, FURNITURE (retail trade) 270.357-030]. ● **GED:** R3, M2, L2 ● **SVP:** 2-30 days ● **Academic:** Ed=N, Eng=G ● **Work Field:** 292 ● **MPSMS:** 881, 460 ● **Aptitudes:** G3, V3, N3, S4, P4, Q4, K4, F4, M4, E5, C4 ● **Temperaments:** I, P ● **Physical:** Stg=L; Freq: T, G, N, X Occas: S, O, R, H, I, A ● **Work Env:** Noise=N; ● **Salary:** 1 ● **Outlook:** 3

GAMBLING DEALER (amuse. & rec.) ● DOT #343.464-010 ● OES: 68014 ● Conducts gambling table, such as dice, roulette, or cards, in gambling establishment: Exchanges paper currency for playing chips or coin money. Ensures that wagers are placed before cards are dealt, roulette wheel is spun, or dice are tossed. Announces winning number or color to players. Computes payable odds to pay winning bets. Pays winning bets and collects losing bets. May be designated according to specialty as Baccarat Dealer (amuse. & rec.); Dice Dealer (amuse. & rec.); Roulette Dealer (amuse. & rec.); Twenty-One Dealer (amuse. & rec.). ● **GED:** R3, M3, L2 ● **SVP:** 6 mos-1 yr ● **Academic:** Ed=N, Eng=G ● **Work Field:** 282, 297 ● **MPSMS:** 919 ● **Aptitudes:** G3, V3, N3, S4, P3, Q3, K3, F2, M3, E5, C4 ● **Temperaments:** J, P, R, T ● **Physical:** Stg=L; Const: R Freq: I, T, V Occas: S, H, E, G, N, A, X ● **Work Env:** Noise=N; ● **Salary:** 1 ● **Outlook:** 3

GAME ATTENDANT (amuse. & rec.) ● DOT #342.657-014 ● OES: 68014 ● Alternate titles: GAME OPERATOR. Induces customers to participate in games at concession booths in parks, carnivals, stadiums,

or similar amusement places: Describes types of games available to passing public to attract customers. Supplies customers with game equipment, such as toss rings or balls, distributes prizes to customers who win games, and collects fees for services. Cleans and repairs booth and keeps equipment in serviceable condition. May be designated according to type of game operated as Shooting Gallery Operator (amuse. & rec.). ● **GED:** R3, M3, L3 ● **SVP:** 1-3 mos ● **Academic:** Ed=N, Eng=S ● **Work Field:** 292 ● **MPSMS:** 919 ● **Aptitudes:** G3, V3, N3, S4, P4, Q4, K4, F4, M3, E5, C5 ● **Temperaments:** I, P ● **Physical:** Stg=L; Const: T Freq: R, H, I, G, N ● **Work Env:** Noise=N; ● **Salary:** 1 ● **Outlook:** 3

HOSPITAL-TELEVISION-RENTAL CLERK (business ser.) ● DOT #295.467-018 ● OES: 49017 ● Rents television sets to hospital patients: Determines, from hospital staff and records, names of patients requesting television rental service. Visits patient's room and unlocks and adjusts television set. Explains operation of remote controls and informs patient of rental fee. Periodically collects rental fees. Keeps records of television rentals and fees due. May deliver and connect portable television sets. ● **GED:** R2, M2, L2 ● **SVP:** 2-30 days ● **Academic:** Ed=N, Eng=S ● **Work Field:** 292 ● **MPSMS:** 884 ● **Aptitudes:** G4, V3, N4, S4, P3, Q3, K4, F4, M4, E5, C4 ● **Temperaments:** P ● **Physical:** Stg=L; Freq: R, H, I, T, G, N Occas: D, A, X ● **Work Env:** Noise=N; ● **Salary:** 2 ● **Outlook:** 3

MANAGER, BRANCH STORE (laundry & rel.) ● DOT #369.467-010 ● OES: 49017 ● Manages store where customers deliver and call for articles to be cleaned, laundered, and pressed and keeps records of same: Receives article from customer. Writes identifying slip or tag giving name of customer, work to be done, and date of completion. Pins or staples tag on article. Delivers finished article to customer and collects amount due. Records cash receipts and articles received and delivered. May examine article in presence of customer to advise of possible damage that might result during processing, such as shrinkage, loss of shape, and fading. May measure garments liable to shrink. May remove ornaments and sew or replace them on finished garment upon return from plant. ● **GED:** R3, M2, L2 ● **SVP:** 1-3 mos ● **Academic:** Ed=N, Eng=S ● **Work Field:** 292 ● **MPSMS:** 906 ● **Aptitudes:** G3, V3, N3, S4, P4, Q3, K4, F4, M4, E5, C4 ● **Temperaments:** D, P, R ● **Physical:** Stg=L; Freq: R, H, I, T, G, N Occas: X ● **Work Env:** Noise=N; Occas: W ● **Salary:** 2 ● **Outlook:** 2

NEWSPAPER CARRIER (retail trade) ● DOT #292.457-010 ● OES: 49998 ● Alternate titles: CARRIER; NEWSPAPER DELIVERER. Delivers and sells newspapers to subscribers along prescribed route and collects money periodically: Purchases newspapers at wholesale price for resale to subscriber at retail rate. Walks or rides bicycle to deliver newspapers to subscribers. Keeps records of accounts. Contacts prospective subscribers along route to solicit subscriptions. May attend training sessions to learn selling techniques. If worker delivers newspapers, using automobile or truck, see NEWSPAPER-DELIVERY DRIVER (wholesale tr.). ● **GED:** R2, M2, L2 ● **SVP:** 2-30 days ● **Academic:** Ed=N, Eng=S ● **Work Field:** 292 ● **MPSMS:** 883 ● **Aptitudes:** G4, V3, N4, S4, P4, Q4, K4, F4, M4, E3, C5 ● **Temperaments:** I, P ● **Physical:** Stg=L; Freq: R, H, I, T, G Occas: N ● **Work Env:** Noise=N; Freq: W ● **Salary:** 1 ● **Outlook:** 4

PARKING-LOT ATTENDANT (automotive ser.) ● DOT #915.473-010 ● OES: 97808 ● Alternate titles: AUTOMOBILE PARKER; PARKING ATTENDANT; PARKING-LOT CHAUFFEUR; PARKING-STATION ATTENDANT; SPOTTER. Parks automobiles for customers in parking lot or storage garage: Places numbered tag on windshield of automobile to be parked and hands customer similar tag to be used later in locating parked automobile. Records time and drives automobile to parking space, or points out parking space for customer's use. Patrols area to prevent thefts from parked automobiles. Collects parking fee from customer, based on charges for time automobile is parked. Takes numbered tag from customer, locates automobile, and surrenders it to customer, or directs customer to parked automobile. May service automobiles with gasoline, oil, and water. When parking automobiles in storage garage, may be designated Storage-Garage Attendant (automotive ser.). May direct customers to parking spaces. ● **GED:** R2, M1, L1 ● **SVP:** 2-30 days ● **Academic:** Ed=N, Eng=S ● **Work Field:** 291 ● **MPSMS:** 961 ● **Aptitudes:** G4, V4, N4, S4, P4, Q4, K4, F4, M3, E3, C5 ● **Temperaments:** P, R ● **Physical:** Stg=L; Freq: R, H, I, N, F, D, A, V Occas: T, G ● **Work Env:** Noise=L; Freq: W ● **Salary:** 1 ● **Outlook:** 3

PERSONAL SHOPPER (retail trade) ● DOT #296.357-010 ● OES: 49998 ● Alternate titles: PROFESSIONAL SHOPPER; SHOPPER'S AID; SPECIAL SHOPPER. Selects and purchases merchandise for department store customers, according to mail or telephone requests. Visits wholesale establishments or other department stores to purchase merchandise which is out-of-stock or which store does not carry. Records and processes mail orders and merchandise returned for exchange. May escort customer through store. ● GED: R4, M3, L3 ● SVP: 6 mos-1 yr ● Academic: Ed=N, Eng=G ● Work Field: 291, 292 ● MPSMS: 880 ● Aptitudes: G3, V3, N3, S4, P4, Q4, K4, F4, M4, E5, C5 ● Temperaments: J, P ● Physical: Stg=L; Freq: R, H, I, T, G, N ● Work Env: Noise=N; ● Salary: 2 ● Outlook: 3

SALES ATTENDANT (retail trade) ● DOT #299.677-010 ● OES: 49011 ● Alternate titles: ATTENDANT, SELF-SERVICE STORE. Performs any combination of following duties to provide customer service in self-service store: Aids customers in locating merchandise. Answers questions from and provides information to customer about merchandise for sale. Obtains merchandise from stockroom when merchandise is not on floor. Arranges stock on shelves or racks in sales area. Directs or escorts customer to fitting or dressing rooms or to cashier. Keeps merchandise in order. Marks or tickets merchandise. Inventories stock. ● GED: R3, M1, L2 ● SVP: 2-30 days ● Academic: Ed=N, Eng=S ● Work Field: 221, 292 ● MPSMS: 881 ● Aptitudes: G3, V4, N4, S4, P4, Q4, K4, F4, M3, E5, C4 ● Temperaments: P ● Physical: Stg=L; Freq: R, H, T, G Occas: S, I, N, X ● Work Env: Noise=N; ● Salary: 2 ● Outlook: 3

SALES ATTENDANT, BUILDING MATERIALS (retail trade) ● DOT #299.677-014 ● OES: 58097 ● Alternate titles: YARD SALES-PERSON. Assists customers and stocks merchandise in building materials and supplies department of self-service store: Answers questions and advises customer in selection of building materials and supplies. Cuts lumber, screening, glass, and related materials to size requested by customer, using power saws, holding fixtures, and various hand-cutting tools. Assists customer to load purchased materials into customer's vehicle. Moves materials and supplies from receiving area to display area, using forklift or hand truck. Marks prices on merchandise or price stickers, according to pricing guides, using marking devices. Straightens materials on display to maintain safe and orderly conditions in sales areas. Covers exposed materials, when required, to prevent weather damage. Counts materials and records totals on inventory sheets. ● GED: R2, M2, L2 ● SVP: 1-3 mos ● Academic: Ed=N, Eng=S ● Work Field: 292, 011 ● MPSMS: 881 ● Aptitudes: G4, V4, N4, S4, P4, Q4, K4, F4, M4, E4, C5 ● Temperaments: P, V ● Physical: Stg=H; Freq: S, O, R, H, I, T, G, V Occas: B, F, D ● Work Env: Noise=N; Occas: W ● Salary: 4 ● Outlook: 3

SALES CLERK (retail trade) ● DOT #290.477-014 ● OES: 49011 ●Obtains or receives merchandise, totals bill, accepts payment, and makes change for customers in retail store such as tobacco shop, drug store, candy store, or liquor store: Stocks shelves, counters, or tables with merchandise. Sets up advertising displays or arranges merchandise on counters or tables to promote sales. Stamps, marks, or tags price on merchandise. Obtains merchandise requested by customer or receives merchandise selected by customer. Answers customer's questions concerning location, price, and use of merchandise. Totals price and tax on merchandise purchased by customer, using paper and pencil, cash register, or calculator, to determine bill. Accepts payment and makes change. Wraps or bags merchandise for customers. Cleans shelves, counters, or tables. Removes and records amount of cash in register at end of shift. May calculate sales discount to determine price. May keep record of sales, prepare inventory of stock, or order merchandise. May be designated according to product sold or type of store. ● GED: R3, M2, L2 ● SVP: 1-3 mos ● Academic: Ed=N, Eng=S ● Work Field: 292, 221 ● MPSMS: 881 ● Aptitudes: G3, V3, N3, S4, P4, Q3, K4, F4, M4, E5, C4 ● Temperaments: P ● Physical: Stg=L; Freq: R, H, I, T, G Occas: S, O, N, F, X ● Work Env: Noise=N; ● Salary: 2 ● Outlook: 3

SALES CLERK, FOOD (retail trade) ● DOT #290.477-018 ● OES: 49011 ● Obtains or prepares food items requested by customers in retail food store, totals customer bill, receives payment, and makes change: Fills customer order, performing duties such as obtaining items from shelves, freezers, coolers, bins, tables, or containers; cleaning poultry; scaling and trimming fish; slicing meat or cheese, using slic-

ing machine; preparing take-out sandwiches and salads; dispensing beverages; and warming food items in oven. Weighs items, such as produce, meat, and poultry to determine price. Lists and totals prices, using paper and pencil, calculator, or cash register. Informs customer of total price of purchases. Receives payment from customer for purchases and makes change. Bags or wraps purchases for customer. Cleans shelves, bins, tables, and coolers. Stamps, marks, or tags price on merchandise. Sets up displays and stocks shelves, coolers, counter, bins, tables, freezers, containers, or trays with new merchandise. May make deliveries to customer home or place of business [DELIVERER, MERCHANDISE (retail trade) 299.477-010]. May write orders, decorate cakes, or describe available specialty products, such as birthday cakes. May order merchandise from warehouse or supplier. May be designated according to type of food sold as Grocery Clerk (retail trade); Meat Counter Clerk (retail trade); Produce Clerk (retail trade) I; Sales Clerk, Fish (retail trade). ● GED: R3, M3, L2 ● SVP: 1-3 mos ● Academic: Ed=N, Eng=S ● Work Field: 292 ● MPSMS: 881 ● Aptitudes: G3, V3, N3, S4, P3, Q3, K3, F3, M4, E5, C5 ● Temperaments: P ● Physical: Stg=L; Freq: R, H, I, T, G, N ● Work Env: Noise=N; Occas: C ● Salary: 1 ● Outlook: 3

SERVICE-ESTABLISHMENT ATTENDANT (laundry & rel.) ● DOT #369.477-014 ● OES: 49017 ● Alternate titles: COUNTER ATTENDANT. Receives articles, such as shoes and clothing, to be repaired or cleaned, in personal-service establishment: Examines articles to determine nature of repair and advises customer of repairs needed. Quotes prices and prepares work ticket. Sends articles to work department. Returns finished articles to customer and collects amount due. May keep records of cash receipts and articles received and delivered. May sell articles, such as cleaner, polish, shoelaces, and accessories. ● GED: R3, M2, L2 ● SVP: 1-3 mos ● Academic: Ed=N, Eng=S ● Work Field: 291 ● MPSMS: 906 ● Aptitudes: G3, V3, N3, S4, P4, Q3, K4, F4, M4, E5, C5 ● Temperaments: J, P ● Physical: Stg=L; Freq: R, H, T, G, N Occas: I, A ● Work Env: Noise=Q; ● Salary: 3 ● Outlook: 2

SELF-SERVICE-LAUNDRY-AND-DRY-CLEANING ATTENDANT (laundry & rel.) ● DOT #369.677-010 ● OES: 49017 ● Alternate titles: ATTENDANT, COIN-OPERATED LAUNDRY; ATTENDANT, LAUNDRY-AND-DRY-CLEANING SERVICE; WASHATERIA ATTENDANT. Assists customer to launder or dryclean clothes, or launders or drycleans clothes for customer paying for complete service, using self-service equipment: Gives instructions to customer in clothes preparation, such as weighing, sorting, fog-spraying spots, and removing perishable buttons. Assigns machine and directs customer or points out posted instructions regarding equipment operation. Weighs soiled items and calculates amount charged customer requiring complete services. Dampens garments with cleaning solvent and rubs with sponge or brush to remove spots or stains. Places clothes, cleaning material, bleach, and coins in laundering or drycleaning equipment, and sets automatic controls to clean or dry clothes. Removes clothes from equipment. Hangs, bags, folds, and bundles clothes for delivery to customer. Receives payment for service. May sell cleansing agents. ● GED: R3, M1, L3 ● SVP: 2-30 days ● Academic: Ed=N, Eng=S ● Work Field: 291, 292 ● MPSMS: 906 ● Aptitudes: G4, V4, N4, S4, P4, Q4, K4, F4, M4, E5, C4 ● Temperaments: P, V ● Physical: Stg=M; Freq: R, H, T, G, N Occas: I, X ● Work Env: Noise=N; ● Salary: 1 ● Outlook: 2

STORAGE-FACILITY RENTAL CLERK (business ser.) ● DOT #295.367-026 ● OES: 49017 ● Leases storage space to customers of rental storage facility: Informs customers of space availability, rental regulations, and rates. Assists customers in selection of storage unit size according to articles or material to be stored. Records terms of rental on rental agreement form and assists customer in completing form. Photographs completed form and customer to establish identification record, using security camera. Computes rental fee and collects payment. Maintains rental status record and waiting list for storage units. Notifies customers when rental term is about to expire or rent is overdue. Inspects storage area periodically to ensure storage units are locked. Observes individuals entering storage area to prevent access to or tampering with storage units by unauthorized persons. Loads film into security and surveillance cameras, records dates of film changes, and monitors camera operations to ensure performance as required. Cleans facility and maintains premises in orderly condition. ● GED: R3, M3, L3 ● SVP: 2-30 days ● Academic: Ed=N, Eng=G ● Work

Field: 292 ● **MPSMS:** 889 ● **Aptitudes:** G3, V3, N3, S4, P4, Q3, K4, F4, M3, E5, C5 ● **Temperaments:** P, V ● **Physical:** Stg=L; Freq: R, H, T, G, F Occas: S, K ● **Work Env:** Noise=N; Occas: W ● **Salary:** 2 ● **Outlook:** 3

TOOL-AND-EQUIPMENT-RENTAL CLERK (business ser.) ● DOT #295.357-014 ● OES: 49017 ● Alternate titles: RENTAL CLERK, TOOL-AND-EQUIPMENT. Rents tools and equipment to customers: Suggests tools or equipment, based on work to be done. Prepares rental form and quotes rental rates to customer. Starts power equipment to ensure performance prior to issuance to customer. Computes rental fee based on hourly or daily rate. Cleans, lubricates, and adjusts power tools and equipment. May drive truck or use handtruck to deliver tools or equipment to customer. ● **GED:** R3, M3, L3 ● **SVP:** 3-6 mos ● **Academic:** Ed=N, Eng=S ● **Work Field:** 292 ● **MPSMS:** 881 ● **Aptitudes:** G3, V3, N3, S4, P3, Q3, K4, F4, M4, E4, C4 ● **Temperaments:** I, J, P ● **Physical:** Stg=M; Freq: R, H, I, T, G, N Occas: X ● **Work Env:** Noise=L; ● **Salary:** 1 ● **Outlook:** 4

TRAILER-RENTAL CLERK (automotive ser.) ● DOT #295.467-022 ● OES: 49017 ● Rents trailers, trucks, and power-driven mobile machinery and equipment: Talks with customer to determine type of equipment needed, such as vacation, boat, or open trailer, or moving truck or moving-van trailer, or cement mixer. Quotes rental rates and collects security deposit. Prepares rental-agreement form. Directs yard personnel to hitch trailer to customer's vehicle or bring truck or power-driven mobile equipment to customer. Computes rental charges, collects money, makes change, and returns deposit. May pull trailer into position and fasten appropriate hitch to customer's vehicle. May splice wires from trailer's taillights onto wires of customer's vehicle's taillights to provide brake and turn signals to trailer. May advise customer on type of equipment to rent, depending on work to be done. May rent power tools and equipment [TOOL-AND-EQUIPMENT-RENTAL CLERK (business ser.; retail trade)]. May be designated according to type of equipment rented as Construction-Machinery-And-Equipment-Rental Clerk (business ser.); Farm-Machinery-And-Equipment-Rental Clerk (business ser.); Truck Rental Clerk (automotive ser.). ● **GED:** R3, M3, L3 ● **SVP:** 3-6 mos ● **Academic:** Ed=N, Eng=G ● **Work Field:** 292 ● **MPSMS:** 881 ● **Aptitudes:** G3, V3, N3, S4, P4, Q3, K4, F4, M4, E5, C5 ● **Temperaments:** P ● **Physical:** Stg=L; Freq: R, H, T, G, N Occas: S, K, O, I, D, A ● **Work Env:** Noise=N; ● **Salary:** 2 ● **Outlook:** 3

Accommodating 09

Attendant Services

09.05

Workers in this group perform services that make life easier and more pleasant for people. They do things that people can't or don't want to do for themselves, like opening doors, delivering messages, carrying luggage and packages, and dishing up food. They find employment in a variety of settings, such as hotels, airports, golf courses, theaters, reducing salons, and gymnasiums.

✓ What kind of work would you do?

Your work activities would depend upon your specific job. For example, you might:

- serve or assist diners at a buffet table.
- carry food to a serving table in a cafeteria.
- carry and deliver messages.
- care for costumes of a theatrical or movie cast.
- carry pails of drinking water to farm or construction workers.
- serve food to cafeteria customers.
- check credentials of those entering a press box and run errands.
- retrieve bats and foul balls from baseball field and supply balls to the umpire.
- massage a customer's muscles to relieve tension.
- clean, shape, and polish fingernails.
- take tickets from persons attending a theater.
- carry baggage on and off trains.

✓ What skills and abilities do you need for this kind of work?

To do this kind of work, you must be able to:

- carry out specific oral or written instructions, frequently following a simple routine.

- do the same task over and over, frequently in the same way.
- get along with all kinds of people.
- stand and walk for long periods of time.
- use hands and fingers skillfully and easily when performing tasks, like giving rubdowns, manicuring fingernails, opening oysters, and bagging groceries.
- lift and carry things like luggage, trays of dishes, and bags of golf clubs.

✓ How do you know if you would like or could learn to do this kind of work?

The following questions may give you clues about yourself as you consider this group of jobs.

- Have you collected tickets or ushered at a play? Do you remain courteous when other people are rude to you?
- Have you served food or beverages in a cafeteria line? Can you walk or stand for long periods of time?
- Have you helped with the wardrobe for a school or community theatrical group? Do you enjoy assisting others?
- Have you been in charge of sports equipment for a team? Do you enjoy caring for other people's property?
- Have you served food in a mess hall as a member of a military force? Did you like doing this?

✓ How can you prepare for and enter this kind of work?

Occupations in this group usually require education and/or training extending from a short demonstration to over three months, depending upon the specific kind of work. Many jobs in this group require only on-the-job training. However, formal training is available. For example, massage techniques may be learned in a few class sessions through a public or private school. Manicurists usually learn their trade in a beauty school.

Some jobs require city or state licenses. Courses in food and beverage service are offered in many vocational schools. Employers usually train inexperienced people.

✓ *What else should you consider about these jobs?*

Income for these workers may be a combination of wages and tips. Their salary sometimes includes room and board. Weekend and evening work is required in some of these jobs. Some workers like Bellhops and Waiters/Waitresses are required to wear uniforms.

If you think you would like to do this kind of work, look at the job titles listed on the following pages.

■ ■ ■

GOE: 09.05.01
Physical Conditioning

COOLING-ROOM ATTENDANT (personal ser.) ● DOT #335.677-010 ● OES: 69998 ● Alternate titles: ALCOHOL RUBBER; SLUMBER-ROOM ATTENDANT. Attends to comfort and needs of thermal bath customers cooling off and resting after bath and massage: Assigns cot to customer. Rubs customer's body with alcohol and oil to soothe skin. Covers customer with sheet. Times length of rest period. Procures beverage, food, or other items on request. May arrange for valet services. May change bedding on cots. May shine shoes [SHOE SHINER (personal ser.)]. May sweep and mop floors and dust furniture [CLEANER, COMMERCIAL OR INSTITUTIONAL (any industry)]. ● **GED:** R2, M1, L2 ● **SVP:** 2-30 days ● **Academic:** Ed=N, Eng=S ● **Work Field:** 291 ● **MPSMS:** 909 ● **Aptitudes:** G4, V4, N4, S4, P4, Q4, K4, F4, M3, E5, C5 ● **Temperaments:** P, R ● **Physical:** Stg=L; Freq: R, H, E, T, G Occas: S, I ● **Work Env:** Noise=Q; ● **Salary:** 1 ● **Outlook:** 2

ELECTROLOGIST (personal ser.) ● DOT #339.371-010 ● OES: 68005 ● Alternate titles: ELECTRIC-NEEDLE SPECIALIST; ELECTROLYSIS OPERATOR; HYPERTRICHOLOGIST. Removes hair from skin of patron by electrolysis: Positions sterile bulbous or round-tipped needles into holders (electrodes) of galvanic or short wave electrical equipment. Places secondary electrode in hand or immerses fingers or hand of patron in water-filled electrode cup to complete circuit and stabilize amount of electricity when equipment is operating. Swabs skin area with antiseptic solution to sterilize it. Inserts needle or needles into hair follicle and into organ beneath hair root (papilla). Presses switch and adjusts timing and rheostat controls of equipment that regulate amount of electricity flowing through needle or needles to decompose cells of papilla. Removes needle or needles, and pulls hair from follicle, using tweezers. ● **GED:** R3, M2, L3 ● **SVP:** 6 mos-1 yr ● **Academic:** Ed=N, Eng=S ● **Work Field:** 294 ● **MPSMS:** 904 ● **Aptitudes:** G3, V3, N4, S4, P2, Q4, K3, F2, M3, E4, C5 ● **Temperaments:** J, P, T ● **Physical:** Stg=L; Const: N, A Freq: S, R, H, I, T, G Occas: D ● **Work Env:** Noise=Q; ● **Salary:** 1 ● **Outlook:** 3

FINGERNAIL FORMER (personal ser.) ● DOT #331.674-014 ● OES: 68008 ● Forms artificial fingernails on customer's fingers: Roughens surfaces of fingernails, using abrasive wheel. Attaches paper forms to tips of customer's fingers to support and shape artificial nails. Brushes coats of powder and solvent onto nails and paper forms with handbrush to extend nails to desired length. Removes paper forms and shapes and smooths edges of nails, using rotary abrasive wheel. Brushes additional powder and solvent onto new growth between cuticles and nails to maintain nail appearance. May soften, trim, or cut cuticles, using oil, water, knife, or scissors, to prepare customer's nails for application of artificial nails. ● **GED:** R2, M1, L2 ● **SVP:** 1-3 mos ● **Academic:** Ed=N, Eng=S ● **Work Field:** 291 ● **MPSMS:** 904 ● **Aptitudes:** G4, V4, N4, S4, P3, Q5, K3, F3, M3, E5, C4 ● **Temperaments:** P, T ● **Physical:** Stg=S; Freq: R, H, I, E, N Occas: A, X ● **Work Env:** Noise=N; ● **Salary:** 1 ● **Outlook:** 2

HOT-ROOM ATTENDANT (personal ser.) ● DOT #335.677-014 ● OES: 69998 ● Alternate titles: ELECTRIC-BATH ATTENDANT; PORTER, BATH; PUBLIC-BATH ATTENDANT; SWEAT-BOX ATTENDANT; TUB ATTENDANT. Serves patrons in dry-heat cabinet or room or steamroom of athletic, bathing, or other establishment: Spreads sheet or towel over seating facility in cabinet or rooms and seats patrons. Supplies drinking water and renders other services requested, such as wrapping cool towels about patron's head, spraying body with water, or timing length of bath. Gives shower baths and furnishes towel or dries patron. Collects soiled linen and cleans bathing area and facilities, such as tubs and showers. May turn valves and switches to adjust heating equipment, regulating amount of steam or temperature. May pour water over heated rocks to prepare steamroom. May be designated according to bath facility served as Dry-Heat-Cabinet Attendant (personal ser.); Dry-Heat-Room Attendant (personal ser.); Shower Attendant (personal ser.); Steam-Room Attendant (personal ser.). ● **GED:** R2, M1, L2 ● **SVP:** 2-30 days ● **Academic:** Ed=N, Eng=S ● **Work Field:** 291 ● **MPSMS:** 909 ● **Aptitudes:** G4, V4, N4, S4, P4, Q4, K4, F4, M3, E5, C5 ● **Temperaments:** P, V ● **Physical:** Stg=L; Freq: R, H, T, G Occas: S, I, E ● **Work Env:** Noise=Q; Occas: H, U ● **Salary:** 1 ● **Outlook:** 2

MANICURIST (personal ser.) ● DOT #331.674-010 ● OES: 68008● Cleans, shapes, and polishes customers' fingernails and toenails: Removes previously applied nail polish, using liquid remover and swabs. Shapes and smooths ends of nails, using scissors, files, and emery boards. Cleans customers' nails in soapy water, using swabs, files, and orange sticks. Softens nail cuticles with water and oil, pushes back cuticles, using cuticle knife, and trims cuticles, using scissors or nippers. Whitens underside of nails with white paste or pencil. Polishes nails, using powdered polish and buffer, or applies clear or colored liquid polish onto nails with brush. May perform other beauty services such as giving facials, and shampooing, tinting, and curling hair [COSMETOLOGIST (personal ser.)]. ● **GED:** R2, M1, L2 ● **SVP:** 1-3 mos ● **Academic:** Ed=N, Eng=S ● **Work Field:** 291 ● **MPSMS:** 904 ● **Aptitudes:** G4, V4, N4, S4, P3, Q5, K3, F3, M3, E5, C3 ● **Temperaments:** J, P ● **Physical:** Stg=S; Const: I, N, A Freq: R, H Occas: X ● **Work Env:** Noise=Q; ● **Salary:** 2 ● **Outlook:** 3

MASSEUR/MASSEUSE (personal ser.) ● DOT #334.374-010 ● OES: 69998 ● Alternate titles: BATH ATTENDANT; BATH-HOUSE ATTENDANT; RUBBER. Massages customers and administers other body conditioning treatments for hygienic or remedial purposes: Applies alcohol, lubricants, or other rubbing compounds. Massages body, using such techniques as kneading, rubbing, and stroking flesh, to stimulate blood circulation, relax contracted muscles, facilitate elimination of waste matter, or to relieve other conditions, using hands or vibrating equipment. Administers steam or dry heat, ultraviolet or infrared, or water treatments on request of customer or instructions of physician. May give directions to clients in activities, such as reducing or remedial exercises. May examine client and recommend body conditioning activities or treatments. May record treatments furnished to customers. ● **GED:** R3, M2, L3 ● **SVP:** 3-6 mos ● **Academic:** Ed=N, Eng=S ● **Work Field:** 291 ● **MPSMS:** 909 ● **Aptitudes:** G3, V3, N4, S3, P3, Q4, K3, F3, M2, E5, C4 ● **Temperaments:** J, P, V ● **Physical:** Stg=M; Freq: R, H, E Occas: I, T, G, X ● **Work Env:** Noise=Q; Occas: U ● **Salary:** 1 ● **Outlook:** 3

REDUCING-SALON ATTENDANT (personal ser.) ● DOT #359.567-010 ● OES: 69998 ● Measures, weighs and records patron's body statistics, refers information to supervisor for evaluation and planning of exercise program, and demonstrates exercises and use of equipment. Monitors member's exercise activities to assure progress toward desired goals. Records patron's measurements periodically for re-evaluation. ● **GED:** R2, M2, L2 ● **SVP:** 2-30 days ● **Academic:** Ed=N, Eng=S ● **Work Field:** 291 ● **MPSMS:** 909 ● **Aptitudes:** G4, V4, N4, S4, P4, Q4, K3, F4, M3, E4, C5 ● **Temperaments:** P ● **Physical:** Stg=M; Freq: S, R, H, I, T, G, N ● **Work Env:** Noise=L; Freq: H, U ● **Salary:** 1 ● **Outlook:** 2

WEIGHT-REDUCTION SPECIALIST (personal ser.) ● DOT #359.367-014 ● OES: 69998 ● Alternate titles: NUTRITION EDUCATOR. Assists clients in devising and carrying out weight-loss plan, using established dietary programs and positive reinforcement procedures: Interviews client to obtain information on weight development history, eating habits, medical restrictions, and nutritional objectives. Weighs and measures client, using measuring instruments, and enters data on client record. Discusses eating habits with client to identify dispensable food items and to encourage increased consumption of high nutrition, low calorie food items, or selects established diet program which matches client goals and restrictions. Explains program and procedures which should be followed to lose desired amount of weight, and answers client questions. Reviews client food diary at regular intervals to identify eating habits which do not coincide with established or agreed upon dietary program, and reviews weight loss statistics to determine progress. Counsels client to promote established goals and to reinforce positive results. May photograph client during therapy to provide visual record of progress. May conduct aversion therapy, utilizing electric shock, rancid odors, and other physical or visual stimuli to promote negative association with food designated for elimination from diet. May conduct positive conditioning therapy sessions, utilizing physical and visual stimuli to promote positive association with foods designated for increase in diet. May give client weight-loss aids, such as calorie counters, or sell nutritional products to be used in conjunction with diet program. ● **GED:** R3, M2, L3 ● **SVP:** 1-3 mos ● **Academic:** Ed=N, Eng=G ● **Work Field:** 291 ● **MPSMS:** 909 ● **Aptitudes:** G3, V3, N4, S5, P4, Q3, K4, F4, M4, E5, C5 ● **Temperaments:** J, P ● **Physical:** Stg=L; Freq: T, G, N Occas: H, I, A ● **Work Env:** Noise=N; ● **Salary:** 4 ● **Outlook:** 2

GOE: 09.05.02
Food Services

CAFETERIA ATTENDANT (hotel & rest.) ● DOT #311.677-010 ● OES: 65014 ● Alternate titles: DINING-ROOM ATTENDANT, CAFETERIA; SERVICE ATTENDANT, CAFETERIA; TABLE ATTENDANT, CAFETERIA; WAITER/WAITRESS, CAFETERIA. Carries trays from food counters to tables for cafeteria patrons. Carries dirty dishes to kitchen. Wipes tables and seats with dampened cloth. Sets tables with clean linens, sugar bowls, and condiments. May wrap clean silver in napkins. May circulate among diners and serve coffee and be designated Coffee Server, Cafeteria or Restaurant (hotel & rest.). ● **GED:** R2, M1, L1 ● **SVP:** 2-30 days ● **Academic:** Ed=N, Eng=S ● **Work Field:** 291 ● **MPSMS:** 903 ● **Aptitudes:** G4, V4, N4, S4, P4, Q5, K4, F4, M3, E4, C5 ● **Temperaments:** R ● **Physical:** Stg=L; Freq: R, H Occas: S, I, T, G, N ● **Work Env:** Noise=N; ● **Salary:** 4 ● **Outlook:** 4

COUNTER ATTENDANT, CAFETERIA (hotel & rest.) ● DOT #311.677-014 ● OES: 65040 ● Alternate titles: SERVER; STEAMTABLE ATTENDANT. Serves food from counters and steamtables to cafeteria patrons: Serves salads, vegetables, meat, breads, and cocktails, ladles soups and sauces, portions desserts, and fills beverage cups and glasses as indicated by customer. Adds relishes and garnishes according to instructions from COUNTER SUPERVISOR (hotel & rest.) 311.137-010. Scrubs and polishes counters, steamtables, and other equipment. May replenish foods at serving stations. May brew coffee and tea. May carve meat. May accept payment for food, using cash register or adding machine to total check. May prepare and serve salads and be known as Salad Counter Attendant (hotel & rest.). May serve food to passenger from steamtable on railroad dining car

and be known as Steamtable Attendant, Railroad (r.r. trans.). ● **GED:** R2, M1, L2 ● **SVP:** 1-3 mos ● **Academic:** Ed=N, Eng=S ● **Work Field:** 291 ● **MPSMS:** 903 ● **Aptitudes:** G4, V4, N4, S4, P3, Q4, K3, F3, M3, E5, C5 ● **Temperaments:** P, R ● **Physical:** Stg=L; Freq: S, R, H, I, N Occas: O, T, G, X ● **Work Env:** Noise=L; Occas: H ● **Salary:** 1 ● **Outlook:** 4

CATERER HELPER (personal ser.) ● DOT #319.677-010 ● OES: 65300 ● Prepares and serves food and refreshments at social affairs, under supervision of CATERER (personal ser.): Arranges tables and decorations. Prepares hors d'oeuvres, fancy and plain sandwiches, and salads. Serves foods and beverages to guests. Washes and packs dishes and utensils for removal to catering establishment. ● **GED:** R3, M2, L2 ● **SVP:** 1-3 mos ● **Academic:** Ed=N, Eng=N ● **Work Field:** 291, 146 ● **MPSMS:** 903 ● **Aptitudes:** G3, V3, N4, S4, P3, Q4, K4, F4, M3, E5, C4 ● **Temperaments:** P ● **Physical:** Stg=L; Freq: R, H, I, T, G Occas: N, X ● **Work Env:** Noise=Q; ● **Salary:** 1 ● **Outlook:** 4

COUNTER SUPERVISOR (hotel & rest.) ● DOT #311.137-010 ● OES: 69998 ● Supervises and coordinates activities of workers engaged in serving food from cafeteria counter: Directs workers engaged in stocking and arranging of food, dishes, silverware, and other supplies at steamtables, ice counters, and serving stations. Inspects serving operations to ensure that supplies are adequate and that food portioning meets prescribed standards. Assigns duties to counter workers. Directs workers engaged in removing food after meals and cleaning counters and work areas. May assist workers in serving customers or in performing other duties. ● **GED:** R3, M2, L3 ● **SVP:** 1-2 yrs ● **Academic:** Ed=N, Eng=S ● **Work Field:** 291, 146 ● **MPSMS:** 903 ● **Aptitudes:** G3, V3, N3, S4, P4, Q4, K4, F4, M4, E4, C4 ● **Temperaments:** D, P, V ● **Physical:** Stg=L; Freq: R, H, T, G, N Occas: S, I, X ● **Work Env:** Noise=N; ● **Salary:** 4 ● **Outlook:** 2

COUNTER-SUPPLY WORKER (hotel & rest.) ● DOT #319.687-010 ● OES: 65014 ● Replenishes food and equipment at steamtables and serving counters of cafeteria to facilitate service to patrons: Carries food, dishes, trays, and silverware from kitchen and supply departments to serving counters. Garnishes foods and positions them on table to ensure their visibility to patrons and convenience in serving. Keeps assigned area and equipment free of spilled foods. Keeps shelves of vending machines stocked with food when working in automat. ● **GED:** R2, M1, L1 ● **SVP:** 2-30 days ● **Academic:** Ed=N, Eng=N ● **Work Field:** 221 ● **MPSMS:** 903 ● **Aptitudes:** G4, V4, N4, S4, P4, Q4, K4, F4, M3, E5, C4 ● **Temperaments:** R ● **Physical:** Stg=M; Freq: S, R, H Occas: I, X ● **Work Env:** Noise=Q; ● **Salary:** 1 ● **Outlook:** 3

DINING ROOM ATTENDANT (hotel & rest.) ● DOT #311.677-018 ● OES: 65014 ● Alternate titles: BUS PERSON. Performs any combination of following duties to facilitate food service: Carries dirty dishes from dining room to kitchen. Wipes table tops and chairs, using damp cloth. Replaces soiled table linens and sets tables with silverware and glassware. Replenishes supply of clean linens, silverware, glassware, and dishes in dining room. Supplies service bar with food, such as soups, salads, and desserts. Serves ice water and butter to patrons. Cleans and polishes glass shelves and doors of service bars and equipment, such as coffee urns and cream and milk dispensers. Makes coffee and fills fruit juice dispensers. May sweep and mop floors. May transfer food and dishes between floors of establishment, using dumbwaiter, and be designated Dumbwaiter Operator (hotel & rest.). May run errands and deliver food orders to offices and be designated Runner (hotel & rest.). May be designated according to type of activity or area of work as Clean-Up Helper, Banquet (hotel & rest.); Counter Dish Carrier (hotel & rest.); Dish Carrier (hotel & rest.); Glass Washer And Carrier (hotel & rest.); Room Service Assistant (hotel & rest.); Steamtable Worker (hotel & rest.); Table Setter (hotel & rest.); Water Server (hotel & rest.). ● **GED:** R2, M1, L1 ● **SVP:** 2-30 days ● **Academic:** Ed=N, Eng=N ● **Work Field:** 291, 031 ● **MPSMS:** 903 ● **Aptitudes:** G4, V4, N4, S4, P4, Q4, K4, F4, M4, E4, C4 ● **Temperaments:** R ● **Physical:** Stg=M; Const: R, H Occas: S, O, I, T, G, F ● **Work Env:** Noise=N; ● **Salary:** 1 ● **Outlook:** 4

FOOD-SERVICE SUPERVISOR (hotel & rest.) ● DOT #319.137-010 ● OES: 69998 ● Supervises employees engaged in serving food in hospital, nursing home, school, or similiar institutions, and in maintaining cleanliness of food service areas and equipment: Trains workers in performance of duties. Assigns and coordinates work of employees to promote efficiency of operations. Supervises serving of meals. Inspects kitchen and dining areas and kitchen utensils and equipment to ensure sanitary standards are met. Keeps records, such as amount and cost of meals served and hours worked by employees. Requisitions and inspects foodstuffs, supplies, and equipment to maintain stock levels and ensure standards of quality are met. Prepares work schedules and evaluates work performance of employees. May direct preparation of foods and beverages. May assist DIETITIAN, CLINICAL (profess. & kin.) 077.127-014 in planning menus. May interview, select, or hire new employees. When supervising workers engaged in tray assembly may be designated Tray-Line Supervisor (medical ser.). ● **GED:** R4, M3, L3 ● **SVP:** 1-2 yrs ● **Academic:** Ed=N, Eng=G ● **Work Field:** 146 ● **MPSMS:** 903 ● **Aptitudes:** G3, V3, N3, S4, P4, Q3, K4, F4, M4, E5, C4 ● **Temperaments:** D, J, P, V ● **Physical:** Stg=L; Freq: R, H, I, T, G, M, N, X ● **Work Env:** Noise=N; Occas: C, H, U, O ● **Salary:** 4 ● **Outlook:** 3

FOOD-SERVICE WORKER, HOSPITAL (medical ser.) ● DOT #319.677-014 ● OES: 65040 ● Alternate titles: DIETARY AIDE; TRAY WORKER. Prepares and delivers food trays to hospital patients, performing any combination of following duties on tray line: Reads production orders on color-coded menu cards on trays to determine items to place on tray. Places items, such as eating utensils, napkins, and condiments on trays. Prepares food items, such as sandwiches, salads, soups, and beverages. Places servings in blender to make foods for soft or liquid diets. Apportions and places food servings on plates and trays according to diet list on menu card. Examines filled tray for completeness and places on cart, dumbwaiter, or conveyor belt. Pushes carts to halls or ward kitchen. Serves trays to patients. Collects and stacks dirty dishes on cart and returns cart to kitchen. Washes dishes and cleans work area, tables, cabinets, and ovens. Collects and places garbage and trash in designated containers. May record amount and types of special food items served to patients. May assemble and serve food items to hospital staff in cafeteria. ● **GED:** R3, M2, L2 ● **SVP:** 2-30 days ● **Academic:** Ed=N, Eng=S ● **Work Field:** 146, 031, 291 ● **MPSMS:** 903 ● **Aptitudes:** G4, V4, N4, S4, P4, Q3, K4, F3, M3, E4, C4 ● **Temperaments:** R, T ● **Physical:** Stg=M; Freq: R, H, N Occas: S, O, I, D, A, X, V ● **Work Env:** Noise=N; Occas: H, U, O ● **Salary:** 1 ● **Outlook:** 2

MESS ATTENDANT (water trans.) ● DOT #350.677-010 ● OES: 65008 ● Serves food to officers and crew aboard ship: Prepares hot and cold drinks, and fruits, for serving, and sets tables for meals. Serves food. Washes glassware and silverware after meals, cleans messroom, and disposes of trash and garbage. Makes beds and cleans bedrooms and bathrooms assigned to ship's officers. May be designated according to area in which work is performed or personnel served as Mess Attendant, Crew (water trans.); Mess Attendant, Officers' Room (water trans.); Mess Attendant, Officers' Salon (water trans.). ● **GED:** R2, M1, L2 ● **SVP:** 1-3 mos ● **Academic:** Ed=N, Eng=S ● **Work Field:** 291 ● **MPSMS:** 903 ● **Aptitudes:** G4, V4, N4, S4, P4, Q4, K3, F4, M3, E4, C5 ● **Temperaments:** P, R ● **Physical:** Stg=M; Freq: R, H, T, G Occas: C, B, S, O, I ● **Work Env:** Noise=N; ● **Salary:** 1 ● **Outlook:** 2

RAW SHELLFISH PREPARER (hotel & rest.) ● DOT #311.674-014 ● OES: 65038 ● Cleans and prepares shellfish for serving to customers: Washes shellfish in water. Inserts blunt-edge knife between halves to open bivalves and cuts out inedible parts. Returns oysters and clams to half shell and arranges them on ice filled dishes or places them in cold storage. Removes shells from shrimp and meat from crab and lobster shells, and arranges meat in special glasses for serving as cocktails. Mixes meat with other ingredients and arranges mixture on plates for salads. Serves customers at bar. May place silverware, napkins, potato chips, and condiments on bar. May mix ketchup, horseradish, lemon juice, and other ingredients to make cocktail sauces. May prepare only oysters for use as food and be designated Oyster Preparer (hotel & rest.). ● **GED:** R2, M1, L2 ● **SVP:** 2-30 days ● **Academic:** Ed=N, Eng=N ● **Work Field:** 146, 291 ● **MPSMS:** 903 ● **Aptitudes:** G4, V4, N4, S4, P4, Q5, K3, F3, M3, E5, C4 ● **Temperaments:** P, R ● **Physical:** Stg=L; Freq: R, H, I, T, G Occas: S, O, X ● **Work Env:** Noise=N; Occas: C, U ● **Salary:** 1 ● **Outlook:** 4

WAITER/WAITRESS, ROOM SERVICE (hotel & rest.) ● DOT #311.477-034 ● OES: 65040 ● Serves meals to guests in their rooms. Carries silverware, linen, and food on tray or uses cart. Sets up table and serves food from cart. Removes equipment from rooms. ● **GED:** R3, M2, L2 ● **SVP:** 1-3 mos ● **Academic:** Ed=N, Eng=S ● **Work**

Field: 291 ● **MPSMS:** 903 ● **Aptitudes:** G3, V4, N4, S4, P4, Q4, K3, F4, M3, E4, C5 ● **Temperaments:** P ● **Physical:** Stg=L; Freq: R, H, T, G ● **Work Env:** Noise=N; ● **Salary:** 1 ● **Outlook:** 4

WAITER/WAITRESS (water trans.) ● DOT #350.677-030 ● OES: 65040 ● Alternate titles: STEWARD/STEWARDESS, DINING ROOM. Serves passengers in ships' dining rooms: Obtains linen, silver, glassware, and china to set tables. Arranges settings on tables. Provides dining room service to passengers [WAITER/WAITRESS, FORMAL (hotel & rest.)]. Maintains assigned station, including table pieces, side stands, and chairs. May be designated according to class of passengers served as Waiter/Waitress, Cabin Class (water trans.); Waiter/Waitress, Economy Class (water trans.); Waiter/Waitress, First Class (water trans.); Waiter/Waitress, Second Class (water trans.); Waiter/Waitress, Third Class (water trans.); Waiter/Waitress, Tourist Class (water trans.). ● **GED:** R3, M1, L2 ● **SVP:** 1-3 mos ● **Academic:** Ed=N, Eng=G ● **Work Field:** 291 ● **MPSMS:** 903 ● **Aptitudes:** G3, V3, N4, S4, P4, Q4, K3, F4, M3, E4, C5 ● **Temperaments:** P, R ● **Physical:** Stg=L; Freq: R, H, T, G Occas: B, I ● **Work Env:** Noise=N; ● **Salary:** 1 ● **Outlook:** 4

WINE STEWARD/STEWARDESS (hotel & rest.) ● DOT #310.357-010 ● OES: 65008 ● Alternate titles: SOMMELIER. Selects, requisitions, stores, sells, and serves wines in restaurant: Keeps inventory and orders wine to replenish stock. Stores wines on racks or shelves. Discusses wines with patrons and assists patrons to make wine selection, applying knowledge of wines. Tastes wines prior to serving and serves wines to patrons. ● **GED:** R3, M3, L3 ● **SVP:** 1-2 yrs ● **Academic:** Ed=N, Eng=S ● **Work Field:** 291, 221 ● **MPSMS:** 903 ● **Aptitudes:** G3, V3, N3, S4, P4, Q3, K4, F4, M4, E5, C3 ● **Temperaments:** J, P ● **Physical:** Stg=L; Freq: R, H, T, G, N, X Occas: I, M ● **Work Env:** Noise=N; ● **Salary:** 1 ● **Outlook:** 3

GOE: 09.05.03
Portering & Baggage Services

BAGGAGE PORTER, HEAD (hotel & rest.) ● DOT #324.137-010 ● OES: 69998 ● Supervises and directs activities of PORTERS, BAGGAGE (hotel & rest.) engaged in handling baggage and related work for hotel patrons: Adjusts work schedules according to work load and makes individual task assignments. Advises PORTERS, BAGGAGE (hotel & rest.) of action to be taken in response to unusual requests. Resolves guests' complaints pertaining to conduct of PORTERS, BAGGAGE (hotel & rest.) and lost or mishandled baggage. May perform personnel duties, such as screening, hiring, giving directions to new workers, and maintaining time records. May give travel information. May act as agent for transportation company. May participate in baggage handling activities and setting up sample rooms. ● **GED:** R3, M3, L3 ● **SVP:** 1-2 yrs ● **Academic:** Ed=N, Eng=G ● **Work Field:** 291 ● **MPSMS:** 905 ● **Aptitudes:** G3, V3, N4, S4, P4, Q3, K4, F4, M4, E4, C5 ● **Temperaments:** D, P, V ● **Physical:** Stg=L; Freq: R, H, T, G Occas: I, N ● **Work Env:** Noise=Q; ● **Salary:** 3 ● **Outlook:** 2

BELL CAPTAIN (hotel & rest.) ● DOT #324.137-014 ● OES: 69998 ● Supervises BELLHOPS (hotel & rest.) engaged in duties, such as paging, running errands, and giving information. Calls BELLHOPS (hotel & rest.) to escort guests to rooms or perform related services. Determines work schedules and keeps time records. Inspects workers for neatness and uniform dress. Instructs workers in procedures regarding requests from guests, utilizing knowledge of hotel facilities and local merchants and attractions. Furnishes information, makes reservations, and obtains tickets for guests to social and recreational events or for travel. May report suspicious behavior of patrons to hotel security personnel. May pick up and bundle guests' laundry for outside cleaning service. May perform duties of subordinates. ● **GED:** R3, M2, L2 ● **SVP:** 1-2 yrs ● **Academic:** Ed=N, Eng=S ● **Work Field:** 291 ● **MPSMS:** 905 ● **Aptitudes:** G3, V3, N4, S4, P4, Q4, K4, F4, M4, E4, C5 ● **Temperaments:** D, P, V ● **Physical:** Stg=M; Freq: R, H, T, G Occas: I, N ● **Work Env:** Noise=Q; ● **Salary:** 3 ● **Outlook:** 4

BELLHOP (hotel & rest.) ● DOT #324.677-010 ● OES: 68023 ● Performs any combination of following duties to serve hotel guests: Escorts incoming hotel guests to rooms, assists with hand luggage, and offers information pertaining to available services and facilities of hotel, points of interest, and entertainment attractions. Inspects guest's room to ensure furnishings are in order and supplies are adequate. Explains features of room, such as operation of radio, television, and nightlock, and how to place telephone calls. Pages guests in lobby, dining room, or other parts of hotel. Delivers messages and runs errands. Delivers room service orders. Picks up articles for laundry and valet service. Calls taxi for guests. Transports guests about premises or local areas in car or motorized cart. Keeps record of calls for service. Delivers packages, suitcases, and trunks, and sets up sample rooms [PORTER, BAGGAGE (hotel & rest.) 324.477-010]. Tidies lobby [HOUSECLEANER (hotel & rest.) 323.687-018]. Operates elevator [ELEVATOR OPERATOR (any industry) 388.663-010]. May be known as Page (hotel & rest.) when paging guests. ● **GED:** R2, M2, L2 ● **SVP:** 2-30 days ● **Academic:** Ed=N, Eng=S ● **Work Field:** 291 ● **MPSMS:** 902 ● **Aptitudes:** G4, V4, N4, S4, P4, Q4, K4, F4, M3, E4, C5 ● **Temperaments:** P, V ● **Physical:** Stg=H; Freq: R, H, T, G Occas: C, S, O, I, F, D, V ● **Work Env:** Noise=N; ● **Salary:** 1 ● **Outlook:** 3

CHECKROOM ATTENDANT (any industry) ● DOT #358.677-010 ● OES: 69998 ● Stores wearing apparel, luggage, bundles, and other articles for patrons of an establishment or employees of business establishment, issuing claim check for articles checked and returning articles on receipt of check. May be designated according to article stored as Baggage Checker (any industry); Coat Checker (any industry); Hat Checker (any industry); Stand-By (motion picture); Wrap Checker (any industry). ● **GED:** R2, M2, L2 ● **SVP:** 2-30 days ● **Academic:** Ed=N, Eng=S ● **Work Field:** 291, 221 ● **MPSMS:** 909 ● **Aptitudes:** G4, V4, N4, S4, P4, Q3, K4, F4, M4, E5, C5 ● **Temperaments:** P, R ● **Physical:** Stg=L; Freq: R, H, T, G, N ● **Work Env:** Noise=N; ● **Salary:** 1 ● **Outlook:** 2

PORTER (air trans.) ● DOT #357.677-010 ● OES: 68023 ● Alternate titles: PORTER, BAGGAGE; REDCAP. Carries baggage for passengers of airline, railroad, or motorbus by hand or handtruck, to waiting or baggage room, onto train or bus, or to taxicab or private automobile. Performs related services, such as calling taxicabs, directing persons to ticket windows and rest rooms, and assisting handicapped passengers upon their arrival or departure. May clean terminal floors; wash walls, windows and counters; and dust furniture. When employed in airline terminal, is designated Skycap (air trans.). ● **GED:** R2, M1, L2 ● **SVP:** 2-30 days ● **Academic:** Ed=N, Eng=S ● **Work Field:** 011, 291 ● **MPSMS:** 905 ● **Aptitudes:** G4, V4, N4, S4, P4, Q4, K4, F4, M4, E4, C5 ● **Temperaments:** P, R ● **Physical:** Stg=M; Freq: S, R, H, T, G ● **Work Env:** Noise=N; Occas: W ● **Salary:** 3 ● **Outlook:** 2

PORTER, BAGGAGE (hotel & rest.) ● DOT #324.477-010 ● OES: 68023 ● Alternate titles: PORTER, LUGGAGE. Delivers luggage to and from hotel rooms, sets up sample rooms for sales personnel and performs related services as requested by guest or BAGGAGE PORTER, HEAD (hotel & rest.). Transfers trunks, packages, and other baggage to room or loading area, using handtruck. Arranges for outgoing freight, express or mail shipments, computes charges, tags article, and records information, such as addressee, addressor, carrier, and charges, on specified forms. Sets up display tables, racks, or shelves and assists sales personnel in unpacking and arranging merchandise display. May supply guests with travel information, such as transportation rates, routes, and schedules. May escort incoming guest to room [BELL-HOP (hotel & rest.)]. May arrange for cleaning, laundering, and repair of guests' clothing and other items. May compute charge slips for services rendered guests and forwards slips to bookkeeping department. ● **GED:** R2, M2, L2 ● **SVP:** 2-30 days ● **Academic:** Ed=N, Eng=S ● **Work Field:** 291, 011 ● **MPSMS:** 905 ● **Aptitudes:** G4, V4, N4, S4, P4, Q4, K4, F4, M3, E4, C5 ● **Temperaments:** P ● **Physical:** Stg=M; Freq: S, R, H, T, G Occas: K, I, N ● **Work Env:** Noise=Q; ● **Salary:** 1 ● **Outlook:** 3

ROOM-SERVICE CLERK (hotel & rest.) ● DOT #324.577-010 ● OES: 69998 ● Alternate titles: DELIVERY-ROOM CLERK; PACKAGE CLERK; RECEIVING-ROOM CLERK; RUNNER. Performs any combination of following tasks related to serving guests in apartment hotels: Delivers and removes packages, laundry, clothes, groceries, and other articles to and from guests rooms or servidors (cabinets built into doors of hotel rooms). Collects supply orders from various departments and delivers to PURCHASING AGENT (profess. & kin.).

Delivers mail to various departments and guests. Records information pertaining to services rendered. May arrange for pressing clothes and shining shoes, sending and receiving packages, and in maintaining valet service. May press clothes and shine shoes [SHOE SHINER (personal ser.)]. May supervise activities of workers engaged in delivering packages to hotel guests. ● **GED:** R2, M2, L2 ● **SVP:** 2-30 days ● **Academic:** Ed=N, Eng=S ● **Work Field:** 291 ● **MPSMS:** 899 ● **Aptitudes:** G4, V4, N4, S4, P4, Q3, K4, F3, M3, E5, C5 ● **Temperaments:** P, V ● **Physical:** Stg=L; Freq: R, H, I Occas: T, G ● **Work Env:** Noise=Q; ● **Salary:** 1 ● **Outlook:** 3

GOE: 09.05.04
Doorkeeping Services

DOORKEEPER (any industry) ● DOT #324.677-014 ● OES: 69998 ● Serves residents, guests, or patrons of hotel, store, apartment building, hospital, or similar establishment by opening doors, hailing taxicabs, answering inquiries, assisting elderly or infirm persons into automobiles, and performing related services. Prevents entrance of unauthorized or undesirable persons. May forcibly eject inebriated or rowdy persons from premises. May notify guests by telephone of delivery of automobiles, packages, or arrival of visitors. May carry baggage. ● **GED:** R2, M1, L2 ● **SVP:** 2-30 days ● **Academic:** Ed=N, Eng=N ● **Work Field:** 291 ● **MPSMS:** 905 ● **Aptitudes:** G4, V4, N4, S4, P4, Q4, K4, F5, M4, E5, C5 ● **Temperaments:** P, V ● **Physical:** Stg=M; Freq: S, R, H, T, G ● **Work Env:** Noise=Q; Occas: W ● **Salary:** 1 ● **Outlook:** 3

DRIVE-IN THEATER ATTENDANT (amuse. & rec.) ● DOT #349.673-010 ● OES: 68021 ● Alternate titles: FIELD ATTENDANT. Performs any combination of following duties in rendering services to patrons of drive-in theaters: Greets patrons desiring to attend theater. Collects admission fee and purchases ticket for patron from TICKET SELLER (clerical). Parks car or directs patron to parking space, indicating available space with flashlight. Patrols theater on foot or bicycle to prevent disorderly conduct, rowdiness, or to detect other infractions of rules. Watches over children in playground during intermission. Serves patrons at refreshment stand during intermission. May attach loudspeaker to automobile door and turn controls to adjust volume. ● **GED:** R2, M1, L2 ● **SVP:** 2-30 days ● **Academic:** Ed=N, Eng=S ● **Work Field:** 291 ● **MPSMS:** 912 ● **Aptitudes:** G4, V3, N4, S4, P4, Q4, K4, F4, M4, E5, C5 ● **Temperaments:** P, R ● **Physical:** Stg=L; Freq: R, H, I, T, G, F, V ● **Work Env:** Noise=N; Freq: W ● **Salary:** 1 ● **Outlook:** 2

GOE: 09.05.05
Card & Game Room Services

BOARD ATTENDANT (amuse. & rec.) ● DOT #249.587-010 ● OES: 59998 ● Alternate titles: GAMBLING BROKER; RACING-BOARD MARKER; WALL ATTENDANT. Writes racing information, such as betting odds, entries, and winning time, on paper sheets affixed to walls or on blackboards of bookmaking establishment. Works from stepladder. ● **GED:** R3, M2, L2 ● **SVP:** 2-30 days ● **Academic:** Ed=N, Eng=S ● **Work Field:** 231 ● **MPSMS:** 913 ● **Aptitudes:** G3, V4, N4, S4, P4, Q2, K4, F4, M4, E4, C5 ● **Temperaments:** R, T ● **Physical:** Stg=L; Freq: B, R, H Occas: I, N ● **Work Env:** Noise=N; ● **Salary:** 2 ● **Outlook:** 2

CARDROOM ATTENDANT II (amuse. & rec.) ● DOT #343.577-010 ● OES: 68014 ● Seats cardroom patrons: Takes name of patron requesting seat at table and adds name, with chalk, to waiting list on board. Pages customer over loudspeaker when notified by SUPERVISOR, CARDROOM (amuse. & rec.) that seat is available. ● **GED:** R2, M1, L2 ● **SVP:** 2-30 days ● **Academic:** Ed=N, Eng=S ● **Work Field:** 291 ● **MPSMS:** 919 ● **Aptitudes:** G4, V4, N4, S4, P4, Q4, K4, F4, M4, E5, C5 ● **Temperaments:** P, R ● **Physical:** Stg=L; Freq: R, H, I, T, G, N ● **Work Env:** Noise=N; ● **Salary:** 1 ● **Outlook:** 3

GOE: 09.05.06
Individualized Services

CADDIE (amuse. & rec.) ● DOT #341.677-010 ● OES: 68014 ● Alternate titles: GOLF CADDIE. Carries golf bags or pushes or pulls cart that holds golf bags around golf course for players, handing clubs to players as requested: Advises players, as requested, on selection of proper club for stroke or concerning peculiarities of course. Locates driven balls and holds marker out of cup while players putt. ● GED: R2, M2, L2 ● SVP: 2-30 days ● Academic: Ed=N, Eng=S ● Work Field: 291 ● MPSMS: 905 ● Aptitudes: G4, V4, N4, S3, P3, Q4, K4, F4, M4, E5, C5 ● Temperaments: P, R ● Physical: Stg=M; Freq: R, H, T, G Occas: S, N, F ● Work Env: Noise=Q; Const: W ● Salary: 2 ● Outlook: 2

DRESSER (amuse. & rec.) ● DOT #346.674-010 ● OES: 69998 ● Aids entertainer to dress and attends to clothing and costumes: Arranges costumes in order of use. Unpacks clothes and costumes and places them for convenient use. Cleans spots from apparel. Presses costumes. Mends ripped seams or makes other minor repairs. May arrange for cleaning, pressing or laundering of costumes. ● GED: R2, M2, L2 ● SVP: 1-3 mos ● Academic: Ed=N, Eng=S ● Work Field: 291, 171 ● MPSMS: 906, 440 ● Aptitudes: G4, V4, N4, S4, P4, Q4, K3, F3, M3, E4, C3 ● Temperaments: P, V ● Physical: Stg=L; Freq: R, H, I Occas: N, A, X ● Work Env: Noise=N; ● Salary: 1 ● Outlook: 2

PERSONAL ATTENDANT (domestic ser.) ● DOT #309.674-014 ● OES: 62061 ● Performs personal services to employer in private household: Brushes, cleans, presses, mends employer's clothing. Lays out employer's clothing, and assists employer to dress. Packs clothing for travel. Cleans employer's quarters. Prepares bath. Purchases clothing and accessories. Answers telephone. Drives car to perform errands. Mixes and serves drinks. May prepare and serve refreshments. May shampoo and groom employer's hair, shave face, manicure nails, give body or facial massages, or apply cosmetics for employer. May change linens, and make employer's bed. ● GED: R2, M2, L2 ● SVP: 1-3 mos ● Academic: Ed=N, Eng=S ● Work Field: 291 ● MPSMS: 906 ● Aptitudes: G4, V4, N4, S4, P4, Q4, K4, F4, M3, E4, C4 ● Temperaments: P, V ● Physical: Stg=L; Freq: S, K, R, H, I, N, F, D, X, V Occas: T, G ● Work Env: Noise=N; ● Salary: 1 ● Outlook: 3

GOE: 09.05.07
General Wardrobe Services

LOCKER-ROOM ATTENDANT (personal ser.) ● DOT #358.677-014 ● OES: 69998 ● Alternate titles: CAGE CLERK; DRESSING-ROOM ATTENDANT; LOCKER ATTENDANT; LOCKER-ROOM CLERK; PERSONAL ATTENDANT; SUIT ATTENDANT. Assigns dressing room facilities, locker space or clothing containers, and supplies to patrons of athletic or bathing establishment: Issues dressing room or locker key. Receives patron's clothing-filled container, furnishes claim check, places container on storage shelf or rack, and returns container upon receipt of claim check. Issues athletic equipment, bathing suit, or supplies, such as soap and towels. May arrange for valet services, such as clothes pressing and shoeshining. May collect soiled linen and perform cleaning tasks, such as mop dressing room floors, wash shower room walls and clean bathroom facilities. May collect fees for use of facilities, equipment, or supplies. May pack athletic uniforms and equipment for individual or team out-of-town sporting events. May attend to needs of athletic team in team clubhouse and be designated Clubhouse Attendant (amuse. & rec.). May provide baseball players with baseball bats, retrieve bats and foul balls from field, and supply balls to game officials and be designated Bat Boy/Girl (amuse. & rec.). ● GED: R2, M2, L2 ● SVP: 2-30 days ● Academic: Ed=N, Eng=S ● Work Field: 291 ● MPSMS: 909, 919 ● Aptitudes: G4, V4, N4, S4, P4, Q4, K4, F4, M4, E5, C5 ● Temperaments: P, V ● Physical: Stg=L; Freq: R, H, I, T, G Occas: S, N ● Work Env: Noise=N; ● Salary: 1 ● Outlook: 2

REST ROOM ATTENDANT (any industry) ● DOT #358.677-018 ● OES: 69998 ● Alternate titles: LAVATORY ATTENDANT; TOILET ATTENDANT; WASHROOM ATTENDANT. Serves patrons of lavatories in store, public building, hotel, or similar establishment by providing soap and towels, brushing patrons' clothing, shining shoes, sewing on loose buttons, and performing related services. Replenishes rest room supplies. May scrub lavatory, floors, walls, mirrors, and fixtures, using brushes, detergent, and water. May administer first aid to ill or injured patrons. ● GED: R2, M1, L1 ● SVP: 2-30 days ● Academic: Ed=N, Eng=S ● Work Field: 291 ● MPSMS: 909 ● Aptitudes: G4, V4, N4, S5, P4, Q5, K4, F4, M4, E5, C5 ● Temperaments: P, R ● Physical: Stg=L; Freq: R, H Occas: S, I ● Work Env: Noise=N; ● Salary: 1 ● Outlook: 2

WARDROBE SUPERVISOR (amuse. & rec.) ● DOT #346.361-010 ● OES: 69998 ● Attends to costumes of members of cast of theatrical production: Examines costumes and cleans and mends them. Presses costumes, using electric iron. Refits costumes as necessary. Assists cast to don completed costumes, or assigns DRESSERS (amuse. & rec.) to assist specific cast members. Arranges costumes, or assigns DRESSERS (amuse. & rec.) to arrange costumes of cast on dress racks in sequence to appearance on stage to facilitate quick changes. Packs costumes for cast when accompanying show on tour. ● GED: R3, M2, L3 ● SVP: 2-4 yrs ● Academic: Ed=N, Eng=G ● Work Field: 031, 032, 171 ● MPSMS: 906, 440 ● Aptitudes: G3, V3, N4, S4, P3, Q4, K3, F2, M3, E4, C3 ● Temperaments: J, P, V ● Physical: Stg=L; Const: R, H, I, E Freq: T, G, N Occas: S, O, A, X ● Work Env: Noise=N; ● Salary: 4 ● Outlook: 2

GOE: 09.05.08
Ticket Taking, Ushering

CHILDREN'S ATTENDANT (amuse. & rec.) ● DOT #349.677-018 ● OES: 68021 ● Monitors behavior of unaccompanied children in children's section of theater to maintain order: Escorts children who are unaccompanied by adult between theater entrance and children's section when children enter or leave theater. Maintains order among children and searches for lost articles. Notes when each child enters section and reminds child to go home after witnessing complete performance. ● GED: R2, M1, L1 ● SVP: 2-30 days ● Academic: Ed=N, Eng=S ● Work Field: 291 ● MPSMS: 911 ● Aptitudes: G4, V4, N4, S4, P4, Q4, K4, F4, M4, E5, C5 ● Temperaments: P ● Physical: Stg=L; Freq: T, G, F Occas: S, K, O, W, R, H, A ● Work Env: Noise=N; ● Salary: 1 ● Outlook: 2

ESCORT (any industry) ● DOT #353.667-010 ● OES: 69998 ● Guides visitors to destinations in industrial establishment: Escorts visitors to office, department, or section of plant. May collect and deliver mail and messages. May issue identification badges and safety devices to visitors. ● GED: R2, M1, L2 ● SVP: 2-30 days ● Academic: Ed=N, Eng=S ● Work Field: 291 ● MPSMS: 909 ● Aptitudes: G4, V3, N4, S4, P4, Q4, K4, F4, M4, E5, C5 ● Temperaments: P ● Physical: Stg=L; Freq: R, H, T, G Occas: I, N ● Work Env: Noise=N; ● Salary: 2 ● Outlook: 3

RIDE ATTENDANT (amuse. & rec.) ● DOT #342.677-010 ● OES: 68014 ● Directs patrons of amusement park in getting on and off riding device: Erects barrier in front of ride, admitting only as many persons to loading platform as can be seated on ride. Keeps order among patrons waiting to ride device. Fastens patrons' safety belts or bars to prevent injuries during ride. Assists children and elderly patrons from ride. Directs patrons from unloading platform to park grounds. May space rides operated in cars or sections to avoid danger of collisions. May collect tickets or cash fares. May clean and polish equipment and perform other minor maintenance work, such as replacing light bulbs. ● GED: R2, M1, L2 ● SVP: 2-30 days ● Academic: Ed=N, Eng=S ● Work Field: 291 ● MPSMS: 919 ● Aptitudes: G4, V4, N4, S4, P4, Q4, K4, F4, M4, E4, C5 ● Temperaments: P, R ● Physical: Stg=L; Const: F, V Freq: R, H, I, T, G Occas: E ● Work Env: Noise=Q; Freq: W ● Salary: 2 ● Outlook: 2

SKI-TOW OPERATOR (amuse. & rec.) ● DOT #341.665-010 ● OES: 68014 ● Alternate titles: SKI-LIFT OPERATOR. Tends gasoline, diesel, or electric lift to transport skiers up slope or mountainside, and collects fares: Pulls levers to start, stop, and adjust speed of lifts, such as rope tow, chair lift, T-bar, or J-bar. Collects or punches ticket for passengers and assists them onto and from lift. May repair and maintain motor and lift equipment. ● **GED:** R3, M2, L3 ● **SVP:** 1-3 mos ● **Academic:** Ed=N, Eng=S ● **Work Field:** 013 ● **MPSMS:** 913 ● **Aptitudes:** G3, V3, N4, S3, P4, Q4, K3, F4, M4, E5, C5 ● **Temperaments:** P, R ● **Physical:** Stg=L; Freq: R, H, I Occas: T, G ● **Work Env:** Noise=Q; Freq: W ● **Salary:** 1 ● **Outlook:** 4

TICKET TAKER (amuse. & rec.) ● DOT #344.667-010 ● OES: 68021 ● Collects admission tickets and passes from patrons at entertainment events: Examines ticket or pass to verify authenticity, using criteria such as color and date issued. Refuses admitance to patrons without ticket or pass, or who are undesirable for reasons, such as intoxication or improper attire. May direct patrons to their seats. May distribute door checks to patrons temporarily leaving establishment. May count and record number of tickets collected. May issue and collect completed release forms for hazardous events, and photograph patron with release form for permanent records file. May be designated Gate Attendant (amuse. & rec.) or Turnstile Attendant (amuse. & rec.) when collecting tickets at open-air event. ● **GED:** R2, M1, L2 ● **SVP:** 2-30 days ● **Academic:** Ed=N, Eng=S ● **Work Field:** 291 ● **MPSMS:** 919 ● **Aptitudes:** G4, V4, N4, S4, P4, Q4, K4, F4, M4, E5, C4 ● **Temperaments:** P, R ● **Physical:** Stg=L; Freq: R, H, T, G, N, X Occas: I ● **Work Env:** Noise=Q; ● **Salary:** 1 ● **Outlook:** 2

USHER (amuse. & rec.) ● DOT #344.677-014 ● OES: 68021 ● Assists patrons at entertainment events to find seats, search for lost articles, and locate facilities, such as restrooms and telephones. Distributes programs to patrons. Assists other workers to change advertising display. ● **GED:** R2, M1, L1 ● **SVP:** 2-30 days ● **Academic:** Ed=N, Eng=S ● **Work Field:** 291 ● **MPSMS:** 910 ● **Aptitudes:** G4, V4, N4, S5, P4, Q4, K4, F4, M4, E5, C5 ● **Temperaments:** P, R ● **Physical:** Stg=L; Freq: T, G, F, V Occas: S, O, R, H, I, A ● **Work Env:** Noise=N; ● **Salary:** 1 ● **Outlook:** 2

USHER, HEAD (amuse. & rec.) ● DOT #344.137-010 ● OES: 69998 ● Supervises and coordinates activities of USHERS (amuse. & rec.) at entertainment events and directs patrons to area of seat location: Directs USHERS (amuse. & rec.) in job duties and assigns to work stations. Directs patrons to area of seat location according to information on ticket stubs. Resolves complaints of patrons. Coordinates activities in emergencies such as fights or fires. May hire and discharge USHERS (amuse. & rec.). May keep records of workers' time. ● **GED:** R3, M2, L3 ● **SVP:** 3-6 mos ● **Academic:** Ed=N, Eng=G ● **Work Field:** 291 ● **MPSMS:** 919 ● **Aptitudes:** G3, V3, N4, S4, P4, Q3, K4, F4, M4, E4, C5 ● **Temperaments:** D, P ● **Physical:** Stg=L; Freq: T, G ● **Work Env:** Noise=Q; Occas: W ● **Salary:** 3 ● **Outlook:** 2

GOE: 09.05.09
Elevator Services

ELEVATOR OPERATOR (any industry) ● DOT #388.663-010 ● OES: 67098 ● Alternate titles: SERVICE-CAR OPERATOR. Operates elevator to transport passengers between floors of office building, apartment house, department store, hotel, or similar establishment: Pushes buttons or moves lever to control movement of elevator on signal or instructions from passengers or others. Opens and closes safety gate and door of elevator at each floor where stop is made. Supplies information to passengers, such as location of offices, merchandise, and individuals. May perform other duties, such as distributing mail to various floors, answering telephone, preventing unauthorized persons from entering building, and assisting other employees to load and unload freight. May sweep or vacuum elevator. May be designated according to location of elevator operated as Front-Elevator Operator (hotel & rest.). ● **GED:** R2, M1, L2 ● **SVP:** 2-30 days ● **Academic:** Ed=N, Eng=N ● **Work Field:** 011, 282 ● **MPSMS:** 969 ● **Aptitudes:** G4, V3, N4, S4, P4, Q4, K3, F4, M3, E5, C5 ● **Temperaments:** P, R ● **Physical:** Stg=L; Freq: R, H, I, T, G ● **Work Env:** Noise=N; ● **Salary:** 1 ● **Outlook:** 2

GOE: 09.05.10
Packaging-Wrapping

BAGGER (retail trade) ● DOT #920.687-014 ● OES: 98710 ● Alternate titles: GROCERY PACKER. Bags groceries at grocery store: Packs grocery items in sacks or cartons, arranging heavy and bulky items at bottom of sack or carton. Verifies price of grocery item in question against price of items on stock shelf, upon request. Carries packed sacks, or places sacks in grocery cart, and pushes cart to customer's vehicle, upon request. Places groceries into customer's vehicle. Collects shopping carts from parking lot and surrounding areas and returns carts to store. Replaces cleaning and packing supplies used at grocery checkout counter. Returns grocery items left at checkout counter to specified stock shelves. Cleans work area and carries empty bottles and trash to storeroom. May price and place grocery articles on shelves. May assist in unloading delivery trucks. ● **GED:** R2, M1, L1 ● **SVP:** 2-30 days ● **Academic:** Ed=N, Eng=S ● **Work Field:** 041 ● **MPSMS:** 881 ● **Aptitudes:** G4, V4, N4, S4, P4, Q5, K4, F4, M3, E5, C5 ● **Temperaments:** R ● **Physical:** Stg=M; Freq: S, R, H, I Occas: N, D, A ● **Work Env:** Noise=N; Occas: W ● **Salary:** 2 ● **Outlook:** 4

Humanitarian 10

An interest in helping individuals with their mental, spiritual, social, physical, or vocational concerns. You can satisfy this interest by work in which caring for the welfare of others is important. Perhaps the spiritual or mental well-being of others concerns you. You could prepare for a job in religion or counseling. You may like to help others with physical problems. You could work in the nursing, therapy, or rehabilitation fields. You may like to provide needed but less difficult care by working as an aide, orderly, or technician.

Social Services 10.01

Workers in this group help people deal with their problems. They may work with one person at a time or with groups of people. Workers sometimes specialize in problems that are personal, social, vocational, physical, educational, or spiritual in nature. Schools, rehabilitation centers, mental health clinics, guidance centers, and churches employ these workers. Jobs are also found in public and private welfare and employment services, juvenile courts, and vocational rehabilitation programs.

✓ What kind of work would you do?

Your work activities would depend upon your specific job. For example, you might:

- observe and interview members of a family to determine their medical or psychological needs.
- help prison parolees find jobs and adjust to society.
- counsel persons about educational and vocational plans.
- promote physical healing or spiritual well-being through prayer or other religious activities.
- help individuals overcome emotional or social problems.
- assist parents with child-rearing problems.

✓ What skills and abilities do you need for this kind of work?

To do this kind of work, you must be able to:

- use logical thinking and special training to counsel others or to help a person define and solve personal problems.

- care about people, their needs, and their welfare enough to want to help in some way.
- understand the way government programs and social service organizations function.
- gain the trust and confidence of people.

✓ How do you know if you would like or could learn to do this kind of work?

The following questions may give you clues about yourself as you consider this group of jobs.

- Have you been active in church or civic groups? Do you like to work with other people toward a common goal?
- Have your friends come to you for advice or help with their personal problems? Did you help them find solutions?
- Have you had courses in psychology, sociology, or other social sciences? Do you like to study human behavior?
- Have you helped to teach someone who had a problem learning something? Are you patient and willing to stay with a task until it is finished?

✓ How can you prepare for and enter this kind of work?

Occupations in this group usually require education and/or training extending from two years to over ten years, depending upon the specific kind of work. More than four years of college study is required for most jobs in this group. Two or more years of graduate level study is often required for jobs in social work or psychology. Some jobs in religion, clinical psychology, or industrial psychology require additional education. School counselors are usually required to have one or more years of teaching experience.

Some workers begin as helpers in social, religious, or welfare organizations and receive on-the-job training. However, formal training is usually required for a worker to become a professional.

Private organizations dealing with problems such as drug addiction and abortion sometimes hire people who can relate to these problems.

✓ *What else should you consider about these jobs?*

Workers in this group sometimes receive community recognition or personal satisfaction from helping others. These jobs may involve irregular working hours and often include weekends and evenings. The work may involve dealing with sensitive people and confidential information.

Knowledge and skills must be updated frequently through reading journals, or attending seminars, summer schools, and workshops.

If you think you would like to do this kind of work, look at the job titles listed on the following pages.

■ ■ ■

GOE: 10.01.01
Religious

CLERGY MEMBER (profess. & kin.) ● DOT #120.107-010 ● OES: 27502 ● Alternate titles: MINISTER; PREACHER; PRIEST; RABBI. Conducts religious worship and performs other spiritual functions associated with beliefs and practices of religious faith or denomination as authorized, and provides spiritual and moral guidance and assistance to members: Leads congregation in worship services. Prepares and delivers sermons and other talks. Interprets doctrine of religion. Instructs people who seek conversion to faith. Conducts wedding and funeral services. Administers religious rites or ordinances. Visits sick and shut-ins, and helps poor. Counsels those in spiritual need and comforts bereaved. Oversees religious education programs. May write articles for publication and engage in interfaith, community, civic, educational, and recreational activities sponsored by or related to interest of denomination. May teach in seminaries and universities. May serve in armed forces, institutions, or industry and be designated Chaplain (profess. & kin.). When in charge of Christian church, congregation, or parish, may be designated Pastor (profess. & kin.) or Rector (profess. & kin.). May carry religious message and medical or educational aid to nonchristian lands and people to obtain converts and establish native church and be designated Missionary (profess. & kin.). ● **GED:** R6, M4, L6 ● **SVP:** 4-10 yrs ● **Academic:** Ed=B, Eng=G ● **Work Field:** 298 ● **MPSMS:** 944 ● **Aptitudes:** G1, V1, N3, S4, P4, Q3, K4, F5, M4, E5, C5 ● **Temperaments:** F, I, J, P, V ● **Physical:** Stg=L; Freq: T, G ● **Work Env:** Noise=Q; ● **Salary:** 2 ● **Outlook:** 1

PASTORAL ASSISTANT (nonprofit org.) ● DOT #129.107-026 ● OES: 39998 ● Assists ordained clergy in conducting worship services; provides spiritual guidance to church members; and plans and arranges educational, social, and recreational programs for congregation: Assists CLERGY MEMBER (profess. & kin.) 120.107-010 in conducting worship, wedding, funeral, and other services and in coordinating activities of lay participants, such as organist, choir, and ushers. Visits church members in hospitals and convalescent facilities or at home to offer spiritual guidance and assistance, such as emergency financial aid or referral to community support services. Assists CLERGY MEMBER (profess. & kin.) and lay teachers in selecting books and reference materials for religious education classes and in adapting content to meet needs of different age groups. May write and deliver sermons. May teach history and doctrine of church to church members. May assist CLERGY MEMBER (profess. & kin.) in coordinating committees that oversee social and recreational programs. ● **GED:** R5, M3, L5 ● **SVP:** 1-2 yrs ● **Academic:** Ed=A, Eng=G ● **Work Field:** 298 ● **MPSMS:** 944 ● **Aptitudes:** G2, V2, N3, S4, P4, Q3, K4, F4, M4, E5, C4 ● **Temperaments:** D, J, P, V ● **Physical:** Stg=L; Freq: T, G, N Occas: R, H, I, X ● **Work Env:** Noise=N; ● **Salary:** 4 ● **Outlook:** 2

GOE: 10.01.02
Counseling & Social Work

ASSISTANT PRINCIPAL (education) ● DOT #091.107-010 ● OES: 15005 ● Administers school student personnel program in primary or secondary school, and counsels and disciplines students, performing any combination of following tasks: Formulates student personnel policies, such as code of ethics. Plans and supervises school student activity programs. Gives individual and group guidance for personal problems, educational and vocational objectives, and social and recreational activities. Talks with and disciplines students in cases of attendance and behavior problems. Supervises students in attendance at assemblies and athletic events. Walks about school building and property to monitor safety and security or directs and coordinates teacher supervision of areas such as halls and cafeteria. Observes and evaluates teacher performance. Maintains records of student attendance. Arranges for and oversees substitute teachers. Works with administrators to coordinate and supervise student teachers program. Teaches courses. Assists PRINCIPAL (education) 099.117-018 to interview and hire teachers. Organizes and administers in-service teacher training. Acts as PRINCIPAL (education) in absence of PRINCIPAL (education). May be required to have certification from state. ● **GED:** R5, M3, L5 ● **SVP:** 4-10 yrs ● **Academic:** Ed=M, Eng=G ● **Work Field:** 295, 298 ● **MPSMS:** 931 ● **Aptitudes:** G2, V2, N3, S4, P4, Q3, K4, F4, M4, E5, C5 ● **Temperaments:** D, I, J, P ● **Physical:** Stg=L; Freq: T, G, N Occas: R, H, I, F ● **Work Env:** Noise=N; ● **Salary:** 5 ● **Outlook:** 2

CASE AIDE (social ser.) ● DOT #195.367-010 ● OES: 27308 ● Alternate titles: COMMUNITY PROGRAM AIDE. Performs community contact work on simpler aspects of programs or cases and assists in providing services to clients and family members, under close and regular supervision and tutorage of CASEWORKER (social ser.) 195.107-010 or CASEWORK SUPERVISOR (social ser.) 195.137-010. Assists in locating housing for displaced individuals and families. Monitors free, supplementary meal program administered by agencies for children and youth from low-income families to ensure cleanliness of facility and that eligibility guidelines are met for persons receiving meals. Assists elderly clients in preparation of forms, such as tax and rent refund forms. Accompanies elderly clients on visits to social, charitable, and government agencies to assist clients with their problems. Submits to and reviews reports and problems with superior. May be designated according to clients serviced as Senior Service Aide (social ser.); Youth Nutritional Monitor (social ser.). ● **GED:** R4, M3, L3 ● **SVP:** 1-3 mos ● **Academic:** Ed=N, Eng=G ● **Work Field:** 271, 282, 298 ● **MPSMS:** 941 ● **Aptitudes:** G3, V3, N3, S5, P4, Q3, K4, M4, E5, C5 ● **Temperaments:** J, P ● **Physical:** Stg=L; Freq: T, G Occas: R, H, I, N ● **Work Env:** Noise=N; ● **Salary:** 1 ● **Outlook:** 3

CASEWORKER (social ser.) ● DOT #195.107-010 ● OES: 27310 ● Alternate titles: COMMUNITY PLACEMENT WORKER; INTAKE WORKER; SOCIAL SERVICE WORKER. Counsels and aids individuals and families requiring assistance of social service agency: Interviews clients with problems, such as personal and family adjustments, finances, employment, food, clothing, housing, and physical and mental impairments to determine nature and degree of problem. Secures information, such as medical, psychological, and social factors contributing to client's situation, and evaluates these and client's capacities. Counsels client individually, in family, or in other small groups regarding plans for meeting needs, and aids client to mobilize inner capacities and environmental resources to improve social functioning. Helps client to modify attitudes and patterns of behavior by increasing understanding of self, personal problems, and client's part in creating them. Refers clients to community resources and other organizations. Compiles records and prepares reports. Reviews service plan and performs follow-up to determine quantity and quality of service provided client and status of client's case. Accesses and records client and community resource information, manually or using computer equipped with keyboard, to input and retrieve information. May secure supplementary information, such as employment, medical records, or school reports. May specialize in providing, monitoring, and evaluating services provided to older adults. May determine client's eligibility for financial assistance. May work in collaboration with other professional disciplines. May be required to visit clients in their homes or in institutions. Usually required to have knowledge and skill in case work method acquired through degree program at school of social work. May be required to possess state license or certificate. When rendering advisory services to agencies, groups, or individuals, may be designated Social-Work Consultant, Casework (social ser.). May aid parents with child rearing problems and children and youth with difficulties in social adjustments [CASEWORKER, CHILD WELFARE (social ser.) 195.107-014]. ● **GED:** R5, M3, L5 ● **SVP:** 2-4 yrs ● **Academic:** Ed=A, Eng=G ● **Work Field:** 271, 298 ● **MPSMS:** 941, 942 ● **Aptitudes:** G2, V2, N3, S4, P4, Q2, K3, F3, M4, E5, C5 ● **Temperaments:** D, I, J, P, V ● **Physical:** Stg=S; Const: T, G, N, A Occas: R, H, I ● **Work Env:** Noise=Q; ● **Salary:** 2 ● **Outlook:** 2

CASEWORKER, CHILD WELFARE (social ser.) ● DOT #195.107-014 ● OES: 27310 ● Aids parents with child rearing problems and children and youth with difficulties in social adjustments: Investigates home conditions to protect children from harmful environment. Evaluates children's physical and psychological makeup to determine needs. Refers child and parent or guardian to community resources according to needs of child. Evaluates foster home environmental factors and personal characteristics of adoption applicants to determine suitability of foster home and adoption applicants. Places and is responsible for children and their well-being in foster or adoptive homes, institutions, and medical treatment centers. Counsels children and parents, guardians, foster parents, or institution staff, concerning adjustment to foster home situation, plans for child's care, interactional behavior modifications needed, or rehabilitation. Places children in adoptive homes and counsels adoptive parents pending legal adoption. Provides service to unmarried parents, including care during pregnancy and planning for child. Arranges for day care or homemaker service. Employed in establishments such as child placement (foster care or adoption), protective service, or institution. Maintains case history records and reports. Usually required to have knowledge and skill in casework methods acquired through degree program at school of social work. May specialize in specific area of child-directed casework and be designated according to work performed as Caseworker, Child Placement (social ser.); Caseworker, Protective Services (social ser.). May interview clients for purpose of screening to determine eligibility for agency services and be designated Caseworker, Intake (social ser.). ● **GED:** R5, M3, L5 ● **SVP:** 2-4 yrs ● **Academic:** Ed=M, Eng=G ● **Work Field:** 271, 298 ● **MPSMS:** 941 ● **Aptitudes:** G2, V2, N3, S5, P4, Q4, K4, F4, M4, E5, C5 ● **Temperaments:** I, J, P ● **Physical:** Stg=L; Freq: T, G Occas: R, H, I, N, A ● **Work Env:** Noise=N; ● **Salary:** 4 ● **Outlook:** 3

CASEWORKER, FAMILY (social ser.) ● DOT #195.107-018 ● OES: 27310 ● Alternate titles: FAMILY COUNSELOR. Aids individuals and families having problems concerning family relationships or other aspects of their social functioning affecting unity of family and welfare of community: Counsels clients on problems, such as unsatisfactory relationships between marriage partners or between parents and children; unwed parenthood; home management; work adjustment; vocational training; need for financial assistance; care of the ill, handicapped, or aged, care of other family members at time of physical or mental

illness; desertion of parent; or difficulties encountered in travel or stabilization in new community. Helps clients to use agency's services, such as homemaker, or day care, and other community resources. In a public assistance or voluntary agency ascertains client's eligibility for financial assistance and determines amount of grant and assumes responsibility for services rendered. May assist travelers, runaways of any age, migrants, transients, refugees, repatriated Americans, and problem families drifting from community to community, encountering difficulty in traveling or needing help toward stabilization. Employed in organizations, such as public assistance, family service, Travelers Aid, and American Red Cross Home Service. Usually required to have knowledge and skill in casework methods acquired through degree program at school of social work. ● **GED:** R5, M4, L5 ● **SVP:** 2-4 yrs ● **Academic:** Ed=A, Eng=G ● **Work Field:** 298, 271 ● **MPSMS:** 941 ● **Aptitudes:** G2, V2, N3, S5, P4, Q4, K5, F4, M4, E5, C5 ● **Temperaments:** I, J, P ● **Physical:** Stg=S; Freq: T, G Occas: R, H, N ● **Work Env:** Noise=N; ● **Salary:** 4 ● **Outlook:** 4

CASEWORK SUPERVISOR (social ser.) ● DOT #195.137-010 ● OES: 27310 ● Alternate titles: CASE SUPERVISOR; SOCIAL WORK UNIT SUPERVISOR. Supervises and coordinates activities of social-service-agency staff and volunteers, and students of school of social work: Assigns caseloads and related duties, and coordinates activities of staff in providing counseling services to assist clients with problems of emergency or crisis nature. Assists agency staff members through individual and group conferences in analyzing case problems and in improving their diagnostic and helping skills. Reviews case records and evaluates performance of staff members and recommends indicated action. Participates in developing and implementing agency administrative policy. Counsels clients individually or in groups on planned or experimental basis and in emergencies. Trains new employees in areas such as agency policy, department procedures, and agency or government regulations. Provides in-service training for experienced workers in areas such as new policies, procedures, and regulations. Represents agency in community or in interagency activities. May conduct or direct staff development programs. May train workers is use of computer. Employed in areas such as child welfare, community welfare councils, family casework, youth services, senior citizen services, health services, public welfare, probation and parole, housing relocation, education, and rehabilitation. Usually required to have master's degree from school of social work. ● **GED:** R5, M3, L5 ● **SVP:** 2-4 yrs ● **Academic:** Ed=M, Eng=G ● **Work Field:** 298 ● **MPSMS:** 940 ● **Aptitudes:** G2, V2, N3, S5, P4, Q4, K4, F4, M4, E5, C5 ● **Temperaments:** D, I, J, P ● **Physical:** Stg=S; Freq: T, G Occas: R, H, I, N, A ● **Work Env:** Noise=N; ● **Salary:** 4 ● **Outlook:** 3

CHILD SUPPORT OFFICER (government ser.) ● DOT #195.267-022 ● OES: 27310 ● Investigates and analyzes child welfare cases and initiates administrative action to facilitate enforcement of child support laws: Reviews application for child support received from client and examines case file to determine that divorce decree and court ordered judgement for payment are in order. Interviews client to obtain information, such as relocation of absent parent, amount of child support previously awarded, and names of persons who can act as witnesses to support client's claim for support. Locates absent parent and interviews parent to gather data, such as support award, and discusses case with parent to resolve issues in lieu of filing court proceedings. Contacts friends and relatives of child's parents to verify gathered information about case. Computes amount of child support payments. Prepares file indicating data, such as wage records of accused, witnesses, and blood test results. Confers with prosecuting attorney to prepare court case. Determines type of court jurisdiction, according to facts and circumstances surrounding case, and files court action. Confers with court clerk to obtain arrest warrant and to schedule court date for hearing or trial. Monitors child support payments awarded by court to ensure compliance and enforcement of child support laws. Prepares report of legal action taken when delinquency in payments occurs. ● **GED:** R5, M3, L5 ● **SVP:** 2-4 yrs ● **Academic:** Ed=H, Eng=G ● **Work Field:** 271, 272, 298 ● **MPSMS:** 941, 949 ● **Aptitudes:** G2, V2, N3, S4, P4, Q3, K4, F4, M4, E5, C5 ● **Temperaments:** J, P, V ● **Physical:** Stg=S; Freq: R, H, I, T, G, N Occas: A ● **Work Env:** Noise=N; Occas: W, O ● **Salary:** 3 ● **Outlook:** 3

CLINICAL PSYCHOLOGIST (profess. & kin.) ● DOT #045.107-022 ● OES: 27108 ● Alternate titles: PSYCHOLOGIST, CLINICAL. Diagnoses or evaluates mental and emotional disorders of individuals, and administers programs of treatment: Interviews patients in clinics, hospitals, prisons, and other institutions, and studies medical and social case histories. Observes patients in play or other situations, and selects, administers, and interprets intelligence, achievement, interest, personality, and other psychological tests to diagnose disorders and formulate plans of treatment. Treats psychological disorders to effect improved adjustments utilizing various psychological techniques, such as milieu therapy, psychodrama, play therapy and hypnosis. Selects approach to use in individual therapy, such as directive, nondirective, and supportive therapy, and plans frequency, intensity, and duration of therapy. May collaborate with PSYCHIATRIST (medical ser.) 070.107-014, and other specialists in developing treatment programs for patients. May instruct and direct students serving psychological internships in hospitals and clinics. May develop experimental designs and conduct research in fields of personality development and adjustment, diagnosis, treatment, and prevention of mental disorders. May serve as consultant to industrial, social, educational, welfare, and other agencies on individual cases or in evaluation, planning, and development of mental health programs. May specialize in behavior problems and therapy, crime and delinquency, group therapy, individual diagnosis and therapy, mental deficiency, objective tests, projective techniques, or speech pathology. ● **GED:** R6, M5, L6 ● **SVP:** 4-10 yrs ● **Academic:** Ed=M, Eng=G ● **Work Field:** 298, 294 ● **MPSMS:** 733 ● **Aptitudes:** G1, V1, N3, S4, P3, Q3, K4, F4, M4, E5, C5 ● **Temperaments:** D, J, P, V ● **Physical:** Stg=S; Const: G Freq: T Occas: R, H, I, N ● **Work Env:** Noise=Q; ● **Salary:** 5 ● **Outlook:** 4

CLINICAL THERAPIST (profess. & kin.) ● DOT #045.107-050 ● OES: 32398 ● Alternate titles: CLINICAL COUNSELOR. Counsels individuals or groups regarding psychological or emotional problems, such as stress, substance abuse, or family situations, using evaluative techniques, and develops and implements therapeutic treatment plan in medical setting: Interviews patient to obtain information concerning medical history or other pertinent information. Observes client to detect indications of abnormal physical or mental behavior. Selects and administers various tests, such as psychological tests, personality inventories, and intelligence quotient tests, to identify behavioral or personality traits and intelligence levels, and records results. Reviews results of tests to evaluate client needs. Plans and administers therapeutic treatment, such as behavior modification and stress management therapy, using biofeedback equipment, to assist patient in controlling disorders and other problems. Changes method and degree of therapy when indicated by client reactions. Discusses progress toward goals with client, such as controlling weight, stress, or substance abuse. Consults with medical doctor or other specialists concerning treatment plan and amends plan as directed. Conducts relaxation exercises, peer counseling groups, and family counseling during clinical therapy sessions. Refers client to supportive services to supplement treatment and counseling. May conduct research in treatment and test validation. May develop evaluative studies of therapy and therapy outcome. ● **GED:** R5, M5, L5 ● **SVP:** 2-4 yrs ● **Academic:** Ed=M, Eng=G ● **Work Field:** 294 ● **MPSMS:** 924 ● **Aptitudes:** G1, V1, N1, S4, P4, Q1, K4, F4, M4, E5, C5 ● **Temperaments:** I, J, P, V ● **Physical:** Stg=S; Freq: T, G, N Occas: R, H, I ● **Work Env:** Noise=N; ● **Salary:** 5 ● **Outlook:** 3

COMMUNITY WORKER (government ser.) ● DOT #195.367-018 ● OES: 27310 ● Investigates problems of assigned community and of individuals disadvantaged because of income, age, or other economic or personal handicaps to determine needs: Seeks out, interviews, and assists persons in need of agency services, under direction of professional staff, or refers persons to specific agencies for service. Visits individuals and families in their homes to explain supportive services and resources available to persons needing special assistance. Speaks before neighborhood groups to establish communication and rapport between persons in community and agency, to publicize supportive services available, and to assist in resolving problems facing community concerning housing, urban renewal, education, welfare, unemployment insurance, and crime prevention. Follows up all contacts and prepares and submits reports of activities. May maintain files and records of work activities to provide access to and retrieval of data. May work for police department for purpose of establishing communication between citizens and police officials to promote understanding of functions, purpose, and goals of police in community and assists in resolution of community problems. ● **GED:** R4, M3, L4 ● **SVP:** 1-2 yrs ● **Academic:** Ed=N, Eng=G ● **Work Field:** 271, 282, 298 ● **MPSMS:** 941

● **Aptitudes:** G3, V3, N3, S4, P4, Q3, K4, F4, M4, E5, C4 ● **Temperaments:** D, I, J, P, V ● **Physical:** Stg=L; Freq: R, H, I, T, G, N Occas: F, D, X, V ● **Work Env:** Noise=N; Occas: W ● **Salary:** 2 ● **Outlook:** 2

COUNSELOR (profess. & kin.) ● DOT #045.107-010 ● OES: 31514 ● Counsels individuals and provides group educational and vocational guidance services: Collects, organizes, and analyzes information about individuals through records, tests, interviews, and professional sources, to appraise their interests, aptitudes, abilities, and personality characteristics, for vocational and educational planning. Compiles and studies occupational, educational, and economic information to aid counselees in making and carrying out vocational and educational objectives. Refers students to placement service. Assists individuals to understand and overcome social and emotional problems. May engage in research and follow-up activities to evaluate counseling techniques. May teach classes. May be designated according to area of activity as Academic Counselor (education); Career Placement Services Counselor (education); Employment Counselor (government ser.); Guidance Counselor (education); Vocational Advisor (education). ● **GED:** R5, M5, L5 ● **SVP:** 2-4 yrs ● **Academic:** Ed=M, Eng=G ● **Work Field:** 298 ● **MPSMS:** 733 ● **Aptitudes:** G2, V2, N3, S4, P4, Q3, K4, F4, M4, E5, C5 ● **Temperaments:** J, P, V ● **Physical:** Stg=S; Freq: T, G, N Occas: R, H, I ● **Work Env:** Noise=Q; ● **Salary:** 4 ● **Outlook:** 2

COUNSELOR, MARRIAGE AND FAMILY (profess. & kin.) ● DOT #045.107-054 ● OES: 31514 ● Provides individual, marital, and family counseling services to adults and children, to assist clients to identify personal and interactive problems, and to achieve effective personal, marital, and family development and adjustment: Collects information about clients (individuals, married couples, or families), using interview, case history, and observation techniques, funnel approach, and appraisal and assessment methods. Analyzes information collected to determine advisability of counseling or referral to other specialists or institutions. Reviews notes and information collected to identify problems and concerns. Consults reference material, such as textbooks, manuals, and journals, to identify symptoms, make diagnoses, and develop therapeutic or treatment plan. Counsels clients, using counseling methods and procedures, such as psychotherapy and hypnosis, to assist clients in gaining insight into personal and interactive problems, to define goals, and to plan action reflecting interests, abilities, and needs. Evaluates results of counseling methods to determine reliability and validity of treatment used. Interacts with other professionals to discuss therapy or treatment, new resources or techniques, and to share information. ● **GED:** R5, M3, L5 ● **SVP:** 4-10 yrs ● **Academic:** Ed=M, Eng=G ● **Work Field:** 298 ● **MPSMS:** 733 ● **Aptitudes:** G2, V1, N3, S4, P4, Q2, K4, F4, M4, E5, C5 ● **Temperaments:** I, J, P, V ● **Physical:** Stg=S; Const: T, G Occas: R, H, I, N ● **Work Env:** Noise=Q; ● **Salary:** 4 ● **Outlook:** 3

DEAN OF STUDENTS (education) ● DOT #090.117-018 ● OES: 15005 ● Alternate titles: DEAN OF STUDENT AFFAIRS; DIRECTOR OF STUDENT SERVICES; VICE PRESIDENT OF STUDENT AFFAIRS. Directs and coordinates student programs of college or university: Formulates and develops student personnel policies. Advises staff members on problems relating to policy, program, and administration. Directs and assists in planning social, recreational, and curricular programs. Counsels or advises individuals and groups on matters pertaining to personal problems, educational and vocational objectives, social and recreational activities, and financial assistance. Reviews reports of student misconduct cases that require disciplinary action to ensure recommendations conform to university policies. Sponsors and advises student organizations. Reviews budget and directs appropriations of student services unit. Represents university in community on matters pertaining to student personnel program and activities. May teach. May direct admissions, foreign student services, health services, student union, and testing services. May be designated Dean Of Men (education); Dean Of Women (education). ● **GED:** R5, M3, L5 ● **SVP:** 4-10 yrs ● **Academic:** Ed=M, Eng=G ● **Work Field:** 295 ● **MPSMS:** 931 ● **Aptitudes:** G2, V2, N2, S4, P3, Q2, K4, F4, M4, E5, C5 ● **Temperaments:** D, I, P ● **Physical:** Stg=S; Freq: R, H, I, T, G, N ● **Work Env:** Noise=N; ● **Salary:** 5 ● **Outlook:** 1

DIRECTOR OF PLACEMENT (education) ● DOT #166.167-014 ● OES: 21511 ● Alternate titles: COORDINATOR OF PLACEMENT; DIRECTOR OF CAREER PLANNING AND PLACEMENT; DIRECTOR OF CAREER RESOURCES; MANAGER OF STUDENT PLACEMENT SERVICE. Coordinates activities of job placement service for students and graduates: Develops placement office procedures. Establishes work loads, assigns tasks, and reviews results. Conducts in-service training program for placement personnel. Interviews applicants to determine qualifications and eligibility for employment. Assists individuals to develop employment plans based on appraisals of aptitudes, interests, and personality characteristics, and to plan curriculums accordingly. Contacts prospective employers to determine needs and to explain placement service. Arranges on-campus interviews between employers and graduating students to facilitate placement of graduates. Collects, organizes, and analyzes occupational, educational, and economic information for use in job placement activities. Directs maintenance of occupational library. Assists in conducting community surveys to gather labor market information, such as prevailing wages, hours, training, and employment possibilities. Coordinates program for analyzing campus jobs. ● **GED:** R6, M5, L5 ● **SVP:** 4-10 yrs ● **Academic:** Ed=B, Eng=G ● **Work Field:** 295 ● **MPSMS:** 943 ● **Aptitudes:** G1, V1, N2, S4, P4, Q3, K4, F4, M4, E5, C5 ● **Temperaments:** D, I, J, P, V ● **Physical:** Stg=S; Freq: R, H, I, T, G, N ● **Work Env:** Noise=N; ● **Salary:** 3 ● **Outlook:** 3

FOOD-MANAGEMENT AIDE (government ser.) ● DOT #195.367-022 ● OES: 27308 ● Alternate titles: NUTRITION AIDE. Advises low-income family members how to plan, budget, shop, prepare balanced meals, and handle and store food, following prescribed standards: Advises clients of advantages of food stamps, how to obtain stamps, and use of stamps during shopping trips. Transports clients to shopping area, using automobile. Observes clients' food selections. Recommends alternate economical and nutritional food choices. Observes and discusses meal preparation. Suggests alternate methods of food preparation. Assists in planning of food budget, utilizing charts and sample budgets. Advises clients on preferred methods of sanitation. Consults with supervisor concerning programs for individual families. Maintains records concerning results of family visits. ● **GED:** R3, M2, L3 ● **SVP:** 1-3 mos ● **Academic:** Ed=N, Eng=G ● **MPSMS:** 282 ● **Aptitudes:** G3, V3, N4, S4, P4, Q3, K4, F4, M4, E4, C5 ● **Temperaments:** P ● **Physical:** Stg=L; Freq: T, G, N Occas: R, H ● **Work Env:** Noise=N; ● **Salary:** 1 ● **Outlook:** 3

FOREIGN-STUDENT ADVISER (education) ● DOT #090.107-010 ● OES: 31514 ● Alternate titles: VISITING-STUDENT COUNSELOR. Assists foreign students in making academic, personal-social, and environmental adjustment to campus and community life: Evaluates students' qualifications in light of admission requirements and makes recommendations relative to admission. Develops and maintains case histories, noting language, educational, social, religious, or physical problems affecting students' adjustments. Provides informal counseling and orientation regarding recreational and religious outlets, study habits, and personal adjustments. Interprets university regulations and requirements. Assists students in complying with government regulations concerning status, immigration, visas, passports, permission to work, and related matters. Represents students in cases involving conflict with regulations. Cooperates with other personnel service bureaus to assist in adjustment of students. Approves students' proposed budgets and requests release of funds from students' home governments to meet financial obligations. Recommends students for scholarships, grants-in-aid, and waivers of tuition fees on basis of scholarship, character, and financial need. Encourages and coordinates activities of groups which promote understanding of foreign cultures. May assist in curriculum planning. ● **GED:** R5, M2, L5 ● **SVP:** 2-4 yrs ● **Academic:** Ed=M, Eng=G ● **Work Field:** 298, 282 ● **MPSMS:** 733, 931 ● **Aptitudes:** G2, V2, N3, S4, P4, Q3, K4, F4, M4, E5, C5 ● **Temperaments:** D, J, P, V ● **Physical:** Stg=S; Freq: R, H, I, T, G, N ● **Work Env:** Noise=N; ● **Salary:** 4 ● **Outlook:** 2

PATIENT-RESOURCES-AND-REIMBURSEMENT AGENT (government ser.) ● DOT #195.267-018 ● OES: 27310 ● Investigates financial assets, properties, and resources of hospitalized retarded and brain-damaged clients to protect financial interests and provide reimbursement of hospital costs: Visits and interviews or contacts by mail or telephone relatives, friends, former employers, pension funds, fraternal and veterans organizations and government agencies. Records documentation of financial resources in patient files. Analyzes data accumulated, such as disability allowances, medicare, medicaid, social security pension, dividends, interest, and insurance, and determines ability to pay for hospitalization. Determines additional sources from which reimbursements can be obtained. Prepares reports and enumer-

ates amounts and sources of reimbursements, including public assistance from social agencies in behalf of patients and families. Reviews patients' records to ensure that reimbursements are maintained. Applies for appointment of conservators to financially protect patients with assets over statutory limits and submits names of appointees to courts. Occasionally attends court hearings to protect patient interests. ● **GED:** R5, M3, L5 ● **SVP:** 2-4 yrs ● **Academic:** Ed=A, Eng=G ● **Work Field:** 271 ● **MPSMS:** 959 ● **Aptitudes:** G3, V3, N3, S4, P4, Q2, K4, F4, M4, E5, C5 ● **Temperaments:** J, P ● **Physical:** Stg=L; Const: T, G, N Freq: R, H, I ● **Work Env:** Noise=N; ● **Salary:** 4 ● **Outlook:** 4

PROBATION-AND-PAROLE OFFICER (profess. & kin.) ● DOT #195.107-046 ● OES: 27310 ● Counsels juvenile or adult offenders in activities related to legal conditions of probation or parole: Confers with offender, legal representatives, family, and other concerned persons, and reviews documents pertaining to legal and social history of offender to conduct prehearing or presentencing investigations and to formulate rehabilitation plan. Compiles reports, testifies in court, and makes recommendations concerning conditional release or institutionalization of offender. Informs offender or guardian of legal requirements of conditional release, such as visits to office, restitution payments, or educational and employment stipulations. Counsels offender and family or guardian, helps offender to secure education and employment, arranges custodial care, and refers offender to social resources of community to aid in rehabilitation. Evaluates offender's progress on follow-up basis including visits to home, school, and place of employment. Secures remedial action by court if necessary. May be employed by correctional institution, parole board, courts system, or separate agency serving court. May specialize in working with either juvenile or adult offenders. May specialize in working with offenders on probation and be designated Probation Officer (profess. & kin.). May specialize in working with offenders on parole and be designated Parole Officer (profess. & kin.). ● **GED:** R5, M3, L5 ● **SVP:** 2-4 yrs ● **Academic:** Ed=B, Eng=G ● **Work Field:** 271, 298 ● **MPSMS:** 949 ● **Aptitudes:** G2, V2, N3, S4, P4, Q4, K4, F4, M4, E5, C5 ● **Temperaments:** D, I, J, P, V ● **Physical:** Stg=L; Freq: T, G Occas: R, H, I, N, A ● **Work Env:** Noise=Q; ● **Salary:** 3 ● **Outlook:** 2

PSYCHOLOGIST, CHIEF (profess. & kin.) ● DOT #045.107-046 ● OES: 27108 ● Plans psychological service programs and directs, coordinates, and participates in activities of personnel engaged in providing psychological services to clients in psychiatric center or hospital: Reviews reports, case management reviews, and psychiatric center's or hospital's procedural manual to assess need for psychological services. Plans psychological treatment programs that meet standards of accreditation. Plans utilization of available staff, assigns staff to treatment units, and recruits professional and nonprofessional psychological staff. Develops, directs, and participates in training programs. Directs testing and evaluation of new admissions and re-evaluation of present clients. Participates in staff conferences to evaluate and plan treatment programs. Interviews clients that present difficult and complex diagnostic problems and assesses their psychological status. Reviews management of cases, assignments, case problems, issues, and methods of treatment. Works with community agencies to develop effective corrective programs and to arrange to provide psychological services. Plans and supervises psychological research. Collaborates with psychiatrists and other professional staff to help develop comprehensive program of therapy, evaluation, and treatment. ● **GED:** R6, M5, L6 ● **SVP:** 4-10 yrs ● **Academic:** Ed=M, Eng=G ● **Work Field:** 294, 295, 251 ● **MPSMS:** 733 ● **Aptitudes:** G1, V1, N2, S4, P3, Q3, K4, F4, M4, E5, C5 ● **Temperaments:** D, I, J, P, V ● **Physical:** Stg=S; Freq: T, G, N Occas: R, H, I ● **Work Env:** Noise=N; ● **Salary:** 5 ● **Outlook:** 2

PSYCHOLOGIST, COUNSELING (profess. & kin.) ● DOT #045.107-026 ● OES: 27108 ● Provides individual and group counseling services in universities and colleges, schools, clinics, rehabilitation centers, Veterans Administration hospitals, and industry, to assist individuals in achieving more effective personal, social, educational, and vocational development and adjustment: Collects data about individual through use of interview, case history, and observational techniques. Selects and interprets psychological tests designed to assess individual's intelligence, aptitudes, abilities, and interests, applying knowledge of statistical analysis. Evaluates data to identify causes of problem of individuals and to determine advisability of counseling or referral to other specialists or institutions. Conducts counseling or therapeutic interviews to assist individual to gain insight into personal problems, define goals, and plan action reflecting interests, abilities, and needs. Provides occupational, educational, and other information to enable individual to formulate realistic educational and vocational plans. Follows up results of counseling to determine reliability and validity of treatment used. May engage in research to develop and improve diagnostic and counseling techniques. May administer and score psychological tests. ● **GED:** R6, M5, L5 ● **SVP:** 4-10 yrs ● **Academic:** Ed=M, Eng=G ● **Work Field:** 298 ● **MPSMS:** 733 ● **Aptitudes:** G1, V1, N3, S4, P3, Q3, K4, F4, M4, E5, C5 ● **Temperaments:** I, J, P, V ● **Physical:** Stg=S; Freq: T, G ● **Work Env:** Noise=Q; ● **Salary:** 5 ● **Outlook:** 4

PSYCHOLOGIST, SCHOOL (profess. & kin.) ● DOT #045.107-034 ● OES: 27108 ● Evaluates needs of average, gifted, handicapped, and disturbed children within educational system or school, and plans and carries out programs to enable children to attain maximum achievement and adjustment: Conducts diagnostic studies to identify child's needs, limitations, and potentials, observing child in classroom and at play, studying school records, consulting with parents and school personnel, and administering and interpreting diagnostic findings. Plans special placement or other treatment programs. Counsels pupils individually and in groups, using psychodrama, play therapy, personal interviews, and other psychological methods to assist pupils to achieve personal, social, and emotional adjustment. Carries out research to aid in introduction of programs in schools to meet current psychological, educational, and sociological needs of children. Advises teachers and other school personnel on methods to enhance school and classroom atmosphere to provide motivating educational environment. Refers individuals to community agencies to secure medical, vocational, or social services for child or family. Participates in planning of remedial classes and testing programs designed to meet needs of students. Serves as consultant to school board, superintendent, administrative committees, and parent-teacher groups in matters involving psychological services within educational system or school. ● **GED:** R6, M5, L5 ● **SVP:** 4-10 yrs ● **Academic:** Ed=M, Eng=G ● **Work Field:** 298 ● **MPSMS:** 733 ● **Aptitudes:** G1, V1, N2, S4, P4, Q4, K4, F4, M4, E5, C5 ● **Temperaments:** I, J, P ● **Physical:** Stg=S; Freq: T, G, N Occas: F, V ● **Work Env:** Noise=Q; ● **Salary:** 4 ● **Outlook:** 3

RESIDENCE COUNSELOR (education) ● DOT #045.107-038 ● OES: 31514 ● Alternate titles: COUNSELOR, DORMITORY; DORMITORY SUPERVISOR; HEAD RESIDENT, DORMITORY. Provides individual and group guidance services relative to problems of scholastic, educational, and personal-social nature to dormitory students: Suggests remedial or corrective actions and assists students in making better adjustments and in planning intelligent life goals. Plans and directs program to orient new students and assists in their integration into campus life. Initiates and conducts group conferences to plan and discuss programs and policies related to assignment of quarters, social and recreational activities, and dormitory living. Supervises dormitory activities. Investigates reports of misconduct and attempts to resolve or eliminate causes of conflict. May interview all dormitory students to determine need for counseling. ● **GED:** R5, M4, L5 ● **SVP:** 2-4 yrs ● **Academic:** Ed=A, Eng=S ● **Work Field:** 298 ● **MPSMS:** 733 ● **Aptitudes:** G1, V1, N4, S4, P4, Q4, K4, F4, M4, E5, C5 ● **Temperaments:** I, J, P, V ● **Physical:** Stg=S; Freq: T, G ● **Work Env:** Noise=Q; ● **Salary:** 4 ● **Outlook:** 5

SOCIAL GROUP WORKER (social ser.) ● DOT #195.107-022 ● OES: 27310 ● Develops program content, organizes, and leads activities planned to enhance social development of individual members and accomplishment of group goals: Interviews individual members to assess social and emotional capabilities and plans group composition in relation to personal and social compatibility of members. Selects program appropriate to particular group goals, level of development, needs, capacities, and interests of group members. Involves members in planning and assuming responsibility for activities. Helps members through group experience to develop attitudes and social skills for improved family relations and community responsibility. May secure supplementary information, such as medical records and school reports. May work

in collaboration with other professional disciplines. Refers members, when indicated, to community resources and other organizations. Employed in agencies, such as community center, settlement house, youth serving organization, institution for children or aged, hospital, or penal institution. Usually required to have skills acquired through degree program at school of social work. ● **GED:** R5, M3, L5 ● **SVP:** 4-10 yrs ● **Academic:** Ed=M, Eng=G ● **Work Field:** 298 ● **MPSMS:** 941 ● **Aptitudes:** G2, V2, N3, S4, P4, Q4, K4, F4, M4, E5, C5 ● **Temperaments:** D, I, J, P, V ● **Physical:** Stg=S; Freq: T, G Occas: R, H, I, N ● **Work Env:** Noise=N; ● **Salary:** 5 ● **Outlook:** 3

SOCIAL-SERVICES AIDE (social ser.) ● DOT #195.367-034 ● OES: 27308 ● Assists professional staff of public social service agency, performing any combination of following tasks: Interviews individuals and family members to compile information on social, educational, criminal, institutional, or drug history. Visits individuals in homes or attends group meetings to provide information on agency services, requirements, and procedures. Provides rudimentary counseling to agency clients. Oversees day-to-day group activities of residents in institution. Meets with youth groups to acquaint them with consequences of delinquent acts. Refers individuals to various public or private agencies for assistance. May care for children in client's home during client's appointments. May accompany handicapped individuals to appointments. ● **GED:** R4, M3, L4 ● **SVP:** 1-2 yrs ● **Academic:** Ed=N, Eng=G ● **Work Field:** 271, 294 ● **MPSMS:** 941 ● **Aptitudes:** G3, V3, N3, S4, P4, Q3, K4, F4, M4, E5, C5 ● **Temperaments:** D, J, P, V ● **Physical:** Stg=L; Freq: T, G, N, A Occas: R, H, I ● **Work Env:** Noise=N; ● **Salary:** 1 ● **Outlook:** 2

SUBSTANCE ABUSE COUNSELOR (profess. & kin.) ● DOT #045.107-058 ● OES: 27310 ● Counsels and aids individuals and families requiring assistance dealing with substance abuse problems, such as alcohol or drug abuse: Interviews clients, reviews records, and confers with other professionals to evaluate condition of client. Formulates program for treatment and rehabilitation of client, using knowledge of drug and alcohol abuse problems and counseling and treatment techniques. Counsels clients individually and in group sessions to assist client in overcoming alcohol and drug dependency. Counsels family members to assist family in dealing with and providing support for client. Refers client to other support services as needed, such as medical evaluation and treatment, social services, and employment services. Monitors condition of client to evaluate success of therapy, and adapts treatment as needed. Prepares and maintains reports and case histories. May formulate and conduct programs to promote prevention of alcohol and drug abuse. May prepare documents for presentation in court and accompany client to court as needed. ● **GED:** R5, M3, L5 ● **SVP:** 4-10 yrs ● **Academic:** Ed=M, Eng=G ● **Work Field:** 298 ● **MPSMS:** 733 ● **Aptitudes:** G2, V2, N3, S4, P4, Q4, K4, F4, M4, E5, C5 ● **Temperaments:** I, J, P ● **Physical:** Stg=S; Const: T Freq: G, N Occas: R, H, I ● **Work Env:** Noise=Q; ● **Salary:** 4 ● **Outlook:** 3

VOCATIONAL REHABILITATION COUNSELOR (government ser.) ● DOT #045.107-042 ● OES: 31514 ● Alternate titles: COUNSELOR, VOCATIONAL REHABILITATION. Counsels handicapped individuals to provide vocational rehabilitation services: Interviews and evaluates handicapped applicants, and confers with medical and professional personnel to determine type and degree of handicap, eligibility for service, and feasibility of vocational rehabilitation. Accepts or recommends acceptance of suitable candidates. Determines suitable job or business consistent with applicant's desires, aptitudes, and physical, mental, and emotional limitations. Plans and arranges for applicant to study or train for job. Assists applicant with personal adjustment throughout rehabilitation program. Aids applicant in obtaining medical and social services during training. Promotes and develops job openings and places qualified applicant in employment. May specialize in type of disability, such as mental illness, alcohol abuse, hearing and visual impairment, or readjustment after prison release. ● **GED:** R5, M3, L5 ● **SVP:** 4-10 yrs ● **Academic:** Ed=M, Eng=G ● **Work Field:** 298 ● **MPSMS:** 733 ● **Aptitudes:** G2, V2, N3, S4, P4, Q3, K4, F4, M4, E5, C5 ● **Temperaments:** D, J, P, V ● **Physical:** Stg=S; Freq: T, G, N Occas: R, H, I ● **Work Env:** Noise=Q; ● **Salary:** 4 ● **Outlook:** 2

Nursing, Therapy, and Specialized Teaching Services   10.02

Workers in this group care for, treat, or train people to improve their physical and emotional well-being. Most workers in this group deal with sick, injured, or handicapped people. Some workers are involved in health education and sickness prevention. Hospitals, nursing homes, and rehabilitation centers hire workers in this group, as do schools, industrial plants, doctors' offices, and private homes. Some sports also have a need for workers in this group.

✓ What kind of work would you do?

Your work activities would depend upon your specific job. For example, you might:

- provide general nursing care to patients in a hospital.
- give medications to patients as prescribed.
- care for and treat patients in a doctor's office.
- observe, record, and report information about the condition of patients in a hospital or clinic.
- plan and carry out a school health program.
- plan, organize, and direct music or art activities to help patients in a mental hospital.
- direct and aid patients in physical therapy exercises.
- provide physical therapy exercises and treatments as directed by a physician.
- train newly blinded people in daily routines, such as grooming, dressing, and using the telephone.

✓ What skills and abilities do you need for this kind of work?

To do this kind of work, you must be able to:

- use common sense and special medical skills to care for or treat sick or handicapped people.
- understand technical information you might get from supervisors, charts, reference books, manuals, or labels.
- use eyes, hands, and fingers with skill.
- work fast in an emergency.
- communicate with people when they are sick, handicapped, or nervous.
- change from one duty to another frequently.
- follow instructions exactly.
- record information accurately.

The above statements may not apply to every job in this group.

✓ How do you know if you would like or could learn to do this kind of work?

The following questions may give you clues about yourself as you consider this group of jobs.

- Have you worked as an aide in a hospital, day care center, nursing home, or other institution? Do you like helping people who are ill or injured?
- Have you had training or school courses in arts, crafts, speech, or music? Can you teach these skills to others?
- Have you assembled a plastic model of a human body? Are you interested in human anatomy?
- Have you taken a first aid course? Do you remember actions you should take in an emergency?
- Have you taken courses which require you to dissect an animal? Can you skillfully handle small instruments such as tweezers or probes?

✓ How can you prepare for and enter this kind of work?

Occupations in this group usually require education and/or training extending from one year to over ten years, depending upon the specific kind of work. People seeking entry into professional nursing and rehabilitation are required to have specialized training. Most schools of professional nursing require a high school education or its equal for admission. A few schools require some college credits for admission.

Most nursing schools offer one or more of the following programs: two-year associate degrees, three-year diploma programs, or four-year baccalaureate degrees. Studies in all programs include biological, physical, and social sciences as well as nursing theory and practice. Two and three year programs prepare graduates for general and private duty nursing. Graduates of four-year baccalaureate programs qualify for general duty nursing, positions in public health agencies, or advancement to supervisory and administrative work.

Jobs in therapy usually require a college degree in a specialized field such as speech, music, recreation, art, or physical education. On-the-job training is also required. People with degrees in other fields may become qualified by taking the necessary academic and clinical courses.

✓ What else should you consider about these jobs?

These jobs involve close physical contact with people. Workers may have to lift, bathe, groom, or massage patients. They may also take blood or apply dressings and medications. Conditions associated with mental, emotional, or physical problems must be tolerated.

Most professionals will work a 40-hour week. However they may be on call or required to work overtime. Workers with seniority usually can be selective about the days and shifts they work.

Jobs may involve direct patient care, research, teaching, or combinations of each. There are many areas of specialization in this field.

If you think you would like to do this kind of work, look at the job titles on the following pages.

■ ■ ■

GOE: 10.02.01
Nursing

NURSE ANESTHETIST (medical ser.) ● DOT #075.371-010 ● OES: 32502 ● Administers local, inhalation, intravenous, and other anesthetics prescribed by ANESTHESIOLOGIST (medical ser.) 070.101-010 to induce total or partial loss of sensation or consciousness in patients during surgery, deliveries, or other medical and dental procedures: Fits mask to patient's face, turns dials and sets gauges of equipment to regulate flow of oxygen and gases to administer anesthetic by inhalation method, according to prescribed medical standards. Prepares prescribed solutions and administers local, intravenous, spinal, or other anesthetic, following specified methods and procedures. Notes patient's skin color and dilation of pupils and observes video screen and digital display of computerized equipment to monitor patient's vital signs during anesthesia. Initiates remedial measures to prevent surgical shock or other adverse conditions. Informs physician of patient's condition during anesthesia. ● **GED:** R5, M5, L5 ● **SVP:** 4-10 yrs ● **Academic:** Ed=B, Eng=G ● **Work Field:** 294 ● **MPSMS:** 924 ● **Aptitudes:** G2, V2, N2, S2, P2, Q2, K4, F2, M2, E5, C3 ● **Temperaments:** P, S, T ● **Physical:** Stg=L; Freq: R, H, I, T, G, N, A, X Occas: S, K, O, E ● **Work Env:** Noise=Q; ● **Salary:** 5 ● **Outlook:** 4

NURSE, CONSULTANT (medical ser.) ● DOT #075.127-014 ● OES: 32502 ● Advises hospitals, schools of nursing, industrial organizations, and public health groups on problems related to nursing activities and health services: Reviews and suggests changes in nursing organization and administrative procedures. Analyzes nursing techniques and recommends modifications. Aids schools in planning nursing curriculums, and hospitals and public health nursing services in developing and carrying out staff education programs. Provides assistance in developing guides and manuals for specific aspects of nursing services. Prepares educational materials and assists in planning and developing health and educational programs for industrial and community groups. Advises in services available through community resources. Consults with nursing groups concerning professional and educational problems. Prepares or furnishes data for articles and lectures. Participates in surveys and research studies. ● **GED:** R5, M4, L5 ● **SVP:** 2-4 yrs ● **Academic:** Ed=B, Eng=G ● **Work Field:** 282 ● **MPSMS:** 924, 926 ● **Aptitudes:** G2, V2, N2, S4, P4, Q3, K4, F4, M4, E5, C5 ● **Temperaments:** D, P, V ● **Physical:** Stg=S; Freq: T, G Occas: R, H, I ● **Work Env:** Noise=N; ● **Salary:** 5 ● **Outlook:** 5

NURSE, GENERAL DUTY (medical ser.) ● DOT #075.364-010 ● OES: 32502 ● Alternate titles: NURSE, STAFF. Provides general nursing care to patients in hospital, nursing home, infirmary, or similar health care facility: Administers prescribed medications and treatments in accordance with approved nursing techniques. Prepares equipment and aids physician during treatments and examinations of patients. Observes patient, records significant conditions and reactions, and notifies supervisor or physician of patient's condition and reaction to drugs, treatments, and significant incidents. Takes temperature, pulse, blood pressure, and other vital signs to detect deviations from normal and assess condition of patient. May rotate among various clinical services of institution, such as obstetrics, surgery, orthopedics, outpatient and admitting, pediatrics, and psychiatry. May prepare rooms, sterile instruments, equipment and supplies, and hand items to SURGEON (medical ser.) 070.101-094; OBSTETRICIAN (medical ser.) 070.101-

054, or other medical practitioner. May make beds, bathe, and feed patients. May serve as leader for group of personnel rendering nursing care to number of patients. ● **GED:** R5, M4, L5 ● **SVP:** 2-4 yrs ● **Academic:** Ed=B, Eng=G ● **Work Field:** 294 ● **MPSMS:** 924 ● **Aptitudes:** G2, V2, N3, S3, P3, Q2, K3, F3, M3, E4, C4 ● **Temperaments:** J, P, S, T ● **Physical:** Stg=M; Freq: R, H, I, E, T, G, N, X Occas: S, A ● **Work Env:** Noise=N; ● **Salary:** 5 ● **Outlook:** 5

NURSE, HEAD (medical ser.) ● DOT #075.137-014 ● OES: 32502 ● Supervises and coordinates nursing activities in hospital unit: Assigns duties and coordinates nursing service. Evaluates nursing activities to ensure patient care, staff relations, and efficiency of service. Observes nursing care and visits patients to ensure that nursing care is carried out as directed, and treatment administered in accordance with physician's instructions. Directs preparation and maintenance of patients' clinical records. Inspects rooms and wards for cleanliness and comfort. Accompanies physician on rounds, and keeps informed of special orders concerning patients. Participates in orientation and training of personnel. Orders, or directs ordering of drugs, solutions, and equipment, and maintains records on narcotics. Investigates and resolves complaints, or refers unusual problems to superior. ● **GED:** R5, M4, L5 ● **SVP:** 2-4 yrs ● **Academic:** Ed=A, Eng=G ● **Work Field:** 294 ● **MPSMS:** 924 ● **Aptitudes:** G2, V2, N2, S3, P3, Q2, K3, F3, M3, E4, C3 ● **Temperaments:** D, P, S, T, V ● **Physical:** Stg=M; Freq: S, R, H, I, T, G, N, X Occas: E ● **Work Env:** Noise=N; ● **Salary:** 4 ● **Outlook:** 4

NURSE, INFECTION CONTROL (medical ser.) ● DOT #075.127-034 ● OES: 32502 ● Directs and coordinates infection control program in hospital: Compares laboratory reports with communicable diseases list to identify conditions that require infection control procedures. Advises and consults with physicians, nurses, and hospital personnel concerning precautions to be taken to protect patients, staff, and other persons from possible contamination or infection. Investigates infection control problems and arranges for follow-up care for persons exposed to infection or disease. Instructs hospital personnel in universal and specific infection control procedures. ● **GED:** R5, M4, L5 ● **SVP:** 2-4 yrs ● **Academic:** Ed=B, Eng=G ● **Work Field:** 294, 271, 296 ● **MPSMS:** 924 ● **Aptitudes:** G2, V2, N2, S4, P3, Q2, K3, F3, M4, E5, C5 ● **Temperaments:** D, J, P ● **Physical:** Stg=L; Const: N Freq: H, I, T, G Occas: R, A ● **Work Env:** Noise=Q; ● **Salary:** 5 ● **Outlook:** 4

NURSE, INSTRUCTOR (medical ser.) ● DOT #075.124-018 ● OES: 31398 ● Demonstrates and teaches patient care in classroom and clinical units to nursing students and instructs students in principles and application of physical, biological, and psychological subjects related to nursing: Lectures to students, conducts and supervises laboratory work, issues assignments, and directs seminars and panels. Supervises student nurses and demonstrates patient care in clinical units of hospital. Prepares and administers examinations, evaluates student progress, and maintains records of student classroom and clinical experience. Participates in planning curriculum, teaching schedule, and course outline. Cooperates with medical and nursing personnel in evaluating and improving teaching and nursing practices. May specialize in specific subject, such as anatomy, chemistry, psychology, or nutrition, or in type of nursing activity, such as nursing of medical or surgical patients. May conduct classes for patients in health practices and procedures. ● **GED:** R5, M4, L5 ● **SVP:** 4-10 yrs ● **Academic:** Ed=B, Eng=G ● **Work Field:** 294, 296 ● **MPSMS:** 924, 931 ● **Aptitudes:** G2, V1, N2, S3, P3, Q2, K4, F3, M4, E5, C4 ● **Temperaments:** D, I, P, V ● **Physical:** Stg=L; Freq: R, H, I, T, G, N Occas: S, K, E, A, X ● **Work Env:** Noise=N; ● **Salary:** 5 ● **Outlook:** 5

NURSE, LICENSED PRACTICAL (medical ser.) ● DOT #079.374-014 ● OES: 32505 ● Provides prescribed medical treatment and personal care services to ill, injured, convalescent, and handicapped persons in such settings as hospitals, clinics, private homes, schools, sanitariums, and similar institutions: Takes and records patients' vital signs. Dresses wounds, gives enemas, douches, alcohol rubs, and massages. Applies compresses, ice bags, and hot water bottles. Observes patients and reports adverse reactions to medication or treatment to medical personnel in charge. Administers specified medication, orally or by subcutaneous or intermuscular injection, and notes time and amount on patients' charts. Assembles and uses such equipment as catheters, tracheotomy tubes, and oxygen suppliers. Collects samples, such as urine, blood, and sputum, from patients for testing and performs routine laboratory tests on samples. Sterilizes equipment and supplies, using germicides, sterilizer, or autoclave. Prepares or examines food trays for prescribed diet and feeds patients. Records food and fluid intake and output. Bathes, dresses, and assists patients in walking and turning. Cleans rooms, makes beds, and answers patients' calls. Washes and dresses bodies of deceased persons. Must pass state board examination and be licensed. May assist in delivery, care, and feeding of infants. May inventory and requisition supplies. May provide medical treatment and personal care to patients in private home settings and be designated Home Health Nurse, Licensed Practical (medical ser.). ● **GED:** R4, M3, L4 ● **SVP:** 1-2 yrs ● **Academic:** Ed=A, Eng=G ● **Work Field:** 294 ● **MPSMS:** 924 ● **Aptitudes:** G3, V3, N4, S3, P3, Q3, K3, F3, M3, E4, C4 ● **Temperaments:** P, S, T, V ● **Physical:** Stg=M; Freq: S, R, H, I, T, G, N Occas: K, O, E, X ● **Work Env:** Noise=N; Occas: O ● **Salary:** 3 ● **Outlook:** 3

NURSE-MIDWIFE (medical ser.) ● DOT #075.264-014 ● OES: 32502 ● Provides medical care and treatment to obstetrical patients under supervision of OBSTETRICIAN (medical ser.), delivers babies, and instructs patients in prenatal and postnatal health practices: Participates in initial examination of obstetrical patient, and is assigned responsibility for care, treatment, and delivery of patient. Examines patient during pregnancy, utilizing physical findings, laboratory test results, and patient's statements to evaluate condition and ensure that patient's progress is normal. Discusses case with OBSTETRICIAN (medical ser.) to assure observation of specified practices. Instructs patient in diet and prenatal health practices. Stays with patient during labor to reassure patient and to administer medication. Delivers infant and performs postpartum examinations and treatments to ensure that patient and infant are responding normally. When deviations from standard are encountered during pregnancy or delivery, administers stipulated emergency measures, and arranges for immediate contact of OBSTETRICIAN (medical ser.). Visits patient during postpartum period in hospital and at home to instruct patient in care of self and infant and examine patient. Maintains records of cases for inclusion in establishment file. Conducts classes for groups of patients and families to provide information concerning pregnancy, childbirth, and family orientation. May direct activities of other workers. May instruct in midwifery in establishment providing such training. ● **GED:** R5, M5, L3 ● **SVP:** 2-4 yrs ● **Academic:** Ed=B, Eng=G ● **Work Field:** 294 ● **MPSMS:** 924 ● **Aptitudes:** G2, V3, N3, S3, P3, Q3, K3, F3, M3, E4, C4 ● **Temperaments:** J, P, V ● **Physical:** Stg=M; Freq: T, G, N, D Occas: B, R, H, I, E, F, A, X ● **Work Env:** Noise=N; ● **Salary:** 1 ● **Outlook:** 3

NURSE, OFFICE (medical ser.) ● DOT #075.374-014 ● OES: 32502 ● Cares for and treats patients in medical office, as directed by physician: Prepares patient for and assists with examinations. Administers injections and medications, dresses wounds and incisions, interprets physician's instructions to patients, assists with emergency and minor surgery, and performs related tasks as directed. Maintains records of vital statistics and other pertinent data of patient. Cleans and sterilizes instruments and equipment, and maintains stock of supplies. May conduct specified laboratory tests. May record and develop electrocardiograms. May act as receptionist, perform secretarial duties, and prepare monthly statements. ● **GED:** R5, M3, L5 ● **SVP:** 2-4 yrs ● **Academic:** Ed=B, Eng=G ● **Work Field:** 294 ● **MPSMS:** 924 ● **Aptitudes:** G2, V3, N3, S3, P3, Q3, K3, F3, M3, E5, C4 ● **Temperaments:** J, P, T ● **Physical:** Stg=L; Freq: R, H, I, T, G, N Occas: E, X ● **Work Env:** Noise=Q; ● **Salary:** 4 ● **Outlook:** 4

NURSE PRACTITIONER (medical ser.) ● DOT #075.264-010 ● OES: 32502 ● Alternate titles: PRIMARY CARE NURSE PRACTITIONER. Provides general medical care and treatment to patients in medical facility, such as clinic, health center, or public health agency, under direction of physician: Performs physical examinations and preventive health measures within prescribed guidelines and instructions of physician. Orders, interprets, and evaluates diagnostic tests to identify and assess patient's clinical problems and health care needs. Records physical findings, and formulates plan and prognosis, based on patient's condition. Discusses case with physician and other health professionals to prepare comprehensive patient care plan. Submits health care plan and goals of individual patients for periodic review and evaluation by physician. Prescribes or recommends drugs or other forms of treatment such as physical therapy, inhalation therapy, or related therapeutic procedures. May refer patients to physician for consultation or to specialized health resources for treatment. May be designated according to field of specialization as Pediatric Nurse Practitioner (medical ser.). Where state law permits, may engage in independent practice. ● **GED:** R5, M5, L5 ● **SVP:** 4-10 yrs ● **Academic:** Ed=M, Eng=G ● **Work Field:** 294 ● **MPSMS:** 924 ● **Aptitudes:** G2, V2, N3, S2, P2, Q2, K3, F3, M3, E5, C3 ● **Temperaments:** D, J, P ● **Physical:** Stg=L; Freq: R, H, I, E, T, G, N, X Occas: S, A ● **Work Env:** Noise=N; ● **Salary:** 5 ● **Outlook:** 4

NURSE, PRIVATE DUTY (medical ser.) ● DOT #075.374-018 ● OES: 32502 ● Alternate titles: NURSE, SPECIAL. Contracts independently to render nursing care, usually to one patient, in hospital or private home: Administers medications, treatments, dressings, and other nursing services, according to physician's instructions and condition of patient. Observes, evaluates, and records symptoms. Applies independent emergency measures to counteract adverse developments and notifies physician of patient's condition. Directs patient in good health habits. Gives information to family in treatment of patient and maintenance of healthful environment. Maintains equipment and supplies. Cooperates with community agencies furnishing assistance to patient. May supervise diet when employed in private home. May specialize in one field of nursing, such as obstetrics, psychiatry, or tuberculosis. ● **GED:** R5, M4, L5 ● **SVP:** 2-4 yrs ● **Academic:** Ed=B, Eng=G ● **Work Field:** 294 ● **MPSMS:** 924 ● **Aptitudes:** G2, V2, N3, S2, P2, Q3, K3, F3, M3, E4, C4 ● **Temperaments:** J, P, S, T ● **Physical:** Stg=M; Freq: R, H, I, T, G, N, A Occas: D, X ● **Work Env:** Noise=N; ● **Salary:** 5 ● **Outlook:** 4

NURSE, SCHOOL (medical ser.) ● DOT #075.124-010 ● OES: 32502 ● Provides health care services to students: Plans school health program, in cooperation with medical authority and administrative school personnel. Participates in medical examinations and reviews findings to evaluate health status of pupils and progress of program. Instructs classes in subjects, such as child care, first aid, and home nursing, and establishes nursing policies to meet emergencies. Cooperates with school personnel in identifying and meeting social, emotional, and physical needs of school children. Administers immunizations, provides first-aid, and maintains health records of students. Counsels students in good health habits. Works with community agencies in planning facilities to meet needs of children outside school situation. May assist in program for care of handicapped children. May work in college and be designated Nurse, College (medical ser.). ● **GED:** R5, M4, L5 ● **SVP:** 2-4 yrs ● **Academic:** Ed=B, Eng=G ● **Work Field:** 294, 296 ● **MPSMS:** 924, 931 ● **Aptitudes:** G2, V2, N3, S3, P3, Q2, K3, F3, M3, E5, C4 ● **Temperaments:** D, I, J, P, S ● **Physical:** Stg=L; Freq: R, H, I, T, G, N Occas: E, A, X ● **Work Env:** Noise=Q; ● **Salary:** 4 ● **Outlook:** 3

NURSE, STAFF, COMMUNITY HEALTH (medical ser.) ● DOT #075.124-014 ● OES: 32502 ● Alternate titles: PUBLIC-HEALTH NURSE. Instructs individuals and families in health education and disease prevention in community health agency: Visits homes to determine patient and family needs, develops plan to meet needs, and provides nursing services. Instructs family in care and rehabilitation of patient, and in maintenance of health and prevention of disease for family members. Gives treatments to patient following physician's instructions. Assists community members and health field personnel to assess, plan for, and provide needed health and related services. Refers patients with social and emotional problems to other community agencies for assistance. Teaches home nursing, maternal and child care, and other subjects related to individual and community welfare. Participates in programs to safeguard health of children, including child health conferences, school health, group instruction for parents, and immunization programs. Assists in preparation of special studies and in research programs. Directs treatment of patient by NURSE, LICENSED PRACTICAL (medical ser.) 079.374-014 and HOME ATTENDANT (personal ser.) 354.377-014. Cooperates with families, community agencies, and medical personnel to arrange for convalescent and rehabilitative care of sick or injured persons. May specialize in one phase of community health nursing, such as clinical pediatrics or tuberculosis. ● GED: R5, M4, L5 ● SVP: 2-4 yrs ● Academic: Ed=B, Eng=G ● Work Field: 294 ● MPSMS: 920 ● Aptitudes: G2, V2, N2, S3, P3, Q3, K4, F3, M3, E4, C3 ● Temperaments: I, J, P, T ● Physical: Stg=M; Const: N Freq: R, H, T, G, D, A, X Occas: I, E ● Work Env: Noise=N; ● Salary: 4 ● Outlook: 4

NURSE, STAFF, OCCUPATIONAL HEALTH NURSING (medical ser.) ● DOT #075.374-022 ● OES: 32502 ● Alternate titles: NURSE, STAFF, INDUSTRIAL. Provides nursing service and first aid to employees or persons who become ill or injured on premises of department store, industrial plant, or other establishment: Takes patient's vital signs, treats wounds, evaluates physical condition of patient, and contacts physician and hospital to arrange for further medical treatment, when needed. Maintains record of persons treated, and prepares accident reports and insurance forms. Develops employee programs, such as health education, accident prevention, alcohol abuse counseling, curtailment of smoking, and weight control regimens. May assist physician in physical examination of new employees. ● GED: R5, M4, L5 ● SVP: 2-4 yrs ● Academic: Ed=B, Eng=G ● Work Field: 294 ● MPSMS: 924 ● Aptitudes: G2, V2, N3, S4, P3, Q3, K3, F3, M3, E5, C4 ● Temperaments: J, P, T, V ● Physical: Stg=L; Freq: R, H, I, T, G, N Occas: E, D, X, V ● Work Env: Noise=N; ● Salary: 4 ● Outlook: 4

NURSE, SUPERVISOR (medical ser.) ● DOT #075.167-010 ● OES: 32502 ● Directs, through head nurses, activities of nursing staff: Plans and organizes activities in nursing services, such as obstetrics, pediatrics, or surgery, or for two or more patient-care units to ensure patient needs are met in accordance with instructions of physician and hospital administrative procedures. Coordinates activities with other patient care units. Consults with NURSE, HEAD (medical ser.) 075.137-014 on nursing problems and interpretation of hospital policies to ensure patient needs are met. Plans and organizes orientation and in-service training for unit staff members, and participates in guidance and educational programs. Assists in formulating budget. Engages in studies and investigations related to improving nursing care. ● GED: R5, M4, L5 ● SVP: 2-4 yrs ● Academic: Ed=A, Eng=G ● Work Field: 294, 295 ● MPSMS: 924 ● Aptitudes: G2, V2, N3, S3, P3, Q3, K3, F3, M3, E4, C3 ● Temperaments: D, P, S, T, V ● Physical: Stg=L; Freq: R, H, I, T, G, N Occas: E, X ● Work Env: Noise=N; ● Salary: 4 ● Outlook: 4

PHYSICIAN ASSISTANT (medical ser.) ● DOT #079.364-018 ● OES: 32511 ● Provides health care services to patients under direction and responsibility of physician: Examines patient, performs comprehensive physical examination, and compiles patient medical data, including health history and results of physical examination. Administers or orders diagnostic tests, such as x ray, electrocardiogram, and laboratory tests, and interprets test results for deviations from normal. Performs therapeutic procedures, such as injections, immunizations, suturing and wound care, and managing infection. Develops and implements patient management plans, records progress notes, and assists in provision of continuity of care. Instructs and counsels patients regarding compliance with prescribed therapeutic regimens, normal growth and development, family planning, emotional problems of daily living, and health maintenance. May have training in particular medical specialty and be designated Anesthesiologist Assistant (medical ser.) or Surgeon Assistant (medical ser.). ● GED: R5, M4, L5 ● SVP: 2-4 yrs ● Academic: Ed=A, Eng=G ● Work Field: 294 ● MPSMS: 924 ● Aptitudes: G2, V2, N3, S2, P2, Q2, K2, F3, M3, E5, C3 ● Temperaments: J, P, T ● Physical: Stg=L; Const: N Freq: R, H, I, T, G, A Occas: S, E, X ● Work Env: Noise=Q; ● Salary: 4 ● Outlook: 4

QUALITY ASSURANCE COORDINATOR (medical ser.) ● DOT #075.167-014 ● OES: 32502 ● Interprets and implements quality assurance standards in hospital to ensure quality care to patients: Reviews quality assurance standards, studies existing hospital policies and procedures, and interviews hospital personnel and patients to evaluate effectiveness of quality assurance program. Writes quality assurance policies and procedures. Reviews and evaluates patients' medical records, applying quality assurance criteria. Selects specific topics for review, such as problem procedures, drugs, high volume cases, high risk cases, or other factors. Compiles statistical data and writes narrative reports summarizing quality assurance findings. May review patient records, applying utilization review criteria, to determine need for admission and continued stay in hospital. May oversee personnel engaged in quality assurance review of medical records. ● GED: R5, M4, L5 ● SVP: 2-4 yrs ● Academic: Ed=B, Eng=G ● Work Field: 294, 271 ● MPSMS: 924 ● Aptitudes: G2, V2, N2, S4, P3, Q2, K3, F3, M4, E5, C5 ● Temperaments: J, P, T ● Physical: Stg=L; Const: N Freq: H, I, T, G Occas: R ● Work Env: Noise=Q; ● Salary: 5 ● Outlook: 4

TRANSPLANT COORDINATOR (medical ser.) ● DOT #079.151-010 ● OES: 32998 ● Alternate titles: ORGAN TRANSPLANT COORDINATOR. Plans and coordinates in-hospital transplant services, solicits organ donors, and assists medical staff in organ retrieval for patients undergoing organ or tissue transplantation: Communicates with donors, patients, and health team members to ensure comprehensive documentation, including informed consent of potential organ donor and transplant recipient, equitable access to transplantation system, and access to treatment alternatives. Analyzes medical data of potential organ donors and transplant recipients from medical and social records, physical examination, and consultation with health team members to perform preliminary physical assessment and screen potential recipients and donors. Schedules recipient and donor laboratory tests to determine histocompatibility of blood or tissue of recipient and donor. Compares collected data to normal values and correlates and summarizes laboratory reports, x rays, and other tests to assist physician to determine medical suitability of procedure, to identify potential complicating factors, and to evaluate recipient and donor compatibility. Solicits medical and community groups for organ donors and assists medical team in retrieval of organs for transplantation, using medical instruments. Coordinates in-hospital services and counsels recipient and donor to alleviate anxieties and assist recipient and donor throughout procedure. Advises post-operative patients on therapies for managing health after transplant and serves as team member to monitor and assess progress of patient and offer advice and assistance to patient following transplant. May coordinate in-hospital services and be known as Clinical Transplant Coordinator (medical ser.). May coordinate organ and tissue procurement services and be known as Procurement Transplant Coordinator (medical ser.). ● GED: R5, M5, L5 ● SVP: 2-4 yrs ● Academic: Ed=A, Eng=G ● Work Field: 294 ● MPSMS: 924 ● Aptitudes: G2, V2, N3, S2, P2, Q2, K3, F2, M3, E5, C4 ● Temperaments: I, P, T ● Physical: Stg=L; Const: T, G, N Freq: R, H, I, E, A Occas: D, X ● Work Env: Noise=Q; ● Salary: 5 ● Outlook: 4

GOE: 10.02.02
Therapy & Rehabilitation

ACUPRESSURIST (medical ser.) ● DOT #079.271-014 ● OES: 32998 ● Examines clients with pain, stress, or tension, determines acupressure techniques required to relieve problems, and demonstrates techniques to client, according to knowledge of acupressure methods and techniques. Directs client to lie on couch and positions client's arms and legs in relaxed position to facilitate examination and demonstration techniques. Questions clients, examines client's muscular system visually, and feels tissue around muscles, nerves, and blood vessels to locate knots and other blockages which indicate excessive accumulations of blood, fluids, and other substances in tissue. Determines cause of accumulations and acupressure techniques needed to increase circulation, according to knowledge of Asian acupuncture and pressure points and Western medical trigger points, bodywork techniques, such as Jin Shin, Do-In, Shiatsu, Swedish, and Esalen, and experience. Feels tissue around muscles, nerves, and blood vessels to locate points and applies specified pressure at specified pressure points or muscles, using thumbs, fingers, palms, or elbows, to redirect accumulated body fluids into normal channels, according to acupressure knowledge, techniques, and experience. Discusses findings with client and explains diet and methods to prevent recurrence of problem. May be known according to specific method or combination of methods used, such as Gia Ahp, Jin Shin, Do-In, or Shiatsu. ● GED: R5, M3, L4 ● SVP: 6

mos-1 yr ● **Academic:** Ed=A, Eng=G ● **Work Field:** 294 ● **MPSMS:** 924 ● **Aptitudes:** G2, V2, N3, S2, P2, Q3, K2, F2, M3, E3, C5 ● **Temperaments:** J, P ● **Physical:** Stg=M; Freq: R, H, I, T, G, N Occas: E, D, A ● **Work Env:** Noise=N; ● **Salary:** 3 ● **Outlook:** 3

ART THERAPIST (medical ser.) ● DOT #076.127-010 ● OES: 32317 ● Plans and conducts art therapy programs in public and private institutions to rehabilitate mentally and physically disabled clients: Confers with members of medically oriented team to determine physical and psychological needs of client. Devises art therapy program to fulfill physical and psychological needs. Instructs individuals and groups in use of various art materials, such as paint, clay, and yarn. Appraises client's art projections and recovery progress. Reports findings to other members of treatment team and counsels on client's response until art therapy is discontinued. Maintains and repairs art materials and equipment. ● **GED:** R5, M4, L5 ● **SVP:** 2-4 yrs ● **Academic:** Ed=B, Eng=G ● **Work Field:** 294 ● **MPSMS:** 924 ● **Aptitudes:** G2, V2, N3, S2, P2, Q3, K4, F3, M3, E4, C3 ● **Temperaments:** D, J, P, V ● **Physical:** Stg=L; Freq: R, H, I, E, T, G, N, X, V ● **Work Env:** Noise=N; ● **Salary:** 4 ● **Outlook:** 1

ATHLETIC TRAINER (amuse. & rec.) ● DOT #153.224-010 ● OES: 34058 ● Evaluates physical condition and advises and treats professional and amateur athletes to maintain maximum physical fitness for participation in athletic competition: Prescribes routine and corrective exercises to strengthen muscles. Recommends special diets to build up health and reduce overweight athletes. Massages parts of players' bodies to relieve soreness, strains, and bruises. Renders first aid to injured players, such as giving artificial respiration, cleaning and bandaging wounds, and applying heat and cold to promote healing. Calls physician for injured persons as required. Wraps ankles, fingers, or wrists of athletes in synthetic skin, protecting gauze, and adhesive tape to support muscles and ligaments. Treats chronic minor injuries and related disabilities to maintain athletes' performance. May give heat and diathermy treatments as prescribed by health service. Workers are identified according to type of sport. ● **GED:** R5, M4, L4 ● **SVP:** 4-10 yrs ● **Academic:** Ed=A, Eng=G ● **Work Field:** 294 ● **MPSMS:** 913 ● **Aptitudes:** G2, V2, N4, S3, P3, Q4, K3, F2, M3, E4, C5 ● **Temperaments:** D, J, P, S ● **Physical:** Stg=M; Freq: S, K, O, R, H, T, G Occas: I, E ● **Work Env:** Noise=N; Freq: W ● **Salary:** 3 ● **Outlook:** 2

CORRECTIVE THERAPIST (medical ser.) ● DOT #076.361-010 ● OES: 32398 ● Provides medically prescribed program of physical exercises and activities designed to prevent muscular deterioration resulting from long convalescence or inactivity due to chronic illness: Collaborates with other members of rehabilitation team in organizing patients' course of treatment. Establishes rapport with patients to motivate them, choosing exercises and activities in accordance with prescription. Utilizes any or combination of resistive, assistive, or free movement exercises, utilizing bars, or hydrogymnastics. Instructs patients in use, function, and care of prostheses and devices, such as braces, crutches, or canes and in use of manually controlled vehicles. Directs blind persons in foot travel. Prepares progress reports of patient's emotional reactions to and progress in training by observing patient during exercises to provide clinical data for diagnosis and prognosis by rehabilitation team. Directs patients in techniques of personal hygiene to compensate for permanent disabilities. ● **GED:** R4, M2, L4 ● **SVP:** 2-4 yrs ● **Academic:** Ed=A, Eng=G ● **Work Field:** 294 ● **MPSMS:** 921 ● **Aptitudes:** G2, V2, N2, S4, P4, Q4, K2, F2, M2, E3, C5 ● **Temperaments:** D, P, V ● **Physical:** Stg=M; Freq: R, H, I, T, G, N ● **Work Env:** Noise=N; Occas: U, A ● **Salary:** 3 ● **Outlook:** 2

DANCE THERAPIST (medical ser.) ● DOT #076.127-018 ● OES: 32317 ● Plans, organizes, and leads dance and body movement activities to improve patients' mental outlooks and physical well-beings: Observes and evaluates patient's mental and physical disabilities to determine dance and body movement treatment. Confers with patient and medical personnel to develop dance therapy program. Conducts individual and group dance sessions to improve patient's mental and physical well-being. Makes changes in patient's program based on observation and evaluation of progress. Attends and participates in professional conferences and workshops to enhance efficiency and knowledge. ● **GED:** R5, M3, L5 ● **SVP:** 4-10 yrs ● **Academic:** Ed=A, Eng=G ● **Work Field:** 294, 263 ● **MPSMS:** 924 ● **Aptitudes:** G2, V2, N3, S2, P3, Q3, K4, F4, M4, E1, C5 ● **Temperaments:** D, J, P, V ● **Physical:** Stg=L; Freq: B, R, H, T, G, F Occas: S, K, N ● **Work Env:** Noise=N; ● **Salary:** 4 ● **Outlook:** 1

DENTAL HYGIENIST (medical ser.) ● DOT #078.361-010 ● OES: 32908 ● Performs dental prophylaxis: Cleans calcareous deposits, accretions, and stains from teeth and beneath margins of gums, using dental instruments. Feels lymph nodes under patient's chin to detect swelling or tenderness that could indicate presence of oral cancer. Feels and visually examines gums for sores and signs of disease. Examines gums, using probes, to locate periodontal recessed gums and signs of gum disease. Applies fluorides and other cavity preventing agents to arrest dental decay. Charts conditions of decay and disease for diagnosis and treatment by dentist. Exposes and develops x-ray film. Makes impressions for study casts. May remove sutures and dressings. May administer local anesthetic agents. May place and remove rubber dams, matrices, and temporary restorations. May place, carve, and finish amalgam restorations. May remove excess cement from coronal surfaces of teeth. May provide clinical services and health education to improve and maintain oral health of school children. May conduct dental health clinics for community groups to augment services of dentist. ● **GED:** R4, M3, L4 ● **SVP:** 1-2 yrs ● **Academic:** Ed=A, Eng=G ● **Work Field:** 294 ● **MPSMS:** 925 ● **Aptitudes:** G2, V3, N3, S2, P3, Q4, K2, F2, M2, E4, C4 ● **Temperaments:** J, P, T ● **Physical:** Stg=L; Freq: R, H, I, E, T, G, N, D, A Occas: S, X ● **Work Env:** Noise=Q; ● **Salary:** 2 ● **Outlook:** 4

DIALYSIS TECHNICIAN (medical ser.) ● DOT #078.362-014 ● OES: 32998 ● Alternate titles: HEMODIALYSIS TECHNICIAN. Sets up and operates hemodialysis machine to provide dialysis treatment for patients with kidney failure: Attaches dialyzer and tubing to machine to assemble for use. Mixes dialysate, according to formula. Primes dialyzer with saline or heparinized solution to prepare machine for use. Transports patient to dialysis room and positions patient on lounge chair at hemodialysis machine. Takes and records patient's predialysis weight, temperature, blood pressure, pulse rate, and respiration rate. Explains dialysis procedure and operation of hemodialysis machine to patient before treatment to allay anxieties. Cleans area of access (fistula, graft, or catheter), using antiseptic solution. Connects hemodialysis machine to access in patient's forearm or catheter site to start blood circulating through dialyzer. Inspects equipment settings, including pressures, conductivity (proportion of chemicals to water), and temperature to ensure conformance to safety standards. Starts blood flow pump at prescribed rate. Inspects venous and arterial pressures as registered on equipment to ensure pressures are within established limits. Calculates fluid removal or replacement to be achieved during dialysis procedure. Monitors patient for adverse reaction and hemodialysis machine for malfunction. Takes and records patient's postdialysis weight, temperature, blood pressure, pulse rate, and respiration rate. May fabricate parts, such as cannulas, tubing, catheters, connectors, and fittings, using handtools. ● **GED:** R4, M3, L3 ● **SVP:** 1-2 yrs ● **Academic:** Ed=A, Eng=S ● **Work Field:** 294 ● **MPSMS:** 925 ● **Aptitudes:** G3, V3, N3, S3, P3, Q3, K2, F2, M3, E4, C4 ● **Temperaments:** P, T ● **Physical:** Stg=L; Const: N Freq: R, H, I, T, G Occas: S, K, E, A, X ● **Work Env:** Noise=Q; Const: O ● **Salary:** 4 ● **Outlook:** 3

EXERCISE PHYSIOLOGIST (medical ser.) ● DOT #076.121-018 ● OES: 32398 ● Develops, implements, and coordinates exercise programs and administers medical tests, under physician's supervision, to program participants to promote physical fitness: Explains program and test procedures to participant. Interviews participant to obtain vital statistics and medical history and records information. Records heart activity, using electrocardiograph (EKG) machine, while participant undergoes stress test on treadmill, under physician's supervision. Measures oxygen consumption and lung functioning, using spirometer. Measures amount of fat in body, using such equipment as hydrostatic scale, skinfold calipers, and tape measure, to assess body composition. Performs routine laboratory test of blood samples for cholesterol level and glucose tolerance, or interprets test results. Schedules other examinations and tests, such as physical examination, chest x ray, and urinalysis. Records test data in patient's chart or enters data into computer. Writes initial and follow-up exercise prescriptions for participants, following physician's recommendation, specifying equipment, such as treadmill, track, or bike. Demonstrates correct use of exercise equipment and exercise routines. Conducts individual and group aerobic, strength, and flexibility exercises. Observes participants during exercise for signs of stress. Teaches behavior modification classes, such as stress management, weight control, and related subjects. Orders material and supplies and calibrates equipment. May supervise work activities of other staff members. ● **GED:** R5, M4, L5 ● **SVP:** 2-4 yrs ● **Academic:** Ed=A, Eng=G ● **Work Field:** 231, 294 ● **MPSMS:** 924 ● **Aptitudes:** G2, V2, N3, S3, P3, Q3, K3, F3, M3, E4, C4 ● **Temperaments:** D, I, J, P ● **Physical:** Stg=M; Freq: R, H, I, E, T, G, N Occas: C, B, S, K, D, A, X, V ● **Work Env:** Noise=Q; ● **Salary:** 5 ● **Outlook:** 4

HORTICULTURAL THERAPIST (medical ser.) ● DOT #076.124-018 ● OES: 32398 ● Plans, coordinates, and conducts therapeutic gardening program to facilitate rehabilitation of physically and mentally handicapped patients: Confers with medical staff and patients to determine patients' needs. Evaluates patients' disabilities to determine gardening programs. Conducts gardening sessions to rehabilitate, train, and provide recreation for patients. Revises gardening program, based on observations and evaluation of patients' progress. ● **GED:** R5, M4, L5 ● **SVP:** 2-4 yrs ● **Academic:** Ed=A, Eng=S ● **Work Field:** 003, 294, 296 ● **MPSMS:** 924, 731 ● **Aptitudes:** G2, V2, N3, S3, P4, Q3, K3, F3, M3, E5, C3 ● **Temperaments:** D, J, P, V ● **Physical:** Stg=L; Freq: S, K, R, H, I, T, G, N, X ● **Work Env:** Noise=L; Freq: W ● **Salary:** 4 ● **Outlook:** 1

HYPNOTHERAPIST (profess. & kin.) ● DOT #079.157-010 ● OES: 32998 ● Induces hypnotic state in client to increase motivation or alter behavior patterns: Consults with client to determine nature of problem. Prepares client to enter hypnotic state by explaining how hypnosis works and what client will experience. Tests subject to determine degree of physical and emotional suggestibility. Induces hypnotic state in client, using individualized methods and techniques of hypnosis based on interpretation of test results and analysis of client's problem. May train client in self-hypnosis conditioning. ● **GED:** R4, M3, L4 ● **SVP:** 2-4 yrs ● **Academic:** Ed=H, Eng=G ● **Work Field:** 294 ● **MPSMS:** 733 ● **Aptitudes:** G2, V2, N4, S4, P4, Q4, K4, F4, M4, E5, C5 ● **Temperaments:** D, J, P ● **Physical:** Stg=S; Freq: T, G, N Occas: R, H ● **Work Env:** Noise=Q; ● **Salary:** 5 ● **Outlook:** 2

INDUSTRIAL THERAPIST (medical ser.) ● DOT #076.167-010 ● OES: 32305 ● Arranges salaried, productive employment in actual work environment for mentally ill patients, to enable patients to perform medically prescribed work activities, and to motivate and prepare patients to resume employment outside hospital environment: Determines work activities for greatest therapeutic value for particular patient within limits of patient's disability. Plans work activities in coordination with other members of rehabilitation team. Assigns patient to work activity and evaluates patient's progress. Processes payroll records and salary distribution. ● **GED:** R5, M5, L5 ● **SVP:** 2-4 yrs ● **Academic:** Ed=A, Eng=G ● **Work Field:** 294 ● **MPSMS:** 920 ● **Aptitudes:** G2, V2, N2, S3, P3, Q3, K3, F3, M3, E4, C5 ● **Temperaments:** D, J, P ● **Physical:** Stg=L; Freq: R, H, I, T, G, N ● **Work Env:** Noise=N; ● **Salary:** 3 ● **Outlook:** 2

INSTRUCTOR, PHYSICAL (amuse. & rec.) ● DOT #153.227-014 ● OES: 31321 ● Teaches individuals or groups beginning or advanced calisthenics, gymnastics, and reducing or corrective exercises, in private health club or gymnasium, evaluating abilities of individual to determine suitable training program: Teaches and demonstrates use of gymnastic apparatus, such as trampolines, corrective weights, and mechanical exercisers. Demonstrates and teaches body movements and skills used in sports. Advises clients in use of heat or ultraviolet treatments and hot baths. Lubricates mechanical equipment and reports malfunctioning equipment to maintenance personnel. ● **GED:** R3, M3, L3 ● **SVP:** 1-2 yrs ● **Academic:** Ed=N, Eng=G ● **Work Field:** 296 ● **MPSMS:** 919, 931 ● **Aptitudes:** G3, V3, N4, S4, P4, Q4, K4, F4, M4, E2, C5 ● **Temperaments:** D, P ● **Physical:** Stg=L; Freq: S, O, R, H, T, G ● **Work Env:** Noise=N; ● **Salary:** 4 ● **Outlook:** 3

MANUAL-ARTS THERAPIST (medical ser.) ● DOT #076.124-010 ● OES: 32398 ● Instructs patients in prescribed manual arts activities to prevent anatomical and physiological deconditioning, and to assist in maintaining, improving, or developing work skills: Collaborates with other members of rehabilitation team in planning and organizing work activities consonant with patients' capabilities and disabilities. Teaches, by means of actual or simulated work situations, activities, such as woodworking, photography, metalworking, agriculture, electricity, and graphic arts. Prepares reports showing development of patient's work tolerance, and emotional and social adjustment to aid medical personnel in evaluating patient's progress and ability to meet physical and mental demands of employment. ● **GED:** R4, M4, L4 ● **SVP:** 2-4 yrs ● **Academic:** Ed=A, Eng=G ● **Work Field:** 296 ● **MPSMS:** 921 ●

Aptitudes: G2, V2, N2, S4, P4, Q4, K2, F2, M2, E3, C5 ● **Temperaments:** D, P, V ● **Physical:** Stg=L; Freq: R, H, I, T, G, N, A ● **Work Env:** Noise=N; Occas: A ● **Salary:** 4 ● **Outlook:** 3

MEDICAL RADIATION DOSIMETRIST (medical ser.) ● DOT #078.261-034 ● OES: 32914 ● Alternate titles: DOSIMETRIST. Measures and calculates radiation dose and develops optimum arrangement of radiation fields and exposures to treat patient: Studies prescription, x rays showing area to be treated, and requirements for dose calculation. Selects beam energy, optimum multiple beam arrangement, beam modifying devices, and other factors, using computer, manuals, and guides. Develops several possible treatment arrangements that meet physician's criteria and submits arrangements for selection by physician. Measures and calculates prescribed radiation dose based upon field sizes, depth of tumor, treatment unit, beam modifying devices, and other information, using manuals, guides, and computer. Calculates and records daily prescribed radiation dose. Explains treatment plan to RADIATION-THERAPY TECHNOLOGISTS (medical ser.) 078.361-034. May operate x-ray equipment to obtain diagnostic x ray of patient in treatment position. May simulate treatment procedure to assist in planning treatment. ● **GED:** R5, M4, L5 ● **SVP:** 4-10 yrs ● **Academic:** Ed=A, Eng=G ● **Work Field:** 294, 201 ● **MPSMS:** 925 ● **Aptitudes:** G2, V2, N2, S2, P2, Q2, K2, F2, M3, E5, C4 ● **Temperaments:** J, P, T ● **Physical:** Stg=L; Const: N, A Freq: R, H, I, T, G Occas: E, X ● **Work Env:** Noise=Q; ● **Salary:** 4 ● **Outlook:** 4

MUSIC THERAPIST (medical ser.) ● DOT #076.127-014 ● OES: 32317 ● Plans, organizes, and directs medically prescribed music therapy activities as part of mental and physical health care and treatment of patients to influence behavorial and psychological changes leading to restoration, maintenance, and improvement of health and increased comprehension of self, environment, and physical ability: Collaborates with other members of rehabilitation team in planning music activities in accordance with patients' physical or psychological needs, capabilities, and interests. Develops treatment plan, using individualized needs assessment, depending on focus of therapy, such as hospice, psychiatric, or obstetrics. Directs and participates in instrumental and vocal music activities designed to meet patients' physical or psychological needs, such as solo or group singing, rhythmic and other creative music activities, music listening, or attending concerts. Instructs patients individually or in groups in prescribed instrumental or vocal music and music projective techniques, such as guided imagery, progressive relaxation, awareness of conscious feelings, or musically intergraded Lamaze Method. Studies and analyzes patients' reactions to various experiences and prepares reports describing symptoms indicative of progress or regression. Submits periodic reports to treatment team or physician to provide clinical data for evaluation. May oversee practicum and approved internships. ● **GED:** R5, M5, L5 ● **SVP:** 2-4 yrs ● **Academic:** Ed=B, Eng=G ● **Work Field:** 294 ● **MPSMS:** 924 ● **Aptitudes:** G2, V2, N2, S4, P4, Q4, K4, F3, M3, E4, C5 ● **Temperaments:** I, J, P ● **Physical:** Stg=L; Freq: T, G, N, V Occas: R, H, I ● **Work Env:** Noise=N; ● **Salary:** 4 ● **Outlook:** 1

NUCLEAR MEDICINE TECHNOLOGIST (medical ser.) ● DOT #078.361-018 ● OES: 32914 ● Prepares, measures, and administers radiopharmaceuticals in diagnostic and therapeutic studies, utilizing variety of equipment and following prescribed procedures: Prepares stock solutions of radiopharmaceutical materials, calculates doses, and administers doses, under direction of physician. Calibrates equipment. Performs diagnostic studies on patients as prescribed by physician, using scanners or scintillation cameras to detect radiation emitted and to produce image of organ on photographic film. Measures radioactivity, using Geiger counters, scalers, and scintillation detecters. Administers therapeutic doses of radiopharmaceuticals under direction of physician. Follows radiation safety techniques in use and disposal of radioactive materials. ● **GED:** R5, M4, L5 ● **SVP:** 2-4 yrs ● **Academic:** Ed=A, Eng=S ● **Work Field:** 294, 201 ● **MPSMS:** 925 ● **Aptitudes:** G2, V2, N2, S2, P2, Q2, K3, F3, M2, E4, C4 ● **Temperaments:** J, P, T, V ● **Physical:** Stg=M; Freq: R, H, I, T, G, N Occas: S, O, E, D, A, X ● **Work Env:** Noise=Q; Const: R, O ● **Salary:** 4 ● **Outlook:** 3

OCCUPATIONAL THERAPIST (medical ser.) ● DOT #076.121-010 ● OES: 32305 ● Plans, organizes, and conducts occupational therapy program in hospital, institution, or community setting to facilitate development and rehabilitation of mentally, physically, or emotionally handicapped: Plans program involving activities, such as manual arts and crafts; practice in functional, prevocational, vocational, and homemaking skills, and activities of daily living; and participation in sensorimotor, educational, recreational, and social activities designed to help patients or handicapped persons develop or regain physical or mental functioning or adjust to handicaps. Consults with other members of rehabilitation team to select activity program consistent with needs and capabilities of individual and to coordinate occupational therapy with other therapeutic activities. Selects constructive activities suited to individual's physical capacity, intelligence level, and interest to upgrade individual to maximum independence, prepare individual for return to employment, assist in restoration of functions, and aid in adjustment to disability. Teaches individuals skills and techniques required for participation in activities and evaluates individual's progress. Designs and constructs special equipment for individual and suggests adaptation of individual's work-living environment. Requisitions supplies and equipment. Lays out materials for individual's use and cleans and repairs tools at end of sessions. May conduct training programs or participate in training medical and nursing students and other workers in occupational therapy techniques and objectives. May plan, direct, and coordinate occupational therapy program and be designated Director, Occupational Therapy (medical ser.). ● **GED:** R5, M4, L5 ● **SVP:** 2-4 yrs ● **Academic:** Ed=B, Eng=G ● **Work Field:** 294 ● **MPSMS:** 924 ● **Aptitudes:** G2, V2, N3, S3, P3, Q3, K4, F3, M3, E4, C4 ● **Temperaments:** D, I, J, P, V ● **Physical:** Stg=M; Freq: R, H, I, T, G, N, D, A Occas: S, K, O, E, X, V ● **Salary:** 4 ● **Outlook:** 4

OCCUPATIONAL THERAPY ASSISTANT (medical ser.) ● DOT #076.364-010 ● OES: 66021 ● Alternate titles: EDUCATIONAL/DEVELOPMENT ASSISTANT. Assists OCCUPATIONAL THERAPIST (medical ser.) 076.121-010 in administering occupational therapy program in hospital, related facility, or community setting for physically, developmentally, mentally retarded, or emotionally handicapped clients: Assists in evaluation of clients daily living skills and capacities to determine extent of abilities amd limitations. Assists in planning and implementing educational, vocational, and recreational programs and activities established by registered OCCUPATIONAL THERAPIST (medical ser.), designed to restore, reinforce, and enhance task performances, diminish or correct pathology, and to promote and maintain health and self-sufficiency. Designs and adapts equipment and working-living environment. Fabricates splints and other assistant devices. Reports information and observations to supervisor. Carries out general activity program for individuals or groups. Assists in instructing patient and family in home programs as well as care and use of adaptive equipment. Prepares work materials, assists in maintenance of equipment, and orders supplies. May be responsible for maintaining observed information in client records and preparing reports. May teach basic living skills to institutionalized, mentally retarded adults. May assist EDUCATIONAL SPECIALIST (education) 099.167-022 or CLINICAL PSYCHOLOGIST (profess. & kin.) 045.107-022 in administering situational or diagnostic tests to measure client's abilities or progress. ● **GED:** R4, M3, L4 ● **SVP:** 1-2 yrs ● **Academic:** Ed=A, Eng=G ● **Work Field:** 294 ● **MPSMS:** 924 ● **Aptitudes:** G3, V3, N3, S3, P3, Q3, K3, F2, M3, E3, C4 ● **Temperaments:** J, P, T ● **Physical:** Stg=M; Freq: R, H, I, T, G, N Occas: S, K, O, F, D, A, X, V ● **Work Env:** Noise=N; ● **Salary:** 3 ● **Outlook:** 3

ORIENTATION AND MOBILITY THERAPIST FOR THE BLIND (education) ● DOT #076.224-014 ● OES: 32398 ● Alternate titles: COUNSELOR, ORIENTATION AND MOBILITY; INSTRUCTOR OF BLIND; ORIENTOR; ORIENTATION THERAPIST FOR BLIND; THERAPIST FOR BLIND. Assists blind and visually impaired clients to achieve personal adjustment and maximum independence through training in techniques of daily living: Interviews clients, analyzes client's lifestyle, and administers assessment tests to determine present and required or desired orientation and mobility skills. Trains clients in awareness of physical environment through sense of smell, hearing, and touch, and to travel alone, with or without cane, through use of variety of actual or simulated travel situations and exercises. Teaches clients personal and home management skills, and communication skills, such as eating, grooming, dressing, coin and money identification, cooking, and use of telephone and bathroom facilities. Teaches clients to protect body, using hands and arms to detect obstacles. Instructs clients in arts, crafts, and recreational skills, such as macrame, leatherworking, sewing, ceramics, and playing piano to improve sense of touch, coordination, and motor skills. Teaches clients to

read and write Braille. Instructs client in use of reading machines and common electrical devices, and in development of effective listening techniques. Instructs clients in group activities, such as swimming, dancing, or playing modified sports activities to encourage and increase capacity for social participation and improve general health. Prepares progress report to allow members of rehabilitation team to evaluate clients' ability to perform varied activities essential to daily living. May develop and implement individualized orientation and mobility instructional program for blind and visually impaired and be designated Orientation And Mobility Instructor (education). ● **GED:** R5, M2, L5 ● **SVP:** 1-2 yrs ● **Academic:** Ed=A, Eng=S ● **Work Field:** 294, 296 ● **MPSMS:** 931 ● **Aptitudes:** G2, V2, N3, S3, P3, Q3, K3, F3, M3, E4, C5 ● **Temperaments:** D, P, V ● **Physical:** Stg=L; Const: T Freq: R, H, I, G, N Occas: E, M, V ● **Work Env:** Noise=N; Occas: W ● **Salary:** 4 ● **Outlook:** 4

ORTHOPTIST (medical ser.) ● DOT #079.371-014 ● OES: 32998 ● Aids persons with correctable focusing defects to develop and use binocular vision (focusing of both eyes): Measures visual acuity, focusing ability, and eye-motor movement of eyes, separately and jointly. Aids patient to move, focus, and coordinate both eyes to aid in visual development. Develops visual skills, near-visual discrimination, and depth perception, using developmental glasses and prisms. Instructs adult patients or parents of young patients in utilization of corrective methods at home. ● **GED:** R4, M4, L4 ● **SVP:** 1-2 yrs ● **Academic:** Ed=A, Eng=G ● **Work Field:** 294 ● **MPSMS:** 929 ● **Aptitudes:** G2, V3, N3, S3, P3, Q4, K4, F3, M3, E5, C4 ● **Temperaments:** I, J, P ● **Physical:** Stg=L; Freq: R, H, I, T, G, N, D, A, X ● **Work Env:** Noise=N; ● **Salary:** 5 ● **Outlook:** 3

PHERESIS SPECIALIST (medical ser.) ● DOT #078.261-042 ● OES: 32998 ● Alternate titles: HEMOTHERAPIST. Collects blood components and provides therapeutic treatments, such as replacement of plasma, or removal of white blood cells or platelets, to patients, using blood cell separator equipment: Compiles and evaluates donor information to ensure that donor meets screening criteria. Connects and installs tubing, transfer pack units, saline solution unit, other solution packs, and collection and separation containers to set up blood cell separator equipment. Explains procedures to donor or patient to reduce anxieties and obtain cooperation of donor or patient. Performs venipuncture on donor or patient to connect donor or patient to tubing of equipment to prepare for procedure. Sets controls and starts equipment that collects specific blood component or adds, reduces, or replaces blood component, and replaces remaining blood in vein of patient or donor. Monitors operation of equipment and observes trouble lights indicating equipment problems. Talks to and observes donor or patient for signs of distress or side effects such as pallor, nausea, fainting, or other problems during procedure. Forwards collection bag to laboratory for testing or further processing. Records information following collection or treatment procedures, such as flow rate, body site at which needle was inserted, anticoagulant rate, amount of fluids used, volume processed, red cells lost, and other information. ● **GED:** R5, M4, L5 ● **SVP:** 2-4 yrs ● **Academic:** Ed=A, Eng=G ● **Work Field:** 294 ● **MPSMS:** 925 ● **Aptitudes:** G2, V2, N2, S3, P2, Q3, K2, F2, M3, E4, C3 ● **Temperaments:** J, P, T ● **Physical:** Stg=L; Const: H, I, N Freq: S, T, G, A, X Occas: R, E ● **Work Env:** Noise=Q; ● **Salary:** 5 ● **Outlook:** 3

PHYSICAL-INTEGRATION PRACTITIONER (medical ser.) ● DOT #076.264-010 ● OES: 32398 ● Conducts physical integration program to improve client's muscular function and flexibility: Determines client's medical history regarding accidents, operations, or chronic health complaints to plan objectives of program, using questionnaire. Photographs client to obtain different views of client's posture to facilitate treatment, using camera. Instructs client to demonstrate arm and leg movement and flexion of spine to evaluate client against established program norms. Determines program treatment procedures and discusses goals of program with client. Applies skin lubricant to section of body specified for treatment and massages muscles to release subclinical adhesions either manually or using hand held tool, utilizing knowledge of anatomy. Demonstrates and directs client's participation in specific exercises designed to fatigue desired muscle groups and release tension. Observes client's progress during program through such factors as increased joint movement, improved posture, or coordination. Records client's treatment, response, and progress. ● **GED:** R3, M1, L2 ● **SVP:** 1-2 yrs ● **Academic:** Ed=A, Eng=G ● **Work Field:**

294 ● **MPSMS:** 929 ● **Aptitudes:** G3, V3, N4, S2, P2, Q4, K3, F3, M3, E4, C4 ● **Temperaments:** J, P ● **Physical:** Stg=L; Freq: R, H, I, E, T, G, N Occas: X ● **Work Env:** Noise=N; ● **Salary:** 3 ● **Outlook:** 1

PHYSICAL THERAPIST (education) ● DOT #076.121-014 ● OES: 32308 ● Alternate titles: PHYSIOTHERAPIST. Plans and administers medically prescribed physical therapy treatment for patients suffering from injuries, or muscle, nerve, joint and bone diseases, to restore function, relieve pain, and prevent disability: Reviews physician's referral (prescription) and patient's condition and medical records to determine physical therapy treatment required. Tests and measures patient's strength, motor development, sensory perception, functional capacity, and respiratory and circulatory efficiency, and records findings to develop or revise treatment programs. Plans and prepares written treatment program based on evaluation of patient data. Administers manual exercises to improve and maintain function. Instructs, motivates, and assists patient to perform various physical activities, such as nonmanual exercises, ambulatory functional activities, daily-living activities, and in use of assistant and supportive devices, such as crutches, canes, and prostheses. Administers treatments involving application of physical agents, using equipment, such as hydrotherapy tanks and whirlpool baths, moist packs, ultraviolet and infrared lamps, and ultrasound machines. Evaluates effects of treatment at various stages and adjusts treatments to achieve maximum benefit. Administers massage, applying knowledge of massage techniques and body physiology. Administers traction to relieve pain, using traction equipment. Records treatment, response, and progress in patient's chart or enters information into computer. Instructs patient and family in treatment procedures to be continued at home. Evaluates, fits, and adjusts prosthetic and orthotic devices and recommends modification to ORTHOTIST (medical ser.) 078.261-018. Confers with physician and other practitioners to obtain additional patient information, suggest revisions in treatment program, and integrate physical therapy treatment with other aspects of patient's health care. Orients, instructs, and directs work activities of assistants, aides, and students. May plan and conduct lectures and training programs on physical therapy and related topics for medical staff, students, and community groups. May plan and develop physical therapy research programs and participate in conducting research. May write technical articles and reports for publications. May teach physical therapy techniques and procedures in educational institutions. May limit treatment to specific patient group or disability or specialize in conducting physical therapy research. In facilities where assistants are also employed, may primarily administer complex treatment, such as certain types of manual exercises and functional training, and monitor administration of other treatments. May plan, direct, and coordinate physical therapy program and be designated Director, Physical Therapy (medical ser.). Must comply with state requirement for licensure. ● **GED:** R5, M4, L5 ● **SVP:** 2-4 yrs ● **Academic:** Ed=B, Eng=G ● **Work Field:** 294 ● **MPSMS:** 924 ● **Aptitudes:** G2, V2, N3, S2, P2, Q3, K2, F2, M2, E4, C4 ● **Temperaments:** D, I, J, P ● **Physical:** Stg=M; Freq: R, H, I, E, T, G, N Occas: C, S, K, O, W, A, X, V ● **Work Env:** Noise=Q; Occas: U, O ● **Salary:** 4 ● **Outlook:** 4

PHYSICAL THERAPIST ASSISTANT (medical ser.) ● DOT #076.224-010 ● OES: 66017 ● Alternate titles: PHYSICAL THERAPY ASSISTANT; PHYSICAL THERAPY TECHNICIAN. Administers physical therapy treatments to patients, working under direction of and as assistant to PHYSICAL THERAPIST (medical ser.) 076.121-014: Administers active and passive manual therapeutic exercises, therapeutic massage, and heat, light, sound, water, and electrical modality treatments, such as ultrasound, electrical stimulation, ultraviolet, infrared, and hot and cold packs. Administers traction to relieve neck and back pain, using intermittent and static traction equipment. Instructs, motivates, and assists patients to learn and improve functional activities, such as preambulation, transfer, ambulation, and daily-living activities. Observes patients during treatments and compiles and evaluates data on patients' responses to treatments and progress and reports orally or in writing to PHYSICAL THERAPIST (medical ser.). Fits patients for, adjusts, and trains patients in use and care of orthopedic braces, prostheses, and supportive devices, such as crutches, canes, walkers, and wheelchairs. Confers with members of physical therapy staff and other health team members, individually and in conference, to exchange, discuss, and evaluate patient information for planning, modifying, and coordinating treatment programs. Gives orientation to new PHYSICAL THERAPIST ASSISTANTS (medical ser.) and directs and gives instructions to PHYSICAL THERAPY AIDES (medical ser.) 355.354-

010. Performs clerical duties, such as taking inventory, ordering supplies, answering telephone, taking messages, and filling out forms. May measure patient's range-of-joint motion, length and girth of body parts, and vital signs to determine effects of specific treatments or to assist PHYSICAL THERAPIST (medical ser.) to compile data for patient evaluations. May monitor treatments administered by PHYSICAL THERAPY AIDES (medical ser.). ● **GED:** R4, M3, L4 ● **SVP:** 1-2 yrs ● **Academic:** Ed=H, Eng=S ● **Work Field:** 294 ● **MPSMS:** 924 ● **Aptitudes:** G2, V2, N3, S3, P3, Q3, K2, F2, M2, E3, C4 ● **Temperaments:** I, J, P, T ● **Physical:** Stg=M; Freq: S, K, O, R, H, I, E, T, G, N, A Occas: C, W, X, V ● **Work Env:** Noise=N; ● **Salary:** 3 ● **Outlook:** 3

PROGRAM AIDE, GROUP WORK (social ser.) ● DOT #195.227-010 ● OES: 27311 ● Alternate titles: GROUP LEADER. Leads group work activities, as directed by agency program staff: Receives instructions from PROGRAM DIRECTOR, GROUP WORK (profess. & kin.) 187.117-046 or GROUP WORKER (social ser.) 195.164-010 prior to initiating therapeutic group activities. Plans program details to meet needs and interests of individual members. Interests participants in various activities, such as arts and crafts and dramatics. Demonstrates techniques for active sports, group dances, and games. Helps develop new skills and interests. May work with part-time or volunteer staff. Works for social service agencies, such as community center, neighborhood house, settlement house, hospital, geriatric residential center, and health care facility. ● **GED:** R5, M3, L4 ● **SVP:** 1-2 yrs ● **Academic:** Ed=A, Eng=S ● **Work Field:** 294, 296 ● **MPSMS:** 941, 924 ● **Aptitudes:** G2, V2, N3, S4, P4, Q4, K4, F4, M4, E5, C5 ● **Temperaments:** D, P ● **Physical:** Stg=L; Freq: R, H, I, T, G, N, V ● **Work Env:** Noise=N; Occas: W ● **Salary:** 3 ● **Outlook:** 3

PSYCHIATRIC TECHNICIAN (medical ser.) ● DOT #079.374-026 ● OES: 32931 ● Provides nursing care to mentally ill, emotionally disturbed, or mentally retarded patients in psychiatric hospital or mental health clinic and participates in rehabilitation and treatment programs: Helps patients with their personal hygiene, such as bathing and keeping beds, clothing, and living areas clean. Administers oral medications and hypodermic injections, following physician's prescriptions and hospital procedures. Takes and records measures of patient's general physical condition, such as pulse, temperature, and respiration, to provide daily information. Observes patients to detect behavior patterns and reports observations to medical staff. Intervenes to restrain violent or potentially violent or suicidal patients by verbal or physical means as required. Leads prescribed individual or group therapy sessions as part of specific therapeutic procedures. May complete initial admittance forms for new patients. May contact patient's relatives by telephone to arrange family conferences. May issue medications from dispensary and maintain records in accordance with specified procedures. May be required to hold state license. ● **GED:** R4, M3, L4 ● **SVP:** 1-2 yrs ● **Academic:** Ed=A, Eng=G ● **Work Field:** 294 ● **MPSMS:** 924 ● **Aptitudes:** G3, V3, N3, S4, P4, Q3, K3, F3, M3, E4, C5 ● **Temperaments:** J, P, S, V ● **Physical:** Stg=M; Freq: R, H, I, E, T, G, N Occas: A, X ● **Work Env:** Noise=N; Occas: U, O ● **Salary:** 4 ● **Outlook:** 3

RADIATION-THERAPY TECHNOLOGIST (medical ser.) ● DOT #078.361-034 ● OES: 32914 ● Provides radiation therapy to patients as prescribed by RADIOLOGIST (medical ser.) 070.101-090, according to established practices and standards: Reviews prescription, diagnosis, patient chart, and identification. Acts as liaison with physicist and supportive care personnel. Prepares equipment, such as immobilization, treatment, and protection devices, and positions patient according to prescription. Enters data into computer and sets controls to operate and adjust equipment and regulate dosage. Observes and reassures patient during treatment and reports unusual reactions to physician. Photographs treated area of patient and processes film. Maintains records, reports, and files as required. Follows principles of radiation protection for patient, self, and others. May assist in dosimetry procedures and tumor localization. May train therapy students. ● **GED:** R5, M4, L5 ● **SVP:** 2-4 yrs ● **Academic:** Ed=A, Eng=S ● **Work Field:** 294, 201 ● **MPSMS:** 925 ● **Aptitudes:** G3, V3, N4, S4, P4, Q3, K3, F4, M4, E5, C4 ● **Temperaments:** J, P, T ● **Physical:** Stg=L; Freq: R, H, I, N Occas: S, O, E, T, G, A, X ● **Work Env:** Noise=Q; Freq: E, R ● **Salary:** 4 ● **Outlook:** 3

RADIOLOGIC TECHNOLOGIST, CHIEF (medical ser.) ● DOT #078.162-010 ● OES: 32916 ● Alternate titles: CHIEF, RADIOLOGY. Directs and coordinates activities of radiology or diagnostic imaging department in hospital or other medical facility: Reviews work schedules and assigns duties to workers to maintain patient flow and achieve production goals. Oversees staff in operation of imaging equipment, such as x-ray machine, fluoroscope, CT (computerized tomography) scanner, or MRI (magnetic resonance imaging) equipment, evaluates accuracy and quality of images, and provides technical assistance. Demonstrates new techniques, equipment, and procedures to staff. Implements and monitors radiation safety measures to ensure safety of patients and staff and compliance with government regulatory requirements. Recommends personnel actions, such as performance evaluations, promotions, and disciplinary measures. Coordinates purchase of supplies and equipment and makes recommendations concerning department operating budget. ● **GED:** R5, M4, L5 ● **SVP:** 4-10 yrs ● **Academic:** Ed=A, Eng=G ● **Work Field:** 294, 295 ● **MPSMS:** 925 ● **Aptitudes:** G2, V2, N2, S2, P2, Q3, K3, F3, M3, E4, C3 ● **Temperaments:** D, P, T ● **Physical:** Stg=L; Freq: R, H, I, T, G, N Occas: D, A, X ● **Work Env:** Noise=N; Occas: E, R ● **Salary:** 5 ● **Outlook:** 2

RADIOLOGIC TECHNOLOGIST (medical ser.) ● DOT #078.362-026 ● OES: 32916 ● Alternate titles: RADIOGRAPHER; X-RAY TECHNOLOGIST. Operates radiologic equipment to produce radiographs (x rays) of body for diagnostic purposes, as directed by RADIOLOGIST (medical ser.) 070.101-090: Positions patient on examining table and adjusts immobilization devices to obtain optimum views of specified area of body requested by physician. Explains procedures to patient to reduce anxieties and obtain patient cooperation. Moves x-ray equipment into specified position and adjusts equipment controls to set exposure factors, such as time and distance, based on knowledge of radiographic exposure techniques and protocols. Practices radiation protection techniques, using beam restrictive devices, patient shielding skills, and knowledge of applicable exposure factors, to minimize radiation to patient and staff. May operate mobile x-ray equipment in operating room, emergency room, or at patient's bedside. May specialize in production of screening and diagnostic x rays for detection of breast tumors and may be known as Radiologic Technologist, Mammogram (medical ser.). ● **GED:** R5, M4, L5 ● **SVP:** 2-4 yrs ● **Academic:** Ed=A, Eng=S ● **Work Field:** 201, 294 ● **MPSMS:** 925 ● **Aptitudes:** G2, V3, N3, S3, P3, Q3, K3, F3, M3, E4, C4 ● **Temperaments:** J, P, T ● **Physical:** Stg=L; Freq: R, H, I, T, G, N Occas: E, D, A, X ● **Work Env:** Noise=Q; Freq: R Occas: O ● **Salary:** 4 ● **Outlook:** 4

RECREATIONAL THERAPIST (medical ser.) ● DOT #076.124-014 ● OES: 32317 ● Alternate titles: THERAPEUTIC RECREATION WORKER. Plans, organizes, and directs medically approved recreation program for patients in hospitals and other institutions: Directs and organizes such activities as sports, dramatics, games, and arts and crafts to assist patients to develop interpersonal relationships, to socialize effectively, and to develop confidence needed to participate in group activities. Regulates content of program in accordance with patients' capabilities, needs and interests. Instructs patients in relaxation techniques, such as deep breathing, concentration, and other activities, to reduce stress and tension. Instructs patients in calisthenics, stretching and limbering exercises, and individual and group sports. Counsels and encourages patients to develop leisure activities. Organizes and coordinates special outings and accompanies patients on outings, such as ball games, sightseeing, or picnics to make patients aware of available recreational resources. Prepares progress charts and periodic reports for medical staff and other members of treatment team, reflecting patients' reactions and evidence of progress or regression. May supervise and conduct in-service training of other staff members, review their assessments and program goals, and consult with them on selected cases. May train groups of volunteers and students in techniques of recreation therapy. May serve as consultant to employers, educational institutions, and community health programs. May prepare and submit requisition for needed supplies. ● **GED:** R4, M2, L4 ● **SVP:** 1-2 yrs ● **Academic:** Ed=A, Eng=G ● **Work Field:** 294 ● **MPSMS:** 924 ● **Aptitudes:** G2, V2, N3, S3, P3, Q2, K3, F3, M3, E4, C5 ● **Temperaments:** D, P, V ● **Physical:** Stg=L; Freq: R, H, I, T, G, N Occas: S, O, F, V ● **Work Env:** Noise=N; ● **Salary:** 3 ● **Outlook:** 4

RESPIRATORY THERAPIST (medical ser.) ● DOT #076.361-014 ● OES: 32302 ● Administers respiratory therapy care and life support to patients with deficiencies and abnormalities of cardiopulmonary system, under supervision of physician and by prescription: Reads prescription, measures arterial blood gases, and reviews patient information to assess patient condition and determine requirements for treatment, such as type and duration of therapy, and medication and dosages. Determines most suitable method of administering inhalants, precautions to be observed, and modifications which may be needed that will be compatible with physician's orders. Sets up and operates devices, such as mechanical ventilators, therapeutic gas administration apparatus, environmental control systems, and aerosol generators. Operates equipment to ensure specified parameters of treatment, such as volume, gas concentration, humidity, and temperature, and to administer medicinal gases and aerosol drugs to patients. Monitors patient's physiological responses to therapy, such as vital signs, arterial blood gases, and blood chemistry changes. Performs bronchopulmonary drainage and assists patient in performing breathing exercises. Performs pulmonary function tests to be used by physician in diagnosis of case. Observes equipment function and adjusts equipment to obtain optimum results to therapy. Consults with physician in event of adverse reactions. Maintains patient's chart that contains pertinent identification and therapy information. Inspects and tests respiratory therapy equipment to ensure equipment is functioning safely and efficiently. Orders repairs when needed. Demonstrates respiratory care procedures to trainees and other health care personnel. ● **GED:** R4, M3, L3 ● **SVP:** 1-2 yrs ● **Academic:** Ed=A, Eng=G ● **Work Field:** 294 ● **MPSMS:** 924 ● **Aptitudes:** G3, V3, N3, S3, P3, Q3, K3, F3, M2, E5, C4 ● **Temperaments:** J, P, T, V ● **Physical:** Stg=M; Freq: R, H, I, T, G, N Occas: S, E, A, X ● **Work Env:** Noise=Q; ● **Salary:** 3 ● **Outlook:** 5

SPECIAL PROCEDURES TECHNOLOGIST, ANGIOGRAM (medical ser.) ● DOT #078.362-046 ● OES: 32916 ● Alternate titles: ANGIOGRAPHER; RADIOGRAPHER, ANGIOGRAM. Operates diagnostic imaging equipment to produce contrast enhanced radiographs of blood vessels to aid physician in diagnosis and treatment of disease: Positions patient in examining position, using immobilization devices, such as head or shoulder braces. Operates fluoroscope to aid physician to view and guide wire or catheter through blood vessel to area of interest. Fills automatic injector with contrast media, sets flow rate, and activates injection of contrast media into blood vessels of patient, as directed by physician. Monitors video display of area of interest and adjusts density and contrast to obtain optimum exposure. Starts filming sequence. Delivers film to dark room to be developed and reviews developed x rays for accuracy of positioning and quality of exposure techniques. ● **GED:** R5, M4, L5 ● **SVP:** 2-4 yrs ● **Academic:** Ed=A, Eng=G ● **Work Field:** 294, 201 ● **MPSMS:** 925 ● **Aptitudes:** G2, V3, N3, S3, P3, Q3, K3, F3, M3, E4, C4 ● **Temperaments:** J, P, T ● **Physical:** Stg=M; Freq: R, H, I, T, G, N, A Occas: E, X ● **Work Env:** Noise=N; Const: R ● **Salary:** 4 ● **Outlook:** 4

SPECIAL PROCEDURES TECHNOLOGIST, CARDIAC CATHETERIZATION (medical ser.) ● DOT #078.362-050 ● OES: 32925 ● Alternate titles: RADIOGRAPHER, CARDIAC CATHETERIZATION; SPECIAL VASCULAR IMAGING TECHNOLOGIST. Operates diagnostic imaging equipment to produce contrast enhanced radiographs of heart and cardiovascular system (angiocardiograms), during cardiac catheterization, to aid physician in diagnostic evaluation and treatment: Positions and immobilizes patient on examining table, using head and shoulder braces and following specified protocols. Enters technical factors determined by protocol such as amount and quality of radiation beam, and specified filming sequence, into computer. Raises and lowers examining table and manipulates and positions x-ray tube in response to instructions from physician. Starts automatic injection of contrast medium into blood vessels of patient. Activates fluoroscope and 35 mm motion picture camera (cinefluorography) to produce images that assist physician in guiding catheter through cardiovascular system of patient. Observes gauges, recorder, and video screens of multichannel data analysis system that indicates blood pressure, cardiac output, and respiration, during imaging of cardiovascular system. Alerts physician to changes in patient responses. May assist physician in interventional procedures, such as instilling enzymes or inserting balloon in blood vessels to remove plaque or other blockage. ● **GED:** R5, M4, L5 ● **SVP:** 2-4 yrs ● **Academic:** Ed=A, Eng=G ● **Work Field:** 201, 294 ● **MPSMS:** 925 ● **Aptitudes:** G2, V2, N3, S2, P3, Q2, K3, F3, M3, E4, C4 ● **Temperaments:** J, P, T ● **Physical:** Stg=M; Freq: R, H, I, N, A Occas: T, G, X ● **Work Env:** Noise=N; Occas: R ● **Salary:** 4 ● **Outlook:** 4

SPECIAL PROCEDURES TECHNOLOGIST, CT SCAN (medical ser.) ● DOT #078.362-054 ● OES: 32916 ● Alternate titles: CT TECHNOLOGIST. Operates computed tomography (CT) scanner to produce cross-sectional radiographs of patient's body for diagnostic purposes: Positions and immobilizes patient on examining table, using supportive devices to obtain precise patient position and following protocols specified by RADIOLOGIST (medical ser.) 070.101-090. Administers contrast media orally or assists physician in intravenous administration. Enters data, such as type of scan requested, slice thickness, scan time, and other technical data into computer, using knowledge of radiologic technology and computed tomography. Starts CT scanner to scan designated anatomical area of patient. Talks to patient over intercom system and observes patient through window of control room to monitor patient safety and comfort. Views images of organs or tissue on video display screen to ensure quality of pictures. Starts camera to produce radiographs. Evaluates radiographs, video tape, and computer generated information for technical quality. ● **GED:** R5, M4, L5 ● **SVP:** 2-4 yrs ● **Academic:** Ed=A, Eng=G ● **Work Field:** 294, 201 ● **MPSMS:** 925 ● **Aptitudes:** G2, V2, N3, S2, P3, Q3, K3, F3, M3, E4, C4 ● **Temperaments:** J, P, T ● **Physical:** Stg=M; Freq: R, H, I, T, G, N, A Occas: E, F, X ● **Work Env:** Noise=Q; Freq: R ● **Salary:** 4 ● **Outlook:** 4

SPECIAL PROCEDURES TECHNOLOGIST, MAGNETIC RESONANCE IMAGING (MRI) (medical ser.) ● DOT #078.362-058 ● OES: 32916 ● Alternate titles: MAGNETIC RESONANCE IMAGING TECHNOLOGIST. Operates magnetic resonance imaging equipment to produce cross-sectional images (photographs) of patient's body for diagnostic purposes: Interviews patient to explain magnetic resonance imaging procedures and to request removal of metal objects which are hazardous to patient and equipment when magnet is activated. Positions patient on examining table and places specified coil (receiver) such as head coil or knee coil, close to area of interest, following protocols requested by RADIOLOGIST (medical ser.) 070.101-090. Demonstrates use of microphone that allows patient and technologist to communicate during examination. Enters data, such as patient history, anatomical area to be scanned, orientation specified, and position of entry into aperture of magnetic resonance imaging equipment (head or feet first), into computer. Keys commands to specify scan sequences, and adjust transmitters and receivers, into computer. Observes patient through window of control room and on closed circuit TV screen to monitor patient safety and comfort. Views images of area being scanned on video display screen to ensure quality of pictures. Keys in data on keyboard of camera to photograph images. Alerts staff entering magnet room to danger of wearing or carrying metal around magnet. ● **GED:** R5, M4, L5 ● **SVP:** 2-4 yrs ● **Academic:** Ed=A, Eng=G ● **Work Field:** 201, 294 ● **MPSMS:** 925 ● **Aptitudes:** G2, V2, N3, S2, P3, Q2, K3, F3, M3, E5, C4 ● **Temperaments:** J, P, T ● **Physical:** Stg=M; Freq: R, H, I, G, N, A Occas: E, T, X ● **Work Env:** Noise=Q; ● **Salary:** 2 ● **Outlook:** 4

GOE: 10.02.03
Specialized Teaching

EVALUATOR (education) ● DOT #094.267-010 ● OES: 31311 ● Assesses type and degree of disability of handicapped children to aid in determining special programs and services required to meet educational needs: Reviews referrals of children having or suspected of having learning disabilities, mental retardation, behaviorial disorders, or physical handicaps to determine evaluation procedure. Confers with school or other personnel and scrutinizes records to obtain additional information on nature and severity of disability. Observes student behavior and rates strength and weakness of factors such as rapport, motivation, cooperativeness, aggression, attention span, and task completion. Selects, administers, and scores variety of preliminary tests to measure individual's aptitudes, educational achievements, perceptual motor skills, vision, and hearing. Reports findings for staff consideration in placement of children in educational programs. May test preschool children to detect learning handicaps and recommend followup activities, consultation, or services. May administer work related tests and review records and other data to assess student vocational interests and abilities. May specialize in evaluating student readiness to transfer from special classes to regular classroom, and in providing supportive services to regular classroom teacher and be designated Mainstreaming Facilitator (education). ● **GED:** R5, M4, L5 ● **SVP:** 2-4 yrs ● **Aca-**

demic: Ed=B, Eng=G ● **Work Field:** 271, 296 ● **MPSMS:** 931 ● **Aptitudes:** G2, V2, N3, S3, P3, Q2, K4, F4, M4, E5, C5 ● **Temperaments:** I, J, P ● **Physical:** Stg=L; Freq: R, H, I, T, G, N ● **Work Env:** Noise=N; ● **Salary:** 2 ● **Outlook:** 3

SUPERVISOR, SPECIAL EDUCATION (education) ● DOT #094.167-010 ● OES: 31398 ● Directs and coordinates activities of teachers and other staff providing home or school instruction, evaluation services, job placement, or other special education services to physically, mentally, emotionally, or neurologically handicapped children: Reviews referrals and diagnoses and participates in conferences with administrators, staff, parents, children, and other concerned parties to formulate recommendations for student placement and provision of services. Monitors staff activities and gives technical assistance in areas, such as assessment, curriculum development, use of materials and equipment, and management of student behavior. Plans and conducts in-service training. Interviews applicants, recommends hirings, and evaluates staff performance. May write grant proposals. May assist program administrators in preparation of budget and development of program policy and goals. May address public to elicit support and explain program objectives. ● **GED:** R5, M4, L5 ● **SVP:** 4-10 yrs ● **Academic:** Ed=M, Eng=G ● **Work Field:** 296, 295 ● **MPSMS:** 931 ● **Aptitudes:** G2, V2, N3, S4, P4, Q2, K4, F4, M4, E5, C5 ● **Temperaments:** D, I, J, P ● **Physical:** Stg=L; Freq: T, G, N Occas: R, H ● **Work Env:** Noise=N; ● **Salary:** 5 ● **Outlook:** 2

TEACHER, EMOTIONALLY IMPAIRED (education) ● DOT #094.227-010 ● OES: 31311 ● Teaches elementary and secondary school subjects to students with emotional impairments in schools, institutions, or other specialized facilities: Plans curriculum and prepares lessons and other instructional materials to meet individual needs of students, considering such factors as physical, emotional, and educational levels of development. Confers with parents, administrators, testing specialists, social workers, and others to develop individual educational plan for student. Instructs students in academic subjects and social interaction skills. Observes students for signs of disruptive behavior, such as violence, verbal outbursts, and episodes of destructiveness. Teaches socially acceptable behavior employing techniques such as behavior modification and positive reinforcement. Confers with other staff members to plan programs designed to promote educational, physical, and social development of students. May be required to have certification from local, state, and federal government. ● **GED:** R5, M4, L5 ● **SVP:** 2-4 yrs ● **Academic:** Ed=B, Eng=G ● **Work Field:** 296 ● **MPSMS:** 931 ● **Aptitudes:** G2, V2, N3, S4, P4, Q2, K4, F4, M4, E5, C5 ● **Temperaments:** D, I, J, P ● **Physical:** Stg=L; Freq: H, I, T, G Occas: R, N ● **Work Env:** Noise=N; ● **Salary:** 4 ● **Outlook:** 3

TEACHER, HEARING IMPAIRED (education) ● DOT #094.224-010 ● OES: 31311 ● Teaches elementary and secondary school subjects to hearing impaired students, using various methods of communication to receive and convey language: Plans curriculum and prepares lessons and other instructional materials according to grade level of students, utilizing visual media, such as computer, films, television, and charts. Confers with committee of parents, administrators, testing specialists, social worker, and others to develop individual educational program. Instructs students in academic subjects. Instructs students in various forms of communication, such as gestures, sign language, finger spelling, and speech cues. Encourages students to participate in verbal communication classroom learning experiences to ensure their comprehension of subject matter, development of social skills, and ability to communicate in situations encountered in daily living. Tests students' hearing aids to ensure hearing aids are functioning. May attend and interpret lectures and instructions for students enrolled in regular classes. May teach parents how to participate in and enhance students' learning experiences. May teach students to use computer. May specialize in teaching lip reading and be designated Teacher, Lip Reading (education). May be required to have certification from state. ● **GED:** R5, M4, L5 ● **SVP:** 2-4 yrs ● **Academic:** Ed=B, Eng=S ● **Work Field:** 296 ● **MPSMS:** 931 ● **Aptitudes:** G2, V2, N3, S4, P4, Q2, K3, F4, M4, E5, C5 ● **Temperaments:** D, I, J, P ● **Physical:** Stg=L; Freq: I, T, G Occas: R, H, E, N ● **Work Env:** Noise=N; ● **Salary:** 4 ● **Outlook:** 3

TEACHER, HOME THERAPY (social ser.) ● DOT #195.227-018 ● OES: 31311 ● Alternate titles: CHILD DEVELOPMENT SPECIALIST; DEVELOPMENT DISABILITY SPECIALIST; INFANT EDU-

CATOR; PARENT TRAINER. Instructs parent of mentally- and physically-handicapped children in therapy techniques and behavior modification: Observes and plays with child and confers with child's parents and other professionals periodically to obtain information relating to child's mental and physical development. Evaluates child's responses to determine levels of child's physical and mental development. Determines parent's ability to comprehend and apply therapeutic and behavior modification techniques and parent's social and emotional needs to formulate teaching plan. Develops individual teaching plan covering self-help, motor, social, cognitive, and language skills development for parents to implement in home. Instructs parents individually or in groups in behavior modification, physical development, language development, and conceptual learning exercises and activities. Revises teaching plan to correspond with child's rate of development. Counsels parents and organizes groups of parents in similar situations to provide social and emotional support for parents. Refers parents and child to social service agencies and facilities for additional services and financial assistance. Consults and coordinates plans with other professionals. Teaches preschool subjects, such as limited vocabulary sign language and color recognition, to children capable of learning such subjects. ● **GED:** R5, M3, L5 ● **SVP:** 2-4 yrs ● **Academic:** Ed=B, Eng=S ● **Work Field:** 296 ● **MPSMS:** 941, 939 ● **Aptitudes:** G2, V2, N3, S4, P4, Q3, K3, F3, M3, E5, C4 ● **Temperaments:** D, I, J, P, V ● **Physical:** Stg=L; Freq: R, H, I, T, G, N Occas: S, K, X ● **Work Env:** Noise=N; ● **Salary:** 4 ● **Outlook:** 3

TEACHER, KINDERGARTEN (education) ● DOT #092.227-014 ● OES: 31302 ● Alternate titles: INSTRUCTOR, KINDERGARTEN. Teaches elemental natural and social science, personal hygiene, music, art, and literature to children from 4 to 6 years old, to promote their physical, mental, and social development: Supervises activities, such as field visits, group discussions, and dramatic play acting, to stimulate students' interest in and broaden understanding of their physical and social environment. Fosters cooperative social behavior through games and group projects to assist children in forming satisfying relationships with other children and adults. Encourages students in singing, dancing, rhythmic activities, and in use of art materials, to promote self-expression and appreciation of esthetic experience. Instructs children in practices of personal cleanliness and self care. Alternates periods of strenuous activity with periods of rest or light activity to avoid overstimulation and fatigue. Observes children to detect signs of ill health or emotional disturbance, and to evaluate progress. Discusses students' problems and progress with parents. ● **GED:** R5, M2, L4 ● **SVP:** 2-4 yrs ● **Academic:** Ed=B, Eng=G ● **Work Field:** 296 ● **MPSMS:** 931 ● **Aptitudes:** G2, V2, N4, S4, P4, Q3, K3, F3, M3, E3, C3 ● **Temperaments:** D, P, V ● **Physical:** Stg=L; Freq: R, H, I, T, G, N Occas: S, O, E, X ● **Work Env:** Noise=L; Occas: W ● **Salary:** 1 ● **Outlook:** 4

TEACHER, LEARNING DISABLED (education) ● DOT #094.227-030 ● OES: 31311 ● Teaches elementary and secondary school subjects in schools, institutions, or other specialized facilities to students with neurological problems in learning: Plans curriculum and prepares lessons and other instructional materials to meet individual need of students, considering state and school requirements, physical, emotional, and educational levels of development. Confers with parents, administrators, testing specialists, social worker, and others to develop individual educational program for student. Instructs students in all academic subjects. Creates learning materials geared to each student's ability and interest. Instructs students, using special educational strategies and techniques, to improve sensory-motor and perceptual-motor development, perception, memory, language, cognition, and social and emotional development. Works with students to increase motivation, provide consistent reinforcement to learning, continuous assessment of level of functioning, and continuous feedback to student for all learning activities. Works with parents to accept and develop skills in dealing with student's learning impairment. May work as consultant, teach in self-contained classroom, or teach in resource room. May be required to hold certification from state. ● **GED:** R5, M4, L5 ● **SVP:** 2-4 yrs ● **Academic:** Ed=B, Eng=G ● **Work Field:** 296 ● **MPSMS:** 931 ● **Aptitudes:** G2, V2, N4, S4, P4, Q3, K4, F4, M4, E5, C5 ● **Temperaments:** D, I, J, P ● **Physical:** Stg=L; Freq: R, H, I, T, G Occas: N, F, V ● **Work Env:** Noise=N; ● **Salary:** 4 ● **Outlook:** 3

TEACHER, MENTALLY IMPAIRED (education) ● DOT #094.227-022 ● OES: 31311 ● Teaches basic academic and living skills to mentally impaired students in schools and other institutions: Plans curriculum and prepares lessons and other instructional materials according to achievement levels of students. Confers with parents, administrators, testing specialists, social workers, and others to develop individual educational program for students who are at different learning ability levels, including educable, trainable, and severely impaired. Instructs students in academic subjects, utilizing various teaching techniques, such as phonetics, multisensory learning, and repetition to reinforce learning. Instructs students in daily living skills required for independent maintenance and economic self-sufficiency, such as hygiene, safety, and food preparation. Observes, evaluates, and prepares reports on progress of students. Meets with parents to provide support and guidance in using community resources. May administer and interpret results of ability and achievement tests. May be required to hold state certification. ● **GED:** R5, M4, L5 ● **SVP:** 2-4 yrs ● **Academic:** Ed=B, Eng=S ● **Work Field:** 296 ● **MPSMS:** 931 ● **Aptitudes:** G2, V2, N3, S4, P4, Q3, K4, F4, M4, E5, C5 ● **Temperaments:** D, I, J, P ● **Physical:** Stg=L; Freq: H, T, G Occas: R, I, N, F, V ● **Work Env:** Noise=N; ● **Salary:** 4 ● **Outlook:** 3

TEACHER, PRESCHOOL (education) ● DOT #092.227-018 ● OES: 31302 ● Instructs children in activities designed to promote social, physical, and intellectual growth needed for primary school in preschool, day care center, or other child development facility. Plans individual and group activities to stimulate growth in language, social, and motor skills, such as learning to listen to instructions, playing with others, and using play equipment. May be required to have certification from state. May be designated Teacher, Child Development Center (education); Teacher, Day Care Center (education); Teacher, Early Childhood Development (education); Teacher, Nursery School (education). ● **GED:** R4, M2, L3 ● **SVP:** 2-4 yrs ● **Academic:** Ed=A, Eng=S ● **Work Field:** 296 ● **MPSMS:** 931 ● **Aptitudes:** G2, V2, N2, S3, P4, Q3, K4, F4, M3, E4, C4 ● **Temperaments:** D, P ● **Physical:** Stg=L; Freq: R, H, T, G Occas: S, K, O, I, N, F, X ● **Work Env:** Noise=N; ● **Salary:** 1 ● **Outlook:** 3

TEACHER, PHYSICALLY IMPAIRED (education) ● DOT #094.224-014 ● OES: 31311 ● Teaches elementary and secondary school subjects to physically impaired students, adapting teaching techniques and methods of instruction to meet individual needs of students in schools, hospitals, and students' homes: Plans curriculum and prepares lessons and other materials, considering factors, such as individual needs, abilities, learning levels, and physical limitations of students. Confers with parents, administrators, testing specialists, social worker, and others to develop educational program for student. Instructs students with observable orthopedic impairments, as well as those with internal impairment, such as heart condition. Arranges and adjusts tools, work aids, and equipment utilized by students in classroom, such as specially equipped worktables, computers, typewriters, and mechanized page turners. Devises special teaching tools, techniques, and equipment. Instructs students in academic subjects and other activities designed to provide learning experience. Confers with other members of staff to develop programs to maximize students' potentials. May assist members of medical staff in rehabilitation programs for students. May be required to have certification from state. ● **GED:** R5, M4, L5 ● **SVP:** 2-4 yrs ● **Academic:** Ed=B, Eng=S ● **Work Field:** 296 ● **MPSMS:** 931 ● **Aptitudes:** G2, V2, N3, S4, P3, Q2, K4, F4, M4, E5, C5 ● **Temperaments:** D, I, J, P, V ● **Physical:** Stg=L; Freq: R, H, T, G Occas: S, K, O, I, N ● **Work Env:** Noise=N; ● **Salary:** 4 ● **Outlook:** 3

TEACHER, VISUALLY IMPAIRED (education) ● DOT #094.224-018 ● OES: 31311 ● Teaches elementary and secondary school subjects and daily living skills to visually impaired students: Instructs students in reading and writing, using magnification equipment and large print material or braille system. Confers with parents, administrator, testing specialists, social worker, and others to develop individual educational program for students. Plans curriculum and prepares lessons and other instructional materials, according to grade level of students. Transcribes lessons and other materials into braille for blind students or large print for low vision students. Reviews and corrects completed assignments, using such aids as braille writer, slate and stylus, or computer. Arranges for and conducts field trips designed to promote experiential learning. Instructs students in academic subject areas and daily living skills, such as hygiene, safety, and food preparation. Encourages students to participate in verbal and sensory classroom learning experiences to ensure their comprehension of subject matter, development of social skills, and ability to identify objects encountered in daily living. Meets with parents to discuss how parents can encourage student's independence and well-being and to provide guidance in using community resources. May counsel students. May teach braille to individuals with sight and be designated Instructor, Braille (education). ● **GED:** R5, M4, L5 ● **SVP:** 2-4 yrs ● **Academic:** Ed=B, Eng=G ● **Work Field:** 296 ● **MPSMS:** 931 ● **Aptitudes:** G2, V2, N3, S4, P3, Q2, K3, F3, M4, E5, C5 ● **Temperaments:** D, I, J, P ● **Physical:** Stg=L; Freq: R, H, I, E, T, G, N Occas: S, K, O, V ● **Work Env:** Noise=N; ● **Salary:** 4 ● **Outlook:** 3

TEACHER, VOCATIONAL TRAINING (education) ● DOT #094.227-026 ● OES: 31311 ● Teaches vocational skills to handicapped students: Confers with students, parents, school personnel, and other individuals to plan vocational training that meets needs, interests, and abilities of students. Instructs students in areas such as personal-social skills and work-related attitudes and behaviors. Develops work opportunities that allow students to experience success in performing tasks of increasing difficulty and that teach work values, such as self-improvement, independence, dependability, productivity, and pride of workmanship. Conducts field trips to enable students to learn about job activities and to explore work environments. May teach academic skills to students. May instruct students in one or more vocational skills, such as woodworking, building maintenance, cosmetology, food preparation, gardening, sewing, or nurse aiding. ● **GED:** R5, M3, L5 ● **SVP:** 2-4 yrs ● **Academic:** Ed=A, Eng=S ● **Work Field:** 296 ● **MPSMS:** 931 ● **Aptitudes:** G2, V2, N3, S4, P4, Q3, K4, F4, M4, E5, C5 ● **Temperaments:** D, J, P ● **Physical:** Stg=L; Freq: R, H, T, G, N Occas: S, O, I ● **Work Env:** Noise=N; ● **Salary:** 4 ● **Outlook:** 4

WORK-STUDY COORDINATOR, SPECIAL EDUCATION (education) ● DOT #094.107-010 ● OES: 31311 ● Plans and conducts special education work and study program for in-school youth: Establishes contacts with employers and employment agencies and surveys newspapers and other sources to locate work opportunities for students. Confers with potential employers to communicate objectives of work study program and to solicit cooperation in adapting work situations to special needs of students. Evaluates and selects program participants according to specified criteria and counsels and instructs selected students in matters such as vocational choices, job readiness, and job retention skills and behaviors. Assists students in applying for jobs and accompanies students to employment interviews. Confers with employer and visits work site to monitor progress of student and to determine support needed to meet employer requirements and fulfill program goals. Counsels students to foster development of satisfactory job performance. Confers with school and community personnel to impart information about program and to coordinate program functions with related activities. ● **GED:** R5, M3, L5 ● **SVP:** 2-4 yrs ● **Academic:** Ed=A, Eng=G ● **Work Field:** 296, 298 ● **MPSMS:** 931 ● **Aptitudes:** G2, V2, N4, S4, P4, Q3, K4, F4, M4, E5, C5 ● **Temperaments:** D, I, J, P ● **Physical:** Stg=L; Freq: T, G, N Occas: R, H, I ● **Work Env:** Noise=N; ● **Salary:** 3 ● **Outlook:** 3

Humanitarian

Child and Adult Care

10

10.03

Workers in this group are concerned with the physical needs and the welfare of others. They assist professionals in treating the sick or injured. They care for the elderly, the very young, or the handicapped. Frequently these workers help people do the things they cannot do for themselves. Jobs are found in hospitals, clinics, day care centers, nurseries, schools, private homes, and centers for helping the handicapped.

✓ What kind of work would you do?

Your work activities would depend upon your specific job. For example, you might:

- help elderly persons bathe, feed, or dress themselves.
- collect medical data, using electronic equipment such as an electrocardiograph.
- assist physical therapists in providing treatment to patients.
- give emergency first aid in a commercial or industrial setting.
- ride in an ambulance and assist the driver in giving first aid and transporting patients.
- entertain and supervise children in a nursery.
- assist a dentist by recording information about patients and doing other simple office and clinical tasks.

✓ What skills and abilities do you need for this kind of work?

To do this kind of work, you must be able to:

- want to help people.
- deal with the young, elderly, sick, or handicapped.
- understand and follow instructions exactly in caring for those who depend on you.
- use arms, eyes, hands, and fingers with skill.
- talk and relate to sick or handicapped people.

The above statements may not apply to every job in this group.

✓ How do you know if you would like or could learn to do this kind of work?

The following questions may give you clues about yourself as you consider this group of jobs.

- Have you cared for children or sick people? Are you patient with and able to relate to those who cannot take care of themselves?
- Have you had courses in first aid? Can you react quickly and calmly in an emergency?
- Have you been a volunteer worker in a hospital? Do you like this kind of work?
- Have you participated in community services or charity work? Are you concerned for the welfare of others?

■ Did you serve in the medical corps in the armed services?

✓ *How can you prepare for and enter this kind of work?*

Occupations in this group usually require education and/or training extending from thirty days to over two years, depending upon the specific kind of work. Employers usually require an applicant to have a high school education or its equal. Hospitals, community agencies, colleges, and public vocational schools offer training courses for many of these jobs. The average program requires about one year to complete. Some jobs in this group require state licenses.

Hospitals and clinics provide on-the-job training for many of these jobs. This training usually includes classroom instruction, demonstration of skills and techniques and practice. The length of training depends upon the job.

Interest and experience in homemaking, child care, or adult care provide good background for working with the aged, blind, or the very young.

✓ *What else should you consider about these jobs?*

Some of these jobs involve close physical contact with people. Workers may have to help lift, bathe, groom, or feed people. Working hours will vary, since health care is given 24 hours a day. The growing demand for health care gives workers in this group security.

The demand for both full- and part-time workers in this area is high. Qualified and experienced workers usually find the jobs that fit their needs.

Personal satisfaction is often received by helping others.

If you think you would like to do this kind of work, look at the job titles listed on the following pages.

GOE: 10.03.01
Data Collection

AUDIOMETRIST (profess. & kin.) ● DOT #078.362-010 ● OES: 32998 ● Alternate titles: AUDIOMETRIC TECHNICIAN; HEARING-TEST TECHNICIAN. Administers audiometric screening and threshold tests, generally pure-tone air conduction, to individuals or groups, under supervision of AUDIOLOGIST (medical ser.) or OTOLARYNGOLOGIST (medical ser.). Fits earphones on subject and provides instruction on procedures to be followed. Adjusts audiometer to control sound emitted and records subjects' responses. Refers individuals to AUDIOLOGIST (medical ser.) for interpretation of test results and need for more definitive hearing examination or to physician for medical examination. ● **GED:** R4, M3, L4 ● **SVP:** 1-2 yrs ● **Academic:** Ed=A, Eng=S ● **Work Field:** 211 ● **MPSMS:** 929 ● **Aptitudes:** G2, V3, N3, S4, P3, Q2, K3, F3, M3, E4, C4 ● **Temperaments:** J, P ● **Physical:** Stg=L; Freq: R, T, G, N Occas: H, I, A ● **Work Env:** Noise=Q; ● **Salary:** 4 ● **Outlook:** 3

CARDIAC MONITOR TECHNICIAN (medical ser.) ● DOT #078.367-010 ● OES: 32998 ● Alternate titles: TELEMETRY TECHNICIAN. Monitors heart rhythm pattern of patients in special care unit of hospital to detect abnormal pattern variances, using telemetry equipment: Reviews patient information to determine normal heart rhythm pattern, current pattern, and prior variances. Observes screen of cardiac monitor and listens for alarm to identify abnormal variation in heart rhythm. Informs supervisor or NURSE, GENERAL DUTY (medical ser.) 075.364-010 of variances to initiate examination of patient. Measures length and height of patient's heart rhythm pattern on graphic tape readout, using calipers, and posts information on patient records. Answers calls for assistance from patients and inquiries concerning patients from medical staff, using intercom and call director. May perform duties as described under ELECTROCARDIOGRAPH TECHNICIAN (medical ser.) 078.362-018. ● **GED:** R3, M2, L2 ● **SVP:** 6 mos-1 yr ● **Academic:** Ed=H, Eng=S ● **Work Field:** 294 ● **MPSMS:** 925 ● **Aptitudes:** G3, V3, N4, S4, P4, Q3, K4, F4, M4, E5, C4 ● **Temperaments:** J, S ● **Physical:** Stg=S; Freq: T, G, N, A Occas: R, H, I, X ● **Work Env:** Noise=N; ● **Salary:** 4 ● **Outlook:** 3

CARDIOPULMONARY TECHNOLOGIST (medical ser.) ● DOT #078.362-030 ● OES: 32925 ● Alternate titles: CARDIOVASCULAR

TECHNOLOGIST. Performs diagnostic tests of cardiovascular and pulmonary systems of patients to aid physician in diagnosis and treatment of heart, lung, and blood vessel disorders: Prepares patient for test and explains procedures to obtain cooperation and reassure patient. Conducts electrocardiogram, phonocardiogram, echocardiogram, stress testing, and other tests to aid in diagnosis of cardiovascular system, using variety of specialized electronic test equipment, recording devices, and laboratory instruments. Conducts tests of pulmonary system to aid physician in diagnosis of pulmonary disorders, using spirometer and other respiratory testing equipment. Operates multichannel physiologic monitor, as part of cardiac catheterization team, to measure and record functions of cardiovascular and pulmonary systems of patient during cardiac catheterization. Alerts physician to instrument readings outside normal ranges during cardiac catheterization procedures. Provides test results to physician. ● **GED:** R4, M4, L4 ● **SVP:** 2-4 yrs ● **Academic:** Ed=H, Eng=S ● **Work Field:** 294 ● **MPSMS:** 925 ● **Aptitudes:** G3, V3, N3, S3, P2, Q2, K3, F3, M3, E5, C4 ● **Temperaments:** J, P, T ● **Physical:** Stg=L; Freq: R, H, I, N Occas: E, T, G, X ● **Work Env:** Noise=Q; Freq: R ● **Salary:** 5 ● **Outlook:** 3

ECHOCARDIOGRAPH TECHNICIAN (medical ser.) ● DOT #078.364-014 ● OES: 32925 ● Alternate titles: DIAGNOSTIC CARDIAC SONOGRAPHER. Produces two-dimensional ultrasonic recordings and Doppler flow analyses of heart and related structures, using ultrasound equipment, for use by physician in diagnosis of heart disease and study of heart: Explains procedures to patient to obtain cooperation and reduce anxieties of patient. Attaches electrodes to patient's chest to monitor heart rhythm and connects electrodes to electrode leads of ultrasound equipment. Adjusts equipment controls according to physician's orders and areas of heart to be examined. Keys patient information into computer keyboard on equipment to record information on video cassette and strip printout of test. Starts ultrasound equipment that produces images of real time tomographic cardiac anatomy, and adjusts equipment to obtain quality images. Moves transducer, by hand, over patient's heart areas, observes ultrasound display screen, and listens to Doppler signals to acquire data for measurement of blood flow velocities. Prints pictures of graphic analysis recordings and removes video cassette for permanent record of internal examination. Measures heart wall thicknesses and chamber sizes recorded on strip printout, using calipers and ruler, or keys commands into computer to measure thicknesses and chamber sizes of heart on video tape, and compares measurement to standard norms to identify abnormalities in heart. Measures blood flow velocities and calculates data, such as cardiac physiology and valve areas for evaluation of cardiac function by physician. Reviews test results with interpreting physician. ● **GED:** R4, M3, L4 ● **SVP:** 2-4 yrs ● **Academic:** Ed=A, Eng=G ● **Work Field:** 294 ● **MPSMS:** 925 ● **Aptitudes:** G3, V3, N3, S2, P2, Q3, K2, F3, M3, E4, C4 ● **Temperaments:** J, P, T ● **Physical:** Stg=L; Const: N, A Freq: R, H, G Occas: I, E, T, X ● **Work Env:** Noise=Q; ● **Salary:** 5 ● **Outlook:** 4

ELECTROCARDIOGRAPH TECHNICIAN (medical ser.) ● DOT #078.362-018 ● OES: 32926 ● Alternate titles: ECG TECHNICIAN; EKG TECHNICIAN. Produces recordings of electromotive variations in patient's heart muscle, using electrocardiograph (ECG), to provide data for diagnosis of heart ailments: Attaches electrodes to chest, arms, and legs of patient. Connects electrode leads to electrocardiograph and starts machine. Moves electrodes along specified area of chest to produce electrocardiogram that records electromotive variations occurring in different areas of heart muscle. Monitors electrocardiogram for abnormal patterns. Keys information into machine or marks tracing to indicate positions of chest electrodes. Replenishes supply of paper and ink in machine and reports malfunctions. Edits and forwards final test results to attending phsyician for analysis and interpretation. May attach electrodes of Holter monitor (electrocardiograph) to patient to record data over extended period of time. ● **GED:** R3, M3, L3 ● **SVP:** 3-6 mos ● **Academic:** Ed=A, Eng=S ● **Work Field:** 294 ● **MPSMS:** 925 ● **Aptitudes:** G3, V3, N3, S3, P3, Q3, K3, F3, M3, E4, C5 ● **Temperaments:** J, P, T ● **Physical:** Stg=L; Freq: R, H, I, T, G, N, A Occas: S, O, E ● **Work Env:** Noise=Q ● **Salary:** 3 ● **Outlook:** 4

ELECTROENCEPHALOGRAPHIC TECHNOLOGIST (medical ser.) ● DOT #078.362-022 ● OES: 32923 ● Alternate titles: EEG TECHNOLOGIST. Measures electrical activity of brain waves, using electroencephalograph (EEG) instrument, and conducts evoked potential response tests for use in diagnosis of brain and nervous system disorders: Measures patient's head and other body parts, using tape measure, and marks points where electrodes are to be placed. Attaches electrodes to predetermined locations, and verifies functioning of electrodes and recording instrument. Operates recording instruments (EEG and evoked potentials) and supplemental equipment and chooses settings for optimal viewing of nervous system. Records montage (electrode combination) and instrument settings, and observes and notes patient's behavior during test. Conducts visual, auditory, and somatosensory evoked potential response tests to measure latency of response to stimuli. Writes technical reports summarizing test results to assist physician in diagnosis of brain disorders. May perform other physiological tests, such as electrocardiogram, electrooculogram, and ambulatory electroencephalogram. May perform video monitoring of patient's actions during test. May monitor patient during surgery, using EEG or evoked potential instrument. May supervise other technologists and be known as Chief Electroencephalographic Technologist (medical ser.). ● **GED:** R4, M4, L4 ● **SVP:** 1-2 yrs ● **Academic:** Ed=A, Eng=S ● **Work Field:** 294 ● **MPSMS:** 925 ● **Aptitudes:** G3, V3, N3, S3, P3, Q3, K3, F3, M4, E4, C4 ● **Temperaments:** J, P, T ● **Physical:** Stg=M; Freq: R, H, I, T, G, N, A Occas: S, K, O, W, E, X ● **Work Env:** Noise=Q; ● **Salary:** 4 ● **Outlook:** 3

ELECTROMYOGRAPHIC TECHNICIAN (medical ser.) ● DOT #078.362-038 ● OES: 32998 ● Alternate titles: EMG TECHNICIAN. Measures electrical activity in peripheral nerves, using electromyograph (EMG) instrument, for use by physician in diagnosing neuromuscular disorders: Explains procedures to patient to obtain cooperation and relieve anxieties during test. Rubs electrode paste on patient's skin to ensure contact of electrodes. Attaches surface recording electrodes to extremity in which activity is being measured to detect electrical impulse. Attaches electrodes to electrode cables or leads connected to EMG instrument and selects nerve conduction mode on EMG. Operates EMG instrument to record electrical activity in peripheral nerves. Presses button on manually held surface stimulator electrode to deliver pulse and send electrical charge along peripheral nerve. Monitors response on oscilloscope and presses button to record nerve conduction velocity. Measures and records time and distance between stimulus and response, manually or using computer, and calculates velocity of electrical impulse in peripheral nerve. Removes electrodes from patient upon conclusion of test and cleans electrode paste from skin, using alcohol and cotton. ● **GED:** R4, M4, L4 ● **SVP:** 6 mos-1 yr ● **Academic:** Ed=A, Eng=G ● **Work Field:** 294 ● **MPSMS:** 925 ● **Aptitudes:** G3, V3, N3, S3, P3, Q3, K3, F3, M3, E5, C4 ● **Tempera-**

ments: J, P, T ● **Physical:** Stg=L; Const: N Freq: R, H, I, T, G, A Occas: S, E, X ● **Work Env:** Noise=Q; ● **Salary:** 3 ● **Outlook:** 3

HOLTER SCANNING TECHNICIAN (medical ser.) ● DOT #078.264-010 ● OES: 32998 ● Alternate titles: HOLTER TECHNICIAN. Analyzes data from cardiac-function monitoring device (Holter monitor) worn by patient for use in diagnosis of cardiovascular disorders: Places magnetic tape or cassette from Holter monitor worn by patient in scanner and starts scanner that produces audio and visual representation of heart activity. Adjusts scanner controls that regulate taped sounds associated with heart activity and focus video representation of sounds on scanner screen. Observes scanner screen to identify irregularities in patient cardiac patterns, utilizing knowledge of regular and irregular cardiac-function patterns, or verifies data provided by computer program that automatically scans, analyzes, identifies, and prints irregular heart patterns. Prints sections of abnormal heart patterns or full disclosure tape for physician. Analyzes information in patient diary to identify incidents that correspond to heart pattern irregularities detected on heart monitor. Records findings on report form and forwards tapes, form, patient diary, and printouts of heart patterns to interpreting physician. May attach electrodes to patient's chest and connect electrodes to heart monitor, following standard procedure. May measure distances between peaks and valleys of heart activity patterns, using calipers, to obtain data for further analysis. May perform other diagnostic procedures, such as electrocardiography and stress testing, to aid in medical evaluation of patient. ● **GED:** R3, M3, L3 ● **SVP:** 1-2 yrs ● **Academic:** Ed=H, Eng=S ● **Work Field:** 294 ● **MPSMS:** 925 ● **Aptitudes:** G3, V3, N3, S4, P3, Q3, K3, F3, M4, E4, C5 ● **Temperaments:** J, T ● **Physical:** Stg=S; Const: N Freq: R, H, I, G, A Occas: E, T ● **Work Env:** Noise=Q; ● **Salary:** 4 ● **Outlook:** 4

OPHTHALMIC TECHNICIAN (medical ser.) ● DOT #078.361-038 ● OES: 32998 ● Tests and measures eye function to assist OPHTHALMOLOGIST (medical ser.) 070.101-058 to diagnose and treat eye disorders and disease: Tests patient's far acuity, near acuity, peripheral vision, depth perception, and color perception to assist OPHTHALMOLOGIST (medical ser.) to diagnose and treat eye disorders and disease. Examines eye, using slit lamp, for abnormalities of cornea, and anterior and posterior chambers. Applies drops to anesthetize, dilate, or medicate eyes. Measures intraocular pressure of eyes (glaucoma test). Tests patient's field of vision, including central and peripheral vision, for defects, and charts test results on graph paper. Measures axial length of eye, using ultrasound equipment. Performs other tests and measurements as requested by physician. Gives instructions to patients concerning eye care. May supervise other technicians and be known as Chief Ophthalmic Technician (medical ser.). ● **GED:** R4, M4, L4 ● **SVP:** 1-2 yrs ● **Academic:** Ed=A, Eng=G ● **Work Field:** 294 ● **MPSMS:** 925 ● **Aptitudes:** G3, V3, N3, S3, P2, Q3, K3, F3, M3, E4, C4 ● **Temperaments:** P, T ● **Physical:** Stg=L; Const: N Freq: H, I, T, G, A Occas: R, E, F, X ● **Work Env:** Noise=Q; ● **Salary:** 4 ● **Outlook:** 3

POLYSOMNOGRAPHIC TECHNICIAN (medical ser.) ● DOT #078.362-042 ● OES: 32998 ● Alternate titles: POLYSOMNOGRAPHIC TECHNOLOGIST. Measures electrical activity of patient's brain waves and other physiological variables, using polysomnograph, to aid physician in diagnosis and treatment of sleep disorders: Applies surface electrodes to patient's head, using adhesive paste or tape, to obtain electroencephalogram (EEG) measurement and applies other combinations of sensors and electrodes to patient to obtain measurements such as electromyogram (EMG), electrooculogram (EOG), electrocardiogram (EKG), air flow respiratory effort, and oxygen saturation, as requested by physician and following established procedures. Operates closed circuit television camera to observe patient during test and to record patient's sleep activities. Operates polysomnograph equipment to record electrical activity of brain waves and other physiological variables and records notes on graph to eliminate from consideration physiological measurements caused by such activities as patient opening eyes, turning head, or turning body. Studies polysomnogram to recognize arrhythmias and abnormal respiratory patterns and calls physician or other emergency personnel if needed. Measures durations of brain waves recorded on polysomnograms, using millimeter ruler. Studies characteristics of completed polysomnogram tracings and summarizes data showing stages of sleep, abnormal breathing events, periodic leg movements, arrhythmias, and other information, applying knowledge of polysomnograph testing principles. Enters data into computer and writes report incorporating patient's medical history, completed patient questionnaires, previous and current polysomnogram information, presence and type of abnormality, and other information for analysis by physician or other health professional. May apply electrodes to patient's head, using pins. May supervise and coordinate activities of other technicians and be known as Chief Polysomnographic Technician (medical ser.). ● **GED:** R4, M4, L4 ● **SVP:** 3-6 mos ● **Academic:** Ed=A, Eng=G ● **Work Field:** 294 ● **MPSMS:** 925 ● **Aptitudes:** G3, V3, N3, S3, P2, Q3, K3, F3, M3, E5, C4 ● **Temperaments:** J, P, T ● **Physical:** Stg=M; Const: N Freq: H, I, G, A Occas: S, R, E, T, X ● **Work Env:** Noise=Q; ● **Salary:** 4 ● **Outlook:** 3

PULMONARY-FUNCTION TECHNICIAN (medical ser.) ● DOT #078.262-010 ● OES: 32998 ● Alternate titles: PULMONARY-FUNCTION TECHNOLOGIST. Performs pulmonary-function, lung-capacity, diffusion capacity, and blood-and-oxygen tests to gather data for use by physician in diagnosis and treatment of pulmonary disorders: Confers with patient in treatment room to explain test procedures. Explains specified methods of breathing to patient and conducts pulmonary-function tests, such as helium dilution and pulmonary mechanics (flow of air rate in lungs), arterial blood gas analyses, and lung-capacity tests, such as vital capacity and maximum breathing capacity tests, using spirometer or other equipment. Measures expired air, using various analyzers. Observes and records readings on metering devices of analysis equipment, and conveys findings of tests and analyses to physician for interpretation. May perform blood analysis tests to measure such factors as oxygen and carbon dioxide tensions, hemoglobin saturation and levels, and pH of blood, using blood gas analyzer. May measure sweat chloride to test for cystic fibrosis, using computerized analyzer. May assist physician in special procedures such as bronchoscopy. ● **GED:** R4, M4, L4 ● **SVP:** 1-2 yrs ● **Academic:** Ed=A, Eng=S ● **Work Field:** 294 ● **MPSMS:** 925 ● **Aptitudes:** G3, V3, N3, S3, P3, Q3, K4, F3, M3, E5, C4 ● **Temperaments:** J, P, T ● **Physical:** Stg=L; Const: T, G, N Freq: R, H, I, A Occas: E, X ● **Work Env:** Noise=Q; Const: O ● **Salary:** 4 ● **Outlook:** 4

STRESS TEST TECHNICIAN (medical ser.) ● DOT #078.362-062 ● OES: 32925 ● Alternate titles: STRESS TECHNICIAN. Produces recordings of electromotive variations in action of heart muscle, using electrocardiograph, while patient walks on treadmill, under direction of physician, to provide data for diagnosis of heart ailments: Attaches electrodes to patient's arms, legs, and chest area, according to specified pattern, and connects electrode leads to electrocardiograph, to obtain electrocardiogram. Explains testing procedures to patient and obtains consent form. Starts treadmill at speed directed by physician. Starts electrocardiograph and records data, such as angle and speed of treadmill, patient's indications of pain, and measurements of blood pressure. Informs physician of wave abnormalities on electrocardiogram. Stands alongside patient during test to lend support if necessary. Removes recorder strip printout from machine upon conclusion of test to obtain permanent record of test. Edits and mounts representative samples of tracings for patient's record, indicating time of test measurement and bodily factors that could have affected recording. May conduct electrocardiograph test of resting patient. ● **GED:** R4, M3, L3 ● **SVP:** 1-2 yrs ● **Academic:** Ed=A, Eng=G ● **Work Field:** 294 ● **MPSMS:** 925 ● **Aptitudes:** G3, V3, N3, S3, P3, Q3, K3, F3, M3, E4, C5 ● **Temperaments:** J, P, T ● **Physical:** Stg=L; Freq: H, I, T, G, N Occas: R, E, A ● **Work Env:** Noise=Q; ● **Salary:** 3 ● **Outlook:** 4

GOE: 10.03.02
Patient Care

AMBULANCE ATTENDANT (medical ser.) ● DOT #355.374-010 ● OES: 66023 ● Accompanies and assists AMBULANCE DRIVER (medical ser.) on calls: Assists in lifting patient onto wheeled cart or stretcher and into and out of ambulance. Renders first aid, such as bandaging, splinting, and administering oxygen. May be required to have Red Cross first-aid training certificate. ● **GED:** R3, M2, L3 ● **SVP:** 1-3 mos ● **Academic:** Ed=A, Eng=G ● **Work Field:** 294 ● **MPSMS:** 929 ● **Aptitudes:** G4, V4, N4, S4, P4, Q4, K3, F3, M3, E4, C4 ● **Temperaments:** J, P, S, V ● **Physical:** Stg=M; Freq: C, B, S, K, O, R, H Occas: I, T, G, N, X ● **Work Env:** Noise=Q; ● **Salary:** 2 ● **Outlook:** 3

BIRTH ATTENDANT (medical ser.) ● DOT #354.377-010 ● OES: 66008 ● Provides assistance to women during childbirth, in absence of medical practitioner. May function under supervision of local or state health department. ● **GED:** R3, M1, L2 ● **SVP:** 3-6 mos ● **Academic:** Ed=A, Eng=G ● **Work Field:** 294 ● **MPSMS:** 929 ● **Aptitudes:** G4, V4, N4, S3, P3, Q4, K3, F3, M3, E5, C5 ● **Temperaments:** J, P ● **Physical:** Stg=M; Freq: R, H, T, G Occas: I, E, N, F, X ● **Work Env:** Noise=Q; ● **Salary:** 4 ● **Outlook:** 3

CERTIFIED MEDICATION TECHNICIAN (medical ser.) ● DOT #355.374-014 ● OES: 66026 ● Administers prescribed medications to patients and maintains related medical records under supervision of NURSE, GENERAL DUTY (medical ser.) 075.364-010: Verifies identity of patient receiving medication and records name of drug, dosage, and time of administration on specified forms or records. Presents medication to patient and observes ingestion or other application, or administers medication, using specified procedures. Takes vital signs or observes patient to detect response to specified types of medications and prepares report or notifies designated personnel of unexpected reactions. Documents reasons prescribed drugs are not administered. Gives direct patient care, such as bathing, dressing, and feeding patients, and assisting in examinations and treatments [NURSE AIDE (medical ser.) 355.674-014]. May receive supply of ordered medications and apportion, mix, or assemble drugs for administration to patient. May record and restock medication inventories. ● **GED:** R3, M3, L3 ● **SVP:** 3-6 mos ● **Academic:** Ed=A, Eng=G ● **Work Field:** 294 ● **MPSMS:** 926 ● **Aptitudes:** G3, V3, N3, S3, P3, Q2, K2, F2, M3, E4, C4 ● **Temperaments:** J, P, T ● **Physical:** Stg=M; Freq: R, H, I, T, G, N Occas: S, E, D, X, V ● **Work Env:** Noise=N; ● **Salary:** 3 ● **Outlook:** 3

CHIROPRACTOR ASSISTANT (medical ser.) ● DOT #079.364-010 ● OES: 66005 ● Aids CHIROPRACTOR (medical ser.) during physical examination of patients, gives specified office treatments, and keeps patients' records: Writes history of patient's accident or illness, and shows patient to examining room. Aids CHIROPRACTOR (medical ser.) in lifting and turning patient under treatment. Gives physiotherapy treatments, such as diathermy, galvanics, or hydrotherapy, following directions of CHIROPRACTOR (medical ser.). Takes and records patient's temperature and blood pressure, assists in x-ray procedures, and gives first aid. Answers telephone, schedules appointments, records treatment information on patient's chart, and fills out insurance forms. Prepares and mails patient's bills. ● **GED:** R4, M3, L4 ● **SVP:** 1-2 yrs ● **Academic:** Ed=H, Eng=G ● **Work Field:** 294, 231 ● **MPSMS:** 923 ● **Aptitudes:** G3, V3, N4, S3, P3, Q3, K2, F3, M3, E5, C5 ● **Temperaments:** P, V ● **Physical:** Stg=M; Freq: R, H, I, T, G, N, A ● **Work Env:** Noise=N; ● **Salary:** 4 ● **Outlook:** 3

DENTAL ASSISTANT (medical ser.) ● DOT #079.361-018 ● OES: 66002 ● Assists dentist during examination and treatment of patients: Prepares patient, sterilizes and disinfects instruments, sets up instrument trays, prepares materials, and assists dentist during dental procedures. Takes and records medical and dental histories and vital signs of patient. Exposes dental diagnostic x rays. Makes preliminary impressions for study casts and occlusal registrations for mounting study casts. Pours, trims, and polishes study casts, fabricates custom impression trays from preliminary impressions, cleans and polishes removable appliances, and fabricates temporary restorations. Assists dentist in management of medical and dental emergencies. Instructs patients in oral hygiene and plaque control programs. Provides postoperative instructions prescribed by dentist. Records treatment information in patient records. Schedules appointments, prepares bills and receives payment for dental services, completes insurance forms, and maintains clerical records, manually or using computer. May clean teeth, using dental instruments. May apply protective coating of fluoride to teeth. ● **GED:** R4, M3, L4 ● **SVP:** 1-2 yrs ● **Academic:** Ed=A, Eng=S ● **Work Field:** 294 ● **MPSMS:** 926, 922 ● **Aptitudes:** G3, V3, N3, S4, P3, Q3, K4, F3, M3, E4, C4 ● **Temperaments:** P, T ● **Physical:** Stg=L; Freq: R, H, I, G, N Occas: S, E, T, D, A, X ● **Work Env:** Noise=Q; ● **Salary:** 2 ● **Outlook:** 3

EMERGENCY MEDICAL TECHNICIAN (medical ser.) ● DOT #079.374-010 ● OES: 32508 ● Administers first-aid treatment to and transports sick or injured persons to medical facility, working as member of emergency medical team: Responds to instructions from emergency medical dispatcher and drives specially equipped emergency vehicle to specified location. Monitors communication equipment to maintain contact with dispatcher. Removes or assists in removal of

420 *The Enhanced Guide for Occupational Exploration*

victims from scene of accident or catastrophe. Determines nature and extent of illness or injury, or magnitude of catastrophe, to establish first aid procedures to be followed or need for additional assistance, basing decisions on statements of persons involved, examination of victim or victims, and knowledge of emergency medical practice. Administers prescribed first-aid treatment at site of emergency, or in specially equipped vehicle, performing such activities as application of splints, administration of oxygen or intravenous injections, treatment of minor wounds or abrasions, or administration of artificial resuscitation. Communicates with professional medical personnel at emergency treatment facility to obtain instructions regarding further treatment and to arrange for reception of victims at treatment facility. Assists in removal of victims from vehicle and transfer of victims to treatment center. Assists treatment center admitting personnel to obtain and record information related to victims' vital statistics and circumstances of emergency. Maintains vehicles and medical and communication equipment and replenishes first-aid equipment and supplies. May assist in controlling crowds, protecting valuables, or performing other duties at scene of catastrophe. May assist professional medical personnel in emergency treatment administered at medical facility. ● **GED:** R4, M3, L4 ● **SVP:** 6 mos-1 yr ● **Academic:** Ed=A, Eng=G ● **Work Field:** 294, 013 ● **MPSMS:** 921, 929 ● **Aptitudes:** G3, V3, N3, S3, P2, Q3, K2, F2, M2, E3, C3 ● **Temperaments:** J, P, S ● **Physical:** Stg=M; Freq: R, H, I, T, G, N, X Occas: C, B, S, K, O, W, E, M, F, D, A, V ● **Work Env:** Noise=N; Freq: W ● **Salary:** 4 ● **Outlook:** 3

FIRST-AID ATTENDANT (any industry) ● DOT #354.677-010 ● OES: 66008 ● Alternate titles: NURSE, FIRST AID. Renders first aid and subsequent treatment to injured or ill employees at industrial plant, commercial establishment, mine, or construction site: Sterilizes, disinfects, anoints, and bandages minor cuts and burns. Applies artificial respiration or administers oxygen, in cases of suffocation and asphyxiation. Administers medications, such as aspirin or antiseptic solution, to relieve pain or prevent infection until patient can receive professional care, and gives prescribed medicines and treatments for illness. Changes beds, cleans equipment, and maintains infirmary for ward patients. Aids physician during emergency situations. Keeps personal and medical records of employees. ● **GED:** R3, M2, L3 ● **SVP:** 1-3 mos ● **Academic:** Ed=A, Eng=G ● **Work Field:** 294 ● **MPSMS:** 929 ● **Aptitudes:** G3, V3, N4, S4, P3, Q3, K3, F3, M3, E5, C4 ● **Temperaments:** J, P, S, V ● **Physical:** Stg=L; Freq: R, H, N Occas: I, E, T, G, A, X ● **Work Env:** Noise=Q; ● **Salary:** 2 ● **Outlook:** 3

MEDICAL ASSISTANT (medical ser.) ● DOT #079.362-010 ● OES: 66005 ● Performs any combination of following duties under direction of physician to assist in examination and treatment of patients: Interviews patients, measures vital signs, such as pulse rate, temperature, blood pressure, weight, and height, and records information on patients' charts. Prepares treatment rooms for examination of patients. Drapes patients with covering and positions instruments and equipment. Hands instruments and materials to doctor as directed. Cleans and sterilizes instruments. Inventories and orders medical supplies and materials. Operates x ray, electrocardiograph (EKG), and other equipment to administer routine diagnostic test or calls medical facility or department to schedule patients for tests. Gives injections or treatments, and performs routine laboratory tests. Schedules appointments, receives money for bills, keeps x ray and other medical records, performs secretarial tasks, and completes insurance forms. May key data into computer to maintain office and patient records. May keep billing records, enter financial transactions into bookeeping ledgers, and compute and mail monthly statements to patients. ● **GED:** R4, M3, L4 ● **SVP:** 1-2 yrs ● **Academic:** Ed=A, Eng=G ● **Work Field:** 294, 231 ● **MPSMS:** 926 ● **Aptitudes:** G3, V3, N4, S4, P4, Q3, K3, F3, M3, E5, C4 ● **Temperaments:** P, T, V ● **Physical:** Stg=L; Freq: R, H, I, T, G, N Occas: E, D, A, X ● **Work Env:** Noise=N; ● **Salary:** 4 ● **Outlook:** 4

MENTAL-RETARDATION AIDE (medical ser.) ● DOT #355.377-018 ● OES: 66014 ● Alternate titles: RESIDENT CARE AIDE. Assists in providing self-care training and therapeutic treatments to residents of mental retardation center: Demonstrates activities such as bathing and dressing to train residents in daily self-care practices. Converses with residents to reinforce positive behaviors and to promote social interaction. Serves meals and eats with residents to act as role model. Accompanies residents on shopping trips and instructs and counsels residents in purchase of personal items. Aids staff in administering therapeutic activities, such as physical exercises, occupational arts and crafts, and recreational games, to residents. Restrains disruptive residents to prevent injury to themselves and others. Observes and documents residents' behaviors, such as speech production, feeding patterns, and toilet training, to facilitate assessment and development of treatment goals. Attends to routine health-care needs of residents under supervision of medical personnel. May give medications as prescribed by physician. May train parents or guardians in care of deinstitutionalized residents. ● **GED:** R4, M3, L3 ● **SVP:** 1-2 yrs ● **Academic:** Ed=H, Eng=G ● **Work Field:** 294, 291 ● **MPSMS:** 926, 942 ● **Aptitudes:** G3, V3, N4, S4, P4, Q4, K4, F4, M4, E5, C4 ● **Temperaments:** J, P, V ● **Physical:** Stg=M; Freq: R, H Occas: S, K, O, I, T, G, N, D, A, X ● **Work Env:** Noise=N; Occas: O ● **Salary:** 3 ● **Outlook:** 3

NURSE AIDE (medical ser.) ● DOT #355.674-014 ● OES: 66008 ● Alternate titles: NURSE AIDE. Performs any combination of following duties in care of patients in hospital, nursing home, or other medical facility, under direction of nursing and medical staff: Answers signal lights, bells, or intercom system to determine patients' needs. Bathes, dresses, and undresses patients. Serves and collects food trays and feeds patients requiring help. Transports patients, using wheelchair or wheeled cart, or assists patients to walk. Drapes patients for examinations and treatments, and remains with patients, performing such duties as holding instruments and adjusting lights. Turns and repositions bedfast patients, alone or with assistance, to prevent bedsores. Changes bed linens, runs errands, directs visitors, and answers telephone. Takes and records temperature, blood pressure, pulse and respiration rates, and food and fluid intake and output, as directed. Cleans, sterilizes, stores, prepares, and issues dressing packs, treatment trays, and other supplies. Dusts and cleans patients' rooms. May be assigned to specific area of hospital, nursing home, or medical facility. May assist nursing staff in care of geriatric patients and be designated Geriatric Nurse Assistant (medical ser.). May assist in providing medical treatment and personal care to patients in private home settings and be designated Home Health Aide (medical ser.). ● **GED:** R3, M2, L2 ● **SVP:** 3-6 mos ● **Academic:** Ed=H, Eng=S ● **Work Field:** 294 ● **MPSMS:** 926 ● **Aptitudes:** G4, V4, N4, S4, P4, Q3, K4, F3, M3, E4, C4 ● **Temperaments:** P, S, V ● **Physical:** Stg=M; Freq: R, H, I, E, T, G, N Occas: S, X ● **Work Env:** Noise=Q; ● **Salary:** 3 ● **Outlook:** 2

NURSE, PRACTICAL (medical ser.) ● DOT #354.374-010 ● OES: 66008 ● Cares for patients and children in private homes, hospitals, sanitoriums, industrial plants, and similar institutions: Bathes and dresses bed patients, combs hair, and otherwise attends to their comfort and personal appearance. Cleans room, and changes bed linen. Takes and records temperature, pulse, and respiration rate. Gives medication as directed by physician or NURSE, GENERAL DUTY (medical ser.) 075.364-010, and makes notation of amount and time given. Gives enemas, douches, massages, and alcohol rubs. Applies hot and cold compresses and hot water bottles. Sterilizes equipment and supplies, using germicides, sterilizer, or autoclave. Prepares food trays, feeds patients, and records food and liquid intake and output. Cooks, washes, cleans, and does other housekeeping duties in private home. May give injections. May care for infants and small children in private home. For practical nurses meeting state licensing requirements see NURSE, LICENSED PRACTICAL (medical ser.) 079.374-014. ● **GED:** R3, M2, L3 ● **SVP:** 3-6 mos ● **Academic:** Ed=A, Eng=G ● **Work Field:** 294 ● **MPSMS:** 924 ● **Aptitudes:** G3, V3, N4, S4, P4, Q4, K3, F4, M3, E4, C5 ● **Temperaments:** P, S, V ● **Physical:** Stg=M; Freq: R, H, T, G, N Occas: S, K, O, I, E ● **Work Env:** Noise=Q; Occas: U ● **Salary:** 4 ● **Outlook:** 4

OCCUPATIONAL THERAPY AIDE (medical ser.) ● DOT #355.377-010 ● OES: 66021 ● Assists OCCUPATIONAL THERAPIST (medical ser.) 076.121-010 or OCCUPATIONAL THERAPY ASSISTANT (medical ser.) 076.364-010 in occupational therapy program in hospital or similar institution: Performs program support services, such as transporting patient, assembling equipment, and preparing and maintaining work areas, as directed by professional staff. Assists in maintaining supplies and equipment. May help professional staff demonstrate therapy techniques, such as manual and creative arts, games, and daily living activities to patients. May assist in selected aspects of patient services as assigned. ● **GED:** R3, M2, L2 ● **SVP:** 3-6 mos ● **Academic:** Ed=H, Eng=G ● **Work Field:** 294 ● **MPSMS:** 926 ● **Aptitudes:** G4, V4, N4, S4, P4, Q4, K4, F3, M3, E5, C5 ● **Temperaments:** P ● **Physical:** Stg=M; Freq: R, H, I, T, G Occas: N ● **Work Env:** Noise=N; ● **Salary:** 1 ● **Outlook:** 3

© 1995, JIST Works, Inc. ● Indianapolis, IN

ORTHOPEDIC ASSISTANT (medical ser.) ● DOT #078.664-010 ● OES: 32998 ● Alternate titles: ORTHOPEDIC CAST SPECIALIST. Applies, adjusts, and removes casts, assembles traction apparatus, and fits strappings and splints for orthopedic patients according to medical staff instructions, using handtools: Covers injured areas with specified protective materials, such as stockinette bandages, gauze, or rubber pads, preparatory to cast application. Wets, wraps, and molds plaster bandages around area of fracture. Trims plaster, using electric cutter. Removes whole and broken casts and alters position of cast to change setting of patient's limb or body part as directed. Assembles wooden, metal, plastic, or plaster material to make orthopedic splints, using handtools. Rigs pulleys, ropes, and frames to assemble fracture beds, using handtools. Attaches traction supports to patient's limb and adjusts support to specified tension. Assembles exercise frames, using handtools. Adjusts crutches and canes to fit patient. Instructs patients in care of and assists patients in walking with casts, braces, and crutches. ● **GED:** R3, M2, L3 ● **SVP:** 3-6 mos ● **Academic:** Ed=N, Eng=S ● **Work Field:** 294 ● **MPSMS:** 929, 604 ● **Aptitudes:** G3, V3, N4, S3, P3, Q4, K4, F3, M3, E5, C5 ● **Temperaments:** J, P, T ● **Physical:** Stg=M; Freq: S, R, H, N Occas: I, T, G, D ● **Work Env:** Noise=N; ● **Salary:** 3 ● **Outlook:** 3

OPTOMETRIC ASSISTANT (medical ser.) ● DOT #079.364-014 ● OES: 32998 ● Performs any combination of following tasks to assist OPTOMETRIST (medical ser) 079.101-018: Obtains and records patient's preliminary case history. Maintains records, schedules appointments, performs bookkeeping, correspondence, and filing. Prepares patient for vision examination; assists in testing for near and far acuity, depth perception, macula integrity, color perception, and visual field, utilizing ocular testing apparatus. Instructs patient in care and use of glasses or contact lenses. Works with patient in vision therapy. Assists patient in frame selection. Adjusts and repairs glasses. Modifies contact lenses. Maintains inventory of materials and cleans instruments. Assists in fabrication of eye glasses or contact lenses. ● **GED:** R4, M4, L4 ● **SVP:** 1-2 yrs ● **Academic:** Ed=H, Eng=G ● **Work Field:** 294, 231 ● **MPSMS:** 929 ● **Aptitudes:** G3, V3, N3, S3, P3, Q3, K4, F3, M3, E3, C3 ● **Temperaments:** J, P ● **Physical:** Stg=S; Freq: R, H, I, T, G, N, D, X Occas: E ● **Work Env:** Noise=N; ● **Salary:** 2 ● **Outlook:** 3

ORDERLY (medical ser.) ● DOT #355.674-018 ● OES: 66008 ● Performs any combination of following tasks, as directed by nursing and medical staff, to care for patients in hospital, nursing home, or other medical facility: Bathes patients and gives alcohol rubs. Measures and records intake and output of liquids, and takes and records temperature, and pulse and respiration rate. Gives enemas. Carries meal trays to patients and feeds patients unable to feed themselves. Lifts patients onto and from bed, and transports patients to other areas, such as operating and x-ray rooms, by rolling bed, or using wheelchair or wheeled stretcher. Sets up equipment, such as oxygen tents, portable x-ray machines, and overhead irrigation bottles. Makes beds and collects soiled linen. Cleans rooms and corridors. Bathes deceased patients, accompanies body to morgue, and places personal belongings in mortuary box. Administers catheterizations and bladder irrigations. Accompanies discharged patients home or to other institutions. ● **GED:** R3, M2, L2 ● **SVP:** 3-6 mos ● **Academic:** Ed=H, Eng=S ● **Work Field:** 294 ● **MPSMS:** 926 ● **Aptitudes:** G4, V4, N4, S4, P4, Q3, K4, F3, M3, E4, C4 ● **Temperaments:** P, S, V ● **Physical:** Stg=H; Freq: R, H Occas: S, O, I, E, T, G, N, X ● **Work Env:** Noise=Q; ● **Salary:** 3 ● **Outlook:** 2

PARAMEDIC (medical ser.) ● DOT #079.364-026 ● OES: 32508 ● Alternate titles: EMT-PARAMEDIC. Administers life support care to sick and injured persons in prehospital setting as authorized and directed by physician: Assesses nature and extent of illness or injury to establish and prioritize medical procedures to be followed or need for additional assistance. Restores and stabilizes heart rhythm on pulseless, nonbreathing patient, using defibrillator, or as directed by physician. Monitors cardiac patient, using electrocardiograph. Initiates intravenous fluids to administer medication or drugs, or to replace fluids lacking in body. Performs endotracheal intubation to open airways and ventilate patient. Administers injections of medications and drugs, following established protocols. Inflates pneumatic anti-shock garment on patient to improve blood circulation. Administers initial treatment at emergency scene and takes and records patient's vital signs. Assists in extricating trapped victims and transports sick and injured persons to treatment center. Observes, records, and reports to physician patient's condition and reaction to drugs, treatments, and significant incidents.

May drive mobile intensive care unit to emergency scene. May serve as team leader for EMERGENCY MEDICAL TECHNICIANS (medical ser.) 079.374-010. May communicate with physician and other medical personnel via radio-telephone. ● **GED:** R4, M3, L4 ● **SVP:** 1-2 yrs ● **Academic:** Ed=A, Eng=G ● **Work Field:** 294 ● **MPSMS:** 929 ● **Aptitudes:** G2, V3, N3, S3, P2, Q2, K2, F2, M2, E3, C3 ● **Temperaments:** J, P, S, T ● **Physical:** Stg=V; Freq: S, K, R, H, I, T, G, N, F, D, A, X, V Occas: C, B, O, W, E, M ● **Work Env:** Noise=L; Const: O Freq: W ● **Salary:** 3 ● **Outlook:** 4

PERFUSIONIST (medical ser.) ● DOT #078.362-034 ● OES: 32998 ● Sets up and operates heart-lung machine in hospital to take over functions of patient's heart and lungs during surgery or respiratory failure: Reviews patient medical history and chart, and consults with surgeon or physician to obtain patient information needed to set up heart-lung machine and associated equipment. Selects, assembles, sets up, and tests heart-lung machine to ensure that machine and associated equipment function according to specifications. Operates heart-lung machine to regulate blood circulation and composition, to administer drugs and anesthetic agents, and to control body temperature during surgery or respiratory failure of patient. Monitors and observes operation of heart-lung machine and patient's physiologic variables such as blood temperature, blood composition, and flow rate, and adjusts equipment to maintain normal body functions. Cleans and adjusts parts of heart-lung machine. ● **GED:** R4, M3, L4 ● **SVP:** 2-4 yrs ● **Academic:** Ed=A, Eng=S ● **Work Field:** 294 ● **MPSMS:** 925 ● **Aptitudes:** G2, V2, N3, S3, P3, Q3, K2, F3, M3, E4, C4 ● **Temperaments:** P, S, T ● **Physical:** Stg=M; Const: R, H, I, G, N, A Freq: T Occas: S, O, E, X ● **Work Env:** Noise=Q; Const: O ● **Salary:** 5 ● **Outlook:** 3

PODIATRIC ASSISTANT (medical ser.) ● DOT #079.374-018 ● OES: 66005 ● Assists PODIATRIST (medical ser.) in patient care. Prepares patients for treatment, sterilizes instruments, performs general office duties, and assists PODIATRIST (medical ser.) in preparing dressings, administering treatments, and developing x rays. ● **GED:** R4, M2, L4 ● **SVP:** 1-2 yrs ● **Academic:** Ed=H, Eng=S ● **Work Field:** 231 ● **MPSMS:** 929 ● **Aptitudes:** G3, V4, N3, S4, P4, Q2, K3, F3, M3, E5, C5 ● **Temperaments:** P, V ● **Physical:** Stg=L; Freq: R, H, I, T, G Occas: N ● **Work Env:** Noise=N; ● **Salary:** 5 ● **Outlook:** 3

PSYCHIATRIC AIDE (medical ser.) ● DOT #355.377-014 ● OES: 66014 ● Alternate titles: ASSISTANT THERAPY AIDE; ASYLUM ATTENDANT; CHARGE ATTENDANT; CHEMICAL DEPENDENCY ATTENDANT; PSYCHIATRIC ATTENDANT; WARD ATTENDANT. Assists patients, working under direction of nursing and medical staff in psychiatric, chemical dependency, or similar setting: Accompanies patients to shower rooms, and assists them in bathing, dressing, and grooming. Accompanies patients to and from wards for examination and treatment, administers prescribed medications, measures vital signs, performs routine nursing procedures, such as collecting laboratory specimens, giving enemas and douches, and drawing blood samples, and records information in patients' charts. Assists patients in becoming accustomed to hospital routine and encourages them to participate in social and recreational activities to promote rehabilitation. Observes patients to ensure that none wanders from ward areas or grounds. Feeds patients or attempts to persuade them to eat, and notes and records reasons for rejection of food. Observes patients to detect unusual behavior, and aids or restrains them to prevent injury to themselves or others. May escort patients off grounds to medical or dental appointments, library, church services, motion pictures, or athletic events. May clean rooms, ward furnishings, walls, and floors, using water, detergents, and disinfectants. May change bed linens. May interview patients upon admission and record data obtained. May be designated Ward Supervisor (medical ser.) when responsible for patient care and other services of single ward. ● **GED:** R3, M2, L3 ● **SVP:** 3-6 mos ● **Academic:** Ed=A, Eng=G ● **Work Field:** 294 ● **MPSMS:** 926 ● **Aptitudes:** G3, V3, N4, S4, P4, Q4, K4, F4, M3, E5, C5 ● **Temperaments:** P, S, V ● **Physical:** Stg=M; Freq: R, H, T, G, N, V Occas: S, I, E ● **Work Env:** Noise=Q; Occas: O ● **Salary:** 4 ● **Outlook:** 3

PHYSICAL THERAPY AIDE (medical ser.) ● DOT #355.354-010 ● OES: 66017 ● Prepares patients for physical therapy treatments, assists PHYSICAL THERAPIST (medical ser.) 076.121-014 or PHYSICAL THERAPIST ASSISTANT (medical ser.) 076.224-010 during administration of treatments, and provides routine treatments: Assists patients to dress, undress, and put on and remove supportive devices, such as braces, splints, and slings, before and after treatments. Secures patients into or onto therapy equipment. Safeguards, motivates, and assists patients practicing exercises and functional activities under direction of professional staff. Provides routine treatments, such as hydrotherapy, hot and cold packs, and paraffin bath. Transports patients to and from treatment area. Cleans work area and equipment after treatment. May record treatment given and equipment used. May inventory and requisition supplies and equipment. May adjust fit of supportive devices for patients, as instructed. May be assigned to specific type of treatment or patient service and be designated Physical Therapy Aide, Hydrotherapy (medical ser.); Physical Therapy Aide, Transport (medical ser.). ● **GED:** R3, M2, L3 ● **SVP:** 3-6 mos ● **Academic:** Ed=A, Eng=G ● **Work Field:** 294 ● **MPSMS:** 926 ● **Aptitudes:** G3, V3, N4, S4, P4, Q4, K3, F3, M3, E4, C4 ● **Temperaments:** P, T ● **Physical:** Stg=M; Freq: R, H, T, G, N Occas: S, K, O, I, X ● **Work Env:** Noise=N; ● **Salary:** 1 ● **Outlook:** 3

RESPIRATORY-THERAPY AIDE (medical ser.) ● DOT #355.674-022 ● OES: 66099 ● Performs any combination of following tasks to assist personnel in Respiratory Therapy Department: Cleans, disinfects, and sterilizes equipment used in administration of respiratory therapy. Examines equipment to detect worn tubes, loose connections, or other indications of disrepair, and notifies supervisor of need for maintenance. Starts equipment and observes gauges measuring pressure, rate of flow, and continuity to test equipment, and notifies supervisor of malfunctions. Assists in preparation of inventory records. Delivers oxygen tanks and other equipment and supplies to specified hospital locations. Assists in administration of gas or aerosol therapy as directed by RESPIRATORY THERAPIST (medical ser.) 076.361-014 and prescribed by physician. ● **GED:** R3, M3, L3 ● **SVP:** 3-6 mos ● **Academic:** Ed=N, Eng=S ● **Work Field:** 231 ● **MPSMS:** 926 ● **Aptitudes:** G4, V4, N4, S3, P3, Q3, K3, F3, M4, E4, C5 ● **Temperaments:** J, V ● **Physical:** Stg=M; Freq: R, H, I, N Occas: S, T, G ● **Work Env:** Noise=N; ● **Salary:** 4 ● **Outlook:** 3

SURGICAL TECHNICIAN (medical ser.) ● DOT #079.374-022 ● OES: 32928 ● Alternate titles: OPERATING-ROOM TECHNICIAN. Performs any combination of following tasks before, during, and after surgery to assist surgical team: Places equipment and supplies in operating room and arranges instruments, according to instructions. Assists team members to place and position patient on table. Scrubs arms and hands and dons gown and gloves. Aids team to don gowns and gloves. Maintains supply of fluids, such as plasma, saline, blood, and glucose for use during operation. Hands instruments and supplies to surgeon, holds retractors, cuts sutures, and performs other tasks as directed by surgeon during operation. Puts dressings on patient following surgery. Counts sponges, needles, and instruments before and after operation. Washes and sterilizes equipment, using germicides and sterilizers. Cleans operating room. ● **GED:** R4, M4, L3 ● **SVP:** 1-2 yrs ● **Academic:** Ed=A, Eng=S ● **Work Field:** 294 ● **MPSMS:** 926 ● **Aptitudes:** G3, V3, N4, S4, P4, Q3, K4, F3, M3, E4, C4 ● **Temperaments:** J, S, T ● **Physical:** Stg=L; Freq: R, H, I, G Occas: S, E, T, N, X ● **Work Env:** Noise=Q; Const: O ● **Salary:** 5 ● **Outlook:** 4

GOE: 10.03.03
Care of Others

ATTENDANT, CHILDREN'S INSTITUTION (any industry) ● DOT #359.677-010 ● OES: 68038 ● Alternate titles: CHILD-CARE ATTENDANT; HOUSE PARENT. Cares for group of children housed in city, county, private, or other similar institution, under supervision of superintendent of home: Awakens children each morning and ensures children are dressed, fed, and ready for school or other activity. Gives instructions to children regarding desirable health and personal habits. Plans and leads recreational activities and participates or instructs children in games. Disciplines children and recommends or initiates other measures to control behavior. May make minor repairs to clothing. May supervise housekeeping activities of other workers in assigned section of institution. May counsel or provide similar diagnostic or therapeutic services to mentally disturbed, delinquent, or handicapped children. May escort child to designated activities. May perform housekeeping duties in children's living area. ● **GED:** R3, M2, L3 ●

SVP: 1-3 mos ● **Academic:** Ed=N, Eng=S ● **Work Field:** 291 ● **MPSMS:** 924, 926 ● **Aptitudes:** G3, V3, N4, S4, P3, Q4, K3, F4, M3, E4, C4 ● **Temperaments:** D, I, J ● **Physical:** Stg=M; Freq: S, O, R, H, T, G, N, F, V Occas: I, X ● **Work Env:** Noise=N; ● **Salary:** 1 ● **Outlook:** 3

BLIND AIDE (personal ser.) ● DOT #359.573-010 ● OES: 68035 ● Alternate titles: CLERK GUIDE; ESCORT, BLIND. Performs any combination of following duties to assist blind persons: Drives motor vehicle to transport blind persons to specified locations according to their personal and business activities. Carries brief or sample cases. Assists client with dressing, moving from one location to another, obtaining information or other personal service. Prepares and maintains records of assistance rendered. May type correspondence and reports [CLERK-TYPIST (clerical)]. May assist teacher of blind in routine classroom activities such as toiletry or group school activities. ● **GED:** R3, M2, L2 ● **SVP:** 1-3 mos ● **Academic:** Ed=N, Eng=G ● **Work Field:** 291 ● **MPSMS:** 909 ● **Aptitudes:** G3, V3, N4, S3, P4, Q3, K3, F4, M3, E3, C4 ● **Temperaments:** P, V ● **Physical:** Stg=L; Freq: R, H, I, T, G, N, F, D, A, X, V ● **Work Env:** Noise=N; Occas: W ● **Salary:** 1 ● **Outlook:** 2

CHILD-CARE ATTENDANT, SCHOOL (personal ser.) ● DOT #355.674-010 ● OES: 68038 ● Attends to personal needs of handicapped children while in school to receive specialized academic and physical training: Wheels handicapped children to classes, lunchrooms, treatment rooms, and other areas of building. Secures children in equipment, such as chairs, slings, or stretchers, and places or hoists children into baths or pools. Monitors children using life support equipment to detect indications of malfunctioning of equipment and calls for medical assistance when needed. Helps children to walk, board buses, put on prosthetic appliances, eat, dress, bathe, and perform other physical activities as their needs require. ● **GED:** R3, M1, L2 ● **SVP:** 2-30 days ● **Academic:** Ed=N, Eng=S ● **Work Field:** 291 ● **MPSMS:** 926 ● **Aptitudes:** G4, V4, N4, S4, P4, Q4, K4, F4, M4, E4, C5 ● **Temperaments:** J, P, V ● **Physical:** Stg=M; Freq: R, H, I Occas: C, S, K, O, E, T, G, N, D ● **Work Env:** Noise=Q; Occas: U ● **Salary:** 1 ● **Outlook:** 4

CHILD MONITOR (domestic ser.) ● DOT #301.677-010 ● OES: 62041 ● Alternate titles: NURSE, CHILDREN'S. Performs any combination of following duties to attend children in private home: Observes and monitors play activities or amuses children by reading to or playing games with them. Prepares and serves meals or formulas. Sterilizes bottles and other equipment used for feeding infants. Dresses or assists children to dress and bathe. Accompanies children on walks or other outings. Washes and irons clothing. Keeps children's quarters clean and tidy. Cleans other parts of home. May be designated Nurse, Infants' (domestic ser.) when in charge of infants. May be designated Baby Sitter (domestic ser.) when employed on daily or hourly basis. ● **GED:** R3, M1, L2 ● **SVP:** 1-3 mos ● **Academic:** Ed=N, Eng=S ● **Work Field:** 291 ● **MPSMS:** 901 ● **Aptitudes:** G4, V4, N5, S5, P5, Q4, K4, F4, M4, E5, C5 ● **Temperaments:** P, V ● **Physical:** Stg=M; Freq: T, G Occas: S, R, H, I, F, V ● **Work Env:** Noise=N; ● **Salary:** 1 ● **Outlook:** 4

CHILDREN'S TUTOR (domestic ser.) ● DOT #099.227-010 ● OES: 31398 ● Cares for children in private home, overseeing their recreation, diet, health, and deportment: Teaches children foreign languages, and good health and personal habits. Arranges parties, outings, and picnics for children. Takes disciplinary measures to control children's behavior. Ascertains cause of behavior problems of children and devises means for solving them. When duties are confined to care of young children may be designated Children's Tutor, Nursery (domestic ser.). ● **GED:** R4, M2, L4 ● **SVP:** 6 mos-1 yr ● **Academic:** Ed=H, Eng=S ● **Work Field:** 291, 296 ● **MPSMS:** 942 ● **Aptitudes:** G3, V3, N3, S4, P4, Q4, K4, F4, M4, E5, C5 ● **Temperaments:** D, P, V ● **Physical:** Stg=L; Freq: R, H, I ● **Work Env:** Noise=N; ● **Salary:** 2 ● **Outlook:** 4

COMPANION (domestic ser.) ● DOT #309.677-010 ● OES: 62061 ● Cares for elderly, handicapped, or convalescent persons: Attends to employer's personal needs [PERSONAL ATTENDANT (domestic ser.)]. Transacts social or business affairs [SOCIAL SECRETARY (clerical)]. Reads aloud, plays cards, or other games to entertain employer. Accompanies employer on trips and outings. May prepare and serve meals to employer. ● **GED:** R3, M2, L3 ● **SVP:** 1-3 mos ● **Academic:** Ed=N, Eng=S ● **Work Field:** 291 ● **MPSMS:** 942 ● **Aptitudes:** G3,

V3, N4, S4, P4, Q4, K4, F4, M3, E4, C5 • **Temperaments:** P, V • **Physical:** Stg=L; Freq: R, H, I, T, G, N • **Work Env:** Noise=N; • **Salary:** 1 • **Outlook:** 3

FOSTER PARENT (domestic ser.) • DOT #309.677-014 • OES: 62041 • Rears homeless or parentless children in own home as members of family: Organizes and schedules activities, such as recreation, rest periods, and sleeping time. Ensures child has nutritious diet. Instructs children in good personal and health habits. Bathes, dresses, and undresses young children. Washes and irons clothing. Accompanies children on outings and walks. Disciplines children when required. May return children to parents' home during weekends and holidays. May work under supervision of welfare agency. May prepare periodic reports concerning progress and behavior of children for welfare agency. • **GED:** R3, M2, L3 • **SVP:** 1-3 mos • **Academic:** Ed=N, Eng=G • **Work Field:** 291 • **MPSMS:** 942 • **Aptitudes:** G4, V4, N4, S4, P4, Q4, K4, F4, M3, E4, C5 • **Temperaments:** D, J, P, V • **Physical:** Stg=M; Freq: R, H, I Occas: S, K, O, T, G • **Work Env:** Noise=N; • **Salary:** 1 • **Outlook:** 1

GUARD, SCHOOL-CROSSING (government ser.) • DOT #371.567-010 • OES: 63044 • Guards street crossings during hours when children are going to or coming from school: Directs actions of children and traffic at street intersections to ensure safe crossing. Records license numbers of vehicles disregarding traffic signals and reports infractions to police. May escort children across street. May place caution signs at designated points before going on duty and remove signs at end of shift. May stop speeding vehicles and warn drivers. • **GED:** R2, M1, L2 • **SVP:** 2-30 days • **Academic:** Ed=N, Eng=S • **Work Field:** 293 • **MPSMS:** 959 • **Aptitudes:** G3, V3, N4, S4, P5, Q4, K4, F5, M4, E4, C4 • **Temperaments:** P • **Physical:** Stg=L; Freq: R, T, G, N Occas: H, F, X, V • **Work Env:** Noise=N; Const: W • **Salary:** 1 • **Outlook:** 2

HOME ATTENDANT (personal ser.) • DOT #354.377-014 • OES: 66011 • Alternate titles: HOME HEALTH AIDE. Cares for elderly, convalescent, or handicapped persons in patient's home, performing any combination of following tasks: Changes bed linens, washes and irons patient's laundry, and cleans patient's quarters. Purchases, prepares, and serves food for patient and other members of family, following special prescribed diets. Assists patients into and out of bed, automobile, or wheelchair, to lavatory, and up and down stairs. Assists patient to dress, bathe, and groom self. Massages patient and applies preparations and treatments, such as liniment or alcohol rubs and heat-lamp stimulation. Administers prescribed oral medications under written direction of physician or as directed by home care nurse. Accompanies ambulatory patients outside home, serving as guide, companion, and aide. Entertains patient, reads aloud, and plays cards or other games with patient. Performs variety of miscellaneous duties as requested, such as obtaining household supplies and running errands. May maintain records of services performed and of apparent condition of patient. May visit several households to provide daily health care to patients. • **GED:** R3, M2, L2 • **SVP:** 1-3 mos • **Academic:** Ed=A, Eng=G • **Work Field:** 294, 291 • **MPSMS:** 942 • **Aptitudes:** G3, V3, N4, S4, P4, Q4, K3, F4, M3, E4, C4 • **Temperaments:** J, P, V • **Physical:** Stg=M; Freq: R, H, T, G Occas: S, O, I, E, N, F, D, A, X, V • **Work Env:** Noise=Q; Occas: W, U • **Salary:** 1 • **Outlook:** 4

NURSERY SCHOOL ATTENDANT (any industry) • DOT #359.677-018 • OES: 68038 • Alternate titles: CHILD-CARE LEADER; CHILD-DAY-CARE CENTER WORKER; DAY CARE WORKER. Organizes and leads activities of prekindergarten children in nursery schools or in playrooms operated for patrons of theaters, department stores, hotels, and similar organizations: Helps children remove outer garments. Organizes and participates in games, reads to children, and teaches them simple painting, drawing, handwork, songs, and similar activities. Directs children in eating, resting, and toileting. Helps children develop habits of caring for own clothing and picking up and putting away toys and books. Maintains discipline. May serve meals and refreshments to children and regulate rest periods. May assist in preparing food and cleaning quarters. • **GED:** R3, M2, L3 • **SVP:** 3-6 mos • **Academic:** Ed=N, Eng=S • **Work Field:** 291 • **MPSMS:** 942 • **Aptitudes:** G3, V3, N4, S4, P4, Q4, K4, F4, M4, E5, C4 • **Temperaments:** P, V • **Physical:** Stg=L; Freq: S, R, H, T, G Occas: K, I, N, F, D, X, V • **Work Env:** Noise=N; • **Salary:** 1 • **Outlook:** 2

PLAYROOM ATTENDANT (any industry) • DOT #359.677-026 • OES: 68038 • Alternate titles: KINDERGARTNER. Entertains children in nursery of department store, country club, or similar establishment as service to patrons. Reads aloud, organizes and participates in games, and gives elementary lessons in arts or crafts. • **GED:** R3, M2, L3 • **SVP:** 1-3 mos • **Academic:** Ed=N, Eng=S • **Work Field:** 297, 291 • **MPSMS:** 942 • **Aptitudes:** G3, V3, N4, S3, P3, Q4, K3, F3, M3, E4, C4 • **Temperaments:** F, P, V • **Physical:** Stg=L; Const: T, G Freq: R, H, N Occas: S, K, O, I, X • **Work Env:** Noise=N; • **Salary:** 1 • **Outlook:** 2

TRANSPORTER, PATIENTS (medical ser.) • DOT #355.677-014 • OES: 66099 • Alternate titles: ESCORT, PATIENTS. Escorts or transports patients within hospital or other medical facility: Determines patient name, destination, mode of travel, time, and other data, following written or oral instructions. Directs or escorts incoming patients from admitting office or reception desk to designated area. Carries patient's luggage. Assists patient in walking to prevent accidents by falling, or transports nonambulatory patient, using wheelchair. Transports patient, alone or with assistance, in bed, wheeled cart, or wheelchair to designated areas within facility during patient stay. Delivers messages, mail, medical records, and other items. • **GED:** R2, M1, L2 • **SVP:** 2-30 days • **Academic:** Ed=N, Eng=S • **Work Field:** 291 • **MPSMS:** 926 • **Aptitudes:** G4, V4, N4, S4, P4, Q4, K4, F4, M4, E4, C5 • **Temperaments:** P, R • **Physical:** Stg=M; Freq: R, H, T, G Occas: S, I, N • **Work Env:** Noise=Q; • **Salary:** 4 • **Outlook:** 3

Leading-Influencing 11

An interest in leading and influencing others by using high-level verbal or numerical abilities. You can satisfy this interest through study and work in a variety of professional fields. You may enjoy the challenge and responsibility of leadership. You could seek work in administration or management. You may prefer working with technical details. You could find a job in finance, law, social research, or public relations. You may like to help others learn. Perhaps working in education would appeal to you.

Mathematics and Statistics

Workers in this group use advanced math and statistics to solve problems and conduct research. They analyze and interpret numerical data for planning and decision making. Some of these workers may first study and then determine how computers may best be used to solve problems or process information. Colleges, large businesses and industries, research organizations, and government agencies use these workers.

✓ What kind of work would you do?

Your work activities would depend upon your specific job. For example, you might:

- apply formulas and mathematical principles to solve technical problems in engineering or the physical sciences.
- develop systems for handling information for businesses and industries.
- design insurance and pension plans and set premiums and benefit rates.
- plan and write computer programs for control of automated operations.
- convert business problems into numbers and symbols for electronic data processing.

✓ What skills and abilities do you need for this kind of work?

To do this kind of work, you must be able to:

- use advanced logic and scientific thinking to solve a variety of complex problems.
- understand and use advanced math and statistics.
- use personal judgment and known facts to make decisions and deal with problems.
- use computer technology to solve problems or process large amounts of information.
- speak and write clearly and accurately.
- use technical terms, math and computer symbols, and complex charts and graphs.

✓ How do you know if you would like or could learn to do this kind of work?

The following questions may give you clues about yourself as you consider this group of jobs.

- Have you had courses in advanced mathematics? Do you enjoy working with complex numerical ideas?
- Have you had experience using a pocket calculator? Can you enter long columns of numbers accurately? Can you use all of the mathematical functions on the machine?
- Do you like to solve written problems in mathematics? Can you easily identify the procedures for solving such problems?

✓ How can you prepare for and enter this kind of work?

Occupations in this group usually require education and/or training extending from two years to over ten years, depending upon the specific kind of work. Almost all jobs in this group require four or more years of study in mathematics and statistics at the college level. Experience in banking, accounting, or a related field is an additional requirement for some jobs. Other jobs require experience and training in a scientific or technical area.

Jobs with the federal government require a civil service examination.

✓ What else should you consider about these jobs?

Workers in this group are expected to keep up with developments and trends in their specific areas. They attend seminars and workshops, or study for advanced degrees.

If you think you would like to do this kind of work, look at the job titles listed on the following pages.

GOE: 11.01.01
Data Processing Design

CHIEF, COMPUTER PROGRAMMER (profess. & kin.) ● DOT #030.167-010 ● OES: 25104 ● Alternate titles: COORDINATOR, COMPUTER PROGRAMMING. Plans, schedules, and directs preparation of programs to process data and solve problems by use of computers: Consults with managerial and systems analysis personnel to clarify program intent, identify problems, suggest changes, and determine extent of programming and coding required. Assigns, coordinates, and reviews work of programming personnel. Develops programs from workflow charts or diagrams, considering factors, such as computer storage capacity and speed, extent of peripheral equipment, and intended use of output data. Converts workflow charts to language processable by computer. Enters program codes into computer. Enters test data into computer. Analyzes test runs on computer to correct or direct correction of coded program and input data. Revises or directs revision of existing programs to increase operating efficiency or adapt to new requirements. Compiles documentation of program development and subsequent revisions. Trains subordinates in programming and program coding. Prescribes standards for terms and symbols used to simplify interpretation of programs. Collaborates with computer manufacturers and other users to develop new programming methods. Prepares records and reports. ● **GED:** R5, M4, L5 ● **SVP:** 4-10 yrs ● **Academic:** Ed=B, Eng=G ● **Work Field:** 233 ● **MPSMS:** 893 ● **Aptitudes:** G2, V2, N2, S4, P4, Q1, K4, F4, M4, E5, C5 ● **Temperaments:** D, J, P, T ● **Physical:** Stg=S; Freq: R, H, I, T, G, N ● **Work Env:** Noise=N; ● **Salary:** 5 ● **Outlook:** 4

COMPUTER PROGRAMMER (profess. & kin.) ● DOT #030.162-010 ● OES: 25104 ● Alternate titles: APPLICATIONS PROGRAMMER; PROGRAMMER, BUSINESS. Converts data from project specifications and statements of problems and procedures to create or modify computer programs: Prepares, or receives from SYSTEMS ANALYST (profess. & kin.) 030.167-014, detailed workflow chart and diagram to illustrate sequence of steps that program must follow and to describe input, output, and logical operations involved. Analyzes workflow chart and diagram, applying knowledge of computer capabilities, subject matter, and symbolic logic. Confers with supervisor and representatives of departments concerned with program to resolve questions of program intent, data input, output requirements, and inclusion of internal checks and controls. Converts detailed logical flow chart to language processable by computer. Enters program codes into computer system. Inputs test data into computer. Observes computer monitor screen to interpret program operating codes. Corrects program errors, using methods such as modifying program or altering sequence of program steps. Writes instructions to guide operating personnel during production runs. Analyzes, reviews, and rewrites programs to increase operating efficiency or to adapt program to new requirements. Compiles and writes documentation of program development and subsequent revisions. May train workers to use program. May assist COMPUTER OPERATOR (clerical) 213.362-010 to resolve problems in running computer program. May work with SYSTEMS ANALYST (profess. & kin.) to obtain and analyze project specifications and flow charts. May direct and coordinate work of others to write, test, and modify computer programs. ● **GED:** R5, M4, L5 ● **SVP:** 2-4 yrs ● **Academic:** Ed=A, Eng=S ● **Work Field:** 233 ● **MPSMS:** 893 ● **Aptitudes:** G2, V2, N2, S4, P4, Q1, K4, F4, M4, E5, C5 ● **Temperaments:** J, P, T ● **Physical:** Stg=S; Freq: R, H, I, N Occas: T, G, A ● **Work Env:** Noise=N; ● **Salary:** 4 ● **Outlook:** 4

DATA BASE ADMINISTRATOR (profess. & kin.) ● DOT #039.162-010 ● OES: 25102 ● Coordinates physical changes to computer data bases; and codes, tests, and implements physical data base, applying knowledge of data base management system: Designs logical and physical data bases [DATA BASE DESIGN ANALYST (profess. & kin.) 039.162-014] or reviews description of changes to data base design to understand how changes to be made affect physical data base (how data is stored in terms of physical characteristics, such as location,

amount of space, and access method). Establishes physical data base parameters. Codes data base descriptions and specifies identifiers of data base to data base management system or directs others in coding data base descriptions. Calculates optimum values for data base parameters, such as amount of computer memory to be used by data base, following manuals and using calculator. Specifies user access level for each segment of one or more data items, such as insert, replace, retrieve, or delete data. Specifies which users can access data bases and what data can be accessed by user. Tests and corrects errors, and refines changes to data base. Enters codes to create production data base. Selects and enters codes of utility program to monitor data base performance, such as distribution of records and amount of available memory. Directs programmers and analysts to make changes to data base management system. Reviews and corrects programs. Answers user questions. Confers with coworkers to determine impact of data base changes on other systems and staff cost for making changes to data base. Modifies data base programs to increase processing performance, referred to as performance tuning. Workers typically specialize in one or more types of data base management systems. May train users. ● **GED:** R5, M4, L5 ● **SVP:** 4-10 yrs ● **Academic:** Ed=A, Eng=G ● **Work Field:** 233 ● **MPSMS:** 893 ● **Aptitudes:** G1, V2, N2, S3, P3, Q1, K4, F4, M4, E5, C5 ● **Temperaments:** J, P, T ● **Physical:** Stg=S; Const: N Freq: T, G Occas: R, H, I, A ● **Work Env:** Noise=Q; ● **Salary:** 5 ● **Outlook:** 5

DATA BASE DESIGN ANALYST (profess. & kin.) ● DOT #039.162-014 ● OES: 25102 ● Designs logical and physical data bases and coordinates data base development as part of project team, applying knowledge of data base design standards and data base management system: Reviews project request describing data base user needs. Estimates time and cost required to accomplish project. Determines if project requires creating series of new programs or modifying existing programs that access data stored in data bases. Attends specification meeting with project team workers to determine scope and limitations of project. Reviews workflow chart developed by PROGRAMMER-ANALYST (profess. & kin.) 030.162-014 to understand tasks computer will perform, such as updating records. Reviews procedures in data base management system manuals for making changes to data base, such as defining, creating, revising, and controlling data base. Revises company definition of data as defined in data dictionary (information about data, including name, description, source of data item, and key words for categorizing and searching for data item descriptions). Determines and enters changes to data dictionary descriptions, including type, structure, and intended use of data within system, using computer or assigns data entry work to programmer. Develops data model describing data elements and how they are used, following procedures and using pen and template or computer software. Creates description to enable PROGRAMMER-ANALYST (profess. & kin.) to understand how programs should access data. Writes description of how user accesses data, referred to as logical data base. Writes physical data base description, such as location, space requirements, and access method, to protect company data resources against unauthorized access and accidental destruction, according to computer industry standards and knowledge of data base management system. May specialize in adding, deleting, and modifying data items in data dictionary and be designated Data Dictionary Administrator (profess. and kin.). Workers typically specialize in one or more types of data base management systems. ● **GED:** R5, M4, L5 ● **SVP:** 4-10 yrs ● **Academic:** Ed=A, Eng=G ● **Work Field:** 233 ● **MPSMS:** 893 ● **Aptitudes:** G1, V2, N2, S3, P3, Q1, K4, F4, M4, E5, C5 ● **Temperaments:** J, P, T ● **Physical:** Stg=S; Const: N Freq: T, G Occas: R, H, I, A ● **Work Env:** Noise=Q; ● **Salary:** 4 ● **Outlook:** 5

DATA COMMUNICATIONS ANALYST (profess. & kin.) ● DOT #031.262-010 ● OES: 25198 ● Researches, tests, evaluates, and recommends data communications hardware and software: Identifies areas of operation which need upgraded equipment, such as modems, fiber optic cables, and telephone wires. Conducts survey to determine user needs. Reads technical manuals and brochures to determine equipment which meets establishment requirements. Visits vendors to learn about available products or services. Tests and evaluates hardware and software to determine efficiency, reliability, and compatibility with existing system, using equipment such as computer terminal and modem. Analyzes test data and recommends hardware or software for purchase. Develops and writes procedures for installation, use, and solving problems of communications hardware and software. Monitors system performance. Trains users in use of equipment. Assists users to identify and solve data communication problems. May write technical specifications to send to vendors for bid. May oversee or assist in installation of communications hardware. May perform minor equipment repairs. ● **GED:** R5, M3, L5 ● **SVP:** 2-4 yrs ● **Academic:** Ed=A, Eng=G ● **Work Field:** 233 ● **MPSMS:** 893 ● **Aptitudes:** G2, V2, N3, S4, P4, Q3, K4, F3, M3, E5, C4 ● **Temperaments:** J, P ● **Physical:** Stg=L; Freq: I, T, G, N Occas: S, K, O, R, H, A, X ● **Work Env:** Noise=N; ● **Salary:** 4 ● **Outlook:** 5

DATA RECOVERY PLANNER (profess. & kin.) ● DOT #033.162-014 ● OES: 21998 ● Alternate titles: DISASTER RECOVERY COORDINATOR. Develops, coordinates implementation of, and tests plan to continue establishment data processing activities at off-site location in case of emergency, such as fire, at main site: Establishes priority of data processing activities according to importance to business. Determines hardware, software, data files, safe storage facilities, and other resources required. Develops plan to meet emergency data processing needs. Identifies personnel needed to implement plan. Presents plan to management and recommends means of obtaining required facilities, such as contracting with off-site vendor. Coordinates implementation of plan. Tests emergency data processing system, using computer and test data. Writes report to document test results and updates emergency recovery procedures. ● **GED:** R5, M3, L5 ● **SVP:** 4-10 yrs ● **Academic:** Ed=A, Eng=G ● **Work Field:** 233 ● **MPSMS:** 893 ● **Aptitudes:** G2, V2, N3, S4, P3, Q2, K4, F4, M4, E5, C5 ● **Temperaments:** D, J, P, T ● **Physical:** Stg=L; Freq: T, G, N Occas: R, H, I ● **Work Env:** Noise=N; ● **Salary:** 4 ● **Outlook:** 5

DIRECTOR, RECORDS MANAGEMENT (profess. & kin.) ● DOT #161.117-014 ● OES: 21905 ● Plans, develops, and administers records management policies designed to facilitate effective and efficient handling of business records and other information: Plans development and implementation of records management policies intended to standardize filing, protecting, and retrieving records, reports, and other information contained on paper, microfilm, computer program, or other media. Coordinates and directs, through subordinate managers, activities of departments involved with records management analysis, reports analysis, and supporting technical, clerical micrographics, and printing services. Evaluates staff reports, utilizing knowledge of principles of records and information management, administrative processes and systems, cost control, governmental recordkeeping requirements, and organizational objectives. Confers with other administrators to assure compliance with policies, procedures, and practices of records management program. ● **GED:** R5, M4, L5 ● **SVP:** 4-10 yrs ● **Academic:** Ed=B, Eng=G ● **Work Field:** 295, 212 ● **MPSMS:** 891 ● **Aptitudes:** G2, V2, N3, S3, P3, Q2, K5, F5, M5, E5, C3 ● **Temperaments:** D, J, P ● **Physical:** Stg=S; Freq: R, H, T, G, N Occas: I, X ● **Work Env:** Noise=N; ● **Salary:** 5 ● **Outlook:** 5

FORMS ANALYST (profess. & kin.) ● DOT #161.267-018 ● OES: 21905 ● Examines and evaluates format and function of business forms to develop new, or improve existing forms format, usage, and control: Reviews forms to evaluate need for revision, consolidation, or discontinuance, using knowledge of form use, workflow, document flow, and compatibility with manual or machine processing. Confers with form users to gather recommendations for improvements, considering such characteristics as form necessity, completeness, design, text, and specifications as to size and color of paper, style of typeface, and number of copies. May design, draft or prepare finished master copy for new or modified form, or confer with printer's representative to specify changes in format and approve proof copies. Prepares and issues written instructions for use of forms in accordance with organizational policies, procedures, and practices. Keeps records to update information concerning form origin, function, necessity, usage, cost, and stock level. ● **GED:** R4, M3, L4 ● **SVP:** 2-4 yrs ● **Academic:** Ed=B, Eng=S ● **Work Field:** 211 ● **MPSMS:** 891 ● **Aptitudes:** G2, V2, N3, S3, P3, Q2, K5, F5, M5, E5, C3 ● **Temperaments:** D, J, V ● **Physical:** Stg=S; Freq: R, H, T, G, N Occas: I, X ● **Work Env:** Noise=N; ● **Salary:** 3 ● **Outlook:** 3

INFORMATION SCIENTIST (profess. & kin.) ● DOT #109.067-010 ● OES: 25102 ● Alternate titles: CHIEF INFORMATION OFFICER; INFORMATION BROKER; INFORMATION MANAGER; INFORMATION RESOURCES DIRECTOR; INFORMATION RESOURCES MANAGER. Designs information system to provide management or clients with specific data from computer storage, utilizing knowledge of electronic data processing principles, mathematics, and computer capabilities: Develops and designs methods and procedures for collecting, organizing, interpreting, and classifying information for input into computer and retrieval of specific information from computer, utilizing knowledge of symbolic language and optical or pattern recognition principles. Develops alternate designs to resolve problems in input, storage, and retrieval of information. May specialize in specific field of information science, such as scientific or engineering research, or in specific discipline, such as business, medicine, education, aerospace, or library science. ● **GED:** R5, M5, L5 ● **SVP:** 2-4 yrs ● **Academic:** Ed=B, Eng=G ● **Work Field:** 233 ● **MPSMS:** 933 ● **Aptitudes:** G2, V2, N1, S2, P4, Q4, K4, F4, M4, E5, C5 ● **Temperaments:** D, J, T ● **Physical:** Stg=S; Freq: N Occas: R, H ● **Work Env:** Noise=N; ● **Salary:** 3 ● **Outlook:** 4

MANAGER, COMPUTER OPERATIONS (profess. & kin.) ● DOT #169.167-082 ● OES: 13017 ● Directs and coordinates activities of workers engaged in computer operations: Plans and develops policies and procedures for carrying out computer operations. Meets with subordinate supervisors to discuss progress of work, resolve problems, and ensure that standards for quality and quantity of work are met. Adjusts hours of work, priorities, and staff assignments to ensure efficient operation, based on work load. Reviews daily logs and reports to detect recurring slowdowns or errors, using computer terminal. Consults with software and hardware vendors and other establishment workers to solve problems impeding computer processing. Meets with users to determine quality of service and identify needs. Meets with data processing managers to determine impact of proposed changes in hardware or software on computer operations and service to users. Evaluates new software and hardware to determine usefulness and compatibility with existing software and hardware. Evaluates proposed data processing projects to assess adequacy of existing hardware, and recommends purchase of equipment. Develops budget and monitors expenditures. May direct and coordinate activities of tape library and supervise TAPE LIBRARIAN (clerical) 206.367-018. ● **GED:** R5, M4, L4 ● **SVP:** 4-10 yrs ● **Academic:** Ed=A, Eng=G ● **Work Field:** 295 ● **MPSMS:** 893 ● **Aptitudes:** G2, V2, N3, S3, P3, Q3, K4, F4, M4, E5, C5 ● **Temperaments:** D, J, P ● **Physical:** Stg=S; Const: T, G Freq: N Occas: R, H, I, A ● **Work Env:** Noise=N; ● **Salary:** 5 ● **Outlook:** 4

MANAGER, DATA PROCESSING (profess. & kin.) ● DOT #169.167-030 ● OES: 13017 ● Alternate titles: DIRECTOR, DATA PROCESSING; DIRECTOR, MANAGEMENT INFORMATION SYSTEMS. Directs and coordinates development and production activities of data processing department: Consults with management to determine information requirements of management, scientists, or engineers, determine boundaries and priorities of new projects, and discuss system capacity and equipment acquisitions. Confers with department heads involved with proposed projects to ensure cooperation and further define nature of project. Consults with COMPUTER SYSTEMS HARDWARE ANALYST (profess. & kin.) 033.167-010 to define equipment needs. Reviews project feasibility studies. Establishes work standards. Assigns and schedules work, or delegates work to subordinate managers and supervisors, and reviews work. Interprets policies, purposes, and goals of organization to subordinates. Prepares progress reports to inform management of project status and deviation from goals. Contracts with management specialists, technical personnel, or vendors to solve problems. Directs COMPUTER PROCESSING SCHEDULER (clerical) 221.362-030 to change computer operating schedule to meet department priorities. Reviews reports of computer and peripheral equipment production, malfunctions, and maintenance to ascertain costs and plan department operating changes. Analyzes department workflow and workers' job duties to recommend reorganization or departmental realignment within company. Participates in decisions concerning staffing and promotions within data processing department. Directs training of subordinates. May prepare proposals and solicit sale of systems analysis, programming, and computer services to outside firms. May assist staff to diagnose and solve computer equipment problems. May participate in technical projects, such as writing equipment specifications or developing computer programs for specified applications. ● **GED:** R5, M4, L5 ● **SVP:** 4-10 yrs

● **Academic:** Ed=B, Eng=G ● **Work Field:** 295 ● **MPSMS:** 893 ● **Aptitudes:** G1, V1, N2, S3, P3, Q3, K4, F4, M4, E5, C5 ● **Temperaments:** D, J, P ● **Physical:** Stg=S; Freq: T, G, N Occas: R, H, I ● **Work Env:** Noise=Q; ● **Salary:** 5 ● **Outlook:** 4

PROGRAMMER-ANALYST (profess. & kin.) ● DOT #030.162-014 ● OES: 25102 ● Alternate titles: APPLICATIONS ANALYST-PROGRAMMER. Plans, develops, tests, and documents computer programs, applying knowledge of programming techniques and computer systems: Evaluates user request for new or modified program, such as for financial or human resource management system, clinical research trial results, statistical study of traffic patterns, or analyzing and developing specifications for bridge design, to determine feasibility, cost and time required, compatibility with current system, and computer capabilities. Consults with user to identify current operating procedures and clarify program objectives. Reads manuals, periodicals, and technical reports to learn ways to develop programs that meet user requirements. Formulates plan outlining steps required to develop program, using structured analysis and design. Submits plans to user for approval. Prepares flowcharts and diagrams to illustrate sequence of steps program must follow and to describe logical operations involved. Designs computer terminal screen displays to accomplish goals of user request. Converts project specifications, using flowcharts and diagrams, into sequence of detailed instructions and logical steps for coding into language processable by computer, applying knowledge of computer programming techniques and computer languages. Enters program codes into computer system. Enters commands into computer to run and test program. Reads computer printouts or observes display screen to detect syntax or logic errors during program test, or uses diagnostic software to detect errors. Replaces, deletes, or modifies codes to correct errors. Analyzes, reviews, and alters program to increase operating efficiency or adapt to new requirements. Writes documentation to describe program development, logic, coding, and corrections. Writes manual for users to describe installation and operating procedures. Assists users to solve operating problems. Recreates steps taken by user to locate source of problem and rewrites program to correct errors. May use computer-aided software tools, such as flowchart design and code generation, in each stage of system development. May train users to use program. May oversee installation of hardware and software. May provide technical assistance to program users. May install and test program at user site. May monitor performance of program after implementation. May specialize in developing programs for business or technical applications. ● **GED:** R5, M5, L5 ● **SVP:** 2-4 yrs ● **Academic:** Ed=B, Eng=S ● **Work Field:** 233 ● **MPSMS:** 893 ● **Aptitudes:** G1, V2, N2, S3, P3, Q1, K3, F3, M4, E5, C5 ● **Temperaments:** J, P, T ● **Physical:** Stg=S; Freq: R, H, I, T, G, N, A ● **Work Env:** Noise=N; ● **Salary:** 5 ● **Outlook:** 5

OPERATIONS-RESEARCH ANALYST (profess. & kin.) ● DOT #020.067-018 ● OES: 25302 ● Conducts analyses of management and operational problems and formulates mathematical or simulation models of problem for solution by computers or other methods: Analyzes problem in terms of management information and conceptualizes and defines problem. Studies information and selects plan from competitive proposals that affords maximum probability of profit or effectiveness in relation to cost or risk. Prepares model of problem in form of one or several equations that relates constants and variables, restrictions, alternatives, conflicting objectives and their numerical parameters. Defines data requirements and gathers and validates information applying judgment and statistical tests. Specifies manipulative or computational methods to be applied to model. Performs validation and testing of model to ensure adequacy, or determines need for reformulation. Prepares reports to management defining problem, evaluation, and possible solution. Evaluates implementation and effectiveness of research. May design, conduct, and evaluate experimental operational models where insufficient data exists to formulate model. May specialize in research and preparation of contract proposals specifying competence of organization to perform research, development, or production work. May develop and apply time and cost networks, such as Program Evaluation and Review Techniques (PERT), to plan and control large projects. May work in association with engineers, scientists, and management personnel in business, government, health, transportation, energy, manufacturing, environmental sciences or other technologies. ● **GED:** R6, M6, L6 ● **SVP:** 2-4 yrs ● **Academic:** Ed=M, Eng=S ● **Work Field:** 251 ● **MPSMS:** 890 ● **Aptitudes:** G1, V1, N1, S2, P3,

Q3, K4, F4, M4, E4, C5 ● **Temperaments:** J, V ● **Physical:** Stg=S; Freq: T, G, N Occas: R, H, I ● **Work Env:** Noise=Q; ● **Salary:** 4 ● **Outlook:** 4

PROGRAMMER, ENGINEERING AND SCIENTIFIC (profess. & kin.) ● DOT #030.162-010 ● OES: 25104 ● Converts scientific, engineering, and other technical problem formulations to format processable by computer: Resolves symbolic formulations, prepares flow charts and block diagrams, and encodes resultant equations for processing by applying extensive knowledge of branch of science, engineering, or advanced mathematics, such as differential equations or numerical analysis, and understanding of capabilities and limitations of computer. Confers with other engineering and technical personnel to resolve problems of intent, inaccuracy, or feasibility of computer processing. Enters program into computer system. Reviews results of computer runs with interested personnel to determine necessity for modifications or reruns. Develops new subroutines or expands program to simplify statement, programming, or coding of future problems. May direct and coordinate activities of COMPUTER PROGRAMMERS (profess. & kin.) 030.162-010 working as part of project team. ● **GED:** R6, M6, L6 ● **SVP:** 4-10 yrs ● **Academic:** Ed=B, Eng=S ● **Work Field:** 233, 244 ● **MPSMS:** 700 ● **Aptitudes:** G1, V1, N1, S2, P3, Q2, K4, F4, M4, E5, C5 ● **Temperaments:** J, T ● **Physical:** Stg=S; Freq: I Occas: R, H, T, G, N, A ● **Work Env:** Noise=N; ● **Salary:** 4 ● **Outlook:** 3

QUALITY ASSURANCE ANALYST (profess. & kin.) ● DOT #033.262-010 ● OES: 25102 ● Evaluates and tests new or modified software programs and software development procedures used to verify that programs function according to user requirements and conform to establishment guidelines: Writes, revises, and verifies quality standards and test procedures for program design and product evaluation to attain quality of software economically and efficiently. Reviews new or modified program, including documentation, diagram, and flow chart, to determine if program will perform according to user request and conform to guidelines. Recommends program improvements or corrections to programmers. Reviews computer operating log to identify program processing errors. Enters instructions into computer to test program for validity of results, accuracy, reliability, and conformance to establishment standards. Observes computer monitor screen during program test to detect error codes or interruption of program and corrects errors. Identifies differences between establishment standards and user applications and suggests modifications to conform to standards. Sets up tests at request of user to locate and correct program operating error following installation of program. Conducts compatibility tests with vendor-provided programs. Monitors program performance after implementation to prevent reoccurrence of program operating problems and ensure efficiency of operation. Writes documentation to describe program evaluation, testing, and correction. May evaluate proposed software or software enhancement for feasibility. May develop utility program to test, track, and verify defects in software program. May write programs to create new procedures or modify existing procedures. May train software program users. ● **GED:** R4, M4, L4 ● **SVP:** 1-2 yrs ● **Academic:** Ed=A, Eng=D ● **Work Field:** 233 ● **MPSMS:** 893 ● **Aptitudes:** G2, V2, N3, S4, P4, Q1, K3, F3, M4, E5, C5 ● **Temperaments:** J, T ● **Physical:** Stg=L; Freq: R, H, I, T, G, N Occas: A ● **Work Env:** Noise=N; ● **Salary:** 4 ● **Outlook:** 5

SOFTWARE ENGINEER (profess. & kin.) ● DOT #030.062-010 ● OES: 25198 ● Researches, designs, and develops computer software systems, in conjunction with hardware product development, for medical, industrial, military, communications, aerospace, and scientific applications, applying principles and techniques of computer science, engineering, and mathematical analysis: Analyzes software requirements to determine feasibility of design within time and cost constraints. Consults with hardware engineers and other engineering staff to evaluate interface between hardware and software, and operational and performance requirements of overall system. Formulates and designs software system, using scientific analysis and mathematical models to predict and measure outcome and consequences of design. Develops and directs software system testing procedures, programming, and documentation. Consults with customer concerning maintenance of software system. May coordinate installation of software system. ● **GED:** R5, M5, L5 ● **SVP:** 4-10 yrs ● **Academic:** Ed=B, Eng=S ● **Work Field:** 233, 244 ● **MPSMS:** 700, 721 ● **Aptitudes:** G1, V2, N1, S2, P2, Q2, K3, F3, M4, E5, C5 ● **Temperaments:** J, T, V ● **Physical:**

Stg=S; Freq: I, N Occas: R, H, T, G ● **Work Env:** Noise=N; ● **Salary:** 5 ● **Outlook:** 5

STATISTICIAN, MATHEMATICAL (profess. & kin.) ● DOT #020.067-022 ● OES: 25312 ● Alternate titles: STATISTICIAN, THEORETICAL. Conducts research into mathematical theories and proofs that form basis of science of statistics and develops statistical methodology: Examines theories, such as those of probability and inference, to discover mathematical bases for new or improved methods of obtaining and evaluating numerical data. Develops and tests experimental designs, sampling techniques, and analytical methods, and prepares recommendations concerning their utilization in statistical surveys, experiments, and tests. Investigates, evaluates, and prepares reports on applicability, efficiency, and accuracy of statistical methods used by physical and social scientists, including STATISTICIANS, APPLIED (profess. & kin.), in obtaining and evaluating data. ● **GED:** R6, M6, L6 ● **SVP:** 4-10 yrs ● **Academic:** Ed=M, Eng=G ● **Work Field:** 251 ● **MPSMS:** 721 ● **Aptitudes:** G1, V1, N1, S1, P2, Q3, K4, F4, M4, E5, C5 ● **Temperaments:** D, J ● **Physical:** Stg=S; Freq: N, A Occas: R, H, I, T, G ● **Work Env:** Noise=Q; ● **Salary:** 4 ● **Outlook:** 3

SYSTEMS ANALYST (profess. & kin.) ● DOT #030.167-014 ● OES: 25102 ● Analyzes user requirements, procedures, and problems to automate processing or to improve existing computer system: Confers with personnel of organizational units involved to analyze current operational procedures, identify problems, and learn specific input and output requirements, such as forms of data input, how data is to be summarized, and formats for reports. Writes detailed description of user needs, program functions, and steps required to develop or modify computer program. Reviews computer system capabilities, workflow, and scheduling limitations to determine if requested program or program change is possible within existing system. Studies existing information processing systems to evaluate effectiveness and develops new systems to improve production or workflow as required. Prepares workflow charts and diagrams to specify in detail operations to be performed by equipment and computer programs and operations to be performed by personnel in system. Conducts studies pertaining to development of new information systems to meet current and projected needs. Plans and prepares technical reports, memoranda, and instructional manuals as documentation of program development. Upgrades system and corrects errors to maintain system after implementation. May assist COMPUTER PROGRAMMER (profess. & kin.) 030.162-010 in resolution of work problems related to flow charts, project specifications, or programming. May prepare time and cost estimates for completing projects. May direct and coordinate work of others to develop, test, install, and modify programs. ● **GED:** R5, M4, L5 ● **SVP:** 2-4 yrs ● **Academic:** Ed=B, Eng=G ● **Work Field:** 233 ● **MPSMS:** 893 ● **Aptitudes:** G2, V2, N2, S4, P4, Q3, K4, F4, M4, E5, C5 ● **Temperaments:** D, J, P ● **Physical:** Stg=S; Freq: I, T, G, N Occas: R, H, A ● **Work Env:** Noise=N; ● **Salary:** 5 ● **Outlook:** 5

SYSTEMS PROGRAMMER (profess. & kin.) ● DOT #030.162-022 ● OES: 25102 ● Coordinates installation of computer operating system software and tests, maintains, and modifies software, using computer terminal: Reads loading and running instructions for system software, such as task scheduling, memory management, computer file system, or controlling computer input and output, and loads tape into tape drive or transfers software to magnetic disk. Initiates test of system program and observes readout on monitor of computer system to detect errors or work stoppage. Enters code changes into computer system to correct errors. Analyzes performance indicators, such as system's response time, number of transactions per second, and number of programs being processed at once, to ensure that system is operating efficiently. Changes system software so that system performance will meet objectives. Reviews computer system capabilities, workflow, and scheduling limitations to determine if requested changes to operating system are possible. Writes description of steps taken to modify system and procedures required to implement new software. Assists users having problems with use of system software. May train users, COMPUTER OPERATOR (clerical) 213.362-010, and COMPUTER PROGRAMMER (profess. & kin.) 030.162-010 to use system software. May prepare workflow charts and diagrams to modify system software. May visit vendors to observe demonstration of systems software. May administer and monitor computer program that controls user access to system. May review productivity reports and problem records to evaluate performance of computer system. ● **GED:** R5, M4,

L5 ● **SVP:** 2-4 yrs ● **Academic:** Ed=B, Eng=S ● **Work Field:** 233 ● **MPSMS:** 893 ● **Aptitudes:** G1, V2, N2, S4, P4, Q2, K3, F3, M3, E5, C5 ● **Temperaments:** J, T ● **Physical:** Stg=S; Freq: I, T, G, N Occas: R, H, A ● **Work Env:** Noise=N; ● **Salary:** 4 ● **Outlook:** 5

TECHNICAL SUPPORT SPECIALIST (profess. & kin.) ● DOT #033.162-018 ● OES: 25198 ● Alternate titles: PROJECT DEVELOPMENT COORDINATOR; TECHNICAL OPERATIONS SPECIALIST. Performs any combination of following duties to provide technical support to workers in information processing departments: Develops work goals and department projects. Assigns and coordinates work projects, such as converting to new hardware or software. Designates staff assignments, establishes work priorities, and evaluates cost and time requirements. Reviews completed projects or computer programs to ensure that goals are met and that programs are compatible with other programs already in use. Evaluates work load and capacity of computer system to determine feasibility of expanding or enhancing computer operations. Makes recommendations for improvements in computer system. Reviews and tests programs written by PROGRAMMER-ANALYST (profess. & kin.) 030.162-014 or COMPUTER PROGRAMMER (profess. & kin.) 030.162-010 to ensure that programs meet objectives and specifications. Consults with QUALITY ASSURANCE ANALYST (profess. & kin.) 033.262-010 to ensure that program follows establishment standards. Modifies, tests, and corrects existing programs. Evaluates and tests vendor-supplied software packages for mainframe computer or microcomputers to determine compatibility with existing system, ease of use, and if software meets user needs. Enters commands into computer to place programs in production status. Inactivates, individually or in combination, each component of computer system, such as central processing unit, tape drives, and mainframe coolers. Tests computer system to determine criticality of component loss. Prioritizes importance of components and writes recommendations for recovering losses and using backup equipment. Assists user to resolve computer-related problems, such as inoperative hardware or software. Trains workers in use of new software or hardware. Reads technical journals or manuals and attends vendor seminars to learn about new computer hardware and software. Writes project reports and documentation for new or modified software and hardware. ● **GED:** R5, M4, L5 ● **SVP:** 2-4 yrs ● **Academic:** Ed=A, Eng=S ● **Work Field:** 233 ● **MPSMS:** 893 ● **Aptitudes:** G2, V2, N3, S3, P3, Q3, K3, F3, M3, E5, C5 ● **Temperaments:** D, J, P, T ● **Physical:** Stg=L; Freq: I, T, G, N Occas: R, H, A ● **Work Env:** Noise=N; ● **Salary:** 4 ● **Outlook:** 3

USER SUPPORT ANALYST (profess. & kin.) ● DOT #032.262-010 ● OES: 25104 ● Alternate titles: CUSTOMER SERVICE REPRESENTATIVE; END USER CONSULTANT; HELP DESK REPRESENTATIVE; INFORMATION CENTER SPECIALIST; OFFICE AUTOMATION ANALYST. Investigates and resolves computer software and hardware problems of users: Receives telephone calls from users having problems using computer software and hardware or inquiring how to use specific software, such as statistical, graphics, data base, printing, word processing, programming languages, electronic mail, and operating systems. Talks to user to learn procedures followed and source of error. Answers questions, applying knowledge of computer software, hardware, and procedures. Asks user with problem to use telephone and participate in diagnostic procedures, using diagnostic software, or by listening to and following instructions. Determines whether problem is caused by hardware, such as modem, printer, cables, or telephone. Talks with coworkers to research problem and find solution. Talks to programmers to explain software errors or to recommend changes to programs. Calls software and hardware vendors to request service regarding defective products. Reads trade magazines and attends computer trade shows to obtain current information about computers. May test software and hardware to evaluate ease of use and whether product will aid user in performing work. May write software and hardware evaluation and recommendation for management review. May write or revise user training manuals and procedures. May develop training materials, such as exercises and visual displays. May train users on software and hardware on-site or in classroom, or recommend outside contractors to provide training. May install microcomputers, software, and peripheral equipment, following procedures and using handtools [MICROCOMPUTER SUPPORT SPECIALIST (profess. & kin.) 039.264-010]. May work as in-house consultant and research alternate approaches to existing software and hardware when standardized approaches cannot be applied. May conduct office automation feasibility studies, including work flow analysis, space design, and cost comparison analysis. May specialize by type of software, computer language, or computer operating system. ● **GED:** R4, M3, L4 ● **SVP:** 2-4 yrs ● **Academic:** Ed=A, Eng=G ● **Work Field:** 233, 282 ● **MPSMS:** 893 ● **Aptitudes:** G2, V2, N3, S3, P3, Q2, K4, F4, M4, E5, C5 ● **Temperaments:** J, P, T ● **Physical:** Stg=S; Const: T, G, N Freq: R, H, I Occas: A ● **Work Env:** Noise=N; ● **Salary:** 4 ● **Outlook:** 4

USER SUPPORT ANALYST SUPERVISOR (profess. & kin.) ● DOT #032.132-010 ● OES: 25104 ● Alternate titles: HELP DESK SUPERVISOR. Supervises and coordinates activities of workers who provide problem-solving support to computer users: Assists USER SUPPORT ANALYST (profess. & kin.) 032.262.010 in solving nonroutine software, hardware, and procedure problems, using computer and manuals. Talks with staff, computer users, supervisors, and managers to determine requirements for new or modified software and hardware. Writes recommendations for management review. Coordinates installation of hardware and software, and implementation of procedure changes. Performs duties described under SUPERVISOR (any industry) Master Title. ● **GED:** R4, M3, L4 ● **SVP:** 4-10 yrs ● **Academic:** Ed=A, Eng=G ● **Work Field:** 233 ● **MPSMS:** 893 ● **Aptitudes:** G2, V2, N2, S3, P3, Q2, K4, F4, M4, E5, C5 ● **Temperaments:** J, P, T ● **Physical:** Stg=S; Const: T, G, N Freq: R, H, I Occas: A ● **Work Env:** Noise=N; ● **Salary:** 4 ● **Outlook:** 5

GOE: 11.01.02
Data Analysis

ACTUARY (profess. & kin.) ● DOT #020.167-010 ● OES: 25313 ● Applies knowledge of mathematics, probability, statistics, principles of finance and business to problems in life, health, social, and casualty insurance, annuities, and pensions: Determines mortality, accident, sickness, disability, and retirement rates; constructs probability tables regarding fire, natural disasters, and unemployment, based on analysis of statistical data and other pertinent information. Designs or reviews insurance and pension plans and calculates premiums. Ascertains premium rates required and cash reserves and liabilities necessary to ensure payment of future benefits. Determines equitable basis for distributing surplus earnings under participating insurance and annuity contracts in mutual companies. May specialize in one type of insurance and be designated Actuary, Casualty (profess. & kin.); Actuary, Life (profess. & kin.). ● **GED:** R5, M5, L5 ● **SVP:** 4-10 yrs ● **Academic:** Ed=B, Eng=G ● **Work Field:** 232, 251 ● **MPSMS:** 721 ● **Aptitudes:** G2, V2, N1, S4, P3, Q1, K4, F4, M4, E5, C5 ● **Temperaments:** D, J, T ● **Physical:** Stg=S; Freq: T, G, N Occas: R, H, I ● **Work Env:** Noise=Q; ● **Salary:** 5 ● **Outlook:** 4

CONSULTANT (profess. & kin.) ● DOT #189.167-010 ● OES: 00000 ● Consults with client to define need or problem, conducts studies and surveys to obtain data, and analyzes data to advise on or recommend solution, utilizing knowledge of theory, principles, or technology of specific discipline or field of specialization: Consults with client to ascertain and define need or problem area, and determine scope of investigation required to obtain solution. Conducts study or survey on need or problem to obtain data required for solution. Analyzes data to determine solution, such as installation of alternate methods and pro-

cedures, changes in processing methods and practices, modification of machines or equipment, or redesign of products or services. Advises client on alternate methods of solving need or problem, and recommends specific solution. May negotiate contract for consulting service. May specialize in providing consulting service to government in field of specialization. May be designated according to field of specialization such as engineering or science discipline, economics, education, labor, or in specialized field of work as health services, social services, or investment services. ● **GED:** R5, M5, L5 ● **SVP:** 4-10 yrs ● **Academic:** Ed=B, Eng=G ● **Work Field:** 244, 271, 251 ● **MPSMS:** 720, 700, 950 ● **Aptitudes:** G2, V2, N2, S2, P3, Q3, K4, F4, M4, E5, C5 ● **Temperaments:** D, J, P ● **Physical:** Stg=S; Freq: T, G, N Occas: R, H, I ● **Work Env:** Noise=N; ● **Salary:** 4 ● **Outlook:** 3

MATHEMATICAL TECHNICIAN (profess. & kin.) ● DOT #020.162-010 ● OES: 24501 ● Alternate titles: DATA-REDUCTION TECHNICIAN. Applies standardized mathematical formulas, principles, and methodology to technological problems in engineering and physical sciences in relation to specific industrial and research objectives, processes, equipment and products: Confers with professional, scientific, and engineering personnel to plan project. Analyzes raw data from computer or recorded on photographic film or other media. Selects most practical and accurate combination and sequence of computational methods, using algebra, trigonometry, geometry, vector analysis and calculus to reduce raw data to meaningful and manageable terms. Selects most economical and reliable combination of manual, mechanical, or data processing methods and equipment consistent with data reduction requirements. Modifies standard formulas to conform to data processing method selected. Translates data into numerical values, equations, flow charts, graphs or other media. Analyzes processed data to detect errors. May operate calculator or computer. ● **GED:** R5, M5, L5 ● **SVP:** 2-4 yrs ● **Academic:** Ed=B, Eng=S ● **Work Field:** 244, 251 ● **MPSMS:** 721 ● **Aptitudes:** G2, V2, N2, S3, P4, Q2, K3, F4, M4, E5, C4 ● **Temperaments:** J, T, V ● **Physical:** Stg=S; Freq: R, H, I, T, G, N Occas: A, X ● **Work Env:** Noise=N; ● **Salary:** 4 ● **Outlook:** 4

STATISTICIAN, APPLIED (profess. & kin.) ● DOT #020.167-026 ● OES: 25312 ● Plans data collection, and analyzes and interprets numerical data from experiments, studies, surveys, and other sources and applies statistical methodology to provide information for scientific research and statistical analysis: Plans methods to collect information and develops questionnaire techniques according to survey design. Conducts surveys utilizing sampling techniques or complete enumeration bases. Evaluates reliability of source information, adjusts and weighs raw data, and organizes results into form compatible with analysis by computers or other methods. Presents numerical information by computer readouts, graphs, charts, tables, written reports or other methods. Describes sources of information, and limitations on reliability and usability. May analyze and interpret statistics to point up significant differences in relationships among sources of information, and prepare conclusions and forecasts based on data summaries. May specialize in specific aspect of statistics or industrial activity reporting and be designated by specialty as Demographer (profess. & kin.) I; Statistician, Analytical (profess. & kin.); Statistician, Engineering And Physical Science (profess. & kin.). ● **GED:** R5, M5, L4 ● **SVP:** 2-4 yrs ● **Academic:** Ed=B, Eng=S ● **Work Field:** 251 ● **MPSMS:** 721 ● **Aptitudes:** G1, V1, N1, S3, P2, Q2, K4, F4, M4, E5, C5 ● **Temperaments:** J ● **Physical:** Stg=S; Freq: R, H, I, T, G, N, A ● **Work Env:** Noise=N; ● **Salary:** 5 ● **Outlook:** 4

Educational and Library Services

Workers in this group do general and specialized teaching, vocational training, advising in agriculture and home economics, and library work of various kinds. Jobs are found in schools, colleges, libraries, and other educational facilities.

✓ **What kind of work would you do?**

Your work activities would depend upon your specific job. For example, you might:

■ teach elementary or secondary school students.

- teach the skills for a specific trade to adults or youth.
- present ideas and information for effective home and farm management to adults.
- teach undergraduate or graduate college courses.
- check out, collect, and shelve books in a library.

✓ What skills and abilities do you need for this kind of work?

To do this kind of work, you must be able to:

- understand and use the basic principles of effective teaching.
- develop special skills and knowledge in one or more academic or vocational subjects.
- use an organized system for storing and using books and other library materials.
- develop a good teacher-student relationship.

✓ How do you know if you would like or could learn to do this kind of work?

The following questions may give you clues about yourself as you consider this group of jobs.

- Have you been a camp or playground instructor? Do you enjoy working with children?
- Have you helped friends or relatives with their homework? Can you explain things and communicate ideas?
- Have you been a member of FTA (Future Teachers of America) or a similar group? Do you have a desire to teach or train others?
- Have you been a school office worker or teacher's helper? Do you enjoy helping and assisting people?
- Have you assisted a librarian in cataloging or shelving books? Did you like this type of activity?

✓ How can you prepare for and enter this kind of work?

Occupations in this group usually require education and/or training extending from two years to over ten years, depending upon the specific kind of work. Four or more years of college is required for most jobs in this group. College and university teachers, supervisors, and librarians must have graduate degrees. Teachers in public schools must obtain state certificates. Requirements for certificates vary among the states, but specific amounts of education and experience are usually included. Vocational teachers are often required to have extensive work experience in their teaching field. Home economics and agricultural extension services workers need special coursework.

✓ What else should you consider about these jobs?

Openings for teachers vary according to the subject area or specialty, the enrollment, and the financial support of each institution. Most teachers are required to work only nine months each year. Therefore, some may have time to further their education or find summer employment.

Teachers and other education workers are frequently required to accept duties outside of the regular work day. These duties may include planning and grading activities; attending conferences, meetings, and workshops; advising students; or supervising student activities. Workers may receive additional pay for some of these duties.

If you think you would like to do this kind of work, look at the job titles listed on the following pages.

■ ■ ■

GOE: 11.02.01
Teaching & Instructing, General

FACULTY MEMBER, COLLEGE OR UNIVERSITY (education) ● DOT #090.227-010 ● OES: 31100 ● Conducts college or university courses for undergraduate or graduate students: Teaches one or more subjects, such as economics, chemistry, law, or medicine, within prescribed curriculum. Prepares and delivers lectures to students. Compiles bibliographies of specialized materials for outside reading assignments. Stimulates class discussions. Compiles, administers, and grades examinations, or assigns this work to others. Directs research of other teachers or graduate students working for advanced academic degrees. Conducts research in particular field of knowledge and publishes findings in professional journals. Performs related duties, such as advising students on academic and vocational curricula, and acting as adviser to student organizations. Serves on faculty committee providing professional consulting services to government and industry.

May be designated according to faculty rank in traditional hierarchy as determined by institution's estimate of scholarly maturity as Associate Professor (education); Professor (education); or according to rank distinguished by duties assigned or amount of time devoted to academic work as Research Assistant (education); Visiting Professor (education). May teach in two-year college and be designated Teacher, Junior College (education); or in technical institute and be designated Faculty Member, Technical Institute (education). May be designated: Acting Professor (education); Assistant Professor (education); Clinical Instructor (education); Instructor (education); Lecturer (education); Teaching Assistant (education). ● **GED:** R6, M5, L5 ● **SVP:** 4-10 yrs ● **Academic:** Ed=M, Eng=G ● **Work Field:** 296 ● **MPSMS:** 931 ● **Aptitudes:** G1, V1, N2, S3, P3, Q2, K4, F4, M4, E5, C5 ● **Temperaments:** D, I, J, P ● **Physical:** Stg=L; Freq: T, G, N, A Occas: R, H, I ● **Work Env:** Noise=N; ● **Salary:** 3 ● **Outlook:** 2

HISTORIC-SITE ADMINISTRATOR (museums) ● DOT #102.167-014 ● OES: 31511 ● Manages operation of historic structure or site: Discusses house or site operation with governing body representatives to form or change policies. Oversees activities of building and grounds maintenance staff and other employees. Maintains roster of volunteer guides, and contacts volunteers to conduct tours of premises according to schedule. Conducts tours, explaining points of interest and answers visitors' questions. Studies documents, books, and other materials to obtain information concerning history of site or structure. Conducts classes in tour presentation methods for volunteer guides. Accepts group reservations for house tours and special social events. Arranges for refreshments, entertainment, and decorations for special events. Collects admission and special event fees, and maintains records of receipts, expenses, and numbers of persons served. Assists in planning publicity, and arranges for printing of brochures or placement of information in media. Inspects premises for evidence of deterioration and need for repair, and notifies governing body of such need. ● **GED:** R5, M4, L5 ● **SVP:** 6 mos-1 yr ● **Academic:** Ed=A, Eng=G ● **Work Field:** 295 ● **MPSMS:** 939 ● **Aptitudes:** G2, V2, N3, S4, P3, Q3, K4, F4, M4, E5, C4 ● **Temperaments:** D, P, V ● **Physical:** Stg=L; Freq: T, G Occas: R, H, I, N, A, X ● **Work Env:** Noise=N; ● **Salary:** 4 ● **Outlook:** 2

INSTRUCTOR, BUSINESS EDUCATION (education) ● DOT #090.222-010 ● OES: 31314 ● Instructs students in commercial subjects, such as typing, filing, secretarial procedures, business mathematics, office equipment use, and personality development, in business schools, community colleges, or training programs: Instructs students in subject matter, utilizing various methods, such as lecture and demonstration, and uses audiovisual aids and other materials to supplement presentations. Prepares or follows teaching outline for course of study, assigns lessons, and corrects homework and classroom papers. Administers tests to evaluate students' progress, records results, and issues reports to inform students of their progress. Maintains discipline in classroom. ● **GED:** R5, M4, L5 ● **SVP:** 4-10 yrs ● **Academic:** Ed=B, Eng=G ● **Work Field:** 296 ● **MPSMS:** 931 ● **Aptitudes:** G2, V2, N3, S5, P4, Q1, K2, F3, M4, E5, C5 ● **Temperaments:** D, I, J, P ● **Physical:** Stg=L; Freq: R, H, I, T, G, N Occas: C, S ● **Work Env:** Noise=N; ● **Salary:** 4 ● **Outlook:** 3

INSTRUCTOR, EXTENSION WORK (education) ● DOT #090.227-018 ● OES: 31398 ● Conducts evening classes for extension service of college or university: Prepares course of study designed to meet community, organization, and student needs. Conducts and corrects examinations, and assigns course grades. ● **GED:** R5, M3, L5 ● **SVP:** 4-10 yrs ● **Academic:** Ed=A, Eng=G ● **Work Field:** 296 ● **MPSMS:** 931 ● **Aptitudes:** G2, V2, N3, S4, P3, Q2, K4, F4, M4, E5, C5 ● **Temperaments:** D, I, P ● **Physical:** Stg=S; Freq: T, G, N Occas: R, H, I ● **Work Env:** Noise=N; ● **Salary:** 3 ● **Outlook:** 3

INSTRUCTOR, PHYSICAL EDUCATION (education) ● DOT #099.224-010 ● OES: 31305 ● Alternate titles: TEACHER, PHYSICAL EDUCATION. Instructs students in physical education activities in educational institution: Plans physical education program to promote development of student's physical attributes and social skills. Teaches individual and team sports to students, utilizing knowledge of sports techniques and of physical capabilities of students. Organizes, leads, instructs, and referees indoor and outdoor games, such as volleyball, baseball, and basketball. Instructs individuals or groups in beginning or advanced calisthenics, gymnastics, or corrective exercises, determining type and level of difficulty of exercises, corrections needed, and prescribed movements, applying knowledge of sports, physiology, and corrective techniques. Teaches and demonstrates use of gymnastic and training apparatus, such as trampolines and weights. Confers with students, parents, and school counselor to resolve student problem. May select, store, order, issue, and inventory equipment, materials, and supplies used in physical education program. May specialize in instructing specific sport, such as tennis, swimming, or basketball. May teach students with disabilities. May be required to have certification from state. ● **GED:** R5, M3, L5 ● **SVP:** 2-4 yrs ● **Academic:** Ed=B, Eng=G ● **Work Field:** 296 ● **MPSMS:** 931 ● **Aptitudes:** G2, V2, N3, S3, P3, Q4, K3, F3, M3, E1, C4 ● **Temperaments:** D, P, V ● **Physical:** Stg=L; Freq: R, H, T, G, F, V Occas: C, B, S, K, O, W, I, E, N, D, A, X ● **Work Env:** Noise=N; Occas: W ● **Salary:** 4 ● **Outlook:** 4

TEACHER (museums) ● DOT #099.227-038 ● OES: 31317 ● Teaches classes, presents lectures, conducts workshops, and participates in other activities to further educational program of museum, zoo, or similar institution: Plans course content and method of presentation, and prepares outline of material to be covered and submits it for approval. Selects and assembles materials to be used in teaching assignment, such as pieces of pottery or samples of plant life, and arranges use of audiovisual equipment or other teaching aids. Conducts classes for children in various scientific, history, or art subjects, utilizing museum displays to augment standard teaching methods and adapting course content and complexity to ages and interests of students. Teaches adult classes in such subjects as art, history, astronomy, or horticulture, using audiovisual aids, demonstration, or laboratory techniques appropriate to subject matter. Presents series of lectures on subjects related to institution collections, often incorporating films or slides into presentation. Conducts seminars or workshops for school system teachers or lay persons to demonstrate methods of using institution facilities and collections to enhance school programs or to enrich other activities. Conducts workshops or field trips for students or community groups and plans and directs activities associated with projects. Plans and presents vacation or weekend programs for elementary or preschool children, combining recreational activities with teaching methods geared to age groups. Conducts classes for academic credit in cooperation with area schools or universities. Teaches courses in museum work to participants in work-study programs. Works with adult leaders of youth groups to assist youths to earn merit badges or fulfill other group requirements. Maintains records of attendance. Evaluates success of courses, basing evaluation on number and enthusiasm of persons participating and recommends retaining or dropping course in future plans. When course is offered for academic credit, evaluates class member performances, administers tests, and issues grades in accordance with methods used by cooperating educational institution. ● **GED:** R5, M4, L5 ● **SVP:** 2-4 yrs ● **Academic:** Ed=B, Eng=G ● **Work Field:** 296 ● **MPSMS:** 931 ● **Aptitudes:** G2, V2, N3, S3, P3, Q3, K4, F4, M4, E5, C3 ● **Temperaments:** D, P ● **Physical:** Stg=L; Freq: R, H, T, G, N Occas: I, F, A, X ● **Work Env:** Noise=N; ● **Salary:** 4 ● **Outlook:** 4

TEACHER AIDE I (education) ● DOT #099.327-010 ● OES: 53904 ● Alternate titles: TEACHER ASSISTANT. Performs any combination of following instructional tasks in classroom to assist teaching staff of public or private elementary or secondary school: Discusses assigned teaching area with classroom teacher to coordinate instructional efforts. Prepares lesson outline and plan in assigned area and submits outline to teacher for review. Plans, prepares, and develops various teaching aids, such as bibliographies, charts, and graphs. Presents subject matter to students, utilizing variety of methods and techniques, such as lecture, discussion, and supervised role playing. Prepares, administers, and grades examinations. Assists students, individually or in groups, with lesson assignments to present or reinforce learning concepts. Confers with parents on progress of students. May specialize in single subject area. May be required to have completed specified number of college education credits. ● **GED:** R4, M3, L4 ● **SVP:** 1-2 yrs ● **Academic:** Ed=H, Eng=G ● **Work Field:** 296 ● **MPSMS:** 931 ● **Aptitudes:** G3, V3, N3, S4, P4, Q3, K4, F4, M3, E5, C4 ● **Temperaments:** J, P ● **Physical:** Stg=L; Freq: R, H, T, G, N Occas: I, F, X ● **Work Env:** Noise=N; ● **Salary:** 2 ● **Outlook:** 1

TEACHER, ADULT EDUCATION (education) ● DOT #099.227-030 ● OES: 31317 ● Instructs out-of-school youths and adults in academic and nonacademic courses in public or private schools or other organizations: Prepares outline of instructional program and studies and assembles material to be presented. Presents lectures and discussions to group to increase students' knowledge or vocational competence. Tests and grades students on achievement in class. Teaches courses, such as citizenship, fine arts, and homemaking, to enrich students' cultural and academic backgrounds. Conducts workshops and demonstrations to teach such skills as driving, sports, and dancing, or to provide training for parenthood. May teach basic courses in American history, principles, ideas, and customs and in English to foreign-born and be designated Teacher, Citizenship (education). ● **GED:** R4, M2, L4 ● **SVP:** 2-4 yrs ● **Academic:** Ed=B, Eng=G ● **Work Field:** 296 ● **MPSMS:** 931 ● **Aptitudes:** G3, V2, N3, S3, P3, Q2, K4, F4, M4, E5, C5 ● **Temperaments:** D, I, J ● **Physical:** Stg=L; Freq: R, H, I, T, G, N Occas: F, D, A, V ● **Work Env:** Noise=N; ● **Salary:** 3 ● **Outlook:** 4

TEACHER, ELEMENTARY SCHOOL (education) ● DOT #092.227-010 ● OES: 31305 ● Teaches elementary school students academic, social, and motor skills in public or private schools: Prepares course objectives and outline for course of study following curriculum guidelines or requirements of state and school. Lectures, demonstrates, and uses audiovisual teaching aids to present subject matter to class. Prepares, administers, and corrects tests, and records results. Assigns lessons, corrects papers, and hears oral presentations. Teaches rules of conduct. Maintains order in classroom and on playground. Counsels pupils when adjustment and academic problems arise. Discusses pupils' academic and behavioral attitudes and achievements with parents. Keeps attendance and grade records as required by school. May coordinate class field trips. May teach combined grade classes. May specialize by subject taught, such as math, science, or social studies. May be required to hold state certification. ● **GED:** R5, M4, L5 ● **SVP:** 2-4 yrs ● **Academic:** Ed=B, Eng=G ● **Work Field:** 296 ● **MPSMS:** 931 ● **Aptitudes:** G2, V2, N3, S4, P4, Q2, K4, F4, M4, E5, C5 ● **Temperaments:** D, I, J, P ● **Physical:** Stg=L; Const: T, G Freq: N Occas: S, R, H, I, F, A, X, V ● **Work Env:** Noise=N; ● **Salary:** 4 ● **Outlook:** 4

TEACHER, RESOURCE (education) ● DOT #099.227-042 ● OES: 31311 ● Teaches basic academic subjects to students requiring remedial work, using special help programs to improve scholastic level: Teaches basic subjects, such as reading and math, applying lesson techniques designed for short attention spans. Administers achievement tests and evaluates test results to discover level of language and math skills. Selects and teaches reading material and math problems related to everyday life of individual student. Confers with school counselors and teaching staff to obtain additional testing information and to gain insight on student behavioral disorders affecting learning process. Designs special help programs for low achievers and encourages parent-teacher cooperation. Attends professional meetings, writes reports, and maintains records. ● **GED:** R5, M5, L5 ● **SVP:** 2-4 yrs ● **Academic:** Ed=B, Eng=G ● **Work Field:** 296 ● **MPSMS:** 931 ● **Aptitudes:** G2, V2, N2, S4, P4, Q2, K4, F4, M4, E5, C5 ● **Temperaments:** D, J, P ● **Physical:** Stg=L; Freq: T, G, N Occas: R, H, I ● **Work Env:** Noise=N; ● **Salary:** 2 ● **Outlook:** 3

TEACHER, SECONDARY SCHOOL (education) ● DOT #091.227-010 ● OES: 31308 ● Alternate titles: HIGH SCHOOL TEACHER. Teaches one or more subjects to students in public or private secondary schools: Instructs students, using various teaching methods, such as lecture and demonstration, and uses audiovisual aids and other materials to supplement presentations. Prepares course objectives and outline for course of study following curriculum guidelines or requirements of state and school. Assigns lessons and corrects homework. Administers tests to evaluate pupil progress, records results, and issues reports to inform parents of progress. Keeps attendance records. Maintains discipline in classroom. Meets with parents to discuss student progress and problems. Participates in faculty and professional meetings, educational conferences, and teacher training workshops. Performs related duties, such as sponsoring one or more activities or student organizations, assisting pupils in selecting course of study, and counseling student in adjustment and academic problems. May be identified according to subject matter taught. May be required to hold certification from state. ● **GED:** R5, M4, L5 ● **SVP:** 2-4 yrs ● **Academic:** Ed=B, Eng=G ● **Work Field:** 296 ● **MPSMS:** 931 ● **Aptitudes:** G2, V2, N3, S4, P3, Q2, K4, F4, M4, E5, C4 ● **Temperaments:** D, I, J, P ● **Physical:** Stg=L; Freq: H, T, G, N Occas: R, I, F, X, V ● **Work Env:** Noise=N; ● **Salary:** 4 ● **Outlook:** 4

TUTOR (education) ● DOT #099.227-034 ● OES: 31398 ● Teaches academic subjects, such as English, mathematics, and foreign languages to pupils requiring private instruction, adapting curriculum to meet individual's needs. May teach in pupil's home. ● **GED:** R5, M3, L5 ● **SVP:** 2-4 yrs ● **Academic:** Ed=A, Eng=G ● **Work Field:** 296 ● **MPSMS:** 931 ● **Aptitudes:** G2, V2, N3, S4, P4, Q2, K4, F4, M4, E5, C5 ● **Temperaments:** J, P ● **Physical:** Stg=L; Freq: R, H, I, T, G, N, A ● **Work Env:** Noise=N; ● **Salary:** 2 ● **Outlook:** 4

GOE: 11.02.02
Teaching, Vocational & Industrial

DIETITIAN, TEACHING (profess. & kin.) ● DOT #077.127-022 ● OES: 32521 ● Plans, organizes, and conducts educational programs in dietetics, nutrition, and institution management for DIETETIC INTERNS (profess. & kin.), nursing students, and other medical personnel: Develops curriculum and prepares manuals, visual aids, course outlines, and other material used in teaching. Lectures students on composition and values of foods, principles of nutrition, menu planning, diet therapy, food cost control, marketing, and administration of dietary department. May engage in research. ● **GED:** R5, M4, L5 ● **SVP:** 4-10 yrs ● **Academic:** Ed=A, Eng=G ● **Work Field:** 296 ● **MPSMS:** 732 ● **Aptitudes:** G2, V2, N3, S3, P3, Q3, K4, F4, M4, E5, C4 ● **Temperaments:** D, J, P ● **Physical:** Stg=L; Freq: T, G, N ● **Work Env:** Noise=N; ● **Salary:** 2 ● **Outlook:** 4

HUMAN RESOURCE ADVISOR (profess. & kin.) ● DOT #166.267-046 ● OES: 21511 ● Provides establishment personnel assistance in identifying, evaluating, and resolving human relations and work performance problems within establishment to facilitate communication and improve employee human relations skills and work performance: Talks informally with establishment personnel and attends meetings of managers, supervisors, and work units to facilitate effective interpersonal communication among participants and to ascertain human relations and work related problems that adversely affect employee morale and establishment productivity. Evaluates human relations and work related problems and meets with supervisors and managers to determine effective remediation techniques, such as job skill training or personal intervention, to resolve human relations issues among personnel. Develops and conducts training to instruct establishment managers, supervisors, and workers in human relation skills, such as supervisory skills, conflict resolution skills, interpersonal communication skills, and effective group interaction skills. Schedules individuals for technical job-related skills training to improve individual work performance. May participate in resolving labor relations issues. May assist in screening applicants for establishment training programs. May write employee newsletter. May operate audio-visual equipment to review or to present audio-visual tapes for training program. ● **GED:** R5, M3, L5 ● **SVP:** 2-4 yrs ● **Academic:** Ed=B, Eng=G ● **Work Field:** 296, 298 ● **MPSMS:** 893 ● **Aptitudes:** G2, V2, N4, S5, P5, Q3, K5, F5, M5, E5, C5 ● **Temperaments:** D, I, J, P ● **Physical:** Stg=L; Const: T, G Freq: N Occas: R, H ● **Work Env:** Noise=N; ● **Salary:** 5 ● **Outlook:** 3

TEACHER, INDUSTRIAL ARTS (education) ● DOT #091.221-010 ● OES: 31308 ● Alternate titles: SHOP TEACHER. Teaches students basic techniques and assists in development of manipulative skills in industrial arts courses in secondary schools: Prepares lesson plans for courses and establishes goals. Lectures, illustrates, and demonstrates when teaching use of handtools; machines, such as lathe, planer, power saws, and drill press; safety practices; precision measuring instruments, such as micrometer; and industrial arts techniques. Evaluates student progress. Talks with parents and counselor to resolve behavioral and academic problems. May teach shop math. May specialize in one or more areas, such as woodworking, metalworking, electricity, graphic arts, automobile repair, or drafting. May teach students with disabilities. May be required to have certification from state. ● **GED:** R5, M4, L5 ● **SVP:** 2-4 yrs ● **Academic:** Ed=B, Eng=G ● **Work Field:** 296 ● **MPSMS:** 931 ● **Aptitudes:** G2, V2, N2, S2, P2, Q3, K3, F3, M3, E5, C4 ● **Temperaments:** D, J, P, V ● **Physical:** Stg=L; Freq: R, H, T, G, N, D, A Occas: S, I, E, F, X, V ● **Work Env:** Noise=L; Occas: M ● **Salary:** 4 ● **Outlook:** 4

INSTRUCTOR, TECHNICAL TRAINING (education) ● DOT #166.221-010 ● OES: 31314 ● Alternate titles: TRAINING SPECIALIST. Develops and conducts programs to train employees or customers of industrial or commercial establishment in installation, programming, safety, maintenance, and repair of machinery and equipment, such as robots, programmable controllers, and robot controllers, following manuals, specifications, blueprints, and schematics, and using handtools, measuring instruments, and testing equipment: Confers with management and staff or TECHNICAL TRAINING COORDINATOR (education) 166.167-054 to determine training objectives. Writes training program, including outline, text, handouts, and tests, and designs laboratory exercises, applying knowledge of electronics, mechanics, hydraulics, pneumatics, and programming, and following machine, equipment, and tooling manuals. Schedules classes based on classroom and equipment availability. Lectures class on safety, installation, programming, maintenance, and repair of machinery and equipment, following outline, handouts, and texts, and using visual aids, such as graphs, charts, videotape, and slides. Demonstrates procedures being taught, such as programming and repair, applying knowledge of electrical wire color coding, programming, electronics, mechanics, hydraulics, and pneumatics, using handtools, measuring instruments, and testing equipment, and following course outline. Observes trainees in laboratory and answers trainees' questions. Administers written and practical exams and writes performance reports to evaluate trainees' performance. Participates in meetings, seminars, and training sessions to obtain information useful to training facility and integrates information into training program. May repair electrical and electronic components of robots in industrial establishments. May install, program, maintain, and repair robots in customer's establishment [FIELD SERVICE TECHNICIAN (machinery mfg.) 638.261-026]. May be designated according to subject taught as Instructor, Programmable Controllers (education); Instructor, Robotics (education). ● **GED:** R5, M4, L5 ● **SVP:** 4-10 yrs ● **Academic:** Ed=A, Eng=G ● **Work Field:** 296, 111, 121 ● **MPSMS:** 931, 560, 580 ● **Aptitudes:** G2, V2, N2, S2, P2, Q3, K3, F3, M2, E5, C4 ● **Temperaments:** D, J, P, T, V ● **Physical:** Stg=L; Const: T, G Freq: R, H, I, N, X Occas: C, D, V ● **Work Env:** Noise=N; Occas: M, E ● **Salary:** 4 ● **Outlook:** 4

INSTRUCTOR, VOCATIONAL TRAINING (education) ● DOT #097.221-010 ● OES: 31314 ● Alternate titles: TEACHER, VOCATIONAL TRAINING. Teaches vocational training subjects to students in public or private schools or in industrial plants: Organizes program of practical and technical instruction, including demonstrations of skills required in trade, and lectures on theory, techniques, and terminology. Instructs students in subject areas, such as mathematics, science, drawing, use and maintenance of tools and equipment, codes or regulations related to trade, and safety precautions. Plans and supervises work of students, individually or in small groups, in shop or laboratory. Tests and evaluates achievement of student in technical knowledge and trade skills. May be identified according to trade or theory taught or type of establishment in which training is conducted, such as plumbing, electronics, or dental assistance. May place students in job training. May teach students with disabilities. May be required to have certification from state. ● **GED:** R4, M4, L4 ● **SVP:** 2-4 yrs ● **Academic:** Ed=A, Eng=G ● **Work Field:** 296 ● **MPSMS:** 931 ● **Aptitudes:** G2, V2, N2, S2, P2, Q3, K3, F3, M3, E5, C4 ● **Temperaments:** D, J, P ● **Physical:** Stg=L; Freq: R, H, I, T, G, N Occas: D, X, V ● **Work Env:** Noise=N; Occas: M, O ● **Salary:** 4 ● **Outlook:** 4

TRAINING REPRESENTATIVE (education) ● DOT #166.227-010 ● OES: 31314 ● Alternate titles: TRAINING INSTRUCTOR. Develops and conducts training programs for employees of industrial, commercial, service, or government establishment: Confers with management to gain knowledge of work situation requiring training for employees to better understand changes in policies, procedures, regulations, and technologies. Formulates teaching outline and determines instructional methods, utilizing knowledge of specified training needs and effectiveness of such methods as individual training, group instruction, lectures, demonstrations, conferences, meetings, and workshops. Selects or develops teaching aids, such as training handbooks, demonstration models, multimedia visual aids, computer tutorials, and reference works. Conducts training sessions covering specified areas such as those concerned with new employee orientation, on-the-job training, use of computers and software, apprenticeship programs, sales techniques, health and safety practices, public relations, refresher training, promotional development, upgrading, retraining displaced workers, and leadership development. Tests trainees to measure progress and to evaluate effectiveness of training. May specialize in developing instructional software. ● **GED:** R5, M4, L5 ● **SVP:** 2-4 yrs ● **Academic:** Ed=A, Eng=G ● **Work Field:** 296, 261 ● **MPSMS:** 931 ● **Aptitudes:** G2, V2, N2, S3, P3, Q3, K4, F4, M4, E5, C4 ● **Temperaments:** D, J, P, T ● **Physical:** Stg=L; Const: T, G Freq: R, H, N Occas: S, K, O, I, F, A, X ● **Work Env:** Noise=N; ● **Salary:** 4 ● **Outlook:** 3

GOE: 11.02.03
Teaching, Home Economics, Agriculture, & Related

COMMUNITY DIETITIAN (profess. & kin.) ● DOT #077.127-010 ● OES: 32521 ● Plans, organizes, coordinates, and evaluates nutritional component of health care services for organization: Develops and implements plan of care based on assessment of nutritional needs and available sources and correlates plan with other health care. Evalu-

ates nutritional care and provides followup continuity of care. Instructs individuals and families in nutritional principles, diet, food selection, and economics and adapts teaching plans to individual life style. Provides consultation to and works with community groups. Conducts or participates in in-service education and consultation with professional staff and supporting personnel of own and related organizations. Plans or participates in development of program proposals for funding. Plans, conducts, and evaluates dietary studies and participates in nutritional and epidemiologic studies with nutritional component. Evaluates food service systems and makes recommendation for conformance level that will provide optional nutrition and quality food if associated with group care institutions. May be employed by public health agency and be designated Nutritionist, Public Health (government ser.). ● **GED:** R5, M4, L5 ● **SVP:** 4-10 yrs ● **Academic:** Ed=B, Eng=G ● **Work Field:** 282 ● **MPSMS:** 732 ● **Aptitudes:** G2, V2, N3, S3, P3, Q3, K4, F4, M4, E5, C5 ● **Temperaments:** J, P, V ● **Physical:** Stg=L; Freq: T, G, N Occas: R, H, I, M, A ● **Work Env:** Noise=N; ● **Salary:** 3 ● **Outlook:** 3

COUNTY-AGRICULTURAL AGENT (government ser.) ● DOT #096.127-010 ● OES: 31323 ● Alternate titles: AGRICULTURAL AGENT; COUNTY ADVISER; COUNTY AGENT; EXTENSION AGENT; EXTENSION-SERVICE AGENT; EXTENSION WORKER; FARM ADVISER; FARM AGENT. Organizes and conducts cooperative extension program to advise and instruct farmers and individuals engaged in agri-business in applications of agricultural research findings: Collects, analyzes, and evaluates agricultural data; plans and develops techniques; and advises farmers to assist in solving problems, such as crop rotation and soil erosion. Delivers lectures and prepares articles concerning subjects, such as farm management and soil conservation. Demonstrates practical procedures used in solving agricultural problems. Discusses extension program with representatives of commercial organizations, county government, and other groups to inform them of program services and to obtain their cooperation in encouraging use of services. Prepares activity, planning, and other reports and maintains program records. Prepares budget requests, or assists in their preparation. May supervise and coordinate activities of other county extension workers. May direct 4-H Club activities. May be designated by specific program assignment as Agri-Business Agent (government ser.); Farm-Management Agent (government ser.); Horticultural Agent (government ser.); Livestock Agent (government ser.); Resource Agent (government ser.). ● **GED:** R5, M3, L5 ● **SVP:** 2-4 yrs ● **Academic:** Ed=A, Eng=S ● **Work Field:** 296, 282 ● **MPSMS:** 959 ● **Aptitudes:** G2, V2, N3, S4, P4, Q3, K4, F4, M4, E5, C3 ● **Temperaments:** D, I, J, P, V ● **Physical:** Stg=L; Freq: R, H, I, T, G, N, A Occas: X ● **Work Env:** Noise=N; Occas: W ● **Salary:** 3 ● **Outlook:** 3

COUNTY HOME-DEMONSTRATION AGENT (government ser.) ● DOT #096.121-010 ● OES: 31323 ● Alternate titles: HOME AGENT; HOME-DEMONSTRATION AGENT; HOME-EXTENSION AGENT. Develops, organizes, and conducts programs for individuals in rural communities to improve farm and family life: Lectures and demonstrates techniques in such subjects as nutrition, clothing, home management, home furnishing, and child care. Visits homes to advise families on problems, such as family budgeting and home remodeling. Organizes and advises clubs, and assists in selecting and training leaders to guide group discussions and demonstrations in subjects, such as sewing, food preparation, and home decoration. Writes leaflets and articles and talks over radio and television to disseminate information. Participates in community activities, such as judging at rural fairs and speaking before parent-teachers associations. May direct 4-H Club activities [FOUR-H CLUB AGENT (education)]. ● **GED:** R5, M3, L5 ● **SVP:** 2-4 yrs ● **Academic:** Ed=A, Eng=S ● **Work Field:** 296, 295 ● **MPSMS:** 959 ● **Aptitudes:** G2, V2, N3, S3, P3, Q3, K4, F3, M3, E4, C3 ● **Temperaments:** D, I, J, P, V ● **Physical:** Stg=L; Freq: R, H, I, T, G, N, D, A Occas: F, X, V ● **Work Env:** Noise=N; ● **Salary:** 4 ● **Outlook:** 2

EXTENSION SERVICE SPECIALIST (government ser.) ● DOT #096.127-014 ● OES: 31323 ● Alternate titles: COOPERATIVE EXTENSION ADVISOR SPECIALIST. Instructs extension workers and develops specialized service activities in area of agriculture or home economics: Plans, develops, organizes, and evaluates training programs in subjects, such as home management, horticulture, and consumer information. Prepares leaflets, pamphlets, and other material for use as training aids. Conducts classes to train extension workers in specialized fields and in teaching techniques. Delivers lectures to commercial and community organizations and over radio and television to promote development of agricultural or domestic skills. Analyzes research data and plans activities to coordinate services with those offered by other departments, agencies, and organizations. May be designated according to field of specialization as Agricultural-Extension Specialist (government ser.); Home Economics Specialist (government ser.). ● **GED:** R5, M3, L5 ● **SVP:** 4-10 yrs ● **Academic:** Ed=A, Eng=G ● **Work Field:** 296 ● **MPSMS:** 959, 931 ● **Aptitudes:** G2, V2, N3, S4, P3, Q2, K4, F4, M4, E5, C3 ● **Temperaments:** D, I, J, P, V ● **Physical:** Stg=L; Freq: R, H, I, T, G, N Occas: X ● **Work Env:** Noise=N; ● **Salary:** 4 ● **Outlook:** 3

HOME ECONOMIST (profess. & kin.) ● DOT #096.121-014 ● OES: 31323 ● Alternate titles: CONSUMER SERVICES CONSULTANT. Organizes and conducts consumer education service or research program for equipment, food, textile, or utility company, utilizing principles of home economics: Advises homemakers in selection and utilization of household equipment, food, and clothing, and interprets homemakers' needs to manufacturers of household products. Writes advertising copy and articles of interest to homemakers, tests recipes, equipment, and new household products, conducts radio and television homemakers' programs, and performs other public relations and promotion work for business firms, newspapers, magazines, and radio and television stations. Advises individuals and families on home management practices, such as budget planning, meal preparation, and energy conservation. Teaches improved homemaking practices to homemakers and youths through educational programs, demonstrations, discussions, and home visits. May engage in research in government, private industry, and colleges and universities to explore family relations or child development, develop new products for home, discover facts on food nutrition, and test serviceability of new materials. May specialize in specific area of home economics and be designated Equipment Specialist (profess. & kin.); Fashion Consultant (profess. & kin.); Home Economist, Consumer Service (profess. & kin.); Nutritionist (profess. & kin.); Product Representative (profess. & kin.); Research-Home Economist (profess. & kin.); Test-Kitchen-Home Economist (profess. & kin.). ● **GED:** R5, M3, L5 ● **SVP:** 2-4 yrs ● **Academic:** Ed=B, Eng=G ● **Work Field:** 282, 296 ● **MPSMS:** 931 ● **Aptitudes:** G2, V2, N3, S3, P3, Q2, K3, F3, M3, E4, C3 ● **Temperaments:** I, J, P, V ● **Physical:** Stg=L; Freq: R, H, I, T, G, N, A, X Occas: E ● **Work Env:** Noise=N; ● **Salary:** 3 ● **Outlook:** 3

HOMEMAKER (social ser.) ● DOT #309.354-010 ● OES: 68035 ● Advises family in private home in dealing with problems, such as nutrition, cleanliness, and household utilities: Advises and assists family members in planning nutritious meals, purchasing and preparing foods, and utilizing commodities from surplus food programs. Assists head of household in training and disciplining children, assigns and schedules housekeeping duties to children according to their capabilities, and encourages parents to take interest in children's schoolwork and assist them in establishing good study habits. Explains fundamental hygiene principles and renders bedside care to individuals who are ill, and trains other family members to provide required care. Participates in evaluating needs of individuals served, and confers with CASEWORKER (social ser.) to plan for continuing additional services. ● **GED:** R4, M2, L4 ● **SVP:** 6 mos-1 yr ● **Academic:** Ed=N, Eng=S ● **Work Field:** 298 ● **MPSMS:** 941 ● **Aptitudes:** G3, V3, N4, S4, P4, Q3, K4, F4, M4, E5, C5 ● **Temperaments:** I, J, P ● **Physical:** Stg=L; Freq: T, G, N Occas: S, R, H, I ● **Work Env:** Noise=N; ● **Salary:** 1 ● **Outlook:** 4

GOE: 11.02.04
Library Services

ACQUISITIONS LIBRARIAN (library) ● DOT #100.267-010 ● OES: 31502 ● Selects and orders books, periodicals, films, and other materials for library: Reviews publishers' announcements and catalogs, and compiles list of publications to be purchased. Compares selections with card catalog and orders-in-process to avoid duplication. Circulates selection lists to branches and departments for comments. Selects vendors on basis of such factors as discount allowance and

delivery dates. Compiles statistics on purchases, such as total purchases, average price, and fund allocations. May recommend acquisition of materials from individuals or organizations or by exchange with other libraries. ● **GED:** R4, M3, L4 ● **SVP:** 1-2 yrs ● **Academic:** Ed=B, Eng=G ● **Work Field:** 221 ● **MPSMS:** 933 ● **Aptitudes:** G2, V2, N2, S4, P4, Q2, K4, F4, M4, E5, C5 ● **Temperaments:** J, V ● **Physical:** Stg=L; Freq: R, H, I, T, G, N, A Occas: S, K ● **Work Env:** Noise=Q; ● **Salary:** 4 ● **Outlook:** 3

AUDIOVISUAL LIBRARIAN (library) ● DOT #100.167-010 ● OES: 31502 ● Alternate titles: FILM LIBRARIAN; RECORDINGS LIBRARIAN. Plans audiovisual programs and administers library of film and other audiovisual materials: Assists patrons in selection of materials, utilizing knowledge of collections. Advises other library personnel on audiovisual materials and appropriate selection for particular needs and uses. Establishes and maintains contact with major film distributors and resources for procurement of tapes and cassettes. Evaluates materials, considering their technical, informational, and aesthetic qualities, and selects materials for library collections. Prepares summaries of acquisitions for catalog. Prepares and arranges audiovisual programs for presentation to groups and may lead discussions after film showings. Advises those planning audiovisual programs on technical problems, such as acoustics, lighting, and program content. Evaluates audiovisual equipment and gives advice in selection of equipment, considering factors, such as intended use, quality, and price. May advise in planning and layout of physical facilities for audiovisual services. May operate film projectors, splicers, rewinders, film inspection equipment, and tape and record playing equipment. May train personnel in operation and maintenance of audiovisual equipment. May select, procure, and maintain framed art prints collection. ● **GED:** R5, M3, L3 ● **SVP:** 2-4 yrs ● **Academic:** Ed=A, Eng=G ● **Work Field:** 221 ● **MPSMS:** 933 ● **Aptitudes:** G2, V2, N3, S3, P2, Q3, K2, F2, M2, E5, C3 ● **Temperaments:** D, I, J, P ● **Physical:** Stg=L; Freq: R, H, I, T, G, N ● **Work Env:** Noise=N; ● **Salary:** 2 ● **Outlook:** 3

BOOKMOBILE LIBRARIAN (library) ● DOT #100.167-014 ● OES: 31502 ● Provides library services from mobile library within given geographical area: Surveys needs and selects books and materials for library. Publicizes visits to area to stimulate reading interest. May prepare special collections for schools and other groups. May arrange bookmobile schedule. May drive bookmobile. ● **GED:** R4, M3, L4 ● **SVP:** 2-4 yrs ● **Academic:** Ed=B, Eng=G ● **Work Field:** 221 ● **MPSMS:** 933 ● **Aptitudes:** G2, V2, N3, S4, P4, Q3, K4, F4, M4, E5, C4 ● **Temperaments:** D, P, V ● **Physical:** Stg=L; Freq: R, H, I, T, G, N Occas: X ● **Work Env:** Noise=N; Occas: W ● **Salary:** 3 ● **Outlook:** 3

CAREER-GUIDANCE TECHNICIAN (education) ● DOT #249.367-014 ● OES: 55347 ● Alternate titles: CAREER-INFORMATION SPECIALIST; CAREER RESOURCE TECHNICIAN. Collects and organizes occupational data to provide source materials for school career information center, and assists students and teachers to locate and obtain materials: Orders, catalogues, and maintains files on materials relating to job opportunities, careers, technical schools, colleges, scholarships, armed forces, and other programs. Assists students and teachers to locate career information related to students' interests and aptitudes, or demonstrates use of files, shelf collections, and other information retrieval systems. Assists students to take and score self-administered vocational interest and aptitude tests. Keeps records of students enrolled in work experience program and other vocational programs to assist counseling and guidance staff. Schedules appointments with school guidance and counseling staff for students requiring professional assistance. May make presentations to parent and other groups to publicize activities of career center. May operate audio-visual equipment, such as tape recorders, record players, and film or slide projectors. ● **GED:** R4, M3, L4 ● **SVP:** 1-2 yrs ● **Academic:** Ed=H, Eng=G ● **Work Field:** 282, 231 ● **MPSMS:** 931 ● **Aptitudes:** G3, V3, N4, S4, P4, Q3, K4, F4, M4, E4, C5 ● **Temperaments:** J ● **Physical:** Stg=L; Freq: R, H, T, G, N Occas: I ● **Work Env:** Noise=N; ● **Salary:** 2 ● **Outlook:** 3

CATALOG LIBRARIAN (library) ● DOT #100.387-010 ● OES: 31505 ● Alternate titles: CATALOGER; DESCRIPTIVE CATALOG LIBRARIAN. Compiles imformation on library materials, such as books and periodicals, and prepares catalog cards to identify materials and to integrate information into library catalog: Verifies author, title, and classification number on sample catalog card received from CLAS-

SIFIER (library) against corresponding data on title page. Fills in additional information, such as publisher, date of publication, and edition. Examines material and notes additional information, such as bibliographies, illustrations, maps, and appendices. Copies classification number from sample card into library material for identification. Files cards into assigned sections of catalog. Tabulates number of sample cards according to quantity of material and catalog subject headings to determine amount of new cards to be ordered or reproduced. Prepares inventory card to record purchase information and location of library material. Requisitions additional cards. Records new information, such as death date of author and revised edition date, to amend cataloged cards. May supervise activities of other workers in unit. ● **GED:** R4, M2, L4 ● **SVP:** 6 mos-1 yr ● **Academic:** Ed=B, Eng=G ● **Work Field:** 221 ● **MPSMS:** 933 ● **Aptitudes:** G3, V3, N3, S4, P3, Q2, K4, F4, M4, E5, C5 ● **Temperaments:** R, T ● **Physical:** Stg=L; Freq: R, H, I, N, A ● **Work Env:** Noise=Q; ● **Salary:** 4 ● **Outlook:** 3

CLASSIFIER (library) ● DOT #100.367-014 ● OES: 31505 ● Classifies library materials, such as books, audiovisual materials, and periodicals, according to subject matter: Reviews materials to be classified and searches information sources, such as book reviews, encyclopedias, and technical publications to determine subject matter of materials. Selects classification numbers and descriptive headings according to Dewey Decimal, Library of Congress, or other classification systems. Makes sample cards containing author, title, and classification number to guide CATALOG LIBRARIAN (library) in preparing catalog cards for books and periodicals. Assigns classification numbers, descriptive headings, and explanatory summaries to book and catalog cards to facilitate locating and obtaining materials. Composes annotations (explanatory summaries) of material content. ● **GED:** R4, M3, L4 ● **SVP:** 1-2 yrs ● **Academic:** Ed=A, Eng=G ● **Work Field:** 221 ● **MPSMS:** 933 ● **Aptitudes:** G2, V2, N4, S4, P3, Q2, K4, F4, M4, E5, C5 ● **Temperaments:** J, R, T ● **Physical:** Stg=L; Freq: R, H, I, N, A ● **Work Env:** Noise=Q; ● **Salary:** 4 ● **Outlook:** 3

FILM-OR-TAPE LIBRARIAN (clerical) ● DOT #222.367-026 ● OES: 58097 ● Classifies, catalogs, and maintains library of motion picture films, photographic slides, and video and audio tapes: Classifies and catalogs items according to contents and purpose and prepares index cards for file reference. Maintains records of items received, stored, issued, and returned. Stores items and records according to classification and catalog number. Delivers and retrieves items to and from departments by hand or push cart. May prepare, store, and retrieve classification and catalog information, lecture notes, or other documents related to documents stored, using computer. May be designated according to items stored as Audio-Tape Librarian (clerical); Film Librarian (motion picture). ● **GED:** R3, M2, L3 ● **SVP:** 6 mos-1 yr ● **Academic:** Ed=N, Eng=S ● **Work Field:** 221 ● **MPSMS:** 898 ● **Aptitudes:** G3, V3, N3, S3, P3, Q2, K3, F4, M4, E5, C5 ● **Temperaments:** R, T ● **Physical:** Stg=L; Freq: R, H Occas: C, O, I, T, G, N, D ● **Work Env:** Noise=N; ● **Salary:** 4 ● **Outlook:** 3

FILM-RENTAL CLERK (business ser.) ● DOT #295.367-018 ● OES: 55323 ● Alternate titles: AUDIO-VISUAL-EQUIPMENT-RENTAL CLERK; FILM BOOKER. Rents films and audio-visual equipment to individuals and organizations, such as schools, churches, clubs, and business firms: Views incoming films to familiarize self with content. Recommends films on specific subjects to show to designated group, utilizing knowledge of film content, availability of film, and rental charge. Determines and quotes rental charges for film, depending on purpose for showing film, number of times to be shown, and size of audience. Writes orders, listing shipping date, show date, and method of shipping film. Posts film rental dates on office records to complete reservation. May write or type correspondence, invoices, and shipping labels. May visit prospective or current customers to sell film-rental and audio-visual-equipment-renting service. ● **GED:** R4, M3, L4 ● **SVP:** 6 mos-1 yr ● **Academic:** Ed=H, Eng=G ● **Work Field:** 292, 221 ● **MPSMS:** 884 ● **Aptitudes:** G3, V3, N3, S4, P3, Q3, K4, F3, M4, E5, C5 ● **Temperaments:** I, J, P ● **Physical:** Stg=L; Freq: R, H, N Occas: T, G ● **Work Env:** Noise=Q; ● **Salary:** 2 ● **Outlook:** 3

LIBRARIAN (library) ● DOT #100.127-014 ● OES: 31502 ● Maintains library collections of books, serial publications, documents, audiovisual, and other materials, and assists groups and individuals in locating and obtaining materials: Furnishes information on library activities, facilities, rules, and services. Explains and assists in use of reference sources, such as card or book catalog or book and periodical indexes to locate information. Describes or demonstrates procedures for searching catalog files. Searches catalog files and shelves to locate information. Issues and receives materials for circulation or for use in library. Assembles and arranges displays of books and other library materials. Maintains reference and circulation materials. Answers correspondence on special reference subjects. May compile list of library materials according to subject or interests, using computer. May select, order, catalog, and classify materials . May prepare or assist in preparation of budget. May plan and direct or carry out special projects involving library promotion and outreach activity and be designated Outreach Librarian (library). May be designated according to specialized function as Circulation Librarian (library); Readers'-Advisory-Service Librarian (library); or Reference Librarian (library). ● **GED:** R5, M3, L4 ● **SVP:** 2-4 yrs ● **Academic:** Ed=B, Eng=G ● **Work Field:** 282, 231, 221 ● **MPSMS:** 933 ● **Aptitudes:** G2, V2, N3, S3, P3, Q2, K4, F4, M4, E5, C5 ● **Temperaments:** J, P, V ● **Physical:** Stg=L; Freq: H, I, T, G, N Occas: S, O, R ● **Work Env:** Noise=Q; ● **Salary:** 4 ● **Outlook:** 3

LIBRARY ASSISTANT (library) ● DOT #249.367-046 ● OES: 53902 ● Alternate titles: BOOK-LOAN CLERK; CIRCULATION CLERK; DESK ATTENDANT; LIBRARY ATTENDANT; LIBRARY CLERK; LIBRARY HELPER. Compiles records, sorts and shelves books, and issues and receives library materials, such as books, films, slides, and phonograph records: Records identifying data and due date on cards by hand or using photographic equipment to issue books to patrons. Inspects returned books for damage, verifies due-date, and computes and receives overdue fines. Reviews records to compile list of overdue books and issues overdue notices to borrowers. Sorts books, publications, and other items according to classification code and returns them to shelves, files, or other designated storage area. Locates books and publications for patrons. Issues borrower's identification card according to established procedures. Files cards in catalog drawers according to system. Repairs books, using mending tape and paste and brush, and places plastic covers on new books. Answers inquiries of nonprofessional nature on telephone and in person and refers persons requiring professional assistance to LIBRARIAN (library) 100.127-014. May type material cards or issue cards and duty schedules. May be designated according to type of library as Bookmobile Clerk (library); Branch-Library Clerk (library); or according to assigned department as Library Clerk, Art Department (library). ● **GED:** R3, M2, L3 ● **SVP:** 6 mos-1 yr ● **Academic:** Ed=H, Eng=G ● **Work Field:** 221, 231, 282 ● **MPSMS:** 933 ● **Aptitudes:** G3, V3, N4, S4, P4, Q2, K3, F3, M3, E5, C5 ● **Temperaments:** P, V ● **Physical:** Stg=L; Freq: R, H, I, T, G, N Occas: S, O ● **Work Env:** Noise=Q; ● **Salary:** 1 ● **Outlook:** 3

LIBRARIAN, SPECIAL LIBRARY (library) ● DOT #100.167-026 ● OES: 31502 ● Manages library or section containing specialized materials for industrial, commercial, or governmental organizations, or for such institutions as schools and hospitals: Selects, orders, catalogs, and classifies special collections of technical books, manufacturers' catalogs and specifications, periodicals, magazines, newspapers, audio-visual material, microforms, journal reprints, and other materials. Searches literature, compiles accession lists, and annotates or abstracts materials. Assists patrons in research problems. May key information into computer to store or search for selected material. May translate or order translation of materials from foreign languages into English. May train other workers engaged in cataloguing, locating, filing, or copying selected material. May be designated according to subject matter, specialty or library, or department as Art Librarian (library); Business Librarian (library); Engineering Librarian (library); Law Librarian (library); Map Librarian (library); Medical Librarian (library). ● **GED:** R5, M4, L5 ● **SVP:** 4-10 yrs ● **Academic:** Ed=B, Eng=G ● **Work Field:** 221, 282 ● **MPSMS:** 933 ● **Aptitudes:** G2, V2, N2, S3, P3, Q2, K4, F4, M4, E5, C5 ● **Temperaments:** D, J, P, V ● **Physical:** Stg=L; Freq: T, G, N Occas: S, R, H, I ● **Work Env:** Noise=Q; ● **Salary:** 3 ● **Outlook:** 4

LIBRARY TECHNICAL ASSISTANT (library) ● DOT #100.367-018 ● OES: 31505 ● Alternate titles: LIBRARY ASSISTANT; LIBRARY TECHNICIAN. Provides information service, such as answering questions regarding card catalogs, and assists public in use of bibliographic tools, such as Library of Congress catalog: Performs routine descriptive cataloging, such as fiction and children's literature. Files cards in catalog drawers according to system used. Answers routine inquiries, and refers persons requiring professional assistance to LIBRARIAN (library). Verifies bibliographic information on order requests. Directs activities of workers in maintenance of stacks or in section of department or division, such as ordering or receiving section of acquisitions department, card preparation activities in catalog department, or limited loan or reserve desk operation of circulation department. ● **GED:** R4, M3, L3 ● **SVP:** 6 mos-1 yr ● **Academic:** Ed=H, Eng=G ● **Work Field:** 221 ● **MPSMS:** 933 ● **Aptitudes:** G3, V3, N2, S4, P3, Q2, K4, F4, M4, E5, C5 ● **Temperaments:** P, V ● **Physical:** Stg=L; Freq: R, H, I, T, G, N Occas: D ● **Work Env:** Noise=N; ● **Salary:** 3 ● **Outlook:** 2

MEDIA SPECIALIST, SCHOOL LIBRARY (library) ● DOT #100.167-030 ● OES: 31502 ● Alternate titles: LIBRARIAN, SCHOOL; MEDIA CENTER DIRECTOR, SCHOOL. Assesses and meets needs of students and faculty for information, and develops programs to stimulate students' interests in reading and use of types of resources: Selects and organizes books, films, tapes, records, and other materials and equipment. Suggests appropriate books to students for classroom assignments and personal readings. Plans and carries out program of instruction in use by school library media center. Prepares and administers budget for media center. Confers with faculty to provide materials for classroom instruction. Confers with parents, faculty, public librarians, and community organizations to develop programs to enrich students' communications skills. Reviews records to compile lists of overdue materials and notifies borrowers to arrange for their return. ● **GED:** R5, M3, L5 ● **SVP:** 4-10 yrs ● **Academic:** Ed=A, Eng=S ● **Work Field:** 221, 282 ● **MPSMS:** 931, 933 ● **Aptitudes:** G2, V2, N3, S4, P4, Q2, K3, F3, M3, E5, C4 ● **Temperaments:** D, I, J, P, V ● **Physical:** Stg=L; Freq: R, H, T, G, N Occas: S, K, I, E, F, X ● **Work Env:** Noise=Q; ● **Salary:** 4 ● **Outlook:** 3

MUSIC LIBRARIAN (radio-tv broad.) ● DOT #100.367-022 ● OES: 31505 ● Alternate titles: LIBRARIAN; MUSIC DIRECTOR. Classifies and files musical recordings, sheet music, original arrangements, and scores for individual instruments. Selects music for subject matter of program or for specific visual or spoken action. Suggests musical selections to DIRECTOR, MUSIC (motion picture; radio-tv broad.) 152.047-018 or DIRECTOR, PROGRAM (radio-tv broad.) 184.167-030 or DISK JOCKEY (radio-tv broad.) 159.147-014. May issue required music to CONDUCTOR, ORCHESTRA (profess. & kin.) 152.047-014, or other studio personnel. May track musical selections broadcasted, using computer. May listen to music, using playback equipment, to verify quality of recordings meet broadcast standards. ● **GED:** R4, M2, L4 ● **SVP:** 1-2 yrs ● **Academic:** Ed=H, Eng=G ● **Work Field:** 221 ● **MPSMS:** 863, 864 ● **Aptitudes:** G3, V3, N3, S4, P3, Q3, K4, F4, M4, E5, C5 ● **Temperaments:** J, T ● **Physical:** Stg=L; Const: H Freq: R, G Occas: C, S, K, O, I, T, N ● **Work Env:** Noise=Q; ● **Salary:** 3 ● **Outlook:** 3

NEWS LIBRARIAN (library) ● DOT #100.167-038 ● OES: 31502 ● Alternate titles: NEWS INFORMATION RESOURCE MANAGER; NEWS LIBRARY DIRECTOR; NEWSPAPER LIBRARY MANAGER. Manages information resources library stored in files, on tape or microfilm, or in computers for use by news and editorial staff in publishing establishments, such as newspaper and magazine publishers, and in broadcasting establishments, such as radio and television stations: Directs activities of workers engaged in clipping, classifying, cataloging, indexing, storing, editing, and retrieving library information, or performs these activities as needed. Researches, retrieves, and disseminates information in resource library or commercial data bases in response to requests from news or editorial staff, using knowledge of classification system or computer data base. Maintains records and statistics on use of data bases and information services provided. May manage in-house data base of news information, assign classification terms to news articles, input news articles into data base, and research news information in in-house data base. May develop data bases for data storage and retrieval, according to needs of news staff. May hire, train, schedule, and evaluate library staff. May prepare library budgets. May promote and market library products and services to public. May coordinate activities of library with activities of other departments. May select and purchase reference books for library collection. May manage graphics library, assign classification terms to graphics, and research graphics and be designated Photo-Graphics Librarian (library). ● **GED:** R5, M4, L5 ● **SVP:** 2-4 yrs ● **Academic:** Ed=B, Eng=G ● **Work Field:** 282, 221 ● **MPSMS:** 933, 481 ● **Aptitudes:** G2, V2, N3, S4, P3, Q2, K3, F3, M3, E5, C5 ● **Temperaments:** D, J, P, V ● **Physical:** Stg=L; Freq: I, T, G, N, A Occas: R, H ● **Work Env:** Noise=N; ● **Salary:** 4 ● **Outlook:** 3

Leading-Influencing   11

Social Research   11.03

Workers in this group gather, study, and analyze information about individuals, specific groups, or entire societies. They conduct research, both historical and current, into all aspects of human behavior, including abnormal behavior, language, work, politics, lifestyle, and cultural expression. They are employed by museums, schools and colleges, government agencies, and private research foundations.

✓ What kind of work would you do?

Your work activities would depend upon your specific job. For example, you might:

- collect and analyze data about jobs, including worker qualifications and characteristics.
- study articles from a historic site to learn about an ancient society.
- conduct research about the mental development of people.
- determine the origins, meanings, and pronun-

ciations of words and define them for a dictionary.
- appraise, assemble, and direct the safekeeping of historic documents.
- conduct research in psychological problems related to engineering projects.
- study the structure of language to understand its social function.
- collect and interpret data on economic conditions.

✓ What skills and abilities do you need for this kind of work?

To do this kind of work, you must be able to:

- analyze and interpret both current and historical information that relates to the research subject.
- understand and use the theories and methods of research in your particular field.
- organize detailed research notes into a logical outline.
- write reports of findings.

✓ How do you know if you would like or could learn to do this kind of work?

The following questions may give you clues about yourself as you consider this group of jobs.

- Have you read magazines concerning world affairs and social problems? Do you keep informed of current events?
- Have you done research projects or surveys for social science classes? Do you enjoy this type of activity?
- Have you taken courses in sociology, psychology, or civics? Do you like to write reports or research papers?
- Have you visited museums or historical sites? Do you enjoy history?

✓ How can you prepare for and enter this kind of work?

Occupations in this group usually require education and/or training extending from two years to over ten years, depending upon the specific kind of work.

Almost all jobs in this group require four or more years of college study in the social sciences. Some jobs require specialization in a particular field such as sociology, history, economics, or archeology. Courses in computer science and statistics are important because these technologies are used to handle research data.

✓ What else should you consider about these jobs?

Employers expect workers in this group to keep up with developments and trends in their specific area. This is done by attending seminars and workshops or studying for advanced degrees.

If you think you would like to do this kind of work, look at the job titles listed on the following pages.

■ ■ ■

GOE: 11.03.01
Psychological

PSYCHOLOGIST, DEVELOPMENTAL (profess. & kin.) ● DOT#045.061-010 ● OES: 27108 ● Investigates problems concerning growth and development of emotional, mental, physical, and social aspects of individuals, to increase understanding of origins of behavior and processes of human growth and decline: Formulates hypothesis or research problem and selects or develops method of investigation to test hypothesis. Studies behavior of children to analyze processes of learning, development of language in children, and parents' influence on children's behavior. Administers intelligence and performance tests to establish and measure patterns of intellectual and psychological growth, development, and decline in children and adults. Observes and records behavior of infants to establish patterns of social, motor, and sensory development. Analyzes growth of social values and attitudes, using information obtained from observation, questionnaires, and interviews. Formulates theories based on research findings for application in such fields as juvenile delinquency, education and guidance of children, parent education, and welfare of aged. Experiments with animals [PSYCHOLOGIST, EXPERIMENTAL (profess. & kin.)], to make comparative studies across species lines to contribute to understanding of human behavior. May specialize in study and treatment of children and be designated Child Psychologist (profess. & kin.). ● **GED:** R6, M6, L5 ● **SVP:** 2-4 yrs ● **Academic:** Ed=M, Eng=G ● **Work Field:** 251 ● **MPSMS:** 733 ● **Aptitudes:** G1, V1, N2, S3, P3, Q4, K3, F3, M3, E5, C5 ● **Temperaments:** J, P, V ● **Physical:** Stg=L; Freq: R, H, I, N Occas: T, G, A ● **Work Env:** Noise=N; ● **Salary:** 4 ● **Outlook:** 3

PSYCHOLOGIST, EDUCATIONAL (profess. & kin.) ● DOT #045.067-010 ● OES: 27108 ● Investigates processes of learning and teaching and develops psychological principles and techniques applicable to educational problems to foster intellectual, social, and emotional development of individuals: Conducts experiments to study importance of motivation in learning, implications of transfer of training in teaching, and nature and causes of individual differences in mental abilities to promote differentiated educational procedures to meet individual needs of students. Analyzes characteristics and adjustment needs of superior and inferior students and recommends educational program to promote maximum adjustment. Formulates achievement, diagnostic, and predictive tests to aid teachers in planning methods and content of instruction. Administers standardized tests to diagnose disabilities and difficulties among students and to develop special methods of remedial instruction. Investigates traits and attitudes of teachers to study conditions that contribute to or detract from optimal mental health of teachers. Studies effects of teachers' feelings and attitudes upon pupils, and characteristics of successful teachers to aid school administrators in selection and adjustment of teachers. Collaborates with education specialists in developing curriculum content and methods of organizing and conducting classroom work. May specialize in educational measurement, school adjustment, school learning, or special education. ● **GED:** R6, M6, L5 ● **SVP:** 4-10 yrs ● **Academic:** Ed=M, Eng=G ● **Work Field:** 296, 251 ● **MPSMS:** 733, 931 ● **Aptitudes:** G1, V1, N2, S3, P3, Q4, K4, F4, M4, E5, C5 ● **Temperaments:** I, J, P, V ● **Physical:** Stg=L; Freq: R, H, I, T, G, N ● **Work Env:** Noise=N; ● **Salary:** 5 ● **Outlook:** 2

PSYCHOLOGIST, ENGINEERING (profess. & kin.) ● DOT #045.061-014 ● OES: 27108 ● Alternate titles: HUMAN FACTORS SPECIALIST. Conducts research, development, application, and evaluation of psychological principles relating human behavior to characteristics, design, and use of environments and systems within which human beings work and live: Collaborates with equipment designers in design, development, and utilization of man-machine systems to obtain optimum efficiency in terms of human capabilities. Advises on human factors to be considered in design of man-machine systems, military equipment, and industrial products. Participates in solving such problems as determining numbers and kinds of workers required to operate machines, allocation of functions to machines and operators, and layout and arrangement of work sites. Analyzes jobs to establish requirements for use in classification, selection, placement, and training of personnel [JOB ANALYST (profess. & kin.)]. Develops training methods and materials, such as curriculums, lectures, and films, and prepares handbooks of human engineering data for use by equipment and system designers. May conduct research to develop psychological theories concerning such subjects as effects of physical factors (temperature, humidity, vibration, noise, and illumination) on worker's behavior; functional design of dials, scales, meters, and other instruments to minimize sensory requirements; specifications for optimal size, shape, direction and speed of motion, and location of equipment controls; and effects of environmental, organismic, and task or job variables on work behavior and life quality. ● **GED:** R6, M6, L6 ● **SVP:** 4-10 yrs ● **Academic:** Ed=M, Eng=G ● **Work Field:** 244 ● **MPSMS:** 733 ●

Aptitudes: G1, V1, N2, S2, P3, Q4, K4, F4, M4, E5, C5 ● **Temperaments:** J, V ● **Physical:** Stg=S; Freq: T, G, N Occas: R, H, I ● **Work Env:** Noise=Q; ● **Salary:** 5 ● **Outlook:** 3

PSYCHOLOGIST, EXPERIMENTAL (profess. & kin.) ● DOT #045.061-018 ● OES: 27108 ● Plans, designs, conducts, and analyzes results of experiments to study problems in psychology: Formulates hypotheses and experimental designs to investigate problems of perception, memory, learning, personality, and cognitive processes. Designs and constructs equipment and apparatus for laboratory study. Selects, controls, and modifies variables in laboratory experiments with humans or animals, and observes and records behavior in relation to variables. Analyzes test results, using statistical techniques, and evaluates significance of data in relation to original hypothesis. Collaborates with other scientists in such fields as physiology, biology, and sociology in conducting interdisciplinary studies of behavior and formulating theories of behavior. Writes papers describing experiments and interpreting test results for publication or for presentation at scientific meetings. May specialize in aesthetics, memory, learning, autonomic functions, electroencephalography, feeling and emotion, motivation, motor skills, perception, or higher order cognitive processes. May conduct experiments to study relationship of behavior to various bodily mechanisms and be designated Psychologist, Physiological (profess. & kin.). May specialize in study of animal behavior to develop theories of animal and human behavior and be designated Psychologist, Comparative (profess. & kin.). ● **GED:** R6, M6, L5 ● **SVP:** 4-10 yrs ● **Academic:** Ed=M, Eng=G ● **Work Field:** 251 ● **MPSMS:** 733 ● **Aptitudes:** G1, V1, N2, S3, P3, Q4, K3, F3, M3, E5, C4 ● **Temperaments:** D, J, V ● **Physical:** Stg=L; Freq: R, H, T, G, N Occas: I ● **Work Env:** Noise=Q; ● **Salary:** 5 ● **Outlook:** 3

PSYCHOLOGIST, INDUSTRIAL-ORGANIZATIONAL (profess. & kin.) ● DOT #045.107-030 ● OES: 27108 ● Develops and applies psychological techniques to personnel administration, management, and marketing problems: Observes details of work and interviews workers and supervisors to establish physical, mental, educational, and other job requirements. Develops interview techniques, rating scales, and psychological tests to assess skills, abilities, aptitudes, and interests as aids in selection, placement, and promotion. Organizes training programs, applying principles of learning and individual differences, and evaluates and measures effectiveness of training methods by statistical analysis of production rate, reduction of accidents, absenteeism, and turnover. Counsels workers to improve job and personal adjustments. Conducts research studies of organizational structure, communication systems, group interactions, and motivational systems, and recommends changes to improve efficiency and effectiveness of individuals, organizational units, and organization. Investigates problems related to physical environment of work, such as illumination, noise, temperature, and ventilation, and recommends changes to increase efficiency and decrease accident rate. Conducts surveys and research studies to ascertain nature of effective supervision and leadership and to analyze factors affecting morale and motivation. Studies consumer reaction to new products and package designs, using surveys and tests, and measures effectiveness of advertising media to aid in sale of goods and services. May advise management on personnel policies and labor-management relations. May adapt machinery, equipment, workspace, and environment to human use. May specialize in development and application of such techniques as job analysis and classification, personnel interviewing, ratings, and vocational tests for use in selection, placement, promotion, and training of workers and be designated Psychologist, Personnel (profess. & kin.). May apply psychological principles and techniques to selection, training, classification, and assignment of military personnel and be designated Psychologist, Military Personnel (profess. & kin.). May conduct surveys and tests to study consumer reaction to new products and package design and to measure effectiveness of advertising media to aid manufacturers in sale of goods and services and be designated Market-Research Analyst (profess. & kin.). II. ● **GED:** R6, M6, L5 ● **SVP:** 4-10 yrs ● **Academic:** Ed=M, Eng=G ● **Work Field:** 251, 271 ● **MPSMS:** 733 ● **Aptitudes:** G1, V1, N2, S3, P3, Q4, K4, F4, M4, E5, C5 ● **Temperaments:** I, J, P, V ● **Physical:** Stg=L; Freq: T, G, N Occas: F, A ● **Work Env:** Noise=N; ● **Salary:** 5 ● **Outlook:** 4

PSYCHOLOGIST, SOCIAL (profess. & kin.) ● DOT #045.067-014 ● OES: 27108 ● Investigates psychological aspects of human interrelationships to gain understanding of individual and group thought, feeling, and behavior, utilizing behavioral observation, experimentation, or survey techniques: Evaluates individual and group behavior, developing such techniques as rating scales and sampling methods to collect and measure data. Conducts surveys and polls to measure and analyze attitudes and opinions as basis for predicting economic, political, and other behavior, using interviews, questionnaires, and other techniques, and adhering to principles of statistical sampling in selecting people. Observes and analyzes relations of individuals to religious, racial, political, occupational, and other groups to evaluate behavior of individuals toward one another in groups, attitudes that exist in groups, and influence of group on individual. Investigates social behavior of individuals to study such problems as origin and nature of prejudice and stereotyping, transmission of values and attitudes in child rearing, and contribution of factors in social environment to individual mental health and illness. Conducts experimental studies on motivation, morale, and leadership, and prepares reports on findings. ● **GED:** R6, M6, L5 ● **SVP:** 4-10 yrs ● **Academic:** Ed=M, Eng=G ● **Work Field:** 251 ● **MPSMS:** 733 ● **Aptitudes:** G1, V1, N2, S4, P4, Q3, K5, F5, M4, E5, C5 ● **Temperaments:** F, P, V ● **Physical:** Stg=S; Freq: R, H, T, G, N Occas: I, E, F ● **Work Env:** Noise=Q; ● **Salary:** 5 ● **Outlook:** 2

PSYCHOMETRIST (profess. & kin.) ● DOT #045.067-018 ● OES: 27108 ● Administers, scores, and interprets intelligence, aptitude, achievement, and other psychological tests to provide test information to teachers, counselors, students, or other specified entitled party: Gives paper and pencil tests or utilizes testing equipment, such as picture tests and dexterity boards, under standard conditions. Times tests and records results. Interprets test results in light of standard norms, and limitations of test in terms of validity and reliability. ● **GED:** R5, M5, L5 ● **SVP:** 2-4 yrs ● **Academic:** Ed=M, Eng=G ● **Work Field:** 271 ● **MPSMS:** 733 ● **Aptitudes:** G2, V2, N2, S3, P3, Q2, K4, F4, M4, E5, C5 ● **Temperaments:** J, P, V ● **Physical:** Stg=S; Freq: R, H, T, G, N Occas: I ● **Work Env:** Noise=Q; ● **Salary:** 4 ● **Outlook:** 2

GOE: 11.03.02
Sociological

CITY PLANNING AIDE (profess. & kin.) ● DOT #199.364-010 ● OES: 39998 ● Alternate titles: PLANNING ASSISTANT. Compiles data for use by URBAN PLANNER (profess. & kin.) in making planning studies: Summarizes information from maps, reports, field and file investigations, and books. Traces maps and prepares statistical tabulations, computations, charts, and graphs to illustrate planning studies in areas, such as population, transportation, traffic, land use, zoning, proposed subdivisions, and public utilities. Prepares and updates files and records. May answer public inquiries, conduct field interviews and make surveys of traffic flow, parking, housing, educational facilities, recreation, zoning, and other conditions which affect planning studies. ● **GED:** R4, M4, L4 ● **SVP:** 1-2 yrs ● **Academic:** Ed=H, Eng=S ● **Work Field:** 271, 231 ● **MPSMS:** 744, 719 ● **Aptitudes:** G3, V3, N3, S3, P2, Q2, K3, F3, M4, E5, C4 ● **Temperaments:** T, V ● **Physical:** Stg=L; Freq: R, H, I, T, G, N, A ● **Work Env:** Noise=N; Occas: W ● **Salary:** 4 ● **Outlook:** 3

PLANNER, PROGRAM SERVICES (government ser.) ● DOT #188.167-110 ● OES: 27105 ● Conducts studies, prepares reports, and advises public and private sector administrators on feasibility, cost-effectiveness, and regulatory conformance of proposals for special projects or ongoing programs in such fields as transportation, conservation, or health care: Consults with administrators or planning councils to discuss overall intent of programs or projects, and determines broad guidelines for studies, utilizing knowledge of subject area, research techniques, and regulatory limitations. Reviews and evaluates materials provided with proposals, such as environmental impact statements, construction specifications, or budget or staffing estimates, to determine additional data requirements. Conducts field investigations, economic or public opinion surveys, demographic studies, or other research to gather required information. Organizes data from all sources, using statistical methods to ensure validity of materials. Evaluates information to determine feasibility of proposals or to identify factors requiring amendment. Develops alternate plans for program or project, incorporating recommendations, for review of officials. Maintains collection of socioeconomic, environmental, and regulatory data related to agency functions, for use by planning and administrative personnel in government and private sectors. Reviews plans and proposals submitted by other governmental planning commissions or private organizations to assist in formulation of overall plans for region. • **GED:** R5, M5, L5 • **SVP:** 2-4 yrs • **Academic:** Ed=B, Eng=G • **Work Field:** 251 • **MPSMS:** 959 • **Aptitudes:** G2, V2, N2, S2, P2, Q2, K3, F4, M4, E5, C5 • **Temperaments:** D, J, P • **Physical:** Stg=L; Freq: H, T, G, N Occas: R, I, F, D, A • **Work Env:** Noise=N; • **Salary:** 3 • **Outlook:** 1

POLITICAL SCIENTIST (profess. & kin.) • DOT #051.067-010 • OES: 27198 • Studies phenomena of political behavior, such as origin, development, operation, and interrelationships of political institutions, to formulate and develop political theory: Conducts research into political philosophy and theories of political systems, utilizing information available on political phenomena, such as governmental institutions, public laws and administration, political party systems, and international law. Consults with government officials, civic bodies, research agencies, and political parties. Analyzes and interprets results of studies, and prepares reports detailing findings, recommendations or conclusions. May organize and conduct public opinion surveys and interpret results. May specialize in specific geographical, political, or philosophical aspect of political behavior. • **GED:** R6, M5, L5 • **SVP:** 4-10 yrs • **Academic:** Ed=M, Eng=G • **Work Field:** 251 • **MPSMS:** 742 • **Aptitudes:** G2, V2, N3, S4, P4, Q2, K4, F4, M4, E5, C5 • **Temperaments:** D, J • **Physical:** Stg=S; Freq: T, G • **Work Env:** Noise=Q; • **Salary:** 5 • **Outlook:** 2

RESEARCH WORKER, SOCIAL WELFARE (profess. & kin.) • DOT #054.067-010 • OES: 27198 • Plans, organizes, and conducts research for use in understanding social problems and for planning and carrying out social welfare programs: Develops research designs on basis of existing knowledge and evolving theory. Constructs and tests methods of data collection. Collects information and makes judgments through observation, interview, and review of documents. Analyzes and evaluates data. Writes reports containing descriptive, analytical, and evaluative content. Interprets methods employed and findings to individuals within agency and community. May direct work of statistical clerks, statisticians, and others. May collaborate with research workers in other disciplines. May be employed in voluntary or governmental social welfare agencies, community welfare councils, and schools of social work. • **GED:** R6, M5, L5 • **SVP:** 2-4 yrs • **Academic:** Ed=B, Eng=G • **Work Field:** 251 • **MPSMS:** 941 • **Aptitudes:** G1, V1, N2, S3, P4, Q4, K4, F4, M4, E5, C5 • **Temperaments:** J • **Physical:** Stg=S; Freq: R, H, T, G, N Occas: I • **Work Env:** Noise=Q; • **Salary:** 4 • **Outlook:** 1

SCIENTIFIC LINGUIST (profess. & kin.) • DOT #059.067-014 • OES: 27198 • Alternate titles: LINGUIST. Studies components, structure, and relationships within specified language to provide comprehension of its social functioning: Prepares description of sounds, forms, and vocabulary of language. Contributes to development of linguistic theory. Applies linguistic theory to any of following areas: development of improved methods in translation, including computerization; teaching of language to other than native speakers; preparation of language-teaching materials, dictionaries, and handbooks; reducing previously unwritten languages to standardized written form; preparation of literacy materials; preparation of tests for language-learning aptitudes and language proficiency; consultation with government agencies regarding language programs; or preparation of descriptions of comparative languages to facilitate improvement of teaching and translation. • **GED:** R6, M5, L6 • **SVP:** 4-10 yrs • **Academic:** Ed=M, Eng=S • **Work Field:** 251 • **MPSMS:** 745 • **Aptitudes:** G2, V2, N3, S2, P2, Q2, K4, F4, M4, E5, C5 • **Temperaments:** J, P • **Physical:** Stg=S; Freq: R, H, T, G, N • **Work Env:** Noise=Q; • **Salary:** 5 • **Outlook:** 2

SOCIOLOGIST (profess. & kin.) • DOT #054.067-014 • OES: 27198 • Conducts research into development, structure, and behavior of groups of human beings and patterns of culture and social organization which have arisen out of group life in society. Collects and analyzes scientific data concerning social phenomena, such as community, associations, social institutions, ethnic minorities, social classes, and social change. May teach sociology, direct research, prepare technical publications, or act as consultant to lawmakers, administrators, and other officials dealing with problems of social policy. May specialize in research on relationship between criminal law and social order in causes of crime

and behavior of criminals and be designated Criminologist (profess. & kin.). May specialize in research on punishment for crime and control and prevention of crime, management of penal institutions, and rehabilitation of criminal offenders and be designated Penologist (profess. & kin.). May specialize in research on group relationships and processes in an industrial organization and be designated Industrial Sociologist (profess. & kin.). May specialize in research on rural communities in contrast with urban communities and special problems occasioned by impact of scientific and industrial revolutions on rural way of life and be designated Rural Sociologist (profess. & kin.). May specialize in research on interrelations between physical environment and technology in spatial distribution of people and their activities and be designated Social Ecologist (profess. & kin.). May specialize in research on social problems arising from individual or group deviation from commonly accepted standards of conduct, such as crime and delinquency, or social problems and racial discrimination rooted in failure of society to achieve its collective purposes and be designated Social Problems Specialist (profess. & kin.). May specialize in research on origin, growth, structure, and demographic characteristics of cities and social patterns and distinctive problems that result from urban environment and be designated Urban Sociologist (profess. & kin.). May specialize in research on social factors affecting health care, including definition of illness, patient and practitioner behavior, social epidemiology, and delivery of health care, and be designated Medical Sociologist (profess. & kin.). May plan and conduct demographic research, surveys, and experiments to study human populations and affecting trends and be designated Demographer (profess. & kin.) II. • **GED:** R6, M5, L5 • **SVP:** 2-4 yrs • **Academic:** Ed=M, Eng=G • **Work Field:** 251 • **MPSMS:** 744 • **Aptitudes:** G1, V1, N3, S4, P4, Q3, K4, F4, M4, E5, C5 • **Temperaments:** D, J • **Physical:** Stg=S; Freq: T, G • **Work Env:** Noise=Q; • **Salary:** 4 • **Outlook:** 1

URBAN PLANNER (profess. & kin.) • DOT #199.167-014 • OES: 27105 • Alternate titles: CITY PLANNER; CITY-PLANNING ENGINEER; LAND PLANNER; TOWN PLANNER. Develops comprehensive plans and programs for utilization of land and physical facilities of cities, counties, and metropolitan areas: Compiles and analyzes data on economic, social, and physical factors affecting land use, and prepares or requisitions graphic and narrative reports on data. Confers with local authorities, civic leaders, social scientists, and land planning and development specialists to devise and recommend arrangements of land and physical facilities for residential, commercial, industrial, and community uses. Recommends governmental measures affecting land use, public utilities, community facilities, and housing and transportation to control and guide community development and renewal. May review and evaluate environmental impact reports applying to specified private and public planning projects and programs. When directing activities of planning department, is known as Chief Planner (profess. & kin.); Director, Planning (profess. & kin.). Usually employed by local government jurisdictions, but may work for any level of government, or private consulting firms. • **GED:** R5, M4, L5 • **SVP:** 4-10 yrs • **Academic:** Ed=B, Eng=G • **Work Field:** 244, 295 • **MPSMS:** 704 • **Aptitudes:** G2, V1, N2, S2, P2, Q3, K4, F3, M4, E5, C4 • **Temperaments:** J, P, V • **Physical:** Stg=S; Freq: T, G Occas: R, H, N • **Work Env:** Noise=N; • **Salary:** 4 • **Outlook:** 2

GOE: 11.03.03
Historical

ANTHROPOLOGIST (profess. & kin.) • DOT #055.067-010 • OES: 27198 • Makes comparative studies in relations to distribution, origin, evolution, and races of humans, cultures they have created, and their distribution and physical characteristics: Gathers, analyzes, and reports data on human physique, social customs, and artifacts, such as weapons, tools, pottery, and clothing. May apply anthropological data and techniques to solution of problems in human relations in fields, such as industrial relations, race and ethnic relations, social work, political administration, education, public health, and programs involving transcultural or foreign relations. May specialize in application of anthropological concepts to current problems and be designated Applied Anthropologist (profess. & kin.). May specialize in study of relationships between language and culture and socialinguistic studies and be designated Anthropological Linguist (profess. & kin.); or in study of relationship between individual personality and culture and be designated Psychological Anthropologist (profess. & kin.); or in study of complex, industrialized societies and be designated Urban Anthropologist (profess. & kin.). ● **GED:** R6, M5, L5 ● **SVP:** 2-4 yrs ● **Academic:** Ed=M, Eng=G ● **Work Field:** 251 ● **MPSMS:** 745 ● **Aptitudes:** G1, V1, N3, S2, P2, Q4, K4, F4, M4, E4, C5 ● **Temperaments:** J ● **Physical:** Stg=L; Freq: T, G, N Occas: R, H ● **Work Env:** Noise=Q; ● **Salary:** 5 ● **Outlook:** 1

ARCHEOLOGIST (profess. & kin.) ● DOT #055.067-018 ● OES: 27198 ● Reconstructs record of extinct cultures, especially preliterate cultures: Studies, classifies, and interprets artifacts, architectural features, and types of structures recovered by excavation in order to determine age and cultural identity. Establishes chronological sequence of development of each culture from simpler to more advanced levels. May specialize in study of literate periods of major civilizations in Near and Middle East and be designated Archeologist, Classical (profess. & kin.). May specialize in study of past Columbian history of the Americas and be designated Historical Archeologist (profess. & kin.). ● **GED:** R6, M5, L5 ● **SVP:** 2-4 yrs ● **Academic:** Ed=B, Eng=S ● **Work Field:** 251 ● **MPSMS:** 745 ● **Aptitudes:** G1, V1, N3, S2, P2, Q4, K4, F4, M4, E4, C5 ● **Temperaments:** J ● **Physical:** Stg=L; Freq: R, H, T, G, N Occas: I, A ● **Work Env:** Noise=Q; Occas: W ● **Salary:** 4 ● **Outlook:** 1

ARCHIVIST (profess. & kin.) ● DOT #101.167-010 ● OES: 31511 ● Appraises and edits permanent records and historically valuable documents, participates in research activities based on archival materials, and directs safekeeping of archival documents and materials: Analyzes documents, such as government records, minutes of corporate board meetings, letters from famous persons, and charters of nonprofit foundations, by ascertaining date of writing, author, or original recipient of letter, to appraise value to posterity or to employing organization. Directs activities of workers engaged in cataloging and safekeeping of valuable materials and directs disposition of worthless materials. Prepares or directs preparation of document descriptions and reference aids for use of archives, such as accession lists, indexes, guides, bibliographies, abstracts, and microfilmed copies of documents. Directs filing and cross indexing of selected documents in alphabetical and chronological order. Advises government agencies, scholars, journalists, and others conducting research by supplying available materials and information according to familiarity with archives and with political, economic, military, and social history of period. Requests or recommends pertinent materials available in libraries, private collllections, or other archives. Selects and edits documents for publication and display, according to knowledge of subject, literary or journalistic expression, and techniques for presentation and display. May be designated according to subject matter specialty as Archivist, Economic History (profess. & kin.); Archivist, Military History (profess. & kin.); Archivist, Political History (profess. & kin.); or according to nature of employing institution as Archivist, Nonprofit Foundation (nonprofit organ.). In smaller organizations, may direct activities of libraries. ● **GED:** R5, M3, L5 ● **SVP:** 4-10 yrs ● **Academic:** Ed=B, Eng=G ● **Work Field:** 211, 251, 293 ● **MPSMS:** 933 ● **Aptitudes:** G2, V1, N2, S3, P2, Q3, K4, F4, M4, E5, C4 ● **Temperaments:** D, F, J, P, V ● **Physical:** Stg=S; Freq: R, H, I, T, G, N, A ● **Work Env:** Noise=N; ● **Salary:** 5 ● **Outlook:** 3

GENEALOGIST (profess. & kin.) ● DOT #052.067-018 ● OES: 27198 ● Conducts research into genealogical background of individual or family in order to establish descent from specific ancestor or to discover and identify forebears of individual or family: Consults American and foreign genealogical tables and publications and documents, such as church and court records, for evidence of births, baptisms, marriages, deaths, and legacies in order to trace lines of descent or succession. Constructs chart showing lines of descent and family relationships. Prepares history of family in narrative form or writes brief sketches emphasizing points of interest in family background. ● **GED:** R5, M2, L5 ● **SVP:** 2-4 yrs ● **Academic:** Ed=A, Eng=G ● **Work Field:** 251 ● **MPSMS:** 743 ● **Aptitudes:** G2, V2, N3, S4, P4, Q2, K4, F4, M4, E5, C5 ● **Temperaments:** D, J ● **Physical:** Stg=S; Freq: R, H, T, G, N ● **Work Env:** Noise=Q; ● **Salary:** 5 ● **Outlook:** 1

HISTORIAN (profess. & kin.) ● DOT #052.067-022 ● OES: 27198 ● Prepares in narrative, brief, or outline form chronological account or record of past or current events dealing with some phase of human activity, either in terms of individuals, or social, ethnic, political, or

geographic groupings: Assembles historical data by consulting sources of information, such as historical indexes and catalogs, archives, court records, diaries, news files, and miscellaneous published and unpublished materials. Organizes and evaluates data on basis of authenticity and relative significance. Acts as adviser or consultant, and performs research for individuals, institutions, and commercial organizations on subjects, such as technological evolution within industry or manners and customs peculiar to certain historical period. May trace historical development within restricted field of research, such as economics, sociology, or philosophy. ● **GED:** R5, M2, L5 ● **SVP:** 2-4 yrs ● **Academic:** Ed=B, Eng=G ● **Work Field:** 251 ● **MPSMS:** 743 ● **Aptitudes:** G2, V2, N3, S4, P4, Q2, K4, F4, M4, E5, C5 ● **Temperaments:** D, J ● **Physical:** Stg=S; Freq: R, H, T, G, N ● **Work Env:** Noise=Q; ● **Salary:** 4 ● **Outlook:** 1

GOE: 11.03.04
Occupational

EMPLOYEE RELATIONS SPECIALIST (profess. & kin.) ● DOT #166.267-042 ● OES: 21511 ● Interviews workers to gather information on worker attitudes toward work environment and supervision received to facilitate resolution of employee relations problems: Explains to workers company and governmental rules, regulations, and procedures, and need for compliance. Gathers information on workers' feelings about factors that affect worker morale, motivation, and efficiency. Meets with management to discuss possible actions to be taken. Inspects work stations to ensure required changes or actions are implemented. Interviews workers to determine reactions to specific actions taken. Prepares reports on workers' comments and actions taken. Enrolls eligible workers in company programs, such as pension and savings plans. Maintains medical, insurance, and other personnel records and forms. May operate computer to compile, store, or retrieve worker related information, such as medical, insurance, pension, and savings plans. ● **GED:** R4, M2, L2 ● **SVP:** 2-4 yrs ● **Academic:** Ed=H, Eng=G ● **Work Field:** 271 ● **MPSMS:** 893 ● **Aptitudes:** G2, V2, N3, S4, P4, Q3, K4, F4, M4, E5, C5 ● **Temperaments:** J, P ● **Physical:** Stg=S; Const: T, G Freq: R, H Occas: I ● **Work Env:** Noise=N; ● **Salary:** 4 ● **Outlook:** 3

EMPLOYMENT INTERVIEWER (profess. & kin.) ● DOT #166.267-010 ● OES: 21508 ● Alternate titles: PERSONNEL INTERVIEWER; PLACEMENT INTERVIEWER. Interviews job applicants to select people meeting employer qualifications: Reviews employment applications and evaluates work history, education and training, job skills, compensation needs, and other qualifications of applicants. Records additional knowledge, skills, abilities, interests, test results, and other data pertinent to selection and referral of applicants. Reviews job orders and matches applicants with job requirements, utilizing manual or computerized file search. Informs applicants of job duties and responsibilities, compensation and benefits, work schedules and working conditions, company and union policies, promotional opportunities, and other related information. Refers selected applicants to person placing job order, according to policy of organization. Keeps records of applicants not selected for employment. May perform reference and background checks on applicants. May refer applicants to vocational counseling services. May conduct or arrange for skills, intelligence, or psychological testing of applicants. May evaluate selection and placement techniques by conducting research or follow-up activities and conferring with management and supervisory personnel. May specialize in interviewing and referring certain types of personnel, such as professional, technical, managerial, clerical, and other types of skilled or unskilled workers. May search for and recruit applicants for open positions [PERSONNEL RECRUITER (profess. & kin.) 166.267-038]. May contact employers in writing, in person, or by telephone to solicit orders for job vacancies for clientele or for specified applicants and record information about job openings on job order forms to describe duties, hiring requirements, and related data. ● **GED:** R5, M3, L5 ● **SVP:** 1-2 yrs ● **Academic:** Ed=B, Eng=G ● **Work Field:** 271 ● **MPSMS:** 893, 943 ● **Aptitudes:** G2, V2, N3, S4, P4, Q3, K4, F4, M4, E5, C5 ● **Temperaments:** I, J, P ● **Physical:** Stg=S; Freq: H, T, G, N Occas: R, I, A ● **Work Env:** Noise=Q; ● **Salary:** 4 ● **Outlook:** 4

JOB ANALYST (profess. & kin.) ● DOT #166.267-018 ● OES: 21511 ● Alternate titles: PERSONNEL ANALYST. Collects, analyzes, and prepares occupational information to facilitate personnel, administration, and management functions of organization: Consults with management to determine type, scope, and purpose of study. Studies current organizational occupational data and compiles distribution reports, organization and flow charts, and other background information required for study. Observes jobs and interviews workers and supervisory personnel to determine job and worker requirements. Analyzes occupational data, such as physical, mental, and training requirements of jobs and workers and develops written summaries, such as job descriptions, job specifications, and lines of career movement. Utilizes developed occupational data to evaluate or improve methods and techniques for recruiting, selecting, promoting, evaluating, and training workers, and administration of related personnel programs. May specialize in classifying positions according to regulated guidelines to meet job classification requirements of civil service system and be known as Position Classifier (government ser.). ● **GED:** R5, M4, L5 ● **SVP:** 1-2 yrs ● **Academic:** Ed=B, Eng=G ● **Work Field:** 295 ● **MPSMS:** 712 ● **Aptitudes:** G2, V2, N2, S3, P3, Q3, K4, F4, M4, E4, C4 ● **Temperaments:** D, J, P ● **Physical:** Stg=L; Freq: R, H, I, T, G, N, A ● **Work Env:** Noise=N; ● **Salary:** 4 ● **Outlook:** 4

JOB DEVELOPMENT SPECIALIST (profess. & kin.) ● DOT #166.267-034 ● OES: 21511 ● Promotes and develops employment and on-the-job training opportunities for disadvantaged applicants: Assists employers in revising standards which exclude applicants from jobs. Demonstrates to employers effectiveness and profitability of employing chronically unemployed by identifying jobs that workers could perform. Establishes relationships with employers regarding problems, complaints, and progress of recently placed disadvantaged applicants and recommends corrective action. Assists employers in establishing wage scales commensurate with prevailing rates. Promotes, develops, and terminates on-the-job training program opportunities with employers and assists in writing contracts. Identifies need for and assists in development of auxiliary services to facilitate bringing disadvantaged applicants into job-ready status. Informs business, labor, and public about training programs through various media. May instruct applicants in resume writing, job search, and interviewing techniques. ● **GED:** R4, M3, L4 ● **SVP:** 6 mos-1 yr ● **Academic:** Ed=H, Eng=G ● **Work Field:** 298, 282 ● **MPSMS:** 943 ● **Aptitudes:** G3, V3, N4, S4, P4, Q4, K4, F5, M4, E5, C5 ● **Temperaments:** I, J, P ● **Physical:** Stg=S; Freq: T, G ● **Work Env:** Noise=N; ● **Salary:** 4 ● **Outlook:** 4

OCCUPATIONAL ANALYST (profess. & kin.) ● DOT #166.067-010 ● OES: 21511 ● Researches occupations and analyzes and integrates data to develop and devise concepts of worker relationships, modify and maintain occupational classification system, and provide business, industry, and government with technical occupational information necessary for utilization of work force: Confers with business, industry, government, and union officials to arrange for and develop plans for studies and surveys. Devises methods and establishes criteria for conducting studies and surveys. Researches jobs, industry and organizational concepts and techniques, and worker characteristics to determine job relationships, job functions and content, worker traits, and occupational trends. Prepares results of research for publication in form of books, brochures, charts, film, and manuals. Identifies need for and develops job analysis tools, such as manuals, reporting forms, training films, and slides. Prepares management tools, such as personnel distribution reports, organization and flow charts, job descriptions, tables of job relationships, and worker trait analysis. Conducts training and provides technical assistance to promote use of job analysis materials, tools, and concepts in areas of curriculum development, career planning, job restructuring, and government and employment training programs. May specialize in providing technical assistance to private, public, or governmental organizations and be designated Industrial Occupational Analyst (profess. & kin.). ● **GED:** R5, M4, L5 ● **SVP:** 2-4 yrs ● **Academic:** Ed=B, Eng=S ● **Work Field:** 251 ● **MPSMS:** 712 ● **Aptitudes:** G1, V1, N2, S3, P3, Q3, K4, F4, M4, E4, C4 ● **Temperaments:** D, J, P ● **Physical:** Stg=L; Freq: R, H, T, G, N Occas: I, A, X ● **Work Env:** Noise=N; ● **Salary:** 4 ● **Outlook:** 3

PERSONNEL RECRUITER (profess. & kin.) ● DOT #166.267-038 ● OES: 21511 ● Seeks out, interviews, screens, and recruits job applicants to fill existing company job openings: Discusses personnel needs with department supervisors to prepare and implement recruitment program. Contacts colleges to arrange on-campus interviews. Provides information on company facilities and job opportunities to potential applicants. Interviews college applicants to obtain work history, education, training, job skills, and salary requirements. Screens and refers qualified applicants to company hiring personnel for follow-up interview. Arranges travel and lodging for selected applicants at company expense. Performs reference and background checks on applicants. Corresponds with job applicants to notify them of employment consideration. Files and maintains employment records for future references. Projects yearly recruitment expenditures for budgetary control. ● **GED:** R5, M3, L5 ● **SVP:** 2-4 yrs ● **Academic:** Ed=B, Eng=G ● **Work Field:** 271 ● **MPSMS:** 943, 893 ● **Aptitudes:** G2, V2, N3, S4, P4, Q3, K4, F4, M4, E5, C5 ● **Temperaments:** I, J, P, V ● **Physical:** Stg=S; Const: T, G Freq: R, H, N Occas: I ● **Work Env:** Noise=N; ● **Salary:** 4 ● **Outlook:** 4

RECRUITER (military ser.) ● DOT #166.267-026 ● OES: 21511 ● Alternate titles: CAREER COUNSELOR. Interviews military and civilian personnel to recruit and inform individuals on matters concerning career opportunities, incentives, military rights and benefits, and advantages of military career: Assists and advises military commands in organizing, preparing, and implementing enlisted recruiting and retention program. Interviews individuals to determine their suitability for placement into specific military occupation. Occasionally lectures to civic and social groups, military dependents, school officials, and religious leaders concerning military career opportunities. ● **GED:** R4, M2, L3 ● **SVP:** 6 mos-1 yr ● **Academic:** Ed=H, Eng=G ● **Work Field:** 282, 295 ● **MPSMS:** 943, 949 ● **Aptitudes:** G3, V3, N4, S4, P4, Q2, K4, F4, M3, E5, C5 ● **Temperaments:** J, P ● **Physical:** Stg=L; Const: T, G Occas: R, H, I ● **Work Env:** Noise=N; ● **Salary:** 4 ● **Outlook:** 4

GOE: 11.03.05
Economic

ECONOMIST (profess. & kin.) ● DOT #050.067-010 ● OES: 27102 ● Alternate titles: ECONOMIC ANALYST. Plans, designs, and conducts research to aid in interpretation of economic relationships and in solution of problems arising from production and distribution of goods and services: Studies economic and statistical data in area of specialization, such as finance, labor, or agriculture. Devises methods and procedures for collecting and processing data, utilizing knowledge of available sources of data and various econometric and sampling techniques. Compiles data relating to research area, such as employment, productivity, and wages and hours. Reviews and analyzes economic data in order to prepare reports detailing results of investigation, and to stay abreast of economic changes. Organizes data into report format and arranges for preparation of graphic illustrations of research findings. Formulates recommendations, policies, or plans to aid in market interpretation or solution of economic problems, such as recommending changes in methods of agricultural financing, domestic, and international monetary policies, or policies that regulate investment and transfer of capital. May supervise and assign work to staff. May testify at regulatory or legislative hearings to present recommendations. May specialize in specific economic area or commodity and be designated Agricultural Economist (profess. & kin.); Commodity-Industry Analyst (profess. & kin.); Financial Economist (profess. & kin.); Industrial Economist (profess. & kin); International-Trade Economist (profess. & kin.); Labor Economist (profess. & kin.); Price Economist (profess. & kin.); Tax Economist (profess. & kin.). ● **GED:** R5, M5, L5 ● **SVP:** 4-10 yrs ● **Academic:** Ed=B, Eng=G ● **Work Field:** 251, 211, 298 ● **MPSMS:** 741 ● **Aptitudes:** G2, V2, N2, S5, P5, Q2, K5, F5, M5, E5, C5 ● **Temperaments:** D, I, J, P, T ● **Physical:** Stg=S; Freq: I, T, G, N Occas: R, H ● **Work Env:** Noise=N; ● **Salary:** 5 ● **Outlook:** 2

Law   **11.04**

Workers in this group advise and represent others in legal matters. Those in small towns and cities conduct criminal or civil cases in court, draw up wills and other legal papers, abstract real estate, and perform related activities. Those in large cities usually specialize in one kind of law, such as criminal, civil, tax, labor, or patent. They work in law firms, unions, government agencies, and commercial and industrial establishments. Some are self-employed and have their own office. Lawyers are frequently elected to public office, particularly as legislators. Many state governors and U.S. presidents have been lawyers.

✓ What kind of work would you do?

Your work activities would depend upon your specific job. For example, you might:

- study court decisions and conduct investigations on claims filed against insurance companies.
- prepare wills, deeds, and other legal documents for people.
- preside in a court of law or at a formal hearing.
- conduct research in technical literature to recommend approval or rejection of patent applications.
- represent union or management in labor negotiations.
- defend people during prosecution under the law.
- represent clients who are suing or being sued for money or legal action.
- give advice concerning federal, state, local, and foreign taxes.

✓ What skills and abilities do you need for this kind of work?

To do this kind of work, you must be able to:

- understand, interpret, and apply legal procedures, principles, and laws.
- define problems, collect information, establish facts, and draw valid conclusions.
- deal with all kinds of clients, juries, judges, and other lawyers in a manner that will influence their opinions, attitudes, and judgments.
- read carefully and listen carefully to identify important details which could help a client win his case.
- use your judgment about how to conduct a case or deal with a problem.

✓ How do you know if you would like or could learn to do this kind of work?

The following questions may give you clues about yourself as you consider this group of jobs.

- Have you taken debate or speech courses? Do you feel at ease presenting a point of view in front of a group?
- Have you taken courses in journalism or composition? Can you communicate complex ideas effectively?
- Have you watched detective or lawyer television programs? Do you understand the legal terminology used?
- Have you attended a trial or court proceeding? Would you like to work in this type of atmosphere?

✓ How can you prepare for and enter this kind of work?

Occupations in this group usually require education and/or training extending from four years to over ten years, depending upon the specific kind of work. Lawyers are required to pass a bar examination and obtain a license for the particular state in which they want to practice. Educational requirements for taking the bar examination vary. Some states require proof of graduation from an approved law school. A four year college degree and completion of a program for law clerks may be accepted. Other states allow persons who study law with a licensed lawyer to take the bar examination. Correspondence courses in law are accepted as preparation for bar examinations in some states. Special requirements and licenses are necessary for those who wish to practice law in certain higher courts.

Entry requirements for law schools vary according to the institution. Some accept students directly from high school. Others require college graduation.

Some jobs in this group require legal education, but not a license. In these jobs, workers need legal knowledge, but do not practice law.

Licensed lawyers enter the field as junior partners in law firms, junior executives in business or industry, or workers in government agencies. A few establish their own law practices. However, self-employment is usually delayed because of the need for money, experience, and reputation. Some jobs in this group are elected or appointed positions.

Lawyers sometimes work long or irregular hours. They may be required to respond to emergency calls from clients. While the ability to see will make the study and practice of law easier, it is not required. There are many successful blind workers in this field.

The field of law is highly competitive, but salaried positions can be found in government agencies, private businesses, and in some law offices. Lawyers in private practice depend on collection of fees for their income. When they have several long-term retainers (fees paid in advance so that service is available when needed), they have a stable income.

If you think you would like to do this kind of work, look at the job titles listed below.

■ ■ ■

GOE: 11.04.01
Justice Administration

APPEALS REFEREE (government ser.) ● DOT #119.267-014 ● OES: 28101 ● Adjudicates social welfare tax or benefit eligibility issues filed by disabled or unemployed claimants or employers: Arranges and conducts hearings to discover pertinent facts bearing on claim in accord with federal and state laws and procedures. Renders decisions affirming or denying previous ruling, based on testimony, claim records, applicable provisions of law, and established precedents. Writes decision explaining ruling and informs interested parties of results. Confers with personnel of employer or agency involved to obtain additional information bearing on appeal, and to clarify future implications of decisions. May participate in court proceedings against claimants attempting to obtain benefits through fraud. May render informal opinions on points of law in questionable cases to facilitate initial determination of benefit eligibility or imposition of penalties. May be required to hold law degree or license to practice law. ● **GED:** R6, M3, L6 ● **SVP:** 4-10 yrs ● **Academic:** Ed=B, Eng=G ● **Work Field:** 271, 272 ● **MPSMS:** 959, 932 ● **Aptitudes:** G2, V2, N3, S4, P3, Q3, K4, F4, M4, E5, C5 ● **Temperaments:** J ● **Physical:** Stg=S; Freq: T, G Occas: R, H, I, N ● **Work Env:** Noise=N; ● **Salary:** 3 ● **Outlook:** 4

HEARING OFFICER (government ser.) ● DOT #119.107-010 ● OES: 28101 ● Alternate titles: APPEALS BOARD REFEREE; REFEREE. Reviews previously adjudicated social welfare tax or eligibility issues, as member of appeals board, utilizing knowledge of regulations, policy, and precedent decisions: Researches laws, regulations, policies, and precedent decisions to prepare for appeal hearings. Schedules hearing, issues subpoenas, counsels parties, and administers oaths to prepare for formal hearing. Conducts hearing to obtain information and evidence relative to disposition of appeal. Questions witnesses and rules on exceptions, motions, and admissibility of evidence. Analyzes evidence and applicable law, regulations, policy, and precedent decisions to determine appropriate and permissible conclusions. Prepares written decision. May hear disability insurance appeals and be designated Disability-Insurance-Hearing Officer (government ser.). May hear unemployment insurance appeals and be designated Unemployment-Insurance-Hearing Officer (government ser.). ● **GED:** R6, M3, L6 ● **SVP:** Over 10 yrs ● **Academic:** Ed=B, Eng=G ● **Work Field:** 272 ● **MPSMS:** 959 ● **Aptitudes:** G1, V2, N3, S4, P3, Q3, K4, F4, M4, E5, C5 ● **Temperaments:** D, J ● **Physical:** Stg=S; Freq: R, H, T, G, N, A Occas: I ● **Work Env:** Noise=N; ● **Salary:** 4 ● **Outlook:** 3

GOE: 11.04.02
Legal Practice

DISTRICT ATTORNEY (government ser.) ● DOT #110.117-010 ● OES: 28108 ● Alternate titles: PROSECUTING ATTORNEY; PROSECUTOR; SOLICITOR, CITY OR STATE; STATE'S ATTORNEY; UNITED STATES ATTORNEY. Conducts prosecution in court proceedings in behalf of city, county, state, or federal government: Gathers and analyzes evidence in case and reviews pertinent decisions, policies, regulations, and other legal matters pertaining to case. Presents evidence against accused to grand jury for indictment or release of accused. Appears against accused in court of law and presents evidence before JUDGE (government ser.) or other judiciary and jury. ●

GED: R6, M4, L6 ● **SVP:** 4-10 yrs ● **Academic:** Ed=M, Eng=G ● **Work Field:** 272 ● **MPSMS:** 932 ● **Aptitudes:** G1, V1, N2, S4, P4, Q3, K4, F4, M4, E5, C5 ● **Temperaments:** I, J, P ● **Physical:** Stg=S; Freq: T, G, N Occas: R, H, I, A ● **Work Env:** Noise=N; ● **Salary:** 5 ● **Outlook:** 1

INSURANCE ATTORNEY (insurance) ● DOT #110.117-014 ● OES: 28108 ● Alternate titles: CLAIM ATTORNEY; INSURANCE COUNSEL. Advises management of insurance company on legality of insurance transactions: Studies court decisions, and recommends changes in wording of insurance policies to conform with law or to protect company from unwarranted claims. Advises claims department personnel of legality of claims filed on company to ensure against undue payments. Advises personnel engaged in drawing up of legal documents, such as insurance contracts and release papers. May specialize in one phase of legal work, such as claims or contracts. ● **GED:** R6, M4, L6 ● **SVP:** 4-10 yrs ● **Academic:** Ed=M, Eng=G ● **Work Field:** 271, 272 ● **MPSMS:** 895, 932 ● **Aptitudes:** G1, V1, N1, S4, P4, Q2, K4, F4, M4, E5, C5 ● **Temperaments:** J, P, V ● **Physical:** Stg=S; Freq: T, G, N Occas: R, H, I, A ● **Work Env:** Noise=N; ● **Salary:** 5 ● **Outlook:** 3

LAWYER (profess. & kin.) ● DOT #110.107-010 ● OES: 28108 ● Alternate titles: ADVOCATE; ATTORNEY; COUNSELOR; COUNSELOR-AT-LAW. Conducts criminal and civil lawsuits, draws up legal documents, advises clients as to legal rights, and practices other phases of law: Gathers evidence in divorce, civil, criminal, and other cases to formulate defense or to initiate legal action. Conducts research, interviews clients, and witnesses and handles other details in preparation for trial. Prepares legal briefs, develops strategy, arguments and testimony in preparation for presentation of case. Files brief with court clerk. Represents client in court, and before quasi-judicial or administrative agencies of government. Interprets laws, rulings, and regulations for individuals and businesses. May confer with colleagues with specialty in area of lawsuit to establish and verify basis for legal proceedings. May act as trustee, guardian, or executor. May draft wills, trusts, transfer of assets, gifts and other documents. May advise corporate clients concerning transactions of business involving internal affairs, stockholders, directors, officers and corporate relations with general public. May supervise and coordinate activities of subordinate legal personnel. May prepare business contracts, pay taxes, settle labor disputes, and administer other legal matters. May teach college courses in law. May specialize in specific phase of law. ● **GED:** R6, M4, L6 ● **SVP:** 4-10 yrs ● **Academic:** Ed=M, Eng=G ● **Work Field:** 272 ● **MPSMS:** 932 ● **Aptitudes:** G1, V1, N1, S4, P4, Q3, K4, F4, M4, E5, C5 ● **Temperaments:** I, J, P, V ● **Physical:** Stg=S; Const: T, G Freq: R, H, I, N Occas: A ● **Work Env:** Noise=N; ● **Salary:** 5 ● **Outlook:** 3

LAWYER, CORPORATION (profess. & kin.) ● DOT #110.117-022 ● OES: 28108 ● Alternate titles: BUSINESS AND FINANCIAL COUNSEL; CORPORATE COUNSEL. Advises corporation concerning legal rights, obligations, and privileges: Studies Constitution, statutes, decisions, and ordinances of quasi-judicial bodies. Examines legal data to determine advisability of defending or prosecuting lawsuit. May act as agent of corporation in various transactions. ● **GED:** R6, M4, L6 ● **SVP:** 4-10 yrs ● **Academic:** Ed=M, Eng=G ● **Work Field:** 272 ● **MPSMS:** 932 ● **Aptitudes:** G1, V1, N1, S4, P4, Q3, K4, F4, M4, E5, C5 ● **Temperaments:** D, I, P, V ● **Physical:** Stg=S; Freq: T, G, N Occas: R, H, I, A ● **Work Env:** Noise=N; ● **Salary:** 5 ● **Outlook:** 4

LAWYER, CRIMINAL (profess. & kin.) ● DOT #110.107-014 ● OES: 28108 ● Specializes in law cases dealing with offenses against society or state, such as theft, murder, and arson: Interviews clients and witnesses to ascertain facts of case. Correlates findings and prepares case. Prosecutes, or defends defendant against charges. Conducts case, examining and cross examining witnesses. Summarizes case to jury. • **GED:** R6, M4, L6 • **SVP:** 4-10 yrs • **Academic:** Ed=M, Eng=G • **Work Field:** 272 • **MPSMS:** 932 • **Aptitudes:** G1, V1, N1, S4, P4, Q3, K4, F4, M4, E5, C5 • **Temperaments:** I, P, V • **Physical:** Stg=S; Freq: T, G, N Occas: R, H, I, A • **Work Env:** Noise=N; • **Salary:** 5 • **Outlook:** 4

LAWYER, PATENT (profess. & kin.) • DOT #110.117-026 • OES: 28108 • Alternate titles: PATENT ATTORNEY; SOLICITOR, PATENT. Specializes in patent law: Advises clients, such as inventors, investors, and manufacturers, concerning patentability of inventions, infringement of patents, validity of patents, and similar items. Prepares applications for patents and presents applications to U.S. Patent Office. Prosecutes or defends clients in patent infringement litigations. May specialize in protecting American trademarks and copyrights in foreign countries. • **GED:** R6, M4, L6 • **SVP:** 4-10 yrs • **Academic:** Ed=M, Eng=G • **Work Field:** 272 • **MPSMS:** 932 • **Aptitudes:** G1, V1, N1, S4, P4, Q3, K4, F4, M4, E5, C5 • **Temperaments:** I, P, V • **Physical:** Stg=S; Freq: T, G, N Occas: R, H, I, A • **Work Env:** Noise=N; • **Salary:** 5 • **Outlook:** 3

LAWYER, PROBATE (profess. & kin.) • DOT #110.117-030 • OES: 28108 • Specializes in settlement and planning of estates: Drafts wills, deeds of trusts, and similar documents to carry out estate planning of clients. Probates wills and represents and advises executors and administrators of estates. • **GED:** R6, M4, L6 • **SVP:** 4-10 yrs • **Academic:** Ed=M, Eng=G • **Work Field:** 272 • **MPSMS:** 932 • **Aptitudes:** G1, V1, N1, S4, P4, Q4, K4, F4, M4, E5, C5 • **Temperaments:** D, I, P, V • **Physical:** Stg=S; Freq: R, H, I, T, G, N, A • **Work Env:** Noise=N; • **Salary:** 5 • **Outlook:** 3

LEGAL INVESTIGATOR (profess. & kin.) • DOT #119.267-022 • OES: 28499 • Alternate titles: LEGAL ASSISTANT. Researches and prepares cases relating to administrative appeals of civil service members: Examines state government, personnel, college, or university rules and regulations. Answers members' questions regarding rights and benefits and advises on how rules apply to individual situations. Presents arguments and evidence to support appeal at appeal hearing. Calls upon witnesses to testify at hearing. • **GED:** R5, M2, L5 • **SVP:** 2-4 yrs • **Academic:** Ed=A, Eng=G • **Work Field:** 271, 272 • **MPSMS:** 932, 959 • **Aptitudes:** G2, V1, N3, S4, P4, Q3, K4, F4, M4, E5, C5 • **Temperaments:** D, I, J, P • **Physical:** Stg=S; Freq: R, H, T, G, N, A Occas: I • **Work Env:** Noise=N; • **Salary:** 4 • **Outlook:** 4

PARALEGAL (profess. & kin.) • DOT #119.267-026 • OES: 28305 • Alternate titles: LAW CLERK; LEGAL AID; LEGAL ASSISTANT. Researches law, investigates facts, and prepares documents to assist LAWYER (profess. & kin.) 110.107-010: Researches and analyzes law sources such as statutes, recorded judicial decisions, legal articles, treaties, constitutions, and legal codes to prepare legal documents, such as briefs, pleadings, appeals, wills, contracts, initial and amended articles of incorporation, stock certificates and other securities, buy-sell agreements, closing papers and binders, deeds, and trust instruments for review, approval, and use by attorney. Appraises and inventories real and personal property for estate planning. Investigates facts and law of case to determine causes of action and to prepare case accordingly. Files pleadings with court clerk. Prepares affidavits of documents and maintains document file. Delivers or directs delivery of subpoenas to witnesses and parties to action. May direct and coordinate activities of law office employees. May prepare office accounts and tax returns. May specialize in litigation, probate, real estate, or corporation law. May prepare real estate closing statement and assist in closing process. May act as arbitrator and liaison between disputing parties. May act as law librarian, keeping and monitoring legal volumes and ensuring legal volumes are up-to-date. May search patent files to ascertain originality of patent application and be designated Patent Clerk (government ser.). • **GED:** R5, M2, L5 • **SVP:** 2-4 yrs • **Academic:** Ed=A, Eng=G • **Work Field:** 271, 272 • **MPSMS:** 932 • **Aptitudes:** G2, V1, N3, S4, P4, Q3, K4, F4, M4, E5, C5 • **Temperaments:** J, P, T, V • **Physical:** Stg=L; Freq: R, H, I, T, G, N Occas: A • **Work Env:** Noise=N; • **Salary:** 4 • **Outlook:** 3

TAX ATTORNEY (profess. & kin.) • DOT #110.117-038 • OES: 28108 • Alternate titles: TAX AGENT; TAX REPRESENTATIVE. Advises individuals, business concerns, and other organizations concerning income, estate, gift, excise, property, and other federal, state, local, and foreign taxes. Prepares opinions on tax liability resulting from prospective and past transactions. Represents clients in tax litigation. • **GED:** R6, M4, L6 • **SVP:** 4-10 yrs • **Academic:** Ed=M, Eng=G • **Work Field:** 272 • **MPSMS:** 932 • **Aptitudes:** G1, V2, N1, S4, P4, Q2, K4, F4, M4, E5, C5 • **Temperaments:** J, V • **Physical:** Stg=S; Freq: R, H, I, T, G, N, A • **Work Env:** Noise=N; • **Salary:** 5 • **Outlook:** 4

GOE: 11.04.03
Conciliation

ADJUDICATOR (government ser.) • DOT #119.167-010 • OES: 28101 • Adjudicates claims filed by government against individuals or organizations: Determines existence and amount of liability, according to law, administrative and judicial precedents and other evidence. Recommends acceptance or rejection of compromise settlement offers. • **GED:** R5, M4, L5 • **SVP:** 2-4 yrs • **Academic:** Ed=B, Eng=G • **Work Field:** 272 • **MPSMS:** 932 • **Aptitudes:** G2, V2, N2, S4, P4, Q4, K4, F4, M5, E5, C5 • **Temperaments:** J, P, V • **Physical:** Stg=S; Freq: T, G Occas: R, H, I, N • **Work Env:** Noise=N; • **Salary:** 4 • **Outlook:** 3

ARBITRATOR (profess. & kin.) • DOT #169.107-010 • OES: 21511 • Arbitrates disputes between labor and management to bind both to specific terms and conditions of labor contract: Conducts hearing to evaluate contentions of parties regarding disputed contract provisions. Analyzes information obtained, using knowledge of facts in issue and industry practices. Renders binding decision to settle dispute, protect public interests, prevent employee wage loss, and minimize business interruptions. Issues report concerning results of arbitration. May serve exclusively for particular case for which selected by parties and be known as Ad Hoc Arbitrator (profess. & kin.). May serve for all disputes concerning specific agreements and be known as Umpire (profess. & kin.); Referee (profess. & kin.). • **GED:** R5, M4, L5 • **SVP:** 4-10 yrs • **Academic:** Ed=M, Eng=G • **Work Field:** 271 • **MPSMS:** 932 • **Aptitudes:** G2, V1, N3, S4, P4, Q3, K5, F5, M5, E5, C5 • **Temperaments:** D, I, J, P • **Physical:** Stg=S; Freq: T, G, N Occas: R, H • **Work Env:** Noise=N; • **Salary:** 5 • **Outlook:** 1

CONCILIATOR (profess. & kin.) • DOT #169.207-010 • OES: 21511 • Alternate titles: MEDIATOR. Mediates and conciliates disputes over negotiations of labor agreements or other labor relations disputes: Promotes use of fact-finding and advisory services to prevent labor disputes and to maintain sound labor relationships. Promotes use of mediation and conciliation services to resolve labor disputes. Advises and counsels parties to solve labor problems. Investigates and mediates labor disputes upon request of any bona fide party, using knowledge of labor law, industry practices, and social policies involved in labor relations. Urges expeditious settlement of negotiations to prevent employee wage loss, to minimize business interruptions, and to achieve labor-management peace. Interrogates parties and clarifies problems to focus discussion on crucial points of disagreement. Assists parties to compromise and settle deadlocked negotiations. Prepares reports of decisions reached or outcome of negotiations. May assist in arranging arbitration. May conduct representation elections according to written consent agreement of concerned parties. May oversee balloting procedures to assist in ratification of labor agreements. • **GED:** R5, M4, L5 • **SVP:** 4-10 yrs • **Academic:** Ed=M, Eng=G • **Work Field:** 271 • **MPSMS:** 733, 899 • **Aptitudes:** G2, V1, N3, S4, P4, Q4, K5, F5, M5, E5, C5 • **Temperaments:** I, J, P • **Physical:** Stg=S; Freq: T, G Occas: R, H, I, N • **Work Env:** Noise=N; • **Salary:** 5 • **Outlook:** 1

GOE: 11.04.04
Abstracting, Document Preparation

ABSTRACTOR (profess. & kin.) • DOT #119.267-010 • OES: 28306 • Alternate titles: ABSTRACT CLERK; ABSTRACT MAKER; ABSTRACT SEARCHER; ABSTRACT WRITER; COURT ABSTRACTOR; TITLE ABSTRACTOR. Analyzes pertinent legal or insurance details or section of statute or case law to summarize for purposes of examination, proof, or ready reference. May search out titles to deter-

mine if title deed is correct [TITLE EXAMINER (profess. & kin.)]. ●
GED: R5, M3, L5 ● **SVP:** 1-2 yrs ● **Academic:** Ed=A, Eng=G ●
Work Field: 271, 231 ● **MPSMS:** 932, 895 ● **Aptitudes:** G2, V1, N4,
S4, P4, Q2, K4, F4, M4, E5, C5 ● **Temperaments:** J, T ● **Physical:**
Stg=S; Freq: R, H, N Occas: I ● **Work Env:** Noise=Q; ● **Salary:** 2 ●
Outlook: 4

CUSTOMS BROKER (financial) ● DOT #186.117-018 ● OES: 19998
● Alternate titles: CUSTOMS-HOUSE BROKER. Prepares and compiles documents required by federal government for discharge of foreign cargo at domestic port to serve as intermediary between importers,
merchant shipping companies, airlines, railroads, trucking companies,
pipeline operators, and the United States Customs Service: Prepares
entry papers from shipper's invoice in accordance with U.S. Customs
Service regulations, and regulations of other federal agencies bearing
on importation of goods, such as Environmental Protection Agency
and Food And Drug Administration. Files papers with Customs Service and arranges for payment of duties. Quotes duty rates on goods to
be imported, based on knowledge of federal tariffs and excise taxes.
Prepares papers for shippers desiring to appeal duty charges imposed

by Customs Service. Provides for storage of imported goods and for
transportation of imported goods from port to final destination. May
register foreign ships with U.S. Coast Guard. Must be licensed by U.S.
Treasury Department or operate under corporate license granted to
employer by Treasury Department. ● **GED:** R5, M4, L5 ● **SVP:** 2-4
yrs ● **Academic:** Ed=A, Eng=S ● **Work Field:** 232 ● **MPSMS:**
859 ● **Aptitudes:** G2, V2, N2, S5, P4, Q3, K4, F4, M4, E5, C4 ●
Temperaments: J, P, T ● **Physical:** Stg=S; Const: T, G, N Freq: A
Occas: S, K, O, R, H, I, X ● **Work Env:** Noise=N; Occas: W ●
Salary: 4 ● **Outlook:** 1

PATENT AGENT (profess. & kin.) ● DOT #119.167-014 ● OES:
28499 ● Prepares and presents patent application to U.S. Patent Office
and in patent courts, according to familiarity with patent law and filing
procedures. Must be registered by U.S. Patent Office. Cannot practice
law or appear in other courts. ● **GED:** R6, M5, L6 ● **SVP:** 2-4 yrs ●
Academic: Ed=B, Eng=G ● **Work Field:** 272 ● **MPSMS:** 932 ● **Aptitudes:** G2, V1, N2, S2, P3, Q4, K4, F4, M5, E5, C4 ● **Temperaments:** F, I, J ● **Physical:** Stg=S; Freq: T, G, N ● **Work Env:** Noise=Q;
● **Salary:** 4 ● **Outlook:** 1

Leading-Influencing   11

Business Administration   **11.05**

Workers in this group are top level adminis-
trators and managers who work through
lower level supervisors to direct all or a part
of the activities in private establishments or
government agencies. They set policies, make
important decisions, and set priorities. These
jobs are found in large businesses, industry,
and government. Labor unions and associa-
tions will also hire these workers.

✓ What kind of work would you do?

Your work activities would depend upon your
specific job. For example, you might:

- serve as president of a company.
- plan and direct operations for an airport.
- administer city government according to
  policies set by city council or other elected
  officials.
- direct the business affairs of a university.
- approve the purchase of goods or services
  needed by a government agency.
- direct all sales activities of a company.
- plan and coordinate conventions, trade
  exhibits, and workshops for a professional
  association.

✓ What skills and abilities do you need for this kind of work?

To do this kind of work, you must be able to:

- think logically to make decisions.
- interpret information in mathematical,
  written, and diagram form, such as statistical
  reports, profit and loss statements, financial
  statements, and credit regulations.
- understand the effect politics and economic
  trends will have on company or agency plans.

- continually make decisions based on experience and personal feelings as well as on facts
  and figures.
- speak to large groups, such as the Chamber
  of Commerce and television audiences.
- deal with all kinds of people ranging from
  civic leaders to employees and from legislators to the general public.
- speak and write clearly and with authority.

✓ How do you know if you would like or could learn to do this kind of work?

The following questions may give you clues about
yourself as you consider this group of jobs.

- Have you been president or treasurer of a
  club or social organization? Can you work
  with others to develop policies and plan
  programs of action?
- Have you taken business administration
  courses? Were you able to understand and
  contribute to class discussions about business
  practices?
- Have you read the business section of news
  magazines or newspapers? Do you understand the terms used?
- Have you supervised the activities of others?
  Were the activities carried out effectively?

✓ How can you prepare for and enter this kind of work?

Occupations in this group usually require education
and/or training extending from two years to over ten
years, depending upon the specific kind of work.
Most jobs in this group require experience in
related positions, usually within the same establishment, industry, or specialization. Degrees in business administration or law provide preparation for

many jobs in this group. However, some administrative jobs require training and experience in such fields as engineering, chemistry, or sociology.

Some businesses offer management-trainee programs to advance employees to management positions. Some employers accept inexperienced college graduates with business degrees and place them in these training programs.

✓ *What else should you consider about these jobs?*

Workers in this group have heavy responsibilities. They may have to work long hours to meet specific situations or to solve problems. They may have to travel to different parts of the country or even to foreign countries to attend meetings and conduct businesses.

These workers sometimes change employers in order to move up the promotion ladder. These changes often require workers to relocate.

If you think you would like to do this kind of work, look at the job titles listed on the following pages.

■ ■ ■

GOE: 11.05.01
Management Services: Nongovernment

ASSOCIATION EXECUTIVE (profess. & kin.) ● DOT #189.117-010 ● OES: 19998 ● Directs and coordinates activities of professional or trade association in accordance with established policies to further achievement of goals, objectives, and standards of profession or association: Directs research surveys, compilation, and analysis of factors, such as average income, benefits, standards, and common problems of profession, for presentation to association committees for action. Confers with officers to ensure that membership roster is current and complete and that members receive equal treatment regarding services and information provided by Board. Directs or participates in preparation of educational and informative materials for presentation to membership or public in newsletters, magazines, news releases, or on radio or television. Provides information and technical assistance to members, clients of members, or public, relating to business operations. Represents association in negotiations with representatives of government, business, labor, and other organizations, and holds news conferences, delivers speeches, and appears before legislative bodies to present association's viewpoints and encourage acceptance of goals and objectives. Oversees finances of Board of Directors, including preparation of long range forecast and monthly and annual budget reports. Plans, develops, and implements new programs and ideas, and confers with committee leaders to evaluate services and recommend methods to promote and increase membership involvement. Directs and coordinates association functions, such as conventions, exhibits, or local or regional workshops, to present membership with committee proposals on goals or objectives, familiarize membership or public with new technology or products, and increase public acceptance of membership objectives. Prepares and updates procedural manual. May conduct investigations on members' professional ethics, competence, or conduct, or financial responsibility of members to enforce quasi-legal standards of membership. May visit members' businesses to maintain goodwill, to encourage greater participation in organization activities, and to offer assistance to businesses experiencing reverses. May be designated according to area of responsibility or activity directed as Director Of Publications (profess. & kin.); Executive Secretary (profess. & kin.); Membership Secretary (profess. & kin.); Representative, Government Relations (profess. & kin.); Research Director (profess. & kin.). ● **GED:** R5, M4, L5 ● **SVP:** 4-10 yrs ● **Academic:** Ed=B, Eng=G ● **Work Field:** 295 ● **MPSMS:** 893 ● **Aptitudes:** G2, V2, N2, S4, P4, Q3, K4, F4, M4, E5, C5 ● **Temperaments:** D, I, P, V ● **Physical:** Stg=L; Freq: T, G, N Occas: R, H, I ● **Work Env:** Noise=N; ● **Salary:** 5 ● **Outlook:** 1

DIRECTOR, TRANSPORTATION (motor trans.) ● DOT #184.117-014 ● OES: 15023 ● Formulates policies, programs, and procedures for transportation system, including schedules, rates, routes, assignment of drivers and vehicles and other terminal operations: Submits recommendations for development of, and compliance with transportation policies, procedures, and programs. Plans, directs, and implements vehicle scheduling, allocation, dispatching, licensing, and communication functions in accordance with established policies and objectives to effect economical utilization of vehicle facilities. Directs compilation and issuance of timetables. Conducts continuous analyses of vehicle and driver assignments and analyzes scheduling for possible consolidation. Reviews and revises driver schedules to ensure increased efficiency and to lower costs. Conducts field surveys to evaluate operations and recommends changes. Directs compilation and preparation of statistical surveys to determine traffic trends. Reviews and analyzes reports, such as revenue and performance records, and seat occupancy patterns to secure information for recommended changes. Analyzes proposed schedules and rates, initiates preparation and distribution of proposed trip schedule changes, and submits analyses of data and rescheduling recommendations to administration. Directs operation and maintenance of communication systems, reviews procedures, provides guidance to resolve technical problems, analyzes costs and recommends cost control measures. Reviews cost statements to locate excessive expenses, and develops plans, policies, and budgets. Selects and recommends personnel for staff positions and trains and assigns personnel for supervisory positions. ● **GED:** R5, M5, L5 ● **SVP:** 4-10 yrs ● **Academic:** Ed=A, Eng=G ● **Work Field:** 295, 013 ● **MPSMS:** 852, 853 ● **Aptitudes:** G2, V2, N2, S4, P4, Q3, K4, F4, M4, E5, C4 ● **Temperaments:** D, J, P ● **Physical:** Stg=S; Freq: T, G, N ● **Work Env:** Noise=N; ● **Salary:** 4 ● **Outlook:** 1

MANAGER, AIRPORT (air trans.) ● DOT #184.117-026 ● OES: 15023 ● Alternate titles: DIRECTOR, AIRPORT; SUPERINTENDENT, AIRPORT. Plans, directs, and coordinates, through subordinate personnel, activities concerned with construction and maintenance of airport facilities and operation of airport in accordance with governmental agency or commission policies and regulations: Consults with commission members, governmental officials, or representatives of airlines to discuss and plan such matters as design and development of airport facilities, formulation of operating rules, regulations, and procedures, and aircraft landing, taxiing, and take-off patterns for various types of aircraft. Negotiates with representatives of airlines, utility companies, or individuals for acquisition of property for development of airport, lease of airport buildings and facilities, or use of rights-of-way over private property. Formulates procedures for use in event of aircraft accidents, fires, or other emergencies. Inspects airport facilities, such as runways, buildings, beacons and lighting, and automotive or construction equipment, or reviews inspection reports, to determine repairs, replacement, or improvements required. Coordinates activities of personnel involved in repair and maintenance of airport facilities, buildings, and equipment to minimize interruption of airport operations and improve efficiency. Directs personnel in investigating violations of aerial or ground traffic regulations, reviews investigation reports, and initiates actions to be taken against violators. Directs studies on noise abatement resulting from complaints of excessive noise from low flying aircraft or other operations. Reviews reports of expenditures for previous fiscal year, proposed improvements to facilities, and estimated increase in volume of traffic, in order to prepare budget estimates for upcoming fiscal year. Represents airport before civic or other organizational groups, courts, boards, and commissions. When management functions are divided at large or international airports, workers may be designated according to activities directed as Director, Airport Operations (air trans.); Manager, Airport-Property-And-Development (air trans.); Superintendent, Airport-Buildings-Maintenance (air trans.); Superintendent, Airport-Facilities-Repair-And-Maintenance (air trans.). ● **GED:** R5, M5, L5 ● **SVP:** 4-10 yrs ● **Academic:** Ed=A, Eng=S ● **Work Field:** 295 ● **MPSMS:** 855 ● **Aptitudes:** G2, V2, N2, S3, P3, Q3, K4, F4, M4, E5, C4 ● **Temperaments:** D, J, P, V ● **Physical:** Stg=L; Freq: R, H, T, G, N Occas: I, F, D, X ● **Work Env:** Noise=N; ● **Salary:** 5 ● **Outlook:** 1

MANAGER, BAKERY (bakery products) ● DOT #189.117-046 ● OES: 19005 ● Directs and coordinates activities involved with production, sale, and distribution of bakery products: Determines variety and quantity of bakery products to be produced, according to orders and sales projections. Develops budget for bakery operation, utilizing experience and knowledge of current market conditions. Directs sales activities, following standard business practices. Plans product distribution to customers, and negotiates with suppliers to arrange purchase and delivery of bakery supplies. Implements, through subordinate managerial personnel, policies to utilize human resources, machines, and materials productively. Hires and discharges employees. May train subordinates in all phases of bakery activities. May manage bakery that produces only specialty products, such as bagels or pastries. May manage bakery that sells products to general public. May prepare bakery products. ● **GED:** R5, M4, L4 ● **SVP:** 4-10 yrs ● **Academic:** Ed=A, Eng=G ● **Work Field:** 295 ● **MPSMS:** 384 ● **Aptitudes:** G2, V2, N2, S4, P4, Q3, K4, F4, M4, E5, C5 ● **Temperaments:** D, I, J, P, V ● **Physical:** Stg=S; Freq: T, G, N Occas: I ● **Work Env:** Noise=N; ● **Salary:** 5 ● **Outlook:** 3

MANAGER, INDUSTRIAL ORGANIZATION (any industry) ● DOT #189.117-022 ● OES: 19005 ● Alternate titles: GENERAL MANAGER, INDUSTRIAL ORGANIZATION; MANAGER, GENERAL; PLANT SUPERINTENDENT, INDUSTRIAL ORGANIZATION. Directs and coordinates activities of industrial organization to obtain optimum efficiency and economy of operations and maximize profits: Plans and develops organization policies and goals, and implements goals through subordinate administrative personnel. Coordinates activities of divisions or departments, such as operating, manufacturing, engineering, planning, sales, maintenance, or research and development, to effect operational efficiency and economy. Directs and coordinates promotion of products manufactured or services performed to develop new markets, increase share of market, and obtain competitive position in industry. Analyzes division or department budget requests to identify areas in which reductions can be made, and allocates operating budget. Confers with administrative personnel, and reviews activity, operating, and sales reports to determine changes in programs or operations required. Directs preparation of directives to division or department administrator outlining policy, program, or operations changes to be implemented. Promotes organization in industry, manufacturing or trade associations. Workers are usually identified according to industry in which employed, such as petroleum production or refining, iron and steel, electrical equipment; type of organization, such as air, rail, motor or water transportation; or type of product, such as paper, chemical, or plastics products. ● **GED:** R5, M4, L5 ● **SVP:** 4-10 yrs ● **Academic:** Ed=A, Eng=G ● **Work Field:** 295 ● **MPSMS:** 893 ● **Aptitudes:** G2, V2, N2, S3, P3, Q3, K4, F4, M4, E5, C5 ● **Temperaments:** D, J, P ● **Physical:** Stg=L; Freq: T, G, N Occas: R, H, I ● **Work Env:** Noise=N; ● **Salary:** 5 ● **Outlook:** 1

MANAGER, LAND DEVELOPMENT (real estate) ● DOT #186.117-042 ● OES: 15011 ● Coordinates activities of land development company and negotiates with representatives of real estate, private enterprise and industrial organizations, and community leaders to acquire and develop land: Supervises staff engaged in such activities as preparing appraisal reports on available land, preparing feasibility studies, showing availability and quality of water resources, mineral deposits, electric power, and labor supply. Prepares or directs preparation of statistical abstracts to reveal trends in tax rates in given communities, and proportion of total work force having specified skills. Plans, oversees, and directs activities of field staff engaged in sampling mineral deposits, surveying land boundaries, and testing water supply to determine optimum usage of land. Negotiates with community, business, and public utility representatives to eliminate obstacles to land purchase, development, sale, or lease. Negotiates mortgage loans. Directs collection and auditing of funds from sale or lease of property. May perform duties of REAL-ESTATE AGENT (profess. & kin.) 186.117-058. May cooperate with representatives of public utilities, universities, and other groups to coordinate research activities. May work for railroad and specialize in industrial development and be designated Manager, Industrial Development (r.r. trans.). May work for government and be designated Property Manager (government ser.). ● **GED:** R5, M5, L5 ● **SVP:** 4-10 yrs ● **Academic:** Ed=H, Eng=G ● **Work Field:** 295, 292 ● **MPSMS:** 895 ● **Aptitudes:** G2, V1, N1, S4, P3, Q2, K4, F4, M4, E5, C5 ● **Temperaments:** D, I, J, P ● **Physical:** Stg=L; Freq: R, H, I, T, G, N Occas: F, D, A, X, V ● **Work Env:** Noise=N; Occas: W ● **Salary:** 1 ● **Outlook:** 2

PRESIDENT (any industry) ● DOT #189.117-026 ● OES: 19005 ● Plans, develops, and establishes policies and objectives of business organization in accordance with board directives and corporation charter: Confers with company officials to plan business objectives, to develop organizational policies to coordinate functions and operations between divisions and departments, and to establish responsibilities and procedures for attaining objectives. Reviews activity reports and financial statements to determine progress and status in attaining objectives and revises objectives and plans in accordance with current conditions. Directs and coordinates formulation of financial programs to provide funding for new or continuing operations to maximize returns on investments, and to increase productivity. Plans and develops industrial, labor, and public relations policies designed to improve company's image and relations with customers, employees, stockholders, and public. Evaluates performance of executives for compliance with established policies and objectives of firm and contributions in attaining objectives. May preside over board of directors. May serve as chairman of committees, such as management, executive, engineering, and sales. ● **GED:** R5, M5, L5 ● **SVP:** 4-10 yrs ● **Academic:** Ed=B, Eng=G ● **Work Field:** 295 ● **MPSMS:** 893 ● **Aptitudes:** G2, V2, N3, S4, P4, Q3, K4, F4, M4, E5, C5 ● **Temperaments:** D, J, P, V ● **Physical:** Stg=S; Freq: T, G Occas: R, H, I, N ● **Work Env:** Noise=N; ● **Salary:** 5 ● **Outlook:** 1

PRESIDENT, FINANCIAL INSTITUTION (financial) ● DOT #186.117-054 ● OES: 19005 ● Plans, develops, and directs financial policies and practices of bank, savings bank, commercial bank, trust company, mortgage company, credit union, or company dealing in consumer credit, such as finance company, to ensure that financial objectives, goals, and institutional growth are met and in accordance with policies of Board of Directors or corporate charter and government regulations: Plans and develops investment, loan, interest, and reserve policies to ensure optimum monetary returns in accordance with availability of investment funds, government restrictions, and sound financial practices. Coordinates communication and reporting activities between divisions, departments, and branch offices to ensure availability of data required for efficient daily operations. Delegates to subordinate corporate officers authority for administering activities and operations under their control. Reviews reports and financial statements to determine policy changes due to changes in economic conditions. May serve as bank representative in professional, business, and community organizations to promote bank services. May plan budget and monitor financial activities, using computer. May serve on Board of Directors. May be designated according to type of financial institution as President, Commercial Bank (financial); President, Credit Union (financial); President, Finance Company (financial); President, Mortgage Company (financial); President, Savings Bank (financial); President, Trust Company (financial). ● **GED:** R6, M5, L5 ● **SVP:** Over 10 yrs ● **Academic:** Ed=B, Eng=G ● **Work Field:** 295 ● **MPSMS:** 894 ● **Aptitudes:** G1, V1, N2, S4, P4, Q3, K4, F4, M4, E5, C5 ● **Temperaments:** D, J, P ● **Physical:** Stg=S; Freq: T, G, N Occas: R, H, I ● **Work Env:** Noise=Q; ● **Salary:** 5 ● **Outlook:** 1

GOE: 11.05.02
Administrative Specialization

ADMINISTRATIVE ASSISTANT (any industry) ● DOT #169.167-010 ● OES: 21998 ● Alternate titles: ADMINISTRATIVE ANALYST; ADMINISTRATIVE OFFICER. Aids executive in staff capacity by coordinating office services, such as personnel, budget preparation and control, housekeeping, records control, and special management studies: Studies management methods in order to improve workflow, simplify reporting procedures, or implement cost reductions. Analyzes unit operating practices, such as recordkeeping systems, forms control, office layout, suggestion systems, personnel and budgetary requirements, and performance standards to create new systems or revise established procedures. Analyzes jobs to delimit position responsibilities for use in wage and salary adjustments, promotions, and evaluation of workflow. Studies methods of improving work measurements or performance standards. Coordinates collection and preparation of operating reports, such as time-and-attendance records, terminations, new hires, transfers, budget expenditures, and statistical records of performance data. Prepares reports including conclusions and recommendations for solution of administrative problems. Issues and interprets operating policies. Reviews and answers correspondence. May assist in preparation of budget needs and annual reports of organization. May interview job applicants, conduct orientation of new employees, and plan training programs. May direct services, such as maintenance, repair, supplies, mail, and files. May compile, store, and retrieve management data, using computer. ● **GED:** R5, M3, L5 ● **SVP:** 2-4 yrs ● **Academic:** Ed=A, Eng=G ● **Work Field:** 295 ● **MPSMS:** 712 ● **Aptitudes:** G2, V2, N3, S4, P4, Q3, K4, F4, M4, E5, C5 ● **Temperaments:** D, J, P, V ● **Physical:** Stg=S; Freq: R, H, I, T, G, N, A ● **Work Env:** Noise=N; ● **Salary:** 3 ● **Outlook:** 4

BUSINESS MANAGER, COLLEGE OR UNIVERSITY (education) ● DOT #186.117-010 ● OES: 15005 ● Administers business affairs of college or university: Prepares operating budget draft for submission through PRESIDENT, COLLEGE OR UNIVERSITY (education) to board of trustees. Directs control of budget upon its approval by board, including collection, custody, investment, disbursement, accounting, and auditing of all college funds. Recruits, supervises, and oversees training of clerical staff. Formulates, with DIRECTOR OF STUDENT AFFAIRS (education), policies and procedures governing financial relations with students, dormitories, cafeterias, bookstores, and recreational and parking facilities. Audits financial status of student organization accounts, campus food service, housing, and bookstores. Administers financial aspects of student loans, scholarships, and student credit. Negotiates with groups, such as foundations, for university loans. Keeps financial records and prepares annual financial report. Formulates and administers policies and procedures for development and management of physical plant, including custodial care, sanitation, and fire and police protection. Negotiates with industry representatives on costs and materials for building construction. Develops policies and procedures for procurement of goods and nonpersonal services for university. Coordinates service operations, such as printing, duplicating, mail and messenger service, bindery, and machine computing and tabulating. ● **GED:** R5, M5, L5 ● **SVP:** 4-10 yrs ● **Academic:** Ed=B, Eng=G ● **Work Field:** 295, 232 ● **MPSMS:** 890, 931 ● **Aptitudes:** G1, V1, N1, S4, P4, Q2, K4, F4, M4, E5, C5 ● **Temperaments:** D, J, P ● **Physical:** Stg=S; Freq: R, H, I, T, G, N ● **Work Env:** Noise=N; ● **Salary:** 4 ● **Outlook:** 4

BUSINESS REPRESENTATIVE, LABOR UNION (profess. & kin.) ● DOT #187.167-018 ● OES: 19998 ● Manages business affairs of labor union: Coordinates and directs such union functions as promoting local membership, placing union members on jobs, arranging local meetings, and maintaining relations between union and employers and press representatives. Visits work sites to ensure management and labor employees adhere to union contract specifications. May assist in developing plant production and safety and health measures. May negotiate with management on hours, wages, individual grievances, and other work-related matters affecting employees. ● **GED:** R5, M3, L4 ● **SVP:** 4-10 yrs ● **Academic:** Ed=N, Eng=G ● **Work Field:** 295 ● **MPSMS:** 890 ● **Aptitudes:** G2, V2, N3, S3, P4, Q4, K4, F4, M4, E4, C5 ● **Temperaments:** P, V ● **Physical:** Stg=S; Freq: R, H, I, T, G, N ● **Work Env:** Noise=N; ● **Salary:** 5 ● **Outlook:** 2

COMMERCIAL LOAN COLLECTION OFFICER (financial) ● DOT #186.167-078 ● OES: 21108 ● Alternate titles: SPECIAL LOAN OFFICER. Coordinates activities to collect delinquent commercial loans: Reviews files of commercial loans in default to determine collateral held by bank. Writes letter to customer to demand payment of loan balance. Calls or visits customer to determine if repayment plan can be established. Computes repayment schedule, using calculator. Determines if status of customer's financial position prevents repayment of

loan and justifies re-classifying loan as non-revenue producing. Initiates collateral liquidation when customer does not repay loan. Petitions court to transfer title and deeds of collateral to bank. Coordinates maintenance and repairs to property. Coordinates activities to maintain income flow related to seized assets, such as notifying renters to mail payments to financial institution. Calls real estate broker to initiate sale of real estate. Calls auctioneer or liquidation specialist to sell specified property, such as machines, equipment, and inventory at public auction. Specifies changes to bank records on value of loan. May testify at legal proceedings. ● **GED:** R5, M4, L5 ● **SVP:** 4-10 yrs ● **Academic:** Ed=H, Eng=G ● **Work Field:** 271 ● **MPSMS:** 894 ● **Aptitudes:** G2, V2, N3, S4, P4, Q3, K4, F4, M4, E5, C5 ● **Temperaments:** I, J, P ● **Physical:** Stg=S; Const: T, G, N Occas: R, H, I ● **Work Env:** Noise=Q; ● **Salary:** 4 ● **Outlook:** 4

DIETITIAN, CHIEF (profess. & kin.) ● DOT #077.117-010 ● OES: 32521 ● Alternate titles: DIETITIAN, ADMINISTRATIVE; DIRECTOR, DIETETICS DEPARTMENT. Directs activities of institution department providing quantity food service and nutritional care: Administers, plans, and directs activities of department providing quantity food service. Establishes policies and procedures, and provides administrative direction for menu formulation, food preparation and service, purchasing, sanitation standards, safety practices, and personnel utilization. Selects professional dietetic staff, and directs departmental educational programs. Coordinates interdepartmental professional activities, and serves as consultant to management on matters pertaining to dietetics. ● **GED:** R5, M4, L5 ● **SVP:** 4-10 yrs ● **Academic:** Ed=B, Eng=G ● **Work Field:** 295 ● **MPSMS:** 903 ● **Aptitudes:** G2, V2, N2, S4, P4, Q3, K4, F4, M4, E4, C5 ● **Temperaments:** D, J, V ● **Physical:** Stg=S; Freq: T, G, N ● **Work Env:** Noise=N; ● **Salary:** 4 ● **Outlook:** 3

DIRECTOR, SERVICE (retail trade) ● DOT #189.167-014 ● OES: 19998 ● Alternate titles: MANAGER, OPERATING AND OCCUPANCY; SUPERINTENDENT, NONSELLING; SUPERINTENDENT, OPERATING. Directs operating and nonselling services, such as building maintenance, warehousing, and payroll, in department store: Controls expenditures for items, such as remodeling and repairing of building, upkeep of elevators and air-conditioning system, and repairing electrical system. Arranges for storage and display space for new merchandise. Acts as liaison for trucking company that delivers merchandise to customers. May hire and train new employees. ● **GED:** R5, M4, L4 ● **SVP:** 2-4 yrs ● **Academic:** Ed=A, Eng=S ● **Work Field:** 295 ● **MPSMS:** 881 ● **Aptitudes:** G2, V2, N3, S4, P3, Q3, K4, F4, M4, E5, C5 ● **Temperaments:** D, J, P ● **Physical:** Stg=S; Freq: T, G Occas: R, H, I, N ● **Work Env:** Noise=N; ● **Salary:** 5 ● **Outlook:** 1

DIRECTOR, QUALITY ASSURANCE (profess. & kin.) ● DOT #189.117-042 ● OES: 15014 ● Alternate titles: DIRECTOR, PRODUCT ASSURANCE. Participates, as member of management team, in formulating and establishing organizational policies and operating procedures for company and develops, implements, and coordinates, through support staff and lower echelon managers, product assurance program to prevent or eliminate defects in new or existing products: Analyzes, evaluates, and presents information concerning factors, such as business situations, production capabilities, manufacturing problems, economic trends, and design and development of new products for consideration by other members of management team. Suggests and debates alternative methods and procedures in solving problems and meeting changing market opportunities. Cooperates with other top management personnel in formulating and establishing company policies, operating procedures, and goals. Develops initial and subsequent modifications of product assurance program to delineate areas of responsibility, personnel requirements, and operational procedures within program, according to and consistent with company goals and policies. Evaluates contents of reports from product assurance program department heads and confers with top management personnel preparatory to formulating fiscal budget for product assurance program. Conducts management meetings with product assurance program department heads to establish, delineate, and review program organizational policies, to coordinate functions and operations between departments, and to establish responsibilities and procedures for attaining objectives. Reviews technical problems and procedures of departments and recommends solutions to problems or changes in procedures. Visits and confers with representatives of material and component vendors to obtain information related to supply quality, capacity of vendor to meet orders, and vendor quality standards. Confers with engineers about quality assurance of new products designed and manufactured products on market to rectify problems. Reviews technical publications, articles, and abstracts to stay abreast of technical developments in industry. ● **GED:** R5, M5, L5 ● **SVP:** 4-10 yrs ● **Academic:** Ed=B, Eng=G ● **Work Field:** 295 ● **MPSMS:** 893 ● **Aptitudes:** G1, V1, N1, S4, P4, Q3, K4, F4, M4, E5, C5 ● **Temperaments:** D, J, P, V ● **Physical:** Stg=L; Freq: T, G, N Occas: R, H, I ● **Work Env:** Noise=N; ● **Salary:** 5 ● **Outlook:** 1

EXECUTIVE CHEF (hotel & rest.) ● DOT #187.161-010 ● OES: 15026 ● Alternate titles: CHEF DE CUISINE; CHEF, HEAD; MANAGER, FOOD PRODUCTION. Coordinates activities of and directs indoctrination and training of CHEFS (hotel & rest.); COOKS (hotel & rest.); and other kitchen workers engaged in preparing and cooking foods in hotels or restaurants to ensure an efficient and profitable food service: Plans or participates in planning menus and utilization of food surpluses and leftovers, taking into account probable number of guests, marketing conditions, popularity of various dishes, and recency of menu. Estimates food consumption, and purchases or requisitions foodstuffs and kitchen supplies. Reviews menus, analyzes recipes, determines food, labor, and overhead costs, and assigns prices to menu items. Directs food apportionment policy to control costs. Supervises cooking and other kitchen personnel and coordinates their assignments to ensure economical and timely food production. Observes methods of food preparation and cooking, sizes of portions, and garnishing of foods to ensure food is prepared in prescribed manner. Tests cooked foods by tasting and smelling them. Devises special dishes and develops recipes. Hires and discharges employees. Familarizes newly hired CHEFS (hotel & rest.) and COOKS (hotel & rest.) with practices of restaurant kitchen and oversees training of COOK APPRENTICES (hotel & rest.). Maintains time and payroll records. Establishes and enforces nutrition and sanitation standards for restaurant. May supervise or cooperate with STEWARD/STEWARDESS (hotel & rest.) in matters pertaining to kitchen, pantry, and storeroom. ● **GED:** R5, M4, L3 ● **SVP:** 4-10 yrs ● **Academic:** Ed=N, Eng=G ● **Work Field:** 146, 295 ● **MPSMS:** 903 ● **Aptitudes:** G2, V2, N3, S4, P3, Q2, K4, F4, M3, E5, C3 ● **Temperaments:** D, J, P, V ● **Physical:** Stg=L; Freq: R, H, T, G Occas: I, N, X ● **Work Env:** Noise=N; Occas: H ● **Salary:** 5 ● **Outlook:** 4

EXECUTIVE VICE PRESIDENT, CHAMBER OF COMMERCE (nonprofit org.) ● DOT #187.117-030 ● OES: 19998 ● Alternate titles: MANAGER, CHAMBER OF COMMERCE. Directs activities of chamber of commerce to promote business, industrial and job development, and civic improvements in community: Administers programs of departments and committees which perform such functions as providing members economic and marketing information, promoting economic growth and stability in community, and counseling business organizations and industry on problems affecting local economy. Coordinates work with that of other community agencies to provide public services. Writes and gives speeches to government, and business organizations to create greater understanding between community, government, and business organizations. Prepares and submits annual budget to elected official for approval. Studies governmental legislation, taxation, and other fiscal matters to determine effect on community interests, and makes recommendations based on organizational policy. ● **GED:** R5, M5, L5 ● **SVP:** 4-10 yrs ● **Academic:** Ed=A, Eng=G ● **Work Field:** 295 ● **MPSMS:** 893 ● **Aptitudes:** G2, V2, N2, S4, P4, Q4, K4, F4, M4, E5, C5 ● **Temperaments:** D, I, J, P ● **Physical:** Stg=S; Freq: T, G Occas: R, I, N ● **Work Env:** Noise=N; ● **Salary:** 5 ● **Outlook:** 1

FREIGHT-TRAFFIC CONSULTANT (business ser.) ● DOT #184.267-010 ● OES: 21905 ● Alternate titles: TRANSPORTATION CONSULTANT. Advises industries, business firms, and individuals concerning methods of preparation of freight for shipment, rates to be applied, and mode of transportation to be used: Consults with client regarding packing procedures and inspects packed or crated goods for conformance to shipping specifications to prevent damage, delay, or penalties. Selects mode of transportation, such as air, water, railroad, or truck without regard to higher rates when speed is necessary. Confers with shipping brokers concerning export and import papers, docking facilities, or packing and marking procedures. Files claims with insurance company for losses, damages, and overcharges of freight shipments. ● **GED:** R5, M4, L4 ● **SVP:** 4-10 yrs ● **Academic:** Ed=N,

Eng=G ● **Work Field:** 282 ● **MPSMS:** 850 ● **Aptitudes:** G2, V2, N2, S4, P4, Q3, K4, F4, M4, E5, C5 ● **Temperaments:** I, J, P ● **Physical:** Stg=S; Freq: R, H, I, T, G, N, A ● **Work Env:** Noise=N; ● **Salary:** 5 ● **Outlook:** 2

GRANT COORDINATOR (profess. & kin.) ● DOT #169.117-014 ● OES: 21998 ● Develops and coordinates grant-funded programs for agencies, institutions, local government, or units of local government, such as school systems or metropolitan police departments: Reviews literature dealing with funds available through grants from governmental agencies and private foundations to determine feasibility of developing programs to supplement local annual budget allocations. Discusses program requirements and sources of funds available with administrative personnel. Confers with personnel affected by proposed program to develop program goals and objectives, outline how funds are to be used, and explain procedures necessary to obtain funding. Works with fiscal officer in preparing narrative justification for purchase of new equipment and other budgetary expenditures. Submits proposal to officials for approval. Writes grant application, according to format required, and submits application to funding agency or foundation. Meets with representatives of funding sources to work out final details of proposal. Directs and coordinates evaluation and monitoring of grant-funded programs, or writes specifications for evaluation or monitoring of program by outside agency. Assists department personnel in writing periodic reports to comply with grant requirements. Maintains master files on grants. Monitors paperwork connected with grant-funded programs. ● **GED:** R5, M4, L5 ● **SVP:** 4-10 yrs ● **Academic:** Ed=B, Eng=G ● **Work Field:** 261, 271 ● **MPSMS:** 941, 959 ● **Aptitudes:** G2, V1, N2, S4, P4, Q4, K4, F4, M4, E5, C5 ● **Temperaments:** D, I, J, P ● **Physical:** Stg=S; Freq: T, G Occas: R, H, I, N ● **Work Env:** Noise=N; ● **Salary:** 5 ● **Outlook:** 1

IMPORT-EXPORT AGENT (any industry) ● DOT #184.117-022 ● OES: 15023 ● Alternate titles: FOREIGN AGENT. Coordinates activities of international traffic division of import-export agency and negotiates settlements between foreign and domestic shippers: Plans and directs flow of air and surface traffic moving to overseas destinations. Supervises workers engaged in receiving and shipping freight, documentation, waybilling, assessing charges, and collecting fees for shipments. Negotiates with domestic customers, as intermediary for foreign customers, to resolve problems and arrive at mutual agreements. Negotiates with foreign shipping interests to contract for reciprocal freight-handling agreements. May examine invoices and shipping manifests for conformity to tariff and customs regulations. May contact customs officials to effect release of incoming freight and resolve customs delays. May prepare reports of transactions to facilitate billing of shippers and foreign carriers. ● **GED:** R5, M4, L5 ● **SVP:** 2-4 yrs ● **Academic:** Ed=H, Eng=S ● **Work Field:** 295 ● **MPSMS:** 850 ● **Aptitudes:** G2, V2, N3, S4, P4, Q3, K5, F5, M4, E5, C5 ● **Temperaments:** D, I, J, P, V ● **Physical:** Stg=S; Freq: T, G Occas: R, H ● **Work Env:** Noise=N; ● **Salary:** 4 ● **Outlook:** 2

MANAGEMENT TRAINEE (any industry) ● DOT #189.167-018 ● OES: 19998 ● Performs assigned duties, under direction of experienced personnel, to gain knowledge and experience required for promotion to management positions: Receives training and performs duties in several departments, such as credit, customer relations, accounting, or sales, to become familiar with line and staff functions, operations, management viewpoints, and company policies and practices that affect each phase of business. Observes experienced workers to acquire knowledge of methods, procedures, and standards required for performance of departmental duties. Workers are usually trained in functions and operations of related departments to facilitate subsequent transferability between departments and to provide greater promotional opportunities. May be required to attend company-sponsored training classes. ● **GED:** R5, M3, L4 ● **SVP:** 1-2 yrs ● **Academic:** Ed=B, Eng=G ● **Work Field:** 295 ● **MPSMS:** 893 ● **Aptitudes:** G2, V2, N3, S4, P4, Q3, K4, F4, M4, E5, C5 ● **Temperaments:** J, P, V ● **Physical:** Stg=L; Freq: T, G, N Occas: R, H, I, F, A ● **Work Env:** Noise=N; ● **Salary:** 4 ● **Outlook:** 1

MANAGER, BENEFITS (profess. & kin.) ● DOT #166.167-018 ● OES: 13005 ● Alternate titles: MANAGER, EMPLOYEE BENEFITS; MANAGER, EMPLOYEE SERVICES; MANAGER, PERSONNEL SERVICES; PERSONNEL ADMINISTRATOR. Manages employee benefits program for organization: Plans and directs implementation and administration of benefits programs designed to insure employees against loss of income due to illness, injury, layoff, or retirement. Directs preparation and distribution of written and verbal information to inform employees of benefits programs, such as insurance and pension plans, paid time off, bonus pay, and special employer sponsored activities. Analyzes existing benefits policies of organization, and prevailing practices among similar organizations, to establish competitive benefits programs. Evaluates services, coverage, and options available through insurance and investment companies, to determine programs best meeting needs of organization. Plans modification of existing benefits programs, utilizing knowledge of laws concerning employee insurance coverage, and agreements with labor unions, to ensure compliance with legal requirements. Recommends benefits plan changes to management. Notifies employees and labor union representatives of changes in benefits programs. Directs performance of clerical functions, such as updating records and processing insurance claims. May interview, select, hire, and train employees. ● **GED:** R4, M4, L4 ● **SVP:** 2-4 yrs ● **Academic:** Ed=A, Eng=G ● **Work Field:** 295, 271 ● **MPSMS:** 893 ● **Aptitudes:** G2, V2, N2, S5, P5, Q2, K4, F4, M4, E5, C5 ● **Temperaments:** D, J, P, T ● **Physical:** Stg=S; Freq: H, T, G, N Occas: R, I ● **Work Env:** Noise=Q; ● **Salary:** 4 ● **Outlook:** 3

MANAGER, BRANCH (any industry) ● DOT #183.117-010 ● OES: 15014 ● Alternate titles: AGENT; MANAGER, AREA; MANAGER, DIVISION; MANAGER, PLANT. Directs production, distribution, and marketing operations for branch plant, or assigned territory of industrial organization: Coordinates production, distribution, warehousing, and sales in accordance with policies, principles, and procedures established by MANAGER, INDUSTRIAL ORGANIZATION (any industry) 189.117-022. Confers with customers and representatives of associated industries to evaluate and promote improved and expanded services in area. Develops plans for efficient use of materials, machines, and employees. Reviews production costs and product quality, and modifies production and inventory control programs to maintain and enhance profitable operation of division. Reviews operations of competing organizations, and plans and directs sales program to develop new markets, using sales aids, advertising, promotional programs, and field services. Directs personnel program. Directs preparation of accounting records. Recommends budgets to management. May be designated according to title of area of jurisdiction as Manager, District (any industry); Manager, Local (any industry); Manager Regional (any industry). ● **GED:** R5, M4, L4 ● **SVP:** 4-10 yrs ● **Academic:** Ed=A, Eng=G ● **Work Field:** 295 ● **MPSMS:** 893 ● **Aptitudes:** G2, V2, N2, S4, P4, Q3, K4, F4, M4, E5, C5 ● **Temperaments:** D, J, P ● **Physical:** Stg=S; Freq: T, G Occas: R, H, I, N ● **Work Env:** Noise=N; ● **Salary:** 4 ● **Outlook:** 1

MANAGER, COMPENSATION (profess. & kin.) ● DOT #166.167-022 ● OES: 21511 ● Alternate titles: WAGE AND SALARY ADMINISTRATOR. Manages compensation program in establishment: Directs development and application of techniques of job analysis, job descriptions, evaluations, grading, and pricing in order to determine and record job factors and to determine and convert relative job worth into monetary values to be administered according to pay-scale guidelines and policy formulated by DIRECTOR, INDUSTRIAL RELATIONS (profess. & kin.). Analyzes company compensation policies, government regulations concerning payment of minimum wages and overtime pay, prevailing rates in similar organizations and industries, and agreements with labor unions, in order to comply with legal requirements and to establish competitive rates designed to attract, retain, and motivate employees. Recommends compensation adjustments according to findings, utilizing knowledge of prevailing rates of straight-time pay, types of wage incentive systems, and special compensation programs for professional, technical, sales, supervisory, managerial, and executive personnel. Approves merit increases permitted within budgetary limits and according to pay policies. Duties may also include administration of employee benefits program [MANAGER, BENEFITS (profess. & kin.)]. ● **GED:** R5, M5, L5 ● **SVP:** 4-10 yrs ● **Academic:** Ed=B, Eng=G ● **Work Field:** 271, 295 ● **MPSMS:** 712 ● **Aptitudes:** G2, V2, N2, S5, P5, Q3, K5, F5, M5, E5, C5 ● **Temperaments:** D, J, P ● **Physical:** Stg=S; Freq: T, G, N Occas: R, H, I ● **Work Env:** Noise=N; ● **Salary:** 5 ● **Outlook:** 2

MANAGER, CONTRACTS (petrol. & gas) ● DOT #163.117-010 ● OES: 21308 ● Alternate titles: SUPPLY REPRESENTATIVE, PETROLEUM PRODUCTS. Negotiates contracts with representatives of oil producers, refiners, and pipeline carriers for purchase, sale, or delivery of crude oil, petroleum distillates, and natural gas and gasoline: Analyzes records of petroleum supply sources, movements of materials from plants to refineries, and current and prospective refinery demands. Coordinates work of sales, production, and shipping departments to implement procurance of products in accordance with refinery needs. Performs liaison work with engineering and production departments concerning contractual rights and obligations. May manage contracts for entire company, department, or for specified product, such as crude oil or natural gas. May be designated according to product contracted as Supply Representative, Dry Gas (petrol. & gas; petrol. refin.; pipe lines); Manager, Natural-Gas Utilization (petrol. & gas). ● **GED:** R5, M5, L5 ● **SVP:** 2-4 yrs ● **Academic:** Ed=A, Eng=G ● **Work Field:** 292 ● **MPSMS:** 501, 856 ● **Aptitudes:** G2, V1, N2, S4, P4, Q3, K4, F4, M4, E5, C5 ● **Temperaments:** D, J, P, V ● **Physical:** Stg=S; Freq: T, G Occas: R, H, I, N ● **Work Env:** Noise=N; ● **Salary:** 5 ● **Outlook:** 4

MANAGER, DEPARTMENT (any industry) ● DOT #189.167-022 ● OES: 19005 ● Alternate titles: DEPARTMENT HEAD; SUPERINTENDENT. Directs and coordinates, through subordinate supervisors, department activities in commercial, industrial, or service establishment: Reviews and analyzes reports, records, and directives, and confers with supervisors to obtain data required for planning department activities, such as new commitments, status of work in progress, and problems encountered. Assigns, or delegates responsibility for, specified work or functional activities and disseminates policy to supervisors. Gives work directions, resolves problems, prepares schedules, and sets deadlines to ensure timely completion of work. Coordinates activities of department with related activities of other departments to ensure efficiency and economy. Monitors and analyzes costs and prepares budget, using computer. Prepares reports and records on department activities for management, using computer. Evaluates current procedures and practices for accomplishing department objectives to develop and implement improved procedures and practices. May initiate or authorize employee hire, promotion, discharge, or transfer. Workers are designated according to functions, activities, or type of department managed. ● **GED:** R5, M4, L4 ● **SVP:** 2-4 yrs ● **Academic:** Ed=H, Eng=G ● **Work Field:** 295 ● **MPSMS:** 893 ● **Aptitudes:** G2, V2, N3, S3, P3, Q3, K4, F4, M4, E5, C5 ● **Temperaments:** D, J, P ● **Physical:** Stg=S; Freq: T, G, N Occas: R, H, I, A ● **Work Env:** Noise=N; ● **Salary:** 5 ● **Outlook:** 3

MANAGER, DEPARTMENT STORE (retail trade) ● DOT #185.117-010 ● OES: 19005 ● Directs and coordinates, through subordinate managerial personnel, activities of department store selling lines of merchandise in specialized departments: Formulates pricing policies for sale of merchandise, or implements policies set forth by merchandising board. Coordinates activities of nonmerchandising departments, as purchasing, credit, accounting, and advertising with merchandising departments to obtain optimum efficiency of operations with minimum costs in order to maximize profits. Develops and implements, through subordinate managerial personnel, policies and procedures for store and departmental operations and customer personnel and community relations. Negotiates or approves contracts negotiated with suppliers of merchandise, or with other establishments providing security, maintenance, or cleaning services. Reviews operating and financial statements and departmental sales records to determine merchandising activities that require additional sales promotion, clearance sales, or other sales procedures in order to turn over merchandise and achieve profitability of store operations and merchandising objectives. ● **GED:** R5, M4, L5 ● **SVP:** 4-10 yrs ● **Academic:** Ed=A, Eng=S ● **Work Field:** 295, 292 ● **MPSMS:** 881 ● **Aptitudes:** G2, V2, N2, S4, P4, Q3, K4, F4, M4, E5, C5 ● **Temperaments:** D, J, P, V ● **Physical:** Stg=S; Freq: R, H, T, G Occas: N ● **Work Env:** Noise=N; ● **Salary:** 5 ● **Outlook:** 1

MANAGER, LABOR RELATIONS (profess. & kin.) ● DOT #166.167-034 ● OES: 13005 ● Alternate titles: LABOR RELATIONS REPRESENTATIVE. Manages labor relations program of organization: Analyzes collective bargaining agreement to develop interpretation of intent, spirit, and terms of contract. Advises management and union officials in development, application, and interpretation of labor relations policies and practices, according to policy formulated by DIRECTOR, INDUSTRIAL RELATIONS (profess. & kin.) 166.117-010. Arranges and schedules meetings between grieving workers, supervisory and managerial personnel, and BUSINESS REPRESENTATIVE,

LABOR UNION (profess. & kin.) 187.167-018, to investigate and resolve grievances. Prepares statistical reports, using records of actions taken concerning grievances, arbitration and mediation cases, and related labor relations activities, to identify problem areas. Monitors implementation of policies concerning wages, hours, and working conditions, to ensure compliance with terms of labor contract. Furnishes information, such as reference documents and statistical data concerning labor legislation, labor market conditions, prevailing union and management practices, wage and salary surveys, and employee benefits programs, for use in review of current contract provisions and proposed changes. May represent management in labor contract negotiations. May supervise employees and be known as Labor Relations Supervisor (profess. & kin.). May be employed by firm offering labor relations advisory services to either management or labor and be known as Labor Relation Consultant (profess. & kin.). May be employed by governmental agency to study, interpret, and report on relations between management and labor and be known as Industrial Relations Representative (government ser.). ● **GED:** R5, M4, L5 ● **SVP:** 4-10 yrs ● **Academic:** Ed=B, Eng=G ● **Work Field:** 271, 295 ● **MPSMS:** 893 ● **Aptitudes:** G2, V2, N3, S4, P4, Q3, K4, F4, M4, E5, C5 ● **Temperaments:** D, I, J, P ● **Physical:** Stg=L; Freq: T, G, N Occas: R, H, I ● **Work Env:** Noise=Q; ● **Salary:** 5 ● **Outlook:** 3

MANAGER, OPERATIONS (air trans.) ● DOT #184.117-050 ● OES: 15023 ● Alternate titles: OPERATIONS MANAGER. Directs and coordinates activities of operations department of air, motor, railroad, or water transportation organization: Confers and cooperates with management personnel in formulating administrative and operational policies and procedures. Directs and coordinates, through subordinate managerial personnel, activities of operations department to obtain optimum use of equipment, facilities, and personnel. Reviews and analyzes expenditure, financial, and operations reports to determine requirements for increasing profits, such as need for increase in fares or tariffs, expansion of existing schedules, or extension of routes or new routes. Prepares recommendations on findings for management evaluation. Recommends capital expenditures for acquisition of new equipment which would increase efficiency and services of operations department. Approves requisitions for equipment, materials, and supplies within limits of operations department budget. Enforces compliance of operations personnel with administrative policies, procedures, safety rules, and governmental regulations. Directs investigations into causes of customer or shipper complaints relating to operations department. May negotiate contracts with equipment and materials suppliers. May act as representative of transportation organization before government commissions or regulatory bodies during hearings for increased fares or tariffs and on extensions of or new routes. ● **GED:** R5, M4, L5 ● **SVP:** 4-10 yrs ● **Academic:** Ed=A, Eng=S ● **Work Field:** 295 ● **MPSMS:** 850 ● **Aptitudes:** G2, V2, N2, S4, P4, Q3, K4, F5, M4, E5, C5 ● **Temperaments:** D, J, P ● **Physical:** Stg=S; Const: T, G Freq: N ● **Work Env:** Noise=N; ● **Salary:** 5 ● **Outlook:** 1

MANAGER, PERSONNEL (profess. & kin.) ● DOT #166.117-018 ● OES: 13005 ● Alternate titles: MANAGER, HUMAN RESOURCES. Plans and carries out policies relating to all phases of personnel activity: Recruits, interviews, and selects employees to fill vacant positions. Plans and conducts new employee orientation to foster positive attitude toward company goals. Keeps record of insurance coverage, pension plan, and personnel transactions, such as hires, promotions, transfers, and terminations. Investigates accidents and prepares reports for insurance carrier. Conducts wage survey within labor market to determine competitive wage rate. Prepares budget of personnel operations. Meets with shop stewards and supervisors to resolve grievances. Writes separation notices for employees separating with cause and conducts exit interviews to determine reasons behind separations. Prepares reports and recommends procedures to reduce absenteeism and turnover. Represents company at personnel-related hearings and investigations. Contracts with outside suppliers to provide employee services, such as canteen, transportation, or relocation service. May prepare budget of personnel operations, using computer terminal. May administer manual and dexterity tests to applicants. May supervise clerical workers. May keep records of hired employee characteristics for governmental reporting purposes. May negotiate collective bargaining agreement with BUSINESS REPRESENTATIVE, LABOR UNION (profess & kin.) 187.167-018. ● **GED:** R5, M5, L5 ● **SVP:** 4-10 yrs ● **Academic:** Ed=B, Eng=G ● **Work Field:** 295, 271 ● **MPSMS:** 893, 943 ● **Aptitudes:** G1, V1, N2, S3, P3, Q3, K4, F4, M4, E5, C5 ●

Temperaments: D, J, P, V ● **Physical:** Stg=S; Freq: R, H, I, T, G, N Occas: A ● **Work Env:** Noise=N; ● **Salary:** 4 ● **Outlook:** 4

MANAGER, PROCUREMENT SERVICES (profess. & kin.) ● DOT #162.167-022 ● OES: 13008 ● Alternate titles: DIRECTOR, PROCUREMENT SERVICES; MANAGER, MATERIAL CONTROL. Directs and coordinates activities of personnel engaged in purchasing and distributing raw materials, equipment, machinery, and supplies in industrial plant, public utility, or other organization: Prepares instructions regarding purchasing systems and procedures. Prepares and issues purchase orders and change notices to PURCHASING AGENTS (profess. & kin.). Analyzes market and delivery conditions to determine present and future material availability and prepares market analysis reports. Reviews purchase order claims and contracts for conformance to company policy. Develops and installs clerical and office procedures and practices, and studies work flow, sequence of operations, and office arrangement to determine expediency of installing new or improved office machines. Arranges for disposal of surplus materials. ● **GED:** R4, M4, L4 ● **SVP:** 2-4 yrs ● **Academic:** Ed=A, Eng=G ● **Work Field:** 292 ● **MPSMS:** 898 ● **Aptitudes:** G2, V2, N2, S4, P4, Q2, K4, F4, M4, E5, C5 ● **Temperaments:** D, J ● **Physical:** Stg=S; Freq: R, H, I, T, G, N, A ● **Work Env:** Noise=N; ● **Salary:** 4 ● **Outlook:** 3

MANAGER, PRODUCTION (radio-tv broad.) ● DOT #184.162-010 ● OES: 34056 ● Coordinates work of various departments to produce radio or television programs and commercial announcements: Trains, assigns duties, and supervises employees engaged in production and taping such programs as game shows, talk broadcasts, and special programs. Ensures that slanderous, libelous, and profane statements are avoided or deleted and that program is in conformance with station or network policy and regulations. Schedules usage of studio and editing facilities needed by PRODUCERS (radio-tv broad.) 159.117-010, and engineering and maintenance staff to maximize use of facilities, according to scheduled events. Operates television broadcasting equipment, such as switcher, video and color monitors, tape decks, lights and microphones to train workers or to substitute for absent employees. Operates portable, shoulder-mounted camera to record or broadcast live programs from location of event. May direct subordinates in auditioning talent and proposed programs. May coordinate audio work, scenes, music, timing, camera work, and script writing, to develop desired production, and review production to ensure objectives are obtained. ● **GED:** R5, M4, L4 ● **SVP:** 2-4 yrs ● **Academic:** Ed=N, Eng=G ● **Work Field:** 281, 295, 297 ● **MPSMS:** 863, 864, 869 ● **Aptitudes:** G2, V2, N4, S4, P4, Q3, K4, F3, M4, E4, C4 ● **Temperaments:** D, J, P, V ● **Physical:** Stg=H; Freq: R, H, T, G, N Occas: S, O, I, F, D, A, X, V ● **Work Env:** Noise=N; Occas: W ● **Salary:** 4 ● **Outlook:** 1

MANAGER, REGIONAL (motor trans.) ● DOT #184.117-054 ● OES: 15023 ● Directs and coordinates regional activities of motor transportation company: Examines and analyzes rates, tariffs, operating costs, and revenues to determine such needs or requirements as increase in rates and tariffs, reduction of operations and maintenance costs, and expansion of or changes in schedules or routes. Prepares, for management evaluation, recommendations designed to increase efficiency and revenues and lower costs. Directs, through subordinate management personnel, compliance of workers with established company policies, procedures, and standards, such as safekeeping of funds and tickets, personnel employment and grievance practices, and enforcement of union contracts and government regulations. Reviews operational records and reports and refers to manuals, company instructions, and government regulations to detect deviations from operational practices and prepares directives to eliminate such infractions. Investigates safeguards and inspects regional premises to ensure that adequate protection exists for company assets, property, and equipment. Participates in union contract negotiations and settling of grievances. Coordinates advertising and sales promotion programs for region. Reviews replies to passenger complaints and settlement of claims for conformance with company public relations policies and procedures. Inspects terminals for conformance with standards for cleanliness, appearance, and need of repair or maintenance, and directs corrective measures required to meet standards. ● **GED:** R5, M5, L5 ● **SVP:** 4-10 yrs ● **Academic:** Ed=A, Eng=S ● **Work Field:** 295 ● **MPSMS:** 852 ● **Aptitudes:** G2, V2, N2, S4, P4, Q3, K4, F4, M4, E5, C5 ● **Temperaments:** D, P, V ● **Physical:** Stg=S; Freq: T, G Occas: R, H, N ● **Work Env:** Noise=N; ● **Salary:** 5 ● **Outlook:** 1

MANAGER, SCHEDULE PLANNING (air trans.) ● DOT #184.117-058 ● OES: 15023 ● Negotiates with governmental regulatory body to change company's route application (fixed schedule for flights) over authorized routes as representative of certificated air carrier: Analyzes documentation on company operations and recommended changes in route application, prepared by subordinates, to determine if company position warrants requesting route application hearing, considering such factors as current and projected traffic load, route application of competitive carriers over same route, and profitability of route operations. Submits current and proposed schedules to Schedule Committee for consideration and approval to request hearing before regulatory body. Prepares company's position and arguments for presentation at route application hearing and negotiates with body for additional route applications or deletion of route applications on unprofitable routes in order to improve efficient utilization of flight personnel and equipment and to reduce losses or increase revenues. Directs and coordinates activities of workers compiling documentation on route application, analyzing data, and preparing recommendations for schedule changes. ● **GED:** R5, M4, L5 ● **SVP:** 4-10 yrs ● **Academic:** Ed=A, Eng=S ● **Work Field:** 295 ● **MPSMS:** 855 ● **Aptitudes:** G1, V1, N3, S4, P3, Q2, K4, F4, M4, E5, C5 ● **Temperaments:** D, P ● **Physical:** Stg=S; Freq: R, H, T, G, N Occas: I ● **Work Env:** Noise=N; ● **Salary:** 5 ● **Outlook:** 1

MANAGER, STATION (radio-tv broad.) ● DOT #184.117-062 ● OES: 15023 ● Directs and coordinates activities of radio or television station, or of cable television franchise: Supervises directly, or through subordinates, personnel engaged in departments, such as sales, program, engineering, and personnel. Observes activities to ensure compliance with government regulations. Discusses plans with marketing personnel to promote sales of programs and time periods to advertisers and their agencies. Confers with owners or company senior management to discuss station policy and administrative procedures. May prepare operational budget and monitor expenses for station or franchise. May negotiate with motion picture companies for purchase of independent film programs. May negotiate cable franchise contract with local issuing authority. May develop strategy to promote sales of new cable television service, or upgraded service, to customers within franchise area. May contact prospective buyers of station time to promote sale of station services. May manage station engaged in transmitting broadcasts to foreign countries and be known as Director, International Broadcasting (radio-tv broad.). May perform different duties and responsibilities, according to station size and network affiliation, and be designated General Manager, Broadcasting (radio-tv broad.). ● **GED:** R5, M4, L5 ● **SVP:** 4-10 yrs ● **Academic:** Ed=A, Eng=G ● **Work Field:** 295 ● **MPSMS:** 863, 864, 869 ● **Aptitudes:** G2, V2, N3, S4, P3, Q4, K4, F4, M4, E5, C5 ● **Temperaments:** D, J, P, V ● **Physical:** Stg=L; Freq: H, T, G Occas: R, I, N ● **Work Env:** Noise=N; ● **Salary:** 5 ● **Outlook:** 1

MANAGER, TRAFFIC (any industry) ● DOT #184.167-094 ● OES: 15023 ● Directs and coordinates traffic activities of organization: Develops methods and procedures for transportation of raw materials to processing and production areas and commodities from departments to customers, warehouses, or other storage facilities. Determines most efficient and economical routing and mode of transportation, using rate and tariff manuals and motor freight and railroad guidebooks. Directs scheduling of shipments and notifies concerned departments or customers of arrival dates. Initiates investigations into causes of damages or shortages in consignments or overcharges for freight or insurance. Conducts studies in areas of packaging, warehousing, and loading of commodities and evaluates existing procedures and standards. Initiates changes designed to improve control and efficiency of traffic department. May negotiate contracts for leasing of transportation equipment or property. May assist in preparing department budget. ● **GED:** R5, M4, L4 ● **SVP:** 4-10 yrs ● **Academic:** Ed=A, Eng=S ● **Work Field:** 221, 013 ● **MPSMS:** 851, 853 ● **Aptitudes:** G2, V2, N3, S4, P3, Q3, K4, F4, M4, E5, C5 ● **Temperaments:** D, J, P ● **Physical:** Stg=S; Freq: R, H, T, G, N Occas: I, A ● **Work Env:** Noise=N; ● **Salary:** 5 ● **Outlook:** 1

MANAGER, WORLD TRADE AND MARITIME DIVISION (nonprofit org.) ● DOT #187.167-170 ● OES: 13011 ● Directs activities of world trade department in chamber of commerce to assist business concerns in developing and utilizing foreign markets: Conducts economic and commercial surveys in foreign countries to locate mar-

kets for products and services. Analyzes data and publishes bulletins concerning business developments in other countries, regulations affecting world trade, and opportunities for selling and buying products. Advises business and other groups on local, national, and international legislation affecting world trade. Advises exporters and importers on documentation procedures and certifies commercial documents that are required by foreign countries. Entertains foreign governmental officials and business representatives to promote trade relations. Promotes travel to other countries. ● **GED:** R5, M4, L5 ● **SVP:** 2-4 yrs ● **Academic:** Ed=A, Eng=G ● **Work Field:** 295, 251 ● **MPSMS:** 741, 894, 959 ● **Aptitudes:** G2, V2, N3, S4, P4, Q4, K4, F4, M4, E5, C5 ● **Temperaments:** D, I, P ● **Physical:** Stg=S; Freq: T, G, N Occas: R, H, I ● **Work Env:** Noise=N; ● **Salary:** 4 ● **Outlook:** 2

PROGRAM MANAGER (profess. & kin.) ● DOT #189.167-030 ● OES: 19005 ● Manages program to ensure that implementation and prescribed activities are carried out in accordance with specified objectives: Plans and develops methods and procedures for implementing program, directs and coordinates program activities, and exercises control over personnel responsible for specific functions or phases of program. Selects personnel according to knowledge and experience in area with which program is concerned, such as social or public welfare, education, economics, or public relations. Confers with staff to explain program and individual responsibilities for functions and phases of program. Directs and coordinates personally, or through subordinate managerial personnel, activities concerned with implementation and carrying out objectives of program. Reviews reports and records of activities to ensure progress is being accomplished toward specified program objective and modifies or changes methodology as required to redirect activities and attain objectives. Prepares program reports for superiors. Controls expenditures in accordance with budget allocations. May specialize in managing governmental programs set up by legislative body or directive and be designated Manager, Governmental Program (government ser.). ● **GED:** R5, M5, L5 ● **SVP:** 4-10 yrs ● **Academic:** Ed=A, Eng=S ● **Work Field:** 295 ● **MPSMS:** 920, 930, 950 ● **Aptitudes:** G2, V2, N2, S3, P3, Q2, K4, F4, M4, E5, C5 ● **Temperaments:** D, J, P ● **Physical:** Stg=S; Freq: R, H, T, G, N Occas: I ● **Work Env:** Noise=N; ● **Salary:** 4 ● **Outlook:** 2

PROGRAM PROPOSALS COORDINATOR (radio-tv broad.) ● DOT #132.067-030 ● OES: 34001 ● Alternate titles: COORDINATOR, PROGRAM PLANNING. Develops, writes, and edits proposals for new radio or television programs: Reviews program proposals submitted by staff, station and independent producers, and other sources to determine proposal feasibility, based on knowledge of station's programming needs, policy and budgetary considerations, and potential underwriting (funding) sources. Edits proposals, or writes proposals for original program concepts, and submits proposals for review of programming, financial, and other departmental personnel. Participates in selection of researchers, consultants, producers, and on-air personalities to facilitate development of program ideas. Authorizes preparation of budget for final proposals. Maintains liaison between program production department and proposal originators to inform originators of status of accepted projects. ● **GED:** R5, M3, L5 ● **SVP:** 2-4 yrs ● **Academic:** Ed=A, Eng=G ● **Work Field:** 261, 211, 295 ● **MPSMS:** 863, 864 ● **Aptitudes:** G1, V1, N3, S4, P4, Q3, K4, F4, M4, E5, C5 ● **Temperaments:** D, J, P, V ● **Physical:** Stg=S; Freq: T, G, N, A Occas: R, H, I ● **Work Env:** Noise=N; ● **Salary:** 3 ● **Outlook:** 3

PROGRAM SPECIALIST, EMPLOYEE-HEALTH MAINTENANCE (profess. & kin.) ● DOT #166.167-050 ● OES: 13005 ● Coordinates activities of area employers in setting up local government funded program within establishments to help employees who are not functioning at satisfactory levels of job performance due to alcoholism or other behavioral medical problems: Writes and prepares newspaper advertisements, newsletters, and questionnaires and speaks before community groups to promote employee assistance program within business community. Analyzes character and type of business establishments in area, and compiles list of prospective employers appropriate for implementing assistance program. Contacts prospective employers, explains program and fees, points out advantages of program, and reaches agreement with interested employers on extent of proposed program. Develops program within establishment. Establishes committee composed of company officials and workers to develop statement of employee assistance program and policy and procedures. Plans and conducts training sessions for company officials to develop skills in identifying and handling employees troubled by alcoholism or other personal problems. Assists employer in setting up in-plant educational program to prevent alcoholism, using posters, pamphlets, and films, and establishes referral network providing for in-plant and out-of-plant group or individual counseling for troubled employees. Confers with team member of assistance program who provides counseling regarding planning and progress of counseling components. Confers with staff of employee assistance program regarding progress and evaluation of current programs and proposals for developing new programs. ● **GED:** R5, M3, L5 ● **SVP:** 1-2 yrs ● **Academic:** Ed=A, Eng=S ● **Work Field:** 282, 295 ● **MPSMS:** 941 ● **Aptitudes:** G2, V1, N3, S4, P4, Q3, K4, F4, M4, E5, C5 ● **Temperaments:** D, I, J, P ● **Physical:** Stg=S; Freq: R, H, I, T, G, N ● **Salary:** 3 ● **Outlook:** 3

PROJECT DIRECTOR (profess. & kin.) ● DOT #189.117-030 ● OES: 19998 ● Alternate titles: PROJECT MANAGER. Plans, directs, and coordinates activities of designated project to ensure that goals or objectives of project are accomplished within prescribed time frame and funding parameters: Reviews project proposal or plan to determine time frame, funding limitations, procedures for accomplishing project, staffing requirements, and allotment of available resources to various phases of project. Establishes work plan and staffing for each phase of project, and arranges for recruitment or assignment of project personnel. Confers with project staff to outline workplan and to assign duties, responsibilities, and scope of authority. Directs and coordinates activities of project personnel to ensure project progresses on schedule and within prescribed budget. Reviews status reports prepared by project personnel and modifies schedules or plans as required. Prepares project reports for management, client, or others. Confers with project personnel to provide technical advice and to resolve problems. May coordinate project activities with activities of government regulatory or other governmental agencies. See PROJECT ENGINEER (profess. & kin.) 019.167-014 for engineering projects. ● **GED:** R5, M5, L5 ● **SVP:** 4-10 yrs ● **Academic:** Ed=A, Eng=G ● **Work Field:** 295 ● **MPSMS:** 720, 730, 740 ● **Aptitudes:** G2, V2, N2, S4, P3, Q3, K4, F4, M4, E5, C5 ● **Temperaments:** D, J, P ● **Physical:** Stg=S; Freq: T, G, N Occas: R, H, I, A ● **Work Env:** Noise=Q; ● **Salary:** 5 ● **Outlook:** 3

RESEARCH ANALYST (insurance) ● DOT #169.267-034 ● OES: 21998 ● Evaluates insurance industry developments to update company products and procedures: Reviews industry publications and monitors pending legislation and regulations to determine impact of new developments on company insurance products. Consults with designated company personnel to disseminate information necessitating changes in language or provisions of insurance contracts and assists in preparation of documents or directives needed to implement changes. Corresponds or consults with agents, brokers, and other interested persons to determine feasibility and marketability of new products to meet competition and increase sales. Develops procedures and materials for introduction and administration of new products, and submits package for review by company personnel and regulatory bodies. May recommend lobbying activities to management. May direct or coordinate activities of other workers. May specialize in analyzing developments in group insurance operations and be designated Group-Contract Analyst (insurance). ● **GED:** R5, M4, L5 ● **SVP:** 4-10 yrs ● **Academic:** Ed=B, Eng=G ● **Work Field:** 271, 251 ● **MPSMS:** 895, 939 ● **Aptitudes:** G2, V2, N3, S4, P4, Q3, K4, F4, M4, E5, C5 ● **Temperaments:** J, P ● **Physical:** Stg=L; Const: R, H Freq: T, G, N, A Occas: I ● **Work Env:** Noise=N; ● **Salary:** 4 ● **Outlook:** 3

SECURITY OFFICER (any industry) ● DOT #189.167-034 ● OES: 21998 ● Plans and establishes security procedures for company engaged in manufacturing products or processing data or material for federal government: Studies federal security regulations and restrictions relative to company operations. Directs activities of personnel in developing company security measures which comply with federal regulations. Consults with local, district, or other federal representatives for interpretation or application of particular regulations applying to company operations. Prepares security manual outlining and establishing measures and procedures for handling, storing, safekeeping, and destroying classified records and documents, and for granting company personnel or visitors access to classified material or entry into restricted areas. Directs and coordinates activities of personnel in revising or updating security measures due to new or revised regulations. May request deviations from restrictive regulations that interfere with normal operations. May interview and hire applicants to fill security guard

vacancies. ● **GED:** R4, M3, L4 ● **SVP:** 2-4 yrs ● **Academic:** Ed=H, Eng=G ● **Work Field:** 293 ● **MPSMS:** 951 ● **Aptitudes:** G2, V2, N3, S4, P4, Q4, K4, F4, M4, E5, C5 ● **Temperaments:** D, J, P ● **Physical:** Stg=S; Freq: R, H, I, T, G, N ● **Work Env:** Noise=N; ● **Salary:** 3 ● **Outlook:** 2

SPECIAL AGENT (insurance) ● DOT #166.167-046 ● OES: 21998 ● Alternate titles: SALES REPRESENTATIVE. Recruits independent SALES AGENTS, INSURANCE (insurance) in field and maintains contact between agent and home office: Selects SALES AGENT, INSURANCE (insurance), based on experience with other insurance companies. Drafts contract between agent and company. Advises agent on matters pertaining to conduct of business, such as cancellations, overdue accounts, and new business prospects. May gather information for UNDERWRITER (insurance). When working in life insurance, is designated Brokerage Manager (insurance). ● **GED:** R5, M3, L5 ● **SVP:** 4-10 yrs ● **Academic:** Ed=H, Eng=G ● **Work Field:** 295 ● **MPSMS:** 895 ● **Aptitudes:** G2, V2, N3, S5, P3, Q2, K4, F4, M4, E5, C5 ● **Temperaments:** D, I, P, T, V ● **Physical:** Stg=S; Freq: R, H, I, T, G, N ● **Work Env:** Noise=N; ● **Salary:** 4 ● **Outlook:** 3

SUPERINTENDENT, PLANT PROTECTION (any industry) ● DOT #189.167-050 ● OES: 19998 ● Alternate titles: PROTECTION CHIEF, INDUSTRIAL PLANT; SECURITY MANAGER. Directs personnel involved in establishing, promoting, and maintaining firm's security and property-protection programs: Establishes and supervises through subordinates, operational procedures for activities, such as fire prevention and firefighting, traffic control, guarding and patrolling physical property, orienting and monitoring of personnel involved with classified information, and investigation of accidents and criminal acts. Confers with representatives of management to formulate policies, determine need for programs, and coordinate programs with plant activities. Confers with representatives of local government to ensure cooperation and coordination of plant activities with law enforcement and firefighting agencies. May direct activities of workers involved in industrial safety programs. May direct activities of workers engaged in performing building maintenance and janitorial services. ● **GED:** R5, M4, L4 ● **SVP:** 4-10 yrs ● **Academic:** Ed=H, Eng=G ● **Work Field:** 293 ● **MPSMS:** 951 ● **Aptitudes:** G2, V2, N3, S4, P4, Q4, K4, F4, M4, E5, C5 ● **Temperaments:** D, J, P, V ● **Physical:** Stg=S; Freq: T, G Occas: S, K, O, R, H, N ● **Work Env:** Noise=N; Occas: O ● **Salary:** 4 ● **Outlook:** 1

SUPERINTENDENT, TRANSPORTATION (any industry) ● DOT #184.167-226 ● OES: 15023 ● Alternate titles: MANAGER, TRANSPORTATION; MOTOR VEHICLES SUPERVISOR; SUPERINTENDENT, AUTOMOTIVE; TRANSPORTATION DEPARTMENT HEAD. Directs and coordinates operational activities of automotive equipment department of an establishment: Procures state-required certificates of title and arranges for registrations and state inspections. Inspects automotive equipment, scheduling needed repair or service work. Coordinates operation and maintenance of equipment, storage facilities, and repair facilities. Directs recording of expenses and analyzes purchase and repair costs to control expenditures. May arrange for insurance coverage on vehicles. May plan and direct safety campaigns. May negotiate with vendors to purchase automotive equipment, materials, and supplies. May assign trucks and passenger cars for use [DISPATCHER, MOTOR VEHICLE (clerical)]. ● **GED:** R5, M4, L5 ● **SVP:** 4-10 yrs ● **Academic:** Ed=N, Eng=G ● **Work Field:** 295, 013 ● **MPSMS:** 850 ● **Aptitudes:** G2, V2, N3, S3, P3, Q3, K4, F4, M4, E5, C5 ● **Temperaments:** D, P, V ● **Physical:** Stg=L; Freq: R, H, I, T, G, N, A ● **Work Env:** Noise=N; ● **Salary:** 5 ● **Outlook:** 2

UTILIZATION COORDINATOR (radio-tv broad.) ● DOT #169.167-078 ● OES: 21998 ● Coordinates subscriber utilization of instructional television programming: Communicates with administrators, teaching staff, audiovisual specialists, and other personnel to assist subscribers in incorporating programs and related materials into planned curricula. Conducts surveys to determine problems in use of programs and materials and develops workshops and other services to address identified needs. Confers with prospective users of programs to elicit interest in subscribing to services. Participates with other station personnel in developing advertising and promotional material. Oversees activities of workers engaged in processing subscriber accounts. ● **GED:** R5, M3, L5 ● **SVP:** 2-4 yrs ● **Academic:** Ed=A, Eng=G ● **Work Field:** 295, 292 ● **MPSMS:** 860, 931 ● **Aptitudes:** G2, V2, N4, S4, P4, Q3, K4, F4, M4, E5, C5 ● **Temperaments:** J, P, V

● **Physical:** Stg=S; Freq: T, G Occas: R, H, I, N ● **Work Env:** Noise=N;
● **Salary:** 4 ● **Outlook:** 4

VICE PRESIDENT, FINANCIAL INSTITUTION (financial) ●
DOT #186.117-078 ● OES: 13002 ● Directs and coordinates, through
subordinate managerial personnel, activities of department, region, administrative division, or specific function of financial institution, such
as lending, trusts, mortgages, investments, acting under authority and
responsibility delegated by corporate executive officer: Coordinates activities of assigned program, such as sales, operations, or electronic
financial services, determines methods and procedures for carrying out
program, and assists in interpreting policies and practices. Directs or
conducts management studies, prepares work load and budget estimates for specified or assigned operations, analyzes operational reports, and submits activity reports. Develops and recommends plans
for expansion of programs, operations, and financial activities. May
solicit new business or participate in community or service organizations. May authorize loans of specified types and amounts when permitted by institution regulations. May be designated according to type
of financial institution as Vice President, Commercial Bank (financial);
or according to activity as Vice President, Lending (financial). ● **GED:**
R5, M5, L5 ● **SVP:** 4-10 yrs ● **Academic:** Ed=B, Eng=G ● **Work
Field:** 295 ● **MPSMS:** 894 ● **Aptitudes:** G1, V1, N2, S4, P4, Q3, K4,
F4, M4, E5, C5 ● **Temperaments:** D, J, P ● **Physical:** Stg=S; Freq: T,
G, N Occas: R, H, I ● **Work Env:** Noise=Q; ● **Salary:** 5 ● **Outlook:** 1

GOE: 11.05.03
Management Services: Government

COURT ADMINISTRATOR (government ser.) ● DOT #188.117-
130 ● OES: 19998 ● Administers nonjudicial functions of court: Coordinates activities such as jury selection, notification, and utilization,
case scheduling and tracking, personnel assignment, and space and
equipment allocation to accomplish orderly processing of court cases.
Investigates problems that affect case flow and recommends or implements corrective measures. Compiles and analyzes data on court activity to monitor management performance and prepare activity reports.
Conducts research to analyze current and alternative personnel, facilities, and data management systems and consults with judicial staff of
court to evaluate findings and recommendations. May oversee accounting of revenues and expenditures and prepare and justify budget. May
resolve questions and complaints raised by court personnel, attorneys,
and members of other organizations and public. ● **GED:** R5, M4, L5 ●
SVP: 4-10 yrs ● **Academic:** Ed=A, Eng=G ● **Work Field:** 295 ●
MPSMS: 959 ● **Aptitudes:** G2, V2, N2, S3, P4, Q2, K4, F4, M4, E5,
C5 ● **Temperaments:** D, I, J, P ● **Physical:** Stg=L; Freq: T, G, N
Occas: R, H, I ● **Work Env:** Noise=N; ● **Salary:** 5 ● **Outlook:** 1

DIRECTOR, REGULATORY AGENCY (government ser.) ● DOT
#188.117-134 ● OES: 19005 ● Directs agency, division, or major func-
tion of agency or division charged with investigating regulated activities to assure compliance with federal, state, or municipal laws: Interprets
and clarifies federal, state, or municipal laws. Represents agency at
meetings, conventions, and other forums to promote and explain agency
objectives. Consults with other governmental agencies, business community, and private organizations to resolve problems. Plans and directs surveys and research studies to ensure effective program operation
and to establish or modify standards. Recommends changes in legislation and administrative procedures to reflect technological and ecological changes and public sentiment. Confers with legislative liaison
individuals or committees to develop legislative bills involving inspection procedures and to obtain wording for proposed inspection codes.
Prepares or directs preparation and release of reports, studies, and other
publications relating to program trends and accomplishments. Reviews
and evaluates work of MANAGER, REGULATED PROGRAM (government ser.) 168.167-090 through conversations, meetings, and reports. Prepares or directs preparation of budget requests. May be required
to testify in court or before control or review board. May be designated
according to function or agency administered as Administrator, Pesticide (government ser.); Administrator, Structural Pest Control (government ser.); Agricultural Commodity Grading Supervisor (government
ser.); Director, Reactor Projects (government ser.); Director, Transportation Utilities Regulation (government ser.); Director, Weights And

Measures (government ser.); Manager For Health, Safety, And Envi-
ronment (government ser.); Petroleum Products Inspection Supervisor
(government ser.). ● **GED:** R5, M4, L5 ● **SVP:** 4-10 yrs ● **Academic:**
Ed=A, Eng=S ● **Work Field:** 295 ● **MPSMS:** 950 ● **Aptitudes:** G2,
V2, N3, S3, P3, Q2, K4, F4, M4, E5, C4 ● **Temperaments:** D, J, P, V
● **Physical:** Stg=S; Freq: R, H, T, G, N Occas: I, X ● **Work Env:**
Noise=N; ● **Salary:** 5 ● **Outlook:** 1

ENVIRONMENTAL ANALYST (government ser.) ● DOT #199.167-
022 ● OES: 19005 ● Directs, develops, and administers state governmental program for assessment of environmental impact of proposed
recreational projects: Directs assessment of environmental impact and
preparation of impact statements required for final evaluation of proposed actions. Directs identification and analysis of alternative proposals for handling projects in environmentally sensitive manner. Plans
for enhancement of environmental setting for each proposed recreational
project. Designs and directs special studies to obtain technical environmental information regarding planned projects, contacting and utilizing various sources, such as regional engineering offices, park region
laboratories, and other governmental agencies. Prepares and controls
budget for functions of impact-statement preparation program. Attends
meetings and represents department on subjects related to program. ●
GED: R5, M3, L4 ● **SVP:** 4-10 yrs ● **Academic:** Ed=B, Eng=G ●
Work Field: 295 ● **MPSMS:** 959 ● **Aptitudes:** G2, V3, N3, S3, P4,
Q2, K4, F4, M4, E5, C5 ● **Temperaments:** D, J, P ● **Physical:** Stg=S;
Freq: T, G, N Occas: R, H, A ● **Work Env:** Noise=N; ● **Salary:** 5 ●
Outlook: 1

HOUSING-MANAGEMENT OFFICER (government ser.) ● DOT
#188.117-110 ● OES: 19005 ● Directs and coordinates activities con-
cerned with providing advice and technical assistance to housing authorities and evaluating housing management programs: Develops policy
and standards for guidance of local housing organizations in establishing and maintaining uniformity in operation of housing projects. Studies operation of housing projects, notes trends and needs, and evaluates
efficiency of housing programs. Prepares regulations, procedures, and
instructions for operation of housing projects based on analysis of operations. Approves or disapproves requests for waivers to policies, standards, and procedures. Consults with and advises housing personnel of
public and private groups concerning needed improvements in housing operations. Advises and assists MANAGERS, HOUSING
PROJECT (profess. & kin.) and staffs of local housing authorities concerning problems, such as eliminating excess costs, improving livabil-
ity features and maintenance care of dwelling units, making more
effective use of project facilities and community services, and promoting satisfactory relationships among tenants, housing project personnel, public officials, and private agencies. Leads public meetings and
serves on committees to stimulate efforts of national, local, and private
housing agencies and to emphasize housing needs of military personnel and low-income families. ● **GED:** R5, M3, L4 ● **SVP:** 4-10 yrs ●
Academic: Ed=B, Eng=G ● **Work Field:** 295 ● **MPSMS:** 959 ● **Aptitudes:** G2, V2, N3, S4, P3, Q2, K4, F4, M4, E5, C5 ● **Temperaments:** D, J ● **Physical:** Stg=L; Freq: I, T, G Occas: R, H, N ● **Work
Env:** Noise=N; ● **Salary:** 5 ● **Outlook:** 1

LEGISLATIVE ASSISTANT (government ser.) ● DOT #169.167-
066 ● OES: 21998 ● Assists legislator in preparation of proposed legislation: Conducts research into subject of proposed legislation and
develops preliminary draft of bill. Analyzes pending legislation and
suggests to legislator action to be taken. Briefs legislator on policy
issues. Attends committee meetings and prepares reports of proceedings. Speaks with lobbyists, constituents, and members of press to gather
and provide information on behalf of legislator. Analyzes voting records
of other legislators and political activity in legislator home district to
derive data for legislator consideration. Maintains liaison with government agencies affected by proposed or pending legislation. Assists in
campaign activities and drafts speeches for legislator. ● **GED:** R5, M3,
L5 ● **SVP:** 2-4 yrs ● **Academic:** Ed=H, Eng=G ● **Work Field:** 251,
261 ● **MPSMS:** 939 ● **Aptitudes:** G2, V2, N3, S4, P4, Q3, K4, F4,
M4, E5, C5 ● **Temperaments:** I, J, P, V ● **Physical:** Stg=S; Freq: T, G,
N Occas: R, H, I ● **Work Env:** Noise=N; ● **Salary:** 4 ● **Outlook:** 1

MANAGER, CITY (government ser.) ● DOT #188.117-114 ● OES:
19002 ● Alternate titles: MANAGER, COUNTY; MANAGER, TOWN.
Directs and coordinates administration of city or county government in
accordance with policies determined by city council or other authorized elected officials: Appoints department heads and staffs as pro-

vided by state laws or local ordinances. Supervises activities of departments performing functions such as collection and disbursement of taxes, law enforcement, maintenance of public health, construction of public works, and purchase of supplies and equipment. Prepares annual budget and submits estimates to authorized elected officials for approval. Plans for future development of urban and nonurban areas to provide for population growth and expansion of public services. May recommend zoning regulation controlling location and development of residential and commercial areas [URBAN PLANNER (profess. & kin.)]. May perform duties of one or more city or county officials as designated by local laws. ● **GED:** R5, M4, L5 ● **SVP:** 4-10 yrs ● **Academic:** Ed=B, Eng=G ● **Work Field:** 295 ● **MPSMS:** 959 ● **Aptitudes:** G2, V2, N3, S4, P4, Q4, K4, F4, M4, E5, C5 ● **Temperaments:** D, J, P, V ● **Physical:** Stg=S; Freq: T, G Occas: R, H, N ● **Work Env:** Noise=N; ● **Salary:** 5 ● **Outlook:** 3

MANAGER, HOUSING PROJECT (profess. & kin.) ● DOT #186.167-030 ● OES: 15011 ● Directs operations of housing project to provide low-income or military families, welfare recipients, or other eligible individuals with furnished or unfurnished housing in single or multiunit dwellings or house trailers: Develops and implements plans for administration of housing project and procedures for making housing assignments. Reviews occupancy reports to ensure that applications, selection of tenants and assignment of dwelling units are in accordance with rules and regulations. Conducts surveys of local rental rates and participates in setting of rental rates according to occupants' income and accommodation requirements. Prepares operational budget requests and receives accounts for and disburses funds. Conducts analyses of management and maintenance costs to determine areas where cost reductions can be effected. Plans long range schedule of major repairs on units, such as reroofing or painting exterior of dwellings. Studies housing demands occupancy and turnover rates and accommodation requirements of applicants to recommend policy and physical requirement changes. Promotes harmonious relations among tenants, housing project personnel, and persons of the community. Directs work activities of office and clerical staff in processing applications, collecting of rents and accounting for monies collected, and assigns building and grounds maintenance personnel to specific duties. Requisitions furnishings and furniture for housing units. May direct activities of other management personnel in housing project having commercial shops, concessions, theater, library, and recreational facilities. May refer applicants to private housing if all available units are occupied or if accommodation requirements are inadequate. ● **GED:** R5, M4, L4 ● **SVP:** 2-4 yrs ● **Academic:** Ed=A, Eng=S ● **Work Field:** 295 ● **MPSMS:** 895 ● **Aptitudes:** G2, V2, N3, S4, P4, Q3, K4, F4, M4, E5, C5 ● **Temperaments:** D, I, P ● **Physical:** Stg=S; Freq: R, H, I, T, G, N ● **Work Env:** Noise=N; ● **Salary:** 4 ● **Outlook:** 2

MANAGER, OFFICE (government ser.) ● DOT #188.167-058 ● OES: 19005 ● Manages local, district, or regional office of governmental agency or department to provide public or other individuals with designated services, or implement laws, codes, programs, or policies prescribed by legislative bodies: Reviews official directives and correspondence to ascertain such data as changes prescribed in agency programs, policies, and procedures, and new assignments or responsibilities delegated to office. Confers with subordinate supervisory personnel and reads staff reports and records to obtain data, such as status of on-going work or projects, cases and investigations pending, indications of probable conclusions, and projected completion dates. Plans office activities and work projects and assigns unit supervisory personnel responsibility for carrying out and completing specific projects and duties. Coordinates activities of various office units in order to provide designated functions or services with minimum delay and optimum efficiency and accuracy. Informs supervisory personnel of changes or interpretations of laws, codes, programs, policies, or procedures. Conducts staff meetings for dissemination of pertinent information. Trains and evaluates performance of supervisory personnel and reviews performance reports prepared on staff. Prepares reports on office activities required by agency. May be designated according to type of office and agency or department managed or by type of work performed by office staff. ● **GED:** R4, M4, L4 ● **SVP:** 4-10 yrs ● **Academic:** Ed=H, Eng=S ● **Work Field:** 295 ● **MPSMS:** 950 ● **Aptitudes:** G2, V2, N2, S3, P3, Q3, K4, F4, M4, E5, C5 ● **Temperaments:** D, J, P, V ● **Physical:** Stg=S; Freq: R, H, I, T, G, N, D, A ● **Work Env:** Noise=N; ● **Salary:** 4 ● **Outlook:** 4

MANAGER, REGULATED PROGRAM (government ser.) ● DOT #168.167-090 ● OES: 19998 ● Directs and coordinates activities of departmental personnel engaged in investigating regulated activities to ensure compliance with federal, state, or municipal laws, utilizing knowledge of agency's purposes, rules, regulations, procedures, and practices: Reviews agency's current work load status, schedules, and individual personnel assignments and expertise to establish priorities and to determine ability to accept and complete future commitments. Assigns specific duties to inspectors or INVESTIGATOR (government ser.) 168.267-062 either directly or through subordinate supervisors. Reviews work reports, papers, rulings, and other records prepared by subordinate personnel for clarity, completeness, accuracy, and conformance with agency policies. Routes approved reports and records to designated individuals, such as DIRECTOR, REGULATORY AGENCY (government ser.) 188.117-134 for action or for information. May participate in or make initial or advanced level investigations, tests, or rulings. May testify in court or before control or review board. May be required to be certified in designated speciality area. May be designated according to function or agency as Business Regulation Investigator (government ser.); Child Day Care Program Supervisor (government ser.); Feed Inspection Supervisor (government ser.); Insurance Licensing Supervisor (government ser.); Meat And Poultry Specialist Supervisor (government ser.); Petroleum Products District Supervisor (government ser.); Poultry Specialist Supervisor (government ser.); Public Utilities Complaint Analyst Supervisor (government ser.); Supervisor, Weights And Measures, Gas And Oil Inspection (government ser.). Workers involved in these activities may be identified by different titles according to classification used by various agencies. ● **GED:** R5, M5, L5 ● **SVP:** 4-10 yrs ● **Academic:** Ed=A, Eng=S ● **Work Field:** 295 ● **MPSMS:** 953 ● **Aptitudes:** G1, V2, N2, S4, P2, Q2, K5, F5, M5, E5, C5 ● **Temperaments:** D, J, P, T, V ● **Physical:** Stg=L; Freq: T, G Occas: C, S, O, R, H, N ● **Work Env:** Noise=N; ● **Salary:** 4 ● **Outlook:** 1

POSTMASTER (government ser.) ● DOT #188.167-066 ● OES: 19998 ● Coordinates activities of workers engaged in postal and related work in assigned post office: Organizes and supervises directly, or through subordinates, such activities as processing incoming and outgoing mail; issuing and cashing money orders; selling stamps, bonds and certificates; and collecting box rents to ensure efficient service to patrons. Resolves customer complaints and informs public of postal laws and regulations. Confers with suppliers to obtain bids for proposed purchases, requisitions supplies, and disburses funds as specified by law. Prepares and submits detailed and summary reports of post office activities to designated superior. Selects, trains, and evaluates performance of employees and prepares work schedules. May perform or participate in post office activities depending on size of post office. May plan and implement labor relations program. May confer with employees to negotiate labor disputes. ● **GED:** R4, M4, L4 ● **SVP:** 2-4 yrs ● **Academic:** Ed=H, Eng=G ● **Work Field:** 295 ● **MPSMS:** 954 ● **Aptitudes:** G2, V2, N3, S4, P3, Q4, K4, F4, M4, E5, C5 ● **Temperaments:** D, J, P, V ● **Physical:** Stg=S; Freq: R, H, T, G, N Occas: I ● **Work Env:** Noise=N; ● **Salary:** 5 ● **Outlook:** 1

SECRETARY OF STATE (government ser.) ● DOT #188.167-082 ● OES: 19005 ● Directs and coordinates activities of Secretary of State office to assist Executive and Legislative Branches of State Government under authority of state statutory and constitutional provisions: Directs activities of workers engaged in preserving records of official acts performed by Governor and Legislative bodies. Directs distribution of laws, resolutions, and other official state documents. Examines corporate articles or corporate statements of qualification to approve or disallow petitions for incorporation, amendments to corporate articles, dissolutions, and agreements of merger or consolidation. Administers Uniform Commercial Code to protect secured interest of retail merchants and lending institutions. Approves licensing of notaries public. Receives for processing, recording, and filing documents, such as deeds to state lands, claims to fraternal names and insignia, manuscripts, oaths of office, organization and boundaries of public districts, administrative rules and regulations adopted by state agencies, and statements of trust receipt financing. Directs activities involved in preserving historical documents and public records in state archives. May interpret and enforce election laws. May tabulate and certify accuracy of election returns. ● **GED:** R5, M4, L5 ● **SVP:** 4-10 yrs ● **Academic:** Ed=M, Eng=G ● **Work Field:** 295 ● **MPSMS:** 959 ● **Aptitudes:** G2, V2, N2, S4, P4, Q3, K4, F4, M4, E5, C5 ● **Temperaments:** J ● **Physical:** Stg=S; Freq: T, G Occas: R, H, N ● **Work Env:** Noise=N; ● **Salary:** 5 ● **Outlook:** 1

GOE: 11.05.04
Sales & Purchasing Management

DIRECTOR, MEDIA MARKETING (radio-tv broad.) ● DOT #163.117-022 ● OES: 13011 ● Plans and administers marketing and distribution of broadcasting television programs and negotiates agreements for ancillary properties, such as copyrights and distribution rights for films and audiovisual materials: Reviews inventory of television programs and films produced and distribution rights of broadcasting station to determine potential markets. Develops marketing strategy, based on knowledge of establishment policy, nature of market, copyright and royalty requirements, and cost and markup factors. Compiles catalog of audiovisual offerings and sets prices and rental fees. Negotiates with media agents to secure agreements for translation of materials into other media. Arranges for reproduction of materials for distribution and examines reproductions for conformity to standards. Edits materials according to specific market or customer requirements. Confers with legal staff to resolve problems, such as copyrights and royalty sharing with outside producers and distributors. ● **GED:** R5, M4, L5 ● **SVP:** 4-10 yrs ● **Academic:** Ed=B, Eng=G ● **Work Field:** 295, 292 ● **MPSMS:** 864, 889 ● **Aptitudes:** G2, V2, N3, S3, P3, Q2, K4, F4, M4, E5, C4 ● **Temperaments:** D, I, J, P, V ● **Physical:** Stg=S; Freq: R, H, I, T, G, N Occas: F, X ● **Work Env:** Noise=N; ● **Salary:** 5 ● **Outlook:** 3

FIELD REPRESENTATIVE (business ser.) ● DOT #163.267-010 ● OES: 13011 ● Alternate titles: DISTRIBUTION MANAGER. Monitors dealers and distributors to ensure efficiency of franchise operation: Surveys proposed locations to determine feasibility of establishing dealerships or distributorships. Advises dealers and distributors of policies and operating procedures to ensure functional effectiveness of business, and also develops information concerning planning and developing of business modifications and expansions. Reviews operations records to evaluate effectiveness. ● **GED:** R5, M4, L3 ● **SVP:** 1-2 yrs ● **Academic:** Ed=A, Eng=S ● **Work Field:** 292, 211 ● **MPSMS:** 899 ● **Aptitudes:** G2, V2, N3, S3, P4, Q3, K4, F4, M4, E5, C5 ● **Temperaments:** D, I, J, P ● **Physical:** Stg=L; Freq: T, G Occas: R, H, N ● **Work Env:** Noise=N; ● **Salary:** 5 ● **Outlook:** 4

MANAGER, BROKERAGE OFFICE (financial) ● DOT #186.117-034 ● OES: 19005 ● Alternate titles: BRANCH MANAGER; OFFICE MANAGER. Directs and coordinates activities concerned with buying or selling investment products and financial services, such as securities, insurance, and real estate, for clients of brokerage firm: Screens, selects, and hires REGISTERED REPRESENTATIVES (financial) 250.257-018 and other employees. Directs inservice training to improve client services and increase sales volume. Develops and implements plans to ensure compliance of workers with established programs, procedures, and practices. Establishes internal control procedures to control margin accounts, short sales, and options and to reduce office errors and client complaints. Reviews recapitulation of daily transactions to ensure accordance with rules and regulations of government agencies, regulatory bodies, and securities exchanges. Analyzes operations to determine areas where cost reductions could be implemented or program improvements initiated. Evaluates profitability of gross sales and transactions. Conducts staff meetings of personnel to discuss changes in policy, redirection of sales emphasis to other programs, or to propose methods and procedures to increase firm's share of local market and trade volume. Explains firm's research and customer service facilities and how use of facilities can promote customer relations and sales. Prepares activity reports for evaluation by management. May be required to have securities agent license. May be required to have experience in certain type of brokerage office managed, such as full-service brokerage office, discount brokerage office, or full-service/discount brokerage office. ● **GED:** R5, M4, L5 ● **SVP:** 4-10 yrs ● **Academic:** Ed=B, Eng=G ● **Work Field:** 295 ● **MPSMS:** 894, 895 ● **Aptitudes:** G2, V2, N2, S5, P5, Q2, K4, F4, M5, E5, C5 ● **Temperaments:** D, I, J, P ● **Physical:** Stg=S; Freq: T, G, N Occas: R, H, I ● **Work Env:** Noise=Q; ● **Salary:** 5 ● **Outlook:** 1

MANAGER, CIRCULATION (print. & pub.) ● DOT #163.167-014 ● OES: 19998 ● Directs sale and distribution of newspapers, books, and periodicals: Directs staffing, training, and performance evaluations to develop and control sales and distribution program. Establishes geographical areas of responsibility for subordinates to coordinate sales and distribution activities. May be designated according to type of circulation activity managed as Manager, Newspaper Circulation (print. & pub.); or area served as Manager, City Circulation (print. & pub.). ● **GED:** R5, M3, L4 ● **SVP:** 4-10 yrs ● **Academic:** Ed=A, Eng=G ● **Work Field:** 292 ● **MPSMS:** 757, 882 ● **Aptitudes:** G2, V2, N2, S3, P3, Q3, K4, F4, M4, E5, C5 ● **Temperaments:** D, J, P, V ● **Physical:** Stg=S; Freq: T, G, N, A Occas: R, H, I ● **Work Env:** Noise=N; ● **Salary:** 5 ● **Outlook:** 3

MANAGER, EXCHANGE FLOOR (financial) ● DOT #186.117-086 ● OES: 13002 ● Alternate titles: MANAGER, FLOOR OPERATIONS; MANAGER, FLOOR SERVICES. Directs floor operations of brokerage firm engaged in buying and selling securities at exchange: Monitors order flow and transactions that brokerage firm executes on floor of exchange. Reviews reports of securities transactions and price lists, using computer, to analyze market conditions. Informs staff of changes affecting firm or exchange. Calculates profit made by firm and estimates business volume lost to competition. Develops plan to increase firm's market share of business. Negotiates business contracts with exchange officials, and represents firm by membership in various exchange committees. Interviews, selects, and hires employees, such as FLOOR BROKER (financial) 162.167-034 and clerical workers. Develops and implements plans to ensure compliance of workers with established programs and procedures. Conducts staff meetings to discuss changes in policy or to propose methods and procedures which could increase profit and trade volume. Monitors employee attendance and takes disciplinary action when regulations are violated. Evaluates employee job performance and promotes or terminates personnel. May place orders with independent trader when additional help is needed to fill orders for brokerage firm. May buy and sell securities on floor of exchange [FLOOR BROKER (financial)]. May specialize according to type of securities traded at exchange and be designated Manager, Commodity Exchange Floor (financial); Manager, Options Exchange Floor (financial); Manager, Stock Exchange Floor (financial). ● **GED:** R5, M4, L5 ● **SVP:** 4-10 yrs ● **Academic:** Ed=B, Eng=G ● **Work Field:** 295 ● **MPSMS:** 894 ● **Aptitudes:** G2, V2, N2, S5, P5, Q2, K4, F4, M4, E5, C4 ● **Temperaments:** D, I, J, P ● **Physical:** Stg=L; Freq: T, G, N, F Occas: C, R, H, I, A, X, V ● **Work Env:** Noise=N; Occas: O ● **Salary:** 5 ● **Outlook:** 3

MANAGER, EXPORT (any industry) ● DOT #163.117-014 ● OES: 13011 ● Directs foreign sales and service outlets of an organization: Negotiates contracts with foreign sales and distribution centers to establish outlets. Directs clerical staff in expediting export correspondence, bid requests, and credit collections. Directs conversion of products from American to foreign standards and specifications to ensure efficient operation under foreign conditions. Arranges shipping details, such as export licenses, customs declarations, and packing, shipping, and routing of product. Directs clerical and technical staff in preparation of foreign language sales manuals. Expedites import-export arrangements and maintains current information on import-export tariffs, licenses, and restrictions. ● **GED:** R5, M5, L5 ● **SVP:** 4-10 yrs ● **Academic:** Ed=H, Eng=G ● **Work Field:** 292 ● **MPSMS:** 880 ● **Aptitudes:** G2, V2, N2, S4, P4, Q3, K4, F4, M4, E5, C5 ● **Temperaments:** D, I, J, P, V ● **Physical:** Stg=S; Freq: T, G Occas: R, H, I, N ● **Work Env:** Noise=N; ● **Salary:** 5 ● **Outlook:** 2

MANAGER, MERCHANDISE (retail trade) ● DOT #185.167-034 ● OES: 13008 ● Alternate titles: DIRECTOR, MERCHANDISE. Formulates merchandising policies and coordinates merchandising activities in wholesale or retail establishment: Determines mark-up and mark-down percentages necessary to ensure profit, based on estimated budget, profit goals, and average rate of stock turnover. Determines amount of merchandise to be stocked and directs buyers in purchase of supplies for resale. Consults with other personnel to plan sales promotion programs. ● **GED:** R4, M3, L4 ● **SVP:** 2-4 yrs ● **Academic:** Ed=H, Eng=G ● **Work Field:** 292 ● **MPSMS:** 881 ● **Aptitudes:** G2, V2, N3, S4, P4, Q4, K4, F4, M4, E5, C5 ● **Temperaments:** D, J, P ● **Physical:** Stg=S; Freq: R, H, I, T, G, N ● **Work Env:** Noise=N; ● **Salary:** 4 ● **Outlook:** 3

MANAGER, PROFESSIONAL EQUIPMENT SALES-AND-SERVICE (business ser.) ● DOT #185.167-042 ● OES: 13011 ● Directs and coordinates activities of establishment engaged in sale of professional equipment and supplies, and providing customer services, to organizations in such fields as medicine and medical services, engineering, and education: Plans and directs sales and service programs to promote new markets, improve competitive position in area, and provide fast and efficient customer service. Confers with potential customer to ascertain equipment, supplies, and service needs. Advises customer on types of equipment to purchase, considering such factors as costs, space availability, and intended use. Directs and coordinates activities of personnel engaged in sales and service accounting and record keeping, and receiving and shipping operations. Reviews articles in trade publications to keep abreast of technological developments in types of professional equipment merchandised. Resolves customer complaints regarding equipment, supplies, and services. Workers are usually classified according to type of firm managed or type of equipment and supplies sold such as dental, hospital, school, medical, or laboratory supply house. ● **GED:** R5, M4, L4 ● **SVP:** 2-4 yrs ● **Academic:** Ed=A, Eng=S ● **Work Field:** 292 ● **MPSMS:** 589, 601, 604 ● **Aptitudes:** G2, V2, N3, S4, P4, Q3, K4, F4, M4, E5, C5 ● **Temperaments:** D, I, P, V ● **Physical:** Stg=S; Freq: R, H, I, T, G, N ● **Work Env:** Noise=N; ● **Salary:** 4 ● **Outlook:** 1

MANAGER, SALES (any industry) ● DOT #163.167-018 ● OES: 13011 ● Manages sales activities of establishment: Directs staffing, training, and performance evaluations to develop and control sales program. Coordinates sales distribution by establishing sales territories, quotas, and goals and advises dealers, distributors, and clients concerning sales and advertising techniques. Assigns sales territory to sales personnel. Analyzes sales statistics to formulate policy and to assist dealers in promoting sales. Reviews market analyses to determine customer needs, volume potential, price schedules, and discount rates, and develops sales campaigns to accommodate goals of company. Directs product simplification and standardization to eliminate unprofitable items from sales line. Represents company at trade association meetings to promote product. Coordinates liaison between sales department and other sales-related units. Analyzes and controls expenditures of division to conform to budgetary requirements. Assists other departments within establishment to prepare manuals and technical publications. Prepares periodic sales report showing sales volume and potential sales. May direct sales for manufacturer, retail store, wholesale house, jobber, or other establishment. May direct product research and development. May recommend or approve budget, expenditures, and appropriations for research and development work. ● **GED:** R5, M3, L5 ● **SVP:** 4-10 yrs ● **Academic:** Ed=B, Eng=G ● **Work Field:** 292, 295 ● **MPSMS:** 860, 880, 890 ● **Aptitudes:** G2, V2, N2, S3, P3, Q3, K4, F4, M4, E5, C5 ● **Temperaments:** D, I, J, P, V ● **Physical:** Stg=S; Freq: H, I, T, G, N Occas: R ● **Work Env:** Noise=N; ● **Salary:** 5 ● **Outlook:** 3

PROPERTY-DISPOSAL OFFICER (any industry) ● DOT #163.167-026 ● OES: 13014 ● Alternate titles: REDISTRIBUTION-AND-MARKETING OFFICER; SURPLUS-PROPERTY DISPOSAL AGENT; SURPLUS SALES OFFICER. Disposes of surplus property, other than real property, using knowledge of merchandising practices: Inspects property to ascertain condition and estimate market value. Investigates market conditions and facilities to determine time, place, type of sale, and whether items shall be sold individually or in lots. Prepares advertising material and selects media for its release. Assigns and directs activities of sales personnel. Determines method of property display and sets prices of items to be sold in conformity with value and market. Advises interested parties of salvage possibilities. Recommends destruction or abandonment of property not deemed possible or practical to sell or salvage. ● **GED:** R5, M5, L5 ● **SVP:** 2-4 yrs ● **Academic:** Ed=A, Eng=G ● **Work Field:** 292, 295 ● **MPSMS:** 959, 572 ● **Apti-**tudes: G2, V2, N3, S3, P4, Q2, K4, F4, M4, E5, C4 ● **Temperaments:** D, J ● **Physical:** Stg=L; Freq: R, H, I, T, G, N Occas: F, D, A, X, V ● **Work Env:** Noise=N; ● **Salary:** 4 ● **Outlook:** 3

PURCHASING AGENT (profess. & kin.) ● DOT #162.157-038 ● OES: 21308 ● Alternate titles: BUYER. Coordinates activities involved with procuring goods and services, such as raw materials, equipment, tools, parts, supplies, and advertising, for establishment: Reviews requisitions. Confers with vendors to obtain product or service information, such as price, availability, and delivery schedule. Selects products for purchase by testing, observing, or examining items. Estimates values according to knowledge of market price. Determines method of procurement, such as direct purchase or bid. Prepares purchase orders or bid requests. Reviews bid proposals and negotiates contracts within budgetary limitations and scope of authority. Maintains manual or computerized procurement records, such as items or services purchased, costs, delivery, product quality or performance, and inventories. Discusses defective or unacceptable goods or services with inspection or quality control personnel, users, vendors, and others to determine source of trouble and take corrective action. May approve invoices for payment. May expedite delivery of goods to users. ● **GED:** R4, M3, L4 ● **SVP:** 2-4 yrs ● **Academic:** Ed=H, Eng=G ● **Work Field:** 292 ● **MPSMS:** 880, 890 ● **Aptitudes:** G2, V2, N3, S4, P3, Q3, K4, F4, M4, E5, C4 ● **Temperaments:** D, I, J, P ● **Physical:** Stg=L; Freq: T, G, N Occas: R, H, I, A, X ● **Work Env:** Noise=Q; ● **Salary:** 2 ● **Outlook:** 4

WHOLESALER I (wholesale tr.) ● DOT #185.167-070 ● OES: 41002 ● Manages establishment engaged in purchasing, wholesaling, and distributing merchandise, such as furniture and home furnishings, construction materials and supplies, metals and minerals, electrical goods, drugs and drug proprietaries, groceries and foodstuffs, and professional equipment and supplies to retailers, industrial and commercial consumers, or professional personnel: Estimates stock requirements based on sales orders, inventory, projected volume of sales, and current condition of economy. Authorizes purchase of merchandise based on estimates. Directs assembly of and storing of merchandise by workers, filling of orders, and distribution to customers according to sales orders. Directs and coordinates activities of workers engaged in wholesaling merchandise and extending credit to purchasers. Advises customers concerning current and future market conditions and availability of merchandise. Workers are classified according to type of merchandise, product, or material wholesaled and distributed. ● **GED:** R5, M5, L4 ● **SVP:** 4-10 yrs ● **Academic:** Ed=N, Eng=G ● **Work Field:** 292 ● **MPSMS:** 882 ● **Aptitudes:** G2, V2, N2, S4, P3, Q4, K4, F4, M4, E5, C5 ● **Temperaments:** D, P ● **Physical:** Stg=S; Freq: R, H, I, T, G, N ● **Work Env:** Noise=N; Occas: W ● **Salary:** 5 ● **Outlook:** 2

WHOLESALER II (wholesale tr.) ● DOT #185.157-018 ● OES: 41002 ● Exports domestic merchandise to foreign merchants and consumers and imports foreign merchandise for sale to domestic merchants or consumers: Arranges for purchase and transportation of imports through company representatives abroad and sells imports to local customers. Sells domestic goods, materials, or products to representatives of foreign companies. May be required to be fluent in language of country in which import or export business is conducted. May specialize in only one phase of foreign trade and be designated Exporter (wholesale tr.); Importer (retail trade; wholesale tr.). ● **GED:** R5, M4, L5 ● **SVP:** 2-4 yrs ● **Academic:** Ed=N, Eng=G ● **Work Field:** 292 ● **MPSMS:** 881, 882 ● **Aptitudes:** G2, V2, N3, S4, P4, Q3, K4, F4, M4, E5, C4 ● **Temperaments:** D, I, J, P, V ● **Physical:** Stg=S; Freq: T, G, N Occas: R, H, I ● **Work Env:** Noise=N; ● **Salary:** 4 ● **Outlook:** 2

Leading-Influencing

11

Finance

11.06

Workers in this group use mathematical and analytical skills to design financial systems and examine and interpret financial records. They are concerned with accounting and auditing activities, records systems analysis, risk and profit analyses, brokering, and budget and financial control. They find employment in banks, loan companies, investment firms, colleges, government agencies, and miscellaneous business

*firms. Some workers, like accountants
and appraisers are self-employed.*

✓ What kind of work would you do?

Your work activities would depend upon your
specific job. For example, you might:

- design an accounting system for a business
  to provide complete financial records.
- analyze financial records to prepare a
  financial status report.
- appraise materials and equipment to determine the total value of a business firm.
- analyze credit information to determine risk
  involved in lending money.
- study information to set schedules and rates
  for the transportation of merchandise and
  passengers.
- administer loan funds of a college or university and make arrangements for repayment.
- provide financial counseling to individuals
  in debt.
- regulate the cash flow in a bank by keeping
  loans, deposits, and Federal Reserve notes in
  balance.

✓ What skills and abilities do you need for this kind of work?

To do this kind of work, you must be able to:

- understand and use mathematical concepts
  in order to design a financial or economic
  system.
- interpret technical information presented in
  mathematical or diagram form in order to
  work with things like real estate property
  values, parimutuel betting systems, and stock
  market reports.
- work math problems quickly and accurately.
- understand and use computers and related
  equipment.
- speak and write clearly to report financial
  information.
- make decisions about the value of real estate
  and personal property based on inspection of
  the property, how you think its location will
  be affected by future plans of the community,
  as well as established facts like past tax
  values.
- plan and direct the work of accounting clerks
  and other workers.

✓ How do you know if you would like or could learn to do this kind of work?

The following questions may give you clues about
yourself as you consider this group of jobs.

- Have you had a checking or savings account?
  Did your balance always agree with the bank
  statement?
- Have you budgeted your own spending?
  Does your budget work?
- Have you had courses in accounting or
  bookkeeping? Do you enjoy this type of
  work?
- Have you been a treasurer of a school or
  community organization? Can you keep
  accurate financial records?
- Have you served in the accounting or payroll
  section of the armed forces?

✓ How can you prepare for and enter this kind of work?

Occupations in this group usually require education
and/or training extending from two years to over ten
years, depending upon the specific kind of work.
Work experience is a major consideration in preparing for jobs in this group. Experience in related
positions for the same employer is often required.
However, courses in accounting, business law,
economics, and investments are helpful. Some of
these courses are available in high schools, but most
are offered by business schools and colleges.

Some jobs in this group require licenses or certificates. Qualifications for credentials vary from state
to state.

✓ What else should you consider about these jobs?

Jobs in this group are in offices which are usually
well-lighted and ventilated. Some workers may be
exposed to the noise of office machines. Other
workers may have private offices.

Most of the work is detailed and workers may
develop eyestrain if proper precautions are not
taken.

The majority of these positions are salaried. Workers are seldom paid for overtime.

If you think you would like to do this kind of work,
look at the job titles listed on the following pages.

■　■　■

GOE: 11.06.01
Accounting & Auditing

ACCOUNTANT (profess. & kin.) ● DOT #160.162-018 ● OES: 21114
● Applies principles of accounting to analyze financial information
and prepare financial reports: Compiles and analyzes financial information to prepare entries to accounts, such as general ledger accounts,
documenting business transactions. Analyzes financial information
detailing assets, liabilities, and capital, and prepares balance sheet, profit

and loss statement, and other reports to summarize current and projected company financial position, using calculator or computer. Audits contracts, orders, and vouchers, and prepares reports to substantiate individual transactions prior to settlement. May establish, modify, document, and coordinate implementation of accounting and accounting control procedures. May devise and implement manual or computer-based system for general accounting. May direct and coordinate activities of other accountants and clerical workers performing accounting and bookkeeping tasks. ● **GED:** R5, M5, L5 ● **SVP:** 4-10 yrs ● **Academic:** Ed=B, Eng=G ● **Work Field:** 232 ● **MPSMS:** 892 ● **Aptitudes:** G2, V2, N2, S4, P4, Q2, K4, F4, M4, E5, C5 ● **Temperaments:** D, J, P, T ● **Physical:** Stg=S; Const: N Freq: I, T, G, A Occas: R, H ● **Work Env:** Noise=N; ● **Salary:** 4 ● **Outlook:** 4

ACCOUNTANT, BUDGET (profess. & kin.) ● DOT #160.162-022 ● OES: 21114 ● Applies principles of accounting to analyze past and present financial operations and estimates future revenues and expenditures to prepare budget: Analyzes records of present and past operations, trends and costs, estimated and realized revenues, administrative commitments, and obligations incurred to project future revenues and expenses, using computer. Documents revenues and expenditures expected and submits to management. Maintains budgeting systems which provide control of expenditures made to carry out activities, such as advertising and marketing, production, maintenance, or to project activities, such as construction of buildings. Advises management on matters, such as effective use of resources and assumptions underlying budget forecasts. Interprets budgets to management. May develop and install manual or computer-based budgeting system. May assist in financial analysis of legislative projects to develop capital improvement budget and be designated Program Analyst (government ser.). May assist communities to develop budget and efficient use of funds and be designated Public Finance Specialist (government ser.) ● **GED:** R5, M5, L5 ● **SVP:** 4-10 yrs ● **Academic:** Ed=A, Eng=S ● **Work Field:** 232 ● **MPSMS:** 892 ● **Aptitudes:** G2, V2, N2, S4, P4, Q2, K4, F4, M4, E5, C5 ● **Temperaments:** J, P, T ● **Physical:** Stg=S; Freq: I, N Occas: R, H, T, G, A ● **Work Env:** Noise=N; ● **Salary:** 3 ● **Outlook:** 4

ACCOUNTANT, COST (profess. & kin.) ● DOT #160.162-026 ● OES: 21114 ● Applies principles of cost accounting to conduct studies which provide detailed cost information not supplied by general accounting systems: Plans study and collects data to determine costs of business activity, such as raw material purchases, inventory, and labor. Analyzes data obtained and records results, using computer. Analyzes changes in product design, raw materials, manufacturing methods, or services provided, to determine effects on costs. Analyzes actual manufacturing costs and prepares periodic report comparing standard costs to actual production costs. Provides management with reports specifying and comparing factors affecting prices and profitability of products or services. May develop and install manual or computer-based cost accounting system. May specialize in analyzing costs relating to public utility rate schedule and be designated Rate Engineer (profess. & kin.). May specialize in appraisal and evaluation of real property or equipment for sale, acquisition, or tax purposes for public utility and be designated Valuation Engineer (profess. & kin.). ● **GED:** R5, M5, L5 ● **SVP:** 4-10 yrs ● **Academic:** Ed=B, Eng=S ● **Work Field:** 232 ● **MPSMS:** 892 ● **Aptitudes:** G2, V2, N2, S4, P4, Q2, K4, F3, M4, E5, C5 ● **Temperaments:** J, P, T ● **Physical:** Stg=S; Const: N Freq: I Occas: R, H, T, G, A ● **Work Env:** Noise=N; ● **Salary:** 4 ● **Outlook:** 4

AUDITOR, DATA PROCESSING (profess. & kin.) ● DOT #160.162-030 ● OES: 21114 ● Alternate titles: AUDITOR, INFORMATION SYSTEMS. Plans and conducts audits of data processing systems and applications to safeguard assets, ensure accuracy of data, and promote operational efficiency: Establishes audit objectives and devises audit plan, following general audit plan and previous audit reports. Interviews workers and examines records to gather data, following audit plan, and using computer. Analyzes data gathered to evaluate effectiveness of controls and determine accuracy of reports and efficiency and security of operations. Writes audit report to document findings and recommendations, using computer. Devises, writes, and tests computer program required to obtain information needed from computer for audit, using computer. Devises controls for new or modified computer application to prevent inaccurate calculations and data loss, and to ensure discovery of errors. ● **GED:** R5, M4, L5 ● **SVP:** 2-4 yrs ● **Academic:** Ed=B, Eng=G ● **Work Field:** 233, 271 ● **MPSMS:** 892 ● **Aptitudes:** G2, V2, N2, S4, P4, Q2, K4, F3, M4, E5, C5 ● **Tempera-**

ments: J, P, T ● **Physical:** Stg=S; Const: N Freq: I, T, G, A Occas: R, H ● **Work Env:** Noise=N; ● **Salary:** 4 ● **Outlook:** 4

ACCOUNTANT, PROPERTY (profess. & kin.) ● DOT #160.167-022 ● OES: 21114 ● Identifies and keeps record of company owned or leased equipment, buildings, and other property: Records description, value, location, and other pertinent information of each item. Conducts periodic inventories to keep records current and ensure that equipment is properly maintained. Distributes cost of maintenance to proper accounts. Examines records to determine that acquisition, sale, retirement, and other entries have been made. Prepares statements reflecting monthly appreciated and depreciated values. Summarizes statements on annual basis for income tax purposes. Prepares schedules for amortization of buildings and equipment. Develops and recommends property accounting methods to provide effective controls. ● **GED:** R5, M5, L5 ● **SVP:** 4-10 yrs ● **Academic:** Ed=A, Eng=S ● **Work Field:** 232 ● **MPSMS:** 892 ● **Aptitudes:** G2, V2, N2, S4, P4, Q2, K4, F4, M4, E5, C5 ● **Temperaments:** D, J, V ● **Physical:** Stg=S; Freq: R, H, N Occas: I ● **Work Env:** Noise=Q; ● **Salary:** 4 ● **Outlook:** 4

ACCOUNTANT, SYSTEMS (profess. & kin.) ● DOT #160.167-026 ● OES: 21114 ● Alternate titles: ACCOUNTING-SYSTEM EXPERT. Devises and installs special accounting systems and related procedures in establishment which cannot use standardized system: Conducts survey of operations to ascertain needs of establishment. Sets up classification of accounts and organizes accounting procedures and machine methods support. Devises forms and prepares manuals required to guide activities of bookkeeping and clerical personnel who post data and keep records. May adapt conventional accounting and recordkeeping functions to machine accounting processes and be designated Accountant, Machine Processing (profess. & kin.). ● **GED:** R5, M5, L5 ● **SVP:** 4-10 yrs ● **Academic:** Ed=A, Eng=G ● **Work Field:** 232 ● **MPSMS:** 892 ● **Aptitudes:** G2, V2, N2, S4, P4, Q2, K4, F4, M4, E5, C5 ● **Temperaments:** D, J, P ● **Physical:** Stg=S; Occas: R, H, T, G, N ● **Work Env:** Noise=N; ● **Salary:** 5 ● **Outlook:** 4

ACCOUNTANT, TAX (profess. & kin.) ● DOT #160.162-010 ● OES: 21114 ● Prepares federal, state, or local tax returns of individual, business establishment, or other organization: Examines accounts and records and computes taxes owed according to prescribed rates, laws, and regulations, using computer. Advises management regarding effects of business activities on taxes, and on strategies for minimizing tax liability. Ensures that establishment complies with periodic tax payment, information reporting, and other taxing authority requirements. Represents principal before taxing bodies. May devise and install tax record systems. May specialize in various aspects of tax accounting, such as tax laws applied to particular industry, or in individual, fiduciary, or partnership income tax preparation. ● **GED:** R5, M5, L5 ● **SVP:** 4-10 yrs ● **Academic:** Ed=B, Eng=G ● **Work Field:** 232 ● **MPSMS:** 892 ● **Aptitudes:** G2, V2, N2, S4, P4, Q2, K3, F3, M4, E5, C5 ● **Temperaments:** J, P, T ● **Physical:** Stg=S; Const: N Freq: I, T, G Occas: R, H, A ● **Work Env:** Noise=N; ● **Salary:** 4 ● **Outlook:** 4

AUDITOR (profess. & kin.) ● DOT #160.167-054 ● OES: 21114 ● Examines and analyzes accounting records to determine financial status of establishment and prepares financial reports concerning operating procedures: Reviews data regarding material assets, net worth, liabilities, capital stock, surplus, income, and expenditures. Inspects items in books of original entry to determine if accepted accounting procedure was followed in recording transactions. Counts cash on hand, inspects notes receivable and payable, negotiable securities, and cancelled checks. Verifies journal and ledger entries of cash and check payments, purchases, expenses, and trial balances by examining and authenticating inventory items. Prepares reports for management concerning scope of audit, financial conditions found, and source and application of funds. May make recommendations regarding improving operations and financial position of company. May supervise and coordinate activities of auditors specializing in specific operations of establishments undergoing audit. May audit banks and financial institutions and be designated Bank Examiner (government ser.). May examine company payroll and personnel records to determine worker's compensation coverage and be designated Payroll Auditor (insurance). ● **GED:** R5, M5, L5 ● **SVP:** 4-10 yrs ● **Academic:** Ed=B, Eng=G ● **Work Field:** 232 ● **MPSMS:** 892 ● **Aptitudes:** G2, V2, N1, S4, P4, Q2, K4, F4, M4, E5, C5 ● **Temperaments:** D, J, T, V ● **Physical:** Stg=S; Freq: R, H, I, T, G, N ● **Work Env:** Noise=Q; ● **Salary:** 4 ● **Outlook:** 4

AUDITOR, COUNTY OR CITY (government ser.) ● DOT #160.167-030 ● OES: 21114 ● Directs activities of personnel engaged in recording deeds and similar legal instruments, keeping records of county or municipal accounts, compiling and transmitting fiscal records to appropriate state officials, preparing financial statements of county or municipal finances for publication in local newspaper, and auditing books of city or county offices and departments. May be designated according to jurisdiction as City Auditor (government ser.); County Auditor (government ser.). In smaller communities or counties, may personally discharge all duties of office. ● **GED:** R5, M5, L5 ● **SVP:** 1-2 yrs ● **Academic:** Ed=A, Eng=G ● **Work Field:** 232 ● **MPSMS:** 892 ● **Aptitudes:** G2, V2, N2, S3, P2, Q3, K4, F4, M4, E5, C5 ● **Temperaments:** D, J, P ● **Physical:** Stg=S; Freq: R, H, N Occas: I ● **Work Env:** Noise=N; ● **Salary:** 4 ● **Outlook:** 3

AUDITOR, INTERNAL (profess. & kin.) ● DOT #160.167-034 ● OES: 21114 ● Conducts audits for management to assess effectiveness of controls, accuracy of financial records, and efficiency of operations: Examines records of departments and interviews workers to ensure recording of transactions and compliance with applicable laws and regulations. Inspects accounting systems to determine their efficiency and protective value. Reviews records pertaining to material assets, such as equipment and buildings, and staff to determine degree to which they are utilized. Analyzes data obtained for evidence of deficiencies in controls, duplication of effort, extravagance, fraud, or lack of compliance with laws, government regulations, and management policies or procedures. Prepares reports of findings and recommendations for management. May conduct special studies for management, such as those required to discover mechanics of detected fraud and to develop controls for fraud prevention. May audit employer business records for governmental agency to determine unemployment insurance premiums, liabilities, and employer compliance with state tax laws. ● **GED:** R5, M5, L5 ● **SVP:** 2-4 yrs ● **Academic:** Ed=B, Eng=G ● **Work Field:** 232, 271 ● **MPSMS:** 892 ● **Aptitudes:** G2, V2, N2, S4, P4, Q2, K4, F4, M4, E5, C5 ● **Temperaments:** J, P, T ● **Physical:** Stg=L; Const: T, G, N Freq: I, A Occas: S, K, O, R, H ● **Work Env:** Noise=N; ● **Salary:** 4 ● **Outlook:** 4

AUDITOR, TAX (profess. & kin.) ● DOT #160.167-038 ● OES: 21114 ● Audits financial records to determine tax liability: Reviews information gathered from taxpayer, such as material assets, income, surpluses, liabilities, and expenditures to verify net worth or reported financial status and identify potential tax issues. Analyzes issues to determine nature, scope, and direction of investigation required. Develops and evaluates evidence of taxpayer finances to determine tax liability, using knowledge of interest and discount, annuities, valuation of stocks and bonds, sinking funds, and amortization valuation of depletable assets. Prepares written explanation of findings to notify taxpayer of tax liability. Advises taxpayer of appeal rights. May conduct on-site audits at taxpayer's place of business and be designated Field Auditor (government ser.). May audit individuals and small businesses through correspondence or by summoning taxpayer to branch office for interview and be designated Office Auditor (government ser.). May perform legal and accounting work in examination of records, tax returns, and related documents pertaining to tax settlement of decedent's estates and be designated Tax Analyst (government ser.). May review most complicated taxpayer accounts and be designated Tax Examiner (government ser.). ● **GED:** R5, M5, L5 ● **SVP:** 4-10 yrs ● **Academic:** Ed=B, Eng=G ● **Work Field:** 271, 232 ● **MPSMS:** 953 ● **Aptitudes:** G2, V2, N1, S4, P4, Q2, K4, F4, M4, E5, C5 ● **Temperaments:** D, J, P ● **Physical:** Stg=L; Freq: R, H, I, T, G, N ● **Work Env:** Noise=N; ● **Salary:** 4 ● **Outlook:** 4

OPERATIONS OFFICER (financial) ● DOT #186.137-014 ● OES: 21998 ● Supervises and coordinates activities of personnel involved in performing internal operations in department or branch office of financial institution: Prepares work schedules and assigns duties to operations personnel to ensure efficient operation of department or branch. Audits accounts, records of proof, and certifications to ensure compliance of workers with established standard procedures and practices. Compiles required and special reports on operating functions of department or branch. Interviews, selects, and hires new employees. Directs employee training to improve efficiency and ensure conformance with standard procedures and practices. Verifies workers' count of incoming cash shipments. Controls supply of money on hand to meet branch's daily needs and legal requirements. Conducts staff meetings

of operations personnel, or confers with subordinate personnel to discuss operational problems or explain procedural changes or practices. May be designated according to type of financial operations supervised as Operations Officer, Branch Office (financial); Operations Officer, Trust Department (financial). ● **GED:** R5, M4, L4 ● **SVP:** 2-4 yrs ● **Academic:** Ed=H, Eng=G ● **Work Field:** 232 ● **MPSMS:** 894 ● **Aptitudes:** G2, V2, N2, S4, P4, Q3, K4, F4, M4, E5, C5 ● **Temperaments:** D, J, P, T ● **Physical:** Stg=S; Freq: T, G, N Occas: R, H, I, A ● **Work Env:** Noise=Q; ● **Salary:** 4 ● **Outlook:** 2

REVENUE AGENT (government ser.) ● DOT #160.167-050 ● OES: 21914 ● Conducts independent field audits and investigations of federal income tax returns to verify or amend tax liabilities: Examines selected tax returns to determine nature and extent of audits to be performed. Analyzes accounting books and records to determine appropriateness of accounting methods employed and compliance with statutory provisions. Investigates documents, financial transactions, operation methods, industry practices and such legal instruments as vouchers, leases, contracts, and wills, to develop information regarding inclusiveness of accounting records and tax returns. Confers with taxpayer or representative to explain issues involved and applicability of pertinent tax laws and regulations. [Workers who investigate and collect federal tax delinquencies are defined under REVENUE OFFICER (government ser.).] Secures taxpayer's agreement to discharge tax assment or submits contested determination to other administrative or judicial conferees for appeals hearings. May participate in informal appeals hearings on contested cases from other agents. May serve as member of regional appeals board to reexamine unresolved issues in terms of relevant laws and regulations and be designated Appellate Conferee (government ser.). ● **GED:** R5, M4, L4 ● **SVP:** 2-4 yrs ● **Academic:** Ed=B, Eng=G ● **Work Field:** 232, 271 ● **MPSMS:** 953 ● **Aptitudes:** G2, V2, N2, S4, P3, Q3, K4, F4, M4, E5, C5 ● **Temperaments:** I, J, P ● **Physical:** Stg=L; Freq: R, H, I, T, G, N ● **Work Env:** Noise=N; ● **Salary:** 4 ● **Outlook:** 3

GOE: 11.06.02
Records Systems Analysis

CONTROLLER (profess. & kin.) ● DOT #160.167-058 ● OES: 13002 ● Alternate titles: COMPTROLLER. Directs financial activities of organization or subdivision of organization: Prepares, using computer or calculator, or directs preparation of, reports which summarize and forecast company business activity and financial position in areas of income, expenses, and earnings, based on past, present, and expected operations. Directs determination of depreciation rates to apply to capital assets. Establishes, or recommends to management, major economic objectives and policies for company or subdivision. May manage accounting department. May direct preparation of budgets. May prepare reports required by regulatory agencies. May advise management on desirable operational adjustments due to tax code revisions. May arrange for audits of company accounts. May advise management about property and liability insurance coverage needed. May direct financial planning, procurement, and investment of funds for organization [TREASURER (profess. & kin.) 161.117-018]. ● **GED:** R5, M5, L4 ● **SVP:** 4-10 yrs ● **Academic:** Ed=B, Eng=G ● **Work Field:** 295, 232 ● **MPSMS:** 892 ● **Aptitudes:** G1, V2, N1, S4, P4, Q3, K4, F4, M4, E5, C5 ● **Temperaments:** D, J, P ● **Physical:** Stg=S; Freq: R, H, T, G, N Occas: I, A ● **Work Env:** Noise=Q; ● **Salary:** 5 ● **Outlook:** 1

REPORTS ANALYST (profess. & kin.) ● DOT #161.267-026 ● OES: 21905 ● Examines and evaluates purpose and content of business reports to develop new, or improve existing format, use, and control: Reviews reports to determine basic characteristics, such as origin and report flow, format, frequency, distribution and purpose or function of report. Confers with persons originating, handling, processing, or receiving reports to identify problems and to gather suggestions for improvements. Evaluates findings, using knowledge of workflow, operating practices, records retention schedules, and office equipment layout. Recommends establishment of new or modified reporting methods and procedures to improve report content and completeness of information. May prepare and issue instructions concerning generation, completion, and distribution of reports according to new or revised practices, procedures, or policies of reports management. ● **GED:** R4,

M3, L4 ● **SVP:** 2-4 yrs ● **Academic:** Ed=B, Eng=S ● **Work Field:** 212 ● **MPSMS:** 891 ● **Aptitudes:** G2, V2, N3, S3, P3, Q2, K5, F5, M5, E5, C3 ● **Temperaments:** D, J, P ● **Physical:** Stg=S; Freq: R, H, T, G, N Occas: I, X ● **Work Env:** Noise=N; ● **Salary:** 3 ● **Outlook:** 3

GOE: 11.06.03
Risk & Profit Analysis

APPRAISER (any industry) ● DOT #191.287-010 ● OES: 49998 ● Appraises merchandise, fixtures, machinery, and equipment of business firms to ascertain values for such purposes as approval of loans, issuance of insurance policies, disposition of estates, and liquidation of assets of bankrupt firms: Examines items and estimates their wholesale or auction-sale values, basing estimate on knowledge of equipment or goods, current market values, and industrial and economic trends. Prepares and submits reports of estimates to clients, such as insurance firms, lending agencies, government offices, creditors, courts, or attorneys. ● **GED:** R5, M5, L5 ● **SVP:** 2-4 yrs ● **Academic:** Ed=A, Eng=S ● **Work Field:** 211 ● **MPSMS:** 899 ● **Aptitudes:** G2, V3, N2, S3, P3, Q3, K4, F4, M4, E5, C5 ● **Temperaments:** J ● **Physical:** Stg=L; Freq: R, H, N Occas: S, I, T, G, F, D, A, X, V ● **Work Env:** Noise=N; ● **Salary:** 5 ● **Outlook:** 1

APPRAISER (government ser.) ● DOT #188.167-010 ● OES: 21998 ● Alternate titles: DEPUTY ASSESSOR. Appraises real and personal property to determine fair value and assesses taxes in accordance with prescribed schedules: Inspects property and considers factors such as current market value, location of property, and building or replacement costs to make property appraisal. Computes amount of tax to be levied, using applicable tax tables, and writes reports of determinations for public record. May interpret laws, formulate policies, and direct activities of assessment office. May be designated according to type of property assessed as Appraiser, Aircraft (government ser.); Appraiser, Auditor (government ser.); Appraiser, Boats And Marine (government ser.); Appraiser, Buildings (government ser.); Appraiser, Land (government ser.); Appraiser, Oil And Water (government ser.); Appraiser, Personal Property (government ser.); Appraiser, Real Estate (government ser.); Appraiser, Timber (government ser.). ● **GED:** R5, M5, L5 ● **SVP:** 2-4 yrs ● **Academic:** Ed=A, Eng=G ● **Work Field:** 211 ● **MPSMS:** 895 ● **Aptitudes:** G2, V2, N2, S3, P3, Q2, K4, F4, M4, E4, C4 ● **Temperaments:** J ● **Physical:** Stg=L; Freq: R, H, I, N Occas: C, F, D ● **Work Env:** Noise=N; Freq: W ● **Salary:** 4 ● **Outlook:** 1

APPRAISER, REAL ESTATE (real estate) ● DOT #191.267-010 ● OES: 43011 ● Appraises improved or unimproved real property to determine value for purchase, sale, investment, mortgage, or loan purposes: Interviews persons familiar with property and immediate surroundings, such as contractors, home owners, and other realtors to obtain pertinent information. Inspects property for construction, condition, and functional design and takes property measurements. Considers factors, such as depreciation, reproduction costs, value comparison of similar property, and income potential, when computing final estimation of property value. Considers location and trends or impending changes that could influence future value of property. Searches public records for transactions, such as sales, leases, and assessments. Photographs interiors and exteriors of property, to assist in estimating property value, to substantiate findings, and to complete appraisal report. Prepares written report, utilizing data collected and submits report to corroborate value established. May direct activities of appraisers. May evaluate staff job performance and recommend measures to improve performance according to establishment policies and procedures. ● **GED:** R5, M4, L4 ● **SVP:** 2-4 yrs ● **Academic:** Ed=A, Eng=S ● **Work Field:** 211 ● **MPSMS:** 895 ● **Aptitudes:** G2, V2, N2, S3, P4, Q2, K4, F4, M4, E5, C5 ● **Temperaments:** J, P, V ● **Physical:** Stg=L; Const: N Freq: R, H, I, T, G Occas: C, S, O, F, D, A, V ● **Work Env:** Noise=N; Occas: W ● **Salary:** 5 ● **Outlook:** 3

BOOKMAKER (amuse. & rec.) ● DOT #187.167-014 ● OES: 19998 ● Alternate titles: BOOKIE. Manages establishment to receive and pay off bets placed by horse racing patrons: Prepares and issues lists of approximate handicap odds on each horse prior to race, from knowledge of previous performance of horse under existing conditions of weather and track. Determines risks on each horse to refuse additional bets after maximum desired limit of liability has been reached. Records bets placed over counter or by telephone or teletype. Issues betting receipts. Pays off bets on track parimutuel basis. May supervise and coordinate activities of CASHIERS, GAMBLING (amuse. & rec.). May balance betting accounts and keep records as required by state or municipal authorities. May place customers' bets with cooperating BOOKMAKERS (amuse. & rec.) to limit liability and apportion risk. May be designated Sports Bookmaker (amuse. & rec.) when taking bets on sports, such as football, boxing, baseball, and hockey. ● **GED:** R4, M3, L3 ● **SVP:** 1-2 yrs ● **Academic:** Ed=H, Eng=G ● **Work Field:** 295 ● **MPSMS:** 913 ● **Aptitudes:** G3, V3, N3, S4, P4, Q3, K4, F3, M3, E5, C5 ● **Temperaments:** D, J, P, V ● **Physical:** Stg=L; Freq: R, H, I, T, G, N ● **Work Env:** Noise=N; ● **Salary:** 2 ● **Outlook:** 1

CREDIT ANALYST (financial) ● DOT #160.267-022 ● OES: 21105 ● Analyzes credit information to determine risk involved in lending money to commercial customers, and prepares report of findings: Selects information, including company financial statements and balance sheet and records data on spreadsheet, using computer. Enters codes for computer program to generate ratios for use in evaluating commercial customer's financial status. Compares items, such as liquidity, profitability, credit history, and cash, with other companies of same industry, size, and geographic location. Analyzes such factors as income growth, quality of management, market share, potential risks of industry, and collateral appraisal. Writes offering sheet (loan application), including results of credit analysis and summary of loan request. Describes credit risk and amount of loan profit. Submits offering sheet to loan committee for decision. May visit company to collect information as part of analysis. ● **GED:** R5, M4, L5 ● **SVP:** 4-10 yrs ● **Academic:** Ed=A, Eng=G ● **Work Field:** 271 ● **MPSMS:** 894 ● **Aptitudes:** G2, V2, N2, S4, P4, Q2, K4, F4, M5, E5, C5 ● **Temperaments:** J, T ● **Physical:** Stg=S; Const: N Occas: R, H, I, T, G ● **Work Env:** Noise=Q; ● **Salary:** 3 ● **Outlook:** 2

DIRECTOR, UTILITY ACCOUNTS (government ser.) ● DOT #160.267-014 ● OES: 21114 ● Evaluates financial condition of electric, telephone, gas, water, and public transit utility companies to facilitate work of regulatory commissions in setting rates: Analyzes annual reports, financial statements, and other records submitted by utility companies, applying accepted accounting and statistical analysis procedures to determine current financial condition of company. Evaluates reports from commission staff members and field investigators regarding condition of company property and other factors influencing solvency and profitability of company. Prepares and presents exhibits and testifies during commission hearings on regulatory or rate adjustments. Confers with company officials to discuss financial problems and regulatory matters. Directs workers engaged in filing company financial records. May conduct specialized studies, such as cost of service, revenue requirement, and cost allocation studies for commission, or design new rates in accordance with findings of commission and be designated Rate Analyst (government ser.). ● **GED:** R5, M5, L5 ● **SVP:** 4-10 yrs ● **Academic:** Ed=B, Eng=G ● **Work Field:** 232 ● **MPSMS:** 894 ● **Aptitudes:** G2, V2, N1, S4, P3, Q3, K4, F4, M4, E5, C5 ● **Temperaments:** J ● **Physical:** Stg=S; Freq: R, H, T, G, N, A Occas: I ● **Work Env:** Noise=Q; ● **Salary:** 4 ● **Outlook:** 3

FACTOR (financial) ● DOT #186.167-082 ● OES: 21998 ● Factors (purchases at discount) accounts receivable from businesses needing operating capital: Directs collection of facts about prospective client's business, such as credit rating of customers, evaluation of past losses, terms of sales, due dates, average amount of invoices, and expected volume and turnover of accounts receivable. Evaluates data collected to determine type of factoring plan to propose and percentage of net face value of accounts to advance which will yield favorable profit margin and alleviate client's cash shortage. Determines charge from fee schedule. Explains factoring agreement to client. Prepares and signs contract specifying terms of agreement and rights and obligations of both parties. May provide clients with other business services, such as credit and collection services, accounts receivable bookkeeping, and management consulting, on contract or fee basis. May specialize in factoring agreements in one or more industries. ● **GED:** R5, M4, L4 ● **SVP:** 4-10 yrs ● **Academic:** Ed=H, Eng=G ● **Work Field:** 232, 295, 271 ● **MPSMS:** 894 ● **Aptitudes:** G1, V2, N2, S4, P4, Q3, K4, F4, M4, E5, C5 ● **Temperaments:** J, P ● **Physical:** Stg=S; Freq: T, G, N Occas: R, H, I ● **Work Env:** Noise=Q; ● **Salary:** 5 ● **Outlook:** 2

FOREIGN-EXCHANGE DEALER (financial) ● DOT #186.117-082 ● OES: 21998 ● Alternate titles: FOREIGN-EXCHANGE TRADER. Maintains bank's balances on deposit in foreign banks to ensure foreign exchange position, and negotiates prices at which such exchanges shall be purchased and sold, based on demand, supply, and stability of currency: Refers to international bank market rate to determine foreign exchange rates. Establishes local rates based upon international bank rates, size of transaction involved, stability of market, and bank's balances available to fund customer requirements. Negotiates purchase and sale of foreign exchange drafts on foreign exchange market and calculates U.S. dollar equivalents, using calculator or computer. Adjusts deposit balances with foreign banks. May direct foreign exchange personnel in transactions relating to international monetary business. ● **GED:** R5, M4, L4 ● **SVP:** 4-10 yrs ● **Academic:** Ed=A, Eng=S ● **Work Field:** 232, 292 ● **MPSMS:** 894 ● **Aptitudes:** G2, V2, N2, S5, P4, Q3, K4, F4, M4, E5, C5 ● **Temperaments:** D, J, P ● **Physical:** Stg=S; Const: T, G, N Occas: R, H, I ● **Work Env:** Noise=Q; ● **Salary:** 5 ● **Outlook:** 1

INVESTIGATOR (clerical) ● DOT #241.267-030 ● OES: 53302 ● Investigates persons or business establishments applying for credit, employment, insurance, loans, or settlement of claims: Contacts former employers, neighbors, trade associations, and others by telephone or in person, to verify employment record and to obtain health history and history of moral and social behavior. Examines city directories and public records to verify residence history, convictions and arrests, property ownership, bankruptcies, liens, and unpaid taxes of applicant. Obtains credit rating from banks and credit services. Analyzes information gathered by investigation and prepares reports of findings and recommendations, using typewriter or computer. May interview applicant on telephone or in person to obtain other financial and personal data to complete report. May be designated according to type of investigation as Credit Reporter (business ser.); Insurance Application Investigator (insurance). ● **GED:** R4, M3, L4 ● **SVP:** 6 mos-1 yr ● **Academic:** Ed=H, Eng=G ● **Work Field:** 271 ● **MPSMS:** 890 ● **Aptitudes:** G3, V2, N3, S5, P5, Q2, K4, F4, M4, E5, C5 ● **Temperaments:** J, P ● **Physical:** Stg=S; Freq: R, H, I, T, G, N ● **Work Env:** Noise=Q; ● **Salary:** 2 ● **Outlook:** 3

INVESTMENT ANALYST (financial) ● DOT #160.267-026 ● OES: 21998 ● Alternate titles: SECURITIES ANALYST; SECURITIES-RESEARCH ANALYST. Analyzes financial information to forecast business, industry, and economic conditions, for use in making investment decisions: Gathers and analyzes company financial statements, industry, regulatory and economic information, and financial periodicals and newspapers. Interprets data concerning price, yield, stability, and future trends of investments. Summarizes data describing current and long term trends in investment risks and economic influences pertinent to investments. Draws charts and graphs to illustrate reports, using computer. Recommends investment timing and buy-and-sell orders to company or to staff of investment establishment for advising clients. May call brokers and purchase investments for company, according to company policy. May recommend modifications to management's investment policy. May specialize in specific investment area, such as bond, commodity, equity, currency, or portfolio management. ● **GED:** R5, M5, L5 ● **SVP:** 4-10 yrs ● **Academic:** Ed=B, Eng=G ● **Work Field:** 271, 232 ● **MPSMS:** 894 ● **Aptitudes:** G2, V2, N2, S4, P4, Q2, K4, F4, M4, E5, C5 ● **Temperaments:** J, T ● **Physical:** Stg=S; Const: N Occas: R, H, I, T, G ● **Work Env:** Noise=Q; ● **Salary:** 4 ● **Outlook:** 4

LETTER-OF-CREDIT DOCUMENT EXAMINER (financial) ● DOT #169.267-042 ● OES: 21105 ● Authorizes payment on letters of credit used in international banking: Examines documents, such as bills of lading, certificates of origin, and shipping manifests, for accuracy and completeness and to ensure that conditions of letters of credit are in accordance with establishment policy and international uniform custom and practice. Verifies document computations, using calculator. Talks with customers and recommends acceptable wording for letters of credit. Explains regulatory and legal implications of terms and conditions, including U.S. trade restrictions. Instructs workers in preparing amendments to letters of credit. Contacts foreign banks, suppliers, or other sources to obtain required documents. Authorizes method of payment against letter of credit in accordance with client instructions. ● **GED:** R5, M4, L4 ● **SVP:** 2-4 yrs ● **Academic:** Ed=H, Eng=G ● **Work Field:** 282, 232 ● **MPSMS:** 894 ● **Aptitudes:** G2, V2, N2, S5, P5, Q2, K4, F4, M4, E5, C5 ● **Temperaments:** J, P ● **Physical:** Stg=S; Const: T, G, N Occas: R, H, I ● **Work Env:** Noise=Q; ● **Salary:** 2 ● **Outlook:** 2

LOAN OFFICER (financial) ● DOT #186.267-018 ● OES: 21108 ● Interviews applicants, and examines, evaluates, and authorizes or recommends approval of customer applications for lines or extension of lines of credit, commercial loans, real estate loans, consumer credit loans, or credit card accounts: Interviews applicant and requests specified information for loan application. Analyzes applicant financial status, credit, and property evaluation to determine feasibility of granting loan or submits application to CREDIT ANALYST (financial) 160.267-022 for verification and recommendation. Corresponds with or interviews applicant or creditors to resolve questions regarding application information. Approves loan within specified limits or refers loan to loan committee for approval. Ensures loan agreements are complete and accurate according to policy. May confer with UNDERWRITER, MORTGAGE LOAN (financial) 186.267-026 to aid in resolving mortgage application problems. May supervise loan personnel. May analyze potential loan markets to develop prospects for loans. May solicit and negotiate conventional or government secured loans on commission basis and be known as Mortgage Loan Originator (financial). May specialize by type of lending activity and be known as Commercial Account Officer (financial); International Banking Officer (financial); Mortgage-Loan Officer (financial; insurance). ● **GED:** R5, M4, L4 ● **SVP:** 2-4 yrs ● **Academic:** Ed=H, Eng=G ● **Work Field:** 271 ● **MPSMS:** 894 ● **Aptitudes:** G2, V2, N3, S4, P4, Q3, K4, F4, M4, E5, C5 ● **Temperaments:** J, P ● **Physical:** Stg=S; Const: T, G, N Freq: R, H Occas: I ● **Work Env:** Noise=Q; ● **Salary:** 4 ● **Outlook:** 3

LOAN REVIEW ANALYST (financial) ● DOT #186.267-022 ● OES: 21108 ● Evaluates quality of commercial loans and assigns risk rating: Selects loans to evaluate for credit risk according to factors, such as geographical location, and type and amount of loan. Records data on work sheet, such as purpose of loan, balance, collateral, and repayment terms. Verifies value of collateral by calling appraisers and auction houses for current value of machinery and equipment. Calls real estate appraiser for new real estate appraisal. Evaluates information to determine whether lending officers have stayed within guidelines of lending authority, if loan is in compliance with banking regulations, and if required documents have been obtained. Identifies problem loans and describes deficiencies. Assigns risk rating indicating borrower's financial strength and probability of loan repayment. Writes summary of analysis and reasons for assigning adverse risk rating. May act as senior analyst and coordinate data collection and evaluations of credit quality of commercial loans, and present loan review information and report to management. ● **GED:** R5, M4, L5 ● **SVP:** 4-10 yrs ● **Academic:** Ed=A, Eng=S ● **Work Field:** 271 ● **MPSMS:** 894 ● **Aptitudes:** G2, V2, N2, S4, P4, Q2, K4, F4, M4, E5, C5 ● **Temperaments:** J, T ● **Physical:** Stg=S; Const: N Freq: T, G Occas: R, H, I ● **Work Env:** Noise=Q; ● **Salary:** 4 ● **Outlook:** 4

MANAGER, CREDIT AND COLLECTION (any industry) ● DOT #169.167-086 ● OES: 13002 ● Directs and coordinates activities of workers engaged in conducting credit investigations and collecting delinquent accounts of customers: Assigns workers, directly or through subordinate supervisors, responsibility for investigating and verifying financial status and reputation of prospective customers applying for credit, preparing documents to substantiate findings, and recommending rejection or approval of applications. Establishes credit limitations on customer account. Assigns responsibility for investigation of fraud cases and possible legal action and collection for worthless checks and delinquent bills. Reviews collection reports to ascertain status of collections-and-balances outstanding and to evaluate effectiveness of current collection policies and procedures. Audits delinquent accounts considered to be uncollectible to ensure maximum efforts have been taken before assigning bad-debt status to account. Coordinates with others, including personnel in company branches and credit card companies, to exchange information and update controls. May submit delinquent accounts to attorney or outside agency for collection. May compile and analyze statistical data on fraudulent use of credit cards to develop procedures designed to deter or prevent use of cards. May specialize in credit and collection activities for credit cards and be designated Manager, Credit Card Operations (any industry). ● **GED:** R4, M4, L4 ● **SVP:** 4-10 yrs ● **Academic:** Ed=A, Eng=S ● **Work Field:** 295,

271 ● **MPSMS:** 894 ● **Aptitudes:** G2, V2, N3, S5, P5, Q2, K4, F4, M5, E5, C5 ● **Temperaments:** D, J, P ● **Physical:** Stg=S; Freq: T, G Occas: R, H, I, N, A ● **Work Env:** Noise=Q; ● **Salary:** 3 ● **Outlook:** 3

MARKET-RESEARCH ANALYST I (profess. & kin.) ● DOT #050.067-014 ● OES: 27102 ● Researches market conditions in local, regional, or national area to determine potential sales of product or service: Establishes research methodology and designs format for data gathering, such as surveys, opinion polls, or questionaires. Examines and analyzes statistical data to forecast future marketing trends. Gathers data on competitors and analyzes prices, sales, and methods of marketing and distribution. Collects data on customer preferences and buying habits. Prepares reports and graphic illustrations of findings. ● **GED:** R5, M5, L5 ● **SVP:** 2-4 yrs ● **Academic:** Ed=A, Eng=G ● **Work Field:** 271, 251 ● **MPSMS:** 741 ● **Aptitudes:** G2, V2, N2, S4, P4, Q2, K4, F4, M4, E5, C5 ● **Temperaments:** J ● **Physical:** Stg=S; Freq: R, H, T, G Occas: N, F ● **Work Env:** Noise=N; ● **Salary:** 4 ● **Outlook:** 3

PERSONAL PROPERTY ASSESSOR (government ser.) ● DOT #191.367-010 ● OES: 21998 ● Alternate titles: DEPUTY ASSESSOR. Prepares lists of personal property owned by householders and merchants in assigned area to facilitate tax assessment, showing number and estimated value of taxable items designated in regulations. ● **GED:** R3, M3, L3 ● **SVP:** 3-6 mos ● **Academic:** Ed=B, Eng=G ● **Work Field:** 211, 232 ● **MPSMS:** 953 ● **Aptitudes:** G3, V3, N3, S4, P4, Q3, K4, F4, M4, E5, C5 ● **Temperaments:** J, P ● **Physical:** Stg=L; Freq: T, G, N Occas: R, H, I ● **Work Env:** Noise=N; ● **Salary:** 4 ● **Outlook:** 2

RISK AND INSURANCE MANAGER (any industry) ● DOT #186.117-066 ● OES: 13002 ● Alternate titles: INSURANCE AND RISK MANAGER. Plans, directs, and coordinates risk and insurance programs of establishment to control risks and losses: Analyzes and classifies risks as to frequency and potential severity, and measures financial impact of risk on company. Selects appropriate technique to minimize loss, such as avoidance (reducing chance of loss to zero), loss prevention and reduction (reducing frequency and severity of loss), retention (including self-insurance and planned noninsurance), grouping of exposure units (to increase predictability of loss), and transfer (placement of property, activity, or risk with other establishment or insurers). Directs insurance negotiations, selects insurance brokers and carriers, and places insurance. Appoints claims and self-insurance administrators, and allocates program costs. Prepares operational and risk reports for management analysis. Manages insurance programs, such as fidelity, surety, liability, property, group life, medical, pension plans, and workers' compensation. Prepares operational and risk reports for management analysis. May direct loss prevention and safety programs. May select and direct activities of safety, engineering, and loss prevention experts. May negotiate with unions for employee benefits. ● **GED:** R5, M4, L4 ● **SVP:** 4-10 yrs ● **Academic:** Ed=B, Eng=G ● **Work Field:** 295 ● **MPSMS:** 895 ● **Aptitudes:** G2, V2, N2, S4, P4, Q3, K4, F4, M4, E5, C5 ● **Temperaments:** D, P ● **Physical:** Stg=S; Freq: R, H, I, T, G, N ● **Work Env:** Noise=N; ● **Salary:** 5 ● **Outlook:** 4

SECURITIES TRADER (financial) ● DOT #162.167-038 ● OES: 43014 ● Alternate titles: BROKER; TRADER. Purchases and sells securities for brokerage firm: Receives sales order ticket from REGISTERED REPRESENTATIVE (financial) 250.257-018, and inspects form to ensure accuracy of information. Contacts market maker (securities exchange or brokerage firm that is trading requested securities) to execute client orders for purchase or sale of securities, or completes transaction independently if brokerage firm is market maker in requested securities. Writes and signs sales order confirmation forms to record and approve securities transactions. Reviews all securities transactions to ensure that trades conform to regulations of Securities and Exchange Commission, National Association of Securities Dealers, and other government agencies. Must pass state examination to receive license and become registered to trade securities. May prepare financial reports to monitor corporate finances. May have management or supervisory responsibility for department employees. May provide clients with information on investments, and sell securities and other financial services [REGISTERED REPRESENTATIVE (financial)]. ● **GED:** R5, M4, L5 ● **SVP:** 2-4 yrs ● **Academic:** Ed=A, Eng=G ● **Work Field:** 292 ● **MPSMS:** 894 ● **Aptitudes:** G2, V2, N2, S5, P5, Q2, K4, F3, M4, E5, C5 ● **Temperaments:** J, P, T ● **Physical:** Stg=S; Freq: I, T, G, N Occas: R, H ● **Work Env:** Noise=Q; ● **Salary:** 5 ● **Outlook:** 3

TREASURER (profess. & kin.) ● DOT #161.117-018 ● OES: 13002 ● Alternate titles: TREASURY REPRESENTATIVE. Directs financial planning, procurement, and investment of funds for an organization: Delegates authority for receipt, disbursement, banking, protection and custody of funds, securities, and financial instruments. Analyzes financial records to forecast future financial position and budget requirements. Evaluates need for procurement of funds and investment of surplus. Advises management on investments and loans for short- and long-range financial plans. Prepares financial reports for management. Develops policies and procedures for account collections and extension of credit to customers. Signs notes of indebtedness as approved by management. May act as CONTROLLER (profess. & kin.) 160.167-058. ● **GED:** R5, M5, L5 ● **SVP:** 4-10 yrs ● **Academic:** Ed=B, Eng=G ● **Work Field:** 295, 232 ● **MPSMS:** 894 ● **Aptitudes:** G2, V2, N2, S4, P4, Q2, K4, F4, M4, E5, C5 ● **Temperaments:** D, J, P ● **Physical:** Stg=S; Freq: T, G Occas: R, H ● **Work Env:** Noise=Q; ● **Salary:** 5 ● **Outlook:** 1

UNDERWRITER (insurance) ● DOT #169.267-046 ● OES: 21102 ● Reviews insurance applications to evaluate, classify, and rate individuals and groups for insurance and accepts or rejects applications, following establishment underwriting standards: Examines such documents as application form, inspection report, insurance maps, and medical reports to determine degree of risk from such factors as applicant financial standing, age, occupation, accident experience, and value and condition of property. Reviews company records to determine amount of insurance in force on single risk or group of closely related risks, and evaluates possibility of losses due to catastrophe or excessive insurance. Writes to field representatives, medical personnel, and other insurance or inspection companies to obtain further information, quote rates, or explain company underwriting policies. Declines excessive risks. Authorizes reinsurance of policy when risk is high. Decreases value of policy when risk is substandard to limit company obligation, and specifies applicable endorsements, or applies rating to ensure safe and profitable distribution of risks, using rate books, tables, code books, computer records, and other reference materials. Workers typically specialize by type of insurance coverage, such as life, health, property and liability, or multiline insurance; and by individual or group underwriting. Within different types of coverage, workers may further specialize in areas, such as pension, workers' compensation, property, marine, automoblile, homeowner, or fire. ● **GED:** R5, M4, L5 ● **SVP:** 2-4 yrs ● **Academic:** Ed=A, Eng=G ● **Work Field:** 271 ● **MPSMS:** 895 ● **Aptitudes:** G1, V2, N2, S4, P4, Q2, K4, F4, M4, E5, C5 ● **Temperaments:** J, T ● **Physical:** Stg=S; Const: N Freq: R, H, T, G Occas: I ● **Work Env:** Noise=Q; ● **Salary:** 4 ● **Outlook:** 3

UNDERWRITER, MORTGAGE LOAN (financial) ● DOT #186.267-026 ● OES: 21108 ● Approves or denies mortgage loans, following mortgage standards: Reviews and evaluates information on mortgage loan documents to determine if buyer, property, and loan conditions meet establishment and government standards. Evaluates acceptability of loan to corporations that buy real estate loans on secondary mortgage markets, where existing mortgages are bought and sold by investors. Approves or rejects loan application, or requests additional information. Records loan rejection specifying investor and institution guidelines and basis for declining application, such as insufficient cash reserves. Assembles documents in loan file, including acceptance or denial, and returns file to originating mortgage loan office. May be authorized by federal agency to certify that mortgage loan applicant and property qualify for mortgage insurance endorsement from federal government and be designated Underwriter, Direct Endorsement (financial). ● **GED:** R5, M4, L5 ● **SVP:** 4-10 yrs ● **Academic:** Ed=A, Eng=G ● **Work Field:** 271 ● **MPSMS:** 894 ● **Aptitudes:** G2, V2, N2, S4, P4, Q2, K4, F4, M4, E5, C5 ● **Temperaments:** J, T ● **Physical:** Stg=S; Const: N Occas: R, H, I, T, G ● **Work Env:** Noise=Q; ● **Salary:** 4 ● **Outlook:** 3

GOE: 11.06.04
Brokering

FLOOR BROKER (financial) ● DOT #162.167-034 ● OES: 43014 ● Alternate titles: BROKER; FLOOR REPRESENTATIVE; FLOOR TRADER; TRADER. Buys and sells securities on floor of securities exchange: Analyzes market conditions and trends to determine best time to execute securities transaction orders. Buys and sells securities based on market quotation and competition in market. Informs REGISTERED REPRESENTATIVE (financial) 250.257-018 of market fluctuations and securities transactions affecting accounts. Must meet exchange requirements, which may include state license, to be member of exchange. May specialize in trading specific securities to stabilize market and be designated Independent Trader (financial) or Specialist (financial). ● **GED:** R5, M3, L4 ● **SVP:** 1-2 yrs ● **Academic:** Ed=B, Eng=G ● **Work Field:** 292 ● **MPSMS:** 894 ● **Aptitudes:** G2, V2, N3, S5, P5, Q2, K4, F4, M4, E5, C4 ● **Temperaments:** I, J, P ● **Physical:** Stg=L; Freq: T, G, N, F Occas: C, R, H, I, A, X, V ● **Work Env:** Noise=N; Occas: O ● **Salary:** 5 ● **Outlook:** 1

REGISTERED REPRESENTATIVE (financial) ● DOT #250.257-018 ● OES: 43014 ● Alternate titles: ACCOUNT EXECUTIVE; BROKER; INVESTMENT EXECUTIVE; SECURITIES BROKER; STOCK-BROKER. Sells financial products and services to clients for investment purposes, applying knowledge of securities, investment plans, market conditions, regulations, and financial situation of clients: Identifies potential clients, using advertising campaigns, mailing lists, and personal contacts. Solicits business from potential clients. Interviews clients to determine financial position, resources, assets available to invest, and financial goals. Provides clients with information and advice on purchase or sale of securities, financial services, and investment plans, based on review of professional publications and other financial literature, and knowledge of securities market and financial services industry. Completes sales order tickets and submits completed tickets to support personnel for processing of client requested transaction. Must pass state examination to receive license and become registered to sell securities. May read status reports and perform calculations to monitor client accounts and verify transactions. May work for firm that offers discounted brokerage fees and does not offer advice to clients. May develop and implement financial plans, and sell insurance, real estate, or securities [FINANCIAL PLANNER (profess. & kin.) 250.257-014]. ● **GED:** R4, M3, L4 ● **SVP:** 2-4 yrs ● **Academic:** Ed=B, Eng=G ● **Work Field:** 292 ● **MPSMS:** 894, 895 ● **Aptitudes:** G2, V2, N2, S5, P5, Q3, K5, F3, M5, E5, C5 ● **Temperaments:** I, J, P ● **Physical:** Stg=S; Freq: T, G, N Occas: R, H, I ● **Work Env:** Noise=Q; ● **Salary:** 4 ● **Outlook:** 3

TICKET BROKER (amuse. & rec.) ● DOT #259.357-034 ● OES: 49998 ● Purchases entertainment tickets in blocks at box-office prices, usually before attraction opens: Prices tickets for profitable resale, based on such factors as availability and demand for tickets and location of seats. Sells tickets to public in accordance with legal regulations concerning amount of profit or place of sale. May trade as well as buy and sell tickets. May pick up and deliver, by automobile, tickets bought, sold, or traded. ● **GED:** R4, M3, L4 ● **SVP:** 1-2 yrs ● **Academic:** Ed=N, Eng=G ● **Work Field:** 292 ● **MPSMS:** 910 ● **Aptitudes:** G3, V3, N3, S3, P3, Q3, K4, F4, M4, E5, C4 ● **Temperaments:** I, J, P ● **Physical:** Stg=L; Freq: T, G Occas: R, H, I, N, X ● **Work Env:** Noise=N; ● **Salary:** 4 ● **Outlook:** 2

GOE: 11.06.05
Budget & Financial Control

BUDGET ANALYST (government ser.) ● DOT #161.267-030 ● OES: 21117 ● Analyzes current and past budgets, prepares and justifies budget requests, and allocates funds according to spending priorities in governmental service agency: Analyzes accounting records to determine financial resources required to implement program and submits recommendations for budget allocations. Recommends approval or disapproval of requests for funds. Advises staff on cost analysis and fiscal allocations. ● **GED:** R5, M3, L4 ● **SVP:** 2-4 yrs ● **Academic:** Ed=B, Eng=G ● **Work Field:** 232 ● **MPSMS:** 892 ● **Aptitudes:** G2, V2, N2, S4, P4, Q2, K4, F4, M4, E5, C5 ● **Temperaments:** D, J, T ● **Physical:** Stg=S; Freq: R, H, T, G, N Occas: I ● **Work Env:** Noise=N; ● **Salary:** 5 ● **Outlook:** 3

BUDGET OFFICER (profess. & kin.) ● DOT #161.117-010 ● OES: 21117 ● Directs and coordinates activities of personnel responsible for formulation, monitoring and presentation of budgets for controlling funds to implement program objectives of public and private organizations: Directs compilation of data based on statistical studies and analyses of past and current years to prepare budgets and to justify funds requested. Correlates appropriations for specific programs with appropriations for divisional programs and includes items for emergency funds. Reviews operating budgets periodically to analyze trends affecting budget needs. Consults with unit heads to ensure adjustments are made in accordance with program changes in order to facilitate long-term planning. Directs preparation of regular and special budget reports to interpret budget directives and to establish policies for carrying out directives. Prepares comparative analyses of operating programs by analyzing costs in relation to services performed during previous fiscal years and submits reports to director of organization with recommendations for budget revisions. Testifies regarding proposed budgets before examining and fund-granting authorities to clarify reports and gain support for estimated budget needs. Administers personnel functions of budget department, such as training, work scheduling, promotions, transfers, and performance ratings. ● **GED:** R5, M5, L5 ● **SVP:** 4-10 yrs ● **Academic:** Ed=A, Eng=S ● **Work Field:** 295, 232 ● **MPSMS:** 892, 893 ● **Aptitudes:** G2, V2, N1, S4, P3, Q2, K4, F4, M4, E5, C5 ● **Temperaments:** D, J, P ● **Physical:** Stg=S; Freq: H, I Occas: T, G, N ● **Work Env:** Noise=N; ● **Salary:** 5 ● **Outlook:** 3

TREASURER, FINANCIAL INSTITUTION (financial) ● DOT #186.117-070 ● OES: 13002 ● Alternate titles: CASHIER. Directs and coordinates programs, transactions, and security measures of financial institution: Examines institution operations to evaluate efficiency. Plans and implements new operating procedures to improve efficiency and reduce costs. Directs receipt and disbursement of funds and acquisition and sale of other assets. Approves agreements affecting capital transactions. Directs safekeeping, control, and accounting of assets and securities. Ensures that institution reserves meet legal requirements. Analyzes financial and operating statements of institution, and reports and makes recommendations to management or board of directors in regard to financial policies and programs. May participate as member of committee deciding on extending lines of credit to commercial enterprises and other organizations. May be designated according to type of financial institution, such as Treasurer, Savings Bank (financial). ● **GED:** R5, M5, L5 ● **SVP:** Over 10 yrs ● **Academic:** Ed=B, Eng=G ● **Work Field:** 295 ● **MPSMS:** 894 ● **Aptitudes:** G2, V2, N2, S4, P4, Q3, K4, F4, M4, E5, C5 ● **Temperaments:** D, J, P ● **Physical:** Stg=S; Const: T, G Freq: N Occas: R, H, I, A ● **Work Env:** Noise=Q; ● **Salary:** 5 ● **Outlook:** 1

TRUST OFFICER (financial) ● DOT #186.117-074 ● OES: 21998 ● Alternate titles: TRUST ADMINISTRATOR. Directs and coordinates activities relative to creating and administering personal, corporate, probate, and court-ordered guardianship trusts in accordance with terms creating trust, will, or court order: Directs drafting of, drafts, or consults with client's attorney who drafts, legal documents specifying details, conditions, and duration of trust. Locates and places funds, securities, and other assets in trust account. Interviews trust beneficiaries of court-ordered guardianship trusts in order to locate probable sources of assets. Negotiates with public agencies, such as Social Security Administration and Worker's Compensation Commission, in effort to accumulate all assets into trust. Directs collection of earnings, dividends, or sale of assets and placement of proceeds in trust account. Directs realization of assets, liquidation of liabilities, and payment of debts for trusts. Directs disbursement of funds according to conditions of trust or needs of court ward or beneficiary. Ensures that excess or surplus funds are invested according to terms of trust and wishes of trust client. May specialize in promoting trust services and establishing new trust accounts. May prepare federal and state tax returns for trusts. May be designated according to type of trust as Corporate Trust Officer (financial); Personal Trust Officer (financial). ● **GED:** R5, M4, L5 ● **SVP:** 2-4 yrs ● **Academic:** Ed=A, Eng=G ● **Work Field:** 272, 295 ● **MPSMS:** 894 ● **Aptitudes:** G2, V2, N2, S4, P4, Q3, K4, F4, M4, E5, C5 ● **Temperaments:** D, I, J, P, T ● **Physical:** Stg=L; Const: T, G Freq: I, N Occas: R, H, A ● **Work Env:** Noise=N; ● **Salary:** 5 ● **Outlook:** 1

Workers in this group manage programs and projects in agencies that provide people with services in such areas as health, welfare, and recreation. They are in charge of program planning, policy making, and other managerial activities. The jobs are found in welfare and rehabilitation agencies and organizations, hospitals, schools, churches, libraries, and museums.

✓ What kind of work would you do?

Your work activities would depend upon your specific job. For example, you might:

- administer the affairs of a public or private school system under the direction of a board of education.
- plan and direct training and staff development programs for a business or government agency.
- serve as president of a college or university.
- direct a city or county welfare program.
- direct workers who classify prisoners and assign them to work and other activities within a prison.
- plan and coordinate community recreation programs.
- direct and coordinate the services and personnel of a hospital.
- coordinate emergency medical services for a city or county.

✓ What skills and abilities do you need for this kind of work?

To do this kind of work, you must be able to do:

- use language and mathematical skills to analyze and interpret financial reports, government funding requirements, and related materials.
- identify problems and make decisions based on your experience and judgment, as well as on established facts like budget allocations and legal requirements.
- deal with all kinds of people.

- speak and write clearly and effectively to influence people's actions and to be sure that your plans will be understood and followed.
- change your activities frequently.
- plan and direct programs and the activities of others.

✓ How do you know if you would like or could learn to do this kind of work?

The following questions may give you clues about yourself as you consider this group of jobs.

- Have you done volunteer work for a hospital or social agency? Do you enjoy helping people in such a setting?
- Have you taken courses in sociology or psychology? Do you enjoy these types of studies?
- Have you supervised the activities of others? Were the activities carried out effectively?

✓ How can you prepare for and enter this kind of work?

Occupations in this group usually require education and/or training extending from two years to over ten years, depending upon the specific kind of work. Most of these jobs require related work experience within the agency or institution involved. Some jobs require four to eight years of college study. In some cases, work experience within an institution or agency may be substituted for a portion of the educational requirements. College level courses in public administration or business administration are often a part of the formal preparation. Typing, while seldom required, will prove to be very useful.

✓ What else should you consider about these jobs?

Workers in this group have heavy responsibility from which they seldom escape, even at home or on vacation.

Some workers transfer to other agencies or institutions in order to move up the promotion ladder.

If you think you would like to do this kind of work, look at the job titles on the following pages.

■ ■ ■

GOE: 11.07.01
Social Services

COMMUNITY ORGANIZATION WORKER (social ser.) ● DOT #195.167-010 ● OES: 27310 ● Alternate titles: COMMUNITY SER-

VICE CONSULTANT; INFORMATION AND REFERRAL DIRECTOR; PROGRAM CONSULTANT. Plans, organizes, and coordinates programs with agencies and groups concerned with social problems of community: Promotes and coordinates activities of agencies, groups, and individuals to meet identified needs. Studies and assesses strength and weakness of existing resources. Interprets needs, programs, and services to agencies, groups, and individuals and provides leadership and assistance. Prepares reports and disseminates information. Maintains contact with representatives of other organizations to exchange and update information on resources and services available. May write proposals to obtain government or private funding for projects designed to meet needs of community. May assist in budget preparation and presentation. May assist in raising funds. Works in specialized fields such as housing, urban renewal and redevelopment, and health or in public or voluntary coordinating agency, such as community welfare or health council, or combined fund raising and welfare planning council. Works with special groups such as elderly, financially disadvantaged, juvenile delinquents, or physically or mentally handicapped. Usually required to have degree from school of social work. May direct and coordinate activities of volunteers or practicum students. ● **GED:** R5, M3, L5 ● **SVP:** 4-10 yrs ● **Academic:** Ed=N, Eng=G ● **Work Field:** 282, 295 ● **MPSMS:** 941 ● **Aptitudes:** G2, V2, N3, S4, P4, Q4, K4, F4, M4, E5, C5 ● **Temperaments:** D, I, J, P ● **Physical:** Stg=S; Freq: T, G, N Occas: R, H, I, A, X, V ● **Work Env:** Noise=N; ● **Salary:** 3 ● **Outlook:** 2

COMMUNITY-RELATIONS-AND-SERVICES ADVISOR, PUBLIC HOUSING (social ser.) ● DOT #195.167-014 ● OES: 27310 ● Alternate titles: TENANT RELATIONS COORDINATOR. Promotes tenant welfare in low income public housing developments: Initiates and maintains liaison between local housing authority and voluntary and public agencies for development and managements of public housing developments. Facilitates establishment of constructive relationships between tenants and housing management, and among tenants. Secures social services, such as health, welfare, and education programs for improving family and community standards. Provides leadership to tenants in development of group activities, such as adult education and recreation. Refers families with personal problems to community resources. Cooperates with other organizations in development of understanding and interest among voluntary and public agencies participating in long range plans for urban improvement. ● **GED:** R5, M3, L5 ● **SVP:** 2-4 yrs ● **Academic:** Ed=A, Eng=G ● **Work Field:** 298 ● **MPSMS:** 941 ● **Aptitudes:** G2, V2, N3, S3, P4, Q4, K4, F4, M4, E5, C5 ● **Temperaments:** D, J, P ● **Physical:** Stg=S; Freq: T, G Occas: R, H, I, N ● **Work Env:** Noise=N; ● **Salary:** 4 ● **Outlook:** 3

COORDINATOR OF REHABILITATION SERVICES (medical ser.) ● DOT #076.117-010 ● OES: 32398 ● Alternate titles: DIRECTOR OF REHABILITATIVE SERVICES. Plans, administers, and directs operation of health rehabilitation programs, such as physical, occupational, recreational, and speech therapies: Consults with medical and professional staff of other departments and personnel from associated health care fields to plan and coordinate joint patient and management objectives. Conducts staff conferences and plans training programs to maintain proficiency of staff in therapy techniques and use of new methods and equipment to meet patients' needs. Allocates personnel on basis of work load, space, and equipment available. Analyzes operating costs and prepares department budget. Recommends patient fees for therapy based on use of equipment and therapy staff. May coordinate research projects to develop new approaches to rehabilitative therapy. May serve as rehabilitative therapy consultant to employers, educational institutions, and community organizations. ● **GED:** R5, M5, L5 ● **SVP:** 4-10 yrs ● **Academic:** Ed=B, Eng=S ● **Work Field:** 295 ● **MPSMS:** 924 ● **Aptitudes:** G2, V2, N3, S4, P4, Q3, K4, F4, M4, E5, C5 ● **Temperaments:** D, J, P ● **Physical:** Stg=L; Freq: I, T, G, N Occas: R, H ● **Work Env:** Noise=N; ● **Salary:** 5 ● **Outlook:** 4

COORDINATOR, VOLUNTEER SERVICES (social ser.) ● DOT #187.167-022 ● OES: 19998 ● Alternate titles: VOLUNTEER COORDINATOR. Coordinates student and community volunteer services program in organizations engaged in public, social, and welfare activities: Consults administrators and staff to determine organization needs for various volunteer services and plans for volunteer recruitment. Interviews, screens, and refers applicants to appropriate units. Orients and trains volunteers prior to assignment in specific units. Arranges for on-the-job and other required training and supervision and evaluation of volunteers. Resolves personnel problems. Serves as liaison between administration, staff, and volunteers. Prepares and maintains procedural and training manuals. Speaks to community groups, explaining organization activities and role of volunteer program. Publishes agency newsletter, and prepares news items for other news media. Maintains personnel records. Prepares statistical reports on extent, nature, and

value of volunteer service. ● **GED:** R5, M3, L5 ● **SVP:** 2-4 yrs ● **Academic:** Ed=N, Eng=G ● **Work Field:** 295 ● **MPSMS:** 940 ● **Aptitudes:** G2, V2, N3, S4, P4, Q2, K4, F4, M3, E5, C5 ● **Temperaments:** D, J, P ● **Physical:** Stg=S; Freq: T, G, N Occas: R, H ● **Work Env:** Noise=N; ● **Salary:** 4 ● **Outlook:** 4

DIRECTOR, COMMUNITY ORGANIZATION (nonprofit org.) ● DOT #187.167-234 ● OES: 19998 ● Alternate titles: COMMUNITY PLANNING DIRECTOR, COMMUNITY CHEST; DIRECTOR, COUNCIL OF SOCIAL AGENCIES; DIRECTOR, FEDERATED FUND; DIRECTOR, UNITED FUND; EXECUTIVE, COMMUNITY PLANNING. Directs activities of organization to coordinate functions of various community health and welfare programs: Organizes and develops planning program to ascertain community requirements and problems in specific fields of welfare work, and to determine agency responsibility for administering program. Surveys functions of member agencies to avoid duplication of efforts and recommends curtailment, extension, modification, or initiation of services. Advises health and welfare agencies in planning and providing services based on community surveys and analyses. Reviews estimated budgets of member agencies. Prepares and releases reports, studies, and publications to promote public understanding of and support for community programs. May recruit and train volunteer workers. May organize and direct campaign for solicitation of funds. May visit agency sites to evaluate effectiveness of services provided. ● **GED:** R5, M3, L4 ● **SVP:** 4-10 yrs ● **Academic:** Ed=A, Eng=G ● **Work Field:** 295, 282 ● **MPSMS:** 941 ● **Aptitudes:** G2, V2, N3, S4, P4, Q3, K4, F4, M4, E5, C5 ● **Temperaments:** D, J, P, V ● **Physical:** Stg=S; Freq: T, G Occas: H, I, N, A ● **Work Env:** Noise=N; ● **Salary:** 4 ● **Outlook:** 1

DIRECTOR, SERVICE (nonprofit org.) ● DOT #187.167-214 ● OES: 19998 ● Directs and coordinates regional program activities of nonprofit agency to provide specialized human services, such as water safety programs, disaster relief, and emergency transportation: Consults with cooperating agencies, such as police, firefighters, and emergency ambulance services, to coordinate efforts and define areas of jurisdiction. Participates in program activities to serve clients of agency. Prepares budgets to control costs and to allocate funds in accordance with provisions and agency charter. May instruct agency staff and volunteers in skills required to provide services. May requisition and arrange for maintenance of equipment, such as two-way radios and agency vehicles. May coordinate services to disaster victims and be designated Disaster Director (nonprofit org.). May coordinate safety programs, such as water safety and emergency first aid, and be designated Safety Director (nonprofit org.). May coordinate transportation of agency clients, blood, and medical supplies and equipment and be designated Transportation Director (nonprofit org.). ● **GED:** R5, M3, L5 ● **SVP:** 4-10 yrs ● **Academic:** Ed=A, Eng=G ● **Work Field:** 295 ● **MPSMS:** 941 ● **Aptitudes:** G1, V2, N3, S3, P4, Q3, K4, F4, M3, E5, C5 ● **Temperaments:** D, J, P, V ● **Physical:** Stg=M; Freq: R, H, T, G, N Occas: I ● **Work Env:** Noise=N; ● **Salary:** 4 ● **Outlook:** 1

EXECUTIVE DIRECTOR, RED CROSS (nonprofit org.) ● DOT #187.117-066 ● OES: 19998 ● Directs and coordinates operations of nonprofit agency to provide blood, medical care, financial aid, and other special services: Oversees agency volunteer operations in areas such as blood donor program, nursing, and financial assistance to assure program adherence to agency charter. Participates in community activities to develop opportunities to ascertain needs, serve clients, and promote agency goals. Establishes and maintains close working relationships with cooperating agencies to avoid duplication of services. Prepares budget in consultation with departmental directors to allocate funds, control costs, and maintain operations at level consistent with agency guidelines. Recommends new policy and procedures to agency governing board. Advises volunteer leaders of potential problems and recommends alternative methods of providing service. Negotiates with community organizations to plan joint fund-raising campaigns. Hires paid staff in consultation with agency head. Confers with staff and disseminates written materials to inform staff of current developments. ● **GED:** R5, M4, L5 ● **SVP:** 4-10 yrs ● **Academic:** Ed=A, Eng=G ● **Work Field:** 295 ● **MPSMS:** 941 ● **Aptitudes:** G1, V1, N3, S4, P4, Q3, K4, F4, M4, E5, C5 ● **Temperaments:** D, I, J, P ● **Physical:** Stg=L; Freq: T, G, N Occas: R, H, I ● **Work Env:** Noise=N; ● **Salary:** 5 ● **Outlook:** 3

FIELD REPRESENTATIVE (profess. & kin.) ● DOT #189.267-010 ● OES: 27310 ● Reviews and evaluates program operations of national or state affiliated or nonaffiliated social service agency or organization, or community group to provide assistance and services in achieving goals: Interprets standards and program goals of national or state agency to assist local boards, committees, groups, or agencies in establishing program goals and standards. Confers with community councils to advise members on matters relating to program. Evaluates capabilities of local or community agencies or groups to achieve goals, considering such factors as administration and program finances, facilities and personnel staffing, and changing community needs. Prepares reports to inform national or state agency on conditions in local agencies or organizations and developing trends in local communities. May organize or conduct training or staff development programs. May organize regional meetings. May plan or conduct studies or surveys of local agency operation. May assist communities in establishing new local affiliates or programs. May confer with field representatives of other national agencies. ● **GED:** R5, M4, L5 ● **SVP:** 4-10 yrs ● **Academic:** Ed=A, Eng=S ● **Work Field:** 211 ● **MPSMS:** 940, 920, 950 ● **Aptitudes:** G2, V2, N3, S4, P4, Q4, K4, F4, M4, E5, C5 ● **Temperaments:** I, J, P ● **Physical:** Stg=S; Freq: T, G Occas: R, H, N ● **Work Env:** Noise=N; ● **Salary:** 4 ● **Outlook:** 3

MANAGER, ANIMAL SHELTER (nonprofit org.) ● DOT #187.167-218 ● OES: 19998 ● Manages animal shelter: Sets standards for and monitors conduct of shelter employees to ensure that humane philosophy is projected to public and implemented in care of animals: Develops work plans and assigns priorities for organizational units. Reviews shelter practices and procedures to ensure efficient and economical use of resources. Recommends to board of directors policy and personnel changes and budget expenditures. Directs actions to provide follow-up on animal neglect and cruelty complaints appearing to justify prosecution. Answers mail and maintains file of documents such as animal adoption and burial contracts and reports of shelter activities. Verifies cash receipts and deposits cash to shelter accounts. Delivers lectures, prepares materials for media broadcasts, and prepares and publishes newsletters to report agency activities and interpret organizational philosophy to public. ● **GED:** R5, M3, L5 ● **SVP:** 1-2 yrs ● **Academic:** Ed=N, Eng=G ● **Work Field:** 295 ● **MPSMS:** 890 ● **Aptitudes:** G2, V2, N3, S4, P3, Q3, K4, F4, M4, E5, C5 ● **Temperaments:** D, J, P, V ● **Physical:** Stg=L; Freq: R, H, T, G, N Occas: I ● **Work Env:** Noise=N; ● **Salary:** 4 ● **Outlook:** 2

PROGRAM DIRECTOR, GROUP WORK (profess. & kin.) ● DOT #187.117-046 ● OES: 19998 ● Plans, organizes, and directs activity program of group work agency or department, or scouting organization: Coordinates activities of program committees and other groups to plan procedures. Studies and analyzes member and community needs for basis of program development. Directs selection and training of staff and volunteer workers. Assigns work and evaluates performance of staff members and recommends indicated actions. Assists staff through individual and group conferences in analysis of specific programs, understanding of program development, and increasing use of individual skills. Interprets agency program and services to individuals or groups in community. May be designated according to agency or program directed as Activities Director, Scouting (nonprofit org.); Director, Teen Post (profess. & kin.); Program Director, Scouting (nonprofit org.). ● **GED:** R5, M5, L5 ● **SVP:** 4-10 yrs ● **Academic:** Ed=A, Eng=S ● **Work Field:** 295 ● **MPSMS:** 941 ● **Aptitudes:** G1, V1, N3, S4, P4, Q4, K4, F4, M4, E5, C5 ● **Temperaments:** D, P ● **Physical:** Stg=L; Freq: R, H, T, G, N Occas: I ● **Work Env:** Noise=N; ● **Salary:** 5 ● **Outlook:** 2

REHABILITATION CENTER MANAGER (government ser.) ● DOT #195.167-038 ● OES: 19998 ● Coordinates activities and provides for physical and emotional needs of public-welfare recipients housed in indigent camp: Cooperates with welfare department investigators, psychologists, and physicians in assigning activities to indigents and in providing specialized attention to them in accordance with recommendations. Appoints leaders of activities, such as food preparation and maintenance of grounds, from camp inmates in accord with democratic leadership principles and welfare department policy. Coordinates sanitation, food management, health, education, spiritual counseling, and vocational activity programs in conformity with available facilities, needs of camp inmates, and policy of department. Interviews inmates and arranges with business and community leaders to place them in jobs. Maintains discipline and arbitrates disputes. Arranges for entertainment, such as movies, lectures, and musical programs. Main-

tains camp records, inventories supplies, and submits requisitions for camp needs. ● **GED:** R5, M4, L5 ● **SVP:** 2-4 yrs ● **Academic:** Ed=S ● **Work Field:** 298, 295 ● **MPSMS:** 941 ● **Aptitudes:** G2, V2, N3, S4, P3, Q3, K4, F4, M4, E5, C5 ● **Temperaments:** D, F, I, J, V ● **Physical:** Stg=L; Freq: T, G Occas: R, H, N ● **Work Env:** Noise=N; Occas: W ● **Salary:** 4 ● **Outlook:** 3

RESIDENCE SUPERVISOR (any industry) ● DOT #187.167-186 ● OES: 39998 ● Alternate titles: ADVISER; CHAPERON; COTTAGE PARENT; HOUSE MANAGER. Coordinates variety of activities for residents of boarding school, college fraternity or sorority house, care and treatment institution, children's home, or similar establishment: Orders supplies and determines need for maintenance, repairs, and furnishings. Assigns rooms, assists in planning recreational activities, and supervises work and study programs. Counsels residents in identifying and resolving social or other problems. Compiles records of daily activities of residents. Chaperones group-sponsored trips and social functions. Ascertains need for and secures services of physician. Answers telephone and sorts and distributes mail. May escort individuals on trips outside establishment for shopping or to obtain medical or dental services. May hire and supervise activities of housekeeping personnel. May plan menus. ● **GED:** R4, M3, L4 ● **SVP:** 1-2 yrs ● **Academic:** Ed=H, Eng=S ● **Work Field:** 295, 291 ● **MPSMS:** 942 ● **Aptitudes:** G3, V3, N3, S4, P4, Q3, K4, F4, M4, E5, C5 ● **Temperaments:** D, P, V ● **Physical:** Stg=S; Freq: R, H, I, T, G Occas: N ● **Work Env:** Noise=N; ● **Salary:** 2 ● **Outlook:** 4

GOE: 11.07.02
Health & Safety Services

ADMINISTRATOR, HEALTH CARE FACILITY (medical ser.) ● DOT #187.117-010 ● OES: 19998 ● Directs administration of hospital, nursing home, or other health care facility within authority of governing board: Administers fiscal operations, such as budget planning, accounting, and establishing rates for health care services. Directs hiring and training of personnel. Negotiates for improvement of and additions to buildings and equipment. Directs and coordinates activities of medical, nursing, and administrative staffs and services. Develops policies and procedures for various establishment activities. May represent establishment at community meetings and promote programs through various news media. May develop or expand programs or services for scientific research, preventive medicine, medical and vocational rehabilitation, and community health and welfare promotion. May be designated according to type of health care facility as Hospital Administrator (medical ser.) or Nursing Home Administrator (medical ser.). ● **GED:** R5, M5, L5 ● **SVP:** 4-10 yrs ● **Academic:** Ed=M, Eng=G ● **Work Field:** 295 ● **MPSMS:** 920 ● **Aptitudes:** G1, V2, N3, S4, P4, Q3, K4, F4, M4, E5, C5 ● **Temperaments:** D, J, P, V ● **Physical:** Stg=L; Freq: T, G, N Occas: R, H, I ● **Work Env:** Noise=N; ● **Salary:** 5 ● **Outlook:** 3

CIVIL PREPAREDNESS TRAINING OFFICER (government ser.) ● DOT #169.127-010 ● OES: 31317 ● Instructs paid and volunteer workers in techniques for meeting disaster situations: Conducts classes in emergency techniques, such as first aid, flood protection, firefighting, shelter management, disaster communications and organization, use of radiological monitoring equipment, and post-attack operations. Confers with local government and federal authorities and with representatives of police, fire, sanitation, and public works departments to coordinate training. May direct or participate in preparation of geographic surveys of local areas to aid in formulating emergency survival plans. May specialize in preparing and distributing emergency preparedness information and be designated Civil Preparedness Public Information Officer (government ser.). ● **GED:** R4, M3, L4 ● **SVP:** 1-2 yrs ● **Academic:** Ed=H, Eng=G ● **Work Field:** 296 ● **MPSMS:** 959 ● **Aptitudes:** G2, V2, N3, S3, P3, Q4, K4, F4, M4, E5, C4 ● **Temperaments:** I, V ● **Physical:** Stg=L; Freq: R, H, I, T, G, N Occas: X ● **Work Env:** Noise=N; ● **Salary:** 3 ● **Outlook:** 3

COMMUNITY-SERVICES-AND-HEALTH-EDUCATION OFFICER (government ser.) ● DOT #079.167-010 ● OES: 19005 ● Plans and directs statewide program of public health education and promotes establishment of local health services: Directs workers engaged in preparation and distribution of health information materials, such as brochures, films, weight charts, and first-aid kits. Promotes establishment or expansion of local health services and provides technical assistance to individuals and groups conducting [health conferences, workshops, and training courses. Answers health information requests received by department or reviews correspondence prepared by others. Coordinates special health education campaigns during epidemics, rabies outbreaks, instances of food poisoning, and similar emergencies. May direct health education activities in public schools. ● **GED:** R6, M5, L6 ● **SVP:** 4-10 yrs ● **Academic:** Ed=B, Eng=S ● **Work Field:** 295 ● **MPSMS:** 920 ● **Aptitudes:** G2, V2, N3, S3, P3, Q4, K4, F4, M5, E5, C5 ● **Temperaments:** D, J, P ● **Physical:** Stg=S; Freq: R, H, I, T, G, N ● **Work Env:** Noise=N; ● **Salary:** 5 ● **Outlook:** 3

DIRECTOR, NURSING SERVICE (medical ser.) ● DOT #075.117-022 ● OES: 19998 ● Administers nursing program in hospital, nursing home, or other medical facility to maintain standards of patient care, and advises medical staff, department heads, and administrators in matters related to nursing service: Recommends establishment or revision of policies and develops organizational structure and standards of performance. Interprets policies and objectives of nursing service to staff and community groups. Promotes working relationships with community agencies and with other establishment departments. Assists in preparation of departmental budget. Establishes personnel qualification requirements, drafts procedure manuals, initiates in-service programs, installs record and reporting system, and performs other personnel management tasks. Initiates studies to evaluate effectiveness of nursing services in relation to their objectives and costs. May assist nursing schools with curricular problems. ● **GED:** R5, M4, L5 ● **SVP:** 4-10 yrs ● **Academic:** Ed=A, Eng=G ● **Work Field:** 295 ● **MPSMS:** 924 ● **Aptitudes:** G2, V2, N2, S4, P4, Q2, K4, F4, M4, E5, C5 ● **Temperaments:** D, P, V ● **Physical:** Stg=S; Freq: T, G, N Occas: R, H, I ● **Work Env:** Noise=N; ● **Salary:** 5 ● **Outlook:** 4

EMERGENCY MEDICAL SERVICES COORDINATOR (medical ser.) ● DOT #079.117-010 ● OES: 19998 ● Directs medical emergency service program: Coordinates activities of persons involved in rescue, transportation, and care of accident or catastrophe victims, and others requiring emergency medical assistance. Arranges for establishment of emergency medical facilities, staffing of facilities by emergency-trained medical and auxiliary personnel, installation of telecommunication network components, and acquisition of emergency vehicles. Maintains records of facilities and personnel, and periodically inspects facilities to ensure capability of meeting area's emergency needs. Maintains telecommunication contact with mobile and stationary units comprising emergency service network to coordinate activities of personnel, enlist services of other protective agencies, or provide alternate directions to onscene emergency personnel when planned procedures are not feasible. Develops, plans, and participates in training programs for ambulance and rescue personnel. Cooperates with schools and community organizations to encourage public interest in and knowledge of basic and advanced first aid training, and assists groups in development and presentation of classes. Maintains records of emergency medical service activities, for coordination with records prepared by cooperating institutions, to provide data for evaluation of program. Prepares reports stating progress, problems, and plans for future implementation of emergency service for community or area, for review by officials of sponsoring agency. Confers with coordinators of emergency programs in other areas to discuss problems, coordinate activities, and cooperate in area or statewide plans. ● **GED:** R4, M4, L4 ● **SVP:** 4-10 yrs ● **Academic:** Ed=A, Eng=G ● **Work Field:** 295 ● **MPSMS:** 920, 929 ● **Aptitudes:** G2, V2, N3, S3, P3, Q3, K4, F4, M4, E5, C5 ● **Temperaments:** D, P ● **Physical:** Stg=L; Freq: T, G, N Occas: R, H ● **Work Env:** Noise=N; ● **Salary:** 5 ● **Outlook:** 4

MEDICAL-RECORD ADMINISTRATOR (medical ser.) ● DOT #079.167-014 ● OES: 19998 ● Plans, develops, and administers health information system for health care facility consistent with standards of accrediting and regulatory agencies and requirements of health care system: Develops and implements policies and procedures for documenting, storing, and retrieving information, and for processing medical-legal documents, insurance data, and correspondence requests, in conformance with federal, state, and local statutes. Supervises staff, directly or through subordinates, in preparing and analyzing medical documents. Participates in development and design of computer software for computerized health information system. Coordinates medi-

cal care evaluation with medical staff and develops criteria and methods for such evaluation. Develops in-service educational materials and conducts instructional programs for health care personnel. Analyzes patient data for reimbursement, facility planning, quality of patient care, risk management, utilization management, and research. May manage medical records department and be known as Director, Medical Records (medical ser.). ● **GED:** R6, M5, L6 ● **SVP:** 4-10 yrs ● **Academic:** Ed=B, Eng=G ● **Work Field:** 295 ● **MPSMS:** 933 ● **Aptitudes:** G1, V2, N2, S3, P3, Q2, K4, F4, M4, E5, C5 ● **Temperaments:** D, J, P ● **Physical:** Stg=L; Freq: R, H, I, T, G, N ● **Work Env:** Noise=Q; ● **Salary:** 3 ● **Outlook:** 4

PUBLIC HEALTH EDUCATOR (profess. & kin.) ● DOT #079.117-014 ● OES: 31398 ● Plans, organizes, and directs health education programs for group and community needs: Conducts community surveys and collaborates with other health specialists and civic groups to ascertain health needs, develop desirable health goals, and determine availability of professional health services. Develops and maintains cooperation between public, civic, professional, and voluntary agencies. Prepares and disseminates educational and informational materials. Promotes health discussions in schools, industry, and community agencies. May plan for and provide educational opportunities for health personnel. ● **GED:** R5, M4, L5 ● **SVP:** 4-10 yrs ● **Academic:** Ed=M, Eng=G ● **Work Field:** 271, 282 ● **MPSMS:** 920 ● **Aptitudes:** G1, V1, N3, S3, P4, Q3, K4, F4, M4, E4, C4 ● **Temperaments:** D, I, J, P ● **Physical:** Stg=L; Freq: T, G ● **Work Env:** Noise=N; Occas: W ● **Salary:** 3 ● **Outlook:** 3

RADIOLOGY ADMINISTRATOR (medical ser.) ● DOT #187.117-062 ● OES: 13014 ● Plans, directs, and coordinates administrative activities of radiology department of hospital medical center: Conducts studies and implements changes to improve internal operations of department. Advises staff and supervisors on administrative changes. Assists hospital officials in preparation of department budget. Conducts specified classes and provides training material to assist in student training program. Directs and coordinates personnel activities of department. Recommends cost saving methods and hospital supply changes to effect economy of department operations. Interprets, prepares, and distributes statistical data regarding department operations. ● **GED:** R5, M5, L5 ● **SVP:** 2-4 yrs ● **Academic:** Ed=A, Eng=G ● **Work Field:** 295 ● **MPSMS:** 925 ● **Aptitudes:** G2, V2, N2, S4, P3, Q2, K5, F4, M4, E5, C4 ● **Temperaments:** D, I, P, V ● **Physical:** Stg=S; Freq: T, G Occas: R, H, I, N, A, X ● **Work Env:** Noise=N; ● **Salary:** 4 ● **Outlook:** 3

UTILIZATION-REVIEW COORDINATOR (medical ser.) ● DOT #079.267-010 ● OES: 32998 ● Analyzes patient records to determine legitimacy of admission, treatment, and length of stay in health-care facility to comply with government and insurance company reimbursement policies: Analyzes insurance, governmental, and accrediting agency standards to determine criteria concerning admissions, treatment, and length of stay of patients. Reviews application for patient admission and approves admission or refers case to facility utilization review committee for review and course of action when case fails to meet admission standards. Compares inpatient medical records to established criteria and confers with medical and nursing personnel and other professional staff to determine legitimacy of treatment and length of stay. Abstracts data from records and maintains statistics. Determines patient review dates according to established diagnostic criteria. May assist review committee in planning and holding federally mandated quality assurance reviews. May supervise and coordinate activities of utilization review staff. ● **GED:** R5, M4, L5 ● **SVP:** 2-4 yrs ● **Academic:** Ed=B, Eng=G ● **Work Field:** 295, 294 ● **MPSMS:** 920 ● **Aptitudes:** G2, V2, N2, S4, P4, Q2, K4, F4, M4, E5, C5 ● **Temperaments:** D, J, P ● **Physical:** Stg=L; Freq: T, G, N Occas: R, H, I ● **Work Env:** Noise=N; ● **Salary:** 4 ● **Outlook:** 4

GOE: 11.07.03

Education Services

ACADEMIC DEAN (education) ● DOT #090.117-010 ● OES: 15005 ● Alternate titles: ACADEMIC VICE PRESIDENT; DEAN OF INSTRUCTION; FACULTY DEAN; PROVOST; UNIVERSITY DEAN;

VICE PRESIDENT FOR INSTRUCTION. Develops academic policies and programs for college or university: Directs and coordinates activities of deans and chairpersons of individual colleges. Advises on personnel matters. Determines scheduling of courses and recommends implementation of additional courses. Coordinates activities of student advisors. Participates in activities of faculty committees, and in development of academic budget. Advises PRESIDENT, EDUCATIONAL INSTITUTION (education) on academic matters. Serves as liaison officer with accrediting agencies which evaluate academic programs. May serve as chief administrative officer in absence of PRESIDENT, EDUCATIONAL INSTITUTION (education). May provide general direction to LIBRARIAN (library); DIRECTOR OF ADMISSIONS (education); and REGISTRAR, COLLEGE OR UNIVERSITY (education). ● **GED:** R5, M3, L5 ● **SVP:** Over 10 yrs ● **Academic:** Ed=M, Eng=G ● **Work Field:** 295 ● **MPSMS:** 931 ● **Aptitudes:** G2, V1, N3, S4, P3, Q2, K4, F4, M4, E5, C5 ● **Temperaments:** D, I, J, P ● **Physical:** Stg=S; Freq: R, H, T, G, N Occas: I ● **Work Env:** Noise=N; ● **Salary:** 5 ● **Outlook:** 1

CONSULTANT, EDUCATION (education) ● DOT #099.167-014 ● OES: 31398 ● Plans and coordinates educational policies for specific subject area or grade level: Develops programs for in-service education of teaching personnel. Confers with federal, state, and local school officials to develop curricula and establish guidelines for educational programs. Confers with lay and professional groups to disseminate and receive input on teaching methods. Reviews and evaluates curricula for use in schools and assists in adaptation to local needs. Interprets and enforces provisions of state education codes and rules and regulations of State Board of Education. Conducts or participates in workshops, committees, and conferences designed to promote intellectual, social, and physical welfare of students. Studies and prepares recommendations on instructional materials, teaching aids, and related equipment. Prepares or approves manuals, guidelines, and reports on state educational policies and practices for distribution to school districts. Advises school officials on implementation of state and federal programs and procedures. Conducts research into areas, such as teaching methods and techniques. May perform tasks at local school district level or as independent consultant in area of expertise. May be designated as consultant in specific area, such as reading, elementary education, or audio-visual education. ● **GED:** R6, M6, L5 ● **SVP:** 4-10 yrs ● **Academic:** Ed=B, Eng=S ● **Work Field:** 296, 251 ● **MPSMS:** 931 ● **Aptitudes:** G2, V1, N2, S4, P4, Q1, K4, F4, M4, E5, C5 ● **Temperaments:** D, J, P ● **Physical:** Stg=S; Freq: T, G, N Occas: R, H, I ● **Work Env:** Noise=N; ● **Salary:** 4 ● **Outlook:** 4

DIRECTOR, ATHLETIC (education) ● DOT #090.117-022 ● OES: 15005 ● Plans, administers, and directs intercollegiate athletic activities in college or university: Interprets and participates in formulating extramural athletic policies. Employs and discharges coaching staff and other department employees on own initiative or at direction of board in charge of athletics. Directs preparation and dissemination of publicity to promote athletic events. Plans and coordinates activities of coaching staff. Prepares budget and authorizes department expenditures. Plans and schedules sports events, and oversees ticket sales activities. Certifies reports of income produced from ticket sales. May direct programs for students of physical education. ● **GED:** R5, M3, L5 ● **SVP:** Over 10 yrs ● **Academic:** Ed=M, Eng=G ● **Work Field:** 295, 296 ● **MPSMS:** 931 ● **Aptitudes:** G2, V2, N3, S4, P3, Q2, K4, F4, M4, E5, C5 ● **Temperaments:** D, J, P, V ● **Physical:** Stg=S; Freq: T, G ● **Work Env:** Noise=N; ● **Salary:** 5 ● **Outlook:** 2

DIRECTOR, DAY CARE CENTER (education) ● DOT #092.167-010 ● OES: 15005 ● Directs activities of preschool, day care center, or other child development facility to provide instruction and care for children: Prepares and submits facility budget to board of trustees, administrative agency, or owner for approval. Authorizes purchase of instructional materials and teaching aids, such as books, toys, and games designed to stimulate learning. Interviews and recommends hiring of teaching and service staff. Confers with parents regarding facility activities, policies, and enrollment procedures. Confers with teaching staff regarding child's behavioral or learning problems, and recommends methods of modifying inappropriate behavior and encouraging learning experiences. Reviews and evaluates facility activities to ensure conformance to state and local regulations. Reviews and approves menu plans and food purchases. May arrange medical attention for ill or injured child in accordance with parental instructions. May perform class-

room teaching duties during absence of regular teacher. May be designated Director, Child Development Center (education); Director, Nursery School (education). ● **GED:** R4, M3, L4 ● **SVP:** 2-4 yrs ● **Academic:** Ed=H, Eng=G ● **Work Field:** 295 ● **MPSMS:** 941 ● **Aptitudes:** G2, V2, N3, S4, P4, Q3, K4, F4, M4, E5, C5 ● **Temperaments:** D, I, P ● **Physical:** Stg=S; Freq: R, H, I, T, G, N ● **Work Env:** Noise=N; ● **Salary:** 4 ● **Outlook:** 1

DIRECTOR, EDUCATIONAL PROGRAM (education) ● DOT #099.117-010 ● OES: 15005 ● Plans, develops, and administers programs to provide educational opportunities for students: Cooperates with business, civic, and other organizations to develop curriculums to meet needs and interests of students and community. Interviews and selects staff members and provides in-service training for teachers. Prepares budget and determines allocation of funds for staff, supplies and equipment, and facilities. Analyzes data from questionaires, interviews, and group discussions to evaluate curriculums, teaching methods, and community participation in educational and other programs. May direct preparation of publicity to promote activities, such as personnel recruitment, educational programs or other services. May specialize in elementary, secondary, adult, or junior college education. ● **GED:** R5, M3, L5 ● **SVP:** 4-10 yrs ● **Academic:** Ed=M, Eng=G ● **Work Field:** 295 ● **MPSMS:** 931 ● **Aptitudes:** G2, V2, N2, S4, P3, Q2, K4, F4, M4, E5, C5 ● **Temperaments:** D, J, P ● **Physical:** Stg=S; Freq: R, H, I, T, G, N, A ● **Work Env:** Noise=N; ● **Salary:** 5 ● **Outlook:** 2

DIRECTOR, SPECIAL EDUCATION (education) ● DOT #094.167-014 ● OES: 15005 ● Alternate titles: ADMINISTRATIVE ASSISTANT, SPECIAL EDUCATION; ASSISTANT SUPERINTENDENT, SPECIAL EDUCATION. Directs and coordinates special education programs in public school systems, public agencies, and state institutions to teach students with mental or physical disabilities: Formulates policies and procedures for new or revised programs or activities, such as screening, placement, education, and training of students. Evaluates special education programs to ensure that objectives for student education are met. Interprets laws, rules, and regulations to students, parents, and staff. Recruits, selects, and evaluates staff. Prepares budget and solicits funds to provide financial support for programs. Prepares reports for federal, state, and local regulatory agencies. May contract with agencies for needed services, such as residential care. May administer achievement tests to measure student level of performance. ● **GED:** R6, M5, L5 ● **SVP:** 4-10 yrs ● **Academic:** Ed=M, Eng=G ● **Work Field:** 295 ● **MPSMS:** 931 ● **Aptitudes:** G2, V2, N2, S4, P4, Q2, K4, F4, M4, E5, C5 ● **Temperaments:** D, J, P ● **Physical:** Stg=S; Freq: T, G Occas: R, H, I, N ● **Work Env:** Noise=N; ● **Salary:** 5 ● **Outlook:** 2

DIRECTOR, VOCATIONAL TRAINING (education) ● DOT #097.167-010 ● OES: 15005 ● Directs and coordinates vocational training programs for public school system, according to board of education policies and state education code: Confers with members of industrial and business communities to determine human resource training needs for apprenticeable and nonapprenticeable occupations. Reviews and interprets federal and state vocational education codes to ensure that program conforms to legislation. Prepares budget and funding allocations for vocational programs. Reviews and approves new programs. Evaluates apprenticeable and nonapprenticeable programs, considering factors, such as selection, training, and placement of enrollees. Plans and develops joint programs in conjunction with other members of education staff. Organizes committees to provide technical and advisory assistance to programs. Coordinates on-the-job training programs with employers, and evaluates progress of enrollees in conjunction with program contract goals. ● **GED:** R5, M3, L5 ● **SVP:** 4-10 yrs ● **Academic:** Ed=B, Eng=G ● **Work Field:** 295, 296 ● **MPSMS:** 931 ● **Aptitudes:** G2, V2, N3, S4, P3, Q2, K4, F4, M4, E5, C5 ● **Temperaments:** D, J, P ● **Physical:** Stg=S; Freq: R, H, I, T, G, N ● **Work Env:** Noise=N; ● **Salary:** 5 ● **Outlook:** 4

DIRECTOR OF ADMISSIONS (education) ● DOT #090.167-014 ● OES: 15005 ● Alternate titles: DEAN OF ADMISSIONS. Directs and coordinates admissions program of public or private college or university, according to policies developed by governing board: Directs program of admissions counseling and reviews exceptional admissions cases. Confers with staff of other schools to explain admission requirements and student transfer credit policies. Evaluates courses offered by other schools to determine their equivalency to courses offered on campus. Directs preparation of printed materials explaining admission requirements and transfer credit policies for dissemination to other schools. May counsel students having problems relating to admissions or may supervise professionally trained admissions counseling staff. May serve on policy making admissions committee. May participate in or conduct student recruitment programs with other members of faculty and staff. May administer financial aid programs. ● **GED:** R5, M3, L5 ● **SVP:** 4-10 yrs ● **Academic:** Ed=M, Eng=G ● **Work Field:** 295 ● **MPSMS:** 931 ● **Aptitudes:** G2, V2, N3, S4, P3, Q2, K4, F4, M4, E5, C5 ● **Temperaments:** D, P ● **Physical:** Stg=S; Freq: T, G, N Occas: R, H, I ● **Work Env:** Noise=N; ● **Salary:** 5 ● **Outlook:** 1

DIRECTOR OF PUPIL PERSONNEL PROGRAM (education) ● DOT #099.167-034 ● OES: 15005 ● Directs pupil information data system program in support of educational services, in accordance with governmental laws and regulations for school district: Develops and maintains compliance program to meet legal requirements concerning students rights to privacy and due process of law in accordance to applicable laws and regulations. Directs and coordinates activities of clerical staff engaged in compiling, maintaining, and releasing pupil records and information. Confers with staff and reviews records management system to recommend changes to improve system, utilizing knowledge of filing methods and coding system, equipment, legal problems, and Board of Education requirements. Provides in-service training on topics, such as legal requirements concerning pupil records and information and to improve quality of report writing. Prepares departmental budget, records, and reports. ● **GED:** R5, M4, L5 ● **SVP:** 4-10 yrs ● **Academic:** Ed=M, Eng=G ● **Work Field:** 231, 295 ● **MPSMS:** 931 ● **Aptitudes:** G2, V2, N3, S4, P4, Q3, K4, F4, M4, E5, C5 ● **Temperaments:** D, J, P ● **Physical:** Stg=S; Freq: R, H, T, G, N Occas: I ● **Work Env:** Noise=N; ● **Salary:** 5 ● **Outlook:** 1

EDUCATIONAL SPECIALIST (education) ● DOT #099.167-022 ● OES: 31398 ● Alternate titles: DIRECTOR, EVALUATION AND RESEARCH. Directs research activities concerned with educational programs and services in school system: Formulates and designs procedures to determine if program objectives are being met. Develops tests to measure effectiveness of curriculum or services and to interpret pupil intellectual and social development and group and school progress. Develops questionnaires and interviews school staff and administrators to obtain information about curriculum. Evaluates data obtained from study and prepares narrative and statistical reports for dissemination to school administrators. Formulates recommendations and procedures for current and proposed units of instruction. Develops in-service training program for staff. May devise questionnaire to evaluate training program. May specialize in research activities concerned with elementary, secondary, college, or other specialized educational programs. May evaluate staff performance. May plan budget. ● **GED:** R6, M5, L5 ● **SVP:** 4-10 yrs ● **Academic:** Ed=B, Eng=G ● **Work Field:** 251 ● **MPSMS:** 931 ● **Aptitudes:** G1, V1, N3, S4, P4, Q2, K4, F4, M4, E5, C5 ● **Temperaments:** D, J, P ● **Physical:** Stg=S; Freq: T, G, N Occas: R, H, I ● **Work Env:** Noise=N; ● **Salary:** 4 ● **Outlook:** 3

FINANCIAL-AIDS OFFICER (education) ● DOT #090.117-030 ● OES: 15005 ● Alternate titles: DIRECTOR OF FINANCIAL AID AND PLACEMENTS; DIRECTOR OF STUDENT AID. Directs scholarship, grant-in-aid, and loan programs to provide financial assistance to students in college or university: Selects candidates and determines types and amounts of aid. Organizes and oversees student financial counseling activities. Coordinates activities with other departmental staff engaged in issuing or collecting student payments. May teach. May select financial aid candidates as members of committee and be designated Chairperson, Scholarship And Loan Committee (education). ● **GED:** R5, M3, L5 ● **SVP:** 4-10 yrs ● **Academic:** Ed=B, Eng=G ● **Work Field:** 295 ● **MPSMS:** 931 ● **Aptitudes:** G2, V2, N2, S4, P4, Q2, K4, F4, M4, E5, C5 ● **Temperaments:** D, P ● **Physical:** Stg=S; Freq: T, G, N Occas: R, H, I ● **Work Env:** Noise=N; ● **Salary:** 4 ● **Outlook:** 4

LABORATORY MANAGER (education) ● DOT #090.164-010 ● OES: 31398 ● Coordinates activities of university science laboratory to assist faculty in teaching and research programs: Consults with faculty laboratory coordinator to determine equipment purchase priorities based on budget allowances, condition of existing equipment, and scheduled laboratory activities. Prepares and puts in place equipment scheduled for use during laboratory teaching sessions. Demonstrates care

and use of equipment to teaching assistants. Builds prototype equipment, applying electromechanical knowledge and using handtools and power tools. Trains teaching staff and students in application and use of new equipment. Diagnoses equipment malfunctions and dismantles and repairs equipment, applying knowledge of shop mechanics and using gauges, meters, handtools, and power tools. Develops methods of laboratory experimentation, applying knowledge of scientific theory and computer capability. Confers with teaching staff periodically to evaluate new equipment and methods. Teaches laboratory sessions in absence of teaching assistant. ● **GED:** R5, M5, L4 ● **SVP:** 2-4 yrs ● **Academic:** Ed=B, Eng=G ● **Work Field:** 296 ● **MPSMS:** 931 ● **Aptitudes:** G2, V2, N2, S2, P2, Q4, K4, F4, M3, E5, C4 ● **Temperaments:** J, P, T ● **Physical:** Stg=L; Freq: R, H, T, G, N Occas: I, D, A, X ● **Work Env:** Noise=L; Occas: M ● **Salary:** 4 ● **Outlook:** 3

MUSIC SUPERVISOR (education) ● DOT #099.167-026 ● OES: 31398 ● Directs and coordinates activities of teaching personnel engaged in instructing students in vocal and instrumental music in school system: Consults with teaching and administrative staff to plan and develop music education curriculum. Observes, evaluates, and recommends changes in work of teaching staff to strengthen teaching skills in classroom. Analyzes music education program to evaluate instructional methods and materials. Orders instructional materials, supplies, equipment, and visual aids designed to meet training needs of students. Authorizes purchase of musical instruments for school system. Inspects and authorizes repair of instruments. Establishes interschool orchestra, band, and choral group to represent schools at civic and community events. ● **GED:** R5, M2, L5 ● **SVP:** 4-10 yrs ● **Academic:** Ed=A, Eng=G ● **Work Field:** 295 ● **MPSMS:** 756, 931 ● **Aptitudes:** G2, V2, N3, S3, P3, Q2, K4, F4, M4, E5, C5 ● **Temperaments:** D, I, J, P ● **Physical:** Stg=S; Freq: T, G, N Occas: R, H, I ● **Work Env:** Noise=N; ● **Salary:** 5 ● **Outlook:** 2

PARK NATURALIST (government ser.) ● DOT #049.127-010 ● OES: 24302 ● Plans, develops, and conducts programs to inform public of historical, natural, and scientific features of national, state, or local park: Confers with park staff to determine subjects to be presented and program schedule. Surveys park to determine forest conditions and distribution and abundance of fauna and flora. Interviews specialists in desired fields to obtain and develop data for programs. Takes photographs and motion pictures to illustrate lectures and publications and to develop displays. Plans and develops audiovisual devices, prepares and presents illustrated lectures, constructs visitor-center displays, and conducts field trips to point out scientific, historic, and natural features of park. Performs emergency duties to protect human life, government property, and natural features of park. May plan, organize, and direct activities of seasonal staff members. May maintain official photographic and informational files for department. ● **GED:** R5, M4, L5 ● **SVP:** 2-4 yrs ● **Academic:** Ed=B, Eng=G ● **Work Field:** 282, 251 ● **MPSMS:** 959, 919 ● **Aptitudes:** G2, V2, N4, S2, P2, Q2, K3, F4, M3, E3, C3 ● **Temperaments:** D, J, P, V ● **Physical:** Stg=M; Freq: R, H, T, G, N Occas: I, F, D, X, V ● **Work Env:** Noise=L; Occas: W, O ● **Salary:** 3 ● **Outlook:** 3

PRESIDENT, EDUCATIONAL INSTITUTION (education) ● DOT #090.117-034 ● OES: 19005 ● Alternate titles: CHANCELLOR. Formulates plans and programs for and directs administration of college, school, or university, within authority delegated by governing board: Confers with board of control to plan and initiate programs concerning organizational, operational, and academic functions of campus, and oversees their execution. Administers fiscal and physical planning activities, such as development of budget and building expansion programs, and recommends their adoption. Negotiates with administrative officials and representatives of business, community, and civic groups to promote educational, research, and public service objectives and policies of institution as formulated by board of control. Establishes operational procedures, rules, and standards relating to faculty and staff classification standards, financial disbursements, and accounting requirements. Represents campus on board of control and at formal functions. May be designated according to type of institution presided over as President, Business School (education); President, College Or University (education). ● **GED:** R5, M3, L5 ● **SVP:** Over 10 yrs ● **Academic:** Ed=M, Eng=G ● **Work Field:** 295 ● **MPSMS:** 931 ● **Aptitudes:** G1, V1, N2, S2, P3, Q2, K4, F4, M4, E5, C5 ● **Temperaments:** D, J, P, V ● **Physical:** Stg=S; Freq: R, H, I, T, G, N ● **Work Env:** Noise=N; ● **Salary:** 5 ● **Outlook:** 1

PRINCIPAL (education) ● DOT #099.117-018 ● OES: 15005 ● Directs and co ordinates educational, administrative, and counseling activities of primary or secondary school: Develops and evaluates educational program to ensure conformance to state and school board standards. Develops and coordinates educational programs through meetings with staff, review of teachers' activities, and issuance of directives. Confers with teachers, students, and parents concerning educational and behavioral problems in school. Establishes and maintains relationships with colleges, community organizations, and other schools to coordinate educational services. Requisitions and allocates supplies, equipment, and instructional material as needed. Directs preparation of class schedules, cumulative records, and attendance reports. Observes and evaluates teacher performance. Interviews and hires teachers. Walks about school building and property to monitor safety and security. Plans and monitors school budget. May plan and direct building maintenance. May develop and administer educational programs for students with mental or physical handicaps. May be required to have certification from state. ● **GED:** R5, M3, L5 ● **SVP:** 4-10 yrs ● **Academic:** Ed=M, Eng=G ● **Work Field:** 295 ● **MPSMS:** 931 ● **Aptitudes:** G2, V2, N2, S4, P4, Q3, K4, F4, M4, E5, C5 ● **Temperaments:** D, J, P, V ● **Physical:** Stg=L; Freq: T, G, N Occas: R, H, I, F ● **Work Env:** Noise=N; ● **Salary:** 5 ● **Outlook:** 4

REGISTRAR, COLLEGE OR UNIVERSITY (education) ● DOT #090.167-030 ● OES: 15005 ● Alternate titles: DIRECTOR OF ADMISSIONS. Directs and coordinates college or university registration activities: Consults with other officials to devise registration schedules and procedures. Analyzes statistical data on registration for administrative use in formulating policies. Exchanges student information with other colleges or universities. Directs preparation of student transcripts. Prepares commencement list. Directs preparation of statistical reports on educational activities for government and educational agencies and interprets registration policies to faculty and students. Directs activities of workers engaged in transcribing and evaluating academic records of students applying for permission to enter college or university. Directs compilation of information, such as class schedules and graduation requirements, for publication in school bulletins and catalogs. Coordinates dissemination of information on courses offered and procedures students are required to follow in order to obtain grade transcripts. Issues official transcripts. Coordinates class schedules with room assignments for optimum use of buildings and equipment. May assign rooms for student activities. ● **GED:** R5, M5, L5 ● **SVP:** 4-10 yrs ● **Academic:** Ed=M, Eng=G ● **Work Field:** 232, 295 ● **MPSMS:** 891, 931 ● **Aptitudes:** G2, V2, N2, S4, P3, Q2, K4, F4, M4, E5, C5 ● **Temperaments:** D, J, P ● **Physical:** Stg=S; Freq: R, H, I, T, G, N, A ● **Work Env:** Noise=N; ● **Salary:** 5 ● **Outlook:** 1

SUPERVISOR, CONTRACT-SHELTERED WORKSHOP (nonprofit org.) ● DOT #187.134-010 ● OES: 27310 ● Supervises and co ordinates activities of handicapped individuals in sheltered workshop to train and improve vocational skills for gainful employment through productive work: Assigns individual to specific tasks, such as cleaning, sorting, assembling, repairing, or hand packing products or components. Demonstrates job duties to handicapped individual and observes worker performing tasks to ensure understanding of job duties. Monitors work performance at each individual's work station to ensure compliance with procedures and safety regulations and to note behavior deviations. Examines workpiece visually to verify adherence to specifications. Confers with individuals to explain or to demonstrate task again to resolve work related difficulties. Reassigns individual to simpler tasks when worker cannot perform assigned tasks, or to tasks containing higher degrees of complexity as level of competence is reached. Performs other duties described under SUPERVISOR (any industry) Master Title. ● **GED:** R4, M3, L3 ● **SVP:** 2-4 yrs ● **Academic:** Ed=A, Eng=G ● **Work Field:** 296 ● **MPSMS:** 931 ● **Aptitudes:** G3, V3, N3, S3, P3, Q3, K3, F3, M3, E4, C5 ● **Temperaments:** D, J, P, V ● **Physical:** Stg=L; Freq: R, H, T, G Occas: I, N ● **Work Env:** Noise=N; ● **Salary:** 4 ● **Outlook:** 1

SUPERINTENDENT, SCHOOLS (education) ● DOT #099.117-022 ● OES: 19005 ● Directs and coordinates activities concerned with administration of city, county, or other school system in accordance with board of education standards: Formulates plans and policies for educational program and submits them to school board for approval. Administers program for selection of school sites, construction of buildings, and provision of equipment and supplies. Directs preparation and presentation of school budget and determines amount of school bond issues required to finance educational program. Addresses community and civic groups to enlist their support. Interprets program and policies of school system to school personnel, to individuals and community groups, and to governmental agencies. Coordinates work of school system with related activities of other school districts and agencies. May ensure that laws applying to attendance of children at school are enforced. May supervise examining, appointing, training, and promotion of teaching personnel. May specialize in areas, such as personnel services, curriculum development, or business administration. ● **GED:** R5, M3, L5 ● **SVP:** Over 10 yrs ● **Academic:** Ed=M, Eng=G ● **Work Field:** 295 ● **MPSMS:** 931 ● **Aptitudes:** G2, V1, N2, S4, P2, Q2, K4, F4, M4, E5, C5 ● **Temperaments:** D, I, J ● **Physical:** Stg=S; Freq: T, G, N Occas: R, H, I ● **Work Env:** Noise=N; ● **Salary:** 5 ● **Outlook:** 1

TECHNICAL TRAINING COORDINATOR (education) ● DOT #166.167-054 ● OES: 21511 ● Coordinates activities of instructors engaged in training employees or customers of industrial or commercial establishment: Confers with managers, instructors, or customer's representative to determine training needs. Assigns instructors to conduct training. Schedules classes, based on availability of classrooms, equipment, and instructors. Evaluates training packages, including outline, text, and handouts written by instructors. Assigns instructors to in-service or out-service training classes to learn new skills as needed. Monitors budget to ensure that training costs do not exceed allocated funds. Writes budget report listing training costs, such as instructors' wages and equipment costs, to justify expenditures. Attends meetings and seminars to obtain information useful to training staff and to inform management of training programs and goals. Monitors instructors during lectures and laboratory demonstrations to evaluate performance. May perform other duties as described under SUPERVISOR (any industry) Master Title. May develop and conduct training programs for employees or customers of industrial or commercial establishment [INSTRUCTOR, TECHNICAL TRAINING (education) 166.221-010]. ● **GED:** R5, M3, L5 ● **SVP:** 4-10 yrs ● **Academic:** Ed=A, Eng=S ● **Work Field:** 295 ● **MPSMS:** 931 ● **Aptitudes:** G2, V2, N3, S4, P3, Q3, K4, F4, M4, E5, C5 ● **Temperaments:** D, J, P ● **Physical:** Stg=L; Const: T, G, N Freq: R, H, I ● **Work Env:** Noise=N; ● **Salary:** 3 ● **Outlook:** 3

VOCATIONAL REHABILITATION CONSULTANT (government ser.) ● DOT #094.117-018 ● OES: 31398 ● Develops and coordinates implementation of vocational rehabilitation programs: Consults with members of local communities and personnel of rehabilitation facilities, such as sheltered workshops and skills training centers, to identify need for new programs or modification of existing programs. Collects and analyzes data to define problems and develops proposals for programs to provide needed services, utilizing knowledge of vocational rehabilitation theory and practice, program funding sources, and government regulations. Provides staff training, negotiates contracts for equipment and supplies, and performs related functions to implement program changes. Monitors program operations and recommends additional measures to ensure programs meet defined needs. ● **GED:** R5, M4, L5 ● **SVP:** 4-10 yrs ● **Academic:** Ed=M, Eng=G ● **Work Field:** 251, 295 ● **MPSMS:** 931, 940 ● **Aptitudes:** G2, V2, N2, S3, P4, Q2, K4, F4, M4, E5, C5 ● **Temperaments:** D, J, P ● **Physical:** Stg=S; Freq: T, G, N Occas: R, H, I ● **Work Env:** Noise=N; ● **Salary:** 4 ● **Outlook:** 4

GOE: 11.07.04
Recreation Services

LIBRARY CONSULTANT (library) ● DOT #100.117-014 ● OES: 21905 ● Advises administrators of public libraries: Analyzes administrative policies, observes work procedures, and reviews data relative to book collections to determine effectiveness of library service to public. Compares allocations for building funds, salaries, and book collections with statewide and national standards, to determine effectiveness of fiscal operations. Gathers statistical data, such as population and community growth rates, and analyzes building plans to determine adequacy of programs for expansion. Prepares evaluation of library systems based on observations and surveys, and recommends measures to improve organization and administration of systems. ● **GED:**

R6, M4, L6 ● **SVP:** 4-10 yrs ● **Academic:** Ed=B, Eng=G ● **Work Field:** 295 ● **MPSMS:** 933 ● **Aptitudes:** G1, V1, N3, S4, P3, Q2, K4, F4, M4, E5, C5 ● **Temperaments:** I, P, V ● **Physical:** Stg=S; Freq: T, G, N ● **Work Env:** Noise=N; ● **Salary:** 1 ● **Outlook:** 3

LIBRARY DIRECTOR (library) ● DOT #100.117-010 ● OES: 15005 ● Alternate titles: LIBRARIAN, HEAD. Plans and administers program of library services: Submits recommendations on library policies and services to governing body, such as board of directors or board of trustees, and implements policy decisions. Analyzes, selects, and executes recommendations of personnel, such as department chiefs or branch supervisors. Coordinates activities of branch or departmental libraries. Analyzes and coordinates departmental budget estimates and controls expenditures to administer approved budget. Reviews and evaluates orders for books and audiovisual materials. Examines trade publications and materials, interviews publishers' representatives, and consults with others to select materials. Administers personnel regulations, interviews and appoints job applicants, rates staff performance, and promotes and discharges employees. Plans and conducts staff meetings and participates in community and professional meetings to discuss and act on library problems. Delivers book reviews and lectures to publicize library activities and services. Provides library public relations services. May examine and select materials to be discarded, repaired, or replaced. May be designated according to governmental subdivision served as City-Library Director (library); County-Library Director (library). ● **GED:** R6, M4, L5 ● **SVP:** 4-10 yrs ● **Academic:** Ed=B, Eng=G ● **Work Field:** 295 ● **MPSMS:** 933 ● **Aptitudes:** G1,

V1, N3, S4, P3, Q2, K4, F4, M4, E5, C5 ● **Temperaments:** D, J, P, V ● **Physical:** Stg=S; Freq: R, H, I, T, G, N ● **Work Env:** Noise=N; ● **Salary:** 5 ● **Outlook:** 3

RECREATION SUPERVISOR (profess. & kin.) ● DOT #187.167-238 ● OES: 27311 ● Alternate titles: AREA SUPERVISOR; DISTRICT DIRECTOR; RECREATION SPECIALIST. Coordinates activities of paid and volunteer recreation service personnel in public department, voluntary agency, or similar type facility, such as community centers or swimming pools: Develops and promotes recreation program, including music, dance, arts and crafts, cultural arts, nature study, swimming, social recreation and games, or camping. Adapts recreation programs to meet needs of individual agency or institution, such as hospital, armed services, institution for children or aged, settlement house, or penal institution. Introduces new program activities, equipment, and materials to staff. Trains personnel and evaluates performance. Interprets recreation service to public and participates in community meetings and organizational planning. May work in team with administrative or other professional personnel, such as those engaged in medicine, social work, nursing, psychology, and therapy, to ensure that recreation is well balanced, coordinated, and integrated with special services. ● **GED:** R5, M3, L5 ● **SVP:** 2-4 yrs ● **Academic:** Ed=A, Eng=G ● **Work Field:** 295 ● **MPSMS:** 941, 919 ● **Aptitudes:** G1, V1, N3, S3, P3, Q4, K4, F4, M4, E4, C4 ● **Temperaments:** D, P, V ● **Physical:** Stg=L; Freq: T, G, N, F, D, A, V Occas: R, H, I, X ● **Work Env:** Noise=N; ● **Salary:** 3 ● **Outlook:** 3

Leading-Influencing   11

Communications   **11.08**

Workers in this group write, edit, report, and translate factual information. They find employment with radio and television broadcasting stations, newspapers, and publishing firms. Government agencies and professional groups provide some opportunities as do large firms which publish company newspapers and brochures.

✓ What kind of work would you do?

Your work activities would depend upon your specific job. For example, you might:

- rush to the scene of important happenings to gather information and write news stories.
- analyze news, attend public gatherings, interview public personalities, and write a column for newspapers.
- examine materials received from foreign broadcasts and select and edit them for local use.
- supervise workers who gather information and write scripts for news, special events, and public affairs broadcasts.
- gather, analyze, select, arrange, and broadcast news for a television station.
- translate spoken or written information from one language into another.

✓ What skills and abilities do you need for this kind of work?

To do this kind of work, you must be able to:

- think logically to analyze written materials, organize facts, and interpret a wide variety of subject matter.
- understand and use a large vocabulary, sometimes in a technical or scientific language.
- speak clearly and easily when interviewing people and broadcasting news events.
- speak and write in a foreign language is an occasional requirement.
- see punctuation and spelling errors in written materials.
- identify the important and newsworthy aspects of a situation.
- change assignments and duties frequently.
- accept responsibility for the direction and planning of an activity.
- use accurate grammar, punctuation, spelling, and sentence structure.
- use words so that your readers and listeners have a clear mental picture of your ideas.

✓ How do you know if you would like or could learn to do this kind of work?

The following questions may give you clues about yourself as you consider this group of jobs.

- Have you worked on a school newspaper? Can you report events accurately?
- Have you had courses in journalism or broadcasting? Did these courses increase your interests in this type of writing?

- Have you proofread term papers or compositions? Can you spot errors in punctuation, spelling, or grammar?
- Have you spoken in front of an audience? Can you speak clearly when presenting a point of view?

✓ How can you prepare for and enter this kind of work?

Occupations in this group usually require education and/or training extending from four years to over ten years, depending upon the specific kind of work. College level courses such as journalism, English, and political science are usually required. In some cases, a four-year college degree is necessary for employment. However, writing or broadcasting experience is sometimes accepted. Some jobs in this group are open to people with experience gained in high school English or journalism courses, or by working on school newspapers. Some

jobs require specific knowledge in areas such as current events, in addition to writing skills. Special courses, such as speech, may be required for some jobs.

✓ What else should you consider about these jobs?

Field work, such as that done by news reporters, will often require standing for long periods of time, walking considerable distance, and being exposed to all kinds of weather. Reporters are also exposed to hazards when reporting on fires, floods, and similar situations.

Workers in this group may be required to work nights or weekends. They are usually required to reflect the policies and points of view of their employers.

If you think you would like to do this kind of work, look at the job titles listed below.

■ ■ ■

GOE: 11.08.01
Editing

EDITOR, CITY (print. & pub.) ● DOT #132.037-014 ● OES: 34001 ● Alternate titles: CITY EDITOR; METROPOLITAN EDITOR. Directs and supervises personnel engaged in selecting, gathering, and editing local news and news photographs for edition of newspaper: Receives information regarding developing news events or originates story ideas and assigns coverage to members of reporting and photography staff. Reviews news copy and confers with executive staff members regarding allocation of news space. Sends copy to copy desk for editing. Reviews edited copy and sends to EDITOR, NEWS (print. & pub.) or composing room. May write or direct writing of headlines. May hire and discharge members of reporting staff. May perform other editorial duties as required. Designated State Editor (print. & pub.) when working with State news and National Editor (print. & pub.) when working with National news. ● **GED:** R6, M3, L6 ● **SVP:** 4-10 yrs ● **Academic:** Ed=B, Eng=G ● **Work Field:** 261 ● **MPSMS:** 757 ● **Aptitudes:** G1, V1, N3, S4, P3, Q3, K4, F4, M4, E5, C5 ● **Temperaments:** D, F, J, P, V ● **Physical:** Stg=S; Freq: R, H, T, G, N, A ● **Work Env:** Noise=Q; ● **Salary:** 4 ● **Outlook:** 3

EDITOR, DEPARTMENT (print. & pub.) ● DOT #132.037-018 ● OES: 34001 ● Supervises personnel engaged in selecting, gathering, and editing news and news photographs for one or more specialized news departments of newspaper: May select submitted material such as letters or articles for publication. May assign cartoons or editorials to staff members. May perform duties of REPORTER (print. & pub.; radio-tv broad.). May edit copy and perform related duties as required. Usually identified according to individual specialty or specialties. ● **GED:** R5, M3, L5 ● **SVP:** 4-10 yrs ● **Academic:** Ed=A, Eng=G ● **Work Field:** 261 ● **MPSMS:** 757 ● **Aptitudes:** G2, V1, N3, S4, P3, Q3, K4, F4, M4, E5, C5 ● **Temperaments:** D, F, J, P, V ● **Physical:** Stg=S; Freq: T, G, N, A ● **Work Env:** Noise=N; ● **Salary:** 4 ● **Outlook:** 2

EDITOR, DICTIONARY (profess. & kin.) ● DOT #132.067-018 ● OES: 34001 ● Alternate titles: LEXICOGRAPHER. Researches information about words that make up language and writes and reviews definitions for publication in dictionary: Conducts or directs research to discover origin, spelling, syllabication, pronunciation, meaning, and usage of words. Organizes research material and writes dictionary definition. May study or conduct surveys to determine factors, such as

frequency of use for a specific word, or word use by particular segment of population in order to select words for inclusion in dictionary. May perform related editorial duties. May select drawings or other graphic material to illustrate word meaning. May specialize in particular type of dictionary, such as medical, electronic, or industrial. ● **GED:** R6, M3, L6 ● **SVP:** 4-10 yrs ● **Academic:** Ed=B, Eng=G ● **Work Field:** 261 ● **MPSMS:** 749, 489 ● **Aptitudes:** G1, V1, N4, S4, P4, Q4, K4, F4, M4, E5, C5 ● **Temperaments:** J, T ● **Physical:** Stg=S; Freq: N ● **Work Env:** Noise=N; ● **Salary:** 5 ● **Outlook:** 2

EDITOR, NEWS (print. & pub.) ● DOT #132.067-026 ● OES: 34001 ● Alternate titles: MAKEUP EDITOR. Plans layout of newspaper edition: Receives news copy, photographs, and dummy page layouts marked to indicate columns occupied by advertising. Confers with management and editorial staff members regarding placement of developing news stories. Determines placement of stories based on relative significance, available space, and knowledge of layout principles. Marks layout sheets to indicate position of each story and accompanying photographs. Approves proofs submitted by composing room. May write or revise headlines. May edit copy. May perform related editorial duties as required. ● **GED:** R5, M3, L5 ● **SVP:** 4-10 yrs ● **Academic:** Ed=A, Eng=G ● **Work Field:** 261, 264 ● **MPSMS:** 757 ● **Aptitudes:** G2, V1, N3, S3, P3, Q3, K3, F4, M4, E5, C5 ● **Temperaments:** D, F, J, T ● **Physical:** Stg=S; Freq: R, H, T, G, N, A Occas: I ● **Work Env:** Noise=N; ● **Salary:** 5 ● **Outlook:** 3

EDITOR, NEWSPAPER (print. & pub.) ● DOT #132.017-014 ● OES: 34001 ● Alternate titles: EDITOR-IN-CHIEF, NEWSPAPER. Formulates editorial policy and directs operation of newspaper: Confers with editorial policy committee and heads of production, advertising, and circulation departments to develop editorial and operating procedures and negotiate decisions affecting publication. Appoints editorial heads and supervises work of their departments in accordance with newspaper policy. Writes leading or policy editorials or notifies editorial department head of position to be taken on specific public issues. Reviews financial reports and takes appropriate action with respect to costs and revenues. Represents publication at professional and community functions. In smaller establishments may perform duties of one or more subordinate editors and direct activities of advertising, circulation, or production personnel. ● **GED:** R6, M3, L6 ● **SVP:** Over 10 yrs ● **Academic:** Ed=B, Eng=G ● **Work Field:** 295, 261 ● **MPSMS:** 757 ● **Aptitudes:** G1, V1, N3, S3, P3, Q3, K4, F4, M4, E5, C5 ● **Temperaments:** D, F, I, J, P ● **Physical:** Stg=S; Freq: R, H, I, T, G, N Occas: A ● **Work Env:** Noise=N; ● **Salary:** 5 ● **Outlook:** 3

EDITOR, TECHNICAL AND SCIENTIFIC PUBLICATIONS (profess. & kin.) ● DOT #132.017-018 ● OES: 34001 ● Alternate titles: MANAGER, TECHNICAL AND SCIENTIFIC PUBLICATIONS; SUPERVISOR, PUBLICATIONS. Directs and coordinates activities of writers engaged in preparing technical, scientific, medical, or other material for publication in conjunction with or independent from manufacturing, research, and related activities: Analyzes developments in specific field to determine need for revisions, corrections, and changes in previously published materials, and development of new material. Confers with customer representatives, vendors, plant executives, or publisher to establish technical specifications, determine specific or general subject material to be developed for publication, and resolve problems concerned with developing and publishing subject material. Assigns staff writer or contracts with specialist in subject area to produce draft of manuscript. Supervises staff writers and delineates standard procedures for gathering data and writing. Reviews draft of manuscript and makes recommendations for changes. May edit and correct final draft to prepare for typesetting. May perform similar duties to those supervised. May select or recommend graphics, such as drawings, diagrams, pictures, and charts to illustrate manuscript. May specialize in particular type of publication, such as manuals, handbooks, articles, or proposals. ● **GED:** R6, M3, L6 ● **SVP:** Over 10 yrs ● **Academic:** Ed=B, Eng=G ● **Work Field:** 261, 295 ● **MPSMS:** 757 ● **Aptitudes:** G1, V1, N3, S3, P3, Q3, K4, F4, M4, E5, C5 ● **Temperaments:** D, F, J, P ● **Physical:** Stg=S; Freq: T, G, N Occas: R, H ● **Work Env:** Noise=Q; ● **Salary:** 5 ● **Outlook:** 2

EDITORIAL ASSISTANT (print. & pub.) ● DOT #132.267-014 ● OES: 34001 ● Alternate titles: ASSISTANT EDITOR; ASSOCIATE EDITOR. Prepares written material for publication, performing any combination of following duties: Reads copy to detect errors in spelling, punctuation, and syntax. Verifies facts, dates, and statistics, using standard reference sources. Rewrites or modifies copy to conform to publication's style and editorial policy and marks copy for typesetter, using standard symbols to indicate how type should be set. Reads galley and page proofs to detect errors and indicates corrections, using standard proofreading symbols. May confer with authors regarding changes made to manuscript. May select and crop photographs and illustrative materials to conform to space and subject matter requirements. May prepare page layouts to position and space articles and illustrations. May write or rewrite headlines, captions, columns, articles, and stories according to publication requirements. May initiate or reply to correspondence regarding material published or being considered for publication. May read and evaluate submitted manuscripts and be designated Manuscript Reader (print. & pub.). May be designated according to type of publication worked on as Copy Reader (print. & pub.) when working on newspaper; Copy Reader, Book (print. & pub.) when working on books. ● **GED:** R5, M3, L5 ● **SVP:** 2-4 yrs ● **Academic:** Ed=A, Eng=G ● **Work Field:** 261 ● **MPSMS:** 757 ● **Aptitudes:** G2, V2, N3, S3, P3, Q2, K4, F4, M4, E5, C5 ● **Temperaments:** J ● **Physical:** Stg=S; Freq: R, H, N Occas: I ● **Work Env:** Noise=Q; ● **Salary:** 4 ● **Outlook:** 3

GOE: 11.08.02
Writing

RESEARCH ASSISTANT II (profess. & kin.) ● DOT #199.267-034 ● OES: 39998 ● Alternate titles: RESEARCHER. Analyzes verbal or statistical data to prepare reports and studies for use by professional workers in variety of areas, such as science, social science, law, medicine, or politics: Searches sources, such as reference works, literature, documents, newspapers, and statistical records, to obtain data on assigned subject. Analyzes and evaluates applicability of collected data. Prepares statistical tabulations, using calculator or computer. Writes reports or presents data in formats such as abstracts, bibliographies, graphs, or maps. May interview individuals to obtain data or draft correspondence to answer inquiries. May be designated Legislative Aide (government ser.) when conducting studies to assist lawmakers. ● **GED:** R5, M3, L5 ● **SVP:** 1-2 yrs ● **Academic:** Ed=B, Eng=G ● **Work Field:** 251, 261 ● **MPSMS:** 939 ● **Aptitudes:** G2, V2, N3, S4, P4, Q2, K4, F4, M4, E5, C4 ● **Temperaments:** J, T ● **Physical:** Stg=S; Freq: H, T, G, N Occas: R, I, X ● **Work Env:** Noise=N; ● **Salary:** 3 ● **Outlook:** 4

REPORTER (print. & pub.) ● DOT #131.262-018 ● OES: 34011 ● Alternate titles: NEWSPERSON. Collects and analyzes information about newsworthy events to write news stories for publication or broadcast: Receives assignment or evaluates news leads and news tips to develop story idea. Gathers and verifies factual information regarding story through interview, observation, and research. Organizes material, determines slant or emphasis, and writes story according to prescribed editorial style and format standards. May monitor police and fire department radio communications to obtain story leads. May take photographs or shoot video to illustrate stories. May edit, or assist in editing, videos for broadcast. May appear on television program when conducting taped or filmed interviews or narration. May give live reports from site of event or mobile broadcast unit. May transmit information to NEWSWRITER (print. & pub.; radio-tv broad.) 131.262-014 for story writing. May specialize in one type of reporting, such as sports, fires, accidents, political affairs, court trials, or police activities. May be assigned to outlying areas or foreign countries and be designated Correspondent (print. & pub.; radio-tv broad.) or Foreign Correspondent (print. & pub.; radio-tv broad.). ● **GED:** R5, M3, L5 ● **SVP:** 2-4 yrs ● **Academic:** Ed=A, Eng=G ● **Work Field:** 261, 271 ● **MPSMS:** 757, 860 ● **Aptitudes:** G2, V1, N3, S4, P3, Q3, K3, F4, M4, E5, C5 ● **Temperaments:** I, J, P ● **Physical:** Stg=L; Freq: R, H, I, T, G Occas: N, A ● **Work Env:** Noise=N; ● **Salary:** 3 ● **Outlook:** 1

WRITER, TECHNICAL PUBLICATIONS (profess. & kin.) ● DOT #131.267-026 ● OES: 34001 ● Develops, writes, and edits material for reports, manuals, briefs, proposals, instruction books, catalogs, and related technical and administrative publications concerned with work methods and procedures, and installation, operation, and maintenance of machinery and other equipment: Receives assignment from supervisor. Observes production, developmental, and experimental activities to determine operating procedure and detail. Interviews production and engineering personnel and reads journals, reports, and other material to become familiar with product technologies and production methods. Reviews manufacturer's and trade catalogs, drawings and other data relative to operation, maintenance, and service of equipment. Studies blueprints, sketches, drawings, parts lists, specifications, mock ups, and product samples to integrate and delineate technology, operating procedure, and production sequence and detail. Organizes material and completes writing assignment according to set standards regarding order, clarity, conciseness, style, and terminology. Reviews published materials and recommends revisions or changes in scope, format, content, and methods of reproduction and binding. May maintain records and files of work and revisions. May select photographs, drawings, sketches, diagrams, and charts to illustrate material. May assist in laying out material for publication. May arrange for typing, duplication, and distribution of material. May write speeches, articles, and public or employee relations releases. May edit, standardize, or make changes to material prepared by other writers or plant personnel and be designated Standard-Practice Analyst (profess. & kin.). May specialize in writing material regarding work methods and procedures and be designated Process-Description Writer (profess. & kin.). ● **GED:** R5, M3, L5 ● **SVP:** 4-10 yrs ● **Academic:** Ed=A, Eng=G ● **Work Field:** 261 ● **MPSMS:** 750 ● **Aptitudes:** G2, V1, N2, S2, P3, Q2, K4, F4, M4, E5, C5 ● **Temperaments:** J, P, T ● **Physical:** Stg=S; Freq: H, I, T, G, N Occas: R ● **Work Env:** Noise=N; ● **Salary:** 5 ● **Outlook:** 4

GOE: 11.08.03
Writing & Broadcasting

COLUMNIST/COMMENTATOR (print. & pub.) ● DOT #131.067-010 ● OES: 34001 ● Analyzes news and writes column or commentary, based on personal knowledge and experience with subject matter, for publication or broadcast: Gathers information and develops subject perspective through research, interview, experience, and attendance at functions, such as political conventions, news meetings, sports events, and social activities. Analyzes and interprets information to formulate and outline story idea. Selects material most pertinent to presentation, organizes material into acceptable media form and format, and writes column or commentary. Records commentary or presents commentary live when working in broadcast medium. May be required to develop material to fit media time or space requirements. May analyze current news items and be designated News Analyst (radio-tv broad.). May be designated according to medium worked in as Columnist (print. & pub.); Commentator (radio-tv broad.). May specialize in particular field, such as sports, fashion, society, or politics. May analyze topics chosen by publication or broadcast facility editorial board. May enter information into computer to prepare commentaries. ● **GED:** R6, M3, L6 ● **SVP:** 2-4 yrs ● **Academic:** Ed=B, Eng=G ● **Work Field:** 261 ● **MPSMS:** 757, 863, 864 ● **Aptitudes:** G1, V1, N3, S4, P3, Q3, K3, F4, M4, E5, C5 ● **Temperaments:** F, I, J, P, V ● **Physical:** Stg=S; Freq: T, G Occas: R, H, I, N, A ● **Work Env:** Noise=N; ● **Salary:** 4 ● **Outlook:** 1

NEWSCASTER (radio-tv broad.) ● DOT #131.262-010 ● OES: 34010 ● Alternate titles: NEWSPERSON. Analyzes and broadcasts news received from various sources: Examines news items of local, national, and international significance to determine selection or is assigned news items for broadcast by editorial staff. Prepares or assists in preparation of script [NEWSWRITER (print. & pub.; radio-tv broad.) 131.262-014]. Presents news over radio or television. May specialize in particular field of news broadcasting, such as political, economic, or military. May gather information about newsworthy events [REPORTER (print. & pub.; radio-tv broad.) 131.262-018]. May introduce broadcasters who specialize in particular fields, such as sports or weather, and be designated Anchorperson (radio-tv broad.) or News Anchor (radio-tv broad.). ● **GED:** R5, M2, L5 ● **SVP:** 2-4 yrs ● **Academic:** Ed=A, Eng=G ● **Work Field:** 261, 282 ● **MPSMS:** 863, 864, 869 ● **Aptitudes:** G2, V1, N3, S4, P4, Q3, K3, F3, M4, E5, C5 ● **Temperaments:** I, J, P, V ● **Physical:** Stg=L; Freq: H, T, G Occas: R, I, N, A ● **Work Env:** Noise=N; ● **Salary:** 5 ● **Outlook:** 1

GOE: 11.08.04
Translating & Interpreting

CODE AND TEST CLERK (financial) ● DOT #209.667-018 ● OES: 59998 ● Verifies and assigns code numbers on telecommunications messages used in banking transactions: Reads code (test) number on incoming messages and compares code number to previously agreed-upon number to verify authenticity of message. Assigns specified code number to outgoing messages, using computer or code sheets. May translate decoded foreign language messages into English. ● **GED:** R4, M3, L4 ● **SVP:** 6 mos-1 yr ● **Academic:** Ed=N, Eng=G ● **Work Field:** 231 ● **MPSMS:** 894 ● **Aptitudes:** G3, V3, N3, S5, P3, Q3, K4, F4, M4, E5, C5 ● **Temperaments:** T ● **Physical:** Stg=S; Const: N Freq: I Occas: R, H, T, G, A ● **Work Env:** Noise=N; ● **Salary:** 1 ● **Outlook:** 3

DIRECTOR, TRANSLATION (profess. & kin.) ● DOT #137.137-010 ● OES: 39998 ● Directs and coordinates activities of INTERPRETERS (profess. & kin.) and TRANSLATORS (profess. & kin.) engaged in translating spoken passages, documents, and other material from one language to another for business establishments, government agencies, and academic institutions: Studies material, using knowledge of language and linguistics, to determine best qualified personnel for specific projects. Assigns projects to personnel and reviews work for quality. Attends meetings of groups and organizations engaged in international relations to promote translation service. Prepares budget for department and determines allocation of funds. Interviews and selects personnel for staff positions. ● **GED:** R5, M3, L5 ● **SVP:** 4-10 yrs ● **Academic:** Ed=B, Eng=G ● **Work Field:** 295 ● **MPSMS:** 749 ● **Aptitudes:** G2, V1, N2, S4, P4, Q2, K4, F4, M4, E5, C5 ● **Temperaments:** D, J, P ● **Physical:** Stg=S; Freq: T, G, N Occas: R, H, I ● **Work Env:** Noise=N; ● **Salary:** 5 ● **Outlook:** 2

INTERPRETER (profess. & kin.) ● DOT #137.267-010 ● OES: 39998 ● Translates spoken passages from one language into another: Provides consecutive or simultaneous translation between languages. In consecutive interpreting listens to complete statements in one language, translates to second, and translates responses from second into first language. Expresses either approximate or exact translation, depending on nature of occasion. In simultaneous interpreting renders oral translation of material at time it is being spoken, usually hearing material over electronic audio system and broadcasting translation to listeners. Usually receives briefing on subject discussed prior to interpreting session. May be designated according to language or languages interpreted. May specialize in specific subject area. ● **GED:** R5, M2, L5 ● **SVP:** 1-2 yrs ● **Academic:** Ed=A, Eng=G ● **Work Field:** 281, 282 ● **MPSMS:** 749 ● **Aptitudes:** G2, V1, N4, S4, P4, Q3, K4, F4, M4, E5, C5 ● **Temperaments:** J, P ● **Physical:** Stg=S; Const: T, G Freq: R, H ● **Work Env:** Noise=N; ● **Salary:** 4 ● **Outlook:** 4

TRANSLATOR (profess. & kin.) ● DOT #137.267-018 ● OES: 39998 ● Translates documents and other material from one language to another: Reads material and rewrites material in specified language or languages, following established rules pertaining to factors, such as word meanings, sentence structure, grammar, punctuation, and mechanics. May specialize in particular type of material, such as news, legal documents, or scientific reports and be designated accordingly. May be identified according to language translated. May represent or spell characters of another alphabet and be designated Transliterator (profess. & kin.). ● **GED:** R6, M3, L6 ● **SVP:** 2-4 yrs ● **Academic:** Ed=B, Eng=G ● **Work Field:** 261 ● **MPSMS:** 749 ● **Aptitudes:** G1, V1, N3, S3, P4, Q3, K4, F4, M4, E5, C5 ● **Temperaments:** J ● **Physical:** Stg=S; Freq: R, H, N Occas: I ● **Work Env:** Noise=Q; ● **Salary:** 3 ● **Outlook:** 2

Leading-Influencing   11

Promotion   11.09

Workers in this group raise money, advertise products and services, and influence people in their actions or thoughts. They find employment in business and industry, with advertising agencies, professional groups, unions, colleges, and government agencies.

✓ What kind of work would you do?

Your work activities would depend upon your specific job. For example, you might:

- promote a business or industry by speaking to groups.
- plan and direct activities in an advertising agency.

- lobby for or against legislation for an industry, organization, or profession.
- develop plans for increasing the membership of an organization.
- write news releases, scripts, and other materials for an advertising campaign.
- develop materials to help dealers and distributors plan sales campaigns.

✓ What skills and abilities do you need for this kind of work?

To do this kind of work, you must be able to:

- originate and carry out sales campaigns.
- create new ways of presenting information that will attract people's attention.

- speak and write clearly and convincingly.
- frequently change from one activity to another, for example, writing a speech, giving a speech, and writing a report of campaign progress.
- understand how different kinds of people react to words, pictures, and color.
- work with all kinds of people.

✓ How do you know if you would like or could learn to do this kind of work?

The following questions may give you clues about yourself as you consider this group of jobs.

- Have you organized and directed ticket sales for a school or community event? Can you lead others in this type of activity?
- Have you made posters for a school or community activity? Did you use your own ideas in making them?
- Have you written advertising copy for a school yearbook or community newspaper?
- Have you worked for a political campaign? Can you understand and influence the public?
- Have you made ideas, products, or services better known and more acceptable to others?

✓ How can you prepare for and enter this kind of work?

Occupations in this group usually require education and/or training extending from four years to over ten years, depending upon the specific kind of work. Education at the college level would assist in entering this field. Another way to enter these jobs is to start at a related job in a public relations agency. Special courses in oral and visual communications may sometimes be required. The time needed to gain the necessary combination of education and experience may be as long as ten years. Typing is rarely a required skill, but being able to type will make many duties easier to perform, especially those concerned with public relations.

Employers often seek workers who have a favorable reputation in the field. Workers sometimes change employers in order to get better jobs.

✓ What else should you consider about these jobs?

Deadlines and performance standards often put pressure on these workers. Long hours and weekend work are not unusual in these situations.

If you think you would like to do this kind of work, look at the job titles below.

■ ■ ■

GOE: 11.09.01
Sales

ACCOUNT EXECUTIVE (business ser.) ● DOT #164.167-010 ● OES: 13011 ● Plans, coordinates, and directs advertising campaign for clients of advertising agency: Confers with client to determine advertising requirements and budgetary limitations, utilizing knowledge of product or service to be advertised, media capabilities, and audience characteristics. Confers with agency artists, copywriters, photographers, and other media-production specialists to select media to be used and to estimate costs. Submits proposed program and estimated budget to client for approval. Coordinates activities of workers engaged in marketing research, writing copy, laying out artwork, purchasing media time and space, developing special displays and promotional items, and performing other media-production activities, in order to carry out approved campaign. ● **GED:** R5, M3, L4 ● **SVP:** 4-10 yrs ● **Academic:** Ed=B, Eng=S ● **Work Field:** 261 ● **MPSMS:** 896 ● **Aptitudes:** G2, V2, N3, S3, P3, Q3, K4, F4, M4, E5, C3 ● **Temperaments:** D, F, I, J, P ● **Physical:** Stg=S; Freq: T, G Occas: R, H, I, N, X ● **Work Env:** Noise=N; ● **Salary:** 5 ● **Outlook:** 1

CIRCULATION-SALES REPRESENTATIVE (print. & pub.) ● DOT #299.167-010 ● OES: 49998 ● Promotes and coordinates sale and distribution of newspapers in areas served by franchised wholesale distributors: Surveys urban and suburban areas to determine newspaper sales potential, using statistical tables, and recommends new outlets and locations for newsstands, street-sale racks, and carrier routes. Schedules delivery and distribution of newspapers and regulates size of orders to maintain maximum sales with minimum return of unsold papers. Evaluates dealer sales and assists dealers through sales promotion and training programs. Inspects routes to ensure prompt and regular delivery of newspapers to distributors, dealers, carriers, and vending machines. Distributes and explains circulation instructions and changes to distributors and dealers, and investigates and adjusts dealer complaints. Examines and investigates applications for sale or transfer of franchises. Investigates delinquent accounts and makes collections. Instructs drivers, dealers, and carriers in sales techniques to improve sales. Lays out home delivery routes and organizes carrier crews. Analyzes sales statistics to assist management in circulation planning. Reports on sales and activities of competitors. Writes promotional bulletins to notify dealers and carriers of special sales promotions and offers. Arranges for sale of newspapers at special events and sale of special issues and editions in case of important news breaks. ● **GED:** R4, M3, L4 ● **SVP:** 1-2 yrs ● **Academic:** Ed=N, Eng=G ● **Work Field:** 292 ● **MPSMS:** 481, 882 ● **Aptitudes:** G3, V3, N4, S4, P4, Q4, K4, F4, M4, E5, C5 ● **Temperaments:** D, I, J, P ● **Physical:** Stg=L; Freq: R, H, I, T, G, N ● **Work Env:** Noise=N; ● **Salary:** 3 ● **Outlook:** 3

FASHION COORDINATOR (retail trade) ● DOT #185.157-010 ● OES: 13011 ● Alternate titles: FASHION STYLIST. Promotes new fashions and coordinates promotional activities, such as fashion shows, to induce consumer acceptance: Studies fashion and trade journals, travels to garment centers, attends fashion shows, and visits manufacturers and merchandise markets to obtain information on fashion trends. Consults with buying personnel to gain advice regarding type of fashions store will purchase and feature for season. Advises publicity and display departments of merchandise to be publicized. Selects garments and accessories to be shown at fashion shows. Provides information on current fashions, style trends, and use of accessories. May contract with models, musicians, caterers, and other personnel to manage staging of shows. May conduct teenage fashion shows and direct activities of store-sponsored club for teenage girls. ● **GED:** R5, M4, L5 ● **SVP:** 2-4 yrs ● **Academic:** Ed=H, Eng=G ● **Work Field:** 292 ● **MPSMS:** 881 ● **Aptitudes:** G2, V2, N3, S4, P3, Q4, K4, F4, M4, E5, C3 ● **Temperaments:** I, J, P ● **Physical:** Stg=L; Freq: R, H, I, T, G, N, F, D, A, X, V Occas: E ● **Work Env:** Noise=N; ● **Salary:** 4 ● **Outlook:** 1

GOODWILL AMBASSADOR (business ser.) ● DOT #293.357-018 ● OES: 49998 ● Alternate titles: WELCOME-WAGON HOST/HOSTESS. Promotes goodwill and solicits trade for local business firms who are members of parent organization: Develops list of prospective clients from such sources as newspaper items, utility companies' records, and local merchants. Visits homes of new residents, prospective parents, recently married couples, engaged persons, and other prospects to explain and sell services available from local merchants. Usually presents token gifts or gift certificates to induce clients to use local services or purchase local merchandise. Prepares reports of services rendered and visits made for parent organization and member firms. May solicit new organization membership. May explain community services available. May organize clubs and plan parties for new residents. ● **GED:** R3, M2, L3 ● **SVP:** 2-30 days ● **Academic:** Ed=N, Eng=G ● **Work Field:** 292 ● **MPSMS:** 896 ● **Aptitudes:** G3, V3, N4, S4, P4, Q3, K4, F4, M4, E5, C5 ● **Temperaments:** I, P ● **Physical:** Stg=L; Freq: R, H, I, T, G, N ● **Work Env:** Noise=N; ● **Salary:** 2 ● **Outlook:** 2

MANAGER, ADVERTISING (any industry) ● DOT #164.117-010 ● OES: 13011 ● Alternate titles: DIRECTOR, ADVERTISING; SALES PROMOTION DIRECTOR. Plans and executes advertising policies of organization: Confers with department heads to discuss possible new accounts and to outline new policies or sales promotion campaigns. Confers with officials of newspapers, radio, and television stations, billboard advertisers, and advertising agencies to negotiate advertising contracts. Allocates advertising space to departments or products of establishment. Reviews and approves television and radio advertisements before release. Reviews rates and classifications applicable to various types of advertising and provides authorization. Directs workers in advertising department engaged in developing and producing advertisements. Directs research activities concerned with gathering information or with compilation of statistics pertinent to planning and execution of advertising sales promotion campaign. May authorize information for publication, such as interviews with reporters or articles describing phases of establishment activity. May serve as establishment representative for geographical district or department. May transact business as agent for advertising accounts. May direct preparation of special promotional features. May monitor and analyze sales promotion results to determine cost effectiveness of promotion campaign. ● **GED:** R6, M5, L5 ● **SVP:** 4-10 yrs ● **Academic:** Ed=B, Eng=S ● **Work Field:** 292, 295 ● **MPSMS:** 880 ● **Aptitudes:** G2, V2, N2, S3, P4, Q4, K4, F4, M4, E5, C5 ● **Temperaments:** D, J, P, V ● **Physical:** Stg=S; Freq: R, H, T, G, N ● **Work Env:** Noise=N; ● **Salary:** 5 ● **Outlook:** 3

MANAGER, ADVERTISING (print. & pub.) ● DOT #163.167-010 ● OES: 13011 ● Directs sale of display and classified advertising services for a publication: Plans sales campaigns. Consults with department heads and other officials to plan special campaigns and to promote sale of advertising services to various industry or trade groups. Corresponds with customers relative to advertising rates and policies, or to solicit new business. May select and train new sales personnel. May be designated according to type of advertising sold as Manager, Classified Advertising (print. & pub.); Manager, Display Advertising (print. & pub.); or area or region served as Manager, Local Advertising (print. & pub.); Manager, National Advertising (print. & pub.). ● **GED:** R5, M3, L5 ● **SVP:** 4-10 yrs ● **Academic:** Ed=A, Eng=G ● **Work Field:** 292 ● **MPSMS:** 896 ● **Aptitudes:** G2, V2, N2, S3, P3, Q3, K4, F4, M4, E5, C5 ● **Temperaments:** D, J, P ● **Physical:** Stg=S; Freq: R, H, I, T, G, N ● **Work Env:** Noise=N; ● **Salary:** 5 ● **Outlook:** 3

MANAGER, ADVERTISING AGENCY (business ser.) ● DOT #164.117-014 ● OES: 13011 ● Directs activities of advertising agency: Formulates plans to extend business with established accounts, to solicit new accounts, and to establish new advertising policies and procedures. Coordinates activities of departments, such as sales, graphic arts, media, finance, and research. Inspects layouts and advertising copy, and edits radio and television scripts for adherence to specifications. Conducts meetings with agency personnel to outline and initiate new advertising policies or procedures. May confer with clients to provide marketing or technical advice. ● **GED:** R5, M3, L4 ● **SVP:** 4-10 yrs ● **Academic:** Ed=H, Eng=G ● **Work Field:** 295 ● **MPSMS:** 896 ● **Aptitudes:** G2, V2, N3, S2, P3, Q3, K4, F4, M4, E5, C3 ● **Temperaments:** D, J, P ● **Physical:** Stg=L; Freq: R, H, T, G, N, X Occas: I, D, A ● **Work Env:** Noise=N; ● **Salary:** 5 ● **Outlook:** 1

MANAGER, PROMOTION (hotel & rest.) ● DOT #163.117-018 ● OES: 13011 ● Alternate titles: DIRECTOR, SALES; MANAGER, BUSINESS PROMOTION; MANAGER, SALES. Plans and administers sales policies and programs to foster and promote hotel patronage: Consults newspapers, trade journals, and other publications to learn about contemplated conventions and social functions. Organizes prospect files by listing information, such as names of officials and plans for conventions, to be used for promotional purposes. Directs workers engaged in preparing promotional correspondence with travel bureaus, business and social groups. Confers with department heads to discuss and formulate plans for soliciting business. Contacts executives of organizations to explain services and facilities offered by hotel and to solicit their business. Supervises and trains service representatives. Plans and prepares advertising and promotional material and arranges for newspaper and other publicity. ● **GED:** R5, M3, L4 ● **SVP:** 4-10 yrs ● **Academic:** Ed=H, Eng=G ● **Work Field:** 295 ● **MPSMS:** 902 ● **Aptitudes:** G2, V2, N3, S4, P4, Q4, K4, F4, M4, E5, C5 ● **Temperaments:** D, J, P, V ● **Physical:** Stg=L; Freq: T, G Occas: R, H, I, N ● **Work Env:** Noise=N; ● **Salary:** 5 ● **Outlook:** 2

MEDIA DIRECTOR (profess. & kin.) ● DOT #164.117-018 ● OES: 13011 ● Plans and administers media programs in advertising department: Confers with representatives of advertising agencies, product managers, and corporate advertising staff to establish media goals, objectives, and strategies within corporate advertising budget. Confers with advertising agents or media representatives to select specific programs and negotiate advertising to ensure optimum use of budgeted funds and long-term contracts. Adjusts broadcasting schedules due to program cancellations. Studies demographic data and consumer profiles to identify target audiences of media advertising. Reads trade journals and professional literature to stay informed of trends, innovations, and changes that affect media planning. ● **GED:** R5, M4, L5 ● **SVP:** 4-10 yrs ● **Academic:** Ed=A, Eng=S ● **Work Field:** 295 ● **MPSMS:** 890 ● **Aptitudes:** G2, V2, N2, S3, P3, Q2, K4, F4, M4, E5, C5 ● **Temperaments:** D, J, P ● **Physical:** Stg=S; Freq: T, G Occas: R, H, I, N ● **Work Env:** Noise=N; ● **Salary:** 5 ● **Outlook:** 1

SALES-SERVICE PROMOTER (any industry) ● DOT #165.167-010 ● OES: 34008 ● Promotes sales and creates goodwill for firm's products or services by preparing displays, touring country, making speeches at retail dealers conventions, and calling on individual merchants to advise on ways and means for increasing sales. May demonstrate products representing technological advances in industry. ● **GED:** R5, M3, L5 ● **SVP:** 2-4 yrs ● **Academic:** Ed=H, Eng=G ● **Work Field:** 295, 292 ● **MPSMS:** 896 ● **Aptitudes:** G2, V2, N3, S3, P3, Q3, K4, F4, M4, E4, C4 ● **Temperaments:** D, F, I, J, P ● **Physical:** Stg=L; Freq: T, G Occas: R, H, I, N, X ● **Work Env:** Noise=N; ● **Salary:** 4 ● **Outlook:** 4

SUPERVISOR OF SALES (business ser.) ● DOT #185.157-014 ● OES: 13011 ● Coordinates and publicizes tobacco marketing activities within specified area: Visits tobacco growers, buyers, and auction warehouses to cultivate interest and goodwill. Develops publicity for tobacco industry. Investigates and confirms eligibility of buyers. Collects membership dues for tobacco Board of Trade. Schedules tobacco auction dates. Records quantity and purchase price of tobacco sold daily, and prepares reports specified by board. May prepare report of marketing activities for state and federal agencies. May review and verify reports for individual warehouses. May examine quality and growth of tobacco in fields of individual growers and inform buyers of results. ● **GED:** R4, M4, L4 ● **SVP:** 2-4 yrs ● **Academic:** Ed=N, Eng=G ● **Work Field:** 292 ● **MPSMS:** 882, 896 ● **Aptitudes:** G2, V2, N2, S4, P4, Q3, K4, F4, M4, E5, C5 ● **Temperaments:** D, I, P ● **Physical:** Stg=L; Freq: R, H, I, T, G, N, A ● **Work Env:** Noise=N; ● **Salary:** 4 ● **Outlook:** 2

GOE: 11.09.02
Fund & Membership Solicitation

BLOOD-DONOR RECRUITER (medical ser.) ● DOT #293.357-010 ● OES: 49998 ● Contacts fraternal, business, and labor organizations by telephone, in person, or by mail to solicit blood donations from employees or members for nonprofit blood bank: Develops list of prospective donor groups by using organizational, professional, and industrial listings and directories. Contacts prospective donor groups to explain requirements and benefits of participation in blood donor program. Visits prospective or participating blood donor group to discuss blood program. Distributes promotional material and uses audio-visual aids to motivate groups to participate in blood-donor program. Keeps records of organizations participating in program. Arranges specific date of blood collection for blood-donor group and confirms appointment in writing. Records information for mobile blood-collection unit, such as space available, staffing required, and number of donors anticipated. Consults blood bank records to answer questions, monitor activity, or resolve problems of blood donor groups. Prepares reports of blood-donor program and recruitment activities. May identify donors with rare-type blood from blood-bank records, and telephone donors to solicit and arrange blood donation. ● **GED:** R4, M2, L4 ● **SVP:** 1-3 mos ● **Academic:** Ed=N, Eng=G ● **Work Field:** 292 ● **MPSMS:** 885 ● **Aptitudes:** G3, V2, N4, S5, P5, Q3, K4, F4, M5, E5, C5 ● **Temperaments:** I, P ● **Physical:** Stg=L; Freq: R, H, I, T, G, N ● **Work Env:** Noise=N; ● **Salary:** 2 ● **Outlook:** 3

DIRECTOR, FUNDRAISING (nonprofit org.) ● DOT #165.117-010 ● OES: 13011 ● Directs and coordinates solicitation and disbursement of funds for community social-welfare organization: Establishes fund-raising goals according to financial need of agency. Formulates policies for collecting and safeguarding contributions. Initiates public relations program to promote community understanding and support for organization's objectives. Develops schedule for disbursing solicited funds. Issues instructions to volunteer and paid workers regarding solicitations, public relations, and clerical duties. ● **GED:** R5, M4, L4 ● **SVP:** 4-10 yrs ● **Academic:** Ed=B, Eng=G ● **Work Field:** 295 ● **MPSMS:** 896, 894 ● **Aptitudes:** G2, V2, N2, S4, P4, Q3, K4, F4, M4, E5, C5 ● **Temperaments:** D, I, J, P, V ● **Physical:** Stg=S; Freq: R, H, I, T, G, N ● **Work Env:** Noise=N; ● **Salary:** 5 ● **Outlook:** 1

DIRECTOR, FUNDS DEVELOPMENT (profess. & kin.) ● DOT #165.117-014 ● OES: 13011 ● Alternate titles: DIRECTOR OF MAJOR OR CAPITAL GIFTS. Plans, organizes, directs, and coordinates ongoing and special project funding programs for museum, zoo, public broadcasting station, or similar institution: Prepares statement of planned activities and enlists support from members of institution staff and volunteer organizations. Develops public relations materials to enhance institution image and promote fund raising program. Identifies potential contributors to special project funds and supporters of institution ongoing operations through examination of past records, individual and corporate contracts, and knowledge of community. Plans and coordinates fund drives for special projects. Assigns responsibilities for personal solicitation to members of staff, volunteer organizations, and governing body according to special interests or capabilities. Organizes direct mail campaign to reach other potential contributors. Plans and coordinates benefit events, such as banquets, balls, or auctions. Organizes solicitation drives for pledges of ongoing support from individuals, corporations, and foundations. Informs potential contributors of special needs of institution, and encourages individuals, corporations, and foundations to establish or contribute to special funds through endowments, trusts, donations of gifts-in-kind, or bequests, conferring with attorneys to establish methods of transferring funds to benefit both donors and institution. Researches public and private grant agencies and foundations to identify other sources of funding for research, community service, or other projects. Supervises and coordinates activities of workers engaged in maintaining records of contributors and grants and preparing letters of appreciation to be sent to contributors. May purchase mailing list of potential donors. May negotiate agreements with representatives of other organizations for exchange of mailing lists, information, and cooperative programs. ● **GED:** R5, M4, L5 ● **SVP:** 2-4 yrs ● **Academic:** Ed=B, Eng=G ● **Work Field:** 292, 295 ● **MPSMS:** 893, 894, 896 ● **Aptitudes:** G2, V2, N2, S4, P4, Q3, K4, F4, M4, E5, C5 ● **Temperaments:** D, I, J, P ● **Physical:** Stg=S; Const: T, G Freq: H Occas: I ● **Work Env:** Noise=Q; ● **Salary:** 5 ● **Outlook:** 3

FUND RAISER I (nonprofit org.) ● DOT #293.157-010 ● OES: 49998 ● Plans fund raising program for charities or other causes, and writes to, telephones, or visits individuals or establishments to solicit funds or gifts-in-kind: Compiles and analyzes information about potential contributors to develop mailing or contact list and to plan selling approach. Writes, telephones, or visits potential contributors and persuades them to contribute funds or gifts-in-kind by explaining purpose and benefits

of fund raising program. Takes pledges or funds from contributors. Records expenses incurred and contributions received. May organize volunteers and plan social functions to raise funds. May prepare fund raising brochures for mail-solicitation programs. May train volunteers to perform certain duties to assist fund raising. ● **GED:** R5, M3, L4 ● **SVP:** 1-2 yrs ● **Academic:** Ed=B, Eng=G ● **Work Field:** 292, 295 ● **MPSMS:** 880, 940 ● **Aptitudes:** G2, V2, N3, S5, P5, Q3, K5, F4, M4, E5, C5 ● **Temperaments:** D, I, J, P, V ● **Physical:** Stg=L; Freq: T, G Occas: R, H, I ● **Work Env:** Noise=N; ● **Salary:** 5 ● **Outlook:** 4

MEMBERSHIP DIRECTOR (profess. & kin.) ● DOT #189.167-026 ● OES: 39998 ● Organizes chapters of fraternal society, lodge, or similar organization and surveys conditions in branches already established: Contacts interested parties to present aims and ideals of organization. Coordinates group efforts in petitioning parent organization for charter and recognition. Advises societies or lodges having financial, organizational, and membership problems. ● **GED:** R5, M4, L4 ● **SVP:** 2-4 yrs ● **Academic:** Ed=A, Eng=S ● **Work Field:** 282, 292 ● **MPSMS:** 896 ● **Aptitudes:** G2, V2, N3, S4, P4, Q4, K4, F4, M4, E5, C5 ● **Temperaments:** D, I, P, V ● **Physical:** Stg=L; Freq: R, H, T, G, N Occas: I ● **Work Env:** Noise=N; ● **Salary:** 4 ● **Outlook:** 1

SUPERVISOR, BLOOD-DONOR RECRUITERS (medical ser.) ● DOT #293.137-010 ● OES: 41002 ● Supervises and coordinates activities of BLOOD-DONOR RECRUITERS (medical ser.) engaged in soliciting blood donations from employees or members of companies, unions, and fraternal organizations: Selects, trains, and assigns BLOOD-DONOR RECRUITERS (medical ser.). Reviews records and reports to evaluate BLOOD-DONOR RECRUITER (medical ser.) performance and recommends personnel action when necessary. Analyzes and resolves work problems, or assists BLOOD-DONOR RECRUITER (medical ser.) in solving problems. Interprets blood-bank policies and procedures to staff. Attends management meetings to exchange ideas and information and discuss problems. Assists in preparation of annual budget by providing data and making recommendations. Serves as liaison between donor-enrollment unit and other units of blood bank. Occasionally answers requests for information from prospective or participating blood-donor groups. Occasionally speaks to interested donor groups about blood-donation program. ● **GED:** R4, M3, L4 ● **SVP:** 1-2 yrs ● **Academic:** Ed=N, Eng=G ● **Work Field:** 282, 292 ● **MPSMS:** 885 ● **Aptitudes:** G3, V2, N3, S5, P5, Q2, K4, F4, M5, E5, C5 ● **Temperaments:** D, J, P ● **Physical:** Stg=S; Freq: R, H, I, T, G, N ● **Work Env:** Noise=N; ● **Salary:** 4 ● **Outlook:** 2

GOE: 11.09.03
Public Relations

EMPLOYER RELATIONS REPRESENTATIVE (profess. & kin.) ● DOT #166.257-010 ● OES: 21511 ● Establishes and maintains working relationships with local employers to promote use of public employment programs and services: Contacts employers new to area or company requiring revisit and arranges appointment to visit company representative or employer responsible for hiring workers. Establishes rapport between Employment Service and company to promote use of agency programs and services. Confers with employer to resolve problems, such as local employment office effectiveness, employer complaints, and alternative employer actions for recruiting qualified applicants. Answers employer questions concerning Employment Service programs or services available. Solicits employers to list job openings with Employment Service. Receives job orders from employers by phone or in person and records information to facilitate selection and referral process. ● **GED:** R5, M2, L4 ● **SVP:** 1-2 yrs ● **Academic:** Ed=A, Eng=G ● **Work Field:** 282 ● **MPSMS:** 896, 943 ● **Aptitudes:** G2, V2, N4, S4, P4, Q3, K4, F4, M4, E5, C5 ● **Temperaments:** I, P ● **Physical:** Stg=L; Freq: R, H, T, G ● **Work Env:** Noise=N; ● **Salary:** 3 ● **Outlook:** 3

FOREIGN-SERVICE OFFICER (government ser.) ● DOT #188.117-106 ● OES: 19005 ● Represents interests of United States Government and Nationals by conducting relations with foreign nations and international organizations; protecting and advancing political, economic, and commercial interests overseas; and rendering personal services to Americans abroad and to foreign nationals traveling to the United States: Manages and administers diplomatic or consular post abroad. Conveys views of U.S. Government to host government. Reports political and other developments in host country to superior or Secretary of State. Analyzes basic economic data, trends, and developments in host country or region. Advances trade by alerting U.S. business personnel to potential foreign trade and investment opportunities. Provides medical, legal, familial, and traveling advice and assistance to U.S. citizens. Issues passports to Americans and visas to foreigners wishing to enter the United States. Offers notarial services and assistance on benefit programs to Americans and eligible foreigners. Determines eligibility of persons to be documented as U.S. citizens. Takes testimony abroad for use in U.S. Courts. May negotiate agreements between host and United States Government. May recommend how American policy can help improve foreign economic conditions. May coordinate American economic assistance programs. May serve in Washington, D.C. as counterpart to outstationed colleagues, relating foreign service administrative needs to Department of State or United States Information Agency. May disseminate information overseas about the United States and its policies by engaging in cultural and educational interaction through United States Information Agency. May be designated according to basic field of specialization as Administrative Officer (government ser.); Commercial Officer (government ser.); Consular Officer (government ser.); Cultural Affairs Officer (government ser.); Diplomatic Officer (government ser.); Economic Officer (government ser.). May be designated: Information Officer (government ser.); Political Officer (government ser.); Public Affairs Officer (government ser.). ● **GED:** R5, M4, L5 ● **SVP:** 4-10 yrs ● **Academic:** Ed=B, Eng=G ● **Work Field:** 295, 271, 211 ● **MPSMS:** 959 ● **Aptitudes:** G2, V1, N3, S3, P3, Q3, K4, F4, M4, E5, C5 ● **Temperaments:** F, I, J, P, V ● **Physical:** Stg=S; Freq: R, H, I, T, G, N ● **Work Env:** Noise=N; ● **Salary:** 5 ● **Outlook:** 1

LOBBYIST (profess. & kin.) ● DOT #165.017-010 ● OES: 34008 ● Alternate titles: LEGISLATIVE ADVOCATE. Contacts and confers with members of legislature and other holders of public office to persuade them to support legislation favorable to client's interest: Studies proposed legislation to determine possible effect on interest of client, who may be person, specific group, or general public. Confers with legislators and officials to emphasize supposed weaknesses or merits of specific bills to influence passage, defeat, or amendment of measure, or introduction of legislation more favorable to client's interests. Contacts individuals and groups having similar interests in order to encourage them also to contact legislators and present views. Prepares news releases and informational pamphlets and conducts news conferences in order to state client's views and to inform public of features of proposed legislation considered desirable or undesirable. Plans and coordinates meetings between members and elected officials to discuss legislative issues and proposals and allow officials to respond to membership concerns. May contact regulatory agencies and testify at public hearings to enlist support for client's interests. May be legally required to register with governmental authorities as lobbyist and to submit reports of regulated expenditures incurred during lobbying activities. May attend and represent local organization at state and national association meetings. May instruct individuals or organization members in lobbying techniques. ● **GED:** R5, M3, L5 ● **SVP:** 2-4 yrs ● **Academic:** Ed=A, Eng=G ● **Work Field:** 282, 271 ● **MPSMS:** 896 ● **Aptitudes:** G2, V2, N2, S4, P4, Q3, K4, F4, M4, E5, C5 ● **Temperaments:** D, I, J, P ● **Physical:** Stg=S; Freq: T, G, N Occas: R, H, I ● **Work Env:** Noise=N; ● **Salary:** 5 ● **Outlook:** 2

MANAGER, AREA DEVELOPMENT (utilities) ● DOT #184.117-030 ● OES: 15023 ● Alternate titles: AREA-DEVELOPMENT CONSULTANT. Negotiates with representatives of industrial, commercial, agricultural, or other interests utilizing electric power or fuel gas to encourage location of facilities in area served by utility: Directs and coordinates activities of workers engaged in preparation of surveys and studies of prospective development area to compile information of interest to companies desirous of relocation. Analyzes compiled data and formulates methods and procedures for developing industrial areas to determine industries that would enhance developmental plan. Plans promotional sales program and advertising to promote maximum utilization of land and consumption of electric power. Contacts companies to persuade them to locate in service area. ● **GED:** R5, M3, L4 ● **SVP:** 4-10 yrs ● **Academic:** Ed=A, Eng=G ● **Work Field:** 292, 295 ● **MPSMS:** 871, 872 ● **Aptitudes:** G2, V2, N2, S4, P4, Q3, K4, F4, M4, E5, C5 ● **Temperaments:** D, I, J, P, V ● **Physical:** Stg=S; Freq: R, H, T, G, N ● **Work Env:** Noise=N; ● **Salary:** 5 ● **Outlook:** 1

PUBLIC-RELATIONS REPRESENTATIVE (profess. & kin.) ● DOT #165.167-014 ● OES: 34008 ● Alternate titles: PUBLIC-RELATIONS PRACTITIONER. Plans and conducts public relations program designed to create and maintain favorable public image for employer or client: Plans and directs development and communication of information designed to keep public informed of employer's programs, accomplishments, or point of view. Arranges for public relations efforts in order to meet needs, objectives, and policies of individual, special interest group, business concern, nonprofit organization, or governmental agency, serving as in-house staff member or as outside consultant. Prepares and distributes fact sheets, news releases, photographs, scripts, motion pictures, or tape recordings to media representatives and other persons who may be interested in learning about or publicizing employer's activities or message. Purchases advertising space and time as required. Arranges for and conducts public-contact programs designed to meet employer's objectives, utilizing knowledge of changing attitudes and opinions of consumers, clients, employees, or other interest groups. Promotes goodwill through such publicity efforts as speeches, exhibits, films, tours, and question/answer sessions. Represents employer during community projects and at public, social, and business gatherings. May research data, create ideas, write copy, lay out artwork, contact media representatives, or represent employer directly before general public. May develop special projects such as campaign fund raisers or public awareness about political issues. May direct activities of subordinates. May confer with production and support personnel to coordinate production of television advertisements and on-air promotions. May prepare press releases and fact sheets, and compose letters, using computer. May disseminate facts and information about organization's activities or governmental agency's programs to general public and be known as Public Information Officer (profess. & kin.). ● **GED:** R5, M4, L5 ● **SVP:** 2-4 yrs ● **Academic:** Ed=B, Eng=G ● **Work Field:** 261, 292, 295 ● **MPSMS:** 896 ● **Aptitudes:** G1, V1, N3, S3, P3, Q3, K4, F4, M4, E5, C4 ● **Temperaments:** D, I, J, P, V ● **Physical:** Stg=S; Freq: R, H, I, T, G, N Occas: A, X ● **Work Env:** Noise=N; ● **Salary:** 5 ● **Outlook:** 3

Leading-Influencing   11

Regulations Enforcement   **11.10**

Workers in this group enforce government regulations and company policies that affect people's rights, health and safety, and finances. They examine records, inspect products, and investigate services, but do not engage in police work. Most workers find employment with government agencies, licensing departments, and health departments. Some are employed by retail establishments, mines, transportation companies, and nonprofit organizations.

✓ *What kind of work would you do?*

Your work activities would depend upon your specific job. For example, you might:

- regulate the entry of people into the United States according to immigration laws.
- investigate employment practices to enforce equal employment opportunity laws.
- observe employees of a bus company to see that company rules are being followed.
- investigate shortages of cash, materials, tools, or equipment in a production or sales company.
- inspect buildings and equipment to detect fire hazards.
- direct the examination of insurance companies to see that state regulations are being followed.
- investigate animal cruelty and neglect complaints.

✓ *What skills and abilities do you need for this kind of work?*

To do this kind of work, you must be able to:

- think logically and apply technical knowledge when making investigations and inspections.
- establish facts and draw conclusions based on information collected.
- read and understand the laws and regulations to be enforced.
- write and speak clearly.
- make decisions based on laws and regulations.
- make decisions based on personal experience and your own opinions.
- cope with a variety of duties, such as questioning people, looking at the physical conditions in a manufacturing plant to identify hazards, and writing reports.
- deal with all kinds of people pleasantly but firmly.
- standing or walking for long periods of time.

✓ *How do you know if you would like or could learn to do this kind of work?*

The following questions may give you clues about yourself as you consider this group of jobs.

- Have you been in charge of a group or class? Can you enforce rules and regulations according to instructions?
- Have you been a member of an environmental or a consumer group? Would you like a job which promotes these interests?
- Have you taken courses in government, political science, or environmental health? Do you think rules and regulations are important?

✓ *How can you prepare for and enter this kind of work?*

Occupations in this group usually require education and/or training extending from one year to over ten years, depending upon the specific kind of work. The education and experience requirements vary greatly among the jobs in this group. Some jobs require prior knowledge of the regulations to be enforced and the procedures to be used. Others require special training such as insurance underwriting. Clerical and other workers within a company or government agency are sometimes promoted to positions in this group. Other jobs require skills and knowledges that are identified by special tests.

Many of the jobs in this group are in government agencies and are filled by those who qualify through civil service examinations. Some jobs are filled by appointment.

✓ *What else should you consider about these jobs?*

Some workers are required to wear uniforms. Some jobs involve shift work. Some workers sit at a desk in a comfortable office most of the day, while others must go from one place to another in order to inspect licenses and determine regulation compliance of people like beauty operators and food service workers. Other workers are stationed at inspection locations, such as port-of-entry and border crossings.

If you think you would like to do this kind of work, look at the job titles listed on the following pages.

■ ■ ■

GOE: 11.10.01
Finance

INVESTIGATOR (government ser.) ● DOT #168.267-062 ● OES: 21911 ● Investigates regulated activities to assure compliance with federal, state, or municipal laws: Locates and interviews plaintiffs, witnesses, or representatives of business or government to gather facts relating to alleged violation. Observes conditions to verify facts indicating violation of law relating to such activities as revenue collection, employment practices, or fraudulent benefit claims. Examines business, personal, or public records and documents to establish facts and authenticity of data. Investigates character of applicant for special license or permit. Investigates suspected misuses of license or permit. Prepares correspondence and reports of investigations for use by administrative or legal authorities. Testifies in court or at administrative proceedings concerning findings of investigation. May serve legal papers. May be required to meet licensing or certification standards established by regulatory agency concerned. May be designated according to function or agency where employed as Inspector, Weights And Measures (government ser.); Investigator, Internal Revenue (government ser.); Investigator, Welfare (government ser.); Postal Inspector (government ser.); Investigator, Claims (government ser.). ● **GED:** R5, M4, L4 ● **SVP:** 1-2 yrs ● **Academic:** Ed=A, Eng=G ● **Work Field:** 271 ● **MPSMS:** 950 ● **Aptitudes:** G2, V2, N3, S3, P3, Q3, K5, F5, M5, E5, C5 ● **Temperaments:** J, P ● **Physical:** Stg=L; Freq: R, H, I, T, G, N, A ● **Work Env:** Noise=N; Occas: W ● **Salary:** 4 ● **Outlook:** 2

INVESTIGATOR, FRAUD (retail trade) ● DOT #376.267-014 ● OES: 63035 ● Investigates cases of fraud involving use of charge cards reported lost or stolen, cash refunds, and nonexistent accounts in retail stores: Receives information from credit, sales, and collection departments regarding suspected fraud cases. Interviews store personnel, and observes and questions suspected customers to obtain evidence. Compiles detailed reports on fraud cases, and submits and discusses cases with police. Consults with postal officials when charge cards are reported stolen in mail. Testifies at court trials of offenders. Prepares reports of fraud cases and submits reports to security department and other store officials. ● **GED:** R4, M4, L3 ● **SVP:** 2-4 yrs ● **Academic:** Ed=H, Eng=G ● **Work Field:** 271 ● **MPSMS:** 969 ● **Aptitudes:** G3, V3, N3, S4, P4, Q3, K4, F4, M4, E5, C4 ● **Temperaments:** J, P ● **Physical:** Stg=S; Freq: R, H, T, G, N Occas: I, F, D, A, X ● **Work Env:** Noise=L; ● **Salary:** 3 ● **Outlook:** 3

REVENUE OFFICER (government ser.) ● DOT #188.167-074 ● OES: 21911 ● Investigates and collects delinquent federal taxes and secures delinquent tax returns from individuals or business firms according to prescribed laws and regulations: Investigates delinquent tax cases referred by agency investigators, as well as leads found in newspapers, trade journals, and public stockbroker records. Confers with individuals or business representatives by telephone, correspondence, or in person to determine amount of delinquent taxes and enforce collection. Examines and analyzes tax assets and liabilities to determine solution for resolving tax problem. Selects appropriate remedy for delinquent taxes when necessary, such as part-payment agreements, offers of compromise, or seizure and sale of property. Directs service of legal documents, such as subpoenas, warrants, notices of assessment, and garnishments. Recommends criminal prosecutions and civil penalties when necessary. Writes reports of determinations and actions taken for departmental files. (Workers who examine and audit tax records to determine tax liabilities are defined under title REVENUE AGENT (government ser.). ● **GED:** R5, M4, L4 ● **SVP:** 2-4 yrs ● **Academic:** Ed=A, Eng=G ● **Work Field:** 232, 271 ● **MPSMS:** 953 ● **Aptitudes:** G2, V2, N2, S4, P3, Q3, K4, F4, M4, E4, C5 ● **Temperaments:** D, I, J, P, S ● **Physical:** Stg=L; Freq: R, H, I, T, G, N ● **Work Env:** Noise=N; ● **Salary:** 4 ● **Outlook:** 1

GOE: 11.10.02
Individual Rights

DIRECTOR, COMPLIANCE (government ser.) ● DOT #188.117-046 ● OES: 19005 ● Directs human relations program: Plans, organizes, and executes compliance programs in areas of employment, housing, and education under authority of federal, state, or local discriminatory legislation. Establishes and coordinates activities of local community relations committees. Conducts investigations to resolve complaints and report violations for adjudication. Plans informational programs to stimulate and maintain community interest and support. Cooperates with local, state, and federal governmental units and other organizations in identifying needs and providing assistance in enforcement of statutes. ● **GED:** R5, M4, L5 ● **SVP:** 2-4 yrs ● **Academic:** Ed=A, Eng=G ● **Work Field:** 295 ● **MPSMS:** 959 ● **Aptitudes:** G2, V2, N2, S4, P4, Q3, K4, F4, M4, E5, C5 ● **Temperaments:** D, P ● **Physical:** Stg=L; Freq: T, G, N Occas: R, H ● **Work Env:** Noise=N; ● **Salary:** 4 ● **Outlook:** 1

EQUAL-OPPORTUNITY REPRESENTATIVE (government ser.) ● DOT #168.167-014 ● OES: 21911 ● Organizes and implements federally funded programs related to equal employment opportunity by providing consultation, encouraging good will between employers and minority communities, and evaluating employment practices: Consults with community representatives to develop technical assistance agreements in accordance with statutory regulations. Informs minority community on civil rights laws. Assists employers to interpret state and federal laws. Develops guidelines for nondiscriminatory employment practices for use by employers. Acts as liaison representative between minority placement agencies and large employers. Investigates existing employment practices to detect and correct discriminatory factors. Conducts surveys and evaluates findings to determine existence of systematic discrimination. ● **GED:** R5, M3, L5 ● **SVP:** 4-10 yrs ● **Academic:** Ed=A, Eng=G ● **Work Field:** 295 ● **MPSMS:** 959 ● **Aptitudes:** G2, V3, N3, S4, P4, Q3, K4, F4, M4, E4, C4 ● **Temperaments:** D, I, J, P ● **Physical:** Stg=S; Freq: R, H, I, T, G, N Occas: X ● **Work Env:** Noise=N; ● **Salary:** 4 ● **Outlook:** 2

GOE: 11.10.03
Health & Safety

ANIMAL TREATMENT INVESTIGATOR (nonprofit org.) ● DOT#379.263-010 ● OES: 63099 ● Alternate titles: ANIMAL CONTROL OFFICER. Investigates animal cruelty and neglect charges and performs related duties to promote compliance with laws regulating animal treatment: Observes areas of alleged violations and interviews available witnesses to determine if laws are being violated. Informs persons perpetrating inhumane acts of laws and penalties for violations. Reports violators to police or requests police to arrest violators. Aids animals in distress by feeding starving animals and freeing trapped animals. Removes animals from inhumane conditions and drives vehicle to transport animals to shelter for treatment and care. Inspects establishments housing or exhibiting animals to ascertain compliance with humane laws. Writes reports of activities. ● **GED:** R3, M1, L3 ● **SVP:** 6 mos-1 yr ● **Academic:** Ed=N, Eng=G ● **Work Field:** 271, 293 ● **MPSMS:** 327, 329, 953 ● **Aptitudes:** G3, V3, N4, S4, P4, Q3, K4, F4, M3, E4, C5 ● **Temperaments:** J, P, S ● **Physical:** Stg=L; Freq: R, H, T, G, N Occas: I, F, D, V ● **Work Env:** Noise=N; Freq: W, O ● **Salary:** 3 ● **Outlook:** 2

CHEMICAL-RADIATION TECHNICIAN (government ser.) ● DOT #015.261-010 ● OES: 24501 ● Tests materials and monitors operations of nuclear-powered electric generating plant, using specialized laboratory equipment and chemical and radiation detection instruments: Collects samples of water, gases, and solids at specified intervals during production process, using automatic sampling equipment. Analyzes materials, according to specified procedures, to determine if chemical components and radiation levels are within established limits. Records test results and prepares reports for review by supervisor. Assists workers to set up equipment and monitors equipment that automatically detects deviations from standard operations. Notifies personnel to adjust processing equipment, quantity of additives, and rate of discharge of waste materials, when test results and monitoring of equipment indicate that radiation levels, chemical balance, and discharge of radionuclide materials are in excess of standards. Carries out decontamination procedures to ensure safety of workers and continued operation of processing equipment in plant. Calibrates and maintains chemical instrumentation sensing elements and sampling system equipment, using handtools. Assists workers in diagnosis and correction of problems in instruments and processing equipment. Advises plant personnel of methods of protection from excessive exposure to radiation. ● **GED:** R4, M3, L3 ● **SVP:** 1-2 yrs ● **Academic:** Ed=H, Eng=S ● **Work Field:** 211, 221 ● **MPSMS:** 715 ● **Aptitudes:** G3, V3, N3, S2, P2, Q4, K2, F3, M3, E5, C3 ● **Temperaments:** J, T ● **Physical:** Stg=L; Freq: R, H, I, N Occas: S, K, O, T, G, X ● **Work Env:** Noise=L; Occas: R ● **Salary:** 4 ● **Outlook:** 2

FIRE INSPECTOR (government ser.) ● DOT #373.267-010 ● OES: 63008 ● Alternate titles: FIELD INSPECTOR. Inspects buildings and equipment to detect fire hazards and enforce local ordinances and state laws: Observes tests of equipment, such as gasoline storage tanks and air compressors, and inspects storage conditions to ensure conformance to fire and safety codes. Issues permits to attest to safe operating conditions. Examines interiors and exteriors of buildings to detect hazardous conditions or violations of fire ordinances and laws. Prepares report of violations or unsafe conditions. Discusses condition with owner or manager and recommends safe methods of storing flammables or other hazardous materials. Informs owner or manager of conditions requiring correction, such as faulty wiring. Issues summons for fire hazards not corrected on subsequent inspection and enforces code when owner refuses to cooperate. Keeps file of inspection records and prepares report of activities. May perform duties of FIRE FIGHTER (any industry) or FIRE CAPTAIN (government ser.). May collect fees for permits and licenses. ● **GED:** R4, M3, L4 ● **SVP:** 2-4 yrs ● **Academic:** Ed=H, Eng=G ● **Work Field:** 271, 293 ● **MPSMS:** 951 ● **Aptitudes:** G3, V3, N4, S3, P3, Q3, K4, F4, M4, E4, C4 ● **Temperaments:** J, P ● **Physical:** Stg=L; Freq: T, G, N Occas: C, S, K, R, H, I, F, D, A, X, V ● **Work Env:** Noise=N; Occas: W ● **Salary:** 4 ● **Outlook:** 3

FOOD AND DRUG INSPECTOR (government ser.) ● DOT #168.267-042 ● OES: 21911 ● Inspects establishment where foods, drugs, cosmetics, and similar consumer items are manufactured, handled, stored, or sold to enforce legal standards of sanitation, purity, and grading: Visits specified establishments to investigate sanitary conditions and health and hygiene habits of persons handling consumer products. Collects samples of products for bacteriological and chemical laboratory analysis. Informs individuals concerned of specific regulations affecting establishments. Destroys subgrades, or prohibits sale of impure, toxic, damaged, or misbranded items. Questions employees, vendors, consumers, and other principals to obtain evidence for prosecuting violators. Ascertains that required licenses and permits have been obtained and are displayed. Prepares reports on each establishment visited, including findings and recommendations for action. May negotiate with marketers and processors to effect changes in facilities and practices, where undesirable conditions are discovered that are not specifically prohibited by law. May grade products according to specified standards. May test products, using variety of specialized test equipment, such as ultraviolet lights and filter guns. May investigate compliance with or violation of public sanitation laws and regulations and be designated Sanitary Inspector (government ser.). ● **GED:** R5, M4, L5 ● **SVP:** 1-2 yrs ● **Academic:** Ed=A, Eng=G ● **Work Field:** 271 ● **MPSMS:** 920 ● **Aptitudes:** G2, V2, N3, S3, P4, Q4, K4, F4, M4, E5, C3 ● **Temperaments:** J, P, T ● **Physical:** Stg=L; Freq: R, H, N Occas: I, T, G, D, A, X ● **Work Env:** Noise=N; ● **Salary:** 3 ● **Outlook:** 3

GAS INSPECTOR (utilities) ● DOT #168.264-018 ● OES: 21911 ● Inspects equipment and facilities used to store, transport, distribute, and measure liquefied petroleum or compressed or natural gas: Examines establishment inspection records to determine that establishment inspection schedule and remedial actions conform to procedures and regulations. Examines containers, piping, tubing, and fittings for leaks and for adherence to government specifications for pressure level, design, construction, and installation. Examines and tests components and support systems, such as relief valves, steam vaporizers, safety devices, electrical equipment, exhaust systems, and vehicles, for conformance with standards and regulations. Connects test equipment, using handtools, and tests calibration of meters and gauges. Inspects above and below ground gas mains to determine that rate of flow, pressure, location, construction, or installation conform to establishment or regulated standards. Maintains records and prepares reports of results of inspections. Discusses and explains procedures and regulations or need for corrective action with establishment or regulatory agency personnel. May be designated according to function, agency, or establishment where employed as Division Field Inspector (utilities); Gas Inspector, Liquefied (government ser.). ● **GED:** R5, M4, L5 ● **SVP:** 2-4 yrs ● **Academic:** Ed=A, Eng=G ● **Work Field:** 271, 231 ● **MPSMS:** 953, 872 ● **Aptitudes:** G2, V2, N2, S4, P3, Q2, K3, F3, M3, E4, C4 ● **Temperaments:** J, P, T, V ● **Physical:** Stg=L; Const: R, H Freq: T, G, F, D, X Occas: C, B, S, O, I ● **Work Env:** Noise=N; Occas: V, X, T ● **Salary:** 5 ● **Outlook:** 2

HAZARDOUS-WASTE MANAGEMENT SPECIALIST (government ser.) ● DOT #168.267-086 ● OES: 21911 ● Conducts studies on hazardous waste management projects and provides information on treatment and containment of hazardous waste: Participates in developing hazardous waste rules and regulations to protect people and environment. Surveys industries to determine type and magnitude of disposal problem. Assesses available hazardous waste treatment and disposal alternatives, and costs involved, to compare economic impact of alternative methods. Assists in developing comprehensive spill prevention programs and reviews facility plans for spill prevention. Par-

ticipates in developing spill-reporting regulations and environmental damage assessment programs. Prepares reports of findings concerning spills and prepares material for use in legal actions. Answers inquiries and prepares informational literature to provide technical assistance to representatives of industry, government agencies, and to general public. Provides technical assistance in event of hazardous chemical spill and identifies pollutant, determines hazardous impact, and recommends corrective action. ● **GED:** R5, M3, L5 ● **SVP:** 2-4 yrs ● **Academic:** Ed=A, Eng=G ● **Work Field:** 271, 282 ● **MPSMS:** 732, 953 ● **Aptitudes:** G2, V2, N2, S4, P4, Q2, K4, F4, M4, E5, C5 ● **Temperaments:** P, T ● **Physical:** Stg=S; Freq: R, H, N Occas: I, T, G ● **Work Env:** Noise=N; ● **Salary:** 4 ● **Outlook:** 2

HEALTH OFFICER, FIELD (government ser.) ● DOT #168.167-018 ● OES: 21911 ● Alternate titles: INVESTIGATOR, COMMUNICABLE DISEASE. Investigates reported cases of communicable diseases and advises exposed persons to obtain medical treatment and to prevent further spread of disease: Locates and interviews exposed person, using information obtained from records of state or local public health departments and from individual already under treatment for communicable disease. Advises person to obtain treatment from private physician or public health clinic. May take blood sample to assist in identifying presence of disease in suspected victim. Questions exposed person to obtain information concerning other persons who may have received exposure. Conducts follow-up interviews with patients and suspected carriers. Writes report of activities and findings. Visits physicians, laboratories, and community health facilities to stimulate reporting of cases and to provide information about government-sponsored health programs concerning immunization efforts, VD control, mosquito abatement, and rodent control. ● **GED:** R5, M3, L5 ● **SVP:** 1-2 yrs ● **Academic:** Ed=B, Eng=G ● **Work Field:** 271 ● **MPSMS:** 920 ● **Aptitudes:** G2, V2, N3, S4, P3, Q3, K4, F5, M4, E5, C4 ● **Temperaments:** D, I, J, P ● **Physical:** Stg=L; Freq: T, G Occas: R, H, I, N, X ● **Work Env:** Noise=N; Occas: O ● **Salary:** 4 ● **Outlook:** 3

INDUSTRIAL HYGIENIST (profess. & kin.) ● DOT #079.161-010 ● OES: 32998 ● Conducts health program in industrial plant or governmental organization to recognize, eliminate, and control occupational health hazards and diseases: Collects samples of dust, gases, vapors, and other potentially toxic materials for analysis. Investigates adequacy of ventilation, exhaust equipment, lighting, and other conditions which may affect employee health, comfort, or efficiency. Conducts evaluations of exposure to ionizing and nonionizing radiation and to noise, and recommends measures to ensure maximum employee protection. Collaborates with INDUSTRIAL-HEALTH ENGINEER (profess. & kin.) and PHYSICIAN, OCCUPATIONAL (medical ser.) to institute control and remedial measures for hazardous and potentially hazardous conditions and equipment. Prepares reports including observations, analysis of contaminants, and recommendations for control and correction of hazards. Participates in educational meetings to instruct employees in matters pertaining to occupational health and prevention of accidents. May specialize in particular area, such as collection and analysis of samples. ● **GED:** R5, M4, L5 ● **SVP:** 4-10 yrs ● **Academic:** Ed=A, Eng=G ● **Work Field:** 244, 271 ● **MPSMS:** 712, 929 ● **Aptitudes:** G1, V2, N1, S1, P1, Q4, K3, F4, M3, E5, C4 ● **Temperaments:** D, J ● **Physical:** Stg=M; Freq: R, H, I, T, G, N, A Occas: F, D, X, V ● **Work Env:** Noise=N; Freq: A ● **Salary:** 5 ● **Outlook:** 3

INDUSTRIAL-SAFETY-AND-HEALTH TECHNICIAN (any industry) ● DOT #168.161-014 ● OES: 21911 ● Plans and directs safety and health activities in industrial plant to evaluate and control environmental hazards: Tests noise levels and measures air quality, using precision instruments. Maintains and calibrates instruments. Administers hearing tests to employees. Trains forklift operators to qualify for licensing. Enforces use of safety equipment. Lectures employees to obtain compliance with regulations. Develops and monitors emergency action plans. Investigates accidents and prepares accident reports. Assists management to prepare safety and health budget. Recommends changes in policies and procedures to prevent accidents and illness. ● **GED:** R5, M4, L4 ● **SVP:** 1-2 yrs ● **Academic:** Ed=A, Eng=G ● **Work Field:** 211 ● **MPSMS:** 953 ● **Aptitudes:** G3, V3, N3, S4, P4, Q3, K3, F3, M3, E4, C4 ● **Temperaments:** D, T ● **Physical:** Stg=L; Freq: R, H, I, T, G, N Occas: A, X ● **Work Env:** Noise=N; ● **Salary:** 2 ● **Outlook:** 3

INSPECTOR, AGRICULTURAL COMMODITIES (government ser.) ● DOT #168.287-010 ● OES: 21911 ● Inspects agricultural commodities, processing equipment, and facilities to enforce compliance with governmental regulations: Inspects horticultural products, such as fruits, vegetables, and ornamental plants to detect disease or infestations harmful to consumers or agricultural economy. Inspects live animals and processing establishments to detect disease or unsanitary conditions. Compares brand with registry to identify owner. Examines, weighs, and measures commodities such as poultry, eggs, mutton, beef, and seafood to certify wholesomeness, grade, and weight. Examines viscera to detect spots or abnormal growths. Collects sample of pests or suspected diseased material and routes to laboratory for identification and analysis. Writes report of findings and advises grower or processor of corrective action. May testify in legal proceedings. May be required to hold U.S. Department of Agriculture license for each product inspected. May be designated according to type of commodity or animal inspected. ● **GED:** R4, M3, L4 ● **SVP:** 2-4 yrs ● **Academic:** Ed=H, Eng=S ● **Work Field:** 211 ● **MPSMS:** 300, 310, 320 ● **Aptitudes:** G2, V3, N3, S3, P2, Q4, K3, F3, M3, E5, C3 ● **Temperaments:** J, V ● **Physical:** Stg=L; Freq: R, H, I, T, G, N Occas: S, K, O, F, D, A, X ● **Work Env:** Noise=L; Occas: W ● **Salary:** 3 ● **Outlook:** 3

INSPECTOR, HEALTH CARE FACILITIES (government ser.) ● DOT #168.167-042 ● OES: 21911 ● Inspects health care facilities, such as hospitals, nursing homes, sheltered care homes, maternity homes, and day care centers, to enforce public health laws and to investigate complaints: Inspects physical facilities, equipment, accommodations, and operating procedures to ensure compliance with laws governing standards of sanitation, acceptability of facilities, record keeping, staff competence qualifications, and ethical practices. Reviews reports concerning staffing, personal references, floor plans, fire inspections, and sanitation. Recommends changes in facilities, standards, and administrative methods in order to improve services and efficiency, utilizing knowledge of good practices and legal requirements. Advises applicants for approval of health care facilities on license application and rules governing operation of such facilities. May testify at hearings or in court. May compile data on conditions of health care facilities, for use in determining construction needs in community or region. ● **GED:** R4, M3, L4 ● **SVP:** 1-2 yrs ● **Academic:** Ed=H, Eng=G ● **Work Field:** 271 ● **MPSMS:** 920 ● **Aptitudes:** G2, V2, N3, S3, P3, Q3, K4, F5, M5, E5, C4 ● **Temperaments:** J, V ● **Physical:** Stg=S; Freq: R, H, I, T, G, N Occas: A ● **Work Env:** Noise=N; ● **Salary:** 3 ● **Outlook:** 3

INSPECTOR, MOTOR VEHICLES (government ser.) ● DOT #168.267-058 ● OES: 21911 ● Alternate titles: AUTOMOBILE INSPECTOR; MOTOR-TRANSPORT INSPECTOR; WEIGH-STATION INSPECTOR. Inspects motor vehicles and cargoes for compliance with statutory regulations: Reviews employer records to determine that accidents, traffic violations, and medical information are recorded according to federal and state regulations. Advises shipper of methods to improve cargo security and record keeping to account for shortage or theft. Interprets applicable regulations and suggests method of self-inspection to accomplish voluntary compliance with code. Inspects vehicle systems, such as lights, brakes, tires, directional signals, exhaust systems, and warning devices, to detect excessive wear or malfunction. Measures interior and exterior noise levels, using decibel meter. Measures efficiency of emission-control devices, using electronic test apparatus. Reviews shipping papers to identify hazardous cargo, such as explosives, poisons, or combustibles. Inspects manner in which hazardous cargo is secured to prevent accidental spillage. Computes and records weight of commercial trucks at highway weigh station or uses portable scale to determine gross weight and distribution of load over axles. Reviews commercial vehicle log to verify driver has not exceeded allowable driving hours and required permits and licenses are displayed. Declares vehicle or driver out-of-service for violation of intra- or interstate commerce regulations. Inspects buses to determine compliance with public transport regulations. May accompany bus drivers to observe conduct and observance with safety precautions. May inspect establishments that rebuild containers used to hold hazardous materials. May testify in legal proceedings. ● **GED:** R4, M3, L4 ● **SVP:** 6 mos-1 yr ● **Academic:** Ed=A, Eng=S ● **Work Field:** 293, 212 ● **MPSMS:** 951, 959 ● **Aptitudes:** G3, V3, N4, S3, P3, Q3, K4, F4, M4, E4, C4 ● **Temperaments:** J ● **Physical:** Stg=L; Freq: R, H, I, N, F, D, A, V Occas: T, G, X ● **Work Env:** Noise=N; Freq: W ● **Salary:** 4 ● **Outlook:** 3

INSPECTOR, WATER-POLLUTION CONTROL (government ser.) ● DOT #168.267-090 ● OES: 21911 ● Inspects sites where discharges enter state waters and investigates complaints concerning water pollution problems: Inspects wastewater treatment facilities at sites, such as mobile home parks, sewage treatment plants, and other sources of pollution. Inspects lagoons and area where effluent enters state waters for such features as obvious discoloration of water, sludge, algae, rodents, and other conditions. Informs owner when unacceptable or questionable conditions are present and recommends corrective action. Notifies mobile laboratory technicians when sampling is required. Advises property owners, facility managers, and equipment operators concerning pollution control regulations. Investigates complaints concerning water pollution problems. Compiles information for pollution control discharge permits. Prepares technical reports of investigations. ● **GED:** R5, M4, L5 ● **SVP:** 2-4 yrs ● **Academic:** Ed=A, Eng=S ● **Work Field:** 211 ● **MPSMS:** 953, 874 ● **Aptitudes:** G2, V2, N3, S4, P3, Q3, K4, F4, M4, E5, C5 ● **Temperaments:** J, P ● **Physical:** Stg=L; Freq: T, G, N Occas: A ● **Work Env:** Noise=N; ● **Salary:** 4 ● **Outlook:** 3

LICENSE INSPECTOR (government ser.) ● DOT #168.267-066 ● OES: 21911 ● Visits establishments licensed by local governments to ascertain that valid licenses and permits are displayed and that licensing standards are being upheld. Prepares report on violators and recommends action. Warns violators of minor or unintentional infractions. May arrest violators. May be designated according to class of establishment visited as Rooming-House Inspector (government ser.); Tavern Inspector (government ser.). ● **GED:** R4, M3, L3 ● **SVP:** 2-4 yrs ● **Academic:** Ed=H, Eng=G ● **Work Field:** 271 ● **MPSMS:** 959 ● **Aptitudes:** G3, V3, N4, S4, P3, Q4, K4, F4, M4, E5, C5 ● **Temperaments:** J, T ● **Physical:** Stg=L; Freq: H, I, T, G, N Occas: R ● **Work Env:** Noise=N; ● **Salary:** 3 ● **Outlook:** 3

MARINE-CARGO SURVEYOR (business ser.) ● DOT #168.267-094 ● OES: 21911 ● Inspects cargoes of seagoing vessels to certify compliance with national and international health and safety regulations in cargo handling and stowage: Reads vessel documents that set forth cargo loading and securing procedures, capacities, and stability factors to ascertain cargo capabilities according to design and cargo regulations. Advises crew in techniques of stowing dangerous and heavy cargo, such as use of extra support beams (deck bedding), shoring, and additional stronger lashings, according to knowledge of hazards present when shipping grain, explosives, logs, and heavy machinery. Inspects loaded, secured cargo in holds and lashed to decks to ascertain that pertinent cargo handling regulations have been observed. Issues certificate of compliance when violations are not detected. Recommends remedial procedures to correct deficiencies. Measures ship holds and depth of fuel and water in tanks, using sounding line and tape measure, and reads draft markings to ascertain depth of vessel in water. Times roll of ship, using stopwatch. Calculates hold capacities, volume of stored fuel and water, weight of cargo, and ship stability factors, using standard mathematical formulas and calculator. Analyzes data obtained from survey, formulates recommendations pertaining to vessel capacities, and writes report of findings. Inspects cargo handling devices, such as boom, hoists, and derricks, to identify need for maintenance. ● **GED:** R4, M4, L4 ● **SVP:** Over 10 yrs ● **Academic:** Ed=H, Eng=S ● **Work Field:** 211, 271 ● **MPSMS:** 953 ● **Aptitudes:** G2, V2, N2, S3, P3, Q2, K4, F4, M4, E5, C5 ● **Temperaments:** J, P, T ● **Physical:** Stg=L; Freq: R, H, T, G, N, F Occas: C, B, S, K, O, D, A ● **Work Env:** Noise=L; Occas: W, O ● **Salary:** 3 ● **Outlook:** 3

MINE INSPECTOR (mine & quarry) ● DOT #168.267-074 ● OES: 21911 ● Alternate titles: CHECK VIEWER; SAFETY INSPECTOR. Inspects underground or open-pit mines to ascertain compliance with contractual agreements and with health and safety laws: Inspects for rotted or incorrectly placed timbers, dangerously placed or defective electrical and mechanical equipment, improperly stored explosives, and other hazardous conditions. Tests air quality to detect toxic or explosive gas or dust, using portable gas-analysis equipment, in order to control health hazards and to reduce injuries and fatalities. Observes mine activities to detect violations of federal and state health and safety standards. Inspects mine workings to verify compliance with contractual agreements concerning production rates or mining within specified limits. May instruct mine workers in safety and first aid procedures. May be designated according to type of mine inspected as Coal-Mine Inspector (mine & quarry); Metal-Mine Inspector (mine & quarry).

May specialize in inspection of specific conditions and be designated Gas Inspector (mine & quarry). When employed by governmental agency (instead of mine operator), conducts periodic mine inspections specifically to enforce federal or state mining laws and is known as Mine Inspector, Federal (government ser.); Mine Inspector, State (government ser.). ● **GED:** R4, M3, L4 ● **SVP:** 1-2 yrs ● **Academic:** Ed=H, Eng=S ● **Work Field:** 212 ● **MPSMS:** 369 ● **Aptitudes:** G3, V3, N4, S3, P3, Q4, K4, F4, M4, E3, C4 ● **Temperaments:** J, T ● **Physical:** Stg=L; Freq: C, R, H, F, A, V Occas: B, S, K, I, N, X ● **Work Env:** Noise=L; Occas: W, A, T, O ● **Salary:** 5 ● **Outlook:** 3

OCCUPATIONAL-SAFETY-AND-HEALTH INSPECTOR (government ser.) ● DOT #168.167-062 ● OES: 21911 ● Alternate titles: OCCUPATIONAL-SAFETY-AND-HEALTH-COMPLIANCE OFFICER. Inspects places of employment to detect unsafe or unhealthy working conditions: Inspects work environment, machinery, and equipment in establishments and other work sites for conformance with governmental standards according to procedure or in response to complaint or accident. Interviews supervisors and employees to obtain facts about work practice or accident. Rates unsafe condition according to factors, such as severity of potential injury, likelihood of recurrence, employers' accident record, and evidence of voluntary compliance. Observes employees at work to determine compliance with safety precautions and safety equipment used. Orders suspension of activity posing threat to workers. Writes new safety order proposal designed to protect workers from work methods, processes, or other hazard not previously covered, using knowledge of safety-engineering practices, available protective devices, safety testing, and occupational safety and health standards. Discusses reason for inspection and penalty rating system with employer. Reviews log of reportable accidents and preventive actions taken to determine employers' attitude toward compliance with regulations. Documents findings and code sections violated. Interprets applicable laws and regulations to advise employer on legal requirements. May specialize in inspection of specific machine, apparatus, or device. May specialize in inspection of specific industry, such as construction, manufacturing, mining, petroleum, or transportation. May testify in legal proceedings. May photograph work environment suspected of endangering workers to provide evidence in legal proceedings. ● **GED:** R5, M5, L5 ● **SVP:** 1-2 yrs ● **Academic:** Ed=A, Eng=S ● **Work Field:** 271, 244 ● **MPSMS:** 712 ● **Aptitudes:** G2, V2, N3, S3, P3, Q3, K4, F4, M4, E5, C4 ● **Temperaments:** J ● **Physical:** Stg=L; Freq: R, H, I, T, G, N, F, A, V Occas: C, B, S, O, E, D ● **Work Env:** Noise=L; Occas: W ● **Salary:** 4 ● **Outlook:** 3

PESTICIDE-CONTROL INSPECTOR (government ser.) ● DOT #168.267-098 ● OES: 21911 ● Inspects operations of distributors and commercial applicators of pesticides to determine compliance with government regulations on handling, sale, and use of pesticides: Inspects premises of wholesale and retail distributors to ensure that registered pesticides are handled in accordance with state and federal regulations. Determines that handlers possess permits and sell restricted pesticides only to authorized users. Evaluates pesticides for correct labeling, misbranding, misrepresentation, or adulteration, and confiscates or quarantines unacceptable pesticides. Inspects operations of commercial applicators of pesticides and observes application methods to ensure correct use of equipment, application procedures, and that applicators possess valid permits. Determines that accurate records are kept to show pesticides used, dosage, times, places, and methods of applications. Inspects premises to ensure that storage and disposal of pesticides conform to regulations. Investigates complaints concerning pesticides and uses. Identifies insect or disease, recommends treatment, and authorizes emergency use of suitable restricted pesticides to respond to emergency situations, such as insect infestations or outbreaks of plant disease. ● **GED:** R4, M2, L3 ● **SVP:** 2-4 yrs ● **Academic:** Ed=H, Eng=S ● **Work Field:** 271 ● **MPSMS:** 953 ● **Aptitudes:** G2, V2, N3, S4, P4, Q2, K4, F4, M4, E4, C4 ● **Temperaments:** J, P ● **Physical:** Stg=L; Freq: R, H, T, G, N Occas: S, K, O, I, A, X ● **Work Env:** Noise=N; ● **Salary:** 2 ● **Outlook:** 3

PUBLIC HEALTH SERVICE OFFICER (government ser.) ● DOT #187.117-050 ● OES: 21911 ● Administers public-health program of county or city: Inspects public facilities for health hazards or directs inspection by others. Negotiates with school, state, federal, or other authorities and with community groups to formulate health standards and legislation affecting jurisdiction. Participates in establishing free clinics, cancer detection centers, and other programs to improve public health. Develops and coordinates public relations campaigns to promote programs and services and participates in radio and television discussions, public meetings, and other activities. Conducts examinations of hospitals, indigent care centers, and other institutions under control of municipality to ensure conformance to accepted standards. Prohibits sale of unsafe milk and other food and dairy products. May impose quarantines on area, animals, or persons with contagious disease. May order closing of establishments not conforming to prescribed health standards. ● **GED:** R5, M5, L5 ● **SVP:** 4-10 yrs ● **Academic:** Ed=B, Eng=G ● **Work Field:** 295 ● **MPSMS:** 920 ● **Aptitudes:** G1, V1, N2, S2, P2, Q3, K3, F4, M4, E4, C4 ● **Temperaments:** D, J, P, V ● **Physical:** Stg=S; Freq: T, G, N Occas: R, H, I, F, D, A, X, V ● **Work Env:** Noise=N; ● **Salary:** 5 ● **Outlook:** 2

RADIATION-PROTECTION SPECIALIST (government ser.) ● DOT #168.261-010 ● OES: 21911 ● Tests x-ray equipment, inspects areas where equipment is used, and evaluates operating procedures to detect and control radiation hazards: Visits hospitals, medical offices, and other establishments to test x-ray machines and fluoroscopes and to inspect premises. Tests equipment to determine that kilovolt potential, alignment of components, and other elements of equipment meet standards for safe operation, using specialized instruments and procedures. Operates equipment to determine need for calibration, repair, or replacement of tubes or other parts. Measures density of lead shielding in walls, using radiometric equipment. Computes cumulative radiation levels and refers to regulations to determine if amount of shielding is sufficient to absorb radiation emissions. Examines license of equipment operator for authenticity and observes operating practices to determine competence of operator to use equipment. Confers with physicians, dentists, and x-ray personnel to explain procedures and legal requirements pertaining to use of equipment. Demonstrates exposure techniques to improve procedures and minimize amount of radiation delivered to patient and operator. Reviews plans and specifications for proposed x-ray installations for conformance to legal requirements and radiation safety practices. Contacts organizations submitting inadequate specifications to explain changes in shielding or layout needed to conform to regulations. ● **GED:** R5, M4, L5 ● **SVP:** 4-10 yrs ● **Academic:** Ed=A, Eng=G ● **Work Field:** 211 ● **MPSMS:** 953 ● **Aptitudes:** G2, V2, N3, S2, P3, Q3, K3, F3, M3, E5, C3 ● **Temperaments:** P, T ● **Physical:** Stg=L; Freq: R, H, I, T, G, N, X Occas: S, K, O, A ● **Work Env:** Noise=N; Occas: R ● **Salary:** 4 ● **Outlook:** 2

REVIEWING OFFICER, DRIVER'S LICENSE (government ser.) ● DOT #168.167-074 ● OES: 21911 ● Evaluates traffic record and other aspects of driver's attitude and behavior to recommend suspension, revocation, or reinstatement of state operator's license: Reviews written record of driver, considering applicable laws and factors, such as number and nature of accidents, interval between accidents or convictions, driver's occupation, and number and gravity of traffic convictions, to evaluate driver's attitude and determine probability of repeated offenses. Recommends probation, suspension, or revocation of license, following rules, regulations, and policies of agency. Conducts hearings at request of persons whose licenses have been suspended or revoked to receive testimony and facts bearing on action. Receives petitions for reinstatement of licenses and approves or disapproves petitions according to evaluation of all pertinent facts. Confers with police and court officials to compile information, facilitate location or punishment of violators, and promote traffic safety. May allocate points for accidents or convictions and mail warnings to violators facing automatic penalties. ● **GED:** R4, M3, L4 ● **SVP:** 2-4 yrs ● **Academic:** Ed=H, Eng=G ● **Work Field:** 211, 271 ● **MPSMS:** 959 ● **Aptitudes:** G2, V2, N4, S4, P4, Q3, K4, F4, M4, E5, C5 ● **Temperaments:** J, P ● **Physical:** Stg=S; Freq: R, H, I, T, G, N ● **Work Env:** Noise=N; ● **Salary:** 3 ● **Outlook:** 3

SAFETY INSPECTOR (insurance) ● DOT #168.167-078 ● OES: 21911 ● Alternate titles: LOSS-CONTROL TECHNICIAN; SAFETY ENGINEER. Inspects insured properties to evaluate physical conditions and promote safety programs: Inspects properties such as buildings, industrial operations, vehicles, and recreational facilities to evaluate physical conditions, safety practices, and hazardous situations according to knowledge of safety and casualty underwriting standards and governmental regulations. Measures insured area, calculates frontage, and records description and amount of stock, and photographs or drafts scale drawings of properties, to identify factors affecting insurance premiums. Analyzes history of accidents and claims against insured and inspects scenes of accidents to determine causes and to develop accident-prevention programs. Prepares written report of findings and recommendations for correction of unsafe or unsanitary conditions. Confers with employees of insured to induce compliance with safety standards, codes, and regulations. Conducts informational meetings among various educational, civic, and industrial groups to promote general safety concepts, utilizing audiovisual aids and insurance statistics. May specialize in specific type of accident-prevention or safety program, such as fire safety or traffic safety. ● **GED:** R5, M4, L5 ● **SVP:** 4-10 yrs ● **Academic:** Ed=A, Eng=G ● **Work Field:** 211, 271 ● **MPSMS:** 895 ● **Aptitudes:** G2, V2, N3, S3, P3, Q3, K4, F4, M4, E5, C4 ● **Temperaments:** D, I, J, P ● **Physical:** Stg=L; Freq: R, H, I, T, G, N Occas: C, B, S, K, O, W, F, D, A, X, V ● **Work Env:** Noise=N; Freq: W ● **Salary:** 4 ● **Outlook:** 3

SAFETY MANAGER (medical ser.) ● DOT #168.167-086 ● OES: 21911 ● Plans, implements, coordinates, and assesses hospital accident, fire prevention, and occupational safety and health programs under general direction of hospital officials, utilizing knowledge of industrial safety-related engineering discipline and operating regulations: Develops and recommends new procedures and approaches to safety and loss prevention based on reports of incidents, accidents, and other data gathered from hospital personnel. Disseminates information to department heads and others regarding toxic substances, hazards, carcinogens, and other safety information. Assists department heads and administrators in enforcing safety regulations and codes. Measures and evaluates effectiveness of safety program, using established goals. Conducts building and grounds surveys on periodic and regular basis to detect code violations, hazards, and incorrect work practices and procedures. Develops and reviews safety training for hospital staff. Maintains administrative control of records related to safety and health programs. Prepares and disseminates memos and reports. Maintains required records. Assists personnel department in administering worker compensation program. ● **GED:** R5, M5, L5 ● **SVP:** 2-4 yrs ● **Academic:** Ed=A, Eng=G ● **Work Field:** 211, 295 ● **MPSMS:** 704, 712 ● **Aptitudes:** G2, V2, N2, S2, P2, Q2, K4, F4, M3, E5, C5 ● **Temperaments:** D, I, J, P, V ● **Physical:** Stg=L; Freq: R, H Occas: I, T, G, N, D, A ● **Work Env:** Noise=N; ● **Salary:** 4 ● **Outlook:** 3

SANITARIAN (any industry) ● DOT #529.137-014 ● OES: 81000 ● Alternate titles: SANITATION SUPERVISOR. Supervises and coordinates activities of workers engaged in duties concerned with sanitation programs in food processing establishment: Inspects products and equipment for conformity to federal and state sanitation laws and plant standards. Directs food handlers and production personnel in sanitary and pest-control procedures. Directs cleaning of equipment and work areas. Inspects premises for unsanitary practices and conditions. Examines incoming shipments of food ingredients for foreign matter, such as insects, poisons, or dirt, and gathers samples of ingredients for laboratory analysis. Confers with management and production personnel on sanitation problems, and recommends changes in equipment, plant layout, lighting, ventilation, or work practices to improve sanitation standards and purity of product. Compiles required reports regarding regular inspections, sanitation violations, and steps taken to resolve deficiencies. Routes reports to designated plant personnel. Performs other duties as described under SUPERVISOR (any industry) Master Title. May be designated according to type of establishment as Supervisor, Bakery Sanitation (bakery products); Supervisor, Dairy Sanitation (dairy products). ● **GED:** R4, M2, L3 ● **SVP:** 2-4 yrs ● **Academic:** Ed=N, Eng=G ● **Work Field:** 031 ● **MPSMS:** 380 ● **Aptitudes:** G3, V3, N3, S3, P3, Q3, K4, F4, M3, E5, C5 ● **Temperaments:** D, P, T ● **Physical:** Stg=L; Freq: C, B, S, K, O, R, H, I, T, G, F Occas: N, D, A ● **Work Env:** Noise=L; ● **Salary:** 4 ● **Outlook:** 2

SANITARIAN (profess. & kin.) ● DOT #079.117-018 ● OES: 21911 ● Plans, develops, and executes environmental health program: Organizes and conducts training program in environmental health practices for schools and other groups. Determines and sets health and sanitation standards and enforces regulations concerned with food processing and serving, collection and disposal of solid wastes, sewage treatment and disposal, plumbing, vector control, recreational areas, hospitals and other institutions, noise, ventilation, air pollution, radiation, and other areas. Confers with government, community, industrial, civil defense, and private organizations to interpret and promote environmental health programs. Collaborates with other health personnel in epidemiological

investigations and control. Advises civic and other officials in development of environmental health laws and regulations. ● **GED:** R6, M5, L6 ● **SVP:** 4-10 yrs ● **Academic:** Ed=B, Eng=G ● **Work Field:** 293, 296 ● **MPSMS:** 874 ● **Aptitudes:** G2, V2, N3, S3, P3, Q4, K4, F4, M4, E5, C3 ● **Temperaments:** D, J, T ● **Physical:** Stg=M; Freq: T, G, N Occas: R, H, F, A, X ● **Work Env:** Noise=L; Freq: W Occas: A, O ● **Salary:** 5 ● **Outlook:** 3

SANITATION INSPECTOR (government ser.) ● DOT #168.267-110 ● OES: 21911 ● Inspects community land areas and investigates complaints concerning neglect of property and illegal dumping of refuse to ensure compliance with municipal code: Inspects designated areas periodically for evidence of neglect, excessive litter, and presence of unsightly or hazardous refuse. Interviews residents and inspects area to investigate reports of illegal dumping and neglected land. Locates property owners to explain nature of inspection and investigation findings and to encourage voluntary action to resolve problems. Studies laws and statutes in municipal code to determine specific nature of code violation and type of action to be taken. Issues notices of violation to land owners not complying with request for voluntary correction of problems. Issues notices of abatement to known violators of dumping regulations and informs other municipal agencies of need to post signs forbidding illegal dumping at designated sites. Prepares case materials when legal action is required to solve problems. Conducts informational meetings for residents, organizes neighborhood cleanup projects, and participates in campaigns to beautify city to promote community interest in eliminating dangerous and unsightly land use practices. ● **GED:** R3, M2, L3 ● **SVP:** 6 mos-1 yr ● **Academic:** Ed=N, Eng=G ● **Work Field:** 271 ● **MPSMS:** 953 ● **Aptitudes:** G3, V3, N4, S3, P4, Q3, K4, F4, M4, E5, C4 ● **Temperaments:** I, J, P ● **Physical:** Stg=L; Freq: R, H, T, G, N Occas: I, A, X ● **Work Env:** Noise=N; Freq: W ● **Salary:** 4 ● **Outlook:** 2

GOE: 11.10.04
Immigration & Customs

CUSTOMS INSPECTOR (government ser.) ● DOT #168.267-022 ● OES: 21911 ● Inspects cargo, baggage, articles worn or carried by persons, and vessels, vehicles, or aircraft entering or leaving United States to enforce customs and related laws: Boards carriers arriving from foreign ports, and inspects and searches carriers to determine nature of cargoes. Superintends loading and unloading of cargo to ensure compliance with customs, neutrality, and commerce laws. Weighs, measures, and gauges imported goods, using calipers, measuring rods, scale, and hydrometer. Examines baggage of passengers arriving from foreign territory to discover contraband or undeclared merchandise. Conducts body search of passengers or crewmembers. Questions suspicious persons to clarify irregularities and explains laws and regulations to tourists or others unfamiliar with customs statutes and procedures. Seals hold and compartments containing sea stores (supplies for ship's personnel) to prevent illegal sale or smuggling of dutiable merchandise. Examines crew and passenger lists, manifests, pratiques, store lists, declarations of merchandise, and ships' documents and issues required permits. Classifies articles and assesses and collects duty on merchandise. Writes reports of findings, transactions, violations, and discrepancies. Seizes contraband and undeclared merchandise and detains or arrests persons involved in violations. May perform preliminary immigration screening of persons entering United States. May take samples of merchandise for appraising. May be designated according to type of inspection performed as Baggage Inspector (government ser.); Border Inspector (government ser.); Cargo Inspector (government ser.). ● **GED:** R4, M4, L4 ● **SVP:** 1-2 yrs ● **Academic:** Ed=A, Eng=G ● **Work Field:** 271 ● **MPSMS:** 953 ● **Aptitudes:** G2, V2, N2, S3, P3, Q2, K3, F3, M3, E3, C3 ● **Temperaments:** J, P ● **Physical:** Stg=L; Freq: R, H, I, T, G, N, A Occas: C, B, S, K, O, W, F, D, X, V ● **Work Env:** Noise=L; Occas: O ● **Salary:** 4 ● **Outlook:** 2

IMMIGRATION INSPECTOR (government ser.) ● DOT #168.167-022 ● OES: 21911 ● Regulates entry of persons into United States at designated port of entry in accordance with immigration laws: Examines applications, visas, and passports and interviews persons to determine eligibility for admission, residence, and travel privileges in United

States. Interprets laws and explains decisions to persons seeking entry. Arrests, detains, paroles, or arranges for deportation of persons according to laws, regulations, and departmental orders. Writes reports of activities and decisions. May patrol border on foot or horseback, or by airplane, automobile, or boat to detect and apprehend persons entering United States illegally and be designated Immigration Patrol Inspector (government ser.). ● **GED:** R4, M3, L4 ● **SVP:** 6 mos-1 yr ● **Academic:** Ed=A, Eng=G ● **Work Field:** 271 ● **MPSMS:** 953 ● **Aptitudes:** G3, V2, N4, S4, P3, Q3, K4, F4, M4, E5, C4 ● **Temperaments:** J, P ● **Physical:** Stg=L; Freq: T, G Occas: R, H, I, N, A ● **Work Env:** Noise=N; Occas: W, O ● **Salary:** 4 ● **Outlook:** 2

GOE: 11.10.05
Company Policy

COMPUTER SECURITY COORDINATOR (profess. & kin.) ● DOT #033.162-010 ● OES: 21998 ● Alternate titles: DATA SECURITY COORDINATOR; INFORMATION SECURITY. Plans, coordinates, and implements security measures to safeguard information in computer files against accidental or unauthorized modification, destruction, or disclosure: Confers with computer user department personnel and COMPUTER PROGRAMMER (profess. & kin.) 030.162-010 to plan data security for new or modified software, discussing issues, such as employee data access needs and risk of data loss or disclosure. Reviews plan to ensure compatibility of planned security measures with establishment computer security system software. Modifies security data files to incorporate new software security into establishment security software, using computer terminal, or meets with SYSTEMS PROGRAMMER (profess. & kin.) 030.162-022 to request needed programming changes. Enters commands into computer in attempt to circumvent new security measures to test system. Reviews employee violations of computer security procedures recorded by computer and reports violations to user department managers or talks with employee to ensure that violation is not repeated. Coordinates implementation of vendor-issued security software update. Develops and writes computer security department policies and procedures. May assign computer access passwords to employees [COMPUTER SECURITY SPECIALIST (profess. & kin.) 033.362-010]. May develop, coordinate implementation of, and test plan to continue establishment data processing activities at off-site location in case of emergency, such as fire, at main site [DATA RECOVERY PLANNER (profess. & kin.) 033.162-014]. ● **GED:** R5, M3, L4 ● **SVP:** 4-10 yrs ● **Academic:** Ed=A, Eng=G ● **Work Field:** 233, 271 ● **MPSMS:** 893 ● **Aptitudes:** G2, V2, N4, S4, P4, Q2, K3, F4, M4, E5, C5 ● **Temperaments:** J, P, T ● **Physical:** Stg=S; Const: N Freq: I, T, G Occas: R, H, A ● **Work Env:** Noise=Q; ● **Salary:** 4 ● **Outlook:** 5

COMPUTER SECURITY SPECIALIST (profess. & kin.) ● DOT #033.362-010 ● OES: 21998 ● Regulates access to computer data files, monitors data file use, and updates computer security files: Enters commands into computer to allow access to computer system for employee who forgot password. Reads computer security files to determine whether denial of data access reported by employee is justified. Modifies security files to correct error, or explains that employee authorization does not permit access. Answers employee questions about computer security. Modifies security files to add new employees, delete former employees, and change employee name, following notice received from computer user departments and personnel office. Sends printouts listing employee data authorization to computer user departments to verify or correct information in security files. Reviews data use records and compares user names listed in records with employee authorization to ensure that all employees who accessed data files were entitled to do so. Deletes data access of unauthorized users, and for users who have not used data for specified time. ● **GED:** R4, M2, L3 ● **SVP:** 1-2 yrs ● **Academic:** Ed=A, Eng=S ● **Work Field:** 233 ● **MPSMS:** 893 ● **Aptitudes:** G2, V2, N4, S4, P4, Q2, K3, F4, M4, E5, C5 ● **Temperaments:** P, T ● **Physical:** Stg=S; Const: N, A Freq: I, T, G Occas: R, H ● **Work Env:** Noise=N; ● **Salary:** 4 ● **Outlook:** 5

DEALER-COMPLIANCE REPRESENTATIVE (retail trade) ● DOT #168.267-026 ● OES: 21911 ● Alternate titles: FIELD REPRESENTATIVE. Inspects franchise dealerships and distributorships to ascertain compliance with company operating policies and procedures and to require adherence in detected instances: Inspects inventory and operating records to ascertain that only approved products are sold and approved operating procedures followed by dealer. Inspects premises and observes working conditions to ensure compliance with company and governmental standards of safety and sanitation. May ascertain that dealers are paying bills due company and may collect monies due. May advise dealers on financial aspects of operating franchise. ● **GED:** R4, M3, L3 ● **SVP:** 1-2 yrs ● **Academic:** Ed=H, Eng=S ● **Work Field:** 211 ● **MPSMS:** 899 ● **Aptitudes:** G3, V3, N3, S4, P4, Q3, K4, F4, M4, E4, C4 ● **Temperaments:** J, P ● **Physical:** Stg=L; Freq: H, I, T, G, N Occas: R, D, X ● **Work Env:** Noise=N; Occas: W ● **Outlook:** 3

RATER, TRAVEL ACCOMMODATIONS (profess. & kin.) ● DOT #168.367-014 ● OES: 21911 ● Inspects and evaluates travel and tourist accommodations in order to rate facilities to be listed in guidebook produced by employing organization, such as automobile club, tourism promoters, or travel guide publishers: Travels to and inspects travel accommodations and tourist facilities, such as hotels, motels, restaurants, campgrounds, vacation resorts, and other similar year-round or seasonal recreational establishments in order to observe conditions and gather data to be used in determining ratings. Rates or re-rates establishment according to predetermined standards concerning quantity and quality of such factors as convenience of location, variety of facilities available, degree of cleanliness maintained, efficiency of services offered, range of rates charged, and other matters of concern to travelers. Reports findings to employer by filling out forms containing ratings and reasons for conclusions and judgments. May sell to establishments concerned advertising space in publication (such as dining guide, tourist magazine, or recreational-area catalogs) in which ratings are to appear. ● **GED:** R3, M3, L3 ● **SVP:** 1-2 yrs ● **Academic:** Ed=H, Eng=S ● **Work Field:** 211 ● **MPSMS:** 896 ● **Aptitudes:** G3, V3, N4, S4, P4, Q4, K4, F4, M4, E4, C4 ● **Temperaments:** D, J, P ● **Physical:** Stg=L; Freq: T, G, N Occas: R, H, I ● **Work Env:** Noise=N; Occas: W ● **Salary:** 4 ● **Outlook:** 3

REGULATORY ADMINISTRATOR (tel. & tel.) ● DOT #168.167-070 ● OES: 15023 ● Directs and coordinates activities of workers engaged in investigating and responding to complaints from telephone subscribers or regulatory agencies concerning rates and services: Directs investigations of telephone company rates and services to ensure that subscribers' complaints are answered and requirements of governmental utility-regulation agencies are met. Analyzes reports of resulting data and recommends response to complaint, considering nature of complaint and company interests and policies. Directs preparation of documents for use by company witnesses summoned to testify at governmental hearings. Reviews governmental rulings to determine changes in legal stipulations and probable effects on company activities. May provide advice and source data to management personnel concerned with preparing applications to regulatory bodies for changes in rates or service. ● **GED:** R5, M5, L5 ● **SVP:** 4-10 yrs ● **Academic:** Ed=B, Eng=G ● **Work Field:** 271 ● **MPSMS:** 861 ● **Aptitudes:** G2, V2, N2, S4, P4, Q3, K4, F4, M4, E5, C5 ● **Temperaments:** D, J, P ● **Physical:** Stg=S; Freq: T, G, N Occas: R, H, I ● **Work Env:** Noise=N; ● **Salary:** 4 ● **Outlook:** 1

SHOPPING INVESTIGATOR (business ser.) ● DOT #376.267-022 ● OES: 63035 ● Alternate titles: INVESTIGATOR; SERVICE AUDITOR; SHOPPING INSPECTOR; SPOTTER. Shops in commercial, retail, and service establishments to test integrity of sales and service personnel, and evaluates sales techniques and services rendered customers: Reviews establishment's policies and standards to ascertain employee-performance requirements. Buys merchandise, orders food, or utilizes services to evaluate sales technique and courtesy of employee. Carries merchandise to check stand or sales counter and observes employee during sales transaction to detect irregularities in listing or calling prices, itemizing merchandise, or handling cash. Delivers purchases to agency conducting shopping investigation service. Writes report of investigations for each establishment visited. Usually works as member of shopping investigation crew. ● **GED:** R3, M3, L3 ● **SVP:** 1-3 mos ● **Academic:** Ed=N, Eng=G ● **Work Field:** 271 ● **MPSMS:** 899 ● **Aptitudes:** G3, V3, N3, S4, P3, Q3, K4, F4, M4, E5, C5 ● **Temperaments:** J, P ● **Physical:** Stg=L; Freq: T, G, N Occas: R, H, I ● **Work Env:** Noise=N; ● **Salary:** 2 ● **Outlook:** 3

TRAFFIC INSPECTOR (motor trans.) ● DOT #184.163-010 ● OES: 21911 ● Alternate titles: DISPATCHER; TRANSPORTATION IN-

SPECTOR. Coordinates scheduled service within assigned territory of streetcar, bus, or railway transportation system: Periodically observes vehicles along route to ensure that service is provided according to schedule. Investigates schedule delays, accidents, equipment failures, and complaints, and files written report. Reports disruptions to service, using radiotelephone. Determines need for changes in service, such as additional coaches, route changes, and revised schedules to increase operating efficiency and improve service. Drives automobile along route to detect conditions hazardous to equipment and passengers, and negotiates with local government personnel to eliminate hazards. Assists in dispatching equipment when necessary. Recommends promotions and disciplinary actions involving transportation personnel. Inspects mechanical malfunctions of vehicles along route and directs repair. ● **GED:** R4, M2, L3 ● **SVP:** 2-4 yrs ● **Academic:** Ed=H, Eng=S ● **Work Field:** 013 ● **MPSMS:** 850 ● **Aptitudes:** G2, V2, N3, S4, P4, Q3, K4, F4, M4, E4, C4 ● **Temperaments:** D, J, P ● **Physical:** Stg=L; Freq: R, H, I, T, G, N, F, D, A, V Occas: X ● **Work Env:** Noise=L; Occas: W ● **Salary:** 4 ● **Outlook:** 3

TRANSPORTATION INSPECTOR (motor trans.) ● DOT #168.167-082 ● OES: 21911 ● Alternate titles: SERVICE INSPECTOR; UNDERCOVER AGENT. Compiles information concerning activities and conduct of employees on railroads, streetcars, and buses and submits written reports of findings: Observes employees performing assigned duties, assuming role of passenger to note their deportment, treatment of passengers, and adherence to company regulations and schedules. Observes and records time required to load and unload passengers or freight, volume of traffic at different stops or stations, and on streetcars and buses, at different times of day. Inspects company vehicles and other property for damage and evidence of abuse. Submits written reports to management with recommendations for improving service. ● **GED:** R4, M3, L4 ● **SVP:** 2-4 yrs ● **Academic:** Ed=H, Eng=G ● **Work Field:** 271 ● **MPSMS:** 852 ● **Aptitudes:** G3, V3, N3, S4, P4, Q3, K5, F4, M4, E5, C5 ● **Temperaments:** J, V ● **Physical:** Stg=L; Freq: H, I, N Occas: S, K, R, T, G ● **Work Env:** Noise=L; Occas: W ● **Salary:** 4 ● **Outlook:** 3

Leading-Influencing   11

Business Management   11.11

Workers in this group manage a business, such as a store or cemetery, a branch of a large company, such as a local office for a credit corporation, or a department within a company, such as a warehouse. They usually carry out operating policies and procedures determined by administrative workers, such as presidents, vice-presidents, and directors. Some managers own their own businesses and are considered self-employed. Managers find employment in all kinds of businesses as well as government agencies.

✓ What kind of work would you do?

Your work activities would depend upon your specific job. For example, you might:

- coordinate the disposal of surplus government property.
- manage a cemetery.
- manage a beauty or barber shop.
- prepare an operating budget for a freight terminal where ships or trucks are unloaded.
- determine the need for hiring additional employees for a hotel or motel.
- operate a branch store according to the policies set by the home office.
- oversee the operation of a recreation establishment, like a skating rink or golf club.

✓ What skills and abilities do you need for this kind of work?

To do this kind of work, you must be able to:

- read and interpret business records and statistical reports.
- use mathematical skills to interpret financial information and prepare budgets.

- analyze and interpret policies established by administrators.
- understand the government regulations covering business operations.
- make business decisions based on production reports and similar facts.
- make business decisions based on your own experience and personal opinions.
- see differences in widths and lengths of lines such as those on graphs.
- deal with the general public, customers, employees, union and government officials with tact and courtesy.
- plan and organize the work of others.
- change activity frequently and cope with interruptions.
- speak and write clearly.
- accept the full responsibility for managing an activity.

✓ How do you know if you would like or could learn to do this kind of work?

The following questions may give you clues about yourself as you consider this group of jobs.

- Have you been in charge of a committee or group activity? Were you able to get others to work well together?
- Have you been class president or treasurer of a club or group? Are you able to use judgment to make decisions?
- Have you planned and organized a project? Do you enjoy this type of activity?

✓ How can you prepare for and enter this kind of work?

Occupations in this group usually require education and/or training extending from one to over ten years, depending upon the specific kind of work.

Nearly all the jobs in this group are entered by promotion or by transfer from related jobs. A college education is not always essential, but may be helpful. Employers usually require applicants to have a high school education or its equal, combined with experience. Experience requirements vary from one to ten years. For some jobs, experience is accepted as a substitute for a high school or college education.

✓ *What else should you consider about these jobs?*

Workers in this group often work more than a standard 40 hour week. They must vary work hours because of emergencies, accidents, or staff shortages. Workers usually are not paid for overtime.

If you think you would like to do this kind of work, look at the job titles listed on the following pages.

■ ■ ■

GOE: 11.11.01
Lodging

CONDOMINIUM MANAGER (real estate) ● DOT #186.167-062 ● OES: 15011 ● Manages condominium complex in accordance with homeowners' property management contract: Confers with representatives of homeowners' association or board of directors to review financial status of association and to determine management priorities. Attends monthly board meetings, records minutes, and prepares copies for distribution to board members. Arranges for and oversees activities of contract service representatives, such as exterminators, trash collector, major repair contractors, utility service repairers, and swimming pool management personnel. Investigates tenant disturbances, violations, or complaints, and resolves problems in accordance with regulations established by board of directors. Directs collection of monthly assessments from residents and payment of incurred operating expenses. Directs maintenance staff in routine repair and maintenance of buildings and grounds of complex. Prepares and maintains record of work assignments, and prepares performance evaluations. Prepares annual budget and activity reports and submits reports to association members. May recruit, hire, train, and supervise maintenance, janitorial, guard, and groundskeeping staff who perform routine repairs, maintain buildings and grounds, and patrol area to maintain secure environment of complex. May maintain contact with insurance carrier, fire protection and police departments, and other agencies having jurisdiction over property to ensure that association is complying with codes and regulations of each agency. May issue and maintain records of special permits, such as vehicle and pet registration, required by condominium association. ● **GED:** R4, M3, L4 ● **SVP:** 2-4 yrs ● **Academic:** Ed=H, Eng=G ● **Work Field:** 295 ● **MPSMS:** 895 ● **Aptitudes:** G2, V2, N3, S4, P3, Q2, K3, F4, M4, E5, C5 ● **Temperaments:** D, J, P ● **Physical:** Stg=L; Freq: T, G, N Occas: S, O, R, H, I ● **Work Env:** Noise=N; Occas: W ● **Salary:** 3 ● **Outlook:** 2

EXECUTIVE HOUSEKEEPER (any industry) ● DOT #187.167-046 ● OES: 15026 ● Alternate titles: CUSTODIAL SERVICES MANAGER; DIRECTOR, HOUSEKEEPING; HOUSEKEEPER, ADMINISTRATIVE; HOUSEKEEPER, HEAD. Directs institutional housekeeping program to ensure clean, orderly, and attractive conditions of establishment: Establishes standards and procedures for work of housekeeping staff, and plans work schedules to ensure adequate service. Inspects and evaluates physical condition of establishment, and submits to management recommendations for painting, repairs, furnishings, relocation of equipment, and reallocation of space. Periodically inventories supplies and equipment. Reads trade journals to keep informed of new and improved cleaning methods, products, supplies, and equipment. Organizes and directs departmental training programs, resolves personnel problems, hires new employees, and evaluates employees performance and working relationship. Maintains records and prepares periodic activity and personnel reports for review by management. Coordinates activities with those of other departments. May select and purchase new furnishings. May evaluate records to forecast department personnel requirements, and to prepare budget. May perform cleaning duties in cases of emergency or staff shortage. ● **GED:** R5, M4, L4 ● **SVP:** 4-10 yrs ● **Academic:** Ed=H, Eng=S ● **Work Field:**

295 ● **MPSMS:** 900 ● **Aptitudes:** G2, V2, N3, S3, P3, Q3, K4, F4, M4, E5, C4 ● **Temperaments:** D, J, P ● **Physical:** Stg=L; Const: T, G Freq: R, H, I, N Occas: X ● **Work Env:** Noise=N; ● **Salary:** 1 ● **Outlook:** 1

MANAGER, APARTMENT HOUSE (real estate) ● DOT #186.167-018 ● OES: 15011 ● Manages apartment house complex or development for owners or property management firm: Shows prospective tenants apartments and explains occupancy terms. Informs prospective tenants of availability of nearby schools, shopping malls, recreational facilities, and public transportation. Rents or leases apartments, collects security deposit as required, and completes lease form outlining conditions and terms of occupancy when required. Collects rents due and issues receipts. Investigates tenant complaints concerning malfunctions of utilities or furnished household appliances or goods, and inspects vacated apartments to determine need for repairs or maintenance. Directs and coordinates activities of maintenance staff engaged in repairing plumbing or electrical malfunctions, painting apartments or buildings, and performing landscaping or gardening work, or arranges for outside personnel to perform repairs. Resolves tenant complaints concerning other tenants or visitors. May arrange for other services, such as trash collection, extermination, or carpet cleaning. May clean public areas of building and make minor repairs to equipment or appliances. ● **GED:** R4, M3, L4 ● **SVP:** 6 mos-1 yr ● **Academic:** Ed=N, Eng=S ● **Work Field:** 295 ● **MPSMS:** 895 ● **Aptitudes:** G3, V3, N3, S4, P4, Q3, K4, F4, M4, E5, C5 ● **Temperaments:** D, J, P, V ● **Physical:** Stg=L; Freq: R, H, T, G, N Occas: I ● **Work Env:** Noise=N; Occas: W ● **Salary:** 4 ● **Outlook:** 4

MANAGER, CONVENTION (hotel & rest.) ● DOT #187.167-078 ● OES: 15026 ● Coordinates activities of staff and convention personnel to make arrangements for group meetings and conventions to be held in hotel: Consults with representatives of group or organization to plan details, such as number of persons expected, display space desired, and food-service schedule. Obtains permits from fire and health departments to erect displays and exhibits and serve food in rooms other than dining rooms. Notifies various department heads of arrangements made. Directs workers in preparing banquet and convention rooms and erecting displays and exhibits. Inspects rooms and displays for conformance to needs and desires of group. Arranges publicity, special functions, adjusts complaints, and performs other duties to promote goodwill. ● **GED:** R5, M4, L4 ● **SVP:** 2-4 yrs ● **Academic:** Ed=N, Eng=G ● **Work Field:** 295 ● **MPSMS:** 902 ● **Aptitudes:** G2, V2, N3, S3, P3, Q3, K4, F4, M4, E5, C4 ● **Temperaments:** D, P, V ● **Physical:** Stg=L; Freq: R, H, I, T, G ● **Work Env:** Noise=N; ● **Salary:** 4 ● **Outlook:** 3

MANAGER, FRONT OFFICE (hotel & rest.) ● DOT #187.137-018 ● OES: 15026 ● Coordinates front-office activities of hotel or motel and resolves problems arising from guests' complaints, reservation and room assignment activities, and unusual requests and inquiries: Assigns duties and shifts to workers and observes performances to ensure adherence to hotel policies and established operating procedures. Confers and cooperates with other department heads to ensure coordination of hotel activities. Answers inquiries pertaining to hotel policies and services. Greets important guests. Arranges for private telephone line and other special services. May patrol public rooms, investigate disturbances, and warn troublemakers. May interview and hire applicants. May receive and process advance registration payments. May send out letters of confirmation or return checks when registration cannot be accepted. ● **GED:** R4, M4, L4 ● **SVP:** 1-2 yrs ● **Academic:**

Ed=H, Eng=G ● **Work Field:** 282, 292 ● **MPSMS:** 902 ● **Aptitudes:** G2, V2, N3, S4, P4, Q2, K4, F4, M4, E5, C5 ● **Temperaments:** D, J, P, V ● **Physical:** Stg=L; Freq: R, H, T, G Occas: I, N ● **Work Env:** Noise=N; ● **Salary:** 3 ● **Outlook:** 3

MANAGER, HOTEL OR MOTEL (hotel & rest.) ● DOT #187.117-038 ● OES: 15026 ● Alternate titles: MANAGER, GENERAL; MANAGER, MOTOR HOTEL; MANAGER, MOTOR INN; MANAGER, RESIDENT. Manages hotel or motel to ensure efficient and profitable operation: Establishes standards for personnel administration and performance, service to patrons, room rates, advertising, publicity, credit, food selection and service, and type of patronage to be solicited. Plans dining room, bar, and banquet operations. Allocates funds, authorizes expenditures, and assists in planning budgets for departments. Interviews, hires, and evaluates personnel. Answers patrons' complaints and resolves problems. Delegates authority and assigns responsibilities to department heads. Inspects guests' rooms, public access areas, and outside grounds for cleanliness and appearance. Processes reservations and adjusts guests' complaints when working in small motels or hotels. ● **GED:** R5, M4, L4 ● **SVP:** 2-4 yrs ● **Academic:** Ed=A, Eng=S ● **Work Field:** 295 ● **MPSMS:** 902, 893 ● **Aptitudes:** G2, V2, N2, S4, P4, Q2, K4, F4, M4, E5, C5 ● **Temperaments:** D, J, P, V ● **Physical:** Stg=S; Freq: T, G Occas: R, H, I, N, F ● **Work Env:** Noise=N; ● **Salary:** 5 ● **Outlook:** 3

MANAGER, LODGING FACILITIES (hotel & rest.) ● DOT #320.137-014 ● OES: 15026 ● Manages and maintains temporary or permanent lodging facilities, such as small apartment houses, motels, small hotels, trailer parks, and boat marinas: Shows and rents or assigns accommodations. Registers guests. Collects rents and records data pertaining to rent funds and expenditures. Resolves occupants' complaints. Purchases supplies and arranges for outside services, such as fuel delivery, laundry, maintenance and repair, and trash collection. Provides telephone answering service for tenants, delivers mail and packages, and answers inquiries concerning travel routes, recreational facilities, scenic attractions, and eating establishments. Cleans public areas, such as entrances, halls, and laundry rooms, and fires boilers. Makes minor electrical, plumbing, and structural repairs. Mows and waters lawns, and cultivates flower beds and shrubbery. Cleans accommodations after guests' departure. Provides daily maid service in overnight accommodations. May rent equipment, such as rowboats, water skis, and fishing tackle. May coordinate intramural activities of patrons of park. May arrange for medical aid for park patron. May sell light lunches, candy, tobacco, and other sundry items. May be designated according to type of establishment managed as Manager, Apartment House (hotel & rest.); Manager, Hotel (hotel & rest.); Manager, Marina (hotel & rest.); Manager, Motel (hotel & rest.); Manager, Tourist Camp (hotel & rest.); Manager, Trailer Park (hotel & rest.). ● **GED:** R4, M3, L4 ● **SVP:** 2-4 yrs ● **Academic:** Ed=N, Eng=G ● **Work Field:** 295 ● **MPSMS:** 902 ● **Aptitudes:** G3, V3, N3, S4, P4, Q3, K4, F4, M4, E4, C5 ● **Temperaments:** D, P, V ● **Physical:** Stg=M; Freq: R, H, T, G ● **Work Env:** Noise=N; ● **Salary:** 5 ● **Outlook:** 3

GOE: 11.11.02
Recreation & Amusement

DIRECTOR, CAMP (social ser.) ● DOT #195.167-018 ● OES: 19998 ● Directs activities of recreation or youth work camp: Plans programs of recreational and educational activities. Hires and supervises camp staff. Arranges for required licenses, certificates, and insurance coverage to meet health, safety, and welfare standards for campers and for camp operation. Keeps records regarding finances, personnel actions, enrollments, and program activities related to camp business operations and budget allotments. ● **GED:** R5, M4, L5 ● **SVP:** 2-4 yrs ● **Academic:** Ed=A, Eng=S ● **Work Field:** 295 ● **MPSMS:** 941 ● **Aptitudes:** G2, V2, N2, S4, P4, Q4, K4, F4, M4, E5, C5 ● **Temperaments:** D, P ● **Physical:** Stg=S; Freq: T, G Occas: R, H, I, N ● **Work Env:** Noise=N; Occas: W ● **Salary:** 3 ● **Outlook:** 3

DIRECTOR, RECREATION CENTER (social ser.) ● DOT #195.167-026 ● OES: 27311 ● Plans, organizes, and directs comprehensive public and voluntary recreation programs at recreation building, indoor center, playground, playfield, or day camp: Studies and

analyzes recreational needs and resources. Oversees and assigns duties to staff. Interprets recreation programs and their philosophy to individuals and groups through personal participation and staff assignments. Schedules maintenance and use of facilities. Coordinates recreation program of host agency, such as settlement house, institution for children or aged, hospital, armed services, or penal institution, with related activity programs of other services or allied agencies. Cooperates with recreation and nonrecreation personnel. Works under direction of RECREATION SUPERVISOR (profess. & kin.). ● **GED:** R5, M3, L5 ● **SVP:** 2-4 yrs ● **Academic:** Ed=A, Eng=S ● **Work Field:** 295 ● **MPSMS:** 941 ● **Aptitudes:** G2, V2, N3, S4, P4, Q4, K4, F4, M4, E5, C5 ● **Temperaments:** D, P ● **Physical:** Stg=L; Freq: T, G Occas: R, H, I, N ● **Work Env:** Noise=L; Occas: W ● **Salary:** 3 ● **Outlook:** 3

MANAGER, BOWLING ALLEY (amuse. & rec.) ● DOT #187.167-222 ● OES: 19998 ● Manages bowling alley: Directs activities of workers engaged in providing services to patrons and in maintaining facilities and equipment. Assigns alleys for use, issues score sheets, and pushes controls to actuate automatic game-scoring equipment. Records number of games played and collects payment. Inspects alleys to ensure equipment is operative and observes patrons to detect disruptive behavior and misuse of alleys and equipment. Rents bowling shoes to patrons. Organizes bowling leagues and informs members of league requirements. Prepares and distributes announcements of league activities, collects member fees, and distributes tournament prizes. May sell bowling equipment. May hire and train workers. ● **GED:** R4, M2, L3 ● **SVP:** 6 mos-1 yr ● **Academic:** Ed=H, Eng=G ● **Work Field:** 295, 211 ● **MPSMS:** 919 ● **Aptitudes:** G3, V2, N3, S3, P4, Q3, K4, F4, M4, E5, C5 ● **Temperaments:** D, P, V ● **Physical:** Stg=L; Freq: T, G Occas: R, H, I, N, F ● **Work Env:** Noise=N; ● **Salary:** 3 ● **Outlook:** 3

MANAGER, GOLF CLUB (amuse. & rec.) ● DOT #187.167-114 ● OES: 19998 ● Manages golf club to provide entertainment for patrons: Directs activities of dining room and kitchen workers and crews that maintain club buildings, equipment, and golf course in good condition. Hires and discharges workers. Estimates quantities and costs of foodstuffs, beverages, and groundskeeping equipment to prepare operating budget. Explains necessity of items on budget to board of directors and requests approval. Inspects club buildings, equipment, and golf course. Requisitions materials, such as foodstuffs, beverages, seeds, fertilizers, and groundskeeping equipment. Keeps accounts of receipts and expenditures. May assist in planning tournaments. ● **GED:** R4, M4, L4 ● **SVP:** 1-2 yrs ● **Academic:** Ed=H, Eng=S ● **Work Field:** 295 ● **MPSMS:** 913 ● **Aptitudes:** G2, V2, N2, S4, P4, Q2, K4, F4, M4, E5, C5 ● **Temperaments:** D, J, P, V ● **Physical:** Stg=S; Freq: R, H, T, G, N Occas: I ● **Work Env:** Noise=N; ● **Salary:** 4 ● **Outlook:** 2

MANAGER, POOL (amuse. & rec.) ● DOT #153.137-010 ● OES: 27311 ● Supervises and coordinates activities of swimming pool staff to prevent accidents and provide assistance to swimmers, and conducts swimming classes: Assigns duties to lifeguards, locker room attendants, and clerical staff. Schedules swimming classes for basic and specialty techniques, according to enrollment, age, and number of instructors. Meets with employees to discuss and resolve work related problems. Completes staff evaluation forms reflecting information such as work habits, effectiveness in interpersonal relations, and acceptance of responsibility. Instructs individuals or groups in swimming classes, principles of water confidence, and lifesaving. Administers first aid, according to prescribed procedures, or calls emergency medical facility, when necessary. Determines chlorine content, pH value, and color of pool water at periodic intervals during day, using testing kit. Completes forms indicating time, date, and pool water test results. Routes forms to supervisor for evaluation and filing. Maintains required forms, such as time and attendance, inventory list, and program of facility activities. ● **GED:** R3, M3, L3 ● **SVP:** 3-6 mos ● **Academic:** Ed=N, Eng=G ● **Work Field:** 293, 296 ● **MPSMS:** 919 ● **Aptitudes:** G3, V3, N3, S3, P3, Q4, K3, F4, M3, E3, C4 ● **Temperaments:** D, P, V ● **Physical:** Stg=H; Freq: R, H, I, T, G, N, F, X Occas: D ● **Work Env:** Noise=N; Occas: W, U ● **Salary:** 3 ● **Outlook:** 2

MANAGER, RECREATION ESTABLISHMENT (amuse. & rec.) ● DOT #187.117-042 ● OES: 19998 ● Manages recreation establishment, such as dancehall, sports arena, or auditorium, to provide entertainment to public: Negotiates with promoters to contract and schedule entertainment. Compiles record of future engagements. Supervises clerical, service, and other employees. Hires and discharges workers. Complies with state and local fire and liquor regulations governing operation of establishment. May order supplies. May oversee workers engaged in keeping premises of establishment clean and in good repair. May be designated according to type of recreational facility directed as Manager, Dance Floor (amuse. & rec.). ● **GED:** R5, M4, L4 ● **SVP:** 2-4 yrs ● **Academic:** Ed=A, Eng=S ● **Work Field:** 295 ● **MPSMS:** 919 ● **Aptitudes:** G2, V2, N3, S4, P4, Q3, K4, F4, M4, E5, C5 ● **Temperaments:** D, P, V ● **Physical:** Stg=L; Freq: R, H, T, G Occas: I, N ● **Work Env:** Noise=L; ● **Salary:** 4 ● **Outlook:** 3

MANAGER, RECREATION FACILITY (amuse. & rec.) ● DOT #187.167-230 ● OES: 19998 ● Manages recreation facilities, such as tennis courts, golf courses, or arcade, and coordinates activities of workers engaged in providing services of facility: Determines work activities necessary to operate facility, hires workers, and assigns specific tasks and work hours, accordingly. Initiates projects, such as promotional mailing or telephone campaigns, to acquaint public with activities of facility. Discusses fees of facility with interested persons. Registers patrons and explains rules and regulations. Confers with patrons to resolve grievances. Hires workers, such as carpenters, plumbers, and electricians, to make needed facility repairs. Maintains financial records. Collects coins from arcade machines. Purchases items such as golf balls, tennis balls, and paper supplies. ● **GED:** R4, M3, L4 ● **SVP:** 1-2 yrs ● **Academic:** Ed=H, Eng=S ● **Work Field:** 295 ● **MPSMS:** 910 ● **Aptitudes:** G2, V2, N3, S4, P4, Q3, K4, F4, M4, E5, C5 ● **Temperaments:** D, P, V ● **Physical:** Stg=L; Freq: T, G ● **Work Env:** Noise=N; ● **Salary:** 3 ● **Outlook:** 1

MANAGER, THEATER (amuse. & rec.) ● DOT #187.167-154 ● OES: 19998 ● Alternate titles: MANAGER, HOUSE. Manages theater for stage productions or motion pictures: Coordinates activities of personnel to ensure efficient operation and to promote patronage of theater. Directs workers in making alterations to and repair of building. Manages financial business of theater. Determines price of admission and promotes theater events. Orders and sells theater tickets. Requisitions or purchases supplies. May book pictures or stage attractions designed to meet tastes of patrons. May negotiate contracts for scripts or performers. May solicit advertisements from business and community groups. May prepare and monitor theater schedules and budget. ● **GED:** R5, M3, L4 ● **SVP:** 2-4 yrs ● **Academic:** Ed=H, Eng=G ● **Work Field:** 295 ● **MPSMS:** 911, 912, 919 ● **Aptitudes:** G2, V2, N3, S4, P4, Q3, K4, F4, M4, E5, C5 ● **Temperaments:** D, I, J, P, V ● **Physical:** Stg=L; Const: T, G Freq: E Occas: R, H, I, N ● **Work Env:** Noise=N; ● **Salary:** 3 ● **Outlook:** 3

GOE: 11.11.03
Transportation

CONDUCTOR, PASSENGER CAR (r.r. trans.) ● DOT #198.167-010 ● OES: 97302 ● Coordinates activities of train crew engaged in transporting passengers on passenger train: Reads train orders, timetable schedules, and other written instructions received from TRAIN DISPATCHER (r.r. trans.) and discusses contents with LOCOMOTIVE ENGINEER (r.r. trans.) and train crew. Compares watch with that of LOCOMOTIVE ENGINEER (r.r. trans.) to ensure that departure time from station or terminal is in accordance with timetable schedules. Assists passengers to board train. Signals LOCOMOTIVE ENGINEER (r.r. trans.) to begin train run, using radiotelephone, giving hand signals, or by waving lantern. Collects tickets, fares, or passes from passengers. Answers passengers' questions concerning train rules and regulations and timetable schedules. Announces names of train stations and terminals to passengers. Supervises workers who inspect air brakes, airhoses, couplings, and journal boxes and who regulate airconditioning, lighting, and heating to ensure safety and comfort to passengers. Assists passengers to get off train at stations or terminals. Prepares reports at end of run to explain accidents, unscheduled stops, or delays. ● **GED:** R4, M3, L4 ● **SVP:** 4-10 yrs ● **Academic:** Ed=H, Eng=G ● **Work Field:** 013 ● **MPSMS:** 851 ● **Aptitudes:** G2, V2, N3, S4, P4, Q2, K3, F4, M4, E3, C4 ● **Temperaments:** D, J, P, V ● **Physical:** Stg=L; Freq: R, H, T, G, N, A Occas: C, B, I, F, D, X ● **Work Env:** Noise=L; Occas: W ● **Salary:** 5 ● **Outlook:** 1

CONDUCTOR, ROAD FREIGHT (r.r. trans.) ● DOT #198.167-018 ● OES: 97302 ● Coordinates activities of train crew engaged in transporting freight on freight train: Reads train orders, schedules, and other written instructions received from TRAIN DISPATCHER (r.r. trans.) and discusses their contents with LOCOMOTIVE ENGINEER (r.r. trans.) and train crew. Inspects couplings and airhoses to ensure that they are securely fastened. Inspects journal boxes to ensure that they are lubricated. Inspects handbrakes on cars to ensure that they are released before train begins to run. Inspects freight cars to ensure that they are securely sealed. Records number of car and corresponding seal number and compares listing with waybill to ensure accuracy of routes and destinations. Compares watch with watch of LOCOMOTIVE ENGINEER (r.r. trans.) to ensure that departure time from station or terminal is in accordance with timetable schedules. Signals LOCOMOTIVE ENGINEER (r.r. trans.) via radiotelephone or by waving lantern to begin train run. Talks to LOCOMOTIVE ENGINEER (r.r. trans.) and traffic control center personnel via telephone during run to give or receive instructions or information concerning stops, delays, or oncoming trains. Instructs workers to set warning signals in front of and at rear of train during emergency stops to warn oncoming trains. Supervises workers engaged in inspection and maintenance of cars and mechanical equipment during run to ensure that train is operating efficiently and safely. Records time of departures and arrivals at all destinations. Prepares reports at end of run to explain accidents, unscheduled stops, or delays. ● **GED:** R4, M3, L3 ● **SVP:** 4-10 yrs ● **Academic:** Ed=H, Eng=G ● **Work Field:** 013 ● **MPSMS:** 851 ● **Aptitudes:** G3, V3, N4, S3, P4, Q3, K4, F4, M4, E3, C4 ● **Temperaments:** D, J, P, V ● **Physical:** Stg=L; Freq: R, H, I, T, G, N, A Occas: C, B, F, D, X, V ● **Work Env:** Noise=L; Occas: W, O ● **Salary:** 5 ● **Outlook:** 2

MANAGER, AUTOMOTIVE SERVICES (any industry) ● DOT #184.117-034 ● OES: 15023 ● Directs and coordinates activities concerned with acquisition of automotive equipment and operation and maintenance of automotive fleet repair and storage facilities for public utility, transportation, commercial, or industrial company: Coordinates activities of staff personnel conducting research and testing program on automotive equipment considered for acquisition for such factors as operational performance, operational and maintenance costs, safety of operation, and compliance with environmental laws and regulations. Reviews and submits staff proposals for modifications to vendor or manufacturer. Directs procurement of all types of company-owned-and-operated automotive equipment, and materials, supplies, and parts required to maintain automotive equipment, garages, and storage facilities. Coordinates automotive repair and maintenance services to obtain maximum utilization of automotive equipment and prevent operational delays in other departments. ● **GED:** R5, M4, L4 ● **SVP:** 4-10 yrs ● **Academic:** Ed=N, Eng=G ● **Work Field:** 295 ● **MPSMS:** 591, 850 ● **Aptitudes:** G2, V2, N2, S3, P3, Q3, K4, F4, M4, E5, C5 ● **Temperaments:** D, J, P ● **Physical:** Stg=S; Freq: T, G Occas: R, H, I, N ● **Work Env:** Noise=N; ● **Salary:** 5 ● **Outlook:** 2

MANAGER, BUS TRANSPORTATION (motor trans.) ● DOT #184.167-054 ● OES: 15023 ● Directs and coordinates activities of motor bus company to provide passengers with fast, efficient, and safe transportation, either performing following duties personally or through subordinate supervisory personnel: Applies for or recommends fare revisions, extension of routes, or changes in schedules in order to improve passenger services and increase revenues. Coordinates terminal and dispatching activities, communication operations, and assignment of driving personnel to obtain optimum use of facilities, equipment, and human resources. Inspects physical facilities of terminal and buses for such factors as cleanliness, safety, and appearance, and takes required actions in order to meet prescribed standards. Processes passenger complaints and initiates corrective actions designed to improve customer relations and services. Initiates investigations into causes of accidents, interviews operators concerned to determine responsibility, and takes actions on findings or submits reports to management. Directs preparation and issuance of new schedules to terminal and operating personnel. Dispatches replacement buses for vehicles involved in accidents and buses and operators for special charter or tours. Directs and participates in training of personnel and issues manuals, bulletins, and technical guides to improve services and operational activities. Reviews operator bids for routes to determine assignments for driving personnel. Checks trip and dispatch logs for conformance with schedules. Verifies cash fares with operator reports and reviews errors with personnel concerned. Directs preparation of and keeping of dispatch and vehicle operations records and reports. ● **GED:** R4, M4, L4 ● **SVP:** 4-10 yrs ● **Academic:** Ed=H, Eng=S ● **Work Field:** 295 ●

MPSMS: 852 ● **Aptitudes:** G2, V3, N3, S4, P4, Q3, K4, F4, M4, E5, C4 ● **Temperaments:** D, P, V ● **Physical:** Stg=S; Freq: R, H, T, G, N Occas: I ● **Work Env:** Noise=Q; ● **Salary:** 3 ● **Outlook:** 1

MANAGER, DISTRIBUTION WAREHOUSE (wholesale tr.) ● DOT #185.167-018 ● OES: 41002 ● Directs and coordinates activities of wholesaler's distribution warehouse: Reviews bills of lading for incoming merchandise and customer orders in order to plan work activities. Assigns workers to specific duties, such as verifying amounts of and storing incoming merchandise and assembling customer orders for delivery. Establishes operational procedures for verification of incoming and outgoing shipments, handling and disposition of merchandise, and keeping of warehouse inventory. Coordinates activities of distribution warehouse with activities of sales, record control, and purchasing departments to ensure availability of merchandise. Directs reclamation of damaged merchandise. ● **GED:** R5, M3, L4 ● **SVP:** 1-2 yrs ● **Academic:** Ed=A, Eng=S ● **Work Field:** 295, 221 ● **MPSMS:** 853 ● **Aptitudes:** G2, V2, N3, S4, P4, Q3, K4, F4, M4, E5, C5 ● **Temperaments:** D, J, P, V ● **Physical:** Stg=S; Freq: R, H, I, T, G, N ● **Work Env:** Noise=N; ● **Salary:** 3 ● **Outlook:** 2

MANAGER, WAREHOUSE (any industry) ● DOT #184.167-114 ● OES: 15023 ● Alternate titles: STOREKEEPER; SUPERINTENDENT, STORAGE AREA; SUPERINTENDENT, WAREHOUSE; WAREHOUSE SUPERVISOR. Directs warehousing activities for commercial or industrial establishment: Establishes operational procedures for activities, such as verification of incoming and outgoing shipments, handling and disposition of materials, and keeping warehouse inventory current. Inspects physical condition of warehouse and equipment and prepares work order for repairs and requisitions for replacement of equipment. Confers with department heads to ensure coordination of warehouse activities with such activities as production, sales, records control, and purchasing. Screens and hires warehouse personnel and issues work assignments. Directs salvage of damaged or used material. May participate in planning personnel-safety and plant-protection activities. ● **GED:** R4, M3, L4 ● **SVP:** 4-10 yrs ● **Academic:** Ed=A, Eng=S ● **Work Field:** 221, 295 ● **MPSMS:** 898 ● **Aptitudes:** G2, V2, N3, S3, P4, Q4, K4, F4, M4, E5, C5 ● **Temperaments:** D, J, P, V ● **Physical:** Stg=L; Freq: R, H, I, T, G Occas: N ● **Work Env:** Noise=N; ● **Salary:** 5 ● **Outlook:** 2

OPERATIONS MANAGER (motor trans.) ● DOT #184.167-118 ● OES: 15023 ● Directs and coordinates activities of workers engaged in crating, moving, and storing household goods and furniture: Inspects warehouse facilities and equipment and recommends changes in allocation of space, and crating procedures to WAREHOUSE SUPERVISOR (motor trans.). Purchases moving equipment such as dollies, pads, trucks, and trailers. Plans pickup and delivery schedules for TRUCK DRIVERS, HEAVY (any industry). Answers such inquiries as type of service offered, rates, schedules, and areas serviced. Examines items to be moved, to ascertain approximate weights and type of crating required. Investigates customers' complaints involving such matters as damaged items, overcharges, and delay in shipment, and makes necessary adjustment. Interviews, selects, trains, and assigns new personnel. May call on customers to solicit new business. May prepare cost estimates for clients. ● **GED:** R4, M3, L3 ● **SVP:** 1-2 yrs ● **Academic:** Ed=H, Eng=S ● **Work Field:** 295, 221 ● **MPSMS:** 853 ● **Aptitudes:** G3, V3, N3, S3, P3, Q3, K3, F4, M3, E3, C5 ● **Temperaments:** D, J ● **Physical:** Stg=L; Freq: R, H, I, T, G, N, F, D Occas: A ● **Work Env:** Noise=N; ● **Salary:** 5 ● **Outlook:** 1

PURSER (water trans.) ● DOT #197.167-014 ● OES: 21998 ● Alternate titles: SHIP PURSER. Coordinates activities of workers aboard ship concerned with shipboard business functions and social activities for passengers: Prepares shipping articles and signs on crew. Maintains payroll records and pays off crews at completion of voyage. Submits passenger and crew sailing lists to governmental agencies as required by regulations. Assists passengers in preparing declarations for customs, arranging for inspections of horticultural items being brought into country, and inspection of documents by immigration authorities. Prepares ship's entrance and clearance papers for foreign ports, and ship's cargo manifests when discharging cargo. Supervises stowage, care, and removal of hold baggage. Arranges for travel and scenic tours at ports of call. Provides banking services and safekeeping of valuables for passengers. Supervises preparing, editing, printing, and distribution of ship's daily newspaper. Plans and conducts games, tournaments, and parties for passengers' enjoyment. May conduct religious services.

May provide first aid for passengers and crew. ● **GED:** R4, M3, L3 ● **SVP:** 2-4 yrs ● **Academic:** Ed=H, Eng=G ● **Work Field:** 232, 013 ● **MPSMS:** 854 ● **Aptitudes:** G2, V2, N2, S4, P3, Q3, K4, F4, M4, E5, C5 ● **Temperaments:** P, V ● **Physical:** Stg=S; Freq: R, H, I, T, G, N, A ● **Work Env:** Noise=N; Occas: O ● **Salary:** 2 ● **Outlook:** 2

STATION MANAGER (r.r. trans.) ● DOT #184.167-130 ● OES: 15023 ● Directs and coordinates activities of railroad station employees and authorizes departure of trains: Notifies employees of changes in arrival and departure times of trains, boarding track numbers, and other information affecting passengers for announcement over loudspeaker and for posting on callboard. Ensures that shift workers and train crews report as scheduled, or that replacements are obtained. Authorizes departure of passenger trains after transfer of mail and baggage is completed, delaying departure for arrival of connecting train if necessary. Authorizes repairs to station facilities and directs activities of custodial and maintenance workers. Investigates passenger service complaints to ensure efficient and courteous service. May negotiate with concessionaires to lease station space or facilities for restaurants, newsstands, advertising displays, and parking. ● **GED:** R4, M3, L3 ● **SVP:** 2-4 yrs ● **Academic:** Ed=H, Eng=S ● **Work Field:** 295 ● **MPSMS:** 851 ● **Aptitudes:** G2, V2, N3, S4, P4, Q3, K4, F4, M4, E5, C5 ● **Temperaments:** D, P, T, V ● **Physical:** Stg=L; Freq: T, G Occas: R, H, N ● **Work Env:** Noise=N; ● **Salary:** 3 ● **Outlook:** 1

GOE: 11.11.04
Services

ASSISTANT BRANCH MANAGER, FINANCIAL INSTITUTION (financial) ● DOT #186.167-070 ● OES: 21998 ● Directs and coordinates activities of workers engaged in providing financial services to customers, and assists in cash management activities: Trains new employees, prepares work schedules, and monitors work performance. Examines documents prepared by subordinates, such as savings bond applications and safe deposit vault entry and exit records, to ensure compliance with establishment policies and procedures. Monitors branch office operations to ensure that security procedures are being followed. Evaluates establishment procedures and recommends changes to MANAGER, FINANCIAL INSTITUTION (financial) 186.167-086. Talks to customers to resolve account-related problems and to ensure positive public relations. Explains services to potential personal and business account customers to generate additional business for establishment. Assists workers to balance daily transactions, using calculator and computer terminal. Manages office in absence of MANAGER, FINANCIAL INSTITUTION (financial). May remove, count, and record cash from automated teller machine. May examine, evaluate, and process loan applications. May prepare, type, and maintain records of financial transactions. ● **GED:** R5, M4, L5 ● **SVP:** 2-4 yrs ● **Academic:** Ed=H, Eng=G ● **Work Field:** 295, 232 ● **MPSMS:** 894 ● **Aptitudes:** G2, V2, N2, S4, P4, Q2, K4, F4, M4, E5, C5 ● **Temperaments:** D, J, P, T ● **Physical:** Stg=L; Const: T, G Freq: N Occas: S, O, R, H, I, F, A ● **Work Env:** Noise=N; ● **Salary:** 4 ● **Outlook:** 2

DIRECTOR, FUNERAL (personal ser.) ● DOT #187.167-030 ● OES: 39011 ● Alternate titles: MANAGER, FUNERAL HOME; MORTICIAN; UNDERTAKER. Arranges and directs funeral services: Coordinates activities of workers to remove body to mortuary for embalming. Interviews family or other authorized person to arrange details, such as preparation of obituary notice, selection of urn or casket, determination of location and time of cremation or burial, selection of PALLBEARERS (personal ser.), procurement of official for religious rites, and transportation of mourners. Plans placement of casket in parlor or chapel and adjusts lights, fixtures, and floral displays. Directs PALLBEARERS (personal ser.) in placement and removal of casket from hearse. Closes casket and leads funeral cortege to church or burial site. Directs preparations and shipment of body for out-of-state burial. May prepare body for interment [EMBALMER (personal ser.)]. ● **GED:** R4, M4, L4 ● **SVP:** 2-4 yrs ● **Academic:** Ed=A, Eng=G ● **Work Field:** 291 ● **MPSMS:** 907 ● **Aptitudes:** G2, V2, N3, S3, P3, Q3, K4, F4, M4, E5, C4 ● **Temperaments:** D, J, P, V ● **Physical:** Stg=L; Freq: R, H, T, G, N Occas: I, D, X ● **Work Env:** Noise=N; Occas: W ● **Salary:** 4 ● **Outlook:** 1

GENERAL MANAGER, ROAD PRODUCTION (amuse. & rec.) ● DOT #187.117-034 ● OES: 19998 ● Directs and coordinates activities concerned with setting up facility for performances of circus, ice skating show, rodeo, or similar touring road show: Plans layout of performance and backstage areas to conform with specification considering such factors, as type and space of facility. Negotiates with local renting agent to arrange personal space for entertainers and animals at each facility used on tour. Coordinates activities of various departments to ensure arrangements are made for providing water and feed for animals and disposal of rubbish and garbage, and to ensure that work crew has equipment and other facilities prepared for each performance. May count daily receipts and verify amount against number of tickets sold. May be designated according to type of show as Superintendent, Circus (amuse. & rec.). ● **GED:** R4, M3, L4 ● **SVP:** 4-10 yrs ● **Academic:** Ed=H, Eng=S ● **Work Field:** 295 ● **MPSMS:** 919 ● **Aptitudes:** G2, V2, N3, S3, P2, Q3, K4, F4, M4, E5, C5 ● **Temperaments:** D, J, P, V ● **Physical:** Stg=L; Freq: T, G Occas: R, H, I, N ● **Work Env:** Noise=N; ● **Salary:** 5 ● **Outlook:** 1

MANAGER, BARBER OR BEAUTY SHOP (personal ser.) ● DOT #187.167-058 ● OES: 69998 ● Manages business operations and directs personal service functions of barber or beauty shop: Confers with employees to ensure quality services for patrons, such as haircuts, facials, hair styling, shaves, massages, shampoos, and manicures. Makes appointments and assigns patrons to BARBERS (personal ser.) or COSMETOLOGIST (personal ser.) to maintain uniform employee schedules. Adjusts customer complaints and promotes new business by expressing personal interest in efficient service for patrons. Directs sanitary maintenance of shop in compliance with health regulations and requires cleanliness, neatness, and courtesy of employees. Negotiates leases and orders equipment and supplies. Keeps accounts of receipts and expenditures and makes up payroll. Performs services of BARBER (personal ser.) or COSMETOLOGIST (personal ser.) in addition to management functions. May supervise on-the-job training and school attendance of apprentice. May train apprentice and master barbers. May supervise MANICURIST (personal ser.); SHOE SHINER (personal ser.) and other workers. ● **GED:** R4, M4, L4 ● **SVP:** 2-4 yrs ● **Academic:** Ed=H, Eng=S ● **Work Field:** 295, 291 ● **MPSMS:** 904 ● **Aptitudes:** G3, V3, N3, S3, P3, Q3, K4, F3, M3, E5, C4 ● **Temperaments:** D, J, P, V ● **Physical:** Stg=L; Freq: R, H, I, T, G, N Occas: E, D, A, X ● **Work Env:** Noise=N; ● **Salary:** 3 ● **Outlook:** 2

MANAGER, EMPLOYMENT AGENCY (profess. & kin.) ● DOT #187.167-098 ● OES: 41002 ● Manages employment services and business operations of private employment agency: Directs hiring, training, and evaluation of employees. Analyzes placement reports to determine effectiveness of EMPLOYMENT INTERVIEWERS (profess. & kin.). Participates in development and utilization of job development methods to promote business for agency. Enforces, through subordinate staff, agency policies, procedures, safety rules, and regulations. Approves or disapproves requests for purchase of new equipment and supplies. Ensures maintenance and repair of facilities and equipment. Prepares budget requests. Investigates and resolves customer complaints. May negotiate leases and order equipment and supplies for agency. ● **GED:** R4, M3, L4 ● **SVP:** 2-4 yrs ● **Academic:** Ed=H, Eng=G ● **Work Field:** 295 ● **MPSMS:** 943 ● **Aptitudes:** G2, V2, N3, S4, P4, Q3, K4, F4, M4, E5, C5 ● **Temperaments:** D, J, V ● **Physical:** Stg=S; Freq: T, G Occas: R, H, I, N ● **Work Env:** Noise=N; ● **Salary:** 4 ● **Outlook:** 2

MANAGER, FAST FOOD SERVICES (retail trade) ● DOT #185.137-010 ● OES: 15026 ● Manages franchised or independent fast food or wholesale prepared food establishment: Directs, coordinates, and participates in preparation of, and cooking, wrapping or packing types of food served or prepared by establishment, collecting of monies from in-house or take-out customers, or assembling food orders for wholesale customers. Coordinates activities of workers engaged in keeping business records, collecting and paying accounts, ordering or purchasing supplies, and delivery of foodstuffs to wholesale or retail customers. Interviews, hires, and trains personnel. May contact prospective wholesale customers, such as mobile food vendors, vending machine operators, bar and tavern owners, and institutional personnel, to promote sale of prepared foods, such as doughnuts, sandwiches, and specialty food items. May establish delivery routes and schedules for supplying wholesale customers. Workers may be known according to type or name of franchised establishment or type

of prepared foodstuff retailed or wholesaled. ● **GED:** R4, M4, L4 ● **SVP:** 6 mos-1 yr ● **Academic:** Ed=H, Eng=G ● **Work Field:** 146 ● **MPSMS:** 881, 882 ● **Aptitudes:** G3, V3, N3, S4, P3, Q3, K4, F4, M4, E5, C5 ● **Temperaments:** D, J, P, V ● **Physical:** Stg=L; Freq: R, H, I, T, G, N, A ● **Work Env:** Noise=N; ● **Salary:** 3 ● **Outlook:** 3

MANAGER, FINANCIAL INSTITUTION (financial) ● DOT #186.167-086 ● OES: 13002 ● Manages branch or office of financial institutions, such as commercial bank, credit union, finance company, mortgage company, savings bank, or trust company: Directs and coordinates activities to implement institution policies, procedures, and practices concerning granting or extending lines of credit, commercial loans, real estate loans, and consumer credit loans. Directs, through subordinate supervisors, activities of workers engaged in implementing establishment services and performing such functions as collecting delinquent accounts, authorizing loans, or opening savings account. Establishes procedures for custody and control of assets, records, loan collateral, and securities to ensure safekeeping. Contacts customers and business, community, and civic organizations to promote goodwill and generate new business. May prepare financial and regulatory reports required by law, regulations, and board of directors. May examine, evaluate, and process loan applications. May recommend securities to board or corporate officers for institution investment. May talk to customers to resolve account problems. May interview and hire workers. May evaluate data pertaining to costs to plan budget. May plan and develop methods and procedures for carrying out activities of establishment. May be designated according to type of financial institution managed, as Manager, Branch Bank (financial); Manager, Commercial Bank (financial); Manager, Credit Union (financial); Manager, Finance Company (financial); Manager, Mortgage Company (financial); Manager, Savings Bank (financial); Manager, Trust Company (financial). ● **GED:** R5, M4, L5 ● **SVP:** 4-10 yrs ● **Academic:** Ed=B, Eng=G ● **Work Field:** 295 ● **MPSMS:** 894 ● **Aptitudes:** G2, V2, N2, S4, P4, Q3, K4, F4, M4, E5, C5 ● **Temperaments:** D, J, P ● **Physical:** Stg=S; Const: T, G Freq: R, H, N Occas: I, F, A ● **Work Env:** Noise=N; ● **Salary:** 5 ● **Outlook:** 2

MANAGER, FOOD SERVICE (hotel & rest.) ● DOT #187.167-106 ● OES: 15026 ● Coordinates food service activities of hotel, restaurant, or other similar establishment or at social functions: Estimates food and beverage costs and requisitions or purchases supplies. Confers with food preparation and other personnel to plan menus and related activities, such as dining room, bar, and banquet operations. Directs hiring and assignment of personnel. Investigates and resolves food quality and service complaints. May review financial transactions and monitor budget to ensure efficient operation, and to ensure expenditures stay within budget limitations. May be designated according to type of establishment or specialty as Caterer (personal ser.); Manager, Banquet (hotel & rest.); Manager, Cafeteria Or Lunchroom (hotel & rest.); Manager, Catering (hotel & rest.); Manager, Food And Beverage (hotel & rest.); Manager, Restaurant Or Coffee Shop (hotel & rest.). ● **GED:** R4, M4, L4 ● **SVP:** 2-4 yrs ● **Academic:** Ed=H, Eng=G ● **Work Field:** 295 ● **MPSMS:** 903 ● **Aptitudes:** G2, V2, N2, S4, P4, Q3, K4, F4, M4, E5, C4 ● **Temperaments:** D, J, P, V ● **Physical:** Stg=L; Freq: R, H, T, G Occas: I, N, X ● **Work Env:** Noise=N; ● **Salary:** 4 ● **Outlook:** 5

MANAGER, INSURANCE OFFICE (insurance) ● DOT #186.167-034 ● OES: 41002 ● Alternate titles: DISTRICT AGENT. Directs and coordinates activities of branch or district office of insurance company, agency or insurance brokerage firm: Hires and trains workers in performing activities, such as selling insurance, processing insurance claims, or underwriting. Reviews activity reports to ensure that personnel have achieved sales quotas, processed claims promptly, or credited collections to policyholders' accounts. Confers with company officials to plan and develop methods and procedures to increase sales, lower costs, and obtain greater efficiency. Interprets, implements, and enforces company policies. Prepares and submits activity reports. May reconcile earned commissions with commission advances on sales personnel. May be designated according to type of office managed as District Branch Manager (insurance); District Claims Manager (insurance); District Sales Manager (insurance); Manager, Farm Underwriters (insurance); Manager, Field Underwriters (insurance); Manager, Insurance Agency (insurance). ● **GED:** R5, M4, L5 ● **SVP:** 4-10 yrs ● **Academic:** Ed=B, Eng=G ● **Work Field:** 295 ● **MPSMS:** 895 ● **Aptitudes:** G1, V1, N2, S5, P5, Q2, K4, F4, M4, E5, C5 ● **Tempera-**

ments: D, J, P ● **Physical:** Stg=S; Const: T, G, N Freq: R, H Occas: I ● **Work Env:** Noise=Q; ● **Salary:** 5 ● **Outlook:** 2

MANAGER, LAUNDROMAT (laundry & rel.) ● DOT #369.167-010 ● OES: 81000 ● Manages coin-operated drycleaning and laundering business: Plans and implements hours of operations, types of services to be provided, and charges for services. Orders machines, equipment, and supplies for operation. Hires, trains, and supervises personnel to provide laundry and drycleaning services. Records and analyzes business data to determine performance record. May clean and perform repair services on machines. ● **GED:** R4, M3, L3 ● **SVP:** 1-2 yrs ● **Academic:** Ed=N, Eng=N ● **Work Field:** 031, 232 ● **MPSMS:** 906 ● **Aptitudes:** G2, V2, N2, S2, P3, Q3, K4, F4, M4, E5, C4 ● **Temperaments:** D, J, P ● **Physical:** Stg=S; Freq: R, H, I, N Occas: B, T, G, A, V ● **Work Env:** Noise=N; ● **Salary:** 3 ● **Outlook:** 2

MANAGER, LIQUOR ESTABLISHMENT (hotel & rest.) ● DOT #187.167-126 ● OES: 15026 ● Alternate titles: MANAGER, CLUB. Coordinates activities of workers engaged in selling alcoholic beverages for consumption on premises: Estimates and orders foodstuffs, liquors, wines, or other beverages, and supplies. Interviews, hires, trains, and discharges workers. Adjusts customer's complaints concerning service, food, and beverages. Inspects establishment and observes workers and patrons to ensure compliance with occupational, health, and safety standards and local liquor regulations. May plan and arrange promotional programs and advertisement. May hire entertainers. May be designated according to kind of establishment managed as Manager, Beer Parlor (hotel & rest.); Manager, Cocktail Lounge (hotel & rest.); Manager, Night Club (hotel & rest.); Manager, Tavern (hotel & rest.). ● **GED:** R4, M4, L4 ● **SVP:** 1-2 yrs ● **Academic:** Ed=N, Eng=G ● **Work Field:** 295, 292 ● **MPSMS:** 903 ● **Aptitudes:** G3, V3, N3, S4, P3, Q3, K4, F4, M4, E5, C5 ● **Temperaments:** D, J, P, V ● **Physical:** Stg=L; Freq: R, H, T, G, N, F Occas: I, D, A, X, V ● **Work Env:** Noise=L; ● **Salary:** 4 ● **Outlook:** 3

MANAGER, PROPERTY (real estate) ● DOT #186.167-046 ● OES: 15011 ● Manages commercial, industrial, or residential real estate properties for clients: Discusses with client terms and conditions for providing management services, and drafts agreement stipulating extent and scope of management responsibilities, services to be performed, and costs for services. Prepares lease or rental agreements for lessees and collects specified rents and impounds. Directs bookkeeping functions, or credits client account for receipts and debits account for disbursements, such as mortgage, taxes, and insurance premium payments, management sevices costs, and upkeep and maintenance costs. Arranges for alterations to, or maintenance, upkeep, or reconditioning of property as specified in management services or lessee's agreement. Employs, or contracts for services of, security, maintenance, and groundskeeping personnel and on-site management personnel if required. Purchases supplies and equipment for use on leased properties. Directs preparation of financial statements and reports on status of properties, such as occupancy rates and dates of expiration of leases. Directs issuance of check for monies due client. May advise client relative to financing, purchasing, or selling property. Usually required to have real estate broker's license and be certified in property management. May prepare periodic inventory of building contents and forward listing to owner for review. May contact utility companies to arrange for transfer of service for tenants. May assist with eviction of tenants in compliance with court order and directions from LAWYER (profess. & kin.) 110.107-010 and owner. ● **GED:** R4, M3, L4 ● **SVP:** 4-10 yrs ● **Academic:** Ed=A, Eng=S ● **Work Field:** 295 ● **MPSMS:** 895 ● **Aptitudes:** G2, V2, N3, S4, P4, Q3, K4, F4, M4, E5, C5 ● **Temperaments:** D, P ● **Physical:** Stg=L; Freq: R, H, I, T, G, N Occas: C, S, O ● **Work Env:** Noise=N; Occas: W ● **Salary:** 4 ● **Outlook:** 2

MANAGER, REAL-ESTATE FIRM (real estate) ● DOT #186.167-066 ● OES: 15011 ● Directs and coordinates activities of sales staff for real estate firm: Screens and hires sales agents. Conducts training sessions to present and discuss sales techniques, ethics, and methods of maintaining sales quotas. Accompanies sales agents and clients to observe sales methods utilized, and counsels agents regarding matters, such as professionalism, financing, and sales closings. Confers with agents and clients to resolve problems, such as adjusting sales price, repairing property, or accepting closing costs. Sells or rents property for clients [SALES AGENT, REAL ESTATE (real estate) 250.357-018]. Manages residential and commercial properties for clients [MAN-

AGER, PROPERTY (real estate) 186.167-046]. May own real estate firm or be employed by nationwide franchise. May confer with legal authority to determine if transactions are handled in accordance with state laws and with regulations governing real estate industry. May assist in negotiating development contracts with land developers, contractors, and architects. May review closing statements and attend closing transactions to represent real estate establishment. ● **GED:** R4, M3, L4 ● **SVP:** 4-10 yrs ● **Academic:** Ed=H, Eng=S ● **Work Field:** 295, 292 ● **MPSMS:** 895 ● **Aptitudes:** G2, V2, N2, S3, P3, Q3, K4, F4, M4, E4, C5 ● **Temperaments:** D, I, J, P ● **Physical:** Stg=L; Freq: R, H, T, G, N Occas: C, I ● **Work Env:** Noise=N; Occas: W ● **Salary:** 4 ● **Outlook:** 1

MANAGER, SALES (laundry & rel.) ● DOT #187.167-138 ● OES: 41002 ● Manages sales functions of drycleaning establishment: Coordinates activities of SERVICE-ESTABLISHMENT ATTENDANT (laundry & rel.; personal ser.) and DRIVERS, SALES ROUTE (retail trade; wholesale tr.). Visits customers to make estimates on proposed work, such as cleaning draperies, rugs, and upholstered furniture. Adjusts customers' complaints. Directs advertising and promotion campaigns. ● **GED:** R4, M4, L4 ● **SVP:** 2-4 yrs ● **Academic:** Ed=H, Eng=S ● **Work Field:** 291, 292 ● **MPSMS:** 906 ● **Aptitudes:** G2, V2, N3, S4, P4, Q4, K4, F5, M5, E5, C4 ● **Temperaments:** D, J, P ● **Physical:** Stg=L; Freq: T, G, A Occas: R, H, I, N ● **Work Env:** Noise=N; ● **Salary:** 4 ● **Outlook:** 2

MANAGER, SERVICE DEPARTMENT (wholesale tr.) ● DOT #187.167-142 ● OES: 81000 ● Alternate titles: MANAGER, SERVICE; SERVICE SUPERVISOR. Manages farm machinery service department and warehouse: Directs workers engaged in servicing equipment, such as mowers, cotton pickers, hay balers, and combines. Analyzes requests for service and records repairs, replacements, or service required. Informs field service personnel of location and work to be done. Authorizes issuance of replacement parts. Provides training for service personnel. May replenish warehouse stock. ● **GED:** R4, M4, L4 ● **SVP:** 2-4 yrs ● **Academic:** Ed=N, Eng=G ● **Work Field:** 121 ● **MPSMS:** 562 ● **Aptitudes:** G2, V2, N3, S3, P3, Q3, K4, F4, M4, E5, C5 ● **Temperaments:** D, J, V ● **Physical:** Stg=L; Freq: I, T, G, N Occas: S, K, O, W, R, H ● **Work Env:** Noise=L; ● **Salary:** 4 ● **Outlook:** 2

MANAGER, TITLE SEARCH (real estate) ● DOT #186.167-090 ● OES: 15011 ● Alternate titles: ABSTRACT MANAGER; CHIEF OF PRODUCTION. Directs and coordinates activities of persons involved in searching, examining, and recording documents to determine status of property titles and participates in real estate closing procedures: Interviews, screens, hires, trains, promotes, and terminates title department personnel to ensure adequate and efficient operation. Evaluates performance of employees for compliance with establishment policies and procedures, prepares performance appraisals, and makes recommendations concerning promotions, separations, or shifting of staff to enhance and provide more efficient environment. Conducts in-service training operations to advise employees of changes or additions to company policies and to introduce new methods implemented to ensure more efficient operation. Confers with employees and assists in solving problems affecting job performance and establishment policies and procedures. Directs preparation of work assignments and work schedules to establish priorities and to ensure completion of assignments in timely manner. Confers with other managers and supervisors to establish new policies and procedures. Oversees preparation of timesheets and reviews data sent to payroll department. Confers with supervisors and other office personnel on status of abstract orders and discusses inconsistencies and discrepancies affecting production or quality of final documents. Receives and reviews data collected by abstractors and title reports prepared for clarity, completeness, accuracy, and conformance to established procedures. Confers with legal counsel to discuss defects in title, such as outstanding liens or judgments, or to explain delays in title search. May coordinate closing activities and review closing documents to determine accuracy of information and need for additional documents. May perform difficult and involved title searches. May attend closing meeting to oversee signing of documents and disbursement of documents and monies held in escrow. May give and receive information related to title searching to other persons involved in real estate transaction. May prepare or direct preparation of periodic reports and complete purchase orders for equipment and supplies. ● **GED:** R4, M4, L4 ● **SVP:** 2-4 yrs ● **Academic:** Ed=H, Eng=G ●

Work Field: 295 ● **MPSMS:** 895 ● **Aptitudes:** G2, V2, N2, S4, P3, Q3, K4, F4, M4, E5, C5 ● **Temperaments:** D, J, P, V ● **Physical:** Stg=S; Freq: R, H, I, T, G, N ● **Work Env:** Noise=N; ● **Salary:** 4 ● **Outlook:** 3

MANAGER, TOURING PRODUCTION (amuse. & rec.) ● DOT #191.117-038 ● OES: 39998 ● Alternate titles: MANAGER, THEATRICAL PRODUCTION; MANAGER, TOURING. Travels with and manages business affairs of theatrical company on tour: Completes various arrangements, such as contracting union agreements, hiring stage hands, and procuring legal permits for performance. Approves budgetary items for advertising and promotional purposes. Audits box-office receipts and files accounting statements according to legal requirements. May compile payroll records and distribute paychecks. When coordinating business affairs of first touring company on road, may be designated Company Manager (amuse. & rec.). When managing second and third road show companies, may be designated Road Manager (amuse. & rec.). ● **GED:** R4, M3, L4 ● **SVP:** 2-4 yrs ● **Academic:** Ed=H, Eng=S ● **Work Field:** 295 ● **MPSMS:** 910 ● **Aptitudes:** G3, V3, N3, S4, P4, Q3, K4, F4, M4, E5, C5 ● **Temperaments:** D, J, P, V ● **Physical:** Stg=S; Freq: T, G, N Occas: R, H, I, A ● **Work Env:** Noise=N; ● **Salary:** 4 ● **Outlook:** 1

MANAGER, TRAVEL AGENCY (business ser.) ● DOT #187.167-158 ● OES: 19998 ● Manages travel agency: Directs, coordinates, and participates in merchandising travel agency services, such as sale of transportation company carrier tickets, packaged or specialized tours, or vacation packages. Plans work schedules for employees. Trains employees in advising customers on current traveling conditions, planning customer travel and itineraries, ticketing and booking functions, and in calculating costs for transportation and accommodations from current transportation schedules and tariff books and accommodation rate books. Sells travel tickets, packaged and specialized tours, and advises customers on travel plans. Reviews employee ticketing and sales activities to ensure cost calculations, booking, and transportation scheduling are in accordance with current transportation carrier schedules, tariff rates, and regulations and that charges are made for accommodations. Reconciles sales slips and cash daily. Coordinates sales promotion activities, approves advertising copy, and travel display work. Keeps employee records and hires and discharges employees. ● **GED:** R4, M4, L4 ● **SVP:** 2-4 yrs ● **Academic:** Ed=H, Eng=S ● **Work Field:** 295 ● **MPSMS:** 850 ● **Aptitudes:** G3, V3, N3, S4, P4, Q3, K4, F4, M4, E5, C4 ● **Temperaments:** D, J, P, V ● **Physical:** Stg=L; Freq: T, G Occas: R, H, I ● **Work Env:** Noise=N; ● **Salary:** 4 ● **Outlook:** 1

SUPERINTENDENT, LAUNDRY (laundry & rel.) ● DOT #187.167-194 ● OES: 19998 ● Manages laundry plant in linen supply establishment or commercial or industrial laundry: Schedules flow of work through sorting, washing, and ironing departments, taking into consideration amount of clothes to be laundered and capacity of equipment. Hires, discharges, and transfers employees according to work performance and production needs. Purchases supplies, such as soap, starch, and bleach. Prepares and analyzes reports on labor cost and production operations to determine whether operating cost standards are being met. Tests strength of bleach, using chemical test kit. Performs other administrative and supervisory duties to ensure efficient and profitable operation. Supervises workers directly or through subordinates. ● **GED:** R4, M3, L3 ● **SVP:** 2-4 yrs ● **Academic:** Ed=N, Eng=G ● **Work Field:** 295 ● **MPSMS:** 906 ● **Aptitudes:** G2, V2, N3, S3, P4, Q3, K4, F4, M4, E5, C5 ● **Temperaments:** D, J, P, V ● **Physical:** Stg=L; Freq: R, H, T, G, N, F, A Occas: I ● **Work Env:** Noise=N; ● **Salary:** 4 ● **Outlook:** 2

GOE: 11.11.05
Wholesale-Retail

AREA SUPERVISOR, RETAIL CHAIN STORE (retail trade) ● DOT #185.117-014 ● OES: 13011 ● Alternate titles: OPERATIONS MANAGER. Directs and coordinates activities of subordinate managerial personnel involved in operating retail chain stores in assigned area: Interviews and selects individuals to fill managerial vacancies. Maintains employment records for each manager. Terminates employment of store managers whose performance does not meet company

standards. Directs, through subordinate managerial personnel, compliance of workers with established company policies, procedures, and standards, such as safekeeping of company funds and property, personnel and grievance practices, and adherence to policies governing acceptance and processing of customer credit card charges. Inspects premises of assigned area stores to ensure that adequate security exists and that physical facilities comply with safety and environmental codes and ordinances. Reviews operational records and reports of store managers to project sales and to determine store profitability. Coordinates sales and promotional activities of store managers. Analyzes marketing potential of new and existing store locations and recommends additional sites or deletion of existing area stores. Negotiates with vendors to enter into contracts for merchandise and determines allocations to each store manager. ● **GED:** R4, M3, L4 ● **SVP:** 2-4 yrs ● **Academic:** Ed=N, Eng=G ● **Work Field:** 295 ● **MPSMS:** 893 ● **Aptitudes:** G2, V2, N2, S3, P4, Q2, K4, F3, M3, E5, C5 ● **Temperaments:** D, I, J, P ● **Physical:** Stg=L; Freq: R, H, I, T, G, N ● **Work Env:** Noise=N; ● **Salary:** 4 ● **Outlook:** 2

COMMISSARY MANAGER (any industry) ● DOT #185.167-010 ● OES: 41002 ● Directs and coordinates activities of commissary store to sell to or provide company employees or other eligible customers with foodstuffs, clothing, or other merchandise: Determines quantities of foodstuffs or other merchandise required to stock commissary, from inventory records, and prepares requisitions or buys merchandise to replenish stock. Sells merchandise to company employees or other eligible customers or issues merchandise upon requisition by authorized personnel. Keeps records pertaining to purchases, sales, and requisitions. May issue foodstuffs and supplies to COOKS, CAMP (any industry) for preparation of meals. ● **GED:** R4, M4, L3 ● **SVP:** 1-2 yrs ● **Academic:** Ed=H, Eng=S ● **Work Field:** 292 ● **MPSMS:** 380, 390 ● **Aptitudes:** G2, V3, N3, S4, P4, Q3, K4, F4, M4, E5, C5 ● **Temperaments:** D, P, V ● **Physical:** Stg=L; Freq: R, H, I, T, G, N, A Occas: S, K ● **Work Env:** Noise=N; ● **Salary:** 3 ● **Outlook:** 2

MANAGER, AUTOMOBILE SERVICE STATION (retail trade) ● DOT #185.167-014 ● OES: 41002 ● Manages automobile service station: Plans, develops, and implements policies for operating station, such as hours of operation, workers required and duties, scope of operations, and prices for products and services. Hires and trains workers, prepares work schedules, and assigns workers to specific duties, such as customer service, automobile maintenance, or repair work. Directs, coordinates, and participates in performing customer service activities, such as pumping gasoline, checking engine oil, tires, battery, and washing windows and windshield. Notifies customer when oil is dirty or low, tires are worn, hoses or fanbelts are defective, or evidece indicates battery defects, to promote sale of products and services, such as oil change and lubrication, tires, battery, or other automotive accessories. Reconciles cash with gasoline pump meter readings, sales slips, and credit card charges. Orders, receives, and inventories gasoline, oil, automotive accessories and parts. May perform automotive maintenance and repair work, such as adjusting or relining brakes, motor tune-ups, valve grinding, and changing and repairing tires. May sell only gasoline and oil on self-service basis and be designated Manager, Self-Service Gasoline Station (retail trade). ● **GED:** R4, M4, L4 ● **SVP:** 2-4 yrs ● **Academic:** Ed=H, Eng=S ● **Work Field:** 292, 121 ● **MPSMS:** 881 ● **Aptitudes:** G3, V3, N3, S3, P3, Q3, K3, F3, M3, E4, C3 ● **Temperaments:** D, J, P, V ● **Physical:** Stg=M; Freq: R, H, T, G, N, D, A Occas: C, B, S, K, O, W, I, E, X ● **Work Env:** Noise=N; Freq: W, H, U, A Occas: C, E, O ● **Salary:** 3 ● **Outlook:** 2

MANAGER, DEPARTMENT (retail trade) ● DOT #299.137-010 ● OES: 41002 ● Alternate titles: DEPARTMENT SUPERVISOR; MANAGER, FLOOR. Supervises and coordinates activities of workers in department of retail store: Interviews job applicants and evaluates worker performance to recommend personnel actions such as hiring, retention, promotion, transfer or dismissal of workers. Assigns duties to workers and schedules break periods, work hours, and vacations. Trains workers in store policies, department procedures, and job duties. Orders merchandise, supplies, and equipment. Records delivery of merchandise, compares record with merchandise ordered, and reports discrepancies to control costs and maintain correct inventory levels. Inspects merchandise to ensure it is correctly priced and displayed. Recommends additions to or deletions of merchandise to be sold in department. Prepares sales and inventory reports. Listens to customer complaints, examines returned merchandise, and resolves problems to restore and promote good public relations. May assist sales workers in completing difficult sales. May sell merchandise. May approve checks written for payment of merchandise purchased in department. May install and remove department cash-register-receipt tape and audit cash receipts. May perform customer service activities and be designated Customer Service Manager (retail trade). May plan department layout or merchandise or advertising display [DISPLAYER, MERCHANDISE (retail trade) 298.081-010]. May be designated according to department managed or type of merchandise sold as Candy-Department Manager (retail trade); Toy-Department Manager (retail trade); Produce-Department Manager (retail trade). ● **GED:** R4, M3, L3 ● **SVP:** 2-4 yrs ● **Academic:** Ed=H, Eng=S ● **Work Field:** 221, 292 ● **MPSMS:** 881 ● **Aptitudes:** G3, V3, N3, S4, P3, Q3, K4, F4, M4, E5, C4 ● **Temperaments:** D, J, P ● **Physical:** Stg=M; Freq: H, T, G Occas: S, O, R, I, N, X ● **Work Env:** Noise=N; ● **Salary:** 4 ● **Outlook:** 1

MANAGER, MACHINERY-OR-EQUIPMENT, RENTAL AND LEASING

(any industry) ● DOT #185.167-026 ● OES: 41002 ● Directs and coordinates activities of establishment engaged in renting or leasing machinery, tools and equipment to companies involved in business operations such as manufacturing, petroleum production, construction or materials handling, or to individuals for personal use: Confers with customer to ascertain article required, duration of rental time, and responsibility for maintenance and repair, in order to determine rental or leasing charges based on such factors as type and cost of article, type of usage, duration of rental or lease, and overhead costs. Prepares rental or lease agreement, specifying charges and payment procedures, for use of machinery, tools, or equipment. Directs activities of workers engaged in bookkeeping, record and inventory keeping, and in checking, handling, servicing or maintaining in-house, leased, or rented machines, tools and equipment. Managers of leasing or renting establishments may be designated according to type or use of machinery, tools or equipment. ● **GED:** R4, M4, L4 ● **SVP:** 1-2 yrs ● **Academic:** Ed=H, Eng=S ● **Work Field:** 292 ● **MPSMS:** 560, 580, 884 ● **Aptitudes:** G3, V3, N3, S4, P4, Q4, K4, F4, M4, E5, C5 ● **Temperaments:** D, P ● **Physical:** Stg=L; Freq: R, H, I, T, G, N, A ● **Work Env:** Noise=N; ● **Salary:** 3 ● **Outlook:** 1

MANAGER, MARKET

(retail trade) ● DOT #186.167-042 ● OES: 15011 ● Directs and coordinates activities of municipal, regional, or state fruit, vegetable, or meat market or exchange: Negotiates contracts between wholesalers and market authority or rents space to food buyers and sellers. Directs through subordinate supervisory personnel collection of fees or monies due market, maintenance and cleaning of buildings and grounds, and enforcement of market sanitation and security rules and regulations. Keeps records of current sales prices of food items and total sales volume. May endeavor to resolve differences arising between buyers and sellers. May prepare market activity reports for management or board. ● **GED:** R4, M3, L3 ● **SVP:** 2-4 yrs ● **Academic:** Ed=H, Eng=S ● **Work Field:** 292 ● **MPSMS:** 880 ● **Aptitudes:** G2, V2, N3, S3, P4, Q3, K4, F4, M4, E5, C5 ● **Temperaments:** D, J, P ● **Physical:** Stg=S; Freq: T, G Occas: R, H, I, N ● **Work Env:** Noise=N; ● **Salary:** 4 ● **Outlook:** 2

SERVICE SUPERVISOR, LEASED MACHINERY AND EQUIPMENT

(any industry) ● DOT #183.167-030 ● OES: 19998 ● Directs and coordinates activities of service department of establishment concerned with providing lessees of machinery and equipment with maintenance and repair services as stipulated in leasing contract: Organizes field service offices and facilities in locations that will provide greatest number of customers with services. Stocks offices with spare parts and supplies to enable offices to provide required services. May arrange for transportation of machinery to and from customer's establishment when repairs cannot be performed on-site. May contact potential customers concerning leasing of machinery and equipment. May negotiate leasing and service contracts for machinery and equipment. ● **GED:** R4, M4, L4 ● **SVP:** 2-4 yrs ● **Academic:** Ed=H, Eng=S ● **Work Field:** 111, 121 ● **MPSMS:** 560, 580 ● **Aptitudes:** G2, V2, N3, S3, P3, Q3, K4, F4, M4, E5, C5 ● **Temperaments:** D, P, V ● **Physical:** Stg=L; Freq: T, G ● **Work Env:** Noise=N; ● **Salary:** 4 ● **Outlook:** 1

MANAGER, MEAT SALES AND STORAGE

(retail trade) ● DOT #185.167-030 ● OES: 41002 ● Coordinates activities of workers engaged in buying, processing, and selling meats and poultry and renting frozen food lockers: Prepares daily schedule and directs activities of employees. Examines products bought for resale or received for storage. Cuts, trims, bones, and cleans meats and poultry. Displays and sells different cuts of meats and poultry to customers and advises customers on quality of food, method of handling, and other factors affecting preparing, freezing, and storing food. Conducts in-service training for employees. ● **GED:** R4, M3, L3 ● **SVP:** 1-2 yrs ● **Academic:** Ed=H, Eng=S ● **Work Field:** 292 ● **MPSMS:** 382, 853 ● **Aptitudes:** G3, V3, N3, S3, P3, Q3, K3, F4, M3, E5, C3 ● **Temperaments:** D, J, P ● **Physical:** Stg=M; Freq: R, H, T, G, N Occas: I, A ● **Work Env:** Noise=Q; Occas: C ● **Salary:** 3 ● **Outlook:** 1

MANAGER, PARTS

(retail trade) ● DOT #185.167-038 ● OES: 41002 ● Alternate titles: MANAGER, STOCKROOM. Manages retail or wholesale automotive parts establishment or department of repair shop or service station: Requisitions new stock. Verifies cash receipts and keeps sales records. Hires, trains, and discharges workers. Confirms credit references of customers by mail or telephone. May sell parts. ● **GED:** R4, M3, L3 ● **SVP:** 2-4 yrs ● **Academic:** Ed=H, Eng=S ● **Work Field:** 292 ● **MPSMS:** 591 ● **Aptitudes:** G2, V2, N3, S4, P3, Q4, K4, F4, M4, E5, C4 ● **Temperaments:** D, P ● **Physical:** Stg=L; Freq: R, H, I, T, G, N, A ● **Work Env:** Noise=N; ● **Salary:** 4 ● **Outlook:** 2

MANAGER, RETAIL STORE

(retail trade) ● DOT #185.167-046 ● OES: 41002 ● Alternate titles: STORE MANAGER. Manages retail store engaged in selling specific line of merchandise, such as groceries, meat, liquor, apparel, jewelry, or furniture; related lines of merchandise, such as radios, televisions, or household appliances; or general line of merchandise, performing following duties personally or supervising employees performing duties: Plans and prepares work schedules and assigns employees to specific duties. Formulates pricing policies on merchandise according to requirements for profitability of store operations. Coordinates sales promotion activities and prepares, or directs workers preparing, merchandise displays and advertising copy. Supervises employees engaged in sales work, taking of inventories, reconciling cash with sales receipts, keeping operating records, or preparing daily record of transactions for ACCOUNTANT (profess & kin.) 160.162-018, or performs work of subordinates, as needed. Orders merchandise or prepares requisitions to replenish merchandise on hand. Ensures compliance of employees with established security, sales, and record keeping procedures and practices. May answer customer's complaints or inquiries. May lock and secure store. May interview, hire, and train employees. May be designated according to specific line of merchandise sold, such as women's apparel or furniture; related lines of merchandise, such as camera and photographic supplies, or gifts, novelties, and souvenirs; type of business, such as mail order establishment or auto supply house; or general line of merchandise, such as sporting goods, drugs and sundries, or variety store. ● **GED:** R4, M4, L4 ● **SVP:** 2-4 yrs ● **Academic:** Ed=H, Eng=G ● **Work Field:** 292 ● **MPSMS:** 881 ● **Aptitudes:** G2, V2, N3, S4, P4, Q3, K4, F4, M4, E5, C5 ● **Temperaments:** D, J, P, V ● **Physical:** Stg=L; Freq: H, T, G Occas: R, I, N ● **Work Env:** Noise=N; ● **Salary:** 4 ● **Outlook:** 2

MANAGER, VEHICLE LEASING AND RENTAL

(automotive ser.) ● DOT #187.167-162 ● OES: 13011 ● Manages automobile and truck leasing business: Directs and evaluates leasing, sales, advertising, and administrative procedures, including collections, inventory financing, and used car sales. Directs and monitors audit of financial accounts to assure compliance with prescribed standards. May visit franchised dealers to stimulate interest in establishment or expansion of leasing programs. ● **GED:** R5, M4, L4 ● **SVP:** 4-10 yrs ● **Academic:** Ed=A, Eng=S ● **Work Field:** 295 ● **MPSMS:** 859 ● **Aptitudes:** G2, V3, N3, S4, P4, Q3, K4, F5, M4, E5, C5 ● **Temperaments:** D, I, J, V ● **Physical:** Stg=L; Freq: T, G Occas: R, H, N ● **Work Env:** Noise=N; ● **Salary:** 3 ● **Outlook:** 2

Contracts and Claims   **11.12**

Workers in this group negotiate contracts and settle claims for companies and individuals. Some make arrangements for agreements between buyers and sellers. Others investigate claims involving damage, injury, and losses. Jobs are found in insurance and transportation companies; businesses; construction companies; and government agencies. Some are found in booking agencies. These agents are frequently self-employed.

✓ What kind of work would you do?

Your work activities would depend upon your specific job. For example, you might:

- interview property holders and settle damage claims resulting from prospecting or drilling for oil.
- negotiate with communities to rent a site for a circus.
- negotiate leases for the use of a city arena or auditorium.
- arrange leases of sites for billboards.
- arrange contracts for the appearance of musicians for a concert or show.
- serve as agent for artists, musicians, or actors and negotiate bookings for them.

✓ What skills and abilities do you need for this kind of work?

To do this kind of work, you must be able to:

- understand laws used in writing contracts and settling claims.
- compute costs and prepare cost estimates.
- understand detailed legal information.
- persuade others to agree to terms.
- speak clearly to avoid misunderstandings.
- use your experience and judgment to make decisions.
- work with all kinds of people.
- make decisions based on repair estimates,

doctors' statements, and other verifiable information.
- keep accurate records and write detailed reports.

✓ How do you know if you would like or could learn to do this kind of work?

The following questions may give you clues about yourself as you consider this group of jobs.

- Have you taken courses in business law? Did you understand the special concepts and terms used in the course?
- Have you argued a point of view in front of a group? Are you persuasive and able to gain the respect and confidence of others?
- Have you helped arrange for a group to entertain at a school or community function? Were the arrangements understood by all parties?

✓ How can you prepare for and enter this kind of work?

Occupations in this group usually require education and/or training extending from two to over ten years, depending upon the specific kind of work. Most jobs in this group require experience in insurance, real estate, and labor relations. Community colleges offer courses in some of these fields. The type and amount of education required varies among the jobs. Some require four or more years of college or university study.

✓ What else should you consider about these jobs?

Some jobs in this group require workers to travel frequently. Pay may be based on salary, commission, or a combination of the two. A civil service examination is usually required for jobs in government.

If you think you would like to do this kind of work, look at the job titles listed on the following below.

■ ■ ■

GOE: 11.12.01
Claims Settlement

APPRAISER, AUTOMOBILE DAMAGE (business ser.) ● DOT #241.267-014 ● OES: 53799 ● Alternate titles: AUTOMOBILE-DAMAGE APPRAISER; ESTIMATOR, AUTOMOBILE DAMAGE. Appraises automobile or other vehicle damage to determine cost of repair for insurance claim settlement and attempts to secure agreement with automobile repair shop on cost of repair: Examines damaged vehicle to determine extent of structural, body, mechanical, electrical, or interior damage. Estimates cost of labor and parts to repair or replace each item of damage, using standard automotive labor and parts cost manuals and knowledge of automotive repair. Determines salvage value on total-loss vehicle. Evaluates practicality of repair as opposed to payment of market value of vehicle before accident. Prepares insurance forms to indicate repair-cost estimates and recommendations. Reviews repair-cost estimates with automobile-repair shop to secure agreement on cost of repairs. Occasionally arranges to have damage appraised by another appraiser to resolve disagreement with repair shop on repair cost. ● **GED:** R4, M2, L4 ● **SVP:** 2-4 yrs ● **Academic:** Ed=H, Eng=G ● **Work Field:** 212, 121 ● **MPSMS:** 961 ● **Aptitudes:** G3, V3, N3, S3, P2, Q3, K4, F4, M4, E5, C5 ● **Temperaments:** J ● **Physical:** Stg=L; Freq: R, H, T, G, N, D, A Occas: I ● **Work Env:** Noise=N; Occas: W ● **Salary:** 3 ● **Outlook:** 4

CLAIM ADJUSTER (business ser.) ● DOT #241.217-010 ● OES: 53302 ● Alternate titles: INSURANCE ADJUSTOR; INSURANCE-CLAIM REPRESENTATIVE; INSURANCE INVESTIGATOR. Investigates claims against insurance or other companies for personal, casualty, or property loss or damages and attempts to effect out-of-court settlement with claimant: Examines claim form and other records to determine insurance coverage. Interviews, telephones, or corresponds with claimant and witnesses; consults police and hospital records; and inspects property damage to determine extent of company's liability, varying method of investigation according to type of insurance. Prepares report of findings and negotiates settlement with claimant. Recommends litigation by legal department when settlement cannot be negotiated. May attend litigation hearings. May be designated according to type of claim adjusted as Automobile-Insurance-Claim Adjuster (business ser.; insurance); Casualty-Insurance-Claim Adjuster (clerical); Fidelity-And-Surety-Bonds-Claim Adjuster (business ser.; insurance); Fire-Insurance-Claim Adjuster (business ser.; insurance); Marine-Insurance-Claim Adjuster (business ser.; insurance); Property-Loss-Insurance-Claim Adjuster (clerical). ● **GED:** R5, M3, L5 ● **SVP:** 1-2 yrs ● **Academic:** Ed=H, Eng=G ● **Work Field:** 271 ● **MPSMS:** 895 ● **Aptitudes:** G2, V2, N3, S3, P3, Q2, K4, F4, M4, E5, C5 ● **Temperaments:** I, J, P ● **Physical:** Stg=L; Freq: R, H, T, G, N, A Occas: I ● **Work Env:** Noise=Q; Occas: W ● **Salary:** 3 ● **Outlook:** 3

CLAIM EXAMINER (business ser.) ● DOT #241.267-018 ● OES: 53302 ● Alternate titles: INSURANCE-CLAIM APPROVER; INSURANCE-CLAIM AUDITOR. Analyzes insurance claims to determine extent of insurance carrier's liability and settles claims with claimants in accordance with policy provisions: Compares data on claim application, death certificate, or physician's statement with policy file and other company records to ascertain completeness and validity of claim. Corresponds with agents and claimants or interviews them in person to correct errors or omissions on claim forms, and to investigate questionable entries. Pays claimant amount due. Refers most questionable claims to INVESTIGATOR (clerical) or to CLAIM ADJUSTER (business ser.; insurance) for investigation and settlement. May investigate claims in field. May be designated according to type of claim handled as Accident-And-Health-Insurance-Claim Examiner (insurance); Automobile-Insurance-Claim Examiner (business ser.; insurance); Death-Claim Examiner (insurance); Disability-Insurance-Claim Examiner (insurance); Fire-Insurance-Claim Examiner (business ser.; insurance); Marine-Insurance-Claim Examiner (business ser.; insurance). ● **GED:** R4, M3, L4 ● **SVP:** 2-4 yrs ● **Academic:** Ed=H, Eng=G ● **Work Field:** 271 ● **MPSMS:** 895 ● **Aptitudes:** G2, V2, N3, S4, P4, Q2, K4, F4, M4, E5, C5 ● **Temperaments:** J ● **Physical:** Stg=S; Freq: R, H, I, T, G, N ● **Work Env:** Noise=Q; ● **Salary:** 3 ● **Outlook:** 3

CLAIMS ADJUDICATOR (government ser.) ● DOT #169.267-010 ● OES: 28101 ● Adjudicates claims for benefits offered under governmental social insurance program, such as those dealing with unemployed, retired, or disabled workers, veterans, dependents, or survivors: Reviews and evaluates data on documents and forms, such as claim applications, birth or death certificates, physician's statements, employer's records, vocational evaluation reports, and other similar records. Interviews or corresponds with claimants or agents to elicit information, correct errors or omissions on claim forms, and to investigate questionable data. Authorizes payment of valid claims, or notifies claimant of denied claim and appeal rights. Reevaluates evidence and procures additional information in connection with claims under appeal or in cases requiring investigation of claimant's continuing eligibility for benefits. Prepares written reports of findings. May specialize in one phase of claim program, such as assisting claimant to prepare forms, rating degree of disability, investigating appeals, or answering questions concerning filing requirements and benefits provided. May be designated according to type of benefit-claim adjudicated. May act as consultant to board rating disability. ● **GED:** R5, M4, L4 ● **SVP:** 2-4 yrs ● **Academic:** Ed=A, Eng=G ● **Work Field:** 271, 282 ● **MPSMS:** 959 ● **Aptitudes:** G2, V2, N3, S5, P5, Q3, K4, F4, M4, E5, C5 ● **Temperaments:** J ● **Physical:** Stg=S; Freq: R, H, I, T, G, N ● **Work Env:** Noise=N; ● **Salary:** 4 ● **Outlook:** 3

GENERAL CLAIMS AGENT (air trans.) ● DOT #186.117-030 ● OES: 21998 ● Directs and coordinates activities involving claims against transportation company for shortages in or damaged freight, accidental death or injury to persons or employees, and private property damages: Directs activities of workers investigating claims to ascertain validity of claims and extent of company liability. Processes freight and property claims for which company is liable and submits claims to head office for settlement, or negotiates settlement with claimant and authorizes payment. Reviews employee accident reports to determine compensation program under which accidents are covered, and doctor reports for type of injury and length of time disabled. Authorizes payment of disability compensation according to state or federal acts. Contacts medical personnel to ascertain need for extension of payments beyond specified recovery date. Negotiates with persons having valid claims against company or death or injury to effect out-of-court settlement and refers cases that cannot be settled to legal department. Represents company at industrial accident or compensation board hearings to present company position on accident liability. May testify at court hearings to present evidence on company liability from investigation documents. ● **GED:** R4, M4, L4 ● **SVP:** 4-10 yrs ● **Academic:** Ed=H, Eng=S ● **Work Field:** 295 ● **MPSMS:** 895 ● **Aptitudes:** G2, V2, N3, S4, P4, Q3, K4, F4, M4, E5, C5 ● **Temperaments:** D, J, P ● **Physical:** Stg=S; Freq: R, H, T, G, N Occas: I ● **Work Env:** Noise=N; ● **Salary:** 3 ● **Outlook:** 3

MANAGER, CUSTOMER SERVICE (tel. & tel.) ● DOT #168.167-058 ● OES: 51002 ● Plans, directs, and coordinates activities of workers engaged in receiving, investigating, evaluating, and settling complaints and claims of telegraph customers: Directs workers to investigate complaints, such as those concerning rates or service in connection with domestic, international, or special-gift telegrams. Analyzes reports of findings and recommends response to complaint, considering nature and complexity of complaint, requirements of governmental utility-regulation agencies, and policies of company. Reviews actions of subordinates to ensure settlements are made correctly. Authorizes retention of data and preparation of documents for use during governmental or customer inquiries. ● **GED:** R5, M5, L5 ● **SVP:** 4-10 yrs ● **Academic:** Ed=A, Eng=G ● **Work Field:** 295, 271 ● **MPSMS:** 862 ● **Aptitudes:** G2, V2, N3, S4, P3, Q3, K4, F4, M4, E5, C5 ● **Temperaments:** D, I, J, P ● **Physical:** Stg=S; Freq: H, T, G, N Occas: R, I ● **Work Env:** Noise=N; ● **Salary:** 4 ● **Outlook:** 3

SERVICE REPRESENTATIVE (auto. mfg.) ● DOT #191.167-022 ● OES: 53123 ● Investigates dealer's claims for reimbursement of defective automotive parts: Reviews claims for labor or material adjustments with automobile dealer, examines parts claimed to be defective, and approves or disapproves dealer's claim. Assists dealers in handling unsettled claims by consulting with service personnel or customers. Prepares reports showing volume, types, and disposition of claims handled, or settlement allowed. May train dealers or service personnel in service operations or construction of products. May study dealers' organizational needs and advise them on matters, such as parts, tools, equipment, and personnel needed to handle service volume. May contact customers to survey customer satisfaction with purchase of new motor vehicle. ● **GED:** R5, M4, L4 ● **SVP:** 2-4 yrs ● **Academic:** Ed=A, Eng=S ● **Work Field:** 271 ● **MPSMS:** 591 ● **Aptitudes:** G2, V2, N3, S4, P4, Q3, K4, F4, M4, E5, C5 ● **Temperaments:** J, P ● **Physical:** Stg=S; Freq: R, H, T, G, N, A Occas: I ● **Work Env:** Noise=Q; ● **Salary:** 3 ● **Outlook:** 3

SUPERVISOR, CLAIMS (insurance) ● DOT #241.137-018 ● OES: 51002 ● Alternate titles: CLAIMS ADMINISTRATOR. Supervises and coordinates activities of workers engaged in examining insurance claims for payment in claims division of insurance company: Analyzes and approves insurance and matured endowment claims. Conducts personal interviews with policy owners and beneficiaries to explain procedure for filing claims. Submits statement of claim liabilities to actuarial department for review. Informs departmental supervisors on claims status. Evaluates job performance of subordinates. Performs duties described under SUPERVISOR (clerical) Master Title. ● **GED:** R4, M3, L4 ● **SVP:** 2-4 yrs ● **Academic:** Ed=H, Eng=G ● **Work Field:** 271, 232 ● **MPSMS:** 895 ● **Aptitudes:** G2, V3, N2, S4, P4, Q2, K4, F4, M4, E5, C5 ● **Temperaments:** D, J, P ● **Physical:** Stg=S; Freq: T, G, N Occas: R, H, I ● **Work Env:** Noise=N; ● **Salary:** 4 ● **Outlook:** 3

GOE: 11.12.02
Rental & Leasing

LEASING AGENT, OUTDOOR ADVERTISING (business ser.) ● DOT #254.357-010 ● OES: 49998 ● Obtains leases to sites for outdoor advertising: Persuades property owners to lease sites for erection of billboard signs used in outdoor advertising. Arranges price and draws up lease. May locate potential billboard sites, using automobile to travel through assigned district. May search legal records for land ownership. ● **GED:** R3, M2, L3 ● **SVP:** 3-6 mos ● **Academic:** Ed=N, Eng=G ● **Work Field:** 292 ● **MPSMS:** 885, 896 ● **Aptitudes:** G3, V3, N3, S4, P4, Q3, K4, F4, M4, E5, C5 ● **Temperaments:** I, J, P ● **Physical:** Stg=L; Freq: T, G Occas: R, H, I, N ● **Work Env:** Noise=N; Occas: W ● **Salary:** 3 ● **Outlook:** 3

LOCATION MANAGER (motion picture) ● DOT #191.167-018 ● OES: 21998 ● Arranges for leasing of suitable property for use as location for television or motion picture production: Confers with production or unit manager and DIRECTOR, TELEVISION (radio-tv broad.) or DIRECTOR, MOTION PICTURE (motion picture) regarding scenic backgrounds, terrain, and other topographical details of locations required for photographing exterior scenes. Searches files for pictures or descriptions of suitable locations or seeks new locations. Contacts property owners and local officials to arrange leasing and use of public and private property, rental of housing facilities, hiring of extras, and to obtain sanction for production activities. Arranges for transportation of troupe to location. ● **GED:** R4, M3, L4 ● **SVP:** 1-2 yrs ● **Academic:** Ed=H, Eng=S ● **Work Field:** 295, 292 ● **MPSMS:** 895 ● **Aptitudes:** G2, V2, N3, S4, P4, Q3, K4, F4, M4, E5, C5 ● **Temperaments:** F, J, V ● **Physical:** Stg=L; Freq: T, G Occas: R, H, N ● **Work Env:** Noise=N; Occas: W ● **Salary:** 4 ● **Outlook:** 1

MANAGER, LEASING (petrol. & gas) ● DOT #186.117-046 ● OES: 15011 ● Alternate titles: GENERAL MANAGER, LAND DEPARTMENT; LAND-AND-LEASES SUPERVISOR; LAND DEPARTMENT HEAD; LEASE AGENT; LEASES-AND-LAND SUPERVISOR; MANAGER, LAND DEPARTMENT; SUPERINTENDENT, LAND DEPARTMENT. Directs land and leasing department of petroleum company to secure leases, options, rights-of-way, and special agreements covering land and mineral rights for drilling wells and producing gas and oil: Studies leases bought, prices paid, and other negotiations of competing companies in specified areas and determines expenditure necessary to obtain leases and other contracts in those areas. Determines and specifies date of termination of lease rentals. Negotiates with brokers or other individuals to sell interests in leases owned. Executes general policies established by company officials. May make final decisions on and sign agreements and contracts for purchase, sale and acquisition of land leases, mineral and royalty rights. May be designated according to area of operations as Manager, Divisional Leasing (petrol. & gas). ● **GED:** R5, M5, L5 ● **SVP:** 4-10 yrs ● **Academic:** Ed=A, Eng=G ● **Work Field:** 295 ● **MPSMS:** 895 ● **Aptitudes:** G1, V2, N2, S4, P4, Q3, K4, F4, M4, E5, C5 ● **Temperaments:** D, J, P ● **Physical:** Stg=S; Freq: R, H, I, T, G, N ● **Work Env:** Noise=N; ● **Salary:** 1 ● **Outlook:** 2

PROPERTY-UTILIZATION OFFICER (government ser.) ● DOT #188.117-122 ● OES: 13014 ● Alternate titles: BUSINESS-SERVICE OFFICER; MANAGER, SURPLUS PROPERTY. Coordinates property procurement and maintenance activities, and negotiates with representatives to effect property transfers and sales, rental, and leasing contracts for government agency: Reviews property-related data, such as inventories, budgets, planning reports, vendor brochures, and excess property and property request reports, to obtain information on property status, needs, and availability. Writes, fills out, and reviews bids, contract specifications, purchase orders and estimates, and transfer forms to effect property transactions. Contacts vendors and potential users, and inspects and inventories acquired and transferred property through visits to government installations and vendor sites. Negotiates and confers with administrators, vendors, or users to effect agreement on property transfer details, such as price, model, packaging, transportation, land boundaries, or building layout. Authorizes expenditures within specified limits for purchases of supplies and equipment, equipment repair and maintenance, and alterations to premises. Fills government agency or other qualifying organization requests from surplus

inventories, considering factors such as donation criteria, actual needs, and justification. Prepares plans, standards, and specifications for building and equipment maintenance, repair, and inspection. May be designated according to property involved as Real-Estate-Utilization Officer (government ser.); State-Surplus-Commodity-And-Property Representative (government ser.). ● **GED:** R5, M4, L4 ● **SVP:** 4-10 yrs ● **Academic:** Ed=A, Eng=S ● **Work Field:** 295 ● **MPSMS:** 959, 890 ● **Aptitudes:** G2, V2, N3, S3, P3, Q3, K4, F4, M4, E5, C4 ● **Temperaments:** D, I, J, P, V ● **Physical:** Stg=L; Freq: R, H, T, G, N Occas: I, F, D ● **Work Env:** Noise=N; ● **Salary:** 4 ● **Outlook:** 1

REAL-ESTATE AGENT (profess. & kin.) ● DOT #186.117-058 ● OES: 15011 ● Alternate titles: LAND AGENT. Coordinates activities of real-estate department of company and negotiates acquisition and disposition of properties in most beneficial manner: Supervises staff engaged in preparing lease agreements, recording rental receipts, and performing other activities necessary to efficient management of company properties, or in performing routine research on zoning ordinances and condemnation considerations. Directs appraiser to inspect properties and land under consideration for acquisition, and recommends acquisition, lease, disposition, improvement, or other action consistent with best interest of company. Authorizes or requests authorization for maintenance of company properties not under control of operating departments, such as dwellings, hotels, or commissaries. Evaluates and promotes industrial-development potential of company properties. Negotiates contracts with sellers of land and renters of properties. ● **GED:** R5, M5, L5 ● **SVP:** 4-10 yrs ● **Academic:** Ed=A, Eng=G ● **Work Field:** 295, 292 ● **MPSMS:** 895 ● **Aptitudes:** G2, V2, N2, S3, P3, Q3, K4, F4, M4, E5, C5 ● **Temperaments:** D, I, J, P ● **Physical:** Stg=L; Freq: T, G, N Occas: R, H, I ● **Work Env:** Noise=N; Occas: W ● **Salary:** 1 ● **Outlook:** 1

RIGHT-OF-WAY AGENT (any industry) ● DOT #191.117-046 ● OES: 15011 ● Alternate titles: CLAIMS AGENT, RIGHT-OF-WAY; PERMIT AGENT. Negotiates with property owners and public officials to secure purchase or lease of land and right-of-way for utility lines, pipelines, and other construction projects: Determines roads, bridges, and utility systems that must be maintained during construction. Negotiates with landholders for access routes and restoration of roads and surfaces. May examine public records to determine ownership and property rights. May be required to know property law. ● **GED:** R5, M4, L5 ● **SVP:** 2-4 yrs ● **Academic:** Ed=B, Eng=G ● **Work Field:** 271, 272 ● **MPSMS:** 870, 895 ● **Aptitudes:** G2, V2, N3, S3, P3, Q3, K4, F4, M4, E5, C5 ● **Temperaments:** I, P, V ● **Physical:** Stg=L; Freq: T, G Occas: R, H, N ● **Work Env:** Noise=N; Occas: W ● **Salary:** 4 ● **Outlook:** 2

GOE: 11.12.03
Booking

ADVANCE AGENT (amuse. & rec.) ● DOT #191.167-010 ● OES: 39998 ● Coordinates business and promotional activities concerned with production of entertainment in advance of touring theatrical company, circus, road show, motion picture, or other attraction: Inspects performance location and reports condition, and if stage presentation, inspects equipment and accommodations of theatre, such as size of stage, seating capacity, and number of dressing rooms. Completes business details, such as advance sale of tickets and lodging for members of touring group. Purchases advertising space or spot announcements in newspapers, radio and television, and other media. Distributes posters, signs, and other displays to stimulate interest in coming attraction and promote box-office sales [PUBLIC-RELATIONS REPRESENTATIVE (profess. & kin.)]. ● **GED:** R4, M4, L4 ● **SVP:** 2-4 yrs ● **Academic:** Ed=N, Eng=G ● **Work Field:** 291 ● **MPSMS:** 910 ● **Aptitudes:** G3, V3, N3, S3, P4, Q3, K4, F4, M4, E5, C5 ● **Temperaments:** D, J, P ● **Physical:** Stg=L; Freq: T, G Occas: R, H, I, N, F ● **Work Env:** Noise=N; ● **Salary:** 4 ● **Outlook:** 2

ARTIST'S MANAGER (amuse. & rec.) ● DOT #191.117-010 ● OES: 39998 ● Alternate titles: ARTIST'S REPRESENTATIVE; ARTIST CONSULTANT; PERSONAL AGENT; PERSONAL MANAGER; TALENT AGENT. Manages affairs of entertainers by participating in negotiations with agents and others concerning contracts and business matters affecting clients' interests, and advises clients on career development and advancement: Represents client in negotiations with officials of unions, motion picture or television studios, theatrical productions, or entertainment house, for favorable contracts and financial fees to be received for engagements. Advises client concerning contracts, wardrobe, and effective presentation of act, according to knowledge of show business. Procures services of professional personnel in particular phase of show business to create or design format of original act, or prepare special material for new act to advance client's career. Manages business details of tours and engagements, such as obtaining reservations for transportation and hotel accommodations, and making disbursements for road expenses. Represents client in public contacts, such as handling fan mail, telephone inquiries, and requests for personal appearances. May audition new talent for representation purposes. May procure bookings for clients. ● **GED:** R5, M4, L5 ● **SVP:** 2-4 yrs ● **Academic:** Ed=B, Eng=G ● **Work Field:** 295 ● **MPSMS:** 919 ● **Aptitudes:** G2, V2, N3, S4, P4, Q3, K4, F4, M4, E5, C5 ● **Temperaments:** D, I, J, P ● **Physical:** Stg=S; Freq: T, G Occas: R, H, I, N ● **Work Env:** Noise=L; ● **Salary:** 4 ● **Outlook:** 1

BOOKING MANAGER (amuse. & rec.) ● DOT #191.117-014 ● OES: 39998 ● Alternate titles: BOOKER; BOOKING AGENT. Books performers, theatrical or ballet productions, variety or nightclub acts, concert or lecture series, trade shows, or other popular or classical attractions for entertainment in various establishments, such as theaters, showplaces, clubs, or halls: Schedules attractions for season, considering such factors as entertainment policy, budget, and tastes of patrons of particular establishment represented. Negotiates with booking representatives or producers of attractions to arrange terms of contract, play dates, and fees to be paid for engagements. Auditions new talent. Arranges for billing in accordance with contract agreement. Books motion pictures for exhibit into theater chains or independent houses. Selects and rents pictures to be exhibited on basis of potential box-office sales, cast of players, advertising allotment allowed by distributor, and similar factors. May specialize in in-house bookings and be designated according to establishment as Concert Or Lecture Hall Manager (amuse. & rec.); Showplace Manager (amuse. & rec.). May specialize in independent bookings and be designated according to type of talent or of entertainment package represented and placed as Artists' Booking Representative (amuse. & rec.); Theatrical Variety Agent (amuse. & rec.). May specialize in rental and distribution of motion pictures and be designated Film Booker (amuse. & rec.). May represent popular or rock musical groups only and be designated Band Booker (amuse. & rec.). When sponsoring, managing, and producing an entertainment, may be designated Impresario (amuse. & rec.). ● **GED:** R4, M4, L4 ● **SVP:** 1-2 yrs ● **Academic:** Ed=B, Eng=G ● **Work Field:** 292 ● **MPSMS:** 910 ● **Aptitudes:** G3, V3, N3, S4, P4, Q2, K4, F4, M4, E5, C5 ● **Temperaments:** I, J, P ● **Physical:** Stg=S; Freq: T, G, N Occas: R, H, I ● **Work Env:** Noise=L; ● **Salary:** 4 ● **Outlook:** 1

BUSINESS MANAGER (amuse. & rec.) ● DOT #191.117-018 ● OES: 39998 ● Alternate titles: BUSINESS AGENT. Manages financial affairs of entertainers and negotiates with agents and representatives for contracts and appearances: Negotiates with officials of unions, motion picture or television studios, stage productions, or entertainment houses for contracts and financial return to be received for engagements. Promotes client's interests by advising on income, investments, taxes, legal, and other financial matters. Provides liaison between client and representatives concerning contractual rights and obligations to settle contracts. Summarizes statements on periodic basis concerning client's investments, property, and financial status. ● **GED:** R5, M4, L5 ● **SVP:** 2-4 yrs ● **Academic:** Ed=A, Eng=S ● **Work Field:** 295 ● **MPSMS:** 910 ● **Aptitudes:** G2, V2, N3, S4, P4, Q2, K4, F4, M4, E5, C4 ● **Temperaments:** D, I, J, P, V ● **Physical:** Stg=S; Freq: T, G Occas: R, H, N ● **Work Env:** Noise=N; ● **Salary:** 5 ● **Outlook:** 3

CIRCUS AGENT (amuse. & rec.) ● DOT #191.117-022 ● OES: 39998 ● Plans and arranges route of circus for following season, coordinating date and location schedules: Obtains information about facilities of new locations to determine feasibility of presenting show. Consults with circus officials to arrange route and obtain approval of tour. Schedules dates of performance for each location, taking into consideration length of travel time to transport circus from one location to another, climatic conditions, budget, and previous year's attendance records. Rearranges tour in event of unexpected occurrences. ● **GED:** R4, M3, L4 ● **SVP:** 2-4 yrs ● **Academic:** Ed=N, Eng=G ● **Work Field:** 295,

297 ● **MPSMS:** 919 ● **Aptitudes:** G2, V2, N3, S4, P3, Q3, K4, F4, M4, E5, C5 ● **Temperaments:** D, J ● **Physical:** Stg=S; Freq: T, G Occas: R, H, N ● **Work Env:** Noise=N; ● **Salary:** 4 ● **Outlook:** 1

JOCKEY AGENT (amuse. & rec.) ● DOT #191.117-026 ● OES: 39998 ● Represents riders of race horses in negotiations with owners to arrange for riding engagements at racetrack: Contacts riders to ascertain races and dates they are available for hire. Confers with owners of horses scheduled to race to inform them of riders available. Negotiates with owners for riding fees. Records name of owner, horse, date, and number of race in engagement book. Notifies riders of contracted engagements, and terms agreed on. Notifies riders to report to owner for briefing on horse's temperament and behavior, and other riding instructions. Collects hiring fees from riders. ● **GED:** R4, M3, L4 ● **SVP:** 6 mos-1 yr ● **Academic:** Ed=N, Eng=G ● **Work Field:** 295 ● **MPSMS:** 913 ● **Aptitudes:** G3, V2, N3, S4, P4, Q3, K4, F4, M4, E5, C5 ● **Temperaments:** I, J, P ● **Physical:** Stg=L; Freq: T, G Occas: R, H, I, N ● **Work Env:** Noise=N; Freq: W ● **Salary:** 3 ● **Outlook:** 1

LITERARY AGENT (business ser.) ● DOT #191.117-034 ● OES: 39998 ● Alternate titles: AUTHOR'S AGENT; WRITER'S REPRESENTATIVE. Markets clients' manuscripts to editors, publishers, and other buyers: Reads and appraises manuscripts and suggests revisions. Contacts prospective purchaser of material, basing selection upon knowledge of market and specific content of manuscript. Negotiates contract between publisher and client. Usually works on commission basis. ● **GED:** R5, M4, L5 ● **SVP:** 2-4 yrs ● **Academic:** Ed=B, Eng=G ● **Work Field:** 292 ● **MPSMS:** 757 ● **Aptitudes:** G2, V2, N3, S3, P3, Q3, K4, F4, M4, E5, C5 ● **Temperaments:** I, P ● **Physical:** Stg=S; Freq: T, G, N Occas: R, H, I ● **Work Env:** Noise=N; ● **Salary:** 5 ● **Outlook:** 1

MANAGER, ATHLETE (amuse. & rec.) ● DOT #153.117-014 ● OES: 34058 ● Manages affairs of PROFESSIONAL ATHLETE (amuse. & rec.) by negotiating with promoters or others to settle contracts and business matters and directs training: Negotiates with team management and promoters to obtain favorable contracts for client [BUSINESS MANAGER (amuse. & rec.)]. May prescribe exercises, rest periods, and diet to be followed by PROFESSIONAL ATHLETE (amuse. & rec.). May direct ATHLETIC TRAINER (amuse. & rec.; education) in conditioning PROFESSIONAL ATHLETE (amuse. & rec.). May give directions to protege in athletic techniques. May determine strategy to be followed by PROFESSIONAL ATHLETE (amuse. & rec.) in competition with others. May be designated according to type of PROFESSIONAL ATHLETE (amuse. & rec.) managed as Manager, Boxer (amuse. & rec.); Manager, Wrestler (amuse. & rec.). ● **GED:** R5, M5, L5 ● **SVP:** 2-4 yrs ● **Academic:** Ed=H, Eng=G ● **Work Field:** 292 ● **MPSMS:** 913 ● **Aptitudes:** G2, V2, N2, S4, P4, Q3, K5, F5, M5, E5, C5 ● **Temperaments:** D, I, J, P, V ● **Physical:** Stg=L; Freq: T, G ● **Work Env:** Noise=Q; Occas: W ● **Salary:** 4 ● **Outlook:** 1

GOE: 11.12.04
Procurement Negotiations

CONTRACT ADMINISTRATOR (any industry) ● DOT #162.117-014 ● OES: 13014 ● Directs activities concerned with contracts for purchase or sale of equipment, materials, products, or services: Examines performance requirements, delivery schedules, and estimates of costs of material, equipment, and production to ensure completeness and accuracy. Prepares bids, process specifications, test and progress reports, and other exhibits that may be required. Reviews bids from other firms for conformity to contract requirements and determines acceptable bids. Negotiates contract with customer or bidder. Requests or approves amendments to or extensions of contracts. Advises planning and production departments of contractual rights and obligations. May compile data for preparing estimates. May coordinate work of sales department with production and shipping department to implement fulfillment of contracts. May act as liaison between company and subcontractors. May direct sales program [MANAGER, SALES (any industry) 163.167-018]. ● **GED:** R5, M3, L5 ● **SVP:** 4-10 yrs ● **Academic:** Ed=A, Eng=G ● **Work Field:** 295 ● **MPSMS:** 894 ● **Aptitudes:** G2, V2, N3, S4, P4, Q3, K4, F4, M4, E5, C5 ● **Temperaments:** D, I, J, P ● **Physical:** Stg=S; Freq: T, G Occas: R, H, I, N ● **Work Env:** Noise=N; ● **Salary:** 5 ● **Outlook:** 4

CONTRACT SPECIALIST (profess. & kin.) ● DOT #162.117-018 ● OES: 21308 ● Alternate titles: CONTRACT COORDINATOR. Negotiates with suppliers to draw up procurement contracts: Negotiates, administers, extends, terminates, and renegotiates contracts. Formulates and coordinates procurement proposals. Directs and coordinates activities of workers engaged in formulating bid proposals. Evaluates or monitors contract performance to determine necessity for amendments or extensions of contracts, and compliance to contractual obligations. Approves or rejects requests for deviations from contract specifications and delivery schedules. Arbitrates claims or complaints occurring in performance of contracts. Analyzes price proposals, financial reports, and other data to determine reasonableness of prices. May negotiate collective bargaining agreements. May serve as liaison officer to ensure fulfillment of obligations by contractors. ● **GED:** R5, M3, L5 ● **SVP:** 4-10 yrs ● **Academic:** Ed=H, Eng=G ● **Work Field:** 295 ● **MPSMS:** 939 ● **Aptitudes:** G2, V2, N3, S4, P4, Q3, K4, F4, M4, E5, C5 ● **Temperaments:** D, I, J, P, V ● **Physical:** Stg=L; Freq: T, G Occas: R, H, I, N ● **Work Env:** Noise=N; ● **Salary:** 5 ● **Outlook:** 4

CONTRACTOR (construction) ● DOT #182.167-010 ● OES: 15017 ● Contracts to perform specified construction work in accordance with architect's plans, blueprints, codes, and other specifications: Estimates costs of materials, labor, and use of equipment required to fulfill provisions of contract and prepares bids. Confers with clients to negotiate terms of contract. Subcontracts specialized craft work, such as electrical, structural steel, concrete, and plumbing. Purchases material for construction. Supervises workers directly or through subordinate supervisors. May be designated according to specialty license or scope of principal activities as Contractor, General Engineering (construction); Contractor, General Building (construction). ● **GED:** R4, M4, L4 ● **SVP:** 2-4 yrs ● **Academic:** Ed=H, Eng=S ● **Work Field:** 102, 295 ● **MPSMS:** 360 ● **Aptitudes:** G3, V3, N2, S2, P2, Q3, K3, F3, M3, E3, C3 ● **Temperaments:** D, J, P, V ● **Physical:** Stg=L; Freq: R, H, I, T, G, N, F, D, A, V Occas: C, B, S, K, O, W, E, X ● **Work Env:** Noise=L; Freq: W ● **Salary:** 4 ● **Outlook:** 1

Physical Performing 12

An interest in physical activities performed before an audience. You can satisfy this interest through jobs in athletics, sports, and the performance of physical feats. Perhaps a job as a professional player or official would appeal to you. You may wish to develop and perform special acts such as acrobatics or wire walking.

Sports 12.01

Workers in this group compete in professional athletic or sporting events, coach players, and officiate at games. They also give individual and group instruction, recruit players, and regulate various aspects of sporting events. Jobs in this group are found in all types of professional sports, such as football, baseball, basketball, hockey, golf, tennis, and horse racing. Some jobs are also available with private recreational facilities, including ski resorts, skating rinks, athletic clubs, and gymnasiums.

✓ What kind of work would you do?

Your work activities would depend upon your specific job. For example, you might:

- coach a professional sports team.
- start, time, or certify winners in a major auto race.
- inspect equipment to see if rules are being followed before an event.
- practice and play on a professional sports team.
- stop a game and penalize players for breaking a rule.
- ride horses in several races each day.
- give karate lessons to an individual or group.
- teach people how to ski.

✓ What skills and abilities do you need for this kind of work?

To do this kind of work, you must be able to:

- master all the rules of a particular game or sport and interpret them accurately.
- make official decisions quickly and enforce them when necessary.
- coordinate eye, hand, body, and foot movements with skill.
- adjust to the physical and mental pressures of competition.

- follow training rules strictly.

✓ How do you know if you would like or could learn to do this kind of work?

The following questions may give you clues about yourself as you consider this group of jobs.

- Have you competed in sports? Do you know the rules of any sport well enough to be a referee, judge, or umpire?
- Have you been an official in intramural games, physical education classes, or sandlot sports? Can you make decisions quickly and firmly?
- Have you coached a team or individual in athletic events? Were your efforts effective?
- Have you competed against others in athletic events? Do you remain calm and alert during competition?
- Have you won any special sports events? Do you excel in any athletic skill? Have others asked you to teach them that skill?

✓ How can you prepare for and enter this kind of work?

Occupations in this group usually require education and/or training extending from six months to over ten years, depending upon the specific kind of work. Professional coaches and officials often obtain the necessary training and experience by working with high school and college athletic teams. Umpires in major league baseball usually receive training in special umpire schools and must have experience in the minor leagues. Officials in horse racing usually have some type of related work experience and receive on-the-job training.

Professional athletes often receive initial training while on high school or college teams. They are recruited by professional clubs or teams and work under a contract. Training continues as long as they remain in active competition.

✓ *What else should you consider about these jobs?*

Often sports officials make decisions that are unpopular with the players or fans. If a player or coach argues about a ruling too strongly, the official in charge must enforce discipline by sending that individual from the game.

Professional athletes must maintain or improve their physical skills to remain in competition. The risk of physical injury is great in all of the contact sports. Some injuries may shorten or end a player's worklife in sports. Also, after reaching a certain age, many competitive players must find work in areas other than team play.

Frequent travel is usually involved for officials and athletes.

If you think you would like to do this kind of work, look at the job titles listed below.

■ ■ ■

GOE: 12.01.01
Coaching & Instructing

HEAD COACH (amuse. & rec.) ● DOT #153.117-010 ● OES: 34058 ● Alternate titles: MANAGER, ATHLETIC TEAM. Plans and directs training and recommends acquisition or trade of players for professional athletic team: Directs conditioning of players to achieve maximum athletic performance. Assesses player's skills and assigns team positions. Evaluates own and opposition team capabilities to determine game strategy. Coaches or directs COACH, PROFESSIONAL ATHLETES (amuse. & rec.) to instruct players in techniques of game. Participates in discussions with other clubs to sell or trade players. May participate on team managed and be designated Coach-Player (amuse. & rec.); Player-Manager (amuse. & rec.). ● **GED:** R5, M4, L4 ● **SVP:** Over 10 yrs ● **Academic:** Ed=B, Eng=G ● **Work Field:** 295 ● **MPSMS:** 913 ● **Aptitudes:** G2, V2, N3, S3, P4, Q4, K4, F4, M4, E5, C5 ● **Temperaments:** D, I, J, P, V ● **Physical:** Stg=L; Freq: T, G ● **Work Env:** Noise=N; Freq: W ● **Salary:** 4 ● **Outlook:** 2

INSTRUCTOR, SPORTS (amuse. & rec.) ● DOT #153.227-018 ● OES: 31321 ● Alternate titles: ATHLETIC COACH. Teaches sport activity to individual or groups at private or public recreational facility or school: Explains and demonstrates use of apparatus and equipment. Explains and demonstrates principles, techniques, and methods of regulating movement of body, hands, or feet to achieve proficiency in activity. Observes students during practice to detect and correct mistakes. Explains and enforces safety rules and regulations. Explains method of keeping score. May organize and conduct competition and tournaments. May participate in competition to demonstrate skill. May purchase, display, sell, maintain, or repair equipment. May keep record of receipts and expenditures. May lecture on history and purpose of sport. Workers are identified according to sport instructed, such as golf, fencing, or tennis. ● **GED:** R4, M3, L4 ● **SVP:** 2-4 yrs ● **Academic:** Ed=H, Eng=S ● **Work Field:** 296 ● **MPSMS:** 913, 931 ● **Aptitudes:** G2, V2, N3, S3, P3, Q4, K2, F3, M2, E2, C4 ● **Temperaments:** D, J, P ● **Physical:** Stg=M; Freq: R, H, I, T, G, F, D Occas: B, S, O, N, A, X, V ● **Work Env:** Noise=N; Occas: W ● **Salary:** 4 ● **Outlook:** 3

SCOUT, PROFESSIONAL SPORTS (amuse. & rec.) ● DOT #153.117-018 ● OES: 34058 ● Evaluates athletic skills of PROFESSIONAL ATHLETES (amuse. & rec.) to determine fitness and potentiality for professional sports and negotiates with them to obtain services: Reviews prospects' exhibitions and past performance records. Negotiates with PROFESSIONAL ATHLETES (amuse. & rec.) to arrange contracts. Reports to team management results of scouting assignments, such as selection or rejection of PROFESSIONAL ATHLETES (amuse. & rec.) scouted and persons and areas sighted for future recruitment. May be designated according to type of sport in which engaged as Baseball Scout (amuse. & rec.); Basketball Scout (amuse. & rec.); Football Scout (amuse. & rec.). ● **GED:** R4, M3, L4 ● **SVP:** 4-10 yrs ● **Academic:** Ed=H, Eng=G ● **Work Field:** 211 ● **MPSMS:** 913 ● **Aptitudes:** G2, V2, N4, S3, P3, Q3, K5, F4, M5, E5, C5 ● **Temperaments:** D, I, J, P, V ● **Physical:** Stg=S; Freq: T, G, N, F, D, A, V Occas: R, H, I ● **Work Env:** Noise=N; Freq: W ● **Salary:** 4 ● **Outlook:** 1

GOE: 12.01.02
Officiating

CHARTER (amuse. & rec.) ● DOT #249.367-018 ● OES: 59998 ● Observes horserace, calls out description of race to other worker, and records statistical and related data on race for use in racing publication: Focuses binoculars on distance markers along track during race and calls out horses' numbers, positions, estimate of distances of horses from inside rail and between horses, and related observable data for other worker to record. Revises record of order and distance between horses at finish line if different from intercom announcement of official results. Copies identifying information, such as horses' names and drivers, from racing form onto record. Transcribes race results, such as winning and intermediate times, purse, and prices paid to bettors from tote board onto record. Contacts judges, using intercom, for decisions on foul claims and notes record accordingly. Computes race completion times for all but winning horses, using formula. Mails completed record to printer for use in printing race results in racing publications. ● **GED:** R3, M2, L3 ● **SVP:** 1-3 mos ● **Academic:** Ed=N, Eng=G ● **Work Field:** 231, 282 ● **MPSMS:** 891 ● **Aptitudes:** G3, V3, N3, S2, P3, Q4, K4, F4, M4, E5, C5 ● **Temperaments:** J ● **Physical:** Stg=S; Freq: T, G, N, F Occas: R, H, I ● **Work Env:** Noise=N; ● **Salary:** 1 ● **Outlook:** 3

FLAGGER (amuse. & rec.) ● DOT #372.667-026 ● OES: 68014 ● Signals with checkered flag when first race horse crosses starting line after release from starting gate to notify racing timer when to start timing race. ● **GED:** R2, M1, L1 ● **SVP:** 2-30 days ● **Academic:** Ed=N, Eng=N ● **Work Field:** 282 ● **MPSMS:** 913 ● **Aptitudes:** G4, V4, N4, S3, P4, Q5, K4, F5, M4, E5, C5 ● **Temperaments:** T ● **Physical:** Stg=L; Freq: R, H, D Occas: T, G ● **Work Env:** Noise=N; Const: W ● **Salary:** 2 ● **Outlook:** 2

GOLF-COURSE RANGER (amuse. & rec.) ● DOT #379.667-010 ● OES: 63047 ● Alternate titles: GOLF-COURSE PATROLLER. Patrols golf course to prevent unauthorized persons from using facilities, keep play running smoothly, and assist injured or ill players: Inspects player and CADDIE (amuse. & rec.) registration and green fee tickets for validity. Prevents players from entering course beyond starting tee. Advises players to speed up or slow down in order to alleviate bottlenecks. Explains rules of game to players to settle disputes. Locates damaged or hazardous areas and marks areas for repair, using lime marker or stake. Cautions players against tearing up turf or otherwise abusing course. Renders first aid to injured or ill players and carries their equipment to clubhouse. Returns lost equipment to owners or to clubhouse. Keeps log of daily activities. May deliver urgent messages to players on course. ● **GED:** R3, M2, L3 ● **SVP:** 3-6 mos ● **Academic:** Ed=N, Eng=S ● **Work Field:** 293 ● **MPSMS:** 913 ● **Aptitudes:** G3, V3, N4, S4, P4, Q4, K4, F4, M4, E5, C5 ● **Temperaments:** P, V ● **Physical:** Stg=L; Freq: R, H, T, G Occas: I, N ● **Work Env:** Noise=N; Const: W ● **Salary:** 1 ● **Outlook:** 2

UMPIRE (amuse. & rec.) ● DOT #153.267-018 ● OES: 34058 ● Alternate titles: FIELD CAPTAIN; JUDGE; REFEREE. Officiates at sporting events: Observes actions of participants to detect infractions

---

of rules. Decides disputable matters according to established regulations. When concerned only with determining validity of goals, finish line order, or out-of-bound plays, may be designated Finish Judge (amuse. & rec.); Goal Umpire (amuse. & rec.); Line Umpire (amuse. & rec.). ● **GED:** R4, M3, L4 ● **SVP:** 4-10 yrs ● **Academic:** Ed=N, Eng=S

● **Work Field:** 295, 211 ● **MPSMS:** 913 ● **Aptitudes:** G2, V2, N3, S2, P3, Q4, K4, F5, M4, E4, C5 ● **Temperaments:** D, J, P ● **Physical:** Stg=L; Const: N, F, D, A, X, V Freq: T, G ● **Work Env:** Noise=Q; Freq: W ● **Salary:** 4 ● **Outlook:** 1

Physical Feats   12.02

Workers in this group perform unusual or daring acts of physical strength or skill to entertain people. They may perform alone or with others. Circuses, carnivals, theaters, and amusement parks hire these workers.

✓ *What kind of work would you do?*

Your work activities would depend upon your specific job. For example, you might:

- demonstrate gymnastic skill on a high wire or trapeze to entertain audiences.
- ski jump in a water show.
- dive from a high platform into a tank of water.
- juggle and balance things such as balls, knives, or plates.
- perform acrobatic stunts on a horse in a circus.
- swim in a water ballet.

✓ *What skills and abilities do you need for this kind of work?*

To do this kind of work, you must be able to:

- coordinate eye, hand, body, and foot movement with skill.
- demonstrate poise and confidence while performing before an audience.
- judge distance, speed, and movement of objects or people.
- follow strict training rules.
- take the risk of physical injury.
- excel in a particular athletic skill.

The above statements may not apply to every job in this group.

✓ *How do you know if you would like or could learn to do this kind of work?*

The following questions may give you clues about yourself as you consider this group of jobs.

- Have you performed stunts that required daring and skill? Did you perform them without great fear?
- Have you had a hobby or specialty act such as juggling, acrobatics, or wire walking? Do you perform well before an audience?

✓ *How can you prepare for and enter this kind of work?*

Occupations in this group usually require education and/or training extending from six months to over ten years, depending upon the specific kind of work. The usual method of training is by observation and practice. Another method is working with and learning from a skilled performer.

Performers of some specialty act such as wire walking, are hired by circuses and other amusement companies. Some workers own their own equipment and contract for individual appearances.

✓ *What else should you consider about these jobs?*

For their own safety, workers must maintain or improve their physical skills. The physical requirements of some jobs may limit the number of years a worker can perform. Frequent travel is usually required.

If you think you would like to do this kind of work, look at the job titles listed below.

■ ■ ■

GOE: 12.02.01
Performing

ACROBAT (amuse. & rec.) ● DOT #159.247-010 ● OES: 34056 ● Alternate titles: TUMBLER. Entertains audience by performing difficult and spectacular feats, such as leaping, tumbling, and balancing, alone or as member of team. Originates act or adapts stock presentations. May use equipment, such as chairs and teeter board. May juggle

various articles [JUGGLER (amuse. & rec.)]. May perform feats requiring bodily contortions and be designated Contortionist (amuse. & rec.). ● **GED:** R3, M2, L2 ● **SVP:** 6 mos-1 yr ● **Academic:** Ed=N, Eng=N ● **Work Field:** 297 ● **MPSMS:** 919 ● **Aptitudes:** G3, V3, N3, S2, P3, Q5, K3, F2, M2, E1, C5 ● **Temperaments:** F, P, V ● **Physical:** Stg=V; Const: C, B, S, K, O Freq: N ● **Work Env:** Noise=N; ● **Salary:** 3 ● **Outlook:** 1

AERIALIST (amuse. & rec.) ● DOT #159.247-014 ● OES: 34056 ● Alternate titles: TRAPEZE ARTIST; TRAPEZE PERFORMER. Performs gymnastic feats of skill and balance while swinging on trapeze, turning somersaults, or executing flying stunts alone or as member of team. ● **GED:** R3, M3, L2 ● **SVP:** 1-2 yrs ● **Academic:** Ed=N, Eng=N ● **Work Field:** 297 ● **MPSMS:** 919 ● **Aptitudes:** G3, V3, N3, S2, P3, Q5, K3, F2, M2, E1, C5 ● **Temperaments:** F, P, S, V ● **Physical:** Stg=V; Const: B Freq: C, S, O, R, H, N, F ● **Work Env:** Noise=N; ● **Salary:** 4 ● **Outlook:** 1

AQUATIC PERFORMER (amuse. & rec.) ● DOT #159.347-014 ● OES: 34056 ● Performs water-ballet routines to entertain audience, utilizing synchronized techniques of swimming: May swim underwater, using air lines. May serve as LIFEGUARD (amuse. & rec.), sell tickets, or perform other duties when not participating in show. ● **GED:** R3, M3, L3 ● **SVP:** 6 mos-1 yr ● **Academic:** Ed=N, Eng=S ● **Work Field:** 297 ● **MPSMS:** 919 ● **Aptitudes:** G3, V3, N4, S2, P2, Q4, K2, F3, M3, E2, C4 ● **Temperaments:** J, P, V ● **Physical:** Stg=M; Freq: R, H, I Occas: C, B ● **Work Env:** Noise=N; ● **Salary:** 3 ● **Outlook:** 1

EQUESTRIAN (amuse. & rec.) ● DOT #159.344-010 ● OES: 34056 ● Rides horses at circus, carnival, exhibition, or horse show, performing acrobatic stunts on saddled or saddleless horse or feats of equestrian skill and daring to entertain audience. When performing stunts on horse without saddle, may be designated Bareback Rider (amuse. & rec.). ● **GED:** R3, M3, L1 ● **SVP:** 1-2 yrs ● **Academic:** Ed=N, Eng=N ● **Work Field:** 297 ● **MPSMS:** 919 ● **Aptitudes:** G3, V3, N3, S3, P4, Q5, K3, F3, M2, E2, C5 ● **Temperaments:** F, J, P, V ● **Physical:** Stg=M; Const: R, H, I Freq: C, B, G, F, V ● **Work Env:** Noise=N; ● **Salary:** 4 ● **Outlook:** 1

JUGGLER (amuse. & rec.) ● DOT #159.341-010 ● OES: 34056 ● Juggles and balances objects, such as balls, knives, plates, tenpins, and hats, to entertain audience. ● **GED:** R3, M2, L2 ● **SVP:** 1-2 yrs ● **Academic:** Ed=N, Eng=S ● **Work Field:** 297 ● **MPSMS:** 919 ● **Aptitudes:** G3, V3, N4, S2, P3, Q4, K2, F2, M2, E1, C5 ● **Temperaments:** J, T ● **Physical:** Stg=L; Const: R, H, I, E, N, F, D, A, X, V ● **Work Env:** Noise=Q; ● **Salary:** 4 ● **Outlook:** 1

RODEO PERFORMER (amuse. & rec.) ● DOT #159.344-014 ● OES: 34056 ● Demonstrates daring and skill by bronc riding, calf roping, bull riding, steer wrestling, or similar feats in rodeo competition to entertain spectators and compete for prize money. ● **GED:** R3, M2, L3 ● **SVP:** 6 mos-1 yr ● **Academic:** Ed=N, Eng=N ● **Work Field:** 297 ● **MPSMS:** 913 ● **Aptitudes:** G3, V3, N4, S2, P3, Q5, K2, F3, M2, E2, C5 ● **Temperaments:** J, S, V ● **Physical:** Stg=H; Freq: C, B, S, K, O, W, R, H, I, E, N, F, D, A, X, V ● **Work Env:** Noise=N; Freq: W ● **Salary:** 3 ● **Outlook:** 1

SHOW-HORSE DRIVER (amuse. & rec.) ● DOT #159.344-018 ● OES: 34056 ● Rides or drives horse before judges in horse show, exercising care to display best points of animal to judges and spectators. ● **GED:** R3, M2, L2 ● **SVP:** 6 mos-1 yr ● **Academic:** Ed=N, Eng=N ● **Work Field:** 297 ● **MPSMS:** 327 ● **Aptitudes:** G3, V3, N4, Q4, K3, F3, M3, E3, C5 ● **Temperaments:** I, P ● **Physical:** Stg=L; Freq: B, R, H, I, E Occas: C ● **Work Env:** Noise=N; Freq: W ● **Salary:** 3 ● **Outlook:** 1

STUNT PERFORMER (amuse. & rec.) ● DOT #159.341-014 ● OES: 34056 ● Performs stunts, such as overturning speeding automobile or falling from runaway horse, and participates in fight-action scenes for motion picture, television, or stage production: Reads script and confers with DIRECTOR, MOTION PICTURE (motion picture) and DIRECTOR OF PHOTOGRAPHY (motion picture; radio-tv broad.) to ascertain positions of cameras and other performers. Examines terrain and inspects equipment, such as harness, rigging bars, or nets to avoid injury. Coordinates body movement and facial expression to simulate giving and receiving violent blows. Rehearses stunt routines alone or with other STUNT PERFORMER (amuse. & rec.; motion picture; radio-tv broad.). May design, build, or repair own safety equipment. ● **GED:** R3, M3, L3 ● **SVP:** 1-2 yrs ● **Academic:** Ed=N, Eng=S ● **Work Field:** 297 ● **MPSMS:** 911 ● **Aptitudes:** G3, V3, N4, S2, P4, Q4, K2, F3, M1, E1, C5 ● **Temperaments:** J, P, S, T ● **Physical:** Stg=M; Freq: N Occas: C, B, S, K, O, W, R, H, I, E, T, G, M, F, D, A, X, V ● **Work Env:** Noise=N; Freq: W, O ● **Salary:** 5 ● **Outlook:** 1

Appendix A
Alphabetical Index of Occupations

Each of the occupations in *The Enhanced Guide for Occupational Exploration* is listed in alphabetical order below. The name is followed by the industry in which it is most commonly found, its DOT number, and its GOE number. Since occupations are arranged in this book by their GOE number, you can use this number to find the occupation's description and obtain additional information.

ABLE SEAMAN (water trans.), 911.364-010, 05.12.03

ABSTRACTOR (profess. & kin.), 119.267-010, 11.04.04

ACADEMIC DEAN (education), 090.117-010, 11.07.03

ACCESS COORDINATOR, CABLE TELEVISION (radio-tv broad.), 194.122-010, 05.03.05

ACCOUNT EXECUTIVE (business ser.), 164.167-010, 11.09.01

ACCOUNT-INFORMATION CLERK (utilities), 210.367-010, 07.02.03

ACCOUNTANT (profess. & kin.), 160.162-018, 11.06.01

ACCOUNTANT, BUDGET (profess. & kin.), 160.162-022, 11.06.01

ACCOUNTANT, COST (profess. & kin.), 160.162-026, 11.06.01

ACCOUNTANT, PROPERTY (profess. & kin.), 160.167-022, 11.06.01

ACCOUNTANT, SYSTEMS (profess. & kin.), 160.167-026, 11.06.01

ACCOUNTANT, TAX (profess. & kin.), 160.162-010, 11.06.01

ACCOUNTING CLERK (clerical), 216.482-010, 07.02.02

ACOUSTICAL CARPENTER (construction), 860.381-010, 05.05.02

ACQUISITIONS LIBRARIAN (library), 100.267-010, 11.02.04

ACROBAT (amuse. & rec.), 159.247-010, 12.02.01

ACTOR (amuse. & rec.), 150.047-010, 01.03.02

ACTUARY (profess. & kin.), 020.167-010, 11.01.02

ACUPRESSURIST (medical ser.), 079.271-014, 10.02.02

ACUPUNCTURIST (medical ser.), 079.271-010, 02.03.04

ADDRESSER (clerical), 209.587-010, 07.07.02

ADDRESSING-MACHINE OPERATOR (clerical), 208.582-010, 05.12.19

ADJUDICATOR (government ser.), 119.167-010, 11.04.03

ADMINISTRATIVE ASSISTANT (any industry), 169.167-010, 11.05.02

ADMINISTRATIVE CLERK (clerical), 219.362-010, 07.01.02

ADMINISTRATIVE SECRETARY (any industry), 169.167-014, 07.01.02

ADMINISTRATOR, HEALTH CARE FACILITY (medical ser.), 187.117-010, 11.07.02

ADMISSIONS EVALUATOR (education), 205.367-010, 07.01.05

ADMITTING OFFICER (medical ser.), 205.162-010, 07.04.01

ADVANCE AGENT (amuse. & rec.), 191.167-010, 11.12.03

ADVERTISING CLERK (business ser.), 247.387-010, 07.02.04

ADVERTISING-DISPATCH CLERK (print. & pub.), 247.387-014, 07.05.01

ADVERTISING-SPACE CLERK (print. & pub.), 247.387-018, 01.06.01

AERIALIST (amuse. & rec.), 159.247-014, 12.02.01

AERODYNAMICIST (aircraft mfg.), 002.061-010, 05.01.01

AERONAUTICAL ENGINEER (aircraft mfg.), 002.061-014, 05.01.07

AERONAUTICAL TEST ENGINEER (aircraft mfg.), 002.061-018, 05.01.04

AERONAUTICAL-DESIGN ENGINEER (aircraft mfg.), 002.061-022, 05.01.07

AERONAUTICAL-RESEARCH ENGINEER (aircraft mfg.), 002.061-026, 05.01.01

AEROSPACE PHYSIOLOGICAL TECHNICIAN (military ser.), 199.682-010, 02.04.02

AGENT-CONTRACT CLERK (insurance), 241.267-010, 07.01.05

AGRICULTURAL ENGINEER (profess. & kin.), 013.061-010, 05.01.08

AGRICULTURAL-ENGINEERING TECHNICIAN (profess. & kin.), 013.161-010, 05.01.07

AGRONOMIST (profess. & kin.), 040.061-010, 02.02.02

AIR ANALYST (profess. & kin.), 012.261-010, 05.01.04

AIR-COMPRESSOR OPERATOR (any industry), 950.685-010, 05.06.02

AIR-CONDITIONING INSTALLER-SERVICER HELPER, WINDOW UNIT (construction), 637.687-010, 05.12.12

AIR-CONDITIONING INSTALLER-SERVICER, WINDOW UNIT (construction), 637.261-010, 05.05.09

AIR-CONDITIONING MECHANIC (automotive ser.), 620.281-010, 05.05.09

AIR-TRAFFIC-CONTROL SPECIALIST, STATION (government ser.), 193.162-014, 05.03.03

AIR-TRAFFIC-CONTROL SPECIALIST, TOWER (government ser.), 193.162-018, 05.03.03

AIRCRAFT BODY REPAIRER (air trans.), 807.261-010, 05.05.06

AIRFRAME-AND-POWER-PLANT MECHANIC (aircraft mfg.), 621.281-014, 05.05.09

AIRFRAME-AND-POWER-PLANT-MECHANIC APPRENTICE (air trans.), 621.281-018, 05.05.09

AIRLINE SECURITY REPRESENTATIVE (air trans.), 372.667-010, 04.02.02

AIRLINE-RADIO OPERATOR (air trans.), 193.262-010, 07.04.05

AIRPLANE INSPECTOR (air trans.), 621.261-010, 05.07.02

AIRPLANE PILOT (agriculture), 196.263-010, 05.04.01

AIRPLANE PILOT, COMMERCIAL (air trans.), 196.263-014, 05.04.01

AIRPLANE-FLIGHT ATTENDANT (air trans.), 352.367-010, 09.01.04

AIRPORT ATTENDANT (air trans.), 912.364-010, 05.10.04

AIRPORT ENGINEER (profess. & kin.), 005.061-010, 05.01.07

AIRPORT UTILITY WORKER (air trans.), 912.663-010, 05.12.06

ALARM INVESTIGATOR (business ser.), 376.367-010, 04.02.04

ALARM OPERATOR (government ser.), 379.162-010, 07.04.05

ALTERATION TAILOR (garment), 785.261-010, 05.05.15

AMBULANCE ATTENDANT (medical ser.), 355.374-010, 10.03.02

AMBULANCE DRIVER (medical ser.), 913.683-010, 05.08.03

AMUSEMENT PARK ENTERTAINER (amuse. & rec.), 159.647-010, 01.07.03

AMUSEMENT PARK WORKER (amuse. & rec.), 349.664-010, 09.01.01

ANALYST, FOOD AND BEVERAGE (hotel & rest.), 310.267-010, 05.05.17

ANESTHESIOLOGIST (medical ser.), 070.101-010, 02.03.01

ANIMAL CARETAKER (any industry), 410.674-010, 03.03.02

ANIMAL KEEPER (amuse. & rec.), 412.674-010, 03.03.02

ANIMAL KEEPER, HEAD (amuse. & rec.), 412.137-010, 03.03.02

ANIMAL SCIENTIST (profess. & kin.), 040.061-014, 02.02.01

ANIMAL TRAINER (amuse. & rec.), 159.224-010, 03.03.01

ANIMAL TREATMENT INVESTIGATOR (nonprofit org.), 379.263-010, 11.10.03

ANIMAL-HOSPITAL CLERK (medical ser.), 245.367-010, 07.04.03

ANIMAL-SHELTER CLERK (nonprofit org.), 249.367-010, 07.04.03

ANNEALER (jewelry-silver.), 504.687-010, 06.04.10

ANNOUNCER (radio-tv broad.), 159.147-010, 01.03.03

ANNOUNCER (amuse. & rec.), 159.347-010, 01.07.02

ANODIZER (any industry), 500.682-010, 06.02.21

ANTENNA INSTALLER, SATELLITE COMMUNICATIONS (any industry), 823.261-022, 05.05.05

ANTHROPOLOGIST (profess. & kin.), 055.067-010, 11.03.03

APPEALS REFEREE (government ser.), 119.267-014, 11.04.01

APPLIANCE REPAIRER (house. appl.), 723.584-010, 05.10.03

APPLIANCE-SERVICE SUPERVISOR (utilities), 187.167-010, 05.02.06

APPRAISER (government ser.), 188.167-010, 11.06.03

APPRAISER (any industry), 191.287-010, 11.06.03

APPRAISER, ART (profess. & kin.), 191.287-014, 01.02.01

APPRAISER, AUTOMOBILE DAMAGE (business ser.), 241.267-014, 11.12.01

APPRAISER, REAL ESTATE (real estate), 191.267-010, 11.06.03

AQUARIST (amuse. & rec.), 449.674-010, 03.03.02

AQUATIC BIOLOGIST (profess. & kin.), 041.061-022, 02.02.03

AQUATIC PERFORMER (amuse. & rec.), 159.347-014, 12.02.01

ARBITRATOR (profess. & kin.), 169.107-010, 11.04.03

ARC CUTTER (welding), 816.364-010, 05.05.06

ARCH-SUPPORT TECHNICIAN (protective dev.), 712.381-010, 05.10.01

ARCHEOLOGIST (profess. & kin.), 055.067-018, 11.03.03

ARCHITECT (profess. & kin.), 001.061-010, 05.01.07

ARCHITECT, MARINE (profess. & kin.), 001.061-014, 05.01.07

ARCHIVIST (profess. & kin.), 101.167-010, 11.03.03

AREA SUPERVISOR, RETAIL CHAIN STORE (retail trade), 185.117-014, 11.11.05

ARMORED-CAR GUARD (business ser.), 372.567-010, 04.02.02

ARMORED-CAR GUARD AND DRIVER (business ser.), 372.563-010, 04.02.02

ART DIRECTOR (profess. & kin.), 141.031-010, 01.02.03

ART DIRECTOR (motion picture), 142.061-062, 01.02.03

ART THERAPIST (medical ser.), 076.127-010, 10.02.02

ARTIFICIAL-FLOWER MAKER (button & notion), 739.684-014, 06.04.34

ARTIST AND REPERTOIRE MANAGER (amuse. & rec.), 159.167-010, 01.04.01

ARTIST'S MANAGER (amuse. & rec.), 191.117-010, 11.12.03

ASBESTOS REMOVAL WORKER (construction), 869.684-082, 05.10.01

ASPHALT-DISTRIBUTOR TENDER (construction), 853.665-010, 05.12.14

ASPHALT-PAVING-MACHINE OPERATOR (construction), 853.663-010, 05.11.01

ASSAYER (profess. & kin.), 022.281-010, 02.04.01

ASSEMBLER I (office machines), 706.684-014, 06.02.23

ASSEMBLER, BICYCLE II (motor-bicycles), 806.687-010, 06.04.22

ASSEMBLER, ELECTROMECHANICAL (aircraft mfg.), 828.381-018, 06.01.04

ASSEMBLER, INTERNAL COMBUSTION ENGINE (engine-turbine), 806.481-014, 06.02.22

ASSEMBLER, METAL BONDING (aircraft mfg.), 806.384-030, 06.02.24

ASSEMBLER, MOLDED FRAMES (optical goods), 713.684-014, 06.04.23

ASSEMBLER, MOTOR VEHICLE (auto. mfg.), 806.684-010, 06.04.22

ASSEMBLER, MUSICAL INSTRUMENTS (musical inst.), 730.684-010, 06.02.23

ASSEMBLER, PLASTIC HOSPITAL PRODUCTS (inst. & app.), 712.687-010, 06.04.24

ASSEMBLER, PRODUCT (machine shop), 706.684-018, 06.02.23

ASSEMBLER, PRODUCTION (any industry), 706.687-010, 06.04.22

ASSEMBLER, SEMICONDUCTOR (electron. comp.), 726.684-034, 06.02.23

ASSEMBLER, SMALL PRODUCTS I (any industry), 706.684-022, 06.04.23

ASSEMBLER, SUBASSEMBLY (aircraft mfg.), 806.384-034, 06.02.22

ASSIGNMENT CLERK (clerical), 249.367-090, 07.05.03

ASSISTANT BRANCH MANAGER, FINANCIAL INSTITUTION (financial), 186.167-070, 11.11.04

ASSISTANT PRESS OPERATOR, OFFSET (print. & pub.), 651.685-026, 05.05.13

ASSISTANT PRINCIPAL (education), 091.107-010, 10.01.02

ASSISTANT-PRESS OPERATOR (print. & pub.), 651.585-010, 05.05.13

ASSOCIATION EXECUTIVE (profess. & kin.), 189.117-010, 11.05.01

ATHLETIC TRAINER (amuse. & rec.), 153.224-010, 10.02.02

ATTENDANCE CLERK (education), 219.362-014, 07.05.03

ATTENDANCE OFFICER (education), 168.367-010, 07.01.06

ATTENDANT, ARCADE (amuse. & rec.), 342.667-014, 09.04.02

ATTENDANT, CAMPGROUND (amuse. & rec.), 329.683-010, 05.12.18

ATTENDANT, CHILDREN'S INSTITUTION (any industry), 359.677-010, 10.03.03

AUCTION ASSISTANT (retail trade), 294.667-010, 07.07.02

AUCTION CLERK (retail trade), 294.567-010, 07.03.01

AUCTIONEER (retail trade), 294.257-010, 08.02.03

AUDIO OPERATOR (radio-tv broad.), 194.262-010, 05.10.05

AUDIO-VIDEO REPAIRER (any industry), 729.281-010, 05.05.10

AUDIOLOGIST (medical ser.), 076.101-010, 02.03.04

AUDIOMETRIST (profess. & kin.), 078.362-010, 10.03.01

AUDIOVISUAL LIBRARIAN (library), 100.167-010, 11.02.04

AUDIOVISUAL PRODUCTION SPECIALIST (profess. & kin.), 149.061-010, 01.02.03

AUDIOVISUAL TECHNICIAN (any industry), 960.382-010, 05.10.05

AUDIT CLERK (clerical), 210.382-010, 07.02.01

AUDITOR (profess. & kin.), 160.167-054, 11.06.01

AUDITOR, COUNTY OR CITY (government ser.), 160.167-030, 11.06.01

AUDITOR, DATA PROCESSING (profess. & kin.), 160.162-030, 11.06.01

AUDITOR, INTERNAL (profess. & kin.), 160.167-034, 11.06.01

AUDITOR, TAX (profess. & kin.), 160.167-038, 11.06.01

AUTO-DESIGN CHECKER (auto. mfg.), 017.261-010, 05.03.02

AUTO-DESIGN DETAILER (auto. mfg.), 017.281-010, 05.03.02

AUTOCLAVE OPERATOR (aircraft mfg.), 553.362-014, 06.02.18

AUTOMATED CUTTING MACHINE OPERATOR (aircraft mfg.), 699.362-010, 06.02.09

AUTOMATED EQUIPMENT ENGINEER-TECHNICIAN (machinery mfg.), 638.261-010, 05.05.05

AUTOMATIC-DOOR MECHANIC (construction), 829.281-010, 05.10.03

AUTOMOBILE DETAILER (automotive ser.), 915.687-034, 05.12.18

AUTOMOBILE LOCATOR (retail trade), 296.367-010, 07.05.03

AUTOMOBILE MECHANIC (automotive ser.), 620.261-010, 05.05.09

AUTOMOBILE RENTAL CLERK (automotive ser.), 295.467-026, 09.04.02

AUTOMOBILE TESTER (automotive ser.), 620.261-014, 05.07.02

AUTOMOBILE UPHOLSTERER (automotive ser.), 780.381-010, 05.05.15

AUTOMOBILE WRECKER (wholesale tr.), 620.684-010, 05.12.15

AUTOMOBILE-ACCESSORIES INSTALLER (automotive ser.), 806.684-038, 05.10.02

AUTOMOBILE-BODY REPAIRER (automotive ser.), 807.381-010, 05.05.06

AUTOMOBILE-BODY-REPAIRER HELPER (automotive ser.), 807.687-010, 05.12.12

AUTOMOBILE-CLUB-SAFETY-PROGRAM COORDINATOR (nonprofit org.), 249.167-010, 07.01.02

AUTOMOBILE-RADIATOR MECHANIC (automotive ser.), 620.381-010, 05.10.02

AUTOMOBILE-REPAIR-SERVICE ESTIMATOR (automotive ser.), 620.261-018, 05.07.02

AUTOMOBILE-SERVICE-STATION ATTENDANT (automotive ser.), 915.467-010, 05.10.02

AUTOMOBILE-SERVICE-STATION MECHANIC (automotive ser.), 620.261-030, 05.05.09

AUTOMOTIVE ENGINEER (auto. mfg.), 007.061-010, 05.01.08

AUTOMOTIVE-COOLING-SYSTEM DIAGNOSTIC TECHNICIAN (automotive ser.), 620.261-034, 05.05.09

AUTOMOTIVE-MAINTENANCE-EQUIPMENT SERVICER (any industry), 620.281-018, 05.05.09

AVIONICS TECHNICIAN (aircraft mfg.), 823.261-026, 05.05.10

BAG-MACHINE OPERATOR (paper goods), 649.685-014, 06.04.04

BAGGAGE HANDLER (r.r. trans.), 910.687-010, 05.12.03

BAGGAGE PORTER, HEAD (hotel & rest.), 324.137-010, 09.05.03

BAGGER (retail trade), 920.687-014, 09.05.10

BAILIFF (government ser.), 377.667-010, 04.02.03

BAKER (hotel & rest.), 313.381-010, 05.10.08

BAKER (bakery products), 526.381-010, 06.02.15

BAKER HELPER (hotel & rest.), 313.684-010, 05.12.17

BAKER HELPER (bakery products), 526.686-010, 06.04.15

BAKER, HEAD (hotel & rest.), 313.131-010, 05.10.08

BAKER, PIZZA (hotel & rest.), 313.381-014, 05.10.08

BALLISTICS EXPERT, FORENSIC (government ser.), 199.267-010, 02.04.01

BANDER, HAND (any industry), 929.687-058, 06.04.38

BARBER (personal ser.), 330.371-010, 09.02.02

BARGE CAPTAIN (water trans.), 911.137-010, 05.12.01

BARTENDER (hotel & rest.), 312.474-010, 09.04.01

BARTENDER HELPER (hotel & rest.), 312.687-010, 05.12.18

BATTER MIXER (bakery products), 520.685-010, 06.04.15

BATTERY ASSEMBLER, DRY CELL (elec. equip.), 727.664-010, 06.04.23

BEACH LIFEGUARD (amuse. & rec.), 379.364-014, 04.02.03

BEAM-WARPER TENDER, AUTOMATIC (knitting), 681.685-018, 06.04.06

BEEKEEPER (agriculture), 413.161-010, 03.01.02

BELL CAPTAIN (hotel & rest.), 324.137-014, 09.05.03

BELLHOP (hotel & rest.), 324.677-010, 09.05.03

BELT REPAIRER (any industry), 630.684-014, 05.12.15

BENCH HAND (bakery products), 520.384-010, 06.02.28

BENCH HAND (jewelry-silver.), 735.381-010, 06.01.04

BENCH WORKER (optical goods), 713.684-018, 06.04.24

BENDING-MACHINE OPERATOR II (any industry), 617.685-010, 06.04.02

BENEFITS CLERK II (clerical), 205.567-010, 07.05.03

BICYCLE REPAIRER (any industry), 639.681-010, 05.10.02

BICYCLE-RENTAL CLERK (retail trade), 295.467-010, 09.04.02

BILLING CLERK (clerical), 214.362-042, 07.02.04

BILLING-CONTROL CLERK (utilities), 214.387-010, 07.02.04

BILLPOSTER (any industry), 299.667-010, 05.12.12

BINDER (any industry), 787.682-010, 06.02.05

BINDERY WORKER (print. & pub.), 653.685-010, 06.04.04

BIOCHEMIST (profess. & kin.), 041.061-026, 02.02.03

BIOCHEMISTRY TECHNOLOGIST (medical ser.), 078.261-010, 02.04.02

BIOGRAPHER (profess. & kin.), 052.067-010, 01.01.02

BIOLOGICAL AIDE (agriculture), 049.364-018, 02.04.02

BIOLOGIST (profess. & kin.), 041.061-030, 02.02.03

BIOLOGY SPECIMEN TECHNICIAN (profess. & kin.), 041.381-010, 02.04.02

BIOMEDICAL ENGINEER (profess. & kin.), 019.061-010, 02.02.01

BIOMEDICAL EQUIPMENT TECHNICIAN (profess. & kin.), 019.261-010, 02.04.02

BIOPHYSICIST (profess. & kin.), 041.061-034, 02.02.03

BIRTH ATTENDANT (medical ser.), 354.377-010, 10.03.02

BLACKSMITH (forging), 610.381-010, 05.05.06

BLANKMAKER (glass mfg.), 579.382-022, 06.02.13

BLASTER (any industry), 859.261-010, 05.10.06

BLIND AIDE (personal ser.), 359.573-010, 10.03.03

BLOCK MAKER (protective dev.), 719.381-018, 05.12.13

BLOOD-DONOR RECRUITER (medical ser.), 293.357-010, 11.09.02

BLOOD-DONOR-UNIT ASSISTANT (medical ser.), 245.367-014, 07.04.01

BLOW-MOLDING-MACHINE TENDER (toy-sport equip.), 556.685-086, 06.04.13

BOARD ATTENDANT (amuse. & rec.), 249.587-010, 09.05.05

BOAT LOADER I (water trans.), 911.364-014, 05.12.06

BOAT PATCHER, PLASTIC (ship-boat mfg.), 807.684-014, 06.02.24

BOAT REPAIRER (ship-boat mfg.), 807.361-014, 05.05.02

BOAT RIGGER (retail trade), 806.464-010, 05.10.01

BOAT-RENTAL CLERK (amuse. & rec.), 295.467-014, 09.04.02

BOATBUILDER, WOOD (ship-boat mfg.), 860.361-010, 05.05.02

BODYGUARD (personal ser.), 372.667-014, 04.02.02

BOILER OPERATOR (any industry), 950.382-010, 05.06.02

BOILERHOUSE MECHANIC (any industry), 805.361-010, 05.05.06

BOILERMAKER I (struct. metal), 805.261-014, 05.05.06

BONDED STRUCTURES REPAIRER (aircraft mfg.), 807.381-014, 06.02.32

BONDING AGENT (business ser.), 186.267-010, 07.04.01

BONER, MEAT (meat products), 525.684-010, 06.04.28

BOOK TRIMMER (print. & pub.), 640.685-010, 06.04.04

BOOKBINDER (print. & pub.), 977.381-010, 05.05.15

BOOKING MANAGER (amuse. & rec.), 191.117-014, 11.12.03

BOOKKEEPER (clerical), 210.382-014, 07.02.01

BOOKMAKER (amuse. & rec.), 187.167-014, 11.06.03

BOOKMOBILE DRIVER (library), 249.363-010, 05.09.01

BOOKMOBILE LIBRARIAN (library), 100.167-014, 11.02.04

BORDER GUARD (government ser.), 375.363-010, 04.02.03

BOTANIST (profess. & kin.), 041.061-038, 02.02.02

BOUNCER (amuse. & rec.), 376.667-010, 04.02.03

BOW MAKER (any industry), 789.684-010, 06.04.27

BOW MAKER, CUSTOM (toy-sport equip.), 732.381-010, 01.06.02

BRAILLE OPERATOR (print. & pub.), 203.582-010, 07.06.02

BRAILLE PROOFREADER (nonprofit org.), 209.367-014, 07.05.02

BRAILLE TYPIST (education), 203.582-014, 07.06.02

BRAILLE-DUPLICATING-MACHINE OPERATOR (print. & pub.), 207.685-010, 05.12.19

BRAKE OPERATOR II (any industry), 619.685-026, 06.02.02

BRAKE REPAIRER (automotive ser.), 620.281-026, 05.10.02

BREWERY CELLAR WORKER (beverage), 522.685-014, 06.04.15

BREWING DIRECTOR (beverage), 183.167-010, 05.02.03

BRICKLAYER (construction), 861.381-018, 05.05.01

BRIGHT CUTTER (jewelry-silver.), 700.684-018, 06.02.24

BRIQUETTE-MACHINE OPERATOR (fabrication, nec), 549.662-010, 06.02.17

BROKERAGE CLERK I (financial), 219.482-010, 07.02.02

BROKERAGE CLERK II (financial), 219.362-018, 07.02.02

BUDGET ANALYST (government ser.), 161.267-030, 11.06.05

BUDGET OFFICER (profess. & kin.), 161.117-010, 11.06.05

BUFFER I (any industry), 705.684-014, 06.04.24

BUFFING-MACHINE TENDER (any industry), 603.665-010, 06.04.02

BUILDING CLEANER (any industry), 891.684-022, 05.10.01

BUILDING CONSULTANT (wholesale tr.), 250.357-010, 08.02.04

BUILDING INSPECTOR (insurance), 168.267-010, 05.03.06

BULLDOZER OPERATOR I (any industry), 850.683-010, 05.11.01

BUS DRIVER (motor trans.), 913.463-010, 09.03.01

BUSINESS MANAGER (amuse. & rec.), 191.117-018, 11.12.03

BUSINESS MANAGER, COLLEGE OR UNIVERSITY (education), 186.117-010, 11.05.02

BUSINESS REPRESENTATIVE, LABOR UNION (profess. & kin.), 187.167-018, 11.05.02

BUSINESS-OPPORTUNITY-AND-PROPERTY-INVESTMENT BROKER (business ser.), 189.157-010, 08.01.03

BUTCHER, ALL-ROUND (meat products), 525.381-014, 06.02.28

BUTCHER, CHICKEN AND FISH (hotel & rest.), 316.684-010, 05.10.08

BUTCHER, FISH (can. & preserv.), 525.684-014, 06.04.28

BUTCHER, MEAT (hotel & rest.), 316.681-010, 05.10.08

BUTLER (domestic ser.), 309.137-010, 09.01.03

BUTTERMAKER (dairy products), 529.362-010, 06.02.15

BUTTONHOLE-AND-BUTTON-SEWING-MACHINE OPERATOR (garment), 786.685-042, 06.04.05

BUYER (profess. & kin.), 162.157-018, 08.01.03

BUYER, ASSISTANT (retail trade), 162.157-022, 08.01.03

BUZZSAW OPERATOR (any industry), 667.685-026, 06.04.03

CABINET ASSEMBLER (furniture), 763.684-014, 06.02.22

CABINETMAKER (woodworking), 660.280-010, 05.05.08

CABLE ENGINEER, OUTSIDE PLANT (tel. & tel.), 003.167-010, 05.01.03

CABLE INSTALLER-REPAIRER (utilities), 821.361-010, 05.05.05

CABLE MAINTAINER (utilities), 952.464-010, 05.06.01

CABLE PULLER (construction), 829.684-018, 05.12.16

CABLE SPLICER (construction), 829.361-010, 05.05.05

CABLE SUPERVISOR (tel. & tel.), 184.161-010, 05.05.05

CABLE TELEVISION INSTALLER (radio-tv broad.), 821.281-010, 05.10.03

CABLE TESTER (tel. & tel.), 822.361-010, 05.05.05

CADDIE (amuse. & rec.), 341.677-010, 09.05.06

CAFETERIA ATTENDANT (hotel & rest.), 311.677-010, 09.05.02

CAKE DECORATOR (bakery products), 524.381-010, 05.05.17

CALCULATING-MACHINE OPERATOR (clerical), 216.482-022, 07.02.02

CALIBRATION LABORATORY TECHNICIAN (aircraft mfg.), 019.281-010, 02.04.01

CALIBRATOR (inst. & app.), 710.381-034, 06.01.04

CALL-OUT OPERATOR (business ser.), 237.367-014, 07.05.03

CAMERA OPERATOR (motion picture), 143.062-022, 01.02.03

CANCELLATION CLERK (insurance), 203.382-014, 07.02.02

CANDLEMAKER (fabrication, nec), 739.664-010, 06.04.32

CANDY DIPPER, HAND (sugar & conf.), 524.684-010, 06.04.28

CANDY MAKER (sugar & conf.), 529.361-014, 06.02.28

CANER II (furniture), 763.684-022, 06.04.25

CANNERY WORKER (can. & preserv.), 529.686-014, 06.04.15

CANTEEN OPERATOR (any industry), 311.674-010, 09.04.01

CANVAS REPAIRER (any industry), 782.684-010, 06.04.27

CANVAS WORKER (ship-boat mfg.), 739.381-010, 06.01.04

CAPTAIN, FISHING VESSEL (fishing & hunt.), 197.133-010, 05.04.02

CAPTION WRITER (motion picture), 203.362-026, 07.05.03

CAR HOP (hotel & rest.), 311.477-010, 09.04.01

CARBURETOR MECHANIC (automotive ser.), 620.281-034, 05.10.02

CARDIAC MONITOR TECHNICIAN (medical ser.), 078.367-010, 10.03.01

CARDIOLOGIST (medical ser.), 070.101-014, 02.03.01

CARDIOPULMONARY TECHNOLO-GIST (medical ser.), 078.362-030, 10.03.01

CARDROOM ATTENDANT II (amuse. & rec.), 343.577-010, 09.05.05

CAREER-GUIDANCE TECHNICIAN (education), 249.367-014, 11.02.04

CARETAKER (domestic ser.), 301.687-010, 05.12.18

CARGO AGENT (air trans.), 248.367-018, 05.09.01

CARPENTER (construction), 860.381-022, 05.05.02

CARPENTER APPRENTICE (construction), 860.381-026, 05.05.02

CARPENTER, MAINTENANCE (any industry), 860.281-010, 05.05.02

CARPENTER, ROUGH (construction), 860.381-042, 05.05.02

CARPET CUTTER (retail trade), 929.381-010, 05.10.01

CARPET CUTTER II (carpet & rug), 585.687-014, 06.04.27

CARPET LAYER (retail trade), 864.381-010, 05.10.01

CARPET SEWER (carpet & rug), 787.682-014, 06.02.05

CARTON-FORMING-MACHINE OPERATOR (any industry), 641.685-022, 06.04.04

CARTON-FORMING-MACHINE TENDER (paper goods), 641.685-026, 06.04.04

CARTOONIST (print. & pub.), 141.061-010, 01.02.03

CARVER (hotel & rest.), 316.661-010, 05.10.08

CASE AIDE (social ser.), 195.367-010, 10.01.02

CASEWORK SUPERVISOR (social ser.), 195.137-010, 10.01.02

CASEWORKER (government ser.), 169.262-010, 07.01.06

CASEWORKER (social ser.), 195.107-010, 10.01.02

CASEWORKER, CHILD WELFARE (social ser.), 195.107-014, 10.01.02

CASEWORKER, FAMILY (social ser.), 195.107-018, 10.01.02

CASH-REGISTER SERVICER (any industry), 633.281-010, 05.05.09

CASHIER I (clerical), 211.362-010, 07.03.01

CASHIER II (clerical), 211.462-010, 07.03.01

CASHIER, COURTESY BOOTH (retail trade), 211.467-010, 09.04.02

CASHIER, GAMBLING (amuse. & rec.), 211.462-022, 07.03.01

CASHIER-CHECKER (retail trade), 211.462-014, 07.03.01

CASHIER-WRAPPER (retail trade), 211.462-018, 09.04.02

CASKET ASSEMBLER (fabrication, nec), 739.684-190, 06.02.22

CASTER (jewelry-silver.), 502.381-010, 06.02.24

CASTER (nonmet. min.), 575.684-018, 06.02.30

CASTING REPAIRER (any industry), 619.281-010, 05.10.01

CATALOG LIBRARIAN (library), 100.387-010, 11.02.04

CATERER HELPER (personal ser.), 319.677-010, 09.05.02

CATHODE RAY TUBE SALVAGE PROCESSOR (electron. comp.), 725.684-026, 06.02.32

CEMENT MASON (construction), 844.364-010, 05.05.01

CEMENTER (optical goods), 711.684-014, 06.02.30

CEMETERY WORKER (real estate), 406.684-010, 03.04.04

CENTER-MACHINE OPERATOR (sugar & conf.), 520.682-014, 06.02.15

CENTRAL-OFFICE EQUIPMENT ENGINEER (tel. & tel.), 003.187-010, 05.01.03

CENTRAL-OFFICE OPERATOR (tel. & tel.), 235.462-010, 07.04.06

CENTRAL-OFFICE REPAIRER (tel. & tel.), 822.281-014, 05.05.05

CENTRAL-SUPPLY WORKER (medical ser.), 381.687-010, 05.12.18

CENTRIFUGE OPERATOR (dairy products), 521.685-042, 06.04.15

CEPHALOMETRIC ANALYST (medical ser.), 078.384-010, 02.04.02

CERAMIC CAPACITOR PROCESSOR (electron. comp.), 590.684-010, 06.04.08

CERAMIC COATER, MACHINE (any industry), 509.685-022, 06.04.21

CERAMIC ENGINEER (profess. & kin.), 006.061-014, 05.01.07

CERTIFIED MEDICATION TECHNI-CIAN (medical ser.), 355.374-014, 10.03.02

CHAIN MAKER, MACHINE (jewelry-silver.), 700.684-022, 06.02.23

CHAIN OFFBEARER (saw. & plan.), 669.686-018, 06.04.03

CHAIN SAW OPERATOR (chemical), 454.687-010, 03.04.02

CHANGE PERSON (amuse. & rec.), 211.467-034, 07.03.01

CHAPERON (personal ser.), 359.667-010, 04.02.03

CHAR-CONVEYOR TENDER (sugar & conf.), 529.685-050, 06.04.40

CHARTER (amuse. & rec.), 249.367-018, 12.01.02

CHAUFFEUR (domestic ser.), 359.673-010, 09.03.02

CHAUFFEUR (any industry), 913.663-010, 09.03.02

CHAUFFEUR, FUNERAL CAR (personal ser.), 359.673-014, 05.08.03

CHECK CASHIER (business ser.), 211.462-026, 07.03.01

CHECK WRITER (retail trade), 219.382-010, 07.06.02

CHECKER (motor trans.), 919.687-010, 05.09.01

CHECKER I (clerical), 222.687-010, 07.07.02

CHECKER, BAKERY PRODUCTS (bakery products), 222.487-010, 05.09.01

CHECKER, DUMP GROUNDS (business ser.), 219.367-010, 05.09.03

CHECKROOM ATTENDANT (any industry), 358.677-010, 09.05.03

CHEESE CUTTER (dairy products), 529.585-010, 06.04.15

CHEESEMAKER (dairy products), 529.361-018, 06.01.04

CHEF (hotel & rest.), 313.131-014, 05.05.17

CHEF DE FROID (hotel & rest.), 313.281-010, 05.05.17

CHEMICAL DESIGN ENGINEER, PROCESSES (profess. & kin.), 008.061-014, 05.01.07

CHEMICAL ENGINEER (profess. & kin.), 008.061-018, 05.01.07

CHEMICAL LABORATORY CHIEF (profess. & kin.), 022.161-010, 02.01.02

CHEMICAL LABORATORY TECHNI-CIAN (profess. & kin.), 022.261-010, 02.04.01

CHEMICAL OPERATOR II (chemical), 558.685-062, 06.04.11

CHEMICAL PREPARER (chemical), 550.685-030, 06.04.11

CHEMICAL RESEARCH ENGINEER (profess. & kin.), 008.061-022, 05.01.01

CHEMICAL-ENGINEERING TECHNI-CIAN (profess. & kin.), 008.261-010, 05.01.08

CHEMICAL-RADIATION TECHNICIAN (government ser.), 015.261-010, 11.10.03

CHEMICAL-TEST ENGINEER (profess. & kin.), 008.061-026, 05.01.04

CHEMIST (profess. & kin.), 022.061-010, 02.01.01

CHEMIST, FOOD (profess. & kin.), 022.061-014, 02.02.04

CHERRY-PICKER OPERATOR (construction), 921.663-014, 05.11.01

CHIEF ENGINEER, WATERWORKS (waterworks), 005.167-010, 05.01.03

CHIEF OPERATOR (chemical), 558.260-010, 06.01.03

CHIEF TECHNOLOGIST, NUCLEAR MEDICINE (medical ser.), 078.131-010, 02.04.02

CHIEF, COMPUTER PROGRAMMER (profess. & kin.), 030.167-010, 11.01.01

CHILD MONITOR (domestic ser.), 301.677-010, 10.03.03

CHILD SUPPORT OFFICER (government ser.), 195.267-022, 10.01.02

CHILD-CARE ATTENDANT, SCHOOL (personal ser.), 355.674-010, 10.03.03

CHILDREN'S ATTENDANT (amuse. & rec.), 349.677-018, 09.05.08

CHILDREN'S TUTOR (domestic ser.), 099.227-010, 10.03.03

CHIMNEY SWEEP (any industry), 891.687-010, 05.12.18

CHIROPRACTOR (medical ser.), 079.101-010, 02.03.04

CHIROPRACTOR ASSISTANT (medical ser.), 079.364-010, 10.03.02

CHOCOLATE MOLDER, MACHINE (sugar & conf.), 529.685-054, 06.04.15

CHOCOLATE-PRODUCTION-MACHINE OPERATOR (sugar & conf.), 529.382-014, 06.02.15

CHOKE SETTER (logging), 921.687-014, 05.12.04

CHRISTMAS-TREE FARM WORKER (forestry), 451.687-010, 03.04.01

CIGARETTE VENDOR (hotel & rest.), 291.457-010, 08.03.01

CIRCULATION-SALES REPRESENTATIVE (print. & pub.), 299.167-010, 11.09.01

CIRCUS AGENT (amuse. & rec.), 191.117-022, 11.12.03

CITY PLANNING AIDE (profess. & kin.), 199.364-010, 11.03.02

CIVIL ENGINEER (profess. & kin.), 005.061-014, 05.01.07

CIVIL ENGINEERING TECHNICIAN (profess. & kin.), 005.261-014, 05.03.02

CIVIL PREPAREDNESS TRAINING OFFICER (government ser.), 169.127-010, 11.07.02

CLAIM ADJUSTER (business ser.), 241.217-010, 11.12.01

CLAIM EXAMINER (insurance), 168.267-014, 07.02.03

CLAIM EXAMINER (business ser.), 241.267-018, 11.12.01

CLAIMS ADJUDICATOR (government ser.), 169.267-010, 11.12.01

CLAIMS CLERK II (insurance), 205.367-018, 07.04.02

CLASSIFICATION CLERK (clerical), 206.387-010, 07.05.03

CLASSIFIED-AD CLERK II (print. & pub.), 247.387-022, 07.05.02

CLASSIFIER (library), 100.367-014, 11.02.04

CLAY MODELER (any industry), 779.281-010, 01.06.02

CLEANER (ordnance), 503.684-010, 06.04.39

CLEANER AND POLISHER (any industry), 709.687-010, 06.04.39

CLEANER II (any industry), 919.687-014, 05.12.18

CLEANER, COMMERCIAL OR INSTITUTIONAL (any industry), 381.687-014, 05.12.18

CLEANER, HOSPITAL (medical ser.), 323.687-010, 05.12.18

CLEANER, HOUSEKEEPING (any industry), 323.687-014, 05.12.18

CLEANER, INDUSTRIAL (any industry), 381.687-018, 05.12.18

CLEANER, LABORATORY EQUIPMENT (any industry), 381.687-022, 05.12.18

CLEANER, WINDOW (any industry), 389.687-014, 05.12.18

CLERGY MEMBER (profess. & kin.), 120.107-010, 10.01.01

CLERK, GENERAL (clerical), 209.562-010, 07.07.03

CLERK, TELEVISION PRODUCTION (radio-tv broad.), 221.367-086, 07.05.01

CLERK-TYPIST (clerical), 203.362-010, 07.06.02

CLINICAL PSYCHOLOGIST (profess. & kin.), 045.107-022, 10.01.02

CLINICAL THERAPIST (profess. & kin.), 045.107-050, 10.01.02

CLOSER (real estate), 186.167-074, 07.01.04

CLOTH DOFFER (textile), 689.686-058, 06.04.06

CLOTH PRINTER (any industry), 652.382-010, 06.02.09

CLOWN (amuse. & rec.), 159.047-010, 01.03.02

COATING EQUIPMENT OPERATOR, PRINTED CIRCUIT BOARDS (electron. comp.), 590.685-066, 06.04.19

CODE AND TEST CLERK (financial), 209.667-018, 11.08.04

CODE INSPECTOR (government ser.), 168.367-018, 05.03.06

COFFEE GRINDER (food prep., nec), 521.685-078, 06.04.15

COFFEE MAKER (hotel & rest.), 317.684-010, 05.12.17

COFFEE ROASTER (food prep., nec), 523.682-014, 06.02.15

COIL WINDER (elec. equip.), 724.684-026, 06.04.23

COIL WINDER, REPAIR (any industry), 724.381-014, 06.02.32

COIN COLLECTOR (business ser.), 292.483-010, 05.08.03

COIN-COUNTER-AND-WRAPPER (clerical), 217.585-010, 05.12.19

COIN-MACHINE COLLECTOR (business ser.), 292.687-010, 07.07.03

COIN-MACHINE-SERVICE REPAIRER (svc. ind. mach.), 639.281-014, 05.10.02

COLD-MILL OPERATOR (steel & rel.), 613.662-018, 06.02.10

COLLATOR OPERATOR (clerical), 208.685-010, 05.12.19

COLLECTION CLERK (financial), 216.362-014, 07.02.02

COLLECTION CLERK (clerical), 241.357-010, 07.04.02

COLLECTOR (clerical), 241.367-010, 07.03.01

COLOR-PRINTER OPERATOR (photofinishing), 976.382-014, 05.10.05

COLUMNIST/COMMENTATOR (print. & pub.), 131.067-010, 11.08.03

COMEDIAN (amuse. & rec.), 159.047-014, 01.03.02

COMMERCIAL DESIGNER (profess. & kin.), 141.061-038, 01.02.03

COMMERCIAL ENGINEER (radio-tv broad.), 003.187-014, 05.01.03

COMMERCIAL LOAN COLLECTION OFFICER (financial), 186.167-078, 11.05.02

COMMISSARY MANAGER (any industry), 185.167-010, 11.11.05

COMMISSION AGENT, AGRICULTURAL PRODUCE (wholesale tr.), 260.357-010, 08.01.03

COMMUNICATIONS COORDINATOR (medical ser.), 239.167-010, 05.03.05

COMMUNICATIONS TECHNICIAN (education), 962.362-010, 01.03.01

COMMUNITY DIETITIAN (profess. & kin.), 077.127-010, 11.02.03

COMMUNITY ORGANIZATION WORKER (social ser.), 195.167-010, 11.07.01

COMMUNITY WORKER (government ser.), 195.367-018, 10.01.02

COMMUNITY-RELATIONS-AND-SERVICES ADVISOR, PUBLIC HOUSING (social ser.), 195.167-014, 11.07.01

COMMUNITY-SERVICES-AND-HEALTH-EDUCATION OFFICER (government ser.), 079.167-010, 11.07.02

COMPANION (domestic ser.), 309.677-010, 10.03.03

COMPARATOR OPERATOR (any industry), 699.384-010, 06.03.01

COMPARISON SHOPPER (retail trade), 296.367-014, 08.01.03

COMPILER (clerical), 209.387-014, 07.05.03

COMPRESSED-GAS-PLANT WORKER (chemical), 549.587-010, 06.04.40

COMPRESSION-MOLDING-MACHINE TENDER (plastic prod.), 556.685-022, 06.04.13

COMPUTER OPERATOR (clerical), 213.362-010, 07.06.01

COMPUTER PERIPHERAL EQUIP-MENT OPERATOR (clerical), 213.382-010, 07.06.01

COMPUTER PROCESSING SCHEDULER (clerical), 221.362-030, 07.05.01

COMPUTER PROGRAMMER (profess. & kin.), 030.162-010, 11.01.01

COMPUTER SECURITY COORDINA-TOR (profess. & kin.), 033.162-010, 11.10.05

COMPUTER SECURITY SPECIALIST (profess. & kin.), 033.362-010, 11.10.05

COMPUTER SYSTEMS HARDWARE ANALYST (profess. & kin.), 033.167-010, 05.01.03

COMPUTER TYPESETTER-KEYLINER (print. & pub.), 979.382-026, 01.06.01

COMPUTERIZED ENVIRONMENTAL CONTROL INSTALLER (electron. comp.), 828.281-026, 05.05.05

CONCILIATOR (profess. & kin.), 169.207-010, 11.04.03

CONCRETE-MIXING-TRUCK DRIVER (construction), 900.683-010, 05.08.03

CONCRETE-PAVING-MACHINE OPERATOR (construction), 853.663-014, 05.11.01

CONDOMINIUM MANAGER (real estate), 186.167-062, 11.11.01

CONDUCTOR, PASSENGER CAR (r.r. trans.), 198.167-010, 11.11.03

CONDUCTOR, ROAD FREIGHT (r.r. trans.), 198.167-018, 11.11.03

CONDUIT MECHANIC (construction), 869.361-010, 05.05.06

CONFIGURATION MANAGEMENT ANALYST (profess. & kin.), 012.167-010, 05.01.06

CONGRESSIONAL-DISTRICT AIDE (government ser.), 209.362-030, 07.04.04

CONSERVATOR, ARTIFACTS (profess. & kin.), 055.381-010, 01.06.02

CONSTRUCTION INSPECTOR (construction), 182.267-010, 05.03.06

CONSTRUCTION WORKER I (construction), 869.664-014, 05.10.01

CONSTRUCTION-EQUIPMENT MECHANIC (construction), 620.261-022, 05.05.09

CONSTRUCTION-EQUIPMENT-MECHANIC HELPER (construction), 620.664-010, 05.12.15

CONSULTANT (profess. & kin.), 189.167-010, 11.01.02

CONSULTANT, EDUCATION (education), 099.167-014, 11.07.03

CONTACT REPRESENTATIVE (government ser.), 169.167-018, 07.01.01

CONTACT WORKER, LITHOGRAPHY (print. & pub.), 976.684-038, 05.10.05

CONTINUITY CLERK (motion picture), 209.382-010, 07.05.03

CONTINUITY DIRECTOR (radio-tv broad.), 132.037-010, 01.01.01

CONTRACT ADMINISTRATOR (any industry), 162.117-014, 11.12.04

CONTRACT CLERK (profess. & kin.), 119.267-018, 07.01.05

CONTRACT CLERK, AUTOMOBILE (retail trade), 219.362-026, 07.02.02

CONTRACT SPECIALIST (profess. & kin.), 162.117-018, 11.12.04

CONTRACTOR (construction), 182.167-010, 11.12.04

CONTROL CLERK (clock & watch), 221.387-018, 05.09.02

CONTROLLER (profess. & kin.), 160.167-058, 11.06.02

CONTROLS DESIGNER (profess. & kin.), 003.261-014, 05.03.02

CONVEYOR FEEDER-OFFBEARER (any industry), 921.686-014, 06.04.40

CONVEYOR-MAINTENANCE ME-CHANIC (any industry), 630.381-010, 05.10.02

CONVEYOR-SYSTEM OPERATOR (any industry), 921.662-018, 05.12.04

COOK (domestic ser.), 305.281-010, 05.10.08

COOK (hotel & rest.), 313.361-014, 05.05.17

COOK (any industry), 315.361-010, 05.10.08

COOK HELPER (hotel & rest.), 317.687-010, 05.12.17

COOK, BARBECUE (hotel & rest.), 313.381-022, 05.10.08

COOK, FAST FOOD (hotel & rest.), 313.374-010, 05.10.08

COOK, FRY, DEEP FAT (can. & preserv.), 526.685-014, 06.04.15

COOK, MEXICAN FOOD (food prep., nec), 526.134-010, 06.01.01

COOK, PASTRY (hotel & rest.), 313.381-026, 05.10.08

COOK, SCHOOL CAFETERIA (hotel & rest.), 313.381-030, 05.10.08

COOK, SHORT ORDER (hotel & rest.), 313.374-014, 05.10.08

COOK, SPECIALTY (hotel & rest.), 313.361-026, 05.10.08

COOK, SPECIALTY, FOREIGN FOOD (hotel & rest.), 313.361-030, 05.10.08

COOLING-ROOM ATTENDANT (personal ser.), 335.677-010, 09.05.01

COORDINATOR OF REHABILITATION SERVICES (medical ser.), 076.117-010, 11.07.01

COORDINATOR, SKILL-TRAINING PROGRAM (government ser.), 169.167-062, 07.01.02

COORDINATOR, VOLUNTEER SERVICES (social ser.), 187.167-022, 11.07.01

COPY WRITER (profess. & kin.), 131.067-014, 01.01.02

COPYIST (any industry), 152.267-010, 01.04.02

CORE-DRILL OPERATOR (any industry), 930.682-010, 05.11.02

COREMAKER (foundry), 518.381-014, 06.01.04

COREMAKER, MACHINE I (foundry), 518.685-014, 06.04.08

CORRECTION OFFICER (government ser.), 372.667-018, 04.02.01

CORRECTIVE THERAPIST (medical ser.), 076.361-010, 10.02.02

CORRESPONDENCE CLERK (clerical), 209.362-034, 07.04.02

CORRESPONDENCE-REVIEW CLERK (clerical), 209.367-018, 07.05.04

CORRUGATED-FASTENER DRIVER (woodworking), 669.685-042, 06.04.20

COSMETOLOGIST (personal ser.), 332.271-010, 09.02.01

COST CLERK (clerical), 216.382-034, 07.02.02

COUNSELOR (profess. & kin.), 045.107-010, 10.01.02

COUNSELOR, CAMP (amuse. & rec.), 159.124-010, 09.01.01

COUNSELOR, MARRIAGE AND FAMILY (profess. & kin.), 045.107-054, 10.01.02

COUNTER ATTENDANT, CAFETERIA (hotel & rest.), 311.677-014, 09.05.02

COUNTER ATTENDANT, LUNCH-ROOM OR COFFEE SHOP (hotel & rest.), 311.477-014, 09.04.01

COUNTER CLERK (photofinishing), 249.366-010, 07.03.01

COUNTER SUPERVISOR (hotel & rest.), 311.137-010, 09.05.02

COUNTER-SUPPLY WORKER (hotel & rest.), 319.687-010, 09.05.02

COUNTY HOME-DEMONSTRATION AGENT (government ser.), 096.121-010, 11.02.03

COUNTY-AGRICULTURAL AGENT (government ser.), 096.127-010, 11.02.03

COUPON CLERK (financial), 219.462-010, 07.02.02

COUPON-REDEMPTION CLERK (retail trade), 290.477-010, 07.03.01

COURT ADMINISTRATOR (government ser.), 188.117-130, 11.05.03

COURT CLERK (government ser.), 243.362-010, 07.01.02

CRACKER-AND-COOKIE-MACHINE OPERATOR (bakery products), 520.682-034, 06.02.15

CRAFT DEMONSTRATOR (museums), 109.364-010, 09.01.02

CRATER (any industry), 920.684-010, 06.04.38

CRATING-AND-MOVING ESTIMATOR (motor trans.), 252.357-010, 08.02.06

CREDIT ANALYST (financial), 160.267-022, 11.06.03

CREDIT ANALYST (clerical), 241.267-022, 07.01.04

CREDIT AUTHORIZER (clerical), 249.367-022, 07.05.02

CREDIT CARD CONTROL CLERK (financial), 249.367-026, 07.05.03

CREDIT CLERK (clerical), 205.367-022, 07.04.01

CREDIT COUNSELOR (profess. & kin.), 160.207-010, 07.01.01

CREDIT REFERENCE CLERK (financial), 209.362-018, 07.05.02

CREDIT REPORTING CLERK (business ser.), 203.362-014, 07.06.01

CREDIT-CARD CLERK (hotel & rest.), 210.382-038, 07.02.02

CREMATOR (personal ser.), 359.685-010, 06.04.19

CREW SCHEDULER (air trans.), 215.362-010, 07.05.01

CRIMINALIST (profess. & kin.), 029.261-026, 02.04.01

CRIMPING-MACHINE OPERATOR (any industry), 616.682-022, 06.02.02

CROSSBAND LAYER (millwork-plywood), 762.687-026, 06.04.25

CROSSING TENDER (any industry), 371.667-010, 05.12.20

CROSSWORD-PUZZLE MAKER (print. & pub.), 139.087-010, 01.01.02

CRUSHER TENDER (any industry), 570.685-022, 06.04.08

CRYPTOGRAPHIC-MACHINE OPERATOR (clerical), 203.582-018, 07.06.02

CURB ATTENDANT (laundry & rel.), 369.477-010, 09.04.02

CURRENCY COUNTER (financial), 217.485-010, 05.12.19

CUSTODIAN, ATHLETIC EQUIPMENT (amuse. & rec.), 969.367-010, 05.09.01

CUSTOM TAILOR (garment), 785.261-014, 05.05.15

CUSTOM VAN CONVERTER (auto. mfg.), 806.381-070, 05.05.02

CUSTOMER SERVICE REPRESENTATIVE (financial), 205.362-026, 07.04.01

CUSTOMER SERVICE REPRESENTATIVE (radio-tv broad.), 239.362-014, 07.04.01

CUSTOMER SERVICES COORDINATOR (print. & pub.), 221.167-026, 05.09.02

CUSTOMER-COMPLAINT CLERK (clerical), 241.367-014, 07.05.02

CUSTOMER-EQUIPMENT ENGINEER (tel. & tel.), 003.187-018, 05.01.08

CUSTOMER-SERVICE CLERK (retail trade), 299.367-010, 09.04.02

CUSTOMS BROKER (financial), 186.117-018, 11.04.04

CUSTOMS INSPECTOR (government ser.), 168.267-022, 11.10.04

CUSTOMS PATROL OFFICER (government ser.), 168.167-010, 04.01.02

CUT-OFF-SAW OPERATOR I (woodworking), 667.682-022, 06.02.03

CUTTER (photofinishing), 976.685-010, 06.04.09

CUTTER OPERATOR (any industry), 699.682-018, 06.02.09

CUTTER, HAND I (any industry), 781.684-074, 06.02.27

CUTTER, MACHINE II (any industry), 699.685-014, 06.04.09

CYLINDER FILLER (chemical), 559.565-010, 06.04.12

CYLINDER-PRESS OPERATOR (print. & pub.), 651.362-010, 05.05.13

CYTOGENETIC TECHNOLOGIST (medical ser.), 078.261-026, 02.04.02

CYTOTECHNOLOGIST (medical ser.), 078.281-010, 02.04.02

DAIRY TECHNOLOGIST (profess. & kin.), 040.061-022, 02.02.04

DAIRY-PROCESSING-EQUIPMENT OPERATOR (dairy products), 529.382-018, 06.02.15

DANCE THERAPIST (medical ser.), 076.127-018, 10.02.02

DANCER (amuse. & rec.), 151.047-010, 01.05.02

DATA BASE ADMINISTRATOR (profess. & kin.), 039.162-010, 11.01.01

DATA BASE DESIGN ANALYST (profess. & kin.), 039.162-014, 11.01.01

DATA COMMUNICATIONS ANALYST (profess. & kin.), 031.262-010, 11.01.01

DATA COMMUNICATIONS TECHNICIAN (any industry), 823.261-030, 05.05.05

DATA ENTRY CLERK (clerical), 203.582-054, 07.06.01

DATA RECOVERY PLANNER (profess. & kin.), 033.162-014, 11.01.01

DATA-EXAMINATION CLERK (clerical), 209.387-022, 07.05.02

DAY WORKER (domestic ser.), 301.687-014, 05.12.18

DEALER-COMPLIANCE REPRESENTATIVE (retail trade), 168.267-026, 11.10.05

DEAN OF STUDENTS (education), 090.117-018, 10.01.02

DECKHAND (water trans.), 911.687-022, 05.08.04

DECKHAND, FISHING VESSEL (fishing & hunt.), 449.667-010, 03.04.03

DECONTAMINATOR (any industry), 199.384-010, 02.04.01

DECORATOR (any industry), 298.381-010, 01.06.02

DECORATOR (bakery products), 524.684-014, 06.04.28

DECORATOR, STREET AND BUILDING (any industry), 899.687-010, 05.12.12

DELI CUTTER-SLICER (retail trade), 316.684-014, 05.12.17

DELIVERER, CAR RENTAL (automotive ser.), 919.663-010, 05.08.03

DELIVERER, MERCHANDISE (retail trade), 299.477-010, 09.04.02

DELIVERER, OUTSIDE (clerical), 230.663-010, 07.07.02

DEMONSTRATOR (retail trade), 297.354-010, 08.02.05

DEMONSTRATOR, ELECTRIC-GAS APPLIANCES (utilities), 297.357-010, 08.02.05

DEMONSTRATOR, KNITTING (retail trade), 297.354-014, 08.02.05

DEMURRAGE CLERK (r.r. trans.), 214.362-010, 07.02.04

DENTAL ASSISTANT (medical ser.), 079.361-018, 10.03.02

DENTAL CERAMIST (protective dev.), 712.381-042, 05.05.11

DENTAL CERAMIST ASSISTANT (protective dev.), 712.664-010, 05.05.11

DENTAL HYGIENIST (medical ser.), 078.361-010, 10.02.02

DENTAL-LABORATORY TECHNICIAN (protective dev.), 712.381-018, 05.05.11

DENTAL-LABORATORY-TECHNICIAN APPRENTICE (protective dev.), 712.381-022, 05.05.11

DENTIST (medical ser.), 072.101-010, 02.03.02

DENTURE WAXER (protective dev.), 712.381-046, 06.02.32

DENTURE-MODEL MAKER (protective dev.), 712.684-046, 05.05.11

DEPUTY, COURT (government ser.), 377.137-018, 04.01.01

DERMATOLOGIST (medical ser.), 070.101-018, 02.03.01

DESIGN DRAFTER, ELECTROMECHANISMS (profess. & kin.), 017.261-014, 05.03.02

DESIGN PRINTER, BALLOON (rubber goods), 651.685-014, 06.04.07

DESIGN TECHNICIAN, COMPUTER-AIDED (electron. comp.), 003.362-010, 05.03.02

DESK OFFICER (government ser.), 375.137-014, 04.01.01

DETAILER (profess. & kin.), 017.261-018, 05.03.02

DETAILER, SCHOOL PHOTOGRAPHS (photofinishing), 976.564-010, 07.05.03

DETECTIVE I (any industry), 376.367-014, 04.02.02

DEVELOPER (photofinishing), 976.681-010, 05.10.05

DEVELOPER, AUTOMATIC (photofinishing), 976.685-014, 06.04.19

DEVELOPMENT MECHANIC (aircraft mfg.), 693.261-014, 06.01.04

DIALYSIS TECHNICIAN (medical ser.), 078.362-014, 10.02.02

DIE CUTTER (any industry), 699.682-022, 06.02.09

DIE MAKER (jewelry-silver.), 601.381-014, 05.05.07

DIE SETTER (forging), 612.360-010, 06.01.02

DIE SINKER (machine shop), 601.280-022, 05.05.07

DIESEL MECHANIC (any industry), 625.281-010, 05.05.09

DIET CLERK (medical ser.), 245.587-010, 07.05.03

DIETETIC TECHNICIAN (profess. & kin.), 077.124-010, 05.05.17

DIETITIAN, CHIEF (profess. & kin.), 077.117-010, 11.05.02

DIETITIAN, CLINICAL (profess. & kin.), 077.127-014, 05.05.17

DIETITIAN, TEACHING (profess. & kin.), 077.127-022, 11.02.02

DIGESTER-OPERATOR HELPER (paper & pulp), 532.686-010, 06.04.18

DINING ROOM ATTENDANT (hotel & rest.), 311.677-018, 09.05.02

DIPPER AND BAKER (any industry), 599.685-030, 06.04.21

DIRECT-MAIL CLERK (clerical), 209.587-018, 07.07.02

DIRECTOR OF ADMISSIONS (education), 090.167-014, 11.07.03

DIRECTOR OF PHOTOGRAPHY (motion picture), 143.062-010, 01.02.03

DIRECTOR OF PLACEMENT (education), 166.167-014, 10.01.02

DIRECTOR OF PUPIL PERSONNEL PROGRAM (education), 099.167-034, 11.07.03

DIRECTOR, ATHLETIC (education), 090.117-022, 11.07.03

DIRECTOR, CAMP (social ser.), 195.167-018, 11.11.02

DIRECTOR, COMMUNITY ORGANIZATION (nonprofit org.), 187.167-234, 11.07.01

DIRECTOR, COMPLIANCE (government ser.), 188.117-046, 11.10.02

DIRECTOR, DAY CARE CENTER (education), 092.167-010, 11.07.03

DIRECTOR, EDUCATIONAL PROGRAM (education), 099.117-010, 11.07.03

DIRECTOR, FUNDRAISING (nonprofit org.), 165.117-010, 11.09.02

DIRECTOR, FUNDS DEVELOPMENT (profess. & kin.), 165.117-014, 11.09.02

DIRECTOR, FUNERAL (personal ser.), 187.167-030, 11.11.04

DIRECTOR, MEDIA MARKETING (radio-tv broad.), 163.117-022, 11.05.04

DIRECTOR, MOTION PICTURE (motion picture), 159.067-010, 01.03.01

DIRECTOR, NURSES' REGISTRY (medical ser.), 187.167-034, 07.01.02

DIRECTOR, NURSING SERVICE (medical ser.), 075.117-022, 11.07.02

DIRECTOR, QUALITY ASSURANCE (profess. & kin.), 189.117-042, 11.05.02

DIRECTOR, RECORDS MANAGEMENT (profess. & kin.), 161.117-014, 11.01.01

DIRECTOR, RECREATION CENTER (social ser.), 195.167-026, 11.11.02

DIRECTOR, REGULATORY AGENCY (government ser.), 188.117-134, 11.05.03

DIRECTOR, RESEARCH AND DEVELOPMENT (any industry), 189.117-014, 05.01.01

DIRECTOR, SERVICE (nonprofit org.), 187.167-214, 11.07.01

DIRECTOR, SERVICE (retail trade), 189.167-014, 11.05.02

DIRECTOR, SOCIAL (hotel & rest.), 352.167-010, 09.01.01

DIRECTOR, SPECIAL EDUCATION (education), 094.167-014, 11.07.03

DIRECTOR, STAGE (amuse. & rec.), 150.067-010, 01.03.01

DIRECTOR, TRANSLATION (profess. & kin.), 137.137-010, 11.08.04

DIRECTOR, TRANSPORTATION (motor trans.), 184.117-014, 11.05.01

DIRECTOR, UTILITY ACCOUNTS (government ser.), 160.267-014, 11.06.03

DIRECTOR, VOCATIONAL TRAINING (education), 097.167-010, 11.07.03

DIRECTORY-ASSISTANCE OPERATOR (tel. & tel.), 235.662-018, 07.04.06

DISBURSEMENT CLERK (financial), 219.367-046, 07.05.02

DISC JOCKEY (radio-tv broad.), 159.147-014, 01.03.03

DISPATCHER (government ser.), 193.262-014, 07.04.05

DISPATCHER (construction), 849.137-010, 05.09.01

DISPATCHER (air trans.), 912.167-010, 05.03.03

DISPATCHER, MAINTENANCE SERVICE (clerical), 239.367-014, 07.04.05

DISPATCHER, MOTOR VEHICLE (clerical), 249.167-014, 07.05.01

DISPATCHER, RADIO (government ser.), 379.362-010, 07.04.05

DISPLAY DESIGNER (profess. & kin.), 142.051-010, 01.02.03

DISPLAY MAKER (fabrication, nec), 739.361-010, 01.06.02

DISPLAY-SCREEN FABRICATOR (electron. comp.), 725.685-010, 06.04.19

DISPLAYER, MERCHANDISE (retail trade), 298.081-010, 01.02.03

DISTILLERY WORKER, GENERAL (beverage), 529.687-066, 06.04.40

DISTRIBUTING CLERK (clerical), 222.587-018, 07.07.02

DISTRIBUTION SUPERVISOR (pipe lines), 914.137-010, 05.09.01

DISTRICT ATTORNEY (government ser.), 110.117-010, 11.04.02

DIVER (any industry), 899.261-010, 05.10.01

DIVIDEND CLERK (financial), 216.482-034, 07.02.02

DOCK HAND (air trans.), 919.683-010, 05.08.04

DOCUMENT PREPARER, MICROFILMING (business ser.), 249.587-018, 07.05.03

DOCUMENTATION ENGINEER (profess. & kin.), 012.167-078, 05.01.06

DOG BATHER (personal ser.), 418.677-010, 03.03.02

DOG CATCHER (government ser.), 379.673-010, 03.04.05

DOG GROOMER (personal ser.), 418.674-010, 03.03.02

DOG LICENSER (nonprofit org.), 249.367-030, 07.04.03

DOLL REPAIRER (any industry), 731.684-014, 05.10.04

DOOR-CLOSER MECHANIC (any industry), 630.381-014, 05.10.02

DOORKEEPER (any industry), 324.677-014, 09.05.04

DOUGH MIXER (bakery products), 520.685-234, 06.02.15

DOUGHNUT MAKER (bakery products), 526.684-010, 06.02.28

DOUGHNUT-MACHINE OPERATOR (bakery products), 526.682-022, 06.02.15

DRAFTER, AERONAUTICAL (aircraft mfg.), 002.261-010, 05.03.02

DRAFTER, ARCHITECTURAL (profess. & kin.), 001.261-010, 05.03.02

DRAFTER, ASSISTANT (profess. & kin.), 017.281-018, 05.03.02

DRAFTER, AUTOMOTIVE DESIGN (auto. mfg.), 017.261-042, 05.03.02

DRAFTER, AUTOMOTIVE DESIGN LAYOUT (auto. mfg.), 017.281-026, 05.03.02

DRAFTER, CARTOGRAPHIC (profess. & kin.), 018.261-010, 05.03.02

DRAFTER, CIVIL (profess. & kin.), 005.281-010, 05.03.02

DRAFTER, COMMERCIAL (profess. & kin.), 017.261-026, 05.03.02

DRAFTER, ELECTRICAL (profess. & kin.), 003.281-010, 05.03.02

DRAFTER, ELECTRONIC (profess. & kin.), 003.281-014, 05.03.02

DRAFTER, GEOLOGICAL (petrol. & gas), 010.281-014, 05.03.02

DRAFTER, GEOPHYSICAL (petrol. & gas), 010.281-018, 05.03.02

DRAFTER, LANDSCAPE (profess. & kin.), 001.261-014, 05.03.02

DRAFTER, MARINE (profess. & kin.), 014.281-010, 05.03.02

DRAFTER, MECHANICAL (profess. & kin.), 007.281-010, 05.03.02

DRAFTER, STRUCTURAL (profess. & kin.), 005.281-014, 05.03.02

DRAGLINE OPERATOR (any industry), 850.683-018, 05.11.04

DRAPERY AND UPHOLSTERY ESTIMATOR (retail trade), 299.387-010, 05.09.02

DRAPERY HANGER (retail trade), 869.484-014, 05.10.01

DRAWINGS CHECKER, ENGINEERING (profess. & kin.), 007.267-010, 05.03.02

DRESSER (amuse. & rec.), 346.674-010, 09.05.06

DRESSMAKER (any industry), 785.361-010, 05.05.15

DRIER OPERATOR (food prep., nec), 523.362-014, 06.02.15

DRIER OPERATOR (chemical), 553.685-042, 06.04.11

DRILL PRESS TENDER (machine shop), 606.685-026, 06.04.02

DRILL-PRESS OPERATOR (machine shop), 606.682-014, 06.02.02

DRILL-PRESS SET-UP OPERATOR, MULTIPLE SPINDLE (machine shop), 606.380-010, 06.01.03

DRILLER, HAND (any industry), 809.684-018, 06.04.34

DRIVE-IN THEATER ATTENDANT (amuse. & rec.), 349.673-010, 09.05.04

DRIVER (motor trans.), 913.663-018, 09.03.01

DRIVER'S LICENSE EXAMINER (government ser.), 168.267-034, 07.01.07

DRIVER, SALES ROUTE (retail trade), 292.353-010, 08.02.07

DROPHAMMER OPERATOR (aircraft mfg.), 610.362-010, 06.02.02

DRY CLEANER (laundry & rel.), 362.382-014, 06.02.16

DRY CLEANER, HAND (laundry & rel.), 362.684-010, 06.04.35

DRY-WALL APPLICATOR (construction), 842.361-030, 05.05.04

DRY-WALL APPLICATOR (construction), 842.684-014, 05.10.01

DUMP OPERATOR (any industry), 921.685-038, 05.11.04

DUMP-TRUCK DRIVER (any industry), 902.683-010, 05.08.01

DUMPER (any industry), 921.667-018, 05.12.03

DUPLICATING-MACHINE OPERATOR I (clerical), 207.682-010, 05.10.05

DYNAMITE-PACKING-MACHINE OPERATOR (chemical), 692.662-010, 06.02.09

EARRING MAKER (jewelry-silver.), 700.684-030, 06.04.23

ECHOCARDIOGRAPH TECHNICIAN (medical ser.), 078.364-014, 10.03.01

ECONOMIST (profess. & kin.), 050.067-010, 11.03.05

EDITOR, CITY (print. & pub.), 132.037-014, 11.08.01

EDITOR, DEPARTMENT (print. & pub.), 132.037-018, 11.08.01

EDITOR, DICTIONARY (profess. & kin.), 132.067-018, 11.08.01

EDITOR, MAP (profess. & kin.), 018.261-018, 05.03.02

EDITOR, NEWS (print. & pub.), 132.067-026, 11.08.01

EDITOR, NEWSPAPER (print. & pub.), 132.017-014, 11.08.01

EDITOR, PUBLICATIONS (print. & pub.), 132.037-022, 01.01.01

EDITOR, TECHNICAL AND SCIENTIFIC PUBLICATIONS (profess. & kin.), 132.017-018, 11.08.01

EDITORIAL ASSISTANT (print. & pub.), 132.267-014, 11.08.01

EDITORIAL WRITER (print. & pub.), 131.067-022, 01.01.02

EDUCATIONAL SPECIALIST (education), 099.167-022, 11.07.03

ELECTION CLERK (government ser.), 205.367-030, 07.04.03

ELECTRIC-GOLF-CART REPAIRER (amuse. & rec.), 620.261-026, 05.10.03

ELECTRIC-METER INSTALLER I (utilities), 821.361-014, 05.05.05

ELECTRIC-METER REPAIRER (utilities), 729.281-014, 05.05.10

ELECTRIC-METER TESTER (utilities), 821.381-010, 05.05.10

ELECTRIC-MOTOR ASSEMBLER (elec. equip.), 721.684-022, 06.04.23

ELECTRIC-MOTOR REPAIRER (any industry), 721.281-018, 05.05.10

ELECTRIC-MOTOR-CONTROL ASSEMBLER (elec. equip.), 721.381-014, 06.01.04

ELECTRIC-ORGAN INSPECTOR AND REPAIRER (musical inst.), 730.281-018, 05.05.12

ELECTRIC-SEALING-MACHINE OPERATOR (any industry), 690.685-154, 06.04.02

ELECTRIC-SIGN ASSEMBLER (fabrication, nec), 729.684-022, 06.02.22

ELECTRIC-TOOL REPAIRER (any industry), 729.281-022, 05.10.03

ELECTRICAL ASSEMBLER (aircraft mfg.), 729.384-026, 06.02.23

ELECTRICAL ENGINEER (profess. & kin.), 003.061-010, 05.01.08

ELECTRICAL ENGINEER, POWER SYSTEM (utilities), 003.167-018, 05.01.03

ELECTRICAL TECHNICIAN (profess. & kin.), 003.161-010, 05.01.01

ELECTRICAL TEST ENGINEER (profess. & kin.), 003.061-014, 05.01.04

ELECTRICAL-APPLIANCE PREPARER (any industry), 827.584-010, 05.12.16

ELECTRICAL-APPLIANCE REPAIRER (any industry), 723.381-010, 05.10.03

ELECTRICAL-APPLIANCE SERVICER (any industry), 827.261-010, 05.05.10

ELECTRICAL-DESIGN ENGINEER (profess. & kin.), 003.061-018, 05.01.07

ELECTRICAL-INSTRUMENT REPAIRER (any industry), 729.281-026, 05.05.10

ELECTRICAL-RESEARCH ENGINEER (profess. & kin.), 003.061-026, 05.01.01

ELECTRICIAN (construction), 824.261-010, 05.05.05

ELECTRICIAN, AIRCRAFT (aircraft mfg.), 825.261-018, 05.05.05

ELECTRICIAN, AUTOMOTIVE (automotive ser.), 825.281-022, 05.05.10

ELECTRICIAN, MAINTENANCE (any industry), 829.261-018, 05.05.05

ELECTRICIAN, POWERHOUSE (utilities), 820.261-014, 05.05.05

ELECTRO-OPTICAL ENGINEER (profess. & kin.), 023.061-010, 05.01.07

ELECTROCARDIOGRAPH TECHNICIAN (medical ser.), 078.362-018, 10.03.01

ELECTROENCEPHALOGRAPHIC TECHNOLOGIST (medical ser.), 078.362-022, 10.03.01

ELECTROLOGIST (personal ser.), 339.371-010, 09.05.01

ELECTROMECHANICAL TECHNICIAN (inst. & app.), 710.281-018, 05.05.11

ELECTROMYOGRAPHIC TECHNICIAN (medical ser.), 078.362-038, 10.03.01

ELECTRONIC EQUIPMENT REPAIRER (comm. equip.), 726.381-014, 05.10.03

ELECTRONIC FUNDS TRANSFER COORDINATOR (financial), 216.362-038, 07.02.01

ELECTRONIC MASKING SYSTEM OPERATOR (print. & pub.), 972.282-018, 01.06.01

ELECTRONIC PREPRESS SYSTEM OPERATOR (print. & pub.), 979.282-010, 01.06.01

ELECTRONIC-COMPONENT PROCESSOR (electron. comp.), 590.684-014, 06.04.19

ELECTRONIC-ORGAN TECHNICIAN (any industry), 828.261-010, 05.05.12

ELECTRONIC-SALES-AND-SERVICE TECHNICIAN (profess. & kin.), 828.251-010, 05.05.05

ELECTRONICS ASSEMBLER (comm. equip.), 726.684-018, 06.02.23

ELECTRONICS ASSEMBLER, DEVELOPMENTAL (any industry), 726.261-010, 05.05.05

ELECTRONICS ENGINEER (profess. & kin.), 003.061-030, 05.01.08

ELECTRONICS INSPECTOR (comm. equip.), 726.381-010, 06.01.05

ELECTRONICS INSPECTOR (electron. comp.), 726.684-022, 06.03.02

ELECTRONICS MECHANIC (any industry), 828.261-022, 05.05.10

ELECTRONICS TECHNICIAN (profess. & kin.), 003.161-014, 05.01.01

ELECTRONICS TESTER (any industry), 726.261-018, 06.01.05

ELECTRONICS TESTER (comm. equip.), 726.684-026, 06.03.02

ELECTRONICS UTILITY WORKER (comm. equip.), 726.364-018, 06.04.34

ELECTRONICS WORKER (electron. comp.), 726.687-010, 06.04.34

ELECTRONICS-DESIGN ENGINEER (profess. & kin.), 003.061-034, 05.01.07

ELECTRONICS-TEST ENGINEER (profess. & kin.), 003.061-042, 05.01.04

ELECTROTYPER (print. & pub.), 974.381-010, 05.05.13

ELEVATOR CONSTRUCTOR (construction), 825.361-010, 05.05.06

ELEVATOR EXAMINER-AND-ADJUSTER (any industry), 825.261-014, 05.07.03

ELEVATOR OPERATOR (any industry), 388.663-010, 09.05.09

ELEVATOR OPERATOR, FREIGHT (any industry), 921.683-038, 05.12.04

ELEVATOR REPAIRER (any industry), 825.281-030, 05.05.05

ELIGIBILITY WORKER (government ser.), 195.267-010, 07.01.01

ELIGIBILITY-AND-OCCUPANCY INTERVIEWER (government ser.), 168.267-038, 07.01.01

EMBALMER (personal ser.), 338.371-014, 02.04.02

EMBOSSER (any industry), 583.685-030, 06.04.02

EMERGENCY MEDICAL SERVICES COORDINATOR (medical ser.), 079.117-010, 11.07.02

EMERGENCY MEDICAL TECHNICIAN (medical ser.), 079.374-010, 10.03.02

EMPLOYEE RELATIONS SPECIALIST (profess. & kin.), 166.267-042, 11.03.04

EMPLOYER RELATIONS REPRESENTATIVE (profess. & kin.), 166.257-010, 11.09.03

EMPLOYMENT CLERK (clerical), 205.362-014, 07.04.01

EMPLOYMENT INTERVIEWER (profess. & kin.), 166.267-010, 11.03.04

EMPLOYMENT-AND-CLAIMS AIDE (government ser.), 169.367-010, 07.04.01

ENERGY-CONTROL OFFICER (education), 199.167-018, 05.03.08

ENGINE-LATHE SET-UP OPERATOR (machine shop), 604.380-018, 06.01.03

ENGINEER (water trans.), 197.130-010, 05.06.02

ENGINEER, SOILS (profess. & kin.), 024.161-010, 05.01.08

ENGINEERING ASSISTANT, MECHANICAL EQUIPMENT (profess. & kin.), 007.161-018, 05.03.02

ENGINEERING MANAGER, ELECTRONICS (profess. & kin.), 003.167-070, 05.01.08

ENGRAVER, HAND, HARD METALS (engraving), 704.381-026, 01.06.01

ENGRAVER, HAND, SOFT METALS (engraving), 704.381-030, 01.06.01

ENGRAVER, MACHINE (print. & pub.), 979.382-014, 05.10.05

ENGRAVER, MACHINE I (engraving), 704.682-010, 05.10.05

ENGRAVING-PRESS OPERATOR (print. & pub.), 651.382-010, 05.10.05

ENVIRONMENTAL ANALYST (profess. & kin.), 029.081-010, 02.01.02

ENVIRONMENTAL ANALYST (government ser.), 199.167-022, 11.05.03

ENVIRONMENTAL EPIDEMIOLOGIST (government ser.), 041.167-010, 02.02.01

EQUAL-OPPORTUNITY REPRESENTATIVE (government ser.), 168.167-014, 11.10.02

EQUESTRIAN (amuse. & rec.), 159.344-010, 12.02.01

EQUIPMENT CLEANER (any industry), 599.684-010, 06.04.39

EQUIPMENT INSTALLER (any industry), 828.381-010, 05.10.04

EQUIPMENT MONITOR, PHOTOTYPESETTING (print. & pub.), 650.682-010, 05.10.05

ESCORT (any industry), 353.667-010, 09.05.08

ESCORT-VEHICLE DRIVER (motor trans.), 919.663-022, 05.08.03

ESCROW OFFICER (profess. & kin.), 119.367-010, 07.01.04

ESTATE PLANNER (insurance), 186.167-010, 08.01.02

ESTIMATOR (profess. & kin.), 169.267-038, 05.03.02

ESTIMATOR AND DRAFTER (utilities), 019.261-014, 05.03.02

ESTIMATOR, PRINTING (print. & pub.), 221.367-014, 05.09.02

ETCHED-CIRCUIT PROCESSOR (electron. comp.), 590.684-018, 06.02.32

ETCHER (engraving), 704.684-010, 01.06.01

EVALUATOR (education), 094.267-010, 10.02.03

EVALUATOR (nonprofit org.), 249.367-034, 05.09.02

EVAPORATIVE-COOLER INSTALLER (any industry), 637.381-010, 05.10.04

EXAMINATION PROCTOR (government ser.), 199.267-018, 07.01.07

EXAMINER (government ser.), 169.267-014, 07.01.05

EXAMINER, QUESTIONED DOCUMENTS (government ser.), 199.267-022, 02.04.01

EXECUTIVE CHEF (hotel & rest.), 187.161-010, 11.05.02

EXECUTIVE DIRECTOR, RED CROSS (nonprofit org.), 187.117-066, 11.07.01

EXECUTIVE HOUSEKEEPER (any industry), 187.167-046, 11.11.01

EXECUTIVE VICE PRESIDENT, CHAMBER OF COMMERCE (nonprofit org.), 187.117-030, 11.05.02

EXERCISE PHYSIOLOGIST (medical ser.), 076.121-018, 10.02.02

EXERCISER, HORSE (amuse. & rec.), 153.674-010, 03.03.01

EXHAUST EQUIPMENT OPERATOR (electron. comp.), 599.382-014, 06.01.03

EXHIBIT ARTIST (museums), 149.261-010, 01.02.03

EXIIIBIT BUILDER (museums), 739.261-010, 01.06.02

EXHIBIT DESIGNER (museums), 142.061-058, 01.02.03

EXHIBIT-DISPLAY REPRESENTATIVE (any industry), 297.367-010, 09.01.02

EXPEDITER (clerical), 222.367-018, 07.05.01

EXPERIMENTAL AIRCRAFT MECHANIC (aircraft mfg.), 621.261-022, 05.05.09

EXPERIMENTAL ASSEMBLER (any industry), 739.381-026, 05.05.11

EXTENSION SERVICE SPECIALIST (government ser.), 096.127-014, 11.02.03

EXTERMINATOR (business ser.), 389.684-010, 05.10.09

EXTERMINATOR, TERMITE (business ser.), 383.364-010, 05.10.09

EXTRA (amuse. & rec.), 159.647-014, 01.08.01

EXTRUDER OPERATOR (grain-feed mills), 520.682-018, 06.02.15

EXTRUDER OPERATOR (plastic prod.), 557.382-010, 06.02.13

EYEGLASS-LENS CUTTER (optical goods), 716.682-010, 06.02.08

FABRICATOR-ASSEMBLER, METAL PRODUCTS (any industry), 809.381-010, 06.02.24

FACILITIES PLANNER (any industry), 019.261-018, 05.01.06

FACTOR (financial), 186.167-082, 11.06.03

FACTORY LAY-OUT ENGINEER (profess. & kin.), 012.167-018, 05.01.06

FACULTY MEMBER, COLLEGE OR UNIVERSITY (education), 090.227-010, 11.02.01

FARM-EQUIPMENT MECHANIC I (agric. equip.), 624.281-010, 05.05.09

FARM-MACHINE OPERATOR (agriculture), 409.683-010, 03.04.01

FARMER, FIELD CROP (agriculture), 404.161-010, 03.01.01

FARMER, FRUIT CROPS, BUSH AND VINE (agriculture), 403.161-014, 03.01.01

FARMER, GENERAL (agriculture),
421.161-010, 03.01.01
FARMWORKER, DIVERSIFIED CROPS
I (agriculture), 407.663-010, 03.04.01
FARMWORKER, FRUIT I (agriculture),
403.683-010, 03.04.01
FARMWORKER, GENERAL II (agricul-
ture), 421.687-010, 03.04.01
FARMWORKER, LIVESTOCK (agricul-
ture), 410.664-010, 03.04.01
FARMWORKER, VEGETABLE II
(agriculture), 402.687-010, 03.04.01
FASHION ARTIST (retail trade),
141.061-014, 01.02.03
FASHION COORDINATOR (retail trade),
185.157-010, 11.09.01
FASHION DESIGNER (profess. & kin.),
142.061-018, 01.02.03
FAST-FOODS WORKER (hotel & rest.),
311.472-010, 09.04.01
FEEDER (print. & pub.), 651.686-014,
05.12.19
FENCE ERECTOR (construction),
869.684-022, 05.10.01
FIBER TECHNOLOGIST (profess. &
kin.), 040.061-026, 05.01.08
FIELD ENGINEER (radio-tv broad.),
193.262-018, 05.03.05
FIELD ENGINEER, SPECIALIST (petrol.
& gas), 010.261-010, 05.03.04
FIELD RECORDER (utilities), 229.367-
010, 05.09.02
FIELD REPRESENTATIVE (business
ser.), 163.267-010, 11.05.04
FIELD REPRESENTATIVE (profess. &
kin.), 189.267-010, 11.07.01
FIELD SERVICE ENGINEER (profess. &
kin.), 828.261-014, 05.05.05
FIELD SERVICE TECHNICIAN
(machinery mfg.), 638.261-026,
05.05.09
FIELD-SERVICE ENGINEER (aircraft
mfg.), 002.167-014, 05.01.04
FILE CLERK I (clerical), 206.387-034,
07.07.01
FILE CLERK II (clerical), 206.367-014,
07.05.03
FILER (jewelry-silver.), 700.684-034,
06.04.24
FILM DEVELOPER (motion picture),
976.382-018, 05.10.05
FILM FLAT INSPECTOR (print. & pub.),
972.284-010, 06.03.02
FILM INSPECTOR (photofinishing),
976.362-010, 05.10.05
FILM LABORATORY TECHNICIAN
(motion picture), 976.684-014,
05.10.05
FILM LABORATORY TECHNICIAN I
(motion picture), 976.381-010,
02.04.01
FILM OR VIDEOTAPE EDITOR (motion
picture), 962.262-010, 01.01.01
FILM-OR-TAPE LIBRARIAN (clerical),
222.367-026, 11.02.04
FILM-RENTAL CLERK (business ser.),
295.367-018, 11.02.04

FILTER OPERATOR (any industry),
551.685-078, 06.04.19
FINAL ASSEMBLER (office machines),
706.381-018, 06.01.04
FINANCIAL-AID COUNSELOR
(education), 169.267-018, 07.01.01
FINANCIAL-AIDS OFFICER (education), 090.117-030, 11.07.03
FINE ARTS PACKER (museums),
102.367-010, 05.03.09
FINGERNAIL FORMER (personal ser.),
331.674-014, 09.05.01
FINGERPRINT CLASSIFIER (government ser.), 375.387-010, 02.04.01
FINGERPRINT CLERK II (government
ser.), 206.387-014, 07.05.03
FINISHER (plastic-synth.), 554.586-010,
06.04.40
FINISHER, DENTURE (protective dev.),
712.381-050, 05.05.11
FIRE CAPTAIN (government ser.),
373.134-010, 04.01.01
FIRE CHIEF (government ser.),
373.117-010, 04.01.01
FIRE FIGHTER (any industry),
373.364-010, 04.02.04
FIRE INSPECTOR (government ser.),
373.267-010, 11.10.03
FIRE INSPECTOR (any industry),
373.367-010, 04.02.02
FIRE LOOKOUT (forestry), 452.367-010,
07.04.05
FIRE MARSHAL (any industry),
373.167-018, 04.01.01
FIRE MARSHAL (government ser.),
373.267-014, 04.01.02
FIRE RANGER (forestry), 452.367-014,
04.02.02
FIRE WARDEN (forestry), 452.167-010,
04.01.02
FIRE-EXTINGUISHER REPAIRER (any
industry), 709.384-010, 05.10.04
FIRE-EXTINGUISHER-SPRINKLER
INSPECTOR (any industry),
379.687-010, 05.07.01
FIRE-PROTECTION ENGINEER
(profess. & kin.), 012.167-026,
05.01.02
FIRE-PROTECTION ENGINEERING
TECHNICIAN (profess. & kin.),
019.261-026, 05.03.02
FIRESETTER (elec. equip.), 692.360-018,
06.01.03
FIREWORKS DISPLAY SPECIALIST
(chemical), 969.664-010, 05.10.06
FIRST-AID ATTENDANT (any industry),
354.677-010, 10.03.02
FISH AND GAME WARDEN (government ser.), 379.167-010, 04.01.02
FISH CLEANER (can. & preserv.),
525.684-030, 06.04.28
FISH FARMER (fishing & hunt.),
446.161-010, 03.01.02
FISHER, DIVING (fishing & hunt.),
443.664-010, 03.04.03
FISHER, LINE (fishing & hunt.),
442.684-010, 03.04.03

FISHING-REEL ASSEMBLER (toy-sport
equip.), 732.684-062, 06.04.23
FITTER I (any industry), 801.261-014,
05.05.06
FIXTURE REPAIRER-FABRICATOR
(any industry), 630.384-010, 05.10.01
FLAGGER (amuse. & rec.), 372.667-026,
12.01.02
FLIGHT ENGINEER (air trans.),
621.261-018, 05.03.06
FLIGHT-INFORMATION EXPEDITER
(air trans.), 912.367-010, 07.04.05
FLIGHT-TEST DATA ACQUISITION
TECHNICIAN (aircraft mfg.),
002.262-010, 05.03.05
FLOOR ATTENDANT (amuse. & rec.),
343.467-014, 09.04.02
FLOOR BROKER (financial),
162.167-034, 11.06.04
FLOOR LAYER (construction),
864.481-010, 05.10.01
FLORAL DESIGNER (retail trade),
142.081-010, 01.02.03
FLOUR BLENDER (grain-feed mills),
520.685-106, 06.04.15
FLUID JET CUTTER OPERATOR
(aircraft mfg.), 699.382-010, 06.02.09
FLUID-POWER MECHANIC (any
industry), 600.281-010, 05.05.07
FOLDING-MACHINE OPERATOR
(clerical), 208.685-014, 05.12.19
FOOD AND DRUG INSPECTOR
(government ser.), 168.267-042,
11.10.03
FOOD ASSEMBLER, KITCHEN (hotel &
rest.), 319.484-010, 05.12.17
FOOD CHECKER (hotel & rest.),
211.482-014, 07.06.02
FOOD ORDER EXPEDITER (hotel &
rest.), 319.467-014, 05.09.03
FOOD TECHNOLOGIST (profess. &
kin.), 041.081-010, 02.02.04
FOOD TESTER (any industry),
029.361-014, 02.04.02
FOOD-MANAGEMENT AIDE (govern-
ment ser.), 195.367-022, 10.01.02
FOOD-SERVICE DRIVER (hotel & rest.),
906.683-010, 05.08.03
FOOD-SERVICE SUPERVISOR (hotel &
rest.), 319.137-010, 09.05.02
FOOD-SERVICE WORKER, HOSPITAL
(medical ser.), 319.677-014, 09.05.02
FOREIGN BANKNOTE TELLER-
TRADER (financial), 211.362-014,
08.01.03
FOREIGN-EXCHANGE DEALER
(financial), 186.117-082, 11.06.03
FOREIGN-EXCHANGE-POSITION
CLERK (financial), 210.367-014,
07.02.01
FOREIGN-SERVICE OFFICER (govern-
ment ser.), 188.117-106, 11.09.03
FOREIGN-STUDENT ADVISER
(education), 090.107-010, 10.01.02
FOREST ECOLOGIST (profess. & kin.),
040.061-030, 02.02.02

FOREST WORKER (forestry),
452.687-010, 03.04.02
FOREST-FIRE FIGHTER (forestry),
452.687-014, 03.04.02
FORESTER (profess. & kin.),
040.167-010, 03.01.04
FORESTER AIDE (forestry),
452.364-010, 03.02.02
FORM BUILDER (construction),
860.381-046, 05.05.02
FORMER, HAND (any industry),
619.361-010, 05.05.06
FORMS ANALYST (profess. & kin.),
161.267-018, 11.01.01
FORMULA-ROOM WORKER (dairy
products), 520.487-014, 05.10.08
FOSTER PARENT (domestic ser.),
309.677-014, 10.03.03
FOUNTAIN SERVER (hotel & rest.),
319.474-010, 09.04.01
FREEZER OPERATOR (dairy products),
529.482-010, 06.02.15
FREIGHT-TRAFFIC CONSULTANT
(business ser.), 184.267-010, 11.05.02
FRETTED-INSTRUMENT MAKER,
HAND (musical inst.), 730.281-022,
05.05.12
FRONT-END LOADER OPERATOR (any
industry), 921.683-042, 05.11.04
FRONT-END MECHANIC (automotive
ser.), 620.281-038, 05.10.01
FUEL ATTENDANT (any industry),
953.362-010, 05.06.02
FUEL-INJECTION SERVICER (any
industry), 625.281-022, 05.05.09
FUMIGATOR (business ser.),
383.361-010, 05.10.09
FUND RAISER I (nonprofit org.),
293.157-010, 11.09.02
FUND RAISER II (nonprofit org.),
293.357-014, 08.02.08
FUNERAL ATTENDANT (personal ser.),
359.677-014, 09.01.04
FURNACE CLEANER (any industry),
891.687-014, 05.12.18
FURNACE INSTALLER (utilities),
862.361-010, 05.05.05
FURNACE INSTALLER-AND-RE-
PAIRER, HOT AIR (any industry),
869.281-010, 05.05.09
FURNITURE ASSEMBLER-AND-
INSTALLER (retail trade),
739.684-082, 05.10.01
FURNITURE CLEANER (laundry & rel.),
362.684-022, 06.04.35
FURNITURE DESIGNER (furniture),
142.061-022, 01.02.03
FURNITURE FINISHER (woodworking),
763.381-010, 05.05.08
FURNITURE RESTORER (museums),
763.380-010, 05.05.08
FURNITURE UPHOLSTERER (any
industry), 780.381-018, 05.05.15
FURNITURE-RENTAL CONSULTANT
(retail trade), 295.357-018, 09.04.02
FUSING-FURNACE LOADER (optical
goods), 573.686-014, 06.04.13

GAMBLING DEALER (amuse. & rec.),
343.464-010, 09.04.02
GAME ATTENDANT (amuse. & rec.),
342.657-014, 09.04.02
GARAGE SERVICER, INDUSTRIAL
(any industry), 915.687-014, 05.12.08
GARBAGE COLLECTOR (motor trans.),
955.687-022, 05.12.03
GARBAGE COLLECTOR DRIVER
(motor trans.), 905.663-010, 05.08.03
GARBAGE-COLLECTION SUPERVI-
SOR (motor trans.), 909.137-014,
05.08.03
GARDE MANGER (hotel & rest.),
313.361-034, 05.10.08
GARMENT INSPECTOR (any industry),
789.687-070, 06.03.02
GAS INSPECTOR (utilities),
168.264-018, 11.10.03
GAS-APPLIANCE SERVICER (any
industry), 637.261-018, 05.10.02
GAS-COMPRESSOR OPERATOR (any
industry), 950.382-014, 05.06.02
GAS-DISTRIBUTION-AND-EMER-
GENCY CLERK (utilities),
249.367-042, 07.04.05
GAS-ENGINE OPERATOR (any indus-
try), 950.382-018, 05.06.01
GAS-ENGINE REPAIRER (any industry),
625.281-026, 05.05.09
GAS-LEAK TESTER (svc. ind. mach.),
827.584-014, 06.03.02
GAS-MAIN FITTER (utilities),
862.361-014, 05.05.03
GAS-WELDING-EQUIPMENT ME-
CHANIC (any industry), 626.381-014,
05.05.09
GATE GUARD (any industry),
372.667-030, 04.02.02
GEM CUTTER (jewelry-silver.),
770.281-014, 05.05.14
GEMOLOGIST (jewelry-silver.),
199.281-010, 05.05.14
GENEALOGIST (profess. & kin.),
052.067-018, 11.03.03
GENERAL CLAIMS AGENT (air trans.),
186.117-030, 11.12.01
GENERAL MANAGER, FARM (agricul-
ture), 180.167-018, 03.01.01
GENERAL MANAGER, ROAD PRO-
DUCTION (amuse. & rec.),
187.117-034, 11.11.04
GENERAL PRACTITIONER (medical
ser.), 070.101-022, 02.03.01
GENERAL-LEDGER BOOKKEEPER
(clerical), 210.382-046, 07.02.01
GEOGRAPHER (profess. & kin.),
029.067-010, 02.01.01
GEOGRAPHER, PHYSICAL (profess. &
kin.), 029.067-014, 02.01.01
GEOLOGICAL AIDE (petrol. & gas),
024.267-010, 02.04.01
GEOLOGIST (profess. & kin.),
024.061-018, 02.01.01
GEOLOGIST, PETROLEUM (petrol. &
gas), 024.061-022, 02.01.02

GEOPHYSICIST (profess. & kin.),
024.061-030, 02.01.01
GIFT WRAPPER (retail trade),
299.364-014, 01.06.03
GILDER (any industry), 749.381-010,
01.06.03
GLASS BLOWER (glass mfg.),
772.381-022, 06.01.04
GLASS CUTTER (any industry),
775.684-022, 06.02.30
GLASS FINISHER (glass products),
775.684-026, 06.04.30
GLASS INSPECTOR (any industry),
579.687-022, 06.03.02
GLASS INSTALLER (automotive ser.),
865.684-010, 05.10.01
GLAZIER (construction), 865.381-010,
05.10.01
GLUING-MACHINE OPERATOR
(woodworking), 569.685-046, 06.04.03
GOLF-COURSE RANGER (amuse. &
rec.), 379.667-010, 12.01.02
GOLF-RANGE ATTENDANT (amuse. &
rec.), 341.683-010, 05.12.18
GOODWILL AMBASSADOR (business
ser.), 293.357-018, 11.09.01
GRADER (woodworking), 669.687-030,
06.03.02
GRADER, MEAT (meat products),
525.387-010, 06.03.01
GRADING CLERK (education),
219.467-010, 07.02.03
GRAINER, MACHINE (any industry),
652.686-014, 06.04.02
GRANT COORDINATOR (profess. &
kin.), 169.117-014, 11.05.02
GRAPHIC DESIGNER (profess. & kin.),
141.061-018, 01.02.03
GRAPHOLOGIST (profess. & kin.),
199.267-038, 02.04.01
GREASE BUFFER (jewelry-silver.),
705.684-022, 06.02.24
GREENSKEEPER I (any industry),
406.137-010, 03.04.04
GREENSKEEPER II (any industry),
406.683-010, 03.04.04
GRINDER (plastic prod.), 555.685-026,
06.04.02
GRINDER OPERATOR (grain-feed mills),
521.682-026, 06.02.15
GRINDER SET-UP OPERATOR (machine
shop), 603.382-034, 06.02.02
GRIP (amuse. & rec.), 962.684-014,
05.10.01
GRIP (motion picture), 962.687-022,
05.12.04
GROUNDSKEEPER, INDUSTRIAL-
COMMERCIAL (any industry),
406.684-014, 03.04.04
GROUP LEADER (agriculture),
180.167-022, 03.01.01
GROUP WORKER (social ser.),
195.164-010, 09.01.01
GROUP-SALES REPRESENTATIVE
(amuse. & rec.), 259.357-010, 08.02.08
GUARD, CHIEF (any industry),
372.167-014, 04.01.01

GUARD, IMMIGRATION (government ser.), 372.567-014, 04.02.01

GUARD, SCHOOL-CROSSING (government ser.), 371.567-010, 10.03.03

GUARD, SECURITY (any industry), 372.667-034, 04.02.02

GUIDE (personal ser.), 353.367-010, 09.01.02

GUIDE, ESTABLISHMENT (any industry), 353.367-014, 09.01.02

GUIDE, HUNTING AND FISHING (amuse. & rec.), 353.161-010, 09.01.01

GUIDE, PLANT (any industry), 353.367-018, 09.01.02

GUIDE, SIGHTSEEING (amuse. & rec.), 353.363-010, 09.01.02

GUIDE, TRAVEL (personal ser.), 353.167-010, 07.05.01

GUNSMITH (any industry), 632.281-010, 05.05.07

HAIR STYLIST (personal ser.), 332.271-018, 09.02.01

HAZARDOUS-WASTE MANAGEMENT SPECIALIST (government ser.), 168.267-086, 11.10.03

HEAD COACH (amuse. & rec.), 153.117-010, 12.01.01

HEAD SAWYER (saw. & plan.), 667.662-010, 06.02.03

HEALTH OFFICER, FIELD (government ser.), 168.167-018, 11.10.03

HEALTH PHYSICIST (profess. & kin.), 015.021-010, 05.01.02

HEALTH-EQUIPMENT SERVICER (medical ser.), 359.363-010, 05.08.03

HEARING AID SPECIALIST (retail trade), 276.354-010, 08.02.02

HEARING OFFICER (government ser.), 119.107-010, 11.04.01

HEAT TREATER I (heat treating), 504.382-014, 06.02.10

HEAT-TRANSFER TECHNICIAN (profess. & kin.), 007.181-010, 05.03.07

HEATING-AND-AIR-CONDITIONING INSTALLER-SERVICER (construction), 637.261-014, 05.05.09

HEMMER (any industry), 787.682-026, 06.02.05

HERBARIUM WORKER (profess. & kin.), 041.384-010, 02.04.02

HIGHWAY-MAINTENANCE WORKER (government ser.), 899.684-014, 05.12.12

HISTOPATHOLOGIST (medical ser.), 041.061-054, 02.02.01

HISTORIAN (profess. & kin.), 052.067-022, 11.03.03

HISTORIC-SITE ADMINISTRATOR (museums), 102.167-014, 11.02.01

HISTOTECHNOLOGIST (medical ser.), 078.261-030, 02.04.02

HOISTING ENGINEER (any industry), 921.663-030, 05.11.04

HOLTER SCANNING TECHNICIAN (medical ser.), 078.264-010, 10.03.01

HOME ATTENDANT (personal ser.), 354.377-014, 10.03.03

HOME ECONOMIST (profess. & kin.), 096.121-014, 11.02.03

HOMEMAKER (social ser.), 309.354-010, 11.02.03

HONEY PROCESSOR (food prep., nec), 522.685-070, 06.04.15

HORIZONTAL-EARTH-BORING-MACHINE-OPERATOR HELPER (construction), 850.684-014, 05.12.02

HORSESHOER (agriculture), 418.381-010, 03.03.02

HORTICULTURAL THERAPIST (medical ser.), 076.124-018, 10.02.02

HORTICULTURAL WORKER I (agriculture), 405.684-014, 03.04.04

HORTICULTURAL WORKER II (agriculture), 405.687-014, 03.04.04

HORTICULTURAL-SPECIALTY GROWER, FIELD (agriculture), 405.161-014, 03.01.03

HORTICULTURIST (profess. & kin.), 040.061-038, 02.02.02

HOSPITAL-ADMITTING CLERK (medical ser.), 205.362-018, 07.04.01

HOSPITAL-INSURANCE REPRESENTATIVE (insurance), 166.267-014, 07.01.05

HOSPITAL-TELEVISION-RENTAL CLERK (business ser.), 295.467-018, 09.04.02

HOST/HOSTESS (any industry), 352.667-010, 09.01.01

HOST/HOSTESS, RESTAURANT (hotel & rest.), 310.137-010, 09.01.03

HOT-CELL TECHNICIAN (profess. & kin.), 015.362-018, 02.04.01

HOT-ROOM ATTENDANT (personal ser.), 335.677-014, 09.05.01

HOTEL CLERK (hotel & rest.), 238.367-038, 07.04.03

HOUSE OFFICER (hotel & rest.), 376.367-018, 04.02.03

HOUSE REPAIRER (construction), 869.381-010, 05.10.04

HOUSECLEANER (hotel & rest.), 323.687-018, 05.12.18

HOUSEHOLD-APPLIANCE INSTALLER (any industry), 827.661-010, 05.10.04

HOUSEKEEPER (hotel & rest.), 321.137-010, 05.12.01

HOUSEKEEPER, HOME (domestic ser.), 301.137-010, 05.12.01

HOUSING-MANAGEMENT OFFICER (government ser.), 188.117-110, 11.05.03

HUMAN RESOURCE ADVISOR (profess. & kin.), 166.267-046, 11.02.02

HUMORIST (profess. & kin.), 131.067-026, 01.01.02

HYDRAULIC ENGINEER (profess. & kin.), 005.061-018, 05.01.03

HYDRAULIC REPAIRER (any industry), 638.281-034, 05.05.09

HYDRO-PNEUMATIC TESTER (any industry), 862.687-018, 06.03.02

HYDROELECTRIC-STATION OPERATOR (utilities), 952.362-018, 05.06.01

HYDROGRAPHER (waterworks), 025.264-010, 02.04.01

HYDROLOGIST (profess. & kin.), 024.061-034, 02.01.01

HYPNOTHERAPIST (profess. & kin.), 079.157-010, 10.02.02

IDENTIFICATION CLERK (clerical), 205.362-022, 07.04.01

IDENTIFICATION CLERK (government ser.), 209.362-022, 07.05.03

IDENTIFICATION OFFICER (government ser.), 377.264-010, 07.01.06

ILLUMINATING ENGINEER (profess. & kin.), 003.061-046, 05.01.03

ILLUSTRATOR (profess. & kin.), 141.061-022, 01.02.03

ILLUSTRATOR, MEDICAL AND SCIENTIFIC (profess. & kin.), 141.061-026, 01.02.03

IMMIGRATION INSPECTOR (government ser.), 168.167-022, 11.10.04

IMMUNOHEMATOLOGIST (medical ser.), 078.261-046, 02.04.02

IMPERSONATOR (amuse. & rec.), 159.047-018, 01.03.02

IMPORT-EXPORT AGENT (any industry), 184.117-022, 11.05.02

INDUSTRIAL DESIGNER (profess. & kin.), 142.061-026, 01.02.03

INDUSTRIAL ENGINEER (profess. & kin.), 012.167-030, 05.01.06

INDUSTRIAL ENGINEERING TECHNICIAN (profess. & kin.), 012.267-010, 05.03.06

INDUSTRIAL HYGIENIST (profess. & kin.), 079.161-010, 11.10.03

INDUSTRIAL THERAPIST (medical ser.), 076.167-010, 10.02.02

INDUSTRIAL-HEALTH ENGINEER (profess. & kin.), 012.167-034, 05.01.02

INDUSTRIAL-ORDER CLERK (clerical), 221.367-022, 05.09.03

INDUSTRIAL-SAFETY-AND-HEALTH TECHNICIAN (any industry), 168.161-014, 11.10.03

INDUSTRIAL-TRUCK OPERATOR (any industry), 921.683-050, 06.04.40

INFORMATION CLERK (clerical), 237.367-022, 07.04.04

INFORMATION CLERK, AUTOMOBILE CLUB (nonprofit org.), 237.267-010, 07.04.04

INFORMATION CLERK-CASHIER (amuse. & rec.), 249.467-010, 07.03.01

INFORMATION SCIENTIST (profess. & kin.), 109.067-010, 11.01.01

INJECTION-MOLDING-MACHINE TENDER (plastic prod.), 556.685-038, 06.04.10

INKER (print. & pub.), 659.667-010, 06.03.02

INSERTING-MACHINE OPERATOR (clerical), 208.685-018, 05.12.19

INSPECTOR (plastic prod.), 559.381-010, 06.03.01

INSPECTOR (pharmaceut.), 559.387-014, 06.03.02

INSPECTOR (office machines), 710.384-014, 06.03.01

INSPECTOR II (pottery & porc.), 774.384-010, 06.03.01

INSPECTOR, AGRICULTURAL COMMODITIES (government ser.), 168.287-010, 11.10.03

INSPECTOR, AIR-CARRIER (government ser.), 168.264-010, 05.03.06

INSPECTOR, ASSEMBLIES AND INSTALLATIONS (aircraft mfg.), 806.261-030, 06.01.05

INSPECTOR, BUILDING (government ser.), 168.167-030, 05.03.06

INSPECTOR, ELECTROMECHANICAL (inst. & app.), 729.361-010, 06.01.05

INSPECTOR, HEALTH CARE FACILI-TIES (government ser.), 168.167-042, 11.10.03

INSPECTOR, HEATING AND REFRIG-ERATION (government ser.), 168.167-046, 05.07.02

INSPECTOR, INDUSTRIAL WASTE (government ser.), 168.267-054, 05.03.06

INSPECTOR, INTEGRATED CIRCUITS (electron. comp.), 726.684-058, 06.03.02

INSPECTOR, MATERIAL DISPOSITION (aircraft mfg.), 806.261-034, 06.01.05

INSPECTOR, METAL FABRICATING (any industry), 619.261-010, 06.01.05

INSPECTOR, MOTOR VEHICLES (government ser.), 168.267-058, 11.10.03

INSPECTOR, OUTSIDE PRODUCTION (aircraft mfg.), 806.261-042, 06.01.05

INSPECTOR, PLASTICS AND COM-POSITES (aircraft mfg.), 806.261-046, 06.01.05

INSPECTOR, PLUMBING (government ser.), 168.167-050, 05.03.06

INSPECTOR, PRINTED CIRCUIT BOARDS (electron. comp.), 726.684-062, 06.03.01

INSPECTOR, PROCESSING (aircraft mfg.), 806.381-074, 06.01.05

INSPECTOR, QUALITY ASSURANCE (government ser.), 168.287-014, 05.03.06

INSPECTOR, RAILROAD (government ser.), 168.287-018, 05.03.06

INSPECTOR, RECEIVING (aircraft mfg.), 222.384-010, 06.03.01

INSPECTOR, SEMICONDUCTOR WAFER (electron. comp.), 726.684-066, 06.03.02

INSPECTOR, TOOL (machine shop), 601.281-022, 05.07.01

INSPECTOR, WATER-POLLUTION CONTROL (government ser.), 168.267-090, 11.10.03

INSTALLER (museums), 922.687-050, 05.12.03

INSTALLER, INTERIOR ASSEMBLIES (aircraft mfg.), 806.381-078, 06.01.04

INSTANT PRINT OPERATOR (print. & pub.), 979.362-010, 05.10.05

INSTRUCTOR, BUSINESS EDUCATION (education), 090.222-010, 11.02.01

INSTRUCTOR, DANCING (education), 151.027-014, 01.05.01

INSTRUCTOR, DRIVING (education), 099.223-010, 09.03.03

INSTRUCTOR, EXTENSION WORK (education), 090.227-018, 11.02.01

INSTRUCTOR, FLYING I (education), 196.223-010, 05.04.01

INSTRUCTOR, FLYING II (education), 097.227-010, 05.04.01

INSTRUCTOR, PHYSICAL (amuse. & rec.), 153.227-014, 10.02.02

INSTRUCTOR, PHYSICAL EDUCA-TION (education), 099.224-010, 11.02.01

INSTRUCTOR, PILOT (air trans.), 196.223-014, 05.04.01

INSTRUCTOR, SPORTS (amuse. & rec.), 153.227-018, 12.01.01

INSTRUCTOR, TECHNICAL TRAINING (education), 166.221-010, 11.02.02

INSTRUCTOR, VOCATIONAL TRAIN-ING (education), 097.221-010, 11.02.02

INSTRUMENT ASSEMBLER (inst. & app.), 710.684-046, 06.02.23

INSTRUMENT INSPECTOR (inst. & app.), 710.684-050, 06.03.02

INSTRUMENT MAKER (any industry), 600.280-010, 05.05.11

INSTRUMENT MECHANIC (any industry), 710.281-026, 05.05.10

INSTRUMENT REPAIRER (any industry), 710.261-010, 05.05.11

INSTRUMENT TECHNICIAN (utilities), 710.281-030, 05.05.11

INSTRUMENT-MAKER AND RE-PAIRER (petrol. & gas), 600.280-014, 05.05.10

INSTRUMENTATION TECHNICIAN (profess. & kin.), 003.261-010, 05.01.01

INSULATION WORKER (construction), 863.364-014, 05.10.01

INSURANCE ATTORNEY (insurance), 110.117-014, 11.04.02

INSURANCE CLERK (medical ser.), 214.362-022, 07.02.04

INSURANCE CLERK (clerical), 219.387-014, 07.05.03

INTEGRATED CIRCUIT FABRICATOR (electron. comp.), 590.684-042, 06.04.34

INTEGRATED CIRCUIT LAYOUT DESIGNER (profess. & kin.), 003.261-018, 05.03.02

INTERIOR DESIGNER (profess. & kin.), 142.051-014, 01.02.03

INTERNIST (medical ser.), 070.101-042, 02.03.01

INTERPRETER (profess. & kin.), 137.267-010, 11.08.04

INTERPRETER, DEAF (profess. & kin.), 137.267-014, 01.03.02

INVENTORY CLERK (clerical), 222.387-026, 05.09.01

INVESTIGATOR (government ser.), 168.267-062, 11.10.01

INVESTIGATOR (clerical), 241.267-030, 11.06.03

INVESTIGATOR (utilities), 376.367-022, 04.01.02

INVESTIGATOR, FRAUD (retail trade), 376.267-014, 11.10.01

INVESTIGATOR, PRIVATE (business ser.), 376.267-018, 04.01.02

INVESTIGATOR, UTILITY-BILL COMPLAINTS (utilities), 241.267-034, 07.05.02

INVESTMENT ANALYST (financial), 160.267-026, 11.06.03

INVOICE-CONTROL CLERK (clerical), 214.362-026, 07.02.04

IRRIGATION ENGINEER (profess. & kin.), 005.061-022, 05.01.03

IRRIGATOR, SPRINKLING SYSTEM (agriculture), 409.685-014, 03.04.05

JAILER (government ser.), 372.367-014, 04.02.01

JANITOR (any industry), 382.664-010, 05.12.18

JEWELER (jewelry-silver.), 700.281-010, 01.06.02

JIG BUILDER (wood. container), 761.381-014, 05.10.01

JIGSAWYER (jewelry-silver.), 700.684-046, 06.04.24

JOB ANALYST (profess. & kin.), 166.267-018, 11.03.04

JOB DEVELOPMENT SPECIALIST (profess. & kin.), 166.267-034, 11.03.04

JOB PRINTER (print. & pub.), 973.381-018, 05.05.13

JOB TRACER (clerical), 221.387-034, 05.09.02

JOCKEY AGENT (amuse. & rec.), 191.117-026, 11.12.03

JUGGLER (amuse. & rec.), 159.341-010, 12.02.01

KEY CUTTER (any industry), 709.684-050, 05.12.13

KICK-PRESS OPERATOR I (any industry), 616.682-026, 06.02.20

KILN WORKER (pottery & porc.), 573.687-022, 06.04.17

KITCHEN HELPER (hotel & rest.), 318.687-010, 05.12.18

KITCHEN SUPERVISOR (hotel & rest.), 319.137-030, 05.10.08

KNITTER MECHANIC (knitting), 685.360-010, 06.01.02

KNITTING-MACHINE FIXER (knitting), 689.260-026, 06.01.02

KNITTING-MACHINE OPERATOR (knitting), 685.665-014, 06.04.06

LABEL CODER (any industry), 920.587-014, 06.04.26

LABOR EXPEDITER (construction), 249.167-018, 07.01.02

LABOR-CREW SUPERVISOR (construction), 899.131-010, 05.12.01

LABORATORY ASSISTANT (petrol. & gas), 024.381-010, 02.04.01

LABORATORY ASSISTANT (utilities), 029.361-018, 02.04.01

LABORATORY ASSISTANT (textile), 029.381-014, 02.04.01

LABORATORY ASSISTANT, BLOOD AND PLASMA (medical ser.), 078.687-010, 02.04.02

LABORATORY ASSISTANT, CULTURE MEDIA (pharmaceut.), 559.384-010, 02.04.02

LABORATORY ASSISTANT, METAL-LURGICAL (steel & rel.), 011.261-022, 02.04.01

LABORATORY CLERK (clerical), 222.587-026, 05.09.01

LABORATORY MANAGER (education), 090.164-010, 11.07.03

LABORATORY SUPERVISOR (profess. & kin.), 022.137-010, 02.04.01

LABORATORY TECHNICIAN (auto. mfg.), 019.261-030, 02.04.01

LABORATORY TECHNICIAN, PHAR-MACEUTICAL (pharmaceut.), 559.361-010, 02.04.02

LABORATORY TESTER (plastic-synth.), 022.281-018, 02.04.01

LABORATORY TESTER (any industry), 029.261-010, 02.04.01

LABORER (pharmaceut.), 559.686-022, 06.04.19

LABORER, CHEMICAL PROCESSING (chemical), 559.687-050, 06.04.40

LABORER, CONCRETE PLANT (concrete prod.), 579.687-042, 06.04.40

LABORER, CONCRETE-MIXING PLANT (construction), 579.665-014, 05.12.04

LABORER, GENERAL (steel & rel.), 509.687-026, 06.04.40

LABORER, GENERAL (plastic-synth.), 559.667-014, 06.04.40

LABORER, GENERAL (motor trans.), 909.687-014, 05.12.18

LABORER, GRINDING AND POLISH-ING (any industry), 705.687-014, 06.04.34

LABORER, LANDSCAPE (agriculture), 408.687-014, 03.04.04

LABORER, PETROLEUM REFINERY (petrol. refin.), 549.687-018, 05.12.03

LABORER, POWERHOUSE (utilities), 952.665-010, 05.12.04

LABORER, SHIPYARD (ship-boat mfg.), 809.687-022, 05.12.03

LABORER, STORES (any industry), 922.687-058, 05.09.01

LAMINATION ASSEMBLER (elec. equip.), 729.684-066, 06.02.23

LAMINATOR (rubber goods), 899.684-018, 06.02.22

LAMINATOR, HAND (furniture), 763.684-050, 06.04.22

LAND SURVEYOR (profess. & kin.), 018.167-018, 05.01.06

LAND-LEASING EXAMINER (government ser.), 237.367-026, 07.04.04

LANDSCAPE ARCHITECT (profess. & kin.), 001.061-018, 05.01.07

LANDSCAPE CONTRACTOR (construction), 182.167-014, 03.01.03

LANDSCAPE GARDENER (agriculture), 408.161-010, 03.01.03

LASER TECHNICIAN (electron. comp.), 019.261-034, 05.03.05

LASER-BEAM-MACHINE OPERATOR (welding), 815.682-010, 06.02.19

LASER-BEAM-TRIM OPERATOR (electron. comp.), 726.682-010, 06.02.02

LATHE OPERATOR, NUMERICAL CONTROL (machine shop), 604.362-010, 06.01.03

LATHE SPOTTER (millwork-plywood), 663.686-022, 06.04.03

LAUNDERER, HAND (laundry & rel.), 361.684-010, 06.04.35

LAUNDRY CLERK (clerical), 221.387-038, 05.09.02

LAUNDRY LABORER (laundry & rel.), 361.687-018, 06.04.35

LAUNDRY OPERATOR (laundry & rel.), 369.684-014, 06.04.35

LAUNDRY WORKER I (any industry), 361.684-014, 05.12.18

LAWN-SERVICE WORKER (agriculture), 408.684-010, 03.04.04

LAWN-SPRINKLER INSTALLER (construction), 869.684-030, 05.10.01

LAWYER (profess. & kin.), 110.107-010, 11.04.02

LAWYER, CORPORATION (profess. & kin.), 110.117-022, 11.04.02

LAWYER, CRIMINAL (profess. & kin.), 110.107-014, 11.04.02

LAWYER, PATENT (profess. & kin.), 110.117-026, 11.04.02

LAWYER, PROBATE (profess. & kin.), 110.117-030, 11.04.02

LAY-OUT WORKER (machine shop), 600.281-018, 05.05.07

LAY-OUT WORKER II (any industry), 809.381-014, 06.02.31

LAYAWAY CLERK (retail trade), 299.467-010, 07.03.01

LEASING AGENT, OUTDOOR ADVER-TISING (business ser.), 254.357-010, 11.12.02

LEASING AGENT, RESIDENCE (real estate), 250.357-014, 08.02.04

LEATHER CLEANER (laundry & rel.), 362.684-026, 06.04.35

LEATHER CUTTER (leather prod.), 783.684-022, 06.02.27

LEATHER WORKER (leather prod.), 783.684-026, 06.02.27

LEGAL INVESTIGATOR (profess. & kin.), 119.267-022, 11.04.02

LEGAL SECRETARY (clerical), 201.362-010, 07.01.03

LEGISLATIVE ASSISTANT (government ser.), 169.167-066, 11.05.03

LENS INSERTER (optical goods), 713.687-026, 06.04.23

LENS MOUNTER II (optical goods), 713.681-010, 05.05.11

LENS-FABRICATING-MACHINE TENDER (optical goods), 716.685-022, 06.04.08

LETTER-OF-CREDIT CLERK (financial), 219.367-050, 07.05.02

LETTER-OF-CREDIT DOCUMENT EXAMINER (financial), 169.267-042, 11.06.03

LIAISON ENGINEER (aircraft mfg.), 012.167-038, 05.01.06

LIBRARIAN (library), 100.127-014, 11.02.04

LIBRARIAN, SPECIAL LIBRARY (library), 100.167-026, 11.02.04

LIBRARY ASSISTANT (library), 249.367-046, 11.02.04

LIBRARY CONSULTANT (library), 100.117-014, 11.07.04

LIBRARY DIRECTOR (library), 100.117-010, 11.07.04

LIBRARY TECHNICAL ASSISTANT (library), 100.367-018, 11.02.04

LIBRETTIST (profess. & kin.), 131.067-030, 01.01.02

LICENSE CLERK (government ser.), 205.367-034, 07.04.03

LICENSE INSPECTOR (government ser.), 168.267-066, 11.10.03

LIFEGUARD (amuse. & rec.), 379.667-014, 04.02.03

LIGHT TECHNICIAN (motion picture), 962.362-014, 05.10.03

LIGHT-FIXTURE SERVICER (any industry), 389.687-018, 05.12.18

LIGHTING-EQUIPMENT OPERATOR (amuse. & rec.), 962.381-014, 05.12.16

LINE ERECTOR (construction), 821.361-018, 05.05.05

LINE INSTALLER-REPAIRER (tel. & tel.), 822.381-014, 05.05.05

LINE MAINTAINER (any industry), 821.261-014, 05.05.05

LINE REPAIRER (utilities), 821.361-026, 05.05.05

LINE WALKER (petrol. & gas), 869.564-010, 05.07.01

LINEN CONTROLLER (laundry & rel.), 299.357-010, 08.02.06

LINEN-ROOM ATTENDANT (hotel & rest.), 222.387-030, 05.09.01

LINEN-ROOM SUPERVISOR (laundry & rel.), 222.137-014, 05.09.01

LITERARY AGENT (business ser.), 191.117-034, 11.12.03

LIVESTOCK-YARD ATTENDANT (any industry), 410.674-018, 03.04.01

LOADER HELPER (any industry),
914.687-014, 05.12.06

LOADER I (any industry), 914.667-010,
06.04.40

LOAN INTERVIEWER, MORTGAGE
(financial), 241.367-018, 07.04.01

LOAN OFFICER (financial),
186.267-018, 11.06.03

LOAN REVIEW ANALYST (financial),
186.267-022, 11.06.03

LOBBYIST (profess. & kin.),
165.017-010, 11.09.03

LOCATION MANAGER (motion picture),
191.167-018, 11.12.02

LOCK ASSEMBLER (cutlery-hrdwr.),
706.684-074, 06.04.23

LOCKER-ROOM ATTENDANT (personal
ser.), 358.677-014, 09.05.07

LOCKSMITH (any industry),
709.281-010, 05.05.09

LOCOMOTIVE ENGINEER (r.r. trans.),
910.363-014, 05.08.02

LOFT WORKER (ship-boat mfg.),
661.281-010, 05.05.08

LOG-CHIPPER OPERATOR (logging),
564.662-010, 06.02.03

LOGGER, ALL-ROUND (logging),
454.684-018, 03.04.02

LOGGING-OPERATIONS INSPECTOR
(forestry), 168.267-070, 03.01.04

LOGGING-TRACTOR OPERATOR
(forestry), 929.663-010, 03.04.02

LOOM FIXER (narrow fabrics),
683.260-018, 06.01.02

LOT ATTENDANT (retail trade),
915.583-010, 05.08.03

LOUNGE-CAR ATTENDANT (r.r. trans.),
291.457-014, 08.03.01

LUBRICATION SERVICER (automotive
ser.), 915.687-018, 05.12.08

LUBRICATION-EQUIPMENT
SERVICER (any industry),
630.381-022, 05.10.02

LUGGAGE REPAIRER (any industry),
365.361-010, 05.10.01

LUNCH-TRUCK DRIVER (hotel & rest.),
292.463-010, 09.04.01

LYRICIST (profess. & kin.), 131.067-034,
01.01.02

MACHINE ASSEMBLER (machinery
mfg.), 638.361-010, 06.02.22

MACHINE BUILDER (machinery mfg.),
600.281-022, 05.05.09

MACHINE CLEANER (any industry),
699.687-014, 06.04.39

MACHINE FEEDER (any industry),
699.686-010, 06.04.09

MACHINE FEEDER, RAW STOCK (tex.
prod., nec), 680.686-018, 06.04.16

MACHINE OPERATOR I (any industry),
616.380-018, 06.01.03

MACHINE OPERATOR II (any industry),
619.685-062, 06.04.02

MACHINE REPAIRER, MAINTENANCE
(any industry), 638.261-030, 05.05.09

MACHINE SET-UP OPERATOR
(machine shop), 600.380-018, 06.01.03

MACHINE SET-UP OPERATOR, PAPER
GOODS (paper goods), 649.380-010,
06.01.02

MACHINE SETTER (machine shop),
600.360-014, 06.01.02

MACHINE SETTER (any industry),
616.360-022, 06.01.02

MACHINE SNELLER (toy-sport equip.),
732.685-026, 06.04.34

MACHINE TESTER (office machines),
706.387-014, 06.03.01

MACHINERY ERECTOR (engine-
turbine), 638.261-014, 05.05.09

MACHINIST (machine shop),
600.280-022, 05.05.09

MACHINIST, EXPERIMENTAL
(machine shop), 600.260-022, 05.05.07

MACHINIST, WOOD (woodworking),
669.380-014, 05.05.08

MAGNETIC-TAPE-COMPOSER
OPERATOR (print. & pub.),
203.382-018, 07.06.02

MAIL CARRIER (government ser.),
230.367-010, 07.05.04

MAIL CLERK (clerical), 209.687-026,
07.05.04

MAIL HANDLER (government ser.),
209.687-014, 07.05.04

MAILER (print. & pub.), 222.587-030,
05.09.01

MAILING-MACHINE OPERATOR
(print. & pub.), 208.462-010, 06.04.38

MAILROOM SUPERVISOR (clerical),
209.137-010, 07.05.04

MAILROOM SUPERVISOR (print. &
pub.), 222.137-022, 07.07.02

MAINTAINABILITY ENGINEER
(profess. & kin.), 019.081-010,
05.01.08

MAINTENANCE MACHINIST (machine
shop), 600.280-042, 05.05.07

MAINTENANCE MECHANIC (construction), 620.281-046, 05.05.09

MAINTENANCE MECHANIC (any
industry), 638.281-014, 05.05.09

MAINTENANCE MECHANIC HELPER
(construction), 620.664-014, 05.10.02

MAINTENANCE MECHANIC, TELE-
PHONE (any industry), 822.281-018,
05.05.05

MAINTENANCE REPAIRER, BUILD-
ING (any industry), 899.381-010,
05.10.01

MAINTENANCE REPAIRER, INDUS-
TRIAL (any industry), 899.261-014,
05.05.09

MAKE-UP ARTIST (amuse. & rec.),
333.071-010, 01.06.02

MANAGEMENT AIDE (social ser.),
195.367-014, 07.01.01

MANAGEMENT ANALYST (profess. &
kin.), 161.167-010, 05.01.06

MANAGEMENT TRAINEE (any
industry), 189.167-018, 11.05.02

MANAGER, ADVERTISING (print. &
pub.), 163.167-010, 11.09.01

MANAGER, ADVERTISING (any
industry), 164.117-010, 11.09.01

MANAGER, ADVERTISING AGENCY
(business ser.), 164.117-014, 11.09.01

MANAGER, AIRPORT (air trans.),
184.117-026, 11.05.01

MANAGER, ANIMAL SHELTER
(nonprofit org.), 187.167-218, 11.07.01

MANAGER, APARTMENT HOUSE (real
estate), 186.167-018, 11.11.01

MANAGER, AREA DEVELOPMENT
(utilities), 184.117-030, 11.09.03

MANAGER, ATHLETE (amuse. & rec.),
153.117-014, 11.12.03

MANAGER, AUTOMOBILE SERVICE
STATION (retail trade), 185.167-014,
11.11.05

MANAGER, AUTOMOTIVE SERVICES
(any industry), 184.117-034, 11.11.03

MANAGER, BAKERY (bakery products),
189.117-046, 11.05.01

MANAGER, BARBER OR BEAUTY
SHOP (personal ser.), 187.167-058,
11.11.04

MANAGER, BENEFITS (profess. & kin.),
166.167-018, 11.05.02

MANAGER, BOWLING ALLEY (amuse.
& rec.), 187.167-222, 11.11.02

MANAGER, BRANCH (any industry),
183.117-010, 11.05.02

MANAGER, BRANCH STORE (laundry
& rel.), 369.467-010, 09.04.02

MANAGER, BROKERAGE OFFICE
(financial), 186.117-034, 11.05.04

MANAGER, BUS TRANSPORTATION
(motor trans.), 184.167-054, 11.11.03

MANAGER, CAMP (construction),
187.167-066, 05.10.04

MANAGER, CHRISTMAS-TREE FARM
(forestry), 180.117-010, 03.01.01

MANAGER, CIRCULATION (print. &
pub.), 163.167-014, 11.05.04

MANAGER, CITY (government ser.),
188.117-114, 11.05.03

MANAGER, COMPENSATION (profess.
& kin.), 166.167-022, 11.05.02

MANAGER, COMPUTER OPERATIONS
(profess. & kin.), 169.167-082,
11.01.01

MANAGER, CONTRACTS (petrol. &
gas), 163.117-010, 11.05.02

MANAGER, CONVENTION (hotel &
rest.), 187.167-078, 11.11.01

MANAGER, CREDIT AND COLLEC-
TION (any industry), 169.167-086,
11.06.03

MANAGER, CUSTOMER SERVICE (tel.
& tel.), 168.167-058, 11.12.01

MANAGER, CUSTOMER SERVICES
(business ser.), 187.167-082, 05.10.02

MANAGER, CUSTOMER TECHNICAL
SERVICES (profess. & kin.),
189.117-018, 05.02.03

MANAGER, DAIRY FARM (agriculture),
180.167-026, 03.01.01

MANAGER, DATA PROCESSING
(profess. & kin.), 169.167-030,
11.01.01

MANAGER, DEPARTMENT (any industry), 189.167-022, 11.05.02

MANAGER, DEPARTMENT (retail trade), 299.137-010, 11.11.05

MANAGER, DEPARTMENT STORE (retail trade), 185.117-010, 11.05.02

MANAGER, DISPLAY (retail trade), 142.031-014, 01.02.03

MANAGER, DISTRIBUTION WARE-HOUSE (wholesale tr.), 185.167-018, 11.11.03

MANAGER, EMPLOYMENT AGENCY (profess. & kin.), 187.167-098, 11.11.04

MANAGER, EXCHANGE FLOOR (financial), 186.117-086, 11.05.04

MANAGER, EXPORT (any industry), 163.117-014, 11.05.04

MANAGER, FAST FOOD SERVICES (retail trade), 185.137-010, 11.11.04

MANAGER, FINANCIAL INSTITUTION (financial), 186.167-086, 11.11.04

MANAGER, FISH HATCHERY (fishing & hunt.), 180.167-030, 03.01.02

MANAGER, FOOD CONCESSION (hotel & rest.), 185.167-022, 09.04.01

MANAGER, FOOD PROCESSING PLANT (can. & preserv.), 183.167-026, 05.02.03

MANAGER, FOOD SERVICE (hotel & rest.), 187.167-106, 11.11.04

MANAGER, FRONT OFFICE (hotel & rest.), 187.137-018, 11.11.01

MANAGER, GOLF CLUB (amuse. & rec.), 187.167-114, 11.11.02

MANAGER, HOTEL OR MOTEL (hotel & rest.), 187.117-038, 11.11.01

MANAGER, HOUSING PROJECT (profess. & kin.), 186.167-030, 11.05.03

MANAGER, INDUSTRIAL ORGANIZA-TION (any industry), 189.117-022, 11.05.01

MANAGER, INSURANCE OFFICE (insurance), 186.167-034, 11.11.04

MANAGER, INTERNAL SECURITY (business ser.), 376.137-010, 04.01.01

MANAGER, LABOR RELATIONS (profess. & kin.), 166.167-034, 11.05.02

MANAGER, LAND DEVELOPMENT (real estate), 186.117-042, 11.05.01

MANAGER, LAND SURVEYING (profess. & kin.), 018.167-022, 05.02.06

MANAGER, LAUNDROMAT (laundry & rel.), 369.167-010, 11.11.04

MANAGER, LEASING (petrol. & gas), 186.117-046, 11.12.02

MANAGER, LIQUOR ESTABLISH-MENT (hotel & rest.), 187.167-126, 11.11.04

MANAGER, LODGING FACILITIES (hotel & rest.), 320.137-014, 11.11.01

MANAGER, MACHINERY-OR-EQUIP-MENT, RENTAL AND LEASING (any industry), 185.167-026, 11.11.05

MANAGER, MARINA DRY DOCK (amuse. & rec.), 187.167-226, 05.02.07

MANAGER, MARINE SERVICE (ship-boat mfg.), 187.167-130, 05.05.09

MANAGER, MARKET (retail trade), 186.167-042, 11.11.05

MANAGER, MEAT SALES AND STORAGE (retail trade), 185.167-030, 11.11.05

MANAGER, MERCHANDISE (retail trade), 185.167-034, 11.05.04

MANAGER, NURSERY (agriculture), 180.167-042, 03.01.03

MANAGER, OFFICE (any industry), 169.167-034, 07.01.02

MANAGER, OFFICE (government ser.), 188.167-058, 11.05.03

MANAGER, OPERATIONS (air trans.), 184.117-050, 11.05.02

MANAGER, PARTS (retail trade), 185.167-038, 11.11.05

MANAGER, PERSONNEL (profess. & kin.), 166.117-018, 11.05.02

MANAGER, POOL (amuse. & rec.), 153.137-010, 11.11.02

MANAGER, PROCUREMENT SER-VICES (profess. & kin.), 162.167-022, 11.05.02

MANAGER, PRODUCTION (radio-tv broad.), 184.162-010, 11.05.02

MANAGER, PROFESSIONAL EQUIP-MENT SALES-AND-SERVICE (business ser.), 185.167-042, 11.05.04

MANAGER, PROMOTION (hotel & rest.), 163.117-018, 11.09.01

MANAGER, PROPERTY (real estate), 186.167-046, 11.11.04

MANAGER, QUALITY CONTROL (profess. & kin.), 012.167-014, 05.02.03

MANAGER, REAL-ESTATE FIRM (real estate), 186.167-066, 11.11.04

MANAGER, RECREATION ESTAB-LISHMENT (amuse. & rec.), 187.117-042, 11.11.02

MANAGER, RECREATION FACILITY (amuse. & rec.), 187.167-230, 11.11.02

MANAGER, REGIONAL (motor trans.), 184.117-054, 11.05.02

MANAGER, REGULATED PROGRAM (government ser.), 168.167-090, 11.05.03

MANAGER, RESERVATIONS (hotel & rest.), 238.137-010, 07.05.01

MANAGER, RETAIL STORE (retail trade), 185.167-046, 11.11.05

MANAGER, SALES (any industry), 163.167-018, 11.05.04

MANAGER, SALES (laundry & rel.), 187.167-138, 11.11.04

MANAGER, SCHEDULE PLANNING (air trans.), 184.117-058, 11.05.02

MANAGER, SERVICE DEPARTMENT (wholesale tr.), 187.167-142, 11.11.04

MANAGER, STAGE (amuse. & rec.), 159.167-018, 01.03.01

MANAGER, STATION (radio-tv broad.), 184.117-062, 11.05.02

MANAGER, THEATER (amuse. & rec.), 187.167-154, 11.11.02

MANAGER, TITLE SEARCH (real estate), 186.167-090, 11.11.04

MANAGER, TOURING PRODUCTION (amuse. & rec.), 191.117-038, 11.11.04

MANAGER, TRAFFIC (any industry), 184.167-094, 11.05.02

MANAGER, TRAFFIC I (motor trans.), 184.167-102, 07.01.02

MANAGER, TRAVEL AGENCY (business ser.), 187.167-158, 11.11.04

MANAGER, VEHICLE LEASING AND RENTAL (automotive ser.), 187.167-162, 11.11.05

MANAGER, WAREHOUSE (any industry), 184.167-114, 11.11.03

MANAGER, WORLD TRADE AND MARITIME DIVISION (nonprofit org.), 187.167-170, 11.05.02

MANICURIST (personal ser.), 331.674-010, 09.05.01

MANUAL-ARTS THERAPIST (medical ser.), 076.124-010, 10.02.02

MANUFACTURER'S REPRESENTA-TIVE (wholesale tr.), 279.157-010, 08.02.01

MANUFACTURING ENGINEER (profess. & kin.), 012.167-042, 05.01.06

MARBLE FINISHER (construction), 861.664-010, 05.05.01

MARGIN CLERK I (financial), 216.362-042, 07.02.02

MARINE ENGINEER (profess. & kin.), 014.061-014, 05.01.03

MARINE SURVEYOR (profess. & kin.), 014.167-010, 05.03.06

MARINE-CARGO SURVEYOR (business ser.), 168.267-094, 11.10.03

MARINE-SERVICES TECHNICIAN (ship-boat mfg.), 806.261-026, 05.05.02

MARKER (retail trade), 209.587-034, 05.09.03

MARKER, SEMICONDUCTOR WA-FERS (electron. comp.), 920.587-026, 06.04.37

MARKET-RESEARCH ANALYST I (profess. & kin.), 050.067-014, 11.06.03

MASKER (any industry), 749.687-018, 06.04.34

MASSEUR/MASSEUSE (personal ser.), 334.374-010, 09.05.01

MASTER CONTROL OPERATOR (radio-tv broad.), 194.262-022, 05.03.05

MAT CUTTER (wood prod., nec), 739.684-126, 06.04.34

MATE, SHIP (water trans.), 197.133-022, 05.04.02

MATERIAL CLERK (clerical), 222.387-034, 05.09.03

MATERIAL COORDINATOR (clerical), 221.167-014, 05.09.02

MATERIAL EXPEDITER (clerical), 221.367-042, 05.09.02

MATERIAL HANDLER (any industry), 929.687-030, 05.12.03

MATERIAL SCHEDULER (aircraft mfg.), 012.167-082, 05.03.03

MATERIALS ENGINEER (profess. & kin.), 019.061-014, 05.01.06

MATERIALS SCIENTIST (profess. & kin.), 029.081-014, 02.01.02

MATHEMATICAL TECHNICIAN (profess. & kin.), 020.162-010, 11.01.02

MATHEMATICIAN (profess. & kin.), 020.067-014, 02.01.01

MEAT CLERK (retail trade), 222.684-010, 05.09.01

MEAT CUTTER (retail trade), 316.684-018, 05.10.08

MEAT GRINDER (meat products), 521.685-214, 06.04.15

MECHANIC, INDUSTRIAL TRUCK (any industry), 620.281-050, 05.05.09

MECHANICAL ENGINEER (profess. & kin.), 007.061-014, 05.01.08

MECHANICAL RESEARCH ENGINEER (profess. & kin.), 007.161-022, 05.01.01

MECHANICAL-DESIGN ENGINEER, FACILITIES (profess. & kin.), 007.061-018, 05.01.07

MECHANICAL-ENGINEERING TECHNICIAN (profess. & kin.), 007.161-026, 05.01.01

MEDIA CLERK (business ser.), 247.382-010, 07.02.04

MEDIA DIRECTOR (profess. & kin.), 164.117-018, 11.09.01

MEDIA SPECIALIST, SCHOOL LIBRARY (library), 100.167-030, 11.02.04

MEDICAL ASSISTANT (medical ser.), 079.362-010, 10.03.02

MEDICAL PHYSICIST (profess. & kin.), 079.021-014, 02.02.01

MEDICAL RADIATION DOSIMETRIST (medical ser.), 078.261-034, 10.02.02

MEDICAL RECORD TECHNICIAN (medical ser.), 079.362-014, 07.05.03

MEDICAL SECRETARY (medical ser.), 201.362-014, 07.01.03

MEDICAL TECHNOLOGIST (medical ser.), 078.261-038, 02.04.02

MEDICAL TECHNOLOGIST, CHIEF (medical ser.), 078.161-010, 02.04.02

MEDICAL-EQUIPMENT REPAIRER (protective dev.), 639.281-022, 05.10.02

MEDICAL-LABORATORY TECHNICIAN (medical ser.), 078.381-014, 02.04.02

MEDICAL-RECORD ADMINISTRATOR (medical ser.), 079.167-014, 11.07.02

MEDICAL-RECORD CLERK (medical ser.), 245.362-010, 07.05.03

MEDICAL-SERVICE TECHNICIAN (military ser.), 079.367-018, 07.05.03

MELTER (jewelry-silver.), 700.687-042, 06.04.24

MEMBERSHIP DIRECTOR (profess. & kin.), 189.167-026, 11.09.02

MEMBERSHIP SECRETARY (nonprofit org.), 201.362-018, 07.01.02

MEMBERSHIP SOLICITOR (any industry), 293.357-022, 08.02.08

MENDER (any industry), 787.682-030, 06.02.05

MENTAL-RETARDATION AIDE (medical ser.), 355.377-018, 10.03.02

MERCHANDISE DISTRIBUTOR (retail trade), 219.367-018, 07.05.04

MESS ATTENDANT (water trans.), 350.677-010, 09.05.02

METAL FABRICATOR (any industry), 619.361-014, 05.05.06

METAL FINISHER (any industry), 705.684-034, 06.04.24

METAL-FINISH INSPECTOR (any industry), 703.687-014, 06.03.02

METALLIZATION EQUIPMENT TENDER, SEMICONDUCTORS (comm. equip.), 590.685-086, 06.04.19

METALLOGRAPHER (profess. & kin.), 011.061-014, 05.01.04

METALLURGICAL TECHNICIAN (profess. & kin.), 011.261-010, 02.04.01

METALLURGIST, EXTRACTIVE (profess. & kin.), 011.061-018, 05.01.06

METEOROLOGICAL-EQUIPMENT REPAIRER (any industry), 823.281-018, 05.05.10

METEOROLOGIST (profess. & kin.), 025.062-010, 02.01.01

METER READER (utilities), 209.567-010, 05.09.03

METER REPAIRER (any industry), 710.281-034, 05.10.02

METROLOGIST (profess. & kin.), 012.067-010, 05.01.04

MICROBIOLOGIST (profess. & kin.), 041.061-058, 02.02.03

MICROBIOLOGY TECHNOLOGIST (medical ser.), 078.261-014, 02.04.02

MICROCOMPUTER SUPPORT SPECIALIST (profess. & kin.), 039.264-010, 05.05.05

MICROELECTRONICS TECHNICIAN (electron. comp.), 590.362-022, 06.01.03

MICROFILM MOUNTER (clerical), 208.685-022, 05.12.19

MICROFILM PROCESSOR (business ser.), 976.385-010, 05.10.05

MIGRANT LEADER (agriculture), 180.167-050, 03.01.01

MILK DRIVER (dairy products), 905.483-010, 05.08.01

MILLER (cement), 570.685-046, 06.04.08

MILLING-MACHINE SET-UP OPERATOR I (machine shop), 605.280-010, 06.01.03

MILLWRIGHT (any industry), 638.281-018, 05.05.06

MINE INSPECTOR (mine & quarry), 168.267-074, 11.10.03

MINERALOGIST (profess. & kin.), 024.061-038, 02.01.01

MINING ENGINEER (mine & quarry), 010.061-014, 05.01.06

MIXER (paint & varnish), 550.685-078, 06.04.11

MIXING-MACHINE OPERATOR (food prep., nec), 520.665-014, 06.04.15

MIXING-MACHINE OPERATOR (any industry), 550.382-022, 06.02.13

MODEL MAKER I (any industry), 777.261-010, 01.06.02

MODEL, ARTISTS' (any industry), 961.667-010, 01.08.01

MOLD DRESSER (any industry), 519.684-018, 06.04.24

MOLD MAKER (smelt. & refin.), 518.664-010, 06.04.32

MOLD MAKER I (jewelry-silver.), 700.381-034, 01.06.02

MOLDER (aircraft mfg.), 518.361-010, 06.01.04

MOLDER (optical goods), 575.381-010, 06.02.30

MONEY COUNTER (amuse. & rec.), 211.467-014, 07.07.02

MORGUE ATTENDANT (medical ser.), 355.667-010, 02.04.02

MORTGAGE CLERK (financial), 249.362-014, 07.01.04

MORTGAGE LOAN CLOSER (financial), 249.362-018, 07.01.04

MORTGAGE LOAN PROCESSOR (financial), 249.362-022, 07.05.02

MORTGAGE-CLOSING CLERK (clerical), 219.362-038, 07.05.02

MORTUARY BEAUTICIAN (personal ser.), 339.361-010, 01.06.02

MOTION-PICTURE PROJECTIONIST (amuse. & rec.), 960.362-010, 05.10.05

MOTORBOAT MECHANIC (engine-turbine), 623.281-038, 05.05.09

MOTORBOAT OPERATOR (any industry), 911.663-010, 05.08.04

MOTORCYCLE ASSEMBLER (motor-bicycles), 806.684-090, 06.02.22

MOTORCYCLE REPAIRER (automotive ser.), 620.281-054, 05.05.09

MOTORCYCLE TESTER (motor-bicycles), 620.384-010, 06.03.01

MOUNTER, AUTOMATIC (photofinishing), 976.685-022, 06.04.20

MUFFLER INSTALLER (automotive ser.), 807.664-010, 05.10.01

MUSEUM ATTENDANT (museums), 109.367-010, 07.04.04

MUSEUM TECHNICIAN (museums), 102.381-010, 01.06.02

MUSIC LIBRARIAN (radio-tv broad.), 100.367-022, 11.02.04

MUSIC SUPERVISOR (education), 099.167-026, 11.07.03

MUSIC THERAPIST (medical ser.), 076.127-014, 10.02.02

MUSICIAN, INSTRUMENTAL (amuse. & rec.), 152.041-010, 01.04.04

NAILER, HAND (any industry), 762.684-050, 06.04.22

NAILING-MACHINE OPERATOR (any industry), 669.682-058, 06.02.03

NAME-PLATE STAMPER (any industry), 652.685-054, 06.04.37

NARRATOR (motion picture), 150.147-010, 01.03.03

NAVIGATOR (air trans.), 196.167-014, 05.03.01

NETWORK CONTROL OPERATOR (any industry), 031.262-014, 07.06.01

NEW-CAR GET-READY MECHANIC (automotive ser.), 806.361-026, 05.10.02

NEWS ASSISTANT (radio-tv broad.), 209.367-038, 07.05.03

NEWS LIBRARIAN (library), 100.167-038, 11.02.04

NEWSCASTER (radio-tv broad.), 131.262-010, 11.08.03

NEWSPAPER CARRIER (retail trade), 292.457-010, 09.04.02

NEWSPAPER-DELIVERY DRIVER (wholesale tr.), 292.363-010, 05.08.03

NIBBLER OPERATOR (any industry), 615.685-026, 06.04.02

NIGHT AUDITOR (hotel & rest.), 210.382-054, 07.02.02

NONDESTRUCTIVE TESTER (profess. & kin.), 011.261-018, 05.07.01

NOTEREADER (clerical), 203.582-078, 07.06.02

NUCLEAR ENGINEER (profess. & kin.), 015.061-014, 05.01.03

NUCLEAR MEDICINE TECHNOLO-GIST (medical ser.), 078.361-018, 10.02.02

NUCLEAR-CRITICALITY SAFETY ENGINEER (profess. & kin.), 015.067-010, 05.01.02

NUCLEAR-FUELS RECLAMATION ENGINEER (profess. & kin.), 015.061-026, 05.01.03

NUMERICAL CONTROL MACHINE OPERATOR (machine shop), 609.362-010, 06.02.02

NUMERICAL CONTROL MACHINE SET-UP OPERATOR (machine shop), 609.360-010, 06.01.03

NUMERICAL-CONTROL DRILL OPERATOR, PRINTED CIRCUIT BOARDS (electron. comp.), 606.382-018, 06.02.09

NUMERICAL-CONTROL ROUTER OPERATOR (aircraft mfg.), 605.382-046, 06.02.09

NURSE ANESTHETIST (medical ser.), 075.371-010, 10.02.01

NURSE ASSISTANT (medical ser.), 355.674-014, 10.03.02

NURSE PRACTITIONER (medical ser.), 075.264-010, 10.02.01

NURSE, CONSULTANT (medical ser.), 075.127-014, 10.02.01

NURSE, GENERAL DUTY (medical ser.), 075.364-010, 10.02.01

NURSE, HEAD (medical ser.), 075.137-014, 10.02.01

NURSE, INFECTION CONTROL (medical ser.), 075.127-034, 10.02.01

NURSE, INSTRUCTOR (medical ser.), 075.124-018, 10.02.01

NURSE, LICENSED PRACTICAL (medical ser.), 079.374-014, 10.02.01

NURSE, OFFICE (medical ser.), 075.374-014, 10.02.01

NURSE, PRACTICAL (medical ser.), 354.374-010, 10.03.02

NURSE, PRIVATE DUTY (medical ser.), 075.374-018, 10.02.01

NURSE, SCHOOL (medical ser.), 075.124-010, 10.02.01

NURSE, STAFF, COMMUNITY HEALTH (medical ser.), 075.124-014, 10.02.01

NURSE, STAFF, OCCUPATIONAL HEALTH NURSING (medical ser.), 075.374-022, 10.02.01

NURSE, SUPERVISOR (medical ser.), 075.167-010, 10.02.01

NURSE-MIDWIFE (medical ser.), 075.264-014, 10.02.01

NURSERY SCHOOL ATTENDANT (any industry), 359.677-018, 10.03.03

OBSTETRICIAN (medical ser.), 070.101-054, 02.03.01

OCCUPATIONAL ANALYST (profess. & kin.), 166.067-010, 11.03.04

OCCUPATIONAL THERAPIST (medical ser.), 076.121-010, 10.02.02

OCCUPATIONAL THERAPY AIDE (medical ser.), 355.377-010, 10.03.02

OCCUPATIONAL THERAPY ASSIS-TANT (medical ser.), 076.364-010, 10.02.02

OCCUPATIONAL-SAFETY-AND-HEALTH INSPECTOR (government ser.), 168.167-062, 11.10.03

OFFICE HELPER (clerical), 239.567-010, 07.07.03

OFFICE-MACHINE SERVICER (any industry), 633.281-018, 05.05.09

OFFSET-DUPLICATING-MACHINE OPERATOR (clerical), 207.682-018, 05.10.05

OFFSET-PRESS OPERATOR I (print. & pub.), 651.382-042, 05.05.13

OILER (any industry), 699.687-018, 05.12.08

OPAQUER (protective dev.), 712.684-030, 06.02.32

OPERATING ENGINEER (construction), 859.683-010, 05.11.01

OPERATIONAL TEST MECHANIC (aircraft mfg.), 806.261-050, 06.01.05

OPERATIONS MANAGER (motor trans.), 184.167-118, 11.11.03

OPERATIONS OFFICER (financial), 186.137-014, 11.06.01

OPERATIONS-RESEARCH ANALYST (profess. & kin.), 020.067-018, 11.01.01

OPHTHALMIC PHOTOGRAPHER (medical ser.), 143.362-014, 02.04.02

OPHTHALMIC TECHNICIAN (medical ser.), 078.361-038, 10.03.01

OPHTHALMOLOGIST (medical ser.), 070.101-058, 02.03.01

OPTICAL ENGINEER (profess. & kin.), 019.061-018, 05.01.07

OPTICAL-EFFECTS-CAMERA OPERA-TOR (motion picture), 143.260-010, 01.02.03

OPTICAL-ELEMENT COATER (optical goods), 716.382-014, 06.02.21

OPTICIAN (optical goods), 716.280-014, 05.05.11

OPTICIAN, DISPENSING (optical goods), 299.361-010, 05.10.01

OPTOMECHANICAL TECHNICIAN (optical goods), 007.161-030, 05.01.01

OPTOMETRIC ASSISTANT (medical ser.), 079.364-014, 10.03.02

OPTOMETRIST (medical ser.), 079.101-018, 02.03.04

ORDER CALLER (clerical), 209.667-014, 05.09.03

ORDER CLERK (clerical), 249.362-026, 07.05.03

ORDER CLERK, FOOD AND BEVER-AGE (hotel & rest.), 209.567-014, 07.04.02

ORDER DEPARTMENT SUPERVISOR (any industry), 169.167-038, 07.05.03

ORDER DETAILER (clerical), 221.387-046, 05.09.02

ORDER FILLER (retail trade), 222.487-014, 05.09.01

ORDERLY (medical ser.), 355.674-018, 10.03.02

ORIENTATION AND MOBILITY THERAPIST FOR THE BLIND (education), 076.224-014, 10.02.02

ORNAMENTAL-IRON WORKER (construction), 809.381-022, 05.05.06

ORNAMENTAL-METAL WORKER (metal prod., nec), 619.260-014, 05.05.06

ORTHODONTIC TECHNICIAN (protective dev.), 712.381-030, 05.05.11

ORTHOPEDIC ASSISTANT (medical ser.), 078.664-010, 10.03.02

ORTHOPTIST (medical ser.), 079.371-014, 10.02.02

ORTHOTICS ASSISTANT (medical ser.), 078.361-022, 05.05.11

ORTHOTICS TECHNICIAN (protective dev.), 712.381-034, 05.05.11

ORTHOTIST (medical ser.), 078.261-018, 05.05.11

OUTPATIENT-ADMITTING CLERK (medical ser.), 205.362-030, 07.04.01

OVEN OPERATOR, AUTOMATIC (bakery products), 526.685-070, 06.04.15

OVERHEAD CRANE OPERATOR (any industry), 921.663-010, 05.11.04

PACKAGE DESIGNER (profess. & kin.), 142.081-018, 01.02.03

PACKAGER, HAND (any industry), 920.587-018, 06.04.38

PACKAGER, MACHINE (any industry), 920.685-078, 06.04.38

PACKAGING ENGINEER (profess. & kin.), 019.187-010, 05.03.09

PACKER, AGRICULTURAL PRODUCE (agriculture), 920.687-134, 03.04.01

PACKER, DENTURE (protective dev.), 712.684-034, 05.05.11

PACKING-LINE WORKER (rubber goods), 753.687-038, 06.04.38

PAINT MIXER, HAND (any industry), 550.684-018, 06.04.34

PAINT MIXER, MACHINE (any industry), 550.485-018, 06.04.11

PAINT-SPRAYER OPERATOR, AUTOMATIC (any industry), 599.382-010, 06.02.21

PAINTER (construction), 840.381-010, 05.10.07

PAINTER, AIRBRUSH (any industry), 741.684-018, 01.06.03

PAINTER, BRUSH (any industry), 740.684-022, 06.04.33

PAINTER, HAND (any industry), 970.381-022, 01.06.03

PAINTER, SIGN (any industry), 970.381-026, 01.06.03

PAINTER, TRANSPORTATION EQUIPMENT (aircraft mfg.), 845.381-014, 05.10.07

PALLETIZER OPERATOR I (any industry), 921.682-014, 06.04.40

PANTRY GOODS MAKER (hotel & rest.), 317.684-014, 05.10.08

PAPERHANGER (construction), 841.381-010, 05.05.04

PARALEGAL (profess. & kin.), 119.267-026, 11.04.02

PARAMEDIC (medical ser.), 079.364-026, 10.03.02

PARASITOLOGIST (profess. & kin.), 041.061-070, 02.02.01

PARCEL POST CLERK (clerical), 222.387-038, 07.05.04

PARIMUTUEL-TICKET CASHIER (amuse. & rec.), 211.467-018, 07.03.01

PARIMUTUEL-TICKET CHECKER (amuse. & rec.), 219.587-010, 07.05.02

PARIMUTUEL-TICKET SELLER (amuse. & rec.), 211.467-022, 07.03.01

PARK AIDE (government ser.), 249.367-082, 07.04.03

PARK NATURALIST (government ser.), 049.127-010, 11.07.03

PARK RANGER (government ser.), 169.167-042, 04.02.03

PARK SUPERINTENDENT (government ser.), 188.167-062, 04.01.01

PARKING ENFORCEMENT OFFICER (government ser.), 375.587-010, 04.02.02

PARKING-LOT ATTENDANT (automotive ser.), 915.473-010, 09.04.02

PARKING-METER SERVICER (government ser.), 710.384-026, 05.10.02

PARTS CLERK (clerical), 222.367-042, 05.09.01

PARTS SALVAGER (any industry), 638.281-026, 05.05.09

PARTS-ORDER-AND-STOCK CLERK (clerical), 249.367-058, 05.09.01

PASSENGER SERVICE REPRESENTATIVE I (r.r. trans.), 352.677-010, 09.01.04

PASSPORT-APPLICATION EXAMINER (government ser.), 169.267-030, 07.01.05

PASTE-UP ARTIST (print. & pub.), 972.381-030, 01.06.01

PASTORAL ASSISTANT (nonprofit org.), 129.107-026, 10.01.01

PASTRY CHEF (hotel & rest.), 313.131-022, 05.10.08

PATENT AGENT (profess. & kin.), 119.167-014, 11.04.04

PATIENT-RESOURCES-AND-REIMBURSEMENT AGENT (government ser.), 195.267-018, 10.01.02

PATTERNMAKER (furniture), 781.361-014, 05.03.02

PATTERNMAKER, METAL (foundry), 600.280-050, 05.05.07

PAWNBROKER (retail trade), 191.157-010, 08.01.03

PAYROLL CLERK (clerical), 215.382-014, 07.02.05

PEDIATRICIAN (medical ser.), 070.101-066, 02.03.01

PERFUSIONIST (medical ser.), 078.362-034, 10.03.02

PERSONAL ATTENDANT (domestic ser.), 309.674-014, 09.05.06

PERSONAL PROPERTY ASSESSOR (government ser.), 191.367-010, 11.06.03

PERSONAL SHOPPER (retail trade), 296.357-010, 09.04.02

PERSONNEL CLERK (clerical), 209.362-026, 07.05.03

PERSONNEL RECRUITER (profess. & kin.), 166.267-038, 11.03.04

PERSONNEL SCHEDULER (clerical), 215.367-014, 07.05.01

PESTICIDE-CONTROL INSPECTOR (government ser.), 168.267-098, 11.10.03

PETROLEUM ENGINEER (petrol. & gas), 010.061-018, 05.01.08

PETROLOGIST (profess. & kin.), 024.061-046, 02.01.01

PHARMACEUTICAL DETAILER (wholesale tr.), 262.157-010, 08.01.01

PHARMACIST (medical ser.), 074.161-010, 02.04.01

PHARMACIST ASSISTANT (military ser.), 074.381-010, 02.04.01

PHARMACOLOGIST (profess. & kin.), 041.061-074, 02.02.01

PHARMACY TECHNICIAN (medical ser.), 074.382-010, 05.09.01

PHERESIS SPECIALIST (medical ser.), 078.261-042, 10.02.02

PHLEBOTOMIST (medical ser.), 079.364-022, 02.04.02

PHOTO CHECKER AND ASSEMBLER (photofinishing), 976.687-014, 06.03.02

PHOTO MASK CLEANER (electron. comp.), 590.684-034, 06.04.34

PHOTO MASK TECHNICIAN, ELECTRON-BEAM (electron. comp.), 972.382-022, 05.10.05

PHOTO-OPTICS TECHNICIAN (profess. & kin.), 029.280-010, 02.04.01

PHOTOCOMPOSING-MACHINE OPERATOR (print. & pub.), 650.582-018, 05.10.05

PHOTOCOMPOSITION-KEYBOARD OPERATOR (print. & pub.), 203.582-046, 07.06.02

PHOTOCOPYING-MACHINE OPERATOR (clerical), 207.685-014, 05.12.19

PHOTOENGRAVER (print. & pub.), 971.381-022, 01.06.01

PHOTOFINISHING LABORATORY WORKER (photofinishing), 976.687-018, 06.03.02

PHOTOGRAMMETRIC ENGINEER (profess. & kin.), 018.167-026, 05.03.01

PHOTOGRAMMETRIST (profess. & kin.), 018.261-026, 05.03.02

PHOTOGRAPH FINISHER (photofinishing), 976.487-010, 05.10.05

PHOTOGRAPHER (amuse. & rec.), 143.457-010, 08.03.01

PHOTOGRAPHER, FINISH (amuse. & rec.), 143.382-014, 05.10.05

PHOTOGRAPHER, LITHOGRAPHIC (print. & pub.), 972.382-014, 01.06.01

PHOTOGRAPHER, SCIENTIFIC (profess. & kin.), 143.062-026, 02.04.01

PHOTOGRAPHER, STILL (profess. & kin.), 143.062-030, 01.02.03

PHOTOGRAPHIC-MACHINE OPERATOR (clerical), 207.685-018, 05.12.19

PHOTOGRAPHIC-PLATE MAKER (electron. comp.), 714.381-018, 05.10.05

PHOTOJOURNALIST (print. & pub.), 143.062-034, 01.02.03

PHOTORESIST LAMINATOR, PRINTED CIRCUIT BOARD (electron. comp.), 554.685-034, 06.04.09

PHOTOTYPESETTER OPERATOR (print. & pub.), 650.582-022, 07.06.02

PHYSICAL THERAPIST (education), 076.121-014, 10.02.02

PHYSICAL THERAPIST ASSISTANT (medical ser.), 076.224-010, 10.02.02

PHYSICAL THERAPY AIDE (medical ser.), 355.354-010, 10.03.02

PHYSICAL-INTEGRATION PRACTITIONER (medical ser.), 076.264-010, 10.02.02

PHYSICIAN ASSISTANT (medical ser.), 079.364-018, 10.02.01

PHYSICIST (profess. & kin.), 023.061-014, 02.01.01

PHYSIOLOGIST (profess. & kin.), 041.061-078, 02.02.03

PICKING-MACHINE OPERATOR (any industry), 680.685-082, 06.04.06

PICTURE FRAMER (retail trade), 739.684-146, 01.06.02

PIE MAKER (hotel & rest.), 313.361-038, 05.10.08

PILE-DRIVER OPERATOR (construction), 859.682-018, 05.11.01

PILOT, SHIP (water trans.), 197.133-026, 05.04.02

PINSETTER ADJUSTER, AUTOMATIC (toy-sport equip.), 829.381-010, 05.05.10

PINSETTER MECHANIC, AUTOMATIC (any industry), 638.261-022, 05.10.04

PIPE FITTER (construction), 862.281-022, 05.05.03

PIPE-FITTER HELPER (construction), 862.684-022, 05.12.12

PLACER (insurance), 239.267-010, 08.01.02

PLAN CHECKER (government ser.), 168.267-102, 05.03.06

PLANETARIUM TECHNICIAN (museums), 962.261-010, 05.10.05

PLANNER, PROGRAM SERVICES (government ser.), 188.167-110, 11.03.02

PLANT ENGINEER (profess. & kin.), 007.167-014, 05.01.08

PLANT OPERATOR (concrete prod.), 570.682-014, 05.11.02

PLANT PATHOLOGIST (profess. & kin.), 041.061-086, 02.02.02

PLANT-CARE WORKER (agriculture), 408.364-010, 03.04.05

PLASTER MAKER (nonmet. min.), 779.684-046, 06.02.30

PLASTER-DIE MAKER (pottery & porc.), 774.684-026, 06.02.30

PLASTERER (construction), 842.361-018, 05.05.04

PLASTIC-TOP ASSEMBLER (furniture), 763.684-062, 06.04.22

PLASTICS FABRICATOR (aircraft mfg.), 754.381-018, 06.01.04

PLATE INSPECTOR (print. & pub.), 972.687-010, 06.03.02

PLATER (electroplating), 500.380-010, 06.02.21

PLATER, PRINTED CIRCUIT BOARD PANELS (electron. comp.), 500.684-026, 06.02.21

PLATER, SEMICONDUCTOR WAFERS AND COMPONENTS (electron. comp.), 500.684-030, 06.04.19

PLATING EQUIPMENT TENDER (electroplating), 500.685-014, 06.04.21

PLAYROOM ATTENDANT (any industry), 359.677-026, 10.03.03

PLAYWRIGHT (profess. & kin.), 131.067-038, 01.01.02

PLUMBER (construction), 862.381-030, 05.05.03

PNEUMATIC-TOOL REPAIRER (any industry), 630.281-010, 05.05.09

PODIATRIC ASSISTANT (medical ser.), 079.374-018, 10.03.02

PODIATRIST (medical ser.), 079.101-022, 02.03.01

POLICE AIDE (government ser.), 243.362-014, 07.04.05

POLICE ARTIST (government ser.), 141.061-034, 01.02.03

POLICE CHIEF (government ser.), 375.117-010, 04.01.01

POLICE CLERK (government ser.), 375.362-010, 07.05.01

POLICE OFFICER I (government ser.), 375.263-014, 04.01.02

POLICE OFFICER III (government ser.), 375.267-038, 04.01.02

POLICY-CHANGE CLERK (insurance), 219.362-042, 07.02.02

POLICY-VALUE CALCULATOR (insurance), 216.382-050, 07.02.03

POLICYHOLDER-INFORMATION CLERK (insurance), 249.262-010, 07.04.04

POLISHER (any industry), 705.684-058, 06.04.24

POLISHING-MACHINE OPERATOR (any industry), 603.682-026, 06.02.02

POLITICAL SCIENTIST (profess. & kin.), 051.067-010, 11.03.02

POLLUTION-CONTROL ENGINEER (profess. & kin.), 019.081-018, 05.01.02

POLLUTION-CONTROL TECHNICIAN (profess. & kin.), 029.261-014, 05.03.08

POLYGRAPH EXAMINER (profess. & kin.), 199.267-026, 02.04.02

POLYSILICON PREPARATION WORKER (electron. comp.), 590.684-038, 06.04.19

POLYSOMNOGRAPHIC TECHNICIAN (medical ser.), 078.362-042, 10.03.01

PORTER (air trans.), 357.677-010, 09.05.03

PORTER, BAGGAGE (hotel & rest.), 324.477-010, 09.05.03

POST-OFFICE CLERK (government ser.), 243.367-014, 07.03.01

POSTMASTER (government ser.), 188.167-066, 11.05.03

POULTRY BONER (meat products), 525.687-066, 06.04.28

POULTRY DRESSER (agriculture), 525.687-070, 06.04.28

POWER-DISTRIBUTION ENGINEER (utilities), 003.167-046, 05.01.03

POWER-PRESS TENDER (any industry), 617.685-026, 06.04.02

POWER-REACTOR OPERATOR (utilities), 952.362-022, 05.06.01

POWER-SHOVEL OPERATOR (any industry), 850.683-030, 05.11.01

POWER-TRANSMISSION ENGINEER (utilities), 003.167-050, 05.01.03

POWERHOUSE MECHANIC (utilities), 631.261-014, 05.05.09

PRECISION-LENS GRINDER (optical goods), 716.382-018, 06.02.08

PREPARER (jewelry-silver.), 700.687-062, 06.04.24

PRESCRIPTION CLERK, LENS-AND-FRAMES (optical goods), 222.367-050, 05.09.02

PRESIDENT (any industry), 189.117-026, 11.05.01

PRESIDENT, EDUCATIONAL INSTITUTION (education), 090.117-034, 11.07.03

PRESIDENT, FINANCIAL INSTITUTION (financial), 186.117-054, 11.05.01

PRESS BUCKER (any industry), 920.686-042, 05.12.03

PRESS OPERATOR (laundry & rel.), 363.685-010, 06.04.35

PRESS OPERATOR, HEAVY DUTY (any industry), 617.260-010, 06.02.02

PRESS OPERATOR, MEAT (meat products), 520.685-182, 06.04.15

PRESSER, ALL-AROUND (laundry & rel.), 363.682-014, 06.04.35

PRESSER, HAND (any industry), 363.684-018, 06.04.35

PRESSER, MACHINE (any industry), 363.682-018, 06.04.05

PRESSURE SEALER-AND-TESTER (aircraft mfg.), 806.384-038, 06.02.24

PREVENTIVE MAINTENANCE COORDINATOR (any industry), 169.167-074, 05.01.06

PRINCIPAL (education), 099.117-018, 11.07.03

PRINT CONTROLLER (photofinishing), 976.360-010, 06.01.02

PRINT DEVELOPER, AUTOMATIC (photofinishing), 976.685-026, 06.04.19

PRINT INSPECTOR (pottery & porc.), 774.687-018, 06.03.02

PRINTED CIRCUIT BOARD ASSEMBLER, HAND (comm. equip.), 726.684-070, 06.02.23

PRINTED CIRCUIT DESIGNER (profess. & kin.), 003.261-022, 05.03.02

PROBATION-AND-PAROLE OFFICER (profess. & kin.), 195.107-046, 10.01.02

PROCESS SERVER (business ser.), 249.367-062, 07.07.02

PROCUREMENT CLERK (clerical), 249.367-066, 07.01.02

PRODUCER (radio-tv broad.), 159.117-010, 01.03.01

PRODUCER (motion picture), 187.167-174, 01.01.01

PRODUCER (amuse. & rec.), 187.167-178, 01.03.01

PRODUCT-SAFETY ENGINEER (profess. & kin.), 012.061-010, 05.01.02

PRODUCTION CLERK (clerical), 221.382-018, 05.03.03

PRODUCTION COORDINATOR (clerical), 221.167-018, 05.09.02

PRODUCTION ENGINEER (profess. & kin.), 012.167-046, 05.01.04

PRODUCTION PLANNER (profess. & kin.), 012.167-050, 05.01.06

PRODUCTION PROOFREADER (print. & pub.), 247.667-010, 07.05.02

PRODUCTION SUPERINTENDENT (any industry), 183.117-014, 05.02.03

PRODUCTION TECHNICIAN, SEMI-CONDUCTOR PROCESSING EQUIPMENT (electron. comp.), 590.384-014, 05.09.01

PROGRAM AIDE, GROUP WORK (social ser.), 195.227-010, 10.02.02

PROGRAM COORDINATOR (amuse. & rec.), 139.167-010, 01.03.03

PROGRAM DIRECTOR, CABLE TELEVISION (radio-tv broad.), 194.162-010, 05.02.04

PROGRAM DIRECTOR, GROUP WORK (profess. & kin.), 187.117-046, 11.07.01

PROGRAM MANAGER (profess. & kin.), 189.167-030, 11.05.02

PROGRAM PROPOSALS COORDINA-TOR (radio-tv broad.), 132.067-030, 11.05.02

PROGRAM SPECIALIST, EMPLOYEE-HEALTH MAINTENANCE (profess. & kin.), 166.167-050, 11.05.02

PROGRAMMER, ENGINEERING AND SCIENTIFIC (profess. & kin.), 030.162-018, 11.01.01

PROGRAMMER-ANALYST (profess. & kin.), 030.162-014, 11.01.01

PROJECT DIRECTOR (profess. & kin.), 189.117-030, 11.05.02

PROJECT ENGINEER (profess. & kin.), 019.167-014, 05.01.08

PROJECT MANAGER, ENVIRONMEN-TAL RESEARCH (profess. & kin.), 029.167-014, 02.01.02

PROJECT-CREW WORKER (any industry), 891.687-018, 05.11.01

PROMPTER (amuse. & rec.), 152.367-010, 01.04.02

PROOF TECHNICIAN (ordnance), 199.171-010, 02.04.01

PROOF-MACHINE OPERATOR (financial), 217.382-010, 07.06.02

PROOF-MACHINE-OPERATOR SUPERVISOR (financial), 217.132-010, 07.06.02

PROOFER, PREPRESS (print. & pub.), 972.381-034, 05.10.05

PROOFREADER (print. & pub.), 209.387-030, 07.05.02

PROP ATTENDANT (amuse. & rec.), 962.684-022, 05.12.16

PROP MAKER (amuse. & rec.), 962.281-010, 01.06.02

PROPERTY CLERK (government ser.), 222.367-054, 07.05.03

PROPERTY-DISPOSAL OFFICER (any industry), 163.167-026, 11.05.04

PROPERTY-UTILIZATION OFFICER (government ser.), 188.117-122, 11.12.02

PROSPECTOR (any industry), 024.284-010, 05.03.04

PROSTHETICS ASSISTANT (medical ser.), 078.361-026, 05.05.11

PROSTHETICS TECHNICIAN (protec-tive dev.), 712.381-038, 05.05.11

PROSTHETIST (medical ser.), 078.261-022, 05.05.11

PROTECTIVE-SIGNAL INSTALLER (business ser.), 822.361-018, 05.05.05

PROTECTIVE-SIGNAL OPERATOR (any industry), 379.362-014, 07.04.05

PROTECTIVE-SIGNAL REPAIRER (business ser.), 822.361-022, 05.05.05

PSYCHIATRIC AIDE (medical ser.), 355.377-014, 10.03.02

PSYCHIATRIC TECHNICIAN (medical ser.), 079.374-026, 10.02.02

PSYCHIATRIST (medical ser.), 070.107-014, 02.03.01

PSYCHOLOGIST, CHIEF (profess. & kin.), 045.107-046, 10.01.02

PSYCHOLOGIST, COUNSELING (profess. & kin.), 045.107-026, 10.01.02

PSYCHOLOGIST, DEVELOPMENTAL (profess. & kin.), 045.061-010, 11.03.01

PSYCHOLOGIST, EDUCATIONAL (profess. & kin.), 045.067-010, 11.03.01

PSYCHOLOGIST, ENGINEERING (profess. & kin.), 045.061-014, 11.03.01

PSYCHOLOGIST, EXPERIMENTAL (profess. & kin.), 045.061-018, 11.03.01

PSYCHOLOGIST, INDUSTRIAL-ORGANIZATIONAL (profess. & kin.), 045.107-030, 11.03.01

PSYCHOLOGIST, SCHOOL (profess. & kin.), 045.107-034, 10.01.02

PSYCHOLOGIST, SOCIAL (profess. & kin.), 045.067-014, 11.03.01

PSYCHOMETRIST (profess. & kin.), 045.067-018, 11.03.01

PUBLIC HEALTH EDUCATOR (profess. & kin.), 079.117-014, 11.07.02

PUBLIC HEALTH PHYSICIAN (medical ser.), 070.101-046, 02.03.01

PUBLIC HEALTH REGISTRAR (government ser.), 169.167-046, 07.04.03

PUBLIC HEALTH SERVICE OFFICER (government ser.), 187.117-050, 11.10.03

PUBLIC-ADDRESS SERVICER (any industry), 823.261-010, 05.05.10

PUBLIC-HEALTH MICROBIOLOGIST (government ser.), 041.261-010, 02.04.02

PUBLIC-RELATIONS REPRESENTA-TIVE (profess. & kin.), 165.167-014, 11.09.03

PUBLIC-SAFETY OFFICER (government ser.), 379.263-014, 04.01.02

PULMONARY-FUNCTION TECHNI-CIAN (medical ser.), 078.262-010, 10.03.01

PUMP INSTALLER (any industry), 630.684-018, 05.10.01

PUMP SERVICER (any industry), 630.281-018, 05.05.09

PUMP-STATION OPERATOR, WATER-WORKS (waterworks), 954.382-010, 05.06.03

PUMPER (any industry), 914.682-010, 05.06.03

PUNCH-PRESS OPERATOR I (any industry), 615.382-010, 06.02.02

PUNCH-PRESS OPERATOR II (any industry), 615.685-030, 06.04.02

PUNCH-PRESS OPERATOR III (any industry), 615.682-014, 06.02.02

PUPPETEER (amuse. & rec.), 159.041-014, 01.03.02

PURCHASING AGENT (profess. & kin.), 162.157-038, 11.05.04

PURSER (water trans.), 197.167-014, 11.11.03

PUTTY GLAZER (any industry), 749.684-042, 06.04.33

QUALITY ASSURANCE ANALYST (profess. & kin.), 033.262-010, 11.01.01

QUALITY ASSURANCE COORDINA-TOR (medical ser.), 075.167-014, 10.02.01

QUALITY ASSURANCE GROUP LEADER (auto. mfg.), 806.367-014, 06.03.02

QUALITY ASSURANCE MONITOR (auto. mfg.), 806.367-018, 06.03.02

QUALITY ASSURANCE SUPERVISOR (auto. mfg.), 806.137-022, 06.01.01

QUALITY CONTROL ENGINEER (profess. & kin.), 012.167-054, 05.01.04

QUALITY CONTROL TECHNICIAN (profess. & kin.), 012.261-014, 02.04.01

QUALITY-CONTROL CLERK (pharmaceut.), 229.587-014, 07.05.03

QUALITY-CONTROL COORDINATOR (pharmaceut.), 168.167-066, 05.02.03

QUALITY-CONTROL INSPECTOR (recording), 194.387-010, 06.03.01

QUALITY-CONTROL TECHNICIAN (photofinishing), 976.267-010, 05.10.05

QUICK SKETCH ARTIST (amuse. & rec.), 149.041-010, 01.02.02

RACKET STRINGER (toy-sport equip.), 732.684-094, 06.02.32

RADIATION MONITOR (profess. & kin.), 199.167-010, 05.03.08

RADIATION-PROTECTION ENGINEER (profess. & kin.), 015.137-010, 05.01.02

RADIATION-PROTECTION SPECIALIST (government ser.), 168.261-010, 11.10.03

RADIATION-THERAPY TECHNOLOGIST (medical ser.), 078.361-034, 10.02.02

RADIO MECHANIC (any industry), 823.261-018, 05.05.10

RADIOGRAPHER (any industry), 199.361-010, 05.03.05

RADIOISOTOPE-PRODUCTION OPERATOR (profess. & kin.), 015.362-022, 02.04.01

RADIOLOGIC TECHNOLOGIST (medical ser.), 078.362-026, 10.02.02

RADIOLOGIC TECHNOLOGIST, CHIEF (medical ser.), 078.162-010, 10.02.02

RADIOLOGICAL-EQUIPMENT SPECIALIST (inst. & app.), 719.261-014, 05.05.11

RADIOLOGIST (medical ser.), 070.101-090, 02.03.01

RADIOLOGY ADMINISTRATOR (medical ser.), 187.117-062, 11.07.02

RADIOPHARMACIST (medical ser.), 074.161-014, 02.04.01

RADIOTELEPHONE OPERATOR (any industry), 193.262-034, 05.03.05

RAILROAD ENGINEER (profess. & kin.), 005.061-026, 05.01.07

RANGE MANAGER (profess. & kin.), 040.061-046, 02.02.02

RATER (insurance), 214.482-022, 07.02.04

RATER, TRAVEL ACCOMMODATIONS (profess. & kin.), 168.367-014, 11.10.05

RAW SHELLFISH PREPARER (hotel & rest.), 311.674-014, 09.05.02

REACTOR OPERATOR, TEST-AND-RESEARCH (profess. & kin.), 015.362-026, 02.04.01

READER (business ser.), 249.387-022, 07.05.02

REAL-ESTATE AGENT (profess. & kin.), 186.117-058, 11.12.02

REAL-ESTATE CLERK (real estate), 219.362-046, 07.01.04

RECEIPT-AND-REPORT CLERK (water trans.), 216.382-054, 07.02.03

RECEIVER-DISPATCHER (nonprofit org.), 239.367-022, 07.04.05

RECEIVING CHECKER (clerical), 222.687-018, 05.09.03

RECEPTIONIST (clerical), 237.367-038, 07.04.04

RECORDING ENGINEER (radio-tv broad.), 194.362-010, 05.10.05

RECORDING STUDIO SET-UP WORKER (recording), 962.664-014, 05.12.03

RECORDIST (motion picture), 962.382-010, 05.10.05

RECREATION AIDE (social ser.), 195.367-030, 09.01.01

RECREATION LEADER (social ser.), 195.227-014, 09.01.01

RECREATION SUPERVISOR (profess. & kin.), 187.167-238, 11.07.04

RECREATION-FACILITY ATTENDANT (amuse. & rec.), 341.367-010, 07.04.03

RECREATIONAL THERAPIST (medical ser.), 076.124-014, 10.02.02

RECRUITER (military ser.), 166.267-026, 11.03.04

REDUCING-SALON ATTENDANT (personal ser.), 359.567-010, 09.05.01

REFERRAL CLERK, TEMPORARY HELP AGENCY (clerical), 205.367-062, 07.05.03

REFERRAL-AND-INFORMATION AIDE (government ser.), 237.367-042, 07.04.02

REFINER (protective dev.), 712.684-038, 06.04.24

REFINERY OPERATOR (petrol. refin.), 549.260-010, 06.01.03

REFRIGERATING ENGINEER (any industry), 950.362-014, 05.06.02

REFRIGERATION MECHANIC (any industry), 637.261-026, 05.05.09

REFRIGERATION MECHANIC (svc. ind. mach.), 827.361-014, 05.05.09

REGISTERED REPRESENTATIVE (financial), 250.257-018, 11.06.04

REGISTRAR (government ser.), 205.367-038, 07.04.03

REGISTRAR, COLLEGE OR UNIVERSITY (education), 090.167-030, 11.07.03

REGISTRATION CLERK (government ser.), 205.367-042, 07.04.01

REGISTRATION CLERK (library), 249.365-010, 07.04.03

REGULATORY ADMINISTRATOR (tel. & tel.), 168.167-070, 11.10.05

REHABILITATION CENTER MANAGER (government ser.), 195.167-038, 11.07.01

REHABILITATION CLERK (nonprofit org.), 205.367-046, 07.04.01

REINSURANCE CLERK (insurance), 219.482-018, 07.02.04

RELIABILITY ENGINEER (profess. & kin.), 019.061-026, 05.01.04

REPAIR-ORDER CLERK (clerical), 221.382-022, 07.05.03

REPAIRER (furniture), 709.684-062, 05.10.01

REPAIRER, ART OBJECTS (any industry), 779.381-018, 01.06.02

REPAIRER, FINISHED METAL (any industry), 809.684-034, 06.02.24

REPAIRER, RECREATIONAL VEHICLE (vehicles, nec), 869.261-022, 05.10.01

REPAIRER, TYPEWRITER (office machines), 706.381-030, 06.02.24

REPORTER (print. & pub.), 131.262-018, 11.08.02

REPORTS ANALYST (profess. & kin.), 161.267-026, 11.06.02

REPOSSESSOR (clerical), 241.367-022, 04.02.03

REPRODUCTION ORDER PROCESSOR (clerical), 221.367-058, 07.05.03

REPRODUCTION TECHNICIAN (any industry), 976.361-010, 05.10.05

RERECORDING MIXER (motion picture), 194.362-014, 05.10.05

RESEARCH ANALYST (insurance), 169.267-034, 11.05.02

RESEARCH ASSISTANT II (profess. & kin.), 199.267-034, 11.08.02

RESEARCH MECHANIC (aircraft mfg.), 002.261-014, 05.01.04

RESEARCH WORKER, SOCIAL WELFARE (profess. & kin.), 054.067-010, 11.03.02

RESERVATION CLERK (clerical), 238.362-014, 07.05.01

RESERVATION CLERK (r.r. trans.), 238.367-014, 07.05.01

RESERVATIONS AGENT (air trans.), 238.367-018, 07.04.03

RESERVES CLERK (financial), 216.362-034, 07.02.01

RESIDENCE COUNSELOR (education), 045.107-038, 10.01.02

RESIDENCE SUPERVISOR (any industry), 187.167-186, 11.07.01

RESOURCE-RECOVERY ENGINEER (government ser.), 019.167-018, 05.01.02

RESPIRATORY THERAPIST (medical ser.), 076.361-014, 10.02.02

RESPIRATORY-THERAPY AIDE (medical ser.), 355.674-022, 10.03.02

REST ROOM ATTENDANT (any industry), 358.677-018, 09.05.07

RETIREMENT OFFICER (government ser.), 166.267-030, 07.01.01

REVENUE AGENT (government ser.), 160.167-050, 11.06.01

REVENUE OFFICER (government ser.), 188.167-074, 11.10.01

REVIEWER (insurance), 209.687-018, 07.05.02

REVIEWING OFFICER, DRIVER'S LICENSE (government ser.), 168.167-074, 11.10.03

RIDE ATTENDANT (amuse. & rec.), 342.677-010, 09.05.08

RIDE OPERATOR (amuse. & rec.), 342.663-010, 05.10.02

RIGGER (any industry), 921.260-010, 05.11.04

RIGHT-OF-WAY AGENT (any industry), 191.117-046, 11.12.02

RING CONDUCTOR (amuse. & rec.), 159.367-010, 01.07.02

RING MAKER (jewelry-silver.), 700.381-042, 06.01.04

RISK AND INSURANCE MANAGER (any industry), 186.117-066, 11.06.03

RIVET HEATER (heat treating), 504.485-010, 05.12.10

RIVETING MACHINE OPERATOR, AUTOMATIC (aircraft mfg.), 806.380-010, 06.01.03

RIVETING-MACHINE OPERATOR I (any industry), 699.482-010, 06.02.02

ROAD-ROLLER OPERATOR (construction), 859.683-030, 05.11.01

ROADABILITY-MACHINE OPERATOR (auto. mfg.), 806.383-010, 06.01.05

ROBOTIC MACHINE OPERATOR (aircraft mfg.), 606.382-026, 06.02.09

ROCKET-ENGINE-COMPONENT MECHANIC (aircraft mfg.), 621.281-030, 05.05.09

ROCKET-MOTOR MECHANIC (aircraft mfg.), 693.261-022, 05.05.07

RODEO PERFORMER (amuse. & rec.), 159.344-014, 12.02.01

ROLL TENDER (print. & pub.), 651.686-022, 05.12.19

ROLLER-SKATE REPAIRER (any industry), 732.684-102, 05.12.15

ROLLING ATTENDANT (steel & rel.), 613.662-010, 06.01.03

ROOFER (construction), 866.381-010, 05.10.01

ROOFING-MACHINE OPERATOR (build. mat., nec), 554.682-022, 06.02.18

ROOM-SERVICE CLERK (hotel & rest.), 324.577-010, 09.05.03

ROTARY DRILLER (petrol. & gas), 930.382-026, 05.11.03

ROTOGRAVURE-PRESS OPERATOR (print. & pub.), 651.362-026, 05.05.13

ROUSTABOUT (petrol. & gas), 869.684-046, 05.10.01

ROUTE-DELIVERY CLERK (clerical), 222.587-034, 07.05.04

ROUTER (clerical), 222.587-038, 07.07.02

ROUTER OPERATOR (woodworking), 665.682-030, 06.02.03

ROUTER OPERATOR, HAND (aircraft mfg.), 806.684-150, 06.02.24

ROUTING CLERK (clerical), 222.687-022, 07.07.02

ROUTING CLERK (nonprofit org.), 249.367-070, 07.05.04

RUBBER CUTTER (rubber goods), 559.685-158, 06.04.07

RUBBER-GOODS ASSEMBLER (rubber goods), 752.684-038, 06.04.23

RUBBER-GOODS REPAIRER (any industry), 759.684-054, 06.02.29

RUG CLEANER, HAND (laundry & rel.), 369.384-014, 06.02.27

RUG CLEANER, MACHINE (laundry & rel.), 361.682-010, 06.02.18

RUG MEASURER (laundry & rel.), 369.367-014, 05.09.02

RUG REPAIRER (laundry & rel.), 782.381-018, 05.05.15

RURAL MAIL CARRIER (government ser.), 230.363-010, 07.05.04

SAFE-AND-VAULT SERVICE MECHANIC (business ser.), 869.381-022, 05.05.06

SAFE-DEPOSIT-BOX RENTAL CLERK (financial), 295.367-022, 07.03.01

SAFETY ENGINEER (profess. & kin.), 012.061-014, 05.01.02

SAFETY INSPECTOR (insurance), 168.167-078, 11.10.03

SAFETY MANAGER (profess. & kin.), 012.167-058, 05.01.02

SAFETY MANAGER (medical ser.), 168.167-086, 11.10.03

SALAD MAKER (water trans.), 317.384-010, 05.10.08

SALES AGENT, BUSINESS SERVICES (business ser.), 251.357-010, 08.02.06

SALES AGENT, INSURANCE (insurance), 250.257-010, 08.01.02

SALES AGENT, REAL ESTATE (real estate), 250.357-018, 08.02.04

SALES ATTENDANT (retail trade), 299.677-010, 09.04.02

SALES ATTENDANT, BUILDING MATERIALS (retail trade), 299.677-014, 09.04.02

SALES CLERK (retail trade), 290.477-014, 09.04.02

SALES CLERK, FOOD (retail trade), 290.477-018, 09.04.02

SALES CORRESPONDENT (clerical), 221.367-062, 05.09.02

SALES ENGINEER, AERONAUTICAL PRODUCTS (aircraft mfg.), 002.151-010, 05.01.05

SALES EXHIBITOR (nonprofit org.), 279.357-010, 08.02.02

SALES REPRESENTATIVE (motor trans.), 250.357-022, 08.02.06

SALES REPRESENTATIVE, ADVERTISING (print. & pub.), 254.357-014, 08.01.02

SALES REPRESENTATIVE, AIRCRAFT (retail trade), 273.253-010, 08.01.01

SALES REPRESENTATIVE, ANIMAL-FEED PRODUCTS (wholesale tr.), 272.357-010, 08.02.01

SALES REPRESENTATIVE, AUTOMO-TIVE-LEASING (business ser.), 273.357-014, 08.02.06

SALES REPRESENTATIVE, BOATS AND MARINE SUPPLIES (retail trade), 273.357-018, 08.02.03

SALES REPRESENTATIVE, CHEMICALS AND DRUGS (wholesale tr.), 262.357-010, 08.01.01

SALES REPRESENTATIVE, COMMUNICATION EQUIPMENT (wholesale tr.), 271.257-010, 08.01.01

SALES REPRESENTATIVE, COMPUTERS AND EDP SYSTEMS (wholesale tr.), 275.257-010, 08.01.01

SALES REPRESENTATIVE, DANCING INSTRUCTIONS (education), 259.357-014, 08.02.05

SALES REPRESENTATIVE, DATA PROCESSING SERVICES (business ser.), 251.157-014, 08.01.02

SALES REPRESENTATIVE, DENTAL AND MEDICAL EQUIPMENT AND SUPPLIES (wholesale tr.), 276.257-010, 08.01.01

SALES REPRESENTATIVE, DOOR-TO-DOOR (retail trade), 291.357-010, 08.02.08

SALES REPRESENTATIVE, EDUCATION COURSES (education), 259.257-010, 08.01.02

SALES REPRESENTATIVE, ELECTRONICS PARTS (wholesale tr.), 271.357-010, 08.01.01

SALES REPRESENTATIVE, FARM AND GARDEN EQUIPMENT AND SUPPLIES (wholesale tr.), 272.357-014, 08.02.01

SALES REPRESENTATIVE, FINANCIAL SERVICES (financial), 250.257-022, 08.01.02

SALES REPRESENTATIVE, FOOD PRODUCTS (wholesale tr.), 260.357-014, 08.02.01

SALES REPRESENTATIVE, FOOTWEAR (wholesale tr.), 261.357-018, 08.02.01

SALES REPRESENTATIVE, FRANCHISE (business ser.), 251.357-022, 08.02.06

SALES REPRESENTATIVE, GRAPHIC ART (business ser.), 254.251-010, 08.01.01

SALES REPRESENTATIVE, HARDWARE SUPPLIES (wholesale tr.), 274.357-034, 08.02.01

SALES REPRESENTATIVE, HOME FURNISHINGS (wholesale tr.), 270.357-010, 08.02.01

SALES REPRESENTATIVE, HOTEL SERVICES (hotel & rest.), 259.157-014, 08.01.02

SALES REPRESENTATIVE, HOUSEHOLD APPLIANCES (wholesale tr.), 270.357-014, 08.02.01

SALES REPRESENTATIVE, LIVESTOCK (wholesale tr.), 260.257-010, 08.01.03

SALES REPRESENTATIVE, MALT LIQUORS (wholesale tr.), 260.357-018, 08.02.01

SALES REPRESENTATIVE, MEN'S AND BOYS' APPAREL (wholesale tr.), 261.357-022, 08.02.01

SALES REPRESENTATIVE, NOVELTIES (wholesale tr.), 277.357-018, 08.02.01

SALES REPRESENTATIVE, OFFICE MACHINES (retail trade), 275.357-034, 08.02.03

SALES REPRESENTATIVE, PETROLEUM PRODUCTS (wholesale tr.), 269.357-014, 08.02.01

SALES REPRESENTATIVE, PRINTING (wholesale tr.), 254.357-018, 08.01.02

SALES REPRESENTATIVE, PRINTING SUPPLIES (wholesale tr.), 274.357-062, 08.02.01

SALES REPRESENTATIVE, PUBLIC UTILITIES (tel. & tel.), 253.357-010, 08.01.02

SALES REPRESENTATIVE, RADIO AND TELEVISION TIME (radio-tv broad.), 259.357-018, 08.01.02

SALES REPRESENTATIVE, RECREATION AND SPORTING GOODS (wholesale tr.), 277.357-026, 08.02.01

SALES REPRESENTATIVE, SECURITY SYSTEMS (business ser.), 259.257-022, 08.01.02

SALES REPRESENTATIVE, SHIPPING SERVICES (motor trans.), 252.357-014, 08.01.02

SALES REPRESENTATIVE, SIGNS AND DISPLAYS (fabrication, nec), 254.257-010, 08.01.01

SALES REPRESENTATIVE, TELEPHONE SERVICES (tel. & tel.), 253.257-010, 08.01.02

SALES REPRESENTATIVE, TELEVISION CABLE SERVICE (radio-tv broad.), 259.357-022, 08.02.06

SALES REPRESENTATIVE, TEXTILES (wholesale tr.), 261.357-030, 08.02.01

SALES REPRESENTATIVE, TOILET PREPARATIONS (wholesale tr.), 262.357-014, 08.02.01

SALES REPRESENTATIVE, UPHOLSTERY AND FURNITURE REPAIR (retail trade), 259.357-026, 08.02.06

SALES REPRESENTATIVE, VIDEOTAPE (wholesale tr.), 271.357-014, 08.02.01

SALES REPRESENTATIVE, WOMEN'S AND GIRLS' APPAREL (wholesale tr.), 261.357-038, 08.02.01

SALES-ENGINEER, ELECTRONICS PRODUCTS AND SYSTEMS (profess. & kin.), 003.151-014, 05.01.05

SALES-PROMOTION REPRESENTATIVE (wholesale tr.), 269.357-018, 08.02.01

SALES-SERVICE PROMOTER (any industry), 165.167-010, 11.09.01

SALES-SERVICE REPRESENTATIVE, MILKING MACHINES (retail trade), 299.251-010, 08.02.02

SALESPERSON, ART OBJECTS (retail trade), 277.457-010, 08.02.02

SALESPERSON, AUTOMOBILE ACCESSORIES (retail trade), 273.357-030, 08.02.03

SALESPERSON, AUTOMOBILES (retail trade), 273.353-010, 08.02.02

SALESPERSON, BOOKS (retail trade), 277.357-034, 08.02.02

SALESPERSON, COSMETICS AND TOILETRIES (retail trade), 262.357-018, 08.02.02

SALESPERSON, CURTAINS AND DRAPERIES (retail trade), 270.357-022, 08.02.02

SALESPERSON, ELECTRIC MOTORS (retail trade), 271.354-010, 08.02.03

SALESPERSON, FLOOR COVERINGS (retail trade), 270.357-026, 08.02.03

SALESPERSON, FLOWERS (retail trade), 260.357-026, 08.02.02

SALESPERSON, FURNITURE (retail trade), 270.357-030, 08.02.02

SALESPERSON, GENERAL HARDWARE (retail trade), 279.357-050, 08.02.03

SALESPERSON, GENERAL MERCHANDISE (retail trade), 279.357-054, 08.02.03

SALESPERSON, HORTICULTURAL AND NURSERY PRODUCTS (retail trade), 272.357-022, 08.02.03

SALESPERSON, HOUSEHOLD APPLIANCES (retail trade), 270.357-034, 08.02.02

SALESPERSON, INFANTS' AND CHILDREN'S WEAR (retail trade), 261.357-046, 08.02.02

SALESPERSON, JEWELRY (retail trade), 279.357-058, 08.02.02

SALESPERSON, MEN'S AND BOYS' CLOTHING (retail trade), 261.357-050, 08.02.02

SALESPERSON, MUSICAL INSTRUMENTS AND ACCESSORIES (retail trade), 277.357-038, 08.02.02

SALESPERSON, ORTHOPEDIC SHOES (retail trade), 276.257-018, 08.02.02

SALESPERSON, PARTS (retail trade), 279.357-062, 08.02.03

SALESPERSON, PETS AND PET SUPPLIES (retail trade), 277.357-042, 08.02.02

SALESPERSON, PHONOGRAPH RECORDS AND TAPE RECORDINGS (retail trade), 277.357-046, 08.02.02

SALESPERSON, PHOTOGRAPHIC SUPPLIES AND EQUIPMENT (retail trade), 277.357-050, 08.02.03

SALESPERSON, PIANOS AND ORGANS (retail trade), 277.354-010, 08.02.02

SALESPERSON, SHEET MUSIC (retail trade), 277.357-054, 08.02.02

SALESPERSON, SHOES (retail trade), 261.357-062, 08.02.02

SALESPERSON, SPORTING GOODS (retail trade), 277.357-058, 08.02.02

SALESPERSON, STAMPS OR COINS (retail trade), 277.357-062, 08.02.03

SALESPERSON, STEREO EQUIPMENT (retail trade), 270.357-038, 08.02.02

SALESPERSON, SURGICAL APPLIANCES (retail trade), 276.257-022, 08.02.02

SALESPERSON, TOY TRAINS AND ACCESSORIES (retail trade), 277.357-066, 08.02.02

SALESPERSON, TRAILERS AND MOTOR HOMES (retail trade), 273.357-034, 08.02.02

SALESPERSON, WIGS (personal ser.), 261.351-010, 08.02.02

SALESPERSON, WOMEN'S APPAREL AND ACCESSORIES (retail trade), 261.357-066, 08.02.02

SALESPERSON, YARD GOODS (retail trade), 261.357-070, 08.02.02

SALESPERSON-DEMONSTRATOR, PARTY PLAN (retail trade), 279.357-038, 08.02.05

SAMPLE MAKER I (jewelry-silver.), 700.381-046, 01.06.02

SAMPLER (mine & quarry), 579.484-010, 02.04.01

SAND MIXER, MACHINE (foundry), 570.682-018, 06.02.10

SANDBLASTER (any industry), 503.687-010, 05.12.18

SANDER (toy-sport equip.), 690.685-346, 06.04.09

SANDWICH MAKER (hotel & rest.), 317.664-010, 05.12.17

SANITARIAN (profess. & kin.), 079.117-018, 11.10.03

SANITARIAN (any industry), 529.137-014, 11.10.03

SANITARY ENGINEER (profess. & kin.), 005.061-030, 05.01.03

SANITARY LANDFILL OPERATOR (sanitary ser.), 955.463-010, 05.11.01

SANITATION INSPECTOR (government ser.), 168.267-110, 11.10.03

SAW FILER (any industry), 701.381-014, 05.05.07

SAWMILL WORKER (saw. & plan.), 667.687-018, 06.04.40

SAWYER (plastic prod.), 690.482-010, 06.02.02

SCALP-TREATMENT OPERATOR (personal ser.), 339.371-014, 09.02.01

SCANNER (profess. & kin.), 015.384-010, 02.04.01

SCHEDULER (museums), 238.367-034, 07.05.01

SCHEDULER, MAINTENANCE (clerical), 221.367-066, 07.05.01

SCHOOL SECRETARY (education), 201.362-022, 07.01.03

SCHOOL-PLANT CONSULTANT (education), 001.167-010, 05.01.08

SCIENTIFIC GLASS BLOWER (glass products), 006.261-010, 05.05.11

SCIENTIFIC LINGUIST (profess. & kin.), 059.067-014, 11.03.02

SCOREBOARD OPERATOR (amuse. & rec.), 349.665-010, 07.04.05

SCOUT, PROFESSIONAL SPORTS (amuse. & rec.), 153.117-018, 12.01.01

SCRAP HANDLER (any industry), 509.685-050, 06.04.09

SCRAPER OPERATOR (construction), 850.683-038, 05.11.01

SCREEN PRINTER (any industry), 979.684-034, 06.04.34

SCREEN WRITER (motion picture), 131.067-050, 01.01.02

SCREEN-PRINTING-EQUIPMENT SETTER (paper goods), 979.360-010, 06.01.02

SCREW-MACHINE OPERATOR, MULTIPLE SPINDLE (machine shop), 604.382-010, 06.02.02

SCREW-MACHINE SET-UP OPERA-TOR, MULTIPLE SPINDLE (machine shop), 604.280-014, 06.01.03

SCROLL-MACHINE OPERATOR (struct. metal), 616.685-062, 06.04.02

SCRUBBER MACHINE TENDER (electron. comp.), 599.685-134, 06.04.39

SEAMLESS-HOSIERY KNITTER (knitting), 684.685-010, 06.04.06

SECRETARY (clerical), 201.362-030, 07.01.03

SECRETARY OF STATE (government ser.), 188.167-082, 11.05.03

SECURITIES CLERK (financial), 219.362-054, 07.01.04

SECURITIES TRADER (financial), 162.167-038, 11.06.03

SECURITY CONSULTANT (business ser.), 189.167-054, 04.02.02

SECURITY OFFICER (any industry), 189.167-034, 11.05.02

SEED ANALYST (profess. & kin.), 040.361-014, 02.04.02

SEED PELLETER (agriculture), 599.685-126, 06.04.21

SEISMOLOGIST (profess. & kin.), 024.061-050, 02.01.01

SELECTOR (glass mfg.), 579.687-030, 06.03.02

SELF-SERVICE-LAUNDRY-AND-DRY-CLEANING ATTENDANT (laundry & rel.), 369.677-010, 09.04.02

SEMICONDUCTOR PROCESSOR (electron. comp.), 590.684-022, 06.04.32

SENIOR RESERVATIONS AGENT (air trans.), 238.137-014, 07.05.01

SERVICE CLERK (clerical), 221.367-070, 07.04.05

SERVICE MANAGER (retail trade), 185.164-010, 05.10.02

SERVICE MANAGER (automotive ser.), 185.167-058, 05.10.02

SERVICE REPRESENTATIVE (auto. mfg.), 191.167-022, 11.12.01

SERVICE REPRESENTATIVE (utilities), 959.574-010, 05.10.01

SERVICE SUPERVISOR, LEASED MACHINERY AND EQUIPMENT (any industry), 183.167-030, 11.11.05

SERVICE-ESTABLISHMENT ATTEN-DANT (laundry & rel.), 369.477-014, 09.04.02

SET DECORATOR (motion picture), 142.061-042, 01.02.03

SET DESIGNER (motion picture), 142.061-046, 01.02.03

SET DESIGNER (amuse. & rec.), 142.061-050, 01.02.03

SETTER, AUTOMATIC-SPINNING LATHE (any industry), 604.360-010, 06.01.02

SEWER, HAND (any industry), 782.684-058, 06.04.27

SEWER-LINE PHOTO-INSPECTOR (sanitary ser.), 851.362-010, 05.07.01

SEWER-LINE REPAIRER (sanitary ser.), 869.664-018, 05.12.12

SEWER-LINE REPAIRER, TELE-GROUT (sanitary ser.), 851.262-010, 05.10.01

SEWER-PIPE CLEANER (business ser.), 899.664-014, 05.12.12

SEWING MACHINE OPERATOR (leather prod.), 783.682-014, 06.02.05

SEWING-MACHINE OPERATOR, SEMIAUTOMATIC (garment), 786.685-030, 06.04.05

SEWING-MACHINE REPAIRER (any industry), 639.281-018, 05.10.02

SHEAR OPERATOR I (any industry), 615.682-018, 06.02.02

SHEET-METAL WORKER (any industry), 804.281-010, 05.05.06

SHELL MOLDER (foundry), 518.685-026, 06.04.17

SHELLFISH DREDGE OPERATOR (fishing & hunt.), 446.663-010, 03.04.03

SHELLFISH GROWER (fishing & hunt.), 446.161-014, 03.01.02

SHERIFF, DEPUTY (government ser.), 377.263-010, 04.01.02

SHIPFITTER (ship-boat mfg.), 806.381-046, 05.05.06

SHIPPING AND RECEIVING CLERK (clerical), 222.387-050, 05.09.01

SHIPPING CHECKER (clerical), 222.687-030, 05.09.01

SHIPPING-AND-RECEIVING WEIGHER (clerical), 222.387-074, 05.09.01

SHIPPING-ORDER CLERK (clerical), 219.367-030, 07.05.04

SHIPWRIGHT (ship-boat mfg.), 860.381-058, 05.05.02

SHOE REPAIRER (personal ser.), 365.361-014, 05.05.15

SHOP ESTIMATOR (automotive ser.), 807.267-010, 05.07.01

SHOP TAILOR (garment), 785.361-022, 05.05.15

SHOPPING INVESTIGATOR (business ser.), 376.267-022, 11.10.05

SHORTHAND REPORTER (clerical), 202.362-010, 07.05.03

SHOW HOST/HOSTESS (radio-tv broad.), 159.147-018, 01.03.03

SHOW-HORSE DRIVER (amuse. & rec.), 159.344-018, 12.02.01

SIGHT-EFFECTS SPECIALIST (amuse. & rec.), 962.267-010, 05.10.03

SIGN ERECTOR I (fabrication, nec), 869.381-026, 05.05.06

SIGN WRITER, HAND (any industry), 970.281-022, 01.06.03

SILK FINISHER (laundry & rel.), 363.681-010, 06.04.35

SILK-SCREEN CUTTER (any industry), 979.681-022, 01.06.01

SILK-SCREEN PRINTER, MACHINE (any industry), 979.685-010, 06.04.09

SILK-SCREEN-FRAME ASSEMBLER (any industry), 709.484-010, 06.04.23

SILVER WRAPPER (hotel & rest.), 318.687-018, 05.12.18

SILVERSMITH II (jewelry-silver.), 700.281-022, 01.06.02

SILVICULTURIST (profess. & kin.), 040.061-050, 02.02.02

SINGER (amuse. & rec.), 152.047-022, 01.04.03

SKI MOLDER (toy-sport equip.), 732.684-114, 06.02.32

SKI PATROLLER (amuse. & rec.), 379.664-010, 04.02.03

SKI REPAIRER, PRODUCTION (toy-sport equip.), 732.684-118, 06.02.24

SKI-TOW OPERATOR (amuse. & rec.), 341.665-010, 09.05.08

SKIFF OPERATOR (fishing & hunt.), 441.683-010, 03.04.03

SKIP TRACER (clerical), 241.367-026, 07.04.01

SLASHER TENDER (textile), 582.562-010, 06.04.16

SMALL-ENGINE MECHANIC (any industry), 625.281-034, 05.05.09

SOAP MAKER (soap & rel.), 559.382-054, 06.02.18

SOCIAL GROUP WORKER (social ser.), 195.107-022, 10.01.02

SOCIAL SECRETARY (clerical), 201.162-010, 07.01.03

SOCIAL-SERVICES AIDE (social ser.), 195.367-034, 10.01.02

SOCIOLOGIST (profess. & kin.), 054.067-014, 11.03.02

SOFT-TILE SETTER (construction), 861.381-034, 05.05.01

SOFTWARE ENGINEER (profess. & kin.), 030.062-010, 11.01.01

SOIL CONSERVATIONIST (profess. & kin.), 040.061-054, 02.02.02

SOIL SCIENTIST (profess. & kin.), 040.061-058, 02.02.02

SOIL-CONSERVATION TECHNICIAN (profess. & kin.), 040.261-010, 02.02.02

SOLAR-ENERGY-SYSTEM INSTALLER (any industry), 637.261-030, 05.05.09

SOLAR-ENERGY-SYSTEMS DE-SIGNER (profess. & kin.), 007.161-038, 05.03.07

SOLAR-FABRICATION TECHNICIAN (machine shop), 809.381-034, 06.02.24

SOLDERER (jewelry-silver.), 700.381-050, 06.01.04

SORTER (clerical), 209.687-022, 07.07.02

SORTER-PRICER (nonprofit org.), 222.387-054, 05.09.03

SOUND CONTROLLER (amuse. & rec.), 194.262-014, 05.10.03

SOUND MIXER (motion picture), 194.262-018, 05.10.05

SOUS CHEF (hotel & rest.), 313.131-026, 05.05.17

SPECIAL AGENT (insurance), 166.167-046, 11.05.02

SPECIAL AGENT (government ser.), 375.167-042, 04.01.02

SPECIAL AGENT, GROUP INSURANCE (insurance), 169.167-050, 08.01.02

SPECIAL EFFECTS SPECIALIST (amuse. & rec.), 962.281-018, 01.06.02

SPECIAL PROCEDURES TECHNOLOGIST, ANGIOGRAM (medical ser.), 078.362-046, 10.02.02

SPECIAL PROCEDURES TECHNOLOGIST, CARDIAC CATHETERIZATION (medical ser.), 078.362-050, 10.02.02

SPECIAL PROCEDURES TECHNOLOGIST, CT SCAN (medical ser.), 078.362-054, 10.02.02

SPECIAL PROCEDURES TECHNOLOGIST, MAGNETIC RESONANCE IMAGING (MRI) (medical ser.), 078.362-058, 10.02.02

SPECIAL TESTER (tobacco), 529.487-010, 06.03.01

SPECIFICATION WRITER (profess. & kin.), 019.267-010, 05.03.02

SPECTROSCOPIST (profess. & kin.), 011.281-014, 02.04.01

SPEECH PATHOLOGIST (profess. & kin.), 076.107-010, 02.03.04

SPINNER (jewelry-silver.), 700.684-074, 06.02.24

SPINNER, HAND (any industry), 619.362-018, 06.02.02

SPORTS-EQUIPMENT REPAIRER (any industry), 732.684-122, 05.10.04

SPOTTER I (laundry & rel.), 361.684-018, 06.02.27

SPRAY-UNIT FEEDER (any industry), 599.686-014, 06.04.21

SPREADER, MACHINE (any industry), 781.685-010, 06.04.05

STABLE ATTENDANT (any industry), 410.674-022, 03.03.02

STACKING-MACHINE OPERATOR I (any industry), 692.682-054, 06.02.20

STAGE TECHNICIAN (amuse. & rec.), 962.261-014, 05.10.04

STAMPING-PRESS OPERATOR (any industry), 652.682-030, 06.04.09

STANDARDS ENGINEER (profess. & kin.), 012.061-018, 05.01.06

STAPLING-MACHINE OPERATOR (any industry), 692.685-202, 06.04.20

STATE-HIGHWAY POLICE OFFICER (government ser.), 375.263-018, 04.01.02

STATEMENT CLERK (financial), 214.362-046, 07.02.02

STATION INSTALLER-AND-REPAIRER (tel. & tel.), 822.261-022, 05.05.05

STATION MANAGER (r.r. trans.), 184.167-130, 11.11.03

STATIONARY ENGINEER (any industry), 950.382-026, 05.06.02

STATISTICAL CLERK (clerical), 216.382-062, 07.02.03

STATISTICIAN, APPLIED (profess. & kin.), 020.167-026, 11.01.02

STATISTICIAN, MATHEMATICAL (profess. & kin.), 020.067-022, 11.01.01

STEAM CLEANER (automotive ser.), 915.687-026, 05.12.18

STENCILER (any industry), 920.687-178, 06.04.37

STENOCAPTIONER (radio-tv broad.), 202.382-010, 07.05.03

STENOGRAPHER (clerical), 202.362-014, 07.05.03

STENOTYPE OPERATOR (clerical), 202.362-022, 07.05.03

STEREO-PLOTTER OPERATOR (profess. & kin.), 018.281-010, 05.03.02

STEREOTYPER (print. & pub.), 974.382-014, 05.05.13

STERILIZER (medical ser.), 599.585-010, 06.04.19

STEVEDORE I (water trans.), 911.663-014, 05.11.04

STEWARD/STEWARDESS (hotel & rest.), 310.137-018, 05.12.01

STILL TENDER (any industry), 552.685-026, 06.04.19

STITCHER, STANDARD MACHINE (boot & shoe), 690.682-082, 06.02.05

STOCK CLERK (clerical), 222.387-058, 05.09.01

STOCK CLERK (retail trade), 299.367-014, 05.09.01

STOCK CONTROL CLERK (clerical), 219.387-030, 07.05.03

STOCK SUPERVISOR (clerical), 222.137-034, 05.09.01

STONE CARVER (stonework), 771.281-014, 01.06.02

STONE SETTER (jewelry-silver.), 700.381-054, 05.05.14

STONECUTTER, HAND (stonework), 771.381-014, 05.05.01

STONEMASON (construction), 861.381-038, 05.05.01

STORAGE-FACILITY RENTAL CLERK (business ser.), 295.367-026, 09.04.02

STRAIGHTENER, HAND (any industry), 709.484-014, 06.02.24

STRAIGHTENING-PRESS OPERATOR II (any industry), 617.482-026, 06.02.02

STRAIGHTENING-ROLL OPERATOR (any industry), 613.662-022, 06.02.02

STREET CLEANER (government ser.), 955.687-018, 05.12.18

STREET-LIGHT SERVICER (utilities), 824.381-010, 05.05.05

STREET-SWEEPER OPERATOR (government ser.), 919.683-022, 05.11.01

STREETCAR OPERATOR (r.r. trans.), 913.463-014, 09.03.01

STRESS ANALYST (aircraft mfg.), 002.061-030, 05.01.04

STRESS ANALYST (profess. & kin.), 007.061-042, 05.01.04

STRESS TEST TECHNICIAN (medical ser.), 078.362-062, 10.03.01

STRIP-CUTTING-MACHINE OPERATOR (textile), 686.685-066, 06.04.05

STRIPER, HAND (any industry), 740.484-010, 01.06.03

STRIPPER (print. & pub.), 971.381-050, 01.06.01

STRIPPER, LITHOGRAPHIC I (print. & pub.), 972.281-022, 01.06.01

STRIPPER-ETCHER, PRINTED CIRCUIT BOARDS (electron. comp.), 590.685-082, 06.04.19

STRUCTURAL ENGINEER (construction), 005.061-034, 05.01.08

STRUCTURAL-STEEL WORKER (construction), 801.361-014, 05.05.06

STUFFER (toy-sport equip.), 731.685-014, 06.04.34

STUNT PERFORMER (amuse. & rec.), 159.341-014, 12.02.01

SUBSTANCE ABUSE COUNSELOR (profess. & kin.), 045.107-058, 10.01.02

SUBSTATION OPERATOR (utilities), 952.362-026, 05.06.01

SUPERINTENDENT, BUILDING (any industry), 187.167-190, 05.02.02

SUPERINTENDENT, CONSTRUCTION (construction), 182.167-026, 05.02.02

SUPERINTENDENT, LAUNDRY (laundry & rel.), 187.167-194, 11.11.04

SUPERINTENDENT, MAINTENANCE (any industry), 189.167-046, 05.05.02

SUPERINTENDENT, PLANT PROTECTION (any industry), 189.167-050, 11.05.02

SUPERINTENDENT, SCHOOLS (education), 099.117-022, 11.07.03

SUPERINTENDENT, TRANSPORTATION (any industry), 184.167-226, 11.05.02

SUPERVISING FILM-OR-VIDEOTAPE EDITOR (motion picture), 962.132-010, 01.01.01

SUPERVISOR (office machines), 706.131-014, 06.02.01

SUPERVISOR I (rubber goods), 759.137-010, 06.02.01

SUPERVISOR OF SALES (business ser.), 185.157-014, 11.09.01

SUPERVISOR, ADVERTISING-MATERIAL DISTRIBUTORS (business ser.), 230.137-010, 07.07.02

SUPERVISOR, AUTOMOBILE BODY REPAIR (automotive ser.), 807.137-010, 05.05.06

SUPERVISOR, BLOOD-DONOR RECRUITERS (medical ser.), 293.137-010, 11.09.02

SUPERVISOR, CASHIERS (hotel & rest.), 211.137-010, 07.03.01

SUPERVISOR, CENTRAL SUPPLY (medical ser.), 381.137-014, 05.12.01

SUPERVISOR, CLAIMS (insurance), 241.137-018, 11.12.01

SUPERVISOR, COMPUTER OPERA-TIONS (clerical), 213.132-010, 07.06.01

SUPERVISOR, CONTRACT-SHEL-TERED WORKSHOP (nonprofit org.), 187.134-010, 11.07.03

SUPERVISOR, CUSTOMER SERVICES (motor trans.), 248.137-018, 07.01.02

SUPERVISOR, FILM PROCESSING (motion picture), 976.131-014, 06.01.01

SUPERVISOR, FOOD CHECKERS AND CASHIERS (hotel & rest.), 211.137-014, 07.03.01

SUPERVISOR, LAUNDRY (laundry & rel.), 361.137-010, 05.09.02

SUPERVISOR, LENDING ACTIVITIES (financial), 249.137-034, 07.01.02

SUPERVISOR, MAIL CARRIERS (government ser.), 230.137-018, 07.05.04

SUPERVISOR, MONEY-ROOM (amuse. & rec.), 211.137-018, 07.02.02

SUPERVISOR, NETWORK CONTROL OPERATORS (any industry), 031.132-010, 07.01.02

SUPERVISOR, POLICY-CHANGE CLERKS (insurance), 219.132-010, 07.02.02

SUPERVISOR, PREPRESS (print. & pub.), 972.137-010, 01.06.01

SUPERVISOR, REAL-ESTATE OFFICE (real estate), 249.137-030, 07.01.04

SUPERVISOR, SAFETY DEPOSIT (financial), 295.137-010, 07.01.02

SUPERVISOR, SHOW OPERATIONS (amuse. & rec.), 969.137-014, 01.03.01

SUPERVISOR, SPECIAL EDUCATION (education), 094.167-010, 10.02.03

SUPERVISOR, STATEMENT CLERKS (financial), 214.137-014, 07.01.04

SUPERVISOR, TRUST ACCOUNTS (financial), 219.132-014, 07.02.02

SUPERVISOR, UNDERWRITING CLERKS (insurance), 219.132-022, 07.02.02

SUPERVISOR, VENDOR QUALITY (any industry), 012.167-062, 05.03.06

SUPPLY CLERK (personal ser.), 339.687-010, 05.09.01

SURGEON (medical ser.), 070.101-094, 02.03.01

SURGICAL TECHNICIAN (medical ser.), 079.374-022, 10.03.02

SURGICAL-DRESSING MAKER (protective dev.), 689.685-130, 06.04.05

SURVEILLANCE-SYSTEM MONITOR (government ser.), 379.367-010, 04.02.03

SURVEY WORKER (clerical), 205.367-054, 07.04.01

SURVEYOR ASSISTANT, INSTRU-MENTS (profess. & kin.), 018.167-034, 05.03.01

SURVEYOR HELPER (any industry), 869.567-010, 05.12.02

SWEEPER-CLEANER, INDUSTRIAL (any industry), 389.683-010, 05.12.18

SWIMMING POOL INSTALLER-AND-SERVICER (construction), 869.463-010, 05.10.01

SWIMMING-POOL SERVICER (any industry), 891.684-018, 05.10.04

SWITCH TENDER (r.r. trans.), 910.667-026, 05.12.05

SWITCHBOARD OPERATOR, POLICE DISTRICT (government ser.), 235.562-014, 07.04.05

SYRUP MAKER (beverage), 520.485-026, 06.02.15

SYSTEMS ANALYST (profess. & kin.), 030.167-014, 11.01.01

SYSTEMS PROGRAMMER (profess. & kin.), 030.162-022, 11.01.01

TAKE-DOWN SORTER (photofinishing), 976.665-010, 05.10.05

TANK CLEANER (any industry), 891.687-022, 05.12.18

TANKER (wood prod., nec) 561.665-010, 06.04.18

TAPE LIBRARIAN (clerical), 206.367-018, 07.05.03

TAPE TRANSFERRER (radio-tv broad.), 194.382-014, 05.10.05

TAPE-RECORDER REPAIRER (any industry), 720.281-014, 05.10.03

TAPER (construction), 842.664-010, 05.10.01

TAX ATTORNEY (profess. & kin.), 110.117-038, 11.04.02

TAX CLERK (clerical), 219.487-010, 07.02.04

TAX PREPARER (business ser.), 219.362-070, 07.02.02

TAXI DRIVER (motor trans.), 913.463-018, 09.03.02

TAXICAB COORDINATOR (motor trans.), 215.367-018, 07.05.03

TAXIDERMIST (profess. & kin.), 199.261-010, 01.06.02

TEACHER (museums), 099.227-038, 11.02.01

TEACHER AIDE I (education), 099.327-010, 11.02.01

TEACHER AIDE II (education), 249.367-074, 07.01.02

TEACHER, ADULT EDUCATION (education), 099.227-030, 11.02.01

TEACHER, ELEMENTARY SCHOOL (education), 092.227-010, 11.02.01

TEACHER, EMOTIONALLY IMPAIRED (education), 094.227-010, 10.02.03

TEACHER, HEARING IMPAIRED (education), 094.224-010, 10.02.03

TEACHER, HOME THERAPY (social ser.), 195.227-018, 10.02.03

TEACHER, INDUSTRIAL ARTS (education), 091.221-010, 11.02.02

TEACHER, KINDERGARTEN (education), 092.227-014, 10.02.03

TEACHER, LEARNING DISABLED (education), 094.227-030, 10.02.03

TEACHER, MENTALLY IMPAIRED (education), 094.227-022, 10.02.03

TEACHER, MUSIC (education), 152.021-010, 01.04.01

TEACHER, PHYSICALLY IMPAIRED (education), 094.224-014, 10.02.03

TEACHER, PRESCHOOL (education), 092.227-018, 10.02.03

TEACHER, RESOURCE (education), 099.227-042, 11.02.01

TEACHER, SECONDARY SCHOOL (education), 091.227-010, 11.02.01

TEACHER, VISUALLY IMPAIRED (education), 094.224-018, 10.02.03

TEACHER, VOCATIONAL TRAINING (education), 094.227-026, 10.02.03

TECHNICAL COORDINATOR (government ser.), 209.132-014, 07.05.03

TECHNICAL ILLUSTRATOR (profess. & kin.), 017.281-034, 05.03.02

TECHNICAL SUPPORT SPECIALIST (profess. & kin.), 033.162-018, 11.01.01

TECHNICAL TRAINING COORDINA-TOR (education), 166.167-054, 11.07.03

TECHNICIAN, NEWS GATHERING (radio-tv broad.), 194.362-022, 05.03.05

TECHNICIAN, SEMICONDUCTOR DEVELOPMENT (profess. & kin.), 003.161-018, 05.01.01

TELECOMMUNICATOR (government ser.), 379.362-018, 07.04.05

TELEPHONE OPERATOR (clerical), 235.662-022, 07.04.06

TELEPHONE OPERATOR, CHIEF (clerical), 235.137-010, 07.04.06

TELEPHONE QUOTATION CLERK (financial), 237.367-046, 07.04.04

TELEPHONE SOLICITOR (any industry), 299.357-014, 08.02.08

TELEPHONE-ANSWERING-SERVICE OPERATOR (business ser.), 235.662-026, 07.04.06

TELEPHONE-DIRECTORY DELIV-ERER (business ser.), 230.667-014, 07.07.02

TELEPHONE-DIRECTORY-DISTRIBU-TOR DRIVER (business ser.), 906.683-018, 05.08.03

TELEVISION INSTALLER (any industry), 823.361-010, 05.10.03

TELEVISION TECHNICIAN (radio-tv broad.), 194.062-010, 01.02.03

TELEVISION-AND-RADIO REPAIRER (any industry), 720.281-018, 05.10.03

TELEVISION-SCHEDULE COORDINA-TOR (radio-tv broad.), 199.382-010, 07.05.01

TELLER (financial), 211.362-018, 07.03.01

TELLER, HEAD (financial), 211.132-010, 07.03.01

TELLER, VAULT (financial), 211.382-010, 07.03.01

TEMPERER (heat treating), 504.682-026, 06.02.10

TEMPLATE MAKER (any industry), 601.381-038, 06.01.04

TEMPLATE MAKER, TRACK (any industry), 809.484-014, 05.10.01

TERMINAL-MAKEUP OPERATOR (print. & pub.), 208.382-010, 07.06.01

TERRAZZO FINISHER (construction), 861.664-014, 05.05.01

TERRAZZO WORKER (construction), 861.381-046, 05.05.01

TEST DRIVER I (auto. mfg.), 806.283-014, 06.03.01

TEST ENGINEER, NUCLEAR EQUIP-MENT (profess. & kin.), 015.061-022, 05.01.04

TEST EQUIPMENT MECHANIC (aircraft mfg.), 710.361-014, 06.01.04

TEST TECHNICIAN (profess. & kin.), 019.161-014, 05.01.04

TEST TECHNICIAN (agric. equip.), 019.261-022, 05.03.07

TEST TECHNICIAN (clerical), 249.367-078, 07.01.07

TEST-ENGINE EVALUATOR (petrol. refin.), 010.261-026, 05.01.04

TESTER (profess. & kin.), 011.361-010, 02.04.01

TESTER (petrol. refin.), 029.261-022, 02.04.01

TESTER, FOOD PRODUCTS (any industry), 199.251-010, 05.05.17

THERMOMETER PRODUCTION WORKER (inst. & app.), 710.685-014, 06.04.19

THERMOSTAT REPAIRER (inst. & app.), 710.381-050, 05.10.02

THREAD CUTTER (any industry), 789.684-050, 06.04.27

THROW-OUT CLERK (retail trade), 241.367-030, 07.05.02

THROWER (pottery & porc.), 774.381-010, 06.02.30

TICKET BROKER (amuse. & rec.), 259.357-034, 11.06.04

TICKET SELLER (clerical), 211.467-030, 07.03.01

TICKET TAKER (amuse. & rec.), 344.667-010, 09.05.08

TICKETING CLERK (air trans.), 248.382-010, 07.02.04

TIER (meat products), 525.687-118, 06.04.28

TILE FINISHER (construction), 861.664-018, 05.05.01

TILE SETTER (construction), 861.381-054, 05.05.01

TIMBER-SIZER OPERATOR (saw. & plan.), 665.482-018, 06.02.03

TIME-STUDY ENGINEER (profess. & kin.), 012.167-070, 05.01.06

TIMEKEEPER (clerical), 215.362-022, 07.02.05

TIRE ADJUSTER (retail trade), 241.367-034, 05.09.01

TIRE MOLDER (rubber tire), 553.685-102, 06.04.13

TIRE MOUNTER (fabrication, nec), 739.684-158, 06.04.23

TIRE REPAIRER (automotive ser.), 915.684-010, 05.12.15

TITLE CLERK (petrol. & gas), 162.267-010, 07.01.05

TITLE EXAMINER (profess. & kin.), 119.287-010, 07.01.05

TITLE SEARCHER (real estate), 209.367-046, 07.05.02

TITLE SUPERVISOR (profess. & kin.), 119.167-018, 07.01.05

TOLL COLLECTOR (government ser.), 211.462-038, 07.03.01

TOOL BUILDER (aircraft mfg.), 693.281-030, 06.01.04

TOOL DESIGN CHECKER (aircraft mfg.), 007.267-014, 05.01.07

TOOL DESIGNER (profess. & kin.), 007.061-026, 05.01.07

TOOL DRESSER (any industry), 601.682-010, 06.04.02

TOOL GRINDER I (any industry), 701.381-018, 05.05.07

TOOL GRINDER II (any industry), 603.664-010, 06.02.01

TOOL PLANNER (any industry), 012.167-074, 05.01.06

TOOL PROGRAMMER, NUMERICAL CONTROL (any industry), 007.167-018, 05.01.06

TOOL PROGRAMMER, NUMERICAL CONTROL (electron. comp.), 609.262-010, 05.01.06

TOOL-AND-DIE MAKER (machine shop), 601.260-010, 05.05.07

TOOL-AND-EQUIPMENT-RENTAL CLERK (business ser.), 295.357-014, 09.04.02

TOOL-CRIB ATTENDANT (clerical), 222.367-062, 05.09.01

TOOL-MACHINE SET-UP OPERATOR (machine shop), 601.280-054, 05.05.07

TORCH-STRAIGHTENER-AND HEATER (any industry), 709.684-086, 05.10.01

TOURIST-INFORMATION ASSISTANT (government ser.), 237.367-050, 07.04.04

TOW-TRUCK OPERATOR (automotive ser.), 919.663-026, 05.08.03

TOWER ERECTOR (construction), 821.361-038, 05.05.05

TOWN CLERK (government ser.), 243.367-018, 07.01.02

TOXICOLOGIST (pharmaceut.), 022.081-010, 02.04.02

TOY ASSEMBLER (toy-sport equip.), 731.687-034, 06.04.23

TRACK LAMINATING MACHINE TENDER (inst. & app.), 692.685-290, 06.04.09

TRACTOR MECHANIC (automotive ser.), 620.281-058, 05.05.09

TRACTOR OPERATOR (any industry), 929.683-014, 05.11.04

TRACTOR-TRAILER-TRUCK DRIVER (any industry), 904.383-010, 05.08.01

TRAFFIC AGENT (air trans.), 252.257-010, 08.01.02

TRAFFIC CHECKER (government ser.), 205.367-058, 07.04.01

TRAFFIC CLERK (clerical), 214.587-014, 07.02.04

TRAFFIC CLERK (business ser.), 221.367-078, 07.05.01

TRAFFIC INSPECTOR (motor trans.), 184.163-010, 11.10.05

TRAILER-RENTAL CLERK (automotive ser.), 295.467-022, 09.04.02

TRAIN DISPATCHER (r.r. trans.), 184.167-262, 07.04.05

TRAINING REPRESENTATIVE (education), 166.227-010, 11.02.02

TRANSCRIBING-MACHINE OPERA-TOR (clerical), 203.582-058, 07.06.02

TRANSFER CLERK (financial), 216.362-046, 07.02.02

TRANSFER CLERK, HEAD (financial), 216.137-014, 07.01.02

TRANSFORMER ASSEMBLER II (elec. equip.), 820.684-010, 06.02.22

TRANSFORMER REPAIRER (any industry), 724.381-018, 05.10.03

TRANSLATOR (profess. & kin.), 137.267-018, 11.08.04

TRANSMISSION MECHANIC (automotive ser.), 620.281-062, 05.10.02

TRANSMITTER OPERATOR (radio-tv broad.), 193.262-038, 05.03.05

TRANSPLANT COORDINATOR (medical ser.), 079.151-010, 10.02.01

TRANSPORTATION AGENT (air trans.), 912.367-014, 07.05.01

TRANSPORTATION ENGINEER (profess. & kin.), 005.061-038, 05.01.08

TRANSPORTATION INSPECTOR (motor trans.), 168.167-082, 11.10.05

TRANSPORTER, PATIENTS (medical ser.), 355.677-014, 10.03.03

TRAVEL AGENT (business ser.), 252.152-010, 08.02.06

TRAVEL CLERK (hotel & rest.), 238.367-030, 07.04.04

TREASURER (profess. & kin.), 161.117-018, 11.06.03

TREASURER, FINANCIAL INSTITU-TION (financial), 186.117-070, 11.06.05

TREE PRUNER (agriculture), 408.684-018, 03.04.05

TREE SURGEON (agriculture), 408.181-010, 03.01.03

TREE TRIMMER (tel. & tel.), 408.664-010, 03.04.05

TRIMMER, MACHINE (garment), 781.682-010, 06.02.05

TRIMMER, MEAT (meat products), 525.684-054, 06.04.28

TROPHY ASSEMBLER (jewelry-silver.),
735.684-018, 06.02.24
TRUCK DRIVER, HEAVY (any industry),
905.663-014, 05.08.01
TRUCK DRIVER, LIGHT (any industry),
906.683-022, 05.08.01
TRUST OFFICER (financial),
186.117-074, 11.06.05
TRUST OPERATIONS ASSISTANT
(financial), 219.362-074, 07.01.03
TUBE ASSEMBLER, CATHODE RAY
(electron. comp.), 725.684-022,
06.02.23
TUBE ASSEMBLER, ELECTRON
(electron. comp.), 725.384-010,
06.02.23
TUBE CLEANER (any industry),
891.687-030, 05.12.18
TUMOR REGISTRAR (medical ser.),
079.362-018, 07.05.03
TUNE-UP MECHANIC (automotive ser.),
620.281-066, 05.05.09
TURBINE ATTENDANT (utilities),
952.567-010, 05.09.03
TURRET-PUNCH-PRESS OPERATOR,
TAPE-CONTROL (any industry),
615.685-042, 06.04.02
TUTOR (education), 099.227-034,
11.02.01
TYPE COPYIST (machinery mfg.),
970.381-042, 01.06.03
TYPIST (clerical), 203.582-066, 07.06.02
ULTRASONIC TESTER (any industry),
739.281-014, 05.07.01
ULTRASOUND TECHNOLOGIST
(medical ser.), 078.364-010, 02.04.01
UMPIRE (amuse. & rec.), 153.267-018,
12.01.02
UNDERWRITER (insurance),
169.267-046, 11.06.03
UNDERWRITER, MORTGAGE LOAN
(financial), 186.267-026, 11.06.03
UNDERWRITING CLERK (insurance),
219.367-038, 07.01.04
UNIT CLERK (medical ser.),
245.362-014, 07.05.03
UPHOLSTERY REPAIRER (furniture),
780.684-122, 05.05.15
URBAN PLANNER (profess. & kin.),
199.167-014, 11.03.02
USED-CAR RENOVATOR (retail trade),
620.684-034, 05.10.04
USER SUPPORT ANALYST (profess. &
kin.), 032.262-010, 11.01.01
USER SUPPORT ANALYST SUPERVI-
SOR (profess. & kin.), 032.132-010,
11.01.01
USHER (amuse. & rec.), 344.677-014,
09.05.08
USHER, HEAD (amuse. & rec.),
344.137-010, 09.05.08
UTILITY CLERK (utilities), 239.367-034,
07.04.05
UTILITY WORKER (mfd. bldgs.),
869.684-074, 06.02.22
UTILITY WORKER, FILM PROCESS-
ING (photofinishing), 976.685-030,
06.04.19

UTILIZATION COORDINATOR (radio-tv
broad.), 169.167-078, 11.05.02
UTILIZATION ENGINEER (utilities),
007.061-034, 05.01.06
UTILIZATION-REVIEW COORDINA-
TOR (medical ser.), 079.267-010,
11.07.02
VACUUM CLEANER REPAIRER (any
industry), 723.381-014, 05.10.03
VALUE ENGINEER (aircraft mfg.),
002.167-010, 05.01.06
VAN DRIVER (motor trans.),
905.663-018, 05.08.03
VARITYPE OPERATOR (clerical),
203.382-026, 07.06.02
VAULT CASHIER (business ser.),
222.137-050, 07.01.04
VAULT WORKER (business ser.),
222.587-058, 07.05.04
VECTOR CONTROL ASSISTANT
(government ser.), 049.364-014,
02.04.02
VENDING-MACHINE ATTENDANT
(hotel & rest.), 319.464-014, 09.04.01
VENDING-STAND SUPERVISOR
(government ser.), 185.167-066,
09.04.01
VENDOR (amuse. & rec.), 291.457-022,
08.03.01
VENTILATION EQUIPMENT TENDER
(any industry), 950.585-010, 05.06.02
VETERINARIAN (medical ser.),
073.101-010, 02.03.03
VETERINARY TECHNICIAN (medical
ser.), 079.361-014, 02.03.03
VICE PRESIDENT, FINANCIAL
INSTITUTION (financial),
186.117-078, 11.05.02
VIDEO OPERATOR (radio-tv broad.),
194.282-010, 05.03.05
VIDEOTAPE OPERATOR (radio-tv
broad.), 194.382-018, 05.03.05
VIOLIN MAKER, HAND (musical inst.),
730.281-046, 05.05.12
VOCATIONAL REHABILITATION
CONSULTANT (government ser.),
094.117-018, 11.07.03
VOCATIONAL REHABILITATION
COUNSELOR (government ser.),
045.107-042, 10.01.02
VOICE PATHOLOGIST (profess. & kin.),
076.104-010, 02.03.04
WAITER/WAITRESS (water trans.),
350.677-030, 09.05.02
WAITER/WAITRESS, BAR (hotel &
rest.), 311.477-018, 09.04.01
WAITER/WAITRESS, CAPTAIN (hotel &
rest.), 311.137-018, 09.01.03
WAITER/WAITRESS, FORMAL (hotel &
rest.), 311.477-026, 09.04.01
WAITER/WAITRESS, HEAD (hotel &
rest.), 311.137-022, 09.01.03
WAITER/WAITRESS, INFORMAL (hotel
& rest.), 311.477-030, 09.04.01
WAITER/WAITRESS, ROOM SERVICE
(hotel & rest.), 311.477-034, 09.05.02
WAITER/WAITRESS, TAKE OUT (hotel
& rest.), 311.477-038, 09.04.01

WARDROBE SUPERVISOR (amuse. &
rec.), 346.361-010, 09.05.07
WASHER, HAND (laundry & rel.),
361.687-030, 06.04.35
WASHER, MACHINE (laundry & rel.),
361.665-010, 06.04.35
WASTE-DISPOSAL ATTENDANT (any
industry), 955.383-010, 05.12.03
WASTE-MANAGEMENT ENGINEER,
RADIOACTIVE MATERIALS
(profess. & kin.), 005.061-042,
05.01.03
WASTE-TREATMENT OPERATOR
(chemical), 955.382-014, 06.02.11
WATER LEAK REPAIRER (auto. mfg.),
807.684-034, 06.03.02
WATER TENDER (any industry),
599.685-122, 05.12.06
WATER-SOFTENER SERVICER-AND-
INSTALLER (business ser.),
862.684-034, 05.10.01
WATER-TREATMENT-PLANT OPERA-
TOR (waterworks), 954.382-014,
05.06.04
WAX MOLDER (foundry), 549.685-038,
06.04.09
WAXER, FLOOR (any industry),
381.687-034, 05.12.18
WEATHER OBSERVER (profess. & kin.),
025.267-014, 02.04.01
WEAVER (nonmet. min.), 683.682-038,
06.02.06
WEB-PRESS OPERATOR (print. & pub.),
651.362-030, 05.05.13
WEDDING CONSULTANT (retail trade),
299.357-018, 08.02.06
WEIGHT-REDUCTION SPECIALIST
(personal ser.), 359.367-014, 09.05.01
WELDER, ARC (welding), 810.384-014,
05.05.06
WELDER, COMBINATION (welding),
819.384-010, 05.05.06
WELDER, EXPERIMENTAL (welding),
819.281-022, 05.05.06
WELDER, GAS (welding), 811.684-014,
05.05.06
WELDER, GUN (welding), 810.664-010,
06.04.31
WELDER, TACK (welding), 810.684-010,
05.10.01
WELDER-ASSEMBLER (machinery
mfg.), 819.381-010, 05.05.06
WELDER-FITTER (welding),
819.361-010, 05.05.06
WELDING ENGINEER (profess. & kin.),
011.061-026, 05.01.08
WELDING TECHNICIAN (profess. &
kin.), 011.261-014, 05.01.01
WELDING-MACHINE OPERATOR,
ARC (welding), 810.382-010, 06.02.19
WELDING-MACHINE OPERATOR,
GAS (welding), 811.482-010, 06.02.19
WHEEL LACER AND TRUER (motor-
bicycles), 706.684-106, 06.02.23
WHOLESALER I (wholesale tr.),
185.167-070, 11.05.04
WHOLESALER II (wholesale tr.),
185.157-018, 11.05.04

WIG DRESSER (fabrication, nec), 332.361-010, 01.06.02

WILDLIFE AGENT, REGIONAL (government ser.), 379.137-018, 04.01.02

WIND TUNNEL MECHANIC (aircraft mfg.), 869.261-026, 05.10.04

WIND-GENERATING-ELECTRIC-POWER INSTALLER (construction), 821.381-018, 05.05.05

WINDOW REPAIRER (any industry), 899.684-042, 05.12.12

WINE MAKER (beverage), 183.161-014, 05.02.03

WINE STEWARD/STEWARDESS (hotel & rest.), 310.357-010, 09.05.02

WIRE DRAWING MACHINE OPERATOR (inst. & app.), 614.382-018, 06.02.02

WIRE-TRANSFER CLERK (financial), 203.562-010, 07.06.02

WIRE-WRAPPING-MACHINE OPERATOR (electron. comp.), 726.682-014, 06.02.09

WIRER, CABLE (comm. equip.), 729.381-022, 05.10.03

WIREWORKER (elec. equip.), 728.684-022, 06.04.34

WOOD CAULKER (ship-boat mfg.), 843.384-010, 05.12.14

WOOD TECHNOLOGIST (profess. & kin.), 040.061-062, 02.02.02

WOODWORKING-SHOP HAND (woodworking), 769.687-054, 06.04.25

WORD PROCESSING MACHINE OPERATOR (clerical), 203.382-030, 07.06.02

WORK-STUDY COORDINATOR, SPECIAL EDUCATION (education), 094.107-010, 10.02.03

WRITER, PROSE, FICTION AND NONFICTION (profess. & kin.), 131.067-046, 01.01.02

WRITER, TECHNICAL PUBLICATIONS (profess. & kin.), 131.267-026, 11.08.02

X-RAY-EQUIPMENT TESTER (any industry), 729.281-046, 06.01.05

YARD CLERK (r.r. trans.), 209.367-054, 07.05.03

YARD LABORER (paper & pulp), 922.687-102, 05.12.03

YARN WINDER (tex. prod., nec), 681.685-154, 06.04.06

ZIPPER SETTER (any industry), 787.682-086, 06.02.05

ZOOLOGIST (profess. & kin.), 041.061-090, 02.02.01

Appendix B

Industry Groupings, Codes, and Abbreviations

One or more abbreviated industry name is listed in parentheses after each job title in *The Enhanced Guide for Occupational Exploration*. The full industry names corresponding to these abbreviations are listed in alphabetical order in the first part of this appendix. In the second part of this appendix, these industries are arranged under broad industry clusters derived from the Standard Industrial Classification system, along with the code numbers assigned to these industries by the Department of Labor. Use the second part of this appendix to find related industries or to find an industry that you have touble finding in the alphabetical listing.

Table of Abbreviations for Industry Designation

agric. equip. = Agricultural Equipment

agriculture = Agriculture and Agricultural Service

air trans. = Air Transportation

aircraft mfg. = Aircraft-Aerospace Manufacturing

amuse. & rec. = Amusement and Recreation

any industry = Any Industry

auto. mfg. = Automobile Manufacturing

automotive ser. = Automotive Services

bakery products = Bakery Products

beverage = Beverage

boot & shoe = Boot and Shoe

brick & tile = Brick, Tile, and Nonclay Refractories

build. mat., nec = Building Materials, Not Elsewhere Classified

business ser. = Business Services

button & notion = Button and Miscellaneous Notions

can. & preserv. = Canning and Preserving

carpet & rug = Carpet and Rug

cement = Cement

chemical = Chemical

clerical = Clerical and Kindred Occupations

clock & watch = Clocks, Watches, and Allied Products

comm. equip. = Radio, Television, and Communication Equipment

concrete prod. = Concrete Products

construction = Construction

cutlery-hrdwr. = Cutlery, Handtools, and Hardware

dairy products = Dairy Products

domestic ser. = Domestic Service

education = Education and Instruction

elec. equip. = Electrical Equipment

electron. comp. = Electronic Components and Accessories

electroplating = Electroplating

engine-turbine = Engine and Turbine

engraving = Engraving, Chasing, and Etching

fabrication, nec = Misc Fabricated Prods, Not Elsewhere Classified

financial = Financial Institutions

fishing & hunt. = Fishing, Hunting, and Trapping

food prep., nec = Food Preparations and Food Specialties, Not Elsewhere Classified

forestry = Forestry

forging = Forging

foundry = Foundry

fur goods = Fur Goods

furniture = Furniture and Fixtures

galvanizing = Galvanizing and Other Coatings

garment = Garment

glass mfg. = Glass Manufacturing

glass products = Glass Products

glove & mit. = Glove and Mitten

government ser. = Government Services

grain-feed mills = Grain and Feed Milling

hat & cap = Hat and Cap

heat treating = Heat Treating

hotel & rest. = Hotel and Restaurant

house. appl. = Household Appliances

inst. & app. = Instruments and Apparatus

insurance = Insurance

jewelry-silver. = Jewelry, Silverware, and Plated Ware

knitting = Knitting

laundry & rel. = Laundry, Cleaning, Dyeing, and Pressing

leather mfg. = Leather Manufacturing

leather prod. = Leather Products

library = Library

light. fix. = Lighting Fixtures

logging = Logging

machine shop = Machine Shop

machine tools = Machine Tool and Accessories

machinery mfg. = Machinery Manufacturing

meat products = Meat Products

medical ser. = Medical Services

metal prod., nec = Fabricated Metal Prods, Not Elsewhere Classified

mfd. bldgs. = Manufactured Buildings

military ser. = Military Services

millwork-plywood = Millwork, Veneer, Plywood, & Structrl Wood Membrs

mine & quarry = Mining and Quarrying

motion picture = Motion Picture

motor trans. = Motor Vehicle Transportation

motor-bicycles = Motorcycles, Bicycles, and Parts

museums = Museums, Art Galleries, & Botan & Zoolog Gardens

musical inst. = Musical Instruments and Parts

narrow fabrics = Narrow Fabrics

nonfer. metal = Nonferrous Metal Alloys and Primary Products

nonmet. min. = Abrasive, Asbestos, & Misc Nonmetal Mineral Prods

nonprofit org. = Nonprofit, Membership, Charitable, & Relig Orgs

nut & bolt = Screw Mach Prods; Bolts, Nuts, Screws, Rivets, & Washers

office machines = Office, Computing, and Accounting Machines

oils & grease = Animal and Vegetable Oils, Fats, and Grease

optical goods = Optical Goods

ordnance = Ord & Accessories, Except Vehs & Guided Missiles

paint & varnish = Paint and Varnish

paper & pulp = Paper and Pulp

paper goods = Paper Goods

pen & pencil = Pen, Pencil, Marking Device, & Artists' Materials

personal ser. = Personal Service

petrol. & gas = Petroleum and Natural Gas Production

petrol. refin. = Petroleum Refining

pharmaceut. = Pharmaceuticals and Related Products

photo. appar. = Photographic Apparatus and Materials

photofinishing = Photofinishing

pipe lines = Pipe Lines

plastic prod. = Fabricated Plastic Products

plastic-synth. = Plastic and Synthetic Materials

plumbing-heat. = Plumbing and Heating Supplies

pottery & porc. = Pottery and Porcelain Ware

print. & pub. = Printing and Publishing

profess. & kin. = Professional and Kindred Occupations

protective dev. = Personal Protective & Medical Devices & Supplies

r.r. trans. = Railroad Transportation

radio-tv broad. = Radio and Television Broadcasting

railroad equip. = Railroad Equipment Building and Repairing

real estate = Real Estate

recording = Recording

retail trade = Retail Trade

rubber goods = Rubber Goods

rubber reclaim. = Rubber Reclaiming

rubber tire = Rubber Tire and Tube

sanitary ser. = Sanitary Services

saw. & plan. = Sawmill and Planing Mill

ship-boat mfg. = Ship and Boat Manufacturing and Repairing

smelt. & refin. = Smelting and Refining

soap & rel. = Soap, Cleaning, and Toilet Preparation

social ser. = Social Services

steel & rel. = Blast Furnace, Steelwork, & Rollng/Finishng Mills

stonework = Stonework

struct. metal = Structural and Ornamental Metal Products

sugar & conf. = Sugar and Confectionery Products

svc. ind. mach. = Servicing Industrial Machines

tel. & tel. = Telephone and Telegraph

tex. prod., nec = Textile Products, Not Elsewhere Classified

textile = Textile

tinware = Tinware and Other Metal Cans and Containers

tobacco = Tobacco

toy-sport equip. = Toys, Games, and Sports Equipment

utilities = Utilities (Light, Heat, and Power)

vehicles, nec = Miscellaneous Vehicles & Transportation Equipment, Not Elsewhere Classified

water trans. = Water Transportation

waterworks = Waterworks

welding = Welding and Related Processes

wholesale tr. = Wholesale Trade

wood prod., nec = Wood Products, Not Elsewhere Classified

wood. container = Wooden Container

woodworking = Woodworking

List of Industries Within Related Clusters

Agriculture, Forestry, and Fishing

116	Agriculture
381	Fisheries
387	Forestry
457	Hunting and Trapping

Mining and Construction

271	Construction
568	Manufactured Buildings
575	Minerals and Earths
578	Mining and Quarrying
677	Petroleum Production

Tobacco, Food, & Related Products

164	Bakery Products
214	Canning and Preserving
234	Cereals
239	Chewing Gum
241	Chocolate and Cocoa
268	Confectionaries
283	Corn Products
313	Dairy Products
317	Distilled Liquors
383	Flavoring Extract and Syrup
385	Food Preparation, n.e.c.
427	Grain and Feed Mills
431	Grease and Tallow
459	Ice
554	Macaroni and Related Products
567	Malt Liquors
639	Nut Processing
646	Oils and Fats
812	Salt Production
831	Slaughtering and Meat Packing
851	Sugar
881	Tabacco
931	Vinous Liquors

Textiles, Leather, Clothing, & Related

176	Boot and Shoe
222	Canvas Goods
226	Carpet and Rug
254	Coated Fabrics

279	Cords and Twine
366	Fabricated Products, n.e.c.
369	Felt Goods
399	Fur Goods
409	Garments
419	Gloves and Mittens
441	Hat and Cap
449	Hosiery
455	Household Furniture
494	Knit Goods
518	Leather Manufacturing
522	Leather Products
615	Narrow Fabrics
871	Textile Bags
873	Textile Products, n.e.c.
875	Textiles
887	Trimming and Embroidery
939	Waste and Batting

Lumber and Wood Products

169	Basketry
185	Building Board
275	Cooperage
281	Cork Products
354	Excelsior
384	Floor Coverings, n.e.c.
514	Lasts and Related Forms
544	Logging
568	Manufactured Buildings
583	Mirror and Picture Frames
689	Planing Mills
817	Sawmills
927	Veneer and Plywood
957	Wooden Boxes
962	Wood Preserving
964	Woodworking

Furniture and Fixtures

401	Furniture
437	Hardware
571	Mattresses and Bedsprings
951	Window Shades and Fixtures
964	Woodworking

Paper, Printing, & Related Products

369	Felt Goods
661	Paper and Pulp

664	Paper Goods
699	Printing and Publishing
937	Wallpaper

Chemicals and Allied Products

174	Bone, Carbon, and Lampblack
237	Chemicals
253	Coal Tar Products
261	Compressed and Liquified Gases
323	Drug Preparations and Related Products
357	Explosives
379	Fireworks
421	Glue
657	Paint and Varnish
835	Soap
858	Synthetic Fibers
891	Turpentine and Rosin
959	Wood Distilling and Charcoal

Petroleum Refining and Related Industries

261	Compressed and Liquified Gases
395	Fuel Briquettes
431	Grease and Tallow
646	Oils and Fats
679	Petroleum Refineries

Rubber and Plastic Products

364	Fabricated Plastics Products
384	Floor Coverings, n.e.c.
691	Plastics Material
754	Rubber Goods
756	Rubber Reclamation
761	Rubber Tires and Tubes

Stone, Clay, Glass, and Concrete Products

114	Abrasive and Polishing Products
145	Asbestos Products
178	Brick and Tile
186	Building Materials, n.e.c.
231	Cement

264 Concrete Products
384 Floor Coverings, n.e.c.
411 Glass Manufacturing
415 Glass Products
429 Graphite
484 Jewelry
537 Lime
575 Minerals and Earths
581 Mirrors
685 Pipe and Boiler Coverings
696 Pottery and Porcelain
843 Statue and Art Goods
845 Stonework

Metal Refining & Working

131 Ammunition
172 Boilermaking
258 Coke Products
294 Cutlery and Tools
345 Electroplating
352 Engraving
362 Fabricated Metal Products, n.e.c.
377 Firearms
391 Forging
393 Foundries
405 Galvanizing
423 Gold Leaf and Foil
437 Hardware
444 Heat Treating
469 Insulated Wire
475 Iron and Steel
484 Jewelry
561 Machine Shop
609 Nails
632 Nonferrous Metal Alloys
636 Nuts and Bolts
651 Ordnance
654 Ore Dressing, Smelting, and Refining
693 Plumbers' Supplies
839 Springs
847 Structural and Ornamental Metalwork
877 Tinware
945 Welding
953 Wire
955 Wirework

Business and Industrial Machinery

121 Agricultural Equipment
166 Balances and Scales

255 Coin Machines
351 Engine and Turbine
557 Machinery Manufacturing
563 Machine Tool and Accessories
644 Office Machines
735 Refrigeration Equipment
894 Type Founding

Electronic/Electrical Equipment

341 Electrical Equipment
343 Electronics
529 Lighting Fixtures
681 Phonographs

Transportation Equipment

123 Aircraft-Aerospace Manu-facturing
151 Automobile Manufacturing
542 Locomotive and Car Building and Repair
592 Motorcycles and Bicycles
824 Ship and Boat Building and Repairs
885 Transportation Equipment

Measuring, Analyzing and Controlling Instruments

166 Balances and Scales
251 Clock and Watch
466 Instruments and Appliances
648 Optical Goods
673 Personal Protection and Medical Devices
683 Photographic Apparatus
829 Silverware

Miscellaneous Manufactur-ing Industries

141 Artificial Flowers
184 Brush and Broom
191 Buttons
218 Candles
366 Fabricated Products, n.e.c.
397 Fur Dressing
434 Hairwork
466 Instruments and Appliances
486 Jewelry Cases
569 Matches
583 Mirror and Picture Frames
585 Models and Patterns

587 Mortuary Goods
595 Musical Instruments
617 Needles, Pins, and Related Products
671 Pens and Pencils
827 Signs
833 Smoking Pipes
837 Sports Equipment
883 Toys and Games
924 Umbrellas

Transportation Services

125 Air Transportation
154 Automobile Services
542 Locomotive and Car Building and Repair
593 Motor Transportation
687 Pipe Lines
751 Railroad Transportation
941 Water Transportation

Communications

699 Printing and Publishing
724 Radio and TV Broadcasting
869 Telegraph and Telephone

Electric, Gas, and Sanitary Services

532 Light, Heat and Power
815 Sanitary Services
943 Waterworks

Trade

741 Retail Trade
948 Wholesale Trade

Finance, Insurance, and Real Estate

375 Financial Institutions
473 Insurance
731 Real Estate

Services

133 Amusement and Recreation
187 Business Services
247 Cleaning, Dyeing, and Pressing
249 Clerical
319 Domestic Service
335 Education
453 Hotel and Restaurant

516 Laundry
524 Library
573 Medical Services
589 Motion Pictures
597 Museums
634 Nonprofit Organizations
674 Personal Service
684 Photofinishing
836 Social Services

Government and Military Services

335 Education
425 Government Services
574 Military Services

Appendix C
2,800 Occupations Within Major Industries

One way to find a job is to select an industry in which you would like to work, then look for a job that you would enjoy in that industry. You may already have valuable knowledge or experience in one industry. Or you may prefer to work for a specific local company, in a fast-growing industry, or in an industry which is known to offer good benefits. This appendix organizes all the occupations in *The Enhanced Guide for Occupational Exploration* under the industry where the occupation is most likely to be found. Use the GOE number preceding each occupation to look up its description in this book. The number following the title is its DOT number, which may be useful if you use other sources of information.

Abrasive, Asbestos, and Miscellaneous Nonmetallic Mineral Products

06.01.02 LOOM FIXER (683.260-018)
06.02.06 WEAVER (683.682-038)
06.02.30 CASTER (575.684-018)
06.02.30 PLASTER MAKER (779.684-046)
06.04.06 BEAM-WARPER TENDER, AUTOMATIC (681.685-018)

Agricultural Equipment

05.03.07 TEST TECHNICIAN (019.261-022)
05.05.09 FARM-EQUIPMENT MECHANIC I (624.281-010)

Agriculture and Agricultural Service

02.04.02 BIOLOGICAL AIDE (049.364-018)
03.01.01 FARMER, FIELD CROP (404.161-010)
03.01.01 FARMER, FRUIT CROPS, BUSH AND VINE (403.161-014)
03.01.01 FARMER, GENERAL (421.161-010)

03.01.01 GENERAL MANAGER, FARM (180.167-018)
03.01.01 GROUP LEADER (180.167-022)
03.01.01 MANAGER, DAIRY FARM (180.167-026)
03.01.01 MIGRANT LEADER (180.167-050)
03.01.02 BEEKEEPER (413.161-010)
03.01.03 HORTICULTURAL-SPECIALTY GROWER, FIELD (405.161-014)
03.01.03 LANDSCAPE GARDENER (408.161-010)
03.01.03 MANAGER, NURSERY (180.167-042)
03.01.03 TREE SURGEON (408.181-010)
03.03.02 HORSESHOER (418.381-010)
03.04.01 FARM-MACHINE OPERATOR (409.683-010)
03.04.01 FARMWORKER, DIVERSIFIED CROPS I (407.663-010)
03.04.01 FARMWORKER, FRUIT I (403.683-010)
03.04.01 FARMWORKER, GENERAL II (421.687-010)
03.04.01 FARMWORKER, LIVESTOCK (410.664-010)
03.04.01 FARMWORKER, VEGETABLE II (402.687-010)
03.04.01 PACKER, AGRICULTURAL PRODUCE (920.687-134)
03.04.04 HORTICULTURAL WORKER I (405.684-014)
03.04.04 HORTICULTURAL WORKER II (405.687-014)
03.04.04 LABORER, LANDSCAPE (408.687-014)

03.04.05 IRRIGATOR, SPRINKLING SYSTEM
(409.685-014)
03.04.05 PLANT-CARE WORKER (408.364-010)
03.04.05 TREE PRUNER (408.684-018)
05.04.01 AIRPLANE PILOT (196.263-010)
06.04.21 SEED PELLETER (599.685-126)
06.04.28 POULTRY DRESSER (525.687-070)

Air Transportation

04.02.02 AIRLINE SECURITY REPRESENTATIVE
(372.667-010)
05.03.01 NAVIGATOR (196.167-014)
05.03.03 DISPATCHER (912.167-010)
05.03.06 FLIGHT ENGINEER (621.261-018)
05.04.01 AIRPLANE PILOT, COMMERCIAL
(196.263-014)
05.04.01 INSTRUCTOR, PILOT (196.223-014)
05.05.05 ELECTRICIAN, AIRCRAFT (825.261-018)
05.05.06 AIRCRAFT BODY REPAIRER (807.261-010)
05.05.09 AIRFRAME-AND-POWER-PLANT
MECHANIC (621.281-014)
05.05.09 AIRFRAME-AND-POWER-PLANT-
MECHANIC APPRENTICE (621.281-018)
05.05.10 AVIONICS TECHNICIAN (823.261-026)
05.07.02 AIRPLANE INSPECTOR (621.261-010)
05.08.04 DOCK HAND (919.683-010)
05.09.01 CARGO AGENT (248.367-018)
05.10.04 AIRPORT ATTENDANT (912.364-010)
05.10.07 PAINTER, TRANSPORTATION EQUIPMENT
(845.381-014)
05.12.06 AIRPORT UTILITY WORKER (912.663-010)
07.02.04 TICKETING CLERK (248.382-010)
07.04.03 RESERVATIONS AGENT (238.367-018)
07.04.05 AIRLINE-RADIO OPERATOR (193.262-010)
07.04.05 FLIGHT-INFORMATION EXPEDITER
(912.367-010)
07.05.01 CREW SCHEDULER (215.362-010)
07.05.01 SENIOR RESERVATIONS AGENT
(238.137-014)
07.05.01 TRANSPORTATION AGENT (912.367-014)
08.01.02 TRAFFIC AGENT (252.257-010)
09.01.04 AIRPLANE-FLIGHT ATTENDANT
(352.367-010)
09.05.03 PORTER (357.677-010)
11.05.01 MANAGER, AIRPORT (184.117-026)
11.05.02 MANAGER, OPERATIONS (184.117-050)
11.05.02 MANAGER, SCHEDULE PLANNING
(184.117-058)
11.12.01 GENERAL CLAIMS AGENT (186.117-030)

Aircraft-Aerospace Manufacturing

02.04.01 CALIBRATION LABORATORY TECHNI-
CIAN (019.281-010)
05.01.01 AERODYNAMICIST (002.061-010)
05.01.01 AERONAUTICAL-RESEARCH ENGINEER
(002.061-026)
05.01.04 AERONAUTICAL TEST ENGINEER
(002.061-018)

05.01.04 FIELD-SERVICE ENGINEER (002.167-014)
05.01.04 RESEARCH MECHANIC (002.261-014)
05.01.04 STRESS ANALYST (002.061-030)
05.01.05 SALES ENGINEER, AERONAUTICAL
PRODUCTS (002.151-010)
05.01.06 LIAISON ENGINEER (012.167-038)
05.01.06 VALUE ENGINEER (002.167-010)
05.01.07 AERONAUTICAL ENGINEER (002.061-014)
05.01.07 AERONAUTICAL-DESIGN ENGINEER
(002.061-022)
05.01.07 TOOL DESIGN CHECKER (007.267-014)
05.03.02 DRAFTER, AERONAUTICAL (002.261-010)
05.03.03 MATERIAL SCHEDULER (012.167-082)
05.03.05 FLIGHT-TEST DATA ACQUISITION TECH-
NICIAN (002.262-010)
05.05.05 ELECTRICIAN, AIRCRAFT (825.261-018)
05.05.07 ROCKET-MOTOR MECHANIC (693.261-022)
05.05.09 AIRFRAME-AND-POWER-PLANT ME-
CHANIC (621.281-014)
05.05.09 EXPERIMENTAL AIRCRAFT MECHANIC
(621.261-022)
05.05.09 ROCKET-ENGINE-COMPONENT
MECHANIC (621.281-030)
05.05.10 AVIONICS TECHNICIAN (823.261-026)
05.10.04 WIND TUNNEL MECHANIC (869.261-026)
05.10.07 PAINTER, TRANSPORTATION EQUIPMENT
(845.381-014)
06.01.03 RIVETING MACHINE OPERATOR, AUTO-
MATIC (806.380-010)
06.01.04 ASSEMBLER, ELECTROMECHANICAL
(828.381-018)
06.01.04 DEVELOPMENT MECHANIC (693.261-014)
06.01.04 INSTALLER, INTERIOR ASSEMBLIES
(806.381-078)
06.01.04 MOLDER (518.361-010)
06.01.04 PLASTICS FABRICATOR (754.381-018)
06.01.04 TEST EQUIPMENT MECHANIC
(710.361-014)
06.01.04 TOOL BUILDER (693.281-030)
06.01.05 INSPECTOR, ASSEMBLIES AND INSTAL-
LATIONS (806.261-030)
06.01.05 INSPECTOR, MATERIAL DISPOSITION
(806.261-034)
06.01.05 INSPECTOR, OUTSIDE PRODUCTION
(806.261-042)
06.01.05 INSPECTOR, PLASTICS AND COMPOSITES
(806.261-046)
06.01.05 INSPECTOR, PROCESSING (806.381-074)
06.01.05 OPERATIONAL TEST MECHANIC
(806.261-050)
06.02.02 DROPHAMMER OPERATOR (610.362-010)
06.02.09 AUTOMATED CUTTING MACHINE OPERA-
TOR (699.362-010)
06.02.09 FLUID JET CUTTER OPERATOR
(699.382-010)
06.02.09 NUMERICAL-CONTROL ROUTER OPERA-
TOR (605.382-046)
06.02.09 ROBOTIC MACHINE OPERATOR
(606.382-026)
06.02.18 AUTOCLAVE OPERATOR (553.362-014)
06.02.22 ASSEMBLER, SUBASSEMBLY
(806.384-034)

06.02.23 ELECTRICAL ASSEMBLER (729.384-026)
06.02.24 ASSEMBLER, METAL BONDING (806.384-030)
06.02.24 PRESSURE SEALER-AND-TESTER (806.384-038)
06.02.24 ROUTER OPERATOR, HAND (806.684-150)
06.02.32 BONDED STRUCTURES REPAIRER (807.381-014)
06.03.01 INSPECTOR, RECEIVING (222.384-010)

Amusement and Recreation

01.02.02 QUICK SKETCH ARTIST (149.041-010)
01.02.03 SET DESIGNER (142.061-050)
01.03.01 DIRECTOR, STAGE (150.067-010)
01.03.01 MANAGER, STAGE (159.167-018)
01.03.01 PRODUCER (187.167-178)
01.03.01 SUPERVISOR, SHOW OPERATIONS (969.137-014)
01.03.02 ACTOR (150.047-010)
01.03.02 CLOWN (159.047-010)
01.03.02 COMEDIAN (159.047-014)
01.03.02 IMPERSONATOR (159.047-018)
01.03.02 PUPPETEER (159.041-014)
01.03.03 PROGRAM COORDINATOR (139.167-010)
01.04.01 ARTIST AND REPERTOIRE MANAGER (159.167-010)
01.04.02 PROMPTER (152.367-010)
01.04.03 SINGER (152.047-022)
01.04.04 MUSICIAN, INSTRUMENTAL (152.041-010)
01.05.02 DANCER (151.047-010)
01.06.02 MAKE-UP ARTIST (333.071-010)
01.06.02 PROP MAKER (962.281-010)
01.06.02 SPECIAL EFFECTS SPECIALIST (962.281-018)
01.07.02 ANNOUNCER (159.347-010)
01.07.02 RING CONDUCTOR (159.367-010)
01.07.03 AMUSEMENT PARK ENTERTAINER (159.647-010)
01.08.01 EXTRA (159.647-014)
03.03.01 ANIMAL TRAINER (159.224-010)
03.03.01 EXERCISER, HORSE (153.674-010)
03.03.02 ANIMAL KEEPER (412.674-010)
03.03.02 ANIMAL KEEPER, HEAD (412.137-010)
03.03.02 AQUARIST (449.674-010)
04.02.03 BEACH LIFEGUARD (379.364-014)
04.02.03 BOUNCER (376.667-010)
04.02.03 LIFEGUARD (379.667-014)
04.02.03 SKI PATROLLER (379.664-010)
05.02.07 MANAGER, MARINA DRY DOCK (187.167-226)
05.09.01 CUSTODIAN, ATHLETIC EQUIPMENT (969.367-010)
05.10.01 GRIP (962.684-014)
05.10.02 RIDE OPERATOR (342.663-010)
05.10.03 ELECTRIC-GOLF-CART REPAIRER (620.261-026)
05.10.03 SIGHT-EFFECTS SPECIALIST (962.267-010)
05.10.03 SOUND CONTROLLER (194.262-014)
05.10.04 STAGE TECHNICIAN (962.261-014)

05.10.05 MOTION-PICTURE PROJECTIONIST (960.362-010)
05.10.05 PHOTOGRAPHER, FINISH (143.382-014)
05.12.16 LIGHTING-EQUIPMENT OPERATOR (962.381-014)
05.12.16 PROP ATTENDANT (962.684-022)
05.12.18 ATTENDANT, CAMPGROUND (329.683-010)
05.12.18 GOLF-RANGE ATTENDANT (341.683-010)
07.02.02 SUPERVISOR, MONEY-ROOM (211.137-018)
07.03.01 CASHIER, GAMBLING (211.462-022)
07.03.01 CHANGE PERSON (211.467-034)
07.03.01 INFORMATION CLERK-CASHIER (249.467-010)
07.03.01 PARIMUTUEL-TICKET CASHIER (211.467-018)
07.03.01 PARIMUTUEL-TICKET SELLER (211.467-022)
07.04.03 RECREATION-FACILITY ATTENDANT (341.367-010)
07.04.05 SCOREBOARD OPERATOR (349.665-010)
07.05.02 PARIMUTUEL-TICKET CHECKER (219.587-010)
07.07.02 MONEY COUNTER (211.467-014)
08.02.08 GROUP-SALES REPRESENTATIVE (259.357-010)
08.03.01 PHOTOGRAPHER (143.457-010)
08.03.01 VENDOR (291.457-022)
09.01.01 AMUSEMENT PARK WORKER (349.664-010)
09.01.01 COUNSELOR, CAMP (159.124-010)
09.01.01 GUIDE, HUNTING AND FISHING (353.161-010)
09.01.02 GUIDE, SIGHTSEEING (353.363-010)
09.04.02 ATTENDANT, ARCADE (342.667-014)
09.04.02 BOAT-RENTAL CLERK (295.467-014)
09.04.02 FLOOR ATTENDANT (343.467-014)
09.04.02 GAMBLING DEALER (343.464-010)
09.04.02 GAME ATTENDANT (342.657-014)
09.05.04 DRIVE-IN THEATER ATTENDANT (349.673-010)
09.05.05 BOARD ATTENDANT (249.587-010)
09.05.05 CARDROOM ATTENDANT II (343.577-010)
09.05.06 CADDIE (341.677-010)
09.05.06 DRESSER (346.674-010)
09.05.07 WARDROBE SUPERVISOR (346.361-010)
09.05.08 CHILDREN'S ATTENDANT (349.677-018)
09.05.08 RIDE ATTENDANT (342.677-010)
09.05.08 SKI-TOW OPERATOR (341.665-010)
09.05.08 TICKET TAKER (344.667-010)
09.05.08 USHER (344.677-014)
09.05.08 USHER, HEAD (344.137-010)
10.02.02 ATHLETIC TRAINER (153.224-010)
10.02.02 INSTRUCTOR, PHYSICAL (153.227-014)
11.06.03 BOOKMAKER (187.167-014)
11.06.04 TICKET BROKER (259.357-034)
11.11.02 MANAGER, BOWLING ALLEY (187.167-222)
11.11.02 MANAGER, GOLF CLUB (187.167-114)
11.11.02 MANAGER, POOL (153.137-010)
11.11.02 MANAGER, RECREATION ESTABLISHMENT (187.117-042)

11.11.02 MANAGER, RECREATION FACILITY (187.167-230)
11.11.02 MANAGER, THEATER (187.167-154)
11.11.04 GENERAL MANAGER, ROAD PRODUC-TION (187.117-034)
11.11.04 MANAGER, TOURING PRODUCTION (191.117-038)
11.12.03 ADVANCE AGENT (191.167-010)
11.12.03 ARTIST'S MANAGER (191.117-010)
11.12.03 BOOKING MANAGER (191.117-014)
11.12.03 BUSINESS MANAGER (191.117-018)
11.12.03 CIRCUS AGENT (191.117-022)
11.12.03 JOCKEY AGENT (191.117-026)
11.12.03 MANAGER, ATHLETE (153.117-014)
12.01.01 HEAD COACH (153.117-010)
12.01.01 INSTRUCTOR, SPORTS (153.227-018)
12.01.01 SCOUT, PROFESSIONAL SPORTS (153.117-018)
12.01.02 CHARTER (249.367-018)
12.01.02 FLAGGER (372.667-026)
12.01.02 GOLF-COURSE RANGER (379.667-010)
12.01.02 UMPIRE (153.267-018)
12.02.01 ACROBAT (159.247-010)
12.02.01 AERIALIST (159.247-014)
12.02.01 AQUATIC PERFORMER (159.347-014)
12.02.01 EQUESTRIAN (159.344-010)
12.02.01 JUGGLER (159.341-010)
12.02.01 RODEO PERFORMER (159.344-014)
12.02.01 SHOW-HORSE DRIVER (159.344-018)
12.02.01 STUNT PERFORMER (159.341-014)

Any Industry

01.04.02 COPYIST (152.267-010)
01.06.01 SILK-SCREEN CUTTER (979.681-022)
01.06.02 CLAY MODELER (779.281-010)
01.06.02 DECORATOR (298.381-010)
01.06.02 MODEL MAKER I (777.261-010)
01.06.02 REPAIRER, ART OBJECTS (779.381-018)
01.06.03 GILDER (749.381-010)
01.06.03 PAINTER, AIRBRUSH (741.684-018)
01.06.03 PAINTER, HAND (970.381-022)
01.06.03 PAINTER, SIGN (970.381-026)
01.06.03 SIGN WRITER, HAND (970.281-022)
01.06.03 STRIPER, HAND (740.484-010)
01.08.01 MODEL, ARTISTS' (961.667-010)
02.04.01 DECONTAMINATOR (199.384-010)
02.04.01 LABORATORY TESTER (029.261-010)
02.04.02 FOOD TESTER (029.361-014)
03.03.02 ANIMAL CARETAKER (410.674-010)
03.03.02 STABLE ATTENDANT (410.674-022)
03.04.01 LIVESTOCK-YARD ATTENDANT (410.674-018)
03.04.04 GREENSKEEPER I (406.137-010)
03.04.04 GREENSKEEPER II (406.683-010)
03.04.04 GROUNDSKEEPER, INDUSTRIAL-COMMERCIAL (406.684-014)
04.01.01 FIRE MARSHAL (373.167-018)
04.01.01 GUARD, CHIEF (372.167-014)
04.02.02 DETECTIVE I (376.367-014)
04.02.02 FIRE INSPECTOR (373.367-010)

04.02.02 GATE GUARD (372.667-030)
04.02.02 GUARD, SECURITY (372.667-034)
04.02.04 FIRE FIGHTER (373.364-010)
05.01.01 DIRECTOR, RESEARCH AND DEVELOP-MENT (189.117-014)
05.01.06 FACILITIES PLANNER (019.261-018)
05.01.06 PREVENTIVE MAINTENANCE COORDI-NATOR (169.167-074)
05.01.06 TOOL PLANNER (012.167-074)
05.01.06 TOOL PROGRAMMER, NUMERICAL CONTROL (007.167-018)
05.02.02 SUPERINTENDENT, BUILDING (187.167-190)
05.02.03 PRODUCTION SUPERINTENDENT (183.117-014)
05.03.04 PROSPECTOR (024.284-010)
05.03.05 RADIOGRAPHER (199.361-010)
05.03.05 RADIOTELEPHONE OPERATOR (193.262-034)
05.03.06 SUPERVISOR, VENDOR QUALITY (012.167-062)
05.05.02 CARPENTER, MAINTENANCE (860.281-010)
05.05.02 SUPERINTENDENT, MAINTENANCE (189.167-046)
05.05.05 ANTENNA INSTALLER, SATELLITE COMMUNICATIONS (823.261-022)
05.05.05 DATA COMMUNICATIONS TECHNICIAN (823.261-030)
05.05.05 ELECTRICIAN, MAINTENANCE (829.261-018)
05.05.05 ELECTRONICS ASSEMBLER, DEVELOP-MENTAL (726.261-010)
05.05.05 ELEVATOR REPAIRER (825.281-030)
05.05.05 LINE MAINTAINER (821.261-014)
05.05.05 MAINTENANCE MECHANIC, TELEPHONE (822.281-018)
05.05.06 BOILERHOUSE MECHANIC (805.361-010)
05.05.06 FITTER I (801.261-014)
05.05.06 FORMER, HAND (619.361-010)
05.05.06 METAL FABRICATOR (619.361-014)
05.05.06 MILLWRIGHT (638.281-018)
05.05.06 SHEET-METAL WORKER (804.281-010)
05.05.07 FLUID-POWER MECHANIC (600.281-010)
05.05.07 GUNSMITH (632.281-010)
05.05.07 SAW FILER (701.381-014)
05.05.07 TOOL GRINDER I (701.381-018)
05.05.09 AUTOMOTIVE-MAINTENANCE-EQUIP-MENT SERVICER (620.281-018)
05.05.09 CASH-REGISTER SERVICER (633.281-010)
05.05.09 DIESEL MECHANIC (625.281-010)
05.05.09 FUEL-INJECTION SERVICER (625.281-022)
05.05.09 FURNACE INSTALLER-AND-REPAIRER, HOT AIR (869.281-010)
05.05.09 GAS-ENGINE REPAIRER (625.281-026)
05.05.09 GAS-WELDING-EQUIPMENT MECHANIC (626.381-014)
05.05.09 HYDRAULIC REPAIRER (638.281-034)
05.05.09 LOCKSMITH (709.281-010)
05.05.09 MACHINE REPAIRER, MAINTENANCE (638.261-030)

05.05.09 MAINTENANCE MECHANIC (638.281-014)
05.05.09 MAINTENANCE REPAIRER, INDUSTRIAL (899.261-014)
05.05.09 MECHANIC, INDUSTRIAL TRUCK (620.281-050)
05.05.09 OFFICE-MACHINE SERVICER (633.281-018)
05.05.09 PARTS SALVAGER (638.281-026)
05.05.09 PNEUMATIC-TOOL REPAIRER (630.281-010)
05.05.09 PUMP SERVICER (630.281-018)
05.05.09 REFRIGERATION MECHANIC (637.261-026)
05.05.09 SMALL-ENGINE MECHANIC (625.281-034)
05.05.09 SOLAR-ENERGY-SYSTEM INSTALLER (637.261-030)
05.05.10 AUDIO-VIDEO REPAIRER (729.281-010)
05.05.10 ELECTRIC-MOTOR REPAIRER (721.281-018)
05.05.10 ELECTRICAL-APPLIANCE SERVICER (827.261-010)
05.05.10 ELECTRICAL-INSTRUMENT REPAIRER (729.281-026)
05.05.10 ELECTRONICS MECHANIC (828.261-022)
05.05.10 INSTRUMENT MECHANIC (710.281-026)
05.05.10 METEOROLOGICAL-EQUIPMENT RE-PAIRER (823.281-018)
05.05.10 PUBLIC-ADDRESS SERVICER (823.261-010)
05.05.10 RADIO MECHANIC (823.261-018)
05.05.11 EXPERIMENTAL ASSEMBLER (739.381-026)
05.05.11 INSTRUMENT MAKER (600.280-010)
05.05.11 INSTRUMENT REPAIRER (710.261-010)
05.05.12 ELECTRONIC-ORGAN TECHNICIAN (828.261-010)
05.05.15 DRESSMAKER (785.361-010)
05.05.15 FURNITURE UPHOLSTERER (780.381-018)
05.05.17 TESTER, FOOD PRODUCTS (199.251-010)
05.06.01 GAS-ENGINE OPERATOR (950.382-018)
05.06.02 AIR-COMPRESSOR OPERATOR (950.685-010)
05.06.02 BOILER OPERATOR (950.382-010)
05.06.02 FUEL ATTENDANT (953.362-010)
05.06.02 GAS-COMPRESSOR OPERATOR (950.382-014)
05.06.02 REFRIGERATING ENGINEER (950.362-014)
05.06.02 STATIONARY ENGINEER (950.382-026)
05.06.02 VENTILATION EQUIPMENT TENDER (950.585-010)
05.06.03 PUMPER (914.682-010)
05.07.01 FIRE-EXTINGUISHER-SPRINKLER INSPECTOR (379.687-010)
05.07.01 ULTRASONIC TESTER (739.281-014)
05.07.03 ELEVATOR EXAMINER-AND-ADJUSTER (825.261-014)
05.08.01 DUMP-TRUCK DRIVER (902.683-010)
05.08.01 TRACTOR-TRAILER-TRUCK DRIVER (904.383-010)
05.08.01 TRUCK DRIVER, HEAVY (905.663-014)
05.08.01 TRUCK DRIVER, LIGHT (906.683-022)

05.08.04 MOTORBOAT OPERATOR (911.663-010)
05.09.01 LABORER, STORES (922.687-058)
05.10.01 BUILDING CLEANER (891.684-022)
05.10.01 CASTING REPAIRER (619.281-010)
05.10.01 DIVER (899.261-010)
05.10.01 FIXTURE REPAIRER-FABRICATOR (630.384-010)
05.10.01 LUGGAGE REPAIRER (365.361-010)
05.10.01 MAINTENANCE REPAIRER, BUILDING (899.381-010)
05.10.01 PUMP INSTALLER (630.684-018)
05.10.01 TEMPLATE MAKER, TRACK (809.484-014)
05.10.01 TORCH-STRAIGHTENER-AND-HEATER (709.684-086)
05.10.02 BICYCLE REPAIRER (639.681-010)
05.10.02 CONVEYOR-MAINTENANCE MECHANIC (630.381-010)
05.10.02 DOOR-CLOSER MECHANIC (630.381-014)
05.10.02 GAS-APPLIANCE SERVICER (637.261-018)
05.10.02 LUBRICATION-EQUIPMENT SERVICER (630.381-022)
05.10.02 METER REPAIRER (710.281-034)
05.10.02 SEWING-MACHINE REPAIRER (639.281-018)
05.10.03 ELECTRIC-TOOL REPAIRER (729.281-022)
05.10.03 ELECTRICAL-APPLIANCE REPAIRER (723.381-010)
05.10.03 TAPE-RECORDER REPAIRER (720.281-014)
05.10.03 TELEVISION INSTALLER (823.361-010)
05.10.03 TELEVISION-AND-RADIO REPAIRER (720.281-018)
05.10.03 TRANSFORMER REPAIRER (724.381-018)
05.10.03 VACUUM CLEANER REPAIRER (723.381-014)
05.10.04 DOLL REPAIRER (731.684-014)
05.10.04 EQUIPMENT INSTALLER (828.381-010)
05.10.04 EVAPORATIVE-COOLER INSTALLER (637.381-010)
05.10.04 FIRE-EXTINGUISHER REPAIRER (709.384-010)
05.10.04 HOUSEHOLD-APPLIANCE INSTALLER (827.661-010)
05.10.04 PINSETTER MECHANIC, AUTOMATIC (638.261-022)
05.10.04 SPORTS-EQUIPMENT REPAIRER (732.684-122)
05.10.04 SWIMMING-POOL SERVICER (891.684-018)
05.10.05 AUDIOVISUAL TECHNICIAN (960.382-010)
05.10.05 REPRODUCTION TECHNICIAN (976.361-010)
05.10.06 BLASTER (859.261-010)
05.10.08 COOK (315.361-010)
05.11.01 BULLDOZER OPERATOR I (850.683-010)
05.11.01 POWER-SHOVEL OPERATOR (850.683-030)
05.11.01 PROJECT-CREW WORKER (891.687-018)
05.11.02 CORE-DRILL OPERATOR (930.682-010)
05.11.04 DRAGLINE OPERATOR (850.683-018)
05.11.04 DUMP OPERATOR (921.685-038)
05.11.04 FRONT-END LOADER OPERATOR (921.683-042)
05.11.04 HOISTING ENGINEER (921.663-030)

05.11.04 OVERHEAD CRANE OPERATOR (921.663-010)

05.11.04 RIGGER (921.260-010)

05.11.04 TRACTOR OPERATOR (929.683-014)

05.12.02 SURVEYOR HELPER (869.567-010)

05.12.03 DUMPER (921.667-018)

05.12.03 MATERIAL HANDLER (929.687-030)

05.12.03 PRESS BUCKER (920.686-042)

05.12.03 WASTE-DISPOSAL ATTENDANT (955.383-010)

05.12.04 CONVEYOR-SYSTEM OPERATOR (921.662-018)

05.12.04 ELEVATOR OPERATOR, FREIGHT (921.683-038)

05.12.06 LOADER HELPER (914.687-014)

05.12.06 WATER TENDER (599.685-122)

05.12.08 GARAGE SERVICER, INDUSTRIAL (915.687-014)

05.12.08 OILER (699.687-018)

05.12.12 BILLPOSTER (299.667-010)

05.12.12 DECORATOR, STREET AND BUILDING (899.687-010)

05.12.12 WINDOW REPAIRER (899.684-042)

05.12.13 KEY CUTTER (709.684-050)

05.12.15 BELT REPAIRER (630.684-014)

05.12.15 ROLLER-SKATE REPAIRER (732.684-102)

05.12.16 ELECTRICAL-APPLIANCE PREPARER (827.584-010)

05.12.18 CHIMNEY SWEEP (891.687-010)

05.12.18 CLEANER II (919.687-014)

05.12.18 CLEANER, COMMERCIAL OR INSTITU-TIONAL (381.687-014)

05.12.18 CLEANER, HOUSEKEEPING (323.687-014)

05.12.18 CLEANER, INDUSTRIAL (381.687-018)

05.12.18 CLEANER, LABORATORY EQUIPMENT (381.687-022)

05.12.18 CLEANER, WINDOW (389.687-014)

05.12.18 FURNACE CLEANER (891.687-014)

05.12.18 JANITOR (382.664-010)

05.12.18 LAUNDRY WORKER I (361.684-014)

05.12.18 LIGHT-FIXTURE SERVICER (389.687-018)

05.12.18 SANDBLASTER (503.687-010)

05.12.18 SWEEPER-CLEANER, INDUSTRIAL (389.683-010)

05.12.18 TANK CLEANER (891.687-022)

05.12.18 TUBE CLEANER (891.687-030)

05.12.18 WAXER, FLOOR (381.687-034)

05.12.20 CROSSING TENDER (371.667-010)

06.01.02 MACHINE SETTER (616.360-022)

06.01.02 SETTER, AUTOMATIC-SPINNING LATHE (604.360-010)

06.01.03 MACHINE OPERATOR I (616.380-018)

06.01.04 TEMPLATE MAKER (601.381-038)

06.01.05 ELECTRONICS TESTER (726.261-018)

06.01.05 INSPECTOR, METAL FABRICATING (619.261-010)

06.01.05 X-RAY-EQUIPMENT TESTER (729.281-046)

06.02.01 TOOL GRINDER II (603.664-010)

06.02.02 BRAKE OPERATOR II (619.685-026)

06.02.02 CRIMPING-MACHINE OPERATOR (616.682-022)

06.02.02 POLISHING-MACHINE OPERATOR (603.682-026)

06.02.02 PRESS OPERATOR, HEAVY DUTY (617.260-010)

06.02.02 PUNCH-PRESS OPERATOR I (615.382-010)

06.02.02 PUNCH-PRESS OPERATOR III (615.682-014)

06.02.02 RIVETING-MACHINE OPERATOR I (699.482-010)

06.02.02 SHEAR OPERATOR I (615.682-018)

06.02.02 SPINNER, HAND (619.362-018)

06.02.02 STRAIGHTENING-PRESS OPERATOR II (617.482-026)

06.02.02 STRAIGHTENING-ROLL OPERATOR (613.662-022)

06.02.03 NAILING-MACHINE OPERATOR (669.682-058)

06.02.05 BINDER (787.682-010)

06.02.05 HEMMER (787.682-026)

06.02.05 MENDER (787.682-030)

06.02.05 ZIPPER SETTER (787.682-086)

06.02.09 CLOTH PRINTER (652.382-010)

06.02.09 CUTTER OPERATOR (699.682-018)

06.02.09 DIE CUTTER (699.682-022)

06.02.13 MIXING-MACHINE OPERATOR (550.382-022)

06.02.20 KICK-PRESS OPERATOR I (616.682-026)

06.02.20 STACKING-MACHINE OPERATOR I (692.682-054)

06.02.21 ANODIZER (500.682-010)

06.02.21 PAINT-SPRAYER OPERATOR, AUTOMATIC (599.382-010)

06.02.24 FABRICATOR-ASSEMBLER, METAL PRODUCTS (809.381-010)

06.02.24 REPAIRER, FINISHED METAL (809.684-034)

06.02.24 STRAIGHTENER, HAND (709.484-014)

06.02.27 CUTTER, HAND I (781.684-074)

06.02.29 RUBBER-GOODS REPAIRER (759.684-054)

06.02.30 GLASS CUTTER (775.684-022)

06.02.31 LAY-OUT WORKER II (809.381-014)

06.02.32 COIL WINDER, REPAIR (724.381-014)

06.03.01 COMPARATOR OPERATOR (699.384-010)

06.03.02 GARMENT INSPECTOR (789.687-070)

06.03.02 GLASS INSPECTOR (579.687-022)

06.03.02 HYDRO-PNEUMATIC TESTER (862.687-018)

06.03.02 METAL-FINISH INSPECTOR (703.687-014)

06.04.02 BENDING-MACHINE OPERATOR II (617.685-010)

06.04.02 BUFFING-MACHINE TENDER (603.665-010)

06.04.02 ELECTRIC-SEALING-MACHINE OPERA-TOR (690.685-154)

06.04.02 EMBOSSER (583.685-030)

06.04.02 GRAINER, MACHINE (652.686-014)

06.04.02 MACHINE OPERATOR II (619.685-062)

06.04.02 NIBBLER OPERATOR (615.685-026)

06.04.02 POWER-PRESS TENDER (617.685-026)

06.04.02 PUNCH-PRESS OPERATOR II (615.685-030)

06.04.02 TOOL DRESSER (601.682-010)

06.04.02 TURRET-PUNCH-PRESS OPERATOR, TAPE-CONTROL (615.685-042)

06.04.03 BUZZSAW OPERATOR (667.685-026)
06.04.04 CARTON-FORMING-MACHINE OPERATOR
    (641.685-022)
06.04.05 PRESSER, MACHINE (363.682-018)
06.04.05 SPREADER, MACHINE (781.685-010)
06.04.06 PICKING-MACHINE OPERATOR
    (680.685-082)
06.04.08 CRUSHER TENDER (570.685-022)
06.04.09 CUTTER, MACHINE II (699.685-014)
06.04.09 MACHINE FEEDER (699.686-010)
06.04.09 SCRAP HANDLER (509.685-050)
06.04.09 SILK-SCREEN PRINTER, MACHINE
    (979.685-010)
06.04.09 STAMPING-PRESS OPERATOR
    (652.682-030)
06.04.11 PAINT MIXER, MACHINE (550.485-018)
06.04.19 FILTER OPERATOR (551.685-078)
06.04.19 STILL TENDER (552.685-026)
06.04.20 STAPLING-MACHINE OPERATOR
    (692.685-202)
06.04.21 CERAMIC COATER, MACHINE
    (509.685-022)
06.04.21 DIPPER AND BAKER (599.685-030)
06.04.21 SPRAY-UNIT FEEDER (599.686-014)
06.04.22 ASSEMBLER, PRODUCTION (706.687-010)
06.04.22 NAILER, HAND (762.684-050)
06.04.23 ASSEMBLER, SMALL PRODUCTS I
    (706.684-022)
06.04.23 SILK-SCREEN-FRAME ASSEMBLER
    (709.484-010)
06.04.24 BUFFER I (705.684-014)
06.04.24 METAL FINISHER (705.684-034)
06.04.24 MOLD DRESSER (519.684-018)
06.04.24 POLISHER (705.684-058)
06.04.26 LABEL CODER (920.587-014)
06.04.27 BOW MAKER (789.684-010)
06.04.27 CANVAS REPAIRER (782.684-010)
06.04.27 SEWER, HAND (782.684-058)
06.04.27 THREAD CUTTER (789.684-050)
06.04.33 PAINTER, BRUSH (740.684-022)
06.04.33 PUTTY GLAZER (749.684-042)
06.04.34 DRILLER, HAND (809.684-018)
06.04.34 LABORER, GRINDING AND POLISHING
    (705.687-014)
06.04.34 MASKER (749.687-018)
06.04.34 PAINT MIXER, HAND (550.684-018)
06.04.34 SCREEN PRINTER (979.684-034)
06.04.35 PRESSER, HAND (363.684-018)
06.04.37 NAME-PLATE STAMPER (652.685-054)
06.04.37 STENCILER (920.687-178)
06.04.38 BANDER, HAND (929.687-058)
06.04.38 CRATER (920.684-010)
06.04.38 PACKAGER, HAND (920.587-018)
06.04.38 PACKAGER, MACHINE (920.685-078)
06.04.39 CLEANER AND POLISHER (709.687-010)
06.04.39 EQUIPMENT CLEANER (599.684-010)
06.04.39 MACHINE CLEANER (699.687-014)
06.04.40 CONVEYOR FEEDER-OFFBEARER
    (921.686-014)
06.04.40 INDUSTRIAL-TRUCK OPERATOR
    (921.683-050)

06.04.40 LOADER I (914.667-010)
06.04.40 PALLETIZER OPERATOR I (921.682-014)
07.01.02 ADMINISTRATIVE SECRETARY
    (169.167-014)
07.01.02 MANAGER, OFFICE (169.167-034)
07.01.02 SUPERVISOR, NETWORK CONTROL
    OPERATORS (031.132-010)
07.04.05 PROTECTIVE-SIGNAL OPERATOR
    (379.362-014)
07.05.03 ORDER DEPARTMENT SUPERVISOR
    (169.167-038)
07.06.01 NETWORK CONTROL OPERATOR
    (031.262-014)
08.02.08 MEMBERSHIP SOLICITOR (293.357-022)
08.02.08 TELEPHONE SOLICITOR (299.357-014)
09.01.01 HOST/HOSTESS (352.667-010)
09.01.02 EXHIBIT-DISPLAY REPRESENTATIVE
    (297.367-010)
09.01.02 GUIDE, ESTABLISHMENT (353.367-014)
09.01.02 GUIDE, PLANT (353.367-018)
09.03.02 CHAUFFEUR (913.663-010)
09.04.01 CANTEEN OPERATOR (311.674-010)
09.05.03 CHECKROOM ATTENDANT (358.677-010)
09.05.04 DOORKEEPER (324.677-014)
09.05.07 REST ROOM ATTENDANT (358.677-018)
09.05.08 ESCORT (353.667-010)
09.05.09 ELEVATOR OPERATOR (388.663-010)
10.03.02 FIRST-AID ATTENDANT (354.677-010)
10.03.03 ATTENDANT, CHILDREN'S INSTITUTION
    (359.677-010)
10.03.03 NURSERY SCHOOL ATTENDANT
    (359.677-018)
10.03.03 PLAYROOM ATTENDANT (359.677-026)
11.05.01 MANAGER, INDUSTRIAL ORGANIZATION
    (189.117-022)
11.05.01 PRESIDENT (189.117-026)
11.05.02 ADMINISTRATIVE ASSISTANT
    (169.167-010)
11.05.02 IMPORT-EXPORT AGENT (184.117-022)
11.05.02 MANAGEMENT TRAINEE (189.167-018)
11.05.02 MANAGER, BRANCH (183.117-010)
11.05.02 MANAGER, DEPARTMENT (189.167-022)
11.05.02 MANAGER, TRAFFIC (184.167-094)
11.05.02 SECURITY OFFICER (189.167-034)
11.05.02 SUPERINTENDENT, PLANT PROTECTION
    (189.167-050)
11.05.02 SUPERINTENDENT, TRANSPORTATION
    (184.167-226)
11.05.04 MANAGER, EXPORT (163.117-014)
11.05.04 MANAGER, SALES (163.167-018)
11.05.04 PROPERTY-DISPOSAL OFFICER
    (163.167-026)
11.06.03 APPRAISER (191.287-010)
11.06.03 MANAGER, CREDIT AND COLLECTION
    (169.167-086)
11.06.03 RISK AND INSURANCE MANAGER
    (186.117-066)
11.07.01 RESIDENCE SUPERVISOR (187.167-186)
11.09.01 MANAGER, ADVERTISING (164.117-010)
11.09.01 SALES-SERVICE PROMOTER (165.167-010)
11.10.03 INDUSTRIAL-SAFETY-AND-HEALTH
    TECHNICIAN (168.161-014)

11.10.03 SANITARIAN (529.137-014)
11.11.01 EXECUTIVE HOUSEKEEPER (187.167-046)
11.11.03 MANAGER, AUTOMOTIVE SERVICES
(184.117-034)
11.11.03 MANAGER, WAREHOUSE (184.167-114)
11.11.05 COMMISSARY MANAGER (185.167-010)
11.11.05 MANAGER, MACHINERY-OR-EQUIPMENT,
RENTAL AND LEASING (185.167-026)
11.11.05 SERVICE SUPERVISOR, LEASED MACHIN-
ERY AND EQUIPMENT (183.167-030)
11.12.02 RIGHT-OF-WAY AGENT (191.117-046)
11.12.04 CONTRACT ADMINISTRATOR
(162.117-014)

Automobile Manufacturing

02.04.01 LABORATORY TECHNICIAN (019.261-030)
05.01.08 AUTOMOTIVE ENGINEER (007.061-010)
05.03.02 AUTO-DESIGN CHECKER (017.261-010)
05.03.02 AUTO-DESIGN DETAILER (017.281-010)
05.03.02 DRAFTER, AUTOMOTIVE DESIGN
(017.261-042)
05.03.02 DRAFTER, AUTOMOTIVE DESIGN LAY-
OUT (017.281-026)
05.05.02 CUSTOM VAN CONVERTER (806.381-070)
06.01.01 QUALITY ASSURANCE SUPERVISOR
(806.137-022)
06.01.05 ROADABILITY-MACHINE OPERATOR
(806.383-010)
06.03.01 TEST DRIVER I (806.283-014)
06.03.02 QUALITY ASSURANCE GROUP LEADER
(806.367-014)
06.03.02 QUALITY ASSURANCE MONITOR
(806.367-018)
06.03.02 WATER LEAK REPAIRER (807.684-034)
06.04.22 ASSEMBLER, MOTOR VEHICLE
(806.684-010)
11.12.01 SERVICE REPRESENTATIVE (191.167-022)

Automotive Services

05.05.02 CUSTOM VAN CONVERTER (806.381-070)
05.05.06 AUTOMOBILE-BODY REPAIRER
(807.381-010)
05.05.06 SUPERVISOR, AUTOMOBILE BODY
REPAIR (807.137-010)
05.05.09 AIR-CONDITIONING MECHANIC
(620.281-010)
05.05.09 AUTOMOBILE MECHANIC (620.261-010)
05.05.09 AUTOMOBILE-SERVICE-STATION ME-
CHANIC (620.261-030)
05.05.09 AUTOMOTIVE-COOLING-SYSTEM DIAG-
NOSTIC TECHNICIAN (620.261-034)
05.05.09 MOTORCYCLE REPAIRER (620.281-054)
05.05.09 TRACTOR MECHANIC (620.281-058)
05.05.09 TUNE-UP MECHANIC (620.281-066)
05.05.10 ELECTRICIAN, AUTOMOTIVE
(825.281-022)
05.05.15 AUTOMOBILE UPHOLSTERER
(780.381-010)
05.07.01 SHOP ESTIMATOR (807.267-010)

05.07.02 AUTOMOBILE TESTER (620.261-014)
05.07.02 AUTOMOBILE-REPAIR-SERVICE ESTIMA-
TOR (620.261-018)
05.08.03 DELIVERER, CAR RENTAL (919.663-010)
05.08.03 TOW-TRUCK OPERATOR (919.663-026)
05.10.01 FRONT-END MECHANIC (620.281-038)
05.10.01 GLASS INSTALLER (865.684-010)
05.10.01 MUFFLER INSTALLER (807.664-010)
05.10.02 AUTOMOBILE-ACCESSORIES INSTALLER
(806.684-038)
05.10.02 AUTOMOBILE-RADIATOR MECHANIC
(620.381-010)
05.10.02 AUTOMOBILE-SERVICE-STATION ATTEN-
DANT (915.467-010)
05.10.02 BRAKE REPAIRER (620.281-026)
05.10.02 CARBURETOR MECHANIC (620.281-034)
05.10.02 NEW-CAR GET-READY MECHANIC
(806.361-026)
05.10.02 SERVICE MANAGER (185.167-058)
05.10.02 TRANSMISSION MECHANIC (620.281-062)
05.10.03 ELECTRIC-GOLF-CART REPAIRER
(620.261-026)
05.10.07 PAINTER, TRANSPORTATION EQUIPMENT
(845.381-014)
05.12.08 LUBRICATION SERVICER (915.687-018)
05.12.12 AUTOMOBILE-BODY-REPAIRER HELPER
(807.687-010)
05.12.15 TIRE REPAIRER (915.684-010)
05.12.18 AUTOMOBILE DETAILER (915.687-034)
05.12.18 STEAM CLEANER (915.687-026)
09.04.02 AUTOMOBILE RENTAL CLERK
(295.467-026)
09.04.02 PARKING-LOT ATTENDANT (915.473-010)
09.04.02 TRAILER-RENTAL CLERK (295.467-022)
11.11.05 MANAGER, VEHICLE LEASING AND
RENTAL (187.167-162)

Bakery Products

05.05.17 CAKE DECORATOR (524.381-010)
05.09.01 CHECKER, BAKERY PRODUCTS
(222.487-010)
06.02.15 BAKER (526.381-010)
06.02.15 CRACKER-AND-COOKIE-MACHINE
OPERATOR (520.682-034)
06.02.15 DOUGH MIXER (520.685-234)
06.02.15 DOUGHNUT-MACHINE OPERATOR
(526.682-022)
06.02.28 BENCH HAND (520.384-010)
06.02.28 DOUGHNUT MAKER (526.684-010)
06.04.15 BAKER HELPER (526.686-010)
06.04.15 BATTER MIXER (520.685-010)
06.04.15 OVEN OPERATOR, AUTOMATIC
(526.685-070)
06.04.28 DECORATOR (524.684-014)
11.05.01 MANAGER, BAKERY (189.117-046)

Beverage

05.02.03 BREWING DIRECTOR (183.167-010)
05.02.03 WINE MAKER (183.161-014)

06.02.15 SYRUP MAKER (520.485-026)
06.04.15 BREWERY CELLAR WORKER
    (522.685-014)
06.04.40 DISTILLERY WORKER, GENERAL
    (529.687-066)

Blast Furnace, Steel Work, and Rolling & Finishing Mill

02.04.01 LABORATORY ASSISTANT, METALLURGI-
    CAL (011.261-022)
06.01.03 ROLLING ATTENDANT (613.662-010)
06.02.10 COLD-MILL OPERATOR (613.662-018)
06.04.40 LABORER, GENERAL (509.687-026)

Boot and Shoe

06.02.05 STITCHER, STANDARD MACHINE
    (690.682-082)

Building Materials

06.02.18 ROOFING-MACHINE OPERATOR
    (554.682-022)

Business Services

04.01.01 MANAGER, INTERNAL SECURITY
    (376.137-010)
04.01.02 INVESTIGATOR, PRIVATE (376.267-018)
04.02.02 ARMORED-CAR GUARD (372.567-010)
04.02.02 ARMORED-CAR GUARD AND DRIVER
    (372.563-010)
04.02.02 SECURITY CONSULTANT (189.167-054)
04.02.04 ALARM INVESTIGATOR (376.367-010)
05.05.05 PROTECTIVE-SIGNAL INSTALLER
    (822.361-018)
05.05.05 PROTECTIVE-SIGNAL REPAIRER
    (822.361-022)
05.05.06 SAFE-AND-VAULT SERVICE MECHANIC
    (869.381-022)
05.08.03 COIN COLLECTOR (292.483-010)
05.08.03 TELEPHONE-DIRECTORY-DISTRIBUTOR
    DRIVER (906.683-018)
05.09.03 CHECKER, DUMP GROUNDS (219.367-010)
05.10.01 WATER-SOFTENER SERVICER-AND-
    INSTALLER (862.684-034)
05.10.02 MANAGER, CUSTOMER SERVICES
    (187.167-082)
05.10.05 MICROFILM PROCESSOR (976.385-010)
05.10.09 EXTERMINATOR (389.684-010)
05.10.09 EXTERMINATOR, TERMITE (383.364-010)
05.10.09 FUMIGATOR (383.361-010)
05.12.12 SEWER-PIPE CLEANER (899.664-014)
07.01.04 VAULT CASHIER (222.137-050)
07.02.02 TAX PREPARER (219.362-070)
07.02.04 ADVERTISING CLERK (247.387-010)
07.02.04 MEDIA CLERK (247.382-010)
07.03.01 CHECK CASHIER (211.462-026)

07.04.01 BONDING AGENT (186.267-010)
07.04.05 AIRLINE-RADIO OPERATOR (193.262-010)
07.04.06 TELEPHONE-ANSWERING-SERVICE
    OPERATOR (235.662-026)
07.05.01 TRAFFIC CLERK (221.367-078)
07.05.02 READER (249.387-022)
07.05.03 CALL-OUT OPERATOR (237.367-014)
07.05.03 DOCUMENT PREPARER, MICROFILMING
    (249.587-018)
07.05.04 VAULT WORKER (222.587-058)
07.06.01 CREDIT REPORTING CLERK (203.362-014)
07.07.02 PROCESS SERVER (249.367-062)
07.07.02 SUPERVISOR, ADVERTISING-MATERIAL
    DISTRIBUTORS (230.137-010)
07.07.02 TELEPHONE-DIRECTORY DELIVERER
    (230.667-014)
07.07.03 COIN-MACHINE COLLECTOR
    (292.687-010)
08.01.01 SALES REPRESENTATIVE, GRAPHIC ART
    (254.251-010)
08.01.02 SALES REPRESENTATIVE, DATA PRO-
    CESSING SERVICES (251.157-014)
08.01.02 SALES REPRESENTATIVE, SECURITY
    SYSTEMS (259.257-022)
08.01.03 BUSINESS-OPPORTUNITY-AND-
    PROPERTY-INVESTMENT BROKER
    (189.157-010)
08.02.06 SALES AGENT, BUSINESS SERVICES
    (251.357-010)
08.02.06 SALES REPRESENTATIVE, AUTOMOTIVE-
    LEASING (273.357-014)
08.02.06 SALES REPRESENTATIVE, FRANCHISE
    (251.357-022)
08.02.06 TRAVEL AGENT (252.152-010)
09.04.02 HOSPITAL-TELEVISION-RENTAL CLERK
    (295.467-018)
09.04.02 STORAGE-FACILITY RENTAL CLERK
    (295.367-026)
09.04.02 TOOL-AND-EQUIPMENT-RENTAL CLERK
    (295.357-014)
11.02.04 FILM-RENTAL CLERK (295.367-018)
11.05.02 FREIGHT-TRAFFIC CONSULTANT
    (184.267-010)
11.05.04 FIELD REPRESENTATIVE (163.267-010)
11.05.04 MANAGER, PROFESSIONAL EQUIPMENT
    SALES-AND-SERVICE (185.167-042)
11.09.01 ACCOUNT EXECUTIVE (164.167-010)
11.09.01 GOODWILL AMBASSADOR (293.357-018)
11.09.01 MANAGER, ADVERTISING AGENCY
    (164.117-014)
11.09.01 SUPERVISOR OF SALES (185.157-014)
11.10.03 MARINE-CARGO SURVEYOR (168.267-094)
11.10.05 SHOPPING INVESTIGATOR (376.267-022)
11.11.04 MANAGER, TRAVEL AGENCY (187.167
    -158)
11.12.01 APPRAISER, AUTOMOBILE DAMAGE
    (241.267-014)
11.12.01 CLAIM ADJUSTER (241.217-010)
11.12.01 CLAIM EXAMINER (241.267-018)
11.12.02 LEASING AGENT, OUTDOOR ADVERTIS-
    ING (254.357-010)
11.12.03 LITERARY AGENT (191.117-034)

Button and Miscellaneous Notions

06.04.34 ARTIFICIAL-FLOWER MAKER
(739.684-014)

Canning and Preserving

05.02.03 MANAGER, FOOD PROCESSING PLANT
(183.167-026)
06.04.15 CANNERY WORKER (529.686-014)
06.04.15 COOK, FRY, DEEP FAT (526.685-014)
06.04.28 BUTCHER, FISH (525.684-014)
06.04.28 FISH CLEANER (525.684-030)

Carpet and Rug

06.02.05 CARPET SEWER (787.682-014)
06.04.27 CARPET CUTTER II (585.687-014)

Cement

06.04.08 MILLER (570.685-046)

Chemical

03.04.02 CHAIN SAW OPERATOR (454.687-010)
05.10.06 FIREWORKS DISPLAY SPECIALIST
(969.664-010)
06.01.03 CHIEF OPERATOR (558.260-010)
06.02.09 DYNAMITE-PACKING-MACHINE OPERA-
TOR (692.662-010)
06.02.11 WASTE-TREATMENT OPERATOR
(955.382-014)
06.04.11 CHEMICAL OPERATOR II (558.685-062)
06.04.11 CHEMICAL PREPARER (550.685-030)
06.04.11 DRIER OPERATOR (553.685-042)
06.04.12 CYLINDER FILLER (559.565-010)
06.04.40 COMPRESSED-GAS-PLANT WORKER
(549.587-010)
06.04.40 LABORER, CHEMICAL PROCESSING
(559.687-050)

Clerical and Kindred Occupations

04.02.03 REPOSSESSOR (241.367-022)
05.03.03 PRODUCTION CLERK (221.382-018)
05.09.01 INVENTORY CLERK (222.387-026)
05.09.01 LABORATORY CLERK (222.587-026)
05.09.01 PARTS CLERK (222.367-042)
05.09.01 PARTS-ORDER-AND-STOCK CLERK
(249.367-058)
05.09.01 SHIPPING AND RECEIVING CLERK
(222.387-050)
05.09.01 SHIPPING CHECKER (222.687-030)
05.09.01 SHIPPING-AND-RECEIVING WEIGHER
(222.387-074)
05.09.01 STOCK CLERK (222.387-058)

05.09.01 STOCK SUPERVISOR (222.137-034)
05.09.01 TOOL-CRIB ATTENDANT (222.367-062)
05.09.02 JOB TRACER (221.387-034)
05.09.02 LAUNDRY CLERK (221.387-038)
05.09.02 MATERIAL COORDINATOR (221.167-014)
05.09.02 MATERIAL EXPEDITER (221.367-042)
05.09.02 ORDER DETAILER (221.387-046)
05.09.02 PRODUCTION COORDINATOR
(221.167-018)
05.09.02 SALES CORRESPONDENT (221.367-062)
05.09.03 INDUSTRIAL-ORDER CLERK (221.367-022)
05.09.03 MATERIAL CLERK (222.387-034)
05.09.03 ORDER CALLER (209.667-014)
05.09.03 RECEIVING CHECKER (222.687-018)
05.10.05 DUPLICATING-MACHINE OPERATOR I
(207.682-010)
05.10.05 OFFSET-DUPLICATING-MACHINE OPERA-
TOR (207.682-018)
05.12.19 ADDRESSING-MACHINE OPERATOR
(208.582-010)
05.12.19 COIN-COUNTER-AND-WRAPPER
(217.585-010)
05.12.19 COLLATOR OPERATOR (208.685-010)
05.12.19 FOLDING-MACHINE OPERATOR
(208.685-014)
05.12.19 INSERTING-MACHINE OPERATOR
(208.685-018)
05.12.19 MICROFILM MOUNTER (208.685-022)
05.12.19 PHOTOCOPYING-MACHINE OPERATOR
(207.685-014)
05.12.19 PHOTOGRAPHIC-MACHINE OPERATOR
(207.685-018)
07.01.02 ADMINISTRATIVE CLERK (219.362-010)
07.01.02 PROCUREMENT CLERK (249.367-066)
07.01.03 LEGAL SECRETARY (201.362-010)
07.01.03 SECRETARY (201.362-030)
07.01.03 SOCIAL SECRETARY (201.162-010)
07.01.04 CREDIT ANALYST (241.267-022)
07.01.07 TEST TECHNICIAN (249.367-078)
07.02.01 AUDIT CLERK (210.382-010)
07.02.01 BOOKKEEPER (210.382-014)
07.02.01 GENERAL-LEDGER BOOKKEEPER
(210.382-046)
07.02.02 ACCOUNTING CLERK (216.482-010)
07.02.02 CALCULATING-MACHINE OPERATOR
(216.482-022)
07.02.02 COST CLERK (216.382-034)
07.02.03 STATISTICAL CLERK (216.382-062)
07.02.04 BILLING CLERK (214.362-042)
07.02.04 INVOICE-CONTROL CLERK (214.362-026)
07.02.04 TAX CLERK (219.487-010)
07.02.04 TRAFFIC CLERK (214.587-014)
07.02.05 PAYROLL CLERK (215.382-014)
07.02.05 TIMEKEEPER (215.362-022)
07.03.01 CASHIER I (211.362-010)
07.03.01 CASHIER II (211.462-010)
07.03.01 COLLECTOR (241.367-010)
07.03.01 TICKET SELLER (211.467-030)
07.04.01 CREDIT CLERK (205.367-022)
07.04.01 EMPLOYMENT CLERK (205.362-014)
07.04.01 IDENTIFICATION CLERK (205.362-022)

07.04.01 SKIP TRACER (241.367-026)
07.04.01 SURVEY WORKER (205.367-054)
07.04.02 COLLECTION CLERK (241.357-010)
07.04.02 CORRESPONDENCE CLERK (209.362-034)
07.04.04 INFORMATION CLERK (237.367-022)
07.04.04 RECEPTIONIST (237.367-038)
07.04.05 DISPATCHER, MAINTENANCE SERVICE
    (239.367-014)
07.04.05 SERVICE CLERK (221.367-070)
07.04.06 TELEPHONE OPERATOR (235.662-022)
07.04.06 TELEPHONE OPERATOR, CHIEF
    (235.137-010)
07.05.01 COMPUTER PROCESSING SCHEDULER
    (221.362-030)
07.05.01 DISPATCHER, MOTOR VEHICLE
    (249.167-014)
07.05.01 EXPEDITER (222.367-018)
07.05.01 PERSONNEL SCHEDULER (215.367-014)
07.05.01 RESERVATION CLERK (238.362-014)
07.05.01 SCHEDULER, MAINTENANCE
    (221.367-066)
07.05.02 CREDIT AUTHORIZER (249.367-022)
07.05.02 CUSTOMER-COMPLAINT CLERK
    (241.367-014)
07.05.02 DATA-EXAMINATION CLERK (209.387-022)
07.05.02 MORTGAGE-CLOSING CLERK
    (219.362-038)
07.05.03 ASSIGNMENT CLERK (249.367-090)
07.05.03 BENEFITS CLERK II (205.567-010)
07.05.03 CLASSIFICATION CLERK (206.387-010)
07.05.03 COMPILER (209.387-014)
07.05.03 FILE CLERK II (206.367-014)
07.05.03 INSURANCE CLERK (219.387-014)
07.05.03 ORDER CLERK (249.362-026)
07.05.03 PERSONNEL CLERK (209.362-026)
07.05.03 REFERRAL CLERK, TEMPORARY HELP
    AGENCY (205.367-062)
07.05.03 REPAIR-ORDER CLERK (221.382-022)
07.05.03 REPRODUCTION ORDER PROCESSOR
    (221.367-058)
07.05.03 SHORTHAND REPORTER (202.362-010)
07.05.03 STENOGRAPHER (202.362-014)
07.05.03 STENOTYPE OPERATOR (202.362-022)
07.05.03 STOCK CONTROL CLERK (219.387-030)
07.05.03 TAPE LIBRARIAN (206.367-018)
07.05.04 CORRESPONDENCE-REVIEW CLERK
    (209.367-018)
07.05.04 MAIL CLERK (209.687-026)
07.05.04 MAILROOM SUPERVISOR (209.137-010)
07.05.04 PARCEL POST CLERK (222.387-038)
07.05.04 ROUTE-DELIVERY CLERK (222.587-034)
07.05.04 SHIPPING-ORDER CLERK (219.367-030)
07.06.01 COMPUTER OPERATOR (213.362-010)
07.06.01 COMPUTER PERIPHERAL EQUIPMENT
    OPERATOR (213.382-010)
07.06.01 DATA ENTRY CLERK (203.582-054)
07.06.01 SUPERVISOR, COMPUTER OPERATIONS
    (213.132-010)
07.06.02 CLERK-TYPIST (203.362-010)
07.06.02 CRYPTOGRAPHIC-MACHINE OPERATOR
    (203.582-018)

07.06.02 NOTEREADER (203.582-078)
07.06.02 TRANSCRIBING-MACHINE OPERATOR
    (203.582-058)
07.06.02 TYPIST (203.582-066)
07.06.02 VARITYPE OPERATOR (203.382-026)
07.06.02 WORD PROCESSING MACHINE OPERA-
    TOR (203.382-030)
07.07.01 FILE CLERK I (206.387-034)
07.07.02 ADDRESSER (209.587-010)
07.07.02 CHECKER I (222.687-010)
07.07.02 DELIVERER, OUTSIDE (230.663-010)
07.07.02 DIRECT-MAIL CLERK (209.587-018)
07.07.02 DISTRIBUTING CLERK (222.587-018)
07.07.02 ROUTER (222.587-038)
07.07.02 ROUTING CLERK (222.687-022)
07.07.02 SORTER (209.687-022)
07.07.03 CLERK, GENERAL (209.562-010)
07.07.03 OFFICE HELPER (239.567-010)
11.02.04 FILM-OR-TAPE LIBRARIAN (222.367-026)
11.06.03 INVESTIGATOR (241.267-030)

Clocks, Watches, and Allied Products

05.09.02 CONTROL CLERK (221.387-018)

Concrete Products

05.11.02 PLANT OPERATOR (570.682-014)
06.01.04 MOLDER (518.361-010)
06.04.40 LABORER, CONCRETE PLANT (579.687-
    042)

Construction

03.01.03 LANDSCAPE CONTRACTOR (182.167-014)
05.01.08 STRUCTURAL ENGINEER (005.061-034)
05.02.02 SUPERINTENDENT, CONSTRUCTION
    (182.167-026)
05.03.06 CONSTRUCTION INSPECTOR (182.267-010)
05.05.01 BRICKLAYER (861.381-018)
05.05.01 CEMENT MASON (844.364-010)
05.05.01 MARBLE FINISHER (861.664-010)
05.05.01 SOFT-TILE SETTER (861.381-034)
05.05.01 STONEMASON (861.381-038)
05.05.01 TERRAZZO FINISHER (861.664-014)
05.05.01 TERRAZZO WORKER (861.381-046)
05.05.01 TILE FINISHER (861.664-018)
05.05.01 TILE SETTER (861.381-054)
05.05.02 ACOUSTICAL CARPENTER (860.381-010)
05.05.02 CARPENTER (860.381-022)
05.05.02 CARPENTER APPRENTICE (860.381-026)
05.05.02 CARPENTER, ROUGH (860.381-042)
05.05.02 FORM BUILDER (860.381-046)
05.05.03 PIPE FITTER (862.281-022)
05.05.03 PLUMBER (862.381-030)
05.05.04 DRY-WALL APPLICATOR (842.361-030)
05.05.04 PAPERHANGER (841.381-010)
05.05.04 PLASTERER (842.361-018)

05.05.05 CABLE SPLICER (829.361-010)
05.05.05 ELECTRICIAN (824.261-010)
05.05.05 LINE ERECTOR (821.361-018)
05.05.05 TOWER ERECTOR (821.361-038)
05.05.05 WIND-GENERATING-ELECTRIC-POWER
INSTALLER (821.381-018)
05.05.06 CONDUIT MECHANIC (869.361-010)
05.05.06 ELEVATOR CONSTRUCTOR (825.361-010)
05.05.06 ORNAMENTAL-IRON WORKER
(809.381-022)
05.05.06 STRUCTURAL-STEEL WORKER
(801.361-014)
05.05.09 AIR-CONDITIONING INSTALLER-
SERVICER, WINDOW UNIT (637.261-010)
05.05.09 CONSTRUCTION-EQUIPMENT MECHANIC
(620.261-022)
05.05.09 HEATING-AND-AIR-CONDITIONING
INSTALLER-SERVICER (637.261-014)
05.05.09 MAINTENANCE MECHANIC (620.281-046)
05.08.03 CONCRETE-MIXING-TRUCK DRIVER
(900.683-010)
05.09.01 DISPATCHER (849.137-010)
05.10.01 ASBESTOS REMOVAL WORKER
(869.684-082)
05.10.01 CONSTRUCTION WORKER I (869.664-014)
05.10.01 DRY-WALL APPLICATOR (842.684-014)
05.10.01 FENCE ERECTOR (869.684-022)
05.10.01 FLOOR LAYER (864.481-010)
05.10.01 GLAZIER (865.381-010)
05.10.01 INSULATION WORKER (863.364-014)
05.10.01 LAWN-SPRINKLER INSTALLER (869.684-
030)
05.10.01 ROOFER (866.381-010)
05.10.01 SWIMMING POOL INSTALLER-AND-
SERVICER (869.463-010)
05.10.01 TAPER (842.664-010)
05.10.02 MAINTENANCE MECHANIC HELPER
(620.664-014)
05.10.03 AUTOMATIC-DOOR MECHANIC
(829.281-010)
05.10.04 HOUSE REPAIRER (869.381-010)
05.10.04 MANAGER, CAMP (187.167-066)
05.10.07 PAINTER (840.381-010)
05.11.01 ASPHALT-PAVING-MACHINE OPERATOR
(853.663-010)
05.11.01 CHERRY-PICKER OPERATOR (921.663-014)
05.11.01 CONCRETE-PAVING-MACHINE OPERA-
TOR (853.663-014)
05.11.01 OPERATING ENGINEER (859.683-010)
05.11.01 PILE-DRIVER OPERATOR (859.682-018)
05.11.01 ROAD-ROLLER OPERATOR (859.683-030)
05.11.01 SCRAPER OPERATOR (850.683-038)
05.11.02 PLANT OPERATOR (570.682-014)
05.12.01 LABOR-CREW SUPERVISOR (899.131-010)
05.12.02 HORIZONTAL-EARTH-BORING-MACHINE-
OPERATOR HELPER (850.684-014)
05.12.04 LABORER, CONCRETE-MIXING PLANT
(579.665-014)
05.12.12 AIR-CONDITIONING INSTALLER-
SERVICER HELPER, WINDOW UNIT
(637.687-010)

05.12.12 PIPE-FITTER HELPER (862.684-022)
05.12.14 ASPHALT-DISTRIBUTOR TENDER
(853.665-010)
05.12.15 CONSTRUCTION-EQUIPMENT-MECHANIC
HELPER (620.664-010)
05.12.16 CABLE PULLER (829.684-018)
07.01.02 LABOR EXPEDITER (249.167-018)
11.12.04 CONTRACTOR (182.167-010)

Cutlery, Handtools, and Hardware

06.04.23 LOCK ASSEMBLER (706.684-074)

Dairy Products

05.08.01 MILK DRIVER (905.483-010)
05.10.08 FORMULA-ROOM WORKER (520.487-014)
06.01.04 CHEESEMAKER (529.361-018)
06.02.15 BUTTERMAKER (529.362-010)
06.02.15 DAIRY-PROCESSING-EQUIPMENT OPERA-
TOR (529.382-018)
06.02.15 FREEZER OPERATOR (529.482-010)
06.04.15 CENTRIFUGE OPERATOR (521.685-042)
06.04.15 CHEESE CUTTER (529.585-010)

Domestic Service

05.10.08 COOK (305.281-010)
05.12.01 HOUSEKEEPER, HOME (301.137-010)
05.12.18 CARETAKER (301.687-010)
05.12.18 DAY WORKER (301.687-014)
09.01.03 BUTLER (309.137-010)
09.03.02 CHAUFFEUR (359.673-010)
09.05.06 PERSONAL ATTENDANT (309.674-014)
10.03.03 CHILD MONITOR (301.677-010)
10.03.03 CHILDREN'S TUTOR (099.227-010)
10.03.03 COMPANION (309.677-010)
10.03.03 FOSTER PARENT (309.677-014)

Education and Instruction

01.03.01 COMMUNICATIONS TECHNICIAN
(962.362-010)
01.04.01 TEACHER, MUSIC (152.021-010)
01.05.01 INSTRUCTOR, DANCING (151.027-014)
05.01.08 SCHOOL-PLANT CONSULTANT
(001.167-010)
05.03.08 ENERGY-CONTROL OFFICER (199.167-018)
05.04.01 INSTRUCTOR, FLYING I (196.223-010)
05.04.01 INSTRUCTOR, FLYING II (097.227-010)
07.01.01 FINANCIAL-AID COUNSELOR
(169.267-018)
07.01.02 TEACHER AIDE II (249.367-074)
07.01.03 SCHOOL SECRETARY (201.362-022)
07.01.05 ADMISSIONS EVALUATOR (205.367-010)
07.01.06 ATTENDANCE OFFICER (168.367-010)
07.02.03 GRADING CLERK (219.467-010)
07.05.03 ATTENDANCE CLERK (219.362-014)
07.06.02 BRAILLE TYPIST (203.582-014)

08.01.02 SALES REPRESENTATIVE, EDUCATION COURSES (259.257-010)

08.02.05 SALES REPRESENTATIVE, DANCING INSTRUCTIONS (259.357-014)

09.03.03 INSTRUCTOR, DRIVING (099.223-010)

10.01.02 ASSISTANT PRINCIPAL (091.107-010)

10.01.02 DEAN OF STUDENTS (090.117-018)

10.01.02 DIRECTOR OF PLACEMENT (166.167-014)

10.01.02 FOREIGN-STUDENT ADVISER (090.107-010)

10.01.02 RESIDENCE COUNSELOR (045.107-038)

10.02.02 ATHLETIC TRAINER (153.224-010)

10.02.02 INSTRUCTOR, PHYSICAL (153.227-014)

10.02.02 ORIENTATION AND MOBILITY THERAPIST FOR THE BLIND (076.224-014)

10.02.02 PHYSICAL THERAPIST (076.121-014)

10.02.03 EVALUATOR (094.267-010)

10.02.03 SUPERVISOR, SPECIAL EDUCATION (094.167-010)

10.02.03 TEACHER, EMOTIONALLY IMPAIRED (094.227-010)

10.02.03 TEACHER, HEARING IMPAIRED (094.224-010)

10.02.03 TEACHER, KINDERGARTEN (092.227-014)

10.02.03 TEACHER, LEARNING DISABLED (094.227-030)

10.02.03 TEACHER, MENTALLY IMPAIRED (094.227-022)

10.02.03 TEACHER, PHYSICALLY IMPAIRED (094.224-014)

10.02.03 TEACHER, PRESCHOOL (092.227-018)

10.02.03 TEACHER, VISUALLY IMPAIRED (094.224-018)

10.02.03 TEACHER, VOCATIONAL TRAINING (094.227-026)

10.02.03 WORK-STUDY COORDINATOR, SPECIAL EDUCATION (094.107-010)

11.02.01 FACULTY MEMBER, COLLEGE OR UNIVERSITY (090.227-010)

11.02.01 INSTRUCTOR, BUSINESS EDUCATION (090.222-010)

11.02.01 INSTRUCTOR, EXTENSION WORK (090.227-018)

11.02.01 INSTRUCTOR, PHYSICAL EDUCATION (099.224-010)

11.02.01 TEACHER AIDE I (099.327-010)

11.02.01 TEACHER, ADULT EDUCATION (099.227-030)

11.02.01 TEACHER, ELEMENTARY SCHOOL (092.227-010)

11.02.01 TEACHER, RESOURCE (099.227-042)

11.02.01 TEACHER, SECONDARY SCHOOL (091.227-010)

11.02.01 TUTOR (099.227-034)

11.02.02 INSTRUCTOR, TECHNICAL TRAINING (166.221-010)

11.02.02 INSTRUCTOR, VOCATIONAL TRAINING (097.221-010)

11.02.02 TEACHER, INDUSTRIAL ARTS (091.221-010)

11.02.02 TRAINING REPRESENTATIVE (166.227-010)

11.02.04 CAREER-GUIDANCE TECHNICIAN (249.367-014)

11.05.02 BUSINESS MANAGER, COLLEGE OR UNIVERSITY (186.117-010)

11.07.03 ACADEMIC DEAN (090.117-010)

11.07.03 CONSULTANT, EDUCATION (099.167-014)

11.07.03 DIRECTOR OF ADMISSIONS (090.167-014)

11.07.03 DIRECTOR OF PUPIL PERSONNEL PROGRAM (099.167-034)

11.07.03 DIRECTOR, ATHLETIC (090.117-022)

11.07.03 DIRECTOR, DAY CARE CENTER (092.167-010)

11.07.03 DIRECTOR, EDUCATIONAL PROGRAM (099.117-010)

11.07.03 DIRECTOR, SPECIAL EDUCATION (094.167-014)

11.07.03 DIRECTOR, VOCATIONAL TRAINING (097.167-010)

11.07.03 EDUCATIONAL SPECIALIST (099.167-022)

11.07.03 FINANCIAL-AIDS OFFICER (090.117-030)

11.07.03 LABORATORY MANAGER (090.164-010)

11.07.03 MUSIC SUPERVISOR (099.167-026)

11.07.03 PRESIDENT, EDUCATIONAL INSTITUTION (090.117-034)

11.07.03 PRINCIPAL (099.117-018)

11.07.03 REGISTRAR, COLLEGE OR UNIVERSITY (090.167-030)

11.07.03 SUPERINTENDENT, SCHOOLS (099.117-022)

11.07.03 TECHNICAL TRAINING COORDINATOR (166.167-054)

12.01.01 INSTRUCTOR, SPORTS (153.227-018)

Electrical Equipment

05.10.03 WIRER, CABLE (729.381-022)

06.01.03 FIRESETTER (692.360-018)

06.01.04 ELECTRIC-MOTOR-CONTROL ASSEMBLER (721.381-014)

06.02.22 TRANSFORMER ASSEMBLER II (820.684-010)

06.02.23 LAMINATION ASSEMBLER (729.684-066)

06.03.01 INSPECTOR, RECEIVING (222.384-010)

06.04.23 BATTERY ASSEMBLER, DRY CELL (727.664-010)

06.04.23 COIL WINDER (724.684-026)

06.04.23 ELECTRIC-MOTOR ASSEMBLER (721.684-022)

06.04.34 WIREWORKER (728.684-022)

Electronic Components and Accessories

02.04.01 CALIBRATION LABORATORY TECHNICIAN (019.281-010)

05.01.06 TOOL PROGRAMMER, NUMERICAL CONTROL (609.262-010)

05.03.02 DESIGN TECHNICIAN, COMPUTER-AIDED (003.362-010)

05.03.05 LASER TECHNICIAN (019.261-034)

05.05.05 COMPUTERIZED ENVIRONMENTAL CONTROL INSTALLER (828.281-026)

05.09.01 PRODUCTION TECHNICIAN, SEMI-CONDUCTOR PROCESSING EQUIPMENT (590.384-014)

05.10.03 ELECTRONIC EQUIPMENT REPAIRER (726.381-014)

05.10.05 PHOTO MASK TECHNICIAN, ELECTRON-BEAM (972.382-022)

05.10.05 PHOTOGRAPHIC-PLATE MAKER (714.381-018)

06.01.03 EXHAUST EQUIPMENT OPERATOR (599.382-014)

06.01.03 FIRESETTER (692.360-018)

06.01.03 MICROELECTRONICS TECHNICIAN (590.362-022)

06.01.04 ASSEMBLER, ELECTROMECHANICAL (828.381-018)

06.01.05 ELECTRONICS INSPECTOR (726.381-010)

06.02.02 LASER-BEAM-TRIM OPERATOR (726.682-010)

06.02.09 NUMERICAL-CONTROL DRILL OPERA-TOR, PRINTED CIRCUIT BOARDS (606.382-018)

06.02.09 NUMERICAL-CONTROL ROUTER OPERA-TOR (605.382-046)

06.02.09 WIRE-WRAPPING-MACHINE OPERATOR (726.682-014)

06.02.21 PLATER, PRINTED CIRCUIT BOARD PANELS (500.684-026)

06.02.23 ASSEMBLER, SEMICONDUCTOR (726.684-034)

06.02.23 ELECTRONICS ASSEMBLER (726.684-018)

06.02.23 LAMINATION ASSEMBLER (729.684-066)

06.02.23 PRINTED CIRCUIT BOARD ASSEMBLER, HAND (726.684-070)

06.02.23 TUBE ASSEMBLER, CATHODE RAY (725.684-022)

06.02.23 TUBE ASSEMBLER, ELECTRON (725.384-010)

06.02.32 CATHODE RAY TUBE SALVAGE PROCES-SOR (725.684-026)

06.02.32 ETCHED-CIRCUIT PROCESSOR (590.684-018)

06.03.01 INSPECTOR, PRINTED CIRCUIT BOARDS (726.684-062)

06.03.01 INSPECTOR, RECEIVING (222.384-010)

06.03.02 ELECTRONICS INSPECTOR (726.684-022)

06.03.02 ELECTRONICS TESTER (726.684-026)

06.03.02 INSPECTOR, INTEGRATED CIRCUITS (726.684-058)

06.03.02 INSPECTOR, SEMICONDUCTOR WAFER (726.684-066)

06.04.08 CERAMIC CAPACITOR PROCESSOR (590.684-010)

06.04.09 PHOTORESIST LAMINATOR, PRINTED CIRCUIT BOARD (554.685-034)

06.04.11 CHEMICAL PREPARER (550.685-030)

06.04.19 COATING EQUIPMENT OPERATOR, PRINTED CIRCUIT BOARDS (590.685-066)

06.04.19 DISPLAY-SCREEN FABRICATOR (725.685-010)

06.04.19 ELECTRONIC-COMPONENT PROCESSOR (590.684-014)

06.04.19 METALLIZATION EQUIPMENT TENDER, SEMICONDUCTORS (590.685-086)

06.04.19 PLATER, SEMICONDUCTOR WAFERS AND COMPONENTS (500.684-030)

06.04.19 POLYSILICON PREPARATION WORKER (590.684-038)

06.04.19 STRIPPER-ETCHER, PRINTED CIRCUIT BOARDS (590.685-082)

06.04.23 COIL WINDER (724.684-026)

06.04.32 SEMICONDUCTOR PROCESSOR (590.684-022)

06.04.34 ELECTRONICS UTILITY WORKER (726.364-018)

06.04.34 ELECTRONICS WORKER (726.687-010)

06.04.34 INTEGRATED CIRCUIT FABRICATOR (590.684-042)

06.04.34 PHOTO MASK CLEANER (590.684-034)

06.04.34 WIREWORKER (728.684-022)

06.04.37 MARKER, SEMICONDUCTOR WAFERS (920.587-026)

06.04.39 SCRUBBER MACHINE TENDER (599.685-134)

Electroplating

06.02.21 PLATER (500.380-010)

06.04.21 PLATING EQUIPMENT TENDER (500.685-014)

Engine and Turbine

05.05.09 MACHINERY ERECTOR (638.261-014)

05.05.09 MOTORBOAT MECHANIC (623.281-038)

06.02.22 ASSEMBLER, INTERNAL COMBUSTION ENGINE (806.481-014)

Engraving, Chasing, and Etching

01.06.01 ENGRAVER, HAND, HARD METALS (704.381-026)

01.06.01 ENGRAVER, HAND, SOFT METALS (704.381-030)

01.06.01 ETCHER (704.684-010)

05.10.05 ENGRAVER, MACHINE I (704.682-010)

Fabricated Metal Products, Not Elsewhere Classified

05.05.06 ORNAMENTAL-METAL WORKER (619.260-014)

Fabricated Plastic Products

06.01.04 PLASTICS FABRICATOR (754.381-018)

06.02.02 SAWYER (690.482-010)

06.02.13 EXTRUDER OPERATOR (557.382-010)

06.03.01 INSPECTOR (559.381-010)

06.04.02 GRINDER (555.685-026)

06.04.10 INJECTION-MOLDING-MACHINE TENDER (556.685-038)

06.04.13 COMPRESSION-MOLDING-MACHINE TENDER (556.685-022)

Financial Institutions

05.12.19 CURRENCY COUNTER (217.485-010)

07.01.02 SUPERVISOR, LENDING ACTIVITIES (249.137-034)

07.01.02 SUPERVISOR, SAFETY DEPOSIT (295.137-010)

07.01.02 TRANSFER CLERK, HEAD (216.137-014)

07.01.03 TRUST OPERATIONS ASSISTANT (219.362-074)

07.01.04 MORTGAGE CLERK (249.362-014)

07.01.04 MORTGAGE LOAN CLOSER (249.362-018)

07.01.04 SECURITIES CLERK (219.362-054)

07.01.04 SUPERVISOR, STATEMENT CLERKS (214.137-014)

07.02.01 ELECTRONIC FUNDS TRANSFER COORDINATOR (216.362-038)

07.02.01 FOREIGN-EXCHANGE-POSITION CLERK (210.367-014)

07.02.01 RESERVES CLERK (216.362-034)

07.02.02 BROKERAGE CLERK I (219.482-010)

07.02.02 BROKERAGE CLERK II (219.362-018)

07.02.02 COLLECTION CLERK (216.362-014)

07.02.02 COUPON CLERK (219.462-010)

07.02.02 DIVIDEND CLERK (216.482-034)

07.02.02 MARGIN CLERK I (216.362-042)

07.02.02 STATEMENT CLERK (214.362-046)

07.02.02 SUPERVISOR, TRUST ACCOUNTS (219.132-014)

07.02.02 TRANSFER CLERK (216.362-046)

07.03.01 SAFE-DEPOSIT-BOX RENTAL CLERK (295.367-022)

07.03.01 TELLER (211.362-018)

07.03.01 TELLER, HEAD (211.132-010)

07.03.01 TELLER, VAULT (211.382-010)

07.04.01 CUSTOMER SERVICE REPRESENTATIVE (205.362-026)

07.04.01 LOAN INTERVIEWER, MORTGAGE (241.367-018)

07.04.04 TELEPHONE QUOTATION CLERK (237.367-046)

07.05.02 CREDIT REFERENCE CLERK (209.362-018)

07.05.02 DISBURSEMENT CLERK (219.367-046)

07.05.02 LETTER-OF-CREDIT CLERK (219.367-050)

07.05.02 MORTGAGE LOAN PROCESSOR (249.362-022)

07.05.03 CREDIT CARD CONTROL CLERK (249.367-026)

07.06.02 PROOF-MACHINE OPERATOR (217.382-010)

07.06.02 PROOF-MACHINE-OPERATOR SUPERVISOR (217.132-010)

07.06.02 WIRE-TRANSFER CLERK (203.562-010)

08.01.02 SALES REPRESENTATIVE, FINANCIAL SERVICES (250.257-022)

08.01.03 FOREIGN BANKNOTE TELLER-TRADER (211.362-014)

11.04.04 CUSTOMS BROKER (186.117-018)

11.05.01 PRESIDENT, FINANCIAL INSTITUTION (186.117-054)

11.05.02 COMMERCIAL LOAN COLLECTION OFFICER (186.167-078)

11.05.02 VICE PRESIDENT, FINANCIAL INSTITUTION (186.117-078)

11.05.04 MANAGER, BROKERAGE OFFICE (186.117-034)

11.05.04 MANAGER, EXCHANGE FLOOR (186.117-086)

11.06.01 OPERATIONS OFFICER (186.137-014)

11.06.03 CREDIT ANALYST (160.267-022)

11.06.03 FACTOR (186.167-082)

11.06.03 FOREIGN-EXCHANGE DEALER (186.117-082)

11.06.03 INVESTMENT ANALYST (160.267-026)

11.06.03 LETTER-OF-CREDIT DOCUMENT EXAMINER (169.267-042)

11.06.03 LOAN OFFICER (186.267-018)

11.06.03 LOAN REVIEW ANALYST (186.267-022)

11.06.03 SECURITIES TRADER (162.167-038)

11.06.03 UNDERWRITER, MORTGAGE LOAN (186.267-026)

11.06.04 FLOOR BROKER (162.167-034)

11.06.04 REGISTERED REPRESENTATIVE (250.257-018)

11.06.05 TREASURER, FINANCIAL INSTITUTION (186.117-070)

11.06.05 TRUST OFFICER (186.117-074)

11.08.04 CODE AND TEST CLERK (209.667-018)

11.11.04 ASSISTANT BRANCH MANAGER, FINANCIAL INSTITUTION (186.167-070)

11.11.04 MANAGER, FINANCIAL INSTITUTION (186.167-086)

Fishing, Hunting, and Trapping

03.01.02 FISH FARMER (446.161-010)

03.01.02 MANAGER, FISH HATCHERY (180.167-030)

03.01.02 SHELLFISH GROWER (446.161-014)

03.04.03 DECKHAND, FISHING VESSEL (449.667-010)

03.04.03 FISHER, DIVING (443.664-010)

03.04.03 FISHER, LINE (442.684-010)

03.04.03 SHELLFISH DREDGE OPERATOR (446.663-010)

03.04.03 SKIFF OPERATOR (441.683-010)

05.04.02 CAPTAIN, FISHING VESSEL (197.133-010)

06.04.28 FISH CLEANER (525.684-030)

Food Preparations and Food Specialties

06.01.01 COOK, MEXICAN FOOD (526.134-010)

06.02.15 COFFEE ROASTER (523.682-014)

06.02.15 DRIER OPERATOR (523.362-014)

06.04.15 COFFEE GRINDER (521.685-078)

06.04.15 HONEY PROCESSOR (522.685-070)

06.04.15 MIXING-MACHINE OPERATOR
(520.665-014)

Forestry

03.01.01 MANAGER, CHRISTMAS-TREE FARM
(180.117-010)
03.01.04 LOGGING-OPERATIONS INSPECTOR
(168.267-070)
03.02.02 FORESTER AIDE (452.364-010)
03.04.01 CHRISTMAS-TREE FARM WORKER
(451.687-010)
03.04.02 FOREST WORKER (452.687-010)
03.04.02 FOREST-FIRE FIGHTER (452.687-014)
03.04.02 LOGGING-TRACTOR OPERATOR
(929.663-010)
04.01.02 FIRE WARDEN (452.167-010)
04.02.02 FIRE RANGER (452.367-014)
07.04.05 FIRE LOOKOUT (452.367-010)

Forging

05.05.06 BLACKSMITH (610.381-010)
06.01.02 DIE SETTER (612.360-010)
06.02.02 DROPHAMMER OPERATOR (610.362-010)

Foundry

05.05.07 PATTERNMAKER, METAL (600.280-050)
06.01.04 COREMAKER (518.381-014)
06.01.04 MOLDER (518.361-010)
06.02.10 SAND MIXER, MACHINE (570.682-018)
06.04.08 COREMAKER, MACHINE I (518.685-014)
06.04.09 WAX MOLDER (549.685-038)
06.04.17 SHELL MOLDER (518.685-026)

Furniture and Fixtures

01.02.03 FURNITURE DESIGNER (142.061-022)
05.03.02 PATTERNMAKER (781.361-014)
05.05.15 UPHOLSTERY REPAIRER (780.684-122)
05.10.01 REPAIRER (709.684-062)
06.02.22 CABINET ASSEMBLER (763.684-014)
06.04.22 LAMINATOR, HAND (763.684-050)
06.04.22 PLASTIC-TOP ASSEMBLER (763.684-062)
06.04.25 CANER II (763.684-022)

Garment

05.03.02 PANMAKER (781.361-014)
05.05.15 ALTERATION TAILOR (785.261-010)
05.05.15 CUSTOM TAILOR (785.261-014)
05.05.15 SHOP TAILOR (785.361-022)
06.02.05 TRIMMER, MACHINE (781.682-010)
06.04.05 BUTTONHOLE-AND-BUTTON-SEWING-
MACHINE OPERATOR (786.685-042)
06.04.05 SEWING-MACHINE OPERATOR, SEMI-
AUTOMATIC (786.685-030)

Glass Manufacturing

06.01.04 GLASS BLOWER (772.381-022)
06.02.13 BLANKMAKER (579.382-022)
06.03.02 SELECTOR (579.687-030)

Glass Products

05.05.11 SCIENTIFIC GLASS BLOWER (006.261-010)
06.04.30 GLASS FINISHER (775.684-026)

Government Services

01.02.03 POLICE ARTIST (141.061-034)
02.02.01 ENVIRONMENTAL EPIDEMIOLOGIST
(041.167-010)
02.04.01 BALLISTICS EXPERT, FORENSIC
(199.267-010)
02.04.01 EXAMINER, QUESTIONED DOCUMENTS
(199.267-022)
02.04.01 FINGERPRINT CLASSIFIER (375.387-010)
02.04.02 PUBLIC-HEALTH MICROBIOLOGIST
(041.261-010)
02.04.02 VECTOR CONTROL ASSISTANT
(049.364-014)
03.04.05 DOG CATCHER (379.673-010)
04.01.01 DEPUTY, COURT (377.137-018)
04.01.01 DESK OFFICER (375.137-014)
04.01.01 FIRE CAPTAIN (373.134-010)
04.01.01 FIRE CHIEF (373.117-010)
04.01.01 PARK SUPERINTENDENT (188.167-062)
04.01.01 POLICE CHIEF (375.117-010)
04.01.02 CUSTOMS PATROL OFFICER (168.167-010)
04.01.02 FIRE MARSHAL (373.267-014)
04.01.02 FISH AND GAME WARDEN (379.167-010)
04.01.02 POLICE OFFICER I (375.263-014)
04.01.02 POLICE OFFICER III (375.267-038)
04.01.02 PUBLIC-SAFETY OFFICER (379.263-014)
04.01.02 SHERIFF, DEPUTY (377.263-010)
04.01.02 SPECIAL AGENT (375.167-042)
04.01.02 STATE-HIGHWAY POLICE OFFICER
(375.263-018)
04.01.02 WILDLIFE AGENT, REGIONAL
(379.137-018)
04.02.01 CORRECTION OFFICER (372.667-018)
04.02.01 GUARD, IMMIGRATION (372.567-014)
04.02.01 JAILER (372.367-014)
04.02.02 PARKING ENFORCEMENT OFFICER
(375.587-010)
04.02.03 BAILIFF (377.667-010)
04.02.03 BORDER GUARD (375.363-010)
04.02.03 PARK RANGER (169.167-042)
04.02.03 SURVEILLANCE-SYSTEM MONITOR
(379.367-010)
05.01.02 RESOURCE-RECOVERY ENGINEER
(019.167-018)
05.03.03 AIR-TRAFFIC-CONTROL SPECIALIST,
STATION (193.162-014)
05.03.03 AIR-TRAFFIC-CONTROL SPECIALIST,
TOWER (193.162-018)

05.03.06 CODE INSPECTOR (168.367-018)
05.03.06 INSPECTOR, AIR-CARRIER (168.264-010)
05.03.06 INSPECTOR, BUILDING (168.167-030)
05.03.06 INSPECTOR, INDUSTRIAL WASTE
   (168.267-054)
05.03.06 INSPECTOR, PLUMBING (168.167-050)
05.03.06 INSPECTOR, QUALITY ASSURANCE
   (168.287-014)
05.03.06 INSPECTOR, RAILROAD (168.287-018)
05.03.06 PLAN CHECKER (168.267-102)
05.07.02 INSPECTOR, HEATING AND REFRIGERA-
   TION (168.167-046)
05.10.02 PARKING-METER SERVICER (710.384-026)
05.11.01 STREET-SWEEPER OPERATOR
   (919.683-022)
05.12.12 HIGHWAY-MAINTENANCE WORKER
   (899.684-014)
05.12.18 STREET CLEANER (955.687-018)
07.01.01 CONTACT REPRESENTATIVE (169.167-018)
07.01.01 ELIGIBILITY WORKER (195.267-010)
07.01.01 ELIGIBILITY-AND-OCCUPANCY INTER-
   VIEWER (168.267-038)
07.01.01 RETIREMENT OFFICER (166.267-030)
07.01.02 COORDINATOR, SKILL-TRAINING
   PROGRAM (169.167-062)
07.01.02 COURT CLERK (243.362-010)
07.01.02 TOWN CLERK (243.367-018)
07.01.05 EXAMINER (169.267-014)
07.01.05 PASSPORT-APPLICATION EXAMINER
   (169.267-030)
07.01.06 CASEWORKER (169.262-010)
07.01.06 IDENTIFICATION OFFICER (377.264-010)
07.01.07 DRIVER'S LICENSE EXAMINER
   (168.267-034)
07.01.07 EXAMINATION PROCTOR (199.267-018)
07.03.01 POST-OFFICE CLERK (243.367-014)
07.03.01 TOLL COLLECTOR (211.462-038)
07.04.01 EMPLOYMENT-AND-CLAIMS AIDE
   (169.367-010)
07.04.01 REGISTRATION CLERK (205.367-042)
07.04.01 TRAFFIC CHECKER (205.367-058)
07.04.02 REFERRAL-AND-INFORMATION AIDE
   (237.367-042)
07.04.03 ELECTION CLERK (205.367-030)
07.04.03 LICENSE CLERK (205.367-034)
07.04.03 PARK AIDE (249.367-082)
07.04.03 PUBLIC HEALTH REGISTRAR
   (169.167-046)
07.04.03 REGISTRAR (205.367-038)
07.04.04 CONGRESSIONAL-DISTRICT AIDE
   (209.362-030)
07.04.04 LAND-LEASING EXAMINER (237.367-026)
07.04.04 TOURIST-INFORMATION ASSISTANT
   (237.367-050)
07.04.05 ALARM OPERATOR (379.162-010)
07.04.05 DISPATCHER (193.262-014)
07.04.05 DISPATCHER, RADIO (379.362-010)
07.04.05 POLICE AIDE (243.362-014)
07.04.05 SWITCHBOARD OPERATOR, POLICE
   DISTRICT (235.562-014)
07.04.05 TELECOMMUNICATOR (379.362-018)
07.05.01 POLICE CLERK (375.362-010)

07.05.03 FINGERPRINT CLERK II (206.387-014)
07.05.03 IDENTIFICATION CLERK (209.362-022)
07.05.03 PROPERTY CLERK (222.367-054)
07.05.03 TECHNICAL COORDINATOR (209.132-014)
07.05.04 MAIL CARRIER (230.367-010)
07.05.04 MAIL HANDLER (209.687-014)
07.05.04 RURAL MAIL CARRIER (230.363-010)
07.05.04 SUPERVISOR, MAIL CARRIERS
   (230.137-018)
09.04.01 VENDING-STAND SUPERVISOR
   (185.167-066)
10.01.02 CHILD SUPPORT OFFICER (195.267-022)
10.01.02 COMMUNITY WORKER (195.367-018)
10.01.02 FOOD-MANAGEMENT AIDE (195.367-022)
10.01.02 PATIENT-RESOURCES-AND-REIMBURSE-
   MENT AGENT (195.267-018)
10.01.02 VOCATIONAL REHABILITATION
   COUNSELOR (045.107-042)
10.03.03 GUARD, SCHOOL-CROSSING (371.567-010)
11.02.03 COUNTY HOME-DEMONSTRATION
   AGENT (096.121-010)
11.02.03 COUNTY-AGRICULTURAL AGENT
   (096.127-010)
11.02.03 EXTENSION SERVICE SPECIALIST
   (096.127-014)
11.03.02 PLANNER, PROGRAM SERVICES
   (188.167-110)
11.04.01 APPEALS REFEREE (119.267-014)
11.04.01 HEARING OFFICER (119.107-010)
11.04.02 DISTRICT ATTORNEY (110.117-010)
11.04.03 ADJUDICATOR (119.167-010)
11.05.03 COURT ADMINISTRATOR (188.117-130)
11.05.03 DIRECTOR, REGULATORY AGENCY
   (188.117-134)
11.05.03 ENVIRONMENTAL ANALYST (199.167-022)
11.05.03 HOUSING-MANAGEMENT OFFICER
   (188.117-110)
11.05.03 LEGISLATIVE ASSISTANT (169.167-066)
11.05.03 MANAGER, CITY (188.117-114)
11.05.03 MANAGER, OFFICE (188.167-058)
11.05.03 MANAGER, REGULATED PROGRAM
   (168.167-090)
11.05.03 POSTMASTER (188.167-066)
11.05.03 SECRETARY OF STATE (188.167-082)
11.06.01 AUDITOR, COUNTY OR CITY (160.167-030)
11.06.01 REVENUE AGENT (160.167-050)
11.06.03 APPRAISER (188.167-010)
11.06.03 DIRECTOR, UTILITY ACCOUNTS
   (160.267-014)
11.06.03 PERSONAL PROPERTY ASSESSOR
   (191.367-010)
11.06.05 BUDGET ANALYST (161.267-030)
11.07.01 REHABILITATION CENTER MANAGER
   (195.167-038)
11.07.02 CIVIL PREPAREDNESS TRAINING
   OFFICER (169.127-010)
11.07.02 COMMUNITY-SERVICES-AND-HEALTH-
   EDUCATION OFFICER (079.167-010)
11.07.03 PARK NATURALIST (049.127-010)
11.07.03 VOCATIONAL REHABILITATION CON-
   SULTANT (094.117-018)

11.09.03 FOREIGN-SERVICE OFFICER (188.117-106)
11.10.01 INVESTIGATOR (168.267-062)
11.10.01 REVENUE OFFICER (188.167-074)
11.10.02 DIRECTOR, COMPLIANCE (188.117-046)
11.10.02 EQUAL-OPPORTUNITY REPRESENTATIVE (168.167-014)
11.10.03 CHEMICAL-RADIATION TECHNICIAN (015.261-010)
11.10.03 FIRE INSPECTOR (373.267-010)
11.10.03 FOOD AND DRUG INSPECTOR (168.267-042)
11.10.03 HAZARDOUS-WASTE MANAGEMENT SPECIALIST (168.267-086)
11.10.03 HEALTH OFFICER, FIELD (168.167-018)
11.10.03 INSPECTOR, AGRICULTURAL COMMODITIES (168.287-010)
11.10.03 INSPECTOR, HEALTH CARE FACILITIES (168.167-042)
11.10.03 INSPECTOR, MOTOR VEHICLES (168.267-058)
11.10.03 INSPECTOR, WATER-POLLUTION CONTROL (168.267-090)
11.10.03 LICENSE INSPECTOR (168.267-066)
11.10.03 OCCUPATIONAL-SAFETY-AND-HEALTH INSPECTOR (168.167-062)
11.10.03 PESTICIDE-CONTROL INSPECTOR (168.267-098)
11.10.03 PUBLIC HEALTH SERVICE OFFICER (187.117-050)
11.10.03 RADIATION-PROTECTION SPECIALIST (168.261-010)
11.10.03 REVIEWING OFFICER, DRIVER'S LICENSE (168.167-074)
11.10.03 SANITATION INSPECTOR (168.267-110)
11.10.04 CUSTOMS INSPECTOR (168.267-022)
11.10.04 IMMIGRATION INSPECTOR (168.167-022)
11.12.01 CLAIMS ADJUDICATOR (169.267-010)
11.12.02 PROPERTY-UTILIZATION OFFICER (188.117-122)

Grain and Feed Milling

06.02.15 EXTRUDER OPERATOR (520.682-018)
06.02.15 GRINDER OPERATOR (521.682-026)
06.04.15 FLOUR BLENDER (520.685-106)

Heat Treating

05.12.10 RIVET HEATER (504.485-010)
06.02.10 HEAT TREATER I (504.382-014)
06.02.10 TEMPERER (504.682-026)

Hotel and Restaurant

04.02.03 HOUSE OFFICER (376.367-018)
05.05.17 ANALYST, FOOD AND BEVERAGE (310.267-010)
05.05.17 CHEF (313.131-014)
05.05.17 CHEF DE FROID (313.281-010)
05.05.17 COOK (313.361-014)

05.05.17 SOUS CHEF (313.131-026)
05.08.03 FOOD-SERVICE DRIVER (906.683-010)
05.09.01 LINEN-ROOM ATTENDANT (222.387-030)
05.09.03 FOOD ORDER EXPEDITER (319.467-010)
05.10.08 BAKER (313.381-010)
05.10.08 BAKER, HEAD (313.131-010)
05.10.08 BAKER, PIZZA (313.381-014)
05.10.08 BUTCHER, CHICKEN AND FISH (316.684-010)
05.10.08 BUTCHER, MEAT (316.681-010)
05.10.08 CARVER (316.661-010)
05.10.08 COOK, BARBECUE (313.381-022)
05.10.08 COOK, FAST FOOD (313.374-010)
05.10.08 COOK, PASTRY (313.381-026)
05.10.08 COOK, SCHOOL CAFETERIA (313.381-030)
05.10.08 COOK, SHORT ORDER (313.374-014)
05.10.08 COOK, SPECIALTY (313.361-026)
05.10.08 COOK, SPECIALTY, FOREIGN FOOD (313.361-030)
05.10.08 GARDE MANGER (313.361-034)
05.10.08 KITCHEN SUPERVISOR (319.137-030)
05.10.08 PANTRY GOODS MAKER (317.684-014)
05.10.08 PASTRY CHEF (313.131-022)
05.10.08 PIE MAKER (313.361-038)
05.12.01 HOUSEKEEPER (321.137-010)
05.12.01 STEWARD/STEWARDESS (310.137-018)
05.12.17 BAKER HELPER (313.684-010)
05.12.17 COFFEE MAKER (317.684-010)
05.12.17 COOK HELPER (317.687-010)
05.12.17 FOOD ASSEMBLER, KITCHEN (319.484-010)
05.12.17 SANDWICH MAKER (317.664-010)
05.12.18 BARTENDER HELPER (312.687-010)
05.12.18 HOUSECLEANER (323.687-018)
05.12.18 KITCHEN HELPER (318.687-010)
05.12.18 SILVER WRAPPER (318.687-018)
06.04.15 COOK, FRY, DEEP FAT (526.685-014)
07.02.02 CREDIT-CARD CLERK (210.382-038)
07.02.02 NIGHT AUDITOR (210.382-054)
07.03.01 SUPERVISOR, CASHIERS (211.137-010)
07.03.01 SUPERVISOR, FOOD CHECKERS AND CASHIERS (211.137-014)
07.04.02 ORDER CLERK, FOOD AND BEVERAGE (209.567-014)
07.04.03 HOTEL CLERK (238.367-038)
07.04.04 TRAVEL CLERK (238.367-030)
07.05.01 MANAGER, RESERVATIONS (238.137-010)
07.06.02 FOOD CHECKER (211.482-014)
08.01.02 SALES REPRESENTATIVE, HOTEL SERVICES (259.157-014)
08.03.01 CIGARETTE VENDOR (291.457-010)
09.01.01 DIRECTOR, SOCIAL (352.167-010)
09.01.03 HOST/HOSTESS, RESTAURANT (310.137-010)
09.01.03 WAITER/WAITRESS, CAPTAIN (311.137-018)
09.01.03 WAITER/WAITRESS, HEAD (311.137-022)
09.04.01 BARTENDER (312.474-010)
09.04.01 CAR HOP (311.477-010)
09.04.01 COUNTER ATTENDANT, LUNCHROOM OR COFFEE SHOP (311.477-014)

09.04.01 FAST-FOODS WORKER (311.472-010)
09.04.01 FOUNTAIN SERVER (319.474-010)
09.04.01 LUNCH-TRUCK DRIVER (292.463-010)
09.04.01 MANAGER, FOOD CONCESSION
(185.167-022)
09.04.01 VENDING-MACHINE ATTENDANT
(319.464-014)
09.04.01 WAITER/WAITRESS, BAR (311.477-018)
09.04.01 WAITER/WAITRESS, FORMAL
(311.477-026)
09.04.01 WAITER/WAITRESS, INFORMAL
(311.477-030)
09.04.01 WAITER/WAITRESS, TAKE OUT
(311.477-038)
09.05.02 CAFETERIA ATTENDANT (311.677-010)
09.05.02 COUNTER ATTENDANT, CAFETERIA
(311.677-014)
09.05.02 COUNTER SUPERVISOR (311.137-010)
09.05.02 COUNTER-SUPPLY WORKER (319.687-010)
09.05.02 DINING ROOM ATTENDANT (311.677-018)
09.05.02 FOOD-SERVICE SUPERVISOR
(319.137-010)
09.05.02 RAW SHELLFISH PREPARER (311.674-014)
09.05.02 WAITER/WAITRESS, ROOM SERVICE
(311.477-034)
09.05.02 WINE STEWARD/STEWARDESS
(310.357-010)
09.05.03 BAGGAGE PORTER, HEAD (324.137-010)
09.05.03 BELL CAPTAIN (324.137-014)
09.05.03 BELLHOP (324.677-010)
09.05.03 PORTER, BAGGAGE (324.477-010)
09.05.03 ROOM-SERVICE CLERK (324.577-010)
11.05.02 EXECUTIVE CHEF (187.161-010)
11.09.01 MANAGER, PROMOTION (163.117-018)
11.11.01 MANAGER, CONVENTION (187.167-078)
11.11.01 MANAGER, FRONT OFFICE (187.137-018)
11.11.01 MANAGER, HOTEL OR MOTEL
(187.117-038)
11.11.01 MANAGER, LODGING FACILITIES
(320.137-014)
11.11.04 MANAGER, FOOD SERVICE (187.167-106)
11.11.04 MANAGER, LIQUOR ESTABLISHMENT
(187.167-126)

Household Appliances

05.10.03 APPLIANCE REPAIRER (723.584-010)

Instruments and Apparatus

05.03.05 LASER TECHNICIAN (019.261-034)
05.05.11 ELECTROMECHANICAL TECHNICIAN
(710.281-018)
05.05.11 RADIOLOGICAL-EQUIPMENT SPECIALIST
(719.261-014)
05.10.02 THERMOSTAT REPAIRER (710.381-050)
06.01.03 FIRESETTER (692.360-018)
06.01.04 ASSEMBLER, ELECTROMECHANICAL
(828.381-018)
06.01.04 CALIBRATOR (710.381-034)

06.01.05 ELECTRONICS INSPECTOR (726.381-010)
06.01.05 INSPECTOR, ELECTROMECHANICAL
(729.361-010)
06.02.02 WIRE DRAWING MACHINE OPERATOR
(614.382-018)
06.02.23 ELECTRONICS ASSEMBLER (726.684-018)
06.02.23 INSTRUMENT ASSEMBLER (710.684-046)
06.02.23 PRINTED CIRCUIT BOARD ASSEMBLER,
HAND (726.684-070)
06.03.02 ELECTRONICS TESTER (726.684-026)
06.03.02 INSTRUMENT INSPECTOR (710.684-050)
06.04.09 TRACK LAMINATING MACHINE TENDER
(692.685-290)
06.04.19 METALLIZATION EQUIPMENT TENDER,
SEMICONDUCTORS (590.685-086)
06.04.19 THERMOMETER PRODUCTION WORKER
(710.685-014)
06.04.24 ASSEMBLER, PLASTIC HOSPITAL PROD-
UCTS (712.687-010)

Insurance

05.03.06 BUILDING INSPECTOR (168.267-010)
07.01.04 UNDERWRITING CLERK (219.367-038)
07.01.05 AGENT-CONTRACT CLERK (241.267-010)
07.01.05 HOSPITAL-INSURANCE REPRESENTATIVE
(166.267-014)
07.02.02 CANCELLATION CLERK (203.382-014)
07.02.02 POLICY-CHANGE CLERK (219.362-042)
07.02.02 SUPERVISOR, POLICY-CHANGE CLERKS
(219.132-010)
07.02.02 SUPERVISOR, UNDERWRITING CLERKS
(219.132-022)
07.02.03 CLAIM EXAMINER (168.267-014)
07.02.03 POLICY-VALUE CALCULATOR
(216.382-050)
07.02.04 RATER (214.482-022)
07.02.04 REINSURANCE CLERK (219.482-018)
07.04.02 CLAIMS CLERK II (205.367-018)
07.04.04 POLICYHOLDER-INFORMATION CLERK
(249.262-010)
07.05.02 REVIEWER (209.687-018)
08.01.02 ESTATE PLANNER (186.167-010)
08.01.02 PLACER (239.267-010)
08.01.02 SALES AGENT, INSURANCE (250.257-010)
08.01.02 SPECIAL AGENT, GROUP INSURANCE
(169.167-050)
11.04.02 INSURANCE ATTORNEY (110.117-014)
11.05.02 RESEARCH ANALYST (169.267-034)
11.05.02 SPECIAL AGENT (166.167-046)
11.06.03 INVESTMENT ANALYST (160.267-026)
11.06.03 LOAN OFFICER (186.267-018)
11.06.03 UNDERWRITER (169.267-046)
11.10.03 SAFETY INSPECTOR (168.167-078)
11.11.04 MANAGER, INSURANCE OFFICE
(186.167-034)
11.12.01 APPRAISER, AUTOMOBILE DAMAGE
(241.267-014)
11.12.01 CLAIM ADJUSTER (241.217-010)
11.12.01 CLAIM EXAMINER (241.267-018)
11.12.01 SUPERVISOR, CLAIMS (241.137-018)

Jewelry, Silverware, and Plated Ware

01.06.02 JEWELER (700.281-010)
01.06.02 MOLD MAKER I (700.381-034)
01.06.02 SAMPLE MAKER I (700.381-046)
01.06.02 SILVERSMITH II (700.281-022)
05.05.07 DIE MAKER (601.381-014)
05.05.14 GEM CUTTER (770.281-014)
05.05.14 GEMOLOGIST (199.281-010)
05.05.14 STONE SETTER (700.381-054)
06.01.04 BENCH HAND (735.381-010)
06.01.04 RING MAKER (700.381-042)
06.01.04 SOLDERER (700.381-050)
06.02.02 WIRE DRAWING MACHINE OPERATOR
    (614.382-018)
06.02.23 CHAIN MAKER, MACHINE (700.684-022)
06.02.24 BRIGHT CUTTER (700.684-018)
06.02.24 CASTER (502.381-010)
06.02.24 GREASE BUFFER (705.684-022)
06.02.24 SPINNER (700.684-074)
06.02.24 TROPHY ASSEMBLER (735.684-018)
06.04.09 WAX MOLDER (549.685-038)
06.04.10 ANNEALER (504.687-010)
06.04.23 EARRING MAKER (700.684-030)
06.04.24 FILER (700.684-034)
06.04.24 JIGSAWYER (700.684-046)
06.04.24 MELTER (700.687-042)
06.04.24 PREPARER (700.687-062)

Knitting

06.01.02 KNITTER MECHANIC (685.360-010)
06.01.02 KNITTING-MACHINE FIXER (689.260-026)
06.02.05 TRIMMER, MACHINE (781.682-010)
06.04.06 BEAM-WARPER TENDER, AUTOMATIC
    (681.685-018)
06.04.06 KNITTING-MACHINE OPERATOR
    (685.665-014)
06.04.06 SEAMLESS-HOSIERY KNITTER
    (684.685-010)

Laundry, Cleaning, Dyeing, and Pressing

05.05.15 RUG REPAIRER (782.381-018)
05.09.01 LINEN-ROOM SUPERVISOR (222.137-014)
05.09.02 RUG MEASURER (369.367-014)
05.09.02 SUPERVISOR, LAUNDRY (361.137-010)
06.02.16 DRY CLEANER (362.382-014)
06.02.18 RUG CLEANER, MACHINE (361.682-010)
06.02.27 RUG CLEANER, HAND (369.384-014)
06.02.27 SPOTTER I (361.684-018)
06.04.35 DRY CLEANER, HAND (362.684-010)
06.04.35 FURNITURE CLEANER (362.684-022)
06.04.35 LAUNDERER, HAND (361.684-010)
06.04.35 LAUNDRY LABORER (361.687-018)
06.04.35 LAUNDRY OPERATOR (369.684-014)
06.04.35 LEATHER CLEANER (362.684-026)
06.04.35 PRESS OPERATOR (363.685-010)
06.04.35 PRESSER, ALL-AROUND (363.682-014)

06.04.35 SILK FINISHER (363.681-010)
06.04.35 WASHER, HAND (361.687-030)
06.04.35 WASHER, MACHINE (361.665-010)
08.02.06 LINEN CONTROLLER (299.357-010)
09.04.02 CURB ATTENDANT (369.477-010)
09.04.02 MANAGER, BRANCH STORE (369.467-010)
09.04.02 SELF-SERVICE-LAUNDRY-AND-DRY-
    CLEANING ATTENDANT (369.677-010)
09.04.02 SERVICE-ESTABLISHMENT ATTENDANT
    (369.477-014)
11.11.04 MANAGER, LAUNDROMAT (369.167-010)
11.11.04 MANAGER, SALES (187.167-138)
11.11.04 SUPERINTENDENT, LAUNDRY
    (187.167-194)

Leather Products

06.02.05 SEWING MACHINE OPERATOR
    (783.682-014)
06.02.27 LEATHER CUTTER (783.684-022)
06.02.27 LEATHER WORKER (783.684-026)

Library

05.09.01 BOOKMOBILE DRIVER (249.363-010)
07.04.03 REGISTRATION CLERK (249.365-010)
11.02.04 ACQUISITIONS LIBRARIAN (100.267-010)
11.02.04 AUDIOVISUAL LIBRARIAN (100.167-010)
11.02.04 BOOKMOBILE LIBRARIAN (100.167-014)
11.02.04 CATALOG LIBRARIAN (100.387-010)
11.02.04 CLASSIFIER (100.367-014)
11.02.04 LIBRARIAN (100.127-014)
11.02.04 LIBRARIAN, SPECIAL LIBRARY
    (100.167-026)
11.02.04 LIBRARY ASSISTANT (249.367-046)
11.02.04 LIBRARY TECHNICAL ASSISTANT
    (100.367-018)
11.02.04 MEDIA SPECIALIST, SCHOOL LIBRARY
    (100.167-030)
11.02.04 NEWS LIBRARIAN (100.167-038)
11.07.04 LIBRARY CONSULTANT (100.117-014)
11.07.04 LIBRARY DIRECTOR (100.117-010)

Logging

03.01.04 LOGGING-OPERATIONS INSPECTOR
    (168.267-070)
03.04.02 CHAIN SAW OPERATOR (454.687-010)
03.04.02 LOGGER, ALL-ROUND (454.684-018)
03.04.02 LOGGING-TRACTOR OPERATOR
    (929.663-010)
05.10.04 MANAGER, CAMP (187.167-066)
05.12.04 CHOKE SETTER (921.687-014)
06.02.03 LOG-CHIPPER OPERATOR (564.662-010)

Machine Shop

05.05.07 DIE SINKER (601.280-022)
05.05.07 LAY-OUT WORKER (600.281-018)

05.05.07 MACHINIST (600.280-022)

05.05.07 MACHINIST, EXPERIMENTAL
(600.260-022)

05.05.07 MAINTENANCE MACHINIST (600.280-042)

05.05.07 TOOL-AND-DIE MAKER (601.260-010)

05.05.07 TOOL-MACHINE SET-UP OPERATOR
(601.280-054)

05.07.01 INSPECTOR, TOOL (601.281-022)

06.01.02 MACHINE SETTER (600.360-014)

06.01.03 DRILL-PRESS SET-UP OPERATOR,
MULTIPLE SPINDLE (606.380-010)

06.01.03 ENGINE-LATHE SET-UP OPERATOR
(604.380-018)

06.01.03 LATHE OPERATOR, NUMERICAL CON-
TROL (604.362-010)

06.01.03 MACHINE SET-UP OPERATOR
(600.380-018)

06.01.03 MILLING-MACHINE SET-UP OPERATOR I
(605.280-010)

06.01.03 NUMERICAL CONTROL MACHINE SET-UP
OPERATOR (609.360-010)

06.01.03 SCREW-MACHINE SET-UP OPERATOR,
MULTIPLE SPINDLE (604.280-014)

06.02.02 DRILL-PRESS OPERATOR (606.682-014)

06.02.02 GRINDER SET-UP OPERATOR (603.382-034)

06.02.02 NUMERICAL CONTROL MACHINE
OPERATOR (609.362-010)

06.02.02 SCREW-MACHINE OPERATOR, MULTIPLE
SPINDLE (604.382-010)

06.02.23 ASSEMBLER, PRODUCT (706.684-018)

06.02.24 SOLAR-FABRICATION TECHNICIAN
(809.381-034)

06.04.02 DRILL PRESS TENDER (606.685-026)

Machine Tools and Accessories

05.05.09 MACHINE BUILDER (600.281-022)

Machinery Manufacturing

01.06.03 TYPE COPYIST (970.381-042)

05.05.05 AUTOMATED EQUIPMENT ENGINEER-
TECHNICIAN (638.261-010)

05.05.06 WELDER-ASSEMBLER (819.381-010)

05.05.09 FIELD SERVICE TECHNICIAN
(638.261-026)

05.05.09 MACHINE BUILDER (600.281-022)

05.05.09 MACHINERY ERECTOR (638.261-014)

06.02.22 MACHINE ASSEMBLER (638.361-010)

Manufactured Buildings

05.10.01 DRY-WALL APPLICATOR (842.684-014)

05.10.01 TAPER (842.664-010)

06.02.22 UTILITY WORKER (869.684-074)

Meat Products

06.02.28 BUTCHER, ALL-ROUND (525.381-014)

06.03.01 GRADER, MEAT (525.387-010)

06.04.15 MEAT GRINDER (521.685-214)

06.04.15 PRESS OPERATOR, MEAT (520.685-182)

06.04.28 BONER, MEAT (525.684-010)

06.04.28 POULTRY BONER (525.687-066)

06.04.28 POULTRY DRESSER (525.687-070)

06.04.28 TIER (525.687-118)

06.04.28 TRIMMER, MEAT (525.684-054)

Medical Services

02.02.01 HISTOPATHOLOGIST (041.061-054)

02.03.01 ANESTHESIOLOGIST (070.101-010)

02.03.01 CARDIOLOGIST (070.101-014)

02.03.01 DERMATOLOGIST (070.101-018)

02.03.01 GENERAL PRACTITIONER (070.101-022)

02.03.01 INTERNIST (070.101-042)

02.03.01 OBSTETRICIAN (070.101-054)

02.03.01 OPHTHALMOLOGIST (070.101-058)

02.03.01 PEDIATRICIAN (070.101-066)

02.03.01 PODIATRIST (079.101-022)

02.03.01 PSYCHIATRIST (070.107-014)

02.03.01 PUBLIC HEALTH PHYSICIAN (070.101-046)

02.03.01 RADIOLOGIST (070.101-090)

02.03.01 SURGEON (070.101-094)

02.03.02 DENTIST (072.101-010)

02.03.03 VETERINARIAN (073.101-010)

02.03.03 VETERINARY TECHNICIAN (079.361-014)

02.03.04 ACUPUNCTURIST (079.271-010)

02.03.04 AUDIOLOGIST (076.101-010)

02.03.04 CHIROPRACTOR (079.101-010)

02.03.04 OPTOMETRIST (079.101-018)

02.04.01 PHARMACIST (074.161-010)

02.04.01 RADIOPHARMACIST (074.161-014)

02.04.01 ULTRASOUND TECHNOLOGIST
(078.364-010)

02.04.02 BIOCHEMISTRY TECHNOLOGIST
(078.261-010)

02.04.02 CEPHALOMETRIC ANALYST (078.384-010)

02.04.02 CHIEF TECHNOLOGIST, NUCLEAR
MEDICINE (078.131-010)

02.04.02 CYTOGENETIC TECHNOLOGIST
(078.261-026)

02.04.02 CYTOTECHNOLOGIST (078.281-010)

02.04.02 HISTOTECHNOLOGIST (078.261-030)

02.04.02 IMMUNOHEMATOLOGIST (078.261-046)

02.04.02 LABORATORY ASSISTANT, BLOOD AND
PLASMA (078.687-010)

02.04.02 MEDICAL TECHNOLOGIST (078.261-038)

02.04.02 MEDICAL TECHNOLOGIST, CHIEF
(078.161-010)

02.04.02 MEDICAL-LABORATORY TECHNICIAN
(078.381-014)

02.04.02 MICROBIOLOGY TECHNOLOGIST
(078.261-014)

02.04.02 MORGUE ATTENDANT (355.667-010)

02.04.02 OPHTHALMIC PHOTOGRAPHER
(143.362-014)

02.04.02 PHLEBOTOMIST (079.364-022)

05.03.05 COMMUNICATIONS COORDINATOR
(239.167-010)

05.05.11 ORTHOTICS ASSISTANT (078.361-022)
05.05.11 ORTHOTIST (078.261-018)
05.05.11 PROSTHETICS ASSISTANT (078.361-026)
05.05.11 PROSTHETIST (078.261-022)
05.08.03 AMBULANCE DRIVER (913.683-010)
05.08.03 HEALTH-EQUIPMENT SERVICER
    (359.363-010)
05.09.01 LINEN-ROOM ATTENDANT (222.387-030)
05.09.01 PHARMACY TECHNICIAN (074.382-010)
05.12.01 HOUSEKEEPER (321.137-010)
05.12.01 SUPERVISOR, CENTRAL SUPPLY
    (381.137-014)
05.12.18 CENTRAL-SUPPLY WORKER (381.687-010)
05.12.18 CLEANER, HOSPITAL (323.687-010)
06.04.19 STERILIZER (599.585-010)
07.01.02 DIRECTOR, NURSES' REGISTRY
    (187.167-034)
07.01.03 MEDICAL SECRETARY (201.362-014)
07.02.04 INSURANCE CLERK (214.362-022)
07.04.01 ADMITTING OFFICER (205.162-010)
07.04.01 BLOOD-DONOR-UNIT ASSISTANT
    (245.367-014)
07.04.01 HOSPITAL-ADMITTING CLERK
    (205.362-018)
07.04.01 OUTPATIENT-ADMITTING CLERK
    (205.362-030)
07.04.03 ANIMAL-HOSPITAL CLERK (245.367-010)
07.05.03 DIET CLERK (245.587-010)
07.05.03 MEDICAL RECORD TECHNICIAN
    (079.362-014)
07.05.03 MEDICAL-RECORD CLERK (245.362-010)
07.05.03 TUMOR REGISTRAR (079.362-018)
07.05.03 UNIT CLERK (245.362-014)
09.05.02 FOOD-SERVICE WORKER, HOSPITAL
    (319.677-014)
10.02.01 NURSE ANESTHETIST (075.371-010)
10.02.01 NURSE PRACTITIONER (075.264-010)
10.02.01 NURSE, CONSULTANT (075.127-014)
10.02.01 NURSE, GENERAL DUTY (075.364-010)
10.02.01 NURSE, HEAD (075.137-014)
10.02.01 NURSE, INFECTION CONTROL
    (075.127-034)
10.02.01 NURSE, INSTRUCTOR (075.124-018)
10.02.01 NURSE, LICENSED PRACTICAL
    (079.374-014)
10.02.01 NURSE, OFFICE (075.374-014)
10.02.01 NURSE, PRIVATE DUTY (075.374-018)
10.02.01 NURSE, SCHOOL (075.124-010)
10.02.01 NURSE, STAFF, COMMUNITY HEALTH
    (075.124-014)
10.02.01 NURSE, STAFF, OCCUPATIONAL HEALTH
    NURSING (075.374-022)
10.02.01 NURSE, SUPERVISOR (075.167-010)
10.02.01 NURSE-MIDWIFE (075.264-014)
10.02.01 PHYSICIAN ASSISTANT (079.364-018)
10.02.01 QUALITY ASSURANCE COORDINATOR
    (075.167-014)
10.02.01 TRANSPLANT COORDINATOR
    (079.151-010)
10.02.02 ACUPRESSURIST (079.271-014)
10.02.02 ART THERAPIST (076.127-010)
10.02.02 CORRECTIVE THERAPIST (076.361-010)

10.02.02 DANCE THERAPIST (076.127-018)
10.02.02 DENTAL HYGIENIST (078.361-010)
10.02.02 DIALYSIS TECHNICIAN (078.362-014)
10.02.02 EXERCISE PHYSIOLOGIST (076.121-018)
10.02.02 HORTICULTURAL THERAPIST
    (076.124-018)
10.02.02 INDUSTRIAL THERAPIST (076.167-010)
10.02.02 MANUAL-ARTS THERAPIST (076.124-010)
10.02.02 MEDICAL RADIATION DOSIMETRIST
    (078.261-034)
10.02.02 MUSIC THERAPIST (076.127-014)
10.02.02 NUCLEAR MEDICINE TECHNOLOGIST
    (078.361-018)
10.02.02 OCCUPATIONAL THERAPIST (076.121-010)
10.02.02 OCCUPATIONAL THERAPY ASSISTANT
    (076.364-010)
10.02.02 ORIENTATION AND MOBILITY THERA-
    PIST FOR THE BLIND (076.224-014)
10.02.02 ORTHOPTIST (079.371-014)
10.02.02 PHERESIS SPECIALIST (078.261-042)
10.02.02 PHYSICAL THERAPIST (076.121-014)
10.02.02 PHYSICAL THERAPIST ASSISTANT
    (076.224-010)
10.02.02 PHYSICAL-INTEGRATION PRACTITIONER
    (076.264-010)
10.02.02 PSYCHIATRIC TECHNICIAN (079.374-026)
10.02.02 RADIATION-THERAPY TECHNOLOGIST
    (078.361-034)
10.02.02 RADIOLOGIC TECHNOLOGIST
    (078.362-026)
10.02.02 RADIOLOGIC TECHNOLOGIST, CHIEF
    (078.162-010)
10.02.02 RECREATIONAL THERAPIST (076.124-014)
10.02.02 RESPIRATORY THERAPIST (076.361-014)
10.02.02 SPECIAL PROCEDURES TECHNOLOGIST,
    ANGIOGRAM (078.362-046)
10.02.02 SPECIAL PROCEDURES TECHNOLOGIST,
    CARDIAC CATHETERIZATION
    (078.362-050)
10.02.02 SPECIAL PROCEDURES TECHNOLOGIST,
    CT SCAN (078.362-054)
10.02.02 SPECIAL PROCEDURES TECHNOLOGIST,
    MAGNETIC RESONANCE IMAGING (MRI)
    (078.362-058)
10.03.01 CARDIAC MONITOR TECHNICIAN
    (078.367-010)
10.03.01 CARDIOPULMONARY TECHNOLOGIST
    (078.362-030)
10.03.01 ECHOCARDIOGRAPH TECHNICIAN
    (078.364-014)
10.03.01 ELECTROCARDIOGRAPH TECHNICIAN
    (078.362-018)
10.03.01 ELECTROENCEPHALOGRAPHIC TECH-
    NOLOGIST (078.362-022)
10.03.01 ELECTROMYOGRAPHIC TECHNICIAN
    (078.362-038)
10.03.01 HOLTER SCANNING TECHNICIAN
    (078.264-010)
10.03.01 OPHTHALMIC TECHNICIAN (078.361-038)
10.03.01 POLYSOMNOGRAPHIC TECHNICIAN
    (078.362-042)

10.03.01 PULMONARY-FUNCTION TECHNICIAN (078.262-010)
10.03.01 STRESS TEST TECHNICIAN (078.362-062)
10.03.02 AMBULANCE ATTENDANT (355.374-010)
10.03.02 BIRTH ATTENDANT (354.377-010)
10.03.02 CERTIFIED MEDICATION TECHNICIAN (355.374-014)
10.03.02 CHIROPRACTOR ASSISTANT (079.364-010)
10.03.02 DENTAL ASSISTANT (079.361-018)
10.03.02 EMERGENCY MEDICAL TECHNICIAN (079.374-010)
10.03.02 MEDICAL ASSISTANT (079.362-010)
10.03.02 MENTAL-RETARDATION AIDE (355.377-018)
10.03.02 NURSE ASSISTANT (355.674-014)
10.03.02 NURSE, PRACTICAL (354.374-010)
10.03.02 OCCUPATIONAL THERAPY AIDE (355.377-010)
10.03.02 OPTOMETRIC ASSISTANT (079.364-014)
10.03.02 ORDERLY (355.674-018)
10.03.02 ORTHOPEDIC ASSISTANT (078.664-010)
10.03.02 PARAMEDIC (079.364-026)
10.03.02 PERFUSIONIST (078.362-034)
10.03.02 PHYSICAL THERAPY AIDE (355.354-010)
10.03.02 PODIATRIC ASSISTANT (079.374-018)
10.03.02 PSYCHIATRIC AIDE (355.377-014)
10.03.02 RESPIRATORY-THERAPY AIDE (355.674-022)
10.03.02 SURGICAL TECHNICIAN (079.374-022)
10.03.03 TRANSPORTER, PATIENTS (355.677-014)
11.07.01 COORDINATOR OF REHABILITATION SERVICES (076.117-010)
11.07.02 ADMINISTRATOR, HEALTH CARE FACILITY (187.117-010)
11.07.02 DIRECTOR, NURSING SERVICE (075.117-022)
11.07.02 EMERGENCY MEDICAL SERVICES COORDINATOR (079.117-010)
11.07.02 MEDICAL-RECORD ADMINISTRATOR (079.167-014)
11.07.02 RADIOLOGY ADMINISTRATOR (187.117-062)
11.07.02 UTILIZATION-REVIEW COORDINATOR (079.267-010)
11.09.02 BLOOD-DONOR RECRUITER (293.357-010)
11.09.02 SUPERVISOR, BLOOD-DONOR RECRUITERS (293.137-010)
11.10.03 SAFETY MANAGER (168.167-086)

Military Services

02.04.01 PHARMACIST ASSISTANT (074.381-010)
02.04.02 AEROSPACE PHYSIOLOGICAL TECHNICIAN (199.682-010)
07.05.03 MEDICAL-SERVICE TECHNICIAN (079.367-018)
11.03.04 RECRUITER (166.267-026)

Millwork, Veneer, Plywood, and Structural Wood Members

03.04.02 CHAIN SAW OPERATOR (454.687-010)
06.04.03 LATHE SPOTTER (663.686-022)
06.04.25 CROSSBAND LAYER (762.687-026)

Mining and Quarrying

02.04.01 SAMPLER (579.484-010)
05.01.06 MINING ENGINEER (010.061-014)
05.11.01 OPERATING ENGINEER (859.683-010)
11.10.03 MINE INSPECTOR (168.267-074)

Miscellaneous Fabricated Products, Not Elsewhere Classified

01.06.02 DISPLAY MAKER (739.361-010)
01.06.02 WIG DRESSER (332.361-010)
05.05.06 SIGN ERECTOR I (869.381-026)
06.02.17 BRIQUETTE-MACHINE OPERATOR (549.662-010)
06.02.22 CASKET ASSEMBLER (739.684-190)
06.02.22 ELECTRIC-SIGN ASSEMBLER (729.684-022)
06.04.23 TIRE MOUNTER (739.684-158)
06.04.32 CANDLEMAKER (739.664-010)
08.01.01 SALES REPRESENTATIVE, SIGNS AND DISPLAYS (254.257-010)

Miscellaneous Vehicles and Transportation Equipment

05.10.01 REPAIRER, RECREATIONAL VEHICLE (869.261-022)
06.02.22 UTILITY WORKER (869.684-074)

Motion Picture

01.01.01 FILM OR VIDEOTAPE EDITOR (962.262-010)
01.01.01 PRODUCER (187.167-174)
01.01.01 SUPERVISING FILM-OR-VIDEOTAPE EDITOR (962.132-010)
01.01.02 SCREEN WRITER (131.067-050)
01.02.03 ART DIRECTOR (142.061-062)
01.02.03 CAMERA OPERATOR (143.062-022)
01.02.03 DIRECTOR OF PHOTOGRAPHY (143.062-010)
01.02.03 OPTICAL-EFFECTS-CAMERA OPERATOR (143.260-010)
01.02.03 SET DECORATOR (142.061-042)
01.02.03 SET DESIGNER (142.061-046)
01.03.01 DIRECTOR, MOTION PICTURE (159.067-010)
01.03.03 NARRATOR (150.147-010)
01.04.03 SINGER (152.047-022)
01.06.02 MAKE-UP ARTIST (333.071-010)
01.06.02 PROP MAKER (962.281-010)
01.06.02 SPECIAL EFFECTS SPECIALIST (962.281-018)

01.08.01 EXTRA (159.647-014)
02.04.01 FILM LABORATORY TECHNICIAN I
 (976.381-010)
05.10.03 LIGHT TECHNICIAN (962.362-014)
05.10.05 FILM DEVELOPER (976.382-018)
05.10.05 FILM LABORATORY TECHNICIAN
 (976.684-014)
05.10.05 MOTION-PICTURE PROJECTIONIST
 (960.362-010)
05.10.05 RECORDIST (962.382-010)
05.10.05 RERECORDING MIXER (194.362-014)
05.10.05 SOUND MIXER (194.262-018)
05.12.04 GRIP (962.687-022)
06.01.01 SUPERVISOR, FILM PROCESSING
 (976.131-014)
07.05.03 CAPTION WRITER (203.362-026)
07.05.03 CONTINUITY CLERK (209.382-010)
11.12.02 LOCATION MANAGER (191.167-018)
12.02.01 STUNT PERFORMER (159.341-014)

Motor Vehicle Transportation

05.08.03 ESCORT-VEHICLE DRIVER (919.663-022)
05.08.03 GARBAGE COLLECTOR DRIVER
 (905.663-010)
05.08.03 GARBAGE-COLLECTION SUPERVISOR
 (909.137-014)
05.08.03 VAN DRIVER (905.663-018)
05.09.01 CHECKER (919.687-010)
05.12.03 GARBAGE COLLECTOR (955.687-022)
05.12.18 LABORER, GENERAL (909.687-014)
07.01.02 MANAGER, TRAFFIC I (184.167-102)
07.01.02 SUPERVISOR, CUSTOMER SERVICES
 (248.137-018)
07.05.03 TAXICAB COORDINATOR (215.367-018)
08.01.02 SALES REPRESENTATIVE, SHIPPING
 SERVICES (252.357-014)
08.01.02 TRAFFIC AGENT (252.257-010)
08.02.06 CRATING-AND-MOVING ESTIMATOR
 (252.357-010)
08.02.06 SALES REPRESENTATIVE (250.357-022)
08.02.06 TRAVEL AGENT (252.152-010)
09.03.01 BUS DRIVER (913.463-010)
09.03.01 DRIVER (913.663-018)
09.03.02 TAXI DRIVER (913.463-018)
09.05.03 PORTER (357.677-010)
11.05.01 DIRECTOR, TRANSPORTATION
 (184.117-014)
11.05.02 MANAGER, OPERATIONS (184.117-050)
11.05.02 MANAGER, REGIONAL (184.117-054)
11.10.05 TRAFFIC INSPECTOR (184.163-010)
11.10.05 TRANSPORTATION INSPECTOR
 (168.167-082)
11.11.03 MANAGER, BUS TRANSPORTATION
 (184.167-054)
11.11.03 OPERATIONS MANAGER (184.167-118)
11.12.01 GENERAL CLAIMS AGENT (186.117-030)

Motorcycles, Bicycles, and Parts

06.02.22 MOTORCYCLE ASSEMBLER (806.684-090)

06.02.23 WHEEL LACER AND TRUER (706.684-106)
06.03.01 MOTORCYCLE TESTER (620.384-010)
06.04.22 ASSEMBLER, BICYCLE II (806.687-010)

Museums, Art Galleries, and Botanical and Zoology Gardens

01.02.03 EXHIBIT ARTIST (149.261-010)
01.02.03 EXHIBIT DESIGNER (142.061-058)
01.06.02 EXHIBIT BUILDER (739.261-010)
01.06.02 MUSEUM TECHNICIAN (102.381-010)
05.03.09 FINE ARTS PACKER (102.367-010)
05.05.08 FURNITURE RESTORER (763.380-010)
05.10.05 PLANETARIUM TECHNICIAN
 (962.261-010)
05.12.03 INSTALLER (922.687-050)
07.04.04 MUSEUM ATTENDANT (109.367-010)
07.05.01 SCHEDULER (238.367-034)
09.01.02 CRAFT DEMONSTRATOR (109.364-010)
11.02.01 HISTORIC-SITE ADMINISTRATOR
 (102.167-014)
11.02.01 TEACHER (099.227-038)

Musical Instruments and Parts

05.05.12 ELECTRIC-ORGAN INSPECTOR AND
 REPAIRER (730.281-018)
05.05.12 FRETTED-INSTRUMENT MAKER, HAND
 (730.281-022)
05.05.12 VIOLIN MAKER, HAND (730.281-046)
06.02.23 ASSEMBLER, MUSICAL INSTRUMENTS
 (730.684-010)

Narrow Fabrics

06.01.02 LOOM FIXER (683.260-018)
06.04.06 BEAM-WARPER TENDER, AUTOMATIC
 (681.685-018)

Nonprofit, Membership, Charitable, and Religious Organizations

05.09.02 EVALUATOR (249.367-034)
05.09.03 SORTER-PRICER (222.387-054)
07.01.02 AUTOMOBILE-CLUB-SAFETY-PROGRAM
 COORDINATOR (249.167-010)
07.01.02 MEMBERSHIP SECRETARY (201.362-018)
07.04.01 REHABILITATION CLERK (205.367-046)
07.04.03 ANIMAL-SHELTER CLERK (249.367-010)
07.04.03 DOG LICENSER (249.367-030)
07.04.04 INFORMATION CLERK, AUTOMOBILE
 CLUB (237.267-010)
07.04.05 RECEIVER-DISPATCHER (239.367-022)
07.05.02 BRAILLE PROOFREADER (209.367-014)
07.05.04 ROUTING CLERK (249.367-070)
07.06.02 BRAILLE TYPIST (203.582-014)
08.02.02 SALES EXHIBITOR (279.357-010)
08.02.08 FUND RAISER II (293.357-014)

10.01.01 PASTORAL ASSISTANT (129.107-026)
10.02.02 ORIENTATION AND MOBILITY THERA-
PIST FOR THE BLIND (076.224-014)
11.05.02 EXECUTIVE VICE PRESIDENT, CHAMBER
OF COMMERCE (187.117-030)
11.05.02 MANAGER, WORLD TRADE AND MARI-
TIME DIVISION (187.167-170)
11.07.01 DIRECTOR, COMMUNITY ORGANIZA-
TION (187.167-234)
11.07.01 DIRECTOR, SERVICE (187.167-214)
11.07.01 EXECUTIVE DIRECTOR, RED CROSS
(187.117-066)
11.07.01 MANAGER, ANIMAL SHELTER
(187.167-218)
11.07.03 SUPERVISOR, CONTRACT-SHELTERED
WORKSHOP (187.134-010)
11.09.02 DIRECTOR, FUNDRAISING (165.117-010)
11.09.02 FUND RAISER I (293.157-010)
11.10.03 ANIMAL TREATMENT INVESTIGATOR
(379.263-010)

Office, Computing, and Accounting Machines

06.01.04 FINAL ASSEMBLER (706.381-018)
06.02.01 SUPERVISOR (706.131-014)
06.02.23 ASSEMBLER I (706.684-014)
06.02.23 PRINTED CIRCUIT BOARD ASSEMBLER,
HAND (726.684-070)
06.02.24 REPAIRER, TYPEWRITER (706.381-030)
06.03.01 INSPECTOR (710.384-014)
06.03.01 MACHINE TESTER (706.387-014)
06.03.02 ELECTRONICS TESTER (726.684-026)

Optical Goods

05.01.01 OPTOMECHANICAL TECHNICIAN
(007.161-030)
05.05.11 LENS MOUNTER II (713.681-010)
05.05.11 OPTICIAN (716.280-014)
05.05.14 STONE SETTER (700.381-054)
05.09.02 PRESCRIPTION CLERK, LENS-AND-
FRAMES (222.367-050)
05.10.01 OPTICIAN, DISPENSING (299.361-010)
06.02.08 EYEGLASS-LENS CUTTER (716.682-010)
06.02.08 PRECISION-LENS GRINDER (716.382-018)
06.02.21 OPTICAL-ELEMENT COATER (716.382-014)
06.02.30 CEMENTER (711.684-014)
06.02.30 MOLDER (575.381-010)
06.04.08 LENS-FABRICATING-MACHINE TENDER
(716.685-022)
06.04.13 FUSING-FURNACE LOADER (573.686-014)
06.04.23 ASSEMBLER, MOLDED FRAMES
(713.684-014)
06.04.23 LENS INSERTER (713.687-026)
06.04.24 BENCH WORKER (713.684-018)

Ordnance and Accessories, Except Vehicles and Guided Missiles

02.04.01 PROOF TECHNICIAN (199.171-010)
06.04.39 CLEANER (503.684-010)

Paint and Varnish

06.04.11 MIXER (550.685-078)

Paper and Pulp

05.12.03 YARD LABORER (922.687-102)
06.04.18 DIGESTER-OPERATOR HELPER
(532.686-010)

Paper Goods

06.01.02 MACHINE SET-UP OPERATOR, PAPER
GOODS (649.380-010)
06.01.02 SCREEN-PRINTING-EQUIPMENT SETTER
(979.360-010)
06.04.04 BAG-MACHINE OPERATOR (649.685-014)
06.04.04 CARTON-FORMING-MACHINE TENDER
(641.685-026)
06.04.18 DIGESTER-OPERATOR HELPER
(532.686-010)

Personal Protective and Medical Devices and Supplies

05.05.11 DENTAL CERAMIST (712.381-042)
05.05.11 DENTAL CERAMIST ASSISTANT
(712.664-010)
05.05.11 DENTAL-LABORATORY TECHNICIAN
(712.381-018)
05.05.11 DENTAL-LABORATORY-TECHNICIAN
APPRENTICE (712.381-022)
05.05.11 DENTURE-MODEL MAKER (712.684-046)
05.05.11 FINISHER, DENTURE (712.381-050)
05.05.11 ORTHODONTIC TECHNICIAN
(712.381-030)
05.05.11 ORTHOTICS TECHNICIAN (712.381-034)
05.05.11 PACKER, DENTURE (712.684-034)
05.05.11 PROSTHETICS TECHNICIAN (712.381-038)
05.10.01 ARCH-SUPPORT TECHNICIAN
(712.381-010)
05.10.02 MEDICAL-EQUIPMENT REPAIRER
(639.281-022)
05.12.13 BLOCK MAKER (719.381-018)
06.02.32 DENTURE WAXER (712.381-046)
06.02.32 OPAQUER (712.684-030)
06.04.05 SURGICAL-DRESSING MAKER
(689.685-130)
06.04.19 STERILIZER (599.585-010)
06.04.24 REFINER (712.684-038)

Personal Service

01.06.02 MORTUARY BEAUTICIAN (339.361-010)
01.06.02 WIG DRESSER (332.361-010)

02.04.02 EMBALMER (338.371-014)
03.03.02 DOG BATHER (418.677-010)
03.03.02 DOG GROOMER (418.674-010)
04.02.02 BODYGUARD (372.667-014)
04.02.02 SECURITY CONSULTANT (189.167-054)
04.02.03 CHAPERON (359.667-010)
05.05.15 ALTERATION TAILOR (785.261-010)
05.05.15 CUSTOM TAILOR (785.261-014)
05.05.15 SHOE REPAIRER (365.361-014)
05.08.03 CHAUFFEUR, FUNERAL CAR (359.673-014)
05.09.01 SUPPLY CLERK (339.687-010)
06.04.19 CREMATOR (359.685-010)
07.05.01 GUIDE, TRAVEL (353.167-010)
08.02.02 SALESPERSON, WIGS (261.351-010)
09.01.02 GUIDE (353.367-010)
09.01.02 GUIDE, SIGHTSEEING (353.363-010)
09.01.04 FUNERAL ATTENDANT (359.677-014)
09.02.01 COSMETOLOGIST (332.271-010)
09.02.01 HAIR STYLIST (332.271-018)
09.02.01 SCALP-TREATMENT OPERATOR
     (339.371-014)
09.02.02 BARBER (330.371-010)
09.04.02 SERVICE-ESTABLISHMENT ATTENDANT
     (369.477-014)
09.05.01 COOLING-ROOM ATTENDANT
     (335.677-010)
09.05.01 ELECTROLOGIST (339.371-010)
09.05.01 FINGERNAIL FORMER (331.674-014)
09.05.01 HOT-ROOM ATTENDANT (335.677-014)
09.05.01 MANICURIST (331.674-010)
09.05.01 MASSEUR/MASSEUSE (334.374-010)
09.05.01 REDUCING-SALON ATTENDANT
     (359.567-010)
09.05.01 WEIGHT-REDUCTION SPECIALIST
     (359.367-014)
09.05.02 CATERER HELPER (319.677-010)
09.05.07 LOCKER-ROOM ATTENDANT (358.677-014)
10.03.03 BLIND AIDE (359.573-010)
10.03.03 CHILD-CARE ATTENDANT, SCHOOL
     (355.674-010)
10.03.03 HOME ATTENDANT (354.377-014)
11.11.04 DIRECTOR, FUNERAL (187.167-030)
11.11.04 MANAGER, BARBER OR BEAUTY SHOP
     (187.167-058)
11.11.04 MANAGER, FOOD SERVICE (187.167-106)

Petroleum and Natural Gas Production

02.01.02 GEOLOGIST, PETROLEUM (024.061-022)
02.04.01 GEOLOGICAL AIDE (024.267-010)
02.04.01 LABORATORY ASSISTANT (024.381-010)
05.01.08 PETROLEUM ENGINEER (010.061-018)
05.03.02 DRAFTER, GEOLOGICAL (010.281-014)
05.03.02 DRAFTER, GEOPHYSICAL (010.281-018)
05.03.04 FIELD ENGINEER, SPECIALIST
     (010.261-010)
05.05.09 MAINTENANCE MECHANIC (620.281-046)
05.05.10 INSTRUMENT-MAKER AND REPAIRER
     (600.280-014)
05.07.01 LINE WALKER (869.564-010)
05.10.01 ROUSTABOUT (869.684-046)

05.10.02 MAINTENANCE MECHANIC HELPER
     (620.664-014)
05.11.03 ROTARY DRILLER (930.382-026)
07.01.05 TITLE CLERK (162.267-010)
11.05.02 MANAGER, CONTRACTS (163.117-010)
11.12.02 MANAGER, LEASING (186.117-046)

Petroleum Refining

02.04.01 TESTER (029.261-022)
05.01.04 TEST-ENGINE EVALUATOR (010.261-026)
05.07.01 LINE WALKER (869.564-010)
05.12.03 LABORER, PETROLEUM REFINERY
     (549.687-018)
06.01.03 REFINERY OPERATOR (549.260-010)
07.01.05 TITLE CLERK (162.267-010)
11.05.02 MANAGER, CONTRACTS (163.117-010)

Pharmaceuticals and Related Products

02.04.02 LABORATORY ASSISTANT, BLOOD AND
     PLASMA (078.687-010)
02.04.02 LABORATORY ASSISTANT, CULTURE
     MEDIA (559.384-010)
02.04.02 LABORATORY TECHNICIAN, PHARMA-
     CEUTICAL (559.361-010)
02.04.02 TOXICOLOGIST (022.081-010)
05.02.03 QUALITY-CONTROL COORDINATOR
     (168.167-066)
06.03.02 INSPECTOR (559.387-014)
06.04.11 DRIER OPERATOR (553.685-042)
06.04.19 LABORER (559.686-022)
06.04.19 STERILIZER (599.585-010)
07.05.03 QUALITY-CONTROL CLERK (229.587-014)

Photofinishing

05.10.05 COLOR-PRINTER OPERATOR (976.382-014)
05.10.05 DEVELOPER (976.681-010)
05.10.05 FILM DEVELOPER (976.382-018)
05.10.05 FILM INSPECTOR (976.362-010)
05.10.05 FILM LABORATORY TECHNICIAN
     (976.684-014)
05.10.05 PHOTOGRAPH FINISHER (976.487-010)
05.10.05 QUALITY-CONTROL TECHNICIAN
     (976.267-010)
05.10.05 TAKE-DOWN SORTER (976.665-010)
06.01.01 SUPERVISOR, FILM PROCESSING
     (976.131-014)
06.01.02 PRINT CONTROLLER (976.360-010)
06.03.02 PHOTO CHECKER AND ASSEMBLER
     (976.687-014)
06.03.02 PHOTOFINISHING LABORATORY
     WORKER (976.687-018)
06.04.09 CUTTER (976.685-010)
06.04.19 DEVELOPER, AUTOMATIC (976.685-014)
06.04.19 PRINT DEVELOPER, AUTOMATIC
     (976.685-026)
06.04.19 UTILITY WORKER, FILM PROCESSING
     (976.685-030)

06.04.20 MOUNTER, AUTOMATIC (976.685-022)
07.03.01 COUNTER CLERK (249.366-010)
07.05.03 DETAILER, SCHOOL PHOTOGRAPHS
(976.564-010)

Photographic Apparatus and Materials

05.01.01 OPTOMECHANICAL TECHNICIAN
(007.161-030)

Pipe Lines

05.05.09 MAINTENANCE MECHANIC (620.281-046)
05.07.01 LINE WALKER (869.564-010)
05.09.01 DISTRIBUTION SUPERVISOR (914.137-010)
05.10.02 MAINTENANCE MECHANIC HELPER
(620.664-014)
07.01.05 TITLE CLERK (162.267-010)
11.05.02 MANAGER, CONTRACTS (163.117-010)

Plastic and Synthetic Materials

02.04.01 LABORATORY TESTER (022.281-018)
06.02.02 SAWYER (690.482-010)
06.02.13 EXTRUDER OPERATOR (557.382-010)
06.03.01 INSPECTOR (559.381-010)
06.04.02 GRINDER (555.685-026)
06.04.40 FINISHER (554.586-010)
06.04.40 LABORER, GENERAL (559.667-014)

Pottery and Porcelain Ware

06.02.30 PLASTER-DIE MAKER (774.684-026)
06.02.30 THROWER (774.381-010)
06.03.01 INSPECTOR II (774.384-010)
06.03.02 PRINT INSPECTOR (774.687-018)
06.04.17 KILN WORKER (573.687-022)

Printing and Publishing

01.01.01 EDITOR, PUBLICATIONS (132.037-022)
01.01.02 CROSSWORD-PUZZLE MAKER
(139.087-010)
01.01.02 EDITORIAL WRITER (131.067-022)
01.02.03 CARTOONIST (141.061-010)
01.02.03 PHOTOJOURNALIST (143.062-034)
01.06.01 ADVERTISING-SPACE CLERK
(247.387-018)
01.06.01 COMPUTER TYPESETTER-KEYLINER
(979.382-026)
01.06.01 ELECTRONIC MASKING SYSTEM OPERA-
TOR (972.282-018)
01.06.01 ELECTRONIC PREPRESS SYSTEM OPERA-
TOR (979.282-010)
01.06.01 PASTE-UP ARTIST (972.381-030)
01.06.01 PHOTOENGRAVER (971.381-022)
01.06.01 PHOTOGRAPHER, LITHOGRAPHIC
(972.382-014)
01.06.01 STRIPPER (971.381-050)

01.06.01 STRIPPER, LITHOGRAPHIC I (972.281-022)
01.06.01 SUPERVISOR, PREPRESS (972.137-010)
05.05.13 ASSISTANT PRESS OPERATOR, OFFSET
(651.685-026)
05.05.13 ASSISTANT-PRESS OPERATOR
(651.585-010)
05.05.13 CYLINDER-PRESS OPERATOR
(651.362-010)
05.05.13 ELECTROTYPER (974.381-010)
05.05.13 JOB PRINTER (973.381-018)
05.05.13 OFFSET-PRESS OPERATOR I (651.382-042)
05.05.13 ROTOGRAVURE-PRESS OPERATOR
(651.362-026)
05.05.13 STEREOTYPER (974.382-014)
05.05.13 WEB-PRESS OPERATOR (651.362-030)
05.05.15 BOOKBINDER (977.381-010)
05.09.01 MAILER (222.587-030)
05.09.02 CUSTOMER SERVICES COORDINATOR
(221.167-026)
05.09.02 ESTIMATOR, PRINTING (221.367-014)
05.10.05 CONTACT WORKER, LITHOGRAPHY
(976.684-038)
05.10.05 ENGRAVER, MACHINE (979.382-014)
05.10.05 ENGRAVING-PRESS OPERATOR
(651.382-010)
05.10.05 EQUIPMENT MONITOR, PHOTOTYPESET-
TING (650.682-010)
05.10.05 INSTANT PRINT OPERATOR (979.362-010)
05.10.05 PHOTOCOMPOSING-MACHINE OPERA-
TOR (650.582-018)
05.10.05 PROOFER, PREPRESS (972.381-034)
05.12.19 BRAILLE-DUPLICATING-MACHINE
OPERATOR (207.685-010)
05.12.19 FEEDER (651.686-014)
05.12.19 ROLL TENDER (651.686-022)
06.03.02 FILM FLAT INSPECTOR (972.284-010)
06.03.02 INKER (659.667-010)
06.03.02 PLATE INSPECTOR (972.687-010)
06.04.04 BINDERY WORKER (653.685-010)
06.04.04 BOOK TRIMMER (640.685-010)
06.04.38 MAILING-MACHINE OPERATOR
(208.462-010)
07.05.01 ADVERTISING-DISPATCH CLERK
(247.387-014)
07.05.02 BRAILLE PROOFREADER (209.367-014)
07.05.02 CLASSIFIED-AD CLERK II (247.387-022)
07.05.02 PRODUCTION PROOFREADER
(247.667-010)
07.05.02 PROOFREADER (209.387-030)
07.06.01 TERMINAL-MAKEUP OPERATOR
(208.382-010)
07.06.02 BRAILLE OPERATOR (203.582-010)
07.06.02 BRAILLE TYPIST (203.582-014)
07.06.02 MAGNETIC-TAPE-COMPOSER OPERATOR
(203.382-018)
07.06.02 PHOTOCOMPOSITION-KEYBOARD
OPERATOR (203.582-046)
07.06.02 PHOTOTYPESETTER OPERATOR
(650.582-022)
07.07.02 MAILROOM SUPERVISOR (222.137-022)
08.01.02 SALES REPRESENTATIVE, ADVERTISING
(254.357-014)

11.05.04 MANAGER, CIRCULATION (163.167-014)
11.08.01 EDITOR, CITY (132.037-014)
11.08.01 EDITOR, DEPARTMENT (132.037-018)
11.08.01 EDITOR, NEWS (132.067-026)
11.08.01 EDITOR, NEWSPAPER (132.017-014)
11.08.01 EDITORIAL ASSISTANT (132.267-014)
11.08.02 REPORTER (131.262-018)
11.08.03 COLUMNIST/COMMENTATOR
      (131.067-010)
11.09.01 CIRCULATION-SALES REPRESENTATIVE
      (299.167-010)
11.09.01 MANAGER, ADVERTISING (163.167-010)

Professional and Kindred Occupations

01.01.02 BIOGRAPHER (052.067-010)
01.01.02 COPY WRITER (131.067-014)
01.01.02 HUMORIST (131.067-026)
01.01.02 LIBRETTIST (131.067-030)
01.01.02 LYRICIST (131.067-034)
01.01.02 PLAYWRIGHT (131.067-038)
01.01.02 WRITER, PROSE, FICTION AND NON-
      FICTION (131.067-046)
01.02.01 APPRAISER, ART (191.287-014)
01.02.03 ART DIRECTOR (141.031-010)
01.02.03 AUDIOVISUAL PRODUCTION SPECIALIST
      (149.061-010)
01.02.03 COMMERCIAL DESIGNER (141.061-038)
01.02.03 DISPLAY DESIGNER (142.051-010)
01.02.03 FASHION DESIGNER (142.061-018)
01.02.03 GRAPHIC DESIGNER (141.061-018)
01.02.03 ILLUSTRATOR (141.061-022)
01.02.03 ILLUSTRATOR, MEDICAL AND SCIEN-
      TIFIC (141.061-026)
01.02.03 INDUSTRIAL DESIGNER (142.061-026)
01.02.03 INTERIOR DESIGNER (142.051-014)
01.02.03 PACKAGE DESIGNER (142.081-018)
01.02.03 PHOTOGRAPHER, STILL (143.062-030)
01.03.02 INTERPRETER, DEAF (137.267-014)
01.06.02 CONSERVATOR, ARTIFACTS (055.381-010)
01.06.02 TAXIDERMIST (199.261-010)
02.01.01 CHEMIST (022.061-010)
02.01.01 GEOGRAPHER (029.067-010)
02.01.01 GEOGRAPHER, PHYSICAL (029.067-014)
02.01.01 GEOLOGIST (024.061-018)
02.01.01 GEOPHYSICIST (024.061-030)
02.01.01 HYDROLOGIST (024.061-034)
02.01.01 MATHEMATICIAN (020.067-014)
02.01.01 METEOROLOGIST (025.062-010)
02.01.01 MINERALOGIST (024.061-038)
02.01.01 PETROLOGIST (024.061-046)
02.01.01 PHYSICIST (023.061-014)
02.01.01 SEISMOLOGIST (024.061-050)
02.01.02 CHEMICAL LABORATORY CHIEF
      (022.161-010)
02.01.02 ENVIRONMENTAL ANALYST (029.081-010)
02.01.02 MATERIALS SCIENTIST (029.081-014)
02.01.02 PROJECT MANAGER, ENVIRONMENTAL
      RESEARCH (029.167-014)
02.02.01 ANIMAL SCIENTIST (040.061-014)
02.02.01 BIOMEDICAL ENGINEER (019.061-010)

02.02.01 MEDICAL PHYSICIST (079.021-014)
02.02.01 PARASITOLOGIST (041.061-070)
02.02.01 PHARMACOLOGIST (041.061-074)
02.02.01 ZOOLOGIST (041.061-090)
02.02.02 AGRONOMIST (040.061-010)
02.02.02 BOTANIST (041.061-038)
02.02.02 FOREST ECOLOGIST (040.061-030)
02.02.02 HORTICULTURIST (040.061-038)
02.02.02 PLANT PATHOLOGIST (041.061-086)
02.02.02 RANGE MANAGER (040.061-046)
02.02.02 SILVICULTURIST (040.061-050)
02.02.02 SOIL CONSERVATIONIST (040.061-054)
02.02.02 SOIL SCIENTIST (040.061-058)
02.02.02 SOIL-CONSERVATION TECHNICIAN
      (040.261-010)
02.02.02 WOOD TECHNOLOGIST (040.061-062)
02.02.03 AQUATIC BIOLOGIST (041.061-022)
02.02.03 BIOCHEMIST (041.061-026)
02.02.03 BIOLOGIST (041.061-030)
02.02.03 BIOPHYSICIST (041.061-034)
02.02.03 MICROBIOLOGIST (041.061-058)
02.02.03 PHYSIOLOGIST (041.061-078)
02.02.04 CHEMIST, FOOD (022.061-014)
02.02.04 DAIRY TECHNOLOGIST (040.061-022)
02.02.04 FOOD TECHNOLOGIST (041.081-010)
02.03.04 SPEECH PATHOLOGIST (076.107-010)
02.03.04 VOICE PATHOLOGIST (076.104-010)
02.04.01 ASSAYER (022.281-010)
02.04.01 CHEMICAL LABORATORY TECHNICIAN
      (022.261-010)
02.04.01 CRIMINALIST (029.261-026)
02.04.01 GRAPHOLOGIST (199.267-038)
02.04.01 HOT-CELL TECHNICIAN (015.362-018)
02.04.01 LABORATORY SUPERVISOR (022.137-010)
02.04.01 METALLURGICAL TECHNICIAN
      (011.261-010)
02.04.01 PHOTO-OPTICS TECHNICIAN (029.280-010)
02.04.01 PHOTOGRAPHER, SCIENTIFIC
      (143.062-026)
02.04.01 QUALITY CONTROL TECHNICIAN
      (012.261-014)
02.04.01 RADIOISOTOPE-PRODUCTION OPERATOR
      (015.362-022)
02.04.01 REACTOR OPERATOR, TEST-AND-
      RESEARCH (015.362-026)
02.04.01 SCANNER (015.384-010)
02.04.01 SPECTROSCOPIST (011.281-014)
02.04.01 TESTER (011.361-010)
02.04.01 WEATHER OBSERVER (025.267-014)
02.04.02 BIOLOGY SPECIMEN TECHNICIAN
      (041.381-010)
02.04.02 BIOMEDICAL EQUIPMENT TECHNICIAN
      (019.261-010)
02.04.02 HERBARIUM WORKER (041.384-010)
02.04.02 POLYGRAPH EXAMINER (199.267-026)
02.04.02 SEED ANALYST (040.361-014)
03.01.04 FORESTER (040.167-010)
05.01.01 CHEMICAL RESEARCH ENGINEER
      (008.061-022)
05.01.01 ELECTRICAL TECHNICIAN (003.161-010)
05.01.01 ELECTRICAL-RESEARCH ENGINEER
      (003.061-026)

05.01.01 ELECTRONICS TECHNICIAN (003.161-014)
05.01.01 INSTRUMENTATION TECHNICIAN (003.261-010)
05.01.01 MECHANICAL RESEARCH ENGINEER (007.161-022)
05.01.01 MECHANICAL-ENGINEERING TECHNICIAN (007.161-026)
05.01.01 TECHNICIAN, SEMICONDUCTOR DEVELOPMENT (003.161-018)
05.01.01 WELDING TECHNICIAN (011.261-014)
05.01.02 FIRE-PROTECTION ENGINEER (012.167-026)
05.01.02 HEALTH PHYSICIST (015.021-010)
05.01.02 INDUSTRIAL-HEALTH ENGINEER (012.167-034)
05.01.02 NUCLEAR-CRITICALITY SAFETY ENGINEER (015.067-010)
05.01.02 POLLUTION-CONTROL ENGINEER (019.081-018)
05.01.02 PRODUCT-SAFETY ENGINEER (012.061-010)
05.01.02 RADIATION-PROTECTION ENGINEER (015.137-010)
05.01.02 SAFETY ENGINEER (012.061-014)
05.01.02 SAFETY MANAGER (012.167-058)
05.01.03 COMPUTER SYSTEMS HARDWARE ANALYST (033.167-010)
05.01.03 HYDRAULIC ENGINEER (005.061-018)
05.01.03 ILLUMINATING ENGINEER (003.061-046)
05.01.03 IRRIGATION ENGINEER (005.061-022)
05.01.03 MARINE ENGINEER (014.061-014)
05.01.03 NUCLEAR ENGINEER (015.061-014)
05.01.03 NUCLEAR-FUELS RECLAMATION ENGINEER (015.061-026)
05.01.03 SANITARY ENGINEER (005.061-030)
05.01.03 WASTE-MANAGEMENT ENGINEER, RADIOACTIVE MATERIALS (005.061-042)
05.01.04 AIR ANALYST (012.261-010)
05.01.04 CHEMICAL-TEST ENGINEER (008.061-026)
05.01.04 ELECTRICAL TEST ENGINEER (003.061-014)
05.01.04 ELECTRONICS-TEST ENGINEER (003.061-042)
05.01.04 METALLOGRAPHER (011.061-014)
05.01.04 METROLOGIST (012.067-010)
05.01.04 QUALITY CONTROL ENGINEER (012.167-054)
05.01.04 RELIABILITY ENGINEER (019.061-026)
05.01.04 STRESS ANALYST (007.061-042)
05.01.04 TEST ENGINEER, NUCLEAR EQUIPMENT (015.061-022)
05.01.04 TEST TECHNICIAN (019.161-014)
05.01.05 SALES-ENGINEER, ELECTRONICS PRODUCTS AND SYSTEMS (003.151-014)
05.01.06 CONFIGURATION MANAGEMENT ANALYST (012.167-010)
05.01.06 DOCUMENTATION ENGINEER (012.167-078)
05.01.06 FACTORY LAY-OUT ENGINEER (012.167-018)
05.01.06 INDUSTRIAL ENGINEER (012.167-030)

05.01.06 LAND SURVEYOR (018.167-018)
05.01.06 MANAGEMENT ANALYST (161.167-010)
05.01.06 MANUFACTURING ENGINEER (012.167-042)
05.01.06 MATERIALS ENGINEER (019.061-014)
05.01.06 METALLURGIST, EXTRACTIVE (011.061-018)
05.01.06 PRODUCTION ENGINEER (012.167-046)
05.01.06 PRODUCTION PLANNER (012.167-050)
05.01.06 STANDARDS ENGINEER (012.061-018)
05.01.06 TIME-STUDY ENGINEER (012.167-070)
05.01.07 AGRICULTURAL-ENGINEERING TECHNICIAN (013.161-010)
05.01.07 AIRPORT ENGINEER (005.061-010)
05.01.07 ARCHITECT (001.061-010)
05.01.07 ARCHITECT, MARINE (001.061-014)
05.01.07 CERAMIC ENGINEER (006.061-014)
05.01.07 CHEMICAL DESIGN ENGINEER, PROCESSES (008.061-014)
05.01.07 CHEMICAL ENGINEER (008.061-018)
05.01.07 CIVIL ENGINEER (005.061-014)
05.01.07 ELECTRICAL-DESIGN ENGINEER (003.061-018)
05.01.07 ELECTRO-OPTICAL ENGINEER (023.061-010)
05.01.07 ELECTRONICS-DESIGN ENGINEER (003.061-034)
05.01.07 LANDSCAPE ARCHITECT (001.061-018)
05.01.07 MECHANICAL-DESIGN ENGINEER, FACILITIES (007.061-018)
05.01.07 OPTICAL ENGINEER (019.061-018)
05.01.07 RAILROAD ENGINEER (005.061-026)
05.01.07 TOOL DESIGNER (007.061-026)
05.01.08 AGRICULTURAL ENGINEER (013.061-010)
05.01.08 CHEMICAL-ENGINEERING TECHNICIAN (008.261-010)
05.01.08 ELECTRICAL ENGINEER (003.061-010)
05.01.08 ELECTRONICS ENGINEER (003.061-030)
05.01.08 ENGINEER, SOILS (024.161-010)
05.01.08 ENGINEERING MANAGER, ELECTRONICS (003.167-070)
05.01.08 FIBER TECHNOLOGIST (040.061-026)
05.01.08 MAINTAINABILITY ENGINEER (019.081-010)
05.01.08 MECHANICAL ENGINEER (007.061-014)
05.01.08 PLANT ENGINEER (007.167-014)
05.01.08 PROJECT ENGINEER (019.167-014)
05.01.08 TRANSPORTATION ENGINEER (005.061-038)
05.01.08 WELDING ENGINEER (011.061-026)
05.02.03 MANAGER, CUSTOMER TECHNICAL SERVICES (189.117-018)
05.02.03 MANAGER, QUALITY CONTROL (012.167-014)
05.02.06 MANAGER, LAND SURVEYING (018.167-022)
05.03.01 PHOTOGRAMMETRIC ENGINEER (018.167-026)
05.03.01 SURVEYOR ASSISTANT, INSTRUMENTS (018.167-034)
05.03.02 CIVIL ENGINEERING TECHNICIAN (005.261-014)

05.03.02 CONTROLS DESIGNER (003.261-014)
05.03.02 DESIGN DRAFTER, ELECTROMECHANISMS (017.261-014)
05.03.02 DETAILER (017.261-018)
05.03.02 DRAFTER, ARCHITECTURAL (001.261-010)
05.03.02 DRAFTER, ASSISTANT (017.281-018)
05.03.02 DRAFTER, CARTOGRAPHIC (018.261-010)
05.03.02 DRAFTER, CIVIL (005.281-010)
05.03.02 DRAFTER, COMMERCIAL (017.261-026)
05.03.02 DRAFTER, ELECTRICAL (003.281-010)
05.03.02 DRAFTER, ELECTRONIC (003.281-014)
05.03.02 DRAFTER, LANDSCAPE (001.261-014)
05.03.02 DRAFTER, MARINE (014.281-010)
05.03.02 DRAFTER, MECHANICAL (007.281-010)
05.03.02 DRAFTER, STRUCTURAL (005.281-014)
05.03.02 DRAWINGS CHECKER, ENGINEERING (007.267-010)
05.03.02 EDITOR, MAP (018.261-018)
05.03.02 ENGINEERING ASSISTANT, MECHANICAL EQUIPMENT (007.161-018)
05.03.02 ESTIMATOR (169.267-038)
05.03.02 FIRE-PROTECTION ENGINEERING TECHNICIAN (019.261-026)
05.03.02 INTEGRATED CIRCUIT LAYOUT DESIGNER (003.261-018)
05.03.02 PHOTOGRAMMETRIST (018.261-026)
05.03.02 PRINTED CIRCUIT DESIGNER (003.261-022)
05.03.02 SPECIFICATION WRITER (019.267-010)
05.03.02 STEREO-PLOTTER OPERATOR (018.281-010)
05.03.02 TECHNICAL ILLUSTRATOR (017.281-034)
05.03.06 INDUSTRIAL ENGINEERING TECHNICIAN (012.267-010)
05.03.06 MARINE SURVEYOR (014.167-010)
05.03.07 HEAT-TRANSFER TECHNICIAN (007.181-010)
05.03.07 SOLAR-ENERGY-SYSTEMS DESIGNER (007.161-038)
05.03.08 POLLUTION-CONTROL TECHNICIAN (029.261-014)
05.03.08 RADIATION MONITOR (199.167-010)
05.03.09 PACKAGING ENGINEER (019.187-010)
05.05.05 ELECTRONIC-SALES-AND-SERVICE TECHNICIAN (828.251-010)
05.05.05 FIELD SERVICE ENGINEER (828.261-014)
05.05.05 MICROCOMPUTER SUPPORT SPECIALIST (039.264-010)
05.05.17 DIETETIC TECHNICIAN (077.124-010)
05.05.17 DIETITIAN, CLINICAL (077.127-014)
05.07.01 NONDESTRUCTIVE TESTER (011.261-018)
07.01.01 CREDIT COUNSELOR (160.207-010)
07.01.04 ESCROW OFFICER (119.367-010)
07.01.05 CONTRACT CLERK (119.267-018)
07.01.05 TITLE EXAMINER (119.287-010)
07.01.05 TITLE SUPERVISOR (119.167-018)
08.01.03 BUYER (162.157-018)
10.01.01 CLERGY MEMBER (120.107-010)
10.01.02 CLINICAL PSYCHOLOGIST (045.107-022)
10.01.02 CLINICAL THERAPIST (045.107-050)
10.01.02 COUNSELOR (045.107-010)

10.01.02 COUNSELOR, MARRIAGE AND FAMILY (045.107-054)
10.01.02 PROBATION-AND-PAROLE OFFICER (195.107-046)
10.01.02 PSYCHOLOGIST, CHIEF (045.107-046)
10.01.02 PSYCHOLOGIST, COUNSELING (045.107-026)
10.01.02 PSYCHOLOGIST, SCHOOL (045.107-034)
10.01.02 SUBSTANCE ABUSE COUNSELOR (045.107-058)
10.02.02 HYPNOTHERAPIST (079.157-010)
10.03.01 AUDIOMETRIST (078.362-010)
11.01.01 CHIEF, COMPUTER PROGRAMMER (030.167-010)
11.01.01 COMPUTER PROGRAMMER (030.162-010)
11.01.01 DATA BASE ADMINISTRATOR (039.162-010)
11.01.01 DATA BASE DESIGN ANALYST (039.162-014)
11.01.01 DATA COMMUNICATIONS ANALYST (031.262-010)
11.01.01 DATA RECOVERY PLANNER (033.162-014)
11.01.01 DIRECTOR, RECORDS MANAGEMENT (161.117-014)
11.01.01 FORMS ANALYST (161.267-018)
11.01.01 INFORMATION SCIENTIST (109.067-010)
11.01.01 MANAGER, COMPUTER OPERATIONS (169.167-082)
11.01.01 MANAGER, DATA PROCESSING (169.167-030)
11.01.01 OPERATIONS-RESEARCH ANALYST (020.067-018)
11.01.01 PROGRAMMER, ENGINEERING AND SCIENTIFIC (030.162-018)
11.01.01 PROGRAMMER-ANALYST (030.162-014)
11.01.01 QUALITY ASSURANCE ANALYST (033.262-010)
11.01.01 SOFTWARE ENGINEER (030.062-010)
11.01.01 STATISTICIAN, MATHEMATICAL (020.067-022)
11.01.01 SYSTEMS ANALYST (030.167-014)
11.01.01 SYSTEMS PROGRAMMER (030.162-022)
11.01.01 TECHNICAL SUPPORT SPECIALIST (033.162-018)
11.01.01 USER SUPPORT ANALYST (032.262-010)
11.01.01 USER SUPPORT ANALYST SUPERVISOR (032.132-010)
11.01.02 ACTUARY (020.167-010)
11.01.02 CONSULTANT (189.167-010)
11.01.02 MATHEMATICAL TECHNICIAN (020.162-010)
11.01.02 STATISTICIAN, APPLIED (020.167-026)
11.02.02 DIETITIAN, TEACHING (077.127-022)
11.02.02 HUMAN RESOURCE ADVISOR (166.267-046)
11.02.03 COMMUNITY DIETITIAN (077.127-010)
11.02.03 HOME ECONOMIST (096.121-014)
11.03.01 PSYCHOLOGIST, DEVELOPMENTAL (045.061-010)
11.03.01 PSYCHOLOGIST, EDUCATIONAL (045.067-010)

11.03.01 PSYCHOLOGIST, ENGINEERING (045.061-014)
11.03.01 PSYCHOLOGIST, EXPERIMENTAL (045.061-018)
11.03.01 PSYCHOLOGIST, INDUSTRIAL-ORGANIZATIONAL (045.107-030)
11.03.01 PSYCHOLOGIST, SOCIAL (045.067-014)
11.03.01 PSYCHOMETRIST (045.067-018)
11.03.02 CITY PLANNING AIDE (199.364-010)
11.03.02 POLITICAL SCIENTIST (051.067-010)
11.03.02 RESEARCH WORKER, SOCIAL WELFARE (054.067-010)
11.03.02 SCIENTIFIC LINGUIST (059.067-014)
11.03.02 SOCIOLOGIST (054.067-014)
11.03.02 URBAN PLANNER (199.167-014)
11.03.03 ANTHROPOLOGIST (055.067-010)
11.03.03 ARCHEOLOGIST (055.067-018)
11.03.03 ARCHIVIST (101.167-010)
11.03.03 GENEALOGIST (052.067-018)
11.03.03 HISTORIAN (052.067-022)
11.03.04 EMPLOYEE RELATIONS SPECIALIST (166.267-042)
11.03.04 EMPLOYMENT INTERVIEWER (166.267-010)
11.03.04 JOB ANALYST (166.267-018)
11.03.04 JOB DEVELOPMENT SPECIALIST (166.267-034)
11.03.04 OCCUPATIONAL ANALYST (166.067-010)
11.03.04 PERSONNEL RECRUITER (166.267-038)
11.03.05 ECONOMIST (050.067-010)
11.04.02 LAWYER (110.107-010)
11.04.02 LAWYER, CORPORATION (110.117-022)
11.04.02 LAWYER, CRIMINAL (110.107-014)
11.04.02 LAWYER, PATENT (110.117-026)
11.04.02 LAWYER, PROBATE (110.117-030)
11.04.02 LEGAL INVESTIGATOR (119.267-022)
11.04.02 PARALEGAL (119.267-026)
11.04.02 TAX ATTORNEY (110.117-038)
11.04.03 ARBITRATOR (169.107-010)
11.04.03 CONCILIATOR (169.207-010)
11.04.04 ABSTRACTOR (119.267-010)
11.04.04 PATENT AGENT (119.167-014)
11.05.01 ASSOCIATION EXECUTIVE (189.117-010)
11.05.02 BUSINESS REPRESENTATIVE, LABOR UNION (187.167-018)
11.05.02 DIETITIAN, CHIEF (077.117-010)
11.05.02 DIRECTOR, QUALITY ASSURANCE (189.117-042)
11.05.02 GRANT COORDINATOR (169.117-014)
11.05.02 MANAGER, BENEFITS (166.167-018)
11.05.02 MANAGER, COMPENSATION (166.167-022)
11.05.02 MANAGER, LABOR RELATIONS (166.167-034)
11.05.02 MANAGER, PERSONNEL (166.117-018)
11.05.02 MANAGER, PROCUREMENT SERVICES (162.167-022)
11.05.02 PROGRAM MANAGER (189.167-030)
11.05.02 PROGRAM SPECIALIST, EMPLOYEE-HEALTH MAINTENANCE (166.167-050)
11.05.02 PROJECT DIRECTOR (189.117-030)
11.05.03 MANAGER, HOUSING PROJECT (186.167-030)

11.05.04 PURCHASING AGENT (162.157-038)
11.06.01 ACCOUNTANT (160.162-018)
11.06.01 ACCOUNTANT, BUDGET (160.162-022)
11.06.01 ACCOUNTANT, COST (160.162-026)
11.06.01 ACCOUNTANT, PROPERTY (160.167-022)
11.06.01 ACCOUNTANT, SYSTEMS (160.167-026)
11.06.01 ACCOUNTANT, TAX (160.162-010)
11.06.01 AUDITOR (160.167-054)
11.06.01 AUDITOR, DATA PROCESSING (160.162-030)
11.06.01 AUDITOR, INTERNAL (160.167-034)
11.06.01 AUDITOR, TAX (160.167-038)
11.06.02 CONTROLLER (160.167-058)
11.06.02 REPORTS ANALYST (161.267-026)
11.06.03 MARKET-RESEARCH ANALYST I (050.067-014)
11.06.03 TREASURER (161.117-018)
11.06.05 BUDGET OFFICER (161.117-010)
11.07.01 FIELD REPRESENTATIVE (189.267-010)
11.07.01 PROGRAM DIRECTOR, GROUP WORK (187.117-046)
11.07.02 PUBLIC HEALTH EDUCATOR (079.117-014)
11.07.04 RECREATION SUPERVISOR (187.167-238)
11.08.01 EDITOR, DICTIONARY (132.067-018)
11.08.01 EDITOR, TECHNICAL AND SCIENTIFIC PUBLICATIONS (132.017-018)
11.08.02 RESEARCH ASSISTANT II (199.267-034)
11.08.02 WRITER, TECHNICAL PUBLICATIONS (131.267-026)
11.08.04 DIRECTOR, TRANSLATION (137.137-010)
11.08.04 INTERPRETER (137.267-010)
11.08.04 TRANSLATOR (137.267-018)
11.09.01 MEDIA DIRECTOR (164.117-018)
11.09.02 DIRECTOR, FUNDS DEVELOPMENT (165.117-014)
11.09.02 MEMBERSHIP DIRECTOR (189.167-026)
11.09.03 EMPLOYER RELATIONS REPRESENTATIVE (166.257-010)
11.09.03 LOBBYIST (165.017-010)
11.09.03 PUBLIC-RELATIONS REPRESENTATIVE (165.167-014)
11.10.03 INDUSTRIAL HYGIENIST (079.161-010)
11.10.03 SANITARIAN (079.117-018)
11.10.05 COMPUTER SECURITY COORDINATOR (033.162-010)
11.10.05 COMPUTER SECURITY SPECIALIST (033.362-010)
11.10.05 RATER, TRAVEL ACCOMMODATIONS (168.367-014)
11.11.04 MANAGER, EMPLOYMENT AGENCY (187.167-098)
11.12.02 REAL-ESTATE AGENT (186.117-058)
11.12.04 CONTRACT SPECIALIST (162.117-018)

Radio and Television Broadcasting

01.01.01 CONTINUITY DIRECTOR (132.037-010)
01.01.01 FILM OR VIDEOTAPE EDITOR (962.262-010)
01.01.01 SUPERVISING FILM-OR-VIDEOTAPE EDITOR (962.132-010)

01.01.02 SCREEN WRITER (131.067-050)
01.02.03 ART DIRECTOR (142.061-062)
01.02.03 CAMERA OPERATOR (143.062-022)
01.02.03 DIRECTOR OF PHOTOGRAPHY
    (143.062-010)
01.02.03 PHOTOJOURNALIST (143.062-034)
01.02.03 SET DECORATOR (142.061-042)
01.02.03 SET DESIGNER (142.061-046)
01.02.03 TELEVISION TECHNICIAN (194.062-010)
01.03.01 MANAGER, STAGE (159.167-018)
01.03.01 PRODUCER (159.117-010)
01.03.03 ANNOUNCER (159.147-010)
01.03.03 DISC JOCKEY (159.147-014)
01.03.03 SHOW HOST/HOSTESS (159.147-018)
01.04.03 SINGER (152.047-022)
01.06.02 MAKE-UP ARTIST (333.071-010)
01.06.02 SPECIAL EFFECTS SPECIALIST
    (962.281-018)
01.08.01 EXTRA (159.647-014)
05.01.03 COMMERCIAL ENGINEER (003.187-014)
05.02.04 PROGRAM DIRECTOR, CABLE TELEVI-
    SION (194.162-010)
05.03.05 ACCESS COORDINATOR, CABLE TELE-
    VISION (194.122-010)
05.03.05 FIELD ENGINEER (193.262-018)
05.03.05 MASTER CONTROL OPERATOR
    (194.262-022)
05.03.05 TECHNICIAN, NEWS GATHERING
    (194.362-022)
05.03.05 TRANSMITTER OPERATOR (193.262-038)
05.03.05 VIDEO OPERATOR (194.282-010)
05.03.05 VIDEOTAPE OPERATOR (194.382-018)
05.10.01 GRIP (962.684-014)
05.10.03 CABLE TELEVISION INSTALLER
    (821.281-010)
05.10.03 LIGHT TECHNICIAN (962.362-014)
05.10.05 AUDIO OPERATOR (194.262-010)
05.10.05 RECORDING ENGINEER (194.362-010)
05.10.05 RERECORDING MIXER (194.362-014)
05.10.05 SOUND MIXER (194.262-018)
05.10.05 TAPE TRANSFERRER (194.382-014)
05.12.04 GRIP (962.687-022)
06.01.01 SUPERVISOR, FILM PROCESSING
    (976.131-014)
07.04.01 CUSTOMER SERVICE REPRESENTATIVE
    (239.362-014)
07.05.01 CLERK, TELEVISION PRODUCTION
    (221.367-086)
07.05.01 TELEVISION-SCHEDULE COORDINATOR
    (199.382-010)
07.05.03 CAPTION WRITER (203.362-026)
07.05.03 NEWS ASSISTANT (209.367-038)
07.05.03 STENOCAPTIONER (202.382-010)
08.01.02 SALES REPRESENTATIVE, RADIO AND
    TELEVISION TIME (259.357-018)
08.02.06 SALES REPRESENTATIVE, TELEVISION
    CABLE SERVICE (259.357-022)
11.02.04 MUSIC LIBRARIAN (100.367-022)
11.05.02 MANAGER, PRODUCTION (184.162-010)
11.05.02 MANAGER, STATION (184.117-062)
11.05.02 PROGRAM PROPOSALS COORDINATOR
    (132.067-030)

11.05.02 UTILIZATION COORDINATOR
    (169.167-078)
11.05.04 DIRECTOR, MEDIA MARKETING
    (163.117-022)
11.08.02 REPORTER (131.262-018)
11.08.03 COLUMNIST/COMMENTATOR
    (131.067-010)
11.08.03 NEWSCASTER (131.262-010)
11.12.02 LOCATION MANAGER (191.167-018)
12.02.01 STUNT PERFORMER (159.341-014)

Radio, Television, and Communication Equipment

05.10.03 ELECTRONIC EQUIPMENT REPAIRER
    (726.381-014)
05.10.03 WIRER, CABLE (729.381-022)
06.01.05 ELECTRONICS INSPECTOR (726.381-010)
06.02.23 ELECTRONICS ASSEMBLER (726.684-018)
06.02.23 PRINTED CIRCUIT BOARD ASSEMBLER,
    HAND (726.684-070)
06.03.02 ELECTRONICS TESTER (726.684-026)
06.04.19 METALLIZATION EQUIPMENT TENDER,
    SEMICONDUCTORS (590.685-086)
06.04.34 ELECTRONICS UTILITY WORKER
    (726.364-018)

Railroad Equipment Building and Repairing

06.02.24 ROUTER OPERATOR, HAND (806.684-150)

Railroad Transportation

05.08.02 LOCOMOTIVE ENGINEER (910.363-014)
05.12.03 BAGGAGE HANDLER (910.687-010)
05.12.05 SWITCH TENDER (910.667-026)
07.02.04 DEMURRAGE CLERK (214.362-010)
07.04.05 TRAIN DISPATCHER (184.167-262)
07.05.01 RESERVATION CLERK (238.367-014)
07.05.03 YARD CLERK (209.367-054)
08.01.02 TRAFFIC AGENT (252.257-010)
08.02.06 CRATING-AND-MOVING ESTIMATOR
    (252.357-010)
08.03.01 LOUNGE-CAR ATTENDANT (291.457-014)
09.01.04 PASSENGER SERVICE REPRESENTATIVE I
    (352.677-010)
09.03.01 STREETCAR OPERATOR (913.463-014)
09.05.03 PORTER (357.677-010)
11.05.02 MANAGER, OPERATIONS (184.117-050)
11.10.05 TRAFFIC INSPECTOR (184.163-010)
11.10.05 TRANSPORTATION INSPECTOR
    (168.167-082)
11.11.03 CONDUCTOR, PASSENGER CAR
    (198.167-010)
11.11.03 CONDUCTOR, ROAD FREIGHT
    (198.167-018)
11.11.03 STATION MANAGER (184.167-130)
11.12.01 GENERAL CLAIMS AGENT (186.117-030)

Real Estate

03.04.04 CEMETERY WORKER (406.684-010)
05.12.01 HOUSEKEEPER (321.137-010)
07.01.04 CLOSER (186.167-074)
07.01.04 REAL-ESTATE CLERK (219.362-046)
07.01.04 SUPERVISOR, REAL-ESTATE OFFICE
    (249.137-030)
07.05.02 TITLE SEARCHER (209.367-046)
08.01.03 BUSINESS-OPPORTUNITY-AND-
    PROPERTY-INVESTMENT BROKER
    (189.157-010)
08.02.04 LEASING AGENT, RESIDENCE
    (250.357-014)
08.02.04 SALES AGENT, REAL ESTATE
    (250.357-018)
11.05.01 MANAGER, LAND DEVELOPMENT
    (186.117-042)
11.06.03 APPRAISER, REAL ESTATE (191.267-010)
11.11.01 CONDOMINIUM MANAGER (186.167-062)
11.11.01 MANAGER, APARTMENT HOUSE
    (186.167-018)
11.11.04 MANAGER, PROPERTY (186.167-046)
11.11.04 MANAGER, REAL-ESTATE FIRM
    (186.167-066)
11.11.04 MANAGER, TITLE SEARCH (186.167-090)

Recording

05.10.05 RECORDING ENGINEER (194.362-010)
05.10.05 SOUND MIXER (194.262-018)
05.10.05 TAPE TRANSFERRER (194.382-014)
05.12.03 RECORDING STUDIO SET-UP WORKER
    (962.664-014)
06.03.01 QUALITY-CONTROL INSPECTOR
    (194.387-010)
06.04.10 INJECTION-MOLDING-MACHINE TENDER
    (556.685-038)

Retail Trade

01.02.03 DISPLAYER, MERCHANDISE (298.081-010)
01.02.03 FASHION ARTIST (141.061-014)
01.02.03 FLORAL DESIGNER (142.081-010)
01.02.03 MANAGER, DISPLAY (142.031-014)
01.06.02 PICTURE FRAMER (739.684-146)
01.06.03 GIFT WRAPPER (299.364-014)
03.01.03 MANAGER, NURSERY (180.167-042)
05.05.01 SOFT-TILE SETTER (861.381-034)
05.05.11 OPTICIAN (716.280-014)
05.05.15 ALTERATION TAILOR (785.261-010)
05.05.15 CUSTOM TAILOR (785.261-014)
05.05.15 SHOP TAILOR (785.361-022)
05.08.03 DELIVERER, CAR RENTAL (919.663-010)
05.08.03 LOT ATTENDANT (915.583-010)
05.09.01 MEAT CLERK (222.684-010)
05.09.01 ORDER FILLER (222.487-014)
05.09.01 STOCK CLERK (299.367-014)
05.09.01 TIRE ADJUSTER (241.367-034)

05.09.02 DRAPERY AND UPHOLSTERY ESTIMATOR
    (299.387-010)
05.09.02 RUG MEASURER (369.367-014)
05.09.03 MARKER (209.587-034)
05.10.01 BOAT RIGGER (806.464-010)
05.10.01 CARPET CUTTER (929.381-010)
05.10.01 CARPET LAYER (864.381-010)
05.10.01 DRAPERY HANGER (869.484-014)
05.10.01 FLOOR LAYER (864.481-010)
05.10.01 FURNITURE ASSEMBLER-AND-
    INSTALLER (739.684-082)
05.10.01 OPTICIAN, DISPENSING (299.361-010)
05.10.02 MANAGER, CUSTOMER SERVICES
    (187.167-082)
05.10.02 MEDICAL-EQUIPMENT REPAIRER
    (639.281-022)
05.10.02 NEW-CAR GET-READY MECHANIC
    (806.361-026)
05.10.02 SERVICE MANAGER (185.164-010)
05.10.04 USED-CAR RENOVATOR (620.684-034)
05.10.08 MEAT CUTTER (316.684-018)
05.12.17 DELI CUTTER-SLICER (316.684-014)
06.02.05 CARPET SEWER (787.682-014)
07.02.02 CONTRACT CLERK, AUTOMOBILE
    (219.362-026)
07.03.01 AUCTION CLERK (294.567-010)
07.03.01 CASHIER-CHECKER (211.462-014)
07.03.01 COUPON-REDEMPTION CLERK
    (290.477-010)
07.03.01 LAYAWAY CLERK (299.467-010)
07.03.01 SUPERVISOR, CASHIERS (211.137-010)
07.05.02 CREDIT REFERENCE CLERK (209.362-018)
07.05.02 PRODUCTION PROOFREADER
    (247.667-010)
07.05.02 THROW-OUT CLERK (241.367-030)
07.05.03 AUTOMOBILE LOCATOR (296.367-010)
07.05.03 CALL-OUT OPERATOR (237.367-014)
07.05.04 MERCHANDISE DISTRIBUTOR
    (219.367-018)
07.06.02 CHECK WRITER (219.382-010)
07.07.02 AUCTION ASSISTANT (294.667-010)
08.01.01 SALES REPRESENTATIVE, AIRCRAFT
    (273.253-010)
08.01.03 BUYER, ASSISTANT (162.157-022)
08.01.03 COMPARISON SHOPPER (296.367-014)
08.01.03 PAWNBROKER (191.157-010)
08.02.02 HEARING AID SPECIALIST (276.354-010)
08.02.02 SALES-SERVICE REPRESENTATIVE,
    MILKING MACHINES (299.251-010)
08.02.02 SALESPERSON, ART OBJECTS
    (277.457-010)
08.02.02 SALESPERSON, AUTOMOBILES
    (273.353-010)
08.02.02 SALESPERSON, BOOKS (277.357-034)
08.02.02 SALESPERSON, COSMETICS AND
    TOILETRIES (262.357-018)
08.02.02 SALESPERSON, CURTAINS AND
    DRAPERIES (270.357-022)
08.02.02 SALESPERSON, FLOWERS (260.357-026)
08.02.02 SALESPERSON, FURNITURE (270.357-030)
08.02.02 SALESPERSON, HOUSEHOLD APPLI-
    ANCES (270.357-034)

08.02.02 SALESPERSON, INFANTS' AND CHILDREN'S WEAR (261.357-046)
08.02.02 SALESPERSON, JEWELRY (279.357-058)
08.02.02 SALESPERSON, MEN'S AND BOYS' CLOTHING (261.357-050)
08.02.02 SALESPERSON, MUSICAL INSTRUMENTS AND ACCESSORIES (277.357-038)
08.02.02 SALESPERSON, ORTHOPEDIC SHOES (276.257-018)
08.02.02 SALESPERSON, PETS AND PET SUPPLIES (277.357-042)
08.02.02 SALESPERSON, PHONOGRAPH RECORDS AND TAPE RECORDINGS (277.357-046)
08.02.02 SALESPERSON, PIANOS AND ORGANS (277.354-010)
08.02.02 SALESPERSON, SHEET MUSIC (277.357-054)
08.02.02 SALESPERSON, SHOES (261.357-062)
08.02.02 SALESPERSON, SPORTING GOODS (277.357-058)
08.02.02 SALESPERSON, STEREO EQUIPMENT (270.357-038)
08.02.02 SALESPERSON, SURGICAL APPLIANCES (276.257-022)
08.02.02 SALESPERSON, TOY TRAINS AND ACCES-SORIES (277.357-066)
08.02.02 SALESPERSON, TRAILERS AND MOTOR HOMES (273.357-034)
08.02.02 SALESPERSON, WIGS (261.351-010)
08.02.02 SALESPERSON, WOMEN'S APPAREL AND ACCESSORIES (261.357-066)
08.02.02 SALESPERSON, YARD GOODS (261.357-070)
08.02.03 AUCTIONEER (294.257-010)
08.02.03 SALES REPRESENTATIVE, BOATS AND MARINE SUPPLIES (273.357-018)
08.02.03 SALES REPRESENTATIVE, OFFICE MACHINES (275.357-034)
08.02.03 SALESPERSON, AUTOMOBILE ACCES-SORIES (273.357-030)
08.02.03 SALESPERSON, ELECTRIC MOTORS (271.354-010)
08.02.03 SALESPERSON, FLOOR COVERINGS (270.357-026)
08.02.03 SALESPERSON, GENERAL HARDWARE (279.357-050)
08.02.03 SALESPERSON, GENERAL MERCHAN-DISE (279.357-054)
08.02.03 SALESPERSON, HORTICULTURAL AND NURSERY PRODUCTS (272.357-022)
08.02.03 SALESPERSON, PARTS (279.357-062)
08.02.03 SALESPERSON, PHOTOGRAPHIC SUP-PLIES AND EQUIPMENT (277.357-050)
08.02.03 SALESPERSON, STAMPS OR COINS (277.357-062)
08.02.05 DEMONSTRATOR (297.354-010)
08.02.05 DEMONSTRATOR, KNITTING (297.354-014)
08.02.05 SALESPERSON-DEMONSTRATOR, PARTY PLAN (279.357-038)
08.02.06 SALES REPRESENTATIVE, UPHOLSTERY AND FURNITURE REPAIR (259.357-026)

08.02.06 TRAVEL AGENT (252.152-010)
08.02.06 WEDDING CONSULTANT (299.357-018)
08.02.07 DRIVER, SALES ROUTE (292.353-010)
08.02.08 SALES REPRESENTATIVE, DOOR-TO-DOOR (291.357-010)
09.04.02 BICYCLE-RENTAL CLERK (295.467-010)
09.04.02 CASHIER, COURTESY BOOTH (211.467-010)
09.04.02 CASHIER-WRAPPER (211.462-018)
09.04.02 CUSTOMER-SERVICE CLERK (299.367-010)
09.04.02 DELIVERER, MERCHANDISE (299.477-010)
09.04.02 FURNITURE-RENTAL CONSULTANT (295.357-018)
09.04.02 NEWSPAPER CARRIER (292.457-010)
09.04.02 PERSONAL SHOPPER (296.357-010)
09.04.02 SALES ATTENDANT (299.677-010)
09.04.02 SALES ATTENDANT, BUILDING MATERIALS (299.677-014)
09.04.02 SALES CLERK (290.477-014)
09.04.02 SALES CLERK, FOOD (290.477-018)
09.04.02 STORAGE-FACILITY RENTAL CLERK (295.367-026)
09.04.02 TOOL-AND-EQUIPMENT-RENTAL CLERK (295.357-014)
09.05.10 BAGGER (920.687-014)
11.02.04 FILM-RENTAL CLERK (295.367-018)
11.05.02 DIRECTOR, SERVICE (189.167-014)
11.05.02 MANAGER, DEPARTMENT STORE (185.117-010)
11.05.04 MANAGER, MERCHANDISE (185.167-034)
11.09.01 FASHION COORDINATOR (185.157-010)
11.10.01 INVESTIGATOR, FRAUD (376.267-014)
11.10.05 DEALER-COMPLIANCE REPRESENTATIVE (168.267-026)
11.11.04 MANAGER, FAST FOOD SERVICES (185.137-010)
11.11.04 MANAGER, TRAVEL AGENCY (187.167-158)
11.11.05 AREA SUPERVISOR, RETAIL CHAIN STORE (185.117-014)
11.11.05 MANAGER, AUTOMOBILE SERVICE STATION (185.167-014)
11.11.05 MANAGER, DEPARTMENT (299.137-010)
11.11.05 MANAGER, MARKET (186.167-042)
11.11.05 MANAGER, MEAT SALES AND STORAGE (185.167-030)
11.11.05 MANAGER, PARTS (185.167-038)
11.11.05 MANAGER, RETAIL STORE (185.167-046)

Rubber Goods

06.02.01 SUPERVISOR I (759.137-010)
06.02.22 LAMINATOR (899.684-018)
06.04.07 DESIGN PRINTER, BALLOON (651.685-014)
06.04.07 RUBBER CUTTER (559.685-158)
06.04.10 INJECTION-MOLDING-MACHINE TENDER (556.685-038)
06.04.23 RUBBER-GOODS ASSEMBLER (752.684-038)
06.04.38 PACKING-LINE WORKER (753.687-038)

Rubber Tire and Tube

06.04.07 RUBBER CUTTER (559.685-158)
06.04.13 TIRE MOLDER (553.685-102)

Sanitary Services

05.07.01 SEWER-LINE PHOTO-INSPECTOR
(851.362-010)
05.10.01 SEWER-LINE REPAIRER, TELE-GROUT
(851.262-010)
05.11.01 SANITARY LANDFILL OPERATOR
(955.463-010)
05.12.12 SEWER-LINE REPAIRER (869.664-018)

Sawmill and Planing Mill

03.04.02 LOGGING-TRACTOR OPERATOR
(929.663-010)
06.02.03 HEAD SAWYER (667.662-010)
06.02.03 TIMBER-SIZER OPERATOR
(665.482-018)
06.04.03 CHAIN OFFBEARER (669.686-018)
06.04.40 SAWMILL WORKER (667.687-018)

Servicing Industrial Machines

05.05.09 REFRIGERATION MECHANIC
(827.361-014)
05.10.02 COIN-MACHINE-SERVICE REPAIRER
(639.281-014)
06.03.02 GAS-LEAK TESTER (827.584-014)

Ship and Boat Manufacturing and Repairing

05.05.02 BOAT REPAIRER (807.361-014)
05.05.02 BOATBUILDER, WOOD (860.361-010)
05.05.02 MARINE-SERVICES TECHNICIAN
(806.261-026)
05.05.02 SHIPWRIGHT (860.381-058)
05.05.06 SHIPFITTER (806.381-046)
05.05.08 LOFT WORKER (661.281-010)
05.05.09 MANAGER, MARINE SERVICE
(187.167-130)
05.05.09 MOTORBOAT MECHANIC (623.281-038)
05.10.01 BOAT RIGGER (806.464-010)
05.12.03 LABORER, SHIPYARD (809.687-022)
05.12.14 WOOD CAULKER (843.384-010)
06.01.04 CANVAS WORKER (739.381-010)
06.02.24 BOAT PATCHER, PLASTIC (807.684-014)

Smelting and Refining

06.04.32 MOLD MAKER (518.664-010)

Soap, Cleaning, and Toilet Preparation

06.02.18 SOAP MAKER (559.382-054)

Social Services

07.01.01 MANAGEMENT AIDE (195.367-014)
09.01.01 GROUP WORKER (195.164-010)
09.01.01 RECREATION AIDE (195.367-030)
09.01.01 RECREATION LEADER (195.227-014)
10.01.02 CASE AIDE (195.367-010)
10.01.02 CASEWORK SUPERVISOR (195.137-010)
10.01.02 CASEWORKER (195.107-010)
10.01.02 CASEWORKER, CHILD WELFARE
(195.107-014)
10.01.02 CASEWORKER, FAMILY (195.107-018)
10.01.02 SOCIAL GROUP WORKER (195.107-022)
10.01.02 SOCIAL-SERVICES AIDE (195.367-034)
10.02.02 PROGRAM AIDE, GROUP WORK
(195.227-010)
10.02.03 TEACHER, HOME THERAPY (195.227-018)
11.02.03 HOMEMAKER (309.354-010)
11.07.01 COMMUNITY ORGANIZATION WORKER
(195.167-010)
11.07.01 COMMUNITY-RELATIONS-AND-SERVICES
ADVISOR, PUBLIC HOUSING (195.167-014)
11.07.01 COORDINATOR, VOLUNTEER SERVICES
(187.167-022)
11.11.02 DIRECTOR, CAMP (195.167-018)
11.11.02 DIRECTOR, RECREATION CENTER
(195.167-026)

Stonework

01.06.02 STONE CARVER (771.281-014)
05.05.01 STONECUTTER, HAND (771.381-014)

Structural and Ornamental Metal Products

05.05.06 BOILERMAKER I (805.261-014)
06.04.02 SCROLL-MACHINE OPERATOR
(616.685-062)

Sugar and Confectionery Products

06.02.15 CENTER-MACHINE OPERATOR
(520.682-014)
06.02.15 CHOCOLATE-PRODUCTION-MACHINE
OPERATOR (529.382-014)
06.02.28 CANDY MAKER (529.361-014)
06.04.15 CHOCOLATE MOLDER, MACHINE
(529.685-054)
06.04.28 CANDY DIPPER, HAND (524.684-010)
06.04.28 DECORATOR (524.684-014)
06.04.40 CHAR-CONVEYOR TENDER (529.685-050)

Telephone and Telegraph

03.04.05 TREE TRIMMER (408.664-010)
05.01.03 CABLE ENGINEER, OUTSIDE PLANT (003.167-010)
05.01.03 CENTRAL-OFFICE EQUIPMENT ENGINEER (003.187-010)
05.01.08 CUSTOMER-EQUIPMENT ENGINEER (003.187-018)
05.05.05 CABLE SPLICER (829.361-010)
05.05.05 CABLE SUPERVISOR (184.161-010)
05.05.05 CABLE TESTER (822.361-010)
05.05.05 CENTRAL-OFFICE REPAIRER (822.281-014)
05.05.05 LINE INSTALLER-REPAIRER (822.381-014)
05.05.05 STATION INSTALLER-AND-REPAIRER (822.261-022)
07.04.01 CUSTOMER SERVICE REPRESENTATIVE (239.362-014)
07.04.06 CENTRAL-OFFICE OPERATOR (235.462-010)
07.04.06 DIRECTORY-ASSISTANCE OPERATOR (235.662-018)
07.07.03 COIN-MACHINE COLLECTOR (292.687-010)
08.01.02 SALES REPRESENTATIVE, PUBLIC UTILITIES (253.357-010)
08.01.02 SALES REPRESENTATIVE, TELEPHONE SERVICES (253.257-010)
11.10.05 REGULATORY ADMINISTRATOR (168.167-070)
11.12.01 MANAGER, CUSTOMER SERVICE (168.167-058)

Textile

02.04.01 LABORATORY ASSISTANT (029.381-014)
06.01.02 LOOM FIXER (683.260-018)
06.02.06 WEAVER (683.682-038)
06.04.05 STRIP-CUTTING-MACHINE OPERATOR (686.685-066)
06.04.06 BEAM-WARPER TENDER, AUTOMATIC (681.685-018)
06.04.06 CLOTH DOFFER (689.686-058)
06.04.06 YARN WINDER (681.685-154)
06.04.16 MACHINE FEEDER, RAW STOCK (680.686-018)
06.04.16 SLASHER TENDER (582.562-010)

Textile Products, Not Elsewhere Classified

05.03.02 PATTERNMAKER (781.361-014)
06.01.04 CANVAS WORKER (739.381-010)
06.04.06 YARN WINDER (681.685-154)
06.04.16 MACHINE FEEDER, RAW STOCK (680.686-018)

Tobacco

06.03.01 SPECIAL TESTER (529.487-010)

Toys, Games, and Sports Equipment

01.06.02 BOW MAKER, CUSTOM (732.381-010)
05.05.10 PINSETTER ADJUSTER, AUTOMATIC (829.381-010)
06.02.24 SKI REPAIRER, PRODUCTION (732.684-118)
06.02.32 RACKET STRINGER (732.684-094)
06.02.32 SKI MOLDER (732.684-114)
06.04.09 SANDER (690.685-346)
06.04.13 BLOW-MOLDING-MACHINE TENDER (556.685-086)
06.04.23 FISHING-REEL ASSEMBLER (732.684-062)
06.04.23 TOY ASSEMBLER (731.687-034)
06.04.34 MACHINE SNELLER (732.685-026)
06.04.34 STUFFER (731.685-014)

Utilities (Light, Heat, and Power)

02.04.01 LABORATORY ASSISTANT (029.361-018)
03.04.05 TREE TRIMMER (408.664-010)
04.01.02 INVESTIGATOR (376.367-022)
05.01.03 ELECTRICAL ENGINEER, POWER SYSTEM (003.167-018)
05.01.03 POWER-DISTRIBUTION ENGINEER (003.167-046)
05.01.03 POWER-TRANSMISSION ENGINEER (003.167-050)
05.01.06 UTILIZATION ENGINEER (007.061-034)
05.02.06 APPLIANCE-SERVICE SUPERVISOR (187.167-010)
05.03.02 ESTIMATOR AND DRAFTER (019.261-014)
05.05.03 GAS-MAIN FITTER (862.361-014)
05.05.05 CABLE INSTALLER-REPAIRER (821.361-010)
05.05.05 CABLE SPLICER (829.361-010)
05.05.05 ELECTRIC-METER INSTALLER I (821.361-014)
05.05.05 ELECTRICIAN, POWERHOUSE (820.261-014)
05.05.05 FURNACE INSTALLER (862.361-010)
05.05.05 LINE ERECTOR (821.361-018)
05.05.05 LINE REPAIRER (821.361-026)
05.05.05 STREET-LIGHT SERVICER (824.381-010)
05.05.05 TOWER ERECTOR (821.361-038)
05.05.05 WIND-GENERATING-ELECTRIC-POWER INSTALLER (821.381-018)
05.05.06 CONDUIT MECHANIC (869.361-010)
05.05.09 POWERHOUSE MECHANIC (631.261-014)
05.05.10 ELECTRIC-METER REPAIRER (729.281-014)
05.05.10 ELECTRIC-METER TESTER (821.381-010)
05.05.11 INSTRUMENT TECHNICIAN (710.281-030)
05.06.01 CABLE MAINTAINER (952.464-010)

05.06.01 HYDROELECTRIC-STATION OPERATOR (952.362-018)
05.06.01 POWER-REACTOR OPERATOR (952.362-022)
05.06.01 SUBSTATION OPERATOR (952.362-026)
05.09.02 FIELD RECORDER (229.367-010)
05.09.03 METER READER (209.567-010)
05.09.03 TURBINE ATTENDANT (952.567-010)
05.10.01 SERVICE REPRESENTATIVE (959.574-010)
05.12.01 LABOR-CREW SUPERVISOR (899.131-010)
05.12.04 LABORER, POWERHOUSE (952.665-010)
05.12.16 CABLE PULLER (829.684-018)
07.02.03 ACCOUNT-INFORMATION CLERK (210.367-010)
07.02.04 BILLING-CONTROL CLERK (214.387-010)
07.04.01 CUSTOMER SERVICE REPRESENTATIVE (239.362-014)
07.04.05 GAS-DISTRIBUTION-AND-EMERGENCY CLERK (249.367-042)
07.04.05 UTILITY CLERK (239.367-034)
07.05.02 INVESTIGATOR, UTILITY-BILL COMPLAINTS (241.267-034)
08.01.02 SALES REPRESENTATIVE, PUBLIC UTILITIES (253.357-010)
08.02.05 DEMONSTRATOR, ELECTRIC-GAS APPLIANCES (297.357-010)
11.09.03 MANAGER, AREA DEVELOPMENT (184.117-030)
11.10.03 GAS INSPECTOR (168.264-018)

Water Transportation

05.02.07 MANAGER, MARINA DRY DOCK (187.167-226)
05.04.02 MATE, SHIP (197.133-022)
05.04.02 PILOT, SHIP (197.133-026)
05.06.02 ENGINEER (197.130-010)
05.08.04 DECKHAND (911.687-022)
05.10.08 SALAD MAKER (317.384-010)
05.11.04 STEVEDORE I (911.663-014)
05.12.01 BARGE CAPTAIN (911.137-010)
05.12.03 ABLE SEAMAN (911.364-010)
05.12.06 BOAT LOADER I (911.364-014)
07.02.03 RECEIPT-AND-REPORT CLERK (216.382-054)
08.01.02 TRAFFIC AGENT (252.257-010)
09.01.01 DIRECTOR, SOCIAL (352.167-010)
09.05.02 MESS ATTENDANT (350.677-010)
09.05.02 WAITER/WAITRESS (350.677-030)
11.05.02 MANAGER, OPERATIONS (184.117-050)
11.11.03 PURSER (197.167-014)
11.12.01 GENERAL CLAIMS AGENT (186.117-030)

Waterworks

02.04.01 HYDROGRAPHER (025.264-010)
05.01.03 CHIEF ENGINEER, WATERWORKS (005.167-010)
05.06.03 PUMP-STATION OPERATOR, WATER-WORKS (954.382-010)

05.06.04 WATER-TREATMENT-PLANT OPERATOR (954.382-014)
05.09.03 METER READER (209.567-010)
05.10.01 SERVICE REPRESENTATIVE (959.574-010)
07.04.01 CUSTOMER SERVICE REPRESENTATIVE (239.362-014)

Welding and Related Processes

05.05.06 ARC CUTTER (816.364-010)
05.05.06 WELDER, ARC (810.384-014)
05.05.06 WELDER, COMBINATION (819.384-010)
05.05.06 WELDER, EXPERIMENTAL (819.281-022)
05.05.06 WELDER, GAS (811.684-014)
05.05.06 WELDER-FITTER (819.361-010)
05.10.01 WELDER, TACK (810.684-010)
06.02.19 LASER-BEAM-MACHINE OPERATOR (815.682-010)
06.02.19 WELDING-MACHINE OPERATOR, ARC (810.382-010)
06.02.19 WELDING-MACHINE OPERATOR, GAS (811.482-010)
06.04.31 WELDER, GUN (810.664-010)

Wholesale Trade

03.01.01 GENERAL MANAGER, FARM (180.167-018)
03.01.03 MANAGER, NURSERY (180.167-042)
05.05.06 SAFE-AND-VAULT SERVICE MECHANIC (869.381-022)
05.08.03 NEWSPAPER-DELIVERY DRIVER (292.363-010)
05.09.01 DISTRIBUTION SUPERVISOR (914.137-010)
05.09.01 ORDER FILLER (222.487-014)
05.09.03 MARKER (209.587-034)
05.10.08 MEAT CUTTER (316.684-018)
05.12.15 AUTOMOBILE WRECKER (620.684-010)
07.03.01 AUCTION CLERK (294.567-010)
07.07.02 AUCTION ASSISTANT (294.667-010)
08.01.01 PHARMACEUTICAL DETAILER (262.157-010)
08.01.01 SALES REPRESENTATIVE, AIRCRAFT (273.253-010)
08.01.01 SALES REPRESENTATIVE, CHEMICALS AND DRUGS (262.357-010)
08.01.01 SALES REPRESENTATIVE, COMMUNICA-TION EQUIPMENT (271.257-010)
08.01.01 SALES REPRESENTATIVE, COMPUTERS AND EDP SYSTEMS (275.257-010)
08.01.01 SALES REPRESENTATIVE, DENTAL AND MEDICAL EQUIPMENT AND SUPPLIES (276.257-010)
08.01.01 SALES REPRESENTATIVE, ELECTRONICS PARTS (271.357-010)
08.01.02 SALES REPRESENTATIVE, PRINTING (254.357-018)
08.01.03 COMMISSION AGENT, AGRICULTURAL PRODUCE (260.357-010)
08.01.03 COMPARISON SHOPPER (296.367-014)
08.01.03 SALES REPRESENTATIVE, LIVESTOCK (260.257-010)

08.02.01 MANUFACTURER'S REPRESENTATIVE
(279.157-010)
08.02.01 SALES REPRESENTATIVE, ANIMAL-FEED
PRODUCTS (272.357-010)
08.02.01 SALES REPRESENTATIVE, FARM AND
GARDEN EQUIPMENT AND SUPPLIES
(272.357-014)
08.02.01 SALES REPRESENTATIVE, FOOD
PRODUCTS (260.357-014)
08.02.01 SALES REPRESENTATIVE, FOOTWEAR
(261.357-018)
08.02.01 SALES REPRESENTATIVE, HARDWARE
SUPPLIES (274.357-034)
08.02.01 SALES REPRESENTATIVE, HOME FUR-
NISHINGS (270.357-010)
08.02.01 SALES REPRESENTATIVE, HOUSEHOLD
APPLIANCES (270.357-014)
08.02.01 SALES REPRESENTATIVE, MALT
LIQUORS (260.357-018)
08.02.01 SALES REPRESENTATIVE, MEN'S AND
BOYS' APPAREL (261.357-022)
08.02.01 SALES REPRESENTATIVE, NOVELTIES
(277.357-018)
08.02.01 SALES REPRESENTATIVE, PETROLEUM
PRODUCTS (269.357-014)
08.02.01 SALES REPRESENTATIVE, PRINTING
SUPPLIES (274.357-062)
08.02.01 SALES REPRESENTATIVE, RECREATION
AND SPORTING GOODS (277.357-026)
08.02.01 SALES REPRESENTATIVE, TEXTILES
(261.357-030)
08.02.01 SALES REPRESENTATIVE, TOILET PREPA-
RATIONS (262.357-014)
08.02.01 SALES REPRESENTATIVE, VIDEOTAPE
(271.357-014)
08.02.01 SALES REPRESENTATIVE, WOMEN'S AND
GIRLS' APPAREL (261.357-038)
08.02.01 SALES-PROMOTION REPRESENTATIVE
(269.357-018)
08.02.03 AUCTIONEER (294.257-010)
08.02.03 SALES REPRESENTATIVE, BOATS AND
MARINE SUPPLIES (273.357-018)
08.02.03 SALES REPRESENTATIVE, OFFICE MA-
CHINES (275.357-034)
08.02.03 SALESPERSON, AUTOMOBILE ACCESSO-
RIES (273.357-030)
08.02.03 SALESPERSON, ELECTRIC MOTORS
(271.354-010)
08.02.03 SALESPERSON, FLOOR COVERINGS
(270.357-026)
08.02.03 SALESPERSON, GENERAL HARDWARE
(279.357-050)
08.02.03 SALESPERSON, GENERAL MERCHAN-
DISE (279.357-054)

08.02.03 SALESPERSON, HORTICULTURAL AND
NURSERY PRODUCTS (272.357-022)
08.02.03 SALESPERSON, PARTS (279.357-062)
08.02.03 SALESPERSON, PHOTOGRAPHIC SUP-
PLIES AND EQUIPMENT (277.357-050)
08.02.03 SALESPERSON, STAMPS OR COINS
(277.357-062)
08.02.04 BUILDING CONSULTANT (250.357-010)
08.02.05 DEMONSTRATOR (297.354-010)
08.02.07 DRIVER, SALES ROUTE (292.353-010)
11.05.04 FIELD REPRESENTATIVE (163.267-010)
11.05.04 MANAGER, MERCHANDISE (185.167-034)
11.05.04 WHOLESALER I (185.167-070)
11.05.04 WHOLESALER II (185.157-018)
11.10.05 DEALER-COMPLIANCE REPRESENTATIVE
(168.267-026)
11.11.03 MANAGER, DISTRIBUTION WAREHOUSE
(185.167-018)
11.11.04 MANAGER, FAST FOOD SERVICES
(185.137-010)
11.11.04 MANAGER, SERVICE DEPARTMENT
(187.167-142)
11.11.05 MANAGER, MARKET (186.167-042)
11.11.05 MANAGER, MEAT SALES AND STORAGE
(185.167-030)
11.11.05 MANAGER, PARTS (185.167-038)

Wood Products, Not Elsewhere Classified

01.06.02 PICTURE FRAMER (739.684-146)
06.04.18 TANKER (561.665-010)
06.04.34 MAT CUTTER (739.684-126)

Wooden Container

05.10.01 JIG BUILDER (761.381-014)

Woodworking

05.05.08 CABINETMAKER (660.280-010)
05.05.08 FURNITURE FINISHER (763.381-010)
05.05.08 MACHINIST, WOOD (669.380-014)
06.02.03 CUT-OFF-SAW OPERATOR I (667.682-022)
06.02.03 ROUTER OPERATOR (665.682-030)
06.03.02 GRADER (669.687-030)
06.04.03 GLUING-MACHINE OPERATOR
(569.685-046)
06.04.20 CORRUGATED-FASTENER DRIVER
(669.685-042)
06.04.25 WOODWORKING-SHOP HAND
(769.687-054)

Appendix D
Listing of Occupations by Educational Level

This index organizes all occupations listed in *The Enhanced Guide for Occupational Exploration* under the minimum formal education required to enter the field. This index is useful for adults with prior work experience who are changing careers. If extensive formal education is not an option for you, this index may help you find occupations that you can enter without retraining or with a short period of retraining. For most jobs, relevant work experience can partially take the place of formal education.

Obtaining specific occupational training is the most common way of entering a new field. While a degree or certificate does not guarantee that you will find a job, employers may prefer applicants who have specific training related to the job. This index does not indicate the amount of education that employers prefer. If further education is in your plans, be sure to seek information from other sources on the amount of training employers prefer.

Use the number preceding each occupation to look up its description in this book. Following the job title is its primary industry, then its DOT number.

Master's Degree or Above

02.01.01 CHEMIST (profess. & kin.), 022.061-010
02.01.01 GEOGRAPHER (profess. & kin.), 029.067-010
02.01.01 GEOGRAPHER, PHYSICAL (profess. & kin.), 029.067-014
02.01.01 GEOLOGIST (profess. & kin.), 024.061-018
02.01.01 GEOPHYSICIST (profess. & kin.), 024.061-030
02.01.01 HYDROLOGIST (profess. & kin.), 024.061-034
02.01.01 MATHEMATICIAN (profess. & kin.), 020.067-014
02.01.01 METEOROLOGIST (profess. & kin.), 025.062-010
02.01.01 MINERALOGIST (profess. & kin.), 024.061-038
02.01.01 PETROLOGIST (profess. & kin.), 024.061-046

02.01.01 PHYSICIST (profess. & kin.), 023.061-014
02.01.01 SEISMOLOGIST (profess. & kin.), 024.061-050
02.01.02 ENVIRONMENTAL ANALYST (profess. & kin.), 029.081-010
02.01.02 GEOLOGIST, PETROLEUM (petrol. & gas), 024.061-022
02.01.02 MATERIALS SCIENTIST (profess. & kin.), 029.081-014
02.01.02 PROJECT MANAGER, ENVIRONMENTAL RESEARCH (profess. & kin.), 029.167-014
02.02.01 ANIMAL SCIENTIST (profess. & kin.), 040.061-014
02.02.01 HISTOPATHOLOGIST (medical ser.), 041.061-054
02.02.01 MEDICAL PHYSICIST (profess. & kin.), 079.021-014

02.02.02 AGRONOMIST (profess. & kin.), 040.061-010

02.02.04 CHEMIST, FOOD (profess. & kin.), 022.061-014

02.03.01 ANESTHESIOLOGIST (medical ser.),
070.101-010

02.03.01 CARDIOLOGIST (medical ser.), 070.101-014

02.03.01 DERMATOLOGIST (medical ser.), 070.101-018

02.03.01 GENERAL PRACTITIONER (medical ser.),
070.101-022

02.03.01 INTERNIST (medical ser.), 070.101-042

02.03.01 OBSTETRICIAN (medical ser.), 070.101-054

02.03.01 OPHTHALMOLOGIST (medical ser.),
070.101-058

02.03.01 PEDIATRICIAN (medical ser.), 070.101-066

02.03.01 PSYCHIATRIST (medical ser.), 070.107-014

02.03.01 PUBLIC HEALTH PHYSICIAN (medical ser.),
070.101-046

02.03.01 RADIOLOGIST (medical ser.), 070.101-090

02.03.01 SURGEON (medical ser.), 070.101-094

02.03.02 DENTIST (medical ser.), 072.101-010

02.03.03 VETERINARIAN (medical ser.), 073.101-010

02.03.04 AUDIOLOGIST (medical ser.), 076.101-010

02.03.04 SPEECH PATHOLOGIST (profess. & kin.),
076.107-010

02.04.01 PHARMACIST (medical ser.), 074.161-010

02.04.01 RADIOPHARMACIST (medical ser.),
074.161-014

02.04.02 CHIEF TECHNOLOGIST, NUCLEAR
MEDICINE (medical ser.), 078.131-010

02.04.02 TOXICOLOGIST (pharmaceut.), 022.081-010

05.01.01 AERODYNAMICIST (aircraft mfg.), 002.061-010

05.01.01 AERONAUTICAL-RESEARCH ENGINEER
(aircraft mfg.), 002.061-026

05.01.02 HEALTH PHYSICIST (profess. & kin.),
015.021-010

05.01.04 METROLOGIST (profess. & kin.), 012.067-010

05.01.04 STRESS ANALYST (aircraft mfg.), 002.061-030

05.01.06 METALLURGIST, EXTRACTIVE (profess. &
kin.), 011.061-018

05.01.07 AERONAUTICAL ENGINEER (aircraft mfg.),
002.061-014

05.01.07 ARCHITECT (profess. & kin.), 001.061-010

05.01.07 ARCHITECT, MARINE (profess. & kin.),
001.061-014

05.01.07 ELECTRO-OPTICAL ENGINEER (profess. &
kin.), 023.061-010

05.01.07 ELECTRONICS-DESIGN ENGINEER (profess.
& kin.), 003.061-034

05.01.08 FIBER TECHNOLOGIST (profess. & kin.),
040.061-026

10.01.02 ASSISTANT PRINCIPAL (education),
091.107-010

10.01.02 CASEWORK SUPERVISOR (social ser.),
195.137-010

10.01.02 CASEWORKER, CHILD WELFARE (social ser.),
195.107-014

10.01.02 CLINICAL PSYCHOLOGIST (profess. & kin.),
045.107-022

10.01.02 CLINICAL THERAPIST (profess. & kin.),
045.107-050

10.01.02 COUNSELOR (profess. & kin.), 045.107-010

10.01.02 COUNSELOR, MARRIAGE AND FAMILY
(profess. & kin.), 045.107-054

10.01.02 DEAN OF STUDENTS (education), 090.117-018

10.01.02 FOREIGN-STUDENT ADVISER (education),
090.107-010

10.01.02 PSYCHOLOGIST, CHIEF (profess. & kin.),
045.107-046

10.01.02 PSYCHOLOGIST, COUNSELING (profess. &
kin.), 045.107-026

10.01.02 PSYCHOLOGIST, SCHOOL (profess. & kin.),
045.107-034

10.01.02 SOCIAL GROUP WORKER (social ser.),
195.107-022

10.01.02 SUBSTANCE ABUSE COUNSELOR (profess.
& kin.), 045.107-058

10.01.02 VOCATIONAL REHABILITATION COUNSE-
LOR (government ser.), 045.107-042

10.02.01 NURSE PRACTITIONER (medical ser.),
075.264-010

10.02.03 SUPERVISOR, SPECIAL EDUCATION
(education), 094.167-010

11.01.01 OPERATIONS-RESEARCH ANALYST
(profess. & kin.), 020.067-018

11.01.01 STATISTICIAN, MATHEMATICAL (profess. &
kin.), 020.067-022

11.02.01 FACULTY MEMBER, COLLEGE OR
UNIVERSITY (education), 090.227-010

11.03.01 PSYCHOLOGIST, DEVELOPMENTAL (profess.
& kin.), 045.061-010

11.03.01 PSYCHOLOGIST, EDUCATIONAL (profess. &
kin.), 045.067-010

11.03.01 PSYCHOLOGIST, ENGINEERING (profess. &
kin.), 045.061-014

11.03.01 PSYCHOLOGIST, EXPERIMENTAL (profess. &
kin.), 045.061-018

11.03.01 PSYCHOLOGIST, INDUSTRIAL-ORGANIZA-
TIONAL (profess. & kin.), 045.107-030

11.03.01 PSYCHOLOGIST, SOCIAL (profess. & kin.),
045.067-014

11.03.01 PSYCHOMETRIST (profess. & kin.),
045.067-018

11.03.02 POLITICAL SCIENTIST (profess. & kin.),
051.067-010

11.03.02 SCIENTIFIC LINGUIST (profess. & kin.),
059.067-014

11.03.02 SOCIOLOGIST (profess. & kin.), 054.067-014

11.03.03 ANTHROPOLOGIST (profess. & kin.),
055.067-010

11.04.02 DISTRICT ATTORNEY (government ser.),
110.117-010

11.04.02 INSURANCE ATTORNEY (insurance),
110.117-014

11.04.02 LAWYER (profess. & kin.), 110.107-010

11.04.02 LAWYER, CORPORATION (profess. & kin.),
110.117-022

11.04.02 LAWYER, CRIMINAL (profess. & kin.),
110.107-014

11.04.02 LAWYER, PATENT (profess. & kin.),
110.117-026

11.04.02 LAWYER, PROBATE (profess. & kin.),
110.117-030

11.04.02 TAX ATTORNEY (profess. & kin.), 110.117-038

11.04.03 ARBITRATOR (profess. & kin.), 169.107-010

11.04.03 CONCILIATOR (profess. & kin.), 169.207-010

11.05.03 SECRETARY OF STATE (government ser.), 188.167-082

11.07.02 ADMINISTRATOR, HEALTH CARE FACILITY (medical ser.), 187.117-010

11.07.02 PUBLIC HEALTH EDUCATOR (profess. & kin.), 079.117-014

11.07.03 ACADEMIC DEAN (education), 090.117-010

11.07.03 DIRECTOR OF ADMISSIONS (education), 090.167-014

11.07.03 DIRECTOR OF PUPIL PERSONNEL PROGRAM (education), 099.167-034

11.07.03 DIRECTOR, ATHLETIC (education), 090.117-022

11.07.03 DIRECTOR, EDUCATIONAL PROGRAM (education), 099.117-010

11.07.03 DIRECTOR, SPECIAL EDUCATION (education), 094.167-014

11.07.03 PRESIDENT, EDUCATIONAL INSTITUTION (education), 090.117-034

11.07.03 PRINCIPAL (education), 099.117-018

11.07.03 REGISTRAR, COLLEGE OR UNIVERSITY (education), 090.167-030

11.07.03 SUPERINTENDENT, SCHOOLS (education), 099.117-022

11.07.03 VOCATIONAL REHABILITATION CONSULTANT (government ser.), 094.117-018

Bachelor's Degree

01.01.01 EDITOR, PUBLICATIONS (print. & pub.), 132.037-022

01.01.01 PRODUCER (motion picture), 187.167-174

01.02.03 ART DIRECTOR (motion picture), 142.061-062

01.02.03 AUDIOVISUAL PRODUCTION SPECIALIST (profess. & kin.), 149.061-010

01.02.03 DIRECTOR OF PHOTOGRAPHY (motion picture), 143.062-010

01.02.03 INDUSTRIAL DESIGNER (profess. & kin.), 142.061-026

01.03.01 PRODUCER (radio-tv broad.), 159.117-010

01.03.01 PRODUCER (amuse. & rec.), 187.167-178

01.04.01 TEACHER, MUSIC (education), 152.021-010

02.01.02 CHEMICAL LABORATORY CHIEF (profess. & kin.), 022.161-010

02.02.01 BIOMEDICAL ENGINEER (profess. & kin.), 019.061-010

02.02.01 ENVIRONMENTAL EPIDEMIOLOGIST (government ser.), 041.167-010

02.02.01 PARASITOLOGIST (profess. & kin.), 041.061-070

02.02.01 PHARMACOLOGIST (profess. & kin.), 041.061-074

02.02.01 ZOOLOGIST (profess. & kin.), 041.061-090

02.02.02 BOTANIST (profess. & kin.), 041.061-038

02.02.02 FOREST ECOLOGIST (profess. & kin.), 040.061-030

02.02.02 HORTICULTURIST (profess. & kin.), 040.061-038

02.02.02 PLANT PATHOLOGIST (profess. & kin.), 041.061-086

02.02.02 RANGE MANAGER (profess. & kin.), 040.061-046

02.02.02 SOIL CONSERVATIONIST (profess. & kin.), 040.061-054

02.02.02 SOIL SCIENTIST (profess. & kin.), 040.061-058

02.02.02 WOOD TECHNOLOGIST (profess. & kin.), 040.061-062

02.02.03 AQUATIC BIOLOGIST (profess. & kin.), 041.061-022

02.02.03 BIOCHEMIST (profess. & kin.), 041.061-026

02.02.03 BIOLOGIST (profess. & kin.), 041.061-030

02.02.03 BIOPHYSICIST (profess. & kin.), 041.061-034

02.02.03 MICROBIOLOGIST (profess. & kin.), 041.061-058

02.02.03 PHYSIOLOGIST (profess. & kin.), 041.061-078

02.02.04 DAIRY TECHNOLOGIST (profess. & kin.), 040.061-022

02.02.04 FOOD TECHNOLOGIST (profess. & kin.), 041.081-010

02.03.01 PODIATRIST (medical ser.), 079.101-022

02.03.04 ACUPUNCTURIST (medical ser.), 079.271-010

02.03.04 CHIROPRACTOR (medical ser.), 079.101-010

02.03.04 OPTOMETRIST (medical ser.), 079.101-018

02.03.04 VOICE PATHOLOGIST (profess. & kin.), 076.104-010

02.04.01 LABORATORY SUPERVISOR (profess. & kin.), 022.137-010

02.04.02 BIOCHEMISTRY TECHNOLOGIST (medical ser.), 078.261-010

02.04.02 IMMUNOHEMATOLOGIST (medical ser.), 078.261-046

02.04.02 MEDICAL TECHNOLOGIST (medical ser.), 078.261-038

02.04.02 MICROBIOLOGY TECHNOLOGIST (medical ser.), 078.261-014

02.04.02 PUBLIC-HEALTH MICROBIOLOGIST (government ser.), 041.261-010

03.01.04 FORESTER (profess. & kin.), 040.167-010

04.01.02 WILDLIFE AGENT, REGIONAL (government ser.), 379.137-018

04.02.03 PARK RANGER (government ser.), 169.167-042

05.01.01 CHEMICAL RESEARCH ENGINEER (profess. & kin.), 008.061-022

05.01.01 DIRECTOR, RESEARCH AND DEVELOPMENT (any industry), 189.117-014

05.01.01 ELECTRICAL-RESEARCH ENGINEER (profess. & kin.), 003.061-026

05.01.01 INSTRUMENTATION TECHNICIAN (profess. & kin.), 003.261-010

05.01.01 MECHANICAL RESEARCH ENGINEER (profess. & kin.), 007.161-022

05.01.02 INDUSTRIAL-HEALTH ENGINEER (profess. & kin.), 012.167-034

05.01.02 NUCLEAR-CRITICALITY SAFETY ENGINEER (profess. & kin.), 015.067-010

05.01.02 POLLUTION-CONTROL ENGINEER (profess. & kin.), 019.081-018

05.01.02 PRODUCT-SAFETY ENGINEER (profess. & kin.), 012.061-010

05.01.02 RADIATION-PROTECTION ENGINEER
(profess. & kin.), 015.137-010

05.01.02 RESOURCE-RECOVERY ENGINEER (government ser.), 019.167-018

05.01.02 SAFETY ENGINEER (profess. & kin.), 012.061-014

05.01.02 SAFETY MANAGER (profess. & kin.), 012.167-058

05.01.03 CABLE ENGINEER, OUTSIDE PLANT (tel. & tel.), 003.167-010

05.01.03 CENTRAL-OFFICE EQUIPMENT ENGINEER (tel. & tel.), 003.187-010

05.01.03 COMMERCIAL ENGINEER (radio-tv broad.), 003.187-014

05.01.03 ELECTRICAL ENGINEER, POWER SYSTEM (utilities), 003.167-018

05.01.03 HYDRAULIC ENGINEER (profess. & kin.), 005.061-018

05.01.03 ILLUMINATING ENGINEER (profess. & kin.), 003.061-046

05.01.03 MARINE ENGINEER (profess. & kin.), 014.061-014

05.01.03 NUCLEAR ENGINEER (profess. & kin.), 015.061-014

05.01.03 NUCLEAR-FUELS RECLAMATION ENGINEER (profess. & kin.), 015.061-026

05.01.03 POWER-DISTRIBUTION ENGINEER (utilities), 003.167-046

05.01.03 POWER-TRANSMISSION ENGINEER (utilities), 003.167-050

05.01.03 SANITARY ENGINEER (profess. & kin.), 005.061-030

05.01.03 WASTE-MANAGEMENT ENGINEER, RADIO-ACTIVE MATERIALS (profess. & kin.), 005.061-042

05.01.04 AERONAUTICAL TEST ENGINEER (aircraft mfg.), 002.061-018

05.01.04 ELECTRICAL TEST ENGINEER (profess. & kin.), 003.061-014

05.01.04 FIELD-SERVICE ENGINEER (aircraft mfg.), 002.167-014

05.01.04 METALLOGRAPHER (profess. & kin.), 011.061-014

05.01.04 QUALITY CONTROL ENGINEER (profess. & kin.), 012.167-054

05.01.04 RELIABILITY ENGINEER (profess. & kin.), 019.061-026

05.01.04 STRESS ANALYST (profess. & kin.), 007.061-042

05.01.04 TEST ENGINEER, NUCLEAR EQUIPMENT (profess. & kin.), 015.061-022

05.01.05 SALES ENGINEER, AERONAUTICAL PRODUCTS (aircraft mfg.), 002.151-010

05.01.06 CONFIGURATION MANAGEMENT ANALYST (profess. & kin.), 012.167-010

05.01.06 FACTORY LAY-OUT ENGINEER (profess. & kin.), 012.167-018

05.01.06 INDUSTRIAL ENGINEER (profess. & kin.), 012.167-030

05.01.06 LIAISON ENGINEER (aircraft mfg.), 012.167-038

05.01.06 MANAGEMENT ANALYST (profess. & kin.), 161.167-010

05.01.06 MANUFACTURING ENGINEER (profess. & kin.), 012.167-042

05.01.06 MATERIALS ENGINEER (profess. & kin.), 019.061-014

05.01.06 MINING ENGINEER (mine & quarry), 010.061-014

05.01.06 PRODUCTION ENGINEER (profess. & kin.), 012.167-046

05.01.06 PRODUCTION PLANNER (profess. & kin.), 012.167-050

05.01.06 STANDARDS ENGINEER (profess. & kin.), 012.061-018

05.01.06 TIME-STUDY ENGINEER (profess. & kin.), 012.167-070

05.01.06 UTILIZATION ENGINEER (utilities), 007.061-034

05.01.06 VALUE ENGINEER (aircraft mfg.), 002.167-010

05.01.07 AERONAUTICAL-DESIGN ENGINEER (aircraft mfg.), 002.061-022

05.01.07 AIRPORT ENGINEER (profess. & kin.), 005.061-010

05.01.07 CERAMIC ENGINEER (profess. & kin.), 006.061-014

05.01.07 CHEMICAL DESIGN ENGINEER, PROCESSES (profess. & kin.), 008.061-014

05.01.07 CHEMICAL ENGINEER (profess. & kin.), 008.061-018

05.01.07 CIVIL ENGINEER (profess. & kin.), 005.061-014

05.01.07 ELECTRICAL-DESIGN ENGINEER (profess. & kin.), 003.061-018

05.01.07 LANDSCAPE ARCHITECT (profess. & kin.), 001.061-018

05.01.07 OPTICAL ENGINEER (profess. & kin.), 019.061-018

05.01.08 AGRICULTURAL ENGINEER (profess. & kin.), 013.061-010

05.01.08 AUTOMOTIVE ENGINEER (auto. mfg.), 007.061-010

05.01.08 CUSTOMER-EQUIPMENT ENGINEER (tel. & tel.), 003.187-018

05.01.08 ELECTRICAL ENGINEER (profess. & kin.), 003.061-010

05.01.08 ELECTRONICS ENGINEER (profess. & kin.), 003.061-030

05.01.08 ENGINEER, SOILS (profess. & kin.), 024.161-010

05.01.08 ENGINEERING MANAGER, ELECTRONICS (profess. & kin.), 003.167-070

05.01.08 MAINTAINABILITY ENGINEER (profess. & kin.), 019.081-010

05.01.08 MECHANICAL ENGINEER (profess. & kin.), 007.061-014

05.01.08 PETROLEUM ENGINEER (petrol. & gas), 010.061-018

05.01.08 PLANT ENGINEER (profess. & kin.), 007.167-014

05.01.08 SCHOOL-PLANT CONSULTANT (education), 001.167-010

05.01.08 STRUCTURAL ENGINEER (construction), 005.061-034

05.01.08 TRANSPORTATION ENGINEER (profess. & kin.), 005.061-038

05.01.08 WELDING ENGINEER (profess. & kin.), 011.061-026

05.02.03 MANAGER, QUALITY CONTROL (profess. & kin.), 012.167-014

05.03.01 PHOTOGRAMMETRIC ENGINEER (profess. & kin.), 018.167-026

05.03.02 CONTROLS DESIGNER (profess. & kin.), 003.261-014

05.03.09 PACKAGING ENGINEER (profess. & kin.), 019.187-010

05.05.11 ORTHOTIST (medical ser.), 078.261-018

05.05.11 PROSTHETIST (medical ser.), 078.261-022

05.05.17 DIETITIAN, CLINICAL (profess. & kin.), 077.127-014

05.12.18 HOUSECLEANER (hotel & rest.), 323.687-018

07.01.01 FINANCIAL-AID COUNSELOR (education), 169.267-018

08.01.01 PHARMACEUTICAL DETAILER (wholesale tr.), 262.157-010

08.01.01 SALES REPRESENTATIVE, DENTAL AND MEDICAL EQUIPMENT AND SUPPLIES (wholesale tr.), 276.257-010

08.02.06 SALES REPRESENTATIVE (motor trans.), 250.357-022

10.01.01 CLERGY MEMBER (profess. & kin.), 120.107-010

10.01.02 DIRECTOR OF PLACEMENT (education), 166.167-014

10.01.02 PROBATION-AND-PAROLE OFFICER (profess. & kin.), 195.107-046

10.02.01 NURSE ANESTHETIST (medical ser.), 075.371-010

10.02.01 NURSE, CONSULTANT (medical ser.), 075.127-014

10.02.01 NURSE, GENERAL DUTY (medical ser.), 075.364-010

10.02.01 NURSE, INFECTION CONTROL (medical ser.), 075.127-034

10.02.01 NURSE, INSTRUCTOR (medical ser.), 075.124-018

10.02.01 NURSE, OFFICE (medical ser.), 075.374-014

10.02.01 NURSE, PRIVATE DUTY (medical ser.), 075.374-018

10.02.01 NURSE, SCHOOL (medical ser.), 075.124-010

10.02.01 NURSE, STAFF, COMMUNITY HEALTH (medical ser.), 075.124-014

10.02.01 NURSE, STAFF, OCCUPATIONAL HEALTH NURSING (medical ser.), 075.374-022

10.02.01 NURSE-MIDWIFE (medical ser.), 075.264-014

10.02.01 QUALITY ASSURANCE COORDINATOR (medical ser.), 075.167-014

10.02.02 ART THERAPIST (medical ser.), 076.127-010

10.02.02 MUSIC THERAPIST (medical ser.), 076.127-014

10.02.02 OCCUPATIONAL THERAPIST (medical ser.), 076.121-010

10.02.02 PHYSICAL THERAPIST (education), 076.121-014

10.02.03 EVALUATOR (education), 094.267-010

10.02.03 TEACHER, EMOTIONALLY IMPAIRED (education), 094.227-010

10.02.03 TEACHER, HEARING IMPAIRED (education), 094.224-010

10.02.03 TEACHER, HOME THERAPY (social ser.), 195.227-018

10.02.03 TEACHER, KINDERGARTEN (education), 092.227-014

10.02.03 TEACHER, LEARNING DISABLED (education), 094.227-030

10.02.03 TEACHER, MENTALLY IMPAIRED (education), 094.227-022

10.02.03 TEACHER, PHYSICALLY IMPAIRED (education), 094.224-014

10.02.03 TEACHER, VISUALLY IMPAIRED (education), 094.224-018

11.01.01 CHIEF, COMPUTER PROGRAMMER (profess. & kin.), 030.167-010

11.01.01 DIRECTOR, RECORDS MANAGEMENT (profess. & kin.), 161.117-014

11.01.01 FORMS ANALYST (profess. & kin.), 161.267-018

11.01.01 INFORMATION SCIENTIST (profess. & kin.), 109.067-010

11.01.01 MANAGER, DATA PROCESSING (profess. & kin.), 169.167-030

11.01.01 PROGRAMMER, ENGINEERING AND SCIENTIFIC (profess. & kin.), 030.162-018

11.01.01 PROGRAMMER-ANALYST (profess. & kin.), 030.162-014

11.01.01 SOFTWARE ENGINEER (profess. & kin.), 030.062-010

11.01.01 SYSTEMS ANALYST (profess. & kin.), 030.167-014

11.01.01 SYSTEMS PROGRAMMER (profess. & kin.), 030.162-022

11.01.02 ACTUARY (profess. & kin.), 020.167-010

11.01.02 CONSULTANT (profess. & kin.), 189.167-010

11.01.02 MATHEMATICAL TECHNICIAN (profess. & kin.), 020.162-010

11.01.02 STATISTICIAN, APPLIED (profess. & kin.), 020.167-026

11.02.01 INSTRUCTOR, BUSINESS EDUCATION (education), 090.222-010

11.02.01 INSTRUCTOR, PHYSICAL EDUCATION (education), 099.224-010

11.02.01 TEACHER (museums), 099.227-038

11.02.01 TEACHER, ADULT EDUCATION (education), 099.227-030

11.02.01 TEACHER, ELEMENTARY SCHOOL (education), 092.227-010

11.02.01 TEACHER, RESOURCE (education), 099.227-042

11.02.01 TEACHER, SECONDARY SCHOOL (education), 091.227-010

11.02.02 HUMAN RESOURCE ADVISOR (profess. & kin.), 166.267-046

11.02.02 TEACHER, INDUSTRIAL ARTS (education), 091.221-010

11.02.03 COMMUNITY DIETITIAN (profess. & kin.),
077.127-010

11.02.03 HOME ECONOMIST (profess. & kin.),
096.121-014

11.02.04 ACQUISITIONS LIBRARIAN (library),
100.267-010

11.02.04 BOOKMOBILE LIBRARIAN (library),
100.167-014

11.02.04 CATALOG LIBRARIAN (library), 100.387-010

11.02.04 LIBRARIAN (library), 100.127-014

11.02.04 LIBRARIAN, SPECIAL LIBRARY (library),
100.167-026

11.02.04 NEWS LIBRARIAN (library), 100.167-038

11.03.02 PLANNER, PROGRAM SERVICES
(government ser.), 188.167-110

11.03.02 RESEARCH WORKER, SOCIAL WELFARE
(profess. & kin.), 054.067-010

11.03.02 URBAN PLANNER (profess. & kin.),
199.167-014

11.03.03 ARCHEOLOGIST (profess. & kin.),
055.067-018

11.03.03 ARCHIVIST (profess. & kin.), 101.167-010

11.03.03 HISTORIAN (profess. & kin.), 052.067-022

11.03.04 EMPLOYMENT INTERVIEWER (profess. &
kin.), 166.267-010

11.03.04 JOB ANALYST (profess. & kin.), 166.267-018

11.03.04 OCCUPATIONAL ANALYST (profess. & kin.),
166.067-010

11.03.04 PERSONNEL RECRUITER (profess. & kin.),
166.267-038

11.03.05 ECONOMIST (profess. & kin.), 050.067-010

11.04.01 APPEALS REFEREE (government ser.),
119.267-014

11.04.01 HEARING OFFICER (government ser.),
119.107-010

11.04.03 ADJUDICATOR (government ser.),
119.167-010

11.04.04 PATENT AGENT (profess. & kin.),
119.167-014

11.05.01 ASSOCIATION EXECUTIVE (profess. & kin.),
189.117-010

11.05.01 PRESIDENT (any industry), 189.117-026

11.05.01 PRESIDENT, FINANCIAL INSTITUTION
(financial), 186.117-054

11.05.02 BUSINESS MANAGER, COLLEGE OR
UNIVERSITY (education), 186.117-010

11.05.02 DIETITIAN, CHIEF (profess. & kin.),
077.117-010

11.05.02 DIRECTOR, QUALITY ASSURANCE
(profess. & kin.), 189.117-042

11.05.02 GRANT COORDINATOR (profess. & kin.),
169.117-014

11.05.02 MANAGEMENT TRAINEE (any industry),
189.167-018

11.05.02 MANAGER, COMPENSATION (profess. & kin.),
166.167-022

11.05.02 MANAGER, LABOR RELATIONS (profess. &
kin.), 166.167-034

11.05.02 MANAGER, PERSONNEL (profess. & kin.),
166.117-018

11.05.02 RESEARCH ANALYST (insurance), 169.267-034

11.05.02 VICE PRESIDENT, FINANCIAL INSTITUTION
(financial), 186.117-078

11.05.03 ENVIRONMENTAL ANALYST (government
ser.), 199.167-022

11.05.03 HOUSING-MANAGEMENT OFFICER
(government ser.), 188.117-110

11.05.03 MANAGER, CITY (government ser.),
188.117-114

11.05.04 DIRECTOR, MEDIA MARKETING
(radio-tv broad.), 163.117-022

11.05.04 MANAGER, BROKERAGE OFFICE (financial),
186.117-034

11.05.04 MANAGER, EXCHANGE FLOOR (financial),
186.117-086

11.05.04 MANAGER, SALES (any industry), 163.167-018

11.06.01 ACCOUNTANT (profess. & kin.), 160.162-018

11.06.01 ACCOUNTANT, COST (profess. & kin.),
160.162-026

11.06.01 ACCOUNTANT, TAX (profess. & kin.),
160.162-010

11.06.01 AUDITOR (profess. & kin.), 160.167-054

11.06.01 AUDITOR, DATA PROCESSING (profess. &
kin.), 160.162-030

11.06.01 AUDITOR, INTERNAL (profess. & kin.),
160.167-034

11.06.01 AUDITOR, TAX (profess. & kin.),
160.167-038

11.06.01 REVENUE AGENT (government ser.),
160.167-050

11.06.02 CONTROLLER (profess. & kin.), 160.167-058

11.06.02 REPORTS ANALYST (profess. & kin.),
161.267-026

11.06.03 DIRECTOR, UTILITY ACCOUNTS (government
ser.), 160.267-014

11.06.03 INVESTMENT ANALYST (financial),
160.267-026

11.06.03 PERSONAL PROPERTY ASSESSOR
(government ser.), 191.367-010

11.06.03 RISK AND INSURANCE MANAGER (any
industry), 186.117-066

11.06.03 TREASURER (profess. & kin.), 161.117-018

11.06.04 FLOOR BROKER (financial), 162.167-034

11.06.04 REGISTERED REPRESENTATIVE (financial),
250.257-018

11.06.05 BUDGET ANALYST (government ser.),
161.267-030

11.06.05 TREASURER, FINANCIAL INSTITUTION
(financial), 186.117-070

11.07.01 COORDINATOR OF REHABILITATION
SERVICES (medical ser.), 076.117-010

11.07.01 REHABILITATION CENTER MANAGER
(government ser.), 195.167-038

11.07.02 COMMUNITY-SERVICES-AND-HEALTH-
EDUCATION OFFICER (government ser.),
079.167-010

11.07.02 MEDICAL-RECORD ADMINISTRATOR
(medical ser.), 079.167-014

11.07.02 UTILIZATION-REVIEW COORDINATOR
(medical ser.), 079.267-010

11.07.03 CONSULTANT, EDUCATION (education),
099.167-014

11.07.03 DIRECTOR, VOCATIONAL TRAINING
(education), 097.167-010

11.07.03 EDUCATIONAL SPECIALIST (education),
099.167-022

11.07.03 FINANCIAL-AIDS OFFICER (education),
090.117-030

11.07.03 LABORATORY MANAGER (education),
090.164-010

11.07.03 PARK NATURALIST (government ser.),
049.127-010

11.07.04 LIBRARY CONSULTANT (library),
100.117-014

11.07.04 LIBRARY DIRECTOR (library), 100.117-010

11.08.01 EDITOR, CITY (print. & pub.), 132.037-014

11.08.01 EDITOR, DICTIONARY (profess. & kin.),
132.067-018

11.08.01 EDITOR, NEWSPAPER (print. & pub.),
132.017-014

11.08.01 EDITOR, TECHNICAL AND SCIENTIFIC
PUBLICATIONS (profess. & kin.),
132.017-018

11.08.02 RESEARCH ASSISTANT II (profess. & kin.),
199.267-034

11.08.03 COLUMNIST/COMMENTATOR (print. & pub.),
131.067-010

11.08.04 DIRECTOR, TRANSLATION (profess. & kin.),
137.137-010

11.08.04 TRANSLATOR (profess. & kin.), 137.267-018

11.09.01 ACCOUNT EXECUTIVE (business ser.),
164.167-010

11.09.01 MANAGER, ADVERTISING (any industry),
164.117-010

11.09.02 DIRECTOR, FUNDRAISING (nonprofit org.),
165.117-010

11.09.02 DIRECTOR, FUNDS DEVELOPMENT
(profess. & kin.), 165.117-014

11.09.02 FUND RAISER I (nonprofit org.), 293.157-010

11.09.03 FOREIGN-SERVICE OFFICER (government
ser.), 188.117-106

11.09.03 PUBLIC-RELATIONS REPRESENTATIVE
(profess. & kin.), 165.167-014

11.10.03 HEALTH OFFICER, FIELD (government ser.),
168.167-018

11.10.03 PUBLIC HEALTH SERVICE OFFICER
(government ser.), 187.117-050

11.10.03 SANITARIAN (profess. & kin.), 079.117-018

11.10.05 REGULATORY ADMINISTRATOR
(tel. & tel.), 168.167-070

11.11.04 MANAGER, FINANCIAL INSTITUTION
(financial), 186.167-086

11.11.04 MANAGER, INSURANCE OFFICE
(insurance), 186.167-034

11.12.02 RIGHT-OF-WAY AGENT (any industry),
191.117-046

11.12.03 ARTIST'S MANAGER (amuse. & rec.),
191.117-010

11.12.03 BOOKING MANAGER (amuse. & rec.),
191.117-014

11.12.03 LITERARY AGENT (business ser.),
191.117-034

12.01.01 HEAD COACH (amuse. & rec.), 153.117-010

Associate Degree or Apprenticeship

01.01.01 CONTINUITY DIRECTOR (radio-tv broad.),
132.037-010

01.01.01 FILM OR VIDEOTAPE EDITOR (motion
picture), 962.262-010

01.01.01 SUPERVISING FILM-OR-VIDEOTAPE
EDITOR (motion picture), 962.132-010

01.01.02 BIOGRAPHER (profess. & kin.), 052.067-010

01.01.02 COPY WRITER (profess. & kin.), 131.067-014

01.01.02 EDITORIAL WRITER (print. & pub.),
131.067-022

01.02.01 APPRAISER, ART (profess. & kin.), 191.287-014

01.02.02 QUICK SKETCH ARTIST (amuse. & rec.),
149.041-010

01.02.03 ART DIRECTOR (profess. & kin.), 141.031-010

01.02.03 COMMERCIAL DESIGNER (profess. & kin.),
141.061-038

01.02.03 DISPLAY DESIGNER (profess. & kin.),
142.051-010

01.02.03 EXHIBIT DESIGNER (museums), 142.061-058

01.02.03 FASHION ARTIST (retail trade), 141.061-014

01.02.03 FASHION DESIGNER (profess. & kin.),
142.061-018

01.02.03 FURNITURE DESIGNER (furniture),
142.061-022

01.02.03 GRAPHIC DESIGNER (profess. & kin.),
141.061-018

01.02.03 ILLUSTRATOR (profess. & kin.), 141.061-022

01.02.03 ILLUSTRATOR, MEDICAL AND SCIENTIFIC
(profess. & kin.), 141.061-026

01.02.03 INTERIOR DESIGNER (profess. & kin.),
142.051-014

01.02.03 MANAGER, DISPLAY (retail trade),
142.031-014

01.02.03 PACKAGE DESIGNER (profess. & kin.),
142.081-018

01.02.03 POLICE ARTIST (government ser.), 141.061-034

01.02.03 SET DECORATOR (motion picture),
142.061-042

01.02.03 SET DESIGNER (motion picture), 142.061-046

01.02.03 SET DESIGNER (amuse. & rec.), 142.061-050

01.02.03 TELEVISION TECHNICIAN (radio-tv broad.),
194.062-010

01.03.01 DIRECTOR, MOTION PICTURE (motion
picture), 159.067-010

01.03.02 ACTOR (amuse. & rec.), 150.047-010

01.03.03 ANNOUNCER (radio-tv broad.), 159.147-010

01.03.03 DISC JOCKEY (radio-tv broad.), 159.147-014

01.03.03 NARRATOR (motion picture), 150.147-010

01.05.01 INSTRUCTOR, DANCING (education),
151.027-014

01.06.02 TAXIDERMIST (profess. & kin.), 199.261-010

02.02.02 SILVICULTURIST (profess. & kin.),
040.061-050

02.02.02 SOIL-CONSERVATION TECHNICIAN
(profess. & kin.), 040.261-010

02.04.01 ASSAYER (profess. & kin.), 022.281-010

02.04.01 BALLISTICS EXPERT, FORENSIC
(government ser.), 199.267-010

02.04.01 CALIBRATION LABORATORY TECHNICIAN (aircraft mfg.), 019.281-010

02.04.01 CHEMICAL LABORATORY TECHNICIAN (profess. & kin.), 022.261-010

02.04.01 CRIMINALIST (profess. & kin.), 029.261-026

02.04.01 EXAMINER, QUESTIONED DOCUMENTS (government ser.), 199.267-022

02.04.01 GEOLOGICAL AIDE (petrol. & gas), 024.267-010

02.04.01 HYDROGRAPHER (waterworks), 025.264-010

02.04.01 LABORATORY ASSISTANT (utilities), 029.361-018

02.04.01 LABORATORY ASSISTANT, METALLURGICAL (steel & rel.), 011.261-022

02.04.01 LABORATORY TECHNICIAN (auto. mfg.), 019.261-030

02.04.01 LABORATORY TESTER (any industry), 029.261-010

02.04.01 METALLURGICAL TECHNICIAN (profess. & kin.), 011.261-010

02.04.01 PHOTO-OPTICS TECHNICIAN (profess. & kin.), 029.280-010

02.04.01 QUALITY CONTROL TECHNICIAN (profess. & kin.), 012.261-014

02.04.01 SPECTROSCOPIST (profess. & kin.), 011.281-014

02.04.01 TESTER (profess. & kin.), 011.361-010

02.04.01 ULTRASOUND TECHNOLOGIST (medical ser.), 078.364-010

02.04.02 BIOLOGY SPECIMEN TECHNICIAN (profess. & kin.), 041.381-010

02.04.02 BIOMEDICAL EQUIPMENT TECHNICIAN (profess. & kin.), 019.261-010

02.04.02 CYTOGENETIC TECHNOLOGIST (medical ser.), 078.261-026

02.04.02 CYTOTECHNOLOGIST (medical ser.), 078.281-010

02.04.02 FOOD TESTER (any industry), 029.361-014

02.04.02 HISTOTECHNOLOGIST (medical ser.), 078.261-030

02.04.02 LABORATORY TECHNICIAN, PHARMACEUTICAL (pharmaceut.), 559.361-010

02.04.02 MEDICAL TECHNOLOGIST, CHIEF (medical ser.), 078.161-010

02.04.02 MEDICAL-LABORATORY TECHNICIAN (medical ser.), 078.381-014

02.04.02 OPHTHALMIC PHOTOGRAPHER (medical ser.), 143.362-014

02.04.02 SEED ANALYST (profess. & kin.), 040.361-014

03.01.01 GENERAL MANAGER, FARM (agriculture), 180.167-018

03.01.04 LOGGING-OPERATIONS INSPECTOR (forestry), 168.267-070

04.01.01 PARK SUPERINTENDENT (government ser.), 188.167-062

04.01.01 POLICE CHIEF (government ser.), 375.117-010

04.01.02 CUSTOMS PATROL OFFICER (government ser.), 168.167-010

04.01.02 FIRE WARDEN (forestry), 452.167-010

04.01.02 SPECIAL AGENT (government ser.), 375.167-042

04.02.02 SECURITY CONSULTANT (business ser.), 189.167-054

05.01.01 ELECTRICAL TECHNICIAN (profess. & kin.), 003.161-010

05.01.01 ELECTRONICS TECHNICIAN (profess. & kin.), 003.161-014

05.01.01 MECHANICAL-ENGINEERING TECHNICIAN (profess. & kin.), 007.161-026

05.01.01 OPTOMECHANICAL TECHNICIAN (optical goods), 007.161-030

05.01.01 TECHNICIAN, SEMICONDUCTOR DEVELOPMENT (profess. & kin.), 003.161-018

05.01.01 WELDING TECHNICIAN (profess. & kin.), 011.261-014

05.01.02 FIRE-PROTECTION ENGINEER (profess. & kin.), 012.167-026

05.01.03 CHIEF ENGINEER, WATERWORKS (waterworks), 005.167-010

05.01.03 COMPUTER SYSTEMS HARDWARE ANALYST (profess. & kin.), 033.167-010

05.01.03 IRRIGATION ENGINEER (profess. & kin.), 005.061-022

05.01.04 AIR ANALYST (profess. & kin.), 012.261-010

05.01.04 CHEMICAL-TEST ENGINEER (profess. & kin.), 008.061-026

05.01.04 ELECTRONICS-TEST ENGINEER (profess. & kin.), 003.061-042

05.01.04 TEST TECHNICIAN (profess. & kin.), 019.161-014

05.01.05 SALES-ENGINEER, ELECTRONICS PRODUCTS AND SYSTEMS (profess. & kin.), 003.151-014

05.01.06 DOCUMENTATION ENGINEER (profess. & kin.), 012.167-078

05.01.06 FACILITIES PLANNER (any industry), 019.261-018

05.01.06 LAND SURVEYOR (profess. & kin.), 018.167-018

05.01.06 TOOL PLANNER (any industry), 012.167-074

05.01.06 TOOL PROGRAMMER, NUMERICAL CONTROL (any industry), 007.167-018

05.01.06 TOOL PROGRAMMER, NUMERICAL CONTROL (electron. comp.), 609.262-010

05.01.07 AGRICULTURAL-ENGINEERING TECHNICIAN (profess. & kin.), 013.161-010

05.01.07 MECHANICAL-DESIGN ENGINEER, FACILITIES (profess. & kin.), 007.061-018

05.01.07 RAILROAD ENGINEER (profess. & kin.), 005.061-026

05.01.07 TOOL DESIGN CHECKER (aircraft mfg.), 007.267-014

05.01.07 TOOL DESIGNER (profess. & kin.), 007.061-026

05.01.08 CHEMICAL-ENGINEERING TECHNICIAN (profess. & kin.), 008.261-010

05.01.08 PROJECT ENGINEER (profess. & kin.), 019.167-014

05.02.03 BREWING DIRECTOR (beverage), 183.167-010

05.02.03 MANAGER, CUSTOMER TECHNICAL SERVICES (profess. & kin.), 189.117-018

05.02.03 MANAGER, FOOD PROCESSING PLANT (can. & preserv.), 183.167-026

05.02.03 QUALITY-CONTROL COORDINATOR
(pharmaceut.), 168.167-066

05.02.03 WINE MAKER (beverage), 183.161-014

05.02.06 MANAGER, LAND SURVEYING (profess. &
kin.), 018.167-022

05.03.01 NAVIGATOR (air trans.), 196.167-014

05.03.01 SURVEYOR ASSISTANT, INSTRUMENTS
(profess. & kin.), 018.167-034

05.03.02 AUTO-DESIGN CHECKER (auto. mfg.),
017.261-010

05.03.02 AUTO-DESIGN DETAILER (auto. mfg.),
017.281-010

05.03.02 CIVIL ENGINEERING TECHNICIAN
(profess. & kin.), 005.261-014

05.03.02 DESIGN DRAFTER, ELECTROMECHANISMS
(profess. & kin.), 017.261-014

05.03.02 DETAILER (profess. & kin.), 017.261-018

05.03.02 DRAFTER, AERONAUTICAL (aircraft mfg.),
002.261-010

05.03.02 DRAFTER, ARCHITECTURAL (profess. & kin.),
001.261-010

05.03.02 DRAFTER, AUTOMOTIVE DESIGN
(auto. mfg.), 017.261-042

05.03.02 DRAFTER, AUTOMOTIVE DESIGN LAYOUT
(auto. mfg.), 017.281-026

05.03.02 DRAFTER, CARTOGRAPHIC (profess. & kin.),
018.261-010

05.03.02 DRAFTER, CIVIL (profess. & kin.),
005.281-010

05.03.02 DRAFTER, COMMERCIAL (profess. & kin.),
017.261-026

05.03.02 DRAFTER, ELECTRICAL (profess. & kin.),
003.281-010

05.03.02 DRAFTER, ELECTRONIC (profess. & kin.),
003.281-014

05.03.02 DRAFTER, GEOLOGICAL (petrol. & gas),
010.281-014

05.03.02 DRAFTER, GEOPHYSICAL (petrol. & gas),
010.281-018

05.03.02 DRAFTER, LANDSCAPE (profess. & kin.),
001.261-014

05.03.02 DRAFTER, MARINE (profess. & kin.),
014.281-010

05.03.02 DRAFTER, MECHANICAL (profess. & kin.),
007.281-010

05.03.02 DRAFTER, STRUCTURAL (profess. & kin.),
005.281-014

05.03.02 DRAWINGS CHECKER, ENGINEERING
(profess. & kin.), 007.267-010

05.03.02 EDITOR, MAP (profess. & kin.), 018.261-018

05.03.02 ENGINEERING ASSISTANT, MECHANICAL
EQUIPMENT (profess. & kin.), 007.161-018

05.03.02 ESTIMATOR (profess. & kin.), 169.267-038

05.03.02 ESTIMATOR AND DRAFTER (utilities),
019.261-014

05.03.02 FIRE-PROTECTION ENGINEERING
TECHNICIAN (profess. & kin.), 019.261-026

05.03.02 INTEGRATED CIRCUIT LAYOUT DESIGNER
(profess. & kin.), 003.261-018

05.03.02 PHOTOGRAMMETRIST (profess. & kin.),
018.261-026

05.03.02 PRINTED CIRCUIT DESIGNER (profess. &
kin.), 003.261-022

05.03.02 SPECIFICATION WRITER (profess. & kin.),
019.267-010

05.03.02 TECHNICAL ILLUSTRATOR (profess. & kin.),
017.281-034

05.03.03 MATERIAL SCHEDULER (aircraft mfg.),
012.167-082

05.03.04 FIELD ENGINEER, SPECIALIST (petrol. &
gas), 010.261-010

05.03.05 FIELD ENGINEER (radio-tv broad.),
193.262-018

05.03.05 FLIGHT-TEST DATA ACQUISITION TECHNI-
CIAN (aircraft mfg.), 002.262-010

05.03.05 LASER TECHNICIAN (electron. comp.),
019.261-034

05.03.05 RADIOGRAPHER (any industry), 199.361-010

05.03.05 TRANSMITTER OPERATOR (radio-tv broad.),
193.262-038

05.03.06 BUILDING INSPECTOR (insurance),
168.267-010

05.03.06 INDUSTRIAL ENGINEERING TECHNICIAN
(profess. & kin.), 012.267-010

05.03.06 INSPECTOR, AIR-CARRIER (government ser.),
168.264-010

05.03.06 INSPECTOR, INDUSTRIAL WASTE (government ser.), 168.267-054

05.03.06 INSPECTOR, PLUMBING (government ser.),
168.167-050

05.03.06 INSPECTOR, QUALITY ASSURANCE
(government ser.), 168.287-014

05.03.06 MARINE SURVEYOR (profess. & kin.),
014.167-010

05.03.06 SUPERVISOR, VENDOR QUALITY
(any industry), 012.167-062

05.03.07 HEAT-TRANSFER TECHNICIAN (profess. &
kin.), 007.181-010

05.03.07 SOLAR-ENERGY-SYSTEMS DESIGNER
(profess. & kin.), 007.161-038

05.03.07 TEST TECHNICIAN (agric. equip.), 019.261-022

05.03.08 POLLUTION-CONTROL TECHNICIAN
(profess. & kin.), 029.261-014

05.04.01 AIRPLANE PILOT (agriculture), 196.263-010

05.04.01 AIRPLANE PILOT, COMMERCIAL (air trans.),
196.263-014

05.04.01 INSTRUCTOR, FLYING I (education),
196.223-010

05.04.01 INSTRUCTOR, FLYING II (education),
097.227-010

05.04.02 MATE, SHIP (water trans.), 197.133-022

05.05.01 CEMENT MASON (construction), 844.364-010

05.05.02 ACOUSTICAL CARPENTER (construction),
860.381-010

05.05.02 BOATBUILDER, WOOD (ship-boat mfg.),
860.361-010

05.05.02 CARPENTER (construction), 860.381-022

05.05.02 CARPENTER, MAINTENANCE (any industry),
860.281-010

05.05.02 FORM BUILDER (construction), 860.381-046

05.05.02 SHIPWRIGHT (ship-boat mfg.), 860.381-058

05.05.03 GAS-MAIN FITTER (utilities), 862.361-014

05.05.03 PIPE FITTER (construction), 862.281-022

05.05.05 ANTENNA INSTALLER, SATELLITE COMMU-
NICATIONS (any industry), 823.261-022

05.05.05 ELECTRICIAN, POWERHOUSE (utilities),
820.261-014

05.05.05 ELEVATOR REPAIRER (any industry),
825.281-030

05.05.05 FURNACE INSTALLER (utilities), 862.361-010

05.05.06 MILLWRIGHT (any industry), 638.281-018

05.05.06 SAFE-AND-VAULT SERVICE MECHANIC
(business ser.), 869.381-022

05.05.06 SHIPFITTER (ship-boat mfg.), 806.381-046

05.05.07 MACHINIST (machine shop), 600.280-022

05.05.07 PATTERNMAKER, METAL (foundry),
600.280-050

05.05.07 TOOL-AND-DIE MAKER (machine shop),
601.260-010

05.05.09 AIRFRAME-AND-POWER-PLANT ME-
CHANIC (aircraft mfg.), 621.281-014

05.05.09 EXPERIMENTAL AIRCRAFT MECHANIC
(aircraft mfg.), 621.261-022

05.05.09 FIELD SERVICE TECHNICIAN (machinery
mfg.), 638.261-026

05.05.09 LOCKSMITH (any industry), 709.281-010

05.05.09 REFRIGERATION MECHANIC (svc. ind.
mach.), 827.361-014

05.05.09 ROCKET-ENGINE-COMPONENT MECHANIC
(aircraft mfg.), 621.281-030

05.05.10 AVIONICS TECHNICIAN (aircraft mfg.),
823.261-026

05.05.10 INSTRUMENT MECHANIC (any industry),
710.281-026

05.05.11 OPTICIAN (optical goods), 716.280-014

05.05.11 RADIOLOGICAL-EQUIPMENT SPECIALIST
(inst. & app.), 719.261-014

05.05.12 ELECTRONIC-ORGAN TECHNICIAN (any
industry), 828.261-010

05.05.13 JOB PRINTER (print. & pub.), 973.381-018

05.05.17 ANALYST, FOOD AND BEVERAGE (hotel &
rest.), 310.267-010

05.05.17 DIETETIC TECHNICIAN (profess. & kin.),
077.124-010

05.06.02 REFRIGERATING ENGINEER (any industry),
950.362-014

05.07.01 NONDESTRUCTIVE TESTER (profess. & kin.),
011.261-018

05.07.02 INSPECTOR, HEATING AND REFRIGERA-
TION (government ser.), 168.167-046

05.07.03 ELEVATOR EXAMINER-AND-ADJUSTER
(any industry), 825.261-014

05.10.01 OPTICIAN, DISPENSING (optical goods),
299.361-010

05.10.03 LIGHT TECHNICIAN (motion picture),
962.362-014

05.10.04 HOUSE REPAIRER (construction), 869.381-010

05.10.05 AUDIOVISUAL TECHNICIAN (any industry),
960.382-010

05.10.05 RECORDING ENGINEER (radio-tv broad.),
194.362-010

05.10.05 RECORDIST (motion picture), 962.382-010

05.10.06 BLASTER (any industry), 859.261-010

05.11.01 ASPHALT-PAVING-MACHINE OPERATOR
(construction), 853.663-010

05.11.01 PILE-DRIVER OPERATOR (construction),
859.682-018

05.11.01 POWER-SHOVEL OPERATOR (any industry),
850.683-030

05.11.03 ROTARY DRILLER (petrol. & gas), 930.382-026

06.01.02 PRINT CONTROLLER (photofinishing),
976.360-010

06.01.03 NUMERICAL CONTROL MACHINE SET-UP
OPERATOR (machine shop), 609.360-010

06.01.05 OPERATIONAL TEST MECHANIC (aircraft
mfg.), 806.261-050

06.02.02 NUMERICAL CONTROL MACHINE OPERA-
TOR (machine shop), 609.362-010

06.02.24 SOLAR-FABRICATION TECHNICIAN (machine
shop), 809.381-034

07.01.01 CONTACT REPRESENTATIVE (government
ser.), 169.167-018

07.01.01 CREDIT COUNSELOR (profess. & kin.),
160.207-010

07.01.01 RETIREMENT OFFICER (government ser.),
166.267-030

07.01.02 ADMINISTRATIVE SECRETARY (any industry),
169.167-014

07.01.02 DIRECTOR, NURSES' REGISTRY (medical
ser.), 187.167-034

07.01.02 MANAGER, TRAFFIC I (motor trans.),
184.167-102

07.01.02 SUPERVISOR, NETWORK CONTROL
OPERATORS (any industry), 031.132-010

07.01.05 TITLE CLERK (petrol. & gas), 162.267-010

07.01.05 TITLE EXAMINER (profess. & kin.),
119.287-010

07.01.05 TITLE SUPERVISOR (profess. & kin.),
119.167-018

07.01.06 CASEWORKER (government ser.), 169.262-010

07.02.03 CLAIM EXAMINER (insurance), 168.267-014

07.05.03 INSURANCE CLERK (clerical), 219.387-014

07.05.03 MEDICAL RECORD TECHNICIAN (medical
ser.), 079.362-014

07.05.03 MEDICAL-SERVICE TECHNICIAN (military
ser.), 079.367-018

07.05.03 TUMOR REGISTRAR (medical ser.),
079.362-018

07.06.01 NETWORK CONTROL OPERATOR (any
industry), 031.262-014

08.01.01 SALES REPRESENTATIVE, CHEMICALS AND
DRUGS (wholesale tr.), 262.357-010

08.01.01 SALES REPRESENTATIVE, COMPUTERS
AND EDP SYSTEMS (wholesale tr.),
275.257-010

08.01.02 SALES REPRESENTATIVE, DATA PROCESS-
ING SERVICES (business ser.), 251.157-014

08.01.02 SALES REPRESENTATIVE, FINANCIAL
SERVICES (financial), 250.257-022

08.02.01 SALES REPRESENTATIVE, NOVELTIES
(wholesale tr.), 277.357-018

08.02.02 SALESPERSON, SURGICAL APPLIANCES
(retail trade), 276.257-022

09.01.01 GROUP WORKER (social ser.), 195.164-010

09.01.01 RECREATION LEADER (social ser.), 195.227-014

09.04.01 VENDING-STAND SUPERVISOR (government ser.), 185.167-066

10.01.01 PASTORAL ASSISTANT (nonprofit org.), 129.107-026

10.01.02 CASEWORKER (social ser.), 195.107-010

10.01.02 CASEWORKER, FAMILY (social ser.), 195.107-018

10.01.02 PATIENT-RESOURCES-AND-REIMBURSE-MENT AGENT (government ser.), 195.267-018

10.01.02 RESIDENCE COUNSELOR (education), 045.107-038

10.02.01 NURSE, HEAD (medical ser.), 075.137-014

10.02.01 NURSE, LICENSED PRACTICAL (medical ser.), 079.374-014

10.02.01 NURSE, SUPERVISOR (medical ser.), 075.167-010

10.02.01 PHYSICIAN ASSISTANT (medical ser.), 079.364-018

10.02.01 TRANSPLANT COORDINATOR (medical ser.), 079.151-010

10.02.02 ACUPRESSURIST (medical ser.), 079.271-014

10.02.02 ATHLETIC TRAINER (amuse. & rec.), 153.224-010

10.02.02 CORRECTIVE THERAPIST (medical ser.), 076.361-010

10.02.02 DANCE THERAPIST (medical ser.), 076.127-018

10.02.02 DENTAL HYGIENIST (medical ser.), 078.361-010

10.02.02 DIALYSIS TECHNICIAN (medical ser.), 078.362-014

10.02.02 EXERCISE PHYSIOLOGIST (medical ser.), 076.121-018

10.02.02 HORTICULTURAL THERAPIST (medical ser.), 076.124-018

10.02.02 INDUSTRIAL THERAPIST (medical ser.), 076.167-010

10.02.02 MANUAL-ARTS THERAPIST (medical ser.), 076.124-010

10.02.02 MEDICAL RADIATION DOSIMETRIST (medical ser.), 078.261-034

10.02.02 NUCLEAR MEDICINE TECHNOLOGIST (medical ser.), 078.361-018

10.02.02 OCCUPATIONAL THERAPY ASSISTANT (medical ser.), 076.364-010

10.02.02 ORIENTATION AND MOBILITY THERAPIST FOR THE BLIND (education), 076.224-014

10.02.02 ORTHOPTIST (medical ser.), 079.371-014

10.02.02 PHERESIS SPECIALIST (medical ser.), 078.261-042

10.02.02 PHYSICAL-INTEGRATION PRACTITIONER (medical ser.), 076.264-010

10.02.02 PROGRAM AIDE, GROUP WORK (social ser.), 195.227-010

10.02.02 PSYCHIATRIC TECHNICIAN (medical ser.), 079.374-026

10.02.02 RADIATION-THERAPY TECHNOLOGIST (medical ser.), 078.361-034

10.02.02 RADIOLOGIC TECHNOLOGIST (medical ser.), 078.362-026

10.02.02 RADIOLOGIC TECHNOLOGIST, CHIEF (medical ser.), 078.162-010

10.02.02 RECREATIONAL THERAPIST (medical ser.), 076.124-014

10.02.02 RESPIRATORY THERAPIST (medical ser.), 076.361-014

10.02.02 SPECIAL PROCEDURES TECHNOLOGIST, ANGIOGRAM (medical ser.), 078.362-046

10.02.02 SPECIAL PROCEDURES TECHNOLOGIST, CARDIAC CATHETERIZATION (medical ser.), 078.362-050

10.02.02 SPECIAL PROCEDURES TECHNOLOGIST, CT SCAN (medical ser.), 078.362-054

10.02.02 SPECIAL PROCEDURES TECHNOLOGIST, MAGNETIC RESONANCE IMAGING (MRI) (medical ser.), 078.362-058

10.02.03 TEACHER, PRESCHOOL (education), 092.227-018

10.02.03 TEACHER, VOCATIONAL TRAINING (education), 094.227-026

10.02.03 WORK-STUDY COORDINATOR, SPECIAL EDUCATION (education), 094.107-010

10.03.01 AUDIOMETRIST (profess. & kin.), 078.362-010

10.03.01 ECHOCARDIOGRAPH TECHNICIAN (medical ser.), 078.364-014

10.03.01 ELECTROCARDIOGRAPH TECHNICIAN (medical ser.), 078.362-018

10.03.01 ELECTROENCEPHALOGRAPHIC TECH-NOLOGIST (medical ser.), 078.362-022

10.03.01 ELECTROMYOGRAPHIC TECHNICIAN (medical ser.), 078.362-038

10.03.01 OPHTHALMIC TECHNICIAN (medical ser.), 078.361-038

10.03.01 POLYSOMNOGRAPHIC TECHNICIAN (medical ser.), 078.362-042

10.03.01 PULMONARY-FUNCTION TECHNICIAN (medical ser.), 078.262-010

10.03.01 STRESS TEST TECHNICIAN (medical ser.), 078.362-062

10.03.02 AMBULANCE ATTENDANT (medical ser.), 355.374-010

10.03.02 BIRTH ATTENDANT (medical ser.), 354.377-010

10.03.02 CERTIFIED MEDICATION TECHNICIAN (medical ser.), 355.374-014

10.03.02 DENTAL ASSISTANT (medical ser.), 079.361-018

10.03.02 EMERGENCY MEDICAL TECHNICIAN (medical ser.), 079.374-010

10.03.02 FIRST-AID ATTENDANT (any industry), 354.677-010

10.03.02 MEDICAL ASSISTANT (medical ser.), 079.362-010

10.03.02 NURSE, PRACTICAL (medical ser.), 354.374-010

10.03.02 PARAMEDIC (medical ser.), 079.364-026

10.03.02 PERFUSIONIST (medical ser.), 078.362-034

10.03.02 PHYSICAL THERAPY AIDE (medical ser.), 355.354-010

10.03.02 PSYCHIATRIC AIDE (medical ser.), 355.377-014

10.03.02 SURGICAL TECHNICIAN (medical ser.),
079.374-022

10.03.03 HOME ATTENDANT (personal ser.),
354.377-014

11.01.01 COMPUTER PROGRAMMER (profess. & kin.),
030.162-010

11.01.01 DATA BASE ADMINISTRATOR (profess. &
kin.), 039.162-010

11.01.01 DATA BASE DESIGN ANALYST (profess. &
kin.), 039.162-014

11.01.01 DATA COMMUNICATIONS ANALYST
(profess. & kin.), 031.262-010

11.01.01 DATA RECOVERY PLANNER (profess. & kin.),
033.162-014

11.01.01 MANAGER, COMPUTER OPERATIONS
(profess. & kin.), 169.167-082

11.01.01 QUALITY ASSURANCE ANALYST (profess. &
kin.), 033.262-010

11.01.01 TECHNICAL SUPPORT SPECIALIST (profess.
& kin.), 033.162-018

11.01.01 USER SUPPORT ANALYST (profess. & kin.),
032.262-010

11.01.01 USER SUPPORT ANALYST SUPERVISOR
(profess. & kin.), 032.132-010

11.02.01 HISTORIC-SITE ADMINISTRATOR
(museums), 102.167-014

11.02.01 INSTRUCTOR, EXTENSION WORK
(education), 090.227-018

11.02.01 TUTOR (education), 099.227-034

11.02.02 DIETITIAN, TEACHING (profess. & kin.),
077.127-022

11.02.02 INSTRUCTOR, TECHNICAL TRAINING
(education), 166.221-010

11.02.02 INSTRUCTOR, VOCATIONAL TRAINING
(education), 097.221-010

11.02.02 TRAINING REPRESENTATIVE (education),
166.227-010

11.02.03 COUNTY HOME-DEMONSTRATION AGENT
(government ser.), 096.121-010

11.02.03 COUNTY-AGRICULTURAL AGENT (government ser.), 096.127-010

11.02.03 EXTENSION SERVICE SPECIALIST (government ser.), 096.127-014

11.02.04 AUDIOVISUAL LIBRARIAN (library),
100.167-010

11.02.04 CLASSIFIER (library), 100.367-014

11.02.04 MEDIA SPECIALIST, SCHOOL LIBRARY
(library), 100.167-030

11.03.03 GENEALOGIST (profess. & kin.), 052.067-018

11.04.02 LEGAL INVESTIGATOR (profess. & kin.),
119.267-022

11.04.02 PARALEGAL (profess. & kin.), 119.267-026

11.04.04 ABSTRACTOR (profess. & kin.), 119.267-010

11.04.04 CUSTOMS BROKER (financial), 186.117-018

11.05.01 DIRECTOR, TRANSPORTATION
(motor trans.), 184.117-014

11.05.01 MANAGER, AIRPORT (air trans.), 184.117-026

11.05.01 MANAGER, BAKERY (bakery products),
189.117-046

11.05.01 MANAGER, INDUSTRIAL ORGANIZATION
(any industry), 189.117-022

11.05.02 ADMINISTRATIVE ASSISTANT (any industry),
169.167-010

11.05.02 DIRECTOR, SERVICE (retail trade), 189.167-014

11.05.02 EXECUTIVE VICE PRESIDENT, CHAMBER
OF COMMERCE (nonprofit org.), 187.117-030

11.05.02 MANAGER, BENEFITS (profess. & kin.),
166.167-018

11.05.02 MANAGER, BRANCH (any industry),
183.117-010

11.05.02 MANAGER, CONTRACTS (petrol. & gas),
163.117-010

11.05.02 MANAGER, DEPARTMENT STORE (retail
trade), 185.117-010

11.05.02 MANAGER, OPERATIONS (air trans.),
184.117-050

11.05.02 MANAGER, PROCUREMENT SERVICES
(profess. & kin.), 162.167-022

11.05.02 MANAGER, REGIONAL (motor trans.),
184.117-054

11.05.02 MANAGER, SCHEDULE PLANNING (air
trans.), 184.117-058

11.05.02 MANAGER, STATION (radio-tv broad.),
184.117-062

11.05.02 MANAGER, TRAFFIC (any industry),
184.167-094

11.05.02 MANAGER, WORLD TRADE AND MARITIME
DIVISION (nonprofit org.), 187.167-170

11.05.02 PROGRAM MANAGER (profess. & kin.),
189.167-030

11.05.02 PROGRAM PROPOSALS COORDINATOR
(radio-tv broad.), 132.067-030

11.05.02 PROGRAM SPECIALIST, EMPLOYEE-
HEALTH MAINTENANCE (profess. & kin.),
166.167-050

11.05.02 PROJECT DIRECTOR (profess. & kin.),
189.117-030

11.05.02 UTILIZATION COORDINATOR (radio-tv
broad.), 169.167-078

11.05.03 COURT ADMINISTRATOR (government ser.),
188.117-130

11.05.03 DIRECTOR, REGULATORY AGENCY (government ser.), 188.117-134

11.05.03 MANAGER, HOUSING PROJECT (profess. &
kin.), 186.167-030

11.05.03 MANAGER, REGULATED PROGRAM (government ser.), 168.167-090

11.05.04 FIELD REPRESENTATIVE (business ser.),
163.267-010

11.05.04 MANAGER, CIRCULATION (print. & pub.),
163.167-014

11.05.04 MANAGER, PROFESSIONAL EQUIPMENT
SALES-AND-SERVICE (business ser.),
185.167-042

11.05.04 PROPERTY-DISPOSAL OFFICER (any industry), 163.167-026

11.06.01 ACCOUNTANT, BUDGET (profess. & kin.),
160.162-022

11.06.01 ACCOUNTANT, PROPERTY (profess. & kin.),
160.167-022

11.06.01 ACCOUNTANT, SYSTEMS (profess. & kin.),
160.167-026

11.06.01 AUDITOR, COUNTY OR CITY (government ser.), 160.167-030

11.06.03 APPRAISER (government ser.), 188.167-010

11.06.03 APPRAISER (any industry), 191.287-010

11.06.03 APPRAISER, REAL ESTATE (real estate), 191.267-010

11.06.03 CREDIT ANALYST (financial), 160.267-022

11.06.03 FOREIGN-EXCHANGE DEALER (financial), 186.117-082

11.06.03 LOAN REVIEW ANALYST (financial), 186.267-022

11.06.03 MANAGER, CREDIT AND COLLECTION (any industry), 169.167-086

11.06.03 MARKET-RESEARCH ANALYST I (profess. & kin.), 050.067-014

11.06.03 SECURITIES TRADER (financial), 162.167-038

11.06.03 UNDERWRITER (insurance), 169.267-046

11.06.03 UNDERWRITER, MORTGAGE LOAN (financial), 186.267-026

11.06.05 BUDGET OFFICER (profess. & kin.), 161.117-010

11.06.05 TRUST OFFICER (financial), 186.117-074

11.07.01 COMMUNITY-RELATIONS-AND-SERVICES ADVISOR, PUBLIC HOUSING (social ser.), 195.167-014

11.07.01 DIRECTOR, COMMUNITY ORGANIZATION (nonprofit org.), 187.167-234

11.07.01 DIRECTOR, SERVICE (nonprofit org.), 187.167-214

11.07.01 EXECUTIVE DIRECTOR, RED CROSS (nonprofit org.), 187.117-066

11.07.01 FIELD REPRESENTATIVE (profess. & kin.), 189.267-010

11.07.01 PROGRAM DIRECTOR, GROUP WORK (profess. & kin.), 187.117-046

11.07.02 DIRECTOR, NURSING SERVICE (medical ser.), 075.117-022

11.07.02 EMERGENCY MEDICAL SERVICES COORDINATOR (medical ser.), 079.117-010

11.07.02 RADIOLOGY ADMINISTRATOR (medical ser.), 187.117-062

11.07.03 MUSIC SUPERVISOR (education), 099.167-026

11.07.03 SUPERVISOR, CONTRACT-SHELTERED WORKSHOP (nonprofit org.), 187.134-010

11.07.03 TECHNICAL TRAINING COORDINATOR (education), 166.167-054

11.07.04 RECREATION SUPERVISOR (profess. & kin.), 187.167-238

11.08.01 EDITOR, DEPARTMENT (print. & pub.), 132.037-018

11.08.01 EDITOR, NEWS (print. & pub.), 132.067-026

11.08.01 EDITORIAL ASSISTANT (print. & pub.), 132.267-014

11.08.02 REPORTER (print. & pub.), 131.262-018

11.08.02 WRITER, TECHNICAL PUBLICATIONS (profess. & kin.), 131.267-026

11.08.03 NEWSCASTER (radio-tv broad.), 131.262-010

11.08.04 INTERPRETER (profess. & kin.), 137.267-010

11.09.01 MANAGER, ADVERTISING (print. & pub.), 163.167-010

11.09.01 MEDIA DIRECTOR (profess. & kin.), 164.117-018

11.09.02 MEMBERSHIP DIRECTOR (profess. & kin.), 189.167-026

11.09.03 EMPLOYER RELATIONS REPRESENTATIVE (profess. & kin.), 166.257-010

11.09.03 LOBBYIST (profess. & kin.), 165.017-010

11.09.03 MANAGER, AREA DEVELOPMENT (utilities), 184.117-030

11.10.01 INVESTIGATOR (government ser.), 168.267-062

11.10.01 REVENUE OFFICER (government ser.), 188.167-074

11.10.02 DIRECTOR, COMPLIANCE (government ser.), 188.117-046

11.10.02 EQUAL-OPPORTUNITY REPRESENTATIVE (government ser.), 168.167-014

11.10.03 FOOD AND DRUG INSPECTOR (government ser.), 168.267-042

11.10.03 GAS INSPECTOR (utilities), 168.264-018

11.10.03 HAZARDOUS-WASTE MANAGEMENT SPECIALIST (government ser.), 168.267-086

11.10.03 INDUSTRIAL HYGIENIST (profess. & kin.), 079.161-010

11.10.03 INDUSTRIAL-SAFETY-AND-HEALTH TECH-NICIAN (any industry), 168.161-014

11.10.03 INSPECTOR, MOTOR VEHICLES (government ser.), 168.267-058

11.10.03 INSPECTOR, WATER-POLLUTION CONTROL (government ser.), 168.267-090

11.10.03 OCCUPATIONAL-SAFETY-AND-HEALTH INSPECTOR (government ser.), 168.167-062

11.10.03 RADIATION-PROTECTION SPECIALIST (government ser.), 168.261-010

11.10.03 SAFETY INSPECTOR (insurance), 168.167-078

11.10.03 SAFETY MANAGER (medical ser.), 168.167-086

11.10.04 CUSTOMS INSPECTOR (government ser.), 168.267-022

11.10.04 IMMIGRATION INSPECTOR (government ser.), 168.167-022

11.10.05 COMPUTER SECURITY COORDINATOR (profess. & kin.), 033.162-010

11.10.05 COMPUTER SECURITY SPECIALIST (profess. & kin.), 033.362-010

11.11.01 MANAGER, HOTEL OR MOTEL (hotel & rest.), 187.117-038

11.11.02 DIRECTOR, CAMP (social ser.), 195.167-018

11.11.02 DIRECTOR, RECREATION CENTER (social ser.), 195.167-026

11.11.02 MANAGER, RECREATION ESTABLISHMENT (amuse. & rec.), 187.117-042

11.11.03 MANAGER, DISTRIBUTION WAREHOUSE (wholesale tr.), 185.167-018

11.11.03 MANAGER, WAREHOUSE (any industry), 184.167-114

11.11.04 DIRECTOR, FUNERAL (personal ser.), 187.167-030

11.11.04 MANAGER, PROPERTY (real estate), 186.167-046

11.11.05 MANAGER, VEHICLE LEASING AND RENTAL (automotive ser.), 187.167-162

11.12.01 CLAIMS ADJUDICATOR (government ser.), 169.267-010

11.12.01 MANAGER, CUSTOMER SERVICE (tel. & tel.), 168.167-058

11.12.01 SERVICE REPRESENTATIVE (auto. mfg.), 191.167-022

11.12.02 MANAGER, LEASING (petrol. & gas), 186.117-046

11.12.02 PROPERTY-UTILIZATION OFFICER (government ser.), 188.117-122

11.12.02 REAL-ESTATE AGENT (profess. & kin.), 186.117-058

11.12.03 BUSINESS MANAGER (amuse. & rec.), 191.117-018

11.12.04 CONTRACT ADMINISTRATOR (any industry), 162.117-014

High School Diploma or GED

01.01.02 SCREEN WRITER (motion picture), 131.067-050

01.01.02 WRITER, PROSE, FICTION AND NON-FICTION (profess. & kin.), 131.067-046

01.02.03 CAMERA OPERATOR (motion picture), 143.062-022

01.02.03 DISPLAYER, MERCHANDISE (retail trade), 298.081-010

01.02.03 FLORAL DESIGNER (retail trade), 142.081-010

01.02.03 OPTICAL-EFFECTS-CAMERA OPERATOR (motion picture), 143.260-010

01.02.03 PHOTOGRAPHER, STILL (profess. & kin.), 143.062-030

01.02.03 PHOTOJOURNALIST (print. & pub.), 143.062-034

01.03.01 COMMUNICATIONS TECHNICIAN (education), 962.362-010

01.03.01 DIRECTOR, STAGE (amuse. & rec.), 150.067-010

01.03.01 MANAGER, STAGE (amuse. & rec.), 159.167-018

01.03.02 INTERPRETER, DEAF (profess. & kin.), 137.267-014

01.03.03 PROGRAM COORDINATOR (amuse. & rec.), 139.167-010

01.04.01 ARTIST AND REPERTOIRE MANAGER (amuse. & rec.), 159.167-010

01.04.02 COPYIST (any industry), 152.267-010

01.04.02 PROMPTER (amuse. & rec.), 152.367-010

01.05.02 DANCER (amuse. & rec.), 151.047-010

01.06.01 COMPUTER TYPESETTER-KEYLINER (print. & pub.), 979.382-026

01.06.01 ELECTRONIC MASKING SYSTEM OPERA-TOR (print. & pub.), 972.282-018

01.06.01 PASTE-UP ARTIST (print. & pub.), 972.381-030

01.06.01 PHOTOENGRAVER (print. & pub.), 971.381-022

01.06.01 PHOTOGRAPHER, LITHOGRAPHIC (print. & pub.), 972.382-014

01.06.01 STRIPPER (print. & pub.), 971.381-050

01.06.01 STRIPPER, LITHOGRAPHIC I (print. & pub.), 972.281-022

01.06.01 SUPERVISOR, PREPRESS (print. & pub.), 972.137-010

01.06.02 CONSERVATOR, ARTIFACTS (profess. & kin.), 055.381-010

01.06.02 JEWELER (jewelry-silver.), 700.281-010

01.06.02 MUSEUM TECHNICIAN (museums), 102.381-010

01.06.03 PAINTER, SIGN (any industry), 970.381-026

01.06.03 TYPE COPYIST (machinery mfg.), 970.381-042

01.07.02 ANNOUNCER (amuse. & rec.), 159.347-010

02.03.03 VETERINARY TECHNICIAN (medical ser.), 079.361-014

02.04.01 FINGERPRINT CLASSIFIER (government ser.), 375.387-010

02.04.01 HOT-CELL TECHNICIAN (profess. & kin.), 015.362-018

02.04.01 LABORATORY ASSISTANT (petrol. & gas), 024.381-010

02.04.01 LABORATORY ASSISTANT (textile), 029.381-014

02.04.01 LABORATORY TESTER (plastic-synth.), 022.281-018

02.04.01 PHARMACIST ASSISTANT (military ser.), 074.381-010

02.04.01 PHOTOGRAPHER, SCIENTIFIC (profess. & kin.), 143.062-026

02.04.01 RADIOISOTOPE-PRODUCTION OPERATOR (profess. & kin.), 015.362-022

02.04.01 REACTOR OPERATOR, TEST-AND-RESEARCH (profess. & kin.), 015.362-026

02.04.01 SCANNER (profess. & kin.), 015.384-010

02.04.01 TESTER (petrol. refin.), 029.261-022

02.04.01 WEATHER OBSERVER (profess. & kin.), 025.267-014

02.04.02 AEROSPACE PHYSIOLOGICAL TECHNICIAN (military ser.), 199.682-010

02.04.02 BIOLOGICAL AIDE (agriculture), 049.364-018

02.04.02 CEPHALOMETRIC ANALYST (medical ser.), 078.384-010

02.04.02 EMBALMER (personal ser.), 338.371-014

02.04.02 HERBARIUM WORKER (profess. & kin.), 041.384-010

02.04.02 LABORATORY ASSISTANT, BLOOD AND PLASMA (medical ser.), 078.687-010

02.04.02 PHLEBOTOMIST (medical ser.), 079.364-022

02.04.02 POLYGRAPH EXAMINER (profess. & kin.), 199.267-026

02.04.02 VECTOR CONTROL ASSISTANT (government ser.), 049.364-014

03.01.01 FARMER, FIELD CROP (agriculture), 404.161-010

03.01.01 FARMER, FRUIT CROPS, BUSH AND VINE (agriculture), 403.161-014

03.01.01 FARMER, GENERAL (agriculture), 421.161-010

03.01.01 MANAGER, DAIRY FARM (agriculture), 180.167-026

03.01.02 FISH FARMER (fishing & hunt.), 446.161-010

03.01.02 SHELLFISH GROWER (fishing & hunt.), 446.161-014

03.01.03 LANDSCAPE CONTRACTOR (construction), 182.167-014

03.01.03 MANAGER, NURSERY (agriculture), 180.167-042

03.01.03 TREE SURGEON (agriculture), 408.181-010

03.02.02 FORESTER AIDE (forestry), 452.364-010

03.03.02 ANIMAL KEEPER, HEAD (amuse. & rec.), 412.137-010

03.04.04 GREENSKEEPER I (any industry), 406.137-010

04.01.01 DEPUTY, COURT (government ser.), 377.137-018

04.01.01 DESK OFFICER (government ser.), 375.137-014

04.01.01 FIRE CAPTAIN (government ser.), 373.134-010

04.01.01 FIRE CHIEF (government ser.), 373.117-010

04.01.01 FIRE MARSHAL (any industry), 373.167-018

04.01.01 MANAGER, INTERNAL SECURITY (business ser.), 376.137-010

04.01.02 FIRE MARSHAL (government ser.), 373.267-014

04.01.02 FISH AND GAME WARDEN (government ser.), 379.167-010

04.01.02 INVESTIGATOR, PRIVATE (business ser.), 376.267-018

04.01.02 POLICE OFFICER I (government ser.), 375.263-014

04.01.02 POLICE OFFICER III (government ser.), 375.267-038

04.01.02 PUBLIC-SAFETY OFFICER (government ser.), 379.263-014

04.01.02 SHERIFF, DEPUTY (government ser.), 377.263-010

04.01.02 STATE-HIGHWAY POLICE OFFICER (government ser.), 375.263-018

04.02.01 CORRECTION OFFICER (government ser.), 372.667-018

04.02.02 FIRE INSPECTOR (any industry), 373.367-010

04.02.03 BAILIFF (government ser.), 377.667-010

04.02.04 FIRE FIGHTER (any industry), 373.364-010

05.01.04 RESEARCH MECHANIC (aircraft mfg.), 002.261-014

05.01.04 TEST-ENGINE EVALUATOR (petrol. refin.), 010.261-026

05.01.06 PREVENTIVE MAINTENANCE COORDINATOR (any industry), 169.167-074

05.02.03 PRODUCTION SUPERINTENDENT (any industry), 183.117-014

05.02.04 PROGRAM DIRECTOR, CABLE TELEVISION (radio-tv broad.), 194.162-010

05.02.06 APPLIANCE-SERVICE SUPERVISOR (utilities), 187.167-010

05.02.07 MANAGER, MARINA DRY DOCK (amuse. & rec.), 187.167-226

05.03.02 DESIGN TECHNICIAN, COMPUTER-AIDED (electron. comp.), 003.362-010

05.03.02 DRAFTER, ASSISTANT (profess. & kin.), 017.281-018

05.03.02 PATTERNMAKER (furniture), 781.361-014

05.03.02 STEREO-PLOTTER OPERATOR (profess. & kin.), 018.281-010

05.03.03 AIR-TRAFFIC-CONTROL SPECIALIST, STATION (government ser.), 193.162-014

05.03.03 AIR-TRAFFIC-CONTROL SPECIALIST, TOWER (government ser.), 193.162-018

05.03.03 PRODUCTION CLERK (clerical), 221.382-018

05.03.05 ACCESS COORDINATOR, CABLE TELEVISION (radio-tv broad.), 194.122-010

05.03.05 MASTER CONTROL OPERATOR (radio-tv broad.), 194.262-022

05.03.05 RADIOTELEPHONE OPERATOR (any industry), 193.262-034

05.03.05 TECHNICIAN, NEWS GATHERING (radio-tv broad.), 194.362-022

05.03.05 VIDEO OPERATOR (radio-tv broad.), 194.282-010

05.03.05 VIDEOTAPE OPERATOR (radio-tv broad.), 194.382-018

05.03.06 CONSTRUCTION INSPECTOR (construction), 182.267-010

05.03.06 FLIGHT ENGINEER (air trans.), 621.261-018

05.03.06 INSPECTOR, RAILROAD (government ser.), 168.287-018

05.03.06 PLAN CHECKER (government ser.), 168.267-102

05.03.08 ENERGY-CONTROL OFFICER (education), 199.167-018

05.03.08 RADIATION MONITOR (profess. & kin.), 199.167-010

05.03.09 FINE ARTS PACKER (museums), 102.367-010

05.04.02 CAPTAIN, FISHING VESSEL (fishing & hunt.), 197.133-010

05.04.02 PILOT, SHIP (water trans.), 197.133-026

05.05.01 BRICKLAYER (construction), 861.381-018

05.05.01 SOFT-TILE SETTER (construction), 861.381-034

05.05.01 STONEMASON (construction), 861.381-038

05.05.01 TERRAZZO WORKER (construction), 861.381-046

05.05.01 TILE SETTER (construction), 861.381-054

05.05.02 CARPENTER APPRENTICE (construction), 860.381-026

05.05.02 CARPENTER, ROUGH (construction), 860.381-042

05.05.02 CUSTOM VAN CONVERTER (auto. mfg.), 806.381-070

05.05.02 MARINE-SERVICES TECHNICIAN (ship-boat mfg.), 806.261-026

05.05.02 SUPERINTENDENT, MAINTENANCE (any industry), 189.167-046

05.05.03 PLUMBER (construction), 862.381-030

05.05.04 PAPERHANGER (construction), 841.381-010

05.05.04 PLASTERER (construction), 842.361-018

05.05.05 AUTOMATED EQUIPMENT ENGINEER-TECHNICIAN (machinery mfg.), 638.261-010

05.05.05 CABLE INSTALLER-REPAIRER (utilities), 821.361-010

05.05.05 CABLE SUPERVISOR (tel. & tel.), 184.161-010

05.05.05 CABLE TESTER (tel. & tel.), 822.361-010

05.05.05 CENTRAL-OFFICE REPAIRER (tel. & tel.), 822.281-014

05.05.05 COMPUTERIZED ENVIRONMENTAL CONTROL INSTALLER (electron. comp.), 828.281-026

05.05.05 DATA COMMUNICATIONS TECHNICIAN (any industry), 823.261-030

05.05.05 ELECTRICIAN (construction), 824.261-010

05.05.05 ELECTRICIAN, AIRCRAFT (aircraft mfg.), 825.261-018

05.05.05 ELECTRICIAN, MAINTENANCE (any industry), 829.261-018

05.05.05 ELECTRONIC-SALES-AND-SERVICE TECHNICIAN (profess. & kin.), 828.251-010

05.05.05 FIELD SERVICE ENGINEER (profess. & kin.), 828.261-014

05.05.05 LINE INSTALLER-REPAIRER (tel. & tel.), 822.381-014

05.05.05 LINE REPAIRER (utilities), 821.361-026

05.05.05 MAINTENANCE MECHANIC, TELEPHONE (any industry), 822.281-018

05.05.05 MICROCOMPUTER SUPPORT SPECIALIST (profess. & kin.), 039.264-010

05.05.05 PROTECTIVE-SIGNAL INSTALLER (business ser.), 822.361-018

05.05.05 PROTECTIVE-SIGNAL REPAIRER (business ser.), 822.361-022

05.05.05 STATION INSTALLER-AND-REPAIRER (tel. & tel.), 822.261-022

05.05.05 TOWER ERECTOR (construction), 821.361-038

05.05.06 AUTOMOBILE-BODY REPAIRER (automotive ser.), 807.381-010

05.05.06 BLACKSMITH (forging), 610.381-010

05.05.06 BOILERMAKER I (struct. metal), 805.261-014

05.05.06 ELEVATOR CONSTRUCTOR (construction), 825.361-010

05.05.06 METAL FABRICATOR (any industry), 619.361-014

05.05.06 ORNAMENTAL-IRON WORKER (construction), 809.381-022

05.05.06 SHEET-METAL WORKER (any industry), 804.281-010

05.05.06 SUPERVISOR, AUTOMOBILE BODY REPAIR (automotive ser.), 807.137-010

05.05.06 WELDER, ARC (welding), 810.384-014

05.05.06 WELDER, COMBINATION (welding), 819.384-010

05.05.06 WELDER-FITTER (welding), 819.361-010

05.05.07 DIE MAKER (jewelry-silver.), 601.381-014

05.05.07 DIE SINKER (machine shop), 601.280-022

05.05.07 FLUID-POWER MECHANIC (any industry), 600.281-010

05.05.07 LAY-OUT WORKER (machine shop), 600.281-018

05.05.07 MACHINIST, EXPERIMENTAL (machine shop), 600.260-022

05.05.07 MAINTENANCE MACHINIST (machine shop), 600.280-042

05.05.07 ROCKET-MOTOR MECHANIC (aircraft mfg.), 693.261-022

05.05.07 TOOL-MACHINE SET-UP OPERATOR (machine shop), 601.280-054

05.05.08 CABINETMAKER (woodworking), 660.280-010

05.05.08 FURNITURE FINISHER (woodworking), 763.381-010

05.05.09 AIR-CONDITIONING INSTALLER-SERVICER, WINDOW UNIT (construction), 637.261-010

05.05.09 AIRFRAME-AND-POWER-PLANT-MECHANIC APPRENTICE (air trans.), 621.281-018

05.05.09 AUTOMOBILE MECHANIC (automotive ser.), 620.261-010

05.05.09 AUTOMOTIVE-MAINTENANCE-EQUIPMENT SERVICER (any industry), 620.281-018

05.05.09 DIESEL MECHANIC (any industry), 625.281-010

05.05.09 FARM-EQUIPMENT MECHANIC I (agric. equip.), 624.281-010

05.05.09 FURNACE INSTALLER-AND-REPAIRER, HOT AIR (any industry), 869.281-010

05.05.09 HEATING-AND-AIR-CONDITIONING INSTALLER-SERVICER (construction), 637.261-014

05.05.09 HYDRAULIC REPAIRER (any industry), 638.281-034

05.05.09 MACHINE BUILDER (machinery mfg.), 600.281-022

05.05.09 MACHINE REPAIRER, MAINTENANCE (any industry), 638.261-030

05.05.09 MAINTENANCE MECHANIC (construction), 620.281-046

05.05.09 MAINTENANCE MECHANIC (any industry), 638.281-014

05.05.09 MANAGER, MARINE SERVICE (ship-boat mfg.), 187.167-130

05.05.09 OFFICE-MACHINE SERVICER (any industry), 633.281-018

05.05.09 POWERHOUSE MECHANIC (utilities), 631.261-014

05.05.09 REFRIGERATION MECHANIC (any industry), 637.261-026

05.05.09 TRACTOR MECHANIC (automotive ser.), 620.281-058

05.05.09 TUNE-UP MECHANIC (automotive ser.), 620.281-066

05.05.10 AUDIO-VIDEO REPAIRER (any industry), 729.281-010

05.05.10 ELECTRIC-MOTOR REPAIRER (any industry), 721.281-018

05.05.10 ELECTRICIAN, AUTOMOTIVE (automotive ser.), 825.281-022

05.05.10 ELECTRONICS MECHANIC (any industry), 828.261-022

05.05.10 INSTRUMENT-MAKER AND REPAIRER (petrol. & gas), 600.280-014

05.05.10 METEOROLOGICAL-EQUIPMENT REPAIRER (any industry), 823.281-018

05.05.10 RADIO MECHANIC (any industry), 823.261-018

05.05.11 DENTAL-LABORATORY TECHNICIAN (protective dev.), 712.381-018

05.05.11 DENTAL-LABORATORY-TECHNICIAN APPRENTICE (protective dev.), 712.381-022

05.05.11 ELECTROMECHANICAL TECHNICIAN (inst. & app.), 710.281-018

05.05.11 INSTRUMENT MAKER (any industry), 600.280-010

05.05.11 INSTRUMENT TECHNICIAN (utilities), 710.281-030
05.05.11 ORTHODONTIC TECHNICIAN (protective dev.), 712.381-030
05.05.11 ORTHOTICS ASSISTANT (medical ser.), 078.361-022
05.05.11 ORTHOTICS TECHNICIAN (protective dev.), 712.381-034
05.05.11 PROSTHETICS ASSISTANT (medical ser.), 078.361-026
05.05.11 PROSTHETICS TECHNICIAN (protective dev.), 712.381-038
05.05.11 SCIENTIFIC GLASS BLOWER (glass products), 006.261-010
05.05.14 GEM CUTTER (jewelry-silver.), 770.281-014
05.05.14 GEMOLOGIST (jewelry-silver.), 199.281-010
05.05.17 CHEF (hotel & rest.), 313.131-014
05.05.17 COOK (hotel & rest.), 313.361-014
05.05.17 TESTER, FOOD PRODUCTS (any industry), 199.251-010
05.06.01 HYDROELECTRIC-STATION OPERATOR (utilities), 952.362-018
05.06.01 POWER-REACTOR OPERATOR (utilities), 952.362-022
05.06.01 SUBSTATION OPERATOR (utilities), 952.362-026
05.06.02 ENGINEER (water trans.), 197.130-010
05.06.02 STATIONARY ENGINEER (any industry), 950.382-026
05.06.04 WATER-TREATMENT-PLANT OPERATOR (waterworks), 954.382-014
05.07.01 INSPECTOR, TOOL (machine shop), 601.281-022
05.07.01 SHOP ESTIMATOR (automotive ser.), 807.267-010
05.07.02 AIRPLANE INSPECTOR (air trans.), 621.261-010
05.07.02 AUTOMOBILE TESTER (automotive ser.), 620.261-014
05.07.02 AUTOMOBILE-REPAIR-SERVICE ESTIMATOR (automotive ser.), 620.261-018
05.08.02 LOCOMOTIVE ENGINEER (r.r. trans.), 910.363-014
05.09.01 DISTRIBUTION SUPERVISOR (pipe lines), 914.137-010
05.09.01 PHARMACY TECHNICIAN (medical ser.), 074.382-010
05.09.01 STOCK SUPERVISOR (clerical), 222.137-034
05.09.02 CONTROL CLERK (clock & watch), 221.387-018
05.09.02 CUSTOMER SERVICES COORDINATOR (print. & pub.), 221.167-026
05.09.02 ESTIMATOR, PRINTING (print. & pub.), 221.367-014
05.09.02 EVALUATOR (nonprofit org.), 249.367-034
05.09.02 MATERIAL COORDINATOR (clerical), 221.167-014
05.09.02 PRODUCTION COORDINATOR (clerical), 221.167-018
05.09.02 SALES CORRESPONDENT (clerical), 221.367-062

05.10.01 MAINTENANCE REPAIRER, BUILDING (any industry), 899.381-010
05.10.01 REPAIRER, RECREATIONAL VEHICLE (vehicles, nec), 869.261-022
05.10.02 MANAGER, CUSTOMER SERVICES (business ser.), 187.167-082
05.10.02 PARKING-METER SERVICER (government ser.), 710.384-026
05.10.02 SERVICE MANAGER (retail trade), 185.164-010
05.10.02 SERVICE MANAGER (automotive ser.), 185.167-058
05.10.02 TRANSMISSION MECHANIC (automotive ser.), 620.281-062
05.10.03 SOUND CONTROLLER (amuse. & rec.), 194.262-014
05.10.03 TELEVISION-AND-RADIO REPAIRER (any industry), 720.281-018
05.10.04 MANAGER, CAMP (construction), 187.167-066
05.10.04 WIND TUNNEL MECHANIC (aircraft mfg.), 869.261-026
05.10.05 AUDIO OPERATOR (radio-tv broad.), 194.262-010
05.10.05 ENGRAVER, MACHINE (print. & pub.), 979.382-014
05.10.05 PHOTOGRAPHIC-PLATE MAKER (electron. comp.), 714.381-018
05.10.05 PLANETARIUM TECHNICIAN (museums), 962.261-010
05.10.05 RERECORDING MIXER (motion picture), 194.362-014
05.10.05 SOUND MIXER (motion picture), 194.262-018
05.11.01 OPERATING ENGINEER (construction), 859.683-010
05.12.01 STEWARD/STEWARDESS (hotel & rest.), 310.137-018
05.12.01 SUPERVISOR, CENTRAL SUPPLY (medical ser.), 381.137-014
05.12.13 BLOCK MAKER (protective dev.), 719.381-018
05.12.18 CENTRAL-SUPPLY WORKER (medical ser.), 381.687-010
06.01.01 QUALITY ASSURANCE SUPERVISOR (auto. mfg.), 806.137-022
06.01.02 DIE SETTER (forging), 612.360-010
06.01.02 SCREEN-PRINTING-EQUIPMENT SETTER (paper goods), 979.360-010
06.01.03 CHIEF OPERATOR (chemical), 558.260-010
06.01.03 DRILL-PRESS SET-UP OPERATOR, MULTIPLE SPINDLE (machine shop), 606.380-010
06.01.03 ENGINE-LATHE SET-UP OPERATOR (machine shop), 604.380-018
06.01.03 LATHE OPERATOR, NUMERICAL CONTROL (machine shop), 604.362-010
06.01.03 MACHINE OPERATOR I (any industry), 616.380-018
06.01.03 MACHINE SET-UP OPERATOR (machine shop), 600.380-018
06.01.03 MICROELECTRONICS TECHNICIAN (electron. comp.), 590.362-022
06.01.03 MILLING-MACHINE SET-UP OPERATOR I (machine shop), 605.280-010

06.01.03 REFINERY OPERATOR (petrol. refin.), 549.260-010

06.01.03 RIVETING MACHINE OPERATOR, AUTOMATIC (aircraft mfg.), 806.380-010

06.01.03 SCREW-MACHINE SET-UP OPERATOR, MULTIPLE SPINDLE (machine shop), 604.280-014

06.01.04 ASSEMBLER, ELECTROMECHANICAL (aircraft mfg.), 828.381-018

06.01.04 CALIBRATOR (inst. & app.), 710.381-034

06.01.04 CHEESEMAKER (dairy products), 529.361-018

06.01.04 DEVELOPMENT MECHANIC (aircraft mfg.), 693.261-014

06.01.04 ELECTRIC-MOTOR-CONTROL ASSEMBLER (elec. equip.), 721.381-014

06.01.04 INSTALLER, INTERIOR ASSEMBLIES (aircraft mfg.), 806.381-078

06.01.04 TEMPLATE MAKER (any industry), 601.381-038

06.01.04 TEST EQUIPMENT MECHANIC (aircraft mfg.), 710.361-014

06.01.04 TOOL BUILDER (aircraft mfg.), 693.281-030

06.01.05 ELECTRONICS INSPECTOR (comm. equip.), 726.381-010

06.01.05 ELECTRONICS TESTER (any industry), 726.261-018

06.01.05 INSPECTOR, ASSEMBLIES AND INSTALLATIONS (aircraft mfg.), 806.261-030

06.01.05 INSPECTOR, MATERIAL DISPOSITION (aircraft mfg.), 806.261-034

06.01.05 INSPECTOR, OUTSIDE PRODUCTION (aircraft mfg.), 806.261-042

06.01.05 INSPECTOR, PLASTICS AND COMPOSITES (aircraft mfg.), 806.261-046

06.02.02 SCREW-MACHINE OPERATOR, MULTIPLE SPINDLE (machine shop), 604.382-010

06.02.09 NUMERICAL-CONTROL DRILL OPERATOR, PRINTED CIRCUIT BOARDS (electron. comp.), 606.382-018

06.02.11 WASTE-TREATMENT OPERATOR (chemical), 955.382-014

06.02.21 PLATER (electroplating), 500.380-010

06.03.01 GRADER, MEAT (meat products), 525.387-010

06.03.01 INSPECTOR (office machines), 710.384-014

06.03.01 QUALITY-CONTROL INSPECTOR (recording), 194.387-010

06.03.02 FILM FLAT INSPECTOR (print. & pub.), 972.284-010

07.01.01 ELIGIBILITY WORKER (government ser.), 195.267-010

07.01.01 ELIGIBILITY-AND-OCCUPANCY INTERVIEWER (government ser.), 168.267-038

07.01.01 MANAGEMENT AIDE (social ser.), 195.367-014

07.01.02 AUTOMOBILE-CLUB-SAFETY-PROGRAM COORDINATOR (nonprofit org.), 249.167-010

07.01.02 COORDINATOR, SKILL-TRAINING PROGRAM (government ser.), 169.167-062

07.01.02 COURT CLERK (government ser.), 243.362-010

07.01.02 MANAGER, OFFICE (any industry), 169.167-034

07.01.02 MEMBERSHIP SECRETARY (nonprofit org.), 201.362-018

07.01.02 SUPERVISOR, CUSTOMER SERVICES (motor trans.), 248.137-018

07.01.02 SUPERVISOR, LENDING ACTIVITIES (financial), 249.137-034

07.01.02 TRANSFER CLERK, HEAD (financial), 216.137-014

07.01.03 LEGAL SECRETARY (clerical), 201.362-010

07.01.03 MEDICAL SECRETARY (medical ser.), 201.362-014

07.01.03 SCHOOL SECRETARY (education), 201.362-022

07.01.03 SECRETARY (clerical), 201.362-030

07.01.04 CLOSER (real estate), 186.167-074

07.01.04 CREDIT ANALYST (clerical), 241.267-022

07.01.04 ESCROW OFFICER (profess. & kin.), 119.367-010

07.01.04 SECURITIES CLERK (financial), 219.362-054

07.01.04 SUPERVISOR, REAL-ESTATE OFFICE (real estate), 249.137-030

07.01.04 SUPERVISOR, STATEMENT CLERKS (financial), 214.137-014

07.01.04 UNDERWRITING CLERK (insurance), 219.367-038

07.01.05 ADMISSIONS EVALUATOR (education), 205.367-010

07.01.05 AGENT-CONTRACT CLERK (insurance), 241.267-010

07.01.05 CONTRACT CLERK (profess. & kin.), 119.267-018

07.01.05 EXAMINER (government ser.), 169.267-014

07.01.05 HOSPITAL-INSURANCE REPRESENTATIVE (insurance), 166.267-014

07.01.05 PASSPORT-APPLICATION EXAMINER (government ser.), 169.267-030

07.01.06 ATTENDANCE OFFICER (education), 168.367-010

07.01.06 IDENTIFICATION OFFICER (government ser.), 377.264-010

07.01.07 DRIVER'S LICENSE EXAMINER (government ser.), 168.267-034

07.01.07 EXAMINATION PROCTOR (government ser.), 199.267-018

07.01.07 TEST TECHNICIAN (clerical), 249.367-078

07.02.01 AUDIT CLERK (clerical), 210.382-010

07.02.01 BOOKKEEPER (clerical), 210.382-014

07.02.01 ELECTRONIC FUNDS TRANSFER COORDINATOR (financial), 216.362-038

07.02.01 FOREIGN-EXCHANGE-POSITION CLERK (financial), 210.367-014

07.02.01 GENERAL-LEDGER BOOKKEEPER (clerical), 210.382-046

07.02.02 ACCOUNTING CLERK (clerical), 216.482-010

07.02.02 BROKERAGE CLERK II (financial), 219.362-018

07.02.02 COLLECTION CLERK (financial), 216.362-014

07.02.02 COST CLERK (clerical), 216.382-034

07.02.02 DIVIDEND CLERK (financial), 216.482-034

07.02.02 MARGIN CLERK I (financial), 216.362-042

07.02.02 SUPERVISOR, MONEY-ROOM (amuse. & rec.), 211.137-018

07.02.02 SUPERVISOR, POLICY-CHANGE CLERKS (insurance), 219.132-010

07.02.02 SUPERVISOR, TRUST ACCOUNTS (financial), 219.132-014

07.02.02 SUPERVISOR, UNDERWRITING CLERKS (insurance), 219.132-022

07.02.02 TAX PREPARER (business ser.), 219.362-070

07.02.02 TRANSFER CLERK (financial), 216.362-046

07.02.03 ACCOUNT-INFORMATION CLERK (utilities), 210.367-010

07.02.03 GRADING CLERK (education), 219.467-010

07.02.03 POLICY-VALUE CALCULATOR (insurance), 216.382-050

07.02.03 RECEIPT-AND-REPORT CLERK (water trans.), 216.382-054

07.02.03 STATISTICAL CLERK (clerical), 216.382-062

07.02.04 BILLING CLERK (clerical), 214.362-042

07.02.04 MEDIA CLERK (business ser.), 247.382-010

07.03.01 CASHIER I (clerical), 211.362-010

07.03.01 COLLECTOR (clerical), 241.367-010

07.03.01 POST-OFFICE CLERK (government ser.), 243.367-014

07.03.01 SAFE-DEPOSIT-BOX RENTAL CLERK (financial), 295.367-022

07.03.01 SUPERVISOR, CASHIERS (hotel & rest.), 211.137-010

07.03.01 SUPERVISOR, FOOD CHECKERS AND CASHIERS (hotel & rest.), 211.137-014

07.03.01 TELLER (financial), 211.362-018

07.03.01 TELLER, VAULT (financial), 211.382-010

07.04.01 ADMITTING OFFICER (medical ser.), 205.162-010

07.04.01 BONDING AGENT (business ser.), 186.267-010

07.04.01 CREDIT CLERK (clerical), 205.367-022

07.04.01 CUSTOMER SERVICE REPRESENTATIVE (financial), 205.362-026

07.04.01 CUSTOMER SERVICE REPRESENTATIVE (radio-tv broad.), 239.362-014

07.04.01 EMPLOYMENT CLERK (clerical), 205.362-014

07.04.01 HOSPITAL-ADMITTING CLERK (medical ser.), 205.362-018

07.04.01 IDENTIFICATION CLERK (clerical), 205.362-022

07.04.01 LOAN INTERVIEWER, MORTGAGE (financial), 241.367-018

07.04.01 OUTPATIENT-ADMITTING CLERK (medical ser.), 205.362-030

07.04.01 REGISTRATION CLERK (government ser.), 205.367-042

07.04.01 REHABILITATION CLERK (nonprofit org.), 205.367-046

07.04.02 CORRESPONDENCE CLERK (clerical), 209.362-034

07.04.03 LICENSE CLERK (government ser.), 205.367-034

07.04.03 PARK AIDE (government ser.), 249.367-082

07.04.03 PUBLIC HEALTH REGISTRAR (government ser.), 169.167-046

07.04.03 REGISTRAR (government ser.), 205.367-038

07.04.03 RESERVATIONS AGENT (air trans.), 238.367-018

07.04.04 CONGRESSIONAL-DISTRICT AIDE (government ser.), 209.362-030

07.04.04 INFORMATION CLERK (clerical), 237.367-022

07.04.04 LAND-LEASING EXAMINER (government ser.), 237.367-026

07.04.04 MUSEUM ATTENDANT (museums), 109.367-010

07.04.04 TOURIST-INFORMATION ASSISTANT (government ser.), 237.367-050

07.04.05 AIRLINE-RADIO OPERATOR (air trans.), 193.262-010

07.04.05 ALARM OPERATOR (government ser.), 379.162-010

07.04.05 DISPATCHER (government ser.), 193.262-014

07.04.05 DISPATCHER, RADIO (government ser.), 379.362-010

07.04.05 GAS-DISTRIBUTION-AND-EMERGENCY CLERK (utilities), 249.367-042

07.04.05 POLICE AIDE (government ser.), 243.362-014

07.04.05 RECEIVER-DISPATCHER (nonprofit org.), 239.367-022

07.04.05 TELECOMMUNICATOR (government ser.), 379.362-018

07.04.05 TRAIN DISPATCHER (r.r. trans.), 184.167-262

07.04.05 UTILITY CLERK (utilities), 239.367-034

07.04.06 TELEPHONE OPERATOR, CHIEF (clerical), 235.137-010

07.05.01 CLERK, TELEVISION PRODUCTION (radio-tv broad.), 221.367-086

07.05.01 COMPUTER PROCESSING SCHEDULER (clerical), 221.362-030

07.05.01 EXPEDITER (clerical), 222.367-018

07.05.01 MANAGER, RESERVATIONS (hotel & rest.), 238.137-010

07.05.01 POLICE CLERK (government ser.), 375.362-010

07.05.01 RESERVATION CLERK (clerical), 238.362-014

07.05.01 SCHEDULER (museums), 238.367-034

07.05.01 SENIOR RESERVATIONS AGENT (air trans.), 238.137-014

07.05.01 TELEVISION-SCHEDULE COORDINATOR (radio-tv broad.), 199.382-010

07.05.02 BRAILLE PROOFREADER (nonprofit org.), 209.367-014

07.05.02 CREDIT REFERENCE CLERK (financial), 209.362-018

07.05.02 CUSTOMER-COMPLAINT CLERK (clerical), 241.367-014

07.05.02 DATA-EXAMINATION CLERK (clerical), 209.387-022

07.05.02 INVESTIGATOR, UTILITY-BILL COMPLAINTS (utilities), 241.267-034

07.05.02 LETTER-OF-CREDIT CLERK (financial), 219.367-050

07.05.02 MORTGAGE-CLOSING CLERK (clerical), 219.362-038

07.05.02 PROOFREADER (print. & pub.), 209.387-030

07.05.02 REVIEWER (insurance), 209.687-018

07.05.03 BENEFITS CLERK II (clerical), 205.567-010

07.05.03 CAPTION WRITER (motion picture), 203.362-026

07.05.03 CLASSIFICATION CLERK (clerical), 206.387-010

07.05.03 FILE CLERK II (clerical), 206.367-014

07.05.03 FINGERPRINT CLERK II (government ser.), 206.387-014

07.05.03 IDENTIFICATION CLERK (government ser.), 209.362-022

07.05.03 NEWS ASSISTANT (radio-tv broad.), 209.367-038

07.05.03 ORDER DEPARTMENT SUPERVISOR (any industry), 169.167-038

07.05.03 PERSONNEL CLERK (clerical), 209.362-026

07.05.03 REFERRAL CLERK, TEMPORARY HELP AGENCY (clerical), 205.367-062

07.05.03 SHORTHAND REPORTER (clerical), 202.362-010

07.05.03 STENOCAPTIONER (radio-tv broad.), 202.382-010

07.05.03 STENOGRAPHER (clerical), 202.362-014

07.05.03 TAPE LIBRARIAN (clerical), 206.367-018

07.05.03 TECHNICAL COORDINATOR (government ser.), 209.132-014

07.05.04 CORRESPONDENCE-REVIEW CLERK (clerical), 209.367-018

07.05.04 MAILROOM SUPERVISOR (clerical), 209.137-010

07.05.04 SUPERVISOR, MAIL CARRIERS (government ser.), 230.137-018

07.06.01 COMPUTER OPERATOR (clerical), 213.362-010

07.06.01 SUPERVISOR, COMPUTER OPERATIONS (clerical), 213.132-010

07.06.02 BRAILLE TYPIST (education), 203.582-014

07.06.02 CRYPTOGRAPHIC-MACHINE OPERATOR (clerical), 203.582-018

07.06.02 NOTEREADER (clerical), 203.582-078

07.06.02 PROOF-MACHINE-OPERATOR SUPERVISOR (financial), 217.132-010

08.01.01 SALES REPRESENTATIVE, GRAPHIC ART (business ser.), 254.251-010

08.01.01 SALES REPRESENTATIVE, SIGNS AND DISPLAYS (fabrication, nec), 254.257-010

08.01.02 ESTATE PLANNER (insurance), 186.167-010

08.01.02 SALES AGENT, INSURANCE (insurance), 250.257-010

08.01.02 SALES REPRESENTATIVE, ADVERTISING (print. & pub.), 254.357-014

08.01.02 SALES REPRESENTATIVE, EDUCATION COURSES (education), 259.257-010

08.01.02 SALES REPRESENTATIVE, HOTEL SERVICES (hotel & rest.), 259.157-014

08.01.02 SALES REPRESENTATIVE, PRINTING (wholesale tr.), 254.357-018

08.01.02 SALES REPRESENTATIVE, PUBLIC UTILI-TIES (tel. & tel.), 253.357-010

08.01.02 SALES REPRESENTATIVE, RADIO AND TELEVISION TIME (radio-tv broad.), 259.357-018

08.01.02 SALES REPRESENTATIVE, SECURITY SYSTEMS (business ser.), 259.257-022

08.01.02 SALES REPRESENTATIVE, TELEPHONE SERVICES (tel. & tel.), 253.257-010

08.01.02 SPECIAL AGENT, GROUP INSURANCE (insurance), 169.167-050

08.01.03 BUYER (profess. & kin.), 162.157-018

08.01.03 BUYER, ASSISTANT (retail trade), 162.157-022

08.01.03 FOREIGN BANKNOTE TELLER-TRADER (financial), 211.362-014

08.02.01 MANUFACTURER'S REPRESENTATIVE (wholesale tr.), 279.157-010

08.02.01 SALES REPRESENTATIVE, FOOTWEAR (wholesale tr.), 261.357-018

08.02.01 SALES REPRESENTATIVE, HARDWARE SUPPLIES (wholesale tr.), 274.357-034

08.02.01 SALES REPRESENTATIVE, PRINTING SUPPLIES (wholesale tr.), 274.357-062

08.02.01 SALES REPRESENTATIVE, TOILET PREPARATIONS (wholesale tr.), 262.357-014

08.02.02 HEARING AID SPECIALIST (retail trade), 276.354-010

08.02.02 SALES-SERVICE REPRESENTATIVE, MILK-ING MACHINES (retail trade), 299.251-010

08.02.02 SALESPERSON, AUTOMOBILES (retail trade), 273.353-010

08.02.02 SALESPERSON, JEWELRY (retail trade), 279.357-058

08.02.03 SALESPERSON, AUTOMOBILE ACCESSO-RIES (retail trade), 273.357-030

08.02.03 SALESPERSON, PHOTOGRAPHIC SUPPLIES AND EQUIPMENT (retail trade), 277.357-050

08.02.04 BUILDING CONSULTANT (wholesale tr.), 250.357-010

08.02.04 SALES AGENT, REAL ESTATE (real estate), 250.357-018

08.02.05 DEMONSTRATOR, KNITTING (retail trade), 297.354-014

08.02.06 SALES AGENT, BUSINESS SERVICES (business ser.), 251.357-010

08.02.06 SALES REPRESENTATIVE, FRANCHISE (business ser.), 251.357-022

08.02.06 TRAVEL AGENT (business ser.), 252.152-010

08.02.06 WEDDING CONSULTANT (retail trade), 299.357-018

09.01.02 CRAFT DEMONSTRATOR (museums), 109.364-010

09.01.02 GUIDE, ESTABLISHMENT (any industry), 353.367-014

09.01.03 BUTLER (domestic ser.), 309.137-010

09.01.03 WAITER/WAITRESS, CAPTAIN (hotel & rest.), 311.137-018

09.01.04 AIRPLANE-FLIGHT ATTENDANT (air trans.), 352.367-010

09.02.01 COSMETOLOGIST (personal ser.), 332.271-010

09.02.02 BARBER (personal ser.), 330.371-010

09.03.03 INSTRUCTOR, DRIVING (education), 099.223-010

10.01.02 CHILD SUPPORT OFFICER (government ser.), 195.267-022

10.02.02 HYPNOTHERAPIST (profess. & kin.),
079.157-010

10.02.02 PHYSICAL THERAPIST ASSISTANT
(medical ser.), 076.224-010

10.03.01 CARDIAC MONITOR TECHNICIAN
(medical ser.), 078.367-010

10.03.01 CARDIOPULMONARY TECHNOLOGIST
(medical ser.), 078.362-030

10.03.01 HOLTER SCANNING TECHNICIAN
(medical ser.), 078.264-010

10.03.02 CHIROPRACTOR ASSISTANT (medical ser.),
079.364-010

10.03.02 MENTAL-RETARDATION AIDE (medical ser.),
355.377-018

10.03.02 NURSE ASSISTANT (medical ser.),
355.674-014

10.03.02 OCCUPATIONAL THERAPY AIDE
(medical ser.), 355.377-010

10.03.02 OPTOMETRIC ASSISTANT (medical ser.),
079.364-014

10.03.02 ORDERLY (medical ser.), 355.674-018

10.03.02 PODIATRIC ASSISTANT (medical ser.),
079.374-018

10.03.03 CHILDREN'S TUTOR (domestic ser.),
099.227-010

11.02.01 TEACHER AIDE I (education), 099.327-010

11.02.04 CAREER-GUIDANCE TECHNICIAN
(education), 249.367-014

11.02.04 FILM-RENTAL CLERK (business ser.),
295.367-018

11.02.04 LIBRARY ASSISTANT (library), 249.367-046

11.02.04 LIBRARY TECHNICAL ASSISTANT (library),
100.367-018

11.02.04 MUSIC LIBRARIAN (radio-tv broad.),
100.367-022

11.03.02 CITY PLANNING AIDE (profess. & kin.),
199.364-010

11.03.04 EMPLOYEE RELATIONS SPECIALIST (profess. & kin.), 166.267-042

11.03.04 JOB DEVELOPMENT SPECIALIST (profess. & kin.), 166.267-034

11.03.04 RECRUITER (military ser.), 166.267-026

11.05.01 MANAGER, LAND DEVELOPMENT
(real estate), 186.117-042

11.05.02 COMMERCIAL LOAN COLLECTION
OFFICER (financial), 186.167-078

11.05.02 IMPORT-EXPORT AGENT (any industry),
184.117-022

11.05.02 MANAGER, DEPARTMENT (any industry),
189.167-022

11.05.02 SECURITY OFFICER (any industry),
189.167-034

11.05.02 SPECIAL AGENT (insurance), 166.167-046

11.05.02 SUPERINTENDENT, PLANT PROTECTION
(any industry), 189.167-050

11.05.03 LEGISLATIVE ASSISTANT (government ser.),
169.167-066

11.05.03 MANAGER, OFFICE (government ser.),
188.167-058

11.05.03 POSTMASTER (government ser.),
188.167-066

11.05.04 MANAGER, EXPORT (any industry),
163.117-014

11.05.04 MANAGER, MERCHANDISE (retail trade),
185.167-034

11.05.04 PURCHASING AGENT (profess. & kin.),
162.157-038

11.06.01 OPERATIONS OFFICER (financial),
186.137-014

11.06.03 BOOKMAKER (amuse. & rec.), 187.167-014

11.06.03 FACTOR (financial), 186.167-082

11.06.03 INVESTIGATOR (clerical), 241.267-030

11.06.03 LETTER-OF-CREDIT DOCUMENT
EXAMINER (financial), 169.267-042

11.06.03 LOAN OFFICER (financial), 186.267-018

11.07.01 RESIDENCE SUPERVISOR (any industry),
187.167-186

11.07.02 CIVIL PREPAREDNESS TRAINING OFFICER
(government ser.), 169.127-010

11.07.03 DIRECTOR, DAY CARE CENTER (education),
092.167-010

11.09.01 FASHION COORDINATOR (retail trade),
185.157-010

11.09.01 MANAGER, ADVERTISING AGENCY (business
ser.), 164.117-014

11.09.01 MANAGER, PROMOTION (hotel & rest.),
163.117-018

11.09.01 SALES-SERVICE PROMOTER (any industry),
165.167-010

11.10.01 INVESTIGATOR, FRAUD (retail trade),
376.267-014

11.10.03 CHEMICAL-RADIATION TECHNICIAN
(government ser.), 015.261-010

11.10.03 FIRE INSPECTOR (government ser.),
373.267-010

11.10.03 INSPECTOR, AGRICULTURAL COMMODI-
TIES (government ser.), 168.287-010

11.10.03 INSPECTOR, HEALTH CARE FACILITIES
(government ser.), 168.167-042

11.10.03 LICENSE INSPECTOR (government ser.),
168.267-066

11.10.03 MARINE-CARGO SURVEYOR (business ser.),
168.267-094

11.10.03 MINE INSPECTOR (mine & quarry),
168.267-074

11.10.03 PESTICIDE-CONTROL INSPECTOR
(government ser.), 168.267-098

11.10.03 REVIEWING OFFICER, DRIVER'S LICENSE
(government ser.), 168.167-074

11.10.05 DEALER-COMPLIANCE REPRESENTATIVE
(retail trade), 168.267-026

11.10.05 RATER, TRAVEL ACCOMMODATIONS
(profess. & kin.), 168.367-014

11.10.05 TRAFFIC INSPECTOR (motor trans.),
184.163-010

11.10.05 TRANSPORTATION INSPECTOR (motor trans.),
168.167-082

11.11.01 CONDOMINIUM MANAGER (real estate),
186.167-062

11.11.01 EXECUTIVE HOUSEKEEPER (any industry),
187.167-046

11.11.01 MANAGER, FRONT OFFICE (hotel & rest.), 187.137-018

11.11.02 MANAGER, BOWLING ALLEY (amuse. & rec.), 187.167-222

11.11.02 MANAGER, GOLF CLUB (amuse. & rec.), 187.167-114

11.11.02 MANAGER, RECREATION FACILITY (amuse. & rec.), 187.167-230

11.11.02 MANAGER, THEATER (amuse. & rec.), 187.167-154

11.11.03 CONDUCTOR, PASSENGER CAR (r.r. trans.), 198.167-010

11.11.03 CONDUCTOR, ROAD FREIGHT (r.r. trans.), 198.167-018

11.11.03 MANAGER, BUS TRANSPORTATION (motor trans.), 184.167-054

11.11.03 OPERATIONS MANAGER (motor trans.), 184.167-118

11.11.03 PURSER (water trans.), 197.167-014

11.11.03 STATION MANAGER (r.r. trans.), 184.167-130

11.11.04 ASSISTANT BRANCH MANAGER, FINANCIAL INSTITUTION (financial), 186.167-070

11.11.04 GENERAL MANAGER, ROAD PRODUCTION (amuse. & rec.), 187.117-034

11.11.04 MANAGER, BARBER OR BEAUTY SHOP (personal ser.), 187.167-058

11.11.04 MANAGER, EMPLOYMENT AGENCY (profess. & kin.), 187.167-098

11.11.04 MANAGER, FAST FOOD SERVICES (retail trade), 185.137-010

11.11.04 MANAGER, FOOD SERVICE (hotel & rest.), 187.167-106

11.11.04 MANAGER, REAL-ESTATE FIRM (real estate), 186.167-066

11.11.04 MANAGER, SALES (laundry & rel.), 187.167-138

11.11.04 MANAGER, TITLE SEARCH (real estate), 186.167-090

11.11.04 MANAGER, TOURING PRODUCTION (amuse. & rec.), 191.117-038

11.11.04 MANAGER, TRAVEL AGENCY (business ser.), 187.167-158

11.11.05 COMMISSARY MANAGER (any industry), 185.167-010

11.11.05 MANAGER, AUTOMOBILE SERVICE STATION (retail trade), 185.167-014

11.11.05 MANAGER, DEPARTMENT (retail trade), 299.137-010

11.11.05 MANAGER, MACHINERY-OR-EQUIPMENT, RENTAL AND LEASING (any industry), 185.167-026

11.11.05 MANAGER, MARKET (retail trade), 186.167-042

11.11.05 MANAGER, MEAT SALES AND STORAGE (retail trade), 185.167-030

11.11.05 MANAGER, PARTS (retail trade), 185.167-038

11.11.05 MANAGER, RETAIL STORE (retail trade), 185.167-046

11.11.05 SERVICE SUPERVISOR, LEASED MACHINERY AND EQUIPMENT (any industry), 183.167-030

11.12.01 APPRAISER, AUTOMOBILE DAMAGE (business ser.), 241.267-014

11.12.01 CLAIM ADJUSTER (business ser.), 241.217-010

11.12.01 CLAIM EXAMINER (business ser.), 241.267-018

11.12.01 GENERAL CLAIMS AGENT (air trans.), 186.117-030

11.12.01 SUPERVISOR, CLAIMS (insurance), 241.137-018

11.12.02 LOCATION MANAGER (motion picture), 191.167-018

11.12.03 MANAGER, ATHLETE (amuse. & rec.), 153.117-014

11.12.04 CONTRACT SPECIALIST (profess. & kin.), 162.117-018

11.12.04 CONTRACTOR (construction), 182.167-010

12.01.01 INSTRUCTOR, SPORTS (amuse. & rec.), 153.227-018

12.01.01 SCOUT, PROFESSIONAL SPORTS (amuse. & rec.), 153.117-018

No Diploma

01.01.02 CROSSWORD-PUZZLE MAKER (print. & pub.), 139.087-010

01.01.02 HUMORIST (profess. & kin.), 131.067-026

01.01.02 LIBRETTIST (profess. & kin.), 131.067-030

01.01.02 LYRICIST (profess. & kin.), 131.067-034

01.01.02 PLAYWRIGHT (profess. & kin.), 131.067-038

01.02.03 CARTOONIST (print. & pub.), 141.061-010

01.02.03 EXHIBIT ARTIST (museums), 149.261-010

01.03.01 SUPERVISOR, SHOW OPERATIONS (amuse. & rec.), 969.137-014

01.03.02 CLOWN (amuse. & rec.), 159.047-010

01.03.02 COMEDIAN (amuse. & rec.), 159.047-014

01.03.02 IMPERSONATOR (amuse. & rec.), 159.047-018

01.03.02 PUPPETEER (amuse. & rec.), 159.041-014

01.03.03 SHOW HOST/HOSTESS (radio-tv broad.), 159.147-018

01.04.03 SINGER (amuse. & rec.), 152.047-022

01.04.04 MUSICIAN, INSTRUMENTAL (amuse. & rec.), 152.041-010

01.06.01 ADVERTISING-SPACE CLERK (print. & pub.), 247.387-018

01.06.01 ELECTRONIC PREPRESS SYSTEM OPERATOR (print. & pub.), 979.282-010

01.06.01 ENGRAVER, HAND, HARD METALS (engraving), 704.381-026

01.06.01 ENGRAVER, HAND, SOFT METALS (engraving), 704.381-030

01.06.01 ETCHER (engraving), 704.684-010

01.06.01 SILK-SCREEN CUTTER (any industry), 979.681-022

01.06.02 BOW MAKER, CUSTOM (toy-sport equip.), 732.381-010

01.06.02 CLAY MODELER (any industry), 779.281-010

01.06.02 DECORATOR (any industry), 298.381-010

01.06.02 DISPLAY MAKER (fabrication, nec), 739.361-010

01.06.02 EXHIBIT BUILDER (museums), 739.261-010

01.06.02 MAKE-UP ARTIST (amuse. & rec.), 333.071-010

01.06.02 MODEL MAKER I (any industry), 777.261-010

01.06.02 MOLD MAKER I (jewelry-silver.), 700.381-034

01.06.02 MORTUARY BEAUTICIAN (personal ser.), 339.361-010

01.06.02 PICTURE FRAMER (retail trade), 739.684-146

01.06.02 PROP MAKER (amuse. & rec.), 962.281-010

01.06.02 REPAIRER, ART OBJECTS (any industry), 779.381-018

01.06.02 SAMPLE MAKER I (jewelry-silver.), 700.381-046

01.06.02 SILVERSMITH II (jewelry-silver.), 700.281-022

01.06.02 SPECIAL EFFECTS SPECIALIST (amuse. & rec.), 962.281-018

01.06.02 STONE CARVER (stonework), 771.281-014

01.06.02 WIG DRESSER (fabrication, nec), 332.361-010

01.06.03 GIFT WRAPPER (retail trade), 299.364-014

01.06.03 GILDER (any industry), 749.381-010

01.06.03 PAINTER, AIRBRUSH (any industry), 741.684-018

01.06.03 PAINTER, HAND (any industry), 970.381-022

01.06.03 SIGN WRITER, HAND (any industry), 970.281-022

01.06.03 STRIPER, HAND (any industry), 740.484-010

01.07.02 RING CONDUCTOR (amuse. & rec.), 159.367-010

01.07.03 AMUSEMENT PARK ENTERTAINER (amuse. & rec.), 159.647-010

01.08.01 EXTRA (amuse. & rec.), 159.647-014

01.08.01 MODEL, ARTISTS' (any industry), 961.667-010

02.04.01 DECONTAMINATOR (any industry), 199.384-010

02.04.01 FILM LABORATORY TECHNICIAN I (motion picture), 976.381-010

02.04.01 GRAPHOLOGIST (profess. & kin.), 199.267-038

02.04.01 PROOF TECHNICIAN (ordnance), 199.171-010

02.04.01 SAMPLER (mine & quarry), 579.484-010

02.04.02 LABORATORY ASSISTANT, CULTURE MEDIA (pharmaceut.), 559.384-010

02.04.02 MORGUE ATTENDANT (medical ser.), 355.667-010

03.01.01 GROUP LEADER (agriculture), 180.167-022

03.01.01 MANAGER, CHRISTMAS-TREE FARM (forestry), 180.117-010

03.01.01 MIGRANT LEADER (agriculture), 180.167-050

03.01.02 BEEKEEPER (agriculture), 413.161-010

03.01.02 MANAGER, FISH HATCHERY (fishing & hunt.), 180.167-030

03.01.03 HORTICULTURAL-SPECIALTY GROWER, FIELD (agriculture), 405.161-014

03.01.03 LANDSCAPE GARDENER (agriculture), 408.161-010

03.03.01 ANIMAL TRAINER (amuse. & rec.), 159.224-010

03.03.01 EXERCISER, HORSE (amuse. & rec.), 153.674-010

03.03.02 ANIMAL CARETAKER (any industry), 410.674-010

03.03.02 ANIMAL KEEPER (amuse. & rec.), 412.674-010

03.03.02 AQUARIST (amuse. & rec.), 449.674-010

03.03.02 DOG BATHER (personal ser.), 418.677-010

03.03.02 DOG GROOMER (personal ser.), 418.674-010

03.03.02 HORSESHOER (agriculture), 418.381-010

03.03.02 STABLE ATTENDANT (any industry), 410.674-022

03.04.01 CHRISTMAS-TREE FARM WORKER (forestry), 451.687-010

03.04.01 FARM-MACHINE OPERATOR (agriculture), 409.683-010

03.04.01 FARMWORKER, DIVERSIFIED CROPS I (agriculture), 407.663-010

03.04.01 FARMWORKER, FRUIT I (agriculture), 403.683-010

03.04.01 FARMWORKER, GENERAL II (agriculture), 421.687-010

03.04.01 FARMWORKER, LIVESTOCK (agriculture), 410.664-010

03.04.01 FARMWORKER, VEGETABLE II (agriculture), 402.687-010

03.04.01 LIVESTOCK-YARD ATTENDANT (any industry), 410.674-018

03.04.01 PACKER, AGRICULTURAL PRODUCE (agriculture), 920.687-134

03.04.02 CHAIN SAW OPERATOR (chemical), 454.687-010

03.04.02 FOREST WORKER (forestry), 452.687-010

03.04.02 FOREST-FIRE FIGHTER (forestry), 452.687-014

03.04.02 LOGGER, ALL-ROUND (logging), 454.684-018

03.04.02 LOGGING-TRACTOR OPERATOR (forestry), 929.663-010

03.04.03 DECKHAND, FISHING VESSEL (fishing & hunt.), 449.667-010

03.04.03 FISHER, DIVING (fishing & hunt.), 443.664-010

03.04.03 FISHER, LINE (fishing & hunt.), 442.684-010

03.04.03 SHELLFISH DREDGE OPERATOR (fishing & hunt.), 446.663-010

03.04.03 SKIFF OPERATOR (fishing & hunt.), 441.683-010

03.04.04 CEMETERY WORKER (real estate), 406.684-010

03.04.04 GREENSKEEPER II (any industry), 406.683-010

03.04.04 GROUNDSKEEPER, INDUSTRIAL-COMMER-CIAL (any industry), 406.684-014

03.04.04 HORTICULTURAL WORKER I (agriculture), 405.684-014

03.04.04 HORTICULTURAL WORKER II (agriculture), 405.687-014

03.04.04 LABORER, LANDSCAPE (agriculture), 408.687-014

03.04.04 LAWN-SERVICE WORKER (agriculture), 408.684-010

03.04.05 DOG CATCHER (government ser.), 379.673-010

03.04.05 IRRIGATOR, SPRINKLING SYSTEM (agriculture), 409.685-014

03.04.05 PLANT-CARE WORKER (agriculture), 408.364-010

03.04.05 TREE PRUNER (agriculture), 408.684-018

03.04.05 TREE TRIMMER (tel. & tel.), 408.664-010

04.01.01 GUARD, CHIEF (any industry), 372.167-014

04.01.02 INVESTIGATOR (utilities), 376.367-022

04.02.01 GUARD, IMMIGRATION (government ser.), 372.567-014

04.02.01 JAILER (government ser.), 372.367-014

04.02.02 AIRLINE SECURITY REPRESENTATIVE (air trans.), 372.667-010

04.02.02 ARMORED-CAR GUARD (business ser.),
372.567-010

04.02.02 ARMORED-CAR GUARD AND DRIVER
(business ser.), 372.563-010

04.02.02 BODYGUARD (personal ser.), 372.667-014

04.02.02 DETECTIVE I (any industry), 376.367-014

04.02.02 FIRE RANGER (forestry), 452.367-014

04.02.02 GATE GUARD (any industry), 372.667-030

04.02.02 GUARD, SECURITY (any industry),
372.667-034

04.02.02 PARKING ENFORCEMENT OFFICER
(government ser.), 375.587-010

04.02.03 BEACH LIFEGUARD (amuse. & rec.),
379.364-014

04.02.03 BORDER GUARD (government ser.),
375.363-010

04.02.03 BOUNCER (amuse. & rec.), 376.667-010

04.02.03 CHAPERON (personal ser.), 359.667-010

04.02.03 HOUSE OFFICER (hotel & rest.), 376.367-018

04.02.03 LIFEGUARD (amuse. & rec.), 379.667-014

04.02.03 REPOSSESSOR (clerical), 241.367-022

04.02.03 SKI PATROLLER (amuse. & rec.), 379.664-010

04.02.03 SURVEILLANCE-SYSTEM MONITOR
(government ser.), 379.367-010

04.02.04 ALARM INVESTIGATOR (business ser.),
376.367-010

05.02.02 SUPERINTENDENT, BUILDING (any industry),
187.167-190

05.02.02 SUPERINTENDENT, CONSTRUCTION
(construction), 182.167-026

05.03.03 DISPATCHER (air trans.), 912.167-010

05.03.04 PROSPECTOR (any industry), 024.284-010

05.03.05 COMMUNICATIONS COORDINATOR
(medical ser.), 239.167-010

05.03.06 CODE INSPECTOR (government ser.),
168.367-018

05.03.06 INSPECTOR, BUILDING (government ser.),
168.167-030

05.04.01 INSTRUCTOR, PILOT (air trans.), 196.223-014

05.05.01 MARBLE FINISHER (construction),
861.664-010

05.05.01 STONECUTTER, HAND (stonework),
771.381-014

05.05.01 TERRAZZO FINISHER (construction),
861.664-014

05.05.01 TILE FINISHER (construction), 861.664-018

05.05.02 BOAT REPAIRER (ship-boat mfg.), 807.361-014

05.05.04 DRY-WALL APPLICATOR (construction),
842.361-030

05.05.05 CABLE SPLICER (construction), 829.361-010

05.05.05 ELECTRIC-METER INSTALLER I (utilities),
821.361-014

05.05.05 ELECTRONICS ASSEMBLER, DEVELOPMEN-
TAL (any industry), 726.261-010

05.05.05 LINE ERECTOR (construction), 821.361-018

05.05.05 LINE MAINTAINER (any industry),
821.261-014

05.05.05 STREET-LIGHT SERVICER (utilities),
824.381-010

05.05.05 WIND-GENERATING-ELECTRIC-POWER
INSTALLER (construction), 821.381-018

05.05.06 AIRCRAFT BODY REPAIRER (air trans.),
807.261-010

05.05.06 ARC CUTTER (welding), 816.364-010

05.05.06 BOILERHOUSE MECHANIC (any industry),
805.361-010

05.05.06 CONDUIT MECHANIC (construction),
869.361-010

05.05.06 FITTER I (any industry), 801.261-014

05.05.06 FORMER, HAND (any industry), 619.361-010

05.05.06 ORNAMENTAL-METAL WORKER (metal
prod., nec), 619.260-014

05.05.06 SIGN ERECTOR I (fabrication, nec),
869.381-026

05.05.06 STRUCTURAL-STEEL WORKER (construction), 801.361-014

05.05.06 WELDER, EXPERIMENTAL (welding),
819.281-022

05.05.06 WELDER, GAS (welding), 811.684-014

05.05.06 WELDER-ASSEMBLER (machinery mfg.),
819.381-010

05.05.07 GUNSMITH (any industry), 632.281-010

05.05.07 SAW FILER (any industry), 701.381-014

05.05.07 TOOL GRINDER I (any industry), 701.381-018

05.05.08 FURNITURE RESTORER (museums),
763.380-010

05.05.08 LOFT WORKER (ship-boat mfg.), 661.281-010

05.05.08 MACHINIST, WOOD (woodworking),
669.380-014

05.05.09 AIR-CONDITIONING MECHANIC (automotive
ser.), 620.281-010

05.05.09 AUTOMOBILE-SERVICE-STATION ME-
CHANIC (automotive ser.), 620.261-030

05.05.09 AUTOMOTIVE-COOLING-SYSTEM DIAG-
NOSTIC TECHNICIAN (automotive ser.),
620.261-034

05.05.09 CASH-REGISTER SERVICER (any industry),
633.281-010

05.05.09 CONSTRUCTION-EQUIPMENT MECHANIC
(construction), 620.261-022

05.05.09 FUEL-INJECTION SERVICER (any industry),
625.281-022

05.05.09 GAS-ENGINE REPAIRER (any industry),
625.281-026

05.05.09 GAS-WELDING-EQUIPMENT MECHANIC
(any industry), 626.381-014

05.05.09 MACHINERY ERECTOR (engine-turbine),
638.261-014

05.05.09 MAINTENANCE REPAIRER, INDUSTRIAL
(any industry), 899.261-014

05.05.09 MECHANIC, INDUSTRIAL TRUCK (any
industry), 620.281-050

05.05.09 MOTORBOAT MECHANIC (engine-turbine),
623.281-038

05.05.09 MOTORCYCLE REPAIRER (automotive ser.),
620.281-054

05.05.09 PARTS SALVAGER (any industry), 638.281-026

05.05.09 PNEUMATIC-TOOL REPAIRER (any industry),
630.281-010

05.05.09 PUMP SERVICER (any industry), 630.281-018

05.05.09 SMALL-ENGINE MECHANIC (any industry),
625.281-034

05.05.09 SOLAR-ENERGY-SYSTEM INSTALLER (any industry), 637.261-030

05.05.10 ELECTRIC-METER REPAIRER (utilities), 729.281-014

05.05.10 ELECTRIC-METER TESTER (utilities), 821.381-010

05.05.10 ELECTRICAL-APPLIANCE SERVICER (any industry), 827.261-010

05.05.10 ELECTRICAL-INSTRUMENT REPAIRER (any industry), 729.281-026

05.05.10 PINSETTER ADJUSTER, AUTOMATIC (toy-sport equip.), 829.381-010

05.05.10 PUBLIC-ADDRESS SERVICER (any industry), 823.261-010

05.05.11 DENTAL CERAMIST (protective dev.), 712.381-042

05.05.11 DENTAL CERAMIST ASSISTANT (protective dev.), 712.664-010

05.05.11 DENTURE-MODEL MAKER (protective dev.), 712.684-046

05.05.11 EXPERIMENTAL ASSEMBLER (any industry), 739.381-026

05.05.11 FINISHER, DENTURE (protective dev.), 712.381-050

05.05.11 INSTRUMENT REPAIRER (any industry), 710.261-010

05.05.11 LENS MOUNTER II (optical goods), 713.681-010

05.05.11 PACKER, DENTURE (protective dev.), 712.684-034

05.05.12 ELECTRIC-ORGAN INSPECTOR AND REPAIRER (musical inst.), 730.281-018

05.05.12 FRETTED-INSTRUMENT MAKER, HAND (musical inst.), 730.281-022

05.05.12 VIOLIN MAKER, HAND (musical inst.), 730.281-046

05.05.13 ASSISTANT PRESS OPERATOR, OFFSET (print. & pub.), 651.685-026

05.05.13 ASSISTANT-PRESS OPERATOR (print. & pub.), 651.585-010

05.05.13 CYLINDER-PRESS OPERATOR (print. & pub.), 651.362-010

05.05.13 ELECTROTYPER (print. & pub.), 974.381-010

05.05.13 OFFSET-PRESS OPERATOR I (print. & pub.), 651.382-042

05.05.13 ROTOGRAVURE-PRESS OPERATOR (print. & pub.), 651.362-026

05.05.13 STEREOTYPER (print. & pub.), 974.382-014

05.05.13 WEB-PRESS OPERATOR (print. & pub.), 651.362-030

05.05.14 STONE SETTER (jewelry-silver.), 700.381-054

05.05.15 ALTERATION TAILOR (garment), 785.261-010

05.05.15 AUTOMOBILE UPHOLSTERER (automotive ser.), 780.381-010

05.05.15 BOOKBINDER (print. & pub.), 977.381-010

05.05.15 CUSTOM TAILOR (garment), 785.261-014

05.05.15 DRESSMAKER (any industry), 785.361-010

05.05.15 FURNITURE UPHOLSTERER (any industry), 780.381-018

05.05.15 RUG REPAIRER (laundry & rel.), 782.381-018

05.05.15 SHOE REPAIRER (personal ser.), 365.361-014

05.05.15 SHOP TAILOR (garment), 785.361-022

05.05.15 UPHOLSTERY REPAIRER (furniture), 780.684-122

05.05.17 CAKE DECORATOR (bakery products), 524.381-010

05.05.17 CHEF DE FROID (hotel & rest.), 313.281-010

05.05.17 SOUS CHEF (hotel & rest.), 313.131-026

05.06.01 CABLE MAINTAINER (utilities), 952.464-010

05.06.01 GAS-ENGINE OPERATOR (any industry), 950.382-018

05.06.02 AIR-COMPRESSOR OPERATOR (any industry), 950.685-010

05.06.02 BOILER OPERATOR (any industry), 950.382-010

05.06.02 FUEL ATTENDANT (any industry), 953.362-010

05.06.02 GAS-COMPRESSOR OPERATOR (any industry), 950.382-014

05.06.02 VENTILATION EQUIPMENT TENDER (any industry), 950.585-010

05.06.03 PUMP-STATION OPERATOR, WATERWORKS (waterworks), 954.382-010

05.06.03 PUMPER (any industry), 914.682-010

05.07.01 FIRE-EXTINGUISHER-SPRINKLER INSPEC-TOR (any industry), 379.687-010

05.07.01 LINE WALKER (petrol. & gas), 869.564-010

05.07.01 SEWER-LINE PHOTO-INSPECTOR (sanitary ser.), 851.362-010

05.07.01 ULTRASONIC TESTER (any industry), 739.281-014

05.08.01 DUMP-TRUCK DRIVER (any industry), 902.683-010

05.08.01 MILK DRIVER (dairy products), 905.483-010

05.08.01 TRACTOR-TRAILER-TRUCK DRIVER (any industry), 904.383-010

05.08.01 TRUCK DRIVER, HEAVY (any industry), 905.663-014

05.08.01 TRUCK DRIVER, LIGHT (any industry), 906.683-022

05.08.03 AMBULANCE DRIVER (medical ser.), 913.683-010

05.08.03 CHAUFFEUR, FUNERAL CAR (personal ser.), 359.673-014

05.08.03 COIN COLLECTOR (business ser.), 292.483-010

05.08.03 CONCRETE-MIXING-TRUCK DRIVER (construction), 900.683-010

05.08.03 DELIVERER, CAR RENTAL (automotive ser.), 919.663-010

05.08.03 ESCORT-VEHICLE DRIVER (motor trans.), 919.663-022

05.08.03 FOOD-SERVICE DRIVER (hotel & rest.), 906.683-010

05.08.03 GARBAGE COLLECTOR DRIVER (motor trans.), 905.663-010

05.08.03 GARBAGE-COLLECTION SUPERVISOR (motor trans.), 909.137-014

05.08.03 HEALTH-EQUIPMENT SERVICER (medical ser.), 359.363-010

05.08.03 LOT ATTENDANT (retail trade), 915.583-010

05.08.03 NEWSPAPER-DELIVERY DRIVER (wholesale tr.), 292.363-010

05.08.03 TELEPHONE-DIRECTORY-DISTRIBUTOR DRIVER (business ser.), 906.683-018

05.08.03 TOW-TRUCK OPERATOR (automotive ser.), 919.663-026

05.08.03 VAN DRIVER (motor trans.), 905.663-018

05.08.04 DECKHAND (water trans.), 911.687-022

05.08.04 DOCK HAND (air trans.), 919.683-010

05.08.04 MOTORBOAT OPERATOR (any industry), 911.663-010

05.09.01 BOOKMOBILE DRIVER (library), 249.363-010

05.09.01 CARGO AGENT (air trans.), 248.367-018

05.09.01 CHECKER (motor trans.), 919.687-010

05.09.01 CHECKER, BAKERY PRODUCTS (bakery products), 222.487-010

05.09.01 CUSTODIAN, ATHLETIC EQUIPMENT (amuse. & rec.), 969.367-010

05.09.01 DISPATCHER (construction), 849.137-010

05.09.01 INVENTORY CLERK (clerical), 222.387-026

05.09.01 LABORATORY CLERK (clerical), 222.587-026

05.09.01 LABORER, STORES (any industry), 922.687-058

05.09.01 LINEN-ROOM ATTENDANT (hotel & rest.), 222.387-030

05.09.01 LINEN-ROOM SUPERVISOR (laundry & rel.), 222.137-014

05.09.01 MAILER (print. & pub.), 222.587-030

05.09.01 MEAT CLERK (retail trade), 222.684-010

05.09.01 ORDER FILLER (retail trade), 222.487-014

05.09.01 PARTS CLERK (clerical), 222.367-042

05.09.01 PARTS-ORDER-AND-STOCK CLERK (clerical), 249.367-058

05.09.01 PRODUCTION TECHNICIAN, SEMI-CONDUCTOR PROCESSING EQUIPMENT (electron. comp.), 590.384-014

05.09.01 SHIPPING AND RECEIVING CLERK (clerical), 222.387-050

05.09.01 SHIPPING CHECKER (clerical), 222.687-030

05.09.01 SHIPPING-AND-RECEIVING WEIGHER (clerical), 222.387-074

05.09.01 STOCK CLERK (clerical), 222.387-058

05.09.01 STOCK CLERK (retail trade), 299.367-014

05.09.01 SUPPLY CLERK (personal ser.), 339.687-010

05.09.01 TIRE ADJUSTER (retail trade), 241.367-034

05.09.01 TOOL-CRIB ATTENDANT (clerical), 222.367-062

05.09.02 DRAPERY AND UPHOLSTERY ESTIMATOR (retail trade), 299.387-010

05.09.02 FIELD RECORDER (utilities), 229.367-010

05.09.02 JOB TRACER (clerical), 221.387-034

05.09.02 LAUNDRY CLERK (clerical), 221.387-038

05.09.02 MATERIAL EXPEDITER (clerical), 221.367-042

05.09.02 ORDER DETAILER (clerical), 221.387-046

05.09.02 PRESCRIPTION CLERK, LENS-AND-FRAMES (optical goods), 222.367-050

05.09.02 RUG MEASURER (laundry & rel.), 369.367-014

05.09.02 SUPERVISOR, LAUNDRY (laundry & rel.), 361.137-010

05.09.03 CHECKER, DUMP GROUNDS (business ser.), 219.367-010

05.09.03 FOOD ORDER EXPEDITER (hotel & rest.), 319.467-010

05.09.03 INDUSTRIAL-ORDER CLERK (clerical), 221.367-022

05.09.03 MARKER (retail trade), 209.587-034

05.09.03 MATERIAL CLERK (clerical), 222.387-034

05.09.03 METER READER (utilities), 209.567-010

05.09.03 ORDER CALLER (clerical), 209.667-014

05.09.03 RECEIVING CHECKER (clerical), 222.687-018

05.09.03 SORTER-PRICER (nonprofit org.), 222.387-054

05.09.03 TURBINE ATTENDANT (utilities), 952.567-010

05.10.01 ARCH-SUPPORT TECHNICIAN (protective dev.), 712.381-010

05.10.01 ASBESTOS REMOVAL WORKER (construction), 869.684-082

05.10.01 BOAT RIGGER (retail trade), 806.464-010

05.10.01 BUILDING CLEANER (any industry), 891.684-022

05.10.01 CARPET CUTTER (retail trade), 929.381-010

05.10.01 CARPET LAYER (retail trade), 864.381-010

05.10.01 CASTING REPAIRER (any industry), 619.281-010

05.10.01 CONSTRUCTION WORKER I (construction), 869.664-014

05.10.01 DIVER (any industry), 899.261-010

05.10.01 DRAPERY HANGER (retail trade), 869.484-014

05.10.01 DRY-WALL APPLICATOR (construction), 842.684-014

05.10.01 FENCE ERECTOR (construction), 869.684-022

05.10.01 FIXTURE REPAIRER-FABRICATOR (any industry), 630.384-010

05.10.01 FLOOR LAYER (construction), 864.481-010

05.10.01 FRONT-END MECHANIC (automotive ser.), 620.281-038

05.10.01 FURNITURE ASSEMBLER-AND-INSTALLER (retail trade), 739.684-082

05.10.01 GLASS INSTALLER (automotive ser.), 865.684-010

05.10.01 GLAZIER (construction), 865.381-010

05.10.01 GRIP (amuse. & rec.), 962.684-014

05.10.01 INSULATION WORKER (construction), 863.364-014

05.10.01 JIG BUILDER (wood. container), 761.381-014

05.10.01 LAWN-SPRINKLER INSTALLER (construction), 869.684-030

05.10.01 LUGGAGE REPAIRER (any industry), 365.361-010

05.10.01 MUFFLER INSTALLER (automotive ser.), 807.664-010

05.10.01 PUMP INSTALLER (any industry), 630.684-018

05.10.01 REPAIRER (furniture), 709.684-062

05.10.01 ROOFER (construction), 866.381-010

05.10.01 ROUSTABOUT (petrol. & gas), 869.684-046

05.10.01 SERVICE REPRESENTATIVE (utilities), 959.574-010

05.10.01 SEWER-LINE REPAIRER, TELE-GROUT (sanitary ser.), 851.262-010

05.10.01 SWIMMING POOL INSTALLER-AND-SERVICER (construction), 869.463-010

05.10.01 TAPER (construction), 842.664-010

05.10.01 TEMPLATE MAKER, TRACK (any industry), 809.484-014

05.10.01 TORCH-STRAIGHTENER-AND HEATER (any industry), 709.684-086

05.10.01 WATER-SOFTENER SERVICER-AND-INSTALLER (business ser.), 862.684-034

05.10.01 WELDER, TACK (welding), 810.684-010

05.10.02 AUTOMOBILE-ACCESSORIES INSTALLER (automotive ser.), 806.684-038

05.10.02 AUTOMOBILE-RADIATOR MECHANIC (automotive ser.), 620.381-010

05.10.02 AUTOMOBILE-SERVICE-STATION ATTENDANT (automotive ser.), 915.467-010

05.10.02 BICYCLE REPAIRER (any industry), 639.681-010

05.10.02 BRAKE REPAIRER (automotive ser.), 620.281-026

05.10.02 CARBURETOR MECHANIC (automotive ser.), 620.281-034

05.10.02 COIN-MACHINE-SERVICE REPAIRER (svc. ind. mach.), 639.281-014

05.10.02 CONVEYOR-MAINTENANCE MECHANIC (any industry), 630.381-010

05.10.02 DOOR-CLOSER MECHANIC (any industry), 630.381-014

05.10.02 GAS-APPLIANCE SERVICER (any industry), 637.261-018

05.10.02 LUBRICATION-EQUIPMENT SERVICER (any industry), 630.381-022

05.10.02 MAINTENANCE MECHANIC HELPER (construction), 620.664-014

05.10.02 MEDICAL-EQUIPMENT REPAIRER (protective dev.), 639.281-022

05.10.02 METER REPAIRER (any industry), 710.281-034

05.10.02 NEW-CAR GET-READY MECHANIC (automotive ser.), 806.361-026

05.10.02 RIDE OPERATOR (amuse. & rec.), 342.663-010

05.10.02 SEWING-MACHINE REPAIRER (any industry), 639.281-018

05.10.02 THERMOSTAT REPAIRER (inst. & app.), 710.381-050

05.10.03 APPLIANCE REPAIRER (house. appl.), 723.584-010

05.10.03 AUTOMATIC-DOOR MECHANIC (construction), 829.281-010

05.10.03 CABLE TELEVISION INSTALLER (radio-tv broad.), 821.281-010

05.10.03 ELECTRIC-GOLF-CART REPAIRER (amuse. & rec.), 620.261-026

05.10.03 ELECTRIC-TOOL REPAIRER (any industry), 729.281-022

05.10.03 ELECTRICAL-APPLIANCE REPAIRER (any industry), 723.381-010

05.10.03 ELECTRONIC EQUIPMENT REPAIRER (comm. equip.), 726.381-014

05.10.03 SIGHT-EFFECTS SPECIALIST (amuse. & rec.), 962.267-010

05.10.03 TAPE-RECORDER REPAIRER (any industry), 720.281-014

05.10.03 TELEVISION INSTALLER (any industry), 823.361-010

05.10.03 TRANSFORMER REPAIRER (any industry), 724.381-018

05.10.03 VACUUM CLEANER REPAIRER (any industry), 723.381-014

05.10.03 WIRER, CABLE (comm. equip.), 729.381-022

05.10.04 AIRPORT ATTENDANT (air trans.), 912.364-010

05.10.04 DOLL REPAIRER (any industry), 731.684-014

05.10.04 EQUIPMENT INSTALLER (any industry), 828.381-010

05.10.04 EVAPORATIVE-COOLER INSTALLER (any industry), 637.381-010

05.10.04 FIRE-EXTINGUISHER REPAIRER (any industry), 709.384-010

05.10.04 HOUSEHOLD-APPLIANCE INSTALLER (any industry), 827.661-010

05.10.04 PINSETTER MECHANIC, AUTOMATIC (any industry), 638.261-022

05.10.04 SPORTS-EQUIPMENT REPAIRER (any industry), 732.684-122

05.10.04 STAGE TECHNICIAN (amuse. & rec.), 962.261-014

05.10.04 SWIMMING-POOL SERVICER (any industry), 891.684-018

05.10.04 USED-CAR RENOVATOR (retail trade), 620.684-034

05.10.05 COLOR-PRINTER OPERATOR (photofinishing), 976.382-014

05.10.05 CONTACT WORKER, LITHOGRAPHY (print. & pub.), 976.684-038

05.10.05 DEVELOPER (photofinishing), 976.681-010

05.10.05 DUPLICATING-MACHINE OPERATOR I (clerical), 207.682-010

05.10.05 ENGRAVER, MACHINE I (engraving), 704.682-010

05.10.05 ENGRAVING-PRESS OPERATOR (print. & pub.), 651.382-010

05.10.05 EQUIPMENT MONITOR, PHOTOTYPESETTING (print. & pub.), 650.682-010

05.10.05 FILM DEVELOPER (motion picture), 976.382-018

05.10.05 FILM INSPECTOR (photofinishing), 976.362-010

05.10.05 FILM LABORATORY TECHNICIAN (motion picture), 976.684-014

05.10.05 INSTANT PRINT OPERATOR (print. & pub.), 979.362-010

05.10.05 MICROFILM PROCESSOR (business ser.), 976.385-010

05.10.05 MOTION-PICTURE PROJECTIONIST (amuse. & rec.), 960.362-010

05.10.05 OFFSET-DUPLICATING-MACHINE OPERATOR (clerical), 207.682-018

05.10.05 PHOTO MASK TECHNICIAN, ELECTRON-BEAM (electron. comp.), 972.382-022

05.10.05 PHOTOCOMPOSING-MACHINE OPERATOR (print. & pub.), 650.582-018

05.10.05 PHOTOGRAPH FINISHER (photofinishing), 976.487-010

05.10.05 PHOTOGRAPHER, FINISH (amuse. & rec.), 143.382-014

05.10.05 PROOFER, PREPRESS (print. & pub.), 972.381-034

05.10.05 QUALITY-CONTROL TECHNICIAN (photofinishing), 976.267-010

05.10.05 REPRODUCTION TECHNICIAN (any industry), 976.361-010

05.10.05 TAKE-DOWN SORTER (photofinishing), 976.665-010

05.10.05 TAPE TRANSFERRER (radio-tv broad.), 194.382-014

05.10.06 FIREWORKS DISPLAY SPECIALIST (chemical), 969.664-010

05.10.07 PAINTER (construction), 840.381-010

05.10.07 PAINTER, TRANSPORTATION EQUIPMENT (aircraft mfg.), 845.381-014

05.10.08 BAKER (hotel & rest.), 313.381-010

05.10.08 BAKER, HEAD (hotel & rest.), 313.131-010

05.10.08 BAKER, PIZZA (hotel & rest.), 313.381-014

05.10.08 BUTCHER, CHICKEN AND FISH (hotel & rest.), 316.684-010

05.10.08 BUTCHER, MEAT (hotel & rest.), 316.681-010

05.10.08 CARVER (hotel & rest.), 316.661-010

05.10.08 COOK (domestic ser.), 305.281-010

05.10.08 COOK (any industry), 315.361-010

05.10.08 COOK, BARBECUE (hotel & rest.), 313.381-022

05.10.08 COOK, FAST FOOD (hotel & rest.), 313.374-010

05.10.08 COOK, PASTRY (hotel & rest.), 313.381-026

05.10.08 COOK, SCHOOL CAFETERIA (hotel & rest.), 313.381-030

05.10.08 COOK, SHORT ORDER (hotel & rest.), 313.374-014

05.10.08 COOK, SPECIALTY (hotel & rest.), 313.361-026

05.10.08 COOK, SPECIALTY, FOREIGN FOOD (hotel & rest.), 313.361-030

05.10.08 FORMULA-ROOM WORKER (dairy products), 520.487-014

05.10.08 GARDE MANGER (hotel & rest.), 313.361-034

05.10.08 KITCHEN SUPERVISOR (hotel & rest.), 319.137-030

05.10.08 MEAT CUTTER (retail trade), 316.684-018

05.10.08 PANTRY GOODS MAKER (hotel & rest.), 317.684-014

05.10.08 PASTRY CHEF (hotel & rest.), 313.131-022

05.10.08 PIE MAKER (hotel & rest.), 313.361-038

05.10.08 SALAD MAKER (water trans.), 317.384-010

05.10.09 EXTERMINATOR (business ser.), 389.684-010

05.10.09 EXTERMINATOR, TERMITE (business ser.), 383.364-010

05.10.09 FUMIGATOR (business ser.), 383.361-010

05.11.01 BULLDOZER OPERATOR I (any industry), 850.683-010

05.11.01 CHERRY-PICKER OPERATOR (construction), 921.663-014

05.11.01 CONCRETE-PAVING-MACHINE OPERATOR (construction), 853.663-014

05.11.01 PROJECT-CREW WORKER (any industry), 891.687-018

05.11.01 ROAD-ROLLER OPERATOR (construction), 859.683-030

05.11.01 SANITARY LANDFILL OPERATOR (sanitary ser.), 955.463-010

05.11.01 SCRAPER OPERATOR (construction), 850.683-038

05.11.01 STREET-SWEEPER OPERATOR (government ser.), 919.683-022

05.11.02 CORE-DRILL OPERATOR (any industry), 930.682-010

05.11.02 PLANT OPERATOR (concrete prod.), 570.682-014

05.11.04 DRAGLINE OPERATOR (any industry), 850.683-018

05.11.04 DUMP OPERATOR (any industry), 921.685-038

05.11.04 FRONT-END LOADER OPERATOR (any industry), 921.683-042

05.11.04 HOISTING ENGINEER (any industry), 921.663-030

05.11.04 OVERHEAD CRANE OPERATOR (any industry), 921.663-010

05.11.04 RIGGER (any industry), 921.260-010

05.11.04 STEVEDORE I (water trans.), 911.663-014

05.11.04 TRACTOR OPERATOR (any industry), 929.683-014

05.12.01 BARGE CAPTAIN (water trans.), 911.137-010

05.12.01 HOUSEKEEPER (hotel & rest.), 321.137-010

05.12.01 HOUSEKEEPER, HOME (domestic ser.), 301.137-010

05.12.01 LABOR-CREW SUPERVISOR (construction), 899.131-010

05.12.02 HORIZONTAL-EARTH-BORING-MACHINE-OPERATOR HELPER (construction), 850.684-014

05.12.02 SURVEYOR HELPER (any industry), 869.567-010

05.12.03 ABLE SEAMAN (water trans.), 911.364-010

05.12.03 BAGGAGE HANDLER (r.r. trans.), 910.687-010

05.12.03 DUMPER (any industry), 921.667-018

05.12.03 GARBAGE COLLECTOR (motor trans.), 955.687-022

05.12.03 INSTALLER (museums), 922.687-050

05.12.03 LABORER, PETROLEUM REFINERY (petrol. refin.), 549.687-018

05.12.03 LABORER, SHIPYARD (ship-boat mfg.), 809.687-022

05.12.03 MATERIAL HANDLER (any industry), 929.687-030

05.12.03 PRESS BUCKER (any industry), 920.686-042

05.12.03 RECORDING STUDIO SET-UP WORKER (recording), 962.664-014

05.12.03 WASTE-DISPOSAL ATTENDANT (any industry), 955.383-010

05.12.03 YARD LABORER (paper & pulp), 922.687-102

05.12.04 CHOKE SETTER (logging), 921.687-014

05.12.04 CONVEYOR-SYSTEM OPERATOR (any industry), 921.662-018

05.12.04 ELEVATOR OPERATOR, FREIGHT (any industry), 921.683-038

05.12.04 GRIP (motion picture), 962.687-022

05.12.04 LABORER, CONCRETE-MIXING PLANT (construction), 579.665-014

05.12.04 LABORER, POWERHOUSE (utilities), 952.665-010

05.12.05 SWITCH TENDER (r.r. trans.), 910.667-026

05.12.06 AIRPORT UTILITY WORKER (air trans.), 912.663-010

05.12.06 BOAT LOADER I (water trans.), 911.364-014

05.12.06 LOADER HELPER (any industry), 914.687-014

05.12.06 WATER TENDER (any industry), 599.685-122

05.12.08 GARAGE SERVICER, INDUSTRIAL (any industry), 915.687-014

05.12.08 LUBRICATION SERVICER (automotive ser.), 915.687-018

05.12.08 OILER (any industry), 699.687-018

05.12.10 RIVET HEATER (heat treating), 504.485-010

05.12.12 AIR-CONDITIONING INSTALLER-SERVICER HELPER, WINDOW UNIT (construction), 637.687-010

05.12.12 AUTOMOBILE-BODY-REPAIRER HELPER (automotive ser.), 807.687-010

05.12.12 BILLPOSTER (any industry), 299.667-010

05.12.12 DECORATOR, STREET AND BUILDING (any industry), 899.687-010

05.12.12 HIGHWAY-MAINTENANCE WORKER (government ser.), 899.684-014

05.12.12 PIPE-FITTER HELPER (construction), 862.684-022

05.12.12 SEWER-LINE REPAIRER (sanitary ser.), 869.664-018

05.12.12 SEWER-PIPE CLEANER (business ser.), 899.664-014

05.12.12 WINDOW REPAIRER (any industry), 899.684-042

05.12.13 KEY CUTTER (any industry), 709.684-050

05.12.14 ASPHALT-DISTRIBUTOR TENDER (construction), 853.665-010

05.12.14 WOOD CAULKER (ship-boat mfg.), 843.384-010

05.12.15 AUTOMOBILE WRECKER (wholesale tr.), 620.684-010

05.12.15 BELT REPAIRER (any industry), 630.684-014

05.12.15 CONSTRUCTION-EQUIPMENT-MECHANIC HELPER (construction), 620.664-010

05.12.15 ROLLER-SKATE REPAIRER (any industry), 732.684-102

05.12.15 TIRE REPAIRER (automotive ser.), 915.684-010

05.12.16 CABLE PULLER (construction), 829.684-018

05.12.16 ELECTRICAL-APPLIANCE PREPARER (any industry), 827.584-010

05.12.16 LIGHTING-EQUIPMENT OPERATOR (amuse. & rec.), 962.381-014

05.12.16 PROP ATTENDANT (amuse. & rec.), 962.684-022

05.12.17 BAKER HELPER (hotel & rest.), 313.684-010

05.12.17 COFFEE MAKER (hotel & rest.), 317.684-010

05.12.17 COOK HELPER (hotel & rest.), 317.687-010

05.12.17 DELI CUTTER-SLICER (retail trade), 316.684-014

05.12.17 FOOD ASSEMBLER, KITCHEN (hotel & rest.), 319.484-010

05.12.17 SANDWICH MAKER (hotel & rest.), 317.664-010

05.12.18 ATTENDANT, CAMPGROUND (amuse. & rec.), 329.683-010

05.12.18 AUTOMOBILE DETAILER (automotive ser.), 915.687-034

05.12.18 BARTENDER HELPER (hotel & rest.), 312.687-010

05.12.18 CARETAKER (domestic ser.), 301.687-010

05.12.18 CHIMNEY SWEEP (any industry), 891.687-010

05.12.18 CLEANER II (any industry), 919.687-014

05.12.18 CLEANER, COMMERCIAL OR INSTITUTIONAL (any industry), 381.687-014

05.12.18 CLEANER, HOSPITAL (medical ser.), 323.687-010

05.12.18 CLEANER, HOUSEKEEPING (any industry), 323.687-014

05.12.18 CLEANER, INDUSTRIAL (any industry), 381.687-018

05.12.18 CLEANER, LABORATORY EQUIPMENT (any industry), 381.687-022

05.12.18 CLEANER, WINDOW (any industry), 389.687-014

05.12.18 DAY WORKER (domestic ser.), 301.687-014

05.12.18 FURNACE CLEANER (any industry), 891.687-014

05.12.18 GOLF-RANGE ATTENDANT (amuse. & rec.), 341.683-010

05.12.18 JANITOR (any industry), 382.664-010

05.12.18 KITCHEN HELPER (hotel & rest.), 318.687-010

05.12.18 LABORER, GENERAL (motor trans.), 909.687-014

05.12.18 LAUNDRY WORKER I (any industry), 361.684-014

05.12.18 LIGHT-FIXTURE SERVICER (any industry), 389.687-018

05.12.18 SANDBLASTER (any industry), 503.687-010

05.12.18 SILVER WRAPPER (hotel & rest.), 318.687-018

05.12.18 STEAM CLEANER (automotive ser.), 915.687-026

05.12.18 STREET CLEANER (government ser.), 955.687-018

05.12.18 SWEEPER-CLEANER, INDUSTRIAL (any industry), 389.683-010

05.12.18 TANK CLEANER (any industry), 891.687-022

05.12.18 TUBE CLEANER (any industry), 891.687-030

05.12.18 WAXER, FLOOR (any industry), 381.687-034

05.12.19 ADDRESSING-MACHINE OPERATOR (clerical), 208.582-010

05.12.19 BRAILLE-DUPLICATING-MACHINE OPERATOR (print. & pub.), 207.685-010

05.12.19 COIN-COUNTER-AND-WRAPPER (clerical), 217.585-010

05.12.19 COLLATOR OPERATOR (clerical), 208.685-010

05.12.19 CURRENCY COUNTER (financial), 217.485-010

05.12.19 FEEDER (print. & pub.), 651.686-014

05.12.19 FOLDING-MACHINE OPERATOR (clerical), 208.685-014

05.12.19 INSERTING-MACHINE OPERATOR (clerical), 208.685-018

05.12.19 MICROFILM MOUNTER (clerical), 208.685-022

05.12.19 PHOTOCOPYING-MACHINE OPERATOR (clerical), 207.685-014

05.12.19 PHOTOGRAPHIC-MACHINE OPERATOR (clerical), 207.685-018

05.12.19 ROLL TENDER (print. & pub.), 651.686-022

05.12.20 CROSSING TENDER (any industry), 371.667-010

06.01.01 COOK, MEXICAN FOOD (food prep., nec), 526.134-010

06.01.01 SUPERVISOR, FILM PROCESSING (motion picture), 976.131-014

06.01.02 KNITTER MECHANIC (knitting), 685.360-010

06.01.02 KNITTING-MACHINE FIXER (knitting), 689.260-026

06.01.02 LOOM FIXER (narrow fabrics), 683.260-018

06.01.02 MACHINE SET-UP OPERATOR, PAPER GOODS (paper goods), 649.380-010

06.01.02 MACHINE SETTER (machine shop), 600.360-014

06.01.02 MACHINE SETTER (any industry), 616.360-022

06.01.02 SETTER, AUTOMATIC-SPINNING LATHE (any industry), 604.360-010

06.01.03 EXHAUST EQUIPMENT OPERATOR (electron. comp.), 599.382-014

06.01.03 FIRESETTER (elec. equip.), 692.360-018

06.01.03 ROLLING ATTENDANT (steel & rel.), 613.662-010

06.01.04 BENCH HAND (jewelry-silver.), 735.381-010

06.01.04 CANVAS WORKER (ship-boat mfg.), 739.381-010

06.01.04 COREMAKER (foundry), 518.381-014

06.01.04 FINAL ASSEMBLER (office machines), 706.381-018

06.01.04 GLASS BLOWER (glass mfg.), 772.381-022

06.01.04 MOLDER (aircraft mfg.), 518.361-010

06.01.04 PLASTICS FABRICATOR (aircraft mfg.), 754.381-018

06.01.04 RING MAKER (jewelry-silver.), 700.381-042

06.01.04 SOLDERER (jewelry-silver.), 700.381-050

06.01.05 INSPECTOR, ELECTROMECHANICAL (inst. & app.), 729.361-010

06.01.05 INSPECTOR, METAL FABRICATING (any industry), 619.261-010

06.01.05 INSPECTOR, PROCESSING (aircraft mfg.), 806.381-074

06.01.05 ROADABILITY-MACHINE OPERATOR (auto. mfg.), 806.383-010

06.01.05 X-RAY-EQUIPMENT TESTER (any industry), 729.281-046

06.02.01 SUPERVISOR (office machines), 706.131-014

06.02.01 SUPERVISOR I (rubber goods), 759.137-010

06.02.01 TOOL GRINDER II (any industry), 603.664-010

06.02.02 BRAKE OPERATOR II (any industry), 619.685-026

06.02.02 CRIMPING-MACHINE OPERATOR (any industry), 616.682-022

06.02.02 DRILL-PRESS OPERATOR (machine shop), 606.682-014

06.02.02 DROPHAMMER OPERATOR (aircraft mfg.), 610.362-010

06.02.02 GRINDER SET-UP OPERATOR (machine shop), 603.382-034

06.02.02 LASER-BEAM-TRIM OPERATOR (electron. comp.), 726.682-010

06.02.02 POLISHING-MACHINE OPERATOR (any industry), 603.682-026

06.02.02 PRESS OPERATOR, HEAVY DUTY (any industry), 617.260-010

06.02.02 PUNCH-PRESS OPERATOR I (any industry), 615.382-010

06.02.02 PUNCH-PRESS OPERATOR III (any industry), 615.682-014

06.02.02 RIVETING-MACHINE OPERATOR I (any industry), 699.482-010

06.02.02 SAWYER (plastic prod.), 690.482-010

06.02.02 SHEAR OPERATOR I (any industry), 615.682-018

06.02.02 SPINNER, HAND (any industry), 619.362-018

06.02.02 STRAIGHTENING-PRESS OPERATOR II (any industry), 617.482-026

06.02.02 STRAIGHTENING-ROLL OPERATOR (any industry), 613.662-022

06.02.02 WIRE DRAWING MACHINE OPERATOR (inst. & app.), 614.382-018

06.02.03 CUT-OFF-SAW OPERATOR I (woodworking), 667.682-022

06.02.03 HEAD SAWYER (saw. & plan.), 667.662-010

06.02.03 LOG-CHIPPER OPERATOR (logging), 564.662-010

06.02.03 NAILING-MACHINE OPERATOR (any industry), 669.682-058

06.02.03 ROUTER OPERATOR (woodworking), 665.682-030

06.02.03 TIMBER-SIZER OPERATOR (saw. & plan.), 665.482-018

06.02.05 BINDER (any industry), 787.682-010

06.02.05 CARPET SEWER (carpet & rug), 787.682-014

06.02.05 HEMMER (any industry), 787.682-026

06.02.05 MENDER (any industry), 787.682-030

06.02.05 SEWING MACHINE OPERATOR (leather prod.), 783.682-014

06.02.05 STITCHER, STANDARD MACHINE (boot & shoe), 690.682-082

06.02.05 TRIMMER, MACHINE (garment), 781.682-010

06.02.05 ZIPPER SETTER (any industry), 787.682-086

06.02.06 WEAVER (nonmet. min.), 683.682-038

06.02.08 EYEGLASS-LENS CUTTER (optical goods), 716.682-010

06.02.08 PRECISION-LENS GRINDER (optical goods), 716.382-018

06.02.09 AUTOMATED CUTTING MACHINE OPERATOR (aircraft mfg.), 699.362-010

06.02.09 CLOTH PRINTER (any industry), 652.382-010

06.02.09 CUTTER OPERATOR (any industry), 699.682-018

06.02.09 DIE CUTTER (any industry), 699.682-022

06.02.09 DYNAMITE-PACKING-MACHINE OPERATOR (chemical), 692.662-010

06.02.09 FLUID JET CUTTER OPERATOR (aircraft mfg.), 699.382-010

06.02.09 NUMERICAL-CONTROL ROUTER OPERATOR (aircraft mfg.), 605.382-046

06.02.09 ROBOTIC MACHINE OPERATOR (aircraft mfg.), 606.382-026

06.02.09 WIRE-WRAPPING-MACHINE OPERATOR (electron. comp.), 726.682-014

06.02.10 COLD-MILL OPERATOR (steel & rel.), 613.662-018

06.02.10 HEAT TREATER I (heat treating), 504.382-014

06.02.10 SAND MIXER, MACHINE (foundry), 570.682-018

06.02.10 TEMPERER (heat treating), 504.682-026

06.02.13 BLANKMAKER (glass mfg.), 579.382-022

06.02.13 EXTRUDER OPERATOR (plastic prod.), 557.382-010

06.02.13 MIXING-MACHINE OPERATOR (any industry), 550.382-022

06.02.15 BAKER (bakery products), 526.381-010

06.02.15 BUTTERMAKER (dairy products), 529.362-010

06.02.15 CENTER-MACHINE OPERATOR (sugar & conf.), 520.682-014

06.02.15 CHOCOLATE-PRODUCTION-MACHINE OPERATOR (sugar & conf.), 529.382-014

06.02.15 COFFEE ROASTER (food prep., nec), 523.682-014

06.02.15 CRACKER-AND-COOKIE-MACHINE OPERATOR (bakery products), 520.682-034

06.02.15 DAIRY-PROCESSING-EQUIPMENT OPERATOR (dairy products), 529.382-018

06.02.15 DOUGH MIXER (bakery products), 520.685-234

06.02.15 DOUGHNUT-MACHINE OPERATOR (bakery products), 526.682-022

06.02.15 DRIER OPERATOR (food prep., nec), 523.362-014

06.02.15 EXTRUDER OPERATOR (grain-feed mills), 520.682-018

06.02.15 FREEZER OPERATOR (dairy products), 529.482-010

06.02.15 GRINDER OPERATOR (grain-feed mills), 521.682-026

06.02.15 SYRUP MAKER (beverage), 520.485-026

06.02.16 DRY CLEANER (laundry & rel.), 362.382-014

06.02.17 BRIQUETTE-MACHINE OPERATOR (fabrication, nec), 549.662-010

06.02.18 AUTOCLAVE OPERATOR (aircraft mfg.), 553.362-014

06.02.18 ROOFING-MACHINE OPERATOR (build. mat., nec), 554.682-022

06.02.18 RUG CLEANER, MACHINE (laundry & rel.), 361.682-010

06.02.18 SOAP MAKER (soap & rel.), 559.382-054

06.02.19 LASER-BEAM-MACHINE OPERATOR (welding), 815.682-010

06.02.19 WELDING-MACHINE OPERATOR, ARC (welding), 810.382-010

06.02.19 WELDING-MACHINE OPERATOR, GAS (welding), 811.482-010

06.02.20 KICK-PRESS OPERATOR I (any industry), 616.682-026

06.02.20 STACKING-MACHINE OPERATOR I (any industry), 692.682-054

06.02.21 ANODIZER (any industry), 500.682-010

06.02.21 OPTICAL-ELEMENT COATER (optical goods), 716.382-014

06.02.21 PAINT-SPRAYER OPERATOR, AUTOMATIC (any industry), 599.382-010

06.02.21 PLATER, PRINTED CIRCUIT BOARD PANELS (electron. comp.), 500.684-026

06.02.22 ASSEMBLER, INTERNAL COMBUSTION ENGINE (engine-turbine), 806.481-014

06.02.22 ASSEMBLER, SUBASSEMBLY (aircraft mfg.), 806.384-034

06.02.22 CABINET ASSEMBLER (furniture), 763.684-014

06.02.22 CASKET ASSEMBLER (fabrication, nec), 739.684-190

06.02.22 ELECTRIC-SIGN ASSEMBLER (fabrication, nec), 729.684-022

06.02.22 LAMINATOR (rubber goods), 899.684-018

06.02.22 MACHINE ASSEMBLER (machinery mfg.), 638.361-010

06.02.22 MOTORCYCLE ASSEMBLER (motor-bicycles), 806.684-090

06.02.22 TRANSFORMER ASSEMBLER II (elec. equip.), 820.684-010

06.02.22 UTILITY WORKER (mfd. bldgs.), 869.684-074

06.02.23 ASSEMBLER I (office machines), 706.684-014

06.02.23 ASSEMBLER, MUSICAL INSTRUMENTS (musical inst.), 730.684-010

06.02.23 ASSEMBLER, PRODUCT (machine shop), 706.684-018

06.02.23 ASSEMBLER, SEMICONDUCTOR (electron. comp.), 726.684-034

06.02.23 CHAIN MAKER, MACHINE (jewelry-silver.), 700.684-022

06.02.23 ELECTRICAL ASSEMBLER (aircraft mfg.), 729.384-026

06.02.23 ELECTRONICS ASSEMBLER (comm. equip.), 726.684-018

06.02.23 INSTRUMENT ASSEMBLER (inst. & app.), 710.684-046

06.02.23 LAMINATION ASSEMBLER (elec. equip.), 729.684-066

06.02.23 PRINTED CIRCUIT BOARD ASSEMBLER, HAND (comm. equip.), 726.684-070

06.02.23 TUBE ASSEMBLER, CATHODE RAY (electron. comp.), 725.684-022

06.02.23 TUBE ASSEMBLER, ELECTRON (electron. comp.), 725.384-010

06.02.23 WHEEL LACER AND TRUER (motor-bicycles), 706.684-106

06.02.24 ASSEMBLER, METAL BONDING (aircraft mfg.), 806.384-030

06.02.24 BOAT PATCHER, PLASTIC (ship-boat mfg.), 807.684-014

06.02.24 BRIGHT CUTTER (jewelry-silver.), 700.684-018

06.02.24 CASTER (jewelry-silver.), 502.381-010

06.02.24 FABRICATOR-ASSEMBLER, METAL PRODUCTS (any industry), 809.381-010

06.02.24 GREASE BUFFER (jewelry-silver.), 705.684-022

06.02.24 PRESSURE SEALER-AND-TESTER (aircraft mfg.), 806.384-038

06.02.24 REPAIRER, FINISHED METAL (any industry), 809.684-034

06.02.24 REPAIRER, TYPEWRITER (office machines), 706.381-030

06.02.24 ROUTER OPERATOR, HAND (aircraft mfg.), 806.684-150

06.02.24 SKI REPAIRER, PRODUCTION (toy-sport equip.), 732.684-118

06.02.24 SPINNER (jewelry-silver.), 700.684-074

06.02.24 STRAIGHTENER, HAND (any industry), 709.484-014

06.02.24 TROPHY ASSEMBLER (jewelry-silver.), 735.684-018

06.02.27 CUTTER, HAND I (any industry), 781.684-074

06.02.27 LEATHER CUTTER (leather prod.), 783.684-022

06.02.27 LEATHER WORKER (leather prod.), 783.684-026

06.02.27 RUG CLEANER, HAND (laundry & rel.), 369.384-014

06.02.27 SPOTTER I (laundry & rel.), 361.684-018

06.02.28 BENCH HAND (bakery products), 520.384-010

06.02.28 BUTCHER, ALL-ROUND (meat products), 525.381-014

06.02.28 CANDY MAKER (sugar & conf.), 529.361-014

06.02.28 DOUGHNUT MAKER (bakery products), 526.684-010

06.02.29 RUBBER-GOODS REPAIRER (any industry), 759.684-054

06.02.30 CASTER (nonmet. min.), 575.684-018

06.02.30 CEMENTER (optical goods), 711.684-014

06.02.30 GLASS CUTTER (any industry), 775.684-022

06.02.30 MOLDER (optical goods), 575.381-010

06.02.30 PLASTER MAKER (nonmet. min.), 779.684-046

06.02.30 PLASTER-DIE MAKER (pottery & porc.), 774.684-026

06.02.30 THROWER (pottery & porc.), 774.381-010

06.02.31 LAY-OUT WORKER II (any industry), 809.381-014

06.02.32 BONDED STRUCTURES REPAIRER (aircraft mfg.), 807.381-014

06.02.32 CATHODE RAY TUBE SALVAGE PROCESSOR (electron. comp.), 725.684-026

06.02.32 COIL WINDER, REPAIR (any industry), 724.381-014

06.02.32 DENTURE WAXER (protective dev.), 712.381-046

06.02.32 ETCHED-CIRCUIT PROCESSOR (electron. comp.), 590.684-018

06.02.32 OPAQUER (protective dev.), 712.684-030

06.02.32 RACKET STRINGER (toy-sport equip.), 732.684-094

06.02.32 SKI MOLDER (toy-sport equip.), 732.684-114

06.03.01 COMPARATOR OPERATOR (any industry), 699.384-010

06.03.01 INSPECTOR (plastic prod.), 559.381-010

06.03.01 INSPECTOR II (pottery & porc.), 774.384-010

06.03.01 INSPECTOR, PRINTED CIRCUIT BOARDS (electron. comp.), 726.684-062

06.03.01 INSPECTOR, RECEIVING (aircraft mfg.), 222.384-010

06.03.01 MACHINE TESTER (office machines), 706.387-014

06.03.01 MOTORCYCLE TESTER (motor-bicycles), 620.384-010

06.03.01 SPECIAL TESTER (tobacco), 529.487-010

06.03.01 TEST DRIVER I (auto. mfg.), 806.283-014

06.03.02 ELECTRONICS INSPECTOR (electron. comp.), 726.684-022

06.03.02 ELECTRONICS TESTER (comm. equip.), 726.684-026

06.03.02 GARMENT INSPECTOR (any industry), 789.687-070

06.03.02 GAS-LEAK TESTER (svc. ind. mach.), 827.584-014

06.03.02 GLASS INSPECTOR (any industry), 579.687-022

06.03.02 GRADER (woodworking), 669.687-030

06.03.02 HYDRO-PNEUMATIC TESTER (any industry), 862.687-018

06.03.02 INKER (print. & pub.), 659.667-010

06.03.02 INSPECTOR (pharmaceut.), 559.387-014

06.03.02 INSPECTOR, INTEGRATED CIRCUITS (electron. comp.), 726.684-058

06.03.02 INSPECTOR, SEMICONDUCTOR WAFER (electron. comp.), 726.684-066

06.03.02 INSTRUMENT INSPECTOR (inst. & app.), 710.684-050

06.03.02 METAL-FINISH INSPECTOR (any industry), 703.687-014

06.03.02 PHOTO CHECKER AND ASSEMBLER (photofinishing), 976.687-014

06.03.02 PHOTOFINISHING LABORATORY WORKER (photofinishing), 976.687-018

06.03.02 PLATE INSPECTOR (print. & pub.), 972.687-010

06.03.02 PRINT INSPECTOR (pottery & porc.), 774.687-018

06.03.02 QUALITY ASSURANCE GROUP LEADER (auto. mfg.), 806.367-014

06.03.02 QUALITY ASSURANCE MONITOR (auto. mfg.), 806.367-018

06.03.02 SELECTOR (glass mfg.), 579.687-030

06.03.02 WATER LEAK REPAIRER (auto. mfg.), 807.684-034

06.04.02 BENDING-MACHINE OPERATOR II (any industry), 617.685-010

06.04.02 BUFFING-MACHINE TENDER (any industry), 603.665-010

06.04.02 DRILL PRESS TENDER (machine shop), 606.685-026

06.04.02 ELECTRIC-SEALING-MACHINE OPERATOR (any industry), 690.685-154

06.04.02 EMBOSSER (any industry), 583.685-030

06.04.02 GRAINER, MACHINE (any industry), 652.686-014

06.04.02 GRINDER (plastic prod.), 555.685-026

06.04.02 MACHINE OPERATOR II (any industry), 619.685-062

06.04.02 NIBBLER OPERATOR (any industry), 615.685-026

06.04.02 POWER-PRESS TENDER (any industry), 617.685-026

06.04.02 PUNCH-PRESS OPERATOR II (any industry), 615.685-030

06.04.02 SCROLL-MACHINE OPERATOR (struct. metal), 616.685-062

06.04.02 TOOL DRESSER (any industry), 601.682-010

06.04.02 TURRET-PUNCH-PRESS OPERATOR, TAPE-CONTROL (any industry), 615.685-042

06.04.03 BUZZSAW OPERATOR (any industry), 667.685-026

06.04.03 CHAIN OFFBEARER (saw. & plan.), 669.686-018

06.04.03 GLUING-MACHINE OPERATOR (woodworking), 569.685-046

06.04.03 LATHE SPOTTER (millwork-plywood), 663.686-022

06.04.04 BAG-MACHINE OPERATOR (paper goods), 649.685-014

06.04.04 BINDERY WORKER (print. & pub.), 653.685-010

06.04.04 BOOK TRIMMER (print. & pub.), 640.685-010

06.04.04 CARTON-FORMING-MACHINE OPERATOR (any industry), 641.685-022

06.04.04 CARTON-FORMING-MACHINE TENDER (paper goods), 641.685-026

06.04.05 BUTTONHOLE-AND-BUTTON-SEWING-MACHINE OPERATOR (garment), 786.685-042

06.04.05 PRESSER, MACHINE (any industry), 363.682-018

06.04.05 SEWING-MACHINE OPERATOR, SEMI-AUTOMATIC (garment), 786.685-030

06.04.05 SPREADER, MACHINE (any industry), 781.685-010

06.04.05 STRIP-CUTTING-MACHINE OPERATOR (textile), 686.685-066

06.04.05 SURGICAL-DRESSING MAKER (protective dev.), 689.685-130

06.04.06 BEAM-WARPER TENDER, AUTOMATIC (knitting), 681.685-018

06.04.06 CLOTH DOFFER (textile), 689.686-058

06.04.06 KNITTING-MACHINE OPERATOR (knitting), 685.665-014

06.04.06 PICKING-MACHINE OPERATOR (any industry), 680.685-082

06.04.06 SEAMLESS-HOSIERY KNITTER (knitting), 684.685-010

06.04.06 YARN WINDER (tex. prod., nec), 681.685-154

06.04.07 DESIGN PRINTER, BALLOON (rubber goods), 651.685-014

06.04.07 RUBBER CUTTER (rubber goods), 559.685-158

06.04.08 CERAMIC CAPACITOR PROCESSOR (electron. comp.), 590.684-010

06.04.08 COREMAKER, MACHINE I (foundry), 518.685-014

06.04.08 CRUSHER TENDER (any industry), 570.685-022

06.04.08 LENS-FABRICATING-MACHINE TENDER (optical goods), 716.685-022

06.04.08 MILLER (cement), 570.685-046

06.04.09 CUTTER (photofinishing), 976.685-010

06.04.09 CUTTER, MACHINE II (any industry), 699.685-014

06.04.09 MACHINE FEEDER (any industry), 699.686-010

06.04.09 PHOTORESIST LAMINATOR, PRINTED CIRCUIT BOARD (electron. comp.), 554.685-034

06.04.09 SANDER (toy-sport equip.), 690.685-346

06.04.09 SCRAP HANDLER (any industry), 509.685-050

06.04.09 SILK-SCREEN PRINTER, MACHINE (any industry), 979.685-010

06.04.09 STAMPING-PRESS OPERATOR (any industry), 652.682-030

06.04.09 TRACK LAMINATING MACHINE TENDER (inst. & app.), 692.685-290

06.04.09 WAX MOLDER (foundry), 549.685-038

06.04.10 ANNEALER (jewelry-silver.), 504.687-010

06.04.10 INJECTION-MOLDING-MACHINE TENDER (plastic prod.), 556.685-038

06.04.11 CHEMICAL OPERATOR II (chemical), 558.685-062

06.04.11 CHEMICAL PREPARER (chemical), 550.685-030

06.04.11 DRIER OPERATOR (chemical), 553.685-042

06.04.11 MIXER (paint & varnish), 550.685-078

06.04.11 PAINT MIXER, MACHINE (any industry), 550.485-018

06.04.12 CYLINDER FILLER (chemical), 559.565-010

06.04.13 BLOW-MOLDING-MACHINE TENDER (toy-sport equip.), 556.685-086

06.04.13 COMPRESSION-MOLDING-MACHINE TENDER (plastic prod.), 556.685-022

06.04.13 FUSING-FURNACE LOADER (optical goods), 573.686-014

06.04.13 TIRE MOLDER (rubber tire), 553.685-102

06.04.15 BAKER HELPER (bakery products), 526.686-010

06.04.15 BATTER MIXER (bakery products), 520.685-010

06.04.15 BREWERY CELLAR WORKER (beverage), 522.685-014

06.04.15 CANNERY WORKER (can. & preserv.), 529.686-014

06.04.15 CENTRIFUGE OPERATOR (dairy products), 521.685-042

06.04.15 CHEESE CUTTER (dairy products), 529.585-010

06.04.15 CHOCOLATE MOLDER, MACHINE (sugar & conf.), 529.685-054

06.04.15 COFFEE GRINDER (food prep., nec), 521.685-078

06.04.15 COOK, FRY, DEEP FAT (can. & preserv.), 526.685-014

06.04.15 FLOUR BLENDER (grain-feed mills), 520.685-106

06.04.15 HONEY PROCESSOR (food prep., nec), 522.685-070

06.04.15 MEAT GRINDER (meat products), 521.685-214

06.04.15 MIXING-MACHINE OPERATOR (food prep., nec), 520.665-014

06.04.15 OVEN OPERATOR, AUTOMATIC (bakery products), 526.685-070

06.04.15 PRESS OPERATOR, MEAT (meat products), 520.685-182

06.04.16 MACHINE FEEDER, RAW STOCK (tex. prod., nec), 680.686-018

06.04.16 SLASHER TENDER (textile), 582.562-010

06.04.17 KILN WORKER (pottery & porc.), 573.687-022

06.04.17 SHELL MOLDER (foundry), 518.685-026

06.04.18 DIGESTER-OPERATOR HELPER (paper & pulp), 532.686-010

06.04.18 TANKER (wood prod., nec), 561.665-010

06.04.19 COATING EQUIPMENT OPERATOR, PRINTED CIRCUIT BOARDS (electron. comp.), 590.685-066

06.04.19 CREMATOR (personal ser.), 359.685-010

06.04.19 DEVELOPER, AUTOMATIC (photofinishing), 976.685-014

06.04.19 DISPLAY-SCREEN FABRICATOR (electron. comp.), 725.685-010

06.04.19 ELECTRONIC-COMPONENT PROCESSOR (electron. comp.), 590.684-014

06.04.19 FILTER OPERATOR (any industry), 551.685-078

06.04.19 LABORER (pharmaceut.), 559.686-022

06.04.19 METALLIZATION EQUIPMENT TENDER, SEMICONDUCTORS (comm. equip.), 590.685-086

06.04.19 PLATER, SEMICONDUCTOR WAFERS AND COMPONENTS (electron. comp.), 500.684-030

06.04.19 POLYSILICON PREPARATION WORKER (electron. comp.), 590.684-038

06.04.19 PRINT DEVELOPER, AUTOMATIC (photofinishing), 976.685-026

06.04.19 STERILIZER (medical ser.), 599.585-010

06.04.19 STILL TENDER (any industry), 552.685-026

06.04.19 STRIPPER-ETCHER, PRINTED CIRCUIT BOARDS (electron. comp.), 590.685-082

06.04.19 THERMOMETER PRODUCTION WORKER (inst. & app.), 710.685-014

06.04.19 UTILITY WORKER, FILM PROCESSING (photofinishing), 976.685-030

06.04.20 CORRUGATED-FASTENER DRIVER (woodworking), 669.685-042

06.04.20 MOUNTER, AUTOMATIC (photofinishing), 976.685-022

06.04.20 STAPLING-MACHINE OPERATOR (any industry), 692.685-202

06.04.21 CERAMIC COATER, MACHINE (any industry), 509.685-022

06.04.21 DIPPER AND BAKER (any industry), 599.685-030

06.04.21 PLATING EQUIPMENT TENDER (electroplating), 500.685-014

06.04.21 SEED PELLETER (agriculture), 599.685-126

06.04.21 SPRAY-UNIT FEEDER (any industry), 599.686-014

06.04.22 ASSEMBLER, BICYCLE II (motor-bicycles), 806.687-010

06.04.22 ASSEMBLER, MOTOR VEHICLE (auto. mfg.), 806.684-010

06.04.22 ASSEMBLER, PRODUCTION (any industry), 706.687-010

06.04.22 LAMINATOR, HAND (furniture), 763.684-050

06.04.22 NAILER, HAND (any industry), 762.684-050

06.04.22 PLASTIC-TOP ASSEMBLER (furniture), 763.684-062

06.04.23 ASSEMBLER, MOLDED FRAMES (optical goods), 713.684-014

06.04.23 ASSEMBLER, SMALL PRODUCTS I (any industry), 706.684-022

06.04.23 BATTERY ASSEMBLER, DRY CELL (elec. equip.), 727.664-010

06.04.23 COIL WINDER (elec. equip.), 724.684-026

06.04.23 EARRING MAKER (jewelry-silver.), 700.684-030

06.04.23 ELECTRIC-MOTOR ASSEMBLER (elec. equip.), 721.684-022

06.04.23 FISHING-REEL ASSEMBLER (toy-sport equip.), 732.684-062

06.04.23 LENS INSERTER (optical goods), 713.687-026

06.04.23 LOCK ASSEMBLER (cutlery-hrdwr.), 706.684-074

06.04.23 RUBBER-GOODS ASSEMBLER (rubber goods), 752.684-038

06.04.23 SILK-SCREEN-FRAME ASSEMBLER (any industry), 709.484-010

06.04.23 TIRE MOUNTER (fabrication, nec), 739.684-158

06.04.23 TOY ASSEMBLER (toy-sport equip.), 731.687-034

06.04.24 ASSEMBLER, PLASTIC HOSPITAL PRODUCTS (inst. & app.), 712.687-010

06.04.24 BENCH WORKER (optical goods), 713.684-018

06.04.24 BUFFER I (any industry), 705.684-014

06.04.24 FILER (jewelry-silver.), 700.684-034

06.04.24 JIGSAWYER (jewelry-silver.), 700.684-046

06.04.24 MELTER (jewelry-silver.), 700.687-042

06.04.24 METAL FINISHER (any industry), 705.684-034

06.04.24 MOLD DRESSER (any industry), 519.684-018

06.04.24 POLISHER (any industry), 705.684-058

06.04.24 PREPARER (jewelry-silver.), 700.687-062

06.04.24 REFINER (protective dev.), 712.684-038

06.04.25 CANER II (furniture), 763.684-022

06.04.25 CROSSBAND LAYER (millwork-plywood), 762.687-026

06.04.25 WOODWORKING-SHOP HAND (woodworking), 769.687-054

06.04.26 LABEL CODER (any industry), 920.587-014

06.04.27 BOW MAKER (any industry), 789.684-010

06.04.27 CANVAS REPAIRER (any industry), 782.684-010

06.04.27 CARPET CUTTER II (carpet & rug), 585.687-014

06.04.27 SEWER, HAND (any industry), 782.684-058

06.04.27 THREAD CUTTER (any industry), 789.684-050

06.04.28 BONER, MEAT (meat products), 525.684-010

06.04.28 BUTCHER, FISH (can. & preserv.), 525.684-014

06.04.28 CANDY DIPPER, HAND (sugar & conf.), 524.684-010

06.04.28 DECORATOR (bakery products), 524.684-014

06.04.28 FISH CLEANER (can. & preserv.), 525.684-030

06.04.28 POULTRY BONER (meat products), 525.687-066

06.04.28 POULTRY DRESSER (agriculture), 525.687-070

06.04.28 TIER (meat products), 525.687-118

06.04.28 TRIMMER, MEAT (meat products), 525.684-054

06.04.30 GLASS FINISHER (glass products), 775.684-026

06.04.31 WELDER, GUN (welding), 810.664-010
06.04.32 CANDLEMAKER (fabrication, nec), 739.664-010
06.04.32 MOLD MAKER (smelt. & refin.), 518.664-010
06.04.32 SEMICONDUCTOR PROCESSOR (electron. comp.), 590.684-022
06.04.33 PAINTER, BRUSH (any industry), 740.684-022
06.04.33 PUTTY GLAZER (any industry), 749.684-042
06.04.34 ARTIFICIAL-FLOWER MAKER (button & notion), 739.684-014
06.04.34 DRILLER, HAND (any industry), 809.684-018
06.04.34 ELECTRONICS UTILITY WORKER (comm. equip.), 726.364-018
06.04.34 ELECTRONICS WORKER (electron. comp.), 726.687-010
06.04.34 INTEGRATED CIRCUIT FABRICATOR (electron. comp.), 590.684-042
06.04.34 LABORER, GRINDING AND POLISHING (any industry), 705.687-014
06.04.34 MACHINE SNELLER (toy-sport equip.), 732.685-026
06.04.34 MASKER (any industry), 749.687-018
06.04.34 MAT CUTTER (wood prod., nec), 739.684-126
06.04.34 PAINT MIXER, HAND (any industry), 550.684-018
06.04.34 PHOTO MASK CLEANER (electron. comp.), 590.684-034
06.04.34 SCREEN PRINTER (any industry), 979.684-034
06.04.34 STUFFER (toy-sport equip.), 731.685-014
06.04.34 WIREWORKER (elec. equip.), 728.684-022
06.04.35 DRY CLEANER, HAND (laundry & rel.), 362.684-010
06.04.35 FURNITURE CLEANER (laundry & rel.), 362.684-022
06.04.35 LAUNDERER, HAND (laundry & rel.), 361.684-010
06.04.35 LAUNDRY LABORER (laundry & rel.), 361.687-018
06.04.35 LAUNDRY OPERATOR (laundry & rel.), 369.684-014
06.04.35 LEATHER CLEANER (laundry & rel.), 362.684-026
06.04.35 PRESS OPERATOR (laundry & rel.), 363.685-010
06.04.35 PRESSER, ALL-AROUND (laundry & rel.), 363.682-014
06.04.35 PRESSER, HAND (any industry), 363.684-018
06.04.35 SILK FINISHER (laundry & rel.), 363.681-010
06.04.35 WASHER, HAND (laundry & rel.), 361.687-030
06.04.35 WASHER, MACHINE (laundry & rel.), 361.665-010
06.04.37 MARKER, SEMICONDUCTOR WAFERS (electron. comp.), 920.587-026
06.04.37 NAME-PLATE STAMPER (any industry), 652.685-054
06.04.37 STENCILER (any industry), 920.687-178
06.04.38 BANDER, HAND (any industry), 929.687-058
06.04.38 CRATER (any industry), 920.684-010
06.04.38 MAILING-MACHINE OPERATOR (print. & pub.), 208.462-010
06.04.38 PACKAGER, HAND (any industry), 920.587-018

06.04.38 PACKAGER, MACHINE (any industry), 920.685-078
06.04.38 PACKING-LINE WORKER (rubber goods), 753.687-038
06.04.39 CLEANER (ordnance), 503.684-010
06.04.39 CLEANER AND POLISHER (any industry), 709.687-010
06.04.39 EQUIPMENT CLEANER (any industry), 599.684-010
06.04.39 MACHINE CLEANER (any industry), 699.687-014
06.04.39 SCRUBBER MACHINE TENDER (electron. comp.), 599.685-134
06.04.40 CHAR-CONVEYOR TENDER (sugar & conf.), 529.685-050
06.04.40 COMPRESSED-GAS-PLANT WORKER (chemical), 549.587-010
06.04.40 CONVEYOR FEEDER-OFFBEARER (any industry), 921.686-014
06.04.40 DISTILLERY WORKER, GENERAL (beverage), 529.687-066
06.04.40 FINISHER (plastic-synth.), 554.586-010
06.04.40 INDUSTRIAL-TRUCK OPERATOR (any industry), 921.683-050
06.04.40 LABORER, CHEMICAL PROCESSING (chemical), 559.687-050
06.04.40 LABORER, CONCRETE PLANT (concrete prod.), 579.687-042
06.04.40 LABORER, GENERAL (steel & rel.), 509.687-026
06.04.40 LABORER, GENERAL (plastic-synth.), 559.667-014
06.04.40 LOADER I (any industry), 914.667-010
06.04.40 PALLETIZER OPERATOR I (any industry), 921.682-014
06.04.40 SAWMILL WORKER (saw. & plan.), 667.687-018
07.01.02 ADMINISTRATIVE CLERK (clerical), 219.362-010
07.01.02 LABOR EXPEDITER (construction), 249.167-018
07.01.02 PROCUREMENT CLERK (clerical), 249.367-066
07.01.02 SUPERVISOR, SAFETY DEPOSIT (financial), 295.137-010
07.01.02 TEACHER AIDE II (education), 249.367-074
07.01.02 TOWN CLERK (government ser.), 243.367-018
07.01.03 SOCIAL SECRETARY (clerical), 201.162-010
07.01.03 TRUST OPERATIONS ASSISTANT (financial), 219.362-074
07.01.04 MORTGAGE CLERK (financial), 249.362-014
07.01.04 MORTGAGE LOAN CLOSER (financial), 249.362-018
07.01.04 REAL-ESTATE CLERK (real estate), 219.362-046
07.01.04 VAULT CASHIER (business ser.), 222.137-050
07.02.01 RESERVES CLERK (financial), 216.362-034
07.02.02 BROKERAGE CLERK I (financial), 219.482-010
07.02.02 CALCULATING-MACHINE OPERATOR (clerical), 216.482-022
07.02.02 CANCELLATION CLERK (insurance), 203.382-014

07.02.02 CONTRACT CLERK, AUTOMOBILE (retail trade), 219.362-026

07.02.02 COUPON CLERK (financial), 219.462-010

07.02.02 CREDIT-CARD CLERK (hotel & rest.), 210.382-038

07.02.02 NIGHT AUDITOR (hotel & rest.), 210.382-054

07.02.02 POLICY-CHANGE CLERK (insurance), 219.362-042

07.02.02 STATEMENT CLERK (financial), 214.362-046

07.02.04 ADVERTISING CLERK (business ser.), 247.387-010

07.02.04 BILLING-CONTROL CLERK (utilities), 214.387-010

07.02.04 DEMURRAGE CLERK (r.r. trans.), 214.362-010

07.02.04 INSURANCE CLERK (medical ser.), 214.362-022

07.02.04 INVOICE-CONTROL CLERK (clerical), 214.362-026

07.02.04 RATER (insurance), 214.482-022

07.02.04 REINSURANCE CLERK (insurance), 219.482-018

07.02.04 TAX CLERK (clerical), 219.487-010

07.02.04 TICKETING CLERK (air trans.), 248.382-010

07.02.04 TRAFFIC CLERK (clerical), 214.587-014

07.02.05 PAYROLL CLERK (clerical), 215.382-014

07.02.05 TIMEKEEPER (clerical), 215.362-022

07.03.01 AUCTION CLERK (retail trade), 294.567-010

07.03.01 CASHIER II (clerical), 211.462-010

07.03.01 CASHIER, GAMBLING (amuse. & rec.), 211.462-022

07.03.01 CASHIER-CHECKER (retail trade), 211.462-014

07.03.01 CHANGE PERSON (amuse. & rec.), 211.467-034

07.03.01 CHECK CASHIER (business ser.), 211.462-026

07.03.01 COUNTER CLERK (photofinishing), 249.366-010

07.03.01 COUPON-REDEMPTION CLERK (retail trade), 290.477-010

07.03.01 INFORMATION CLERK-CASHIER (amuse. & rec.), 249.467-010

07.03.01 LAYAWAY CLERK (retail trade), 299.467-010

07.03.01 PARIMUTUEL-TICKET CASHIER (amuse. & rec.), 211.467-018

07.03.01 PARIMUTUEL-TICKET SELLER (amuse. & rec.), 211.467-022

07.03.01 TELLER, HEAD (financial), 211.132-010

07.03.01 TICKET SELLER (clerical), 211.467-030

07.03.01 TOLL COLLECTOR (government ser.), 211.462-038

07.04.01 BLOOD-DONOR-UNIT ASSISTANT (medical ser.), 245.367-014

07.04.01 EMPLOYMENT-AND-CLAIMS AIDE (government ser.), 169.367-010

07.04.01 SKIP TRACER (clerical), 241.367-026

07.04.01 SURVEY WORKER (clerical), 205.367-054

07.04.01 TRAFFIC CHECKER (government ser.), 205.367-058

07.04.02 CLAIMS CLERK II (insurance), 205.367-018

07.04.02 COLLECTION CLERK (clerical), 241.357-010

07.04.02 ORDER CLERK, FOOD AND BEVERAGE (hotel & rest.), 209.567-014

07.04.02 REFERRAL-AND-INFORMATION AIDE (government ser.), 237.367-042

07.04.03 ANIMAL-HOSPITAL CLERK (medical ser.), 245.367-010

07.04.03 ANIMAL-SHELTER CLERK (nonprofit org.), 249.367-010

07.04.03 DOG LICENSER (nonprofit org.), 249.367-030

07.04.03 ELECTION CLERK (government ser.), 205.367-030

07.04.03 HOTEL CLERK (hotel & rest.), 238.367-038

07.04.03 RECREATION-FACILITY ATTENDANT (amuse. & rec.), 341.367-010

07.04.03 REGISTRATION CLERK (library), 249.365-010

07.04.04 INFORMATION CLERK, AUTOMOBILE CLUB (nonprofit org.), 237.267-010

07.04.04 POLICYHOLDER-INFORMATION CLERK (insurance), 249.262-010

07.04.04 RECEPTIONIST (clerical), 237.367-038

07.04.04 TELEPHONE QUOTATION CLERK (financial), 237.367-046

07.04.04 TRAVEL CLERK (hotel & rest.), 238.367-030

07.04.05 DISPATCHER, MAINTENANCE SERVICE (clerical), 239.367-014

07.04.05 FIRE LOOKOUT (forestry), 452.367-010

07.04.05 FLIGHT-INFORMATION EXPEDITER (air trans.), 912.367-010

07.04.05 PROTECTIVE-SIGNAL OPERATOR (any industry), 379.362-014

07.04.05 SCOREBOARD OPERATOR (amuse. & rec.), 349.665-010

07.04.05 SERVICE CLERK (clerical), 221.367-070

07.04.05 SWITCHBOARD OPERATOR, POLICE DISTRICT (government ser.), 235.562-014

07.04.06 CENTRAL-OFFICE OPERATOR (tel. & tel.), 235.462-010

07.04.06 DIRECTORY-ASSISTANCE OPERATOR (tel. & tel.), 235.662-018

07.04.06 TELEPHONE OPERATOR (clerical), 235.662-022

07.04.06 TELEPHONE-ANSWERING-SERVICE OPERATOR (business ser.), 235.662-026

07.05.01 ADVERTISING-DISPATCH CLERK (print. & pub.), 247.387-014

07.05.01 CREW SCHEDULER (air trans.), 215.362-010

07.05.01 DISPATCHER, MOTOR VEHICLE (clerical), 249.167-014

07.05.01 GUIDE, TRAVEL (personal ser.), 353.167-010

07.05.01 PERSONNEL SCHEDULER (clerical), 215.367-014

07.05.01 RESERVATION CLERK (r.r. trans.), 238.367-014

07.05.01 SCHEDULER, MAINTENANCE (clerical), 221.367-066

07.05.01 TRAFFIC CLERK (business ser.), 221.367-078

07.05.01 TRANSPORTATION AGENT (air trans.), 912.367-014

07.05.02 CLASSIFIED-AD CLERK II (print. & pub.), 247.387-022

07.05.02 CREDIT AUTHORIZER (clerical), 249.367-022

07.05.02 DISBURSEMENT CLERK (financial),
219.367-046
07.05.02 MORTGAGE LOAN PROCESSOR (financial),
249.362-022
07.05.02 PARIMUTUEL-TICKET CHECKER (amuse. &
rec.), 219.587-010
07.05.02 PRODUCTION PROOFREADER (print. & pub.),
247.667-010
07.05.02 READER (business ser.), 249.387-022
07.05.02 THROW-OUT CLERK (retail trade),
241.367-030
07.05.02 TITLE SEARCHER (real estate), 209.367-046
07.05.03 ASSIGNMENT CLERK (clerical), 249.367-090
07.05.03 ATTENDANCE CLERK (education),
219.362-014
07.05.03 AUTOMOBILE LOCATOR (retail trade),
296.367-010
07.05.03 CALL-OUT OPERATOR (business ser.),
237.367-014
07.05.03 COMPILER (clerical), 209.387-014
07.05.03 CONTINUITY CLERK (motion picture),
209.382-010
07.05.03 CREDIT CARD CONTROL CLERK (financial),
249.367-026
07.05.03 DETAILER, SCHOOL PHOTOGRAPHS
(photofinishing), 976.564-010
07.05.03 DIET CLERK (medical ser.), 245.587-010
07.05.03 DOCUMENT PREPARER, MICROFILMING
(business ser.), 249.587-018
07.05.03 MEDICAL-RECORD CLERK (medical ser.),
245.362-010
07.05.03 ORDER CLERK (clerical), 249.362-026
07.05.03 PROPERTY CLERK (government ser.),
222.367-054
07.05.03 QUALITY-CONTROL CLERK (pharmaceut.),
229.587-014
07.05.03 REPAIR-ORDER CLERK (clerical),
221.382-022
07.05.03 REPRODUCTION ORDER PROCESSOR
(clerical), 221.367-058
07.05.03 STENOTYPE OPERATOR (clerical),
202.362-022
07.05.03 STOCK CONTROL CLERK (clerical),
219.387-030
07.05.03 TAXICAB COORDINATOR (motor trans.),
215.367-018
07.05.03 UNIT CLERK (medical ser.), 245.362-014
07.05.03 YARD CLERK (r.r. trans.), 209.367-054
07.05.04 MAIL CARRIER (government ser.),
230.367-010
07.05.04 MAIL CLERK (clerical), 209.687-026
07.05.04 MAIL HANDLER (government ser.),
209.687-014
07.05.04 MERCHANDISE DISTRIBUTOR (retail trade),
219.367-018
07.05.04 PARCEL POST CLERK (clerical), 222.387-038
07.05.04 ROUTE-DELIVERY CLERK (clerical),
222.587-034
07.05.04 ROUTING CLERK (nonprofit org.), 249.367-070
07.05.04 RURAL MAIL CARRIER (government ser.),
230.363-010

07.05.04 SHIPPING-ORDER CLERK (clerical),
219.367-030
07.05.04 VAULT WORKER (business ser.), 222.587-058
07.06.01 COMPUTER PERIPHERAL EQUIPMENT
OPERATOR (clerical), 213.382-010
07.06.01 CREDIT REPORTING CLERK (business ser.),
203.362-014
07.06.01 DATA ENTRY CLERK (clerical), 203.582-054
07.06.01 TERMINAL-MAKEUP OPERATOR (print. &
pub.), 208.382-010
07.06.02 BRAILLE OPERATOR (print. & pub.),
203.582-010
07.06.02 CHECK WRITER (retail trade), 219.382-010
07.06.02 CLERK-TYPIST (clerical), 203.362-010
07.06.02 FOOD CHECKER (hotel & rest.), 211.482-014
07.06.02 MAGNETIC-TAPE-COMPOSER OPERATOR
(print. & pub.), 203.382-018
07.06.02 PHOTOCOMPOSITION-KEYBOARD OPERA-
TOR (print. & pub.), 203.582-046
07.06.02 PHOTOTYPESETTER OPERATOR (print. &
pub.), 650.582-022
07.06.02 PROOF-MACHINE OPERATOR (financial),
217.382-010
07.06.02 TRANSCRIBING-MACHINE OPERATOR
(clerical), 203.582-058
07.06.02 TYPIST (clerical), 203.582-066
07.06.02 VARITYPE OPERATOR (clerical), 203.382-026
07.06.02 WIRE-TRANSFER CLERK (financial),
203.562-010
07.06.02 WORD PROCESSING MACHINE OPERATOR
(clerical), 203.382-030
07.07.01 FILE CLERK I (clerical), 206.387-034
07.07.02 ADDRESSER (clerical), 209.587-010
07.07.02 AUCTION ASSISTANT (retail trade),
294.667-010
07.07.02 CHECKER I (clerical), 222.687-010
07.07.02 DELIVERER, OUTSIDE (clerical), 230.663-010
07.07.02 DIRECT-MAIL CLERK (clerical), 209.587-018
07.07.02 DISTRIBUTING CLERK (clerical), 222.587-018
07.07.02 MAILROOM SUPERVISOR (print. & pub.),
222.137-022
07.07.02 MONEY COUNTER (amuse. & rec.),
211.467-014
07.07.02 PROCESS SERVER (business ser.), 249.367-062
07.07.02 ROUTER (clerical), 222.587-038
07.07.02 ROUTING CLERK (clerical), 222.687-022
07.07.02 SORTER (clerical), 209.687-022
07.07.02 SUPERVISOR, ADVERTISING-MATERIAL
DISTRIBUTORS (business ser.), 230.137-010
07.07.02 TELEPHONE-DIRECTORY DELIVERER
(business ser.), 230.667-014
07.07.03 CLERK, GENERAL (clerical), 209.562-010
07.07.03 COIN-MACHINE COLLECTOR (business ser.),
292.687-010
07.07.03 OFFICE HELPER (clerical), 239.567-010
08.01.01 SALES REPRESENTATIVE, AIRCRAFT (retail
trade), 273.253-010
08.01.01 SALES REPRESENTATIVE, COMMUNICA-
TION EQUIPMENT (wholesale tr.), 271.257-010
08.01.01 SALES REPRESENTATIVE, ELECTRONICS
PARTS (wholesale tr.), 271.357-010

08.01.02 PLACER (insurance), 239.267-010

08.01.02 SALES REPRESENTATIVE, SHIPPING SERVICES (motor trans.), 252.357-014

08.01.02 TRAFFIC AGENT (air trans.), 252.257-010

08.01.03 BUSINESS-OPPORTUNITY-AND-PROPERTY-INVESTMENT BROKER (business ser.), 189.157-010

08.01.03 COMMISSION AGENT, AGRICULTURAL PRODUCE (wholesale tr.), 260.357-010

08.01.03 COMPARISON SHOPPER (retail trade), 296.367-014

08.01.03 PAWNBROKER (retail trade), 191.157-010

08.01.03 SALES REPRESENTATIVE, LIVESTOCK (wholesale tr.), 260.257-010

08.02.01 SALES REPRESENTATIVE, ANIMAL-FEED PRODUCTS (wholesale tr.), 272.357-010

08.02.01 SALES REPRESENTATIVE, FARM AND GARDEN EQUIPMENT AND SUPPLIES (wholesale tr.), 272.357-014

08.02.01 SALES REPRESENTATIVE, FOOD PRODUCTS (wholesale tr.), 260.357-014

08.02.01 SALES REPRESENTATIVE, HOME FURNISHINGS (wholesale tr.), 270.357-010

08.02.01 SALES REPRESENTATIVE, HOUSEHOLD APPLIANCES (wholesale tr.), 270.357-014

08.02.01 SALES REPRESENTATIVE, MALT LIQUORS (wholesale tr.), 260.357-018

08.02.01 SALES REPRESENTATIVE, MEN'S AND BOYS' APPAREL (wholesale tr.), 261.357-022

08.02.01 SALES REPRESENTATIVE, PETROLEUM PRODUCTS (wholesale tr.), 269.357-014

08.02.01 SALES REPRESENTATIVE, RECREATION AND SPORTING GOODS (wholesale tr.), 277.357-026

08.02.01 SALES REPRESENTATIVE, TEXTILES (wholesale tr.), 261.357-030

08.02.01 SALES REPRESENTATIVE, VIDEOTAPE (wholesale tr.), 271.357-014

08.02.01 SALES REPRESENTATIVE, WOMEN'S AND GIRLS' APPAREL (wholesale tr.), 261.357-038

08.02.01 SALES-PROMOTION REPRESENTATIVE (wholesale tr.), 269.357-018

08.02.02 SALES EXHIBITOR (nonprofit org.), 279.357-010

08.02.02 SALESPERSON, ART OBJECTS (retail trade), 277.457-010

08.02.02 SALESPERSON, BOOKS (retail trade), 277.357-034

08.02.02 SALESPERSON, COSMETICS AND TOILETRIES (retail trade), 262.357-018

08.02.02 SALESPERSON, CURTAINS AND DRAPERIES (retail trade), 270.357-022

08.02.02 SALESPERSON, FLOWERS (retail trade), 260.357-026

08.02.02 SALESPERSON, FURNITURE (retail trade), 270.357-030

08.02.02 SALESPERSON, HOUSEHOLD APPLIANCES (retail trade), 270.357-034

08.02.02 SALESPERSON, INFANTS' AND CHILDREN'S WEAR (retail trade), 261.357-046

08.02.02 SALESPERSON, MEN'S AND BOYS' CLOTHING (retail trade), 261.357-050

08.02.02 SALESPERSON, MUSICAL INSTRUMENTS AND ACCESSORIES (retail trade), 277.357-038

08.02.02 SALESPERSON, ORTHOPEDIC SHOES (retail trade), 276.257-018

08.02.02 SALESPERSON, PETS AND PET SUPPLIES (retail trade), 277.357-042

08.02.02 SALESPERSON, PHONOGRAPH RECORDS AND TAPE RECORDINGS (retail trade), 277.357-046

08.02.02 SALESPERSON, PIANOS AND ORGANS (retail trade), 277.354-010

08.02.02 SALESPERSON, SHEET MUSIC (retail trade), 277.357-054

08.02.02 SALESPERSON, SHOES (retail trade), 261.357-062

08.02.02 SALESPERSON, SPORTING GOODS (retail trade), 277.357-058

08.02.02 SALESPERSON, STEREO EQUIPMENT (retail trade), 270.357-038

08.02.02 SALESPERSON, TOY TRAINS AND ACCESSORIES (retail trade), 277.357-066

08.02.02 SALESPERSON, TRAILERS AND MOTOR HOMES (retail trade), 273.357-034

08.02.02 SALESPERSON, WIGS (personal ser.), 261.351-010

08.02.02 SALESPERSON, WOMEN'S APPAREL AND ACCESSORIES (retail trade), 261.357-066

08.02.02 SALESPERSON, YARD GOODS (retail trade), 261.357-070

08.02.03 AUCTIONEER (retail trade), 294.257-010

08.02.03 SALES REPRESENTATIVE, BOATS AND MARINE SUPPLIES (retail trade), 273.357-018

08.02.03 SALES REPRESENTATIVE, OFFICE MACHINES (retail trade), 275.357-034

08.02.03 SALESPERSON, ELECTRIC MOTORS (retail trade), 271.354-010

08.02.03 SALESPERSON, FLOOR COVERINGS (retail trade), 270.357-026

08.02.03 SALESPERSON, GENERAL HARDWARE (retail trade), 279.357-050

08.02.03 SALESPERSON, GENERAL MERCHANDISE (retail trade), 279.357-054

08.02.03 SALESPERSON, HORTICULTURAL AND NURSERY PRODUCTS (retail trade), 272.357-022

08.02.03 SALESPERSON, PARTS (retail trade), 279.357-062

08.02.03 SALESPERSON, STAMPS OR COINS (retail trade), 277.357-062

08.02.04 LEASING AGENT, RESIDENCE (real estate), 250.357-014

08.02.05 DEMONSTRATOR (retail trade), 297.354-010

08.02.05 DEMONSTRATOR, ELECTRIC-GAS APPLIANCES (utilities), 297.357-010

08.02.05 SALES REPRESENTATIVE, DANCING INSTRUCTIONS (education), 259.357-014

08.02.05 SALESPERSON-DEMONSTRATOR, PARTY PLAN (retail trade), 279.357-038

08.02.06 CRATING-AND-MOVING ESTIMATOR
(motor trans.), 252.357-010

08.02.06 LINEN CONTROLLER (laundry & rel.),
299.357-010

08.02.06 SALES REPRESENTATIVE, AUTOMOTIVE-
LEASING (business ser.), 273.357-014

08.02.06 SALES REPRESENTATIVE, TELEVISION
CABLE SERVICE (radio-tv broad.),
259.357-022

08.02.06 SALES REPRESENTATIVE, UPHOLSTERY
AND FURNITURE REPAIR (retail trade),
259.357-026

08.02.07 DRIVER, SALES ROUTE (retail trade),
292.353-010

08.02.08 FUND RAISER II (nonprofit org.), 293.357-014

08.02.08 GROUP-SALES REPRESENTATIVE (amuse. &
rec.), 259.357-010

08.02.08 MEMBERSHIP SOLICITOR (any industry),
293.357-022

08.02.08 SALES REPRESENTATIVE, DOOR-TO-DOOR
(retail trade), 291.357-010

08.02.08 TELEPHONE SOLICITOR (any industry),
299.357-014

08.03.01 CIGARETTE VENDOR (hotel & rest.),
291.457-010

08.03.01 LOUNGE-CAR ATTENDANT (r.r. trans.),
291.457-014

08.03.01 PHOTOGRAPHER (amuse. & rec.), 143.457-010

08.03.01 VENDOR (amuse. & rec.), 291.457-022

09.01.01 AMUSEMENT PARK WORKER (amuse. &
rec.), 349.664-010

09.01.01 COUNSELOR, CAMP (amuse. & rec.),
159.124-010

09.01.01 DIRECTOR, SOCIAL (hotel & rest.),
352.167-010

09.01.01 GUIDE, HUNTING AND FISHING (amuse. &
rec.), 353.161-010

09.01.01 HOST/HOSTESS (any industry), 352.667-010

09.01.01 RECREATION AIDE (social ser.), 195.367-030

09.01.02 EXHIBIT-DISPLAY REPRESENTATIVE
(any industry), 297.367-010

09.01.02 GUIDE (personal ser.), 353.367-010

09.01.02 GUIDE, PLANT (any industry), 353.367-018

09.01.02 GUIDE, SIGHTSEEING (amuse. & rec.),
353.363-010

09.01.03 HOST/HOSTESS, RESTAURANT (hotel & rest.),
310.137-010

09.01.03 WAITER/WAITRESS, HEAD (hotel & rest.),
311.137-022

09.01.04 FUNERAL ATTENDANT (personal ser.),
359.677-014

09.01.04 PASSENGER SERVICE REPRESENTATIVE I
(r.r. trans.), 352.677-010

09.02.01 HAIR STYLIST (personal ser.), 332.271-018

09.02.01 SCALP-TREATMENT OPERATOR (personal
ser.), 339.371-014

09.03.01 BUS DRIVER (motor trans.), 913.463-010

09.03.01 DRIVER (motor trans.), 913.663-018

09.03.01 STREETCAR OPERATOR (r.r. trans.),
913.463-014

09.03.02 CHAUFFEUR (domestic ser.), 359.673-010

09.03.02 CHAUFFEUR (any industry), 913.663-010

09.03.02 TAXI DRIVER (motor trans.), 913.463-018

09.04.01 BARTENDER (hotel & rest.), 312.474-010

09.04.01 CANTEEN OPERATOR (any industry),
311.674-010

09.04.01 CAR HOP (hotel & rest.), 311.477-010

09.04.01 COUNTER ATTENDANT, LUNCHROOM OR
COFFEE SHOP (hotel & rest.), 311.477-014

09.04.01 FAST-FOODS WORKER (hotel & rest.),
311.472-010

09.04.01 FOUNTAIN SERVER (hotel & rest.),
319.474-010

09.04.01 LUNCH-TRUCK DRIVER (hotel & rest.),
292.463-010

09.04.01 MANAGER, FOOD CONCESSION (hotel &
rest.), 185.167-022

09.04.01 VENDING-MACHINE ATTENDANT (hotel &
rest.), 319.464-014

09.04.01 WAITER/WAITRESS, BAR (hotel & rest.),
311.477-018

09.04.01 WAITER/WAITRESS, FORMAL (hotel & rest.),
311.477-026

09.04.01 WAITER/WAITRESS, INFORMAL (hotel &
rest.), 311.477-030

09.04.01 WAITER/WAITRESS, TAKE OUT (hotel & rest.),
311.477-038

09.04.02 ATTENDANT, ARCADE (amuse. & rec.),
342.667-014

09.04.02 AUTOMOBILE RENTAL CLERK (automotive
ser.), 295.467-026

09.04.02 BICYCLE-RENTAL CLERK (retail trade),
295.467-010

09.04.02 BOAT-RENTAL CLERK (amuse. & rec.),
295.467-014

09.04.02 CASHIER, COURTESY BOOTH (retail trade),
211.467-010

09.04.02 CASHIER-WRAPPER (retail trade), 211.462-018

09.04.02 CURB ATTENDANT (laundry & rel.),
369.477-010

09.04.02 CUSTOMER-SERVICE CLERK (retail trade),
299.367-010

09.04.02 DELIVERER, MERCHANDISE (retail trade),
299.477-010

09.04.02 FLOOR ATTENDANT (amuse. & rec.),
343.467-014

09.04.02 FURNITURE-RENTAL CONSULTANT
(retail trade), 295.357-018

09.04.02 GAMBLING DEALER (amuse. & rec.),
343.464-010

09.04.02 GAME ATTENDANT (amuse. & rec.),
342.657-014

09.04.02 HOSPITAL-TELEVISION-RENTAL CLERK
(business ser.), 295.467-018

09.04.02 MANAGER, BRANCH STORE (laundry & rel.),
369.467-010

09.04.02 NEWSPAPER CARRIER (retail trade),
292.457-010

09.04.02 PARKING-LOT ATTENDANT (automotive ser.),
915.473-010

09.04.02 PERSONAL SHOPPER (retail trade),
296.357-010

09.04.02 SALES ATTENDANT (retail trade), 299.677-010

09.04.02 SALES ATTENDANT, BUILDING MATERIALS (retail trade), 299.677-014

09.04.02 SALES CLERK (retail trade), 290.477-014

09.04.02 SALES CLERK, FOOD (retail trade), 290.477-018

09.04.02 SELF-SERVICE-LAUNDRY-AND-DRY-CLEANING ATTENDANT (laundry & rel.), 369.677-010

09.04.02 SERVICE-ESTABLISHMENT ATTENDANT (laundry & rel.), 369.477-014

09.04.02 STORAGE-FACILITY RENTAL CLERK (business ser.), 295.367-026

09.04.02 TOOL-AND-EQUIPMENT-RENTAL CLERK (business ser.), 295.357-014

09.04.02 TRAILER-RENTAL CLERK (automotive ser.), 295.467-022

09.05.01 COOLING-ROOM ATTENDANT (personal ser.), 335.677-010

09.05.01 ELECTROLOGIST (personal ser.), 339.371-010

09.05.01 FINGERNAIL FORMER (personal ser.), 331.674-014

09.05.01 HOT-ROOM ATTENDANT (personal ser.), 335.677-014

09.05.01 MANICURIST (personal ser.), 331.674-010

09.05.01 MASSEUR/MASSEUSE (personal ser.), 334.374-010

09.05.01 REDUCING-SALON ATTENDANT (personal ser.), 359.567-010

09.05.01 WEIGHT-REDUCTION SPECIALIST (personal ser.), 359.367-014

09.05.02 CAFETERIA ATTENDANT (hotel & rest.), 311.677-010

09.05.02 CATERER HELPER (personal ser.), 319.677-010

09.05.02 COUNTER ATTENDANT, CAFETERIA (hotel & rest.), 311.677-014

09.05.02 COUNTER SUPERVISOR (hotel & rest.), 311.137-010

09.05.02 COUNTER-SUPPLY WORKER (hotel & rest.), 319.687-010

09.05.02 DINING ROOM ATTENDANT (hotel & rest.), 311.677-018

09.05.02 FOOD-SERVICE SUPERVISOR (hotel & rest.), 319.137-010

09.05.02 FOOD-SERVICE WORKER, HOSPITAL (medical ser.), 319.677-014

09.05.02 MESS ATTENDANT (water trans.), 350.677-010

09.05.02 RAW SHELLFISH PREPARER (hotel & rest.), 311.674-014

09.05.02 WAITER/WAITRESS (water trans.), 350.677-030

09.05.02 WAITER/WAITRESS, ROOM SERVICE (hotel & rest.), 311.477-034

09.05.02 WINE STEWARD/STEWARDESS (hotel & rest.), 310.357-010

09.05.03 BAGGAGE PORTER, HEAD (hotel & rest.), 324.137-010

09.05.03 BELL CAPTAIN (hotel & rest.), 324.137-014

09.05.03 BELLHOP (hotel & rest.), 324.677-010

09.05.03 CHECKROOM ATTENDANT (any industry), 358.677-010

09.05.03 PORTER (air trans.), 357.677-010

09.05.03 PORTER, BAGGAGE (hotel & rest.), 324.477-010

09.05.03 ROOM-SERVICE CLERK (hotel & rest.), 324.577-010

09.05.04 DOORKEEPER (any industry), 324.677-014

09.05.04 DRIVE-IN THEATER ATTENDANT (amuse. & rec.), 349.673-010

09.05.05 BOARD ATTENDANT (amuse. & rec.), 249.587-010

09.05.05 CARDROOM ATTENDANT II (amuse. & rec.), 343.577-010

09.05.06 CADDIE (amuse. & rec.), 341.677-010

09.05.06 DRESSER (amuse. & rec.), 346.674-010

09.05.06 PERSONAL ATTENDANT (domestic ser.), 309.674-014

09.05.07 LOCKER-ROOM ATTENDANT (personal ser.), 358.677-014

09.05.07 REST ROOM ATTENDANT (any industry), 358.677-018

09.05.07 WARDROBE SUPERVISOR (amuse. & rec.), 346.361-010

09.05.08 CHILDREN'S ATTENDANT (amuse. & rec.), 349.677-018

09.05.08 ESCORT (any industry), 353.667-010

09.05.08 RIDE ATTENDANT (amuse. & rec.), 342.677-010

09.05.08 SKI-TOW OPERATOR (amuse. & rec.), 341.665-010

09.05.08 TICKET TAKER (amuse. & rec.), 344.667-010

09.05.08 USHER (amuse. & rec.), 344.677-014

09.05.08 USHER, HEAD (amuse. & rec.), 344.137-010

09.05.09 ELEVATOR OPERATOR (any industry), 388.663-010

09.05.10 BAGGER (retail trade), 920.687-014

10.01.02 CASE AIDE (social ser.), 195.367-010

10.01.02 COMMUNITY WORKER (government ser.), 195.367-018

10.01.02 FOOD-MANAGEMENT AIDE (government ser.), 195.367-022

10.01.02 SOCIAL-SERVICES AIDE (social ser.), 195.367-034

10.02.02 INSTRUCTOR, PHYSICAL (amuse. & rec.), 153.227-014

10.03.02 ORTHOPEDIC ASSISTANT (medical ser.), 078.664-010

10.03.02 RESPIRATORY-THERAPY AIDE (medical ser.), 355.674-022

10.03.03 ATTENDANT, CHILDREN'S INSTITUTION (any industry), 359.677-010

10.03.03 BLIND AIDE (personal ser.), 359.573-010

10.03.03 CHILD MONITOR (domestic ser.), 301.677-010

10.03.03 CHILD-CARE ATTENDANT, SCHOOL (personal ser.), 355.674-010

10.03.03 COMPANION (domestic ser.), 309.677-010

10.03.03 FOSTER PARENT (domestic ser.), 309.677-014

10.03.03 GUARD, SCHOOL-CROSSING (government ser.), 371.567-010

10.03.03 NURSERY SCHOOL ATTENDANT (any industry), 359.677-018

10.03.03 PLAYROOM ATTENDANT (any industry), 359.677-026

10.03.03 TRANSPORTER, PATIENTS (medical ser.), 355.677-014

11.02.03 HOMEMAKER (social ser.), 309.354-010

11.02.04 FILM-OR-TAPE LIBRARIAN (clerical), 222.367-026

11.05.02 BUSINESS REPRESENTATIVE, LABOR UNION (profess. & kin.), 187.167-018

11.05.02 EXECUTIVE CHEF (hotel & rest.), 187.161-010

11.05.02 FREIGHT-TRAFFIC CONSULTANT (business ser.), 184.267-010

11.05.02 MANAGER, PRODUCTION (radio-tv broad.), 184.162-010

11.05.02 SUPERINTENDENT, TRANSPORTATION (any industry), 184.167-226

11.05.04 WHOLESALER I (wholesale tr.), 185.167-070

11.05.04 WHOLESALER II (wholesale tr.), 185.157-018

11.06.04 TICKET BROKER (amuse. & rec.), 259.357-034

11.07.01 COMMUNITY ORGANIZATION WORKER (social ser.), 195.167-010

11.07.01 COORDINATOR, VOLUNTEER SERVICES (social ser.), 187.167-022

11.07.01 MANAGER, ANIMAL SHELTER (nonprofit org.), 187.167-218

11.08.04 CODE AND TEST CLERK (financial), 209.667-018

11.09.01 CIRCULATION-SALES REPRESENTATIVE (print. & pub.), 299.167-010

11.09.01 GOODWILL AMBASSADOR (business ser.), 293.357-018

11.09.01 SUPERVISOR OF SALES (business ser.), 185.157-014

11.09.02 BLOOD-DONOR RECRUITER (medical ser.), 293.357-010

11.09.02 SUPERVISOR, BLOOD-DONOR RECRUITERS (medical ser.), 293.137-010

11.10.03 ANIMAL TREATMENT INVESTIGATOR (nonprofit org.), 379.263-010

11.10.03 SANITARIAN (any industry), 529.137-014

11.10.03 SANITATION INSPECTOR (government ser.), 168.267-110

11.10.05 SHOPPING INVESTIGATOR (business ser.), 376.267-022

11.11.01 MANAGER, APARTMENT HOUSE (real estate), 186.167-018

11.11.01 MANAGER, CONVENTION (hotel & rest.), 187.167-078

11.11.01 MANAGER, LODGING FACILITIES (hotel & rest.), 320.137-014

11.11.02 MANAGER, POOL (amuse. & rec.), 153.137-010

11.11.03 MANAGER, AUTOMOTIVE SERVICES (any industry), 184.117-034

11.11.04 MANAGER, LAUNDROMAT (laundry & rel.), 369.167-010

11.11.04 MANAGER, LIQUOR ESTABLISHMENT (hotel & rest.), 187.167-126

11.11.04 MANAGER, SERVICE DEPARTMENT (wholesale tr.), 187.167-142

11.11.04 SUPERINTENDENT, LAUNDRY (laundry & rel.), 187.167-194

11.11.05 AREA SUPERVISOR, RETAIL CHAIN STORE (retail trade), 185.117-014

11.12.02 LEASING AGENT, OUTDOOR ADVERTISING (business ser.), 254.357-010

11.12.03 ADVANCE AGENT (amuse. & rec.), 191.167-010

11.12.03 CIRCUS AGENT (amuse. & rec.), 191.117-022

11.12.03 JOCKEY AGENT (amuse. & rec.), 191.117-026

12.01.02 CHARTER (amuse. & rec.), 249.367-018

12.01.02 FLAGGER (amuse. & rec.), 372.667-026

12.01.02 GOLF-COURSE RANGER (amuse. & rec.), 379.667-010

12.01.02 UMPIRE (amuse. & rec.), 153.267-018

12.02.01 ACROBAT (amuse. & rec.), 159.247-010

12.02.01 AERIALIST (amuse. & rec.), 159.247-014

12.02.01 AQUATIC PERFORMER (amuse. & rec.), 159.347-014

12.02.01 EQUESTRIAN (amuse. & rec.), 159.344-010

12.02.01 JUGGLER (amuse. & rec.), 159.341-010

12.02.01 RODEO PERFORMER (amuse. & rec.), 159.344-014

12.02.01 SHOW-HORSE DRIVER (amuse. & rec.), 159.344-018

12.02.01 STUNT PERFORMER (amuse. & rec.), 159.341-014

Appendix E
Listing of Occupations by Skills Required with Data, People, and Things

This index organizes all occupations listed in *The Enhanced Guide for Occupational Exploration* in numerical order of the third through sixth digits of their *Dictionary of Occupational Titles* (*DOT*) code number. These digits correspond to the levels of skill required for each occupation in terms of data, people, and things. This list provides a useful way to look for occupations that require skills that are similar to yours.

The first number listed to the left of each job title is its GOE number. Use this number to find that job's description in this book. The number that follows each job title is its DOT number. The jobs are lised in numerical order of the fourth through sixth DOT digits, beginning with the fourth digit, having to do with data. This system avoids duplicate listings of the same job in multiple locations but does make it somewhat more difficult to find all jobs listed with similar fifth digits (people) and sixth digits (things). For example, if you wanted to find jobs that require high level skills with people but relatively lower skills with data and things, you would have to begin by finding occupations listed by the fourth DOT digit (data) within the range you find acceptable, then for occupations within each of these data codes that require higher levels of skills with people (fifth digit) and then those with lower skill requirements with things (sixth digit).

Chapter 2 provides additional details on the meaning of the DOT code number but here is a summary that may help you use this index:

DATA (high = 0, low = 6): This refers to the fourth digit in the DOT code number. 0 = Synthesizing, 1 = Coordinating, 2 = Analyzing, 3 = Compiling, 4 = Computing, 5 = Copying, 6 = Comparing

PEOPLE (high = 0, low = 8): This refers the fifth digit in the DOT code number. 0 = Mentoring, 1 = Negotiating, 2 = Instructing, 3 = Supervising, 4 = Diverting, 5 = Persuading, 6 = Speaking-Signaling, 7 = Serving, 8 = Taking Instructions-Helping

THINGS (high = 0, low = 7): This refers to the sixth digit in the DOT code number. 0 = Setting Up, 1 = Precision Working, 2 = Operating-Controlling, 3 = Driving-Operating, 4 = Manipulating, 5 = Tending, 6 = Feeding-Offbearing, 7 = Handling

Data = Synthesizing

017 (Synthesizing, Negotiating, Handling)

11.08.01 EDITOR, NEWSPAPER (print. & pub.) 132.017-014

11.08.01 EDITOR, TECHNICAL AND SCIENTIFIC PUBLICATIONS (profess. & kin.) 132.017-018

11.09.03 LOBBYIST (profess. & kin.) 165.017-010

021 (Synthesizing, Instructing, Precision)

01.04.01 TEACHER, MUSIC (education) 152.021-010

02.02.01 MEDICAL PHYSICIST (profess. & kin.) 079.021-014

05.01.02 HEALTH PHYSICIST (profess. & kin.) 015.021-010

027 (Synthesizing, Instructing, Handling)

01.05.01 INSTRUCTOR, DANCING (education) 151.027-014

031 (Synthesizing, Supervising, Precision)

01.02.03 ART DIRECTOR (profess. & kin.) 141.031-010

01.02.03 MANAGER, DISPLAY (retail trade) 142.031-014

037 (Synthesizing, Supervising, Handling)

01.01.01 CONTINUITY DIRECTOR (radio-tv broad.) 132.037-010

01.01.01 EDITOR, PUBLICATIONS (print. & pub.) 132.037-022

11.08.01 EDITOR, CITY (print. & pub.) 132.037-014

11.08.01 EDITOR, DEPARTMENT (print. & pub.) 132.037-018

041 (Synthesizing, Diverting, Precision)

01.02.02 QUICK SKETCH ARTIST (amuse. & rec.) 149.041-010

01.03.02 PUPPETEER (amuse. & rec.) 159.041-014

01.04.04 MUSICIAN, INSTRUMENTAL (amuse. & rec.) 152.041-010

047 (Synthesizing, Diverting, Handling)

01.03.02 ACTOR (amuse. & rec.) 150.047-010

01.03.02 CLOWN (amuse. & rec.) 159.047-010

01.03.02 COMEDIAN (amuse. & rec.) 159.047-014

01.03.02 IMPERSONATOR (amuse. & rec.) 159.047-018

01.04.03 SINGER (amuse. & rec.) 152.047-022

01.05.02 DANCER (amuse. & rec.) 151.047-010

051 (Synthesizing, Persuading, Precision)

01.02.03 DISPLAY DESIGNER (profess. & kin.) 142.051-010

01.02.03 INTERIOR DESIGNER (profess. & kin.) 142.051-014

061 (Synthesizing, Speaking-Signaling, Precision)

01.02.03 ART DIRECTOR (motion picture) 142.061-062

01.02.03 AUDIOVISUAL PRODUCTION SPECIALIST (profess. & kin.) 149.061-010

01.02.03 CARTOONIST (print. & pub.) 141.061-010

01.02.03 COMMERCIAL DESIGNER (profess. & kin.) 141.061-038

01.02.03 EXHIBIT DESIGNER (museums) 142.061-058

01.02.03 FASHION ARTIST (retail trade) 141.061-014

01.02.03 FASHION DESIGNER (profess. & kin.) 142.061-018

01.02.03 FURNITURE DESIGNER (furniture) 142.061-022

01.02.03 GRAPHIC DESIGNER (profess. & kin.) 141.061-018

01.02.03 ILLUSTRATOR (profess. & kin.) 141.061-022

01.02.03 ILLUSTRATOR, MEDICAL AND SCIENTIFIC (profess. & kin.) 141.061-026

01.02.03 INDUSTRIAL DESIGNER (profess. & kin.) 142.061-026

01.02.03 POLICE ARTIST (government ser.) 141.061-034

01.02.03 SET DECORATOR (motion picture) 142.061-042

01.02.03 SET DESIGNER (motion picture) 142.061-046

01.02.03 SET DESIGNER (amuse. & rec.) 142.061-050

02.01.01 CHEMIST (profess. & kin.) 022.061-010

02.01.01 GEOLOGIST (profess. & kin.) 024.061-018

02.01.01 GEOPHYSICIST (profess. & kin.) 024.061-030

02.01.01 HYDROLOGIST (profess. & kin.) 024.061-034

02.01.01 MINERALOGIST (profess. & kin.) 024.061-038

02.01.01 PETROLOGIST (profess. & kin.) 024.061-046

02.01.01 PHYSICIST (profess. & kin.) 023.061-014

02.01.01 SEISMOLOGIST (profess. & kin.) 024.061-050

02.01.02 GEOLOGIST, PETROLEUM (petrol. & gas) 024.061-022

02.02.01 ANIMAL SCIENTIST (profess. & kin.) 040.061-014

02.02.01 BIOMEDICAL ENGINEER (profess. & kin.) 019.061-010

02.02.01 HISTOPATHOLOGIST (medical ser.) 041.061-054

02.02.01 PARASITOLOGIST (profess. & kin.) 041.061-070

02.02.01 PHARMACOLOGIST (profess. & kin.) 041.061-074

02.02.01 ZOOLOGIST (profess. & kin.) 041.061-090

02.02.02 AGRONOMIST (profess. & kin.) 040.061-010

02.02.02 BOTANIST (profess. & kin.) 041.061-038

02.02.02 FOREST ECOLOGIST (profess. & kin.) 040.061-030

02.02.02 HORTICULTURIST (profess. & kin.) 040.061-038

02.02.02 PLANT PATHOLOGIST (profess. & kin.) 041.061-086

02.02.02 RANGE MANAGER (profess. & kin.) 040.061-046

02.02.02 SILVICULTURIST (profess. & kin.) 040.061-050

02.02.02 SOIL CONSERVATIONIST (profess. & kin.) 040.061-054

02.02.02 SOIL SCIENTIST (profess. & kin.) 040.061-058

02.02.02 WOOD TECHNOLOGIST (profess. & kin.) 040.061-062

02.02.03 AQUATIC BIOLOGIST (profess. & kin.) 041.061-022

02.02.03 BIOCHEMIST (profess. & kin.) 041.061-026

02.02.03 BIOLOGIST (profess. & kin.) 041.061-030

02.02.03 BIOPHYSICIST (profess. & kin.) 041.061-034

02.02.03 MICROBIOLOGIST (profess. & kin.) 041.061-058

02.02.03 PHYSIOLOGIST (profess. & kin.) 041.061-078

02.02.04 CHEMIST, FOOD (profess. & kin.) 022.061-014

02.02.04 DAIRY TECHNOLOGIST (profess. & kin.) 040.061-022

05.01.01 AERODYNAMICIST (aircraft mfg.) 002.061-010

05.01.01 AERONAUTICAL-RESEARCH ENGINEER (aircraft mfg.) 002.061-026

05.01.01 CHEMICAL RESEARCH ENGINEER (profess. & kin.) 008.061-022

05.01.01 ELECTRICAL-RESEARCH ENGINEER (profess. & kin.) 003.061-026

05.01.02 PRODUCT-SAFETY ENGINEER (profess. & kin.) 012.061-010

05.01.02 SAFETY ENGINEER (profess. & kin.) 012.061-014

05.01.03 HYDRAULIC ENGINEER (profess. & kin.) 005.061-018

05.01.03 ILLUMINATING ENGINEER (profess. & kin.) 003.061-046

05.01.03 IRRIGATION ENGINEER (profess. & kin.) 005.061-022

05.01.03 MARINE ENGINEER (profess. & kin.) 014.061-014

05.01.03 NUCLEAR ENGINEER (profess. & kin.) 015.061-014

05.01.03 NUCLEAR-FUELS RECLAMATION ENGINEER (profess. & kin.) 015.061-026

05.01.03 SANITARY ENGINEER (profess. & kin.) 005.061-030

05.01.03 WASTE-MANAGEMENT ENGINEER, RADIOACTIVE MATERIALS (profess. & kin.) 005.061-042

05.01.04 AERONAUTICAL TEST ENGINEER (aircraft mfg.) 002.061-018

05.01.04 CHEMICAL-TEST ENGINEER (profess. & kin.) 008.061-026

05.01.04 ELECTRICAL TEST ENGINEER (profess. & kin.) 003.061-014

05.01.04 ELECTRONICS-TEST ENGINEER (profess. & kin.) 003.061-042

05.01.04 METALLOGRAPHER (profess. & kin.) 011.061-014

05.01.04 RELIABILITY ENGINEER (profess. & kin.) 019.061-026

05.01.04 STRESS ANALYST (aircraft mfg.) 002.061-030

05.01.04 STRESS ANALYST (profess. & kin.) 007.061-042

05.01.04 TEST ENGINEER, NUCLEAR EQUIPMENT (profess. & kin.) 015.061-022

05.01.06 MATERIALS ENGINEER (profess. & kin.) 019.061-014

05.01.06 METALLURGIST, EXTRACTIVE (profess. & kin.) 011.061-018

05.01.06 MINING ENGINEER (mine & quarry) 010.061-014

05.01.06 STANDARDS ENGINEER (profess. & kin.) 012.061-018

05.01.06 UTILIZATION ENGINEER (utilities) 007.061-034

05.01.07 AERONAUTICAL ENGINEER (aircraft mfg.) 002.061-014

05.01.07 AERONAUTICAL-DESIGN ENGINEER (aircraft mfg.) 002.061-022

05.01.07 AIRPORT ENGINEER (profess. & kin.) 005.061-010

05.01.07 ARCHITECT (profess. & kin.) 001.061-010

05.01.07 ARCHITECT, MARINE (profess. & kin.) 001.061-014

05.01.07 CERAMIC ENGINEER (profess. & kin.) 006.061-014

05.01.07 CHEMICAL DESIGN ENGINEER, PROCESSES (profess. & kin.) 008.061-014

05.01.07 CHEMICAL ENGINEER (profess. & kin.) 008.061-018

05.01.07 CIVIL ENGINEER (profess. & kin.) 005.061-014

05.01.07 ELECTRICAL-DESIGN ENGINEER (profess. & kin.) 003.061-018

05.01.07 ELECTRO-OPTICAL ENGINEER (profess. & kin.) 023.061-010

05.01.07 ELECTRONICS-DESIGN ENGINEER (profess. & kin.) 003.061-034

05.01.07 LANDSCAPE ARCHITECT (profess. & kin.) 001.061-018

05.01.07 MECHANICAL-DESIGN ENGINEER, FACILITIES (profess. & kin.) 007.061-018

05.01.07 OPTICAL ENGINEER (profess. & kin.) 019.061-018

05.01.07 RAILROAD ENGINEER (profess. & kin.) 005.061-026

05.01.07 TOOL DESIGNER (profess. & kin.) 007.061-026

05.01.08 AGRICULTURAL ENGINEER (profess. & kin.) 013.061-010

05.01.08 AUTOMOTIVE ENGINEER (auto. mfg.) 007.061-010

05.01.08 ELECTRICAL ENGINEER (profess. & kin.) 003.061-010

05.01.08 ELECTRONICS ENGINEER (profess. & kin.) 003.061-030

05.01.08 FIBER TECHNOLOGIST (profess. & kin.) 040.061-026

05.01.08 MECHANICAL ENGINEER (profess. & kin.) 007.061-014

05.01.08 PETROLEUM ENGINEER (petrol. & gas) 010.061-018

05.01.08 STRUCTURAL ENGINEER (construction) 005.061-034

05.01.08 TRANSPORTATION ENGINEER (profess. & kin.) 005.061-038

05.01.08 WELDING ENGINEER (profess. & kin.) 011.061-026

11.03.01 PSYCHOLOGIST, DEVELOPMENTAL (profess. & kin.) 045.061-010

11.03.01 PSYCHOLOGIST, ENGINEERING (profess. & kin.) 045.061-014

11.03.01 PSYCHOLOGIST, EXPERIMENTAL (profess. & kin.) 045.061-018

062 (Synthesizing, Speaking-Signaling, Operating-Controlling)

01.02.03 CAMERA OPERATOR (motion picture) 143.062-022

01.02.03 DIRECTOR OF PHOTOGRAPHY (motion picture) 143.062-010

01.02.03 PHOTOGRAPHER, STILL (profess. & kin.) 143.062-030

01.02.03 PHOTOJOURNALIST (print. & pub.) 143.062-034

01.02.03 TELEVISION TECHNICIAN (radio-tv broad.) 194.062-010

02.01.01 METEOROLOGIST (profess. & kin.) 025.062-010

02.04.01 PHOTOGRAPHER, SCIENTIFIC (profess. & kin.) 143.062-026

11.01.01 SOFTWARE ENGINEER (profess. & kin.) 030.062-010

067 (Synthesizing, Speaking-Signaling, Handling)

01.01.02 BIOGRAPHER (profess. & kin.) 052.067-010

01.01.02 COPY WRITER (profess. & kin.) 131.067-014

01.01.02 EDITORIAL WRITER (print. & pub.) 131.067-022

01.01.02 HUMORIST (profess. & kin.) 131.067-026

01.01.02 LIBRETTIST (profess. & kin.) 131.067-030

01.01.02 LYRICIST (profess. & kin.) 131.067-034

01.01.02 PLAYWRIGHT (profess. & kin.) 131.067-038

01.01.02 SCREEN WRITER (motion picture) 131.067-050

01.01.02 WRITER, PROSE, FICTION AND NON-FICTION (profess. & kin.) 131.067-046

01.03.01 DIRECTOR, MOTION PICTURE (motion picture) 159.067-010

01.03.01 DIRECTOR, STAGE (amuse. & rec.) 150.067-010

02.01.01 GEOGRAPHER (profess. & kin.) 029.067-010

02.01.01 GEOGRAPHER, PHYSICAL (profess. & kin.) 029.067-014

02.01.01 MATHEMATICIAN (profess. & kin.) 020.067-014

05.01.02 NUCLEAR-CRITICALITY SAFETY ENGINEER (profess. & kin.) 015.067-010

05.01.04 METROLOGIST (profess. & kin.) 012.067-010

11.01.01 INFORMATION SCIENTIST (profess. & kin.) 109.067-010

11.01.01 OPERATIONS-RESEARCH ANALYST (profess. & kin.) 020.067-018

11.01.01 STATISTICIAN, MATHEMATICAL (profess. & kin.) 020.067-022

11.03.01 PSYCHOLOGIST, EDUCATIONAL (profess. & kin.) 045.067-010

11.03.01 PSYCHOLOGIST, SOCIAL (profess. & kin.) 045.067-014

11.03.01 PSYCHOMETRIST (profess. & kin.) 045.067-018

11.03.02 POLITICAL SCIENTIST (profess. & kin.) 051.067-010

11.03.02 RESEARCH WORKER, SOCIAL WELFARE (profess. & kin.) 054.067-010

11.03.02 SCIENTIFIC LINGUIST (profess. & kin.) 059.067-014

11.03.02 SOCIOLOGIST (profess. & kin.) 054.067-014

11.03.03 ANTHROPOLOGIST (profess. & kin.) 055.067-010

11.03.03 ARCHEOLOGIST (profess. & kin.) 055.067-018

11.03.03 GENEALOGIST (profess. & kin.) 052.067-018

11.03.03 HISTORIAN (profess. & kin.) 052.067-022

11.03.04 OCCUPATIONAL ANALYST (profess. & kin.) 166.067-010

11.03.05 ECONOMIST (profess. & kin.) 050.067-010

11.05.02 PROGRAM PROPOSALS COORDINATOR (radio-tv broad.) 132.067-030

11.06.03 MARKET-RESEARCH ANALYST I (profess. & kin.) 050.067-014

11.08.01 EDITOR, DICTIONARY (profess. & kin.) 132.067-018

11.08.01 EDITOR, NEWS (print. & pub.) 132.067-026

11.08.03 COLUMNIST/COMMENTATOR (print. & pub.) 131.067-010

071 (Synthesizing, Serving, Precision)

01.06.02 MAKE-UP ARTIST (amuse. & rec.) 333.071-010

081 (Synthesizing, Taking Instructions-Helping, Precision)

01.02.03 DISPLAYER, MERCHANDISE (retail trade) 298.081-010
01.02.03 FLORAL DESIGNER (retail trade) 142.081-010
01.02.03 PACKAGE DESIGNER (profess. & kin.) 142.081-018
02.01.02 ENVIRONMENTAL ANALYST (profess. & kin.) 029.081-010
02.01.02 MATERIALS SCIENTIST (profess. & kin.) 029.081-014

02.02.04 FOOD TECHNOLOGIST (profess. & kin.) 041.081-010
02.04.02 TOXICOLOGIST (pharmaceut.) 022.081-010
05.01.02 POLLUTION-CONTROL ENGINEER (profess. & kin.) 019.081-018
05.01.08 MAINTAINABILITY ENGINEER (profess. & kin.) 019.081-010

087 (Synthesizing, Taking Instructions-Helping, Handling)

01.01.02 CROSSWORD-PUZZLE MAKER (print. & pub.) 139.087-010

Data = Coordinating

101 (Coordinating, Mentoring, Precision)

02.03.01 ANESTHESIOLOGIST (medical ser.) 070.101-010
02.03.01 CARDIOLOGIST (medical ser.) 070.101-014
02.03.01 DERMATOLOGIST (medical ser.) 070.101-018
02.03.01 GENERAL PRACTITIONER (medical ser.) 070.101-022
02.03.01 INTERNIST (medical ser.) 070.101-042
02.03.01 OBSTETRICIAN (medical ser.) 070.101-054
02.03.01 OPHTHALMOLOGIST (medical ser.) 070.101-058
02.03.01 PEDIATRICIAN (medical ser.) 070.101-066
02.03.01 PODIATRIST (medical ser.) 079.101-022
02.03.01 PUBLIC HEALTH PHYSICIAN (medical ser.) 070.101-046
02.03.01 RADIOLOGIST (medical ser.) 070.101-090
02.03.01 SURGEON (medical ser.) 070.101-094
02.03.02 DENTIST (medical ser.) 072.101-010
02.03.03 VETERINARIAN (medical ser.) 073.101-010
02.03.04 AUDIOLOGIST (medical ser.) 076.101-010
02.03.04 CHIROPRACTOR (medical ser.) 079.101-010
02.03.04 OPTOMETRIST (medical ser.) 079.101-018

104 (Coordinating, Mentoring, Manipulating)

02.03.04 VOICE PATHOLOGIST (profess. & kin.) 076.104-010

107 (Coordinating, Mentoring, Handling)

02.03.01 PSYCHIATRIST (medical ser.) 070.107-014
02.03.04 SPEECH PATHOLOGIST (profess. & kin.) 076.107-010
10.01.01 CLERGY MEMBER (profess. & kin.) 120.107-010
10.01.01 PASTORAL ASSISTANT (nonprofit org.) 129.107-026

10.01.02 ASSISTANT PRINCIPAL (education) 091.107-010
10.01.02 CASEWORKER (social ser.) 195.107-010
10.01.02 CASEWORKER, CHILD WELFARE (social ser.) 195.107-014
10.01.02 CASEWORKER, FAMILY (social ser.) 195.107-018
10.01.02 CLINICAL PSYCHOLOGIST (profess. & kin.) 045.107-022
10.01.02 CLINICAL THERAPIST (profess. & kin.) 045.107-050
10.01.02 COUNSELOR (profess. & kin.) 045.107-010
10.01.02 COUNSELOR, MARRIAGE AND FAMILY (profess. & kin.) 045.107-054
10.01.02 FOREIGN-STUDENT ADVISER (education) 090.107-010
10.01.02 PROBATION-AND-PAROLE OFFICER (profess. & kin.) 195.107-046
10.01.02 PSYCHOLOGIST, CHIEF (profess. & kin.) 045.107-046
10.01.02 PSYCHOLOGIST, COUNSELING (profess. & kin.) 045.107-026
10.01.02 PSYCHOLOGIST, SCHOOL (profess. & kin.) 045.107-034
10.01.02 RESIDENCE COUNSELOR (education) 045.107-038
10.01.02 SOCIAL GROUP WORKER (social ser.) 195.107-022
10.01.02 SUBSTANCE ABUSE COUNSELOR (profess. & kin.) 045.107-058
10.01.02 VOCATIONAL REHABILITATION COUNSELOR (government ser.) 045.107-042
10.02.03 WORK-STUDY COORDINATOR, SPECIAL EDUCATION (education) 094.107-010
11.03.01 PSYCHOLOGIST, INDUSTRIAL-ORGANIZATIONAL (profess. & kin.) 045.107-030
11.04.01 HEARING OFFICER (government ser.) 119.107-010
11.04.02 LAWYER (profess. & kin.) 110.107-010
11.04.02 LAWYER, CRIMINAL (profess. & kin.) 110.107-014
11.04.03 ARBITRATOR (profess. & kin.) 169.107-010

117 (Coordinating, Negotiating, Handling)

01.03.01 PRODUCER (radio-tv broad.) 159.117-010
03.01.01 MANAGER, CHRISTMAS-TREE FARM (forestry) 180.117-010
04.01.01 FIRE CHIEF (government ser.) 373.117-010
04.01.01 POLICE CHIEF (government ser.) 375.117-010
05.01.01 DIRECTOR, RESEARCH AND DEVELOPMENT (any industry) 189.117-014
05.02.03 MANAGER, CUSTOMER TECHNICAL SERVICES (profess. & kin.) 189.117-018
05.02.03 PRODUCTION SUPERINTENDENT (any industry) 183.117-014
10.01.02 DEAN OF STUDENTS (education) 090.117-018
11.01.01 DIRECTOR, RECORDS MANAGEMENT (profess. & kin.) 161.117-014
11.04.02 DISTRICT ATTORNEY (government ser.) 110.117-010
11.04.02 INSURANCE ATTORNEY (insurance) 110.117-014
11.04.02 LAWYER, CORPORATION (profess. & kin.) 110.117-022
11.04.02 LAWYER, PATENT (profess. & kin.) 110.117-026
11.04.02 LAWYER, PROBATE (profess. & kin.) 110.117-030
11.04.02 TAX ATTORNEY (profess. & kin.) 110.117-038
11.04.04 CUSTOMS BROKER (financial) 186.117-018
11.05.01 ASSOCIATION EXECUTIVE (profess. & kin.) 189.117-010
11.05.01 DIRECTOR, TRANSPORTATION (motor trans.) 184.117-014
11.05.01 MANAGER, AIRPORT (air trans.) 184.117-026
11.05.01 MANAGER, BAKERY (bakery products) 189.117-046
11.05.01 MANAGER, INDUSTRIAL ORGANIZATION (any industry) 189.117-022
11.05.01 MANAGER, LAND DEVELOPMENT (real estate) 186.117-042
11.05.01 PRESIDENT (any industry) 189.117-026
11.05.01 PRESIDENT, FINANCIAL INSTITUTION (financial) 186.117-054
11.05.02 BUSINESS MANAGER, COLLEGE OR UNIVERSITY (education) 186.117-010
11.05.02 DIETITIAN, CHIEF (profess. & kin.) 077.117-010
11.05.02 DIRECTOR, QUALITY ASSURANCE (profess. & kin.) 189.117-042
11.05.02 EXECUTIVE VICE PRESIDENT, CHAMBER OF COMMERCE (nonprofit org.) 187.117-030
11.05.02 GRANT COORDINATOR (profess. & kin.) 169.117-014
11.05.02 IMPORT-EXPORT AGENT (any industry) 184.117-022
11.05.02 MANAGER, BRANCH (any industry) 183.117-010
11.05.02 MANAGER, CONTRACTS (petrol. & gas) 163.117-010

11.05.02 MANAGER, DEPARTMENT STORE (retail trade) 185.117-010
11.05.02 MANAGER, OPERATIONS (air trans.) 184.117-050
11.05.02 MANAGER, PERSONNEL (profess. & kin.) 166.117-018
11.05.02 MANAGER, REGIONAL (motor trans.) 184.117-054
11.05.02 MANAGER, SCHEDULE PLANNING (air trans.) 184.117-058
11.05.02 MANAGER, STATION (radio-tv broad.) 184.117-062
11.05.02 PROJECT DIRECTOR (profess. & kin.) 189.117-030
11.05.02 VICE PRESIDENT, FINANCIAL INSTITUTION (financial) 186.117-078
11.05.03 COURT ADMINISTRATOR (government ser.) 188.117-130
11.05.03 DIRECTOR, REGULATORY AGENCY (government ser.) 188.117-134
11.05.03 HOUSING-MANAGEMENT OFFICER (government ser.) 188.117-110
11.05.03 MANAGER, CITY (government ser.) 188.117-114
11.05.04 DIRECTOR, MEDIA MARKETING (radio-tv broad.) 163.117-022
11.05.04 MANAGER, BROKERAGE OFFICE (financial) 186.117-034
11.05.04 MANAGER, EXCHANGE FLOOR (financial) 186.117-086
11.05.04 MANAGER, EXPORT (any industry) 163.117-014
11.06.03 FOREIGN-EXCHANGE DEALER (financial) 186.117-082
11.06.03 RISK AND INSURANCE MANAGER (any industry) 186.117-066
11.06.03 TREASURER (profess. & kin.) 161.117-018
11.06.05 BUDGET OFFICER (profess. & kin.) 161.117-010
11.06.05 TREASURER, FINANCIAL INSTITUTION (financial) 186.117-070
11.06.05 TRUST OFFICER (financial) 186.117-074
11.07.01 COORDINATOR OF REHABILITATION SERVICES (medical ser.) 076.117-010
11.07.01 EXECUTIVE DIRECTOR, RED CROSS (nonprofit org.) 187.117-066
11.07.01 PROGRAM DIRECTOR, GROUP WORK (profess. & kin.) 187.117-046
11.07.02 ADMINISTRATOR, HEALTH CARE FACILITY (medical ser.) 187.117-010
11.07.02 DIRECTOR, NURSING SERVICE (medical ser.) 075.117-022
11.07.02 EMERGENCY MEDICAL SERVICES COORDINATOR (medical ser.) 079.117-010
11.07.02 PUBLIC HEALTH EDUCATOR (profess. & kin.) 079.117-014
11.07.02 RADIOLOGY ADMINISTRATOR (medical ser.) 187.117-062
11.07.03 ACADEMIC DEAN (education) 090.117-010
11.07.03 DIRECTOR, ATHLETIC (education) 090.117-022

11.07.03 DIRECTOR, EDUCATIONAL PROGRAM (education) 099.117-010

11.07.03 FINANCIAL-AIDS OFFICER (education) 090.117-030

11.07.03 PRESIDENT, EDUCATIONAL INSTITUTION (education) 090.117-034

11.07.03 PRINCIPAL (education) 099.117-018

11.07.03 SUPERINTENDENT, SCHOOLS (education) 099.117-022

11.07.03 VOCATIONAL REHABILITATION CONSULTANT (government ser.) 094.117-018

11.07.04 LIBRARY CONSULTANT (library) 100.117-014

11.07.04 LIBRARY DIRECTOR (library) 100.117-010

11.09.01 MANAGER, ADVERTISING (any industry) 164.117-010

11.09.01 MANAGER, ADVERTISING AGENCY (business ser.) 164.117-014

11.09.01 MANAGER, PROMOTION (hotel & rest.) 163.117-018

11.09.01 MEDIA DIRECTOR (profess. & kin.) 164.117-018

11.09.02 DIRECTOR, FUNDRAISING (nonprofit org.) 165.117-010

11.09.02 DIRECTOR, FUNDS DEVELOPMENT (profess. & kin.) 165.117-014

11.09.03 FOREIGN-SERVICE OFFICER (government ser.) 188.117-106

11.09.03 MANAGER, AREA DEVELOPMENT (utilities) 184.117-030

11.10.02 DIRECTOR, COMPLIANCE (government ser.) 188.117-046

11.10.03 PUBLIC HEALTH SERVICE OFFICER (government ser.) 187.117-050

11.10.03 SANITARIAN (profess. & kin.) 079.117-018

11.11.01 MANAGER, HOTEL OR MOTEL (hotel & rest.) 187.117-038

11.11.02 MANAGER, RECREATION ESTABLISHMENT (amuse. & rec.) 187.117-042

11.11.03 MANAGER, AUTOMOTIVE SERVICES (any industry) 184.117-034

11.11.04 GENERAL MANAGER, ROAD PRODUCTION (amuse. & rec.) 187.117-034

11.11.04 MANAGER, TOURING PRODUCTION (amuse. & rec.) 191.117-038

11.11.05 AREA SUPERVISOR, RETAIL CHAIN STORE (retail trade) 185.117-014

11.12.01 GENERAL CLAIMS AGENT (air trans.) 186.117-030

11.12.02 MANAGER, LEASING (petrol. & gas) 186.117-046

11.12.02 PROPERTY-UTILIZATION OFFICER (government ser.) 188.117-122

11.12.02 REAL-ESTATE AGENT (profess. & kin.) 186.117-058

11.12.02 RIGHT-OF-WAY AGENT (any industry) 191.117-046

11.12.03 ARTIST'S MANAGER (amuse. & rec.) 191.117-010

11.12.03 BOOKING MANAGER (amuse. & rec.) 191.117-014

11.12.03 BUSINESS MANAGER (amuse. & rec.) 191.117-018

11.12.03 CIRCUS AGENT (amuse. & rec.) 191.117-022

11.12.03 JOCKEY AGENT (amuse. & rec.) 191.117-026

11.12.03 LITERARY AGENT (business ser.) 191.117-034

11.12.03 MANAGER, ATHLETE (amuse. & rec.) 153.117-014

11.12.04 CONTRACT ADMINISTRATOR (any industry) 162.117-014

11.12.04 CONTRACT SPECIALIST (profess. & kin.) 162.117-018

12.01.01 HEAD COACH (amuse. & rec.) 153.117-010

12.01.01 SCOUT, PROFESSIONAL SPORTS (amuse. & rec.) 153.117-018

121 (Coordinating, Instructing, Precision)

10.02.02 EXERCISE PHYSIOLOGIST (medical ser.) 076.121-018

10.02.02 OCCUPATIONAL THERAPIST (medical ser.) 076.121-010

10.02.02 PHYSICAL THERAPIST (education) 076.121-014

11.02.03 COUNTY HOME-DEMONSTRATION AGENT (government ser.) 096.121-010

11.02.03 HOME ECONOMIST (profess. & kin.) 096.121-014

122 (Coordinating, Instructing, Operating-Controlling)

05.03.05 ACCESS COORDINATOR, CABLE TELEVISION (radio-tv broad.) 194.122-010

124 (Coordinating, Instructing, Manipulating)

05.05.17 DIETETIC TECHNICIAN (profess. & kin.) 077.124-010

09.01.01 COUNSELOR, CAMP (amuse. & rec.) 159.124-010

10.02.01 NURSE, INSTRUCTOR (medical ser.) 075.124-018

10.02.01 NURSE, SCHOOL (medical ser.) 075.124-010

10.02.01 NURSE, STAFF, COMMUNITY HEALTH (medical ser.) 075.124-014

10.02.02 HORTICULTURAL THERAPIST (medical ser.) 076.124-018

10.02.02 MANUAL-ARTS THERAPIST (medical ser.) 076.124-010

10.02.02 RECREATIONAL THERAPIST (medical ser.) 076.124-014

127 (Coordinating, Instructing, Handling)

05.05.17 DIETITIAN, CLINICAL (profess. & kin.) 077.127-014

10.02.01 NURSE, CONSULTANT (medical ser.) 075.127-014

10.02.01 NURSE, INFECTION CONTROL (medical ser.) 075.127-034

10.02.02 ART THERAPIST (medical ser.) 076.127-010

10.02.02 DANCE THERAPIST (medical ser.) 076.127-018

10.02.02 MUSIC THERAPIST (medical ser.) 076.127-014

11.02.02 DIETITIAN, TEACHING (profess. & kin.) 077.127-022

11.02.03 COMMUNITY DIETITIAN (profess. & kin.) 077.127-010

11.02.03 COUNTY-AGRICULTURAL AGENT (government ser.) 096.127-010

11.02.03 EXTENSION SERVICE SPECIALIST (government ser.) 096.127-014

11.02.04 LIBRARIAN (library) 100.127-014

11.07.02 CIVIL PREPAREDNESS TRAINING OFFICER (government ser.) 169.127-010

11.07.03 PARK NATURALIST (government ser.) 049.127-010

130 (Coordinating, Supervising, Setting Up)

05.06.02 ENGINEER (water trans.) 197.130-010

131 (Coordinating, Supervising, Precision)

02.04.02 CHIEF TECHNOLOGIST, NUCLEAR MEDICINE (medical ser.) 078.131-010

05.05.17 CHEF (hotel & rest.) 313.131-014

05.05.17 SOUS CHEF (hotel & rest.) 313.131-026

05.10.08 BAKER, HEAD (hotel & rest.) 313.131-010

05.10.08 PASTRY CHEF (hotel & rest.) 313.131-022

05.12.01 LABOR-CREW SUPERVISOR (construction) 899.131-010

06.01.01 SUPERVISOR, FILM PROCESSING (motion picture) 976.131-014

06.02.01 SUPERVISOR (office machines) 706.131-014

132 (Coordinating, Supervising, Operating -Controlling)

01.01.01 SUPERVISING FILM-OR-VIDEOTAPE EDITOR (motion picture) 962.132-010

07.01.02 SUPERVISOR, NETWORK CONTROL OPERATORS (any industry) 031.132-010

07.02.02 SUPERVISOR, POLICY-CHANGE CLERKS (insurance) 219.132-010

07.02.02 SUPERVISOR, TRUST ACCOUNTS (financial) 219.132-014

07.02.02 SUPERVISOR, UNDERWRITING CLERKS (insurance) 219.132-022

07.03.01 TELLER, HEAD (financial) 211.132-010

07.05.03 TECHNICAL COORDINATOR (government ser.) 209.132-014

07.06.01 SUPERVISOR, COMPUTER OPERATIONS (clerical) 213.132-010

07.06.02 PROOF-MACHINE-OPERATOR SUPERVISOR (financial) 217.132-010

11.01.01 USER SUPPORT ANALYST SUPERVISOR (profess. & kin.) 032.132-010

133 (Coordinating, Supervising, Driving-Operating)

05.04.02 CAPTAIN, FISHING VESSEL (fishing & hunt.) 197.133-010

05.04.02 MATE, SHIP (water trans.) 197.133-022

05.04.02 PILOT, SHIP (water trans.) 197.133-026

134 (Coordinating, Supervising, Manipulating)

04.01.01 FIRE CAPTAIN (government ser.) 373.134-010

06.01.01 COOK, MEXICAN FOOD (food prep., nec) 526.134-010

11.07.03 SUPERVISOR, CONTRACT-SHELTERED WORKSHOP (nonprofit org.) 187.134-010

137 (Coordinating, Supervising, Handling)

01.03.01 SUPERVISOR, SHOW OPERATIONS (amuse. & rec.) 969.137-014

01.06.01 SUPERVISOR, PREPRESS (print. & pub.) 972.137-010

02.04.01 LABORATORY SUPERVISOR (profess. & kin.) 022.137-010

03.03.02 ANIMAL KEEPER, HEAD (amuse. & rec.) 412.137-010

03.04.04 GREENSKEEPER I (any industry) 406.137-010

04.01.01 DEPUTY, COURT (government ser.) 377.137-018

04.01.01 DESK OFFICER (government ser.) 375.137-014

04.01.01 MANAGER, INTERNAL SECURITY (business ser.) 376.137-010

04.01.02 WILDLIFE AGENT, REGIONAL (government ser.) 379.137-018

05.01.02 RADIATION-PROTECTION ENGINEER (profess. & kin.) 015.137-010

05.05.06 SUPERVISOR, AUTOMOBILE BODY REPAIR (automotive ser.) 807.137-010

05.08.03 GARBAGE-COLLECTION SUPERVISOR (motor trans.) 909.137-014

05.09.01 DISPATCHER (construction) 849.137-010

05.09.01 DISTRIBUTION SUPERVISOR (pipe lines) 914.137-010

05.09.01 LINEN-ROOM SUPERVISOR (laundry & rel.) 222.137-014

05.09.01 STOCK SUPERVISOR (clerical) 222.137-034

05.09.02 SUPERVISOR, LAUNDRY (laundry & rel.) 361.137-010

05.10.08 KITCHEN SUPERVISOR (hotel & rest.) 319.137-030

05.12.01 BARGE CAPTAIN (water trans.) 911.137-010
05.12.01 HOUSEKEEPER (hotel & rest.) 321.137-010
05.12.01 HOUSEKEEPER, HOME (domestic ser.)
    301.137-010
05.12.01 STEWARD/STEWARDESS (hotel & rest.)
    310.137-018
05.12.01 SUPERVISOR, CENTRAL SUPPLY (medical
    ser.) 381.137-014
06.01.01 QUALITY ASSURANCE SUPERVISOR (auto.
    mfg.) 806.137-022
06.02.01 SUPERVISOR I (rubber goods) 759.137-010
07.01.02 SUPERVISOR, CUSTOMER SERVICES
    (motor trans.) 248.137-018
07.01.02 SUPERVISOR, LENDING ACTIVITIES
    (financial) 249.137-034
07.01.02 SUPERVISOR, SAFETY DEPOSIT (financial)
    295.137-010
07.01.02 TRANSFER CLERK, HEAD (financial)
    216.137-014
07.01.04 SUPERVISOR, REAL-ESTATE OFFICE (real
    estate) 249.137-030
07.01.04 SUPERVISOR, STATEMENT CLERKS
    (financial) 214.137-014
07.01.04 VAULT CASHIER (business ser.) 222.137-050
07.02.02 SUPERVISOR, MONEY-ROOM (amuse. &
    rec.) 211.137-018
07.03.01 SUPERVISOR, CASHIERS (hotel & rest.)
    211.137-010
07.03.01 SUPERVISOR, FOOD CHECKERS AND
    CASHIERS (hotel & rest.) 211.137-014
07.04.06 TELEPHONE OPERATOR, CHIEF (clerical)
    235.137-010
07.05.01 MANAGER, RESERVATIONS (hotel & rest.)
    238.137-010
07.05.01 SENIOR RESERVATIONS AGENT (air trans.)
    238.137-014
07.05.04 MAILROOM SUPERVISOR (clerical)
    209.137-010
07.05.04 SUPERVISOR, MAIL CARRIERS (govern-
    ment ser.) 230.137-018
07.07.02 MAILROOM SUPERVISOR (print. & pub.)
    222.137-022
07.07.02 SUPERVISOR, ADVERTISING-MATERIAL
    DISTRIBUTORS (business ser.) 230.137-010
09.01.03 BUTLER (domestic ser.) 309.137-010
09.01.03 HOST/HOSTESS, RESTAURANT (hotel &
    rest.) 310.137-010
09.01.03 WAITER/WAITRESS, CAPTAIN (hotel &
    rest.) 311.137-018
09.01.03 WAITER/WAITRESS, HEAD (hotel & rest.)
    311.137-022
09.05.02 COUNTER SUPERVISOR (hotel & rest.)
    311.137-010
09.05.02 FOOD-SERVICE SUPERVISOR (hotel & rest.)
    319.137-010
09.05.03 BAGGAGE PORTER, HEAD (hotel & rest.)
    324.137-010
09.05.03 BELL CAPTAIN (hotel & rest.) 324.137-014
09.05.08 USHER, HEAD (amuse. & rec.) 344.137-010
10.01.02 CASEWORK SUPERVISOR (social ser.)
    195.137-010

10.02.01 NURSE, HEAD (medical ser.) 075.137-014
11.06.01 OPERATIONS OFFICER (financial)
    186.137-014
11.08.04 DIRECTOR, TRANSLATION (profess. & kin.)
    137.137-010
11.09.02 SUPERVISOR, BLOOD-DONOR RECRUIT-
    ERS (medical ser.) 293.137-010
11.10.03 SANITARIAN (any industry) 529.137-014
11.11.01 MANAGER, FRONT OFFICE (hotel & rest.)
    187.137-018
11.11.01 MANAGER, LODGING FACILITIES (hotel &
    rest.) 320.137-014
11.11.02 MANAGER, POOL (amuse. & rec.)
    153.137-010
11.11.04 MANAGER, FAST FOOD SERVICES (retail
    trade) 185.137-010
11.11.05 MANAGER, DEPARTMENT (retail trade)
    299.137-010
11.12.01 SUPERVISOR, CLAIMS (insurance)
    241.137-018

147 (Coordinating, Diverting, Handling)

01.03.03 ANNOUNCER (radio-tv broad.) 159.147-010
01.03.03 DISC JOCKEY (radio-tv broad.) 159.147-014
01.03.03 NARRATOR (motion picture) 150.147-010
01.03.03 SHOW HOST/HOSTESS (radio-tv broad.)
    159.147-018

151 (Coordinating, Persuading, Precision)

05.01.05 SALES ENGINEER, AERONAUTICAL
    PRODUCTS (aircraft mfg.) 002.151-010
05.01.05 SALES-ENGINEER, ELECTRONICS PROD-
    UCTS AND SYSTEMS (profess. & kin.)
    003.151-014
10.02.01 TRANSPLANT COORDINATOR (medical
    ser.) 079.151-010

152 (Coordinating, Persuading, Operating -Controlling)

08.02.06 TRAVEL AGENT (business ser.) 252.152-010

157 (Coordinating, Persuading, Handling)

08.01.01 PHARMACEUTICAL DETAILER (wholesale
    tr.) 262.157-010
08.01.02 SALES REPRESENTATIVE, DATA PRO-
    CESSING SERVICES (business ser.)
    251.157-014
08.01.02 SALES REPRESENTATIVE, HOTEL SER-
    VICES (hotel & rest.) 259.157-014
08.01.03 BUSINESS-OPPORTUNITY-AND-PROP-
    ERTY-INVESTMENT BROKER (business
    ser.) 189.157-010
08.01.03 BUYER (profess. & kin.) 162.157-018
08.01.03 BUYER, ASSISTANT (retail trade)
    162.157-022

08.01.03 PAWNBROKER (retail trade) 191.157-010
08.02.01 MANUFACTURER'S REPRESENTATIVE
(wholesale tr.) 279.157-010
10.02.02 HYPNOTHERAPIST (profess. & kin.)
079.157-010
11.05.04 PURCHASING AGENT (profess. & kin.)
162.157-038
11.05.04 WHOLESALER II (wholesale tr.) 185.157-018
11.09.01 FASHION COORDINATOR (retail trade)
185.157-010
11.09.01 SUPERVISOR OF SALES (business ser.)
185.157-014
11.09.02 FUND RAISER I (nonprofit org.) 293.157-010

161 (Coordinating, Speaking-Signaling, Precision)

02.01.02 CHEMICAL LABORATORY CHIEF (profess.
& kin.) 022.161-010
02.04.01 PHARMACIST (medical ser.) 074.161-010
02.04.01 RADIOPHARMACIST (medical ser.)
074.161-014
02.04.02 MEDICAL TECHNOLOGIST, CHIEF (medical ser.) 078.161-010
03.01.01 FARMER, FIELD CROP (agriculture) 404.161-
010
03.01.01 FARMER, FRUIT CROPS, BUSH AND VINE
(agriculture) 403.161-014
03.01.01 FARMER, GENERAL (agriculture)
421.161-010
03.01.02 BEEKEEPER (agriculture) 413.161-010
03.01.02 FISH FARMER (fishing & hunt.) 446.161-010
03.01.02 SHELLFISH GROWER (fishing & hunt.)
446.161-014
03.01.03 HORTICULTURAL-SPECIALTY GROWER,
FIELD (agriculture) 405.161-014
03.01.03 LANDSCAPE GARDENER (agriculture)
408.161-010
05.01.01 ELECTRICAL TECHNICIAN (profess. & kin.)
003.161-010
05.01.01 ELECTRONICS TECHNICIAN (profess. &
kin.) 003.161-014
05.01.01 MECHANICAL RESEARCH ENGINEER
(profess. & kin.) 007.161-022
05.01.01 MECHANICAL-ENGINEERING TECHNI-
CIAN (profess. & kin.) 007.161-026
05.01.01 OPTOMECHANICAL TECHNICIAN (optical
goods) 007.161-030
05.01.01 TECHNICIAN, SEMICONDUCTOR DEVEL-
OPMENT (profess. & kin.) 003.161-018
05.01.04 TEST TECHNICIAN (profess. & kin.)
019.161-014
05.01.07 AGRICULTURAL-ENGINEERING TECHNI-
CIAN (profess. & kin.) 013.161-010
05.01.08 ENGINEER, SOILS (profess. & kin.)
024.161-010
05.02.03 WINE MAKER (beverage) 183.161-014
05.03.02 ENGINEERING ASSISTANT, MECHANICAL
EQUIPMENT (profess. & kin.) 007.161-018

05.03.07 SOLAR-ENERGY-SYSTEMS DESIGNER
(profess. & kin.) 007.161-038
05.05.05 CABLE SUPERVISOR (tel. & tel.)
184.161-010
09.01.01 GUIDE, HUNTING AND FISHING (amuse. &
rec.) 353.161-010
11.05.02 EXECUTIVE CHEF (hotel & rest.)
187.161-010
11.10.03 INDUSTRIAL HYGIENIST (profess. & kin.)
079.161-010
11.10.03 INDUSTRIAL-SAFETY-AND-HEALTH
TECHNICIAN (any industry) 168.161-014

162 (Coordinating, Speaking-Signaling, Operating-Controlling)

05.02.04 PROGRAM DIRECTOR, CABLE TELEVI-
SION (radio-tv broad.) 194.162-010
05.03.03 AIR-TRAFFIC-CONTROL SPECIALIST,
STATION (government ser.) 193.162-014
05.03.03 AIR-TRAFFIC-CONTROL SPECIALIST,
TOWER (government ser.) 193.162-018
07.01.03 SOCIAL SECRETARY (clerical) 201.162-010
07.04.01 ADMITTING OFFICER (medical ser.)
205.162-010
07.04.05 ALARM OPERATOR (government ser.)
379.162-010
10.02.02 RADIOLOGIC TECHNOLOGIST, CHIEF
(medical ser.) 078.162-010
11.01.01 COMPUTER PROGRAMMER (profess. &
kin.) 030.162-010
11.01.01 DATA BASE ADMINISTRATOR (profess. &
kin.) 039.162-010
11.01.01 DATA BASE DESIGN ANALYST (profess. &
kin.) 039.162-014
11.01.01 DATA RECOVERY PLANNER (profess. &
kin.) 033.162-014
11.01.01 PROGRAMMER, ENGINEERING AND
SCIENTIFIC (profess. & kin.) 030.162-018
11.01.01 PROGRAMMER-ANALYST (profess. & kin.)
030.162-014
11.01.01 SYSTEMS PROGRAMMER (profess. & kin.)
030.162-022
11.01.01 TECHNICAL SUPPORT SPECIALIST
(profess. & kin.) 033.162-018
11.01.02 MATHEMATICAL TECHNICIAN (profess. &
kin.) 020.162-010
11.05.02 MANAGER, PRODUCTION (radio-tv broad.)
184.162-010
11.06.01 ACCOUNTANT (profess. & kin.) 160.162-018
11.06.01 ACCOUNTANT, BUDGET (profess. & kin.)
160.162-022
11.06.01 ACCOUNTANT, COST (profess. & kin.)
160.162-026
11.06.01 ACCOUNTANT, TAX (profess. & kin.)
160.162-010
11.06.01 AUDITOR, DATA PROCESSING (profess. &
kin.) 160.162-030
11.10.05 COMPUTER SECURITY COORDINATOR
(profess. & kin.) 033.162-010

163 (Coordinating, Speaking-Signaling, Driving-Operating)

11.10.05 TRAFFIC INSPECTOR (motor trans.) 184.163-010

164 (Coordinating, Speaking-Signaling, Manipulating)

05.10.02 SERVICE MANAGER (retail trade) 185.164-010
09.01.01 GROUP WORKER (social ser.) 195.164-010
11.07.03 LABORATORY MANAGER (education) 090.164-010

167 (Coordinating, Speaking-Signaling, Handling)

01.01.01 PRODUCER (motion picture) 187.167-174
01.03.01 MANAGER, STAGE (amuse. & rec.) 159.167-018
01.03.01 PRODUCER (amuse. & rec.) 187.167-178
01.03.03 PROGRAM COORDINATOR (amuse. & rec.) 139.167-010
01.04.01 ARTIST AND REPERTOIRE MANAGER (amuse. & rec.) 159.167-010
02.01.02 PROJECT MANAGER, ENVIRONMENTAL RESEARCH (profess. & kin.) 029.167-014
02.02.01 ENVIRONMENTAL EPIDEMIOLOGIST (government ser.) 041.167-010
03.01.01 GENERAL MANAGER, FARM (agriculture) 180.167-018
03.01.01 GROUP LEADER (agriculture) 180.167-022
03.01.01 MANAGER, DAIRY FARM (agriculture) 180.167-026
03.01.01 MIGRANT LEADER (agriculture) 180.167-050
03.01.02 MANAGER, FISH HATCHERY (fishing & hunt.) 180.167-030
03.01.03 LANDSCAPE CONTRACTOR (construction) 182.167-014
03.01.03 MANAGER, NURSERY (agriculture) 180.167-042
03.01.04 FORESTER (profess. & kin.) 040.167-010
04.01.01 FIRE MARSHAL (any industry) 373.167-018
04.01.01 GUARD, CHIEF (any industry) 372.167-014
04.01.01 PARK SUPERINTENDENT (government ser.) 188.167-062
04.01.02 CUSTOMS PATROL OFFICER (government ser.) 168.167-010
04.01.02 FIRE WARDEN (forestry) 452.167-010
04.01.02 FISH AND GAME WARDEN (government ser.) 379.167-010
04.01.02 SPECIAL AGENT (government ser.) 375.167-042
04.02.02 SECURITY CONSULTANT (business ser.) 189.167-054

04.02.03 PARK RANGER (government ser.) 169.167-042
05.01.02 FIRE-PROTECTION ENGINEER (profess. & kin.) 012.167-026
05.01.02 INDUSTRIAL-HEALTH ENGINEER (profess. & kin.) 012.167-034
05.01.02 RESOURCE-RECOVERY ENGINEER (government ser.) 019.167-018
05.01.02 SAFETY MANAGER (profess. & kin.) 012.167-058
05.01.03 CABLE ENGINEER, OUTSIDE PLANT (tel. & tel.) 003.167-010
05.01.03 CHIEF ENGINEER, WATERWORKS (waterworks) 005.167-010
05.01.03 COMPUTER SYSTEMS HARDWARE ANALYST (profess. & kin.) 033.167-010
05.01.03 ELECTRICAL ENGINEER, POWER SYSTEM (utilities) 003.167-018
05.01.03 POWER-DISTRIBUTION ENGINEER (utilities) 003.167-046
05.01.03 POWER-TRANSMISSION ENGINEER (utilities) 003.167-050
05.01.04 FIELD-SERVICE ENGINEER (aircraft mfg.) 002.167-014
05.01.04 QUALITY CONTROL ENGINEER (profess. & kin.) 012.167-054
05.01.06 CONFIGURATION MANAGEMENT ANALYST (profess. & kin.) 012.167-010
05.01.06 DOCUMENTATION ENGINEER (profess. & kin.) 012.167-078
05.01.06 FACTORY LAY-OUT ENGINEER (profess. & kin.) 012.167-018
05.01.06 INDUSTRIAL ENGINEER (profess. & kin.) 012.167-030
05.01.06 LAND SURVEYOR (profess. & kin.) 018.167-018
05.01.06 LIAISON ENGINEER (aircraft mfg.) 012.167-038
05.01.06 MANAGEMENT ANALYST (profess. & kin.) 161.167-010
05.01.06 MANUFACTURING ENGINEER (profess. & kin.) 012.167-042
05.01.06 PREVENTIVE MAINTENANCE COORDINATOR (any industry) 169.167-074
05.01.06 PRODUCTION ENGINEER (profess. & kin.) 012.167-046
05.01.06 PRODUCTION PLANNER (profess. & kin.) 012.167-050
05.01.06 TIME-STUDY ENGINEER (profess. & kin.) 012.167-070
05.01.06 TOOL PLANNER (any industry) 012.167-074
05.01.06 TOOL PROGRAMMER, NUMERICAL CONTROL (any industry) 007.167-018
05.01.06 VALUE ENGINEER (aircraft mfg.) 002.167-010
05.01.08 ENGINEERING MANAGER, ELECTRONICS (profess. & kin.) 003.167-070
05.01.08 PLANT ENGINEER (profess. & kin.) 007.167-014
05.01.08 PROJECT ENGINEER (profess. & kin.) 019.167-014
05.01.08 SCHOOL-PLANT CONSULTANT (education) 001.167-010

05.02.02 SUPERINTENDENT, BUILDING (any industry) 187.167-190

05.02.02 SUPERINTENDENT, CONSTRUCTION (construction) 182.167-026

05.02.03 BREWING DIRECTOR (beverage) 183.167-010

05.02.03 MANAGER, FOOD PROCESSING PLANT (can. & preserv.) 183.167-026

05.02.03 MANAGER, QUALITY CONTROL (profess. & kin.) 012.167-014

05.02.03 QUALITY-CONTROL COORDINATOR (pharmaceut.) 168.167-066

05.02.06 APPLIANCE-SERVICE SUPERVISOR (utilities) 187.167-010

05.02.06 MANAGER, LAND SURVEYING (profess. & kin.) 018.167-022

05.02.07 MANAGER, MARINA DRY DOCK (amuse. & rec.) 187.167-226

05.03.01 NAVIGATOR (air trans.) 196.167-014

05.03.01 PHOTOGRAMMETRIC ENGINEER (profess. & kin.) 018.167-026

05.03.01 SURVEYOR ASSISTANT, INSTRUMENTS (profess. & kin.) 018.167-034

05.03.03 DISPATCHER (air trans.) 912.167-010

05.03.03 MATERIAL SCHEDULER (aircraft mfg.) 012.167-082

05.03.05 COMMUNICATIONS COORDINATOR (medical ser.) 239.167-010

05.03.06 INSPECTOR, BUILDING (government ser.) 168.167-030

05.03.06 INSPECTOR, PLUMBING (government ser.) 168.167-050

05.03.06 MARINE SURVEYOR (profess. & kin.) 014.167-010

05.03.06 SUPERVISOR, VENDOR QUALITY (any industry) 012.167-062

05.03.08 ENERGY-CONTROL OFFICER (education) 199.167-018

05.03.08 RADIATION MONITOR (profess. & kin.) 199.167-010

05.05.02 SUPERINTENDENT, MAINTENANCE (any industry) 189.167-046

05.05.09 MANAGER, MARINE SERVICE (ship-boat mfg.) 187.167-130

05.07.02 INSPECTOR, HEATING AND REFRIGERATION (government ser.) 168.167-046

05.09.02 CUSTOMER SERVICES COORDINATOR (print. & pub.) 221.167-026

05.09.02 MATERIAL COORDINATOR (clerical) 221.167-014

05.09.02 PRODUCTION COORDINATOR (clerical) 221.167-018

05.10.02 MANAGER, CUSTOMER SERVICES (business ser.) 187.167-082

05.10.02 SERVICE MANAGER (automotive ser.) 185.167-058

05.10.04 MANAGER, CAMP (construction) 187.167-066

07.01.01 CONTACT REPRESENTATIVE (government ser.) 169.167-018

07.01.02 ADMINISTRATIVE SECRETARY (any industry) 169.167-014

07.01.02 AUTOMOBILE-CLUB-SAFETY-PROGRAM COORDINATOR (nonprofit org.) 249.167-010

07.01.02 COORDINATOR, SKILL-TRAINING PROGRAM (government ser.) 169.167-062

07.01.02 DIRECTOR, NURSES' REGISTRY (medical ser.) 187.167-034

07.01.02 LABOR EXPEDITER (construction) 249.167-018

07.01.02 MANAGER, OFFICE (any industry) 169.167-034

07.01.02 MANAGER, TRAFFIC I (motor trans.) 184.167-102

07.01.04 CLOSER (real estate) 186.167-074

07.01.05 TITLE SUPERVISOR (profess. & kin.) 119.167-018

07.04.03 PUBLIC HEALTH REGISTRAR (government ser.) 169.167-046

07.04.05 TRAIN DISPATCHER (r.r. trans.) 184.167-262

07.05.01 DISPATCHER, MOTOR VEHICLE (clerical) 249.167-014

07.05.01 GUIDE, TRAVEL (personal ser.) 353.167-010

07.05.03 ORDER DEPARTMENT SUPERVISOR (any industry) 169.167-038

08.01.02 ESTATE PLANNER (insurance) 186.167-010

08.01.02 SPECIAL AGENT, GROUP INSURANCE (insurance) 169.167-050

09.01.01 DIRECTOR, SOCIAL (hotel & rest.) 352.167-010

09.04.01 MANAGER, FOOD CONCESSION (hotel & rest.) 185.167-022

09.04.01 VENDING-STAND SUPERVISOR (government ser.) 185.167-066

10.01.02 DIRECTOR OF PLACEMENT (education) 166.167-014

10.02.01 NURSE, SUPERVISOR (medical ser.) 075.167-010

10.02.01 QUALITY ASSURANCE COORDINATOR (medical ser.) 075.167-014

10.02.02 INDUSTRIAL THERAPIST (medical ser.) 076.167-010

10.02.03 SUPERVISOR, SPECIAL EDUCATION (education) 094.167-010

11.01.01 CHIEF, COMPUTER PROGRAMMER (profess. & kin.) 030.167-010

11.01.01 MANAGER, COMPUTER OPERATIONS (profess. & kin.) 169.167-082

11.01.01 MANAGER, DATA PROCESSING (profess. & kin.) 169.167-030

11.01.01 SYSTEMS ANALYST (profess. & kin.) 030.167-014

11.01.02 ACTUARY (profess. & kin.) 020.167-010

11.01.02 CONSULTANT (profess. & kin.) 189.167-010

11.01.02 STATISTICIAN, APPLIED (profess. & kin.) 020.167-026

11.02.01 HISTORIC-SITE ADMINISTRATOR (museums) 102.167-014

11.02.04 AUDIOVISUAL LIBRARIAN (library) 100.167-010

11.02.04 BOOKMOBILE LIBRARIAN (library) 100.167-014

11.02.04 LIBRARIAN, SPECIAL LIBRARY (library) 100.167-026

11.02.04 MEDIA SPECIALIST, SCHOOL LIBRARY
(library) 100.167-030

11.02.04 NEWS LIBRARIAN (library) 100.167-038

11.03.02 PLANNER, PROGRAM SERVICES (government ser.) 188.167-110

11.03.02 URBAN PLANNER (profess. & kin.)
199.167-014

11.03.03 ARCHIVIST (profess. & kin.) 101.167-010

11.04.03 ADJUDICATOR (government ser.)
119.167-010

11.04.04 PATENT AGENT (profess. & kin.)
119.167-014

11.05.02 ADMINISTRATIVE ASSISTANT (any
industry) 169.167-010

11.05.02 BUSINESS REPRESENTATIVE, LABOR
UNION (profess. & kin.) 187.167-018

11.05.02 COMMERCIAL LOAN COLLECTION
OFFICER (financial) 186.167-078

11.05.02 DIRECTOR, SERVICE (retail trade)
189.167-014

11.05.02 MANAGEMENT TRAINEE (any industry)
189.167-018

11.05.02 MANAGER, BENEFITS (profess. & kin.)
166.167-018

11.05.02 MANAGER, COMPENSATION (profess. &
kin.) 166.167-022

11.05.02 MANAGER, DEPARTMENT (any industry)
189.167-022

11.05.02 MANAGER, LABOR RELATIONS (profess. &
kin.) 166.167-034

11.05.02 MANAGER, PROCUREMENT SERVICES
(profess. & kin.) 162.167-022

11.05.02 MANAGER, TRAFFIC (any industry)
184.167-094

11.05.02 MANAGER, WORLD TRADE AND MARI-
TIME DIVISION (nonprofit org.) 187.167-170

11.05.02 PROGRAM MANAGER (profess. & kin.)
189.167-030

11.05.02 PROGRAM SPECIALIST, EMPLOYEE-
HEALTH MAINTENANCE (profess. & kin.)
166.167-050

11.05.02 SECURITY OFFICER (any industry) 189.167-
034

11.05.02 SPECIAL AGENT (insurance) 166.167-046

11.05.02 SUPERINTENDENT, PLANT PROTECTION
(any industry) 189.167-050

11.05.02 SUPERINTENDENT, TRANSPORTATION
(any industry) 184.167-226

11.05.02 UTILIZATION COORDINATOR (radio-tv
broad.) 169.167-078

11.05.03 ENVIRONMENTAL ANALYST (government
ser.) 199.167-022

11.05.03 LEGISLATIVE ASSISTANT (government ser.)
169.167-066

11.05.03 MANAGER, HOUSING PROJECT (profess. &
kin.) 186.167-030

11.05.03 MANAGER, OFFICE (government ser.)
188.167-058

11.05.03 MANAGER, REGULATED PROGRAM
(government ser.) 168.167-090

11.05.03 POSTMASTER (government ser.) 188.167-066

11.05.03 SECRETARY OF STATE (government ser.)
188.167-082

11.05.04 MANAGER, CIRCULATION (print. & pub.)
163.167-014

11.05.04 MANAGER, MERCHANDISE (retail trade)
185.167-034

11.05.04 MANAGER, PROFESSIONAL EQUIPMENT
SALES-AND-SERVICE (business ser.)
185.167-042

11.05.04 MANAGER, SALES (any industry)
163.167-018

11.05.04 PROPERTY-DISPOSAL OFFICER (any
industry) 163.167-026

11.05.04 WHOLESALER I (wholesale tr.) 185.167-070

11.06.01 ACCOUNTANT, PROPERTY (profess. & kin.)
160.167-022

11.06.01 ACCOUNTANT, SYSTEMS (profess. & kin.)
160.167-026

11.06.01 AUDITOR (profess. & kin.) 160.167-054

11.06.01 AUDITOR, COUNTY OR CITY (government
ser.) 160.167-030

11.06.01 AUDITOR, INTERNAL (profess. & kin.)
160.167-034

11.06.01 AUDITOR, TAX (profess. & kin.) 160.167-038

11.06.01 REVENUE AGENT (government ser.)
160.167-050

11.06.02 CONTROLLER (profess. & kin.) 160.167-058

11.06.03 APPRAISER (government ser.) 188.167-010

11.06.03 BOOKMAKER (amuse. & rec.) 187.167-014

11.06.03 FACTOR (financial) 186.167-082

11.06.03 MANAGER, CREDIT AND COLLECTION
(any industry) 169.167-086

11.06.03 SECURITIES TRADER (financial)
162.167-038

11.06.04 FLOOR BROKER (financial) 162.167-034

11.07.01 COMMUNITY ORGANIZATION WORKER
(social ser.) 195.167-010

11.07.01 COMMUNITY-RELATIONS-AND-SERVICES
ADVISOR, PUBLIC HOUSING (social ser.)
195.167-014

11.07.01 COORDINATOR, VOLUNTEER SERVICES
(social ser.) 187.167-022

11.07.01 DIRECTOR, COMMUNITY ORGANIZA-
TION (nonprofit org.) 187.167-234

11.07.01 DIRECTOR, SERVICE (nonprofit org.)
187.167-214

11.07.01 MANAGER, ANIMAL SHELTER (nonprofit
org.) 187.167-218

11.07.01 REHABILITATION CENTER MANAGER
(government ser.) 195.167-038

11.07.01 RESIDENCE SUPERVISOR (any industry)
187.167-186

11.07.02 COMMUNITY-SERVICES-AND-HEALTH-
EDUCATION OFFICER (government ser.)
079.167-010

11.07.02 MEDICAL-RECORD ADMINISTRATOR
(medical ser.) 079.167-014

11.07.03 CONSULTANT, EDUCATION (education)
099.167-014

11.07.03 DIRECTOR OF ADMISSIONS (education)
090.167-014

11.07.03 DIRECTOR OF PUPIL PERSONNEL PRO-
GRAM (education) 099.167-034

11.07.03 DIRECTOR, DAY CARE CENTER (education)
092.167-010

11.07.03 DIRECTOR, SPECIAL EDUCATION (education) 094.167-014

11.07.03 DIRECTOR, VOCATIONAL TRAINING
(education) 097.167-010

11.07.03 EDUCATIONAL SPECIALIST (education)
099.167-022

11.07.03 MUSIC SUPERVISOR (education)
099.167-026

11.07.03 REGISTRAR, COLLEGE OR UNIVERSITY
(education) 090.167-030

11.07.03 TECHNICAL TRAINING COORDINATOR
(education) 166.167-054

11.07.04 RECREATION SUPERVISOR (profess. & kin.)
187.167-238

11.09.01 ACCOUNT EXECUTIVE (business ser.)
164.167-010

11.09.01 CIRCULATION-SALES REPRESENTATIVE
(print. & pub.) 299.167-010

11.09.01 MANAGER, ADVERTISING (print. & pub.)
163.167-010

11.09.01 SALES-SERVICE PROMOTER (any industry)
165.167-010

11.09.02 MEMBERSHIP DIRECTOR (profess. & kin.)
189.167-026

11.09.03 PUBLIC-RELATIONS REPRESENTATIVE
(profess. & kin.) 165.167-014

11.10.01 REVENUE OFFICER (government ser.)
188.167-074

11.10.02 EQUAL-OPPORTUNITY REPRESENTATIVE
(government ser.) 168.167-014

11.10.03 HEALTH OFFICER, FIELD (government ser.)
168.167-018

11.10.03 INSPECTOR, HEALTH CARE FACILITIES
(government ser.) 168.167-042

11.10.03 OCCUPATIONAL-SAFETY-AND-HEALTH
INSPECTOR (government ser.) 168.167-062

11.10.03 REVIEWING OFFICER, DRIVER'S
LICENSE (government ser.) 168.167-074

11.10.03 SAFETY INSPECTOR (insurance)
168.167-078

11.10.03 SAFETY MANAGER (medical ser.)
168.167-086

11.10.04 IMMIGRATION INSPECTOR (government
ser.) 168.167-022

11.10.05 REGULATORY ADMINISTRATOR (tel. &
tel.) 168.167-070

11.10.05 TRANSPORTATION INSPECTOR (motor
trans.) 168.167-082

11.11.01 CONDOMINIUM MANAGER (real estate)
186.167-062

11.11.01 EXECUTIVE HOUSEKEEPER (any industry)
187.167-046

11.11.01 MANAGER, APARTMENT HOUSE (real
estate) 186.167-018

11.11.01 MANAGER, CONVENTION (hotel & rest.)
187.167-078

11.11.02 DIRECTOR, CAMP (social ser.) 195.167-018

11.11.02 DIRECTOR, RECREATION CENTER (social
ser.) 195.167-026

11.11.02 MANAGER, BOWLING ALLEY (amuse. &
rec.) 187.167-222

11.11.02 MANAGER, GOLF CLUB (amuse. & rec.)
187.167-114

11.11.02 MANAGER, RECREATION FACILITY
(amuse. & rec.) 187.167-230

11.11.02 MANAGER, THEATER (amuse. & rec.)
187.167-154

11.11.03 CONDUCTOR, PASSENGER CAR (r.r. trans.)
198.167-010

11.11.03 CONDUCTOR, ROAD FREIGHT (r.r. trans.)
198.167-018

11.11.03 MANAGER, BUS TRANSPORTATION (motor
trans.) 184.167-054

11.11.03 MANAGER, DISTRIBUTION WAREHOUSE
(wholesale tr.) 185.167-018

11.11.03 MANAGER, WAREHOUSE (any industry)
184.167-114

11.11.03 OPERATIONS MANAGER (motor trans.)
184.167-118

11.11.03 PURSER (water trans.) 197.167-014

11.11.03 STATION MANAGER (r.r. trans.) 184.167-130

11.11.04 ASSISTANT BRANCH MANAGER, FINAN-
CIAL INSTITUTION (financial) 186.167-070

11.11.04 DIRECTOR, FUNERAL (personal ser.)
187.167-030

11.11.04 MANAGER, BARBER OR BEAUTY SHOP
(personal ser.) 187.167-058

11.11.04 MANAGER, EMPLOYMENT AGENCY
(profess. & kin.) 187.167-098

11.11.04 MANAGER, FINANCIAL INSTITUTION
(financial) 186.167-086

11.11.04 MANAGER, FOOD SERVICE (hotel & rest.)
187.167-106

11.11.04 MANAGER, INSURANCE OFFICE (insurance) 186.167-034

11.11.04 MANAGER, LAUNDROMAT (laundry & rel.)
369.167-010

11.11.04 MANAGER, LIQUOR ESTABLISHMENT
(hotel & rest.) 187.167-126

11.11.04 MANAGER, PROPERTY (real estate)
186.167-046

11.11.04 MANAGER, REAL-ESTATE FIRM (real
estate) 186.167-066

11.11.04 MANAGER, SALES (laundry & rel.)
187.167-138

11.11.04 MANAGER, SERVICE DEPARTMENT
(wholesale tr.) 187.167-142

11.11.04 MANAGER, TITLE SEARCH (real estate)
186.167-090

11.11.04 MANAGER, TRAVEL AGENCY (business
ser.) 187.167-158

11.11.04 SUPERINTENDENT, LAUNDRY (laundry &
rel.) 187.167-194

11.11.05 COMMISSARY MANAGER (any industry)
185.167-010

11.11.05 MANAGER, AUTOMOBILE SERVICE
STATION (retail trade) 185.167-014

11.11.05 MANAGER, MACHINERY-OR-EQUIPMENT, RENTAL AND LEASING (any industry) 185.167-026

11.11.05 MANAGER, MARKET (retail trade) 186.167-042

11.11.05 MANAGER, MEAT SALES AND STORAGE (retail trade) 185.167-030

11.11.05 MANAGER, PARTS (retail trade) 185.167-038

11.11.05 MANAGER, RETAIL STORE (retail trade) 185.167-046

11.11.05 MANAGER, VEHICLE LEASING AND RENTAL (automotive ser.) 187.167-162

11.11.05 SERVICE SUPERVISOR, LEASED MACHINERY AND EQUIPMENT (any industry) 183.167-030

11.12.01 MANAGER, CUSTOMER SERVICE (tel. & tel.) 168.167-058

11.12.01 SERVICE REPRESENTATIVE (auto. mfg.) 191.167-022

11.12.02 LOCATION MANAGER (motion picture) 191.167-018

11.12.03 ADVANCE AGENT (amuse. & rec.) 191.167-010

11.12.04 CONTRACTOR (construction) 182.167-010

171 (Coordinating, Serving, Precision)

02.04.01 PROOF TECHNICIAN (ordnance) 199.171-010

181 (Coordinating, Taking Instructions-Helping, Precision)

03.01.03 TREE SURGEON (agriculture) 408.181-010

05.03.07 HEAT-TRANSFER TECHNICIAN (profess. & kin.) 007.181-010

187 (Coordinating, Taking Instructions-Helping, Handling)

05.01.03 CENTRAL-OFFICE EQUIPMENT ENGINEER (tel. & tel.) 003.187-010

05.01.03 COMMERCIAL ENGINEER (radio-tv broad.) 003.187-014

05.01.08 CUSTOMER-EQUIPMENT ENGINEER (tel. & tel.) 003.187-018

05.03.09 PACKAGING ENGINEER (profess. & kin.) 019.187 010

Data = Analyzing

207 (Analyzing, Mentoring, Handling)

07.01.01 CREDIT COUNSELOR (profess. & kin.) 160.207-010

11.04.03 CONCILIATOR (profess. & kin.) 169.207-010

217 (Analyzing, Negotiating, Handling)

11.12.01 CLAIM ADJUSTER (business ser.) 241.217-010

221 (Analyzing, Instructing, Precision)

11.02.02 INSTRUCTOR, TECHNICAL TRAINING (education) 166.221-010

11.02.02 INSTRUCTOR, VOCATIONAL TRAINING (education) 097.221-010

11.02.02 TEACHER, INDUSTRIAL ARTS (education) 091.221-010

222 (Analyzing, Instructing, Operating-Controlling)

11.02.01 INSTRUCTOR, BUSINESS EDUCATION (education) 090.222-010

223 (Analyzing, Instructing, Driving-Operating)

05.04.01 INSTRUCTOR, FLYING I (education) 196.223-010

05.04.01 INSTRUCTOR, PILOT (air trans.) 196.223-014

09.03.03 INSTRUCTOR, DRIVING (education) 099.223-010

224 (Analyzing, Instructing, Manipulating)

03.03.01 ANIMAL TRAINER (amuse. & rec.) 159.224-010

10.02.02 ATHLETIC TRAINER (amuse. & rec.) 153.224-010

10.02.02 ORIENTATION AND MOBILITY THERAPIST FOR THE BLIND (education) 076.224-014

10.02.02 PHYSICAL THERAPIST ASSISTANT (medical ser.) 076.224-010

10.02.03 TEACHER, HEARING IMPAIRED (education) 094.224-010

10.02.03 TEACHER, PHYSICALLY IMPAIRED (education) 094.224-014

10.02.03 TEACHER, VISUALLY IMPAIRED (education) 094.224-018

11.02.01 INSTRUCTOR, PHYSICAL EDUCATION (education) 099.224-010

227 (Analyzing, Instructing, Handling)

05.04.01 INSTRUCTOR, FLYING II (education) 097.227-010

09.01.01 RECREATION LEADER (social ser.) 195.227-014

10.02.02 INSTRUCTOR, PHYSICAL (amuse. & rec.) 153.227-014

10.02.02 PROGRAM AIDE, GROUP WORK (social ser.) 195.227-010

10.02.03 TEACHER, EMOTIONALLY IMPAIRED (education) 094.227-010

10.02.03 TEACHER, HOME THERAPY (social ser.) 195.227-018

10.02.03 TEACHER, KINDERGARTEN (education) 092.227-014

10.02.03 TEACHER, LEARNING DISABLED (education) 094.227-030

10.02.03 TEACHER, MENTALLY IMPAIRED (education) 094.227-022

10.02.03 TEACHER, PRESCHOOL (education) 092.227-018

10.02.03 TEACHER, VOCATIONAL TRAINING (education) 094.227-026

10.03.03 CHILDREN'S TUTOR (domestic ser.) 099.227-010

11.02.01 FACULTY MEMBER, COLLEGE OR UNIVERSITY (education) 090.227-010

11.02.01 INSTRUCTOR, EXTENSION WORK (education) 090.227-018

11.02.01 TEACHER (museums) 099.227-038

11.02.01 TEACHER, ADULT EDUCATION (education) 099.227-030

11.02.01 TEACHER, ELEMENTARY SCHOOL (education) 092.227-010

11.02.01 TEACHER, RESOURCE (education) 099.227-042

11.02.01 TEACHER, SECONDARY SCHOOL (education) 091.227-010

11.02.01 TUTOR (education) 099.227-034

11.02.02 TRAINING REPRESENTATIVE (education) 166.227-010

12.01.01 INSTRUCTOR, SPORTS (amuse. & rec.) 153.227-018

247 (Analyzing, Diverting, Handling)

12.02.01 ACROBAT (amuse. & rec.) 159.247-010
12.02.01 AERIALIST (amuse. & rec.) 159.247-014

251 (Analyzing, Persuading, Precision)

05.05.05 ELECTRONIC-SALES-AND-SERVICE TECHNICIAN (profess. & kin.) 828.251-010

05.05.17 TESTER, FOOD PRODUCTS (any industry) 199.251-010

08.01.01 SALES REPRESENTATIVE, GRAPHIC ART (business ser.) 254.251-010

08.02.02 SALES-SERVICE REPRESENTATIVE, MILKING MACHINES (retail trade) 299.251-010

253 (Analyzing, Persuading, Driving-Operating)

08.01.01 SALES REPRESENTATIVE, AIRCRAFT (retail trade) 273.253-010

257 (Analyzing, Persuading, Handling)

08.01.01 SALES REPRESENTATIVE, COMMUNICATION EQUIPMENT (wholesale tr.) 271.257-010

08.01.01 SALES REPRESENTATIVE, COMPUTERS AND EDP SYSTEMS (wholesale tr.) 275.257-010

08.01.01 SALES REPRESENTATIVE, DENTAL AND MEDICAL EQUIPMENT AND SUPPLIES (wholesale tr.) 276.257-010

08.01.01 SALES REPRESENTATIVE, SIGNS AND DISPLAYS (fabrication, nec) 254.257-010

08.01.02 SALES AGENT, INSURANCE (insurance) 250.257-010

08.01.02 SALES REPRESENTATIVE, EDUCATION COURSES (education) 259.257-010

08.01.02 SALES REPRESENTATIVE, FINANCIAL SERVICES (financial) 250.257-022

08.01.02 SALES REPRESENTATIVE, SECURITY SYSTEMS (business ser.) 259.257-022

08.01.02 SALES REPRESENTATIVE, TELEPHONE SERVICES (tel. & tel.) 253.257-010

08.01.02 TRAFFIC AGENT (air trans.) 252.257-010

08.01.03 SALES REPRESENTATIVE, LIVESTOCK (wholesale tr.) 260.257-010

08.02.02 SALESPERSON, ORTHOPEDIC SHOES (retail trade) 276.257-018

08.02.02 SALESPERSON, SURGICAL APPLIANCES (retail trade) 276.257-022

08.02.03 AUCTIONEER (retail trade) 294.257-010

11.06.04 REGISTERED REPRESENTATIVE (financial) 250.257-018

11.09.03 EMPLOYER RELATIONS REPRESENTATIVE (profess. & kin.) 166.257-010

260 (Analyzing, Speaking-Signaling, Setting Up)

01.02.03 OPTICAL-EFFECTS-CAMERA OPERATOR (motion picture) 143.260-010

05.05.06 ORNAMENTAL-METAL WORKER (metal prod., nec) 619.260-014

05.05.07 MACHINIST, EXPERIMENTAL (machine shop) 600.260-022

05.05.07 TOOL-AND-DIE MAKER (machine shop) 601.260-010

05.11.04 RIGGER (any industry) 921.260-010
06.01.02 KNITTING-MACHINE FIXER (knitting) 689.260-026
06.01.02 LOOM FIXER (narrow fabrics) 683.260-018
06.01.03 CHIEF OPERATOR (chemical) 558.260-010
06.01.03 REFINERY OPERATOR (petrol. refin.) 549.260-010
06.02.02 PRESS OPERATOR, HEAVY DUTY (any industry) 617.260-010

261 (Analyzing, Speaking-Signaling, Precision)

01.02.03 EXHIBIT ARTIST (museums) 149.261-010
01.06.02 EXHIBIT BUILDER (museums) 739.261-010
01.06.02 MODEL MAKER I (any industry) 777.261-010
01.06.02 TAXIDERMIST (profess. & kin.) 199.261-010
02.02.02 SOIL-CONSERVATION TECHNICIAN (profess. & kin.) 040.261-010
02.04.01 CHEMICAL LABORATORY TECHNICIAN (profess. & kin.) 022.261-010
02.04.01 CRIMINALIST (profess. & kin.) 029.261-026
02.04.01 LABORATORY ASSISTANT, METALLURGICAL (steel & rel.) 011.261-022
02.04.01 LABORATORY TECHNICIAN (auto. mfg.) 019.261-030
02.04.01 LABORATORY TESTER (any industry) 029.261-010
02.04.01 METALLURGICAL TECHNICIAN (profess. & kin.) 011.261-010
02.04.01 QUALITY CONTROL TECHNICIAN (profess. & kin.) 012.261-014
02.04.01 TESTER (petrol. refin.) 029.261-022
02.04.02 BIOCHEMISTRY TECHNOLOGIST (medical ser.) 078.261-010
02.04.02 BIOMEDICAL EQUIPMENT TECHNICIAN (profess. & kin.) 019.261-010
02.04.02 CYTOGENETIC TECHNOLOGIST (medical ser.) 078.261-026
02.04.02 HISTOTECHNOLOGIST (medical ser.) 078.261-030
02.04.02 IMMUNOHEMATOLOGIST (medical ser.) 078.261-046
02.04.02 MEDICAL TECHNOLOGIST (medical ser.) 078.261-038
02.04.02 MICROBIOLOGY TECHNOLOGIST (medical ser.) 078.261-014
02.04.02 PUBLIC-HEALTH MICROBIOLOGIST (government ser.) 041.261-010
05.01.01 INSTRUMENTATION TECHNICIAN (profess. & kin.) 003.261-010
05.01.01 WELDING TECHNICIAN (profess. & kin.) 011.261-014
05.01.04 AIR ANALYST (profess. & kin.) 012.261-010
05.01.04 RESEARCH MECHANIC (aircraft mfg.) 002.261-014
05.01.04 TEST-ENGINE EVALUATOR (petrol. refin.) 010.261-026
05.01.06 FACILITIES PLANNER (any industry) 019.261-018

05.01.08 CHEMICAL-ENGINEERING TECHNICIAN (profess. & kin.) 008.261-010
05.03.02 AUTO-DESIGN CHECKER (auto. mfg.) 017.261-010
05.03.02 CIVIL ENGINEERING TECHNICIAN (profess. & kin.) 005.261-014
05.03.02 CONTROLS DESIGNER (profess. & kin.) 003.261-014
05.03.02 DESIGN DRAFTER, ELECTROMECHANISMS (profess. & kin.) 017.261-014
05.03.02 DETAILER (profess. & kin.) 017.261-018
05.03.02 DRAFTER, AERONAUTICAL (aircraft mfg.) 002.261-010
05.03.02 DRAFTER, ARCHITECTURAL (profess. & kin.) 001.261-010
05.03.02 DRAFTER, AUTOMOTIVE DESIGN (auto. mfg.) 017.261-042
05.03.02 DRAFTER, CARTOGRAPHIC (profess. & kin.) 018.261-010
05.03.02 DRAFTER, COMMERCIAL (profess. & kin.) 017.261-026
05.03.02 DRAFTER, LANDSCAPE (profess. & kin.) 001.261-014
05.03.02 EDITOR, MAP (profess. & kin.) 018.261-018
05.03.02 ESTIMATOR AND DRAFTER (utilities) 019.261-014
05.03.02 FIRE-PROTECTION ENGINEERING TECHNICIAN (profess. & kin.) 019.261-026
05.03.02 INTEGRATED CIRCUIT LAYOUT DESIGNER (profess. & kin.) 003.261-018
05.03.02 PHOTOGRAMMETRIST (profess. & kin.) 018.261-026
05.03.02 PRINTED CIRCUIT DESIGNER (profess. & kin.) 003.261-022
05.03.04 FIELD ENGINEER, SPECIALIST (petrol. & gas) 010.261-010
05.03.05 LASER TECHNICIAN (electron. comp.) 019.261-034
05.03.06 FLIGHT ENGINEER (air trans.) 621.261-018
05.03.07 TEST TECHNICIAN (agric. equip.) 019.261-022
05.03.08 POLLUTION-CONTROL TECHNICIAN (profess. & kin.) 029.261-014
05.05.02 MARINE-SERVICES TECHNICIAN (ship-boat mfg.) 806.261-026
05.05.05 ANTENNA INSTALLER, SATELLITE COMMUNICATIONS (any industry) 823.261-022
05.05.05 AUTOMATED EQUIPMENT ENGINEER-TECHNICIAN (machinery mfg.) 638.261-010
05.05.05 DATA COMMUNICATIONS TECHNICIAN (any industry) 823.261-030
05.05.05 ELECTRICIAN (construction) 824.261-010
05.05.05 ELECTRICIAN, AIRCRAFT (aircraft mfg.) 825.261-018
05.05.05 ELECTRICIAN, MAINTENANCE (any industry) 829.261-018
05.05.05 ELECTRICIAN, POWERHOUSE (utilities) 820.261-014
05.05.05 ELECTRONICS ASSEMBLER, DEVELOPMENTAL (any industry) 726.261-010

05.05.05 FIELD SERVICE ENGINEER (profess. & kin.) 828.261-014

05.05.05 LINE MAINTAINER (any industry) 821.261-014

05.05.05 STATION INSTALLER-AND-REPAIRER (tel. & tel.) 822.261-022

05.05.06 AIRCRAFT BODY REPAIRER (air trans.) 807.261-010

05.05.06 BOILERMAKER I (struct. metal) 805.261-014

05.05.06 FITTER I (any industry) 801.261-014

05.05.07 ROCKET-MOTOR MECHANIC (aircraft mfg.) 693.261-022

05.05.09 AIR-CONDITIONING INSTALLER-SERVICER, WINDOW UNIT (construction) 637.261-010

05.05.09 AUTOMOBILE MECHANIC (automotive ser.) 620.261-010

05.05.09 AUTOMOBILE-SERVICE-STATION ME-CHANIC (automotive ser.) 620.261-030

05.05.09 AUTOMOTIVE-COOLING-SYSTEM DIAG-NOSTIC TECHNICIAN (automotive ser.) 620.261-034

05.05.09 CONSTRUCTION-EQUIPMENT MECHANIC (construction) 620.261-022

05.05.09 EXPERIMENTAL AIRCRAFT MECHANIC (aircraft mfg.) 621.261-022

05.05.09 FIELD SERVICE TECHNICIAN (machinery mfg.) 638.261-026

05.05.09 HEATING-AND-AIR-CONDITIONING INSTALLER-SERVICER (construction) 637.261-014

05.05.09 MACHINE REPAIRER, MAINTENANCE (any industry) 638.261-030

05.05.09 MACHINERY ERECTOR (engine-turbine) 638.261-014

05.05.09 MAINTENANCE REPAIRER, INDUSTRIAL (any industry) 899.261-014

05.05.09 POWERHOUSE MECHANIC (utilities) 631.261-014

05.05.09 REFRIGERATION MECHANIC (any industry) 637.261-026

05.05.09 SOLAR-ENERGY-SYSTEM INSTALLER (any industry) 637.261-030

05.05.10 AVIONICS TECHNICIAN (aircraft mfg.) 823.261-026

05.05.10 ELECTRICAL-APPLIANCE SERVICER (any industry) 827.261-010

05.05.10 ELECTRONICS MECHANIC (any industry) 828.261-022

05.05.10 PUBLIC-ADDRESS SERVICER (any industry) 823.261-010

05.05.10 RADIO MECHANIC (any industry) 823.261-018

05.05.11 INSTRUMENT REPAIRER (any industry) 710.261-010

05.05.11 ORTHOTIST (medical ser.) 078.261-018

05.05.11 PROSTHETIST (medical ser.) 078.261-022

05.05.11 RADIOLOGICAL-EQUIPMENT SPECIALIST (inst. & app.) 719.261-014

05.05.11 SCIENTIFIC GLASS BLOWER (glass products) 006.261-010

05.05.12 ELECTRONIC-ORGAN TECHNICIAN (any industry) 828.261-010

05.05.15 ALTERATION TAILOR (garment) 785.261-010

05.05.15 CUSTOM TAILOR (garment) 785.261-014

05.07.01 NONDESTRUCTIVE TESTER (profess. & kin.) 011.261-018

05.07.02 AIRPLANE INSPECTOR (air trans.) 621.261-010

05.07.02 AUTOMOBILE TESTER (automotive ser.) 620.261-014

05.07.02 AUTOMOBILE-REPAIR-SERVICE ESTIMA-TOR (automotive ser.) 620.261-018

05.07.03 ELEVATOR EXAMINER-AND-ADJUSTER (any industry) 825.261-014

05.10.01 DIVER (any industry) 899.261-010

05.10.01 REPAIRER, RECREATIONAL VEHICLE (vehicles, nec) 869.261-022

05.10.02 GAS-APPLIANCE SERVICER (any industry) 637.261-018

05.10.03 ELECTRIC-GOLF-CART REPAIRER (amuse. & rec.) 620.261-026

05.10.04 PINSETTER MECHANIC, AUTOMATIC (any industry) 638.261-022

05.10.04 STAGE TECHNICIAN (amuse. & rec.) 962.261-014

05.10.04 WIND TUNNEL MECHANIC (aircraft mfg.) 869.261-026

05.10.05 PLANETARIUM TECHNICIAN (museums) 962.261-010

05.10.06 BLASTER (any industry) 859.261-010

06.01.04 DEVELOPMENT MECHANIC (aircraft mfg.) 693.261-014

06.01.05 ELECTRONICS TESTER (any industry) 726.261-018

06.01.05 INSPECTOR, ASSEMBLIES AND INSTAL-LATIONS (aircraft mfg.) 806.261-030

06.01.05 INSPECTOR, MATERIAL DISPOSITION (aircraft mfg.) 806.261-034

06.01.05 INSPECTOR, METAL FABRICATING (any industry) 619.261-010

06.01.05 INSPECTOR, OUTSIDE PRODUCTION (aircraft mfg.) 806.261-042

06.01.05 INSPECTOR, PLASTICS AND COMPOSITES (aircraft mfg.) 806.261-046

06.01.05 OPERATIONAL TEST MECHANIC (aircraft mfg.) 806.261-050

10.02.02 MEDICAL RADIATION DOSIMETRIST (medical ser.) 078.261-034

10.02.02 PHERESIS SPECIALIST (medical ser.) 078.261-042

11.10.03 CHEMICAL-RADIATION TECHNICIAN (government ser.) 015.261-010

11.10.03 RADIATION-PROTECTION SPECIALIST (government ser.) 168.261-010

262 (Analyzing, Speaking-Signaling, Operating-Controlling)

01.01.01 FILM OR VIDEOTAPE MDITOR (motion picture) 962.262-010

© 1995, JIST Works, Inc. • Indianapolis, IN

05.01.06 TOOL PROGRAMMER, NUMERICAL
CONTROL (electron. comp.) 609.262-010
05.03.05 FIELD ENGINEER (radio-tv broad.)
193.262-018
05.03.05 FLIGHT-TEST DATA ACQUISITION TECH-
NICIAN (aircraft mfg.) 002.262-010
05.03.05 MASTER CONTROL OPERATOR (radio-tv
broad.) 194.262-022
05.03.05 RADIOTELEPHONE OPERATOR (any
industry) 193.262-034
05.03.05 TRANSMITTER OPERATOR (radio-tv broad.)
193.262-038
05.10.01 SEWER-LINE REPAIRER, TELE-GROUT
(sanitary ser.) 851.262-010
05.10.03 SOUND CONTROLLER (amuse. & rec.)
194.262-014
05.10.05 AUDIO OPERATOR (radio-tv broad.)
194.262-010
05.10.05 SOUND MIXER (motion picture)
194.262-018
07.01.06 CASEWORKER (government ser.)
169.262-010
07.04.04 POLICYHOLDER-INFORMATION CLERK
(insurance) 249.262-010
07.04.05 AIRLINE-RADIO OPERATOR (air trans.)
193.262-010
07.04.05 DISPATCHER (government ser.)
193.262-014
07.06.01 NETWORK CONTROL OPERATOR (any
industry) 031.262-014
10.03.01 PULMONARY-FUNCTION TECHNICIAN
(medical ser.) 078.262-010
11.01.01 DATA COMMUNICATIONS ANALYST
(profess. & kin.) 031.262-010
11.01.01 QUALITY ASSURANCE ANALYST (profess.
& kin.) 033.262-010
11.01.01 USER SUPPORT ANALYST (profess. & kin.)
032.262-010
11.08.02 REPORTER (print. & pub.) 131.262-018
11.08.03 NEWSCASTER (radio-tv broad.)
131.262-010

263 (Analyzing, Speaking-Signaling, Driving-Operating)

04.01.02 POLICE OFFICER I (government ser.)
375.263-014
04.01.02 PUBLIC-SAFETY OFFICER (government ser.)
379.263-014
04.01.02 SHERIFF, DEPUTY (government ser.)
377.263-010
04.01.02 STATE-HIGHWAY POLICE OFFICER
(government ser.) 375.263-018
05.04.01 AIRPLANE PILOT (agriculture) 196.263-010
05.04.01 AIRPLANE PILOT, COMMERCIAL (air
trans.) 196.263-014
11.10.03 ANIMAL TREATMENT INVESTIGATOR
(nonprofit org.) 379.263-010

264 (Analyzing, Speaking-Signaling, Manipulating)

02.04.01 HYDROGRAPHER (waterworks) 025.264-010
05.03.06 INSPECTOR, AIR-CARRIER (government
ser.) 168.264-010
05.05.05 MICROCOMPUTER SUPPORT SPECIALIST
(profess. & kin.) 039.264-010
07.01.06 IDENTIFICATION OFFICER (government
ser.) 377.264-010
10.02.01 NURSE PRACTITIONER (medical ser.)
075.264-010
10.02.01 NURSE-MIDWIFE (medical ser.) 075.264-014
10.02.02 PHYSICAL-INTEGRATION PRACTITIONER
(medical ser.) 076.264-010
10.03.01 HOLTER SCANNING TECHNICIAN (medical
ser.) 078.264-010
11.10.03 GAS INSPECTOR (utilities) 168.264-018

267 (Analyzing, Speaking-Signaling, Handling)

01.03.02 INTERPRETER, DEAF (profess. & kin.)
137.267-014
01.04.02 COPYIST (any industry) 152.267-010
02.04.01 BALLISTICS EXPERT, FORENSIC (government ser.) 199.267-010
02.04.01 EXAMINER, QUESTIONED DOCUMENTS
(government ser.) 199.267-022
02.04.01 GEOLOGICAL AIDE (petrol. & gas)
024.267-010
02.04.01 GRAPHOLOGIST (profess. & kin.)
199.267-038
02.04.01 WEATHER OBSERVER (profess. & kin.)
025.267-014
02.04.02 POLYGRAPH EXAMINER (profess. & kin.)
199.267-026
03.01.04 LOGGING-OPERATIONS INSPECTOR
(forestry) 168.267-070
04.01.02 FIRE MARSHAL (government ser.)
373.267-014
04.01.02 INVESTIGATOR, PRIVATE (business ser.)
376.267-018
04.01.02 POLICE OFFICER III (government ser.)
375.267-038
05.01.07 TOOL DESIGN CHECKER (aircraft mfg.)
007.267-014
05.03.02 DRAWINGS CHECKER, ENGINEERING
(profess. & kin.) 007.267-010
05.03.02 ESTIMATOR (profess. & kin.) 169.267-038
05.03.02 SPECIFICATION WRITER (profess. & kin.)
019.267-010
05.03.06 BUILDING INSPECTOR (insurance)
168.267-010
05.03.06 CONSTRUCTION INSPECTOR (construction)
182.267-010
05.03.06 INDUSTRIAL ENGINEERING TECHNICIAN
(profess. & kin.) 012.267-010

05.03.06 INSPECTOR, INDUSTRIAL WASTE (government ser.) 168.267-054

05.03.06 PLAN CHECKER (government ser.) 168.267-102

05.05.17 ANALYST, FOOD AND BEVERAGE (hotel & rest.) 310.267-010

05.07.01 SHOP ESTIMATOR (automotive ser.) 807.267-010

05.10.03 SIGHT-EFFECTS SPECIALIST (amuse. & rec.) 962.267-010

05.10.05 QUALITY-CONTROL TECHNICIAN (photofinishing) 976.267-010

07.01.01 ELIGIBILITY WORKER (government ser.) 195.267-010

07.01.01 ELIGIBILITY-AND-OCCUPANCY INTERVIEWER (government ser.) 168.267-038

07.01.01 FINANCIAL-AID COUNSELOR (education) 169.267-018

07.01.01 RETIREMENT OFFICER (government ser.) 166.267-030

07.01.04 CREDIT ANALYST (clerical) 241.267-022

07.01.05 AGENT-CONTRACT CLERK (insurance) 241.267-010

07.01.05 CONTRACT CLERK (profess. & kin.) 119.267-018

07.01.05 EXAMINER (government ser.) 169.267-014

07.01.05 HOSPITAL-INSURANCE REPRESENTATIVE (insurance) 166.267-014

07.01.05 PASSPORT-APPLICATION EXAMINER (government ser.) 169.267-030

07.01.05 TITLE CLERK (petrol. & gas) 162.267-010

07.01.07 DRIVER'S LICENSE EXAMINER (government ser.) 168.267-034

07.01.07 EXAMINATION PROCTOR (government ser.) 199.267-018

07.02.03 CLAIM EXAMINER (insurance) 168.267-014

07.04.01 BONDING AGENT (business ser.) 186.267-010

07.04.04 INFORMATION CLERK, AUTOMOBILE CLUB (nonprofit org.) 237.267-010

07.05.02 INVESTIGATOR, UTILITY-BILL COMPLAINTS (utilities) 241.267-034

08.01.02 PLACER (insurance) 239.267-010

10.01.02 CHILD SUPPORT OFFICER (government ser.) 195.267-022

10.01.02 PATIENT-RESOURCES-AND-REIMBURSEMENT AGENT (government ser.) 195.267-018

10.02.03 EVALUATOR (education) 094.267-010

11.01.01 FORMS ANALYST (profess. & kin.) 161.267-018

11.02.02 HUMAN RESOURCE ADVISOR (profess. & kin.) 166.267-046

11.02.04 ACQUISITIONS LIBRARIAN (library) 100.267-010

11.03.04 EMPLOYEE RELATIONS SPECIALIST (profess. & kin.) 166.267-042

11.03.04 EMPLOYMENT INTERVIEWER (profess. & kin.) 166.267-010

11.03.04 JOB ANALYST (profess. & kin.) 166.267-018

11.03.04 JOB DEVELOPMENT SPECIALIST (profess. & kin.) 166.267-034

11.03.04 PERSONNEL RECRUITER (profess. & kin.) 166.267-038

11.03.04 RECRUITER (military ser.) 166.267-026

11.04.01 APPEALS REFEREE (government ser.) 119.267-014

11.04.02 LEGAL INVESTIGATOR (profess. & kin.) 119.267-022

11.04.02 PARALEGAL (profess. & kin.) 119.267-026

11.04.04 ABSTRACTOR (profess. & kin.) 119.267-010

11.05.02 FREIGHT-TRAFFIC CONSULTANT (business ser.) 184.267-010

11.05.02 RESEARCH ANALYST (insurance) 169.267-034

11.05.04 FIELD REPRESENTATIVE (business ser.) 163.267-010

11.06.02 REPORTS ANALYST (profess. & kin.) 161.267-026

11.06.03 APPRAISER, REAL ESTATE (real estate) 191.267-010

11.06.03 CREDIT ANALYST (financial) 160.267-022

11.06.03 DIRECTOR, UTILITY ACCOUNTS (government ser.) 160.267-014

11.06.03 INVESTIGATOR (clerical) 241.267-030

11.06.03 INVESTMENT ANALYST (financial) 160.267-026

11.06.03 LETTER-OF-CREDIT DOCUMENT EXAMINER (financial) 169.267-042

11.06.03 LOAN OFFICER (financial) 186.267-018

11.06.03 LOAN REVIEW ANALYST (financial) 186.267-022

11.06.03 UNDERWRITER (insurance) 169.267-046

11.06.03 UNDERWRITER, MORTGAGE LOAN (financial) 186.267-026

11.06.05 BUDGET ANALYST (government ser.) 161.267-030

11.07.01 FIELD REPRESENTATIVE (profess. & kin.) 189.267-010

11.07.02 UTILIZATION-REVIEW COORDINATOR (medical ser.) 079.267-010

11.08.01 EDITORIAL ASSISTANT (print. & pub.) 132.267-014

11.08.02 RESEARCH ASSISTANT II (profess. & kin.) 199.267-034

11.08.02 WRITER, TECHNICAL PUBLICATIONS (profess. & kin.) 131.267-026

11.08.04 INTERPRETER (profess. & kin.) 137.267-010

11.08.04 TRANSLATOR (profess. & kin.) 137.267-018

11.10.01 INVESTIGATOR (government ser.) 168.267-062

11.10.01 INVESTIGATOR, FRAUD (retail trade) 376.267-014

11.10.03 FIRE INSPECTOR (government ser.) 373.267-010

11.10.03 FOOD AND DRUG INSPECTOR (government ser.) 168.267-042

11.10.03 HAZARDOUS-WASTE MANAGEMENT SPECIALIST (government ser.) 168.267-086

11.10.03 INSPECTOR, MOTOR VEHICLES (government ser.) 168.267-058

11.10.03 INSPECTOR, WATER-POLLUTION CONTROL (government ser.) 168.267-090

11.10.03 LICENSE INSPECTOR (government ser.)
168.267-066

11.10.03 MARINE-CARGO SURVEYOR (business ser.)
168.267-094

11.10.03 MINE INSPECTOR (mine & quarry)
168.267-074

11.10.03 PESTICIDE-CONTROL INSPECTOR (government ser.) 168.267-098

11.10.03 SANITATION INSPECTOR (government ser.)
168.267-110

11.10.04 CUSTOMS INSPECTOR (government ser.)
168.267-022

11.10.05 DEALER-COMPLIANCE REPRESENTATIVE (retail trade) 168.267-026

11.10.05 SHOPPING INVESTIGATOR (business ser.)
376.267-022

11.12.01 APPRAISER, AUTOMOBILE DAMAGE (business ser.) 241.267-014

11.12.01 CLAIM EXAMINER (business ser.)
241.267-018

11.12.01 CLAIMS ADJUDICATOR (government ser.)
169.267-010

12.01.02 UMPIRE (amuse. & rec.) 153.267-018

271 (Analyzing, Serving, Precision)

02.03.04 ACUPUNCTURIST (medical ser.) 079.271-010

09.02.01 COSMETOLOGIST (personal ser.)
332.271-010

09.02.01 HAIR STYLIST (personal ser.) 332.271-018

10.02.02 ACUPRESSURIST (medical ser.) 079.271-014

280 (Analyzing, Taking Instructions-Helping, Setting Up)

02.04.01 PHOTO-OPTICS TECHNICIAN (profess. & kin.) 029.280-010

05.05.07 DIE SINKER (machine shop) 601.280-022

05.05.07 MACHINIST (machine shop) 600.280-022

05.05.07 MAINTENANCE MACHINIST (machine shop) 600.280-042

05.05.07 PATTERNMAKER, METAL (foundry)
600.280-050

05.05.07 TOOL-MACHINE SET-UP OPERATOR (machine shop) 601.280-054

05.05.08 CABINETMAKER (woodworking)
660.280-010

05.05.10 INSTRUMENT-MAKER AND REPAIRER (petrol. & gas) 600.280-014

05.05.11 INSTRUMENT MAKER (any industry)
600.280-010

05.05.11 OPTICIAN (optical goods) 716.280-014

06.01.03 MILLING-MACHINE SET-UP OPERATOR I (machine shop) 605.280-010

06.01.03 SCREW-MACHINE SET-UP OPERATOR, MULTIPLE SPINDLE (machine shop)
604.280-014

281 (Analyzing, Taking Instructions-Helping, Precision)

01.06.01 STRIPPER, LITHOGRAPHIC I (print. & pub.)
972.281-022

01.06.02 CLAY MODELER (any industry) 779.281-010

01.06.02 JEWELER (jewelry-silver.) 700.281-010

01.06.02 PROP MAKER (amuse. & rec.) 962.281-010

01.06.02 SILVERSMITH II (jewelry-silver.)
700.281-022

01.06.02 SPECIAL EFFECTS SPECIALIST (amuse. & rec.) 962.281-018

01.06.02 STONE CARVER (stonework) 771.281-014

01.06.03 SIGN WRITER, HAND (any industry)
970.281-022

02.04.01 ASSAYER (profess. & kin.) 022.281-010

02.04.01 CALIBRATION LABORATORY TECHNICIAN (aircraft mfg.) 019.281-010

02.04.01 LABORATORY TESTER (plastic-synth.)
022.281-018

02.04.01 SPECTROSCOPIST (profess. & kin.)
011.281-014

02.04.02 CYTOTECHNOLOGIST (medical ser.)
078.281-010

05.03.02 AUTO-DESIGN DETAILER (auto. mfg.)
017.281-010

05.03.02 DRAFTER, ASSISTANT (profess. & kin.)
017.281-018

05.03.02 DRAFTER, AUTOMOTIVE DESIGN LAYOUT (auto. mfg.) 017.281-026

05.03.02 DRAFTER, CIVIL (profess. & kin.)
005.281-010

05.03.02 DRAFTER, ELECTRICAL (profess. & kin.)
003.281-010

05.03.02 DRAFTER, ELECTRONIC (profess. & kin.)
003.281-014

05.03.02 DRAFTER, GEOLOGICAL (petrol. & gas)
010.281-014

05.03.02 DRAFTER, GEOPHYSICAL (petrol. & gas)
010.281-018

05.03.02 DRAFTER, MARINE (profess. & kin.)
014.281-010

05.03.02 DRAFTER, MECHANICAL (profess. & kin.)
007.281-010

05.03.02 DRAFTER, STRUCTURAL (profess. & kin.)
005.281-014

05.03.02 STEREO-PLOTTER OPERATOR (profess. & kin.) 018.281-010

05.03.02 TECHNICAL ILLUSTRATOR (profess. & kin.) 017.281-034

05.05.02 CARPENTER, MAINTENANCE (any industry) 860.281-010

05.05.03 PIPE FITTER (construction) 862.281-022

05.05.05 CENTRAL-OFFICE REPAIRER (tel. & tel.)
822.281-014

05.05.05 COMPUTERIZED ENVIRONMENTAL CONTROL INSTALLER (electron. comp.)
828.281-026

05.05.05 ELEVATOR REPAIRER (any industry)
825.281-030

05.05.05 MAINTENANCE MECHANIC, TELEPHONE (any industry) 822.281-018

05.05.06 MILLWRIGHT (any industry) 638.281-018

05.05.06 SHEET-METAL WORKER (any industry) 804.281-010

05.05.06 WELDER, EXPERIMENTAL (welding) 819.281-022

05.05.07 FLUID-POWER MECHANIC (any industry) 600.281-010

05.05.07 GUNSMITH (any industry) 632.281-010

05.05.07 LAY-OUT WORKER (machine shop) 600.281-018

05.05.08 LOFT WORKER (ship-boat mfg.) 661.281-010

05.05.09 AIR-CONDITIONING MECHANIC (automotive ser.) 620.281-010

05.05.09 AIRFRAME-AND-POWER-PLANT MECHANIC (aircraft mfg.) 621.281-014

05.05.09 AIRFRAME-AND-POWER-PLANT-MECHANIC APPRENTICE (air trans.) 621.281-018

05.05.09 AUTOMOTIVE-MAINTENANCE-EQUIPMENT SERVICER (any industry) 620.281-018

05.05.09 CASH-REGISTER SERVICER (any industry) 633.281-010

05.05.09 DIESEL MECHANIC (any industry) 625.281-010

05.05.09 FARM-EQUIPMENT MECHANIC I (agric. equip.) 624.281-010

05.05.09 FUEL-INJECTION SERVICER (any industry) 625.281-022

05.05.09 FURNACE INSTALLER-AND-REPAIRER, HOT AIR (any industry) 869.281-010

05.05.09 GAS-ENGINE REPAIRER (any industry) 625.281-026

05.05.09 HYDRAULIC REPAIRER (any industry) 638.281-034

05.05.09 LOCKSMITH (any industry) 709.281-010

05.05.09 MACHINE BUILDER (machinery mfg.) 600.281-022

05.05.09 MAINTENANCE MECHANIC (construction) 620.281-046

05.05.09 MAINTENANCE MECHANIC (any industry) 638.281-014

05.05.09 MECHANIC, INDUSTRIAL TRUCK (any industry) 620.281-050

05.05.09 MOTORBOAT MECHANIC (engine-turbine) 623.281-038

05.05.09 MOTORCYCLE REPAIRER (automotive ser.) 620.281-054

05.05.09 OFFICE-MACHINE SERVICER (any industry) 633.281-018

05.05.09 PARTS SALVAGER (any industry) 638.281-026

05.05.09 PNEUMATIC-TOOL REPAIRER (any industry) 630.281-010

05.05.09 PUMP SERVICER (any industry) 630.281-018

05.05.09 ROCKET-ENGINE-COMPONENT MECHANIC (aircraft mfg.) 621.281-030

05.05.09 SMALL-ENGINE MECHANIC (any industry) 625.281-034

05.05.09 TRACTOR MECHANIC (automotive ser.) 620.281-058

05.05.09 TUNE-UP MECHANIC (automotive ser.) 620.281-066

05.05.10 AUDIO-VIDEO REPAIRER (any industry) 729.281-010

05.05.10 ELECTRIC-METER REPAIRER (utilities) 729.281-014

05.05.10 ELECTRIC-MOTOR REPAIRER (any industry) 721.281-018

05.05.10 ELECTRICAL-INSTRUMENT REPAIRER (any industry) 729.281-026

05.05.10 ELECTRICIAN, AUTOMOTIVE (automotive ser.) 825.281-022

05.05.10 INSTRUMENT MECHANIC (any industry) 710.281-026

05.05.10 METEOROLOGICAL-EQUIPMENT REPAIRER (any industry) 823.281-018

05.05.11 ELECTROMECHANICAL TECHNICIAN (inst. & app.) 710.281-018

05.05.11 INSTRUMENT TECHNICIAN (utilities) 710.281-030

05.05.12 ELECTRIC-ORGAN INSPECTOR AND REPAIRER (musical inst.) 730.281-018

05.05.12 FRETTED-INSTRUMENT MAKER, HAND (musical inst.) 730.281-022

05.05.12 VIOLIN MAKER, HAND (musical inst.) 730.281-046

05.05.14 GEM CUTTER (jewelry-silver.) 770.281-014

05.05.14 GEMOLOGIST (jewelry-silver.) 199.281-010

05.05.17 CHEF DE FROID (hotel & rest.) 313.281-010

05.07.01 INSPECTOR, TOOL (machine shop) 601.281-022

05.07.01 ULTRASONIC TESTER (any industry) 739.281-014

05.10.01 CASTING REPAIRER (any industry) 619.281-010

05.10.01 FRONT-END MECHANIC (automotive ser.) 620.281-038

05.10.02 BRAKE REPAIRER (automotive ser.) 620.281-026

05.10.02 CARBURETOR MECHANIC (automotive ser.) 620.281-034

05.10.02 COIN-MACHINE-SERVICE REPAIRER (svc. ind. mach.) 639.281-014

05.10.02 MEDICAL-EQUIPMENT REPAIRER (protective dev.) 639.281-022

05.10.02 METER REPAIRER (any industry) 710.281-034

05.10.02 SEWING-MACHINE REPAIRER (any industry) 639.281-018

05.10.02 TRANSMISSION MECHANIC (automotive ser.) 620.281-062

05.10.03 AUTOMATIC-DOOR MECHANIC (construction) 829.281-010

05.10.03 CABLE TELEVISION INSTALLER (radio-tv broad.) 821.281-010

05.10.03 ELECTRIC-TOOL REPAIRER (any industry) 729.281-022

05.10.03 TAPE-RECORDER REPAIRER (any industry) 720.281-014

05.10.03 TELEVISION-AND-RADIO REPAIRER (any industry) 720.281-018

05.10.08 COOK (domestic ser.) 305.281-010
06.01.04 TOOL BUILDER (aircraft mfg.) 693.281-030
06.01.05 X-RAY-EQUIPMENT TESTER (any industry)
729.281-046

282 (Analyzing, Taking Instructions-Helping, Operating-Controlling)

01.06.01 ELECTRONIC MASKING SYSTEM
OPERATOR (print. & pub.) 972.282-018
01.06.01 ELECTRONIC PREPRESS SYSTEM
OPERATOR (print. & pub.) 979.282-010
05.03.05 VIDEO OPERATOR (radio-tv broad.)
194.282-010

283 (Analyzing, Taking Instructions-Helping, Driving-Operating)

06.03.01 TEST DRIVER I (auto. mfg.) 806.283-014

284 (Analyzing, Taking Instructions-Helping, Manipulating)

05.03.04 PROSPECTOR (any industry) 024.28-.010
06.03.02 FILM FLAT INSPECTOR (print. & pub.)
972.284-010

287 (Analyzing, Taking Instructions-Helping, Handling)

01.02.01 APPRAISER, ART (profess. & kin.)
191.287-014
05.03.06 INSPECTOR, QUALITY ASSURANCE
(government ser.) 168.287-014
05.03.06 INSPECTOR, RAILROAD (government ser.)
168.287-018
07.01.05 TITLE EXAMINER (profess. & kin.)
119.287-010
11.06.03 APPRAISER (any industry) 191.287-010
11.10.03 INSPECTOR, AGRICULTURAL COMMODI-
TIES (government ser.) 168.287-010

Data = Compiling

327 (Compiling, Instructing, Handling)

11.02.01 TEACHER AIDE I (education) 099.327-010

341 (Compiling, Diverting, Precision)

12.02.01 JUGGLER (amuse. & rec.) 159.341-010
12.02.01 STUNT PERFORMER (amuse. & rec.)
159.341-014

344 (Compiling, Diverting, Manipulating)

12.02.01 EQUESTRIAN (amuse. & rec.) 159.344-010
12.02.01 RODEO PERFORMER (amuse. & rec.)
159.344-014
12.02.01 SHOW-HORSE DRIVER (amuse. & rec.)
159.344-018

347 (Compiling, Diverting, Handling)

01.07.02 ANNOUNCER (amuse. & rec.) 159.347-010
12.02.01 AQUATIC PERFORMER (amuse. & rec.)
159.347-014

351 (Compiling, Persuading, Precision)

08.02.02 SALESPERSON, WIGS (personal ser.)
261.351-010

353 (Compiling, Persuading, Driving-Operating)

08.02.02 SALESPERSON, AUTOMOBILES (retail
trade) 273.353-010
08.02.07 DRIVER, SALES ROUTE (retail trade)
292.353-010

354 (Compiling, Persuading, Manipulating)

08.02.02 HEARING AID SPECIALIST (retail trade)
276.354-010
08.02.02 SALESPERSON, PIANOS AND ORGANS
(retail trade) 277.354-010
08.02.03 SALESPERSON, ELECTRIC MOTORS (retail
trade) 271.354-010
08.02.05 DEMONSTRATOR (retail trade) 297.354-010
08.02.05 DEMONSTRATOR, KNITTING (retail trade)
297.354-014
10.03.02 PHYSICAL THERAPY AIDE (medical ser.)
355.354-010
11.02.03 HOMEMAKER (social ser.) 309.354-010

357 (Compiling, Persuading, Handling)

07.04.02 COLLECTION CLERK (clerical) 241.357-010
08.01.01 SALES REPRESENTATIVE, CHEMICALS
AND DRUGS (wholesale tr.) 262.357-010

08.01.01 SALES REPRESENTATIVE, ELECTRONICS PARTS (wholesale tr.) 271.357-010

08.01.02 SALES REPRESENTATIVE, ADVERTISING (print. & pub.) 254.357-014

08.01.02 SALES REPRESENTATIVE, PRINTING (wholesale tr.) 254.357-018

08.01.02 SALES REPRESENTATIVE, PUBLIC UTILITIES (tel. & tel.) 253.357-010

08.01.02 SALES REPRESENTATIVE, RADIO AND TELEVISION TIME (radio-tv broad.) 259.357-018

08.01.02 SALES REPRESENTATIVE, SHIPPING SERVICES (motor trans.) 252.357-014

08.01.03 COMMISSION AGENT, AGRICULTURAL PRODUCE (wholesale tr.) 260.357-010

08.02.01 SALES REPRESENTATIVE, ANIMAL-FEED PRODUCTS (wholesale tr.) 272.357-010

08.02.01 SALES REPRESENTATIVE, FARM AND GARDEN EQUIPMENT AND SUPPLIES (wholesale tr.) 272.357-014

08.02.01 SALES REPRESENTATIVE, FOOD PRODUCTS (wholesale tr.) 260.357-014

08.02.01 SALES REPRESENTATIVE, FOOTWEAR (wholesale tr.) 261.357-018

08.02.01 SALES REPRESENTATIVE, HARDWARE SUPPLIES (wholesale tr.) 274.357-034

08.02.01 SALES REPRESENTATIVE, HOME FURNISHINGS (wholesale tr.) 270.357-010

08.02.01 SALES REPRESENTATIVE, HOUSEHOLD APPLIANCES (wholesale tr.) 270.357-014

08.02.01 SALES REPRESENTATIVE, MALT LIQUORS (wholesale tr.) 260.357-018

08.02.01 SALES REPRESENTATIVE, MEN'S AND BOYS' APPAREL (wholesale tr.) 261.357-022

08.02.01 SALES REPRESENTATIVE, NOVELTIES (wholesale tr.) 277.357-018

08.02.01 SALES REPRESENTATIVE, PETROLEUM PRODUCTS (wholesale tr.) 269.357-014

08.02.01 SALES REPRESENTATIVE, PRINTING SUPPLIES (wholesale tr.) 274.357-062

08.02.01 SALES REPRESENTATIVE, RECREATION AND SPORTING GOODS (wholesale tr.) 277.357-026

08.02.01 SALES REPRESENTATIVE, TEXTILES (wholesale tr.) 261.357-030

08.02.01 SALES REPRESENTATIVE, TOILET PREPARATIONS (wholesale tr.) 262.357-014

08.02.01 SALES REPRESENTATIVE, VIDEOTAPE (wholesale tr.) 271.357-014

08.02.01 SALES REPRESENTATIVE, WOMEN'S AND GIRLS' APPAREL (wholesale tr.) 261.357-038

08.02.01 SALES-PROMOTION REPRESENTATIVE (wholesale tr.) 269.357-018

08.02.02 SALES EXHIBITOR (nonprofit org.) 279.357-010

08.02.02 SALESPERSON, BOOKS (retail trade) 277.357-034

08.02.02 SALESPERSON, COSMETICS AND TOILETRIES (retail trade) 262.357-018

08.02.02 SALESPERSON, CURTAINS AND DRAPERIES (retail trade) 270.357-022

08.02.02 SALESPERSON, FLOWERS (retail trade) 260.357-026

08.02.02 SALESPERSON, FURNITURE (retail trade) 270.357-030

08.02.02 SALESPERSON, HOUSEHOLD APPLIANCES (retail trade) 270.357-034

08.02.02 SALESPERSON, INFANTS' AND CHILDREN'S WEAR (retail trade) 261.357-046

08.02.02 SALESPERSON, JEWELRY (retail trade) 279.357-058

08.02.02 SALESPERSON, MEN'S AND BOYS' CLOTHING (retail trade) 261.357-050

08.02.02 SALESPERSON, MUSICAL INSTRUMENTS AND ACCESSORIES (retail trade) 277.357-038

08.02.02 SALESPERSON, PETS AND PET SUPPLIES (retail trade) 277.357-042

08.02.02 SALESPERSON, PHONOGRAPH RECORDS AND TAPE RECORDINGS (retail trade) 277.357-046

08.02.02 SALESPERSON, SHEET MUSIC (retail trade) 277.357-054

08.02.02 SALESPERSON, SHOES (retail trade) 261.357-062

08.02.02 SALESPERSON, SPORTING GOODS (retail trade) 277.357-058

08.02.02 SALESPERSON, STEREO EQUIPMENT (retail trade) 270.357-038

08.02.02 SALESPERSON, TOY TRAINS AND ACCESSORIES (retail trade) 277.357-066

08.02.02 SALESPERSON, TRAILERS AND MOTOR HOMES (retail trade) 273.357-034

08.02.02 SALESPERSON, WOMEN'S APPAREL AND ACCESSORIES (retail trade) 261.357-066

08.02.02 SALESPERSON, YARD GOODS (retail trade) 261.357-070

08.02.03 SALES REPRESENTATIVE, BOATS AND MARINE SUPPLIES (retail trade) 273.357-018

08.02.03 SALES REPRESENTATIVE, OFFICE MACHINES (retail trade) 275.357-034

08.02.03 SALESPERSON, AUTOMOBILE ACCESSORIES (retail trade) 273.357-030

08.02.03 SALESPERSON, FLOOR COVERINGS (retail trade) 270.357-026

08.02.03 SALESPERSON, GENERAL HARDWARE (retail trade) 279.357-050

08.02.03 SALESPERSON, GENERAL MERCHANDISE (retail trade) 279.357-054

08.02.03 SALESPERSON, HORTICULTURAL AND NURSERY PRODUCTS (retail trade) 272.357-022

08.02.03 SALESPERSON, PARTS (retail trade) 279.357-062

08.02.03 SALESPERSON, PHOTOGRAPHIC SUPPLIES AND EQUIPMENT (retail trade) 277.357-050

08.02.03 SALESPERSON, STAMPS OR COINS (retail trade) 277.357-062

08.02.04 BUILDING CONSULTANT (wholesale tr.) 250.357-010

08.02.04 LEASING AGENT, RESIDENCE (real estate) 250.357-014

08.02.04 SALES AGENT, REAL ESTATE (real estate) 250.357-018

08.02.05 DEMONSTRATOR, ELECTRIC-GAS APPLIANCES (utilities) 297.357-010

08.02.05 SALES REPRESENTATIVE, DANCING INSTRUCTIONS (education) 259.357-014

08.02.05 SALESPERSON-DEMONSTRATOR, PARTY PLAN (retail trade) 279.357-038

08.02.06 CRATING-AND-MOVING ESTIMATOR (motor trans.) 252.357-010

08.02.06 LINEN CONTROLLER (laundry & rel.) 299.357-010

08.02.06 SALES AGENT, BUSINESS SERVICES (business ser.) 251.357-010

08.02.06 SALES REPRESENTATIVE (motor trans.) 250.357-022

08.02.06 SALES REPRESENTATIVE, AUTOMOTIVE-LEASING (business ser.) 273.357-014

08.02.06 SALES REPRESENTATIVE, FRANCHISE (business ser.) 251.357-022

08.02.06 SALES REPRESENTATIVE, TELEVISION CABLE SERVICE (radio-tv broad.) 259.357-022

08.02.06 SALES REPRESENTATIVE, UPHOLSTERY AND FURNITURE REPAIR (retail trade) 259.357-026

08.02.06 WEDDING CONSULTANT (retail trade) 299.357-018

08.02.08 FUND RAISER II (nonprofit org.) 293.357-014

08.02.08 GROUP-SALES REPRESENTATIVE (amuse. & rec.) 259.357-010

08.02.08 MEMBERSHIP SOLICITOR (any industry) 293.357-022

08.02.08 SALES REPRESENTATIVE, DOOR-TO-DOOR (retail trade) 291.357-010

08.02.08 TELEPHONE SOLICITOR (any industry) 299.357-014

09.04.02 FURNITURE-RENTAL CONSULTANT (retail trade) 295.357-018

09.04.02 PERSONAL SHOPPER (retail trade) 296.357-010

09.04.02 TOOL-AND-EQUIPMENT-RENTAL CLERK (business ser.) 295.357-014

09.05.02 WINE STEWARD/STEWARDESS (hotel & rest.) 310.357-010

11.06.04 TICKET BROKER (amuse. & rec.) 259.357-034

11.09.01 GOODWILL AMBASSADOR (business ser.) 293.357-018

11.09.02 BLOOD-DONOR RECRUITER (medical ser.) 293.357-010

11.12.02 LEASING AGENT, OUTDOOR ADVERTISING (business ser.) 254.357-010

360 (Compiling, Speaking-Signaling, Setting Up)

06.01.02 DIE SETTER (forging) 612.360-010

06.01.02 KNITTER MECHANIC (knitting) 685.360-010

06.01.02 MACHINE SETTER (machine shop) 600.360-014

06.01.02 MACHINE SETTER (any industry) 616.360-022

06.01.02 PRINT CONTROLLER (photofinishing) 976.360-010

06.01.02 SCREEN-PRINTING-EQUIPMENT SETTER (paper goods) 979.360-010

06.01.02 SETTER, AUTOMATIC-SPINNING LATHE (any industry) 604.360-010

06.01.03 FIRESETTER (elec. equip.) 692.360-018

06.01.03 NUMERICAL CONTROL MACHINE SET-UP OPERATOR (machine shop) 609.360-010

361 (Compiling, Speaking-Signaling, Precision)

01.06.02 DISPLAY MAKER (fabrication, nec) 739.361-010

01.06.02 MORTUARY BEAUTICIAN (personal ser.) 339.361-010

01.06.02 WIG DRESSER (fabrication, nec) 332.361-010

02.03.03 VETERINARY TECHNICIAN (medical ser.) 079.361-014

02.04.01 LABORATORY ASSISTANT (utilities) 029.361-018

02.04.01 TESTER (profess. & kin.) 011.361-010

02.04.02 FOOD TESTER (any industry) 029.361-014

02.04.02 LABORATORY TECHNICIAN, PHARMACEUTICAL (pharmaceut.) 559.361-010

02.04.02 SEED ANALYST (profess. & kin.) 040.361-014

05.03.02 PATTERNMAKER (furniture) 781.361-014

05.03.05 RADIOGRAPHER (any industry) 199.361-010

05.05.02 BOAT REPAIRER (ship-boat mfg.) 807.361-014

05.05.02 BOATBUILDER, WOOD (ship-boat mfg.) 860.361-010

05.05.03 GAS-MAIN FITTER (utilities) 862.361-014

05.05.04 DRY-WALL APPLICATOR (construction) 842.361-030

05.05.04 PLASTERER (construction) 842.361-018

05.05.05 CABLE INSTALLER-REPAIRER (utilities) 821.361-010

05.05.05 CABLE SPLICER (construction) 829.361-010

05.05.05 CABLE TESTER (tel. & tel.) 822.361-010

05.05.05 ELECTRIC-METER INSTALLER I (utilities) 821.361-014

05.05.05 FURNACE INSTALLER (utilities) 862.361-010

05.05.05 LINE ERECTOR (construction) 821.361-018

05.05.05 LINE REPAIRER (utilities) 821.361-026

05.05.05 PROTECTIVE-SIGNAL INSTALLER (business ser.) 822.361-018

05.05.05 PROTECTIVE-SIGNAL REPAIRER (business ser.) 822.361-022

05.05.05 TOWER ERECTOR (construction) 821.361-038

05.05.06 BOILERHOUSE MECHANIC (any industry) 805.361-010

05.05.06 CONDUIT MECHANIC (construction)
869.361-010

05.05.06 ELEVATOR CONSTRUCTOR (construction)
825.361-010

05.05.06 FORMER, HAND (any industry) 619.361-010

05.05.06 METAL FABRICATOR (any industry)
619.361-014

05.05.06 STRUCTURAL-STEEL WORKER (construction) 801.361-014

05.05.06 WELDER-FITTER (welding) 819.361-010

05.05.09 REFRIGERATION MECHANIC (svc. ind.
mach.) 827.361-014

05.05.11 ORTHOTICS ASSISTANT (medical ser.)
078.361-022

05.05.11 PROSTHETICS ASSISTANT (medical ser.)
078.361-026

05.05.15 DRESSMAKER (any industry) 785.361-010

05.05.15 SHOE REPAIRER (personal ser.) 365.361-014

05.05.15 SHOP TAILOR (garment) 785.361-022

05.05.17 COOK (hotel & rest.) 313.361-014

05.10.01 LUGGAGE REPAIRER (any industry)
365.361-010

05.10.01 OPTICIAN, DISPENSING (optical goods)
299.361-010

05.10.02 NEW-CAR GET-READY MECHANIC
(automotive ser.) 806.361-026

05.10.03 TELEVISION INSTALLER (any industry)
823.361-010

05.10.05 REPRODUCTION TECHNICIAN (any
industry) 976.361-010

05.10.08 COOK (any industry) 315.361-010

05.10.08 COOK, SPECIALTY (hotel & rest.)
313.361-026

05.10.08 COOK, SPECIALTY, FOREIGN FOOD (hotel
& rest.) 313.361-030

05.10.08 GARDE MANGER (hotel & rest.) 313.361-034

05.10.08 PIE MAKER (hotel & rest.) 313.361-038

05.10.09 FUMIGATOR (business ser.) 383.361-010

06.01.04 CHEESEMAKER (dairy products)
529.361-018

06.01.04 MOLDER (aircraft mfg.) 518.361-010

06.01.04 TEST EQUIPMENT MECHANIC (aircraft
mfg.) 710.361-014

06.01.05 INSPECTOR, ELECTROMECHANICAL (inst.
& app.) 729.361-010

06.02.22 MACHINE ASSEMBLER (machinery mfg.)
638.361-010

06.02.28 CANDY MAKER (sugar & conf.) 529.361-014

09.05.07 WARDROBE SUPERVISOR (amuse. & rec.)
346.361-010

10.02.02 CORRECTIVE THERAPIST (medical ser.)
076.361-010

10.02.02 DENTAL HYGIENIST (medical ser.)
078.361-010

10.02.02 NUCLEAR MEDICINE TECHNOLOGIST
(medical ser.) 078.361-018

10.02.02 RADIATION-THERAPY TECHNOLOGIST
(medical ser.) 078.361-034

10.02.02 RESPIRATORY THERAPIST (medical ser.)
076.361-014

10.03.01 OPHTHALMIC TECHNICIAN (medical ser.)
078.361-038

10.03.02 DENTAL ASSISTANT (medical ser.)
079.361-018

362 (Compiling, Speaking-Signaling, Operating-Controlling)

01.03.01 COMMUNICATIONS TECHNICIAN (education) 962.362-010

02.04.01 HOT-CELL TECHNICIAN (profess. & kin.)
015.362-018

02.04.01 RADIOISOTOPE-PRODUCTION OPERATOR
(profess. & kin.) 015.362-022

02.04.01 REACTOR OPERATOR, TEST-AND-
RESEARCH (profess. & kin.) 015.362-026

02.04.02 OPHTHALMIC PHOTOGRAPHER (medical
ser.) 143.362-014

05.03.02 DESIGN TECHNICIAN, COMPUTER-AIDED
(electron. comp.) 003.362-010

05.03.05 TECHNICIAN, NEWS GATHERING (radio-tv
broad.) 194.362-022

05.05.13 CYLINDER-PRESS OPERATOR (print. &
pub.) 651.362-010

05.05.13 ROTOGRAVURE-PRESS OPERATOR (print.
& pub.) 651.362-026

05.05.13 WEB-PRESS OPERATOR (print. & pub.)
651.362-030

05.06.01 HYDROELECTRIC-STATION OPERATOR
(utilities) 952.362-018

05.06.01 POWER-REACTOR OPERATOR (utilities)
952.362-022

05.06.01 SUBSTATION OPERATOR (utilities)
952.362-026

05.06.02 FUEL ATTENDANT (any industry)
953.362-010

05.06.02 REFRIGERATING ENGINEER (any industry)
950.362-014

05.07.01 SEWER-LINE PHOTO-INSPECTOR (sanitary
ser.) 851.362-010

05.10.03 LIGHT TECHNICIAN (motion picture)
962.362-014

05.10.05 FILM INSPECTOR (photofinishing)
976.362-010

05.10.05 INSTANT PRINT OPERATOR (print. & pub.)
979.362-010

05.10.05 MOTION-PICTURE PROJECTIONIST
(amuse. & rec.) 960.362-010

05.10.05 RECORDING ENGINEER (radio-tv broad.)
194.362-010

05.10.05 RERECORDING MIXER (motion picture)
194.362-014

06.01.03 LATHE OPERATOR, NUMERICAL CON-
TROL (machine shop) 604.362-010

06.01.03 MICROELECTRONICS TECHNICIAN
(electron. comp.) 590.362-022

06.02.02 DROPHAMMER OPERATOR (aircraft mfg.)
610.362-010

06.02.02 NUMERICAL CONTROL MACHINE
OPERATOR (machine shop) 609.362-010

06.02.02 SPINNER, HAND (any industry) 619.362-018

06.02.09 AUTOMATED CUTTING MACHINE OPERA-
TOR (aircraft mfg.) 699.362-010

06.02.15 BUTTERMAKER (dairy products)
529.362-010

06.02.15 DRIER OPERATOR (food prep., nec)
523.362-014

06.02.18 AUTOCLAVE OPERATOR (aircraft mfg.)
553.362-014

07.01.02 ADMINISTRATIVE CLERK (clerical)
219.362-010

07.01.02 COURT CLERK (government ser.)
243.362-010

07.01.02 MEMBERSHIP SECRETARY (nonprofit org.)
201.362-018

07.01.03 LEGAL SECRETARY (clerical) 201.362-010

07.01.03 MEDICAL SECRETARY (medical ser.)
201.362-014

07.01.03 SCHOOL SECRETARY (education)
201.362-022

07.01.03 SECRETARY (clerical) 201.362-030

07.01.03 TRUST OPERATIONS ASSISTANT (financial)
219.362-074

07.01.04 MORTGAGE CLERK (financial) 249.362-014

07.01.04 MORTGAGE LOAN CLOSER (financial)
249.362-018

07.01.04 REAL-ESTATE CLERK (real estate)
219.362-046

07.01.04 SECURITIES CLERK (financial) 219.362-054

07.02.01 ELECTRONIC FUNDS TRANSFER COOR-
DINATOR (financial) 216.362-038

07.02.01 RESERVES CLERK (financial) 216.362-034

07.02.02 BROKERAGE CLERK II (financial)
219.362-018

07.02.02 COLLECTION CLERK (financial)
216.362-014

07.02.02 CONTRACT CLERK, AUTOMOBILE (retail
trade) 219.362-026

07.02.02 MARGIN CLERK I (financial) 216.362-042

07.02.02 POLICY-CHANGE CLERK (insurance)
219.362-042

07.02.02 STATEMENT CLERK (financial) 214.362-046

07.02.02 TAX PREPARER (business ser.) 219.362-070

07.02.02 TRANSFER CLERK (financial) 216.362-046

07.02.04 BILLING CLERK (clerical) 214.362-042

07.02.04 DEMURRAGE CLERK (r.r. trans.)
214.362-010

07.02.04 INSURANCE CLERK (medical ser.)
214.362-022

07.02.04 INVOICE-CONTROL CLERK (clerical)
214.362-026

07.02.05 TIMEKEEPER (clerical) 215.362-022

07.03.01 CASHIER I (clerical) 211.362-010

07.03.01 TELLER (financial) 211.362-018

07.04.01 CUSTOMER SERVICE REPRESENTATIVE
(financial) 205.362-026

07.04.01 CUSTOMER SERVICE REPRESENTATIVE
(radio-tv broad.) 239.362-014

07.04.01 EMPLOYMENT CLERK (clerical)
205.362-014

07.04.01 HOSPITAL-ADMITTING CLERK (medical
ser.) 205.362-018

07.04.01 IDENTIFICATION CLERK (clerical)
205.362-022

07.04.01 OUTPATIENT-ADMITTING CLERK (medical
ser.) 205.362-030

07.04.02 CORRESPONDENCE CLERK (clerical)
209.362-034

07.04.04 CONGRESSIONAL-DISTRICT AIDE (government ser.) 209.362-030

07.04.05 DISPATCHER, RADIO (government ser.)
379.362-010

07.04.05 POLICE AIDE (government ser.) 243.362-014

07.04.05 PROTECTIVE-SIGNAL OPERATOR (any
industry) 379.362-014

07.04.05 TELECOMMUNICATOR (government ser.)
379.362-018

07.05.01 COMPUTER PROCESSING SCHEDULER
(clerical) 221.362-030

07.05.01 CREW SCHEDULER (air trans.) 215.362-010

07.05.01 POLICE CLERK (government ser.)
375.362-010

07.05.01 RESERVATION CLERK (clerical) 238.362-014

07.05.02 CREDIT REFERENCE CLERK (financial)
209.362-018

07.05.02 MORTGAGE LOAN PROCESSOR (financial)
249.362-022

07.05.02 MORTGAGE-CLOSING CLERK (clerical)
219.362-038

07.05.03 ATTENDANCE CLERK (education)
219.362-014

07.05.03 CAPTION WRITER (motion picture)
203.362-026

07.05.03 IDENTIFICATION CLERK (government ser.)
209.362-022

07.05.03 MEDICAL RECORD TECHNICIAN (medical
ser.) 079.362-014

07.05.03 MEDICAL-RECORD CLERK (medical ser.)
245.362-010

07.05.03 ORDER CLERK (clerical) 249.362-026

07.05.03 PERSONNEL CLERK (clerical) 209.362-026

07.05.03 SHORTHAND REPORTER (clerical)
202.362-010

07.05.03 STENOGRAPHER (clerical) 202.362-014

07.05.03 STENOTYPE OPERATOR (clerical)
202.362-022

07.05.03 TUMOR REGISTRAR (medical ser.)
079.362-018

07.05.03 UNIT CLERK (medical ser.) 245.362-014

07.06.01 COMPUTER OPERATOR (clerical)
213.362-010

07.06.01 CREDIT REPORTING CLERK (business ser.)
203.362-014

07.06.02 CLERK-TYPIST (clerical) 203.362-010

08.01.03 FOREIGN BANKNOTE TELLER-TRADER
(financial) 211.362-014

10.02.02 DIALYSIS TECHNICIAN (medical ser.)
078.362-014

10.02.02 RADIOLOGIC TECHNOLOGIST (medical
ser.) 078.362-026

10.02.02 SPECIAL PROCEDURES TECHNOLOGIST,
ANGIOGRAM (medical ser.) 078.362-046

10.02.02 SPECIAL PROCEDURES TECHNOLOGIST,
CARDIAC CATHETERIZATION (medical
ser.) 078.362-050

10.02.02 SPECIAL PROCEDURES TECHNOLOGIST, CT SCAN (medical ser.) 078.362-054

10.02.02 SPECIAL PROCEDURES TECHNOLOGIST, MAGNETIC RESONANCE IMAGING (MRI) (medical ser.) 078.362-058

10.03.01 AUDIOMETRIST (profess. & kin.) 078.362-010

10.03.01 CARDIOPULMONARY TECHNOLOGIST (medical ser.) 078.362-030

10.03.01 ELECTROCARDIOGRAPH TECHNICIAN (medical ser.) 078.362-018

10.03.01 ELECTROENCEPHALOGRAPHIC TECH-NOLOGIST (medical ser.) 078.362-022

10.03.01 ELECTROMYOGRAPHIC TECHNICIAN (medical ser.) 078.362-038

10.03.01 POLYSOMNOGRAPHIC TECHNICIAN (medical ser.) 078.362-042

10.03.01 STRESS TEST TECHNICIAN (medical ser.) 078.362-062

10.03.02 MEDICAL ASSISTANT (medical ser.) 079.362-010

10.03.02 PERFUSIONIST (medical ser.) 078.362-034

11.10.05 COMPUTER SECURITY SPECIALIST (profess. & kin.) 033.362-010

363 (Compiling, Speaking-Signaling, Driving-Operating)

04.02.03 BORDER GUARD (government ser.) 375.363-010

05.08.02 LOCOMOTIVE ENGINEER (r.r. trans.) 910.363-014

05.08.03 HEALTH-EQUIPMENT SERVICER (medical ser.) 359.363-010

05.08.03 NEWSPAPER-DELIVERY DRIVER (whole-sale tr.) 292.363-010

05.09.01 BOOKMOBILE DRIVER (library) 249.363-010

07.05.04 RURAL MAIL CARRIER (government ser.) 230.363-010

09.01.02 GUIDE, SIGHTSEEING (amuse. & rec.) 353.363-010

364 (Compiling, Speaking-Signaling, Manipulating)

01.06.03 GIFT WRAPPER (retail trade) 299.364-014

02.04.01 ULTRASOUND TECHNOLOGIST (medical ser.) 078.364-010

02.04.02 BIOLOGICAL AIDE (agriculture) 049.364-018

02.04.02 PHLEBOTOMIST (medical ser.) 079.364-022

02.04.02 VECTOR CONTROL ASSISTANT (govern-ment ser.) 049.364-014

03.02.02 FORESTER AIDE (forestry) 452.364-010

03.04.05 PLANT-CARE WORKER (agriculture) 408.364-010

04.02.03 BEACH LIFEGUARD (amuse. & rec.) 379.364-014

04.02.04 FIRE FIGHTER (any industry) 373.364-010

05.05.01 CEMENT MASON (construction) 844.364-010

05.05.06 ARC CUTTER (welding) 816.364-010

05.10.01 INSULATION WORKER (construction) 863.364-014

05.10.04 AIRPORT ATTENDANT (air trans.) 912.364-010

05.10.09 EXTERMINATOR, TERMITE (business ser.) 383.364-010

05.12.03 ABLE SEAMAN (water trans.) 911.364-010

05.12.06 BOAT LOADER I (water trans.) 911.364-014

06.04.34 ELECTRONICS UTILITY WORKER (comm. equip.) 726.364-018

09.01.02 CRAFT DEMONSTRATOR (museums) 109.364-010

10.02.01 NURSE, GENERAL DUTY (medical ser.) 075.364-010

10.02.01 PHYSICIAN ASSISTANT (medical ser.) 079.364-018

10.02.02 OCCUPATIONAL THERAPY ASSISTANT (medical ser.) 076.364-010

10.03.01 ECHOCARDIOGRAPH TECHNICIAN (medical ser.) 078.364-014

10.03.02 CHIROPRACTOR ASSISTANT (medical ser.) 079.364-010

10.03.02 OPTOMETRIC ASSISTANT (medical ser.) 079.364-014

10.03.02 PARAMEDIC (medical ser.) 079.364-026

11.03.02 CITY PLANNING AIDE (profess. & kin.) 199.364-010

365 (Compiling, Speaking-Signaling, Tending)

07.04.03 REGISTRATION CLERK (library) 249.365-010

366 (Compiling, Speaking-Signaling, Feeding-Offbearing)

07.03.01 COUNTER CLERK (photofinishing) 249.366-010

367 (Compiling, Speaking-Signaling, Handling)

01.04.02 PROMPTER (amuse. & rec.) 152.367-010

01.07.02 RING CONDUCTOR (amuse. & rec.) 159.367-010

04.01.02 INVESTIGATOR (utilities) 376.367-022

04.02.01 JAILER (government ser.) 372.367-014

04.02.02 DETECTIVE I (any industry) 376.367-014

04.02.02 FIRE INSPECTOR (any industry) 373.367-010

04.02.02 FIRE RANGER (forestry) 452.367-014

04.02.03 HOUSE OFFICER (hotel & rest.) 376.367-018

04.02.03 REPOSSESSOR (clerical) 241.367-022

04.02.03 SURVEILLANCE-SYSTEM MONITOR (government ser.) 379.367-010

04.02.04 ALARM INVESTIGATOR (business ser.) 376.367-010

05.03.06 CODE INSPECTOR (government ser.)
168.367-018
05.03.09 FINE ARTS PACKER (museums) 102.367-010
05.09.01 CARGO AGENT (air trans.) 248.367-018
05.09.01 CUSTODIAN, ATHLETIC EQUIPMENT
(amuse. & rec.) 969.367-010
05.09.01 PARTS CLERK (clerical) 222.367-042
05.09.01 PARTS-ORDER-AND-STOCK CLERK
(clerical) 249.367-058
05.09.01 STOCK CLERK (retail trade) 299.367-014
05.09.01 TIRE ADJUSTER (retail trade) 241.367-034
05.09.01 TOOL-CRIB ATTENDANT (clerical)
222.367-062
05.09.02 ESTIMATOR, PRINTING (print. & pub.)
221.367-014
05.09.02 EVALUATOR (nonprofit org.) 249.367-034
05.09.02 FIELD RECORDER (utilities) 229.367-010
05.09.02 MATERIAL EXPEDITER (clerical)
221.367-042
05.09.02 PRESCRIPTION CLERK, LENS-AND-
FRAMES (optical goods) 222.367-050
05.09.02 RUG MEASURER (laundry & rel.)
369.367-014
05.09.02 SALES CORRESPONDENT (clerical)
221.367-062
05.09.03 CHECKER, DUMP GROUNDS (business ser.)
219.367-010
05.09.03 INDUSTRIAL-ORDER CLERK (clerical)
221.367-022
06.03.02 QUALITY ASSURANCE GROUP LEADER
(auto. mfg.) 806.367-014
06.03.02 QUALITY ASSURANCE MONITOR (auto.
mfg.) 806.367-018
07.01.01 MANAGEMENT AIDE (social ser.)
195.367-014
07.01.02 PROCUREMENT CLERK (clerical)
249.367-066
07.01.02 TEACHER AIDE II (education) 249.367-074
07.01.02 TOWN CLERK (government ser.)
243.367-018
07.01.04 ESCROW OFFICER (profess. & kin.)
119.367-010
07.01.04 UNDERWRITING CLERK (insurance)
219.367-038
07.01.05 ADMISSIONS EVALUATOR (education)
205.367-010
07.01.06 ATTENDANCE OFFICER (education)
168.367-010
07.01.07 TEST TECHNICIAN (clerical) 249.367-078
07.02.01 FOREIGN-EXCHANGE-POSITION CLERK
(financial) 210.367-014
07.02.03 ACCOUNT-INFORMATION CLERK
(utilities) 210.367-010
07.03.01 COLLECTOR (clerical) 241.367-010
07.03.01 POST-OFFICE CLERK (government ser.)
243.367-014
07.03.01 SAFE-DEPOSIT-BOX RENTAL CLERK
(financial) 295.367-022
07.04.01 BLOOD-DONOR-UNIT ASSISTANT (medical
ser.) 245.367-014
07.04.01 CREDIT CLERK (clerical) 205.367-022

07.04.01 EMPLOYMENT-AND-CLAIMS AIDE
(government ser.) 169.367-010
07.04.01 LOAN INTERVIEWER, MORTGAGE
(financial) 241.367-018
07.04.01 REGISTRATION CLERK (government ser.)
205.367-042
07.04.01 REHABILITATION CLERK (nonprofit org.)
205.367-046
07.04.01 SKIP TRACER (clerical) 241.367-026
07.04.01 SURVEY WORKER (clerical) 205.367-054
07.04.01 TRAFFIC CHECKER (government ser.)
205.367-058
07.04.02 CLAIMS CLERK II (insurance) 205.367-018
07.04.02 REFERRAL-AND-INFORMATION AIDE
(government ser.) 237.367-042
07.04.03 ANIMAL-HOSPITAL CLERK (medical ser.)
245.367-010
07.04.03 ANIMAL-SHELTER CLERK (nonprofit org.)
249.367-010
07.04.03 DOG LICENSER (nonprofit org.) 249.367-030
07.04.03 ELECTION CLERK (government ser.)
205.367-030
07.04.03 HOTEL CLERK (hotel & rest.) 238.367-038
07.04.03 LICENSE CLERK (government ser.)
205.367-034
07.04.03 PARK AIDE (government ser.) 249.367-082
07.04.03 RECREATION-FACILITY ATTENDANT
(amuse. & rec.) 341.367-010
07.04.03 REGISTRAR (government ser.) 205.367-038
07.04.03 RESERVATIONS AGENT (air trans.)
238.367-018
07.04.04 INFORMATION CLERK (clerical)
237.367-022
07.04.04 LAND-LEASING EXAMINER (government
ser.) 237.367-026
07.04.04 MUSEUM ATTENDANT (museums)
109.367-010
07.04.04 RECEPTIONIST (clerical) 237.367-038
07.04.04 TELEPHONE QUOTATION CLERK (financial) 237.367-046
07.04.04 TOURIST-INFORMATION ASSISTANT
(government ser.) 237.367-050
07.04.04 TRAVEL CLERK (hotel & rest.) 238.367-030
07.04.05 DISPATCHER, MAINTENANCE SERVICE
(clerical) 239.367-014
07.04.05 FIRE LOOKOUT (forestry) 452.367-010
07.04.05 FLIGHT-INFORMATION EXPEDITER (air
trans.) 912.367-010
07.04.05 GAS-DISTRIBUTION-AND-EMERGENCY
CLERK (utilities) 249.367-042
07.04.05 RECEIVER-DISPATCHER (nonprofit org.)
239.367-022
07.04.05 SERVICE CLERK (clerical) 221.367-070
07.04.05 UTILITY CLERK (utilities) 239.367-034
07.05.01 CLERK, TELEVISION PRODUCTION (radio-
tv broad.) 221.367-086
07.05.01 EXPEDITER (clerical) 222.367-018
07.05.01 PERSONNEL SCHEDULER (clerical)
215.367-014
07.05.01 RESERVATION CLERK (r.r. trans.)
238.367-014

07.05.01 SCHEDULER (museums) 238.367-034
07.05.01 SCHEDULER, MAINTENANCE (clerical) 221.367-066
07.05.01 TRAFFIC CLERK (business ser.) 221.367-078
07.05.01 TRANSPORTATION AGENT (air trans.) 912.367-014
07.05.02 BRAILLE PROOFREADER (nonprofit org.) 209.367-014
07.05.02 CREDIT AUTHORIZER (clerical) 249.367-022
07.05.02 CUSTOMER-COMPLAINT CLERK (clerical) 241.367-014
07.05.02 DISBURSEMENT CLERK (financial) 219.367-046
07.05.02 LETTER-OF-CREDIT CLERK (financial) 219.367-050
07.05.02 THROW-OUT CLERK (retail trade) 241.367-030
07.05.02 TITLE SEARCHER (real estate) 209.367-046
07.05.03 ASSIGNMENT CLERK (clerical) 249.367-090
07.05.03 AUTOMOBILE LOCATOR (retail trade) 296.367-010
07.05.03 CALL-OUT OPERATOR (business ser.) 237.367-014
07.05.03 CREDIT CARD CONTROL CLERK (financial) 249.367-026
07.05.03 FILE CLERK II (clerical) 206.367-014
07.05.03 MEDICAL-SERVICE TECHNICIAN (military ser.) 079.367-018
07.05.03 NEWS ASSISTANT (radio-tv broad.) 209.367-038
07.05.03 PROPERTY CLERK (government ser.) 222.367-054
07.05.03 REFERRAL CLERK, TEMPORARY HELP AGENCY (clerical) 205.367-062
07.05.03 REPRODUCTION ORDER PROCESSOR (clerical) 221.367-058
07.05.03 TAPE LIBRARIAN (clerical) 206.367-018
07.05.03 TAXICAB COORDINATOR (motor trans.) 215.367-018
07.05.03 YARD CLERK (r.r. trans.) 209.367-054
07.05.04 CORRESPONDENCE-REVIEW CLERK (clerical) 209.367-018
07.05.04 MAIL CARRIER (government ser.) 230.367-010
07.05.04 MERCHANDISE DISTRIBUTOR (retail trade) 219.367-018
07.05.04 ROUTING CLERK (nonprofit org.) 249.367-070
07.05.04 SHIPPING-ORDER CLERK (clerical) 219.367-030
07.07.02 PROCESS SERVER (business ser.) 249.367-062
08.01.03 COMPARISON SHOPPER (retail trade) 296.367-014
09.01.01 RECREATION AIDE (social ser.) 195.367-030
09.01.02 EXHIBIT-DISPLAY REPRESENTATIVE (any industry) 297.367-010
09.01.02 GUIDE (personal ser.) 353.367-010
09.01.02 GUIDE, ESTABLISHMENT (any industry) 353.367-014
09.01.02 GUIDE, PLANT (any industry) 353.367-018

09.01.04 AIRPLANE-FLIGHT ATTENDANT (air trans.) 352.367-010
09.04.02 CUSTOMER-SERVICE CLERK (retail trade) 299.367-010
09.04.02 STORAGE-FACILITY RENTAL CLERK (business ser.) 295.367-026
09.05.01 WEIGHT-REDUCTION SPECIALIST (personal ser.) 359.367-014
10.01.02 CASE AIDE (social ser.) 195.367-010
10.01.02 COMMUNITY WORKER (government ser.) 195.367-018
10.01.02 FOOD-MANAGEMENT AIDE (government ser.) 195.367-022
10.01.02 SOCIAL-SERVICES AIDE (social ser.) 195.367-034
10.03.01 CARDIAC MONITOR TECHNICIAN (medical ser.) 078.367-010
11.02.04 CAREER-GUIDANCE TECHNICIAN (education) 249.367-014
11.02.04 CLASSIFIER (library) 100.367-014
11.02.04 FILM-OR-TAPE LIBRARIAN (clerical) 222.367-026
11.02.04 FILM-RENTAL CLERK (business ser.) 295.367-018
11.02.04 LIBRARY ASSISTANT (library) 249.367-046
11.02.04 LIBRARY TECHNICAL ASSISTANT (library) 100.367-018
11.02.04 MUSIC LIBRARIAN (radio-tv broad.) 100.367-022
11.06.03 PERSONAL PROPERTY ASSESSOR (government ser.) 191.367-010
11.10.05 RATER, TRAVEL ACCOMMODATIONS (profess. & kin.) 168.367-014
12.01.02 CHARTER (amuse. & rec.) 249.367-018

371 (Compiling, Serving, Precision)

02.04.02 EMBALMER (personal ser.) 338.371-014
09.02.01 SCALP-TREATMENT OPERATOR (personal ser.) 339.371-014
09.02.02 BARBER (personal ser.) 330.371-010
09.05.01 ELECTROLOGIST (personal ser.) 339.371-010
10.02.01 NURSE ANESTHETIST (medical ser.) 075.371-010
10.02.02 ORTHOPTIST (medical ser.) 079.371-014

374 (Compiling, Serving, Manipulating)

05.10.08 COOK, FAST FOOD (hotel & rest.) 313.374-010
05.10.08 COOK, SHORT ORDER (hotel & rest.) 313.374-014
09.05.01 MASSEUR/MASSEUSE (personal ser.) 334.374-010
10.02.01 NURSE, LICENSED PRACTICAL (medical ser.) 079.374-014
10.02.01 NURSE, OFFICE (medical ser.) 075.374-014
10.02.01 NURSE, PRIVATE DUTY (medical ser.) 075.374-018
10.02.01 NURSE, STAFF, OCCUPATIONAL HEALTH NURSING (medical ser.) 075.374-022

10.02.02 PSYCHIATRIC TECHNICIAN (medical ser.) 079.374-026

10.03.02 AMBULANCE ATTENDANT (medical ser.) 355.374-010

10.03.02 CERTIFIED MEDICATION TECHNICIAN (medical ser.) 355.374-014

10.03.02 EMERGENCY MEDICAL TECHNICIAN (medical ser.) 079.374-010

10.03.02 NURSE, PRACTICAL (medical ser.) 354.374-010

10.03.02 PODIATRIC ASSISTANT (medical ser.) 079.374-018

10.03.02 SURGICAL TECHNICIAN (medical ser.) 079.374-022

377 (Compiling, Serving, Handling)

10.03.02 BIRTH ATTENDANT (medical ser.) 354.377-010

10.03.02 MENTAL-RETARDATION AIDE (medical ser.) 355.377-018

10.03.02 OCCUPATIONAL THERAPY AIDE (medical ser.) 355.377-010

10.03.02 PSYCHIATRIC AIDE (medical ser.) 355.377-014

10.03.03 HOME ATTENDANT (personal ser.) 354.377-014

380 (Compiling, Taking Instructions-Helping, Setting Up)

05.05.08 FURNITURE RESTORER (museums) 763.380-010

05.05.08 MACHINIST, WOOD (woodworking) 669.380-014

06.01.02 MACHINE SET-UP OPERATOR, PAPER GOODS (paper goods) 649.380-010

06.01.03 DRILL-PRESS SET-UP OPERATOR, MULTIPLE SPINDLE (machine shop) 606.380-010

06.01.03 ENGINE-LATHE SET-UP OPERATOR (machine shop) 604.380-018

06.01.03 MACHINE OPERATOR I (any industry) 616.380-018

06.01.03 MACHINE SET-UP OPERATOR (machine shop) 600.380-018

06.01.03 RIVETING MACHINE OPERATOR, AUTOMATIC (aircraft mfg.) 806.380-010

06.02.21 PLATER (electroplating) 500.380-010

381 (Compiling, Taking Instructions-Helping, Precision)

01.06.01 ENGRAVER, HAND, HARD METALS (engraving) 704.381-026

01.06.01 ENGRAVER, HAND, SOFT METALS (engraving) 704.381-030

01.06.01 PASTE-UP ARTIST (print. & pub.) 972.381-030

01.06.01 PHOTOENGRAVER (print. & pub.) 971.381-022

01.06.01 STRIPPER (print. & pub.) 971.381-050

01.06.02 BOW MAKER, CUSTOM (toy-sport equip.) 732.381-010

01.06.02 CONSERVATOR, ARTIFACTS (profess. & kin.) 055.381-010

01.06.02 DECORATOR (any industry) 298.381-010

01.06.02 MOLD MAKER I (jewelry-silver.) 700.381-034

01.06.02 MUSEUM TECHNICIAN (museums) 102.381-010

01.06.02 REPAIRER, ART OBJECTS (any industry) 779.381-018

01.06.02 SAMPLE MAKER I (jewelry-silver.) 700.381-046

01.06.03 GILDER (any industry) 749.381-010

01.06.03 PAINTER, HAND (any industry) 970.381-022

01.06.03 PAINTER, SIGN (any industry) 970.381-026

01.06.03 TYPE COPYIST (machinery mfg.) 970.381-042

02.04.01 FILM LABORATORY TECHNICIAN I (motion picture) 976.381-010

02.04.01 LABORATORY ASSISTANT (petrol. & gas) 024.381-010

02.04.01 LABORATORY ASSISTANT (textile) 029.381-014

02.04.01 PHARMACIST ASSISTANT (military ser.) 074.381-010

02.04.02 BIOLOGY SPECIMEN TECHNICIAN (profess. & kin.) 041.381-010

02.04.02 MEDICAL-LABORATORY TECHNICIAN (medical ser.) 078.381-014

03.03.02 HORSESHOER (agriculture) 418.381-010

05.05.01 BRICKLAYER (construction) 861.381-018

05.05.01 SOFT-TILE SETTER (construction) 861.381-034

05.05.01 STONECUTTER, HAND (stonework) 771.381-014

05.05.01 STONEMASON (construction) 861.381-038

05.05.01 TERRAZZO WORKER (construction) 861.381-046

05.05.01 TILE SETTER (construction) 861.381-054

05.05.02 ACOUSTICAL CARPENTER (construction) 860.381-010

05.05.02 CARPENTER (construction) 860.381-022

05.05.02 CARPENTER APPRENTICE (construction) 860.381-026

05.05.02 CARPENTER, ROUGH (construction) 860.381-042

05.05.02 CUSTOM VAN CONVERTER (auto. mfg.) 806.381-070

05.05.02 FORM BUILDER (construction) 860.381-046

05.05.02 SHIPWRIGHT (ship-boat mfg.) 860.381-058

05.05.03 PLUMBER (construction) 862.381-030

05.05.04 PAPERHANGER (construction) 841.381-010

05.05.05 LINE INSTALLER-REPAIRER (tel. & tel.) 822.381-014

05.05.05 STREET-LIGHT SERVICER (utilities) 824.381-010

05.05.05 WIND-GENERATING-ELECTRIC-POWER INSTALLER (construction) 821.381-018

05.05.06 AUTOMOBILE-BODY REPAIRER (automotive ser.) 807.381-010
05.05.06 BLACKSMITH (forging) 610.381-010
05.05.06 ORNAMENTAL-IRON WORKER (construction) 809.381-022
05.05.06 SAFE-AND-VAULT SERVICE MECHANIC (business ser.) 869.381-022
05.05.06 SHIPFITTER (ship-boat mfg.) 806.381-046
05.05.06 SIGN ERECTOR I (fabrication, nec) 869.381-026
05.05.06 WELDER-ASSEMBLER (machinery mfg.) 819.381-010
05.05.07 DIE MAKER (jewelry-silver.) 601.381-014
05.05.07 SAW FILER (any industry) 701.381-014
05.05.07 TOOL GRINDER I (any industry) 701.381-018
05.05.08 FURNITURE FINISHER (woodworking) 763.381-010
05.05.09 GAS-WELDING-EQUIPMENT MECHANIC (any industry) 626.381-014
05.05.10 ELECTRIC-METER TESTER (utilities) 821.381-010
05.05.10 PINSETTER ADJUSTER, AUTOMATIC (toy-sport equip.) 829.381-010
05.05.11 DENTAL CERAMIST (protective dev.) 712.381-042
05.05.11 DENTAL-LABORATORY TECHNICIAN (protective dev.) 712.381-018
05.05.11 DENTAL-LABORATORY-TECHNICIAN APPRENTICE (protective dev.) 712.381-022
05.05.11 EXPERIMENTAL ASSEMBLER (any industry) 739.381-026
05.05.11 FINISHER, DENTURE (protective dev.) 712.381-050
05.05.11 ORTHODONTIC TECHNICIAN (protective dev.) 712.381-030
05.05.11 ORTHOTICS TECHNICIAN (protective dev.) 712.381-034
05.05.11 PROSTHETICS TECHNICIAN (protective dev.) 712.381-038
05.05.13 ELECTROTYPER (print. & pub.) 974.381-010
05.05.13 JOB PRINTER (print. & pub.) 973.381-018
05.05.14 STONE SETTER (jewelry-silver.) 700.381-054
05.05.15 AUTOMOBILE UPHOLSTERER (automotive ser.) 780.381-010
05.05.15 BOOKBINDER (print. & pub.) 977.381-010
05.05.15 FURNITURE UPHOLSTERER (any industry) 780.381-018
05.05.15 RUG REPAIRER (laundry & rel.) 782.381-018
05.05.17 CAKE DECORATOR (bakery products) 524.381-010
05.10.01 ARCH-SUPPORT TECHNICIAN (protective dev.) 712.381-010
05.10.01 CARPET CUTTER (retail trade) 929.381-010
05.10.01 CARPET LAYER (retail trade) 864.381-010
05.10.01 GLAZIER (construction) 865.381-010
05.10.01 JIG BUILDER (wood. container) 761.381-014
05.10.01 MAINTENANCE REPAIRER, BUILDING (any industry) 899.381-010
05.10.01 ROOFER (construction) 866.381-010
05.10.02 AUTOMOBILE-RADIATOR MECHANIC (automotive ser.) 620.381-010

05.10.02 CONVEYOR-MAINTENANCE MECHANIC (any industry) 630.381-010
05.10.02 DOOR-CLOSER MECHANIC (any industry) 630.381-014
05.10.02 LUBRICATION-EQUIPMENT SERVICER (any industry) 630.381-022
05.10.02 THERMOSTAT REPAIRER (inst. & app.) 710.381-050
05.10.03 ELECTRICAL-APPLIANCE REPAIRER (any industry) 723.381-010
05.10.03 ELECTRONIC EQUIPMENT REPAIRER (comm. equip.) 726.381-014
05.10.03 TRANSFORMER REPAIRER (any industry) 724.381-018
05.10.03 VACUUM CLEANER REPAIRER (any industry) 723.381-014
05.10.03 WIRER, CABLE (comm. equip.) 729.381-022
05.10.04 EQUIPMENT INSTALLER (any industry) 828.381-010
05.10.04 EVAPORATIVE-COOLER INSTALLER (any industry) 637.381-010
05.10.04 HOUSE REPAIRER (construction) 869.381-010
05.10.05 PHOTOGRAPHIC-PLATE MAKER (electron. comp.) 714.381-018
05.10.05 PROOFER, PREPRESS (print. & pub.) 972.381-034
05.10.07 PAINTER (construction) 840.381-010
05.10.07 PAINTER, TRANSPORTATION EQUIPMENT (aircraft mfg.) 845.381-014
05.10.08 BAKER (hotel & rest.) 313.381-010
05.10.08 BAKER, PIZZA (hotel & rest.) 313.381-014
05.10.08 COOK, BARBECUE (hotel & rest.) 313.381-022
05.10.08 COOK, PASTRY (hotel & rest.) 313.381-026
05.10.08 COOK, SCHOOL CAFETERIA (hotel & rest.) 313.381-030
05.12.13 BLOCK MAKER (protective dev.) 719.381-018
05.12.16 LIGHTING-EQUIPMENT OPERATOR (amuse. & rec.) 962.381-014
06.01.04 ASSEMBLER, ELECTROMECHANICAL (aircraft mfg.) 828.381-018
06.01.04 BENCH HAND (jewelry-silver.) 735.381-010
06.01.04 CALIBRATOR (inst. & app.) 710.381-034
06.01.04 CANVAS WORKER (ship-boat mfg.) 739.381-010
06.01.04 COREMAKER (foundry) 518.381-014
06.01.04 ELECTRIC-MOTOR-CONTROL ASSEMBLER (elec. equip.) 721.381-014
06.01.04 FINAL ASSEMBLER (office machines) 706.381-018
06.01.04 GLASS BLOWER (glass mfg.) 772.381-022
06.01.04 INSTALLER, INTERIOR ASSEMBLIES (aircraft mfg.) 806.381-078
06.01.04 PLASTICS FABRICATOR (aircraft mfg.) 754.381-018
06.01.04 RING MAKER (jewelry-silver.) 700.381-042
06.01.04 SOLDERER (jewelry-silver.) 700.381-050
06.01.04 TEMPLATE MAKER (any industry) 601.381-038
06.01.05 ELECTRONICS INSPECTOR (comm. equip.) 726.381-010

06.01.05 INSPECTOR, PROCESSING (aircraft mfg.) 806.381-074

06.02.15 BAKER (bakery products) 526.381-010

06.02.24 CASTER (jewelry-silver.) 502.381-010

06.02.24 FABRICATOR-ASSEMBLER, METAL PRODUCTS (any industry) 809.381-010

06.02.24 REPAIRER, TYPEWRITER (office machines) 706.381-030

06.02.24 SOLAR-FABRICATION TECHNICIAN (machine shop) 809.381-034

06.02.28 BUTCHER, ALL-ROUND (meat products) 525.381-014

06.02.30 MOLDER (optical goods) 575.381-010

06.02.30 THROWER (pottery & porc.) 774.381-010

06.02.31 LAY-OUT WORKER II (any industry) 809.381-014

06.02.32 BONDED STRUCTURES REPAIRER (aircraft mfg.) 807.381-014

06.02.32 COIL WINDER, REPAIR (any industry) 724.381-014

06.02.32 DENTURE WAXER (protective dev.) 712.381-046

06.03.01 INSPECTOR (plastic prod.) 559.381-010

382 (Compiling, Taking Instructions-Helping, Operating-Controlling)

01.06.01 COMPUTER TYPESETTER-KEYLINER (print. & pub.) 979.382-026

01.06.01 PHOTOGRAPHER, LITHOGRAPHIC (print. & pub.) 972.382-014

05.03.03 PRODUCTION CLERK (clerical) 221.382-018

05.03.05 VIDEOTAPE OPERATOR (radio-tv broad.) 194.382-018

05.05.13 OFFSET-PRESS OPERATOR I (print. & pub.) 651.382-042

05.05.13 STEREOTYPER (print. & pub.) 974.382-014

05.06.01 GAS-ENGINE OPERATOR (any industry) 950.382-018

05.06.02 BOILER OPERATOR (any industry) 950.382-010

05.06.02 GAS-COMPRESSOR OPERATOR (any industry) 950.382-014

05.06.02 STATIONARY ENGINEER (any industry) 950.382-026

05.06.03 PUMP-STATION OPERATOR, WATER-WORKS (waterworks) 954.382-010

05.06.04 WATER-TREATMENT-PLANT OPERATOR (waterworks) 954.382-014

05.09.01 PHARMACY TECHNICIAN (medical ser.) 074.382-010

05.10.05 AUDIOVISUAL TECHNICIAN (any industry) 960.382-010

05.10.05 COLOR-PRINTER OPERATOR (photofinishing) 976.382-014

05.10.05 ENGRAVER, MACHINE (print. & pub.) 979.382-014

05.10.05 ENGRAVING-PRESS OPERATOR (print. & pub.) 651.382-010

05.10.05 FILM DEVELOPER (motion picture) 976.382-018

05.10.05 PHOTO MASK TECHNICIAN, ELECTRON-BEAM (electron. comp.) 972.382-022

05.10.05 PHOTOGRAPHER, FINISH (amuse. & rec.) 143.382-014

05.10.05 RECORDIST (motion picture) 962.382-010

05.10.05 TAPE TRANSFERRER (radio-tv broad.) 194.382-014

05.11.03 ROTARY DRILLER (petrol. & gas) 930.382-026

06.01.03 EXHAUST EQUIPMENT OPERATOR (electron. comp.) 599.382-014

06.02.02 GRINDER SET-UP OPERATOR (machine shop) 603.382-034

06.02.02 PUNCH-PRESS OPERATOR I (any industry) 615.382-010

06.02.02 SCREW-MACHINE OPERATOR, MULTIPLE SPINDLE (machine shop) 604.382-010

06.02.02 WIRE DRAWING MACHINE OPERATOR (inst. & app.) 614.382-018

06.02.08 PRECISION-LENS GRINDER (optical goods) 716.382-018

06.02.09 CLOTH PRINTER (any industry) 652.382-010

06.02.09 FLUID JET CUTTER OPERATOR (aircraft mfg.) 699.382-010

06.02.09 NUMERICAL-CONTROL DRILL OPERA-TOR, PRINTED CIRCUIT BOARDS (electron. comp.) 606.382-018

06.02.09 NUMERICAL-CONTROL ROUTER OPERA-TOR (aircraft mfg.) 605.382-046

06.02.09 ROBOTIC MACHINE OPERATOR (aircraft mfg.) 606.382-026

06.02.10 HEAT TREATER I (heat treating) 504.382-014

06.02.11 WASTE-TREATMENT OPERATOR (chemical) 955.382-014

06.02.13 BLANKMAKER (glass mfg.) 579.382-022

06.02.13 EXTRUDER OPERATOR (plastic prod.) 557.382-010

06.02.13 MIXING-MACHINE OPERATOR (any industry) 550.382-022

06.02.15 CHOCOLATE-PRODUCTION-MACHINE OPERATOR (sugar & conf.) 529.382-014

06.02.15 DAIRY-PROCESSING-EQUIPMENT OPERA-TOR (dairy products) 529.382-018

06.02.16 DRY CLEANER (laundry & rel.) 362.382-014

06.02.18 SOAP MAKER (soap & rel.) 559.382-054

06.02.19 WELDING-MACHINE OPERATOR, ARC (welding) 810.382-010

06.02.21 OPTICAL-ELEMENT COATER (optical goods) 716.382-014

06.02.21 PAINT-SPRAYER OPERATOR, AUTOMATIC (any industry) 599.382-010

07.02.01 AUDIT CLERK (clerical) 210.382-010

07.02.01 BOOKKEEPER (clerical) 210.382-014

07.02.01 GENERAL-LEDGER BOOKKEEPER (clerical) 210.382-046

07.02.02 CANCELLATION CLERK (insurance) 203.382-014

07.02.02 COST CLERK (clerical) 216.382-034

07.02.02 CREDIT-CARD CLERK (hotel & rest.) 210.382-038

07.02.02 NIGHT AUDITOR (hotel & rest.) 210.382-054
07.02.03 POLICY-VALUE CALCULATOR (insurance)
    216.382-050
07.02.03 RECEIPT-AND-REPORT CLERK (water
    trans.) 216.382-054
07.02.03 STATISTICAL CLERK (clerical) 216.382-062
07.02.04 MEDIA CLERK (business ser.) 247.382-010
07.02.04 TICKETING CLERK (air trans.) 248.382-010
07.02.05 PAYROLL CLERK (clerical) 215.382-014
07.03.01 TELLER, VAULT (financial) 211.382-010
07.05.01 TELEVISION-SCHEDULE COORDINATOR
    (radio-tv broad.) 199.382-010
07.05.03 CONTINUITY CLERK (motion picture)
    209.382-010
07.05.03 REPAIR-ORDER CLERK (clerical)
    221.382-022
07.05.03 STENOCAPTIONER (radio-tv broad.)
    202.382-010
07.06.01 COMPUTER PERIPHERAL EQUIPMENT
    OPERATOR (clerical) 213.382-010
07.06.01 TERMINAL-MAKEUP OPERATOR (print. &
    pub.) 208.382-010
07.06.02 CHECK WRITER (retail trade) 219.382-010
07.06.02 MAGNETIC-TAPE-COMPOSER OPERATOR
    (print. & pub.) 203.382-018
07.06.02 PROOF-MACHINE OPERATOR (financial)
    217.382-010
07.06.02 VARITYPE OPERATOR (clerical) 203.382-026
07.06.02 WORD PROCESSING MACHINE OPERA-
    TOR (clerical) 203.382-030

383 (Compiling, Taking Instructions-Helping, Driving-Operating)

05.08.01 TRACTOR-TRAILER-TRUCK DRIVER (any
    industry) 904.383-010
05.12.03 WASTE-DISPOSAL ATTENDANT (any
    industry) 955.383-010
06.01.05 ROADABILITY-MACHINE OPERATOR
    (auto. mfg.) 806.383-010

384 (Compiling, Taking Instructions-Helping, Manipulating)

02.04.01 DECONTAMINATOR (any industry)
    199.384-010
02.04.01 SCANNER (profess. & kin.) 015.384-010
02.04.02 CEPHALOMETRIC ANALYST (medical ser.)
    078.384-010
02.04.02 HERBARIUM WORKER (profess. & kin.)
    041.384-010
02.04.02 LABORATORY ASSISTANT, CULTURE
    MEDIA (pharmaceut.) 559.384-010
05.05.06 WELDER, ARC (welding) 810.384-014
05.05.06 WELDER, COMBINATION (welding)
    819.384-010
05.09.01 PRODUCTION TECHNICIAN, SEMI-
    CONDUCTOR PROCESSING EQUIPMENT
    (electron. comp.) 590.384-014

05.10.01 FIXTURE REPAIRER-FABRICATOR (any
    industry) 630.384-010
05.10.02 PARKING-METER SERVICER (government
    ser.) 710.384-026
05.10.04 FIRE-EXTINGUISHER REPAIRER (any
    industry) 709.384-010
05.10.08 SALAD MAKER (water trans.) 317.384-010
05.12.14 WOOD CAULKER (ship-boat mfg.)
    843.384-010
06.02.22 ASSEMBLER, SUBASSEMBLY (aircraft mfg.)
    806.384-034
06.02.23 ELECTRICAL ASSEMBLER (aircraft mfg.)
    729.384-026
06.02.23 TUBE ASSEMBLER, ELECTRON (electron.
    comp.) 725.384-010
06.02.24 ASSEMBLER, METAL BONDING (aircraft
    mfg.) 806.384-030
06.02.24 PRESSURE SEALER-AND-TESTER (aircraft
    mfg.) 806.384-038
06.02.27 RUG CLEANER, HAND (laundry & rel.)
    369.384-014
06.02.28 BENCH HAND (bakery products) 520.384-010
06.03.01 COMPARATOR OPERATOR (any industry)
    699.384-010
06.03.01 INSPECTOR (office machines) 710.384-014
06.03.01 INSPECTOR II (pottery & porc.) 774.384-010
06.03.01 INSPECTOR, RECEIVING (aircraft mfg.)
    222.384-010
06.03.01 MOTORCYCLE TESTER (motor-bicycles)
    620.384-010

385 (Compiling, Taking Instructions-Helping, Tending)

05.10.05 MICROFILM PROCESSOR (business ser.)
    976.385-010

387 (Compiling, Taking Instructions-Helping, Handling)

01.06.01 ADVERTISING-SPACE CLERK (print. &
    pub.) 247.387-018
02.04.01 FINGERPRINT CLASSIFIER (government
    ser.) 375.387-010
05.09.01 INVENTORY CLERK (clerical) 222.387-026
05.09.01 LINEN-ROOM ATTENDANT (hotel & rest.)
    222.387-030
05.09.01 SHIPPING AND RECEIVING CLERK
    (clerical) 222.387-050
05.09.01 SHIPPING-AND-RECEIVING WEIGHER
    (clerical) 222.387-074
05.09.01 STOCK CLERK (clerical) 222.387-058
05.09.02 CONTROL CLERK (clock & watch)
    221.387-018
05.09.02 DRAPERY AND UPHOLSTERY ESTIMATOR
    (retail trade) 299.387-010
05.09.02 JOB TRACER (clerical) 221.387-034
05.09.02 LAUNDRY CLERK (clerical) 221.387-038
05.09.02 ORDER DETAILER (clerical) 221.387-046

05.09.03 MATERIAL CLERK (clerical) 222.387-034

05.09.03 SORTER-PRICER (nonprofit org.) 222.387-054

06.03.01 GRADER, MEAT (meat products) 525.387-010

06.03.01 MACHINE TESTER (office machines) 706.387-014

06.03.01 QUALITY-CONTROL INSPECTOR (recording) 194.387-010

06.03.02 INSPECTOR (pharmaceut.) 559.387-014

07.02.04 ADVERTISING CLERK (business ser.) 247.387-010

07.02.04 BILLING-CONTROL CLERK (utilities) 214.387-010

07.05.01 ADVERTISING-DISPATCH CLERK (print. & pub.) 247.387-014

07.05.02 CLASSIFIED-AD CLERK II (print. & pub.) 247.387-022

07.05.02 DATA-EXAMINATION CLERK (clerical) 209.387-022

07.05.02 PROOFREADER (print. & pub.) 209.387-030

07.05.02 READER (business ser.) 249.387-022

07.05.03 CLASSIFICATION CLERK (clerical) 206.387-010

07.05.03 COMPILER (clerical) 209.387-014

07.05.03 FINGERPRINT CLERK II (government ser.) 206.387-014

07.05.03 INSURANCE CLERK (clerical) 219.387-014

07.05.03 STOCK CONTROL CLERK (clerical) 219.387-030

07.05.04 PARCEL POST CLERK (clerical) 222.387-038

07.07.01 FILE CLERK I (clerical) 206.387-034

11.02.04 CATALOG LIBRARIAN (library) 100.387-010

Data = Computing

457 (Computing, Persuading, Handling)

08.02.02 SALESPERSON, ART OBJECTS (retail trade) 277.457-010

08.03.01 CIGARETTE VENDOR (hotel & rest.) 291.457-010

08.03.01 LOUNGE-CAR ATTENDANT (r.r. trans.) 291.457-014

08.03.01 PHOTOGRAPHER (amuse. & rec.) 143.457-010

08.03.01 VENDOR (amuse. & rec.) 291.457-022

09.04.02 NEWSPAPER CARRIER (retail trade) 292.457-010

462 (Computing, Speaking-Signaling, Operating-Controlling)

06.04.38 MAILING-MACHINE OPERATOR (print. & pub.) 208.462-010

07.02.02 COUPON CLERK (financial) 219.462-010

07.03.01 CASHIER II (clerical) 211.462-010

07.03.01 CASHIER, GAMBLING (amuse. & rec.) 211.462-022

07.03.01 CASHIER-CHECKER (retail trade) 211.462-014

07.03.01 CHECK CASHIER (business ser.) 211.462-026

07.03.01 TOLL COLLECTOR (government ser.) 211.462-038

07.04.06 CENTRAL-OFFICE OPERATOR (tel. & tel.) 235.462-010

09.04.02 CASHIER-WRAPPER (retail trade) 211.462-018

463 (Computing, Speaking-Signaling, Driving-Operating)

05.10.01 SWIMMING POOL INSTALLER-AND-SERVICER (construction) 869.463-010

05.11.01 SANITARY LANDFILL OPERATOR (sanitary ser.) 955.463-010

09.03.01 BUS DRIVER (motor trans.) 913.463-010

09.03.01 STREETCAR OPERATOR (r.r. trans.) 913.463-014

09.03.02 TAXI DRIVER (motor trans.) 913.463-018

09.04.01 LUNCH-TRUCK DRIVER (hotel & rest.) 292.463-010

464 (Computing, Speaking-Signaling, Manipulating)

05.06.01 CABLE MAINTAINER (utilities) 952.464-010

05.10.01 BOAT RIGGER (retail trade) 806.464-010

09.04.01 VENDING-MACHINE ATTENDANT (hotel & rest.) 319.464-014

09.04.02 GAMBLING DEALER (amuse. & rec.) 343.464-010

467 (Computing, Speaking-Signaling, Handling)

05.09.03 FOOD ORDER EXPEDITER (hotel & rest.) 319.467-010

05.10.02 AUTOMOBILE-SERVICE-STATION ATTENDANT (automotive ser.) 915.467-010

07.02.03 GRADING CLERK (education) 219.467-010

07.03.01 CHANGE PERSON (amuse. & rec.) 211.467-034

07.03.01 INFORMATION CLERK-CASHIER (amuse. & rec.) 249.467-010

07.03.01 LAYAWAY CLERK (retail trade) 299.467-010

07.03.01 PARIMUTUEL-TICKET CASHIER (amuse. & rec.) 211.467-018

07.03.01 PARIMUTUEL-TICKET SELLER (amuse. & rec.) 211.467-022

07.03.01 TICKET SELLER (clerical) 211.467-030

07.07.02 MONEY COUNTER (amuse. & rec.)
211.467-014

09.04.02 AUTOMOBILE RENTAL CLERK (automotive ser.) 295.467-026

09.04.02 BICYCLE-RENTAL CLERK (retail trade)
295.467-010

09.04.02 BOAT-RENTAL CLERK (amuse. & rec.)
295.467-014

09.04.02 CASHIER, COURTESY BOOTH (retail trade)
211.467-010

09.04.02 FLOOR ATTENDANT (amuse. & rec.)
343.467-014

09.04.02 HOSPITAL-TELEVISION-RENTAL CLERK (business ser.) 295.467-018

09.04.02 MANAGER, BRANCH STORE (laundry & rel.) 369.467-010

09.04.02 TRAILER-RENTAL CLERK (automotive ser.)
295.467-022

472 (Computing, Serving, Operating-Controlling)

09.04.01 FAST-FOODS WORKER (hotel & rest.)
311.472-010

473 (Computing, Serving, Driving-Operating)

09.04.02 PARKING-LOT ATTENDANT (automotive ser.) 915.473-010

474 (Computing, Serving, Manipulating)

09.04.01 BARTENDER (hotel & rest.) 312.474-010
09.04.01 FOUNTAIN SERVER (hotel & rest.)
319.474-010

477 (Computing, Serving, Handling)

07.03.01 COUPON-REDEMPTION CLERK (retail trade) 290.477-010

09.04.01 CAR HOP (hotel & rest.) 311.477-010

09.04.01 COUNTER ATTENDANT, LUNCHROOM OR COFFEE SHOP (hotel & rest.) 311.477-014

09.04.01 WAITER/WAITRESS, BAR (hotel & rest.)
311.477-018

09.04.01 WAITER/WAITRESS, FORMAL (hotel & rest.) 311.477-026

09.04.01 WAITER/WAITRESS, INFORMAL (hotel & rest.) 311.477-030

09.04.01 WAITER/WAITRESS, TAKE OUT (hotel & rest.) 311.477-038

09.04.02 CURB ATTENDANT (laundry & rel.)
369.477-010

09.04.02 DELIVERER, MERCHANDISE (retail trade)
299.477-010

09.04.02 SALES CLERK (retail trade) 290.477-014

09.04.02 SALES CLERK, FOOD (retail trade)
290.477-018

09.04.02 SERVICE-ESTABLISHMENT ATTENDANT (laundry & rel.) 369.477-014

09.05.02 WAITER/WAITRESS, ROOM SERVICE (hotel & rest.) 311.477-034

09.05.03 PORTER, BAGGAGE (hotel & rest.)
324.477-010

481 (Computing, Taking Instructions-Helping, Precision)

05.10.01 FLOOR LAYER (construction) 864.481-010
06.02.22 ASSEMBLER, INTERNAL COMBUSTION ENGINE (engine-turbine) 806.481-014

482 (Computing, Taking Instructions-Helping, Operating-Controlling)

06.02.02 RIVETING-MACHINE OPERATOR I (any industry) 699.482-010

06.02.02 SAWYER (plastic prod.) 690.482-010

06.02.02 STRAIGHTENING-PRESS OPERATOR II (any industry) 617.482-026

06.02.03 TIMBER-SIZER OPERATOR (saw. & plan.)
665.482-018

06.02.15 FREEZER OPERATOR (dairy products)
529.482-010

06.02.19 WELDING-MACHINE OPERATOR, GAS (welding) 811.482-010

07.02.02 ACCOUNTING CLERK (clerical) 216.482-010

07.02.02 BROKERAGE CLERK I (financial)
219.482-010

07.02.02 CALCULATING-MACHINE OPERATOR (clerical) 216.482-022

07.02.02 DIVIDEND CLERK (financial) 216.482-034

07.02.04 RATER (insurance) 214.482-022

07.02.04 REINSURANCE CLERK (insurance)
219.482-018

07.06.02 FOOD CHECKER (hotel & rest.) 211.482-014

483 (Computing, Taking Instructions-Helping, Driving-Operating)

05.08.01 MILK DRIVER (dairy products) 905.483-010
05.08.03 COIN COLLECTOR (business ser.)
292.483-010

484 (Computing, Taking Instructions-Helping, Manipulating)

01.06.03 STRIPER, HAND (any industry) 740.484-010
02.04.01 SAMPLER (mine & quarry) 579.484-010
05.10.01 DRAPERY HANGER (retail trade)
869.484-014
05.10.01 TEMPLATE MAKER, TRACK (any industry)
809.484-014

05.12.17 FOOD ASSEMBLER, KITCHEN (hotel & rest.)
319.484-010
06.02.24 STRAIGHTENER, HAND (any industry)
709.484-014
06.04.23 SILK-SCREEN-FRAME ASSEMBLER (any
industry) 709.484-010

485 (Computing, Taking Instructions-Helping, Tending)

05.12.10 RIVET HEATER (heat treating) 504.485-010
05.12.19 CURRENCY COUNTER (financial) 217.485-010
06.02.15 SYRUP MAKER (beverage) 520.485-026
06.04.11 PAINT MIXER, MACHINE (any industry)
550.485-018

Data = Copying

562 (Copying, Speaking-Signaling, Operating-Controlling)

06.04.16 SLASHER TENDER (textile) 582.562-010
07.04.05 SWITCHBOARD OPERATOR, POLICE
DISTRICT (government ser.) 235.562-014
07.06.02 WIRE-TRANSFER CLERK (financial)
203.562-010
07.07.03 CLERK, GENERAL (clerical) 209.562-010

563 (Copying, Speaking-Signaling, Driving-Operating)

04.02.02 ARMORED-CAR GUARD AND DRIVER
(business ser.) 372.563-010

564 (Copying, Speaking-Signaling, Manipulating)

05.07.01 LINE WALKER (petrol. & gas) 869.564-010
07.05.03 DETAILER, SCHOOL PHOTOGRAPHS
(photofinishing) 976.564-010

565 (Copying, Speaking-Signaling, Tending)

06.04.12 CYLINDER FILLER (chemical) 559.565-010

567 (Copying, Speaking-Signaling, Handling)

04.02.01 GUARD, IMMIGRATION (government ser.)
372.567-014

487 (Computing, Taking Instructions-Helping, Handling)

05.09.01 CHECKER, BAKERY PRODUCTS (bakery
products) 222.487-010
05.09.01 ORDER FILLER (retail trade) 222.487-014
05.10.05 PHOTOGRAPH FINISHER (photofinishing)
976.487-010
05.10.08 FORMULA-ROOM WORKER (dairy products)
520.487-014
06.03.01 SPECIAL TESTER (tobacco) 529.487-010
07.02.04 TAX CLERK (clerical) 219.487-010

04.02.02 ARMORED-CAR GUARD (business ser.)
372.567-010
05.09.03 METER READER (utilities) 209.567-010
05.09.03 TURBINE ATTENDANT (utilities)
952.567-010
05.12.02 SURVEYOR HELPER (any industry)
869.567-010
07.03.01 AUCTION CLERK (retail trade) 294.567-010
07.04.02 ORDER CLERK, FOOD AND BEVERAGE
(hotel & rest.) 209.567-014
07.05.03 BENEFITS CLERK II (clerical) 205.567-010
07.07.03 OFFICE HELPER (clerical) 239.567-010
09.05.01 REDUCING-SALON ATTENDANT (personal
ser.) 359.567-010
10.03.03 GUARD, SCHOOL-CROSSING (government
ser.) 371.567-010

573 (Copying, Serving, Driving-Operating)

10.03.03 BLIND AIDE (personal ser.) 359.573-010

574 (Copying, Serving, Manipulating)

05.10.01 SERVICE REPRESENTATIVE (utilities)
959.574-010

577 (Copying, Serving, Handling)

09.05.03 ROOM-SERVICE CLERK (hotel & rest.)
324.577-010
09.05.05 CARDROOM ATTENDANT II (amuse. & rec.)
343.577-010

582 (Copying, Taking Instructions-Helping, Operating-Controlling)

05.10.05 PHOTOCOMPOSING-MACHINE OPERA-
TOR (print. & pub.) 650.582-018
05.12.19 ADDRESSING-MACHINE OPERATOR
(clerical) 208.582-010
07.06.01 DATA ENTRY CLERK (clerical) 203.582-054
07.06.02 BRAILLE OPERATOR (print. & pub.)
203.582-010
07.06.02 BRAILLE TYPIST (education) 203.582-014
07.06.02 CRYPTOGRAPHIC-MACHINE OPERATOR
(clerical) 203.582-018
07.06.02 NOTEREADER (clerical) 203.582-078
07.06.02 PHOTOCOMPOSITION-KEYBOARD
OPERATOR (print. & pub.) 203.582-046
07.06.02 PHOTOTYPESETTER OPERATOR (print. &
pub.) 650.582-022
07.06.02 TRANSCRIBING-MACHINE OPERATOR
(clerical) 203.582-058
07.06.02 TYPIST (clerical) 203.582-066

583 (Copying, Taking Instructions-Helping, Driving-Operating)

05.08.03 LOT ATTENDANT (retail trade) 915.583-010

584 (Copying, Taking Instructions-Helping, Manipulating)

05.10.03 APPLIANCE REPAIRER (house. appl.)
723.584-010
05.12.16 ELECTRICAL-APPLIANCE PREPARER (any
industry) 827.584-010
06.03.02 GAS-LEAK TESTER (svc. ind. mach.)
827.584-014

585 (Copying, Taking Instructions-Helping, Tending)

05.05.13 ASSISTANT-PRESS OPERATOR (print. &
pub.) 651.585-010
05.06.02 VENTILATION EQUIPMENT TENDER (any
industry) 950.585-010

05.12.19 COIN-COUNTER-AND-WRAPPER (clerical)
217.585-010
06.04.15 CHEESE CUTTER (dairy products)
529.585-010
06.04.19 STERILIZER (medical ser.) 599.585-010

586 (Copying, Taking Instructions-Helping, Feeding-Offbearing)

06.04.40 FINISHER (plastic-synth.) 554.586-010

587 (Copying, Taking Instructions-Helping, Handling)

04.02.02 PARKING ENFORCEMENT OFFICER
(government ser.) 375.587-010
05.09.01 LABORATORY CLERK (clerical) 222.587-026
05.09.01 MAILER (print. & pub.) 222.587-030
05.09.03 MARKER (retail trade) 209.587-034
06.04.26 LABEL CODER (any industry) 920.587-014
06.04.37 MARKER, SEMICONDUCTOR WAFERS
(electron. comp.) 920.587-026
06.04.38 PACKAGER, HAND (any industry)
920.587-018
06.04.40 COMPRESSED-GAS-PLANT WORKER
(chemical) 549.587-010
07.02.04 TRAFFIC CLERK (clerical) 214.587-014
07.05.02 PARIMUTUEL-TICKET CHECKER (amuse.
& rec.) 219.587-010
07.05.03 DIET CLERK (medical ser.) 245.587-010
07.05.03 DOCUMENT PREPARER, MICROFILMING
(business ser.) 249.587-018
07.05.03 QUALITY-CONTROL CLERK (pharmaceut.)
229.587-014
07.05.04 ROUTE-DELIVERY CLERK (clerical)
222.587-034
07.05.04 VAULT WORKER (business ser.) 222.587-058
07.07.02 ADDRESSER (clerical) 209.587-010
07.07.02 DIRECT-MAIL CLERK (clerical) 209.587-018
07.07.02 DISTRIBUTING CLERK (clerical)
222.587-018
07.07.02 ROUTER (clerical) 222.587-038
09.05.05 BOARD ATTENDANT (amuse. & rec.)
249.587-010

Data = Comparing

647 (Comparing, Diverting, Handling)

01.07.03 AMUSEMENT PARK ENTERTAINER
(amuse. & rec.) 159.647-010
01.08.01 EXTRA (amuse. & rec.) 159.647-014

657 (Comparing, Persuading, Handling)

09.04.02 GAME ATTENDANT (amuse. & rec.)
342.657-014

661 (Comparing, Speaking-Signaling, Precision)

05.10.04 HOUSEHOLD-APPLIANCE INSTALLER
(any industry) 827.661-010
05.10.08 CARVER (hotel & rest.) 316.661-010

662 (Comparing, Speaking-Signaling, Operating-Controlling)

05.12.04 CONVEYOR-SYSTEM OPERATOR (any industry) 921.662-018

06.01.03 ROLLING ATTENDANT (steel & rel.) 613.662-010

06.02.02 STRAIGHTENING-ROLL OPERATOR (any industry) 613.662-022

06.02.03 HEAD SAWYER (saw. & plan.) 667.662-010

06.02.03 LOG-CHIPPER OPERATOR (logging) 564.662-010

06.02.09 DYNAMITE-PACKING-MACHINE OPERATOR (chemical) 692.662-010

06.02.10 COLD-MILL OPERATOR (steel & rel.) 613.662-018

06.02.17 BRIQUETTE-MACHINE OPERATOR (fabrication, nec) 549.662-010

07.04.06 DIRECTORY-ASSISTANCE OPERATOR (tel. & tel.) 235.662-018

07.04.06 TELEPHONE OPERATOR (clerical) 235.662-022

07.04.06 TELEPHONE-ANSWERING-SERVICE OPERATOR (business ser.) 235.662-026

663 (Comparing, Speaking-Signaling, Driving-Operating)

03.04.01 FARMWORKER, DIVERSIFIED CROPS I (agriculture) 407.663-010

03.04.02 LOGGING-TRACTOR OPERATOR (forestry) 929.663-010

03.04.03 SHELLFISH DREDGE OPERATOR (fishing & hunt.) 446.663-010

05.08.01 TRUCK DRIVER, HEAVY (any industry) 905.663-014

05.08.03 DELIVERER, CAR RENTAL (automotive ser.) 919.663-010

05.08.03 ESCORT-VEHICLE DRIVER (motor trans.) 919.663-022

05.08.03 GARBAGE COLLECTOR DRIVER (motor trans.) 905.663-010

05.08.03 TOW-TRUCK OPERATOR (automotive ser.) 919.663-026

05.08.03 VAN DRIVER (motor trans.) 905.663-018

05.08.04 MOTORBOAT OPERATOR (any industry) 911.663-010

05.10.02 RIDE OPERATOR (amuse. & rec.) 342.663-010

05.11.01 ASPHALT-PAVING-MACHINE OPERATOR (construction) 853.663-010

05.11.01 CHERRY-PICKER OPERATOR (construction) 921.663-014

05.11.01 CONCRETE-PAVING-MACHINE OPERATOR (construction) 853.663-014

05.11.04 HOISTING ENGINEER (any industry) 921.663-030

05.11.04 OVERHEAD CRANE OPERATOR (any industry) 921.663-010

05.11.04 STEVEDORE I (water trans.) 911.663-014

05.12.06 AIRPORT UTILITY WORKER (air trans.) 912.663-010

07.07.02 DELIVERER, OUTSIDE (clerical) 230.663-010

09.03.01 DRIVER (motor trans.) 913.663-018

09.03.02 CHAUFFEUR (any industry) 913.663-010

09.05.09 ELEVATOR OPERATOR (any industry) 388.663-010

664 (Comparing, Speaking-Signaling, Manipulating)

03.04.01 FARMWORKER, LIVESTOCK (agriculture) 410.664-010

03.04.03 FISHER, DIVING (fishing & hunt.) 443.664-010

03.04.05 TREE TRIMMER (tel. & tel.) 408.664-010

04.02.03 SKI PATROLLER (amuse. & rec.) 379.664-010

05.05.01 MARBLE FINISHER (construction) 861.664-010

05.05.01 TERRAZZO FINISHER (construction) 861.664-014

05.05.01 TILE FINISHER (construction) 861.664-018

05.05.11 DENTAL CERAMIST ASSISTANT (protective dev.) 712.664-010

05.10.01 CONSTRUCTION WORKER I (construction) 869.664-014

05.10.01 MUFFLER INSTALLER (automotive ser.) 807.664-010

05.10.01 TAPER (construction) 842.664-010

05.10.02 MAINTENANCE MECHANIC HELPER (construction) 620.664-014

05.10.06 FIREWORKS DISPLAY SPECIALIST (chemical) 969.664-010

05.12.03 RECORDING STUDIO SET-UP WORKER (recording) 962.664-014

05.12.12 SEWER-LINE REPAIRER (sanitary ser.) 869.664-018

05.12.12 SEWER-PIPE CLEANER (business ser.) 899.664-014

05.12.15 CONSTRUCTION-EQUIPMENT-MECHANIC HELPER (construction) 620.664-010

05.12.17 SANDWICH MAKER (hotel & rest.) 317.664-010

05.12.18 JANITOR (any industry) 382.664-010

06.02.01 TOOL GRINDER II (any industry) 603.664-010

06.04.23 BATTERY ASSEMBLER, DRY CELL (elec. equip.) 727.664-010

06.04.31 WELDER, GUN (welding) 810.664-010

06.04.32 CANDLEMAKER (fabrication, nec) 739.664-010

06.04.32 MOLD MAKER (smelt. & refin.) 518.664-010

09.01.01 AMUSEMENT PARK WORKER (amuse. & rec.) 349.664-010

10.03.02 ORTHOPEDIC ASSISTANT (medical ser.) 078.664-010

665 (Comparing, Speaking-Signaling, Tending)

05.10.05 TAKE-DOWN SORTER (photofinishing) 976.665-010

05.12.04 LABORER, CONCRETE-MIXING PLANT (construction) 579.665-014

05.12.04 LABORER, POWERHOUSE (utilities) 952.665-010

05.12.14 ASPHALT-DISTRIBUTOR TENDER (construction) 853.665-010

06.04.02 BUFFING-MACHINE TENDER (any industry) 603.665-010

06.04.06 KNITTING-MACHINE OPERATOR (knitting) 685.665-014

06.04.15 MIXING-MACHINE OPERATOR (food prep., nec) 520.665-014

06.04.18 TANKER (wood prod., nec) 561.665-010

06.04.35 WASHER, MACHINE (laundry & rel.) 361.665-010

07.04.05 SCOREBOARD OPERATOR (amuse. & rec.) 349.665-010

09.05.08 SKI-TOW OPERATOR (amuse. & rec.) 341.665-010

667 (Comparing, Speaking-Signaling, Handling)

01.08.01 MODEL, ARTISTS' (any industry) 961.667-010

02.04.02 MORGUE ATTENDANT (medical ser.) 355.667-010

03.04.03 DECKHAND, FISHING VESSEL (fishing & hunt.) 449.667-010

04.02.01 CORRECTION OFFICER (government ser.) 372.667-018

04.02.02 AIRLINE SECURITY REPRESENTATIVE (air trans.) 372.667-010

04.02.02 BODYGUARD (personal ser.) 372.667-014

04.02.02 GATE GUARD (any industry) 372.667-030

04.02.02 GUARD, SECURITY (any industry) 372.667-034

04.02.03 BAILIFF (government ser.) 377.667-010

04.02.03 BOUNCER (amuse. & rec.) 376.667-010

04.02.03 CHAPERON (personal ser.) 359.667-010

04.02.03 LIFEGUARD (amuse. & rec.) 379.667-014

05.09.03 ORDER CALLER (clerical) 209.667-014

05.12.03 DUMPER (any industry) 921.667-018

05.12.05 SWITCH TENDER (r.r. trans.) 910.667-026

05.12.12 BILLPOSTER (any industry) 299.667-010

05.12.20 CROSSING TENDER (any industry) 371.667-010

06.03.02 INKER (print. & pub.) 659.667-010

06.04.40 LABORER, GENERAL (plastic-synth.) 559.667-014

06.04.40 LOADER I (any industry) 914.667-010

07.05.02 PRODUCTION PROOFREADER (print. & pub.) 247.667-010

07.07.02 AUCTION ASSISTANT (retail trade) 294.667-010

07.07.02 TELEPHONE-DIRECTORY DELIVERER (business ser.) 230.667-014

09.01.01 HOST/HOSTESS (any industry) 352.667-010

09.04.02 ATTENDANT, ARCADE (amuse. & rec.) 342.667-014

09.05.08 ESCORT (any industry) 353.667-010

09.05.08 TICKET TAKER (amuse. & rec.) 344.667-010

11.08.04 CODE AND TEST CLERK (financial) 209.667-018

12.01.02 FLAGGER (amuse. & rec.) 372.667-026

12.01.02 GOLF-COURSE RANGER (amuse. & rec.) 379.667-010

673 (Comparing, Serving, Driving-Operating)

03.04.05 DOG CATCHER (government ser.) 379.673-010

05.08.03 CHAUFFEUR, FUNERAL CAR (personal ser.) 359.673-014

09.03.02 CHAUFFEUR (domestic ser.) 359.673-010

09.05.04 DRIVE-IN THEATER ATTENDANT (amuse. & rec.) 349.673-010

674 (Comparing, Serving, Manipulating)

03.03.01 EXERCISER, HORSE (amuse. & rec.) 153.674-010

03.03.02 ANIMAL CARETAKER (any industry) 410.674-010

03.03.02 ANIMAL KEEPER (amuse. & rec.) 412.674-010

03.03.02 AQUARIST (amuse. & rec.) 449.674-010

03.03.02 DOG GROOMER (personal ser.) 418.674-010

03.03.02 STABLE ATTENDANT (any industry) 410.674-022

03.04.01 LIVESTOCK-YARD ATTENDANT (any industry) 410.674-018

09.04.01 CANTEEN OPERATOR (any industry) 311.674-010

09.05.01 FINGERNAIL FORMER (personal ser.) 331.674-014

09.05.01 MANICURIST (personal ser.) 331.674-010

09.05.02 RAW SHELLFISH PREPARER (hotel & rest.) 311.674-014

09.05.06 DRESSER (amuse. & rec.) 346.674-010

09.05.06 PERSONAL ATTENDANT (domestic ser.) 309.674-014

10.03.02 NURSE ASSISTANT (medical ser.) 355.674-014

10.03.02 ORDERLY (medical ser.) 355.674-018

10.03.02 RESPIRATORY-THERAPY AIDE (medical ser.) 355.674-022

10.03.03 CHILD-CARE ATTENDANT, SCHOOL (personal ser.) 355.674-010

677 (Comparing, Serving, Handling)

03.03.02 DOG BATHER (personal ser.) 418.677-010
09.01.04 FUNERAL ATTENDANT (personal ser.)
 359.677-014
09.01.04 PASSENGER SERVICE REPRESENTATIVE I
 (r.r. trans.) 352.677-010
09.04.02 SALES ATTENDANT (retail trade)
 299.677-010
09.04.02 SALES ATTENDANT, BUILDING
 MATERIALS (retail trade) 299.677-014
09.04.02 SELF-SERVICE-LAUNDRY-AND-DRY-
 CLEANING ATTENDANT (laundry & rel.)
 369.677-010
09.05.01 COOLING-ROOM ATTENDANT (personal
 ser.) 335.677-010
09.05.01 HOT-ROOM ATTENDANT (personal ser.)
 335.677-014
09.05.02 CAFETERIA ATTENDANT (hotel & rest.)
 311.677-010
09.05.02 CATERER HELPER (personal ser.)
 319.677-010
09.05.02 COUNTER ATTENDANT, CAFETERIA (hotel
 & rest.) 311.677-014
09.05.02 DINING ROOM ATTENDANT (hotel & rest.)
 311.677-018
09.05.02 FOOD-SERVICE WORKER, HOSPITAL
 (medical ser.) 319.677-014
09.05.02 MESS ATTENDANT (water trans.)
 350.677-010
09.05.02 WAITER/WAITRESS (water trans.)
 350.677-030
09.05.03 BELLHOP (hotel & rest.) 324.677-010
09.05.03 CHECKROOM ATTENDANT (any industry)
 358.677-010
09.05.03 PORTER (air trans.) 357.677-010
09.05.04 DOORKEEPER (any industry) 324.677-014
09.05.06 CADDIE (amuse. & rec.) 341.677-010
09.05.07 LOCKER-ROOM ATTENDANT (personal ser.)
 358.677-014
09.05.07 REST ROOM ATTENDANT (any industry)
 358.677-018
09.05.08 CHILDREN'S ATTENDANT (amuse. & rec.)
 349.677-018
09.05.08 RIDE ATTENDANT (amuse. & rec.)
 342.677-010
09.05.08 USHER (amuse. & rec.) 344.677-014
10.03.02 FIRST-AID ATTENDANT (any industry)
 354.677-010
10.03.03 ATTENDANT, CHILDREN'S INSTITUTION
 (any industry) 359.677-010
10.03.03 CHILD MONITOR (domestic ser.)
 301.677-010
10.03.03 COMPANION (domestic ser.) 309.677-010
10.03.03 FOSTER PARENT (domestic ser.) 309.677-014
10.03.03 NURSERY SCHOOL ATTENDANT (any
 industry) 359.677-018
10.03.03 PLAYROOM ATTENDANT (any industry)
 359.677-026

10.03.03 TRANSPORTER, PATIENTS (medical ser.)
 355.677-014

681 (Comparing, Taking Instructions-Helping, Precision)

01.06.01 SILK-SCREEN CUTTER (any industry)
 979.681-022
05.05.11 LENS MOUNTER II (optical goods)
 713.681-010
05.10.02 BICYCLE REPAIRER (any industry)
 639.681-010
05.10.05 DEVELOPER (photofinishing) 976.681-010
05.10.08 BUTCHER, MEAT (hotel & rest.) 316.681-010
06.04.35 SILK FINISHER (laundry & rel.) 363.681-010

682 (Comparing, Taking Instructions-Helping, Operating-Controlling)

02.04.02 AEROSPACE PHYSIOLOGICAL TECHNI-
 CIAN (military ser.) 199.682-010
05.06.03 PUMPER (any industry) 914.682-010
05.10.05 DUPLICATING-MACHINE OPERATOR I
 (clerical) 207.682-010
05.10.05 ENGRAVER, MACHINE I (engraving)
 704.682-010
05.10.05 EQUIPMENT MONITOR, PHOTOTYPE-
 SETTING (print. & pub.) 650.682-010
05.10.05 OFFSET-DUPLICATING-MACHINE OPERA-
 TOR (clerical) 207.682-018
05.11.01 PILE-DRIVER OPERATOR (construction)
 859.682-018
05.11.02 CORE-DRILL OPERATOR (any industry)
 930.682-010
05.11.02 PLANT OPERATOR (concrete prod.)
 570.682-014
06.02.02 CRIMPING-MACHINE OPERATOR (any
 industry) 616.682-022
06.02.02 DRILL-PRESS OPERATOR (machine shop)
 606.682-014
06.02.02 LASER-BEAM-TRIM OPERATOR (electron.
 comp.) 726.682-010
06.02.02 POLISHING-MACHINE OPERATOR (any
 industry) 603.682-026
06.02.02 PUNCH-PRESS OPERATOR III (any industry)
 615.682-014
06.02.02 SHEAR OPERATOR I (any industry)
 615.682-018
06.02.03 CUT-OFF-SAW OPERATOR I (woodworking)
 667.682-022
06.02.03 NAILING-MACHINE OPERATOR (any
 industry) 669.682-058
06.02.03 ROUTER OPERATOR (woodworking)
 665.682-030
06.02.05 BINDER (any industry) 787.682-010
06.02.05 CARPET SEWER (carpet & rug) 787.682-014
06.02.05 HEMMER (any industry) 787.682-026
06.02.05 MENDER (any industry) 787.682-030
06.02.05 SEWING MACHINE OPERATOR (leather
 prod.) 783.682-014

06.02.05 STITCHER, STANDARD MACHINE (boot & shoe) 690.682-082
06.02.05 TRIMMER, MACHINE (garment) 781.682-010
06.02.05 ZIPPER SETTER (any industry) 787.682-086
06.02.06 WEAVER (nonmet. min.) 683.682-038
06.02.08 EYEGLASS-LENS CUTTER (optical goods) 716.682-010
06.02.09 CUTTER OPERATOR (any industry) 699.682-018
06.02.09 DIE CUTTER (any industry) 699.682-022
06.02.09 WIRE-WRAPPING-MACHINE OPERATOR (electron. comp.) 726.682-014
06.02.10 SAND MIXER, MACHINE (foundry) 570.682-018
06.02.10 TEMPERER (heat treating) 504.682-026
06.02.15 CENTER-MACHINE OPERATOR (sugar & conf.) 520.682-014
06.02.15 COFFEE ROASTER (food prep., nec) 523.682-014
06.02.15 CRACKER-AND-COOKIE-MACHINE OPERATOR (bakery products) 520.682-034
06.02.15 DOUGHNUT-MACHINE OPERATOR (bakery products) 526.682-022
06.02.15 EXTRUDER OPERATOR (grain-feed mills) 520.682-018
06.02.15 GRINDER OPERATOR (grain-feed mills) 521.682-026
06.02.18 ROOFING-MACHINE OPERATOR (build. mat., nec) 554.682-022
06.02.18 RUG CLEANER, MACHINE (laundry & rel.) 361.682-010
06.02.19 LASER-BEAM-MACHINE OPERATOR (welding) 815.682-010
06.02.20 KICK-PRESS OPERATOR I (any industry) 616.682-026
06.02.20 STACKING-MACHINE OPERATOR I (any industry) 692.682-054
06.02.21 ANODIZER (any industry) 500.682-010
06.04.02 TOOL DRESSER (any industry) 601.682-010
06.04.05 PRESSER, MACHINE (any industry) 363.682-018
06.04.09 STAMPING-PRESS OPERATOR (any industry) 652.682-030
06.04.35 PRESSER, ALL-AROUND (laundry & rel.) 363.682-014
06.04.40 PALLETIZER OPERATOR I (any industry) 921.682-014

683 (Comparing, Taking Instructions-Helping, Driving-Operating)

03.04.01 FARM-MACHINE OPERATOR (agriculture) 409.683-010
03.04.01 FARMWORKER, FRUIT I (agriculture) 403.683-010
03.04.03 SKIFF OPERATOR (fishing & hunt.) 441.683-010
03.04.04 GREENSKEEPER II (any industry) 406.683-010

05.08.01 DUMP-TRUCK DRIVER (any industry) 902.683-010
05.08.01 TRUCK DRIVER, LIGHT (any industry) 906.683-022
05.08.03 AMBULANCE DRIVER (medical ser.) 913.683-010
05.08.03 CONCRETE-MIXING-TRUCK DRIVER (construction) 900.683-010
05.08.03 FOOD-SERVICE DRIVER (hotel & rest.) 906.683-010
05.08.03 TELEPHONE-DIRECTORY-DISTRIBUTOR DRIVER (business ser.) 906.683-018
05.08.04 DOCK HAND (air trans.) 919.683-010
05.11.01 BULLDOZER OPERATOR I (any industry) 850.683-010
05.11.01 OPERATING ENGINEER (construction) 859.683-010
05.11.01 POWER-SHOVEL OPERATOR (any industry) 850.683-030
05.11.01 ROAD-ROLLER OPERATOR (construction) 859.683-030
05.11.01 SCRAPER OPERATOR (construction) 850.683-038
05.11.01 STREET-SWEEPER OPERATOR (government ser.) 919.683-022
05.11.04 DRAGLINE OPERATOR (any industry) 850.683-018
05.11.04 FRONT-END LOADER OPERATOR (any industry) 921.683-042
05.11.04 TRACTOR OPERATOR (any industry) 929.683-014
05.12.04 ELEVATOR OPERATOR, FREIGHT (any industry) 921.683-038
05.12.18 ATTENDANT, CAMPGROUND (amuse. & rec.) 329.683-010
05.12.18 GOLF-RANGE ATTENDANT (amuse. & rec.) 341.683-010
05.12.18 SWEEPER-CLEANER, INDUSTRIAL (any industry) 389.683-010
06.04.40 INDUSTRIAL-TRUCK OPERATOR (any industry) 921.683-050

684 (Comparing, Taking Instructions-Helping, Manipulating)

01.06.01 ETCHER (engraving) 704.684-010
01.06.02 PICTURE FRAMER (retail trade) 739.684-146
01.06.03 PAINTER, AIRBRUSH (any industry) 741.684-018
03.04.02 LOGGER, ALL-ROUND (logging) 454.684-018
03.04.03 FISHER, LINE (fishing & hunt.) 442.684-010
03.04.04 CEMETERY WORKER (real estate) 406.684-010
03.04.04 GROUNDSKEEPER, INDUSTRIAL-COMMERCIAL (any industry) 406.684-014
03.04.04 HORTICULTURAL WORKER I (agriculture) 405.684-014
03.04.04 LAWN-SERVICE WORKER (agriculture) 408.684-010

03.04.05 TREE PRUNER (agriculture) 408.684-018

05.05.06 WELDER, GAS (welding) 811.684-014

05.05.11 DENTURE-MODEL MAKER (protective dev.) 712.684-046

05.05.11 PACKER, DENTURE (protective dev.) 712.684-034

05.05.15 UPHOLSTERY REPAIRER (furniture) 780.684-122

05.09.01 MEAT CLERK (retail trade) 222.684-010

05.10.01 ASBESTOS REMOVAL WORKER (construction) 869.684-082

05.10.01 BUILDING CLEANER (any industry) 891.684-022

05.10.01 DRY-WALL APPLICATOR (construction) 842.684-014

05.10.01 FENCE ERECTOR (construction) 869.684-022

05.10.01 FURNITURE ASSEMBLER-AND-INSTALLER (retail trade) 739.684-082

05.10.01 GLASS INSTALLER (automotive ser.) 865.684-010

05.10.01 GRIP (amuse. & rec.) 962.684-014

05.10.01 LAWN-SPRINKLER INSTALLER (construction) 869.684-030

05.10.01 PUMP INSTALLER (any industry) 630.684-018

05.10.01 REPAIRER (furniture) 709.684-062

05.10.01 ROUSTABOUT (petrol. & gas) 869.684-046

05.10.01 TORCH-STRAIGHTENER-AND HEATER (any industry) 709.684-086

05.10.01 WATER-SOFTENER SERVICER-AND-INSTALLER (business ser.) 862.684-034

05.10.01 WELDER, TACK (welding) 810.684-010

05.10.02 AUTOMOBILE-ACCESSORIES INSTALLER (automotive ser.) 806.684-038

05.10.04 DOLL REPAIRER (any industry) 731.684-014

05.10.04 SPORTS-EQUIPMENT REPAIRER (any industry) 732.684-122

05.10.04 SWIMMING-POOL SERVICER (any industry) 891.684-018

05.10.04 USED-CAR RENOVATOR (retail trade) 620.684-034

05.10.05 CONTACT WORKER, LITHOGRAPHY (print. & pub.) 976.684-038

05.10.05 FILM LABORATORY TECHNICIAN (motion picture) 976.684-014

05.10.08 BUTCHER, CHICKEN AND FISH (hotel & rest.) 316.684-010

05.10.08 MEAT CUTTER (retail trade) 316.684-018

05.10.08 PANTRY GOODS MAKER (hotel & rest.) 317.684-014

05.10.09 EXTERMINATOR (business ser.) 389.684-010

05.12.02 HORIZONTAL-EARTH-BORING-MACHINE-OPERATOR HELPER (construction) 850.684-014

05.12.12 HIGHWAY-MAINTENANCE WORKER (government ser.) 899.684-014

05.12.12 PIPE-FITTER HELPER (construction) 862.684-022

05.12.12 WINDOW REPAIRER (any industry) 899.684-042

05.12.13 KEY CUTTER (any industry) 709.684-050

05.12.15 AUTOMOBILE WRECKER (wholesale tr.) 620.684-010

05.12.15 BELT REPAIRER (any industry) 630.684-014

05.12.15 ROLLER-SKATE REPAIRER (any industry) 732.684-102

05.12.15 TIRE REPAIRER (automotive ser.) 915.684-010

05.12.16 CABLE PULLER (construction) 829.684-018

05.12.16 PROP ATTENDANT (amuse. & rec.) 962.684-022

05.12.17 BAKER HELPER (hotel & rest.) 313.684-010

05.12.17 COFFEE MAKER (hotel & rest.) 317.684-010

05.12.17 DELI CUTTER-SLICER (retail trade) 316.684-014

05.12.18 LAUNDRY WORKER I (any industry) 361.684-014

06.02.21 PLATER, PRINTED CIRCUIT BOARD PANELS (electron. comp.) 500.684-026

06.02.22 CABINET ASSEMBLER (furniture) 763.684-014

06.02.22 CASKET ASSEMBLER (fabrication, nec) 739.684-190

06.02.22 ELECTRIC-SIGN ASSEMBLER (fabrication, nec) 729.684-022

06.02.22 LAMINATOR (rubber goods) 899.684-018

06.02.22 MOTORCYCLE ASSEMBLER (motor-bicycles) 806.684-090

06.02.22 TRANSFORMER ASSEMBLER II (elec. equip.) 820.684-010

06.02.22 UTILITY WORKER (mfd. bldgs.) 869.684-074

06.02.23 ASSEMBLER I (office machines) 706.684-014

06.02.23 ASSEMBLER, MUSICAL INSTRUMENTS (musical inst.) 730.684-010

06.02.23 ASSEMBLER, PRODUCT (machine shop) 706.684-018

06.02.23 ASSEMBLER, SEMICONDUCTOR (electron. comp.) 726.684-034

06.02.23 CHAIN MAKER, MACHINE (jewelry-silver.) 700.684-022

06.02.23 ELECTRONICS ASSEMBLER (comm. equip.) 726.684-018

06.02.23 INSTRUMENT ASSEMBLER (inst. & app.) 710.684-046

06.02.23 LAMINATION ASSEMBLER (elec. equip.) 729.684-066

06.02.23 PRINTED CIRCUIT BOARD ASSEMBLER, HAND (comm. equip.) 726.684-070

06.02.23 TUBE ASSEMBLER, CATHODE RAY (electron. comp.) 725.684-022

06.02.23 WHEEL LACER AND TRUER (motor-bicycles) 706.684-106

06.02.24 BOAT PATCHER, PLASTIC (ship-boat mfg.) 807.684-014

06.02.24 BRIGHT CUTTER (jewelry-silver.) 700.684-018

06.02.24 GREASE BUFFER (jewelry-silver.) 705.684-022

06.02.24 REPAIRER, FINISHED METAL (any industry) 809.684-034

06.02.24 ROUTER OPERATOR, HAND (aircraft mfg.) 806.684-150

06.02.24 SKI REPAIRER, PRODUCTION (toy-sport equip.) 732.684-118

06.02.24 SPINNER (jewelry-silver.) 700.684-074

06.02.24 TROPHY ASSEMBLER (jewelry-silver.) 735.684-018

06.02.27 CUTTER, HAND I (any industry) 781.684-074

06.02.27 LEATHER CUTTER (leather prod.) 783.684-022

06.02.27 LEATHER WORKER (leather prod.) 783.684-026

06.02.27 SPOTTER I (laundry & rel.) 361.684-018

06.02.28 DOUGHNUT MAKER (bakery products) 526.684-010

06.02.29 RUBBER-GOODS REPAIRER (any industry) 759.684-054

06.02.30 CASTER (nonmet. min.) 575.684-018

06.02.30 CEMENTER (optical goods) 711.684-014

06.02.30 GLASS CUTTER (any industry) 775.684-022

06.02.30 PLASTER MAKER (nonmet. min.) 779.684-046

06.02.30 PLASTER-DIE MAKER (pottery & porc.) 774.684-026

06.02.32 CATHODE RAY TUBE SALVAGE PROCESSOR (electron. comp.) 725.684-026

06.02.32 ETCHED-CIRCUIT PROCESSOR (electron. comp.) 590.684-018

06.02.32 OPAQUER (protective dev.) 712.684-030

06.02.32 RACKET STRINGER (toy-sport equip.) 732.684-094

06.02.32 SKI MOLDER (toy-sport equip.) 732.684-114

06.03.01 INSPECTOR, PRINTED CIRCUIT BOARDS (electron. comp.) 726.684-062

06.03.02 ELECTRONICS INSPECTOR (electron. comp.) 726.684-022

06.03.02 ELECTRONICS TESTER (comm. equip.) 726.684-026

06.03.02 INSPECTOR, INTEGRATED CIRCUITS (electron. comp.) 726.684-058

06.03.02 INSPECTOR, SEMICONDUCTOR WAFER (electron. comp.) 726.684-066

06.03.02 INSTRUMENT INSPECTOR (inst. & app.) 710.684-050

06.03.02 WATER LEAK REPAIRER (auto. mfg.) 807.684-034

06.04.08 CERAMIC CAPACITOR PROCESSOR (electron. comp.) 590.684-010

06.04.19 ELECTRONIC-COMPONENT PROCESSOR (electron. comp.) 590.684-014

06.04.19 PLATER, SEMICONDUCTOR WAFERS AND COMPONENTS (electron. comp.) 500.684-030

06.04.19 POLYSILICON PREPARATION WORKER (electron. comp.) 590.684-038

06.04.22 ASSEMBLER, MOTOR VEHICLE (auto. mfg.) 806.684-010

06.04.22 LAMINATOR, HAND (furniture) 763.684-050

06.04.22 NAILER, HAND (any industry) 762.684-050

06.04.22 PLASTIC-TOP ASSEMBLER (furniture) 763.684-062

06.04.23 ASSEMBLER, MOLDED FRAMES (optical goods) 713.684-014

06.04.23 ASSEMBLER, SMALL PRODUCTS I (any industry) 706.684-022

06.04.23 COIL WINDER (elec. equip.) 724.684-026

06.04.23 EARRING MAKER (jewelry-silver.) 700.684-030

06.04.23 ELECTRIC-MOTOR ASSEMBLER (elec. equip.) 721.684-022

06.04.23 FISHING-REEL ASSEMBLER (toy-sport equip.) 732.684-062

06.04.23 LOCK ASSEMBLER (cutlery-hrdwr.) 706.684-074

06.04.23 RUBBER-GOODS ASSEMBLER (rubber goods) 752.684-038

06.04.23 TIRE MOUNTER (fabrication, nec) 739.684-158

06.04.24 BENCH WORKER (optical goods) 713.684-018

06.04.24 BUFFER I (any industry) 705.684-014

06.04.24 FILER (jewelry-silver.) 700.684-034

06.04.24 JIGSAWYER (jewelry-silver.) 700.684-046

06.04.24 METAL FINISHER (any industry) 705.684-034

06.04.24 MOLD DRESSER (any industry) 519.684-018

06.04.24 POLISHER (any industry) 705.684-058

06.04.24 REFINER (protective dev.) 712.684-038

06.04.25 CANER II (furniture) 763.684-022

06.04.27 BOW MAKER (any industry) 789.684-010

06.04.27 CANVAS REPAIRER (any industry) 782.684-010

06.04.27 SEWER, HAND (any industry) 782.684-058

06.04.27 THREAD CUTTER (any industry) 789.684-050

06.04.28 BONER, MEAT (meat products) 525.684-010

06.04.28 BUTCHER, FISH (can. & preserv.) 525.684-014

06.04.28 CANDY DIPPER, HAND (sugar & conf.) 524.684-010

06.04.28 DECORATOR (bakery products) 524.684-014

06.04.28 FISH CLEANER (can. & preserv.) 525.684-030

06.04.28 TRIMMER, MEAT (meat products) 525.684-054

06.04.30 GLASS FINISHER (glass products) 775.684-026

06.04.32 SEMICONDUCTOR PROCESSOR (electron. comp.) 590.684-022

06.04.33 PAINTER, BRUSH (any industry) 740.684-022

06.04.33 PUTTY GLAZER (any industry) 749.684-042

06.04.34 ARTIFICIAL-FLOWER MAKER (button & notion) 739.684-014

06.04.34 DRILLER, HAND (any industry) 809.684-018

06.04.34 INTEGRATED CIRCUIT FABRICATOR (electron. comp.) 590.684-042

06.04.34 MAT CUTTER (wood prod., nec) 739.684-126

06.04.34 PAINT MIXER, HAND (any industry) 550.684-018

06.04.34 PHOTO MASK CLEANER (electron. comp.) 590.684-034

06.04.34 SCREEN PRINTER (any industry) 979.684-034

06.04.34 WIREWORKER (elec. equip.) 728.684-022

06.04.35 DRY CLEANER, HAND (laundry & rel.) 362.684-010

06.04.35 FURNITURE CLEANER (laundry & rel.) 362.684-022

06.04.35 LAUNDERER, HAND (laundry & rel.) 361.684-010

06.04.35 LAUNDRY OPERATOR (laundry & rel.) 369.684-014

06.04.35 LEATHER CLEANER (laundry & rel.) 362.684-026

06.04.35 PRESSER, HAND (any industry) 363.684-018

06.04.38 CRATER (any industry) 920.684-010

06.04.39 CLEANER (ordnance) 503.684-010

06.04.39 EQUIPMENT CLEANER (any industry) 599.684-010

---

685 (Comparing, Taking Instructions-Helping, Tending)

03.04.05 IRRIGATOR, SPRINKLING SYSTEM (agriculture) 409.685-014

05.05.13 ASSISTANT PRESS OPERATOR, OFFSET (print. & pub.) 651.685-026

05.06.02 AIR-COMPRESSOR OPERATOR (any industry) 950.685-010

05.11.04 DUMP OPERATOR (any industry) 921.685-038

05.12.06 WATER TENDER (any industry) 599.685-122

05.12.19 BRAILLE-DUPLICATING-MACHINE OPERATOR (print. & pub.) 207.685-010

05.12.19 COLLATOR OPERATOR (clerical) 208.685-010

05.12.19 FOLDING-MACHINE OPERATOR (clerical) 208.685-014

05.12.19 INSERTING-MACHINE OPERATOR (clerical) 208.685-018

05.12.19 MICROFILM MOUNTER (clerical) 208.685-022

05.12.19 PHOTOCOPYING-MACHINE OPERATOR (clerical) 207.685-014

05.12.19 PHOTOGRAPHIC-MACHINE OPERATOR (clerical) 207.685-018

06.02.02 BRAKE OPERATOR II (any industry) 619.685-026

06.02.15 DOUGH MIXER (bakery products) 520.685-234

06.04.02 BENDING-MACHINE OPERATOR II (any industry) 617.685-010

06.04.02 DRILL PRESS TENDER (machine shop) 606.685-026

06.04.02 ELECTRIC-SEALING-MACHINE OPERATOR (any industry) 690.685-154

06.04.02 EMBOSSER (any industry) 583.685-030

06.04.02 GRINDER (plastic prod.) 555.685-026

06.04.02 MACHINE OPERATOR II (any industry) 619.685-062

06.04.02 NIBBLER OPERATOR (any industry) 615.685-026

06.04.02 POWER-PRESS TENDER (any industry) 617.685-026

06.04.02 PUNCH-PRESS OPERATOR II (any industry) 615.685-030

06.04.02 SCROLL-MACHINE OPERATOR (struct. metal) 616.685-062

06.04.02 TURRET-PUNCH-PRESS OPERATOR, TAPE-CONTROL (any industry) 615.685-042

06.04.03 BUZZSAW OPERATOR (any industry) 667.685-026

06.04.03 GLUING-MACHINE OPERATOR (woodworking) 569.685-046

06.04.04 BAG-MACHINE OPERATOR (paper goods) 649.685-014

06.04.04 BINDERY WORKER (print. & pub.) 653.685-010

06.04.04 BOOK TRIMMER (print. & pub.) 640.685-010

06.04.04 CARTON-FORMING-MACHINE OPERATOR (any industry) 641.685-022

06.04.04 CARTON-FORMING-MACHINE TENDER (paper goods) 641.685-026

06.04.05 BUTTONHOLE-AND-BUTTON-SEWING-MACHINE OPERATOR (garment) 786.685-042

06.04.05 SEWING-MACHINE OPERATOR, SEMIAUTOMATIC (garment) 786.685-030

06.04.05 SPREADER, MACHINE (any industry) 781.685-010

06.04.05 STRIP-CUTTING-MACHINE OPERATOR (textile) 686.685-066

06.04.05 SURGICAL-DRESSING MAKER (protective dev.) 689.685-130

06.04.06 BEAM-WARPER TENDER, AUTOMATIC (knitting) 681.685-018

06.04.06 PICKING-MACHINE OPERATOR (any industry) 680.685-082

06.04.06 SEAMLESS-HOSIERY KNITTER (knitting) 684.685-010

06.04.06 YARN WINDER (tex. prod., nec) 681.685-154

06.04.07 DESIGN PRINTER, BALLOON (rubber goods) 651.685-014

06.04.07 RUBBER CUTTER (rubber goods) 559.685-158

06.04.08 COREMAKER, MACHINE I (foundry) 518.685-014

06.04.08 CRUSHER TENDER (any industry) 570.685-022

06.04.08 LENS-FABRICATING-MACHINE TENDER (optical goods) 716.685-022

06.04.08 MILLER (cement) 570.685-046

06.04.09 CUTTER (photofinishing) 976.685-010

06.04.09 CUTTER, MACHINE II (any industry) 699.685-014

06.04.09 PHOTORESIST LAMINATOR, PRINTED CIRCUIT BOARD (electron. comp.) 554.685-034

06.04.09 SANDER (toy-sport equip.) 690.685-346

06.04.09 SCRAP HANDLER (any industry) 509.685-050

06.04.09 SILK-SCREEN PRINTER, MACHINE (any industry) 979.685-010

06.04.09 TRACK LAMINATING MACHINE TENDER (inst. & app.) 692.685-290

06.04.09 WAX MOLDER (foundry) 549.685-038

06.04.10 INJECTION-MOLDING-MACHINE TENDER (plastic prod.) 556.685-038

06.04.11 CHEMICAL OPERATOR II (chemical) 558.685-062

06.04.11 CHEMICAL PREPARER (chemical) 550.685-030

06.04.11 DRIER OPERATOR (chemical) 553.685-042

06.04.11 MIXER (paint & varnish) 550.685-078

06.04.13 BLOW-MOLDING-MACHINE TENDER (toy-sport equip.) 556.685-086

06.04.13 COMPRESSION-MOLDING-MACHINE TENDER (plastic prod.) 556.685-022

06.04.13 TIRE MOLDER (rubber tire) 553.685-102

06.04.15 BATTER MIXER (bakery products) 520.685-010

06.04.15 BREWERY CELLAR WORKER (beverage) 522.685-014

06.04.15 CENTRIFUGE OPERATOR (dairy products) 521.685-042

06.04.15 CHOCOLATE MOLDER, MACHINE (sugar & conf.) 529.685-054

06.04.15 COFFEE GRINDER (food prep., nec) 521.685-078

06.04.15 COOK, FRY, DEEP FAT (can. & preserv.) 526.685-014

06.04.15 FLOUR BLENDER (grain-feed mills) 520.685-106

06.04.15 HONEY PROCESSOR (food prep., nec) 522.685-070

06.04.15 MEAT GRINDER (meat products) 521.685-214

06.04.15 OVEN OPERATOR, AUTOMATIC (bakery products) 526.685-070

06.04.15 PRESS OPERATOR, MEAT (meat products) 520.685-182

06.04.17 SHELL MOLDER (foundry) 518.685-026

06.04.19 COATING EQUIPMENT OPERATOR, PRINTED CIRCUIT BOARDS (electron. comp.) 590.685-066

06.04.19 CREMATOR (personal ser.) 359.685-010

06.04.19 DEVELOPER, AUTOMATIC (photofinishing) 976.685-014

06.04.19 DISPLAY-SCREEN FABRICATOR (electron. comp.) 725.685-010

06.04.19 FILTER OPERATOR (any industry) 551.685-078

06.04.19 METALLIZATION EQUIPMENT TENDER, SEMICONDUCTORS (comm. equip.) 590.685-086

06.04.19 PRINT DEVELOPER, AUTOMATIC (photofinishing) 976.685-026

06.04.19 STILL TENDER (any industry) 552.685-026

06.04.19 STRIPPER-ETCHER, PRINTED CIRCUIT BOARDS (electron. comp.) 590.685-082

06.04.19 THERMOMETER PRODUCTION WORKER (inst. & app.) 710.685-014

06.04.19 UTILITY WORKER, FILM PROCESSING (photofinishing) 976.685-030

06.04.20 CORRUGATED-FASTENER DRIVER (woodworking) 669.685-042

06.04.20 MOUNTER, AUTOMATIC (photofinishing) 976.685-022

06.04.20 STAPLING-MACHINE OPERATOR (any industry) 692.685-202

06.04.21 CERAMIC COATER, MACHINE (any industry) 509.685-022

06.04.21 DIPPER AND BAKER (any industry) 599.685-030

06.04.21 PLATING EQUIPMENT TENDER (electroplating) 500.685-014

06.04.21 SEED PELLETER (agriculture) 599.685-126

06.04.34 MACHINE SNELLER (toy-sport equip.) 732.685-026

06.04.34 STUFFER (toy-sport equip.) 731.685-014

06.04.35 PRESS OPERATOR (laundry & rel.) 363.685-010

06.04.37 NAME-PLATE STAMPER (any industry) 652.685-054

06.04.38 PACKAGER, MACHINE (any industry) 920.685-078

06.04.39 SCRUBBER MACHINE TENDER (electron. comp.) 599.685-134

06.04.40 CHAR-CONVEYOR TENDER (sugar & conf.) 529.685-050

686 (Comparing, Taking Instructions-Helping, Feeding-Offbearing)

05.12.03 PRESS BUCKER (any industry) 920.686-042

05.12.19 FEEDER (print. & pub.) 651.686-014

05.12.19 ROLL TENDER (print. & pub.) 651.686-022

06.04.02 GRAINER, MACHINE (any industry) 652.686-014

06.04.03 CHAIN OFFBEARER (saw. & plan.) 669.686-018

06.04.03 LATHE SPOTTER (millwork-plywood) 663.686-022

06.04.06 CLOTH DOFFER (textile) 689.686-058

06.04.09 MACHINE FEEDER (any industry) 699.686-010

06.04.13 FUSING-FURNACE LOADER (optical goods) 573.686-014

06.04.15 BAKER HELPER (bakery products) 526.686-010

06.04.15 CANNERY WORKER (can. & preserv.) 529.686-014

06.04.16 MACHINE FEEDER, RAW STOCK (tex. prod., nec) 680.686-018

06.04.18 DIGESTER-OPERATOR HELPER (paper & pulp) 532.686-010

06.04.19 LABORER (pharmaceut.) 559.686-022

06.04.21 SPRAY-UNIT FEEDER (any industry) 599.686-014

06.04.40 CONVEYOR FEEDER-OFFBEARER (any industry) 921.686-014

687 (Comparing, Taking Instructions-Helping, Handling)

02.04.02 LABORATORY ASSISTANT, BLOOD AND PLASMA (medical ser.) 078.687-010

03.04.01 CHRISTMAS-TREE FARM WORKER (forestry) 451.687-010

03.04.01 FARMWORKER, GENERAL II (agriculture) 421.687-010

03.04.01 FARMWORKER, VEGETABLE II (agriculture) 402.687-010

03.04.01 PACKER, AGRICULTURAL PRODUCE (agriculture) 920.687-134

03.04.02 CHAIN SAW OPERATOR (chemical) 454.687-010

03.04.02 FOREST WORKER (forestry) 452.687-010

03.04.02 FOREST-FIRE FIGHTER (forestry) 452.687-014

03.04.04 HORTICULTURAL WORKER II (agriculture) 405.687-014

03.04.04 LABORER, LANDSCAPE (agriculture) 408.687-014

05.07.01 FIRE-EXTINGUISHER-SPRINKLER INSPECTOR (any industry) 379.687-010

05.08.04 DECKHAND (water trans.) 911.687-022

05.09.01 CHECKER (motor trans.) 919.687-010

05.09.01 LABORER, STORES (any industry) 922.687-058

05.09.01 SHIPPING CHECKER (clerical) 222.687-030

05.09.01 SUPPLY CLERK (personal ser.) 339.687-010

05.09.03 RECEIVING CHECKER (clerical) 222.687-018

05.11.01 PROJECT-CREW WORKER (any industry) 891.687-018

05.12.03 BAGGAGE HANDLER (r.r. trans.) 910.687-010

05.12.03 GARBAGE COLLECTOR (motor trans.) 955.687-022

05.12.03 INSTALLER (museums) 922.687-050

05.12.03 LABORER, PETROLEUM REFINERY (petrol. refin.) 549.687-018

05.12.03 LABORER, SHIPYARD (ship-boat mfg.) 809.687-022

05.12.03 MATERIAL HANDLER (any industry) 929.687-030

05.12.03 YARD LABORER (paper & pulp) 922.687-102

05.12.04 CHOKE SETTER (logging) 921.687-014

05.12.04 GRIP (motion picture) 962.687-022

05.12.06 LOADER HELPER (any industry) 914.687-014

05.12.08 GARAGE SERVICER, INDUSTRIAL (any industry) 915.687-014

05.12.08 LUBRICATION SERVICER (automotive ser.) 915.687-018

05.12.08 OILER (any industry) 699.687-018

05.12.12 AIR-CONDITIONING INSTALLER-SERVICER HELPER, WINDOW UNIT (construction) 637.687-010

05.12.12 AUTOMOBILE-BODY-REPAIRER HELPER (automotive ser.) 807.687-010

05.12.12 DECORATOR, STREET AND BUILDING (any industry) 899.687-010

05.12.17 COOK HELPER (hotel & rest.) 317.687-010

05.12.18 AUTOMOBILE DETAILER (automotive ser.) 915.687-034

05.12.18 BARTENDER HELPER (hotel & rest.) 312.687-010

05.12.18 CARETAKER (domestic ser.) 301.687-010

05.12.18 CENTRAL-SUPPLY WORKER (medical ser.) 381.687-010

05.12.18 CHIMNEY SWEEP (any industry) 891.687-010

05.12.18 CLEANER II (any industry) 919.687-014

05.12.18 CLEANER, COMMERCIAL OR INSTITUTIONAL (any industry) 381.687-014

05.12.18 CLEANER, HOSPITAL (medical ser.) 323.687-010

05.12.18 CLEANER, HOUSEKEEPING (any industry) 323.687-014

05.12.18 CLEANER, INDUSTRIAL (any industry) 381.687-018

05.12.18 CLEANER, LABORATORY EQUIPMENT (any industry) 381.687-022

05.12.18 CLEANER, WINDOW (any industry) 389.687-014

05.12.18 DAY WORKER (domestic ser.) 301.687-014

05.12.18 FURNACE CLEANER (any industry) 891.687-014

05.12.18 HOUSECLEANER (hotel & rest.) 323.687-018

05.12.18 KITCHEN HELPER (hotel & rest.) 318.687-010

05.12.18 LABORER, GENERAL (motor trans.) 909.687-014

05.12.18 LIGHT-FIXTURE SERVICER (any industry) 389.687-018

05.12.18 SANDBLASTER (any industry) 503.687-010

05.12.18 SILVER WRAPPER (hotel & rest.) 318.687-018

05.12.18 STEAM CLEANER (automotive ser.) 915.687-026

05.12.18 STREET CLEANER (government ser.) 955.687-018

05.12.18 TANK CLEANER (any industry) 891.687-022

05.12.18 TUBE CLEANER (any industry) 891.687-030

05.12.18 WAXER, FLOOR (any industry) 381.687-034

06.03.02 GARMENT INSPECTOR (any industry) 789.687-070

06.03.02 GLASS INSPECTOR (any industry) 579.687-022

06.03.02 GRADER (woodworking) 669.687-030

06.03.02 HYDRO-PNEUMATIC TESTER (any industry) 862.687-018

06.03.02 METAL-FINISH INSPECTOR (any industry) 703.687-014

06.03.02 PHOTO CHECKER AND ASSEMBLER (photofinishing) 976.687-014

06.03.02 PHOTOFINISHING LABORATORY WORKER (photofinishing) 976.687-018

06.03.02 PLATE INSPECTOR (print. & pub.) 972.687-010

06.03.02 PRINT INSPECTOR (pottery & porc.) 774.687-018

06.03.02 SELECTOR (glass mfg.) 579.687-030

06.04.10 ANNEALER (jewelry-silver.) 504.687-010

06.04.17 KILN WORKER (pottery & porc.) 573.687-022

06.04.22 ASSEMBLER, BICYCLE II (motor-bicycles) 806.687-010

06.04.22 ASSEMBLER, PRODUCTION (any industry) 706.687-010

06.04.23 LENS INSERTER (optical goods) 713.687-026

06.04.23 TOY ASSEMBLER (toy-sport equip.) 731.687-034

06.04.24 ASSEMBLER, PLASTIC HOSPITAL
    PRODUCTS (inst. & app.) 712.687-010
06.04.24 MELTER (jewelry-silver.) 700.687-042
06.04.24 PREPARER (jewelry-silver.) 700.687-062
06.04.25 CROSSBAND LAYER (millwork-plywood)
    762.687-026
06.04.25 WOODWORKING-SHOP HAND (wood-
    working) 769.687-054
06.04.27 CARPET CUTTER II (carpet & rug)
    585.687-014
06.04.28 POULTRY BONER (meat products)
    525.687-066
06.04.28 POULTRY DRESSER (agriculture)
    525.687-070
06.04.28 TIER (meat products) 525.687-118
06.04.34 ELECTRONICS WORKER (electron. comp.)
    726.687-010
06.04.34 LABORER, GRINDING AND POLISHING
    (any industry) 705.687-014
06.04.34 MASKER (any industry) 749.687-018
06.04.35 LAUNDRY LABORER (laundry & rel.)
    361.687-018
06.04.35 WASHER, HAND (laundry & rel.)
    361.687-030
06.04.37 STENCILER (any industry)
    920.687-178
06.04.38 BANDER, HAND (any industry)
    929.687-058

06.04.38 PACKING-LINE WORKER (rubber goods)
    753.687-038
06.04.39 CLEANER AND POLISHER (any industry)
    709.687-010
06.04.39 MACHINE CLEANER (any industry)
    699.687-014
06.04.40 DISTILLERY WORKER, GENERAL (bever-
    age) 529.687-066
06.04.40 LABORER, CHEMICAL PROCESSING
    (chemical) 559.687-050
06.04.40 LABORER, CONCRETE PLANT (concrete
    prod.) 579.687-042
06.04.40 LABORER, GENERAL (steel & rel.)
    509.687-026
06.04.40 SAWMILL WORKER (saw. & plan.)
    667.687-018
07.05.02 REVIEWER (insurance) 209.687-018
07.05.04 MAIL CLERK (clerical) 209.687-026
07.05.04 MAIL HANDLER (government ser.)
    209.687-014
07.07.02 CHECKER I (clerical) 222.687-010
07.07.02 ROUTING CLERK (clerical) 222.687-022
07.07.02 SORTER (clerical) 209.687-022
07.07.03 COIN-MACHINE COLLECTOR (business ser.)
    292.687-010
09.05.02 COUNTER-SUPPLY WORKER (hotel & rest.)
    319.687-010
09.05.10 BAGGER (retail trade) 920.687-014

Appendix F
Occupational Employment Statistics (OES) Codes

The Bureau of Labor Statistics and most public employment agencies use Occupational Employment Statistics (OES) codes when they publish data about the number of people currently working in each occupation and projections of future employment. An OES code is provided for every occupation in *The Enhanced Guide for Occupational Exploration*. This appendix lists the titles that correspond to these codes.

Code	Title
13002	Financial managers
13005	Personnel, training, and labor relations managers
13008	Purchasing managers
13011	Marketing, advertising, and public relations managers
13014	Administrative services managers
13017	Engineering, mathematical, and natural science managers
15005	Education administrators
15011	Property and real estate managers
15014	Industrial production managers
15017	Construction managers
15023	Communication, transportation, and utilities operations managers
15026	Food service and lodging managers
19002	Government chief executives and legislators
19005	General managers and top executives
19998	All other managers and administrators
21102	Underwriters
21105	Credit analysts
21108	Loan officers and counselors
21114	Accountants and auditors
21117	Budget analysts
21302	Wholesale and retail buyers, except farm products
21308	Purchasing agents, except wholesale, retail, and farm products
21508	Employment interviewers, private or public employment service
21511	Personnel, training, and labor relations specialists
21902	Cost estimators
21905	Management analysts
21908	Construction and building inspectors
21911	Inspectors and compliance officers, except construction
21914	Tax examiners, collectors, and revenue agents
21921	Claims examiners, property and casualty insurance
21998	All other management support workers
22102	Aeronautical and astronautical engineers
22105	Metallurgists and metallurgical, ceramic, & materials engineers
22108	Mining engineers, including mine safety engineers
22111	Petroleum engineers
22114	Chemical engineers
22117	Nuclear engineers
22121	Civil engineers, including traffic engineers
22126	Electrical and electronics engineers
22128	Industrial engineers, except safety engineers
22135	Mechanical engineers
22198	All other engineers
22302	Architects, except landscape and marine
22308	Landscape architects
22310	Surveyors
22505	Electrical and electronic technicians/technologists
22512	Drafters
24102	Physicists and astronomers
24105	Chemists
24108	Meteorologists
24111	Geologists, geophysicists, and oceanographers
24198	All other physical scientists
24302	Foresters and conservation scientists

24305	Agricultural and food scientists
24308	Biological scientists
24311	Medical scientists
24398	All other life scientists
24501	Science and mathematics technicians
25101	Systems analysts and computer scientists
25104	Computer programmers
25111	Programmers, numerical, tool, and process control
25302	Operations research analysts
25312	Statisticians
25313	Actuaries
25317	Mathematicians and all other mathematical scientists
27102	Economists
27105	Urban and regional planners
27108	Psychologists
27198	All other social scientists
27308	Human services workers
27310	Social workers
27311	Recreation workers
27502	Clergy
27505	Directors, religious activities and education
28101	Judges, magistrates, and other judicial workers
28108	Lawyers
28305	Paralegals
28306	Title examiners and searchers
28499	All other legal assistants, including law clerks
31100	College and university faculty
31302	Teachers, preschool and kindergarten
31305	Teachers, elementary
31308	Teachers, secondary school
31311	Teachers, special education
31314	Teachers and instructors, vocational education and training
31317	Instructors, adult (nonvocational) education
31321	Instructors and coaches, sports and physical training
31323	Farm and home management advisors
31398	All other teachers and instructors
31502	Librarians, professional
31505	Technical assistants, library
31511	Curators, archivists, museum technicians, and restorers
31514	Counselors
32102	Physicians
32105	Dentists
32108	Optometrists
32111	Podiatrists
32114	Veterinarians and veterinary inspectors
32302	Respiratory therapists
32305	Occupational therapists
32308	Physical therapists
32314	Speech-language pathologists and audiologists
32317	Recreational therapists
32398	All other therapists
32502	Registered nurses
32505	Licensed practical nurses
32508	Emergency medical technicians
32511	Physician assistants
32514	Opticians, dispensing and measuring
32517	Pharmacists
32521	Dietitians and nutritionists
32908	Dental hygienists
32910	Clinical lab technologists and technicians
32911	Medical records technicians
32914	Nuclear medicine technologists
32916	Radiologic technologists and technicians
32923	EEG technologists
32926	EKG technicians
32928	Surgical technologists
32998	All other health professionals, paraprofessionals, & technicians
34001	Writers and editors, including technical writers
34008	Public relations specialists and publicity writers
34010	Radio and TV announcers and newscasters
34011	Reporters and correspondents
34023	Photographers
34026	Camera operators, television, motion picture, video
34028	Broadcast technicians
34035	Artists and commercial artists
34038	Designers, except interior designers
34041	Interior designers
34050	Musicians
34053	Dancers and choreographers
34056	Producers, directors, actors, and entertainers
34058	Athletes, coaches, umpires, and referees
35199	All other engineering technicians and technologists
39002	Air traffic controllers
39011	Funeral directors and morticians
39099	All other technicians
39998	All other professional workers
43002	Insurance sales workers
43005	Brokers, real estate
43008	Sales agents, real estate
43011	Real estate appraisers
43014	Securities and financial services sales workers
43021	Travel agents
49011	Salespersons, retail
49017	Counter and rental clerks
49021	Stock clerks, sales floor
49023	Cashiers
49998	All other sales and related workers
51002	Clerical supervisors and managers
53102	Bank tellers
53105	New accounts clerks, banking
53111	Loan interviewers
53114	Credit authorizers
53117	Credit checkers
53121	Loan and credit clerks
53123	Adjustment clerks
53126	Statement clerks
53128	Brokerage clerks
53302	Insurance adjusters, examiners, and investigators
53311	Insurance claims clerks
53314	Insurance policy processing clerks
53502	Welfare eligibility workers and interviewers
53508	Bill and account collectors
53702	Court clerks
53705	Municipal clerks
53799	All other adjusters and investigators
53808	Hotel desk clerks
53810	Reservation and transportation ticket agents and travel clerks
53902	Library assistants and bookmobile drivers
53904	Teacher aides and educational assistants
53908	Advertising clerks
53911	Proofreaders and copy markers
53914	Real estate clerks
55102	Legal secretaries
55105	Medical secretaries
55198	Secretaries, except legal and medical
55302	Stenographers
55305	Receptionists and information clerks
55307	Typists and word processors
55314	Personnel clerks, except payroll and timekeeping
55317	Correspondence clerks

55321	File clerks
55323	Order clerks, materials, merchandise, and service
55326	Procurement clerks
55328	Statistical clerks
55332	Interviewing clerks, except personnel and social welfare
55335	Customer service representatives, utilities
55338	Bookkeeping, accounting, and auditing clerks
55341	Payroll and timekeeping clerks
55344	Billing, cost, and rate clerks
55347	General office clerks
56002	Billing, posting, and calculating machine operators
56011	Computer operators, except peripheral equipment
56014	Peripheral EDP equipment operators
56017	Data entry keyers, except composing
56021	Data entry keyers, composing
56200	Duplicating, mail, and other office machine operators
57102	Switchboard operators
57105	Directory assistance operators
57108	Central office operators
57198	All other communications equipment operators
57302	Mail clerks, except mail machine operators and postal service
57305	Postal mail carriers
57308	Postal service clerks
57311	Messengers
58002	Dispatchers, police, fire, and ambulance
58005	Dispatchers, except police, fire, and ambulance
58008	Production, planning, and expediting clerks
58014	Meter readers, utilities
58017	Weighers, measurers, checkers, and samplers, recordkeeping
58023	Stock clerks, stockrooom, warehouse, or yard
58026	Order fillers, wholesale and retail sales
58028	Traffic, shipping, and receiving clerks
58098	All other material recording, scheduling, & distribution workers
59998	All other clerical and administrative support workers
61002	Fire fighting and prevention supervisors
61005	Police and detective supervisors
61008	Institutional cleaning supervisors
62021	Cooks, private household
62031	Housekeepers and butlers
62041	Child care workers, private household
62061	Cleaners and servants, private household
63001	Fire inspection occupations
63008	Fire fighters
63009	Police detectives and investigators
63014	Police patrol officers
63017	Correction officers
63032	Sheriffs and deputy sheriffs
63033	Other law enforcement occupations
63035	Detectives, except public
63044	Crossing guards
63047	Guards
63099	All other protective service workers
65002	Hosts and hostesses, restaurant, lounge, or coffee shop
65005	Bartenders
65008	Waiters and waitresses
65014	Dining room and cafeteria attendants and bar helpers
65021	Bakers, bread and pastry
65026	Cooks, restaurant
65028	Cooks, institution or cafeteria
65030	Cooks, short order and fast food
65038	Food preparation workers
65040	Food counter, fountain, and related workers

65300	All other food preparation and service workers
66002	Dental assistants
66005	Medical assistants
66008	Nursing aides, orderlies, and attendants
66011	Home health aides
66014	Psychiatric aides
66017	Physical and corrective therapy assistants and aides
66021	Occupational therapy assistants and aides
66023	Ambulance drivers and attendants, except EMTs
66026	Pharmacy assistants
66099	All other health service workers
67001	Janitors and cleaners, including maids and house-keeping cleaners
67008	Pest controllers and assistants
67098	All other clean and building service workers
68002	Barbers
68005	Hairdressers, hairstylists, and cosmetologists
68008	Manicurists
68011	Shampooers
68014	Amusement and recreation attendants
68021	Ushers, lobby attendants, and ticket takers
68023	Baggage porters and bellhops
68026	Flight attendants
68035	Personal and home care aides
68038	Child care workers
69998	All other service workers
71002	Farmers
71005	Farm managers
72000	Supervisors, farming, forestry, & agricultural related occs
73002	Fallers and buckers
73008	Log handling equipment operators
73011	Logging tractor operators
73098	All other timber cutting and related logging workers
74002	Farm workers
77002	Captains and other officers, fishing vessels
77005	Fishers, hunters, and trappers
79002	Forest and conservation workers
79005	Nursery workers
79014	Gardeners and groundskeepers, except farm
79017	Animal caretakers, except farm
79998	All other agricultural, forestry, fishing, and related workers
81000	Blue collar worker supervisors
83000	Inspectors, testers, and graders, precision
85109	Industrial machinery mechanics
85123	Millwrights
85132	Maintenance repairers, general utility
85302	Automotive mechanics
85305	Automotive body and related repairers
85308	Motorcycle repairers
85311	Bus and truck mechanics and diesel engine specialists
85314	Mobile heavy equipment mechanics
85321	Farm equipment mechanics
85323	Aircraft mechanics
85326	Aircraft engine specialists
85328	Small engine specialists
85502	Central office and PBX installers and repairers
85505	Frame wirers, central office
85511	Signal or track switch maintainers
85514	Radio mechanics
85598	All other comm equip mechanics, installers, & repairers
85702	Telephone and cable TV line installers and repairers
85705	Data processing equipment repairers
85708	Electronic home entertainment equipment repairers

85710	Home appliance and power tool repairers
85717	Electronics repairers, commercial and industrial equipment
85720	All other elec & electronic equip mechs, installers, & repairers
85723	Electrical powerline installers and repairers
85726	Station installers and repairers, telephone
85902	Heat, air conditioning, & refrigeration mechanics and installers
85905	Precision instrument repairers
85908	Electromedical and biomedical equipment repairers
85911	Electric meter installers and repairers
85914	Camera and photographic equipment repairers
85917	Watchmakers
85921	Musical instrument repairers and tuners
85926	Office machine and cash register servicers
85932	Elevator installers and repairers
85935	Riggers
85947	Coin and vending machine servicers and repairers
85951	Bicycle repairers
85953	Tire repairers and changers
85998	All other mechanics, installers, and repairers
87105	Ceiling tile installers and acoustical carpenters
87110	Carpenters
87120	Drywall installers and finishers
87202	Electricians
87308	Hard tile setters
87310	Bricklayers and stone masons
87311	Concrete and terrazzo finishers
87317	Plasterers
87320	Structural and reinforcing metal workers
87402	Painters and paperhangers, construction and maintenance
87502	Plumbers, pipefitters, and steamfitters
87510	Pipelayers and pipelaying fitters
87602	Carpet installers
87708	Paving, surfacing, and tamping equipment operators
87711	Highway maintenance workers
87802	Insulation workers
87808	Roofers
87811	Glaziers
87823	Sheet metal workers and duct installers
87898	All other construction trades workers
87921	Roustabouts
87929	All other oil and gas extraction occupations
87930	Mining, quarrying, and tunneling occupations
87988	All other extraction and related workers
89102	Tool and die makers
89108	Machinists
89121	Shipfitters
89123	Jewelers and silversmiths
89135	Boilermakers
89198	All other precision metal workers
89308	Wood machinists
89311	Cabinetmakers and bench carpenters
89314	Furniture finishers
89398	All other precision woodworkers
89502	Patternmakers and layout workers, fabric and apparel
89505	Custom tailors and sewers
89508	Upholsterers
89511	Shoe and leather workers and repairers, precision
89598	All other precision textile, apparel, and furnishings workers
89702	Compositors and typesetters, precision
89705	Job printers
89706	Paste-up workers
89707	Electronic pagination systems workers

89712	Photoengravers
89713	Camera operators
89716	All other printing workers, precision
89717	Strippers, printing
89718	Platemakers
89721	Bookbinders
89803	Butchers and meatcutters
89805	Bakers, manufacturing
89898	All other precision food and tobacco workers
89914	Photographic process workers, precision
89917	Optical goods workers, precision
89921	Dental lab technicians, precision
89998	All other precision workers
91105	Lathe & turning mach tool setters & setup opers, metal/plastic
91108	Drilling & boring mach tool setters & setup opers, metal/plastic
91114	Grinding machine setters and set-up operators, metal and plastic
91117	Machine tool cutting operators and tenders, metal and plastic
91302	Punching machine setters and set-up operators, metal and plastic
91321	Machine forming operators and tenders, metal and plastic
91399	All other machine tool cutting and forming etc.
91502	Numerical control machine tool opers & tenders, metal/plastic
91510	Combination machine tool setters, setup opers, opers, & tenders
91710	Soldering and brazing machine operators and tenders
91714	Metal fabricators, structural metal products
91750	Welding machine setters, operators, and tenders
91910	Metal molding machine operators & tenders, setters & setup opers
91914	Foundry mold assembly and shakeout workers
91920	Elec plating opers & tenders, setters & setup opers, metal/plast
91928	Heating equipment setters and set-up operators, metal/plastic
91930	Nonelec platng opers & tenders, setters & setup opers, metl/plas
91932	Heat treating machine operators and tenders, metal and plastic
91935	Furnace operators and tenders
91938	Heaters, metal and plastic
91950	Plastic molding mach operators & tenders, setters & setup opers
92100	All other metal/plastic mach setters, opers, & related workers
92305	Head sawyers & saw mach opers & tenders, setters & setup opers
92310	Woodworking machine operators and tenders, setters & setup opers
92512	Offset lithographic press operators
92515	Letterpress operators
92519	All other printing press setters and set-up operators
92524	Screen printing machine setters and set-up operators
92540	Bindery machine operators and set-up operators
92541	Typesetting and composing machine operators and tenders
92542	Printing press machine setters, operators and tenders
92545	Photoengraving and lithographic machine operators and tenders
92599	All other printing, binding, and related workers
92702	Textile machine setters and set-up operators
92708	Extruding & forming mach opers & tenders, synthetic/glass fibers

92710	Textile draw-out and winding machine operators and tenders
92714	Textile bleaching and dyeing machine operators and tenders
92717	Sewing machine operators, garment
92721	Sewing machine operators, non-garment
92723	Shoe sewing machine operators and tenders
92726	Laundry & drycleaning mach operators & tenders, except pressing
92728	Pressing mach opers/tenders, textile, garment, & relatd material
92902	Electronic semiconductor processors
92905	Motion picture projectionists
92908	Photographic processing machine operators and tenders
92910	Cooking and roasting machine operators & tenders, food & tobacco
92911	Tire building machine operators
92914	Paper goods machine setters and set-up operators
92923	Furnace, kiln, or kettle operators and tenders
92926	Boiler operators and tenders, low pressure
92930	Chemical equipment controllers, operators and tenders
92932	Dairy processing equipment operators, including setters
92940	Cutting and slicing machine setters, operators and tenders
92947	Painters, transportation equipment
92956	Cement and gluing machine operators and tenders
92960	Coat, paint, & spray mach opers, tenders, setters, & setup opers
92962	Separating and still machine operators and tenders
92965	Crushing and mixing machine operators and tenders
92970	Extruding and forming machine setters, operators and tenders
92974	Packaging and filling machine operators and tenders
92999	All other machine operators, tenders, setters, & setup operators
93102	Aircraft assemblers, precision
93105	Machine builders and other precision machine assemblers
93108	Fitters, structural metal, precision
93111	Electromechanical equipment assemblers, precision
93114	Electrical and electronic equipment assemblers, precision
93196	All other precision assemblers
93902	Machine assemblers
93905	Electrical and electronic assemblers
93908	Coil winders, tapers, and finishers
93914	Welders and cutters
93917	Solderers and brazers
93921	Pressers, hand
93923	Sewers, hand

93926	Cutters and trimmers, hand
93928	Portable machine cutters
93935	Cannery workers
93938	Meat, poultry, and fish cutters and trimmers, hand
93941	Metal pourers and casters, basic shapes
93947	Painting, coating, and decorating workers, hand
93953	Grinders and polishers, hand
93997	All other assemblers and fabricators
93998	All other hand workers
95002	Water and liquid waste treatment plant and system operators
95008	Chemical plant and system operators
95010	Gas and petroleum plant and system occupations
95028	Power distributors and dispatchers
95032	Stationary engineers
95098	All other plant and system operators
95200	Power generating and reactor plant operators
97001	Truck drivers light and heavy
97108	Bus drivers
97111	Bus drivers, school
97114	Taxi drivers and chauffeurs
97117	Driver/sales workers
97199	All other motor vehicle operators
97302	Railroad conductors and yardmasters
97305	Locomotive engineers
97308	Rail yard engineers, dinkey operators, and hostlers
97310	All other rail vehicle operators
97314	Subway and streetcar operators
97317	Railroad brake, signal, and switch operators
97504	Able seamen, ordinary seamen, and marine oilers
97505	Mates, ship, boat, and barge
97510	Captains and pilots, ship
97521	Ship engineers
97702	Aircraft pilots and flight engineers
97805	Service station attendants
97808	Parking lot attendants
97898	All other transportation and related workers
97910	All other material moving equipment operators
97923	Excavation and loading machine operators
97938	Grader, dozer, and scraper operators
97941	Hoist and winch operators
97944	Crane and tower operators
97947	Industrial truck and tractor operators
97956	Operating engineers
97999	All other transportation and material moving equipment operators
98310	Helpers, construction trades
98502	Machine feeders and offbearers
98705	Refuse collectors
98710	Freight, stock, and material movers, hand
98902	Hand packers and packagers
98905	Vehicle washers and equipment cleaners
98998	All other helpers, laborers, and material movers, hand

Appendix G
Materials, Products, Subject Matter, and Services (MPSMS) Codes

Each job in *The Enhanced Guide for Occupational Exploration* lists up to three of these codes. They tell you with which materials (M), products (P), subject matter (SM), or services (S) you would work. Knowledge of the MPSMS category or categories listed for each job is often an important requirement for getting the job. More information about these categories can be found in *The Revised Handbook for Analyzing Jobs*.

300 Plant Farm Crops
301 Grains
302 Field Crops, Except Grain
303 Vegetables and Melons
304 Citrus Fruits
305 Fruits, Except Citrus
306 Tree Nuts
309 Plant Farm Crops, N.E.C.
310 Horticultural Specialties, Forest Trees/Products
311 Floricultural and Related Nursery Products
312 Ornamental Trees
313 Standing Timber
314 Forest Nursery Products
319 Horticultural Specialties, Forest Trees/Products, N.E.C.
320 Animals
321 Cattle
322 Hogs
323 Sheep and Goats
324 Poultry and Other Fowl
325 Captive Fur-Bearing Animals
326 Game and Wildlife
327 Horses and Other Equines
329 Animals, N.E.C.
330 Marine Life
331 Finfish
332 Shellfish

339 Marine Life, N.E.C.
340 Raw Fuels and Nonmetallic Minerals
341 Coal and Lignite
342 Crude Petroleum and Natural Gas
343 Stone, Dimension
344 Stone, Crushed and Broken
345 Sand and Gravel
346 Clay
347 Chemical and Fertilizer Minerals
349 Raw Fuels and Nonmetallic Minerals, N.E.C.
350 Raw Metallic Minerals
351 Iron Ores
352 Copper Ores
353 Lead and Zinc Ores
354 Gold and Silver Ores
355 Bauxite and Other Aluminum Ores
356 Ferroalloy Ores, Except Vanadium
357 Mercury Ores
358 Uranium, Radium and Vanadium Ores
359 Raw Metallic Minerals, N.E.C.
360 Structures
361 Buildings, Except Prefabricated
362 Highways and Streets
363 Bridges, Tunnels, Viaducts, and Elevated Highways
364 Water/Gas/Sewer Mains, Pipelines, & Communication/Power Lines

365 Marine Construction
366 Power Plant Projects
367 Railroads and Subways
368 Oil Refineries
369 Structures, N.E.C.
370 Ordnance
371 Guns, Howitzers, Mortars, and Related Equipment
372 Ammunition, Except Small Arms
373 Small Arms
374 Small Arms Ammunition
375 Guided Missiles
379 Ordnance and Accessories, N.E.C.
380 Food Staples and Related
381 Grain Mill Products
382 Meat Products, Processed
383 Dairy Products
384 Bakery Products
385 Oils and Fats, Edible

386 Seafoods, Processed
387 Fruits and Vegetables, Processed
389 Food Staples and Related, N.E.C.
390 Food Specialties
391 Coffee, Tea, and Spices
392 Sugar and Syrup
393 Confectionery and Related Products
394 Flavoring Extracts and Flavoring Syrups
395 Beverages, Alcoholic
396 Soft Drinks and Carbonated Waters
397 Macaroni, Spaghetti, Vermicelli, Noodles
398 Vinegar and Cider
399 Food Specialties, N.E.C.
400 Tobacco Products
401 Cigarettes
402 Cigars
403 Tobacco, Chewing, Smoking, and Snuff
404 Tobacco, Stemmed and Redried
409 Tobacco Products, N.E.C.
410 Textile Fibers and Related
411 Yarn
412 Thread
413 Cordage and Twine
414 Fiber Stock
419 Textile Fibers and Related, N.E.C.
420 Fabrics and Related
421 Fabric, Broad Woven Cotton, Synthetic/Glass, & Silk
422 Fabrics, Broad Woven Wool
423 Narrow Fabrics and Related Smallwares
424 Fabrics, Knitted
425 Fabrics, Nonwoven
429 Fabrics and Related, N.E.C.
430 Textile Products
431 Carpet and Rugs
432 Textiles, Fancy
433 Paddings and Upholstery Filling
434 Impregnated and Coated Fabrics
435 Housefurnishings
436 Canvas and Related Products
439 Textile Products, N.E.C.
440 Apparel
441 Men's and Boys' Suites, Coats, and Overcoats
442 Men's/Boys' Furnishings, Work Clothing, & Allied Products
443 Women's, Girls', and Infants' Outerware
444 Women's, Girls', and Infants' Undergarments

445 Hats
446 Hosiery
447 Fur Goods
449 Apparel, N.E.C.
450 Lumber and Wood Products
451 Logs and Hewn Timber Products, Untreated
452 Sawmill, Planing Mill, and Treated Wood Products
453 Veneer and Plywood
454 Wood Containers
455 Prefabricated Wood Buildings, Mobile Homes, & Structural Wood Members
456 Particleboard
457 Wood Articles
459 Lumber and Wood Products, N.E.C.
460 Furniture and Fixtures
461 Wood Household Furniture (Except Upholstered)
462 Wood Household Furniture (Upholstered)
463 Metal Household Furniture
464 Mattresses, Bedsprings, and Sofa Beds
465 Wood Office, Public Building, and Related Furniture
466 Metal Office, Public Building, & Related Furniture
467 Wood and Metal Fixtures
468 Plastic, Glass, and Fiberglass Furniture & Fixtures
469 Furniture and Fixtures, N.E.C.
470 Paper and Allied Products
471 Pulp
472 Nonconverted Paper and Paperboard, Except Building
473 Nonconverted Building Paper and Building Board
474 Convertd Paper/Paperboard Products, Except Containers/Boxes
475 Paperboard Containers and Boxes
479 Paper and Allied Products, N.E.C.
480 Printed and Published Products
481 Newspapers
482 Periodicals
483 Books and Pamphlets
484 Manifold Business Forms
485 Greeting Cards
486 Blankbooks, Looseleaf Binders, and Related Products
489 Published and Printed Products, N.E.C.
490 Chemical and Allied Products
491 Chemicals, Inorganic

492 Plastics Materials/Synthetic Resin; Synthetic Rubber/Fiber, Except Glass
493 Drugs
494 Soaps, Detergents, & Cleaning Preparations; Perfumes/Cosmetics
495 Paints, Varnishes/Lacquers, Enamels, & Allied Products
496 Chemicals, Organic
497 Agricultural Chemicals
499 Chemical and Allied Products, N.E.C.
500 Petroleum and Related Products
501 Petroleum Products
502 Paving Materials
503 Roofing Materials
504 Fuel Briquettes, Packaged Fuel, and Powdered Fuel
505 Coke
509 Petroleum and Related Products, N.E.C.
510 Rubber and Miscellaneous Plastic Products
511 Tires and Tubes
512 Rubber and Plastic Footwear
513 Reclaimed Rubber
514 Rubber and Plastic Hose and Belting
519 Rubber and Miscellaneous Plastic Products, N.E.C.
520 Leather and Leather Products
521 Hides, Skins, and Leather
522 Footwear, Except Rubber
523 Leather Gloves and Mittens
524 Luggage of Any Material
525 Handbags and Related Accessories of Any Material
529 Leather and Leather Products, N.E.C.
530 Stone, Clay, and Glass Products
531 Flat, Pressed, or Blown Glass and Glassware
532 Glass Products Made of Purchased Glass
533 Cement, Hydraulic
534 Structural Clay Products
535 Pottery and Related Products
536 Concrete, Gypsum, and Plaster Products
537 Cut Stone and Stone Products
538 Abrasive, Asbestos, and Related Products
539 Stone, Clay, and Glass Products, N.E.C.
540 Metal, Ferrous and Nonferrous
541 Blast Furnace, Steelworks, & Rolling/Finishing Mill Products
542 Metal Castings

543 Nonferrous Metals, Smelted and Refined

544 Nonferrous Metals, Rolled, Drawn, and Extruded

549 Metal, Ferrous and Nonferrous, N.E.C.

550 Fabricated Metal Products, Except Ordnance, Machinery, & Transportation Equipment

551 Metal Cans and Containers

552 Cutlery, Handtools, and General Hardware

553 Nonelectric Heating Equipment and Plumbing Fixtures

554 Fabricated Structural Metal Products

555 Screw-Machine Products

556 Metal Forgings and Stampings

557 Fabricated Wire Products

559 Fabricated Metal Products, Except Ordnance, Machinery, & Transportation Equipment N.E.C.

560 Machinery and Equipment, Except Electrical

561 Engines and Turbines

562 Farm and Garden Machinery and Equipment

563 Construction Machinery and Equipment

564 Mining and Oil Field Machinery and Equipment

565 Materials-Handling Machinery and Equipment

566 Metalworking Machinery and Equipment

567 Special Industrial Machinery

568 General Industrial Machinery and Equipment

571 Office, Computing, and Accounting Machines

572 Service-Industry Machinery

573 Refrigeration and Air-Conditioning Equipment

579 Machinery and Equipment, Except Electrical, N.E.C.

580 Electrical and Electronic Machinery, Equipment, & Supplies

581 Electrical Transmission and Distribution Equipment

582 Electrical Industrial Apparatus

583 Household Appliances

584 Electric Lighting and Wiring Equipment

585 Home-Entertainment Electric Equipment

586 Communication and Related Equipment

587 Electronic Components and Accessories

589 Electrical/Electronic Machine, Equipment, & Supplies, N.E.C

590 Transportation Equipment

591 Motor Vehicles and Motor-Vehicle Equipment

592 Aircraft and Parts

593 Ships and Boats

594 Railroad Equipment

595 Motorcycles, Bicycles, and Parts

596 Space Vehicles and Parts

597 Travel Trailers and Campers

598 Military Tanks and Tank Components

599 Transportation Equipment, N.E.C.

600 Measuring, Analyzing, & Controlling Instruments; Photographic, Medical, & Optical Goods; & Watches & Clocks

601 Engineering, Labatory, Scientific, & Research Instruments & Equipment

602 Measuring and Controlling Instruments

603 Optical Instruments and Lenses

604 Surgical, Medical, & Dental Instruments & Supplies

605 Ophthalmic Goods

606 Photographic Equipment and Supplies

607 Watches, Clocks, Clockwork-Operated Devices, & Parts

609 Measuring, Analyzing, Controlling Instruments; Photographic, Medical, Optical Goods, N.E.C

610 Miscellaneous Fabricated Products

611 Jewelry, Precious Metal

612 Silverware, Plated Ware, and Stainless Steel Ware

613 Jewelers' Findings and Materials and Lapidary Work

614 Musical Instruments and Parts

615 Games and Toys

616 Sporting & Athletic Goods, Except Firearms & Apparel

617 Pens, Pencils, & Other Office & Artists' Materials

618 Costume Jewelry and Novelties, Buttons, and Notions

619 Miscellaneous Fabricated Products, N.E.C.

700 Architecture and Engineering

701 Architectural Engineering

702 Aeronautical Engineering

703 Electrical, Electronic Engineering

704 Civil Engineering

705 Ceramic Engineering

706 Mechanical Engineering

707 Chemical Engineering

708 Mining and Petroleum Engineering

711 Metallurgical Engineering

712 Industrial Engineering

713 Agricultural Engineering

714 Marine Engineering

715 Nuclear Engineering

716 Surveying, Cartographic Engineering

719 Architecture and Engineering, N.E.C.

720 Mathematical and Physical Sciences

721 Mathematics

722 Astronomy

723 Chemistry

724 Physics

725 Geology and Geophysics

729 Mathematics and Physical Sciences, N.E.C.

730 Life Sciences

731 Agriculture, Horticulture, and Forestry

732 Biological Sciences

733 Psychology

739 Life Sciences, N.E.C.

740 Social Sciences

741 Economics

742 Political Science

743 History

744 Sociology

745 Anthropology

749 Social Sciences, N.E.C.

750 Arts and Literature

751 Fine Arts

752 Graphic Arts

753 Photography

754 Dramatics

755 Rhythmics

756 Music

757 Literature and Journalism

759 Arts and Literature, N.E.C.

850 Transportation Services

851 Interurban Railroad Transportation

852 Local/Suburban Transit & Inter-urban Highway Passenger Transportation

853 Motor Freight Transportation and Warehousing

854 Water Transportation

855 Air Transportation

856 Pipeline Transportation

859 Transportation Services, N.E.C.

860 Communication Services
861 Telephone Communication
862 Telegraph Communication
863 Radio Broadcasting
864 Television Broadcasting
869 Communication Services, N.E.C.
870 Electric , Gas, and Sanitary Services
871 Electric Services
872 Gas Production and Distribution
873 Water Supply and Irrigation Services
874 Sanitation Services
875 Steam Supply
879 Electric, Gas, and Sanitary Services, N.E.C.
880 Merchandising Services
881 Retail Trade
882 Wholesale Trade
883 Route Sales and Delivery Services
884 Auctioneering, Vending, and Rental Services
885 Sales Promotion Services
889 Merchandising Services, N.E.C.
890 General Business, Finance, Insurance, & Real Estate Services
891 Clerical Services, Except Bookkeeping
892 Accounting, Auditing, and Bookkeeping Services
893 General Administration & Administrative Specialties
894 Financial Services
895 Insurance and Real Estate
896 Advertising and Public Relations Services

897 Blueprinting, Photocopying, Photofinishing, & Printing Services
898 Production Services
899 General Business, Finance, Insurance, & Real Estate Services, N.E.C
900 Domestic, Building, and Personal Services
901 Domestic Services
902 Lodging Services
903 Meal Services, Except Domestic
904 Beauty and Barbering Services
905 Janitorial and Portering Services
906 Apparel and Furnishings Services
907 Funeral and Crematory Services
909 Domestic, Building, and Personal Services, N.E.C.
910 Amusement and Recreation Services
911 Motion Picture Services
912 Theater Services
913 Sports Services
919 Amusement and Recreation Services, N.E.C.
920 Medical and Other Health Services
921 Physician Services, Including Surgical
922 Dental Services, Including Surgical
923 Optometric, Chiropractic, and Related Services
924 Nursing, Dietetic, and Therapeutic Services
925 Health Technological Services
926 Medical Assistant, Aide, and Attendant Services

929 Medical and Other Health Services, N.E.C.
930 Educational, Legal, Museum, Library, & Archival Services
931 Educational Services
932 Legal Services
933 Museum, Library, and Archival Services
939 Educational, Legal, Museum, Library, & Archival Services, N.E.C
940 Social, Employment, and Spiritual Services
941 Social and Welfare Services
942 Child and Adult Residential and Day-Care Services
943 Employment Services
944 Spiritual Services
949 Social, Employment, and Spiritual Services, N.E.C.
950 Regulation, Protection, & Related Government Services
951 Protective Services, Except Military
952 Military Services
953 Regulatory Law Investigation and Control Services
954 Postal Services
959 Regulation, Protection, & Related Government Services, N.E.C
960 Miscellaneous Services
961 Motor-Vehicle Services, Except Maintenance & Repair
962 Deodorizing, Exterminating, & Decontaminating Services
969 Miscellaneous Services, N.E.C.

Appendix H
Work Fields

Each job in *The Enhanced Guide for Occupational Exploration* lists up to three of these codes. They tell you which work fields (skills) are most important for the job. The titles of the 96 work fields are listed here in numerical order. Notice that the numbering system begins with physical skills and ends with intellectual and interpersonal skills. More information about these categories can be found in *The Revised Handbook for Analyzing Jobs*.

001 Hunting-Fishing
002 Animal Propagating
003 Plant Cultivating
004 Logging
005 Mining-Quarrying-Earth Boring
007 Excavating-Clearing-Foundation Building
011 Material Moving
013 Transporting
014 Pumping
021 Stationary Engineering
031 Cleaning
032 Surface Finishing
033 Lubricating
034 Butchering-Meat Cutting
041 Filling-Packing-Wrapping
051 Abrading
052 Chipping
053 Boring
054 Shearing-Shaving
055 Milling-Turning-Planing
056 Sawing
057 Machining
061 Fitting-Folding
062 Fastening
063 Gluing-Laminating
071 Bolting-Screwing
072 Nailing
073 Riveting
081 Welding
082 Flame Cutting-Arc Cutting-Beam Cutting
083 Soldering-Brazing
091 Masoning

092 Laying-Covering
094 Caulking
095 Paving
101 Upholstering
102 Structural Fabricating-Installing-Repairing
111 Electrical-Electronic Fabricating-Installing-Repairing
121 Mechanical Fabricating-Installing-Repairing
131 Melting
132 Casting
133 Heat Conditioning
134 Pressing-Forging
135 Die Sizing
136 Molding
141 Baking-Drying
142 Crushing-Grinding
143 Mixing
144 Distilling
145 Separating
146 Cooking-Food Preparing
147 Processing-Compounding
151 Immersing-Coating
152 Saturating
153 Brushing-Spraying
154 Electroplating
161 Combing-Napping
162 Spinning
163 Winding
164 Weaving
165 Knitting
166 Tufting
171 Sewing-Tailoring

182 Etching
183 Engraving
191 Printing
192 Imprinting
201 Photographing
202 Developing-Printing
211 Appraising
212 Inspecting-Measuring-Testing
221 Stock Checking
231 Verbal Recording-Recordkeeping
232 Numerical Recording-Recordkeeping
233 Data Processing
241 Laying Out
242 Drafting
243 Surveying
244 Engineering
251 Researching
261 Writing
262 Artistic Painting-Drawing
263 Composing-Choreographing
264 Styling
271 Investigating
272 Litigating
281 System Communicating
282 Information-Giving
291 Accommodating
292 Merchandising-Sales
293 Protecting
294 Health Caring-Medical
295 Administering
296 Teaching
297 Entertaining
298 Advising-Counseling

JIST Customer Information

JIST specializes in publishing the very best results-oriented career and self-directed job search material. Since 1981 we have been a leading publisher in career assessment devices, books, videos, and software. We continue to strive to make our materials the best there are so that people can stay abreast of what's happening in the labor market, and so they can clarify and articulate their skills and experiences for themselves as well as for prospective employers. **Our products are widely available through your local bookstores, wholesalers, and distributors.**

The World Wide Web

For more occupational or book information, get online and see our Web site at **www.jist.com**. Advance information about new products, services, and training events is continually updated.

Quantity Discounts Available!

Quantity discounts are available for businesses, schools, and other organizations.

The JIST Guarantee

We want you to be happy with everything you buy from JIST. If you aren't satisfied with a product, return it to us within 30 days of purchase along with the reason for the return. Please include a copy of the packing list or invoice to guarantee quick credit to your order.

How to Order

For your convenience, the last page of this book contains an order form.

24-Hour Consumer Order Line:
Call toll free 1-800-648-JIST
Please have your credit card (VISA, MC, or AMEX) information ready!

Mail: Mail your order to the address listed on the order form to:

JIST Works, Inc.
8902 Otis Avenue
Indianapolis, IN 46216
Fax: Toll free 1-800-JIST-FAX

JIST Order Form

Please copy this form if you need more lines for your order.

Purchase Order #: _____ (Required by some organizations)

Billing Information

Organization Name: _____

Accounting Contact: _____

Street Address: _____

_____

City, State, Zip: _____

Phone Number: ( ) _____

Shipping Information with Street Address (If Different from Above)

Organization Name: _____

Contact: _____

Street Address: (We *cannot* ship to P.O. boxes) _____

_____

City, State, Zip: _____

Phone Number: ( ) _____

```
┌─────────────────────────────────────────┐
│ Phone: 1-800-648-JIST                    │
│ Fax: 1-800-JIST-FAX                      │
│ World Wide Web Address:                  │
│ http://www.jist.com                      │
└─────────────────────────────────────────┘
```

Credit Card Purchases: VISA_____ MC_____ AMEX_____

Card Number: _____

Exp. Date: _____

Name As on Card: _____

Signature: _____

Quantity	Order Code	Product Title	Unit Price	Total

Subtotal	
+5% Sales Tax *Indiana Residents*	
+Shipping / Handling / Ins. (See left)	
TOTAL	

Shipping / Handling / Insurance Fees

In the continental U.S. add 7% of subtotal:
- Minimum amount charged = $4.00
- Maximum amount charged = $100.00
- FREE shipping and handling on any prepaid orders over $40.00.

Above pricing is for regular ground shipment only. For rush or special delivery, call JIST Customer Service at 1-800-648-JIST for the correct shipping fee.

Outside the continental U.S. call JIST Customer Service at 1-800-648-JIST for an estimate of these fees.

Payment in U.S. funds only!

JIST Works, Inc.
8902 Otis Avenue
Indianapolis, IN 46216

Practical, self-directed tools and training for career explorers and job seekers of all ages!

JIST thanks you for your order!